AF580456

Mandeville's

USED BOOK PRICE GUIDE

An Aid In Ascertaining Current Prices

RETAIL PRICES OF RARE, SCARCE, USED AND
OUT-OF PRINT BOOKS

This Volume May Be Used As a Separate
Reference Work
Or in Conjunction with the Previous
5 YEAR EDITIONS

Editor
Richard L. Collins

Assistant Editor
Alea M. Collins

5 YEAR EDITION

1994

Prices through July 1993 catalogues

PRICE GUIDE PUBLISHERS
PO Box 82525, Kenmore,Washington 98028

ISBN 0-911182-94-5

PRICE GUIDE PUBLISHERS

International Standard Book Number **ISBN 0-911182-94-5**

Printed in the U.S.A

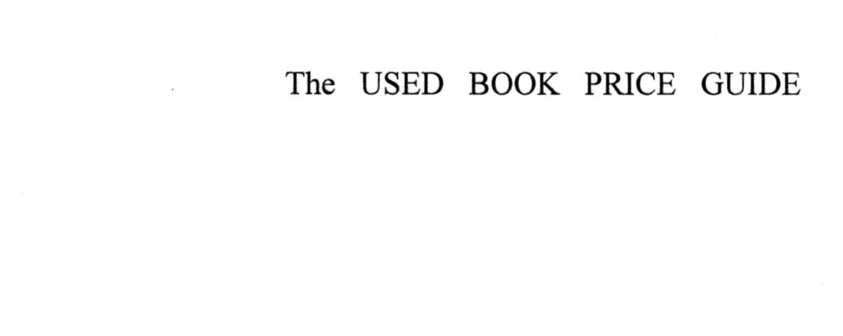

The USED BOOK PRICE GUIDE

CONTENTS

Asterisk (*) after price indicates CANADIAN DOLLARS

USED BOOK PRICE GUIDE ©

ABBREVIATIONS

a/c - aircraft
ad; adv(s) - advertisement(s)
a.e.g. - all edges gilt
ALs; als - autographed letter(s)
anon- anonymous
anr - another
auth; authr - author
autg; autog - autographed
authzd ed - authorized edition
bdg; bdng - binding, bound
bds - boards
bk - book, back
bkplt- bookplate
bkstrp - backstrip
blk - black
blu - blue
brok - broken
brn; brwn - brown
btw - between
buck - buckram
bul; bull - bulletin
bx - box, boxed
c - copy (after nbr of copies ie: 1,000c); copyrite ; (sometime circa)
ca - circa
cat - catolog
chip - chipped
cl - cloth
co - country, company
col - color
copyr pg - copyright page
corr - correct
cov - cover
cpy - copy
cwo - cash with order
dec - decoration, decorated
dedic - dedicated
def - defective
defac - defaced
dict - dictionary
dif - different, difference
disbnd - disbound
dj - dust jacket, dust wrapper
dup - duplicate
ea- each
ed- edition, editor
eleph - elephant folio
Eng - English
engr - engraved, engraving
enlgd ed - enlarged edition
e.p. - end paper
errata; errat - errata slip
ex - extra
ex-lib - ex-library copy
f - fine
f bndg - fine binding
fab - fabricoid
facs - facsimile
1st - first edition
fldg; fold - folding, folded
Fr - French
front (is) - frontpiece
fx; fox - foxed, foxing
g - good (condition)
g. - gold, gilt
g.e. - gilt edges
g.t. - gilt top
g. stmpd - gold stamped
grn - green
hf t; h.t. - half title
handcol - handcolored
hndbk - handbook
hng - hinge
illus - illustrated, illustrations
imprt - imprint
incor - incorrect
inscr - inscribed,inscription
Jap ppr - Japan paper
Jn - John
l.; li. - line
l.p. - large paper
lab; labl - label
lacks - missing
lea - leather
lev - levant (polished lea)
lf - leaf
lg ppr - large paper
lib; libr - library
lin - linen
litho; liths - lithograph
ls; l.s. - letter signed
lt - light
ltd - limited
lvs - leaves
missg - missing
mor - Morocco
motld - mottled
mrbld - marbled
ms (s) - manuscript (s)
mtd; mntd - mounted
mult - multigraph, multilith
nbr - number (d)
n.d. - no date
n.p. - no place
n.y. - no year
oblg; obl - oblong
o.p. - out of print
p.; pgs - page (s)
papr; pap; ppr - paper
pamph - pamphlet
parch - parchment
pebld - pebbled
photo - photograph
pic; pict - picture
plns - plans
plts - plates
port - portrait
p.p.; pp - post paid
pr - press
pres; pres cpy - presentation copy
priv prntd - privately printed
prtd; prntd - printed
prntg - printing
prntr imp - printer's imprin
ptd - printed
pub; publ - publisher
purpl - purple
rag - rag paper
rbkd - rebacked
rbnd - rebound
reprnt - reprint
rev - revised
rprd - repaired
rub - rubbed
sig - signature
sgnd - signed copy
sl - slip, slight, slightly
sml; sm - small
sp - spine
spec bndg - special bindin
spot - spotted
sq - square
stmpd - stamped
stns - stains
supl - supplement (s)
t - tall
t. - title
t.e.g - top edges gilt
t.p. - title page
th; thk - thick
tip in - tipped in
tn - torn
tr - tear
unbd; unbnd - unbound
unfin - unfinished
untrmd - untrimmed
v.d. - various dates
vf - very fine
v.p. - various places
vel - vellum
vignt - vignette
vo; 8vo - (size)
vol; vols - volume(s)
wi - with
wk - work(s)
wn - worn
wr - wear
wrps - wrapper(s) (paper cov)
wtrstn - waterstained
yel; yell - yellow
yr - year(s)

PREFACE

The USED BOOK PRICE GUIDE, 5 YEAR EDITION, 1994, is part of a series of volumes containing retail prices asked by book dealers throughout the United States and Canada. The total of over 135,000 entries in the 4 FIVE YEAR editions of 1994, 1989, 1983, 1977, plus additional pertinent information contained in each volume produce a basic reference work for pricing used books.

The 1994 FIVE YEAR EDITION contains many new listings as well as updating and/or supplying additional identifying points for the other listings. Each FIVE YEAR EDITION may be used separately or in conjunction with the other FIVE YEAR EDITIONS.

The GUIDES are compiled from many hundreds of catalogs received from United States and Canadian used book dealers. Prices are taken from the latest catalogs. When specific listings were not found in a later catalog, an attempt has been made to take entries from earlier catalogs. Books listed are assumed to be in good or very good condition unless stated otherwise.

When possible the condition of the book listed is described as stated in the dealer's catalog. Each description has been taken by the dealer from the copy of the book he has on hand and therefore may vary from known bibliographer's descriptions. Researchers and collectors will find many interesting variants, hitherto unknown, listed within these pages. Where there is a wide variant of price of one particular edition, we assumed the conditions of the books justified the prices,

The guide is specifically produced for the use of the USED BOOK DEALER, BOOK SCOUT, LIBRARIAN, AUCTIONEER and BOOK COLLECTOR to assist in the evaluation of rare, scarce, old and used books. The information herein, plus auction records, plus experience, should provide a background for determining the current market value of books.

The contents of this book have been checked many times, but with a work of this size errors will be found. Modern computer technology has aided us in making this edition as accurate and orderly as can be, within the bounds of all those who helped in its compilation. We have done our utmost to produce a current, efficient reference work. It has been a long, but very enjoyable project, which we hope will translate into a pleasurable experience for all you book people out there.

Prices from 1989 through July 1993 catalogues.

Richard L. Collins
Kenmore ,Washington

September 1993

HOW TO USE THIS BOOK - Listings are alphebetical according to author, compiler or editor. When anonymous the book is listed by the title or, sometimes, subject. As a general rule the listings read as follows:

Author-title-place of publication-date of publication-size-kind of binding-other identifying points where possible-(dealer's code number and condition)-Price in dealer's catalog.

Or,

HUDSON RIVER-Letters About...& Its Vicinity-1836-by a Citizen of NY-209p-(Freeman Hunt)
(5ff2,bkstrp tn) 10.00

The letter and number in ( ) immediately preceding each price is our identification of dealer's catalog from which that price was taken. Occasionally a dealer will cite a bibliographical reference such as Howes or BAL. This reference is usually place at the end of the listing and before the dealer's code.

CONDITIONS

(Condition of the book is an important factor in a book's value)

Conditions are usually defined as follows:

Mint - as new, same as when published. Dust jacket without tears and in new condition.

Fine - no defects but yet not quite as new

Very good - no defects but does show some wear. No tears.

Good - average used book. No pages missing.

Fair - well worn but complete text. May lack end papers. Jacket and binding may be badly worn.

Poor - badly worn but complete text legible.

ABBREVIATIONS FOR CONDITION OF BOOK

(Used with dealers code number - immediately before price)

autog - autographed
bkstrp - backstrip
brok - broken
bx; box - boxed
chip - chipped
cv; cov - cover
def - defaced
defac - defaced
disb - disbound
dj - dust jacket; dust wrapper
ex-lib - ex-library copy
f - fine
fx; fox - foxed; foxing
g - good
hng - hinge
inscr - inscribed
lf - leaf
mssg - missing
p - poor
pres - presentation copy
rbkd; rebkd - rebacked
rebnd; rbnd - rebound
reprd; rprd - repaired
rub - rubbed
sl - slight(ly)
sp - spine
spot - spotted, spots
stns - stains, stained
vf - very fine
vg - very good
unct - uncut
wn - worn

Asterisk (*) after price indicates CANADIAN DOLLARS.

BOOK SIZES

4to (quarto)	12"	32mo	4-5"	double elephant folio	50"
8vo	9"	48mo	4"	atlas folio	25"
12mo	7-8"	64mo	3"	elephant folio	23"
16mo	6-7"	folio-over	13"	below 1" - miniature	
24mo	5-6"				

USED BOOK PRICE GUIDE©

A KEMPIS,THOMAS-Of the Imitation of Jesus Christ-Lond-1828-Pickering and Major-lea (l9,fox,sl scuff) 300.00

A.E.G.-Modern Art at Venice & Other Notes-NY-1910-J M Bowles-8vo-ltd to 175c-scarce (h10,sl chip sp labl) 100.00

AARON,DANIEL-Unwritten War-NY-(1973)-Knopf-(19),385,(14)p-1st ed (m4,vf,dj) 16.50

AARTS,DOROTHY-Ghost Towns of the Republic of Texas-(1939)-J M Hill Tex Hist Essay Award-22p-wrps-1st prtg (a9) 45.00

AATEL AND JONES-How to Set a Table-(Phila)-1946-(priv prtd)-19p-wrps,illus (l6) 10.00

ABBATE,FRANCESCO-ED.-American Art...-Lond-(1972)-158p-cl-87 col picts (d1,f,dj) 12.50

ABBEY,EDWARD-Appalachian Wilderness-NY-1970-Dutton-4to-col photos by E Porter-1st ed (bb1,f,dj) 175.00

ABBEY,EDWARD-Cactus Country-NY-1973-Time Life-1st ed (y1,f,sl tn dj) 100.00

ABBEY,EDWARD-Desert Images-NY-1979-HBJ-lg folio-photos,D Muench-1st ed (d8,f,box) 200.00

ABBEY,EDWARD-Desert Solitaire-(1968)-McGraw Hill-1st ed so stated (v8,sm spot to t.e.,f dj) 125.00

ABBEY,EDWARD-Monkey Wrench Gang-Phila-(1975)-Lippincott-1st ed (p1,f,sl tn dj) 150.00

ABBEY,EDWARD-Slickrock-SF-1971-Sierra Club-1st ed (c8,f,dj) 250.00

ABBEY,EDWARD-Sunset Canyon-Lond-1971-Talmy,Franklin Ltd-8vo-159p-1st Brit ed (z4,dj) 95.00

ABBEY,EDWARD-Sunset Canyon-Lond-1971-Talmy,Franklin-1st Brit ed (e8,f,f dj) 125.00

ABBOT,ANTHONY-About the Murder of Geraldine Foster-NY-1930-Covici-1st ed (g4,sl wn sp) 12.50

ABBOT,ANTHONY-Shudders-1943-F&R-1st ed (x7,dj) 15.00

ABBOT,ANTHONY-Shudders-NY-1943-Farrar-1st ed (f4,chip dj) 20.00

ABBOT,BRIG GEN HENRY L-Problems of the Panama Canal-NY-1905-MacMillan-8vo-248p-red cl,fldg map,chrts,15 woodcts-(1st ed is smaller than 2nd ed & has no photo plts)-1st ed (p8,pres) 45.00

ABBOT,WILLIS J-Battlefields and Camp Fires-NY-(1889)-356p-pict cl,illus-1st ed (c4) 40.00

ABBOTT,BERENICE-World of Atget-NY-1964-Horizon-lg 4to-cl,174 photos,Atget-1st ed (y3,dj) 115.00

ABBOTT,C-South African Butterflies-1984-Macmillan-100p-24 col plts-1st ed (bb3,f,dj) 25.00

ABBOTT,CHARLES C,M.D.-Primitive Industry-Salem-1881-Geo A Bates-560p-illus-1st ed (cc4,ex-libr) 30.00

ABBOTT,CHARLES C-Travels in a Tree Top-Phila-1894-215,(1)p-cl-1st ed (aa6) 40.00

ABBOTT,G F-Macedonian Folklore-Lond-1903-Cambridge Univ-cl-1st ed (o8) 45.00

ABBOTT,JACK H-In the Belly of the Beast-NY-(1981)-Random-auth 1st bk-1st ed (b5,as new in dj) 20.00

ABBOTT,JACOB-Harper Establishment-NY-(1850)-Harper & Bros-12mo-160p-orig blnd stmpd red cl,gilt,engrvngs (hh9,sp ends wn) 75.00

ABBOTT,LAWRENCE-Impressions of Theodore Roosevelt-GC-1919-8vo-315p-photos (m3) 25.00

ABBOTT,LYMAN-Reminiscences-NY-1915-509p-cl-1st ed (b1) 20.00

ABBOTT,MABEL-Life of William T Davis-Ithaca-1949-Cornell Univ Pr-xviii+321p-grn cl,18 figs on plts-1st ed (b2) 20.00

ABBOTT,MAE-Oklahoma Indian Cook Book-Tulsa-1956-auth-30p-wrps,illus-1st ed (mm6,sl soil cov,pg taped) 30.00

ABBOTT,MAUDE-Classified and Annotated Bibliography of Sir William Osler's Publications-Montreal-1939-163p-2nd ed (dd3) 100.00

ABDILL,GEORGE B-Locomotive Engineer's Album-Seattle-1965-190p-Old RR Ser.No.5-1st ed (n4,f,dj) 25.00

ABDILL,GEORGE B-Pacific Slope Railroads from 1854 to 1900-Seattle-(1959)-Superior-182p-gry cl,illus-1st ed (mm10,dj) 25.00

ABDILL,GEORGE B-Rails West-Seattle-1960-190p-1st ed (n4,f,dj) 30.00

ABDILL,GEORGE B-This Was Railroading-Seattle-1958-192p-photos-1st ed (n4,f,dj) 27.50

ABE,KOBO-Secret Rendevous-NY-1979-Knopf-1st US ed (b10,as new in dj) 15.00

ABE,KOBO-Secret Rendevous-NY-1979-Knopf-1st US ed (b5,as new in dj) 15.00

ABEL,ANNIE H-ED.-Chardon's Journal at Fort Clark 1834 thru 1839-Pierre-1932-Dept of Hist-458p-cl,2 pltd-Howes c303-1st ed (d7) 100.00

ABELL,MRS. L G-Woman in Her Various Relations-NY-(1851)-Wm Holdredge-319p-cl,col t.p. preceding reg t.p. (d1) 60.00

ABERNATHY,ALONZO-Dedication of Monuments Erected by the State of Iowa-Des Moines-1908-E H English,State Prtr-301p-3/4 lea,frntis,illus,fldg maps (o7,hng weak) 50.00

ABERNATHY,JOHN R-Catch 'Em Alive Jack-NY-1936-Assoc-224p-1st ed (a9) 80.00

ABERNATHY,JOHN R-In the Camp with Theodore Roosevelt-Okla City-1933-279p-wrps,frntis,photos-Herd,scarce-1st ed (t7) 75.00

ABERNETHY,FRANCIS-ED.-Observations & Reflections on Texan Folklore-Austin-1972-1st ed (a6,f,dj) 35.00

ABERT,JAMES W-Through the Country of Comanche Indians in Fall of Year 1845-SF-1970-73p+pre pgs-col plts,fldg map,illus-1st ed (u7,f) 55.00

ABERT,JAMES W-Western America in 1846,1847-SF-1966-folio-116p-cl,plastic dj,2 fldg maps,15 wtrcols-1st ed (z1,f,dj) 100.00

ABISH,WALTER-Alphabetical Africa-(NY)-(1974)-New Directions-1st ed (a10,as new in dj) 20.00

ABISH,WALTER-Minds Meet-(NY)-(1975)-New Directions-8vo-cl-1st ed (jj8,as new in dj) 20.00

ABOSCH,HEINZ-Menace of the Miracle-NY-1963-Monthly Review-277p-1st US ed (r1,dj) 20.00

ABRAHAM,DOROTHY-Lone Cone-Victoria-nd-auth-63p-prtd wrps-1st ed (aa2) 25.00*

ABRAHAM,GERALD-ED.-Music of Shubert-NY-1947-Norton-1st ed (u4,chip dj) 12.00

ABRAHAM,JAMES J-Lettsom-Lond-1933-Heinemann-lg 8vo-xx+498p-blu cl,illus-1st ed (g2) 85.00

ABRAHAMS,PETER-Night of Their Own-NY-1965-Knopf-1st US ed (cc1,dj) 25.00

ABRAHAMS,PETER-Path of Thunder-NY-1948-Harper-1st ed (f8,edgewn dj) 50.00

ABRAMOWITZ,I-ED.-Great Prisoners, Anthology of Literature Written in Prison-NY-1946-879p-1st ed (y7,fray dj) 60.00

ABRAMS,GARY-Prince Albert the First Century, 1866 to 1966-Saskatoon-1966-Modern Pr-8vo-vii,389p-14 illus,12 maps-1st ed (cc7,sl rub dj) 20.00*

ABRAMS,LOUIS E-Rabbits by the Acre-NY-(1954)-McBride-8vo-208p-1st ed (gg5,dj) 15.00

ABREU,MARGARET-Food of the Conquerors-Santa Fe-(1954)-Rydal Pr-51p-wrps (o6) 18.00

ABZUG,MARTIN-Spearhead-NY-1946-Dial-auth 1st bk-1st ed (hh5,sl tn dj) 15.00

ACKART,ROBERT C-To Set Before the King-NY-(1967)-Brussel-333p-tan bds,drwngs-1st ed (q8,dj) 17.50

ACKERMAN,BILL-Handbook of Fishes of the Atlantic Seaboard-Wash D.C.-1951-8vo-144p-col plts-1st ed (m3) 17.50

ACKERMAN,CARL W-George Eastman-Bost-1930-Houghton-4to-grn cl-1st ed (y3) 45.00

ACKERMAN,DIANE-Wife of Light-NY-1978-Morrow-1st ed (k7,dj) 20.00

ACKERMAN,PHYLLIS-Wall Paper-NY-1923-Stokes-8vo-268p wi index,dec tan cl-1st ed (t1,few pencil mrks) 45.00

ACOSTA,OSCAR Z-Autobiography of a Brown Buffalo-SF-1972-Straight Arrow-1st ed (f8,f,f dj) 50.00

ACTON,ELIZA-People's Book of Modern Cookery-Lond-nd(ca.1900?)-SMHK & Co-500p-blu bds,dec sp,frntis,8p of carving illus & 3 plts-34th ed,rvsd & enlgd (n6) 60.00

ACTON,HAROLD-Memoirs of an Aesthete 1939 to 1969-NY-1970-1st US ed (n5,f,f dj) 35.00

ACTON,HAROLD-Nancy Mitford-NY-1975-Harper & Row-252p-wht cl-1st US ed (z9,dj) 10.00

ACTON,WILLIAM-Functions and Disorders of the Reproductive Organs in Childhood, Youth, Adult Age, and Advanced Life-Phila-1865-Lindsay & Blakiston-269p-blk cl-presumed 1st Amer ed (c2,sl discol sp) 30.00

ACWORTH,B-Cuckoo and Other Bird Mysteries-Lond-1946(1944)-8vo-202p-cl,col frntis,e.p. map (y8,fade,dj wn) 25.00

ADAIR'S HISTORY OF THE AMERICAN INDIANS-NY-ca.1960-508p (ll3,f,dj) 40.00

ADAIR,F E S-Summer in High Asia-Lond-1899-286p-dec cov & sp,photos,fldg map-scarce (gg3,sl tn sp) 275.00

ADAIR,JAMES R-Man From Steamtown-Chig-1967-224p-1st ed (n4,f,dj) 15.00

ADAIR,JOHN-People's Health, Anthropolgy and Medicine in a Navajo Community-NY-(1970)-188p-maps-1st ed (v7,dj) 15.00

ADAIR,W-Lure of the Iron Trail-1912-Assoc Pr-1st ed (x2,sp lettrng flakng) 25.00

ADAM,HELEN-Gone Sailing-West Branch-1980-Toothpaste Pr-ltd to 150c,2 autg,drwngs,A Mikolowski-1st ed (w6,f) 30.00

ADAMI,G-ED.-Letters of Giacomo Puccini-Phila-1931-Lippincott-8vo-illus-1st Amer ed (s1,f,dj) 40.00

ADAMIC, LOUIS-House In Antigua-NY,Lond-1937-illus-1st ed (l5,brwnd sp,wn dj) 12.50

ADAMIC,LOUIS-Robinson Jeffers, a Portrait-Covelo-(1983)-Yolla Bolly Pr-orig glassine,ltd to 265c,nbrd,autg (x3,f,dj) 115.00

ADAMIC,LOUIS-Robinson Jeffers-Seattle-1929-U of Wash-wrps,U of Wash Chapbook Ser #27-1st ed (h8,f) 30.00

ADAMS,A D-Great Britain and the American Civil War-NY-1958-340p-illus,ports (z10,soil dj) 22.50

ADAMS,A-Daniel Chester French, Sculptor-Bost-1932-32 illus-1st ed (kk4,sl chip dj) 85.00

ADAMS,ALEXANDER B-Geronimo, a Biography-NY-(1971)-381p-e.p. maps,illus-1st ed (n3,dj chip) 27.50

ADAMS,ALEXANDER B-Sunlight and Storm-NY-1977-479p-photos-1st ed (t7,f,dj) 17.50

ADAMS,ALICE-Beautiful Girls-1979-Knopf-1st ed (m9,f,sl soil dj) 25.00

ADAMS,ALICE-Families and Survivors-NY-1974-Knopf-1st ed (a10,f,dj) 45.00

ADAMS,ALICE-Families and Survivors-NY-1974-Knopf-1st ed (l7,dj) 35.00

ADAMS,ALICE-Listening to Billie-NY-1978-Knopf-1st ed (bb2,f,dj) 35.00

ADAMS,ALICE-Rich Rewards-1980-Knopf-1st ed (m9,f,dj) 20.00

ADAMS,ALICE-To See You Again-1982-Knopf-1st ed (o9,vf,dj) 15.00

ADAMS,ANDY-Reed Anthony, Cowman-Bost-1907-Houghton Mifflin-1st ed (k8,sl soil) 25.00

ADAMS,ANDY-Reed Anthony, Cowman-Bost-1907-Riverside Pr-12mo-384p+(4p)ads-illus tan cl,1907 on t.p.-3rd imprssn (b6) 35.00

ADAMS,ANDY-Why the Chisholm Trail Forks-Austin-1956-U of Tex Pr-296p-illus by Thurgood-1st ed (bb4) 45.00

ADAMS,ANSEL-Examples-Bost-1983-Little,Brown-4to-178p-blk cl,illus-4th prtg (r10,f dj) 20.00

ADAMS,ANSEL-Fiat Lux-NY-(1967)-McGraw Hill-folio-192p-blu cl,photos-1st ed (r10,tattrd dj,autg) 100.00

ADAMS,ANSEL-Fiat Lux-NY-(1967)-McGraw Hill-folio-cl-1st ed (y3,sl fox,dj) 75.00

ADAMS,ANSEL-Illustrated Guide to Yosemite-SF-1963-191p-39 photos-1st ed (q10,f,dj) 35.00

ADAMS,ANSEL-Images 1923 to 1974-Bost-(1974)-NYGS-ltd to 1000c,nbrd,autg-1st ed (w5,f,f dj,sun box) 250.00

ADAMS,ANSEL-Images 1923 to 1974-Bost-(1974)-NYGS-oblng folio-cl-1st ed (y3,dj) 135.00

ADAMS,ANSEL-Making a Photograph-Lond,NY-1935-Studio-cl & illus bds-"How To Do It" Ser.No.8-2nd ed (y3,dj) 95.00

ADAMS,ANSEL-Polaroid Land Photography Manual-NY-(1963)-Morgan-8vo-cl-1st ed (y3,f,dj) 55.00

ADAMS,ANSEL-Portfolios of...-Bost-1977-NYGS-124p-90 photos-1st prtg (cc9,as new in dj) 75.00

ADAMS,ANSEL-Taos Pueblo-Bost-1977-NYGS-lg folio-1/2 lea & cl,12 photos,ltd to 950c,nbrd,autg-facs of 1930 ed (y3,f,f box) 850.00

ADAMS,ANSEL-These We Inherit-SF-(1962)-Sierra Club-folio-cl-1st ed (y3,sl soil dj) 125.00

ADAMS,ANSEL-This is American Earth-SF-1960-Sierra Club-lg 4to-xx,90p-grn buckram,photos-1st ed (u1,dj) 50.00

ADAMS,ANSEL-Yosemite and the Range of Light-Bost-1979-NYGS-144p-116 photos-1st prtg (cc9,as new in dj) 150.00

ADAMS,ANSEL-Yosemite and the Range of Light-Bost-1979-NYGS-2nd prtg (w5,f,dj) 75.00

ADAMS,CHARLOTTE-1001 Questions Answered About Cooking-NY-(1963)-Dodd,Mead-frntis (m6,dj) 15.00

ADAMS,CHAS C-Middletown Upper Houses-NY-1908-847p-illus (a3) 75.00

ADAMS,CLINTON-Fritz Scholder Lithographs-Bost-1975-160p-frntis,photos-1st ed (t7,f,dj) 15.00

ADAMS,DANIEL-Scholar's Arithmetic-Keene-1824-prntd by John Prentiss-224p-bds-stereotype ed,revsd & corrected wi add (k1,wn) 25.00

ADAMS,DOUGLAS-Hitchhiker's Guide to the Galaxy-1980-Harmony-1st Amer ed (w4,dj) 30.00

ADAMS,DOUGLAS-Life, the Universe and Everything-NY-(1982)-Harmony-1st US ed (h3,f,dj) 20.00

ADAMS,DOUGLAS-Restaurant at the End of the Universe-1980-Harmony-1st Amer ed (m9,f,dj) 25.00

ADAMS,DOUGLAS-So Long, and Thanks For the Fish-NY-(1980)-Harmony-1st US ed (h3,f,dj) 20.00

ADAMS,EDWARD D-Niagara Power-1927-Niagara Falls Power Co-4to-2 vols-blu cl,photos,maps,diagrams-1st ed (g2) 90.00

ADAMS,EDWARD D-Niagara Power-1928-2 vols-277 illus-1st ed (h6) 110.00

ADAMS,EMMA H-Digging the Top Off-SF-1892-Pacific Pr-8vo-174p-prntd gry cl-3rd ed (w6) 125.00

ADAMS,EMMA H-To and Fro in Southern California-Cin-1887-W M B C Pr-288p-cl,sketches-1st ed (d1,sl wn) 60.00

ADAMS,EPHRAIM D-Great Britain and the American Civil War-NY-1925-2 vols-illus-1st Amer ed (n3,sl wtrstnd cov,sp chip) 45.00

ADAMS,F-Kidnapped Millionaires-1901-Lothrop-pict cl-1st ed (x7) 30.00

ADAMS,FRANKLIN P-Diary of Our Own Samuel Pepys 1911 to 25-NY-1935-S&S-1st ed (z9) 20.00

ADAMS,FRANKLIN P-Tobogganing on Parnassus-GC-1912-142p-cl (b1) 15.00

ADAMS,FREDERICK B-Fourth Annual Report to the Fellows of the Pierpont Morgan Library-NY-1953-78p-cl,illus-ltd to 350c (jj4) 30.00

ADAMS,FREDERICK U-John Henry Smith-NY-1905-Dbldy,Page-grn pict cl-illus,A B Frost-1st ed (f2,sl rub edges) 25.00

ADAMS,FREDERICK U-Plot That Failed-np-nd-24p-wrps-(Chig,1912) (g1) 15.00

ADAMS,HENRY-Degradation of the Democratic Dogma-NY-1919-1st ed (r2,sl sun sp) 35.00

ADAMS,HENRY-Mont St.Michel and Chartres-Bost-1913-Houghton Mifflin-4to-1st trd ed (pp3) 30.00

ADAMS,HERBERT-Golden Ape-Phila-1930-Lippincott-1st US ed (f4) 12.50

ADAMS,HERBERT-Rogues Fall Out-1928-Lippincott-1st Amer ed (s10) 12.50

ADAMS,J DONALD-Speaking of Books and Life-NY-(1965)-HR&W-279p-bds-1st ed so stated (l1,dj) 15.00

ADAMS,JOHN-Railway Picture Gallery-Lond-1962-96p-1st ed (n4,f,dj) 14.00

ADAMS,JOSEPH-Ten Thousand Miles Through Canada-Lond-(1912)-xx,310p-orig cl,50 photos (a7) 50.00

ADAMS,KRAMER A-Covered Bridges of the West-Berkeley-1963-Howell North-4to-146p-cl,illus-1st ed (e2,chp & tn dj) 25.00

ADAMS,L A-Intro to Vertebrates-1933-8vo-414p-cl-1st ed (y8) 36.00

ADAMS,LEON-Striped Bass Fishing-Palo Alto-1953-8vo-224p-illus-1st ed (m3,fray dj) 11.00

ADAMS,MRS LELA-Spark Lid Top Gas Stove Cook Book-(Santa Rosa)-1925-Press Democrat-176p-papr wrps,frntis,illus (n6) 25.00

ADAMS,NEHEMIAH-South Side View of Slavery-Bost-1855(1854)-T R Marvin-12mo-viii,222,4,4p-cl-3rd ed (n2,sp chip) 50.00

ADAMS,P-Arctic Island Hunter-GB-1961-136p-photos (gg3,vf,dj) 40.00

ADAMS,RAMON F-Burs Under the Saddle-Norman-(1964)-U of Okla-1st ed (a9,dj) 200.00

ADAMS,RAMON F-Burs Under the Saddle-Norman-(1964)-U of Okla-xii,610p-cl-1st ed (v1,dj) 125.00

ADAMS,RAMON F-Charles M Russell-Pasadena-1948-350p-13 col illus by Russell,photos-1st ed (n10,dj) 75.00

ADAMS,RAMON F-Come An' Get It-Norman-(1952)-U of Okla Pr-170p-drwngs,N Eggenhoffer-1st ed (o6,dj) 50.00

ADAMS,RAMON F-Come An' Get It-Norman-(1952)-U of Okla Pr-170p-illus by Eggenhofer-Herd 12-1st ed (a9,dj) 40.00

ADAMS,RAMON F-Come An'Get It-(1952)-U of Okla-xii,170p-cl-1st ed (v1,dj) 45.00

ADAMS,RAMON F-Cowboy and His Humor-1968-Encino Pr-71p-ltd to 850c,nbrd,autg (r8,f) 50.00

ADAMS,RAMON F-Cowman Says It Salty-Tucson-(1971)-U of Ariz Pr-163p-drwngs by Donahue-1st ed (bb4,dj) 35.00

ADAMS,RAMON F-ED.-Best of the American Cowboy-Norman-(1957)-U of Okla Pr-289p-illus,N Eggenhofer-Six Guns 13-1st ed (ff4) 45.00

ADAMS,RAMON F-Fitting Death for Billy the Kid-Norman-(1960)-310p-illus-1st ed (c7,f,dj) 50.00

ADAMS,RAMON F-Fitting Death for Billy the Kid-Norman-(1960)-U of Okla Pr-310p-illus-1st ed (cc4,dj) 40.00

ADAMS,RAMON F-Language of the Railroader-Norman-(1977)-U of Okla Pr-180p-1st ed (ff4,dj) 40.00

ADAMS,RAMON F-More Burs Under the Saddle-Norman-(1979)-Univ of Okla-xvi,182p-cl-1st ed (v1,dj) 35.00

ADAMS,RAMON F-Old Time Cowhand-NY-1961-Macmillan-354p-illus by Eggenhofer-Six Guns 12-1st ed (bb4,dj) 35.00

ADAMS,RAMON F-Rampaging Herd-Cleve-(1982)-Zubal-xx,463p-cl,illus (v1,dj) 45.00

ADAMS,RAMON F-Six Guns and Saddle Leather-Norman-1969-807p-cl-1st prtg of rvsd ed (z1,f,dj) 150.00

ADAMS,RICHARD-Girl in a Swing-(Lond)-(1980)-Lane-8vo-bds-1st ed,1st iss (jj8,f,dj) 125.00

ADAMS,RICHARD-Iron Wolf and Other Stories-Lond-(1980)-Allen Lane-1st ed (g3,f,dj) 20.00

ADAMS,RICHARD-Plague Dogs-(Lond)-(1977)-Allen Lane-1st Brit ed (a10,f,dj) 20.00

ADAMS,RICHARD-Shardik-NY-(1974)-S&S-1st US ed (a10,f,dj) 20.00

ADAMS,ROBERT H-White Churches From the Plains-(1970)-Colo Assoc U Pr-4to-57p photos-1st ed (l10,edge wn dj) 17.50

ADAMS,RUFUS W-Young Gentleman and Lady's Explanatory Monitor-Columbus-1818-E Griswold,Jun.,prntr-260p-bds,leaf A5 from preface is lacking wi no indication it was ever present-fifth ed (k1) 125.00

ADAMS,SAMUEL H-Average Jones-Indpls-1911-Bobbs-1st ed (f4) 120.00

ADAMS,SAMUEL H-Incredible Era-Bost-1939-Houghton,Mifflin-456,(1)p-cl (d1) 15.00

ADAMS,SAMUEL H-Revelry-NY-1926-Boni & Liveright-318p-cl-1st ed (f1) 15.00

ADAMS,SAMUEL-Writings of ...-NY-1904-Putnam's-4 vols-grn cl,lea sp labl-ltd to 750 sets,nbrd-1st ed (h2,labls wn) 175.00

ADAMS,TOM-Agatha Christie-NY-1981-Everest-col illus-1st Amer ed (r4,f,dj) 35.00

ADAMS,W DAVENPORT-Dictionary of English Literature-Lond-nd(ca.1880)-Cassell Petter & Galpin-(4),708p-1/2 mor,g,raised bnds,mrbld e.p.-rvsd ed (m4) 30.00

ADAMSON,H C-Eddie Rickenbacker-NY-1946-8vo-cl,12p plts-1st ed (s2,sl chip dj) 45.00

ADAMSON,HANS C-Rebellion in Missouri: 1861-Phila-1961-Chilton-305p-e.p. maps,illus-1st ed (v2,dj) 55.00

ADAMSON,HELEN L-Grandmother in the Kitchen-Phila-(1963)-Chilton Bks-320p-brwn cl bds-1st ed (k6) 18.00

ADAMSON,W A-Enterprising Angler-Lond-1950-8vo-268p-illus-1st ed (m3) 17.50

ADDAMS,CHARLES-Homebodies-NY-1954-col illus e.p.s-1st ed (s5,sl wn dj) 40.00

ADDAMS,CHAS-Dear Dead Days-NY-(1959)-4to-photos,drwngs,cartoons-1st ed (f5,sl wn dj) 25.00

ADDINGTON,ROBERT M-History of Scott County, Virginia-Kingsport-1932-xiv,364p (jj3,dj taped) 47.50

ADDISON,ALBERT C-Romantic Story of the Puritan Fathers and their Founding of New Boston...-Bost-1912-243p-cl,50p illus,dec cov & sp-1st Imprssn so stated (m1,f) 15.00

ADDISON,THOMAS-Collection of the Published Writings-Lond-1868-242p-1st ed (dd3,ex-libr) 250.00

ADE,GEORGE-Artie-Chig-1896-Herbert S Stone-t.e.g.,pics by J T McCutcheon-auth 1st reg publ bk-1st ed (r2,uncut,sl sun sp) 40.00

ADE,GEORGE-Bang! Bang!-NY-1928-Sears-1st ed (l4,f) 20.00

ADE,GEORGE-Breaking Into Society-NY-1904-12mo-drwngs-1st ed (m4,sp fade) 10.00

ADE,GEORGE-Fables in Slang-1900-H Stone-illus,C Newman-1st ed (x2,sl soil) 28.00

ADE,GEORGE-Fables in Slang-Westvaco-Christmas 1972-8vo-172p-cl-1st ed (t3,f,box) 45.00

ADE,GEORGE-Girl Proposition-NY-1902-192p-cl wi lg pict labl,illus-1st ed (hh1) 15.00

ADE,GEORGE-Letters of ...-W Lafayette-1973-1st ed (l5,sl wrnkld pgs,f dj) 12.50

ADE,GEORGE-More Fables-Chig,NY-1900-218p-cl-1st ed (m1) 15.00

ADE,GEORGE-Stories of the Streets and of the Town-Chig-1941-Caxton Club/Lakeside Pr-illus,iss w/o dj-ltd to 500c-1st ed (y1,f) 100.00

ADE,GEORGE-True Bills-NY-1904-Harper & Bros-154p-illus-1st ed (ll2) 15.00

ADELMANN,HOWARD-Marcello Malpighi and the Evolution of Embryology-Ithaca-1966-4to-5 vols-1st ed (dd3,box) 200.00

ADELPHIAN BOOK OF RECIPES-By the Ladies of Omar M. E. Aid Society, Omar, Ohio-np-1905-143,(2)p-linen wrps (b1) 17.50

ADES,D-Dada & Surrealism Reviewed-1978-Arts Cncl of Grt Brit-wrps,illus(incl col)-1st ed (ee1,sl stnd cov) 175.00

ADHEMAR,JEAN-Toulouse Lautrec-NY-1965-Abrams-lg 4to-369p-orng cl,b&w & col plts (r10,f,dj) 100.00

ADIRONDACK LEAGUE CLUB-NY-1915-priv prtd-red cl,fldg maps,photos (dd6) 40.00

ADLER,FRIEDRICH-Moscow Trial and the Labour and Socialist International-Lond-1931-Labour Prty-wrps,photo illus cov-1st ed (v5) 20.00

ADLER,RENATA-Toward a Radical Middle-NY-(1969)-Random-1st ed (b5,f,dj) 25.00

ADLER,TERRY-On Murder's Skirts-Phoenix-1947-1st ed (s10,dj) 12.50

ADLER,WARREN-War of the Roses-NY-(1981)-Warner-1st ed (e3,f,dj) 25.00

ADNEY & CHAPELLE-Bark Canoes & Skin Boats of North America-Wash D.C.-1964-U.S. Nat'l Mus-4to-242p-illus-1st ed (f7) 40.00

ADNEY,E T-Bark Canoes & Skin Boats of North America-Wash D.C.-1964-4to-242p-photos-scarce-1st ed (m3) 35.00

ADOFF,ARNOLD-ED.-I Am the Darker Brother...-NY-1968-Macmillan-pict bds-1st ed (w5,f,dj) 25.00

ADOMEIT,RUTH E-Three Centuries of Thumb Bibles-NY,Lond-1980-Garland-390p-cl,photos (c1,f) 60.00

ADVENTURE: THE WORLD OF MUSIC-Bost-(1938)-Ginn-4to-cl,4 col plts,N C Wyeth-1st ed (s3) 35.00

ADYE,JOHN-Recollections of a Military Life-NY-1895-382p-blu cl,illus-1st Amer ed (b7) 125.00

AFLALO,F G-British Salt Water Fish-Lond-1904-4to-328p-12 col plts-v scarce-1st ed (m3) 50.00

AFLALO,F G-Sunset Playgrounds-NY-1909-8vo-251p-photos (m3) 35.00

AFTANDILIAN,GREGORY L-Armenia, Vision of a Republic-Bost-1981-Charles River Bks-cl-1st ed (m8,f,dj) 10.00

AGASSIZ,L-Principles of Zoology...Part 1-NY-1875-8vo-250p-orig cl,frntis-rvsd ed (y8) 35.00

AGASSIZ,LOUIS-Bibliographia Zoologiae Et Geologiae-NY-1968-4 vols-(facs of 1848-1854 ed) (dd3) 150.00

AGATE,JAMES-Kingdoms for Horses-Lond-1936-Gollancz-decs by R Whistler-1st ed (f10) 45.00

AGEE,JAMES-Agee on Film-NY-1958-McDowell,Obolensky-1st ed (f8,f,f dj) 75.00

AGEE,JAMES-Death in the Family-Lond-1965-1st Brit ed (q5,f,sl rub dj) 45.00

AGEE,JAMES-Death in the Family-NY-1957-1st ed,1st iss (p5,sl sunned sp,dj) 90.00

AGEE,JAMES-Letters of...to Father Flye-1962-Braziller-1st ed (x2,vf,dj) 35.00

AGEE,JAMES-Way of Seeing-NY-(1965)-Viking-oblng 8vo-cl,photos by H Levitt-1st ed (u10,f,f dj) 200.00

AGRICULTURAL ALMANAC, FOR...1893...-Lancaster-(1892)-John Baer's Sons-18p-wrps (g1) 12.50

AGUILERA-MALTA,DEMETRIO-Seven Serpents and Seven Moons-Austin,Lond-(1979)-U of Tex Pr-1st ed (a10,as new in dj) 35.00

AHLBERG,H-Swedish Architecture of the 20th Century-Lond-1925-folio-152 plts (h10) 250.00

AI-Cruelty-Bost-1973-HM-auth(Florence Ogawa) 1st bk-1st ed (z3) 17.50

AI-Killing Floor-Bost-1979-HMCo-1st ed (e8,f,f dj) 45.00

AICKMAN,ROBERT-Cold Hand In Mine-NY-(1975)-Scribner's-1st US ed (k3,f,dj) 25.00

AICKMAN,ROBERT-Painted Devils-(1979)-Scribner's-dj designed & illus,E Gorey-1st US ed (q9,vf,dj) 20.00

AICKMAN,ROBERT-Painted Devils-NY-(1979)-Scribner's-1st US ed (k3,f,dj) 25.00

AICKMAN,ROBERT-Power of Darkness-Lond-1966-Collins-1st ed (k3,dj chip & wrnkld) 40.00

AIKEN,ALBERT W-Fresh of Frisco-NY-Sept 24,1879-Beadle & Adams-21,(3)P-self wrps(punched along bndg edge)-New York Dime Library No.77 (b1) 22.50

AIKEN,ALBERT W-Winged Whale-NY-(1879)-Beadle & Adams-44,(4)p-self wrps(punched along bndg edge)-N.Y. Dime Library No.63 (b1) 25.00

AIKEN,CONRAD-Brownstone Eclogues & Other Poems-NY-1942-DS&P-1st ed (y1,f,f dj) 40.00

AIKEN,GEORGE D-Pioneering with Wild Flowers-Putney-1933-Auth-122p-dec cov,illus-1st ed (mm4) 25.00

AIKEN,JOAN-Crystal Crow-1968-Dbldy-1st Amer ed (s10,dj) 12.50

AIKEN,JOAN-Dark Interval-NY-1967-Dbldy-1st US ed (e4,dj) 15.00

AIKEN,JOAN-Nightbirds on Nantucket-NY-1966-DD-illus-1st ed (y1,f,dj) 22.50

USED BOOK PRICE GUIDE©

AIKEN,JOAN-Skin Spinners-NY-(1976)-Viking-83p-cl & bds-1st ed (r3,f,dj) 25.00

AIKEN,JOAN-Wolves of Willoughby Chase-GC-(1963)-Dbldy-drwngs-1st US ed (pp10,dj wn,chip) 40.00

AIKMAN,DUNCAN-ED.-Taming of the Frontier-NY-1925-319p-cl-1st ed (l1) 15.00

AILSWORTH,T S-ET AL-Charlotte County Rich Indeed-Charlotte-1979-588p-illus,fldg map (z10,wn dj) 50.00

AINSLIE,CAPTAIN KENNETH-Pacific Ordeal-NY-1956-Norton-8vo-251p-blu cl-1st ed (p8,tn dj) 20.00

AINSWORTH,ED-Cowboy in Art-NY,Cleve-1968-World-sm folio-242p wi index,illus-1st ed (t1,dj) 45.00

AINSWORTH,ED-Pot Luck-Hollywood-1940-frntis,photos-1st ed (t7,dj,2 autgs) 42.50

AINSWORTH,WILLIAM H-Ballads-Lond-1855-1/2 calf,g sp,raised bnds,t.e.g.,illus by J Gilbert-1st ed (r2,sl rub) 60.00

AIR NEWS YEARBOOK-NY-(1942)-sm oblng 4to-264p-cl,plts,text illus-1st ed,1st iss (t2,sl wn sp,dj missing pcs) 60.00

AIR POWER-NY-(1943)-editors of Look Mag-4to-98p-cl,illus t.p.,col & b&w plts,col illus e.p.-1st ed (t2,chip dj) 30.00

AIRD,CATHERINE-Henrietta Who-NY-1968-Dbldy CC-1st US ed (g4,dj) 15.00

AIRD,CATHERINE-Slight Mourning-NY-1976-Dbldy CC-1st US ed (g4,dj) 15.00

AIRD,CATHERINE-Some Die Eloquent-Lond-1979-Collins-1st ed (p4,vf,dj) 25.00

AIRD,CATHERINE-Stately Home Murder-NY-1970-Dbldy CC-1st Amer ed (h4,dj) 15.00

AIRLIE,MABELL-ED.-With the Guards We Shall Go-Lond-1933-322p-blk cl,illus-1st ed (b7) 50.00

AITCHISON,CHARLES-Lord Lawrence-Oxford-1892-216p-blu cl,fldg map-1st ed (b7,f) 25.00

AITKEN,RUSSELL-Great Game Animals of the World-NY-nd(c.1968)-folio-192p-photos-scarce (m3,f,dj) 60.00

AITKEN,SIR MAX-Canada in Flanders-Lond-1916-Hodder & Stoughton-sm 8vo-xx,243p-orng cl,g sp titles,emboss frnt bd,2 maps (cc7,sun cl) 20.00*

AJAYI,J F A-ED.-History of Africa-NY-(1971)-Columbia U Pr-lg 8vo-2 vols-wrps-2nd ed (y5) 30.00

AKEHURST,RICHARD-Sporting Guns-NY-1968-8vo-120p-photos (m3,f,dj) 10.00

AKELEY,M L J-Congo Eden-NY-1961-356p-photos (gg3,f,chip dj) 15.00

AKELEY,M L J-Restless Jungle-NY-1936-313p-photos (gg3,f,pres cpy) 40.00

AKELEY,M L J-Rumble of a Distant Drum-NY-1946-364p-photos,fldg map (gg3,f,chip dj) 30.00

AKERMAN,JOHN Y-Spring Tide-Lond-1850-12mo-192p-illus-scarce (m3,rebckd) 75.00

AKERS,DWIGHT-Drivers Up-NY-1947-Putnam-2nd ed rvsd (h9,dj) 25.00

AKERS,DWIGHT-Sleepy Tom-NY-1939-Putnam-1st ed (j9,dj wn) 58.00

AKERS,FLOYD-Boy Fortune Hunters in Alaska-Chig-1908-Reilly & Britton-1st ed,3rd iss (y2,wn,stnd) 125.00

AKERS,FLOYD-Boy Fortune Hunters in China-Chig-(1909)-Reilly & Britton-1st ed,2nd iss (y2,wn,lacks ffep) 150.00

AKERS,FLOYD-Boy Fortune Hunters in Panama-Chig-1908-Reilly & Britton-1st ed (y2,sl slant sp) 200.00

AKERS,FLOYD-Boy Fortune Hunters in the South Seas-Chig-1911-Reilly & Britton-scarce-1st ed (y2,cov sl rub,spot) 400.00

AKERSTROM,JENNY-Princesses Cook Book from the Original Swedish "Prinsessornas Kokbok"-NY-1936-A Bonnier-315p-illus-scarce (mm6,f) 55.00

AKINJOGBIN,I A-Dahomey and Its Neighbours:1708 to 1818-Cambridge-1967-Univ Pr-8vo-234p-cl-1st ed (y5,f,f dj) 27.00

AKUTAGAWA,R-Exotic Japanese Stories-1964-Liveright-22 illus,incl 6 col,M Kuwata-1st Amer ed (x2,vf,vf dj) 45.00

ALADDIN HOUSES-Bay City-1914-No Amer Constr-8vo-96p-illus wrps,illus-trade cat-3rd ed (r10,sp tn) 27.50

ALAIN-FOURNIER-Wanderer-Bost-1928-Houghton Mifflin-1st ed (w5,sl discol bds,dj) 75.00

ALAN,MARJORIE-Dark Prophecy-NY-1945-Mill-1st US ed (g4,chip dj) 10.00

ALBANO,JUDGE M W-Souls Judgement Day-Paterson-1940-Lorecraft-1st ed (w5,f,dj) 25.00

ALBARET,CELESTE-Monsieur Proust: A Memoir-NY et al-(1976)-McGraw-Hill-photos-1st US ed (bb1,as new in dj) 17.50

ALBAUGH,W A-Confederate Handguns-NY-nd-250p-illus,rprnt of 1963 ed-scarce (z10,dj) 75.00

ALBEE,EDWARD-American Dream-NY-1961-1st ed (q5,f,dj) 75.00

ALBEE,EDWARD-Malcolm-NY-1966-Atheneum-1st ed (f3,sl chip dj) 20.00

ALBEE,EDWARD-Tiny Alice-NY-1965-Atheneum-1st ed (u4,f,dj) 15.00

ALBEE,EDWARD-Who's Afraid of Virginia Woolf-NY-1962-1st ed (p5,wn dj) 60.00

ALBEE,FRED H-Bone Graft Surgery-Phila-1915-417p-3 col illus-1st ed (g10) 275.00

ALBEE,HELEN R-Hardy Plants for Cottage Gardens-NY-1910-vi,309p-g dec sp,t.e.g.,67 photos,1 plan-1st ed (m10) 15.00

ALBEE,LOUISE R-Bartlett Collection-Cambridge-1896-8vo-180p (m3,e.p. tape stns) 80.00

ALBERT,LILLIAN-Complete Button Book...-GC,NY-1949-Dbldy-xix,409p-cl,col frntis,illus-1st ed (dd10,f,rprd dj) 85.00

ALBERTS,ROBERT C-Benjamin West-Bost-1978-Houghton Mifflin-(16)525p-photos-1st ed (l10,vf,dj) 12.50

ALBERTS,ROBERT-Most Extraordinary Adventures of Major Robert Stobo-Bost-1965-422p-illus-1st ed (b7,dj) 35.00

ALBERY,F F D-Michael Ryan, Capitalist-Columbus-1913-Rowfant-163p-cl (n1) 20.00

ALBION,ROBERT G-Rise of New York Port, 1815 to 1860-NY-1939-Scribners-illus-1st ed (pp4,dj) 25.00

ALBRIGHT,NANCY-Rodale Cookbook-1977-Rodale (v6,wn dj) 12.00

ALBRIGHT,VERNE R-Peruvian Paso and His Classic Equitation-Ft.Collins-1975-Caballus-4to-1st ed (h9,dj) 45.00

ALBUCASIS-On Surgery and Instruments-Lond-1973-850p-plts-1st ed (dd3,dj) 100.00

ALCOFORADO,MARIANNA-Portuguese Letters-Switzerland-(April,1948)-H L Mermod-3/4 lea,illus,Modigliani-ltd to 3500c (l9,f) 125.00

ALCOTT,A BRONSON-Letters of...-Ames-(1969)-Iowa St Univ Pr-xl+846p-tan cl,plts-1st ed (b2,dj) 35.00

ALCOTT,LOUISA M-Aunt Jo's Scrap Bag. My Girls...-Bost-1878-Roberts-12mo-229p+ads-grn cl,vol 4 in ser-BAL 186-1st ed (w6,2 lvs oxidized) 100.00

ALCOTT,LOUISA M-Aunt Jo's Scrap Bag. Shawl Straps-Bost-1872-Roberts-grn cl,brn coated e.p.s-BAL 171-1st ed (w6,sl warped,dusted) 125.00

ALCOTT,LOUISA M-Life, Letters, and Journals-Bost-1890-Roberts Bros-1st Amer ed (y2,rprd sp,stnd cov & frntis) 75.00

ALCOTT,LOUISA M-Under the Lilacs-Bost-1878-Roberts-1st ed (pp10,hng weak,stns) 35.00

ALCOTT,LOUISA M-Work-Bost-1873-Roberts Bros-1st Amer ed (y2,sp wn) 65.00

ALCOTT,WILLIAM A-Young Housekeeper...-Bost-1849-Strong & Brodhead-424p-bds-Bitting 6-9th stereotype ed (l6,sp wn) 75.00

ALCOTT,WILLIAM A-Young Woman's Book of Health-Phila-nd(late 1860s?)-Keystone Publ-311p-cl (o1) 17.50

ALDAM,W H-Quaint Treatise on Flies & Flymaking by an Old Fisherman-Lond-1876-4to-91p text-2pg chromolitho plts,25 flies + add materials in 22 sunken mnts-orig grn cl gilt (m3,f) 1,550.00

ALDANOV,MARK-Tenth Symphony-NY-1948-Scribner's-viii,149p-cl-1st Amer ed (kk1,chip dj) 20.00

ALDIS,BRIAN W-Billion Year Spree-Lond-(1973)-Weidenfeld And Nicholson-1st ed (j3,f,dj) 30.00

ALDIS,BRIAN W-Greybeard-NY-(1964)-Harcourt Brace-1st ed (j3,sp wn dj) 50.00

ALDIS,BRIAN W-Malacia Tapestry-NY-(1976)-Harper & Row-1st US ed (l3,f,dj) 15.00

ALDISS,BRIAN W-Helliconia Spring-NY-1982-Atheneum-iss simultaneously wi Brit ed-1st US ed (bb1,f,dj) 30.00

ALDISS,BRIAN W-Soldier Erect-NY-(1971)-Coward,McCann & Geoghegan-1st US ed (b10,sl rub dj) 25.00

ALDRICH,CHILSON D-Real Log Cabin-NY-1946-8vo-278p-illus,photos (m3,f) 9.00

ALDRICH,LORENZO-Journal of the Overland Route to California and the Gold Mines-La-1950-93p-cl & bds,fldg map rear e.p. pckt (t7,f) 45.00

ALDRICH,THOMAS B-Ballad of Babie Bell and Other Poems-NY-1859-Rudd & Carleton-brwn cl,5p ads in rear-1st state wi publ Broadway addr-BAL 253-1st ed (f2) 40.00

ALDRICH,THOMAS B-Sea Turn & Other Matters-Bost-1902-HMCO-1st ed (x1,lacks dj) 30.00

ALDRIDGE,ALAN-ED.-Beatles Illustrated Lyrics-NY-1969-Delacorte-1st US ed (v5,dj) 35.00

ALDRIDGE,ALAN-Ship's Cat-NY-1977-Knopf-4to-pict glossy bds,col illus-1st US ed (s3,as new in dj) 20.00

ALDRIDGE,PAUL-Living Egypt-Lond-(1969)-MacGibbon-4to-cl-1st ed (y3,f,f dj) 185.00

ALDRIDGE,REGINALD-Ranch Notes in Kansas,Colorado, the Indian Territory and Northern Texas-Lond-1884-332p-illus,publ emboss pres stamp on title leaf-Graff #30-rare (t7,f) 450.00

ALDROVANDI,ULISSE-Aldrovandi on Chickens-Norman-(1963)-U of Okla Pr-8vo-447p-drwngs-1st US ed (gg5,f,chip,tape rprd dj) 30.00

ALEXANDER,CHRISTOPHER-Production of Houses-NY-1985-Oxford U Pr-8vo-381,(2)p-cl,illus(incl col)-1st prtg (cc10,dj) 45.00

ALEXANDER,DAVID-Sound of Horses-Indpls-1966-Bobbs Merrill-1st ed (h9,dj) 40.00

ALEXANDER,DRURY B-Texas Homes of the 19th Century-Austin-1966-UTP-folio-276p-photos-1st ed (a9,dj) 30.00

ALEXANDER,E P-Iron Horses-NY-(1941)-Bonanza-4to-239p-cl (m1,dj) 12.50

ALEXANDER,E P-Iron Horses-NY-1941-239p-1st ed (n4,f,dj) 40.00

ALEXANDER,E P-Military Memoirs of a Confederate-NY-1907-Scribners-634p-frntis,illus,maps,fldg map-1st ed (cc6,ex-libr) 70.00

ALEXANDER,EDWIN P-American Locomotives-NY-1950-256p-1st ed (n4,f,dj) 30.00

ALEXANDER,EDWIN P-Collector's Book of the Locomotive-1966-Bramhall Hs-4to-197p-illus-rprnt (d3,dj) 15.00

ALEXANDER,EDWIN P-Collector's Book of the Locomotive-NY-1966-197p-illus(44 col)-1st ed (n4,f,dj) 25.00

ALEXANDER,EDWIN P-Down at the Depot-NY-(1970)-Potter-sm folio-320p-photos-1st ed (p1,dj) 45.00

ALEXANDER,GILCHRIST-From the Middle Temple to the South Seas-Lond-1927-J Murray-8vo-xiv,287p+1p ads-blu cl,photos-1st ed (pp1,sp fade,bump,sl fox) 65.00

ALEXANDER,HARTLEY B-Cooke Daniels Lectures-(Denver)-1927-43p-photos-1st ed (v7,rbnd) 27.50

ALEXANDER,JAMES E-Transatlantic Sketches-Lond-1833-Richard Bentley-8vo-2 vols-mod cl cov vel bckd bds,papr labls,map,10 etched plts-Howes A117-1st ed (u3,rbnd) 450.00

ALEXANDER,MARC-Man Who Exorcised the Bermuda Triangle-So Brunswick-1980-Barnes-cl,frntis,illus-1st Amer ed (l8,as new in dj) 12.50

ALEXANDER,MARC-Phantom Britain-Lond-1975-F Muller Ltd-8vo-256p-frntis,44 illus-1st ed (cc7,dj) 15.00*

ALEXANDER,MARY C-Punahou, 1841 to 1941-Berkeley-1941-U of Cal Pr-xiv+577p-beige cl,plts-1st ed (b2) 60.00

ALEXANDER,MARY C-William Patterson Alexander in Kentucky, the Marquesas, Hawaii-Honolulu-1934-priv prtd wi Yale U Pr-xviii,516p-grn bds,plts-1st ed (mm10) 40.00

ALEXANDER,MICHAEL-ED.-Discovering the New World-NY-1976-Harper & Row-1st US ed (v4,as new) 20.00

ALEXANDER,MICHAEL-Queen Victoria's Maharajah-NY-(1980)-Taplinger-8vo-326p-16p photos-1st US ed (dd5,f,f dj) 15.00

ALEXANDER,W B-Birds of the Ocean-NY-1928-12mo-428p-cl,88 plts (y8,dj wn) 21.00

ALEXANDER,W D-Brief History of the Hawaiian People-(1891)-Amer Bk Co-341p-dec cov,illus,col maps-assumed 1st ed (u8,sl wn sp,few discol pgs) 45.00

ALEXANDROV,VICTOR-Kremlin, Nerve Centre of Russian History-NY-(1963,60)-St.Martin's-8vo-335p-15 illus-1st US ed (jj5,sl wn dj) 15.00

ALFALFA-Nashville-1917-24p-wrps (j1) 12.50

ALFIERI,BERNARD-Where to Catch Salmon & Trout in England,Scotland,Wales & Ireland-Lond-1937-8vo-198p-photos,map-1st ed (m3,f) 17.50

ALFORD,T G-Paul Bunyan & Resinous Rhymes of the North Woods-1934-Derrydale-137p-ltd to 332c (gg3,pres cpy,cov spots) 100.00

ALGER,HORATIO,JR.-Rough and Ready-Bost-(1869)-Loring-300p-orig g grn cl,illus-1st ed,1st issue wi latr titles listed in ads as due Apr & Dec,& plt facing p217 (hh9,sl rub & fox) 175.00

ALGER,HORATIO,JR.-Young Explorer-Bost-(1880)-Loring-8vo-285p-orig g grn cl,illus-1st ed,1st issue(3rd title in Pacific Ser,only 2 prev titles listed in ads) (hh9,f) 175.00

ALGONKIANS-(Ottawa)-1938-Nat Mus of Can-8p-prtd wrps,illus,map-Anthro lflt #1 (k10) 10.00*

ALGREN,NELSON-Chicago-NY-1951-1st ed (s5,dj) 45.00

ALGREN,NELSON-Chicago-NY-1951-Dbldy-1st ed (h8,chip & edge wn dj) 35.00

ALGREN,NELSON-ED.-Own Book of Lonesome Monsters-NY-(1963)-1st ed (m4,wn dj) 15.00

ALGREN,NELSON-Last Carousel-NY-(1973)-Putnam's-435p-1st ed (f1,f,sp rub dj) 15.00

ALGREN,NELSON-Last Carousel-NY-(1973)-Putnam-1st ed (j3,f,dj) 20.00

ALGREN,NELSON-Man with the Golden Arm-GC-1949-Dbldy-1st ed (v5,f,dj sl wn,chip) 100.00

ALGREN,NELSON-Neon Wilderness-GC-1947-Dbldy-1st ed,1st state dj (c10,sl soil dj) 100.00

ALGREN,NELSON-Never Come Morning-NY-1942-Harper-1st ed (d8,f,sl chip dj) 250.00

ALGREN,NELSON-Notes From a Sea Diary-NY-1965-1st ed (n5,sl wn dj) 15.00

ALGREN,NELSON-Walk on the Wild Side-NY-1956-FSC-1st ed (x9,dj) 20.00

ALHAMBRA-(Alhambra)-nd-Board of Trade-(10)p-wrps-frnt cov photos (l1) 15.00

ALI SHAH,SIRDAR IKBAL-ED.-Book of Oriental Literature-NY-1938-Garden City Publ-cl-1st ed (l8,dj) 12.50

ALISON,F-Charles Rennie Mackintosh as a Designer of Chairs-Milan-1974-wrps,illus(incl col)-1st transl ed (ee1) 40.00

ALL FOR HER-NY,Lond-1877-429p-cl-Wright 67-1st ed (g1,sl wn,sp flecked) 22.50

ALLAIN,MARCEL-Lord of Terror-Phila-1925-McKay-1st US ed (d4,wk inner hng,sl wn sp) 15.00

ALLAN,D-Safari-NY-1963-214p (gg3,vf,dj) 12.00

ALLAN,E R P-March Past-Richmond-1938-274p-illus-1st ed (z10,covs soil) 60.00

ALLAN,IRIS-White Sioux-Sidney-1969-Gray's Publ-209p-e.p. maps,photo plts-1st ed (o2) 20.00

ALLAN,MEA-Hookers of Kew: 1785 to 1911-Lond-1967-M Joseph-273p-col frntis,plts,fldg tbl-scarce-1st ed (mm4,f,dj) 75.00

ALLAN,P B M-Trout Heresy-NY-1936-8vo-206p (m3) 25.00

ALLARD,WILLIAM A-Vanishing Breed-Bost-(1982)-Little,Brown-photos-1st ed (m7,f,dj) 50.00

ALLBEURY,TED-Choice of Enemies-Lond-1973-Davies-auth 1st bk-1st ed (r4,dj) 27.50

ALLBEURY,TED-Snowball-Phila-1974-Lippincott-1st Amer ed (h4,f,dj) 15.00

ALLEN & GINTER-Game Bird Album-(Richmond)-nd(ca.1880)-8 1/2 x 6-14p-hvy papr,card bnd & prtd on facing pgs only,col plts-scarce (ee3,vf) 120.00

ALLEN COUNTY-A GUIDE TO LIMA AND ...,OHIO-np-nd(1938)-WPA-64p-1st ed (e1,f,wrps) 40.00

ALLEN,A A-Book of Bird Life-NY-1954(1930)-8vo-426p-cl,illus (y8) 10.00

ALLEN,A A-Stalking Birds with Color Camera-Wash-1951-8vo-328p-cl,col & b&w photos (y8,dj) 18.50

ALLEN,ALBERT H-Arkansas Imprints, 1821 to 1876-NY-1947-R R Bowker-xx+236p-maroon cl-1st ed (m2) 50.00

ALLEN,ALBERT-Dakota Imprints 1858 thru 1889-NY-1947-221p-1st ed (t7) 30.00

ALLEN,C B-Wonder Book of the Air-Chig-(1936)-roy 8vo-xii,340p-illus cl g,frntis,illus-1st ed (t2) 35.00

ALLEN,C L-Bulbs and Tuberous Rooted Plants-NY-1919-Orange Judd-vi,311p (m10,soil,cov spots) 10.00

ALLEN,CECIL J-Locospotters Annual 1970-Lond-1970-64p-1st ed (n4) 12.00

ALLEN,CECIL J-Modern Railways-Lond-1959-307p-1st ed (n4,f,dj) 30.00

ALLEN,CECIL J-Titled Trains of Great Britain-Lond-1953-240p-3rd ed (n4,dj) 22.00

ALLEN,CHARLES D-American Bookplates-Lond-1895-Geo Bell & Sons-8vo-xv,437p-orig cl,t.e.g.,illus-1st Brit ed (w2,cov wn) 45.00

ALLEN,D L-ED.-Pheasants in North America-1956-Stackpole/Wldlf Mgmt Inst-490p-photos (bb3,f,dj) 38.00

ALLEN,D L-Michigan Fox Squirrel Management-Lansing-1943-8vo-404p-cl,frntis,photos (y8) 35.00

ALLEN,DAVID E-Victorian Fern Craze-Lond-(1969)-Hutchinson-8vo-83p-illus-1st Brit ed (gg5,f,dj) 20.00

ALLEN,DOUGLAS-Frederic Remington & the Spanish American War-NY-(1971)-4to-178p-illus-1st ed (h7,dj) 35.00

ALLEN,DR.WILLIAM A-Adventures with Indians and Game or Twenty Years in the Rocky Mountains-Chig-1903-Bowen-8vo-302p-lea sp over cl bds,illus-Six Guns #26-scarce-1st ed (b3,sp rprd) 125.00

ALLEN,DURWARD L-ED.-Pheasants in North America-Harrisburg-1956-Stackpole,Wildlife Inst-490p-frntis,drwngs (c9) 15.00

ALLEN,DURWARD L-Our Wildlife Legacy-NY-1954-8vo-422p-photos (m3) 10.00

ALLEN,E A-Jolly Trip-Cin-nd-W H Ferguson-266p-cl,illus (e1,sp chip) 22.50

ALLEN,EDWARD W-Mysterious Disappearance of Laperouse, the Vanishing Frenchman-Rutland-(1959)-Tuttle-8vo-321p-1st ed (cc5,sl chip dj,pres) 20.00

ALLEN,EDWARD W-Vanishing Frenchman, La Perouse-Rutland-(1959)-321p-illus-1st ed (f7,f,rprd dj,autg) 35.00

ALLEN,G FREEMAN-Last Years of British Steam: First Series-Lond-1968-1st ed (n4,f,dj) 18.00

ALLEN,G FREEMAN-Luxury Trains of the World-NY-1979-192p-1st ed (n4,f,dj) 24.00

ALLEN,G M-Birds and Their Attributes-Francestown-1948(1925)-8vo-338p-cl,col frntis,31 plts (y8,dj) 16.00

ALLEN,G-Hilda Wade-1900-Putnam-pict cl,illus-1st ed (x7,few stnd pgs) 100.00

ALLEN,GARDNER W-Papers of Francis Gregory Dallas-NY-1917-Naval Hist Scty-bds,frntis,3 illus (nn1,soil bds) 85.00

ALLEN,GAY-Two Poets of Leaves of Grass-Westwood-1969-Kindle Pr-8vo-wrps (x3) 20.00

ALLEN,GERALD-Architectural Drawing-NY-1981-Whitney Libr of Design-4to-200p-beige cl,col illus-1st prtg (r10,f,f dj) 30.00

ALLEN,GRANT-An African Millionaire-Lond-1897-Grant Richards-1st ed (w5) 300.00

ALLEN,H WARNER-Romance of Wine-NY-(1932)-264,(1)p-cl (d1) 15.00

ALLEN,H WARNER-Romance of Wine-NY-1932-Dutton-264p-1st ed (n6) 35.00

ALLEN,H-Story of the Airship-Akron-1942-8vo-x,74p-cl,illus (t2) 30.00

ALLEN,HERVEY-Action at Aquilla-NY-(1938)-369p-1st ed (c4,sl chip dj) 22.50

ALLEN,IDA B-Gastronomique-NY-1958-Dbldy-384p-red cl,drwngs-1st ed (q8,dj) 17.50

ALLEN,IDA B-Luscious Luncheons and Tasty Teas-Mpls-nd(ca.1928)-Buzza Co-59p-illus wrps,silken cord & tassels (l6) 22.00

ALLEN,J A-History of North American Pinnipeds-Wash-1880-785p-60 figs (bb3,ex-libr) 45.00

ALLEN,J A-History of North American Pinnipeds-Wash-1880-8vo-785p-cl,illus (y8,wn) 47.00

ALLEN,JAMES L-Reign of Law-NY-1900-Macmillan-385p-cl,dec cov-1st ed (aa1,sl spot cov) 15.00

ALLEN,JAMES S-Atomic Energy & Society-NY-1949-International-90p-wrps (r1,sl dmpstnd,sp wn) 15.00

ALLEN,JOHN H-San Juan-np-(1945)-J H Allen-53p-illus,Bugbee,ltd to 420c-v scarce (f9,sp wn) 50.00

ALLEN,JOHN H-Southwest-Phila-(1952)-Lippincott-220p-Herd 29-1st ed (cc4,sl wn dj) 25.00

ALLEN,JOHN L-Passage Through the Garden-1975-U of Ill Pr-lg 8vo-xxvi,412p-47 maps(incl dbl pg)-1st ed (aa3,f,dj) 45.00

ALLEN,JOHN L-Passage Through the Garden-Urbana-1975-412p-maps-1st ed (t7,f,dj) 35.00

ALLEN,JOHN W-It Happened in Southern Illinois-Carbondale-1968-400p-cl (g1) 15.00

ALLEN,LEE-Giants & the Dodgers-1964-Putnam-1st ed (ff2,dj) 60.00

ALLEN,LEE-Hot Stove League-1955-Barnes-1st ed (r7,brwng pgs,dj) 185.00

ALLEN,LEE-World Series-1969-Putnam-1st ed (p7,f,dj) 25.00

ALLEN,LUCY G-Choice Recipes for Clever Cooks-Bost-1924-Little,Brown-282p-1st ed (mm6,edgewn,sl soil,sl fox) 85.00

ALLEN,LUCY G-Table Service-Bost-1929-Little,Brown-128p-photos (l6) 20.00

ALLEN,MARGARET V-Achievement of Margaret Fuller-Univ Park-(1979)-Penn State U Pr-1st ed (k7,f,rub dj) 10.00

ALLEN,MAURY-Bo, Pitching and Wooing-1973-Dial-1st ed (r7,dj) 12.50

ALLEN,MAURY-Now Wait a Minute Casey-1965-Dbldy-1st ed (r7,f,dj) 15.00

ALLEN,MAURY-Where Have You Gone, Joe DiMaggio-1975-Dutton-1st ed (p7,f,dj) 15.00

ALLEN,MEL-You Can't Beat the Hours-1964-Harper-1st ed (ff2,dj) 12.50

ALLEN,PERRY-Navajoland USA-Window Rock-1968-Navajo Tribe-4to-1st ed (a6,f) 25.00

ALLEN,PHILIP S-Romanesque Lyric-Chapel Hill-1928-UNC Pr-cl-1st ed (l8) 35.00

ALLEN,R P-Roseate Spoonbill-NY-1942-4to-142p-wrps,col frntis,R T Peterson,plts (y8,fade) 37.00

ALLEN,R P-Roseate Spoonbill-NY-1942-Nat Audubon Soc-4to-xviii,142p-wrps,col frntis,20 plts-Rsrch Rprt No.2-Orig issue (jj10) 45.00

ALLEN,ROBERT F-Rugged Man's Life-Phila-(1968)-191p-cl-1st ed (g1,dj) 15.00

ALLEN,ROBERT J-Clubs of Augustan London-Cambridge-1933-Harvard-viii,305p-cl,frntis,plts-1st ed (dd10,f) 45.00

ALLEN,Robert P-Birds of the Caribbean-NY-1961-4to-256p-cl,98 col plts (y8,soil,dj chip) 45.00

ALLEN,ROBERT P-Birds of the Caribbean-NY-1961-Viking-256p-col photos (c9,sl wn dj) 25.00

ALLEN,ROBERT P-Whooping Crane-NY-1952-Nat Audubon Soc-246p-orig wrps-Rsrch Rprt No.3 (c9,sp top tn) 35.00

ALLEN,ROBERT T-Great Lakes-Tor-1970-oblng 8vo-160p-photos (m3,f,dj) 12.50

ALLEN,STEVE-Talk Show Murders-NY-1982-Delacorte-1st ed (r4,f,dj) 17.50

ALLEN,T B-Vanishing Wildlife of North Am-Wash-1974-8vo-207p-cl,col illus (y8) 13.00

ALLEN,T D-Navahos Have Five Fingers-Norman-(1963)-241p-illus,map e.p.-1st ed (v7,f,dj,review cpy) 25.00

ALLEN,T D-Navahos Have Five Fingers-Norman-1965-U of Okla-8vo-249p-cl (z4,f,dj) 13.50

ALLEN,WALTER F-English Walnuts-Lawrenceville-1912-priv prtd by auth-12mo-29p-4 half tone plts (jj7) 32.50

ALLEN,WILLIAM C-Quaker Diary in the Orient-San Jose-1915-Wright Eley-8vo-101p (y6,wn,cov soil,sl fox) 14.00

ALLEN,WOODY-Don't Drink the Water-NY-1967-Random-auth 1st bk-1st ed (z2,f,sl wn dj) 45.00

ALLEN,WOODY-Floating Light Bulb-NY-(1982)-Random-cl bckd bds-1st ed (jj8,as new in dj) 35.00

ALLEN,WOODY-Getting Even-NY-(1971)-Random-1st ed (b10,as new in dj) 50.00

ALLEN,WOODY-Getting Even-NY-1971-1st ed (s5,dj) 35.00

ALLEN,WOODY-Play It Again, Sam-NY-1969-1st ed (t5,sl dmpstnd pg cor,dj) 45.00

ALLEN,WOODY-Side Effects-NY-(1980)-1st ed (q5,f,dj) 15.00

ALLEN,WOODY-Side Effects-NY-(1980)-Random-1st ed (b5,as new in dj) 25.00

ALLEN,WOODY-Without Feathers-NY-(1975)-1st ed (s5,f,dj) 22.50

ALLEN,WOODY-Without Feathers-NY-(1975)-Random-1st ed (b5,as new in dj) 30.00

ALLER,PAUL-Build Your Own Adobe-(1947)-Stanford-110p-photos-2nd prtg (u7,dj) 20.00

ALLERTON,JAMES M-Tom Quick, the Avenger-Port Jervis-1888-(2),49p-wrps (aa6) 60.00

ALLERTON,R G-Brook Trout Fishing-NY-1869-12mo-61p+ads-illus-rare (m3,lacks trple fldout plt,vf) 400.00

ALLEVI,BAPTISTIN-Savarin Cookbook-NY-1929-Harper & Bros-262p-red bds,photo plts (l6,wn bds) 25.00

ALLEY,FREDERICK-Myopia Races and Riders 1879 to 1930-Hamilton-1931-Myopia Hunt Club-sm 4to-bds-1st ed (j9) 35.00

ALLGOOD,MARY B-Demonstration Techniques-NY-1947-Prentice Hall-147p-b&w photos (n6) 20.00

ALLHANDS,J L-Gringo Builders-1931-priv prtd-283p+indx-photos-1st ed (a9,autg) 150.00

ALLHANDS,J L-Tools of the Earthmover-Huntsville-1951-362p-emboss sim lea,photos-scarce (n10) 125.00

ALLHANDS,J L-Uriah Lott-San Antonio-1949-Naylor-187p-maps,photos (n10,pres,dj wn & tn) 75.00

ALLHUSEN,DOROTHY-Book of Scents and Dishes-Lond-1927-Williams & Norgate-257p-blu cl sp,pattrnd bds (m6,sl wn) 36.00

ALLINGHAM,MARGERY-Allingham Minibus-Lond-1973-Chatto-1st ed (f4,f,dj) 25.00

ALLINGHAM,MARGERY-Black Dudley Murder-GC-1929-Dbldy CC-1st Amer ed (w9,vf dj) 200.00

ALLINGHAM,MARGERY-Black Dudley Murder-NY-1929-Dbldy CC-1st Amer ed (f4,cov stns) 10.00

ALLINGHAM,MARGERY-Black Plumes-NY-1940-Dbldy CC-1st US ed (e4,dj) 30.00

ALLINGHAM,MARGERY-Cargo of Eagles-NY-1968-Morrow-1st Amer ed (q4,sl wn dj) 22.50

ALLINGHAM,MARGERY-China Governess-Lond-1963-Chatto-1st Brit ed (k4,f,dj) 25.00

ALLINGHAM,MARGERY-Gyrth Chalice Mystery-NY-1931-Dbldy CC-1st US ed (g4,f,sl stnd dj) 75.00

ALLINGHAM,MARGERY-Mystery Mile-NY-1930-Dbldy CC-1st US ed (f4) 15.00

ALLINGHAM,MARGERY-Oaken Heart-NY-1941-Dbldy-1st Amer ed (f4,f,sp rprd dj) 30.00

ALLINGHAM,MARGERY-Police at the Funeral-NY-1932-Dbldy CC-1st US ed (h4,sp fade) 15.00

ALLINSON,FRANCESCA-Childhood-Lond-1937-Hogarth Pr-187p-cl,engrvngs-Woolmer 404-1st ed (nn4,dj) 40.00

ALLISON,WILLIAM-Memories of Men and Horses-NY-1924-Brentano-1st US ed (j9,ex-libr) 35.00

ALLSOP,KENNETH-Hard Travellin'-NY-1967-NAL-1st ed (r1,chip dj) 25.00

ALLSOP,KENNETH-Hard Travellin'-NY-1967-NAL-1st ed (w5,f,sl chip dj) 20.00

ALLSOPP,FRED W-Folklore of Romantic Arkansas-np-1931-Grolier Soc-2 vols-cl,scarce (a1,uncut) 85.00

ALLYN,RUBE-Dictionary of Fishes-St.Petersburg-1948-4to-100p-col plts,photos,illus-scarce-1st ed (m3,vf,pres cpy) 25.00

ALMANAC FOR NEW YORKERS 1938-NY-(1937)-Modern Age Bks/WPA-118p+ads-pict wrps-scarce-1st ed (p1,f) 50.00

ALNER,JAMES Z-Capital Murder-1932-Knopf-1st ed (s10,dj) 30.00

ALPERN,A-Apartments for the Affluent-NY-1975-illus-1st ed (h10,dj) 75.00

ALPERS,ANTONY-Legends of the South Seas-NY-(1970)-Crowell-8vo-416p-cl-1st ed (y5,chip dj) 20.00

ALSOP,JOSEPH-Rare Art Traditions-NY-1982-Harper & Row-thk 4to-691p-grn cl,illus-Bollingen ser-1st ed (r10,f dj) 25.00

ALSOP,JOSEPH-We Accuse-NY-1954-S&S-4to-88p-wrps-1st ed (c2) 25.00

ALSOP,KENNETH-Bootleggers and Their Era-GC-1961-Dbldy-8vo-383p-photos-1st ed (b3,f,dj) 25.00

ALSTON,WALT-Year at a Time-1976-Word-1st ed (ff2,dj) 17.50

ALTER,J CECIL-James Bridger-SLC-1925-546p-pict cl,frntis,photos-Howes A191-1st ed (t7,autg) 175.00

ALTER,J CECIL-Through the Heart of the Scenic West-SLC-1927-Shepard Bk-220p-65 illus-ltd to 1000c,autg (dd4) 45.00

ALTHER,LISA-Kin Flicks-NY-1976-Knopf-auth 1st bk-1st ed (a5,as new in dj) 25.00

ALTHER,LISA-Original Sins-NY-1981-Knopf-1st ed (a5,as new in dj) 17.50

ALTICK,RICHARD D-To Be In England-NY-1969-Norton-illus-1st ed (y10,f,dj) 18.00

ALTROCCHI,JULIA C-Snow Covered Wagons-NY-1936-Macmillan-203p-map e.p.-1st ed (dd4) 25.00

ALTRURIAN COOK BOOK-Piqua-1910-Troy,Altrurian Club-246p-bds-3rd ed (n1) 17.50

ALTSCHUL,SIRI-Genus Anandenanthera in Amerindian Cultures-Cambridge-1972-Harvard-96p-cl (x6) 30.00

ALTSHULER,CONSTANCE W-Latest from Arizona!-Tucson-1969-Ariz Pioneers Hist Scty-(vi)+293p-orng cl,fldg map-1st ed (e2,dj) 25.00

ALVAREZ,A-Lost-Lond-1968-Turret Bks-8vo-cl-ltd to 250c,nbrd,autg-1st ed (u10,f) 35.00

ALVAREZ,A-Savage God-NY-(1972)-1st ed (g5,f,dj) 25.00

ALVORD JR,THOMAS G-Paul Bunyan & Resinous Rhymes of the North Woods-Derrydale-1934-8vo-137p-illus by auth-ltd to 332c,nbrd,autg-grn bndg (m3) 175.00

ALVORD JR.,THOMAS G-Paul Bunyan & Resinous Rhymes of the North Woods-Derrydale-1934-8vo-137p-illus by auth,ltd to 166c,nbrd-scarce-blu cl (m3,f) 225.00

ALY,BOWER-Rhetoric of Alexander Hamilton-NY-1941-Columbia Univ-x+226p-gry cl-1st ed (e2) 20.00

AMADO,JORGE-Tent of Miracles-NY-1971-Knopf-1st US ed (o5,dj sl tn & sl chip) 30.00

AMARAL,ANTHONY A-Commanche-LA-1961-86p-Dowd #12-ltd 1st ed (c7,f,dj) 35.00

AMAU,FRANK-Art of the Faker-Bost-1961-Little,Brown-illus-1st ed (y10,dj sl chip,tn) 25.00

AMBA,ACHMED-I Was Stalin's Bodyguard-Lond-1952-F Muller-256p-1st ed so stated (r1,dj wn,tape rprd) 17.00

AMBASZ,EMILIO-Architecture of Luis Barragan-NY-1976-MOMA(NYGS,Bost)-sm folio-128p-cl,94 illus(28 col) (cc10,as new in dj) 75.00

AMBLER,CHARLES H-History of Transportation in the Ohio Valley-Glendale-1932-Arthur Clark Publ-465p-t.e.g.,illus,fldg map-Amer Waterways Ser, Vol.3-1st ed (e7,unopened,f) 95.00

AMBLER,ERIC-Cause For Alarm-NY-1939-Knopf-1st Amer ed (w9,dj chip & tn) 85.00

AMBLER,ERIC-Coffin For Dimitrios-Cleve-1944-World-Photoplay ed wi movie scenes (f4,yel pgs,dj) 12.50

AMBLER,ERIC-Epitaph for a Spy-1952-Knopf-1st Amer ed (s10,dj) 25.00

AMBLER,ERIC-Judgement on Deltchev-NY-1951-1st US ed (q5,dj) 25.00

AMBLER,ERIC-Kind of Anger-Lond-1974-Bodley Head-1st ed (g4,dj) 12.50

AMBLER,ERIC-King of Anger-1974-Bodley Head-1st ed (n9,f,wn dj) 25.00

AMBLER,ERIC-Nightcomers-Lond-1956-1st Brit ed (q5,dj) 35.00

AMBLER,Eric-Passage of Arms-1960-Knopf-1st Amer ed (x7,2 djs) 35.00

AMBLER,Eric-Schirmer Inheritance-1953-Knopf-1st Amer ed (x7,f,dj) 22.00

AMBLER,ERIC-Schirmer Inheritance-NY-1953-Knopf-1st Amer ed (w1,f,dj) 25.00

AMBLER,ERIC-Send No More Roses-Lond-1977-Weidenfeld-1st ed (p4,sl wn cov,dj) 25.00

AMBROSE,GORDON-Hypnotherapy with Children-Lond-(1956)-Staples Pr Ltd-sm 8vo-(136)p-thatched blk cl-1st ed (y9,f,dj) 25.00

AMBROSE,STEPHEN E-Crazy Horse and Custer-GC-1975-486p-illus-1st ed (h7,f,dj) 45.00

AMBRUS,VICTOR-Mishka-1978-Warne-24p-1st Amer ed (v8,f,f dj) 22.00

AMENT,PAT-Master of Rock-Boulder-1977-197p-1st ed (a4,f,dj) 70.00

AMERICAN ALPS, OTHER SUMMER HAUNTS AND WINTER RETREATS-Bethlehem-1893-40p-pict wrps-prntd at Office of the White Mtn Echo (j1) 15.00

AMERICAN ANGLER'S GUIDE...-NY-1849-Long-sm 8vo-224p+ads-g dec grn cl,illus-4th ed,rvsd (t1,tn frnt e.p.) 100.00

AMERICAN BELL TEL CO-Deposition of Alexander Graham Bell in the Suit brought by the US to Annul the Bell Patents-Bost-1908-Amer Bell Tel-iv+469p-red cl,plts (c2,lacks e.p.) 85.00

AMERICAN CAN COMPANY-Canned Food Reference Manual-NY-(1939)-Amer Can Co-242p (l6) 20.00

AMERICAN CARAVAN-NY-1927-lg 8vo-843p-gilt grn cl (p2) 17.50

AMERICAN HERITAGE BOOK OF GREAT ADVENTURES OF THE OLD WEST-NY-1969-384p-photos,maps,illus-1st ed (t7,dj) 15.00

AMERICAN ORNITHOLOGISTS' UNION-Check List of North American Birds-1957-blu cl-5th ed (e9) 25.00

AMERICAN ORNITHOLOGISTS' UNION-Code of Nomenclature and Check List of North American Birds-NY-1886-AOU-392p-scarce (b9,hng sl crack) 95.00

AMERICAN ORNITHOLOGY-Vol.2,Jan. Dec.-Worcester-1902-8vo-wrps,col illus (y8) 18.50

AMERICAN PETROLEUM INSTITUTE-History of Petroleum Engineering-NY-1961-API-x+1241p-gry cl,illus-1st ed (g2) 75.00

AMERICAN STUFF: AN ANTHOLOGY OF PROSE & VERSE BY MEMBERS OF THE FEDERAL WRITERS' PROJECT-NY-1937-Viking/WPA-8vo-cl,illus-scarce-1st ed (p1) 50.00

AMERICAN TROTTING TURF-By Laws and Rules and Regulations...-NY-1873-73p-wrps (t7) 35.00

AMERICAN TYPE FOUNDERS CO.-Specimen Book and Catalogue-(Jersey City)-1923-1148p-cl,illus,622p type styles+256p of dec,etc. (z1,cov soil,sp rprd) 100.00

AMERINE,MAYNARD A-Check List of Books and Pamphlets on Grapes and Wines and Related Subjects. 1938 to 1948-Berkeley-1951-U of Cal Pr-240p (m6) 35.00

AMES,AZEL-Mayflower and Her Log, July 16,1620 to May 6, 1621-Bost-1901-Houghton Mifflin-8vo-xviii+376p-maps,illus-Howes A218-1st ed (b2,pres) 150.00

AMES,CHARLES E-Pioneering the Union Pacific-NY-1969-591p-1st ed (n4,f,dj) 33.00

AMES,DELANO-Death of a Fellow Traveler-NY-1950-Rinehart-1st US ed (f4,f,sl wn dj) 25.00

AMES,DELANO-Man with Three Chins-Chig-1968-Regnery-1st US ed (f4,f,sl wn dj) 12.50

AMES,DELANO-Man with Three Jaguars-Chig-1967-Regnery-1st US ed (f4,f,dj) 12.50

AMES,DELANO-Murder,Maestro,Please-NY-1952-Rinehart-1st US ed (f4,f,dj) 25.00

AMES,DELANO-No Mourning for the Matador-NY-1953-Washburn-1st US ed (f4,sp fade dj) 15.00

AMES,EVELYN-In Time Like Glass-Bost-1974-Houghton Mifflin-8vo-xvi,174p-cl-1st ed (ee9,dj) 16.00

AMES,EVELYN-Wind from the West-Bost-1970-Houghton Mifflin-1st ed (u4,dj) 10.00

AMES,FISHER,JR.-American Red Cross Work Among the French People-NY-1921-178p-photos-1st ed (dd3) 40.00

AMES,FRANCIS-Fishing the Oregon Country-Caldwell-1966-8vo-324p-photos-1st ed (m3,f,dj,pres cpy) 19.00

AMES,MARY C-Ten Years in Washington-Cin-1874-Queen City Publ-587p-lea,30p engrvd plts (d1,joints crckng) 20.00

AMIET,ERNEST-Palmer House-Chig-(1940)-John Willy-318p-blk cl,art deco cov illus,col & b&w photos-1st ed (q8) 17.50

AMIS,KINGSLEY-Anti Death League-NY-1966-1st US ed (p5,dj) 15.00

AMIS,KINGSLEY-Ending Up-NY-(1974)-Harcourt Brace-1st US ed (j3,f,dj) 20.00

AMIS,KINGSLEY-Every Day Drinking-Lond-(1983)-1st ed (e3,f,dj) 25.00

AMIS,KINGSLEY-Green Man-NY-1970-1st US ed (p5,dj) 15.00

AMIS,KINGSLEY-I Like It Here-NY-1958-1st US ed (p5,dj) 25.00

AMIS,KINGSLEY-James Bond Dossier-Lond-1965-1st Brit ed (r5,dj) 50.00

AMIS,KINGSLEY-On Drink-Lond-(1972)-Cape-16mo-107p-red cl,cartoons-1st ed (q8,dj) 12.50

AMIS,KINGSLEY-Riverside Villa Murders-Lond-1973-Cape-1st ed (p4,dj) 22.50

AMIS,KINSLEY-Green Man-NY-1970-HB&W-1st US ed (y1,f,f dj) 25.00

AMIS,MARTIN-Dead Babies-NY-1976-1st US ed (o5,dj) 45.00

AMIS,MARTIN-Other People-1981-Viking-1st US ed (m9,f,dj) 35.00

AMIS,MARTIN-Other People-NY-1981-1st US ed (p5,f,dj) 22.50

AMIS,MARTIN-Rachel Papers-NY-1974-Knopf-auth 1st bk-1st Amer ed (x10,f,f dj) 45.00

AMMONS,A R-Briefings-NY-(1971)-Norton-1st ed (l7,f,f dj) 40.00

AMORY,CLEVELAND-ED.-Celebrity Register-NY-1963-Harper-thk 4to-677p-photos-1st ed (b3) 45.00

AMORY,CLEVELAND-Home Town-NY-(1950)-Harper-1st ed (hh5,edgewn dj,autg) 15.00

AMORY,MARTHA B-Domestic and Artistic Life of John Singleton Copley-Bost-1882-Houghton Mifflin-8vo-cl-1st ed (oo6,wn cov & sp) 60.00

AMOS,ALAN-Fatal Harvest-NY-1957-Dbldy CC-1st ed (f4,f,sl wn dj) 12.50

AMOSOFF,N-Notes From the Future-NY-(1970)-S&S-1st US ed (j3,f,dj) 10.00

AMRAM,DAVID-Vibrations-NY-1968-1st ed (x8,sl wn dj) 45.00

AMSDEN,CHARLES A-Navaho Weaving-Santa Ana-1934-Fine Arts Pr-261p-orig dec cl,map e.p.,123 plts,some in col,(incl lg fldg plt)-scarce-1st ed (z1,cov rub,sunned,hng crack) 250.00

AMSHEY,EDWARD P-Picnic in November-NY-1956-Pageant-1st ed (g4,f,dj) 15.00

AMUNDSEN,R-First Crossing of the Polar Sea-GC-1928-Dbldy,Doran-8vo-324p-cl,frntis,18p plts,1 fldg map (t2,dj) 35.00

AMUNDSEN,R-First Crossing of the Polar Sea-NY-1927-Doran-roy 8vo-324p-cl,frntis,22p plts,1 fldg map-1st ed (t2,sl stnd,sp sl wn) 50.00

AMUNDSEN,R-Our Polar Flight-NY-1925-8vo-x,374p-illus cl g,frntis,35p plts,3p maps-1st ed (t2,uncut) 60.00

AN APPEAL TO PHARAOH. THE NEGRO PROBLEM, AND ITS RADICAL SOLUTION-NY-1889-Fords,Howrd & Hulbert-205p-cl-scarce-1st ed (b1) 50.00

ANDERS,CURT-Fighting Confederates-NY-(1968)-315p-maps-1st ed (n3,f,dj) 35.00

ANDERSCH BROS HUNTERS & TRAPPERS GUIDE-MN-1906-431p-illus (gg3,f) 12.00

ANDERSEN,HANS C-Danish Fairy Tales and Legends-Lond-1897-Bliss & Sands-332p-pict red cl gilt,16 tip in plts by W Heath Robinson(2 of which have been used for cov & sp illus)-1st ed thus (oo10,sp fade,sl rub,hng rprd) 150.00

ANDERSEN,HANS C-Fairy Tales-Lond-(1932)-Harrap-orig pict g cl,illus by A Rackham-1st trd ed (aa9) 350.00

ANDERSEN,HANS C-Hans Clodhopper-Phila-(1975)-Lippincott-retold & illus by L Shtainmets,col illus-1st ed (oo10,dj) 15.00

ANDERSON,A I-Artistic Side of Photography-NY-1911-Dodd,Mead-8vo-360p-cl,12 gravures,illus-1st ed (q3) 100.00

ANDERSON,A-How to Do the Black Art-NY-(1895)-Frank Tousey-12mo-orig pict wrps,illus (jj9,sl fray,pgs sl brwng) 75.00

ANDERSON,ALEX D-Silver Country or the Great Southwest-NY-1877-221p-rbnd wi part of orig cov laid on,fldg map-1st ed (t7,rbnd) 55.00

ANDERSON,ALICE S-Our Garden Heritage-NY-1961-Dodd-622p (x6,dj wn) 20.00

ANDERSON,ARLOW W-Salt of the Earth-Nashville-(1962)-Parthenon-8vo-338p-8p photos-1st ed (gg5,f,dj) 20.00

ANDERSON,C W-Deep Through the Heart-NY-1940-Macmillan-oblng 4to-1st prtg (h9,wn dj) 45.00

ANDERSON,C W-Miracle of Greek Sculpture-NY-1970-Dutton-sm 4to-112p-47 drwngs-1st ed (h9,dj) 45.00

ANDERSON,C W-Thoroughbreds-NY-1942-Macmillan-oblng 4to-1st prtg (h9,dj) 45.00

ANDERSON,CAPT ROBERT P-Personal Journal of the Siege of Lucknow-Lond-1858-110p-orng cl-scarce-1st ed (b7,cov fade & soil) 300.00

ANDERSON,E L-Modern Horsemanship-Edinburgh-1884-bds,photos-1st ed (j9) 35.00

ANDERSON,E L-Riding and Driving-NY-1905-Macmlln Amer Sprtsmn Libr-1st ed (f10) 40.00

ANDERSON,E T-Quarter Inch of Rain-Emporia-1964-220p-pict cl (t7) 30.00

ANDERSON,EDWARD-Thieves Like Us-1937-Stokes-1st ed (s10,sp chip dj) 35.00

ANDERSON,EVA G-Chief Seattle-Caldwell-1943-390p-e.p. maps-Tweney #2-1st ed (h7) 40.00

ANDERSON,FRANK J-An Illustrated History of the Herbals-NY-(1977)-Columbia Univ Pr-270p-illus (m6) 25.00

ANDERSON,FRANK J-Riches of the Earth-NY-1981-Rutledge Pr-223p-col illus-1st prtg (u5,f,f dj) 28.50

ANDERSON,FRANK W-Bill Miner Train Robber-Calgary-nd-56p-stiff pict wrps,photos,maps-1st ed (t7) 35.00

ANDERSON,HENRY-Medical and Surgical Aspects of Aviation...with Chapters...by Martin Flack-Lond-1919-255p-photo plts-1st ed (dd3,ex-libr) 300.00

ANDERSON,ISABEL-Odd Corners-NY-1917-Dodd Mead-8vo-368p-illus-1st ed (ff5,wn,dj wn,chip) 20.00

ANDERSON,J R L-Death in the Channel-NY-1976-Stein-1st Amer ed (r4,vf,dj) 17.50

ANDERSON,J R L-Death in the Thames-Lond-1974-Gollancz-1st ed (s4,dj) 20.00

ANDERSON,J R L-Vinland Voyage-Lond-(1967)-Eyre & Spottiswoode-8vo-278p-18 photos-1st Brit ed (cc5,dj) 17.50

ANDERSON,JAMES-Abolition of Death-NY-1975-Walker-1st Amer ed (p4,sl rub dj) 17.50

ANDERSON,JAMES-Assault & Matrimony-Lond-1980-Muller-1st ed (r4,dj) 17.50

ANDERSON,JOHN J-United States Reader...-NY-1884-Clark & Maynard-420p-1/2 lea (k1,sl wn sp) 12.50

ANDERSON,JOHN L-COMP.-15th Century Cookry Boke-NY-(1962)-Scribners-93p-blu cl,col illus-1st ed (q8,dj) 20.00

ANDERSON,JOHN Q-ED.-Tales of Frontier Texas 1830 to 1860-Dallas-1966-315p-1st ed (t7,f,dj) 12.50

ANDERSON,JOHN Q-Southwestern American Literature-Chig-(1980)-Swallow Pr-445p-cl-1st ed so stated (g1,dj) 15.00

ANDERSON,JOHN R L-Death in the Channel-NY-1976-Stein-1st US ed (g4,f,dj) 12.50

ANDERSON,JOHN R L-Death in the North Sea-NY-1976-Stein-1st US ed (g4,f,sl wn dj) 12.50

ANDERSON,K-Man Eaters & Jungle Killers-NY-1957-199p-photos (gg3,f,dj) 35.00

ANDERSON,MARGARET B-Robert Frost and John Bartlett-NY-(1963)-224p-cl-1st ed so stated (e1,dj) 15.00

ANDERSON,MARGARET-Unknowable Gurdjieff-Lond-1962-Routledge & K Paul-cl-1st ed (l8,chip dj) 25.00

ANDERSON,MARY E-Scenes in the Hawaiian Islands & California-Bost-(1865)-Amer Tract Scty-16mo-238p-col frontis-1st ed (u8,sl wn) 110.00

ANDERSON,MARY E-Scenes in the Hawaiian Islands and California-NY-(1865)-Amer Tract Scty-238p-grn cl,frontis-Sabin 1413-1st ed (h2,sl fox) 135.00

ANDERSON,MAXWELL-Knickerbocker Holiday-NY-(1938)-Anderson Hs-1st ed (aa10,fade,dj sl wn) 100.00

ANDERSON,MAXWELL-Night Over Taos-NY-1932-French-1st ed (a6,cov wn,sp fade) 20.00

ANDERSON,MAXWELL-Winterset-Wash D.C.-1935-cl cov bds-1st ed (r5,sl stnd bds,dj) 15.00

ANDERSON,MAYBELLE H-Appleton Harmon Goes West-Berkeley-1946-Gillick Pr-xvi+208p-blu cl-1st ed (k2) 25.00

ANDERSON,MAYBELLE HARMON-ED.-Journals of Appleton Milo Harmon-Glendale-1946-Arthur H Clark-sm 4to-xiv+208p-leatherette,col plt following t.p.-1st ed (z4) 35.00

ANDERSON,NEIL-Freckle Face-NY-(1957)-Crowell-33p-cl,illus by B Cooney-1st ed (oo10,f dj) 25.00

ANDERSON,PAUL L-Fine Art of Photography-Phila-1919-Lippincott-315p-24 photos-3rd impr (cc9,f,dj) 50.00

ANDERSON,PAUL L-Fine Art of Photography-Phila-1919-Lippincott-8vo-315p-illus-2nd prtg (t3) 60.00

ANDERSON,PAUL L-Fine Art of Photography-Phila-1919-Lippincott-8vo-cl-1st ed (y3,sl dmpstnd,dj) 45.00

ANDERSON,POUL-Avatar-NY-(1978)-Putnam-1st ed (j3,f,dj,autg) 30.00

ANDERSON,POUL-Fire Time-GC-1974-Dbldy-1st ed (k3,f,dj) 30.00

ANDERSON,POUL-Homeward and Beyond-GC-1975-Dbldy-1st ed (k3,f,dj) 30.00

ANDERSON,POUL-Midsummer Temptest-GC-1974-Dbldy-1st ed (k3,dj) 30.00

ANDERSON,POUL-Murder Bound-1962-Macmillan-1st ed (s10,brwnd pgs,dj sl soil) 67.50

ANDERSON,R V-Geology in Coastal Atlas of Western Algeria-1936-Geol Soc Amer Mem 4-450p-19 plts(incl fldg map & structure sects in pckt) (bb3,cov spot) 35.00

ANDERSON,ROBERT T-Old Timer and Other Poems-1909-Edmonton Prtg & Publ Co-8vo-103p-1/2 lea,mrbld covs & e.p.,9 illus-1st ed (cc7,sl wtrstnd,rbnd) 25.00*

ANDERSON,ROMOLA-Sailing Ship: Six Thousand Years of History-Lond-1926-Harrap (v4,sl fade) 50.00

ANDERSON,RUDOLPH M-Birds of Iowa-1907-Davenport Academy of Sci-417p-wrps (b9) 45.00

ANDERSON,RUDOLPH M-Birds of Iowa-Davenport-1907-Acad of Sci-8vo-(125-)417p-wrps,1 map (y8,chip wrps) 35.00

ANDERSON,RUFUS-Hawaiian Islands-Bost-1864-Gould & Lincoln-450p+ads-frntis,illus,fldg map-2nd ed (u8,sp sunned,sl wn) 200.00

ANDERSON,RUFUS-History of the Sandwich Islands-Bost-1870-Congregational Publ Scty-xxiv+408p-brwn cl,frontis,map,t.e.g.-1st ed (m2) 150.00

ANDERSON,SHERWOOD-Dark Laughter-1925-Boni & Liveright-1st ed (n9,sl sunned sp) 45.00

ANDERSON,SHERWOOD-Hello Towns-1929-Liveright-1st ed (q9) 35.00

ANDERSON,SHERWOOD-Jargon 45-Highlands-(1964)-Nantahala Fndtn-oblng 8vo-illus spiral bnd bds,11 photos by Sinsabaugh-ltd to 1550c (y3) 375.00

ANDERSON,SHERWOOD-Kit Brandon-NY-1936-1st ed (s5,sl chip dj) 50.00

ANDERSON,SHERWOOD-Letters of ...-Bost-(1953)-Little,Brown-photos-1st ed (d10,dj) 35.00

ANDERSON,SHERWOOD-Perhaps Women-NY-1931-1st ed (s5,sl curved rear bd,dj) 75.00

ANDERSON,SHERWOOD-Sherwood Anderson Reader-Bost-1947-Houghton Mifflin-1st ed (e10,dj) 40.00

ANDERSON,SHERWOOD-Tar-1926-Boni & Liveright-1st ed (s9,f) 45.00

ANDERSON,SHERWOOD-Triumph of the Egg-1921-Huebsch-1st ed (s9) 40.00

ANDERSON,SPARKY-Main Spark-1978-Dbldy-photos-1st ed (s8,f,dj) 10.00

ANDERSON,SUSANNE-Song of the Earth Spirit-NY-nd(ca.1973)-126p-dbl col,photo plts(incl col)-1st ed (v7,f,dj) 25.00

ANDERSON,T MCCLURG-Human Kinetics and Analysing Body Movements-Lond-1951-Heinemann-8vo-287p-245 illus-1st Brit ed (gg5,f,f dj) 20.00

ANDERSON,WILLIAM C-Bat 21-Englewood Cliffs-1980-1st ed (v9,f,f dj) 40.00

ANDERSON,WILLIAM M-They Died to Make Men Free-Berrien Spgs-1980-Hardscrabble Bks-320p-illus,maps (o7,f,f dj) 25.00

ANDERSON,WING-Prophetic Years 1947 to 1953-LA-1946-Kosmon Pr-234p-cl (h1) 15.00

ANDERSSON, C J-Lake Ngami-1967-Struik-546p-56 illus,lg fldg map-ltd to 750c,nbrd-facs of 2nd(1856)ed (bb3,f,rub dj) 75.00

ANDREE,S A-Andree's Story-NY-1930-Swede Scty Anthro & Geog-roy 8vo-xvi,390p-illus cl,frntis,42p plts,4p diags,5 maps incl 2 fldg-1st ed (t2,sp fade) 75.00

ANDREN,ERIK-Swedish Silver-NY-1950-Barrows-160p-frntis,photos-1st prtg (u5) 16.50

ANDREWS,BESSIE A-Colonial and Old Houses of Greenwich, New Jersey-Vineland-1907-priv prtd-87p-cl,plts-ltd to 500c (aa6) 50.00

ANDREWS,C L-Eskimo & His Reindeer in Alaska-1939-Caxton-253p-photos-1st ed (u8,chip dj) 60.00

ANDREWS,C L-Story of Sitka-Seattle-c.1922-Lowman & Hanford-108p-grn cl,frntis,plts,fldg map in rear-Ricks p.25-1st ed (oo1,few cov spots) 85.00

ANDREWS,E A-Young of the Crayfishes Astacus and Cambarus-1907-Smith Inst-79p-binder bd cov,9 plts (bb3) 20.00

ANDREWS,EDWARD D-Community Industries of the Shakers-Albany-1933-Univ of St of NY-322p-wrps-NY St Mus Hndbk 15-1st ed (v5,cor crease) 40.00

ANDREWS,FRANK D-Beginning of the Temperance Movement in Vineland-Vineland-1911-priv prtd-17p-wrps-ltd to 100c (aa6) 40.00

ANDREWS,KENNETH R-ED.-English Privateering Voyages to the West Indies-Cambridge-1959-Hakluyt Scty-8vo-xxvii,421p-blu cl,g,maps,illus,2nd Ser.No.CXI (nn1,dj soil & wn) 55.00

ANDREWS,KENNETH R-ED.-Last Voyage of Drake and Hawkins-Cambridge-1972-Hakluyt Scty-8vo-xiv,283p-blu cl,g,maps,plts-2nd Ser,Vol.142 (nn1,vf,vf dj) 40.00

ANDREWS,KEVIN-Flight of Ikaros-Lond-(1959)-Weidenfeld & Nicolson-8vo-255p-1st Brit ed (jj5,dj) 15.00

ANDREWS,MARY R S-Joy in the Morning-NY-1919-Scribner's-8vo-dec grn cl in 3 cols,frntis by N C Wyeth-1st ed (p1) 75.00

ANDREWS,MATTHEW P-Dixie Book of Days-Phila-1912-294p (hh3) 25.00

ANDREWS,MATTHEW P-Virginia the Old Dominion-1937-Dbldy,Doran-2 vols-blu lea wi gold coat of arms-1st ed (dd9,sl rub,box broken) 60.00

ANDREWS,MATTHEW P-Women of the South in War Times-Balt-1920-466p-cl-2nd prntg (l1) 20.00

ANDREWS,MYRTLE-Red Chili-Santa Fe-1941-Rydal-1st ed (a6,dj) 75.00

ANDREWS,RALPH W-Glory Days of Logging-Seattle-(1956)-4to-176p-illus-ltd ed (j7,chip dj,autg) 35.00

ANDREWS,RALPH W-Indian Primitive-Seattle-1960-Superior-4to-175p-photos-1st ed (d3,dj) 35.00

ANDREWS,RALPH W-Photographers of the Frontier West-Seattle-(1965)-Superior-4to-181p-1st ed (cc4,sl wn dj) 25.00

ANDREWS,RALPH W-Picture Gallery Pioneers, 1850 to 1875-Seattle-1964-Superior-4to-192p-illus,ports,photos-1st ed (k10,dj) 30.00*

ANDREWS,RALPH W-Redwood Classic-Seattle-1958-Superior-174p-photos-1st ed (d3,dj) 25.00

ANDREWS,RALPH W-This Was Seafaring-(1955)-Superior-4to-168p-photos-1st ed (r8,sl wn dj) 35.00

ANDREWS,RALPH-This Was Logging-(1954)-Superior-4to-157p-photos by D Kinsey-1st ed (r8,dj sl chip,crease) 35.00

ANDREWS,ROGER-Old Fort Mackinac on the Hill of History-Menominee-1938-Herald Leader Pr-188p-pict cl,maps,photos-1st ed (gg4) 20.00

ANDREWS,ROY C-An Explorer Comes Home-GC-1947-8vo-276p-illus,T Voter-1st ed (m3,f,dj) 25.00

ANDREWS,ROY C-ED.-My Favorite Stories of the Great Outdoors-NY-1950-8vo-404p (m3,fray dj) 17.50

ANDREWS,ROY C-On the Trail of Ancient Man-NY/Lond-1926-Putnam's-xxiv,375p-grn cl wi g titles,dec e.p.,port,58 photos,J B Shackelford,errata & erratum tip in-1st ed (ll1) 65.00

ANDREWS,RUTH H-First Thirty Years-Lubbock-1956-Tex Tech Pr-392p-photos-ltd to 2000c,nbrd,autg-1st ed (v3) 35.00

ANDREWS,V C-My Sweet Andrina-NY-(1982)-Poseidon-1st ed (h3,f,dj) 15.00

ANDREWS,WAYNE-American Gothic-NY-1975-92 illus-1st ed (h10,dj) 35.00

ANDRICH,DON-Steelhead, Steelheaders, Steelheading-Hoodriver-1971-8vo-44p-wrps,illus (m3,vf) 15.00

ANDRIEU,PIERRE-Fine Bouche-Lond-(1956)-Gassell-274p-blu cl,errata slip-1st ed (q8) 30.00

ANDRIST,RALPH K-Long Death-NY-(1964)-Macmillan-371p-illus,maps-1st ed (gg4,dj) 30.00

ANDRIST,RALPH K-Long Death-NY-(1964)-Macmillan-sm 4to-ix+371p-cl,illus,maps-1st ed (z4,sp fade dj) 35.00

ANDROUET,PIERRE-Complete Encyclopedia of French Cheese-NY-(1973)-Harper's Mag-545p-illus-1st ed (o6) 30.00

ANDRY,NICOLAS-Orthopaedia-Phila-1961-2 vols-leatherette-(facs of Lond 1743 ed) (dd3,box) 150.00

ANESAKI,MASAHARU-Art,Life and Nature in Japan-Bost-1933-Marshall Jones Co-178p-illus (c3,wn dj) 40.00

ANGELL,ROGER-Day in the Life of ...-1970-Viking-1st ed (s8,f,dj) 25.00

ANGELL,ROGER-Five Seasons-1977-S&S-1st ed (r7,dj) 15.00

ANGELL,ROGER-Five Seasons-1977-S&S-1st ed (s8,f,dj) 17.50

ANGELL,ROGER-Late Innings-1982-S&S-1st ed (r7,f,f dj) 15.00

ANGELL,ROGER-Stone Arbor-1960-Little,Brown-dj illus,E Gorey,auth 1st bk-1st ed (x2,vf,dj) 35.00

ANGELL,ROGER-Summer Game-1972-Viking-1st ed (ff2,dj) 25.00

ANGELL,TONY-Ravens,Crows,Magpies,and Jays-Seattle-1978-U of Wash-112p-drwngs (c9,sl spot cov) 15.00

ANGELO,VALENTI-Hill of Little Miracles-NY-1942-Viking-200p-cl,drwngs,auth-1st ed (r3,f,dj) 35.00

ANGELO,VALENTI-Nino-NY-1938-Viking-244p-cl,mono illus,auth-1st ed (s3,cov tan,sl soil) 20.00

ANGELOU,MAYA-And Still I Rise-NY-(1978)-Random Hs-1st ed (c10,f,dj) 20.00

ANGELOU,MAYA-Heart of a Woman-NY-1981-Random-1st ed (y1,f,dj) 30.00

ANGELOU,MAYA-I Know Why a Caged Bird Sings-NY-1969-auth 1st bk-1st ed (n5,sl chip dj) 45.00

ANGELOU,MAYA-Oh Pray My Wings are Gonna Fit Me Well-NY-1975-Random-1st ed (v5,f,f dj) 15.00

ANGELOU,MAYA-Shaker, Why Don't You Sing?-NY-(1983)-Random-1st ed (k7,f,dj) 30.00

ANGELOU,MAYA-Singin' and Swingin' and Gettin' Marry Like Christmas-NY-1976-Random-1st ed (y1,f,dj) 35.00

ANGELUCCI,ENZO-Ships-NY-1983-Greenwich Hs-4to-336p-cl over bds,illus-1st ed thus (p8,f,f dj) 25.00

ANGIER,BRADFORD-Wilderness Cookery-Harrisburg-(1961)-Stackpole-sm 8vo-256p-illus (u6) 15.00

ANGIER,R H-Firearm Blueing & Browning-Harrisburg-nd-8vo-151p-illus (m3,vf,dj) 12.50

ANGIER,R H-Firearm Blueing and Browning-Harrisburg-1936-152p-illus-1st ed (t7,dj) 30.00

ANGLE,PAUL M-Great Chicago Fire...-Chig-1946-Chig Hist Soc-85p-gry cl,drwngs (cc3,dj) 30.00

ANGLE,PAUL M-Here I Have Lived-Springfield-1935-A Lincoln Assoc-xvi+313p-blu cl,illus,fldg map-1st ed (h2) 20.00

ANGLE,PAUL M-Tragic Years, 1860 to 1865-NY-1960-2 vols-maps-1st ed (c4,sl soil box,sp labl wn) 37.50

ANGLER'S CLUB OF NEW YORK-Well Dressed Lines Stripped From the Reels of Five New Englanders-1962-priv prntd-8vo-82p-one of 500c-scarce (m3,f) 110.00

ANGLO,MICHAEL-Penny Dreadfuls and Other Victorian Horrors-Lond-(1977)-Jupiter-4to-125p-bds,illus-1st ed (x4,dj) 35.00

ANGUS,MARK-Modern Stained Glass in British Churches-Mowbray-1984-120p-pict wrps,col illus-1st ed (cc8) 30.00

ANLEY,GWENDOLYN-Irises-Lond-1946-xx,115p-32 b&w photo plts,e.p. maps-1st ed (j10,drknd,dj tattrd) 20.00

ANN AND HER LITTLE BOOK-Phila-nd-Amer Sunday-Schl Union-7,(1)p+wrps,wdcuts (n1) 15.00

ANNABEL,R-Tales of a Big Game Guide-NY-1938-Derrydale-198p-red cl wi tan buckr sp & cor,g title on lea sp labl,g decs-ltd to 950c,nbrd (ee3,vf) 400.00

ANNABEL,RUSSELL-Hunting & Fishing in Alaska-NY-1948-8vo-341p+index-photos,col frontis-1st ed (m3,fray dj) 90.00

ANNABEL,RUSSELL-Tales of a Big Game Guide-(1938)-Derrydale-8vo-198p-ltd to 950c,nbrd-photos-scarce (m3,sl fade sp label) 325.00

ANNABEL,RUSSELL-Tales of a Big Game Guide-NY-(1938)-Derrydale-8vo-cl,photos-ltd to 950c,nbrd-1st ed (u10,f) 450.00

ANNO,M-Anno's Counting Book-NY-1977-Crowell-sm 4to-unpgd-col illus-1st US ed (nn8,f,dj sp chip) 35.00

ANNO,MITSUMASA-Anno's Italy-NY-(1971)-Collins-sm 4to-unpgd-pict glossybds-1st US ed (r3,f,f dj) 30.00

ANNO,MITSUMASA-Upside Downers-NY & Tokyo-(1971)-Weatherhill-sm 4to-pict cl-1st US ed (s3,f dj) 40.00

ANONYMOUS-Master of Mysteries-Indpls-1912-Bobbs-auth is Gelett Burgess-1st ed (d4,sm sp tr,sl fox & fade) 85.00

ANONYMOUS-President Vanishes-NY-1934-Farrar-auth is Rex Stout-1st ed (d4,dj sp chip,rprd) 250.00

ANSON,GEORGE-Anson's Voyages-Lond-1776-Bowers & Nichols-bds,rbkd in mor,orig nameplate on sp,42 plts(1 bnd out of order)-15th ed (z2,rbkd,cor wn) 875.00

ANSON,GEORGE-Voyage Round the World-Lond-1748-Knapton-contemp polished calf,g sp,3 fldg maps-Sabin 1626-3rd ed (dd7) 650.00

ANSTEY,F-Baboo Jabberjee, B.A.-Lond-1897-Dent-272p-t.e.g.,illus-1st ed (ll2) 25.00

ANTARCTIC BIBLIOGRAPHY.-Vol.I-Wash D.C.-1965-GPO-4to-506p-blu cl (ee7) 45.00

ANTHOLOGY OF VERSE-Columbus-1926-Ohio St Univ-1st ed (cc2) 150.00

ANTHONY,IRVIN-Paddle Wheels and Pistols-Phila-(1929)-329p-cl-1st ed so stated (e1) 15.00

ANTHONY,KATHARINE-Lambs-NY-1945-Knopf-1st ed (hh5,dj) 10.00

ANTHONY,KATHERINE-Queen Elizabeth-NY-1929-Knopf-8vo-263p-16 illus-1st ed (jj5,edgewn dj) 17.50

ANTHONY,SUSAN B-Ghost in My Life-NY-(1971)-Chosen Bks-221p-cl (d1,f,dj) 15.00

ANTIGUA AND THE ANTIGUANS-1967-Spottiswood Ballantyne-2 vols-rprnt of rare 1844 ed (bb3,f) 45.00

ANTIN,MARY-Promised Land-Bost,NY-1912-373p-cl-1st ed (aa1) 30.00

ANTIOCH BOOKPLATES-Yellow Springs-nd-Antioch Bkplt Co.-32p-trade cat-wrps,illus,incl col & tip in (f1) 32.50

ANTIQUARIAN AND TOPOGRAPHICAL CABINET-Lond-1807-W Clarke-10 vols-3/4 lea,engrvngs (l9) 1,650.00

APEL,WILLI-Harvard Dictionary of Music-1969-Belknap/Harvard-2nd rvsd ed (u4,sl wn & sp fade,dj) 30.00

APICUS-Roman Cookery Book-Lond-(1958)-Harrap-240p-grn cl,photos,drwngs-1st ed thus (q8,edgewn dj) 30.00

APOLLINAIRE,G-Apollinaire on Art-1972-Viking-1st Engl lang ed (h10,dj) 45.00

APOLLINAIRE,GUILLAUME-Poet Assassinated-NY-1923-Broom-ltd to 1250c,nbrd (v5) 35.00

APPEL,B-Four Roads to Death-1935-Knopf-1st ed (x7,dj) 65.00

APPEL,B-Raw Edge-1958-Random-1st ed (x7,f,dj) 17.00

APPEL,BENJAMIN-Four Roads to Death-NY-1935-Knopf-1st ed (d4,sl stnd cov) 20.00

APPEL,MARTIN-Baseball's Best-1977-McGraw Hill-photos-1st ed (s8,f,dj) 25.00

APPLE,MAX-Oranging of America-NY-1976-Grossman-auth 1st bk-1st ed (b5,as new in dj) 35.00

APPLE,MAX-Zip-NY-(1978)-Viking-1st ed (bb1,as new in dj) 20.00

APPLEGATE,FRANK G-Indian Stories from the Pueblos-Phila-1929-178p-col illus-scarce-1st ed (v7) 45.00

APPLEGATE,FRANK G-Indian Stories from the Pueblos-Phila-1929-Lippincott-col illus-1st ed (a6) 60.00

APPLEGATE,FRANK G-Native Tales of New Mexico-Phila-(1932)-263p-col illus-Adams Guns#66-1st ed (u7,dj) 45.00

APPLEGATE,JESSE A-Day with the Cow Column in 1843-Chig-1934-207p-pict cl,illus,Ltd to 300c-Herd #108-scarce-1st ed (t7) 135.00

APPLER,A C-Younger Brothers-NY-(1955)-F Fell-245p-Six Guns 69-1st ed (gg4,dj) 15.00

APPLETON,LEROY H-Indian Art of the Americas-NY-(1950)-tall-270p-75 col plts,map-1st ed (u7) 65.00

APPLETON,TONY-COMP.-Typological Tally-Brighton-1973-Dolphin Pr-94p-ltd to 1250c-1st ed (k9,vf,dj) 17.50

APPLETON-Dictionary of Machines, Mechanics, Engine Work and Engineering-NY-1866-Appleton-2 vols-half blk lea,illus (c2,sl rub) 165.00

APPLEYARD,ROLLO-Tribute to Michael Faraday-1931-204p-30 illus-rare-1st ed (h6,f) 25.00

APPLIN,ARTHUR-Philandering Angler-Lond-nd-8vo-176p-illus,Watkins-Pitchford-1st ed (m3,dj) 15.00

APPLIN,ARTHUR-Stories of the Russian Ballet-NY-nd-John Lane-4to-97p-beige papr sp,red cl,t.e.g.,deckled edges,21 photos (r10) 50.00

APSLEY,ALDY-Bridleways Through History-Lond-1948-Hutchinson-2nd ed rvsd (h9,dj) 45.00

APTE,STU-Fishing in the Florida Keys & Flamingo-Miami-1976-8vo-80p-wrps-photos,maps-1st prntng (m3,f) 15.00

APTHEKER,HERBERT-Colonial Era-NY-1959-Int'l-158p (r1,dj) 20.00

APTHEKER,HERBERT-Laureates of Imperialism-NY-1954-Masses & Mainstream-96p-wrps (r1) 15.00

APTHEKER,HERBERT-Mission to Hanoi-NY-(1966)-Intl Publ-wrps,photos-1st ed (ff3) 30.00

APTHEKER,HERBERT-Negro in the Abolitionist Movement-NY-1941-Int'l-wrps-1st ed (w5) 15.00

APTHEKER,HERBERT-Negro Today-NY-nd-Marzani & Munsell-wrps-1st ed (w5,f) 15.00

ARAGON,LOUIS-Bells of Basel-NY-1936-Harcourt-1st ed (w5,f,dj) 60.00

ARALDO,JOSEPHINE-Cooking with Josephine-SF-1977-Strawberry Hill Pr-218p-wrps-1st prtg (l6) 15.00

ARBAUGH,GEORGE B-Revelation in Mormonism-Chig-(1932)-U of Chig Pr-xii+252p-blu cl-1st ed (h2,chip dj) 35.00

ARBER,AGNES-Herbals-Cambridge-1912-Univ Pr-253p-illus (m6,soil) 100.00

ARBERRY,A J-TRANSL.-Discourse of Rumi-Lond-1961-J Murray-cl-1st prtg (l8,f) 35.00

ARBONA,FRED L-Mayflies, The Angler & The Trout-Tulsa-1980-4to-188p-illus-1st ed (m3,f,dj) 35.00

ARBUTHNOT,T S-African Hunt-NY-1964-269p-photos (gg3,f,dj,autg) 45.00

ARCHER,GLEASON L-History of Radio to 1926-1938-421p-20 photos-rare-1st ed (h6,f) 65.00

ARCHER,JEFFREY-Prodigal Daughter-1982-Linden Pr-1st Amer ed (s10,dj) 12.50

ARCHITECTURAL BEAUTY IN JAPAN-NY-(1956)-Studio Publ-lg 4to-164p-illus-1st US ed (ee5) 25.00

ARCINIEGAS,GERMAN-Caribbean, Sea of the New World-NY-1946-Knopf-8vo-464p-16 illus-1st US ed (jj5,dj) 15.00

ARCTANDER,JOHN W-Apostle of Alaska-NY,Chig,Tor-(1909)-395p+4p ads-illus-1st ed (d7,sl spot sp) 100.00

ARD,WILLIAM-As Bad As I Am-NY,Tor-(1959)-Rinehart-1st ed (bb1,dj) 20.00

ARD,WILLIAM-Hell is a City-NY-1955-Rinehart-1st ed (g4,pgs yel,sp chip dj) 15.00

ARD,WILLIAM-Root of His Evil-NY-(1957)-Rinehart-1st ed (l3,f,dj) 20.00

ARDENNE,MANFRED VON-Television Reception-1936-121p-50 photos,46 illus-rare-1st Engl language ed (h6) 55.00

ARDIZZONE,EDWARD-Ship's Cook Ginger-NY-(1978)-Macmillan-4to-48p-pict bds,col & b&w illus-1st US ed (nn10,as new in dj) 40.00

ARDIZZONE,EDWARD-Tim's Last Voyage-Lond-1972-Bodley Head-4to-unpgd-pict bds,illus,auth-1st ed (r3,f,dj) 40.00

ARDREY,ROBERT-Worlds Beginning-NY-(1944)-1st ed (q5,sl wn dj) 25.00

ARDREY,ROBERT-Worlds Beginning-NY-(1944)-DSP-1st ed (hh5,dj) 20.00

ARENDT,HANNAH-Men in Dark Times-1968-HB&W-1st ed (s9,f,dj) 25.00

ARENSBERG,ANN-Sister Wolf-NY-1980-Knopf-auth 1st bk-1st ed (a10,as new in dj) 20.00

ARENSBERG,ANN-Sister Wolf-NY-1980-Knopf-auth 1st bk-1st ed (k7,f,dj) 30.00

ARESTY,ESTHER B-Delectable Past-(1964)-S&S-254p-gry bds,photos-1st prtg (q8) 17.50

ARESTY,ESTHER B-Delectable Past-NY-(1964)-S&S-254p-1st prtg (m6,dj) 20.00

ARESTY,ESTHER B-Exquisite Table-Indpls-(1980)-Bobbs Merrill-257p-orng cl,photos-1st prtg (q8,dj) 15.00

ARETZ,GERTRUDE-Napoleon and His Women Friends-Phila-1927-Lippincott-8vo-375p-16 illus-1st US ed (jj5) 15.00

ARGENZIO,VICTOR-Diamonds Eternal-NY-(1974)-McKay-290p-illus-1st ed (u5,f,f dj) 35.00

ARGYLL,DUKE OF-Reign of Law-NY-1884-265p-cl (m1) 15.00

ARIS,GEORGE-Fifth British Division 1939 to 1945-Lond-1959-266p-maps,illus-1st ed (gg2,f,dj) 125.00

ARKIN,FRIEDA-Cook's Companion-NY-1968-Dbldy-172p-1st ed (m6,tn dj) 9.00

ARKLE,WILLIAM-Geography of Consciousness-Lond-1974-Neville Spearman-cl-1st ed (o8,f,dj) 17.50

ARLEN,MICHAEL-Babes in the Wood-NY-1929-Dbldy-1st ed (t4,f,dj) 15.00

ARMER,LAURA A-Forest Pool-NY-(1938)-Longmans,Green-4to-40p-dec cl,illus,8 paintings,auth-1st ed (s3,dj sp wn & chip) 50.00

ARMER,LAURA A-In Navajo Land-NY-1962-107p-photos-1st ed (v7,f,dj) 20.00

ARMER,LAURA A-Waterless Mountain-NY-1931-Longmans,Green-sm 4to-212p-pict cl,illus,S Armer-1st ed (r3) 30.00

ARMES,COL.GEORGE A-Ups and Downs of an Army Officer-Wash D.C.-1900-784p-illus,lea title labl-1st ed (cc4,rbckd) 200.00

ARMES,ETHEL-Stratford Hall-1936-Garrett & Massie-575p-illus-1st ed (dd9,sl tn dj) 120.00

ARMES,JAY J-Jay J Armes, Investigator-NY-(1976)-Macmillan-8vo-234p-16p photos-1st ed (bb5,dj,autg) 15.00

ARMISTEAD,J J-An Angler's Paradise & How to Obtain it-Scarborough-1895-8vo-304p-illus (m3) 30.00

ARMISTEAD,J J-An Angler's Paradise and How to Obtain It-Scarborough-1895-Engl,Angler Ltd-tall 8vo-xvi,304p-orig cl,illus-1st ed (pp8,sp fade) 75.00*

ARMISTEAD,WILSON-Trout Waters-Lond-1908-8vo-203p-1st ed (m3) 25.00

ARMITAGE,ALBERT B-Two Years in the Antarctic-Lond-1905-Edw Arnold-8vo-315p+16p ads-grn cl,fldg map,illus-1st ed (dd7,sp fade,sl fox) 650.00

ARMITAGE,ETHEL-Country Garden-NY-1936-Macmillan-226p-wood engrvngs (x6,vf,dj) 25.00

ARMITAGE,ETHEL-Country Garden-NY-1936-Macmillan-4to-(4),226p-cl,24 illus (cc10,sun cl,dj) 45.00

ARMITAGE,FLORA-Desert and the Stars-NY-1955-1st ed (b7,f,dj) 30.00

ARMITAGE,MERLE-Dance Memoranda-NY-1946-DS&P-4to-242p-cl,illus-2nd ed (t3) 45.00

ARMITAGE,MERLE-Fit for a King-(1939)-DS&P-258p-blk cl,4 photos by E Weston,drnwgs-1st prtg (q8,cov soil) 40.00

ARMITAGE,MERLE-Merle Armitage's Accent on Life-Iowa-1965-Iowa St U Pr-8vo-386p-cl-1st ed (t3,f,dj) 75.00

ARMITAGE,MERLE-Operations: Santa Fe-1948-DS&P-263p-1st ed (d3) 35.00

ARMITAGE,MERLE-Operations: Santa Fe-NY-1948-252p+index-illus,maps-1st ed (v7,dj) 50.00

ARMITAGE,MERLE-Rendevous with the Book-Brklyn-1949-Geo McKibbin & Son-8vo-30p-cl,illus-1st ed (x4) 20.00

ARMITAGE,MERLE-Stella Dysart of Ambrosia Lake-NY-1959-162p-photos,map e.p.-1st ed (t7,dj) 12.50

ARMOUR,J OGDEN-Packers, the Private Car Lines and the People-Phila-(1906)-Altemus-380p-cl-Rampaging Herd 167 (b1) 75.00

ARMOUR,J OGDEN-Packers, the Private Car Lines and the People-Phila-(1906)-Altemus-380p-cl-Reese(Six Score)#6 (f1) 65.00

ARMOUR,MARGARET-TRANSL-Fall of the Nibelungs-Lond-1897-J M Dent-cl,illus & decs,W B Macdougall-1st ed (o8,edge wn) 25.00

ARMOUR,RICHARD-Golf is a Four Letter Word-NY-1962-1st ed (ll7,f,f dj,autg) 25.00

ARMS,D N-Fishing Memories-NY-1938-184p-illus (gg3,f) 20.00

ARMSTRONG,A N-Oregon-Fairfield-1969-Ye Galleon Pr-147p-e.p. maps-rprnt (j7) 30.00

ARMSTRONG,CHARLOTTE-Duo-NY-1959-Coward-1st ed (h4,dj) 15.00

ARMSTRONG,DR NELSON-Nuggets of Experience-np-1906-257p-pict cl,illus-1st ed (c4) 55.00

ARMSTRONG,G H-Origin and Meaning of Place Names in Canada-Tor-1930-Macmillan-8vo-vii,312p,1p errata-red cl-1st ed (cc7,ex-libr) 75.00*

ARMSTRONG,HARRY-Principles and Practice of Aviation Medicine-Balt-1941-496p-photos-1st ed,3rd prtg (dd3) 100.00

ARMSTRONG,JAMES E-Life of a Woman Pioneer as Illustrated in the Life of Elsie Strawn Armstrong 1789 to 1871...-Chig-1931-127p-cl (m1,pres cpy) 22.50

ARMSTRONG,LE ROY-An Indiana Man-Chig-1891-Schulte-218p-cl-Wright 129 (n1,bndg sl askew) 17.50

ARMSTRONG,LOUIS-Satchmo: My Life in New Orleans-NY-(1954)-Prentice Hall-1st ed (w1,f,dj) 30.00

ARMSTRONG,M K-History and Resources of Dakota, Montana, and Idaho-Pierre-1928-62p-wrps,orig publ in 1866 (t7) 30.00

ARMSTRONG,MARGARET-Fanny Kemble-NY-1938-387p-cl-1st ed (d1,sl wn dj) 15.00

ARMSTRONG,MARGARET-Murder in Stained Glass-1939-Random Hs-1st ed (s10,dj rprd,sp wn) 25.00

ARMSTRONG,MOSES K-Early Empire Builders of the Great West-St.Paul-1901-E W Porter-456p-illus-1st ed (ff4) 50.00

ARMSTRONG,NEVILL A D-After Big Game in the Upper Yukon-Lond-1937-J Long-8vo-287p+8p ads-blk cl,map e.p.,photos,maps (ee7) 150.00

ARMSTRONG,PERRY A-Sauks and Black Hawk War-Springfield-1887-H W Rokker-726p-brwn cl-Howes A324-1st ed (h2,sl rub cov) 165.00

ARMSTRONG,REV LEBBEUS-Temperance Reformation-NY-1853-Fowler & Wells-orig cl (u2,sl fox) 30.00

ARMSTRONG,T-ET AL-200 Years of American Sculpture-NY-1976-Whitney Mus/Godine-folio-353 illus(incl col)-1st ed (h10,dj) 75.00

ARMSTRONG,W H-Warriors in Two Camps-Syracuse-1978-195p-illus (z10,f) 17.50

ARMY HORSE IN ACCIDENT AND DISEASE-Wash-1909-GPO-1st ed thus (h9) 35.00

ARMY TIMES-ED.-History of the U.S. Signal Corps-NY-(1961)-Putnam-lg 8vo-192p-illus-1st ed (gg5,dj chip,tn) 12.50

ARNDT,J W-Early History of Green Bay and the Fox River Valley-De Pere-1894-Democrat Print-57p-wrps,dbl cols-rare (l1,sp pc lacking frnt wrpr) 75.00

ARNHEIM,R-Art & Visual Perception-Berkeley-1954-UC Pr-3 col plts-1st ed (h10,dj) 85.00

ARNO,PETER-Whoops Dearie-NY-1927-S&S-auth 1st bk-1st ed (w5,new frnt e.p.) 25.00

ARNOLD,ANNA E-History of Kansas-Topeka-1914-State of Ks-250p-illus-1st ed (v8) 10.00

ARNOLD,E C-British Waders-Cambridge-1924-4to-102p-cl,51 col plts (y8,sp fade,e.p. soil) 85.00

ARNOLD,H H-Army Flyer-NY-(1942)-8vo-xiv,300p-cl,frntis-1st ed (t2,chip dj) 20.00

ARNOLD,H H-Global Mission-NY-(1949)-8vo-xii,626p-cl,plts-1st ed (t2,dj) 40.00

ARNOLD,H H-This Flying Game-NY-(1938)-8vo-xx,308p-cl,frntis,64p plts-2nd ed rvsd & enlgd (t2,chip dj) 40.00

ARNOLD,H H-Winged Warfare-NY-(1941)-8vo-xviii,266p-cl,plts,e.p. maps-1st ed (t2) 25.00

ARNOLD,H J P-William Henry Fox Talbot-Lond-(1977)-Hutchinson Benham-4to-cl-1st ed (y3,dj) 45.00

ARNOLD,JOSE-Golden Swords and Pots and Pans-NY-(1963)-HBW-8vo-240p-8p photos-1st ed (gg5,sl rub dj) 12.50

ARNOLD,LLOYD-High on the Wild with Hemingway-Caldwell-1968-4to-343p-photos-1st ed (m3,pres cpy) 40.00

ARNOLD,MATTHEW-Note Books of...-1952-Oxford Pr-1st ed (y1,sl wn dj) 50.00

ARNOLD,MATTHEW-Poems. Second Series-Lond-1855-polished calf,g sp & dentelles,t.e.g.-1st ed (hh1,sl wn & fox) 100.00

ARNOLD,OREN-Hot Irons-NY-1940-Macmillan-(xii),242p-cl,illus-1st prtg (v1) 45.00

ARNOLD,OREN-Hot Irons-NY-1940-Macmillan-1st prtg (f10) 58.00

ARNOLD,OREN-Sun in Your Eyes-Albuq-(1947)-U of NM Pr-253p-illus-Herd 169-1st ed (ff4,dj) 15.00

ARNOLD,R ROSS-Indian Wars of Idaho-Caldwell-1932-268p-illus-1st ed (c7,f,rprd dj) 110.00

ARNOLD,R ROSS-Indian Wars of Idaho-Caldwell-1932-Caxton-268p-cl,photos,map,dec e.p.-Smith 296-scarce-1st ed (v1) 125.00

ARNOLD,THOMAS K-Practical Introduction to Greek Prose Composition...Revised and Corrected by Rev. J A Spencer-NY-1872-D Appleton-237p-lea bckd cl-from fifth Lond ed (k1,covs flecked) 15.00

ARNOTT,JAMES-Petit Trianon Versailles-NY-1929-Helburn-folio-blk cl sp,beige bds,97 drwngs & photos (r10,sl spot bds,sl chip) 85.00

ARNOW,HARRIETTE S-Seedtime on the Cumberland-NY-1960-Macmillan-xx+449p-grn cl,6 maps-1st ed (k2,dj) 35.00

ARNOW,HARRIETTE-Hunter's Horn-NY-1949-1st ed (t5,f,dj) 60.00

ARONOVICI,CAROL-Housing the Masses-NY-1939-John Wiley-xvi+291p-gry cl,plts-1st ed (g2,cov fade,pnclng,sl soil) 20.00

ARONS,HARRY-Hypnosis in Criminal Investigation-Springfield-(1967)-Chas C Thomas Publ-(xxviii)+(212)p-blu buckram-1st ed (y9,dj) 28.50

ARONSON,JOSEPH-Encyclopedia of Furniture-NY-(1941)-202p-cl,illus-4th prtg (aa1,dj) 20.00

ARRINGTON,LEONARD-ET AL-Building the City of God-SLC-1976-497p-cl,illus-1st ed (bb8,dj) 25.00

ARROWSMITH,JAMES-Paper-Hanger's Companion-Phila-1903-H C Baird-108p+32p publ cat.-cl (e1) 22.50

ART OF ANGLING-Princeton-1956-12mo-66p-1st ed (m3,vf) 40.00

ARTAUD,ANTONIN-Peyote Dance-NY-1976-Farrar-1st ed (w5,f,sp tn dj) 25.00

ARTHUR,ELIZABETH-Island Soujourn-NY-(1980)-H&R-8vo-220p-auth 1st bk-1st ed (ff5,f,dj) 12.50

ARTHUR,GEORGE-ED.-Letters of Lord and Lady Wolseley-NY-1922-440p-blu cl-1st Amer ed (gg2,f) 75.00

ARTHUR,S C-Birds of Louisiana-New Orleans-1931-State of La.,Bull.20-598p-stiff papr cov,illus(incl col)-scarce (z1,rub) 40.00

ARTHUR,S C-ET AL-Birds of Louisiana-New Orleans-1931-8vo-598p-wrps,col plts,photos (y8,sp chip) 50.00

ARTHUR,S C-Fur Animals of Louisiana-New Orleans-1928-8vo-433p-wrps,photos (y8,wrps tn) 19.00

ARTHUR,T S-Ten Nights in a Barroom-Phila-1861-Bradley & Co-240p-brn bds,blnd stmpd & g decs,frntis,pict half t.p. (n6,sl wn) 55.00

ARTS AND CRAFTS EXHIBITION SOCIETY-Arts and Crafts Essays by Members of...-Lond-1899-Longmans,Green-stout 16mo-xvii,(1),419,(1)p-qtr linen/bds (pp7,edge rub,sp drknd,fray) 100.00

ARTZYBASHEFF,BORIS-As I See-NY-1954-Dodd,Mead-4to-gry cl,illus-1st ed (x10,f,dj edges wn & tn) 45.00

ARTZYBASHEFF,BORIS-Poor Shaydullah-NY-1931-Macmillan-8vo-unpgd-pict cl,b&w illus-1st ed (s3,edge fade,dj sl chip) 75.00

ASBURY,HERBERT-French Quarter-NY-1936-Knopf-illus-1st ed (w1,f,f dj) 50.00

ASBURY,HERBERT-Gangs of New York-NY-1928-Knopf-xx+382p-cl sp,illus-1st ed (m2,sl edge-wn bds) 20.00

ASBURY,HERBERT-Gem of the Prairie-NY-1940-Knopf-xiv+378+xx pgs-cl & pap cov bds,illus-1st ed (e2,dj) 20.00

ASH,W-Ride a Paper tiger-1969-Walker-1st Amer ed (x7,f,rub dj) 18.00

ASHBAUGH,DON-Nevada's Turbulent Yesterday...-1963-Westernlore-346p-photos,illus-1st ed (t7,f,dj) 32.50

ASHBEE,C R-Craftsmanship in Competitive Industry-Lond-Essex Hs Pr-258,(6)p-qtr cl/bds,illus (pp7) 125.00

ASHBERY,JOHN-Double Dream of Spring-NY-1970-Dutton-1st ed (x10,f,dj) 20.00

ASHBERY,JOHN-Self Portrait in a Convex Mirror-NY-(1975)-Viking-1st ed (b5,as new in dj) 20.00

ASHBROOK,H-Murder of Sigurd Sharon-1933-Coward-1st ed (s10,dj) 30.00

ASHBROOK,H-Murder of Sigurd Sharon-NY-1933-Coward-1st ed (h4,f) 15.00

ASHBURNER,JOHN-Notes and Studies in the Philosophy of Animal Magnetism...-Lond-1867-H Bailliere-xxiv+444p+4p ads-embossed mauve cl-1st ed (y9) 250.00

ASHCRAFT,C ALLAN-Texas in the Civil War-Odessa-1962-W Tex Office Spply-53p-wrps-1st ed (w3,f) 15.00

ASHE,PENELOPE-Naked Came the Stranger-NY-(1969)-Lyle Stuart-1st ed (hh5,dj) 10.00

ASHENDEN-Mountains of My Life-Lond-1954-lg 8vo-212p-28 plts-1st ed (q10,f,chip dj) 35.00

ASHLEY,FREDERICK W-Story of the Vollbehr Collection of Incunabula-Providence-nd-priv prtd-12mo-50,(2)p-bds-ltd to 485c,nbrd (w2) 25.00

ASHLEY-MONTAGU,M F-Coming Into Being Among the Australian Aborigines-Lond-1937-Routledge-xxxv,362p-blu cl,4 plts-1st ed (pp1,edgewn,dj wn) 95.00

ASHTON,DORE-Rosa Bonheur-NY-1981-Viking/Studio Bk-sm 4to-1st prtg (f10,dj) 65.00

ASHTON,LEIGH-Chinese Arts-NY-1953-Beechhurst Pr-366p-col frntis,map,144p plts-1st Amer ed (c3,f,dj) 35.00

ASHTON,RUTH E-Plants of Rocky Mountain National Park-1933-GPO-iv,157p-wrps,photos,fldg ident key (m10,cors bent) 7.00

ASHTON-WARNER,SYLVIA-Myself-NY-1967-S&S-239p-red cl-1st ed (z9,f,dj) 10.00

ASIMOV,ISAAC-Asimov's Sherlockian Limericks-NY-1978-Mysterious Pr-1st ed (o3,f,dj) 15.00

ASIMOV,ISAAC-Foundation's Edge-Binghamton-1982-Whisper Pr-ltd to 1000c,two autgs (k3,f,box) 60.00

ASIMOV,ISAAC-Murder at the ABA-NY-1976-Dbldy-1st ed (h4,f,dj) 15.00

ASIMOV,ISAAC-Whiff of Death-NY-1968-Walker-1st hdbk ed (d4,sl sp slant,dj) 200.00

ASINOF,ELIOT-Bedfellow-1967-S&S-1st ed (ff2,f,dj) 50.00

ASINOF,ELIOT-Bleeding Between the Lines-1979-Holt Rinehart-1st ed (s7,f,dj) 16.00

ASINOF,ELIOT-Bleeding Between the Lines-1979-HR&W-1st ed (s8,f,dj) 17.50

ASINOF,ELIOT-Craig and Joan-NY-(1971)-Viking-1st ed (ff3,sl spot pgs,dj) 55.00

ASINOF,ELIOT-Eight Men Out-1963-HR&W-photos-1st ed (s8,f,sl wn dj) 50.00

ASINOFF,ELIOT-Eight Men Out-1963-HR&W-1st ed (n9,f,chip dj) 45.00

ASKINS,CHARLES-American Shotgun-NY-1910-Outing Publ-321p-brwn cl,dec cov,illus (ee3,f) 70.00

ASKINS,CHARLES-Art of Handgun Shooting-NY-1941-8vo-219p-photos-1st ed (m3,f) 15.00

ASKINS,CHARLES-Asian Jungle, African Bush-1959-Stackpole-258p-photos (gg3,f,tn dj) 65.00

ASKINS,CHARLES-Modern Shotguns & Loads-Marshalltown-1929-8vo-416p-illus,photos (m3) 25.00

ASKINS,CHARLES-Texans, Guns & History-NY-(1970)-246p-photos (gg3,f,dj) 30.00

ASKINS,CHARLES-Texans,Guns & History-NY-(1970)-Winchester Pr-x,246p-cl,photos-1st ed (v1,dj) 35.00

ASKINS,CHARLES-Wing & Trap Shooting-NY-1928-12mo-168p-illus (m3) 12.50

ASPINALL,JAMES-Roscoe's Library-Lond/Liverpool-1853-Whittaker/Dghtn & Lghtn-77p-orig blnd & g dec cl,port-1st ed (dd10,cov sl soil,fade & wn) 45.00

ASQUITH,CYNTHIA-This Mortal Coil-Sauk City-1947-Arkham-245p-ltd to 2609c-1st ed (k5,f,sl wn dj) 40.00

ASTAIRE,FRED-Steps in Time-NY-1959-photos-1st ed (s5,f,sl chip dj) 40.00

ASTON,JAMES-Wrought Iron-Pitt-1937-Byers-59p (h9) 18.00

ASTOR,GERALD-New York Cops-NY-1971-Scribner's-1st ed (z9,dj) 8.50

ASTOR,JOHN J-Journey in Other Worlds-NY-1894-Appleton-1st ed (w5) 85.00

ATHEARN,ROBERT G-Forts of the Upper Missouri-Englewood Cliffs-(1967)-Prentice Hall-339p-map e.p.,illus-1st ed (bb4,dj) 50.00

ATHEARN,ROBERT G-Union Pacific Country-1971-Rand McNally-8vo-480p-illus-1st ed (nn7,dj tn) 12.00

ATHERN,ROBERT G-Westward the Briton-NY-1953-Scribners-8vo-206p,index,photos-1st ed (t1,dj) 50.00

ATHERTON,GERTRUDE-American Wives and English Husbands-1898-Heinemann-1st Brit ed (x2,sl fade sp) 75.00

ATHERTON,GERTRUDE-Ancestors-NY-1907-Harper-8vo-709p-1st ed (w6) 20.00

ATHERTON,GERTRUDE-California-NY-1914-Harper-8vo-(330p)-red cl,wi "K-O" on cpyrght pg-1st ed (w6,uncut) 45.00

ATHERTON,GERTRUDE-Dido, Queen of Hearts-NY-1929-Liveright-8vo-384p-1st ed (w6,uncut,f,dj) 75.00

ATHERTON,GERTRUDE-Foghorn...-Bost-1934-Houghton,Mifflin-8vo-198p-1st ed (w6,dj) 85.00

ATHERTON,GERTRUDE-Jealous Gods-NY-1928-Liveright-8vo-452p-1st ed (w6,f,dj) 75.00

ATHERTON,GERTRUDE-Rulers of Kings-NY/Lond-1904-Harper & Bros-413p-brwn cl-1st ed (x9) 15.00

ATHERTON,JOHN-Fly & the Fish-NY-1951-8vo-195p-illus by auth-1st trd ed (m3,fray dj) 75.00

ATHERTON,LEWIS-Cattle Kings-Bloomington-(1961)-Ind U Pr-308p-e.p. maps,illus-Six Guns 92-1st ed (gg4,dj) 40.00

ATHOLL,JUSTIN-Shadow of the Gallows-Lond-1954-J Long-1st ed (z9,f,dj) 15.00

ATIL,ESIN-ED.-Turkish Art-NY-1980-Smithsonian & Abrams-4to-cl,289 illus incl 65 col plts & 3 maps-1st ed (m8,vf,dj) 75.00

ATIYA,AZIZ S-Crusade in the Later Middle Ages-Lond-1938-604p-blu cl,maps,illus-1st ed (gg2) 75.00

ATIYEH,WADEEHA-Scheherazade Cooks!-(NY)-(1960)-Gramercy Publ-189p-illus,J Alcorn (o6) 10.00

ATKESON,RAY-Cascade Range-Portland-(1969)-Belding-lg 4to-181p-150 col photos-1st ed (bb5,dj) 35.00

ATKIN,RONALD-Revolution! Mexico 1910 to 20-NY-(1970)-John Day-354p-maps,illus-1st Amer ed (cc4,dj) 25.00

ATKINS,WM-ED.-Art and Practice of Printing...-Lond-1932-Sir Isaac Pitman & Sons-8vo-6 vols-cl (x4) 150.00

ATKINSON,BROOKS-Cingalese Prince-GC-1934-Dbldy,Doran-8vo-303p-yel cl,e.p. maps-1st ed (p8,soil bds) 10.00

ATKINSON,C T-South Wales Borderers 24th Foot 1689 to 1937-Cambridge-1937-601p-dec grn cl,fldg maps,illus-1st ed (b7) 600.00

ATKINSON,JENNIFER-Eugene O'Neill: A Descriptive Bibliography-Pitt-1974-UP Pr-w/o dj as iss-1st ed (x9,f) 55.00

ATKINSON,JOSEPH-History of Newark, New Jersey-Newark-1878-xiv,344p-cl,plts (aa6) 125.00

ATKINSON,M E-Production of 300 Eggers and Better by Line Breeding-Dayton-(1923)-Reliable Poultry Journal-415p-red cl,186 illus-1st ed (d2,sl soil cov) 45.00

ATKINSON,MARY J-Texas Indians-S.A.-1935-345p-map e.p.,illus-1st ed (a9) 75.00

ATKINSON,THOMAS W-Oriental and Western Siberia-NY-1858-Harper & Bros-8vo-533p+2p ads-brwn cl,fldg map,52 illus-1st ed (ll1) 125.00

ATLANTIC COUNTY-EARLY HISTORY OF...NEW JERSEY-Kutztown-(1915)-Atl Cnty Hist Soc-178p-cl,illus (aa6) 125.00

ATTENBOROUGH,D-Journeys to the Past-1981-Lutterworth-384p-114 col & b&w photos-1st ed (bb3,f,dj) 20.00

ATTERDIGE,A HILLIARD-Towards Khartoum-Lond-1897-357p-dec grn cl,illus-1st ed (gg2) 175.00

ATTERIDGE,A HILLIARD-Wars of the 'Nineties-Lond-1899-qto-836p-dec red cl,illus-1st ed (b7,recased) 200.00

ATWATER,CALEB-An Essay on Education-Cin-1841-Kendall & Henry-123p-lea & mrbld bds (k1,upper jnts sl tender) 75.00

ATWATER,CALEB-Remarks Made on a Tour to Prairie Du Chien-Columbus-1831-Jenkins & Grover-296p-Howes A379-1st ed (cc4,ex-libr) 300.00

ATWOOD,E BAGBY-Regional Vocabulary of Texas-Austin-1962-UTP-273p-illus-1st ed (a9,dj) 75.00

ATWOOD,MARGARET-Dancing Girls and Other Stories-Lond-1982-1st ed (r2,f,dj,autg) 45.00

ATWOOD,MARGARET-Edible Woman-Tor-1969-M&S-1st ed (g8,f,sl rub dj) 225.00

ATWOOD,MARGARET-Encounters with the Element Man-Concord-1982-Wm B Ewert-wrps(100c in wrps),engrvngs by M McCurdy-ltd to 160c,two autg-1st ed (pp2,f) 85.00*

ATWOOD,MARGARET-Interlunar-Tor-1984-OUP-glossy wrps-1st ed (pp2,f) 15.00*

ATWOOD,MARGARET-Journals of Susanna Moodie, Poems-Tor-1970-OUP-wrps-1st ed,1st prtg(wi no numerical code on the verso of the title)-1st ed (pp2) 50.00*

ATWOOD,MARGARET-Journals of Susanna Moodie-1970-OUP-pict stiff wrps-1st ed (ee2,f,autg) 50.00

ATWOOD,MARGARET-Lady Oracle-(Tor)-1976-M&S-1st ed (l7,f,edgewn dj) 40.00

ATWOOD,MARGARET-Lady Oracle-1976-M&S-1st ed (o9,f,dj sl rub,sm tr) 35.00

ATWOOD,MARGARET-Lady Oracle-1976-S&S-1st Amer ed (n9,rmdr mrk,dj) 25.00

ATWOOD,MARGARET-Life Before Man-(Tor)-(1979)-M&S-1st ed (l7,f,dj) 40.00

ATWOOD,MARGARET-Life Before Man-Lond-(1980)-J Cape-1st Brit ed (f3,f,dj) 30.00

ATWOOD,MARGARET-Power Politics-NY-(1971)-Harper & Row-1st US ed (pp2,f dj) 25.00*

ATWOOD,MARGARET-Procedures for Underground-Bost-(1970)-Little,Brown-4to-cl-1st Amer ed (x3,f,dj) 70.00

ATWOOD,MARGARET-Second Words-Tor-(1982)-Anansi-1st Can ed (cc2,f,dj) 40.00

ATWOOD,MARGARET-Surfacing-NY-1972-S&S-1st ed (d8,dj) 60.00

ATWOOD,MARGARET-True Stories-NY-(1981)-S&S-1st ed (ee2,f,dj) 30.00

ATWOOD,MARGARET-You Are Happy-Tor-1974-Oxford-wrps-1st ed (v5) 20.00

ATWOOD,REV A-Glimpses in Pioneer Life on Puget Sound-Seattle-1903-Denny Corvell-483p-cl,illus (b6,sl loose) 42.00

AUBIER,DOMINIQUE-Fiesta in Seville-NY-(1956)-Studio-4to-blu cl,140 photo plts by Brassai-1st US ed (y3,sl chip dj) 75.00

AUBREY,EDMUND-Sherlock Holmes in Dallas-NY-1980-Dodd-1st Amer ed (p4,f,dj) 20.00

AUBREY,PHILIP-Defeat of James Stuarts Armada-Leicester-1979-194p-illus-1st ed (b7,f,dj) 15.00

AUCHINCLOSS,LOUIS-Dark Lady-1977-Houghton Mifflin-1st ed (t9,f,dj) 25.00

AUCHINCLOSS,LOUIS-Portrait in Brownstone-Bost-1962-Houghton Mifflin-1st ed (cc2,f,dj) 40.00

AUCHINCLOSS,LOUIS-Reflections of a Jacobite-Lond-1961-Gollancz-1st Brit ed (q2,dj) 35.00

AUCHINCLOSS,LOUIS-Rereading Henry James-Mpls-1975-UM Pr-illus-1st ed (z3,f,dj) 7.50

AUCHINCLOSS,LOUIS-Venus in Sparta-Bost-1958-Houghton Mifflin-1st ed (cc2,f,sl rub dj) 40.00

AUCHINCLOSS,LOUIS-Winthrop Covenant-Bost-1976-Houghton Mifflin-1st ed (h3,f,dj) 15.00

AUCHINCLOSS-Portrait in Brownstone-Bost-1962-HMCo-1st ed (hh5,dj) 10.00

AUDEMARS,PIERRE-Host for Dying-Lond-1970-Long-1st ed (g4,f,dj) 10.00
AUDEN,W H-Certain World, A Commonplace Book-Lond-1971-1st ed (y7,sl soil dj) 30.00
AUDEN,W H-Look, Stranger-Lond-(1936)-Faber-8vo-cl-ltd to 2300c-1st ed (ll10,f,sl rub dj) 200.00
AUDEN,W H-Magic Flute-NY-1956-1st US ed (p5,dj) 40.00
AUDEN,W H-Nones-1952-Faber-1st Brit ed (jj6,dj) 70.00
AUDEN,W H-Nones-Lond-1952-1st Brit ed (y7,dj) 65.00
AUDEN,W H-On the Frontier-Lond-1938-1st ed (r2,f,dj sl rub,sp sun) 200.00
AUDEN,W H-Shield of Achilles-NY-(1955)-Random-1st ed (a10,sl soil dj) 50.00
AUDEN,W H-Spain-(Lond)-(1937)-Faber-8vo-prtd wrps-1st ed (ll10,f) 100.00
AUDEN,W H-Thank You, Fog-NY-(1974)-Random-1st ed (b5,as new in dj) 15.00
AUDIGIER,ELEANOR D-Art Collection-Knoxville-(1937)-U of Tenn Libr-4to-51p (ll3,sl soil) 22.50
AUDSLEY,GEO A-Artistic & Decorative Stencilling-Lond-1911-80p-red cl,illus,27 plts(incl 4 col) (a3,sl fade sp) 145.00
AUDUBON,J J-1826 Journal of...-Norman-(1967)-409p-illus-1st ed (e7,f,dj) 45.00
AUDUBON,J J-Birds of America-NY-1937-4to-half cl & mrbld bds,frntis port,500 col plts-rag papr-ltd ed (y8,f) 175.00
AUDUBON,J J-Birds of America-NY-1937-Macmillan-folio-xxvi p+500 col plts,cl (ll4,sl rub edges) 95.00
AUDUBON,J J-Birds of America-NY-1978-4to-120,(1)p-cl,59 col plts (y8,dj) 12.50
AUDUBON,J J-Delineations of American Scenery and Character-1926-Baker-349p (bb3) 30.00
AUDUBON,J J-Delineations of American Scenery and Character-NY-1926-G A Baker-349p-1st ed (c9,shaken,frnt e.p. crack) 25.00
AUDUBON,J J-Letters of...1826 to 1840-Bost-1930-Club of Odd Vols-8vo-cl/bds-ltd to 225 sets-1st ed (v10,f,box) 250.00
AUDUBON,J J-Original Water Color Paintings by...for the Birds of America-NY-1966-Amer Heritage-2 vols-brwn buckrm (c9,f,box) 115.00
AUDUBON,J J-Original Watercolor Paintings by...for the Birds of America-NY-1966-tall 4to-2 vols-cl,col port frntis,431 col plts(several fldg) (y8,f,box) 135.00
AUDUBON,J J-Selected Birds of North America-Kent-1977-Volair Ltd-2 vols-lea,a.e.g.,g dec,col illus,ltd to 5000c,nbrd-rprnt (f9) 200.00
AUEL,JEAN-Clan of the Cave Bear-NY-(1980)-auth 1st bk-1st ed (l5,as new in dj) 50.00
AUEL,JEAN-Clan of the Cave Bear-NY-(1980)-Crown-1st ed (a5,as new in dj) 60.00
AUEL,JEAN-Clan of the Cave Bear-NY-(1980)-Crown-auth 1st bk-1st ed (ff6,f,dj) 65.00
AUEL,JEAN-Mammoth Hunters-NY-(1985)-Crown-1st ed (bb1,as new in dj) 15.00
AUEL,JEAN-Valley of Horses-NY-1982-1st ed (t5,f,dj) 25.00
AUER,MICHEL-Illustrated History of the Camera-Bost-1975-NYGS-285p-605 photos(70 col)-1st ed (cc9,as new in dj,box) 150.00
AUGHEY,JOHN H-Fighting Preacher-Chig-1899-Rhodes & McClure-361p-cl (m1) 17.50
AUGHEY,REV JOHN H-Tupelo-Lincoln-1888-595p+ads-grn cl-1st ed (mm10) 45.00
AUGUR,HELEN-Passage to Glory. John Ledyard's America-GC-1946-Dbldy-8vo-310p-blu cl,map e.p.,illus-1st ed (nn1,wn dj) 25.00
AUGUST,JOHN-Troubled Star-Bost-1939-Little-1st ed (h4,f,rprd dj) 20.00
AUK,THE QURTLY JOUR.,VOL.13 THRU VOL.99-1896 to 1982-8vo-total of 80 vols-tan buckr,illus (y8,lacks 7 vols,rbnd) 1,150.00
AULT,PHIL-Wires West-NY-1974-176p-illus,maps,photos-1st ed (t7,dj) 17.50
AUROBINDO,SRI-Essays on the Gita-NY-1950-Sri Aurobindo Libr-cl-1st ed,2nd prtg (n8,f,edge wn dj) 25.00
AUROBINDO,SRI-Human Cycle-NY-1950-Dutton-cl-1st ed (n8,f,dj) 20.00
AUROBINDO,SRI-Ideal of Human Unity-NY-1950-Dutton-cl-1st ed (n8,f,dj) 20.00
AUROBINDO,SRI-Ideal of the Karmayogin-Calcutta-1945-Arya Publ Hs-66p-wrps-scarce-6th ed (n8) 10.00
AUSTEN,CAROLINE-My Aunt Jane Austen-Alton-1952-Austen Soc-ix,22p-pict card covs,glassine dj,5 plts-1st ed (ll5,dj) 55.00
AUSTEN,JANE-Sense and Sensibility-Lond-1899-Geo Allen-grn & gold dec bndg,t.e.g.,illus by C Hammond-1st in Cranford Ser (ff6) 125.00
AUSTIN & KANE-ET AL-Yearbook of Landscape Architecture-NY-1983-Reinhold-192p (x6,f,dj tn) 20.00
AUSTIN,GABRIEL-Library of Jean Grolier-NY-1971-Grolier Club-t.e.g.,illus,iss w/o dj-1st ed (hh10,f) 85.00
AUSTIN,HUGH-Cock's Tail Murder-NY-1938-Dbldy CC-1st ed (k4,sl stnd cov,dj) 20.00
AUSTIN,HUGH-Drink the Green Water-NY-1948-Scribners-1st ed (g4,wn dj) 10.00
AUSTIN,HUGH-Murder in Triplicate-NY-1935-Dbldy CC-1st ed (f4,f) 17.50
AUSTIN,LEONARD-Around the World in San Francisco-np-1940-J L Delkin/Stanford-111p-linen sp,pattrnd bds,picts by P Vinson-Grabhorn Pr-ltd to 500c (q6,soil,fade) 75.00
AUSTIN,MARY-American Rhythm-Bost/NY-1930-Houghton Mifflin-8vo-x,(1),3-174p-purple cl wi cov & sp labl paste-ons-new & enlgd ed (mm1,wn dj) 40.00
AUSTIN,MARY-American Rhythm-NY-(1923)-155p-frntis-1st ed (u7) 40.00
AUSTIN,MARY-American Rhythm-NY-(1923)-Harcourt-8vo-155p-brwn cl-1st ed (oo7,uncut,dj sl chip & soil) 75.00
AUSTIN,MARY-Can Prayer Be Answered-NY-1934-Farrar-sm 8vo-55p-dj & illus by L Ward-1st ed (p1,dj) 50.00
AUSTIN,MARY-Can Prayer be Answered?-NY-1934-55p-scarce-1st ed (u7,sp wn) 40.00
AUSTIN,MARY-Earth Horizon, Autobiography-NY-1932-381p-frntis (t7,stnd bds) 7.50
AUSTIN,MARY-Everyman's Genius-Indpls-(1925)-Bobbs Merrill-8vo-365p-1st ed (w6) 35.00
AUSTIN,MARY-Isidro-Bost-1905-HMCo-col frntis-1st ed (a6) 60.00
AUSTIN,MARY-Man Jesus-NY-(1915)-Harper-8vo-215p-1st ed (w6) 35.00
AUSTIN,MARY-Man Jesus-NY-1915-Harper & Bros-8vo-215p (z4) 15.00
AUSTIN,MARY-One Smoke Stories-Bost-1934-Houghton Mifflin-295p-drwngs-1st ed (bb4,wn) 35.00
AUSTIN,MARY-Santa Lucia-NY-1908-346p-1st ed (u7) 65.00
AUSTIN,O L-Birds of the World-1961-Golden Pr-319p-300 col illus (bb3,f,tn dj) 25.00

AUSTIN,OLIVER L,JR.-Birds of Newfoundland-Cambridge-1932-Nuttall Ornith Club-4to-229p-map-Memoirs No.VII (c9) 60.00

AUSTIN,OLIVER L,JR.-Birds of the World-NY-1961-Golden Pr-316p-col illus,deluxe bndg,Orig ed (d9) 30.00

AUSTIN,ROBERT B-Early American Medical Imprints, 1668 to 1820-Wash D.C.-1961-US Dept HEW-x+240p-gry wrps-1st ed (a2) 35.00

AUSTING,G R-World of the Great Horned Owl-1966-Lippincott-158p-photos (bb3,f,dj) 35.00

AUSTING,G R-World of the Red Tailed Hawk-Phila & NY-1964-4to-128p-cl,frntis,map,photos (y8,dj) 16.00

AUTHORS CLUB-NY-1894-Auth Club/De Vinne Pr-sm 8vo-85p-orig 1/2 prchmnt over bds,papr sp labl-ltd to 250c (w2,cov soil) 15.00

AUTOBIOGRAPH OF AN ENGLISH SOLDIER IN THE UNITED STATES ARMY-NY-1853-288p-dec brwn cl,engrvd frntis-Howes B77-1st ed (gg2,sl fox) 100.00

AVEDON,RICHARD-Photographs, 1947 to 1977-Tor-1978-McGraw Hill-sm folio-160p-cl,plastic dj-1st ed (t3,f,dj) 175.00

AVEDON,RICHARD-Portraits-NY-1976-FS&G-sm folio-164p-cl-1st ed (t3,dj) 85.00

AVERELL,WILLIAM W-Ten Years in the Saddle-San Rafael-(1978)-443p-illus,maps-1st ed (c4,f,dj) 30.00

AVERILL,MARY-Japanese Flower Arrangement-Lond-1914-J Lane the Bodley Head-218p-g pict cl,t.e.g.,col frntis,illus-1st ed (dd10,sl scuff,cor bump) 40.00

AVERY,BENJAMIN P-Californian Pictures-Cambridge-1878(1877)-Riverside Pr-344p-dec grn cl,a.e.g.,13p illus (d3) 50.00

AXELSON,G W-Commy-1919-Reilly & Lee-red cov,photos-2nd prtg (s8) 85.00

AXFORD,H WM-Gilpin Country Gold, Peter McFalane 1848 to 1929-Chig-1976-210p-frntis,photos,map e.p.-1st ed (t7,f,dj) 15.00

AXFORD,JOSEPH-Around Western Campfires-Tucson-(1969)-U of Ariz Pr-266p-1st ed (cc4,dj) 15.00

AXFORD,LAVONNE B-English Language Cookbooks. 1600 to 1974-Detr-(1976)-Gale Rsrch-675p (m6) 150.00

AXTELL,S MARGARET-Goals,Gumption and Grit-Phoenix-1975-Hist Bk Project Comm-117p-cl,photos-1st ed (w3,dj) 20.00

AYER COLLECTION-Narratives of Captivity Among the Indians of North America-Chig-1912-120p-wrps-(with supplmnt I,Chig, 1928, 49p) (t7) 50.00

AYER,I WINSLOW-Life in the Wilds-Grand Rapids-1880-Central Publ-528p-cl-Rampaging Herd 188-1st ed (c1) 75.00

AYER,JACQUELINE-Wish for Little Sister-NY-(1960)-Harcourt,Brace-oblng 8vo-unpgd-pict bds,col illus,auth-1st ed (r3,f,dj) 15.00

AYLETT,MARY-Country Wines-Lond-(1953)-Odhams-16mo-192p-grn cl-1st ed (q8,dj) 15.00

AYLING,K,R.A.F.-Story of a British Fighting Pilot-NY-(1941)-H Holt-8vo-xvi,332p-cl,12p plts-1st ed (t2,dj) 25.00

AYLWARD,J D-English Master of Arms-Lond-1956-284p-illus-1st ed (gg2,f,dj) 20.00

AYMAR,GORDON-Bird Flight-GC-1938-234p-200 photos-Deluxe ed (b9,dj) 15.00

AYMAR,GORDON-Bird Flight-GC-1938-4to-234p-photos-"De Luxe" ed (m3) 12.50

AYMAR,GORDON-Treasury of Sea Stories-NY-1948-Barnes-8vo-303p-grn cl,illus by R Kent-1st ed (p8) 25.00

AYRTON,MICHAEL-Fabrications-NY-1973-HR&W-silv foil cov dj-1st US ed (y1,f,dj) 40.00

AZEMA,M A-Conquest of Fitzroy-Lond-1957-237p-1st ed (a4,f,dj) 60.00

BABAYAN,LEVON-Romance of the Oriental Rug-Tor-1925-Babayan's Ltd-sm 4to-80p-red cl,frntis,illus,19 col plts-1st ed (mm8,sl bump,dj chip) 50.00*

BABBIT,CHARLES-Early Days at Council Bluffs-Wash D.C.-1916-Byron Adams-Howes B4-1st ed (a6) 75.00

BABCOCK,HAVILAH-Best of Babcock-NY-1974-8vo-262p-1st ed (m3,f,sl soil dj) 35.00

BABCOCK,HAVILAH-Education of a Pretty Boy-NY-1960-8vo-160p-illus-1st ed (m3,f,sl wn dj) 200.00

BABCOCK,HAVILAH-I Don't Want to Shoot an Elephant-NY-1958-184p-illus (gg3,f,dj) 75.00

BABCOCK,HAVILAH-I Don't Want to Shoot an Elephant-NY-1958-8vo-284p-1st ed (m3,f,dj) 105.00

BABCOCK,HAVILAH-Jaybirds Go to Hell on Friday-NY-1965-149p-grn cl,dec cov-1st ed so stated (ee3,vf,dj) 80.00

BABCOCK,HAVILAH-Jaybirds go to Hell on Friday-NY-1965-8vo-149p-2nd prntng (m3,f,dj) 50.00

BABCOCK,HAVILAH-My Health is Better in November-Columbia-1948-8vo-284p-2nd prntng (m3,f,sl wn dj) 80.00

BABCOCK,HAVILAH-My Health is Better in November-NY-1952-284p-illus (gg3,f) 45.00

BABCOCK,HAVILAH-Tales of Quails `N Such-NY-1951-237p-illus (gg3,f,dj) 60.00

BABCOCK,HAVILAH-Tales of Quails `N Such-NY-1951-8vo-237p-decs by Wm Schaldach-2nd prntng (m3,f,dj) 65.00

BABCOCK,JOHN P-Game Fishes of British Columbia-Vict-1908-(62)p-orig wrps,illus-1st ed (a7) 50.00

BABCOCK,JOHN P-Game Fishes of British Columbia-Vict-1910-4to-(70)p-orig dec wrps,photos-scarce-"Special Edition" (a7,sl soil cov) 75.00

BABER,D F-Longest Rope-Caldwell-1959-320p-illus,e.p. maps (h7,f,dj) 35.00

BABINGTON,S H-Navaho, Gods, Tom Toms-NY-1950-246p-photos,map e.p.-1st ed (t7,dj,pres) 17.50

BABINGTON-SMITH,C-Testing Time-(NY)-(1961)-8vo-xiv,226p-cl bkd bds,24p plts,3 text illus-1st ed (t2,dj) 25.00

BABITZ,EVE-Eve's Hollywood-NY-1974-auth 1st bk,photos-1st ed (o5,dj) 25.00

BABITZ,EVE-Slow Days, Fast Company-NY-1977-Knopf-1st ed (b5,as new in dj) 17.50

BABITZ,EVE-Slow Days,Fast Company-1977-Knopf-1st ed (t9,vf,dj) 15.00

BACA,MANUEL-Vincente Silva & His 40 Bandits-Wash D.C.-1947-MacLean-folio-illus,ltd to 300c,case bnd,2 autg (a6,dj,unopened) 200.00

BACH,RICHARD-Stranger to the Ground-NY-1963-auth 1st bk-1st ed (s5,dj) 35.00

BACHELLER,IRVING-Coming Up the Road-Indpls-1928-Bobbs Merrill-316p-frntis port-1st ed (o2,sl rub) 15.00

BACHELLER,IRVING-Keeping Up with Lizzie-NY & Lond-1911-Harper & Bros-157,(1)p-cl,illus,W H D Koerner-1st ed (b1) 15.00

BACHMAN,JUL-New Directions in Swiss Architecture-NY-1969-Braziller-4to-128p-cl-1st ed (t3,dj) 35.00

BACHMANN,LAWRENCE P-Kiss of Death-NY-1946-1st solo bk-1st ed (h5,bndg dull,dj sl wn,soil) 25.00

BACHMANN,LAWRENCE P-Kiss of Death-NY-1946-Knopf-1st ed (h4,dj) 15.00

BACK,JOE-Horses, Hitches & Rocky Trails-Denver-1959-Sage-illus-1st ed (a6,f,dj) 27.50

BACK,SIR GEORGE-Narrative of the Arctic Land Expedition to the Mouth of the Great Fish River...1833,1834 and 1835-Lond-1836-J Murray-8vo-x,11p,663,(1)p-1/2 blk lea,mrbld papr,16 illus,fldg map-Arctic Biblio 851 (dd7,map rprd,sl rub) 495.00

BACKUS,TRUMAN J-Outlines of Literature English and American based upon Shaw's Manual of English Literature-NY-(1897)-Butler,Sheldon & Co-481p-lea-bckd cl (k1) 12.50

BACON,GEORGE B-Siam: the Land of the White Elephant as it Was and Is-NY-1893-Scribners Illus Libr Trvl-12mo-296p-engrvngs (c3) 34.00

BAD BOY'S DIARY-NY-(1880)-Ogilvie-276p-cl (f1,fade,sl wn) 25.00

BADEN-POWELL,B H-Indian Village Community-Lond,NY,Bombay-1896-Longmans,Green-8vo-xiv,465p+32p ads-blu cl (ll1,part unopened) 85.00

BADER,BARBARA-American Picture Books from Noah's Ark to the Beast Within-NY-(1976)-Macmillan-4to-572p-cl,illus(incl 130 col)-1st ed (nn10,f,f dj) 95.00

BADGER,JOSEPH E,JR.-Big George, the Giant of the Gulch-NY-Feb.25,1880-Beadle & Adams-30,(2)p-self wrps(punched along bndg edge)-N.Y. Dime Library No.88 (b1) 25.00

BADHAM,ALEXANDER-Wonders of Alaska-SF-1890-Bancroft-152p-dec gry cl,photos-1st ed (w1) 100.00

BADURA-SKODA,PAUL-Interpreting Mozart on the Keyboard-NY-1962-St.Martin's (u4,dj) 25.00

BAEKLAND,GEORGE-Gunner's Guide-NY-1948-12mo-115p-illus (m3,f,fray dj) 17.50

BAERG,W J-Birds of Arkansas-Fayetteville-1931-8vo-197p-wrps,frntis,photos (y8,sl soil wrps) 18.50

BAEZ,JOAN-Daybreak-1968-Dial-1st ed (t9,dj) 20.00

BAGBY,GEORGE W-Old Virginia Gentleman and Other Sketches-Richmond-1948-318p (aa4) 10.00

BAGBY,GEORGE-Corpse with the Purple Thighs-NY-1939-Dbldy CC-1st ed (k4,sp chip dj) 20.00

BAGBY,GEORGE-Innocent Bystander-Lond-1978-Hale-1st Brit ed (r4,f,dj) 17.50

BAGBY,GEORGE-Ring Around a Murder-NY-1936-Covici-1st ed (h4,sl fox,dj) 30.00

BAGG,A C-Birds of the Connecticut Valley in Massachusetts-Northampton-1937-4to-(20),813p-cl,col frntis,Fuertes,plts (y8,pres cpy) 145.00

BAGG,A C-Birds of the Connecticut Valley in Massacusetts-1937-Hampshire Bkshp-813p-col frntis,plts,photos,e.p. map (bb3,f) 165.00

BAGLEY,CLARENCE B-Acquisition and Pioneering of Old Oregon-Seattle-1924-4to-60p-wrps,illus (d7,sl chip) 75.00

BAGLEY,CLARENCE B-History of Seattle From the Earliest Settlement to the Present Time-Chig-1916-Clarke-4to-3 vols-g stmpd lea over cl-1st ed (t1) 650.00

BAGLEY,DESMOND-Enemy-Lond-1977-Collins-1st ed (q4,sl stnd rear cov,dj) 30.00

BAGLEY,DESMOND-Freedom Trap-NY-1972-Dbldy-1st Amer ed (r4,f,sl wn dj) 22.50

BAGLEY,HELEN-Sand in My Shoe-Twentynine Palms-(1978)-268,(1)p-cl-1st ed so stated (f1,f,dj) 15.00

BAGNOLD,ENID-National Velvet-NY-1935-Morrow-8vo-303p-1st US ed (bb5,dj) 40.00

BAGNOLD,ENID-National Velvet-NY-1935-Morrow-drwngs,L. Jones-1st US ed (e10,sl wn dj) 50.00

BAGSHAWE,EDWARD-COMP.-Le Walke Mysteries-Lond-nd-60p-wrps (l1) 15.00

BAHM,A J-Philosophy of the Buddha-NY-1958-Harper & Bros-cl-1st ed (n8,f,dj) 12.50

BAILEY,A M-Birds of Cape Prince of Wales, Alaska-1943-Col Mus Nat Hist,V.18,#1-113p-wrps,photos,map (b9) 15.00

BAILEY,A M-Birds of Colorado-1965-Denver Mus of Nat Hist-2 vols-col plts,b&w photos (c9,f,vol.2 lacks dj) 175.00

BAILEY,A M-Birds of Colorado-1965-Denver Mus-4to-2 vols-124 col plts,b&w photos,e.p. map (bb3,f,dj) 170.00

BAILEY,A M-Pictorial Checklist of Colorado Birds-Denver-1967-Mus. of Nat. Hist.-4to-168p-cl,124 col plts,photos (y8,dj chip) 75.00

BAILEY,A M-Subantarctic Campbell Island-1962-Denver Mus-305p-232 photos (bb3,f) 35.00

BAILEY,ADRIAN-Blessings of Bread-NY-(1975)-Paddington Pr-4to-287p-brwn cl,photos-1st US ed (q8) 17.50

BAILEY,ALFRED G-Conflict of European and Eastern Algonkian Cultures-1969-U of Tor Pr-xxiii,218p-2nd ed (bb7,dj) 25.00*

BAILEY,ALMIRA-Seattle-Sea-(1925)-38p-pict wrps,tip in col plt,photos (r8) 12.00

BAILEY,B H-Raptorial Birds of Iowa-1918-Iowa Geol Survey-238p-93 figs (bb3,ex-libr) 40.00

BAILEY,CAROLYN S-Children of the Handcrafts-NY-1935-JLG,Viking-188p-pict cl,lithos-1st ed (nn10,f,dj) 30.00

BAILEY,CAROLYN S-Tops and Whistles-1937-Jr Lit Guild/Viking-193p-pict cl,lithos-1st ed thus (oo10,f,dj sl chip) 25.00

BAILEY,CAROLYN S-Tops and Whistles-NY-1937-Viking-8vo-193p-illus-1st ed (dd5,chip dj) 35.00

BAILEY,EBENEZER-Young Ladies' Class Book-Bost-1837-Gould,Kendall & Lincoln-408p-lea-Amer Imprnts 42911-16th Stereotype ed (d1) 25.00

BAILEY,EBENEZER-Young Ladies' Class Book-Bost-1837-Gould,Kendall & Lincoln-408p-lea-Amer Imprnts 42911-16th stereotype ed (k1) 25.00

BAILEY,ERIC-Christmas Island Story-Lond-1977-Stacey Int'l-88p-map e.p.,illus-1st ed (nn1,dj) 20.00

BAILEY,F M-Among the Birds in the Grand Canyon Country-Wash D.C.-1939-US Dept of Interior-211p-wrps,photos,drwngs (d9) 20.00

BAILEY,F M-Among the Birds in the Grand Canyon-Wash-1939-8vo-211p-wrps,map,illus (y8) 30.00

BAILEY,F M-Birds of New Mexico-Santa Fe-1928-8vo-807p-cl,79 plts(25 col),60 maps (y8,dj chip) 160.00

BAILEY,F M-Birds of New Mexico-Socorro-1928-NM Dept Game & Fish-sm 4to-illus-1st ed (a6) 150.00

BAILEY,F M-Handbook of Birds of the Western United States-1902-Houghton Mifflin-512p-33 plts-1st ed (bb3) 30.00

BAILEY,H C-Honour Among Thieves-NY-1947-Dbldy-1st US ed (d4,dj) 20.00

BAILEY,H C-Merchant Prince-1929-Dutton-1st ed (x7,sl chip dj) 55.00

BAILEY,H C-Mr.Clunk's Text-NY-1939-Dbldy CC-1st Amer ed (h4,f,dj sl rub) 35.00

BAILEY,H C-Mr.Clunk's Text-NY-1939-Dbldy CC-1st Amer ed (hh2,f,dj) 50.00

BAILEY,H C-Orphan Ann-NY-1941-Dbldy CC-1st US ed (e4,sp top wn,dj) 20.00

BAILEY,H C-Queen of Spades-1944-DD-1st Amer ed (x7,dj) 24.00

BAILEY,H C-Queen of Spades-NY-1944-Dbldy CC-1st Amer ed (h4,dj) 12.50

BAILEY,H C-Red Castle Mystery-NY-1932-Dbldy CC-1st US ed (f4) 20.00

BAILEY,H H-Birds of Floirda-Balt-1925-4to-146p-cl,76 col plts,fldg map (y8) 135.00

BAILEY,H H-Birds of Virginia-Lynchburg-1913-8vo-362p-cl,14 col plts,1 map,108 half-tones (y8) 70.00

BAILEY,JAMES H-Henrico Home Front 1861 to 1865-(Richmond)-1963-275p (ll3) 35.00

BAILEY,JEAN-Cherokee Bill Oklahoma Pacer-NY-1952-191p-illus-1st ed (t7,dj,pres,crd,photo pstd in) 12.50

BAILEY,JESSIE B-Diego de Vargas and Reconquest of New Mexico-Albuq-(1940)-270p-1st ed (u7) 100.00

BAILEY,JOSIAH-ED.-Fishery Resources of the United States-Wash D.C.-1945-4to-135p-wrps-illus,maps (m3) 12.50

BAILEY,KENNETH K-Southern White Protestantism in the Twentieth Century-NY-(1964)-180p-1st ed (aa4,sl soil dj) 10.00

BAILEY,L H-Cultivated Evergreens-NY-1925-Macmillan-434p-cl (x6) 20.00

BAILEY,L H-Cyclopedia of American Agriculture-NY-1917-Macmillan-4 vols-cl-scarce-5th ed (x6) 275.00

BAILEY,L H-Farm and Garden Rule Book-NY-1911-Macmillan-587p-bds (o6,sl wn bds) 35.00

BAILEY,L H-Garden of Pinks-NY-1938-Macmillan-142p-cl,illus (x6,cl spot,dj chip,sl wn) 28.00

BAILEY,L H-Horticulturist's Rule Book-NY-1908-ix+312p+ads-3rd ed (x5,sl soil & stnd cov) 12.00

BAILEY,L H-Hortus Third-NY-1976-4to-xiv,1290p-illus (jj7) 97.50

BAILEY,L H-Hortus-NY-1930-652p-16 photos-1st ed (m10,edgewn dj,promo laid in) 45.00

BAILEY,L H-Manual of Cultivated Plants-NY-1968-Macmillan-1116p (x6,sp tn) 40.00

BAILEY,L H-Manual of Gardening-NY-1910-Macmillan-539p-cl (x6,edges fox) 10.00

BAILEY,L H-Manual of Gardening-NY-1939-xvi,539p-blu dec cl,32 b&w photo plts,figs (x5,sl wn) 12.00

BAILEY,L H-Principles of Fruit Growing-NY-1911-Macmillan-516p-cl (x6,wn,rub) 18.00

BAILEY,L H-Standard Cyclopedia of Horticulture-NY-1914-6 vols-96 plts(incl col) (m10,cov spots,hngs split) 160.00

BAILEY,LYNN R-If You Take My Sheep...-Pasadena-1980-293p-photos,maps-1st ed (v7,f,dj) 20.00

BAILEY,LYNN R-Long Walk-LA-1964-254p-e.p. maps,illus-1st ed (c4,f,dj) 32.50

BAILEY,MARGARET E-Robin Hood's Barn-NY-(1922)-Doran-8vo-301p-sketches-1st ed (bb5,unopened,dj) 30.00

BAILEY,N BETH-Meal Planning and Table Service in the American Home-Peoria-(1923)-Manual Arts Pr-128p-grn bds,illus (l6,sl sunned sp) 18.00

BAILEY,PAUL-Claws of the Hawk-LA-1966-358p-1st ed (n3,f,dj) 25.00

BAILEY,PEARL-Duey's Tale-NY-(1975)-HBJ-59p-photos-1st ed (oo10,f,dj) 15.00

BAILEY,RALPH E-An American Colossus-Bost-(1933)-318p-cl (g1) 15.00

BAILEY,ROBERT G-Hell's Canyon-Lewiston-1943-R G Bailey Prtg-575p-photos,illus e.p.-ltd to 1500c,autg-1st ed (gg4,sl fade sp) 140.00

BAILEY,ROBERT G-River of No Return-Lewiston-1935-515p-illus-ltd ed,autg-scarce-1st ed (g7,sp rub) 100.00

BAILEY,ROBERT G-River of No Return-Lewiston-1935-Bailey Blake Prtg-515p-photos-ltd to 1400c,,autg-1st ed (gg4,sl wn sp) 145.00

BAILEY,SIBYLLA A-Glances at the Treasures of the Old World-(Bost)-1880-prntd,not publ,no copyrt-92p-cl (e1) 25.00

BAILEY,TEMPLE-Burning Beauty-Phila-(1929)-Penn-1st ed (hh5,dj) 10.00

BAILEY,V-Animal Life of the Carlsbad Cavern-Balt-1928-8vo-195p-cl,illus,maps (y8,dj chip) 40.00

BAILLIE SCOTT,M H-Houses & Gardens-Lond-1933-illus (ee1) 350.00

BAILY,W L-Our Own Birds-Phila-1869-12mo-265p-cl,frntis,9 plts (y8,chip) 35.00

BAINBRIDGE,HENRY C-Peter Carl Faberge-Lond-1949-Batsford-4to-xxiv,169,(1)p-126 plts(incl 16 col)-1st ed (u5,dj) 135.00

BAINBRIDGE,HENRY C-Peter Carl Faberge-Lond-1971-Spring Bks-4to-176p-blk cl,col illus (r10,f,f dj) 22.50

BAINBRIDGE,W G-Fly Fisher's Guide to Aquatic Flies-Lond-1936-12mo-87p-illus-1st ed (m3) 22.50

BAIRD,NEWTON-Key to Frederic Brown's Wonderland-1981-Talisman Lit Resrch-63p-prntd wrps,ltd to 360c,of which 275c are wrps-1st ed (g9) 50.00

BAIRD,R D-Trout Rose-Lond-nd-8vo-160p-illus-1st ed (m3) 15.00

BAIRD,S F-Birds-Wash-1858-4to-1005p-cl (bb3,rbnd) 150.00

BAIRD,W D-Quapaw Indians-1980-U of Okla-290p-photos,maps-1st ed (bb3,f,dj) 35.00

BAIRD,W D-Quapaw Indians-Norman-1980-290p-photos,illus,maps-1st ed (t7,f,dj) 22.50

BAKARICH,SARAH G-Gun Smoke-np-1947-18mo-152p-pict wrps-Six Guns #118-1st ed (dd4) 25.00

BAKELESS,J-Spies of the Confederacy-Phila-1970-456p (z10,fade dj) 35.00

BAKELESS,JOHN-Eyes of Discovery-Phila-1950-439p-illus,maps,map e.p.-1st ed (t7,dj) 15.00

BAKELESS,JOHN-Eyes of Discovery-Phila-1950-Lippincott-1st ed (v4,frnt cov stnd,dj) 20.00

BAKELESS,JOHN-Lewis & Clark, Partners in Discovery-NY-1947-498p-illus,fldg map (f7,dj) 30.00

BAKER'S BIOGRAPHICAL DICTIONARY OF MUSICIANS-NY-1919-Schirmer-3rd rvsd ed (u4) 20.00

BAKER,B GRANVILLE-Winter Holiday in Portugal-NY-nd(ca.1910)-James Pott-8vo-324p-illus,fldg map-1st US ed(?) (ff5) 50.00

BAKER,CAROLYN-Forty Years of Pulitzer Prizes-NY-1956-Grolier Club-pale grn wrps-1st ed (dd2) 30.00

BAKER,CHARLES H-Gentleman's Companion-Derrydale-1939-8vo-2 vol-ltd to 1250sets,nbrd-photos-scarce (m3,f,wn box) 120.00

BAKER,CLYDE-Modern Gunsmithing-Plantersville-1933-529p-dec cl,frntis,photos (t7) 20.00

BAKER,DENYS VAL-Face in the Mirror-Sauk City-1971-ltd to 2045c-1st ed (k5,as new in dj) 22.50

BAKER,DOROTHY-Cassandra at the Wedding-1962-Houghton Mifflin-1st ed (x2,f,dj) 27.00

BAKER,DOROTHY-Young Man with a Horn-Bost-1938-HMCO-1st ed (u10,f,edgewn dj) 30.00

BAKER,E T-Sheep Diseases-Chig-1920-Amer Vet Publ-8vo-299p-illus-2nd ed (gg5) 10.00

BAKER,EZEKIEL-Remarks on Rifle Guns-Huntington-nd-8vo-267p+tbls & plts,illus-facsimile of 11th ed of 1835 (m3,f) 15.00

BAKER,FRANK C-Molluscan Family Planorbidae-Urbana-1945-U of Ill Pr-xxxvi+530p-brwn cl,141 plts-1st ed (c2) 30.00

BAKER,G-ET AL-Century of Service-Wash D.C.-1963-GPO-560p-cl (x6,as new) 12.00

BAKER,GEN L C-History of the United States Secret Service-Phila-1867-704p+ads-illus-1st ed (n3,rbnd) 60.00

BAKER,JOSEPHINE-Josephine-NY-1977-Harper-1st ed (w5,f,dj) 25.00

BAKER,L C-History of the United States Secret Service-Phila-1867-Auth publ-704p-illus-1st ed (n2,cors wn) 45.00

BAKER,MARCUS-Geographic Dictionary of Alaska-Wash D.C.-1906-GPO-Geo Srvy,Bull.#299,ser.F-690p-2nd ed,enlgd (oo1,rbnd) 95.00

BAKER,MARY-Florida Wild Flowers-NY-1926-Macmillan-256p-cl (x6) 15.00

BAKER,MICHAEL-Doyle Diary-NY-(1978)-oblng 4to-col & b&w illus,Chas A Doyle-1st ed (k9,f,dj) 17.50

BAKER,PEARL-Wild Bunch at Robbers Roost-LA-1965-Wstrnlore Pr-255p-illus-Six Guns 121-1st ed (gg4,wn dj) 25.00

BAKER,RICHARD M-Death Stops the Manuscript-NY-1936-Scribner's-auth 1st bk-1st ed (hh2,dj chip & rnfrcd) 125.00

BAKER,ROBERT A-Blossoming Desert a Concise History of Texas Baptists-Waco-1970-Word Bks-282p-cl-1st ed (w3,f,dj) 22.50

BAKER,RONALD L-Indiana Place Names-Bloomington-(1975)-196p+map in pocket-wrps (j1) 10.00

BAKER,S JOSEPHINE-Division of Child Hygiene of the Department of Health of the City of New York-NY-1912-103p-wrps,fldg chrts,photos-1st ed (dd3,ex-libr) 100.00

BAKER,SAMUEL W-Eight Years' Wanderings in Ceylon-Phila-1877-Lippincott-323p-orig dec grn cl (ll1,pgs fox & soil) 65.00

BAKER,SAMUEL W-Exploration of the Nile Tributaries of Abyssinia-Hartford-1868-O D Case-fldg map,illus-1st ed (gg7,sp stnd) 75.00

BAKER,SAMUEL W-Exploration of the Nile Tributaries of Abyssinia...-1868-Case-608p-21 engrvngs,map (bb3,cov sl wn) 145.00

BAKER,SAMUEL W-Nile Tributaries pf Abyssinia and the Sword Hunters of the Hamran Arabs-Lond-1871-2 col maps,24 b&w illus,grn half calf wi 5 raised bands on sp-4th ed (d5) 100.00

BAKER,SAMUEL W-Wild Beasts and Their Ways-Lond-1890-Macmillan-8vo-errata,455p-burgundy cl,tiger,back cov two horned beasts in combat,29 illus (gg6) 185.00

BAKER,VIRGINIA-History of Warren, Rhode Island, in the War of the Revolution,1776 to 1783-Warren-1901-68p-maroon cl-1st ed (h2) 25.00

BAKER,W J-History of the Marconi Company-NY-(1972)-St.Martin's-414p-blk cl,illus-1st ed (l2,dj) 35.00

BAKER,WM A-Engine Powered Vessel from Paddle Wheeler to Nuclear Ship-NY-(1965)-lg folio-268p-225 illus(incl 50 col)-1st ed (pp4) 35.00

BAKER,WM A-Maritime History of Bath, Maine and the Kennebec River Region-Bath-1973-Maritime Rsrch Soc-2 vols-red cl,64 plts,18 plans-1st ed (b2,box) 90.00

BALCHEN,B-Come North with Me-NY-1958-8vo-318p-cl,frntis,22p plts,2p maps-1st ed (t2,dj) 25.00

BALD,F CLEVER-Michigan in Four Centuries-NY-1954-Harper & Bros-498p-cl,photos,maps-1st ed (z7,dj) 27.50

BALDRIDGE,LETITIA-Roman Candle-Bost-1956-Houghton Mifflin-308p-1st prtg (ff8,dj rub & chip) 18.00

BALDUCCI,CAROLYN-Self Made Woman-Bost-(1975)-200p-cl-1st ed (d1,f,dj) 15.00

BALDWIN LOCOMOTIVE WORKS-HISTORY OF...1831 TO 1923-c.1931-Baldwin-8vo-210p-cl,illus-Orig ed (nn7) 75.00

BALDWIN,FAITH-Letty and the Law-NY-(1940)-F&R-1st ed (hh5,f,f dj) 15.00

BALDWIN,JAMES-Blues for Mr.Charlie-NY-1964-Dial-1st ed (bb2,f,dj) 50.00

BALDWIN,JAMES-Blues for Mr.Charlie-NY-1964-1st ed (p5,sl rub dj) 35.00

BALDWIN,JAMES-Devil Finds Work-NY-1976-Dial-1st ed (bb2,f,dj) 35.00

BALDWIN,JAMES-Giovanni's Room-1956-Dial-1st ed (kk6,sl spot,dj sl chip) 100.00

BALDWIN,JAMES-Going to Meet the Man-NY-1965-Dial-1st ed (j6,dj) 65.00

BALDWIN,JAMES-If Beale Street Could Talk-NY-1974-Dial-1st ed (b5,as new in dj) 25.00

BALDWIN,JAMES-Just Above My Head-NY-(1979)-1st ed (f5,f,dj) 20.00

BALDWIN,JAMES-Nothing Personal-NY-(1964)-Atheneum-folio-wht bds,photos by Avedon-1st ed (x3,sl scuff,soil cov) 110.00

BALDWIN,JAMES-Rap on Race-Phila-1971-1st ed (t5,dj) 20.00

BALDWIN,JAMES-Tell Me How Long the Train's Been Gone-NY-1968-Dial-1st ed (b5,f,sp tan dj) 30.00

BALDWIN,JAMES-Tell Me How Long the Train's Been Gone-NY-1968-Dial-1st ed (bb2,f,dj) 50.00

BALDWIN,LELAND D-Pittsburgh, the Story of a City-1937-U of Pitt Pr-illus-1st ed (r2,f) 45.00

BALDWIN,MARY H-Marigold Cook Book-NY-1938-Dbldy,Doran-126p-hvy wrps,plastic comb bndg (l6,sl scuff) 25.00

BALDWIN,STAN-Bad Henry-Radnor-(1974)-205p-cl-Smith 9804 (n1) 15.00

BALDWIN-SMITH,E-Egyptian Architecture as Cultural Expression-NY-1938-D Appleton-4to-xviii,264p-grn cl wi g decs,78 plts-1st ed (y4,dj) 75.00

BALDY,LIZZIE F-California Pioneer...-SF-1879-Bacon-8vo-159p-stmpd cl-1st ed (w6) 75.00

BALES,WILLIAM A-Tiger in the Streets-NY-1962-Dodd Mead-8vo-212p-16 illus-1st ed (gg5,sl rub dj) 12.50

BALFOUR,G-Armored Train-Lond-1981-168p-illus,maps-1st ed (jj2,f,dj) 25.00

BALFOUR,HAROLD-Folk,Fish & Fun-Suffolk-1978-8vo-106p-photos (m3,f,dj) 10.00

BALFOUR-KINNEAR,G P R-More About Trout & Salmon-Lond-1963-8vo-139p-photos-1st ed (m3,f,dj) 35.00

BALJEU,JOOST-Theo Van Doesburg-NY-(1974)-Macmillan-4to-232p-illus-1st US ed (ee5,f,f dj) 30.00

BALL,ANNETTE C-History of the Parsippany Prebysterian Church-(Parsippany)-(1915)-22p-wrps (aa6,chip,brittle) 30.00

BALL,ANNETTE C-History of the Parsippany, New Jersey Presbyterian Church-(Parsippany)-(1928)-(5)-57p-wrps,illus fldg facs (aa6) 30.00

BALL,BONNIE-Red Trails and White-NY-(1955)-62p-1st ed (jj3) 17.50

BALL,BRIAN-Death of a Low Handicap Man-NY-1978-Walker-1st Amer ed (w9,f,dj) 30.00

BALL,DON,JR.-Portrait of the Rails-Greenwich-1972-304p-1st ed (n4,sl tn dj) 29.00

BALL,DON,JR.-Portrait of the Rails:From Steam to Rail-NY-1972-295p-1st ed (n4,dj) 25.00

BALL,DON,JR.-Railroads:An American Journey-Bost-1975-288p-1st ed (n4,f,dj) 27.50

BALL,IAN M-Pitcairn: Children of Mutiny-Bost,Tor-(1973)-380p-e.p. maps,illus,photos-1st ed (d7,dj) 45.00

BALL,J DYER-Chinese at Home-NY-1912-370p-plts(incl 7 col) (a3) 37.50

BALL,JOHN W-One Man's Overalls-Coburg-1974-8vo-67p-wrps (m3,f) 14.00

BALL,JOHN W-Teaching Your Fly to Fly-Coburg-1972-8vo-17p-wrps-photos (m3,f) 17.50

BALL,JOHN-ED.-Mystery Story-San Diego/Del Mar-(1976)-U of Cal/Publ Inc-390p-1st ed (g9,dj wn,tape rprd) 40.00

BALL,JOHN-In the Heat of the Night-1963-Harper & Row-1st ed (n9,sp chip dj) 60.00

BALL,JOHN-Mark One:The Dummy-Bost-1974-Little-1st ed (g4,f,dj) 10.00

BALL,KATHERINE M-Bamboo-Berkeley-1945-Gillick Pr-109p-blk cl,papr cov labl,paintings,W Tseng Tsu-ltd to 500c,autg-1st ed (ll1,f,dj) 125.00

BALL,LARRY-United States Marshals of New Mexico and Arizona Territories, 1846 thru 1912-Albuq-1978-315p-photos-1st ed (t7,f,dj,pres) 45.00

BALL,W W R-History of the Study of Mathematics at Cambridge-Cambridge-1889-Cambridge U Pr-xvi+264p+ads-grn cl (j2) 35.00

BALLANTINE,BILL-Horses & Their Bosses-Phila-1964-Lippincott-1st ed (h9,dj) 25.00

BALLANTYNE,R M-Blue Lights or Hot Work in the Soudan-Lond-1888-Nisbet & Co-pict grn,gold & red bndg,5 plts,illus identified for p.217 bnd as frntis-1st Brit ed (aa8) 175.00

BALLARD,C R-Kitchener-NY-1930-340p-maps-1st ed (b7,dj) 30.00

BALLARD,H C-Poems-Chig-1870-Church,Goodman,Donnelley-164p-cl (l1,sl wn sp) 20.00

BALLARD,J G-High Rise-NY-1975-1st US ed (n5,f,dj) 30.00

BALLARD,J G-Love & Napalm-NY-1972-1st US ed (p5,f,dj) 50.00

BALLARD,J G-Unlimited Dream Company-Lond-1979-1st Brit ed (n5,vf,vf dj) 45.00

BALLARD,J G-Unlimited Dream Company-Lond-1979-Cape-1st ed (kk5,f,dj) 60.00

BALLARD,VICE ADMIRAL G A-Influence of the Sea on the Political History of Japan-NY-1921-Dutton-8vo-311p-9 illus-1st US ed (ff5) 40.00

BALLENGER,EDGAR G-ET AL-History of Urology-Balt-1933-2 vols-illus (g10,ex-libr) 195.00

BALLIETT,WHITNEY-Such Sweet Thunder-(1966)-Bobbs Merrill-1st ed (w1,f,dj) 20.00

BALLIETT,WHITNEY-Super Drummer-(1968)-Bobbs Merrill-sm oblng 8vo-128p-1st ed (p1,dj) 85.00

BALLINGER,BILL S-49 Days of Death-LA-1969-Sherbourne-1st ed (s4,f,sl soil dj) 20.00

BALLINGER,BILL S-Fourth of Forever-NY-1963-Harper-1st ed (h4,dj) 10.00

BALLINGER,RAYMOND A-Layout-NY-(1956)-Reinhold Publ-4to-244p-cl,illus-1st ed (w2) 25.00

BALLOU,MATURIN M-Aztec Land-Bost,NY-(1890)-355p-cl-Smith B18 (j1) 15.00

BALLOU,WILLIAM-Compend of Equine Anatomy and Physiology-Phila-1896-Blakiston-29 illus (j9) 18.00

BALMER,E-Achievements of Luther Trant-1910-SM-illus-1st ed (x7,sp fade & lttrng gone) 375.00

BALMER,EDWIN-Keeban-Bost-1923-Little,Brown-1st ed (bb1,sl chip dj) 75.00

BALNEAVES,ELIZABETH-Mountains of the Murcha Zerin-Lond-(1972)-Gifford-8vo-239p-col photos-1st ed (ff5,dj) 25.00

BALTZELL,E DIGBY-Protestant Establishment-NY-1964-Random-xviii,429p-1st prtg (o2,tn dj) 15.00

BALTZELL,ISAIAH-Golden Songs-Dayton-1874-174,(2)p-bds (h1,sp wn) 12.50

BALTZER,ADOLF C G-Recollections of Missouri-Bred Preacher-Rio de Janeiro-1939-91,xi p-cl (h1) 20.00

BALZER,ROBERT L-California's Best Wines-(1948)-Ward Ritchie-154p-pict bds,col illus-1st ed (q8,dj wn) 15.00

BALZER,ROBERT L-Discovering Italian Wines-(1971)-Ward Ritchie-4to-136p-dec wht cl,col map e.p.,col plts-1st ed (q8) 20.00

BALZER,ROBERT L-Robert Lawrence Balzer's Book of Wines & Spirits-(1973)-Ward Ritchie-4to-118p-red cl,col plts-1st ed (q8,wn dj) 20.00

BAMBARA,TONI C-Salt Eaters-1980-Random-1st ed (n9,rmdr mrk,dj) 15.00

BAMBARA,TONI C-Sea Birds are Still Alive-NY-1977-1st ed (p5,f,dj) 30.00

BAMBURG,L-Beads of Silence-1927-Dutton-1st ed (x7,f,chip dj) 27.00

BANCROFT,CAROLINE-Gulch of Gold-Denver-(1958)-376p-photos,maps-1st ed (v7,rprd dj) 20.00

BANCROFT,CAROLINE-Six Racy Madams of Colorado-Boulder-1965-Johnson-64p-prtd wrps,illus-1st ed (oo7) 15.00

BANCROFT,H H-History of Arizona and New Mexico-SF-1889-829p-orig tan calf,fldg map-vol.17 of "Works"-1st ed (z1,f) 195.00

BANCROFT,H H-History of the Northwest Coast-SF-1886-2 vols-deluxe 3/4 lea,mrbld bds,e.p. & page edges-text maps-Tweney #4 (h7) 175.00

BANCROFT,H H-History of Washington, Idaho & Montana-SF-1890-836p-3/4 calf,raised sp bands,mrbld bds & e.p.,text maps-Tweney #4-1st ed (d7) 110.00

BANCROFT,H H-Literary Industries, a Memoir-SF-1891-Hist Co-thk 8vo-vii,808p-cl,papr sp labl-1st separately iss vol (x4,few stnd pgs) 85.00

BANCROFT,HUBERT H-New Pacific-NY-1915-Bancroft Co-8vo-blu cl,map-3rd rvsd ed (nn1) 65.00

BANDEL,EUGENE-Frontier Life in the Army 1854-61-Phila-1974-330p-frntis,illus,fldg map (t7,f) 20.00

BANDELIER,A F-An Outline of the Documentary History of the Zuni Tribe-Bost-1892-115p-Vol.III of Jour of Amer Ethn & Arch,Hemenway SW Arch Exped-1st ed (v7,rbnd) 150.00

BANDELIER,A F-Delight Makers-NY-(1890)-490p-1st ed (v7) 125.00

BANDELIER,A F-Final Report of Investigations among the Indians of the Southwestern US...1880 thru 1885-Cambridge-1890,1892-Arch Inst of Amer-Amer Ser.III & IV-2 vols-wrps,photos,maps-rare (v7,chip,box) 275.00

BANDELIER,ADOLPHE F-Gilded Man-NY-1893-Appleton-302p+ads-g emboss dec blk cl-1st ed (d3) 100.00

BANDELIER,FANNY-Journey of Alvar Nunez Cabeza De Vaca-NY-1905-Barnes-231p-Trail Makers Ser-1st ed (d3) 70.00

BANDINI,HELEN-History of California-1908-Amer Bk Co-302p-illus-1st ed (d3) 25.00

BANDINI,RALPH-Veiled Horizons-NY-(1939)-Derrydale Pr-4to-illus-ltd to 950c,nbrd (jj4) 125.00

BANFIELD,E J-Confessions of a Beachcomber-NY-1924-Knopf-8vo-336p-1st US ed (jj5,sp wn) 15.00

BANGAY,R D-Elementary Principles of Wireless Telegraphy-1917-241p-302 illus-2nd ed (h6) 30.00

BANGOR & AROOSTOOK RAILROAD-In the Maine Woods-Bangor-1936-8vo-160p-wrps-photos,fldg map (m3) 17.50

BANGS,FRANCIS H-John Kendrick Bangs, Humorist of the Nineties-NY-1941-Knopf-1st ed (hh5,sl chip dj) 17.50

BANGS,JOHN K-Bicyclers and Three Other Farces-NY-1896-Harper & Bros-176p-frntis,plts-1st ed (ll2) 22.50

BANGS,JOHN K-Booming of Acre Hill-NY-1900-Harper-1st ed (hh5) 15.00

BANGS,JOHN K-Booming of Acre Hill...-NY-1900-Harper & Bros-265p-frntis,1 plt-1st ed (ll2) 25.00

BANGS,JOHN K-Cobwebs from a Library Corner-NY-1899-Harper & Bros-illus-1st ed (y10) 32.00

BANGS,JOHN K-Coffee and Repartee and the Idiot-NY-1900-Harper & Bros-221p-frntis,plts-ltd to 500c,nbrd,autg-auth autg ed (ll2,sp wn) 20.00

BANGS,JOHN K-Dreamers-NY-1899-Harper & Bros-246p-frntis,plts-1st ed (ll2,f) 25.00

BANGS,JOHN K-Enchanted Typewriter-NY-1899-Harper & Bros-170p-frntis,illus by P Newell-1st ed (ll2,sm stn on sp) 25.00

BANGS,JOHN K-House Boat on the River Styx-1896-Harpers-scarce in dj-1st ed (x7,rnfrcd dj) 275.00

BANGS,JOHN K-Mr.Munchausen-Bost-1901-Noyes,Platt-180p-col frntis,plts-1st ed (ll2) 29.50

BANGS,JOHN K-Over the Plum Pudding-NY,Lond-1901-Harper-1st ed (e10,sl wn) 17.50

BANGS,JOHN K-Paste Jewels-NY-1897-Harper & Bros-202p-1st ed (ll2) 29.50

BANGS,JOHN K-Pursuit of the House Boat-NY-1897-Harper & Bros-1st ed (h3) 15.00

BANGS,JOHN K-Pursuit of the House Boat-NY-1897-Harper-1st ed (d4) 20.00

BANKO,W E-Trumpeter Swan-Wash-1963-8vo-214p-wrps,frntis,illus-N A Fauna,No.63 (y8) 22.50

BANKS,ELEANOR-Wandersong-Caldwell-1950-309p-illus-1st ed (u7,dj) 45.00

BANKS,ERNIE-Mr.Cub-1971-Follet-photos-1st ed (s8,dj) 20.00

BANKS,ERNIE-Mr.Cub-1971-Follett-1st ed (ff2,dj) 30.00

BANKS,LOUIS A-Immortal Songs of Camp and Field-Cleve-1899-Burrows Bros-298p-cl (a1) 40.00

BANKS,LOUIS A-Seven Times Around Jericho-NY-1896-134p-cl (a1) 20.00

BANKS,MIKE-Commando Climber-Lond-1955-240p-1st Brit ed (p10,f,dj) 35.00

BANKS,RUSSELL-New World-Urbana-1978-U of Ill-1st ed (v5,f,f dj) 30.00

BANKS,RUSSELL-Relation of My Imprisonment-College Pk-1983-Sun & Moon-1st ed (v5,f,f dj) 15.00

BANKS,RUSSELL-Trailerpark-Bost-1981-1st ed (t5,f,dj) 20.00

BANKS,RUSSELL-Waiting to Freeze-Northwood Narrows-1969-Lillabulero-wrps-1st ed (v5,f) 50.00

BANKS,SIR JOSEPH-Journal of the Right Hon...During Captain Cook's First Voyage in H.M.S. Endeavour 1768-71...-Lond-1896-Macmillan-8vo-orig blu cl,5 chrts(on 4 sheets),2 ports (nn1,sp fade,fr cov sticker) 295.00

BANNERMAN,D A-Birds of West and Equatorial Africa-1953-Oliver Boyd-2 vols-30 col & 24 b&w plts-1st ed (bb3,fray dj) 165.00

BANNERMAN,D A-Birds of West and Equatorial Africa-Edinburgh-1953-Oliver & Boyd-2 vols-red cl-abridgement of 8 vol ed (b9,f,f dj) 175.00

BANNISTER,DON-Sam Chard-NY-1979-Knopf-auth 1st bk-1st US ed (bb1,as new in dj) 25.00

BANNON,JOHN F-ED.-Bolton and the Spanish Borderlands-Norman-(1964)-U of Okla Pr-346p-1st ed (cc4) 35.00

BANNON,JOHN F-ED.-Bolton and the Spanish Borderlands-Norman-(1964)-U of Okla Pr-346p-1st ed (d3,dj) 40.00

BANTON,MICHAEL-West African City-Lond-1957-OUP-8vo-228p-cl-1st ed (y5,dj chip,sun) 25.00

BAR-DAVID,MOLLY L-Jewish Cooking for Pleasure-Lond-(1967)-Hamlyn-4to-col & b&w photos-1st ed (q8,dj) 15.00

BARAKA,AMIRI-Motion of History and Other plays-NY-1978-Morrow-1st ed (w5,f,f dj) 25.00

BARBARY,JAMES-Puritan & Cavalier-NY-1977-192p-illus-1st ed (b7,f,dj) 30.00

BARBE,WAITMAN-In the Virginias-Akron-1896-Werner Co-184p-gry cl-1st ed (z9,f) 10.00

BARBEAU,MARIUS-Downfall of Temlaham-Tor-1928-MacMillan-xii,253p-dec cov,frntis,12 col illus-1st ed (mm8,bump,dj chip & wn) 85.00*

BARBEAU,MARIUS-Haida Carvers in Argillite-(1957)-Nat'l Mus of Canada-214p-stiff wrps,illus-Bull. No.139,Anthro Ser No.38 (bb4) 65.00

BARBEAU,MARIUS-Haida Carvers in Argillite-Ottawa-(1957)-Nat Mus Canada-sm 4to-viii,214p-wrps,229 photos-1st ed (ll8) 55.00

BARBEAU,MARIUS-Jongleur Songs of Old Quebec-Tor-1962-Ryerson Pr-8vo-xxi,202p-decs by A Price-1st transl ed (cc7,sl scuff dj) 25.00*

BARBEAU,MARIUS-Medicine Men on the North Pacific Coast-(1973)-Canadian Mus-95p-wrps,illus-rprnt (c7) 35.00

BARBER,G M-Interest Tables at Six Percent-Sandusky,Cin-1850-Johnson,Derby-122,(1)p-bds (e1,joints crckng) 50.00

BARBER,H-Aeroplane Speaks-NY-1929-roy 8vo-x,278p-cl,52p plts,text illus (t2) 25.00

BARBER,J-Wild Fowl Decoys-Dover-1954-156p-4 col illus (gg3,f,dj) 35.00

BARBER,JOEL-Wild Fowl Decoys-GC-1937-4to-151p-Illus by auth (m3,dj) 75.00

BARBER,JOHN W-Historical Collections of New Jersey-New Haven-1868-543,(1)p-buckram,2 col plts,col map-t.p.:"New Haven, Conn./Published by subscription, by John W Barber./1868" (aa6,rbnd) 150.00

BARBER,JOHN W-Historical Collections of the State of New Jersey-NY-1844-512p-mod cl,plts(incl 2 col)-1st ed (aa6,rbnd,fox) 150.00

BARBER,NOEL-From the Land of Lost Content-Bost-1970-Houghton Mifflin-235p-1st Amer ed (r1,dj wn,tn,chip) 17.00

BARBER,NOEL-Sinister Twilight-1968-Houghton Mifflin-1st ed (dd8,dj) 12.00

BARBER,RED-1947, When All Hell Broke Loose in Baseball-1982-Dbldy-1st ed (p7,f,f dj) 35.00

BARBER,RED-Broadcasters-1971-Dial (q7,dj) 20.00

BARBER,RED-Rhubarb in the Catbird Seat-1968-Dbldy-1st ed (p7,dj) 50.00

BARBER,RED-Walk in the Spirit-1969-Dial-1st ed (ff2,f,dj) 25.00

BARBER,W A-Murder Draws a Line-1940-DD-1st ed (x7,sl chip dj) 45.00

BARBER,WILLETTA A-Deed is Drawn-1949-Scribners-1st ed (s10,dj) 20.00

BARBER,WILLETTA A-Drawback to Murder-NY-1947-Scribners-illus-1st ed (f4,f,dj) 20.00

BARBER,WILLETTA A-Drawback to Murder-NY-1947-Scribners-illus-1st ed (k4,f,dj) 20.00

BARBER,WILLETTA A-Pencil Points to Murder-1941-CC-1st ed (s10,fox,dj) 25.00

BARBER,WILLETTA A-Pencil Points to Murder-GC-1941-Dbldy CC-1st ed (w9,f,sl tn dj) 45.00

BARBOUR,PHILIP-ED.-Jamestown Voyages Under the First Charter 1606 to 1609...-Cambridge-1969-Hakluyt Soc-8vo-2 vols-blu cl,fldg maps & plts (p1) 65.00

BARBOUR,R W-Mammals of Kentucky-Lexington-1974-8vo-(1),322p-cl,photos(66 col),maps (y8,dj chip) 25.00

BARBOUR,RALPH H-Double Play-1909-Appleton-pict cov-1st ed (s8) 30.00

BARBOUR,T-Cuban Ornithology-Cambridge-1943-4to-144p-cl,2 plts-Nutall Ornith Cl No.9 (y8) 55.00

BARCLAY,C N-London Scottish in the Second World War 1939 to 1945-Lond-1952-459p-maps,illus-1st ed (b7,f,dj) 75.00

BARCSAY,J-Anatomy for the Artist-Budapest-1958-folio-illus-2nd rvsd ed (h10) 45.00

BARCSAY,J-Drapery and the Human Form-Budapest-(1958)-folio-102p-68 drwngs (l10,dj) 25.00

BARD,FLOYD C-Horse Wrangler-Norman-(1960)-U of Okla Pr-296p-illus,map-Six Guns 136-1st ed (bb4) 50.00

BARD,FLOYD-Dude Wrangler,Hunter,Line Rider-nd-Sage Bks-100p-stiff wrps,illus (r8) 15.00

BARDI,P M-Tropical Gardens of Burle Marx-NY-1964-4to-160p-photos(incl 60 col)-scarce (jj7,dj tn,chip) 195.00

BARDON,FRED B-Historical Recapitulation-(Madison)-1910-64p-wrps,illus (aa6,tape rnfrcd) 30.00

BARE,J E-Wildflowers and Weeds of Kansas-1979-Regents Pr-4to-509p-132 col & 680 b&w photos (bb3,f,dj) 40.00

BAREA,ARTURO-Broken Root-NY-1951-1st US ed (p5,dj) 20.00

BAREA,ARTURO-Lorca-NY-1949-1st US ed (p5,dj) 30.00

BARICH,BILL-Laughing In the Hills-1980-Viking-1st ed (q9,sl wn dj) 15.00

BARING-GOULD,WILLIAM S-Nero Wolfe of West Thirty Fifth Street-NY-1969-Viking-1st ed (j4,f,dj) 35.00

BARING-GOULD,WILLIAM-Nero Wolfe of West Thirty Fifth Street-1969-Viking-1st ed (x2,f,sl tn dj) 25.00

BARINGER,WILLIAM E-Lincoln's Vandalia-New Brunswick-1949-141p-e.p. maps,illus-1st ed (n3,f,dj) 22.50

BARK,CONRAD V-See the Living Crocodiles-NY-1968-Walker-1st Amer ed (q4,sl wn & brwng,dj sl soil) 20.00

BARK,CONRAD V-Shepherd File-NY-1966-Dutton-1st Amer ed (s4,sl soil,dj) 20.00

BARKER,ALAN-Civil War in America-GC-1961-182p-map-1st Amer ed (c4,f,dj) 20.00

BARKER,CAPT F C-Lake & Forest As I Have Known Them-Bost-1903-12mo-230p-photo frontis-1st ed (m3) 50.00

BARKER,ELLIOTT S-Beatty's Cabin-Albuq-1953-UNM-1st ed (a6,dj) 45.00

BARKER,ELLIOTT S-Beatty's Cabin-Albuq-1953-UNM-220p-photos-1st ed (d3,dj) 40.00

BARKER,ELLIOTT S-When the Dogs Bark Treed-Albuq-1946-8vo-209p-photos (m3,f) 35.00

BARKER,ELSA-C.I.D. of Dexter Drake-NY-1929-Sears-1st ed (f4) 15.00

BARKER,EUGENE C-Life of Stephen F Austin-Nashville-1925-Cokesbury-551p-t.e.g.-ltd to 250c,nbrd,autg-scarce (a9) 200.00

BARKER,EUGENE C-Life of Stephen F Austin-Nashville-1925-Cokesbury-blu cl-Basic TX #7,Howes B137-1st ed (a6) 125.00

BARKER,GEORGE-Poems-Lond-(1935)-Faber-1st ed (x10,dj) 75.00

BARKER,H M-Camels and the Outback-Melbourne-(1964)-Pitman-8vo-225p-illus-1st Austr (gg5,dj) 25.00

BARKER,J ELLIS-British Socialism-Lond-1908-Smith,Elder-522p (r1) 30.00

BARKER,NANCY-French Legation in Texas-Austin-(1971)-2 vols,illus,vol.1 wi glassine dj as issued-Basic Texas Bks #9 (t8,dj sl rub & f,dj) 85.00

BARKER,R-Verdict on a Lost Flyer-NY-(1971)-roy 8vo-238p-cl,32 illus,4 maps,e.p. maps (t2,dj) 40.00

BARKHAU,ROY L-Great Steamboat Race Between the Natchez and the Rob't E Lee-(Cin)-(1952)-priv prntd-46,(2)p-pict wrps,photos (l1) 12.50

BARLAND,ADA-John Opie and His Circle-Lond-1911-t.e.g.,51 illus-1st ed (r2) 60.00

BARLOW,MARJORIE D-Notes on Woman Printers in Colonial America and the United States, 1639 to 1975-NY-1976-Hroswitha Club-tall 8vo-xi,89,(3)p-cl bckd dec bds-ltd to 600c (x4,dj) 35.00

BARLOW,NORA-ED.-Charles Darwin's Diary of the Voyage of H.M.S. Beagle-1933-Cambridge U Pr-451p-cl,fldg maps (x6,vf) 40.00

BARLOWE,WAYNE D-Barlowe's Guide to Extraterestrials-NY-(1979)-Workman-1st ed (o3,f,dj) 15.00

BARNARD,EVAN G-Rider of the Cherokee Strip-Bost-1936-Houghton Mifflin-233p-illus,map e.p.-Herd 207-1st ed (cc4,sl sun sp) 45.00

BARNARD,GEO-Theory & Practice of Landscape Painting in Water Colours-Lond-1855-g dec cov,a.e.g.,26 col plts,43 woodcts & figs (ee1) 175.00

BARNARD,GEORGE P-Selenium Cell, Its Properties and Applications-1930-331p-258 illus-1st ed (h6) 55.00

BARNARD,HARRY-Eagle Forgotten-Indpls-1938-Bobbs Merrill-1st ed (w5) 35.00

BARNARD,HENRY-School Architecture-NY-1849-Barnes-8vo-384p+ads-brwn cl,illus-3rd ed (r10,sl wn) 95.00

BARNARD,INMAN-Cities and Men-NY-1940-Dutton-8vo-256p-8 illus-1st ed (jj5,edgewn dj) 20.00

BARNARD,J L-ET AL-Abyssal Crustacea-1962-Columbia U-4to-223p-158 figs (bb3,dj) 20.00

BARNARD,J-Decorative Tradition-Princeton-1973-1st ed (h10,dj) 30.00

BARNARD,MARY-Mythmakers-Athens-1966-Ohio Univ Pr-cl-1st ed (n8,f,dj) 15.00

BARNARD,ROBERT-Death & the Princess-NY-1982-Scribner's-1st US ed (d4,dj) 12.50

BARNARD,ROBERT-Death of a Literary Widow-NY-1980-Scribner's-1st US ed (d4,f,dj) 15.00

BARNARD,ROBERT-Death of an Old Goat-NY-1977-Walker-1st US ed (e4,rub dj) 45.00

BARNARD,ROBERT-Sheer Torture-Lond-1981-Collins CC-1st ed (w9,vf,dj) 45.00

BARNES & DE MAZIA-Art of Henri Matisse-NY-1933-Scribners-464p-135 plts-1st ed (l10) 16.50

BARNES,AL-Vinegar Pie and Other Tales of the Grand Traverse Region-Detr-(1971)-Harlo Pr-cl,Special ltd ed,photos (z7,dj) 25.00

BARNES,CLARE-John F Kennedy: Scrimshaw Collector-Bost-1969-Little,Brown-4to-129p-cl,photos-1st ed (v3,sl tn dj) 25.00

BARNES,DJUNA-Ladies Almanack-NY-1972-Harpers-illus by auth-1st US ed (y1,f,sl soil dj) 50.00

BARNES,GEORGE W-How to Make Bamboo Fly Rods-NY-1977-4to-110p-photos-1st ed (m3,f,dj) 17.50

BARNES,HENRY A-Man with the Red and Green Eyes-NY-1965-Dutton-8vo-252p-illus-1st ed (gg5,dj) 15.00

BARNES,MAUDE F-Renaissance Vistas-NY-(1930)-223p-bds,ltd to 500c,nbrd (m1) 15.00

BARNES,R MONEY-Military Uniforms of Britain & the Empire-Lond-1960-347p-engrvngs,col plts-1st ed (b7,f,dj) 65.00

BARNES,VALERIE-Strange and Mysterious Past in the Somerset Hills Area-(Bernardsville)-(1975)-(8),84,(2)p-wrps (aa6) 20.00

BARNES,WALTER-English in the Country School-Chig,NY-(1913)-Row,Peterson-286p+ads-cl (k1) 17.50

BARNES,WILL C-Arizona Place Names-Tucson-1935-U of Arizona-502p-fldg illus (b6) 42.50

BARNES,WILL C-Tales from the X Bar Horse Camp-Chig-1920-218p-pict cl,bds,photos,illus-Herd #212-1st ed (t7,cor wn,hng weak) 125.00

BARNETT,AVROM-Foundations of Feminism-NY-1921-McBride-8vo-245p-1st ed (oo7) 45.00

BARNETT,DONALD L-Mau Mau From Within-Lond-(1966)-MacGibbon & Kee-8vo-512p-17 illus-1st Brit ed (jj5,f,dj) 15.00

BARNETT,H G-Indian Shakers-Carbondale-1957-SIU Pr-378p-illus-1st ed (ff4) 25.00

BARNEY,W L-Secessionist Impulse-Princeton-1974-371p-maps (z10,dj) 17.50

BARNHART,PERCY S-Marine Fishes of Southern California-Berkeley-1936-8vo-209p-illus-scarce (m3) 25.00

BARNS,T ALEXANDER-Wonderland of the Eastern Congo-Lond-(1922)-Putnam's-photos-1st ed (p6) 125.00

BARNUM,H L-American Farrier...-Phila-1845-Uriah Hunt-lea (f10,scuff,sp top tn) 45.00

BARNUM,P T-Struggles and Triumphs-Buffalo-1880-Courier Co-327p-orig cl-Authors Ed.-"revsd,enlgd & newly illus" (j1,f) 20.00

BARON,MARGARET E-Origins of Infinitesimal Calculus-Oxford-(1969)-Pergamon Pr-viii+304p-blck cl-1st ed (a2,dj) 25.00

BARON,S-End of the Line-1951-Knopf-auth 1st bk-1st ed (x7,f,dj) 25.00

BARON,STANLEY-Brewed in America-Bost-(1962)-Little Brown-lg 8vo-424p wi index,illus-1st ed (t1,dj) 30.00

BARON,STANLEY-Brewed in America-Bost-(1962)-Little,Brown-424p-illus-1st ed (p2,dj) 22.50

BARONI,D-Furniture of Gerrit Thomas Rietveld-Woodbury-1978-oblng 8vo-illus-1st Amer ed (kk4,dj) 75.00

BARR,ALWYN-Polignac's Texas Brigade-Houston-1964-Tex Gulf Coast Hist Assoc-72p-wrps,photos-1st ed (w3,f) 45.00

BARR,BERYL-Artists and Writers' Cookbook-Sausalito-(1961)-Contact Eds-sm 4to-288,(20)p-designed by N Sidjakov (o6,box) 45.00

BARR,BERYL-Artists' and Writers' Cookbook-Sausalito-1961-Contact Eds-iss w/o dj-1st ed (w5,f,sl wn box) 50.00

BARR,E OSMUN-Flying Men and Medicine-NY-1943-Funk & Wagnalls-8vo-254p-1st ed (gg5,f,dj,autg) 25.00

BARR,STRINGFELLOW-Kitchen Garden Book-NY-1956-Viking-372p-yel cl-1st prtg (q8,dj) 15.00

BARRATT,GLYNN-Russia in Pacific Waters 1715 thru 1825-Vancouver,Lond-(1981)-300p-illus-1st ed (h7,f,dj) 35.00

BARRETT,C-Op Art-NY-1970-54 illus(incl col),illus glassine dj-1st ed (h10,sl tn dj) 85.00

BARRETT,ELIZABETH-Seraphim, and Other Poems-Lond-1838-Saunders & Otley-8vo-xxi,360p-orig blnd stmpd prpl cl,sp g lttrd-1st ed (hh4,sl fade sp) 950.00

BARRETT,HARRISON D-Life Work of Mrs.Cora L V Richmond-Chig-1895-Hack & Anderson-xviii+759p+ads-brwn cl,3 plts-1st ed (h2) 35.00

BARRETT,HARRY B-19th Century Journals and Paintings of William Pope-Tor-(1976)-M F Fehely-lg 4to-175p-36 col plts-1st Can ed (bb5,sl tn dj) 25.00

BARRETT,J L M-Practical Horsemanship-NY-1930-McBride-1st US ed (h9) 20.00

BARRETT,J PRESSLEY-ED.-Centennial of Religious Journalism-Dayton-1908-656p-cl (l1) 25.00

BARRETT,JAY A-History and Government of Nebraska-Lincoln-1892-171p-cl (k1) 15.00

BARRETT,JOSEPH H-Life of Abraham Lincoln-NY-1865-842p+ads-lea,illus (n3) 37.50

BARRETT,MONTE-Smoke Up the Valley-Indpls-1949-Bobbs Merrill-ltd to 1000c,nbrd,autg-1st ed (j9,dj) 25.00

BARRETT,PETER-ED.-Great True Hunts-NJ-1967-4to-278p-photos (m3,f,dj) 40.00

BARRETT,PETER-ED.-Treasury of African Hunting-NY-nd-4to-261p-photos (m3,f,dj) 60.00

BARRETT,PETER-In Search of Trout-NJ-1973-8vo-223p-illus,photos (m3,f,dj) 20.00

BARRETT,WALTER H-Fisherman's Methods & Memories-Lond-nd-8vo-176p-photos (m3,f,sl chip dj) 22.50

BARRETT,WALTER-Old Merchants of New York City-NY-1865-Carleton-8vo-351p+ads-blk cl,third series-1st ed (w1) 50.00

BARRIE,J M-Admiral Crichton-Lond-(1914)-Hodder & Stoughton-4to-viii,235p-orig g pict cl,frntis,20 tip in col illus-1st ed (dd10) 125.00

BARRIE,J M-Little Minister-NY-(1891)-Lovell,Coryell & Co-pict cov gilt,illus-1st Amer ed (r2,sl rub) 40.00

BARRIE,J M-Little White Bird-NY-1902-Scribner's-map-1st US ed (pp10) 15.00

BARRIE,J M-Peter and Wendy-(1911)-Scribners-stmpd pict cl,scarce dj-1st Amer ed (x2,dj sl wn & soil) 325.00

BARRIE,J M-Peter and Wendy-NY-(1911)-Scribner's-13 b&w plts,F.D. Bedford-gld stmpd grn cl-1st Amer ed (e10) 75.00

BARRIE,J M-Peter and Wendy-NY-(1911)-Scribner's-g pict cl,12 plts (pp10,sp g dull) 40.00

BARRIE,J M-Peter Pan in Kensington Gardens-NY-1925-Scribner's-sq 8vo-cl,lg col pict labl frnt cov,illus,incl 16 col plts by A Rackham (a3,sl tn sp) 47.50

BARRIE,J M-Plays-Lond-1928-1st ed (y7,e.p. fox,dj) 45.00

BARRIE,J M-Plays-NY-1930-Scribner's-871p-cl (m1) 12.50

BARRIE,J M-Tommy and Grizel-NY-1900-Scribner-1st US ed (hh5) 20.00

BARRIE,J M-Window in Thrums-Lond-1889-dk blu cl,t.e.g.-1st ed (hh1,sl wn) 25.00

BARRIE,JAMES M-George Meredith 1909-Lond-nd-Constable-1st ed (l9,discol) 150.00

BARRINGER,DR PAUL B-Natural Bent-Chapel Hill-1949-UNC Pr-280p (o7) 20.00

BARRINGTON,PAMELA-Gentle Killer-Lond-1961-Hammond-1st ed (r4,f,sl soil dj) 22.50

BARROW,EDWARD-My 50 Years in Baseball-1951-Coward McCann-1st ed (ff2,dj) 75.00

BARROW,EDWARD-My 50 Years in Baseball-1951-Coward McCann-photos-1st ed (s8,dj) 65.00

BARROW,JOHN-ED.-Description of Pitcairn's Island and its Inhabitants...Subsequent Fortunes of the Mutineers-NY-nd-J & J Harper-brwn cl,g sp titles,2 plts-Harper's Family Libr No.31 (nn1) 95.00

BARROW,JOHN-Mutiny and Piratical Seizure of H M S Bounty-Lond-1976-Folio Soc-261p-e.p. maps,illus (d7,f,box) 50.00

BARROW,JOHN-Mutiny of the Bounty-Bost-1980-Godine-208p-grn cl,g titles,dec e.p.,9 col plts,maps,b&w ullus-1st US ed (nn1,sl wn dj) 35.00

BARROW,JOHN-Travels in China-Lond-1806-Cadell & Davis-4to-calf,8 plts(5 col incl frntis)-2nd ed (gg6,rebkd) 950.00

BARROW,JOHN-Voyage to Cochinchina in Years 1792 and 1793...Account of a Journey Made in Years 1801 and 1802...-Lond-1806-prtd for Cadell & Davies-(11),447p-lea,20 col plts(1 fldg),1 fldg map-1st ed (gg6,rebkd) 1,450.00

BARROWS,JOHN H-World Pilgrimage-Chig-1897-McClurg-8vo-479p-g dec cl,photos (ll1,sl soil) 25.00

BARROWS,JOHN R-Ubet-Caldwell-1934-Caxton Pr-278p-cl,illus,R H Hall-Howes B185-1st ed (v1) 95.00

BARROWS,R M-COMP.-Kit Book for Soldiers, Sailors and Marines-Chig-1943-Consolidtd Bk Publ-pict pap-cov bds,iss w/o dj-1st ed,2nd iss (a10,pg margins brnd) 100.00

BARROWS,R M-ED.-Kit Book for Soldiers, Sailors, and Marines-Chig-1943-Consol Bk Publ-pict bds (dd2,wn,scuff,pgs brwnd) 150.00

BARROWS,W B-Michigan Bird Life-Lansing-1912-8vo-822p-cl,70 plts (y8,hng weak) 35.00

BARRY,CHAS-Shot From the Door-NY-1935-Dutton-1st US ed (d4,fade sp) 12.50

BARRY,FLORENCE-Century of Children's Books-NY-(ca.1922)-Doran-vii,257p-orig blind stmpd cl (dd10) 35.00

BARRY,IRIS-D W Griffith-NY-1940-MOMA-thin 4to-illus beige bds,illus-ltd to 8000c-MOMA Film Libr Ser No.1 (r10) 30.00

BARRY,JOSEPH-Strange Story of Harper's Ferry with Legends of the Surrounding Country-Shepherdtown-1958-216p-photos (t7) 7.50

BARRY,LOUISE-Beginning of the West-Topeka-(1972)-Kansas St Hist Soc-1296p-map e.p.-1st ed (cc4,dj) 30.00

BARSALI,ISA B-European Enamels-Lond-1969-Hamlyn-158p-71 col plts (u5,f,f dj) 25.00

BARSKE,P-Black Duck-1968-Brew Prtg-Atlntc Wtrfowl Cncl,publ-193p-wrps,photos (gg3,f) 15.00

BARSLEY,MICHAEL-Orient Express-NY-1967-204p-1st Amer ed (n4,dj) 21.00

BARSNESS,L-Heads, Hides & Horns-1985-TCU-233p-illus (bb3,f,dj) 40.00

BARTELS,ALBERT-Fighting the French in Morocco-Lond-1932-255p-blu cl,illus-1st ed (b7) 60.00

BARTH,JOHN-Chimera-NY-(1972)-1st ed (p5,f,dj) 15.00

BARTH,JOHN-Chimera-NY-(1972)-Random-ltd to 300c,autg,orig acetate dj-1st ed (l9,f,dj,box) 110.00

BARTH,JOHN-End of the Road-Lond-1962-1st Brit ed (s5,dj sl brwng) 75.00

BARTH,JOHN-Floating Opera-Lond-(1962)-Secker & Warburg-1st Brit ed (ee2,f,dj) 60.00

BARTH,JOHN-Lost in the Fun House-GC-1968-Dbldy-1st ed (ee2,f,dj) 75.00

BARTH,JOHN-Sot Weed Factor-GC-1960-E Gorey dj-1st ed (s5,dj sl chip,tape reinfrcd) 225.00

BARTH,JOHN-Sot Weed Factor-Lond-1961-illus dj-1st Brit ed (s5,pgs sl fox & brwnd,dj) 50.00

BARTH,JOHN-Sot Weed Factor-Lond-1961-Secker & Warburg-1st Brit ed (ee2,f,dj) 100.00

BARTH,LOIS-Run From the River-1965-Avalon-1st ed (s10,dj) 12.50

BARTHEL,THOMAS S-Eighth Land-Honolulu-1978-U Pr of Hawaii-8vo-xi,372p-1st English ed (nn1,dj) 30.00

BARTHELL,E E-Mystery of the Merrimack-Muskegon-1959-54p-illus,ports,facs (z10,wn dj) 20.00

BARTHELME,DONALD-Amateurs-NY-1976-1st ed (r5,f,dj) 15.00

BARTHELME,DONALD-City Life-NY-(1970)-FS&G-1st ed (a10,f,dj) 35.00

BARTHELME,DONALD-City Life-NY-(1970)-FS&G-1st ed (g3,f,dj) 30.00

BARTHELME,DONALD-Come Back, Dr. Caligari-1966-E & S-auth 1st bk-1st Brit ed (x2,sl tn dj) 65.00

BARTHELME,DONALD-Come Back, Dr.Caligari-1964-Little,Brown-auth 1st bk-1st ed (jj6,f,dj) 125.00

BARTHELME,DONALD-Dead Father-NY-(1975)-FS&G-1st ed (b5,as new in dj) 15.00

BARTHELME,DONALD-Great Days-NY-(1979)-FS&G-1st ed (b5,as new in dj) 12.50

BARTHELME,DONALD-Guilty Pleasures-NY-(1974)-FS&G-1st ed (b5,as new in dj) 25.00

BARTHELME,DONALD-Sadness-NY-1972-FS&G-1st ed (g3,sl soil dj) 15.00

BARTHELME,DONALD-Snow White-1967-Atheneum-1st ed (x2,f,dj) 70.00

BARTHELME,DONALD-Snow White-NY-1967-1st ed (s5,dj) 65.00

BARTHELME,DONALD-Unspeakable Practices, Unnatural Acts-NY-(1968)-FS&G-1st ed (b5,f,dj) 45.00

BARTHOLOMEW,ED-Kill of Be Killed-Houston-1953-Frontier Pr-(iv),148p+8p photos plts,cl-1st ed (v1) 40.00

BARTHOLOMEW,ED-Western Hard Cases-Ruidoso-1960-Frontier-Six Guns #154-1st ed (a6,dj) 37.50

BARTHOLOW,ROBERTS-Spermatorrhoea-NY-1870-120p-3rd ed (g10) 65.00

BARTLETT,ALICE H-Facism and Poetry-NY-nd-Italian Hist Soc-wrps-1st ed (v5,f) 35.00

BARTLETT,ARTHUR-Baseball and Mr.Spalding-1951-FS&Y-1st ed (s8,dj) 22.00

BARTLETT,ARTHUR-Game Legs-NY-1928-Cupples & Leon-1st ed (h9,dj) 20.00

BARTLETT,ARTHUR-General Jim-NY-1931-Cupples & Leon-1st ed (h9) 15.00

BARTLETT,D W-Life of Gen. Franklin Pierce...-Auburn-1852-300p-cl (n1) 30.00

BARTLETT,ELISHA-History, Diagnosis, and Treatment of the Fevers of the U.S.-Phila-1856-610p-4th ed (dd3) 125.00

BARTLETT,EVAN A-Love Murders of Harry F Powers-NY-(1931)-Sheftel Pr-221(1)p-cl (e1) 27.50

BARTLETT,JOHN-Personal Narrative of Exploration & Incidences...-NY-1854-Appelton-2 vols-maps,plts-Howes B201-1st ed (a6,top sp chip & rprd) 825.00

BARTLETT,NORMAN-Pearl Seekers-NY-1954-Coward McCann-312p-blk cl,g titles,e.p. maps,57 illus (nn1,sl spot cov) 25.00

BARTLETT,RICHARD A-Nature's Yellowstone-Albuquerque-1974-8vo-250p-photos-1st ed (m3) 15.00

BARTLETT,RICHARD-New Country-1974-Oxford-487p-illus,maps-1st ed (r8,sl chip dj) 20.00

BARTLEY,DAVID-Man Redeemed from Sin and Death-Greenfield-1887-Goble-342p-cl (j1,rub,faded) 15.00

BARTMAN,WILLIAM-John Bartman His Garden and His House-Phila-1938-J Bartman Assc-35p-pamphlet-scarce (x6) 25.00

BARTOK,EVA-Worth Living For-NY-1959-Univ Bks-cl,illus-1st ed (n8,f,dj) 12.50

BARTON,F T-Pheasant in Covert & Aviary-Lond-1912-288p-red dec cl,4 col & 37 b&w plts (ee3,f) 40.00

BARTON,FRED-Charles M Russell-(LA)-(nd)-16p-wrps,sketches,photos (j7,f) 30.00

BARTON,GEORGE-Bell Haven Eleven-1915-Winston (ff2,dj) 25.00

BARTON,GEORGE-Bell Haven Nine-1914-Winston (ff2,dj) 50.00

BARTON,GEORGE-Thrilling Triumphs of Crime Detection-Phila-1937-McKay-1st ed (h4,f,dj) 15.00

BARTON,W E-Life in the Hills of Kentucky-Oberlin-1890-295p-cl-Coleman 2521-Wright 369 (g1,pres cpy) 30.00

BARTON,WILLIAM E-Beautiful Blunder-Indpls-(1926)-Bobbs Merrill-136p-blu cl,ltd to 500c,nbrd,autg-1st ed (m2,t.p. fox) 40.00

BARTON,WILLIAM E-Life of Abraham Lincoln-Lond-(1925)-2 vols-illus-1st Brit ed (n3,dj chip,tn) 35.00

BARTOV,HANOCH-Brigade-NY-1968-Jewish Publ Soc-1st ed (x1,f,dj) 25.00

BARTRAM,A-Lettering on Architecture-1976-Whitney Libr Design-300 photos-1st ed (h10,dj) 65.00

BARZUN,JACQUES-Birthday Tribute to Rex Stout-(NY)-Dec 1,1965-Viking-15p-prtd wrps-1st ed (g9) 50.00

BARZUN,JACQUES-Catalogue of Crime-NY-1971-Harper-1st ed (d4,dj) 65.00

BARZUN,JACQUES-ED.-Delights of Detection-NY-1961-Criterion Bks-1st ed (hh2,dj) 45.00

BASCOM,JOE-Malcolm's Job-Phila-(1959)-Lippincott (s3,f,dj) 12.00

BASEBALL ENCYCLOPEDIA-(NY)-(1969)-2348p-cl (n1,box) 25.00

BASHLINE,JAMES-ED.-Eastern Trail-Rockville Centre-1972-8vo-320p-illus (m3,f,dj) 10.00

BASKIN,LEONARD-Ars Anatomica-NY-(1972)-Medicina Rara-lea sp,cl box,ltd to 2500c,autg (l9,f,box) 150.00

BASKIN,LEONARD-Hosie's Zoo-NY-(1981)-Viking-4to-unpgd-cl & bds,illus,auth-1st ed (r3,f,f dj) 20.00

BASKIN,LEONARD-Portrait of Artists-1963-Mass Review-stiff brwn wrps-1st ed (bb2,f) 30.00

BASNETT,FRED-Travels of a Capitalist Lackey-S Brunswick-(1965)-Barnes-8vo-224p-8p photos-1st ed (jj5,f,dj) 12.50

BASON,FRED-Fred Bason's Diary-Lond-(1950)-Wingate-1st ed (w1,f,dj) 20.00

BASS,ALTHEA-Arapaho Way-NY-1966-80p-frntis,col illus-1st ed (t7,f) 12.50

BASS,FERIS A,JR.-ED-Fragile Empires-Austin-1978-Shoal Creek Publ-384p-cl-1st ed (w3,vf) 15.00

BASS,FLORENCE-Stories of Early Times in the Great West-Indpls-1927-197p-pict cl,illus-1st ed (t7) 12.50

BASS,RICK-Deer Pasture-College Sta-1985-Tex A&M-auth 1st bk-1st ed (b8,f,f dj) 65.00

BASSETT,JOHN-William Faulkner-NY-1972-D Lewis-1st ed (x9,f,dj) 20.00

BASSNETT,T-Outlines of a Mechanical Theory of Storms...-NY-1854-D Appleton-246p+ads-Purple cl,25 text figs-1st ed (j2,sl fade sp) 35.00

BAST,WILLIAM-James Dean-NY-1956-Ballantine (z2,f,sl fade dj) 375.00

BATCHELOR,DENZIL-English Inn-NY-1963-1st ed (y7,dj) 20.00

BATEMAN,ED,SR.-Rawhide Bound-Seattle-1950-Carl Wilson-1st ed (a6,dj,pres) 35.00

BATEMAN,MICHAEL-Cooking People-Lond-1966-Leslie Frewin-296p-gry cl-1st ed (q8,dj) 16.50

BATEMAN,WALTER L-Navajo of the Painted Desert-Bost-(1970)-124p-drwngs,photos-1st ed (v7,f,dj) 15.00

BATES,COL CHARLES F-Custer's Indian Battles-NY-1936-prtd by auth-sm folio-36p-pict wrps,illus-1st ed (dd4) 30.00

BATES,ELISHA-Doctrines of Friends-Mt.Pleasant-1825-publ by auth-320p-Amer Imprnts 19626-2nd ed (aa1,sm sp chip) 50.00

BATES,H E-Daffodil Sky-1955-Little,Brown-1st Amer ed (x2,f,dj) 35.00

BATES,H E-Day of the Tortoise-Lond-1961-Michael Joseph-illus-1st ed (y1,f,dj) 30.00

BATES,H E-Nature of Love-1954-Little,Brown-1st Amer ed (x2,f,dj) 30.00

BATES,J LEONARD-Tom Walsh in Dakota Territory-Urbana-1966-301p-photos-1st ed (t7,f,dj) 10.00

BATES,JOE-Atlantic Salmon Flies & Fishing-Harrisburg-1970-8vo-363p-drwngs,M Weiler-1st ed (m3,f,sl wn dj) 100.00

BATES,JOE-Fishing-NY-1974-8vo-716p-illus (m3,f,dj) 12.00

BATES,JOE-How to Find Fish & Make Them Strike-NY-1974-8vo-216p-photos (m3,as new in dj) 12.00

BATES,JOE-Spinning for American Game Fish-Bost-1947-8vo-247p-illus-1st ed (m3,f,dj) 12.50

BATES,JOE-Spinning for American Game Fish-Bost-1947-Little,Brown-xix,247p-cl,illus-1st ed (pp8,f,sl wn dj) 35.00*

BATES,JOE-Spinning for Fresh Water Game Fish-Bost-1954-8vo-254p-illus-1st ed (m3,f,fray dj) 9.50

BATES,JOE-Streamer Fly Fishing in Fresh & Salt Water-NY-1950-8vo-402p-col plts-drwngs by M Weiler-1st ed (m3) 42.50

BATES,JOE-Streamer Fly Tying & Fishing-Harrisburg-1966-8vo-368p-illus-1st ed (m3,f,dj) 27.50

BATES,JOE-Streamer Fly Tying & Fishing-PA-1966-368p-photos (ee3,f,dj) 25.00

BATES,JOE-Trout Waters & How to Fish Them-Bost-1949-8vo-316p-photos,illus-1st ed (m3,fray dj) 40.00

BATES,KENNETH F-Enameling Principles and Practice-Cleve,NY-(1951)-World-208p-col frntis,3 col plts,illus-1st ed (u5,f) 24.50

BATES,KENNETH-Brackman-Noank-1951-Noank Publ Studio-4to-61p text+26 plts,red cl wi pasteon cov illus,tip in col frntis (r10) 12.50

BATES,L VERNON-Tackle Making For Anglers-Lond-1938-12mo-221p-illus-1st ed (m3) 20.00

BATES,MRS D B-Incidents on Land and Water-Bost-1857-James French-336p-illus-1st ed (gg4,rebackd wi orig cl) 100.00

BATES,ORIC-Eastern Libyans-(Lond)-1970-Frank Cass-4to-xxii,298p-red cl,plts,2 fldg maps-new imprssn (t10,dj) 40.00

BATHE,GREVILLE-An Engineer's Miscellany-Phila-1938-Patterson & White-4to-xii+136p-red & gry cl,illus-ltd to 500c-1st ed (l2,sl fox) 65.00

BATSON,WADE T-Wild Flowers in South Carolina-1964-U of S Carolina Pr-146p-col photo cov,198 col photos,e.p. maps (x5) 12.00

BATTELL,JOSEPH-Ellen...-Middlebury/Lond-1909-Amer Publ/Arthur Bird-2 vols-2nd ed,rvsd & enlgd (f10) 85.00

BATTEN,J-Best of Shep Hunting-1981-Amwell-584p-photos-2nd ed (gg3,box) 75.00

BATTEN,J-Skyline Pursuits-1981-Amwell-318p-blu lea,a.e.g.,frntis,photos,ltd to 1000c,2 autg,box-High Country Heritage Bk (gg3,vf,box) 250.00

BATTEN,J-Skyline Pursuits-Clinton-1981-Amwell Press-8vo-318p-ltd to 1000c,nbrd,autg-frontis,illus-deluxe ed (m3,as new in box) 200.00

BATTERBURY,MICHAEL-Children's Homage to Picasso-NY-1974-Abrams-4to-27p text-cl,drwngs (r10,f) 22.50

BATTISCOMB,GEORGIA-English Picnic-Lond-1949-Harvill Pr Ltd-212p (a8) 35.00

BATTLE,KEMP P-Memories of an Old Time Tar Heel-Chapel Hill-1945-UNC Pr-xii+296p-maroon cl,illus-1st ed (m2,dj) 30.00

BATTY,J H-Practical Taxidermy & Home Decoration...-NY-1897-12mo-203p-illus (m3) 25.00

BAUDELAIRE,CHARLES-Conquest of Solitude-Chig-1982-U of Chig-1st ed (t4,f,f dj) 20.00

BAUDELAIRE,CHARLES-Flowers of Evil-NY-1947-priv prtd for Sylvan Pr-lg 8vo-140p-blk dec buckrm wi glassine dj,drwngs,Egan & Alcock-ltd ed (aa7) 150.00*

BAUDELAIRE,CHARLES-My Heart Laid Bare and Other Prose Writings-NY-(1951)-Vanguard-225p-trans by N Cameron-1st ed thus (m4,f,dj) 25.00

BAUER,ERWIN-Bass in America-NY-1955-4to-137p-illus-1st ed (m3,f,dj) 15.00

BAUER,HELEN-California Rancho Days-1953-Dbldy-4to-128p-photos-1st ed (d3,dj) 20.00

BAUER,JOSEF M-As Far as My Feet Will Carry Me-NY-(1957)-Random-8vo-347p-1st US ed (jj5,f,dj) 12.50

BAUER,K JACK-Mexican War, 1846 to 1848-NY-(1974)-MAcmillan-454p-maps,illus-1st ed (cc4,dj) 50.00

BAUER,PAUL-Siege of Nanga Parbat-Lond-211p-1st Brit ed (o10) 30.00

BAUGHMAN,A J-History of Seneca County, Ohio-Chig,NY-1911-2 vols,3/4 lea (n1,scuff sp) 100.00

BAUGHMAN,A J-Past and Present of Wyandot County, Ohio-Chig-1913-3/4 lea-2 vols (l1,rbkd) 100.00

BAUGHMAN,HAROLD E-Baughman's Aviation Dictionary and Reference Guide. Aero-Thesaurus-Glendale-(1940)-Aero Publ-8vo-600p-cl,col frntis,illus-1st ed,2nd prtg (t2,two autg) 45.00

BAUGHMAN,THEODORE-Baughman, the Oklahoma Scout-Chig-1886-215p-imi lea,lea labl,11 plts-rare-1st ed (z1,rbnd) 250.00

BAUGHMAN,THEODORE-Oklahoma Scout-Chig-(1886)-Conkey Co-215p-cl,illus-Howes B244 (w3) 50.00

BAUGHMAN,THEODORE-Oklahoma Scout-Chig-nd(ca.1886)-216p+ads-pict cl,illus (n3,pgs brwnd) 27.50

BAUM,L FRANK-American Fairy Tales-Chig-1901-Geo M Hill-illus-1st ed (y2,sl rub) 600.00

BAUM,L FRANK-Annotated Wizard of Oz-NY-(1973)-Clarkson Potter-oblng 4to-362p-cl,wi orig col illus,Denslow-1st ed (r3,f,f dj) 25.00

BAUM,L FRANK-Babes in Birdland-Chig-1917-Reilly & Britton-col pict bds,8 col illus,M W Enright,1917 ed wi Baum's name on t.p. (y2,sl spot cov) 300.00

BAUM,L FRANK-Emerald City of Oz-Chig-(1910)-Reilly & Britton-dk blu cl,cov plt wi metallic grn highlights+16 plts-1st ed,1st state (pp10,rub,bump,sl bow) 200.00

BAUM,L FRANK-L Frank Baum's Juvenile Speaker-Chig-1910-Reilly & Britton-illus,Neill & Enright-1st ed (y2) 750.00

BAUM,L FRANK-Laughing Dragon of Oz-Racine-1934-Whitman-1st ed (y2) 225.00

BAUM,L FRANK-Magic of Oz-Chig-(1919)-Reilly & Lee-12 col plts-1st ed (y2,f) 600.00

BAUM,L FRANK-Magic of Oz-Chig-(1919)-Reilly & Lee-sm 4to-grn cl,pict cov labl,pict dj,illus by J R Neill-1st ed,1st state (kk8,vf,dj sl chip & tn) 1,500.00

BAUM,L FRANK-Magical Monarch of Mo-Indpls-1903-Bobbs Merrill-illus,F Verbeck-1st ed,2nd state (y2,sp sl fade,hng rprd) 400.00

BAUM,L FRANK-Master Key-Indpls-1901-Bowen Merrill-col & b&w illus,Fannie Cory-all 1st iss points satisfied-1st ed (q2,rub) 295.00

BAUM,L FRANK-Navy Alphabet-Chig-1900-Geo M HIll-orig bds,illus,H Kennedy-scarce-1st & only ed (y2,wn,sl scratched,hng rprd) 500.00

BAUM,L FRANK-Ozma of Oz-Chig-(1907)-Reilly & Britton-lg 8vo-270p-tan cl wi pict stmpng,illus,incl 40p col illus,J R Neill,plain e.p.s-1st ed,4th prntg (s3,rbkd,cor rub,text wn) 130.00

BAUM,L FRANK-Queen Zixi of IX-NY-1905-Century-16 col plts,illus,F Richardson-1st ed,1st iss (y2) 600.00

BAUM,L FRANK-Sky Island-Chig-Reilly & Britton-col plts-1st ed (z2,sp fray,cor bump) 225.00

BAUM,L FRANK-Visitors from Oz-(1960)-Reilly & Lee-tll 8vo-95p-pict bds,illus(incl col),D Martin-1st & only ed (v8,sl wn cov) 85.00

BAUM,L FRANK-Wizard of Oz-NY-1982-HR&W-4to-219p-pict glossy laminated bds,pict e.p.,col illus by M Hague-1st ed thus (nn8,dj) 45.00

BAUM,L FRANK-Woggle Bug Book-Chig-1905-Reilly & Britton-illus,Morgan-1st ed,2nd state (l9,soil,pres) 2,000.00

BAUMAN,R-ED.-And Other Neighborly Names-(1981)-U of Tex-321p-illus-1st ed (t8,sl tn dj) 25.00

BAUMGARDT,JOHN P-Bulbs for Summer Bloom-NY-1970-Hawthorn-232p-cl,125 col illus (x6,dj) 12.00

BAUR,J I H-New Art in America-Greenwich-1957-illus(incl col)-1st ed (ee1,dj) 100.00

BAXTER,E V-Birds of Scotland-Edinburgh-1953-8vo-2 vols-cl,2 col plts,24 photos plts (y8,sl underlines,dj) 160.00

BAXTER,GREGORY-Murder Could not Kill-NY-1934-Macaulay-1st US ed (d4,dj) 20.00

BAXTER,GREGORY-Murder Could Not Kill-NY-1934-Macaulay-1st US ed (j4,dj) 20.00

BAXTER,KATHERINE S-In Beautiful Japan-NY-1904-Hobart Co-381p-cl,illus (a1,f) 20.00

BAXTER,NANCY N-ED.-Hoosier Farm Boy in Lincoln's Army, the Civil War Letters of Private John R McClure-np-1971-priv prtg-72p-cl,photos-1st ed (z7,f,f dj) 25.00

BAXTER,W T-House of Hancock-Cambridge-1945-Harvard Univ Pr-xviii+321p-illus-1st ed (b2) 15.00

BAXTER,WILLIAM-Life of Knowles Shaw, the Singing Evangelist-Cin,Oskaloosa-1879-237p+ads-cl (pp6) 25.00

BAY,KENNETH-Salt Water Flies-Phila-1972-8vo-150p-photos-1st ed (m3,f,dj) 12.50

BAYARD,SAMUEL J-Sketch of the Life of Com. Robert F Stockton-NY-1856-Derby & Jackson-blu emboss cl-Howes B259-1st ed (gg7) 65.00

BAYER,GROPIUS & GROPIUS-EDS.-Bauhaus 1919 to 1928-NY-1938-MOMA-4to-224p-dec yel cl,photos-1st ed (oo8) 75.00

BAYER,H-ED.-Bauhaus 1919 to 1928-NY-1938-1st ed (h10) 175.00

BAYER,OLIVER W-No Little Enemy-GC-1944-Dbldy CC-1st ed (w9,f,sl tn dj) 25.00

BAYLEN,JOSEPH-ED.-Soldier Surgeon-Knoxville-1968-158p-1st ed (b7,f,dj) 25.00

BAYLESS,RAYMOND-Enigma of the Poltergeist-W Nyack-(1967)-Parker-8vo-210p-1st ed (gg5,f,dj) 12.50

BAYLEY,BARRINGTON J-Garments of Caen-GC-1976-Dbldy-1st ed (f3,f,dj) 20.00

BAYLEY,BARRINGTON J-Soul of the Robot-GC-1974-Dbldy-1st ed (g3,f,dj) 20.00

BAYLEY,MONICA-Black Africa Cook Book-(SF)-(1971)-Determined Prdctns-24mo-66p-illus,A Le Foll (o6,dj) 14.00

BAYLIS,D-California Houses of Gordon Drake-NY-1956-illus-1st ed (h10,sl tn dj) 60.00

BAYLIS,SAMUEL M-Camp & Lamp-Montreal-1897-8vo-316p-ltd to 500c,nbrd,autg-photos frntis-scarce (m3) 85.00

BAYLISS,MARGUERITE F-Bolinvar-NY-1937-Derrydale Pr-2 vols-cl,publ box,ltd to 950c,nbrd (aa6,box) 200.00

BAYLOR,FRANCES C-On Both Sides-Phila-1886-478p-cl-Wright III #414-1st ed (f1) 20.00

BAYLY,WILLIAM-Collection of the Several Writings-Phila-1830-Marcus T C Gould-8vo-400p-20th cent libr bndg,rprnt of 1676 ed (y6,rbnd,cov scuff,pgs fox) 25.00

BAYNES,ERNEST-Sprite-NY-1924-Macmillan-1st prtg (f10,sp fade) 35.00

BAYNES,KEN-Art of the Engineer-Woodstock-1981-Overlook Pr-240p-grn cl wi g cov dec & sp titles,244 illus-1st ed (mm1,sl wn dj,box) 65.00

BAYROS,MARQUIS VON-Amorous Drawings-NY-1968-Cythera Pr-4to-240p-(two vols in one)-dec blk cl,photos,drwngs-1st ed (aa7,sl scuff cl) 35.00*

BAZ,GUSTAVO-History of the Mexican Railway-Mex-1876-Gallo & Co,ed.-folio-211p-col frntis,32 chromo plts,fldg map-Geo F Henderson,transl-1st ed (gg4,sp chip) 1,500.00

BAZIN,GERMAIN-Avant Garde in Painting-NY-1969-S&S-4to-323p-red cl,256 illus(incl 52 col) (r10,tape rprd dj) 32.50

BEACH,ALLEN C-Centennial Celebrations of the State of New York-Albany-1879-Weed Parsons & Co-lg 8vo-459p-17 illus-1st ed (gg5) 40.00

BEACH,BELLE-Riding and Driving for Women-NY-1912-Scribner-deluxe bndg-1st ed (h9) 95.00

BEACH,P-Personal Exposure, His Own Stories-NY-1940-303p-photos (gg3,f,dj) 12.00

BEACH,REX-Auction Block-NY-1914-Harper-1st ed (hh5) 12.50

BEACH,REX-Auction Block-NY-1914-Harpers-28 illus by Gibson-1st ed (y1,sl soil e.p.,sp chip dj) 65.00

BEACH,REX-Net-NY & Lond-1912-Harper & Bros-332,(1)p-cl,full col frnt cov,3p b&w illus-1st ed (b1) 20.00

BEACH,REX-Oh Shoot!-1921-Harpers-8vo-281p-photos-1st ed (m3,f) 25.00

BEACH,REX-Pardners-GC-1905-Dbldy-278p-bds (z7) 25.00

BEACH,REX-Silver Horde-NY-1909-Harpers-silv & gold stmpd cov dec,illus by H Dunn-1st ed (y1,f,sl wn dj) 125.00

BEACH,REX-Spoilers-NY,Lond-1906-Harper & Bros-pict bndg,1st iss-1st ed (b10,sp sl cocked & sl dull) 35.00

BEACH,REX-Winds of Chance-NY-1918-Harpers-illus by J Henry-1st ed (y1,sl soil dj) 75.00

BEACH,SYLVIA-Shakespeare and Company-NY-1959-1st ed (n5,dj) 40.00

BEACH,SYLVIA-Shakespeare and Company-NY-1959-Harcourt-1st ed (v5,f,dj) 35.00

BEACHAM,H-Architecture of Mexico-NY-1969-illus-1st ed (h10,sl chip dj) 45.00

BEADLE,J H-Life in Utah-Phila-1870-Nat'l Publ Co-8vo-540p+4p ads-orig emboss lea wi sp labl,2 frntis,fldg map,illus,plts,ports,facs-1st ed,1st iss (mm1) 185.00

BEADLE,J H-Life in Utah-Phila-1874-Natl Publ-608p-fldg map,illus (d3,sl wn cov) 90.00

BEADLE,J H-Life in Utah; or, the Mysteries and Crimes of Mormonism, Being an Expose...-Phila-(c.1870)ca.1875-Nat'l Publ-thk 8vo-540p+ads-grn cl,illus,fldg map-later prtg (t1,fox) 60.00

BEAGLE,PETER S-Fantasy World of...-NY-1978-1st ed (q5,dj sl chip & soil) 22.50

BEAGLE,PETER S-Fantasy Worlds of...-NY-1978-Viking-1st ed (z3,f,sl sun dj) 25.00

BEAGLE,PETER S-Fine and Private Place-1960-Viking-auth 1st bk-1st ed (x2,dj) 70.00

BEAGLE,PETER S-Fine and Private Place-NY-1960-Viking-auth 1st bk-1st ed (g8,f,dj) 100.00

BEAGLE,PETER S-I See By My Outfit-NY-1965-1st ed (q5,f,dj) 40.00

BEAGLEHOLE,ERNEST-Ethnology of Pukapuka-Honolulu-1938-Bishop Mus/Bull.150 (y5,sp rprd) 65.00

BEAGLEHOLE,ERNEST-Social Change in the South Pacific-NY-(1957)-Macmillan-8vo-268p-cl (y5) 25.00

BEAGLEHOLE,J C-Life of Captain James Cook-Stanford-1974-Stanford Univ-thk 8vo-760p-blu cl,g titles-1st Amer ed (nn1,lacks dj) 55.00

BEAL,M D-History of Southeastern Idaho-Caldwell-1942-443p-maps,illus (a7) 60.00

BEAL,MERRILL D-I Will Fight No More Forever-Seattle-1963-357p-illus,map-1st ed (v7,dj) 35.00

BEAL,MERRILL D-Intermountain Railroads: Standard and Narrow Gauge-Caldwell-1962-252p-1st ed (n4,f,dj) 32.00

BEALE,LIONEL S-Bioplasm-Lond-1872-Churchill-12mo-xvi+345p-tan cl,22 plts-1st ed (a2,cov sl wn,sl crack hng) 40.00

BEALE,LIONEL S-Microscope in its Application to Practical Medicine-Phila-1867-Lindsay & Blakiston-xxiv+320p-lilac cl,58 plts-3rd ed (a2,sl wn,sp fade) 75.00

BEALLE,MORRIS-Washington Senators-1947-Columbia Pub-photos-1st ed (s8,f,dj) 150.00

BEALS,CARLETON-Crime of Cuba-Phila-(1933)-Lippincott-8vo-silv stmpd blk cl,31 illus,W Evans-1st ed (y3) 90.00

BEALS,CARLETON-Great Circle-Phila-(1940)-Lippincott-8vo-358p-1st ed (jj5,f,sl tn dj) 20.00

BEAMISH,RICHARD-Memoir of the Life of Sir Marc Isambard Brunel, Civil Engineer-Lond-1862-LGL&R-xviii+359p-grn cl,9 plts-1st ed (c2,ex-libr) 80.00

BEAN,L L-Hunting,Fishing & Camping-Freeport-1942-8vo-96p-illus,photos-1st ed (m3,as new) 17.50

BEAN,MONTE L-These Mortal Years-Seattle-1977-465p-red cl,illus (b6,f,dj,autg) 10.00

BEANE,WILHELMINA-Texas Thirties-S.A.-1963-Naylor-176p-1st ed (a9,dj) 28.00

BEAR,F-Fred Bear's Field Notes-NY-1976-288p-photos (gg3,f,dj,autg) 25.00

BEAR,F-Fred Bear's World of Archery-NY-1979-402p-photos (gg3,f,dj) 15.00

BEARD,DAN-Book of Camp-Lore & Woodcraft-GC-1920-8vo-270p-illus (m3) 22.50

BEARD,GEORGE-Sexual Neurasthenia...-NY-1972-308p-(facs of 1898 ed)-5th ed (dd3) 40.00

BEARD,GORDON-Birds on the Wing-1967-Dbldy-1st ed (s7,dj) 22.50

BEARD,JAMES-Beard on Food-NY-1974-Knopf-316p-dec e.p.,illus,B Greer,prntd in two inks-1st ed (o6,dj) 20.00

BEARD,JAMES-Delights and Prejudices-Lond-1964-Gollancz-337p-illus,E Thollander (o6,dj) 30.00

BEARD,JAMES-Fireside Cookbook-NY-1949-S&S-4to-222p-pict cl-1st ed (r3,f,tattrd dj) 25.00

BEARD,JAMES-Hors D'Oeuvre and Canapes-NY-Barrows-photos-6th prtg (q8,dj) 26.50

BEARD,JAMES-How to Eat (and Drink) Your Way Through a French (and Italian) Menu-NY-1971-Atheneum-thin 8vo-192p-pict wht cl-1st ed (q8,dj) 17.50

BEARD,JAMES-James Beard's American Cookery-Bost-(1972)-Little,Brown-877p-illus,E Thollander-1st ed (o6) 25.00

BEARD,JAMES-James Beard's Theory and Practice of Good Cooking-NY-1977-Knopf-465p-1st ed (o6,dj) 19.00

BEARD,JAMES-Paris Cuisine-NY-(1952)-Little,Brown-272p-illus,V Bobri,dec e.p. (o6,dj) 25.00

BEARD,P-End of the Game-NY-1965-255p-photos (gg3,cov stnd) 100.00

BEARD,PATTEN-Jolly Book of Boxcraft-Lond-1918-Harrap-sm 4to-203p-blu cl,col illus,photos-1st ed (h10) 75.00

BEARD,PATTEN-Jolly Book of Playcraft-NY-(1916)-227p-blu cl,pict papr labl,illus,plts (a3,sl fox) 27.50

BEARDSLEE,CLARK S-Birds of the Niagara Frontier Region-1965-Buff Soc Nat Sci,Vol.22-478p-orig stiff wrps (b9) 40.00

BEARDSLEY,AUBREY-Early Work of...and the Later Work of...-NY-1967-DeCapo Pr-4to-2 vols-blu cl,331 plts (r10,f,sl wn dj) 32.50

BEARDSLEY,AUBREY-Selected Drawings-1967-Grove-120 plts-1st prtg (h10,dj) 45.00

BEARDSLEY,AUBREY-Under the Hill-NY-(1959)-Grove-illus-1st ed (t4,f,f dj) 15.00

BEARDSLEY,AUBREY-Under the Hill-NY-(1959)-illus-1st ed (m4,dj) 10.00

BEARDSLEY,JOHN-Probing the Earth-(1977)-Smithsonian-4to-111p-col photos-1st ed (ee5,f,f dj) 12.50

BEARSS,EDWIN C-Fort Smith-Norman-(1969)-U of Okla Pr-349p-illus-1st ed (dd4,dj) 30.00

BEASLEY,HENRY-Druggists' General Receipt Book-Lond-1857-John Churchill-503p-pebbld brwn cl-4th ed (q8,cov edgewn) 75.00

BEATH,ROBERT B-Grand Army Blue Book-Phila-1889-255p-5th ed (c4,cov sl wn & soil) 40.00

BEATIE,RUSSEL-Saddles-Norman-1981-UOP-4to-391p-illus-1st ed (a9,dj) 40.00

BEATON,CECIL-British Photographers-Lond-1944-Wm Collins-48p-32 photos-1st ed (cc9,dj) 45.00

BEATON,CECIL-Fair Lady-1964-HRW-photos-1st ed (x2,f,dj) 24.00

BEATON,CECIL-Images-NY-1964-Lond Hs & Maxwell-unpgd-60 photos-1st Amer ed (cc9,f,tn dj) 40.00

BEATON,CECIL-Japanese-NY-1959-John Day-drwngs,132 photo plts-1st ed (c3,f,dj) 65.00

BEATON,CECIL-Memoirs of the `40s-NY-(1972)-McGraw Hill-1st US ed (hh5,f,f dj) 10.00

BEATON,CECIL-Photobiography-GC-1951-Dbldy-lg 8vo-255p-photos-1st Amer ed (u1,dj) 50.00

BEATTIE,ANN-Burning House-NY-(1982)-Random-1st ed (a5,f,dj) 15.00

BEATTIE,ANN-Burning House-NY-(1982)-Random-1st ed (m7,f,dj) 25.00

BEATTIE,ANN-Chilly Scenes of Winter-GC-1976-Dbldy-auth co 1st bk issued simultaneously wi "Distortions"-1st ed (b5,as new in dj) 100.00

BEATTIE,ANN-Distortions-GC-1976-Dbldy-auth co 1st bk issued simultaneously wi "Chilly Scenes of Winter"-1st ed (b5,as new in dj) 100.00

BEATTIE,ANN-Distortions-NY-1976-Dbldy-auth 1st bk-1st ed (g8,f,sl wn dj) 75.00

BEATTIE,ANN-Falling In Place-NY-(1980)-Random-1st ed (a5,f,dj) 15.00

BEATTIE,ANN-Falling in Place-NY-(1980)-Random-1st ed (g3,f,dj) 25.00

BEATTIE,ANN-Secrets and Surprises-Lond-1979-1st Brit ed (r5,f,dj) 20.00

BEATTIE,ANN-Secrets and Surprises-NY-(1978)-Random-1st ed (a10,as new in dj) 30.00

BEATTIE,ANN-Secrets and Surprises-NY-(1978)-Random-1st ed (cc1,as new in dj,autg) 50.00

BEATTIE,GEORGE W-Heritage of the Valley-Pasadena-1939-San Pasqual Pr-459p-map,illus-Six Guns #176-1st ed (cc4,sl wn dj) 150.00

BEATTY,RICHARD C-ED.-Contemporary Southern Prose-Bost-1940-1st ed (n5,sl chip dj) 50.00

BEATTY,RICHMOND-William Byrd of Westover-NY-1932-Houghton Mifflin-233p-cl (x6,edge wn) 15.00

BEAUCHAMP,H-Lost Emeralds of Zarintha-1900-Knight & Millet-pict cov-v scarce-1st ed (x7) 45.00

BEAUCHAMP,REV WM M-Moravian Journals Relating to Central New York 1745 to 66-Syracuse-1916-Dehler Pr (dd6,few sm sp holes) 60.00

BEAUCHAMP,WILLIAM M-History of the New York Iroquois-Albany-1905-NY State Museum-(ii)+125-462p-grn cl,18 plts,one fldg pckt map-bulletin 78,Archlgy 9 (e2,sl nick,sm sp spot) 65.00

BEAUCHAMP,WILLIAM-Essay on the Truth of the Christian Religion-Marietta-1811-223,iiip-orig lea-prntd for auth,by J Israel-Ohio Imprnts 125-Amer Imprnts 22314 (g1) 275.00

BEAUCLERK,HELEN-Green Lacquer Pavilion-NY-(1926)-9 drwngs & frntis by E.Dulac-1st ed (l5,chip dj) 15.00

BEAUCLERK,HELEN-Love of the Foolish Angel-Lond-1929-Collins-decs by E Dulac-1st Brit ed (hh5) 10.00

BEAUDRY,EVIEN G-Puppy Stories-Akron-1934-Saalfield-4to-unpgd-cl & bds,8p col illus (r3) 20.00

BEAUFORT,DUKE OF-Driving-Lond-1894-Badminton Libr-4th ed (f10,e.p. fox) 45.00

BEAUMONT,A-My Three Big Flights-NY-1912-8vo-xii,156p-illus cl g,frntis,plts-1st ed (t2,lacks frnt e.p.,sl fox) 75.00

BEAUMONT,CYRIL W-First Score-NY-nd(1979)-illus-1st ed (hh10,f,dj sp sun,sl tn) 35.00

BEAUMONT,FRANCIS-Maides Tragedy-NY-1932-Cheshire Hs-t.e.g.,engrvngs-ltd to 1200c,nbrd (r2,sl spot cov,uncut) 60.00

BEAUMONT,ROGER A-Military Elites-Indpls-1974-Bobbs Merrill-1st ed (z2,f,dj) 20.00

BEAUMONT-Houston-nd(1939)-Anson Jones Pr-167p-illus bds,photos,illus-Fed Writers Project-1st ed (ee10,f) 32.00

BEAUREGARD,NETTIE H-COMP.-Illustrations of Colonel Lindbergh's Decorations and Some of His Trophies ...Trans-Atlanic Flight...-St.Louis-(1928)-(52)p-wrps-2pg text,the remainder photos-scarce (h1) 17.50

BEAVER,HERBERT-Reports & Letters of...1836 to 1838-Champoeg-1959-148p+index-ltd to 750c (e7,f) 85.00

BEAVER,ROY C-Bessemer and Lake Erie Railroad, 1869 to 1969-San Marino-1969-184p-1st ed (n4,f,dj) 26.00

BEAZLEY,C RAYMOND-Dawn of Modern Geography, Vol.III-Oxford-1906-Clarendon Pr-8vo-xvi,638p-maroon cl,fldg map,7 fldg plts-1st ed (t10) 60.00

BEAZLEY,J D-Development of Attic Black Figure-Berkeley-1951-UC Pr-49 plts-1st ed (h10) 65.00

BECERRA,FRANCISCO-Mexican Sergeant's Recollections of the Alamo & San Jacinto-Austin-1980-Jenkins-45p-1st ed (a9,dj) 50.00

BECHDOLT,JACK-Trusty-NY-1947-Dutton-1st ed (h9,dj) 18.00

BECHET,SIDNEY-Treat it Gentle-Lond-(1950)-Cassel-1st Brit ed (ll9,f,dj) 50.00

BECHET,SIDNEY-Treat It Gentle-NY-(1960)-Hill & Wang-8vo-245p-photos-1st ed (p1,f,f dj) 50.00

BECHTOLD,FRITZ,B-Nanga Parbat Adventure-Lond-1935-lg 8vo-93p-80 plts,3 maps-1st ed (o10,f) 36.00

BECK,ERNEST-Horse-Cedarburg-1971-Animal Tech Publ-spiralbnd bds,col illus (j9) 35.00

BECK,ETHEL F-Lummi Indian How Stories-Caldwell-1955-Caxton Pr-124p-brn cl,illus-1st ed (b6) 15.00

BECK,HENRY H-History of South Africa and the Boer British War-Phila-1900-536p-dec blu cl,maps,illus-1st ed (gg2,f) 35.00

BECK,L C-Fighter Pilot-Huntington Park-(1946)-publ by auth-8vo-200p-cl,frntis,8p plts-1st ed (t2,dj) 25.00

BECK,LEWIS C,M.D.-Botany of the United States North of Virginia-NY-1848-Harper-480p-lea-2nd ed,rvsd (x6,rub sp,sl fox) 85.00

BECK,LOUIS J-New York's Chinatown-NY-(1898)-Bohemia Publ-xii+332p-blk dec cl,illus-presume 1st ed (e2) 100.00

BECK,WALTER-Self Development in Drawing as Interpreted by the Genius of Romano Dazzi and other Children-NY-1928-Putnam's-lg 8vo-xiv+281p-cl,119 illus-1st ed (j2,dj) 35.00

BECK,WARREN A-Historical Atlas of New Mexico-Norman-1969-74p-illus,maps-1st ed (t7) 20.00

BECKER,A C,JR.-Decoying Waterfowl-S Brunswick-1973-4to-247p-photos-1st ed (m3,f,dj) 20.00

BECKER,BOB-Bob Becker's Dog Digest-Chig-1947-4to-130p-wrps-photos (m3) 20.00

BECKER,BOB-Memo-Go Fishing-Indpls-1931-8vo-349p-illus-1st ed (m3) 10.00

BECKER,BOB-Practical Wood Craft-1929-Chig Trib-8vo-40p-wrps-photos (m3) 12.50

BECKER,ETHEL A-Here Comes the Polly-Seattle-(1971)-Superior-128p-brwn simulated lea,illus-1st ed (oo1,f,dj) 35.00

BECKER,ETHEL A-Here Comes the Polly-Seattle-(1971)-Superior-4to-128p-brwn cl-1st ed (m2,dj) 20.00

BECKER,GEORGE F-Reconnaissance of the Gold Fields of Southern Alaska...-1898-4to-86p txt-31 plts,6 dblpg maps-3/4 lea,mrbld bds-(vol from 18th annual US Geo Survey Rprt) (u8) 225.00

BECKER,JOSEPH-Prof. Becker's Cooking Recipes-St.Louis-nd(1906)-Skinner & Kennedy-83p-wrps wi photos of auth (n6) 22.00

BECKER,STEPHEN-Juice-NY-1958-1st ed (r5,f,dj) 20.00

BECKETT,DR.JAMES-Sport Americana Baseball Card Price Guide-1979-photos(incl col)-1st ed,1st prntg (s8,pencl & ink notes) 20.00

BECKETT,JAMES-Sport Americana Baseball Price Guide No.1-1979-Collins-wrps (s7) 20.00

BECKETT,JAMES-Sport Americana Baseball Price Guide No.2-1980-Collins-wrps (s7) 15.00

BECKETT,SAMUEL-All That Fall-NY-(1957)-Grove-wrps,iss as a holiday greeting from publ-1st ed (z8,f) 70.00

BECKETT,SAMUEL-Collected Poems in English and French-1977-Grove-1st Amer ed (m9,f,dj) 25.00

BECKETT,SAMUEL-End and Odds-Lond-1977-1st Brit ed (n5,dj) 15.00

BECKETT,SAMUEL-First Love and Other Shorts-1974-Grove-1st Amer ed (m9,f,dj) 25.00

BECKETT,SAMUEL-I Can't Go On, I'll Go On-NY-1976-1st US ed (t5,f,dj) 15.00

BECKETT,SAMUEL-Ill Seen, Ill Said-1981-Grove-1st Amer ed (m9,f,dj) 20.00

BECKETT,SAMUEL-Mercier and Camier-NY-(1974)-Grove Pr-1st US ed (a10,dj) 20.00

BECKETT,SAMUEL-Molloy, Malone Dies, The Unnamable-NY-1959-Grove-1st US ed (h8,dj) 100.00

BECKETT,SAMUEL-Murphy-NY-(1957)-Grove-8vo-wht buckrm-1st ed (u10,f,f dj) 100.00

BECKETT,SAMUEL-Not I-Lond-(1973)-Faber-wrps as iss-1st ed (z8,vf) 32.50

BECKETT,SAMUEL-Poems in English-Lond-(1961)-J Calder-1st ed (z8,vf,dj) 45.00

BECKETT,SAMUEL-Rockaby-1981-Grove-1st Amer ed (m9,f,dj) 20.00

BECKETT,SAMUEL-Unnamable-1958-Grove Pr-1st Amer ed (x2,vf,f dj) 80.00

BECKETT,SAMUEL-Waiting for Godot-Lond-(1956)-Faber & Faber-1st Brit ed (l9,dj) 200.00

BECKETT,SAMUEL-Watt-1958-Olympia Pr-1st hdbk ed (x2,dj sl wn & tn) 350.00

BECKEY,FRED-Challenge of the North Cascades-Seattle-1969-280p-wrps,photos,maps-1st ed (o10,f,dj) 75.00

BECKEY,FRED-Climbers Guide to the Cascades & Olympic Mountains of Washington-1949-271p-fldg map-1st ed (q10,f) 95.00

BECKEY,FRED-Mountains of North America-SF-1982-4to-256p-140 col plts-1st ed (p10,as new in dj) 30.00

BECKWITH,MARTHA W-Hawaiian Romance of Laieikawai-Wash D.C.-1911-12-GPO-4to-677p-orig olive cl,g titles-1st ed (nn1) 100.00

BECKWITH,PAUL-Creoles of St.Louis-St.Louis-1893-Nixon Jones Prtg-maroon cl,5 fldg chrts in rear (u2) 65.00

BEDE,CUTHBERT-Mr.Verdant Green Married and Done For-Lond-1857-Blackwood-112p-illus-1st ed (ll2,sp fade) 29.50

BEDE,ELBERT-Fabulous Opal Whiteley-Portland-1954-Binford & Mort-181p-red cl (b6,pres cpy) 18.00

BEDFORD,H W-Parrots and Parrot Like Birds in Aviculture-1929-White-298p-8 col plts-1st ed (bb3) 85.00

BEDFORD-JONES-This Fiction Business-NY-1929-Covici Friede-8vo-179p-cl-"New Enlarged ed" (pp2) 65.00*

BEE,CLAIR-Fourth Down Showdown-1956-G&D (q7,dj) 17.50

BEE,CLAIR-Pay Off Pitch-1958-G&D-pict cov-Hilton #16 (ff2) 20.00

BEE,CLAIR-Strike Three-1943-G&D-#3 in ser-1st ed (s8,f,chip dj) 15.00

BEE,CLAIR-Strike Three-1949-G&D (r7,dj) 20.00

BEE,JAMES-Mammals of Northern Alaska-1956-U of KS-309p-wrps-col frntis,131 plts & figs-1st ed (u8) 10.00

BEEBE,F L-North American Falconry and Hunting Hawks-1976-priv publ-4to-331p-14 col plts (bb3,f,dj) 45.00

BEEBE,LUCIUS-20th Century-Berkeley-1962-180p-1st ed (n4,f,dj) 30.00

BEEBE,LUCIUS-Age of Steam-Berkeley-304p-2nd ed (n4,f,dj) 32.00

BEEBE,LUCIUS-American West-NY-1955-Dutton-4to-511p-illus-1st ed (bb4,dj) 25.00

BEEBE,LUCIUS-American West-NY-1955-Dutton-4to-511p-illus-1st ed (d3,dj) 40.00

BEEBE,LUCIUS-Bibliography of the Writings of Edwin Arlington Robinson-Cambridge-1931-Dunster Hs Bkshp-sm 8vo-59,(3)p-bds,papr cov labl-ltd to 300c,nbrd (w2) 45.00

BEEBE,LUCIUS-Cable Car Carnival-Oakland-1951-130p-illus-2nd prtg (n4,f,dj) 29.50

BEEBE,LUCIUS-Cable Car Carnival-Oakland-1951-G Hardy-4to-130p+appndx,illus-1st ed (d3) 50.00

BEEBE,LUCIUS-Comstock Commotion-Stanford-(1954)-Stanford U Pr-129p-illus-1st ed (cc4,dj) 20.00

BEEBE,LUCIUS-Hear the Train Blow-NY-(1952)-G&D-407;(8)p-cl (j1,sl wn dj) 15.00

BEEBE,LUCIUS-Hear the Train Blow-NY-1952-415p-10 drwngs by E S Hammack,860 illus-1st ed (n4,f,dj) 32.00

BEEBE,LUCIUS-Hear the Train Blow-NY-1952-Dutton-4to-860 illus-1st ed (d3) 40.00

BEEBE,LUCIUS-High Iron-NY-1938-225p-1st ed (n4,sl tn dj,pres) 60.00

BEEBE,LUCIUS-Highball, a Pageant of Trains-1945-Appleton Century-4to-223p-photos-1st ed (d3,dj) 30.00

BEEBE,LUCIUS-Highball-NY-1945-223p-1st ed (n4,f,dj) 35.00

BEEBE,LUCIUS-Highliners-NY-1941-103 plts-1st ed (n4) 40.00

BEEBE,LUCIUS-Mixed Train Daily-1947-Dutton-4to-368p-illus-1st ed (d3) 45.00

BEEBE,LUCIUS-Mixed Train Daily-1947-Dutton-4to-368p-photos-2nd ed (d3) 25.00

BEEBE,LUCIUS-Narrow Gauge in the Rockies-Berkeley-1970-e.p. map,250 photos,illus-6th ed (n4,dj) 45.00

BEEBE,LUCIUS-Narrow Guage in the Rockies-Berkeley-1958-Howell,North-sm folio-224p-col frntis,e.p. maps,2 col illus-1st ed (gg4,dj) 45.00

BEEBE,LUCIUS-Overland Limited-1963-Howell North-4to-157p-photos-1st ed (d3,dj) 30.00

BEEBE,LUCIUS-Overland Limited-Berkeley-1963-157p-1st ed (n4,f,dj) 28.50

BEEBE,LUCIUS-Steamcars to the Comstock-Berkeley-1958-100p-2nd ed (n4,f,dj) 26.00

BEEBE,LUCIUS-Trains in Transition-1938-Appleton-4to-225p-photos-3rd impr (d3,dj) 35.00

BEEBE,LUCIUS-Trains in Transition-NY-1942-210p-1st ed (n4) 39.50

BEEBE,LUCIUS-Trains We Rode Volume 1-1965-Howell North-4to-465p-illus-1st ed (nn7,dj wn) 42.00

BEEBE,LUCIUS-Trains We Rode Volume 2-1966-Howell North-4to-511p-illus-1st ed (nn7,f,f dj) 45.00

BEEBE,LUCIUS-Trains We Rode-Vol 2: Northern Pacific,Wabash-1966-Howell North-4to-750 illus-1st ed (d3,dj) 40.00

BEEBE,LUCIUS-Virginia & Truckee-1949-Hardy-8vo-58p-illus-1st ed (nn7,dj tn) 22.00

BEEBE,LUCIUS-When Beauty Rode the Rails-GC-1962-223p-1st ed (n4,f,dj) 25.00

BEEBE,WILLIAM-Arcturus Adventure-NY-1926-Putnam's-grn cl,dec e.p.,t.e.g.,col plts,photos,maps-later prtg (p8) 25.00

BEEBE,WILLIAM-Arcturus Adventure-NY-1926-Putnam's-lg 8vo-xix,439p-dec e.p.,77 illus incl col plts,photos,maps (nn1) 65.00

BEEBE,WILLIAM-Beneath Tropic Seas-NY-1928-8vo-234p-illus-1st ed (m3) 12.50

BEEBE,WILLIAM-ET AL-Tropical Wild Life in British Guiana,Vol.I-NY-1917-NY Zoological Soc-504p-photos,other vols not iss (d9) 50.00

BEEBE,WILLIAM-Nonsuch Land of Water-NY-1932-8vo-259p-photos-1st ed (m3,f) 10.00

BEEBE,WILLIAM-Nonsuch: Land of Water-NY-1932-Brewer,Warren & Putnam-259p-blu cl,photo e.p.,frntis,illus (p8) 15.00

BEEBE,WILLIAM-Pheasants-1931-Dbldy,Doran-4to-2 vols-64 plts (bb3) 110.00

BEEBE,WILLIAM-Pheasants-1936-Dbldy,Doran-4to-(2 vols in one)-64 plts (bb3,f,fray dj) 80.00

BEEBE,WILLIAM-Pheasants-GC-1931(1926)-4to-2 vols-cl,64 plts(mostly col) (y8,lt spot) 115.00

BEECHER,HENRY W-Star Papers-NY-1855-12mo-359p-scarce (m3,ex-lib) 20.00

BEECHER,HENRY W-Star Papers-NY-1855-359p-cl-1st ed (c1,fox,lacks f.e.p.) 20.00

BEECHER,LYMAN-Sermon, Containing a General History of the Town of East Hampton...-Sag Harbor-1806-prntd by A Spooner-40p-sewed as iss(title-leaf mounted)-Amer Imprnts 9945 (l1) 50.00

BEECHEY,FREDERICK W-Narrative of a Voyage to the Pacific and Beering's Strait to Cooperate with Polar Expeditions...-Lond-1831-Colburn & Bentley-orig 3/4 lea & mrbld bds,e.p.& edges,23 plts,3 maps(2 fldg)-2nd ed (d8) 850.00

BEECHING,JACK-Chinese Opium Wars-NY-1976-352p-illus-1st Amer ed (gg2,f,dj) 25.00

BEEDE,A M-Sitting Bull, Custer-Bismarck-(1913)-Bismarck Trib-50p-tan suede,illus (nn6) 175.00

BEEDING,FRANCIS-Death Walks in Eastrepps-NY-1931-Myst League-1st US ed (z9) 15.00

BEEDING,FRANCIS-Death Walks in Eastrepps-NY-1931-Mystery League-1st US ed (bb1,sp bow,dj edgewn,chip) 75.00

BEEDING,FRANCIS-Death Walks in Eastrepps-NY-1931-Mystery League-1st US ed (f4) 10.00

BEEDING,FRANCIS-He Could Not Have Slipped-NY-1939-Harpers-1st US ed (e4,chip dj) 20.00

BEEDING,FRANCIS-House of Dr.Edwards-1928-Little,Brown-1st Amer ed (s10) 12.50

BEEDOME,THOMAS-Select Poems Divine and Humane-Bloomsbury-1928-Nonesuch Pr-51,iv,(4)p-vel-ltd to 1250c,nbrd (a1,box) 50.00

BEEKMAN,E M-Poison Tree-1981-U of Mass-260p-16 illus-1st ed (bb3,f,dj) 17.00

BEEKMAN,E M-Poison Tree-Amherst-1981-U of Mass-260p-cl (x6,as new in dj) 20.00

BEEKMAN,GEORGE C-Early Dutch Settlers of Monmouth County, New Jersey-Freehold-(1915)-(4),155,(1),xix p-cl,plts,1st publ in 1901-v scarce-2nd ed (aa6) 225.00

BEELER,JOE-Cowboys & Indians-Norman-1967-U of Okla Pr-4to-80p+index,illus-1st ed (d3,dj) 30.00

BEELER,JOE-Cowboys & Indians-Norman-1967-U of Okla-lg 8vo-illus-1st ed (a6,dj) 35.00

BEELER,JOHN-Warfare in England 1066 to 1189-Ithaca-1966-493p-maps-1st ed (jj2,f,dj) 75.00

BEER,RUDIGER R-Unicorn. Myth and Reality-NY-1977-Mason/Charter-cl,illus-1st Amer ed (n8,f,dj) 13.50

BEER,THOMAS-Mauve Decade-NY-1936-Knopf-8vo-cl & mbrld bds,tiss dj-ltd to 150c,nbrd,autg-1st ed (u10,sl rub edges,dj,box) 75.00

BEER,THOMAS-Road to Heaven-NY-1928-Knopf-8vo-blu cl-ltd to 200c,nbrd,autg-1st ed (u10,f,damaged box) 60.00

BEER,THOMAS-Stephen Crane: A Study in American Letters-Lond-1924-Heinemann-1st ed (w1,f,dj) 45.00

BEERBOHM,MAX-And Even Now-Lond-1920-1st ed (y7,cov nick,dj wn,drknd) 30.00

BEERBOHM,MAX-Christmas Garland-Lond et al-(1950)-new ed wi added material-1st ed thus (c5,dj sl soil,brwnd sp) 25.00

BEERBOHM,MAX-Happy Hypocrite-NY,Lond-1897-John Lane:Bodley Head-sq 12mo-olive grn wrps,fldg box,No.1 of Bodley Bklts-1st ed (bb2,covs wn,detached) 195.00

BEERBOHM,MAX-Rossetti and His Circle-Lond-1922-Heinemann-4to-blu cl,23 tip in col plts (r10,cov sl soil) 60.00

BEERBOHM,MAX-Rossetti and His Circle-Lond-1922-Heinemann-lg 8vo-ix,22p-beige cl,g titles,22 tip in col prnts-ltd to 380c,nbrd,autg(of which 350c for sale & 30c for pres) (bb7,soil cl) 250.00*

BEERBOHM,MAX-Works of...-Lond,NY-1896-John Lane-12mo-red cl wi papr labl-auth 1st bk publ in own name-1st ed (bb2,bump,rub,dupe labl tip-in 200.00

BEERS,HENRY A-Initial Studies in American Letters-NY-1891-Chautauqua-1st ed (y10) 18.00

BEERY,CHARLES-Black Bass Manual-Modesto-1972-4to-63p-wrps-ltd to 1000c,nbrd,autg-handpntd plts by auth-scarce (m3,f) 35.00

BEETON'S SHILLING GARDENING-Lond-nd(ca.1910)-drk grn cl,e.p. ads,350 illus (m10,sp rub,tips wn,hng split) 50.00

BEETON,MRS ISABELLA-Beeton's Book of Household Management-NY-(1969)-FS&G-1112p-facs of first bnd ed of 1861 (u6,dj) 40.00

BEEVE,A C-Original Collection of War Poems and War Songs of Amer Civil War, 1860 to 1865-Red Wing-(ca.1903)-96p-wrps,col plts,ports (z10,soil wrps) 30.00

BEGER,JOHN W-Annals of Elder Horn-NY-1930-R Smith-225p (ff8,dj) 78.00

BEHAN,BRENDAN-Hostage-Lond-1958-1st ed (r2,sl chip dj) 75.00

BEHM,MARC-Queen of the Night-Bost-1977-auth 1st bk-1st ed (p5,f,dj) 30.00

BEHN,JACK-.45-.70 Rifles-Harrisburg-1956-8vo-137p-photos-1st ed (m3,f,fray dj) 40.00

BEHRENDS,A J F-Socialism and Christianity-NY-1886-Baker & Taylor-1st ed (v5) 30.00

BEILENSON,PETER-Story of Frederic W Goudy-Mt.Vernon-1965-Peter Pauper Pr-12mo-68p-cl-ltd to 1950c (x4,vf) 15.00

BEISER,ARTHUR-Sailor's World-NY-1978-Random-4to-250p-lt blu gry cl,col photos-1st prtg (p8,f,f dj) 25.00

BEKKER,C-Luftwaffe War Diaries-Lond-(1967)-8vo-400p-cl,illus (t2) 40.00

BEKOFF,M-ED.-Coyotes-NY-1978-8vo-384p-cl,illus (y8,dj) 53.00

BEL GEDDES,NORMAN-Horizons-Bost-1932-1st ed (ee1,dj) 150.00

BEL GEDDES,NORMAN-Magic Motorways-NY-(1940)-Random-4to-297p-photos-1st ed (p1,dj) 125.00

BELANEY,GEORGE S-Adventures of Sajo and Her Beaver People-Lond-1935-Lovat Dickson & Thompson-xv,256p-red cl,frntis port,illus,plts-Peel #3438 (k10) 35.00*

BELANEY,GEORGE S-Men of the Last Frontier-Lond-(1935)-Country Life-xii,253p-frntis port,plts (k10,sp fade) 25.00*

BELANEY,GEORGE S-Pilgrim of the Wild-Lond-1937-Lovat Dickson-xxii,282p-frntis port,plts-Peel #3383-9th prtg (k10,sl fox) 20.00*

BELCHER,LADY-Mutineers of the Bounty and Their Descendants in Pitcairn and Norfolk Islands-NY-1871-Harper & Bros-377p+6p ads,orig cl,9 illus (nn1,sp drknd) 195.00

BELDEAN,MURIEL W-To and From the Ottawa Valley-Dallas-1964-Book Craft-111p-cl (z7,dj,autg) 25.00

BELKNAP,GEORGE N-Oregon Imprints, 1845 to 1870-Eugene-(1968)-U of Ore-sm 4to-305p-cl (w2,dj) 65.00

BELKNAP,WILLIAM W-History of the Fifteenth Regiment Iowa Veteran Volunteer Infantry-Keokuk-1887-Ogden & Son-644p-frntis port,illus (n7,ex-libr) 100.00

BELL,A N-Climatology and Mineral Waters of the U.S.-NY-1885-386p-1st ed (g10) 75.00

BELL,A N-Climatology and Mineral Waters of the U.S.-NY-1885-386p-chrts,maps-1st ed (dd3) 125.00

BELL,ALEXANDER-Daughter of Maryland was the Mother of Texas-Wash D.C.-nd(ca.1920)-142p-1st ed (a9) 125.00

BELL,ARCHIE-Sunset Canada-Bost-1918-xii,320p-orig dec cl,map,illus (bb9,sl edgewn) 85.00

BELL,ARCHIE-Trip to Lotus Land-NY-1917-287p-cl,photos (a1,sl discol cov) 15.00

BELL,C N-Henry's Journal...1799 to 1801-Winnipeg-1888-9p-wrps-1st prtg (bb9) 40.00

BELL,CHARLES-Anatomy and Philosophy of Expression as Connected with the Fine Arts-Lond-1888-254p-plts-7th ed (dd3) 75.00

BELL,CHARLES-Manuscript of Drawings of the Arteries-NY-1971-48p+12 col plts-ltd ed (dd3,box) 60.00

BELL,CHARLES-Portrait of the Dalai Lama-Lond-1946-414p-1st Brit ed (p10,f) 40.00

BELL,CURRIER-Professor-NY-1857-Harper-8vo-330p-publs cl-1st US ed (w6,cor last 30p wtrstnd) 150.00

BELL,ERNEST A-Fighting the Traffic in Young Girls or War on the White Slave Trade-Chig-(1911)-Nat'l Bible Hs-95,(2)p-pict wrps (c1,sl wn) 17.50

BELL,ERNEST A-Fighting the Traffic in Young Girls...-np-(1911)-482p-cl (d1) 15.00

BELL,I LOWTHIAN-Principles of the Manufactures of Iron and Steel-Lond-1884-Routledge-xx+744p-grn cl,10 plts-1st ed (c2) 40.00

BELL,JOHN C-Pilgrim and the Pioneer-Lincoln-1906-Int'l Publ Assoc-8vo-531p-cl-1st ed (z4,frnt hng cracked) 12.50

BELL,JOHN T-Tramps and Triumphs of the Second Iowa Infantry-Des Moines-1961-Vlly Bank & Trust-54p-wrps,illus (v2) 30.00

BELL,JULIAN-Winter Movement and Other Poems-Lond-1930-Chatto & Windus-61p-cl-auth 1st bk-1st ed (nn4,sp bump,dj) 115.00

BELL,LANDON C-Old Free State...-Richmond-(1927)-2 vols-3 maps,4 plts,illus-Howes B328-1st ed (hh3,f,dj) 125.00

BELL,LILLIAN-Little Sister to the Wilderness-Chig-1895-Stone & Kimball-bndg designed by Bruce Rogers-1st ed (dd6,sl tn sp) 50.00

BELL,LOUISE P-Kitchen Fun-Cleve-1932-Harter-28p-pict cov by Jessie W Smith (mm6) 75.00

BELL,MAJ HORACE-On the Old West Coast-NY-1930-Morrow-336p-illus-Six Guns #188-1st ed (cc4) 35.00

BELL,MAJ HORACE-Reminiscences of a Ranger-Santa Barbara-1927-Wallace Hebberd-499p-pict cl-Howes B325 (cc4) 35.00

BELL,QUENTIN-Virginia Woolf-NY-(1972)-HBJ-photos-1st US ed (bb1,as new in dj) 25.00

BELL,R C-Diaries From the Days of Sail-NY-1974-HR&W-8vo-160p-photos,drwngs (nn1,dj) 35.00

BELL,THOMAS-In the Midst of Life-NY-1961-Atheneum-1st ed (v5,f,dj) 25.00

BELL,W D M-Karamojo Safari-NY-1949-8vo-298p-1st ed (m3,f,sl chip dj) 100.00

BELL,W D M-Wanderings of an Elephant Hunter-Lond-1923-4to-187p-illus-scarce-1st ed (m3) 400.00

BELL,W S-Old Fort Benton-Helena-1909-31p-stiff pict wrps,frntis,photos-Howes B331-1st ed (t7,f) 55.00

BELL,WALTER G-Great Plague in London in 1665-Lond-1924-374p-illus-1st ed (dd3) 100.00

BELL,WILLIAM G-Will James-Flagstaff-(1982)-Northland Pr-130p-col plts (ff4,dj) 30.00

BELL,WILLIAM-New Tracks in North America-Lond-1869-Chapman & Hall-2 vols-plans,maps-Rittenhouse 31-1st ed (a6,cov wn,hng crack) 350.00

BELLAIRS,GEORGE-An Old Man Dies-Lond-1980-Gifford-1st ed (s4,f,dj) 20.00

BELLAIRS,GEORGE-Close All Roads to Sospel-Lond-1976-Gifford-1st ed (r4,f,dj) 20.00

BELLAIRS,GEORGE-Death in the Night Watches-NY-1946-Macmillan-1st US ed (f4,chip dj) 12.50

BELLAIRS,GEORGE-Fear Round About-NY-1981-Walker-1st US ed (g4,f,dj) 15.00

BELLAIRS,JOHN-House With a Clock In Its Walls-NY-(1973)-Dial-drwngs,E Gorey-1st ed (a10,edge-tn dj) 20.00

BELLAMY,JOE D-New Fiction-Urbana,Chig,Lond-(1974)-Univ of Ill-1st ed (b5,f,sp fade dj) 12.50

BELLARD,ALFRED-Gone for a Soldier-Bost-1975-Little,Brown-298p-frntis,illus,e.p. maps-1st ed so stated (o7,sl dmpstnd edge,chip dj) 35.00

BELLASIS,M-Honourable Company-Lond-1952-286p-illus-1st ed (b7,dj) 30.00

BELLOC,H-Emerald of Katherine the Great-1926-Harpers-21 drwngs by G K Chesterton-1st Amer ed (x7,sl chip dj) 100.00

BELLOC,HILAIRE-Advice-Lond-(1960)-Harvill-38p-red bds,drwngs-1st ed (q8,dj tn) 25.00

BELLOC,HILAIRE-Conversation with a Cat and Others-NY-1931-Harper-8vo-227p-1st US ed (ee5,dj) 35.00

BELLOC,HILAIRE-Joan of Arc-Lond-1929-1st ed (y7,sl fray dj) 50.00

BELLOC,HILAIRE-Road-Lond-(1924)-Unwin's "Popular Ed."-8vo-218p (f10,sp drknd,cor bump) 65.00

BELLOCQ,E J-Storyville Portraits-NY-(1970)-MOMA-4to-cl,photos-1st ed (y3,dj) 65.00

BELLOW,SAUL-Adventures of Augie March-NY-1953-Viking-1st ed (z2,dj) 75.00

BELLOW,SAUL-Dean's December-NY et al-(1982)-Harper & Row-1st ed (b5,as new in dj) 15.00

BELLOW,SAUL-Dean's December-NY-(1982)-Harper & Row-1st ed (e3,f,sl tn dj) 20.00

BELLOW,SAUL-Henderson the Rain King-NY-1959-1st ed (p5,f,dj sp sl chip) 90.00

BELLOW,SAUL-Humboldt's Gift-NY-(1975)-Viking-1st ed (ee2,f,dj) 35.00

BELLOW,SAUL-Humboldt's Gift-NY-(1975)-Viking-1st ed (k3,sl tn dj) 25.00

BELLOW,SAUL-Last Analysis-NY-1965-1st ed (n5,dj) 40.00

BELLOW,SAUL-Mosby's Memoirs and Other Stories-NY-(1968)-Viking-1st ed (ee2,f,dj) 40.00

BELLOW,SAUL-Mosby's Memoirs-NY-(1968)-1st ed (p5,dj) 20.00

BELLOW,SAUL-Mr Sammler's Planet-NY-(1970)-Viking-1st ed (ee2,f,dj) 40.00

BELLOW,SAUL-Mr. Sammler's Planet-NY-(1970)-Viking-1st ed (e3,dj) 35.00

BELLOW,SAUL-Seize the Day-NY-1956-1st ed (r5,sp sunned dj) 40.00

BELLOW,SAUL-To Jerusalem and Back-NY-1976-Viking-1st ed (w5,f,f dj) 25.00

BELLWOOD,P-Man's Conquest of the Pacific-1979-Oxford Univ-462p-27 col & 238 b&w photos,maps (bb3,f,dj) 35.00

BELOTE,JAMES H-Typhoon of Steel-NY-1970-Harper & Row-1st ed (z2,f, f dj) 25.00

BEMELMANS,LUDWIG-Best of Times-NY-(1948)-S&S-1st ed (hh5,dj) 20.00

BEMELMANS,LUDWIG-Castle Number Nine-NY-1937-Viking-4to-unpgd-col illus-1st ed (r3,sl wn,lacks dj) 40.00

BEMELMANS,LUDWIG-Eye of God-NY-1949-Viking/Brown-1st ed (hh5,dj) 12.00

BEMELMANS,LUDWIG-Golden Basket-NY-(1936)-JLG,Viking-sm 4to-96p-pict cl,col & b&w illus-Bader #60-1st ed (nn10,sp wn,dj sp sl wn) 100.00

BEMELMANS,LUDWIG-Italian Holiday-Bost-1961-Houghton,Mifflin-4to-102p-cl & bds,drwngs,auth-1st ed (r3,f,sl tanned dj) 35.00

BEMELMANS,LUDWIG-La Bonne Table-1964-S&S-446p-blu bds,drwngs & e.p. by auth-1st prtg (q8,dj) 30.00

BEMELMANS,LUDWIG-Madeline-Lond-(1952)-Verschoyle-lg 4to-unpgd-pict bds-1st Brit ed (nn10,dj rub) 100.00

BEMELMANS,LUDWIG-Now I Lay Me Down to Sleep-NY-1943-1st ed (j5,dj) 15.00

BEMELMANS,LUDWIG-On Board Noah's Ark-Lond-(1962)-Collins-188p-red cl,col & b&w illus-1st ed (q8,dj) 17.50

BEMELMANS,LUDWIG-On Board Noah's Ark-NY-(1962)-14 col illus-1st ed (j5,f,sp chip dj) 10.00

BEMELMANS,LUDWIG-Parsley-NY-(1955)-Harper-oblng 4to-46p-cl,col illus-1st ed (r3,dj sl tn & chip) 65.00

BEMELMANS,LUDWIG-World of Bemelmans-NY-1955-Viking-1st ed thus (hh5,dj) 10.00

BEMENT,C N-American Poulterer's Companion-1863-Harper-304p,120p (bb3,sp fade,fray,sl fox) 45.00

BEMENT,R B-Kingdom of Brass-Cin-1860-Moore,Wilstach,Keys-312p-cl,frntis,5p illus (c1) 25.00

BEMIS,A F-Evolving House-1933,1934,1936-MIT-3 vols (h10,v.2 cov sl soil) 250.00

BENAVIDES,ALONSO DE-Memorial of Fray Alonso de Benevides-Chig-1916-priv prtd-285p-photos,facs,ltd to 300c,pres by Chas Lummis-Rader#332-rare-1st ed (u7,f) 350.00

BENCH,JOHNNY-From Behind the Plate-1972-Rutledge-photos-1st ed (s8,dj) 15.00

BENCHLEY,NATHANIEL-Sail a Crooked Ship-NY-1960-McGraw Hill-1st ed (y1,f,dj) 25.00

BENCHLEY,NATHANIEL-Winter's Tale-NY-1964-McGraw Hill-1st ed (y1,f,f dj) 25.00

BENCHLEY,ROBERT-After 1903-NY-1938-Harper-1st ed (ee2,dj wn & chip) 35.00

BENCHLEY,ROBERT-Benchley or Else-NY-1947-illus,G Williams-1st ed (p5,sl chip dj) 35.00

BENCHLEY,ROBERT-Benchley Roundup-NY-1954-drwngs,Gluyas Williams-1st ed (q5,dj sp sl sunned) 25.00

BENCHLEY,ROBERT-Benchley, Or Else-NY-1947-illus,G Williams-1st ed (o5,sl chip dj) 35.00

BENCHLEY,ROBERT-Chips off the Old Benchley-NY-(1949)-Harper-1st ed (hh5,dj) 15.00

BENCHLEY,ROBERT-Chips Off the Old Benchley-NY-(1949)-illus,G Williams-1st ed (p5,dj) 30.00

BENCHLEY,ROBERT-Of All Things-NY-1921-Holt-drwngs,G.Williams-1st ed (d10,sl wn,fox e.p.) 50.00

BENDA,W T-Masks-NY-1944-Watson Guptill-128p-illus-1st ed (w1,f,dj) 75.00

BENDANN,E-Death Customs-Lond-1930-K Paul,Trench,Trubner-cl-1st ed (l8,f,dj) 65.00

BENDER,AVERAM-March of Empire-Lawrence-1952-U of Kansas-1st ed (a6,dj,pres) 45.00

BENDER,C J-Twenty Years among the African Negroes-Girard-nd-Haldeman Julius-64p-Little Blu Bk #797-nine illus (f1,wrps) 12.50

BENDER,HELEN C-Variations on the Cooking Theme-Honolulu-(1957)-Pacific Publ-149p-bds-ltd ed (l6) 25.00

BENECKE,AMY M-Cannes and Its Surroundings-Lond-nd(ca.1910)-Allen & Unwin-8vo-94p-16 tip-in col plts-1st ed (jj5,dj sp chip,sl tn) 35.00

BENEDICT,B-Phonographics-NY-1977-folio-col illus-1st ed (h10,dj) 35.00

BENEDICT,BRAD-Fame-NY-1980-Harmony-sm 4to-120p-blk cl,col illus-1st ed (r10,f,f dj) 12.50

BENEDICT,C G-Vermont in the Civil War, Vol.II-Burlington-1888-808p-illus-1st ed (c4) 35.00

BENEDICT,LEONARD-Waifs of the Slums and Their Way Out-NY-1907-Revell-1st ed (v5) 40.00

BENEDICT,ROY G-Interurban to Milwaukee-Chig-1962-168p-spiral bndg-Bull.#106-1st ed (n4) 27.00

BENEDICT,ROY G-Route of the Electroliners-Chig-1963-188p-spiral bndg-Bull.#107-1st ed (n4) 24.00

BENEDICT,RUTH-Tales of the Cochiti Indians-Wash D.C.-1931-Smith Inst-256p-wrps-Bur of Amer Ethn,Bull#98-scarce-1st ed (v7,sl chip) 30.00

BENEDICT,RUTH-Zuni Mythology-NY-1935-2 vols-Columbia U Contbs to Anthrop,Vol.21-1st ed (v7) 250.00

BENEDICT,WILLIAM H-New Brunswick in History-New Brunswick-1925-391p-cl,2 fldg maps (aa6) 100.00

BENELL,JULIE-Let's Eat at Home-NY-(1981)-Crowell-385p-red cl-1st ed (q8,dj) 15.00

BENESCH,O-Drawings of Rembrandt-Lond-1973-Phaidon-6 vols-t.e.g.,illus-enlgd ed (h10) 750.00

BENET,JAMES-Knife Behind You-NY-1950-Harper-1st ed (g4,dj) 10.00

BENET,LAURA-Thackeray-NY-1947-Dodd Mead-1st ed (hh5,tn dj) 10.00

BENET,SULA-Song,Dance, and Customs of Peasant Poland-NY-(1951)-Roy-8vo-247p-16 illus-1st US ed (gg5,dj) 25.00

BENFORD,GREGORY-If the Stars are Gods-NY-(1977)-1st ed (bb10,f,dj) 40.00

BENFORD,ROBERT-Doctors in the Sky-Springfield-1955-326p-1st ed (dd3,dj) 50.00

BENHAM,CLARENCE-Pearl Diver's Luck-NY-(1950)-Norton-286p-1st US ed (u5) 18.50

BENHAM,HERVEY-Codbangers-Colchester-1979-Essex Cnty Newspapers-8vo-207p-illus-1st ed (gg5,f,dj) 17.50

BENHAM,W GURNEY-Playing Cards-Lond-(1931)-Ward,Lock-4to-195p-grn cl,illus(incl col)-1st ed (b3) 90.00

BENHAM,W GURNEY-Playing Cards-Lond-nd-Spring Bks-4to-vii,196p-cl,illus(incl col) (ll4,dj sl chip) 75.00

BENJAMIN FRANKLIN PRIMER-Bost-1880-Bost School Suppy Co-24p-wrps (g1) 20.00

BENJAMIN FRANKLIN SHAMBAUGH AS IOWA REMEMBERS HIM 1871-1940-Iowa City-1941-Torch Pr-229p-cl (e1) 15.00

BENJAMIN,MRS. M G-Missionary Sisters-Bost-1860-Amer Tract Scty-cl,frntis-rare-1st ed (m8) 45.00

BENJAMIN,S G W-Atlantic Islands as Resorts of Health & Pleasure-NY-1878-Harper & Bros-274p+ads-dec brwn cl wi blk & gilt,illus-1st ed (p2,wn cors & sp) 80.00

BENNET,JOSEPHINE-Measure for Measure as Royal Entertainment-NY-1966-Columbia U Pr-1st ed (x9,dj rub) 12.50

BENNET,ROBERT A-Bowl of Baal-W Kingston-1975-Grant-1st ed (g3,f,dj) 15.00

BENNET,ROBERT A-Sheepman's Gold-1939-Washburn-1st Amer ed (r9,sl wn dj) 35.00

BENNETT,ARNOLD-Our Women-NY-(1920)-Doran-8vo-264p-1st US ed (oo7) 45.00

BENNETT,ARNOLD-Riceyman Steps-1923-Doran-1st Amer ed (x2,sl chip dj) 65.00

BENNETT,DOROTHY-How Strange a Thing-Caldwell-1935-Caxton Pr-102p-grn cl-1st ed (b6) 15.00

BENNETT,EDNA M-Turquoise and the Indian-Chig-(1970)-Sage Bks/Swallow Pr-152p-12 col illus-rvsd ed (u5,f,dj) 24.00

BENNETT,EDNA M-Turquoise and the Indian-Chig-(1970)-Swallow-8vo-152p (z4,dj) 15.00

BENNETT,EDNA M-Turquoise Jewelry of the Indians of the Southwest-Col Spgs-1974-Turq Bks-4to-148p-illus covs,40 col plts,51 b&w photos-2nd prtg (u5,f,sl chip dj) 30.00

BENNETT,EDWARD T-Society for Psychical Research-Lond-1903-R Brimley Johnson-thin 8vo-(ii)+58+(2)p-prntd grn cl,illus-1st ed (y9) 45.00

BENNETT,ESTELLINE-Old Deadwood Days-NY-(1928)-J H Sears-300p-illus-1st ed (cc4,sp wn) 35.00

BENNETT,GEOFFREY-Battle of Trafalgar-Annapolis-1977-256p-maps,illus-1st Amer ed (b7,f,dj) 25.00

BENNETT,H S-English Books & Readers 1475 to 1557-Cambridge-1952-Univ Pr-1st ed (w1) 30.00

BENNETT,IAN-COMP.-Sotheby Parke Benet Guide to Pricing Antiques from 25 to 2500 Dollars-1975-Studio Bk-240p-illus (cc8,dj) 40.00

BENNETT,J G-Image of God in Work-Sherbourne-1976-Coombe Springs Pr-wrps in dj,Transf of Man Ser No.5-1st ed (l8,dj) 10.00

BENNETT,JOAN-Virginia Woolf-NY-(1945)-Harcourt-8vo-1st Amer ed (x3,dj) 30.00

BENNETT,L J-Training Grouse & Woodcock Dogs-NY-1948-146p-photos (gg3,f) 60.00

BENNETT,MARGOT-Long Way Back-Lond-1954-Bodley Head-1st ed (e4,wn spot e.p.,dj) 30.00

BENNETT,NOEL-Weaver's Pathway-Flagstaff-(1974)-64p-illus-1st ed (v7,f,dj) 25.00

BENNETT,RICHARD R-Aviation, Its Commercial and Financial Aspects-NY-(1929)-Ronald Pr-127p-cl (m1) 12.50

BENNETT,ROBERT-Wrath of John Steinbeck-LA-1939-Albertson Pr-ltd to 1000c,nbrd,autg,tip-in frntis by Artemis,red bds wi gold labl,iss w/o dj (a10,sl scuff & wn edges) 125.00

BENNETT,ROSS-ED.-Visiting Our Past-(Wash)-(1977)-Nat'l Geographic Scty-400p-cl,11 maps,400 col illus-1st ed so stated (l1,f,dj) 17.50

BENNETT,TINY-Art of Angling-NY-1970-8vo-288p-photos (m3,f,dj) 10.00

BENNETT,VICTOR-Around the World in a Salad Bowl-SF-(1961)-Hesperian-212p-pict wht pebbld cl,6 col plts-1st ed (q8,dj) 16.50

BENNETT,WENDELL-Tarahumara-1935-U of Chig-412p-photos-scarce-1st ed (a9) 200.00

BENNETT,WHITMAN-Practical Guide to American Book Collecting-NY-(1941)-Bennett Bk Studios-8vo-254p-cl-ltd to 1250c (x4) 50.00

BENRIMO,DOROTHY-Camposantos-Ft.Worth-(1968)-76p-dbl col,photos-1st ed (u7) 45.00

BENSON,ALLAN L-Daniel Webster-NY-1929-402p-cl-1st ed (c1) 20.00

BENSON,CAPT N P-Log of the El Dorado-SF-1914-James H Barry-66p-gry prtd wrps,6 photo plts-1st complete ed (pp1,chip wrps,sl fox) 75.00

BENSON,E F-Spook Stories-Lond-nd(1928)-1st ed (m5,sl wn sp) 25.00

BENSON,L-Cacti of the United States and Canada-1983-Stanford-4to-1044p-photos,maps (bb3,f,dj) 90.00

BENSON,RICHARD M-Steamships and Motorships of the West Coast-NY-1968-Bonanza-175p-1/2 cl,illus (p8,dj) 8.50

BENT,A C-Life Histories of N Amer Blackbirds, Orioles, Tanagers, and Allies-Wash-1958-8vo-549p-orig wrps,37 plts (y8) 19.00

BENT,A C-Life Histories of N Amer Cuckoos, Goatsuckers, Hummingbirds, and their Allies-NY-1964-8vo-2 vols-wrps,73 plts (y8) 15.00

BENT,A C-Life Histories of N Amer Diving Birds-NY-1946-8vo-237p-cl,32p illus (y8,dj chip) 30.00

BENT,A C-Life Histories of N Amer Diving Birds-Wash-1919-8vo-245p-cl,55 plts(12 col) (y8,rbnd) 75.00

BENT,A C-Life Histories of N Amer Flycatchers, Larks, Swallows, and Their Allies-Wash-1942-8vo-555p-wrps,70 plts (y8,fade) 25.00

BENT,A C-Life Histories of N Amer Gallinaceous Birds-1932-USNM Bull.162-490p-93 plts (bb3) 35.00

BENT,A C-Life Histories of N Amer Gulls and Terns-NY-1947-8vo-(1),333p-cl-Dodd ed (y8,dj) 21.00

BENT,A C-Life Histories of N Amer Jays, Crows, and Titmice-Wash-1946-8vo-495p-wrps,68 plts (y8) 27.00

BENT,A C-Life Histories of N Amer Marsh Birds-NY-1963-Dover-8vo-392p-wrps,98 b&w plts (y8,rprnt) 9.50

BENT,A C-Life Histories of N Amer Shore Birds-NY-1962-Dover-8vo-2 vols-wrps,121 b&w plts (y8,rprnt) 18.50

BENT,A C-Life Histories of N Amer Thrushes, Kinglets, and Their Allies-Wash-1949-8vo-454p-orig wrps,51 b&w plts (y8) 25.00

BENT,A C-Life Histories of N Amer Wagtails, Shrikes, Vireos, and Their Allies-Wash-1950-8vo-411p-orig wrps,48 b&w plts (y8) 25.00

BENT,A C-Life Histories of N Amer Wild Fowl-NY-1962-Dover-8vo-2 vols-wrps,106 plts-orig Dover ed (y8) 15.00

BENT,A C-Life Histories of N Amer Wildfowl-1962-Dover-2 vols-106 plts-rprnt (bb3,f) 35.00

BENT,A C-Life Histories of N Amer Wood Warblers-Wash-1953-8vo-734p-orig wrps,83 plts (y8) 27.00

BENT,A C-Life Histories of N Amer Woodpeckers-1939-USNM-334p-wrps,37plts (bb3) 26.00

BENT,A C-Life Histories of N Amer Woodpeckers-Wash-1939-8vo-334p-orig wrps,39 b&w plts (y8,spots) 30.00

BENT,A C-Life Histories on N Amer Blackbirds, Orioles, Tanagers, and Allies-NY-1965-Dover-8vo-(2),549p-wrps,37 plts-rprnt (y8) 9.50

BENTLEY,E C-Elephant's Work-1951-Knopf-1st Amer ed (x7,dj) 20.00

BENTLEY,E C-Trent's Case Book-1953-Knopf-1st ed (x7,f,dj) 33.00

BENTLEY,E C-Trent's Own Case-1936-Knopf-1st Amer ed (n9,sl fade sp) 20.00

BENTLEY,NICHOLAS-ED.-Russell's Despatches from the Crimea 1854 to 1856-Lond-1966-287p-illus-1st ed (b7,f,dj) 25.00

BENTLEY,THOMAS-False Honor-NY-1879-Walker-270p-cl-Wright-1st ed (c1) 27.50

BENTON,CHARLES E-As Seen From the Ranks-NY-1902-292p (o7,hngs weak,cov wn & soil) 75.00

BENTON,CHARLES W-Four Days on the Webutuck River-Amenia-1925-Troutbeck Pr-soft brwn wrps,ltd to 200c-1st ed (ee2) 175.00

BENTON,KENNETH-Craig & the Midas Touch-NY-1976-Walker-1st Amer ed (r4,f,dj) 17.50

BENTON,PEGGIE-Finnish Food for Your Table-Oxford-(1960)-Bruno Cassirer-116p-illus,auth (o6,dj) 20.00

BENTON,THOMAS H-Thirty Years in the Senate-NY-1854-Appleton-2 vols-1st ed (a6,cov dull,sl fox) 175.00

BENUZZI,FELICE-No Picnic on Mount Kenya-NY-1953-239p-1st US ed,2nd prtg (o10,f,dj) 25.00

BENWELL,GWEN-Sea Enchantress-Lond-(1961)-Hutchinson-287p-cl,16 plts,illus-1st ed (dd10) 35.00

BENY,ROLOFF-Time of Gods-NY-(1962)-Viking-4to-272p-132 plts+16 tip-in b&w plts-1st US ed (jj5,f,dj) 35.00

BERCKMAN,EVELYN-Be All and End All-Lond-1976-Hamilton-1st ed (r4,dj) 17.50

BERCKMAN,EVELYN-Nelson's Dear Lord-Lond-1962-274p-illus-1st ed (b7,f,dj) 25.00

BERDYAEV,NICHOLAS-Christianity & Class War-NY-1933-Sheed & Ward-123p (r1) 15.00

BERE,R-Antelopes-Lond-1970-96p-col illus (gg3,f,dj) 10.00

BERE,RENNIE-Way to the Mountains of the Moon-Lond-1966-147p-5 maps,16p photos-1st ed (a5,f,dj) 75.00

BERENDT,JOACHIM-New Jazz Book-NY-(1962)-Hill & Wang-1st Amer ed (w1,f,dj) 25.00

BERESFORD,J D-Peckover-1935-Putnam-1st Amer ed (x7,f,dj sl tn & chip) 65.00

BERESFORD,MAURICE-Lost Villages of England-NY-(1954)-Philos Libr-8vo-445p-31 illus+tabular mater-1st US ed (gg5,sl tn dj) 30.00

BERESFORD-HOWE,CONSTANCE-Invisible Gate-NY-(1949)-Dodd,Mead-scarce-1st ed (pp2,sl chip dj) 85.00*

BERG,A SCOTT-Max Perkins-NY-1978-1st ed (p5,dj) 20.00

BERG,B-To Africa with Migratory Birds-NY-1930-8vo-274p-cl,75 photos-1st ed (y8) 20.00

BERG,NORAH-Lady on the Beach-NY-(1952)-Prentice-Hall-251p (b6) 10.00

BERGE,VICTOR-Pearl Diver-GC-1930-Dbldy,Doran-368p-illus e.p.,illus by Haweis-1st US ed (u5) 20.00

BERGEN COUNTY HISTORICAL SOCIETY-Papers and Proceedings, Number Ten, 1914 to 1915-(Hackensack)-(1915)-85p-wrps,plts (aa6) 20.00

BERGEN COUNTY PANAORAMA-Hackensack-1941-Fed Writers Project/WPA-x,356p-cl,plts (aa6) 45.00

BERGEN,FANNY D-ED.-Animals and Plants Lore-Bost,NY-1899-Amer Folk-Lore Scty-cl,ltd to 500c,nbrd-1st ed (n8) 65.00

BERGER,A J-Hawaiian Birdlife-1972-U of Hawaii-4to-270p-59 col plts,maps-1st prtg (bb3,f,dj) 38.00

BERGER,A J-Hawaiian Birdlife-Honolulu-1972-4to-270p-cl,59 col plts,photos-1st ed (y8,dj) 40.00

BERGER,CHARLES-Image Tibet-SF-1973-Artisan Pr-sm folio-cl,col photo silk screen prnts-1st ed (q3,dj) 85.00

BERGER,JOHN A-Franciscan Missions of California-NY-1941-Putnam's-392p-photos-1st ed (d3,dj) 30.00

BERGER,JOHN-Another Way of Telling-NY-(1982)-300p-photos-1st Amer ed (l10,f,dj) 16.50

BERGER,JOHN-Pig Earth-NY-1979-Pantheon-1st US ed (h8,f,f dj) 40.00

BERGER,THOMAS-Arthur Rex-NY-1978-1st ed (s5,f,dj) 25.00

BERGER,THOMAS-Crazy in Berlin-NY-1958-Scribners-auth 1st bk-1st ed (w5,f,sl tn dj) 125.00

BERGER,THOMAS-Killing Time-NY-1967-Dial-1st ed (b5,edge rub dj) 20.00

BERGER,THOMAS-Little Big Man-NY-(1964)-Dial-1st ed (d6,dj) 150.00

BERGER,THOMAS-Neighbors-(NY)-(1980)-Delacorte/Lawrence-1st ed (b5,as new in dj) 20.00

BERGER,THOMAS-Reinhart in Love-1962-Scribners-scarce-1st ed (n9,f,dj chip,sl wn) 90.00

BERGER,THOMAS-Vital Parts-NY-1970-Baron-1st ed (h3,chip dj) 15.00

BERGER,THOMAS-Who is Teddy Villanova-np-(1977)-Delacorte/Lawrence-1st ed (a5,as new in dj) 30.00

BERGER,WM M-Berger's Tourists' Guide to New Mexico-KC-1883-39p+interspersed ads,wrps-rare-1st ed (v7,backstrip chipped away) 750.00

BERGET,A-Conquest of the Air-NY-(1911)-8vo-xx,250p-illus cl,frntis,46p plts,83 text figs-new & rvsd ed (t2,sl wn sp) 30.00

BERGH,KIT-Minnesota Fish & Fishing-Mpls-1958-8vo-318p-photos (m3) 13.00

BERGH,KIT-Northern Pike Fishing-Mpls-1975-8vo-272p-photos (m3,f,dj) 20.00

BERGH,VANDEN-On the Trial of the Pigmies-NY-1921-McCann-8vo-xiv,264p-orig cl,61 plts-1st ed (bb6) 15.00

BERGMAN,ANDREW-Big Kiss Off of 1944-NY-(1974)-Holt-1st ed (w1,dj) 30.00

BERGMAN,INGMAR-Scenes From a Marriage-NY-1974-Pantheon-1st US ed (z9,dj) 10.00

BERGMAN,RAY-Fresh Water Bass-NY-1947-436p-photos,illus by Hildebrandt (ee3,soil dj) 10.00

BERGMAN,RAY-Fresh-Water Bass-Phila-1942-8vo-436p-illus,Fred Hildebrandt-14 col plts-1st ed (m3,f) 35.00

BERGMAN,RAY-Just Fishing-NY-1942-418p-photo,illus (gg3,f) 12.00

BERGMAN,RAY-Just Fishing-Phila-1933-8vo-418p-illus-2nd prntng (m3) 15.00

BERGMAN,RAY-Trout-Lond-1950-4to-295p (m3) 65.00

BERGMAN,RAY-With Fly,Plug & Bait-NY-1947-8vo-640p-illus,6 col plts-1st trd ed (m3,f,sl chip dj) 35.00

BERGOLD,LILIAN C-Abraham Lincoln Centennial-Bost-(1908)-61p-cl (k1,few spots frnt cov) 12.50

BERGTOLD,W H-Guide to Colorado Birds-np-1928-8vo-207p-cl (y8) 20.00

BERHOLZER,RUTH-Victory Binding of the American Woman's Cook Book-Chig-(1942)-Consldtd Bk Publ-816p+70p wartime spplmnt,frntis,thumb index-Wartime ed (n6,dj) 35.00

BERKELEY,ANTHONY-Dead Mrs. Stratton-1933-Dbldy CC-1st US ed (e4,rub dj) 45.00

BERKELEY,ANTHONY-Mr.Pidgeon's Island-1934-Dbldy CC-1st Amer ed (s10) 20.00

BERKELEY,ANTHONY-Mr.Pidgeon's Island-NY-1934-Dbldy CC-1st Amer ed (k4,sl rub e.p.,dj chip) 45.00

BERKELEY,ANTHONY-Piccadilly Murder-1930-Dbldy CC-1st US ed (s10) 12.50

BERKELEY,ANTHONY-Piccadilly Murder-NY-1930-Dbldy CC-1st US ed (f4,sl chip sp) 15.00

BERKELEY,ANTHONY-Second Shot-GC-1931-Dbldy CC-wraparound-1st Amer ed (w9,cov stnd,vf dj) 150.00

BERKELEY,ANTHONY-Silk Stocking Murders-1928-CC-1st Amer ed (s10,chip dj) 37.50

BERKELEY,ANTHONY-Wychford Poisoning Case-GC-1930-Dbldy CC-wraparound-1st Amer ed (w9,f,vf dj) 175.00

BERKELEY,ED-John Clayton Pioneer of American Botany-Chapel Hill-1963-U of NC-236p-cl (x6,as new in dj) 32.00

BERKELEY,EDMUND C-Giant Brains or Machines That Think-1949-270p-75 illus-1st ed (h6,f) 65.00

BERKELEY,GRANTLEY-Month in the Forests of France-Lond-1857-8vo-286p-1/2 mor,gilt-mrbld bds & e.p.s,handcol frontis-1st ed (m3) 75.00

BERKELEY,GRANTLEY-Reminiscences of a Huntsman-Lond-1897-8vo-344p-1/2 vel,mrbld bds & e.p.s,lea labl-col illus,J Leech-scarce (m3,sl chip lea labl) 75.00

BERKELEY,HASTINGS-Mysticism in Modern Mathematics-Lond-1910-OUP-xii+264p-blu cl-1st ed (l2,cov fade & soil) 20.00

BERKMAN,ALEXANDER-Prison Memoirs-Pitt-1970-Frontier Pr-538p (r1,dj) 20.00

BERLEPSCH,H VON-On the Birds of the Orinoco Region-Tring-1902-4to-134p-half mor,1 hand-col plt-scarce (y8,scuff) 125.00

BERLIN,SVEN-Jonah's Dream-Lond-1964-8vo-119p-illus-1st ed (m3,f,dj) 20.00

BERLINGER,B-Danger Down the Sights-NY-1964-priv prtd-202p-photos-scarce (ee3,vf,vf dj) 135.00

BERLITZ,CHARLES-Without a Trace-GC-1977-Dbldy-illus-1st ed (p8,dj) 5.00

BERNARD,ART-Dog Days-Caldwell-1969-8vo-204p-illus (m3,dj) 15.00

BERNARD,CLAUDE-An Introduction to the Study of Experimental Medicine-NY-1927-1st Engl ed (r2) 75.00

BERNARD,J-Fly Dressing-Lond-1932-12mo-199p-illus,col plts (m3,f,chip dj) 37.50

BERNARD,JOHN-Retrospections of America,1797 to 1811-NY-1887-Harper & Bros-xvi+380p+ads-brwn cl-1st ed (h2) 45.00

BERNARD,KENNETH A-Lincoln and the Music of the Civil War-Caldwell-1966-333p-illus-1st ed (c4,f,dj) 27.50

BERNARD,KENNETH A-Lincoln and the Music of the Civil War-Caldwell-1966-Caxton-333p-frntis port,illus (n7,dj) 35.00

BERNARD,THEOS-Heaven Lies Within Us-NY-1939-Scribner-8vo-326p-illus-1st ed (gg5,f,dj) 30.00

BERNARD,THEOS-Hindu Philosophy-NY-1947-Philo Libr-cl-1st Amer ed (o8,dj) 20.00

BERNAYS,ANNE-Growing Up Rich-Bost-1975-Little,Brown-1st ed (w5,f,f dj) 30.00

BERNAYS,ANNE-New York Ride-NY-1965-Trident-1st ed (w5,f,dj) 35.00

BERNERI,MARIE L-Journey Through Utopia-Bost-1950-Beacon-399p (r1,edgewn dj) 28.00

BERNERS,DAME JULIANA-An American Edition of the Treatyse of Fysshynge Wyth an Angle from the Boke of St.Albans-NY-1875-12mo-118p-hdbk issue-illus-1st Amer ed (m3) 90.00

BERNERS,DAME JULIANA-Treatyse of Fishing Wyth an Angle-NY-1903-Wm Loring Andrews-8vo-86p-one of 150c,vel,gilt,red lettered signatures,illus-scarce (m3,lacks ties) 150.00

BERNHARD,THOMAS-Gargoyles-NY-1970-Knopf-1st US ed (b5,f,dj) 40.00

BERNHARD,THOMAS-Lime Works-NY-1973-Knopf-1st US ed (a10,f,dj) 30.00

BERNHEIM-Suggestive Therapeutics-NY/Lond-1889-Putnam's/Knickerbocker-(ii)+xvi+420+(2)p-grn cl-1st ed in Engl (y9,cancel t.p.,sl loose hng) 100.00

BERNIER,R L-Art in California-SF-1916-t.e.g.,332 plts-Orig ed (h10,sp labl chip) 950.00

BERNSTEIN,JEREMY-Ascent-NY-1965-124p-8 plts-1st prtg (o10,f,dj) 14.00

BERRA,T M-William Beebe. An Annotated Bibliography-1977-Archon-157p-photos-1st ed (bb3,f,dj) 18.00

BERRA,YOGI-Yogi Berra's Baseball Guidebook-NY,et al-(1966)-80p-wrps,spiral bnd-1st ed so stated (n1) 12.50

BERRALL,JULIA S-Garden-NY-(1966)-lg 8vo-388p-grn cl,over 200 b&w & col plts-1st ed (j10,sl wn dj) 35.00

BERRIAULT,GINA-Conference of Victims-NY-1962-1st ed (p5,f,dj) 20.00

BERRIAULT,GINA-Descent-NY-1960-Atheneum-1st ed (g8,sl wn dj) 30.00

BERRIAULT,GINA-Descent-NY-1960-auth 1st bk-1st ed (p5,dj) 25.00

BERRIDGE,P S A-Couplings to the Khyber-Newton Abbot-1969-320p-1st ed (n4,f,dj) 22.00

BERRIGAN,DANIEL-Night Flight to Hanoi-NY-(1968)-Macmillan-1st ed (k3,f,sl fray dj) 20.00

BERRILL,N J-Tunicata with an Account of the British Species-1950-Ray Soc-354p-120 figs (bb3,f) 30.00

BERRY,ADRIAN-Next Ten Thousand Years-NY-1974-Sat Rev/Dutton-250p-1st prtg (hh6,sl chip dj) 10.00

BERRY,CHARLES W-Viniana-Lond-1929-Constable-141p-red cl,8 illus-1st ed (q8,soil dj) 35.00

BERRY,CHARLES W-Viniana-NY-1930-Knopf-sm 8vo-140p-mrbld bds,8 illus (o6) 35.00

BERRY,DON-Majority of Scoundrels-NY-1961-432p-photos-1st ed (t7,dj) 50.00

BERRY,DON-Majority of Scoundrels-NY-1961-Harpers-pckt maps-1st ed (a6,dj) 85.00

BERRY,DON-Moontrap-NY-1962-Viking-1st ed (e8,dj edge-wn & chip) 30.00

BERRY,DON-Trask-NY-1960-Viking-auth 1st bk-1st ed (d8,dj edge wn & chip) 45.00

BERRY,EDWARD W-Tree Ancestors-Balt-1923-Williams & Wilkins-vi+270p-maroon cl,48 text illus(incl maps)-1st ed (j2,sl fox) 30.00

BERRY,ERICK-Seven Beaver Skins-Phila-(1948)-Winston-275p-cl,auth illus-1st ed (oo10,dj) 15.00

BERRY,JOHN-Flight of White Crows-1961-Macmillan-1st ed (t4,f,dj) 10.00

BERRY,ROBERT E-Yankee Stargazer-NY-1941-McGraw Hill-xi,234p-illus-1st ed (o2) 20.00

BERRY,THOMAS S-Western Prices Before 1861-Cambridge-1943-645p-chrts,graphs-1st ed (t7,dj) 20.00

BERRY,WENDELL-Broken Ground-NY-(1964)-Harcourt,Brace-8vo-cl/bds-1st ed (ll10,f,dj) 65.00

BERRY,WENDELL-Findings-Iowa City-1969-Prairie Pr-scarce-1st ed (y1,f,f dj) 100.00

BERRY,WENDELL-Hidden Wound-Bost-1970-Houghton Mifflin-1st ed (ee2,f,dj) 35.00

BERRY,WENDELL-Nathan Coulter-Bost-1960-HM-auth 1st bk-1st ed (g8,f,sl tn dj) 150.00

BERRY,WENDELL-Nathan Coulter-Bost-1960-Houghton Mifflin-auth 1st bk-1st ed (q2,dj soil,chip & wrnkld) 175.00

BERRY,WENDELL-November Twenty Six Nineteen Hundred Sixty Three-1964-Braziller-illus,B Shahn-1st ed (x2,f,box) 30.00

BERRY,WENDELL-Openings-NY-1968-1st ed (s5,dj sl rub) 35.00

BERRY,WENDELL-There is Singing Around Me-Austin-1976-Cold Mtn Pr-prtd wrps,ltd to 300c,autg-1st ed (ee2,f) 45.00

BERRY,WENDELL-Traveling at Home-SF-1979-North Point-grn pattrnd bds & cl,wood engrvngs,no dj as iss-1st ed (dd2,f) 25.00

BERRY,WM D-Buffalo Land-NY-1961-46p-frntis,col illus-1st ed (t7,dj) 12.50

BERRYMAN,JOHN-Delusions, Etc-(1972)-FS&G-1st ed (t9,f,dj) 20.00

BERRYMAN,JOHN-Disposessed-NY-(1948)-Sloane-1st ed (w1,f,dj) 250.00

BERRYMAN,JOHN-Dream Songs-(1969)-FS&G-1st ed (s9,f,sp chip dj) 35.00

BERRYMAN,JOHN-Dream Songs-NY-(1969)-FS&G-1st ed (e6,f,dj) 60.00

BERRYMAN,JOHN-Freedom of the Poet-NY-(1976)-FS&G-1st ed (b5,as new in dj) 25.00

BERRYMAN,JOHN-Henry's Fate & Other Poems,1967 to 1972-NY-1977-FS&G-1st ed (b5,as new in dj) 17.50

BERRYMAN,JOHN-His Toy, His Dream, His Rest-NY-(1968)-FS&G-1st ed (b5,as new in dj) 35.00

BERRYMAN,JOHN-Love & Fame-NY-1970-FS&G-1st ed (bb1,as new in dj) 25.00

BERRYMAN,JOHN-Love and Fame-Lond-1971-Faber-1st Brit ed (y1,f,f dj) 50.00

BERRYMAN,JOHN-Short Poems-NY-(1967)-FS&G-1st ed (x10,f,f dj) 35.00

BERRYMAN,JOHN-Stephen Crane-NY-1950-Wm Sloane-347p-1st prtg (v3,dj) 18.00

BERSON,FRED-After the Big House-NY-(1952)-Crown-8vo-238p-1st ed (gg5,dj) 20.00

BERSTEIN,JEREMY-Wildest Dreams of KEW-NY-1969-186p-1st prtg (q10,as new in dj) 30.00

BERTHOLF,JACK-Men and Mutualty-Seattle-1951-illus cl-1st ed (b6,f,dj,autg) 10.00

BERTHRONG,DONALD-Cheyenne & Arapaho Ordeal-Norman-1976-U of Okla (a6,f,f dj) 24.95

BERTIN,JACK-Blood of Helios-NY-(1966)-Arcadia-1st ed (e3,sp fade dj) 10.00

BERTO,HAZEL-North to Alaska's Shining River-Indpls-1959-Bobbs Merrill-224p-gry bds,e.p. maps-1st ed (p2,dj) 15.00

BERTON,PIERRE-Impossible Railway-NY-1972-574p-1st Amer ed (n4,f,dj) 35.00

BERTON,PIERRE-Klondike-Tor-1958-McClelland & Stewart-457p-illus e.p.-1st ed (ff4,dj wn,chip) 20.00

BERTON,RALPH-Remembering Bix-NY-1974-Harper-1st ed (w1,f,dj) 15.00

BERTRAM,COLIN-In Search of Mermaids-NY-(1964,63)-Crowell-8vo-183p-1st US ed (gg5,dj) 20.00

BERTRAND,GABRIELLE-Jungle People-Lond-nd(ca.1960)-Hale Ltd-190p-photos (c3) 16.00

BERTRAND,GENERAL-Napoleon at St.Helena-GC-1952-318p-1st ed (d7,dj) 30.00

BERVE,H-Greek Temples, Theatres & Shrines-NY-1962-Abrams-212 illus(incl 36 col),photos-1st ed (h10) 250.00

BERZELIUS,J J-Use of the Blowpipe in Chemistry and Mineralogy-Bost-1845-237p-illus,3 fldg plts-4th enlgd & corrected ed (cc8,sl fox) 75.00

BESANT,ANNIE-Place of Peace-Lond-1894-Theosophical Publ-14p-wrps (d1) 12.50

BESKOW,ELSA-Adventures of Peter and Lotta-NY-nd(1931)-Harper-oblng 4to-unpgd-cl-bkd pict bds,col illus,auth (r3,sl soil cov) 75.00

BESKOW,ELSA-Sun-Egg-NY,Lond-1933-Harper-oblng 4to-cl bkd pict bds,12p col illus,auth (s3) 70.00

BESSET,M-Le Corbusier-Geneva/NY-1976-Skira/Rizzoli-sq folio-illus (kk4,dj) 100.00

BESSEY,ERNST A-Morphology and Taxonomy of Fungi-Phila-1950-Blakiston-xiii,791p-cl (x6) 25.00

BESSIE,ALVAH-Men in Battle-NY-1939-Scribners-1st ed (w5) 25.00

BESSIE,ALVAH-Symbol-NY-(1966)-Random-1st ed (hh5,f,dj) 10.00

BESSON,MAURICE-Scourge of the Indies-NY-1929-Random Hs-4to-5 hand col agetreated drwng & maps,140 illus,one of 1040c (nn1,sp lttrng fade,sl wn bds) 125.00

BEST,GERALD M-Mexican Narrow Gauge-Berkeley-1968-180p-1st ed (n4,f,dj) 18.50

BEST,GERALD M-Nevada County Narrow Gauge-1965-Howell North-4to-214p-photos,maps-1st ed (d3,dj) 40.00

BEST,GERALD M-Nevada County Narrow Gauge-Berkeley-1965-214p-1st ed (n4,f,dj) 25.00

BEST,GERALD M-Ships and Narrow Gauge Rails-Berkeley-1964-153p-1st ed (n4,f,dj) 16.00

BEST,GERALD M-Ulster and Delaware...Railroad Through the Catskills-San Marino-1972-210p-illus,maps-1st ed (n4,f,dj) 27.50

BESTER,A-Demolished Man-1953-Shasta-1st ed (x7,f,sp chip dj) 165.00

BESTER,ALFRED-Golem 100-NY-(1980)-S&S-1st ed (j3,f,dj) 15.00

BESTERMAN,THEODORE-Besterman World Bibliographies, Medicine...-Totowa-1971-409p (dd3) 45.00

BETENSON,LULU P-Butch Cassidy, My Brother-Provo-(1975)-BYU Pr-xiv,265p-cl,photos-1st ed (v1,dj) 45.00

BETHAM,GEOFFREY-Golden Galley-Oxford-1956-330p-maps,illus-1st ed (b7,f,dj) 95.00

BETHUNE,W C-Canada's Eastern Arctic-Ottawa-1934-King's Prtr/NW Terr Cncl-166p-prtd wrps,ports,tabls,fldg map-Arctic Bibl.#1507 (k10) 30.00*

BETJEMAN,JOHN-Antiquarian Prejudice-Lond-1939-Hogarth Pr-wrps-Sixpenny Pamphlets No.5-Woolmer 443-1st ed (nn4,f) 35.00

BETTELHEIM,BRUNO-Empty Fortress-NY-(1967)-Free Pr-8vo-484p-33 photos-1st ed (gg5,f,dj) 12.50

BETTELHEIM,BRUNO-Uses of Enchantment-NY-1976-Knopf-cl-1st ed (n8,f,dj) 20.00

BETTEMBOURG,GEORGE-White Death-Seattle-1981-310p-illus-1st ed (o10,as new in dj) 35.00

BETTINA-Cocolo Comes to America-NY-(1949)-Harper & Jr Lit Guild-folio-pict cl,illus,auth (s3,dj) 30.00

BETTS,DORIS-Astronomer-1966-H & R-1st ed (x2,vf,dj) 30.00

BETTS,DORIS-Gentle Insurrection-NY-(1954)-Putnam's-auth 1st bk-1st ed (ff6,dj sl soil & sp wn) 125.00

BETTS,DORIS-Heading West-NY-1981-Knopf-1st ed (ff6,f,dj) 20.00

BETTS,DORIS-River to Pickle Beach-NY-1972-1st ed (n5,f,f dj) 25.00

BETTS,EDWIN M-Thomas Jefferson's Farm Book-Princeton-1953-Amer Philos Soc-552p (x6,f,dj) 40.00

BETTS,EDWIN-Thomas Jefferson's Flower Garden at Monticello-Richmond-1941-Dietz-4to-56p-cl (x6,dj) 32.00

BETTY CROCKER'S NEW PICTURE COOK BOOK-NY-1961-McGraw Hill-455p-illus bds-1st ed,2nd prtg (o6) 25.00

BETTY CROCKER'S PICTURE COOK BOOK-Mpls-1950-Gen Mills-448p-1st ed,2nd prtg (k6,sl wn,soil) 35.00

BETZINEZ,JASON-I Fought With Geronimo-Harrisburg-(1959)-Stackpole-(viii),214p-cl,photos,map e.p.-1st ed (v1,chip dj) 45.00

BEUDANT,E-Horse Training-NY-1931-Scribner-wi "A"-1st ed (h9) 45.00

BEURLING,G F-Malta Spitfire-NY-(1943)-8vo-xiv,236p-cl,frntis,9p illus,text illus,illus e.p.-1st ed (t2,sp fade,dj tn & pc mssng) 25.00

BEVERIDGE,W I B-Art of Scientific Investigation-NY-1951-Norton-171p-cl (x6) 15.00

BEWICK,T-History of British Birds-Newcastle-1826-8vo-2 vols-1/2 calf,mrbld e.p.-6th ed (y8,sl scuff & fox) 250.00

BEWICK,THOMAS-Selection of Engravings on Wood by...-Lond-1947-King Penguin Bks-tall 12mo-56p-bds (w2,spot cov) 20.00

BEY,PILAFF-Venus in the Kitchen-NY-1953-Viking-192p (q6) 35.00

BEYER,WILLIAM G-Minions of the Moon-NY-(1950)-Gnome Pr-1st ed (f3,dj) 20.00

BEZA,M-Byzantine Art in Romania-NY-1940-22 col & 46 b&w plts-1st ed (ee1) 85.00

BIALIK,HAYYIM N-And It Came to Pass-NY-(1938)-Hebrew Publ-8vo-281p-woodcts-1st US ed (bb5,f,dj) 25.00

BIANCE,MARGERY-Poor Cecco-NY-1935-Jr Lit Guild/Dbldy,Doran-pict cl,7 col plts by A Rackham (oo10) 60.00

BIART,LUCIEN-Aztecs-Chig-1887-McClurg-cl,illus,J L Garner,Transl-1st ed (l8,sp wn) 35.00

BIBBY,GEOFFREY-Four Thousand Years Ago-NY-1961-Knopf-8vo-398p-32 plts-1st ed (jj5,sl tn dj) 17.50

BIBBY,GEOFFREY-Looking for Dilmun-NY-1969-Knopf-8vo-383p-32 photos-1st ed (jj5,f,dj) 15.00

BIBBY,GEOFFREY-Testimony of the Spade-NY-1956-Knopf-8vo-414p-photos,maps-1st ed (jj5,f,dj) 20.00

BIBLIOGRAPHY OF HOOKWORM DISEASE-NY-1922-417p-1st ed (dd3) 20.00

BICKEL,LENNARD-Mawson's Will-NY-1977-Stein & Day-8vo-237p-e.p. maps,24 illus-1st ed thus (cc7,dj) 15.00*

BICKERSTAFF,LAURA M-Pioneer Artists of Taos-Denver-1955-93p-photos-1st ed (t7,f,dj) 150.00

BICKMORE,ALBERT S-Travels in the East Indian Archipelago-NY-1869-Appleton-lg 8vo-553p+ads-grn cl wi g sp titles & cov dec,fldg map,illus (ll1,sm rpr to sp) 275.00

BICKNELL,FRANK M-Blitzen the Conjurer-Phila-(1906)-Altemus-sm 8vo-col pict cl-1st ed (oo8) 35.00

BICKNELL,RALPH E-Ralph's Scrap Book-Lawrence-1905-priv prtd-452p-lea wi satin liners,photos (d3) 100.00
BIDDLE,C J-Fighting Airman-GC-(1968)-8vo-xxii,290p-cl,44 illus,19 text illus-1st ed (t2,dj) 25.00
BIDDLE,GEORGE-Tahitian Journal-(1968)-U of Minn Pr-4to-cl-1st ed (oo6,dj) 50.00
BIDDLE,W EARL-Hypnosis in the Psychoses-Springfield-(1967)-Thomas-(xii)+(140)p-pebbled blu fabrikoid-1st prntg (y9,dj) 22.50
BIDWELL,GEN JOHN-Echoes of the Past About California,together with In Camp and Cabin by Rev John Steele-Chig-377p-frntis,map-Lakeside Classics (cc4) 30.00
BIDWELL,SHELFORD-Gunners at War-Lond-1970-244p-illus-1st ed (b7,f,dj) 25.00
BIEBER,MARGARETE-Sculpture of the Hellenistic Age-NY-1967-Columbia U Pr-folio-illus-rvsd ed (r2) 100.00
BIEBER,RALPH-ED.-Marching with the Army of the West 1846 thru 1848...-Phila-1974-369p-frntis,fldg map,illus (t7,f) 20.00
BIEGELEISEN,J I-Book of 60 Hand Lettered Alphabets-Cin-1976-Sign of Times Publ-sm 8vo-(viii),127p-stiff wrps-1st ed (w2) 10.00
BIEK,LEO-Archaeology and the Miscroscope-NY-(1963)-Praeger-8vo-287p-26 plts,12 figs-1st US ed (gg5,f,dj) 25.00
BIENSTOCK,GREGORY-Struggle for the Pacific-NY-1937-Macmillan-8vo-299p-red cl,maps (gg6,sp fade) 15.00
BIERCE,AMBROSE-Ambrose Bierce Satanic Reader-NY-1968-Dbldy-1st ed thus (d8,f dj) 40.00
BIERCE,AMBROSE-Collected Works of ...-NY & Wash D.C.-1909-Neale Publ-12 vols,gry cl (f2,sl discol,rub sps,wk hngs) 250.00
BIERMANN,BERTHOLD-ED.-Goethe's World-NY-1949-New Directions-cl-1st ed (n8) 25.00
BIERSTADT,EDWARD H-What Do You Know About Crime-NY-1935-Stokes-sm 8vo-103p-photos-1st ed (b3,f,dj) 15.00
BIGELOW,GEORGE H-Cancer and Other Chronic Diseases in Massachusetts-Bost-1933-Houghton Mifflin-xxii+355p-blu cl,tbls-1st ed (l2,sp lettrng fade) 15.00
BIGELOW,H-Flying Feathers-VA-1937-95p-burlap bds wi sp & cov labl,photo e.p. (ee3,vf) 80.00
BIGELOW,H-Gunnerman's Gold-WV-1943-128p-dec e.p.,photos,ltd to 1000c (gg3,sl wn) 85.00
BIGELOW,H-Gunnerman-NY-1939-Derrydale-246p-red cl,gilt dec,photos (gg3,f) 125.00
BIGELOW,H-Scatter Gun Sketches-1922-Hazleton-128p-navy blu cl,g sp & cov dog decs,photos-scarce (ee3,f) 250.00
BIGELOW,HORATIO-An International System of Electro Therapeutics-Phila-1895-1179p-woodcut illus-1st ed (dd3) 250.00
BIGELOW,JACOB-Nature in Disease-Bost-1854-391p-scarce-1st ed (dd3,vf) 200.00
BIGELOW,JOHN-Memoir of the Life and Public Services of John Charles Fremont...-NY-1856-Derby & Jackson-480p-cl-Wagner Camp 271a-Sabin 5306-1st ed (j1,sl wn sp,fox) 25.00
BIGGER,DAVID D-Millionaire Tom-Dayton-1914-325p-cl (d1,sl spot cov) 17.50
BIGGER,DAVID D-Ohio's Silver-Tongued Orator-Dayton-1901-558p-one vol in two parts-cl (f1) 35.00
BIGGERS,DON H-German Pioneers in Texas-Fredericksburg-1925-Gillespie Cnty Ed-230p-cl,photos-1st ed (a9) 145.00
BIGGERS,DON H-German Pioneers in Texas-Fredericksburg-1925-Pr of Fredericksburg Publ-230p-cl,photos,Herd #259-1st ed (w3) 125.00
BIGGERS,EARL D-Behind That Curtain-1928-Bobbs Merrill-1st ed (o9) 15.00
BIGGERS,EARL D-Charlie Chan Solves a New Mystery-Racine-1940-Whitman-Better Little Bks #1459-1st ed (d4,edge wn) 75.00
BIGGERS,EARL D-Chinese Parrot-1927-Harrap-1st Brit ed (x7,f) 35.00
BIGGERS,EARL D-Chinese Parrot-Indpls-(1926)-Bobbs Merrill-1st ed (m4,f,sl wn dj) 150.00
BIGGERS,EARL D-Chinese Parrot-NY-(1926)-Grosset-reprint (e4,dj) 25.00
BIGGERS,EARL D-House Without a Key-Indpls-1925-Bobbs-1st ed (d4) 25.00
BIGGERS,EARL D-House Without a Key-NY-(1925)-Grosset-reprint (f4,yel pgs,dj) 10.00
BIGGERS,EARL D-Love Insurance-Indpls-1914-Bobbs-1st ed (j4,f) 20.00
BIGGLE,JACOB-Biggle Orchard Book-Phila-1911-24mo-144p-20 col photo plts-Biggle Farm Libr ser-3rd ed (m10,sl wn) 16.00
BIGGLE,LLOYD-World Menders-Yorkshire-(1973)-Enfeld Pr-1st Brit ed (g3,f,dj) 20.00
BIHALJI-MERIN,O-Modern Primitves-Lond-1971-folio-204 col plts-1st ed (h10,dj) 85.00
BIHALY,ANDREW-Journal of...-NY-1973-Crowell-1st ed (y1,dj) 30.00
BILIK,S E-Athletic Training-(Champaign)-(1918)-109,(2)p-cl (j1) 15.00
BILL,ALFRED H-Beleaguered City-NY-1946-Knopf-332p-cl,frntis,illus,fldg maps-1st ed (o7) 20.00
BILL,EDWARD L-Sword of the Pyramids-NY-nd-Empire Publ-363p-cl (d1) 22.50
BILLCLIFFE,R-Macintosh Textile Designs-NY-1982-69 illus(incl col)-1st ed (h10,dj) 45.00
BILLEB,EMIL-Mining Camp Days-1968-Howell North-229p-photos-1st ed (d3,dj) 25.00
BILLINGS,C K G-Memories of Blue and Gold-1927-priv prtd-12mo-56p-lea,a.e.g. (j9,f) 135.00
BILLINGS,JOHN D-Hardtack and Coffee-1982-Time Life-408p-illus(incl col)-rprnt of 1887 ed (z10,f) 30.00
BILLINGS,JOHN D-Hardtack and Coffee-Chig-1960-Lakeside Pr-483p-frntis port,illus,glassine dj,Lakeside Classic (o7,f,dj) 35.00
BILLINGS,JOHN D-Hardtack and Coffee-Lakeside Classic-483p-dec cl,frntis,illus (t7,f) 17.50
BILLINGS,JOHN S-Report on the Hygiene of the U.S. Army with Descriptions of Military Posts-NY-1974-4to-567p-plts,chrts,maps-(facs of 1875 ed) (dd3) 150.00
BILLINGS,JOHN S-Selected Papers of...-Chig-1965-300p-1st ed (dd3) 75.00
BILLINGTON,RAY A-Land of Savagery, Land of Promise-NY-(1981)-364p-1st ed (c4,dj) 20.00
BILLINGTON,RAY A-Protestant Crusade, 1800 to 1860-NY-1938-Macmillan-xiv+514p-brwn cl,illus-1st ed (m2,dj) 15.00
BILLON,STAIR-Story of the 29th Division-Lond-1925-276p-frntis port,illus-1st ed (b7,frntis clipped) 150.00
BILLROTH,T-Medical Sciences in the German Universities-NY-1924-Macmillan-xiv+292p-grn cl-1st ed in Engl (a2,dj) 25.00

BINCHI,JOHN-Blue Steel & Gun Leather-No Hollywood-1979-8vo-214p-photos (m3,f) 12.50

BINFORD,LEWIS R-Archaeology at Hatchery West-Wash D.C.-1970-Scty for Amer Archlgy-25cm 4to-brwn papr wrps,chrts,tbls,drwngs (mm1) 15.00

BINFORD-FLEMING,NELIA-Sketches of Early High Prairie-Portland-nd(1949)-61p-blu cl,illus (b6) 10.00

BINGAY,MALCOLM W-Detroit is My Own Hometown-Indpls-1946-Bobbs,Merrill-360p-cl-1st ed (z7,dj) 15.00

BINGAY,MALCOLM W-Detroit is My Own Hometown-Indpls-1946-Bobbs-Merrill-360p-3/4 grn lea,gilt dec,ltd to 199c,autg-Tiger Town ed (z7,f) 100.00

BINGHAM,CALEB-American Preceptor-Troy-1803-prntd by O Penniman-228p-pap-cov wooden bds (k1) 35.00

BINGHAM,CALEB-Columbian Orator-Bost-1807-Manning & Loring-300p-lea-Amer Imprnts 12150-8th ed (k1,lacks f.e.p.s,wn) 40.00

BINGHAM,H-An Explorer in the Air Service-New Haven-1920-Yale Univ Pr-8vo-xiv,260p-cl bkd bds,t.e.g,other edges untrimmed-1st ed (t2) 50.00

BINGHAM,HIRAM-Inca Land-NY-1922-365p-photos-scarce-1st ed (o10,f) 140.00

BINGHAM,HIRAM-Residence Twenty One Years in the Sandwich Island-Hartford/NY-1848-Huntington/Converse-8vo-xvi,(17)-616p-orig emboss brwn cl,frntis,fldg map,6 wdcuts,plt called for at p.473,bnd at p.580-2nd ed (nn1,sp wn,sl fox) 200.00

BINGHAM,JOHN H-Short History of Brule County-np-1947-184p-wrps,photos-1st ed (t7) 30.00

BINNEY,GEORGE-With Seaplane and Sledge in the Arctic-Lond-nd(ca.1920s)-Hutchinson-g dec blu cl,frntis,1 fldg map,40 illus (mm8) 75.00*

BINNS,ARCHIE-Mighty Mountains-Portland-(1940)-Binsford & Mort-1st ed (b10,chip dj) 12.50

BINNS,ARCHIE-Northwest Gateway-Seattle-1945-313p-photos,map e.p. (t7,dj) 7.50

BINNS,ARCHIE-Peter Skene Ogden, Fur Trader-Portland-(1967)-353p-illus,e.p. maps-1st ed (h7,f,dj) 35.00

BINNS,ARCHIE-Sea in the Forest-GC-1953-256p-e.p. maps-1st ed (h7,dj sl tn & nick) 20.00

BINYON,LAURENCE-English Water Colours-Lond-1933-col frntis,24 photos-1st ed (r2) 45.00

BIRCHLEY,S W-British Birds for Cages, Aviaries & Exhibition-Lond-1909-2 vols-illus (gg3,f) 35.00

BIRD LORE-BI-MONTHLY MAGAZINE,ED BY CHAPMAN-VOL.16-Harrisburg-1914-8vo-565p-cl,col plts,photos (y8) 22.00

BIRD,ANNIE L-Boise, the Peace Valley-Caldwell-1934-408p-illus-v scarce-1st ed (t7,dj) 125.00

BIRD,ISABELLA B-Among the Tibetians-NY,Tor-1894-159p-g pict cov,illus by E Whymper-1st ed (a4) 95.00

BIRD,ISABELLA L-Unbeaten Tracks in Japan-NY-1881-Putnam's-8vo-2 vols-orig brwn cl,illus,fldg map-2nd ed (gg6,cov wn,stns) 150.00

BIRD,ISABELLA L-Unbeaten Tracks in Japan-NY-nd(1880)-Putnam's-(2 vols in 1)-engrvngs,fldg map (c3) 65.00

BIRD,ISABELLA-Lady's Life in the Rocky Mountains-Lond-1885-Murray-8vo-296p+ads-illus-5th ed (oo7,hng weak) 65.00

BIRD,J MALCOLM-Margery the Medium-Bost-(1921)-Small,Maynard-(iii)-(xii)+518p+20 hlftones-prntd ruled blu cl-1st ed (y9) 30.00

BIRD,JOSEPH-Protection Against Fire...the Best Means of Putting Out Fires in Cities, Towns and Villages...-NY-1873-Hurd-8vo-278p-dec tan cl-1st ed (y4,vf) 150.00

BIRD,MICHAEL J-Town That Died-NY-(1963,62)-Putnam-8vo-192p-22 illus-1st US ed (gg5,f,dj) 15.00

BIRD,T H-Hundred Grand Nationals-Lond-1937-Country Life-sm 4to-1st prtg (f10) 30.00

BIRD,WILL R-Atlantic Anthology-Tor-1959-M&S-8vo-310p-1st ed (aa7,sl chip dj) 20.00*

BIRD,WILL R-This is Novia Scotia-Tor-1951(1950)-Ryerson Pr-299p-e.p. maps,photos-2nd prtg (p2) 10.00

BIRDWELL,CLEO-Amazons-1980-Holt-1st ed (s9,dj) 22.50

BIRDWOOD,FIELD MARSHALL LORD-Khaki and Gown-Lond-1941-456p-blu cl,maps,illus-1st ed (gg2) 75.00

BIRDWOOD,GEORGE C M-Industrial Arts of India-Lond-1971-344p-plts (mm3) 22.50

BIRKELAND,CAPT TORGER-Echoes of Puget Sound-Caldwell-1960-Caxton Pr-251p-blu cl,col frntis,illus (b6) 16.00

BIRKET-SMITH,KAJ-Eskimos-Lond-1959-Methuen-8vo-262p-blu cl,map e.p.,photos-enlgd & rvsd ed (oo1,dj wn) 45.00

BIRKIN,ANDREW-J M Barrie & the Lost Boys-NY-1979-C Potter-1st ed (x9,f,dj) 12.50

BIRKLELAND,CAPT TORGER-Echoes of Puget Sound-Caldwell-1961-251p-illus,map in rear pckt-2nd prtg (c7,chip dj) 25.00

BIRMINGHAM,GEORGE A-Wild Justice-Indpls-1930-Bobbs-1st US ed (h4) 12.50

BIRMINGHAM,STEPHEN-Life at the Dakota-NY-(1979)-Random-1st ed (hh5,dj) 15.00

BIRNBAUM,M-Jacovleff & Other Artists-NY-1924-60 plts-ltd ed-1st ed (h10,sl chip dj) 40.00

BIRNEY,EARLE-Strait of Anian-Tor-1948-Ryerson-viii,84p-1st ed (aa2,dj) 35.00*

BIRRELL,AUGUSTINE-Essays About Men,Women,and Books-Lond-1894-Elliot Stock-1st ed (kk5) 55.00

BIRRELL,AUGUSTINE-Essays about Men,Women,and Books-NY-1894-234p-cl (d1) 17.50

BIRRELL,AUGUSTINE-Res Judicatae, Papers and Essays-Lond-1892-Elliot Stock-sm 8vo-(viii),280p-1/2 prchmnt over cl-1st ed (w2,sl soil prchmnt) 17.50

BIRRELL,FRANCIS-Letter From a Black Sheep-Lond-1932-Hogarth Pr-wrps-Letters No.5-Woolmer 281-1st ed (nn4,f) 55.00

BISCHOFF,CHARITAS-Hard Road-Lond-1931-Hopkinson-8vo-317p-1st Brit ed (aa5,dj) 25.00

BISCHOFF,HENRY-From Pioneer Settlement to Suburb-So Brunswick-(1979)-386p-cl,illus (aa6) 35.00

BISHER,FURMAN-Miracle in Atlanta-1966-World-photos-1st ed (s8,f,sl wn dj) 15.00

BISHOP THE BIRD MAN'S TREATISE ON BIRDS AND AQUARIA...-(Balt)-(1911?)-84p-wrps (d1) 20.00

BISHOP,CARLTON T-Structural Details of Hip and Valley Rafters-NY-1912-Wiley & Sons-obng 8vo-72p (r10) 20.00

BISHOP,CAROL-Book of Home Remedies and Herbal Cures-Lond-(1979)-Octopus-4to-224p-brwn cl,decs,plts-1st ed (q8,dj) 20.00

BISHOP,ELIZABETH-ED. & TRANSL.-Diary of Helena Morley-NY-(1957)-Farrar-8vo-1st ed (u1,f,sl wn dj) 75.00

BISHOP,ELIZABETH-Questions of Travel-NY-(1965)-FS&G-8vo-blu cl-1st ed (v10,dj) 25.00

BISHOP,MICHAEL-And Strange at Ecbatan the Trees-NY-1976-Harper-1st ed (w5,f,f dj) 15.00

BISHOP,MORRIS-Champlain, The Life of Fortitude-NY-1948-364p-lg fldg map,illus-1st ed (t7,dj) 12.50

BISHOP,MORRIS-Odyssey of Cabeza De Vaca-NY-1933-306p-frntis,photo plts-1st ed (t7) 25.00

BISHOP,MORRIS-St.Francis of Assisi-Bost-(1974)-Little,Brown-1st ed (u10,f,f dj) 15.00

BISHOP,NATHANIEL H-Four Months in a Sneak Box-Bost-1879-Lee & Shepard-xii,322,(2)p-illus-1st ed (n2,rebckd,sl wn) 100.00

BISHOP,R E-Bishop's Birds-1936-Lippincott-4to-unpgd-73 etchngs-ltd to 1000c for sale,nbrd (bb3,sl stnd) 195.00

BISHOP,R E-Bishop's Wildfowl-MN-1948-282p-lea,12 col plts (gg3,f) 175.00

BISHOP,R E-Ways of the Wildfowl-1971-Ferguson-4to-260p-64 col illus,maps-1st ed (bb3,f,dj) 95.00

BISHOP,R E-Ways of Wildfowl-Chig-1971-folio-256p-deluxe ed,blu lea-illus by auth-scarce-1st ed (m3,f,box) 200.00

BISHOP,ROBERT-Folk Painters of America-NY-1979-1st ed (ff10,dj) 45.00

BISHOP,ROBERT-Folk Painters of America-NY-1979-Dutton-4to-255p-col & b&w plts-1st ed (n2,f,dj) 30.00

BISHOP,W A-Winged Peace-NY-1944-8vo-xxii,176p-illus cl g,8p plts-1st ed (t2,dj) 30.00

BISHOP,W A-Winged Warfare-Lond-nd(ca.1920)-sm 8vo-vi,302p-cl,frntis,5p plts-1st ed (t2,dj mssng pcs) 25.00

BISLAND,JAMES-Common Sense in the Rock Garden-NY-1932-De La Mare-217p-cl (x6) 10.00

BISNAM,RON-Cardigan Bay-So Brunswick-1972-Barnes-1st US ed (f10,dj) 25.00

BISPHAM,DAVID-Quaker Singer's Recollections-NY-1920-Macmillan-8vo-401p-1st ed (y6,wn,sl soil & fox) 18.00

BISS,HAROLD C J-Relief of Kumasi-Lond-1901-315p-red cl,fldg map,illus-2nd ed (b7) 125.00

BITS OF SILVER-Hastings-(1961)-306p-1st ed (t8,f,dj) 15.00

BITTING,KATHERINE G-Gastronomic Bibliography-1981-Holland Pr-718p-ltd to 500c-reprnt ed (m6) 85.00

BITTING,KATHERINE G-Gastronomic Bibliography-SF-1939-priv prntd-718p-blu buckram bds,lea labl,illus-ltd to 500c-1st ed (m6) 275.00

BJERRE,JENS-Last Cannibals-NY-1957-Morrow-8vo-192p-1/2 cl,e.p. maps,48 plts-1st US ed (p8,wn dj) 25.00

BJERRE,JENS-Last Cannibals-NY-1957-Morrow-8vo-192p-1/2 cl,e.p. maps,76 photos (nn1) 25.00

BJORNVIG,THORKILD-Pact-Baton Rouge-1974-LSU Pr-1st ed (z9,f,dj,revw slip laid in) 15.00

BLACK HAWK-Life of..., Dictated by Himself-Chig-1916-Donnelley-196p-frntis,fldg map (cc4) 35.00

BLACK,A P-End of the Long Horn Trail-Selfridge-nd-Selfridge Journal-59p-wrps,illus (ff4) 20.00

BLACK,A-ED.-R.A.F. in Action-NY-1941-roy 8vo-108p-cl,frntis,62p plts (t2,sp fade,dj) 20.00

BLACK,COLETTE-French Provincial Cookery-NY-(1963)-Crowell Collier-189p-gry cl,illus-1st ed (q8,dj) 15.00

BLACK,ELEANORA-Gold Rush Song Book-SF-1940-Colt Pr-oblng 8vo-55p-dec bds,illus-1st ed (t1) 45.00

BLACK,FORREST R-Ill Starred Prohibition Cases-Bost-(1931)-Richard G Badger-162p (n6,fade sp) 25.00

BLACK,GLENN A-Angel Site-Indpls-1967-Indiana Hist Soc-2 vols (p6,f,box) 100.00

BLACK,J B-Reign of Elizabeth-Oxford-1936-Oxford Hist Engl/Univ Pr-448p-blu cl over bds,10 fldg maps (gg6) 35.00

BLACK,JOHN L-Crumbling Defenses-Macon-1960-Editor-133p-gry cl-1st ed (oo5,sl rub & soil) 75.00

BLACK,MARTHA L-My Seventy Years-Lond-(1938)-317p-port-Smith 865 (bb9,f,dj wn) 75.00

BLACK,MARY-American Folk Painting-NY-1966-86 col plts-1st ed (h10,sl chip dj) 60.00

BLACK,MARY-American Folk Painting-NY-1966-Clarkson Potter-4to-244p-beige cl,86 col plts,146 b&w illus-1st ed (r10,sl wn dj) 32.50

BLACK,MRS-Household Cookery and Laundry Work-Lond-nd(preface 1898)-Wm Collins-144p-grn bds,frntis-Bitting 42 (n6,sl wn bds) 20.00

BLACK,ROBERT L-Little Miami Railroad-Cin-nd(1936?)-priv publ-191p-cl-scarce (o1,dj wn,rprd) 35.00

BLACK,SAMUEL-Journal of a Voyage from Rocky Mountain Portage in Peace River to...Finlays Branch...1824-Lond-1955-Hudson's Bay Rec Soc-8vo-blu cl,3 plts,fldg map in rear (oo1,sl fade,cor bump) 150.00

BLACK,WILLIAM-Madcap Violet-Chig-1879-Belfords,Clarke-541p-cl (n1,sl wn) 12.50

BLACKBEARD,BILL-Sherlock Holmes in America-NY-1981-Abrams-1st ed (g4,as new in dj) 35.00

BLACKBURN,HENRY-Randolph Caldecott-Lond-1886-Sampson Low,M,S & R-lg 8vo-grn g cl,photo frntis,illus-1st ed (v10,bndg sl loose) 65.00

BLACKBURN,JOHN-Broken Boy-NY-1962-Morrow-1st US ed (e4,dj) 15.00

BLACKBURN,JOHN-Children of the Night-1969-Putnam-1st Amer ed (s10,dj) 17.50

BLACKBURN,JOHN-Hundred Miles, a Hundred Heartbreaks-np-1972-294p-illus (n7,chip dj) 35.00

BLACKBURN,PAUL-Nets-NY-1961-Trobar-wrps-1st ed (v5,sl drknd sp) 60.00

BLACKFOOT CATECHISM AND PRAYERS-(Calgary)-(1920)-iv,120p-orig wrps-rare-Peel 4288 (bb9) 100.00

BLACKFOOT HYMNS-np-(1924)-72,26p-stiff wrps-Peel 4392 (bb9) 75.00

BLACKFOOT PRAYERS-np-(1921)-32p-wrps-Peel 4390 (bb9) 75.00

BLACKMAN,F F-Analytic Studies in Plant Respiration-Cambridge-1954-Cambridge Univ Pr-x+231p-grn cl,chrts-1st ed (l2,dj) 25.00

BLACKMAR,FRANK W-Spanish Institutions of the Southwest-Balt-1891-344p-orig cl,photos-Howes#B-496-1st ed (u7) 100.00

BLACKMORE,R D-Slain by the Doones & Other Stories-1895-D,M-1st ed (x2,f) 75.00

BLACKSTOCK,CHARITY-Knock at Midnight-NY-1967-Coward-1st US ed (h4,f,dj) 10.00

BLACKSTOCK,CHARITY-Mr.Christopoulos-NY-1964-London House-Edw Gorey dj-1st US ed (g4,f,sl wn dj) 12.50

BLACKSTOCK,LEE-All Men are Murderers-NY-1958-Dbldy-1st ed (r4,f,dj) 20.00

BLACKWELDER,BERNICE-Great Westerner-Caldwell-1962-Caxton-373p-frntis,map e.p.-1st ed (gg4,dj) 25.00

BLACKWELL,BUNYAN-ED.-Tales from the Bush Country-San Antonio-1963-183p-illus-1st ed (t7,f,dj) 15.00

BLACKWOOD,ALGERNON-Doll and One Other-Sauk City-1946-Arkham Hs-ltd to 3490c-1st ed (l7,f,dj) 45.00

BLACKWOOD,ALGERNON-Fruit Stoners-NY-1935-Dutton-8vo-Mauve cl-1st ed (v10,f,dj) 45.00

BLACKWOOD,ALGERNON-Promise of Air-Lond-1918-275p-1st ed (m4) 15.00

BLACKWOOD,ALGERNON-Shocks-Lond-(1935)-1st ed (m5) 20.00

BLACKWOOD,CAROLINE-For All That I Forgot There-NY-(1974)-Braziller-1st Amer ed (z8,vf,dj) 15.00

BLADES,W F-Fishing Flies & Fly Tying-Harrisburg-1951-8vo-234p-photos,illus-1st ed (m3,fray dj) 85.00

BLADES,W F-Fishing Flies & Fly Tying-PA-1951-234p-photos (ee3,f) 55.00

BLADES,WILLIAM-Pentateuch of Printing, with a Chapter on Judges-Lond-1891-Stock-sm 4to-dec grn cl stmpd in g & blk,illus-1st ed (w1) 125.00

BLAFFER,SARAH C-Black Man of Zinacantan-Austin-1972-U of Tex Pr-8vo-194p-dec brwn cl,39 illus,7 plts,3 maps & 20 tabls-1st ed (mm1,f,dj) 30.00

BLAIKIE,THOMAS-Diary of a Scotch Gardener-NY-1932-Dutton-256p-cl (x6,sp sun) 25.00

BLAINE,JAMES G-Twenty Years of Congress-Norwich-1884,1886-2 vols,cl (o1) 20.00

BLAINE,JAMES G-Twenty Years of Congress-Norwich-1884,1886-2 vols-illus,fldg map (n3) 45.00

BLAINE,MARTHA R-Ioway Indians-Norman-(1979)-364p-illus,maps-1st ed (c4,dj) 25.00

BLAINE,WM E-Ride Through the Garden of Canada-Grimsby-1967-26p+pict sect-papr wrps-1st ed (n4) 10.00

BLAIR & MEINE-EDS-Half Horse Half Alligator-Chig-(1956)-U of Chig Pr-8vo-289p-1st ed (b3,f,dj) 45.00

BLAIR,C F-Red Ball in the Sky-NY-(1969)-8vo-xii,204p-cl,8p plts (t2,dj) 30.00

BLAIR,CLAY,JR.-Atomic Submarine & Admiral Rickover-NY-1954-Holt-277p-photos-1st ed (p2,dj) 12.50

BLAIR,DOROTHEA-Roger, a Most Unusual Rabbit-Phila-(1952)-Lippincott-63p-pict cl,illus,H Knight (r3,dj) 20.00

BLAIR,FRED-Ashes of Six Million Jews-Milw-1946-People's Bk Shop-wrps-1st ed (w5) 25.00

BLAIR,ROBERT-Tales of the Superstitions-Tempe-1975-167p-photos,maps-1st ed (v7) 20.00

BLAIR,WALTER A-Raft Pilot's Log-Cleve-1930-Arthur Clark Publ-328p-illus-1st ed (f7,f,autg) 160.00

BLAIR,WALTER A-Raft Pilot's Log-Cleve-1930-Arthur H Clark-328p-illus,fldg map-1st ed (nn6,hng weak) 125.00

BLAIR,WALTER-Half Horse, Half Alligator-Chig-1956-289p-illus-1st ed (t7,dj) 25.00

BLAIS,MARIE-CLAIRE-St.Lawrence Blues-NY-1974-FS&G-1st ed (y1,sl fade dj) 25.00

BLAISDELL,GUS-Park City-NY-1980-Castelli Graphics-sq sm folio-246p-cl,photos by L Baltz-1st ed (t3,f,dj) 75.00

BLAISDELL,HAROLD F-Tricks That Take Fish-NY-1954-8vo-299p-illus (m3,f,dj) 16.00

BLAISE,CLARK-North American Education-Tor & GC-1973-Dbldy-auth 1st bk-1st ed (bb1,as new in dj) 25.00

BLAKE, MOFFITT & TOWNE-Pioneers in Paper-np(Seattle?)-stiff wrps,illus (b6,dj) 12.00

BLAKE,BEN-Awakening of the American Theatre-NY-1935-Tomorrow Publ-wrps-1st ed (v5,sp sunned) 35.00

BLAKE,CLAGETTE-Charles Elliot R.N. 1801 thru 1875-Lond-1960-130p-frntis,map-1st ed (t7,f) 12.50

BLAKE,E R-Birds of Mexico-Chig-1959(1953)-8vo-644p-cl,col frntis,.e.p. maps (y8,dj chip) 30.00

BLAKE,E VALE-ED.-Arctic Experiences-NY-1874-486p+6p ads-illus-1st ed (g7,sl fox) 85.00

BLAKE,ELEANOR-Wherever I Choose-NY-1938-Putnam-271p-cl-1st ed (z7,dj) 35.00

BLAKE,FORRESTER-Riding the Mustang Trail-NY-1935-261p-illus-1st ed (u7,f,dj) 35.00

BLAKE,HENRY-Talking with Horses-NY-1976-Dutton-1st US ed (f10,dj) 35.00

BLAKE,JOHN H-Tea Hints for Retailers-Denver-1903-Williamson Haffner Engrv-275p-grn illus bds,maps,photos-Bitting 42 (l6,soil bds) 35.00

BLAKE,JOHN-Short Title Catalog of Eighteenth Century Books in the National Library of Medicine-Bethesda-1979-501p-1st ed (dd3) 75.00

BLAKE,N-Beast Must Die-1938-Harper-1st Amer ed (x7,sl tn dj) 165.00

BLAKE,N-Beast Must Die-NY-1938-Harper-1st Amer ed (k4,f,sp chip dj) 150.00

BLAKE,N-End of Chapter-1957-Harper-1st US ed (x7,f,sl stnd dj) 27.00

BLAKE,N-End of Chapter-NY-1957-Harper-1st US ed (v5,f,wn dj) 20.00

BLAKE,N-Penknife in My Heart-1958-Harper-wi publ prntd band offering a refund if book is returned wi seal unbroken-1st ed (x7,vf,dj,band) 35.00

BLAKE,N-Tangled Web-1956-Harper-1st ed (x7,f,f dj) 28.00

BLAKE,N-Widow's Cruise-1959-Harper-1st ed (x7,f,dj) 28.00

BLAKE,N-Widow's Cruise-Lond-1959-Collins CC-1st ed (k4,f,dj) 25.00

BLAKE,N-Worm of Death-1961-Harper-1st US ed (x7,f,dj) 25.00

BLAKE,N-Worm of Death-NY-1961-Harper-1st US ed (h4,f,dj) 15.00

BLAKE,PETER-Architecture for the New World-Sydney-1973-sq 4to-illus-1st ed (ee1,dj) 100.00

BLAKE,ROBERT-Disraeli-NY-1967-St.Martin's-thk 8vo-819p-brwn cl,16 illus-bk club ed (gg6,dj) 9.50

BLAKE,W H-Brown Waters-Tor-1940-8vo-168p-Deluxe Memorial ed (1000c prntd)-frontis of auth-col illus,C A Gagnon-scarce (m3,f) 200.00

BLAKE,W H-Fisherman's Creed-Tor-1923-16mo-40p (m3,autg) 30.00

BLAKE,W H-In a Fishing Country-Tor-1922-8vo-262p (m3,f) 25.00

BLAKE,WILLIAM-Letters of...-Cambridge-1968-Harvard Univ Pr-cl,frntis,illus-1st Amer prtg (n8,f,dj) 35.00

BLAKE,WILLIAM-Poetry and Prose of...-1927-Nonesuch Pr-orig g titled cl over bev bds (aa9,sp fade) 75.00

BLAKEMORE,KENNETH-Book of Gold-NY-1971-Stein & Day-224p-col illus (u5,dj) 28.50

BLAKESLEE,ALBERT-Trees in Winter-NY-1926-Macmillan-446p-cl (x6) 20.00

BLAKNEY,RAYMOND B-Meister Eckhart-NY-1941-Harper & Bros-cl-1st ed (n8) 25.00

BLANCH,LESLEY-Sabres of Paradise-NY-(1960)-Viking-8vo-495p-26 illus-1st ed (cc5,dj) 25.00

BLANCH,LESLEY-Wilder Shores of Love-NY-1954-S&S-8vo-332p-16p illus-1st ed (cc5,f,dj) 20.00

BLANCHAN,N-How to Attract the Birds-NY-1903(1902)-8vo-224p-cl,photos (y8) 20.00

BLANCHARD,CHARLES E-Nut Cracker and Other Human Ape Fables-NY-(1911)-109p-cl (aa1) 15.00

BLANCHARD,J P-First Air Voyage in America-Phila-1943-8vo-cl,frntis,4p plts (t2) 30.00

BLANCHARD,LESLIE-Trolley Days in Seattle-LA-1965-48p-wrps-2nd prtg (n4) 10.00

BLAND,J O P-China Under the Empress Dowager...Life and Times of Tzu Hsi...-Phila-1910-Lippincott-8vo-xv,525p-1/2 lea,mrbld e.p.,dblpg map,30 illus-1st Amer ed (ll1,sl fox) 125.00

BLANKENSHIP,MRS GEORGE-Tillicum Tales of Thurston County-Olympia-1914-292+4p-illus-1st ed (d7,sl spot cov) 85.00

BLANTON,BURT C-400,000 Miles by Rail-Berkeley-1972-183p-1st ed (n4,f,dj) 22.00

BLANTON,WYNDHAM-Medicine in Virginia in the Nineteenth Century-Richmond-1933-466p-scarce-1st ed (dd3) 200.00

BLASDALE,WALTER C-Cultivated Species of Primula-Berkeley & LA-1948-8vo-xii,284p-grn cl,col frntis,41 b&w photo plts,8 figs,map (j10,sl bowed,dj tattrd) 50.00

BLASER,M-Mies Van Der Rohe: Furniture & Interiors-Lond-1982-220 illus-1st ed (h10,dj) 60.00

BLASIG,ANNE-Wends of Texas-S.A.-1954-Naylor-123p-1st ed (a9,dj) 50.00

BLASINGAME,IKE-Dakota Cowboy-NY-(1958)-Putnam's-317p-cl,map e.p.,illus,J Mariani-1st ed (v1) 45.00

BLASINGAME,IKE-Dakota Cowboy-NY-(1958)-Putnam's-317p-e.p. maps-1st ed (cc4,dj) 95.00

BLASIO,JOSE L-Maximillian, Emperor of Mexico-New Haven-1934-235p-cl,photos-scarce-1st ed (n10,sl fade sp) 50.00

BLATCHFORD,ROBERT-Merrie England-NY-1895-Commonwealth Co-wrps,Cmmwlth Libr Ser No.1-1st US ed (v5) 35.00

BLATCHFORD,THOMAS W-Observations on Equivocal Generation-Albany-1844-J Munsell-14p-prtd wrps (u2,sl tn wrps) 185.00

BLATCHLEY,W S-In Days Agone-Indpls-1932-Nature Publ-338p-grn cl,plts-1st ed (mm10) 50.00

BLATTY,WILLIAM P-John Goldfarb, Please Come Home-GC-1963-Dbldy-1st ed (hh5,sp fade dj) 15.00

BLATTY,WILLIAM P-Which Way to Mecca, Jack?-(NY)-(1960)-Bernard Geis-auth 1st bk-1st ed (e10,dj) 35.00

BLATZ,WILLIAM E-Five Sisters-NY-1938-Morrow-xii+209p-gry cl,photos-1st ed (d2,chip & soil dj) 40.00

BLAU,E E-Queens Falcon-1947-McKay-auth 1st & only bk-1st ed (x7,f,dj) 35.00

BLAU,MILTON-Brief Journey-NY-1949-Int'l-wrps-1st ed (w5) 20.00

BLAVATSKY,H P-Studies in Occultism-Pasadena-1946-Theosophical Univ Pr-cl-1st ed (n8,f,chip dj) 15.00

BLAWIS,PATRICIA B-Tijerina & the Land Grants-NY-1971-Int Publ-1st ed (a6,dj) 45.00

BLAWIS,PATRICIA B-Tijerina and the Land Grants-NY-(1971)-188p-wrps,photos-1st ed (u7,pres) 25.00

BLEECK,OLIVER-Highbinders-NY-1974-Morrow-1st ed (e4,tn dj) 40.00

BLEGEN,THEODORE-ED.-Peter Testman's Account of His Experiences in North America-Northfield-1927-60p-wrps-Howes T108-rprnt (aa1) 25.00

BLENCOWE,ANN-Receipt Book of Mrs.Ann Blencowe, A.D.1694-Lond-1925-Adelphi-60p-g dec bds-ltd to 625c,nbrd-1st ed (q8,dj) 75.00

BLESH,RUDI-Combo U.S.A.:Eight Lives in Jazz-(1971)-Chilton-1st ed (w1,f,dj) 25.00

BLEVINS,WINFRED-Give Your Heart to the Hawks-LA-1973-349p-photos,map,map e.p.-1st ed (t7,f,dj) 35.00

BLEW,W C-Brighton and Its Coaches-Lond-1894-Nimmo-1/2 lea & mrbld bds,20 handcol illus-1st ed (h9) 425.00

BLEWETT,WILLIAM E,JR.-Always Good Ships-Newcomen Address-1960-28p (kk3) 10.00

BLIGH,WILLIAM-Log of H.M.S. Providence. 1791 to 1793-Guilford-1976-Genesis Publ-951p-3/4 lea wi raised bnds,g sp titles & decs,col frntis,fldg chrt,illus,ltd ed of 500c (nn1,f,sl rub box) 750.00

BLIGH,WILLIAM-Mutiny on Board H.M.S. Bounty-Guilford/Melbourne-1981-Pageminster/Argot,Beazley-illus by R Williams (dd7,f,dj) 140.00

BLIGH,WILLIAM-Voyage to the South Sea...In His Majesty's Ship the Bounty...Including an Account of the Mutiny-Lond-1792-Geo Nicol-4to-264p-mor,8 plts-1st ed (p8,rbnd,sl fox) 3,000.00

BLIGH,WILLIAM-Voyage to the South Seas-Honolulu-1967-4to-264p-illus,fldg maps-facs of 1792 1st ed (f7) 50.00

BLISH,HELEN H-Pictographic History of the Oglala Sioux-(1967)-U of Nebr Pr-4to-xxii,530p-32 col plts,421 b&w illus-1st ed (aa3,f,box) 65.00

BLISH,HELEN H-Pictographic History of the Oglala Sioux-Lincoln-(1967)-U of Nebr Pr-4to-530p-col illus-1st ed (dd4,box) 95.00

BLISH,HELEN H-Pictographic History of the Oglala Sioux-Lincoln-(1967)-U of Nebr Pr-4to-xxii+530p,blk & ochre cl,415p illus(incl 32 col)-1st ed (k2,sl rippling of pgs) 50.00

BLISH,JAMES-Black Easter-Lond-1968-Faber-1st ed (v5,f,sl soil dj) 25.00

BLISH,JAMES-Case of Conscience-Lond-1959-Faber & Faber-1st Brit & 1st hdcov ed (dd8,dj) 60.00

BLISH,JAMES-Earthman Come Home-NY-1955-Putnam-1st ed (v5,sl stnd e.p.,dj) 40.00

BLISH,JAMES-Jack of Eagles-NY-(1952)-Greenberg Publ-auth 1st bk-1st ed (a10,sl tn dj) 100.00

BLISH,JAMES-Star Trek Reader III-NY-(1977)-Dutton-1st hdbk ed (k3,f,sl tn dj) 20.00

BLISH,JAMES-Star Trek Reader IV-NY-(1978)-Dutton-1st hdbk ed (f3,f,dj) 20.00

BLISS,CHARLES R-New West-Bost-1879-16p-1/4 lea,full pg map,2 sm drwngs-rare-not in Howes-1st ed (u7,lacks wrapper,rbnd) 250.00

BLISS,FRANK E-Life of Hon William F Cody Known as Buffalo Bill...-Hartford-1879-365p-pict cl,frntis,photos-Graff #786-1st ed (t7) 175.00

BLISS,MICHAEL-Discovery of Insulin-Chig-1982-304p-1st ed (dd3,dj) 45.00

BLITS,PROFESSOR H-...METHODS OF CANNING FRUITS AND VEGETABLES BY HOT AIR AND STEAM...-Brklyn-1890-auth-106p-blu bds-new ed & spplmnt (n6) 75.00

BLOCH,IWAN-Sexual Life of Our Time in its Relations to Modern Civilization-NY-1928-790p (dd3) 35.00

BLOCH,MAURICE-Placing the Dead-Lond-1971-Seminar Pr-8vo-240p-cl-1st ed (y5,dj) 30.00

BLOCH,ROBERT-Blood Runs Cold-NY-1961-S&S-1st ed (d10,dj) 75.00

BLOCH,ROBERT-Opener of the Way-Sauk City-1945-Arkham Hs-ltd to 2000c-1st ed (ee6,dj) 125.00

BLOCH,ROBERT-Psycho-NY-1959-Simon-1st ed (k4,sl yel pgs,sl tn dj) 275.00

BLOCH,ROBERT-Scarf-1947-Dial-1st ed (s10,brwnd pgs,dj sl wn) 80.00

BLOCHMAN,LAWRENCE G-Clues for Dr.Coffee-Phila-1964-Lippincott-1st ed (j4,f,dj) 40.00

BLOCHMAN,LAWRENCE G-Diagnosis:Homicide-Phila-1950-Lippincott-1st ed (f4,f,dj) 60.00

BLOCK,EUGENE B-Great Stagecoach Robbers of the West-GC-(1962)-Dbldy-262p-illus,e.p. maps-1st ed (cc4,sl wn dj) 20.00

BLOCK,LAWRENCE-Ariel-NY-(1980)-1st ed (r2,sl nick dj) 25.00

BLOCK,LAWRENCE-Ariel-NY-(1980)-Arbor-1st ed (l3,f,dj) 30.00

BLOCK,LAWRENCE-Burglar Who Studied Spinoza-NY-1980-Random-1st ed (h4,f,dj sp sl fade) 15.00

BLOCK,LAWRENCE-Burglar Who Studied Spinoza-NY-1980-Random-1st ed (w9,vf,dj) 25.00

BLOCK,LAWRENCE-Code of Arms-NY-(1981)-Marek-1st ed (j3,f,dj) 15.00

BLOCK,LAWRENCE-Death Pulls a Double Cross-NY-1961-Fawcett-pict wrps(pbk orig)-1st ed (hh2,f) 85.00

BLOCK,LAWRENCE-Me Tanner, You Jane-1970-Macmillan-1st ed (x7,f,dj) 28.00

BLOCK,LAWRENCE-Mona-NY-1961-Fawcett-pict wrps(pbk orig)-1st ed (hh2,f) 85.00

BLOCK,LAWRENCE-Mr.Rhodenbarr, Bookseller, Advises a Young Customer on Seeking a Vocation-New Castle-1980-Oak Knoll-prtd wrps-ltd to 250c,nbrd-1st ed (hh2,as new) 150.00

BLOCK,LAWRENCE-Specialists-Greenwich-1969-Gold Medal-pbk orig-1st ed (g4,f,wrps) 12.50

BLOGG,MINNIE-Bibliography of the Writings of Sir William Osler-Balt-1921-96p-2nd ed (dd3) 60.00

BLOGG,PERCY T-There are No Dull Dark Days-Balt-1944-8vo-92p-illus,photos-scarce (m3,vf,dj) 100.00

BLOME,RICHARD-Hawking or Falconry-1929-Cresset Pr-8vo-xxxii,123p-qtr wht prchmnt,tan bds,t.e.g.,lg fldg plt,ltd to 650c,nbrd (t10,f,unopened) 150.00

BLOMFIELD,JAMES-Rod,Gun & Palette in the High Rockies-Chig-1914-4to-116p-1/2 lea & bds,illus by auth (m3) 250.00

BLOMFIELD,R-History of French Architecture-Lond-1921-2 vols-illus (h10) 150.00

BLOMFIELD,REGINALD-History of Renaissance Architecture in England, 1500 to 1800-Lond-1897-Geo Bell & Sons-4to-2 vols-cl,t.e.g.,illus,plts(2 dbl-pg) (pp7) 300.00

BLONG,R J-Time of Darkness-Seattle,Lond-1982-U of Wash Pr-8vo-xi,257p (pp1,as new in dj) 30.00

BLOODGOOD,LIDA F-Hoofs in the Distance-NY-1953-Van Nostrand-ltd to 985c,autg,glassine dj (h9,f,dj,box) 125.00

BLOOMVILLE, OHIO-Bloomville-1965-60p-wrps (h1) 12.50

BLOSS,G M D-Historic and Literary Miscellany-Cin-1875-468p-cl (g1) 17.50

BLOSSFELDT,KARL-Art Forms in Nature-NY-1967-Univ Bks-4to-112p-cl (t3,f,dj) 65.00

BLOT,PIERRE-Hand Book of Practical Cookery-NY-1868-Appleton-478p-grn bds-Bitting 45 (n6,rprd e.p.) 125.00

BLOWER,JAMES M-N.O.T. & L. Story-Chig-1966-269p-1st ed (n4,f,dj) 27.50

BLOXOM,MARGUERITE-Pickaxe and Pencil-Wash-1982-Libr of Congress-87p-wrps (c1) 17.50

BLUE,HERBERT T O-Centennial History of Hardin County, Ohio...-(Canton)-(1933)-180p-wrps (j1) 22.50

BLUE,HERBERT T O-History of Canton Lodge No.60...1821 to 1946-Canton-1946-360p-cl (j1) 15.00

BLUM,ARLENE-Annapurna, a Woman's Place-SF-1980-lg 8vo-256p-8 col plts-1st prtg (p10,f,dj) 25.00

BLUM,RICHARD-Utopiates-NY-1965-Atherton Pr-xvi+303p-blu/grn cl-1st ed (c2,dj) 35.00

BLUNT,DON-Dead Giveaway-1963-Avalon-1st ed (s10,dj) 12.50

BLUNT,WILFRID-Art of Botanical Illustration-Lond-1950-Collins-xxvi,304p-47 col & 32 b&w plts-scarce-1st ed (mm4,f) 140.00

BLUNT,WILFRID-Illustrated Herbal-Lond-(1979)-Thames & Hudson-folio-191p (m6) 50.00

BLUNT,WILFRID-Illustrated Herbal-NY-(1979)-Thames & Hudson-folio-191p-grn cl,64 col plts-1st Amer ed (q8,dj) 30.00

BLUNT,WILFRID-Illustrated Herbal-NY-1979-Thames & Hudson-4to-191p-col & b&w plts (r10,f,f dj) 35.00

BLUNT,WILFRID-Persian Spring-Lond-1957-Barrie-1st ed (y1,f,sl rub dj) 25.00

BLUNT,WILFRID-Tulipomania-Harmondsworth-(1950)-King Penguin-32p+16 col plts,pict bds-1st ed (x5,sl wn sp,dj) 25.00

BLY,CAROL-Letters From the Country-NY-1981-Harper & Row-1st ed (g8,sl wn dj) 25.00

BLY,ROBERT-Light Around the Body-NY-1967-Harepr & Row-1st ed (c8,f dj) 75.00

BLY,ROBERT-Man in the Black Coat Turns-NY-1981-1st ed (t5,dj) 12.50

BLY,ROBERT-Teeth Mother Naked at Last-(Madison)-(1970)-(Amer Writers)-wrps-1st ed (ff3,f) 65.00

BLY,ROBERT-Teeth Mother Naked at Last-1970-City Lights-wrps-1st ed thus (t9) 15.00

BLYTH,R H-Haiku. Vol.I:Eastern Culture-np-1962-Hokuseido-buckram,col frntis,col & b&w plts-10th prtg (l8,f,dj) 35.00

BLYTH,R H-Zen in English Literature and Oriental Classics-Tokyo-1942-Hokuseido Pr-cl,frntis,illus-1st ed (n8) 35.00

BLYTHE,RONALD-From the Headlands-Lond-1982-1st ed (y7,dj) 12.00

BOAK,DENNIS-Andre Malraux-Oxford-1968-OUP-1st ed (z9,f,dj) 10.00

BOARDMAN,HARVEY-Complete and Accurate Guide to and Around the White Mountains-Bost-1859-Crosby,Nichols-26p-emboss blu cl,2 fldg maps-1st ed (k8) 65.00

BOARDMAN,PETER-Sacred Summits-Seattle-1982-264p-1st US ed (o10,as new in dj) 40.00

BOAS,FRANZ-Ethnology of the Kwakiutl,British Columbia-Wash D.C.-1913,14-GPO-4to-two vols,orig olive cl,g titles,Bureau of Amer Ethnology,35th Annual Report-1st ed (mm1) 195.00

BOAS,FRANZ-Ethnology of the Kwakiutl-1921-Bur Amer Ethnol 35th Ann Rept-2 vols-figs (bb3,cor wn) 95.00

BOAS,FRANZ-Ethnology of the Kwakiutl-Wash-1921-GPO/Bur Amer Ethnol-1481p-3/4 lea-35th Annual Report (ff4,ex-libr) 100.00

BOAS,FRANZ-Kathlamet Texts-Wash-1901-BAE Bull.#26-sm 4to-261p-text in Engl & Kathlamet-1st ed (g7,fade bds) 45.00

BOAS,FRANZ-Kathlamet Texts-Wash-1901-GPO/Bur Amer Ethno-261p-frntis-Bull.26 (bb4) 25.00

BOAS,FRANZ-Keresan Texts. Parts 1 & 2-NY-1925 & 1928-Amer Ethn Soc,Vol.VIII-2 vols (v7,vol.1 lacks f.e.p.) 85.00

BOAS,FRANZ-Tsimshian Mythology-Wash-1916-GPO/Bur Amer Ethnol-1037p-3/4 lea-31st Annual Report (ff4,ex-libr) 75.00

BOAS,FRANZ-Tsimshian Texts-Wash-1902-GPO/Bur Amer Ethno-244p-Bull.27 (bb4) 30.00

BOAS,GEORGE-ED.-Romanticism in America-Balt-1940-(13),202p-15 plts-1st ed (l10,f,dj) 15.00

BOATNER,MARK M-Civil War Dictionary-NY-(1959)-974p-maps (c4,f,dj) 25.00

BOATRIGHT,MODY C-Folk Travellers-Dallas-1953-SMU-Tex Folklore Soc,No.25-1st ed (a6,dj) 35.00

BOATRIGHT,MODY-ED.-And Horns on the Toads-Dallas-1959-237p-Tex Folklore Scty Publ 29-1st ed (t8,f,sl tn dj sp) 22.00

BOATRIGHT,MODY-ED.-Golden Log-(1962)-SMU-168p-Tex Folklore Scty XXXI-1st ed (t8,f,sl chip dj) 30.00

BOATRIGHT,MODY-ED.-Golden Log-Dallas-(1962)-SMU-168p-1st ed (a9,dj) 25.00

BOCCA,GEOFFREY-La Legion-NY-1964-307p-illus-1st ed (b7,f,dj) 15.00

BOCCACCIO,GIOVANNI-Decameron-Phila-1928-J P Horn-2 vols-3/4 lea-ltd to 1550 sets-rprnt of Villon Soc ed of 1886 (f1) 35.00

BOCCIUS,GOTTLIEB-Treatise on the Managment of the Fish in Rivers & Streams-Lond-1848-8vo-38p+ads-orig bndg-scarce (m3) 50.00

BOCK,C E-Atlas of the Human Anatomy-NY-1881-Wm Wood-lg folio-orig cl,38 col plts (dd10,f) 85.00

BOCKRIS,VICTOR-With William Burroughs-NY-(1981)-Seaver Bks-photos-1st ed (ff6,f,dj) 20.00

BODDAM-WHETHAM,J W-Western Wanderings, a Record of Travel in the Evening Land-Lond-1874-Richard Bentley & Son-8vo-xii+364p-cl (z4,sp cocked,cov wn,bump) 25.00

BODDE,DEREK-Peking Diary-NY-(1950)-Schuman-8vo-292p-28 photos-1st ed (ff5,dj) 15.00

BODENHEIM,MAXWELL-King of Spain and Other Poems-NY-1928-Boni & Liveright-1st ed (v5,f,dj sl wn) 65.00

BODSWORTH,FRED-Atonement of Ashley Morden-NY-1964-Dodd Mead-1st ed (y1,f,f dj) 30.00

BOEGLI,LINA-Forward-Phila,Lond-1904-Lippincott-8vo-320p-dec stmpd cl,t.e.g.,frntis,1 ilus-1st ed (ee9) 25.00

BOELL,JAQUES-High Heaven-Lond-1947-126p-photos-1st Brit ed (p10,f,dj) 18.00

BOELTER,HOMER H-Portfolio of Hopi Kachinas-Hollywood-(1969)-H H Boelter-61p+16 col plts,sep suite of plts accompany portfolio,both in box-ltd to 1000c,nbrd,autg-1st ed (gg4) 350.00

BOELTER,HOMER H-Portfolio of Hopi Kachinas-Hollywood-1969-Boelter Litho-folio-16 col plts wi 16 sep plts in cardbd fldr-1st ed (a6,f,fldr tn,sl wn) 250.00

BOERICKE,ART-Handmade Houses-SF-1973-Scrimshaw Pr-sq 4to-blu & grn cl,col photos-2nd prtg (r10,dj) 20.00

BOESEN,VICTOR-Edward S Curtis: Photographer of the North American Indian-NY-1977-Dodd,Mead-8vo-191p-cl,photos-1st ed (z4,dj) 25.00

BOGAN,LOUISE-Body of This Death-NY-1923-McBride-auth 1st bk-1st ed (q2) 195.00

BOGAN,LOUISE-Body of This Death-NY-1923-McBride-beige cl sp,blu bds-auth 1st bk-scarce-1st ed (f2,sm pc tape on dj sp) 275.00

BOGART,W H-Daniel Boone & the Hunters of Kentucky-Auburn,Buffalo-1854-8vo-390p-orig bndg-illus-scarce-1st ed (m3) 75.00

BOGGS,LUCINDA P-Chinese Womanhood-Cin-(1915)-Jennings & Graham-sm 8vo-129p-orng cl-1st ed (s1) 45.00

BOHEMIAN FLATS-Mpls-nd(ca.1940)-U of Minn/WPA-sm 8vo-52p-ltd to 1000c,nbrd (p1,f,dj) 40.00

BOHLKE,J E-Fishes of the Bahamas and Adjacent Tropical Waters-Wynnewood-1968-cl,36 plts(32 col),text illus-scarce (jj10,f) 175.00

BOHR,NEILS-Atomic Physics and Human Knowledge-NY-1958-101p-1st ed (dd3,dj) 35.00

BOK,EDWARD W-Successward-NY,et al-1895-184p-cl,auth 1st bk-1st ed (m1) 17.50

BOKSER,RABBI BEN ZION-From the World of the Cabbalah-NY-1954-Philo Libr-cl-1st ed (l8,f,dj) 15.00

BOLIN,ROLF-Review of the Marine Cottid Fishes of California-1944-Stanford-8vo-135p-wrps,illus-scarce (m3,f) 75.00

BOLINDER,GUSTAF-Indians on Horseback-Lond-(1957)-Dobson-8vo-189p-6 col illus-1st Brit ed (ff5,sl chip dj) 17.50

BOLITHO,HECTOR-ED.-Glorious Oyster-NY-1961-Horizon-174p-red cl,17 illus-1st Amer ed (q8,dj) 30.00

BOLITHO,HECTOR-Galloping Third-Lond-1963-341p-maps,illus-1st ed (gg2,f,dj) 100.00

BOLITHO,WILLIAM-Italy Under Mussolini-NY-1926-Macmillan-129p (r1) 15.00

BOLITHO,WILLIAM-Murder for Profit-NY-1926-Harpers-8vo-332p-1st ed (b3,f,dj) 35.00

BOLLER,HENRY A-Among the Indians-Chig-1959-Donnelley & Sons-illus,maps-Lakeside Classics (ff4) 20.00

BOLLER,WILLY-Masterpieces of the Japanese Color Woodcut-Bost-nd-Bost Bk & Art Shop-folio-174p-col illus-1st US ed (bb5,dj) 75.00

BOLLINGER,EDWARD T-Coronado Knight of Pueblos and Plains-Albuq-1949-491p-map e.p. (t7) 20.00

BOLLINGER,EDWARD T-Moffat Road-Denver-1962-359p-frntis,photos,maps-1st ed (t7,dj) 27.50

BOLLINGER-SAVELLI,ANTONELLA-Knitted Cat-NY-1971-Macmillan-sq 8vo-unpgd-cl,wordless pic bk-1st US ed (r3,f,dj) 20.00

BOLLMAN,DON-Run for the Roses-1975-Canadian Lakes-photos-1st ed (s8,f,dj) 25.00

BOLTON,ARTHUR T-Architecture of Robert & James Adam-Lond-1922-Cntry Life-folio-2 vols-cl wi g cameos on cov,illus (pp7,sl shaken) 450.00

BOLTON,ETHEL S-American Samplers-NY-1973-Weathervane-viii,416p-76 plts-1st prtg (o2,sl chip dj) 17.50

BOLTON,HERBERT E-Anza's California Expeditions-Berkeley-1930-UCP-5 vols-illus,maps-1st ed (d3) 500.00

BOLTON,HERBERT E-Coronado-(1949)-Whittlesey Hs-491p-maps,map e.p.-1st ed (cc4,sl wn dj) 40.00

BOLTON,HERBERT E-ED.-Arredondo's Historical Proof of Spain's Title to Georgia-Berkeley-1925-382p-cl-1st ed (j1,autg) 35.00

BOLTON,HERBERT E-ED.-Historical Memoirs of New California by Fray Francisco Palou, O.F.M.-NY-1966(1926)-Russell & Russell-4 vols (d3) 200.00

BOLTON,HERBERT E-Font's Complete Diary-Berkeley-1931-U of Cal Pr-8vo-xix,552p-blu cl,maps,plts,facs-Howes B585 (mm1,ex-libr) 100.00

BOLTON,HERBERT E-Fray Juan Crespi, Missionary Explorer on the Pacific Coast: 1769 to 1774-Berkeley-1927-UCP-402p-errata-1st ed (d3) 145.00

BOLTON,HERBERT E-Outpost of Empire-NY-1931-Knopf-8vo-334p+xvii index-blk cl,g titles,frntis,illus,4 fldg maps-1st ed (mm1,rprd fldg map) 75.00

BOLTON,HERBERT E-Padre on Horseback-SF-1932-Sonora-90p-mrbld bds,suede sp labl,map e.p.,illus-1st ed (d3,dj) 75.00

BOLTON,HERBERT E-Rim of Christendom-NY-1936-Macmillan-644p-maps-1st ed (cc4,ex-libr) 75.00

BOLTON,HERBERT E-Rim of Christendom-NY-1936-Macmillan-8vo-xiv,(21),3-644p-blu cl,8 fldg maps,12 plts,3 facs-1st ed (mm1) 85.00

BOLTON,SARAH K-Famous Voyagers and Explorers-NY-(1893)-509p-cl (g1) 17.50

BOLTON,SARAH K-Lives of Girls Who Became Famous-NY-(1886)-Crowell-347p+ads-cl (d1) 20.00

BOND,ALLEN-When the Hopkins Came to Baltimore-Balt-1927-84p-1st ed (dd3) 25.00

BOND,GEORGE-ED.-African Christianity-NY-(1979)-Academic-8vo-175p-cl-1st ed (y5,dj) 35.00

BOND,HORATIO-Fire and the Air War-Bost-(1946)-Nat Fire Protection Assn-xii+262p-red cl,photos,maps-1st ed (dd1,edgewn dj) 30.00

BOND,J-Birds of the West Indies-Bost-1971-sm 8vo-256p-cl,9 col plts-3rd Amer ed (y8) 16.00

BOND,JIM-From Out of the Yukon-Portland-1948-8vo-220p-photos-1st ed (m3,f,dj,pres) 45.00

BOND,JIM-Hold that Tiger & Other Stories-Portland-1958-4to-67p+photos-wrps (m3,autg,f) 35.00

BOND,JIM-Mule Deer-Portland-nd-4to-125p-wrps-photos (m3,autg,as new) 25.00

BOND,JIM-Rifleman in Alaska-Portland-1953-4to-46p+photos-wrps-1st ed (m3,autg) 25.00

BOND,MARSHALL,JR.-Gold Hunter-Albuq-1969-UNM-1st ed (a6,dj) 35.00

BOND,MICHAEL-Bear Called Paddington-Bost-1960-Houghton Mifflin-drwngs-1st US ed (oo10,lacks dj) 20.00

BOND,NELSON-COMP.-Postal Stationery of Canada-Shrub Oak-1953-H Herst,Jr.-xii,132p-illus (k10) 30.00*

BOND,NELSON-Nightmares and Daydreams-Sauk City-1968-Arkham-269p-ltd to-1st ed (k5,as new in dj) 35.00

BOND,NELSON-Thirty First of February-NY-(1949)-Gnome-8vo-272p-1st ed (ee5,dj) 30.00

BOND,W H-ED.-Houghton Library, 1942 to 1967-Cambridge-1967-folio-256p-1st ed (dd3) 100.00

BONEHILL,CAPTAIN RALPH-Out With Gun and Camera-NY-1910-8vo-258p-illus (m3) 12.50

BONI,ADA-Italian Regional Cooking-1969-Dutton-folio-305p-blk cl,144p col plts-1st US ed (q8,dj) 25.00

BONI,ALBERT-Photographic Literature, 1960 to 1970-Hastings,NY-1972-Morgan & Morgan-535p (cc9,as new in dj) 75.00

BONI,MARGARET B-Fireside Book of Folk Songs-NY-1947-S&S (u4,dj) 32.00

BONIFACE,MARJORIE-Murder as an Ornament-1940-CC-1st ed (s10,sp wn dj) 25.00

BONINGTON,CHRIS-Annapurna South Face-Lond-1971-334p-48 col plts-1st Brit ed (p10,f,dj) 40.00

BONINGTON,CHRIS-ET AL-Changabang-NY-1976-118p-1st US ed (p10,f,dj) 28.00

BONINGTON,CHRIS-Everest Southwest Face-Lond-1973-351p-56 plts,fldg map,illus-1st Brit ed (q10,f,dj) 40.00

BONINGTON,CHRIS-Everest the Hard Way-Lond-1976-238p-80 col plts-1st Brit ed (p10,f,dj) 45.00

BONINGTON,CHRIS-Everest the Hard Way-NY-1976-1st US ed (p10,f,dj) 20.00

BONINGTON,CHRIS-Kongur-Lond-1982-Hodder & Stoughton-8vo-224p-col illus-1st ed (cc7,dj) 35.00*

BONINGTON,CHRIS-Ultimate Challenge-NY-1973-Stein & Day-8vo-352p-blu cl,56 photos-1st US ed (gg6,f,dj) 40.00

BONNAMY,FRANCIS-Portrait of the Artist as a Dead Man-NY-1947-Duell-1st ed (g4,chip dj) 12.50

BONNELL,FISHER-Texas Emigrant Guides 1840 to 1841-Waco-1964-Texian-3 vols (a9,box) 75.00

BONNELL,JAMES F-Death Over Sunday-1940-Scribners-1st ed (s10,tape rprd dj) 25.00

BONNER,M G-Baseball Rookies Who Made Good-1954-Knopf-photos-1st ed (s8,f,dj) 25.00

BONNER,PAUL H-Aged in the Woods-NY-1958-8vo-157p-illus-1st ed (m3) 12.50

BONNER,PAUL H-Aged in the Woods-NY-1958-Scribner's-1st ed (ff7,dj) 25.00

BONNER,PAUL H-Glorious Mornings-NY-1954-8vo-228p-illus-1st ed (m3,fray dj) 17.50

BONNER,T D-Life & Adventures of James P Beckwourth-NY-1931-405p-1st rprnt (f7,sl chip dj) 75.00

BONNER,T D-Life and Adventures of James P Beckwourth-Mpls-(1965)-Ross & Haines-547p-illus-ltd to 1500c-Howes B601 (bb4,dj) 15.00

BONNER,T D-Smiling Pioneer-LA-1932-87p-dec cl,frntis-1st ed (t7) 15.00

BONNER,WILLARD H-Pirate Laureate-New Brunswick-1947-Rutgers U Pr-8vo-xvi,239p-grn cl-1st ed (pp1,dj wn) 45.00

BONNEY,CECIL-Looking Over My Shoulder-Roswell-1971-235p-cl,photos,cov illus & e.p. maps by J Cisneros-1st ed (w3,f) 45.00

BONNEY,CECIL-Looking Over My Shoulder-Roswell-1971-cl-1st ed (z1,vf) 40.00

BONNEY,CECIL-Looking Over My Shoulder-Roswell-1971-Hall Poorb-1st ed (a6,f,dj) 60.00

BONNEY,ORRIN H-Battle Drums and Geysers-Chig-(1970)-Sage Books/Swallow Pr-thk 8vo-xxvi,622p-cl,fldg maps,maps,illus-1st ed (v1,dj) 65.00

BONNEY,T G-Building of the Alps-NY-1912-384p-g lttrng,t.e.g.,32 plts-1st US ed (o10) 50.00

BONOSKY,PHILLIP-Beyond the Borders of Myth-NY-1967-Praxis-scarce-1st ed (ff3,insect damgd dj) 45.00

BONTEMPS,ARNA-Lonesome Boy-Bost-1955-Houghton Mifflin-28p-cl,illus-1st ed (oo10,f,dj) 35.00

BONTEMPS,ARNA-Lonesome Boy-Bost-1955-Houghton Mifflin-illus,F Topolski-1st ed (c10,dj wn & sp drknd) 50.00

BONTEMPS,ARNA-We Have Tomorrow-Bost-1945-Houghton Mifflin-photos by M Palfi-1st ed (w5,f,sl tn dj) 100.00

BONVALOT,GABRIEL-Through the Heart of Asia, Over the Pamir to India-Lond-1889-Chapman & Hall-8vo-2 vols-pict dec blu cl,250 illus,A Pepin (ll1,ex-libr) 275.00

BOOKBINDING IN AMERICA, THREE ESSAYS-Portland-1941-Southworth Anthoensen Pr-8vo-xix,293p-cl backd bds-1st ed (w2,sp fade,cov soil) 85.00

BOOKER,ANTON S-Wildcats in Petticoats-Girard-(1945)-Haldeman Julius-24p-wrps (d1) 15.00

BOOKMEN'S HOLIDAY...IN TRIBUTE TO HARRY MILLER LYDENBERG-NY-1943-NY Public Libr-thk 8vo-573p-cl-ltd to 1000c-1st ed (w2,sp spot) 30.00

BOOKWALTER,JOHN W-If Not Silver What?-Springfield-1896-138p-cl (g1) 17.50

BOOMER,PETE-Operating Manual for Model Railroaders-Milw-1954-153p-spiral bndg-4th prtg (n4) 12.00

BOONE & CROCKETT CLUB-American Big Game in Its Haunts-NY-1904-497p-photos (gg3,sp fade) 95.00

BOONE & CROCKETT CLUB-An American Crusade for Wildlife-NY-1975-8vo-409p-J B Trefethen,Ed.-photos (m3,dj) 15.00

BOONE & CROCKETT CLUB-Crusade for Wildlife-Harrisburg-1961-8vo-344p+biblio-J B Trefethen,Ed.-Col plts,C Rungius-drwngs,B Hines-1st ed (m3,f,dj) 50.00

BOONE & CROCKETT CLUB-Hunting at High Altitudes-NY-1913-8vo-511p-photos-scarce-1st ed (m3,sp lettrng gone) 125.00

BOONE & CROCKETT CLUB-Hunting in Many Lands-NY-1895-8vo-447p-illus-1st ed (m3) 125.00

BOONE & CROCKETT CLUB-North American Big Game-NY-1939-8vo-533p-illus,photos-scarce (m3,f) 450.00

BOONE & CROCKETT CLUB-Records of North American Big Game 1964 Edition-NY-1964-Holt-8vo-398p-1st ed (p1,f,dj) 225.00

BOONE & CROCKETT CLUB-Records of North American Big Game Hunting 1971 Edition-Pitt-1971-Boone & Crockett-8vo-402p-1st ed (p1,f,dj) 175.00

BOONE & CROCKETT CLUB-Records of North American Big Game-NY-1952-8vo-174p+photos-scarce-1st ed (m3,f,fray dj) 325.00

BOONE & CROCKETT CLUB-Records of North American Big Game-NY-1958-264p-gilt antlers on fr cov,photos-1st ed so stated (ee3,f) 225.00

BOONE & CROCKETT CLUB-Records of North American Big Game-NY-1981-409p-photos (gg3,f,dj) 30.00

BOORSE,J W,JR.-Rapid Transit in Canada-Phila-1968-104p-1st ed (n4,f,dj) 16.00

BOOTH,ABRAHAM-Glad Tidings to Perishing Sinners...-Phila-1833-162p-bds-Amer Imprnts 17874 (b1,sp chip) 22.50

BOOTH,ABRAHAM-Reign of Grace-NY-1809-prntd for John Tiebout-306,(1)p-lea-Amer Imprnts 17062-2nd Amer ed (h1) 20.00

BOOTH,LOUIS F-Bak Vault Mystery-1933-Dodd-1st ed (s10,chip dj) 15.00

BOOTHBY,G-Beautiful White Devil-NY-1897-Appleton-1st US ed (f4,f) 35.00

BOOTHBY,G-Bid for Fortune-1895-Appleton-1st Amer ed (x7) 65.00

BOOTHBY,G-Dr Nikola's Experiment-1899-Appleton-1st Amer ed (x7) 60.00

BOOTHBY,G-Dr Nikola's Experiment-1899-Appleton-v scarce in wrps iss-1st Amer ed (x7,sl tn wrps) 100.00

BOOTHBY,G-Farewell, Nikola-1901-Lippincott-pict stmpd cl-1st Amer ed (x7) 50.00

BOOTHBY,G-Farewell, Nikola-1901-WL-1st ed (x7,sl sunned sp) 75.00

BOOTHBY,G-Marriage of Esther-1895-Appleton-1st Amer ed (x7) 25.00

BOOY,D M-Rock of Exile-NY-1958-Devin-Adair Co-8vo-xi,196p-15p photos,map,line drwngs (nn1,dj) 30.00

BOR,ELEANOR-Adventures of a Botanist's Wife-Lond-1952-Hurst & Blackett-8vo-204p-e.p. maps,35 photos,6 drwngs-1st ed (ff9,dj) 25.00*

BORDEAUX,HENRY-Knight of the Air-New Haven-1918-Yale Univ Pr-8vo-256p-dec bds,col frntis,4 plts-1st ed (t2) 75.00

BORDEAUX,W J-Conquering the Mighty Sioux-Sioux Falls-1929-211p-illus-1st ed (nn6) 150.00

BORDEN,MARY-Forbidden Zone-Lond-(1929)-Heinemann-8vo-199p-1st ed (w6,f,dj) 45.00

BORDEN,MRS JOHN-Cruise of the Northern Light-NY-1928-xi,317p-illus-Smith 958 (a7) 50.00

BORDEN,SPENCER-Arab Horse-NY-1906-Dbldy,Page-1st ed (j9,t.p. detached) 58.00

BORDEN,W C-Use of the Roentgen Ray...in the War with Spain-Wash-1900-4to-98p+38 plts(x-rays)-1st ed (dd3,hng crack,sl stnd,shaken) 400.00

BORDER AND THE BUFFALO-Chig-1938-Donnelley-480p-frntis (dd4,cov spot) 20.00

BOREIN,EDWARD-Borein's West-Santa Barbara-1952-Schaeur Prtg-4to-col frntis,10p text,sketches-1st ed (a6,dj) 75.00

BORGER,GARY-Naturals-Harrisburg-1980-8vo-223p-illus-1st ed (m3,f,dj) 15.00

BORGERS'S FIFTIETH BIRTHDAY, 1926 TO 1976-Borger-1976-47p-wrps,photos-1st ed (w3,vf) 15.00

BORGES,JORGE L-Book of Sand-NY-1977-1st US ed (n5,f,f dj) 35.00

BORGES,JORGE L-Book of Sand-NY-1977-Dutton-1st US ed (e10,f,dj) 40.00

BORGES,JORGE L-Chronicles of Bustos Domecq-NY-1976-1st US ed (p5,f,dj) 35.00

BORGES,JORGE L-Chronicles of Bustos Domecq-NY-1976-Dutton-1st US ed (y1,f,f dj) 50.00

BORGES,JORGE L-Dreamtigers-Lond-1973-Souvenir Pr-1st Brit ed (d8,f,f dj) 50.00

BORGES,JORGE L-Extaordinary Tales-1971-Herder & Herder-1st ed (x2,f,dj) 75.00

BORGES,JORGE L-Introduction to American Literature-Lexington-1971-Univ Pr/KY-1st ed (h8,f,sl tn dj) 50.00

BORGES,JORGE L-Universal History of Infamy-NY-1972-Dutton-1st ed (h8,f,sl tn dj) 45.00

BORGES,JORGE L-Universal History of Infamy-NY-1972-Dutton-1st US ed (y1,dj) 50.00

BORING,EDWIN-History of Experimental Psychology-NY-1929-699p-1st ed (dd3) 45.00

BORLAND,HAL-Sundial of the Seasons-Phila,NY-(1964)-Lippincott-350p-bds (m1,dj) 12.50

BORLAND,HAL-When the Legends Die-Phila-1963-Lippincott-1st ed (d8,dj) 50.00

BORLAND,J NELSON-First Medical and Surgical Report of the Boston City Hospital-Bost-1870-688p-photos-1st ed (dd3,hng crack,few secs strtng 325.00

BORLASE,G W-By Twinkling Streams-Salisbury-1950-8vo-160p-photos (m3) 15.00

BORN,MAX-My Life-NY-(1978)-Scribner's-x+308p-tan bds,illus-1st ed (a2,dj) 15.00

BORN,MAX-Natural Philosophy of Cause and Chance-Oxford-1949-Clarendon Pr-viii+215p-blu cl-1st ed (g2,dj) 100.00

BORN,WOLFGANG-Still Life Painting in America-NY-1947-Oxford-folio-cl-1st ed (oo6,dj tn) 50.00

BORNEMAN,WALTER R-Marshall Pass-Colo Spgs-(1980)-187p-dbl col,photos,maps-1st ed (u7,f,dj) 25.00

BORNSTEIN,M-Manual of Instruction in the Use of Dumb Bells...Indian Clubs and Other Exercises-NY-(1880)-M Borstein-128p+ads-cl,frontis (j1,frnt inner hng weak) 25.00

BOROWITZ,ALBERT-Innocence & Arsenic-NY-(1977)-Harper-1st ed (r4,f,sl soil dj) 27.50

BOROWITZ,ALBERT-Innocence and Arsenic-NY-(1977)-Harper & Row-170p-1st ed (g9,sl soil dj) 25.00

BORRETT,WILLIAM C-East Coast Port and Other Tales Told Under the Old Town Clock-Halifax-1946-Imperial Publ-ix,237p-illus (k10) 20.00*

BOSE,SIR JAGADIS C-Plant Autographs and their Revelations-NY-1927-Macmillan-xviii+240p-grn cl-1st Amer ed (c2) 35.00

BOSSERT,HELMUT-An Encyclopedia of Colour Decoration from the Earliest Times to the Middle of the XIX Century-Lond-1928-Gollancz-lg 4to-35p+120 col plts,cl (ll4) 250.00

BOSTON,CHARLES K-Silver Jackass-NY-1941-Reynal & Hitchcock-1st ed (w9,f,dj) 90.00

BOSTON,L M-Stones of Green Knowe-NY-(1976)-Atheneum-118p-drwngs,P Boston-1st US ed (r3,f,dj) 25.00

BOSTON,NOEL-Old Guns & Pistols-Lond-1958-8vo-159p-illus (m3) 17.50

BOSTON,THOMAS-Human Nature in Its Fourfold State...-Pitt-1831-Richard Hanna-400p-lea-Amer Imprnts 6208-5th ed (h1,sp chip,upper jnts crckng) 25.00

BOSWELL,JAMES-Boswell on the Grand Tour-Lond-1955-Wm Heinemann-1/4 vel-ltd to 400c,nbrd-deluxe ed (p6,f) 200.00

BOSWELL,JAMES-Life of Samuel Johnson, LLD-Lond-1835-Murray-sm 8vo-ten vols-3/4 brn mor over mrbld bds,illus (t1) 375.00

BOSWELL,JAMES-On the Grand Tour: Germany and Switzerland, 1764-Lond-1953-Wm Heinemann-1/4 vel-ltd to 1000c,nbrd-deluxe ed (p6,f) 150.00

BOSWELL,PEYTON-Wine Makers Manual-NY-1935-Orange Judd Publ-96p-illus (o6,wn & soil) 20.00

BOSWELL,THOMAS-How Life Imitates the World Series-1982-Dbldy-1st ed (q7,f,dj) 25.00

BOSWORTH,A S-History of Randolph County, West Virginia-(Elkin)-1916-448p-1st ed (jj3) 100.00

BOSWORTH,ALLAN R-Ozona Country-NY-1964-238p-dec cl,photos-1st ed (t7) 12.50

BOSWORTH,CLARENCE E-Breeding Your Own-Derrydale-1939-8vo-245p-ltd to 1250c,nbrd-photos (m3) 65.00

BOSWORTH,CLARENCE E-Breeding Your Own-NY-1939-Derrydale Pr-illus-ltd to 1250c (jj4) 75.00

BOTAFOGO,DOLORES-Art of Brazilian Cookery-GC-1960-Dbldy-240p-1st ed (o6) 15.00

BOTKIN,B A-ED.-Folk Say IV-Norman-1932-U of Okla Pr-295p-1st ed (ff4) 45.00

BOTKIN,B A-ED.-New York City Folklore-NY-1956-Random-red cl,plts-1st ed (mm10,dj) 25.00

BOTKIN,B A-ED.-Treasury of Railroad Folklore-NY-1953-530p-1st ed (n4,f,dj) 18.00

BOTSFORD,HARRY T-Fish & Game Cookbook-NY-(1947)-Cornell Maritime Pr-290p-tan cl-1st ed (q8,sp tn dj) 15.00

BOTT,A,CAPT.-Eastern Nights - and Flights-GC-1919-8vo-xii,298p-cl,frntis,2p illus-1st ed (t2,wn) 35.00

BOTT,A-Cavalry of the Clouds-GC-1918-8vo-xii,266p-illus cl,frntis (t2,sp fade,sl wn) 35.00

BOTTING,DENNIS-Island of the Dragon's Blood-NY-(1958)-Funk-8vo-251p-photos-1st ed (cc5,dj) 15.00

BOTTOME,PHYLLIS-Danger Signal-1939-Little-1st Amer ed (s10,dj) 25.00

BOTTONE,S R-Wireless Telegraphy and Hertzian Waves-1901-123p-37 illus-v rare-2nd ed (h6) 150.00

BOUCHER,ANTHONY-Case of the Seven of Calvary-NY-1937-Simon-1st ed (e4,sl stnd pgs) 40.00

BOUCHER,ANTHONY-Compleat Werewolf-1969-S&S-1st ed (x7,f,dj) 58.00

BOUCHER,ANTHONY-ED.-Four & Twenty Bloodhounds-1950-Simon-1st ed (s10,f,dj) 25.00

BOUCHER,E S-Notes on the Stained Glass of the Oxford District-Oxford-1918-106p-wrps (cc8) 45.00

BOUCHER,JONATHON-Reminiscences of an American Loyalist, 1738 to 1789-Bost-1925-Houghton Mifflin-xii+201p-grn bds,sp labl-ltd to 575c-Howes B640-1st ed (b2,sl bump) 75.00

BOUDON,P-Lived In Architecture-1972-MIT-8vo-70 illus-1st Amer transl ed (ee1,dj) 30.00

BOUDREAUX,H B-Arthropod Phylogeny with Special Reference to Insects-1979-Wiley-320p-80 figs-1st ed (bb3,f,dj) 20.00

BOUGHAN,ROLLA-Shotgun Ballistics for Hunters-NY-1965-8vo-159p-photos (m3,f,dj) 12.50

BOULENGER,E G-British Anglers' Natural History-Lond-1946-8vo-47p-illus-1st ed (m3,f,dj) 12.50

BOULESTIN,X MARCEL-What Shall We Have Today-Lond-(1931)-Heinemann-251p-brwn cl-1st prtg (q8) 15.00

BOULLE,PIERRE-Planet of the Apes-NY-1963-Vanguard-1st ed (h8,f,dj) 100.00

BOULTON,W H-Railways of Britain-Lond-1950-384p-1st ed (n4,dj) 19.50

BOURINOT,J G-How Canada is Governed-Tor-1897-Copp,Clark Co-8vo-xiv,344p-brwn cl,illus-3rd ed (aa7,bump) 20.00*

BOURJAILY,VANCE-End of My Life-1947-Scribners-1st ed (p9,f,dj) 90.00

BOURJAILY,VANCE-Unnatural Enemy-NY-1963-182p-illus (gg3,f) 10.00

BOURJAILY,VANCE-Unnatural Enemy-NY-1963-8vo-182p-illus,D Levine (m3,f,sl chip dj) 16.00

BOURKE,JOHN G-An Apache Campaign in the Sierra Madre-NY-1958-128p-rprnt (n3,f,dj) 25.00

BOURKE,JOHN G-Apache Campaign-NY-1886-Scribners-Howes B652-1st ed (a6,cov wn,hng crack) 175.00

BOURKE,JOHN G-On the Border with Crook-1962-Rio Grande-491p-illus-(facs rprnt of 1891 1st ed) (r8) 25.00

BOURKE-WHITE,MARGARET-Dear Fatherland Rest Quietly-NY-1946-S&S-4to-gry cl-1st ed (qq1,dj chip) 45.00

BOURKE-WHITE,MARGARET-Eyes on Russia-NY-1931-Simon-4to-cl-dj scarce-1st ed (qq1,dj chip) 300.00

BOURKE-WHITE,MARGARET-One Thing Leads to Another-Bost-1936-Houghton Mifflin-8vo-106p-cl,photos-1st ed (t3,chip dj) 45.00

BOURKE-WHITE,MARGARET-Portrait of Myself-NY-1963-S&S-383p-65 photos-1st prtg (cc9,f,sl tn dj) 50.00

BOURKE-WHITE,MARGARET-You Have Seen Their Faces-NY-1937-Viking-cl,scarce in dj-1st ed (y3,dj pc missing) 195.00

BOURNE CO.,RICHARD A-Public Auction of Rare American Decoys,etc-Aug 3,1971 catalog-wrps wi prices (gg3,f) 10.00

BOURNE CO.,RICHARD A-Very Rare & Important Amer Bird Decoys from Collection of Wm J Mackey,Jr.-July 17,18, 1973-sessns 1 & 2-wrps,prices (gg3,f) 20.00

BOURNE,EULALIA-Woman in Levi's-(1967)-U of Ariz Pr-208p-illus-1st ed (ee4,dj,autg) 20.00

BOURNE,G H-ED.-Rhesus Monkey. Vol.1-1975-8vo-432p (y8,box) 115.00

BOURNE,G H-ED.-Rhesus Monkey. Vol.2-1975-8vo-456p (y8,box) 115.00

BOURNE,PETER G,M.D.-Men,Stress, and Vietnam-Bost-(1970)-Little,Brown-1st ed (ff3,f,dj) 55.00

BOURNE,RANDOLPH-History of a Literary Radical-NY-1920-Huebsch-1st ed (w5) 35.00

BOURNE,RANDOLPH-History of a Literary Radical-NY-1920-Huebsch-grn cl,sp labl-1st ed (mm10,sl wn) 50.00

BOURNE,RANDOLPH-Untimely Papers-NY-1919-Huebsch-1st ed (v5) 30.00

BOUTELL'S MANUAL OF HERALDRY: RVSD & ILLUS-Lond-1931-332p-32 col plts (cc8,cov scuff) 50.00

BOUTON,EMILY S-Health and Beauty-Toledo-(1884)-Locke Publ-288p-cl (d1) 25.00

BOUTON,JIM-Ball Four-1970-World-photos-1st ed (s8,f,dj) 25.00

BOUTON,JIM-I Managed Good, But Boy Did They Play Bad-(1973)-Playboy-1st ed (s8,dj) 13.00

BOUTON,JIM-I Managed Good, But Boy Did They Play Bad-Chig-(1973)-325,(3)p-cl-Smith 9558-1st ed so stated (n1,f,dj) 15.00

BOUTON,JIM-I'M Glad You Didn't Take It Personally-1971-Morrow-1st ed (s8,f,dj) 12.00

BOUYER,LOUIS-Liturgy and Architecture-Notre Dame-1967-UND Pr-8vo-127p-11 illus-1st ed (ee5,f,dj) 15.00

BOVA,BEN-As on a Darkling Plain-NY-(1972)-1st ed (h5,f,sl wn dj) 20.00

BOVA,BEN-Starcrossed-Radnor-(1975)-Chilton-1st ed (j3,f,sl tn dj) 20.00

BOVEY,M-Saga of the Waterford-DC-1949-Wildlife Mngmnt Inst-141p-photos (gg3,f,dj) 17.00

BOVEY,MARTIN-Whistling Wings-GC-1947-4to-162p-illus,F L Jaques-1st ed (m3,f,fray dj) 40.00

BOWDEN,ANGIE B-Early Schools of Washington Territory-Seattle-1935-631p-illus-1st ed (j7,f,chip dj) 45.00

BOWDEN,EDWIN T-James Thurber: A Bibliography-(1968)-Ohio St-1st ed (w1,f,f dj) 20.00

BOWDEN,J J-Spanish and Mexican Land Grants in Chihuahuan Acquisition-EL Paso-1971-223p-maps-1st ed (u7,dj) 30.00

BOWDITCH,HENRY I-ED.-First Annual Report of the State Board of Health,Lunacy,and Charity of Massachusetts, 1879-Bost-1880-277p+fldg maps-1st ed (dd3) 150.00

BOWEN,ASHLEY-Journals of...(1728-1813)of Marblehead-Salem-1973-Peabody Mus-8vo-2 vols,red cl,g sp titles,Vol.I:3 col plts,24 b&w plts.Vol.II:1 col plt,16 b&w plts-ltd to 500c (nn1,box) 135.00

BOWEN,CROSWELL-Curse of the Misbegotten-Lond-1960-Rupert Hart-Davis-8vo-384p-5 illus-1st Brit ed (ee5,dj) 12.50

BOWEN,ELBERT R-Theatrical Entertainments in Rural Missouri before the Civil War-Columbia-(1959)-141p-cl (h1,pres cpy) 15.00

BOWEN,ELIZABETH-Cat Jumps, and Other Stories-Lond-(1949)-Cape-frntis,J Hassall-1st ed thus (z8,dj) 25.00

BOWEN,ELIZABETH-Collected Impressions-NY-1950-Knopf-1st US ed (v5,f,sl soil dj) 25.00

BOWEN,ELIZABETH-Demon Lover, and Other Stories-Lond-(1945)-Cape-1st ed (z8,f,sp rprd dj) 22.50

BOWEN,ELIZABETH-Eva Trout or Changing Scenes-1968-Knopf-1st ed (t9,f,dj) 15.00

BOWEN,ELIZABETH-Hotel-NY-1928-Lincoln Mac Veagh/Dial-1st US ed (ff6,dj sp chip,sl tn) 60.00

BOWEN,ELIZABETH-House in Paris-NY-1936-Knopf-1st US ed (hh5,chip dj) 20.00

BOWEN,ELIZABETH-Ivy Gripped the Steps...-NY-1946-Knopf-1st Amer ed (z8,stnd dj) 15.00

BOWEN,ELIZABETH-Ivy Gripped the Steps...-NY-1946-Knopf-8vo-233p-1st Amer ed (w6,dj) 35.00

BOWEN,ELIZABETH-Little Girls-Lond-(1964)-J Cape-1st ed (ee2,f,dj) 50.00

BOWEN,ELIZABETH-Little Girls-NY-1964-Knopf-8vo-307p-1st Amer ed (w6,dj) 20.00

BOWEN,ELIZABETH-Look at All Those Roses-NY-1941-Knopf-1st US ed (w5,f,sl tn dj) 45.00

BOWEN,ELIZABETH-Pictures and Conversations-Lond-(1975)-Lane-1st ed (z8,vf,sp tn dj) 15.00

BOWEN,ELIZABETH-Seven Winters and Afterthoughts-NY-1962-Knopf-1st Amer ed (ee2,dj) 35.00

BOWEN,ELIZABETH-Time in Rome-NY-1960-Knopf-1st US ed (hh5,f,sl tn dj) 12.50

BOWEN,F W-History of Port Elizabeth, Cumberland County, New Jersey, Down to the Present Time-Phila-1885-58p-cl,plts (aa6) 90.00

BOWEN,MARJORIE-Kecksies and Other Twilight Tales-Sauk City-(1976)-Arkham-1st ed (f3,f,dj) 15.00

BOWER,DONALD E-Roaming the American West-Harrisburg-(1971)-Stackpole-4to-256p-illus-1st ed (cc4,dj) 20.00

BOWER,URSULA G-Hidden Land-NY-1953-Morrow-8vo-260p-16p photos-1st ed (jj5,sl tn dj) 15.00

BOWERS,ALFRED W-Hidatsa Social and Ceremonial Organization-Wash-1965-BAE Bull 194-528p+12 plts,cl (a1,emboss stmp on t.p.) 25.00

BOWERS,ALFRED W-Mandan Social and Ceremonial Organization-Chig-1950-407p-photos,illus-1st ed (t7,dj) 47.50

BOWERS,CLAUDE G-Tragic Era-Cambridge-(1929)-567p-1st ed (n3,dj) 32.50

BOWES,GORDON E-ED.-Peace River Chronicles-(Vancouver)-(1963)-Prescott Publ-557p-cl,illus,map(1 fldg),ports (aa2,dj) 35.00*

BOWIE,NAN-Mick Bowie-Wellington-1969-196p-1st ed (p10,f,dj) 25.00

BOWKER,PIERPONT F-Indian Vegetable Family Instructor-Bost-1836-auth-180p-lea sp,mrbld bds-scarce (x6,sl stnd pgs) 200.00

BOWLES,E A-Handbook of Crocus & Colchicum for Gardeners-Lond-1952-Bodley-222p-col plts (x6,dj wn) 25.00

BOWLES,E A-Handbook of Crocus and Colchicum-Lond-1952-222p-col & b&w plts-rev ed (x5,sl scraped dj) 30.00

BOWLES,E A-My Garden in Autumn and Winter-Lond-1915-Jack-272p (x6,sp soil) 30.00

BOWLES,JANE-Collected Works of ...-NY-(1966)-FSG-1st ed (m7,dj) 35.00

BOWLES,JANE-Collected Works of...-NY-(1966)-1st ed (p5,dj) 30.00

BOWLES,JANE-In the Summer House-NY-(1954)-1st ed (t5,dj) 75.00

BOWLES,JANE-Plain Pleasures-Lond-(1966)-1st ed (t5,dj) 50.00

BOWLES,JANE-Plain Pleasures-Lond-(1966)-P Owen-1st ed (j6,stnd t.e.,dj) 100.00

BOWLES,PAUL-Delicate Prey and Other Stories-(NY)-(1950)-1st ed (q5,dj) 95.00

BOWLES,PAUL-Delicate Prey and Other Stories-(NY)-(1950)-Random-8vo-cl-1st ed (ll10,f,dj sp fade,sl tn & wn) 65.00

BOWLES,PAUL-Hours After Noon-Lond-1959-1st Brit ed (r5,dj) 50.00

BOWLES,PAUL-Let It Come Down-(1952)-Random-1st ed (x2,dj wn) 40.00

BOWLES,PAUL-Let It Come Down-NY-(1952)-1st ed (t5,dj) 75.00

BOWLES,PAUL-Let It Come Down-Santa Barbara-1980-ltd to 350c,nbrd,autg,acetate dj (t5,f,dj) 60.00

BOWLES,PAUL-Little Stone-1950-J Lehmann-not publ in US-1st ed (x2,f,dj,auth photo laid in) 125.00

BOWLES,PAUL-Pages From Cold Point-Lond-1968-1st Brit ed (r5,dj) 35.00

BOWLES,PAUL-Spider's House-NY-(1955)-1st ed (t5,dj) 65.00

BOWLES,PAUL-Spider's House-NY-(1955)-Random-8vo-cl-1st ed (x3,dj) 75.00

BOWLES,PAUL-Their Heads are Green and Their Hands are Blue-NY-(1963)-1st ed (o5,dj) 45.00

BOWLES,PAUL-Their Heads are Green and Their Hands are Blue-NY-(1963)-Random-1st ed (y1,f,dj) 50.00

BOWLES,PAUL-Time of Friendship-NY-1967-1st ed (t5,dj) 30.00

BOWLES,PAUL-Up Above the World-NY-(1966)-1st ed (t5,dj) 40.00

BOWLES,PAUL-Up Above the World-NY-(1966)-Simon-8vo-cl-1st ed (x3,dj) 70.00

BOWLES,PAUL-Without Stopping-NY-(1972)-photos-1st ed (t5,dj) 40.00

BOWLES,PAUL-Without Stopping-NY-(1972)-Putnam-1st ed (v10,f,f dj) 35.00

BOWLES,PAUL-Yallah-NY-1957-McDowell Obolensky-83 photos by P Haeberlin-1st ed (h8,sl wn dj) 200.00

BOWLES,SAMUEL-Summer Vacation in the Parks & Mountains of Colorado-Springfield-1869-16mo-166p+ads-g brwn cl-1st ed (p2,sp fade,sl rub) 60.00

BOWMAN,COL S M-Sherman and His Campaigns-NY-1865-512p+ads-1/2 lea,illus-1st ed (n3,edgewn) 47.50

BOWMAN,HEATH & JEFFERSON-Crusoe's Island in the Caribbean-Indpls-1939-Bobbs Merrill-e.p. maps-1st ed (v4) 25.00

BOWMAN,HEATH-Westward From Rio-Chig-1936-Willett Clark-8vo-351p-100 block prnts-1st ed (jj5,dj sl tn,wn) 17.50

BOWMAN,ISAIAH-Andes of Southern Peru-NY-1916-336p-maps,7 fldg topos,107 illus,51 plts-1st ed (o10) 45.00

BOWMAN,ISAIAH-Desert Trails of Atacama-NY-1924-362p-illus,maps-1st ed (o10,f) 45.00

BOWMAN,LORENE-Hope Chest-Chig-(1922)-Reilly & Lee-162p-brn leather-like bds,decs,J Weage (n6,chip sp) 15.00

BOWMAN,W E-Ascent of Rum Doddle-Lond-1956-141p-1st Brit ed (q10,f) 55.00

BOWMAN,W E-Ascent of Rum Doodle-Lond-1956-1st Brit ed (a4,vf,vf dj) 80.00

BOWMAN,W E-Ascent of Rum Doodle-NY-1956-141p-illus-1st US ed (o10,f,dj) 50.00

BOWNESS,A-ED.-Complete Sculpture of Barbara Hepworth 1960 to 69-Lond-1971-1st ed (h10,dj) 135.00

BOWNOCKER,JOHN A-Occurrence and Exploitation of Petroleum and Natural Gas in Ohio-Columbus-1903-325p-cl-9 fldg maps + 5 plts-Geo Survey of Ohio,4th Ser.,Bulletin 1 (j1) 15.00

BOWRING,DAVE-How to Fish Streams-NY-1977-8vo-251p-photos-1st ed (m3,f,dj) 10.00

BOWSER,FREDERICK P-African Slave in Colonial Peru 1524 to 1650-1974-Stanford U Pr-8vo-xiv,11,439p-drk beige cl-1st ed (mm1,vf,sl wn dj) 35.00

BOXER,C R-ED.-Further Selections From the Tragic History of the Sea 1559 to 1565-Cambridge-1968-Hakluyt Soc-8vo-x,170p-blu cl,illus,fldg maps-Second Ser.CXXXII-1st Engl Transl (nn1,sp fade) 45.00

BOXER,C R-ED.-Further Selections From the Tragic History of the Sea 1559 to 1565...-Cambridge-1968-Hakluyt Soc-8vo-170p-blu cl,plts,fldg map (p1) 35.00

BOXER,C R-South China in the Sixteenth Century-Lond-1953-Hakluyt Scty-8vo-xci,388p-blu cl,g sp titles & cov dec,8 maps,12 illus(some fldg) (ll1,partially unopened) 40.00

BOYCE,BEN S-Dear Dad Letters From New Guinea-Chig-1928-Boyce-8vo-xviii,124p-orig cl,illus,2 col maps rear e.p.-1st ed (bb6) 15.00

BOYCE,BURKE-Around the World on the Belgenland-NY-1925-Knickerbocker Pr-8vo-x,323p-orig cl,t.e.g.,48 illus,map e.p. (bb6,sl fray sp) 18.00

BOYCE,CHRIS-Extraterrestrial Encounters-Secaucus-(1979)-Chartwell-1st US ed (h3,f,dj) 10.00

BOYCE,RUBERT-Mosquito or Man-Lond-1910-280p-photos-2nd ed (dd3,sl chip) 100.00

BOYD,BEVERLY-Chaucer and the Medieval Book-np-1973-Huntington Libr-tall 8vo-xi,165p-cl-1st ed (w2,dj) 30.00

BOYD,BLANCHE M-Mourning the Death of Magic-NY-(1977)-Macmillan-1st ed (k7,f,f dj) 25.00

BOYD,BLANCHE M-Redneck Way of Knowledge-NY-1982-Knopf-1st ed (k7,f,dj) 20.00

BOYD,BRENDAN-Great American Baseball Card Flipping,Trading and Bubble Gum Book-1973-Little,Brown-col photos-1st ed (s8,f,chip & tn dj) 25.00

BOYD,BRENDON-Great American Baseball Card Flipping,Trading and Bubble Gum Book-1973-Little,Brown-1st ed (s7,f,f dj) 30.00

BOYD,BUD-Hunting & Fishing in California-SF-1960-4to-95p-illus (m3,f,dj) 20.00

BOYD,E-Popular Arts of Spanish New Mexico-Santa Fe-1974-500p+index-photos(some col)-1st ed (u7,f,dj) 35.00

BOYD,E-Saints & Saint Makers of New Mexico-Santa Fe-(1946)-139p-illus-1st ed (u7,dj) 200.00

BOYD,ELIZABETH F-Bloomsbury Heritage-NY-1976-Taplinger-1st ed (t4,f,f dj) 15.00

BOYD,ELIZABETH F-First Quarter Millenium-(New Brunswick)-(1976)-127p-cl (aa6) 25.00

BOYD,JAMES-Life and Public Services of Hon. James G Blaine...-np-1893-Publisher's Union-704p-cl (m1) 15.00

BOYD,JAMES-Life of General William T Sherman-np-1891-Publishers' Union-608p-cl (d1) 20.00

BOYD,JAMES-Marching On-NY-1927-Scribners-426p-1st ed (o7) 20.00

BOYD,JAMES-Military and Civil Life of Gen Ulysses S Grant-Phila-1885-734p-pict cl,illus,maps-1st ed (n3) 50.00

BOYD,JAMES-Recent Indian Wars Under the Lead of Sitting Bull and Other Chiefs-np-1891-320p-pict cl,illus-1st ed (n3) 55.00

BOYD,JAMES-Recent Indian Wars...-np-1891-320p-cl (c1,few cov spots) 50.00

BOYD,JOHN-Andromeda Gun-NY-(1974)-Berkley-1st ed (p3,f,dj) 15.00

BOYD,JOHN-ET AL-Images of Steam-Lond-1968-192p-1st ed (n4,f,dj) 22.00

BOYD,JOHN-Girl With the Jade Green Eyes-1978-Viking-1st ed (t9,f,sl tn dj sp) 20.00

BOYD,JOHN-Sex and the High Command-NY-(1970)-Weybright & Talley-1st ed (f3,f,dj) 20.00

BOYD,NANCY-Distressing Dialogues-NY-(1924)-Harper-8vo-290p-scarce-1st ed (w6,chip dj) 125.00

BOYD,ROBIN-Kenzo Tange-NY-1962-Braziller-sm 4to-125p-illus-1st ed (ee5,f,sl tn dj) 20.00

BOYD,THOMAS-Through the Wheat-NY-1923-Scribners-1st ed (w5) 35.00

BOYD,WILLIAM K-Some Eighteenth Century Tracts Concerning North Carolina-Raleigh-1927-Edwards & Broughton-viii+508p-maroon cl,plts-1st ed (b2) 50.00

BOYD,WILLIAM-Good Man in Africa-NY-1982-auth 1st bk-1st US ed (q5,f,dj) 35.00

BOYER,CHARLES S-Early Forges and Furnaces in New Jersey-Phila-1931-U of Penn Pr-xvi+287p-red cl,plts-1st ed (mm10) 50.00

BOYER,CHARLES S-Old Mills of Camden County-(Camden)-1962-(8),66p-wrps,frntis,fldg map (aa6) 30.00

BOYER,CHARLES S-Rambles Through Old Highways and Byways of West Jersey-Camden-1967-xvii,284p-cl,plts (aa6) 40.00

BOYER,RICHARD O-Legend of John Brown-NY-1973-611p-illus-1st ed (c4,f,dj wn) 25.00

BOYER,WARREN E-Vanishing Trails of Romance-Denver-1923-94p-stiff pict wrps,frntis-1st ed (t7,f) 25.00

BOYES,W-No Custer Survivors or the Unveiling of Frank Finkel-Rockville-1977-16p-stiff wrps-1st ed (t7,f) 20.00

BOYLAN,LEONA D-Spanish Colonial Silver-(Santa Fe)-(1974)-198p+index-wrps,photos-1st ed (u7,f) 20.00

BOYLE,HARRY J-Mostly in Clover-NY-(1964)-227p-cl-1st Amer ed (h1,dj) 12.50

BOYLE,KAY-Collected Poems-NY-1962-Knopf-1st ed (bb2,f,dj) 50.00

BOYLE,KAY-Long Walk at San Francisco State-NY-1970-photos-1st ed (r5,f,dj) 35.00

BOYLE,KAY-Nothing Ever Breaks Except the Heart-NY-1966-Dbldy-8vo-357p-1st ed (w6,dj) 15.00

BOYLE,KAY-Primer For Combat-NY-1942-8vo-320p-1st ed (w6,sl wn dj) 25.00

BOYLE,KAY-Short Stories-Paris-1929-Black Sun Pr-orig prtd wrps,gold foil folder,red ribbon ties,glassine dj-ltd to 150c on Holland papr-auth 1st bk-1st ed (ll10,fldr sl rub,dj sl wn) 450.00

BOYLE,KAY-Three Short Novels-Bost-(1940)-Beacon-stiff pict wrps(publ only in this ed)-1st ed (cc2,f) 35.00

BOYLE,R H-Second Fly-Tyer's Almanac-Phila-1978-4to-224p-photos,illus-1st ed (m3,f) 12.50

BOYLE,SUNA-Hungry Housewife & Her Family-Lond-(1974)-Arlington-tall qto-96p-blk cl,drwngs-1st prtg (q8,dj) 20.00

BOYLE,T CORAGHESSAN-Water Music-Bost-1981-1st ed (p5,f,dj) 75.00

BOYLE,T CORAGHESSAN-Water Music-Lond-1982-Gollancz-1st Brit ed (ee2,f,dj) 40.00

BOYLE,TERRY-Under This Roof-Tor-c.1980-Dbldy Can-oblng 4to-129p-map e.p.,illus (k10) 20.00*

BOYNTON,H V-National Military Park, Chickamauga Chattanooga-Cin-1895-307p-illus,maps-1st ed (n3) 32.50

BOYNTON,M F-ED.-Louis Agassiz Fuertes-1956-Oxford Univ-317p-illus (bb3,f,dj) 35.00

BOYNTON,REV C B-Journey Through Kansas with Sketches of Nebraska...-Cin-1855-Moore,Wilstach,Keys & Co-x+216p-brwn cl,fldg map-1st ed (k2,some foxing) 325.00

BOYS' LIFE BOOK OF BASEBALL STORIES-1964-Random-pict cov-1st ed (p7) 10.00

BRACE,TIMOTHY-Murder Goes Fishing-NY-1936-Dutton-1st ed (e4) 15.00

BRACE,TIMOTHY-Murder Goes to the World's Fair-NY-1939-Dutton-1st ed (d4) 15.00

BRACEWELL,RONALD N-ED.-Paris Symposium on Radio Astronomy-1959-Stanford U Pr-xii+612p-blu cl-1st ed (c2,dj) 25.00

BRACKEN,DOROTHY K-Early Texas Homes-Dallas-1956-SMU Pr-qto-188p-illus-1st ed (bb4) 30.00

BRACKENRIDGE,W D-Brackenridge Journal for the Oregon Country-1931-U of Wash-70p-bds (r8,ex-libr) 50.00

BRACKENRIDGE,W D-Brackenridge Journal for the Oregon Country-Seattle-1931-70p-wrps-scarce (j7) 65.00

BRACKETT,LEIGH-Best of ...-GC-(1977)-Dbldy-1st ed (l3,f,dj) 10.00

BRACKETT,LEIGH-Silent Partner-1969-Putnam-1st ed (x7,dj) 60.00

BRACKETT,LEIGH-Starman-NY-(1952)-Gnome-1st ed (k3,fray dj) 50.00

BRACKETT,LEIGH-Tiger Among Us-1957-Dbldy-1st ed (x7,dj) 45.00

BRACKMAN,ARNOLD C-Delicate Arrangement-NY-1980-Times Bks-8vo-370p-blck cl,map illus-Book Club ed (p8,dj) 25.00

BRADBURN,JOHN-Breeding and Driving the Trotter-Bost-1906-Amer Horse Breeder-1st ed (h9) 45.00

BRADBURY,FREDERICK-History of Old Sheffield Plate-Sheffield-1968-4to-539p-gold dec blu cl,illus (a3) 100.00

BRADBURY,RAY-Dark Carnival-1948-H Hamilton-auth 1st bk-1st Brit ed (jj6,sl cocked sp,sl chip dj) 225.00

BRADBURY,RAY-Fahrenheit 451-Lond-1954-1st Brit ed (d5,dj) 175.00

BRADBURY,RAY-Golden Apples of the Sun-GC-1953-Dbldy-8vo-cl,drwngs-1st ed (x3,f,sp chip dj) 85.00

BRADBURY,RAY-Haunted Computer and the Android Pope-NY-1981-Knopf-1st ed (k3,f,dj) 18.00

BRADBURY,RAY-Last Circus & the Electrocution-Northridge-1980-Lord John Pr-1st trd ed (ff6,as new in dj) 25.00

BRADBURY,RAY-Long After Midnight-NY-1976-1st ed (d5,as new in dj) 30.00

BRADBURY,RAY-Long After Midnight-NY-1976-Knopf-1st ed (v5,dj crease) 25.00

BRADBURY,RAY-Machineries of Joy-NY-1964-1st ed (p5,dj chip,sp sunned) 30.00

BRADBURY,RAY-Stories of...-NY-1980-Knopf-1st ed (a10,f,dj) 50.00

BRADBURY,RAY-When Elephants Last in the Dooryard Bloomed-Lond-(1975)-Hart Davis,MacGibbon-1st Brit ed (a5,as new in dj) 25.00

BRADBURY,RAY-Where Robot Mice and Robot Men Run Round in Robot Towns-NY-1977-Knopf-1st ed (a5,f,sl soil dj) 15.00

BRADBURY,WILLIAM B-Gold Censer-NY-(1864)-128p-bds (n1) 15.00

BRADDON,R-New Wings for a Warrior-NY-(1954)-8vo-240p-cl,27 illus-1st ed (t2,dj) 25.00

BRADDON,RUSSELL-Seige-NY-1970-352p-illus-1st Amer ed (b7,f,dj) 35.00

BRADFORD ,EDWARD H-Orthopedic Surgery-NY-1911-410p-illus-1st ed (g10) 120.00

BRADFORD,CHARLES B-Angler's Guide-Long Island-1908-12mo-155p+ads-wrps-illus (m3,sl chip sp) 60.00

BRADFORD,CHARLES B-Angler's Secret-NY & Lond-1904-12mo-206p-1st ed (m3) 35.00

BRADFORD,CHARLES B-Brook Trout & the Determined Angler-NY-1900-12mo-71p-illus-1st ed (m3) 40.00

BRADFORD,E-Four Centuries of European Jewellery-1967-Spring Bks-226p-photo plts (u5,f,f dj) 45.00

BRADFORD,EDWARD H-Treatise on Orthopedic Surgery-NY-1890-783p-789 wood engrvngs-1st ed (g10,cov wn) 150.00

BRADFORD,EDWARD H-Treatise on Orthopedic Surgery-NY-1907-669p-592 engrvngs-3rd ed (g10) 85.00

BRADFORD,GAMALIEL-Union Portraits-Bost-1916-Houghton Mifflin-330p-frntis,ports (cc6) 25.00

BRADFORD,NED-Boston's Locke-Ober Cafe-NY-1978-Atheneum-tall 8vo-207p-red bds,col frntis,photos-1st ed (q8,edgewn dj) 27.50

BRADFORD,ROARK-John Henry-NY-1931-patterned bds,dec e.p.s,25 wdcuts by J J Lankes-1st ed (r5,sl chip dj) 45.00

BRADLEY,A G-Clear Waters-Bost-1914-8vo-380p-photos (m3) 15.00

BRADLEY,A G-Gateway of Scotland-Bost-1912-Little,Brown-8vo-452p-8 col plts-1st US ed (ff5,sl fox) 25.00

BRADLEY,BILL-Last of the Great Stations-LA-1979-110p-wrps-Interurban spec #72-1st ed (n4) 26.00

BRADLEY,CAROL W-Pocketful of Tansy-SF-1975-24mo-21p-pap cov bds,col wdcuts,ltd to 200c,nbrd (x5) 20.00

BRADLEY,DAVID-Chaneysville Incident-NY-1981-Harper-1st ed (w5,f,f dj) 30.00

BRADLEY,ERWIN S-Simon Cameron, Lincoln's Secretary of War-Phila-(1966)-451p-1st ed (c4,dj) 35.00

BRADLEY,GEORGE K-Fort Wayne and Wabash Valley Trolleys-Chig-1983-288p-Bull.#122-1st ed (n4,f,f dj) 28.00

BRADLEY,GLENN D-Story of the Pony Express-Chig-1928-175p-illus (t7,auth wife autg) 12.50

BRADLEY,HOWARD A-Daniel Webster and the Salem Murder-Columbia-1956-230,(3)p-cl (c1) 30.00

BRADLEY,JAMES H,LT-March of the Montana Column-Norman-(1961)-182p-illus,Luther 50-1st Okla ed (c7,f,chip dj) 45.00

BRADLEY,JAMES-Confederate Mail Carrier...An Unwritten Leaf of The Civil War-Mexico-1894-auth-275p-frntis port,illus-scarce-1st ed (n7) 200.00

BRADLEY,JOHN H-Farewell Thou Busy World-LA-1935-12mo-102p-illus,P Landacre-scarce (m3,f) 35.00

BRADLEY,JOHN W-Illuminated Manuscripts-Lond-(1905)-Methuen-12mo-xiv,290p-cl,t.e.g.,col frntis (w2,sl fox) 25.00

BRADLEY,O C-Structure of the Fowl-rvsd by Graham-Lond-1950-8vo-128p-cl,23 plts-3rd ed (y8,dj chip) 35.00

BRADLEY,OMAR N-Soldier's Story-NY-1951-HR&W-618p-frntis,illus,maps,e.p. maps (o7,f,pres) 50.00

BRADLEY,REV G S-Star Corps-Milw-1865-Jermain & Brightman-304p-frntis port-Coulter 49 (v2,sl soil cl,fox) 165.00

BRADLEY,VAN ALLEN-Book Collector's Handbook of Values-NY-(1978)-Putnam's-xviii,590p-cl,illus-3rd ed (v1,dj) 65.00

BRADLEY,VAN ALLEN-Music for the Millions-Chig-1957-Regnery-8vo-334p-30 illus-1st ed (dd5,dj edgewn,soil) 15.00

BRADNA,FRED-Big Top-1952-S&S-332p-illus-1st ed (v8,sl rub dj sp) 30.00

BRADNER,ENOS-Northwest Angling-Portland-1950-8vo-239p-illus,photos,2 col plts-1st ed (m3,f,dj) 25.00

BRADSHAW,GILLIAN-Kingdom of Summer-NY-(1981)-S&S-1st ed (bb1,dj) 20.00

BRADSHAW,HENRY-Collected Papers of...-Cambridge-1889-Univ Pr-8vo-viii,500p-orig cl-1st ed (w2) 85.00

BRADSHAW,P V-Art in Advertising-Lond-nd(ca.1925)-lg 4to-gry linen bds,illus (ee1,sl soil bds) 250.00

BRADY,CHARLES-Seven Games in October-1979-Little,Brown-1st ed (r7,f,dj) 15.00

BRADY,CYRUS-Border Fights and Fighters-NY-1902-382p-pict cl,illus-1st ed (n3) 37.50

BRADY,CYRUS-Indian Fights and Fighters-NY-1913-423p-frntis,photos (t7,f,dj chip) 30.00

BRADY,CYRUS-Northwestern Fights & Fighters-NY-1913-Dbldy,Page-373p-pict cl,drwngs,maps,photos-Howes B713 (dd4) 35.00

BRADY,CYRUS-Northwestern Fights and Fighters-NY-1907-McClure-8vo-373p-27 illus,9 maps-Amer Fights & Fighter ser-1st ed (cc5,sp tn) 25.00

BRADY,JAMES F-Modern Turkey Hunting-NY-1973-4to-160p-illus-1st ed (m3,f,dj) 20.00

BRADY,L-Edge of Doom-1949-Dutton-1st ed (x7,f,dj) 12.00

BRAGDON,CLAUDE-Beautiful Necessity-NY-1927-Knopf-cl,illus,auth-2nd ed (n8,sl wn) 35.00

BRAGDON,CLAUDE-Frozen Fountain-NY-1932-Knopf-sm 4to-125p-blk cl,illus-1st ed (oo8,f) 45.00

BRAGDON,CLAUDE-More Lives Than One-NY-1938-1st ed (h10,dj) 75.00

BRAGDON,CLAUDE-More Lives Than One-NY-1938-Knopf-cl,frntis,illus-1st ed (n8) 45.00

BRAGDON,CLAUDE-Old Lamps for New-NY-1925-Knopf-cl,illus,auth-1st ed (l8,dj) 45.00

BRAHAM,TREVOR-Himalayan Odyssey-Lond-1974-243p-1st ed (o10,f,f dj) 50.00

BRAID,JAMES-Neurypnology-Lond/Edinburgh-1843-Churchill/Black-sm 8vo-xii+266p-publ emboss grn cl,rebkd wi orig sp laid down-scarce-1st ed (y9,rebkd) 1,500.00

BRAINE,JOHN-Crying Game-Lond-(1968)-1st ed (m5,f,dj) 15.00

BRAINE,JOHN-Jealous God-Lond-1964-1st ed (m5,f,sl chip dj) 10.00

BRAINE,JOHN-Life at the Top-Lond-1962-1st ed (m5,dj) 20.00

BRAINE,JOHN-Vodi-np(Lond)-(1959)-1st ed (m5,dj) 50.00

BRAINE,JOHN-Vodi-np(Lond)-(1959)-Eyre & Spottiswoode-1st Brit ed (bb1,dj) 50.00

BRAISLIN,W C-List of Birds of Long Island N.Y-NY-1907-Linnaean Soc-8vo-136p-wrps,4 photos (y8,sp chip,stnd) 27.00

BRAITHWAITE,CECIL-Fishing Vignettes-Lond-nd-8vo-240p-illus,photos (m3) 30.00

BRAITHWAITE,E R-To Sir, With Love-1959-P&H-auth 1st bk-1st ed (x2,f,dj) 45.00

BRAITHWAITE,ROBERT-Sphagnaceae or Peat Mosses of Europe and North America-Lond-1880-David Bogue-91p-cl,29p b&w illus(some sources call for part col plts) (x6,f) 100.00

BRAIVE,MICHEL-Photograph-NY-1966-McGraw Hill-4to-366p-cl-1st ed (t3,dj sl chip) 125.00

BRAKE,BRIAN-Art of the Pacific-NY-(1980)-Abrams-4to-unpgd-cl,174 illus(incl 84 col) (y5,f,f dj) 85.00

BRAKE,HEZEKIAH-On Two Continents-Topeka-1896-Van-Rittenhouse 80-1st ed (a6,lacks ffep) 95.00

BRAKEFIELD,TOM-Hunting Big Game Trophies-NY-1976-8vo-446p-illus (m3,f,dj) 13.00

BRAKHAGE,STAN-Metaphors On Vision-np-1963-Film Culture Inc-4to-corrugated wrps,photos-scarce (l10) 20.00

BRAMAH,E-Mirror of Kong Ho-1930-DD-1st Amer ed (x7,dj) 65.00

BRAMAH,ERNEST-Kai Lung Unrolls his Mat-NY-1928-Dbldy-pict cov`-1st US ed (g4) 10.00

BRAMAH,ERNEST-Kai Lung's Golden Hours-1923-Doran-dec cov-1st Amer ed (n9) 15.00

BRAMWELL,BYROM-Diseases of the Spinal Cord-NY-1886-298p-53 col plts-2nd ed (g10) 85.00

BRANCH,E DOUGLAS-Hunting of the Buffalo-NY-1929-Appleton-12mo-239p-cl-1st ed (mm7,f,f dj) 75.00

BRANCH,E DOUGLAS-Hunting of the Buffalo-NY-1929-Appleton-12mo-vi,239p-photos,illus-1st ed (aa3,f,dj) 85.00

BRANCH,E DOUGLAS-Hunting of the Buffalo-NY-1929-D Appleton-239p-illus-1st ed (bb4,dj) 50.00

BRANCH,E DOUGLAS-Westward-NY-1930-Appleton-627p-woodcts,map e.p.-Six Guns #260-1st ed (cc4) 25.00

BRANCH,LOUIS L-Los Bilitos...-NY-1980-Carlton Pr-225p-cl,photos-1st ed (w3,vf,dj) 40.00

BRAND BOOK OF THE DENVER WESTERNERS-Boulder-(1966)-Johnson Publ-411p-illus-ltd to 735c,nbrd-Six Guns 2362-1st ed (ff4,dj) 50.00

BRAND BOOK OF THE LOS ANGELES CORRAL-np-(1950)-illus-ltd to 400c-Six Guns 2364-1st ed (ff4,dj) 175.00

BRAND,CHRISTIANA-Tour de Force-NY-1955-Scribners-1st US ed (h4,sp chip dj) 15.00

BRAND,CHRISTIANNA-Fog of Doubt-Bost-1979-Gregg-1st ed (r4,f,dj) 20.00

BRAND,MAX-Streak-NY-1937-Dodd-1st ed (k4,dj) 35.00

BRAND,MILLEN-Outward Room-NY-1937-S&S-auth 1st bk-1st ed (x9,f,chip dj) 12.50

BRANDAU,ROBERTA S-History of Homes and Gardens of Tennessee-Nashville-1964(1936)-Garden Study Club-503p-cl-ltd to 3000c-scarce-2nd ed (x6) 100.00

BRANDEL,MARC-Survivor-Lond-1976-Hamilton-1st ed (s4,f,dj) 20.00

BRANDER,MICHAEL-Scottish & Border Battles & Ballads-NY-1976-300p-illus-1st Amer ed (gg2,f,dj) 25.00

BRANDES,RAY-ED.-Troopers West-San Diego-1970-4to-206p-illus by DeGrazia-ltd to 1000c,nbrd-1st ed (h7,f,dj) 50.00

BRANDON,HEATHER-Casualties-NY-(1984)-St.Martin's-1st ed (ff3,f,dj) 30.00

BRANDON,JOHN G-One Minute Murder-NY-1935-Dial-1st ed (w9,f,dj sp chip & tn) 30.00

BRANDON,WILLIAM-Dangerous Dead-NY-1943-Dodd,Mead-auth 1st bk-1st ed (bb1,sl chip dj) 30.00

BRANDON,WM-Men and the Mountain-NY-1955-337p-maps-1st ed (t7,f,dj) 30.00

BRANDOW,JOHN H-Story of Old Saratoga-ALbany-1919-Brandow Prntg Co-xxiv+528p,red cl,illus,2 fldg maps in rear-2nd ed (k2,sl spot cov,dj) 30.00

BRANDT,BILL-Nudes 1945 to 1980-NY-1980-NYGS-unpgd-100 photos-1st ed (cc9,as new in dj) 50.00

BRANDT,HERBERT-Alaska Bird Trails-1943-Bird Rsrch Found.-464p-12 col plts,photos,drwngs,e.p. map-v scarce-1st ed (bb3) 150.00

BRANDT,HERBERT-Arizona and Its Bird Life-Cleve-1951-Bird Rsrch Fndtn-725p-illus (b9,ex-libr) 160.00

BRANDT,HERBERT-Texas Bird Adventures-Cleve-1940-8vo-192p-cl,17 b&w plts,photos (y8,dj chip,pres,autg photo) 150.00

BRANDT,HERBERT-Texas Bird Adventures-Cleve-1940-Bird Rsrch Fndtn-192p-blu cl,sketches by G M Sutton (e9) 65.00

BRANDT,JOHANNA-Grape Cure-NY-(1950)-Harmony Cntr-16mo-191p-grn cl-17th ed (q8,dj) 17.50

BRANDT,RICHARD B-Hopi Ethics-Chig-1954-398p-Laird#254-scarce-1st ed (t7) 25.00

BRANGWYN,FRANK-Book of Bridges-Lond-1915-dec cov,t.e.g.,illus (h10) 75.00

BRANGWYN,FRANK-Windmills-Lond-1923-Bodley Head-4to-126p-dec yel cl,12p col plts-1st ed (oo8,sl soil) 125.00

BRANNER,JOHN C-Bibliography of Clays and the Ceramic Arts-Wash-1906-Amer Ceramic Soc-8vo-451p-cl-2nd ed (w2) 145.00

BRANSON,H C-Pricking Thumb-NY-1942-Simon-1st ed (j4,f,dj) 35.00

BRANT,CHARLES S-Jim Whitewolf-NY-1969-144p-stiff pict wrps-1st ed (t7) 12.50

BRANT,IRVING-Bill of Rights-Indpls-1965-Bobbs Merrill-567p-blu cl wi silv-1st prtg (p2) 17.50

BRANT,IRVING-James Madison: Secretary of State-(1953)-Bobbs Merrill-533p-illus-1st ed (dd9,dj) 25.00

BRANTLY,J E-History of Oil Well Drilling-Houston-1971-Gulf Publ-xxvi+1525p-olive cl,illus-1st ed (l2,dj) 75.00

BRASHLER,WILLIAM-Bingo Long Traveling All Stars and Motor Kings-NY-1973-Harper-auth 1st bk-1st ed (w5,f,f dj) 45.00

BRASHLER,WILLIAM-Bingo Long Travelling All Stars-1973-Harper & Row-1st ed (s8,f,dj) 40.00

BRASHLER,WILLIAM-Josh Gibson-1978-Harper & Row-1st ed (s7,f,f dj) 75.00

BRASS,ALLISTER-Bleeding Earth-Melbourne-(1968)-Heinemann-1st ed (ff3,dj) 45.00

BRASSEY,LADY-Last Voyage-Lond-1889-Longmans,Green-8vo-xxiv,490p-3/4 lea,mrbld papr,2 col fldg maps,plts (ee7,sl rub) 125.00

BRASSEY,MRS-Around the World in the Yacht Sunbeam-NY-1889-Holt-8vo-479p-g dec brwn cl-illus (s1,vf) 65.00

BRATT,GEORGE-On the Boss's Time-SF-1958-Bay Region-wrps-1st ed (w5,crease rear wrps,sl rub) 20.00

BRATT,JOHN-Trails of Yesterday-Chig-1921-302p-pict cl,frntis,photos-Howes B725-1st ed (t7) 150.00

BRATTON,FRED G-History of Egyptian Archaeology-NY-(1968)-Crowell-8vo-313p-brwn cl,54 illus & maps (t10) 25.00

BRAUDEL,FERNAND-Mediterranean and the Mediterranean World in the Age of Philip II-NY,Evanston,SF,Lond-(1972-73)-Harper & Row-8vo-2 vols-red cl,illus,maps-1st Amer ed (t10,dj) 40.00

BRAUN,E LUCY-Woody Plants of Ohio-Columbus-1961-(7),362p-col frntis,illus,maps,prtd on glossy papr-1st ed (jj7,dj) 54.00

BRAUN,LILLIAN JACKSON-Cat Who Ate Danish Modern-Lond-1967-Collins CC-1st Brit (f4,sl fox,dj) 25.00

BRAUN,WERNHER VON-Mars Project-Urbana-1953-U of Illinois-(vi)+91p-gry cl,9 text figs,36 tbls-1st ed (d2,sl soil dj) 175.00

BRAUTIGAN,RICHARD-All Watched Over By Machines of Loving Grace-(SF)-(1967)-Comm Co-pict wrps-ltd to 1,500c-"None of the copies are for sale. They are all free."-1st ed (m7) 300.00

BRAUTIGAN,RICHARD-Confederate General From Big Sur-NY-1964-1st ed (s5,dj lacks sm pc rear flylf) 85.00

BRAUTIGAN,RICHARD-Dreaming of Babylon-NY-1977-1st ed (o5,dj) 35.00

BRAUTIGAN,RICHARD-Hawkline Monster-1974-S&S-1st ed (x2,dj) 28.00

BRAUTIGAN,RICHARD-Hawkline Monster-NY-1974-1st ed (s5,dj) 15.00

BRAUTIGAN,RICHARD-In Watermelon Sugar...-SF-1968-sftbnd orig,wrps-1st ed (t5,f) 35.00

BRAUTIGAN,RICHARD-Loading Mercury with a Pitchfork-NY-1976-S&S-1st ed (j8,remndr mrk,f,dj) 40.00

BRAUTIGAN,RICHARD-Loading Mercury with a Pitchfork-NY-1976-S&S-1st ed (mm5,f,f dj) 20.00

BRAUTIGAN,RICHARD-Pill Versus the Springhill Mine Disaster-SF-(1968)-Four Seasons Foundation-1st ed (s6,sl rub wrps) 45.00

BRAUTIGAN,RICHARD-Revenge of the Lawn-1971-S&S-1st ed (t9,dj sp sunned) 25.00

BRAUTIGAN,RICHARD-Rommel Drives on Deep Into Egypt-NY-1970-1st ed (s5,dj) 60.00

BRAUTIGAN,RICHARD-Sombrero Fallout-NY-(1976)-S&S-1st ed (b5,as new in dj) 15.00

BRAUTIGAN,RICHARD-Tokyo Montana Express-1980-Delacorte-1st ed (x2,vf,dj) 17.00

BRAUTIGAN,RICHARD-Tokyo Montana Express-NY-(1979)-Targ Eds-ltd to 350c,autg,orig glassine dj-1st ed (l9,f,dj) 75.00

BRAUTIGAN,RICHARD-Tokyo Montana Express-NY-1980-1st ed (s5,dj) 22.50

BRAUTIGAN,RICHARD-Willard and His Bowling Trophies-NY-(1975)-S&S-1st ed (b10,as new in dj) 20.00

BRAUTIGAN,RICHARD-Willard and His Bowling Trophies-NY-1975-1st ed (p5,f,dj) 25.00

BRAVERMAN,KATE-Lithium for Medea-NY-(1979)-Harper & Row-auth 1st bk-1st ed (g3,f,dj) 25.00

BRAY,M-Mystic Seaport Museum Watercraft-Mystic-(1979)-4to-280p-illus-1st ed (w10,dj) 25.00

BRAYER,GARNET M-American Cattle Trails 1540 to 1900-NY-1952-Wstrn Rng Cattle Indstry-128p-illus-1st ed (gg4,dj) 50.00

BRAYER,HERBERT-Pueblo Indian Land Grants of the "Rio Abajo",New Mexico-Albuq-1938-U of NM Bul,Hist Ser Vol 1,No.1-128p-wrps,2 maps-1st ed (v7,f) 15.00

BRAYER,HERBERT-To Form a More Perfect Union-Albuq-1941-UNM-illus-ltd to 350c-1st ed (a6,sp soil) 50.00

BRAYER,HERBERT-William Blackmore-Denver-1949-2 vols-illus,maps,ltd to 500c-v scarce-1st ed (u7,box) 200.00

BRAYER,HERBERT-William Blackmore-Denver-1949-Bradford Rob-2 vols-1st ed (a6,box) 150.00

BREAM,HERBERT-ED.-Mystery Writers' Handbook-NY-1956-1st ed (t5,dj) 45.00

BREAN,HERBERT-Traces of Brillhart-Lond-1961-Heinemann-1st Brit ed (s4,sl wn dj) 20.00

BREARD,WALTER R-Modern Bait & Spincasting-NY-1959-12mo-207p-photos (m3,f,dj) 25.00

BREARLY,HARRY C-Time Telling Through the Ages-NY-1919-Dbldy,Page-4to-294p-cl,photos by Hiller-rare-1st ed (q3) 50.00

BREBNER,PERCY J-Master Detective-NY-1916-Dutton-1st ed (g4,fade sp) 20.00

BRECHER,RUTH-Rays-NY-1969-484p-1st ed (dd3) 100.00

BRECK,JOSEPH-New Book of Flowers-NY-1866(1851)-Orange Judd-480p-cl (x6,rub,hng rnfrcd) 40.00

BRECK-MRS.ALAN...RECIPE BOOK-Glasgow-1921-Cooper & Co-154p-blu bds (n6,wn bds) 15.00

BREDER JR,CHARLES M-Field Book of Marine Fishes of the Atlantic Coast-NY-1929-12mo-332p-photos,illus-1st ed (m3,dj sl chip & soil) 30.00

BREE,C R-History of the Birds of Europe not Observed in the British Isles-Lond-1867-8vo-4 vols-mod 1/2 lea,mrbld bds & e.p.,t.e.g.,180 hand-col plts,58 col plts of eggs (y8,edges sl rub,rbnd) 750.00

BREED,W P-Theatre-Phila-1868-16mo-35p (aa4) 45.00

BREEDEN,MARSHALL-Romantic Southland of California-LA-1928-Kenmore-207p-photos-1st ed (d3) 20.00

BREHM,A E-From the North Pole to Equator-Lond-(1895)-Blackie & Son-g stmpd red buckrm,83 illus (p6) 100.00

BREIHAN,CARL W-Badmen of the Frontier Days-NY-(1957)-Robt M McBride-315p-pict e.p.,illus-Six Guns 263-1st ed (gg4,dj) 20.00

BREIHAN,CARL W-Day Jesse James was Killed-NY-(1961)-F Fell-223p+index-illus-Six Guns #265-1st ed (cc4,dj) 20.00

BREIHAN,CARL W-Great Lawmen of the West-Lond-(1963)-John Long-190p-Six Guns #267-1st Brit ed (dd4,dj) 25.00

BREIHAN,CARL W-Quantrill and His Civil War Guerillas-NY-1959-Promontory Pr-174p-illus (v2,f,dj) 20.00

BREIHAN,CARL-Complete & Authentic Life of Jesse James-NY-(1953)-287p-illus-Six Guns #264-1st ed (h7,f,dj) 25.00

BREMER,CHARLOTTE-ED.-Life, Letters and Posthumous Works of Frederika Bremer-NY-1869-Hurd-439p-cl (x6,cl soil) 30.00

BRENAN,GERALD-Personal Record 1920 to 1972-NY-1975-Knopf-1st US ed (x9,f,dj) 12.50

BREND,G-My Dear Holmes-1951-A&U-1st ed (x7,f,dj) 40.00

BREND,G-My Dear Holmes-1951-Allen-1st ed (s10,f,dj) 55.00

BRENNAN,JOSEPH P-Act of Providence-W Kingston-(1979)-Donald M Grant-illus,R Arrington-1st trd ed (a10,as new in dj) 25.00

BRENNAN,JOSEPH P-Casebook of Lucius Leffing-1973-Macabre Hs-1st ed (x7,f,dj) 70.00

BRENNAN,JOSEPH P-Casebook of Lucius Leffing-New Haven-1973-Macabre Hs-1st ed (k3,f,dj) 65.00

BRENNAN,JOSEPH P-Nine Horrors and a Dream-Sauk City-1958-Arkham-120p-ltd to 1336c-auth 1st bk-1st ed (k5,f,dj sp sl wn) 100.00

BRENNAN,JOSEPH P-Stories of Darkness and Dread-Sauk City-1973-Arkham-1st ed (j3,f,dj) 15.00

BRENNAN,JOSEPH P-Stories of Darkness and Dread-Sauk City-1973-ltd to 4138c-1st ed (k5,as new in dj) 10.00

BRENNER,ANITA-Wind That Swept Mexico-Austin-(1976)-U of Tex Pr-310p-photos (cc4,dj) 25.00

BRENT,P-Charles Darwin-1981-Harper Row-536p-illus,map-1st ed (bb3,f,dj) 23.00

BRENTANO,FRANCES-ED.-Big Cats-Lond-1949-8vo-344p-illus-1st ed (m3,f,dj) 27.50

BRERETON,L H-Brereton Diaries-NY-1946-8vo-cl,e.p. maps-1st ed (t2) 30.00

BRESLIN,JIMMY-Can't Anyone Here Play This Game-1963-Viking-1st ed (s8,dj) 25.00

BRESLIN,JIMMY-Sunny Jim-GC-1962-Dbldy-1st ed (f10,dj) 25.00

BRESSON,H C-Europeans-1955-S&S-orig cov design,J Miro-1st Amer ed (x2) 450.00

BRETHREN'S FAMILY ALMANAC FOR ...1875-Somerset Co. & Huntingdon-(1874)-(36)p-wrps (h1) 15.00

BRETON,ANDRE-Manifestoes of Surrealism-Ann Arbor-1969-U of Mich-304p-1st ed thus (j8,f,dj) 35.00

BRETON,ANDRE-Odes to Charles Fourier-NY-1970-Grossman-1st US ed (x9,f,dj) 10.00

BRETT,DOROTHY-Lawrence and Brett-Phila-(1933)-301p-col frntis,photos-1st Amer ed (u7) 40.00

BRETT,DOROTHY-Lawrence and Brett-Phila-(1933)-Lippincott-col frntis,12 b&w photos-1st Amer ed (b10) 25.00

BRETT,S-Cast, In Order of Disappearance-1975-Scribners-auth 1st bk-1st Amer ed (x7,vf,dj) 25.00

BRETT,W H-Indian Tribes of Guiana: Their Condition and Habits-Lond-1868-Bell & Daldy-fldg map,8 col lithos,plts-1st ed (p6,hngs weak) 350.00

BRETZ,J H-Grand Coulee-1932-Am Geo Soc Spec Pub 15-86p-illus,lg col fldg map,8 stereoscopic views in rear pckt (r8,cov soil,spot) 35.00

BREUER,JOSEF-Studies on Hysteria-NY-(1957)-Basic Books-8vo-335p-Strachey transl.-1st US ed (gg5,f,dj) 25.00

BREWER,LEIGHTON-Virgin Water-NY-1941-8vo-223p-photos (m3,fray dj) 21.00

BREWER,REGINALD-Delightful Diversion-NY-1935-Macmillan-1st ed (w1,f,dj) 25.00

BREWER,REV. E COBHAM-Character Sketches of Romance Fiction and the Drama-NY-1892-lg 4to-4 vols-1/2 lea,mrbld e.p.,illus incl 4 chromolithos-1st ed (k9) 75.00

BREWER,WILLIAM H-Up and Down California in 1860 to 1864-New Haven-1930-Yale U Pr-570p+itinerary-illus,fldg map-Howes B754-1st ed (ff4) 150.00

BREWER,WILLIAM H-Up and Down California in 1860 to 1864-New Haven-1930-Yale U Pr-8vo-xxx,601p-blu cl,g sp titles,maps,illus-Howes B754-1st ed,2nd prtg (mm1,dj chip & drknd) 120.00

BREWERTON,G DOUGLAS-War in Kansas-NY-1856-Derby & Jackson-400p+ads-cl-Sabin 7765-1st ed (l1) 60.00

BREWERTON,GEORGE D-Fitz Poodle at Newport-Cambridge-1869-1st ed (m4) 17.50

BREWERTON,GEORGE D-Overland with Kit Carson-NY-(1930)-Burt-301p-illus,fldg map (dd4) 20.00

BREWINGTON,M V-Shipcarvers of North America-NY-1962-Dover-8vo-173p-illus wrps,illus (r10) 10.00

BREWSTER,EDWIN T-Life and Letters of Josiah Dwight Whitney-Bost-1916-Houghton Mifflin-xiv+411p-blu cl-1st ed (a2,sl wn) 25.00

BREWSTER,KATE-Little Garden for Little Money-Bost-1924-Atlantic-108p (x6,dj wn) 10.00

BREWSTER,SIR DAVID-Stereoscope-Hastings on Hudson-1971-Morgan & Morgan-236p-illus,facs rprnt of 1856 1st ed (cc9,as new in dj) 35.00

BRIAND,RENA-Waifs-Melbourne-(1973)-Phuong Hoang-wrps,photos-1st ed (ff3,vf) 85.00

BRICKHILL,P-Dambusters-Lond-(1951)-8vo-270p-cl,frntis,12p plts-1st ed (t2,dj) 30.00

BRICKHILL,P-Reach for the Sky-Lond-1954-8vo-384p-cl,frntis,plts (t2) 30.00

BRICKHILL,PAUL-War of Nerves-1963-Morrow-1st Amer ed (s10,dj) 10.00

BRIDENBAUGH,CARL-Peter Harrison, First American Architect-Chapel Hill-1949-UNC Pr-8vo-195p-41 illus-1st ed (ee5) 25.00

BRIDENBAUGH,CARL-Vexed and Troubled Englishmen 1590 to 1642-NY-1968-Oxford U Pr-8vo-487p-1st ed (cc5,sl tn dj) 20.00

BRIDGEMAN,THOMAS-Kitchen Gardener's Instructor-NY-1840-Auth-144p-orig papr cov bds,cl sp-ltd to 5000c-rvsd ed (x6,f) 80.00

BRIDGEMAN,THOMAS-Kitchen Gardener's Instructor-NY-1865-vi,164p-grn cl,catalogue-new ed (m10,wn,scrape,few spot pgs) 25.00

BRIDGES,ANTHONY-Modern Salmon Fishing-Lond-1939-8vo-236p-photos-1st ed (m3) 30.00

BRIDGES,H P-Woodmont Story-NY-1953-209p-photos-Wdmnt Gun Cl of Hancock (gg3,f,dj) 50.00

BRIDGES,HENRY P-Woodmont Story-NY-1953-folio-209p-photos-1st ed (m3,f,dj) 50.00

BRIDGES,RAYMOND-Climbing-NY-1977-402p-1st ed (q10,as new in dj) 18.00

BRIDGETT,R C-By Loch & Stream-Lond-1922-8vo-300p+ads-photos (m3) 25.00

BRIDGETT,R C-Dry Fly Fishing-Lond-1922-8vo-316p-illus,col plts (m3,f) 35.00

BRIDGETT,R C-Loch Fishing in Theory & Practice-Lond-1924-8vo-320p-2 col plts,photos (m3) 25.00

BRIDGETT,R C-Tight Lines-Lond-1926-8vo-320p-photos (m3) 27.50

BRIDGMAN,HELEN B-Within My Horizon-Bost-(1920)-Small,Maynard-8vo-262p-photos-1st ed (aa5,dj) 25.00

BRIDGMAN,JON M-Revolt of Hereros-Berkeley-(1981)-U of Cal-8vo-184p-cl-1st ed (y5,dj) 25.00

BRIDGMAN,P W-Thermodynamics of Electrical Phenomena in Metals-NY-1934-Macmillan-viii+200p-maroon cl-1st ed (dd1) 60.00

BRIDGMAN,RICHARD-Gertrude Stein in Pieces-NY-1970-Oxford-1st ed (z3,f,dj sl rub) 15.00

BRIER,HOWARD-Sawdust Empire-1958-Knopf-269p+index-illus-1st ed (r8) 22.00

BRIGGS,CHARLES F-Story of the Telegraph and a History of the Great Atlantic Cable-NY-1858-Rudd & Carleton-255p+ads-purple cl,col fldg map,illus-1st ed (j2,sp fade) 100.00

BRIGGS,CHARLES L-Wood Carvers of Cordova, New Mexico-Knoxville-(1980)-240p+index-col photos,maps-1st ed (u7,dj) 35.00

BRIGGS,ELLIS O-Shots Heard Round the World-NY-1957-Viking-8vo-149p-sketches-1st ed (ff5,f,dj) 15.00

BRIGGS,F S-Joysticks and Fiddlesticks-Lond-nd(1936)-Hutchinson & Co-8vo-222p-cl,frntis,plts (t2,f,dj) 100.00

BRIGGS,G A-Audio Biographies-1961-343p-90 photos-1st ed (h6,dj) 45.00

BRIGGS,G A-Stereo Handbook-1959-146p-photos,illus-1st ed (h6,f,dj) 20.00

BRIGGS,HAROLD E-Frontiers of the Northwest-NY-1940-Appleton Century-629p-illus,maps,e.p. maps-Six Guns 275-1st ed (bb4) 35.00

BRIGGS,JEAN L-Never in Anger-Cambridge-1970-Harvard U Pr-8vo-377p-4p photos-1st ed (dd5,f,dj rub) 20.00

BRIGGS,KATHERINE-Encyclopedia of Fairies-NY-(1976)-Pantheon-1st US ed (oo10,as new in dj) 20.00

BRIGGS,L VERNON-History of Shipbuilding on North River, Plymouth Co.,Mass-Bost-1889-priv prtd-xv,(1),421p-maps,illus,photos-1st ed (o2,cors bump,sl wn sp) 100.00

BRIGGS,M S-Christopher Wren-Lond-1951-8vo-1st ed (h10,dj) 20.00

BRIGGS,RAYMOND-White Land-Lond-(1963)-Hamish Hamilton-oblng 8vo-48p-pict bds,19p col illus,b&w drwngs,auth-1st ed (r3,sl mottld bds,drknd dj) 55.00

BRIGGS,WALTER-Without Noise of Arms-Flagstaff-(1976)-202p,dbl col,lea,box,col illus,maps,deluxe,ltd to 100c-1st ed (u7,f,box,2 autg) 175.00

BRIGGS,WALTER-Without Noise of Arms-Flagstaff-(1976)-Northland-oblng 8vo-x,212p-maps,col plts-1st ed (v1,sl soil dj) 60.00

BRIGHAM,CLARENCE S-Paul Revere's Engravings-Worcester-1954-Amer Antiq Soc-4to-77 plts-1st ed (ff7,f,dj) 100.00

BRIGHAM,L-Box Furniture-NY-1910-dec col cov,100 illus,8 photos in rear (kk4) 30.00

BRIGHT,ARTHUR A-Electric-Lamp Industry-NY-1949-Macmillan-xxviii+526p-gry cl,43 text figs,tbls-1st ed (d2,chip dj) 30.00

BRIGHT,ARTHUR-Electric Lamp Industry-NY-1949-Macmillan-xxviii+526p-gry bds,43 text illus (a2,dj sl stnd,tn) 20.00

BRIGHT,JAMES R-Automation and Management-Bost-1958-Harvard Grad School-4to-xvi+270p-blu cl,plts-1st ed (j2,dj) 35.00

BRIGHT,WILLIAM-Karok Language-Berkeley-1957-U of Cal-xii+457p-wrps,map-1st ed (e2) 35.00

BRIGMAN,ANNE-Songs of a Pagan-Caldwell-1949-Caxton-4to-90p-cl,photos-1st ed (t3,dj) 250.00

BRIGNANO,RUSSELL-Black Americans in Autobiography-Durham-1974-Duke Univ-x+118p-brwn cl-1st ed (e2,dj) 20.00

BRILL,CHARLES J-Conquest of the Southern Plains-Millwood-1975-323p-frntis,photos (t7) 20.00

BRILL,CHARLES J-Conquest of the Southern Plains-Okla City-(1938)-323p-cl-1st ed (aa1,sl stnd cov) 50.00

BRILL,JOHN A-Development of the Streetcar-Montreal-1968-Traction Coll Libr:Vol.1-38p-wrps-rprnt of 1899 Cassier Mag (n4) 4.00

BRILL,NORMAN Q-Follow-Up Study of War Neuroses-Wash D C-1955-V A Med Mono-xviii+393p-blu cl,tbls-1st ed (d2) 25.00

BRILLAT-SAVARIN,JEAN A-Handbook of Gastronomy-1915-Houghton Mifflin-394p-dec red cl,6p engrvngs wi tiss guards-Riverside Pr,ltd to 375c,nbrd (q8) 125.00

BRILLAT-SAVARIN,JEAN A-Physiology of Taste-(c.1949)-Heritage Pr-471p-pict bds,col illus by S Sauvage,transl by M F K Fisher (q8,box) 50.00

BRILLAT-SAVARIN,JEAN A-Physiology of Taste-Lond-1925-Davies-4to-326p-mrbld bds,vel sp-ltd to 750c,nbrd (q8,edgewn cov) 85.00

BRILLAT-SAVARIN,JEAN A-Physiology of Taste-NY-(1949)-Heritage Pr-471p-illus,S Sauvage (o6,box) 60.00

BRILLAT-SAVARIN-Handbook of Dining-NY-1865-Appleton-12mo-200+(4)p ads-orig drk grn pebbld cl (t10,f) 175.00

BRIMLOW,GEORGE F-Bannock Indian War of 1878-Caldwell-1938-Caxton-241p-e.p. maps-1st ed (f7,dj,autg) 100.00

BRIMLOW,GEROGE-Cavalryman Out of the West-Caldwell-1944-442p-frntis,photos-1st ed (t7,f,dj) 67.50

BRININSTOOL,E A-Crazy Horse-LA-1949-87p-illus-1st ed (c7,f,dj,pres) 50.00

BRININSTOOL,E A-Crazy Horse-LA-1949-Wetzel-87p-cl,photos-1st ed (v1,rprd dj) 75.00

BRININSTOOL,E A-Fighting Red Cloud's Warriors-Columbus-1926-Hunter,Trader,Trapper Co-241p-pict cl,illus-1st ed (dd4) 50.00

BRININSTOOL,E A-Trooper with Custer-Columbus-1925-12mo-214p+6p ads-illus-scarce-1st ed (c7) 60.00

BRININSTOOL,E A-Troopers with Custer-Harrisburg-(1952)-343p-illus-rvsd & enlgd ed-1st ed thus (c4,dj) 37.50

BRININSTOOL,E A-Troopers with Custer-Harrisburg-(1952)-Stackpole-343p-illus-Dowd #97-rvsd & enlgd ed (c7,f,dj) 40.00

BRINK,CAROL-Chateau Saint Barnabe-NY-(1963)-Macmillan-1st ed (hh5,f,dj sl soil) 8.50

BRINKERHOFF,GEN ROELIFF-Recollections of a Lifetime-Cin-1900-Robert Clarke Co-448p-cl (h1) 35.00

BRINLEY,GORDON-Away to the Rocky Mountains and British Columbia-NY-1938-Dodd,Mead-x,301p-red cl,col frntis,plts(incl col),map lining papers-Edwards & Lort #323 (k10) 25.00*

BRINNIN,JOHN M-Sextet-NY-1981-1st ed (z6,vf,sl tn dj) 20.00

BRINSMEAD,EDGAR-History of the Pianoforte...and Also of the Music and Musical Instruments of the Ancients-Lond-1879-Novello-sm 8vo-201p-g dec blu cl,illus-1st ed (s1) 75.00

BRINTON,HOWARD H-Children of Light-NY-1938-Macmillan-8vo-416p-1st ed (y6,fox cov & e.p.) 16.00

BRIOL,PAUL-City of Rivers and Hills-Cin-1925-Book Shelf-limp cl,photos (cc3) 40.00

BRION,MARCEL-Story of the Huns-NY-(1931)-McBride-8vo-286p-8 photos-1st US ed (jj5,dj) 15.00

BRISBIN,JAMES S-Beef Bonanza-(1959)-U of Ok-208p-illus-Herd #322-1st ed thus (t8,dj) 25.00

BRISSENDEN,PAUL F-I.W.W. a Study of American Syndicalism-NY-1919-Columbia Univ-Studies in Hist,Econ & Public Law Vol.LXXXIII,Whole No.193-1st ed (v5,sl tn sp) 65.00

BRISSENDEN,ROSEMARY-Joys & Subtleties-NY-(1971)-Pantheon-262p-orng cl-1st Amer ed (q8,dj) 15.00

BRISSMAN,BARRY-Swing Low-NY-1972-H&R-auth 1st bk-1st ed (y1,f,f dj) 17.50

BRISTER,BOB-Moss,Mallards & Mules-NY-1974-8vo-216p-illus (m3,f,dj) 10.00

BRISTOW,GWEN-Gutenberg Murders-NY-1931-Mystery League-1931 (f4,wn dj) 12.50

BRISTOW,GWEN-Invisible Host-NY-1930-Mystery League-1st ed (g4,sl wn, f dj) 15.00

BRISTOW,GWEN-Louisiana Trilogy-NY-1948-3 vols-rprnts (m4,f,wn box) 17.50

BRITISH ACADEMY-Proceedings of the...-Lond-1956 to 1972-Oxford U Pr-8vo-13 vols-maroon cl-1st ed (t10,ex-libr) 250.00

BRITON,E VINCENT-Some Account of Amyot Brough...-Lond-1885-Seeley-8vo-2 vols-orig grn cl-auth 1st bk-1st ed (pp2,sl rub) 185.00*

BRITT,ALBERT-Toward the Western Ocean-Barre-1963-164p-pict cl,maps,illus-1st ed (t7) 12.50

BRITTAN,BELLE-Belle Brittan on a Tour,at Newport and Here and There-NY-1858-Derby & Jackson-359p-brwn cl-1st ed (h2,sp sunned,sl wn sp) 30.00

BRITTON,NAN-Honesty or Politics-NY-1932-Elizabeth Ann Guild-374p-cl (d1) 35.00

BRITTON,NAN-President's Daughter-NY-1927-Elizabeth Ann Guild-437(2)p-cl (d1,sl wn dj) 15.00

BRITTON,NATHANIEL L-An Illustrated Flora of the Northern United States, Canada and the British Possessions-NY-1943(1923)-lg 8vo-3 vols-blnd stmpd maroon cl,drwngs-2nd rvsd ed (jj7,sl bump cor) 97.50

BRITTON,WILEY-Memoirs of the Rebellion on the Border 1863-Chig-1882-458p-scarce-1st ed (t7) 185.00

BRITTON,WILEY-Union Indian Brigade in the Civil War-KC-1922-474p-pict cl,frntis,photos-Dornbusch K 26-scarce-1st ed (t7) 225.00

BROOKS,A-Distributional List of the Birds of British Columbia-Berkeley-1925-8vo-158p-wrps,2 col plts (y8,sl dmpstns) 18.50

BROBECK,FLORENCE-Chafing Dish Cookery-NY-1950-M Barrows-221p (u6,dj) 14.00

BROBECK,FLORENCE-Cook it in a Casserole-(1943)-Barrows-183p-tan cl,frntis,4p plts-1st ed (q8,sl stnd,dj sl tn) 12.50

BROCH,HERMANN-Sleepwalkers-Bost-1932-Little,Brown-scarce-auth 1st bk-1st US ed (d10,dj soil,sl chip,tn) 150.00

BROCK,ALAN-History of Fireworks-Lond-(1949)-Harrap-8vo-8 col & 32 halftone plts,dec dj-1st ed (jj9,sm hole dj) 60.00

BROCK,ALICE M-Alice's Restaurant Cookbook-(NY)-(1969)-Random Hs-148p-illus bds,record,A Guthrie-1st prtg (m6,dj) 22.00

BROCK,LYNN-Colonel Gore's Second Case-NY-1926-Harper-1st US ed (h4) 12.50

BROCK,LYNN-Kink-NY-1927-Harper-1st US ed (d4) 15.00

BROCKBANK,ELISABETH-Edward Burrough-Lond-1949-Bannisdale Pr-12mo-176p-1st ed (y6,chip dj) 15.00

BROCKETT,L P-Epidemic and Contagious Diseases-NY-1873-507p-lea,col plts-1st ed (dd3,rub) 250.00

BROCKETT,L P-Woman-Cin-1869-Howe's Subscrptn Bk Cncrn-447p-cl,18p illus (d1,ex-lib) 50.00

BROCKHOUS,ALBERT-Netsukes-1924-Duffield-175p-g dec cov,16 plts-1st Amer ed (v8) 65.00

BROCKLESBY,JOHN-Views of the Microscopic World-NY-1851-Pratt,Woodford-146p+ads-cl,illus (k1) 27.50

BROCKMAN,C FRANK-Flora of Mount Rainier NAtional Park-Wash D.C.-(1947)-Nat'l Prk Serv-8vo-170p-wrps,illus (gg5) 12.50

BRODER,BILL-Sacred Hoop-SF-(1979)-Sierra Club-1st ed (e3,f,sl creased dj) 15.00

BRODER,PATRICIA J-Bronzes of the American West-NY-(1974)-Abrams-sm oblng folio-429p-illus-1st ed (dd4,dj) 200.00

BRODER,PATRICIA J-Bronzes of the American West-NY-1973-Abrams-oblng folio-431p-illus-1st ed (a9,dj) 150.00

BRODER,PATRICIA-Great Paintings of the American West-NY-1979-Abbeville-4to-1st ed (a6,f,dj) 35.00

BRODERICK,ALAN H-Father of Prehistory-NY-1963-Morrow-8vo-306p-16 photos-1st ed (jj5,dj) 15.00

BRODERICK,HENRY-Commandment Breakers of Walla Walla-Seattle-1934-Dogwood Pr-sm 4to-prison denim bndg-1st ed (w1,f) 75.00

BRODEUR,PAUL-Sick Fox-Bost,Tor-(1963)-Little,Brown-auth 1st bk-1st ed (c10,f,sl soil dj) 35.00

BRODEUR,PAUL-Stunt Man-NY-1970-Atheneum-1st ed (c10,dj) 25.00

BRODHEAD,L W-Delaware Water Gap-Phila-1867-xii,(9)-220p-cl,10 photos on lttrd mnts-1st ed (aa6,wn) 150.00

BRODIE,FAWN-Devil Drives-NY-1967-390p-illus-1st ed (b7,dj) 20.00

BRODIE,FAWN-Devil Drives-NY-1967-Norton-cl,illus-1st ed (l8,fray dj) 25.00

BRODKEY,HAROLD-First Love and Other Sorrows-NY-(1957)-Dial-auth 1st bk-1st ed (b5,f,sl wn dj) 125.00

BRODKEY,HAROLD-First Love and Other Stories-NY-(1957)-auth rare 1st bk-1st ed (n5,f,dj) 200.00

BRODMAN,ESTELLE-Development of Medical Bibliography-Balt-1954-226p (dd3) 75.00

BRODSKY,ALYN-Madame Lynch and Friend-NY-(1975)-H&R-8vo-312p-1st ed (cc5,f,dj) 17.50

BRODY,J J-Indian Painters & White Patrons-Albuq-1971-UNM-4to-238p-beige cl,8 col,92 b&w illus,2 maps (r10,sl wn dj) 40.00

BROEG,BOB-Stan Musial's "How the Majors Play Baseball"-1953-Rawlings-48p-TP orig,Musial photos on cov-1st ed (s8) 20.00

BROEG,BOB-Stan Musial's "How the Majors Play Baseball"-St.Louis-(1957)-Rawlings-48p-wrps (n1) 12.50

BROGGER,W C-Fridtjof Nansen. 1861 to 1893-Lond-1896-Longmans,Green-8vo-x,402p+24p ads-drk cl,3 maps,8 plts-Arctic Biblio 2225-1st Brit ed (oo1,sl wn sp) 125.00

BROMFIELD,L-Strange Case of Miss Annie Spragg-1928-Stokes-1st ed (x7,dj sl wn & tn) 20.00

BROMFIELD,LOUIS-ET AL-Flat Top Ranch-Norman-(1957)-U of Okla Pr-232p-illus-Herd 327-1st ed (ff4) 45.00

BROMFIELD,LOUIS-Twenty Four Hours-NY-1930-Stokes-ltd to 500c,nbrd,autg,silv foil dj,orig dec box-Autg ed (y2,f,dj,sl wn box) 65.00

BROMLEY,GEORGE T-Long Ago & Later On-SF-1904-289p-illus blu cl (b6) 35.00

BRONGERSMA,L D-To the Mountains of the Stars-NY-1963-318p-48 plts-1st US ed (o10,f,dj) 25.00

BRONK,WILLIAM-Light and Dark-(Ashland)-1956-Origin Pr-sm 8vo-dec wrps-auth 1st bk-1st ed (kk8,sl fade) 150.00

BRONSON,WILFRED-Water People-NY-(1935)-Wise Parslow-104p-g pict cl,col illus (oo10) 30.00

BRONTE,PATRICIA-Vittles and Vice-Chig-(1952)-Regnery-192p-blk cl-1st prtg (q8,dj) 15.00

BROOKE,HENRY-Leslie Brooke & Johnny Crow-Lond-1982-F Warne-4to-143p-brwn cl,col & b&w illus-1st ed (nn8,f,f dj) 30.00

BROOKE,IRIS-Four Walls Adorned-Lond-(1952)-Methuen-4to-120p-8 col plts (l10,dj) 10.00

BROOKE,RUPERT-Letters From America-NY-1916-frntis port-1st ed (hh10,sl sun sp,sl stnd cov) 25.00

BROOKE,STOPFORD-Need and Use of Getting Irish into the English Tongue-Lond-1893-66p (m4,rbnd) 35.00

BROOKES,GEORGE S-Friend Anthony Benezet-Phila-1937-U of Penn-8vo-516p-1st ed (y6,sl fade dj) 18.50

BROOKES,OWEN-Gatherer-NY-(1982)-HRW-1st ed (hh5,f,f dj) 20.00

BROOKNER,ANITA-Debut-1981-Linden-1st Amer ed (t9,vf,dj) 20.00

BROOKNER,ANITA-Jacques-Louis David: a Personal Interpretation-1974-Oxford U Pr-wrps-1st ed (jj6,vf) 75.00

BROOKS,A D-History of Ellis County Baptist Assoc-Hillsboro-(1907)-Tex Prtg & Sply Co-200p-illus-rare-1st ed (f9) 750.00

BROOKS,A H-ET AL-Mineral Resources of Alaska-1919-US Geo Srvy,Bull.714-244p-wrps,4 fldg maps in text,1 fldg map rear pckt (u8) 20.00

BROOKS,A H-ET AL-Mineral Resources-1920-US Geo Srvy,Bull.722-266p-wrps,3 fldg maps (u8) 20.00

BROOKS,CHARLES E-Nymph Fishing for Larger Trout-NY-1976-4to-184p-illus,photos-1st ed (m3,f,dj) 22.50

BROOKS,CHARLES E-Trout and the Stream-NY-1974-4to-216p-photos,illus-1st ed (m3,f,dj) 20.00

BROOKS,CHARLES S-Chimney Pot Papers-New Haven-1919-Yale U Pr-1st ed (hh5) 10.00

BROOKS,CHARLES-Siege of New Orleans-Seattle-1961-334p-1st ed (jj2,f,dj) 45.00

BROOKS,CLINTON-Forts and Forays-Albuq-1948-85p-frntis,photos,fldg map-Rittenhouse#34-1st ed (t7,dj) 65.00

BROOKS,DR W E-Northwest Turnpike, and West Virginia-Newcomen Address-1943-24p-wrps,frntis,illus-1st ed (kk3) 12.50

BROOKS,GEORGE-ED.-Southwest Expedition of Jedediah S Smith-Glendale-1977-259p-1 fldg map,plain dj-v scarce-1st ed (e7,vf,dj) 150.00

BROOKS,GWENDOLYN-Maud Martha-NY-1953-1st ed (v9,f,sl tn dj) 225.00

BROOKS,GWENDOLYN-Report From Part One-Detr-1982-Broadside Pr-iss w/o dj-1st ed (w5,f) 30.00

BROOKS,JOE-Bass Bug Fishing-NY-1947-8vo-69p-illus-1st prntng (m3,f) 70.00

BROOKS,JOE-Bermuda Fishing-Harrisburg-1957-8vo-166p-photos (m3) 18.00

BROOKS,JOE-Complete Book of Fly Fishing-NY-1958-8vo-352p-illus-1st ed (m3,f) 15.00

BROOKS,JOE-Complete Book of Fly Fishing-NY-1968-405p-photos,illus (gg3,f,dj) 10.00

BROOKS,JOE-Complete Guide to Fishing Across North America-NY-1966-8vo-613p-illus-1st ed (m3,f,dj) 10.00

BROOKS,JOE-Complete Illustrated Guide to Casting-GC-1963-4to-192p-photos-1st ed (m3,f,chip dj) 18.50

BROOKS,JOE-Greatest Fishing-Harrisburg-1957-8vo-228p-photos-1st ed (m3,f,dj) 14.00

BROOKS,JOE-Salt Water Game Fishing-NY-1968-8vo-346p-photos-1st ed (m3,f,dj) 20.00

BROOKS,JOE-Trout Fishing-NY-1972-8vo-302p-photos-1st ed (m3,f,dj) 32.50

BROOKS,JOE-World of Fishing-NY-1964-8vo-375p-photos-1st ed (m3,dj) 20.00

BROOKS,JOHN G-Labor's Challenge to the Social Order-NY-1920-Macmillan-1st ed (w5,f) 35.00

BROOKS,JUANITA-John Doyle Lee-Glendale-1962-404p-illus-scarce-1st ed (c7,f,folded dj) 95.00

BROOKS,JUANITA-John Doyle Lee-Glendale-1964-404p-cl,deckle edge pgs,plts (bb8,dj) 55.00

BROOKS,JUANITA-Mountain Meadows Massacre-(1950)-Stanford U Pr-243p-map frntis,map e.p. (gg4,dj) 50.00

BROOKS,JUANITA-Mountain Meadows Massacre-Norman-1962-U of Okla Pr-8vo-xiii+316p-cl-1st rprnt ed (z4,dj) 35.00

BROOKS,LAKE-Science of Fishing-Columbus-1912-12mo-258p-illus-1st ed (m3) 15.00

BROOKS,RICHARD A E-ED.-Diary of Michael Floy Jr., Bowery Village, 1833 to 1837-New Haven-1941-Yale Univ-xii+270p-red cl-1st ed (e2,sl rub sp) 20.00

BROOKS,THOMAS R-Communications Workers of America-NY-1977-Mason/Charter-257p-1st ed (r1,sl tn dj) 25.00

BROOKS,V-Tilly from Tillamook-Portland-(1925)-126p-wrps (bb9,sl wn) 25.00

BROOKS,WILLIAM E-Grant of Appomattox-Indpls-1942-347p-frntis port,maps-1st ed (o7) 35.00

BROOKSHIER,FRANK-Burro-1974-U of Okla-370p-photos-1st ed (bb3,f,rub dj) 25.00

BROOKSHIER,FRANK-Burro-Norman-1974-U of Okla-8vo-xiii+370p-1st ed (z4,sl tn dj) 50.00

BROPHY,BRIGID-Adventures of God in His Search for the Black Girl-Bost-1974-Little Brown-1st US ed (z9,dj rub) 10.00

BROPHY,BRIGID-Hackenfeller's Ape-NY-(1954)-Random-1st ed (bb1,cor bump,dj lt soil) 20.00

BROSNAN,C J-Jason Lee-1932-Macmillan-348p-1st ed (r8,rub dj) 35.00

BROSNAN,CORNELIUS J-Jason Lee, Prophet of the New Oregon-NY-1932-Macmillan-348p-frntis-1st ed (cc4,dj) 20.00

BROSNAN,CORNELIUS J-Jason Lee-NY-1932-348p-frntis-Smith #1148-1st ed (t7,f,dj tn) 15.00

BROSNAN,JIM-Long Season-(1960)-Harper-1st ed (p7,dj) 30.00

BROSNAN,JIM-Long Season-NY-(1960)-273p-cl-1st ed (n1,f,dj) 20.00

BROSNAN,JIM-Pennant Race-1962-Harper-1st ed (p7,dj) 35.00

BROSS,WILLIAM-Legend of the Delaware-Chig-1887-195p-cl-Wright 693-1st ed (d1,frnt cov sl dmpstnd,flckd) 20.00

BROSSARD,CHANDLER-Bold Saboteurs-NY-(1953)-FS&Y-1st ed (c10,sl wn dj) 30.00

BROSSARD,CHANDLER-ED.-I Want More of This-NY-1967-Dell-wrps-1st ed (w5) 15.00

BROSSARD,CHANDLER-Who Walk in Darkness-(NY)-(1952)-auth 1st bk-1st ed (x8,sl chip & rub dj) 100.00

BROSSARD,CHANDLER-Who Walk in Darkness-(NY)-(1952)-New Directions-auth 1st bk-1st ed (c10,dj sp sl wn) 85.00

BROTHERHEAD,WILLIAM-Forty Years among the Old Booksellers of Philadelphia-Phila-1891-A P Brotherhead-sm sq 8vo-122p-orig red cl,papr cov labl-1st ed (t10) 90.00

BROTHERSTON,R P-Book of the Carnation-Lond-1914-95p+ads-17 plts (x5,sl tn frntis) 10.00

BROUDE,N-ED.-Feminism & Art History-NY-1982-306 illus-1st ed (h10,dj) 40.00

BROUGHTON,COL JACK-Thud Ridge-Phila-(1969)-Lippincott-1st ed (ff3,dj) 85.00

BROUGHTON-MAINWARING,MAJ R-Historical Record of the Royal Welch Fusiliers-Lond-1889-372p-dec blk cl,24 col plts-1st ed (b7) 300.00

BROUN,M-Hawks Aloft-NY-1949-8vo-222p-cl,photos (y8,wn,tn dj) 20.00

BROW,JAMES-Vedda Villages of Anuradhapura-Seattle/Lond-1978-U of Wash Pr-xv,268,(3)p-brwn cl,maps,photos,figs,illus (ll1,f) 25.00

BROWDER,EARL-Build the United People's Front-NY-1936-Workers Library-70p-stapled wrps (r1) 19.00

BROWDER,EARL-Communist Party of the USA-NY-1941-Workers Library-47p-wrps (r1) 17.00

BROWDER,EARL-Meaning of Social Facism-NY-1933-Workers Library-48p-stapled wrps (r1,rust stpls) 20.00

BROWDER,EARL-Moscow Cairo Teheran-NY-1944-Workers Library-23p-stapled wrps-Seidman B605 (r1) 12.00

BROWDER,EARL-Production for Victory-NY-1942-Workers Library-stapled wrps (r1) 17.00

BROWDER,EARL-Road to Victory-NY-1941-Workers Library-46p-stapled wrps (r1) 14.00

BROWDER,EARL-Why America is Interested in the Chinese Communists-NY-1945-New Century-16p-wrps (r1) 15.00

BROWER,DAVID-Gentle Wilderness of the Sierra Nevada-1967-4to-167p-col photos-1st ed (p10,f,dj) 30.00

BROWER,K-Song for Satawal-1983-Harper Row-218p-1st ed (bb3,f,dj) 16.00

BROWER,KENNETH-With Their Island Around Them-NY-1974-HR&W-8vo-216p-1/2 wht cl & dec bds,12p drwngs,T Suzuki-1st ed (nn1,f,sl wn dj) 30.00

BROWN & POLSON, LTD-Light Fare Recipes for Corn Flour and "Raisley Cookery"-Paisley,Lond-nd(ca.1920)-16mo-121p-pict bds,illus (q8) 15.00

BROWN COUNTY-FIFTY YEARS IN ... CONVENT-Cin-1895-McDonald & Co-294p-cl-scarce (j1,sl spot cov,rprd inn hngs) 32.50

BROWN DERBY COOKBOOK-GC-1949-Dbldy-272p (l6) 35.00

BROWN,A W-Flying the Atlantic in Sixteen Hours-NY-(1920)-8vo-x,178p-illus cl,frntis,11p plts-1st ed (t2,wn) 20.00

BROWN,ALFRED-Old Masterpieces in Surgery-Omaha-1928-priv prtd-263p-57 plts-v scarce-1st ed (dd3) 225.00

BROWN,ALICE C-Early American Herb Recipes-Rutland-(1966)-Tuttle-152p-b&w illus-1st ed (m6,box) 35.00

BROWN,ALICE-Children of the Earth...-NY-1915-Macmillan-8vo-212p-1st ed (w6) 25.00

BROWN,ALICE-Golden Ball-NY-1929-Macmillan-8vo-92p-1st ed (w6,uncut) 25.00

BROWN,ALICE-King's End-Bost-1901-8vo-246p-1st ed (w6) 35.00

BROWN,ALICE-Meadow Grass-Bost-1895-Copeland & Day-12mo-315p-untrim-1st ed (w6) 65.00

BROWN,ALICE-Old Crow-NY-1922-Macmillan-8vo-534p-1st ed (w6) 25.00

BROWN,ALICE-Paradise-Bost-1905-Houghton,Mifflin-8vo-388p-1st ed (w6) 35.00

BROWN,ALICE-Road to Castaly...-NY-1917-Macmillan-8vo-170p-1st ed (w6,sl rub) 35.00

BROWN,ALICE-Story of Thyrza-Bost,NY-1909-Houghton Mifflin-8vo-327p-frntis,A B Stephen-1st ed (w6) 35.00

BROWN,BOB-Complete Book of Cheese-(1955)-Random-316p-pict bds,illus-1st prtg (q8,dj) 15.00

BROWN,BRUCE-Mountain in the Clouds-NY-1982-S&S-auth 1st bk-1st ed (d8,f,dj) 30.00

BROWN,C BARRINGTON-Canoe and Camp Life in British Guiana-Lond-1876-Edw Stanford-8vo-x,11,400p-3/4 calf & mrbld papr,5 raised bnds & g dentelle on sp,fldg map at rear,10 col litho plts-1st ed (mm1,rehngd) 395.00

BROWN,CHARLES E-When the Trumpet Sounded-Anderson-(1951)-402p-cl (g1) 15.00

BROWN,CHARLES-Correspondent's War-NY-1967-478p-illus-1st ed (gg2,dj) 20.00

BROWN,CHRISTY-Background Music-Lond-1973-Secker & Warburg-8vo-66p-1st ed (aa7,sl rub dj) 25.00*

BROWN,CHRISTY-My Left Foot-Lond-1954-Secker & Warburg-sm 8vo-193p-frntis,3 photos,1 drwng-1st ed (aa7,dj chip) 50.00*

BROWN,CHRISTY-Shadow on Summer-NY-(1975,74)-Stein & Day-1st US ed (hh5,sl tn dj) 12.50

BROWN,CLARA S-Life at Shut In Valley and Other Pacific Coast Tales-Franklin-1895-Editor Publ-188p-blu cl (mm1,sp wn) 15.00

BROWN,CLAUDE-Manchild in the Promised Land-NY & Lond-(1965)-Macmillan/Collier-Macmlln-auth 1st bk-1st ed (b10,sl fade dj sp) 40.00

BROWN,CORA-Country Cookbook-Weston-(1937)-Countryman Pr-224p-red plaid bds (o6,dj) 25.00

BROWN,DEE-Hear That Lonesome Whistle Blow-NY-(1977)-311p-1st ed (n4,f,dj) 20.00

BROWN,DEE-Hear That Lonesome Whistle Blow-NY-(1977)-HR&W-311p-illus,map e.p.-1st ed (cc4,dj) 25.00

BROWN,DEE-Trail Driving Days-NY-(1952)-Scribner-4to-264p-229 illus-1st ed (cc5,sl tn dj) 40.00

BROWN,DEE-Trail Driving Days-NY-(1952)-Scribners-4to-264p-photos,sketches-Herd 340-1st ed (cc4,sl chip dj) 50.00

BROWN,E K-On Canadian Poetry-Tor-(1943)-Ryerson-1st ed (r2,f,dj sp sun,sl rub) 25.00

BROWN,ELEANOR-Culinary Americana-NY-(1961)-Roving Eye Pr-417p (m6) 55.00

BROWN,ELI F-Eclectic Physiology for Use in Schools-Cin,NY-(1884)-Van Antwerp,Bragg & Co-189p-cl (e1) 15.00

BROWN,ELI F-New Tocology-Chig-(1921)-Laird & Lee-398p-cl (d1) 15.00

BROWN,ELI-Real Billy Sunday-1914-Otterbein-pict cov (p7) 45.00

BROWN,ELMER E-Making of our Middle Schools-NY-1903-547p-cl (k1,pres cpy) 25.00

BROWN,ELTON T-History of the Great Minnesota Forest Fires...-St.Paul-(1894)-Brown Bros-233,(5)p-cl cov bds (aa1,sl wn & soil) 40.00

BROWN,F M-Jamaica and Its Butterflies-1972-Classey-4to-478p-9 col plts,maps (bb3,f,dj) 115.00

BROWN,FRANK-Contingent Ditties and Other Soldier Songs of the Great War-Lond-1915-S Low,Marston-Watters p.26-1st ed (pp2,f,dj chip) 35.00*

BROWN,FREDRIC-Angels & Spaceships-Lond-1955-wi scarce wraparound band-1st ed (g5,f,sl soil dj) 125.00

BROWN,FREDRIC-Compliments of a Fiend-NY-1950-Dutton-1st ed (k4,sml tape mrks e.p. & dj) 85.00

BROWN,FREDRIC-Deep End-NY-1952-Dutton-1st ed (a5,sl wn dj) 100.00

BROWN,FREDRIC-Far Cry-NY-1951-Dutton-1st ed (hh2,f,sl tn dj) 125.00

BROWN,FREDRIC-Here Comes a Candle-1950-Dutton-1st ed (x7,dj) 120.00

BROWN,FREDRIC-Here Comes a Candle-NY-1950-Dutton-1st ed (aa8,dj) 200.00

BROWN,FREDRIC-Honeymoon in Hell-1958-Bantam-wrps-1st ed (x7) 15.00

BROWN,FREDRIC-Mind Thing-NY-1961-Bantam-pbk orig-1st prtg (bb1) 35.00

BROWN,FREDRIC-Mostly Murder-1953-Dutton-1st ed (x7,f,sl tn dj) 125.00

BROWN,FREDRIC-Mrs.Murphy's Underpants-NY-1963-1st ed (p5,wn dj) 75.00

BROWN,FREDRIC-Murderers-NY-1961-Dutton-1st ed (c10,dj) 85.00

BROWN,FREDRIC-Office-1961-Dutton-1st ed (x7,f,dj) 175.00

BROWN,FREDRIC-Screaming Mimi-NY-1949-Dutton-1st ed (h4,sl fox,dj sl brwnd) 60.00

BROWN,FREDRIC-Shaggy Dog and Other Stories-Lond-(1963)-T V Boardman & Co-1st Brit ed (q1,sl scuff dj) 75.00

BROWN,FREDRIC-Space on My Hands-1951-Shasta-1st ed (x7,dj) 195.00

BROWN,FREDRIC-We All Killed Grandma-NY-1952-Dutton-1st ed (d4,chip dj) 45.00

BROWN,FREDRIC-Wench is Dead-NY-1955-Dutton-1st ed (e4,sl stnd cov,dj rear stnd) 120.00

BROWN,G W-Baltimore and the Nineteenth of April, 1861-Balt-1887-176p-map-1st ed (z10,sl soil & scuff) 60.00

BROWN,GEORGE A-Harold the Klansman-KC-1923-Wstrn Baptist-303p-blu cl wi red Klan cross-scarce (v8,sl stnd cov) 50.00

BROWN,GEORGE-Melanesians and Polynesians-Lond-1910-Macmillan-8vo-xv,451p-g grn cl,70 photos (pp1,sl wn,cov spot) 150.00

BROWN,H RAP-Die Nigger Die!-NY-1969-Dial-photos-auth 1st bk-1st ed (d10,sl tn dj) 40.00

BROWN,H RAP-Die, Nigger, Die-NY-1969-Dial-145p-2nd prtg (r1,dj snag,tn) 25.00

BROWN,HELEN D-Talks to Freshman Girls-Bost-1914-Houghton Mifflin-8vo-90p-1st ed (oo7) 25.00

BROWN,HELEN E-Breakfasts and Brunches for Every Occasion-(1961)-Dbldy-260p-red cl-1st ed (q8,dj) 12.50

BROWN,HELEN E-Complete Book of Outdoor Cookery-1955-Dbldy-255p-tan cl-1st ed (q8,edgewn dj) 15.00

BROWN,HELEN E-Shrimp and Other Shellfish Recipes-(1966)-Ward Ritchie-16mo-152p-dec grn cl (q8,dj) 12.50

BROWN,HELEN E-Some Oyster Recipes-Pasadena-1951-Ampersand Pr-16mo-28p-pict gry bds,illus (q8) 20.00

BROWN,HELEN-...WEST COAST COOK BOOK-Bost-1952-Little,Brown-443p-1st ed (o6,dj) 25.00

BROWN,HELEN-Helen Brown's West Coast Cook Book-Bost-1952-Little,Brown-443p-1st ed (k6) 30.00

BROWN,HENRY C-Glimpses of Old New York-NY-1917-Anderson Galleries-sm folio-381p-dec blu cl,illus,incl col,"Priv Prntd for Subscribers" (w1) 90.00

BROWN,J HAMMOND-ED.-Great Hunting & Fishing Stories-NY-1947-8vo-343p-illus (m3,f,dj) 15.00

BROWN,J P S-Forests of the Night-NY-1974-1st ed (p5,f,dj) 25.00

BROWN,J S-Vocabulary of Mute Signs-Baton Rouge-1856-Morning Comet Office-50p-prntd wrps (k1) 30.00

BROWN,JAMES A-ED.-Approaches to the Social Dimensions of Mortuary Practices-np-1971-Scty of Amer Archeology-8vo-112p-prntd yel wrps (mm1) 15.00

BROWN,JENNIE B-Fort Hall on the Oregon Trail-Caldwell-1932-466p-frntis,photos-1st ed (t7) 65.00

BROWN,JESSE-Black Hills Trails-Rapid City-1924-Rapid City Journal-572p-cl,frntis port,photo plts-1st ed (v1,innr hngs weak) 165.00

BROWN,JESSE-Black Hills Trails-Rapid City-1924-Rapid City Journal-572p-illus-Howes B850-Herd 342-1st ed (nn6) 195.00

BROWN,JOHN H-Life of Henry Smith-Dallas-1887-395p-frntis-1st ed (f9) 100.00

BROWN,JOHN H-Life of Henry Smith-Dallas-1887-395p-frntis-1st ed (jj1) 125.00

BROWN,JOHN M-Beyond the Present-Mpls-1948-Ampersand Club-12mo-cl-ltd to 650c (w2) 10.00

BROWN,JOHN M-Worlds of Robert E Sherwood-NY-(1965)-409p-cl (l1,f,sl wn dj) 12.50

BROWN,JOHN-Spare Hours. First Series-Bost-1883-458p-1st Amer ed (dd3) 45.00

BROWN,JOHN-Spare Hours. Third Series-Bost-1883-373p-1st Amer ed (dd3) 45.00

BROWN,K S-ET AL-United States Army and AIr Force Fighters 1916 to 1961-(1961)-Letchworth,Herts-4to-256p-cl,col frntis,illus (t2,dj) 35.00

BROWN,KENNETH-Medchester Club-Derrydale-1938-8vo-224p-ltd to 950c,nbrd-illus (m3) 50.00

BROWN,L-African Birds of Prey-1971-Houghton Mifflin-320p-12p photos,maps-1st Amer ed (bb3,f,dj) 45.00

BROWN,L-African Birds of Prey-Bost-1971-Houghton Mifflin-320p-illus-1st Amer ed (d9,f,dj) 40.00

BROWN,L-Eagles of the World-NY-1979-Universe Bks-224p-illus-2nd prtg (d9,dj) 15.00

BROWN,L-Eagles, Hawks and Falcons of the World-NY-1968-4to-2 vols-cl,165 plts(mostly col)+15 under-wing plt,94 maps-1st Amer ed (y8,scuff) 175.00

BROWN,L-ET AL-Birds of Africa. Vol.1-1983-Academic Pr-4to-521p-32p plts(most col),maps-2nd prtg wi corrections (bb3,f,dj) 110.00

BROWN,LAWRENCE L-Episcopal Church in Texas, 1838 to 1874-Austin-1963-Church Hist Scty-271p-lea,photos,illus,deluxe ed ltd to 100c,autg-v scarce (w3,vf,box) 125.00

BROWN,LEWIS-Horse Anatomy-Pelham-1948-Bridgman-oblng 4to-1st ed (j9) 30.00

BROWN,LLOYD A-Early Maps of the Ohio Valley-Pitt-1959-U of Pitt Pr-4to-xvi+132p-ltd to 1000c,52p maps-1st ed (k2,f,dj) 65.00

BROWN,LLOYD A-Early Maps of the Ohio Valley-Pitt-1959-U of Pitt Pr-ltd to 1000c (v4,as new) 35.00

BROWN,MARGARET W-Christmas in the Barn-NY-(1952)-Crowell-oblng 8vo-unpgd-dec cl,B Cooney illus-1st ed (nn10,f,dj) 40.00

BROWN,MARGARET W-Duck-NY-(1953)-Harper-4to-unpgd-cl bckd pict bds,photos-1st ed (oo10,edgewn,cov rub) 15.00

BROWN,MARGARET W-Fox Eyes-Lond-(1979)-Collins-4to-unpgd-glossy pict bds,col illus,G Williams,reissue (r3,f) 12.00

BROWN,MARGARET W-Willie's Adventure-NY-(1954)-Scott-8vo-68p-pict bds,illus,C Johnson-presumed 1st ed (s3,fade,dj) 35.00

BROWN,MARION-Pickles and Preserves-NY-1955-Avenel-281p (l6) 18.00

BROWN,MARION-Southern Cook Book-Chapel Hill-(1951)-UNC Pr-371p-grn bds (l6) 30.00

BROWN,MARK H-Flight of the Nez Perce-NY-(1967)-Putnams-480p-maps-1st ed (cc4,dj) 25.00

BROWN,MARK H-Plainsman of the Yellowstone-NY-(1961)-480p-e.p. maps-1st ed (e7,f,dj) 30.00

BROWN,MARK-Plainsmen of the Yellowstone-NY-(1961)-Putnam's-480p-illus,e.p. maps-Six Guns #299-1st ed (dd4,dj) 35.00

BROWN,MARY A-Dainty Dining-Lewiston-1908-Reed Pr-144p-grn bds,cov title "The Lady of the Manor"-Bitting 63 (n6,sp wn) 55.00

BROWN,MRS HUGH-Lady in Boomtown-Palo Alto-(1968)-Amer West Publ-127p-illus (cc4,dj) 15.00

BROWN,NIGEL-Ice Skating-Lond-1959-N Kaye-8vo-220p-41 illus-1st ed (bb7,sl chip dj) 20.00*

BROWN,O PHELPS-Dr.O Phelps Brown's Shakespearian Annual Almanac, 1880-(Jersey City)-(1879)-32p-wrps,illus (aa6) 40.00

BROWN,PAUL-Polo-NY-1949-Scribner (h9,dj) 45.00

BROWN,R J E-Permafrost in Canada-1970-U of Tor Pr-8vo-viii,234p-fldg map,illus,chrts-1st ed (aa7,sl scuff dj) 20.00*

BROWN,RICHARD-London Bookshop. Part Two-Lond-1977-oblng 4to-ltd to 2000c,illus-1st ed (w1,f) 25.00

BROWN,RITA MAE-In Her Day-Plainfield-1976-softbnd orig,wrps-1st ed (s5) 22.50

BROWN,RITA MAE-Plain Brown Rapper-Oakland-(1976)-Diana Pr-brwn wrps-1st ed (k7) 40.00

BROWN,ROBERT B-Sportsman's Books-Michigan-1950-4to-6p-wrps (m3) 10.00

BROWN,ROBERT C-Canada's National Policy, 1883 to 1900-1964-Princeton U Pr-ix,436p (k10,f,dj) 25.00*

BROWN,ROBERT L-Colorado Ghost Towns-Caldwell-1972-322p-photos,map e.p.-1st ed (t7,dj) 25.00

BROWN,ROBERT L-Jeep Trails to Colorado Ghost Towns-Caldwell-1963-239p-photos,map e.p.-1st ed (t7,dj) 20.00

BROWN,ROSELLEN-Autobiography of My Mother-GC-1976-Dbldy-1st ed (a10,as new in dj) 20.00

BROWN,ROSELLEN-Autobiography of My Mother-GC-1976-Dbldy-1st ed (b5,as new in dj) 20.00

BROWN,ROSELLEN-Cora Fry-NY-(1977)-Norton-1st ed (a10,as new in dj) 20.00

BROWN,ROSELLEN-Some Deaths in the Delta & Other Poems-np-(1970)-U of Mass Pr-auth 1st bk-1st ed (a10,vf,vf dj) 40.00

BROWN,ROSELLEN-Tender Mercies-NY-1978-Knopf-1st ed (a10,as new in dj) 15.00

BROWN,STERLING A-Last Ride of Wild Bill-Detr-1975-Broadside Pr-wrps-1st ed (v5,f) 35.00

BROWN,T-Taxidermist's Manual-1883-Putnams-199p-6 plts (bb3) 15.00

BROWN,THEODORE M-Margaret Bourke White Photojournalist-Ithaca-(1972)-Cornell-4to-illus bds,orig glassine dj-1st ed (y3,dj tn) 45.00

BROWN,VINSON-Explorer Naturalist-Harrisburg-1976-Stackpole-8vo-288p-75 maps & drwngs-1st ed (ff9,dj) 18.00*

BROWN,W F-Albert Frederick Hochwalt-OH-1939-346p-photos (gg3,f,dj) 15.00

BROWN,W R-Horse of the Desert-NY-1947-Macmillan-4to-1st trd ed (h9,dj) 95.00

BROWN,WALTER C-Cross Over Nine-NY-1934-Macaulay-1st ed (d4,fox,chip dj) 40.00

BROWN,WARREN-Chicago Cubs-1946-Putnam-1st ed (s8,dj chip & wn) 40.00

BROWN,WARREN-Chicago White Sox-1952-Putnam-photos-1st ed (s8) 30.00

BROWN,WILFRED G-Angler's Almanac-Lond-1949-8vo-140p-illus-1st ed (m3,f,dj) 10.00

BROWN,WILLIAM C-Indian Side of the Story-Spokane-(1961)-priv prtd-469p-illus-v scarce-1st ed (d7) 100.00

BROWN,WILLIAM F-Beat, Beat, Beat-NY-1959-wrps-1st ed (x8,f) 20.00

BROWN,WILLIAM F-Field Trial Primer-Chig-1934-12mo-80p+ads-illus-1st ed (m3,fray dj) 35.00

BROWN,WILLIAM F-National Field Trial Champions 1956 to 1966-So Brunswick-1966-8vo-252p-illus,photos (m3) 40.00

BROWN,WILLIAM H-On the South African Frontier-NY-1899-430p-grn cl,fldg map,plts-1st ed (b7) 100.00

BROWN,WILLIAM N-Art of Enameling on Metal-Tor-1900-28 illus (ll3,dmpstnd cov) 22.50

BROWN,WILLIAM R-Horse of the Desert-np-1936-Maynesboro Ed-4to (j9,edge wn,hng broken) 185.00

BROWN,WILLIAM R-Our Forest Heritage-Concord-1958-NH Hist Scty-xvi+341p-grn cl,illus-1st ed (h2,dj) 22.00

BROWN,WILLIAM S-California Northeast, the Bloody Ground, Annals of Modoc-Oakland-1951-Biobooks-8vo-207p-cl,fldg map-ltd to 750c (mm7) 65.00

BROWN,WILLIAM-Suggestion and Mental Analysis-Lond-1922-U of Lond Pr-1st ed (y9) 25.00

BROWN,WM-Natural History of the Salmon-Glasgow-1862-16mo-136p-blndstmpd blu cl,2 plts (hh1,sl wn cov) 55.00

BROWNE,BELMORE-Conquest of Mount McKinley-Bost-1956-rprnt (o10,f,dj) 50.00

BROWNE,C R-Maori Witchery-Lond-(1920)-Dent-209p-cl-1st ed (y5) 25.00

BROWNE,CHARLES-Gun Club Drink Book-(1939)-190p-dec red cl,illus-1st ed (q8,edgewn,sl soil) 15.00

BROWNE,J GILBERT-Iraq Levies 1915 to 1932-Lond-1932-88p-dec tan cl,maps,plts-1st ed (b7,f) 80.00

BROWNE,J ROSS-Apache Country-NY-1869-Harpers-illus-Howes N875-1st ed (a6,sl wn sp) 295.00

BROWNE,J ROSS-Crusoe's Island-NY-1864-Harper & Bros-436p-brwn cl,text illus-1st ed (mm10,sl soil) 150.00

BROWNE,J ROSS-His Letters, Journals, and Writings-(1969)-UNM Pr-419p-illus-1st ed (cc4,dj) 25.00

BROWNE,JUNIUS H-Great Metropolis-Hartford-1869(1868)-Amer Publ-700p-22 plts (o2,sl rub,fade) 30.00

BROWNE,LEWIS-Wisdom of Israel-NY-1945-Random-cl-1st ed (o8) 15.00

BROWNE,LINA F-ED.-J Ross Browne: His Letters, Journals & Writings-Albuq-1969-UNM-xxi,419p-illus-1st ed (o2,f,f dj) 25.00

BROWNE,MOSES-Angling Sports in Nine Piscatory Ecologues-Lond-1773-12mo-136p-full brwn calf gilt-red lea lettering piece-frontis-3rd ed (m3) 150.00

BROWNE,NINA E-Bibliography of Nathaniel Hawthorne-Bost-1905-Houghton Mifflin-ltd to 550c-1st ed (w1,f,box) 60.00

BROWNE,NOEL-Horse in Ireland-Lond-1967-Pelham-1st ed (h9,dj) 35.00

BROWNE,PHYLLIS-Dictionary of Dainty Breakfasts-Lond-1899-Cassell-139p-brn bds-Bitting 64 (n6,sl soil) 75.00

BROWNE,THOMAS-Hydriotaphia Urn Burial-Lond-1893-109p-Japanese vel-ltd to 50c (dd3) 100.00

BROWNE,THOMAS-Religio Medici and Other Works-Oxford-1964-383p (dd3,dj) 50.00

BROWNE,THOMAS-Religio Medici-NY-1903-187p-prtd on hand made papr-ltd ed (dd3) 100.00

BROWNE,TURNER-Macmillan Biographical Cyclopedia of Photographic Artists & Innovators-NY-1983-Macmillan-722p-illus-1st prtg (cc9,as new in dj) 75.00

BROWNING,ELIZABETH B-Last Poems-Lond-1862-Chapman & Hall-8vo-xi,142,(2)p-1st ed (hh4,sl fade sp,part unopened) 425.00

BROWNING,J-John M Browning, American Gunmaker-NY-1964-323p-photos (gg3,f,dj) 15.00

BROWNING,MESHACK-Forty-Four Years of the Life of a Hunter-Winston-Salem-1942-8vo-400p-illus (m3,f,dj) 50.00

BROWNING,ROBERT-Pied Piper of Hamelin-Chig-(1910)-Rand McNally-4to-56p-g cl wi pict pasteon,col & monotone illus,H Dunlap-1928 ed (s3) 45.00

BROWNING,ROBERT-Pied Piper of Hamelin-Phila-nd-Lippincott-8vo-illus(incl 4 col)-1st ed (v10,f,sl chip dj) 75.00

BROWNLOW,W G-Sketches of the Rise, Progress, and Decline of Secession-Phila-1862-Geo W Childs-12mo-458,(8)p-frntis,13 plts-1st ed (n2,cov sl dull) 45.00

BROWNLOW,W G-Sketches of the Rise,Progress, and Decline of Secession-Phila-1862-458p+ads-cl-1st ed (j1,sp side reglued,cov spot) 15.00

BROWNSON,JAMES I-An Address Commemorative of the Life and Character of the Rev. David Elliot...-Pitt-1874-Robert S Davis & Co-85p-cl (j1,sl spot cov,sl wn sp) 17.50

BROWSE,L-Degas Dancers-Lond-1949-plts(incl 12 col)-1st Brit ed (ee1,dj sl tn) 225.00

BROYARD,ANATOLE-Aroused by Books-1974-Random-1st ed (m9,f,dj sp sl sunned) 20.00

BROYARD,ANATOLE-Aroused By Books-NY-1974-Random-1st ed (c10,as new in dj) 17.50

BRUAN,LIONEL H-Fanny Hill's Cook Book-NY-(1971)-Taplinger-137p-illus (q6) 20.00

BRUCCOLI,MATTHEW J-ED.-Raymond Chandler-Pitt-1979-U of Pitt-iss w/o dj-1st ed (h4,as new) 25.00

BRUCCOLI,MATTHEW J-James Gould Cozzens: A Life Apart-SD,NY,Lond-(1983)-HBJ-photos-1st ed (bb1,as new in dj) 10.00

BRUCCOLI,MATTHEW J-John O'Hara: A Descriptive Bibliography-Pitt-1978-324p-cl (a1) 20.00

BRUCCOLI,MATTHEW J-John O'Hara: A Descriptive Bibliography-Pitt-1978-UP Pr-w/o dj as iss-1st ed (x9,f) 45.00

BRUCE,ALFRED-Steam Locomotive in North America-1952-Bonanza-8vo-443p-illus (nn7,dj wn) 35.00

BRUCE,C G-Assault on Mount Everest-Lond-1923-339p-33 photos,2 fldg maps-1st Brit ed (a4) 165.00

BRUCE,CHARLES-Tomorrow's Tide-Tor-1932-MacMillan-sm 8vo-28p-grn cl,rag papr-1st ed (aa7) 25.00*

BRUCE,GEORGE-Sea Battles of the 20th Century-Lond-1975-Hamlyn-160p-illus (p8,sl spot,dj) 10.00

BRUCE,HENRY-Life of General Houston 1793-1863-NY-(1891)-232p-cl (e1) 25.00

BRUCE,J C-Cougar Killer-NY-1953-172p-photos (gg3,vf,dj) 45.00

BRUCE,J M-British Aeroplanes 1914 to 1918-NY-(1969)-thk 4to-viii,742p-cl,illus (t2) 85.00

BRUCE,LENNY-How to Talk Dirty and Influence People-Chig-1965-Playboy Pr-1st ed (oo2,f,dj) 70.00

BRUCE,LEO-Death in Albert Park-NY-1979-Scribner-1st Amer ed (q4,f,dj) 22.50

BRUCE,LEO-Death with Blue Ribbons-1970-London Hs-1st Amer ed (s10,dj) 20.00

BRUCE,LEO-Furious Old Women-Lond-1960-Davies-1st ed (s4,dj) 20.00

BRUCE,MINER-Alaska-Seattle-1895-Lowman & Hanford-128p-pict cl,photos,lg col fldg map in rear-v scarce-1st ed (f9,sl spot,wn) 150.00

BRUCE,ROBERT-Fighting Norths and Pawnee Scouts-Lincoln-1932-4to-72p-wrps,triple cols,illus-1st ed (mm10) 65.00

BRUCE,SIR MICHAEL-No Escape from Adventure-NY-(1954)-Hasting Hs-8vo-263p-18 illus-1st US ed (cc5,dj) 15.00

BRUCE,WILLIAM B-Letters Home 1859 to 1906-Moonbeam-1982-Penumbra Pr-8vo-254p-frntis,plts-1st ed (aa7) 15.00*

BRUCKER,HERBERT-Changing American Newspaper-NY-1937-Columbia Univ Pr-111p-cl-14p illus (l1) 12.50

BRUETTE,DR WM-American Duck,Goose & Brant Shooting-NY-1929-Watt Publ-415p-illus grn cl,col frntis,col plts,Davis,t.e. stnd grn (b6) 42.00

BRUETTE,DR.WILLIAM A-ED.-Sportsmen's Encyclopedia-NY-1923-12mo-233p-illus (m3) 10.00

BRUFF,J GOLDSBOROUGH-Gold Rush, the Journals, Drawings, and Other Papers of...-1949(1944)-Columbia U Pr-794p-Cal Centennial ed (d3,dj) 75.00

BRUMFIELD,KIRBY-This Was Wheat Farming-Seattle-(1968)-Superior-4to-191p-beige cl,illus (mm10,dj) 25.00

BRUNDAGE,BURR C-Phoenix of the Western World, Quetzalcoatl and the Sky Religion-Norman-1982-U of Okla Pr-xiv,2,3-349p-36 figs,map-1st ed (mm1,f,f dj) 35.00

BRUNDAGE,CARTWRIGHT-Two Earths Two Heavens-Albuquerque-1975-U of N Mex Pr-128p-gry cl-1st ed (mm1,f,f dj) 30.00

BRUNING,H F,JR.-Venetian Cooking-NY-(1973)-Macmillan-256p-1st prtg (q6) 20.00

BRUNN,H O-Story of the Original Dixieland Jazz Band-(1960)-Louisiana St-1st ed (w1,f,dj) 30.00

BRUNNER,JOHN-Foreign Constellations-NY-(1980)-Everest Hs-1st ed (k3,f,sp fray dj) 15.00

BRUNNER,JOHN-Into the Slave Nebula-NY-1968-Lancer-wrps-1st ed (v5,f) 15.00

BRUNNER,JOHN-Shockwave Rider-NY-(1975)-Harper & Row-1st ed (g3,f,dj) 20.00

BRUNNER,JOHN-Stand on Zanzibar-GC-1968-Dbldy-1st ed (g3,f,dj sl creased & rub) 85.00

BRUNO,H-Wings Over America-NY-(1942)-roy 8vo-cl,frntis,96p plts-1st ed (t2) 40.00

BRUNS,HANK-Angling Books of the Americas-Atlanta-1975-4to-543p-illus (m3,as new) 95.00

BRUNS,HANK-Angling Books of the Americas-Atlanta-1975-543p-grn cl,photos,ltd to 500c (ee3,as new) 85.00

BRUNS,URSULA-Connemara-Lond-1971-Harrap-transl by A Dent-1st ed in Engl (j9,dj) 35.00

BRUNS,URSULA-Ponies-Princeton-1961-Van Nostrand-4to-1st ed (j9,dj) 25.00

BRUNTON,PAUL-Message from Arunachala-Phila-1943-Blakiston-cl-2nd ed (n8) 20.00

BRUNTON,T LAUDER-Pharmacology and Therapeutics-Lond-1880-212p-scarce-1st ed (dd3) 125.00

BRUSKE,PAUL H-Story of a Pathfinding Expedition That Made its Own Path...From the Log of the Trip by P E Sands-Detr-nd(1911)-Studebaker Corp-(32)p-pict wrps,photos,W T Curtis-rare (b1) 125.00

BRUSKE,PAUL H-Story of a World's Record Setting Feat by a 20 Horse Power Motor Car...-Detr-nd(1911)-Studebaker Corp-(32)p-pict wrps,photos,auth-rare (b1) 125.00

BRUTON,ERIC-Diamonds-Phila-(1971)-Chilton-xi,373p-illus (u5,dj wn) 30.00

BRUUN,B-Birds of Europe-NY-1969-4to-321p-cl,col drwngs (y8,scuff) 30.00

BRY,DORIS-Alfred Stieglitz, Photographer-Bost-1965-Mus of Fine Arts-unpgd-62 photos-1st ed (cc9,as new in dj) 75.00

BRYAN,C D B-Friendly Fire-NY-(1976)-Putnam's-1st ed (b5,as new in dj) 40.00

BRYAN,E A-Historical Sketch of the State College of Washington 1890 to 1925-Pullman-(1928)-556p-illus (r8) 50.00

BRYAN,GEORGE S-Great American Myth-NY-(1940)-Carrick & Evans-xii+436p-blu cl,illus-1st ed (h2,dj) 50.00

BRYAN,GEORGE-ED.-Camper's Own Book-NY-1913-8vo-191p+ads-illus,photos (m3) 12.00

BRYAN,MARY E-Wild Work-NY-1881-410p-cl-Wright 745-1st ed (d1) 22.50

BRYAN,PEARL-THE MYSTERIOUS MURDER OF...THE HEADLESS HORROR-Cin-nd-Barclay-111p-pict wrps (l1,sl wn,few dog-eared lvs) 65.00

BRYAN,WM JENNINGS-Old World and Its Ways-St.Louis-1907-Thompson-8vo-574p-1st ed (ff5) 50.00

BRYAN,WM JENNINGS-Old World and Its Ways...-St.Louis-1907-574p-cl (l1) 17.50

BRYAN,WM S-History of the Pioneer Families of Missouri-Columbia-(1935)-Lucas Bros-569p-frntis-Howes B901 (ee4) 125.00

BRYANT,ARTHUR-Forest Trees, for Shelter, Ornament and Profit-NY-1871-Williams-247p-cl (x6) 22.50

BRYANT,ARTHUR-Great Duke-NY-1972-492p-maps,illus-1st Amer ed (b7,f,dj) 15.00

BRYANT,CHARLES S-History of the Great Massacre by the Sioux Indians-Cin-1864-Rickey & Carroll-504p+ads-illus-Howes B902 (dd4,fox) 75.00

BRYANT,H STAFFORD,JR.-Georgian Locomotive-Barre-1962-89p-1st ed (n4,f,dj) 20.00

BRYANT,KENNETH E-Poems to the Child God-Berkeley-1978-U of Cal Pr-cl-1st ed (n8,dj) 20.00

BRYANT,LORINDA M-Children's Book of Recent Pictures-NY-1934-Appleton Century-4to-100p-cl,illus-1st ed (r3) 15.00

BRYANT,NELSON-Fresh Air Bright Water-NY-1971-8vo-283p (m3,f,dj) 10.00

BRYANT,SETH-Shoe and Leather Trade of the Last Hundred Years-Bost-1891-S Bryant-136p-red cl,a.e.g.-1st ed (mm10,sl soil) 40.00

BRYCE,DR GEORGE-Romantic Settlement of Lord Selkirk's Colonists-Tor-1909-Musson Bk Co-8vo-328p-illus grn cl,frntis,illus-Peel 2038-1st ed (mm8,sp fade) 50.00*

BRYCE,GEORGE-Remarkable History of the Hudson's Bay Company-Lond-1902-Sampson Low Marston-501p-illus,maps-2nd issue (ll8,hng weak) 65.00

BRYCE,GEORGE-Remarkable History of the Hudson's Bay Company...Astor Fur Companies-Tor-1900-xx,501p-orig cl,illus,maps-Smith 1230 (a7,sl rub) 85.00

BRYCE,JAMES-South America-NY-1914-611p-rprnt (o10) 15.00

BRYK,F-Voodo Eros-1964-United Bk Guild-251p-photos-ltd to 500c (bb3) 10.00

BUBEL,MIKE-Root Cellaring-Emmaus-(1979)-Rodale Pr-297p-1st ed (l6) 20.00

BUBER,MARTIN-Good and Evil-NY-1953-Scribner's-cl-1st ed (l8,f) 20.00

BUCH,LEOPOLD VON-Travels Through Norway and Lapland, During the Years 1806, 1807...-Lond-1813-prtd for Henry Colburn-4to-460p-calf,fldg map-1st Brit ed (gg6) 450.00

BUCHAN,JOHN-Castle Gay-Lond-1930-Hodder & Stoughton-1st Brit ed (e10,sl soil dj) 150.00

BUCHAN,JOHN-Castle Gay-Lond-1930-Hodder & Stoughton-pict dj-1st ed (kk5,dj) 85.00

BUCHAN,JOHN-Comments and Characters-Lond et al-(1940)-T Nelson-1st Brit ed (e10,sl soil dj) 50.00

BUCHAN,JOHN-Dancing Floor-1926-HM-1st Amer ed (x7,dj sl wn & chip) 125.00

BUCHAN,JOHN-Free Fishers-1934-HM-1st Amer ed (x7,chip dj) 75.00

BUCHAN,JOHN-Green Mantle-1916-Doran-1st Amer ed (x7) 65.00

BUCHAN,JOHN-Greenmantle-Lond et al-1916-Hodder & Stoughton-scarce-1st Brit ed (e10,sml cov bruise) 175.00

BUCHAN,JOHN-Half Hearted-Lond-1900-Isbister-1st Brit ed (e10,sl fray,bk cov sl mottld) 45.00

BUCHAN,JOHN-House of the Four Winds-Bost-1935-Houghton-1st US ed (j4,sl fade sp,dj) 35.00

BUCHAN,JOHN-Island of Sheep-Lond-(1936)-Hodder & Staughton-1st Brit ed (e10,cor bump,chip dj) 95.00

BUCHAN,JOHN-King's Grace 1910 to 1935-Lond-(1935)-Hodder & Stoughton-1st Brit ed (e10,sp tan,dj sl spot,rprd) 50.00

BUCHAN,JOHN-Kirk in Scotland, 1560 to 1929-Lond-(1930)-Hodder & Stoughton-12mo-244p-4 illus-1st Brit ed (dd5,sp chip dj) 50.00

BUCHAN,JOHN-Lost Lady of Old Years-Lond & NY-1899-J Lane:Bodley Head-scarce-1st Brit ed (e10,sp brwnd,fray) 125.00

BUCHAN,JOHN-Magic Walking Stick-Lond-1932-Hodder & Stoughton-6 b&w plts,M Sale-1st Brit ed (e10,lt fox e.p.,dj soil,chip) 150.00

BUCHAN,JOHN-Massacre of Glencoe-np-1933-Peter Davies-1st Brit ed (e10,sp sl tan,dj) 125.00

BUCHAN,JOHN-Memory Hold the Door-Lond-1940-8vo-327p-photos-1st ed (m3) 17.50

BUCHAN,JOHN-Montrose-NY-1928-384p-illus-1st Amer ed (b7,f,dj) 50.00

BUCHAN,JOHN-Mountain Meadow-Bost-1941-Houghton-Rockwell Kent dj-1st ed (d4,f,dj) 20.00

BUCHAN,JOHN-Oliver Cromwell-Lond-(1934)-Hodder & Stoughton-gravure frontis,10 maps-1st Brit ed (e10,dj soil,sp brwnd & chip) 85.00

BUCHAN,JOHN-Prester John-(1910)-Doran-1st Amer ed (x7) 28.00

BUCHAN,JOHN-Runagates Club-Lond-1928-1st ed (f5) 75.00

BUCHAN,JOHN-Runagates Club-Lond-1928-Hodder & Stoughton-1st ed (gg8,chip dj) 45.00

BUCHAN,JOHN-Salute to Adventures-(1917)-HM (x7,f,dj) 30.00

BUCHAN,JOHN-Salute to Adventures-1915-Doran-1st Amer ed (x7) 30.00

BUCHAN,JOHN-Scholar Gipsies-Lond,NY-1896-J Lane:Bdly Hd/Macmillan-1st Brit ed (e10) 200.00

BUCHAN,JOHN-Scholar Gipsies-Lond-1896-8vo-206p-illus-2nd prntng (m3) 65.00

BUCHAN,JOHN-Sick Heart River-Lond-(1941)-Hodder & Stoughton-1st Brit ed (e10,sl wn dj) 85.00

BUCHAN,JOHN-Sir Quixote of the Moors-Lond-1895-scarce-1st issue bndg-auth 1st bk-1st ed (f5) 300.00

BUCHAN,JOHN-Thirty Nine Steps-Edinburgh,Lond-1915-1st ed (f5,frnt hng loose,brwnd pgs) 175.00

BUCHAN,JOHN-Three Hostages-1924-HM-pict dj-1st Amer ed (x7,dj) 135.00

BUCHAN,JOHN-Witch Wood-Cambridge-1927-Houghton Mifflin-pict dj,wi rare wrap around band-1st Amer ed (gg8,dj) 250.00

BUCHAN,JOHN-Witch Wood-Lond-(1927)-1st ed (f5,dj sp sl tan,sl tn) 150.00

BUCHAN,WILLIAM-Domestic Medicine-Leominster-1804-Isaiah Thomas,Jr.-484p-lea-scarce (dd3,lacks frnt e.p.,fox) 100.00

BUCHANAN,A R-ED.-Navy's Air War-NY-nd(ca.1946)-Harper-8vo-xvi,432p-cl,32p photos,3 maps (s2) 75.00

BUCHANAN,ANGUS-Wild Life in Canada-Lond-1920-xx,264p-illus (a7,sl soil) 45.00

BUCHANAN,GEORGE-Bodily Responses-Lond-(1958)-Gaberbocchus-1st ed (z8,f,dj) 22.50

BUCHANAN,LAMONT-Street Trails and Iron Horses-NY-1955-159p-1st ed (n4,f,dj) 18.00

BUCHANAN,LAMONT-World Series & Highlights of Baseball-1951-Dutton-photos-1st ed (s8,dj) 35.00

BUCHEN,GUSTAVE W-Historical Sheboygan County-(Sheboygan)-(1944)-347p-cl (c1) 32.50

BUCHENHOLZ,BRUCE-Doctor in the Zoo-NY-1974-Viking/Studio Bk-4to-191p-photos-1st prtg (f10,dj) 35.00

BUCHER,ELMER E-Practical Wireless Telegraphy-1917-336p-334 photos & illus-2nd ed (h6) 20.00

BUCHER,ELMER E-Vacuum Tubes in Wireless Communication-1919-202p-148 illus-1st ed (h6) 20.00

BUCK,ALBERT-Treatise on Hygiene and Public Health-Lond-1879-2 vols-scarce-1st Brit ed (dd3) 250.00

BUCK,B-Burning up the Sky-NY-1931-8vo-x,178p-cl,frntis,7p plts-1st ed (t2) 25.00

BUCK,DANIEL-Indian Outbreaks-Mankato-1904-284p-illus-Howes B914-1st ed (cc4,ex-libr) 100.00

BUCK,DANIEL-Indian Outbreaks-Mpls-1965-Ross & Haines-284p-illus-Howes B914 (dd4,dj) 20.00

BUCK,F-Animals are Like That-1939-McBride-240p-photos-1st ed (bb3,f) 32.00

BUCK,FRANK-On Jungle Trails-NY-1936-8vo-280p-photos (m3) 20.00

BUCK,J D-Mystic Masonry or the Symbols of Freemasonry and the Greater Mysteries of Antiquity-Cin-1897-Clarke Co-cl,frntis,illus-2nd ed (n8) 35.00

BUCK,PEARL S-Far and Near-NY-1947-John Day-1st ed (y1,dj) 40.00

BUCK,PEARL S-Patriot-1939-J Day-1st ed (x2,dj) 25.00

BUCK,PEARL-Fighting Angel-NY-(1936)-Day-1st ed (h3,chip dj) 15.00

BUCKBEE,EDNA B-Pioneer Days of Angel's Camp-Angel's Camp-(1932)-Calaveras Californian-(viii),80p-wrps,photos-1st ed (v1) 35.00

BUCKEYE COOKERY-Mpls-1881-Buckeye Publ Co-536p-grn bds-rvsd & enlgd ed (n6) 90.00

BUCKINGHAM AND CHANDOS,DUCHESS OF-Willy Wind and Jock and the Cheese-Lond-1905-A C Black-59p-illus by Eland(incl 8 tip in col plts) (oo10) 40.00

BUCKINGHAM,NASH-Best of ...-NY-1973-4to-320p-photos (m3,f) 20.00

BUCKINGHAM,NASH-De Shootinest Gent'man-Derrydale-1934-8vo-240p-ltd to 950c,nbrd-photos-scarce (m3,f) 525.00

BUCKINGHAM,NASH-De Shootinest Gent'man-NY-1943-Putnam-222p-photos (gg3,f) 50.00

BUCKINGHAM,NASH-Game Bag-NY-(1945)-Putnam's-illus by Hoecker-ltd to 1250c,nbrd,autg (p6,f) 300.00

BUCKINGHAM,NASH-Game Bag-NY-1945-8vo-186p-illus,Hoecker-1st trd ed (m3,f,fray dj) 47.50

BUCKINGHAM,NASH-Game Bag-NY-1945-Putnam-187p-illus (gg3,f) 45.00

BUCKINGHAM,NASH-Hallowed Years-Harrisburg-1953-8vo-209p-scarce-1st ed (m3) 80.00

BUCKINGHAM,NASH-Mark Right-NY-1936-Derrydale-250p-red cl,col medallion frnt cov,ltd to 1250c,nbrd,illus,E Burke (ee3,f) 225.00

BUCKINGHAM,NASH-Mark Right-NY-1936-Derrydale-8vo-red cl,cov medallion by E Burke-ltd to 1250c,nbrd-1st ed (u10) 350.00

BUCKINGHAM,NASH-Ole Miss'-NY-1946-Putnam-178p-photos (gg3,f) 45.00

BUCKINGHAM,NASH-Tattered Coat-NY-1944-8vo-210p-illus-3rd imprssn of trd ed (m3,f,chip dj) 50.00

BUCKINGHAM,NASH-Tattered Coat-NY-1944-8vo-210p-ltd to 995c,nbrd,autg-illus,A Fuller (m3,f) 200.00

BUCKINGHAM,NASH-Tattered Coat-NY-1944-Putnam-210p-photos (gg3,sl cov spot) 45.00

BUCKLAND,FRANK M-Fish Hatching-Lond-1863-8vo-268p-scarce-1st ed (m3) 35.00

BUCKLAND,FRANK M-Rhymes of the Stream & Forest-NY-1909-8vo-90p-frontis (m3,f) 25.00

BUCKLAND,GAIL-Reality Recorded-Greenwich-1974-NYGS-128p-205 photos-1st ed (cc9,as new in dj) 40.00

BUCKLER,ERNEST-Ox Bells and Fireflies-NY-1968-Knopf-8vo-302p-sketches-1st ed (jj5,sl scuff dj) 12.50

BUCKLEY,WILFRED-Art of Glass-1939-Phaidon Pr-142 plts-1st ed (cc8,covs scuff) 125.00

BUCKLEY,WILLIAM F,JR.-Cruising Speed-NY-(1971)-Putnam-8vo-257p-1st ed (jj5,dj,pres) 15.00

BUCKMAN,WILLIAMSON-Under the Southern Cross in South America-NY-1914-Book Publ Pr-8vo-blu dec cl,photos-1st ed (ee7,sp fade,sl wn) 35.00

BUDD,GEORGE-On the Organic Diseases and Functional Disorders of the Stomach-NY-1856-S & W Wood-283p-grn cl-1st Amer ed (j2,cov rub,sl fade sp) 45.00

BUDD,THOMAS-Good Order Established in Pennsylvania and New Jersey-Cleve-1902-80p-bds,plt (aa6,fox) 60.00

BUDD,WILLIAM-Typhoid Fever-NY-1931-184p-(facs of 1873 ed) (dd3) 100.00

BUDE,JOHN-Night the Fog Came Down-NY-1958-Washburn-1st US ed (g4,dj) 10.00

BUDGE,E A WALLIS-Osiris-New Hyde Park-1961-Univ Bks-illus-1st ed thus (y10,dj) 50.00

BUECHNER,FREDERICK-Entrance to Porlock-NY-1970-1st ed (s5,f,dj) 22.50

BUECHNER,FREDERICK-Long Day's Dying-NY-1950-auth 1st bk-1st ed (t5,as new in dj) 65.00

BUECHNER,FREDERICK-Season's Difference-NY-1952-Knopf-1st ed (b5,f,dj) 40.00

BUECHNER,FREDERICK-Treasure Hunt-NY-1977-Atheneum-1st ed (hh5,f,f dj) 15.00

BUECHNER,H K-Bighorn Sheep in the U S-1960-8vo-174p-wrps,frntis,illus (y8) 12.50

BUECHNER,THOMAS-Norman Rockwell-NY-(1970)-Abrams-lg folio-cl,fldg & tip in plts-1st ed (oo6,sl soil dj) 95.00

BUEL,J W-Fighting in Africa-NY-(1887)-502p-cl (f1,sl wn) 22.50

BUELL,AUGUSTUS C-Memoirs of Charles H Cramp-Phila-1906-Lippincott-269p-blu cl,plts-1st ed (l2,cov sl dmpstnd) 35.00

BUELL,AUGUSTUS-Cannoneer-Wash D.C.-1897-Nat'l Trib-384p-buckr(orig in wrps),maps,illus-Old Glory Libr (o7,rbnd,chip t.p.,yel pgs) 25.00

BUFFALO HISTORICAL SOCIETY-Peace Episodes on the Niagara-Buffalo-1914-BHS-x+383p-blu cl,plts-1st ed (m2) 25.00

BUFFET-CHALLIE,LAURENCE-Entertaining Today-Lond-(1971)-oblng 4to-212p-red cl,col drwngs-1st Engl lang ed (q8,dj) 30.00

BUGBEE,H D-Black Bull-Clarendon-1966-Clarendon Pr-yel wrps-1st ed (a9) 35.00

BUHL,HERMANN-Nanga Parbat Pilgrimage-Lond-1956-18 photos,3 maps-1st Brit ed (a4,f,dj) 150.00

BUICK,T LINDSAY-Moa Hunters of New Zealand-New Plymouth-1937-T Avery-12mo-260p-cl-scarce (y5) 20.00

BUICK,T LINDSAY-New Zealand's First War-Wellington-1926-304p-illus,maps-scarce (jj2,dj) 100.00

BUILDING WITH ASSURANCE-NY-1923-Morgan Woodwork Org-4to-439p-limp maroon cl,col illus-trade cat-2nd ed (r10,sl wn,1p tn) 85.00

BUIST,H M-Aircraft in the German War-Lond-1914-sm 8vo-128;8p-cl,frntis,5p plts-1st ed (t2) 25.00

BUIST,ROBERT-American Flower Garden Directory-NY-1865-Orange Judd-342p-cl (x6) 65.00

BUIST,ROBERT-Buist Garden Guide-Phila-1919-Buist-148p-col prntd cov,photos (x6) 25.00

BUIST,ROBERT-Family Kitchen Gardener-NY-1858(1847)-Moore-216p-cl (x6,lacks ffep,cl wn,brwng) 55.00

BUIST,ROBERT-Family Kitchen Gardener-NY/SF-1860-Saxton,Barker/Bancroft-8vo-vi,216,10p-stmpd grn cl,25 engrvngs (t10,sl rub) 75.00

BUKHARI,EMIR-Napoleon's Cavalry-San Rafael-1979-folio-illus,40 col plts-1st ed (gg2,f,dj) 50.00

BUKOWSKI,CHARLES-Bukowski Stories-SF-1972-City Lights-orig wrps (z2,f) 50.00

BUKOWSKI,CHARLES-Dangling in the Tournefortia-Santa Barbara-1981-illus bds-ltd to 350c,autg-1st ed (p5,f) 100.00

BUKOWSKI,CHARLES-Factotum-Lond-1981-WH Allen-1st Brit ed (f8,f,f dj) 45.00

BUKOWSKI,CHARLES-Poems Written Before Jumping Out of an 8 Story Window-Berkeley-nd-sftbnd orig,wrps-1st ed (s5) 85.00

BUKOWSKI,CHARLES-Post Office-Lond-1974-1st Brit ed (p5,f,dj) 40.00

BUKOWSKI,CHARLES-What a Man I Was-(1969)-Caterpillar-pict wrps-1st ed (hh10,f) 35.00

BULEY,E C-Glorious Deeds of Australasians in the Great War-Lond-1915-337p-blu dec cl,illus-1st ed (jj2) 45.00

BULEY,R C-American Life Convention,1906 to 1952-NY-1953-Appleton Century Crofts-2 vols-cl-1st ed (c2) 25.00

BULEY,R CARLYLE-Old Northwest Pioneer Period 1815 to 1840-Indpls-1950-2 vols-frntis,maps-1st ed (t7,box) 35.00

BULEY,R CARLYLE-Old Northwest Pioneer Period 1815 to 1840-Indpls-1950-2 vols-illus-1st ed (jj4,sl soil cov) 40.00

BULFINCH,T-Legends of Charlemagne-1924-Cosmopolitan-9p col plts,col pict e.p.,N C Wyeth-1st ed (x2) 125.00

BULGAKOV,MIKHAIL-Master & Margarita-NY-1967-Grove-1st US ed (z9,dj) 20.00

BULGAKOV,MIKHAIL-White Guard-NY-1971-McGraw Hill-1st ed (f8,f,dj) 45.00

BULL,J-Birds of the New York Area-NY-1964-8vo-540p-cl,drwngs,maps-1st ed (y8,sp fade) 14.00

BULL,RICE C-Soldiering, the Civil War Diary of...123rd New York Volunteer Infantry-San Rafael-(1977)-259p-illus,maps-1st ed (c4,f,dj) 30.00

BULLA,CLYDE R-White Bird-NY-(1966)-Crowell-drwngs,L Weisgard-1st ed (r3,f,fade dj) 18.00

BULLARD,F LAURISTON-Lincoln in Marble and Brass-New Brunswick-(1952)-353p-1st ed (c4,f,dj sl wn,chip) 27.50

BULLEN,FRANK T-Cruise of the Cachalot,Round the World After Sperm Whales-NY-1899-Appleton-grn cl wi g titles & cov dec,8 illus,(1st ed was Lond 1898)-Authorized ed (nn1,sl drknd sp,soil cov) 35.00

BULLEN,FRANK-Cruise of the Cachalot...-NY-1899-Intrn'l Bk & Publ-illus,fldg map (s3,cl dmpstnd) 12.00

BULLETT,GERALD-George Eliot-New Haven-1948-Yale-1st ed (z9,dj chip,tn) 15.00

BULLINS,ED-How Do You Do-Mill Valley-1967-Illuminations-wrps,auth 1st publ work-1st ed (v5) 25.00

BULLITT,ORVILLE-Search for Sybaris-Phila-(1969)-Lippincott-8vo-238p-18 photos,4 maps-1st ed (cc5,dj) 15.00

BULLOCK,BARBARA-Wynn Bullock-(SF)-(1971)-Scrimshaw Pr-sm folio-cl,plastic dj-1st ed (t3,dj) 225.00

BULLOCK,BARBARA-Wynn Bullock-(SF)-(1971)-Scrimshaw-4to-cl wi photo,orig glassine dj-1st ed (y3,dj) 185.00

BULLOCK,HELEN D-COMP.-National Treasury of Cookery-(1967)-Heirloom Publ-16mo-5 vols-pict bds,col plts by Chas Wysocki,intro by V Price (q8,rprd box) 25.00

BULLOCK,MOTIER A-Congregational Nebraska-Lincoln-1905-West Publ & Engrv Co-359p-cl (h1) 22.50

BULLOCK,PAUL-ED.-Watts: The Aftermath-NY-(1969)-Grove Pr-8vo-285p-1st ed (dd5,dj) 15.00

BULLOUGH,CHARLES-Song of the Salmon-Cambrdg,Lond-1903-oblng 8vo-unpgd-wrps-illus-scarce (m3) 25.00

BULPIN,T V-Ivory Trail-Capetown-1981-235p-dec bds (gg3,vf) 35.00

BULPIN,T V-Shaka's Country-Cape Town-1952-306p-illus-1st ed (b7,f,dj) 75.00

BUMP,G-ET AL-Ruffed Grouse-1947-NY Conserv Dept-915p-4 col plts,photos,drwngs-1st ed (bb3) 105.00

BUMP,G-ET AL-Ruffed Grouse-1947-NY State Conserv Dept-915p-4 painting by F Everett,127 sketches (c9,few cov mrks) 80.00

BUMP,G-ET AL-Ruffed Grouse-NY-1947-915p-red bds,gilt dec,coated papr,photos (gg3,f) 65.00

BUMSTEAD,JOHN-On the Wing-NY-1869-12mo-274p-illus-scarce-1st ed (m3,pres cpy) 35.00

BUNBURY,C J-Journal of a Residence at the Cape of Good Hope with Excursions into the Interior...-1969-Negro Univ-297p-illus-rprnt of 1848 ed (bb3,f) 35.00

BUNCE,WILLIAM K-ED.-Religions in Japan-Rutland/Tokyo-1955-Tuttle-xi,194p-grn cl-1st ed (ll1,wn dj) 10.00

BUND,J W WILLIS-Salmon Problems-Lond-1885-12mo-215p-scarce-1st ed (m3,ex-lib) 35.00

BUNDY,C LYNN-Maritime Association of the Port of New York-(1923)-Maritime Assn of NY-143p-illus-1st ed (pp4) 18.00

BUNIN,I A-Gentleman from San Francisco and Other Stories-Richmond-1922-Hogarth Pr-8vo-86p-bds,labls,errata-Woolmer 19-1st ed (nn4,sp drknd) 190.00

BUNKER,ROBERT-Other Men's Skies-Bloomington-1956-256p-drwngs,map-1st ed (v7,dj) 12.50

BUNN,MATTHEW-Journal of the Adventures of...-Chig-1962-Newberry Libr-wrps,ltd to 2000c prtd by Stinehour Pr (w3,vf) 15.00

BUNNING,JIM-ET AL-Grand Slam-1965-Viking-photos-1st ed (s8,f,dj) 20.00

BUNT,CYRIL G E-Goldsmiths of Italy-Lond-1926-M Hopkinson-xv,182p-g blu cl,t.e.g,tip-in col frntis,21 plts-1st ed (u5,ex-libr) 200.00

BUNTON,MARY T-Bride on the Old Chisholm Trail in 1886-San Antonio-1939-77p-frntis,illus-Herd #354-1st ed (t7,f,sl chip dj) 75.00

BUNTS,FRANK E-Letters From the Asiatic Station, 1881 to 1883-Cleve-1938-Caxton-219p-blu cl-ltd to 350c (z9,sp sunned) 20.00

BUNYAN,JOHN-Pilgrim's Progress...with notes, by the Rev. J Newton, Dr.Hawker, and Others.-Cin-1813-prtd by J W Browne & Co-282p-lea-Ohio Imprnts 174,Amer Imprnts 28044 (b1,rbkd,wn) 300.00

BUNYARD,GEORGE-Fruit Garden-Lond-1904-Country Life-sm 4to-xiii,507p-photos,drwngs-scarce-1st ed (mm4) 85.00

BUNZEL,RUTH L-Pueblo Potter-NY-1928-Columbia U Pr-tall-130p-dbl col,photos-Zuni sect in 2 col-rare-1st ed (u7) 300.00

BUNZEL,RUTH L-Zuni Texts-NY-1933-Amer Ethno Soc,Vol.XV-285p-Boas,ed.-v scarce (u7,f) 200.00

BUONASSISSI,VINCENZO-Pasta-Wilton-(1976)-Lyceum-371p-dec wht cl,col illus-1st US ed (q8,f,dj) 20.00

BURANELLI,PROSPER-Big Nick-GC-1931-Dbldy-1st ed (w5,sl chip dj) 35.00

BURBANK,LUTHER-Training of the Human Plant-NY-1907-Century-12mo-(vi)+99p-grn cl-1st ed (g2,sl rub) 25.00

BURBANK,W H-Photographic Negative-NY-1888-Scovill Mfg-198p-1st ed (cc9,sp wn) 75.00

BURBANK,W H-Photographic Printing Methods-NY-1887-Scovill Mfg-221p-1st ed (cc9,sp wn) 125.00

BURCH,JOHN P-Charles W Quantrell-(Vega)-(1923)-pict cl,illus-Six Guns 323-1st ed (gg4) 45.00

BURCHETT,WILFRED-Vietnam: Inside Story of Guerilla War-NY-1965-Int'l Publ-1st ed (c8,f,f dj) 45.00

BURD,CLARA M-Mother Goose and Her Goslings Pictured in Colors by ...-(NY)-nd-Hartman Farm Dairy-16p-col pict wrps-12 col illus by Burd (h1) 15.00

BURDEKIN,HAROLD-London Night-Lond-1934-Collins-sm folio-112p-cl,gravures-2nd impr (q3,dj) 75.00

BURDEKIN,K-Children's Country-1929-Morrow-8p col plts-1st ed (x2,dj sl wn & chip) 55.00

BURDEN,W A M-Struggle for the Airways in Latin America-NY-(1943)-4to-xxiv,246p-cl,8p plts,39 text illus,11 maps incl one in rear pckt,errata slip (t2,stnd e.p.) 50.00

BURDEN,W DOUGLAS-Dragon Lizards of Komodo-NY-1927-8vo-221p-photos,e.p. maps-1st ed (m3) 70.00

BURDETT,CHARLES-Life of Kit Carson-NY-1902-376p-col frntis-Rader #539 (t7,dj) 20.00

BURDICK,JOEL W-Our World Tour, 1922 to 23...-Pitt-1923-priv prtd-134p-lea-1st ed (pp4,edge rub) 15.00

BURDICK,USHER L-Jacob Horner and the Indian Campaigns of 1876 and 1877-Balt-1942-Wirth Bros-30p-wrps,illus,map-1st ed (dd4) 25.00

BURDICK,USHER L-Last Battle of the Sioux Nation-Stevens Point-(1929)-Worzalla Publ-164p-illus-1st ed (bb4) 75.00

BURDICK,USHER L-Last Battle of the Sioux Nation-Stevens Pt-(1929)-Worzalla-12mo-2 maps,24 illus-v scarce-1st ed (a6,edgewn) 60.00

BURDICK,USHER L-Life and Exploits of John Goodall-Watford City-1931-McKenzie Cnty Farmer-29p-wrps-Herd 360-1st ed (dd4) 30.00

BURDICK,USHER L-Tragedy in the Great Sioux Camp-Balt-1936-15p-prtd wrps,illus,map-scarce-1st ed (t7,f) 40.00

BURESH,LUMIR F-October 25th and the Battle of Mine Creek-KC-1977-Lowell Pr-265p-maps,e.p. maps,illus (cc6,dj) 55.00

BURESH,LUMIR-October 25th and the Battle of Mine Creek-KC-1977-Lowell Pr-265p-maps,e.p. maps,illus (v2,as new in dj) 60.00

BURET,F-Syphillis in Ancient and Prehistoric Times. Vol.1-Phila-1891-226p-1st Engl transl (dd3) 75.00

BURGE,C G-ED.-Encyclopedia of Aviation-Lond-1935-sm 4to-642p-cl,plts incl one col,text illus,illus e.p.-1st ed (t2,dj missing pcs) 45.00

BURGER,J F-African Buffalo Trails-Lond-1967-221p-grn cl,illus (ee3,f) 130.00

BURGER,J F-Horned Death-WV-1947-342p-dec covs-1st ed (gg3,f) 75.00

BURGES,ARNOLD-American Kennel & Sporting Field-Brklyn-1876-8vo-201p-illus-1st ed (m3) 70.00

BURGESS,AL-Everest Canada-Tor-1983-214p-115 col plts-1st ed (o10,f,dj) 35.00

BURGESS,ANTHONY-1985-Bost-(1978)-Little,Brown-1st ed (j3,f,dj) 20.00

BURGESS,ANTHONY-Clockwork Orange-1962-Heinemann-1st ed (x2,f,dj) 675.00

BURGESS,ANTHONY-Clockwork Testament or Enderby's End-NY-1975-13 drwngs-1st Amer ed (hh10,f,dj) 25.00

BURGESS,ANTHONY-Cyrano De Bergerac-NY-1971-1st US ed (s5,dj) 22.50

BURGESS,ANTHONY-Ernest Hemingway and His World-Lond-(1978)-116 illus-1st ed (r2,f,dj) 30.00

BURGESS,ANTHONY-Honey for the Bears-NY-1964-1st US ed (t5,dj) 30.00

BURGESS,ANTHONY-Napoleon Symphony-NY-1974-1st US ed (n5,chip dj) 12.50

BURGESS,ANTHONY-On Going to Bed-NY-(1982)-Abbeville Pr-95p-illus-1st US ed (k6) 25.00

BURGESS,ANTHONY-Rejoyce-1965-Norton-1st Amer ed (x2,vf,vf dj) 28.00

BURGESS,ANTHONY-Right to Answer-NY-1961-1st US ed (p5,sp sunned dj) 30.00

BURGESS,ANTHONY-Tremor of Intent-1966-Norton-1st ed (m9,dj sp drknd) 30.00

BURGESS,FREW W-Old Prints and Engravings-NY-1948-Tudor-thk 8vo-79 illus-1st ed (w1,f,dj) 20.00

BURGESS,G H O-Eccentric Ark-NY-(1967)-Horizon-8vo-242p-15 photos-1st US ed (dd5,f,dj) 20.00

BURGESS,GELETT-Maxims of Methuselah...in Regard to Women-NY-(1907)-Stokes-cl sp,pict bds-illus,L D Fancher-1st ed (f2,sl wn) 20.00

BURGESS,GELETT-Maxims of Noah derived from his Experiences with Women...-NY-(1913)-Stokes-cl sp,pict bds-illus,L D Fancher-1st ed (f2,sl wn) 20.00

BURGESS,GELETT-Rubaiyat of Omar Cayenne-NY-(1904)-1st ed (hh10) 30.00

BURGESS,JAMES A-Burgess, Mullins, Browning, Brown and Allied Families-Parsons-1978-262p-cl (j1,f) 20.00

BURGESS,P H E-Diamonds Unlimited-Lond-1960-Adventurers Club-191p-plts (u5,dj) 20.00

BURGESS,THORNTON W-Adventures of Bobby Coon-Bost-1918-Little,Brown-12mo-117p-pict cl,illus by H Cady-1st ed (hh9) 65.00

BURGESS,THORNTON W-Adventures of Chatterer the Red Squirrel-Bost-1916-Little,Brown-12mo-120p-pict cl,illus by H Cady-early rprnt (hh9) 35.00

BURGESS,THORNTON W-Adventures of Jimmy Skunk-Bost-1918-Little,Brown-12mo-118p-pict cl,illus by H Cady-1st ed (hh9) 60.00

BURGESS,THORNTON W-Adventures of Ol'Mistah Buzzard-Bost-1919-Little,Brown-12mo-119p-pict cl,illus by H Cady-1st ed (hh9) 60.00

BURGESS,THORNTON W-Adventures of Poor Mrs.Quack-Bost-1917-Little,Brown-12mo-119p-pict cl,illus by H Cady-1st ed (hh9) 65.00

BURGESS,THORNTON W-Adventures of Prickly Porky-Bost-1916-Little,Brown-12mo-116p-pict cl,illus by H Cady-1st ed (hh9) 65.00

BURGESS,THORNTON W-Adventures of Sammy Jay-Bost-1915-Little,Brown-12mo-119p-pict cl,illus by H Cady-1st ed (hh9,cov sl soil) 75.00

BURGESS,THORNTON W-Now I Remember-Bost-1960-Little,Brown-8vo-viii,340p-frntis-1st ed (ff9,dj tn) 25.00*

BURK,JOHN N-Life and Works of Beethoven-NY-(1943)-Random-8vo-483p-1st ed (bb5,f,dj) 25.00

BURKE,CARLETON-Symphony Iroquoian-NY-1937-Rochstr Mus Arts & Sci-70p-1st ed (gg4) 15.00

BURKE,DR.EDGAR-American Dry Flies & How to Tie Them-Derrydale-1931-12mo-25p-ltd to 500c-photos,errata slip-scarce (m3) 400.00

BURKE,E-History of Archery-NY-1957-224p-photos (gg3,f,dj) 25.00

BURKE,EDMUND-Philosophical Inquiry into the Origin of Our Ideas of the Sublime and Beautiful-Ehittingham-1825-Chiswick Pr-16mo-158p-orig cl,papr labl (x6,stnd,wn,chip labl,sl fox) 125.00

BURKE,HELEN-Kippers to Caviar-Lond-(1965)-Evans-263p-pebbld grn cl,wood engrvngs-1st ed (q8,dj) 15.00

BURKE,JAMES L-Half of Paradise-Bost-1965-Houghton Mifflin-auth 1st bk-scarce-1st ed (a10,sl tn dj) 500.00

BURKE,JOHN-Beatles, A Hard Day's Night-1964-Dell-wrps,photos-1st ed (x2) 15.00

BURKE,JOHN-Buffalo Bill-NY-(1973)-320p-1st ed (n3,f,dj) 22.50

BURKE,JOHN-Legend of Baby Doe-NY-(1974)-Putnam's-8vo-273p-cl-1st ed (z4,f,dj) 20.00

BURKE,JOHN-Legend of Baby Doe-NY-(1974)-Putnam-8vo-273p-8p photos-1st ed (gg5,dj) 10.00

BURKE,RICHARD-Red Gate-Chig-1947-Ziff-1st ed (g4,f,dj) 12.00

BURKE,T-East of Mansion House-1926-Doran-1st ed (x7,sl chip dj) 55.00

BURKE,THOMAS-Limehouse Nights-NY-1917-McBride-1st US ed (g4,sl fray) 10.00

BURKE,THOMAS-Murder at Elstree-Lond-1936-Longmans,Green-1st ed (w9,tape rprd dj) 90.00

BURKE,THOMAS-Wind and the Rain: a Book of Confessions-Lond-1924-T Butterworth-greenish brwn prtd cl-Colonial or "overseas issue"-1st ed (gg8,fox,dj sl chip & tn) 65.00

BURKHALTER,LOIS-Seth Eastman Sketchbook-San Antonio-1961-M Koogler-4to-1st ed (a6,f,dj) 35.00

BURKHARDT,FRANK A-Pioneer Days of George H A Burkhardt-(LA)-1935-31,(1)p-wrps (j1) 17.50

BURL,AUBREY-Prehistoric Avebury-New Haven-1979-Yale U Pr-4to-275p-13 col plts-1st ed (cc5,f,tape rprd dj) 20.00

BURLEIGH,BENNET-Two Campaigns: Madagascar and Ashantee-Lond-1896-555p-gry dec cl,plts-1st ed (kk2) 150.00

BURLEIGH,T D-Birds of Idaho-Caldwell-1972(c.1971)-8vo-467p-cl,12 col plts,photos,1 map (y8,dj) 30.00

BURLEIGH,T D-Birds of Idaho-Caldwell-1972-Caxton Pr-467p-photos (d9) 35.00

BURLEIGH,T D-Georgia Birds-Norman-1958-lg 8vo-746p-cl,35 col plts,15 maps-1st ed (y8,dj) 80.00

BURLESON,HUGH L-Conquest of the Continent-NY-1911-212p-stiff wrps,illus,col fldg map,dblpg map-3rd ed (r8) 25.00

BURLINGAME,H J-Magician's Handbook-Chig-(1942)-298p-pict wrps (g1) 15.00

BURLINGAME,MERRILL G-Montana Frontier-Helena-(1942)-State Publ.-xvi,418p-cl,illus,maps,map e.p.-Montana's Best Bks#45-1st ed (v1) 35.00

BURLINGHAM,DOROTHY-Twins-Lond-(1952)-Imago Publ-x+94p-grn cl,30 charts-1st ed (j2) 30.00

BURLINGTON-Constitution and Act of Incorporation of the Endeavour Fire Company of...Instituted 1795...-Burlington-1857-14,(2)p-wrps (aa6) 75.00

BURNAP,GEORGE W-Lectures on the Sphere and Duties of Woman and Other Subjects-Balt-1841-John Murphy-272p+ads-cl (j1) 35.00

BURNE,LT COL ALFRED H-Art of War on Land-Lond-1944-Methuen-illus-1st ed (z2,f) 20.00

BURNE,LT COL ALFRED H-Strategy in World War Two-Harrisburg-1947-Military Serv Publ-1st ed (z2,f) 20.00

BURNELL,ROY-Gundogs for Field or Trial-Wollstonecraft-1972-4to-198p-photos-1st ed (m3,f,dj) 27.50

BURNETT,ALF-Incidents of the War-Cin-1863-Rickey & Carroll-310p-cl-scarce (h1,edge wn,sp sl wn & chip) 75.00

BURNETT,AVIS-Gertrude Stein-NY-1972-Atheneum-1st ed (z9,f,dj) 10.00

BURNETT,FRANCES H-Editha's Burglar-Bost-1888-Jordan Marsh-sq 8vo-red cl stmpd in blk & gilt,illus by Sandham-1st ed,1st state (x3) 55.00

BURNETT,FRANCES H-Good Wolf-NY-1908-Moffat,Yard-125p-pict cl,5 tip in col plts by H Sichel-1st ed (oo10) 50.00

BURNETT,FRANCES H-Hawworth's-NY-1879-Scribner-8vo-374p+ads-brwn cl-BAL 2051-1st ed (w6) 35.00

BURNETT,FRANCES H-In the Closed Room-NY-1904-McClure,Phillips-130p-g cl,8 col plts,Jessie Willcox Smith-2nd prtg (s3,few pgs stnd) 45.00

BURNETT,FRANCES H-Sara Crewe-NY-(1981)-Putnam's-sm 4to-79p-cl & bds,col & b&w illus,M Tomes-1st ed thus (r3,f,dj sl chip & tn) 20.00

BURNETT,W R-Adobe Walls-NY-1953-Knopf-279p-bds-1st ed so stated (b1,dj) 15.00

BURNETT,W R-Asphalt Jungle-NY-1949-Knopf-1st ed (kk9,f,f dj) 150.00

BURNETT,W R-Captain Lightfoot-NY-1954-Knopf-1st ed (f4,f,dj) 15.00

BURNETT,W R-Dark Hazard-1933-Harper-1st ed (x7,sl tn dj) 30.00

BURNETT,W R-Giant Swing-NY-1932-art deco e.p.s-1st ed (s5,dj) 90.00

BURNETT,W R-Good Bye Chicago-NY-1981-St.Martin's-1st ed (g4,f,dj) 12.50

BURNETT,W R-Goodhues of Sinking Creek-NY-1934-Harper & Row-5p col wdcuts,J J Lankes-1st ed (q2,dj chip,sm pcs missng) 35.00

BURNETT,W R-Iron Man-1930-Dial-1st ed (x7,sp chip dj) 35.00

BURNETT,W R-Iron Man-Tor-1930-Longman's,Green-pict dj-1st Can ed (gg8,f,sl wn dj) 65.00

BURNETT,W R-Little Men, Big World-NY-1951-1st ed (n5,dj) 35.00

BURNETT,W R-Nobody Lives Forever-NY-1943-Knopf-1st ed (g4,dj) 25.00

BURNETT,W R-Pale Moon-NY-1956-1st ed (r5,dj) 35.00

BURNETT,W R-Pale Moon-NY-1956-1st ed (s5,dj) 35.00

BURNETT,W R-Roar of the Crowd-1964-Potter-drwngs,R Hoban-1st ed (s8,dj) 12.50

BURNETT,W R-Tomorrow's Another Day-NY-1945-Knopf-1st ed (w5,f,f dj) 35.00

BURNETT,W R-Vanity Row-1952-Knopf-1st ed (s10,sp wn dj) 20.00

BURNETT,W.R.-Romelle-NY-1946-Knopf-1st ed (a5,sl soil dj) 40.00

BURNETTE,ROBERT-Tortured Americans-Englewood Cliffs-(1971)-Prentice Hall-176p,index+photo portfolio-1st ed (cc4,dj) 15.00

BURNEY,COMMANDER SIR C D-World, the Air and the Future-Lond-1929-8vo-xxvi,356p-cl,g sp,frntis,22p plts,2 maps (t2) 75.00

BURNEY,JAMES-History of the Buccaneers of America-NY,Lond-1891-Aberdeen U Pr-8vo-xv,382p-blu cl,g sp title,t.e.g.-rprnt of 1816 ed (p8,hngs weak) 45.00

BURNEY,JAMES-With Capt Cook in the Antarctic & the Pacific-Canberra-(1975)-illus-1st ed (g7,f,dj) 45.00

BURNHAM,CAPT. GEO P-Memoirs of the United States Secret Service-Bost-1872-Laban Heath-8vo-viii+436p,illus,Bricher & Conant,presumed 1st ed (z4,wn cov,fr hng sl split) 85.00

BURNHAM,CLARA L-Dr.Latimer, a Story of Casco Bay-Bost,NY-1893-Houghton,Mifflin-384p-cl-Wright 821-1st ed (g1) 15.00

BURNHAM,FREDERICK R-Scouting on Two Continents-GC-1926-Dbldy,Page-370p-illus-Six Guns #333 (ee4) 35.00

BURNHAM,FREDERICK R-Scouting on Two Continents-GC-1926-Dbldy,Page-8vo-xxii,370p-photos,illus-Graff 498-1st ed (aa3) 50.00

BURNHAM,FREDERICK R-Scouting on Two Continents-GC-1927(1926)-Dbldy,Page-370p-g brwn cl,illus (p2) 25.00

BURNS,ANNALEE-Gone are the Days-S.A.-1960-Naylor-95p-1st ed (a9,dj) 25.00

BURNS,EUGENE-Advanced Fly Fishing-Harrisburg-1953-8vo-268p-photos,illus,F Everett-1st ed (m3,f) 80.00

BURNS,EUGENE-Complete Book of Fresh & Salt Water Spinning-NY-1955-8vo-256p-illus (m3,f,dj) 12.00

BURNS,EUGENE-ED.-An ANgler's Anthology-Harrisburg-1952-4to-147p-illus (m3,dj) 14.00

BURNS,EUGENE-Last King of Paradise-NY-1952-Pellegrini & Cudahy-8vo-xxv,345p-grn cl (nn1,fade) 20.00

BURNS,JOHN H-Gallery-NY-1947-auth 1st bk-1st ed (t5,dj) 45.00

BURNS,JOHN-Dissertations on Inflammation-Albany-1812-E F Backus-2 vols in one-calf,red sp labl-Austin 357-1st Amer ed (c2,sl rub) 115.00

BURNS,REX-Angle of Attack-NY-(1979)-Harper & Row-1st ed (f3,f,dj) 30.00

BURNS,REX-Fansworth Score-NY-(1977)-Harper & Row-1st ed (f3,f,dj) 40.00

BURNS,REX-Fansworth Score-NY-(1977)-Harper & Row-1st ed (p3,f,dj) 25.00

BURNS,ROBERT H-ET AL-Wyoming's Pioneer Ranches-Laramie-1955-Top of The World Pr-752p-cl,photos,ltd to 1000c,nbrd-Herd #377-v scarce-1st ed (w3,f,two autg,ancmnt laid in) 300.00

BURNS,ROBERT-Complete Poems of...-Bost-1926-Houghton Mifflin-8vo-ten vols-cl sp wi labls over pap bds,Lg Pap Ed,ltd to 750 sets (t1,f) 350.00

BURNS,S J-Jesuits & the Indian Wars of the Northwest-New Haven,Lond-1966-512p+16p illus-Yale Wstrn Amer Ser #11-1st ed (d7,f,dj) 75.00

BURNS,W J-Crevice-1915-Watt-auth 1st bk-scarce in dj-1st ed (x7,dj) 95.00

BURNS,WALTER N-Robin Hood of El Dorado-NY-(1932)-Coward-McCann-304p-Six Guns #336-1st ed (cc4,sm cov spot) 15.00

BURNS,WALTER N-Robin Hood of Eldorado-NY-(1932)-304p (t7,dj) 20.00

BURNS,WALTER N-Saga of Billy the Kid-NY-1926-322p-pict e.p.-Dykes #107 (t7,dj) 20.00

BURNS,WALTER N-Tombstone-GC-1927-Dbldy,Page-388p-Six Guns 338-1st ed (gg4) 25.00

BURNS,WILLIAM-ED.-Natural History of the Southwest-NY-1960-Watts-4to-1st ed (a6,chip dj) 35.00

BURNS,WM A-Practical Sheep Husbandry-Chig-1931-Exch Bldg/U.S. YDS-96p-illus (bb4) 15.00

BURNT TOAST-LA-1940-Women's Aux of Cal...Hosp-223p-bds-1st ed (q6) 25.00

BURPEE,LAWRENCE J-Among the Canadian Alps-Tor-1918-MG&S-239p-g red cl,4 col illus,45 photos,5 maps (cc7,sl bump) 50.00*

BURPEE,LAWRENCE J-ED.-Flowers From a Canadian Garden-Tor-(1909)-Musson-24mo-pict wrps-scarce-1st ed (pp2) 75.00*

BURR,AGNES R-Alaska-Bost-1919-Page-8vo-xii,428p-pict grn cl,fldg map,54plts(incl 6 col)-1st ed (y4) 45.00

BURR,AGNES-Alaska: Our Beautiful Northland of Opportunity-Bost-1919-Page-lg 8vo-428p-dec & g cl,illus,fldg map,"See America First" series-1st ed (w1) 75.00

BURR,FRANK A-Life of Gen Philip H Sheridan-Providence-1888-Reid-445p-pict cl,frntis,illus (o7,hngs weak) 25.00

BURR,GEORGE L-Narratives of the Witchcraft Cases 1648 yo 1706-NY-1914-Scribner's-xviii+467+(3)p+ 3 facs plts,grn cl-1st ed (y9) 50.00

BURR,MAJOR DANGERFIELD-Buffalo Bill, the Buckskin King-NY-April 21,1880-Beadle & Adams-23,(1)p-self wrps(punched along bndg edge)-N.Y. Dime Library No.92 (b1) 25.00

BURR,NELSON R-Education in New Jersey, 1630 to 1871-Princeton-1942-(12),355p-cl,plts (aa6) 45.00

BURRAGE,HENRY S-Maine in the Northeastern Boundary Controversy-Portland-1919-Marks Prntg Hs-xvi+398p-blu cl,illus,4 fldg maps-1st ed (h2) 65.00

BURRAGE,HENRY S-Thomas Hamlin Hubbard-Portland-1923-66p (hh3,cov spot) 37.50

BURRAGE,WALTER L-History of the Massachusetts Medical Society-(Bost)-1923-priv prtd-505p-illus (g10) 50.00

BURRARD,G-Modern Shotgun-NY-1964-2 vols-photos (ee3,vf,box) 100.00

BURRARD,MAJ GERALD-Fly Tying Principles & Practice-Lond-1940-12mo-216p-illus (m3) 30.00

BURRARD,MAJ GERALD-Guns & Shooting-NY-1962-12mo-147p (m3,f,soil dj) 12.50

BURRARD,MAJ GERALD-In the Gunroom-Lond-1951-12mo-147p-revsd & enlrgd ed (m3) 30.00

BURRILL,KATHERINE-Amateur Cook-Lond-nd(ca.1910)-Chambers-296p-pict grn cl,e.p. & 12 illus by M L Atwell,red bordered text (q8,edgewn,hngs weak) 75.00

BURRO BOOK-Pueblo-(1900)-S M McCandless-39p-tied,wrps-photos (f1) 35.00

BURROUGHS,ALAN-Art Criticism from a Laboratory-Bost-1938-Little,Brown-xxiv+277p-gry cl,133 figs on plts-1st ed (d2,dj) 30.00

BURROUGHS,ALAN-Limners & Likenesses-Cambridge-1936-4to-191p (a3) 55.00

BURROUGHS,EDGAR R-At Earth's Core-NY-nd-G&D-8 plts-early rprnt (v5,f,dj sp sl tn) 40.00

BURROUGHS,EDGAR R-At the Earth's Core-NY-nd(1923)-G&D-8 plts by J A St.John-1st G&D ed (ff6,cov sl wrnkld,dj sl chip) 85.00

BURROUGHS,EDGAR R-Beasts of Tarzan-Chig-1916-McClurg-illus by St.John-scarce-1st ed (bb1) 500.00

BURROUGHS,EDGAR R-Beasts of Tarzan-NY-nd-G&D-frontis,illus by J A St.John (d5,dj edges sl wn) 85.00

BURROUGHS,EDGAR R-Carson of Venus-Tarzana-(1939)-1st ed (bb10,dj chip,tape rnfrcd) 175.00

BURROUGHS,EDGAR R-Carson of Venus-Tarzana-(1939)-ERB,Inc-6 plts by J C Burroughs-1st ed (b10,f,dj) 325.00

BURROUGHS,EDGAR R-Carson of Venus-Tarzana-(1939)-ERB-1st ed (v5,f,sl chip dj) 175.00

BURROUGHS,EDGAR R-Deputy Sheriff of Comanche County-Tarzana-(1940)-Burroughs-1st ed (k4,dj) 350.00

BURROUGHS,EDGAR R-Deputy Sheriff of Comanche County-Tarzana-(1940)-ERB,Inc-illus,J C Burroughs-1st ed (b10,sl drknd sp,dj sl tn,chip 400.00

BURROUGHS,EDGAR R-Fighting Man of Mars-Tarzana-(1948)-ERB-frntis by Hutton-orig publ in 1931 (bb1,dj) 45.00

BURROUGHS,EDGAR R-Girl From Hollywood-NY-(1923)-Macauley-frntis by P J Monahan-1st ed,1st iss (bb1,sm sp hole,sl fray cor) 75.00

BURROUGHS,EDGAR R-Jungle Tales of Tarzan-1919-McClurg-1st ed (x2,dj sl chip & soil) 1,750.00

BURROUGHS,EDGAR R-Jungle Tales of Tarzan-Chig-1919-McClurg-St.John,illus wi frontis & 4 plts,1st bndg-1st ed (a5,sl soil,lacks dj) 300.00

BURROUGHS,EDGAR R-Land of Terror-Tarzana-(1944)-ERB,Inc-1st ed (b10,f,dj) 500.00

BURROUGHS,EDGAR R-Llana of Gathol-Tarzana-(1948)-ERB,Inc-1st ed (dd2,publ slip pasted in,f,dj) 135.00

BURROUGHS,EDGAR R-Mad King-NY-nd(1927)-G&D-frntis by St.John-1st G&D ed (ff6,f,sl chip dj) 85.00

BURROUGHS,EDGAR R-Princess of Mars-NY-1917-McClurg-illus by Schoonover-1st ed (m4,sl crease sp) 400.00

BURROUGHS,EDGAR R-Savage of Pellucidar-NY-1963-Canaveral-1st ed (l3,f,dj) 40.00

BURROUGHS,EDGAR R-Tarzan and the Castaways-NY-1975-Canaveral Pr-6 b&w drwngs,F Frazetta-reissue of 1964 ed (b10,as new in dj) 50.00

BURROUGHS,EDGAR R-Tarzan and the Foreign Legion-Tarzana-(1947)-Burroughs-1st ed (k3,f,sl wn dj) 55.00

BURROUGHS,EDGAR R-Tarzan and the Golden Lion-NY-nd-G&D-rprnt (j8,f,dj) 45.00

BURROUGHS,EDGAR R-Tarzan and the Jewels of Opar-1918-McClurg-1st ed (x2,dj sp fade & sl chip) 2,875.00

BURROUGHS,EDGAR R-Tarzan and the Jewels of Opar-NY-nd-G&D-rprnt (j8,f,dj) 45.00

BURROUGHS,EDGAR R-Tarzan Lord of the Jungle-Chig-1928-McClurg-1st ed (o3,sunned sp,lacks dj) 45.00

BURROUGHS,EDGAR R-Tarzan of the Apes-Chig-1914-McClurg-auth 1st bk-red cl-"W.F. Hall Printing Co. Chicago" at bot of cpyrt pg in two lines old Engl type-1st ed,1st bndg (d5,sm rear cov spt,sl fd sp) 1,000.00

BURROUGHS,EDGAR R-Tarzan the Terrible-NY-nd-G&D-rprnt (j8,f,dj) 45.00

BURROUGHS,EDGAR R-Tarzan Triumphant-Tarzana-(1932)-frontis,S Burroughs-1st ed (d5,cor bump,dj sp sl chip) 275.00

BURROUGHS,J-Harriman Alaska Expedition-NY-1901-lg 8vo-2 vols-grn cl,t.e.g.,16 col plts,Fuertes,2 by Knight,7 by Walpole,14 of landscapes & 85 plts,5 maps-1st ed (y8,cors wn,vol.2 jnts crackd) 365.00

BURROUGHS,JOHN R-Steamboat in the Rockies-Ft.Collins-1974-208p-illus-1st ed (t7,dj) 12.50

BURROUGHS,JOHN-Burroughs' Complete Works-1921-Houghton Mifflin-12 vols (bb3) 65.00

BURROUGHS,JOHN-Camping & Tramping with Roosevelt-Bost-1907-12mo-111p-photos (m3) 14.00

BURROUGHS,WILLIAM S-Cities of the Red Night-NY-(1981)-HRW-1st ed (e8,f,f dj) 25.00

BURROUGHS,WILLIAM S-Cities of the Red Night-NY-(1981)-HRW-1st ed (q1,vf,dj) 40.00

BURROUGHS,WILLIAM S-Exterminator-NY-(1973)-Viking-1st ed (q1,sl wn dj) 40.00

BURROUGHS,WILLIAM S-Last Words of Dutch Schultz-NY-1975-1st ed (o5,dj) 40.00

BURROUGHS,WILLIAM S-Naked Lunch-NY-(1962)-Grove-blk cl/bds-1st US ed (c5,dj) 100.00

BURROUGHS,WILLIAM S-Nova Express-NY-(1964)-1st US ed (o5,dj) 25.00

BURROUGHS,WILLIAM S-Nova Express-NY-(1964)-Grove-orng cl-1st ed (f2,dj) 30.00

BURROUGHS,WILLIAM S-Soft Machine-1966-Grove Pr-1st ed (kk6,f,sl nick dj) 35.00

BURROUGHS,WILLIAM S-Soft Machine-NY-1966-Grove Pr-1st ed (q2,sl tn dj) 45.00

BURROUGHS,WILLIAM S-Third Mind-Lond-(1979)-John Calder-1st Brit ed (q1,f,dj) 30.00

BURROUGHS,WILLIAM S-Ticket That Exploded-NY-1967-1st US ed (o5,f,dj) 50.00

BURROWS,ABE-Songs-NY-1955-Dbldy-1st ed (u4,sl chip dj) 20.00

BURROWS,V E-Tramways in Metropolitan Essex Vol.1-Huddersfield-1967-163p-1st ed (n4,f,dj) 14.00

BURRUS,ERNEST J-ED.-Kino's Biography of Francisco Javier Saeta-1971-Jesuit Hist Inst-363p-fldg map (d3) 45.00

BURRUS,ERNEST J-ED.-Wencelaus Linck's Reports and Letters 1762 thru 1778-LA-1967-Dawson Bk Shp,trav ser.#9-94p-frntis,maps-1st ed (t7,f) 12.50

BURT,ELINOR-Olla Podrida-Caldwell-1941-Caxton-277p-dec red cl-2nd prtg (q8) 35.00

BURT,MARY E-ED.-Boy General-NY-1901-204p-dec cl,photos-1st ed (t7,ex-libr) 15.00

BURT,OLIVE-John Charles Fremont-NY-(1955)-Messner-192p-illus-1st ed (bb4,dj) 20.00

BURT,STRUTHERS-Diary of a Dude Wrangler-1924-Scribner-331p-frntis-Six Guns #343-1st ed (r8) 40.00

BURT,STRUTHERS-Powder River, Let 'er Buck-NY-1938-Farrar-389p-illus by Ross Santee-1st ed (d3) 25.00

BURT,W H-Field Guide to the Mammals-Bost-1959-12mo-(2),200p-cl,24 col plts (y8,dj chip) 12.50

BURTON,E MILBY-Charleston Furniture 1700 to 1825-Charleston-1955-Charleston Mus-4to-150p-rust cl,illus (r10) 30.00

BURTON,J A-ED.-Owls of the World-1973-A&W-4to-216p-wrps,col plts,photos (bb3) 40.00

BURTON,J A-ED.-Owls of the World-NY-1973-4to-216p-col illus,90 col photos,maps (y8,dj) 45.00

BURTON,J-Lectures on Female Education and Manners-Elizabeth Town-1799-S Kollock for C Davis-280,(4)p-contemp sheep-5th Amer ed (aa6,sp chip) 300.00

BURTON,JEAN-Heyday of a Wizard-NY-(1944)-Knopf-sm 8vo-(x)+275+(7)p+frntis port-dec grn cl-1st ed (y9,dj) 22.50

BURTON,JEAN-Sir Richard Burton's Wife-NY-1941-378p-illus-1st ed (b7,dj) 15.00

BURTON,JIMALEE-Indian Heritage, Indian Pride-Norman-1974-U of Okla Pr-4to-176p-cl,illus,auth-1st ed (z4,sl spot t.e.,dj) 35.00

BURTON,JOHN A-ED.-Owls of the World-NY-1973-Dutton-216p-illus by J Rignall,photos,maps (c9,chip dj) 30.00

BURTON,KATHERINE-Make the Way Known-NY-(1959)-291p-cl-1st prntng (f1,f,dj) 17.50

BURTON,MAURICE-Animal Courtship-Lond-(1953)-Hutchinson-8vo-268p-22 photos,sketches-1st ed (dd5,dj) 15.00

BURTON,MAURICE-Encyclopedia of Fish-Lond-1975-4to-253p-photos (m3,f,dj) 20.00

BURTON,MAURICE-Systematic Dictionary of Mammals of the World-NY-1962-8vo-307p-illus (y8,dj stnd) 15.00

BURTON,MILES-Hardway Diamonds Mystery-1930-Mystery League-1st Amer ed (s10,slant,dj) 20.00

BURTON,MILES-Hardway Diamonds Mystery-NY-1930-Mystery League-1st US ed (l4,dj) 15.00

BURTON,MILES-Look Alive-NY-1950-Dbldy CC-1st US ed (f4,yel pgs,dj) 20.00

BURTON,MILES-Platinum Cat-1938-DD CC-1st ed (x7,rnfrcd dj) 65.00

BURTON,MILES-Written in Dust-1940-DD CC-1st ed (x7,dj) 65.00

BURTON,R-Carnivores of Europe-1979-Batsford-176p-col & b&w photos,maps-1st ed (bb3,f,dj) 23.00

BURTON,RICHARD-Christmas Story-NY-1964-Morrow-8vo-31p-drwngs by Fruhauf-1st ed (bb7,chip dj) 25.00*

BURTON,RICHARD-City of Saints and Across the Rocky Mountains to California-NY-1963-Knopf-1st Borzoi ed (v4,vf,wn dj) 25.00

BURTON,RICHARD-City of the Saints, and Across the Rocky Mountains to California-NY-1862-Harper & Bros-574p-illus,map-1st ed (d3,rebckd) 90.00

BURTON,RICHARD-Selected Papers on Anthropology, Travel & Exploration-Lond-1924-A M Philpot Ltd-8vo-240p-tan calf,maroon mor sp labls-1st ed (t10,rbnd) 200.00

BURTON,RICHARD-TRANSL.-Kama Sutra of Vatsyayana-Lond-1963-Allen & Unwin-cl-3rd imprssn (l8,f,dj) 25.00

BURTON,RICHARD-TRANSL.-Kasidah of Haji Abdu El Yezdi-Phila-1931-McKay-dec cov,g lettrng,12p illus,W Pogany-1st ed (y10) 75.00

BURTON,RICHARD-TRANSL.-Kasidah of Haji Abdu El-Yezdi-Phila-(1931)-David McKay-219p-cl,frntis & 11p plts,Willy Pogany (c1) 20.00

BURTON,ROBERT-Anatomy of Melancholy...-Bost-1859-3 vols-engrvd frntis (dd3,vf) 200.00

BUSBEY,HAMILTON-Trotting & the Pacing Horse in America-NY-1904-Macmillan-1st ed (h9) 45.00

BUSBEY,L WHITE-Uncle Joe Cannon...-NY-(1927)-362p-cl-1st ed (n1) 15.00

BUSCH,FREDERICK-Manual Labor-NY-1974-New Directions-1st ed (y1,f,f dj) 50.00

BUSENBARK,ERNEST-Symbols,Sex, and the Stars in Popular Beliefs-NY-1949-Truth Seeker Co-cl,88 plts-1st ed (n8,dj) 25.00

BUSEY,JOHN W-Regimental Strengths at Gettysburg-Balt-1982-258p-ltd to 1000c,nbrd-1st ed (c4,f) 25.00

BUSGEN,M-Structure and Life of Forest Trees-1929-Chapman Hall-436p-173 figs (bb3) 36.00

BUSH,CHRISTOPHER-Case of the Deadly Diamonds-NY-1969-Macmillan-1st US ed (g4,f,dj) 10.00

BUSH,CHRISTOPHER-Case of the Good Employer-NY-1966-Macmillan-1st Amer ed (s4,f,dj) 20.00

BUSH,CHRISTOPHER-Case of the Russian Cross-NY-1958-Macmillan-1st US ed (g4,dj) 10.00

BUSH,CHRISTOPHER-Case of the Triple Twist-NY-1958-Macmillan-1st US ed (f4,f,sl wn dj) 10.00

BUSH,CHRISTOPHER-Dancing Death-NY-1931-Dbldy CC-1st US ed (f4,f) 10.00

BUSH,CHRISTOPHER-Tea Tray Murders-NY-1934-Morrow-1st US ed (g4) 12.50

BUSH,W L-Saga of Duck & Goose Hunting-1978-Am Wildlife Art Galleries-223p-coated papr,col plts (gg3,vf,dj,2 autg) 75.00

BUSH,WESLEY A-Paradise to Leeward-NY-1954-4to-140p-photos-1st ed (m3) 35.00

BUSHICK,FRANK H-Glamorous Days-San Antonio-1934-Naylor-308p-photos-Six Guns #349-1st ed (cc4,edges wn) 65.00

BUSHNELL,G H-From Bricks to Books, a Miscellany-Lond-1949-Grafton-8vo-160p-cl-1st ed (w2,dj sp pc missng) 10.00

BUSS,CLAUDE A-Asia in the Modern World-NY,Lond-1964-Macmillan/Collier Macmll-xiii,767p-mustard col cl,maps (ll1,wn dj) 20.00

BUSTARD,R-Sea Turtles-1972-Collins-220p-24 photos-1st ed (bb3,f,dj) 25.00

BUTCHER,BERNARD L-Genealogical and Personal History of the Upper Monongahela Valley, West Virginia-NY-1912-3 vols (jj3) 175.00

BUTCHER,D-Exploring Our National Wildlife Refuges-Bost-1963-8vo-(1),340p-wrps,photos-2nd ed (y8) 15.00

BUTKOVSKY-HEWITT,ANNA-With Gurdjieff in St.Petersburg and Paris-NY-1978-Samuel Weiser-1st Amer ed (n8,f,dj) 25.00

BUTLER,A C-Persimmons-Taylorville-(1915)-Parker Publ-189p-cl-revsd ed (k1) 15.00

BUTLER,ARTHUR G-Birds of Great Britain and Ireland-Lond-(1904,08)-Caxton-2 vols-cl,lea labls,115 col plts (p6,rbnd) 450.00

BUTLER,ARTHUR-TRANSL-Memoirs of Baron De Marbot-Lond-1892-2 vols-3/4 grn calf,g tooled sp,linen e.p.,t.e.g.,maps,plts-1st Brit ed (kk2,sp sun) 225.00

BUTLER,E M-Heinrich Heine-Lond-1956-Hogarth Pr-1st ed (z9,sl cocked,dj chip,tn) 12.50

BUTLER,E M-Ritual Magic-Lond-1949-Cambridge U Pr-cl,plts,text figs-1st ed (o8) 95.00

BUTLER,E M-Silver Wings-1953-Putnams-1st ed (x7,dj) 25.00

BUTLER,ELLIS P-Josephus & the Jet Hackle-1927-priv prntd-12mo-11p-wrps-scarce (m3) 60.00

BUTLER,FRANCES A-Star of Seville-Lond-1837-Saunders & Otley-8vo-146p-3/4 calf & mrbld bds-rare-1st Brit ed (w6,sp wn) 300.00

BUTLER,FRANK H-Wines and the Wine Lands of the World-Lond-(1926)-T Fisher Unwin-271p-blu bds wi tip in bkplt,illus (n6) 50.00

BUTLER,FREDERICK-Farmer's Manual-Hartford-1819-Goodrich-224p-1/2 lea,mrbld cov bds (x6,rub) 225.00

BUTLER,GWENDOLINE-Nameless Coffin-Lond-1966-Bles-1st ed (r4,f,dj) 25.00

BUTLER,HAL-Al Kaline and the Detroit Tigers-1973-Regnery-1st ed (ff2,dj) 50.00

BUTLER,HAL-Al Kaline and the Detroit Tigers-Chig-(1973)-271,(1)p-cl (n1,dj wn & rprd) 12.50

BUTLER,HAL-Bob Allison Story-1966-Messner (r7,f,dj) 25.00

BUTLER,HAL-Harmon Killebrew Story-1966-Messner (r7,dj) 30.00

BUTLER,HAL-Harmon Killebrew Story-1966-Messner-1st ed (q7,dj) 45.00

BUTLER,HOWARD R-Painter and Space-NY-1923-39 illus(7 col)-1st ed (r2) 40.00

BUTLER,JAMES D-Incentives to Mental Culture Among Teachers-Bost-1852-TR&F-33p-prntd wrps (k1) 15.00

BUTLER,JOHN-Text Book of Electro Therapeutics and Electro Surgery...-NY,Phila-1880-Boericke & Tafel-323,(1)p+publ catlg-cl,wdct illus-2nd ed (m1) 20.00

BUTLER,JUNE-Floralia-Chapel Hill-1938-U of NC-187p-cl-ltd to 500c (x6,lacks box) 25.00

BUTLER,M B-My Story of the Civil War and the Under Ground Railroad-Huntington-1914-United Brethren Publ-390p-illus-1st ed (ee4,cor bump) 100.00

BUTLER,RAGAN-Captain Nash & the Wroth Inheritance-1975-Harwood-1st ed (s10,dj) 12.50

BUTLER,SAMUEL-Erewhon Revisited-1901-G Richards-1st ed (x2) 75.00

BUTLER,SIR W F-Wild North Land-Lond-1907-illus-1st ed (r2) 35.00

BUTLER,WILLIAM V-Durable Desperadoes-Lond-(1973)-Macmillan-288p-1st ed (g9,dj) 30.00

BUTLER,WILLIAM-An Autobiography-Lond-1911-476p-blk cl,illus,maps-1st ed (gg2,sl wn sp) 100.00

BUTLIN,MARTIN-Turner Watercolours-NY-1965-Watson Guptill-4to-84p-red cl,32 col illus (r10,f,f dj) 22.50

BUTTERBAUGH,WAYNE E-Atlas of Traffic Maps-Chig-1924-LaSalle Ext Univ-43 fldg maps (gg9,sl spot bds) 100.00

BUTTERFIELD,CONSUL W-History of Seneca County-Sandusky-1848-Campbell-251,(1)p-cl (l1,sl wn sp,sl dmpstnd) 100.00

BUTTERFIELD,CONSUL W-History of the Girtys-Cin-1890-Robert Clarke-426p-cl-Howes B1066-scarce-1st ed (a1) 150.00

BUTTERWORTH,HEZEKIAH-Log School House on the Columbia-1890-Appleton-250p-silv dec cov,illus-1st ed (r8) 25.00

BUTTERWORTH,W E-Soldiers on Horseback-NY-1967-141p-photos,illus-1st ed (t7,dj) 25.00

BUTTERY,MRS ORVILLE-Llano County Centennial-Llano-1956-Cent Assoc-36p-wrps,photos,ads-1st ed (w3) 25.00

BUTTON,SUSAN S-Poems-Litchfield-1858-8vo-336p-stmpd cl,engrvd port-1st ed (w6) 45.00

BUTTREE,JULIA M-Rhythm of the Redman-NY-(1930)-Barnes-280p-pict cl,col illus-1st ed (ff4) 50.00

BUXTON,ANTHONY-Happy Year-Lond-1950-8vo-191p-photos (m3,f,dj) 10.00

BUXTON,ANTHONY-Traveling Naturalist-Lond-1948-12mo-224p-photos (m3,vf,dj) 10.00

BUXTON,AUBREY-King in His Country-Lond-1955-8vo-139p-photos-1st ed (m3,f,fray dj) 15.00

BUXTON,E N-Short Stalks, Second Series-Lond-1898-226p-photos,pckt maps frnt & rear (gg3,cov sl spot,sl fox) 75.00

BUXTON,SYDNEY-Fishing & Shooting-NY-1903-8vo-268p-illus,A Thorburn (m3,f) 25.00

BUZZACOTT,FRANCIS H-Buzzacott's Masterpiece...-Mlwk-1913-12mo-544p-illus,photos (m3,f) 25.00

BUZZACOTT,FRANCIS H-Complete American & Canadian Sportsman's Encyclopedia-Chig-1908-12mo-521p-illus (m3) 22.50

BYAS,HUGH-Japanese Enemy-NY-1942-Knopf,Borzoi-107p-1st ed (c3,sl fox,dj) 12.00

BYATT,A S-Still Life-NY-(1985)-Scribners-1st Amer ed (dd2,f,dj) 45.00

BYBEE,CORA B-History of Syracuse-Springville-1965-255p-pict cl,frntis,photos-1st ed (t7) 25.00

BYERS,S H M-Happy Isles and Other Poems-Chig-1901-Rand,McNally-162p-3rd ed (o7,pres) 25.00

BYFIELD,BARBARA N-Eating in Bed Cookbook-NY-(1962)-Macmillan-103p-bds dec in mattress ticking design,illus e.p. (m6) 25.00

BYLES,MARIE B-Paths to Inner Calm-Lond-1965-Allen & Unwin-cl-1st ed (n8) 15.00

BYNE,A-Majorcan Houses & Gardens-1928-Helburn-lg folio-188 plts-1st ed (h10,sl soil sp) 300.00

BYNE,A-Provincial Houses in Spain-NY-1925-Wm Helburn-folio-(8)p text,190 plts,cl (cc10) 135.00

BYNE,A-Spanish Gardens & Patios-Phila-1924-175 illus,4 col plts (h10,sl tn dj) 150.00

BYNE,MILDRED-Spanish Gardens and Patios-NY-1928-Archit Rec-305p-cl,4 col plts (x6) 125.00

BYNNER,WITTER-Jouney with Genius-NY-(1951)-356p-photo-1st ed (u7) 45.00

BYRD,CECIL K-Bibliography of Illinois Imprints, 1814 to 1858-Chig-(1966)-U of Chig-xxvi+601p-brwn cl-1st ed (h2,dj) 55.00

BYRD,RICHARD E-Alone-NY-1938-Putnam's-8vo-xii,296p-cl,text illus,R E Harrison (t2,chip dj) 20.00

BYRD,RICHARD E-Discovery-NY-1935-8vo-xxiv,406p-cl,g dj,frntis,plts,map,e.p. maps-1st ed (t2,sp fade,stnd,dj chip,autg) 100.00

BYRD,RICHARD E-Discovery: the Story of the Second Byrd Antarctic Expedition-NY-1935-Putnam's-illus,maps-1st ed (v4,dj) 25.00

BYRD,RICHARD E-Little America-NY-1930-422p-cl-maps,photos-1st ed so stated (e1) 17.50

BYRD,RICHARD E-Little America-NY-1930-8vo-xvi,422p-g cl,port,col t.p.,55p plts,4 maps(2 fldg),illus e.p.-1st ed (t2,dj missing pcs,autg) 100.00

BYRD,RICHARD E-Skyward-NY-1928-8vo-xvi,360p-g cl,frntis,46 illus,e.p. maps,1st iss wi photogravure port of auth-1st ed (t2) 75.00

BYRD,RICHARD E-Skyward...-Chig-1981-Lakeside Pr-388p-cl-Lakeside Classic ed (j1,f) 15.00

BYRD,WILLIAM-London Diary-NY-1958-OUP-viii+647p-blu cl-1st ed (h2,dj) 30.00

BYRNE,DONN-Hangman's House-NY,Lond-(1926)-Century-illus,J R Flanagan-1st ed (a10,dj) 20.00

BYRNE,P E-Soldiers of the Plains-NY-1926-Milton,Balch-xii,260p-red cl-1st ed (v1,sl stnd bndg) 65.00

BYRNE,REV STEPHEN-Irish Emigration to the United States-NY-1873-Catholic Publ Scty-165p+ads-purple cl-1st ed (h2) 60.00

BYRNE,W E R-Tale of the Elk-Richwood-1940-priv prntd-8vo-455p-scarce (m3,vf) 100.00

BYRON,HON JOHN-Byron's Journal of His Circumnavigation 1764 to 1766-Cambridge-1964-Hakluyt Scty-8vo-lxxxii,230p-blu cl,illus,fldg map (nn1,dj) 45.00

BYRON,LORD-Hebrew Melodies-Lond-1815-John Murray-1/2 lea-1st ed,2nd iss w/o ads (l9,sl fox,rbnd) 250.00

BYRON,LORD-Marino Faliero Doge of Venice and the Prophecy of Dante, a Poem-Lond-1821-John Murray-lea-1st ed,2nd issue (l9,sp wn) 500.00

BYRON,LORD-Selected Letters and Journals-Cambridge-1982-Harvard U Pr-400p-1st ed (j8,f,dj) 25.00

BYRON,LORD-Works of...-Phila-1825-Pomeroy-16mo-8 vols in 4-g stmpd 1/2 lea,16 engrvngs (m4,edge rub) 50.00

BYRON,ROBERT-Station; Athos: Treasures and Men-NY-1949-Knopf-cl,frntis,illus-1st Amer ed (o8,fray dj) 17.50

BYRON-CURTISS,A L-Life and Adventures of Nat Foster...-Utica-1897-12mo-286p-illus,photos-scarce-1st ed (m3) 75.00

CABANNE,P-Brothers Duchamp-Bost-1976-NYGS-50 col & 130 b&w illus-1st ed (ee1,dj) 185.00

CABELL,G A-Safari, Pan Am's Guide to Hunting with Gun & Camera...-NY-1968-319p-photos,maps (gg3,f,dj) 12.00

CABELL,JAMES B-Devil's Own Dear Son-NY-1949-1st ed (r2,f,dj sp sl sun) 30.00

CABELL,JAMES B-Jurgen-NY-1919-1st state-1st ed (l5) 100.00

CABELL,JAMES B-Line of Love-NY-1905-Harper & Bros-grn cl wi gold lttrng,wht decs,col illus on frnt,col plts by H Pyle-1st ed (k8,f) 65.00

CABELL,JAMES B-Music From Behind the Moon-NY-1926-John Day Co-4to-55p-cl,8 wood engrvngs-1st ed (q3) 85.00

CABELL,JAMES B-Silver Stallion-NY-1926-McBride-1st ed (k8,dj) 20.00

CABELL,JAMES B-Taboo-NY-1921-McBride-ltd to 920c,nbrd-1st ed (t4) 25.00

CABELL,JAMES B-There Were Two Pirates-NY-1946-Farrar Straus-dec e.p.,illus-1st ed (t4,dj) 25.00

CABELL,JAMES B-Way of Ecben-1929-McBride-1st Trd ed (r9) 30.00

CABELL,JAMES B-Way of Ecben-NY-1929-209p-bds-1st impr so stated (e1,box wn & tn) 20.00

CABINET COOK BOOK-Springfield-(1901)-Phelps Publ-440p-illus wrps (n6) 25.00

CABLE,B-Air Men O' War-Lond-1918-sm 8vo-x,246p-illus cl-1st ed (t2,sp fade) 25.00

CABLE,GEORGE W-Amateur Garden-NY-1914-Scribner's-12mo-ix,199p-cl,39 plts-1st ed (cc10) 35.00

CABLE,GEORGE W-Bonaventure-NY-1888-Scribner's-maroon cl-BAL 2346-1st ed (f2) 50.00

CABOT,JOHN-Cabot Voyages and Bristol Discovery Under Henry VII-Cambridge-1962-Hakluyt Scty-8vo-xvi,330p-blu cl,maps,illus,Second Ser:No.CXX (nn1,drknd dj) 50.00

CABOT,RICHARD C-Layman's Handbook of Medicine with Special Reference to Social Workers-Bost-1916-524p-1st ed (g10) 20.00

CABRERA INFANTE,G-Three Trapped Tigers-NY-1971-Harper & Row-auth 1st bk-1st US ed (g8,f,dj) 40.00

CADDY,EILEEN-Spirit of Findhorn-NY-1976-Harper & Row-cl,illus-1st ed (n8,f,dj) 12.50

CADELL,ELIZABETH-Corner Shop-1967-Morrow-1st Amer ed (s10,dj) 15.00

CADFRYN-ROBERTS,JOHN-ED.-British Sporting Prints-Lond-1963-8vo-14p+plts-illus (m3,f,dj) 17.50

CADY,JACK-Burning-Iowa City-(1972)-U of Iowa Pr-8vo-157p-1st ed (bb5,dj rub,sl tn) 15.00

CADY,JOHN H-Civic and Architectural Development of Providence-Providence-1957-Book Shop-4to-xvi+320p-blu cl,illus,maps-1st ed (m2,sl spot dj) 75.00

CAELIUS AURELIANUS-On Acute Diseases and on Chronic Diseases-Chig-(1950)-U of Chig-xxviii+viii+1019p-red cl-1st ed (d2,dj) 75.00

CAESAR,GENE-King of the Mountain Men-NY-1961-317p-illus-1st ed so stated (c7,f,dj) 35.00

CAESAR,GENE-King of the Mountain Men-NY-1961-317p-photos,maps-1st ed (t7,dj) 20.00

CAFFREY,NANCY-Scene From the Saddle-NY-1958-Dutton-1st ed (f10,dj) 18.00

CAGE,JOHN-Silence-Middletown-1961-Wesleyan Pr-auth 1st bk-1st ed (y1,f,dj) 100.00

CAGE,JOHN-Year From Monday-Middletown-1967-Wesleyan Pr-1st ed (y1,dj) 75.00

CAGLE,MALCOLM W-Sea War in Korea-Annapolis-(1957)-US Naval Inst-xx+555p-blu cl,illus,maps-presumed 1st ed (k2,dj) 25.00

CAHN,ROBERT-American Photographers & the National Parks-NY-1981-Viking-sm folio-col & b&w photos-1st ed (a6,f,box) 50.00

CAIDIN,M-Air Force-NY-(1957)-4to-viii,232p-cl,illus t.p.,plts,text illus (t2,sp fade,dj) 25.00

CAIDIN,M-Golden Wings-NY-(1960)-4to-8;232p-cl bkd bds,illus t.p.,illus (t2,dj) 35.00

CAIDIN,M-Spaceport U.S.A.-NY-1959-Dutton-380p-photos,drwngs,diags-1st ed (hh6,dj chip,sp tn & drknd) 35.00

CAIDIN,M-Tigers are Burning-NY-(1974)-Hawthorn-8vo-243p-16p photos-1st ed (cc5,dj) 20.00

CAIDIN,M-Vanguard-NY-1957-Dutton-8vo-288p-illus-1st ed (dd5,sl tn dj) 20.00

CAIDIN,M-War for the Moon-NY-1959-8vo-258p-cl,illus (t2,dj) 30.00

CAIN,JAMES M-Baby in the Icebox-NY-(1981)-HR&W-1st ed (a5,f,dj) 15.00

CAIN,JAMES M-Baby in the Icebox-NY-(1981)-HR&W-1st ed (cc2,f,dj) 25.00

CAIN,JAMES M-Butterfly-NY-1947-1st ed (t5,dj) 25.00

CAIN,JAMES M-Butterfly-NY-1947-Knopf-1st ed (e4,dj) 20.00

CAIN,JAMES M-Cloud Nine-NY-(1984)-Mysterious Pr-1st ed (bb1,f,sl wn dj) 15.00

CAIN,JAMES M-Institute-NY-1976-Mason/Charter-1st ed (c10,f,dj) 25.00

CAIN,JAMES M-Love's Lovely Counterfeit-1942-Knopf-1st ed (x7,rnfrcd dj) 110.00

CAIN,JAMES M-Love's Lovely Counterfeit-NY-1942-Knopf-1st ed (z2,f,dj) 250.00

CAIN,JAMES M-Magician's Wife-1965-Dial-1st ed (s10,dj) 15.00

CAIN,JAMES M-Mignon-1962-Dial-1st ed (r9,f,sp wn dj) 20.00

CAIN,JAMES M-Mildred Pierce-NY-1941-1st ed (t5,sl wn dj) 130.00

CAIN,JAMES M-Moth-NY-1948-Knopf-1st ed (bb2,dj) 55.00

CAIN,JAMES M-Moth-NY-1948-Knopf-1st ed (z2,f,f dj) 85.00

CAIN,JAMES M-Our Government-1930-Knopf-auth 1st bk-1st ed (x7,sl fade sp) 85.00

CAIN,JAMES M-Past All Dishonor-NY-1946-Knopf-1st ed (cc2,f,rub dj) 50.00

CAIN,JAMES M-Past All Dishonor-NY-1946-Knopf-1st ed (e4,f,dj) 35.00

CAIN,JAMES M-Rainbow's End-NY-1975-Mason/Charter-1st ed (a5,f,sl chip dj) 12.50

CAIN,JAMES M-Serenade-NY-1937-red iss of dec dj-1st ed (t5,dj) 150.00

CAIN,JAMES M-Three of a Kind-NY-1943-1st ed (t5,dj) 100.00

CAIN,JULIEN-Lithographs of Chagall 1962 thru 1968-Bost-(1969)-Bost Bk & Art Shop-1st Amer ed (l9,sl creased dj) 350.00

CAINE,LOU S-Game Fish of the South & How to Catch Them-NY-1935-8vo-259p-illus (m3,fray dj) 12.50

CAINE,LOU S-North American Fresh Water Sport Fish-NY-1949-8vo-212p-illus (m3,vf,dj) 10.50

CAIRD,JANET-Murder Scholastic-1968-CC-1st Amer ed (s10,dj) 12.50

CAIRIS,NICHOLAS T-North Atlantic Passenger Liners Since 1900-Lond-(1972)-224p-1st ed (pp4) 25.00

CAIRNS,BILL-Fly Casting with ...-Lexington-1974-4to-107p-photos-1st prntng (m3,vf,dj) 15.00

CAIRNS,KATE-Bobbie-Richmond-1899-B F Johnson Publ-134,(1)p-cl-1st ed (l1) 22.50

CAIRNS,MARY L-Grand Lake in the Olden Days-(Denver)-(1971)-308p-cl (c1) 25.00

CAIRNS,MARY L-Grand Lakes-Denver-1946-295p-frntis,photos,map e.p.-scarce-1st ed (t7,f,chip dj) 27.50

CAKE,PATRICK-Pro Am Murders-Aptos-1979-Proteus-illus-1st ed (w9,f,dj) 30.00

CALDECOTT,MOYRA-Lily and the Bull-NY-(1979)-Hill & Wang-1st US ed (l3,f,dj) 15.00

CALDECOTT,RANDOLPH-Great Panjandrum Himself-Lond-nd-F Warne-sq 4to-24p-pale gold pict bds,col illus-early rprnt (nn8) 45.00

CALDER,JENNI-Women and Marriage in Victorian Fiction-NY-1976-Oxford-223p-cl,illus-1st ed (z5,dj) 25.00

CALDER,ROBERT-Dogs-np-(1976)-Delacorte/Quicksilver-1st ed (bb1,as new in dj) 15.00

CALDERWOOD,W L-Salmon Rivers & Lochs of Scotland-Lond-1909-4to-442p-ltd to 250c,nbrd,deluxe lg pap ed-illus,photogrvr plts,col frontis by E Briggs (m3,f) 250.00

CALDWELL,CAPT. D S-Incidents of War, and Southern Prison Life-Dayton-1864-United Brethren-61p-wrps-rare-Dornbusch 412 (n1,sl dmpstnd) 150.00

CALDWELL,ERSKINE-Afternoons in Mid America-NY-1976-Dodd,Mead-1st ed (h8,f,dj) 40.00

CALDWELL,ERSKINE-Around About America-NY-1964-Farrar-1st ed (v5,dj rub) 20.00

CALDWELL,ERSKINE-Gretta-Bost,Tor-(1955)-1st ed (c5,dj sp sl wn) 35.00

CALDWELL,ERSKINE-Jenny by Nature-NY-(1961)-1st ed (c5,dj) 25.00

CALDWELL,ERSKINE-Journeyman-(NY)-(1935)-Viking-ltd to 1475c,nbrd-1st ed (aa10,f,rprd box) 125.00

CALDWELL,ERSKINE-Kneel to the Rising Sun-Lond-1961-Heinemann-1st Brit ed (h8,f,dj) 35.00

CALDWELL,ERSKINE-Molly Cottontail-Bost-1958-Little,Brown-1st ed (h8,sl tn dj) 30.00

CALDWELL,ERSKINE-Place Called Estherville-NY-(1949)-DS&P-1st ed (h3,chip dj) 15.00

USED BOOK PRICE GUIDE©

CALDWELL,ERSKINE-Say, Is This the U.S.A.-NY-(1941)-Duell-4to-illus bds-1st ed (x3,sl chip dj) 150.00

CALDWELL,ERSKINE-Stories of Life North & South-NY-1983-Dodd, Mead-1st ed (c8,f,f dj) 30.00

CALDWELL,ERSKINE-We Are the Living-1933-Viking-1st ed (x2,sl sun sp,dj sl wn & chip) 68.00

CALDWELL,JOSEPH-In Such Dark Places-NY-(1978)-FS&G-auth 1st bk-1st ed (bb1,as new in dj) 20.00

CALDWELL,N-Fangs of the Sea-Sydney,Lond-1939-12mo-310p (m3,sp fade) 10.00

CALDWELL,ROBERT G-Red Hannah, Delaware's Whipping Post-Phila-1947-U of Penn Pr-xvi+144p-gry cl,plts-1st ed (b2,dj) 20.00

CALHOUN,MARY-Houn' Dog-NY-1959-Morrow-4to-cl,one & two col illus-1st ed (s3,dj) 20.00

CALHOUN,MARY-Medicine Show, Conning People and Making Them Like It-NY-1976-136p-1st ed (dd3,dj) 35.00

CALIF,RUTH-World on Wheels-NY-(1983)-Cornwall-4to-176p-photos-1st ed (gg5,f,dj) 15.00

CALIFORNIA HERITAGE COOKBOOK-GC-1976-Dbldy-424p-Jr. League of Pasadena-1st ed (k6,dj) 18.00

CALIFORNIA STORY BOOK-Berkeley-1909-Engl Club of U of Cal-12mo-195p-tan cl (mm1) 20.00

CALIFORNIA THE BEAUTIFUL-SF-1911-Paul Elder-4to-76p-cl,72 tip in photos-1st ed (t3,f) 100.00

CALIFORNIA-RECORDS OF...MEN IN THE WAR OF THE REBELLION 1861 TO 1867-Sacramento-1890-887p (c4,sm tr sp top) 195.00

CALISHER,HORTENSE-False Entry-Bost-(1961)-Little,Brown-1st ed (u10,f,f dj) 20.00

CALISHER,HORTENSE-Journal From Ellipsia-Bost-(1965)-Little,Brown-1st ed (h3,f,dj) 15.00

CALISHER,HORTENSE-Journal From Ellipsia-Bost-(1965)-Little,Brown-1st ed (z3,dj sl rub,soil) 10.00

CALISHER,HORTENSE-Tale for the Mirror-Bost-(1962)-Little,Brown-1st ed (hh5,dj) 20.00

CALISHER,HORTENSE-Textures of Life-Bost-(1963)-Little,Brown-1st ed (hh5,f.dj) 15.00

CALKINS,FAY-CIO & the Democratic Party-Chig-1952-U of Chig-162p (ff1,dj) 25.00

CALKINS,FRANK-Jackson Hole-NY-1973-Knopf-8vo-299p-cl,16p photos-1st ed (z4,dj nicked & tn) 12.50

CALKINS,FRANKLIN W-My Host the Enemy and Other Tales-Chig-1901-302p-cl-1st ed (l1,sm wn spot frnt cov) 15.00

CALKINS,R H-High Tide-Seattle-1952-Marine Digest Publ-8vo-356p-32p photos-1st ed (cc5,dj) 15.00

CALLAGHAN,MORLEY-Fine and Private Place-Tor-(1975)-Macmillan-1st ed (pp2,f,dj) 20.00*

CALLAGHAN,MORLEY-Lost and Found Stories of...-(Tor)-(1985)-Lester & O Dennys/Exile-1st ed (pp2,f,dj) 15.00*

CALLAGHAN,MORLEY-Loved and the Lost-1951-Macmillan-1st ed (dd8,dj) 10.00

CALLAGHAN,MORLEY-Many Colored Coat-Tor-1960-Macmillan-1st Can ed (pp2,sl chip dj) 45.00*

CALLAGHAN,MORLEY-Passion in Rome-Tor-1961-Macmillan-1st ed (pp2,f,dj) 45.00*

CALLAGHAN,MORLEY-That Summer in Paris-Lond-1963-Macgibbon & Kee-secondary bndg,lttrd in blk,8 plts-1st ed (ll5,f,dj) 30.00

CALLAGHAN,MORLEY-They Shall Inherit the Earth-NY-1935-1st US ed (q5,edge chip dj) 35.00

CALLAGHAN,MORLEY-Varsity Story-Tor-1948-Macmillan-8vo-172p-illus-1st ed (cc7,chip dj) 35.00*

CALLAHAN,GENEVIEVE-Sunset All,Western Foods-SF-(1947)-Lane Publ-284p-grn bds,illus-1st prtg (o6,sl wn bds) 20.00

CALLAHAN,HARRY-Harry Callahan-NY-1967-MOMA-84p-61 photos-1st ed (cc9,as new in dj) 40.00

CALLAHAN,HARRY-Harry Callahan: Color 1941 thru 1980-Providence-(1980)-Matrix-sq folio-brwn cl stmpd in yel,box wi photo cov-1st ed (y3,f,f box) 75.00

CALLAHAN,HARRY-Water's Edge-Lyme-1980-Callaway Ed-1st trd ed (mm9,f,dj) 50.00

CALLEN,A-Women Artists of the Arts & Crafts Movement 1870 to 1914-NY-1979-lg 4to-illus-1st Amer ed (h10,dj) 75.00

CALLEN,A-Women of the Arts and Crafts Movement-1979-Pantheon-illus,wrps-1st Amer ed (cc8) 35.00

CALLINGHAM,JAMES-Sign Writing and Glass Embossing-Phila-1895 (aa4,rprd) 75.00

CALLWELL,C E-Dardanelles-Lond-1919-361p-red cl,maps-1st ed (b7) 45.00

CALMAN,W T-Life of Crustacea-1911-Methuen-289p-32 plts-1st ed (bb3) 24.00

CALTHROP,DION-Charm of Gardens-Lond-1910-Black-239p-cl,32p col plts (x6,sl fox) 20.00

CALUMET BAKING POWDER CO-Master Baker's Manual-Chig-(1930)-127p-grn cl,col & b&w photos (q8,wn dj) 20.00

CALVER,WILLIAM L-History Written with Pick and Shovel-NY-1950-NY Hist Scty-xiv+320p-blu cl,illus-1st ed (k2) 45.00

CALVERLEY,CHARLES S-Literary Remains-Lond-1885-1st ed (y7) 28.00

CALVERT,ALBERT F-Discovery of Australia-Lond-1902-Dean & Son-lg 8vo-xii,184p-g dec grn cl,a.e.g.,maps,illus-2nd ed,rvsd (y4) 125.00

CALVERTON,V F-Man Inside-NY-1936-Scribners-1st ed (v5,f,dj) 45.00

CALVIN COLLEGE-Semi Centennial Volume, Theological School and...1876 to 1926-Grand Rapids-1926-Calvin Coll-317p-blu cl,photos (cc3,f) 60.00

CALVIN,ROSS-River of the Sun-1946-UNM-8vo-dec end sheets,photos,map-Herd 399-1st ed (aa3,f,sl chip dj) 50.00

CALVIN,ROSS-River of the Sun-Albuq-1946-illus-1st ed (j7,poor dj,pres) 60.00

CALVIN,ROSS-Sky Determines-NY-1934-Macmillan-354p-cl,illus-1st ed (z1,f,wn dj) 60.00

CALVINO,ITALO-Baron in the Trees-NY-1959-Random-scarce-1st ed (y1,dj sl fade & soil) 200.00

CALVINO,ITALO-Path to the Nest of Spiders-Bost-1957-Beacon-auth 1st bk-1st ed (d8,f,f dj) 125.00

CALVINO,ITALO-T Zero-NY-1969-Harcourt-1st ed (w5,f,dj) 45.00

CAMBELL,MARY M-Betty Crocker's Kitchen Gardens-(1971)-Scribners-170p-pict bds,col & b&w illus by T Tudor-Home Libr ser (q8,dj) 17.50

CAMBRIDGE UNIV PRESS-History of American Literature-Cambridge-1918-21-Cambridge Univ Pr-4 vols-red cl-1st ed (f2) 75.00

CAMDEN,J-Hundredth Acre-1905-Turner-pict cl-1st ed (x7) 30.00

CAMERON,A-Nightwatchers-NY-1972(1971)-4to-111p-cl,drwngs (y8,dj chip) 23.00

CAMERON,AGNES D-New North-NY-1910-398p-paste down map fr cov,photos-1st ed (o10,hngs loose) 60.00

CAMERON,AGNES D-New North-NY-1910-Appleton-8vo-xix,398p-illus grn cl,frntis,114 illus-1st ed (mm8,sl bump) 110.00*

CAMERON,ELEANOR-Time and Mr.Bass-Bost-(1967)-Little,Brown-illus-1st ed (oo10,f,f dj) 35.00
CAMERON,I-Mountains of the Gods-1984-Facts on File-248p-col & b&w photos-1st ed (bb3,f,dj) 25.00
CAMERON,IAN-To the Farthest Ends of the Earth-NY-1980-Dutton-1st Amer ed (v4,as new in dj) 30.00
CAMERON,JULIA M-Victorian Album-NY-1975-Da Capo-lg 4to-1st Amer ed (y3,dj sp sunned) 55.00
CAMERON,RODERICK-Golden Haze-Cleve,NY-(1964)-283p-col illus-1st ed (f7,dj) 35.00
CAMERON,W J-Ford Sunday Evening Hour Talks...1937-1938-Dearborn-1938-135p-fourth ser (e1,wrps) 12.50
CAMM,F J-Newnes Television and Shortwave Handbook-1934-256p-61 photos,169 illus-1st ed (h6,f) 25.00
CAMM,F J-Newnes Wireless Constructor's Encyclopedia-1932-392p-490 illus-1st ed (h6) 20.00
CAMP,C L-ED.-James Clyman, Frontiersman-Portland-(1960)-352p-fldg maps,illus,glassine dj-ltd ed (d7,f,dj) 125.00
CAMP,CHARLES-ED.-George C Yount & His Chronicles of the West-Denver-1966-280p-pict bndg,clear dj,illus-ltd ed (f7,f,mar dj) 110.00
CAMP,CHARLES-Muggins the Cow Horse-Denver-1928-Welch Haffner Prtg-110p-extended wrps,photos-Herd#401-scarce-1st ed (w3,f) 95.00
CAMP,R R-Duck Boats, Blinds, Decoys & Eastern Seaboard Wildfowling-NY-1925-240p-photos-scarce (gg3,vf.dj) 75.00
CAMP,RAY-All Seasons Afield with Rod & Gun-NY-1939-8vo-352p-illus (m3,vf,sl chip dj) 12.50
CAMP,RAY-Collier's Book of Hunting & Fishing-NY-1954-8vo-223p-illus (m3,as new in dj) 10.00
CAMP,RAY-Duck Boats:Blinds:Decoys-1952-Borzoi-8vo-240p+index-illus,photos (m3,vf,dj) 110.00
CAMP,RAY-ED.-Fireside Book of Fishing-NY-1959-8vo-500p-illus-1st prntng (m3,vf,dj) 25.00
CAMP,RAY-ED.-Fireside Book of Fishing-NY-1959-S&S-500p-cl/bds-1st ed (pp8,dj) 45.00*
CAMP,RAY-ED.-Fireside Book of Fishing-NY-1959-S&S-8vo-500p-illus-1st ed (bb5,dj tn) 17.50
CAMP,RAY-ED.-Hunter's Encyclopedia-Harrisburg-1948-4to-1152p-illus,photos-1st ed (m3,fray dj) 27.50
CAMP,RAY-ED.-Hunting Trails-NY-1961-8vo-502p-illus (m3,vf,dj) 14.50
CAMP,RAY-Fishing the Surf-Bost-1941-12mo-223p-illus-1st ed (m3) 15.00
CAMP,SAMUEL G-Angler's Handbook-Ohio-1925-12mo-201p-illus (m3) 10.00
CAMP,SAMUEL G-Fine Art of Fishing-NY-1911-12mo-177p-grn cl wi drk grn stmpng (m3,lacks photos) 20.00
CAMP,SAMUEL G-Fishing Kits and Equipment-NY-1933-12mo-145p-photos (m3) 12.50
CAMP,SAMUEL G-Taking Trout with the Dry Fly-NY-1930-12mo-143p-illus-1st ed (m3) 20.00
CAMP,WALTER-Custer in `76-(1976)-BYU Pr-303p-illus-Dowd 426 (c7,f,dj) 25.00
CAMP,WALTER-Walter Camp's Book of College Sports-NY-1893-Century-329p-dec cl,prntd dj,illus-1st ed (w1,f,dj) 175.00
CAMPA,ARTHUR-Hispanic Culture in the Southwest-Norman-(1979)-310p-dbl col,photos,maps-1st ed (u7,f,dj) 35.00
CAMPA,ARTHUR-Spanish Folk Poetry in New Mexico-Albuq-1946-224p-poems reproduced in Spanish-1st ed (u7) 50.00
CAMPA,ARTHUR-Spanish Folk Poetry in New Mexico-Albuq-1946-UNM-1st ed (a6,dj) 37.50
CAMPA,ARTHUR-Treasure of the Sangre de Cristo-Norman-1963-214p+index-illus-1st ed (u7,f,dj) 25.00
CAMPA,ARTHUR-Treasure of the Sangre de Cristos-Norman-1963-223p-illus-1st ed (t7,f,dj) 20.00
CAMPANELLA,ROY-It's Good To Be Alive-1959-Little,Brown-1st ed (s8,dj) 20.00
CAMPBELL,ALEXANDER-Memoirs of Elder Thomas Campbell-Cinn-1861-H S Bosworth-319p-cl (f1) 35.00
CAMPBELL,ARCHIBALD-Voyage Round the World from 1806 to 1812-Roxbury-1825-Allen & Watts-orig 1/2 calf,bds-Howes C88-Sabin 10210-4th Amer ed (v4,wn,leaves chip,lacks chrt) 350.00
CAMPBELL,B-Dictionary of Birds in Color-NY-1974-4to-352p-col photos (y8,dj chip) 25.00
CAMPBELL,BLANCHE-Gourmet's Gamble-San Antonio-(1962)-Naylor-199p-dec red cl,e.p. & illus by D M Yena-1st ed (q8,dj) 16.50
CAMPBELL,CAPT GEORGE F-Soldier of the Sky-Chig-1918-232p-blu cl,illus (jj2) 50.00
CAMPBELL,DONALD-Arabian Medicine and Its Influence on the Middle Ages-Lond-1926-2 vols-1st ed (dd3,vf) 250.00
CAMPBELL,DOUGLAS H-Evolution of the Land Plants-(1940)-Stanford Univ-x+731p-grn cl,351 text figs-1st ed (d2,dj tn & chip) 25.00
CAMPBELL,HARRIETTE R-String Glove Murder-1936-Knopf-1st ed (s10,sp wn) 10.00
CAMPBELL,HELEN-ET AL-Darkness and Daylight-Hartford-1895-Hartford Publ-740p-250 engrvngs-1st ed (n2,sl rub) 35.00
CAMPBELL,IAIN-Ian Fleming-Liverpool-(1978)-auth publ-71p-wrps-1st ed (g9) 20.00
CAMPBELL,J F-Popular Tales of the West Highlands, Orally Collected-Lond-1890 thru 1893-Alexander Gardner-4 vols-1/2 lea (p6) 500.00
CAMPBELL,J RAMSEY-ED.-New Tale of the Cthulhu Mythos-(Sauk City)-1980-Arkham Hs-1st ed (aa8,as new in dj) 100.00
CAMPBELL,J RAMSEY-Inhabitant of the Lake & Less Welcome Tenants-Sauk City-1964-Arkham Hs-auth 1st bk-ltd to 2009c-1st ed (ff6,dj sp sl wn) 125.00
CAMPBELL,JOHN W,JR-Cloak of Aesir-Chig-(1952)-Shasta-1st ed (j3,sl scuff & fray dj) 35.00
CAMPBELL,JOSEPH-Masks of God:Occidental Mythology-NY-1964-Viking-cl-1st ed (l8,f,dj) 27.50
CAMPBELL,JOSEPH-Masks of God:Primitive Mythology-NY-1959-Viking-cl-1st ed (l8,f,dj) 27.50
CAMPBELL,JOSEPH-Skeleton Key to Finnegan's Wake-NY-(1944)-Harcourt Brace-1st ed (cc2,f,dj) 40.00
CAMPBELL,JUDITH-Police Horses-Abbot-(1967)-D & C Newton-8vo-184p-illus-1st Brit ed (gg5,dj) 15.00
CAMPBELL,LEON-Story of Variable Stars-Phila-(1941)-Blakiston-vi+226p-red cl,82 text figs-1st ed (d2,f,dj,two autg) 20.00
CAMPBELL,MARJORIE W-North West Company-NY-1957-St.Martin's Pr-295p-e.p. maps,illus-1st ed (gg4,dj) 35.00
CAMPBELL,P J-In the Cannon's Mouth-Lond-1979-146p-1st ed (b7,f,dj) 20.00
CAMPBELL,RAMSEY-ED.-New Tales of the Cthulhu Mythos-Sauk City-1980-ltd to 3647c-1st ed (k5,as new in dj) 75.00

CAMPBELL,RAMSEY-Height of the Scream-Sauk City-1976-Arkham-1st ed (g3,f,sl wn dj) 12.00

CAMPBELL,RAMSEY-Parasite-NY-(1980)-Macmillan-1st US ed (e3,f,dj) 20.00

CAMPBELL,RAMSEY-Parasite-NY-(1980)-Macmillan-1st US ed (v5,f,f dj) 25.00

CAMPBELL,RODNEY-Luciano Project-NY-1977-McGraw Hill-299p-photos-1st prtg (p2,chip dj) 15.00

CAMPBELL,ROY-Flowering Reeds, Poems-Lond-1933-1st ed (y7,dj) 60.00

CAMPBELL,ROY-Talking Bronco-Lond-1946-1st ed (y7,dj fray) 30.00

CAMPBELL,ROY-TRANSL-Poems of St.John of the Cross-Lond-1951-1st ed (y7,dj) 50.00

CAMPBELL,SAM-Tippy Canoe and Canada Too-Indpls,NY-1946-8vo-250p-illus (m3) 25.00

CAMPBELL,T J-Upper Tennessee-Chattanooga-1932-the Author-(8),144,(1)p-illus (hh8,fox,cov soil) 30.00

CAMPBELL,THOMAS-Life of Mrs.Siddons-Lond-1839-Edward Moxon-lea-1st ed (l9,sp wn,weak hngs) 125.00

CAMPBELL,WILFRED-Scotsman in Canada-Lond-nd(c.1911)-Sampson Low,Marston-2 vols-grn cl,orig djs,16 illus-presumed 1st ed (bb7,sl fox,dj chip,sl discol) 175.00*

CAMUS,ALBERT-Caligula and 3 Other Plays-NY-1958-1st US ed (t5,dj) 15.00

CAMUS,ALBERT-Exile and the Kingdom-NY-1958-1st US ed (t5,dj) 20.00

CAMUS,ALBERT-Fall-NY-1957-1st US ed (t5,dj) 15.00

CAMUS,ALBERT-Lyrical and Critical Essays-NY-1968-1st US ed (t5,f,dj) 12.50

CAMUS,ALBERT-Myth of Sisyphus...-NY-1955-1st US ed (t5,dj) 20.00

CAMUS,ALBERT-Notebooks:1935-1942-NY-1963-1st US ed (t5,dj) 12.50

CAMUS,ALBERT-Notebooks:1942-1951-NY-1965-1st US ed (t5,dj) 12.50

CAMUS,ALBERT-Rebel-NY-1955-Knopf-1st ed (h8,f,dj) 75.00

CAMUS,ALBERT-Resistance, Rebellion, and Death-NY-1961-1st US ed (t5,tape reinfrcd dj) 12.50

CANADA-ATLAS OF WESTERN...-Ottawa-1902-Minister of Interior-4to-40p-illus card covs,photos,col maps-scarce (bb7,wn,fray,gov't stamps) 250.00*

CANADIAN PACIFIC RAILWAY CO-Your Journey Through the Canadian Rockies from Calgary, Alberta, to Vancouver and Victoria in B.C.-(Montr)-1937-News Dept-62p-prtd wrps,illus,maps-Edwards & Lort #748 (k10) 20.00*

CANADIAN PACIFIC RAILWAY-Game Fishes of Canada-Montreal-1928-8vo-45p-col plts (m3) 20.00

CANCIAN,FRANK-Change and Uncertainty in a Peasant Economy-1972-Stanford U Pr-8vo-beige cl,map e.p.,maps,chrts,photos (mm1,sl wn dj) 30.00

CANDLER,EDMUND-Long Road to Baghdad-Lond-1919-2 vols-dec gry cl,illus-1st ed (b7) 80.00

CANER,PERCY-Modern Gardens, British & Foreign-Lond-1927-Studio-166p-cl,180 plts,8 col photos (x6,vf) 45.00

CANETTI,ELIAS-Human Province-NY-(1978)-Seabury Pr-1st ed in Engl (bb1,as new in dj) 35.00

CANETTI,ELIAS-Tongue Set Free-NY-(1979)-Seabury Pr-1st ed in Engl (bb1,as new in dj) 35.00

CANFIELD,DWIGHT R-Poems of the Maumee Valley-Fostoria-1943-107p-cl (h1) 12.50

CANFIELD,FREDERICK A-History of Thomas Canfield and of Mathew Camfield with a Genealogy of...Descendants in New Jersey-Dover-1897-200p-cl,plts,28 charts (aa6) 150.00

CANFIELD,WILLIAM W-Legends of the Iroquois Told by "The Cornplanter"-NY-1902-Wessels-211p-red cl sp,papr over bds wi papr labls,col frntis plt,1 b&w photo-ltd to 500c,nbrd-scarce-1st ed (n2,sp flecked) 115.00

CANNING,VICTOR-Black Flamingo-1963-Sloan-1st Amer ed (s10,dj) 12.50

CANNING,VICTOR-Doubled in Diamonds-1967-Morrow-1st Amer ed (s10,dj) 12.50

CANNING,VICTOR-Python Project-1968-Morrow-1st Amer ed (r9,dj) 15.00

CANNING,VICTOR-Python Project-NY-1968-Morrow-1st Amer ed (g4,f,dj) 10.00

CANNON,CARL L-American Book Collectors...-NY-1941-Wilson-thk 8vo-1st ed (w1,f) 75.00

CANNON,CARL L-American Book Collectors...-NY-1941-Wilson-thk 8vo-xii,391p-cl-1st ed (w2) 65.00

CANNON,MILES-Waiilatpu, It's Rise and Fall-Boise-1915-171p-wrps,illus-Tweney #7-1st ed (d7,sl chip) 50.00

CANNON,POPPY-Poppy Cannon's Eating European Abroad & at Home-1961-Dbldy-460p-blk cl (q8,dj) 15.00

CANNON,RAY-Sea of Cortez-Menlo Park-1967-4to-264p-col photos,maps (m3,f,fray dj) 22.50

CANNON,WALTER B-Mechanical Factors in Digestion-Lond-1911-227p-illus-1st ed (g10,ex-libr) 75.00

CANSE,JOHN-Pilgrim and Pioneer-(1930)-Abingdon-306p-illus,e.p. map-1st ed (r8,wn,sp fade) 25.00

CANTON,FRANK M-Frontier Trails-Bost-1930-Houghton Mifflin-xviii,237p-cl,photos-Howes C118-1st ed (v1,innr hngs weak) 65.00

CANTWELL,J S-Thirty Days Over the Sea-Cin-1873-Williamson & Cantwell-230p-orig emboss cl-1st ed (p8,fade,sl fox) 20.00

CANTWELL,R-Alexander Wilson-1961-Lippincott-4to-319p-16 plts-1st ed (bb3,dj wn) 47.00

CANTWELL,R-Alexander Wilson-Phila-1961-4to-319p-cl,8 col repro & 12 b&w-1st ed (y8,dj chip) 35.00

CANTWELL,ROBERT-Nathaniel Hawthorne. The American Years-NY-1948-Rinehart-1st ed (v5,f,dj rnfrcd) 35.00

CANU,F-Bryozoa of the Philippine Region-1929-USNM-685p-224 figs (bb3,f) 35.00

CANU,F-Fossil and Recent Bryozoa of the Gulf of Mexico Region-1928-USNM-199p-34 plts (bb3,f) 15.00

CAPA,ROBERT-Images of War-NY-1964-Grossman-lg 4to-cl-1st ed (y3,sl soil) 60.00

CAPA,ROBERT-Report on Israel-NY-(1950)-Simon-4to-cl & bds-1st ed (y3,dj) 75.00

CAPA,ROBERT-Slightly Out of Focus-NY-(1947)-Holt-sm 4to-243p-photos-1st ed (b3,chip dj) 40.00

CAPE MAY-Book of...New Jersey-Cape May-1937-Albert Hand Co-(10),196,48p-contemp buckram,illus-1st publ in 1857 (aa6) 100.00

CAPEK,KAREL-I Had a Dog and a Cat-NY-1941-Macmillan-drwngs-1st ed (y1,dj) 25.00

CAPEK,KAREL-Letters From Spain-NY-1932-Putnam's-1st ed (a10,sp drknd,dj sp sl chip) 50.00

CAPLAN,RUTH B-Psychiatry and the Community in Nineteenth Century America-NY-(1969)-Basic Bks-xx+360p-tan cl-1st ed (d2,dj) 25.00

CAPONIGRO,PAUL-Wise Silence-Bost-(1983)-NYGS-4to-cl/bds-1st ed (y3,dj sl scuff) 95.00

CAPOTE,TRUMAN-Breakfast at Tiffany's-NY-(1958)-Random-8vo-1st ed (x3,sl chip dj) 140.00

CAPOTE,TRUMAN-Breakfast at Tiffanys-NY-(1958)-1st ed (t5,dj) 100.00

CAPOTE,TRUMAN-Christmas Memory-NY-(1966)-1st separate bk publ-1st ed thus (o5,f,box) 50.00

CAPOTE,TRUMAN-Dogs Bark-NY-(1973)-1st ed (p5,f,sl tn dj) 25.00

CAPOTE,TRUMAN-Dogs Bark-NY-(1973)-Random-8vo-cl-1st ed (x3,dj) 30.00

CAPOTE,TRUMAN-Grass Harp-NY-(1951)-1st ed (o5,f,sl chip dj) 150.00

CAPOTE,TRUMAN-Grass Harp-NY-(1951)-Random-1st state bndg wi rough cl-1st ed (x3,dj) 125.00

CAPOTE,TRUMAN-In Cold Blood-1965-Random-1st ed (x7,dj) 23.00

CAPOTE,TRUMAN-In Cold Blood-NY-(1965)-Random-1st issue dj wi "1/66" on frnt flap-1st ed (a5,dj) 30.00

CAPOTE,TRUMAN-In Cold Blood-NY-(1965)-Random-4to-cl-1st ed (x3,f,dj) 35.00

CAPOTE,TRUMAN-Local Color-NY-(1950)-Random-8vo-94p-cl,photos-1st ed (q3,tape dj) 90.00

CAPOTE,TRUMAN-Local Color-NY-(1950)-Random-photos-1st ed (a10,dj wn & sp chip) 95.00

CAPOTE,TRUMAN-Local Color-NY-(1950)-Random-tall 8vo-cl/pict bds,photos-1st ed (kk8,dj sp wn) 100.00

CAPOTE,TRUMAN-Muses are Heard-NY-1956-1st ed (t5,dj) 50.00

CAPOTE,TRUMAN-Observations-NY-1959-S&S-sm folio-bds,Avedon photos-1st ed (t3,sl wn box) 300.00

CAPOTE,TRUMAN-One Christmas-NY-(1983)-Random-ltd to 500c,autg (bb2,f,unopened box) 300.00

CAPOTE,TRUMAN-Other Voices, Other Rooms-NY-(1948)-Random-auth 1st bk-1st ed (cc1,dj,autg) 400.00

CAPOTE,TRUMAN-Other Voices,Other Rooms-NY-(1948)-Random-auth 1st bk-1st ed (b5,tan sp,dj wn) 175.00

CAPOTE,TRUMAN-Thanksgiving Visitor-NY-(1967)-Random (n6,box) 20.00

CAPOTE,TRUMAN-Thanksgiving Visitor-NY-(1967)-Random-4to-cl & bds-1st ed (x3,f,box) 40.00

CAPOTE,TRUMAN-Tree of Night-NY-(1949)-Random-1st ed (bb2,dj) 95.00

CAPOTE,TRUMAN-Tree of Night-NY-(1949)-Random-blk cl-1st ed (f2,sl wn dj) 75.00

CAPPON,LESTER J-Bibliography of Virginia History Since 1865-1930-U.Va,Inst Rsrch Soc Sci-900p-wrps-(Mono no.5) (dd9) 40.00

CAPPS & JOHNSON-Ellamar District, Alaska-1915-US Geo Srvy,Bull.605-125p-wrps,photo plts,figs,2 fldg maps in pckt (u8) 20.00

CAPPS,BENJAMIN-Warren Wagontrain Raid-NY-1974-Dial-xvi,304p-cl,photos,map-1st prtg (v1,dj) 35.00

CAPPY DICK'S STAY AT HOME BOOK-NY-(1944)-Greenberg-218p-1/2 lea & bds,illus (oo10,sl rub) 25.00

CAPRON,ELISHA S-History of California-Bost-1854-J P Jewett-fldg col map frntis-Howes C127-1st ed (dd6,f) 300.00

CAPSTICK,P H-Death in the Silent Places-NY-1981-258p-photos (gg3,f,dj) 10.00

CAPSTICK,PETER H-Death in the Long Grass-NY-(1977)-St.Martin's-8vo-297p-illus-1st ed (jj5,f,dj) 20.00

CAPTAIN KANGAROO'S STORYBOOK-NY-(1963)-Random-lg 4to-92p-pict bds,col illus (oo10,tips wn,sl peel joints) 20.00

CAPUTO,PHILIP-DelCorso's Gallery-NY-1983-352p-bds-1st ed so stated (c1,f,dj) 22.50

CAPUTO,PHILIP-Rumor of War-NY-(1977)-Holt Rinehart-1st ed (h8,f,dj) 45.00

CAR BUILDERS CYCLOPEDIA-1943-Simmons Boardman-4to-1324p-cl,illus-16th ed (nn7) 125.00

CARAS,R A-Venomous Animals of the World-1974-Prentice Hall-4to-362p-col & b&w photos-1st ed (bb3,dj) 18.00

CARAS,ROGER-Monarch of Deadman Bay-1969-Little,Brown-1st ed (r9,f,dj) 20.00

CARAS,ROGER-Monarch of Deadman Bay-Bost-1969-8vo-185p-illus-1st ed (m3,vf,dj) 10.00

CARCO,FRANCIS-Perversity-Chig-1928-Pascal Covici-1st US ed (e3,dj sl chip & sp sunned) 20.00

CARDELL,WILLIAM S-Happy Family-Phila-1828-Thomas T. Ash-177p-prntd bds-frontis,map between pgs 50 & 51-2nd ed (j1,weak uppr jnts,sm sp chip) 100.00

CARDWELL,K H-Bernard Maybeck, Artisan, Architect, Artist-Santa Barbara-1977-illus-1st ed (h10,dj) 125.00

CARE AND TRAINING OF TROTTERS-Chig-1914-The Horseman-Vol.1,"The Horseman Library"-scarce (j9) 95.00

CAREW,ROD-Carew-1979-S&S-photos-1st ed (s8,f,dj) 15.00

CAREY,A MERWYN-American Firearms Makers-NY-(1953)-Crowell-8vo-146p-photos-1st ed (s1) 45.00

CAREY,ALICE-Clovernook...-NY-1852-Redfield-8vo-342p-1st ed (w6) 45.00

CAREY,PETER-Bliss-NY-1981-1st US ed (p5,f,dj) 45.00

CAREY,PETER-Fat Man in History-NY-(1980)-Random-auth 1st bk-1st US ed (bb1,f,dj) 35.00

CARHART,ARTHUR-Fishing in the West-NY-1950-8vo-144p-photos (m3,f,dj) 14.00

CARIGIET,ALOIS-Pear Tree, the Birch Tree and the Barbary Bush-NY-1967-oblng 4to-cl,col illus,auth-1st US ed (s3,f) 20.00

CARL,LOUIS-Mountains in the Desert-GC-1954-Dbldy-8vo-318p-16p photos-1st ed (ff5,dj) 15.00

CARL,LOUIS-Mountains in the Desert-NY-1954-318p-photos,maps-1st US ed (p10,as new in dj) 25.00

CARLETON,GEORGE-Memoirs of Captain Carleton-NY-1929-Dutton-8vo-301p-4 illus-1st US ed thus (jj5,dj sl tn,chip) 20.00

CARLETON,LT J HENRY-Prairie Logbook-Chig-1943-295p-maps-ltd to 350c-1st ed (c4,f,box) 150.00

CARLETON,MARJORIE-Bride Regrets-NY-1950-Morrow-1st ed (f4,f,dj) 12.50

CARLETON,WILL-City Ballads-NY-1886-180p-cl-BAL 2495-1st ed (m1) 15.00

CARLETON,WILL-City Festivals-NY-1892-164p-cl-BAL 2511-1st ed (e1,rub) 15.00

CARLETON,WILL-City Legends-NY-1890-170p-cl-BAL 2504-1st ed (e1) 15.00

CARLETTI,FRANCESCO-My Voyage Around the World-NY-1964-Random Hs-8vo-xv,270p-1/2 cl,dbl pg map-1st prtg (nn1,wn dj) 30.00

CARLEY,KENNETH-Minnesota in the Civil War-Mpls-1961-Ross & Haines-168p-illus-1st ed (o7,f,dj) 20.00

CARLEY,KENNETH-Sioux Uprising of 1862-St.Paul-1961-Minn Hist Soc-80p-illus (dd4,dj) 20.00

CARLISLE,BILL-Bill Carlisle Lone Bandit-Pasadena-(1946)-Trail's End-220p-photos,map e.p.,illus,C M Russell-1st ed (f9,brwng,dj chip,rprd) 50.00

CARLISLE,D T-Belvedere Hounds-NY-1935-Derrydale-4to-bds,ltd to 1250c (j9) 65.00

CARLISLE,N-ED.-Air Forces Reader-NY-(1944)-8vo-406p-cl,31p plts-1st ed (t2,sl stnd & wn) 25.00

CARLISLE,NORMAN-Modern Wonder Book of Trains-1946-Winston-289p-photos-1st ed (d3) 25.00

CARLISLE,NORMAN-Wonder Book of Trains-Phila-1957-313p-rvsd ed (n4,f,dj) 17.50

CARLISLE,ROBERT-An Account of Bellevue Hospital with a Catalogue of the Medical and Surgical Staff from 1736 to 1894-NY-1893-381p-photos-1st ed (dd3) 150.00

CARLSON,NATALIE S-Happy Orpheline-NY-(1957)-Harper-4to-96p-pict cl,drwngs,G Williams-presumed 1st ed (s3,f,dj) 35.00

CARLSON,PAUL-Texas Woollybacks-College Sta-1982-Tex A&M-1st ed (f10,dj) 35.00

CARLSON,STEPHEN P-PCC: the Car that Fought Back-Glendale-1980-250p-1st ed (n4,f,dj) 36.00

CARLTON,W N C-Notes on the Bridgewater Library-NY-1918-priv prtd-tall 12mo-20p-papr wrps (w2) 20.00

CARLYLE,JANE W-Letters and Memorials of...-Lond-1883-Longmans,Green-8vo-3 vols-1st ed (w6) 125.00

CARLYLE,THOMAS-ED.-Oliver Cromwell's Letters and Speeches-NY-nd(ca.1900)-4 vols-red cl (b7) 25.00

CARLYLE,THOMAS-Reminiscences...-Lond-1881-Longmans,Green-2 vols-3/4 tan calf,cl,grn lea labls on panneled sp,t.e.g.,frntis-1st ed (dd10) 75.00

CARMAN,BLISS-Poems-Bost-1905-L C Page-lg 8vo-two vols-ltd to 350 sets,autg-Ltd deluxe ed (t1) 250.00

CARMAN,HARRY-American Husbandry-NY-1939-Columbia Univ-582p-cl (x6) 35.00

CARMER,CARL-Farm Boy and the Angel-GC-1970-Dbldy-1st ed (nn3,dj) 10.00

CARMICHAEL,GERTRUDE-History of the West Indian Islands of Trinidad and Tobago 1498 to 1900-Lond-(1961)-Redman-8vo-463p-8 illus-1st ed (jj5,f,dj) 15.00

CARMICHAEL,HOAGY-Sometimes I Wonder-NY-(1965)-Farrar-photos-1st ed (w1,f,dj) 20.00

CARMICHAEL,HOAGY-Stardust Road-NY,Tor-(1946)-photos-1st ed (c5,sl wn dj) 40.00

CARMICHAEL,HOAGY-Stardust Road-NY-(1946)-Rinehart-1st ed (w1,f,dj) 45.00

CARMICHAEL,JOHN-COMP.-My Greatest Day in Baseball...47 Dramatic Stories by 47 Famous Stars-NY-(1951)-G&D-250p-cl (n1) 12.50

CARMICHAEL,JOHN-My Greatest Day in Baseball-1945-Barnes-1st ed (ff2,dj) 25.00

CARMICHEL,JIM-Compleat Just Jim-Prescott-1973-8vo-117p-ltd to 202c,nbrd,autg-illus-1st ed (m3,vf) 30.00

CARMICHEL,JIM-Modern Rifle-NY-1975-8vo-342p-photos (m3,vf,dj) 10.00

CARNAC,CAROL-It's Her Own Funeral-NY-1952-Dbldy CC-1st US ed (f4,yel pgs,dj intrn taped) 15.00

CARNAC,CAROL-Upstairs and Downstairs-NY-1950-Dbldy CC-1st US ed (f4,yel pgs,chip dj) 15.00

CARNACINA,LUIGI-Great Italian Cooking-NY-nd(ca.1968)-Abradale Pr-851p (q6) 45.00

CARNACINA,LUIGI-Luigi Carnacina's Great Italian Cooking-NY-(1968)-Abradale-thk 4to-851p-pict wht cl,col photos & drwngs (q8,dj) 45.00

CARNEGIE,ANDREW-An American Four in Hand in Britain-NY-1884-Scribner (j9) 45.00

CARNEY,MABEL-Country Life and the Country School-Chig,NY-(1912)-Row,Peterson-408p-cl (k1) 20.00

CAROSSO,VINCENT P-California Wine Industry-Berkeley-1951-U of Cal Pr-241p (o6,dj) 35.00

CARPENTER,CAROLE H-Many Voices-Ottawa-1979-Nat Mus Can-x,483p-blu prtd wrps,photos (oo1) 45.00

CARPENTER,DON-Hard Rain Falling-NY-(1966)-HB&W-auth 1st bk-1st ed (a10,f,dj) 30.00

CARPENTER,DON-Hard Rain Falling-NY-(1966)-HBW-auth 1st bk-1st ed (hh5,dj) 15.00

CARPENTER,DON-Murder of the Frogs...-NY-(1969)-Harcourt-1st ed (s6,dj) 30.00

CARPENTER,EDMUND S-They Became What They Beheld-NY-1970-Outerbridge & Dienstfrey-unpgd-86 photos by K Heyman-1st ed (cc9,f,dj) 30.00

CARPENTER,EDMUND-Eskimo Realities-NY-(1973)-HR&W-216p-illus,photos,maps-1st ed (ll8,dj) 25.00

CARPENTER,EDWARD-Drama of Love and Death-NY-1912-M Kennerley-cl-1st ed (n8) 27.50

CARPENTER,F A-Aviator and the Weather Bureau-San Diego-1917-12mo-54p-bds,frntis,22 plts,chrts (t2) 25.00

CARPENTER,FRANK D Y-Round About Rio-Chig-1884-Jansen,McClurg-8vo-415p-drk grn pict cl-1st ed (t10) 22.50

CARPENTER,FRANK D-Adventures in Geyser Land-1935-Caxton-319p-illus,fldg map.e.p. maps-rprnt of 1878 1st ed wi add material (r8,f) 75.00

CARPENTER,FRANK G-Alaska, Our Northern Frontier-GC-1923-Dbldy-lg 8vo-xviii,320p-multi col dec cov,123 illus,2 maps-1st ed (y4) 40.00

CARPENTER,WILLIAM-Angler's Assistant-Lond-1848-12mo-153p-pict gilt cl-illus-rare (m3,chip sp) 125.00

CARPENTIER,GEORGES-My Fighting Life-Lond-1920-Cassell-8vo-253p-grn cl,frntis,10 illus-1st ed (mm8,bump,sp fade) 35.00*

CARPENTIER,WESLEY M-So Long, Ohio-Bost-1935-Meadow Publ-261p-cl (l1,dj) 20.00

CARPER,ROBERT S-American Railroads in Transition-NY-1968-260p-1st ed (n4,f,dj) 20.00

CARPER,ROBERT S-Focus: the Railroad in Transition, 1947 to 1967-NY-1968-260p-1st ed (n4,f,dj) 25.00

CARPUE,J C-An Account of Two Successful Operations for Restoring a Lost Nose...Biography by Frank McDowell-Birmingham-1981-103p-lea-(facs of 1816 ed) (dd3) 75.00

CARR,ALBERT-Juggernaut, the Path of Dictatorship-NY-1939-Viking-531p-cl-1st ed (m1,dj) 15.00

CARR,CHARLES C-Alcoa-NY-1952-Rinehart-292p-maps,illus-1st ed (p2,sl rub dj) 10.00

CARR,EMILY-Autobiography of...-Tor-1946-OUP-8vo-brwn cl,col frntis,17 plts-1st ed (cc7,sl scuff,bump) 45.00*

CARR,EMILY-Book of Small-Tor-1942-Oxford Univ Pr-1st ed (h8,dj missing chips) 50.00

CARR,EMILY-House of All Sorts-Tor-1944-OUP-8vo-221p-brwn cl,col frntis-1st ed (cc7,new e.p.) 35.00*

CARR,EMILY-Hundreds and Thousands-Tor-(1966)-Clarke,Irwin & Co-8vo-x,332p-12p col illus-1st ed (aa7,dj) 40.00*

CARR,EMILY-Hundreds and Thousands-Tor-(1966)-Clarke-1st ed (e3,f,chip dj) 20.00

CARR,GLYN-Death on Milestone Buttress-1951-Bles-no US ed-1st ed (s10,dj) 40.00

CARR,GLYN-Swing Away, Climber-1959-Washburn-1st Amer ed (s10,chip dj) 25.00

CARR,H GRESHAM-ED.-Flags of the World-Lond-(1956)-F Warne-8vo-286p-32 col plts-1st ed (cc5,dj) 50.00

CARR,HERBERT-Irvine Diaries-UK-1979-143p-1st ed (o10,as new in dj) 30.00

CARR,HERBERT-Mountains of Snowdonia-Lond-1925-405p-58 illus & diagrams-1st ed (o10,sl fox) 30.00

CARR,JOHN D-Arabian Nights Murder-NY-1936-Harper-1st ed (j4) 35.00

CARR,JOHN D-Blind Barber-1934-Harper-1st ed (s10) 35.00

CARR,JOHN D-Captain Cut Throat-NY-1955-Harper-1st ed (k4,f,dj) 15.00

CARR,JOHN D-Captain Cut-Throat-NY-1955-Harper-1st ed (f4,f,dj) 12.50

CARR,JOHN D-Crooked Hinge-NY-1938-Harper-1st ed (d4,rear dj tpe stn,word frnt) 400.00

CARR,JOHN D-Demoniacs-NY-1962-Harper-1st ed (g4,sl soil dj) 15.00

CARR,JOHN D-Door to Doom...-Lond-1980-Hamilton-1st Brit ed (p4,vf,dj) 35.00

CARR,JOHN D-Fire,Burn-NY-1957-Harper-1st ed (f4,dj) 10.00

CARR,JOHN D-Ghosts' High Noon-NY-1969-Harper & Row-1st ed (w9,f,dj) 45.00

CARR,JOHN D-Hungry Goblin-NY-1972-Harper-1st ed (g4,dj) 20.00

CARR,JOHN D-It Walks By Night-1930-Harper-auth 1st bk-1st ed (s10) 55.00

CARR,JOHN D-It Walks By Night-NY-1930-Harper-auth 1st bk-1st ed (f4) 35.00

CARR,JOHN D-Life of Sir Arthur Conan Doyle-1949-Harper-1st ed (s10,f,f dj) 30.00

CARR,JOHN D-Life of Sir Arthur Conan Doyle-NY-1949-Harper-1st ed (f4,dj) 20.00

CARR,JOHN D-Most Secret-1964-Harper-1st ed (s10,sp fray dj) 25.00

CARR,JOHN D-Murder of Sir Edmund Godfrey-NY-1936-Harper & Bros-1st ed (w9,spottng,dj sp fade,rprd) 350.00

CARR,JOHN D-Nine Wrong Answers-NY-1952-1st ed (q5,sl wn dj) 50.00

CARR,JOHN D-Patrick Butler for the Defence-1956-HH-1st ed (x7,dj) 18.00

CARR,JOHN D-Scandal at High Chimneys-NY-(1959)-Harper-1st ed (a5,f,dj) 20.00

CARR,JOHN D-Sleeping Sphinx-1947-Harper-1st ed (s10,dj) 30.00

CARR,JOHN D-Witch of the Low-Tide-NY-1961-Harper-1st ed (f4,f,dj) 12.50

CARR,LORRAINE-To the Philippines with Love-LA-1966-Shelbourne Pr-254p-1st ed (c3,f,dj) 10.00

CARRA,MASSIMO-Ivories of the West-Lond-1970-Hamlyn-159p-71 col plts,dbl pg map-Cameo Bk (u5,f,f dj) 20.00

CARRADINE,B-Mississippi Stories-Chig-(1904)-254p-cl (f1) 15.00

CARREL,FRANK-Canada's West and Farther West-Tor-1911-xvi,258p-orig cl wi photo cov (a7) 75.00

CARRIE,AUNT-COMP.-Popular Pastimes for Field and Fireside-1867-Milton Bradley-emboss pict cov,illus-1st ed (s8) 250.00

CARRIER,ROBERT-Connoisseur's Cookbook-(c.1965)-Random-thk 4to-513p-pict bds,col plts & drwngs-1st Amer ed (q8,dj) 30.00

CARRIER,ROBERT-Food, Wine & Friends-Lond-(1980)-Sidgwick & Jackson-qto-207p-blk cl,col photos-1st ed (q8,dj) 30.00

CARRIER,ROBERT-Great Dishes of the World-(1964)-Random-folio-279p-tan cl,col photos-1st US ed (q8,f,edgewn dj) 25.00

CARRIERE,JOE-Yankee Batboy-1955-Prentice Hall-1st ed (p7,f,dj) 35.00

CARRIGHAR,SALLY-Home to the Wilderness-Bost-1973-Houghton Mifflin-330p-cl,illus-1st ed (z5,dj) 17.00

CARRIGHAR,SALLY-Icebound Summer-NY-1953-drwngs,H B Kane-1st ed (g5,sl wn dj) 12.50

CARRIGHAR,SALLY-One Day at Teton Marsh-NY-1947-drwngs,Geo & P Mattson-1st ed (g5,sl wn dj) 20.00

CARRIGHAR,SALLY-Twilight Seas-NY-(1975)-Weybright & Talley-drwngs-1st ed (b5,as new in dj) 15.00

CARRIGHAR,SALLY-Wild Heritage-Bost-1965-drwngs,R S Horne-1st ed (g5,f,dj) 12.50

CARRIKER,ROBERT C-Kalispel People-Phoenix-1973-104p-frntis,photos-1st ed (t7,f,autg) 20.00

CARRINGTON,FRANCES C-My Army Life and the Fort Phil. Kearney Massacre with...the Celebration of "Wyoming Opened"-Phila-1910-Lippincott-318p-cl,maps,plts-1st ed (v1) 75.00

CARRINGTON,FRANCES-Army Life on the Plains-Phila-1911-318p-illus,maps,fldg maps (t7,ex-libr) 35.00

CARRINGTON,GEN HENRY B-Indian Question-NY-1973-Sol Lewis-52p-illus,fldg map-Howes C174 (bb4) 30.00

CARRINGTON,HEREWARD-Modern Psychical Phenomena-NY-1919-Dodd,Mead-(xvi)+231+(5)p+23 plts,prntd blu cl-1st Amer ed (y9,sp fade) 28.50

CARRINGTON,LEONORA-Hearing Trumpet-NY-1976-St.Martin's-1st ed (t4,f,sl rub dj) 15.00

CARRINGTON,R-Elephants-NY-1959-272p-photos (gg3,f,dj) 25.00

CARROLL,CAMPBELL-Three Bar-Vancouver-1958-Mitchell Pr-sm 4to-111p-cl,map e.p.,frntis map,illus,ports (aa2) 35.00*

CARROLL,DANIEL B-Henri Mercier and the American Civil War-Princeton-1971-396p-illus-1st ed (c4,f,dj) 30.00

CARROLL,DIXIE-Goin' Fishin'-Cin-1920-8vo-357p-photos-1st ed (m3,f) 22.50

CARROLL,DIXIE-Lake & Stream Game Fishing-Cin-1917-8vo-251p-illus-1st ed (m3,f) 15.00

CARROLL,JAMES-Madonna Red-Bost-1976-auth 1st bk-1st ed (r5,dj) 25.00

CARROLL,JAMES-Mortal Friends-Bost-(1978)-Little,Brown-1st ed (g3,f,dj) 20.00

CARROLL,JOHN A-ED.-Reflections of Western Historians-Tucson-1969-U of Ariz Pr-314p-1st ed (ll1,as new in dj) 20.00

CARROLL,JOHN J-Filipino Manufacturing Entrepreneur-Ithaca-1965-Cornell-230p-tbls-1st ed (c3,f,rub dj) 15.00

CARROLL,JOHN M-Custer in Texas-NY-1975-288p-illus-1st ed (n3,f) 30.00

CARROLL,JOHN M-Custer in Texas-NY-1975-Sol Lewis/Liveright-288p-illus (ff4,dj) 35.00

CARROLL,JOHN M-ED.-Papers of the Order of Indian Wars-Ft.Collins-(1975)-287p-illus-1st ed (n3,f,dj) 27.50

CARROLL,JOHN M-Roll Call on the Little Big Horn-Ft.Collins-1974-168p-vol.3 Source Custeriana Ser.-1st ed (t7,f) 45.00

CARROLL,JONATHAN-Land of Laughs-1980-Viking-auth 1st bk-1st Amer ed (t9,f,dj) 30.00

CARROLL,JONATHAN-Land of Laughs-NY-1980-Viking-auth 1st bk-1st ed (p3,f,dj) 50.00

CARROLL,JONATHAN-Voice of Our Shadow-NY-1983-Viking-1st ed (b8,f,sl tn dj) 65.00

CARROLL,LEWIS-Alice in Wonderland-NY-nd-Gregg-154p-wrps,prntd in Gregg shorthand,dbl cols,illus (f1,sm stn on pg cors) 50.00

CARROLL,LEWIS-Alice's Adventures in Wonderland and Through the Looking Glass-NY-1928-Macmillan-cl,illus,Tenniel,col frntis,Macmillan Children's Classic (s3) 15.00

CARROLL,LEWIS-Alice's Adventures in Wonderland-NY-1901-Harper & Bros-xvii,192,(1)p-g stmpd Japanese vel,illus by Peter Newell-1st ed thus (o4,dj) 300.00

CARROLL,LEWIS-Hunting of the Snark-Lond-(1970)-Heinemann-4to-48p-pict cl,col & b&w illus,H Oxenbury-1st ed (s3,f,dj) 30.00

CARROLL,LEWIS-Hunting of the Snark-Los Altos-(1981)-Wm Kaufmann-4to-linen cl,lea labl,43 plts-ltd to 1955c-Centennial ed (m4,vf) 25.00

CARROLL,LEWIS-Hunting of the Snark...-1903-Harpers-40 illus,P Newell-1st ed thus (x2,sl drknd sp) 125.00

CARROLL,LEWIS-Hunting of the Snark...-NY-1903-t.e.g.,illus by P Newell-1st Amer ed (hh10,f,dj sp sun) 200.00

CARROLL,LEWIS-Jabberwocky-NY-(1977)-Warne-unpgd-cl,watercol illus-1st ed (pp10,f,dj) 20.00

CARROLL,LEWIS-Letters of...-NY-1979-Oxford U Pr-2 vols-blu cl-1st ed (kk10,f,box) 25.00

CARROLL,LEWIS-Picture Book-Lond-1909-Unwin-8vo-g dec red cl-1st ed (y3,sl fray,hng crack) 95.00

CARROLL,LEWIS-Through the Looking Glass-Lond,NY-1889-Macmillan-224p-red cl,blk & g dec floral stmpg,50 illus by Tenniel-50th thousand (nn10) 90.00

CARSE,ROBERT-Blockade, the Civil War at Sea-NY-(1958)-279p-illus,map-1st ed (n3,dj) 25.00

CARSE,ROBERT-Department of the South-Columbia-1961-156p-e.p. maps,illus(incl col)-1st ed (c4,f,pc tn dj) 40.00

CARSON,CHRISTOPHER-THE LIFE AND TIMES OF...THE ROCKY MOUNTAIN SCOUT AND GUIDE-NY,Lond-nd-Beadle-94p-pict wrps-rare-1st ed (l1) 150.00

CARSON,GERALD-Social History of Bourbon-NY-(1963)-Dodd,Mead-8vo-280p-20 photos-1st ed (bb5,dj) 20.00

CARSON,RACHEL-Edge of the Sea-Bost-1956-8vo-276p-illus,B Hines (m3) 12.50

CARSON,RACHEL-Silent Spring-Bost-1962-Hougton Mifflin-1st ed (ee2,f,sl tn dj) 40.00

CARSON,RACHEL-Under the Sea Wind-NY-1941-auth 1st bk-illus-1st ed (g5,chip dj) 125.00

CARSON,ROBERT-ED.-Waterfront Writers-NY-1979-Harper-198p-1st ed (r1,f,f dj) 20.00

CARSON,THOMAS-Ranching Sport and Travel-NY,Lond-1911-319p-pict cl,illus by C M Russell-Herd #422-1st ed (t7) 175.00

CARSPECKEN,PHIL-Fishin' Poems & Others-Iowa-1922-12mo-104p (m3,f) 20.00

CARSWELL,EDWARD-Let It Alone and It Won't Hurt You-NY-(1886)-Nat Temp Soc & Publ Hs-286p-cl (a1,hngs weak) 20.00

CARSWELL,JOHN-Romantic Rogue-NY-(1950)-Dutton-8vo-278p-7 plts-1st US ed (dd5,sl dmpstnd,dj sl wn) 25.00

CARTER,ANGELA-Bloody Chamber-NY et al-(1979)-Harper & Row-1st US ed (bb1,vf,vf dj) 25.00

CARTER,ANGELA-Fireworks-NY-(1981)-Harper & Row-1st US ed (cc2,f,dj) 25.00

CARTER,ANGELA-Fireworks-NY-(1981)-Harper & Row-1st US ed (h3,f,dj) 15.00

CARTER,ANGELA-Passion of New Eve-1977-HBJ-1st Amer ed (r9,f,dj) 17.50

CARTER,BENJAMIN F-Historical Address-Woodbury-1873-51p-wrps (aa6,chip,detchd) 75.00

CARTER,CHARLES F-When Railroads Were New-NY-1909-324p-1st ed (n4) 34.00

CARTER,CHARLES S-ED.-Protestant Dictionary-Lond-(1933)-Harrison Trust-tall 8vo-xix,805p-blk cl,14 plts-new ed (t10,hng split) 90.00

CARTER,CHICKERING-ED.-Clarice, the Woman Detective-NY-1907-28(4)p-col pict wrps,Nick Carter Weekly No.528 (d1,sl wn) 12.50

CARTER,D-Butterflies and Moths in Britain and Europe-1982-Heinemann-4to-192p-col photos-1st ed (bb3,f,dj) 32.00

CARTER,GWENDOLEN M-Expanding Horizons in African Studies-Evanston-1969-Nrthwstrn U Pr-8vo-384p-cl (y5,f) 55.00

CARTER,HODDING-Doomed Road of Empire-NY-(1963)-McGraw Hill-408p-illus-Amer Trails ser-1st ed (bb4,wn dj) 30.00

CARTER,HODDING-Southern Legacy-1950-LSU Pr-1st ed (kk6,f,dj) 50.00

CARTER,JAMES D-ED.-First Century of Scottish Rite Masonry in Texas, 1867 to 1967-Waco-1967-Tex Scot Rite Bodies-508p-g dec purple cl,photos-1st prtg (ff8) 42.00

CARTER,JAMES-In the Wake of the Setting Sun-Lond-1908-Hurt & Blackett-lg 8vo-456p+4p ads-g dec orng cl,frntis,29 illus-1st ed (mm8,cl fade & wn) 50.00*

CARTER,JOHN-Books and Book Collectors-NY-(1957)-World-1st Amer ed (w1,f,f dj) 30.00

CARTER,JOHN-ED.-New Paths in Book Collecting-Lond-1934-Constable-1st ed (w5,sl tn dj) 125.00

CARTER,LIN-Dreams From R'Lyeh-Sauk City-1975-ltd to 3152c-1st ed (k5,as new in dj) 10.00

CARTER,MARY L-Two Story Book-Lamoni-1913-122p-illus-1st ed (t7) 15.00

CARTER,MARY N-North Carolina Sketches-Chig-1900-McClurg-313p-cl-Wright 929-1st ed (h1,few spot pgs) 20.00

CARTER,NICHOLAS-Just One Slip-NY-1915-Street & Smith-1st ed (h4,wrps) 15.00

CARTER,PAUL A-Little America-NY-1979-Columbia U Pr-301p-blk cl/bds,4 maps,illus-1st ed (dd7,dj) 28.50

CARTER,R G-Four Brothers in Blue-Austin-1978-537p (z10,dj) 45.00

CARTER,R G-On the Border with Mackenzie-Wash D.C.-(1935)-542p-frntis,2 photos-Howes #C195-rare-1st ed (u7) 500.00

CARTER,R S-British Railways Main Line Diesels-Lond-1963-47p-spiral bndg-1st ed (n4) 20.00

CARTER,ROBERT-Summer Cruise on the Coast of New England-Bost-1864-Crosby & Nichols-viii+261p-lilac cl-1st ed (e2,sl fade cov) 80.00

CARTER,SAMUEL,III-Incredible Great White Fleet-NY-1977-Crowell Collier-184p-blu cl,map-1st Amer ed (nn1,dj soil & wn) 20.00

CARTER,SAMUEL-Cowboy Capital of the World-GC-1973-Dbldy-280p-cl,photos-1st ed (w3,vf,dj) 20.00

CARTER,SAMUEL-Final Fortress-NY-(1980)-355p-illus,e.p. maps-1st ed (c4,f,dj) 32.50

CARTER,TOM-ED.-Pacific Northwest Steelhead-Portland-1955-folio-70p-wrps-photos-scarce (m3,vf) 30.00

CARTER,W H-Horses of the World-Wash-1923-Nat'l Geographic Scty-118p-fabrikoid-95 illus(incl 24p col) (l1) 15.00

CARTER,W H-Horses, Saddles and Bridles-Balt-1906-Lord Balt Pr-3rd ed (j9,sp wn) 65.00

CARTER,W N-Tragedy of the Plains-Chig-1913-296p-col pict wrps,frntis,photos,illus (t7) 45.00

CARTER,WILLIAM-Middle West Country-Bost-1975-Houghton,Mifflin-278p-cl-photos-1st ed (e1,dj) 15.00

CARTHY,J D-Behavior of Arthropods-1965-Oliver Boyd-148p-41 figs-1st ed (bb3,f,dj) 18.00

CARTIER,JOHN O-ED.-20 Great Trophy Hunts-NY-1980-8vo-269p-photos (m3,vf,dj) 30.00

CARTIER-BRESSON,HENRI-Europeans: Photographs-NY-1955-S&S-folio-dec papr bds-1st Amer ed (y4,sp bump) 125.00

CARTIER-BRESSON,HENRI-Man and Machine-NY-(1971)-Viking-4to-cl-1st ed thus (y3,f,dj) 65.00

CARTIER-BRESSON,HENRI-People of Moscow-NY-1955-S&S-4to-163p-cl,gravures-1st ed (q3,sl chip dj) 90.00

CARTIER-BRESSON,HENRI-Photographs of...-text by Kirstein & Newhall-NY-1947-MOMA-4to-56p-wrps-third in MOMA ser-1st ed (t3) 30.00

CARTOONIST COOKBOOK-NY-(1966)-Hobbs,Dorman & Co-189p+index,photos,Newspaper Comic Council (n6,dj) 35.00

CARTWRIGHT,B W-Sports Afield Treasury of Waterfowl-NY-1957-142p-col illus (gg3,f,dj) 20.00

CARVALHO,DAVID N-Forty Centuries of Ink-NY-1904-Banks Law Publ-viii+374p-maroon cl-1st ed (g2,sl discol frnt cov) 100.00

CARVER,C-Brann and the Iconoclast-Austin-(1957)-illus-1st ed (f9,dj) 35.00

CARVER,JONATHAN-Three Years' Travels throughout the Interior Parts of North America...-Walpole-1813-Isaiah Thomas,publ-280p-lea-Howes C 215,a later ed (o1) 65.00

CARVER,RAYMOND-Cathedral-NY-1983-1st ed (c5,as new in dj) 35.00

CARVER,RAYMOND-Cathedral-NY-1983-Knopf-1st ed (q2,dj) 45.00

CARVER,RAYMOND-Furious Seasons and Other Stories-Santa Barbara-1977-Capra Pr-ltd to 3000c in wrps-1st ed (d8,f) 100.00

CARVER,RAYMOND-Furious Seasons and Other Stories-Santa Barbara-1977-Capra Pr-pict wrps-1st ed (l7) 150.00

CARVER,RAYMOND-Put Yourself in My Shoes-Santa Barbara-1974-Capra Pr-ltd to 1000c in wrps-1st ed (d8,f) 100.00

CARVER,RAYMOND-What We Talk About When We Talk About Love-NY-1981-Knopf-1st ed (cc2,f,dj) 45.00

CARVER,RAYMOND-Winter Insomnia-Santa Cruz-1970-wrps,prnts by Robt Chesney,auth 1st reg publ bk-1st ed (t5,f) 125.00

CARVIC,HERON-Miss Seeton Draws the Line-1970-Harper-1st Amer ed (s10,dj) 15.00

CARY,ALAN L-Mail Liners of the World-NY-(1937)-Appleton-8vo-144p-photos-1st Amer ed (u1,dj) 50.00

CARY,JOYCE-Horse's Mouth-NY-1944-Harper & Bros-1st ed (h8,f,sp chip dj) 75.00

CARY,KATHARINE T-Arranging Flowers Throughout the Year-NY-1934-vii,230p-60 hlftones (x5,sl fray,scrtchd cov) 12.00

CASALS,PABLO-Joys and Sorrows-1970-S&S (u4,f,sl drknd dj) 18.00

CASANOVA,GIACOMO-History of My Life-NY-1966-HBW-1st ed thus (x9,f,box) 15.00

CASAS,PENELOPE-Food & Wines of Spain-1982-Knopf-456p-pict tan cl,e.p. & drwngs by Ochoa-1st ed (q8,edgewn dj) 18.50

CASATI,GAETANO-Ten Years in Equatoria and the Return with Emin Pasha-Lond,NY-1891-Warne-8vo-2 vols-orig cl,illus(incl col),2 fldg maps rear pckts-1st ed (bb6,ex-libr) 145.00

CASE,DAVID-Third Grave-Sauk City-(1981)-Arkham-1st ed (g3,f,dj) 15.00

CASE,ROBERT O-Empire Builders-NY-1947-333p-map e.p.-1st ed (t7,dj) 6.50

CASE,ROBERT-Last Mountains-1945-Dbldy-236p-illus-1st ed (r8,chip dj) 12.00

CASE,ROBERT-Last Mountains-Portland-1945-8vo-236p-photos (m3,f) 10.00

CASEWIT,CURTIS-Mountaineering Handbook-NY-1968-222p-1st ed (q10,f,dj) 11.00

CASEY,CLIFFORD-Brewster County Texas-Hereford-1972-Pioneer-4to-485p-photos-1st ed (a9) 60.00

CASEY,JOHN-An American Romance-NY-1977-auth 1st bk-1st ed (n5,f,f dj) 50.00

CASEY,JOHN-Testimony and Demeanor-NY-1979-1st ed (o5,f,dj) 40.00

CASEY,JUANITA-Circus Nantucket-1978-Longship Pr-1st Amer ed (z8,vf,dj) 20.00

CASEY,JUANITA-Horse of Selene-NY-1972-Grossman-1st Amer ed (z8,f,dj) 20.00

CASEY,ROBERT J-Black Hills and their Incredible Characters-Indpls-(1949)-Bobbs Merrill-383p-grn cl,plts-1st ed (h2,dj) 35.00

CASEY,ROBERT J-Cambodian Quest-1931-BM-pict dj-1st ed (x7,dj sl soil & tn) 75.00

CASEY,ROBERT J-Easter Island-1931-Bobbs Merrill-337p-photo plts,pict dj-1st ed (u8,chip dj) 35.00

CASEY,ROBERT J-Easter Island-Indpls-1931-Bobbs Merrill-tall 8vo-337p-g dec,blu cl,pict e.p.,43 photos-1st ed (p8,few cov spots) 30.00

CASEY,ROBERT J-Lackawanna Story-NY-(1951)-(8),223p-cl,plts (aa6) 40.00

CASEY,ROBERT J-Lost Kingdom of Burgandy-NY-1923-Century-8vo-399p-46 illus-1st ed (ff5,sl tn dj) 30.00

CASEY,ROBERT J-Midwesterner-Chig-(1948)-Wilcox & Follett-8vo-311p-photos-1st ed (gg5,sl tn dj) 15.00

CASEY,ROBERT J-Pioneer Railroad-1948-Whittlesey Hs-8vo-334p (nn7,tn dj) 29.00

CASEY,ROBERT J-Secret of 37 Hardy Street-Indpls-1929-Bobbs-1st ed (h4) 10.00

CASEY,ROBERT J-Third Owl-Indpls-1934-Bobbs-1st ed (g4) 10.00

CASH,WILBUR J-Mind of the South-1941-Knopf-1st ed (dd9,fox) 25.00

CASHMAN,TONY-Edmonton Story-Edmonton-1956-Inst of Applied Arts-8vo-284p-blu cl,frntis,photos-1st prtg (cc7) 10.00*

CASHMAN,TONY-Singing Wires-Edmonton-(1972)-Alberta Govt Tele Comm-496p-yel cl,illus-1st ed (dd1,bump pgs,dj) 25.00

CASPER,LEONARD-New Writings From the Philippines-1966-Syracuse U Pr-411p-1st ed (c3,f) 24.00

CASS,A R HARRIS-Catching the Wily Sea-Trout-Lond-nd-12mo-128p-photos,illus-1st prntng so stated (m3) 15.00

CASS,A R HARRIS-Sea Fishing from the Shore-Lond-1940-12mo-126p-illus-1st prntng (m3) 10.00

CASSADY,NEIL-First Third-SF-1971-wrps-1st ed (x8,f) 10.00

CASSELS,LAVENDER-Struggle for the Ottoman Empire 1717 to 1740-NY-1967-226p-illus-1st Amer ed (b7,dj) 45.00

CASSERIUS,JULIUS-Tabulae Anatomicae & De Formato Foetu Tabulae-NY-c.1970-folio-(facs of 1627 ed) (dd3) 90.00

CASSERLEY,H C-British Locomotive Names of the Twentieth Century-Lond-1963-177p-1st ed (n4,f,dj) 22.00

CASSERLEY,H C-Midlands: Railway History in Pictures-NY-1969-109p-1st ed (n4,f,dj) 16.00

CASSERLEY,H C-Preserved Locomotives-Lond-1969-312p-2nd ed (n4,f,dj) 18.00

CASSIDY,JOHN-Station in the Delta-NY-1979-1st ed (v9,f,dj) 50.00

CASSIDY,PATRICK S-Borrowed Bride-NY-1892-dec covs gilt,a.e.g.,illus-1st Amer ed (r2,rub) 60.00

CASSIN,J-Birds(of Chile)...In U.S. Naval Astron. Exped...Vol.2-Wash-1855-4to-300p-buckr,13 col plts,3 col plts antiquities,13 plain plts,2 maps(1 fldg) (y8,rbnd) 150.00

CASSIN,RICCARDO-50 Years of Alpinism-Seattle-1981-205p-1st US ed (o10,as new in dj) 18.00

CASSON,LIONEL-Illustrated History of Ships and Boats-GC-1964-Dbldy-1st ed (v4,vf,sl chip dj) 40.00

CASSON,MICHAEL-Pottery in Britain Today-Lond-1967-Titanti-4to-unpgd-224 photos-1st ed (ee5,f,sl tn dj) 20.00

CASTANEDA,CARLOS E-Our Catholic Heritage-1936 to 1958-Von Boeckmann Jones-7 vols-1st ed (a9,ex-libr) 1,000.00

CASTANEDA,CARLOS-Journey to Ixtlan-NY-(1972)-1st ed (c5,dj) 17.50

CASTANEDA,CARLOS-Second Ring of Power-NY-(1977)-1st ed (c5,f,dj) 10.00

CASTANEDA,CARLOS-Tales of Power-NY-(1974)-1st ed (c5,f,dj) 15.00

CASTEL,ALBERT-General Sterling Price-Baton Rouge-(1968)-LSU Pr-300p-illus,maps-1st ed (ee4,dj) 50.00

CASTIGLIONI,ARTURO-Adventuress of the Mind-NY-1946-Knopf-cl-1st Amer ed (n8,dj) 17.50

CASTIGLIONI,ARTURO-History of Medicine-NY-1941-1013p-1st ed (dd3,sp dull) 150.00

CASTILLO-PUCHE,JORGE LUIS-Hemingway in Spain-NY-1974-(15),388p-photos-1st ed (k9,chip dj) 15.00

CASTLE,CORA-Statistical Study of Eminent Women-1913-90p-1st ed (dd3) 75.00

CASTLE,MOLLY-Round the World with an Appetite-Lond-(1936)-H&S-254p (n6,wn dj) 18.00

CASTLE,MRS V-My Husband-NY-1919-8vo-xii,264p-cl,frntis,23p plts (t2) 30.00

CASTLE,WILLIAM R,JR.-Hawaii Past & Present-1913-Dodd,Mead-242p-pict cov,photo plts-1st ed (u8,cov rub) 25.00

CASTLE,WILLIAM R-Hawaii Past and Present-NY-1917-Dodd,Mead-lg 12mo-xii,260p-illus,col map-rvsd & enlgd ed (o2) 20.00

CASTLEMAN,HARVEY N-Bald Knobbers-Girard-(1944)-Haldeman Julius-29p-wrps (m1) 15.00

CASTLEMAN,HARVEY N-Texas Rangers-Girard-(1944)-Haldeman Julius-24p (e1,wrps) 15.00

CASTLEMAN,HARVEY N-Texas Rangers-Girard-1944-Haldemann Julius-24p-wrps-1st ed (w3,f) 25.00

CASTLEMAN,RIVA-Technics and Creativity: Gemini Gel-NY-1971-MOMA-4to-108p-col wrps,illus (r10) 10.00

CASTLEMON,HARRY-Sportsman's Club Afloat-Phila-1874-12mo-277p-frontis (m3) 12.50

CASTLEMON,HARRY-Winged Arrow's Medicine-Akron-1901-Saalfield Publ-293p-cl,frontis+3 illus by W H Fry (d1) 15.00

CASTRO,FIDEL-Cuba Confronts the Future-(ca.1964)-Fair Play for Cuba Comm-wrps-1st ed (w5,f) 20.00

CASTRO,J I-Sharks of North American Waters-1983-Texas A&M-180p-col photos-1st ed (bb3,f,dj) 20.00

CASWELL,JEAN-Coutumes of France in the Library of Congress-Wash-1977-80p-cl,7 tip-in col illus (n1,f) 15.00

CASWELL,JOHN E-Arctic Frontiers-(1956)-U of Okla-232p-wrps,illus,maps-1st ed (u8,dj sl soil & wn) 35.00

CASWELL,JOHN E-Arctic Frontiers-Norman-(1956)-U of Okla Pr-232p-photos-1st ed (ll8,f,dj) 25.00

CATHEDRAL OF COMMERCE-(NY)-(1918)-(28)p-wrps (c1) 10.00

CATHER,WILLA-Alexander's Bridge-Bost,NY-1912-Houghton Mifflin-1st ed,2nd iss wi half title after t.p.-1st ed (ff6) 250.00

CATHER,WILLA-April Twilights-Bost-1903-Badger/Gorham Pr-8vo-52p-pap cov bds,pap sp labl,auth 1st bk-scarce-1st ed (w6,spot cov,uncut) 700.00

CATHER,WILLA-Death Comes to the Archbishop-NY-1927-Knopf-8vo-303p-1st ed,trd iss (w6,f) 50.00

CATHER,WILLA-Lost Lady-1923-Knopf-1st ed (x2,f,dj) 250.00

CATHER,WILLA-Lucy Gayheart-NY-1935-Knopf-ltd to 749c,autg-1st ed (cc1,dj chip,box) 325.00

CATHER,WILLA-My Mortal Enemy-NY-1926-Knopf-4to-cl & illus bds-1st ed (x3,dj sunned,chip) 40.00

CATHER,WILLA-Not Under Forty-1936-Knopf-1st ed (dd8,sp sun dj) 37.50

CATHER,WILLA-Not Under Forty-NY-1936-Knopf-ltd to 333c,autg-1st ed (e10,f,chip dj,sl wn box) 375.00

CATHER,WILLA-Novels and Stories of...-Bost-1937 to 41-13 vols-cl,lea sp labls,orig prtd papr fold over wrps-ltd to 975 sets,nbrd,autg (gg1,f,djs) 1,500.00

CATHER,WILLA-Obscure Destinies-1932-Knopf-1st ed (x2,sl fade sp,dj) 125.00

CATHER,WILLA-Obscure Destinies-NY-1932-Knopf-8vo-230p-1st ed (w6,sp fade,sp fade dj) 75.00

CATHER,WILLA-Old Beauty and Others-NY-1948-1st ed (t5,dj) 35.00

CATHER,WILLA-On Writing-NY-1949-Knopf-8vo-126p-1st ed (z4,dj) 45.00

CATHER,WILLA-On Writing-NY-1949-Knopf-grn cl-1st ed (f2,dj) 30.00

CATHER,WILLA-Shadows on the Rock-NY-1931-Knopf-8vo-280p-1st ed so stated (z4,sp fade,dj sp fade,pc msg) 45.00

CATHER,WILLA-Shadows on the Rock-NY-1931-Knopf-grn bds-1st ed (cc2,f,dj) 50.00

CATHER,WILLA-Song of the Lark-1915-Houghton Mifflin-1st ed,1st iss (x2) 275.00

CATLIN'S NORTH AMERICAN INDIAN PORTFOLIO-Chig-1970-Swallow Pr-25 two tone plts-20p description-(repro of 1844 ed)-ltd to 1000c (nn6) 200.00

CATLIN,GEORGE-George Catlin: Episodes From Life Among the Indians and Last Rambles-Norman-1959-U of Okla Pr-4to-xxv+357p-cl,illus-1st ed (z4,dmpstnd dj) 35.00

CATLIN,GEORGE-Illustrations of the Manners, Customs, and Condition of the North Amer Indians-Lond-1851-H G Bohn-2 vols-3/4 lea,360 engrvngs-8th ed (l9,sl scuff,wn & fox) 525.00

CATLIN,GEORGE-Letters and Notes on the Manners...North American Indian-Lond-1841-2 vols-custom box-orig cl,papr sp labls,3 maps,drwngs,errata slip,plt 113/114-"publ. by the auth",uncor error p104-1st ed,1st iss (o4,sp chip,labl rub) 2,000.00

CATLIN,GEORGE-Letters and Notes on the Manners...North American Indians-Mpls-1965-Ross & Haines-2 vols-illus-Howes C241 (cc4,box) 45.00

CATLIN,GEORGE-North American Indians-Edinburgh-1926-2 vols-col plts,2 fldg maps-rprnt of Howes#C241 (u7) 150.00

CATON,J D-Antelope & Deer of America-1877-426p-illus-2nd ed (ee3,soil) 40.00

CATON,J D-Antelope and Deer of America-NY-1877-8vo-426p-g cl,port,engrvngs-1st ed (y8,wn,fade) 135.00

CATTON,BRUCE-America Goes to War-Middletown-1966-Wesleyan U Pr-126p-illus (o7,dj) 10.00

CATTON,BRUCE-Banners at Shenandoah-GC-1955-245p-e.p. maps-1st ed (n3,f,dj) 25.00

CATTON,BRUCE-ED.-American Heritage Picture History of the Civil War-NY-1960-Amer Heritage Publ-2 vols+spplmnt-deluxe box set in maroon cl,illus,maps (o7,sl soil,fray,box wn) 20.00

CATTON,BRUCE-Grant Takes Command-Bost-(1968)-556p-illus,maps-1st ed (c4,f,dj) 25.00

CATTON,BRUCE-War Lords of Washington-NY-(1948)-Harcourt Brace-313p-cl-1st ed (l1,dj) 15.00

CAUCCI,AL-Hatches-NY-1975-4to-320p-illus-1st ed (m3,vf,dj) 30.00

CAUDWELL,SARAH-Thus Was Adonis Murdered-NY-1981-Scribner's-auth 1st bk-1st US ed (e4,dj) 35.00

CAUGHEY,JOHN W-Gold is the Cornerstone-Berkeley-1948-U Cal Pr-321p-1st ed (d3,dj) 30.00

CAUGHEY,JOHN-Gold is the Cornerstone-Berkeley-1948-U of Cal Pr-321p-illus-1st ed (cc4,dj) 25.00

CAULFIELD,MAX-Easter Rebellion-NY-1963-Holt Rinehart-375p-1st ed (r1,dj) 20.00

CAVAICK,WEMYSS-Uprooted Heather-Vancouver-1967-Mitchell Pr-8vo-221p-e.p. maps-1st ed (cc7,scuff dj) 10.00*

CAVALCADE OF THE AMERICAN NEGRO-Chig-1940-WPA-95p-wrps (f1,sp wn,sl wn) 20.00

CAVAN,SHERRI-Hippies of the Haight-St.Louis-1972-New Critics Pr-1st ed (e8,f,f dj) 45.00

CAVANAGH,HELEN M-Funk of Funk's Grove-Bloomington-1952-Pantagraph Prtg-208p-illus-1st ed (cc4,dj) 25.00

CAVE,C J P-Structure of the Atmosphere in Clear Weather-Cambridge-1912-Cambridge U Pr-4to-xii+144p-photos,maps,tbls-1st ed (a2) 50.00

CAVE,F O-Birds of the Sudan-1955-Oliver Boyd-444p-12 col plts,drwngs,photos,maps-v scarce-1st ed (bb3,tattrd dj) 295.00

CAVE,H B-Wings Across the World-NY-1945-sm 4to-viii,176p-illus cl,plts,illus e.p.-1st ed (t2) 30.00

CAWS,MARY ANN-Presence of Rene Char-1976-Princeton U Pr-1st ed (x9,f,dj) 20.00

CAYWOOD,LOUIS R-Green Spring Plantation Archeological Report-Yorktown-1955-29p-6 maps,17 plts (jj3) 20.00

CAYWOOD,LOUIS R-Restored Mission of Nuestra Senora de Guadalupe de Zuni-(St.Michaels)-1972-101p-wrps,photos,plts-1st ed (v7) 20.00

CECIL,HENRY-Asking Price-NY-1966-Harper-1st US ed (g4,f,sl wn dj) 10.00

CECIL,HENRY-Friends at Court-NY-1956-Harper-1st US ed (h4,dj) 15.00

CECIL,HENRY-No Bail for the Judge-NY-1952-Harper-1st US ed (h4,dj) 15.00

CECIL,HENRY-Settled Out of Court-NY-1959-Harper-1st US ed (g4,dj) 10.00

CELLINI,BENVENUTO-Life of...Written By Himself-NY-1906-Brentano's-2 vols-g dec,t.e.g.40 plts (u5,sl drknd sp,vol.1 uncut) 50.00

CENTAUR ALMANAC AND COOK BOOK. 1886-np-(1885)-36p-wrps (o1) 12.50

CENTENNIAL COOKERY BOOK-Marietta-1887-Woman's Cent'l Assoc-145p+16p blanks,grn bds (q6,v wn,items pasted blnks) 50.00

CEPEDA,ORLANDO-My Ups and Downs in Baseball-1968-Putnam-1st ed (p7,f,dj) 30.00

CERF,BENNETT-At Random-NY-(1977)-Random-1st ed (w1,f,box) 17.50

CERULLI,DOM-ET AL-Jazz Word-NY-1960-Ballantine-wrps-1st ed (v5) 15.00

CESCINSKY,HERBERT-Early English Furniture & Wooodwork-Lond-1922-sm folio-2 vols-col frntis,photos (aa4) 175.00

CHABOT,FREDERICK C-San Antonio of the 17th, 18th and 19th Centuries-S.A.-1929-16p-pict wrps-1st ed (a9) 25.00

CHABOT,FREDERICK C-Texas Letters-San Antonio-Yanaguana Soc Vol.V-188p-ltd to 250c,nbrd (a9) 150.00

CHADWICK,ALBERT A-Little Churches of France..-NY-1930-Harper & Bros-folio-125 free photo plts-1st ed (gg6) 175.00

CHADWICK,LESTER-Baseball Joe at Yale-1913-Cupples & Leon-third in ser-1st ed (s8) 23.50

CHADWICK,LESTER-Baseball Joe in the Big League...-NY-(1915)-Cupples & Leon-250p-cl (c1) 15.00

CHADWICK,LESTER-Baseball Joe in the Big Leagues-(1915)-Cupples & Leon-later prntg (s8,dj) 35.00

CHADWICK,LESTER-Baseball Joe in the Central League-(1914)-Cupples & Leon-4th in ser-later prntg (s8,dj) 45.00

CHADWICK,LESTER-Baseball Joe in the Central League-NY-(1914)-Cupples & Leon-246p+ads-cl (n1,f,dj wn) 20.00

CHADWICK,LESTER-Baseball Joe of the Silver Stars-1912-Cupples & Leon-1st in ser-1st ed (s8) 25.00

CHADWICK,LESTER-Batting to Win-NY-(1911)-Cupples & Leon-308p+ads-cl-1st ed (n1) 15.00

CHADWICK,LESTER-Rival Pitchers-Cupples & Leon-illus (s8,dj) 55.00

CHADWICK,W-Women Artists & the Surrealist Movement-Bost-1985-20 col & 200 b&w illus-1st ed (h10,dj) 35.00

CHAFFEE,DON-Indiana's Big Top-Grand Rapids-(1969)-79p-Illus-1st ed (v8,dj) 15.00

CHAGALL,BELLA-Burning Lights-NY-1946-Schocken Bks-8vo-268p-blu cl,36 drwngs,M Chagall-1st ed (u1,dj) 75.00

CHALFANT,W A-Death Valley, the Facts-1930-Stanford Univ Pr-155p-pict bds,illus-1st ed (cc4) 25.00

CHALFRONT,LORD-ED.-Waterloo, Battle of Three Armies-NY-1980-239p-col & b&w illus-1st Amer ed (d7,f,dj) 35.00

CHALKLEY,LYMAN-Chronicles of the Scotch Irish Settlement in Virginia...Records of Augusta Co.-1965-Genealogical Publ-3 vols-rprnt of 1912 ed (dd9) 100.00

CHALLIS,GEORGE-Splendid Rascal-Lond-1927-Cassell-1st Brit ed (x1,sl cocked,dj edgewn) 75.00

CHALMERS,IAN-Salmon Fishing in Little Rivers-Lond-1938-8vo-133p-frontis-scarce-1st ed (m3,f) 35.00

CHALMERS,PATRICK-Angler's England-Phila-1938-8vo-254p-photos (m3,f) 20.00

CHALMERS,PATRICK-At the Tail of the Weir-Glasgow-1932-8vo-277p-woodcts-1st ed (m3) 30.00

CHALMERS,PATRICK-Fisherman's Angles-Lond-1931-4to-91p-etchings,N Wilkinson-1st ed (m3) 30.00

CHALMERS,PATRICK-Rhymes of Flood & Field-Lond,NY-1931-4to-96p-one of 1500c-t.e.g.,illus (m3) 20.00

CHALMERS,RADM W S-Life and Letters of David Beatty, Admiral of the Fleet-Lond-(1951)-Hodder & Stoughton-8vo-488p-23 illus-1st ed (cc5,dj) 30.00

CHALON,JEAN-Portrait of a Seductress-NY-(1979)-Crown-8vo-248p-cl,illus-1st US ed (z5,dj tn & chip) 22.00

CHAMBERLAIN & LIVINGSTON-COMP-Bibliography of the First Editions in Book Form of the Writings of Henry Wadsworth Longfellow-NY-(1968)-Burt Franklin-(14),131p-port-facs of 1908 ed (m4) 17.50

CHAMBERLAIN,CHARLES-Methods in Plant Histology-Chig-1905-U of Chig-262p-cl-2nd ed (x6) 22.00

CHAMBERLAIN,F M-Some Observations on Salmon & Trout in Alaska-Wash-1907-8vo-112p-wrps,5 plts,fldg map (m3,ex-lib) 15.00

CHAMBERLAIN,HARRY-Training Hunters, Jumpers & Hacks-Derrydale-1937-8vo-329p-ltd to 1250c,nbrd-illus,photos (m3,f,dj) 75.00

CHAMBERLAIN,NARCISSE-Chamberlain Sampler of American Cooking in Recipes and Pictures-(1961)-Hastings Hs-232p-red cl,photos (q8,dj) 15.00

CHAMBERLAIN,RUDOLPH W-There Is No Truce-NY-1935-420p-cl-1st ed (c1,sl wn dj) 17.50

CHAMBERLAIN,SAMUEL E-Recollections of a Rogue-Lond-(1957)-302p-col illus-1st ed (j7,dj) 35.00

CHAMBERLAIN,SAMUEL E-Recollections of a Rogue-Lond-(1957)-302p-frntis,16p col paintings,auth-1st ed (t7,dj) 17.50

CHAMBERLAIN,SAMUEL-British Bouquet-1963-Gourmet (v6) 14.00

CHAMBERLAIN,SAMUEL-Frontier of Freedom-NY-(1957)-Hastings Hs-b&w photos-revsd & enlgd ed (a10,dj) 12.50

CHAMBERLAIN,SAMUEL-Italian Bouquet-Lond-(1938)-H Hamilton-591p-Italian cols on wht vel cov,prnts,drwngs,photos (q8,soil cov) 30.00

CHAMBERLAIN,SAMUEL-Nantucket-NY-(1955)-71,(1)p-bds,photos (d1) 12.50

CHAMBERLAIN,SAMUEL-Soft Skies of France-NY-(1953)-Hastings Hs-140 photos by auth-1st ed (a10,dj) 20.00

CHAMBERLAIN,SAMUEL-Tudor Homes of England-NY-1929-folio-orig engrvng frntis,illus (h10) 300.00

CHAMBERLIN,HARRY-Riding and Schooling Horses-Wash-1934-Armored Cavalry Journal (f10,dj) 35.00

CHAMBERLIN,HARRY-Training Hunters Jumpers and Hacks-NY-1952-Van Nostrand-1st trd ed (f10) 35.00

CHAMBERLIN,WILBUR-Ordered to China-NY-1903-340p-red dec cl-scarce-1st ed (jj2,hngs weak) 100.00

CHAMBERS,ANDREW J-Recollections-np-1947-47p-stapled in plain wrps as iss-Howes C270(aa) (mm1,f) 80.00

CHAMBERS,CAPT ERNEST J-ED.-Unexploited West-Ottawa-1914-lg 8vo-xv,361p-card covs,frntis map,52 illus-1st ed (mm8,sl wn cov) 125.00*

CHAMBERS,E T D-Quananiche & Its Canadian Environment-NY-1896-8vo-357p-illus (m3) 40.00

CHAMBERS,HOMER S-Enduring Rock-Blackwell-1954-120p-frntis,photos-1st ed (t7,ex-libr) 50.00

CHAMBERS,J S-Conquest of Cholera-NY-1938-Macmillan-xvi+366p-grn cl,plts-1st ed (a2,edgewn dj) 25.00

CHAMBERS,JOHN R-Arctic Bush Mission-Seattle-(1970)-174p+2p index-illus-1st ed (j7,f,dj) 30.00

CHAMBERS,JOHN-Autobiography-Iowa City-1908-St Hist Soc of Iowa-xiv+49p-red cl,2 plts-ltd to 400c-Howes C271-1st ed (b2,sp tips wn) 55.00

CHAMBERS,MARY D-Table Etiquette-Bost-1929-Bost Cooking Sch Mag Co-263p-red bds-Axford p.385-2nd prtg (a8) 25.00

CHAMBERS,PETER-Blonde Wore Black-1968-Roy-1st Amer ed (s10,soil dj) 12.50

CHAMBERS,R-In Secret-1919-Doran-1st ed (x7,f,sl chip dj) 75.00

CHAMBERS,RAYMOND W-Thomas More-Lond,Tor-(1935)-J Cape-8vo-416p-brwn cl,frntis port,7 plts-1st ed (t10) 50.00

CHAMBERS,ROBERT W-In Search of the Unknown-NY-1904-Harper & Bros-dec blu/gry cl-1st ed (k8,sl rub) 17.50

CHAMBERS,ROBERT W-Mystery of Choice-NY-1897-Appleton-1st ed (d4) 75.00

CHAMBERS,ROBERT W-River Land-NY-1904-Harper-4to-92p-pict cl,8 inserted col plts,E S Green-1st ed (r3,sl rub,few smudges) 80.00

CHAMBERS,THEODORE F-Early Germans of New Jersey-Balt-1969-viii,667p-cl,illus-rprnt of 1895 ed (aa6) 50.00

CHAMBERS,W-Coast of Intrigue-1928-I F L (x7,sp chip dj) 18.00

CHAMBERS,WHITMAN-Navy Murders-NY-1932-Dodd-1st ed (f4) 10.00

CHAMBLISS,WILLIAM-On the Take-Bloomington-1978-IU Pr-1st ed (z9,f,dj) 12.50

CHAMIER,CAPT FREDERIC-Life of a Sailor-Lond-1833-Richard Bentley-3 vols-3/4 lea,raised bnds-2nd ed (p8,f,box) 150.00

CHAMPION,F W-With a Camera in Tiger Land-1928-Dbldy Doran-226p-73 photos-1st ed (bb3,f) 65.00

CHAMPION,F W-With a Camera in Tiger Land-GC-1928-4to-226p-photos (m3,badly fray dj) 28.50

CHAMPLAIN,SAMUEL DE-Works of...-Tor-1971-U of Tor Pr-thk 8vo-6 vols + map portfolio,red cl wi g titles,t.e.g.,in French & Engl,illus-rprnt of 1922 ed (mm1,f) 895.00

CHAMPNEY,ELIZABETH W-Romance of Old Belgium-NY-1915-Putnam-8vo-432p-90 illus-1st ed (jj5) 20.00

CHAMPNEY,ELIZABETH W-Three Vassar Girls in France-Bost-(1888)-Estes & Lauriat-240p-pict bds,b&w illus by "Champ" (r3,sl wn & rub,few spot pgs) 75.00

CHANCE,FRANK-Bride and the Pennant-1910-Laird & Lee-pict cov,drwngs-1st ed (s8) 950.00

CHANCE,JOSEPH E-Second Texas Infantry-Austin-(1984)-216p-illus-1st ed (n3,vf,dj) 17.50

CHANDLER,C D-How Our Army Grew Wings-NY-(1943)-8vo-xiv,334p-cl,36p plts-1st ed (t2) 100.00

CHANDLER,DAVID-Campaigns of Napoleon-NY-(1966)-1172p-illus,two col text & fldg maps (d7,f,dj) 60.00

CHANDLER,DAVID-Waterloo, the Hundred Days-NY-(1981)-224p-e.p. maps,illus-1st Amer ed (d7,f,dj) 35.00

CHANDLER,HATCHETT-Little Gems from Fort Morgan-(Foley)-(1953)-105p-wrps (b1) 12.50

CHANDLER,LT COL M C-Of Garryowen in Glory-np-(1960)-458p-illus,fldg map-Dowd #174-1st ed (c7,nick dj) 65.00

CHANDLER,PELEG W-American Criminal Trials. Vol.II-Bost-1844-Little,Brown-orig cl-publ separately two yrs after vol.1-1st ed (ee6,sp sun,sl fox) 55.00

CHANDLER,RAYMOND-Big Sleep-Clev,NY-(1946)-World-165p-cl,photos,Forum Motion Pict Ed-1st ed so stated (o1,lacks dj) 15.00

CHANDLER,RAYMOND-Big Sleep-Cleve,NY-(1946)-World-165p-cl-Forum Bk Motion Picture Ed-photos-1st ed thus (g1,dj sl wn,stnd frnt panel) 35.00

CHANDLER,RAYMOND-Big Sleep-Lond-(1939)-Hamish Hamilton-301,(1)p-cl-1st Brit ed (o1,lt fox,sl fade sp) 35.00

CHANDLER,RAYMOND-Big Sleep-NY-1939-Knopf-277p-cl,Chandler's 1st novel,wi dj would be ten times this price-1st ed (o1,lacks dj) 175.00

CHANDLER,RAYMOND-Der Tiefe Schlaf-(Frankfurt/Main)-nd(1940s?)-Ullstein Bucher-274p-wrps (o1) 15.00

CHANDLER,RAYMOND-Farewell, My Lovely-Cleve,NY-(1944)-World-203p-cl-1st prntg Tower Bks ed (o1,lacks dj) 15.00

CHANDLER,RAYMOND-Farewell, My Lovely-NY-1940-Knopf-275p-cl-1st ed (o1,dj blurb pasted to e.p.) 75.00

CHANDLER,RAYMOND-Finger Man and Other Stories-NY-(1946)-Avon Bk Co-122p+ads-wrps-v scarce-1st ed (o1) 125.00

CHANDLER,RAYMOND-Finger Man and Other Stories-NY-(1950)-Avon Publ-153p+ads-wrp,New Avon Library 219-2nd ed (o1,f) 25.00

CHANDLER,RAYMOND-Five Murders-NY-(latest cpyrt 1944)-New Avon Library 63-286p+ads-wrps-2nd ed (o1) 20.00

CHANDLER,RAYMOND-Five Sinister Characters-NY-(1945)-Avon Bk Co-168p-wrps-1st ed (o1,sp wn,marg dmpstns) 65.00

CHANDLER,RAYMOND-High Window-Cleve,NY-(1946)-World-240p-cl-Bruccoli A3.1.d.-1st prntng Tower Bks ed-1st ed thus (g1,dj) 25.00

CHANDLER,RAYMOND-High Window-NY-1942-Knopf-240p-cl-1st ed (o1,e.p. discol) 35.00

CHANDLER,RAYMOND-Killer in the Rain-Bost-1964-Houghton Mifflin-1st Amer ed (c10,dj sl chip,sl wn & tn) 125.00

CHANDLER,RAYMOND-Killer in the Rain-Bost-1964-Houghton Mifflin-394p-cl-1st Amer ed (o1,f,dj) 85.00

CHANDLER,RAYMOND-Lady in the Lake-NY-1943-Knopf-216p-cl-1st ed (o1,sl fade sp,lacks dj) 75.00

CHANDLER,RAYMOND-Letters:Raymond Chandler to James M Fox-Santa Barbara-1978-Neville and Yellin-blu bds stmpd in silv,ltd to 350c,nbrd,autg(Fox)-1st ed (cc2,f) 45.00

CHANDLER,RAYMOND-Little Sister-Bost-1949-1st Amer ed (f5,dj sl chip,wn) 250.00

CHANDLER,RAYMOND-Little Sister-Bost-1949-Houghton-1st Amer ed (d4,tape mrks on dj flaps) 200.00

CHANDLER,RAYMOND-Long Goodbye-Bost-(1954)-Houghton Mifflin-256p-cl,"Book Club Ed"(on frnt dj)-Book Club ed (o1,dj) 12.50

CHANDLER,RAYMOND-Long Goodbye-Bost-1954-HM-1st Amer ed (x7,dj sl wn & chip) 155.00

CHANDLER,RAYMOND-Long Goodbye-Bost-1954-Houghton-1st Amer ed (e4,dj sl chip,sl rub) 250.00

CHANDLER,RAYMOND-Long Goodbye-Lond-(1953)-Hamish Hamilton-1st ed (x2,dj sl wn,tn & soil) 195.00

CHANDLER,RAYMOND-Long Goodbye-Lond-(1953)-Hamish Hamilton-319,(1)P-cl,preceded 1st Amer ed-1st ed (o1,lacks dj) 75.00

CHANDLER,RAYMOND-Long Goodbye-Lond-(1953)-Hamish Hamilton-320p-preceded 1st Amer ed-1954 Edgar award-1st ed (h5,f,sl tn dj) 275.00

CHANDLER,RAYMOND-Midnight Raymond Chandler-Bost-1971-1st ed (n5,f,dj) 45.00

CHANDLER,RAYMOND-Midnight Raymond Chandler-Bost-1971-Houghton Mifflin-734p-cl-1st prntg so stated (o1,f,dj) 30.00

CHANDLER,RAYMOND-Notebooks of Raymond Chandler & English Summer-NY-1976-illus,E Gorey-1st ed (t5,f,dj) 20.00

CHANDLER,RAYMOND-Notebooks of...& English Summer-Lond-(1977)-Weidenfeld & Nicholson-photos,3 drwngs by E.Gorey-1st Brit ed (b5,cor sl bump,dj) 30.00

CHANDLER,RAYMOND-Pearls are a Nuisance-Lond-(1958)-H Hamilton-1st Brit ed (ff6,f,soil dj) 150.00

CHANDLER,RAYMOND-Playback-Bost-1958-Houghton Mifflin-1st Amer ed (x7,vf,f dj) 165.00

CHANDLER,RAYMOND-Playback-Lond-(1958)-HH-207,(1)p-cl,preceded Amer ed-1st ed (o1,lacks dj) 25.00

CHANDLER,RAYMOND-Playback-Lond-(1958)-HH-8vo-orng cl wi silv sp lettrng-1st ed,1st iss (x3,sl chip dj) 150.00

CHANDLER,RAYMOND-Playback-Lond-(1958)-HH-precedes 1st Amer ed-1st ed (z2,sl fox,dj sl rub) 175.00

CHANDLER,RAYMOND-Playback-Lond-1958-HH-1st ed (x7,dj) 145.00

CHANDLER,RAYMOND-Raymond Chandler Speaking-Bost-1962-Houghton Mifflin-1st Amer ed (h8,f,dj) 100.00

CHANDLER,RAYMOND-Raymond Chandler Speaking-Bost-1962-Houghton Mifflin-1st Amer ed (y2,f,dj) 85.00

CHANDLER,RAYMOND-Raymond Chandler Speaking-Bost-1962-Houghton Mifflin-271p-cl,photos-Bruccoli A13.1.b.-1st ed,1st Amer prtg (c1,f,dj) 80.00

CHANDLER,RAYMOND-Raymond Chandler Speaking-Lond-(1962)-HH-1st ed (r5,dj) 60.00

CHANDLER,RAYMOND-Raymond Chandler's Mystery Omnibus-1944-World-1st ed (x7,f,sl chip dj) 20.00

CHANDLER,RAYMOND-Red Wind-Cleve,NY-(1946)-World-253p-cl,Tower Bk ed-1st prntg (o1) 15.00

CHANDLER,RAYMOND-Second Chandler Omnibus-Lond-(1962)-H Hamilton-1st ed thus (bb1,f,dj) 90.00

CHANDLER,RAYMOND-Selected Letters of...-NY-1981-1st ed (t5,f,dj) 30.00

CHANDLER,RAYMOND-Simple Art of Murder-Bost-1950-Houghton Mifflin-1st ed (d4,sp chip dj) 400.00

CHANDLER,RAYMOND-Simple Art of Murder-Bost-1950-Houghton Mifflin-533p-cl-1st ed (o1) 50.00

CHANDLER,RAYMOND-Smart Aleck Kill-1958-Hamish Hamilton-1st ed (x2,sl bump,dj sl wn & tn) 125.00

CHANDLER,RAYMOND-Spanish Blood-Cleve,NY-(1946)-World-1st ed (f5,brwnd pgs,dj) 40.00

CHANDLER,RAYMOND-Spanish Blood-Cleve,NY-(1946)-World-221p-cl,Tower Bks ed-1st prntg (o1,spot cov,wn dj) 25.00

CHANDLER,Z M-Class Book of English Grammar and Analysis-Zanesville-(1862)-Beer & Hurd-228p-prntd bds (k1,wn bds) 15.00

CHANG,HSIN PAO-Commissioner Lin and the Opium War-1964-Harvard-319p-maps-1st ed (b7,f,dj) 35.00

CHANLER,MRS.WINTHROP-Autumn in the Valley-Bost-1936-293p-cl-1st ed (d1,wn dj) 15.00

CHANNING,GRACE E-Sister of a Saint...-Chig-1895-Stone & Kimball-12mo-261p-Lakeside Pr,Carnation Ser.-1st ed (w6,uncut) 45.00

CHANSLER,W D-River Trapper-OH-1928-214p-photos (gg3) 15.00

CHANSLER,WALTER S-River Trapper-Columbus-(1928)-214p+ads-cl (n1) 20.00

CHANTRAINE,CHARLES-La Cuisine Chantraine-1966-Barrows-174p-tan cl-1st ed (q8,dj) 17.50

CHAPEL,CHARLES E-Field, Skeet & Trapshooting-NY-1949-8vo-288p-illus (m3,vf,fray dj) 12.50

CHAPEL,CHARLES E-Gun Collector's Handbook of Values-NY-(1947)-412p-cl-1st revised ed (g1,sl rub) 15.00

CHAPEL,CHARLES E-Gun Collector's Handbook of Values-NY-1970-398p-frntis,photos (t7,dj) 12.50

CHAPELLE,DICKEY-What's a Woman Doing Here-NY-1962-Morrow-2nd prtg (ff3,dj) 45.00

CHAPELLE,H I-Boat Building-Handbook of Wooden Boat Construction-NY-1941-624p-photos (gg3,f) 30.00

CHAPELLE,H I-History of American Sailing Ships-NY-1935-Norton-400p-beige cl,frntis,16 plts,photos-2nd prtg (p8,sp drknd) 50.00

CHAPELLE,H I-National Watercraft Collection-Wash D.C.-1960-GPO-xi,327p-lt blu cl wi wht cov title & dec,drwngs,b&w photos (nn1,cors bump) 50.00

CHAPELLE,H I-Search for Speed Under Sail, 1700 to 1855-NY-1967-Norton-36 halftones,136 plts(incl 16 fldg)-1st ed (v4,f,dj) 95.00

CHAPIN,C-Bird Lovers' Book of Verse-Lond-1937-12mo-188p-half cl,illus (y8,dj) 27.00

CHAPIN,CARL M-Three Died Beside the Marble Pool-NY-1936-Dbldy CC-1st ed (g4,dj) 12.50

CHAPIN,HENRY-Ocean River-NY-1954(1952)-Scribners-8vo-325p-4p photos-latr prtg (dd5,dj,autg) 15.00

CHAPIN,HOWARD M-Documentary History of Rhode Island-Providence-1916,19-Preston & Rounds-2 vols-blu cl,maps,illus-ltd to 250c-1st ed (b2) 75.00

CHAPIN,HOWARD M-Privateer Ships and Sailors-Toulon-1926-G Mouton-258p-blu cl,illus-1st ed (e2) 100.00

CHAPLIN,CHARLES-My Autobiography-NY-(1964)-S&S-8vo-512p-illus-1st US ed (bb5,dj) 17.50

CHAPLIN,CHARLIE-Charlie Chaplin's Own Story-1916-B M-photos,v scarce-1st ed (x2) 1,000.00

CHAPLIN,H D-Queen's Own Royal West Kent Regiment 1920 to 1950-Lond-1954-510p-blu cl,27 maps,illus-1st ed (b7,f) 80.00

CHAPLIN,LITA G-My Life With Chaplin-1966-Bernard Geis Assoc-1st ed (s9,dj) 20.00

CHAPLIN,RALPH-Somewhat Barbaric-Seattle-1944-Dogwood Pr-95p-lt brn cl (b6,autg) 28.00

CHAPLIN,RUTH A-Little Details-Brklyn-(1949)-Geo McKibbin & Son-8vo-13p-cl bckd bds-ltd to 2000c-1st ed (x4) 10.00

CHAPMAN,A-Bird life of the Borders...-Lond-1907-8vo-458p-buckr,col fldg map,60 plts-2nd ed (y8) 80.00

CHAPMAN,ARTHUR-Pony Express-NY,Lond-1932-319p-illus,e.p. maps-1st ed (g7,chip dj) 60.00

CHAPMAN,CHARLES E-History of California: the Spanish Period-NY-1921-Macmillan-527p-maps,illus-1st ed (cc4,hngs rprd) 25.00

CHAPMAN,CHARLES F-How to Build Thirty Five Modern Motor Boats-NY-1929-4to-115p-blu cl,illus (p8) 35.00

CHAPMAN,CHARLES F-Piloting, Seamanship and Small Boat Handling-NY-1972-Motor Boat & Sailing-4to-638p-blu cl over bds,illus (p8) 10.00

CHAPMAN,CHARLES F-Twenty Easy To Build Motor Boats-NY-1922-Motor Boating-4to-79p-blu cl,illus (p8) 25.00

CHAPMAN,F M-Autobigraphy of a Bird Lover-NY-1933-Appleton Century-420p-1st prtg (e9,sp drknd) 30.00

CHAPMAN,F M-Bird Life-NY-1897-Appleton-269p-75p plts by E S Thompson-1st ed (d9) 25.00

CHAPMAN,F M-Bird Life-NY-1901-8vo-88p-cl,75 col plts-Popular col ed (y8,cracked) 25.00

CHAPMAN,F M-Camp and Cruises of an Ornithologist-1908-Appleton-432p-250 photos-1st ed (bb3) 35.00

CHAPMAN,F M-Color Key to North American Birds-1912-Appleton-356p-illus(incl col)-rvsd ed (bb3) 21.00

CHAPMAN,F M-Distribution of Bird Life in Ecuador-NY-1926-8vo-(1),784p-cl,raised bands,27 plts(5 col plts+col map),fldg map-Bull Am Muse of Nat Hist,Vol.LV (y8,rbnd) 160.00

CHAPMAN,F M-Handbook of Birds of Eastern North America-NY-1934(1932)-8vo-581p-cl,29 plts-2nd ed (y8,hng crack) 23.00

CHAPMAN,F M-Travels of Birds-NY-1916-sm 8vo-(6),160p-cl,drwngs (y8,papr yellowed) 18.50

CHAPMAN,F M-Warblers of North America-NY-1907-Appleton-306p-24p col plts by Fuertes-1st ed (e9) 40.00

CHAPMAN,F M-Warblers of North America-NY-1914-Appleton-306p-24 col plts by Fuertes-scarce-2nd ed (c9) 75.00

CHAPMAN,F M-Warblers of North America-NY-1923(1907)-8vo-306p-cl,24 col plts+12 half-tone plts-3rd ed (y8) 45.00

CHAPMAN,F SPENCER-Helvellyn to Himalya-NY-1940-284p-fldg map-1st US ed (p10,f) 25.00

CHAPMAN,F SPENCER-Lightest Africa-Lond-1953-288p-38 plts(mostly col)-1st ed (o10,dj chip) 20.00

CHAPMAN,KENNETH M-Pottery of Santo Domingo Pueblo-Albuq-1977-192p-cl,69 col plts-reiss of 1953 rvsd ed (z1,f) 65.00

CHAPMAN,KENNETH-Pottery of San Ildefonso Pueblo-Albuq-1970-UNMP-4to-260p-wrps,174 plts-1st ed (d3) 30.00

CHAPMAN,MRS.WOODALLEN-In Her Teens-NY-(1914)-Revell-62p-cl (d1) 15.00

CHAPMAN,R W-ET AL-Book Collecting, Four Broadcast Talks-Cambridge-(1950)-Bowes & Bowes-sm 8vo-45p-cl-1st ed (w2,dj,fox e.p.) 25.00

CHAPMAN,V-Victor Chapman's Letters from France-NY-1917-8vo-10;198;6p-cl bkd bds-prntd labl on sp & fr cov,frntis,7p plts-1st ed (t2,sp fade) 30.00

CHAPMAN,WALKER-Search for El Dorado-Indpls-(1967)-Bobbs Merrill-8vo-272p-5 illus-1st ed (jj5,dj) 12.50

CHAPPELL,GORDON-Rails to Carry Copper-Boulder-1973-243p-1st ed (n4,f,dj) 35.00

CHAPPELL,GORDON-Scenic Line of the World-Golden-1970-131p-1st ed (n4,f,dj) 22.00

CHAPPELL,WARREN-Short History of the Printed Word-NY-1970-Knopf-8vo-xviii,255,xv,(v)p-cl,illus-1st ed (x4) 20.00

CHAPPLE,JOE M-To Bagdad and Back-Bost-1928-Chapple-8vo-298p-frntis,col illus-1st ed (jj5,sp rub) 20.00

CHAPUT,DONALD-Francois X Aubry-Glendale-1975-249p-frntis,photos,maps(incl fldg)-1st ed (t7,f) 12.50

CHARAKA CLUB-PROCEEDINGS OF THE...VOLUME 4-NY-1916-153p-ltd ed-dd3 (dd3) 100.00

CHARAKA CLUB-PROCEEDINGS OF THE...VOLUME 5-NY-1919-101p-ltd ed-scarce (dd3) 150.00

CHARAKA CLUB-PROCEEDINGS OF THE...VOLUME 7-NY-1931-190p-ltd ed (dd3) 75.00

CHARCOT,JEAN M-Clinical Lectures on the Diseases of Old Age-NY-1881-280p (g10) 50.00

CHARDIN,SIR JOHN-Travels in Persia-Lond-1927-Argonaut Pr-xxx,287p-1/2 vel/g blu cl,illus-ltd to 975c,nbrd (pp1,cor bump,sl soil) 250.00

CHARHADI,DRISSBEN H-Life Full of Holes-NY-1964-P Bowles,transl-1st ed (t5,f,dj) 20.00

CHARLES,DR J-Wonders of Electricity-Richmond-1890-T E De Yarmon,prntr-64p-pict wrps (l1,sm tr rprd frnt wrps) 20.00

CHARLTON,E HARPER-Railway Car Builders of the United States & Canada-1957-Interurban spec #24-92p-wrps-1st ed (n4) 12.00

CHARNAS,SUZY M-Motherlines-NY-1978-Berkley/Putnam-1st ed (v5,f,f dj) 15.00

CHARNEY,HANNA-Detective Novel of Manners-E Brunswick-1981-Fairleigh Dickinson U-1st ed (d4,f,dj) 25.00

CHARPENTIER,HENRI-Henri Charpentier Cookbook-LA-(1970)-PS&S-4to-414p-blu cl,col & b&w photos-1st trd ed (q8,f,dj) 25.00

CHARTERIS,EVAN-William Augustus Duke of Cumberland and the Seven Years' War-Lond-(1925)-334p-illus-scarce-1st ed (b7,cov spot,dj) 100.00

CHARTERIS,LESLIE-Ace of Knaves-NY-(1944)-Avon/Muder Myst Mo 22-161p+ads-pict wrps (a1) 12.50

CHARTERIS,LESLIE-Angels of Doom-1932-DD-1st Amer ed (x7,sl tn dj) 175.00

CHARTERIS,LESLIE-Brighter Buccaneer-NY-1933-Dbldy CC-1st ed (d4,sl chip dj) 250.00

CHARTERIS,LESLIE-Happy Highwayman-NY-1939-Dbldy-1st US ed (d4,sl chip dj) 40.00

CHARTERIS,LESLIE-Saint in Miami-NY-1940-Dbldy-(precedes Brit ed)-1st ed (hh2,dj) 100.00

CHARTERIS,LESLIE-Saint Sees It Through-NY-1946-Dbldy CC-1st ed (d4,chip dj) 20.00

CHARTERIS,LESLIE-Thieves' Picnic-GC-1937-Dbldy CC-1st Amer ed (w5,dj) 60.00

CHARTERS,ANN-Bibliography of Works by Jack Kerouac-NY-1975-iss w/o dj-rvsd ed (x8,f) 20.00

CHARTERS,ANN-Kerouac: A Biography-SF-1973-1st ed (x8,dj) 18.00

CHARTERS,SAMUEL B-Country Blues-NY-1959-Rinehart-1st ed (v5,f,dj) 35.00

CHARYK,JOHN C-Little White Schoolhouse-Saskatoon-1968-Prairie Bks,Wstrn Prod-8vo-302p-1st ed (aa7,sl chip dj) 15.00*

CHARYN,JEROME-Education of Patrick Silver-1976-Arbor-1st ed (r9,vf,dj) 15.00

CHARYN,JEROME-Eisenhower, My Eisenhower-1971-HRW-1st ed (m9,f,dj) 25.00

CHARYN,JEROME-Franklin Scare-NY-(1977)-Arbor-1st ed (a5,as new in dj) 12.50

CHARYN,JEROME-Franklin Scare-NY-(1977)-Arbor-1st ed (h3,f,dj) 15.00

CHARYN,JEROME-Once Upon a Droshky-NY-(1964)-McGraw Hill-8vo-cl bckd bds-auth 1st bk-1st ed (jj8,f,dj) 45.00

CHARYN,JEROME-Once Upon a Droshky-NY-(1964)-McGraw Hill-auth 1st bk-1st ed (y1,f,f dj) 50.00

CHARYN,JEROME-Pinochio's Nose-NY-(1983)-1st ed (bb10,f,dj) 15.00

CHARYN,JEROME-Seventh Babe-1979-Arbor Hs-1st ed (ff2,dj) 40.00

CHARYN,JEROME-Seventh Babe-1979-Arbor Hs-1st ed (o9,f,sl chip dj) 25.00

CHARYN,JEROME-Tar Baby-1973-Holt-1st ed (m9,f,dj) 15.00

CHASE,A W-Dr Chase's Third and Last Receipt Book and Household Physician-Detr-1891-Dickerson-865p-cl (z7,clippings on cov) 20.00

CHASE,C M-Editor's Run in New Mexico and Colorado-Lyndon-(1882)-232p+3p ads-3/4 lea,drwngs-rare-1st ed (u7,rbnd,rub) 250.00

CHASE,DON M-Pioneers-Redding-1945-Auth-sm 8vo-31p-wrps,map,illus (cc4) 15.00

CHASE,ERNEST D-Romance of Greeting Cards-Cambridge-1956-Univ Pr-8vo-252p-gold cl,col illus,50th Anniversary Rust Craft-scarce (b6,f,chip dj,autg) 20.00

CHASE,EVELYN-Mountain Climber: George B Bayley 1840 to 1894-Palo Alto-1981-173p-illus,map-1st ed (q10,f,dj) 14.00

CHASE,J SMEATON-California Desert Trails-Bost-1919-387p-pict cl,frntis,photos-1st ed (t7) 45.00

CHASE,JAMES H-No Orchids for Miss Blandish-NY-1942-Howell-1st US ed (e4,sp chip dj) 75.00

CHASE,JAMES H-You Have Yourself a Deal-NY-1968-Walker-1st US ed (v5,f,f dj) 25.00

CHASE,OWEN-ET AL-Narratives of the Wreck of the Whale Ship Essex-Lond-1935-Golden Cockerel Pr-4to-88p-12 engrvngs,iss w/o dj-ltd to 275c,nbrd (bb5) 400.00

CHASE,W H-Alaska's Mammoth Brown Bears-MO-1947-129p-photos (gg3,vf,dj) 65.00

CHASE,WILL H-Pioneers of Alaska-KC-1952-203p-pict cl,frntis,photos-1st ed (t7,f) 12.50

CHASTAIN,THOMAS-Pandora's Box-NY-(1974)-Mason & Lipscomb-1st ed (ff3,dj) 40.00

CHATFIELD,CHARLES H-Airplane and Its Engine-NY-1928-McGraw Hill-329p-cl,illus-1st ed so stated (m1) 15.00

CHATHAM,RUSSELL-Angler's Coast-GC-1976-8vo-158p-illus by auth-1st ed (m3,vf,dj) 27.50

CHATHAM,RUSSELL-Striped Bass on the Fly-SF-1977-8vo-96p-illus-1st ed (m3,f) 12.50

CHATHAM-Centennial of the Village Church in...Known as the Ogden Memorial Presbyterian Church...-(Chatham)-1923-60p-cl,illus (aa6) 30.00

CHATTANOOGA, ITS HISTORY AND GROWTH-Chattanooga-nd(1929?)-35p-wrps,illus (aa1) 15.00

CHATTERTON,E K-Chats on Naval Prints-NY-nd-208p-col frntis,34 illus on glossy plts-1st Amer ed (w10) 24.00

CHATTERTON,E K-Old East Indiamen-Lond-nd-T Werner Laurie Ltd-8vo-343p-illus blu cl,illus (p8,sl fox & wn) 40.00

CHATTERTON,E K-Sailing Ships-Lond-(1914)-sq 8vo-362p-col papr cov labl,illus,plts,2 fldg plans-2nd prtg (w10,sl snag sp) 27.50

CHATTERTON,E K-Ship Models-Lond-1923-Studio Ltd-hvy 4to-53p text-g cov dec,dec e.p.,142 plts(incl col tip-in)-ltd to 1000c (pp1,fade,hng weak) 225.00

CHATTERTON,E K-Ships & Ways of Other Days-Phila-(1924)-wht lettrd,dec blu cl wi col papr labl on cov,plts,illus,3 fldg plans-2nd prtg (w10,sp lettrng wn) 24.00

CHATTERTON,E K-Steamship Models-Lond-1924-T Werner Laurie-tip in col plts,ltd to 1000c,autg (l9,sl fox,cov sl soil) 300.00

CHATWIN,BRUCE-In Patagonia-1977-Summit Bks-auth 1st bk-1st Amer ed (x2,f,dj) 125.00

CHATWIN,BRUCE-In Patagonia-Lond-1978-204p-map frntis,photos (t7,dj) 20.00

CHATWIN,BRUCE-On the Black Hill-Lond-(1982)-J Cape-1st ed (j6,f,f dj) 85.00

CHATWIN,BRUCE-On the Black Hill-NY-(1983)-Viking-1st US ed (cc2,f,dj) 30.00

CHATWIN,BRUCE-On the Black Hill-NY-(1983)-Viking-1st US ed (q2,dj) 20.00

CHATWIN,BRUCE-Viceroy of Ouidah-1980-J Cape-1st ed (s9,vf,dj) 40.00

CHATWIN,BRUCE-Viceroy of Ouidah-NY-(1980)-Summit-1st US ed (h3,f,dj) 20.00

CHAUVELOT,ROBERT-Mysterious India-NY-1921-Century-8vo-277p-60 photos-1st US ed (jj5,f,sl chip dj) 30.00

CHAVEZ,ANELICO-Coronado's Friars-Wash D.C.-1968-102p-4 photos,frntis-1st ed (v7,f) 45.00

CHAVEZ,ANGELICO-My Penitente Land-Albuq-(1975)-272p-1st ed (u7,wn dj) 35.00

CHAVEZ,ANGELICO-Origins of New Mexico Families in the Spanish Colonial Period...-Santa Fe-1954-337p-dbl col,4 illus,Cisneros-scarce (u7) 100.00

CHAVEZ,TIBO J-New Mexican Folklore of the Rio Abajo-(Portales)-(1972)-(Bishop Prtg Co)-67p (m6) 20.00

CHAYEFSKY,PADDY-Altered States-NY-(1978)-H&R-1st ed (hh5,f,f dj) 15.00

CHAYTOR,A H-Letters to a Salmon Fisher's Son-Lond-1919-8vo-304p-photos (m3) 45.00

CHECK LIST OF N AMER BIRDS-(A.O.U.)-Lancaster-1931-8vo-526p-cl-4th ed (y8) 50.00

CHEEVER,GEORGE B-God Against Slavery-NY-1857-J H Ladd-1st ed (u2) 60.00

CHEEVER,JOHN-Brigadier and the Golf Widow-(1964)-Harper & Row-1st ed (q9,sl rub dj) 35.00

CHEEVER,JOHN-Brigadier and the Golf Widow-NY-(1964)-Harper-1st ed (m7,wn dj) 20.00

CHEEVER,JOHN-Bullet Park-NY-1969-Knopf-1st ed (k3,f,dj) 25.00

CHEEVER,JOHN-Bullet Park-NY-1969-Knopf-1st ed (m7,f,dj) 45.00

CHEEVER,JOHN-Enormous Radio-NY-1953-Funk & Wagnalls-1st ed (m7,sl wn dj) 175.00

CHEEVER,JOHN-Enormous Radio-NY-1953-Funk & Wagnalls-wi "1" on cpyrt pg-1st ed (ee2,dj) 125.00

CHEEVER,JOHN-Falconer-NY-1977-Knopf-1st ed (j3,f,dj) 25.00

CHEEVER,JOHN-Homage to Shakespeare-Stevenson-(1968)-Country Squires Bk-ltd to 150c,nbrd,autg-1st ed (m7,f,f dj) 250.00

CHEEVER,JOHN-Housebreaker of Shady Hill-NY-(1958)-Harper-1st ed (ee2,f,dj) 85.00

CHEEVER,JOHN-Housebreaker of Shady Hill-NY-(1958)-Harper-1st ed (l7,sl wn dj) 65.00

CHEEVER,JOHN-Oh What a Paradise it Seems-NY-1982-Knopf-1st ed (b5,as new in dj) 12.50

CHEEVER,JOHN-Oh What a Paradise it Seems-NY-1982-Knopf-1st ed (u10,as new in dj) 15.00

CHEEVER,JOHN-Some People,Places & Things That Will Not Appear In My Next Novel-NY-(1961)-Harper-1st ed (d10,dj) 75.00

CHEEVER,JOHN-Some People,Places & Things That Will Not Appear in My Next Novel-NY-(1961)-Harper-1st ed (m7,f,sl rub dj) 65.00

CHEEVER,JOHN-Stories of...-NY-1978-Knopf-1st ed (u10,f,f dj) 25.00

CHEEVER,JOHN-Wapshot Scandal-NY-(1964)-Harper & Row-1st ed (ee2,f,sl chip dj) 35.00

CHEEVER,REV HENRY T-Reel in a Bottle, for Jack in the Doldrums, Being the Adventures of the Two King's Seamen...-NY-1852-Scribner-purple cl-Wright II,494-1st ed (f2,sl fade sp) 65.00

CHEEVER,SUSAN-Looking For Work-Lond-(1979)-Weidenfeld & Nicolson-1st ed (k7,dj) 15.00

CHEKHOV,ANTON-Sea Gull-1939-Scribners-S Young,transl.-1st Amer ed (x2,dj) 45.00

CHELEY,F H-Camping with Henry-NY-1918-12mo-137p (m3) 25.00

CHELEY,F H-Little Camp Fires-Bost-1938-12mo-248p-photos (m3,f) 17.50

CHENEVIX-TRENCH,CHARLES-History of Horsemanship-GC-1970-Dbldy-1st US prtg (j9,dj) 40.00

CHENEY,EDNAH D-Louisa May Alcott, the Children's Friend-Bost-(1888)-L Prang-oblng 8vo-58p-dec gry cl prtd in blu & silv,chromolitho frntis,illus-scarce (hh9,cov sl soil) 200.00

CHENEY,P-Dames Don't Care-1938-CM-1st Amer ed (x7,dj) 65.00

CHENEY,SHELDON-Stage Decoration-NY-1928-John Day-sm 4to-138p-blk cl sp,prple bds,126 illus (r10,poor box) 75.00

CHERNAIK,JUDITH-Daughter-NY-1979-Harper-216p-1st ed (ff1,sl chip dj) 15.00

CHERNIAVSKY,L S-ED.-Moscow Theatre for Children-Moscow-1934-Coop Publ Co-oblng 8vo-pict cov,illus-1st ed (jj9) 65.00

CHERNICHEWSKI,VLADIMIR-Anthropological Report on a London Suburb-Lond-(1935)-Grayson-68p-cl-1st ed (dd10,dj soil & sl wn) 25.00

CHERRY,KELLY-Augusta Played-Bost-1979-Houghton Mifflin-1st ed (j6,f,dj) 20.00

CHERRY-GARRARD,APSLEY-Worst Journey in the World-Lond-1952-612p-9 illus,4 maps (o10,vf) 70.00

CHESBRO,GEORGE C-City of Whispering Stone-1978-Simon-1st ed (s10,dj) 15.00

CHESBRO,GEORGE C-City of Whispering Stone-NY-1978-Simon-1st ed (g4,f,dj) 20.00

CHESELDEN,WILLIAM-Anatomy of the Human Body-Lond-1741-8vo-336p-qtr tan linen wi Ingres papr over bds,39p engrvngs-6th ed (g10,recased) 275.00

CHESELDINE,R M-Ohio in the Rainbow-Columbus-1924-528p-cl (l1) 20.00

CHESHAM,SALLIE-Born to Battle-Chig-(1965)-Rand McNally-8vo-286p-64p photos-1st ed (gg5,cor wn,sl chip dj) 10.00

CHESHIRE,FRANK-Scientific Temperance Hand Book-Lond-c.1890-285p-1st ed (dd3) 60.00

CHESLER,PHYLLIS-Women and Madness-GC-1972-Dbldy-8vo-359p-cl,illus-1st ed (ee9,f,dj) 15.00

CHESNEL,PAUL-History of Cavelier De La Salle, 1643 to 1687-NY-1932-Putnam-vii,232p-frntis port,maps(2 fldg) (k10,wn dj) 30.00*

CHESNEY,W-Founderd Galleon-1902-Methuen-1st ed (x7,sl fade sp) 125.00

CHESNUT,MARY-Diary From Dixie-Bost-1949-572p-illus (n3,dj) 32.50

CHESNUTT,CHARLES W-Conjure Woman-Bost,NY-1899-auth 1st bk-1st ed (d5,few stnd pgs) 250.00

CHESTER,G R-Wallingford in His Prime-1913-BM-1st ed (x7) 15.00

CHESTER,GIRARD-Embattled Maiden-NY-1951-Putnam-8vo-307p-13 illus-1st ed (gg5,dj sl tn) 20.00

CHESTERTON,G K-Alarms and Discursions-NY-1911-Dodd,Mead-1st US ed (e10,drknd cov) 20.00

CHESTERTON,G K-Ball and the Cross-1910-Wells,Gardner,Darton & Co-1st Brit ed (x2) 65.00

CHESTERTON,G K-Ballad of the White Horse-NY-1911-1st ed (y7) 45.00

CHESTERTON,G K-Club of Queer Trades-1905-Harpers-1st ed (x7,cov spots) 150.00

CHESTERTON,G K-Coloured Lands-1938-S&W-col & b&w illus-1st ed (x7,f,vf dj) 150.00

CHESTERTON,G K-Coloured Lands-NY-1938-Sheed & Ward-illus by auth-1st ed (y1,dj sl wn) 50.00

CHESTERTON,G K-Innocence of Father Brown-NY-1911-Lane-1st US ed (d4) 10.00

CHESTERTON,G K-Man Who Knew Too Much-1922-Harpers-1st Amer ed (x7,f,dj) 185.00

CHESTERTON,G K-Man Who Was Thursday-1908-DM-1st Amer ed (x7) 70.00

CHESTERTON,G K-Napoleon of Notting Hill-1906-J Lane-t.p. is a cancel-1st Amer ed (x2,f) 70.00

CHESTERTON,G K-Napoleon of Notting Hill-Lond-1904-J Lane,Bodley Head-illus by W G Robertson-1st ed (kk5) 135.00

CHESTERTON,G K-Paradoxes of Mr Pond-1937-DM-1st Amer ed (x7,dj sl wn & tn) 55.00

CHESTERTON,G K-Return of Don Quixote-1927-DM-1st Amer ed (x7,f,sl chip dj) 125.00

CHESTERTON,G K-Secret of Father Brown-NY-1927-Harper-1st US ed (f4,dj) 150.00

CHESTERTON,G K-St.Francis of Assisi-Lond-(1926)-illus by F Cayley Robinson-1st ed (y7,dj) 75.00

CHESTERTON,G K-What's Wrong with the World-1910-D,M-1st Amer ed (x2) 35.00

CHESTNUT,ROBERT-Syndicate-Chig-1960-Newsstand Libr-wrps-1st ed (v5,f) 40.00

CHETLAIN,AUGUSTUS L-Recollections of Seventy Years-Galena-1899-Gazette Publ-304p-errata-Nevins II,145-1st ed (ee4,pres) 80.00

CHETWYND,SIR GEORGE-Racing Reminiscences and Experiences of the Turf-Lond-1891-Longmans,Green-2 vols-2nd ed (p6) 150.00

CHEVIGNY,HECTOR-Lord of Alaska-NY-1942-Viking-320p-e.p. maps-1st Amer ed (p2,sl rub) 12.50

CHEVIGNY,HECTOR-Lord of Alaska-NY-1942-Viking-8vo-320p-cl,map e.p.-1st Amer ed (ll1,wn dj) 30.00

CHEW,PETER-Kentucky Derby-Bost-1974-Houghton Mifflin-4to-1st ed (f10,dj) 65.00

CHEYNEY,PETER-Dark Hero-Lond-1946-Collins-1st ed (w9,f,dj) 25.00

CHEYNEY,PETER-No Ordinary Cheyney-Lond-1948-Faber-1st ed (g4,sl yel pgs,dj) 15.00

CHEZ MAXIM'S-NY-(1962)-McGraw Hill-253p-red cl bds,photos (l6,dj) 65.00

CHICAGO AMERICAN INDIAN CENTER COOKBOOK-Chig-1970-Amer Indian Cntr-unpgd-wrps,illus-1st ed (k6,sl sun) 26.00

CHICAGO-Reminiscences of...During the Forties and Fifties-Chig-1913-Donnelley-137p-frntis-Lakeside Classics (cc4) 35.00

CHICAGO-Reminiscences of...During the Great Fire-Chig-1915-Donnelley-140p-fldg plt-Lakeside Classics (cc4) 35.00

CHIDESTER,OTIS-ED.-Brand Book 1 of the Tucson Corral of Westerners-1967-4to-204p-illus-1st ed (d3) 35.00

CHIDESTER,OTIS-ED.-Brand Book 2 of the Tucson Corral of Westerners-Tucson-1971-4to-261p-illus,maps-1st ed (d3) 25.00

CHIDSEY,DONALD B-Lewis and Clark, the Great Adventure-NY-(1970)-191p-illus-1st ed (c7,f,dj) 30.00

CHIERA,EDWARD-They Wrote on Clay-1938-U of Chig Pr-cl,illus-1st ed (n8,f) 15.00

CHILD,C M-Patterns and Problems of Development-Chig-(1941)-U of Chig Pr-x+811p-brwn cl-1st ed (a2) 25.00

CHILD,DAPHNE-ED.-Zulu War Journal of Col Henry Harford-Hamden-1980-88p-illus-1st Amer ed (b7,f,dj) 35.00

CHILD,GEORGIE B-Efficient Kitchen-NY-1914-McBride,Nast & Co-242p-bds,photos plts,drwngs-Bitting 86 (n6) 20.00

CHILD,J M-Early Mathematical Manuscripts of Leibniz-Chig-1920-Open Court-238p-grn cl,text illus (hh6,cor bump) 45.00

CHILD,JULIA-ET AL-Mastering the Art of French Cooking. Vol.1-1963-Knopf-4to-684p+34p index,pict wht bds,drwngs-4th prtg (q8) 20.00

CHILD,JULIA-From Julia Child's Kitchen-1975-Knopf-687p+26p index,pict bds,photos,drwngs-1st ed (q8,dj) 18.50

CHILD,JULIA-Julia Child & Company-1978-Knopf-4to-244p-dec wht bds,col photos-1st ed (q8,dj) 20.00

CHILD,JULIA-Mastering the Art of French Cooking. Vol.2-1970-Knopf-555p+54p index,dec wht bds,illus-1st ed (q8,dj) 22.50

CHILD,LYDIA M-Letters From New York. Second Series-NY-1845-Francis-8vo-287p+ads-publ cl-1st ed (w6) 75.00

CHILD,RICHARD W-Blue Wall-Bost-1912-Houghton Mifflin-dbl spread pict t.p.-1st ed (gg8,vf) 40.00

CHILD,STEPHEN-Landscape Architecture-1927-Stanford Univ-4to-xiv,(2),279p-cl,14 illus,14 plts(3 fldg)-1st ed (cc10) 150.00

CHILDE,V GORDON-New Light on the Most Ancient East-NY-1934-Appleton-cl,32 plts,drwngs-1st ed (o8) 25.00

CHILDERNESS,GEORGE-Murder in False Face-NY-1943-Phoenix-1st ed (g4,dj) 15.00

CHILDERS,E-Riddle of the Sands-1915-DM-1st Amer ed (x7) 185.00

CHILDERS,G S-War Eagles-NY-1943-8vo-xiv,352p-illus cl,frntis,64p plts,3 dbl-pg plts,illus e.p.-1st ed (t2) 35.00

CHILDRESS,ALICE-Like One of the Family-Brklyn-(1956)-Independence Publ-auth scarce 1st bk-1st ed (cc1,dj chip,sl tn) 100.00

CHILDRESS,ALICE-Rainbow Jordan-NY-(1981)-CM&G-1st ed (cc1,f,dj) 25.00

CHILDRESS,ALICE-Short Walk-NY-(1979)-CM&G-1st ed (cc1,dj sl tn) 50.00

CHILDRESS,ALICE-Short Walk-NY-(1979)-Coward-1st ed (w5,f,f dj) 30.00

CHILDS,MARILYN C-Training Your Colt to Ride and Drive-NY-1972-Arco (h9,dj) 30.00

CHILDS,TIMOTHY-Cold Turkey-1979-Harper & Row-1st ed (r9,f,dj) 10.00

CHILTON,JOHN-Who's Who in Jazz-1978-Time Life Records-Special Ed (u4,f) 18.00

CHILVERS,H A-Huberta Goes South-South Africa-1931-8vo-174p (m3) 20.00

CHILVERS,HEDLEY A-Out of the Crucible-Lond-1929-Cassell-xiii,274p-gilt,frntis,15 plts (u5,f) 50.00

CHINDAHL,GEORGE L-History of the Circus in America-1959-Caxton-279p-Illus-1st ed (v8,dj) 35.00

CHINESE LOVE POEMS-Mount Vernon-(1942)-Peter Pauper Pr-8vo-unpgd-bds,papr sp labl-ltd to 1650c (x4,box) 35.00

CHINIQUY,FATHER-Priest,the Woman and the Confessional-Chig-1890-296p-cl-36th ed (h1,sl wn sp) 15.00

CHIPMAN,GEN NORTON P-Tragedy of Andersonville-Sacramento-(1911)-N P Chipman-529p-illus-1st ed (dd4) 60.00

CHIPPENDALE,THOMAS-Gentleman and Cabinet Maker's Director-NY-1938-Towse Publ-folio-red/beige cl,200 plts,99p ads,40 photos (r10,chip dj) 100.00

CHIPPERFIELD,JIMMY-My Wild Life-1976-Putnam-219p-Illus-1st Amer ed (v8,dj) 12.00

CHIROL,VALENTINE-Indian Unrest-Lond-1910-371p-red cl-1st ed (b7) 25.00

CHISHOLM,JAMES-South Pass 1868-1960-U of Nebr-244p-drwngs-Six Guns #1016-1st ed (r8,dj chip & wn) 35.00

CHISHOLM,JAMES-South Pass 1868-1960-U of Nebr-244p-illus-1st ed (g7,poor dj) 30.00

CHISHOLM,JOE-Brewery Gulch-San Antonio-(1949)-Naylor-xii,180p-cl,frntis plt-1st ed (v1,dj) 35.00

CHISHOLM,LAWRENCE W-Fenollosa-New Haven-1963-Yale Univ Pr-cl-1st ed (o8,dj) 22.50

CHITTENDEN,HIRAM-American Fur Trade of the Far West-NY-(1935)-2 vols-illus,fldg map rear pckt-2nd ed (f7,fade sp,rprd box) 225.00

CHITTENDEN,HIRAM-American Fur Trade of the Far West-NY-1902-Francis P Harper-3 vols-illus,fldg map rear pckt vol.3-Howes C390-1st ed (cc4,hngs rprd) 600.00

CHITTENDEN,HIRAM-History of the American Fur Trade of the Far West-Stanford-1954(1902)-Academic Rprnts-2 vols-Howes C390 (d3,as new in dj) 60.00

CHITTENDEN,HIRAM-History of the American Fur Trade of the Far West.Vol.I & II-Stanford-1954-1029p-frntis (t7,f,dj) 75.00

CHITTENDEN,HIRAM-Yellowstone National Park-Cin-1895-Robt Clarke Co-xvi+397p-grn cl,illus,maps(incl lg fldg map)-1st ed (b2) 25.00

CHITTENDEN,HIRAM-Yellowstone National Park-St.Paul-(1927)-J E Haynes-356p-illus,map in rear-new & enlgd ed (cc4) 15.00

CHITTENDEN,HIRAM-Yellowstone National Park-Stanford-1933-286p-cl,fldg map-rvsd ed (x6) 20.00

CHITTENDEN,RUSSELL-Development of Physiological Chemistry in the United States-NY-1930-427p-1st ed (dd3) 85.00

CHITTENDEN,WILLIAM L-Ranch Verses-NY,Lond-1925-228p+ads-cl (l1) 12.50

CHITTENDON,LUCIUS E-Invisible Shield-San Diego-(1969)-133p-ltd to 1500c-1st ed (n3,f,box) 15.00

CHOICE RECIPES...DIVISION ONE,ZION LUTHERAN CHURCH...-Wooster-(1921)-48p-wrps (f1,sl wn) 10.00

CHOLMONDELEY,LIONEL B-History of the Bonin Islands-Lond-1915-Constable-178p-e.p. maps,photos (c3,sl fox) 75.00

CHOLMONDELEY-PENNELL,H-Angler-Naturalist-Lond-1863-8vo-425p+ads-illus (m3,f) 35.00

CHOLMONDELEY-PENNELL,H-Book of the Pike-Lond-1865-12mo-254p+ads-col frontis,illus-1st ed (m3) 40.00

CHONZ,SELINA-Bell for Ursli-NY-(1950)-OUP-oblng 4to-unpgd-cl bckd bds,col illus,A Carigiet-1st US ed (r3,dj) 40.00

CHOPIN,KATE-Bayou Folk-Bost-1894-Houghton Mifflin-8vo-313p-BAL 3244-scarce-1st ed (w6,sp fade,frnt fly separate) 400.00

CHOPIN,KATE-Night in Acadie-Chig-1897-Way & Williams-1st ed (w5,f) 275.00

CHORLTON,WM-American Grape Grower's Guide-NY-1865-Orange Judd-204p-cl,illus (x6,edge rub) 45.00

CHOUINARD,YVON-Climbing Ice-SF-1978-4to-192p-166 photos-1st ed (o10,f,dj) 35.00

CHOUKAS,MICHAEL-Black Angels of Athos-Brattleboro-1934-Stephen Daye Pr-cl,frntis,illus-1st ed (n8,f,dj) 25.00

CHOUKRI,MOHAMED-Jean Genet in Tangier-NY-1974-1st US ed (s5,dj) 20.00

CHRISMAN,ARTHUR B-Shen of the Sea-NY-(1925)-Dutton-252p-pict cl,over 50 silhouettes,E Hasselriis-6th prtg (s3,sp top wn,g rub) 12.00

CHRISMAN,HARRY-1001 Most Asked Questions About the American West-(1982)-Ohio U Pr-349p-illus,e.p. map-1st ed (r8,f,sl tn dj) 20.00

CHRISMAN,HARRY-Fifty Years on the Owl Hoot Trail-Chig-(1969)-Sage Bks-355p-cl,photos-1st ed (w3,vf) 45.00

CHRISMAN,HARRY-Ladder of Rivers-(1962)-Sage-426p-illus-Six Guns 420-1st ed (t8,sl wn) 35.00

CHRISMAN,HARRY-Ladders of Rivers-Denver-(1962)-Sage Bks-426p-illus-Six Guns 420-1st ed (ff4,dj) 45.00

CHRIST,JAY F-An Irregular Guide to Sherlock Holmes-NY-1947-Argus-1st ed (l4,sl fray) 35.00

CHRISTENSEN,CLYDE M-Common Edible Mushrooms-Mpls-(1943)-U of Minn Pr-124p-col frntis,3 plts,b&w photos (u6) 25.00

CHRISTENSEN,ERWIN O-Index of American Design-NY-1950-Macmillan-4to-xviii,229p-cl,illus-1st ed (x4) 40.00

CHRISTIAN,FRANCIS A-Homes & Gardens in Old Virginia-NY-(1931)-Bonanza-(2),367p-photos-4th ed (o2,sl rub dj) 15.00

CHRISTIAN,GLYNN-Fragile Paradise-Bost/Tor-1982-Little,Brown-sm 4to-256p-illus,maps-1st Amer ed (nn1,dj) 35.00

CHRISTIAN,MRS.EUGENE-Uncooked Food-NY-(1904)-Health Culture Co-246p-blk cl bds,gold lttrs,frntis-Bitting 88 (m6) 30.00

CHRISTIANSEN,HARRY-Lake Shore Electric Railway 1893 to 1938-(Cleve)-(1963)-51,(31)p-wrps,photos (d1) 15.00

CHRISTIANSEN,HARRY-Ride the Red Devils Along Ohio's Trolley Trails-1971-Transit Hs-4to-152p-wrps,illus (nn7) 24.00

CHRISTIE,AGATHA-13 at Dinner-1933-Dodd-1st Amer ed (s10,sl chip dj) 225.00

CHRISTIE,AGATHA-Agatha Christie Mystery Collection-1983-Bantam-74 vols-lea wi gold stmpg,a.e.g.,mrbld e.p. (x7) 375.00

CHRISTIE,AGATHA-Agatha Christie's Crime Reader-1944-World-1st ed (x7,dj) 24.00

CHRISTIE,AGATHA-And Then There Were None-1940-Dodd-1st Amer ed (s10,dj sp fade) 175.00

CHRISTIE,AGATHA-At Bertram's Hotel-1965-Collins-1st ed (x2,dj) 28.00

CHRISTIE,AGATHA-At Bertram's Hotel-NY-1966-Dodd-1st US ed (k4,f,dj) 12.50

CHRISTIE,AGATHA-Big Four-1927-DM-1st Amer ed (x7) 90.00

CHRISTIE,AGATHA-By the Pricking of My Thumbs-Lond-1968-Collins CC-1st ed (f4,f,dj) 15.00

CHRISTIE,AGATHA-By the Pricking of My Thumbs-Lond-1968-Collins CC-1st ed (w9,f,dj) 25.00

CHRISTIE,AGATHA-Carribean Mystery-Lond-1954-Collins-1st ed (z2,f,f dj) 50.00

CHRISTIE,AGATHA-Cat Among the Pigeons-Lond-1959-Collins CC-1st ed (k4,dj) 25.00

CHRISTIE,AGATHA-Cat Among the Pigeons-Lond-1959-Collins-1st ed (z2,f,dj) 40.00

CHRISTIE,AGATHA-Clocks-Lond-1963-Collins CC-1st ed (f4,f,dj) 35.00

CHRISTIE,AGATHA-Dead Man's Folly-NY-1956-Dodd,Mead-1st Amer ed (z2,f,sl soil dj) 35.00

CHRISTIE,AGATHA-Death Comes as the End-Lond-1945-Collins CC-1st Brit ed (w9,f,dj sp sl fade) 250.00

CHRISTIE,AGATHA-Destination Unknown-1954-Collins-1st ed (x7,dj) 50.00

CHRISTIE,AGATHA-Double Sin and Other Stories-NY-1961-Dodd-1st ed (j4,f,dj) 25.00

CHRISTIE,AGATHA-Easy to Kill-NY-1939-Dodd Mead-1st Amer ed (gg8,dj) 125.00

CHRISTIE,AGATHA-Elephants Can Remember-Lond-1972-Collins CC-1st ed (g4,f,dj) 17.50

CHRISTIE,AGATHA-Elephants Can Remember-Lond-1972-Collins-1st ed (r4,dj) 25.00

CHRISTIE,AGATHA-Endless Night-1968-Dodd-1st Amer ed (s10,dj) 15.00

CHRISTIE,AGATHA-Endless Night-Lond-1967-Collins-1st ed (q4,dj sl tn & soil) 22.50

CHRISTIE,AGATHA-Hallow'en Party-Lond-1969-Collins CC-1st Ed (f4,dj) 12.50

CHRISTIE,AGATHA-Hercule Poirot's Early Cases-NY-1974-Dodd-1st US ed (f4,f,dj) 15.00

CHRISTIE,AGATHA-Hickory Dickory Dock-1955-Collins-1st ed (x2,dj) 45.00

CHRISTIE,AGATHA-Hound of Death and Other Stories-Lond-1933-Odhams-1st ed (w9,sl spot,fade,dj chip,stnd) 185.00

CHRISTIE,AGATHA-Labors of Hercules-NY-1947-Dodd-1st US ed (f4,dj missing sm chips) 85.00

CHRISTIE,AGATHA-Mirror Crack'd From Side to Side-Lond-1962-Collins-1st ed (z2,f,f dj) 35.00

CHRISTIE,AGATHA-Miss Marple's 6 Final Cases-Lond-1979-Collins CC-1st ed (w9,f,dj) 30.00

CHRISTIE,AGATHA-Moving Finger-1943-Collins-1st Brit ed (x7,dj) 325.00

CHRISTIE,AGATHA-Moving Finger-NY-1942-Dodd Mead-1st Amer ed (gg8,dj chip & creased) 85.00

CHRISTIE,AGATHA-Moving Finger-NY-1942-Dodd-1st Amer ed (e4,sp wn dj) 135.00

CHRISTIE,AGATHA-Murder in the Calais Coach-NY-1934-Dodd,Mead-lt yel cl-1st Amer ed (gg7) 50.00

CHRISTIE,AGATHA-Mystery of the Blue Train-NY-1928-Dodd-1st US ed (e4,sl fade sp) 30.00

CHRISTIE,AGATHA-Nemesis-Lond-1971-Collins CC-1st ed (h4,f,dj) 15.00

CHRISTIE,AGATHA-Partner's in Crime-NY-1929-Dodd-1st US ed (g4,sl fade sp) 35.00

CHRISTIE,AGATHA-Pocket Full of Rye-1953-CCC-1st ed (s10,dj) 20.00

CHRISTIE,AGATHA-Pocket Full of Rye-NY-1953-Dodd-1st US ed (h4,f,sl wn dj) 35.00

CHRISTIE,AGATHA-Postern of Fate-Lond-1973-Collins CC-1st ed (k4,dj) 15.00

CHRISTIE,AGATHA-Remembered Death-1945-DM-1st ed (x7,dj sl wn & tn) 78.00

CHRISTIE,AGATHA-Secret Adversary-NY-1922-Dodd-1st US ed (d4,fade sp) 125.00

CHRISTIE,AGATHA-There is a Tide-1948-Dodd,Mead-1st Amer ed (n9,dj missing sm chips) 65.00

CHRISTIE,AGATHA-They Do It With Mirrors-Lond-1952-Collins-1st ed (z2,f,dj) 45.00

CHRISTIE,AGATHA-Third Girl-1967-DM-1st Amer ed (x7,dj) 18.00

CHRISTIE,AGATHA-Third Girl-NY-1967-Dodd-1st Amer ed (h4,f,sl wn dj) 15.00

CHRISTIE,AGATHA-Towards Zero-Lond-1944-Collins CC-1st ed (w9,drknd pgs,sl creased dj) 250.00

CHRISTIE,AGATHA-Triple Threat-1943-DM-1st ed (x7,dj) 85.00

CHRISTIE,AGATHA-Under Dog and Other Stories-NY-1951-Dodd-1st US ed (e4,sp chip dj) 50.00

CHRISTIE,AGATHA-Under Dog-1929-Readers Libr-scarce in dj-1st ed (x7,dj) 325.00

CHRISTIE,AGATHA-Witness for the Prosecution-NY-1948-Dodd-1st ed (j4,f,sl tn dj) 100.00

CHRISTOPHER,MATT-Fox Steals Home-1978-Little,Brown-1st ed (s7,f,dj) 10.00

CHRISTOPHER,MILBOURNE-Illustrated History of Magic-NY-1973-Crowell-4to-452p-frntis,6 col plts (aa7,dj) 45.00*

CHRISTOVICH-ED.-New Orleans Architecture Volume Three: The Cemeteries-Gretna-(1974)-Pelican-sm folio-198p-col photos-1st ed (p1,f,dj) 45.00

CHRISTY,E V A-Modern Side Saddle Riding-lond-1907-Vinton-3rd ed rvsd (h9) 65.00

CHRISTY,THOMAS-Road Across the Plains-Denver-1969-4to-94 maps-1st ed (r8,f,f dj) 60.00

CHRISTY,THOMAS-Road Across the Plains-Denver-1969-Old West Publ-94p-illus (cc4,dj) 50.00

CHRISTY,THOMAS-Road Across the Plains-Denver-1969-Rosenstock Publ-4to-unpgd-frntis port,94 maps-1st ed (g7,unopened,f,dj) 85.00

CHROMAN,NATHAN-Treasury of American Wines-(1976)-Crown-folio-256p-red bds,col & b&w illus (q8,dj) 22.50

CHRYSLER,M-Ferns of New Jersey-New Bruns-1947-Rutgers-201p-cl,photos,maps (x6,f,dj chip,wn) 35.00

CHU,ARTHUR-Collector's Book of Jade-NY-1978-Crown-xvi,144p-illus (u5,f,f dj) 22.50

CHURCH,ALBERT C-American Fisherman-NY-(1940)-Norton-192p-cl,photos-1st ed so stated (aa1,dj) 30.00

CHURCH,ELLA R-Money-Making for Ladies-NY-1882-221p-cl (c1) 22.50

CHURCH,PEGGY P-House at Otowi Bridge-(Albuq)-(1966)-149p-drwngs-scarce-1st ed (v7,dj) 35.00

CHURCH,RICHARD-Portrait of Canterbury-Lond-1953-Hutchinson-cl,frntis,illus-1st ed (n8,f,dj) 20.00

CHURCH,RUTH E-American Guide to Wines-Chig-(1963)-Quadrangle-272p-dec gry cl,photos,drwngs,maps-1st ed (q8,dj) 15.00

CHURCH,RUTH E-Mary Meade's Sausage Cookbook-(1967)-Rand McNally-223p-pink cl-1st prtg (q8,dj) 12.50

CHURCH,THOMAS D-Gardens are for People-NY-(1955)-Reinhold-sm folio-248p wi index,photos-1st ed (t1,f,dj) 60.00

CHURCH,WILLIAM C-Life of John Ericsson-NY-1890-Scribner's-2 vols,blu cl,illus,t.e.g.-1st ed (m2) 75.00

CHURCHILL,ALLEN-Improper Bohemians-Lond-1961-Cassell-1st Brit ed (f8,f,dj) 30.00

CHURCHILL,ALLEN-Improper Bohemians-NY-1959-Dutton-1st ed (h8,f,dj) 40.00

CHURCHILL,ALLEN-Literary Decade-Englewood Cliffs-(1971)-Prentice Hall-8vo-346p-cl-1st ed (w2,dj) 20.00

CHURCHILL,CHARLES W-Fortunes are For the Few-Pasadena-1977-San Diego Hist Scty-xiv+136p-brwn cl,illus-1st ed (h2,dj) 25.00

CHURCHILL,R-Churchill's Shotgun Book-NY-1955-277p-photos (gg3,f,dj) 20.00

CHURCHILL,ROBERT-Game Shooting-Harrisburg-1963-4to-252p-photos-revsd ed (m3,f,dj) 25.00

CHURCHILL,WINSTON-Dawn od Liberation-1945-Cassell-War Speeches #5-1st ed (x2,f,dj sl wn & tn) 85.00

CHURCHILL,WINSTON-Europe Unite-1950-Cassell-1st ed (x2,f,dj) 100.00

CHURCHILL,WINSTON-Frontiers and Wars-NY-1962-567p-maps,illus-1st Amer ed (b7,f,dj) 50.00

CHURCHILL,WINSTON-Ian Hamilton's March-NY-1900-409p-red cl,frntis,fldg map-scarce-1st ed (jj2) 600.00

CHURCHILL,WINSTON-My African Journey-Lond-1908-Hodder & Stoughton-8vo-maroon cl-1st ed,2nd bndg (t1,sl fade) 550.00

CHURCHILL,WINSTON-My African Journey-NY-(1908)-226p-red cl,photos-1st Amer ed (b7,sp tn,sl wn) 375.00

CHURCHILL,WINSTON-Savrola-NY-1900-rare-1st ed (b7,f) 900.00

CHURCHILL,WINSTON-Second World War-1948 to 1954-Cassell-6 vols-1st eds (x2,dj) 225.00

CHURCHILL,WINSTON-Second World War-Lond-1948 to 1954-6 vols-1st eds (b7,sl fox,dj) 200.00

CHURCHILL,WINSTON-Stemming the Tide-1953-Cassell-1st ed (x2,f,dj) 85.00

CHURCHILL,WINSTON-Step by Step-1939-Thorton Butterworth-1st ed (x2,f,dj missng sm sp chip) 425.00

CHURCHILL,WINSTON-Unrelenting Struggle-Bost-1942-1st Amer ed (b7,f,dj) 75.00

CHURCHILL,WINSTON-Victory-1946-Cassell-War Speeches #6-1st ed (x2,f,dj) 75.00

CHUTE,MARCHETTE-Rhymes About the Country-NY-1941-Macmillan-4to-74p-pict cl,illus,auth-1st ed (r3,f,dj) 40.00

CHUTE,MARCHETTE-Rhymes about the Country-NY-1941-Macmillan-sm 4to-74p-pict cl,silhouettes-1st ed (oo10,f,dj) 40.00

CIARDI,JOHN-39 Poems-New Brunswick-1959-Rutgers Univ-1st ed (f8,f,dj) 45.00

CIARDI,JOHN-An Alphabestiary-Phila,NY-(1966)-illus,M Hebald-1st ed (j5,f,rprd box) 15.00

CIARDI,JOHN-For Instance-NY-1979-Norton-1st ed (h8,f,dj) 35.00

CIARDI,JOHN-Someone Could Win a Polar Bear-Phila-1970-Lippincott-illus by E Gorey-1st ed (y1,f,f dj) 40.00

CIKOVSKY,NICOLAI-George Inness-NY-1971-Praeger-4to-159p-tan cl,b&w & col illus (r10,dj) 32.50

CIPRIANI,COUNT LEONETTO-California & Overland Diaries of...-1962-Champoeg Pr-148p+5p index-frntis-ltd to 750c-1st ed (j7,f) 70.00

CIRCLE,HOMER-Art of Plug Fishing-Harrisburg-1965-8vo-224p-photos (m3,f,sl fray dj) 17.50

CIST,CHARLES-Sketches and Statistics of Cincinnati in 1851-Cin-1851-WM H Moore & Co-363p-cl-illus (j1,sl wn,cov sl spot,fox) 75.00

CJECHANOWSKA,PAOLA-Le Pur Sang Francais-Lond-1969-Allen-4to-text in French & Engl-1st ed (h9,dj) 40.00

CLABBY,J-History of the Royal Army Veterinary Corps 1919 to 1961-Lond-1963-244p-illus,tissue dj-1st ed (jj2,f,dj) 100.00

CLABBY,J-History of the Royal Army Veterinary Corps 1919 to 1961-Lond-1963-244p-illus-1st ed (b7,f) 75.00

CLAFLIN,BERT-American Waterfowl-NY-1952-Borzoi Bks for Sportsmen-8vo-285p-col frontis,photos-1st ed (m3,f,fray dj) 40.00

CLAFLIN,BERT-Blazed Trails for Anglers-NY-1949-Knopf-8vo-xii,238p+index & 17 photo plts-1st ed (u1,dj) 45.00

CLAIR,COLIN-Chronology of Printing-NY-(1969)-Prager-228p wi index-1st ed (w1,f,dj) 35.00

CLAIR,COLIN-Of Herbs and Spices-Lond-(1961)-Abelard Schuman-275p-col plts,illus (m6) 30.00

CLAIRE,LORETTA-Caldwell, 1776 to 1976-Caldwell-1976-(8),48,(1)p-wrps,illus (aa6) 15.00

CLAMPITT,JOHN W-Echoes From the Rocky Mountains-Chig-1890-671p-red cl,pict gilt,frntis wi tiss,illus-(1st was 1888)-Smith 1771 (z1) 100.00

CLANCY,FOGHORN-My Fifty Years in Rodeo-S.A.-1952-Naylor-285p-illus-scarce-1st ed (a9,dj) 85.00

CLANCY,JUDITH S-Not a Station But a Place-SF-(1949)-Synergistic Pr-4to-72p-drwngs,collages,ltd to 250c,nbrd (o6,as new in box) 40.00

CLANCY,LEO-Fix-NY-1979-Knopf-auth 1st bk-1st ed (bb1,as new in dj) 20.00

CLANCY,TOM-Hunt for Red October-Annapolis-(1984)-Naval Inst-8vo-cl-1st ed,1st iss (x3,f,f dj) 650.00

CLAP,THOMAS-Religious Constitution of College...-New London-1754-prntd & sold by T Green-20p-lea & mrbld bds (k1,upper jnts crckng) 150.00

CLAPHAM,RICHARD-Fishing for Sea Trout in Tidal Water-Lond-1950-8vo-98p-photos-1st ed (m3,fray dj) 12.50

CLARK CO,ARTHUR H-Catalog of Books on U.S. History-Cleve-(1920)-321p+51p Clark Publs+10p prospectus-cl-ltd to 150c (j7) 75.00

CLARK CO.,ARK-GARDEN SPOT OF THE SUNNY SOUTH-np(Little Rock?)-nd(ca 1877)-23,(1)p-unbnd as iss,map (o1,unbnd) 40.00

CLARK,AMASA G-Reminiscences of a Centenarian-S.A.-1972-Naylor-84p-1st ed (a9,dj) 30.00

CLARK,ANN-In My Mother's House-NY-1941-56p-col drwngs-v scarce-1st ed (v7,chip dj,pres) 75.00

CLARK,ANN-Journey to the People-NY-1969-128p-1st ed (v7,f,dj,pres) 20.00

CLARK,ANN-These Were the Valiant-Albuq-1969-150p-1st ed (t7,f,dj) 17.50

CLARK,ANN-Young Hunter of Picuris-Chilocco-1943-oblng-56p-wrps,drwngs-1st ed (v7) 10.00

CLARK,ATWOOD-For Fisherman Only-Lond-1934-8vo-274p (m3) 17.50

CLARK,ATWOOD-Those Were the Days-Lond-1933-8vo-283p-illus-1st ed (m3) 15.00

CLARK,DALE-Country Coffins-NY-1961-Mystery House-1st ed (d4,dj) 20.00

CLARK,DANIEL A-Reminiscences of a Ruined Generation-NY-1841-106p-cl (a1,sl chip sp,sl wn) 25.00

CLARK,DICK-To Goof or Not To Goof-1963-Bernard Geis-212p (r1,ink date bot edge,dj wn) 12.00

CLARK,E WARREN-Life and Adventure in Japan-NY-(1878)-247p-cl,illus (m1) 20.00

CLARK,ELEANOR-Oysters of Locmariaquer-(1964)-Pantheon-203p-grn cl,drwngs-1st prtg (q8,dj) 15.00

CLARK,ELLERY H,JR-Boston Red Sox-1975-Exposition-64p illus-1st ed (s8,dj) 20.00

CLARK,ELLERY H,JR-Red Sox Forever-1977-Exposition-photos-1st ed (s8,f,dj) 30.00

CLARK,GALEN-Big Trees of California-Yosemite Vlly-1907-Clark-104p-cl (x6,cl wn,innr hngs rnfrcd) 10.00

CLARK,GEO L-History of Connecticut...-NY-1914-609p-100 illus & maps (a3) 27.50

CLARK,GEORGE R-Conquest of Illinois-1920-Donnelley-190p-2 illus-Lakeside Classics (cc4) 35.00

CLARK,GEORGE-Line on Fishing-Tor-1941-oblng 12mo-36p-spiral bnd,col plts (m3,f) 12.50

CLARK,GRACE G-Best Cookery in the Middle West-1956-Dbldy-355p-yel cl,illus e.p.-1st ed (q8,dj) 12.50

CLARK,GREGORY-Fishing with ...-Montreal-1975-8vo-192p-photos (m3,f,dj) 12.50

CLARK,GREGORY-With Rod & Reel in Canada-Ottawa-1947-12mo-40p-wrps,col illus (m3,vf) 25.00

CLARK,H L-North Pacific Ophiurans in the Collection of the United States National Museum-1911-USNM-302p-144 figs (bb3) 25.00

CLARK,J L-Good Hunting-1966-U of Okla-242p-photos-1st ed (bb3,f,fray dj) 30.00

CLARK,JAMES L-Trails of the Hunted-NY-1932-8vo-310p-photos-Blue Ribbon ed (m3,f) 25.00

CLARK,JAMES-Spindletop-(1952)-Random-306p-illus,e.p. maps-1st prtg so stated (t8,sl tn & chip dj) 40.00

CLARK,JAMES-Treatise on the Prevention of Diseases Incidental to Horses-Phila-1791-Wm Spotswood-xvi+208+(iv)p-calf-Austin 469-1st Amer ed (c2) 375.00

CLARK,JOHN G-Frontier Challenge-Wichita-1971-307p-1st ed (t7,dj) 7.50

CLARK,JOHN W-Life and Letters of the Reverend Adam Sedgwick-Cambridge-1890-U of Cambridge Pr-2 vols-brwn cl,plts-1st ed (a2,sl crack hngs) 125.00

CLARK,JOSEPH L-Thank God We Made It-1969-U of Tex-564p-photos-1st ed (a9,dj) 40.00

CLARK,LAVERNE H-They Sang for Horses-(1966)-U of Ariz-4to-225p-col plts-1st ed (d3,dj) 65.00

CLARK,M-Roadhouse Tales: Or Nome in 1909-Girard-1902-Appeal Publ-263p+index,tan cl,photos-1st ed (w1,f) 150.00

CLARK,MARIAN B-Model Corpse-1942-Hale-1st ed (s10,dj) 25.00

CLARK,MARJORIE-Captive on the Ho Chi Minh Trail-Chig-(1974)-Moody Pr-wrps-1st ed (ff3) 45.00

CLARK,MARY H-Cradle Will Fall-1980-S&S-1st ed (x2,f,dj) 30.00

CLARK,MARY H-Where are the Children-NY-1975-1st ed (o5,f,dj) 40.00

CLARK,ROLAND-Gunner's Dawn-NY-1937-Derrydale-4to-frontis autg,14 b&w & 5 col plts-ltd to 950c,nbrd-1st ed (u10,sl rub) 600.00

CLARK,ROLAND-Pot Luck-NY-1945-8vo-101p-one of 5000c-illus,auth-1st ed (m3,f,box) 27.50

CLARK,ROLAND-Roland Clark's Etchings-NY-(1938)-Derrydale Pr-folio-3/4 mor,2 orig signed drypoint etchings+69 reproductions-de luxe ed,ltd to 50c,nbrd,autg (o4,vf) 5,000.00

CLARK,ROLAND-Rowland Clark's Etchings-NY-1938-Derrydale-maroon cl,beige cl sp & cor,frntis orig pencil signed etching,69 plts,ltd to 800c,glssn dj,nbrd box (gg3,vf,sl wn box,dj) 600.00

CLARK,RONALD-Men, Myths, and Mountains-NY-1976-292p-illus-1st US ed (q10,as new in dj) 18.00

CLARK,SIMON-Puma's Claw-Bost-1959-223p-22 photos,4 maps-1st US ed (o10,f,dj) 20.00

CLARK,THOMAS D-Frontier America-NY-1959-Scribner's-4to-xi+832p-cl,map e.p.-1st ed (z4,dj sl wn & sp fade) 20.00

CLARK,THOMAS D-Three American Frontiers-Lexington-1968-330p-cl (b1,f,dj) 15.00

CLARK,TOM-Blue-1974-Black Sparrow-ltd to 200c,nbrd,autg (s7,f) 85.00

CLARK,TOM-Champagne and Baloney-1976-Harper & Row-photos,drwngs-1st ed (s8,f,dj) 12.50

CLARK,TOM-Jack Kerouac-San Diego-(1984)-Harcourt Brace-1st ed (q1,vf,dj) 30.00

CLARK,W P-Indian Sign Language-Lincoln-1982-443p-rprnt of Howes C449-1st Bison ed (t7,f) 35.00

CLARK,WALTER VAN TILBURG-City of Trembling Leaves-NY-1945-1st ed (s5,dj) 50.00

CLARK,WALTER VAN TILBURG-Ox Bow Incident-NY-(1940)-Random-1st ed (aa10,sl chip dj) 250.00

CLARK,WALTER VAN TILBURG-Track of the Cat-NY-(1949)-1st ed (s5,sl chip dj) 25.00

CLARK,WALTER VAN TILBURG-Track of the Cat-NY-(1949)-Random-1st ed (d10,dj sl wn,sp chip) 15.00

CLARK,WALTER VAN TILBURG-Watchful Gods-NY-(1950)-Random-1st ed (e10,sl bump,dj sl wn) 50.00

CLARK,WALTER VAN TILBURG-Watchful Gods-NY-(1950)-Random-1st ed (u10,f,f dj) 45.00

CLARK,WILLIAM B-First Saratoga-Baton Rouge-(1953)-LSU Pr-8vo-199p-1st ed (gg5,dj chip,tn) 20.00

CLARK,WILLIAM P-Indian Sign Language-Phila-1885-Hamersley-443p+4p ads-orig cl,fldg frntis map-1st ed (bb7,hngs crack,map taped in) 150.00*

CLARKE,A B-Travels in Mexico and California-Bost-1952-Wright & Hasty's Steam Pr-orig prntd wrps in custom made gry cl box & chemise-Howes C451,Graff 746,Sabin 13393-1st ed (mm1,vf) 2,400.00

CLARKE,A C-Exploration of Space-NY-(1951)-8vo-x,200p-cl,col frntis,14p plts(3 col),18 text illus,illus e.p.-1st ed (t2) 30.00

CLARKE,A C-Interplanetary Flight-NY-nd(ca.1950)-sm 8vo-viii,164p-cl,frntis,14p plts,15 text illus (t2) 25.00

CLARKE,ARTHUR C-2001: A Space Odyssey-NY-(1968)-NAL-1st ed (l3,f,dj) 100.00

CLARKE,ARTHUR C-City and the Stars-NY-(1956)-Harcourt,Brace-1st ed (c5,sl chip dj) 150.00

CLARKE,ARTHUR C-Coast of Coral-NY-(1956)-Harper & Bros-208p-e.p. maps,40p photos(incl 8p col)-1st US ed (u5,sl chip dj) 45.00

CLARKE,ARTHUR C-Fountains of Paradise-NY,Lond-(1979)-1st US ed (h5,as new in dj) 20.00

CLARKE,ARTHUR C-Fountains of Paradise-NY-(1979)-Harcourt Brace-1st US ed (h3,f,dj) 15.00

CLARKE,ARTHUR C-Glide Path-NY-1963-HB&W-1st US ed (x1,f,sl tn dj) 25.00

CLARKE,ARTHUR C-Imperial Earth-NY-(1976)-Harcourt Brace-1st US ed (h3,f,dj) 15.00

CLARKE,AUSTIN-Cattledrive in Connaught, and Other Poems-Lond-(1925)-Allen & Unwin-scarce-1st ed (z8,f,sl chip dj) 250.00

CLARKE,AUSTIN-Collected Plays-Dublin-(1963)-Dolmen Pr-1st ed (z8,"j" stamp on t.p.,dj) 85.00

CLARKE,AUSTIN-Collected Poems-Dublin-(1974)-Dolmen Pr/OUP-1st collected ed (z8,vf,dj) 45.00

CLARKE,AUSTIN-Echo at Coole & Other Poems-(Dublin)-(1968)-Dolmen Pr-1st ed (z8,as new in dj) 22.50

CLARKE,AUSTIN-Mnemosyne Lay in Dust-Dublin-1966-Dolmen Pr-(Dolmen Eds III),ltd to 1000c-1st ed (z8,f,sl tn dj) 40.00

CLARKE,AUSTIN-Penny in the Clouds-Lond-(1968)-Routledge & K Paul-1st ed (z8,vf,dj) 25.00

CLARKE,AUSTIN-Selected Poems-Dublin/Winston Salem-1976-Dolmen Pr/Wake Forest U-1st ed (z8,vf,dj) 27.50

CLARKE,AUSTIN-Son of Learning-Lond-(1927)-Allen & Unwin-ltd to 1000c-1st ed (z8,f,f dj) 200.00

CLARKE,BRIAN-Architectural Stained Glass-1973-McGraw Hill-234p-158 plts(30 col) (cc8,dj) 65.00

CLARKE,CHARLES-Men of the Lewis & Clark Expedition-Glendale-1970-351p-illus,fldg map-scarce-1st ed (d7,vf) 150.00

CLARKE,DONALD H-Joe and Jennie-NY-(1949)-Vanguard-1st ed (hh5,dj) 12.50

CLARKE,EDWARD H-Visions-Bost-1878-Houghton,Osgood-xxii+315p-grn cl,photos frntis-BAL 8926-1st ed (d2,f) 150.00

CLARKE,EDWIN-ED.-Modern Methods in the History of Medicine-Lond-1971-389p-1st ed (dd3,dj) 90.00

CLARKE,EDWIN-Human Brain and Spinal Cord-Berkeley-1968-U of Cal-lg 8vo-xiv+926p-yel cl,plts-1st ed (a2,dj) 135.00

CLARKE,ELIOT C-Main Drainage Works of the City of Boston-Bost-1888-Rockwell & Church-4to-217p-bds,31 plts(8 fldg,8 dbl fldg)-3rd ed (cc10) 80.00

CLARKE,GEORGE H-ED.-New Treasury of War Poetry-Bost-(1943)-Houghton Mifflin-1st ed (dd2,f,dj) 40.00

CLARKE,JAMES M-Life and Adventures of John Muir-San Diego-1980-326p-illus,map e.p. (t7,f,dj) 12.50

CLARKE,JAMES-Life and Adventures of John Muir-San Diego-1979-lg 8vo-324p-handbnd ltd ed of 1000c,nbrd-1st ed (o10,f,dj) 35.00

CLARKE,JAMES-Man is the Prey-NY-1969-8vo-318p-photos (m3,f,dj) 13.00

CLARKE,MARY W-David G Burnet-Austin-1969-Pemberton Pr-303p-cl,fldg map,photos-1st ed (w3,f) 30.00

CLARKE,S J-History of McDonough County, Illinois ...-Springfield-1878-692p-cl-Flake 2404 (h1,cov spot,sl wn) 100.00

CLARKE,TOM E-Big Road-NY-(1965)-LL&S-1st ed (hh5,dj) 12.50

CLARKSON,JOAN-Back Casts & Backchat-Lond-1936-8vo-128p-photos-1st ed (m3,vf,dj) 15.00

CLARKSON,ROSETTA E-Herbs-NY-1945-Macmillan-226p-grn bds (m6,dj) 35.00

CLASON,CLYDE B-Ark of Venus-NY-1955-Knopf-1st ed (h3,f,chip dj) 15.00

CLASON,CLYDE B-Man From Tibet-1938-Dbldy-1st ed (r9,f) 25.00

CLASON,CLYDE B-Purple Parrot-NY-1937-Dbldy CC-1st ed (f4) 15.00

CLASPY,EVERETT-Negro in Southwestern Michigan-np-1967-Dowagiac-112p-wrps,photos (z7,f) 30.00

CLAUSEN,C A-ED.-Lady with the Pen, Elise Woerenskjold in Texas-Northfield-1961-Norwegian Amer Hist Assn-183p-1st ed (a9) 35.00

CLAUSEN,CONNIE-I Love You Honey But the Seasons Over-(1961)-HRW-240p-1st ed (v8,spot f.e.,dj wn & sl chip) 10.00

CLAVELL,JAMES-King Rat-Lond-1962-auth 1st bk-1st Brit ed (t5,dj) 60.00

CLAVELL,JAMES-Noble House-NY-(1981)-1st trd ed (f5,sp tn dj) 20.00

CLAVELL,JAMES-Shogun-1975-Atheneum-1st ed (o9,dj sl tn,sp sl sunned) 45.00

CLAVELL,JAMES-Shogun-NY-1975-1st ed (f5,bowed sp,dj sl chip) 50.00

CLAVELL,JAMES-Tai Pan-NY-1966-1st ed (f5,dj) 85.00

CLAVELL,JAMES-Tai Pan-NY-1966-Atheneum-1st ed (hh5,dj) 60.00

CLAY,JEHU C-Annals of the Swedes on the Delaware, from their First Settlement in 1636, to the Present Time-Phila-1858-H Hooker & Co-179p-cl,plts-revsd 2nd ed (aa6,rub,sp chip) 45.00

CLAY,JOHN-My Recollections of Ontario-Chig-1918-60p-frntis,col plts,fldg plt,photo-scarce-Herd #476-1st ed (t7) 150.00

CLAY,ROBERT-Chequer Board-Phila-1927-Lippincott-1st ed (x1,dj soil & chip) 35.00

CLAY,ROTHA-Mediaeval Hospitals of England-Lond-1966-357p-(facs of 1909 ed) (dd3) 50.00

CLAY,SAMPSON-Present-Day Rock Garden-Lond-1937-4to-681p-blu cl,56 half tones-1st ed (j10,wn) 75.00

CLAYPOOLE,H G C-Witchery of Water-Lond-1970-4to-125p-photos-1st ed (m3,vf,dj) 17.50

CLEARE,JOHN-Mountaineering-Poole-1980-169p-photos-1st Brit ed (q10,as new in dj) 10.00

CLEARE,JOHN-Mountains-NY-1975-256p-photos-1st US ed (q10,f,dj) 20.00

CLEARE,JOHN-World Guide to Mountains & Mountaineering-NY-1979-4to-208p-maps,illus(incl col)-1st US ed (p10,f,dj) 30.00

CLEARY,BEVERLY-Dear Mr.Henshaw-NY-1983-Morrow-1st ed (pp10,as new) 25.00

CLEARY,BEVERLY-Ralph S Mouse-NY-1982-Morrow-160p-cl/bds,illus-1st ed (nn10,sl fade,dj) 20.00

CLEARY,J-Flight of Chariots-1963-Morrow-1st ed (x2,dj sl sunned,missng sm pc) 35.00

CLEARY,JON-Pulse of Danger-1966-Morrow-1st Amer ed (q9,f,dj) 15.00

CLEATON,IRENE-Books & Battles-Bost-1937-282p-illus,ports-1st ed (mm3,f,dj) 12.50

CLEATON,IRENE-Books & Battles-Bost-1937-Houghton Mifflin-282p-cl,frntis port,plts-1st ed (dd10,fray dj) 35.00

CLEAVELAND,AGNES M-No Life For a Lady-Bost-1941-Houghton Mifflin-356p-map e.p.,illus,pict dj-1st ed (f9,dj) 55.00

CLEAVELAND,AGNES M-Satan's Paradise-Bost-1952-274p-cl,later prtg (z1,chip dj) 25.00

CLEAVER,ELDRIDGE-Soul on Ice-NY-1968-Ramparts/McGraw-1st ed (w5,f,dj rprd) 35.00

CLEEK,CHARLES-Story of Ebird-(1938)-Morrow-93p-illus-1st ed (r8,dj) 15.00

CLEGG,ANTHONY-Canadian National Steam Power-Montreal-1969-128p-1st ed (n4) 35.00

CLELAND,ROBERT G-History of Phelps Dodge, 1834 thru 1950-NY-1952-307p-1st ed (v7,dj) 20.00

CLELAND,ROBERT G-This Reckless Breed of Men-NY-1963-381p-dec cl,col frntis,illus (t7,f) 15.00

CLEMEN,CARL-Religions of the World-NY-1931-Harcourt,Brace-482p-135 illus-1st ed (gg6,sp fade) 40.00

CLEMENS,FRED-Three Hundred Years Along the Rothrock Trail-Spokane-(1954)-240p-photos-1st ed (r8,pres by Rothrock) 40.00

CLEMENS,JERE-Rivals-Phila-1860-286p-cl-Wright 545-1st ed (a1) 20.00

CLEMENS,W A-Fishes of the Pacific Coast of Canada-Ottawa-1946-4to-368p-col & b&W illus-1st ed (m3,f) 40.00

CLEMENS,W A-Fishes of the Pacific Coast of Canada-Ottawa-1946-Fish Rsrch Bd of Can-sm 4to-368p-col frntis-1st ed (ff9) 35.00*

CLEMENT,ERNEST W-Handbook of Modern Japan-Chig-1907-McClurg-423p+7p ads-pict cov,2 maps,72 illus-7th ed,rvsd (c3) 35.00

CLEMENT,HAL-Needle-GC-1950-Dbldy-auth 1st bk-1st ed (a5,sl chip dj) 60.00

CLEMENT,JOHN-Historical Sketch of the Baptist Church in Haddonfield, New Jersey-Camden-1883-30p-wrps (aa6) 40.00

CLEMENT,JOHN-Sketches of the First Emigrant Settlers in Newton Township, Old Gloucester County, West New Jersey-Camden-1877-442,(2)p-cl,port,3 fldg maps (aa6) 100.00

CLEMENTS LIBRARY-Michigan Through Three Centuries-Ann Arbor-1937-U of Mich-20p-wrps (cc3) 50.00

CLEMENTS,FRANK-Kariba-NY-(1960,59)-Putnam-8vo-223p-22 illus,2 maps-1st US ed (dd5,dj) 15.00

CLEMENTS,FREDERIC E-Flower Families and Ancestors-NY-1928-x,156p-stmpd g,red & grn cov,col chrt,64 b&w illus (x5,2 autgs) 45.00

CLEMENTS,FREDERIC E-Rocky Mountain Flowers-1945-Wilson-390p-26 col & 21 b&w plts (bb3) 20.00

CLEMONS,WALTER-Poison Tree & Other Stories-Bost-1959-Houghton Mifflin-auth 1st bk-1st ed (ff6,f,dj) 50.00

CLENDENING,LOGAN-Handbook to Pickwick Papers-NY-1936-Knopf-25 illus,2 maps-1st ed (cc2,f,dj) 30.00

CLENDENNING,SHEILA-Emily Dickinson a Bibliography-(1968)-Kent St U Pr-(30),145p-cl-1st ed (m4) 20.00

CLER,GEN-Reminiscences of an Officer of Zouaves-NY-1860-317p-brwn cl (gg2) 75.00

CLERK,MRS. GODFREY-'Ilam-En-Nas-Lond-1873-Henry S King Co-cl-1st ed (o8) 35.00

CLERKE,AGNES M-System of the Stars-Lond-1905-Black-xvi+403p-grn cl,20 plts,38 text illus,fldg chrt-2nd ed (d2) 35.00

CLERMONT COUNTY,OHIO-HISTORY OF...-Phila-1880-557p-cl,dbl cols,illus,scarce (n1,rbnd,dmpstnd cov) 100.00

CLEVELAND,GROVER-Fishing & Shooting Sketches-NY-1906-12mo-209p-illus,H S Watson-1st ed (m3,f) 27.50

CLEVELAND,H W S-Hints to Riflemen-NY-1948-12mo-262p+ads-illus-reprnt of 1864 ed (m3) 15.00

CLEVELAND,H W S-Hints to Riflemen-NY-1948-262p+ads & addendum-grn cl,illus,deluxe cpy ltd to 500c,nbrd (ee3,vf) 35.00

CLEVELAND,R M-Air Transport at War-NY-(1946)-8vo-xii,324p-cl,32p plts-1st ed (t2,chip dj) 40.00

CLEVELAND,R M-Coming Air Age-NY-(1944)-8vo-360p-cl,16p plts-1st ed (t2,chip dj) 25.00

CLEVELAND,RAY L-An Ancient South Arabian Necropolis-Balt-(1965)-John Hopkins-8vo-x,188p-qtr blk cl,red bds,120 plts,fldg plan-1st ed (t10,f) 35.00

CLEVELAND,ROSE E-Long Run-Detr-1886-Dickerson-8vo-146p-red stmpd crm cl-scarce-1st ed (w6) 95.00

CLEVER COOKING-Seattle-1896-Metropolitan Prtg & bndg-318p-limp cov,illus ads-publ by Women's Guild of St.Mark's Church-Bitting 531 (n6,sl shaky) 130.00

CLEVER,CHARLES P-New Mexico, Her Resources,etc.-Wash D.C.-1868-47p-wrps,rare-Howes#C488-1st ed (u7,chip) 250.00

CLEVER,CHARLES P-New Mexico-Wash D.C.-1868-47p-wrps-Adams Herd#491-rare-1st ed (v7,chip) 250.00

CLEYRE,VOLTAIRINE DE-Anarchism and American Traditions-Chig-1932-Free Soc Grp-wrps-1st ed (v5,f) 30.00

CLIFFORD,DEREK-History of Garden Design-Lond-1962-Faber & Faber-sm 4to-232p-1st ed (mm4,f,dj) 95.00

CLIFFORD,FRANCIS-Drummer in the Dark-Lond-1976-Hodder-1st ed (r4,sl wn dj) 17.50

CLIFFORD,H T-Identifying Grasses-1977-Queensland Univ-sq 4to-146p-33 plts (bb3,f,dj) 20.00

CLIFFORD,JAMES-Person and Myth-Berkeley-(1982)-U of Cal-8vo-270p-cl-1st ed (y5,f,f dj) 20.00

CLIFFORD,MRS W K-Love Letters of a Worldly Woman-Chig-nd-256p-cl (d1) 15.00

CLIFFORD,W G-Books in Bottles-Lond-(1926)-G Bles-185p-cl bckd bds,papr sp labl,frntis,illus-1st ed (dd10) 25.00

CLIFTON,HARRY-Walls of Carthage-Dublin-(1977)-Gallery Pr-cl,ltd ed-1st ed (z8,f,dj) 40.00

CLIFTON,VIOLET-Book of Talbot-NY-(c.1933)-Harcourt,Brace-439p-cl,frntis,ports,fldg maps-Arctic Bibl #3228 (k10) 40.00*

CLINCH,NICHOLAS-Walk in the Sky-Seattle-1982-214p-1st ed (o10,as new in dj) 17.00

CLINE,ISAAC M-Tropical Cyclones...1900 to 1924...-NY-1926-Macmillan-301p-grn cl,chrts,maps,tbls-1st ed (hh6,sl wn cor) 40.00

CLINE,W M-Muzzle Loading Rifle, Then & Now-Huntington-1942-4to-162p-photos-1st ed (m3,f,dj) 70.00

CLINE,W M-Muzzle Loading Rifle, Then & Now-WV-1942-162p-photos (ee3,vf,dj) 55.00

CLINTON COUNTY-History of...Ohio...-Chig-1882-W H Beers-1180p-cl (a1,rbckd) 125.00

CLINTON,GEORGE-Public Papers of...First Governor of New York-NY-1900-Wynkoop,Hllnbck,Crawford-3 vols-cl-"War of the Revolution Ser." (gg7) 60.00

CLINTON-BADDELEY,V C-My Foe Outstretch'd Beneath the Tree-NY-1968-Morrow-1st US ed (h4,f,dj) 20.00

CLINTON-BADDELEY,V C-No Case for the Police-NY-1970-Morrow-1st US ed (k4,f,dj) 15.00

CLOAK,E-Glass Paperweights of the Bergstrom Art Center-1969-Crown-196p-col illus (cc8) 60.00

CLOSE,A W-Mysteries of the Kingdom-Traverse City-1952-Way to Life-129p-cl (z7,f) 25.00

CLOSE,UPTON-In the Land of the Laughing Buddha-NY/Lond-1924-Putnam's-8vo-xxiii,359p-blu cl,g titles,33 photos-1st ed (ll1) 30.00

CLOSSON,ERNEST-History of the Piano-Lond-1947-Paul Elek-8vo-168p-qtr blk cl & red bds,illus-1st Brit ed (t10) 25.00

CLOUSTON,J S-Adventures of M D'Haricot-1902-Harpers-pict cl,illus-1st ed (x7) 85.00

CLOUSTON,J S-Lunatic at Large-1910-Brentanos-authorized ed (x7) 15.00

CLUM,WOODWORTH-Apache Agent-Bost-1936-Houghton Mifflin-297p-illus-Six Guns #446-1st ed (ee4,new frnt fly) 95.00

CLUM,WOODWORTH-Apache Agent-Bost-1936-Houghton Mifflin-297p-illus-Six Guns 446-1st ed (gg4,dj) 50.00

CLUTE,WILLARD N-Agronomy a Course in Practical Gardening for High Schools-Bost-1913-Ginn-296p-cl,illus,photos (x6) 16.00

CLUTE,WILLARD-Dictionary of American Plant Names-1923-Clute-215p-cl (x6,edge rub) 22.00

CLYDESDALE,MARQUESS OF-Pilots' Book of Everest-NY-1936-Dbldy,Doran-8vo-(1),267p-emboss DC3 on blu cl,17 photos & maps-1st Amer ed (gg6) 45.00

CLYMER,R SWINBURNE-Occult Initiation-Quakertown-1938-Philo Publ-48p-wrps-1st ed (n8) 25.00

CLYMER,R SWINBURNE-Science of the Soul-Quakertown-1944-Philo Publ-cl-1st ed (n8,f) 25.00

CLYNE,GERALDYNE-Jolly Jump Ups Vacation Trips-(1942)-McLoughlin Bros-oblng 8vo-unpgd-cl/pict bds,bound at top,6 pop ups (nn8) 42.00

COAD,ORAL S-New Jersey in Travelers' Accounts, 1524 to 1971-Metuchen-1972-x,211p-cl (aa6) 25.00

COALE,ANSLEY J-Problem of Reducing Vulnerability to Atomic Bombs-Princeton-1947-Princeton Univ Pr-xvi+116p-gry cl-1st ed (dd1,sl soil dj) 30.00

COAN,CHARLES F-Shorter History of New Mexico-Ann Arbor-1928-2 vols-wrps,mimeographed,maps-1st ed (u7,underlining) 165.00

COAST,JOHN-Dancers of Bali-NY-(1953)-Putnam-8vo-250p-24p photos-1st ed (ff5,dj) 25.00

COATES,HAROLD-Stories of Kentucky Feuds-Cinn-(1924)-41p-wrps (f1) 15.00

COATES,HENRY-American Trotting and Pacing Horse-Phila-1901-Coates-1st ed (f10) 45.00

COATES,JAMES-How to Read Heads and Faces-Phila-nd(ca.early 1900s)-McKay-sm 8vo-126p-illus card cov,illus-new & rvsd ed (aa7) 25.00*

COATES,ROBERT M-All the Year Round-NY-(1943)-Harcourt,Brace-1st ed (d10,dj sl soil,sp chip) 45.00

COATES,ROBERT M-Farther Shore-NY-(1955)-Harcourt,Brace-1st ed (d10,dj) 17.50

COATES,ROBERT M-Outlaw Years-NY-1930-Lit Guild-308p-illus (o2) 15.00

COATS,ALICE-Flowers and Their Histories-Lond-(1968)-xiii,346p-4 col illus (m10,chip dj) 40.00

COATS,ALICE-Garden Shrubs and Their Histories-NY-1965-Dutton-416p-cl (x6,vf,dj sun) 45.00

COATS,ALICE-Quest for Plants-Lond-(1969)-Studio Vista-400p-cl,illus-1st ed (dd10,f,dj) 35.00

COATS,ALICE-Shrubs and Their Histories-Lond-1963-Vista Bks-416p-4 col plts,11 b&w,5 drwngs-1st ed (mm4,f,dj) 60.00

COATS,ALICE-Treasury of Flowers-NY-(1975)-8vo-116p-119 illus incl 33 col (j10,f,dj) 30.00

COATS,PETER-Great Gardens of the Western World-Lond-(1968)-sm folio-288p-illus,40 col plts (x5,rear cov scrtchd,rprd dj) 40.00

COATS,PETER-Roses-NY-1962-Putnam-128p (x6,as new in box) 12.00

COATSWORTH,ELIZABETH-Alice All by Herself-NY-1937-Macmillan-181p-picts by M De Angeli-1st ed (hh9,f,sl wn dj) 45.00

COATSWORTH,ELIZABETH-Children Came Running-NY-(1960)-Golden-illus,Unicef bk-1st ed (s3,f,dj) 30.00

COATSWORTH,ELIZABETH-Mouse Chorus-(1955)-Pantheon-sq 12mo-unpgd-every pg illus,G Vaughan Jackson-1st ed (v8,sl wn) 25.00

COATSWORTH,ELIZABETH-Night and the Cat-NY-1950-Macmillan-sm 4to-55p-cl,12 drwngs,Foujita-1st ed (s3,f,edgewn dj) 30.00

COBB,BOB-ED.-Best of Bassmaster-Montgomery-1980-4to-384p-illus,photos (m3,f) 17.50

COBB,HUMPHREY-Paths of Glory-NY-1935-Viking-auth 1st & only bk-1st ed (b10,sl chip dj) 25.00

COBB,IRVIN S-All Aboard-NY-1928-Cosmopolitan-1st ed (x1,f,dj) 50.00

COBB,IRVIN S-Down Yonder with Judge Priest and Irvin S Cobb-1932-Long & Smith-1st ed (x7,dj) 75.00

COBB,JOHN-Pacific Salmon Fisheries-Wash D.C.-1930-8vo-295p-photos-4th ed (m3) 20.00

COBB,LYMAN-Cobb's Juvenile Reader, No.2-Balt-1831-J Jewett-144p-prntd bds (k1,rub) 27.50

COBB,LYMAN-Cobb's Juvenile Reader, No.3-Balt-1831-J Jewett-212p+ads-bds-Amer Imprnts 6572 (k1,rub) 25.00

COBB,THOMAS-House by the Common-Lond-1891-Ward-col pict wrps-illus-1st ed (d4,wrps sp chip & wn) 35.00

COBB,TY-My Life in Baseball-1961-Dbldy-1st ed (p7,f,f dj) 75.00

COBB,WM H-Monument To and History Of the Mingo Indians-np-1921-32p-illus-1st ed (t7) 25.00

COBBETT,WM-French Grammar-Lond-1824-Clement-300p-lea sp,mrbld bds (x6,sp crack,bds rub) 75.00

COBLENTZ,STANTON-Next to the Sun-NY-(1960)-Avalon-1st ed (j3,f,sl wn dj) 30.00

COBLENTZ,STANTON-Villains and Vigilantes-NY-1936-Wilson Erickson-261p-illus,pict dj-1st ed (f9,sp spot,dj) 45.00

COBURN,ALVIN L-Alvin Langdon Coburn, Photographer-NY-(1966)-Praeger-4to-cl-1st ed (y3,f,dj sl soil & tn) 100.00

COBURN,ALVIN L-Door in the Wall-NY,Lond-1911-Kennerley-folio-cl/bds,1 gravure,9 aquatones,ltd to 600c(only 300c had full set of gravures)-1st ed (y3,sl spot,lacks sp labl) 875.00

COBURN,ALVIN L-Men of Mark-Lond-1913-Duckworth-33 gravures-1st ed (y3) 1,850.00

COBURN,ALVIN L-More Men of Mark-NY-1922-Knopf-4to-cl & patterned bds-1st ed (y3,sp tn) 375.00

COBURN,F D-Alfalfa-NY-1905-Orange Judd-163p-cl (x6,f) 20.00

COBURN,WALT-Pioneer Cattleman in Montana-Norman-1968-338p-frntis,illus,photos,map-1st ed (t7,dj) 50.00

COCANNOUER,JOSEPH A-Trampling Out the Vintage-1945-U of Okla-221p (x6,dj) 15.00

COCHRAN,E WINSTON-Deer Tales and Pen Feathers-San Antonio-1975-8vo-64p-illus-1st ed (m3,vf,dj) 15.00

COCHRAN,HAMILTON-Scudders in the American Revolution-(np)-1976-xiv,140p-cl,illus (aa6) 35.00

COCHRAN,JOHN S-Bonnie Belmont-(Wheeling)-(1907)-291p-cl,only 1000c prtd,Six-Guns 450-scarce (b1) 85.00

COCHRAN,LOUIS-Son of Haman-Caldwell-1937-Caxton-1st ed (hh5,dj) 15.00

COCHRANE,HUGH-Gateway to Oblivion, the Great Lakes' Bermuda Triangle-GC-1980-Dbldy-183p-cl,photos-1st ed (cc3,dj) 32.50

COCHRANE,IAN-F For Ferg-Lond-1980-Gollancz-1st ed (z8,vf,dj) 37.50

COCHRANE,IAN-Gone in the Head-Lond-(1974)-Routledge & K Paul-1st ed (z8,vf,dj) 20.00

COCHRANE,IAN-Jesus on a Stick-Lond-(1975)-Routledge & K Paul-1st ed (z8,f,dj) 17.50

COCKADAY,LAURENCE M-Radio Experimenters' Handbook-1932-Radio News-136p-illus-1st ed (h6) 10.00

COCKAINE,T-Short Treatise on Hunting, 1591-Lond-1932-Shakespeare Assoc Facs #5-unpgd-illus (gg3,f) 17.00

COCKER,W J-Civil Government of Michigan...-Detr-1883-223p-cl (k1) 15.00

COCKING,W T-Television Receiving Equipment-1944-298p-14 photos,100 illus-1st ed (h6,f) 35.00

COCTEAU,JEAN-Blood of a Poet-NY-(1949)-Bodley Pr-oblng 4to-blk cl-1st ed (x10,dj chip,tn,soil) 25.00

COCTEAU,JEAN-Call to Order-Lond-1926-Faber & Gwyer-1st ed (x10,f,dj) 75.00

COCTEAU,JEAN-Children of the Game-Lond-1955-1st ed (y7,dj) 30.00

COCTEAU,JEAN-Difficulty of Being-NY-(1967)-Coward McCann-1st Amer ed (x10,f,dj) 15.00

COCTEAU,JEAN-Miscreant-Lond-1958-Peter Owen-1st ed (v5,chip dj) 20.00

COCTEAU,JEAN-Professional Secrets-NY-1970-FSG-1st ed (f8,f,dj) 30.00

COCTEAU,JEAN-Typewriter-Lond-1947-Dobson-1st ed (w5,f,dj sl tn,chip) 45.00

CODDINGTON,E B-Gettysburg Campaign-NY-1968-866p-illus,maps,ports-1st ed (z10,soil dj) 60.00

CODMAN,JOHN T-Brook Farm-Bost-1894-Arena Publ-335p-cl (j1,cov sl dull,rub & spot) 20.00

CODMAN,JOHN-Round Trip by Way of Panama through California, Oregon,Nevada,Utah,Idaho and Colorado-NY-1879-Putnam's-xiv+331p+ads-grn cl-Adams,Herd 496-1st ed (mm10) 65.00

COADMAN,JOHN-Round Trip-NY-1879-Putnam-1st ed (gg7) 40.00

CODY,MORRILL-Favorite Restaurants of an American in Paris-Paris-(1966)-Nouveau Quartier Latin-225p-wht wrps,illus,Man Ray (l6,sl wn wrps) 15.00

COE,BRIAN-History of Movie Photography-Westfield-1981-Eastview Eds-176p-illus-1st Amer ed (cc9,as new in dj) 35.00

COE,CHARLES H-Juggling a Rope-Pendleton-1927-12mo-114p-photos-Howes C533-1st ed (aa3,sl rub) 55.00

COE,ELMER-Fort Scott as I Knew It-Ft.Scott-1940-94p-stiff pict wrps,frntis,photos-1st ed (t7,f) 10.00

COE,HAMLIN-Mine Eyes Have Seen the Glory-Rutherford-(1975)-240p-illus-1st ed (n3,f,dj) 25.00

COE,TUCKER-Murder Among Children-NY-1967-Random-1st ed (d8,f,f dj) 30.00

COE,TUCKER-Wax Apple-NY-1970-Random-1st ed (w9,f,dj) 35.00

COE,URLING C-Frontier Doctor-NY-1939-Macmillan-264p-Six Guns #459-1st ed (dd4) 25.00

COE,W R-Nemerteans of the West and Northwest Coasts of America-1905-Harvard-318p-25 plts(incl 3 col) (bb3,f) 25.00

COFFEY,BRIAN-Surrounded-Indpls-1974-Bobbs Merrill-1st ed (w9,f,sl wn dj) 150.00

COFFEY,D J-Dolphins, Whales and Porpoises-1977-Macmillan-223p-photos-1st US ed (bb3,f,dj) 20.00

COFFEY,L S-Wilds of Alaska Big Game Hunting-NY-1963-172p-photos (gg3,vf,dj) 35.00

COFFIN,CHARLES C-War of the Rebellion-NY-1888 to 1891-4 vols-pict cl,illus,maps (c4) 75.00

COFFIN,LEWIS-ET AL-Small French Buildings-NY-1926-Scribner's-4to-275p-lt blu cl,183 illus (r10,sp sl sun) 45.00

COFFIN,MARIAN C-Trees and Shrubs for Landscape Effects-NY-1940-Scribner-169p (x6,dj wn) 20.00

COFFIN,ROBERT P T-John Dawn-NY-1936-Macmillan-1st ed (hh5,dj) 15.00

COFFIN,ROBERT P T-Saltwater Farm-NY-1937-Macmillan-5 wdcuts,J J Lankes-1st ed (a10,sp chip dj) 30.00

COFFIN,TRISTRAM-Old Ball Game-1971-Herder-1st ed (p7,dj) 15.00

COFFIN,VICTOR-Province of Quebec and the Early American Revolution-Madison-1896-Univ of Wisc-xviii+275-562p-lt grn wrps-1st ed (e2,covs soil & sl chip) 15.00

COFIELD,THOMAS R-Training the Hunting Retriever-NY-1959-Van Nostrand-8vo-138p-photos-1st ed (m3,dj) 35.00

COFIELD,TOM-Fisherman's Guide to North America-NY-1976-4to-336p-photos,illus (m3,f,dj) 12.50

COGGESHALL,WILLIAM T-Poets and Poetry of the West-Columbus-1860-Follett,Foster-688p-later cl (l1,rbnd) 50.00

COGGINS,CAROLYN-Company Cook Book-(1954)-Hanover Hs-394p-yel cl-1st ed (q8) 15.00

COGGINS,CAROLYN-Fabulous Foods for People You Love-Lond-(1956)-Arco-308p-prpl cl-1st ed (q8,dj) 17.50

COGHLAN,MRS.-Memoirs of...-Lond,Dublin-1794-reprntd by Z Jackson-8vo-x,(1)-171p-contemp calf-Howes C-543-1st Irish ed (w6) 350.00

COGLEY,JOHN-Blacklisting-(np)-(1956)-2 vols-prtd wrps-1st ed (r2) 60.00

COGSWELL,H L-Water Birds of California-Berkeley-1977-8vo-399p-cl,12 col plts-1st ed (y8) 13.00

COHAN,GEORGE M-Broadway Jones-1913-Dillingham-scarce in dj-1st ed (x2,f,sl chip dj) 225.00

COHEN,ABNER-Custom & Politics in Urban Africa-Berkeley-(1969)-U of Cal-8vo-452p-cl (y5) 40.00

COHEN,ANTHEA-Angel of Vengeance-Lond-1982-Quartet-1st ed (r4,vf,dj) 35.00

COHEN,ANTHEA-Angel Without Mercy-Lond-1982-Quartet-auth 1st bk-1st ed (r4,dj) 30.00

COHEN,DAVID S-Folklore and Folklife of New Jersey-New Brunswick-(1983)-xviii,253p-cl,illus (aa6) 30.00

COHEN,DAVID S-Ramapo Mountain People-New Brunswick-(1974)-xvi,285p-cl,plts (aa6) 35.00

COHEN,I BERNARD-ED.-Isaac Newton's Papers and Letters on Natural Philosophy and Related Documents-Cambridge-1958-Harvard U Pr-xiv+501p-brwn cl-1st ed (c2,dj) 35.00

COHEN,I BERNARD-Franklin and Newton-Phila-1956-Amer Philo Soc-xxvi+657p-blu cl,24 plts-1st ed (g2,dj) 85.00

COHEN,I BERNARD-Introduction to Newton's `Principia'-Cambridge-1971-Cambridge Univ Pr-4to-xxx+380p-blu cl-1st ed (g2,dj) 135.00

COHEN,ISABEL E-COMP.-Legends and Tales in Prose and Verse-Phila-1905-Jewish Publ Scty-12mo-260p-1st ed (w6,hngs tender) 45.00

COHEN,JULIUS H-An American Labor Policy-NY-1919-Macmillan-1st ed (w5,f) 25.00

COHEN,LEONARD-Beautiful Losers-NY-1966-Viking-243p-1st Amer ed (cc7,scuff dj) 50.00*

COHEN,LEONARD-Energy of Slaves-NY-1972-Viking-8vo-127p-1st Amer ed (cc7,dj) 50.00*

COHEN,LEONARD-Favorite Game-NY-(1963)-1st US ed (r5,f,dj) 50.00

COHEN,LEONARD-Favorite Game-NY-(1963)-Viking-1st US ed (c10,dj) 75.00

COHEN,LEONARD-Selected Poems, 1956 to 1968-NY-1968-1st US ed (r5,f,dj) 40.00

COHEN,LEONARD-Selected Poems, 1956 to 1968-Tor-(1968)-M&S-8vo-x,245p-1st ed (cc7,dj) 65.00*

COHEN,LEONARD-Selected Poems, 1956 to 1968-Tor-(1968)-M&S-scarce in cl-1st Can ed (pp2,f,dj) 75.00*

COHEN,LEONARD-Spice Box of Earth-(Tor)-(1961)-(M&S)-drwngs-1st ed (pp2,f,dj) 175.00*

COHEN,LEONARD-Spice Box of Earth-NY-(1961)-Viking-1st US ed (pp2,f,dj) 100.00*

COHEN,LESTER-Oscar Wilde, a Play-NY-1928-Boni & Liveright-1st ed (w5,f,dj wn,sl chip) 35.00

COHEN,MARVIN-Self Devoted Friend-NY-1967-New Directions-1st ed (w5,f,f dj) 25.00

COHEN,MORTON-Rider Haggard, His Life and Works-Lond-(1960)-Hutchinson-photos-1st Brit ed (aa8,sl soil dj) 35.00

COHEN,OCTAVUS R-Florian Slappey Goes Abroad-Bost-1928-Little,Brown-8vo-1st ed (b3,f,dj) 50.00

COHRS,TIMOTHY-Fort Selden, New Mexico-Santa Fe-1974-24p-pict wrps,photos,maps-1st ed (t7) 12.50

COIGNE,C-Money-NY-1877-113;213;206p-cl (h1,sl spot cov) 15.00

COIT,DANIEL W-Digging for Gold, Without a Shovel-(SF)-1967-Old West Publ-sm folio-116p-drwngs,ltd to 1250c (cc4) 50.00

COIT,THOMAS W-Puritanism-NY-1845-527,(1)p-cl (h1) 20.00

COKE,VAN DEREN-Photographs 1956 to 1973-Albuq-1973-UNM-1st ed (pp9,dj chip) 65.00

COKE,VAN DEREN-Photography in New Mexico-Albuq-1979-UNM-1st ed (pp9,f,rprd dj) 50.00

COKER,W C-Boletaceae of North Carolina-1943-UNC-96p-65 plts(incl 6 col) (bb3,f,dj) 35.00

COLBOURNE,MAURICE-Meaning of Social Credit-Alberta-1935-Soc Credit Bd-sm 8vo-284p-grn cl (cc7,sl bump,dj tattrd) 25.00*

COLBRATH,M TARBOX-What To Get For Breakfast-Bost-1883(c.1882)-James H Earle-268p-g trim grn bds,interleaved wi ruled papr-Bitting p.93 (a8) 65.00

COLBURN,WARREN-An Introduction to Algebra, Upon the Inductive Method of Instruction-Bost-1841-276p-lea (k1) 20.00

COLBURN,WARREN-Colburn's First Lessons-Hallowell-1828-Glazier-172p+ads-bds-Amer Imprnts 32758 (k1,sl wn,lacks f.e.p.s) 20.00

COLBURN,WARREN-Key Containing the Answers to Examples in the Introduction to Algebra...-Bost-1835-Hilliard,Gray-50p-bds-Amer Imprnts 31042 (k1) 20.00

COLBY,C B-Six Shooter-NY-1956-4to-48p-photos (m3,sl fray dj) 12.50

COLBY,CONSTANCE TABER-Skunk in the House-Phila-(1973)-Lippincott-8vo-144p-photos-1st ed (dd5,dj) 12.50

COLBY,HARRIET-Where is Johnny?-np-(1944)-Howell,Soskins-oblng 16mo-pict bds,spiral bnd,col illus,R Davis (r3) 10.00

COLBY,WILLIAM-ED.-John Muir Studies in the Sierra-SF-1960-103p-drwngs-rvsd ed (o10,f,dj) 25.00

COLE,A C-Pogonomyrmex Harvester Ants-1968-U of Tenn-222p-photos-1st ed (bb3,f,dj) 14.00

COLE,C-ED.-Royal Flying Corps. 1915 to 1916-(Lond)-(1969)-roy 8vo-352p-cl,24p plts (t2,dj) 40.00

COLE,CYRENUS-I Am a Man, the Indian Black Hawk-Iowa City-1938-312p-pict cl,illus,map-1st ed (n3,f) 75.00

COLE,D-From Tipi to Skyscraper-NY-1973-illus-1st ed (h10,dj) 35.00

COLE,ERNEST-House of Bondage-NY-(1967)-Random-187p-1st US ed (gg10,dj) 75.00

COLE,G D H-Brooklyn Murders-NY-1924-Seltzer-1st US ed (d4) 50.00

COLE,G D H-Dead Man's Watch-NY-1932-Dbldy CC-1st US ed (f4) 12.50

COLE,G D H-Double Blackmail-1939-CCC-1st ed (s10,sp chip dj) 40.00

COLE,G D H-Missing Aunt-1937-CCC-1st ed (s10,sp soil) 20.00

COLE,G D H-Walking Corpse-NY-1931-Morrow-1st US ed (g4) 15.00

COLE,GEORGE E-Early Oregon-np(Spokane)-nd(1905)-95p-cl,frntis port wi tiss-scarce-1st ed (z1,f,chip dj) 75.00

COLE,HARRY E-Stagecoach & Tavern Tales of the Old Northwest-Cleve-1930-Arthur H Clark Co-376p-illus,map-1st ed (cc4) 100.00

COLE,HARRY E-Stagecoach & Tavern Tales of the Old Northwest-Cleve-1930-Arthur H Clarke Co-376p-illus-1st ed (f7,vf,chip dj) 120.00

COLE,HERBERT-Heraldry and Floral Forms as Used in Decoration-1922-Dent-245p-illus (cc8) 65.00

COLE,JEAN M-Exile in the Wilderness-1979-Burns & MacEachern Ltd-8vo-xviii,268p-15 illus,e.p. maps-1st ed (cc7,sl rub dj) 35.00*

COLE,JOHN N-Striper-Bost-1978-8vo-269p-illus,M Kuhn-1st ed (m3,vf,dj) 12.50

COLE,M R-Los Pastores, a Mexican Play-Bost & NY-1907-Am Folk-Lore Soc,Vol.IX-234p-illus,music-v scarce-1st ed (u7) 100.00

COLE,MRS MARY-Lady's Complete Guide-Lond-1791-G Kearsly-460p-lea sp & mrbld bds-Bitting 94-3rd ed (n6,rbnd) 450.00

COLE,PHILIP G-Montana in Miniature-Kalispell-1966-4to-216p-illus-1st ed (g7,f) 70.00

COLE,PHILIP G-Montana in Miniature-Kalispell-1966-O'Neil Pr-sm folio-216p-col illus-Six Guns 464-1st ed (bb4) 60.00

COLE,RALPH D-Thirty Seventh Division in the World War 1917 to 1918-Columbus-1926-404p-cl-Dornbusch 1530 (m1) 15.00

COLE,SONIA-Prehistory of East Africa-NY-(1963)-Macmillan-lg 8vo-382p-cl,photos,maps-1st prtg (y5,dj) 15.00

COLEMAN,A P-Canadian Rockies-Lond-1911-T Fisher Unwin-8vo-379p-blu cl,col pict pasteon,31 photo plts,4 maps(3 fldg)-(t.p. calls for 31 plts & 3 maps) (oo1,few spots,maps sl tn) 125.00

COLEMAN,FREDERIC-With Cavalry in the Great War-Phila-1917-296p-illus-1st ed (b7,dj) 25.00

COLEMAN,J WINSTON,JR.-Pistols at Eight Paces-(Cin)-(1962)-35p-cl-Christmas keepsake by Krehbiel Co. (j1) 12.50

COLEMAN,MARION M-Polish Circuit Rider-Cheshire-1971-Cherry Hill Bks-49p-wrps-1st ed (w3,vf) 15.00

COLEMAN,MAX M-From Mustanger to Lawyer-Lubbock-1952-auth-156p-Book One-cl,photos,ltd to 500c,autg (w3,f) 30.00

COLEMAN,MAX M-From Mustanger to Lawyer. Parts A & B-Abilene-1952,1953-2 vols-dec cl-both ltd to 500c,autg-Herd #500-scarce (n10,f) 90.00

COLEMAN,MCALISTER-Men and Coal-NY-1943-Farrar-1st ed (w5,f,sl tn dj) 35.00

COLEMAN,WILLIAM-ED.-Studies in the History of Biology-Balt-1977 to 1984-7 vols-1st ed (dd3) 150.00

COLERIDGE,MRS S T-Minnow Among Tritons...-Bloomsbury-1934-Nonesuch Pr-8vo-185p-water mrkd laid pap,3 ports,facs-ltd to 675c,nbrd-1st ed (w6,uncut,part unopened) 65.00

COLES,C-Game Birds-1983-Dodd,Mead-folio-119p-24p col plts-1st US ed (bb3,f,dj) 55.00

COLES,MANNING-Fifth Man-NY-1946-Dbldy CC-1st US ed (f4,f,dj) 12.50

COLES,MANNING-Night Train to Paris-Lond-1952-Hodder-1st ed (h4,dj) 15.00

COLES,MANNING-They Tell No Tales-NY-1942-Dbldy CC-1st US ed (f4,dj missing sm chips) 20.00

COLES,MANNING-Toast to Tomorrow-GC-1941-Dbldy CC-1st Amer ed (w9,f,sl wn dj) 45.00

COLES,MANNING-Toast to Tomorrow-Tor-1943-Musson-1st Can ed (g4,f,dj) 15.00

COLES,MANNING-Without Lawful Authority-NY-1943-Dbldy CC-1st US ed (f4,f,dj) 20.00

COLES,ROBERT-Old Ones of New Mexico-Albuq-(1973)-74p-photos-1st ed (u7,f,dj) 25.00

COLETTE-Cheri-NY-1929-Boni-10 illus-transl by J Flanner-1st Amer ed (m4,f,dj) 50.00

COLETTE-Claudine Married-1960-FS&C-1st Amer ed (t9,f,sp chip dj) 30.00

COLETTE-Earthly Paradise-NY-1966-FSG-1st US ed (z9,f,dj sl chip,tn) 17.50

COLETTE-My Mother's House and Sido-NY-1953-FS&Y-8vo-219p-1st US ed (w6,f,dj) 25.00

COLETTE-Other One-NY-(1960)-FS&C-8vo-160p-1st US ed (w6,dj) 25.00

COLETTE-Ripening Seed-NY-(1955)-FS&C-8vo-186p-1st US ed (w6,f,sl wn dj) 25.00

COLIO,Q-American Decoys-Ephrata-1972-Science Pr-96p-wrps prtd same time as hdbk,col photo decoy on cov-scarce (gg3,f) 150.00

COLIO,Q-American Decoys-Ephrata-1972-Science Pr-oblng-96p-blu cl,gilt dec,coated papr,col illus,ltd to 550c (gg3,f) 250.00

COLLADAY,MORRISON-When the Moon Fell-NY-(1929)-Stellar Publ-24p-wrps-"Science Fiction No.6" (c1) 10.00

COLLECTION OF NURSERY RHYMES-Lond-1916-Poetry Bkshp-sm 24mo-60p-papr bds (a8) 25.00

COLLEDGE,ERIC-Mediaeval Mystics of England-NY-1961-Scribner's-cl-1st ed (n8,f,dj) 35.00

COLLES,JAMES,JR.-Journal of a Hunting Excursion to Louis Lake-Blu Mt. Lake-1961-Adirondack Mus-4to-glassine dj-ltd to 1000c (dd6,f,wn dj) 45.00

COLLIAS,JOE G-Last of Steam-Berkeley-1960-269p-1st ed (n4,dj) 24.00

COLLIAS,JOE G-Search for Steam-Berkeley-1972-360p-1st ed (n4,f,dj) 32.00

COLLIER,BASIL-Take Forty Eggs-Lond-1938-Gollancz-117p-blu bds (l6,wn bds) 22.00

COLLIER,JANE F-Law and Social Change in Zinacantan-1973-Stanford U Pr-8vo-281p-brwn cl (mm1,as new in dj) 30.00

COLLIER,JOHN-Defy the Foul Fiend-NY-1934-Knopf-1st US ed (w5,f,dj sl wn,tn) 35.00

COLLIER,JOHN-Patterns and Ceremonials of the Indians of the Southwest-NY-1949-192p-lithos,drwngs-ltd to 1475c,nbrd,2 autg-1st ed (v7,tn dj) 100.00

COLLIER,JOHN-Presenting Moonshine-NY-1941-Viking-1st ed (w5,f,dj chip) 45.00

COLLIER,MAJ CALVIN L-First In, Last Out-Little Rock-1961-Pioneer Pr-162p-illus,maps (o7,f,dj) 150.00

COLLIER,R-Eagle Day-NY-1966-8vo-316p-cl,24p plts,e.p. maps-1st ed (t2,dj) 35.00

COLLIER,RICHARD-River That God Forgot-NY-1968-Dutton-8vo-288p-41 photos-1st ed (ff5,f,dj) 17.50

COLLIER,WILLIAM R-Dave Cook of the Rockies-NY-1936-R R Wilson-224p-illus-Six Guns #466-1st ed (cc4,sl chip dj) 40.00

COLLIER,WILLIAM R-Reign of Soapy Smith-GC,NY-1935-Dbldy,Doran-299p-illus e.p.,illus-Six Guns 467-1st ed (bb4) 35.00

COLLIN,RODNEY-Theory of Celestial Influence-Lond-1954-V Stuart-cl-1st ed (l8) 55.00

COLLINGS,ELLSWORTH-101 Ranch-Norman-1938-249p-illus-2nd prtg (z1,chip dj) 25.00

COLLINGWOOD,G H-Knowing Your Trees-Wash D.C.-(1947)-4to-312p-photos (x5) 10.00

COLLINS,A FREDERICK-Experimental Television-1932-313p-illus cov,185 illus-rare-1st ed (h6,f) 175.00

COLLINS,ANNA C-History of the Methodist Episcopal Church on Port Republic and Smithville Charge-(np)-1892-56p-wrps-scarce (aa6) 60.00

COLLINS,CAPT GEO K-Memoirs of the 149th Regiment New York Volunteers Infantry-Syracuse-1891-publ by auth-426p-pict cl,illus-(Nevins I,p.72)-1st ed (nn6,sp wn) 165.00

COLLINS,CARVEL-ED.-Sam Ward in the Gold Rush-(1949)-Stanford Univ Pr-x+189p-beige cl,illus-1st ed (m2,dj) 35.00

COLLINS,DEAN-Stars of Oregon-1943-Binfords & Mort-4to-117p-illus-1st ed (r8,chip dj) 30.00

COLLINS,ELIZABETH-Memoirs of...of Upper Evesham, NJ-Phila-1833-Nathan Kite-18mo-144p-1/4 lea-1st ed (y6,sl fox) 18.00

COLLINS,F A-Air Man-NY-1918-8vo-xiv,242p-illus cl,frntis,31p plts (t2) 75.00

COLLINS,FREDERICK L-Money Town-NY-(1946)-Putnam-8vo-327p-37 illus-1st ed (gg5,dj) 20.00

COLLINS,FREDERICK-Book of Wireless-1915-222p-219 illus-1st ed (h6) 30.00

COLLINS,FREDERICK-Manual of Wireless Telegraphy and Telephony-1913-300p-129 illus-rare-3rd ed (h6) 65.00

COLLINS,FREDERICK-Wireless Telegraphy-1905-299p-122 photos,200 illus-v rare-1st ed (h6) 195.00

COLLINS,HENRY H,JR.-Familiar Garden Birds of America-NY-1965-Harper & Row-viii,309p-col plts (o2,sl chip dj) 17.50

COLLINS,HUBERT E-Warpath and Cattle Trail-NY-1928-296p-illus-Herd 506-1st ed (g7) 40.00

COLLINS,HUBERT E-Warpath and Cattle Trail-NY-1928-Morrow-296p-Illus-Herd 506-1st ed (cc4) 65.00

COLLINS,J T-Amphibians and Reptiles in Kansas-1982-U of Kans-356p-179 photos,91 maps-rvsd ed (bb3,f) 20.00

COLLINS,J-Test Pilot-NY-(1935)-8vo-xiv,178p-cl-1st ed (t2,sl wn sp,dj chip) 35.00

COLLINS,JOHN S-My Experiences in the West-1970-Lakeside-252p-illus,fldg map-1st ed thus (r8,f) 18.00

COLLINS,JOHN S-My Experiences in the West-Chig-1970-Donnelley & Sons-frntis,illus,map-Lakeside Classics (ff4) 20.00

COLLINS,MARY-Sister of Cain-NY-1943-Scribners-1st ed (f4,dj) 15.00

COLLINS,RANDALL-Case of the Philosopher's Ring-Brighton-1980-Harvester-illus-1st Brit ed (p4,f,dj) 20.00

COLLINS,RANDALL-Case of the Philosopher's Ring-NY-1978-Crown-1st ed (d4,f,dj) 20.00

COLLINS,ROBERT F-History of the Daniel Boone National Forest, 1770 to 1970-Lexington-1975-Betty B Ellison-xi+349p-yel cl,maps-1st ed (k2,sl soil) 20.00

COLLINS,ROBERT O-Land Beyond the Rivers-New Haven-1971-Yale U Pr-lg 8vo-368p-cl-1st ed (y5,dj) 25.00

COLLINS,TOM-Such is Life-Chig-(1948,03)-U of Chig-facs rprnt of 1st Aussie ed publ 1903-1st US ed (hh5,dj) 15.00

COLLINS,VARNUM L-Continental Congress at Princeton-Princeton-1908-xiii,295p-cl,plts (aa6) 75.00

COLLINS,VARNUM L-Princeton-NY-1914-vii,416p-cl,plts (aa6) 25.00

COLLINS,WILKIE-Miss or Mrs? and Other Stories-Phila-(1872)-Peterson & Bros-wrps-1st US ed (a10,edge-wn,chip,cov stnd) 200.00

COLLINS,WILLIAM A-At Long and Short Range-Phila,Lond-1893-Lippincott-198p-cl,ltd to 500c (c1,sl wn) 15.00

COLLIS,EDGAR L-Health of the Industrial Worker-Lond-1921-450p-illus (g10,ex-libr) 30.00

COLLIS,MAURICE-Foreign Mud-NY-1947-Knopf-8vo-300p-24 illus-1st US ed (ff5,dj tn,chip) 25.00

COLLISON,ROBERT-Book Collecting-1957-Essential Bks-photos-1st Amer ed (w1,f,dj) 25.00

COLLISON,ROBERT-Story of Street Literature-Lond-1973-Dent-1st ed (ll5,f,dj) 40.00

COLLISON,T-ED.-This Winged World-NY-(1943)-Coward,McCann-8vo-xxiv,520p-cl,illus e.p.-1st ed (t2,rear cov sl stnd) 25.00

COLLISON,T-Flying Fortress-NY-1943-sm 4to-viii,168p-cl,illus t.p.,plts,text illus,e.p. maps-1st ed (t2,chip dj) 40.00

COLLISON,T-Superfortress is Born-NY-(1945)-8vo-6;218p-cl,32p plts,text illus,illus e.p.-1st ed (t2,dj) 40.00

COLLODI,C-Adventures of Pinocchio-NY-1929-Macmillan-4to-pict cl,col & b&w illus,A Mussino-3rd prtg of 1st US ed thus (s3,sp fade,sl soil,rub) 85.00

COLLODI,C-Pinocchio-NY-(1940)-Platt & Munk-4to-122p-pict cl,col illus(incl 8 col plts) by T Sarg (oo10,f,dj rprd,creased) 50.00

COLONIAL AND EARLY ENGLISH HARDWARE-New Britain-1931-Corbin-4to-95p-brwn bds,cl sp,photos-trade cat (r10,sl wn) 40.00

COLQUHOUN,ARCHIBALD R-Overland to China-Lond,NY-1900-Harper & Bros-8vo-465p-blu cl,4 fldg maps,33 illus (gg6) 125.00

COLQUHOUN,MAJ J A S-With the Kurram Field Force 1878 to 79-Lond-1881-419p-red cl,fldg maps,plts-scarce-1st ed (kk2,sl sun sp) 150.00

COLSON,ELIZABETH-Makah Indians-Mpls-(1953)-308p (g7) 40.00

COLSON,ELIZABETH-Marriage & the Family Among the Plateau Tonga of Northern Rhodesia-Manchester-1967-U of Mnchstr-8vo-379p-cl,map,plts-rprnt (y5,sl tn dj) 35.00

COLSON,ELIZABETH-Plateau Tonga of Northern Rhodesia-Manchester-1970-Mnchstr U Pr-8vo-237p-cl,map-rprnt (y5,dj) 35.00

COLT PATENT FIREARMS CO-Makers of History-Hartford-1926-16mo-64p-wrps-illus (m3) 35.00

COLT,MRS S S-Tourist's Guide Through the Empire State-Albany-1871-Colt-wood engrvngs-1st ed (dd6,f) 80.00

COLTON,HAROLD S-Hopi Katchina Dolls-Albuq-1971-150p-stiff pict wrps,frntis,col photos (t7,f) 10.00

COLTON,WALTER-Deck and Port-1850-Barnes-408p-col lithos,map-Howes C624-1st ed (d3,rebckd) 65.00

COLTON,WALTER-Deck and Port-NY-1850-408p-cl,map on pg 12,four col plts litho by Sarony & Major,prntd e.p.-variant iss,Howes C 624-1st ed (b1,sl fox) 100.00

COLTON,WALTER-Deck and Port-NY-1850-Barnes-408p-frntis,4 col plts-Howes C624-1st ed (gg4,fox) 75.00

COLUM,PADRAIC-Adventures of Odysseus and the Tale of Troy-Lond-(1920)-Harrap-8 col plts & b&w illus,Pogany-pict bndg & e.p.-1st Brit ed (e10,sl rub edges) 35.00

COLUM,PADRAIC-At the Gateways of the Day-New Haven-1924-Yale U Pr-tall 8vo-217p-cl,decs,J MayFraser,5p drwngs,vol.1(vol 2 in prep)-1st ed (s3,sp tanned,sp lttrs flaked) 35.00

COLUM,PADRAIC-At the Gateways of the Day-New Haven-1924-Yale Univ Pr-cl-1st ed (n8) 27.50

COLUM,PADRAIC-Boy Apprenticed to an Enchanter-NY-1920-Macmillan-cl,illus,D S Walker-1st ed (z8,f) 50.00

COLUM,PADRAIC-Bright Island-1925-Yale-233p-g dec cov,e.p. maps,illus by J M Fraser-1st ed (u8) 45.00

COLUM,PADRAIC-Children of Odin-NY-(1920)-Macmillan-cl,illus,W Pogany-1st ed (z8,f,autg) 75.00

COLUM,PADRAIC-ED.-Anthology of Irish Verse-NY-1922-Boni & Liveright-cl-1st ed (z8,f) 30.00

COLUM,PADRAIC-Golden Fleece, and the Heroes Who Lived Before Achilles-NY-(1921)-Macmillan-cl,illus,W Pogany-1st ed (z8,f) 75.00

COLUM,PADRAIC-Half Day's Ride, or Estates in Corsica-NY-1932-Macmillan-1st ed (z8,vf,dj) 65.00

COLUM,PADRAIC-Images of Departure-Dublin-(1969)-Dolmen Pr-1st ed (z8,vf,dj) 32.50

COLUM,PADRAIC-Legend of Saint Columba-NY-1935-Macmillan-illus,E Mackinstry-1st ed (z8,vf,dj) 50.00

COLUM,PADRAIC-Legends of Hawaii-1937-Yale-220p-yel cl,grn pict pastedown on cov & sp,decs by D Forrer-1st ed (u8,sl wn cov) 45.00

COLUM,PADRAIC-Legends of Hawaii-New Haven-1937-Yale U-xiv,220p-1st ed (o2,dj sun,chip) 30.00

COLUM,PADRAIC-Moytura-Dublin-(1963)-Dolmen Pr-1st ed (z8,vf,dj) 40.00

COLUM,PADRAIC-Old Pastures-NY-1930-Macmillan-1st ed (z8,vf,dj missing sm pc) 55.00

COLUM,PADRAIC-White Sparrow-NY-1933-Macmillan-sq 8vo-46p-dec cl,illus by L Ward-1st ed (oo10,fade,cor wn) 25.00

COLUM,PADRAIC-Wild Earth-Dublin-1907-Maunsel-papr cov bds,linen sp-1st ed (z8) 45.00

COLUMBIA BASIN PROJECT-Olympia-1920-53p-wrps,photos,5 fldg maps (r8) 8.00

COLUMBIA'S EMBLEM. INDIAN CORN-Bost-1893-Houghton Mifflin-16mo-62p-yel cl,frntis,5 plts (o6,wn,soil cl,chip fr f.e.p.) 45.00

COLUMBUS,CHRISTOPHER-Letter of Columbus on the Discovery of America-NY-1892-Lenox Libr-12mo-g dec red cl (p8,f) 50.00

COLVIN,FRED H-60 Years with Man and Machines-NY-(1947)-Whittlesey Hs-ltd to 1000c,nbrd,autg-1st ed (g2,dj) 25.00

COLVIN,H M-Biographical Dictionary of English Architects 1660 to 1840-Lond-1954-1st ed (h10) 75.00

COLWIN,LAURIE-Dangerous French Mistress & Other Stories-Lond-1975-Chatto & Windus-1st ed (z9,f,f dj) 20.00

COLWIN,LAURIE-Family Happiness-NY-1982-Knopf-1st ed (x9,f,dj) 12.50

COLWIN,LAURIE-Happy All the Time-NY-1978-Knopf-1st ed (m7,f,dj) 20.00

COLWIN,LAURIE-Lone Pilgrim-NY-1981-Knopf-1st ed (l7,dj) 20.00

COLWIN,LAURIE-Passion and Affect-1974-Viking-auth 1st bk-1st ed (p9,f,dj) 45.00

COLWIN,LAURIE-Shine On, Bright & Dangerous Object-1975-Viking-1st ed (p9,dj) 45.00

COMAN,DALE REX-Pleasant River-NY-1966-8vo-169p-illus-1st ed (m3,vf,dj) 20.00

COMBE,GEORGE-System of Phrenology-Bost-1837-Marsh,Capen & Lyon-(xvi)+664p+2 plts,publ emboss mauve cl,papr sp labl (y9,sl fox) 65.00

COMBS,BARRY B-Westward to Promontory-Palo Alto-1969-79p-1st ed (n4,f,dj) 20.00

COMBS,TREY-Steelhead Fly Fishing & Flies-Portland-1979-4to-118p-wrps-photos (m3,f) 11.00

COMIC ALBUM-Lond-1844-3/4 lea,orig frnt wrps bnd in,illus-1st ed (l9,rbnd) 200.00

COMINI,A-Fantastic Art of Vienna-NY-1978-folio-40 col plts-1st ed (h10,dj) 35.00

COMMONWEALTH V. GORDON ET AL: THE OPINION OF JUDGE BOK-SF-1949-Grabhorn Pr/Knopf-4to-dec bds,cl sp-ltd to 500c (w1) 75.00

COMMUNIST PARTY USA-Resolutions of the Ninth Covention of the...-NY-1936-Workers Libr-64p-wrps-Seidman C468 (r1) 30.00

COMMUNIST PARTY-HISTORY OF THE ... OF THE SOVIET UNION-NY-(1939)-Internat'l Publ-364p-wrps (g1) 12.50

COMMUNITY COOK BOOK-Lake Grove-1924-PTA-64p-sm booklet,illus wrps (n6,sl soil) 10.00

COMPTON,D G-Ascendencies-NY-(1980)-Berkley-1st US ed (g3,f,sl soil dj) 15.00

COMSTOCK,ANDREW-System of Elocution, with Special Reference to Gesturing...Defective Articulation-Phila-1845-Butler & Williams-364;32p-mod lea-illus (g1,rbnd) 50.00

COMSTOCK,ANTHONY-Frauds Exposed-NY-(1880)-J Howard Brown-576p-cl-auth 1st bk-scarce (f1,sl wn) 50.00

COMSTOCK,HENRY B-Iron Horse-NY-1971-228p-200 illus-1st ed (n4,f,dj) 32.00

CONANT,PAUL-Dr.Gatskill's Blue Shoes-NY-1952-Wyn-1st ed (h4,f,dj) 15.00

CONANT,ROGER-Mercer's Belles-Seattle-1960-190p-illus-1st ed (h7,dj) 30.00

CONANT,ROGER-Mercer's Belles-Seattle-1960-UW Pr-1st ed (w1,f,dj) 40.00

CONARD,HENRY-Water Lilies and How to Grow Them-GC,NY-1914-xii,228p (x5,wn,sl stnd cor) 20.00

CONARD,HOWARD L-Uncle Dick Wooton-1957-Lakeside Classic (t7,f) 20.00

CONARD,HOWARD L-Uncle Dick Wooton-Columbus-1950-472p-frntis,illus,ltd ed (t7,f,dj chip) 45.00

CONCAS Y PALAU,CAPT VICTOR M-Squadron of Admiral Cervera-Wash-1900-GPO-117p-pnk wrps,offc of Naval Intell War Notes No.VIII-1st ed (k2,sl chip sp) 25.00

CONDICT,JEMIMA-Jemima Condict, Her Book-Newark-1930-Carteret Bk Club-73,(1)p-cl backed bds-ltd to 200c,plts (aa6,as new) 90.00

CONDIT,CARL W-American Building Art-NY-1960,61-OUP-4to-2 vols-cl,illus (pp7) 100.00

CONDIT,CARL W-Rise of the Skyscraper-Chig-(1952)-U of Chig Pr-8vo-255p-108 illus-1st ed (bb5,dj) 30.00

CONDIT,CARL W-Rise of the Skyscraper-Chig-(1952)-U of Chig Pr-x+255p-red cl,108 plts-1st ed (dd1,dj) 35.00

CONDIT,JOTHAM H-Genealogical Record of the Condit Family-(np)-1916-470p-cl,illus-rvsd & enlgd from 1885 ed (aa6) 150.00

CONDOMINAS,GEORGES-We Have Eaten the Forest-NY-(1977,57)-Hill & Wang-8vo-423p-photos-1st US ed (aa5,sl tn dj) 25.00

CONDON,DAVE-Go Go Chicago White Sox-1960-Coward McCann-1st ed (q7,f,dj) 40.00

CONDON,R-Manchurian Candidate-1960-M Joseph-1st Brit ed (x7,f,dj) 95.00

CONDON,RICHARD-Manchurian Candidate-NY,Tor,Lond-(1959)-McGraw-Hill-1st ed (a10,sl cocked sp,dj) 125.00

CONDOR,THE-MAGAZINE-Santa Clara-1912 to 59-Cooper Ornith Cl of Cal-8vo-vols.14 thru 61 wi first 6 ten year indexes-orig wrps (y8,lacks Sept-Oct,1954) 685.00

CONGDON,HERBERT W-Early American Homes for Today-Rutland-1963-Tuttle-lg 4to-cl,illus-1st prtg (cc10,dj) 50.00

CONGDON,HERBERT W-Old Vermont Houses-NY-1946-Knopf-4to-cl,col frntis,140 illus-new ed,rvsd,enlgd (cc10,wn dj) 40.00

CONGDON,HERBERT W-Old Vermont Houses-NY-1946-Knopf-8vo-192p-grn cl,col frntis,b&w illus-rvsd ed (r10,chip dj) 25.00

CONGER,HORRACE O-Obstetrics and Womanly Beauty-Chig-nd-Amer Publ Hs-541p-cl-32p pamphlet "Obstetrics...Scientifically Illustrated" in rear pckt (d1) 20.00

CONIL,JEAN-Gastronomic Tour De France-(1960)-Dutton-lg 8vo-376p-blk cl,photos,maps-1st US ed (q8,dj) 16.50

CONIL,JEAN-Haute Cuisine-Lond-(1953)-Faber-lg 8vo-579p-gry cl,photos-1st prtg (q8) 35.00

CONKLIN,GEORGE-Ways of the Circus-NY-(1921)-Harper & Bros-illus-1st ed (jj9) 35.00

CONKLIN,GROFF-ED.-Best of Science Fiction-NY-(1946)-1st ed (bb10,chip dj) 10.00

CONKLING,ALFRED-Young Citizen's Manual-Albany-1836-Oliver Steele-221p-cl-Amer Imprnts 36883 (n1) 22.50

CONN,GEORGE-Some Common Diseases of Cattle-NY-1946-Orange Judd-176p-cl (x6,as new in dj) 20.00

CONNECTICUT-MODERN...HOMES AND HOMECRAFTS-NY-1921-Amer Homecrafts-4to-160p+6p ads-tan bds wi papr labl (r10) 75.00

CONNELL,CHARLES-Aphrodisiacs in Your Garden-NY-(1966)-12mo-143p-1st Amer ed (m10,dj chip,sl soil) 10.00

CONNELL,EVAN S,JR.-Anatomy Lesson and Other Stories-NY-1957-Viking-8vo-cl/bds-auth 1st bk-1st ed (ll10,f,dj) 125.00

CONNELL,EVAN S,JR.-Connoisseur-NY-1974-Knopf-1st ed (b5,f,dj) 20.00

CONNELL,EVAN S,JR.-Mr.Bridge-NY-1969-Knopf-1st ed (h8,f,dj) 65.00

CONNELL,EVAN S,JR.-Mrs.Bridge-NY-1959-Viking-1st ed (b5,sl rub dj) 75.00

CONNELL,EVAN S,JR.-Points for a Compass Rose-1973-Knopf-1st ed (o9,sl wn dj) 20.00

CONNELL,EVAN S,JR.-Points for a Compass Rose-NY-1973-Knopf-1st ed (b5,as new in dj) 30.00

CONNELL,EVAN S,JR.-Saint Augustine's Pigeon-SF-1980-North Point-1st ed (b5,as new in dj) 15.00

CONNELL,EVAN S,JR.-White Lantern-NY-(1980)-Holt-1st ed (k7,f,dj) 15.00

CONNELL,J H-Canaigre, a New Tanning Plant-Austin-1896-Agri Exp St-10p-wrps (x6) 12.00

CONNELLEY,WILLIAM E-Quantrill and the Border Wars-Cedar Rapids-1910-Torch Pr-539p-frntis,illus,maps-1st ed (cc6) 165.00

CONNELLEY,WILLIAM E-Quantrill and the Border Wars-Cedar Rapids-1910-Torch Pr-539p-maps,illus,errata-Six Guns 479-1st ed (gg4,fade sp lttrng) 75.00

CONNELLEY,WILLIAM E-War with Mexico, 1846-1847-KC-1907-649p-2 fldg maps,photos-1st ed (v7,1 map rprd) 100.00

CONNELLEY,WILLIAM E-Wild Bill and His Era-NY-1933-Pr of Pioneers-229p-illus-Six Guns #480-1st ed (dd4) 100.00

CONNELLEY,WILLIAM E-Wild Bill and His Era-NY-1933-Pr of the Pioneers-229p+11 leaves plts,pict g red cl-scarce-Howes C690-1st ed (z1,sunned sp) 135.00

CONNELLEY,WILLIAM E-Wild Bill and His Era-NY-1933-Pr of the Pioneers-229p-cl (h1) 35.00

CONNELLY,MARC-Green Pastures-NY-(1929)-Farrar & Rinehart-grn cl-1st ed (f2,dj) 65.00

CONNERS,DANIEL E-Confederate in the Colorado Gold Fields-Norman-1970-186p-photos-Rittenhouse #126-1st ed (t7,f,dj) 15.00

CONNETT,EUGENE V-Any Luck?-NY-1933-8vo-240p-illus,R Boyer-1st ed (m3) 25.00

CONNETT,EUGENE V-Duck Decoys-NY-1953-8vo-116p-illus-scarce-1st ed (m3,f,dj) 50.00

CONNETT,EUGENE V-Duck Shooting Along the Atlantic Tidewater-NY-1947-4to-308p-red mor,gilt-ltd to 149c,nbrd,autg-deluxe ed-rare (m3,sl dull sp,sl wn box) 950.00

CONNETT,EUGENE V-ED.-Wildfowling the Mississippi Flyway-NY-1949-8vo-387p-photos-1st ed (m3,f,chip dj) 150.00

CONNETT,EUGENE V-ED.-Yachting in North America-NY-1948-Van Nostrand-sm 4to-photos,drwngs,maps-1st ed (ee6,dj) 40.00

CONNETT,EUGENE V-Feathered Game From a Sporting Journal-NY-(1929)-Derrydale-4to-illus,E Burke-ltd to 500c,this one unnumbered-1st ed (u10) 300.00

CONNETT,EUGENE V-Fishing a Trout Stream-NY-(1934)-Derrydale-8vo-blu cl,photos-ltd to 950c,nbrd-1st ed (u10,sp drknd) 175.00

CONNETT,EUGENE V-Random Casts-Derrydale-1939-8vo-195p-ltd to 1075c,nbrd-illus,Boyer & Weiler-orig glassine dj (m3,vf,dj) 200.00

CONNICK,C J-Adventures in Light & Color-NY-1937-lg thk 4to-tip in col illus on cov,42 plts & 48 collotypes(incl col tip-in)-1st ed (ee1,hngs weak,sp labl wn) 250.00

CONNINGHAM,F A-Currier & Ives-Cleve-(1950)-World-sm 8vo-63p-cl,col illus-ltd to 950c,nbrd (x4,box) 15.00

CONNINGTON,J J-Boathouse Riddle-Bost-1931-Little-1st US ed (f4) 15.00

CONNINGTON,J J-Death at Swaythling Court-Bost-1926-Little-1st US ed (g4,f,dj missing sp pc) 35.00

CONNINGTON,J J-Murder Will Speak-1938-Little,Brown-1st Amer ed (s10,dj fray & sp crease) 35.00

CONNINGTON,J J-Nemesis at Raynham Parva-1929-Gollancz-1st ed (s10) 15.00

CONNINGTON,J J-Sweepstake Murders-1932-Little,Brown-1st Amer ed (s10) 17.50

CONNOLLY,CHRISTOPHER P-Devil Learns to Vote-NY-(1938)-Covici,Friede-310p-1st ed (ff4,sl tn sp) 18.00

CONNOLLY,CYRIL-Les Pavillons-NY-1962-MacMillan-4to-211p-beige cl,col frntis,photos,sketches-1st prtg (r10,wn dj) 30.00

CONNOLLY,CYRIL-Les Pavillons-NY-1962-Macmillan-4to-cl,col frntis,illus-1st prtg (cc10,dj,autg) 45.00

CONNOLLY,J-P G Wodehouse, An Illustrated Biography-1979-Orbis-1st ed (x2,f,dj) 50.00

CONNOLLY,JAMES B-Between Shipmates-Ormond Beach-1953-G A Zabriskie-ltd to 750c (x1,f,dj) 35.00

CONNOLLY,JAMES B-Port of Gloucester-NY-1940-Dbldy,Doran-ix,333p-g blu cl,illus-1st ed (p2) 22.50

CONNOLLY,JAMES B-Trawler-NY-1914-Scribners-scarce in dj-1st ed (x1,dj sl fade & soil) 50.00

CONNOLLY,JOSEPH P-Tertiary Mineralization of the Northern Black Hills-Rapid City-1927-SD Sch Mine Bull.#15-149p-wrps,frntis,photos-1st ed (t7) 10.00

CONNOLLY,JOSEPH-Modern First Editions-Lond-(1984)-Orbis-1st ed (dd2,f,dj) 40.00

CONNOR,D RUSSELL-BG-On the Record-(1969)-Arlington Hs-photos-1st ed (w1,f,dj) 50.00

CONNOR,RALPH-Corporal Cameron of the North West Mounted Police-Tor-1912-Westminster-454p-Peel #2298-1st ed (k10) 20.00*

CONNOR,RALPH-Sky Pilot-Chig-1899-Revell-300p-1st ed (k10) 20.00*

CONNOR,SEYMOUR-Peters Colony of Texas-Austin-1959-Tx St Hist-473p-illus,maps,chrts-1st ed (a9) 90.00

CONOT,ROBERT-Streak of Luck-NY-(1979)-Seaview-xviii+565p-brwn cl-1st ed (a2,dj) 20.00

CONOVER,DAVID-Once Upon an Island-NY-1967-Crown-8vo-242p-illus-1st ed (cc7,dj) 20.00*

CONRAD,BARNABY-How to Fight a Bull-GC-1968-Dbldy-pict e.p.,illus-1st ed (y10,sl wn dj) 25.00

CONRAD,JOSEPH-Inheritors-NY-1901-McClure,Phillips-8vo-beige pict cl-1st bndg wi sky in gold,wi corrected dedication-1st ed (ll10,sp drknd,sl soil,hng wea 350.00

CONRAD,JOSEPH-Letters of...to Richard Curle-NY-1928-Crosby Gaige-grn bds bckd in cl wi labl,lg papr ed,ltd to 850c (cc2) 125.00

CONRAD,JOSEPH-Nature of a Crime-Lond-1924-Duckworth-magenta bds-1st ed (cc2) 50.00

CONRAD,JOSEPH-Nature of a Crime-Lond-1924-Duckworth-red/pnk bndg-1st ed (a10,fade,brnd e.p.s,soil dj) 100.00

CONRAD,JOSEPH-Nature of a Crime-Lond-1924-Duckworth-sm 8vo-119p-orng cl-1st ed (mm8,fade) 75.00*

CONRAD,JOSEPH-Nigger of "Narcissus"-Lond-1898-Heinemann-cl-1st ed,1st iss (hh4,sl rub) 400.00

CONRAD,JOSEPH-Nostromo-NY,Lond-1904-Harper & Bros-8vo-dec grn cl-1st Amer ed (ll10,f) 150.00

CONRAD,JOSEPH-Rescue-Lond-1920-Dent-grn bds stmpd in gold,pict dj-1st Brit ed (cc2,f,rub dj) 175.00

CONRAD,JOSEPH-Rover-GC-1923-Dbldy Page-1st trd ed after ltd ed of 377c & preceding Brit ed (bb2,f,dj) 175.00

CONRAD,JOSEPH-Rover-GC-1923-Dbldy,Page-1st trd ed (a10,sl cocked sp,sl rub) 35.00

CONRAD,JOSEPH-Secret Agent-1907-Harpers-pict cl,ltd to 4000c-1st Amer ed (x7,sp fade) 135.00

CONRAD,JOSEPH-Suspense-Lond-1925-frntis-1st ed (r2,sl rub sp,sl fox) 65.00

CONRAD,JOSEPH-Tales of Hearsay-Lond-(1925)-T Fisher Unwin-1st ed (cc2) 50.00

CONRAD,JOSEPH-Typhoon-Lond-1902-Heinemann-gold stmpd gry bds,ltd to 1500c-1st ed,1st iss (bb2,sl cocked) 150.00

CONRAD,JOSEPH-Typhoon-NY,Lond-1902-Putnam's-sm 8vo-dec grn cl-1st ed,1st issue(wi publ 4p ads in rear) (ll10,sl rub) 250.00

CONRAD,JOSEPH-Under Western Eyes-Lond-(1911)-Methuen-red bds stmpd in gold,1st iss wi publ catalogue incl-1st ed (cc2) 150.00

CONRAD,JOSEPH-Within the Tides-Lond-1915-J M Dent-gold stmpd grn bds-1st ed (bb2) 175.00

CONRADS,U-Archtecture of Fantasy-NY-1966-Praeger-illus (h10,sl tn dj) 100.00

CONRADY,A E-ET AL-Photography as a Scientific Implement-NY-1923-Van Nostrand-viii+549p-blu cl,21 plts-1st ed (c2) 50.00

CONROTTO,EUGENE-Lost Desert Bonanzas-1963-Palm Desert-278p-91 maps-1st ed (d3,dj) 30.00

CONROY,FRANK-Stop Time-Lond-1968-1st Brit ed (s5,chip dj) 25.00

CONROY,FRANK-Stop Time-NY-1967-auth 1st bk-1st ed (s5,dj) 45.00

CONROY,JACK-Disinherited-NY-1933-Covici Friede-orng cl,art deco dj-2nd prtg (w5,f,dj sp wn,chip) 20.00

CONROY,JACK-ED.-Writers in Revolt-NY-1973-1st ed (n5,f,f dj) 15.00

CONROY,JACK-ED.-Writers in Revolt-NY-1973-Lawrence Hill-234p (r1,f,dj) 25.00

CONROY,PAT-Lords of Discipline-Bost-1980-1st ed (s5,f,sl soil dj) 35.00

CONROY,PAT-Lords of Discipline-Bost-1980-HMCo-1st ed (h8,f,f dj) 50.00

CONSIDINE,BOB-Toots-1969-Meredith Pr-photos-1st ed (s7,dj) 20.00

CONSTANTINE,K C-Always a Body to Trade-Bost-(1983)-Godine-1st ed (aa10,f,dj) 40.00

CONSTANTINE,K C-Fix Like This-1975-Sat Review-1st ed (p9,f,dj) 25.00

CONSTANTINE,K C-Fix Like This-NY-(1975)-Sat Rev-1st ed (aa10,f,f dj) 45.00

CONSTANTINE,K C-Man Who Liked Slow Tomatoes-Bost-1982-Godine-1st ed (w9,f,dj) 50.00

CONSTANTINE,K C-Man Who Liked to Look at Himself-1973-Sat Rev Pr/Dutton-1st ed (x7,dj) 55.00

CONSTANTINE,K C-Man Who Liked to Look at Himself-NY-1973-Sat Rev/Dutton-1st ed (w9,f,dj) 65.00

CONTINI,M-Fashion from Ancient Egypt to Present Day-NY-1965-folio-550 illus-1st ed (h10,dj) 45.00

CONVERSATIONS ON COMMON THINGS-Bost-1824-Munroe & Francis-263p-bds-Amer Imprnts 15983 (d1,sl wn) 125.00

CONVERSATIONS ON NATURAL PHILOSOPHY-Phila-1826-220p-lea,auth is Jane Marcet,plts-Amer Imprnts 25225 (d1,rbckd) 30.00

CONVERSE,FLORENCE-Into the Void-Bost-1926-Little-1st ed (e4) 15.00

CONVERSE,FLORENCE-Story of Wellesley-Bost-1915-Little,Brown-284p-cl (k1) 17.50

CONVERSION OF THE WORLD-Andover-1818-84p-lea-Amer Imprnts 44225 (g1,wk lower joints,sl wn sp) 15.00

CONWAY,AINSLIE-Enchanted Islands-NY-(1947)-Putnam-8vo-280p-1st ed (cc5,f,f dj) 25.00

CONWAY,J GREGORY-Flowers East West-NY-1938-lg 4to-(10),336p+7p index-100p photos-1st ed (l10,f,dj) 17.50

CONWAY,M-Bolivian Andes-NY-1901-403p-wht/blu pict cov of mtns,photos-1st US ed (o10,f) 195.00

CONWAY,MARTIN-Episodes in a Varied Life-Lond-1932-276p-40 photos-1st ed (a4,f) 150.00

CONWAY,W M-Alps from End to End-Westminster-1895-403p-t.e.g.,100 illus-1st Brit ed (a4) 175.00

CONWAY,W M-Climbing and Exploration in the Karakoram Himalayas-Lond-1894-T Fisher Unwin-lg 8vo-709p+1p ads-brwn dec cl,fldg map,illus (gg6,fade,soil,sp weak) 250.00

CONWAY,W M-Mountain Memories-Lond-1920-lg 8vo-282p-16 plts-scarce-1st Brit ed (o10) 40.00

CONWELL,RUSSELL H-Life, Speeches, and Public Services of James A Garfield-Portland-1881-384p-1/2 lea,illus-1st ed (c4,ex-libr) 30.00

CONZE,EDWARD-Spain To Day-NY-nd-Greenberg-1st ed (v5) 25.00

COOK,A J-Birds of Michigan-np-1893-8vo-(2),148p-wrps,engrvngs (y8,autg) 27.00

COOK,A J-Nine Days-Lond-1926-Cook/Coop-wrps-1st ed (v5) 30.00

COOK,BRUCE-Beat Generation-NY-1971-Scribner's-1st ed (bb1,f,dj) 25.00

COOK,BRUCE-Beat Generation-NY-1971-Scribner's-1st ed (c8,dj) 45.00

COOK,CLARENCE-Girl's Life Eighty Years Ago-NY-1887-Scribner-239p-cl (x6) 20.00

COOK,D J-Hands Up-Denver-1882-Republican Publ Co-285p-cl-plts-Howes C 728,Six-Guns 483-rare-1st ed (j1,sl shaken,one illus raggd) 400.00

COOK,EDMUND V-Chronicles of the Little Tot-NY-(1905)-Dodge-115p-cl wi pict pasteon,8 col plts (r3) 65.00

COOK,FRED J-Nightmare Decade-NY-1971-Random Hs-626p-1st ed (r1,dj) 20.00

COOK,FREDERICK A-My Attainment of the Pole...1907 to 1909-NY-1911-Polar Publ-4to-599p wi index,photos,dec brwn cl-1st ed (t1) 110.00

COOK,FREDERICK A-Return From the Pole-NY-1931-335p-1st ed (q10,f) 35.00

COOK,FREDERICK A-Through the First Antarctic Night 1898 to 1899-NY-1900-Dbldy,McCLure-8vo-xxiv,478p-dec cl,t.e.g.,spec ed wi autg photo before col frntis,4 col plts,map,photos-ltd ed (oo1,cov spot,hngs weak) 1,250.00

COOK,FREDERICK A-To the Top of the Continent-NY-1908-321p-pict grn cl,gold stmpd sp-scarce-1st ed (a4,vf) 485.00

COOK,FREDERICK F-Reminiscences of Chicago During the Civil War-Chig-1914-Donnelley-194p-frntis-Lakeside Classics (cc4) 35.00

COOK,GEORGE H-Geology of New Jersey-Newark-1868-xxiv,899,(1)p-cl,fldg maps,plts (aa6) 175.00

COOK,J H-Fifty Years on the Old Frontier-1923-Yale-291p-photos(1 dbl-fld)-Six Guns #484-1st ed (r8) 75.00

COOK,J H-Fifty Years on the Old Frontier-New Haven-1923-Yale U Pr-291p-illus-Herd 569-1st ed (dd4) 95.00

COOK,JAMES-Bibliography of Captain James Cook, R.N., F.R.S., Circumnavigator-NY-1968-Burt Franklin-172p-drk blu cl,g sp titles,(rprnt of Sydney 1928) (nn1,as new) 25.00

COOK,JAMES-Captain Cook's Journal During His First Voyage Round the World...H.M. Bark Endeavor,1768 to 71-Lond-1893-4to-lvi,400p-maps,illus-scarce-1st prtg (bb9,sl rub sp) 450.00

COOK,JAMES-Journal of H.M.S. Resolution-Guilford-1981-Genesis Publ-g dec red lea/cl,bands,a.e.g.,ribbon mrkrs,mrbld e.p.,col plts wi guards-ltd to 500c (dd7,f,box) 750.00

COOK,JAMES-Voyages of Captain...Round the World-Lond-1813-Sherwood,Neely & Jones-7 vols-orig calf,separate t.p.s (bb9) 850.00

COOK,JOSEPH-Heredity, with Preludes on Current Events-Bost-1879-268p-1st ed (dd3,f) 75.00

COOK,MARC-Wilderness Cure-NY-1881-153p-1st ed (dd3) 75.00

COOK,MARGARET-America's Charitable Cooks-Kent-1971-315p-blu cl (q8) 35.00

COOK,MARGARET-America's Charitable Cooks-Kent-1971-auth-315p (m6) 45.00

COOK,MRS E T-From a Woman's Note Book-Lond-1903-Allen-8vo-237p+ads-1st ed (oo7) 45.00

COOK,O F-Origin & Distribution of Cocoa Palm-Wash-1901-GPO/US Nat Herb-37p-wrps (x6) 15.00

COOK,O F-Three New Genera of Stilt Palms from Colombia-Wash-1913-GPO/US Nat Herb-20p-wrps (x6) 15.00

COOK,OLIVE-English Cottages and Farmhouses-Lond-1954-1st ed (y7,dj fray,tn) 30.00

COOK,OLIVE-Movement in Two Dimensions-Lond-1963-Hutchison-142p-illus-1st ed (cc9,dj fray & tn) 45.00

COOK,RICHARD J-Super Power Steam Locomotives-San Marino-1966-144p-1st ed (n4,f,dj) 25.00

COOK,SIR THEODORE A-Twenty Five Great Houses of France-Lond-nd-Country Life-folio-1/2 mor & cl (y3,hngs weak) 195.00

COOK,THEO M-Father Abraham's Boys in Blue S.E. Iowa Co "F" 14th Iowa Infantry-Keosauqua-1973-Auth-46p-wrps,illus,map-scarce (o7,f) 25.00

COOK,WARREN L-Flood Tide of Empire-New Haven,Lond-1973-620p-illus-1st ed (c7,vf,sl chip dj) 60.00

COOK,WARREN L-Flood Tide of Empire-New Haven,Lond-1973-620p-illus-1st ed (g7,f,f dj) 60.00

COOK,WILLIAM A-By Horse, Canoe and Float Through the Wilderness of Brazil-Akron-1909-Werner Co-iv,487p-lt blu cl,wht sp & cov titles,photos (mm1,sl soil & sp fade) 75.00

COOKE,ALISTAIR-Christmas Eve-NY-(1952)-Knopf-57p-dec bds,col illus-1st ed (s3,dj) 25.00

COOKE,ALISTAIR-Douglas Fairbanks-NY-(1940)-MOMA-8vo-35p-prtd bds,frntis,Film Libr Ser,No.2-scarce (t10) 25.00

COOKE,CHARLES-Big Show-1938-Harper-360p-1st ed (v8,dj wn & chip missing) 15.00

COOKE,D C-War Wings-NY-(1941)-8vo-218p-illus cl,frntis,text illus-1st ed (t2) 25.00

COOKE,EDMUND VANCE-Baseballogy-Chig-1912-88p-bds (n1) 35.00

COOKE,G W-Fertilizing for Maximum Yield-NY-(1972)-xxiv,296p-bds (x5,sp fade) 10.00

COOKE,H LESTER-Fletcher Martin-NY-1977-Abrams-232p-orng cl,b&w & col illus (r10,f,f dj) 45.00

COOKE,J E-Outlines From the Outpost-Chig-1961-Harwell,ed.-413p-illus (z10) 40.00

COOKE,JOHN E-Outlines From the Outpost-Chig-1961-Donnelley & Sons-frntis-Lakeside Classics (ff4) 20.00

COOKE,JOHN ESTEN-Pretty Mrs.Gaston, and Other Stories-NY-(1874)-Orange Judd-288p-cl-Wright 624-1st ed (g1) 17.50

COOKE,M C-Rust,Smut,Mildew, and Mould-Lond-1878-Hardwicke & Bogue-12mo-viii+262p-brwn cl,16plts(12 col)-4th ed (j2,sl wn) 55.00

COOKE,P ST.G-Scenes and Adventures in the Army-Phila-1857-432p-cl-Howes#C740-1st ed (u7,cov wn) 275.00

COOKE,P ST.GEORGE-Conquest of New Mexico and California-NY-1878-307p-fldg map-1st ed (v7,map rprd) 275.00

COOKE,P ST.GEORGE-Conquest of New Mexico and California-NY-1878-Putnam's-307p-fldg map-Howes C738-1st ed (gg4,ex-libr) 95.00

COOKE,ROSE T-Poems-Bost-1861-Ticknor & Fields-8vo-231+16p ads-brwn cl-BAL 3770-1st ed (w6,vf) 150.00

COOKERY MADE EASY-Lond-nd(ca.1850's)-Thomas Dean & Son-174p+ publ catlg,brn hvy papr wrps wi embossed design-"By A Lady"-10th ed improved (n6) 110.00

COOKING BY GAS-Detr-nd(1902)-Detr Stove Works-95p-art nouveau wrps,illus (n6,sl chip sp) 25.00

COOKING BY GAS-Lond-1910-Cassell & Co-270p-blu pict bds (n6) 18.00

COOKING THE SEPHARDIC WAY-LA-1971-Sephardic Sisterhood-illus papr wrps,comb bndg (n6) 30.00

COOKRIDGE,E H-Baron of Arizona-NY-1967-John Day-8vo-ix,304p-illus-1st ed (z4,sp & t.e. spot,sl wn dj) 20.00

COOKRIDGE,E H-Net That Covers the World-NY-1955-H Holt-315p-1st ed (r1,dj sl chip) 25.00

COOLEY,THOMAS M-Michigan, a History of Governments-Bost-1885-Houghton,Mifflin-376p-cl,fldg map-Amer Commonwealth Ser(Vol.5)-Streeter 811 (z7) 40.00

COOLIDGE,DANE-Arizona Cowboys-NY-1938-Dutton-160p-photos,col pict dj-1st ed (f9,uncut,dj sl wn & chip) 50.00

COOLIDGE,DANE-Last of the Seris-NY-1939-Dutton-8vo-264p-red cl,photos,drwngs-1st ed (mm1,sl fade & fox) 37.00

COOLIDGE,DANE-Texas Cowboys-NY-1937-Dutton-photos-2nd prtg (a9,dj) 45.00

COOLIDGE,MARY R-Rain-Makers-Bost-(1929)-316p-photos,map e.p.-1st ed (v7) 25.00

COOLIDGE,RICHARD-Statistical Report on the Sickness and Mortality...Army of the U.S....January,1839 to January,1855-Wash-1856-4to-703p-1st ed (dd3,rebkd wi lea labl) 275.00

COOLIDGE,RICHARD-Statistical Report on the Sickness and Mortality...Army of the U.S....January,1855 to January,1860-Wash-1860-4to-515p-hand col fldg map-1st ed (dd3) 250.00

COOMARASWAMY,ANANDA-Buddha and the Gospel of Buddhism-New Hyde Park-1964-Univ Bks-cl,plts-1st prtg (o8,dj edge wn) 22.50

COOMARASWAMY,ANANDA-Why Exhibit Works of Art?-Lond-1943-Luzac & Co-wrps-scarce-1st ed (o8) 75.00

COOMBS,J V-Religious Delusions-Cinn-(1904)-Standard Publ-185p-cl (f1) 25.00

COOMBS,JOHN W-Baseball Individual Play and Team Strategy-NY-1938-Prentice-Hall-278p-cl-1st ed (n1) 20.00

COOMBS,L MADISON-Indian Child Goes to School-1957-Bur of Indian Affairs-249p-pict wrps-1st ed (cc4,autg) 15.00

COOMBS,SARAH V-South African Plants for American Gardens-NY-(1936)-364p-col plts (w10) 24.00

COON,NELSON-Complete Book of Violets-NY-1977-Barnes-147p (x6,dj wn) 18.00

COONS,FREDERICA B-Trail to Oregon-Portland-(1954)-Binfords & Mort-183p-illus,fldg map (cc4,dj) 25.00

COOPER,COURTNEY R-High Country-Bost-1926-Little,Brown-294p-pict cl,illus-Six Guns #491-1st ed (ee4) 25.00

COOPER,COURTNEY R-With The Circus-1930-Little,Brown-212p-illus (v8) 20.00

COOPER,ELIZABETH-Harim and the Purdah-NY-nd(c.1900)-Century-8vo-gold dec blu cl,32 photo plts (ll1) 60.00

COOPER,ELIZABETH-My Lady of the Chinese Courtyard-NY-1914-Stokes-8vo-262p-cl,31 photos by D Mennie-latr prtg (t3) 35.00

COOPER,ERIC-Modern Sea Fishing From Bass to Tunny-Lond-1937-12mo-247p-photos (m3,f,fray dj) 15.00

COOPER,FRANCK C-Stirring Lives of Buffalo BIll-NY-(1912)-Parson-223p-pict cl,illus-Six Guns 492 (gg4) 25.00

COOPER,GORDON-Isles of Romance and Mystery-Lond-(1949)-Lutterworth-8vo-180p-40 photos-1st ed (ff5,dj) 25.00

COOPER,HOWARD M-Some Account of Camden's Rise and Growth-Camden-1899-23p-wrps (aa6,chip,taped) 25.00

COOPER,J M-Analytical and Critical Bibliography of the Tribes of Tierra Del Fuego and Adjacent Territory-1917-Bur Amer Ethnol Bull.63-233p-fldg map (bb3) 25.00

COOPER,J W-Experienced Botanist or Indian Physician-Ebensburg-1833-prtd by Canan & Scott-xxiv,(25)-301p-lea-rare (b1,f f.e.p. detchd,but prsnt) 500.00

COOPER,JAMES F-Technique of Contraception-NY-1928-271p-4th prtg (g10) 20.00

COOPER,JEFF-Fireworks-Rogue River-1980-8vo-191p-illus (m3,vf,dj) 20.00

COOPER,JOE-With or Without Beans-Dallas-1952-Henson-247p-1st ed (a9) 25.00

COOPER,JOHN R-Art of the Compleat Angler-Durham-1968-8vo-200p-1st ed (m3,vf,dj) 12.50

COOPER,JOHN-First Base Jinx-GC-1952-Mel Martin ser.#4-1st ed (q7,dj) 17.50

COOPER,LINN F-Time Distortion in Hypnosis-Balt-1954-Williams & Wilkins-(xvi)+192+(3)p-beige cl-1st ed (y9,f,dj) 36.50

COOPER,LT A-In & Out of Rebel Prisons-Oswego-1888-335p-illus (a3) 50.00

COOPER,MATTHEW-German Army 1933 to 1945-NY-(1978)-598p-bds-1st Amer ed (m1,f,dj) 15.00

COOPER,PARLEY J-My Lady Evil-NY-(1973)-S&S-1st ed (p3,f,dj) 15.00

COOPER,PAUL F-Island of the Lost-NY-(1961)-Putnam-8vo-256p-1st ed (jj5,dj) 15.00

COOPER,REV-History of North America-Catskill-1810-Shaw-267p-calf (x6,rub,hng weak) 75.00

COOPER,SAMUEL-Dictionary of Practical Surgery-NY-1830-2 vols-lea (dd3) 150.00

COOPER,SUSAN F-Rural Hours-Syracuse-(1968)-xxxviii; 337p-cl-reprint (h1,f,dj) 15.00

COOPER,SUSAN-Seaward-NY-1983-Atheneum-167p-cl-1st ed (r3,f,f dj) 20.00

COOPER,SUSAN-Silver on the Tree-NY-1977-Atheneum-cl,fifth & final bk in ser-1st ed (r3,dj) 30.00

COOPLAND,G W-Nicole Oresme and the Astrologers-Cambridge-1952-Harvard-cl-1st prtg (l8,dj) 25.00

COOTE,WILLIAM A-Vision and Its Fulfilment-Lond-nd-189p-cl (d1,sl wn) 15.00

COOVER,ROBERT-Charlie in the House of Rue-(Lincoln)-(1980)-Penmaen Pr-illus,J Kaplan-1st ed (c10,as new in dj) 25.00

COOVER,ROBERT-Charlie in the House of Rue-(Lincoln)-(1980)-Penmaen-illus by J Kaplan-1st ed (b5,as new in dj) 25.00

COOVER,ROBERT-Origin of the Brunists-(1966)-Putnam-auth 1st bk-1st ed (m9,f,dj sp wn,rear pnl soil) 140.00

COOVER,ROBERT-Origin of the Brunists-NY-(1966)-Putnam's-auth 1st bk-1st ed (b5,f,dj) 125.00

COOVER,ROBERT-Pricksongs & Descants-1969-Dutton-1st ed (m9,f,dj) 40.00

COOVER,ROBERT-Pricksongs & Descants-1969-Dutton-1st ed (x2,f,dj) 45.00

COOVER,ROBERT-Public Burning-NY-(1977)-Viking-1st ed (b5,as new in dj) 20.00

COOVER,ROBERT-Public Burning-NY-(1977)-Viking-1st ed (j3,f,dj) 15.00

COOVER,ROBERT-Theological Position-NY-1972-scarce-1st ed (j5,as new in dj) 65.00

COOVER,ROBERT-Universal Baseball Association, Inc.-NY-(1968)-Random-1st ed (b5,f,sl tn dj) 65.00

COOVER,ROBERT-Universal Baseball Association-(1968)-Random-1st ed (x2,f,dj) 95.00

COOVER,ROBERT-Universal Baseball Association-(1970)-Hart Davis-glossary of bb terms-1st Brit ed (s8,f,dj) 80.00

COPE,E D-Report Upon Extinct Vertebrata Obtained in New Mexico by Parties of the Expedition of 1874-Wash-1877-4to-370p-plts (bb3,cov wn) 100.00

COPE,E D-Vertebrata of Cretaceous Formations of the West-Wash-1875-4to-303p-57p plts,dbl pg & 1 fldg plt (bb3,cov wn,sl soil) 135.00

COPE,GERTRUDE V-Heritage of the Quest-Bost-1936-Marshall Jones-1st ed (t4) 30.00

COPE,ZACHARY-History of the Acute Abdomen-Lond-1965-123p-1st ed (dd3,dj) 75.00

COPEMAN,W S C-Short History of the Gout and the Rheumatic Diseases-Berkeley-1964-236p-1st ed (dd3,dj) 75.00

COPLEY,HUGH-Letters of Two Fishermen-Lond-1950-8vo-150p-photos-1st ed (m3,f,dj) 20.00

COPPEE,HENRY-General Thomas-NY-1893-Appleton-332p-frntis port,maps-1st ed (o7,f) 50.00

COPPENS,CHARLES-Moral Principles and Medical Practice, the Basis of Medical Jurisprudence-Cin-1897-222p-1st ed (dd3) 100.00

COPPER,BASIL-And Afterward the Dark-Sauk City-1977-Arkham-1st ed (f3,f,dj) 15.00

COPPER,BASIL-And Afterward, The Dark-Sauk City-1977-ltd to 4259c-1st ed (k5,as new in dj) 10.00

COPPER,BASIL-From Evil's Pillow-Sauk City-1973-Arkham-1st ed (f3,f,dj) 15.00

COPPER,BASIL-From Evil's Pillow-Sauk City-1973-ltd to 3468c-1st ed (k5,as new in dj) 10.00

COPPER,BASIL-Necropolis-Sauk City-(1980)-Arkham-ltd to 4050c-Fabian,illus-1st ed (a5,as new in dj) 50.00

COPPING,ARTHUR E-Canada Today and To Morrow-Lond-1911-Cassell-275p-g olive grn cl,6p col plts,34 b&w photos,fldg map (p2,sl wn) 20.00

CORBET,A S-Butterflies of the Malay Peninsula-1956-Oliver Boyd-537p-8 col plts,maps,27 photos-2nd ed rvsd & enlgd (bb3,sl stnd cov,dj) 90.00

CORBETT,J-Jungle Lore-NY-1953-172p-photos (gg3,vf,dj) 40.00

CORBETT,J-Man Eaters of India-NY-1957-619p-3 vols in one (gg3,vf,dj) 58.00

CORBETT,J-Man Eaters of Kumaon-NY-1946-8vo-235p-cl wi bds,5 photos (y8,dj chip) 15.00

CORBETT,J-Man Eating Leopard of Rudraprayag-NY-1948-188p-photos (gg3,f,dj) 35.00

CORBETT,J-My India-NY-1952-163p-photos (gg3,f) 35.00

CORBETT,J-Temple Tiger & More Man Eaters of Kumaon-NY-1955-197p-photos (gg3,f,dj) 38.00

CORBETT,J-Tree Tops-NY-1956-30p-illus (gg3,f,dj) 35.00

CORBETT,LUCY-Long Windows-(1948)-Harper-208p-blk cl,drwngs-1st ed (q8,dj) 15.00

CORBETT,SCOTT-Sea Fox-NY-(1956)-Crowell-8vo-244p-1st ed (cc5,sl chip dj) 20.00

CORBITT,HELEN-Cooks for Looks-1967-Houghton Mifflin-115p-grn cl-1st ed (q8,sl tn dj) 10.00

CORBITT,HELEN-Helen Corbitt Cooks for Company-Bost-1974-Houghton Mifflin-434p-1st prtg (k6,dj) 18.00

CORCORAN,FRED-Unplayable Lies-NY-1965-photos-1st ed (ll7,f,dj) 35.00

CORDASCO,F-Bibliography of Robert Watt,M.D. with his Catalogue of Medical Books-Detr-1968-70p-(facs of 1950 ed) (dd3) 30.00

CORDEAUX,E H-Bibliography of Printed Works Relating to the University of Oxford-Oxford-1968-809p-1st ed (dd3,dj) 25.00

CORDELIER,JEANNE-Life-NY-(1978,76)-Viking-8vo-368p-1st US ed (gg5,f,dj) 10.00

CORDELL,EUGENE-Medical Annals of Maryland 1799 to 1899-Balt-1903-888p-1st ed (dd3) 40.00

CORDILLERA INDIANS-(Ottawa)-1939-Nat Mus of Can-11p-prtd wrps,illus,map-Anthro lflt #7 (k10) 10.00*

CORELL,CHARLES J-Here They are Amos 'n Andy-NY-1931-Long & Smith-sm 8vo-174p-prntd dj-1st ed (b3,f,dj) 125.00

COREY,C B-Mammals of Illinois and Wisconsin-Chig-1912-8vo-502p-wrps,plts,maps (y8,sp chip,unopened) 40.00

COREY,DONALD W-ED.-21 Variations on a Theme-NY-(1953)-Greenberg-1st ed (p1,dj) 40.00

COREY,LEWIS-Crisis of the Middle Class-NY-1935-Covici Friede-1st ed (v5,f,dj) 30.00

CORLE,EDWIN-Coarse Gold-NY-1942-1st ed (n5,sl chip dj) 15.00

CORLE,EDWIN-Death Valley and the Creek Called Furnace-1962(1941)-Ward Ritchie-4to-59p+photos by A Adams-1st ed thus (d3,dj) 125.00

CORLE,EDWIN-Fig Tree John-NY-1935-Liveright-1st ed (y1,sl chip dj) 150.00

CORLE,EDWIN-Royal Highway-Indpls-(1949)-Bobbs Merrill-351p-illus,maps,map e.p.-1st ed (bb4,dj) 25.00

CORLE,EDWIN-Solitaire-NY-1940-Dutton-1st ed (y1,dj) 100.00

CORLET,WILLIAM-Dark Side of the Moon-NY-(1977)-Bradbury Pr-1st US ed (h3,f,sl tn dj) 10.00

CORLETT,WM THOS-Medicine Man of American Indian and His Cultural Background-Springfield-(1935)-354p-photos-scarce-1st ed (u7,unopened,f,dj) 85.00

CORMIER,ROBERT-I Am the Cheese-NY-(1977)-Pantheon-1st ed (nn10,f,sl tn dj) 30.00

CORN,WANDA-Art of Andrew Wyeth-Greenwich-1973-NYGS-oblng 4to-cl-1st ed (oo6,dj) 50.00

CORNELL LABORATORY OF ORNITHOLGY-Enjoying Birds Around New York City-Bost-1966-Houghton Mifflin-171p-wrps,illus (d9) 10.00

CORNELL,LEE H-Tale of the Kicking Mule-Wichita-1949-60p-stiff pict wrps,frntis,photos-1st ed (t7,autg) 17.50

CORNELL,RALPH D-Conspicuous California Plants-Pasadena-1938-192p-dec brick col cl,46 photos,drwngs-ltd to 1500c-scarce-1st ed (jj7) 60.00

CORNER,BETSY C-William Shippen,Jr.-Phila-1951-Amer Philos Scty-xiv+161p-blu cl,8 plts-1st ed (d2,chip dj) 20.00

CORNER,GEORGE W-Doctor Kane of the Arctic Seas-Phila-1971-Temple U Pr-8vo-xiii,306p-frntis,36 illus,6 maps-1st ed (bb7,dj) 25.00*

CORNER,GEORGE-Two Centuries of Medicine-Phila-1965-363p-1st ed (dd3,dj) 60.00

CORNISH,NELLIE C-Miss Aunt Nellie, the Autobiography of...-Seattle-1964-Univ of Wash-283p-blk cl,photos,red illus dj (b6,f,sl tn dj) 18.00

CORNISH,SAM-Generations-Bost-1971-Beacon Pr-1st ed (w5,f,dj) 25.00

CORNWALLIS,KINAHAN-New Eldorado-Lond-1858-xxviii,405p-1/2 lea,fldg map,illus-Lowther 61 (a7) 1,250.00

CORNWALLIS-WEST,G-Edwardians Go Fishing-Lond,NY-1932-8vo-218p-photos (m3,f) 20.00

CORODIUMUS,PETER-ED.-In Trout Country-Bost-1971-8vo-300p-illus-1st ed (m3,vf,dj) 15.00

CORONA CLUB COOK BOOK-(SF)-(1925)-John Kitchen Jr. Co-235p-wht oilcl (u6) 40.00

COROTIS,A CHARLES-Camden County Centennial, 1844 to 1944-(Camden)-(1944)-4to-144p-wrps,illus (aa6) 35.00

CORRELL,A BOYD-Murder is an Art-NY-1950-Phoenix-1st ed (h4,f,dj) 12.50

CORRELL,CHARLES-All About Amos`n'Andy and Their Creators-1930-R,M-scarce in pict dj,photos (x2,sl chip dj) 150.00

CORREVON,HENRY-Rock Garden and Alpine Plants-NY-1930-xiv,544p-8 col & 8 b&w plts (x5,fray,cov soil) 15.00

CORSER,H P-Legendary Lore of the Alaska Totems-Juneau-1910-unpgd-wrps,15 tip-in photos-1st ed (e7,sl chip) 75.00

CORSON,JULIET-Cooking Manual-NY-1877-Dodd,Mead-144p-Bitting 102 (k6,soil,fox) 75.00

CORTAZAR,JULIO-62: a Model Kit-1972-Pantheon-1st US ed (kk6,vf,sl tn dj) 50.00

CORTAZAR,JULIO-Change of Light & Other Stories-NY-1980-Knopf-1st ed (b5,f,dj) 22.50

CORTAZAR,JULIO-End of the Game-NY-(1963)-Pantheon-1st ed (c10,dj) 125.00

CORTAZAR,JULIO-Hopscotch-1967-Collins-1st Brit ed (kk6,f,dj) 65.00

CORTAZAR,JULIO-Manual for Manuel-NY-(1978)-Pantheon-1st ed (b5,as new in dj) 25.00

CORTAZAR,JULIO-Winners-NY-1965-Pantheon-auth 1st bk-1st Amer ed (z2,f,dj) 75.00

CORTISSOZ,ROYAL-An Introduction to the Mellon Collection-Bost-1937-priv prtd/Merrymount Pr-g covs,illus-1st ed (r2) 35.00

CORWIN,EDWARD T-Historical Discourse...Centennial Anniversary of the Reformed Dutch Church, of Millstone, 1866-NY-1866-113p-cl,fldg map (aa6,sp chip) 60.00

CORWIN,EDWARD T-Manual of the Reformed Church in America-NY-1869-Bd of Publ of R C of A-viii+397p-purple cl,ports-2nd ed (k2,fade sp) 25.00

CORY,C B-Birds of Illinois and Wisconsin-1908-Field Mus-764p-wrps,illus (bb3,cov chip & stnd) 45.00

CORY,C B-How to Know the Ducks,Geese & Swans of North America-Bost-1897-8vo-95p-wrps-illus-scarce (m3) 40.00

CORY,ESTHER B-Mediterranean Specialties for the Modern Cook-(1963)-Crowell-148p-wht vel,map e.p.-1st prtg (q8,dj) 15.00

CORY,FANNY Y-Our Baby Book-Indpls-(1907)-Bobbs Merrill-unpgd-bds,illus (a8,sl wn) 75.00

CORY,HARPER-Bears of Jasper-Lond-1946-8vo-119p-photos (m3) 14.00

COSGROVE,RACHEL R-Hidden Valley of Oz-Chig-1951-Reilly & Lee-illus,Dirk-1st ed (z2,cor bump,sl rub) 100.00

COSSLEY-BATT,JILL L-Last of the California Rangers-NY-(1928)-Funk & Wagnells-299p-illus,illus e.p.-Six Guns 499 (gg4,wn dj) 25.00

COSTAKIS,GEO-Russian Avant Garde Art-NY-1981-Abrams-illus(incl col)-1st ed (h10,dj) 285.00

COSTELLO,DAVID F-World of the Gull-Phila-1971-Lippincott-157p-photos-1st ed (b9,dj) 17.50

COSTELLO,J A-Siwash Their Life Legends and Tales-Seattle-1895-Calvery-8vo-(xviii),169p-blk cl,plts-Smith 2062-1st ed (kk9) 165.00

COSTON,TOWNER-Water Symphony-Lond-1948-4to-53p-photos (m3,f,fray dj) 15.00

COSULICH,BERNICE-Tucson-Tucson-1953-310p-frntis,map e.p.,illus-1st ed (t7,dj) 25.00

COTT,H B-Adaptive Coloration in Animals-Lond-1957-8vo-508p-cl,col frntis,48 half-tone plts (y8,dj chip) 85.00

COTTAGE GARDEN ALMANAC...FOR 1873-Phila-(1872)-33,(1)p+wrps (o1) 20.00

COTTAM,C-Food Habits of North American Diving Ducks-Wash-1939-8vo-140p-wrps,10 plts(4 col) (y8) 20.00

COTTAM,CLARENCE-ED.-Whitewings-Princeton-1968-Van Nostrand-348p (c9) 30.00

COTTAM,CLARENCE-Food Habits of North American Diving Ducks-Wash D.C.-1939-8vo-140p-wrps,photos,4 col plts by A Brooks-scarce (m3) 35.00

COTTER,OLIVER-Adulteration of Liquors-NY-1874-Barnes-45p-stiff cl cov,col frntis (u2,sp wn) 35.00

COTTERILL,G F-Climax of a World Quest-Seattle-nd(c.1927)-226p-2 maps (r8) 25.00

COTTERILL,G F-Climax of a World Quest-Seattle-nd-Olympic Publ Co-226p-grn cl,illus (h2,dj) 18.00

COTTERILL,R S-Southern Indians-Norman-1954-255p-1st ed (n10,dj wn,fade) 45.00

COTTON,CHARLES-Compleat Gamester-Barre-1970-Imprint Scty-176p-lea,illus,J Low-ltd ed,autg (n6,box) 50.00

COTTON,LEO-COMP.-Old Mr.Boston De Luxe Official Bartender's Guide-Bost-(1963)-16mo-150p-dec red cl,prntd in red & blk-22nd ed (q8) 12.50

COTTON,PHEBE-Phebe in Wonderland-Holland-1983-4to-77p-wrps (z7,autg) 30.00

COTTRELL,LEONARD-Madame Tussaud-Lond-(1951)-Evans-8vo-194p-28 illus-1st ed (dd5,dj) 30.00

COUDY,JULIEN-ED.-Huguenot Wars-NY-1969-405p-illus-1st ed (kk2,f,dj) 25.00

COUES,E-Birds of the Colorado Valley. Part I-Wash-1878-807p-cl,70 illus (bb3,rbnd) 115.00

COUES,E-Birds of the Northwest-Wash-1874-791p-cl (bb3,rbnd,sl dmpstnd) 95.00

COUES,E-Birds of the Northwest-Wash-1874-8vo-791p-cl (y8,wn,crack,soil) 47.00

COUES,E-ED.-Forty Years a Fur Trader on the Upper Missouri-NY-1898-2 vols-illus,ltd to 950c,nbrd (d7,f) 325.00

COUES,E-ED.-Journal of Jacob Fowler-Mpls-1965-183p-ltd ed (t7,f,dj) 15.00

COUES,E-ED.-Journal of Jacob Fowler...-NY-1898-Francis P Harper-183p+ads-blu cl,fldg frntis,ltd to 950c-v scarce-1st ed (z1) 195.00

COUES,E-Field Ornithology-Salem-1874-Naturalists' Agency-137p-g dec blu cl on bds (b9) 70.00

COUES,E-Key to North American Birds-Bost-1903-Estes-2 vols-col frntis by Fuertes-5th ed (b9) 95.00

COUES,E-Monograph of North American Rodentia-1877-US Geol Surv of Terr-4to-1091p-cl,7 plts (bb3,rbnd) 90.00

COUES,E-On the Trail of a Spanish Pioneer...-NY-1900-Francis P Harper-8vo-2 vols,orig blu cl,18 maps,views & facs,ltd to 950c (mm1,f,mostly unopened) 295.00

COUFFIGNALK,HUGETTE-Peoples' Cook Book-NY-(1977)-St.Martin's-burlap cov bds-1st ed in English (m6) 20.00

COUGHLIN,CHARLES E-Father Coughlin's Radio Discourses 1931 to 1932-Royal Oak-1932-239p-wrps (d1,sl wn & soil) 10.00

COUGHLIN,CHARLES E-Father Coughlin's Radio Discourses, 1931 to 1932-Royal Oak-1932-Radio League of Little-239p-cl (z7) 30.00

COUGHLIN,CHARLES E-Series of Lectures of Social Justice-Royal Oak-1935-Radio League of Little-244p-wrps (z7) 30.00

COULSON,ZOE-Good Housekeeping Cookbook-NY-1973-Good Hskpng Bks-811p-drwngs,M Tinkelman,photos,J Viles (o6) 18.00

COULTER,E M-Civil War and Readjustment in Kentucky-Chapel Hill-(1926)-468p-maps-1st ed (c4,dj chip) 125.00

COULTER,E M-Confederate States of America-Baton Rouge-1950-644p-illus-1st ed (n3,f,dj wn) 37.50

COULTER,E M-Daniel Lee Agriculturist-Athens-1972-U of Ga-165p (x6,sl wn dj) 42.00

COULTER,JOHN M-Plant Relations-NY-1905-viii,266p-214 figs-3rd rvsd ed (m10,loose signatures) 12.00

COULTER,JOHN-Complete Story of Galveston Horror-np-1900-United Publ-8vo-386p (z4,hngs weak,cov rub) 12.50

COUNSELMAN,MARY-Half in Shadow-Sauk City-(1978)-Arkham-1st US ed (f3,f,dj) 15.00

COUNSELOR,JIM-Wild,Wooly and Wonderful-NY-(1954)-392p-1st ed (v7,sl wn dj) 25.00

COUNTRY KITCHEN COOK BOOK-St.Paul-(1948)-Webb Publ-213p-bds,plastic comb bndg (o6) 25.00

COUPLAND,REGINALD-Zulu Battle Piece: Isandhlwana-Lond-1948-144p-map,illus-scarce-1st ed (jj2,f,dj) 125.00

COURLANDER,HAROLD-Hopi Voices-Albuq-1982-255p-1st ed (t7,f,dj) 15.00

COURTINE,ROBERT J-Madame Maigret's Recipes-(1975)-Harcourt-183p-g dec bds,drwngs-1st ed (q8,dj) 25.00

COURTINE,ROBERT J-Madame Maigret's Recipes-NY-(1975)-HBJ-1st ed (w9,f,dj) 45.00

COURVILLE,CYRIL B-Intracranial Tumors, Their Pathology, Symptomatology, Diagnosis and Prognosis-Providence-1931-158p-illus (g10,sl soil) 75.00

COUSIN ALICE-"All's not Gold that Glitters"-NY-1853-D Appleton-214p+ads-cl-3 illus,chromolitho t.p. preceding reg t.p.-1st ed (h1) 50.00

COUSINS,F-Colonial Architecture of Salem-Bost-1919-illus,ltd ed,nbrd-1st ed (h10) 75.00

COUSINS,FRANK-Colonial Architecture of Philadelphia-Bost-1920-Little,Brown-4to-xix,248p-cl,t.e.g.,95 plts-ltd to 975c,nbrd (pp7) 180.00

COUSINS,JAMES H-Collected Poems-Madras-1940-Kalakshetra-1st ed (z8,f,sl tn dj) 45.00

COUSTEAU,JACQUES-IVES-Dolphins-GC-1975-Dbldy-sm 4to-1st US ed (f10,dj) 25.00

COUSTILLAS,PIERRE-George Gissing at Alderley Edge-Lond-1969-Enitharmon Pr-ii+39p-ltd to 250c,nbrd-1st ed (kk5,f,dj) 25.00

COUTANT,C G-History of Wyoming-NY-1966-Argonaut Pr-2 vols-illus-rprnt of 1899 ed (g7) 50.00

COUZINOS,EFTHIMIOS N-Twenty Three Years in Asia Minor-NY-1969-Vantage Pr-illus-1st ed (m8,f,dj) 16.50

COVARRUBIAS,M-Indian Art of Mexico & Central America-NY-1957-64 plts(incl col)-1st ed (ee1,dj sl chip) 125.00

COVARRUBIAS,MIGUEL-Eagle, the Jaguar, and the Serpent-NY-1954-Knopf-buckram,12 col plts,112 b&w illus-1st ed (o8,f,dj) 45.00

COVARRUBIAS,MIGUEL-Indian Art of Mexico & Central America-NY-1957-Knopf-4to-xvi,360,xx p-pict cl,12 col plts,64p photo "album"-1st ed (y4,f,dj) 45.00

COVELL,C V-Field Guide to the Moths of Eastern North America-1984-Houghton Mifflin-496p-64 plts-1st ed (bb3,f,dj) 15.00

COVEY,A DALE-Secrets of the Specialists-Detr-1905-330p-illus-2nd ed (g10) 35.00

COVILL,WILLIAM E-Ink Bottles and Inkwells-1971-Wm S Sullwold-430p-photos-1st ed (cc8,dj) 50.00

COWAN,BUD-Range Rider-GC-(1930)-Sun Dial Pr-289p-illus-Six Guns 503 (gg4) 25.00

COWAN,DR J MACQUEEN-Journeys and Plant Introductions of George Forrest-Lond-1952-OUP-252p-fldg map-scarce (x6,sp sun) 50.00

COWAN,JOHN-Science of a New Life-NY-1869-405p-1st ed (g10,pgs brwng) 45.00

COWAN,ROBERT E-Bibliography of the History of California and the Pacific West, 1510 to 1906-Columbus-1952(1914)-Long's-4to-279p+index (d3) 75.00

COWAN,ROBERT E-Bibliography of the History of California, 1510 to 1930-SF-1933-John Henry Nash-vi+926p-cl sp,dec bds,sp labl,3 vols in one-1st ed (e2) 125.00

COWAN,SAM-Sergeant York-NY-(1922)-G&D-Photoplay ed (s1,f,dj) 20.00

COWARD,NOEL-Bon Voyage-NY-1968-1st US ed (y7,dj) 15.00

COWARD,NOEL-Bon Voyage-NY-1968-Dbldy-1st US ed (hh5,f,f dj) 10.00

COWARD,NOEL-Noel Coward Diaries-Bost-1982-LB-1st US ed (x9,f,dj) 15.00

COWARD,NOEL-Not Yet the Dodo & Other Verses-Lond-(1967)-Heinemann-1st Brit ed (e10,f,sl wn dj) 25.00

COWARD,NOEL-Pomp and Circumstance-GC-1960-Doubleday-1st US ed (e10,dj) 20.00

COWARD,NOEL-Present Laughter-GC-1946-Dbldy-1st ed (ee2,f,dj) 35.00

COWARD,NOEL-This Happy Breed-GC-1947-Dbldy-1st ed (ee2,dj) 35.00

COWBOY ARTISTS OF AMERICA-15th Annual Exhib-Flagstaff-72p-dec cl wi box,photos,col plts,ltd to 75c (t7,f,box,autg by all artists) 150.00

COWELL,F R-Garden as a Fine Art from Antiquity to Modern Times-Bost-1978-Houghton Mifflin-4to-232p-cl,illus(Incl col)-1st Amer prtg (cc10) 35.00

COWIE,ISAAC-Company of Adventures-Tor-1913-Wm Briggs-8vo-515p-dec blk cl,frntis,41 illus-Peel 2382-1st ed (mm8,sl scuff) 75.00*

COWLES,HARRY-Art of Squash Racquets-NY-1935-photos-1st ed (r2) 30.00

COWLEY,MALCOLM-Dream of the Golden Mountains-NY-1980-Viking-1st ed (z9,f,dj) 12.50

COWLEY,MALCOLM-ED.-Books That Changed Our Minds-NY-1939-Dbldy,Doran-1st ed (a10,sm tape mrks e.p.s,dj) 35.00

COWLEY,MALCOLM-Exile's Return-NY-1981-LEC-ltd to 2000c,three autgs (w1,f,box) 100.00

COWLEY,MALCOLM-Faulkner Cowley File-Lond-1966-1st Brit ed (s5,dj) 20.00

COWLEY,MALCOLM-Faulkner Cowley Files-NY-1966-Viking-184p-1st ed (j8,f,dj missing sm chip) 45.00

COWLEY,MALCOLM-Second Flowering-NY-1973-Viking-1st ed (z3,f,dj) 20.00

COWLEY,MALCOLM-Think Back on Us-Carbondale-1967-S Illinois Univ-1st ed (h8,f,dj) 45.00

COWPER,L I-ED.-King's Own-Oxford-1939-2 vols-blu cl,maps,plts-1st ed (b7,f) 275.00

COWPER,WILLIAM-Poetical Works of-Lond-1861-Routledge-12mo-(48),631p-ornate red mor,g stmpd,a.e.g.,tiss cov plts-New ed (m4,f) 30.00

COWTAN,ROBERT-Memories of the British Museum-Lond-1872-R Bentley & Son-vii,428p-orig g pict cl,frntis-1st ed (dd10,hng crack,sl soil) 45.00

COX'S MANUAL OF GELATINE COOKERY-Edinburgh-1913-J & G Cox Co-64p-pict wrps (q8) 15.00

COX,ALEX-Deer Hunting in Texas-San Antonio-1947-12mo-105p-illus-1st ed (m3) 25.00

COX,CHARLES E-John Tobias, Sportsman-NY-1937-Derrydale-204p-lt blu cl,prtd drk blu sp,cov labls,illus by Ripley,ltd to 950c (ee3,vf) 80.00

COX,DONALD W-Space Race-Phila-1963(1962)-Chilton-393p-illus-2nd prtg (hh6,dj) 30.00

COX,E H M-Rhododendrons for Amateurs-Lond-1924-xv,112p-16 hlf tones,map (x5,tips bump) 22.00

COX,E S-World Steam in the Twentieth-Lond-1969-191p-1st ed (n4,f,dj) 17.50

COX,E-Exploits of Kesho Naik, Dacoit-1912-Constable-1st ed (x7) 55.00

COX,FLORENCE M A-ED.-Kiss Josey for Me-Santa Clara-1874-Friis Pioneer Pr-250p (n7,dj) 45.00

COX,HAROLD E-Road from Upper Darby-NY-1967-46p-wrps-1st ed (n4) 9.50

COX,HELEN-Food, Flowers and Wine Cookbook-Lond-1964-Odhams-224p-dec red cl,photos,7p col plts-1st ed (q8,dj) 16.50

COX,IAN-Scallop-1957-Shell Trading-4to-135p-g dec red cl,col illus (bb3,f) 25.00

COX,IAN-Scallop-Lond-1957-Shell Trnsprt & Trdng Co-red emboss bds (a8) 35.00

COX,J CHARLES-Pulpits, Lecturns and Organs-Lond-1915-OUP-8vo-228p-blu cl,155 illus (r10) 35.00

COX,JAMES-Cattle Industry of Texas and Adjacent Territory-NY-1959-Antiquarian Pr-4to-2 vols-cowhide wi Bancroft buckrm,stmpd wi gold leaf,t.e.g,illus-ltd to 500c,nbrd,(rprnt of 1895 1st ed)-Howes C820 (y4,box) 250.00

COX,JAMES-Classics in the Literature of Mountaineering and Mountain Travel from Francis F Farquhar...-LA-1980-sm 4to-58p-ltd to 500c-1st ed (o10,f) 50.00

COX,MARY L-History of Hale County Texas-Plainview-1937-230p-1st ed (a9) 100.00

COX,MIKE-Fred Gipson, Texas Storyteller-Austin-1980-Shoal Creek-233p-photos-1st ed (a9,dj) 20.00

COX,REV JOHN E-Five Years in the United States Army-Owensville-1973-171p-illus-ltd to 500c-rprnt (c4,f) 30.00

COX,ROSS-Columbia River-(1957)-U of Okla-398p-illus-1st ed thus (r8,dj) 45.00

COX,SAMUEL S-Why We Laugh-NY-1876-Harper & Bros-387p-cl (d1) 20.00

COX,THOMAS R-Mills and Markets-Seattle-1974-U of Wash Pr-8vo-xx,332p-cl,photos,illus-1st ed (y4,dj) 30.00

COX,TOM-Damned Englishman-NY-(1975)-Expo Pr-374p-1st ed (g9) 30.00

COX,WILLIAM R-Luke Short and His Era-GC-1961-Dbldy-214p-cl,pict dj-1st ed (v1,dj) 35.00

COX,WILLIAM-Battery Mates-1978-Dodd Mead-1st ed (s7,dj) 10.00

COXE,DR JOHN R-Short Account of the Occurrences Which Led to the Removal of...from the Chair of Materia...U of Penn-Phila-1835-12p-prtd tan wrps (u2,fld mark) 100.00

COXE,GEORGE H-Lady Killer-1949-Knopf-1st ed (s10,dj) 15.00

COXE,GEORGE H-Murder for Two-NY-1943-Knopf-1st ed (d4,sp creased dj) 25.00

COXE,GEORGE H-Silent Witness-NY-1973-Knopf-1st ed (h4,f,dj) 10.00

COXE,GEORGE H-Uninvited Guest-NY-1953-Knopf-1st ed (g4,f,dj) 10.00

COXE,JOHN R-Philadelphia Medical Dictionary-Phila-1808-433p-lea-1st ed (dd3,rub bndg,fox,stnd) 200.00

COXE,MARGARET-Floral Emblems-Cin/NY-1845-Derby/Appleton-144p-cl,col frontis+3p col plts-rare (d1,sl wn,sl fox) 125.00

COXE,MARGARET-Young Lady's Companion-Columbus-1839-I N Whiting-342p-cl-Amer Imprnts 55182 (d1) 175.00

COXE,MARGARET-Young Lady's Companion-Columbus-1839-I N Whiting-342p-new 3/4 lea & mrbld bds-rare-Amer Imprnts 55182 (b1,dmpstnd pgs,rbnd) 150.00

COXERE,EDWARD-Adventures by Sea of...-NY,Lond-1946-Oxford U-xxxviii,190p-1/2 cl,dec bds,fldg map,illus-1st Amer ed (p8) 25.00

COY,OWEN C-Gold Days-SF-(1929)-Powell Publ-381p-illus,maps,Califonia ser-1st ed (ff4,sl wn dj) 25.00

COY,OWEN C-Great Trek-SF-(1931)-Powell Publ-349p-illus,maps,California ser-1st ed (ff4,dj) 25.00

COY,WALTER THERON,SR.-My Uncle Sam Don't Like Me-NY-1980-Vantage Pr-333p-blu cl-1st ed (b6,f,dj,pres cpy) 10.00

COYKENDALL,R-Duck Decoys & How to Rig Them-NY-1955-125p-photos,illus,dec e.p. (gg3,vf,dj) 20.00

COYKENDALL,RALF-Duck Decoys & How to Rig Them-NY-1955-8vo-125p-photos,illus-1st ed (m3,vf,dj) 50.00

COYKENDALL,RALF-Wildfowling at a Glance-Harrisburg-1968-12mo-94p-illus (m3,vf) 22.50

COYLE,LILLIAN S-Our American Heritage from Wilderness to Nation-NY,Lond-(1934)-303p-cl (k1) 10.00

COYLE,WILLIAM-Ohio Authors and their Books-Cleve-(1962)-World-xxiv+741p-red/brwn cl-1st ed (h2,tn dj) 65.00

COYNER,DAVID H-Lost Trappers-Cin-1847-J A & U P James-255p+1p ads-mod cl-rare-Howes C836-Graff 897-Wagner-Camp 130-1st ed (g1,rbnd,fox) 175.00

COZZENS,FREDERIC S-Sparrowgrass Papers-NY-1856-BAL 3998-1st ed,1st state (r2) 65.00

COZZENS,JAMES G-Cock Pit-NY-1928-map e.p.s-1st ed (r5,lacks dj) 15.00

COZZENS,JAMES G-Just and the Unjust-NY-1942-Harcourt-1st ed (l4,f,dj) 25.00

CRABTRE,A D-Funny Side of Physic-Hartford-1880-816p-woodcuts-scarce-1st ed (dd3) 225.00

CRABTREE,P E-First Belgian Hare Course of Instruction-Bost-1901-New Engl Belgian Hare Co-246p-red bds,t.e.g.,illus-rvsd ed (n6,few cov spots) 45.00

CRADDOCK,HARRY-Savoy Cocktail Book-1976-Arno Pr-287p-yel cl,col plts-rvsd ed (q8,f,dj) 20.00

CRAFT,ROBERT-Prejudices in Disguise-NY-1974-Knopf-1st ed (u4,sl rub dj) 15.00

CRAFTS,WILBUR-Intoxicants & Opium in All Lands and Times-Wash-1900-288p-wrps-6th ed (dd3) 50.00

CRAFTS,WILLIAM A-Pioneers in the Settlement of America-Bost-(1876)-Estes & Lauriat-2 vols-3/4 lea,illus (gg4) 150.00

CRAHAN,MARCUS-Early American Inebriatis-LA-1964-Zamorano Club-tall thin 8vo-62p-pict bds,drwngs (q8) 50.00

CRAIG,ALEC-Suppressed Books-NY-(1963)-World-1st ed (w1,dj) 20.00

CRAIG,CHARLES F-Amebiasis and Amebic Dysentery-Springfield-(1934)-Chas C Thomas-viii+315p-grn cl,54 illus-1st ed (a2,sl fray sp) 50.00

CRAIG,CHARLES F-Parasitic Amoebae of Man-Phila-1911-Lippincott-x+253p-maroon cl,30 plts-1st ed (g2,sl rub) 65.00

CRAIG,EDWARD-Gordon Craig-Lond-1968-Gollancz-8vo-398p-36 photos-1st ed (aa7,sl chip dj) 20.00*

CRAIG,ELIZABETH-Entertaining with...-(1933)-Collins-322p-dec red cl,pict t.p. & e.p.,32p col plts-2nd prtg (q8,sp tn dj) 15.00

CRAIG,ELIZABETH-Wine in the Kitchen-Lond-(1934)-Constable-16mo-140p-blu cl-1st ed (q8,edgewn) 15.00

CRAIG,H STANLEY-South Jersey Marriages-Merchantville-(ca.1930?)-163,(1)p-cl (aa6) 90.00

CRAIG,REGINALD S-Fighting Parson-LA-1959-284p-illus,map-1st ed (n3,f,dj) 42.50

CRAIG,RICHARD B-Bracero Program,Interest Groups and Foreign Policy-Austin-1971-U of Tex Pr-8vo-233p-red cl (mm1,f,dj) 30.00

CRAIG,ROBERT-Storm & Sorrow in the High Pamirs-Seattle-1977-171p-wrps,16 col plts,maps,illus-preceded hdbk ed-1st ed (q10,sl stnd) 20.00

CRAIG,ROBERT-Storm & Sorrow in the High Pamirs-Seattle-1980-223p-rvsd ed (q10,f,dj) 30.00

CRAIGHEAD,F C-Tracks of the Grizzly-CA-1979-261p-photos,illus (gg3,f,dj) 17.00

CRAIGHEAD,FRANK-Hawks in the Hand-Bost-1939-Houghton Mifflin-290p-57 photos-scarce-1st ed (b9,sl soil cov) 120.00

CRAIGHEAD,FRANK-Hawks in the Hand-Bost-1939-Riverside Pr-290p-photos-1st ed (gg3,f,wn dj) 110.00

CRAIL,CHARLES S-My Twin Joe-GC-1932-Country Life-8vo-404p-1st ed (dd5,dj edgewn,chip) 20.00

CRAINE,E R-Chronicles of Michoacan-1970-U of Okla-259p-44 plts-1st ed (bb3,f,dj) 20.00

CRAM,RALPH A-Walled Towns-Bost-1919-Marshall Jones-8vo-105p-bds,t.e.g.-1st prtg (cc10,dj) 35.00

CRAMER,M J-Ulysses S Grant:Conversations and Unpublished Letters-NY-1897-207p-port (z10,soil,stnd,scuff) 20.00

CRAMER,S S-ED.-Through Hell & High Water by Members of the Explorers Club-NY-(1941)-385p-1st ed (r8,cor bump) 30.00

CRAMOND,MICHAEL-Big Game Hunting in the West-Vancouver,B.C.-1965-8vo-164p+ads-illus (m3,vf,dj) 20.00

CRAMOND,MICHAEL-Fishin' Holes of the West-Vancouver,B.C.-1972-8vo-173p-wrps,photos,maps (m3,f) 12.50

CRAMOND,MICHAEL-Game Bird Hunting in the West-Vancouver,B.C.-1967-8vo-246p+index-illus (m3,vf,dj) 18.50

CRAMP,ARTHUR-Nostrums and Quackery...Vol.2-Chig-1921-832p-1st ed (dd3) 75.00

CRAMPTON,C GREGORY-Zunis of Cibola-SLC-(1977)-194p-photos-1st ed (v7,dj) 25.00

CRAMPTON,H E-Doctrine of Evolution-1924-Columbia Univ-320p (bb3,f) 20.00

CRAN,MARION-Gardens in America-NY-1932-320p-grn cl,papr labl,16 halftones (m10,wtrspots,sl soil) 15.00

CRAN,MRS-Garden of Experience-Lond-1922-Jenkins-316p-cl (x6,sl fox) 20.00

CRANDALL,DANIEL-Columbian Spelling-Book-Cooperstown-1833-H & E Phinney-168p-bds,illus-Amer Imprnts 18448 (k1) 35.00

CRANDALL,JULIE V-Story of Pacific Salmon-Portland-1946-8vo-59p-illus (m3,vf,dj) 12.00

CRANDALL,L S-Management of Wild Mammals in Captivity-Chig-1964-8vo-769p-cl,11 plts (y8) 40.00

CRANDALL,LATHAN-Days in the Open-NY-1914-8vo-270p-illus,L Rhead (m3,vf,chip dj) 25.00

CRANE,ALBERT L-Race Differences in Inhibition-1923-Arch of Psych Rprnt 63-wrps-1st ed (v5,f) 20.00

CRANE,FRANCES-Applegreen Cat-1943-Lippincott-1st ed (s10,hng tender,dj) 27.50

CRANE,FRANCES-Buttercup Case-NY-1959-Random-1st ed (f4,f,sl wn dj) 25.00

CRANE,FRANCES-Cinnamon Murder-NY-1946-Random-1st ed (k4,dj) 25.00

CRANE,FRANCES-Coral Princess Murders-NY-1954-Random-1st ed (f4,f,sl wn dj) 25.00

CRANE,FRANCES-Daffodil Blond-NY-1950-Random-1st ed (w5,f,dj sl chip) 20.00

CRANE,FRANCES-Daffodil Blonde-1950-Random Hs-1st ed (s10,dj) 25.00

CRANE,FRANCES-Death in Lilac Time-1955-Random Hs-1st ed (s10,dj) 25.00

CRANE,FRANCES-Death-Wish Green-1960-Random Hs-1st ed (s10,dj) 15.00

CRANE,FRANCES-Golden Box-Phila-1942-Lippincott-1st ed (k4,dj) 50.00

CRANE,FRANCES-Thirteen White Tulips-1953-Random Hs-1st ed (s10,dj) 25.00

CRANE,HART-Letters of...1916 to 1932-NY-(1952)-Hermitage Hs-8vo-1st ed (p1,f,dj) 50.00

CRANE,J-Fiddler Crabs of the World-1975-Princeton-4to-736p-photos,illus (bb3,f,dj) 90.00

CRANE,L H-Flowers and Folk Lore from Far Korea-Seoul-1970-folio-93p-45 tip in col plts (bb3,f) 55.00

CRANE,LEO-Desert Drums, the Pueblo Indians of New Mexico 1540 thru 1928-Bost-1928-393p-photos,fldg map-1st ed (v7,dj) 45.00

CRANE,LEO-Indians of the Enchanted Desert-Bost-1925-364p-photos,fldg map-1st ed (u7,f,rprd dj) 45.00

CRANE,STEPHEN-Little Regiment, and Other Episodes of the American Civil War-NY-1896-Appleton-196p-cl-1st ed (cc6,cl soil) 200.00

CRANE,STEPHEN-Little Regiment-NY-1896-Appleton-8vo-tan cl stmpd in red,blk & gilt-1st iss wi "Gilbert Parker's Best Books" at top of ads-BAL 4076-1st ed (x3,rear hng weak) 110.00

CRANE,STEPHEN-Sullivan County Sketches of ...-Syracuse-(1949)-Syracuse Univ Pr-viii+85p-grn cl-BAL 4112-1st ed (f2,edge-wn dj) 30.00

CRANE,STEPHEN-Third Violet-NY-1897-Appleton-8vo-tan cl stmpd in red,blk & gilt-BAL 4077-1st ed (x3,sp drknd,cov soil) 110.00

CRANE,WALTER-Claims of Decorative Art-Bost,NY-1892-Houghton Mifflin-sm 4to-191p-dec grn cl-1st Amer ed (p1,sp rub) 90.00

CRAPANZANO,VINCENT-Fifth World of Enoch Maloney-NY-(1969)-242+1p-1st ed (v7,f,dj) 15.00

CRAPANZANO,VINCENT-Fifth World of Forster Bennett-NY-(1972)-245p-1st ed (v7,f,dj) 15.00

CRAPO,CAPT THOMAS-Strange, But True-New Bedford-1893-Thomas Crapo-151p-brwn cl-1st ed (h2) 25.00

CRARY,C S-ED.-Dear Belle-Middletown-1965-256p-illus,ports (z10,soil dj) 30.00

CRASHAW,RICHARD-Verse in English of...-NY-1949-Grove Pr-Grove Pr No.1,errata slip-1st ed (w5,f,sl wn dj) 50.00

CRATON,MICHAEL-History of the Bahamas-Lond-1973-Collins-e.p. maps,illus-rvsd ed (v4,f,dj) 25.00

CRAVEN,MARGARET-Walk Gently This Good Earth-NY-(1977)-Putnam-1st ed (hh5,dj) 10.00

CRAWFORD,ANN-ED.-Eagle-Austin-1967-Pemberton-299p-1st ed (a9,dj) 75.00

CRAWFORD,BENJAMIN F-William Holmes McGuffey, the Schoolmaster to Our Nation-Delaware,Ohio-(1963)-priv prntd-105p-cl (k1,sl spot sp) 15.00

CRAWFORD,CAPT JACK-Lariattes-Sigourney-1904-Wm A Bell-84p-wrps,photos-scarce-1st ed (w3,sm wtrstn,sp wn) 20.00

CRAWFORD,CAPTAIN JACK-Broncho Book-East Aurora-1908-Roycrofter-143,(1)p-suede (l1,minor sp rpr) 17.50

CRAWFORD,CHARLES H-Scenes of Earlier Days-Chig-(1962)-facs rprnt of 1898 1st ed-Smith 2098 (e7,stnd dj) 35.00

CRAWFORD,E MAY-By the Equator's Snowy Peak-Lond-1913-176p-25 photos-1st ed (o10) 40.00

CRAWFORD,F MARION-Khaled-Lond,NY-1891-Macmillan-1st ed (a5) 25.00

CRAWFORD,F MARION-White Sister-NY-(1913)-G&D-Photoplay ed (s1,dj) 45.00

CRAWFORD,F-Girl of the Desert-NY-1961-124p (gg3,f,dj,autg) 35.00

CRAWFORD,HOWARD L-Rekindling Camp Fires-Bismarck-1926-324p-cl,map.illus-1st ed (n10,f) 65.00

CRAWFORD,J R-Witchcraft and Sorcery in Rhodesia-Lond-1967-OUP-8vo-312p-cl-1st ed (y5,dj) 25.00

CRAWFORD,JACK R-Philosopher's Murder Case-NY-1931-Sears-1st ed (h4,f) 15.00

CRAWFORD,LEWIS F-Badlands and Broncho Trails-Bismarck-(1926)-Capital Bk-99p-illus-Herd 604 (cc4) 20.00

CRAWFORD,LEWIS F-Medora Deadwood Stage Line-Bismarck-1925-Capital Bks-17p-wrps,illus-1st ed (dd4) 35.00

CRAWFORD,LEWIS F-Rekindling Camp Fires-Bismarck-(1926)-Capital Bk-8vo-324p-blu cl,illus-Six Guns #509-1st ed (p1) 90.00

CRAWFORD,LEWIS F-Rekindling Camp Fires-Bismarck-1926-Torch Pr-324p-cl,9 plts-1st trd ed after ltd ed (z1) 80.00

CRAWFORD,MARY C-Little Pilgrimages Among Old New England Inns...-Bost-1907-Page-1st ed (f10) 45.00

CRAWFORD,MARY C-Romance of Old New England Rooftrees-Bost-1922-390p-cl (e1) 15.00

CRAWFORD,MARY C-Romantic Days in Old Boston-Bost-1910-Little,Brown-411p-dec gry/grn cl wi wht & gilt,port on frnt,t.e.g.,illus-1st ed (p2) 20.00

CRAWFORD,MAX-Waltz Across Texas-NY-(1975)-auth 1st bk-1st ed (p5,f,dj) 20.00

CRAWFORD,MAX-Waltz Across Texas-NY-(1975)-FS&G-auth 1st bk-1st ed (b10,as new in dj) 30.00

CRAWFORD,MEDOREM-Journal of...-Eugene-1897-26p-wrps-Sources of Hist of Oregon Vol.1,No.1-Tweney #11-1st ed (c7) 75.00

CRAWFORD,O G S-Said and Done-Lond-(1955)-Weidenfeld & Nicolson-8vo-316p-12 illus-1st ed (jj5,dj) 20.00

CRAWFORD,ROSELLE W-Survival of Legends-S.A.-1952-Naylor-94p-1st ed (a9,dj) 35.00

CRAWFORD,SAMUEL J-Kansas in the Sixties-Chig-1911-McClurg-440p-blk cl,frntis port-1st ed (b6) 65.00

CRAWFORD,T S-History of the Umbrella-Abbot-(1970)-D & C Newton-8vo-220p-illus-1st Brit ed (gg5,dj) 25.00

CRAWFORD,THOMAS E-West of the Texas Kid, 1881 to 1910-Norman-(1962)-U of Okla Pr-202p-drwngs by Eggenhofer-Six Guns 510-1st ed (ff4) 25.00

CRAWFURD,OSWALD-Revelations of Inspector Morgan-NY-1907-Dodd-1st US ed (d4) 75.00

CRAWHALL,JOSEPH-Compleatest Angling Book That Ever Was Writ-1970-Freshet Pr-4to-235p-illus,auth-facsimile of 2nd ed (m3,as new in box) 40.00

CRAWHALL,JOSEPH-ED.-Collection of Right Merrie Garlands for North Country Anglers-Newcastle-On-Tyne-1864-8vo-312p-1/4 lea,gilt-illus-scarce (m3,wn) 55.00

CRAYON,J PERCY-Rockaway Records of Morris County...-Rockaway-1902-(2),300,(4)p-cl,plts (aa6,ex-libr) 150.00

CREAMER,ROBERT-Babe-1974-S&S-1st ed (ff2,dj) 30.00

CREAMER,ROBERT-Babe-1974-S&S-1st ed (s8,dj) 25.00

CREASEY,JOHN-Give a Man a Gun-NY-(1953)-Harper & Bros-1st US ed (bb1,dj) 15.00

CREASEY,JOHN-Inferno-1966-Walker-1st Amer ed (s10,dj) 10.00

CREASEY,JOHN-So Young to Burn-NY-1968-Scribners-1st US ed (f4,f,dj) 10.00

CREASEY,JOHN-Theft of Magna Carta-NY-1973-Scribners-1st US ed (f4,f,dj) 12.50

CREASEY,JOHN-Toff on Fire-1966-Walker-1st Amer ed (s10,dj) 10.00

CREASEY,JOHN-Toff Proceeds-NY-(1968)-Walker-1st US ed (a5,f,dj) 7.50

CRECELIUS,OWEN L-Reminiscences of a Small Town Hoosier-np-nd(1975?)-79p-wrps (a1) 12.50

CREE,DR EDWARD H-Naval Surgeon-NY-1982-Dutton-276p-map e.p.,illus-1st Amer ed (p8,as new in dj) 20.00

CREELEY,ROBERT-Gold Diggers-np-1954-Divers Pr-sm 8vo-illus wrps-1st ed (x3) 100.00

CREELEY,ROBERT-Island-NY-1963-Scribner's-1st ed (h8,f,sl wn dj) 50.00

CREMER,JAN-Jan Cremer Writes Again-1969-Grove-1st ed (t9,dj) 15.00

CREMER,JAN-Jan Cremer Writes Again-NY-1969-Grove-1st ed (z3,f,dj) 10.00

CREMONY,JOHN C-Life Among the Apaches-SF-1868-A Roman & Co-12mo-322p-cl-Graff 915-Howes C879-1st ed (mm7,f) 300.00

CREPEAU,RICHARD-Baseball, America's Diamond Mind 1919 to 1941-1980-U of Central Fl-1st ed (r7,f,f dj) 25.00

CRESPELLE,J P-Fauves-Greenwich-1962-NYGS-100p col plts (ee1,dj) 150.00

CRESSMAN,L S-Sandal and the Cave-Portland-1962-81p-stiff prntd wrps,illus,e.p. maps (r8,rear cov crease) 15.00

CRESSWELL,BEATRIX F-Mavericks of Devonshire and Massachusetts-Exeter-1929-Jas Commin-64p-photos-1st ed (a9) 75.00

CRESTI,C-Le Corbusier-Lond-1970-46 col plts,36 b&w illus-1st Brit ed (h10,dj) 35.00

CRESWICK,PAUL-Robin Hood-1917-D McKay-9p col plts & col pict e.p.,N C Wyeth-1st ed thus (x2) 125.00

CREW,PETER-Dictionary of Mountaineering-Harrisburg-1969-Stackpole-140p-1st ed (j8,sm stn ffep,dj) 27.50

CREW,PETER-Encyclopedic Dictionary of Mountaineering-Lond-1968-140p-16 plts-1st Brit ed (p10,f,dj) 16.00

CREWS,CALLOWAY S-Ox Cart Days in Old Helena...-Helena-1968-Old Helena Fndtn-26p-wrps,photos-1st ed (w3,vf) 17.50

CREWS,HARRY-Blood and Grits-NY-1979-1st ed (p5,f,dj wi sm tr) 55.00

CREWS,HARRY-Car-Lond-(1973)-Secker & Warburg-1st Brit ed (e6,sl wn dj) 50.00

CREWS,HARRY-Car-NY-1972-1st ed (q5,f,dj) 85.00

CREWS,HARRY-Childhood-1978-Harper & Row-1st ed (p9,f,dj) 30.00

CREWS,HARRY-Childhood-NY-1978-1st ed (n5,dj) 45.00

CREWS,HARRY-Enthusiast-np(Winston-Salem)-(1981)-Palaemon Pr-ltd to 200c,autg,iss w/o dj-1st ed (cc1,as new) 175.00

CREWS,HARRY-Feast of Snakes-NY-1976-Atheneum-1st ed (c10,f,dj) 85.00

CREWS,HARRY-Feast of Snakes-NY-1976-Atheneum-1st ed (dd2,f,dj) 60.00

CREWS,HARRY-Florida Frenzy-Gainesville-(1982)-Univ of Fl-wrps-1st ed (c10,as new in wrps) 30.00

CREWS,HARRY-Gospel Singer-NY-1968-Morrow-auth 1st bk-1st ed (bb1,covs blotchy,f dj) 700.00

CREWS,HARRY-Gypsy's Curse-NY-1974-Knopf-1st ed (a10,f,dj) 100.00

CREWS,HARRY-Gypsy's Curse-NY-1974-Knopf-1st ed (m7,f,dj rear panel soiled) 75.00

CREWS,HARRY-Hawk is Dying-NY-(1973)-Knopf-1st ed (e6,f,dj) 60.00

CREWS,HARRY-Hawk is Dying-NY-1973-Knopf-1st ed (a10,f,dj) 100.00

CREWS,HARRY-Hawk is Dying-NY-1973-Knopf-1st ed (m7,f,dj) 75.00

CREWS,HARRY-Karate is a Thing of the Spirit-Lond-(1972)-Secker & Warburg-1st Brit ed (a10,f,dj) 200.00

CREWS,HARRY-Karate is a Thing of the Spirit-NY-1971-Morrow-1st ed (a10,f,dj) 175.00

CREWS,HARRY-Naked in the Garden Hills-NY-(1969)-Morrow-1st issue dj-1st ed (e6,dj) 150.00

CREWS,HARRY-This Thing Don't Lead to Heaven-NY-1970-Morrow-1st ed (a10,f,tn dj) 150.00

CREWS,HARRY-This Thing Don't Lead to Heaven-NY-1970-Morrow-1st ed (q2,dj) 145.00

CRICHTON,KYLE S-Law and Order, Ltd.-Santa Fe-1928-New Mexican Publ Corp-viii,219p,cl,photos-1st ed (v1) 85.00

CRICHTON,M-Jasper Johns-1977-Abrams-orig col litho cov,128 plts(incl 61 col & 6 fldg)-1st ed (h10,dj) 100.00

CRICHTON,MICHAEL-Andromeda Strain-NY-1969-Knopf-1st ed (j3,dj) 10.00

CRICHTON,MICHAEL-Terminal Man-NY-1972-Knopf-1st ed (p3,f,dj) 15.00

CRICK,BERNARD-George Orwell-Bost-(1980)-Little,Brown-photos-1st US ed (bb1,f,dj) 20.00

CRIEP,LEO H-Essentials of Allergy-Phila-1945-381p-illus (g10) 15.00

CRISFIELD,THOS-Value of Hypnotism-Lond-1893-thin 8vo-40p-blu cl-scarce-1st prntg (y9) 75.00

CRISP,LUCY C-Spring Fever and Other Dialect Verse-Greensboro-1935-Joseph Stone-1st ed (l7,sl wn & soil wrps) 15.00

CRISP,N J-Brink-1982-Viking-1st Amer ed (s10,dj) 15.00

CRISPIN,EDMUND-Beware of the Trains-1962-Walker-1st Amer ed (x7,f,dj) 75.00

CRISPIN,EDMUND-Dead and Dumb-Phila-1947-Lippincott-1st US ed (k4,f,dj) 50.00

CRISPIN,EDMUND-Fen Country-1979-Gollancz-1st ed (s10,dj) 20.00

CRISPIN,EDMUND-Fen Country-Lond-1979-Gollancz-1st ed (q4,f,dj) 27.50

CRISPIN,EDMUND-Frequent Hearses-Lond-1950-Gollancz-1st ed (w9,dj sp drknd,tape rnfrcd) 125.00

CRISPIN,EDMUND-Glimpses of the Moon-NY-1977-Walker-1st US ed (f4,f,dj) 20.00

CRISPIN,EDMUND-Holy Disorders-1946-Lippincott-1st Amer ed (s10,sp wn dj) 50.00

CRISPIN,EDMUND-Holy Disorders-1946-Lippincott-1st Amer ed (x7,f,dj) 75.00

CRISPIN,EDMUND-Love Lies Bleeding-1948-Lippincott-1st Amer ed (x7,f,f dj) 75.00

CRISPIN,EDMUND-Moving Toyshop-Phila-1946-Lippincott-1st US ed (f4,dj missing chips) 35.00

CRISPIN,EDMUND-Moving Toyshop-Phila-1946-Lippincott-1st US ed (g4,f,dj sl wn,sl sp fade) 75.00

CRISPIN,EDMUND-Obsequies at Oxford-1945-Lippincott-auth 1st bk-1st Amer ed (x7,f,dj) 95.00

CRISPIN,EDMUND-Sudden Vengeance-NY-1950-Dodd Mead-1st Amer ed (w9,f,dj chip & wn) 25.00

CRISPIN,EDMUND-Sudden Vengeance-NY-1950-Dodd-1st US ed (d4,rprd dj) 45.00

CRISSEY,FORREST-Alexander Legge 1866-1933-Chig-1936-priv prntd-232p-cl-Rampaging Herd 611 (c1) 20.00

CRITCHLEY,MACDONALD-Shipwreck Survivors, a Medical Study-Lond-1943-119p-photos-scarce (dd3) 50.00

CRITTENDEN,H H-Crittenden Memoirs-NY-1936-Putnam's-542p-cl,photos-1st ed (v1,spot covs,chip dj) 80.00

CRITTENDEN,H H-Crittenden Memoirs-NY-1936-Putnam's-8vo-xv,(1),17-542p-brwn cl,illus-1st ed (mm1,sl wn sp) 175.00

CROCKETT,DAVID-A NARRATIVE OF THE LIFE OF..., OF THE STATE OF TENNESSEE-1834-Carey & Hart-210p-rare-Howes C900-1st ed though it states 6th (a9,lacks papr sp labl) 250.00

CROCKETT,LAWRENCE J-Wildly Successful Plants-NY-(1977)-Macmillan-268p-illus-1st prtg (m6,dj) 20.00

CROCKETT,S R-Sir Toady Crusoe-NY-1905-Stokes-illus-1st ed (oo10) 12.00

CROFT,HELEN D-Downs, The Rockies and Desert Gold-Caldwell-1961-Caxton-8vo-247p-1st ed (z4,rnfrcd dj wn & tn) 15.00

CROFT,P J-ED.-Autograph Poetry in the English Language-NY-(1973)-McGraw Hill-sm folio-2 vols-ltd to 1500c (p1,f,dj,box) 125.00

CROFT-COOKE,RUPERT-Sherry-Lond-(1955)-Putnam-232p-orng cl,map e.p.-1st ed (q8,dj) 20.00

CROFTS,FREEMAN W-Crime at Nornes-1935-Dodd-1st ed (s10,dj sp chip) 80.00

CROFTS,FREEMAN W-Inspector French's Greatest Case-1925-Seltzer-1st Amer ed (s10,dj sp chip) 250.00

CROFTS,FREEMAN W-Pit Prop Syndicate-NY-1925-Seltzer-1st US ed (h4) 20.00

CROFTS,FREEMAN W-Starvel Hollow Tragedy-NY-1927-Harper-1st US ed (f4,f) 20.00

CROFUTT,GEORGE A-Crofutt's New Overland Tourist and Pacific Coast Guide-Chig-1878,79-322p-Vol.1-1st ed (n4) 135.00

CROFUTT,GEORGE A-Crofutt's New Overland Tourist and Pacific Coast Guide-Chig-1879,80-273p-Vol.2-1st ed (n4) 125.00

CROFUTT,GEORGE A-Crofutt's New Overland Tourist and Pacific Coast Guide-Omaha-1880-282p-1st ed (n4) 100.00

CROGHAN,COL GEORGE-Army Life on the Western Frontier-Norman-(1958)-187p-illus-1st ed (c4,dj) 30.00

CROKER,RICHARD S-ED.-Report of the Governor's Conference on Pacific Salmon-Olympia-1963-4to-66p-wrps,photos (m3,vf) 10.00

CROLY,DAVID G-Seymour and Blair-NY-1868-Richardson & Co-275p-cl (m1,sp wn,edge-wn) 15.00

CROMB,JAMES-Highland Brigade-Edinburgh-1893-320p-gry dec cl,illus (gg2) 85.00

CRON,G-Roaring Veldt-NY-1930-286p-photos,fldg map (gg3,f,pres cpy) 30.00

CRONIN,A J-Keys of the Kingdom-Bost-1941-Little,Brown-1st US ed (hh5,dj) 15.00

CRONIN,EDWARD W,JR.-Arun-Bost-1979-HMCo-8vo-236p-illus-1st ed (dd5,dj) 15.00

CRONISE,TITUS F-Natural Wealth of California-SF-1868-lg 8vo-696p+12p ads-grn cl-1st ed (kk7,sp & cor wn) 35.00

CROOK,GEN GEORGE-General Crook-Norman-1946-U of Okla Pr-326p-e.p. maps,illus-1st ed (gg4,sl chip dj) 50.00

CROOKER,JOSEPH H-Shall I Drink-Bost-(1914)-Pilgrim Pr-257p-cl (a1,few pencil mrks) 15.00

CROOKSHANK,EDGAR-ED.-History and Pathology of Vaccination. Volume 2-Lond-1889-610p-scarce-1st ed (dd3) 150.00

CROSBY,ALEXANDER-ED.-Steamboat Up the Colorado-1965-Little,Brown-112p-illus-1st ed (d3,dj) 20.00

CROSBY,CARESSE-ED.-Portfolio V-(Paris)-1947-Black Sun Pr-slim folio-orig prtd gry wrps,text & 11 b&w plts laid in loose as iss-1st trd ed (x3,edge sunned,sl wn & soil) 100.00

CROSBY,CARESSE-Graven Images-Bost,NY-1926-Houghton Mifflin-sm 8vo-papr cov bds-1st ed (x3,sl sunned,sp chip) 100.00

CROSBY,CARESSE-Passionate Years-NY-(1953)-Dial-8vo-cl & bds-1st US ed (x3,sl chip dj) 45.00

CROSBY,ELISHA O-Memoirs of...-1945-Huntington-119p-1st ed (d3,dj) 25.00

CROSBY,HARRY-Shadows of the Sun-1977-Black Sparrow-8vo-cl/bds-ltd to 200c,nbrd-1st ed (v10,f,acetate dj) 50.00

CROSBY,LEE-Midsummer Night's Murder-1942-Dutton-1st ed (s10,dj) 25.00

CROSBY,LEE-Terror by Night-1938-Dutton-1st ed (s10,dj) 30.00

CROSBY,W W-Some Western Fishing-Balt-1926-12mo-128p-photos (m3,f) 25.00

CROSKEY,JOHN W-History of Blockley-Phila-1929-765p-illus (g10) 65.00

CROSS,AMANDA-Death in a Tenured Position-1981-Dutton-1st ed (s9,dj) 15.00

CROSS,AMANDA-Death in a Tenured Position-NY-1981-Dutton-1st ed (s4,sl edgewn,dj) 20.00

CROSS,AMANDA-Death in the Faculty-Lond-1981-Gollancz-1st Brit ed (kk5,f,dj) 35.00

CROSS,AMANDA-In the Last Analysis-1964-Macmillan-auth 1st novel-1st ed (x7,f,dj) 85.00

CROSS,AMANDA-In the Last Analysis-NY-1964-Macmillan-1st ed (e4,soil pg tops,dj sp sl fde) 90.00

CROSS,AMANDA-James Joyce Murder-NY-1967-1st ed (q5,dj) 100.00

CROSS,AMANDA-Theban Mysteries-1971-Knopf-1st ed (m9,f,sl wn dj) 25.00

CROSS,AMANDA-Theban Mysteries-1971-Knopf-1st ed (x7,vf,dj) 45.00

CROSS,DOROTHY-Archaeology of New Jersey-Trenton-1941-sm folio-xii,271p-3/4 mor,73 plts+fldg map & fldg plan in pckt-ltd to 150c,nbrd-Vol.1(2nd vol not publ until 1956) (aa6) 150.00

CROSS,DOROTHY-Archaeology of New Jersey-Trenton-1941-sm folio-xii,271p-cl,73 plts,fldg map & plan in pckt-Vol.1(2nd vol publ in 1956) (aa6) 125.00

CROSS,GEORGE N-Randolph Old and New-Randolph-1924-(xii)+260p-grn cl,plts-1st ed (h2,dj) 35.00

CROSS,K G W-Bibliography of Yeats Criticism, 1887 to 1965-NY-(1971)-Macmillan-1st Amer ed (z8,vf,dj) 12.50

CROSS,MILTON-Milton Cross New Encyclopedia of the Great Composers and Their Music-NY-1969-Dbldy-2 vols-rvsd & enlgd (u4,f,box) 25.00

CROSS,RALPH H-Early Inns of California 1844 to 1869-SF-1954-(viii)+vi+302p-cl sp,plts-ltd to 500c-1st ed (e2) 65.00

CROSS,RUBE-Fur,Feathers & Steel-NY-1946-12mo-78p-illus-3rd prntng (m3,vf,dj) 35.00

CROSSEN,FOREST-Switzerland Trail of America-1962-Pruett-4to-417p-illus-ltd ed,nbrd,autg (nn7,wn dj) 87.00

CROSSLEY,FRED H-English Church Craftsmanship-Lond-1941-Batsford Ltd-cl,col frntis,illus-1st ed (l8) 25.00

CROSSMAN,E C-Military & Sporting Rifle Shooting-Onslow Cnty-1932-8vo-499p-1st ed (m3,f) 40.00

CROTHERS,SAMUEL M-Miss Muffet's Christmas Party-Bost-1904-Houghton,Mifflin-106p-red bds wi gold decs,illus,O M Long (n6,sm trs in text) 30.00

CROTTY,DR.JOHN-Treatise on the Horse...-Cleve-(1893)-M Ernst-128p-cl (n1) 15.00

CROUCH,CARRIE J-History of Young County, Texas-Austin-1956-326p-e.p. maps (n10,f,dj) 65.00

CROUSE,NELLIS M-La Verendrye-Ithaca-(1956)-Cornell U Pr-247p-illus,fldg map-1st ed (ee4,ex-libr) 20.00

CROUSE,RUSSELL-Life With Father: a Play-NY-1940-Knopf-8vo-illus-1st ed (s1,f,dj) 45.00

CROUSE,RUSSELL-Mr.Currier and Mr.Ives-GC-1941-138p-16 col & 16 b&w plts (e1,dj) 17.50

CROWCROFT,P-Mice All Over-Lond-1966-8vo-121p-9 plts (y8,dj) 20.00

CROWE,CAMERON-Fast Times at Ridgegmont High-NY-(1981)-S&S-auth 1st bk-1st ed (bb1,f,dj) 25.00

CROWE,JOHN-Book of Trout Lore-NY-1947-8vo-233p-photos-1st ed (m3,sl fray dj) 20.00

CROWE,KEITH J-History of the Original Peoples of Northern Canada-Montreal-1974-Arctic Inst-xiii,226p-illus bds,13 figs,11 maps-1st ed (bb7) 15.00*

CROWE,MAJ J H V-Problems in Manoeuvre Tactics-NY-1905-Macmillan-4 maps (z2,ex-libr) 35.00

CROWE,P K-Sporting Journeys in Asia & Africa-MA-1966-183p-photos,ltd to 2500c (gg3,f,dj,pres) 25.00

CROWE,PHILIP K-World Wildlife-NY-1970-8vo-308p-photos-1st ed (m3,f,chip dj) 20.00

CROWE,SYLVIA-Garden Design-NY-1959-Hearthside Pr-4to-229p-61 plts-1st Amer ed (cc10,sl fox e.p.,dj) 50.00

CROWELL,NORMAN H-Sportsman's Primer-NY-1907-8vo-189p-illus (m3) 10.00

CROWELL,WILLIAM-Church Members Hand Book-Cin-(1849)-D Anderson-144p+ads-cl (l1) 35.00

CROWLEY,JOHN-Beasts-GC-1976-Dbldy-1st ed (a5,f,dj) 40.00

CROWNINSHIELD,B B-Fore And Afters-Bost/Cambridge-1940-Houghton Mifflin-tall 4to-wht cl wi red cl titles pasted on,plts,7 text illus-1st ed (nn1,sl soil cov) 145.00

CROY,HOMER-Corn Country-NY-(1947)-DS&P-325p-map e.p.-Amer Folkways Ser-1st ed (bb4) 20.00

CROY,HOMER-Last of the Great Outlaws-NY-(1956)-DS&P-242p-illus-Six Guns #524-1st ed (cc4,dj) 35.00

CROY,HOMER-Our Will Rogers-NY-(1953)-DS&P-377p-1st ed (bb4,dj) 25.00

CROY,HOMER-Trigger Marshal-NY-(1958)-DS&P-267p-illus-Six Guns 525-1st ed (gg4,dj) 35.00

CROYDON,M-Ivan Albright-1978-Abbeville Pr-lg folio-170 plts(83 col)-1st ed (h10,dj) 100.00

CROZIER,EMMET-Yankee Reporters 1861 to 1865-NY-1956-OUP-441p-maps,e.p. maps (o7,sm underlining,wn dj) 15.00

CROZIER,R H-Golden Rule a Tale of Texas-Richmond-1900-Whittet & Shepperson-179p-cl-1st ed (w3) 25.00

CRUESS,W V-Fermentation Organisms of California Grapes-Berkeley-1918-U of Cal Pr-66p-wrps,uncut (n6) 30.00

CRUICKSHANK'S-POCKET GUIDE TO THE BIRDS, EASTERN AND CENTRAL N AMER-NY-1953-sm 8vo-216p-cl,72 col photos (y8,dj chip) 10.00

CRUICKSHANK,A D-Birds Around New York City-NY-1942-Amer Muse of Nat Hist-8vo-489p-cl,35 photos (y8) 20.00

CRUICKSHANK,HELEN G-Paradise of Birds-NY-(1968)-Dodd,Mead-8vo-398p-48 photos-1st ed (aa5,dj) 12.50

CRUIKSHANK,GEORGE-Comic Almanac-Lond-1835 thru 1853-19 years bnd in 5 vols,3/4 grn lea,numerous G C plts(few hand-col) (l9,hngs wn,rbnd) 500.00

CRUIKSHANK,GEORGE-Italian Tales-Lond-1824-orig brwn bds,16p woodcts on India papr by G C,in cl fldg cov & cl box wi lea sp-1st ed,1st issue (l9,sp wn,fldg cov,box) 300.00

CRUM,MASON-Gullah-Durham-1940-Duke Univ Pr-xvi+351p-brwn cl,plts-1st ed (b2,dj chip,discol) 45.00

CRUME,PAUL-World of...-(1980)-SMU-290p-1st ed (t8,dj) 10.00

CRUMLEY,JAMES-Dancing Bear-NY-1983-1st ed (n5,f,f dj) 25.00

CRUMLEY,JAMES-Last Good Kiss-NY-1978-Random-1st ed (h4,f,dj) 30.00

CRUMLEY,JAMES-Last Good Kiss-NY-1978-Random-1st ed (w9,vf,dj) 45.00

CRUMLEY,JAMES-One to Count Cadence-1969-Random-auth 1st bk-1st ed (x7,f,dj) 250.00

CRUMLEY,JAMES-One to Count Cadence-NY-(1969)-auth 1st bk-1st ed (c5,f,sl wn dj) 225.00

CRUMLEY,JAMES-One to Count Cadence-NY-(1969)-Random-auth 1st bk-1st ed (cc2,f,f dj) 200.00

CRUMLEY,JAMES-One To Count Cadence-NY-(1969)-Random-auth 1st bk-1st ed (e6,f,dj) 250.00

CRUMP,SPENCER-Ride the Big Red Cars-1962-Crest-4to-240p-illus-1st ed (nn7,f,dj) 17.00

CRUMP,SPENCER-Ride the Big Red Cars-LA-1962-240p-1st ed (n4,f,dj) 27.50

CULBERT,DICK-Climber's Guide to the Coast Range of British Columbia-1969-426p-scarce-2nd ed (q10,f) 80.00

CULLEN,COUNTEE-Medea and Some Poems-NY-1935-1st ed (v9,dj sl soil,edgewn) 150.00

CULLEN,COUNTEE-On These I Stand-NY,Lond-(1947)-1st ed (c5,f,dj sp sl chip,sl soil) 75.00

CULLIMORE,C-Santa Barbara Adobes-Santa Barbara-1948-illus-1st ed (h10,sl tn dj) 50.00

CULLIMORE,C-Santa Barbara Adobes-Santa Barbara-1948-illus-1st ed (kk4,sl tn dj) 50.00

CULLING,LOUIS T-Complete Magick Curriculum of the Secret Order of G B G-St.Paul-1969-Llewellyn Publ-sm 4to-130p-frntis,wi add col frntis,illus,photos-1st prtg (aa7,sl scuff dj) 35.00*

CULLUM,RIDGWELL-Vampire of N'Gobi-1936-Lippincott-1st Amer ed (s10,fox pgs) 15.00

CULP,EDWARD C-25th Ohio Vet. Vol. Infantry in the War for the Union-Topeka-1885-Geo W Crane-168,(1)p-cl (l1,cov dull,sl rub,few spots) 150.00

CULVER,HENRY B-Forty Famous Ships-NY-1938-Garden City Publ-xiv,320p-grn cl,dec e.p.,col & line drwngs (nn1,sl fade & wn) 45.00

CUMBERLAND COUNTY-Biographical Review...Sketches of Leading Citizens of...New Jersey-Bost-1896-4to-557p-mod buckram,ports (aa6,rbnd) 200.00

CUMBERLAND,CHARLES C-Mexican Revolution: Genesis Under Madero-Austin-(1974)-U of Tex Pr-298p-map,illus (cc4,dj) 20.00

CUMBERLAND,CHARLES C-Mexican Revolution: the Constitutionalist Years-Austin-(1972)-U of Tex Pr-449p-map,illus (cc4,dj) 25.00

CUMBERLAND,MARTEN-Knife Will Fall-1944-CC-1st Amer ed (s10,dj) 12.50

CUMBERLAND,MARTEN-Murmurs in the Rue Morgue-NY-1959-London House-1st US ed (f4,f,dj) 12.50

CUMMING,A M-California for the Sportsman-SF-1911-8vo-162p-wrps,photos (m3) 35.00

CUMMING,JOHN-ED.-Gold Rush-Mt.Pleasant-(1974)-priv prntd-154p-cl-ltd to 487c (g1) 25.00

CUMMING,K-Journal of Kate Cumming-Savannah-1975-288p (z10,ex-libr,dj) 50.00

CUMMING,R G-Five Year's Hunting Adventure in South Africa-Lond-ca.1850-349p-illus (ee3,sl fox) 100.00

CUMMINGS,E E-73 Poems-1962-Harcourt-1st ed (kk6,f,dj sp sl fade) 75.00

CUMMINGS,E E-Complete Poems 1913 to 1962-NY-(1972)-HBJ-1st ed (k7,dj wn) 15.00

CUMMINGS,E E-Complete Poems,1910 to 1962-Lond-1981-Granada-8vo-2 vols-rvsd,enlgd ed (mm8,f,sl bump box) 50.00*

CUMMINGS,E E-Complete Poems-(Lond)-(1968)-MacGibbon & Kee-8vo-2 vols-blu cl,ltd to 150 sets,glassine dj (x3,f,chip dj,bump box) 150.00

CUMMINGS,E E-Enormous Room-NY-(1922)-Boni-8vo-cl,scarce in dj-1st ed wi word uncensored on p 219 (x3,chip,sunned,rprd dj) 250.00

CUMMINGS,E E-Is 5-NY-1926-(10),115p-cl bckd bds-ltd to 75c,autg (gg1,chip,sl fade sp) 475.00

CUMMINGS,E E-Is 5-NY-1926-Boni & Liveright-8vo-cl/bds-Firmage A6a-1st ed (x3) 115.00

CUMMINGS,E E-One Times One-NY-1944-Henry Holt-1st ed (h8,f,dj) 65.00

CUMMINGS,E E-Santa Claus-NY-(1946)-Holt-4to-cl-1st ed (ll10,cov sl soil,dj edgewn) 45.00

CUMMINGS,E E-Santa Claus-NY-(1946)-Holt-tall 4to-cl-total ed of 1500c-1st trd ed (x3,dj sl chip & creased) 65.00

CUMMINGS,E E-Selected Poems 1923 to 1958-Lond-1960-Faber-1st Brit ed (c8,f,dj) 75.00

CUMMINGS,E E-Tom-(Santa Fe)-(1935)-Arrow Eds-sl 8vo-brwn cl,silv sp lettrng,col frntis by Ben Shahn,total ed of 1500c-Firmage A15-1st ed (x3,f,tattrd dj) 75.00

CUMMINGS,E E-Tulips and Chimneys-NY-1923-Seltzer-8vo-canvas bckd bds,papr sp labl-auth 1st bk-1st ed (kk8,sl fox,sp labl rub) 125.00

CUMMINGS,O R-Maine's Fast Electric Railroad: Portland and Lewiston Interurban-Manchester-1967-88p-wrps-Bull.#3 (n4) 14.00

CUMMINGS,PARKE-Dictionary of Baseball-1950-Barnes-drwngs-1st ed (s8,f,dj) 20.00

CUMMINS,D DUANE-William Robinson Leigh-Norman-(1980)-U of Okla Pr-204p-col illus-1st ed (cc4,dj) 27.00

CUMMINS,J S-ED.-Travels and Controversies of Friar Domingo Navarette 1618 to 1686-Cambridge-1962-Hakluyt Soc-8vo-2 vols-blu cl,plts,fldg maps (p1) 65.00

CUNARD,NANCY-These Were the Hours-Carbondale-(1969)-photos-1st ed (s5,f,dj) 22.50

CUNARD,NANCY-These Were the Hours-Carbondale-(1969)-So Illinois U Pr-8vo-xxiv,216p-cl-1st ed (w2,dj) 15.00

CUNDIFF,WILLARD-Panoramic Automobile Road Map and Tourist Guide Book of Southern California, Season 1914 to 15-LA-1914-Cadmus Pr-tall,narrow 8vo-brwn cl wi compass inlaid on frnt cov,fldg map in rear,drwngs-1st ed (ee6) 100.00

CUNNINGHAM,A B-Death Haunts the Dark Lane-NY-1958-Dutton-1st ed (q4,dj sl wn & soil) 25.00

CUNNINGHAM,A B-Death Rides a Sorrel Horse-1946-Dutton-1st ed (s10,dj) 12.50

CUNNINGHAM,A B-Murder at Deer Lick-1939-Dutton-1st ed (s10,dj) 45.00

CUNNINGHAM,A B-Murder at Deer Lick-NY-1939-Dutton-auth 1st bk-1st ed (z3,sl cocked,dj chip) 60.00

CUNNINGHAM,A B-One Man Must Die-1946-Dutton-1st ed (s10,dj) 15.00

CUNNINGHAM,A B-Who Killed Pretty Becky Low?-1951-Dutton-1st ed (s10,dj) 15.00

CUNNINGHAM,ALBERT B-Old Black Bass-NY-1922-12mo-111p-illus-1st ed (m3) 30.00

CUNNINGHAM,D-Antietam-(Springfield)-(1904)-150,(1)p-cl-Ryan 535 (g1) 35.00

CUNNINGHAM,E V-Case of the Kidnapped Angel-NY-1982-Delacorte-1st ed (r4,f,dj) 20.00

CUNNINGHAM,E V-Case of the One Penny Orange-1977-Holt-1st ed (n9,f,dj) 15.00

CUNNINGHAM,E V-Case of the Poisoned Eclairs-Lond-1980-Deutsch-1st Brit ed (q4,f,dj) 20.00

CUNNINGHAM,E V-Cynthia-1968-Morrow-1st ed (s10,dj) 20.00

CUNNINGHAM,E V-Penelope-NY-1965-Dbldy-1st ed (h4,f,dj) 12.50

CUNNINGHAM,E V-Sally-NY-1967-Morrow-1st ed (l4,f,dj) 15.00

CUNNINGHAM,EUGENE-Gun Bulldogger-1939-Houghton Mifflin-1st ed (r9,dj chip & wn) 35.00

CUNNINGHAM,EUGENE-Triggernometry, Gallery of Gunfighter-NY-1934-441p-illus-Howes C954-1st ed (g7,sl rub) 65.00

CUNNINGHAM,F-Sky Master-Phila-(1943)-8vo-332p-cl,frntis,50p plts,illus e.p.-1st ed (t2,chip dj) 100.00

CUNNINGHAM,FRANK-General Stand Watie's Confederate Indians-S.A.-1959-Naylor-242p-1st ed (a9,dj) 75.00

CUNNINGHAM,IMOGEN-Photographs-Seattle-(1970)-U of Wash-4to-cl-1st ed (y3,dj) 135.00

CUNNINGHAM,J T-Sexual Dimorphism in the Animal Kingdom-Lond-1900-Black-xii+317p+ads-olive cl,32 text illus-1st ed (c2) 25.00

CUNNINGHAM,JULIA-Dear Rat-Bost-1961-Houghton Mifflin-8vo-126p-cl,line drwngs,W Lorraine-1st ed (s3,f,dj) 25.00

CUNNINGHAM,MERCE-Changes: Notes on Choreography-NY-1968-Something Else Pr-photos-ltd to 3761c-1st ed (q2,dj) 35.00

CUNNINGHAM,T M-Hugh Wilson-np(Dallas)-(1938)-150p-illus-scarce-1st ed (jj1,sm spot) 75.00

CUNNINGHAM,W G-Aircraft Industry-LA-(1951)-8vo-xviii,248p-cl,illus t.p.,8p plts,11p maps-1st ed (t2,dj) 40.00

CUNNINGHAME GRAHAM,R B-Horses of the Conquest-Norman-1949-U of Okla-4to-1st US ed (f10) 40.00

CUNNINGHAME GRAHAM,R B-Rodeo-NY-1936-Literary Guild (h9,dj) 15.00

CUNYNGHAME,ARTHUR T-Travels in the Eastern Caucasus, on the Caspian and Black Seas...During the Summer of 1871-Lond-1872-John Murray-27 drwngs,maps-1st ed (p6) 200.00

CUPPY,WILL-How to Tell Your Friends From the Apes-NY-1931-picts by Jacks,pict dj-1st ed (r5,dj) 35.00

CURLE,RICHARD-Wanderings-NY-1920-Dutton-8vo-350p-1st US ed (cc5,dj) 30.00

CURLEY,D N-ED.-Library of Literary Criticism-NY-1969-Ungar-3 vols-blu cl-4th ed (z3,f,dj) 65.00

CURRAN,JIM-Trango-Sheffield-1978-174p-1st Brit ed (o10,f,dj) 40.00

CURRENT,KAREN-Photography and the Old West-NY-(1977)-Abrams-oblng 8vo-cl wi photo cov-1st ed (y3,sl soil cov) 50.00

CURRENT,W R-Greene & Greene-Ft.Worth-1974-oblng 4to-1st ed (ee1,dj) 100.00

CURRENT-GARCIA,EUGENE-ED.-Shem Ham & Japheth-1973-U of Ga Pr-8vo-361p-illus e.p.,fldg map-1st ed (cc7,dj) 35.00*

CURRIE,BARTON-Fishers of Books-Bost-1931-2 vols-illus,ltd to 365 sets,nbrd,autg (r2,uncut,sp rub,sunned) 75.00

CURRIE,BARTON-Fishers of Books-Bost-1931-photos-1st ed (s5,dj) 35.00

CURRIER,THOMAS F-Bibliography of Oliver Wendell Holmes-NY-1953-Bibliog Soc of Amer-707p-illus (g10,edge rprd dj) 100.00

CURRY,MANFRED-Yacht Racing-NY-1927-H Holt-(vi)+308p,illus-1st Amer ed (dd1,cov sl soil,spot) 65.00

CURTIN,JEREMIAH-Creation Myths of Primitive America...-Bost-1898-Little,Brown-xl+532p+ads-maroon cl-1st ed (b2,sl soil) 45.00

CURTIN,L S M-Healing Herbs of the Upper Rio Grande-LA-(1965)-258p-errata pg,photos-rprnt (u7,f) 20.00

CURTIS,A-Lectures on Midwifery...to the Members of the Botanico-Medical College of the state of Ohio...-Cin-1846-prntd for auth by C Nagle-447p+fldg plt-lea-3rd ed corrctd & enlgd (d1,joints crckd,sp chip) 85.00

CURTIS,ALBERT-Fabulous San Antonio-San Antonio-1954-Waylor Co-298p-cl,photos-1st ed (w3,f,dj) 12.50

CURTIS,ASAHEL-Photos-Seattle-July,1925-Prgrm & Souvenir Bklt 36th Triennial Conclave of Knights Templar-blu wrps,col illus cov,photos,ports (b6) 12.00

CURTIS,BRIAN-Life Story of the Fish-NY-1938-8vo-260p-illus-scarce-1st ed (m3,dj) 55.00

CURTIS,BRIAN-Warm Water Game Fishes of California-Sacramento-1949-8vo-22p-wrps,col plts (m3,vf) 10.00

CURTIS,C H-Orchids for Everyone-Lond-1910-Dutton-4to-xii,234p-orig g pict cl,t.e.g.,col t.p.,50p col illus-scarce-1st ed (mm4,spot cov,uncut) 85.00

CURTIS,C P-Hunting in Africa East & West-NY-1925-281p-photos (gg3,cov wn) 40.00

CURTIS,CAROLINE-Keola, A Boy of Old Hawaii-Honolulu-(1941)-Tongg-159p-illus,E Myhre-1st ed (u8) 15.00

CURTIS,D A-Queer Luck-1899-Brentanos-pict cl,scarce-1st ed (x2) 75.00

CURTIS,EDWARD S-Portraits from North American Indian Life-NY-1972-Mus Nat Hist-folio-176p-cl-1st ed (q3) 150.00

CURTIS,ELIZABETH G-Gateways and Doorways of Charleston,South Carolina...-NY-1926-Archi Bk Publ-4to-68p-brwn cl-1st ed (oo5,bump,rub,sl fray sp) 75.00

CURTIS,GEORGE T-Creation of Evolution-NY-1887-D Appleton-xxii+564p-red cl-1st ed (g2,sl rub cov) 25.00

CURTIS,L PERRY,JR.-Apes and Angels-Wash D.C.-(1971)-Smithsonian-4to-126p-cartoons-1st ed (gg5,chip dj) 12.50

CURTIS,NATALIE-Indians' Book-NY-(1935)-572p-illus-3rd ed (v7) 35.00

CURTIS,O B-History of the Twenty Fourth Michigan of the Iron Brigade-Detr-1891-Winn & Hammond-483p-illus,maps,errata-Nevins I,77-1st ed (bb4,sl soil cov) 175.00

CURTIS,PAUL A-American Game Shooting-NY-1927-8vo-279p-photos (m3) 20.00

CURTIS,PAUL A-Sportsmen All-1938-Derrydale-8vo-160p-ltd to 950c,nbrd-illus (m3,f) 100.00

CURTIS,PAUL A-Sportsmen All-NY-1938-Derrydale-160p-blk cl,g dec,frntis+11 plts-ltd to 950c (ee3,vf) 145.00

CURTIS,THOMAS S-High Frequency Apparatus-1920-269p-150 illus-2nd ed (h6) 65.00

CURTIS,WILLIAM E-Children of the Sun-Chig-1883-154p+ads-v scarce-1st ed (v7,pres) 150.00

CURTIS-BENNETT,SIR NOEL-Food of the People-Lond-(1959)-Faber-320p-brwn cl,30 photos-1st ed (q8) 25.00

CURTISS,MINA-Bizet and His World-NY-1958-Knopf-8vo-477p-38 illus-1st ed (ee5,f,sl chip dj) 25.00

CURTISS,URSULA-Voice Out of Darkness-NY-1948-Dodd-auth 1st bk-1st ed (f4,f,dj) 30.00

CURWEN,HENRY-History of Booksellers, the Old and the New-Lond-(1873)-g dec covs-1st ed (r2,sl fox,hng weak) 75.00

CURWOOD,JAMES O-Ancient Highway-Tor-1925-Copp,Clark-illus-1st Can ed (pp2,f,dj chip,tape rprd) 45.00*

CURWOOD,JAMES O-Black Hunter-Tor-1926-Copp,Clark-illus-1st Can ed (pp2) 20.00*

CURWOOD,JAMES O-Flaming Forest-NY-1921-296p-cl-1st ed (b1) 15.00

CURWOOD,JAMES O-Hunted Woman-GC-1926-Dbldy-324p-cl (z7) 15.00

CUSHING,CALEB-Territory of Oregon-Wash-1839-25th Congress,Hs Rprt 101-(Ser.351)-61p-Howes C-970-rare (z1,disbnd) 200.00

CUSHING,FRANK H-My Adventures in Zuni-Santa Fe-(1941)-178p-illus,ltd to 400c-1st publ in book format-rare (u7,sl chip dj) 350.00

CUSHING,FRANK H-Zuni Folk Tales-NY-1901-474p-illus-1st ed (u7,cov spots) 75.00

CUSHING,FRANK H-Zuni. Selected Writings of...-Lincoln-(1979)-436p-photos,map e.p.-1st ed (v7,f,dj) 20.00

CUSHING,HARVEY-Chiasmal Syndrome of Primary Optic Atrophy and Bitemporal Field Defects in Adult Patients...-Leiden-1929-184p-orig prtd wrps,76 figs (g10,sl dmpstnd) 75.00

CUSHING,HARVEY-Consecratio Medici and Other Papers-Bost-1928-276p-1st ed,1st prtg (dd3) 150.00

CUSHING,HARVEY-From a Surgeon's Journal 1915 to 1918-Bost-1936-534p-illus-1st ed (g10) 25.00

CUSHING,HARVEY-Life of Sir William Osler-Oxford-1925-2 vols-illus-1st prtg (g10,sl wn,sp tn) 125.00

CUSHMAN,DAN-Great North Trail-(1966)-McGraw HIll-383p-maps-Six Guns #537-1st ed (r8,chip dj) 15.00

CUSHMAN,DAN-Great North Trail-NY-(1966)-McGraw-Hill-383p-1st ed (cc4,dj) 25.00

CUSHMAN,J A-Monograph of the Foraminifera of the North Pacific-1914-USNM-229p-89 plts (bb3) 25.00

CUST,LIONEL-Cenci-Lond-1929-Mandrake-124p-blk cl & snakeskin papr over bds-1st ed (z9,sp labl chip,edgewn) 15.00

CUSTER,ELIZABETH-Boots and Saddles-1885-Harper & Bros-312p-orig g stmpd pict brwn cl,wi map & port added-Howes C980-1st ed (d3) 100.00

CUSTER,ELIZABETH-Boots and Saddles-NY-(1885)-Harper & Bros-312p-pict cl,frntis,map-Howes C980 (dd4,sp wn) 40.00

CUSTER,ELIZABETH-Following the Guidon-1890-Harper & Bros-341p-orig g stmpd dec grn cl,illus-1st ed (d3) 50.00

CUSTER,ELIZABETH-Following the Guidon-NY-1890-Harper & Bros-1st ed (l9,f,dj soil & sl tn) 300.00

CUSTER,ELIZABETH-Following the Guidon-NY-1890-Harper & Bros-341p-pict cl cov,illus-1st ed (dd4) 50.00

CUSTER,ELIZABETH-Tenting on the Plains or General Custer in Kansas and Texas-NY-1887-Chas Webster-702p-orig g stmpd dec bndg,illus-1st ed (d3) 200.00

CUSTER,ELIZABETH-Tenting on the Plains or General Custer in Kansas and Texas-NY-1887-Webster-thk 8vo-702p-dec cl-1st ed (s1) 175.00

CUSTER,ELIZABETH-Tenting on the Plains-NY-1895-C L Webster-403p-pict cl,illus (dd4) 30.00

CUSTER,GEORGE A-My Life on the Plains-Norman-(1962)-418p-illus-Dowd #236-1st Okla ed (c7,f,chip dj) 40.00

CUSTER,GEORGE A-My Life on the Plains-Norman-(1962)-U of Okla-8vo-418p-1st ed thus (z4,dj) 35.00

CUTCLIFFE,H C-Art of Trout Fishing on Rapid Streams-Barnstaple-1970-16mo-206p (m3,vf) 35.00

CUTLER,CARL C-Descriptive Catalogue of the Marine Collection at India House-Middleton-1973-India Hs-4to-144p-12 col plts,39 monochr plts-ltd to 1250c-2nd ed (p8,as new in box) 125.00

CUTRIGHT,PAUL R-Lewis & Clark-Urbana,Chig,Lond-1969-506p-illus-1st ed (f7,f,dj) 95.00

CUTTEN,GEORGE-Three Thousand Years of Mental Healing-NY-1911-318p-scarce-1st ed (dd3) 100.00

CUTTER,DONALD C-California Coast-Norman-1969-U of Okla-8vo-xxv,(3),4-278p-illus,bilingual ed (mm1,f,dj) 85.00

CUTTER,MRS. B H-Practical Recipes-NY-1909-Duffield & Co-177p-grn bds-Bitting 111 (n6) 40.00

CUTTER,W R-Genealogical & Personal Memoirs, Relating to the Families of the State of Mass-NY-1910-4to-4 vols-3/4 lea,ports,illus (a3,sl wn) 65.00

CUVIER,GEORGES-Discourse on the Revolutions of the Surface of the Globe and Changes...in the Animal Kingdom-Phila-1831-Carey & Lea-iv+252p+ads-orig gry bds,lilac cl sp,6 plts-1st Amer ed (l2,sl wn,fox,few pencil mrks) 150.00

CUVIER-Animal Kingdom Arranged in Conformity...-NY-1831-8vo-4 vols-calf,errata,20 plts-v scarce (y8,wn,fox) 350.00

D'AGNEAU,MARCEL-Curse of the Nibelung-Lond-1981-Arlington-1st ed (w9,f,dj) 40.00

D'ANNUNZIO,GABRIELE-Francesca Da Rimini-NY-(1902)-Stokes-12mo-223p-photos-1st US ed (ee5) 35.00

D'AULAIRE,INGRI-ED.-East of the Sun and West of the Moon-NY-1938-Viking-4to-188p-pict linen cl,22p illus-1st ed (s3,cl tanned,hngs strngthnd) 30.00

D'AULAIRE,INGRI-Wings for Per-NY-(1944)-Dbldy/Jr Lit Guild-4to-unpgd-pict cl,col illus-1st ed thus (oo10,dj) 45.00

D'ERIGNY,SIMONE-Mysterious Madame S...-Phila-1934-Lippincott-1st US ed (e4,sp chip dj) 20.00

D'OMBRAIN,ATHEL-Game Fishing off the Australian Coast-Sydney-1957-4to-230p-photos,illus-1st ed (m3,tape mrks on e.p.s) 60.00

D'ORLEANS,PRINCE HENRI-From Tonkin to India...-NY-1898-Dodd,Mead-tall 8vo-xii,467p-fldg map,illus,G Vuillier-1st Amer ed (ll1,sl soil,rprd e.p.) 250.00

D'REMUSAT,JEAN T-Autobiography of...-Bost-1935-Meador Publ-230p-blk cl,frntis port-scarce-1st ed (b6,f) 35.00

DABBS,EDITH M-Face of an Island-NY-1971-Grossman-unpgd-94 photos by L Miner-1st ed (cc9,f,dj) 60.00

DABNEY,CHARLES W-Universal Education in the South-Chapel Hill-(1936)-Univ of NC Pr-2 vols,red cl,plts-presumed 1st ed (k2,sl fox,dj) 65.00

DABNEY,OWEN P-Lost Shackle-np(Salem)-1897-vi,98p-orig blu prtd wrps-Smith 2200-Graff 966 (gg9,wrps sl chip & tn) 60.00

DABOLL,DAVID A-New England Almanac...1880...-New London-(1879)-Chas Allyn-48,(16)p-wrps (g1) 12.50

DABOLL,NATHAN-Daboll's Schoolmaster's Assistant, Improved and Enlarged-Norwich-1818-R Hubbard-240p-lea-Amer Imprnts 43796-Stereotype ed (k1) 27.50

DAFOE,JOHN W-Laurier-Tor-1922-Thos Allen-12mo-182p-g grn cl (p2) 12.50

DAGGETT,CARLEEN M-Noah McCuiston-Waco-1975-308p-photos-1st ed (n10,f,dj) 45.00

DAGLISH,ERIC F-Birds of the British Isles-Lond-1948-Dent-222p-48 engrvngs(25 hand col),orig jacket-ltd ed (d9,dj) 100.00

DAHINDEN,J-Urban Structures for the Future-1972-Praeger-illus-1st Amer ed (h10) 45.00

DAHL,ROALD-Charlie and the Great Glass Elevator-NY-(1972)-Knopf-illus-1st ed (nn10,f,f dj) 15.00

DAHL,ROALD-Danny the Champion of the World-NY-(1975)-Knopf-illus by J Bennett-1st ed (nn10,f,f dj) 15.00

DAHL,ROALD-Fantastic Mr.Fox-NY-(1970)-Knopf-sm 4to-62p-pict cl,b&w illus,D Chaffin-1st ed (s3,f,dj) 35.00

DAHL,ROALD-George's Marvellous Medicine-NY-(1982)-Knopf-cl/bds,illus by Q Blake-1st US ed (oo10,f,dj) 20.00

DAHL,ROALD-Gremlins, From the Walt Disney Production...A Royal Air Force Story-NY-(1943)-Random Hs-4to-prntd pap bds in col,col illus,auth 1st bk-rare-1st ed (t1) 750.00

DAHL,ROALD-Kiss Kiss-NY-1960-1st ed (z6,vf,dj) 60.00

DAHL,ROALD-Kiss Kiss-NY-1960-Knopf-1st ed (a5,f,dj) 45.00

DAHL,ROALD-Over To You-NY-(1946)-scarce-1st ed (z6,f,tn & chip dj) 250.00

DAHL,ROALD-Someone Like You-NY-1953-Knopf-1st ed (z9,f,dj) 125.00

DAHL,ROALD-Switch Bitch-NY-1974-1st ed (z6,vf,dj) 45.00

DAHL,ROALD-Switch Bitch-NY-1974-Knopf-1st ed (hh5,f dj) 10.00

DAHL,ROALD-Witches-NY-(1982)-FS&G-tall 8vo-202p-line drwngs-1st US ed (nn10,dj) 20.00

DAHLBERG,B L-White-Tailed Deer in Wisconsin-Madison-1956-8vo-282p-photos (m3) 10.00

DAHLBERG,EDWARD-Bottom Dogs-NY-1930-S&S-1st US ed (w5,sunned sp) 20.00

DAHLBERG,EDWARD-Confessions of ...-1971-Braziller-1st ed (t9,f,dj) 25.00

DAHLBERG,EDWARD-Confessions of...-NY-1971-linen cov bds,iss w/o dj,ltd to 200c,nbrd,autg-1st ed (r5,f,box) 75.00

DAHLBERG,EDWARD-Do These Bones Live-NY-(1941)-Harcourt Brace-8vo-158p-1st ed (ee5,tape rprd dj) 35.00

DAHLBERG,EDWARD-Do These Bones Live-NY-(1941)-Harcourt,Brace-8vo-1st ed (jj8,f,dj) 65.00

DAHLBERG,EDWARD-Epitaphs of Our Times-1967-Brazillier-1st ed (o9,sl tn dj) 15.00

DAHLBERG,EDWARD-Flea of Sodom-(Norfolk)-(1950)-Direction 18(New Dirctns)-1st US ed (a10,edge-wn dj) 17.50

DAHLBERG,EDWARD-Olive of Minerva or the Comedy of a Cuckold-NY-(1976)-Crowell-1st ed (g3,f,dj) 25.00

DAHLGREN,MADELEINE V-Memoir of John A Dahlgren...-Bost-1882-James R Osgood-xii+660p-grn cl,fldg map,illus-1st ed (b2) 100.00
DAICHES,DAVID-James Boswell and His World-NY-1976-1st ed (y7,dj) 12.00
DAICHES,DAVID-Scotch Whiskey-NY-(1970)-Macmillan-168p-red cl,map e.p.,col photos-1st Amer ed (q8,dj) 20.00
DAICHES,DAVID-Virginia Woolf-Norfolk-(1942)-New Directions-8vo-cl-1st ed (x3,dj) 30.00
DAILEY,ABRAM H-Mollie Francher, The Brooklyn Enigma-Brklyn-1894-8vo-262p-illus-1st ed (w6,soil cl) 45.00
DAILEY,GARDNER A-Memorial Gardens for the Manila Cemetary-SF-(c.1954)-Amer Battle Mnmnts Comm-folio-orig brwn wrps,fldg frntis (p8) 50.00
DAIN,MARTIN J-Faulkner's County: Yoknapatawpha-NY-(1964)-Random-4to-photos-1st ed (ff6,f,dj) 50.00
DAINELLI,GIOTTO-Buddhists & Glaciers of Western Tibet-Lond-1933-304p-31 photos,map-1st Brit ed (q10,f) 175.00
DAINTY AND ARTISTIC DESSERTS-Bost-c.1920-J Burnett Co-48p-wrps (k6) 15.00
DAKE,H C-ET AL-Quartz Family Minerals-NY-(1938)-Whittlesey Hs,McGraw Hill-xvi,304p-g,col frntis,photos-10th prtg (u5,f,dj) 32.50
DAKIN,SUSANNA B-Lives of William Hartnell-Stanford-1949-Stanford Univ Pr-308p-illus orng cl (b6,vf,sl tn dj) 22.50
DAKIN,SUSANNA B-Published Writings of Francis Peloubet Farquhar-SF-1954-lg 8vo-17p-untrmmd-1st ed (o10,vf) 40.00
DAL,ERIK-ED.-Danish Ballads and Folk Songs-Copenhagen & NY-1967-Amer Scandi Fndtn-cl,wdcuts,M Rasmussen-1st prtg (l8,f,dj) 15.00
DALE,CHARLES W-Familiar Laws as Adapted Principally from the Ohio Supreme Court Decisions...-Dayton-1888-79,(1)p-cl (e1) 15.00
DALE,EDWARD E-Cherokee Cavaliers-Norman-1939-U of Okla Pr-319p-illus-1st ed (nn6,dj) 75.00
DALE,EDWARD E-Pioneer Judge-Cedar Rapids-(1958)-Torch Pr-433p-frntis-1st ed (cc4,dj,autg) 40.00
DALE,HENRY-Adventures in Physiology with Excursions into Autopharmacology-Lond-1953-652p-1st ed (dd3) 75.00
DALEY,ARTHUR-Kings of the Home Run-1962-Putnam-photos-1st ed (s8,f,tn dj) 16.00
DALEY,ARTHUR-Times at Bat-1950-Random-1st ed (s8,dj) 27.50
DALGLIESH,ALICE-ED.-Will James Cowboy Book-NY-1938-158p-pict cl,frntis,illus-scarce-1st ed (t7,cov soil) 75.00
DALI,SALVADOR-Diary of a Genius-GC-1965-illus-1st Amer ed (h10,dj) 45.00
DALI,SALVADOR-Fifty Secrets of Magic Craftsmanship-1948-Dial (h10,dj) 300.00
DALI,SALVADOR-Les Diners de Gala-Paris-1973-Draeger-folio-323p-dec tan cl,col illus-1st ed (q8,f,dj,box) 80.00
DALI,SALVADOR-Wines of Gala-1978-Abrams-124 col illus,dec col dj-1st Amer ed (h10,dj) 150.00
DALLAS,E S-Kettner's Book of the Table-(Lond)-(1968)-Centaur Pr-500p-first publ 1877 (k6) 35.00
DALLAS,E S-Kettner's Book of the Table-Lond-(1968)-Centaur Pr-500p-wht cl-facs of 1877 ed (q8,dj) 25.00
DALLAS,SANDRA-Sacred Paint-Santa Fe-(1979)-Fenn Galleries-135p-col illus,plts-1st ed (bb4,dj) 45.00
DALLY,JOSEPH W-Woodbridge and Vicinity-New Brunswick-1873-391,(1)p-cl (aa6,sl wn) 150.00
DALRYMPLE,BYRON W-Hunting Across North America-NY-1947-8vo-848p-photos (m3,vf,dj) 12.50
DALRYMPLE,BYRON W-Light Tackle Fishing-NY-1947-8vo-398p-illus (m3,vf,fray dj) 12.50
DALRYMPLE,BYRON W-North American Big Game Hunting-NY-1974-8vo-384p-photos (m3,vf,dj) 11.50
DALRYMPLE,BYRON W-North American Game Animals-NY-1978-4to-516p-illus,D Allen (m3,vf,dj) 15.00
DALRYMPLE,BYRON W-Panfish-NY-1947-8vo-398p-illus (m3,f,tn dj) 16.00
DALRYMPLE,JEAN-Pinafore Farm Cookbook-NY-(1971)-Bobbs Merrill-238p-grn cl (q8,dj) 20.00
DALTON BROTHERS-And Their Astounding Career of Crime by an Eyewitness-NY-1954-F Fell-251p-pict e.p.,drwngs-Six Guns 546-1st ed (gg4,dj) 20.00
DALTON,JOHN-History of the College of Physicians and Surgeons in the City of New York-NY-1888-208p-scarce (dd3) 100.00
DALTON,VAN B-Genesis of Dental Education in the U.S.-Cin-1946-216p-blu cl,illus-1st ed (a2,dj) 40.00
DALY,CARROLL J-Murder Won't Wait-1933-Washburn-1st ed (s10,sp fade) 40.00
DALY,ELIZABETH-Any Shape or Form-1945-Farrar-1st ed (s10,dj chip) 30.00
DALY,ELIZABETH-Book of the Crime-NY-1951-Rinehart-1st ed (f4,dj) 35.00
DALY,ELIZABETH-Book of the Lion-1948-Rinehart-1st ed (x7,vf,f dj) 75.00
DALY,ELIZABETH-Death and Letters-1950-Rinehart-1st ed (x7,vf,f dj) 58.00
DALY,ELIZABETH-Death and Letters-NY-1950-Rinehart-1st ed (f4,dj) 35.00
DALY,ELIZABETH-Evidence of Things Seen-NY-1943-Farrar-1st ed (f4,dj sp sl wn) 45.00
DALY,HUGH-Memoirs of General Sir Henry Dermot Daly-Lond-1905-388p-red cl,illus-1st ed (gg2) 80.00
DALY,JOSEPH F-Life of Augustin Daly-NY-1917-Macmillan-thick 8vo-xi,672,(4)p-g stmpd blu cl,t.e.g.-1st ed (w2) 35.00
DALZELL,KATHLEEN E-Queen Charlotte Islands 1774 to 1966-(Terrace)-(1968)-340p-illus,map-1st ed (h7,chip dj) 25.00
DAMASE,JACQUES-Carriages-NY-1968-Putnam-1st US ed (h9,dj) 35.00
DAMAZ,PAUL-Art in European Architecture-NY-1956-266p-col illus-1st ed (cc8,dj) 50.00
DAMON,ETHEL M-Sanford Ballard Dole & His Hawaii-(1957)-Pacific Bks-394p-photo plts,facs-1st ed (u8,dj) 35.00
DAMPIER,ROBERT-To the Sandwich Islands on H.M.S. Blonde-Honolulu-1971-oblng 4to-131p-dbl col,illus,clear dj-1st ed (f7,f,dj) 50.00
DAMPIER,WILLIAM-New Voyage Round the World-Lond-1927-Argonaut Pr-4to-376p-1/2 vel-ltd to 975c (p8,unopened) 165.00
DAMPIER,WILLIAM-Voyages and Discoveries-Lond-1931-Argonaut Pr-orig gold emboss red bds,vel sp-ltd to 974c,nbrd (v4,f) 225.00
DAN,JACK-Starhiker-NY-(1977)-Harper & Row-1st ed (j3,f,dj) 20.00
DANA,EDWARD S-Minerals and How to Study Them-NY-1901-Wiley & Sons-vi,380p+16p publ catlg-dec cov,gilt,frntis photo,illus-2nd rvsd ed (u5) 30.00
DANA,H W L-Handbook on Soviet Drama-NY-1938-Amer Russ Inst-pict bds,pict dj-1st ed (jj9,sl wn dj) 25.00

DANA,JAMES D-Corals and Coral Islands-1872-Dodd,Mead-398p-dec blu cl,t.e.g.,engrvngs,3 maps-1st ed (bb3,new e.p.,cor wn) 165.00

DANA,JAMES D-Corals and Coral Islands-NY-1872-Dodd,Mead-398p-maps,illus (p8,rbnd) 175.00

DANA,JAMES D-Text-Book of Geology-Phila-1867-Bliss-354p-cl,375 wdcts (k1) 17.50

DANA,JOSEPH-Quaestiones Grammaticae-Bost-1828-HGL&W-70p-plain wrps-Amer Imprnts 32885-2nd ed (k1) 20.00

DANA,JULIAN-Sutter of California-NY-1934-Pr of Pioneers-423p-illus-1st ed (cc4,wn dj) 35.00

DANA,MARSHALL N-Newspaper Story-Portland-1951-226,(4)p-cl (e1,sl wn dj) 15.00

DANA,MRS WM S-According to Season-NY-1894-Scribner-159p-dec cl (x6) 16.00

DANA,MRS WM S-How to Know the Wild Flowers-NY-1895-Scribner-373p-M Armstrong cov,cl,illus-rvsd ed (x6) 18.00

DANA,RICHARD H,JR.-Journal of...-Cambridge-1968-Belknap Pr of Harvard-8vo-3 vols,mustard yel cl,illus (nn1,f,box) 125.00

DANA,RICHARD H,JR.-Journal of...-Cambridge-1968-Harvard Univ Pr-3 vols,olive cl,illus-1st ed (k2,box) 65.00

DANA,RICHARD H,JR.-Two Years Before the Mast-Chig-1930-Lakeside Pr-ltd to 1000c-illus,Edw A Wilson-1st ed thus (e10,lacks orig box) 95.00

DANA,RICHARD H,JR.-Two Years Before the Mast-LA-1964-Ward Ritchie Pr-2 vols-illus-Howes D49 (cc4,box) 85.00

DANA,RICHARD H,JR.-Two Years Before the Mast-NY-(1947)-Heritage Pr-col engrv,H A Mueller (e10,f,box) 15.00

DANA,RICHARD H,JR.-Two Years Before the Mast-NY-1968-Collier & Son-404p-frntis,Harvard Classics Registered ed-"Deluxe Edition" (nn1) 15.00

DANA,RICHARD H-Richard Henry Dana, Architect-NY-1965-priv prtd-oblng 4to-unpgd-cl,74 plts-ltd to 500c,nbrd (cc10) 95.00

DANA,RICHARD-Old Canterbury on the Quinnebaug-St.Paul-1923-White Pine Monos-4to-16p-wrps,photos (l10) 9.50

DANCE,S PETER-Shell Collecting-Berkeley-1966-U of Cal-8vo-344p-35 plts(3 col)-1st ed (gg5,f,dj) 30.00

DANCE,STANLEY-World of Count Basie-NY-(1980)-Scribners-1st ed (w1,f,f dj) 25.00

DANCE,STANLEY-World of Earl Hines-NY-(1977)-Scribners-lg 4to-photos-1st ed (w1,f,dj) 25.00

DANCKAERTS,JASPER-Diary of Our Second Trip from Holland to New Netherland-Upper Saddle River-1969-Gregg Pr-62p-orng cl,22 illus,text in Engl & Dutch (nn1) 35.00

DANCKAERTS,JASPER-Journal of...1679 to 1680-NY-1913-xxxi,313p+ads-cl,plts (aa6) 40.00

DANDY ANDY BOOK-np-(1916)-no publ-lg 8vo-cl wi pict pasteon,13p col plts,incl cov (s3) 45.00

DANE,CLEMENCE-Enter Sir John-NY-1928-Cosmopolitan-illus-1st US ed (h4,sl tn e.p.,dj) 35.00

DANE,CLEMENCE-London Has a Garden-NY-(1964)-Norton-8vo-211p-illus-1st US ed (gg5,sl rub dj) 12.50

DANE,G EZRA-Ghost Town-NY-1941-Knopf-311p-illus-Six Guns 553-1st ed (gg4,dj) 25.00

DANIEL,DAN-Babe Ruth-1930-Whitman-pict cov,photos-1st ed (s8,top sp taped) 45.00

DANIEL,GLYN-Hungry Archaeologist in France-Lond-(1963)-Faber & Faber-198p (k6) 20.00

DANIEL,GLYN-Megalith Builders of Western Europe-Lond-1958-Hutchinson-cl,illus-1st ed (n8,dj) 35.00

DANIELL,DAVID-Cap of Honour-Lond-1951-344p-illus-1st ed (b7,f,dj) 100.00

DANIELS,BEBE-282 Ways of Making a Salad-Lond-(1950)-Cassell-206p-grn cl,drwngs-1st prtg (q8,fade dj) 15.00

DANIELS,BRADFORD K-Outer Edge-1943-Caxton-326p-illus-1st ed (r8,chip dj) 25.00

DANIELS,JONATHAN-Prince of Carpetbaggers-Phila-(1958)-Lippincott-319p-red cl-1st ed (b2,chip dj) 25.00

DANIELS,LES-Comix, A History of Comic Books in America-NY-(1971)-Outerbridge & Dienstfrey-4to-198p-col illus-1st ed (ee5,dj) 25.00

DANIELS,ZEKE-Life and Death of Julia C Bullette-Va.City-1958-65p-illus-1st ed (t7,dj) 15.00

DANIELSON,RICHARD E-Martha Doyle-NY-(1938)-Derrydale Pr-illus,glassine dj-1st Amer ed (r2,uncut,dj) 125.00

DANIELSSON,BENGT-What Happened on the Bounty-Lond-1963-223p-frntis,map-1st English ed (d7,dj) 25.00

DANKER,DONALD F-Mollie-1959-U of Nebr-201p-pict bds & cl-1st ed (t7) 15.00

DANKER,DONALD F-Mollie-Lincoln-1959-U of Nebr Pr-8vo-ix,201p-1st ed (mm1,f,chip dj) 40.00

DANN,JACK-Future Power-NY-(1976)-Random-1st ed (h3,f,dj) 15.00

DANN,JACK-Starhiker-NY-(1977)-Harper & Row-1st ed (l3,f,dj) 20.00

DANNALDSON,JAMES-Trek in the Amazon Jungles-Culver City-1947-8vo-90p-photos (m3,pres cpy) 15.00

DANNENBAUM,JULIE-Creative Cooking School-(1971)-McCall-266p-dec prpl cl,drwngs-1st ed (q8,dj) 20.00

DANNER'S POCKET GUIDE BOOK-Gettysburg-1889-W J Cook-15p-pict wrps,fldg map (c1,sl wn) 32.50

DANVERS HISTORICAL SOCIETY-Old Anti Slavery Days-Danvers-1893-Danvers Mirror Prnt-xxviii+151p-blk cl-1st ed (h2) 35.00

DANZIGER,EDMUND J-Chippewas of Lake Superior-Norman-(1978)-U of Okla Pr-263p-illus-1st ed (gg4,dj) 20.00

DARBEE,HARRY-Catskill Fly Tier-Phila-1977-8vo-174p-photos-1st ed (m3,f,dj) 55.00

DARBY,JOHN C-Science and the Healing Art, or a New Book on Old Facts-Louisville-1880-403p-scarce-1st ed (dd3) 100.00

DARBY,R-Death Boards the "Lazy Lady"-1939-DD CC-auth 1st bk-1st ed (x7,dj) 35.00

DARDEN,NORMA J-Spoonbread and Strawberry Wine-GC-(1978)-Anchor Pr-288p-line drwngs,D Jamieson (o6) 30.00

DARGAN,OLIVE T-Highland Annals-NY-1925-Scribners-1st ed (w5) 30.00

DARGAN,OLIVE T-Welsh Pony-Bost-1913-priv prtd-12mo-ltd to 500c (h9) 45.00

DARING,HOPE-Paul Crandal's Charge-NY-(1900)-Amer Tract Society-48p-cl (h1) 10.00

DARK,ALVIN-When In Doubt, Fire the Manager-1980-Dutton-1st ed (s8,f,f dj) 16.00

DARLEY,GEORGE M-Pioneering the San Juan-Chig-1899-Revell-8vo-226p-photos (z4) 35.00

DARLING,ESTHER B-Baldy of Nome-Phila-1923(1916)-Penn Publ-301p-17 photos (o2,sp wn,sl rub) 15.00

DARLING,ESTHER B-Baldy of Nome-SF-1913-A M Robertson-12mo-76p-cl-1st ed (mm7,f) 45.00

DARLING,F FRASER-Seasons & the Fisherman-Cambridge-1941-8vo-70p-illus,C F Tunnicliffe (m3,f,dj) 20.00

DARLING,JAY N-In Peace and War-Des Moines-1916-12 x 9-unpgd-wrps-cartoons (g1,sp wn) 15.00

DARLINGTON,C D-Recent Advances in Cytology-Lond-1932-J & A Churchill-xviii+559p,cl,109 text figs-1st ed (j2) 35.00

DARLINGTON,HENRY-ET AL-Some Important Michigan Weeds-E Lansing-Dec. 1940-8vo-216p-wrps,94 figs (x5) 12.00

DARLINGTON,WILLIAM-American Weeds & Useful Plants-NY-1859-Orng Judd-12mo-xvi,460p-illus-2nd ed wi add by Geo Thurber (o2,sl chip sp) 35.00

DARLOW,T H-William Robertson Nicoll-Lond-1925-Hodder & Stoughton-cl-1st ed (l8) 13.50

DARNTON,ROBERT-Business of Enlightenment-Cambridge-1979-Belknap Pr/Harvard U Pr-thk 8vo-xiv,624p-1st ed (x4,dj) 35.00

DARRAH,JUANITA E-Modern Baking Powder-Chig-1927-Commonwealth Pr-125p-Bitting 662 (o6) 15.00

DARRAH,WILLIAM C-Powell of the Colorado-1951-Princeton Univ Pr-426p-illus-1st ed (cc4,dj) 35.00

DARRAH,WILLIAM C-Stereographs-Gettysburg-1977-Darrah-4to-246p-cl-1st ed (t3,f,dj) 65.00

DARROW,CLARENCE S-Persian Pearl and Other Essays-East Aurora-1899-Roycroft-175p-bds wi suede sp,ltd to 980c,nbrd,auth 1st bk-1st ed (c1,sl edge-wn) 250.00

DARROW,CLARENCE-Ordeal of Prohibition-Girard-(1925)-Haldeman-Julius-60p+4p ads-wrps-Little Blu Bk 974 (n1) 10.00

DARROW,GEORGE M-Strawberry-1966-Holt,Rinehart-447p-50 col plts,photos-1st ed (bb3,wn dj) 25.00

DARROW,GEORGE M-Strawberry-NY-1966-Holt-447p-cl (x6,sl wn dj) 30.00

DARWIN,CHARLES-Charles Darwin 1809 to 1882. A Centennial Commerorative-Wellington-1982-Nova Pac-lg thk folio-xii,376p-blk 1/2 calf & drk blu buckram,lea labls,inlaid red lea lttrng fr cov,matchng box,28 col tip in plts-ltd to 750c-1st ed (nn1,f,box) 750.

DARWIN,CHARLES-Descent of Man, and Selection in Relation to Sex-NY-1871-Appleton-2 vols-terra cotta cl-1st Amer ed (a2,sl drknd sp,sl fray sp) 135.00

DARWIN,CHARLES-Different Forms of Flowers on Plants of the Same Species-Lond-1877-John Murray-viii+352p+32p ads,grn cl,text illus,ads dated March, 1877(no priority Mar or Jan)-1st ed (g2,sl fox t.p.) 475.00

DARWIN,CHARLES-Expression of the Emotions in Man and Animals-NY-1873-Appleton-iv+374p-terra cotta cl,7 plts,21 text figs-1st Amer ed (d2,sl wn sp) 175.00

DARWIN,CHARLES-Formation of Vegetable Mould through the Action of Worms, with Observations on their Habits-NY-1882-Appleton-viii+326p-Terra cotta cl-1st Amer ed (d2,sl bump cor,few cov speck) 75.00

DARWIN,CHARLES-Insectivorous Plants-NY-1915-Appleton-xiv,376p-cl (x6) 22.00

DARWIN,CHARLES-Journal of Researches...During the Voyage Around the World of the H.M.S. "Beagle"...-NY-1890-Appleton-8vo-xvi,551p+ads-col & g vignette dec grn cl,frntis,illus,R T Prichett,publ claims 1st illus ed-"A New Edition" (nn1,soil,edge wn) 65.00

DARWIN,CHARLES-Life and Letters of...-NY-1887-Appleton-8vo-2 vols-dec red cl,Vol.I:frntis,3 illus,Vol.II:errata,frntis,1 illus-1st Amer ed (aa7) 200.00*

DARWIN,CHARLES-Life and Letters of...Including an Autobiographical Chapter-NY-1898-Appleton-2 vols,burgandy cl wi g sp titles,Vol.1:frntis,3 illus,Vol.2:frntis,facs-authrzd ed (nn1) 95.00

DARWIN,CHARLES-On the Origin of Species-NY-1887-Appleton-8vo-ix,458p+1p ad-red dec cl-new ed from 6th Engl ed, wi add & corr (aa7) 40.00*

DARWIN,CHARLES-Structure and Distribution of Coral Reefs-NY-1897-344p-1/2 lea,fldg maps-3rd ed (dd3,1 map tn) 45.00

DATIG,FRED-Luger Pistol-Alhambra-1962-8vo-328p-illus-revsd & enlrgd ed (m3,vf,chip dj) 45.00

DAUMAL,RENE-Mount Analogue-NY-1960-157p-1st US ed (p10,f,dj) 35.00

DAUMAS,E-Horses of the Sahara and the Manners of the Desert...-Lond-1863-Allen-1st ed in Engl (f10,sl wn) 225.00

DAUMIER,HONORE-Hunting & Fishing-Paris,NY-1975-folio-145p-illus (m3,vf,dj) 40.00

DAUNT,ACHILLES-In the Land of the Moose, the Bear and the Beaver-Lond-1885-Nelson-8vo-viii,328,(10)p ads-orig g dec pict cl-1st ed (pp2) 100.00*

DAVENPORT,GUY-Tatlin-NY-(1974)-Scribner's-1st ed (u10,f,f dj) 20.00

DAVENPORT,GWEN-Tall Girl's Handbook-GC-1959-Dbldy-8vo-185p-cl bckd bds,drwngs (ee9,dj) 20.00

DAVENPORT,HOMER-My Quest of the Arabian Horse-Lond-1911-Grant Richards-1st Brit ed (j9) 65.00

DAVENPORT,HOMER-My Quest of the Arabian Horse-NY-1909-Dodge-1st ed (f10,few cov spots) 195.00

DAVENPORT,JOHN-Aphrodisiacs and Anti Aphrodisiacs-Lond-1869-priv prtd-154p+7 plts-qtr lea-rare-1st ed (dd3,hng crack,sp pcs missng) 150.00

DAVENPORT,JOHN-Curiositates Eroticae Physiologiae-Lond-1875-priv prtd-216p-qtr lea-1st ed (dd3,rub) 200.00

DAVEY,JOCELYN-Capitol Offense-NY-1956-Knopf-1st Amer ed (g4,f,dj) 15.00

DAVEY,JOCELYN-Capitol Offense-NY-1956-Knopf-auth 1st bk-1st Amer ed (s4,dj) 22.50

DAVEY,K G-Reproduction in Insects-1965-Oliver Boyd-96p-21 figs-1st ed (bb3,f,dj) 20.00

DAVEY,RICHARD-Sultan and His Subjects-Lond-1897-Chapman & Hall-2 vols-buckram,frntis,maps-1st ed (m8,pgs 31-37 removed) 65.00

DAVID,C L-Our Presidents-Ontario-1897-42p-wrps (m1,sl wn) 12.50

DAVID-NEEL,A-Magic and Mystery in Tibet-NY-1958-Univ Bks-8vo-xiv,320p-17 illus-1st ed (aa7,dj) 15.00*

DAVID-NEEL,A-Magic and Mystery in Tibet-NY-1958-Univ Bks-cl-1st ed thus (n8,f,dj) 25.00

DAVIDOFF,ZINO-Connoisseur's Book of the Cigar-NY-(1969)-McGraw Hill-cigar box like cov,e.p. show cigars & inside of box,illus,w/o dj as iss-1st ed (y10) 28.00

DAVIDS,THADDEUS-History of Ink-NY-(1860)-T Davids-sm 8vo-72,4p-orig brwn cl,gilt,a.e.g.,chromolitho half title,17 plts(1 col)-1st ed (t10,sm dmpstn) 200.00

DAVIDSON,ART-Minus 148-NY-1969-218p-16 photos-1st prtg (p10,f,dj) 50.00

DAVIDSON,AVRAM-Joyleg-NY-(1971)-Walker-1st ed (j3,f,dj) 25.00

DAVIDSON,AVRAM-Peregrine:Primus-NY-(1971)-Walker-1st ed (j3,f,dj) 15.00

DAVIDSON,AVRAM-Phoenix and the Mirror-GC-1969-Dbldy-1st ed (k3,f,dj) 15.00

DAVIDSON,DONALD-An Essay and a Bibliography-Nashville-1965-Vanderbilt U Pr-1st ed (cc2,f,dj) 25.00

DAVIDSON,DONALD-An Outland Piper-Bost-1924-HMCO-8vo-dec bds,auth 1st bk-1st ed (v10,vf,lacks dj) 75.00

DAVIDSON,DONALD-Caught Short-1972-Atheneum-1st ed (s7,f,dj) 15.00

DAVIDSON,DONALD-Spyglass, Views & Reviews 1924 to 1930-Nashville-1963-Vanderbilt U Pr-1st ed (y1,dj) 22.50

DAVIDSON,DONALD-Tennessee-NY-1946 & 1948-Rinehart-2 vols-1st ed (y4,f,djs) 125.00

DAVIDSON,ELLIS A-Practical Manual of Housepainting, Graining, Marbling and Sign Writing-Lond-1888-394p-9 col plts,ads-5th ed (ff10) 100.00

DAVIDSON,HAROLD G-Edward Borein, Cowboy Artist-NY-1974-Dbldy-4to-189p-col illus-1st ed (dd4,dj) 30.00

DAVIDSON,HOMER K-Black Jack Davidson-Glendale-1974-273p-illus,fldg map-1st ed (n3,f,dj) 35.00

DAVIDSON,HOMER K-Black Jack Davidson-Glendale-1974-A H Clark-273p-illus,fldg map-1st ed (dd4,dj) 30.00

DAVIDSON,J THAIN-City Youth-NY-1893-291p+ads-cl,dec frnt cov (b1) 20.00

DAVIDSON,K L-Gardens Past and Present-Lond-nd(ca 1915)-232p-dec cov wi pict onlay,14 b&w photo plts,col frntis (x5,sm sp tr,sl fox,soil pgs) 18.00

DAVIDSON,L S-South of Joplin-NY-(1939)-Norton-290p-illus-1st ed (nn6,wn dj) 35.00

DAVIE,O-Naturalist's Manual-Columbus-1882-12mo-127p-cl,engrvngs (y8,stains) 35.00

DAVIE,O-Nest and Eggs of North American Birds-Columbus-1889-8vo-(7),455p-cl,13 plts-4th ed (y8,nbr on sp) 85.00

DAVIE,OLIVER-Methods in the Art of Taxidermy-Columbus-1894-Hann & Adair-150p-90p engrvngs-1st ed (d9) 100.00

DAVIE,W GALSWORTHY-Old Cottages and Farmhouses in Surrey-Lond-1908-Batsford-sm 4to-69p text-g dec grn cl,100 plts (r10,sp fade) 65.00

DAVIES,A MERVYN-Strange Destiny-NY-(1935)-Putnam-8vo-468p-13 illus-1st US ed (dd5,dj) 45.00

DAVIES,A TEGLA-Friends Ambulance Unit: The Story of the F.A.U. in the Second World War 1939 to 1946-(Lond)-(1947)-Allen & Unwin-tan cl,61 photos,6 maps-1st ed (p6) 60.00

DAVIES,CHARLES-Elements of Geometry and Trigonometry...-NY,Chig-(1851)-Barnes-262;62p-cl (k1) 20.00

DAVIES,G-Early History of the Cold Stream Guards-Oxford-1924-160p-blu cl,fldg map,illus-1st ed (b7) 125.00

DAVIES,J-Douglas of the Forests-1981-U of Wash-189p-photos,maps (bb3,f,dj) 20.00

DAVIES,JOHN-History of the Tahitian Mission 1799 to 1830-Cambridge-1961-Hakluyt Soc-8vo-blu cl,fldg frntis,fldg map in rear,21 illus & maps in all (pp1) 85.00

DAVIES,K G-ED.-Northern Quebec and Labrador Journals and Correspondence-Lond-1963-Hudson Bay Rec Soc-8vo-2 fldg maps-Vol.XXIV-1st ed,ltd (dd7,f,dj) 125.00

DAVIES,L P-Paper Dolls-1966-CC-1st Amer ed (s10,dj) 20.00

DAVIES,R E G-Airlines of the United States since 1914-Lond-(1972)-8vo-xiv,746p-cl,frntis,maps,chrts,text illus-1st ed (t2,dj) 40.00

DAVIES,RAYMOND A-Great Mackenzie-Tor-1947-Ryerson Pr-8vo-x,139p-grn cl,99 photos-1st ed (mm8,sl chip dj) 25.00*

DAVIES,ROBERTSON-Diary of Samuel Marchbanks-Tor-1947-Clarke,Irwin-1st ed (pp2,dj sp drknd,sl chip) 75.00*

DAVIES,ROBERTSON-Jig for the Gypsy-Tor-1954-Clarke,Irwin-1st ed (pp2,f,dj sl wn & chip) 75.00*

DAVIES,ROBERTSON-Leaven of Malice-Tor-(1954)-Clarke,Irwin-1st ed (pp2,f,dj) 85.00*

DAVIES,ROBERTSON-Manticore-Lond-1973-1st Brit ed (t5,sl tn dj) 40.00

DAVIES,ROBERTSON-Manticore-NY-1972-1st US ed (p5,f,dj) 40.00

DAVIES,ROBERTSON-Marchbanks' Almanack-Tor-(1967)-M&S-1st ed (pp2,f,sl tn dj) 75.00*

DAVIES,ROBERTSON-Mixture of Frailties-NY-1958-1st US ed (p5,sl chip dj) 60.00

DAVIES,ROBERTSON-Mixture of Frailties-NY-1958-Scribners-1st US ed (f8,f,chip dj) 90.00

DAVIES,ROBERTSON-One Half of Robertson Davies-Tor-1977-Macmlln of Can-8vo-286p (aa7,dj,autg) 45.00*

DAVIES,ROBERTSON-Rebel Angels-NY-(1982)-1st US ed (s5,f,dj) 25.00

DAVIES,ROBERTSON-Rebel Angels-NY-(1982)-Viking-1st US ed (b5,as new in dj) 17.50

DAVIES,ROBERTSON-Rebel Angels-Tor-1981-Macmillan-1st ed (z2,f,f dj) 85.00

DAVIES,ROBERTSON-Table Talk of Samuel Marchbanks-Lond-1951-1st Brit ed (o5,dj sp sl drknd) 75.00

DAVIES,ROBERTSON-Table Talk of Samuel Marchbanks-Tor-1949-Clarke,Irwin-1st ed (q2,sp drknd dj) 295.00

DAVIES,ROBERTSON-Table Talk of Samuel Marchbanks-Tor-1949-Clarke,Irwin-1st ed (z2,f,dj) 200.00

DAVIES,ROBERTSON-Voice From the Attic-Tor-1960-1st Can ed (p5,dj) 90.00

DAVIES,ROBERTSON-Voice from the Attic-Tor-1960-M&S-1st Can ed (pp2,f,dj sl rub) 50.00*

DAVIES,ROBERTSON-World of Wonders-NY-(1976)-Viking-1st US ed (z9,f,dj) 30.00

DAVIES,THURSTON-Anglers Atlas of California-Long Bch-1948-4to-91p+index-wrps,maps (m3) 12.50

DAVIES,VALENTINE-It Happens Every Spring-1949-Farrar Strauss-scarce (ff2,dj) 150.00

DAVIES,WILLIAM H-Collected Poems of ...-NY-1916-190p-bds-1st Amer ed (h1) 15.00

DAVIES,WM-Tropical Pastures-Lond-1966-Faber-215p-cl (x6) 20.00

DAVIS,ANGELA-If They Come in the Morning-NY-(1971)-Third Press-281p-1st prtg so stated (q1,f,sl tn,rub dj) 40.00

DAVIS,ARLON B-Offings and Musing of A. Nutt-Sherman-1937-Courier-249p-ltd to 1000c,nbrd,autg (a9) 45.00

DAVIS,BRITTON-Truth About Geronimo-New Haven-1929-253p-illus,map-Quaife,ed.-1st ed (u7) 45.00

DAVIS,BRITTON-Truth about Geronimo-New Haven-1929-Yale U Pr-xviii+253p-blu cl,plts-1st ed (h2,sl fade sp) 65.00

DAVIS,BURKE-Our Incredible Civil War-NY-1960-HRW-249p-illus-1st ed (o7,f,dj) 25.00

DAVIS,C L-Our Presidents-Ontario-1897-42,(2)p (e1,wrps) 12.50

DAVIS,CAPT W E-Ziba Foote-(New Vienna)-1877-publ by auth-241p-cl (a1,sl wn sp) 40.00

DAVIS,CHARLES G-Built Up Ship Model-Salem-1933-Marine Rsrch Soc-206p+ads-blu cl,photos,plts-1st ed (p8,sl wn) 65.00

DAVIS,CHARLES G-Ship Model Builders Assistant-Salem-1926-Marine Rsrch Soc-275p+ads-blu cl-1st ed (p8,sl wn) 50.00

DAVIS,CHARLES G-Shipping and Craft in Silhouette-Salem-1929-Marine Rsrch Soc-4to-red cl-1st ed (s1) 75.00

DAVIS,CHARLES G-Shipping and Craft in Silhouette-Salem-1929-Marine Rsrch Soc-red cl,102 silhouettes-ltd to 950c (pp1) 95.00

DAVIS,D D-Giant Panda-Chig-1964-4to-339p-cl,frntis,col illus (y8,sl wtrstnd) 125.00

DAVIS,DEERING-Georgetown Houses of the Federal Period 1780 to 1830-1944-Architect Bk Publ-130p-illus (dd9,dj) 25.00

DAVIS,DEERING-Georgetown Houses of the Federal Period-NY-1944-Arch Bk Publ-tall 4to-130p-cl,e.p. map,illus-1st ed (cc10,dj) 60.00

DAVIS,DOROTHY S-Death in the Life-NY-1976-Scribners-1st ed (g4,f,dj) 10.00

DAVIS,DOROTHY S-Death of an Old Sinner-NY-1957-Scribners-1st ed (h4,f,dj wn) 15.00

DAVIS,DOROTHY S-Enemy and Brother-NY-1966-Scribners-1st ed (f4,dj) 12.50

DAVIS,DOROTHY S-Judas Cat-NY-1949-Scribners-auth 1st bk-1st ed (w5,f,laminated dj,sl chip) 45.00

DAVIS,E W-Pioneering with Taconite-St.Paul-1964-Minn Hist Soc-8vo-246p-photos-1st ed (gg5,sl tn dj) 20.00

DAVIS,ELLIS A-ED.-New Encyclopedia of Texas, Historical Encyclopedia of Texas-nd(ca.1936)-Tex Hist Soc-2 vols-photos (a9) 175.00

DAVIS,ERNEST-Forty Years on the Road-Richmond-1954-75p-wrps (c1) 17.50

DAVIS,F HADLAND-Myths and Legends of Japan-Bost-nd(c.1930)-David D Nickerson-cl,col frntis,col illus,one of 1000c,nbrd-1st Amer ed (o8) 30.00

DAVIS,FRANK-How to Collect a Doctor Bill-Newark-1913-98p-1st ed (dd3) 50.00

DAVIS,H E-American Wild Turkey-1949-Samworth-328p+9p ads-yel cl,col frntis,gravures (ee3,vf,sl tn dj) 250.00

DAVIS,H L-Distant Music-NY-1957-Morrow-1st ed (y1,f,sl wn dj) 40.00

DAVIS,H L-Winds of Morning-NY-1952-Morrow-1st ed (hh5,dj) 10.00

DAVIS,H P-ET AL-Plant Life of South West Asia-Edinburgh-1971-Univ Pr-335p-cl,illus,maps (x6,dj) 25.00

DAVIS,HASSOLDT-Jungle and the Damned-NY/Bost-(1952)-DSP/Little,Brown-8vo-306p-16p photos-1st ed (jj5,sl tn dj) 15.00

DAVIS,HASSOLDT-Land of the Eye-NY-(1940)-Holt-8vo-415p-photos-1st ed (jj5,f,dj) 30.00

DAVIS,HASSOLDT-World Without a Roof-NY-(1957)-DSP-8vo-436p-1st ed (jj5,dj) 12.50

DAVIS,HENRY P-Training Your Own Bird Dog-NY-1948-8vo-175p-photos-1st ed (m3,sl chip dj) 17.50

DAVIS,HORACE B-Shoes-NY-(1940)-Int'l (r1) 22.00

DAVIS,HORACE B-Shoes-NY-(1940)-Intern'tl Publ-256p-tan cl (k2,sl wn dj) 30.00

DAVIS,J CHARLES-California Saltwater Fishing-NY-1949-8vo-271p-illus (m3,vf,sl chip dj) 15.00

DAVIS,J CHARLES-Salt Water Fishing on the Pacific Coast-NY-1964-8vo-262p-photos,illus (m3,f,dj) 12.50

DAVIS,J-ED.-Choice and Change-NY-1974-Athlone Pr-8vo-259p-cl-Lond Sch of Econ Mono of Soc Anthro No.50-1st ed (y5,sl wn dj) 30.00

DAVIS,JEFFERSON-Short History of the Confederate States of America-NY-1890-Belford Co-505p-illus-Nevins II,172-1st ed (ee4,innr hngs rnfrcd) 125.00

DAVIS,JOHN-Travels of...In the United States of America, 1798 to 1802-Bost-1910-Bibliophile Soc-2 vols-edit by J V Cheney-Howes D123 (cc4) 95.00

DAVIS,KEITH F-Desire Charnay Expeditionary Photographer-(1981)-UNM Pr-4to-212p wi photos,index-1st ed (t1,f,dj) 40.00

DAVIS,KENNETH S-Hero-GC-1959-Dbldy-roy 8vo-528p-cl,illus e.p.-1st ed (s2,dj) 45.00

DAVIS,KENNETH S-Soldier of Democracy-GC-1945-Dbldy,Doran-566p-cl-1st ed so stated (h1,dj wn,tn) 12.50

DAVIS,L P-What Did I Do Tomorrow-GC-1973-Dbldy-1st US ed (h3,dj) 10.00

DAVIS,LAVINIA R-Reference to Death-NY-1950-Dbldy CC-1st ed (l4,yel pgs,dj) 25.00

DAVIS,LAVINIA-Pony Jungle-GC-1941-Doran-1st ed (h9,dj) 25.00

DAVIS,LYNN-Na Pa`i Ki`i-Honolulu-(1980)-1st ed (t10) 12.50

DAVIS,MARY L-Alaska, The Great Bear's Cub-(1930)-Wilde-314p-1st ed (u8) 12.00

DAVIS,MARY L-Sourdough Gold-Bost-1933-W A Wilde-351p-cl,frntis,fldg map,illus,ports-Smith #2326 (aa2) 40.00*

DAVIS,MARY L-We Are Alaskans-1931-W A Wilde-8vo-335p-1st ed (oo4,sl tn dj) 30.00

DAVIS,MARY L-We Are Alaskans-Bost-1931-335p-frntis,photos-Smith #2328-1st ed (t7,dj) 15.00

DAVIS,MATTHEW L-Memoirs of Aaron Burr-NY-1836-Harper & Bros-2 vols-cl,sp labls,frntis-Howes D126-1st ed (h2,sp yel,cov sl spot,pg fox) 90.00

DAVIS,MICHAEL-Image of Lincoln in the South-Knoxville-(1971)-205p-1st ed (n3,dj) 22.50

DAVIS,OSCAR K-William Howard Taft the Man of the Hour-Phila-(1908)-406p-cl-Miles 896 (g1) 17.50

DAVIS,PARIS M-An Authentick History of the Late War Between the United States and Great Britain-Ithaca-1829-Davis & Sounders-12mo-360p-orig calf,blk labl-Howes D128-1st ed (u3,sl fox) 100.00

DAVIS,RICHARD B-Colonial Southern Bookshelf-Athens-(1979)-(10),140p-1st ed (k9,vf,dj) 10.00

DAVIS,RICHARD H-In the Fog-NY-1901-Russell-illus,F D Steele-1st ed (h4) 15.00

DAVIS,RICHARD H-Our English Cousins-NY-1894-Harper-228p-cl,frontis,33 plts-1st ed (e1,sl wn) 20.00

DAVIS,RICHARD H-West From a Car Window-NY & Lond-1904-242p-cl,illus,Remington (b6) 22.00

DAVIS,ROY E-Darshan-Lakemont-1971-CSA Pr-cl-1st ed (n8,f,dj) 15.00

DAVIS,TECH-Full Fare for a Corpse-NY-1937-Dbldy CC-1st ed (e4,chip dj) 20.00

DAVIS,W C-Orphan Brigade-NY-1980-318p-plts,maps (t7,f,dj) 25.00

DAVIS,W J-Air Conquest-LA-(1930)-8vo-xiv,234p-illus cl,frntis,5p plts,e.p. maps-1st ed (t2,sp fade & sl wn) 25.00

DAVIS,W J-World's Wings-NY-(1927)-8vo-xviii,210p-cl bkd bds wi sp labl,frntis,22p plts-1st ed (t2) 35.00

DAVIS,W W H-El Gringo-NY-1857-432p-gry cl,plts-Howes D139-1st ed (z1,box) 250.00

DAVIS,W W H-El Gringo-Santa Fe-1962-334p-illus (y7,f) 20.00

DAVIS,WALLACE-Corduroy Road-Houston-1951-Anson Jones-282p-photos-1st ed (a9,tn dj) 40.00

DAVIS,WATSON-ET AL-Atomic Bombing-NY-1950-186p-cl (c1,sl wn dj) 15.00

DAVIS,WILLIAM C-Duel Between the First Ironclads-NY-1975-Dbldy-201p-illus-1st ed (o7,f,dj) 20.00

DAVIS,WILLIAM H-Seventy Five Years in California-SF-1967-John Howell Bks-lg 8vo-354p-illus,col fldg plts-ltd to 2500c-Howes D136 (cc4,dj) 65.00

DAVISON,G M-Fashionable Tour in 1825-Saratoga Spgs-1825-G M Davison-12mo-orig qtr lea & mrbld bds (u2,sl wn,fox,new box) 135.00

DAVISON,GRACE L-Gates of Memory-Solvang-(1955)-Santa Ynez Valley News-(viii)+101p-red cl,illus-1st ed (k2,dj,pres cpy) 15.00

DAVISON,VERNE E-Homemade Fishing-Harrisburg-1953-8vo-205p-illus,W Hughes (m3) 12.00

DAVITT,MICHAEL-Boer Fight for Freedom-NY-1902-603p-orng cl,maps,illus-1st ed (gg2) 100.00

DAVY,GYPSY-Himalayan Letters of...and Lady Ba-Bost-1927-lg 8vo-280p-4 fldg maps-1st US ed (o10,f) 95.00

DAVY,M J B-Handbook of the Collections Illustrating Aeronautics - I. Heavier-Than-Air Craft-Lond-1929-roy 8vo-116p-prntd wrps,22p plts (t2,sp damaged wrps) 30.00

DAVY,NORMAN-British Scientific Literature in the Seventeenth Century-Lond-1953-244p-1st ed (dd3,dj) 25.00

DAVY,SIR HUMPHREY-Salmonia, or Days of Fly Fishing-Lond-1828-12mo-273p-orig bds wi pap sp labl-illus-scarce-1st ed (m3,extrnl hngs cracked) 85.00

DAWES,RUFUS R-Service with the Sixth Wisconsin Volunteers-Marietta-1890-Alderman-330p-illus-Nevins I,79-1st ed (bb4) 150.00

DAWSON,CONINGSBY-Auctioning of Mary Angel-NY-1930-Dbldy-emboss cov-1st ed (t4,f,dj) 10.00

DAWSON,E-Texas Wildlife-1955-Banks Upshaw-4to-174p-30 col illus-1st ed (bb3) 23.00

DAWSON,EMMA F-Gracious Visitation-SF-1921-Bk Club of Cal-mrbld cov,deckld paprs-ltd to 300c,nbrd-rare-1st ed (t4) 35.00

DAWSON,FIELDING-Great Day for a Ballgame-1973-Bobbs Merrill-1st ed (m9,f,dj sl rub,sp sunned) 25.00

DAWSON,GEORGE F-Life and Services of Gen John A Logan-Chig-1887-Bedford, Clarke-580p-pict cl,frntis port,illus (v2,few dmpstnd pgs,sl soil) 25.00

DAWSON,GEORGE-Pleasures of Angling with Rod and Reel for Trout and Salmon-NY-1876-Sheldon-8vo-264p-g dec tan cl,illus-1st ed (t1,sl fox) 225.00

DAWSON,GILES E-Elizabethan Handwriting 1500 to 1650-NY-(1966)-Norton-lg 8vo-1st ed (w1,f,f dj) 20.00

DAWSON,J M-Spiritual Conquest of the Southwest-Nashville-1927-180p-illus-1st ed (a9) 50.00

DAWSON,KENNETH-Casts From a Salmon Reel-Lond-nd-12mo-158p-photos-1st ed so stated (m3,sl fade sp) 17.50

DAWSON,KENNETH-From Major to Minor-Lond-1928-4to-289p-illus (m3,f,fray dj) 15.00

DAWSON,KENNETH-Modern Salmon & Sea Trout Fishing-Lond-1938-8vo-191p-photos-1st ed (m3,dj) 20.00

DAWSON,KENNETH-Salmon & Trout in Moorland Streams-Lond-1928-12mo-240p-photos-1st prntng (m3) 25.00

DAWSON,KENNETH-Son of a Gun-Lond-1929-4to-155p-illus,Chas Simpson (m3,vf,dj) 35.00

DAWSON,KENNETH-Two Anglers-Lond-1933-12mo-216p-1st ed (m3,sl fox) 12.50

DAWSON,LIONEL-Sport in War-NY-1937-folio-98p-grn cl,6 col plts (jj2,sp sun) 75.00

DAWSON,MILES M-Ethical Religion of Zoroaster-NY-1931-Macmillan-cl-1st ed (n8) 65.00

DAWSON,NICHOLAS-Narrative of Nicholas "Cheyenne" Dawson-1933-Grabhorn Pr-100p+notes-dec bds,col drwngs,drk brwn dj,ltd to 500c-Rare Amer Ser No.7-1st prtg thus (r8,f,sl chip dj) 150.00

DAWSON,S J-Report on the Exploration of the Country Between Lake Superior and the Red River Settlement...-NY-1968-Greenwood Pr-folio-brwn cl,plts,maps,rprnt of 1859 Toronto ed (mm1,as new) 65.00

DAWSON,W L-Birds of California-San Diego-1923-4to-4 vols-grn fabri bndg wi gulls stmpd on cov & sp,plts-Booklovers' Edition,ltd to 1000c (y8) 325.00

DAWSON,W L-Birds of California-San Diego-1923-So Moulton-4 vols-dec grn cov,photos,col plts-ltd to 1000c,nbrd-"Booklovers' Edition" (e9) 400.00

DAWSON,W L-Birds of Ohio-Columbus-1903-4to-671p-blu buckr,80 col plts-ltd to 1000c (y8,sp fade) 100.00

DAWSON,W L-Birds of Washington...-Seattle-1909-Occidental Publ-2 vols-grn g stmpd mor,t.e.g.,col illus,ltd to 250 sets(of 1250 total)in this format-Author's Ed (w1) 400.00

DAWSON,WARREN-Beginnings: Egypt & Assyria-NY-1930-86p-1st ed (dd3) 45.00

DAY LEWIS,CECIL-Buried Day-NY-(1960)-Harper-1st Amer ed (z8,f,dj) 15.00

DAY LEWIS,CECIL-Christmas Eve-Lond-(1954)-Faber-in envelope,illus,E Ardizzone-1st ed (z8) 22.50

DAY LEWIS,CECIL-Collected Poems 1929 to 1936-Lond-1948-Hogarth Pr-1st ed (z8,f,f dj) 125.00

DAY LEWIS,CECIL-Noah and the Waters-Lond-1936-Hogarth Pr-cl-1st ed (z8,f.e.p. sl mottld) 18.50

DAY LEWIS,CECIL-Time to Dance-Lond-1935-Hogarth Pr-8vo-cl-ltd to 750c-1st ed (jj8,vf,dj) 100.00

DAY,A GROVE-Coronado and the Discovery of SW-NY-(1967)-184p-maps,photos-1st ed (u7,f,dj) 20.00

DAY,A GROVE-Hawaii and Its People-NY-(1955)-DS&P-8vo-338p-cl-1st ed (y5,chip dj) 27.00

DAY,ALBERT M-North American Waterfowl-Harrisburg-1949-8vo-329p-illus,photos-1st ed (m3,vf,dj) 35.00

DAY,ALBERT M-North American Waterfowl-PA-1949-329p-photos (gg3,f,dj) 17.00

DAY,ALLEN-Goddesses in Slacks-NY-1945-House of Field-8p illus by W Pogany-1st ed (dd8,dj) 20.00

DAY,AVANELLE-Spice Cookbook-NY-1964-David White-4to-623p-tan cl,drwngs-3rd prtg (q8,dj) 18.50

DAY,B-Glacier Pilot-NY-1965-346p-photos-4th prtg (o10,f,dj) 22.00

DAY,BUNNY-Crazy Quilt Cookery-1964-Dbldy-156p-rust cl,drwngs-1st ed (q8,dj) 16.50

DAY,CAROLINE B-Study of Some Negro White Families in the United States-Cambridge-1932-Harvard Peabody Mus-4to-xii+127p-orng cl,58 plts-1st ed (j2,dj) 65.00

DAY,DONALD-Will Rogers-NY-(1962)-370p-cl-1st ed (d1,f,sl wn dj) 15.00

DAY,DOROTHY-Long Loneliness-NY-1952-Harper & Bros-cl,illus,F Eichenberg-1st ed (o8,chip dj) 17.50

DAY,HARVEY-Complete Book of Curries-NY-(1966)-Barnes-252p (m6,tattrd dj) 18.00

DAY,HARVEY-Curries of India-Lond-(1955)-Kaye-64p-pict bds-1st ed (q8) 15.00

DAY,IRENE F-Kitchen in the Kasbah-(Lond)-(1976)-Deutsch-155p-brwn cl (q8,dj) 16.50

DAY,J R-More Unusual Railways-Lond-1960-214p-1st ed (n4,f,dj) 20.00

DAY,J R-Railways of Southern Africa-Lond-1963-143p-1st ed (n4,f,dj) 19.00

DAY,J-Hunting & Exploration Adventures of Theodore Roosevelt-NY-1955-431p (gg3,f) 10.00

DAY,JAMES-Maps of Texas, 1527 to 1900-Austin-1964-178p-grn cl wi labls-scarce-1st ed (jj1) 100.00

DAY,JAMES-Maps of Texas-Austin-1964-178p-cl wi labls,ltd ed-1st ed (f9) 75.00

DAY,JAMES-Texas Indian Papers-Austin-1959 thru 1961-Tex St Libr-5 vols-(incl rare vol.5 spplmnt)-Basic Tex Bks 219-1st ed (a9) 600.00

DAY,LARAINE-Day with the Giants-1952-Dbldy-1st ed (p7,dj) 30.00

DAY,LOUIS F-Windows: a Book About Stained and Painted Glass-Lond-1909-Batsford-419p-257 illus-3rd ed (cc8,sl scuff,fray) 125.00

DAY,SARAH J-Man on a Hill Top-Phila-(1931)-319p-cl (b1,f,dj) 20.00

DAY,STELLA-100 Years of History of Millard County-Provo-1951-808p-photos (t7,f) 40.00

DAY,SUSAN DE FOREST-Cruise of the Scythian in the West Indies-Lond-1899-F Tennyson Neely-8vo-299p-dec blu cl,b&w photos (nn1,soil,fade) 30.00

DAYTON,EDSON C-Dakota Days-Clifton Spgs-1937-128p-map,plt-ltd to 300c,nbrd-Howes D165-1st ed (gg4) 500.00

DAYTON,ELDOROUS L-Walter Reuther-NY-1958-Devon-Adair-280p (r1,dj edge tn) 15.00

DAYTON,FRED E-Steamboat Days-NY-(1939)-Tudor Publ-436p (cc4) 35.00

DAYTON,FRED E-Steamboat Days-NY-1925-Stokes-436p-tiss guard col frntis,86 illus (p8) 55.00

DAYTON,WILLIAM L-Historical Sketch of the Trenton Academy, Read at Centennial Anniversary of its Foundation...-Trenton-1881-43p-prtd wrps (aa6,soil,chip cor) 40.00

DAYTON,WM-Important Western Browse Plants-Wash-GPO/USDA-213p-wrps,illus (x6) 15.00

DAZAI,OSAMU-Setting Sun-NY-1956-New Directions-1st ed (g8,f,dj) 35.00

DE AMICIS,EDMONDO-Heart of Boyhood-Racine-(1918)-Whitman-198p-cl wi pict pasteon,8 col plts,24 b&w,A Carsey (r3) 35.00

DE ANDREA,WILLIAM L-Five O'Clock Lightning-1982-St.Martin's-1st ed (s10,dj) 12.50

DE ANDREA,WILLIAM L-Killed in the Ratings-NY-1978-Harcourt-1st ed (g4,f,dj) 15.00

DE ANGELI,MARGUERITE-Thee, Hannah-NY-1940-Dbldy,Doran-sq 8vo-unpgd-col & b&w illus-1st ed (nn10,dj) 40.00

DE ANGELI,MARGUERITE-Yonie Wondernose-GC-1944-Dbldy,Doran-sq 4to-cl bkd pict bds,col & b&w illus,auth-1st ed (s3,sl wn dj) 50.00

DE ARMENT,ROBERT K-Bat Masterson-Norman-(1979)-U of Okla Pr-441p-illus-1st ed (gg4,dj) 30.00

DE BARANT,BLANCHE Z-Cuban Cookery-Havana-nd(ca.1935)-lg 16mo-158p-blk cl (q8) 22.50

DE BEAUVOIR,SIMONE-Brigitte Bardot and the Lolita Syndrome-NY-(1960)-Reynal-oblng 8vo-37p+87 photos-pict wrps-scarce-1st US ed (oo7,sl wn) 75.00

DE BEAUVOIR,SIMONE-Djamila Boupacha-NY-1962-Macmillan-1st US ed (x9,f,sl rub dj) 20.00

DE BEAUVOIR,SIMONE-Force of Circumstance-NY-(1965)-Putnam-1st US ed (f3,f,dj) 20.00

DE BEAUVOIR,SIMONE-Long March-Cleve,NY-(1958)-World-8vo-513p-1st ed (oo7,sl soil dj) 65.00

DE BEAUVOIR,SIMONE-Mandarins-Cleve-(1956)-World-silv stmpd red bds & blu cl,ltd to 500c,autg-1st ed (ee2,f,box) 150.00

DE BEAUVOIR,SIMONE-Marquis De Sade-NY-(1953)-Grove-1st ed (b10,dj) 25.00

DE BEAUVOIR,SIMONE-Prime of Life-1962-World-1st Amer ed (m9,f,dj sp sl sunned) 25.00

DE BECKER,J E-Sexual Life of Japan-NY-nd-Amer Anthro Soc-386p-yel cl,illus-3rd ed (c3,lacks dj) 95.00

DE BEER,G R-Development of the Vertebrate Skull-1937-Oxford Univ-552p-143 plts (bb3,f,dj) 70.00

DE BETHEL,DAVID-Bouquet Garni Good Dishes from La Belle France-(1939)-Medici Soc-54p-dec bds,illus-1st prtg (q8) 16.50

DE BOTH,JESSIE-It's Easy to be a Good Cook-(1951)-Garden City-254p-grn cl-1st prtg (q8,dj) 12.50

DE BOTH,JESSIE-Modern Household Encyclopedia-Chig-1946-Ferguson & Assoc-339p-red bds (m6) 35.00

DE BROGLIE,MAURICE-X Rays-Lond-(1925)-Methuen-xiv+204p-blu cl,7 plts-1st ed (a2,dj sl wn & fox) 65.00

DE BRUNHOFF,JEAN-Babar and Father Christmas-Lond-1947-Methuen-folio-unpgd-cl/pict bds-3rd Brit prtg (nn10,cov wn) 65.00

DE BUNSEN,VICTORIA-Soul of a Turk-Lond-1910-John Lane the Bodley Head-cl,illus-1st ed (m8) 65.00

DE BUSSIGNY,HENRY-Equitation-Bost-1922-Houghton Mifflin-1st ed (h9) 38.00

DE CAMP,L SPRAGUE-Castle of Iron-NY-1950-Gnome Pr-1st ed (v5,f,dj) 75.00

DE CAMP,L SPRAGUE-Continent Makers & Other Tales of the Viagens-NY-(1953)-Twayne-1st ed (a5,f,sl wn dj) 40.00

DE CAMP,L SPRAGUE-ED.-Conan Grimoire-Balt-1972-Mirage-1st ed (g3,f,dj) 45.00

DE CAMP,L SPRAGUE-Genus Homo-Reading-1950-Fantasy Pr-1st ed (b10,f,dj sl wn & sp fade) 85.00

DE CAMP,L SPRAGUE-Glory That Was-NY-(1960)-Avalon-1st ed (a5,f,dj) 60.00

DE CAMP,L SPRAGUE-Golden Wind-GC-1969-Dbldy-1st ed (v5,sl sun,dj sl wn) 25.00

DE CAMP,L SPRAGUE-Lovecraft: A Biography-Lond-1976-New Engl Libr-1st Brit ed (v5,f,f dj) 25.00

DE CAMP,L SPRAGUE-Rogue Queen-GC-1951-Dbldy-1st ed (a5,f,sl wn,sp fade dj) 85.00

DE CAMP,L SPRAGUE-Solomon's Stone-NY-(1957)-Avalon Bks-1st ed (b10,f,dj sp sl fade) 75.00

DE CAMP,L SPRAGUE-Tales From Gavagan's Bar-NY-(1953)-Twayne-1st ed (a5,dj sp sl chip) 30.00

DE CAMP,L SPRAGUE-Tower of Zanid-NY-(1958)-Avalon-1st ed (bb1,f,dj) 75.00

DE CAMP,L SPRAGUE-Undesired Princess-LA-1951-Fantasy Publ-1st ed (b10,sl chip dj sp) 65.00

DE CAMP,L SPRAGUE-Wall of Serpents-NY-(1960)-Avalon-1st ed (bb1,f,dj) 150.00

DE CAUX,LEN-Labor Radical-Bost-1970-Beacon-548p (r1,dj) 18.00

DE CHAMBRUN,CLARA L-Shadows Lengthen-NY-1949-296p-cl-1st ed (l1,sl wn dj) 15.00

DE COCK,LILIANE-Ansel Adams-Bost-1972-NYGS-1st ed (w5,f,f dj) 75.00

DE COU,MAY A-Destiny-Cin-1898-Editor Publ Co-305p-cl-Wright 1456 (l1) 30.00

DE FILIPPI,FILIPPO-Ruwenzori-NY-1908-Dutton-403p-32 plts,5 maps-1st US ed (q10,ex-libr) 425.00

DE FOREST,JOHN W-Union Officer in the Reconstruction-1948-Yale-211p-1st ed (dd9,wn,wn dj) 30.00

DE FOREST,JOHN W-Union Officer in the Reconstruction-New Haven-1948-Yale U Pr-211p-1st ed (o7,soil dj) 40.00

DE FOREST,JOHN W-Volunteer's Adventure-New Haven-1946-Yale U Pr-237p-frntis port,facs,maps-2nd prtg (o7,chip dj) 35.00

DE GOUY,LOUIS P-Ice Cream Desserts for Every Occasion-(1938)-Hastings Hs-283p-tan cl-1st ed (q8,sl discol pgs) 15.00

DE GOUY,LOUIS P-Oyster Book-(1951)-Greenberg-175p-grn cl,photos-1st prtg (q8,dj) 20.00

DE GOUY,LOUIS-Derrydale Game Cookbook-NY-1950-8vo-308p-reprnt (m3,f,dj) 25.00

DE GOYLER,E-Bibliography on the Petroleum Industry-College Sta-1944-Ag & Mech Coll of Tex-730p-wrps (ee10,f) 40.00

DE GROOT,ROY A-Feasts for All Seasons-(1966)-Knopf-4to-750p+33p index,dec tan cl,drwngs (q8,dj) 25.00

DE HAURANNE,ERNEST D-Frenchman in Lincoln's America-Chig-1974-Lakeside Classic-2 vols-illus-1st Amer ed (n3) 30.00

DE HEVESY,ANDRE-Discoverer-NY-1928-Macaulay-8vo-285p-blu cl,dec e.p.,illus (dd7,gilt fade,dj fade & wn) 35.00

DE HUFF,ELIZABETH W-Blue Wings Flying-(Reading)-(1977)-57 & 3p-illus,Sierra-1st ed (v7,f,dj) 20.00

DE JONG,DOLA-Level Land-NY-1943-Scribner's-164p-bds,b&w illus,J Hoowig-1st ed (s3,dj) 15.00

DE KORNE,JAMES B-Aspen Art in the New Mexico Highlands-Santa Fe-1970-71p-photos (u7,f) 15.00

DE KORNE,JOHN C-ED.-Navaho and Zuni for Christ-Grand Rapids-1947-208p-illus (v7,lacks fr f.e.p.) 15.00

DE KRUIF,PAUL-Hunger Fighters-NY-(1928)-Harcourt Brace-8vo-376p-illus-1st ed (gg5,dj) 25.00

DE KUBINYI,VICTOR-As We Are-NY-1929-Stokes-8vo-unpgd-63 plts-1st ed (ee5,dj chip,sl tn) 30.00

DE LA CIERVA,J-Wings of Tomorrow-np-(1931)-Brewer,Warren & Putnam-8vo-284p-cl,frntis,30p plts,illus e.p.-1st ed (t2,chip dj) 125.00

DE LA MARE,WALTER-Listeners and Other Poems-NY-1916-1st ed (s5,dj) 30.00

DE LA MARE,WALTER-Magic Jacket-NY-(1962)-Knopf-277p-cl,illus,P Kennedy (s3,f,dj) 30.00

DE LA MARE,WALTER-Peacock Pie-Lond-(1946)-Faber & Faber-8vo-107p-pict cl,b&w drwngs,Ardizzone-1st ed thus (s3,tattrd dj) 45.00

DE LA MARE,WALTER-Selection From His Writings-Lond-1966-Faber-1st ed (t4,f,dj) 15.00

DE LA MARE,WALTER-Winged Chariot-NY-1951-Viking-8vo-160p-1st US ed-ee5 (dd5,tn dj) 10.00

DE LA RHUE,T-Spanish Trails to California-Caldwell-1937-Caxton Pr-285p-e.p. maps-1st ed (cc4) 35.00

DE LA TORRE,LILLIAN-Dr.Sam: Johnson, Detector-NY-1946-Knopf-1st ed (w9,f,dj) 45.00

DE LA TORRE,LILLIAN-Heir of Douglas-NY-1952-Knopf-1st ed (z9,f,dj) 15.00

DE LA VEGA,GARCILASO-Florida of the Inca-Austin-1951-U of Tex-lg 8vo-xlv,655p-1st ed (o2,rub dj) 30.00

DE LAUBENFELS,D J-Mapping the World's Vegetation-1975-Syracuse Univ-246p-38 photos,28 flora maps-1st ed (bb3,f,dj) 20.00

DE LEEUW,HENDRIK-Holland: Crossroads of the Zuider Zee-Phila-(1938)-Lippincott-8vo-377p-1st ed (jj5,sp chip dj) 20.00

DE LEON,DANIEL-?What Means This Strike?...-NY-1903-NY Labor News Co-31p+ads-wrps (f1,sl wn) 15.00

DE LINT,J G-Atlas of the History of Medicine, Anatomy-NY-1926-folio-96p-199 illus-1st ed (dd3) 200.00

DE LONG,EMMA-ED.-Voyage of the Jeanette-Bost-1884-Houghton Mifflin-thick 8vo-2 vols-dec cl,maps,ports,illus-1st ed (y4) 200.00

DE MIERRE,H C-Long Voyage-NY-(1963)-Walker-8vo-306p-20 illus incl fldg sheet of plans,gear-1st US ed (cc5,f,dj) 20.00

DE MILLE,JAMES-Strange Manuscript Found in a Copper Cylinder-NY-1888-Harper & Bros-grn cl wi gold lttrng,illus by G Gaul-1st ed (k8) 75.00

DE MORGAN,AUGUSTUS-Budget of Paradoxes-Chig-1915-Open Court-2 vols,red cl-2nd ed,but 1st Amer ed (l2) 75.00

DE MORGAN,WILLIAM-Old Madhouse-1919-Holt-1st Amer ed (s10,tn dj) 35.00

DE OCA,M-Hummingbirds and Orchids of Mexico-1963-Editorial Fournier-folio-34p text-59p col plts-ltd to 1500c in Engl (bb3,cors bump,dj rprd) 165.00

DE PACKMAN,ANA B-Early California Hospitality-Fresno-1952-Acad Libr Guild-182p-dec tan cl,illus,prtd glassine dj-1st ed (q8,few creased pgs,dj,pres) 50.00

DE PAOLA,TOMIE-Clown of God-NY-(1978)-HBJ-4to-unpgd-dec cl,col illus-1st ed (r3,f,dj) 25.00

DE POURTALES,COUNT-On Western Tour with Washington Irving-Norman-(1968)-U of Okla Pr-96p-illus-1st ed (dd4,dj) 20.00

DE PROFT,MELANIE-ED.-American Family Cookbook-Chig-(1974)-Culinary Arts Inst-4to-800p-pict bds,16 col photos-rvsd ed (q8,f,dj) 17.50

DE PUY,HENRY W-Ethan Allen and the Green Mountain Heroes of '76-Buffalo-1853-Phinney-12mo-xvii,428p-emboss cov,frntis engrvngs-Howes D265-1st ed (n2,cov dull,sp sl fade) 40.00

DE QUINCEY,THOMAS-Recollections of the Lake Poets-Lond-1948-J Lehmann-1st ed in book form (kk5,dj tn) 70.00

DE REGNIERS,BEATRICE-Child's Book of Dreams-NY-(1947)-Harcourt,Brace-pict cl,b&w illus,B Sokol (s3,f,dj) 15.00

DE REGNIERS,BEATRICE-Something Special-NY-(1958)-Harcourt,Brace-cl,line drwngs,I Haas-1st US ed (s3,f,dj) 30.00

DE RICCI,SEYMOUR-English Collectors of Books & Manuscripts(1530-1930) and Their Marks of Ownership-Lond-1960-Holland Pr (w1,f,f dj) 35.00

DE ROOS,WILLY-North West Passage-Camden-(1980)-Int'l Marine-8vo-207p-15 illus,3 maps-1st US ed (jj5,vf,vf dj) 12.50

DE ROPP,ROBERT S-Science and Salvation-NY-1962-St.Martin's-cl-1st ed (n8,f,dj) 15.00

DE ROPP,ROBERT S-Warrior's Way-Lond-1980-Allen & Unwin-cl,frntis-1st Brit ed (o8,f,dj) 45.00

DE SAINT-AMAND,IMBERT-Famous Women of the French Court-NY-(1893 to 1902)-Scribner's-19 vols-blu cl,frntis (gg6,cov wn) 135.00

DE SALIS,MRS-Gardening A La Mode Vegetables-Lond-1895-Longmans-119p-papr cov bds-scarce (x6,sp rub) 20.00

DE SCHAUENSEE,R M-Guide to the Birds of South America-Wynnewood-1970-8vo-(1),470p-cl,50 plts(31 col)-1st ed (y8,3p laid in,dj) 135.00

DE SHAZO,EDITH-Everett Shinn 1876 to 1953-NY-1974-Clarkson Potter-4to-236p-red cl sp,blk bds,b&w & col illus (r10,f,f dj) 40.00

DE SOUSA,BARETTO-Principles of Equitation-NY-1929-Dutton (h9) 18.00

DE SOUZA,BARETTO-Horseback Riding Made Easy-NY-1935-Dutton-1st ed (h9,dj) 25.00

DE TERRE,H-Humboldt-1955-Knopf-386p-illus,maps-1st ed (bb3,tn dj) 30.00

DE TOLNAY,CHARLES-Hieronymus Bosch-NY-1966-Reynal-4to-312p-wht cl,b&w & col illus (r10,f dj) 45.00

DE VERE,M SCHELE-Americanisms-NY-1872-Scribner's-685p+ads-terra cotta cl-1st ed (k2) 35.00

DE VIGHNE,HARRY C-Time of My Life-Phila-1942-Lippincott-336p-Arctic Bibl #3927 (k10) 20.00*

DE VILLIERS,S J A-Cook and Enjoy It-(Capetown)-1968-546p-grn cl,col & b&w photos-2nd ed,rvsd & enlgd (q8,dj) 20.00

DE VOL,E T-Farmer's Practical Treatise on the Fermentation, Distillation & General Manufacture of Alcohol-Omaha-(1921)-16mo-68p-blk cl-1st ed (q8) 25.00

DE VRIES,HUGO-Intracellular Pangenesis Including a Paper on Fertilization and Hybridization-Chig-1910-270p-1st Engl transl (dd3) 100.00

DE VRIES,HUGO-Plant Breeding-Chig-1907-Open Court Publ-xvi+360p+ads-red cl,t.e.g.,114 illus-1st ed (j2,sp tip wn) 90.00

DE VRIES,LEONARD-Flowers of Delight-Tor-1965-McClelland & Stewart-232p-pict cl,frntis,illus-1st ed (dd10,f,dj) 65.00

DE WAAL,RONALD B-World Bibliography of Sherlock Holmes and Dr.Watson-Bost-1974-NYGS-1st ed (k4,sp fade,sl wn box) 35.00

DE ZAVALA,ADINA-History and Legends of the Alamo and Other Missions...-S.A.-1917-publ by auth-219p-wrps,photos-1st ed (a9) 75.00

DEACOCK,ANTONIA-No Purdah in Padam-Lond-1960-206p-11 plts-1st ed (o10,f,dj) 30.00

DEAK,ISTVAN-Lawful Revolution-NY-1979-Columbia U Pr-8vo-415p-21 illus,6 maps-1st ed (cc5,f,dj) 20.00

DEAL,ALONZO,SR.-Locomotive Operation, Questions & Answers...-1918-Deal-12mo-346p-cl,illus (nn7,sl rub) 42.00

DEAN,ABNER-Abner Dean's Naked People-NY-1963-Stein & Day-207p+1 loose orig drwng,oblng blu cl,brn backstrip,illus,ltd to 1000c (b6,as new in box) 18.00

DEAN,AMBER-Collectors' Item-1953-CC-1st ed (s10,brwng pgs,dj chip) 12.50

DEAN,ROBERT G-Body Was Quite Cold-NY-1951-Dutton-1st ed (g4,f,dj) 20.00

DEAN,ROBERT G-Case of Joshua Locke-NY-1951-Dutton-1st ed (g4,f,sl wn dj) 20.00

DEAN,ROBERT G-Layoff-NY-1942-Scribners-1st ed (g4,f,sl wn dj) 35.00

DEAN,ROBERT G-What Gentleman Strangles a Lady?-NY-1936-Dbldy CC-1st ed (f4,rprd dj) 17.50

DEAN,SARA-Travers, a Story of the San Francisco Earthquake-(Racine)-(1923)-Western Prntng & Litho-287p-cl-no col illus as promised on t.p.-orig publ 1907 (j1) 12.50

DEANE,CHARLES W-Phonetic Reader-NY-1896-Morse Co.-165p-cl,illus (k1) 15.00

DEANE,DOROTHY N-Sierra Railway-1960-Howell North-181p-photos-1st ed (d3,dj) 25.00

DEANE,DOROTHY N-Sierra Railway-Berkeley-1960-Howell North-(x)+181p-crm cl,photos-1st ed (mm10,dj) 30.00

DEARBORN,L S F-Mayflower, Pilgrim Pioneers-Seattle-1910-Lindsay Publ-143+(3)p-oblng blu wrps,photos,Alaska-Yukon-Pacific Expo (b6,autg) 20.00

DEARBORNE,FREDERICK-American Homeopathy in the World War-Chig-1923-447p-1st ed (dd3,ex-libr) 25.00

DEBARTHE,JOE-Life & Adventures of Frank Grouard, Chief of Scouts, USA-St.Joseph-1894-Combe-cl,photos-Howes D183-Six Guns 574-1st ed (pp9,rbnd) 250.00

DEBARTHE,JOE-Life and Adventures of Frank Grouard-Norman-(1958)-U of Okla Pr-268p-illus,maps-Howes D183 (ee4,dj) 45.00

DEBARTHE,JOE-Life and Adventures of Frank Grouard-Norman-(1958)-U of Okla-(28),268p-cl,maps,illus,(orig prtd in 1894)-1st prtg thus (v1,dj) 50.00

DEBARTHE,JOSEPH-Answer-(Marion)-(1928)-"The Answer" Publishers-238p-cl-many pgs prntd on recto only (e1) 150.00

DEBO,ANGIE-ED.-Cowman's Southwest Being the Reminiscences of Oliver Nelson-Glendale-1953-Arthur H Clark Co-343p-cl,photos-1st ed (w3,vf) 95.00

DEBO,ANGIE-Prairie City-NY-1944-245; viii p-cl-1st ed so stated (b1,sl wn dj) 15.00

DEBUIGNE,GERARD-Larousse Dictionary of Wines of the World-Lond-(1976)-Hamlyn-4to-272p-red cl,col plts & maps-1st Brit ed (q8,dj) 30.00

DEBYE,PETER-Polar Molecules-NY-1929-Chemical Catlg Co-172p-maroon cl,33 text figs-1st ed (l2) 75.00

DECKER,AMELIA S-That Ancient Trail-(np)-1942-151p-cl,illus (aa6) 40.00

DECKER,GEORGE C-Bows & Arrows for Boys-Mlwk-1930-8vo-48p-wrps,photos (m3) 20.00

DECOU,GEORGE-Historic Rancocas-(Moorestown)-(1949)-ix,269p-cl,plts (aa6) 45.00

DECOU,GEORGE-Moorestown and Her Neighbors-Phila-(1929)-ix,146p-cl,plts (aa6) 35.00

DEDERA,DON-Navajo Rugs-Flagstaff-1975-114p-pict stiff wrps,col & b&w illus-1st ed (n10,f) 15.00

DEDIJER,VLADIMIR-Beloved Land-NY-1961-S&S-8vo-382p-20 illus-1st ed (jj5,f,dj) 12.50

DEEPING,J B-Evenings Entertainments-Lond-1817-N Hailes-sm 8vo-viii,338p+2p ads-lea,dec sp,frntis,3p engrvngs-3rd ed (bb7,sl shaken,wn) 35.00*

DEEPING,WARWICK-Corn in Egypt-NY-1941-Knopf-1st ed (x1,f,sl tn dj) 25.00

DEFENBACH,BYRON-Red Heroines of the Northwest-Caldwell-1930-303p-frntis,illus (t7,dj) 25.00

DEFORD,MIRIAM A-Elsewhere, Elsewhen, Elsehow-NY-(1971)-1st ed (bb10,f,dj) 25.00

DEFOREST,JOHN W-History of the Indians of Connecticut from the Earliest Known Period to 1850-Hartford-1851-Wm Jas Hamersley-6p engrvngs,fldg map-1st ed (p6,rebckd,restored,sl fox) 150.00

DEFOREST,JOHN W-History of the Indians of Connecticut from the Earliest Known Period-Hartford-1852-509p-lea & mrbld bds,fldg map (t7) 45.00

DEFOREST,JOHN W-Union Officer in the Reconstruction-New Haven-1948-Yale U Pr-211p-1st ed (v2,soil dj) 40.00

DEGOLYER,E-Journey of Three Englishmen Across Texas in 1568-El Paso-1947-Peripatetic Pr-illus by J Cisneros-ltd to 235c,all rag papr wi laurel dj (a9,dj) 500.00

DEGRAFF,E V-School-Room Guide...-Syracuse-1878-457p-cl-2nd ed,revsd (k1) 22.50

DEGREGORIO,GEORGE-Joe DiMaggio-1981-Stein & Day-1st ed (p7,dj) 10.00

DEGROOT,IRENE-ED.-Sailing Ships-NY-1980-Viking-284p-blk cl,250 engrvngs & etchngs-1st Amer ed (nn1,dj) 75.00

DEIGHTON,LEN-Airshipwreck-Lond-1978-Cape-illus,wi special postcard laid in-1st ed (s4,f,dj) 35.00

DEIGHTON,LEN-An Expensive Place to Die-NY-1967-Putnam-1st US ed (f4,dj) 10.00
DEIGHTON,LEN-Basic French Cooking-Lond-(1979)-Cape-oblng 8vo-222p-grn cl,illus-1st ed (q8,dj) 20.00
DEIGHTON,LEN-Billion Dollar Brain-Lond-1966-Cape-silv foil dj-1st ed (z2,f,dj sl soil,creased) 100.00
DEIGHTON,LEN-Billion Dollar Brain-Lond-1966-J Cape-1st ed (w9,f,dj nick & sl tn) 85.00
DEIGHTON,LEN-Declarations of War-Lond-1971-J Cape-1st ed (w9,f,dj) 65.00
DEIGHTON,LEN-Funeral in Berlin-Lond-1964-Cape-1st ed (z2,f,dj sp brwnd) 125.00
DEIGHTON,LEN-Funeral in Berlin-NY-1965-Putnam-1st US ed (g4,f,sl soil dj) 20.00
DEIGHTON,LEN-Horse Under Water-NY-1968-Putnam-1st US ed (g4,f,dj) 20.00
DEIGHTON,LEN-SS-GB-Lond-1978-Cape-1st ed (f4,f,dj) 15.00
DEIGHTON,LEN-XPD-NY-1981-Knopf-1st US ed (g4,f,dj) 10.00
DEIGHTON,LEN-Yesterday's Spy-Lond-1975-Cape-1st ed (q4,f,dj) 35.00
DEIGNAN,H G-Type Specimens of Birds in U S Nat'l Museum-Wash-1961-8vo-718p-wrps (y8) 40.00
DEIGNAN,HERBERT-Checklist of the Birds of Thailand-Wash-1963-USNM Bull 226-263p-orig wrps (b9,f) 30.00
DEINDORFER,ROBERT G-Incompleat Angler-Lond-1977-8vo-155p-illus (m3,as new in dj) 10.00
DEINDORFER,ROBERT G-Positive Fishing-NY-1981-8vo-205p-illus-1st ed (m3,vf,dj) 10.00
DEITE,DR C-Practical Treatise on the Manufacture of Perfumery...-Phila-1892-H C Baird-358p+ads-brwn cl,28 text illus-1st Amer ed (g2,sl soil) 60.00
DEKNATEL,F B-Edvard Munch-Bost-1950-Inst Contemp Art-ltd ed-1st ed (h10,dj) 40.00
DEKORNE,JOHN C-ED.-Navaho and Zuni for Christ-Grand Rapids-1947-208p-pict cl,illus-1st ed (t7) 15.00
DEL REY,LESTER-Cave of Spears-NY-1957-Knopf-206p-cl,b&w illus,F Nicholas-1st ed (s3,dj) 15.00
DEL REY,LESTER-Early Del Rey-GC-1975-Dbldy-1st ed (a5,dj) 15.00
DEL REY,LESTER-ED.-Best Science Fiction of the Year-NY-1974-Dutton-1st ed (h3,f,dj) 15.00
DEL VECCHIO,JOHN M-13th Valley-NY-(1982)-Bantam Bks-1st ed (u10,f,f dj) 35.00
DELABARRE,EDMUND B-Dighton Rock-NY-1928-Walter Neale-xvi+369p-grn cl,108 illus-1st ed (m2,sl speckld sp,dj) 35.00
DELACOUR,J-Birds of Maylasia-NY-1947-8vo-382p-cl,drwngs (y8,ex-libr) 35.00
DELACOUR,J-Pheasants of the World-1984-Spur-4to-395p-18 col & 15 b&w plts,maps-2nd rvsd ed (bb3,f,dj) 95.00
DELACOUR,J-Pheasants of the World-Surrey-1977-Spur Publ,Wrld Phsnt Assn-395p-32 plts by J C Harrison-2nd ed (c9,as new in dj) 75.00
DELACOUR,J-Waterfowl of the World-Lond-1954 to 59-8vo-3 vols(of 4)-cl,maps (y8,autg) 225.00
DELACOUR,J-Waterfowl of the World-Lond-1954 to 64-8vo-4 vols-cl,66 col plts,Scott,maps (y8,lt scuff,dj sl chip) 400.00
DELACOUR,J-Waterfowl of the World-NY-1973-Arco-4 vols-glassine wrps,col plts by Scott,maps-5th impr (c9,as new) 200.00
DELAFIELD,FRANCIS-Hand Book of Post Mortem Examinations and of Morbid Anatomy-NY-1872-376p-1st ed (g10,ex-libr) 75.00
DELAMER,EUGENE S-Kitchen Garden-Lond-nd(ca.1870)-Routledge-16mo-184p-brn cl (u6) 75.00
DELAMOTTE,F-Signist's Book of Modern Alphabets plain and ornamental,ancient and mediaeval...with numerals...-Chig-(1906)-Frederick J Drake-unpgd-cl (j1) 17.50
DELAND,MARGARET-An Old Chester Secret-NY-(1920)-Harper-8vo-126p-stmpd cl-1st ed (w6,dj) 45.00
DELAND,MARGARET-Voice-NY-1912-Harper-8vo-85p-stmpd bndg-1st ed (w6) 35.00
DELANGE,JACQUELINE-Art and Peoples of Black Africa-NY-1974-Dutton-8vo-354p-wrps,illus-1st ed (y5) 25.00
DELANO,ALONZO-Across the Plains and Among the Diggins-NY-1936-Wilson Erickson-sm folio-192p-photos-Howes D230 (bb4) 50.00
DELANO,ALONZO-Old Block's Sketch Book-Santa Ana-1947-Fine Arts Pr-89p-cl,drwngs,Chas Nahl (w3,f) 15.00
DELAY,JEAN-Youth of Andre Gide-Chig-1963-UC Pr-1st ed (z9,f,dj) 12.50
DELAY,PETER J-History of Yuba and Sutter Counties, California...-LA-1924-Hist Rec Co-1328p-3/4 lea,illus-scarce-Six Guns 579-1st ed (bb4) 250.00
DELBANCO,NICHOLAS-Grasse 3/23/66-Phila-1967-1st ed (q5,sl rub dj) 20.00
DELCROIX,EUGENE-Patios, Stairways and Iron Lace Balconies of Old New Orleans-New Orleans-1941-thin 4to-94p-illus wrps,41 photos-3rd prtg (r10) 25.00
DELDERFIELD,R F-Seven Men of Gascony-NY-(1973)-1st ed (y7,dj) 15.00
DELDERFIELD,R F-Seven Men of Gascony-NY-(1973)-S&S-1st ed (b5,f,dj) 12.50
DELEEUW,HENDRIK-Java Jungle Tales-Lond-1956-Arco Publ-cl,illus,K Wiese-1st Amer ed (n8) 15.00
DELEON,T C-Joseph Wheeler-Kennesaw-1960-142p-frntis,photos (t7,f) 22.50
DELEUZE,J P F-Practical Instruction-Lond-1845-J Cleave-12mo-(ii)+270+(2)p-patterned Victorian cl-1st Brit ed (y9,tn lower sp,labl chip) 125.00
DELEVOY,RBT L-Symbolists & Symbolism-1978-Skira/Rizzoli-folio-83 tip in col & 228 b&w plts (h10,dj) 85.00
DELGER,FRANK-Joseph Culbertson, Famous Indian Scout who Served Under General Miles in 1876 thru 1895-1958-103p-stiff pict wrps-scarce-1st ed (t7) 85.00
DELICACIES BY THURSDAY CLUB MEMBERS-San Diego-1927-160p-red wrps (q6,sl spot wrps) 35.00
DELILLO,DON-Americana-1971-Houghton,Mifflin-auth 1st bk-1st ed (x2,f,dj) 150.00
DELILLO,DON-Americana-Bost-1971-Houghton Mifflin-auth 1st bk-1st ed (bb1,dj) 125.00
DELILLO,DON-End Zone-Bost-1972-Houghton Mifflin-1st ed (s1,f,dj) 45.00
DELILLO,DON-Great Jones Street-(Lond)-(1974)-A Deutsch/Wildwood Hs-1st Brit ed (bb1,f,dj) 30.00
DELILLO,DON-Great Jones Street-Bost-1973-Houghton Mifflin-1st ed (v5,f,dj) 35.00
DELILLO,DON-Names-NY-1982-Knopf-1st ed (b5,as new in dj) 20.00
DELILLO,DON-Ratner's Star-NY-1976-1st US ed (n5,f,f dj) 30.00
DELILLO,DON-Ratner's Star-NY-1976-Knopf-1st ed (a10,f,dj) 25.00
DELINEATOR HOME INSTITUTE-Delineator Cook Book-NY-(1928)-Butterick Publ-788p+6p publ ads,photos-rvsd by Rose & Van Renssalaer (q8) 25.00

DELL'ISOLA,FRANK-Merton: A Bibliography-(1975)-KSU Pr-1st ed (ee2) 40.00

DELL'ISOLA,FRANK-Thomas Merton-Kent-(1975)-KSU Pr-1st ed (z3,f) 20.00

DELL,A-Llama Land-1927-Doran-248p-24 photo plts (bb3) 38.00

DELL,FLOYD-Diana Stair-NY-(1932)-F&R-1st ed (hh5,dj wn) 20.00

DELL,FLOYD-Love in the Machine Age-NY-(1930)-8vo-vii,428p-1st ed (oo7) 45.00

DELLENBAUGH,FREDERICK S-North Americans of Yesterday-NY-1906-Putnams-487p-pict cl,illus (dd4,sp wn) 50.00

DELORIA,VINE,JR.-ED.-Of Utmost Good Faith-SF-(1971)-Straight Arrow-262p-1st ed (gg4,dj) 25.00

DELVAN,DR.JAMES-Gold Rush-Mt.Pleasant-1976-Cumming Pr-ltd to 487c (o2,f) 37.50

DELVING,MICHAEL-Bored to Death-NY-1975-Scribners-1st ed (f4,dj) 12.50

DEMAREST,ANN-Murder on Every Floor-1939-Hillman-1st ed (s10,chip dj) 20.00

DEMBY,WILLIAM-Catacombs-NY-(1965)-Pantheon-1st ed (c10,f,dj) 35.00

DEMCKER,ROBERT-Course in Systematic and Progressive Drawing-Cin-(1868)-Ehrgott,Forbriger-6 vols,bds,84 plts (k1) 75.00

DEMENT'EV,G P-ET AL-Birds of the Soviet Union. Vol.1-Jerusalem-1966-8vo-704p-wrps,maps,plts (y8,lt wn) 75.00

DEMENT'EV,G P-ET AL-Birds of the Soviet Union. Vol.III-Jerusalem-1969-8vo-756p-wrps,118 maps,4 plts (y8,lt staining) 75.00

DEMENY,JABOS-ED.-Bela Bartok Letters-NY-1971-St.Martin's-1st ed (u4,as new in dj) 30.00

DEMIDOFF,E-After Wild Sheep in the Altai & Mongolia-1966-A & F Libr-324p-photos,fldg map-rprnt (gg3,vf) 125.00

DEMOND,ROBERT O-Loyalists in North Carolina during the Revolution-Durham-1940-Duke Univ Pr-x+286p-gry cl-1st ed (k2) 22.00

DEMPEWOLFF,RICHARD-Famous Old New England Murders and Some that are Infamous-Brattleboro-(1942)-Stephen Daye Pr-293+(ix)p-yel cl,illus-1st ed (k2,dj) 20.00

DEMPSEY,DAVID-Triumphs and Trials of Lotta Crabtree-NY-1968-Morrow-8vo-341p-1st ed (z4,sl stnd dj) 12.50

DEMPSEY,HUGH A-ED.-History in Their Blood-Vancouver-1982-Douglas & McIntyre-4to-124p-illus e.p.,64 ports-1st ed (bb7,dj) 40.00*

DEMPSEY,HUGH A-History In Their Blood-NY-1982-Hudson Hills Pr-lg 4to-124p-ports-1st US ed (z4,dj) 50.00

DEMPSEY,MARY V-Occupational Progress of Women, 1910 to 1930-Wash-1933-Dept of Labor/USGPO-wrps,Bull. of Women's Bur,No.104-1st ed (w5,ex-libr) 20.00

DEMPSTER,J H-Pathfinders of Physiology-Detr-1914-66p-illus (g10) 30.00

DENBY,EDWIN-Mrs W's Last Sandwich-NY-1972-Horizon Pr-1st ed (y1,f,f dj) 20.00

DENE,SHAFTO-Trail Blazing in the Skies-Akron-1943-Goodyear Tire & Rubber-78p+32p photos,bds (b1) 15.00

DENHAM,FRANK-Shaping of Our Alphabet-NY-1955-Knopf-lg 8vo-228p-illus-1st ed (aa5,dj) 40.00

DENHARDT,ROBERT M-Horse of the Americas-1947-U of Okla Pr-8vo-xvii,286p-photos,illus-Herd 675-1st ed (aa3,f,dj) 45.00

DENHARDT,ROBERT M-Horse of the Americas-Norman-1947-U of Okla Pr-286p-illus-1st ed (a9,dj) 35.00

DENIG,EDWIN T-Five Indian Tribes of the Upper Missouri-Norman-(1961)-217p-illus-1st ed (e7,f,dj) 45.00

DENIG,EDWIN T-Five Indian Tribes of the Upper Missouri-Norman-(1961)-217p-illus-1st ed (g7,f,dj) 45.00

DENIS,A-Cats of the World-1964-Houghton Mifflin-144p-36 col & b&w photos-1st prtg (bb3,f,fray dj) 30.00

DENIS,ARMAND-On Safari-NY-1963-8vo-320p-photos (m3,vf,dj) 15.00

DENIS,MICHAELA-Ride a Rhino-GC-1960-8vo-215p-photos (m3,f,dj) 10.00

DENISON,MERRILL-Klondike Mike, an Alaskan Odyssey-NY-1943-Morrow-8vo-393p-22 illus-1st ed (ff5,dj sp rprd) 25.00

DENISON,MERRILL-Klondike Mike-Seattle-1948-L O Johnson-393p-Six Guns 299-1st ed (u8,sl wn dj) 18.00

DENKER,HENRY-Kingmaker-NY-1972-1st ed (r5,dj) 30.00

DENLEY,C F-Ornamental Pheasants-(Wash)-1935-8vo-93p-cl,11 plts (y8,fox) 45.00

DENLINGER,M G-Complete Saint Bernard-Richmond-1952-127p-illus-1st ed (v8,f) 20.00

DENLINGER,MILO-Complete Dalmation-Wash-1947-Denlinger-wht bndg-1st ed (f10,sl soil bndg) 45.00

DENMAN,EARL-Alone to Everest-NY-1954-255p-1st US ed (p10,f,dj) 25.00

DENNETT,MARY W-Birth Control Laws-NY-1926-F H Hitchcock-x+309p-blu cl-1st ed (j2,dj) 55.00

DENNEY,JOHN D,JR.-Trains of the Pennsylvania Dutch Country-Columbia-1966-60p-wrps-1st ed (n4) 10.00

DENNEY,JOHN D,JR.-Trolleys of the Pennsylvania Dutch Country-Columbia-1970-56p-wrps-1st ed (n4) 16.00

DENNIS,PATRICK-3D-NY-1972-1st ed (q5,dj) 15.00

DENNIS,PATRICK-Around the World with Auntie Mame-NY-(1958)-1st ed (m5,dj) 10.00

DENNIS,PATRICK-First Lady-NY-1964-172 photos-1st ed (n5,dj) 15.00

DENNIS,PATRICK-First Lady-NY-1964-Morrow-1st ed (hh5,edgewn dj) 17.50

DENNIS,PATRICK-Joyous Season-NY-1965-1st ed (q5,dj) 20.00

DENNIS,PATRICK-Little Me-NY-(1961)-Dutton-1st ed (hh5,dj) 20.00

DENNIS,WAYNE-Hopi Child-1940-Appleton-204p-photos-1st ed (d3) 35.00

DENNISON,GEORGE-Oilers and Sweepers-NY-(1979)-Random-1st ed (bb1,as new in dj) 20.00

DENNISON,L-Devil Mountain-NY-1942-271p-1st ed (o10,f,sl chip dj) 26.00

DENNY,ARTHUR A-Pioneer Days on Puget Sound-Seattle-1888-C B Bagley,Prntr-83p wi errara slip at pg 83,brwn cl-rare-Smith 2408-1st ed (w1) 250.00

DENNY,GEORGE H-Dread Fishwish-NY-1975-4to-222p-illus (m3,vf,dj) 10.00

DENNYS,JOHN-Secrets of Angling-Edinburgh-1885-12mo-2 vols,orig wrps,specially made box (m3,uncut,box) 80.00

DENSMORE,FRANCES-Chippewa Music-Wash-1910-GPO/Bur Amer Ethn,Bull.45-2 vols-illus (dd4) 50.00

DENSMORE,FRANCES-Music of Acoma, Isleta, Cochiti and Zuni Pueblos-Wash D.C.-1957-Bur of Amer Ethno No.165-117p+6 photo plts-orig cl-1st ed (v7) 20.00

DENSMORE,FRANCES-Music of Santo Domingo Pueblo, New Mexico-LA-1938-SW Mus Paprs No.12-186p-wrps,illus-1st ed (v7,f) 30.00

DENSMORE,FRANCES-Papago Music-Wash-1929-GPO/Bur Amer Ethno-229p-illus-Bull.90 (bb4) 25.00

DENSMORE,FRANCES-Pawnee Music-Wash-1929-GPO/Bur Amer Ethno-129p-illus (bb4) 25.00

DENT,ALAN-Burns in His Time-Lond-1966-Thos Nelson-1st ed (z9,f,dj) 12.50

DENTON,CLARA J-Twinkling Fingers and Swaying Figures-Chig-(1903)-T S Denison & Co-117p-blu wrps (n6,wn wrps) 15.00

DENTON,V L-Far West Coast-Tor-1924-Dent-ix,297p-pict bds,illus,maps,ports-Strathern #142 (k10) 35.00*

DENVER POSSE-1956 Brand Book(No.XII)-Denver-1957-375p-photos,maps,ltd to 500c-Adams Guns#2356-1st reg ed (v7) 50.00

DENVER WESTERNERS 1953 BRAND BOOK:IX-Denver-(1954)-315p-photos-Herd#2485-1st ed (u7,f,dj) 65.00

DENYS,F WARD-Our Summer in the Vale of Kashmir-Wash D.C.-(1915)-J W Bryan Pr-lg 8vo-233p-g cl,col & b&w illus-1st ed (v10) 30.00

DEODENE,FRANK-Black American Poetry Since 1944-Chatham-1971-Chatham-wrps-1st ed (c10,f) 35.00

DERBEC,ETIENNE-French Journalist in the California Gold Rush-Georgetown-1964-Talisman Pr-258p-map e.p.-ltd to 750c (ee4,dj) 75.00

DERBY,J C-Fifty Years Among Authors, Books and Publishers-NY-1884-Carteton-thk 8vo-739p-bev cl bds wi dec g,sketches-1st ed (w1) 50.00

DERLETH,AUGUST-Adventure of the Unique Dickensians-Sauk City-1968-Mycroft & Moran-stapled wrps-1st ed (w9,f,wrps) 45.00

DERLETH,AUGUST-Bright Journey-NY-1940-Scribner's-1st ed (bb1,dj) 25.00

DERLETH,AUGUST-Case Book of Solar Pons-Sauk City-1965-Mycroft Moran-1st ed (k3,f,dj) 45.00

DERLETH,AUGUST-Chronicles of Solar Pons-Sauk City-1973-ltd to 4176c-1st ed (k5,as new in dj) 10.00

DERLETH,AUGUST-Chronicles of Solar Pons-Sauk City-1973-Mycroft Moran-1st ed (f3,f,dj) 20.00

DERLETH,AUGUST-Collected Poems 1937 to 1967-NY-1967-1st ed (c5,as new in dj) 20.00

DERLETH,AUGUST-Countryman's Journal-NY-(1963)-DS&P-illus-1st ed (bb1,f,dj) 17.50

DERLETH,AUGUST-Dark of the Moon-Sauk City-1947-Arkham-xvi,418p-ltd to 2,634c-scarce 1st state dj designed by F Utpatel-1st ed (f5,f,dj sp sl creased) 100.00

DERLETH,AUGUST-Dwellers in Darkness-Sauk City-1976-Arkham-1st ed (k3,f,dj) 15.00

DERLETH,AUGUST-Dwellers in Darkness-Sauk City-1976-ltd to 3926c-1st ed (k5,as new in dj) 10.00

DERLETH,AUGUST-Harrigan's File-Sauk City-1975-Arkham-1st ed (k3,f,dj) 15.00

DERLETH,AUGUST-Harrigan's File-Sauk City-1975-ltd to 4102c-1st ed (k5,as new in dj) 10.00

DERLETH,AUGUST-Narracong Riddle-NY-1940-Scribners-1st ed (h4,dj missing sm chips) 25.00

DERLETH,AUGUST-New Poetry Out of Wisconsin-Sauk City-1969-1st ed (c5,dj) 20.00

DERLETH,AUGUST-Praed Street Dossier-Sauk City-1968-Mycroft & Moran-108p-illus,F Utpatel-ltd to 2904c-1st ed (g4,f,dj) 25.00

DERLETH,AUGUST-Prince Goes West-NY-(1968)-Meredith Pr-1st ed (bb1,f,dj) 20.00

DERLETH,AUGUST-Shadow in the Glass-NY-1963-1st ed (n5,dj,pres) 30.00

DERLETH,AUGUST-Shield of the Valiant-NY-1945-1st ed (c5,f,dj) 25.00

DERLETH,AUGUST-Tent Show Summer-(NY)-(1963)-DS&P-1st ed (e10,f,dj) 25.00

DERLETH,AUGUST-Thirty Years of Arkham House-Sauk City-1970-Arkham-1st ed (l3,f,dj) 60.00

DERLETH,AUGUST-Three Straw Men-NY-1970-Candlelight Pr-1st ed (bb1,dj) 17.50

DERLETH,AUGUST-Village Daybook-Chig-(1947)-map e.p. by Skuldt,illus by Utpatel-1st ed (c5,edge rub dj) 20.00

DERLETH,AUGUST-Wilbur, the Trusting Whippoorwill-Sauk City-1959-Stanton & Lee-drwngs,C V Dwiggins-1st ed (e10,f,dj cov glue mrks) 35.00

DERLETH,AUGUST-Wind Leans West-NY-1969-Candlelight Pr-1st ed (bb1,as new in dj) 25.00

DERMAN,WILLIAM-Serfs, Peasants, and Socialists-Berkeley-(1973)-U of Cal Pr-8vo-282p-cl (y5,dj) 30.00

DERRYDALE PRESS-Decade of American Sporting Books & Prints-Derrydale-1937-8vo-71p-ltd to 950c,nbrd-illus (m3) 100.00

DERSHOWITZ,ALAN-Best Defense-NY-1982-Random-1st ed (x9,dj) 15.00

DES MONTAIGNES,FRANCOIS-Plains-Norman-(1972)-U of Okla Pr-182p-illus-1st ed (gg4,dj) 25.00

DESANTI,DOMINIQUE-Woman in Revolt-NY-1972-Crown-281p (r1,dj) 18.00

DESCAMPS,MATHILDE-La Cuisine Exquise-(Chig)-(1947)-147p-dec grn cl (q8) 20.00

DESCARTES,RENATO-Geometria-Amsterdam-1659-Ludovicum & Elzevirios-vel bndg,in Latin-2nd ed (l9,soil) 700.00

DESCENDENT-NY-1897-Harper-orig olive grn pattrnd bds,gold stmpd,wi all iss points-Ellen Glasgow's 1st bk-1st ed (ee2,e.p. restored) 125.00

DESCHARNES,RBT-World of Salvador Dali-NY-1962-folio-col & tip in illus-1st ed (h10,dj) 100.00

DESCHIN,JACOB-Exakta Photography-SF-(1955)-Camera Craft-192p-photos-1st ed (l10,dj) 10.00

DESCHIN,JACOB-Rollei Photography-SF-1952-Camera Craft-192p-1st ed (cc9) 35.00

DESERET FIRST BOOK...-(SLC)-1868-36,(2)p-orig prtd salmon bds,cl sp,scarce wi errata slip-Flake 2817 (bb8) 65.00

DESERET SECOND BOK-by Regents...Deseret Yiouniversiti-SLC-1868-Deseret Univ-72p-cl sp,prtd papr over bds-1st ed (z1) 100.00

DESHIELDS,JAMES T-Border Wars of Texas-Waco-1976-400p-rprnt of 1912 ed (n10,f,dj) 50.00

DESIO,ARDITO-Victory Over K2-NY-1956-273p-1st US ed (a4,f,dj) 65.00

DESMAISON,RENE-Total Alpinism-Lond-1982-202p-16 plts-1st Brit ed (p10,f) 25.00

DETROIT SCHOOL OF LETTERING-Lettering Plates-1908-oblng folio-qtr lea,illus-scarce (b6,rear cov stnd) 75.00

DEUCHER,SYBIL-Giotto Tended the Sheep-(NY)-(1938)-Dutton-4to-96p-pict cl,col illus,D Bayley-1st ed (r3,dj sp wn,sl chip & tn) 20.00

DEUTE,ARTHUR H-200 Dishes for Men to Cook-(1944)-Barrows-254p-dec blk cl-1st prtg (q8,dj) 15.00

DEUTSCH,ALBERT-Mentally Ill in America-GC-1937-530p-1st ed (dd3,dj) 75.00

DEUTSCH,BABETTE-One Part Love-NY-1939-1st ed (p5,f,dj) 25.00

DEUTSCH,BABETTE-Poetry in Our Time-NY-1952-1st ed (p5,chip dj) 25.00

DEUTSCH,BABETTE-TRANSL.-Twelve-NY-1920-Huebsch-wrps-1st Amer ed (r2,sl sunned) 25.00

DEUTSCH,BABETTE-Walt Whitman, Builder for America-NY-(1941)-Messner-8vo-278p-1st ed (ee5,dj sl fade,tn) 25.00

DEUTSCH,JORDAN-Scrapbook History of Baseball-1975-Bobbs Merril-photos-1st ed (s8,f,dj) 20.00

DEVAS,NICOLETTE-Two Flamboyant Fathers-NY-1967-Morrow-8vo-287p-16p photos-1st US ed (gg5,dj) 10.00

DEVEREUX,GEORGE-Mohave Ethnopsychiatry and Suicide-Wash-1961-BAE Bull 175-567p+10 photo plts,cl (a1) 25.00

DEVERY,ELIZABETH C-Story of Four Mile Colony-New Lisbon-1939-120p-wrps,illus (aa6) 35.00

DEVOTO,BERNARD-Across the Wide Missouri-Bost-1947-483p-col illus-1st ed (d7,f,chip dj) 50.00

DEVOTO,BERNARD-ED.-Journals of Lewis and Clark-Bost-1953-Houghton Mifflin-sm 8vo-iii,504p-map e.p.,6 maps-1st ed thus (aa3,dj) 35.00

DEVOTO,BERNARD-Year of Decision-Bost-1943-524p-map e.p. (y7,dj) 15.00

DEVOTO,BERNARD-Year of Decision-Bost-1943-538p-cl,maps-1st ed (z1,dj) 35.00

DEVRIES,PETER-But But Who Wakes the Bugler?-Bost-1940-C.Addams illus,scarce,auth's 1st bk-1st ed (l5,f,sl wn dj) 300.00

DEVRIES,PETER-Let Me Count the Ways-Bost,Tor-(1965)-1st ed (l5,sp faded dj) 10.00

DEVRIES,PETER-Reuben, Reuben-Bost-1964-Little,Brown-1st ed (x9,f,sl rub dj) 17.50

DEW,ROBB F-Dale Loves Sophie to Death-NY-(1981)-FSG-auth 1st bk-1st ed (j6,dj) 30.00

DEW-SMITH,A-Confidences of an Amateur Gardener-Lond-1897-Sheeley-299p-g dec cl (x6) 18.00

DEWAR,D-Jungle Folk-1912-Lane-271p (bb3) 20.00

DEWART,EDWARD H-Selections From Canadian Poets-Montreal-1864-J Lovell-8vo-xix,(21),304p-orig brwn cl-Watters p.57-1st ed (pp2,lacks ffep,sl wn sp) 65.00*

DEWEES,REBECCA-MEMOIR OF...LATE OF PENNSVILLE, OHIO-Phila-1883-104p-cl (n1) 15.00

DEWEES,REBECCA-Memoir of...Late of Pennsville,Ohio-Phila-1883-Wm H Pile-16mo-104p (y6,hng cracking) 14.00

DEWEESE,H D-Coercion and Perversion or Primeval Degenerates-Columbus-1904-90p-cl (n1) 12.50

DEWEY,JOHN-Schools of Tomorrow-NY-1915-(11),316p-1st ed (k9,vf,dj) 25.00

DEWEY,THOMAS B-Chased and the Unchaste-NY-1958-Simon-1st ed (e4,yel pgs,dj sp sl wn) 15.00

DEWEY,THOMAS B-Chased and the Unchaste-NY-1959-Random-1st ed (w5,brwng pgs,f dj) 20.00

DEWEY,THOMAS B-Death and Taxes-NY-1967-Putnam-1st ed (f4,f,dj) 12.50

DEWEY,THOMAS B-You've Got Him Cold-1958-Simon-1st ed (s10,dj) 10.00

DEWOLFE HOWE,M A-Life and Labors of Bishop Hare-NY-1911-Sturgis & Walton-417p-illus-1st ed (dd4) 50.00

DEXTER,COLIN-Service for All the Dead-NY-1980-St.Martin's-1st US ed (j4,f,dj) 35.00

DEXTER,COLIN-Silent World of Nicholas Quinn-NY-1977-St.Martin's-1st Amer ed (w9,vf,dj) 90.00

DEXTER,DAVE-Jazz Story: From the 90's to the 60's-(1964)-Prentice Hall-1st ed (w1,f,dj) 20.00

DEXTER,F THEODORE-Thirty-Five Years Scrapbook of Antique Arms-Topeka-1947-4to-unpgd-2 vols-ltd to 2000 sets,nbrd,autg-photos (m3,f) 60.00

DEY,HARYOT-Story of Washday-Phila-nd(ca.1905)-Standard Oil-44p-wrps (q8) 15.00

DI FATE,VINCENT-Di Fate Catalog of Science Fiction Hardware-NY-(1980)-Workman-1st ed (l3,f,dj) 15.00

DI PRIMA,DIANE-Dinners and Nightmares-NY-1961-Corinth-1st ed (v5) 20.00

DI PRIMA,DIANE-Dinners and Nightmares-NY-1961-Corinth-wrps-1st ed (c10) 10.00

DI PRIMA,DIANE-Freddie Poems-1974-Eidolon-wrps-1st ed (t9,vf) 20.00

DI PRIMA,DIANE-Loba, Part 1-1973-Capra Pr-wrps-1st ed (r2,f) 25.00

DI PRIMA,DIANE-Seven Love Songs From the Middle Latin-NY-1965-Poets Pr-wrps-1st prtg (v5,few spots) 30.00

DIAMOND,STANLEY-ED.-Transformation of East Africa-NY-(1966)-Basic Bks-8vo-623p-cl,maps-1st ed (y5,f,sl sun dj) 15.00

DIAMONSTEIN,B-Buildings Reborn-NY-1978-331 illus-1st ed (h10,dj) 40.00

DIAMONSTIEN,BARBARALEE-Art World-(NY)-(1977)-Artnews Bks-tall 4to-cl-1st ed (oo6,dj) 60.00

DIAZ DEL CASTILLO,BERNAL-Discovery and Conquest of Mexico. 1517 to 1521-Mexico-1942-LED,Loera Y Chavez-263p-lea,sp labls wi g lettrng,illus,M Covarrubias,3 autg (mm1,f,box sl rub & wn) 175.00

DIBDIN,MICHAEL-Last Sherlock Holmes Story-1978-Pantheon-1st Amer ed (r9,f,dj) 20.00

DIBDIN,MICHAEL-Last Sherlock Holmes Story-NY-1978-Pantheon-1st US ed (g4,f,dj) 12.50

DIBNER,BERN-Atlantic Cable-Norwalk-1959-Burndy Libr-4to-96p-wrps,fldg map,illus-1st ed (g2,sl soil) 20.00

DICHMAN,E W-This Aviation Business-NY-1929-8vo-xiv,274p-illus cl,24p plts-1st ed (t2,sp fade) 35.00

DICK,LENOX-Art & Science of Fly Fishing-NY-1966-8vo-103p-photos-1st ed (m3,dj) 15.00

DICK,PHILIP K-Divine Invasion-1981-Timescape-1st ed (p9,vf,dj) 25.00

DICK,PHILIP K-Transmigration of Timothy Archer-Lond-1982-Gollancz-1st Brit ed (f3,f,dj) 30.00

DICK,STEWART-Arts and Crafts of Old Japan-Chig-1905-McClurg-152p-cl/pict bds,frntis,plts-1st ed (kk1,sl soil cov) 30.00

DICK,STEWART-Arts and Crafts of Old Japan-Edinburgh-1908-Foulis-cl,illus-scarce-1st ed (l8) 55.00

DICKENS,CEDRIC-Drinking with Dickens-(1980)-127p-yel bds,facs illus-ltd to 2000c,nbrd-1st ed (q8,dj,pres) 20.00

DICKENS,CHARLES-Battle of Life. A Love Story-Cin-1847-Robinson & J-16p-wrps,dbl cols-rare (b1,t.p. tn & cor pc missng) 30.00

DICKENS,CHARLES-Bleak House-Lond-1853-3/4 lea-1st ed in book form (l9,rbnd,sl fox) 135.00

DICKENS,CHARLES-Chimes-Lond-1931-LED-4to-tan cl stmpd in blk & gold,ltd to 1500c,nbrd,autg by illus Rackham (x3,sp drknd,lacks box) 250.00

DICKENS,CHARLES-Christmas Carol-Lond-1843-Chapman & Hall-orig bndg,grn e.p.,illus by J Leech,1st ed,1st state wi red & blu t.p.,heading "Stave I" 1st pg text (l9,sl wn,box) 3,000.00

DICKENS,CHARLES-Christmas Carol-Phila/Lond-nd-Lippincott/Heinemann-rbnd in cl gilt,English sheets,a.e.g.,12 inserted col plts wi prntd guards,17 line drwngs,A Rackham (s3,rbnd) 65.00

DICKENS,CHARLES-Hard Times for These Times-NY-1966-LED-illus by Chas Raymond,ltd to 1500c,nbrd,autg by Raymond in colophon (x3,f,f box,monthly lttr) 60.00

DICKENS,CHARLES-Life and Adventures of Martin Chuzzlewit-Lond-1844-Chapman & Hall-8vo-drk grn calf & mrbld bds,rebkd in pbbld cl wi orig g bkstrp,new mrbld e.p.,extra engrvd title-1st ed,1st state (x3,rbkd,new e.p.,sl fox) 145.00

DICKENS,CHARLES-Life and Adventures of Nicholas Nickleby-Lond-1839-lea by Riviere wi silk e.p.,orig fr wrps bnd in,illus,Phiz,lea surround-1st ed,1st iss bnd frm parts (l9,wn,rbnd,surround,box) 700.00

DICKENS,CHARLES-Little Dorrit-Lond-1857-3/4 lea-1st ed in bk form (l9,rbnd,sl fox) 150.00

DICKENS,CHARLES-Little Nell retold for boys and girls by Alice F Jackson-Lond-nd-Jack-8vo-dec cl wi pict pasteon,8 col plts,F M B Blaikie (r3,sl fox) 15.00

DICKENS,CHARLES-Personal History of David Copperfield-NY-1924-Dodd,Mead-lg 8vo-850p-giltstamped cl,16 col plts,G D Hammond (r3,sm tr at crwn) 15.00

DICKENS,CHARLES-Pictures From Italy-1846-Bradbury & Evans-orig cl-1st ed (x2,rprd sp) 275.00

DICKENS,CHARLES-Pictures from Italy-Lond-1846-3/4 lea in cl box,vignette illus,S Palmer-1st ed (l9,box) 300.00

DICKENS,CHARLES-Posthumous Papers of the Pickwick Club-Lond-1837-Chapman & Hall-3/4 mor bndg by Bayntun,43 illus,R Seymour & Phiz-1st book ed,1st iss (w1,rbnd,sl wn) 450.00

DICKENS,CHARLES-Posthumous Papers of the Pickwick Club...-Paris-1839-8vo-2 vols-g stmpd lea sp over mrbld bds,lea cors (b3) 225.00

DICKENS,CHARLES-Short Stories of...-NY-1971-LED-4to-1/2 cl & mrbld bds,ltd to 1500c,nbrd,two autg (x3,f,f box,monthly lttr) 80.00

DICKENS,CHARLES-Writings of...-Bost-1894-Houghton Mifflin-8vo-32 vols-grn cl wi lea sp labls,illus (p1,sl fox) 550.00

DICKERSON,M C-Frog Book-1906-Dbldy,Page-253p-16 col & 96 b&w plts-1st ed (bb3) 55.00

DICKERSON,PHILIP A-History of the Osage Nation-Pawhuska-1906-143p-stiff pict wrps,photos-Howes P321-1st ed (t7) 100.00

DICKEY,ESTHER-Passport to Survival-SLC-1970-Bookcraft-180p-g dec grn cl,col frntis,photos-4th prtg (q8,dj) 18.50

DICKEY,GLENN-History of American League Baseball Since 1901-NY-(1980)-319p-bds-1st ed (n1,f,dj) 22.50

DICKEY,GLENN-History of National League Baseball Since 1876-1979-Stein & Day-photos-1st ed (s8,f,dj) 17.50

DICKEY,JAMES-Deliverance-Bost-(1970)-Houghton Mifflin-1st ed (s6,dj) 35.00

DICKEY,JAMES-Deliverance-Lond-1970-1st Brit ed (s5,sl chip dj) 30.00

DICKEY,JAMES-Enemy From Eden-Northridge-1978-Lord John-ltd to 275c,autg,w/o dj as iss-1st ed (j3,f) 35.00

DICKEY,JAMES-Eye Beaters, Blood, Victory, Madness, Buckhead and Mercy-GC-1970-Dbldy-1st ed (cc2,f,sl chip dj) 35.00

DICKEY,JAMES-Poems 1957 to 1967-Middletown-(1967)-Wesleyan U Pr-1st ed (cc2,f,dj) 45.00

DICKEY,JAMES-Self Interviews-1970-Dbldy-1st ed (t9,f,dj) 25.00

DICKEY,JAMES-Tucky the Hunter-NY-1978-1st ed (s5,f,dj) 17.50

DICKEY,ROLAND F-New Mexico Village Arts-Albuq-1949-260p+index-col drwngs-1st ed (u7,f,dj) 50.00

DICKINSON,ANNA E-Ragged Register-NY-1879-Harper-12mo-286p-orig cl-1st ed (w6,sl rub) 75.00

DICKINSON,C E,LIEUT.-Flying Guns-NY-1942-8vo-x,196p-cl-1st ed (t2) 25.00

DICKINSON,C-Encyclopedia of Mushrooms-1979-Putnams-4to-280p-col photos-1st US ed (bb3,f,dj) 25.00

DICKINSON,CHARLES-Waltz in Marathon-NY-1983-Knopf-auth 1st bk-1st ed (bb1,as new in dj) 25.00

DICKINSON,EMILY-Bolts of Melody-NY-1945-Harper-8vo-352p-BAL 4695-1st ed (w6) 35.00

DICKINSON,EMILY-Emily Dickinson's Letters-Cambridge-1951-Harvard U Pr-1st ed (bb2,f,dj) 30.00

DICKINSON,EMILY-Further Poems of...-Bost-1929-Little,Brown-1st ed (u2,chip dj) 45.00

DICKINSON,EMILY-Unpublished Poems of...-Bost-1936-Little,Brown-grn cl-1st trd ed (f2,dj) 85.00

DICKINSON,H W-Matthew Boulton-Cambridge-1937-Cambridge Univ Pr-xiv+218p-orng cl,15 plts,6 text figs-1st ed (j2,dj) 40.00

DICKINSON,PETER-Blue Hawk-Bost-(1976)-Little,Brown-1st US ed (h3,f,dj) 25.00

DICKINSON,PETER-Poison Oracle-1974-Hodder & Stoughton-1st ed (r9,f,dj) 15.00

DICKINSON,PETER-Sleep and His Brother-NY-1971-Harper-1st US ed (v5,f,dj) 25.00

DICKSON,ARTHUR J-Covered Wagon Days-Cleve-1929-Arthur Clark Publ-287p-illus-1st ed (c7) 135.00

DICKSON,CARTER-Cavalier's Cup-1953-Morrow-1st ed (s10,dj) 20.00

DICKSON,CARTER-Death in Five Boxes-NY-1938-Morrow-1st ed (h4) 35.00

DICKSON,CARTER-Department of Queer Complaints-NY-1940-Morrow-1st ed (f4,sl wn,sl stnd e.p.) 75.00

DICKSON,CARTER-Department of Queer Complaints-NY-1940-Morrow-scarce-1st ed (d4,dj creased,tape reinfrcd) 500.00

DICKSON,CARTER-Fear is the Same-NY-1956-Morrow-1st ed (f4,dj sl tn,chip) 25.00

DICKSON,CARTER-Graveyard to Let-NY-1949-Morrow-1st ed (e4,dj) 50.00

DICKSON,CARTER-Judas Window-1938-Morrow-1st ed (s10,dj) 450.00

DICKSON,CARTER-White Priory Murders-NY-1934-Morrow-1st ed (l4,f) 50.00

DICKSON,LEONARD E-Algebraic Invariants-NY-1914-John Wiley-x+100p-grn cl-Math Mono #14-1st ed (c2) 30.00

DICKSTEIN,MORRIS-Gates of Eden-NY-(1977)-Basic-photos-1st ed (d10,f,dj) 17.50

DIDELOT,ROGER-FRANCIS-Murder in the Bath-Phila-1933-Lippincott-1st US ed (d4) 15.00

DIDEROT,DENIS-Rameau's Nephew and Other Works-Lond-1926-Chapman & Hall/Curwen Pr-ltd to 1000c-1st ed thus (m4) 15.00

DIDION,JOAN-Book of Common Prayer-NY-(1977)-S&S-1st ed (e3,f,dj) 30.00

DIDION,JOAN-Play It As It Lays-1970-FSG-1st ed (x2,f,dj) 20.00

DIDION,JOAN-Play It As It Lays-NY-(1970)-FS&G-1st ed (a10,f,dj) 25.00

DIDION,JOAN-Run River-NY-1963-auth 1st bk-1st ed (t5,dj wn,tape reprd) 55.00

DIDION,JOAN-Salvador-NY-(1983)-S&S-1st ed (bb1,as new in dj) 15.00

DIDION,JOAN-Slouching Toward Bethlehem-NY-(1968)-FS&G-1st ed (g6,sl wn dj) 75.00

DIDION,JOAN-White Album-NY-(1979)-S&S-1st ed (bb1,as new in dj) 20.00

DIDUSCH,WILLIAM P-Collection of Urogenital Drawings-NY-1952-222p-243 illus (g10) 50.00

DIEBEL,J H-Arithmetic by Analysis-West Unity-(1891)-publ by auth-100p-cl cov wrps (k1) 12.50

DIEDERICH,BERNARD-Papa Doc-NY-(1969)-McGraw Hill-8vo-393p-1st ed (jj5,dj) 12.50

DIEHL,EDITH-Bookbinding Its Background and Technique-NY-1946-Rinehart-2 vols-1st ed (w1,f,box) 75.00

DIETZGEN,JOSEPH-Positive Outcome of Philosophy-Chig-1906-Kerr-444p (ff1) 20.00

DIGBY,GEORGE-Down Wind-NY-1939-Dutton-1st ed (p8,chip dj) 10.00

DIGBY,SIR KENELM-Closet of Sir Kenelm Digby Knight Opened-Lond-1910-P L Warner-8vo-lv,291p-brwn blind stmpd buckram,t.e.g.,frntis port-newly ed by A MacDonell (t10,f) 150.00

DILELLO,RICHARD-Longest Cocktail Party-1972-Playboy-1st ed (o9,f,tn dj) 45.00

DILG,WILL-ED.-Tragic Fishing Moments-Chig-1922-8vo-266p-illus (m3) 15.00

DILLARD,ANNIE-Holy the Firm-NY-(1977)-Harper & Row-1st ed (k7,f,dj) 35.00

DILLARD,ANNIE-Holy the Firm-NY-(1977)-Harper & Row-1st ed (v10,as new in dj) 25.00

DILLARD,ANNIE-Holy the Firm-NY-1977-1st ed (p5,f,edge chip dj) 15.00

DILLARD,ANNIE-Pilgrim at Tinker Creek-Lond-(1975)-J Cape-intro by Richard Adams-1st Brit ed (m7,f,dj) 40.00

DILLARD,ANNIE-Pilgrim at Tinker Creek-Lond-(1975)-J Cape-R Adams intro-1st Brit ed (u10,f,f dj) 35.00

DILLARD,ANNIE-Pilgrim at Tinker Creek-NY-(1974)-Harper's Mag Pr-1st ed (b8,f,sl tn dj) 65.00

DILLARD,ANNIE-Pilgrim at Tinker Creek-NY-(1974)-Harper's Mag Pr-1st ed (g8,f,dj) 45.00

DILLARD,ANNIE-Teaching a Stone to Talk-NY et al-(1982)-Harper & Row-1st ed (m5,as new in dj) 15.00

DILLARD,ANNIE-Teaching a Stone To Talk-NY-(1982)-Harper & Row-1st ed (g3,f,dj) 20.00

DILLARD,R H W-Book of Changes-GC-1974-Dbldy-1st ed (cc2,f,sp sunned dj) 35.00

DILLARD,R H W-Day I Stopped Dreaming About Barbara Steele-Chapel Hill-1966-UNC-1st ed (k7,f,dj) 25.00

DILLER,J S-ET AL-Guidebook of the Western United States. Part D. The Shasta Route and Coast Line-Wash D.C.-1916-GPO-146p-burgandy cl,15 figs,33 plts,19 route maps-Bulletin 614 Dept of Interior/U S Geo Survey (mm1) 45.00

DILLEY,A U-Key to Oriental Rugs-NY-1909-illus (kk4) 35.00

DILLEY,J W-History of the Scofield Mine Disaster...-(Provo)-(1900)-298p-orig tan dec cl,ports,illus-1st ed (bb8) 95.00

DILLIN,CAPT JOHN-Kentucky Rifle-NY-1946-136p-blu cl,g dec,illus-3rd ed (ee3,vf,box) 125.00

DILLIN,CAPT JOHN-Kentucky Rifle-Wash-1924-NRA-124p+index-plts-Howes D342-1st ed (dd4,cor bump) 95.00

DILLING,ELIZABETH-Red Network-Chig-1934-publ by auth-338p-Seidman D200-4th prtg (r1,sl tn dj) 20.00

DILLION,RICHARD-We Have Met the Enemy-NY-1978-231p-maps-1st ed (b7,f,dj) 25.00

DILLON,ELIZABETH-Manual of Common Beetles of Eastern North America-Evanston-(1961)-Row Peterson-8vo-884p-4p col illus-1st ed (gg5) 20.00

DILLON,JOHN B-History of Indiana-Indpls-1859-637p-lea,2 fldg maps,5 plts-Howes D 343 (d1,rbnd) 75.00

DILLON,MILLICENT-Little Original Sin-NY-(1981)-HRW-1st ed (m7,dj) 15.00

DILLON,RICHARD-ED.-Journal of Private Joshua M Rice, 1851-Denver-1970-123p-frntis,illus-1st ed (t7,f,dj) 25.00

DILLON,RICHARD-INTRO-Narrative of the Life and Adventures of Major C Bolin, Alias David Butler-Palo Alto-1966-87p-dec cl,illus,map e.p. (t7,dj) 35.00

DILLON,RICHARD-J Ross Browne: Confidential Agent in Old California-Norman-1965-U of Okla Pr-218p-1st ed (d3,dj) 20.00

DILLON,RICHARD-Legend of Grizzly Adams-NY-1966-223p-photos-1st ed (t7,f,dj) 17.50

DILLON,RICHARD-Meriwether Lewis-NY-(1965)-365p-e.p. maps,illus-2nd prtg (c7,chip dj) 25.00

DILS,LENORE-Horny Toad Man-(El Paso)-(1966)-183p-photos-scarce-1st ed (v7,dj,autg) 65.00

DIMAGGIO,JOE-Baseball For Everyone-1948-Whittlesey Hs-photos,drwngs-1st ed (s8,dj) 35.00

DIMAGGIO,JOE-Lucky to be a Yankee-1946-Rudolph Field-1st ed (ff2,dj pc missng) 60.00

DIMAGGIO,JOE-Lucky to be a Yankee-1946-Rudolph Field-1st ed (r7,lacks dj) 25.00

DIME DETECTIVE MAGAZINE-(Chig)-(1937)-Popular Publ-128p-col pict wrps,Nov.1937 orig issue containing R Chandler's "Mandarin Jade"-rare (o1,sl wn) 75.00

DIME DETECTIVE MAGAZINE-(Chig)-(1939)-Popular Publ-128p-col pict wrps,complt iss for Jan.1939,contains R Chandler's "Lady in the Lake"-rare (o1,chip,pc lackng frnt cov) 75.00

DIMOCK,A W-Wall Street & the Wilds-NY-1915-8vo-476p-photos-scarce-1st ed (m3,cov soil & wn) 30.00

DIMOCK,EDWARD C-TRANSL.-Thief of Love-1963-U of Chig Pr-cl-1st ed (n8,f) 20.00

DIMSDALE,THOMAS-Vigilantes of Montana-Helena-(1915)-290p-illus-Howes H345-scarce (c7) 95.00

DIN,GILBERT C-Imperial Osages-Norman-(1983)-432p-cl-1st ed so stated (aa1,f,dj) 25.00

DINER,HELEN-Mothers and Amazons-NY-1965-Julian Pr-8vo-308p wi index-1st Amer ed (t1,f,dj) 45.00

DINESEN,ISAK-Anecdotes of Destiny-1958-M Joseph-1st ed (n9,sl tn & wn dj) 30.00

DINESEN,ISAK-Ehrengard-1963-Random-1st Amer ed (n9,f,sl wn dj) 35.00

DINESEN,ISAK-Last Tales-NY-1957-Random-1st ed (j8,f,sl chip dj) 50.00

DINESEN,ISAK-Seven Gothic Tales-1934-Harrison Smith-auth 1st bk-1st US ed (jj6,dj) 125.00

DINESEN,ISAK-Seven Gothic Tales-NY-1934-Harrison Smith/Robt Haas-auth 1st bk-1st ed (g8,f,chip dj) 150.00

DINESEN,ISAK-Shadows on the Grass-NY-(1961)-149p-photos (gg3,vf,dj) 35.00

DINESEN,ISAK-Shadows on the Grass-NY-(1961)-Random-1st US ed (x9,f,sp sun dj) 20.00

DINGEE & CONARD CO.,WEST GROVE-New Guide to Rose Culture 1887...-(Phila)-1887-87p-col pict wrps,2p col plts (o1) 25.00

DINGLE,EDWIN J-My Life in Tibet-LA-1939-cl-1st ed (o8,dj) 10.00

DINGMAN,LARRY-Bibliography of Limited and Signed Editions in Literature, 20th Century American Authors-Stillwater-(1973)-issued w/o dj-1st ed (e5,as new) 25.00

DINSDALE,ALFRED-Television: Seeing By Wireless-Lond-1926-Sir Isaac Pitman-sm 8vo-62p-pap bds,frntis,illus-v rare-1st ed (w1,f,dj) 1,000.00

DION,JOSEPH F-My Tribe the Crees-Calgary-1979-Glenbow Alberta Inst-8vo-x,194p-16 illus-1st ed (cc7,scuff dj) 25.00*

DIPESO,CHARLES C-Casa Grandes-Flagstaff-1974-3 vols-2 col drwngs,Wesche,photos,maps-1st ed (t7,f) 75.00

DIPESO,CHARLES C-Casa Grandes-supplemented by Vol 4 thru 8-Flagstaff-8vols-illus,maps (t7,f) 250.00

DIPPIE,BRIAN W-ED.-Nomad-Austin,Lond-(1980)-174p-illus-1st ed thus (g7,f,dj) 30.00

DIRINGER,DAVID-Illuminated Book, Its History and Production-Lond-(1958)-Faber & Faber-thick 8vo-524p-cl,col illus-1st ed (w2,cov rub) 95.00

DIRINGER,DAVID-Writing-NY-(1962)-Praeger-8vo-261p-cl,78 photos,49 line drwngs-Ancient Peoples & Places ser-1st US ed (x4,dj) 95.00

DISCH,T-Black Alice-1968-Dbldy-1st ed (x7,dj) 85.00

DISCH,THOMAS M-ED.-Bad Moon Rising-NY-(1973)-Harper & Row-1st ed (j3,f,dj) 20.00

DISCH,THOMAS M-On Wings of Song-NY-(1979)-St.Martin's-1st ed (bb1,as new in dj) 20.00

DISHER,MAURICE W-Victorian Song-Lond-(1955)-Phoenix Hs-8vo-256p-31 plts-1st Brit ed (ee5,sl tn dj) 20.00

DISNEY,DORIS M-At Some Forgotten Door-1966-CC-1st ed (s10,dj) 12.50

DISNEY,DORIS M-Chandler Policy-NY-1971-Putnam-1st ed (g4,dj) 15.00

DISNEY,DORIS M-Dark Lady-NY-1960-Dbldy CC-1st ed (f4,dj) 10.00

DISNEY,DORIS M-Do Not Fold, Spindle or Mutilate-NY-1970-Dbldy CC-1st ed (f4,f,sl wn dj) 12.50

DISNEY,DORIS M-Don't Go Into the Woods Today-NY-1974-Dbldy CC-1st ed (f4,f,dj) 15.00

DISNEY,DORIS M-Hospitality of the House-NY-1964-Dbldy CC-1st ed (f4,f,dj) 17.50

DISNEY,DORIS M-Last Straw-NY-1954-Dbldy CC-1st ed (g4,sl fox,yel,dj) 12.50

DISNEY,DORIS M-Murder on a Tangent-NY-1945-Dbldy CC-1st ed (k4,f,dj) 25.00

DISNEY,DORIS M-Night of Clear Choice-NY-1967-Dbldy CC-1st ed (h4,f,dj) 12.50

DISNEY,DORIS M-That Which is Crooked-NY-1948-Dbldy CC-1st ed (f4,sl yel pgs,dj sl wn) 20.00

DISNEY,DORIS M-Who Rides A Tiger-NY-1946-Dbldy CC-1st ed (j4,f,sl wn dj) 25.00

DISNEY,DOROTHY C-17th Letter-1945-Random-1st ed (x7,f,dj) 20.00

DISNEY,DOROTHY C-Crimson Friday-NY-1943-Random-1st ed (g4,f,dj) 20.00

DISNEY,DOROTHY C-Hangman's Tree-1949-Random Hs-1st ed (s10,chip dj) 10.00

DISNEY,DOROTHY C-Thirty Days Hath September-NY-1942-Random-1st ed (k4,f,sp chip dj) 20.00

DISNEY,WALT-Ave Maria-1940-Random-col illus,lyrics,R Field-1st ed (x2) 15.00

DISNEY,WALT-Mickey Mouse Story Book-1931-McKay-col paste-down on frnt panel,illus-scarce-1st ed (x2) 375.00

DISPLAYING AUSTRALIA AND NEW GUINEA-Sydney-c.1945-Australia Story Trust-folio-256p-blu cl,photos (p8,edges wn) 55.00

DISRAELI,BENJAMIN-Letters of...-1929-Appleton-2 vols,illus-1st ed (x2,sl fade sp) 55.00

DISRAELI,BENJAMIN-Lord George Bentinck-Lond-1852-Colburn & Co (l9,sl fox & wn) 65.00

DISTURNELL'S,JOHN-Disturnell's Treaty Map-Santa Fe-1965-20p-lg fldg col map-text by J Rittenhouse-1st ed (t7,f) 35.00

DITCHFIELD,P H-Manor Houses of England-NY-1910-Scribner's-sm 4to-211p-blu cl,t.e.g.,col frntis,illus (r10,rub,sl shaken) 22.50

DITMARS,R L-Reptiles of the World-1926-Macmillan-373p-200 photos-2nd prtg (bb3) 20.00

DITMARS,R L-Strange Animals I Have Known-NY-1931-8vo-375p-1/2 cl,28 sepia photos-1st ed (y8,edges wn) 24.00

DIX,MORGAN-Memoirs of John Adams Dix-NY-1883-2 vols,cl-1st ed (l1,partly unopened) 17.50

DIXON,CAPT GEORGE-Voyage Round the World But More Particularly to the Northwest Coast of America-Amsterdam-(1968)-360p+47p-illus,fldg maps,clear dj-facs rprnt (f7,f,dj) 225.00

DIXON,CAPT GEORGE-Voyage Round the World-Lond-1789-Geo Goulding-4to-xxix,errata,360,47p-orig mrbld bds,1/2 lea,5 fldg maps,17 plts(7 hand col)-Howes D365-1st ed (u3,rebckd,recornrd,rprd pg) 1,985.00

DIXON,CAPT GEORGE-Voyage Round the World-Lond-1789-George Goulding-4to-22 plts & maps(incl lg fldg map as frntis)-Streeter 3484-1st ed (p8,rbnd,lacks half title) 1,500.00

DIXON,CHARLES-Game Birds and Wild Fowl of the British Islands-Lond-1895-Chapman & Hall-13 col drwngs by A T Elwes (p6) 300.00

DIXON,DR JOSEPH K-Vanishing Race-NY-nd-231p-illus-Dowd #267-rprnt (c7,chip dj) 25.00

DIXON,H N-Student's Handbook of British Mosses-1904-Sumfield-583p+65 plain plts (bb3,new e.p.) 48.00

DIXON,JOSEPH-Wildlife Portfolio of the Western National Parks-Wash D.C.-1957-4to-121p-photos (m3,vf) 10.00

DIXON,JOSEPH-Wildlife Portfolio of the Western National Parks-Wash-1942-121p-pict cl,plts-1st ed (t7) 20.00

DIXON,KEITH-Hidden House-Flagstaff-1956-Mus of N Ariz Bull.#29-90p-stiff wrps,frntis,photos,maps-1st ed (t7,f) 12.50

DIXON,PETER L-Men and Waves-1966-Coward McCann-2nd ed (p9,sl tn dj) 25.00

DIXON,ROLAND B-Mythology of All Races.Vol.IX:Oceanic-Bost-1916-Marshall Jones-buckram,plts,fldg map-1st ed (l8) 45.00

DIXON,THOMAS,JR.-Life Worth Living-NY-1905-140p-cl,illus-1st ed (n1) 20.00

DIXON,WILLIAM H-New America-Phila-1867-Lippincott-495p+ads-grn cl,plts-1st Amer ed (m2) 75.00

DIXON,WILLIAM S-Men,Horses and Hunting-NY-nd(1931)-Payson-1st US ed (h9,wn dj) 45.00

DOANE,GEORGE W-Ends and Objects of Burlington College-Burlington-1848-16p-wrps (aa6) 40.00

DOANE,PELAGIE-First Day-Phila-(1956)-Lippincott-oblng 8vo-unpgd-pict cl,col illus,auth (s3,dj) 25.00

DOBIE,J FRANK-Apache Gold and Yaqui Silver-Bost-(1939)-Little,Brown-1st trd ed (aa10,f,dj) 185.00

DOBIE,J FRANK-Ben Lilly Legend-Bost-1950-Little,Brown-1st ed (ee2,f,dj) 45.00

DOBIE,J FRANK-Coronado's Children-Dallas-(1930)-SW Pr-367p-illus,e.p. maps-Howes D374 (ff4) 15.00

DOBIE,J FRANK-Cow People-Bost-(1964)-Little,Brown-xii,305p-cl,photos-1st ed (v1,dj) 40.00

DOBIE,J FRANK-ED.-Follow De Drinkin' Gou'd-Austin-1928-201p-Tx Folklore Scty VII-1st ed (t8,sl wn sp) 55.00

DOBIE,J FRANK-ED.-Publications of the Texas Folk Lore Society-Austin-May 1925-Tex Folk Lore Soc,No.IV-133p-1st ed (cc4) 75.00

DOBIE,J FRANK-ED.-Southwestern Lore-Dallas-(1931)-199p-stiff dec wrps-Six Guns #607-1st ed (t7) 50.00

DOBIE,J FRANK-ED.-Southwestern Lore-Dallas-(1931)-SW Pr-199p-Tex Folk Lore Soc,No.IX-Herd 706 (cc4) 65.00

DOBIE,J FRANK-ED.-Spur of the Cock-Austin-1933-Folk Lore Soc/publ XI-1st ed (a9) 35.00

DOBIE,J FRANK-ED.-Texas and Southwestern Lore-Austin-(July,1934)-Tex Folk Lore Soc,No.VI-259p (cc4) 50.00

DOBIE,J FRANK-ED.-Tone the Bell Easy-Austin-1932-Tx Folklore Soc-1st ed (pp9) 65.00

DOBIE,J FRANK-Flavor of Texas-Dallas-1936-287p-illus-1st ed (jj1,sl soil) 150.00

DOBIE,J FRANK-Mustangs and Cow Horses-Dallas-1965-SMU Pr-later prtg (h9,dj) 28.00

DOBIE,J FRANK-Mustangs-Bost-(1952)-Little,Brown-sm 8vo-pict cl,illus-Graff 1100-Herd 696-1st ed (aa3,f,f dj) 45.00

DOBIE,J FRANK-Mustangs-Bost-(1952)-Little,Brown-xviii,376p-cl,illus & col frntis,Chas B Wilson-1st ed (v1) 50.00

DOBIE,J FRANK-On the Open Range-Dallas-(1931)-312p-pict cl,col frntis-1st ed (t7,sp fade) 150.00

DOBIE,J FRANK-On the Open Range-Dallas-(1931)-Southwest Pr-312p-col frntis,illus,Mead,dec e.p.-rare-1st ed (f9,cov wn & fade) 350.00

DOBIE,J FRANK-On the Open Range-Dallas-(1931)-Southwest Pr-sm 8vo-312p-dec blu cl,illus-ltd to 750c-scarce-1st ed (oo8,sl wn) 150.00

DOBIE,J FRANK-Prefaces-Bost-(1975)-Little,Brown-1st ed (ee2,f,dj) 35.00

DOBIE,J FRANK-Some Part of Myself-(1967)-Little,Brown-282p-illus-1st ed (t8,sl chip dj) 30.00

DOBIE,J FRANK-Some Part of Myself-Bost-(1967)-Little,Brown-1st ed (ee2,f,dj) 35.00

DOBIE,J FRANK-Stories of Christmas and the Bowie Knife-Austin-1953-Steck-62p-illus by W Hunter-1st ed (a9,box) 75.00

DOBIE,J FRANK-Tales of Old Time Texas-Bost-(1955)-Little,Brown-xvi,336p-cl,illus-1st ed (v1,wn dj) 30.00

DOBIE,J FRANK-Texan in England-Bost-1945-Little,Brown-xvi,285p-cl-1st ed (v1,dj) 45.00

DOBIE,J FRANK-Tongues of the Monte-1948-Hammond,Hammond-224p-g. sombrero on cov,engvngs by E Knight-1st Brit ed (t8,chip dj) 75.00

DOBIE,J FRANK-Tongues of the Monte-GC-1935(date on t.p.)-Dbldy,Doran-301p-pict cl-1st ed (z1,f) 75.00

DOBIE,J FRANK-Vaquero of the Brush Country-Dallas-1929-South West Pr-orig pattrnd bds,auth 1st bk-Howes D376-scarce-1st ed (dd2,rub,clipping pasted in) 195.00

DOBIE,J FRANK-Voice of the Coyote-Bost-1949-Little,Brown-1st ed (pp9,dj wn,chip) 40.00

DOBIE,J FRANK-Voice of the Coyote-Bost-1949-Little,Brown-xx,386p-cl,illus-1st prtg (v1,sl chip dj) 65.00

DOBLE,JOHN-Journal and Letters from the Mines-Denver-(1962)-304p-illus,fldg map,celuloid dj-ltd to 1000c-ltd 1st ed (f7,f,chip dj) 75.00

DOBREE,BONAMY-English Literature in the Early 18th Century, 1700 to 1740-NY-1959-Oxford-1st US ed (hh5,dj) 30.00

DOBYNS,STEPHEN-Saratoga Swimmer-1981-Atheneum-1st ed (s9,f,dj) 15.00

DOBYNS,W S-California Gardens-NY-1931-208 illus-1st ed (h10,fade) 175.00

DOBYNS,W S-California Gardens-NY-1931-scarce in dj-1st ed (kk4,dj tn) 225.00

DOBZHANSKY,THEODOSIUS G-Dobzhansky's Genetics of Natural Populations, I to XLIII-NY-1981-Columbia Univ Pr-942p-red cl,illus-1st ed (l2,dj) 45.00

DOCK,PHYLLIS-Little Hawk-Hampden Highlands-1967-Highland Pr-1st ed (j9) 25.00

DOCKSTADER,FREDERICK J-Great North American Indians-NY-1977-Van Nostrand-4to-ix+386p-cl,photos,illus-1st ed (z4,f dj) 30.00

DOCKSTADER,FREDERICK J-Indian Art in America-NY-1973-Promontory Pr-4to-224p-yel bds,b&w & col illus (r10,dj) 25.00

DOCKSTADER,FREDERICK J-Indian Art of the Americas-1973-NY Mus Amer Ind/Heye Fnd-tall 8vo-304p-pict cov,col photos-1st ed (cc4) 40.00

DOCTOR,JOSEPH E-Shotguns on Sunday-LA-(1958)-Westernlore-230p-cl,illus-1st ed (v1,dj) 35.00

DOCTOR,JOSEPH E-Shotguns on Sunday-LA-1958-230p-pict cl,photos (t7) 25.00

DOCTOROW,E L-Big as Life-NY-1966-1st ed (q5,f,dj) 250.00

DOCTOROW,E L-Big as Life-NY-1966-red cl bds-1st ed (n5,sl dmpstnd,dj edgewn) 125.00

DOCTOROW,E L-Book of Daniel-NY-(1971)-1st ed (c5,f,dj) 40.00

DOCTOROW,E L-Loon Lake-NY-(1980)-Random-1st ed (f3,f,dj) 20.00

DOCTOROW,E L-Loon Lake-NY-(1980)-Random-1st trd ed (d10,as new in dj) 15.00

DOCTOROW,E L-Ragtime-NY-(1975)-ltd to 150c,autg-1st ed (c5,as new in box) 150.00

DOCTOROW,E L-Ragtime-NY-(1975)-Random-1st ed (bb1,as new in dj) 30.00

DODD,ANNA B-In and Out of Three Normandy Inns-NY-(1892)-Lovell,Coryell-394p-blu/gry bds,dec wi 3 coat of arms,illus (l6) 30.00

DODD,L E-History of the Odd Fellows' Home of Ohio-(Greenville)-1916-523p-cl (h1,wk hngs,ldge stmp few pgs) 15.00

DODD,RUTH-Cocky Cocker Book-Bost-1934-Bruce Humphries-8vo-86p-1st ed (bb5,f,dj) 15.00

DODD,WILLIAM E-Life of Nathaniel Macon-Raleigh-1903-Edwards & Broughton-443p-grn cl-1st ed (oo5,bump,rub,sl fox) 75.00

DODDRIDGE,AMELIA-Liberty Recipes-Cin-1918-Stewart & Kidd-106p-blu bds,frntis,6 b&w plts-Bitting 125 (m6,tattrd dj) 18.00

DODDS,GORDON B-Hiram Martin Chittenden, His Public Career-(Lexington)-(1973)-220p-cl (g1) 15.00

DODGE,BERTHA S-Road West-Albuq-(1980)-218p-photos-1st ed (u7,f,dj) 20.00

DODGE,D-It Ain't Hay-1946-S&S-1st ed (x7,dj) 33.00

DODGE,DAVID-Angel's Ransom-NY-(1956)-Random-1st ed (bb1,sl chip dj) 20.00

DODGE,DAVID-Hooligan-NY-(1969)-Macmillan-1st ed (bb1,dj) 20.00

DODGE,DAVID-Lights of Skaro-Lond-1954-Joseph-1st Brit ed (r4,f,dj) 22.50

DODGE,DAVID-Lights of Skaro-NY-(1954)-Random-1st ed (bb1,dj) 25.00

DODGE,ERNEST S-Beyond the Capes-Bost-1971-Little,Brown-1st ed (v4,as new in dj) 30.00

DODGE,ERNEST S-New England and the South Seas-Cambridge-1965-Harvard U Pr-8vo-xv,(1),216p-grn cl,e.p. maps,53 drwngs & photos-1st ed (nn1,f,f dj) 40.00

DODGE,ERNEST S-Northwest by Sea-NY-1961-348p-map e.p.-1st ed (t7,f,dj) 12.50

DODGE,G M-How We Built the Union Pacific Railway-Wash-1910-GPO-136p-wrps,illus-Howes D393 (cc4,wrps wn) 35.00

DODGE,G M-Union Pacific Railroad-NY-1867-Bryant-33p-wrps-Howes D395-scarce (nn6,sl chip) 200.00

DODGE,HARRISON H-Mount Vernon-Phila-1932-Lippincott-31 illus (p2) 15.00

DODGE,MARY E-Hans Brinker-NY-1866-James O'Kane-lea,illus,Darley & Nast-1st ed (l9,sl chip & fragile sp) 300.00

DODGE,MARY M-Hans Brinker and the Silver Skates-Phila-(1925)-Winston-325p-cl wi pict pasteon,4 col plts,b&w illus,C Burd (s3) 12.00

DODGE,MARY M-Theophilus-NY-1876-Scribner,Armstrong-8vo-247p-BAL 4769-1st ed (w6,f) 65.00

DODGE,MARY M-When Life is Young-NY-1894-Century-8vo-255p-pnk & gld stmpd grn cl,t.e.g.,illus-BAL 4787-1st ed (w6,f) 65.00

DODGE,ORVIL-ED.-Heros of Battle Rock or the Miner's Reward, a Short Story of Thrilling Interest...-(Portland)-1904-21p-wrps-scarce (p1) 75.00

DODGE,RICHARD I-Black Hills-Mpls-(1965)-Ross & Haines-156p-illus,map-Howes D401 (cc4,dj) 15.00

DODGE,RICHARD I-Plains of the Great West and Their Inhabitants-NY-1877-447p-pict cl,illus,fldg map-Howes D404-1st ed (t7,sp wn) 45.00

DODGE,RICHARD V-Rails of the Silver Gate-San Marino-1962-143p-3rd prtg (n4,f,dj) 20.00

DODRILL,CHARLES T-Heritage of a Pioneer-Huntington-1967-782p-cl (m1,f,sl soil dj) 30.00

DOE,JANET-Bibliography of the Works of Ambroise Pare-Chig-1937-266p-illus-scarce-1st ed (dd3,dj) 175.00

DOGGETT,HENRY S-Sketch of the Life and Professional Services of Isaac Sams...-Cin-1880-83p-cl (k1) 20.00

DOHERTY,EDDIE-Matt Talbot-Milw-(1953)-Bruce-8vo-200p-1st ed (aa5,dj) 15.00

DOIG,IVAN-This House of Sky-NY-(1978)-Harcourt Brace-auth 1st bk-1st ed (b3,f,dj) 40.00

DOIG,IVAN-This House of Sky-NY-(1978)-HBJ-auth 1st bk-1st ed (g8,f,dj wi sm stn frnt cov) 50.00

DOIG,IVAN-Winter Brothers-NY-1980-1st ed (t5,f,dj) 20.00

DOIG,IVAN-Winter Brothers-NY-1980-HBJ-1st ed (j8,f,dj) 35.00

DOISNEAU,ROBERT-My Paris-NY-1972-Macmillan-sm folio-text by M Chevalier-1st ed (q3,dj) 75.00

DOLCI,DANILO-Outlaws-NY-(1961)-Orion-8vo-296p-1st US ed (jj5,dj) 12.50

DOLE,EDMUND P-Hiwa-NY,Lond-1900-Harper & Bros-sm 8vo-107p-lt tan pict cl,t.p. in red & blk-1st ed (t10) 75.00

DOLE,SANFORD B-Memoirs of the Hawaiian Revolution-Honolulu-1936-Adv Publ Co-8vo-xxiii,188p-`lea look' red cl,12 plts-1st ed (nn1,g fade,sl wn) 95.00

DOLFIN,J-Bringing the Gospel in Hogan and Pueblo-Grand Rapids-1921-376p-frntis,photos-scarce-1st ed (t7) 40.00

DOLFIN,J-Bringing the Gospel in Hogan and Pueblo-Grand Rapids-1921-376p-photos-scarce-1st ed (u7,e.p. tn) 45.00

DOLFIN,J-Bringing the Gospel in Hogan and Pueblo-Grand Rapids-1921-376p-photos-scarce-1st ed (v7,fr f.e.p. cut) 45.00

DOLGE,ERNEST-Industrial Douglas Fir-Tacoma-1927-auth-8vo-235p-wrps,photos-ltd to 250c,nbrd-1st ed (gg5) 20.00

DOLINGER,JANE-Inca Gold-Chig-(1968,67)-Regnery-8vo-189p-1st US ed (ff5,dj) 12.50

DOLL,EDGAR A-ED.-Twenty Five Years-Vineland-1932-xxi,135p-bds,plts (aa6) 45.00

DOLL,EDGAR A-ET AL-Mental Deficiency Due to Birth Injuries-NY-1932-Macmillan-xvi+289p-red cl,plts,illus-1st ed (d2,sl wn dj) 20.00

DOLMETSCH,CARL R-Smart Set-NY-1966-Dial-4to-262p-col illus-1st ed (bb5,dj sl tn,soil) 20.00

DOLSON,HILDEGARDE-Guess Whose Hair I'm Wearing-NY-(1963)-Random-8vo-206p-cl,illus-1st ed (z5,dj) 14.00

DOMINIC,R B-Attending Physician-Lond-1980-Macmillan-1st Brit ed (f4,f,dj) 12.50

DOMINIC,R B-Attending Physician-NY-1980-Harper-1st ed (q4,dj) 25.00

DOMINIC,R B-There is No Justice-NY-1971-Dbldy CC-1st ed (f4,f,sl yel dj) 25.00

DONAHEY,VIC-Beak and Claws of America-Waynesfield-(1931)-129p-cl (n1,pres cpy) 12.50

DONALDSON,IVAN J-Fishwheels on the Columbia-Portland-(1971)-Binfords & Mort-4to-124p-photos,maps,sketches-1st ed (aa5,dj rub) 30.00

DONALDSON,STEPHEN R-One Tree-NY-(1982)-Ballantine-1st ed (k3,f,dj) 25.00

DONALDSON,THOMAS-Extra Census Bulletin, Indians, Six Nations of New York-Wash D.C.-1892-89p-wrps,fldg map frntis,photos,fldg maps-1st ed (t7) 100.00

DONAN,P-Webfoot Bonanzas-Portland-(1900)-Ore RR & Navigation Co-15p-col map on verso (bb9) 75.00

DONATH,DOROTHY C-Buddhism for the West-NY-1971-Julian Pr-cl-1st ed (o8,f) 17.50

DONAVAN,FRANK P,JR.-ED.-Headlights and Markers-NY-1946-406p-1st ed (n4) 16.00

DONAVAN,JOHN-Case of the Beckoning Dead-NY-1938-HIllman-1st US ed (d4) 12.50

DONLEAVY,J P-Beastly Beatitudes of Balthazar B-1968-Delacorte-1st ed (s9,f,dj) 20.00

DONLEAVY,J P-Ginger Man-NY-(1958)-McDowell Obolensky-1st ed (cc2,f,dj) 75.00

DONLEAVY,J P-Singular Man-Bost-(1963)-Little,Brown-1st ed (k3,f,dj) 25.00

DONLEAVY,J P-Unexpurgated Code-NY-1975-drwngs,auth-1st ed (r5,f,dj) 20.00

DONNELL,DICK-Dupus Boomer-Kennewick-1947 & 1948-79p-wrps,cartoons (b6) 10.00

DONNELL,DICK-You Asked For It-Kennewick-(1946)-63,(1)p-red illus wrps,cartoons (b6) 10.00

DONNELLY,MARIAN C-New England Meeting Houses of the 17th Century-(1968)-Wesleyan U Pr-165p-bds wi cl sp,illus-1st ed (a3,sl wn dj) 25.00

DONNELLY,SHRILEY-Notable Mine Disasters of Fayette County, West Virginia-(Oak Hill)-(1951)-33p-wrps (aa1) 15.00

DONON,JOSEPH-Classic French Cuisine-NY-1959-Knopf-1st ed (l6) 30.00

DONOSO,JOSE-Coronation-Lond-(1965)-Bodley Head-1st Brit ed (u10,f,f dj) 30.00

DONOSO,JOSE-Coronation-NY-1965-1st US ed (n5,f,dj) 35.00

DONOSO,JOSE-Sacred Families-NY-1977-Knopf-1st US ed (a10,as new in dj) 20.00
DONOSO,JOSE-This Sunday-NY-1967-1st US ed (q5,f,dj) 30.00
DONOVAN,FRANK,JR.-Railroads of America-1949-Kalmbach-8vo-244p-maps (nn7,wn dj) 18.00
DONOVAN-Dry Songs and Scribbles-GC-(1971)-Dbldy-1st ed (q1,dj) 35.00
DOOLEN,RICHARD S-Michigan's Polar Bears-Ann Arbor-1965-U of Mich-28p-wrps,photos (z7) 25.00
DOOLIN,JOHN B-Field,Forest & Stream in Oklahoma-Guthrie-1913-4to-159p-photos-scarce (m3) 50.00
DOONER,MILDRED-Last Post-Lond-(1903)-446p-gry cl-scarce (b7) 150.00
DOORLY,J W-God and Science-Lond-1949-Muller Ltd-8vo-227p-1st ed (aa7,dj sl soil,chip) 15.00*
DORCUS,ROY M-ED.-Hypnosis and Its Therapeutic Applications-NY-1956-McGraw Hill-(x)+300+(16)p-beige cl-1st prntg (y9) 31.50
DORE,RONALD P-Shinohata-NY-1978-Pantheon Bks-322p-grn cl,18 photos-1st Amer ed (ll1,dj) 20.00
DOREMUS,GEORGE S-American Revolution and Morris County-Rockaway-1926-(10),110,(1)p-cl,illus (aa6) 45.00
DOREN,MARK-Travels of William Bartram-NY-1940-Macy-Masius-414p (x6,sp sun) 20.00
DORESSE,JEAN-Secret Book of the Egyptian Gnostics-NY-1960-Viking-cl,illus-1st Amer ed (n8,fray dj) 45.00
DORGELES,ROLAND-On the Mandarin Road-NY-1926-Century-332p-photos (c3) 45.00
DORIN,PATRICK C-Canadian Pacific Railway-Seattle-1974-175p-1st ed (n4,f,f dj) 24.00
DORIN,PATRICK C-Commuter Railroads-Seattle-1970-192p-1st ed (n4,f,dj) 23.50
DORLAND,WAYNE-Fragrance and Flavor Industry-Mendham-1977-W Dorland Co-xvi+444p-cl sp-1st ed (c2,box) 25.00
DORMAN,C C-COMP.-Northwestern Album-Lond-1965-100p-1st ed (n4,f,dj) 16.00
DORMAN,C C-LMS Album-Lond-1967-1st ed (n4,f,dj) 16.50
DORMAN,SONYA-Planet Patrol-NY-(1978)-Coward McCann-1st ed (f3,f,dj) 20.00
DORN,EDWARD-Songs Set Two, A Short Count-Buffalo-1970-Frontier Pr-wrps-1st ed (w5,f) 15.00
DORN,EDWARD-Twenty-Four Love Songs-1969-Frontier-wrps-1st ed (t9,vf) 20.00
DORN,FRANK-Frank Dorn Cookbook-Chig-1953-Regnery Co-341p (l6) 18.00
DORN,FRANK-Good Cooking with Herbs and Spices-Irvington-on Hudson-(1958)-Harvey Hs-176p-illus,G Dorn (m6) 18.00
DORN,MICHAEL-Tycoons in the Kitchen-(NY)-(1968)-(Dorn Pr)-199p-1st prtg (l6) 18.00
DORNBUSCH,C E-Regimental Publications and Personal Narratives of the Civil War-NY-1961,1967-2 vols-wrps & bds (t7,ex-libr) 100.00
DORR,JOS W-On the Sunset Shore-Seattle-1908-Souvenir Publ Co-211p-illus cov,photos,frntis port-1st ed (b6,tn e.p.) 20.00
DORR,NELL-Bare Feet-NY-1962-NYGS-unpgd-74 photos-1st ed (cc9,chip & tn dj) 60.00
DORR,RHETA C-Woman of Fifty-NY-1924-Funk & Wagnalls-(vi)+451p-brwn cl-1st ed (b2) 35.00
DORRINGTON,A-Radium Terrors-1912-DP-1st Amer ed (x7) 45.00
DORSEY,MRS.SARAH A-Panola, a Tale of Louisiana-Phila-(1877)-261p+ads-cl-Wright 1600-1st ed (h1) 17.50
DORSON,RICHARD M-British Folklorists-Lond-1968-Routledge & Kegan Paul-cl,illus-1st ed (n8) 25.00
DORSON,RICHARD M-ED.-Davy Crockett, American Comic Legend-NY-1939-171p-frntis,illus-scarce-1st ed (t7) 35.00
DORSON,RICHARD M-ED.-Peasant Customs and Savage Myths-1968-U of Chig Pr-2 vols,cl-1st prtg (n8,as new in dj) 35.00
DORST,J-Migration of Birds-Bost-1963-8vo-476p-cl,drwngs (y8,dj) 37.50
DOS PASSOS,JOHN-1919-NY-1932-illus dj-1st ed (n5,dj) 150.00
DOS PASSOS,JOHN-42nd Parallel-1930-Harper-1st ed (jj6) 35.00
DOS PASSOS,JOHN-Best Times-NY-1966-1st ed (t5,dj) 20.00
DOS PASSOS,JOHN-Big Money-NY-1936-1st ed (o5,sl wn dj wi tape mrks) 90.00
DOS PASSOS,JOHN-Chosen Country-Bost-1951-Houghton Mifflin-8vo-cl bckd bds-1st ed (jj8,f,dj) 35.00
DOS PASSOS,JOHN-Ground We Stand On-1941-Harcourt,Brace-1st ed (x2,f,sl fade sp) 55.00
DOS PASSOS,JOHN-Head and Heart of Thomas Jefferson-GC-1954-Dbldy-vi+442p-blk cl-1st ed (k2,dj) 20.00
DOS PASSOS,JOHN-Midcentury-Bost-1961-Houghton Mifflin-8vo-cl-1st ed (jj8,dj) 25.00
DOS PASSOS,JOHN-Midcentury-Lond-(1961)-Andre Deutsch-1st Brit ed (cc2,f,dj) 40.00
DOS PASSOS,JOHN-Most Likely to Succeed-NY-(1954)-Prentice-ltd to 1000c,autg (w1,f,dj) 75.00
DOS PASSOS,JOHN-Number One-1943-Houghton,Mifflin-1st ed (x2,f,dj) 30.00
DOS PASSOS,JOHN-Panama-or the Adventures of My Seven Uncles-1931-Harpers-wrps,one of 300c,two autg,col illus by Dos Passos-1st ed (x2,sl sunned) 225.00
DOS PASSOS,JOHN-Portugal Story-GC-(1969)-Dbldy-1st ed (bb2,f,dj) 35.00
DOS PASSOS,JOHN-Pushcart at the Curb-1922-Doran-1st ed (jj6,sl chip dj) 330.00
DOS PASSOS,JOHN-Rosinante-NY-1922-Doran-1st ed (z2,dj wn & chip) 150.00
DOS PASSOS,JOHN-Three Soldiers-NY-(1921)-Doran-cl-1st ed,3rd state (x3,hng weak) 35.00
DOS PASSOS,JOHN-Three Soldiers-NY-1921-1st iss wi misprnt on pg 213,2nd iss dj-1st ed (r5,sl wn dj) 200.00
DOS PASSOS,JOHN-Tour of Duty-1946-Houghton,Mifflin-1st ed (x2,f,dj) 20.00
DOS PASSOS,JOHN-U.S.A.-Bost-1946-3 vols,illus by R Marsh-1st illus ed (t5,1 dj chip,wn box) 75.00
DOS PASSOS,JOHN-U.S.A.-Bost-1946-Houghton Mifflin-tan cl,lea labls,illus by R Marsh-ltd to 350 sets,two autg (w1,sl wn box) 550.00
DOS PASSOS,JOHN-Villages are the Heart of Spain-Chig-(1937)-Esquire Coronet-sm 8vo-cl wi prtd labl,illus-ltd to 1200c,nbrd-1st ed (ll10,sl sun sp) 85.00
DOSSENBACH,H D-Family Life of Birds-NY-1971-4to-192p-col photos (y8,dj chip) 22.00
DOSTOEVSKY,F M-Stavrogin's Confession-NY-1947-Lear-8vo-136p-transl by V Woolf & S S Koteliansky-1st US ed (w6,f,sl chip dj) 125.00
DOSTOEVSKY,F-Winter Notes on Summer Impressions-1955-Criterion-1st Amer ed & 1st in Engl (x2,f,dj) 55.00
DOSTOIEFFSKAYA,L F-Emigrant-NY-1916-Brentano's-8vo-320p-red cl-1st US ed (w6) 35.00

DOTEN,ALFRED-Journals of...1849 to 1903-Reno-1973-U of Nev Pr-3 vols-gry cl,plts-1st ed (b2,box) 50.00

DOTY,ROBERT-Photo Secession-Rochester-(1960)-Eastman-tall 4to-cl-1st ed (y3,f,dj) 95.00

DOUBLEDAY,F N-Memoirs of a Publisher-1972-Dbldy-1st ed (t9,vf,dj) 45.00

DOUBLEDAY,RUSSELL-Cattle Ranch to College-NY-1899-McClure-347p+24 lvs photos-pict cl-1st ed (z1) 35.00

DOUCETTE,EARL-Fisherman's Guide to Maine-NY-1951-12mo-308p-maps (m3) 15.00

DOUGHTY,A G-Quebec of Yester Year-Tor-1932-198p-illus (a7,sl fade) 60.00

DOUGHTY,J-Cabinet of Natural History & American Rural Sports-Barre-1973-4to-150p-ltd to 1950c-col plts-facsimile ed (m3,vf,box) 65.00

DOUGHTY,J-Some Early American Hunters-Derrydale-1928-8vo-41p-ltd to 375c,nbrd-hand col frntis-scarce (m3) 135.00

DOUGLAS,BYRD-Science of Baseball-NY,Chig,SF-(1922)-190p+ads-cl (n1) 22.50

DOUGLAS,BYRD-Steamboatin' on the Cumberland-Nashville-(1961)-Tenn Bk Co-xvi+407p-gry cl-presumed 1st ed (k2,dj,pres cpy) 35.00

DOUGLAS,C L-James Bowie-Dallas-1944-Banks Upshaw-216p-1st ed (a9) 60.00

DOUGLAS,C L-Life Story of W Lee O'Daniel-Dallas-1938-Regional Pr-176p-cl,photos-1st ed (w3,autg) 65.00

DOUGLAS,C L-Thunder on the Gulf-Dallas-1936-Turner-128p-blu cl,plts-1st ed (n10) 175.00

DOUGLAS,C L-Thunder on the Gulf-Dallas-1936-Turner-1st ed (pp9,dj chip,rub) 100.00

DOUGLAS,ELLEN-Apostles of Light-Bost-(1973)-Houghton Mifflin-1st ed (s6,dj) 50.00

DOUGLAS,FREDERIC H-Indian Art of the United States-1941-MOMA-4to-204p-illus-1st ed (d3,dj) 40.00

DOUGLAS,FREDERIC H-Indian Art of the United States-NY-1941-MOMA-cl,208 plts incl 8 col-1st ed (l8,f,dj) 85.00

DOUGLAS,GEORGE B-ET AL-Ship Model Book-NY-1926-Rudder Publ Co-4to-47 nbrd pgs+plans+ads,fldg patterns(single sheet) in rear pckt,blu cl-3rd ed (nn1,sl fox) 45.00

DOUGLAS,GEORGE M-Lands Forlorn-NY-1914-Putnam's-8vo-xv,285p-illus blu cl,col frntis,180 photos,2 fldg col maps at rear-1st ed (mm8,sl scuff & wn) 90.00*

DOUGLAS,MARY-ED.-Man in Africa-Lond-(1969)-Tavistock-8vo-372p-cl,maps,plts-1st ed (y5,dj) 25.00

DOUGLAS,MARY-Lele of the Kasai-Lond-1963-OUP-8vo-268p-cl,illus,maps-1st ed (y5,dj) 22.00

DOUGLAS,MARY-Natural Symbols-NY-(1970)-Pantheon Bks-8vo-127p-cl-1st ed (y5,dj) 18.00

DOUGLAS,MIKE-Mike Douglas Cookbook-(1969)-Funk & Wagnalls-180p-dec blk cov,photos-1st prtg (q8,dj) 12.50

DOUGLAS,NORMAN-An Alamanac-Lond-(1945)-Chatto & Windus-8vo-cl-1st ed (jj8,f,dj) 25.00

DOUGLAS,NORMAN-ED.-Venus in the Kitchen-1953-Viking-192p-blu cl-1st prtg (q8,dj) 16.50

DOUGLAS,NORMAN-Footnotes on Capri-Lond-1952-Sidgwick & Jackson-48 photos-1st ed (y1,dj) 50.00

DOUGLAS,NORMAN-Paneros-Lond-1931-Chatto & Windus-8vo-cl bckd bds,frntis-ltd to 650c-1st Brit ed (jj8,vf,dj) 85.00

DOUGLAS,NORMAN-South Wind-Chig-1929-Argus Bks-2 vols-t.e.g.,illus by John Austen-1st ed thus (w5,f,sl tn dj,box) 60.00

DOUGLAS,R D-Three Boy Scouts in Africa-NY-1928-8vo-149p-photos (m3) 35.00

DOUGLAS,R W-History of Glassmaking-1972-Foulis-213p-illus (cc8,dj) 55.00

DOUGLAS,ROY-Who Is Nemo?-Phila-1937-Lippincott-1st US ed (g4,dj) 25.00

DOUGLAS,WILLIAM O-Beyond the High Himalayas-NY-1952-352p-16 plts,e.p. maps-1st ed (o10,sm cov stn,autg) 10.00

DOUGLAS,WILLIAM O-My Wilderness the Pacific Northwest-GC-1960-8vo-206p-illus,F L Jaques-1st ed (m3,sp tn dj) 12.50

DOUGLAS,WILLIAM O-Russian Journey-GC-1956-Dbldy-255p-cl,plts-1st ed (kk1,f,dj sl soil & creased) 25.00

DOUSSER-LEENHARDT,ROSENE-Le Grande Case-Paris-(1965)-Buchet/Chastel-8vo-198p-photo illus wrps,4 plts (p8) 30.00

DOW,ALDEN B-Reflections-Midland-1970-lg sq folio-illus-1st ed (ee1) 225.00

DOW,EDSON-Passes to the North-(1963)-Wenatchee-255p-illus,e.p. map (r8,f,dj) 30.00

DOW,GEORGE F-Pirates of the New England Coast 1630 to 1730-Salem-1923-Marine Rsrch Soc-lg 8vo-xxii,plt,394p-red buckrm,map e.p.,45 illus-Howes 437-1st ed (pp1,sp fade) 155.00

DOW,GEORGE F-Whale Ships and Whaling-Salem-1925-Marine Rsrch Soc-4to-dec e.p.,photos-1st ed (p8,sp fade) 200.00

DOW,GEORGE-British Steam Horses-Lond-1950-128p-1st ed (n4,f) 16.00

DOW,GEORGE-Great Central Album-Lond-1969-128p-fldg map-1st ed (n4,f,dj) 20.00

DOW,GEORGE-North Staffordshire Album-Lond-1970-112p-1st ed (n4,f,dj) 17.50

DOW,HELEN J-Art of Alex Colville-Tor-1972-McGraw Hill Ryerson-4to-231p-col plts-1st ed (aa7,dj) 35.00*

DOW,NEAL-Reminiscences of...-Portland-1898-769p-g stmpd illus frnt cov (a1,f) 25.00

DOWD,CLEMENT-Life of Zebulon B Vance-Charlotte-1897-493p-1st ed (n3) 35.00

DOWD,JAMES P-Custer Lives-Fairfield-1982-263p-1st ed (n3,vf,dj) 17.50

DOWD,JAMES P-Custer Lives-Fairfield-1982-Ye Galleon-(vi),263p-cl,illus,col illus e.p.-1st ed (v1) 25.00

DOWELL,COLEMAN-Island People-NY-(1976)-New Directions-1st US ed (hh5,f,f dj) 12.50

DOWELL,COLEMAN-Mrs October Was Here-NY-(1974)-New Directions-1st US ed (hh5,f,f dj) 12.50

DOWER,WALTER-Trout Trouble & Other Trouble-NY-1948-8vo-90p-illus-1st ed (m3,f,dj) 27.50

DOWLING,PHIL-Mountaineers-Edmonton-1979-258p-1st ed (p10,f,dj) 15.00

DOWNES,ALFRED M-Firefighters and Their Pets-NY-1907-Harper & Bros-xvi+185p-red cl,photos-1st ed (b2,cov soil & wn) 45.00

DOWNES,RANDOLPH C-Frontier Ohio, 1788-1803-Columbus-1935-280p-cl-Ohio Hist Collections (j1,sl spot frnt cov) 22.50

DOWNEY,FAIRFAX-Guns at Gettysburg-NY-(1958)-290p-illus,maps-1st ed (n3,f,dj) 35.00

DOWNEY,FAIRFAX-Indian Fighting Army-NY-1941-Scribner-xiv,329p-blu cl,paintings-1st prtg (v1) 90.00

DOWNEY,FAIRFAX-Indian Wars of the U.S. Army-GC-1963-248p-illus-1st ed (n3,dj missing pcs) 25.00

DOWNEY,FAIRFAX-Seventh's Staghound-NY-1948-230p-fiction-illus-1st ed (t7,wn dj) 30.00

DOWNEY,JOSEPH T-Cruise of the Portsmouth, 1845 to 1847...-New Haven/Lond-1963-Yale U Pr-8vo-xxi,246p-blu pict g dec cl,col frntis,5 maps (mm1,f,publ card laid in) 50.00

DOWNIE,RALPH E-Pictorial History of the State of Washington-Seattle-1939-lg 8vo-163p-photos,fldg map (r8,cov wn,soil,autg) 15.00

DOWNIE,WILLIAM-Hunting for Gold-Palo Alto-(1971)-Amer West Publ-412p-photos,drwngs-Howes D448 (bb4,dj) 20.00

DOWNIE,WILLIAM-Hunting for Gold-Palo Alto-1971-412p-photos,illus (t7,f,dj) 15.00

DOWNIE,WILLIAM-Hunting for Gold-SF-1893-407p-orig 1/2 lea,port,illus-Lowther 1036 (a7,chip sp top,mar cov) 150.00

DOWNING,A J-Fruits and Fruit Trees of America-NY-1852-Wiley-594p-14th ed (x6,sp sun,wn,sl fox) 62.50

DOWNING,ANDREW J-Treatise on the Theory and Practice of Landscape Gardening-NY-1855-Saxton-532p-cl-5th ed (x6,wn,stns,hngs rnfrcd) 50.00

DOWNING,ANTOINETTE F-Architectural Heritage of Newport, Rhode Island, 1640 to 1915-Cambridge-1952-Harvard-lg 4to-cl,230 plts (cc10,dj) 150.00

DOWNING,ANTOINETTE F-Early Homes of Rhode Island-Richmond-1937-Garret & Massie-4to-480p-cl,frntis,209 plts,80 illus (cc10,dj) 95.00

DOWNING,CENTURY-Conspirators' Cookbook-NY-1967-Knopf-250p (r6) 11.00

DOWNING,DAVID-Devil's Virtuosos-NY-1977-St.Martin's-1st ed (z2,f,f dj) 15.00

DOWNING,ELIOT R-Naturalist in the Great Lakes Region-Chig-1922-U of Chig Pr-328p-limp cl,photos,maps (z7) 30.00

DOWNS,JOSEPH-American Furniture Queen Anne and Chippendale Periods-NY-(1977)-lg 4to-10 col plts (l10,dj) 30.00

DOWSE,THOMAS S-Brain and the Nerves-NY-1884-150p (g10) 85.00

DOYLE,A CONAN-Adventures of Gerard-1903-McClure-1st Amer ed (s10,sp lettrng flaked) 20.00

DOYLE,A CONAN-Adventures of Sherlock Holmes-1892-Harper-1st iss wi "if had" on pg 65 line 4-1st Amer ed (x7) 1,500.00

DOYLE,A CONAN-Case Book of Sherlock Holmes-1927-Doran-1st Amer ed (x7) 55.00

DOYLE,A CONAN-Casebook of Sherlock Holmes-NY-1971-Union Carbide-story by H Waugh on dj reverse (e4,dj) 25.00

DOYLE,A CONAN-Danger! and Other Stories-1919-Doran-1st ed (x7) 55.00

DOYLE,A CONAN-Desert Drama, Being the Tragedy of the Korosko-1898-Lippincott-pict cl-1st ed (x7) 90.00

DOYLE,A CONAN-Doings of Raffles Haw-1892-Cassell-1st ed (x7) 375.00

DOYLE,A CONAN-Duet-1899-Appleton-1st Amer ed (x7) 65.00

DOYLE,A CONAN-Edge of the Unknown-1930-Putnam-1st ed (x7,sp chip dj) 225.00

DOYLE,A CONAN-ET AL-Strange Secrets-1895-Fenno-1st ed (x7) 125.00

DOYLE,A CONAN-Exploits of Brigadier Gerard-NY-1896-Appleton-1st Amer ed (y2,f) 100.00

DOYLE,A CONAN-Great Boer War-Cape Town-1976-768p-maps-ltd to 1000c,nbrd (kk2,f,dj) 75.00

DOYLE,A CONAN-Great Shadow and Beyond the City-Bristol/Lond-(1893)-Arrowsmith/Simpkin,Mrshll-brwn dec cl,gilt,illus-1st ed,1st iss (ll5,sl spot rear cov) 285.00

DOYLE,A CONAN-Great Shadow-NY-1893-Harpers-1st US ed (d4,edge wn) 40.00

DOYLE,A CONAN-Hound of the Baskervilles-1902-G Newnes-1st ed (x7) 1,250.00

DOYLE,A CONAN-Hound of the Baskervilles-NY-1902-McClure,Phillips & Co-salmon pnk bds-inserted lf pasted to stub of cancelled t.p.-1st ed,third issue (t9) 35.00

DOYLE,A CONAN-Land of Mist-1926-Doran-1st Amer ed (x2,dj sl wn & tn) 825.00

DOYLE,A CONAN-Lost World-(1912)-Burt-b&w photos-photo play ed (x7) 38.00

DOYLE,A CONAN-Lost World-NY-1912-Doran-g stmpd brwn cl,16 plts(only 8 in Brit ed)-1st Amer ed (gg8,sl rub sp) 75.00

DOYLE,A CONAN-Maracot Deep-NY-1929-Dbldy-1st ed (g4) 30.00

DOYLE,A CONAN-Memoirs of Sherlock Holmes-NY-(1894)-Harper-8vo-g dec pale blu cl-w/o add story-1st Amer ed thus (x3,sl wn & soil) 100.00

DOYLE,A CONAN-Micah Clarke-1894-Harper & Bros-1st Amer hdcov ed (x7,sl sunned sp) 65.00

DOYLE,A CONAN-New Revalation-NY-1918-Doran-1st US ed (d4) 25.00

DOYLE,A CONAN-Poison Belt-NY-(1913)-Hodder & Stoughton/Doran-frontis,15 plts-1st US ed (e10,sl fray,rub,2 loose plts) 30.00

DOYLE,A CONAN-Refugees-NY-(1893)-illus by Thulstrup-2nd prtg (m4) 22.50

DOYLE,A CONAN-Return of Sherlock Holmes-NY-1905-McClure-precedes Brit ed-1st ed (f4,weak hngs) 20.00

DOYLE,A CONAN-Round the Fire Stories-NY-1908-McClure-1st US ed (j4) 75.00

DOYLE,A CONAN-Sir Nigel-NY-1906-6 illus-1st Amer ed (m4) 20.00

DOYLE,A CONAN-Songs of Action-NY-1898-8vo-144p-g stmpd red cl-1st ed (kk7) 25.00

DOYLE,A CONAN-Stark Munro Letters-NY-1895-Appleton-dec maroon cl,illus-1st Amer ed (k8) 25.00

DOYLE,A CONAN-Uncle Bernac-Lond-1897-Smith-1st ed (d4,sp wn,cut in sp) 40.00

DOYLE,A CONAN-Uncle Bernac-NY-1897-Appleton-8vo-red cl stmpd in silv & gilt-1st Amer ed (x3) 40.00

DOYLE,A CONAN-Valley of Fear-1914-Doran-1st ed (s10) 50.00

DOYLE,A CONAN-Visit to Three Fronts-NY-1916-93p-brwn papr cov bds-1st Amer ed (kk2) 25.00

DOYLE,ADRIAN C-Heaven Has Claws-NY-(1953)-1st ed (jj4,dj) 15.00

DOYLE,J E P-Plymouth Church and its Pastor-Hartford-1874-Park Publ-566p+ads-brwn cl,plts-1st ed (mm10,edge wn & soil) 75.00

DOYLE,JOSEPH B-Frederick William Von Steuben and the American Revolution-Steubenville-1913-399p-cl,ltd to 600c,nbrd-1st ed (n1) 35.00

DOYLE,JOSEPH B-Frederick William von Steuben and the American Revolution-Steubenville-1913-H C Cook-xx+399p-red cl,plts-ltd to 600c,nbrd-1st ed (mm10,sm cov spot,sl fox) 85.00

DOYLE,LYNN-Babel Babble-Dublin-(1945)-Talbot Pr-1st ed (z8,f,dj) 75.00

DOYLE,MARTIN-Flower Garden or Monthly Calendar-NY-1835-Moore-180p-cl,col frntis,3 handcol plts (x6,sp rbckd,cl wn,fox) 85.00

DOZIER,EDWARD P-Hano-NY-(April,1966)-104p-wrps,photos-1st ed (v7) 10.00

DOZIER,EDWARD P-Mountain Arbiters-Tuscon-(1966)-U of Ariz Pr-8vo-297p-cl,illus-1st ed (y5,f) 20.00

DOZIER,EDWARD P-Pueblo Indians of North America-NY-(1970)-224p-wrps,photos,maps-1st prtg (v7) 15.00

DOZOIS,GARDNER-ED.-Best Science Fiction of the Year-NY-(1979)-Dutton-1st ed (o3,f,dj) 15.00

DRABBLE,MARGARET-Needle's Eye-1972-Knopf-1st Amer ed (o9,dj sl rub & chip) 30.00

DRABBLE,MARGARET-Summer Bird Cage-1964-Morrow-auth 1st bk-1st Amer ed (x2,vf,f dj) 65.00

DRABBLE,MARGARET-Waterfall-NY-1969-1st US ed (t5,f,dj) 22.50

DRABBLE,MARGARET-Writer's Britain-NY-1979-photos-1st US ed (d5,f,dj) 30.00

DRACHMAN,JULIAN-Studies in the Literature of Natural Science-NY-1930-Macmillan-xii+487p-blu cl-1st ed (l2,dj) 20.00

DRAGO,HARRY S-Great American Cattle Trails-(1965)-Dodd,Mead-274p-illus,maps-Six Guns 624-1st ed (t8,sl wn dj) 25.00

DRAGO,HARRY S-Great American Cattle Trails-NY-(1965)-Dodd,Mead-274p-illus e.p.,photos-1st ed (d3,dj) 30.00

DRAGO,HARRY S-Red River Valley-NY-(1962)-Potter-328p-map e.p.-Six Guns 627-1st ed (gg4,dj) 35.00

DRAGO,HARRY S-Wild, Woolly & Wicked-(1960)-Potter-354p-Six Guns 629-1st ed (t8,sl chip dj) 40.00

DRAGO,HARRY S-Wild, Wooly & Wicked-NY-(1960)-354p-e.p. maps-1st ed (j7,wn dj) 30.00

DRAGO,HARRY-River of Gold-NY-1945-233p-1st ed (t7,dj) 10.00

DRAGO,HENRY S-Great Range Wars-NY-1970-Dodd,Mead-307p-photos-1st ed (d3,dj) 20.00

DRAIN,BROOKS-Essentials of Systematic Pomology-NY-1925-Wiley-284p-cl (x6,sl wn) 25.00

DRAIN,JAMES A-Stories of Some Shoots-1912-priv prntd-8vo-114p-rare (m3) 45.00

DRAKE,BENJAMIN-Life and Adventures of Black Hawk-Cin-1841-Geo. Conclin-288p-cl-6th ed-improved (j1) 60.00

DRAKE,DANIEL-Pioneer Education & Life-Cedar Rapids-1939-Torch-55p-cl-ltd to 400c (x6,vf) 30.00

DRAKE,F V-Vertical Warfare-GC-1943-roy 8vo-xiv,142p-cl,61p plts,illus e.p.-1st ed (t2,uncut) 50.00

DRAKE,FRANCIS-World Emcompassed and Analagous Contemporary Documents...-Lond-1926-Argonauts-orig blu bds,gold emboss dec,vel sp-ltd to 975c,nbrd (v4,sl fade bds) 150.00

DRAKE,G S-Old Indian Chronicle...-Bost-1836-woodcts-1st Amer ed (r2,rbnd) 175.00

DRAKE,H B-Cursed be the Treasure-1928-Macy Masius-1st Amer ed (x7,f,dj) 135.00

DRAKE,JAMES M-Historical Sketches of the Revolutionary and Civil Wars-NY-1908-272p-cl,illus,port (aa6) 75.00

DRAKE,M-History of English Glass Painting-Lond-1912-folio-36 illus-scarce (ee1,sl fade bds) 225.00

DRAKE,MAURICE-History of English Glass Painting-1912-T Werner Laurie Ltd-208p-col illus-salesman's sample wi bndg choices on rear cov (cc8,sl fox) 75.00

DRAKE,MRS.EMMA F A-What a Woman of Forty-Five Ought to Know-Phila-(1902)-Vir Publ Co-211p-cl (d1,sl dull covs) 20.00

DRAKE,SAMUEL A-Benefactors of the World-Chig-(1902)-622(1)p-cl (d1) 15.00

DRAKE,STILLMAN-Unsung Journalist and the Origin of the Telescope-LA-1976-Zeitlin & Ver Brugge-8vo-19p-red prtd wrps,ltd to 530c (t10,f) 25.00

DRANEY,JOHN-Diesel Locomotives Mechanical Equipment-1947-Am Tech Soc-8vo-472p-cl,illus (nn7) 17.00

DRANNAN,CAPT W F-31 Years on the Plains and in the Mountains-Chig-1901-585p+8p ads-illus (g7) 35.00

DRANNAN,CAPT W F-31 Years on the Plains and in the Mountains-Chig-1908-586p+ads-illus-rprnt (c4) 32.50

DRANNAN,W F-Chief of Scouts-Chig-(1910)-407p-dec maroon cl,illus-Six Guns #630 (r8,sl wn,sm pg soil) 20.00

DRAPER,C-Mad Major-(Letchworth)-(1962)-8vo-232p-cl,frntis,32p plts-1st ed (t2,dj) 25.00

DRAPER,JOHN S-Shams or Uncle Ben's Experience with Hypocrites...and Sharpers of the Metropolitan World-Chig-(1899)-Thompson & Thomas-412p-cl-Wright III, 1646 (g1) 15.00

DRAPER,JOHN W-Thoughts on the Future Civil Policy of America-NY-1865-Harper & Bros-vii,325p-1st ed (n2) 35.00

DRAPER,MURIEL-Music at Midnight-NY-1929-Harper-photos-1st ed (t4,f,f dj) 25.00

DRAPER,WM R-Stories About Indian Maidens-Girard-(1946)-Haldeman Julius-32p-wrps,Big Blu Bk B-507 (d1) 15.00

DRAX,P-Crime Within Crime-1938-AC-1st Amer ed (x7,dj) 35.00

DRAYSON,LIEUT.-COL.-Cause of the Supposed Proper Motion of the Fixed Stars...Moon's Mean Motion...-Lond-1874-Chapman & Hall-xxiv+311p-purple cl,text diagrams,errata slip-1st ed (g2) 55.00

DREIER,THOMAS-Power of Print and Men-NY-1936-Mergenthaler Linotype-4to-166p-dec papr over bds,dec & design by Dwiggins-1st ed (t3) 45.00

DREISER,THEODORE-Symbolic Drawings of Hubert Davis for An American Tragedy by...-(NY)-(1930)-Horace Liveright-folio-dec bds-ltd to 525c,two autg (p1,f,box) 200.00

DREPPERD,CARL-American Pioneer Arts & Artists-Springfield-1942-Pond Ekberg-4to-cl-1st ed (oo6,dj tn) 80.00

DRESDEN,DONALD-Marquis De More-Norman-(1970)-U of Okla Pr-282p-illus,map-1st ed (ff4,dj) 35.00

DRESSER,ANNETTA G-Philosophy of P P Quimby-Bost-1895-114p-grn cl-1st ed (m2) 25.00

DRESSER,H E-Eggs of the Birds of Europe-Lond-(1905)1910-lg 4to-2 vols-1/2 mor,bands,g.t.,106 col plts (y8,rbnd) 1,250.00

DRESSLER,ALBERT-ED.-California's Pioneer Circus-SF-(1926)-98p-illus-ltd to 1250c,nbrd-scarce (v8) 85.00

DREW,C S-Communication From...Late Adjutant...Oregon Mounted Volunteers...Indian War in Oregon-Wash-1860-GPO-8vo-(1),48p-mod cl,g cov & sp titles-36th Congress,1st session.Mis.Doc. No.59-Howes 497,Graff 1150 (mm1,f,rbnd) 150.00

DREXLER,ARTHUR-Architecture of Japan-NY-1955-MOMA-4to-288p-235 plts-1st ed (c3) 36.00

DREYFUSS,HENRY-10 Years of Industrial Design 1929 to 1939-NY-1939-Pynson Prt-8vo-32p-red cl,photos (r10,autg) 25.00

DRIGGS,FRANK-Black Beauty, White Heat-NY-1982-Morrow-photos-1st ed (w5,f,f dj) 50.00

DRIGGS,HOWARD R-Old West Speaks-Englewood Cliffs-(1956)-Prentice-Hall-4to-220p-37 col plts,b&w photos-1st ed (cc5,sl tn dj) 35.00

DRIGGS,HOWARD R-Westward America-NY-c.1942-Auth's Autg Ed-312p-cl,ltd to 500c(not nbrd),2 autg,col illus (z1,f,box) 200.00

DRINKER,ELIZABETH-Extracts from the Journal of...From 1759 to 1807,A.D.-Phila-1889-Lippincott-8vo-423p-cl (y6,ex-libr) 45.00

DRINKER,FREDERICK E-Radio, Miracle of the 20th Century-1922-320p-illus cov,30 photos,55 illus-1st ed (h6) 20.00

DRINKWATER,H-Lecture on Mendelism-Lond-1910-Dent-31p-cl (x6) 15.00

DRINKWATER,JOHN-History of the Siege of Gibraltar 1779 to 1783-Lond-1871-172p-grn cl,fldg map (gg2) 45.00

DRINKWATER,PENNY-To Set Before a King-Lond-1960-Hart Davis-200p-pict blu bds,photos-1st ed (q8,edgewn dj) 17.50

DRINNON,RICHARD-White Savage-NY-1972-282p-frntis,map e.p.-1st ed (t7,f,dj) 10.00

DRINNON,RICHARD-White Savage-NY-1972-Schocken Bks-grn cl,frntis port (b6,vf,f dj) 15.00

DRIVER,CHRISTOPHER-Pepys at Table-1984-UC Berkeley-120p-tan bds,illus-1st US ed (q8,dj) 15.00

DRUCKER,P-Ceramic Sequences at Tres Zapotes, Veracruz, Mexico-1943-Bur Amer Ethnol Bull.140-155p-papr wrps,1 col & 64 b&w plts (bb3,f) 18.00

DRUCKER,PHILIP-Native Brotherhoods-Wash-1958-BAE Bull 168-194p-wrps (a1) 25.00

DRUMMOND,ALISON-Married and Gone to New Zealand-Hamilton/Lond-1960-Paul's/Oxford-192p-blu cl,illus-1st ed (dd7,dj) 45.00

DRUMMOND,H-Ascent of Man-1894-Pott-346p (bb3) 13.00

DRUMMOND,HENRY-Natural Law in the Spiritual World-NY-1890-John B Alden-8vo-285p-blu cl,g sp titles-1st ed (aa7,bump,wn) 15.00*

DRUMMOND,HENRY-Tropical Africa-NY-1888-Scribner & Welford-sm 8vo-xi,228p-orig cl,5 col fldg maps(4&5 on same fold-out),illus (bb6,wn,sp chip & tn) 50.00

DRUMMOND,JUNE-Murder on a Bad Trip-1968-Holt-1st Amer ed (s10,dj) 10.00

DRUMMOND,WILLIAM H-Habitant and Other French Canadian Poems-NY,Lond-1897-Putnam's-12mo-137p-g blu cl,illus-1st ed (p2,sl rub) 17.50

DRUON,MAURICE-Tistou of the Green Thumbs-NY-(1958)-Scribner's-178p-pict cl,b&w drwngs,J Duheme-1st US ed (r3,f,fade dj) 25.00

DRURY,ALLEN-Throne of Saturn-GC-1971-Dbldy-1st ed (h3,dj,autg) 20.00

DRURY,CLIFFORD M-Diaries and Letters of Henry H Spalding and Asa Bowen Smith...the Nez Perce Mission 1838 thru 1842-Glendale-1958-379p-col frntis-1st ed (t7,f,uncut,autg) 40.00

DRURY,CLIFFORD M-First White Women Over the Rockies-Glendale-1963,1966-A H Clark Co-3 vols,blu cl,illus-scarce-1st eds (v1) 150.00

DRURY,CLIFFORD M-Nine Years with the Spokane Indians-1976-Arthur Clark-547p-col & sepia illus-NW Hist Ser XIII-1st ed (r8) 45.00

DRURY,CLIFFORD M-Nine Years with the Spokane Indians-Glendale-1976-547p-frntis,col plts-1st ed (t7,f) 22.50

DRURY,CLIFFORD M-Pioneer of Old Oregon-Caldwell-1936-438p-pict cl,col frntis,photos,map e.p. (t7,pres) 25.00

DRURY,CLIFFORD M-Tepee in His Front Yard-Portland-(1949)-206p-illus,e.p. map-1st ed (r8,sl tn dj) 30.00

DRURY,CLIFFORD M-William Anderson Scott-Glendale-1967-352p-illus-1st ed (h7,f,dj) 30.00

DRURY,CLIFFORD-ED.-Diary of Titian Ramsay Peale-LA-1957-85p-tip-in col frntis,illus,e.p. map,ltd to 300c (d7,f) 35.00

DRURY,JAMES-Rare and Well Done-Chig-(1966)-Quadrangle Bks-186p (u6) 20.00

DRURY,JOHN-Historic Midwest Houses-Mpls-1947-U of Minn Pr-4to-246p-illus bds,illus (cc10) 45.00

DRYBOROUGH,T B-Polo-Lond-1898-Vinton-1st ed (j9) 85.00

DRYDEN,CECIL-Give All to Oregon-(1968)-Hastings-256p-illus-1st ed (r8,dj chip,rub) 20.00

DRYFHOUT,JOHN-Work of Augustus Saint Gaudens-Hanover-1982-U Pr of New Engl-folio-cl-1st ed (oo6,dj) 60.00

DU BOIS,W E B-Black Flame: Mansart Builds a School-NY-1959-Mainstream-367p-1st ed (ff1,dj sl scuff) 30.00

DU BOIS,W E B-Gift of Black Folk-Bost-1924-Stratford-8vo-349p-coated blu cl-(K of C Racial Contrib Ser)-1st ed (oo8,sp sl spot) 300.00

DU BOIS,WILLIAM P-21 Balloons-NY-1947-Viking-tall 8vo-180p-cl & dec bds,illus,auth-1st ed (r3,dj sl rub & chip) 50.00

DU BOIS,WILLIAM P-Forbidden Forest-NY-(1978)-Harper & Row-4to-56p-pict bds,col illus-1st ed (s3,vf,dj) 25.00

DU BOIS,WILLIAM P-Porko von Popbutton-NY-(1969)-Harper & Row-80p-rnfrcd bndg,pict cl,col illus,auth (r3,dj) 30.00

DU BOIS,WILLIAM P-Squirrel Hotel-NY-1952-Viking-sm 4to-48p-cl,b&w illus,auth-1st ed (r3,f,dj) 30.00

DU BOIS,WILLIAM P-Three Policeman, or Young Botsford of Farbe Island-NY-1938-Viking-sm 4to-92p-cl,illus,auth-1st ed (s3,fade,soil,ink price) 35.00

DU BREUIL,A-Vineyard Culture-Cin-1867-Robt Clarke & Co-337p-grn bds,144 illus (n6,sl wn) 150.00

DU CANE,FLORENCE-Flowers and Gardens of Madeira-Lond-1909-A & C Black-vii,150+(6)p ads-g dec cl,t.e.g.,col frntis,col plts guarded-1st ed (dd10,sl soil sp) 50.00

DU CANE,FLORENCE-Flowers and Gardens of Madeira-Lond-1909-A & C Black-vii,150,(2)p-g emboss wht cl,t.e.g.,24 guarded col plts (cc10,cov sl soil,sp drknd) 60.00

DU CANE,PETER-High Speed Small Craft-Cambridge-c.1951-Cornell Maritime Pr-8vo-ix,278p-drk grn cl,dec e.p.,18 photo plts (p8,dj) 45.00

DU CHAILLU,PAUL-Land of the Long Night-NY-1936-8vo-266p-illus (m3) 10.00

DU MAURIER,DAPHNE-Not After Midnight and Other Stories-Lond-1971-1st ed (y7,dj) 18.00

DU MAURIER,DAPHNE-Parasites-GC-1950-Dbldy-lt grn dj-1st US ed (hh5,dj) 15.00

DU MAURIER,DAPHNE-Parasites-Lond-1949-Gollancz-1st Brit ed (a10,edge-wn dj) 15.00

DU MAURIER,DAPHNE-Rebecca-Tor-1945-Ryerson-1st Can ed (l4,dj sl chip,sl tn) 35.00

DU MAURIER,DAPHNE-Rule Britannia-Lond-1972-1st ed (y7,dj) 15.00

DU MONCEL,COUNT-Electric Lighting-1882-318p-76 illus-v rare-1st ed (h6,f) 115.00

DU MONCEL,COUNT-Telephone, the Microphone, and the Phonograph-1879-277p-74 illus-rare-1st Brit ed (h6,sl wn) 110.00

DU PLESSIS,CAPT J H-Diamonds are Dangerous-NY-1961-John Day-250p-map-1st Amer ed (u5,f,dj wn,chip) 20.00

DU PRATZ,LE PAGE-History of Louisiana-New Orleans-nd-J S W Harmanson-(xvi)+xxviii+376p-tan cl,maps,illus,ltd to 600c-rprnt of 1774 Engl ed-1st Amer ed (k2,sl soil & bump) 25.00

DU PUY,W A-Uncle Sam Detective-1916-Stokes-1st ed (x7) 25.00

DUBE,JEAN-PAUL-Let's Save Our Salmon-Ottawa-1972-brwn cl,col frntis,drwng-ltd to 700c,nbrd,autg-1st ed (kk10,box) 60.00

DUBERMAN,MARTIN-Visions of Kerouac-Bost-1977-Little Brown-1st ed (e8,f,f dj) 30.00

DUBINSKY,DAVID-David Dubinsky: A Life with Labor-NY-1977-S&S-351p-1st ed (r1,dj) 18.00

DUBOIS,DONALD-Fisherman's Handbook of Trout Flies-NY-1960-8vo-340p-photos-1st ed (m3,f,dj) 35.00

DUBOIS,FELIX-Timbuctoo the Mysterious-NY-1896-Longmans,Green-8vo-xii,377p-orig cl,t.e.g.,153 illus,11 maps (bb6,rub,soil,fray sp,sl fox) 65.00

DUBOIS,THEODORA-Case of the Perfumed Mouse-1944-CC-1st Amer ed (s10,dj sl wtrstnd) 25.00

DUBOIS,THEODORA-Death Sails in a High Wind-NY-1945-Dbldy CC-1st ed (d4,dj) 25.00

DUBOIS,THEODORA-McNeills Chase a Ghost-Bost-1941-Houghton-1st ed (d4,chip dj) 50.00

DUBOIS,THEODORA-Seeing Red-NY-1954-Dbldy CC-1st ed (e4,brwng pgs,dj) 15.00

DUBOSE,J W-Alabama's Tragic Decade-Birmingham-1940-435p-illus,maps,ports (z10,wn dj) 35.00

DUBUS,ANDRE-Adultery & Other Choices-Bost-1977-Godine-1st ed (c8,f,f dj) 45.00

DUBUS,ANDRE-Finding a Girl in America-Bost-1980-1st ed (t5,dj) 25.00

DUBUS,ANDRE-Separate Flights-Bost-1975-1st ed (q5,dj) 25.00

DUCA,LO-Bayard-Paris-1943-Prisma-4to-g dec bds,ltd to 1500c,nbrd (y3,hngs weak,pgs brwnd) 225.00

DUCANE,FLORENCE-Flowers and Gardens of Japan-Lond-1908-A & C Black-lg 8vo-249p+ads-g stmpd pict cl,50 col plts-1st ed (mm4,f) 80.00

DUCASSE,C J-Critical Examination of the Belief in a Life After Death-Springfield-1961-Chas C Thomas-cl-1st ed (o8,dj fray) 20.00

DUCHENNE,G B-Physiology of Motion Demonstrated by Means of Electrical Stimulation and Clinical Observation...-Phila-1949-612p-qtr lea-ltd ed-1st Engl transl (dd3) 250.00

DUCK,L G-Survey of the Game and Furbearing Animals of Oklahoma-Ponca City-nd-4to-144p-photos,charts,maps (m3) 30.00

DUCKETT,J-Fly-Tying Dictionary-Medford-nd-16mo-56p-wrps (m3,vf) 20.00

DUDLEY,ALBERTUS T-With Mask and Mitt-Bost-(1906)-Lothrop,Lee & Shepard-300p+ads-1st ed (n1,sl soil cov,hngs weak) 25.00

DUDLEY,DARLE W-Evolution of the Gear Art-Wash D.C.-1969-Amer Gear Mfg Assoc-x+93p-grn cl,61 figs-1st ed (g2) 15.00

DUDLEY,GEORGINA,COUNTESS OF-Second Dudley Book of Recipes-(1914)-Hutchinson-418p-blu cl,8 photo plts (q8,cov wn,hngs weak) 45.00

DUDLEY,UNCLE-Fifty Thousand Miles with Uncle Sam's Army-Waynesville-1912-Enterprise Publ-95p-wrps,fldg map,photos (c3,pg tn,wn wrps) 35.00

DUDLEY-GORDON,T-I Seek My Prey in the Waters-NY-1943-8vo-xiv,298p-cl,8p plts-1st ed (t2) 25.00

DUFF,DOUGLAS V-Spunyarn-Lond-1957-Jarrolds-8vo-200p-maroon cl-1st ed (p8,sl wn dj) 15.00

DUFFEE,MAY M-As I Remember Washington Court House and My Autobiography-Wilmington-(1953)-publ by auth-185p-wrps (g1,f) 12.50

DUFFEY,DAVID MICHAEL-Hunting Hounds-NY-1972-8vo-186p-photos (m3,dj) 12.50

DUFFEY,K-Black Elephant Hunter-Lond-1960-208p-photo,illus (gg3,f,autg) 25.00

DUFFUS,R L-Santa Fe Trail-Lond-(Feb 1931)-Longmans,Green-283p-illus (ff4) 20.00

DUFFUS,R L-Valley and Its People-NY-1944-Knopf-4to-167p-qtr cl,illus bds,illus dbl pg map-1st ed (cc10,sl fox e.p.,dj) 40.00

DUFFY,FRANCIS P-Father Duffy's Story-NY-c.1919-Doran-8vo-381p-orig grn cl,fldg map (gg6,hng weak) 30.00

DUFRESNE,FRANK-Alaska's Animals & Fishes-(1946)-Barnes-lg 8vo-297p-drwngs-1st ed (u8,dj sp sl sunned,sl chip) 55.00

DUFRESNE,FRANK-Alaska's Animals & Fishes-1946-Countryman Press-4to-297p-illus,B Hines-1st ed (m3,f,dj) 35.00

DUFRESNE,FRANK-Alaska's Animals & Fishes-1946-Countryman Press-4to-297p-ltd to 475c,nbrd,autg (m3,box crckd & Wn) 100.00

DUFRESNE,FRANK-My Way Was North-NY-1966-8vo-274p-illus-1st ed (m3,f,dj) 25.00

DUFRESNE,FRANK-No Room for Bears-NY-1965-8vo-252p-illus-1st ed (m3,vf,dj) 16.50

DUGGAR,BEN-Fungous Diseases of Plants-Bost-1909-Ginn-508p-drwngs,photos-Cntry Educ Ser (x6) 16.00

DUGMORE,A R-African Jungle life-Lond-1928-8vo-246p-cl,col frntis,7 col plts (y8,lt wear) 35.00

DUGMORE,A R-Romance of the Beaver-Lond-1914(1914)-8vo-(1),225p-cl,frntis,90 half tone plts (y8,fox) 40.00

DUGMORE,A R-Romance of the Newfoundland Caribou-Phila-1913-4to-191p-cl,col frntis,72 photos,2 maps(1 fldg) (y8,fray,hng weak) 50.00

DUGMORE,A RADCLYFFE-Wild Life & the Camera-Phila-1912-8vo-332p-photos-1st ed (m3) 17.50

DUGMORE,A RADCLYFFE-Wonderland of Big Game-Lond-(1925)-Arrowsmith-sm 4to-288p-photos-1st ed (ff5,wn,hngs weak) 45.00

DUGUID,J-Green Hell-NY-1931-339p-photos (gg3,f,dj) 25.00

DUGUID,J-Tiger Man-NY-1932-287p-photos (gg3,vf,dj) 15.00

DUHAYS,CHARLES-Percheron Horse-Balt-1886-priv prtd-4to-bds,ltd ed,transl by W T Walters,orig tiss dj-scarce (j9,ffep tn,dj) 725.00

DUIKER,WILLIAM-Cultures in Collision-San Rafael-1978-226p-illus-1st ed (b7,f,dj) 35.00

DUKE,DONALD-ED.-Water Trails West-NY-1978-271p-photos,illus-1st ed (t7,f,dj) 17.50

DUKE,DONALD-Night Train-1961-PRJ-4to-127p-illus (nn7,f,f dj) 35.00

DUKE,DONALD-Night Train-San Marino-1961-127p-1st ed (n4) 15.00

DUKE,DONALD-Santa Fe...Steel Rails Through California-San Marino-1963-184p-1st ed (n4,f,dj) 29.00

DUKE,DONALD-Southern Pacific Steam Locomotives-San Marino-1962-88p-2nd ed (n4,f,dj) 19.50

DUKE,WILLIAM W-Allergy, Asthma, Hay Fever, Urticaria and Allied Manifestations of Reaction-St.Louis-1926-344p-illus-2nd ed (g10) 20.00

DULAC,EDMUND-Dulac-1975-Scribners-40p col plts-1st ed (x2,f,dj) 45.00

DULAC,EDMUND-Edmund Dulac-1976-Scribners-181 illus,incl 32 col-1st Amer ed (x2,f,dj) 85.00

DUMAS ON FOOD-Lond-1978-Folio Soc-324p-pict prpl cl,illus (q8,box) 25.00

DUMAS,ALEXANDRE-Twenty Years After...-NY-1958-LED-496p-cl,ltd to 1500c,nbrd,autg,hand col illus,E Legrand (m1,f,box) 35.00

DUMFRIESSHIRE COOKERY BOOK-Dumfries-(1935)-Courier Pr-247p-wrps (q6) 30.00

DUMONT,ETIENNE-Recollections of Mirabeau-Lond-1832-Edw Bull-3/4 lea,extra illus (l9,sl wn) 100.00

DUNBAR & PHILLIPS-ED.-Journals and Letters of Major John Owen-NY-1927-2 vols-illus,fldg maps,celophane dj,ltd to 550c-Tweney #58-1st ed (d7,f,poor dj) 300.00

DUNBAR,ALICE M-ED.-Masterpieces of Negro Eloquence-NY-(1914)-Bookery Publ-512p-grn & red cl,plts-1st ed (m2,few bent pgs) 75.00

DUNBAR,CHARLES S-Buses, Trolleys & Trams-Lond-1967-141p-1st ed (n4,f,dj) 27.00

DUNBAR,ERNEST-Black Expatriates-NY-1968-Dutton-1st ed (w5,f,sl wn dj) 40.00

DUNBAR,H FLANDERS-Emotions and Bodily Changes-NY-1935-Columbia U Pr-xviii+595p-grn cl-1st ed (g2,wn dj) 50.00

DUNBAR,MAURICE-Fundamentals of Book Collecting-Los Altos-1976-Hermes-illus-1st ed (y10,f,f dj) 20.00

DUNBAR,PATRICIA-Cadbury's Novelty Cookbook-Lond-(1983)-Hamlyn-128p-pict blu bds,col illus-2nd prtg (q8,f,dj) 15.00

DUNBAR,SEYMOUR-History of Travel in America-Indpls-1915-Bobbs Merrill-8vo-4 vols-blu lea sp,mrbld papr over bds,2 maps,12 col plts,illus (ee7) 250.00

DUNBAR,WILLIS F-All Aboard-Grand Rapids-1969-308p-1st ed (n4,f,dj) 19.00

DUNCAN,ALASTAIR-Tiffany Windows-1980-S&S-114 col illus-1st ed (cc8,dj) 75.00

DUNCAN,BOB-Buffalo Country-1959-Dutton-256p-drwngs-1st ed (v8,dj) 20.00

DUNCAN,BOB-Dicky Bird was Singing-NY-1952-Rinehart-282p-cl-1st ed (ee10,dj) 20.00

DUNCAN,D-Madrone Tree-1949-Macmillan-1st ed (x7,f,dj) 30.00

DUNCAN,D-Shade of Time-1946-Random-1st ed (x7,f,dj) 60.00

DUNCAN,DAVID D-Goodbye Picasso-NY-1974-G&D-4to-300p-orng cl,b&w & col illus-1st ed (r10,f,f dj) 45.00

DUNCAN,DAVID D-I Protest-NY-1968-NAL-8vo-124p-wrps,photos-1st ed (t3) 35.00

DUNCAN,DAVID D-Private World of Pablo Picasso-NY-1958-Ridge Pr-176p-300 photos by Duncan-1st ed (cc9,sl wn dj) 35.00

DUNCAN,DAVID D-Self Portrait: U.S.A.-NY-(1969)-Abrams-lg 4to-240p-325 photos-1st ed(?) (gg5,f,dj) 30.00

DUNCAN,DAVID D-Self Portrait: USA-NY-1969-Abrams-240p-325 photos-1st ed (cc9,f,dj) 50.00

DUNCAN,DAVID D-Yankee Nomad, a Photographic Odessey-NY-1967-HR&W-4to-480p-red cl,col photos-2nd ed (p8,wn dj) 75.00

DUNCAN,FRANCIS-History of the Royal Regiment of Artillery-Lond-1879-2 vols-blu cl-3rd ed (b7) 350.00

DUNCAN,H O-World on Wheels-Paris-1907-publ by auth-4to-2 vols-1/2 orng mor wi linen bds,illus (a3,rbnd) 235.00

DUNCAN,J BARKER-Manual of the General Acts of Parliament Relating to the Salmon Fisheries of Scotland-Ednbrgh,Lond-1886-12mo-200p (m3) 25.00

DUNCAN,NORMAN-Billy Topsail & Company-NY-1910-Revell-pict cov-1st ed (x1,lacks dj) 25.00

DUNCAN,S-Complete Wildfowler Ashore & Afloat-Lond-1911-360p-gilt cov dec,photos (gg3,sp discol) 100.00

DUNCAN,THOMAS W-Big River, Big Man-Phila-1959-Lippincott-8vo-cl-1st ed so stated (z4,sl wn dj) 12.50

DUNGLISON,ROBLEY-History of Medicine from the Earliest Ages to the Commencement of the Nineteenth Century-Phila-1872-287p-1st ed (dd3) 150.00

DUNGLISON,ROBLEY-Medical Lexicon-Phila-1845-771p-lea-5th ed (dd3) 100.00

DUNGLISON,ROBLEY-Medical Lexicon-Phila-1874-1131p-New ed,enlgd & rvsd by Richard J Dunglison (dd3) 75.00

DUNHAM,CAPTAIN JACOB-Journal of Voyages-NY-1850-priv prtd-12mo-243p-orig emboss cl,12 plts-Howes D567-1st ed (p8,rbckd,fox) 150.00

DUNHAM,DICK-Our Strip of Land, a History of Daggett County, Utah-(Lusk)-nd-106p-orig yel wrps-2nd ed (bb8) 25.00

DUNIWAY,ABIGAIL S-David and Anna Matson-NY-1876-Wells-8vo-194p-orig cl,a.e.g.-scarce-1st ed (w6,soil,wn cl) 100.00

DUNIWAY,ABIGAIL S-Path Breaking-(Portland)-(1914)-xviii+297p-yel cl,illus-2nd ed (mm10) 65.00

DUNKELMAN,MARK H-Hardtack Regiment-Rutherford-(1981)-211p-illus-1st ed (n3,f,dj) 20.00

DUNLAP,LESLIE W-ED.-Your Affectionate Husband, J F Culver-Iowa City-1978-Friends of Iowa Libr-467p-illus,maps (o7,f) 20.00

DUNLAP,ORRIN E-Marconi-1937-360p-15 photos-1st ed (h6,f) 45.00

DUNLAP,ROY-Gunsmithing-Georgetown-1950-Small Arms Tech Publ-x+714p+ads-grn cl,illus-1st ed (l2) 35.00

DUNLAP,ROY-Gunsmithing-Georgetown-1955-8vo-714p-illus (m3,vf) 25.00

DUNLAP,WILLIAM-History of the Rise and Progress of the Arts of Design in the United States-NY-1834-2 vols-orig cl bckd bds-Howes D571-BAL 5026-1st ed (o4,sl rub,fox) 450.00

DUNLAY,THOMAS W-Wolves for the Blue Soldiers-Lincoln-1982-U of Neb Pr-304p-maps,illus-1st ed (dd4,dj) 33.00

DUNLOP,W S-Lee's Sharpshooters-Dayton-1982-Morningside Bkshp-499p-port-ltd to 500c,nbrd (o7,f) 30.00

DUNMORE,JOHN-Expedition of the St.Jean-Baptiste to the Pacific 1769 to 1770...Jean De Surville and Guillaume Labe-Lond-1981-Hakluyt Scty-8vo-x,310p-blu cl,g titles & cov dec (nn1,vf,sl wn dj) 45.00

DUNN,DOROTHY-American Indian Painting-1968-U of NM Pr-qto-429p-col & b&w plts-1st ed (nn6,dj) 175.00

DUNN,E B-Weather-NY-1902-Dodd,Mead-grn cl-1st ed (pp3) 20.00

DUNN,HELEN-COMP.-Celebrity Recipes-(NY)-(1958)-(Grayson)-234p-dec wht cl,photos-1st prtg (q8,dj) 15.00

DUNN,J P-Massacres of the Mountains-NY-1886-784p-dec cl,frntis,illus-Howes D575-1st ed (t7,ex-libr) 30.00

DUNN,JOHN-Violin Playing-NY-1909-Scribner's-Strad Libr No.4-2nd ed (u4,sl rub) 20.00

DUNN,KATHERINE-Truck-(1971)-Harper & Row-1st ed (p9,f,dj) 25.00

DUNN,LAURENCE-Passenger Liners-Southhampton-1961-Adlard Coles Ltd-476p-illus (p8,sl wn) 35.00

DUNN,ROBERT-Shameless Diary of an Explorer-NY-1907-Outing Publ-photos-1st ed (p6,sl wn sp) 60.00

DUNN,SHIRLEY-Historic Homes and Old Buildings of Lincoln County, Kentucky-np-nd-59p-wrps (n1) 12.50

DUNNE,BERT-Play Ball!-GC-1947-274p-cl-Smith 6188-1st ed (n1,sl wn dj) 17.50

DUNNE,PETER M-Black Robes in Lower California-Berkeley-1952-UCP-540p-fldg map-1st ed (d3,dj) 50.00

DUNNETT,DOROTHY-Photogenic Soprano-Bost-1968-Houghton-1st ed (h4,dj) 15.00

DUNNING,CHARLES H-Arizona's Golden Road-Phoenix-1961-185p-illus-1st ed (t7,f,dj) 12.50

DUNNING,JOHN-Tune in Yesterday-NY-(1976)-Prentice Hall-lg 8vo-703p wi index,photos-1st ed (u1,f,dj) 125.00

DUNRAVEN,EARL OF-Canadian Nights...Life and Sport in the Rockies, the Prairies, and the Canadian Woods-NY-1914-296p (a7,sl soil cov) 75.00

DUNRAVEN,EARL OF-Hunting in the Yellowstone-NY-1917-333p (gg3,scribbling,sl soil) 25.00

DUNSANY,LORD-Fourth Book of Jorkens-Sauk City-1948-Arkham Hs-ltd to 3118c-1st ed (l7,sl wn dj) 60.00

DUNSANY,LORD-Ghosts of the Heaviside Layer...-Phila-(1980)-Owlswick-col frontis & 18p b&w plts by Tim Kirk-1st ed (a5,as new in dj) 25.00

DUNSANY,LORD-Mirage Water-Phila-(1939)-Dorrance-1st Amer ed (z8,vf,sp fade dj) 50.00

DUNSANY,LORD-Night at an Inn-NY-1916-Sunwise Turn-8vo-dec wrps-1st ed (jj8,f) 45.00

DUNSANY,LORD-Tales of Three Hemispheres-Lond-1920-T Fisher Unwin Ltd-1st Brit ed (aa8) 35.00

DUNSANY,LORD-Tales of War-Bost-1918-Little,Brown-1st US ed (ff6,sp fade) 50.00

DUNTHORNE,GORDON-Flower and Fruit Prints of the 18th and Early 19th Centuries...-Wash D.C.-1938-the auth-sm folio-275p-cl wi lea labls,col illus-orig ed (p1,f,box) 325.00

DUPONT,E I-DuPont the Autobiography of an American Enterprise-Wilmington-1952-138p-col frntis,photos,col plts & illus-1st ed (t7,dj) 7.50

DUPONT,SAMUEL F-Samuel Francis Dupont, a Selection from His Civil War Letters-Ithica-(1969)-3 vols-illus-1st ed (c4,f,box) 115.00

DUPREE,A HUNTER-Asa Gray 1810 to 1888-Cambridge-1959-Harvard-505p-cl (x6,vf) 35.00

DUPREE,MORRISON-Tap on the Shoulder-NY-1929-Dbldy CC-1st ed (e4) 15.00

DUPUY,WILLIAM A-Hawaii and Its Race Problem-Wash D.C.-1932-GPO-8vo-x,132p-pict cl,illus-1st ed (y4,pres) 35.00

DUPUY,WM ATHERTON-Uncle Sam Detective-NY-1916-Stokes-pict cov-1st ed (d4) 35.00

DURAND,ALGERNON-Making of a Frontier-Lond-1899-298p-blu cl,fldg map,plts-1st ed (b7) 125.00

DURAND,HERBERT-My Wild Flower Garden-NY-1927-Putnam-242p (x6,dj wn) 12.00

DURAND,RALPH-Oxford Its Buildings and Gardens-Lond-1909-Richards-238p-cl,32 col plts (x6,cl wn,sl fox) 45.00

DURAND,SIR EDWARD-Ponies Progress-NY-1935-Scribner-1st US ed (j9) 30.00

DURANT,C F-Exposition...-NY-1982-Da Capo Pr-sm 8vo-(vii)+xi+(14)-225+(2)p-prntd red cl-(facs reprnt of 1837 ed) (y9,f) 25.00

DURANT,JOHN-Highlights of the World Series-1963-Hastings Hs (q7,f,dj) 15.00

DURANT,JOHN-Pictorial History of the American Circus-(1957)-Barnes-4to-328p-illus-1st ed (v8,dj wn & sl chip) 25.00

DURANT,WILL-Duel Autobiography-NY-1977-S&S-420p-photos-1st ed (o2,f,dj) 15.00

DURATSCHEK,SISTER MARY C-Crusading Along Sioux Trails-Yankton-(1947)-Benedictine Convent-334p-illus-1st ed (gg4) 25.00

DURATSCHEK,SISTER MARY C-Crusading Along Sioux Trails-Yankton-(1947)-Grail Publ-xiv+334p-brwn cl,photos-presumed 1st ed (b2) 45.00

DURDEN,CHARLES-No Bugles, No Drums-NY-(1976)-Viking-auth 1st bk-1st ed (a10,f,dj) 35.00

DUREN,RYNE-Comeback-1978-Lorenz-1st ed (q7,dj) 15.00

DURFEE,JOB-Discourse-Providence-1847-Chas Burnett,Jr.-32p-wrps (d1) 15.00

DURHAM,GEORGE-Taming the Nueces Strip-Austin-1962-U Tex-178p-1st ed (a9,dj) 35.00

DURHAM,MARILYN-Man Who Loved Cat Dancing-NY-(1972)-HBJ-auth 1st bk-1st ed (b10,f dj) 20.00

DURHAM,PHILIP-Down These Mean Streets a Man Must Go-Chapel Hill-1963-1st ed (s5,dj) 75.00

DURHAM,PHILIP-Down These Mean Streets a Man Must Go-Chapel Hill-1963-UNC Pr-1st ed (v5,f,f dj) 65.00

DURHAM,PHILIP-Negro Cowboys-NY-(1965)-Dodd,Mead-278p-illus-Six Guns 653 (gg4,dj) 15.00

DURIE,ALISTAIR-Weird Tales-Lond-1979-Jupiter-illus-1st ed (q4,f,dj) 35.00

DURIEN,PAUL-Chinook Bible History-Kamloops-1899-112p-orig wrps,2 ports,in Chinook shorthand (a7,wrps stnd) 100.00

DURKIN,JOSEPH T-General Sherman's Son-NY-1959-276p-illus-1st ed (c4,dj wn,chip) 17.50

DURLING,RICHARD-Cataglogue of Sixteenth Century Printed Books in the National Library of Medicine-Bethesda-1967-698p-1st ed (dd3) 150.00

DURNFORD,REV RICHARD-Diary of a Test Fisherman 1809-1819-Lond-1911-8vo-112p-frontis port,col plt (m3,sl dmpstnd cov edge) 45.00

DUROCHER,LEO-Dodgers and Me-1948-Ziff Davis-1st ed (s8,f,dj) 40.00

DUROCHER,LEO-Nice Guys Finish Last-1975-S&S-1st ed (r7,f,f dj) 25.00

DUROCHER,LEO-Nice Guys Finish Last-1975-S&S-photos-1st ed (s8,f,f dj) 20.00

DUROV,V L-My Circus Animals-1936-Houghton Mifflin-114p-illus,R Murray-1st Amer ed (v8,dj) 28.00

DURRANT,THEO-Marble Forest-NY-1951-Knopf-1st ed (k4,dj) 35.00

DURRELL,G M-Golden Bats and Pink Pigeons-1977-S&S-190p-photos-1st ed (bb3,f,dj) 17.00

DURRELL,G M-Whispering Land-1962-Viking-235p-illus-1st ed (bb3,dj) 12.00

DURRELL,GERALD-Birds, Beasts, and Relatives-NY-(1969)-Viking-8vo-244p-1st US ed (aa5,f,dj) 12.50

DURRELL,GERALD-Catch Me a Colobus-1972-Viking-1st Amer ed (t9,f,dj) 25.00

DURRELL,L-White Eagles over Serbia-1957-Criterion Bks-1st Amer ed (x7,vf,dj) 125.00

DURRELL,LAWRENCE-Bitter Lemons-1957-Dutton-1st Amer ed (x2,vf,dj) 100.00

DURRELL,LAWRENCE-Dark Labyrinth-1962-Dutton-1st Amer hdbk ed (x2,vf,dj) 50.00

DURRELL,LAWRENCE-Down the Styx-Santa Barbara-1971-Capricorn Pr-ltd to 200c,autg (l9) 150.00

DURRELL,LAWRENCE-Livia or Buried Alive-Lond-1978-1st ed (y7,dj) 12.00

DURRELL,LAWRENCE-Mountolive, a Novel-Lond-1958-1st ed (y7,dj) 75.00

DURRELL,LAWRENCE-Nunquam-1970-Dutton-1st Amer ed (q9,f,dj) 15.00

DURRELL,LAWRENCE-Nunquam-NY-1970-Dutton-1st Amer ed (hh5,f,f dj) 10.00

DURRELL,LAWRENCE-Red Limbo Lingo-NY-1971-Dutton-ltd to 1200c,autg (l9,f,box) 100.00

DURRELL,LAWRENCE-Sappho-1958-Dutton-1st Amer ed (x2,f,dj) 45.00

DURRELL,LAWRENCE-Sebastian or Ruling Passions-Lond-(1983)-1st ed (bb10,f,dj) 20.00

DURRELL,LAWRENCE-Sicilian Carousel-NY-(1977)-1st ed (d5,f,dj) 15.00

DURRELL,LAWRENCE-White Eagles Over Serbia-1957-Criterion Bks-1st Amer ed (x2,vf,dj) 125.00

DURSO,JOSEPH-Amazing-1970-Houghton Mifflin-1st ed (s8,dj) 13.00

DURSO,JOSEPH-Casey-1967-Prentice Hall-photos-1st ed (s8,dj) 18.00

DURSO,JOSEPH-Days of Mr.McGraw-Englewood Cliffs-(1969)-243p-cl (n1,f,dj) 17.50

DURSO,JOSEPH-Yankee Stadium, 50 Years of Drama-1972-Houghton Mifflin-1st ed (r7,f,dj) 35.00

DUTAUD,HANNAH-Glorious Art of Home Cooking-Chig-(1935)-Assoc Auth-282p (r6,autg,) 14.00

DUTTON,BERTHA P-ED.-Pocket Handbook-Santa Fe-1960-112p-wrps,dbl col,photos,maps-1st ed (v7) 10.00

DUTTON,BERTHA P-Indians of the American Southwest-Englewood Cliffs-(1975)-289p-photos,map-1st ed (v7,f,dj,autg) 25.00

DUTTON,BERTHA P-Sun Father's Way-Albuq-1963-228p-dbl col,photos,color drwngs-1st ed (u7,dj) 45.00

DUTTON,CHARLES J-Flying Clues-NY-1927-Dodd-1st ed (d4) 12.50

DUTTON,JOAN P-Flower World of Williamsburg-NY-(1962)-viii,148p-8 col & 54 b&w photos (m10,tattrd dj) 15.00

DUTTON,MARGIT S-German Pastry Bakeout-Radnor-(1977)-Chilton-lg 8vo-182p-brwn cl,col plts-1st ed (q8,dj) 16.50

DUVAL,J C-Early Times in Texas-Austin-1892-Gammel & Co-253p-Howes D603-1st ed (ee4,ex-libr) 100.00

DUVAL,JOHN C-Adventures of Big Foot Wallace-Austin-1947-291p-frntis,illus (t7) 25.00

DUVAL,MARGUERITE-King's Garden-Charlottesville-(1982)-U Pr of Va-ix,214p-illus (x5,dj) 16.00

DUVAL,P-Four Decades-Tor-1972-folio-128 col & 69 b&w illus-1st ed (h10,dj) 85.00

DUVAL,PAUL-Art of Glen Loates-Canada-1977-folio-189,(2)p-brn cl,col illus-2nd prtg (b6,f,dj) 25.00

DUVEEN,DENIS-Bibliography of the Works of Antoine Laurent Lavoisier, 1743 to 1794-Lond-1954,1965-2 vols-1st ed (dd3) 200.00

DUVEEN,JAMES H-Rise of the House of Duveen-NY-1957-Knopf-8vo-293p-10 illus-1st US ed (dd5,f,dj) 15.00

DUVOISIN,ROGER-Three Sneezes and Other Swiss Tales-NY-1941-Knopf-245p-pict cl,col & b&w illus,auth-1st ed (s3) 15.00

DVORKIN,DAVID-Time for Sherlock Holmes-NY-1983-Dodd,Mead-1st ed (z3,dj) 10.00

DWIGGINS,D-Air Devils-Phila-(1966)-8vo-226p-cl bkd bds,frntis,plts-1st ed (t2,dj) 25.00

DWIGHT,J-Ipswich Sparrow and its Summer Home-Cambridge-1895-4to-(1),56p-cl,col frntis (y8) 30.00

DWIGHT,MARGARET-Journey to Ohio in 1810-New Haven-1912-64p-bds,papr labls-ltd to 600c-scarce-1st ed (jj4) 40.00

DWIGHT,THEODORE-Character of Thomas Jefferson, as Exhibited in His Own Writings-Bost-1839-Weeks,Jordan & Co-371p-cl-Sabin 21535-1st ed (h1) 35.00

DWIGHT,TIMOTHY-Sermons-New Haven-1828-Howe,Durrie & Peck-2 vols-calf,sp labls-1st ed (h2,sl fox) 150.00

DWORACZYK,REV EDWARD J-First Polish Colonies of America in Texas-1936-Naylor-201p-wrps,photos-1st ed (a9) 100.00

DWYER,C P-Immigrant Builder-(1884)-Hurst-145p-illus-10th ed (r8,fray,lacks ffep,rprd hng) 40.00

DWYER,J P-Traditional Art of Africa, Oceania & the Americas-1973-F A Mus of SF-wrps,illus-1st ed (h10) 25.00

DWYER,K R-Dragonfly-NY-1975-Random-1st ed (w9,f,dj wi sm tr) 125.00

DWYER,K R-Shattered-NY-1973-Random-1st ed (y2,f,f dj) 125.00

DWYER,WILLIAM M-Day is Ours-NY-(1983)-xiii,426p-cl bckd bds (aa6) 30.00

DYAR,HARRISON G-Mosquitoes of the U.S.-Wash-1922-119p-orig prtd wrps (g10) 15.00

DYCHE,JOHN A-Bolshevism in American Labor Unions-NY-1926-Boni & Liveright-1st ed (w5) 20.00

DYCHE,L L-Ponds,Pond Fish & Pond Fish Culture-Topeka-1914-8vo-208p-photos,illus (m3) 15.00

DYE,EVA-McDonald of Oregon-1906-McClurg-395p-grn cl,oval cov pict,illus by W Enright-1st ed (r8) 35.00

DYE,EVA-McLoughlin and Old Oregon-1900-McClurg-381p-2nd ed (r8) 45.00

DYE,JOHN H,M.D.-Painless Childbirth-Buffalo-1888-Baker,Jones-451p-cl-7th ed,rvsd & enlrgd (m1,fade,sl wn) 15.00

DYER AND COLOUR MAKER'S COMPANION-Phila-1850-Henry C Baird-sm 12mo-104p (m6,sp tn) 75.00

DYER,JOHN L-Snow Shoe Itinerant-Cin-1890-Cranston & Stowe-362p-illus-Howes D622-1st ed (dd4) 40.00

DYER,MARY M-Rise and Progress of the Serpent from the Garden of Eden to the Present Day-Concord-1847-prtd for auth-268p-calf,blk sp labl-1st ed (b2,sl wn) 150.00

DYK,WALTER-Navaho Autobiography-NY-1947-Viking Publ Anthro No.8-218p+16 photo plts,stiff wrps,map-1st ed (v7,f) 35.00

DYKES,J C-Billy the Kid, the Bibliography of a Legend-Albuq-1952-186p-cl,Russell frntis-ltd to 500c-scarce-2nd prtg of 1st ed (jj1,sl fade & scuff) 125.00

DYKES,JEFF C-Law on a Wild Frontier-Wash D.C.-1969-25p-wrps,illus-Potomac Corral,Westerners #5-1st ed (c7,f) 35.00

DYKES,JEFF-Rare Western Outlaw Books-Albuq-1985-Albuq Corral of Wstrnrs-wrps,ltd to 535c,autg-1st ed (dd4) 25.00

DYKES,JEFF-Western High Spots-1977-Northland Pr-192p-photo,illus-1st ed (t7,pres,dj) 60.00

DYKES,JEFF-Western High Spots-np-(1977)-Northland Pr-(xvi),192p-illus-1st ed (v1,dj) 35.00

DYLAN,BOB-Tarantula-1971-MacMillan-1st ed (x2,f,dj) 35.00

DYLAN,BOB-Tarantula-NY-1971-1st trd ed (s5,dj) 15.00

DYMOND,J R-Trout & Other Game Fishes of British Columbia-Ottawa-1932-8vo-51p-7 col plts,text illus-1st ed (m3) 23.00

EAGER,EDWARD-Seven Day Magic-NY-(1962)-HB&W-pict cl,illus,N M Bodecker (s3,f,dj) 25.00

EAMES,HUGH-Sleuths, Inc.-Phila-1978-Lippincott-1st ed (d4,f,sl wn dj) 15.00

EARHART,AMELIA-Last Flight-NY-(1937)-8vo-xvi,230p-cl,illus t.p.,26p plts,1 dbl-pg plt-1st ed (t2,wtrstnd) 30.00

EARL,GEORGE W-Eastern Seas...-Lond-1837-Allen-8vo-xii,461p-mod 1/2 lea,mrbld bds & e.p.,g sp labls-1st ed (ll1,rbnd) 800.00

EARL,LAWRENCE-Crocodile Fever-NY-1953-Knopf-1st ed (f8,f,sl wn dj) 35.00

EARLE,ALICE M-Stagecoach and Tavern Days-NY-1900-Macmillan-1st ed (h9) 45.00

EARLE,ALICE M-Sun Dials and Roses of Yesterday-NY-1902-Macmillan-xxiii,461p-g pict cl,t.e.g.,44 plts-1st ed (mm4,vf) 65.00

EARLE,ALICE M-Sun Dials and Roses of Yesterday-NY-1902-Macmillan-xxiv+461p-grn dec cov,illus-1st ed (a2) 55.00

EARLE,C-More Potpourri From a Surrey Garden-Lond-1904-Elder-453p (x6,sp sun) 22.00

EARLE,MRS C W-Potpourri Mixed by Two-Lond-1914-xiii,456p-cl backd grn bds,,photos-1st ed (m10,sp rub,split) 22.00

EARLE,PETER-Monmouth's Rebels-NY-1978-293p-illus-1st ed (b7,f,dj) 35.00

EARLE,PLINY-Memoirs of...-Bost-1898-Damrell & Upham-xvi+409p-grn cl-1st ed (g2) 90.00

EARLY DAWN-NY-1866-Dodd-sm 8vo-441p-1st US ed (w6,sl fox,loose hngs) 35.00

EARLY,ELEANOR-Adirondack Tales-Bost-1939-Little Brown-Plum 7286-1st ed (dd6,dj) 40.00

EARLY,ELEANOR-New England Cookbook-NY-(1954)-Random-236p-1st ed (k6) 20.00

EARP,S A-Blue Water Bait Book-Bost-1974-8vo-177p-photos-1st ed (m3,vf,dj) 15.00

EAST,ANDY-Agatha Christie Quizbook-NY-1975-Drake-1st ed (g4,f,dj) 12.50

EAST,BEN-Survival-NY-1967-8vo-371p-illus (m3,f,dj) 17.50

EASTLAKE,WILLIAM-Bamboo Bed-Lond-1970-1st Brit ed (t5,f,dj) 20.00

EASTLAKE,WILLIAM-Bronc People-NY-1958-1st ed (p5,dj wn & chip) 45.00

EASTLAKE,WILLIAM-Castle Keep-NY-1965-1st ed (t5,chip dj) 22.50

EASTLAKE,WILLIAM-Child's Garden of Verses for the Revolution-NY-(1970)-Grove-1st ed (cc2,f,dj) 50.00

EASTLAKE,WILLIAM-Dancers in the Scalp House-NY-(1975)-Viking-1st ed (cc2,f,dj) 40.00

EASTLAKE,WILLIAM-Go in Beauty-NY-(1956)-Harper & Bros-auth 1st bk-1st ed (ff6,f,dj) 175.00

EASTLAKE,WILLIAM-Long Naked Descent Into Boston-NY-(1977)-Viking-1st ed (k3,f,dj) 20.00

EASTLAKE,WILLIAM-Portrait of an Artist with 26 Horses-NY-1960-S&S-8vo-221p-1st ed (z4,dj) 27.50

EASTLAKE,WILLIAM-Portrait of an Artist with 26 Horses-NY-1963-221p-1st ed (u7,dj) 40.00

EASTLAKE,WILLIAM-Portrait of an Artist with 26 Horses-NY-1963-S&S-1st ed (ee2,f,dj) 50.00

EASTMAN,BUELL-United States Farriery...-Cin-1853-Cropper-2nd ed,rvsd & enlgd (f10) 58.00

EASTMAN,CHARLES A-Indian Heroes and Great Chieftains-Bost-1918-Little,Brown-241p-pict cl,illus-1st ed (dd4,cov spots) 25.00

EASTMAN,CHARLES A-Indian Scout Talks-Bost-1914-Little,Brown-190p-pict cl,illus-1st ed (ee4) 40.00

EASTMAN,CHARLES A-Red Hunters and the Animal People-NY-1904-Lond-249p-pict cl,illus-1st ed (ff4,sp lettrng fade) 20.00

EASTMAN,CHARLES A-Soul of the Indian-Bost-(1911)-Houghton Mifflin-170p-frntis (dd4) 25.00

EASTMAN,ELAINE G-Pratt-Norman-1935-U of Okla Pr-285p-illus-1st ed (ee4,sp wn) 50.00

EASTMAN,GEORGE-Chronicles of an African Trip-1927-priv prntd-8vo-87p+28 photos,M Johnson (m3,vf) 80.00

EASTMAN,GEORGE-Chronicles of an African Trip-1927-priv prtg-87p-photos (gg3,f) 50.00

EASTMAN,GEORGE-Chronicles of an African Trip-Rochester-1927-priv prtd-8vo-cl bkd bds-1st ed (y3) 65.00

EASTMAN,MAX-Heroes I Have Known-NY-1942-S&S-1st ed (v5,f,dj sp sl chip,drknd) 35.00

EASTMAN,ROY-Mysteries of Blair House-Detr-(1948)-Conjure Hs-auth 1st bk-1st ed (a5,dj) 35.00

EASTON,CAROL-Straight Ahead-NY-1973-Morrow-1st ed (w1,f,f dj) 20.00

EASTON,MALCOLM-Artists and Writers in Paris-Lond-1964-Edw Arnold-viii+205p-wrps,vignetted dj,7 plts-1st ed (kk5,dj) 25.00

EASTON,ROBERT-Guns,Gold & Caravans-1978-Capra-256p-illus-1st ed (u8,f,f dj) 15.00

EASTON,ROBERT-Lord of Beasts-(Lond)-(1964)-287p-bds-1st Brit ed (m1,f,sl wn dj) 15.00

EASTON,ROBERT-Lord of Beasts-Tucson-(1961)-U of Ariz Pr-287p-illus-1st ed (cc4,dj) 15.00

EASTWOOD,DOROTHEA-River Diary-Bost-1950-8vo-256p-1st ed (m3,f,dj) 15.00

EASUM,CHESTER-Americanization of Carl Schurz-Chig-1929-U of Chig-374p (o7,soil dj) 20.00

EAT RIGHT TO WORK AND WIN-Chig-1942-Swift & Co-14p-illus papr wrps,illus (n6) 25.00

EATON,A H-Beauty Behind Barbed Wire-NY-(1952)-Harper & Bros-xiv+209p-grn cl,plts-presumed 1st ed (b2,dj) 30.00

EATON,A H-Handicrafts of New England-NY-1949-Harper-illus-1st ed (h10,dj) 50.00

EATON,A H-Handicrafts of the Southern Highlands-NY-1937-Russell Sage Fndtn-8vo-370p-cl,58 illus by Ulmann-2nd prtg (q3) 50.00

EATON,AMOS-Botanical Exercises...-Albany-1820-Websters & Skinners-171,(1)p-bds-1st ed (k1,rub,chip sp top) 50.00

EATON,D H-Trapshooting the Patriotic Sport-Cin-1920-16mo-365p-photos,illus-revsd 2nd ed (m3) 35.00

EATON,E H-Birds of New York-1910,1914-NY State Mus-4to-2 vols-106 col plts,photos,maps-1st ed (bb3,sl wn) 110.00

EATON,E H-Birds of New York. Vol.1 & 2-Albany-1910,1914-NY State Mus,Memoir 12-2 vols-106 plts by Fuertes (e9) 125.00

EATON,HARRIET P-Jersey City and Its Historic Sites-Jersey City-(1899)-144p-cl,plts (aa6) 35.00

EATON,JOHN H-Life of Andrew Jackson, Major General in the Service of the United States-Cin-1827-Hatch & Nichols-454p-lea-Howes R 171,Sabin 21731 (j1,sl wn sp,lacks f.e.p.,fox) 65.00

EATON,L K-American Architecture Comes of Age-1972-MIT-142 illus-1st ed (ee1,dj) 65.00

EATON,L K-American Architecture Comes of Age-1972-MIT-142 illus-1st ed (h10,dj) 65.00

EATON,L K-Landscape Artist in America-Chig-1964-Chig U Pr-illus,1 fldg plt (h10,dj) 150.00

EATON,L K-New England Hospitals, 1790 to 1833-Ann Arbor-(1957)-U of Mich-xiv+282p-blu cl,plts-1st ed (mm10,dj) 30.00

EATON,R C-ED.-Where to Fish 1953-1954-Lond-1953-8vo-386p-photos,fldg map (m3) 15.00

EATON,R L-Cheetah-1974-Van Nostrand-178p-photos-1st ed (bb3,f,dj) 30.00

EATON,THELMA L-Five Generations of Fun-Quanah-1973-auth-37p-cl,illus-1st ed (w3,vf) 15.00

EATON,WALTER P-Green Trails and Upland Pastures-1917-Dbldy,Page-303p-col plts-1st ed (r8,sl wn,bump) 12.00

EATON,WALTER P-Skyline Camps-(1922)-Wilde-245p-photos-1st ed (r8) 45.00

EATON,WALTER P-Skyline Camps-US-(1922)-245p-pict cov,17 photos-1st ed (o10,f) 25.00

EAVENSON,HOWARD N-First Century and a Quarter of American Coal Industry-Pitt-1942-priv prtd-xiv+701p-blk cl,14 fldg maps-1st ed (mm10) 75.00

EBERHARD,F-Microbe Murders-1935-Macaulay-pict dj-1st ed (x7,f,dj sp fade) 95.00

EBERHARD,WOLFRAM-Chinese Festivals-NY-1952-H Schuman-cl,illus-1st ed (l8,f,dj) 15.00

EBERHART,MIGNON G-Chiffon Scarf-NY-1939-Dbldy-1st ed (g4,dj) 10.00

EBERHART,MIGNON G-El Rancho Rio-1970-Random-1st ed (s10,dj tn) 10.00

EBERHART,MIGNON G-Enemy in the House-NY-1962-Random-1st ed (h4,f,dj) 10.00

EBERHART,MIGNON G-Fair Warning-1936-Dbldy-1st ed (s10,sp wn dj) 25.00

EBERHART,MIGNON G-Hangman's Whip-NY-1940-Dbldy-1st ed (e4,dj) 30.00

EBERHART,MIGNON G-Postmark Murder-NY-1956-Random-1st ed (g4,dj) 10.00

EBERHART,MIGNON G-Two Little Rich Girls-NY-1971-Random-1st ed (f4,f,dj) 10.00

EBERHART,MIGNON G-Unidentified Woman-NY-1943-Random-1st ed (h4,f,dj) 15.00

EBERHART,MIGNON G-Unknown Quantity-NY-1953-Random-1st ed (g4,dj) 10.00

EBERHART,MIGNON G-Wings of Fear-NY-1945-Random-1st ed (f4,f,dj) 15.00

EBERHART,PERRY-Guide to the Colorado Ghost Towns and Mining Camps-Denver-1959-479p-photos,maps-1st ed (t7,dj) 22.50

EBERHART,RICHARD-Collected Poems 1930 to 1960 Including 51 New Poems-NY-1960-Oxford U Pr-8vo-228p-1st ed (ee5,dj) 25.00

EBERHART,RICHARD-Reading the Spirit-NY-1937-Oxford U Pr-8vo-cl bckd bds-1st Amer ed (jj8,f,sp tan dj) 50.00

EBERLEIN,H D-English Inn Past & Present-Phila-1926-Lippincott-4to-308p-red cl,illus-1st ed (r10,sl wn) 45.00

EBERLEIN,HAROLD D-Manor Houses and Historic Homes of Long Island and Staten Island-Phila-1928-11,318p-frntis,75 illus-1st ed (pp4) 50.00

EBERLEIN,HAROLD D-Manors and Historic Homes of the Hudson Valley-Phila-1924-Lippincott-thk 4to-xvi,(2),327p-cl,82 plts (cc10) 60.00

EBERLEIN,HAROLD D-Practical Book of Chinaware-NY-(1925)-Halcyon Hs-325p-blu bds,illus-rprnt ed (l6) 30.00

EBERLEIN,HAROLD D-Rabelaisian Princess-NY-1931-Brentano's-8vo-304p-19 illus-1st ed (jj5,sp chip dj) 20.00

EBERLEIN,HAROLD-Seventeenth Century Connecticut House-St.Paul-1919-White Pine Monos-4to-16p-wrps,photos (l10) 9.50

EBERLEIN,HAROLD-Villas of Florence and Tuscany-Phila-1922-Lippincott-4to-411p-blu cl,t.e.g.,col frntis,illus (r10,dj wn,tape rprd) 60.00

EBERSOHN,WESSEL-Divide the Night-NY-1981-Pantheon-1st Amer ed (p4,f,dj) 20.00

EBERSTADT,EDWARD-Catalogue 162:Texas-NY-(1963)-stiff papr covs,950 items-1st ed (z1,f) 85.00

EBIED,R Y-Bibliography of Mediaeval Arabic and Jewish Medicine and Allied Sciences-Lond-1971-150p-wrps-1st ed (dd3) 60.00

EBIN,DAVID-ED.-Drug Experience-NY-(1961)-385p-1st ed (dd3,dj) 50.00

EBIN,DAVID-ED.-Drug Experience-NY-(1961)-Orion Pr-xii+385p-gry cl-1st ed (a2,dj) 25.00

EBSEN,BUDDY-Polynesian Concept-Englewood Cliffs-(1972)-Prentice Hall-sm 4to-142p-photos-1st ed (ff5,dj) 12.50

EBY,HENRY H-Observations of an Illinois Boy in Battle, Camp and Prisons 1861 to 1865-Mendota-1910-publ by auth-284p-frntis,illus (o7,weak hngs) 95.00

EBY,LOIS-Velvet Fleece-NY-1947-Dutton-1st ed (h4,f,dj) 12.50

ECCLESTON,ROBERT-Mariposa Indian War. 1850 to 1851. Diaries of...-SLC-1957-U of Utah Pr-vii,168p-brwn cl,tip-in frntis photos,fldg map,one of 500c (mm1) 65.00

ECKENHOFF,JAMES E-Anesthesia from Colonial Times-Phila-(1966)-Lippincott-95p-maroon & blk cl,illus-1st ed (j2) 15.00

ECKENRODE,HAMILTON J-List of the Revolutionary Soldiers of Virginia-1912-V.S.L-488p (dd9,rbnd,pgs brwng) 45.00

ECKERT,ALLAN W-Time of Terror-Bost-(1965)-Little,Brown-8vo-341p-8p photos-1st ed (gg5,dj) 17.50

ECKERT,ALLAN W-Wading Birds of North America-GC-1981-Dbldy-4to-xviii,252p-32 col plts,illus-1st ed (ff9,f,sl wn dj) 55.00*

ECKERT,EDWARD K-ED.-Ten Years in the Saddle-San Rafael-1978-Presidio Pr-8vo-xiv+443p-leatherette-1st ed (z4,smudge foredges,dj) 12.50

ECKHARDT,GEORGE H-Pennsylvania Clocks and Clockmakers-NY-1955-Bonanza-229p-gry cl sp,blu bds,illus (r10,sl wn dj) 15.00

ECKSTORM,F H-Woodpeckers-Bost-1901-sm 8vo-(5),131p-cl,5 col plts (y8,cov spots) 18.50

ECLECTIC ELEMENTARY GEOGRAPHY-NY,et al-(1911)-Amer Bk Co-82p-bds,illus,col maps (k1) 15.00

ECO,U-Name of the Rose-1980-HBJ-1st ed (x7,f,dj) 50.00

ECONOMY COOK BOOK...-Streator-1910-Ladies of Neighbrhd Guild-127p-wrps (f1,sl wn,few bent pgs) 17.50

EDBERG,ROLF-Dream of Kilimanjaro-NY-(1977)-Pantheon-8vo-179p-1st US ed (aa5,sl tn dj) 12.50

EDDINGS,DAVID-High Hunt-NY-(1973)-Putnam-1st ed (e3,sm spot t.e.,sl chip dj) 35.00

EDDISON,E R-Styrbiorn the Strong-Lond-(1926)-J.Cape-illus,Keith Henderson-scarce-1st Brit ed (b5) 75.00

EDDY,A J-Cubists & Post Impressionism-Chig-1919-McClurg-47 b&w illus,22 col plts,matted & tip in-new & rvsd ed (h10) 225.00

EDDY,DAVID B-What Next in Turkey-Bost-1913-Amer Board-illus-1st ed (m8) 45.00

EDDY,J W-Hunting the Alaska Brown Bear-1930-Putnam-253p-photos-scarce (gg3,f,chip dj) 225.00

EDDY,S-Northern Fishes with Special Reference to Upper Mississippi Valley-Mass-1943-8vo-276p-illus-1st ed (m3,f,fray dj) 12.50

EDE,CHARLES-ED.-Art of the Book-Lond-1951-Studio Publ-illus-1st ed (hh10,dj sl chip & tn) 50.00

EDE,CHARLES-ED.-Art of the Book-NY-1951-Studio Publ-4to-214p-cl,multi col pgs-1st ed (q3,dj) 60.00

EDEL,LEON-Bibliography of Henry James-Lond-1957-frntis port,illus-1st ed (r2,dj) 75.00

EDEL,LEON-Bloomsbury-Lond-1979-Hogarth-11 illus-1st ed (kk5,f,dj) 40.00

EDEN'S PARADISICAL LIBERTY-Benton Harbor-(1915)-House of David-33,(1)p-wrps,frntis port-rare (a1) 25.00

EDEY,M-Cats of Africa-NY-1968-4to-192p-cl,col photos (y8) 20.00

EDGAR,IRVING-Shakespeare, Medicine and Psychiatry-NY-1970-382p-1st ed (dd3,dj) 45.00

EDGAR,WILLIAM C-Story of a Grain of Wheat-NY-1902-12mo-195p-lea bkd cl cov bds,40 b&w illus (x5) 18.00

EDGEWORTH,MARIA-Tales and Novels-Lond-1857-Simkin et al-12mo-10 vols-3/4 mor,frntis engrvngs on steel (w6,fade,sl rub) 200.00

EDGLEY,LESLIE-Fear No More-NY-1946-Simon-1st ed (g4,yel pgs,dj) 12.50

EDISON,THOMAS-Diary and Sundry Observations of...-NY-(1948)-Philos Libr-xii+247p-grn cl (c2,dj) 25.00

EDISONIA-NY-1904-Assoc of Edison Illum Co-213p-grn cl,photos-1st ed (c2,cov soil & wn) 45.00

EDMINSTER,ALLEN-Gardening as a Hobby-NY-1938-Harper-184p (x6,dj chip,wn) 12.00

EDMINSTER,F C-American Game Birds of Field & Forest-NY-1954-4to-490p-illus (m3,f) 29.00

EDMINSTER,F C-Fish Ponds for the Farm-NY-1947-4to-114p-photos-1st ed (m3,vf,fray dj) 27.50

EDMINSTER,F C-Hunting Whitetails-NY-1954-192p-photos (gg3,f) 20.00

EDMINSTER,F C-Ruffed Grouse-1947-Macmillan-385p-photos-1st prtg (bb3,cors bump) 45.00

EDMINSTER,F C-Ruffed Grouse-NY-1947-8vo-(1),385p-cl,56 plts (y8,tn dj) 47.00

EDMINSTER,F C-Ruffed Grouse-NY-1947-8vo-385p-illus-1st ed (m3,f,sl chip dj) 55.00

EDMINSTER,F C-Ruffed Grouse-NY-1947-Macmillan-385p-photos by A A Allen-1st prtg (b9,f dj) 45.00

EDMINSTER,HENRY-Curse of Malvern-Columbus-1892-295p-cl-Wright 1701 (g1) 17.50

EDMONDS,EMMA-Nurse and Spy in the Union Army-Hartford-1865-384p-1st ed (dd3) 125.00

EDMONDS,W D-They Fought with What They Had-Bost-1951-8vo-xvi,532p-cl,13 maps,e.p. maps-1st ed (t2,chip dj) 35.00

EDMONDS,WALTER D-Tom Whipple-NY-1942-Dodd,Mead-illus by P Lantz-1st ed (y1,f,f dj) 50.00

EDMONSON,HAROLD-World Steam in Action-Lond-1970-160p-1st ed (n4,f,dj) 22.00

EDMONSON,MUNRO S-ED.-Sixteenth Century Mexico,The Work of Sahagun-Albuquerque-1974-UNM Pr-8vo-xv,1,292p-grn cl-1st ed (mm1,as new in dj) 30.00

EDMONSTON,WILLIAM E,JR.-Hypnosis and Relaxation-NY-(1981)-John Wiley & Sons-(xvi)+255p-1st ed (y9) 19.50

EDMUNDS,JOHN-ED.-Williamsburg Songbook-NY-1964-Holt-linen & mrbld bndg,illus-1st ed (u4,as new) 30.00

EDMUNDS,LOWELL-Silver Bullet-Westport-(1981)-Greenwood Pr-149p-1st ed (k6) 21.00

EDMUNDS,R DAVID-Otoe-Phoenix-1976-100p-frntis,photos-1st ed (t7,f,autg) 20.00

EDMUNDSON,SARAH E-Nurse and Spy in the Union Army-Hartford-1865-W S Williams-384p-orig cl,frntis port,illus (v2,lacks ffep,sl wn,fox) 30.00

EDSON,LELAH J-Fourth Corner-(Bellingham)-(1951)-298p-illus,nbrd,autg(most copies were signed & nbrd by the auth)-Tweney #19-1st ed (j7,rprd dj) 45.00

EDSON,LELAH J-Fourth Corner-Bellingham-(1951)-298p-photos,nbrd,autg-scarce (r8,dj rub,sl chip) 60.00

EDSON,RUSSELL-Appearances-(1961)-Thing Pr-8vo-stapled dec wrps-1st ed (x10,f) 25.00

EDSON,RUSSELL-Stone is Nobody's-1961-Thing Pr-8vo-dec wrps-ltd to 1000c-1st ed (x10,f) 35.00

EDWARDES,MICHAEL-Battle of Plassy-NY-1963-167p-illus-1st ed (gg2,f,dj) 35.00

EDWARDES,MICHAEL-East West Passage-NY-(1971)-Taplinger-8vo-248p-54 illus-1st US ed (jj5,dj) 12.50

EDWARDES,MICHAEL-Last Years of British India-Cleve-1964-World-8vo-viii,248p-cl-1st Amer ed (ll1,wn dj) 12.50

EDWARDES,MICHAEL-Last Years of British India-Lond-1963-Cassell-250p-1st ed (gg6,dj) 15.00

EDWARDS,AMELIA B-Outlines of English History-Bost-1861-SB&T-106p+ads-prntd bds-Amer ed,revsd & corrctd (k1) 15.00

EDWARDS,CARL I-Pequannock Township, 1740 to 1956-(Pequannock Twnshp)-(1956)-68p-wrps,illus (aa6) 25.00

EDWARDS,CECIL-Persian Caravan-NY-1928-Harper & Bros-cl,illus-1st ed (n8,f,dj) 25.00

EDWARDS,CHARLES-History and Poetry of Finger Rings-NY-1894-John W Lovell-cl,illus-1st ed (o8) 35.00

EDWARDS,E P-Field Guide to the Birds of Mexico-Sweet Briar-1972-300p-stiff wrps,24 col plts-1st ed (b9,as new) 10.00

EDWARDS,E P-Finding Birds in Mexico-Sweet Briar-1968-8vo-(1),282p-cl,15 plts(4 col),8 maps-2nd ed (y8,dj) 20.00

EDWARDS,ELWYN H-ED.-Encyclopedia of the Horse-Lond-1983-Octopus-folio-256p (h9,dj) 35.00

EDWARDS,ETHEL-Carver of Tuskegee-(1971)-Psyche Pr of Cin-ltd to 200c,nbrd (a10,f) 40.00

EDWARDS,FRANK-Campaign in New Mexico with Colonel Doniphan-Phila-1847-Carey & Hart-cl wi orig sp labl,map-Howes E52-Wagner Camp 123:1-1st ed (pp9,rbnd,map split) 500.00

EDWARDS,GEORGE W-Rome-(1928)-Penn-344p-blk dec cl,24p col plts pntng,28 plts drwngs (v8,corners wn) 60.00

EDWARDS,GLADYS B-Photographic History of the Polish Arabian-Rockville-nd(1978)-Arab Ink-4to-1st ed (j9) 195.00

EDWARDS,GUS C-Legal Laughs...-Clarksville-(1915)-Legal Publ Co-416p-cl-2nd prntng (c1) 17.50

EDWARDS,IRENE-Short Portage to Lillooet and Other Tales and Trails-Lillooet-1978-Auth-sm 4to-289p-prtd wrps,maps,ports (k10) 15.00*

EDWARDS,J B-Early Days in Abilene-np-nd(ca.1938)-16p-pict wrps,photos,illus-Herd #746-scarce (t7,f) 175.00

EDWARDS,JOHN N-Noted Guerillas, or the Warfare of the Border-Dayton-1976-488p-frntis port,illus,e.p. maps (o7,as new) 20.00

EDWARDS,LIONEL-Reminiscences of a Sporting Artist-Lond-1947-Putnam-col plts-1st ed (u2,dj) 50.00

EDWARDS,LIONEL-Sketches in Stable and Kennel-Lond,NY-1933-Putnam,Scribner-4to-1st US ed (f10,dj) 125.00

EDWARDS,MICHAEL-Battles of the Indian Mutiny-NY-1963-216p-illus-1st ed (b7,f,dj) 40.00

EDWARDS,OLIVER-Talking of Books-Lond-(1957)-Heinemann-8vo-306p-1st Brit ed (bb5,dj) 15.00

EDWARDS,PAUL-English Garden Ornament-(1965)-Barnes-sq 4to-110p-16 col & 40 b&w photos,73 drwngs (x5,f,rprd dj) 18.00

EDWARDS,PAUL-English Garden Ornament-So Brunswick-1965-Barnes-sq 4to-110p-grn cl,illus (r10,wn dj) 22.50

EDWARDS,PERMELIA-Table and its Service-Spokane-nd(ca.1905)-auth-oblng 12mo-488p-bds-Bitting 141 (o6,spot bds,dmpstnd pgs) 85.00

EDWARDS,PHILIP L-California in 1837-Sacramento-1890-A J Johnston-12mo-47p-orig prtd wrps-Adams Herd 747,Howes E66-1st ed (mm1) 325.00

EDWARDS,PHILIP LEGET-Diary of...-SF-1932-Grabhorn Pr-47p-col litho frntis,Wagner-Camp #48-ltd ed (e7,f,box) 85.00

EDWARDS,ROSS-Fiddle Dust-Denver-1965-102p-frntis,photos-1st ed (t7,pres) 17.50

EDWARDS,RUTH D-Corridors of Death-Lond-1981-Quartet-1st ed (p4,dj) 25.00

EDWORDS,CLARENCE-Bohemian San Francisco-SF-(1914)-Paul Elder-138p-cl cov bds,prntd in red & blk,tip in frntis-Bitting 141 (l6,dj) 85.00

EELES,FRANCISE C-Ancient Stained and Painted Glass in the Churches of Surrey-1930-Surrey Archae Soc-141p-bds,17 col plts (cc8) 75.00

EELES,H H-Dressing Flies for Trout and Salmon-Lond-nd-12mo-96p-illus,col plts (m3,f) 20.00

EELES,H H-Tackle Making for Fishermen-Lond-1954-12mo-101p-illus-1st ed (m3) 10.00

EELLS,MYRON-Hyms of the Chinook Jargon-Portland-1889-Steel-12mo-40p-pnk wrps-2nd ed,rvsd & enlgd (w1,f) 100.00

EELLS,MYRON-Marcus Whitman: Pathfinder and Patriot-Seattle-1909-Alice Harriman Co-lg 8vo-349p-illus-Smith 2763-1st ed (v1,chip dj) 75.00

EELLS,MYRON-Reply to Professor Bourne's "The Whitman Legend"-Walla Walla-1902-122p+errata,wrps-Smith#2766 (v7) 25.00

EFFLER,DR.LOUIS R-Aztec-Land-Toledo-(1944)-priv prntd-80p-wrps (c1) 15.00

EFFLER,DR.LOUIS R-Totem Land-Toledo-(1943)-56,(1)p-wrps,illus-scarce (d1) 20.00

EFFLER,LOUIS R-My Trip to Hopi Land or a Trip to Oraibi-Toledo-(1941)-priv publ-100p-wrps,illus (d1) 22.50

EGAN,FEROL-El Dorado Trail-NY-(1970)-McGraw Hill-313p-maps-1st ed (gg4,dj) 25.00

EGAN,FEROL-El Dorado Trail-NY-(1970)-McGraw Hill-xvi+313p-red cl,Amer Trails Ser-1st ed (e2,dj) 20.00

EGAN,FEROL-Sani in a Whirlwind-NY-1972-316p-map e.p.-1st ed (t7,f,dj) 20.00

EGAN,HOWARD-Pioneering the West 1846 to 1878-Richmond-1917-302p-pict cl,photos-Howes E76-1st ed (t7) 75.00

EGAN,HOWARD-Pioneering the West 1846 to 1878-Richmond-1917-H Egan-photos,illus-Howes E76-1st ed (pp9) 100.00

EGAN,LESLEY-Choice of Crimes-1980-Crime Club-1st ed (r9,vf,dj) 20.00

EGAN,LESLEY-Random Death-Lond-1982-Gollancz-1st Brit ed (q4,vf,dj) 20.00

EGAN,MAURICE F-Recollections of a Happy Life-NY-1924-374p-cl (n1) 15.00

EGAN,PIERCE-Life in London-Lond-1830-2 vols-3/4 lea,36 handcol illus,I & G Cruikshank-New ed (l9,fragile & sl wn sp) 275.00

EGELER,C G-Challenge of the Andes-NY-1955-203p-32 photos,9 maps-1st US ed (p10,f,dj) 30.00

EGERTON,GEORGE-Keynotes-Bost/Lond-1894-Roberts/Matthews & Lane-8vo-192p-grn cl,tp illus,A Beardsley-1st US ed (w6,sl soil cl) 75.00

EGERTON,JUDY-British Sporting and Animal Paintings 1655 to 1867-Lond-1978-Tate Gallery-4to-382p-43 col & 120 b&w plts-1st ed (j9,f,f dj) 95.00

EGG HARBOR TOWNSHIP-Sketches of...Atlantic County, New Jersey-Egg Harbor-1964-(7),96p-cl,illus,fldg map (aa6) 40.00

EGGAN,FRED-American Indian-Chig-(1966)-Aldine-8vo-193p-cl-2nd prtg (y5,sl wn dj) 28.00

EGGAN,FRED-ED.-Social Anthropology of North American Tribes-Chig-1937-456p-scarce-1st ed (t7,f) 22.50

EGGAN,FRED-Social Organization of the Western Pueblos-Chig-(1950)-367p+index-map frntis-scarce-1st ed (v7,f,dj) 45.00

EGGAN,FRED-Social Organization of the Western Pueblos-Chig-(1950)-373p-map frntis-scarce-1st ed (t7,dj) 40.00

EGGENHOFFER,NICK-Horses, Horses Always Horses-Cody-1981-oblng 8vo-213p-lea,col illus-1st ed (f7,f,dj) 110.00

EGGENHOFFER,NICK-Wagons, Mules and Men-NY-1961-184p-plts-1st ed (t7,cov sl flecked) 45.00

EGGLER,ALBERT-Everest Lhotse Adventure-Lond-1957-Allen & Unwin-8vo-222p-col frntis,24 photos-1st Brit ed (ll1,chip dj) 22.50

EGGLER,ALBERT-Everest Lhotse Adventure-NY-1957-222p-24 photos-1st US ed (p10,f,dj) 35.00

EGGLER,ALBERT-Everest Lhotse Adventure-NY-1957-Harper-222p-24p photos-Neate 240-1st ed (j8,f,dj) 40.00

EGGLESTON,EDWARD-Hoosier School-Master-NY-(1871)-Orange Judd-226p+(2)p ads-cl-1st ed,6th prntg (k1,sl wn sp) 17.50

EGGLESTON,GEORGE C-Big Brother-NY-1875-Putnam's-182p-cl-1st ed (d1) 22.50

EGGLESTON,GEORGE C-History of the Confederate War-NY-1910-Sturgis & Walton-2 vols-(Nevins II,p.173)-1st ed (nn6,ex-libr) 80.00

EGGLESTON,GEORGE C-Man of Honor-NY-(1873)-Orange Judd Co-222p+ads-cl-Wright 845-1st ed (h1) 20.00

EGGLESTON,GEORGE C-Rebel's Recollections-NY-1887-260p (z10,cov speck) 45.00

EGLESTON,THOMAS-Life of John Paterson-NY-1894-Putnam's-xii+293p-blu cl,maps,charts-1st ed (h2,sl wn cor) 85.00

EHERNBERGER,JAMES L-Smoke Across the Prairie-Golden-1964-64p-1st ed (n4) 27.50

EHERNBERGER,JAMES L-Smoke Along the Columbia-Callaway-1968-64p-no dj as iss-1st ed (n4) 27.50

EHERNBERGER,JAMES L-Smoke Down the Canyons-Callaway-1966-64p-1st ed (n4) 27.50

EHERNBERGER,JAMES L-Smoke Over the Divide-Callaway-1965-64p-1st ed (n4) 27.50

EHLE,JOHN-Free Men-NY-(1965)-Harper & Row-photos-1st ed (k7,dj soil) 25.00

EHLE,JOHN-Journey of August King-1971-Harper & Row-1st ed (s9,f,dj) 20.00

EHLE,JOHN-Road-NY-1967-1st ed (r5,dj) 30.00

EHLE,JOHN-Winter People-NY-(1982)-Harper Row-1st ed (a5,f,dj) 25.00

EHRLICH,BLAKE-London on the Thames-Bost-1966-Little,Brown-1st ed (z9,dj) 10.00

EHRLICH,MAX-Reincarnation in Venice-NY-(1979)-S&S-1st ed (e3,f,dj) 20.00

EHRMANN,HERBERT B-Untried Case-1933-Vanguard-1st ed (s10) 15.00

EHWA,CARL,JR.-Book of Pipes & Tobacco-NY-(1974)-Ridge Pr-lg sq 8vo-239p-cl,col plts,photos-1st ed (l10,f,dj) 20.00

EIBL-EIBEFELDT,I-Galapagos-Lond-1960-MacGibbon & Kee-8vo-192p-map e.p.,5 col plts,16 b&w plts-1st Engl ed (p8,wn dj) 35.00

EIDE,INGVARD H-American Odyssey-Chig-1969-Rand McNally-4to-241p-cl,260 photos-1st ed (z4,dj sl wn & soil) 20.00

EIDE,INGVARD H-Oregon Trail-Chig-1973-Rand McNally-4to-244p-cl,photos-1st ed (z4,sl wn dj) 15.00

EILOART,A-Flight of the Small World-NY-(1959)-8vo-256p-cl,20p plts-1st ed (t2,dj) 25.00

EINARSEN,A S-Pronghorn Antelope and Its Management-1948-Wldlf Mgmt Inst-238p-photos (bb3,f,dj) 35.00

EINARSEN,A S-Pronghorn Antelope-MD-1948-Wildlife Mgmt Inst-238p-photos (gg3,f,dj) 35.00

EINARSEN,A S-Pronghorn Antelope...-Wash-(1948)-8vo-238p-cl,col frntis,col plt,photos (y8,dj chip) 40.00

EINERSEN,ARTHUR S-Black Brant-Seattle-1965-8vo-142p-illus-1st ed (m3,vf,dj,pres cpy) 20.00

EINERSEN,ARTHUR S-Pronghorn Antelope-Wash D C-1948-8vo-238p-illus-1st ed (m3,vf) 27.50

EINSENSTEIN,PHYLLIS-Born to Exile-Sauk City-1978-Arkham-1st ed (f3,f,dj) 15.00

EINSTEIN,CHARLES-ED.-Fireside Book of Baseball-1956-S&S-illus-1st ed (s8,dj) 45.00

EINSTEIN,CHARLES-ED.-Second Fireside Book of Baseball-1958-S&S-1st ed (r7,dj) 40.00

EINSTEIN,CHARLES-ED.-Third Fireside Book of Baseball-1968-S&S-1st ed (r7,f,dj nick & edgetn) 75.00

EINSTEIN,CHARLES-Flag for San Francisco-1962-S&S-1st ed (s7,dj) 16.00

EINSTEIN,CHARLES-Only Game in Town-1955-Dell-pbk orig-1st ed (s8) 20.00

EINSTEIN,CHARLES-Willie's Time-1979-Lippincott-1st ed (ff2,dj) 20.00

EIPPER,PAUL-Circus-NY-1931-Viking-8vo-213p-48 photos-1st US ed (jj5,dj) 60.00

EISELE,WILBERT E-Real Wild Bill Hickok-Denver-1931-Wm H Andre-364p-illus-Six Guns 668-1st ed (gg4,dj) 35.00

EISELEY,LOREN-Firmanent of Time-NY-1960-Atheneum-12mo-184p-1st ed (aa5,chip dj) 20.00

EISELEY,LOREN-Immense Journey-NY-1957-Random-auth 1st bk-1st ed (g8,f,chip dj) 75.00

EISELIN,MAX-Ascent of Dhaulagiri-Lond-1961-159p-1st ed (a4,f,dj) 110.00

EISENBERG,LARRY-Best Laid Schemes-NY-(1971)-Macmillan-auth 1st bk-1st ed (bb1,f,dj) 20.00

EISENHOWER,DWIGHT D-Crusade in Europe-GC-1948-Dbldy-559p-maps,photos-1st trd ed (p2,sl rub dj) 17.50

EISENHOWER,DWIGHT D-Mandate for Change-GC-1963-Dbldy-e.p. maps,photos-1st trd ed (p2,f,dj) 15.00

EISENHOWER,DWIGHT D-Papers of...the War Years-Balt-1971-Johns Hopkins-5 vols-illus-2nd prtg (y10,f) 60.00

EISENSCHIML,OTTO-American Iliad-Indpls-(1947)-720p-illus-1st ed (n3,f,dj chip) 27.50

EISENSCHIML,OTTO-Hidden Face of the Civil War-Indpls-1961-Bobbs Merrill-319p-maps-1st ed (v2) 20.00

EISENSCHIML,OTTO-Why the Civil War-Indpls-1958-Bobbs Merrill-208p-1st ed (cc6,dj) 30.00

EISENSTAEDT,ALFRED-Witness to Nature-NY-1971-Viking-144p-1st ed (cc9,sl tn dj) 40.00

EISENSTAEDT,ALFRED-Witness to Our Time-NY-1966-Viking-343p-photos-1st ed (cc9,f,dj) 85.00

EKBERG,CARL-Failure of Louis XIV's Dutch War-Chapel Hill-1979-240p-maps,illus-1st ed (b7,f,dj) 40.00

EKIN,C-Howard Hill, the Man & the Legend-priv prtd-231p-photos (gg3,vf,dj,autg) 30.00

EKVALL,ROBERT B-Tibetan Sky Lines-NY-(1952)-FS&Y-8vo-240p-8 photos-1st ed (ff5,dj) 25.00

EL COMANCHO-Old Timer's Tale-Chig-1929-114p-dec cov,illus-1st ed(w/o errata slips) (r8,sm stn rear cov) 50.00

EL COMANCHO-Old Timer's Tale-Chig-1929-114p-pict bds,frntis,photos-Herd #752-1st ed (t7) 55.00

ELDER,NORMAN-Thing of Darkness-NY-(1979)-Everest-4to-151p-col photos-1st ed (jj5,f,dj rub) 15.00

ELDER,PAUL-COMP.-California the Beautiful-SF-(1911)-P Elder & Co-72,(1)p-bds,frntis,36 mounted plts (aa1) 75.00

ELDER,PAUL-Nature & Science on the Pacific Coast-SF-1915-Paul Elder & Co-12mo-illus cl cov,photos,6 fldg maps (b6) 25.00

ELDER,PAUL-Old Spanish Missions of California-SF-1913-Paul Elder-4to-vi,89p-burlap on bds,photos-Spec ed (n2,sl wn) 100.00

ELDERFIELD,JOHN-Modern Drawing-NY-1983-MOMA-4to-216p-beige cl,100 col plts (r10,f) 30.00

ELDREDGE,ZOETH S-Beginnings of San Francisco from the Expedition of Anza...-SF-1912-Z S Eldredge-8vo-2 vols-cl,t.e.g.,illus,maps (ee7,sp fade) 125.00

ELDRIDGE,ELLEANOR-Memoirs of ...-Providence-1840-prntd by B T Albro-128p-bds-Amer Imprnts 40-4216-1st ed wi this title (d1,inner hngs tp rnfrcd) 125.00

ELDRIDGE,ROBERT L-History of Overton County, Tennessee, 1776 to 1976-Livingston-1976-Enterprise Prtg-226p-cl,photos (v3,dj) 28.00

ELDRIDGE,ROGER-Shadow of the Gloom World-NY-(1978)-Dutton-auth 1st bk-1st US ed (s3,f,dj) 15.00

ELEK,STEPHEN D-Staphylococcus Pyogenes and its Relation to Disease-Edinburgh-1959-Livingstone-viii+767p-grn cl,44 illus-1st ed (d2) 50.00

ELEY,JAMES-American Florist-Hartford-1845-Geer-12mo-183p-cl (x6,rebckd,sl fox) 100.00

ELFER,MAURICE-Madam Candelaria-Houston-1933-Rein-23p-wrps,frntis port-scarce-1st ed (a9) 75.00

ELFLANDSSON,GALAD-Black Wolf-W Kingston-1979-illus,R Broecker-auth 1st bk-ltd to 1000c-1st ed (k5,f,dj) 20.00

ELGOOD,CYRIL-Medical History of Persia and the Eastern Caliphate from the Earliest Times until the Year A.D.1932-Cambridge-1951-617p-5 plts-1st ed (g10,dj) 75.00

ELIADE,MIRCEA-Myth of the Eternal Return-NY-1954-Pantheon Bks-buckram,Bollingen Ser.XLVI-1st ed (l8,f) 45.00

ELIAS,SOL P-Stories of Stanislaus-Modesto-(1924)-Sol P Elias-344p-1st ed (ff4,autg) 50.00

ELIN,STANLEY-Dark Fantastic-1983-Mysterious Pr-one of 250c,autg-1st ed (x2,f,dj) 75.00

ELIOT,ALEXANDER-Three Hundred Years of American Painting-NY-1957-Time-folio-cl-1st ed (oo6,box) 45.00

ELIOT,CHARLES-Charles Eliot Landscape Architect-Cambridge-1924-Harvard Pr-770p-cl,fldg plans-latr prtg (x6,cov sl soil) 100.00

ELIOT,CHARLES-Charles Eliot Landscape Architect-Freeport-1971(1902)-Bks for Libr Rprnt-xxiv,770p-photos,fldg plans (mm4,f) 55.00

ELIOT,CHAS W-Harvard Memories-Cambridge-1923-Harvard-vii,145p-illus-3rd prtg (o2) 17.50

ELIOT,GEORGE-Essays and Leaves From a Notebook-Edinburgh & Lond-1884-Blackwood-8vo-382p-brwn cl-1st ed (w6,sl wn,hngs tender) 125.00

ELIOT,GEORGE-Impressions of Theophrastus Such-NY-1879-Harper & Bros-dec cl-1st Amer ed (k8) 50.00

ELIOT,GEORGE-Legend of Jubal-Edinburgh & Lond-1875-Blackwood-sm 8vo-242+16p ads-orig cl,wi errata slip-1st ed (w6) 150.00

ELIOT,GEORGE-Mill on the Floss-NY-1860-Harper-8vo-464p-1st US ed (w6) 200.00

ELIOT,GEORGE-Silas Marner-Lond-1907-Macmillan-grn & gold pict bndg,a.e.g.,24 col plts by H Thomson-1st in Cranford Ser (ff6,f) 150.00

ELIOT,GEORGE-Silas Marner-NY-1861-Harpers-8vo-265p+ads-publ blk cl-1st Amer ed (b3,edges & cors wn,scuff) 75.00

ELIOT,GEORGE-Spanish Gypsy-Bost-1868-Ticknor & Fields-8vo-287p-orig cl-1st US ed (w6,hng tender) 25.00

ELIOT,GEORGE-Works of...-Bost-1886-Estes & Lauriat-24 vols-dec lea bndg-Edition deLuxe (l9) 4,000.00

ELIOT,T S-Cocktail Party-NY-(1950)-Harcourt,Brace-blk cl,cancel on pg 35,36-Gallup A55b-1st Amer ed (f2,f,dj) 55.00

ELIOT,T S-Cultivation of Christmas Trees-Lond-(1954)-Faber-sewn wrps,illus,orig envelope-1st ed (v5,f,envelope) 20.00

ELIOT,T S-Cultivation of Christmas Trees-NY-(1956)-Farrar,Straus-8vo-illus bds-1st Amer ed (x3) 40.00

ELIOT,T S-Cultivation of Christmas Trees-NY-(1956)-FS&C-8vo-dec blk bds-1st Amer ed (ll10,f) 35.00

ELIOT,T S-Dante-Lond-(1929)-Faber-sm 8vo-gry bds,1st state dj wi no reviews,ltd to 2000c-Gallup A13-1st ed (x3,sl sunned & tattrd dj) 100.00

ELIOT,T S-Elder Statesman-NY-(1959)-Farrar-8vo-cl-1st ed (x3,dj) 40.00

ELIOT,T S-Family Reunion-Lond-(1939)-Faber-8vo-cl-1st ed (ll10,f,sl soil dj) 75.00

ELIOT,T S-Family Reunion-Lond-(1939)-Faber-8vo-gry cl-Gallup A33a-1st ed (x3,sl chip dj) 70.00

ELIOT,T S-Family Reunion-NY-(1939)-Harcourt,Brace-blk cl-1st Amer ed (f2,dj) 50.00

ELIOT,T S-Film of the Murder in the Cathedral-1952-Harcourt,Brace-illus,photos-1st Amer ed (x2,f,dj sl wn & tn) 20.00

ELIOT,T S-Idea of a Christian Society-Lond-(1939)-Faber-8vo-blu cl,ltd to 2000c-Gallup A35a-1st ed (x3,sl chip dj) 70.00

ELIOT,T S-Journey of the Magi-NY-1927-Wm E Rudge-gry papr wrps,untrimmed-27c prtd,of which 12 were for sale-Gallup A9c-1st Amer ed (hh4,f) 1,650.00

ELIOT,T S-Little Gidding-Lond-(1942)-Faber-8vo-wrps-Gallup A42-1st ed (x3,sl stnd cov) 75.00

ELIOT,T S-Notes Toward the Definition of Culture-NY-(1949)-HBCo-128p-1st Amer ed (j8,dj) 40.00

ELIOT,T S-Notes Towards the Definition of Culture-NY-(1949)-Harcourt,Brace-128p-blk cl-1st Amer ed (f2,sl wn dj sp) 25.00

ELIOT,T S-On Poetry and Poets-NY-1957-FS&C-blk cl-1st Amer ed (f2,sl wn dj) 15.00

ELIOT,T S-Poems 1909-1925-1932-Harcourt,Brace-1st Amer ed (x2,sl wn & fade sp) 37.00

ELIOT,T S-Sweeney Agonistes-1932-Faber-1st ed (kk6,sl fox,sp chip,dj sl chip 125.00

ELIOT,WILLARD A-Forest Trees of the Pacific Coast-NY-1938-Putnam's-8vo-568p-248 photos-1st ed (ff9) 30.00*

ELKIN,STANLEY-Bad Man-NY-(1967)-Random-1st ed (u10,f,f dj) 40.00

ELKIN,STANLEY-Criers and Kibitzers-1965-Random-1st ed (x2,f,dj) 75.00

ELKIN,STANLEY-Franchiser-NY-(1976)-1st ed (d5,f,dj) 12.50

ELKIN,STANLEY-Living End-NY-(1979)-Dutton-1st ed (b5,as new in dj) 15.00

ELKIN,STANLEY-Living End-NY-(1979)-Dutton-1st ed (h3,f,dj) 20.00

ELLENBERGER,HENRI-Discovery of the Unconscious-NY-(1970)-Basic Bks-thk 8vo-(xvi)+932p-blu cl-1st ed (y9,dj) 50.00

ELLET,ELIZABETH F-Pioneer Women of the West-1873-Porter & Coates-434p (d3,hng crack) 40.00

ELLET,MRS E F-Court Circles of the Republic-Phila-1872-Phila Publ Co-586p-cl,frntis+12p engrvngs (d1) 25.00

ELLET,MRS E-Poems-Phila-1835-Key & Biddle-12mo-229p-orig cl-scarce (w6) 85.00

ELLET,MRS ELIZABETH F-Pioneer Women of the West-Phila-1873-Porter & Coates-434p-cl,frntis (w3) 30.00

ELLET,MRS-Queens of American Society-Phila-(1867)-Porter & Coates-464p-cl (m1) 15.00

ELLIN,STANLEY-Eighth Circle-Bost-1979-Gregg-1st ed (r4,f,dj) 20.00

ELLIN,STANLEY-House of Cards-1967-Random-1st ed (x7,f,dj) 33.00

ELLIN,STANLEY-Mystery Stories-1956-S&S-1st ed (n9,wn dj) 25.00

ELLIN,STANLEY-Mystery Stories-1956-S&S-1st ed (x7,f,dj) 55.00

ELLIN,STANLEY-Panama Portrait-NY-(1962)-Random-8vo-242p-1st ed (ee5,soil dj) 15.00

ELLIN,STANLEY-Star Light Star Bright-NY-1979-Random-1st ed (g4,f,dj) 10.00

ELLIN,STANLEY-Winter After This Summer-NY-(1960)-Random-1st ed (p3,f,chip dj) 10.00

ELLIOT,BOB-All About Brook Trout from Maine to California-Orange-1954-8vo-242p-col plts,photos (m3,f,sl fray dj) 27.50

ELLIOT,BOB-Bass Fishing in New England-Lexington-1973-8vo-117p-photos (m3,f,dj) 12.50

ELLIOT,BOB-Eastern Brook Trout-NY-1950-242p-grn cl,col frntis,photos (ee3,sl soil) 20.00

ELLIOT,BOB-Eastern Brook Trout-NY-1950-8vo-242p-photos-1st ed (m3,f,fray dj) 40.00

ELLIOT,BOB-Making of an Angler-NY-1975-8vo-209p-illus-1st ed (m3,vf,dj) 12.00

ELLIOT,D G-Catalogue of the Collection of Mammals in the Field Columbian Museum-Chig-1907-8vo-694p-wrps,drwngs (y8,tear rprd) 65.00

ELLIOT,D G-Game Birds of North America-NY-1897-8vo-220p-col chrts inside rear cov-2nd prntng (m3) 20.00

ELLIOT,D G-Land and Sea Mammals of Middle America and the West Indies-Chig-1904-8vo-2 vols-wrps,68 plts-Zoological Series (y8) 98.00

ELLIOT,D G-Review of the Primates-NY-1913-4to-3 vols-mor,28 col plts,140 plain plts-rare (y8,sl scuff) 950.00

ELLIOT,DAVID-Training Gun Dogs to Retrieve-NY-1952-12mo-128p-illus-1st ed (m3) 12.50

ELLIOT,F-Hand Book of Practical Landscape Gardening-NY-1877-Dewey-96p-cl,chromo litho frntis,plans-scarce (x6) 175.00

ELLIOT,GEORGE P-Parktilden Village-Beacon Hill-(1958)-Beacon Pr-auth 1st bk-1st ed (f3,chip dj) 25.00

ELLIOT,MAUD H-Three Generations-Bost-1923-Little,Brown-8vo-418p-18 illus-1st ed (gg5) 20.00

ELLIOT,W J-Spurs-Spur-1939-Texas Spur-274p-cl,illus,photos-v scarce-1st ed (w3,sp fade,pres cpy) 175.00

ELLIOTT,CHARLES B-Philippines-Indpls-1917-Bobbs Merrill-2 vols-ports (c3) 48.00

ELLIOTT,CHARLES W-Winfield Scott-NY-1937-Macmillan-817p-maps,illus-1st ed (cc4,sun sp) 40.00

ELLIOTT,CHARLES-Fading Trails-NY-1942-8vo-279p-illus-1st ed (m3,f,sl fray dj) 12.50

ELLIOTT,CHARLES-Gone Fishin-Harrisburg-1953-8vo-291p-illus-1st ed (m3,dj) 15.00

ELLIOTT,CLAUDE-Leathercoat-S.A.-1938-Standard-315p-photos-1st ed (a9,dj) 100.00

ELLIOTT,EDWARD-Biographical Story of the Constitution-NY,Lond-(1910)-Putnam's-400p-cl (f1) 15.00

ELLIOTT,F R-Western Fruit Book or American Fruit Grower's Guide-NY-1860-Saxton-528p-cl-4th ed (x6,sp wn) 80.00

ELLIOTT,HENRY W-Our Arctic Province-1887-Scribner-465p-pict cov,sp g,red,orange on blk,plts,drwngs,fldg map,-1st ed (u8,sl wn,sp fray,map split) 65.00

ELLIOTT,JAMES W-Transport to Disaster-NY-(1962)-247p-1st ed (n3,f,dj) 25.00

ELLIOTT,RICHARD S-Notes Taken in Sixty Years-St.Louis-1883-R P Studley-(iv)+336p-grn cl,1st iss wi port as frnts-1st ed (k2) 165.00

ELLIS,C HAMILTON-Lore of the Train-1971-G&D-folio-240p-col illus-1st ed (d3,dj) 30.00

ELLIS,C HAMILTON-Picture History of Railways-Lond-1956-408p-1st ed (n4,f,dj) 24.00

ELLIS,C HAMILTON-Railway Carriages in the British Isles from 1830 to 1914-Lond-1965-179p-1st rvsd & enlgd ed of 1949 ed (n4,f,dj) 23.00

ELLIS,CHARLES-ET AL-California Gold Rush Voyages, 1848 to 1849-1954-Huntington-246p-map-1st ed (d3,dj) 25.00

ELLIS,CLARENCE-Hubert De Burgh-Lond-(1952)-Phoenix Hs-8vo-240p-9 plts,3 maps-1st ed (jj5,dj) 17.50

ELLIS,DAVID M-ED.-Frontier in American Development-Ithaca-(1969)-Cornell U Pr-425p-1st ed (dd4) 15.00

ELLIS,EDWARD S-Indian Wars of the United States-Chig-(1902)-J D Kenyon-484p-illus (ff4) 50.00

ELLIS,EDWARD S-Life of Kit Carson-NY-1889-260p-col frntis (t7,dj) 10.00

ELLIS,ELMER-Defender of the West-Caldwell-1941-409p-frntis,photos-1st ed (t7,dj) 20.00

ELLIS,F H-Atlantic Air Conquest-Lond-(1963)-roy 8vo-224p-cl,51 illus-1st ed (t2,dj) 25.00

ELLIS,F H-In Canadian Skies-Tor-1959-Ryerson-x,230p-cl,illus (aa2,dj) 25.00*

ELLIS,HAMILTON-Pictorial Encyclopedia of Railroads-NY-1968-591p-1st ed (n4,f,dj) 19.50

ELLIS,HAVELOCK-More Essays of Love and Virtue-Lond-1931-Constable-xii,218p-cl-1st ed (dd10,f) 35.00

ELLIS,JOHN-Cavalry-NY-(1978)-192p-illus(incl col)-1st ed (n3,f,dj) 25.00

ELLIS,MARTHA D-Bell Ranch Places and People-Clarendon-1963-Clarendon Pr-75p-red cl,photos,drwngs-ltd to 500c (ff8) 45.00

ELLIS,MARTHA D-Bell Ranch Recollections-Clarendon-1965-Clarendon Pr-95p-cl,photos,illus,R E Lougheed,ltd to 500c (w3,f) 45.00

ELLIS,RICHARD N-General Pope and U.S. Indian Policy-Albuq-(1970)-U of NM Pr-287p-illus-1st ed (cc4,dj) 25.00

ELLIS,RUTH-Shakespeare Memorial Theatre-Lond-1948-Winchester Publ-1st ed (z9) 10.00

ELLIS,W ASHTON-ED.-Richard to Minna Wagner: Letters to his First Wife-Lond-1909-Grevel-8vo-2 vols-blu cl-1st Brit ed (s1) 75.00

ELLIS,WILLIAM T-Billy Sunday-1914-Winston (s8) 65.00

ELLIS,WILLIAM-Narraative of a Tour Through Hawaii...-Lond-1826-for the auth-(8),442p-mod blu 1/2 mor,7 litho plts,fldg map-1st Brit ed (o4,f,rbnd) 750.00

ELLIS,WILLIAM-Polynesian Researches...-Lond-1829-Fisher,Son & Jackson-8vo-2 vols-calf,gilt,raised bnds,2 maps(1 fldg),9 plts(incl map),16 wood engrvngs-1st ed (p8,sl rub) 950.00

ELLIS,WILLIAM-Polynesian Researches...-NY-1833-Harper-4 vols-3 fldg maps,6 plts-1st Amer ed (p8,ex-libr,fox) 850.00

ELLIS,WILLIAM-Three Visits to Madagascar During the Years 1853,1854,1856-NY-1859-Harper-8vo-xvi,514p-orig cl,plts,illus,1 map-1st ed (bb6,sp fade,chip,tn) 35.00

ELLISON,DOUGLAS W-Sole Survivor-Aberdeen-(1983)-128p-pict cl,illus-ltd to 1000c-1st ed (c4,f) 35.00

ELLISON,HARLAN-Alone Against Tomorrow-NY-1971-Macmillan-1st ed (q2,dj) 45.00

ELLISON,HARLAN-Deathbead Stories-NY-1975-Harper & Row-1st ed (y2,dj) 45.00

ELLISON,HARLAN-ED.-Again, Dangerous Visions-GC-1972-Dbldy-1st ed (w5,dj tn) 100.00

ELLISON,HARLAN-Golden Spike-1952-Ballantine-1st ed (x2,sl chip dj) 65.00

ELLISON,HARLAN-Strange Wine-NY et al-(1978)-Harper & Row-1st ed (b5,f,dj) 65.00

ELLISON,JEROME-Dam-NY-(1941)-Random-1st ed (hh5,dj) 15.00

ELLISON,JEROME-Prisoner Ate a Hearty Breakfast-NY-(1939)-Random-auth 1st bk-1st ed (hh5,dj) 15.00

ELLISON,R S-Pawnee Naming Ceremonial-NY-1933-36p-pict wrps,photos-scarce-1st ed (t7) 20.00

ELLISON,RALPH-Invisible Man-NY-1952-Random-auth 1st bk-1st ed (w5,sl rub,sp drknd) 45.00

ELLISON,RALPH-Shadow & Act-NY-(1964)-Random-1st ed (q2,dj sl tn & soil) 75.00

ELLISON,RALPH-Shadows and Act-NY-(1964)-1st ed (k5,sl soil dj) 60.00

ELLISON,WILLIAM H-Self Governing Dominion, California 1849 to 1860-Berkeley-1950-U Cal Pr-8vo-335p-1st ed (cc5,f,dj) 25.00

ELLMAN,RICHARD-James Joyce-NY-1959-illus-1st ed (m5,sl wn dj) 45.00

ELLMANN,RICHARD-Eminent Domain-NY-1967-OUP-1st ed (z8,vf,dj) 15.00

ELLSON,HAL-Duke-NY-1947-Scribners-1st ed (y1,f,dj) 40.00

ELLSWORTH,HENRY W-Valley of the Upper Wabash, Indiana, with Hints for its Agricultural Advantages-NY-1838-Pratt-175p-cl (x6,rbckd,lacks map) 125.00

ELLSWORTH,L-Search-NY-1932-8vo-xxviii,184p-cl,frntis,30p plts,1 fldg map-1st ed (t2) 25.00

ELLSWORTH,LYMAN R-Halibut Schooner-(1953)-McKay-242p-e.p. maps-1st ed (u8,chip dj) 20.00

ELLWANGER,GEORGE H-Idylists of the Country Side-NY-1896-16mo-263p-scarce (m3) 40.00

ELLWANGER,GEORGE H-In Gold & Silver-NY-1892-8vo-156p-lg pap ed,ltd to 200c,nbrd-1/2 brn mor gilt bndg-scarce (m3,f) 80.00

ELLWANGER,GEORGE H-Story of My House-NY-1891-D Appleton-286p-bev bds,ribbon marker,t.e.g.,frntis (k6,hng crack) 50.00

ELLWANGER,H B-Rose-NY-1893-16mo-310p-pap labl frnt cov (x5,fox,edge-wn,soil) 20.00

ELLWOOD,G M-English Furniture and Decoration 1680 to 1800-Lond-nd-B T Batsford-4to-201p-grn cl,photos-3rd ed (r10,sp fade,spot cov,sl fox) 45.00

ELMAN,ROBERT-Atlantic Flyway-NY-1980-4to-203p-photos (m3,vf,dj) 20.00

ELMAN,ROBERT-ED.-Great American Shooting Prints-NY-1972-obl folio-160p-80 col plts (m3,f,dj) 40.00

ELMER,LUCIUS Q C-History of the Early Settlement and Progress of Cumberland County, New Jersey-(Greenwich)-(1976)-142p-cl-rprnt of 1869 ed (aa6) 30.00

ELMINA,AUNT-Little Lessons for Little Folks-NY-(1887)-Truth Seeker Co-98,(4)p-bds-scarce (k1,rub) 27.50

ELMSLIE,KENWARD-Pavilions-NY-1961-Tibor De Nagy-8vo-stapled wrps,auth 1st bk-ltd to 300c-1st ed (u10) 100.00

ELPHICK,RICHARD-Kraal and Castle-New Haven-1977-Yale-8vo-266p-5 maps-1st ed (jj5,vf,f dj) 20.00

ELSBERG,CHARLES A-Diagnosis and Treatment of Surgical Diseases of the Spinal Cord and its Membranes-Phila-1916-330p-158 illus(3 col)-1st ed (g10) 350.00

ELSEN,ALBERT E-Rodin-NY-1963-Dbldy-4to-228p-rust cl,b&w illus (r10,f,f dj) 10.00

ELSEN,ALBERT-Seymour Lipton-NY-(1974)-Abrams-folio-cl,tip in plts-1st ed (oo6,dj) 75.00

ELSNER,ELEANOR-Romance of the Basque Country and the Pyrenees-NY-nd(ca.1920)-Dodd Mead-8vo-319p-18 illus-1st US ed (ff5) 20.00

ELSON,BOB-ED.-Major League Baseball Facts and Figures and Official Rules-Racine-(1938)-240,(2)p-wrps,photos (n1,sl wn) 12.50

ELSTON,ALLAN-Saddle Up For Sunlight-1952-Lippincott-1st ed (r8,sl wn sp,dj) 15.00

ELTON,C-Voles,Mice and Lemmings-Codicote-1965(1942)-8vo-(6),496p-cl,frntis,maps (y8) 53.00

ELTON,CHARLES-Voles, Mice, and Lemmings-Oxford-1942-Clarendon Pr-(viii)+496p-blu cl,tbls-1st ed (a2,sl fade sp) 65.00

ELTON,LORD-Gordon of Khartoum-NY-1955-376p-illus-1st Amer ed (b7,dj) 25.00

ELVERSON,VIRGINIA T-Cooking Legacy-NY-1975-Walker & Co-108p-illus,B Duson (o6,dj) 22.00

ELVILLE,E M-English and Irish Cut Glass-1964-Cntry Life Bks-91p-62 photos (cc8) 35.00

ELWOOD,ROGER-ED.-Future Kin-GC-1974-Dbldy-1st ed (h3,f,dj) 10.00

ELWOOD,ROGER-ED.-Signs and Wonders-Old Tappen-(1972)-Revel-1st ed (g3,f,dj) 10.00

ELWOOD,ROGER-ED.-Tomorrow-NY-(1975)-Evans-1st ed (g3,f,dj) 10.00

ELY,HELENA R-Woman's Hardy Garden-NY-1903-Macmillan-xv,216p-orig dec bds,t.e.g.,illus,plans-1st ed (cc10) 50.00

ELY,ROBERT T-Labor Movement in America-NY-1886-Crowell-1st ed (v5,sp wn) 45.00

ELY,SIMS-Lost Dutchman Mine-NY-1953-Morrow-179p-e.p. maps-1st ed (ff4,wn dj) 25.00

EMANUEL,WALTER-Dog Day-NY-1919-Dutton-12mo-bds,illus by C Aldin-1st US ed (f10,edgewn,hng crack) 40.00

EMBICK,MILTON A-Military History of the 3rd Division, 9th Corps, Army of the Potomac-Harrisburg-1913-C E Aughinbaugh-100p-pict cl,illus (v2,f) 45.00

EMERSON,A I-Our Trees & How to Know Them-GC-1936-295p-cl,photos-5th ed (x6) 15.00

EMERSON,B D-First Class Reader-St.Louis-1836-Meach & Dennis-276p-lea (k1,upper jnts crckng,sp chip) 35.00

EMERSON,B D-First Class Reader...-Claremont-1841-Claremont Mfg-276p-cl (k1) 22.50

EMERSON,EDWARD R-Beverages Past and Present-NY-1908-Putnam-8vo-2 vols,maroon cl-1st ed (u1,vf,dj) 250.00

EMERSON,ELLEN T-Letters of...-Kent-1982-KSU Pr-2 vols-1st ed (x9,box marked) 37.50

EMERSON,L O-Harp of Judah-Bost-(1863)-Oliver Ditson-384p-bds (j1) 15.00

EMERSON,L O-Jubilate-Bost-(1866)-Oliver Ditson-384p-bds (j1) 15.00

EMERSON,NATHANIEL B-Unwritten Literature of Hawaii-Wash-1909-Bur of Amer Ethn,Bull.38-288p-grn cl,24 plts,3 figs,14 music pcs (u8,cov sl wn.sl soil) 50.00

EMERSON,NATHANIEL B-Unwritten Literature of Hawaii-Wash-1909-GPO-8vo-288p-orig blk cl,frntis,24 plts-Smiths Inst Bur Amer Ethno Bull.#38-1st ed (t10,f) 65.00

EMERSON,OLIVER P-Pioneer Days in Hawaii-GC-1928-Dbldy,Doran-8vo-xiii,257p-tan cl,map e.p.,9 photos (p8,sp fade) 30.00

EMERSON,RALPH W-Essays of...-SF-1934-John Henry Nash/LEC-folio-cl sp wi papr labl over papr bds-ltd to 1500c,autg (y4,sl wn box) 90.00

EMERSON,RALPH W-Letters of...-NY-1939-Columbia Univ-6 vols,red/brwn cl,facs-1st ed (e2) 200.00

EMERSON,RALPH W-Representative Men-Bost-1850-Phillips,Sampson-lea-1st ed, 1st issue (l9,fragile sp) 250.00

EMERSON,RALPH W-Society and Solitude-Bost-1870-Fields Osgood-lea-1st ed,1st issue (l9,sl wn) 250.00

EMERTON,J H-Common Spiders of the United States-1902-Ginn-225p-501 figs-1st ed (bb3) 23.00

EMME,E M-Aeronautics and Astronautics-Wash D.C.-1961-8vo-xii,240p-cl-1st ed (t2) 30.00

EMME,EUGENE-ED.-History of Rocket Technology-Detr-1964-Wayne St U Pr-x+321p-wht cl,plts-1st ed (a2,dj) 30.00

EMMERSON,JOAN-ED.-Catalogue of the Pybus Collection of Medical Books, Letters and Engravings-Manchester-1981-4to-271p-1st ed (dd3) 75.00

EMMETT,CHRIS-Fort Union and the Winning of the Southwest-Norman-1965-Univ of Okla Pr-xvi+436p-blu cl,plts-1st ed (e2,dj) 35.00

EMMETT,CHRIS-Shanghai Pierce-Norman-(1953)-326p-illus-1st ed (j7) 40.00

EMMETT,CHRIS-Shanghai Pierce-Norman-(1953)-U of Okla-xiv,326p-cl,photos,illus,N Eggenhofer-1st ed (v1,dj) 50.00

EMMITT,ROBERT-Last War Trail-Norman-(1954)-Univ of Okla-x+333p-turq cl,3 maps-1st ed (m2,dj) 35.00

EMMONS,DELLA G-Leschi of the Nisquallies-Mpls-(1965)-416p-e.p. maps-1st ed (f7,f,dj) 35.00

EMMONS,FREDERICK-Atlantic Liners-NY-1972-Bonanza-160p-1st Crown ed (p8,f,sl tn dj) 8.00

EMMONS,SAMUEL B-Vegetable Family Physician-Bost-1842-B Adams-180p-blind stmpd cl,g lttrs (x6,cl rub) 125.00

EMMONS,WILLIAM-Battle of Bunker Hill-Bost-(cpyrt 1839)-144p-cl-10th ed (j1) 15.00

EMPSON,WILLIAM-Seven Types of Ambiguity-Lond-1930-1st ed (y7,dj fray,soil) 100.00

EMSWILER,GEORGE P-Poems and Sketches-Richmond-1897-435p-cl (l1,sl rub) 25.00

ENCYCLOPEDIA BRITANNICA-NY-1910-pebble-grain brn lea,8 1/2" x 6 1/2" "Handy Edition" format-11th ed (w1) 250.00

ENDICOTT,WENDELL-Adventures with Rod & Harpoon Along the Florida Keys-NY-1925-8vo-273p-photos (m3,f) 35.00

ENDICOTT,WILLIAM-Wrecked Among the Cannibals in the Fijis-Salem-1923-Marine Rsrch Soc-76p-13 illus-1st ed (ee7,sl soil bds & e.p.) 125.00

ENFIELD,DR J E-Man from Packsaddle-Hollywood-1951-186p-pict cl-Herd #767-1st ed (t7) 40.00

ENFIELD,DR J E-Man From Packsaddle-Hollywood-1951-House Warven Publ-Six Guns 680-Herd 767-1st ed (bb4,dj) 75.00

ENFIELD,EDWARD-Indian Corn-NY-1866-Appleton-308p-cl-scarce (x6,cl dull,fade) 110.00

ENFIELD,WILLIAM-Speaker-Bost-1795-prntd by J Bumstead-323,(5)p-lea-1st Amer ed (k1,sp rprd,lacks frnt f.e.p.) 100.00

ENGEL,CLAIRE-Mont Blanc, an Anthology-Chig-1965-Rand McNally-232p-69 illus-1st Amer ed (gg6,fade) 35.00

ENGEL,CLAIRE-Mont Blanc-Lond-1965-232p-48 plts-1st Brit ed (q10,f,dj) 18.00

ENGEL,D H-Japanese Gardens for Today-Rutland-1959-illus-1st ed (h10,dj) 75.00

ENGEL,HOWARD-Murder on Location-NY-(1982)-St.Martin's-1st US ed (l3,f,dj) 15.00

ENGEL,HOWARD-Suicide Murders-Tor-1980-Clarke Irwin-auth 1st bk-1st ed (gg8,f,dj) 35.00

ENGEL,MARIAN-No Clouds of Glory-NY-(1968)-HB&W-auth 1st bk-1st US ed (pp2,dj) 50.00*

ENGELHARDT,ZEPHYRIN-San Luis Rey Mission-SF-1921-266p-pict cl,frntis,photos,maps-1st ed (t7) 15.00

ENGINEER'S REPORT ON THE PRELIMINARY SURVEYS OF THE ILLINOIS,INDIANA AND MICHIGAN RAILROAD-Toledo-1854-8p-wrps (d1) 25.00

ENGINEERING RESEARCH ASSOCIATES-High-Speed Computing Devices-NY-1950-McGraw-Hill-xiv+451p-blu cl,text figs-1st ed (d2) 75.00

ENGLAND,G A-Alibi-1916-S&M-v scarce in dj-1st ed (x7,sl tn dj) 135.00

ENGLAND,GEORGE A-Pod, Bender & Co-NY-1916-McBride-1st ed (w5,f) 40.00

ENGLAND,JOSEPH W-ED.-First Century of the Philadelphia College of Pharmacy, 1821 to 1921-1922-Phila Coll of Phmcy & Sci-728p-blu cl-1st ed (j2,sl soil text) 45.00

ENGLE,ELOISE-America's Maritime Heritage-Annapolis-1975-Naval Inst Pr-sm 4to-371p-dec cl,col illus (p8,as new) 10.00

ENGLISH FORESTS & FOREST TREES-Lond-1853-406p-dec red cl,illus (a3,sl tan sp) 45.00

ENGLISH,WILLIAM-Conquest of the Northwest 1778 to 83-Indpls-1896-2 vols-brwn dec cl,illus-Howes E157-1st ed (jj2) 150.00

ENNIS,JOHN-Drink of Spring-Dublin-(1979)-Gallery Pr-1st ed (z8,f,dj) 35.00

ENNIS,JOHN-Night On Hibernia-Dublin-(1976)-Gallery Pr-cl,ltd ed,autg,auth 1st bk-1st ed (z8,f,dj) 37.50

ENOCK,G R-Andes and the Amazon-1910-Unwin-379p-58 illus (bb3) 19.00

EPHRON,NORA-Wallflower at the Orgy-NY-1970-1st ed (o5,dj) 22.50

EPOSITO,VINCENT-Military History and Atlas of the Napoleonic Wars-NY-1968-oblng folio-169p maps-3rd ed (kk2,f) 125.00

EPPENSTEIN,LOUISE-Sally Goes Shopping Alone-NY-(1940)-Platt & Munk-4to-44p-cl,illus (s3) 10.00

EPSTEIN,BRIAN-Cellarful of Noise-Lond-1964-photos-1st Brit ed (r5,dj) 75.00

EPSTEIN,EDWARD J-Rise and Fall of Diamonds-NY-(1982)-S&S-301p-1st prtg (u5,f,f dj) 22.50

EPSTEIN,LADY-Epstein: Drawings-Lond-1962-64 plts-1st ed (h10,dj) 75.00

EPSTEIN,LESLIE-King of the Jews-NY-(1979)-CM&G-1st ed (bb1,as new in dj) 20.00

EPSTEIN,LESLIE-P.D. Kimerakov-Bost,Tor-(1975)-Little,Brown-auth 1st bk-1st ed (b5,as new in dj) 25.00

EPSTEIN,LESLIE-Steinway Quintet Plus Four-Bost,Tor-(1976)-Little,Brown-1st ed (b5,as new in dj) 25.00

ERBSTEIN,C-Show Up-1926-PC-pict dj-v scarce-1st ed (x7,f,dj sl chip & soil) 95.00

ERCOLI,M-Inside Italy-NY-1942-Workers Libr-31p-wrps (r1) 10.00

ERDBERG,ELEANOR VON-Chinese Influence on European Garden Structure-Cambridge-1936-Harvard-4to-221p-cl,94 illus-Harvard Landscape Arch Mono,#1-v scarce (cc10,dj) 165.00

ERICKSON,ARTHUR-Architecture...-Montreal-1975-sq lg 4to-illus-1st ed (h10,dj) 100.00

ERICKSON,MILTON H-Collected Papers of...on Hypnosis-NY-1980-4 vols-purple cl-1st trd ed (y9,chip dj) 126.50

ERLANGER,MICHAEL-Silence in Heaven-NY-(1961)-Atheneum-1st ed (h3,dj sp fray & sl tn) 15.00

ERLICH,MAX-Reincarnation in Venice-NY-(1979)-S&S-1st ed (e10,f,dj) 10.00

ERNST,ALICE H-Trouping in the Oregon Country-Portland-(1961)-Ore Hist Soc-197p-illus-1st ed (cc4,dj) 15.00

ERNST,BERNARD M L-Houdini and Conan Doyle-NY-(1932)-A & C Boni-1st ed (g3) 30.00

ERRINGTON,P L-Muskrat Populations-IA-1963-665p-photos (gg3,f) 12.00

ERSKINE,JOHN E-Journal of a Cruise Among the Islands of the Western Pacific...-Lond-1853-John Murray-vi,11,488p-qtr lea,red mrbld papr,col frntis,6 plts(3 col),fldg map (p8,rbckd,map rprd) 550.00

ERSKINE,MARGARET-Brood of Folly-NY-1971-Dbldy CC-1st US ed (f4,f,dj) 10.00

ERSKINE,MARGARET-Harriet Farewell-Lond-1975-Hodder-1st Brit ed (q4,dj) 17.50

ERTE-Costumes & Sets for Der Rosenkavalier in Full Color-1980-Dover-81 col designs-ltd ed,nbrd,autg-1st ed (h10,dj) 200.00

ERWIN,ALICE C-Nature Talks, a Book of Days-Harbor Springs-1939-Fay Erwin-399p-tan cl,illus-1st ed (cc3) 30.00

ERWIN,ALLEN A-Southwest of John H Slaughter 1841 to 1922-Glendale-1965-A H Clark-368p-cl,fldg map,illus,Wstrn Frntr Ser Vol.10-1st ed (v1,sl stnd f.e.p.) 65.00

ERWIN,ALLEN A-Southwest of John H Slaughter, 1841 to 1922...-Glendale-1965-Arthur H Clark Co-368p-cl,photos-1st ed (w3,f,dj) 125.00

ESCOBOSA,HECTOR-Here's Seatle-Seattle-1948-McCaffrey Publ-135,(1)p-illus grn cl,photos-1st ed (b6,f,sl tn dj) 10.00

ESCOFFIER-Escoffier Cook Book-1969-Crown (v6,dj rub) 10.00

ESDAILE,JAMES-Hypnosis in Medicine and Surgery-NY-(1957)-Julian Pr (y9) 30.00

ESDAILE,JAMES-Natural and Mesmeric Clairvoyance...-Lond-1852-Hippolyte Bailliere-12mo-4+xx+272p-pebbled blu cl-rare-1st ed (y9,edge tn) 375.00

ESHBACH,LLOYD A-Tyrant of Time-Reading-(1955)-Fantasy Pr-1st ed (l3,f,dj) 20.00

ESKEW,GARNETT L-Willards of Washington-NY-(1954)-240p-illus-1st ed (c4,f,sl wn dj) 30.00

ESKIMO-(Ottawa)-1939-Nat Mus of Can-12p-prtd wrps,illus,map-Anthro lflt #5 (k10) 10.00*

ESKRIDGE,ROBERT L-Manga Reva-(1931)-Bobbs Merrill-286p-illus,col e.p.s-1st ed (u8) 15.00

ESKRIDGE,ROBERT L-Umi the Hawaiian Boy Who Became King-(1936)-Winston-104p-blu cl,pict cov,illus by auth-1st ed (u8,edge wn) 22.00

ESMONDE,SIR T H GRATTAN-More Hunting Memories-Dublin-1930-12mo-194p-photos (m3,f,sl chip dj) 40.00

ESPINOSA,CARMEN G-Freeing of the Deer and Other New Mexican Indian Myths-Albuq-(1985)-83p-drwngs-1st ed (v7,f,dj) 10.00

ESPINOSA,CARMEN-Shawls, Crinolines, Filigree-El Paso-(1970)-58p-photos(some col),Carl Hertzog book-1st ed (u7,f,dj) 20.00

ESPINOSA,GILBERTO-Heroes, Hexes and Haunted Halls-Albuq-(1972)-41p-1st ed (u7,f,dj) 15.00

ESPINOSA,J MANUEL-Crusaders of the Rio Grande-Chig-1942-390p-frntis port,4 maps-1st ed (u7) 75.00

ESPINOSA,J MANUEL-First Expedition of Vargas into New Mexico, 1692-Albuq-1940-Coronado Ser.,Vol.10-319p-cl-v scarce-1st of this ed (z1,f) 150.00

ESPINOSA,JOSE E-Saints in the Valleys-1960-UNMP-folio-122p-illus-1st ed (d3,dj) 100.00

ESPINOSA,JOSE M-Spanish Folk Tales from New Mexico-NY-1937-Am Folk Lore Soc,Vol.XXX-222p-1st ed (u7,spot rear cov) 45.00

ESPOSITO,VINCENT J-West Point Atlas of America Wars-NY-(1978)-Praeger-10" x 14"-2 vols-maps-6th ed (b2) 75.00

ESPY,WILLARD R-Oysterville-NY-1977-Clarkson N Potter-300p-beige cl,illus-1st ed (dd7,f,dj) 35.00

ESQUEMELING,JOHN-Buccaneers of America-Lond-1911-Geo Allen (z2,sl fox) 85.00

ESSAME,MAJ GEN H-43rd Wessex Division at War 1944 to 1945-Lond-1952-292p-maps,illus-1st ed (gg2,f,dj) 125.00

ESSE,JAMES-Hunger-Dublin-1918-Candle Pr-wrps,(Candle Pr prose bklts,no.2)-1st ed (z8,f) 100.00

ESSERY,R J-British Goods Wagons from 1887 to the Present Day-NY-1970-144p-1st ed (n4,f,dj) 22.00

ESTABROOK,EMMA F-Ancient Lovers of Peace-Bost-1959-priv prtd-90p-illus-1st ed (v7,pres) 25.00

ESTABROOK,EMMA F-Givers of Life-Albuq-1931-101p-illus-1st ed (v7) 25.00

ESTERGREEN,M-Kit Carson-Norman-(1962)-320p-illus-1st ed (c7,f,dj nick) 45.00

ESTERGREEN,M-Kit Carson-Norman-(1962)-320p-photos,maps-1st ed (t7,dj) 30.00

ESTEY,P C-Woodchuck Hunter-NY-1936-Samworth Bk-135p+ads-blu cl,gilt t,photo frntis-scarce (gg3,f) 40.00

ESTLEMAN,L-Glass Highway-1983-HM-1st ed (x7,f,dj) 23.00

ESTLEMAN,LOREN D-Dr.Jekyll and Mr.Holmes-NY-1979-Dbldy-1st ed (f4,f,dj) 25.00

ESTLEMAN,LOREN D-Hider-GC-1978-Dbldy-8vo-184p-auth 1st bk-1st ed (z4,autg,dj) 20.00

ESTLEMAN,LOREN D-Midnight Man-Bost-1982-Houghton-1st ed (h4,f,sl wn dj) 35.00

ESTLEMAN,LOREN D-Sherlock Holmes vs. Dracula...-1978-Dbldy-1st ed (s10,f dj) 30.00

ETCHEN,FRED-Common Sense Shotgun Shooting-Huntington-1946-8vo-187p-photos (m3,f) 35.00

ETTINGHAUSEN,MAURICE L-Rare Books and Royal Collectors-NY-1966-S&S-8vo-220p-cl-1st ed (w2,dj) 55.00

EUSTIS,HELEN-Fool Killer-1954-Dbldy-1st ed (s10,sp fade dj) 15.00

EVANOFF,VLAD-Making Your Own Fishing Lures-S Brunswick-nd-4to-158p-illus (m3,vf,dj) 15.00

EVANOFF,VLAD-Natural Salt Water Fishing Baits-NY-1953-8vo-96p-illus-1st ed (m3,vf,dj) 10.00

EVANS,B R-Story of Durocs-Peoria-(1946)-United Duroc Record Assn-xii+558p-red cl,illus (c2) 50.00

EVANS,BILLY-ED-Baseball Records Southern Association 1901 to 1945-1945-So.Assoc-wrps-1st ed (s8,chip cor,discol pgs) 40.00

EVANS,BROCK-Alpine Lakes-Seattle-1971-lg 4to-128p-92 col photos-1st ed (p10,f,dj) 28.00

EVANS,CERINDA W-Collis Potter Huntington-Newport News-1954-Mariner's Museum-2 vols,grn cl,plts-1st ed (m2,fade sp) 55.00

EVANS,CHARLES-Eye on Everest-Lond-1955-122p-cartoons-1st Brit ed (p10,f,dj) 25.00

EVANS,DONALD-Hanover-So Brunswick-1976-Barnes-1st ed (h9,dj) 15.00

EVANS,DONALD-Rambling Willie-San Diego-1981-Barnes-1st ed (h9,dj) 35.00

EVANS,EDNA-Written with Fire-NY-1962-HR&W-1st ed (h9,dj) 25.00

EVANS,F W-Shakers-New Lebanon-1867-12mo-192p-yel wrps-4th ed (b2,f) 75.00

EVANS,G B-ED.-Best of Nash Buckingham-Winchester-1973-320p-photos,dec e.p. (gg3,f,dj) 22.00

EVANS,G B-Upland Shooting Life-NY-1971-301p-photos (gg3,f) 20.00

EVANS,G E-Ask the Fellows Who Cut the Hay-Lond-1956-Faber & Faber-1st ed (j9,dj) 58.00

EVANS,G E-Horse Power and Magic-Lond,Bost-1979-Faber & Faber-1st US ed (j9) 35.00

EVANS,G H-Elephants and Their Diseases-Rangoon-1961-8vo-(6),(1),323p-cl & bds-scarce (y8,fade) 75.00

EVANS,GEORGE B-An Affair with Grouse-Old Hemlock-1982-8vo-213p-ltd to 1000c,nbrd,autg (m3,vf,box) 150.00

EVANS,GEORGE B-Upland Shooting Life-NY-1971-8vo-301p-photos,illus-1st ed (m3,f,dj) 20.00

EVANS,H E-Wasp Farm-1963-Nat Hist Pr-178p-illus (bb3,f,dj) 14.00

EVANS,H MUIR-Sting-fish & Seafarer-Lond-1963-8vo-180p-illus,photos (m3) 10.00

EVANS,HUBERT-Silent Call-NY-1930-8vo-248p-illus (m3) 20.00

EVANS,HUMPHREY-Falconry-NY-1978-Arco-2nd prtg (c9,f,f dj) 30.00

EVANS,LUTHER H-Texas Centennial Exhibition-Wash-1946-USGPO-54p-tip in plts-1st ed (a9) 50.00

EVANS,MARTIN-Atlantic Era: British Atlantic Locomotives-Lond-1961-94p-1st ed (n4,f,dj) 15.50

EVANS,MICHELE-Fearless Cooking for Men-NY-(1977)-Van Nostrand Reinhold-288p-illus,B Goldsmith (l6) 23.00

EVANS,PHILIP S-History of Connecticut Baptist State Convention 1823 to 1907-Hartford-1909-297p-cl (d1,sl tn sp bottom) 15.00

EVANS,ROBLEY D-Sailor's Log-NY-1902-407p-pict cl,frntis,illus-1st ed (t7) 25.00

EVANS,THOMAS-Examples of Youthful Piety...-Phila-1830-Thomas Kite-12mo-215p-lea-1st ed (y6,wn,scuff,fox) 18.00

EVANS,WALKER-Message from the Interior-NY-1966-Eakins Pr-sm sq folio-32p-cl,12 illus-1st ed (t3) 325.00

EVANS,WILL F-Border Skylines-1940-Cecil Baugh-588p-photos-scarce-1st ed (a9) 100.00

EVANS,WILLIAM B-Jonathan Evans and His Time 1759 to 1839, Bicentennial Biography-Bost-1959-Christopher Publ-8vo-192p-1st ed (y6,chip dj) 10.00

EVANS-PRITCHARD,E E-Azande-Oxford-1971-Clarendon Pr-8vo-444p-cl,plts-1st ed (y5,dj) 40.00

EVANS-PRITCHARD,E E-Kinship and Marriage Among the Nuer-Oxford-1951-Clarendon Pr-8vo-cl-1st ed (y5,dj tn) 28.00

EVANS-PRITCHARD,E E-Witchcraft, Oracles and Magic Among the Azande-Oxford-1977-Clarendon Pr-8vo-558p-cl,35 plts,map-rprnt (y5,dj) 35.00

EVANS-WENTZ,W Y-Tibetan Book of the Dead-NY-1973-Causeway Bks-cl,illus-1st prtg thus (o8,f,dj) 15.00

EVARTS,R C-Alice's Adventures in Cambridge-1913-Harvard Lampoon-papr bds,illus,E L Barron-1st ed (x2) 85.00

EVELYN,GEORGE P-Diary of the Crimea-Lond-1954-148p-illus-1st ed (b7,f,dj) 35.00

EVELYN,JOHN-Acetaria-Brklyn-1937-Brklyn Botanic garden-148p+index-brn cl bds,lea sp labl,rprnt of 1699 ed (m6,sunned) 30.00

EVENSON,NORMA-Le Corbusier: the Machine and the Grand Design-NY-1969-Braziller-4to-(12),128p-bds,102 illus,plans-1st prtg (cc10,f,dj) 35.00

EVENTFUL NARRATIVES: THE THIRTEENTH BOOK OF THE FAITH PROMOTING SERIES-SLC-1887-Juv Instr Office-97p-grn cl (w1) 75.00

EVERDS,JOHN-Spectacular Trains-Northbrook-1973-64p-1st ed (n4,f) 10.00

EVEREST,F K,JR.-Fastest Man Alive-Lond-(1958)-8vo-xiv,204p-cl,frntis,12p plts-1st ed (t2,dj) 30.00

EVEREST,KELVIN-Coleridge's Secret Ministry-Sussex/NY-1979-Harvester/Barnes-1st Amer ed (t4,f,dj) 15.00

EVEREST,THOMAS-Popular View of Homoeopathy...Survey of the Progress and Homoeopathia in Europe by A. Gerald Hull-NY-1842-243p-1st Amer ed (dd3) 150.00

EVERETT,ERASTUS-System of English Versification...-NY-1848-198p-cl (k1,wn cov) 20.00

EVERETT,FRED-Fun with Game Birds-Harrisburg-1954-4to-287p-1st trd ed (m3,f) 22.50

EVERETT,FRED-Fun with Game Birds-Harrisburg-1954-4to-287p-ltd ed,nbrd,autg,full lea,a.e.g. (m3,f) 100.00

EVERETT,PERCIVAL L-Suder-NY-1983-auth 1st bk-1st ed (n5,f,f dj) 20.00

EVERHART,W HARRY-Fishes of Maine-Augusta-1950-8vo-53p-wrps-col photos (m3) 17.50

EVERITT,C-Birds of the Edward Marshall Boehm Aviaries-Trenton-1973-4to-297p-cl,photos(incl col),maps (y8,sp tn) 50.00

EVERITT,CHARLES P-Adventures of a Treasure Hunter-Bost-1951-Little,Brown-1st ed (c8,f,dj missng chips) 45.00

EVERITT,CHARLES P-Adventures of a Treasure Hunter-Bost-1951-Little,Brown-1st ed (w1,f,dj) 30.00

EVERMANN,B W-An Annotated List of the Fishes Known from the State of Vermont-Wash D.C.-1896-8vo-25p-wrps (m3) 20.00

EVERS,JOHN J-Baseball in the Big Leagues-1913-Reilly & Britton-photos-(reiss of 1910 bk "Touching Second")-rprnt (s8,cov soil) 80.00

EVERSON,WILLIAM-Blowing of the Seed-New Haven-1966-Wenning-8vo-qtr calf-ltd to 218c,nbrd,autg (x3,sl rub sp) 135.00

EVERSON,WILLIAM-Man's Fate-NY-(1974)-New Directions-1st ed (cc2,f,dj) 40.00

EVERSON,WILLIAM-Rose of Solitude-GC-1967-Dbldy-1st ed (dd2,f,dj,autg) 45.00

EVERSON,WILLIAM-War Elegies-Waldport-1944-Untide Pr-pict wrps,illus-ltd to 975c-1st enlgd ed (b3,sl sun wrps) 85.00

EVERSON,WM K-Detective in Film-Secaucas-1972-Citadel-1st ed (d4,dj) 35.00

EVERTS,TRUMAN C-Thirty Seven Days of April-SF-1923-57p-bds,illus-Graff #1227-1st ed (t7,f) 100.00

EVERY,EDWARD V-Sins of America as "Exposed" by the Police Gazette-NY-1931-297p-frntis,illus-Six Guns #688-Scarce-1st ed (t7,sl fade sp) 35.00

EWAN,JOSEPH-John Bannister and His Natural History of Virginia-1970-U of Ill-485p-cl (x6,as new in dj) 15.00

EWEN,DAVID-Life and Death of Tin Pan Alley-NY-(1964)-Funk-1st ed (w1,f,dj) 25.00

EWEN,DAVID-Men of Popular Music-Chig-1944-Ziff Davis-1st ed (w1,f,dj) 20.00

EWERS,JOHN C-Blackfeet-(1958)-348p-illus-1st ed (c7,chip dj,autg) 45.00

EWERS,JOHN C-Blackfeet-Norman-(1958)-U of Okla-xviii,348p-cl,illus-1st ed (v1,chip dj) 45.00

EWERS,JOHN C-Horse in Blackfoot Indian Culture with Comparative Material from Other Western Tribes-Wash-1955-BAE Bull 159-374p+17 plts,cl (a1) 22.50

EWERS,JOHN C-Horse in Blackfoot Indian Culture-Wash-1955-GPO-Bur Amer Ethnol,Bull.159-374p-illus (gg4) 45.00

EWERS,JOHN C-Indian Life on the Upper Missouri-Norman-(1968)-U of Okla Pr-222p-illus-1st ed (cc4,dj) 30.00

EWING,SARAH W R-Along Absecon Creek-(np)-(1965)-325p-cl,illus-ltd to 1000c,nbrd (aa6) 45.00

EWING,THOMAS-England-Cin-1866-R W Carroll-40p-wrps (g1) 15.00

EXLEY,FREDERICK-Fan's Notes-NY-1968-auth 1st bk-1st ed (q5,f,dj) 90.00

EXLEY,FREDERICK-Pages From a Cold Island-NY-(1975)-Random Hs-1st ed (e3,f,dj) 20.00

EXLINE,J W-ED.-Afternoon of Life-Canal Dover-1881-W W Scott's Rptr Stm Nwsp-498;v;iv p-cl (j1,sl weak inner hng) 15.00

EYLER & YEAGER-Many Roads to Highline-np(Seattle)-1972-4to-92p-red cl wi gold dec,dbl col,illus,e.p. map-1st ed (h7,2 autg) 40.00

EYRE,EDWARD J-Autobiographical Narrative of Residence and Exploration in Australia 1832 to 1839 by...-Lond-1984-Caliban Bks-8vo-230p-port frntis,6 maps-1st ed (p8,as new in dj) 35.00

F,M T-My Chinese Marriage-NY-1921-Duffield-8vo-169p-cl bkd bds,t.e.g.,Katherine A Porter's 1st bk,ghost written for Mai Taim Fran King-1st ed (w6) 200.00

FAANES,CRAIG A-Birds of the St.Croix River Valley-Wash-1981-US Fish & Wildlife Serv-196p-orig wrps-No Amer Fauna No.73 (c9,as new) 15.00

FABB,JOHN-Victorian and Edwardian Army from Old Photographs-Lond-1975-154 photos-1st ed (b7,f,dj) 35.00

FABER,WILLIAM F-Fifty Years, a History of St.John's Church...-Detr-1909-Richmond & Backus-174p (z7) 40.00

FABES,GILBERT H-Romance of a Bookshop, 1904 to 1938-np-1938-priv prtd-8vo-64p-cl,10 plts-rvsd ed (w2,rub) 45.00

FABRI,RALPH-History of the American Watercolor Society-np-1969-Amer Watercol Soc-4to-90p-lt blu cl,b&w & col illus-1st ed (r10,sl spot edges,f dj) 25.00

FADIMAN,CLIFTON-Joys of Wine-NY-(1974)-Abrams-thk folio-450p wi index,emboss wht cl-1st ed (u1) 40.00

FAGAN,B-Elusive Treasure-1977-Scribners-369p-photos-1st ed (bb3,f,dj) 22.00

FAGERSTROM,STAN-Catch More Black Bass-Caldwell-1973-4to-167p-wrps-photos (m3,vf) 15.00

FAGERSTROM,STAN-Catch More Crappie-Seattle-1977-4to-111p-wrps (m3,f) 12.50

FAGG,WILLIAM-Yoruba Sculpture of West Africa-NY-1982-Knopf-4to-xiv,210p-cl,col plts-1st ed (y4) 35.00

FAHEY,JOHN-Days of the Hercules-Moscow-324p-illus-1st ed (c7,dj) 40.00

FAHEY,JOHN-Inland Empire D.C. Corbin and Spokane-1965-U of Wash-8vo-270p-illus (nn7,dj) 36.00

FAHIE,J J-History of Electric Telegraphy to the Year 1837-1974-Arno Pr-542p-35 illus-rprnt (h6,f) 35.00

FAHY,CAROLE-Cooking with Beer-Lond-(1972)-Elm Tree Bks-144p-red cl,4 col plts-1st ed (q8,dj) 15.00

FAIR,A A-All Grass Isn't Green-NY-1970-Morrow-1st ed (f4,f,dj) 20.00

FAIR,A A-Beware the Curves-NY-1956-Morrow-1st ed (f4,dj) 15.00

FAIR,A A-Cats Prowl at Night-1943-Morrow-1st ed (s10,sp chip dj) 65.00

FAIR,A A-Cats Prowl at Night-NY-1943-Morrow-1st ed (g4,dj missing sm chips) 100.00

FAIR,A A-Cut Thin to Win-NY-1965-Morrow-1st ed (g4,f,dj) 25.00

FAIR,A A-Give'Em the Ax-NY-1944-Morrow-1st ed (j4,chip dj) 50.00

FAIR,A A-Pass the Gravy-NY-1959-Morrow-1st ed (d4,sp tn dj) 20.00

FAIR,A A-Some Slips Don't Show-NY-1957-Morrow-1st ed (g4,dj) 12.00

FAIR,A A-Top of the Heap-Melbrn,Lond,Tor-(1957)-Heinemann-1st Brit ed (bb1,sl soil dj) 20.00

FAIR,A A-You Can Die Laughing-NY-1957-Morrow-1st ed (h4,chip dj) 12.50

FAIR,JAMES R-North Arkansas Line-Berkeley-1969-304p-1st ed (n4,f,dj) 27.50

FAIR,RONALD-We Can't Breathe-NY-1972-Harper-1st ed (w5,f,f dj) 20.00

FAIRCHILD,DAVID-Garden Islands of the Great East-NY-1943-Scribner-8vo-239p-photos-1st ed (jj5,dj sl tn,edgewn) 25.00

FAIRCHILD,DAVID-Golden Islands of the Great East-NY-1943-Scribner's-8vo-239p-red cl,photos (p8,bump,wn) 18.50

FAIRCHILD,DAVID-World Grows Round My Door-NY-(1947)-xii,347p-123 hlf tones-1st ed (x5,edge-wn dj) 36.00

FAIRCHILD,DAVID-World Was My Garden-NY-1941-xiv,494p-grn cl,hlf tones (x5) 20.00

FAIRCHILD,L H-Cats and All About Them-NY-1942-8vo-231p-cl,photos (y8,wn,soil) 11.00

FAIRCLOUGH,M A-Ideal Cookery Book-Lond-1950-K Paul-thk 4to-945p-g dec red cl,247 illus,48 col plts-1st ed (q8) 60.00

FAIRLEY,JAMES-Irish Whales and Whaling-Belfast-1981-Blackstaff Pr-8vo-218p-cream cl,46 plts,6 ports-1st ed (p8,as new in dj) 25.00

FAIRLIE,GERARD-Bulldog Drummond on Dartmoor-NY-1939-Hillman-Curl-1st US ed (f4) 15.00

FAIRLIE,GERARD-Yellow Munro-Bost-1929-Little-1st US ed (k4) 10.00

FAIRRIE,GEOFFREY-Sugar-Liverpool-1925-Fairrie & Co-8vo-xiv,234p-red cl,62 plts & diags-1st ed (y4) 45.00

FAKHRY,AHMED-Pryamids-(1961)-U of Chig Pr-8vo-260p-photos-1st ed (p1,f,dj) 35.00

FALCONER,THOMAS-Texan Santa Fe Expedition-NY-1930-Dauber & Pine-Howes F14-1st ed thus (pp9,cov spot) 100.00

FALK,JOHN R-Practical Hunter's Dog Book-NY-1973-8vo-314p-photos (m3,f,fray dj) 10.00

FALKINER,RICHARD-Investing in Antique Jewelry-NY-1968-Clarkson Potter-160p-16 col plts,b&w illus (u5,f,f dj) 42.50

FALKIRK,RICHARD-Blackstone on Broadway-Lond-1977-Eyre-1st ed (s4,f,dj) 30.00

FALKIRK,RICHARD-Blackstone-Lond-1972-Eyre-1st ed (r4,dj) 20.00

FALL,BERNARD B-Hell in a Very Small Place-Phila-1967-Lippincott-1st ed (ff3,f,dj) 150.00

FALL,BERNARD B-Street Without Joy-Harrisburg-(1967)-Stackpole-4th ed,rvsd (ff3,dj) 85.00

FALL,BERNARD B-Viet Nam Witness 1953 to 1966-Lond-1966-Pall Mall-1st Brit ed (e8,f,sl tn dj) 50.00

FALLA,R A-ET AL-Field Guide to the Birds of New Zealand-Bost-1967-12mo-254p-cl,6 col & 12 b&w plts (y8,dj) 25.00

FALLACI,ORIANA-Egotists-Chig-1968-Regnery-1st US ed (z3,f,dj) 15.00

FALLACI,ORIANA-Letter to a Child Never Born-NY-1976-1st ed (y7,dj) 15.00

FALLACI,ORIANA-Man-NY-(1980)-S&S-1st ed (b10,f,dj) 10.00

FALLIS,RICHARD-Irish Renaissance-1977-Syracuse Univ Pr-1st ed (z8,vf,dj) 27.50

FALLON,GABRIEL-Sean O'Casey, the Man I Knew-Bost-(1965)-Little, Brown-1st Amer ed (z8,vf,dj) 12.50

FALLON,JACK-All About Surf Fishing-NY-1975-8vo-288p-photos (m3,f,dj) 20.00

FALLON,JACK-Teaching Your Children to Fish-NY-1974-8vo-243p-photos-1st ed (m3,as new in dj) 12.50

FALLOW,L M-Ugglians-NY-(1956)-Philosophical Libr-1st ed (e3,dj) 20.00

FALLS,CYRIL-Royal Irish Rifles in the Great War-Aldershot-1925-189p-grn cl,maps,illus-scarce (b7,f) 175.00

FAMILY SECRETS...-Lond-(1843)-Fisher-8vo-3 vols,3/4 red mor & mrbld bds,g sp,a.e.g.,engrvd t.p.s,29 engrvd plts-1st ed (w6) 225.00

FAMULARO,JOE-Festive Famularo Kitchen-1977-Atheneum-464p-g dec red cl-1st ed (q8,dj) 25.00

FANE,R A B-Kyoto...-Hong Kong-1931-Rumford Prntg Pr-434p-cl,illus,4 fldg plts (m1,f,dj) 35.00

FANNING,EDMUND-Voyages & Discoveries in the South Seas 1792 to 1832-Salem-1924-Marine Research Scty-8vo-355p-blu cl,g titles,dec e.p.,32 plts (ll1,sl fox) 115.00

FANNING,EDMUND-Voyages Round the World...-Upper Saddle River-1970-Gregg Pr-lg 8vo-xii,499p-dec wht cl,illus-facs of 1833 ed (p8,sl soil) 25.00

FANNING,EDMUND-Voyages to the South Seas,Indian and Pacific Oceans,China Sea...Between the Years 1830 to 1837-Upper Saddle River-1970-Gregg Pr-8vo-324p-beige cl wi brwn/blu title decs,frntis,rprnt of 1838 ed (nn1,sl soil) 32.50

FANNING,PETE-Great Crimes of the West-SF-(1929)-P Fanning-292p-frntis-Six Guns #694-1st ed (cc4) 35.00

FANTE,JOHN-Brotherhood of the Grape-Bost-1977-1st ed (p5,f,dj sl chip & rub) 45.00

FANTE,JOHN-Brotherhood of the Grape-Bost-1977-Houghton Mifflin-1st ed (g3,f,sl chip dj) 25.00

FANTE,JOHN-Dago Red-NY-1940-illus,V Angelo-1st ed (s5,sl chip dj) 200.00

FANTE,JOHN-Dreams From Bunker Hill-1982-Black Sparrow-wi acetate dj as issued-1st ed (m9,f,dj) 45.00

FANTE,JOHN-Dreams From Bunker Hill-Santa Barbara-1982-illus bds-ltd to 200c,autg-1st ed (p5,f) 150.00

FANTE,JOHN-Full of Life-Bost-1952-1st ed (r5,wn dj) 60.00

FANTIN,MARIO-Mani Rimdu Nepal, the Buddhist Dance Drama of Tengpoche-New Delhi-1976-sm 4to-170p-111 col photos,60 drwngs,maps-1st ed (a4,f,dj) 150.00

FARAGO,LADISLAS-Abyssinia on the Eve-Lond-1935-Putnam-8vo-x,286p-orig cl,photo plts,e.p. maps-1st ed (bb6) 30.00

FARAGO,LADISLAS-Broken Seal-NY-1967-Random-439p-1st ed (j8,f,dj) 15.00

FARB,PETER-Man's Rise to Civilization...-NY-1968-Dutton-332p-illus-1st ed (cc4,dj) 20.00

FARBER,JAMES-Texans with Guns-San Antonio-(1950)-Naylor Co-196p-illus by R L McCollister-Six Guns 695-1st ed (gg4,dj) 20.00

FARBER,JAMES-Texans with Guns-San Antonio-(1950)-Naylor-196p-1st ed (n10,f,f dj) 45.00

FARBER,NORMA-There Goes Feathertop!-NY-(1979)-Dutton-b&w illus,M Brown-1st ed (s3,f,dj) 15.00

FARBER,THOMAS-Tales For the Son of My Unborn Child-1971-Dutton-1st ed (m9,f,sl wn dj) 15.00

FAREWELL,BYRON-Prisoners of the Mahdi-NY-1967-356p-illus-1st Amer ed (b7,f,dj) 30.00

FARINA,RICHARD-Been Down So Long It Looks Like Up To Me-NY-1966-auth 1st bk-1st ed (r5,dj) 75.00

FARINA,RICHARD-Been Down So Long, It Looks Like Up to Me-1966-Random-auth 1st bk-1st ed (x2,f,dj) 90.00

FARINA,RICHARD-Long Time Coming and a Long Time Gone-(1969)-Random-1st ed (n9,dj sl chip,sl tn) 25.00

FARINA,RICHARD-Long Time Coming and Long Time Gone-NY-(1969)-Random-1st ed (e3,f,dj) 55.00

FARIS,JOHN T-Historic Shrines of America-NY-(1918)-Doran-8vo-421p-illus-1st ed (ff5,unopened) 25.00

FARIS,JOHN T-Old Gardens In and About Philadelphia and Those Who Made Them-Indpls-1932-Bobbs Merrill-4to-311p-cl,illus e.p.,54 illus-1st ed (cc10,dj chip & tn) 60.00

FARIS,JOHN T-Old Gardens In and About Philadelphia-Indpls-(1932)-sm 4to-311p-pict e.p.s,31p hlf tones (x5,bump,sp wn) 35.00

FARIS,JOHN T-Seeing Canada-Phila,Lond-1924-Lippincott-265p-dec tan cl wi drk grn & blu,col frntis,150 photos-1st ed (p2) 20.00

FARIS,JOHN T-Seeing the Far West-Phila-1920-Lippincott-1st ed (cc4) 25.00

FARIS,JOHN T-Seeing the Far West-Phila-1920-pict cl,frntis,photos,fldg map-Smith #2980-1st ed (t7) 15.00

FARIS,JOHN-Roaming the Eastern Mountains-NY-1932-327p-50 photos-1st ed (o10) 13.00

FARIS,N A-Arab Archery-Princeton-1945-8vo-182p-photos-scarce-1st ed (m3) 60.00

FARISH,THOMAS E-History of Arizona-np(Phoenix)-1915-2 vols-illus (ee4) 40.00

FARJEON,ELEANOR-Ameliaranne's Prize Packet-Lond-(1933)-Harrap-8vo-cl wi pasteon,col & b&w illus-1st ed (pp10,sl shaken) 45.00

FARJEON,ELEANOR-Little Bookroom-NY,Lond-1956(1955)-OUP-illus by Ardizzone-Bader #575-1st US ed (nn10,f,dj) 60.00

FARJEON,ELEANOR-Ten Saints-NY-(1936)-OUP-sm 4to-124p-pict cl,col illus,H Sewell-1st ed (s3,fade t.e.,dj) 40.00

FARJEON,JEFFERSON-Friday the Thirteenth-Indpls-1940-Bobbs-1st US ed (g4,dj) 12.50

FARLEY,BARNEY-How to Catch Fish in the Gulf of Mexico-Corpus Christi-1965-8vo-32p-wrps-illus-1st ed (m3,vf) 10.00

FARM JOURNAL CHRISTMAS BOOK-Phila-1970-Countryside Pr-folio-176p-wht bds,illus (n6) 15.00

FARMBOROUGH,FLORENCE-With the Armies of the Tsar-NY-(1975)-Stein & Day-8vo-422p-48 photos-1st US ed (cc5,dj) 20.00

FARMER,FANNIE M-Boston Cooking School Cook Book-Bost-1938-Little,Brown-838p-later ed (j8,f) 40.00

FARMER,FANNIE M-Boston Cooking School Cookbook-Bost-1924-Little,Brown-806p+32p ads,tan cl,122 halftone illus-new,rvsd ed (q8,edgewn cov,hngs weak) 35.00

FARMER,FANNIE M-Boston Cooking School Cookbook-Bost-1937-Little,Brown-838p+24p ads,tan cl,illus e.p.,illus-6th ed (q8) 30.00

FARMER,FANNIE M-Chafing Dish Possibilities-Bost-1905-Little,Brown-161p-bds-Bitting 153 (u6,sp drknd) 30.00

FARMER,FANNIE M-Dinner Calendar-NY-1915-Sully & Kleinteich-unpgd-illus wrps (n6,wrps sl curled,chip,spot) 25.00

FARMER,LYDIA H-Girls' Book of Famous Queens-NY-(1887)-495p-cl (d1) 20.00

FARMER,PHILIP J-Dark Design-np-(1977)-Berkley-1st ed (b5,f,dj sp sl rub) 15.00

FARMER,PHILIP J-Dark Design-NY-(1977)-Berkley-1st ed (f3,f,dj) 20.00

FARMER,PHILIP J-Fabulous Riverboat-NY-1971-Putnam-1st ed (h8,vf,f dj) 300.00

FARMER,PHILIP J-Lord Tyger-GC-1970-Dbldy-1st ed (p3,f,dj) 100.00

FARMER,PHILIP J-Magic Labyrinth-np-(1980)-Berkley-1st ed (b5,f,dj) 12.50

FARMER,PHILIP J-Maker of Universes-NY-1965-Ace-wrps-1st ed (v5,f) 20.00

FARMER,PHILIP J-Tarzan Alive-NY-1972-Dbldy-312p-1st ed (g9,discol cov,dj sl wn) 65.00

FARMER,PHILIP J-Unreasoning Mask-NY-(1981)-Putnam-1st ed (h3,f,dj) 20.00

FARMER,ROBERT E L-From Florida to the Far West-(Bartow?)-(1936)-photos,12 plts (hh8,few cov spots,sl fox) 28.00

FARNHAM,A B-Home Taxidermy for Pleasure and Profit-1916-Harding-246p-illus (bb3) 10.00

FARNHAM,ALBERT B-Home Manufacture of Furs & Skins-Columbus-1916-16mo-285p-illus (m3) 12.50

FARNHAM,CHARLES H-Life of Francis Parkman-Bost-1902-394p-cl (n1) 15.00

FARNSWORTH,SAMUEL-Ferret Book-Cleve-1899-30p-wrps (n1,sl wn wrps) 12.50

FARQUHAR,CARLEY-Sportsman Almanac-NY-1965-8vo-493p-illus-1st ed (m3,f,dj) 10.00

FARQUHAR,FRANCIS-History of the Sierra Nevada-Berkeley-1965-262p-photos-1st ed (p10,f,sl chip dj) 100.00

FARQUHAR,FRANCIS-Yosemite, the Big Trees and the High Sierra-Berkeley,LA-1948-U of Cal Pr-tall 8vo-xi,104p-gry cl,9 illus-1st ed (t10,f,dj,autg) 175.00

FARQUHAR,FRANCIS-Yosemite, the Big Trees, & the High Sierra-Berkeley-1948-lg 8vo-103p-1st ed (o10,vf,vf dj) 225.00

FARQUHAR,FRANKLIN S-History of Livingston, California-Livingston-1945-Chronicle-168p-stiff wrps-Six Guns 697-scarce (nn6) 35.00

FARQUHAR,WILLIAM G-Enjoy Europe by Rail-Lond-1965-222p-1st ed (n4) 12.00

FARR,F-Rickenbacker's Luck-Bost-1979-8vo-xvi,366p-cl-1st ed (s2,dj) 20.00

FARR,WILLIAM E-Montana-Boulder-(1978)-Pruett-oblng 8vo-iv,279p-cl,photos-1st ed (v1,dj) 40.00

FARRAR,CAPT CHARLES A J-Through the Wilds-Bost-1892-8vo-415p-illus-scarce (m3,cracked hngs) 27.50

FARRAR,EMMIE F-Old Virginia Houses Along the Fall Line-(1971)-Hastings Hs-236p-photos-1st ed (dd9,dj) 35.00

FARRAR,EMMIE F-Old Virginia Houses: Shenandoah-(1976)-Delmar-217p-photos-1st ed (dd9,dj) 35.00

FARRAR,GERALDINE-Such Sweet Compulsion-NY-1938-Greystone Pr-1st ed (u4,sp fade) 18.00

FARRAR,JOHN-Elements of Electricity, Magnetism, and Electro Dynamics-1842-336p-193 illus(incl 7 fldg plts)-v rare-3rd ed (h6,few drwngs on e.p.) 150.00

FARRAR,STEWART-Sword of Orley-NY-(1977)-St.Martin's-1st US ed (j3,f,dj) 15.00

FARRE,HENRY-Sky Fighters of France-Bost-1919-4to-xviii,144p-cl & dec bds,col frntis,24p plts by auth-1st ed (t2,uncut) 150.00

FARRE,HENRY-Sky Fighters of France-Bost-1919-qto-143p-yel cl,gry papr cov bds,25 plts-1st Amer trd ed (kk2,1 plt tn) 225.00

FARRELL,H-What Ever Happened to Baby Jane-1960-Rinehart-1st ed (x7,f,dj) 70.00

FARRELL,JAMES T-$1,000 a Week...-NY-(1942)-1st ed (d5,top dj sp wn,cor tape mks) 50.00

FARRELL,JAMES T-An American Dream Girl-NY-(1950)-1st ed (l5,f,sl chip dj) 25.00

FARRELL,JAMES T-Bernard Clare-NY-(1946)-Vanguard-1st ed (hh5,dj) 15.00

FARRELL,JAMES T-Bernard Clare-NY-1946-Vanguard-367p-brwn cl-1st ed (x9,chip dj) 17.50

FARRELL,JAMES T-Dangerous Woman-NY-1957-Vanguard-1st ed (z2,f,dj) 35.00

FARRELL,JAMES T-Ellen Rogers-NY-1941-Vanguard-1st ed (z2,f,dj) 45.00

FARRELL,JAMES T-French Girls are Vicious & Other Stories-NY-(1955)-1st ed (l5,sl soil dj) 25.00

FARRELL,JAMES T-Gas House McGinty-NY-1933-cl-1st ed (d5,brwng e.p.,dj chip,tp mrk) 125.00

FARRELL,JAMES T-Guillotine Party & Other Stories-NY-(1935)-1st ed (l5,tape mrkd dj) 75.00

FARRELL,JAMES T-League of Frightened Philistines-NY-(1945)-1st ed (l5,tape mrkd dj) 25.00

FARRELL,JAMES T-League of Frightened Philistines-NY-(1945)-Vanguard-xiv+210p-gry cl-1st ed (f2,sp chip dj) 30.00

FARRELL,JAMES T-Life Adventures-NY-1953-Vanguard-1st ed (z2,f,f dj) 50.00

FARRELL,JAMES T-Misunderstanding-NY-1949-House of Bks-8vo-cl,tissue dj-ltd to 300c,autg-1st ed (jj8,vf,dj) 65.00

FARRELL,JAMES T-My Days of Anger-Lond-1945-Routledge-300p-1st Brit ed (r1,dj sl tn,chip) 20.00

FARRELL,JAMES T-My Days of Anger-NY-1943-Vanguard-1st ed (z2,f,sl chip dj) 35.00

FARRELL,JAMES T-Olive and Mary Jane-NY-1977-Stonehill-1st ed (z2,f,dj) 10.00

FARRELL,JAMES T-Reflections at Fifty-NY-1954-Vanguard-1st ed (z2,f,f dj) 45.00

FARRELL,JAMES T-Road Between-NY-(1949)-1st ed (l5,sl chip dj) 10.00

FARRELL,JAMES T-This Man and This Woman-NY-(1951)-1st ed (l5,sl wn dj) 10.00

FARRELL,JAMES T-This Man and This Woman-NY-(1951)-Vanguard-8vo-205p-1st ed (ee5,dj) 20.00

FARRELL,JAMES T-To Whom it May Concern...-NY-1944-1st ed (s5,chip dj) 15.00

FARRELL,JAMES T-What Time Collects-GC-1964-1st ed (l5,f,dj) 17.50

FARRELL,JAMES T-When Time Was Born-NY-1966-drwngs,S Dwoskin-1st ed (s5,dj) 15.00

FARRELL,JAMES-My Baseball Diary-1957-Barnes-1st ed (s8,f,f dj) 45.00

FARRELL,M J-Devoted Ladies-Bost-1934-Little,Brown-1st US ed (hh5,dj) 30.00

FARRELL,M J-Devoted Ladies-Bost-1934-Little,Brown-1st US ed (z8,f,f dj) 55.00

FARRELL,MICHAEL R-Who Made All Our Streetcars Go-Balt-1973-319p-1st ed (n4,f,dj) 27.50

FARRELLY,M J-Settlement After the War in South Africa-NY-1900-323p-red cl-1st ed (b7,sl fade sp) 35.00

FARRELLY,MIDGET-Surfing Life-1967-Arco-photos-1st ed (p9,f,sl wn dj) 35.00

FARRER,REGINALD-Dolomites-Lond-1913-vii,207p-pict cl cov,fldg map,20 col plts-1st & only ed (jj7) 79.00

FARRER,REGINALD-Rainbow Bridge-Lond-1926-383p-gold emboss lt blu cl,16 photos,fldg map-3rd impr (hh7,f,publ card laid in) 115.00

FARRINGTON,CHISIE-Women Can Fish-NY-1951-8vo-238p-photos (m3,vf,dj) 25.00

FARRINGTON,EDWARD I-Vegetable Garden-(Lexington)-(1939)-HC&F-8vo-139p-grn cl,8 plts-"Gardener's Library" ser-1st ed (t10,dj) 15.00

FARRINGTON,EDWARD-Gardener's Travel Book-(1938)-Mass Horticultural Scty-390p-photos-1st prntg (x5,dj wn,tn) 18.00

FARRINGTON,S KIP-Atlantic Game Fishing-NY-1937-Kennedy Bros-7 col illus by L B Hunt-1st ed (z3) 75.00

FARRINGTON,S KIP-Book of Fishes-Phila-1946-8vo-88p-88 col illus,L B Hunt-1st ed (m3,f,v fray dj) 12.50

FARRINGTON,S KIP-Ducks Came Back-NY-1945-4to-138p-illus,L B Hunt (m3,f) 25.00
FARRINGTON,S KIP-Fishing the Atlantic Offshore & On-NY-1949-8vo-312p-photos-1st ed (m3) 25.00
FARRINGTON,S KIP-Fishing the Atlantic Offshore and On-NY-1949-312p-blu cl,dec e.p.,photos,illus,L B Hunt (ee3,vf,dj) 30.00
FARRINGTON,S KIP-Fishing the Pacific Offshore & On-NY-1953-8vo-297p-photos-1st ed (m3,f,fray dj) 25.00
FARRINGTON,S KIP-Fishing with Hemingway & Glassell-NY-1971-8vo-118p-photos-1st ed (m3,vf,dj) 25.00
FARRINGTON,S KIP-Interesting Birds of Our Country-GC-1945-oblng 4to-unpgd-illus,L B Hunt (m3,f,fray dj) 32.50
FARRINGTON,S KIP-Pacific Game Fish-NY-1942-4to-290p-illus by L B Hunt,photos-1st ed (m3) 45.00
FARRINGTON,S KIP-Railroading Around the World-NY-1955-230p-1st ed (n4,f,dj) 24.00
FARRINGTON,S KIP-Railroading Coast to Coast-NY-1976-305p-1st ed (n4,f,dj) 30.00
FARRINGTON,S KIP-Railroading from the Head End-GC-1943-296p-1st ed (n4) 23.00
FARRINGTON,S KIP-Railroading From the Rear End-1946-Coward,McCann-430p-photos-2nd ed (d3) 20.00
FARRINGTON,S KIP-Railroading the Modern Way-NY-1951-395p-1st ed (n4,f,dj) 28.00
FARRINGTON,S KIP-Railroads at War-NY-(1944)-Coward McCann-8vo-320p-photos-1st ed (p1,f,dj) 35.00
FARRINGTON,S KIP-Railroads of Today-1949-Coward McCann-306p-72p photos-1st ed (d3,dj) 25.00
FARRIS,A L-Ring-Necked Pheasant in Iowa-Des Moines-1977-8vo-147p-frontis by M Reece,photos (m3,vf) 25.00
FARRIS,J-Sharp Practice-1974-S&S-1st ed (x7,f,dj) 65.00
FARRIS,JOHN-King Windom-1967-Trident Pr-1st ed (n9,dj sl wn & rub) 60.00
FARRIS,JOHN-King Windom-NY-1967-Trident Pr-1st ed (k3,sl tn dj) 40.00
FARROW,W MILTON-How I Became a Crack Shot-Newport-1882-18mo-206p-illus-rare (m3) 75.00
FARSHLER,EARL-American Saddle Horse-Louisville-1934-2nd ed,1st prtg this ed (j9) 40.00
FARSHLER,EARL-Riding and Training-Princeton-1959-Van Nostrand (j9,dj wn) 18.00
FARSON,NEGLEY-Going Fishing-Lond-1942-4to-144p-illus,Tunnifcliff-1st ed (m3,dj) 28.00
FARWELL,BYRON-Queen Victoria's Little Wars-NY-1972-394p-illus-1st Amer ed (b7,f,dj) 50.00
FASHIONABLE AMERICAN LETTER WRITER-Bost-1823-James Loring-179,(1)p-prntd bds-Amer Imprnts 12520 (l1,sl chip sp) 50.00
FAST,HOWARD-American-NY-(1946)-DSP-1st ed (hh5,f,dj) 12.50
FAST,HOWARD-Children-NY-1947-Duell-1st ed (v5,f,dj) 30.00
FATHER CHRISTMAS-NY,Buff-(1895)-W B Perkins-lg 4to-unpgd-cl bckd pict bds,5 lg chromos,drwngs (r3,sl loose,few tape mrks) 60.00
FATOUT,PAUL-Ambrose Bierce and the Black Hills-Norman-(1956)-U of Okla Pr-180p-illus-1st ed (bb4,dj) 40.00
FAUBION,NINA L-Some Edible Mushrooms...-Portland-(1938)-Binfords & Mort-127p-illus,auth (u6) 20.00
FAUGHNAN,THOMAS-Stirring Incidents in the Life of a British Soldier-Tor-1879-336p-dec grn cl,frntis-1st ed (b7) 40.00
FAULK,ODIE-Arizona, A Short History-Norman-1970-267p-photos,maps-1st ed (t7,autg,dj) 12.50
FAULK,ODIE-Crimson Desert-NY-1974-237p-photos-1st ed (t7,dj) 15.00
FAULK,ODIE-Geronimo Campaign-NY-1969-Oxford-12mo-ix,245p-pict cl,map e.p.,photos-1st ed (aa3,f,dj) 25.00
FAULK,ODIE-Land of Many Frontiers-NY-1968-358p-map e.p.-1st ed (t7,dj) 12.50
FAULK,ODIE-Too Far North...Too Far South-LA-1967-Westernlore Pr-8vo-xiii+186p-cl,map e.p.,illus,Great West & Indian Series XXXV-1st ed (z4,dj) 50.00
FAULKNER,D-Living Corals-1979-Potter-sq 4to-310p-194 col photos-1st ed (bb3,f,dj) 35.00
FAULKNER,JOSEPH P-Eighteen Months on a Greenland Whaler-NY-1878-publ by auth-317p-grn cl,frntis-1st ed (h2,some pencil mrks) 150.00
FAULKNER,JOSEPH-Life of Philip Henry Sheridan-NY-1888-Hurst & Co-149p-frnts,illus (o7) 20.00
FAULKNER,WILLIAM-Big Woods-NY-(1955)-Random Hs-decs by Edw Shenton-1st ed (bb2,f,f dj) 100.00
FAULKNER,WILLIAM-Big Woods-NY-(1955)-Random-1st ed (l9,sl wn dj) 150.00
FAULKNER,WILLIAM-Big Woods-NY-(1955)-Random-4to-cl-1st ed (x3,sl chip dj) 95.00
FAULKNER,WILLIAM-Collected Stories-Lond-1951-Chatto & Windus-1st Brit ed (z2,f,dj chip,rnfrcd) 125.00
FAULKNER,WILLIAM-Fable-1955-Chatto & Windus-392p-1st Brit ed (v8,dj chip,sl soil,sl tn) 80.00
FAULKNER,WILLIAM-Fable-NY-(1954)-Random-1st ed (b10,sl tn dj) 75.00
FAULKNER,WILLIAM-Fable-NY-(1954)-Random-1st ed (ee2,f,f dj) 100.00
FAULKNER,WILLIAM-Fable-NY-1954-ltd to 1000c,nbrd,autg,rag pap,stmpd bds (t5,f,box) 500.00
FAULKNER,WILLIAM-Faulkner at West Point-NY-(1964)-Random-8vo-cl,illus-1st ed (jj8,f,dj) 35.00
FAULKNER,WILLIAM-Faulkner at West Point-NY-1964-(Random)-1st ed (h8,f,f dj) 55.00
FAULKNER,WILLIAM-Faulkner Cowley File-NY-(1966)-Viking-1st ed (ee2,f,dj) 35.00
FAULKNER,WILLIAM-Go Down Moses-NY-(1942)-Random-grn stmpd blu bds-Massey 44-1st ed (bb2,dj sl chip) 300.00
FAULKNER,WILLIAM-Hamlet-NY-1940-1st ed (t5,sl wn dj) 250.00
FAULKNER,WILLIAM-Intruder in the Dust-NY-(1948)-1st ed (k9,sp lettrng flaked,dj) 150.00
FAULKNER,WILLIAM-Intruder in the Dust-NY-(1948)-Random-8vo-cl-1st ed (ll10,f,sl tan dj) 125.00
FAULKNER,WILLIAM-Intruder in the Dust-NY-(1948)-Random-8vo-cl-1st ed (x3,tape rnfrcd dj) 135.00
FAULKNER,WILLIAM-Knight's Gambit-(1949)-Random-1st ed (x2,f,dj) 185.00
FAULKNER,WILLIAM-Knight's Gambit-NY-(1949)-Random-8vo-cl-1st ed (ll10,f,sl chip dj) 100.00
FAULKNER,WILLIAM-Knight's Gambit-NY-(1949)-Random-8vo-cl-1st ed (x3,weak hng,dj sl chip) 135.00
FAULKNER,WILLIAM-Mansion-NY-(1959)-Random Hs-1st ed (b10,sl wn dj) 75.00
FAULKNER,WILLIAM-Mansion-NY-(1959)-Random-1st ed (a5,f,sl wn dj) 75.00
FAULKNER,WILLIAM-Mansion-NY-(1959)-Random-1st ed (ee2,f,dj) 125.00

FAULKNER,WILLIAM-Mansion-NY-(1959)-Random-ltd to 500c,nbrd,autg-1st ed (f6,f) 850.00

FAULKNER,WILLIAM-Mayday-1978-Notre Dame-1st trd ed (t5,f,dj) 15.00

FAULKNER,WILLIAM-Mosquitoes-1964-C&W-1st Brit ed (x2,f dj) 95.00

FAULKNER,WILLIAM-Mosquitoes-NY-1927-patterned bds-1st ed (t5,lacks dj) 200.00

FAULKNER,WILLIAM-New Orleans Sketches-1953-Hokuseido Pr-wrps-1st ed (x2) 185.00

FAULKNER,WILLIAM-New Orleans Sketches-Lond-1959-Sidgwick & Jackson-1st Brit ed (h8,dj missing sm chip) 50.00

FAULKNER,WILLIAM-New Orleans Sketches-NY-(1968)-Random-1st ed thus (l9,f,dj) 80.00

FAULKNER,WILLIAM-Notes on a Horsethief-Greenville-1950-Levee Pr-ltd to 950c,nbrd,autg (v5,sl wn sp) 450.00

FAULKNER,WILLIAM-Reivers-NY-(1962)-1st ed (j5,sp chip dj) 25.00

FAULKNER,WILLIAM-Reivers-NY-(1962)-1st ed (t5,dj) 45.00

FAULKNER,WILLIAM-Requiem for a Nun-NY-(1951)-Random-1st ed (l9,dj sp fade) 150.00

FAULKNER,WILLIAM-Requiem for a Nun-NY-(1951)-Random-1st ed (w1,f,dj) 85.00

FAULKNER,WILLIAM-Requiem for a Nun-NY-1951-1st ed (p5,sl chip dj) 100.00

FAULKNER,WILLIAM-Sanctuary-1931-C&W-1st Brit ed (x7,dj sl wn & sp fade) 375.00

FAULKNER,WILLIAM-Sanctuary-NY-1931-1st ed (t5,sp chip dj) 600.00

FAULKNER,WILLIAM-Sartoris-NY-1929-Harcourt-1st ed (w5) 150.00

FAULKNER,WILLIAM-Soldier's Pay-1930-C&W-1st Brit ed (x2,dj sl wn & tn & sp fade) 685.00

FAULKNER,WILLIAM-Soldier's Pay-NY-1926-Boni & Liveright-1st ed (t6,sl spot cov,pg miss sm pc) 450.00

FAULKNER,WILLIAM-Soldier's Pay-NY-1926-Boni & Liveright-yel stmpd orig blu cl-1st prtg wi "borders on borders upon" pg.60-1st ed (ee2,bndg strngthnd,lacks dj) 500.00

FAULKNER,WILLIAM-Sound and the Fury-NY-1929-patterned bds & e.p.s-1st ed (t5,bds sl wn,lacks dj) 350.00

FAULKNER,WILLIAM-These Thirteen: Stories-NY-(1931)-Cape & Smith-1st ed (u1,dj drknd,sp chip) 350.00

FAULKNER,WILLIAM-Town-NY-(1957)-Random-1st ed (ee2,f,dj) 85.00

FAULKNER,WILLIAM-Town-NY-(1957)-Random-orng cl,t.e. grn-Petersen A34d-1st ed (v10,f,dj) 35.00

FAULKNER,WILLIAM-Town-NY-1957-Random-1st ed,1st iss (q2,dj) 95.00

FAULKNER,WILLIAM-Town-NY-1957-var 2nd iss of 1st ed wi t.e. stnd grn (r2,dj) 40.00

FAULKNER,WILLIAM-Uncollected Stories of...-NY-(1979)-1st ed (t5,f,dj) 20.00

FAULKNER,WILLIAM-Uncollected Stories of...-NY-(1979)-Random-1st ed (l9,f,dj) 30.00

FAULKNER,WILLIAM-Unvanquished-NY-(1938)-Random-4to-cl-1st ed (x3,sp sunned dj) 300.00

FAULKNER,WILLIAM-Wild Palms-NY-(1939)-Random-4to-cl,stmpd in gold & grn on sp-1st ed,1st iss (x3,sl chip dj) 250.00

FAUNCE,HILDA-Desert Wife-Bost-1934-305p-drwngs-1st ed (v7) 25.00

FAUNCE,HILDA-Desert Wife-Bost-1934-305p-drwngs-2nd prtg (v7) 10.00

FAURE,GABRIEL-Gardens of Rome-Lond-Medici Soc Ltd-100p-cl,14p tip in col repro's,photos (x6) 85.00

FAUSSET,HUGH-Samuel Taylor Coleridge-Lond-1926-J Cape-350p-brwn cl-1st ed (z9,f,dj sp sunned,rub) 20.00

FAUSTER,CARL U-COMP.-Libbey Glass Since 1818-Toledo-(1979)-quarto-415p-cl,illus incl 24p col (m1,f,dj,autg) 30.00

FAUX,RONALD-High Ambition-Lond-1982-177p-3rd impr (o10,f,dj) 50.00

FAVORITE FAIRY TALES-NY-1907-Harper-355p-Japan vel wi emboss g fig,16 plts by P Newell-1st ed (nn10,cov rub,sp sl drknd) 150.00

FAVOUR,ALPHEUS H-Old Bill Williams Mountain Man-Norman-1962-U of Okla Pr-8vo-xv+234p-cl,illus-1st rprnt ed (z4,sl fade dj sp) 45.00

FAVOUR,ALPHEUS H-Old Bill Williams-Chapel Hill-(1936)-UNC Pr-(x),229p-cl,fldg map,col frntis,photos,illus-1st ed (v1) 75.00

FAVOUR,ALPHEUS H-Old Bill Williams-Chapel Hill-(1936)-UNC-229p-illus,fldg map-scarce-1st ed (f7) 65.00

FAWCETT,BRIAN-Railways of the Andes-Lond-1963-328p-1st ed (n4,f,dj) 26.00

FAWCETT,CLAIRE H-We Fell In Love With The Circus-1949-Lindquist-198p-drwngs,photos-1st prntg (v8) 20.00

FAWCETT,CLARA H-Dolls-Bost-(1964)-Brandford-8vo-282p-photos-1st ed (gg5,sl tn dj) 17.50

FAWCETT,COL P H-Lost Trails, Lost Cities-NY-(1953)-Funk & Wagnalls-8vo-332p-8p photos-1st ed (jj5,sl tn dj) 17.50

FAY,CHARLES E-Mary Celeste-Salem-1942-Peabody Mus-xxvii,261p-blu buckrm,t.e.g.,14 plts,9 illus(incl maps,facs)-ltd to 850c,nbrd (pp1,sp fade) 95.00

FAY,F M-Windows of Merchant Taylors' Hall-1934-Cheswick Pr-17p text-col frntis,plts (cc8) 75.00

FAY,JAY-American Psychology before William James-New Brunswick-1939-Rutgers U Pr-x+240p-blu cl-1st ed (c2,soil dj) 20.00

FAY,PETER W-Opium War-Chapel Hill-1975-406p-maps-1st ed (b7,f,dj) 25.00

FEAGANS,RAYMOND J-Railroad that Ran by the Tide-Berkeley-1972-146p-1st ed (n4,f,dj) 26.00

FEARING,DANIEL B-Catalog of an Exhibition of Angling Bookplates Forming the Collection of ...-NY-1918-8vo-84p-one of 500c,frontis-scarce (m3,f) 80.00

FEARING,KENNETH-Big Clock-1946-Harcourt-1st ed (s10,dj) 50.00

FEARING,KENNETH-Big Clock-NY-1946-Harcourt-1st ed (l4,dj sl tn,sl chip) 35.00

FEARING,KENNETH-Crozart Story-GC-1960-Dbldy-1st ed (w9,f,sl wn dj) 65.00

FEARING,KENNETH-Dead Reckoning-NY-1938-Random-1st ed (v5,f,dj) 50.00

FEARING,KENNETH-Loneliest Girl in the World-NY-1951-Harcourt-1st ed (w5,sl chip dj) 40.00

FEARS,J WAYNE-Wild Turkey Book-1981-Amwell Press-8vo-274p-ltd to 100c,nbrd,autg-illus,T Hennessey (m3,as new in box) 125.00

FEATHER,LEONARD-Encyclopedia of Jazz-1955-Horizon-photos-1st ed (o9,dj wn & chip) 45.00

FEATHER,LEONARD-Encyclopedia Yearbook of Jazz-1956-Horizon-illus-1st ed (m9,dj chip,wn & sl tn) 45.00

FEATHERSTONE,DONALD-Bowmen of England-NY-1968-200p-illus-1st Amer ed (b7,wn dj) 30.00

FEATHERSTONHAUGH,G W-Report of a Geological Reconnoissance Made in 1835-Wash-1836-GPO-168p-illus-1st ed (cc4,sl fox) 150.00

FECHET,J E-Flying-Balt-1933-sm 8vo-cl g,frntis,"Century of Progress Ser."-1st ed (t2,sl fade) 20.00

FEDDEN,ROBIN-Alpine Ski Tour-Lond-1956-4to-93p-fldg map,24 plts-1st Brit ed (q10,sp fray) 25.00

FEDDEN,ROMILLY-Food and Other Frailties-Lond-(1948)-Seeley-143p-red cl,drwngs-1st prtg (q8,dj) 20.00

FEDER,NORMAN-American Indian Art-nd-Abrams-folio-445p-g stmpd red silk bndg,242 illus,60 tip in col plts-1st ed (d3,dj) 100.00

FEDER,NORMAN-American Indian Art-NY-1969-Abrams-4to-446p-red cl,b&w & tip in col plts (r10,f,f dj) 75.00

FEDERMANN,REINHARD-Royal Art of Alchemy-Phila-1964-Chilton-cl,illus-1st ed (n8,fray dj) 20.00

FEE,CHESTER A-Chief Joseph-NY-1936-Wilson Erickson-8vo-346p wi map,illus,index-1st ed (t1,f,dj) 125.00

FEHRENBACH,T R-Lone Star-NY-1968-751p-map e.p.-1st ed (t7,f,dj) 40.00

FEHRENBACH,T R-San Antonio Story-Tulsa-1978-Heritage-240p-photos-1st ed (a9,dj) 35.00

FEIED,FREDERICK-No Pie in the Sky-NY-1964-Citadel-wrps-1st ed (v5) 15.00

FEIED,FREDERICK-No Pie in the Sky-NY-1964-wrps-1st ed (x8,f) 10.00

FEIFFER,JULES-Feiffer on Nixon-NY-(1974)-RH-oblng 8vo-wrps-1st ed (ff3,f) 25.00

FEIFFER,JULES-Little Murders-Lond-1970-1st Brit ed (n5,f,f dj) 25.00

FEIN,HARRY H-Flying Chinaman-1938-Knopf-1st ed (s10,dj) 45.00

FEININGER,ANDREAS-Andreas Feininger-Dobbs Ferry-1973-Morgan & Morgan-160p-128 photos-1st ed (cc9,as new in dj) 35.00

FEJES,CLAIRE-People of the Noatak-1966-Knopf-368p-1st ed (u8,dj) 25.00

FELCE,W-Apes-Lond-1948-8vo-90p-cl,16 plts (y8) 16.00

FELCONE,JOSEPH J-Abstracts of New Jersey Manuscripts in the Sol Feinstone Collection of the American Revolution-Wash Cross-1976-39p-wrps (aa6) 10.00

FELCONE,JOSEPH J-An Index to John F Hageman's History of Princeton and its Institutions-Princeton-1976-55p-wrps (aa6) 10.00

FELCONE,JOSEPH J-Books, Pamphlets & Broadsides Printed in Trenton, New Jersey, 1778 to 1800-Princeton-1978-73p-wrps-ltd to 100c (aa6) 40.00

FELCONE,JOSEPH J-Guide to the Manuscript Collections in the Historical Society of Princeton, New Jersey-Princeton-1982-62p-wrps (aa6) 10.00

FELCONE,JOSEPH J-Trenton Index-Princeton-1976-87p-wrps-2nd ed (aa6) 10.00

FELDMAN,EDDY S-Art of Street Lighting in Los Angeles-LA-1972-Dawson's-55p+photos (d3) 30.00

FELDMAN,GENE-Beat Generation and the Angry Young Men-NY-1958-1st ed (x8,wn dj) 40.00

FELIX,DAVID-Protest-Bloomington-1965-Indiana Univ-274p (ff1,dj) 25.00

FELLEGY,JOE-Classic Minnesota Fishing Stories-Mpls-1982-8vo-238p-wrps-illus-1st prntng (m3) 10.00

FELLOWS,HENRY P-Boating Trips on New England Rivers-Bost-1884-Cupples,Upham-176p+ads-tan bds,illus-1st ed (m2,ex-lib) 55.00

FELOW,R-Game of Croquet-NY-1865-Hurd & Houghton-sm 8vo-31p-flex g stmpd cl,illus-1st ed (t1) 125.00

FELT,EPHRAIM A-Memorial of Life & Entomological Work of Joseph A Lintner-Albany-1899-U of NY-308p-wrps (x6) 25.00

FENADY,ANDREW J-Man with Bogart's Face-Chig-1977-Regnery-1st ed (f4,dj) 10.00

FENADY,ANDREW J-Secret of Sam Marlowe-Chig-1980-Contemporary-1st ed (q4,f,dj) 20.00

FENISONG,R-Snare for Sinners-1949-Dbldy-1st ed (x7,dj) 14.00

FENISONG,RUTH-Dead Weight-NY-1962-Dbldy CC-1st ed (f4,f,sm spot dj sp) 10.00

FENISONG,RUTH-Dead Yesterday-NY-1951-Dbldy CC-1st ed (e4,dj sp sl wn) 15.00

FENLEY,FLORENCE-Oldtimers of Southwest Texas-Uvalde-1957-319p-photos-1st ed (t7,dj) 35.00

FENNING,DANIEL-Ready Reckoner...-Phila-1801-prtd by Henry Sweitzer-192p-bds-Amer Imprnts 493 (a1) 40.00

FENSCH,THOMAS-Steinbeck and Covici...-Middlebury-(1979)-Paul S Eriksson-1st ed (d5,f,dj) 20.00

FENTON,ROBERT W-Big Swingers-Englewood-(1967)-Prentice Hall-1st ed (k3,wn dj) 20.00

FENTON,WILLIAM N-American Indian and White Relations to 1830-Chapel Hill-1957-U of NC Pr-138p-1st ed (ff4) 20.00

FENWICK,E P-Two Names for Death-NY-1945-Farrar-1st ed (k4,dj) 25.00

FERBER,EDNA-American Beauty-GC-1931-Dbldy,Doran-woodcuts by R Ruzicka-1st ed (bb1,drknd,fray sp,dj) 35.00

FERBER,EDNA-Cimarron-GC-1930-illus e.p.-1st ed (n5,sp chip dj) 35.00

FERBER,EDNA-Giant-GC-1952-Dbldy-1st ed (b10,sl chip dj) 25.00

FERBER,EDNA-Ice Palace-GC-1958-Dbldy-1st ed (e3,dj) 20.00

FERBER,EDNA-Ice Palace-GC-1958-Dbldy-1st ed (hh5,dj) 10.00

FERBER,EDNA-Saratoga Trunk-GC-1941-Dbldy,Doran-1st ed (bb1,dj) 25.00

FERBER,EDNA-Stage Door-GC-1936-1st ed (n5,sl chip dj) 45.00

FERET,BARBARA L-Gastronomical and Culinary Literature-Metuchen-1970-Scarecrow Pr-124p (m6,as new) 20.00

FERGUSON,CHARLES D-Experiences of a Forty Niner During Thirty Four Years' Residence in California and Australia-Cleve-1888-Williams Publ-dec brwn cl-1st ed (k8) 85.00

FERGUSON,DAVID L-Cleopatra's Barge-Bost-(1976)-Little,Brown-8vo-293p-illus-1st ed (cc5,f,dj) 20.00

FERGUSON,DUGALD-Vicissitudes of Bush Life in Australia and New Zealand-Lond-1891-Swan Sonnenschein-8vo-vii,(1),327p-dec papr bds,blu cl sp wi papr labl (p8,bds soil,wn,hng crack) 75.00

FERGUSON,HENRY L-English Springer Spaniel in America-Derrydale-1932-8vo-106p-one of 850c,photos (m3,f) 110.00

FERGUSON,JOHN C-Mythology of All Races.Vol.VIII:Chinese by...Japanese, by Masaharu Anesaki-Bost-1928-Marshall Jones-buckram,col frntis,plts,drwngs-1st ed (l8) 45.00

FERGUSON,JOHN-Bibliotheca Chemica-Lond-1954-Vandenhoeck & Ruprecht-lg 8vo-2 vols-gry buckrm,(rprnt of 1906 ed) (y9,cor bump) 200.00

FERGUSON,MUNGO-Printed Books in the Library of the Hunterian Museum in the University of Glasgow: a Catalogue-Glasgow-1930-folio-396p-1st ed (dd3) 150.00

FERGUSON,T J-Zuni Atlas-Norman-(1985)-150p-photos,maps-1st ed (v7,f,dj) 25.00

FERGUSON,W J-I Saw Booth Shoot Lincoln-Bost-1930-Houghton Mifflin-viii+63p-blk cl,illus-ltd to 1000c-1st ed (h2) 50.00

FERGUSON,W M-Maya Ruins in Central America in Color-1984-UNM-4to-387p-413 illus(incl col photos)-1st ed (bb3,f,dj) 35.00

FERGUSSON,BERNARD-Black Watch and the King's Enemies-NY-1950-384p-dec cl,maps-1st ed (b7) 50.00

FERGUSSON,BERNARD-Eton Portrait-Lond-1937-Miles-4to-grn cl-1st ed (y3,cov sl soil) 150.00

FERGUSSON,ERNA-Dancing Gods-NY-1931-276p-drwngs-1st ed (u7) 40.00

FERGUSSON,ERNA-Murder & Mystery in New Mexico-Albuq-(1948)-M Armitage Eds-193p+8p photos,frntis-Six Guns 710-1st ed (bb4,dj) 45.00

FERGUSSON,HARVEY-Home in the West-NY-(1945)-247p-1st ed (v7,sl fade dj) 25.00

FERGUSSON,HARVEY-Rio Grande-NY-1933-Knopf-1st ed (pp9,dj sl chip) 45.00

FERGUSSON,JAMES-Illustrated Handbook of Architecture-Lond-1855-J Murray-8vo-2 vols-lea,mrbld edges & e.p.,g titles & emboss,bands,850 woodcts-1st ed (mm8,scuff,edgewn) 200.00*

FERLATTE,WILLIAM-Flora of the Trinity Alps of Northern California-Berkeley-1974-U of Cal Pr-8vo-xii,212p-14 photos,map-1st ed (ff9) 38.00*

FERLINGHETTI,LAWRENCE-Populist Manifestos Plus an Interview with Jean Jacques Lebel-SF-(1981)-Grey Fox Pr-1st ed (l7,wrps) 10.00

FERN,FANNY-Folly As It Flies-NY-1868-G W Carleton-355p-cl-1st ed (d1) 20.00

FERNALD,CHARLES-County Judge in Arcady-Glendale-1954-Arthur H Clark-268p-illus-Six Guns 1887-1st ed (bb4,uncut) 50.00

FERNIE,F-Dry-Fly Fishing in Border Waters-Lond-1912-12mo-136p-illus (m3) 17.50

FERRARS,E X-Count the Cost-NY-1957-Dbldy CC-1st US ed (j4,f,rprd dj) 15.00

FERRARS,E X-Doubly Dead-1963-CC-1st Amer ed (s10,dj) 12.50

FERRARS,E X-Drowned Rat-NY-1975-Dbldy CC-1st US ed (g4,f,dj) 12.50

FERRARS,E X-March Hare Murders-NY-1949-Dbldy CC-1st US ed (f4,sl yel pgs,dj) 25.00

FERRERO,FELICE-Valley of Aosta-NY-1910-t.e.g.,35 illus,4 fldg maps (o10,ex-libr) 20.00

FERREZ,GILBERTO-Pioneer Photographers of Brazil-NY-1976-Cntr Intr Amer Relations-143p-92 photos-1st ed (cc9,f,dj) 45.00

FERRI,ENRICO-Criminal Sociology-NY-1900-Appleton-284p-cl (f1) 17.50

FERRIMAN,Z DUCKETT-East and West of Hellespont-Bost-1926-Houghton Mifflin-cl,frntis,illus-1st Amer ed (m8,sp sunned) 25.00

FERRIS,BENJAMIN G-Utah and the Mormons-NY-1854-Harper & Bros-347p-brwn cl,illus-Howes F98-1st ed (m2) 135.00

FERRIS,BENJAMIN-History of the Original Settlements on the Delaware...-Wilmington-1846-312p-cl,plts,maps (aa6) 150.00

FERRIS,C D-ED.-Butterflies of the Rocky Mountain States-1981-U of Okla-442p-4 col plts,photos-1st ed (bb3,f,dj) 40.00

FERRIS,PAUL-Dylan Thomas-NY-1977-1st ed (y7,dj) 12.00

FERRIS,ROBERT G-American West-Santa Fe-1963-287p-1st ed (t7,f,dj) 30.00

FERRIS,ROBERT-ED.-Prospector, Cowhand and Sodbuster-Wash-1967-320p-photos,e.p. map-1st ed (r8,cor bump) 18.00

FERRIS,W A-Life in the Rocky Mountains-Denver-1940-Rosenstock/Old West Publ-(100),365p-maroon cl,maps,illus-Howes F100-1st ed (v1) 200.00

FERRISS,HUGH-Metropolis of Tomorrow-1929-Washburn-59 drwngs (h10) 250.00

FERRISS,HUGH-Metropolis of Tomorrow-NY-1929-Ives Washburn-folio-140,(4)p-cl,illus-scarce-1st prtg (pp7) 175.00

FERRY & CO,D M-SEED ANNUAL 1883-Detr-1883-164p-wrps,6 col plts by Calvert Lith.,early catlg (o1,wn,marg trs frnt wrp rprd) 45.00

FETHERSTONHAUGH,R C-13th Battallion Royal Highlanders of Canada 1914 to 1919-1925-The Regiment-344p-blk cl,maps,illus-1st ed (gg2,sp fade,lacks ffep) 150.00

FETHERSTONHAUGH,R C-ED.-Royal Montreal Regiment 14th Battalion, C.E.F. 1914 to 1925-Montreal-1927-Gazette Prtg Co-8vo-334p-brgndy cl,g dec & sp titles,frntis,20 illus,6 maps (cc7) 45.00*

FETRIDGE,WM H-ED.-Navy Reader-Indpls-1943-Bobbs Merrill-443p-red cl,photos,maps,drwngs (p8) 15.00

FEUERLICHT,ROBERTA S-Justice Crucified-NY-1977-McGraw-480p-1st ed (ff1,tn dj) 20.00

FEW WORDS ON BEHALF OF THE LOYAL WOMEN OF THE UNITED STATES, BY ONE OF THEMSELVES-NY-1863-Wm Bryant-23p-prntd wrps (c1) 40.00

FEW,SMITH J-Fiftieth Anniversary of the Second Presbyterian Church, Newark,N.J.-Newark-1861-75p-wrps (aa6,ex-libr) 50.00

FEWKES,J WALTER-Prehistoric Mesa Verde Pueblo and Its People-Wash-1917-26p-pict wrps,illus,maps-1st ed (t7) 10.00

FEWSMITH,WILLIAM-Grammar of the English Language...-Phila-(1866)-Sower,Potts-228p-bds-revsd ed (k1,wn) 15.00

FFOULKES,CHARLES-Gun Founders of England-Cambridge-1937-Cambridge Univ Pr-4to-xvi+134p-15 plts,38 text illus-1st ed (l2,dj) 65.00

FFRENCH,YVONNE-Great Exhibition: 1851-Lond-(1950)-Harvell-8vo-297p-9 plts-1st ed (gg5,dj) 30.00

FICKEN,ROBERT-Lumber and Politics-(1979)-U of Wash-264p-illus-1st ed (r8,f,f dj) 12.00

FIEDLER,A-Squadron 303-NY-1943-8vo-182p-cl,frntis,16p illus (t2,dj) 25.00

FIEDLER,LESLIE-Being Busted-NY-(1969)-Stein & Day-1st ed (e3,f,dj) 25.00

FIELD,AL-Watch Yourself Go By-Columbus-1912-593p-cl (h1,sp fade,sl spot) 15.00

FIELD,BEN-Last Freshet-GC-1948-Dbldy-1st ed (w5,f,dj) 30.00

FIELD,CHARLES D-Three Years in the Saddle-Sylvania-nd-Borderland Bks-74p-wrps,frntis,(rprnt of 1898 Goldfield, Iowa ed) (o7) 20.00

FIELD,EDWARD-Revolutionary Defenses in Rhode Island-Providence-1896-Preston & Rounds-xvi+161p+ads-red cl,illus,plans,2 fldg maps-1st ed (k2,rub cov) 40.00

FIELD,EUGENE-Branches Green-NY-1934-Macmillan-8vo-pict cl,illus by D Lathrop-1st ed (pp10,sp fade,dj fade,sl chip) 40.00

FIELD,EUGENE-House-NY-1896-1st ed (m4) 9.50

FIELD,EUGENE-In Wink A Way Land-Chig-(1904)-Donahue-sm 8vo-148p-g pict cl (s3) 25.00

FIELD,EUGENE-Little Book of Profitable Tales-NY-1895-Scribners-243p-t.e.g.-1st ed (v3,cors rub) 65.00

FIELD,EUGENE-Songs of Childhood-1906-Scribner's (u4) 18.00

FIELD,EUGENE-Works of...-NY-1903-Scribner's/Devinne Pr-12 vols-g cl,frntis ea vol (m4,f) 50.00

FIELD,HENRY-Track of Man-GC-1953-Dbldy-8vo-448p-28 illus-1st ed (jj5,dj) 17.50

FIELD,JOHN P-Richard Wilbur-Kent-1971-Kent State U Pr-iss w/o dj-1st ed (w5,f) 20.00

FIELD,MATTHEW C-Prairie & Mountain Sketches-Norman-(1957)-239p-illus-1st ed (j7,sl chip dj) 35.00

FIELD,MATTHEW-Prairie & Mountain Sketches-Norman-1957-U of Okla Pr-8vo-239p-1st ed (z4,dj) 30.00

FIELD,MICHAEL-All Manner of Food-NY-1970-Knopf-382p+index,illus-1st ed (u6,dj) 16.00

FIELD,MICHAEL-Prevailing Wind-Lond-1965-Methuen-1st Brit ed (c8,f,f dj) 40.00

FIELD,PETER-Dig the Spurs Deep-NY-1953-Jefferson Hs-8vo-215p-1st ed (z4,sl tn dj) 10.00

FIELD,RACHEL-All This, and Heaven Too-NY-1938-Macmillan-1st ed (b10,sl chip dj) 25.00

FIELD,RACHEL-Calico Bush-NY-1931-Macmillan-1st ed (hh5,sl tn dj) 20.00

FIELD,RACHEL-Calico Bush-NY-1931-Macmillan-213p-cl,wood engrvngs,A Lewis-1st ed (s3,rub) 25.00

FIELD,RICHARD S-Provincial Courts of New Jersey, with Sketches of the Bench and Bar-NY-1849-xi,311,(1)p-cl (aa6,sl chip) 60.00

FIELD,SARA B-Barabbas-NY-1932-Boni-1st ed (w5,dj wn) 40.00

FIELD,WOOSTER B-Architectural Drawing-NY-1922-folio-buckrm,col frntis,illus-1st ed (ff10,cor bump) 45.00

FIELD,WOOSTER B-Architectural Drawing-NY-1922-McGraw Hill-4to-161p-brwn cl,col frntis,sketches,photos (r10) 30.00

FIELDER,MILDRED-Wild Bill and Deadwood-Seattle-(1965)-Superior-160p-dj illus by N C Wyeth,photos-Six Guns #715-1st ed (dd4,wn dj) 25.00

FIELDING,A-Upfold Farm Mystery-1932-Kinsey-1st Amer ed (s10,rprd dj) 25.00

FIELDING,MICHAEL-Parenthood-NY-1935-239p (g10) 20.00

FIELDING,SARAH-Governess, or, Little Female Academy-Lond-(1968)-OUP-facs of 1749 1st ed (s3,f,f dj) 15.00

FIELDING,WILLIAM J-What Every Married Woman Should Know-Girard-(1924)-Haldeman Julius-64p-wrps,Little Blu Bk 657 (d1) 10.00

FIELDS,JOSEPH-ET AL-Wonderful Town-NY-(1953)-1st ed (b10,f dj) 40.00

FIFE,AUSTIN-Saints of Sage and Saddle-Bloomington-1956-Indiana U Pr-367p-map e.p.-1st ed (cc4,dj) 25.00

FIFE,G B-Lindbergh. The Lone Eagle-NY-(1928)-8vo-iv,284p-cl,frntis,30p plts (s2,sp fade) 25.00

FIFTH BATTALION HIGHLAND LIGHT INFANTRY IN THE WAR 1914 TO 1918-Glasgow-1921-priv prtd-250p-blu dec cl,illus,fldg pckt map-scarce (jj2) 175.00

FIFTY TEXAS RARITIES-Ann Arbor-1946-Clements Libr-40p-wrps-1st ed (a9) 45.00

FIGHTING THE WHALES-NY-1869-Appleton-16mo-169p+ads-orig red cl,gilt,4 chromo plts-1st ed (hh9) 75.00

FIGUEROA,DON J-Manifesto to the Mexican Republic-Oakland-1952-103p-ltd to 750c-1st ed (t7) 15.00

FILBEE,MARJORIE-Dictionary of Country Furniture-NY-1977-Hearst Bks-4to-200p-gry bds,illus (r10,f,f dj) 10.00

FILBY,FREDERICK A-History of Food Adulteration and Analysis-Lond-(1934)-Allen & Unwin-269p-1st ed (l6) 30.00

FILLMORE,JAMES H-Hours of Song-Cin-(1879)-Fillmore Bros-127,(1)p-bds-revised ed (g1) 15.00

FINAUGHTY,W-Recollections of Wm. Finaughty, Elephant Hunter-Capetown-1957-127p (gg3,f,dj) 35.00

FINCH,CHRISTOPHER-Art of Walt Disney-NY-(1973)-Abrams-lg 4to-458p-351 col plts-1st ed(wi cut-out Mickey on cov) (bb5,tn & chip dj) 55.00

FINCH,I-Travels in the United States of America and Canada-Lond-1833-L,R,O,B,G & L-ornate 1/2 lea-Howes F131-1st ed (ee6) 175.00

FINCH,JAMES K-Topographic Maps and Sketch Mapping-NY-(1920)-Wiley & Sons-8vo-xi,175p-grn cl,col frntis,2 col plts,fldg map laid in-1st ed (t10) 30.00

FINCHER,JACK-Sinister People-NY-(1977)-Putnam-8vo-221p-1st ed (gg5,f,sl wn dj) 15.00

FINCK,HENRY T-Musical Progress-Phila-(1923)-Presser-8vo-422p-1st ed (ee5,dj) 25.00

FINCK,HENRY T-Primitive Love and Love Stories-NY-1899-Scribner's-cl-1st ed (n8) 75.00

FINDLAY,HUGH-Garden Making & Keeping-NY-1928-252p (x6) 12.00

FINDLAY,HUGH-Garden Making and Keeping-NY-1932-Dbldy-252p-cl (x6) 10.00

FINDLEY,PALMER-Priests of Lucina, the Story of Obstetrics-Bost-1939-421p-1st ed (dd3,sp spot) 75.00

FINDLEY,TIMOTHY-Butterfly Plague-NY-1969-1st US ed (p5,f,dj) 30.00

FINDLEY,TIMOTHY-Last of the Crazy People-Lond-1967-auth 1st bk-1st Brit ed (p5,sl rub dj) 60.00

FINDLEY,TIMOTHY-Wars-NY-1977-1st US ed (p5,dj) 15.00

FINE,NATHAN-Labor and Farmer Parties in the United States 1828 to 1928-NY-1928-Rand Schl-1st ed (v5,hng crack,dj sp chip) 40.00

FINEGAN,JACK-Light from the Ancient Past-1946-Princeton U Pr-cl,illus-2nd prtg (n8) 27.50

FINERTY,JOHN F-War Path and Bivouac-Chig-1955-Lakeside Pr-379p-illus,maps-Lakeside Classics-Howes F136 (ff4) 25.00

FINGER,CHARLES J-Sailor Chanties and Cowboy Songs-Girard-(1923)-Haldeman-Julius-64p-wrps-Little Blu Bk 301 (j1) 15.00

FINGER,CHARLES-Heroes from Hakluyt-NY-(1928)-Holt-sm 4to-331p-cl,10 col woodcts-1st ed (s3) 20.00

FINGER,ERNEST-Gonorrhoea-NY-1894-Wm Wood-7p col plts,36 engrvngs-3rd ed (p6,sp chip) 75.00

FINGER-POST TO PUBLIC BUSINESS-NY-(1864)-Dick & Fitzgerald-377p-cl (g1) 25.00

FINK,BRUCE-Lichens of Minnesota-Wash-1910-GPO/US Nat Herb-269p-wrps,illus (x6,wrps wn) 30.00

FINK,EDITH-Hot Birds & Cold Bottles-(1972)-Delacorte-392p-dec wht bds-1st prtg (q8,dj) 27.50

FINKELSTEIN,SIDNEY-Jazz-(1948)-Citadel-1st ed (o9,f,dj rub,sl chip & tn) 45.00

FINKELSTEIN,SIDNEY-Jazz-NY-(1948)-Citadel-1st ed (w1,f,dj) 20.00

FINLAYSON,H H-Red Centre-Sydney/Lond-1943-Angus & Robertson-8vo-153p-blk cl,52 plts-5th ed (p8,hng weak) 35.00

FINLEY,FLORENCE-Oldtimers of Southwest Texas-Uvalde-1957-Hornby Pr-318p-illus-v scarce-1st ed (f9,dj sl chip & wn) 65.00

FINLEY,JAMES B-History of the Wyandott Mission at Upper Sandusky...-Cin-1840-432p-lea-Howes F144-scarce-1st ed (pp6,sl crack & sp wn) 250.00

FINLEY,MARTHA-Elsie and Her Namesakes-NY-1905-Dodd,Mead-sm 8vo-1st ed (s1) 45.00

FINLEY,MARTHA-Elsie's Journey on Inland Waters-NY-1895-Dodd,Mead-sm 8vo-blndstmpd maroon cl-1st ed (s1) 45.00

FINLEY,REV JAMES B-Autobiography of...-Cin-1853-R P Thompson-455p-illus-Howes F143-1st ed (nn6,fox,rbnd wi orig cov & sp 125.00

FINLEY,REV JAMES B-Sketches of Western Methodism-Cin-1854-Methdst Bk Cncrn-551p-grn cl,frnts-Howes F146-1st ed (k2,sl rub) 65.00

FINLEY,RUTH E-Lady of Godey's-Phila-(1931)-Lippincott-318p-bds,illus-1st ed (n6,sl mar frnt cov) 25.00

FINN,MOLLY-Summer Feasts-(1979)-S&S-293p-bds-1st prtg (q8,dj) 15.00

FINN,WILLIAM J-Conductor Raises His Baton-NY-(1944)-Harper-8vo-302p-1st ed (ee5,f,dj) 20.00

FINNEY,BEN R-Polynesian Peasants and Proletarians-Cambridge-(1973)-Schenkman Publ-8vo-147p-cl-1st ed (y5,dj tn) 20.00

FINNEY,BRIAN-Christopher Isherwood-NY-1979-OUP-1st ed (z9,f,dj) 12.50

FINNEY,CHARLES G-Circus of Dr.Lao-NY-1982-LED-illus,C Van Vliet,autg by illus (f3,f,box) 75.00

FINNEY,HUMPHREY-Stud Farm Diary-Middleburg-1959-Amer Racing-16mo-1st ed (j9,dj) 30.00

FINNEY,J-House of Numbers-1957-Eyre & Spottiswoode-1st Brit & 1st hdbk ed (x7,sl cocked sp,dj) 175.00

FINNEY,JACK-Body Snatchers-1955-E&S-1st Brit & hdbk ed (x2,dj) 325.00

FINNEY,JACK-Night People-GC-1977-1st ed (t5,sl chip dj) 20.00

FINNEY,JACK-Time and Again-NY-(1970)-S&S-1st ed (cc2,f,dj) 100.00

FINNEY,JACK-Unholy City-NY-(1937)-Vanguard Pr-orng bds wi labs on sp & recto-1st ed (cc2,sl rub) 35.00

FINNEY,PATRICIA-Shadow of Gulls-Lond-1977-Collins-1st ed (z8,vf,dj) 12.50

FIREBAUGH,ELLEN-Physician's Wife and the Things That Pertain to Her Life-Phila-1900-186p-woodcut illus (dd3) 60.00

FIREMAN,JANET-Spanish Royal Corps of Engineers in the Western Borderlands-Glendale-1977-250p-plain dj,text maps-Spain in the West Ser.,Vol.12 (e7,vf,dj) 65.00

FIRESTONE,O J-Other A Y Jackson-Tor-1979-M&S-8vo-272p-illus-1st ed (bb7,rub dj) 20.00*

FIRSOFF,V A-On Foot in the Cairngroms-Edinburgh-1965-12mo-113p-maps,photos (o10,f,dj) 18.00

FIRST PRESIDENCY-AN EPISTLE OF THE...-SLC-1886-19p-orig gry prtd wrps-Flake 1662-1st ed (bb8) 85.00

FIRTH,RAYMOND-We, The Tikopia-Lond-1961-G Allen-8vo-606p-cl,plts-3rd impr (y5,sun dj) 35.00

FIRTH,RAYMOND-Work of the Gods in Tikopia-Lond-1967-Athlone Pr-8vo-490p-cl,plts-Lond Sch Econ Mono on Soc Anthro 1 & 2-2nd ed (y5,sl wn dj) 38.00

FISCHER,JOHN-From the High Plains-NY-1978-181p-illus-1st ed (t7,f,dj) 15.00

FISCHER,L H-Lincoln's Gadfly, Adam Gurowski-(1964)-U of Ok-301p-illus-1st ed (v8,sl rub dj) 25.00

FISCHER,LOUIS-ED.-Thirteen Who Fled-NY-(1949)-Harper & Bros-244p-cl-1st ed (kk1,sl tn dj) 20.00

FISCHER,MAUDIE-ED.-Boonton Years, 1867 to 1967-(Boonton)-(1967)-4to-(2),67,(31)p-wrps,illus (aa6) 20.00

FISH,ROBERT L-Brazilian Sleigh Ride-NY-1965-1st ed (t5,f,dj) 35.00

FISH,ROBERT L-Diamond Bubble-NY-1965-Simon-1st ed (f4,dj) 10.00

FISH,ROBERT L-Fugitive-NY-1962-auth 1st bk-1st ed (t5,dj) 50.00

FISH,ROBERT L-Fugitive-NY-1962-Simon-auth 1st bk-1st ed (f4,dj) 20.00

FISH,ROBERT L-Hochmann Miniatures-NY-1967-1st ed (t5,dj) 30.00

FISH,ROBERT L-Incredible Schlock Homes-1966-S&S-1st ed (x7,dj sp sl wn,sunned) 85.00

FISH,ROBERT L-Isle of the Snakes-NY-1963-1st ed (t5,dj) 40.00

FISH,ROBERT L-Memoirs of Schlock Holmes-NY-1974-Bobbs-1st ed (e4,f,dj) 35.00

FISH,ROBERT L-Murder League-NY-1968-1st ed (t5,dj) 25.00

FISH,ROBERT L-Pursuit-GC-1978-1st ed (t5,f,dj) 30.00

FISH,ROBERT L-Rub A Dub Dub-1971-S&S-1st ed (x7,f,dj) 12.00

FISH,ROBERT L-Shrunken Head-1963-Simon-1st ed (s10,dj) 25.00

FISH,ROBERT L-Shrunken Head-NY-1963-1st ed (t5,sl chip dj) 35.00

FISHER,AILEEN-Going Barefoot-NY-(1960)-Crowell-4to-unpgd-pict cl,col & b&w illus,A Adams-1st ed (r3,f,dj) 16.00

FISHER,DOROTHY C-Vermont Tradition-Bost-1953-Little,Brown-later prtg (h9,wn dj) 15.00

FISHER,GERARD-Hospitality for Murder-NY-1959-Washburn-1st US ed (g4,f,dj) 10.00

FISHER,J-Fulmar-Lond-1952-New Naturalist,No.6-8vo-496p-cl,col plt,82 photos(4 col),70 maps-1st ed (y8,dj chip) 125.00

FISHER,J-Sea Birds-Bost-1954-8vo-320p-cl,77 photos(9 col),66 maps (y8,sp spot,wn dj) 60.00

FISHER,J-World of Birds-1964-MacDonald-4to-288p-col illus-1st ed (bb3,cov spots,dj) 35.00

FISHER,J-World of Birds-GC-(1964)-4to-288p-cl,photos,maps (y8,underlinings,dj) 40.00

FISHER,JOEL-Bibliography of American Mountain Ascents-NY-1946-297p-1st ed (p10) 45.00

FISHER,JOHN-World of the Forsytes-Lond-(1976)-Secker & Warburg-sm 4to-224p-red cl,col & b&w photos-1st prtg (q8,dj) 20.00

FISHER,KATHARINE-Good Meal and How to Prepare Them-1929-Good Hskpng-7th ed (v6,sl soil cov) 12.00

FISHER,M F K-Among Friends-NY-1971-Knopf-306p-1st ed (o6,dj) 20.00

FISHER,M F K-An Alphabet for Gourmets-1949-Viking-255p-dec red cl,drwngs-1st ed (q8,dj) 45.00

FISHER,M F K-An Alphabet for Gourmets-NY-1949-Viking-255p-illus,M Bileck-1st ed (o6) 25.00

FISHER,M F K-Art of Eating-(1954)-World-750p-grn bds (q8,dj) 35.00

FISHER,M F K-As They Were-NY-1982-1st ed (q5,f,dj) 20.00

FISHER,M F K-Cordiall Water-Bost-(1961)-Little,Brown-16mo-178p-1st ed (o6,sl tn dj) 40.00

FISHER,M F K-Here Let Us Feast-1946-Viking-491p-blu cl-1st ed (q8,dj) 40.00

FISHER,M F K-Here Let Us Feast-NY-1946-Viking-1st ed (e8,dj) 50.00

FISHER,M F K-Map of Another Town-Bost-(1964)-Little,Brown-273p-1st ed (o6,tn dj) 35.00

FISHER,M F K-Not Now, But Now-NY-1947-Viking-1st ed (mm5,f,f dj) 60.00
FISHER,M F K-Serve it Forth-NY-1937-Harper & Bros-253p-auth 1st bk-1st ed (o6,dj) 45.00
FISHER,M F K-Sister Age-NY-1983-1st ed (m4,f,dj) 17.50
FISHER,M F K-Sister Age-NY-1983-1st ed (q5,f,dj) 20.00
FISHER,M F K-With Bold Knife & Fork-NY-1969-1st ed (p5,sl chip dj) 40.00
FISHER,MAJ A T-Through the Stable and Saddle Room-Lond-1890-Bentley-1st ed (j9) 65.00
FISHER,O C-King Fisher-(1966)-U of Okla Pr-12mo-xvii,157p-Wstrn Frntr Libr Ser-1st ed (aa3,f,dj) 35.00
FISHER,O C-King Fisher-(1966)-U of Okla Pr-157p-Six Guns 724-1st ed (t8,f,dj) 30.00
FISHER,R A-Contributions to Mathematical Statistics-NY-1950-J Wiley & Sons-4to-blu cl-1st ed (c2,dj) 40.00
FISHER,RALPH-Guide to Javelina-Tex-1957-8vo-208p (m3,vf,dj) 25.00
FISHER,REV H D-Gun and the Gospel-KC-1902-Hudson Kimberly-347p-illus-4th ed (v2) 45.00
FISHER,ROBIN-Captain James Cook and His Times-Canberra-1979-Austr Nat'l U Pr-8vo-278p-gry cl,wht sp titles,map e.p.,31 illus,11 maps,4 tabls-1st ed (nn1,dj) 40.00
FISHER,STEVE-Hell Black Night-LA-1970-Sherbourne-1st ed (s4,f,dj) 37.50
FISHER,STEVE-Hell Black Night-LA-1970-Sherbourne-auth 1st bk-1st ed (p4,f,dj) 37.50
FISHER,STEVE-Hell-Black Night-1970-Sherbourne Pr-1st ed (s10,dj) 20.00
FISHER,STEVE-Image of Hell-1961-Dutton-1st ed (s10,sl chip dj) 25.00
FISHER,VARDIS-April-Caldwell,GC-(1937)-1st trd ed (j5,f,dj) 50.00
FISHER,VARDIS-City of Illusion-NY-(1941)-382p-pict cl-1st ed (t7) 15.00
FISHER,VARDIS-In Tragic Life-Caldwell-1932-Caxton-1st ed (w1,f,f dj) 60.00
FISHER,VARDIS-Neurotic Nightingale-1935-Casanova-ltd to 300c,autg (pp9,dj chip,wn) 125.00
FISHER,VARDIS-Suicide or Murder-Denver-(1962)-Alan Swallow-288p-illus,map e.p.-1st ed (ff4) 40.00
FISHER,VARDIS-Tale of Valor-1958-Dbldy-456p-1st ed (r8,dj chip,edgewn) 55.00
FISHER,VARDIS-Tale of Valor-NY-1958-Dbldy-1st ed (h8,f,f dj) 65.00
FISHER,VARDIS-We Are Betrayed-GC-1935-1st ed (r5,f,dj) 125.00
FISHER,W H-Top of the World-NY-1926-178p-pict cov-1st ed (q10,f) 25.00
FISHER,WELTHY H-Top of the World-NY/Cin-1926-Abingdon Pr-178p-g dec pict cl,32 photos plts-1st ed (ll1) 35.00
FISHMAN,ALFRED P-Circulation of the Blood-NY-1964-Oxford U Pr-lg 8vo-xiv+859p-brwn cl,illus-1st ed (c2) 75.00
FISHWICK,MARSHALL W-Lee After the War-NY-(1963)-242p-illus-1st ed (n3,f,dj sl wn,chip) 22.50
FISK,MAY I-Eternal Feminine-NY-1911-Harper & Bros-239p-cl (c1) 15.00
FISK,NICHOLAS-Rag a Bone and a Hank of Hair-NY-(1982)-Crown-1st US ed (h3,f,dj) 15.00
FISKE,JOHN-Mississippi Valley in the Civil War-Bost-(1900)-368p-maps-1st ed (c4,cov sl wn) 40.00
FISKE,JOHN-Witchcraft in Salem Village-Bost-1923-Houghton Mifflin-16mo-(iv)+60p-rprntd frm "New France and New England"-1st separate ed (y9) 25.00
FISKE,TURBESE LUMMIS-Charles F Lummis-Norman-(1975)-226p-dbl-col,photos,illus,col plt-1st ed (v7,f,dj) 25.00
FITCH,A H-Junipero Serra-Chig-1914-364p-frntis,illus,fldg map-Howes F3590-1st ed (t7) 28.00
FITCH,GEORGE H-Comfort Found in Good Old Books-SF-(1911)-Paul Elder-sm 8vo-xxi,172p-cl (w2) 15.00
FITCH,GEORGE H-Critic in the Occident-SF-1913-Paul Elder-8vo-178p-tan cl,tip in plts (r10) 25.00
FITCH,MICHAEL H-Chattanooga Campaign-Madison-1911-Wisc Hist Comm-255p-frntis map,maps-ltd 1st ed (o7,sp soil) 50.00
FITCH,MICHAEL H-Chattanooga Campaign-np-1911-255p-maps-ltd to 2500c-1st ed (n3,sp sl discol) 42.50
FITCH,NOEL R-Sylvia Beach and the Lost Generation-Lond-1983-Souvenir-447p-illus-1st Brit ed (kk5,dj cor bump) 25.00
FITCHET,W H-ED.-Wellington's Men-Lond-1900-1st ed (k5,sl drknd bndg) 20.00
FITCHETT,CARLTON-Rimes of a Reporter-Seattle-1946-Superior Publ-157p-blk cl-Memorial ed (b6) 10.00
FITCHETT,W H-ED.-Wellington's Men-Lond-1900-419p-red dec cl-1st ed (b7,f) 40.00
FITE,GILBERT C-Mount Rushmore-Norman-1952-272p-photos-1st ed (t7,dj) 15.00
FITHIAN,PHILIP V-Journal & Letters of Philip Vickers Fithian, 1773 to 1774-Williamsburg-1943-xlv,323p-cl,plts (aa6) 35.00
FITHIAN,PHILIP V-Philip Vickers Fithian Journal and Letters, 1767 to 1774-Princeton-1900-xxi,(3),320p-cl,plts (aa6) 100.00
FITHIAN,PHILIP V-Philip Vickers Fithian, 1775 to 1776-Princeton-1934-xviii,279p-cl,fldg maps (aa6) 50.00
FITTER,R S R-Pocket Guide to British Birds-NY-1953-8vo-240p-cl,112 plts(64 col) (y8,dj) 15.00
FITTS,JAMES F-Bartered Birthright-Springfield-(1890)-Mast,Crowell & Kirkptrck-85p-wrps-Farm & Fireside Library #65 (j1) 12.50
FITTS,JAMES F-Sharp Night's Work-Chig-(1888)-Laird & Lee-170p+ads-cl-rare (a1,rear cov spots,hng wn) 40.00
FITZ,G-N. American Head Hunting-NY-1957-188p (gg3,f,dj) 10.00
FITZ,GRANCEL-How to Measure & Score Big-Game Trophies-NY-1963-4to-88p-wrps,illus,photos-1st ed (m3,f) 25.00
FITZGERALD,C P-Barbarian Beds-So Brunswick-1965-17 plts-1st Amer ed (kk4,dj) 45.00
FITZGERALD,CAPT HUGH-Sam Steele's Adventures on Land and Sea-Chig-1906-Reilly & Britton (y2) 450.00
FITZGERALD,E A-Highest Andes-NY-1899-390p-45 photos(1 fldg),2 fldg maps-1st US ed (a4,sl fox) 190.00
FITZGERALD,ED-Ballplayer-1957-Barnes-1st ed (p7,f,dj) 35.00
FITZGERALD,ED-ED.-Book of Major League Clubs-1952-Barnes-2 vols,orig box-1st ed (s8,pgs brnd,f dj,box) 65.00
FITZGERALD,EDWARD-Fitzgerald Friendship-Lond-1932-Faber & Faber-ltd to 750c-1st ed (x9) 40.00
FITZGERALD,F SCOTT-Afternoon of an Author-NY-1957-1st ed (s5,dj) 60.00
FITZGERALD,F SCOTT-Afternoon of an Author-NY-1957-Scribners-1st ed (bb2,dj) 45.00
FITZGERALD,F SCOTT-All the Sad Young Men-NY-1926-Scribner's-1st issue wi perfect type-1st ed (c10) 125.00
FITZGERALD,F SCOTT-All the Sad Young Men-NY-1926-Scribners-8vo-grn cl-1st ed (oo8) 100.00

FITZGERALD,F SCOTT-Basil and Josephine Stories-NY-1973-Scribner's-1st ed (e10,sl soil dj) 50.00

FITZGERALD,F SCOTT-Basil and Josephine Stories-NY-1973-Scribner's-1st ed thus (j8,f,dj) 40.00

FITZGERALD,F SCOTT-Beautiful and Damned-NY-1922-Scribner-8vo-grn cl-1st iss wi "Published March 1922" on cpyrt pg-1st ed (x3,sl rub) 125.00

FITZGERALD,F SCOTT-Beautiful and Damned-NY-1922-Scribner-8vo-grn cl-2nd iss wi ads-1st ed (x3) 75.00

FITZGERALD,F SCOTT-Beautiful and Damned-NY-1922-Scribners-1st iss w/o Scribner's seal-1st ed (aa8,sp dull,cors sl wn) 100.00

FITZGERALD,F SCOTT-Bits of Paradise-1973-Scribner's-1st ed (x2,dj) 38.00

FITZGERALD,F SCOTT-Bits of Paradise-NY-1973-Scribner's-1st ed (e8,f,f dj) 50.00

FITZGERALD,F SCOTT-Crack Up-(NY)-(1945)-New Directions-8vo-cl/dec bds,prtd sp labl-1st ed (ll10,f,dj sp sl wn) 150.00

FITZGERALD,F SCOTT-Crack-Up-(NY)-(1945)-New Directions-347p-1st prtg wi t.p. in red & blk-1st ed (e5,e.p. sl brwnd,dj) 175.00

FITZGERALD,F SCOTT-Dear Scott/Dear Max-Lond-(1973)-Cassell-1st Brit ed (e10,f,dj) 50.00

FITZGERALD,F SCOTT-Dear Scott/Dear Max-NY-1971-Scribner's-1st ed (e10,f,sp spot dj) 25.00

FITZGERALD,F SCOTT-Flappers and Philosophers-NY-1920-Scribners-orig cl-wi all points-1st ed (ee2,sl fade sp) 350.00

FITZGERALD,F SCOTT-Great Gatsby-NY-1925-Scribner's-1st ed,1st issue (c10) 275.00

FITZGERALD,F SCOTT-Last Tycoon-NY-1941-Scribner's-476p-blu cl,t.e. red-1st ed (k5,brwnd e.p.,dj sp sl chip) 350.00

FITZGERALD,F SCOTT-Pat Hobby Stories-1962-Scribners-1st ed (m9,dj sl chip & tn) 45.00

FITZGERALD,F SCOTT-Pat Hobby Stories-NY-1962-Scribner's-1st ed (c10,f dj) 60.00

FITZGERALD,F SCOTT-Stories-NY-1951-Scribner's-8vo-cl-1st ed (ll10,f,dj spot,soil) 75.00

FITZGERALD,F SCOTT-Tales of the Jazz Age-NY-1922-Scribner's-8vo-grn cl-Bruccoli A9-1st ed (jj8) 225.00

FITZGERALD,F SCOTT-Taps at Reveille-NY-(1935)-Scribner's-1st ed,2nd state(pgs 349-352 tip-in) (aa10,sl tn dj) 750.00

FITZGERALD,F SCOTT-Taps at Reveille-NY-1935-Scribner's-2nd state-1st ed (b10,dj) 800.00

FITZGERALD,F SCOTT-Taps at Reveille-NY-1935-Scribner's-8vo-grn cl-1st state wi p 349 to 52 not canceled & p 351,lines 29,30 "Oh,catch it--oh, catch it..."-1st ed (x3,dj sl chip,folded) 1,000.00

FITZGERALD,F SCOTT-Tender is the Night-Lond-(1953)-Grey Walls Pr-new ed,revised (m7,f dj) 100.00

FITZGERALD,F SCOTT-Three Comrades-Carbondale-1978-1st ed (p5,dj) 25.00

FITZGERALD,F SCOTT-Vegetable-NY-1923-Scribner's-1st ed,1st iss (aa8,sp drknd) 125.00

FITZGERALD,JOHN D-Papa Married a Mormon-Englewood-1955-298p-photos-Six Guns #728-1st ed (t7,dj) 12.50

FITZGERALD,ZELDA-Save Me the Waltz-Lond-(1953)-Grey Walls-1st Brit ed (w6,dj) 95.00

FITZGIBBON,THEODORA-Art of British Cooking-1965-Dbldy-366p-red cl,map e.p.-1st Amer ed (q8,dj) 12.50

FITZGIBBON,THEODORA-COMP.-Pleasures of the Table-1981-Oxford U Pr-16mo-92p-grn cl-1st prtg (q8,dj) 12.50

FITZHUGH,LESTER N-Canon Smoke-Hillsboro-1971-209p-1st ed (n10,f,dj) 75.00

FITZHUGH,LESTER N-Texas Batteries, Battalions, Regiments, Commanders...Confederate States Army 1861 to 1865-Midlothian-1959-Mirror Pr-33p-wrps-1st ed (w3,f) 27.50

FITZPATRICK,J P-Transvaal from Within-NY-1899-452p-grn cl-1st Amer ed (gg2) 75.00

FITZROY,V M-Eat and Be Merry-Lond-nd(ca.1930)-Allen & Unwin-211p (r6) 10.00

FITZROY,YVONNE-Canadian Panorama-Lond-1929-Methuen-grn cl,e.p. maps,19 photos-1st ed (ff7,sl sun sp) 25.00

FITZSIMMONS,BERNARD-150 Years of North American Railroads-Secaucus-1982-224p-1st ed (n4,f,f dj) 15.50

FITZSIMMONS,CORTLAND-70,000 Witnesses-NY-1931-McBride-1st ed (e4) 10.00

FITZSIMMONS,CORTLAND-Death Rings a Bell-1942-Lipincott-1st ed (s10,dj) 15.00

FITZSIMMONS,CORTLAND-Evil Men Do-NY-1941-Stokes-1st ed (k4,dj) 30.00

FITZSIMMONS,CORTLAND-Tied for Murder-Phila-1943-Lippincott-1st ed (f4,sl rprd dj) 20.00

FITZSIMONS,F W-Natural History of South Africa:Birds-Lond-1923-8vo-2 vols-cl,10 col plts,photos (y8) 90.00

FIVE-STAR FAVORITE RECIPES FROM FRIENDS OF MAMIE AND IKE-NY-(1974)-Golden Pr-272p-prpl cl,col photos-1st ed (q8,f,dj) 25.00

FLACK,MARJORIE-Angus and the Cat-GC-1931-Dbldy,Doran-1st ed (pp10,sl soil,edgewn) 60.00

FLACK,MARJORIE-Away Goes Jonathan Wheeler-GC-1944-GC Publ-oblng 8vo-unpgd-pict bds,cov illus,H Larsson-1st ed (s3,cov wn) 25.00

FLAGG,A L-Rockhounds and Arizona Minerals-Phoenix-1944-82p-col frntis,col plts(2 tip-in)-1st ed (t7,autg) 32.50

FLAGG,FANNIE-Coming Attractions-NY-1981-Morrow-1st ed (j6,dj) 50.00

FLAGG,FANNIE-Coming Attractions-NY-1981-Morrow-auth 1st bk-1st ed (bb1,f,sl creased dj) 75.00

FLAGG,OSCAR-Review of the Cattle Business in Johnson Co.,Wyoming since 1892...-NY-1969-82p-pict cl-Six Guns #2481-scarce-1st ed thus (t7) 30.00

FLAHERTY,FRANCIS-Elephant Dance-NY-1937-8vo-136p-photos-1st ed (m3,fray dj) 12.50

FLAHERTY,TOM-Masters-1961-HR&W-1st ed (dd8,dj) 15.00

FLAKE,CHAD-ED.-Mormon Bibliography 1830 to 1930-SLC-1978-825p-cl-1st ed (bb8,as new) 150.00

FLAMMARION,CAMILLE-Unknown-NY-1905-Harper & Bros-cl-1st Amer ed (o8,sp sunned) 17.50

FLANAGAN,CATHLEEN C-American Folklore-Metuchen-1977-406p-cl-1st ed (aa1,f) 15.00

FLANDERS,ALLAN-Management & Unions-Lond-1970-Faber & Faber-317p-1st ed (ff1,edgetn dj) 15.00

FLANDRAU,GRACE-Historic Northwest Adventure Land-np-nd-32p-wrps,photos,maps-Smith #3135-1st ed (t7) 17.50

FLANNAGAN,ROY C-Story of Lucky Strike-np-1938-(Amer Tobacco Co)-illus-publ for 1939 World's Fair-1st ed (y10,sl soil) 23.00

FLANNER,JANET-Stronger Sex as Seen by Vertes-NY-1941-Hyperion Pr-orig acetate dj-ltd to 1750c (l9,sl soil cov,sl fox,dj) 145.00

FLANNER,JANET-Stronger Sex as Seen by Vertes-NY-1941-Hyperion Pr-oversized-24 handcol plts-ltd to 1750c,nbrd (o5) 150.00

FLATTER,RICHARD-Hamlet's Father-New Haven-1949-Yale-1st ed (x9,f,dj) 10.00

FLEAY,D-Nightwatchmen of Bush and Plain-1968-Jacaranda-163p-col & b&w photos-1st ed (bb3,f,dj) 35.00

FLEAY,D-Nightwatchmen of Bush and Plain-Melbourne-1968-8vo-(10),163p-photos (y8,dj) 40.00

FLEET,B-ED.-Virginia Plantation Family During the Civil War-Charlottesville-1977-374p-illus,ports,map (z10,as new in dj) 20.00

FLEISCHLI,JOSEPH-Saint Bernard-Chig-1936-Judy-106p-photos,drwngs-1st ed (v8,dj sunned & sl chip) 20.00

FLEISCHMAN,PAUL-Graven Images-NY-(1982)-Harper & Row-85p-cl bckd pict bds,illus,A Glass-1st ed (r3,f,dj) 20.00

FLEITMANN,LIDA L-Comments on Hacks and Hunters-NY-1921-Scribner-1st ed (h9) 45.00

FLEMING,ALEXANDER-Recent Advances in Vaccine and Serum Therapy-Lond-1934-J & A Churchill-x+463p+ads-grn cl,5 diagrams-1st ed (g2,some pnclng) 65.00

FLEMING,CLINT-When the Fish are Rising-NY-1947-8vo-205p-frontis-1st ed (m3) 12.00

FLEMING,DONALD-William H Welch and the Rise of Modern Medicine-Bost-1954-216p-1st ed (g10,dj) 25.00

FLEMING,G H-Unforgettable Season-1981-Holt Rinehart-1st ed (r7,dj) 22.50

FLEMING,G H-Unforgettable Season-1981-HR&W-photos-1st ed (s8,f,chip dj) 30.00

FLEMING,HOWARD-Narrow Gauge Railways in America-1949-Hardy-8vo-101p-illus (nn7,dj tn) 43.00

FLEMING,IAN-Bonded Fleming-NY-1965-Viking-1st ed thus (g4,f,dj) 15.00

FLEMING,IAN-Casino Royale-1954-Macmillan-1st Amer ed (s10,dj tn & sp chip) 375.00

FLEMING,IAN-Chitty Chitty Bang Bang-1964-Random-1st Amer ed (x7,dj) 45.00

FLEMING,IAN-Diamond Smugglers-(1957)-Cape-1st ed (x7,dj) 135.00

FLEMING,IAN-Diamonds are Forever-Lond-(1956)-Cape-1st ed (aa10,f,dj) 1,000.00

FLEMING,IAN-Doctor No-1958-Macmillan-1st Amer ed (x7,f,dj) 175.00

FLEMING,IAN-Dr.No-Lond-(1958)-J Cape-girl's silhouette on frnt cov-1st ed (g6,sl wn dj) 175.00

FLEMING,IAN-For Your Eyes Only-NY-1960-Viking-1st US ed (h4,dj fray,sl chip) 35.00

FLEMING,IAN-From Russia With Love-(1957)-Cape-1st ed (x2,dj) 245.00

FLEMING,IAN-From Russia with Love-NY-1957-Macmillan-1st US ed (h4,dj missing chips) 50.00

FLEMING,IAN-Gilt Edged Bonds-NY-1961-Macmillan-thck 8vo-cl-1st ed (x10,f,sp sunned dj) 35.00

FLEMING,IAN-Goldfinger-Lond-(1959)-J Cape-1st Brit ed (s6,sl rub dj) 175.00

FLEMING,IAN-Goldfinger-NY-1959-Macmillan-1st Amer ed (w9,f,dj sl nick & tn) 150.00

FLEMING,IAN-Live and Let Die-1955-Macmillan-1st Amer ed (x7,f,sl tn dj) 265.00

FLEMING,IAN-Man with the Golden Gun-Lond-(1965)-1st Brit ed (q5,dj) 40.00

FLEMING,IAN-Man with the Golden Gun-Lond-(1965)-J Cape-1st Brit ed (bb1,dj) 45.00

FLEMING,IAN-Man With the Golden Gun-NY-1965-NAL-1st Amer ed (s9,dj) 20.00

FLEMING,IAN-Man with the Golden Gun-NY-1965-NAL-1st US ed (g4,f,dj) 15.00

FLEMING,IAN-More Gilt Edged Bonds-1965-Macmillan-1st ed thus (s10,dj) 17.50

FLEMING,IAN-Octopussy & the Living Daylights-Lond-(1966)-Cape-1st ed (q4,f,dj) 35.00

FLEMING,IAN-Octopussy & the Living Daylights-Lond-(1966)-J Cape-1st Brit ed (a5,f,dj) 45.00

FLEMING,IAN-On Her Majesty's Secret Service-NY-1963-1st US ed (t5,dj) 25.00

FLEMING,IAN-Spy Who Loved Me-NY-1962-Viking-1st US ed (e4,sp chip dj) 15.00

FLEMING,IAN-Thrilling Cities-Lond-(1963)-J Cape-1st ed (w9,f,dj) 75.00

FLEMING,IAN-Thrilling Cities-NY-1964-1st ed (j5,dj) 20.00

FLEMING,IAN-Thunderball-(1961)-Cape-1st ed (x2,dj) 115.00

FLEMING,IAN-Thunderball-NY-1961-Viking-1st US ed (w5,f,dj) 60.00

FLEMING,IAN-You Only Live Twice-Lond-1964-1st ed (q5,dj) 45.00

FLEMING,IAN-You Only Live Twice-Lond-1964-Cape-1st ed (x2,dj) 55.00

FLEMING,IAN-You Only Live Twice-NY-1964-NAL-1st US ed (f4,f,dj) 15.00

FLEMING,IAN-You Only Live Twice-NY-1964-NAL-1st US ed (s9,sl tn dj) 20.00

FLEMING,J A-Fifty Years of Electricity-1921-371p-110 photos,167 illus-rare-1st ed (h6,f) 110.00

FLEMING,J A-Principles of Electric Wave Telegraphy-Lond-1906-Longmans,Green-xx+671p-grn cl,illus-1st ed (j2) 150.00

FLEMING,JOAN-Screams from a Penny Dreadful-Lond-1971-Hamish-1st ed (e4,dj) 15.00

FLEMING,JOHN A-Principles of Electric Wave Telegraphy-1906-671p-photos,illus-rare-1st ed (h6,rprd) 110.00

FLEMING,P-News From Tartary-Lond-1936-384p-1st Brit ed (o10,f) 25.00

FLEMING,PETER-Bayonets to Lhasa-NY-1961-319p-illus-1st Amer ed (kk2,f,dj) 30.00

FLEMING,PETER-Brazilian Adventure-NY-1934-Scribner's-1st US ed (j3,dj) 20.00

FLEMING,V M-Campaigns of the Army of Northern Virginia including the Jackson Valley Campaign, 1861 to 1865-Richmond-1928-167p-fldg maps(1 col) (z10,pres cpy) 100.00

FLEMING,WALTER L-ED.-Documentary History of Reconstruction-(1966)-McGraw Hill-2 vols (dd9,dj) 35.00

FLETCHER,BOB-Corral Dust-Helena-(1936)-State Publ Co-87p-illus cov,illus (b6,autg) 17.50

FLETCHER,DANIEL C-Reminiscences of California and the Civil War-Ayer-1894-Huntley S Turner-196p-maroon cl,ports-Howes F188-1st ed (e2,f) 150.00

FLETCHER,FRANK-My Out-of-Doors-Littleton-1937-12mo-178p-photos (m3) 15.00

FLETCHER,H GEORGE-ED.-Miscellany for Bibliophiles-NY-1979-Grastoft & Long-1st ed (hh2,f,dj) 65.00

FLETCHER,HORACE-New Glutton or Epicure-NY-1908-Stokes-328p-grn bds-Bitting 160 (n6) 15.00

FLETCHER,J S-Behind the Monocle-1930-DD-1st ed (x7,wn dj) 17.00

FLETCHER,J S-Cartwright Gardens Murder-NY-1926-Knopf-1st US ed (e4,dj sp tn,wn) 45.00

FLETCHER,J S-Charing Cross Mystery-NY-1923-Putnam-1st US ed (e4) 15.00

FLETCHER,J S-Middle Temple Murder-1919-Knopf-1st Amer ed (s10,sp lettrng fade) 15.00

FLETCHER,J S-Mill House Murder-1937-Knopf-1st Amer ed (s10,sp chip dj) 25.00

FLETCHER,J S-Murder in the Squire's Pew-NY-1932-Knopf-1st US ed (k4,f,dj) 20.00

FLETCHER,J S-Murder of a Banker-1933-Knopf-1st Amer ed (s10,fade,dj) 25.00

FLETCHER,J S-Murder of the Secret Agent-NY-1934-Knopf-1st US ed (e4,rprd dj) 30.00

FLETCHER,J S-Passenger to Folkestone-NY-1927-Knopf-1st US ed (k4,f,chip dj) 20.00

FLETCHER,J S-South Foreland Murder-NY-1930-Knopf-1st US ed (f4,dj sl wn,intrnl taped) 20.00

FLETCHER,JEFFERSON B-Religion of Beauty in Woman ...-NY-1911-205p-cl (d1) 20.00

FLETCHER,PHINEAS-Piscatory Eclogues with Other Poetical Miscellanies-Ednbrgh-1771-12mo-151p+index-full calf-rare (m3,poorly rebkd) 135.00

FLETCHER,ROBERT H-Free Grass to Fences-NY-(1960)-Univ Publ-lg 8vo-236p-col frntis & e.p.,62 illus by C M Russell (bb4,dj) 50.00

FLETCHER,ROBERT S-From Cleveland by Ship to California,1849 to 1850-Durham-1959-145p-photos,map e.p.-1st ed (t7,dj) 13.50

FLETCHER,S W-Strawberry Growing-NY-1917-Macmillan-illus-Rural Life Ser-1st ed (y10,sl soil,cor bump) 30.00

FLETCHER,S W-Strawberry in North America-NY-1917-Macmillan-xvi+234p+ads-grn cl-1st ed (l2,few bent pgs) 18.00

FLETCHER,SYDNEY-Cowboy and His Horse-(1951)-G&D-4to-159p-drwngs-Herd #813-1st ed (t8,sl wn) 18.00

FLETCHER,WILLIAM-English and American Steam Carriages and Traction Engines-Lond-1904-Longmans,Green-xx+428p+ads-grn cl,250 illus-1st ed (c2) 125.00

FLEXNER,ABRAHAM-Medical Education: a Comparative Study-NY-1925-334p-1st ed (dd3) 100.00

FLEXNER,JAMES T-Lord of the Mohawks-Bost-(1979)-Little,Brown-400p-illus (ff4,dj) 20.00

FLEXNER,MARION-Out of Kentucky Kitchens-(1949)-F Watts-319p-tan cl-1st prtg (q8,dj fray) 20.00

FLEXNER,MARION-Out of Kentucky Kitchens-NY-(1949)-Franklin Watts-319p-1st ed (u6) 20.00

FLICK,ART-Art Flick's New Streamside Guide to Naturals & Their Imitations-NY-1969-12mo-173p-illus-1st trd ed (m3,f,dj) 20.00

FLICK,ART-Master Fly Tying Guide-NY-1972-4to-207p-photos,illus-1st prntng (m3,vf,dj) 37.50

FLINT,H M-Life of Stephen A Douglas-NY-1860-215p-pict wrps-1st ed (t7) 40.00

FLINT,MARTHA B-Garden of Simples-Lond-1901-David Nutt-307p-bds (m6,wn bds,soil) 35.00

FLINT,TIMOTHY-Recollections of the Last Ten Years in the Valley of the Mississippi-Carbondale-1968-SIU Pr-343p-cl,illus (w3,vf,dj) 15.00

FLOOD,CHARLES B-Lee, the Last Years-Bost-(1981)-308p-illus-1st ed (c4,f,dj) 20.00

FLOOD,CHARLES B-War of the Innocents-NY-(1970)-McGraw Hill-1st ed (ff3,f,dj) 35.00

FLORA,SNOWDEN D-Hailstorms of the United States-Norman-(1956)-U of Okla-8vo-201p-30 illus-1st ed (gg5,dj) 30.00

FLORIN,LAMBERT-Boot Hill-(1966)-Superior-4to-192p-illus-Six Guns #738-1st ed (r8,dj) 30.00

FLORIN,LAMBERT-Ghost Town Album-Seattle-(1962)-184p-dbl col,photos,sm maps-1st ed (u7,f,dj) 25.00

FLORIN,LAMBERT-Ghost Town El Dorado-Seattle-(1968)-192p-dbl col,photos,drwngs,sm maps-1st ed (u7,f,dj) 25.00

FLORIN,LAMBERT-Ghost Town Eldorado-(1968)-Superior-4to-192p-illus-1st ed (r8,dj) 30.00

FLORIN,LAMBERT-Ghost Town Trails-Seattle-(1963)-192p-dbl col,photos,map-1st ed (u7,f,dj) 25.00

FLORIN,LAMBERT-Ghost Town Treasures-Seattle-(1965)-192p-photos,sm maps-1st ed (u7,f,dj) 25.00

FLORIN,LAMBERT-Tales the Western Tombstones Tell-Seattle-nd-Superior-191p-illus-1st ed (bb4,dj) 15.00

FLORIN,LAMBERT-Victorian West-Seattle-1978-Superior-4to-photos-1st ed (t1,dj) 35.00

FLORIN,LAMBERT-Western Ghost Town Shadows-Seattle-(1964)-189 & 1 dbl col pgs,photos,sm maps-1st ed (u7,f,dj) 25.00

FLORIN,LAMBERT-Western Ghost Towns-(1961)-Superior-176p-illus-1st ed (r8,dj) 32.00

FLORIN,LAMBERT-Western Ghost Towns-Seattle-(1961)-174 & 2 dbl col pgs,photos(col frntis),maps-1st ed (u7,f,chip dj) 25.00

FLORIN,LAMBERT-Western Wagon Wheels-(1970)-Superior-4to-183p-illus-1st ed (r8,dj) 35.00

FLORIS,MARIA-Cooking for Love-Lond-(1959)-Putnam-217p-1st prtg (q8,dj) 16.50

FLORY,M A-Book about Fans-NY-1895-Macmillan-xiii,141p-pict cl,t.e.g.,plts,illus-1st ed (dd10,cov soil) 50.00

FLOURNOY,THEODORE-From India to the Planet Mars-New Hyde Park-1963-Univ Bks-cl-1st prtg (n8) 25.00

FLOURNOY,THEODORE-From India to the Planet Mars-NY/Lond-1900-Harper & Bros-sm 8vo-(xx)+446+(2)p-prntd dec grn cl-1st ed in Engl (y9,few chip pgs,shelfwn) 50.00

FLOURNOY,THEODORE-Spiritism and Psychology-NY-1911-Harper & Bros-cl-1st Amer ed (n8) 35.00

FLOWER,FRANK A-Edwin McMasters Stanton, the Autocrat of Rebellion, Emancipation and Reconstruction-Akron-1905-425,(1)p+(19)p index-cl (j1,sl spot cov,reinfrcd hngs) 20.00

FLOWER,JOHN-Moonlight Serenade-New Rochelle-1972-Arlington Hs-2nd prtg (u4,vf) 345.00

FLOWER,OLIVE-History of Oxford College for Women 1830 to 1928-(Hamilton)-(1949)-329p-cl (d1,f,dj) 20.00

FLOWER,WILLIAM-Horse, a Study in Natural History-Lond-1891-Kegan Paul-1st ed (j9) 25.00

FLOWERS,A W-Forty Years of Steam 1926 to 1966-Lond-1969-144p-1st ed (n4,f,dj) 24.95

FLOWERS,RALPH-Education of a Bear Hunter-NY-1975-8vo-277p-photos-1st ed (m3,vf,dj) 15.00

FLUCKIGER,F-Pharmacographia-Lond-1874-704p-qtr lea-1st ed (dd3) 200.00

FLYNN,BRIAN-Mystery of the Peacock's Eye-NY-1930-Macrae-1st US ed (g4) 10.00

FLYNN,ELIZABETH G-Daughters of America, Ella Reeve Bloor and Anita Whitney-NY-1942-Workers Libr-wrps-1st ed (v5) 30.00

FLYNN,ELIZABETH G-I Speak My Own Piece-NY-1955-Masses & Mainstream-325p-wrps-1st ed (r1,cov wrnkld,edgewn) 15.00

FLYNN,GEORGE L-ED.-Vince Lombardi on Football-NY-1973-NYGS-2 vols-g lettrng,padded bndg wi pict box,incl 33 1/3 rpm record,8x10 prnt-1st ed (y10,box sl soil,scrtchd) 40.00
FLYNN,JOHN T-Smear Terror-NY-(1947)-30p-wrps,dbl cols (a1) 10.00
FLYNN,PAUL V-History of St.John's Church-Newark-(1908)-xvii,217p-cl,plts (aa6) 35.00
FLYNN,WARREN-ED.-J B S Anthology-St.Louis-(1929)-John Burroughs Sch-pap-cov bds-1st ed (a10,sl soil bds) 75.00
FOCILLON,HENRI-Year 1000-NY-(1969)-Ungar-8vo-190p-20 illus-1st US ed (dd5,f,dj) 17.50
FODOR,NANDOR-Freud, Jung, and Occultism-New Hyde Park-1971-Univ Bks-cl-1st ed (o8,vf,dj) 25.00
FOESIG,HARRY-Trolleys of Montgomery County Pennsylvania-Forty Fort-1968-107p-wrps,map-1st ed (n4) 10.00
FOGDALL,ALBERTA B-Royal Family of the Columbia-Fairfield-1978-Ye Galleon-4to-330p-illus-1st ed (gg5,f,sl tn dj,autg) 30.00
FOISY,J ALBERT-Sentinellist Agitation in New England,1925 to 1928-Providence-(1930)-Prvdnce Visitor Pr-viii+234p-red cl-1st ed (h2) 45.00
FOLEY,D J-ED.-Flowering World of "Chinese" Wilson-1969-Macmillan-334p-photos-1st prtg (bb3,f,dj) 30.00
FOLEY,DANIEL J-Complete Book of Garden Ornaments,Complements and Accessories-NY-(1972)-tall 8vo-247p-400 b&w,25 col photos (x5,rprd dj) 19.00
FOLEY,JOHN P-ED.-Jeffersonian Encyclopedia-NY-1900-Funk & Wagnalls-xiv+1009p-calf-1st ed (b2) 50.00
FOLEY,RAE-Wake the Sleeping Wolf-NY-1952-Dodd-1st ed (f4,f,dj) 25.00
FOLLETT,J B-COMP.-Legal Tender Decision of the Supreme Court of the United States, Delivered by Judge Strong-St.Louis-1879-Hackstaff's Prnt-35p-cl cov wrps (d1) 15.00
FOLSOM,JOSEPH F-ED.-Municipalities of Essex County, New Jersey, 1666 to 1924-NY-1925-4to-4 vols-cl,plts (aa6) 125.00
FOLSOM,JOSEPH F-Lucas George-Somerville-1915-23p-wrps-rprntd from Somerset Cnty Hist Qtrly (aa6) 20.00
FOLSOM,W H C-Fifty Years in the Northwest-(St.Paul)-1888-Pioneer Pr-blk simulated lea-1st ed (p6,rbnd) 150.00
FONSECA,ESTHER H-Death Below the Dam-NY-1936-Dbldy CC-1st ed (g4,f) 15.00
FONSECA.LEW-Want to be a Baseball Champion-(Mpls)-(1945)-Wheaties Libr of Sports-29p-wrps (aa1) 15.00
FONTANA,BERNALD-ET AL-Papago Indian Pottery-Seattle-1962-156p-illus-1st ed (u7,dj) 25.00
FONTANA,BERNARD-ET AL-Papago Indian Pottery-Seattle-1962-163p-cl-1st ed (a1,dj sl wn,sm pc missng) 20.00
FOOTE,HARRIET-Mrs. Foote's Rose Book-Bost-1948-Branford-168p (x6,dj wn) 20.00
FOOTE,HENRY-Bench and Bar of the Southwest-St.Louis-1876-264p-rare-1st ed (jj1,sl wn & chip) 150.00
FOOTE,HORTON-Chase-NY-1956-1st ed (t5,dj) 30.00
FOOTE,HORTON-Harrison, Texas-NY-(1956)-Harcourt,Brace-auth co-1st bk iss same day as "The Chase"-1st ed (a10,dj) 75.00
FOOTE,J T-Anglers All-NY-1947-212p-illus,Weiler-1st ed (ee3,vf,vf dj) 35.00
FOOTE,J T-Anglers All-NY-1947-8vo-212p-1st ed (m3,sl chip dj) 40.00
FOOTE,J T-Dumb-Bell and Others-NY-1946-8vo-309p-1st ed (m3) 17.50
FOOTE,J T-Dumbell of Brookfield-NY-1917-261p (gg3) 25.00
FOOTE,J T-Fatal Gesture-NY-1933-12mo-68p-1st ed (m3,dj) 25.00
FOOTE,J T-Hoofbeats-NY-1950-8vo-243p (m3) 12.50
FOOTE,J T-Jing-Derrydale-1936-8vo-37p-ltd to 950c,nbrd-illus,A Ripley (m3) 70.00
FOOTE,J T-Pocono Shot-NY-1924-12mo-143p-1st ed (m3) 35.00
FOOTE,J T-Pocono Shot-NY-1938-143p (gg3,f) 23.00
FOOTE,J T-Trub's Diary-NY-1935-270p-grn cl,g dec (ee3,vf,vf dj) 32.00
FOOTE,J T-Wedding Gift-NY-1924-12mo-63p-1st ed (m3) 25.00
FOOTE,SHELBY-Follow Me Down-NY-1950-Dial-1st ed (t6,wn dj missing sm sp pc) 95.00
FOOTE,SHELBY-Jordan County-NY-1954-1st ed (r5,dj) 45.00
FOOTNER,HULBERT-Madame Storey-NY-1926-Doran-1st ed (d4) 20.00
FORBES,ALEXANDER-California-Lond-1839-xvi,352p-contemp calf,10 litho plts,fldg map,explanation slip-Howes F242-Graff 1377-1st ed (o4,rebkd,cov soil,sl fox) 900.00
FORBES,ALLAN-Sport in Norfolk County-Bost-1938-8vo-274p-ltd to 65oc,nbrd,autg-photos-scarce (m3,as new in dj & Box) 80.00
FORBES,ARCHIBALD-Afghan Wars-Lond-1896-337p-orng/brwn cl,illus-3rd ed (gg2,scribblings on e.p.) 85.00
FORBES,ARCHIBALD-Camps, Quarters and Casual Places-Lond-1896-344p-red cl-1st ed (b7) 40.00
FORBES,COLIN-Stockholm Syndicate-Lond-1981-Collins-1st ed (p4,f,dj) 27.50
FORBES,COLIN-Target Five-Lond-1973-Collins-1st ed (r4,f,dj) 35.00
FORBES,COSMO-Where the Cobra Sings-NY-(1932)-Macauley-pict dj-1st ed (ff3,vf,dj) 100.00
FORBES,ELIZABETH L-Wild Roses at Their Feet-(Vancouver)-(1971)-(Evergreen Pr)-prtd wrps,ports-Edwards & Lort #1384 (k10) 15.00*
FORBES,ESTHER-America's Paul Revere-Bost-1946-Houghton Mifflin-4to-46p-pict cl,col & b&w illus,Lynd Ward-1st ed (s3,vf,f dj) 35.00
FORBES,FREDERICK E-Dahomey and the Dahomians-Lond-1851-Longman,Brown,Green-2 vols-orig cl,10 tinted plts(4 handcol),3 plts-1st ed (bb6,ex-libr) 195.00
FORBES,GRAHAM-Boys of Columbia High on the Diamond-1911-G&D-pict cov (p7) 10.00
FORBES,H O-Hand Book of the Primates-Lond-1894-8vo-2 vols-half cl,29 col plts,8 fldg maps (y8,fade,cor wn) 65.00
FORBES,JACK D-Apache Navaho and Spaniard-Norman-1960-304p-photos-1st ed (t7,dj) 25.00
FORBES,JACK D-Apache, Navaho and Spaniard-Norman-(1960)-293p-illus,maps-1st ed (v7,f,dj,autg) 30.00
FORBES,JACK D-Warriors of the Colorado-Norman-(1965)-378p-illus-1st ed (e7,f,creased dj) 40.00
FORBES,R J-Technical Development of the Royal Dutch/Shell 1890-1940-Leiden-1957-E J Brill-4to-(x)+670p-blu cl,326 text figs,fldg plt & map,glossy pgs-1st ed (d2) 65.00
FORBES,ROBERT E-Transactions of Oliver Prince-NY-1924-Holt-1st US ed (d4) 30.00
FORBES,S A-Fishes of Illinois-1920-Ill Nat Hist Survey-2 vols-71 col plts,103 maps (bb3,cov sl wn & soil) 65.00

FORBES,S A-Fishes of Illinois-Danville-1908-4to-488p-col plts-scarce (m3,f) 150.00

FORBES-ROBERTSON,DIANA-Battle of Waterloo Road-NY-(1941)-Random-4to-cl,photos,Capa-1st ed (y3) 55.00

FORBUSH,E H-Birds of Massachusetts and Other New England States-1925,1929-Mass Dept of Agri-3 vols-col plts by Fuertes (d9) 175.00

FORBUSH,E H-Birds of Massachusetts and Other New England States-Norwood-1925,29,29(1925,27,29)-4to-3 vols-cl,col plts,photos (y8) 250.00

FORBUSH,E H-Natural History of the Birds of Eastern & Central North America-Bost-1939-4to-553p+plts,col illus (m3,f,badly fray dj) 40.00

FORBUSH,E H-Natural History of the Birds of Eastern & Central North America-Bost-1939-HM-553p-97 col plts by Fuertes (x6,sp fade) 25.00

FORBUSH,E H-Useful Birds and Their Protection-1913-451p-illus-4th ed (b9) 20.00

FORCE,GEN MANNING F-General Sherman-NY-1899-Appleton-353p-frntis,illus,maps-1st ed (cc6,uncut) 35.00

FORD,A-1826 Journal of John James Audubon-1967-U of Okla-409p-illus-1st ed(1st unabridged version) (bb3,f,dj) 20.00

FORD,ALICE-Pictorial Folk Art: New England to California-NY,Lond-1949 (ff10,dj edge rub,sl tn) 100.00

FORD,C-Where the Sea Breaks Its Back-1966-Little,Brown-206p-illus (gg3,vf,dj) 35.00

FORD,CHARLES H-Overturned Lake-Cin-1941-Little Man Pr-col illus by Matta-ltd to 400c-1st ed (w5,f,dj) 85.00

FORD,COREY-Best of ...-NY-1975-8vo-266p-illus-1st ed (m3,vf,dj) 30.00

FORD,COREY-Coconut Oil-NY-1931-8vo-217p-photos (m3) 25.00

FORD,COREY-Coconut Oil-NY-1931-Putnam-8vo-1st ed (u1,dj) 45.00

FORD,COREY-Corey Ford's Guide to Thinking-GC-1961-8vo-95p-illus-1st ed (m3,f,dj) 18.00

FORD,COREY-Day Nothing Happened-GC-1959-8vo-59p-photos (m3,f,dj) 11.00

FORD,COREY-From the Ground Up-NY-1943-Scribner-8vo-197p-5 illus-1st ed (dd5,sl tn dj) 30.00

FORD,COREY-Gazelle's Ears-NY-1926-8vo-306p-illus,Frueh-1st ed (m3) 30.00

FORD,COREY-Has Anybody Seen Me Lately-GC-1958-8vo-380p-illus,W Darrow Jr.-1st ed (m3,vf,dj) 15.00

FORD,COREY-Horse of Another Color-NY-1946-8vo-unpgd-illus,J Falter (m3,f,chip dj) 15.00

FORD,COREY-Minutes of the Lower Forty-NY-1962-HRW-8vo-1st ed (m3,f,dj) 70.00

FORD,COREY-Salt Water Taffy-NY,Lond-1929-8vo-206p-photos-1st ed (m3) 20.00

FORD,COREY-Uncle Perk's Jug-NY-1965-8vo-150p-illus,W Dower-2nd prntng (m3,vf) 45.00

FORD,COREY-You Can Always Tell a Fisherman But You Can't Tell Him Much-NY-1958-8vo-159p-Illus,W Dower-1st ed (m3,vf,dj) 65.00

FORD,CORYDON-Child of Democracy-Ann Arbor-1894-J V Sheehan-283p+app-wrps (z7) 75.00

FORD,DANIEL-Incident at Muc Wa-NY-1967-1st ed (v9,f,sl tn dj) 100.00

FORD,E B-Butterflies-1945-Collins-368p-48 col & 24 b&w plts-1st ed (bb3,cov stns) 30.00

FORD,FORD M-Fifth Queen-NY-nd-Vanguard-1st ed (f8,f,dj) 45.00

FORD,FORD M-Great Trade Route-NY-1937-Oxford-1st iss w/o illustrator's name-1st ed (cc2,f,dj) 75.00

FORD,FORD M-New York Essays-NY-1927-Wm Rudge-8vo-cl/bds-ltd to 750c,autg-1st ed (u10) 100.00

FORD,HENRY-Ford Ideals-Dearborn-1926-Dearborn Publ-456p-grn cl (cc3) 45.00

FORD,HUGH-Published in Paris-Lond-1975-Garnstone Pr-illus-1st ed (ll5,dj) 55.00

FORD,HUGH-Published in Paris-NY-(1975)-1st ed (s5,dj) 35.00

FORD,HUGH-Published in Paris-NY-(1975)-Macmillan-8vo-xviii,453p-cl-1st ed (x4,dj) 25.00

FORD,JAMES A-Tchefuncte Culture, An Early Occupation of the Lower Mississippi Valley-Menasha-1945-Scty for Amer Archeology-113p-prtd wrps,23 figs,12 plts (mm1,chip sp,sl soil,bent pgs) 15.00

FORD,JOHN D-An American Cruiser in the East-NY-1898-Barnes-8vo-xiii,468p-blu cl,g sp titles & pasteon cov dec,photos-1st ed (ll1) 95.00

FORD,JOHN S-ED.-Rip Ford's Texas-Austin-1963-UTP-519p-illus-1st ed (a9,tn dj) 100.00

FORD,LAUREN-Little Book about God-GC-(1934)-Dbldy-16mo-unpgd-pict bds,dbl pgs,col illus,auth (r3,f,dj) 20.00

FORD,LESLIE-All for the Love of a Lady-NY-1944-Scribner's-1st ed (d4,dj) 25.00

FORD,LESLIE-Bahamas Murder Case-NY-1952-Scribner's-1st ed (e4,dj) 17.50

FORD,LESLIE-By the Watchman's Clock-NY-1932-Farrar-1st ed (f4) 20.00

FORD,LESLIE-Date with Death-NY-1949-Scribners-1st ed (g4,dj) 15.00

FORD,LESLIE-Old Lover's Ghost-1940-Scribners-1st ed (x7,dj) 25.00

FORD,LESLIE-Philadelphia Murder Story-NY-1945-Scribners-1st ed (f4,f,dj) 25.00

FORD,MARY F-Dude Ranch Murders-1965-Avalon-1st ed (s10,soil dj) 12.50

FORD,PAUL L-Great K and A Train Robbery-NY-1897-Dodd Mead-blu pict cl-1st iss wi "train" absent from t.p.-BAL 6213-1st ed (f2,sl flecked cov) 35.00

FORD,PAUL L-His Version of It...-NY-1905-Dodd,Mead-109p-dec frnt cov,partly floral in grn,gold & rose on gry cl,decs,T B Hapgood,illus,H Hutt-1st ed (b1) 17.50

FORD,RICHARD-Piece of My Heart-NY-1976-Harper & Row-auth 1st bk-1st ed (g8,f,f dj) 250.00

FORD,ROBERT-Wind Between the Worlds-1957-McKay-1st ed (r9,sl tn dj) 30.00

FORD,SIMEON-Few Remarks-NY-1903-Dbldy,Page-8vo-340p-1st ed (p1) 30.00

FORD,WHITEY-Whitey and Mickey-1977-Viking-photos-1st ed (s8,f,f dj) 15.00

FORDE,DARYLL-Yako Studies-Lond-1964-OUP-8vo-288p-cl,illus,maps-1st ed (y5,dj) 30.00

FORDHAM,PETA-Villains-NY-(1972)-H&R-8vo-196p-1st US ed (dd5,dj) 10.00

FOREL,DR.AUGUST-Hypnotism, or Suggestion and Psychotherapy-NY-1906-Rebman-xii+370p-gry cl-1st ed in Engl (d2,sl fade cov) 75.00

FOREMAN,GRANT-ED.-Pathfinder in the Southwest-Norman-1941-298p-fldg map,illus-1st ed (e7,rprd dj) 65.00

FOREMAN,GRANT-Indian Removal-Norman-1932-U of Okla Pr-415p-illus,maps-Howes F258-1st ed (bb4) 100.00

FOREMAN,GRANT-Marcy and the Gold Seekers-Norman-1939-U of Okla Pr-8vo-433p-fldg map-1st ed (b3,f,dj) 45.00

FOREMAN,GRANT-Sequoyah-Norman-1938-90p-photos-1st ed (t7) 35.00

FORESTER,C S-Age of Fighting Sail-GC-(1956)-Dbldy-1st ed (aa10,dj) 100.00

FORESTER,C S-Bedchamber Mystery-Tor-1944-S J Reginald Saunders-pict papr bds-1st ed (gg8,f,sl chip dj) 125.00

FORESTER,C S-General-Bost-1936-Little,Brown-ltd to 2000c publ in US-1st ed (y1,f,sl wn dj) 300.00

FORESTER,C S-Gold From Crete-Bost-1970-Little,Brown-1st ed (x1,f,dj) 40.00

FORESTER,C S-Hornblower and the Hotspur-Bost-1962-Little,Brown-1st ed (z2,f,dj) 45.00

FORESTER,C S-Hornblower and the Hotspur-Lond-(1962)-M Joseph-1st ed (aa10,f,dj) 125.00

FORESTER,C S-Hornblower Companion-Bost-1964-Little,Brown-maps-1st ed (y1,dj) 100.00

FORESTER,C S-Hornblower Companion-Lond-(1964)-M Joseph-illus,30 maps-1st ed (aa10,f,dj) 200.00

FORESTER,C S-Lord Hornblower-Lond-(1946)-Joseph-1st Brit ed (a10,dj sl creased & soil) 30.00

FORESTER,C S-To The Indies-1940-Little,Brown-1st ed (x2,sl chip dj) 65.00

FORESTER,C S-To the Indies-Bost-1940-Little,Brown-1st ed (z2,f,dj sl tn & chip) 85.00

FORESTER,F-Dog by Dinks, Mayhew & Hutchinson-NY-1857-655p-illus (gg3,crease) 30.00

FORESTER,FRANK-Deer Stalkers-Derrydale-1930-8vo-185p-ltd to 750c-vol#4 of 4 of "Hitchcock Edition" (m3,f) 60.00

FORESTER,FRANK-ED.-Old Forest Ranger-NY-1856-12mo-383p-1/2 calf,gilt,frontis (m3,rebnd) 40.00

FORESTER,FRANK-ED.-Sporting Scenes & Sundry Sketches...Writings of J Cypress Jr.-NY-1842-Gould,Banks & Co-12mo-2vols-illus-scarce-1st ed (m3) 175.00

FORESTER,FRANK-Field Sports of the United States & British Provinces of North America-NY-1864-8vo-2 vols-illus (m3) 65.00

FORESTER,FRANK-Frank Forester On Upland Shooting-NY-1951-8vo-276p-illus (m3,vf,dj) 18.50

FORESTER,FRANK-Frank Forester's Fish & Fishing-NY-nd-Excelsior-8vo-512p-illus (m3) 60.00

FORESTER,FRANK-Frank Forester's Sporting Scenes & Characters-1857-T B Peterson-12mo-2 vols-illus-scarce-1st ed (m3,fair,bndg wn) 90.00

FORESTER,FRANK-Hints to Horse Keepers-NY-1901-Orange Judd-12mo-425p-illus (m3,f) 35.00

FORESTER,FRANK-My Shooting Box-Derrydale-1941-8vo-187p-ltd to 250c,nbrd-hand col illus,Robt Ball-scarce (m3,f) 190.00

FORESTER,FRANK-Quorndon Hounds-Derrydale-1930-8vo-145p-ltd to 750c-vol #3 of 4 of "Hitchcock Edition" (m3,f) 60.00

FORESTER,FRANK-Supplement to ... Fish & Fishing of the United States & British Provinces of North America-NY-1850-8vo-86p-col frontis-rare-1st ed (m3) 130.00

FORESTER,JOSEPH-Fishing-British Columbia's Commercial Fishing History-Saanichton-1975-4to-224p-photos,illus (m3,vf,dj) 12.50

FORKERT,OTTO M-From Gutenberg to the Cuneo Press-Chig-1933-Cuneo Press-31p-woodcuts (e1,wrps) 10.00

FORKNER,JOHN L-Historical Sketches and Reminiscences of Madison County, Indiana-Anderson-1897-1038,(1)p-cl (h1,sm holes joints,sl wn sp) 85.00

FORMAN,H-Tidewater Maryland Architecture & Gardens-NY-1956-208p (x6,dj) 20.00

FORMAN,W-Benin Art-Lond-1960-Paul Hamlyn-4to-58p text-dec tan bds,92 photos (r10,sl wn dj) 40.00

FORREST,EARLE R-Arizona's Dark and Bloody Ground-Caldwell-1936-370p-photos,map e.p.-Howes F265-scarce-1st ed (t7) 85.00

FORREST,EARLE R-Arizona's Dark and Bloody Ground-Caldwell-1936-Caxton-370p-red cl,map e.p.-1st ed (v1,sl edgewn) 75.00

FORREST,EARLE R-Arizona's Dark and Bloody Ground-Caldwell-1952-Caxton-382p-illus,map e.p.-Six Gun #747-rvsd & enlgd ed (cc4) 45.00

FORREST,EARLE R-Lone War Trail of Apache Kid-Pasadena-(1947)-Trail's End-143,(1)p-cl,col plt by C M Russell,map e.p.,illus-1st ed (v1) 60.00

FORREST,EARLE R-Missions and Pueblos of the Old Southwest-1929-A C Clark Co-386p-photos-1st ed (d3) 200.00

FORREST,GEORGE-Life of Lord Roberts, V.C.-Lond-1914-372p-blu cl,illus-1st ed (gg2) 75.00

FORREST,J R-Retribution. A Border Mystery-NY-(1906)-Ogilvie Publ-262p-cl (b1) 15.00

FORREST,RICHARD-Dew at Yew Corner-NY-1980-Holt-1st ed (q4,vf,dj) 17.50

FORREST,RICHARD-Wizard of Death-Indpls-1977-Bobbs-1st ed (l4,f,dj) 15.00

FORRESTER,FRANCIS-Arthur's Triumph-Bost-1864-Taggard & Thompson-64p-illus-cl (e1) 20.00

FORSEE,AYLESA-William Henry Jackson Pioneer Photographer of the West-NY-1964-205p-photos,illus-1st ed (t7,f,dj) 30.00

FORSHAW JOS M-Parrots of the World-NY-(1973)-thk folio-584p-illus by Wm T Cooper,col pict dj (w10,f,dj) 300.00

FORSHAW,J M-Australian Parrots-1981-Lansdowne-4to-312p-56 col plts,maps,photos (bb3) 80.00

FORSHAW,J M-Parrots of the World-1978-Landsdowne-4to-616p-col plts-2nd rvsd ed (bb3,f,dj) 70.00

FORSTER,E M-Albergo Empedocle...-NY-(1971)-Liveright-1st ed (x10,f,sl rub dj) 15.00

FORSTER,E M-Collected Tales-NY-1946-Knopf-1st Amer ed (cc2,sl fox dj) 30.00

FORSTER,E M-Hill of Devi-NY-(1953)-Harcourt Brace-1st US ed (hh5,dj) 15.00

FORSTER,E M-Life to Come and Other Stories-Lond-1972-1st ed (y7,dj) 30.00

FORSTER,E M-Maurice-Lond-1971-1st ed (r2,f,edge rub dj) 35.00

FORSTER,E M-Maurice-NY-(1971)-Norton-1st Amer ed (cc2,f,dj) 30.00

FORSTER,E M-Two Cheers for Democracy-NY-(1951)-Harcourt Brace-1st Amer ed (cc2,f,sl rub dj) 30.00

FORSTER,E M-What I Believe-Lond-1939-Hogarth-sm 8vo-prtd wrps-1st ed (ll10,papr drknd) 45.00

FORSTER,J-Studies in Black and Red-1896-W & D-pict cl stmpd in red & gold-scarce-1st ed (x7) 125.00

FORSTER,JOHAN R-Resolution Journal of...1772 to 1775-Lond-1982-Hakluyt Scty-8vo-4 vols-blu cl,g titles,plts,maps-1st ed (nn1,as new in dj) 125.00

FORSTER,JOHN R-History of the Voyages and Discoveries Made in the North-Lond-1786-Robinson-4to-contemp calf,3 lg fldg maps-Howes F269-1st Brit ed (w1,rbkd,fox) 1,500.00

FORSTER,R K-Postmark on a Letter-Lond-nd-Chambers-blk cl (w1) 20.00

FORSTER,WILLIAM-Memoirs of...-Lond-1865-Alfred W Bennett-8vo-394p+400p-1st ed (y6,shaken,lacks e.p.,fox) 25.00

FORSYTH,FREDERICK-Dogs of War-1974-Viking-1st Amer ed (x2,f dj) 18.00

FORSYTH,FREDERICK-Shepherd-Lond-1975-1st Brit ed (q5,dj) 22.50

FORSYTHE,GEORGE A-Story of the Soldier-NY-1900-389p-pict cl,frntis,illus-Graff #1381-1st ed (t7) 100.00

FORSYTHE,W E-ED.-Measurement of Radiant Energy-NY-1937-McGraw Hill-452p-grn cl,illus-1st ed (hh6,few sm scrapes) 50.00

FORT,CHARLES-Book of the Damned-NY-1919-Boni & Liveright-cl-1st ed (o8) 55.00

FORT,CHARLES-Books of...-NY-(1941)-Holt-(26),1125p-1st ed thus (m4,f,chip dj) 35.00

FORT,CHARLES-Lo!-NY-1931-Claude Kendall-cl,illus,A King-scarce-1st ed (n8) 65.00

FORT,CHARLES-New Lands-NY-1923-Boni & Liveright-cl-rare-1st ed (n8) 75.00

FORTES,MEYER-Dynamics of Clanship Among the Tallensi-Lond-1945-OUP-8vo-270p-cl,illus,map (y5) 25.00

FORTES,MEYER-ED.-Marriage in Tribal Societies-Cambridge-1962-Univ Pr-lg 8vo-157p-cl-Cambr Paprs in Soc Anthro No.3-1st ed (y5) 18.00

FORTES,MEYER-Time and Social Structure...-Lond-1970-Athlone Pr-8vo-287p-cl,illus-Lond Sch Econ Mono on Soc Anthro No.40-1st ed (y5,sl wn dj) 30.00

FORTESCUE,JOHN-Last Poet-Lond-1934-320p-1st ed (b7,f,dj) 35.00

FORTUINE,ROBERT-Health of the Eskimos a Bibliography 1857 to 1967-Hanover-1968-87p-wrps-1st ed (dd3) 25.00

FORTUNE,R F-Sorcerers of Dobu-Lond-1932-Routledge-8vo-xxviii,318p-blu cl,8 photo plts,text drwngs & map-1st ed (nn1,sl fox,fade dj) 125.00

FOSBURGH,HUGH-One Man's Pleasure-NY-1960-Morrow-Plum 10428-1st ed (dd6,dj) 30.00

FOSTER,GEORGE M-Medical Anthropology-NY-(1978)-J Wiley-8vo-354p-cl-1st ed (y5) 18.00

FOSTER,J C-20th century Dog Breeding with the American Pointer & His Family Tree-TX-1939-301p-photos (gg3) 35.00

FOSTER,JOHN B-ED.-How to Pitch-NY-1912-Spaldings Athletic Libr-90p+(42)p ads (nn2,lacks rear wrp) 55.00

FOSTER,JOHN Y-New Jersey and the Rebellion-Newark-1868-viii,872p-cl,port (aa6,rbkd wi orig sp,new e.p.) 200.00

FOSTER,JOSEPH-D H Lawrence in Taos-Albuq-1972-344p-cl,illus-1st ed (z1,f,dj) 35.00

FOSTER,MAXIMILIAN-Trap-1920-Appleton-1st ed (s10,sp sl tn & fade,dj) 25.00

FOSTER,MICHAEL-Lectures on the History of Physiology-Cambridge-1901-310p-frntis-1st ed (g10,ex-libr) 50.00

FOSTER,MURIEL-Days on Sea,Loch & River-Lond-1979-18mo-unpgd-illus,auth-1st ed (m3,vf) 15.00

FOSTER,MURIEL-Muriel Foster's Fishing Diary-NY-1980-oblng 16mo-unpgd-illus (m3,as new in box) 15.00

FOSTER,MYLES B-Anthems and Anthem Composers...-Lond & NY-1901-Novello-blu cl,frntis,illus-1st ed (w1) 25.00

FOSTER,ROBERT D-North American Indian Doctor...-Canton-1838-154,(2)p-bds-prntd for auth by Smith & Bevin-rare-Amer Imprnts 50367 (j1,sl wn) 300.00

FOSTER,S DAMON-Day after Christmas-NY-1930-Boni-205p-pict cl & bds,illus,V Bock-1st ed (s3,dj) 15.00

FOSTER,STEPHEN C-Old Folks at Home-Troy-1890-Nims & Knight-"The Swanee River" is listed title on sp & frnt cov,12 engrvd drwngs-1st ed (a10,sl drknd sp,rear cov soil 25.00

FOSTER,W H-New England Grouse Shooting-NY-1970-193p-illus (gg3,vf,chip dj) 20.00

FOSTER,W H-New England Grouse Shooting-NY-1970-4to-193p-illus,auth (m3,as new in dj) 35.00

FOSTER,WILLIAM Z-Communism versus Facism-NY-1941-Workers Libr-31p-wrps-Seidman F399-2nd prtg (r1) 13.00

FOSTER,WILLIAM Z-Your Questions Answered-NY-1939-Workers Libr-127p-stapled wrps-Seidman F341-2nd prtg (r1) 17.00

FOSTER-HARRIS-Look of the Old West-NY-1955-Viking-4to-316p-illus-1st ed (d3,dj) 25.00

FOTHERGILL,JOHN-My Three Inns-Lond-1951-Readers Union-242p-brwn cl,illus (q8,dj) 16.50

FOUGERA,KATHERINE G-With Custer's Cavalry-Caldwell-1942-285p-illus-2nd prtg (c4,f,dj) 70.00

FOUGERA,KATHERINE G-With Custer's Cavalry-Caldwell-1942-285p-illus-Dowd #358-Scarce-2nd prtg (c7) 75.00

FOUGERA,KATHERINE G-With Custer's Cavalry-Caldwell-1942-Caxton-285p-photos (ee4,dj wn,chip) 85.00

FOUGNER,G SELMER-Gourmet Dinners-NY-1941-M Barrows-358p-illus (l6) 35.00

FOUNTAIN,ALBERT J-Bur of Immigration of Territory of New Mex,Report of Dona Ana Co-Santa Fe-1882-34p-wrps-Adams Herd#830-v rare-1st ed (v7) 400.00

FOUNTAIN,PAUL-Great North West and the Great Lake Region of North America-Lond-1904-Longmans,Green-viii,355p+42p ads-red cl,dec sp-1st ed (bb7,sl scuff) 125.00*

FOWKE,GERARD-Archeological History of Ohio-Columbus-nd-760p-cl (m1,few spots frnt cov) 50.00

FOWLER & WELLS-New Illustrated Rural Manuals, The House, The Garden, The Farm, Domestic Animals-NY-1859-12mo-176p,166p,156p,165p-brn cl,g illus sp,illus-v scarce (b6) 145.00

FOWLER,ALBERT-ED.-Cranberry Lake from Wilderness to Adirondack Park-Syracuse-1968-8vo-207p-illus (m3,vf,dj) 15.00

FOWLER,FRANK-Bronco Riderboys Down in Arizona...-NY-1914-A L Burt-249p-dec tan cl,frntis,illus (ff8,chip dj) 46.00

FOWLER,GENE-Salute to Yesterday-NY-1937-Random-8vo-365p-1st ed (z4,dj sl chip & tn) 15.00

FOWLER,GENE-Schnozzola-NY-1951-1st ed (s5,f,dj) 20.00

FOWLER,HARLAN D-Camels to California-Stanford-(1950)-93p-photos,map e.p.-1st ed (t7,dj) 35.00

FOWLER,HARLAN D-Camels to California-Stanford-(1950)-Stanford U Pr-93p-illus,map e.p.-1st ed (ff4,dj) 20.00

FOWLER,HARLAN D-Three Caravans to Yuma-Glendale-1980-173p-illus-ltd to 750c-1st ed (h7,vf,dj) 55.00

FOWLER,HENRY W-Description of Fossil Fish Remains of the Cretaceous, Eocene and Miocene Formations of New Jersey-Trenton-1911-Geo Survey of NJ,Bull.#4-192p-cl,illus,fldg plts (aa6) 40.00

FOWLER,JACOB-Journal of...-NY-1898-183p-fldg frntis-ltd to 950c,nbrd-1st ed (f7,sl spot) 150.00

FOWLER,O S-Creative and Sexual Science-np-(1875)-1040p-cl (d1,rear inner hng rprd) 20.00

FOWLER,O S-Sexual Science...as Taught by Phrenology-Phila-(1870)-Nat Publ Co-xxx+11-930p+ads-terra cotta cl,woodcts (a2) 35.00

FOWLER,ORSON S-Hereditary Descent-NY-1849-288p-illus (g10,fox) 45.00

FOWLER,RUSSELL-Operating Room and the Patient-Phila-1907-284p-33 photos-2nd ed (dd3) 75.00

FOWLER,WILLIAM W-Ten Years in Wall Street...-Hartford-1870-Worthington,Dustin-536p-grn cl,plts-1st ed (k2,cov sl flecked & wn) 50.00

FOWLER,WILLIAM W-Woman on the American Frontier-Hartford-1881-Scranton-lg thk 8vo-527p-g dec grn cl,illus-rprnt of 1876 ed (oo8) 90.00

FOWLES,JOHN-Aristos-Bost-1964-1st US ed (s5,dj) 85.00

FOWLES,JOHN-Collector-Bost,Tor-(1963)-auth 1st bk-1st Amer ed (j5,sl wn dj sp) 90.00

FOWLES,JOHN-Collector-Bost-(1963)-Little,Brown-1st Amer ed (ee2,dj) 100.00

FOWLES,JOHN-Collector-Bost-(1963)-Little,Brown-1st Amer ed (x10,f,f dj) 125.00

FOWLES,JOHN-Ebony Tower-Bost-1974-1st US ed (s5,f,sl chip dj) 20.00

FOWLES,JOHN-Enigma of Stonehenge-1980-Summit-1st Amer ed (s9,f,dj) 17.50

FOWLES,JOHN-French Lieutenant's Woman-Lond-(1969)-Cape-8vo-1st ed (x3,f,f dj) 175.00

FOWLES,JOHN-Islands-Bost,Tor-(1978)-Little,Brown-photos-1st US ed (b10,as new in dj) 12.50

FOWLES,JOHN-Magus-Bost-(1965)-Little,Brown-1st US ed (k3,chip dj) 20.00

FOWLES,JOHN-Mantissa-Bost-(1982)-Little,Brown-1st US ed (l3,f,dj) 15.00

FOWLES,JOHN-Poems-NY-(1973)-1st ed (q5,f,dj) 50.00

FOWLES,JOHN-Poems-NY-(1973)-Ecco Pr-1st ed (bb2,f,dj) 40.00

FOWLES,JOHN-Shipwreck-Bost-(1975)-Little,Brown-oblng 4to-cl & bds,pict dj,photos-1st Amer ed (x10,f,sl tn dj) 30.00

FOWLES,JOHN-Short History of Lime Regis-(1982)-Devecote Pr-w/o dj as iss-1st ed (f3,autg) 50.00

FOWLES,JOHN-Tree-Bost,Tor-(1979)-Little,Brown-col photos-1st Amer ed (b5,f,dj) 25.00

FOX,CHARLES F-New Hampshire Book-Nashua/Bost-1842-D Marshall/J Munroe (u2,sp chip) 75.00

FOX,CHARLES K-Advanced Bait Casting-NY-1950-8vo-204p-illus,F Everett-1st ed (m3,vf,dj) 30.00

FOX,CHARLES K-Advanced Bait Casting-NY-1950-Putnam-204p-dec e.p.,illus (gg3,f) 40.00

FOX,CHARLES K-Book of Lures-1975-Freshet Press-4to-256p-photos (m3,as new in dj) 25.00

FOX,CHARLES K-Wonderful World of Trout-Carlisle-1963-8vo-296p-ltd ed,nbrd,autg-illus,F Everett-1st ed (m3,f) 60.00

FOX,CHARLES P-Pictorial History of Performing Horses-Seattle-1960-Superior-4to-ltd to 250c,autg (f10,dj) 45.00

FOX,CHARLES P-Ticket to the Circus-(1959)-Superior-184p-photos-1st ed (v8,dj) 35.00

FOX,CHARLES-Legal Advice and Instructions to Business Men...-Cin-1869-144p-cl (d1,f) 25.00

FOX,FRANK-Royal Inniskilling Fusiliers in the Second World War-Aldershot-1951-204p-illus-1st ed (gg2,f,dj) 125.00

FOX,G V-An Attempt to Solve the Problem of the First Landing of Columbus in the New World-Wash D.C.-1882-GPO-4to-68p-US Coast & Geo Survey,Appdx No.18-Rprt for 1880-blk cl,lg fldg map in rear pckt (h2,sp wn,cov spots,ink notes) 35.00

FOX,GEORGE H-Reminiscences-NY-1926-Med Life Pr-xiv+248p-red cl,illus-1st ed (l2) 15.00

FOX,GEORGE-Works of...-Phila-1831-Marcus T Gould-12mo-lea-1st ed (y6,hngs crkng,fox,lacks labl) 250.00

FOX,H B-2,000 Mile Turtle-Austin-1975-128p-1st ed (t8,dj) 10.00

FOX,HELEN M-Garden Cinderellas-NY-1928-xii,269p-grn cl,4 col & 39 b&w photo plts-1st ed (x5,scratched sp) 20.00

FOX,HELEN M-Gardening for Good Eating-NY-1943-Macmillan-262p-dec bds,illus,L Mansfield (m6,dj) 24.00

FOX,HELEN M-Gardening with Herbs for Flavor and Fragrance-NY-1933-Macmillan-334p-dec bds,papr labl,illus,L Mansfield (m6,sunned sp) 22.00

FOX,HELEN M-Patio Gardens-NY-1929-illus-1st ed (ee1,dj) 125.00

FOX,JAMES M-Code Three-Bost-1953-Little-1st ed (e4,f,dj) 12.50

FOX,JOHN,JR.-"Hell Fer Sartain" and Other Stories-NY-1897-Harper & Bros-118,(1)p-cl-BAL 6244-1st ed (g1) 20.00

FOX,LARRY-Last to First-1970-Harper & Row-1st ed (s8,f,dj) 25.00

FOX,LAWRENCE K-Who's Who Among South Dakotans, Vol I and Vol II-Pierre-1924,1928-2 vols-1st ed (t7) 35.00

FOX,LITT D-Threshold of the Pacific-Lond-1924-K Paul-blu cl,g titles & cov dec,maps,14 photos (p8,ex-libr) 45.00

FOX,LITT D-Threshold of the Pacific-NY-1925-K Paul-xvi,379p-drk red cl,g sp titles,maps,14 photos (p8,sl fox) 45.00

FOX,M W-ED.-Wild Canids-1975-Van Nostrand-508p-illus-1st ed (bb3,f,dj) 40.00

FOX,MARIA-Memoirs of...-Lond-1846-Chas Gilpin-8vo-493p-cl-1st ed (y6,wn,frnt hng splttng) 20.00

FOX,ROBIN L-Search for Alexander-Bost-1980-1st ed (y7,dj) 15.00

FOX,S-John Muir and His Legacy-1981-Little,Brown-436p-illus-1st ed (bb3,f,dj) 18.00

FOX,W S-Silken Lines & Silver Hooks-Tor-1954-149p-illus (gg3) 10.00

FOX,W SHERWOOD-Silken Lines & Silver Hooks-Tor-1954-8vo-152p-illus,C Bice-1st ed (m3,f,dj) 20.00

FOX,WILLIAM P-Dixiana Moon-NY-(1981)-Viking-1st ed (a10,f,dj) 12.50

FOX,WILLIAM P-Doctor Golf-(1963)-Lippincott-illus,C Rodrigues-1st ed (x10,f,edge-tn dj) 35.00

FOX,WILLIAM P-Doctor Golf-Phila,NY-(1963)-Lippincott-1st ed (a10,f,sl wn dj) 40.00

FOXX,JACK-Freebooty-Indpls-1976-Bobbs-1st ed (h4,f,dj) 15.00

FRACASTORIUS,H-Contagion, Contagious Diseases and Their Treatment-NY-1930-356p-1st Engl transl (dd3) 150.00

FRACKELTON,DR WILL-Sagebrush Dentist-Chig-(1941)-McClur-246p-Herd 834-1st ed (ee4) 35.00

FRACKELTON,DR.WILL-Sagebrush Dentist-Chig-(1941)-McClurg-246p-Six Guns 755-1st ed (ff4,autg) 35.00

FRAENKEL,G S-Orientation of Animals-Oxford-1940-8vo-(2),352p-cl,illus (y8,ex-libr) 28.00

FRALEY,OSCAR-Pictorial Guide to Casting & Spinning-NY-1954-4to-68p+photos (m3,f,dj) 12.50

FRANCATELLI,CHARLES E-Modern Cook: a Practical Way to the Culinary Art-Lond-1883-Bently-560p-ribbed grn cl,frntis port,60 text illus-27th ed,rvsd & enlgd (q8,sl fox e.p & discol text) 65.00

FRANCE,ANATOLE-In All France-Chig-(1930)-Whitman-110p-cl wi pict pasteon,col illus,L Enders-1st ed (s3,tips wn) 20.00

FRANCE,L B-Mountain Trails and Parks in Colorado-Denver-1888-Chain,Hardy-dec drk grn cl-2nd ed (u2) 35.00

FRANCE,LEWIS B-Pine Valley-Denver-1891-38p-pict cl,frntis,photos-1st ed (t7) 25.00

FRANCESCO,GRETE DE-Power of the Charlatan-New Haven-1939-Yale Univ-viii+288p-grn cl,68 illus-1st Amer ed (l2,dj) 30.00

FRANCHERE,GABRIEL-Adventure at Astoria 1810 to 1814-1967-U of OK-190p-illus,map-1st ed (r8,f,dj) 22.00

FRANCHERE,GABRIEL-Adventure at Astoria, 1810 to 1814-Norman-1967-190p-maps-1st ed (t7,f,dj) 18.00

FRANCHERE,GABRIEL-Narrative of a Voyage to Northwest Coast of America...1811,1812,1813,1814-NY-1854-Redfield-376p+8p ads-orig blindstmpd blk cl,3 plts wi tiss-rare-Howes F310-1st ed in Engl (z1,lacks f.e.p,box) 495.00

FRANCHERE,GABRIEL-Narrative of a Voyage to the Northwest Coast of America...1811,1812,1813 and 1814-NY-1854-Redfield-376p+8p ads-orig grn cl,g lettrd sp,3 plts(incl frntis)-Graff 1400-1st ed in Engl (bb7,sl tn,chip sp,sl fox) 650.00

FRANCHERE,GABRIEL-Voyage to the Northwest Coast of America-Chig-1954-Donnelley & Sons-illus,maps-Lakeside Classics (ff4) 20.00

FRANCIS,DICK-Banker-Lond-1982-Joseph-1st ed (q4,f,dj) 30.00

FRANCIS,DICK-Blood Sport-NY-(1968)-Harper & Row-1st Amer ed (u10,f,dj) 35.00

FRANCIS,DICK-Bonecrack-1971-M Joseph-1st ed (n9,f,sp rub dj) 75.00

FRANCIS,DICK-Bonecrack-NY-1971-Harper-1st US ed (e4,dj) 25.00

FRANCIS,DICK-Dead Cert-NY-1962-Harper-auth 1st mystery-1st US ed (w5,sl rub dj) 400.00

FRANCIS,DICK-Flying Finish-1966-M Joseph-1st ed (x7,sl tn dj) 185.00

FRANCIS,DICK-Flying Finish-NY-1967-Harper-1st US ed (f4,f,dj) 75.00

FRANCIS,DICK-Forfeit-NY-1969-1st US ed (o5,f,dj) 60.00

FRANCIS,DICK-Forfeit-NY-1969-Harper-1st US ed (e4,f,sl wn dj) 40.00

FRANCIS,DICK-High Stakes-1975-Harper-1st Amer ed (p9,f,dj) 25.00

FRANCIS,DICK-In the Frame-Lond-1976-M Joseph-1st ed (g4,f,sl wn dj) 40.00

FRANCIS,DICK-In the Frame-Lond-1976-M Joseph-1st ed (o9,f,dj) 50.00

FRANCIS,DICK-In the Frame-NY-(1976)-Harper & Row-1st Amer ed (u10,f,dj) 20.00

FRANCIS,DICK-In the Frame-NY-(1976)-Harper-1st Amer ed (p9,f,dj) 15.00

FRANCIS,DICK-Knock Down-Lond-1974-M Joseph-1st ed (x2,f,dj) 55.00

FRANCIS,DICK-Knockdown-Lond-1974-M Joseph-1st ed (q4,f,dj) 75.00

FRANCIS,DICK-Knockdown-NY-(1975)-Harper-1st Amer ed (p9,f,dj) 25.00

FRANCIS,DICK-Nerve-Lond-1964-M Joseph-scarce-1st ed (hh2,f,dj sl tn,sl fade sp) 850.00

FRANCIS,DICK-Nerve-NY-(1964)-Harper-1st Amer ed (w1,f,dj) 125.00

FRANCIS,DICK-Odds Against-NY-1966-Harper-1st US ed (f4,sl stnd dj) 20.00

FRANCIS,DICK-Rat Race-1971-Harper-1st Amer ed (m9,dj sp sunned) 35.00

FRANCIS,DICK-Reflex-1981-Putnam-1st Amer ed (m9,f,dj) 15.00

FRANCIS,DICK-Risk-Lond-1977-Joseph-1st ed (r4,f,dj) 45.00

FRANCIS,DICK-Risk-Lond-1977-M Joseph-1st ed (p9,f,sl chip dj) 30.00

FRANCIS,DICK-Risk-NY-1978-Harper-1st US ed (f4,f,dj) 15.00

FRANCIS,DICK-Slay-Ride-Lond-1973-M Joseph-1st ed (x2,dj) 50.00

FRANCIS,DICK-Slayride-NY-(1974)-Harper & Row-1st Amer ed (o9,f,dj) 25.00

FRANCIS,DICK-Slayride-NY-(1974)-Harper & Row-1st Amer ed (u10,dj) 20.00

FRANCIS,DICK-Smoke Screen-NY-(1973)-Harper & Row-1st Amer ed (u10,f,f dj) 25.00

FRANCIS,DICK-Smokescreen-1972-M Joseph-1st ed (p9,f,dj) 55.00

FRANCIS,DICK-Trial Run-NY-(1978)-Harper & Row-1st Amer ed (u10,f,dj) 20.00

FRANCIS,DICK-Twice Shy-Lond-1981-Joseph-1st ed (r4,f,dj) 37.50

FRANCIS,DICK-Whip Hand-Lond-1979-Joseph-1st ed (q4,sl creased dj) 30.00

FRANCIS,PHIL-Salt Water Fishing From Maine to Texas-NY-1963-8vo-243p-photos-1st prntng (m3,vf,dj) 14.00

FRANCIS,REV. P H-Mechanical Biology-Lond-nd(ca.1940)-Mitre Pr-688p-turq cl,72 text figs (l2,dj) 50.00

FRANCISCONO,MARCEL-Walter Gropius and the Creation of Bauhaus in Weimar-Urbana-(1971)-U of Ill-8vo-336p-42 illus-1st ed (ee5,dj) 30.00

FRANCK,HARRY A-East of Siam-NY-1939-Appleton Century-photos-scarce-1st ed (ff3,lacks dj) 65.00

FRANCK,HARRY A-Vagabonding Down the Andes-NY-1917-Century-8vo-xxi,612p-dec grn cl,photo plts,col fldg map (dd7,cor bump,sp fade,sl soil) 30.00

FRANCOIS,YVES R-CTZ Paradigm-GC-1975-Dbldy-1st ed (e3,f,dj) 10.00

FRANCOIS,YVES R-CTZ Paradigm-GC-1975-Dbldy-1st ed (o3,f,dj) 15.00

FRANGSMYR,T-ED.-Linnaeus-1983-U of Cal-203p-illus-1st ed (bb3,f,dj) 28.00

FRANK,ADAM-History of the Several Branches of the I O O F of Germantown, Ohio-Dayton-1910-276p-cl (aa1,cov crease) 25.00

FRANK,JEANIE M-History of the District of El Paso in Texas and New Mexico-El Paso-1947-107p-wrps,photos-1st ed (t7) 30.00

FRANK,WALDO-Jew in Our Day-NY-1944-Duell-1st ed (v5,f,dj) 30.00

FRANK,WALDO-Our America-NY-1919-Boni & Liveright-1st ed (v5) 25.00

FRANK,WALDO-Salvos-NY-(1924)-Boni-1st ed (w1,f,dj) 60.00

FRANKE,H W-Computer Graphics, Computer Art-NY-(1971)-Phaidon-134p-orng cl,plts-1st ed (dd1,dj) 25.00

FRANKE,H W-Computer Graphics-1971-Phaidon-sq 4to-100 illus-1st ed (h10,dj) 35.00

FRANKE,PAUL-They Plowed up Hell in Old Cochise-Douglas-1950-Douglas Climate Club-60p-stiff wrps,illus-Six Guns 758-1st ed (gg4) 15.00

FRANKEL,FRED H-ED.-Hypnosis at its Bicentennial-NY-(1978)-Plenum Med Bk Co-(xiv)+306p-brwn cl-1st ed (y9,dj) 27.50

FRANKENSTEIN,ALFRED-William Sidney Mount-NY-(1975)-Abrams-folio-cl-1st ed (oo6,dj) 100.00

FRANKFURTER,MARION D-ED.-Letters of Sacco and Vanzetti-NY-1928-Viking-1st ed (v5,sl wn,sp labl chip) 35.00

FRANKLIN COUNTY-INVENTORY OF THE COUNTY ARCHIVES OF OHIO. NO.25 ...-Columbus-1942-Ohio Hist Rcrds Survey-528,(2)p-wrps (d1) 20.00

FRANKLIN,BENJAMIN-Anais Nin: A Bibliography-Kent-1973-KSU Pr-115p-yel cl-1st ed (z3) 10.00

FRANKLIN,CHARLES A H-Bearing of Coat Armour by Ladies-Lond-1923-144p-col illus (cc8) 65.00

FRANKLIN,EUGENE-Money Murders-NY-1972-Stein-1st ed (f4,f,dj) 10.00

FRANKLIN,JIMMIE L-Born Sober-Norman-(1971)-Univ of Okla-xviii+212p-brwn bds-1st ed (k2,dj) 20.00

FRANKLIN,JOHN-Narrative of a Second Expedition to the Shores of the Polar Sea in the Years 1825, 1826 and 1827-Edmonton-(1971)-4to-plts,maps-rprnt of orig ed (a7,f,dj) 125.00

FRANKLIN,K J-De Venarum Ostiolis 1603 of Hieronymus Fabricius of Aquapendente-Springfield-1933-98p-1st Enlg transl (dd3) 50.00

FRANKLIN,RENA-Soups of Hakafri Restaurant-Gainesville-(1981)-Triad-136p-dec brwn bds,drwngs-1st Amer ed (q8) 15.00

FRANKLIN,VINCENT P-Education of Black Philadelphia-1979-Univ of Penn-298p-cl (g1,f,dj) 15.00

FRANKLIN,WAYNE-Discoverers, Explorers, Settlers-Chig-(1979)-U of Chig-8vo-252p-30 illus-1st ed (cc5,vf,vf dj) 12.50

FRANKLING,ELEANOR-Popular Dalmation-Lond-1964-Popular Dogs-1st ed (f10,dj) 25.00

FRANTZ,JOE B-Texas-(1976)-Norton-222p-1st ed (t8,dj sp chip,sl tn) 15.00

FRANZWA,GREGORY-Oregon Trail Revisited-St.Louis-(1972)-417p-illus,maps (r8) 18.00

FRARY,I T-Early Homes of Ohio-Richmond-1936-illus (h10,dj) 40.00

FRARY,I T-Thomas Jefferson Architect & Builder-Richmond-1931-1st ed (h10,dj sl tn & wn) 75.00

FRARY,I T-Thomas Jefferson Architect and Builder-Richmond-1931-139p-cl,96p plts-1st ed (m1) 25.00

FRARY,I T-Thomas Jefferson Architect and Builder-Richmond-1931-Garret & Massie-4to-xv,(3),139p-cl,96p plts-1st ed (pp7) 100.00

FRARY,MICHAEL-Impressions of the Texas Panhandle-College Station-1977-Texas A & M-112p-paintings-1st ed (z4,sl scuff dj) 17.50

FRASCONE,JON PAUL-Aphrodisiac Cook Book-np(Dallas)-1975-Emerson Hs-188p-illus (q6) 18.00

FRASER,ANTONIA-History of Toys-np-(1966)-Delacorte-qto-256p-cl,illus(incl col)-1st ed (dd10,f,dj) 45.00

FRASER,C M-Hydroids of the Pacific Coast of Canada and the United States-1937-U of Tor-207p-44 plts (bb3,f) 35.00

FRASER,C-Story of Aircraft-NY-(1933)-8vo-x,510p-illus cl,frntis,plts,text illus (t2,sl wn sp) 25.00

FRASER,COLIN-Avalanches & Snow Safety-NY-1978-269p-24 plts-1st US ed (o10,as new in dj) 22.00

FRASER,ESTHER-Canadian Rockies-Edmonton-(c.1969)-Hurtig-xvi,252p-col illus & maps(lining papers),ports-Edwards & Lort #1409 (k10,dj) 40.00*

FRASER,ESTHER-Wheeler-Banff-1978-164p-1st Can ed (q10,as new in dj) 25.00

FRASER,G M-General Danced at Dawn-1973-Knopf-1st Amer ed (x7,f,dj) 45.00

FRASER,GEORGE F-Steel Bonnets-NY-1972-395p-1st Amer ed (b7,f,dj) 75.00

FRASER,GEORGE M-Flash for Freedom-NY-1972-Knopf-1st US ed (k4,f,dj) 30.00

FRASER,GEORGE M-Flashman and the Lady-Lond-1977-1st ed (z2,f,f dj) 85.00

FRASER,GEORGE M-Flashman-Lond-1969-auth 1st bk-1st Brit ed (t5,f,dj) 75.00

FRASER,GEORGE M-Flashman-NY-1969-1st ed (b7,f,f dj) 65.00

FRASER,GEORGE M-Flashman-NY-1969-256p-1st Amer ed (v8,dj) 70.00

FRASER,GEORGE M-Mr.American-NY-1980-Simon-1st US ed (f4,f,sl wn dj) 15.00

FRASER,GEORGE M-Royal Flash-NY-1970-1st Amer ed (b7,f,f dj) 50.00

FRASER,GEORGE M-Royal Flash-NY-1970-1st Amer ed (q5,f,dj) 40.00

FRASER,GEORGE M-Steel Bonnets-NY-1972-395p-1st Amer ed (kk2,f,f dj) 75.00

FRASER,HUGH-Seven Years on the Pacific Slope-1914-Dodd,Mead-391p-dec sp,illus-Six Guns #761 (r8) 60.00

FRASER,JAMES-Cock Pit of Roses-NY-1970-Harcourt-1st US ed (h4,dj) 10.00

FRASER,JAMES-Death in a Pheasant's Eye-NY-1972-Walker-1st US ed (e4,f,dj) 15.00

FRASER,SHELAGH-Cheeses of Old England-Lond-(1960)-Abelard Schuman-139p-yel cl,col frntis,photos,map-1st prtg (q8,dj) 10.00

FRASER,W A-Outcasts-Tor-1901-Wm Briggs-illus by A Heming-1st ed (pp2) 50.00*

FRASER,WILLIAM-Red Book of Grandtully-Edinburgh-1868-2 vols-plts,illus-ltd to 100c,nbrd-rare (pp9,sl wn cov,sl fox) 750.00

FRASER-BRUNNER,ALEC-Danger in the Sea-Lond-1975-4to-128p-photos (m3,dj) 15.00

FRASSANITO,W A-Antietam-NY-1978-304p-illus-1st ed (c4,f,dj) 30.00

FRASSANITO,W A-Gettysburg:A Journey in Time-NY-1975-248p-illus,maps,ports (z10,soil dj) 45.00

FRASSANITO,W A-Grant and Lee-NY-(1983)-442p-illus-1st ed (n3,f,dj) 30.00

FRAZEE,STEVE-Hellsgrin-NY-1960-Rinehart-1st ed (f4,dj) 10.00

FRAZER,ELIZABETH-Old Glory and Verdun-NY-1918-Duffield-8vo-303p-g stmpd blu cl,frntis,photos-1st book publ (ee9) 17.00

FRAZER,PERRY D-Amateur Rodmaking-NY-1931-12mo-220p-1st ed (m3,vf) 20.00

FRAZER,PERRY D-Angler's Workshop-Rodmakings for Beginners-NY-1908-12mo-179p-photos,illus-1st ed (m3) 50.00

FRAZER,PERRY D-Elementary Gunsmithing-Plantersville-1946-12mo-208p-illus-1st prntng (m3,f) 15.00

FRAZER,ROBERT W-ED.-New Mexico in 1850-Norman-1968-222p-1st ed (t7,f,dj) 17.50

FRAZER,ROBERT W-Forts of the West-Norman-(1965)-U of Okla-(28),246p-cl,maps,photos-1st ed (v1,dj) 40.00

FREAR,M-Our Familiar Island Trees-Bost-1929-161p (x6) 10.00

FREDDI,CRIS-Pork and Others-NY-1981-Knopf-auth 1st bk-1st US ed (bb1,as new in dj) 30.00

FREDDI,CRIS-Pork-Lond,Henley-(1982)-Routledge & K Paul-auth 1st bk-1st Brit ed (bb1,as new in dj) 35.00

FREDERICK II OF HOHENSTAUFEN-1969-Stanford-4to-637p-g dec grn cl,186 plts(incl col) (bb3,f,sl soil dj) 110.00

FREDERICK,J V-Ben Holladay-Glendale-1940-Arthur H Clark Co-334p-illus,map-Six Guns #762-1st ed (cc4) 175.00

FREDERICK,JOHN V-Siege of Oxford-Lond-1932-179p-map,illus-scarce-1st ed (gg2) 75.00

FREDERICKS,A-Blue Lights-1915-Watt-pict bndg-1st ed (x7) 55.00

FREDERICKS,A-Ivory Snuff Box-1912-Watt-1st ed (x7) 18.00

FREDERICKS,PIERCE G-Sepoy and the Cosack-NY-1971-274p-illus-1st ed (b7,f,dj) 20.00

FREDERICKSON,GEORGE M-Inner Civil War-NY-(1965)-277p-1st ed (n3) 20.00

FREDGE,FREDERIQUE-Cooking Round the World with a Wooden Spoon-1965-Dbldy-213p-grn cl,drwngs-1st ed (q8,dj) 15.00

FREDRICKSON,OLIVE-Silence of the North-NY-1972-8vo-209p-photos (m3,vf,dj) 12.50

FREDRICKSON,OLIVE-Silence of the North-NY-1972-Crown-8vo-209p-cl,photos (z7) 20.00

FREE,JAMES L-Training Your Retriever-Richmond-1949-8vo-236p-photos-1st ed (m3,vf) 15.00

FREEDOM SCHOOL POETRY-Atlanta-1965-SNCC-wrps-1st ed (v5,f) 30.00

FREEHAND,JULIANNA-Seafaring Legacy-NY-1981-Random-209p-2nd prtg (p8,as new in dj) 15.00

FREELAND,L S-Central Sierra Miwok Dictionary with Texts-Berkeley-1960-Univ of Cal-x+71p-wrps-1st ed (e2) 15.00

FREELING,NICOLAS-Arlette-1981-Pantheon-1st Amer ed (r9,f,dj) 15.00

FREELING,NICOLAS-Arlette-NY-1981-Pantheon-1st Amer ed (g4,f,dj) 10.00

FREELING,NICOLAS-Aupres De Ma Blonde-1972-Harper-1st Amer ed (m9,f,dj) 15.00

FREELING,NICOLAS-Bugles Blowing-NY-1976-Harper-1st US ed (h4,f,dj) 10.00

FREELING,NICOLAS-Double Barrel-NY-1964-1st US ed (r5,f,dj) 20.00

FREELING,NICOLAS-Dressing of Diamond-NY-1974-1st US ed (r5,dj) 10.00

FREELING,NICOLAS-King of the Rainy Country-1965-Harper-1st Amer ed (p9,f,dj) 15.00

FREELING,NICOLAS-Kitchen Book-Lond-(1970)-H Hamilton-192p-grn cl,drwngs-1st ed (q8,dj) 17.50

FREELING,NICOLAS-Kitchen-NY-1970-Harper-1st Amer ed (w9,f,dj) 45.00

FREELING,NICOLAS-Lake Isle-Lond-1976-Heinemann-1st ed (q4,dj) 20.00

FREELING,NICOLAS-Long Silence-1972-H Hamilton-1st ed (q9,f,dj) 25.00

FREELING,NICOLAS-Night Lords-NY-1978-1st US ed (r5,f,dj) 12.50

FREELING,NICOLAS-Question of Loyalty-NY-1963-Harper & Row-1st Amer ed (gg8,dj) 40.00

FREELING,NICOLAS-Sabine-(1976)-Harper-1st Amer ed (m9,f,dj) 15.00

FREELING,NICOLAS-Tsing Boom-1969-Harper-1st Amer ed (p9,f,dj) 15.00

FREELING,NICOLAS-Tsing-Boom-NY-1969-Harper-1st Amer ed (f4,f,sl wn dj) 10.00

FREELING,NICOLAS-Widow-1979-Pantheon-1st Amer ed (p9,vf,dj) 20.00

FREEMAN,BUD-You Don't Look Like a Musician-Detr-1974-Balamp Publ-1st ed (v5,f,dj) 20.00

FREEMAN,CAPT HENRY B-Freeman Journal-San Rafael-(1977)-104p-illus,maps-ltd to 1000c-1st ed (c4,f,dj) 27.50

FREEMAN,DAN A-Four Years with the Utes-Waco-1962-W M Morrison-7p-papr over bds,illus,ltd to 125c,nbrd (w3,rear hng cracked) 60.00

FREEMAN,DENNE H-Hook 'Em Horns-Huntsville-1974-Strode Publ-224p-cl,photos-1st ed (w3,f,dj) 15.00

FREEMAN,DOUGLAS S-R E Lee: A Biography-NY-1945 to 1947-Scribners-4 vols-frntis,illus,maps-1st ed (o7,sl stnd covs) 200.00

FREEMAN,EDWARD A-How to Hunt Deer-Harrisburg-1960-8vo-243p-illus (m3,vf,dj) 10.50

FREEMAN,G D-Midnight and Noonday or the Incidental History of Southern Kansas and the Indian Territory-Caldwell-1892-406p-red dc cl,frntis,illus,photos-Howes F353-Six Guns #763-rare (t7) 200.00

FREEMAN,HARRY C-Brief History of Butte, Montana-Chig-1900-H O Shepard Co-sm folio-123p-illus by Russell,photos-1st ed (bb4) 125.00

FREEMAN,JAMES W-ED.-Prose and Poetry of the Live Stock Industry of the United States-NY-1959-Antiquarian Pr-757p-illus-ltd to 550c,nbrd (ff4,box) 200.00

FREEMAN,JAMES-Practical Steelhead Fishing-So Brunswick-1966-8vo-230p-photos (m3,vf,sl tn dj) 30.00

FREEMAN,JOHN R-Earthquake Damage and Earthquake Insurance-NY-1932-McGraw-Hill-xiv+904p-maroon cl,illus-1st ed (d2) 60.00

FREEMAN,KATHLEEN-Ancilla to the Pre-Socratic Philosphers-Oxford-1948-Blackwell-8vo-x,162p-grn cl-1st ed (t10) 15.00

FREEMAN,LEWIS R-Sea Hounds-NY-1919-Dodd,Mead-8vo-309p-blu cl,13 photos (p8) 45.00

FREEMAN,LEWIS R-Waterways of Westward Wanderings-NY-1927-Dodd,Mead-xii,368p-photos-1st ed (n2,sl fox) 25.00

FREEMAN,LUCY-Story of Anna O-NY-(1971)-Walker-8vo-268p-1st ed (gg5,sl tn dj) 12.50

FREEMAN,R A-Cat's Eye-1927-DM-1st Amer ed (x7) 45.00

FREEMAN,R A-Mr Polton Explains-1940-DM-1st Amer ed (x7,dj) 150.00

FREEMAN,R AUSTIN-Cat's Eye-NY-1927-Dodd-1st US ed (g4) 45.00

FREEMAN,R AUSTIN-Dr. Thorndyke's Discovery-1932-Dodd-1st Amer ed (s10) 20.00

FREEMAN,R AUSTIN-Dr.Thorndyke Omnibus-NY-1932-Dodd-1st US ed (h4,chip dj) 95.00

FREEMAN,R AUSTIN-Magic Casket-NY-1927-Dodd-1st US ed (f4,sl stnd cov) 20.00

FREEMAN,R AUSTIN-Mr.Pottermack's Oversight-NY-1930-Dodd Mead-1st Amer ed (w9,f,vf dj) 350.00

FREEMAN,R AUSTIN-Puzzle Lock-NY-1926-Dodd-1st US ed (l4) 45.00

FREEMAN,R AUSTIN-Silent Witness-1915-Winston-1st Amer ed (s10,pg ends drknd,dj sp chip) 475.00

FREEMAN,R AUSTIN-Silent Witness-Phila-1915-Winston-pict cov,illus-1st Amer ed (j4,sl fray,sl wn hnge) 35.00

FREEMAN,R AUSTIN-Social Decay and Regeneration-Bost-1921-Houghton-1st US ed (g4) 40.00

FREEMAN,R AUSTIN-Vanishing Man-NY-1912-Dodd-pict cov-1st US (d4) 125.00

FREEMAN,R B-Works of Charles Darwin-Lond-(1977)-Dawson & Archon Bks-8vo-235p-grn cl,frntis-2nd ed,rvsd & enlgd (t10,f) 45.00

FREEMAN,RUTH-American Dolls-Watkins Glen-1952-Century Hs-71,(29)p-cl,illus-1st ed (dd10,f) 30.00

FREEMAN,WILLIAM H-Thermal Baths of Bath-Lond-1888-Hamilton,Adams-xxiv+3-382p+xxi-blu cl,fldg maps & plans-1st ed (g2,sp faded) 35.00

FREEMANTLE,BRIAN-Inscrutable Charlie Muffin-Lond-1979-Cape-1st ed (q4,dj) 25.00

FREMANTLE,ANNE-Desert Calling, the Story of Charles Foucauld-NY-(1949)-Holt-8vo-364p-1st ed (jj5,dj) 15.00

FREMANTLE,ANNE-Three Cornered Heart-NY-1971-Viking-cl,illus-2nd prtg (n8,f,dj) 15.00

FREMANTLE,ARTHUR J-Fremantle Diary-Bost-1954-Little,Brown-304p-e.p. maps (v2) 15.00

FREMANTLE,HON. T F-Book of the Rifle-Lond-1901-558p-drk grn cl wi g stmpngs,fldg illus (ee3,f) 150.00

FREMONT AND SANDUSKY COUNTY-(Columbus & Fremont)-(1940)-WPA-115p-wrps,fldg map- Writer's Program of Ohio (j1) 35.00

FREMONT,JESSIE B-Souvenirs of My Time-Bost-(1887)-393p (bb9,sp fade) 50.00

FREMONT,JESSIE B-Will and the Way Stories-Bost-(C.1891)-Lothrop Co-182p+ads-orig blu cl,frntis port wi tiss-rare-1st ed (z1,ex-libr) 90.00

FREMONT,JESSIE B-Year of American travel-NY-1878-Harpers-12mo-190p+ads-grn cl-Howes F363-1st ed (w1) 45.00

FREMONT,JOHN C-Expeditions of...(Vol I)+Map Portfolio-Urbana-1970-U of Ill-rust col cl,2 vols(incl map portfolio in box) (mm1,as new) 55.00

FREMONT,JOHN C-Expeditions of...-Urbana-var dates-3 vol in 4 + map portfolio(11 fldg maps boxed)-1st ed (c7,f,djs) 275.00

FREMONT-LIFE OF COL...-(NY)-(1856)-Greeley & M'Elrath-32p-sewed as issued,dbl cols,port on top half of first pg-scarce (b1,frst few lvs fox) 25.00

FRENCH,CAVID HEATH-Factionalism in Isleta Pueblo-Columbia-(1947)-48+1p-plain wrps (v7) 20.00

FRENCH,FIONA-King Tree-NY-1973-Walck-4to-cl,col illus (s3,f,f dj) 25.00

FRENCH,GILES-Cattle Country of Peter French-1965-Binfords & Mort-167p-photos,maps-2nd ed (r8,dj edgewn,sl chip) 30.00

FRENCH,GILES-Cattle Country of Peter French-Portland-1964-Binfords & Mort-8vo-167p-photos-1st ed (cc5,f,f dj,map poster laid in 12.50

FRENCH,HERBERT-ED.-An Index of Differential Diagnosis of Main Symptons by Various Writers-NY-1913-1017p-1st Amer ed (dd3) 50.00

FRENCH,J C-Passenger Pigeon in Pennsylvania-Altoona-1919-258p-photos-scarce (gg3,hngs weak,cl bulged) 45.00

FRENCH,JAMES W-Modern Power Generators-1908-2 vols-emboss covs,500 illus-rare-1st ed (h6) 150.00

FRENCH,JOSEPH L-ED.-Gallery of Old Rogues-NY-(1931)-King-285p-red cl-1st ed (v1) 45.00

FRENCH,LILLIE H-House Dignified-NY-1908-Putnam's-4to-orig dec cl,t.e.g.,60 plts (cc10) 50.00

FRENCH,SAMUEL L-Reminiscences of Plymouth, Luzerne County, Penna.-(NY)-1914-Lotus Pr-94p+5p plts & Frntis,,cl (n1) 20.00

FRENCH,WILLIAM-Some Recollections of a Western Ranchman, New Mexico: 1883 to 1889-NY-(1928)-F Stokes-283p-Howes F375-Herd 847-1st Amer ed (d3,ex-libr) 200.00

FRENEAU,PHILIP-Poems Written and Published During the American Revolutionary War...-Phila-1809-2 vols-mod cl,lea labls-3rd ed (aa6,rbnd) 300.00

FRERICHS,DR.F T-Clinical Treatise on Diseases of the Liver-NY-1879-Wood & Co-8vo-3 vols-maroon cl,illus-1st Amer ed (y4) 100.00

FREUCHEN,PETER-Arctic Adventure-NY-(1935)-Farrar & Rinehart-467p-cl (m1,f,dj) 12.50

FREUCHEN,PETER-Book of the Eskimos-NY-1961-441p-pict cl,photos,map e.p. (t7,f) 7.50

FREUCHEN,PETER-Men of the Frozen North-Cleve-1962-World-8vo-315p-dec wht cl,map e.p.,illus-1st ed (ee7,dj) 25.00

FREUD,CLEMENT-Freud on Food-Lond-(1978)-Dent-lg 8vo-256p-grn cl,cartoons-1st ed (q8,dj) 25.00

FREUD,SIGMUND-Collected Papers-NY-(1959)-Basic Bks-5 vols-lt brwn cl-1st Amer ed (dd1,box) 75.00

FREUD,SIGMUND-Delusion and Dream-Lond-(1921)-Allen & Unwin-1st Brit ed (w5) 40.00

FREUD,SIGMUND-Delusion and Dream-Lond-(1921)-Allen & Unwin-213p+ads-lilac cl-1st Brit ed (g2,sl fade covs) 25.00

FREUD,SIGMUND-Selected Papers on Hysteria and Other Psychoneuroses-NY-1909-200p-blk buckram-transl by A A Brill (g10,ex-libr) 75.00

FREUND,GISELE-James Joyce in Paris-NY-(1965)-Harcourt Brace-qto-88 photos-1st ed (cc2,f,dj) 50.00

FREUNDLICH,AUGUST L-Richard Florsheim-NY-1976-Barnes-4to-blu cl,b&w & col illus (r10,wn dj) 25.00

FREYTAG,FREDERICKA F-Hypnoanalysis of an Anxiety Hysteria-NY-1959-Julian Pr-xiv+412p-1st ed (y9,dj) 25.00

FRIED,FREDERICK-Artists in Wood-NY-1970-folio-illus-1st ed (ff10) 65.00

FRIEDAN,BETTY-Second Stage-1981-Summit-1st ed (r9,vf,dj,pres) 15.00

FRIEDENWALD,HARRY-Jews and Medicine, Essays-NY-1967-2 vols-2nd ed (dd3) 75.00

FRIEDENWALD,HARRY-Jews and Medicine: Essays-Balt-1944-Johns Hopkins Pr-2 vols-blu cl,plts-1st ed (dd1) 135.00

FRIEDLAENDER,WALTER-Claude Lorrain-Berlin-1921-3/4 lea,t.e.g.,illus-1st ed (r2) 100.00

FRIEDLANDER,ELIZABETH-Vaulting-Brattleboro-1970-Stephen Greene-1st ed (f10,dj) 25.00

FRIEDLANDER,LEE-American Monument-NY-(1976)-Eakins-oblng 4to-cl wi lea sp,ltd to 150c,specially bnd wi orig signed prnt-1st ed (y3,f) 1,150.00

FRIEDLANDER,SAUL-Pius XII and the Third Reich-NY-1966-Knopf-8vo-238p-1st US ed (jj5,dj) 15.00

FRIEDLANDER,SAUL-Prelude to Downfall-NY-1967-Knopf-1st ed (j8,f,dj) 20.00

FRIEDMAN,B H-Alfonso Ossorio-NY-(1973)-Abrams-folio-cl-1st ed (oo6,dj) 75.00

FRIEDMAN,BRUCE J-Far From the City of Class-NY-1963-Frommer Pasmantier-1st ed (r5,f,dj) 45.00

FRIEDMAN,BRUCE J-Far From the City of Class-NY-1963-Frommer/Pasmantier-1st ed (y1,dj) 50.00

FRIEDMAN,BRUCE J-Stern-NY-1962-auth 1st bk-1st ed (r5,f,dj) 50.00

FRIEDMAN,I K-Autobiography of a Beggar-Bost-1903-Small,Maynard-1st ed (v5,autg) 60.00

FRIEDMAN,JOSEPH S-History of Color Photography-Bost-1944-Amer Photo Publ-514p-scarce-1st ed (cc9,sl wn dj) 100.00

FRIEDMAN,M-Charles Sheeler-NY-1975-lg 4to-48 col plts & b&w plts-1st prtg (h10,dj) 150.00

FRIEDMAN,MYRA-Buried Alive-NY-(1973)-Morrow-12p photo insert-1st prtg (q1,sm stn t.e.,dj) 28.00

FRIEDMANN,H-Distributional Checklist of Birds of Mexico. Parts I & II-Berkeley-1950,57-8vo-2 vols-wrps,9 col plts (y8) 75.00

FRIEDMANN,H-Distributional Checklist of Birds of Mexico.2 parts(in 1)-Berkeley-1950,57-Cooper Ornith Club-8vo-202;436p-cl,9 col plts (y8,spot sp) 75.00

FRIEDMANN,H-Honey Guides-Wash D.C.-1958-USNM Bull 208-292p-wrps (d9) 30.00

FRIEDMANN,H-Honey Guides-Wash-1955-8vo-292p-wrps,5 col plts,20 b&w plts (y8) 45.00

FRIEDMANN,H-Host Relations of the Parasitic Cowbirds-Wash D.C.-1963-USNM Bull.233-274p-wrps (d9) 12.50

FRIEND OF THE FAMILY-Adventures of a Salmon in the River Dee...Fly-Fisher in North Wales-Lond-1853-16mo-104p-rebnd in pap wrps wi orig wrps bnd in-illus-rare (m3,rebnd) 125.00

FRIEND,J NEWTON-Iron in Antiquity-Lond-1926-Chas Griffin-viii+221p-red cl,18 text figs-1st ed (j2) 35.00

FRIEND,LLERENA-Sam Houston, the Great Designer-Austin-1954-UTP-394p-illus-1st ed (a9,dj) 50.00

FRIEND,W H-Plants of Ornamental Value for the Rio Grande Valley of Texas-1942-Agr Exp-156p-wrps (x6,as new) 15.00

FRIENDLY,ALFRED-Beaufort of the Admiralty-NY-1977-Random-1st US ed (v4,as new in dj) 20.00

FRIENDS OF FRANCE-The Field Service of the American Ambulance Described by its Members-Bost,NY-1916-295p (g10) 25.00

FRIENDS OF FRANCE: FIELD SERVICE OF THE AMERICAN AMBULANCE DESCRIBED BY ITS MEMBERS-Bost-1916-297p-photos-1st ed (dd3) 50.00

FRIESEN,G-Flamethrowers-1936-Caxton Pr-auth 1st bk-1st ed (x2,sl chip dj) 45.00

FRIIS,HERMAN R-ED.-Arctic Diary of Russell Williams Porter-1976-U Pr of VA-1st ed (oo4,f,dj) 20.00

FRIIS,LEO J-Orange County Through Four Centuries-Santa Ana-1965-Pioneer-225p-1st ed (d3,dj) 30.00

FRIMMER,STEVEN-Dead Matter-NY-1982-Holt-1st ed (s4,vf,dj) 22.50

FRINK,MAURICE-Cow Country Cavalcade-1954-Old West Publ-243p-photos,drwngs,map-Herd 852-1st ed (r8,f,f dj) 35.00

FRINK,MAURICE-Cow Country Cavalcade-Denver-1954-Old West-1st ed (pp9,dj) 45.00

FRISBIE,CHARLOTTE J-Kinaalda-Middletown-1967-437p-photos-1st ed (t7,dj) 32.50

FRISCH,KARL VON-Bees:Their Vision, Chemical Senses & Language-1950-Cornell Univ-xiii,119p-illus (hh1) 17.50

FRISCH,MAX-Bluebeard-SD,NY,Lond-(1983)-HBJ-1st US ed (bb1,f,dj) 15.00

FRISCH,MAX-Homo Faber-Lond,NY-1959-1st ed in Engl (s5,dj) 25.00

FRISCH,MAX-Montauk-NY,Lond-(1976)-HBJ-1st ed (b5,as new in dj) 15.00

FRISCH,MAX-Sketchbook 1946 to 1949-NY,Lond-(1977)-HBJ-1st ed (bb1,f,dj) 12.50

FRISCH,MAX-Sketchbook 1966 to 1971-NY-(1974)-HBJ-1st ed (bb1,f,dj) 15.00

FRISCH,MAX-Wilderness of Mirrors-NY-1966-1st US ed (s5,dj) 20.00

FRISON-ROCHE,ROGER-Mont Blanc and Seven Valleys-Paris-1961-Arthaud-267p-blu cl,photos,fldg map (gg6,f,dj) 40.00

FRISON-ROCHE,ROGER-Mont Blanc and the Seven Valleys-Paris-1961-267p-illus,fldg map-1st ed (q10,f,dj) 30.00

FRISTRUP,BORGE-Greenland Ice Cap-(1966)-U of Wash-sq 4to-312p-tip in col & b&w plts-1st Amer ed (u8,pg sl bump,sl soil cov) 60.00

FRITZ,HENRY E-Movement for Indian Assimilation, 1860 to 1890-Phila-(1963)-U of Penn Pr-244p-illus (dd4,dj) 15.00

FRITZ,LEAH-Dreamers & Dealers-Bost-(1979)-Beacon Pr-293p-cl-1st ed (d1,f,dj) 15.00

FROHAWK,F W-British Birds-NY-1958-8vo-256p-cl,31 col plts (y8,speckld sp) 35.00

FROHMAN,CHARLES E-Sandusky's Yesterdays-Col-(1968)-177p-cl (l1) 12.50

FROISSART,SIR JOHN-Chronicles of England, France, Spain, and the Adjoining Countries...-NY-(1843)-J Winchester-4to-634p-qtr lea,illus-v scarce-1st US ed (jj5,rbnd) 750.00

FROLOV,WANDA L-Katish, Our Russian Cook-1947-Farrar,Straus-208p-brwn cl,drwngs-1st ed (q8,wn dj) 15.00

FROM DANISH KITCHENS-(Seattle)-(1941)-(Annex Club,St.Johannes)-150p-wht wrps,plastic comb bndg (n6) 25.00

FROME,DAVID-Homicide House-1950-Rinehart-1st ed (s10,f,f dj) 30.00

FROME,DAVID-Mr Pinkerton at the Old Angel-NY-1939-Farrar-1st ed (e4,f,dj sp sl fade) 35.00

FROME,DAVID-Mr.Pinkerton Grows a Beard-1935-Farrar-1st ed (s10,dj) 30.00

FROME,DAVID-Mr.Pinkerton Grows a Beard-NY-1935-Farrar-1st ed (k4,f,dj) 35.00

FROME,DAVID-Mr.Pinkerton Has the Clue-NY-1936-Farrar-1st ed (d4) 15.00

FROME,DAVID-Strange Death of Martin Green-NY-1931-Dbldy CC-1st ed (e4) 15.00

FROMMER,HARVEY-New York City Baseball-1980-MacMillan-1st ed (s7,f,dj) 17.50

FRONCEK,THOMAS-ED.-Voices From the Wilderness-NY-1974-McGraw Hill-sm 4to-xv+360p-cl,not Spec. ed (z4,dj) 25.00

FRONCEK,THOMAS-Frontierman's Own Story-NY-1974-360p-maps-1st ed (t7,dj) 10.00

FROST,A B-Book of Drawings by ...-NY-1904-elephant folio-unpgd-illus,auth-scarce (m3) 70.00

FROST,A B-Book of Drawings by...-NY-1904-oversize-dec frnt bd,illus (ee3) 75.00

FROST,CLARK-Long Riders-1941-Phoenix-1st ed (r9,dj) 35.00

FROST,J-ED.-Class Book of Nature...-Hartford-1839-Belknap & Hamersley-283p-bds-4th ed (k1,wn) 17.50

FROST,JOHN-Pictorial Life of General Marion-Phila-1847-Lindsay & Blakiston-208p-red cl-scarce-1st ed (oo5,sp chip,fox) 65.00

FROST,L A-Phil Sheridan Album-Seattle-1978-176p-illus,ports-1st ed (z10,soil dj) 25.00

FROST,LAWRENCE A-Custer Album-Seattle-(1964)-Superior-192p-1st ed (gg4,dj) 30.00

FROST,LAWRENCE A-General Custer's Libbie-Seattle-(1976)-Superior Publ-336p-photos,drwngs-1st ed (ee4,dj) 50.00

FROST,LAWRENCE A-General Custer's Libbie-Seattle-(1976)-Superior-336p-cl-1st ed so stated (j1,f,dj) 30.00

FROST,MAX-ED.-New Mexico-Santa Fe-1894-New Mex Prtg Co-343,(1)p+lg fldg map-wrps-Rampaging Herd 857 (b1,sl wn) 45.00

FROST,MAX-New Mexico-Santa Fe-1894-343p+1p index,photos,fldg map-Adams Herd#857-2nd ed (v7,cov sl soil,sp wn) 150.00

FROST,NINA HOLT-From Shore to Shore...-Montpelier-1893-Argus & Patriot Prntng Hs-32p-wrps (h1) 45.00

FROST,ROBERT-An Unstamped Letter in Our Rural Letter Box-(NY)-Dec 1944-H Holt-sm 8vo-(16)p-mauve wrps,prtd cov labl,t.p. illus,T W Nason,ltd ed-scarce (t10,f) 125.00

FROST,ROBERT-Boy's Will-NY-1915-Holt-1st state wi "Aind"-1st ed (ll6,f) 300.00

FROST,ROBERT-Collected Poems 1939-NY-1939-Halcyon-"Halcyon House Edition, March, 1939" on cpyrght pg-1st ed,1st prtg (ll6,f,dj) 100.00

FROST,ROBERT-Come In and Other Poems-NY-1943-Holt-1st ed,1st prtg (ll6,dj) 50.00

FROST,ROBERT-Complete Poems of...-Lond-1951-Cape-1st Brit ed (ll6,f,dj) 200.00

FROST,ROBERT-Complete Poems of...-NY-1949-Holt-1st ed,1st prtg (ll6,dj wn) 75.00

FROST,ROBERT-From Snow to Snow-NY-1936-Holt-bndg B-1st ed (ll6,dj) 100.00

FROST,ROBERT-Further Range-NY-1936-Holt-1st ed,1st state wi "First Printing" (ll6) 25.00

FROST,ROBERT-Further Range-NY-1936-Holt-8vo-cl-1st ed (x3,sl chip dj) 60.00

FROST,ROBERT-In the Clearing-NY-1962-Holt-1st ed,1st prtg (ll6,f,dj) 35.00

FROST,ROBERT-Lone Striker-NY-1933-Knopf-wrps,No.8 of Borzoi Chap bks-Crane H17-1st ed (bb2,f) 65.00

FROST,ROBERT-Lovely Shall be Choosers-NY-1929-Random-pict wrps,ltd to 475c,Poetry Quartos-Crane A12-1st ed (dd2,f) 65.00

FROST,ROBERT-Masque of Mercy-NY-(1947)-1st ed (c5,dj) 30.00

FROST,ROBERT-Masque of Reason-NY-1945-Holt-1st ed,1st prtg (ll6,f,dj) 50.00

FROST,ROBERT-North of Boston-Lond-1914-Nutt-bndg A-1st ed,1st issue (ll6) 2,000.00

FROST,ROBERT-Robert Frost: Farm Poultryman-Hanover-1963-Dartmouth-1st ed,1st prtg (ll6,dj) 25.00

FROST,ROBERT-Selected Poems 1928-NY-1928-Holt-1st ed,1st prtg (ll6,f,dj) 300.00

FROST,ROBERT-Selected Poems 1936-Lond-1936-Cape-1st Brit ed (ll6,f,dj) 200.00

FROST,ROBERT-Steeple Bush-NY-1947-Holt-1st ed,1st prtg (ll6,dj) 40.00

FROST,ROBERT-Steeple Bush-NY-1947-Holt-8vo-cl-1st ed (x3,dj) 60.00

FROST,ROBERT-West Running Brook-NY-1928-Holt-1st ed,1st state (ll6,f,dj) 100.00

FROST,ROBERT-West Running Brook-NY-1928-Holt-slim 8vo-cl/bds-1st state,w/o "first edition" on cpyrt pg-1st ed (x3,sp chip dj) 95.00

FROST,ROBERT-Witness tree-NY-1942-Holt-1st ed,1st prtg (ll6,f,dj) 50.00

FROST,ROBERT-You Come Too-NY-1959-Holt-1st ed,1st prtg (ll6,f,dj) 50.00

FROST,S ANNIE-Ladies Guide to Needle Work, Embroidery, Etc...-NY-(1877)-Henry T Williams-158p+ads-cl,illus (l1,sl wn sp) 25.00

FROST,THOMAS-Circus Life and Circus Celebrities-Detr-1970-328p-facs of 1875 Lond ed (v8) 20.00

FROSTIC,GWEN-My Michigan-(Benzonia)-(1957)-unpgd-pict bds,col drwngs (m1) 12.50

FROSTIC,GWEN-Walk with Me-(Benzonia)-(1958)-unpgd-bds,illus (n1) 10.00

FROTHINGHAM,A W-Barcelona Glass in Venetian Style-NY-1965-Hispanic Soc Amer-42p text-wrps,col frntis,38 illus (cc8) 40.00

FROTHINGHAM,A W-Hispanic Glass-1941-Hispanic Soc-204p-wrps,illus (cc8) 55.00

FROTHINGHAM,A W-Spanish Glass-1964-Faber & Faber-96p-96 plts+4 col (cc8,dj) 40.00

FROTHINGHAM,OCTAVIUS B-Transcendentalism in New England-NY-1876-Putnams-x+395p+ads-brwn cl-Howes F397-1st ed (b2) 65.00

FROTHINGHAM,ROBERT-Trails Through the Garden West-NY-1932-272p-pict e.p.-1st ed (t7,dj) 17.50

FROUD,NINA-Home Book of Russian Cookery-Lond-(1958)-Faber-266p-red cl-1st ed (q8,dj) 15.00

FROUDE,JAMES A-English Seamen in the Sixteenth Century-NY-1895-Scribner's-228p-dec brwn cl,t.e.g. (pp1,sl wn) 75.00

FROUDE,JAMES A-Oceana, or England and her Colonies-Lond-1886-Longmans,Green-8vo-viii,341p+(1)p ads-orig pict bds,9 plts-1st ed (t10,f) 150.00

FROUDE,JAMES-ED.-Letters and Memorials of Jane Welsh Carlyle-Lond-1883-Longmans,Green-3 vols-3/4 lea-1st ed (l9,sl wn & chip) 200.00

FRY,M-Art in a Machine Age-Lond-1969-1st ed (h10,sl chip dj) 45.00

FRY,ROGER-Transformations-NY-1926-Brentano's-4to-230p-grn cl,prpl labl,illus (r10,sl fox,sp fade,nbrs on sp 45.00

FRY,W H-ED.-Complete Treatise on Artificial Fish-Breeding-NY-1866-12mo-188p-illus-later prntng (m3) 45.00

FRYER,DONALD S-Songs and Sonnets Atlantean-Sauk City-1971-Arkham-1st ed (g3,f,dj) 30.00

FRYER,DONALD S-Songs and Sonnets Atlantean-Sauk City-1971-ltd to 2045c-1st ed (k5,as new in dj) 20.00

FRYER,PETER-Secrets of the British Museum-NY-(1966)-Citadel-1st Amer ed (w1,f,dj) 17.50

FRYMAN,JOHN F-From the Mountains to the Valley-(Oxford)-(1971)-115p-cl (g1,sl wn dj,autg) 15.00

FRYMIR,ALICE W-Basket Ball for Women-NY-1930-260p-cl (h1) 12.50

FRYXELL,FRITIOF-ED.-Francois Matthes and the Marks of Time-SF-1962-sm 4to-189p-e.p. map,illus,photos-1st ed (a4,f,f dj) 65.00

FRYXELL,FRITIOF-Teton Peaks and Their Ascents-Wyoming-1932-105p-18 photos,fldg map-1st ed (p10,vf) 150.00

FUCHIDA,M-Midway-(Annapolis)-(1957)-U.S. Naval Inst-roy 8vo-xxiv,266p-cl,frntis,36 illus,e.p. maps (t2) 35.00

FUCHS,VIVIAN-Crossing of Antartica-Lond-1958-337p-30 col & 63 b&w photos-1st Brit ed (p10,sl fox,dj) 25.00

FUENTES,CARLOS-Hydra Head-(1978)-Farrar-1st Amer ed (s9,f,dj) 17.50

FUENTES,CARLOS-Hydra Head-NY-(1978)-FS&G-1st Amer ed (b5,as new in dj) 25.00

FUENTES,CARLOS-Terra Nostra-Lond-1977-1st Brit ed (q5,f,dj) 25.00

FUENTES,CARLOS-Terra Nostra-NY-(1976)-FSG-1st Amer ed (ee2,f,dj) 40.00

FUENTES,CARLOS-Where the Air is Clear-NY-(1960)-Obolensky-auth 1st bk-1st Amer ed (b5,dj sl soil & sp chip) 35.00

FUENTES,CARLOS-Where the Air is Clear-NY-(1960)-Obolensky-auth 1st bk-1st Amer ed (ee2,dj) 50.00
FUERMAN,GEORGE-Houston: Land of the Big Rich-GC-1951-Dbldy-253p-cl,illus,L Collins-1st ed (w3,f,dj) 15.00
FUERTES,L A-Portraits of New England Birds-1932-Mass Dept Agri-4to-2p txt & indx-93 col plts (bb3,sl wn) 65.00
FUGARD,ATHOL-Blood Knot-NY-1964-auth 1st bk-1st US ed (o5,f,dj sl rub & chip) 90.00
FUGARD,ATHOL-Lesson From Aloes-NY-(1981)-Random-1st ed (bb1,as new in dj) 20.00
FUGARD,ATHOL-Master Harold...and the Boys-NY-1982-Knopf-1st ed (bb1,as new in dj) 20.00
FUGARD,ATHOL-Tsotsi-1981-Random-1st Amer ed (m9,vf,dj) 20.00
FUHRER,C-Mysteries of Montreal-Montreal-1881-245p-rare-1st ed (dd3) 200.00
FUKURAI,T-Clairvoyance and Thoughtography-Lond-1931-Rider & Co-247p-red cl,119 illus-1st ed (dd1) 65.00
FULD,JAS J-Pictorial Bibliography of the First Editions of Stephen C Foster-Phila-1857-tall folio-col illus (a3) 100.00
FULLER,A S-Small Fruit Culturist-1904-Orng Judd-298p-125 figs-new & enlgd ed (bb3) 38.00
FULLER,ANDREW-...LETTERS TO MR.VIDLER,ON THE DOCTRINE OF UNIVERSAL SALVATION...-Wash-1832-prntd by Yeoman & Lydy-115p-bds-Amer Imprnts 12536 (d1) 75.00
FULLER,ANDREW-Grape Culturist-NY-1866-OJ-262p-cl-7th thousand (x6) 45.00
FULLER,C E-Firearms of the Confederacy-Lawrence-1977-333p-illus,rprnt of 1944 ed (z10,dj) 60.00
FULLER,C F-Springfield Shoulder Arms, 1795 to 1865-NY-1931-176p-photos (gg3,f) 35.00
FULLER,GEO-History of the Pacific Northwest-NY-1966-383p+index,tan cl,frntis,fldg map-2nd ed rvsd (b6) 12.50
FULLER,GEORGE W-Bibliography of Bookplate Literature-Spokane-1926-Spokane Publ Libr-8vo-151p-cl-ltd to 500c,nbrd,autg-1st ed (w2) 95.00
FULLER,GEORGE W-Report on the Investigations into the Purification of the Ohio River Water at Louisville, KY...-NY-1898-Van Nostrand-4to-vii+461p-blck cl,8 plts in rear-1st ed (a2,sl crack hng) 85.00
FULLER,HARVEY A-Where Dark Shadows Play-Mlwk-(1890)-H A Fuller-134,(1)p-cl-wi Will Carleton intro (h1) 17.50
FULLER,HENRY B-Bertram Cope's Year-Chig-1919-R F Seymour/Alderbrink Pr-314p-cl-1st ed (j1) 15.00
FULLER,HENRY C-Texas Sheriff-Nacogdoches-1931-Baker Prtg-80p-pict wrps-1st ed (gg4) 95.00
FULLER,HENRY C-Texas Sheriff-Nacogdoches-1931-Baker Prtg-8vo-80p-pict wrps,photos-1st ed (aa3) 125.00
FULLER,JOHN G-Day of St.Anthony's Fire-NY-(1968)-Macmillan-8vo-310p-1st ed (gg5,dj) 12.50
FULLER,O E-Brave Men and Women-Chig,Phila-1887-H F Smith-512p-cl (d1) 27.50
FULLER,R BUCKMINSTER-Tetrascroll-NY-1982-St.Martin's-4to-illus,auth-1st ed (q2,dj) 30.00
FULLER,R BUCKMINSTER-Untitled Epic Poem on the History of Industrialization-Highlands-1962-Jargon Soc 44-8vo-dec wrps,prtd glassine dj-1st ed (jj8,f,dj) 65.00
FULLER,SARA-ED.-Ohio Black History Guide-Columbus-1975-Ohio Hist Soc-221p-cl (e1) 12.50
FULLERTON,B M-Select Bibliography of American Literature; 1775 to 1900-NY-1932-327p (w10) 15.00
FULLERTON,LADY GEORGIANA-Stormy Life-NY-1868-Appleton-8vo-304p-cl,illus,G Fay-1st US ed (w6,sl wn) 60.00
FULLMER,JANE-Sir Humphry Davy's Published Works-Cambridge-1969-112p-1st ed (dd3,dj) 30.00
FULSHER,K-Hair-Wing Atlantic Salmon Flies-N Conway-1981-4to-181p-ltd to 500c,nbrd,two autg,col plts,photos (m3,vf,dj) 85.00
FULTON,J A-Peach Culture-1870-Orng Judd-190p-illus (bb3,cov wn) 23.00
FULTON,JOHN F-Harvey Cushing, a Biography-Springfield-1946-754p-illus-1st ed (g10,dj wn) 60.00
FULTON,JOHN F-Harvey Cushing, a Biography-Springfield-1946-Chas C Thomas-8vo-xii,754,(2)p-1st ed (x4,sp fade) 35.00
FULTON,JOHN-Bibliography of Two Oxford Physiologists-Oxford-1935-62p-wrps-1st ed (dd3) 75.00
FULTON,JOHN-Great Medical Bibliographers-Phila-1951-106p+37 plts-1st ed (dd3) 100.00
FULTON,JOHN-Selected Readings in the History of Physiology-Springfield-1930-317p-1st ed (dd3) 100.00
FULTON,JOHN-Yale Medical Library-New Haven-1962-29p-wrps-1st ed (dd3) 15.00
FULTON,MAURICE G-History of the Lincoln County War-Tucson-(1968)-U of Arizona-(iv),433p-cl,maps,photos,map e.p.-1st ed (v1,sl wn dj) 50.00
FULTON,MAURICE G-New Mexico's own Chronicle-Dallas-(1937)-364p-Adams Guns#396-v scarce-1st ed (u7,dj chip) 100.00
FULTZ,HOLLIS-Famous Northwest Manhunts and Murder Mysteries-Elma-(1955)-229p-photos-Six Guns #789 (r8) 45.00
FUNDERBURK,T R-Fighters-NY-(1965)-4to-xx,200p-cl,frntis,plts,1 dbl-pg map,text illus,col illus e.p.-1st ed (t2,dj) 25.00
FUNKHOUSER,W D-Archaeological Survey of Kentucky-Lexington-1932-U of KY-viii,463p-wrps,65 photo plts,maps-scarce-1st ed (ll9,f) 125.00
FUNKHOUSER,W D-Wild Life in Kentucky-Frankfort-1925-8vo-(11),385p-cl,col frntis,illus,ltd to 1000c (y8,cor wn) 65.00
FUNSTON,FREDERICK-Memories of Two Wars-NY-1911-Scribners-451p-photo frntis,drwngs-1st ed (c3,cor rub) 36.00
FURGUSON,T J-Negro Education the Future of the Race...to which is Appended the Emancipation Proclamation...-Marietta-1866-Register Office Power-20p-prntd wrps-rare (c1,sl soil wrps) 250.00
FURLAN,WILLIAM P-In Charity Unfeigned-1952-Diocese of St.Cloud-270p-map e.p.,illus-1st ed (gg4,chip dj) 20.00
FURLONG,CHARLES W-Let 'er Buck-NY-1921-Putnam's-242p-photo paste down on cov,photos-Herd 866-1st ed (cc4) 40.00
FURMAN,LAURA-Shadow Line-NY-(1982)-Viking-1st ed (j6,f,f dj) 20.00
FURMAN,LAURA-Watch Time Fly-NY-(1983)-Viking-1st ed (j6,f,f dj) 15.00
FURMAN,MOORE-Letters of...Deputy Quarter Master General of New Jersey in the Revolution-NY-1912-xiii,162p-cl-ltd to 350c (aa6) 50.00
FURNAS,J C-Late Demon Rum-Lond-1965-Allen-381p-blk cl,facs illus-1st Brit ed (q8,dj) 15.00
FURNEAUX,RUPERT-Money Pit Mystery-NY-(1972)-Dodd,Mead-8vo-158p-1st ed (jj5,f,dj) 15.00
FURZER,BRIAN-Flyfishing-NY-1980-12mo-125p-col photos & plts (m3,vf) 10.00

FUSSELL,BETTY-Masters of American Cookery-(1983)-Times Bks-424p-blk cl-1st ed (q8,dj) 22.50

FUSSELL,EDWIN-Frontier: American Literature and the American West-1965-Princeton-sm 4to-xv+450p-cl-1st ed (z4) 20.00

FUSSELL,G E-Old English Farming Books From Fitzherbert to Tull 1523 to 1730-Lond-1947-C Lockwood-1st ed (w1,f,dj) 20.00

FUTCHER,WINNIFRED M-ED.-Great North Road to the Cariboo-(Vancouver)-1938-Roy Wrigley-113p-dec bds,photos,illus,fldg map (aa2) 60.00*

FUTRELLE,JACQUES-Chase of the Golden Plate-NY-1907-Dodd-pict cov-1st ed (h4,sl soil pg edges) 75.00

FUTRELLE,JACQUES-Diamond Master-Indpls-1909-Bobbs-col frontis-1st ed (h4,sl fox) 20.00

FUTRELLE,JACQUES-High Hand-Indpls-1911-Bobbs Merrill-1st ed (w5) 35.00

FUTRELLE,JACQUES-Thinking Machine-NY-1907-Dodd-1st ed (d4,frnt hng weak) 100.00

FYLEMAN,ROSE-Fairies and Chimneys-NY-(1920)-Doran-sm 8vo-62p-cl,col frntis-1st ed (r3,f,dj) 25.00

FYLEMAN,ROSE-Fairies and Chimneys-NY-(1920)-Doran-sm 8vo-pict cl,col frntis-1st ed (pp10,f,chip dj) 40.00

FYSH,H-Qantas at War-(Sydney)-(1968)-roy 8vo-xii,244p-cl,frntis,24p plts-1st ed (t2,dj) 75.00

FYSH,H-Qantas Rising-(Sydney)-(1966)-roy 8vo-xii,296p-cl,frntis,24p plts (t2,dj) 50.00

GABEL,CREIGHTON-ED.-Reconstructing African Culture History-Bost-1967-Bost U Pr-8vo-264p-cl & bds-1st ed (y5,dj) 15.00

GABLER,HANS-ET AL-Ulysses, a Critical and Synoptic Editon-NY,Lond-1984-Garland Publ-3 vols-iss w/o djs-1st ed (bb1,as new) 170.00

GABLIK,SUZI-Magritte-Greenwich-1970-NYGS-1st ed (v5,f,sl tn dj) 30.00

GABRIELSON,I N-Birds of Alaska-Harrisburg-1959-8vo-922p-cl,12 col plts,map (y8,dj chip) 165.00

GABRIELSON,I N-Birds of Oregon-Corvallis-1940-8vo-650p-cl,col frntis,97 b&w plts (y8,sp drknd) 70.00

GABRIELSON,I N-Birds of the Pacific NW-NY-1970(1940)-8vo-(1),650p-wrps,97 plts,fldg map (y8) 20.00

GABRIELSON,I N-Wildlife Management-NY-1951-8vo-274p-cl,24 plts (y8,dj chip) 22.00

GABRIELSON,IRA N-ED.-Fisherman's Encyclopedia-Harrisburg-1954-4to-730p-photos,illus-1st ed (m3,dj) 22.50

GADDIS,WILLIAM-JR-NY-1975-Knopf-1st ed (b5,as new in dj) 100.00

GADDIS,WILLIAM-Recognitions-NY-(1955)-Harcourt,Brace-auth 1st bk-1st ed (ff6,sl soil dj) 200.00

GADDY,JERRY-Texas in Revolt-Ft.Collins-1973-139p-col frntis,col plts-1st ed (t7,dj) 20.00

GADE,JOHN A-Book Plates, Old and New-NY-1898-Manfield-sm 8vo-52p-cl backd bds,t.e.g.,plts-1st ed (w2,sp wn,spot cov) 30.00

GADE,JOHN-Life and Times of Tycho Brahe-1947-Princeton U Pr/Amer Scand-xii+209p-grn cl,plts-1st ed (g2,sl spot cov,dj) 15.00

GAG,WANDA-Millions of Cats-NY-1928-Coward McCann-oblng 8vo-unpgd-pict bds & e.p.,illus by auth-1st ed (nn8,scuff,edge fray,sl soil) 95.00

GAG,WANDA-Three Gay Tales from Grimm-NY-(1943)-Coward McCann-sm sq 8vo-63p-pict bds,illus,auth-1st ed (r3,wn) 25.00

GAGE,EDWIN-Phoenix No More-NY-1978-Harper-1st ed (g4,f,dj) 10.00

GAGE,JACK-Johnson County War is a Pack of Lies-Cheyenne-1967-Flintlock-xviii,89;xvi,79p-photos,book needs to be turned over & read from reverse end for other side of story-1st ed (v1,dj) 65.00

GAGE,JACK-Tensleep and No Rest-Casper-(1958)-Prairie Publ-(vi),222,(4)p-cl,illus-1st ed (v1,chip dj) 30.00

GAGE,JACK-Tensleep and No Rest-Casper-(1958)-Prairie-222p-Six Guns #792-1st ed (r8) 35.00

GAGE,WILLIAM-Cully Cully and the Bear-NY-(1983)-Greenwillow-4to-unpgd-cl-1st ed (r3,dj) 15.00

GAIL,MARZIEH-Persia and the Victorians-Lond-1951-Allen & Unwin-1st ed (t4,f,f dj) 30.00

GAINES,ERNEST J-Autobiography of Miss Jane Pittman-NY-1971-Dial-1st ed (f8,f,dj) 100.00

GAINES,ERNEST J-Catherine Carmier-NY-1964-auth 1st bk-1st ed (r5,sl chip dj) 100.00

GAIR,MALCOLM-Sapphires on Wednesday-Lond-(1957)-Collins-auth 1st bk-1st ed (bb1,dj) 17.50

GAISBERG,F W-Music Goes Round-NY-1942-Macmillan-1st ed (w1,f,dj) 35.00

GALBRAITH,JOHN S-Hudson's Bay Company as an Imperial Factor, 1821 to 1869-Berkeley,LA-1957-U of Cal Pr-8vo-grn cl (oo1,dj wn) 125.00

GALBREATH,CHARLES B-Benjamin Russel Hanby, Author of "Darling Nelly Gray"-Columbus-1905-43p-wrps (l1) 12.50

GALBREATH,CHARLES B-Daniel Decatur Emmett, Author of "Dixie"-Columbus-1904-66p-cl (l1) 15.00

GALDOS,B PEREZ-Dona Perfecta-NY-1896-Harper & Bros-xiii;319p-cl-BAL 9702-1st Amer ed (j1) 15.00

GALDSTON,IAGO-Behind the Sulfa Drugs: a Short History of Chemotherapy-NY-1943-174p-1st ed (dd3) 40.00

GALDSTON,IAGO-ED.-Panic and Morale-NY-(1958)-Int'l Univ Pr-xx+340p-blu cl-1st ed (l2,dj) 15.00

GALE,ZONA-Friendship Village Love Stories-NY-1909-Macmillan-8vo-321p+ads-1st ed (w6) 35.00

GALE,ZONA-Miss Lulu Bett-NY-1921-Appleton-grn cl-1st ed (f2,dj chip & sl tn) 25.00

GALE,ZONA-Portage,Wisconsin...-Tor-1928-Longmans,Green-8vo-214p-bndg by W A Dwiggins-1st Can ed (w6,f,dj) 35.00

GALEN-On Anatomical Procedures-Lond-1956-289p-1st Engl transl (dd3) 150.00

GALEN-Translation of Galen's Hygiene-Springfield-1951-277p-1st Engl transl (dd3,dj) 50.00

GALENA GUIDE-Galena-1937-WPA-fldg map tip in rear-1st ed (v5,f) 100.00

GALES,R L-Dwellers in Arcady-Lond-1931-Sheldon Pr-cl-1st ed (n8,f,dj) 25.00

GALILEI-ET AL-Controversy on the Comets of 1618-Phila-1960-U of Penn Pr-380p (hh6,dj) 40.00

GALLAGHER,M-Birds of Oman-1980-Quartet-4to-310p-wrps,120 col plts,maps-1st ed (bb3,f) 95.00

GALLAGHER,SARAH A-Early History of Lambertville-Trenton-1903-55p-cl,plts (aa6) 35.00

GALLAHER,W W-Black Bass Lore-NY-1937-236p-illus (gg3,f,chip dj) 20.00

GALLAHER,WALLACE-Black Bass Lore-NY-1937-8vo-236p-illus-1st ed (m3,fray dj) 25.00

GALLANT,MAVIS-From the Fifteenth District-NY-1979-Random-1st ed (w5,f,f dj) 20.00

GALLANT,MAVIS-Pegnitz Junction-NY-1973-Random-1st ed (w5,f,f dj) 20.00

GALLATIN,A E-American Water Colourists-1922-Dutton-30 illus-ltd to 950c (h10,sl rub cov,uncut) 125.00

GALLATIN,A E-Art & the Great War-1919-Dutton-folio-illus-1st ed (ee1) 100.00

GALLATIN,JAMES-Diary of James Gallatin Secretary to Albert Gallatin-NY-1916-Scribner's-xiii,314p-illus-New ed (n2) 25.00

GALLAWAY,B P-ED.-Dark Corner of the Confederacy-Dubuque-1968-Wm C Brown-188p-wrps-1st ed (w3) 25.00

GALLERY,DANIEL V-Pueblo Incident-GC-(1970)-Dbldy-1st ed (ff3,dj) 30.00

GALLICO,PAUL-All the Brave-NY-(1939)-Modern Age Bks-qto-pict wrps,drwngs,Quintanilla-1st ed (bb2,sl wn) 45.00

GALLICO,PAUL-Coronation-Lond-1962-1st ed (y7,dj) 15.00

GALLICO,PAUL-Honorable Cat-NY-(1972)-Crown-73 col photos-1st ed (bb1,f,dj) 12.50

GALLICO,PAUL-Hurricane Story-GC-1960-Dbldy-1st ed (bb1,sp wn dj) 25.00

GALLICO,PAUL-Manxmouse-NY-(1968)-Coward McCann-J & A Grahame Johnstone,illus-1st ed (b5,dj) 30.00

GALLICO,PAUL-Scruffy-GC-1962-Dbldy-1st ed (hh5,f,dj) 15.00

GALLICO,PAUL-Small Miracle-Lond-1951-Michael Joseph-illus by E Norfield-1st ed (y1,f,dj) 25.00

GALLICO,PAUL-Snowflake-NY-1953-DD-1st US ed (y1,f,dj) 17.50

GALLOWAY,JOHN D-First Transcontinental Railroad-NY-1950-319p-1st ed (n4,f,dj) 20.00

GALLOWAY,KATHERINE-Owensville-Hearne-1974-Robco Pr-7 one sided pgs-wrps-1st ed (w3,f) 17.50

GALLUP,DONALD-T S Eliot, a Bibliography-NY-(1953)-Harcourt Brace-8vo-xi,177p-cl-1st US ed (w2,dj chip) 35.00

GALLUP,JOSEPH A-Sketches of Epidemic Disease in the State of Vermont-Bost-1815-419p-calf-Austin #809 (g10,hngs split,chip,wn) 250.00

GALSWORTHY,JOHN-Awakenings-1920-Scribners-illus,R H Sauter-1st ed (x2,f,sl chip dj) 95.00

GALSWORTHY,JOHN-Eldest Son-1912-Scribners-scarce in dj-1st ed (x2,f,sl chip dj) 65.00

GALTON,FRANCIS-Hereditary Genius-NY-1870-390p-buckrm-1st Amer ed (dd3,rbnd) 200.00

GALVAYNE,SIDNEY-XXth Century Book on the Horse-Lond-1907-Balliere Tindall & Cox-4to-2nd ed (h9) 48.00

GALVIN,MAJ JOHN R-Minute Men-NY-(1967)-Hawthorn-8vo-286p-1st ed (ff5,f,dj) 15.00

GALWAY,THOMAS F-Valiant Hours-Harrisburg-(1961)-262p-maps-1st ed (c4,f,dj) 50.00

GAMBIER,CAPTAIN J W-Links In My Life On Land and Sea-NY-1906-Dutton-thk 8vo-451p wi index,dec tan cl-1st Amer ed (t1) 50.00

GAMBINO,RICHARD-Vendetta-GC-1977-Dbldy-198p (r1,dj) 15.00

GAMBLE,ELIZA B-Evolution of Woman-NY,Lond-1894-Putnam's-356p-cl (d1) 40.00

GAMBLE,JAY M-Steamboats on the Muskingum-Staten Island-(1971)-Stmshp Hist Soc of Amer-xii+143p-brwn cl,illus-1st ed (e2,dj) 20.00

GAMBRILL,RICHARD-Sporting Stables and Kennels-NY-1935-Derrydale Pr-4to-ltd to 950c (f10,sp drknd) 275.00

GAMMETT,JAMES-Nevada Post Offices-Las Vegas-1983-176p-frntis,photos,maps-1st ed (t7,f,dj) 25.00

GANDHI,MAHATMA-Sermon on the Sea-Chig-1924-Univ Publ Hs-128p-1st ed so stated (m4,cl dusty) 15.00

GANDHI,MAHATMA-Young India 1924 to 1926-NY-1927-Viking-(16),984p-1st ed (m4,spot cl) 15.00

GANN,E K-Getting Them Into the Blue-NY-(1942)-roy 8vo-vi,154p-cl,plts,text illus-1st ed (t2,dj) 30.00

GANN,ERNEST K-Antagonists-NY-(1970)-S&S-1st ed (d10,f,dj) 12.50

GANN,ERNEST K-Flying Circus-NY-1974-Macmillan-illus-1st prtg (b6,f,sl tn dj) 35.00

GANN,T-Maya Indians of Southern Yucatan and Northern British Honduras-1918-Bur Amer Ethnol Bull.64-146p-6 col & 22 b&w plts (bb3) 38.00

GANN,WALTER-Tread of the Longhorns-San Antonio-(1949)-188p-1st ed (v7,dj) 35.00

GANN,WALTER-Tread of the Longhorns-San Antonio-(1949)-Naylor Co-188p-illus by R L McCollister-Six Guns #794-1st ed (dd4,dj) 30.00

GANNETT,LEWIS-John Steinbeck Personal and Bibliographical Notes-1937-1st iss (bb2,f) 60.00

GANZHORN,JACK-I've Killed Men-NY-1959-Devin-Adair-256p-illus-Six Guns #796-1st Amer ed (ee4,dj) 30.00

GAPEN,DAN-River Fishing a Happy World-1978-priv prntng-8vo-281p-illus (m3,vf,dj) 12.50

GARAGIOLA,JOE-Baseball is a Funny Game-1960-Lippincott-1st ed (q7,f,f dj) 20.00

GARAGIOLA,JOE-Baseball is a Funny Game-Phila,NY-(1960)-192p-cl-1st ed so stated (n1,sl wn dj,pres cpy) 22.50

GARAVAGLIA,LOUIS A-Firearms of the American West,1803 to 1865,1866 to 1894-Albuq-1984,1985-UNM-4to-2 vols,cl,photos,illus-1st eds (v1,dj) 75.00

GARCES,FRANCISCO-Record of Travels in Arizona and California 1775 to 76-SF-1965-John Howell Bks-4to-113p-cl,glassine dj-ltd to 1500c (mm7,f,dj) 55.00

GARCIA,ANDREW-Tough Trip Through Paradise 1878 to 1879-Bost-1967-446p-illus,e.p. maps-1st ed (d7,f,dj) 65.00

GARCIA,ANDREW-Tough Trip Through Paradise, 1878 to 1879-Bost-1967-Houghton Mifflin-8vo-xvii,446p-map e.p.,photos,dbl pg map-1st ed (aa3,f,dj) 85.00

GARCIA,EUGENE C-Shem Ham and Japeth-Athens-1973-361p-illus-1st ed (t7,f,dj) 12.50

GARCIA,JERRY-Garcia-1972-Straight Arrow-1st ed (r9,f,sl tn dj) 35.00

GARCILASO DE LA VEGA-Florida of the Inca-Austin-1951-Univ of Tex-xlviii+656p-1st ed (m2,dj) 35.00

GARD,R E-Wild Goose Country-Madison-1975-4to-(5),146p-cl,photos(incl col) (y8,autg,sl tn dj) 35.00

GARD,WAYNE-Chisholm Trail-Norman-(1954)-U of Okla Pr-drwngs by Eggenhofer,maps,photos-Herd 875-1st ed (dd4,dj) 65.00

GARD,WAYNE-Great Buffalo Hunt-NY-1959-8vo-324p-illus-1st ed (m3,vf) 15.00

GARD,WAYNE-Great Buffalo Hunt-NY-1959-Knopf-324p-illus-1st ed (f9,dj) 35.00

GARD,WAYNE-Rawhide Texas-Norman-(1965)-U of Okla Pr-236p-illus-1st ed (f9,sl chip dj) 35.00

GARD,WAYNE-Sam Bass-Bost,NY-1936-262p-illus,e.p. maps-Six Guns 803-scarce-1st ed (e7) 70.00

GARDI,R-Indigenous African Architecture-NY-1974-folio-illus-1st ed (h10,dj) 125.00

GARDINER,ALAN H-Egyptian Grammar-Lond-1927-Oxford U-illus-1st ed (y10,sp fade) 115.00

GARDINER,ALEXANDER-Canfield, the True Story of the Greatest Gambler-NY-1930-frntis,illus-1st ed (t7) 20.00

GARDINER,ALLEN F-Visit to the Indians on the Frontiers of Chili-Lond-1841-(4),194,(2)p-cl,map,3 litho plts-1st ed (o4,sp ends rprd) 600.00

GARDINER,SAMUEL-HIstory of the Great Civil War-Lond-1886 to 1891-3 vols-1/2 red lea,mrbld bds & e.p.,g dec sp,t.e.g.,fldg maps-1st ed (gg2) 250.00

GARDNER,ALBERT T E-History of Water Color Painting in America-NY-1966-Reinhold-oblng 4to-cl-1st ed (oo6,dj chip) 50.00

GARDNER,ALBERT T E-Winslow Homer, American Artist-NY-(1961)-262,(1)p-cl-frontis & 35 illus in col + b&w illus-1st ed so stated (g1,dj) 35.00

GARDNER,ALICE-Short History of Newnham College, Cambridge-Cambridge-1921-Bowes & Bowes-8vo-vi,144p-cl,frntis,illus-1st ed (z5) 35.00

GARDNER,ARTHUR-Britain's Mountain Heritage and Its Preservation as National Parks-Lond-1942-51p-128 photos,fldg map-1st Brit ed (q10,dj) 40.00

GARDNER,BRIAN-African Dream-NY-1970-314p-maps-1st Amer ed (b7,f,dj) 20.00

GARDNER,DAVID L-Adventures & Misadventures with Rod & Gun-Baker-1981-8vo-183p-wrps-photos (m3,vf,autg) 22.50

GARDNER,E C-Homes, & How to Make Them-Bost-1874-Osgood-8vo-g cov & sp,30 wood engr-1st ed (h10) 125.00

GARDNER,ERLE S-Case of the Angry Mourner-NY-1951-Morrow-1st ed (f4,f,dj) 25.00

GARDNER,ERLE S-Case of the Angry Mourner-NY-1951-Morrow-1st ed (z2,dj wn,sp chip) 35.00

GARDNER,ERLE S-Case of the Backward Mule-NY-1946-Morrow-1st ed (f4,f,dj) 25.00

GARDNER,ERLE S-Case of the Bigamous Spouse-NY-1961-Morrow-1st ed (d4,dj) 17.50

GARDNER,ERLE S-Case of the Black Eyed Blonde-1944-Morrow-1st ed (x7,dj) 65.00

GARDNER,ERLE S-Case of the Borrowed Brunette-NY-1946-Morrow-1st ed (d4,f,sl tn dj) 30.00

GARDNER,ERLE S-Case of the Cautious Coquette-NY-1949-Morrow-1st ed (z2,dj) 40.00

GARDNER,ERLE S-Case of the Crimson Kiss-NY-1970-Morrow-1st ed (d4,f,dj) 20.00

GARDNER,ERLE S-Case of the Crooked Candle-NY-1944-Morrow-1st ed (k4,f,dj sp sl wn) 45.00

GARDNER,ERLE S-Case of the Crying Swallow-NY-1971-Morrow-1st ed (j4,f,dj) 15.00

GARDNER,ERLE S-Case of the Daring Divorcee-NY-1964-Morrow-1st ed (f4,f,dj) 20.00

GARDNER,ERLE S-Case of the Demure Defendant-NY-1956-Morrow-1st ed (g4,f,dj) 30.00

GARDNER,ERLE S-Case of the Fabulous Fake-NY-1969-Morrow-1st ed (f4,f,dj) 20.00

GARDNER,ERLE S-Case of the Half Wakened Wife-1945-Mill-1st ed (s10,dj) 30.00

GARDNER,ERLE S-Case of the Lucky Loser-NY-1957-Morrow-1st ed (f4,f,chip dj) 20.00

GARDNER,ERLE S-Case of the Moth Eaten Mink-NY-1952-Morrow-1st ed (f4,dj) 12.50

GARDNER,ERLE S-Case of the One Eyed Witness-NY-1950-Morrow-1st ed (z2,dj) 45.00

GARDNER,ERLE S-Case of the Runaway Corpse-NY-1954-Morrow-1st ed (f4,f,sl wn dj) 25.00

GARDNER,ERLE S-Case of the Sun Bather's Diary-NY-1955-Morrow-1st ed (h4,f,dj) 25.00

GARDNER,ERLE S-Case of the Terrified Typist-NY-1956-Morrow-1st ed (e4,dj) 25.00

GARDNER,ERLE S-Case of the Vagabond Virgin-NY-1948-Morrow-1st ed (h4,f,sp chip dj) 25.00

GARDNER,ERLE S-Case of the Velvet Claws-NY-(1933)-Grosset-reprint (h4,dj) 15.00

GARDNER,ERLE S-Case of the Waylaid Wolf-NY-1959-Morrow-1st ed (z2,dj) 20.00

GARDNER,ERLE S-Case of the Worried Waitress-NY-1966-Morrow-1st ed (f4,dj) 20.00

GARDNER,ERLE S-Court of Last Resort-NY-1952-Sloan-1st ed (z2,f,dj) 40.00

GARDNER,ERLE S-D.A. Breaks a Seal-1946-Morrow-1st ed (s10,dj) 30.00

GARDNER,ERLE S-D.A. Calls It Murder-NY-1937-Morrow-1st ed (hh2,f,rub dj) 475.00

GARDNER,ERLE S-D.A. Draws a Circle-NY-1939-Morrow-1st ed (hh2,sl soil cl,dj) 325.00

GARDNER,ERLE S-D.A. Holds a Candle-NY-1938-Morrow-1st ed (hh2,f,sl tn dj) 335.00

GARDNER,ERLE S-Hidden Heart of Baja-NY-1962-Morrow-1st ed (z2,f,dj) 45.00

GARDNER,ERLE S-Hovering Over Baja-NY-1961-Morrow-1st ed (z2,dj) 45.00

GARDNER,ERLE S-Hunting the Desert Whale-1960-Morrow-208p-photos (bb3) 15.00

GARDNER,ERLE S-Neighborhood Frontiers-(1954)-Morrow-photos,auth-1st ed (cc1,sl chip dj,autg) 125.00

GARDNER,F B-How to Paint-NY-1875-Samuel R Wells-126p+18p ads-cl (m1,sl wn sp) 20.00

GARDNER,G-Travels in the Interior of Brazil...During the Years 1836 to 1841-1970-AMS-562p-map-rprnt of 1846 ed (bb3,f) 35.00

GARDNER,JOHN-Construction of Christian Poetry in Old English-Carbondale-(1975)-So Ill U Pr-1st ed (cc2,f,dj) 40.00

GARDNER,JOHN-Construction of the Wakefield Cycle-Carbondale-1974-SIU Pr-1st ed (b8,f,f dj) 125.00

GARDNER,JOHN-Every Night's a Bullfight-1971-Joseph-1st ed (s10,dj) 12.50

GARDNER,JOHN-For Special Services-Lond-1982-Cape & Hodder-1st ed (q4,dj) 27.50

GARDNER,JOHN-For Special Services-Lond-1982-Cape-1st ed (f4,f,dj) 35.00

GARDNER,JOHN-Forms of Fiction-NY-1962-prntd bds,iss w/o dj,auth 1st bk-1st ed (t5,sl sunned sp) 80.00

GARDNER,JOHN-Forms of Fiction-NY-1962-Random-auth 1st bk,w/o dj as issued-1st ed (g8) 125.00

GARDNER,JOHN-Freddy's Book-NY-1980-Knopf-illus,D Biamonte-1st ed (a10,as new in dj) 15.00

GARDNER,JOHN-Gawain Poet-Lincoln-1967-Cliff's Notes-wrps-1st ed (v5) 35.00

GARDNER,JOHN-Grendel-NY-1971-1st ed (o5,f,dj) 175.00

GARDNER,JOHN-Grendel-NY-1971-Knopf-14 drwngs,E Antonucci-1st ed (a10,f,sl fade dj) 200.00

GARDNER,JOHN-In the Suicide Mountains-NY-1977-illus,J Servello-1st ed (e5,f,dj) 25.00

GARDNER,JOHN-In the Suicide Mountains-NY-1977-Knopf-illus,J Servello-1st ed (r3,f,dj) 20.00

GARDNER,JOHN-Jason & Medeia-NY-1973-1st ed (o5,f,dj) 50.00

GARDNER,JOHN-Jason & Medeia-NY-1973-Knopf-1st ed (q2,dj) 55.00

GARDNER,JOHN-King of the Hummingbirds-NY-1977-illus,M Sporn,illus bds,no dj issued-1st ed (q5,f) 25.00

GARDNER,JOHN-King's Indian-NY-1974-Knopf-Fink,illus-1st ed (b5,as new in dj) 35.00

GARDNER,JOHN-Life and Times of Chaucer-NY-1977-Knopf-1st ed (h8,f,f dj) 50.00

GARDNER,JOHN-Nickel Mountain-NY-1973-Knopf-O'Donohue,illus-1st ed (b5,as new in dj) 20.00

GARDNER,JOHN-Nickelson's Ghost-NY-1982-Knopf-1st ed (g3,f,dj) 20.00

GARDNER,JOHN-October Light-NY-1976-Knopf-illus-1st ed (b5,as new in dj) 35.00

GARDNER,JOHN-On Moral Fiction-NY-(1978)-1st ed (s5,dj) 30.00

GARDNER,JOHN-On Moral Fiction-NY-(1978)-Basic Bks-1st ed (b5,as new in dj) 35.00

GARDNER,JOHN-Resurrection-(NY)-(1966)-NAL-scarce 1st novel-1st ed (a10,dj sl soil & tape rprd) 450.00

GARDNER,JOHN-Revenge of Moriarty-NY-1975-Putnam-1st US ed (f4,f,sl wn dj) 15.00

GARDNER,JOHN-Sunlight Dialogues-1972-Knopf-1st ed (x2,f,dj) 58.00

GARDNER,JOHN-Sunlight Dialogues-NY-1972-illus,J Napper-1st ed (o5,dj) 40.00

GARDNER,JOHN-Vlemk the Box Painter-Northridge-1979-1st ed (p5,f,dj) 25.00

GARDNER,JOHN-Vlemk the Box-Painter-Northridge-1979-ltd to 300c,autg,spec pap & patterned bds,illus by C Kanner-1st ed (s5,f,dj) 65.00

GARDNER,JOHN-Werewolf Trace-NY-1977-Dbldy-1st US ed (f4,rem mrk,dj) 12.50

GARDNER,JOHN-Wreckage of Agathon-NY et al-(1970)-Harper & Row-1st ed (a10,f,dj) 150.00

GARDNER,JOHN-Wreckage of Agathon-NY-1970-Harper & Row-1st ed (z2,f,f dj) 100.00

GARDNER,LEONARD-Fat City-NY-(1969)-FS&G-auth 1st bk-1st ed (b5,f,dj) 30.00

GARDNER,MATTHEW-Autobiography of Elder ..., a Minister in the Christian Church Sixty-Three Years-Dayton-1875-Christian Publ Assoc-286p-cl (g1) 37.50

GARDNER,PAUL-Glass of Frederick Carder-1976-Crown-373p-400 photos(80 col) (cc8,dj) 35.00

GARDNER,RICHARD-Grito-Indpls-(1970)-292p-photos,maps-1st ed (u7,dj) 35.00

GARDNER,RICHARD-Grito-Indpls-(1970)-292p-photos-1st ed (n10,f,dj) 30.00

GARDNER,ROBERT-Gardens of War-NY-(1968)-Random-4to-184p-337 photos incl col-1st ed (ff5,f,f dj) 25.00

GARDYNE,A D GREENHILL-Scottish Salmon Law-Manchester-1935-8vo-45p-wrps (m3,f) 10.00

GARFIELD,BRIAN-Line of Succession-NY-1972-Delacorte-1st ed (y1,f,f dj) 25.00

GARFIELD,LEON-King Nimrod's Tower-NY-(1982)-Lothrop,Lee & Shepard-4to-unpgd-pict cl,col illus,M Bragg-1st US ed (r3,as new in dj) 25.00

GARFIELD,SIDNEY-Teeth Teeth Teeth-NY-1969-S&S-8vo-448p-illus e.p.,illus-1st ed (cc7,dj) 25.00*

GARFIELD,VIOLA-Wolf and the Raven-Seattle-1948-151p-frntis,photos-1st ed (t7,f,dj) 27.00

GARFIELD,VIOLA-Wolf and the Raven-Seattle-1971-U of Wash Pr-156p-wrps,illus-6th prntg (j8,f,wrps) 25.00

GARLAND,HAMLIN-Back Trailers From the Middle Border-NY-1928-Macmillan-1st ed (hh5) 12.50

GARLAND,HAMLIN-Back Trailers From the Middle Border-NY-1928-Macmillan-1st ed (z2,f,sp chip dj) 45.00

GARLAND,HAMLIN-Book of the American Indian-NY,Lond-(1923)-lg 4to-274p+2p ads-35 illus by Remington (f7,f,dj) 165.00

GARLAND,HAMLIN-Book of the American Indian-NY-(1923)-Harper & Bros-sm folio-274p-illus by Remington-Howes G66 (dd4,dj) 150.00

GARLAND,HAMLIN-Book of the American Indian-NY-1923-Harper-4to-(viii),274p-pict pap cov bds,col frntis & illus,F Remington-1st ed (v1,dj,box wn) 185.00

GARLAND,HAMLIN-Captain of the Gray Horse Troop-1902-Harper-415p-1st ed (r8,cov wn) 40.00

GARLAND,HAMLIN-Crumbling Idols-Chig-1894-Stone & Kimball-gold stmpd cov,t.e.g.-1st ed (y1,as new) 100.00

GARLAND,HAMLIN-Hesper-NY-1903-Harpers-1st ed (hh5,sl cocked sp) 15.00

GARLAND,HAMLIN-Light of the Star-NY,Lond-1904-Harper & Bros-277,(1)p-cl-1st ed (g1) 17.50

GARLAND,HAMLIN-Light of the Star-NY-1904-Harper-1st ed (hh5,f) 25.00

GARLAND,HAMLIN-Main Travelled Roads-Cambridge,Chig-1893-Stone & Kimball-g dec covs,t.e.g.-1st ed (r2,f) 50.00

GARLAND,HAMLIN-Moccasin Ranch-NY-1909-Harpers-col dec cov,frntis-1st ed (y1,hng rprd) 50.00

GARLAND,HAMLIN-My Friendly Contemporaries-NY-1932-MacMillan-1st ed (pp9,sl chip dj) 45.00

GARLAND,HAMLIN-Spirit of Sweetwater-Phila,NY-1898-Curtis,DD Page-t.e.g.-1st ed (y1) 75.00

GARLAND,JAMES-Private Stable-Bost-1903-Little,Brown-2nd ed (j9) 375.00

GARLAND,JOSEPH E-Eastern Point-Peterborough-(1971)-Wm L Bauhan-xiv+424p-wht cl,illus-presume 1st ed (k2,dj) 35.00

GARLAND,JOSEPH E-Lone Voyager-Bost-(1963)-Little,Brown-8vo-272p-12p photos-1st ed (jj5,dj) 12.50

GARLAND,JOSEPH E-Lone Voyager-Bost-(1963)-Little,Brown-8vo-map e.p.-1st ed (nn1,wn dj) 25.00

GARLICK,THEODATUS-Treatise on the Artificial Propagation of Certain Kinds of Fish...-Cleve-1857-Tho. Brown,Publ-142p+ads-cl (j1,fox,pres cpy) 75.00

GARNEAU,JOS,JR.-Nebraska-Omaha-1892-24p-wrps-Herd 881-rare-1st ed (aa3,soil) 50.00

GARNER,R L-Speech of Monkeys-NY-1892-217p+ads-cl (c1,cov cor sl dmpstnd) 20.00

GARNER,S G-Going Nowhere Fast-1979-Vantage Pr-1st ed (t4,f,rub dj) 15.00

GARNER,WILLIAM R-Letters of...from California 1846 to 1847-Berkeley-1970-U of Cal-xiii,262p-photos,engrvngs-1st ed (o2,f,dj) 37.50

GARNETT,D-War in the Air-NY-1941-8vo-xii,292p-cl,9p plts-1st ed (t2,chip dj) 35.00

GARNETT,DAVID-ED.-Letters of T E Lawrence-NY-1939-1st ed (b7,f,dj) 45.00

GARNETT,DAVID-Flowers of the Forest-Lond-1955-Chatto & Windus-photos-1st Brit ed (e10,sl chip & soil dj) 15.00

GARNETT,DAVID-Golden Echo-NY-(1954)-Harcourt,Brace-photos-1st US ed (e10,f,dj) 20.00

GARNETT,DAVID-Grasshoppers Come-np(NY)-(1931)-Brewer,Warren & Putnam-woodcts-1st Us ed (ff6,sp drknd,f dj) 50.00

GARNETT,P-Stately Homes of California-Bost-1915-illus-1st ed (ee1,rub) 225.00

GARNETT,PORTER-Stately Homes of California-Bost-1915-Little,Brown-4to-xx,95p-qtr cl/bds,25p plts(5 col),guarded-scarce (pp7,sl rub & fox) 150.00

GARRAGHAN,GILBERT J-Jesuits of the Middle United States-NY-1938-America Pr-3 vols-blu cl,plts (mm10) 75.00

GARRARD,LEWIS H-Wah To Yah & the Taos Trail-Cin-1850-H W Derby-orig cl-Howes G70-Rittenhouse 236-1st ed (pp9,cl rub & wn,box) 1,600.00

GARRETT,EDMUND H-Romance and Reality of the Puritan Coast-Bost-1897-Little,Brown-grn lea,dec bndg,a.e.g.,illus-1st ed (dd6) 45.00

GARRETT,GEORGE-Death of the Fox-GC-1971-1st ed (r5,dj) 20.00

GARRETT,GEORGE-King of the Mountain-NY-1957-1st ed (r5,dj) 40.00

GARRETT,PAT F-Authentic Life of Billy the Kid-NY-1927-233p-col frntis,illus-1st ed thus (e7) 50.00

GARRETT,R-Too Many Magicians-1967-Dbldy-scarce-1st ed (x7,f,dj) 195.00

GARRETT,RICHARD-General Gordon-Lond-(1974)-Arthur Barker-8vo-240p-8p photos-1st ed (cc5,dj) 15.00

GARRETT,THEODORE F-Encyclopedia of Practical Cookery-Lond-nd(ca.1890's)-L Upcott Gill-8 vols,rose red cl,a.e.g.,col plts,engrvngs-Bitting 177 (o6) 275.00

GARRETT,WENDELL-ET AL-Arts in America-NY-1969-Scribner's-4to-412p-rust/beige cl (r10,sl wn dj) 30.00

GARRISON,FIELDING-An Introduction to the History of Medicine-Phila-1917-905p-2nd ed (dd3) 75.00

GARRISON,FIELDING-Principles of Anatomic Illustration Before Vesalius-NY-1926-58p-1st ed (dd3,ex-libr) 125.00

GARRISON,OMAR V-Hidden Story of Scientology-Lond-1974-Arlington Bks-8vo-231p-1st ed (aa7,rub dj) 25.00*

GARRO,ELENA-Recollections of Things to Come-Austin-1969-U of Tex Pr-8vo-289p-blk cl,drwngs,A Beltrain (mm1,f,f dj) 30.00

GARSTIN,CROSBIE-Samuel Kelly, an Eighteenth Century Seaman-NY-1925-Stokes-lg papr 8vo-320p-grn ribbed cl,g titles,t.e.g,24 plts-1st ed (p8,f) 60.00

GARTNER,JOHN-ED.-Western Outdoor News Almanac for California Sportsmen-LA-1957-8vo-544p-wrps-photos,illus,maps-1st ed (m3) 15.00

GARVAN,ANTHONY N B-Architecture and Town Planning in Colonial Connecticut-New Haven-1951-Yale U Pr(Hist Publ,31)-4to-xiv,166p-cl,illus (pp7) 70.00

GARVE,ANDREW-Ascent of D 13-1969-Harper-1st Amer ed (s10,dj) 12.50

GARVE,ANDREW-Ascent of D 13-NY-1969-187p-1st ed (o10,f,dj) 25.00

GARVE,ANDREW-Ashes of Loda-1964-Harper-1st Amer ed (s10,dj) 12.50

GARVE,ANDREW-Boomerang-1970-1st Amer ed (s10,dj) 12.50

GARVE,ANDREW-Case of Robert Quarry-NY-1972-Harper-1st US ed (g4,dj) 10.00

GARVE,ANDREW-Counterstroke-Lond-1978-Collins-1st ed (p4,f,dj) 22.50

GARVE,ANDREW-Frame Up-NY-1964-Harper-1st US ed (h4,f,dj) 10.00

GARVE,ANDREW-Home to Roost-NY-1976-Crowell-1st US ed (e4,f,sl wn dj) 10.00

GARVE,ANDREW-Prisoner's Friend-NY-1962-Harper-1st US ed (f4,f,dj) 10.00

GARVE,ANDREW-Riddle of Samson-Lond-1954-Gollancz-1st ed (g4,f,sl wn dj) 20.00

GARVIN,RICHARD-Crystal Skull-GC-1973-Dbldy-8vo-108p-35 photos-1st ed (gg5,f,dj) 15.00

GARVIN,RICHARD-Midnight Special: The Legend of Leadbelly-NY-(1971)-Geis-1st ed (w1,f,dj) 25.00

GARWOOD,DARRELL-Crossraods of America-NY-1948-8vo-331p-map e.p.,photos,illus-1st ed (aa3,f,sl chip dj) 22.50

GARWOOD,DARRELL-Crossroads of America-NY-(1948)-331p-cl-1st ed (e1,dj) 15.00

GARWOOD,DARRELL-Crossroads of America-NY-(1948)-Norton-322p-illus-Six Guns 814-1st ed (ff4,sl wn dj) 20.00

GARY-THE STORY OF ...,INDIANA-np-1908-(24)p-wrps-illus (j1) 15.00

GASCOYNE,D-Short Survey of Surrealism-1935-Cobden Sanderson-scarce-1st ed (ee1,sp fade) 150.00

GASH,JONATHAN-Grail Tree-1979-Harper-1st ed (s10,f dj) 35.00

GASH,JONATHAN-Sleepers of Erin-NY-1983-Dutton-1st Amer ed (s4,vf,dj) 30.00

GASH,JONATHAN-Spend Game-New Haven-1981-Ticknor-1st US ed (e4,f,sl wn dj) 35.00

GASK,ARTHUR-Gentlemen of Crime-NY-1933-Macaulay-1st US ed (d4,rear cov sl stnd,dj) 75.00

GASK,LILIAN-True Stories of Big Game and Jungles-Lond-1933-8vo-236p-16 col plts (m3) 25.00

GASK,NORMAN-Old Silver Spoons of England-Lond-1926-4to-189p-1/4 lea,32 plts,illus (a3,rbnd) 125.00

GASKELL,JANE-Sweet Sweet Summer-1972-St.Martin's-1st Amer ed (t9,vf,dj) 35.00

GASKELL,WILLIAM-Involuntary Nervous System-Lond-1920-178p-2nd ed (dd3) 100.00

GASKILL,NELSON B-Imprints from the Press of Stephen C Ustick-Wash-1940-viii,93p-wrps,frntis (aa6) 60.00

GASKIN,CATHERINE-Edge of Glass-1967-Dbldy-1st Amer ed (s10,dj) 12.50

GASPER,HOWLAND-Complete Sportsman-NY-1893-277p-illus (m3,f) 22.50

GASQUE,JIM-Bass Fishing-NY-1945-8vo-204p-3 col plts,photos-1st ed (m3,dj) 20.00

GASS,PATRICK-Journal of the Voyages and Travels of a Corps of Discovery-Mpls-1958-317p-frntis,photos,fldg frnt e.p. map-ltd ed (t7,f) 45.00

GASS,PATRICK-Journals of the Lewis & Clark Expedition-Mpls-1958-Ross & Haines-317p-illus,fldg e.p. map-ltd rprnt (d7,f,discol dj) 50.00

GASS,WILLIAM H-Fiction and the Figures of Life-NY-1970-1st ed (s5,f,dj) 40.00

GASS,WILLIAM H-Fiction and the Figures of Life-NY-1970-Knopf-1st ed (bb1,as new in dj) 35.00

GASS,WILLIAM H-Fiction and the Figures of Life-NY-1970-Knopf-1st ed (h8,sl soil dj) 45.00

GASS,WILLIAM H-In the Heart of the Country-NY-(1968)-Harper & Row-1st ed (bb2,f,dj) 65.00

GASS,WILLIAM H-In the Heart of the Heart of the Country-NY et al-(1968)-Harper & Row-1st ed (bb1,f,dj) 60.00

GASS,WILLIAM H-Omensetter's Luck-Lond-1967-Collins-auth 1st bk-1st Brit ed (b5,f,sl stnd dj) 65.00

GASS,WILLIAM H-Omensetter's Luck-NY-1966-NAL-auth 1st bk-1st ed (g8,f,dj) 200.00

GASS,WILLIAM H-On Being Blue-Bost-nd-Godine-1st trd ed (b5,as new in dj) 40.00

GASS,WILLIAM H-Willie Masters' Lonesome Wife-NY-1971-1st hdbk ed (j5,as new in dj) 35.00

GASS,WILLIAM H-Willie Masters' Lonesome Wife-NY-1971-Knopf-1st trd ed (h8,f,f dj) 45.00

GASS,WILLIAM H-World Within the Word-NY-1978-Knopf-1st ed (bb1,as new in dj) 30.00

GASSET,J O-Meditations on Hunting-NY-1972-152p-drwngs (gg3,cor sl wn,chip dj) 100.00

GASSNER,JULIUS S-TRANSL-Voyages & Adventures of LaPerouse-Honolulu-1969-162p-dbl pg illus-1st ed (f7,vf,dj) 35.00

GATES,ALFRED A-War Recollections-np-nd(ca.1920)-prtd for family & friends-(36)p-wrps (a1) 100.00

GATES,JOSEPHINE S-More About Live Dolls-Toledo-(1903)-Franklin-105p-cl,pict pasteon,illus,V Keeping,col frntis-presumed 1st ed (s3) 40.00

GATHORNE-HARDY,A E-Salmon-Lond-1898-8vo-267p-deluxe lg pap ed,ltd to 157c,nbrd,1/4 vel bndng (m3,uncut) 135.00

GATHORNE-HARDY,JONATHAN-Unnatural History of the Nanny-NY-1973(1972)-Dial-lg 8vo-350p-cl,illus-1st Amer ed (ee9,f,dj) 25.00

GATHORNE-HARDY,ROBERT-Three Acres and a Mill-NY-1939-Macmillan-361p-cl (x6,sl fade) 16.00

GATHORNE-HARDY,ROBERT-Wild Flowers in Britain-NY-1938-Scribner-120p-cl,photos,4 col lithos (x6,fox) 15.00

GATTI,A-Killers All-Lond-1951-8vo-219p (m3) 15.00

GATTI,A-Killers All-NY-1943-245p-photos (gg3,f,chip dj) 25.00

GATTI,CARLO-Verdi the Man and His Music-NY-1955-Putnam (u4,dj) 16.00

GATTI,GUIDO M-Ildebrando Pizzetti-Lond-(1951)-Dobson-8vo-124p-8 illus-1st Brit ed (ee5,dj) 20.00

GATTI-CASAZZA,GIULIO-Memories of Opera-NY-1941-Scribner-1st ed (w1,f,dj) 25.00

GATTY,MRS.ALFRED-Book of Sundials-Lond-1900-Geo Bell-4to-529p-red cl,t.e.g.,9 plts-4th ed,enlgd (r10) 120.00

GAUL,ALBRO T-Complete Book of Space Travel-Cleve-1956-World-159p-silv/g illus blk cl,illus-1st ed (hh6,lacks sp labl,bump) 28.00

GAULT,WILLIAM C-County Kill-1962-Inner Sanctum-1st ed (r9,dj) 30.00

GAULT,WILLIAM C-Death Out of Focus-NY-1959-Random-1st ed (e4,dj) 20.00

GAUVREAU,E-Billy Mitchell-NY-1942-306p-illus cl,frntis port,map.,illus e.p.-1st ed (s2,chip dj) 40.00

GAUVREAU,E-Wild Blue Yonder-NY-1944-8vo-386p-cl-1st ed (t2,sp fade,sl wn) 25.00

GAVELIN,GUNNAR-Fourdrinier Paper Making-NY-1963-Lockwood Trade Journal-8vo-(viii),181p-cl,illus-1st ed (x4) 35.00

GAVITT,ELNATHAN C-Crumbs from My Saddle Bags-Toledo-1884-298p-cl (f1) 65.00

GAY,AUGUSTE-New Presentation of Cooking with Timed Recipes-SF-(1924)-Ringsmith & Wellman-500p-red leatherette bds-Bitting 178 (n6) 24.00

GAY,AUGUSTE-New Presentation of Cooking, With Timed Recipes-SF-(1924)-Ringsmith & Wellman-500p-maroon cl (q8) 50.00

GAY,JOHN-Beggars's Opera-Larchmont-1961-Argonaut Bks-reprod of 1729 ed (u4,f,sl rub box) 28.00

GAY,ZHENYA-Shire Colt-GC-1931-Dbldy,Doran-folio-cl/pict bds,lithos-1st trd ed (pp10,f,dj sl chip,one mrk) 65.00

GEAUGA COUNTY-INVENTORY OF THE COUNTY ARCHIVES OF OHIO. NO.28...-Columbus-1942-Ohio Hist Rcds Srvy-323,(3)p-wrps,WPA (d1) 20.00

GEBHARD,PAUL-ET AL-Pregnancy, Birth and Abortion-NY-(1958)-Harper & Bros-xvi+282p-gry cl,tbls-1st ed (d2,dj) 35.00

GEDDES,ANNE E-Trends in Relief Expenditures 1910 to 1935-Wash-1937-USGPO-WPA-Rsrch Mono X-wrps-1st ed (v5) 25.00

GEDDES,PATRICK-Cities in Evolution-Lond-1949-Williams & Norgate-sm 4to-241p-cl,illus,maps-1st prtg of "New Edition" (c10) 65.00

GEDNEY,LIDA C-Town Records of Hopewell, New Jersey-(np)-1931-197p-cl,frntis (aa6) 40.00

GEE,E P-Wild Life of India-NY-1964-8vo-192p-cl,12 col & b&w plts (y8,sm tears dj) 20.00

GEE,E P-Wildlife of India-1964-Dutton-192p-col & b&w photos-1st US ed (bb3,f,fray dj) 30.00

GEE,ERNEST R-Early American Sporting Books 1734 to 1844-Derrydale-1928-8vo-61p-one of the first 100 copies,illus-(Frazer State g-2-10)-rare (m3) 450.00

GEE,ERNEST R-Early American Sporting Books 1734-1844-Derrydale-1928-8vo-61p-one of 500c,illus (m3) 175.00

GEE,ERNEST R-Sportsman's Library-NY-1940-8vo-158p-one of 600c,frontis (m3,pres cpy) 120.00

GEE,MARJORY-Captain Fraser's Voyages-NY-1979-Norton-219p-photos-1st Amer ed (dd7,f,f dj) 17.50

GEE,NANCIE-Reflections in Pike Place Markets-Seattle-(1968)-4to-128p-photos-1st ed (r8) 25.00

GEELHAAR,C-Paul Klee & the Bauhaus-1973-NYGS-sq 4to-24 col & 108 b&w illus-1st Amer ed (ee1,dj) 145.00

GEER,CAPT J J-Beyond the Lines-Phila-1863-Daughaday-285p-frntis,illus (o7,cov wn,fox) 100.00

GEER,T T-Fifty Years in Oregon-NY-1912-536p-frntis,photos-1st ed (t7,cor bump,hng rnfrcd) 45.00

GEERTY,HILDRED-Javanese Family-Glencoe-(1961)-Free Pr-8vo-176p-cl-1st ed (y5,sl sun,dj tn) 15.00

GEHERIN,DAVID-John D MacDonald-NY-1982-Ungar-1st ed (e4,as new in dj) 25.00

GEHLBACK,F R-Mountain Islands and Desert Seas-1981-Tex A&M-298p-3 maps,65 col & 36 b&w photos-1st ed (bb3,f,dj) 25.00

GEIGER,MAYNARD J-Life and Times of Fray Junipero Serra O.F.M.-Wash-(1959)-Acad Amer Franciscan Hist-8vo-2 vols-blu cl,frntis,12 plts,6 maps-1st ed (t10,ex-libr) 50.00

GEIGER,MAYNARD-Life and Times of Fray Junipero Serra, O.F.M.-(1959)-Acad Amer Frncscn Hist-2 vols-illus,maps (d3) 85.00

GEIKIE,JAMES-Antiquity of Man in Europe-Edinburgh-1914-Oliver & Boyd-xx+328p-grn cl,21 plts,4 fldg maps-1st ed (c2) 35.00

GEIKIE,JOHN C-ED.-Adventures in Canada-Phila-ca1875-Porter & Coates-16mo-408p-pict covs,illus (dd4) 40.00

GEISER,S W-Naturalists on the Frontier-1948-SMU-296p-maps-2nd ed rvsd & enlgd (bb3,f,dj) 25.00

GELD,ELLEN B-Strangers in the Valley-NY-1957-Dodd Mead-8vo-229p-sketches-1st ed (ff5,rub dj) 15.00

GELDER,WILLIAM DE-Dutch Homestead on the Prairies-1973-U of Tor Pr-8vo-xv,92p-1st ed (cc7,dj) 15.00*

GELEY,DR. GUSTAVE-Clairvoyance and Materialism-NY-1927-Doran-401p wi index,lg thck grn cl,photos-1st Amer ed (t1,sl spot) 100.00
GELLHORN,MARTHA-Face of War-NY-1959-S&S-1st ed (d8,f,dj) 40.00
GELLHORN,MARTHA-Honeyed Peace-GC-1953-Dlbdy-1st ed (k8,dj) 30.00
GELLHORN,MARTHA-Pretty Tales for Tired People-NY-1965-1st ed (v9,f,sun dj) 35.00
GELLHORN,MARTHA-Travels with Myself and Another-NY-1978-Dodd,Mead-1st ed (d8,f,f dj) 40.00
GELLHORN,MARTHA-Wine of Astonishment-NY-1948-Scribner's-1st ed (a10,bump cor,dj) 20.00
GENAUER,E-Chagall at the "Met"-NY-1971-Met Opera Assoc-col illus (ee1,dj,box) 125.00
GENDERS,ROY-Polyanthus-Newton-(1963)-231p-col frntis,45 b&w photos (x5) 16.00
GENERAL ELECTRIC-Century of Progress-Schenectady-1981-4to-4 vols in one,red cl,illus (j2) 25.00
GENERAL FOODS KITCHENS COOKBOOK-1959-Random-1st ed (v6,dj wn) 10.00
GENERAL MILLS-Picture Cook Book-1950-McGraw Hill-463p-col & b&w illus-1st ed,3rd prtg (mm6,dj) 65.00
GENERALS AND BATTLES OF THE CIVIL WAR-(Canton)-(1891)-30p-cl,30p of views,fldg style (c1,few minor rprs) 100.00
GENESEE PURE FOOD CO-Jell-o and the Kewpies-Buffalo-1918-22p(wi 4p insert)-pict wrps,col plts (q8) 20.00
GENET,JEAN-Miracle of the Rose-NY-1966-1st US ed (q5,f,dj) 12.50
GENET,JEAN-Miracle of the Rose-NY-1966-Grove-1st US ed (x9,f,dj) 17.50
GENET,JEAN-Thief's Journal-NY-1964-Grove-268p-red cl-1st ed (z3,f,dj) 20.00
GENTHE,ARNOLD-As I Remember-NY-(1936)-Reynal & Hitchcock-4to-cl,112 photos-1st ed (y3) 65.00
GENTHE,ARNOLD-Book of the Dance-Bost-1920-Int'l-4to-cl-2nd ed (y3) 55.00
GENTILE,MRS MARIA-Italian Cook Book-NY-(1919)-Italian Bk Co-160p-red bds (q6) 25.00
GENTLEMAN ANGLER CONTAINING SHORT,PLAIN & EASY INSTRUCTIONS...IN ANGLING FOR SALMON-PEAL,TROUT...-Lond-1726-16mo-183p+index & ads-v old 1/4 calf & mrbld bds-rare-1st ed (m3,frnt hng cracked) 450.00
GEORGE,HENRY-Perplexed Philosopher-NY-1892-Chas L Webster-iv+319p+ads-brwn cl-1st ed (b2) 45.00
GEORGE,HENRY-Protection or Free Trade-NY-1886-Henry George-viii+359p+ads-red cl-1st ed (b2) 35.00
GEORGE,JEAN C-Julie of the Wolves-NY-1972-Harper & Row-170p-pict bds,illus-1st ed (nn10,f,dj) 40.00
GEORGE,L-Air, Men and Wings-NY-1930-8vo-xii,264p-cl,frntis,24p plts,text illus (t2,sp fade,sl wn,uncut) 30.00
GEORGE,MARIAN M-Little Journey to Canada-Chig-(1901)-A Flanagan-106,(8)p-wrps-col frontis & map,illus-Plan Book Series,May, 1901 (j1) 15.00
GEORGE,MARY-Mary Bonner: Impressions of a Print Maker-S.A.-1982-Trinity-125p-1st ed (a9,dj) 30.00
GEORGE,W L-Literary Chapters-Bost-1918-241p-1st ed (g1) 15.00
GEORGE,W-Animals and Maps-Berkeley-1969-8vo-235p-cl,illua (y8,dj) 20.00
GEPHART,RONALD M-Periodical Literature on the American Revolution-Wash-1971-Library of Congress-93p-wrps (h1) 12.50
GERARD,FRANCIS-Fatal Friday-NY-1937-Holt-1st US ed (g4,dj) 20.00
GERARD,FRANCIS-Prince of Paradise-1941-Dutton-1st US ed (s10,sp chip dj) 25.00
GERARD,FRANCIS-Prince of Paradise-NY-1941-Dutton-1st US ed (h4,dj) 12.50
GERDTS,WILLIAM H-Painting and Sculpture in New Jersey-Princeton-1964-xix,276p-cl,illus (aa6) 35.00
GERHARD,PETER-Pirates on the West Coast of New Spain-Glendale-1960-274p-illus-1st ed (g7,f) 75.00
GERLACH,LARRY R-Blazing Crosses in Zion-Logan-1982-Utah St Univ Pr-8vo-248p (z4,dj) 12.50
GERLACH,REX-Creative Fly Tying & Fly Fishing-NY-1974-4to-231p-photos,illus-1st ed (m3,vf,dj) 20.00
GERLACH,REX-Fly Fishing the Lakes-NY-1972-8vo-163p-photos-1st ed (m3,vf,dj) 12.50
GERMAN AVIATION MEDICINE, WORLD WAR II-Wash-1950-2 vols-illus-1st ed (dd3,ex-libr) 200.00
GERMINO,DANTE L-Italian Facist Party in Power-Mpls-1959-U of Minn-181p (r1,dj wn,tn,chip) 20.00
GERNSBACH,HUGO-Ralph 124C41, a Romance of the Year 2660-1925-293p-16 illus-v rare-1st ed (h6) 245.00
GERNSBACK,HUGO-Ultimate World-NY-(1971)-Walker-1st ed (h3,f,dj) 10.00
GERNSHEIM,HELMUT-Beautiful London-Lond-1950-Phaidon-4to-cl,103 photos-1st ed (y3,sl chip dj) 60.00
GERNSHEIM,HELMUT-Creative Photography-Bost-1962-Bost BK & Art Shop-258p-244 photos-1st Amer ed (cc9,f,dj) 60.00
GERNSHEIM,HELMUT-Lewis Carroll Photographer-NY-1949-Chanticleer-64 gravures-1st ed (y3,sl fox,dj sp chip,wn) 125.00
GERNSHEIM,HELMUT-Man Behind the Camera-Lond-1948-Fountain Pr-4to-144p-cl,illus-1st ed (t3) 45.00
GERNSHEIM,HELMUT-Roger Fenton-Lond-1954-106p-85 photos-1st ed (b7,dj) 50.00
GEROULD,KATHERINE F-Hawaii-1916-Scribners-181p-photo plts-1st ed (u8) 30.00
GERRARD,FRANK-Small Goods Production-Lond-(1946)-L Hill-150+xv p-red cl,photos-3rd prtg (q8,cov spot) 22.50
GERSHAW,SENATOR F W-Brief History of Southern Alberta-nd(1950's)-priv prtd-8vo-123p-g red cl,illus (cc7) 35.00*
GERSON,NOEL B-Kit Carson-NY-1964-255p-1st ed (t7,f,dj) 10.00
GERSTACKER,FRIEDRICH-Wild Sports in the Far West-Durham-1958-409p-illus (m3,vf,dj) 17.50
GERSTAECKER,FREDERICh-Wild Sports in the Far West-Bost-1864-Crosby & Nichols-396p-illus-Howes G142 (cc4,lacks fr fly) 50.00
GERSTAECKER,FRIEDRICH-Wild Sports in the Far West-Lond-1854-396p-dec red cl,8 plts-Howes G142-1st ed in Engl (z1,lacks e.p.) 200.00
GETLEIN,FRANK-Chaim Gross-NY-(1974)-Abrams-sm folio-cl-1st ed (oo6,dj) 75.00
GETTYSBURG-Annual Report of...National Military Park Commission to the Secretary of War, 1893 to 1904-Wash-1905-107p+illus (n3) 42.50
GEUE,ETHEL H-New Homes in a New Land-Waco-1970-116p-1st ed (n10,f,dj) 50.00
GEYER,FRANK P-Holmes Pitezel Case-np(Phila)-(1896)-512p-cl (d1,sl rub & soil,wk rear hng) 100.00
GHENT,W F-Early Far West-NY-1936-411p-frntis,maps (t7) 10.00

GHENT,W J-Road to Oregon-NY-1929-Longmans,Green-8vo-274p-cl-1st ed (mm7,f,chip dj) 75.00

GHOSE,SUDHIN N-Folk Tales and Fairy Stories from India-NY-1964-T Yoseloff-cl,illus,S E Carlile-1st Amer ed (l8,f,edge wn dj) 20.00

GHYKA,MATILA-World Mine Oyster-Lond-(1961,56)-Heinemann-8vo-330p-7 illus-1st Brit ed (gg5,dj) 15.00

GIAP,GENERAL VO NGUYEN-How We Won the War-Phila-1976-Recon-wrps-1st ed (c8,f) 25.00

GIBB,JAMES A-Shipwrecks of the Pacific Coast-Portland-(1957)-312p-illus,e.p. map-1st ed (r8,sp chip dj) 35.00

GIBBINGS,ROBERT-Trumpets From Montparnasse-NY-(1955)-8 col plts,40 wood engrv by auth-1st ed (c5,sl wn dj) 25.00

GIBBON,EDWARD-History of the Decline and Fall of the Roman Empire-Phila-(1845)-Porter & Coates-8vo-6 vols-brwn cl wi blk & g decs-rprnt (cc5) 75.00

GIBBON,J-Artillerist's Manual-Glendale-1970-568p-illus,plts-rprnt of 1860 ed (z10,cov soil) 75.00

GIBBON,JOHN M-Our Old Montreal-Tor-1947-M&S-8vo-xiii,266p-frntis,30 illus,illus e.p.-1st ed (cc7,dj) 50.00*

GIBBON,JOHN M-Romance of the Canadian Canoe-Tor-1951-Ryerson Pr-xiv,145p-col frntis,col illus-1st ed (bb7,sl chip dj) 50.00*

GIBBON,JOHN M-Steel of Empire-Indpls-1935-Bobbs Merrill-423p-blu cl,frntis port,col plts,ports(3 fldg) (k10) 45.00*

GIBBON,JOHN-Personal Recollections of the Civil War-Dayton-1977-Morningside Bkshp-426p-e.p. map (o7,f) 25.00

GIBBON,LEWIS G-Niger-Edinburgh-1934-Porpoise Pr-8vo-307p-cl,map e.p.,frntis port (dd7,cov soil & wn) 45.00

GIBBONS,COLIN-They Rode in Spaceships-Lond-(1957)-Spearman-8vo-217p wi index,illus,pict dj-1st ed (t1,f,dj) 30.00

GIBBONS,CROMWELL-Murder in Hollywood-NY-1936-Kemp-1st ed (f4,f,dj) 35.00

GIBBONS,GAVIN-They Rode in Spaceships-Lond-(1957)-Neville Spearman-8vo-xx,217p-cl-1st ed (y4,f,dj) 25.00

GIBBONS,J S-Banks of New York...and the Panic of 1857-NY-1858-D Appleton-399p-brwn cl,plts by Herrick-1st ed (h2) 100.00

GIBBONS,WILLIAM-Practical Logic, or an Assistant to Theme Writers-Cleve-1840-prntd by Sanford & Lott-100p-cl (h1,fox) 45.00

GIBBS,A HAMILTON-Need We Have-Bost-1936-Little,Brown-1st ed (hh5,dj) 15.00

GIBBS,A HAMILTON-Rivers Glide On-Bost-1934-Little,Brown-1st ed (hh5,dj) 15.00

GIBBS,A HAMILTON-Undertow-Bost-1932-Little,Brown-1st ed (hh5,dj) 15.00

GIBBS,E L-Gibbs' Western Reserve Almanac, for 1852...-Cleve-(1851)-prntd by Harris,Fairbanks-28,(4)p-sewed (o1) 40.00

GIBBS,GEORGE-Castle Rock Mystery-NY-1927-Appleton-1st ed (h4) 10.00

GIBBS,GEORGE-Out of the Dark-NY-1934-Appleton-1st ed (h4) 10.00

GIBBS,GEORGE-Sleeper Wakes-NY-1941-Appleton-1st ed (g4,dj) 25.00

GIBBS,GEORGE-Yellow Diamond-NY-1935-Appleton-1st ed (f4,f,chip dj) 25.00

GIBBS,J F-Lights and Shadows of Mormonism-(1909)-(Salt Lake Trib Publ)-535p-illus (bb4,sl fade sp) 75.00

GIBBS,J WILLARD-Collected Works-New Haven-(1948)-Yale U Pr-2 vols-blu cl (a2,djs wn & tn) 50.00

GIBBS,J WILLARD-Collected Works-New Haven-(1957)-Yale U Pr-2 vols-blk cl-rprnt of 2nd ed (c2,dj) 85.00

GIBBS,JAMES A-Pacific Graveyard-1950-Binfords & Mort-173p-illus-1st ed (r8,tattrd dj) 45.00

GIBBS,JERRY-Bass Myths Exploded-NY-1978-8vo-200p-photos (m3,as new in dj) 10.00

GIBBS,JIM-Shipwrecks in Paradise-Seattle-(1977)-Superior-183p-photos-1st ed (ee8,f,dj wn & tn) 24.00

GIBBS,JIM-West Coast Lighthouses-Seattle-1974-207p-maps,photos-1st ed (p2,f,f dj) 17.50

GIBBS,JOSIAH-Lights and Shadows of Mormonism-SLC-1909-535p-frntis,photos-Flake #3552-1st ed (t7) 85.00

GIBBS,W M-Spices and How to Know Them-Buffalo-1909-179p-14 col plts,40 photos,fldg maps (hh7,f) 65.00

GIBBS,W M-Spices and How to Know Them-Buffalo-1909-Matthews Northrup Works-179p-grn bds,illus,fldg map (m6) 45.00

GIBBS,WINIFRED S-Economical Cooking-NY-(1912)-NY Book Co-illus red bds,frntis,chrts-Bitting 182 (m6) 25.00

GIBNEY,VERGIL P-Hip and Its Diseases-NY-1884-412p-64 wood engrvngs (g10,soil) 125.00

GIBONEY,EZRA-Life of Mark A Matthew-Grand Rapids-1948-134p-tan cl,frntis port (b6) 10.00

GIBRAN,KAHLIL-Love Letters of...and Mary Haskell, and Her Private Journal-NY-1972-Knopf-cl-1st ed (n8,f,dj) 15.00

GIBSON,A M-ED.-Frontier Historian-(1975)-Univ of Ok-367p-1st ed (t8,rub dj) 20.00

GIBSON,A M-ED.-Frontier Historian-Norman-1975-367p-frntis-1st ed (t7,dj) 12.50

GIBSON,A M-Life and Death of Colonel Albert Jennings Fountain-1965-U of Okla Pr-8vo-xi,301p-photos,illus,map-1st ed (aa3,vf,f dj) 30.00

GIBSON,A M-Political Crime-NY-1885-Gottsberger-vii,402p-1st ed (o2,sl wn sp) 20.00

GIBSON,CHARLES DANA-Sketches in Egypt-NY-1899-Dbldy & McClure-4to-115p-dec cl,illus,auth-1st ed (w1) 75.00

GIBSON,CHARLES-Aztecs Under Spanish Rule-1976-Stanford U Pr-8vo-x,21,657p-gry cl,16 plts,17 figs,12 maps (mm1,vf,sl wn dj) 45.00

GIBSON,CHARLINE-Wife's Guide to Baseball-1970-Viking-1st ed (p7,dj) 15.00

GIBSON,DALE-Attorney For the Frontier-(1983)-U of Manitoba Pr-180p-map e.p. (cc4,dj) 20.00

GIBSON,J M-Those 163 Days-NY-1961-317p-illus,map,ports (z10,dj) 25.00

GIBSON,JAMES E-Dr.Bodo Otto and the Medical Background of the American Revolution-Springfield-(1937)-Chas C Thomas-x+345p-blu cl,plts-1st ed (dd1,chip dj) 35.00

GIBSON,JOHN-Ship of the '45-Lond-1967-172p-illus-1st ed (b7,f,dj) 35.00

GIBSON,KATHARINE-Golden Bird...-NY-1927-Macmillan-cl,col frntis,illus-1st ed (o8) 15.00

GIBSON,LANGHORNE-Riddle of Jutland,An Authentic History-NY-1934-Coward-McCann-xvi,416p-brgndy cl wi g sp,12 illus,14 diags-4th imprssn (nn1) 45.00

GIBSON,LOUIS H-Convenient Houses with Fifty Plans for the Housekeeper-NY-(1889)-Crowell-iv+321p-dec tan cl,50 plans,38 text figs-1st ed (j2) 110.00

GIBSON,RALPH-Days at Sea-NY-1974-Lustrum Pr-4to-56p-wrps-1st ed (t3) 35.00

GIBSON,SIR CHRISTOPHER-Enchanted Trails-Lond-1948-8vo-272p-frontis photo (m3) 12.00

GIBSON,TOM-Wiltshire Regiment-Lond-1969-146p-illus-Famous Regiment ser-1st ed (gg2,f,dj) 25.00

GIBSON,W H-Sharp Eyes-NY-1892-8vo-(2),322p-dec cl (y8,marg dampstaining) 25.00

GIBSON,WALTER B-Complete Illustrated Book of Divination and Prophecy-NY-1973-Dbldy-8vo-xii,336p-drwngs,figs,tbls-1st ed (aa7,sl chip dj) 15.00*

GIBSON,WALTER B-Science of Numerology-NY-1927-Sully & Co-sm 8vo-186p-red cl,illus-1st ed (aa7,rub,bump) 35.00*

GIBSON,WALTER B-Witchcraft-Lond-(1973)-Barker Ltd-two lines inked out by publ on cpyrt pg,photos-1st Brit ed (bb1,f,dj) 20.00

GIBSON,WALTER M-Diaries of Walter Murray Gibson 1886,1887-1973-U of Hawaii-tall 8vo-illus-1st ed (pp1,f) 30.00

GIBSON,WALTER-Shadow,Crime Over Casco & the Mother Goose Murders-NY-1979-Dbldy-1st ed (s4,f,dj) 25.00

GIDDENS,PAUL-Birth of the Oil Industry-NY-1938-Macmillan-8vo-xxxix,216p-frntis,31 illus,5 maps-1st ed (bb7,sl rub dj) 35.00*

GIDDINGS,J L-Archeology of Cape Denbigh-1964-Brown Univ-lg 8vo-331p+73 plts & add photos,plans & 1 fldg plan-1st ed (u8,dj) 60.00

GIDDINGS,JOSHUA R-Exiles of Florida-Columbus-1858-338p-cl-Sabin 27327-1st ed (j1,sl fox,sl wn sp) 45.00

GIDDINGS,JOSHUA R-Exiles of Florida-Columbus-1858-Follett,Foster-viii+338p-brwn cl,woodcts-1st ed (b2) 85.00

GIDE,ANDRE-Fruits of the Earth-NY-1949-Knopf-1st Amer ed (v10,f,f dj) 15.00

GIDE,ANDRE-If It Die...-NY-1935-ltd to 1500c,nbrd-1st US ed (p5,sl chip dj) 45.00

GIDE,ANDRE-My Theater-NY-1952-1st US ed (s5,dj) 20.00

GIDE,ANDRE-So Be It-NY-1959-Knopf-1st ed (y1,sl soil dj) 30.00

GIDLEY,M-With One Sky Above Us-NY-(1979)-Putnam's-259p-photos (dd4,dj) 15.00

GIES,JOSEPH-Stars of the Series-1964-Crowell-1st ed (s8,f,dj) 17.50

GIFFORD,BARRY-Jack's Book-NY-(1978)-St.Martin's Pr-photos-1st ed (ff6,f,dj) 20.00

GIFFORD,BARRY-Jack's Book-NY-(1978)-St.Martin's-1st ed (q1,f,dj) 25.00

GIFFORD,BARRY-Jack's Book-NY-1978-St.Martin's-1st ed (v5,f,f dj) 15.00

GIFFORD,BARRY-Kerouac's Town-Berkeley-1977-Creative Arts-wrps,photos,M Clements-1st rvsd ed (e8,f) 20.00

GIFFORD,BARRY-Kerouac's Town-Santa Barbara-1973-wrps-1st ed (x8) 15.00

GIFFORD,COLIN T-Decline of Steam-Lond-1966-3rd prtg (n4,dj) 22.00

GIFFORD,JOHN-Everglades and Other Essays Relating to Southern Florida...-Miami-(1912)-226,(6)p-cl-2nd ed (g1,spots on rear cov) 20.00

GIFFORDS,GLORIA KAY-Mexican Folk Retablos, Masterpieces on Tin-Tucson-(1974)-oblng-152p+index,dbl col,photos(some col)-1st ed (u7,f,dj) 45.00

GILBERT,A C-Man Who Lives in Paradise-NY-(1954)-Rinehart-8vo-374p-8p photos-1st ed (dd5,dj) 75.00

GILBERT,ANTHONY-By Hook or By Crook-NY-1947-Barnes-1st ed (v5,f,sp fade dj) 25.00

GILBERT,ANTHONY-By Hook or By Crook-NY-1947-Barnes-1st US ed (e4,dj) 20.00

GILBERT,ANTHONY-Case Against Andrew Fane-NY-1931-Dodd-1st US ed (l4) 15.00

GILBERT,ANTHONY-Case for Mr.Crook-NY-1952-Random-1st US ed (g4,dj) 12.50

GILBERT,ANTHONY-Death Casts a Long Shadow-NY-1959-Random-1st US ed (h4,dj) 10.00

GILBERT,ANTHONY-Death in the Wrong Room-NY-1947-Barnes-1st ed (v5,f,dj) 20.00

GILBERT,ANTHONY-Death in the Wrong Room-NY-1947-Barnes-1st US ed (e4,dj) 22.50

GILBERT,ANTHONY-Death Won't Wait-NY-1954-Random-1st US ed (e4,dj) 15.00

GILBERT,ANTHONY-Looking Glass Murder-NY-1966-Random-1st US ed (h4,dj) 12.50

GILBERT,ANTHONY-Murder Anonymous-NY-1968-Random-1st US ed (e4,dj) 10.00

GILBERT,ANTHONY-Murder by Experts-NY-1937-Dial-1st US ed (f4) 15.00

GILBERT,ANTHONY-Nice Little Killing-NY-1973-Random-1st US ed (j4,dj) 10.00

GILBERT,ANTHONY-No Dust in the Attic-NY-1963-Random-1st US ed (f4,dj) 10.00

GILBERT,ANTHONY-Thirty Days to Live-NY-1944-Smith & Durrell-1st ed (e4,chip dj) 15.00

GILBERT,ANTHONY-Visitor-NY-1967-Random-1st US ed (j4,dj) 10.00

GILBERT,BIL-Westering Man-NY-1983-339p-1st ed (t7,f,dj) 30.00

GILBERT,BIL-Westering Man-NY-1983-339p-text maps-1st ed (e7,f,dj) 40.00

GILBERT,BILL-Chulo-NY-1973-Knopf-8vo-290p-10 illus-1st ed (gg5,dj) 12.50

GILBERT,DOUGLAS-American Vaudeville, Its Life and Times-NY-(1940)-428p-cl (h1,sl wn sp) 15.00

GILBERT,E W-Exploration of Western America 1800 to 1850-1933-Cambridge Univ-scarce-1st ed (pp9,chip dj) 75.00

GILBERT,G K-Report on the Geology of the Henry Mountains-Wash D C-1877-Dept of the Interior-4to-x+160p-brwn cl,73 text illus,5 fldg maps (d2,cov sl edge-wn) 90.00

GILBERT,H A-Tale of a Wye Fisherman-Lond-1929-8vo-160p+ads-photos-1st ed (m3) 40.00

GILBERT,J WARREN-Blue and Gray-np-(1922)-166,(2)p + fldg map-col pict wrps (j1,sl wn) 15.00

GILBERT,J-Great Planes-NY-(1970)-4to-252p-cl,col illus t.p.,col & b&w plts,text illus (t2,dj) 25.00

GILBERT,JAMES-Flier's World-NY-(1979)-G&D/Ridge Pr-4to-252p-col illus-1st ed (bb5,dj) 12.50

GILBERT,JOHN F-ED.-Crossties over Saluda-Raleigh-1971-36p-wrps-1st ed (n4) 10.00

GILBERT,JOHN-ED.-Crossties Through Carolina-Raleigh-1969-88p-1st ed (n4) 16.00

GILBERT,MICHAEL-Be Shot for Sixpence-NY-1956-Harper-1st US ed (g4,f,sl wn dj) 25.00

GILBERT,MICHAEL-Blood and Judgement-NY-1959-Harper-1st US ed (h4,f,dj) 25.00

GILBERT,MICHAEL-Body of a Girl-NY-1972-Harper-1st US ed (h4,dj) 12.50

GILBERT,MICHAEL-Overdrive-NY-1967-Harper-1st US ed (j4,f,dj) 20.00

GILBERT,MICHAEL-Petrella at Q-Lond-1977-Hodder-1st ed (s4,dj) 20.00
GILBERT,MICHAEL-Petrella at Q-NY-1977-Harper-1st US ed (g4,dj) 15.00
GILBERT,O P-Men in Women's Guise-Lond-(1926)-(15),284p-g cl,6 illus-1st ed (m4) 25.00
GILBERT,ROBERT-Moose Mousse and Other Exotic Recipes-(NY)-(1964)-S&S-92p-picts,N Langner-1st ed (m6) 14.00
GILBERT,W S-Bab Ballads-Lond-1869-Hotten-orig grn cl,g decs,illus by auth-1st ed,1st iss(wi Hotten Imprnt on t.p.) (hh9,hngs weak) 150.00
GILBERT,W S-Patience-NY-1902-Page-ltd to 100c,nbrd-1st US ed (k3,hng weak,cor bump) 30.00
GILBEY,SIR WALTER-Ponies Past and Present-Lond-1900-Vinton-1st ed (j9) 65.00
GILBEY,SIR WALTER-Small Horses in Warfare-Lond-1900-Vinton-1st ed (h9) 45.00
GILBRETH,FRANK,JR.-Of Whales and Women-NY-(1956)-Crowell-8vo-242p-sketches-1st ed (cc5,dj) 15.00
GILCHRIST,ELLEN-Annunciation-Bost-1983-Little,Brown-1st ed (q2,dj) 35.00
GILCHRIST,ELLEN-In the Land of Dreamy Dreams-(Lond)-(1982)-Faber & Faber-auth 1st bk-1st Brit ed (k7,dj) 50.00
GILCHRIST,ELLEN-In the Land of Dreamy Dreams-Lond-(1982)-Faber-1st Brit ed (v10,as new in dj) 45.00
GILCHRIST,ELLEN-Victory Over Japan-Bost-1984-Little,Brown-1st ed (v5,f,f dj) 35.00
GILES,DOROTHY-Singing Valleys-NY-(1940)-Random-361p-1st ed (cc4,dj) 15.00
GILES,HARRY F-Homeseekers' Guide to the State of Washington-Olympia-1915-120p+fldg map,wrps-2nd issue (a1) 15.00
GILES,JANICE H-Kinta Years-1973-Houghton Mifflin-337p-1st ed (d3,dj) 17.50
GILES,JANICE H-Kinta Years-Bost-1973-337p-cl-1st ed so stated (j1,f,dj) 15.00
GILES,KENNETH-Death Among the Stars-NY-1968-Walker-1st US ed (e4,dj) 10.00
GILES,REV CHARLES-Convention of Drunkards-NY-1840-Scofield & Voorhies-16mo-126p-2nd ed (dd6,sl fox) 60.00
GILES,ROSENA A-Shasta County California, a History-Oakland-1949-Biobooks-4to-301p-cl,map,illus-ltd to 1000c (mm7,f) 55.00
GILES,W E-Cruize in a Queensland Labour Vessel to the South Seas-Honolulu-1968-U of Hawaii-thin 8vo-124p-blu cl,gilt,6 plts,map-1st ed (p8,as new in dj) 15.00
GILL,B-Dream Come True-NY-1980-illus-1st Amer ed (h10,dj) 40.00
GILL,BARTHOLOMEW-McGarr and the Politician's Wife-NY-1977-Scribners-1st ed (f4,f,sl wn dj) 12.50
GILL,BARTHOLOMEW-McGarr and the Sienese Conspiracy-1977-Scribners-1st Amer ed (m9,f,dj sp sunned) 35.00
GILL,BARTHOLOMEW-McGarr at the Dublin Horse Show-NY-1979-Scribners-1st Amer ed (j4,f,dj) 10.00
GILL,BRENDAN-Here at the New Yorker-NY-(1975)-Random-illus-1st ed (b5,f,dj) 20.00
GILL,ELIZABETH-Crime Coast-1931-CC-1st Amer ed (s10,sp fade dj) 20.00
GILL,ELIZABETH-Crime Coast-NY-1931-Dbldy CC-wi orig wrap-around band-1st ed (j4,f,rprd dj) 30.00
GILL,EMLYN-Practical Dry Fly Fishing-NY-1912-12mo-216p-illus-1st ed (m3,vf) 50.00
GILL,ERIC-Clothes-Lond-1931-Cape-grn bds blind stmpd,10 diagrams,auth-1st ed (bb2) 75.00
GILL,ERIC-Engravings of...-Wellingborough-1983-C Skelton-buckram bkd bds,publ box-1st ed (l8,as new in box) 85.00
GILL,ERIC-First Nudes-Lond-1954-illus-1st ed (h10,dj tn) 25.00
GILL,ERIC-Letters-Lond-(1947)-Cape-1st ed (bb2,f,dj sl chip) 50.00
GILL,WALTER-Petermann Journey-Adelaide-(1968)-Rigby-8vo-183p-illus-1st ed (ff5,f,f dj) 15.00
GILLELAN,G H-Complete Book of the Bow & Arrow-Harrisburg-1971-8vo-320p-photos-1st ed (m3,f,dj) 10.00
GILLESPIE,G CURTIS-Rumford Fireplaces and How They are Made-NY-1906-Comstock-8vo-193p+ads-cl,illus-scarce-1st ed (ll9) 75.00
GILLETT,JAMES B-Six Years with the Texas Rangers 1875 to 1881-Chig-1943-Lakeside Pr-364p-frontis,fldg map-Six Guns 829 (t8) 28.00
GILLETT,JAMES B-Six Years with the Texas Rangers 1875 to 1881-New Haven-1925-Yale U Pr-259p-illus-Six Guns #829 (ee4,dj) 50.00
GILLETT,JAMES B-Six Years with the Texas Rangers 1875 to 1881-New Haven-1925-Yale U Pr-xvi,259p-photos (p2,dj) 75.00
GILLETT,JAMES-Texas Rangers-NY-1927-223p-pict cl,frntis,illus-1st ed (t7,f) 25.00
GILLETTE,BERTHA-Homesteading with the Elk-Idaho Falls-1967-75p-1st ed (t7) 30.00
GILLETTE,MRS F L-New Temperance Cookery Book-Vancouver-nd-Thomson Stationery Co-337p-red bds (n6) 30.00
GILLETTE,MRS F L-Presidential Cook Book-Akron-1904-Saalfield-440p+4p ads,pict bds,frntis port (q8,text brwng) 55.00
GILLETTE,MRS F L-White House Cookbook-Chig-(1897)-Peale-4to-521p-gry cl,frntis port+4 port plts-2nd ed (q8,cov wn & soil) 90.00
GILLEY,W-Bird Carving, A Guide ...-NY-1961-115p-coated papr,photos (gg3,f,dj) 15.00
GILLHAM,C E-Medicine Men of Hooper Bay-Lond-1955-Batchworth Pr-8vo-142p-brwn cl,18 illus-1st ed (cc7) 15.00*
GILLIAM,ANN-Voices for the Earth-SF-1979-567p-1st ed (q10,f,dj) 24.00
GILLIAM,ANN-Voices for the Earth-SF-1979-592p-photos-1st ed (t7,dj) 18.00
GILLIATT,PENELOPE-One by One-Lond-(1965)-auth 1st bk-1st ed (h5,f,sl tn dj) 45.00
GILLIES,HAROLD-Plastic Surgery of the Face Based on Selected Cases of War Injuries...with Original Illustrations-Lond-1983-4to-408p-photos-(facs of 1920 ed) (dd3) 200.00
GILLIES,JOHN W-Principles of Pictorial Photography-NY-(1923)-Falk-4to-red cl stmpd in gilt-1st ed (y3,sl soil cov) 50.00
GILLINGHAM,JOHN-Richard the Lionheart-NY-(1978)-Times Bks-8vo-318p-17 illus-1st US ed (cc5,f,dj) 15.00
GILLMAN,PETER-Direttissima-NY-1966-Harper & Row-174p-38 photos-1st ed (j8,f,dj) 30.00
GILLMOR,FRANCES-Traders to the Navajos-Albuq-1952-265p-photos (t7,dj) 30.00
GILLMOR,FRANCES-Traders to the Navajos-Bost-1934-Houghton Mifflin-263p-illus-1st ed (dd4,wn) 30.00
GILLMOR,FRANCES-Traders to the Navajos-Bost-1934-Houghton,Mifflin-(vi),265p-orng cl,photos-1st ed (v1,dj) 60.00
GILLMORE,PARKER-Gun,Rod and Saddle-Lond-1869-12mo-295p (m3) 22.50

GILLMORE,PARKER-Prairie and Forest-NY-1874-Harper-278p-35 illus-1st ed (d3) 75.00

GILLMORE,PARKER-Ride Through Hostile Africa-Lond-1881-380p-blu cl,illus-2nd ed (jj2) 200.00

GILLMORE,Q A-Practical Treatise on Roads, Streets, and Pavements...-NY-1882-258p-cl-4th ed (j1) 15.00

GILLON,EDMUND V,JR.-Early New England Gravestone Rubbings-NY-(1966)-Dover-(207)p-wrps,195 plts (m1) 10.00

GILLY,ANTOINE-Feast of France-Lond-1974-Cassell-387p-blu bds,photos,drwngs-1st ed (q8,dj) 20.00

GILMAN,CAROLINE-Recollections of a Southern Matron-NY-1839-272p+ads-cl-Amer Imprnts 55873 (aa1,sl wn,cov fade) 50.00

GILMAN,DOROTHY-Amazing Mrs.Pollifax-GC-1970-Dbldy-1st ed (w9,stnd bottom edge,dj) 30.00

GILMAN,DOROTHY-Clairvoyant Countess-NY-1975-Dbldy-1st ed (j4,dj) 10.00

GILMAN,DOROTHY-Palm for Mrs.Pollifax-1973-Dbldy-1st ed (s10,dj) 15.00

GILMAN,DOROTHY-Palm for Mrs.Pollifax-NY-1973-Dbldy-1st ed (g4,dj) 10.00

GILMAN,DOROTHY-Tightrope Walker-NY-1979-Dbldy-1st ed (g4,dj) 10.00

GILMAN,SANDER-Seeing the Insane-NY-1982-4to-242p-287 illus-1st ed (dd3,dj) 75.00

GILMORE,ALBERT F-Yes 'Tis Round-Bost-(1932)-Stratford-8vo-393p-1st ed (ff5,f,dj) 17.50

GILMORE,BERTHA C-Days of Then-Cuyahoga Falls-1975-Ohio Adv Co-64p-wrps,photos (w3,vf,pres cpy) 20.00

GILMORE,JAMES A-Practice and Precedents in the Probate Courts of Ohio in Civil and Criminal Proceedings...-Cin-1884-Robt Clarke-445p-lea (n1,sl scuff lea) 15.00

GILMORE,MELVIN R-Prairie Smoke-NY-1929-Columbia U Pr-208p-illus-1st ed (ff4) 45.00

GILPATRIC,GUY-Mr.Glencannon Ignores the War-NY-1944-Dutton-1st ed (a10,dj soil & sl wn) 30.00

GILPIN,LAURA-Pueblos: A Camera Chronicle-NY-1941-Hastings Hs-8vo-unpgd-1st ed (z4,dj wn & sp chip) 200.00

GILPIN,LAURA-Rio Grande, River of Destiny-NY-(1940)-244p-illus,photos,map e.p.-1st ed,1st prtg (u7,dj) 100.00

GILPIN,LAURA-Temples in Yucatan-NY-1948-Hastings-photos-1st ed (pp9,f,dj sl soil & tn) 195.00

GILPIN,LAURA-Will Rogers Shrine of the Sun-Col Sprngs-1937-Broadmoor-grn wrps wi orig tie,10 photos(incl 2 fldg)-rare-1st ed (pp9,f) 200.00

GINGER,RAY-Bending Cross-New Brunswick-1949-459p+index,cl (n1,sl creased sp) 12.50

GINGRICH,ARNOLD-ED.-American Trout Fishing-NY-1966-8vo-247p-illus (m3,f,dj) 25.00

GINGRICH,ARNOLD-ED.-Armchair Esquire-NY-(1958)-Putnam's-1st ed (b10,sl chip dj) 25.00

GINGRICH,ARNOLD-Fishing in Print-NY-1974-4to-344p-illus,J Groth (m3,as new in dj) 25.00

GINGRICH,ARNOLD-Joys of Trout-1973-Crown-1st ed (dd8,dj) 18.00

GINGRICH,ARNOLD-Joys of Trout-NY-1973-8vo-275p-photos (m3,vf,dj) 30.00

GINGRICH,ARNOLD-Well Tempered Angler-NY-1973-331p-illus (gg3,f) 30.00

GINSBERG,ALLEN-Airplane Dreams-Tor-1968-Anansi-wrps,errata slip laid in-1st ed (v5,sl sun,soil) 15.00

GINSBERG,ALLEN-Chicago Trial Testimony-(SF)-(1975)-City Lights-wrps-1st ed (l9,autg) 140.00

GINSBERG,ALLEN-Empty Mirror-NY-1961-Totem/Corinth-wrps-1st ed (f8,f) 35.00

GINSBERG,ALLEN-Fall of America, Poems of These States 1965 to 1971-SF-1972-City Lights-wrps-1st ed (e8) 35.00

GINSBERG,ALLEN-Gates of Wrath-Bolinas-1972-Grey Fox Pr-#2 of 100c,autg,acetate dj-1st ed (g8,f,dj) 150.00

GINSBERG,ALLEN-Gates of Wrath-Bolinas-1972-Grey Fox Pr-wrps-1st ed (e8,autg) 45.00

GINSBERG,ALLEN-Moments Return-SF-1970-Grabhorn Hoyem-3 drwngs by La Vigne,orig acetate dj-ltd to 200c,autg (l9,f,dj) 125.00

GINSBERG,ALLEN-Planet News 1961 to 1967-SF-(1968)-City Lights-wrps-1st ed thus (e8) 35.00

GINSBERG,ALLEN-Planet News, 1961 to 1967-SF-(1968)-City Lights Bks-wrps-1st ed thus (f2) 25.00

GINSBERG,ALLEN-Sad Dust Glories-Berkeley-1975-Workingmans Pr-wrps-1st ed (d8,f) 25.00

GINSBURG,NORTON-Malaya-Seattle-1958-U of Wash-8vo-532p-papr over bds,maps-AES Publ-1st ed (y5) 22.00

GINZBURG,EUGENIA-Journey Into the Whirlwind-NY-(1967)-HBW-8vo-418p-1st US ed (jj5,dj) 20.00

GINZBURG,NATALIA-Road to the City-Lond-1952-Hogarth Pr-8vo-149p-1st Brit ed (w6,f,dj) 25.00

GINZBURG,R-An Unhurried View of Erotica-1958-Helmsman Pr-1st ed (x2,f,box) 35.00

GINZBURG,RALPH-ED.-Eros-Spring 1962-folio-4 vols-Vol.1,Nmbrs 1 thru 4-papr cov bds (y3) 150.00

GIONO,JEAN-Harvest-NY-1939-Viking-cl-1st Amer ed (o8) 20.00

GIOVANNI,NIKKI-Black Feeling Black Talk Black Judgement-NY-1970-Morrow-1st hdcov ed of auth 1st bk-1st ed (y1,f,dj) 75.00

GIOVANNI,NIKKI-Cotton Candy on a Rainy Day-NY-1978-Wm Morrow-1st ed (c10,dj) 20.00

GIOVANNI,NIKKI-My House-NY-1972-1st ed (n5,sl tn dj) 22.50

GIOVANNI,NIKKI-My House-NY-1972-Morrow-1st ed (ee2,f,dj) 40.00

GIOVANNI,NIKKI-Re:Creation-Detr-(1970)-Broadside Pr-8vo-48p-stapled pict wrps-1st ed (z5) 28.00

GIOVANNI,NIKKI-Women and the Men-NY-1975-Morrow-1st ed (cc1,f,dj) 35.00

GIOVANNI,NIKKI-Women and the Men-NY-1975-Morrow-1st ed (v5,f,f dj) 20.00

GIPSON,FRED-Fabulous Empire-Bost-1946-Houghton Mifflin-411p-Six Guns #835-1st ed (cc4,dj) 35.00

GIPSON,FRED-Fabulous Frontier-Bost-1946-411p-Herd #898-1st ed (t7,dj) 30.00

GIRAUD,J P-Birds of Long Island-NY-1844-8vo-(1),397p-half lea,mrbld bds & e.p.,1 plt (y8,rub) 175.00

GIROUARD,MARK-Robert Smythson and the Architecture of the Elizabethan Era-NY-1967-Barnes-sm 4to-232p-blu cl,illus (r10,sl wn dj) 25.00

GISH,ANTHONY-American Bandits-Girard-(1938)-Haldeman Julius-101p,ads-stiff wrps-1st ed (v1) 30.00

GISH,ANTHONY-American Bandits-Girard-(1938)-Haldeman-Julius-101p+11p ads-wrps,Six-Guns 836 (n1) 20.00

GISSING,GEORGE-In the Year of Jubilee-NY-1895-1st Amer ed (r2,cl sl soil & rub) 50.00

GISSING,GEORGE-Victim of Circumstance...-Bost-1927-1st ed (t5,chip dj) 30.00

GIST,B D-High Sierra Adventure-Visalia-1950-8vo-108p-photos-1st ed (m3,f) 20.00

GITHENS,THOMAS-Drug Plants of Africa-Phila-1948-125p-wrps-1st ed (dd3) 40.00

GITTINGS,ROBT-Nature of Biography-Seattle-(1978)-U of Wash-1st ed (d10,f,dj) 12.50

GIVENS,JOHN-Friend in the Police-1980-HBJ-1st ed (t9,f,dj) 15.00

GIVENS,JOHN-Sons of the Pioneers-(1977)-HBJ-auth 1st bk-1st ed (t9,dj) 25.00

GIVENS,JOHN-Sons of the Pioneers-NY,Lond-(1977)-HBJ-auth 1st bk-1st ed (a10,as new in dj) 15.00

GJEVRE,JOHN A-Chili Line-(Espanola)-(1969)-82p-wrps,photos,maps-1st ed (v7,f,autg) 15.00

GLADDEN,WASHINGTON-From the Hub to the Hudson-Bost-1869-New England News-illus-1st ed (dd6) 40.00

GLADDEN,WASHINGTON-Ultima Veritas and Other Verses-Bost-1912-Pilgrim Pr-1st ed (w5,f) 30.00

GLADWIN,HAROLD S-History of the Ancient Southwest-Portland-1957-Bond Wheelwright-xx+383p-illus-1st ed (mm10,dj) 65.00

GLADWIN,HAROLD-ET AL-Excavations at Snaketown-Globe-1937-4to-2 vols-wrps-scarce (pp9) 275.00

GLARUM,SIVERT N-Our Land and Lakes, Michigan Benzie County, Lower Herring Lake-Manistee-1983-West Graf-70p-wrps (z7) 22.50

GLASER,LYNN-Counterfeiting in America-np-(1968)-Clarkson N Potter-xii+274p-beige cl,illus-1st ed (b2,dj) 15.00

GLASER,MILTON-Graphic Design-Woodstock-(1973)-Overlook Pr-344 plts(incl 97 col)-1st ed (bb1,as new in dj) 50.00

GLASGOW,ELLEN-Deliverance-NY-1904-Dbldy,Page-col illus by Schoonover-1st ed (m4) 12.50

GLASGOW,ELLEN-In This Our Life-NY-(1941)-Harcourt Brace-1st ed (ee2,f,dj) 35.00

GLASGOW,ELLEN-In This Our Life-NY-(1941)-Harcourt Brace-8vo-467p-1st ed (w6,dj) 50.00

GLASGOW,ELLEN-Letters-NY-(1958)-Harcourt Brace-1st ed (dd2,f,dj) 25.00

GLASGOW,ELLEN-Phases of an Inferior Planet-NY,Lond-1898-Harper & Bros-324,(1)p-cl-Wright 2191-1st ed (c1,sm cov spots) 25.00

GLASGOW,ELLEN-Romantic Comedians-NY-1926-Dbldy-8vo-346p-1st ed (w6,dj) 75.00

GLASGOW,ELLEN-They Stooped to Folly-GC-1929-Dbldy-8vo-351p-1st trd ed (w6,f,dj) 75.00

GLASGOW,ELLEN-They Stooped to Folly-NY-1929-1st ed (m4) 14.50

GLASGOW,ELLEN-Virginia-GC-1913-Dbldy-8vo-526p-1st ed (w6,tender hngs) 45.00

GLASIER,PHILIP-As the Falcon Her Bells-NY-1964-Dutton-223p-illus,photos (d9) 15.00

GLASPELL,SUSAN-Ambrose Holt and Family-NY-1931-Stokes-1st ed (hh5,sl tn dj) 20.00

GLASS,MAJ E L N-Tenth Cavalry-Ft.Collins-1972-147p-stiff pict wrps,frntis,photos-1st ed (t7) 22.50

GLASSCOCK,C B-Gold in Them Hills-Indpls-(1932)-330p-dec cl,frntis (t7) 15.00

GLASSCOCK,C B-Gold in Them HIlls-Indpls-(1932)-Bobbs Merrill-330p-frntis-Six Guns 839 (gg4) 20.00

GLASSCOCK,C B-Here's Death Valley-NY-1940-329p-frntis,photos,map e.p.-1st ed (t7) 15.00

GLASSCOCK,C B-Man Hunt Bandits and the Southern Pacific-NY-1929-294p-frntis,photos (t7) 20.00

GLASSCOCK,C B-War of the Copper Kings-NY-1935-314p-frntis,photos (t7) 10.00

GLASSCOCK,G B-Golden Highway-Indpls-(1934)-Bobbs Merrill-333p-map e.p.,illus-Six Guns 840-1st ed (bb4,sp fade) 15.00

GLASSER,RONALD J-365 Days-NY-1971-Braziller-1st ed (v5,f,sl tn dj) 25.00

GLATTHAAR,JOSEPH T-March to the Sea and Beyond-NY-1985-318p-illus-1st ed (n3,f,dj) 25.00

GLAZIER,CAPT WILLARD-Down the Great River-Phila-1891-Hubbard Bros-443p-illus,fldg map (gg4) 20.00

GLEASON,C W-Seven Lectures on the Philosophy of Life and the Art of Preserving Health-Columbus-1852-prntd by Scott & Bascom-252,(1)p-cl,plts (d1,sl wn,fox) 30.00

GLEASON,GENE-Hong Kong-NY-(1963)-John Day-8vo-318p-16p photos-1st ed (gg5,dj) 12.50

GLEASON,H A-Plants of the Vicinity of New York-NY-1935-NY Botanical Grdn-12mo-lxxxvi,198p-flex leatherette,drwngs-1st ed (o2) 12.50

GLEASON,HENRY A-Manual of Vascular Plants of Northeastern United States and Adjacent Canada-(1963)-Van Nostrand-11,810p (x5,dj) 30.00

GLEASON,OSCAR-How to Handle and Educate Vicious Horses-NY-1886-Orange Judd-1st ed (j9) 35.00

GLEASON,RALPH-ED.-Jam Session-NY-(1958)-Putnam-1st ed (w1,f,dj) 25.00

GLENN,LOIS-Charles W S Williams. A Checklist-1975-Kent State U Pr-cl-1st ed (o8,f) 15.00

GLENN,W W-Between North and South-Rutherford-1976-430p (z10,f,dj) 20.00

GLESS,ELEANOR G-Murder at Tall Tip-1964-Avalon-1st ed (s10,dj) 12.50

GLEYSTEEN,JAN-Symphony in Steam-Scottdale-1966-112p-1st ed (n4,f,dj) 16.00

GLICK,ALLEN-Winters Coming, Winters Gone-NY-(1984)-Pinnacle Bks-auth 1st bk-1st ed (bb1,as new in dj) 40.00

GLINES,C V,JR.-Grand Ole Lady-(Cleve)-(1959)-8vo-250p-illus cl,24p plts-1st ed (t2,dj) 25.00

GLINES,C V-Compact History of the United States Air Force-NY-(1963)-roy 8vo-342p-cl,14p illus,illus e.p.,Gil Walker-1st ed (t2,cl) 25.00

GLINES,C V-Doolittle's Tokyo Raiders-Princeton-(1964)-8vo-xiv,448p-cl,plts,text illus-1st ed (t2,dj) 35.00

GLINES,C V-Four Came Home-Princeton-(1966)-roy 8vo-xiv,228p-cl,text illus (t2,dj) 20.00

GLINES,LT COL C V-Polar Aviation-NY-(1964)-F Watts Aerospace Libr-xii,289p-cl,photos-1st ed (kk9,dj) 35.00

GLOAG,JOHN-Manna-Lond-(1940)-Cassell-280p-1st ed (q1,dj sl wn,chip) 40.00

GLOAG,M-Book of English Gardens-Lond-1906-Methuen-340p-cl,24 wtrcols by Wyatt (x6) 22.00

GLOUCESTER COUNTY SERIES-Transcriptions of Early County Records of New Jersey-Newark-1940-Hist Rec Survey/WPA-4to-xiv,144,(1)p-wrps,map (aa6) 35.00

GLOVER,GRAHAM-British Locomotive Design 1825 to 1960-Lond-1967-113p-1st ed (n4,f,dj) 19.50

GLOVER,H CLAY-Diseases of the Dog-NY-1897-18mo-30p-wrps (m3) 17.50

GLOVER,MICHAEL-Napoleonic Wars, an Illustrated History-NY-(1979)-232p-col illus-1st Amer ed (d7,f,dj) 25.00

GLOVER,MICHAEL-Rorke's Drift-Lond-1975-146p-illus-1st ed (gg2,f,dj) 50.00

GLOVER,ROBERT-Tyler to Sharpsburg-Waco-1960-22p-stiff pict wrps-Dornbusch II #1069-1st ed (t7) 25.00

GLOZER,LISELOTTE F-California in the Kitchen-(Berkeley)-1960-(priv prntd)-43p-ltd to 500c (m6) 75.00

GLOZER,LISELOTTE F-Librarian's Cook Book-Berkeley-1965-Peacock Pr-16mo-30p-stiff red wrps-1st ed (q8) 12.50

GLUCKMAN,ARCADI-United States Martial Pistols & Revolvers-NY-1956-8vo-249p+appndcs-illus (m3,vf,dj) 15.00

GLUCKMAN,ARCADI-United States Muskets,Rifles & Carbines-Buffalo-1948-8vo-441p+Appendix & plts-illus-1st ed (m3) 35.00

GLUCKMAN,MAX-ED.-Essays on the Ritual of Social Relations-(1962)-Manchester U Pr-8vo-190p-cl-1st ed (y5,dj wn) 22.00

GLUCKMAN,MAX-ED.-Ideas and Procedures in African Customary Law-Lond-1969-OUP-8vo-361p-cl-1st ed (y5,dj) 20.00

GLUCKMAN,MAX-Ideas in Barotse Jurisprudence-New Haven-1965-Yale U Pr-lg 8vo-299p-cl,photos-1st ed (y5,dj tn) 30.00

GLUCKMAN,MAX-Judicial Process Among the Barotse of Northern Rhodesia-(1955)-Manchester U Pr-8vo-386p-cl,maps,plts-1st ed (y5,dj) 28.00

GLUCKMAN,MAX-Order and Rebellion in Tribal Africa-Lond-(1963)-Cohen & West-8vo-273p-cl-1st ed (y5,dj) 25.00

GNADINGER,C B-Pyrethrum Flowers-1936-McLaughlin Gormley King-380p-photos-2nd ed wi spplmnt laid in (bb3) 20.00

GOBLE,PAUL-Red Hawk's Account of Custer's Battle-NY-(1969)-Pantheon Bks-sm folio-59p-1st ed (gg4,dj) 25.00

GODDARD,ABBOTT-Selection of Hymns and Spirituals Songs, Designed for the use of the Pious-Cin-1838-E Morgan-224p-lea (g1,sm t.p. pc miss,crckd jnt) 50.00

GODDARD,CHRIS-Jazz Away From Home-NY-(1979)-Paddington-photos-1st ed (w1,f,f dj) 20.00

GODDARD,FREDERICK B-Where to Emigrate, and Why-NY-1869-F B Goddard-591p-buckrm,maps,illus-1st ed (bb4,rbnd) 50.00

GODDARD,HENRY H-Criminal Imbecile-NY-1915-Macmillan-x+157p+ads-blu cl-1st ed (dd1) 25.00

GODDARD,HENRY H-Kallikak Family-NY-1912-xv,(1),121p+ads-cl,plts-1st ed (aa6) 60.00

GODDARD,JOHN-Trout Flies of Stillwater-Lond-1969-8vo-263p-photos-1st ed (m3,f,dj) 25.00

GODDARD,JOHN-Trout Fly Recognition-Lond-1966-8vo-202p-illus,col photos-1st ed (m3,vf) 40.00

GODDARD,PLINY E-Indians of the Northwest Coast-NY-1934-lg 12vo-175p-dec bds,illus,fldg map-2nd ed (d7) 35.00

GODDARD,ROBERT H-Papers of...-NY-(1970)-McGraw-Hill-3 vols,illus-1st ed (d2,v 3 cov sl spot,box) 200.00

GODDARD,RUTH-Porfirio Salinas-Austin-1975-Rock Hs-oblng 4to-95p-27 illus-1st ed (a9) 50.00

GODDEN,RUMER-Fairy Doll-NY-1956-Viking-68p-pict cl,col illus,A Adams-1st ed (s3,f,sp fade dj) 30.00

GODDEN,RUMER-In This House of Brede-NY-1969-Viking-cl-1st Amer ed (o8,dj) 10.00

GODDEN,RUMER-Kitchen Madonna-NY-(1967)-Viking-89p-cl bckd bds,col illus,C Barker-1st ed (s3,f,dj) 25.00

GODDEN,RUMER-Miss Happiness and Miss Flower-NY-(1961)-Viking-73p-pict cl,col & b&w illus,J Primrose-1st ed (r3,dj) 25.00

GODDEN,RUMER-Valiant Chatti Maker-NY-(1983)-Viking-61p-bds,b&w illus,J Roy-1st US ed (r3,as new in dj) 20.00

GODFREY,CAPT E S-An Account of Custer's Last Campaign and the Battle of the Little Big Horn-Palo Alto-1968-Lewis Osborne-87p-illus,map e.p.-ltd to 2100c,nbrd (ee4,dj) 60.00

GODFREY,CARLOS E-Mechanics Bank, 1834 to 1919-(Trenton)-1919-164p-cl,plts(incl fldg) (aa6) 35.00

GODFREY,E L B-History of the Medical Profession of Camden County,NJ-Phila-1896-303p-1st ed (dd3,ex-libr) 60.00

GODFREY,EDWARD S-Diary of the Little Big Horn-Champoeg-1957-74p-illus,fldg maps & plts-Dowd #393-ltd 1st ed (c7) 85.00

GODFREY,ELEANOR S-Development of English Glassmaking 1560 to 1640-Chapel Hill-U of NC Pr-288p-5 plts (cc8,dj) 35.00

GODFREY,JOE-ED.-Great Outdoors-St.Paul-1947-4to-376p-mission lea,illus-1st ed (m3) 20.00

GODFREY,JOE-Popular Mechanics Guide to Good Hunting & Trapping-NY-1952-4to-160p-illus (m3,fray dj) 10.00

GODFREY,LT EDWARD SETTLE-Field Diary of...-Portland-1957-Champoeg Pr-74p-pict cl (dd4,uncut) 95.00

GODFREY,W E-Birds of Canada-1979-Can Nat Mus-4to-428p-68 col plts,maps (bb3,f,dj) 40.00

GODFREY,W E-Birds of Canada-Ottawa-1974(1966)-4to-428p-cl,69 col plts,maps (y8,dj) 35.00

GODINE,DAVID R-Lyric Verse, a Printer's Choice-np-1966-priv prtd/Stinehour Pr-8vo-(ii),75,(3)p-cl backd mrbl cov bds-ltd to 500c (x4,box) 45.00

GODMAN,JOHN D-Rambles of a Naturalist with a Memoir of the Author-Phila-1859-Assn of Friends-12mo-124p-cl-1st ed (y6,sl cl damaged,fox e.p.) 12.00

GODOLPHIN,MARY-RETOLD BY-Pilgrim's Progress-NY-1939-Stokes-4to-120p-pict cl,b&w illus,map e.p.-1st ed (s3,dj wn,sp chip) 45.00

GODSELL,JEAN W-I Was No Lady-Tor-1959-Ryerson-8vo-xiv,212p-frntis,map,15 illus-1st ed (aa7,dj) 20.00*

GODWIN,GAIL-Dream Children-1976-Knopf-1st ed (o9,f,dj) 30.00

GODWIN,GAIL-Odd Woman-1974-Knopf-1st ed (p9,dj) 35.00

GODWIN,GAIL-Perfectionists-Lond-(1971)-J Cape-auth 1st bk-1st Brit ed (m7,f,dj) 60.00

GODWIN,GAIL-Perfectionists-NY-(1970)-auth 1st bk-1st ed (p5,f,dj) 60.00

GODWIN,GAIL-Perfectionists-NY-(1970)-Harper & Row-auth 1st bk-1st ed (k7,dj) 100.00

GODWIN,GAIL-Violet Clay-1978-Knopf-1st ed (o9,f,dj) 25.00

GODWIN,GEORGE-Eternal Forest-NY-1929-Appleton-318p-cl (aa2) 25.00*

GOEDICKE,HANS-Protocol of Neferyt-Balt-1977-John Hopkins-1st ed (y10,f) 50.00

GOELET,FRANCIS-Voyages and Travels of...1746 to 1758-np-1970-Queens College/Gregg Pr-unpgd-blk dec cl,illus-1st ed (nn1,sl rub) 35.00

GOERNER,F-Search for Amelia Earhart-GC-1966-8vo-x,326p-cl,16p plts-1st ed (t2,dj) 30.00

GOETZ,HERMAN-India, 5000 Years of Indian Art-Lond-1960-Methuen-276p-tip in col plts-series-2nd prtg (gg6,f,box) 35.00

GOETZMANN,WM H-Army Exploration in the American West, 1803 thru 1863-Lincoln-1979-489p-photos,maps-1st Bison ed (t7,f) 40.00

GOETZMANN,WM H-Looking Far North-Princeton-1982-Viking-8vo-244p-1/2 cl,illus-1st ed (ee7,dj) 35.00

GOFF,BRUCE-Architecture: 30 Plates-Billings-1978-Yellowstone Art Cntr-oblng folio-ltd ed (h10,box) 175.00

GOFF,RICHARD D-Confederate Supply-Durham-1969-Duke U Pr-275p (o7,f,dj) 20.00

GOFF,RICHARD-Century in the Saddle-Denver-(1967)-Colo Cattlmn's Cent Comm-365p-illus-1st ed (gg4,dj) 50.00

GOFFIN,ROBERT-Horn of Plenty-NY-1947-Allen,Towne & Heath-1st ed (v5,f,f dj) 50.00

GOFFIN,ROBERT-Jazz From the Congo to the Metropolitan-GC-1944-Dbldy-1st ed (w1,f,sl chip dj) 35.00

GOGAN,HIRAM J-Modern Bow Hunting-Harrisburg-1958-8vo-163p-photos-1st ed (m3,dj) 22.50

GOGARTY,OLIVER ST.JOHN-Collected Poems-NY-(1954)-Devin Adair-1st Amer ed (z8,vf,dj) 35.00

GOGARTY,OLIVER ST.JOHN-It Isn't This Time of Year At All-GC-1954-Dbldy-1st Amer ed (z8,vf,sl wn dj) 20.00

GOGARTY,OLIVER ST.JOHN-It Isn't This Time of Year at All-Lond-1954-MacGibbon & Kee-1st ed (z8,vf,dj) 25.00

GOGARTY,OLIVER ST.JOHN-Mr. Petunia-Lond-(1946)-Constable-1st Brit ed (z8,dj) 37.50

GOGARTY,OLIVER ST.JOHN-Rolling Down the Lea-Lond-1950-Constable-wi errata tip in-1st ed (z8,f,dj) 65.00

GOLD,ALEC-ED.-Wines and Spirits of the World-Lond-(1968)-Virtue-4to-708p-wht bds,25 col plts,35 col maps,photos-1st ed (q8,edgewn dj) 40.00

GOLD,HERBERT-Love & Like-NY-1960-1st ed (d5,f,dj) 17.50

GOLD,HERBERT-My Last Two Thousand Years-NY-(1972)-Random-1st ed (d10,dj) 15.00

GOLD,HERBERT-Salt-NY-1963-Dial-1st ed (d10,dj) 15.00

GOLD,ROBERT S-Jazz Lexicon-NY-1964-Knopf-1st ed (w5,f,sl tn dj) 25.00

GOLD,S M-Short Account of the Life and Work of John Rowell-1965-Ranelagh Pr-71p-23 plts (cc8,dj) 65.00

GOLDBERG,A-ED.-History of the United States Air Force. 1907 to 1957-Princeton-(1958)-4to-x,278p-cl,plts,text illus (t2,sl chip dj) 40.00

GOLDBERG,HOWARD-Angler's Book on Fly Tying & Fishing-NY-1973-4to-107p-photos (m3,vf,dj) 10.00

GOLDBERG,HYMAN-Our Man in the Kitchen-NY-(1964)-Odyssey Pr-386p-illus,Wm Hogarth (u6) 15.00

GOLDBERG,LEO-Atoms, Stars, and Nebulae-Phila-(1943)-Blakiston-vi+323p-red cl-presume 1st ed (c2,sl fox,dj) 20.00

GOLDEN NUGGETS OF PIONEER DAYS-Panguitch-1949-374p-frntis,photos-1st ed (t7) 30.00

GOLDEN VASE-Bost-(1851)-J Buffum-96p-miniature bk,approx 3 x 2 inches-orig red cl (f1) 17.50

GOLDEN,HARRY-Carl Sandburg-Cleve,NY-(1961)-World-pict cl-1st ed (aa9,f,sl wn dj) 15.00

GOLDEN,HARRY-Mr.Kennedy and the Negroes-Cleve,NY-(1964)-World-319p-cl,frntis-1st ed (dd10,sl fade sp,dj) 25.00

GOLDEN,JANE-Botanic Manuscript of...-NY-1963-Chanticleer-205p (x6) 30.00

GOLDER,FRANK A-March of the Mormon Battalion from Council Bluffs to California-NY-1928-295p-frntis,photos,map e.p.-Rittenhouse #245-1st ed (t7) 55.00

GOLDHURST,RICHARD-Many are the Hearts-NY-1975-297p-illus-1st ed (n3,dj) 20.00

GOLDING,H-ED.-Wonder Book of Aircraft-Lond-1927-roy 8vo-256p-cl & col illus bds,col frntis,plts incl 11 col,text illus,illus e.p.-1st ed (t2) 30.00

GOLDING,WILLIAM-Free Fall-Lond-(1959)-Faber & Faber-1st ed (c10,f,dj) 85.00

GOLDING,WILLIAM-Hot Gates-Lond-(1965)-Faber & Faber-1st ed (c10,dj) 50.00

GOLDING,WILLIAM-Hot Gates-NY-1966-1st US ed (o5,dj) 22.50

GOLDING,WILLIAM-Hot Gates-NY-1966-HBW-1st US ed (z9,f,dj) 20.00

GOLDING,WILLIAM-Inheritors-NY-(1962)-1st Amer ed (t5,sl wn dj) 15.00

GOLDING,WILLIAM-Inheritors-NY-(1962)-HB&W-1st Amer ed (u10,f,f dj) 40.00

GOLDING,WILLIAM-Moving Target-NY-(1982)-FSG-1st ed (ee2,f,dj) 30.00

GOLDING,WILLIAM-Rites of Passage-Lond-1980-Faber & Faber-1st ed (p3,f,dj) 25.00

GOLDMAN,ALBERT-Grass Roots-NY-(1979)-H&R-8vo-262p-1st ed (dd5,sl soil dj) 15.00

GOLDMAN,E A-Mammals of Panama-Wash-1920-8vo-(2),309p-wrps,39 plts,fldg map(col) (y8,chip) 45.00

GOLDMAN,EMMA-Place of the Individual in Society-Chig-nd-Free Soc Forum-wrps-1st ed (v5,pgs brwng) 35.00

GOLDMAN,EMMA-Social Significance of the Modern Drama-Bost-1914-Badger-1st ed (w5,sl soil,sp wn) 65.00

GOLDMAN,IRVING-Mouth of Heaven-NY-(1975)-John Wiley-265p-map e.p.-1st ed (bb4,dj) 25.00

GOLDMAN,LAUREL-Sounding the Territory-NY-1982-Knopf-1st ed (w5,f,f dj) 20.00

GOLDMAN,LAUREL-Sounding the Territory-NY-1982-Knopf-auth 1st bk-1st ed (bb1,sl stnd dj) 25.00

GOLDMAN,PETER-Charlie Company: What Vietnam Did to Us-NY-1983-Morrow-1st ed (ff3,f,dj) 30.00

GOLDMAN,WILLIAM-Boys and Girls Together-NY-1964-1st ed (q5,f,dj) 25.00

GOLDMAN,WILLIAM-Marathon Man-NY-1974-1st ed (q5,dj) 20.00

GOLDMAN,WILLIAM-Marathon Man-NY-1974-Delacorte-1st ed (v5,f,f dj) 25.00

GOLDMAN,WILLIAM-Soldier in the Rain-NY-1960-1st ed (r2,f,sl rub dj) 30.00

GOLDMAN,WILLIAM-Thing of It Is...-NY-1967-1st ed (s5,sl chip dj) 15.00

GOLDMAN,WILLIAM-Wigger-NY-1974-illus,E LeCain-1st ed (o5,f,dj) 45.00

GOLDNER,SANFORD-Jewish People & the Fight for Negro Rights-LA-1953-Comm Negro-Jewish Relatns-56p-wrps (r1) 18.00

GOLDSCHMIDT,WALTER-Culture and Behavior of the Sebei-Berkeley-(1976)-U of Cal Pr-sm 4to-395p-cl,illus,maps (y5,dj) 45.00

GOLDSMITH,ALFRED N-Radio Telephony-1918-247p-110 photos,116 illus-1st ed (h6) 25.00

GOLDSMITH,ALFRED N-Radio Telephony-NY-(1918)-Wireless Pr-viii+247p-red cl,226 illus (l2,cov spot,soil,sm sp hole) 60.00

GOLDSMITH,J-An Easy Grammar of Geography-Phila-1810-Johnson & Warner-144p-bds (k1) 25.00

GOLDSMITH,JOEL S-Contemplative Life-NY-1963-Univ Bks-cl-1st ed (o8,f,dj) 15.00

GOLDSMITH,MARGARET-Designs for Outdoor Living-NY-1941-Stewart-358p-cl (x6,dj wn) 25.00

GOLDSMITH,MARGARET-Franz Anton Mesmer-Lond-(1934)-Arthur Barker-(x)+308+(2)p-grn cl,frntis-1st ed (y9) 25.00

GOLDSTEIN,DAVID-Suicide Bent-St.Paul-(1945)-Radio Replies Pr-x+244p-brwn cl (b2) 20.00

GOLDSTEIN,RICHARD-Spartan Seasons-1980-Macmillan-photos-1st ed (s8,f,dj) 20.00

GOLDSTEIN,SHELDON-ED.-Coca Cola Collectibles with Current Prices and Photographs in Full Color-Woodland Hills-1971 to 1975-the Auth-sm 4to-4 vols-pict cl cov over bds,col photos (y4) 150.00

GOLDSTROM,JOHN-Narrative History of Aviation-NY-1930-8vo-xii,320p-g cl,frntis,plts (t2) 75.00

GOLLMAR,ROBERT-My Father Owned a Circus-1965-Caxton-205p-photos-1st ed (v8,dj) 35.00

GOLOVNIN,V M-Around the World on the Kamchatka, 1817 to 1819-Honolulu-1979-Hawaiian Hist Soc/U Pr-8vo-353p-map e.p.,col frntis,maps,illus-1st Engl ed (ee7,as new in dj) 25.00

GOMBRICH,E H-Heritage of Apelles-(1976)-Cornell U Pr-(8)250p-plts,photos-1st ed (l10,f,dj) 16.50

GOMBROWICZ,WITOLD-Ferdydurke-1961-HB&W-1st Amer ed (r9,f,wn dj) 30.00

GOMBROWICZ,WITOLD-Pornografia-NY-(1966)-Grove-1st ed (s6,dj) 35.00

GOMERY,PERCY-Motor Scamper 'Cross Canada-Tor-1922-Ryerson Pr-xx,208p-cl (aa2) 40.00*

GONCHAROV,IVAN-Voyage of the Frigate Pallada-Lond-1965-Folio Soc-8vo-266p-blu dec cl,e.p. map,4 maps,8 illus (p8,sp drknd,box) 35.00

GONZALEZ,LUIS J-Great Rebel-NY-1969-Grove-1st ed (w5,f,sl wn dj) 25.00

GOOCH,BOB-In Search of the Wild Turkey-Waukegon-1978-8vo-182p-photos (m3,vf,dj) 10.00

GOODALE,JANE C-Tiwi Wives-Seattle-(1971)-U of Wash Pr-8vo-368p-cl-1st ed (y5) 23.00

GOODALL,CHARLES S-Complete English Springer Spaniel-Middleburg-1958-8vo-128p-photos-1st ed (m3) 30.00

GOODALL,DAPHNE-British Native Ponies-Lond-1963-Country Life-1st ed (j9) 25.00

GOODALL,DAPHNE-History of Horse Breeding-Lond-1977-Hale-1st ed (j9,dj) 35.00

GOODALL,DAPHNE-Ponies-So Brunswick-1963-Barnes-1st US ed (j9,dj) 22.00

GOODALL,JOHN S-An Edwardian Christmas-Lond-(1977)-Macmillan-oblng 16mo-dec cl-1st ed (s3,f,f dj) 20.00

GOODALL,JOHN S-Shrewbettina Goes to Work-NY-(1981)-Atheneum-oblng 16mo-glossy pict bds,pop up wi 6 movable openings-1st US ed (s3,f) 20.00

GOODALL,JOHN S-Victorians Abroad-NY-(1981)-Atheneum-oblng 12mo-unpgd-cl,rnfrcd bndg-1st US ed (r3,as new in dj) 15.00

GOODCHILD,GEORGE-Jack O'Lantern-1930-Mystery League-1st Amer ed (s10,dj) 15.00

GOODE,G BROWN-American Fishes-Bost-1903-8vo-562p-illus-new ed revsd & enlgd (m3) 35.00

GOODE,G BROWN-Game Fishes of the United States-NY-nd-elephant folio-46p text-ltd to 1000c,nbrd,20 paintings by Kilbourne-reprnt (m3,vf) 100.00

GOODE,JOHN-World Guide to Cooking with Fruits & Vegetables-(1974)-Dutton-oblng 4to-200p-pict grn cl,col plts-1st US ed (q8,dj) 15.00

GOODENOW,EARL-Cow Voyage-NY-(1953)-Knopf-4to-cl,col & b&w illus,auth-1st ed (s3,dj) 20.00

GOODHUE,BERTRAM G-Book of Architectural & Decorative Drawings-NY-1924-folio (ee1,edge rub) 125.00

GOODHUE,BERTRAM G-Book of Architectural & Decorative Drawings-NY-1924-folio (h10,edge rub) 125.00

GOODHUE,BERTRAM G-Book of Architecture & Decorative Drawings-NY-1924-folio-illus (kk4,edge rub) 125.00

GOODHUE,ISABEL-Good Things and Graces-SF-(1905)-P Elder-16mo-30p-suede,bordered text (q8,sl fade cov) 20.00

GOODMAN,DAVID M-Western Panorama 1849 to 1875-Glendale-1966-Arthur H Clark Co-328p-illus (cc4) 30.00

GOODMAN,JAMES M-Navajo Atlas-Norman-(1982)-103p-dbl col,photos,maps-1st ed (v7,f,dj) 20.00

GOODMAN,JOHN K-Ross Stefen-Flagstaff-1977-91p-col frntis & illus,photos-1st ed (t7,f,dj) 27.50

GOODMAN,PAUL-Breaking Up of Our Camp-Norfolk-1949-New Directions-Direction Ser #14-1st ed (y1,f,dj) 25.00

GOODMAN,PAUL-Communitas-(1947)-U of Chig Pr-oblng 4to-illus-1st ed (kk4,dj sl chip) 150.00

GOODMAN,PAUL-ED.-Seeds of Liberation-NY-1964-Braziller-551p-1st ed (ff1,chip dj) 18.00

GOODMAN,PAUL-Growing Up Absurd-NY-(1960)-1st ed (y7,dj) 28.00

GOODMAN,PAUL-Growing Up Absurd-NY-(1960)-Random-1st ed (hh5,f,dj) 25.00

GOODMAN,PAUL-Homespun of Oatmeal Gray-NY-(1970)-Random-8vo-120p-1st ed (ee5,dj) 10.00

GOODMAN,PAUL-Like a Conquered Province-NY-1967-Random-Massey Lectures,6th ser-1st ed (y1,f,f dj) 25.00

GOODMAN,PAUL-Lordly Hudson-NY-1962-prtd wrps-1st ed (r2) 25.00

GOODMAN,PAUL-Making Do-(1963)-Macmillan-1st ed (n9,f,sl rub dj sp) 20.00

GOODMAN,PAUL-Making Do-NY-(1963)-Macmillan-1st ed (y1,f,dj) 25.00

GOODMAN,PAUL-Utopian Essays & Practical Proposals-NY-(1962)-Random-1st ed so stated (q1,sl tn dj) 25.00

GOODMAN,WALTER-Committee-NY-1968-Farrar-1st ed (v5,f,f dj) 25.00

GOODRICH,A L-Birds in Kansas-1946-Kan Agri Bd-340p-wrps,6 col plts,maps (bb3) 25.00

GOODRICH,CASPAR-Report on the British Naval and Military Operations in Egypt, 1882-Wash-1883-340p-1/2 blk calf & mrbld bds,edges & e.p.,engrvngs-scarce-1st ed (jj2,rub) 200.00

GOODRICH,CHARLES A-Child's History of the United States...-Phila-1883-Cowperthwait-158p-rvsd by Berard-bds,woodcuts (e1) 15.00

GOODRICH,EDWIN S-Structure and Development of Vertebrates-Lond-1930-Macmillan-xxxii+837p,errata slip-grn cl-1st ed (a2) 40.00

GOODRICH,JEREMIAH-Murray's English Reader-Saratoga Springs-1825-S Newton-304p-lea-Amer Imprnts 21569 (k1) 22.50

GOODRICH,L-Max Weber-NY-1949-37 illus-1st ed (h10,sl tn dj) 45.00

GOODRICH,LLOYD-Winslow Homer-NY-1959-127p-cl (n1,dj) 15.00

GOODRICH,NORMA L-Priestesses-NY-1898-Franklin Watts-8vo-428p-1st ed (gg5,vf,f dj) 12.50

GOODRICH,S-Illustrative Anecdotes of the Animal Kingdom-Bost-1845-12mo-336p-1/2 lea,frntis (y8,lea scuff,sp split) 30.00

GOODRIDGE,HARRY-Seal Called Andre-NY-(1975)-Pantheon-8vo-181p-16p photos-1st ed (gg5,dj) 12.50

GOODRUM,CHARLES-Dewey Decimated-NY-1977-Crown-1st ed (g4,dj) 17.50

GOODSELL,DANIEL A-Nature and Character at Granite Bay-NY-1901-Eatin & Mains-xv,219p-dec cov,22 photo plts-1st ed (o2) 20.00

GOODSPEED,CHARLES E-ED.-Treasury of Fishing Stories-NY-1946-4to-600p-illus-1st ed (m3) 30.00

GOODSPEED,CHARLES E-Yankee Bookseller-Bost-1937-8vo-325p-photos-1st ed (m3,f,badly fray dj) 45.00

GOODSPEED,CHARLES E-Yankee Bookseller-Bost-1937-Houghton Mifflin-1st trd ed (w1,lacks dj) 30.00

GOODSPEED,EDGAR J-Curse in the Colophon-Chig-1935-Willett,Clark-1st ed (e4) 15.00

GOODSPEED,T HARPER-Plant Hunters in the Andes-NY-(1941)-xvi,429p-e.p. maps,76 photos (m10,sp fade,pres) 50.00

GOODWIN,C C-Comstock Club-SLC-1891-314p-cl-Wright 2205-1st ed (m1) 32.50

GOODWIN,CARDINAL-Trans Mississippi West(1803 to 1853)-NY-1922-Appleton-xiv+528p-blu cl,6 maps-Howes G247-1st ed (e2) 55.00

GOODWIN,CARDINAL-Trans Mississippi West(1803 to 1853)-NY-1924-Appleton-528p-maps-Howes G247 (gg4) 35.00

GOODWIN,CHARLES H-Treatment of Diseases of Women, Puerperal and Non-Puerperal...-NY-1884-C H Goodwin-436p-cl (d1) 25.00

GOODWIN,D-Crows of the World-1976-Cornell Univ-4to-354p-3 col plts,maps-1st ed (bb3,f) 35.00

GOODWIN,GRENVILLE-Social Organization of the Western Apache-Chig-1942-701p-pict cl,illus,maps(incl fldg)-1st ed (t7,f) 60.00

GOODWIN,MAUD W-Dutch and English on the Hudson-New Haven-1920-Yale-qtr cl,papr cov bds,fldg map-Chron of Amer Ser,Vol.7 (nn3) 20.00

GOODY,JACK-Comparative Studies in Kinship-Stanford-1969-Stanford U Pr-8vo-261p-cl (y5,dj) 29.00

GOODY,JACK-Death, Property and the Ancestors-Lond-(1962)-Tavistock-8vo-452p-cl,illus (y5,dj wn) 38.00

GOODY,JACK-Literacy in Traditional Societies-Cambridge-1968-Univ Pr-lg 8vo-340p-cl-1st ed (y5,f dj) 55.00

GOODY,JACK-Technology, Tradition and the State in Africa-Lond-1971-OUP-8vo-88p-cl,plts,maps-1st ed (y5,f,dj) 30.00

GOODYKOONTZ,COLIN B-Home Missions on the American Frontier-Caldwell-1939-Caxton-460p-1st ed (cc4,dj) 40.00

GOOLD,WILLIAM-Portland in the Past-Portland-1886-B Thurston,prntr-543p-blk cl,plts-1st ed (k2,sl wn cov) 65.00

GOOLRICK,JOHN-Old Homes and History Around Fredericksburg, the Northern Neck...Stafford and Spotsylvania Counties-Richmond-(1929)-105p-cl (d1) 15.00

GOOSSEN,E C-Ellsworth Kelly-NY-1973-MOMA-4to-128p-b&w wrps,b&w & col illus (r10) 12.50

GORDEN,JOHN V-Missing,Presumed Dead-1976-North Country-1st ed (s10,dj,autg) 10.00

GORDIMER,NADINE-Burger's Daughter-NY-(1979)-Viking-1st ed (m7,f,dj) 25.00

GORDIMER,NADINE-Conservationist-1975-Viking-1st Amer ed (q9,f,dj) 20.00

GORDIMER,NADINE-Friday's Footprint-NY-1960-Viking-1st Amer ed (cc2,f,dj rub,chip) 50.00

GORDIMER,NADINE-Guest of Honor-NY-(1971)-Viking-504p-1st US ed (gg10,dj) 35.00

GORDIMER,NADINE-Late Bourgeois World-NY-(1966)-1st US ed (p5,f,dj) 45.00

GORDIMER,NADINE-Late Bourgeois World-NY-(1966)-Viking-120p-1st US ed (gg10,dj) 50.00

GORDIMER,NADINE-Livingtone's Companions-NY-1971-Viking-1st ed (q2,sl tn dj) 45.00

GORDIMER,NADINE-Occasion for Loving-NY-(1963)-1st US ed (s5,f,dj) 35.00

GORDIMER,NADINE-Occasion for Loving-NY-(1963)-Viking-1st US ed (u10,f,dj) 30.00

GORDIMER,NADINE-Selected Stories-NY-1976-1st US ed (s5,f,dj) 22.50

GORDIMER,NADINE-Soft Voice of the Serpent-NY-(1952)-S&S-scarce-1st US ed (ee2,dj sl wn & chip) 100.00

GORDIMER,NADINE-Soft Voice of the Serpent...-NY-(1952)-1st US ed (k5,sl soil dj) 75.00

GORDIMER,NADINE-Soldier's Embrace-NY-(1980)-1st US ed (o5,f,dj) 15.00

GORDIMER,NADINE-Soldier's Embrace-NY-(1980)-Viking-1st Amer ed (ee2,f,dj) 30.00

GORDIMER,NADINE-Soldier's Embrace-NY-(1980)-Viking-1st US ed (y1,f,f dj) 25.00

GORDIMER,NADINE-World of Strangers-NY-1958-1st US ed (o5,dj) 60.00

GORDIMER,NADINE-World of Strangers-NY-1958-1st US ed (t5,sl rub dj) 35.00

GORDIMER,NADINE-World of Strangers-NY-1958-S&S-312p-1st US ed (gg10,dj) 50.00

GORDON,ANNA A-Beautiful Life of Frances E Willard-Chig-(1898)-416p-cl (a1,sl soil cov) 17.50

GORDON,ANTOINETTE K-Iconography of Tibetan Lamaism-Rutland-1959-Tuttle-4to-131p txt-blk/yel cl,b&w & col illus-2nd ed (r10,sl wn & soil dj) 75.00

GORDON,CAROLINE-Collected Stories-NY-(1981)-1st ed (t5,dj) 25.00

GORDON,CAROLINE-Collected Stories-NY-(1981)-FS&G-1st ed (cc2,f,dj) 30.00

GORDON,CAROLINE-Forest of the South-NY-1945-Scribner's-1st ed (ff6,sl chip dj) 200.00

GORDON,CAROLINE-Garden of Adonis-NY-1937-Scribner's-1st ed (k7,dj sl wn) 150.00

GORDON,CAROLINE-Malefactors-NY-(1956)-Harcourt Brace-1st ed (ee2,f,dj) 70.00

GORDON,CAROLINE-Malefactors-NY-(1956)-Harcourt,Brace-1st ed (a5,dj) 50.00

GORDON,CAROLINE-Strange Children-NY-1951-Scribner's-1st ed (ff6,f,dj) 125.00

GORDON,CAROLINE-Woman on the Porch-NY-1944-1st ed (q5,2 mrks pg edge bttm,dj wn) 50.00

GORDON,CHARLES W-Life of James Robertson-NY-(1908)-Revell-403p-illus (cc4) 15.00

GORDON,DR W E-Socialism-Cleve-1903-Suggestive New Thought-wrps-1st ed (v5,sl chip) 35.00

GORDON,ELIZABETH-Cuisines of the Western World-(1965)-Golden Pr-folio-204p-tan cl,col plts,promo bk (q8,wn dj) 12.50

GORDON,H LAING-Sir James Young Simpson and Chloroform-NY-1898-233p-1st ed (dd3) 75.00

GORDON,J E H-Practical Treatise on Electrical Lighting-1884-228p-94 illus-rare-1st ed (h6) 115.00

GORDON,JEAN-Coffee Recipes-Woodstock-(1963)-Red Rose Publ-16mo-97p-brwn cl,photos,drwngs-1st prtg (q8) 15.00

GORDON,JEAN-Immortal Roses-Woodstock-1959-ix,170p-pbk,6 illus-1st prtg (m10) 8.00

GORDON,JEAN-Orange Recipes-(1962)-Red Rose-16mo-101p-orng cl,photos,drwngs-1st prtg (q8,dj) 16.50

GORDON,JEAN-Orange Recipes-Woodstock-(1962)-Red Rose-101p-bds-1st ed (u6,dj) 12.00

GORDON,JESSE E-ED.-Handbook of Clinical and Experimental Hypnosis-NY/Lond-(1967)-Macmillan/Collier,MacMlln-(ii)+viii+653+(9)p-prntd blk cl-1st ed (y9,chip dj) 31.50

GORDON,JOHN-My Six Years with the Black Watch-Bost-1929-362p-blu cl-1st ed (gg2,lacks ffep) 200.00

GORDON,LESLEY-Country Herbal-Lond-(1980)-Peerage-208p-dec grn cl,col & b&w plts-1st ed (q8,dj) 22.50

GORDON,LESLIE-Peepshow Into Paradise-NY-nd(ca.1953)-John De Graff-264p-illus(incl col) (a8,tattrd dj) 35.00

GORDON,LYDIA L-From Lady Washington to Mrs Cleveland-Bost-1889-448p-cl (d1) 35.00

GORDON,MARY-Final Payments-NY-(1978)-Random-auth 1st bk-1st ed (b5,f,dj) 30.00

GORDON,MAURICE B-Aesculapius Comes to the Colonies-Ventnor-(1949)-xiv,560p-cl,plts(1 fldg) (aa6) 90.00

GORDON,NEIL-Professor's Poison-NY-1928-Harcourt-1st US ed (h4) 10.00

GORDON,PIERRE-Sex and Religion-NY-1949-Soc Sci Publ-cl-1st Amer ed (n8,f,dj) 15.00

GORDON,SID-How to Fish From Top to Bottom-Harrisburg-1955-8vo-384p-photos,illus-1st ed (m3,vf) 60.00

GORDON,T-American Trout Fishing-NY-1972-247p-illus (gg3,f,dj) 35.00

GORDON,WILLIAM R-Maniton Beach Trolley Days 1895 to 1925-Rochester-1957-111p+maps-1st ed (n4) 12.50

GORDON,WILLIAM R-Rochester Syracuse and Eastern "Travelectric" 1906 to 1931-Rochester-1961-191p-wrps-1st ed (n4) 18.50

GORDON,WILLIAM R-Stories and History of the Erie Railroad, Rochester Division-Rochester-1965-144p-wrps-1st ed (n4) 15.00

GORDON,WILLIAM R-Trolleys Down the Mohawk Valley-Rochester-208p-wrps-1st ed (n4) 12.00

GORDONS,THE-Undercover Cat-1963-Dbldy-1st ed (s10,dj) 15.00

GORES,JOE-Final Notice-1973-Random Hs-1st ed (s10,dj) 30.00

GORES,JOE-Final Notice-NY-1973-1st ed (s5,f,dj) 40.00

GORES,JOE-Gone, No Forwarding-NY-1978-Random-1st ed (h4,f,sl wn dj) 20.00

GORES,JOE-Hammett-NY-(1975)-Putnam's-1st ed (a5,as new in dj) 30.00

GORES,JOE-Interface-NY-1974-Evans-1st ed (e4,f,dj) 20.00

GORES.JOE-Time of Predators-NY-1969-auth 1st bk-1st ed (s5,f,dj) 100.00

GOREY,EDGAR-Vinegar Works...-1963-S&S-3 vols,w/o dj as iss-1st ed (x2,f,box) 145.00

GOREY,EDWARD-Amphigorey Also-NY-(1983)-Congdon & Weed-1st ed so stated (q1,dj) 40.00

GOREY,EDWARD-Broken Spoke-NY-1976-Dodd,Mead-1st ed (v5,f,dj) 20.00

GOREY,EDWARD-Dwindling Party-1982-Random-pop-up bk-1st ed (x2,f) 40.00

GOREY,EDWARD-Fletcher & Zenobia Save the Circus-NY-1971-illus,V Chess-1st ed (z6,vf,dj) 10.00

GOREY,EDWARD-Glorious Nosebleed: Fifth Alphabet-NY-1974-1st ed (z6,vf,dj) 15.00

GOREY,EDWARD-Gorey Cats Paper Dolls-SF-1982-wrps,full col fldover cov,40p illus-1st ed (z6,vf,sl rub wrps) 15.00

GOREY,EDWARD-Listing Attic & the Unstrung Harp-Lond-1974-laminated yel pict bds-1st Brit & 1st combined ed (z6,vf) 20.00

GOREY,EDWARD-Listing Attic-NY-(1954)-sm 8vo-pict bds-1st ed (x3,dj sl tn & chip) 65.00

GOREY,EDWARD-Object Lesson-1958-Dbldy-oblng 8vo-bds-1st ed (v10,f,soil dj) 50.00

GOREY,EDWARD-Secrets, Volume One: The Other Statue-NY-1968-S&S-1st ed (v5,f,dj wn,rprd) 25.00

GOREY,EDWARD-Unstrung Harp-NY,Bost-(1953)-auth 1st bk-illus by auth-1st ed (e5,f,sl wn dj) 150.00

GOREY,EDWARD-Water Flowers-NY-(1982)-Congdon & Weed-1st ed (bb2,f,dj,autg) 45.00

GORHAM,BOB-ED.-Churchill Downs 100th Kentucky Derby...1875 to 1974-4to-hdbk-1st ed (f10) 45.00

GORKY,MAXIM-Foma Gordeyev-Lond-1956-Lawrence & Wishart-1st ed thus (z9,dj chip,sp sunned) 12.50

GORMAN,HERBERT S-James Joyce. His First Forty Years-NY-1924-Huebsch-sm 8vo-(viii),238p-1st ed (u1,dj) 45.00

GORMAN,TOM-Three and Two-1979-Scribners-1st ed (s8,f,f dj) 15.00

GOSNELL,H ALLEN-Guns on the Western Waters-Baton Rouge-(1949)-LSU Pr-273p-illus,maps,ports-Nevins I,224 (ee4) 35.00

GOSNELL,HARPUR A-Before the Mast in the Clippers-NY-1937-Derrydale-tall 8vo-ix,(3),283p-qtrbnd in red cl,plts,fldg chrts-ltd to 950c,nbrd (p8,f) 200.00

GOSS,HELEN R-Life and Death of a Quicksilver Mine-LA-1958-150p-pict cl,frntis,photos-Hist Soc So Cal Spec Bk Publ #3-1st ed (t7) 15.00

GOSS,N S-History of the Birds of Kansas: Illustrating 529 Birds-Topeka-1891-G Crane-photos-1st ed (oo9,cov wn) 60.00

GOSS,N S-Revised Catalogue of the Birds of Kansas-Topeka-1886-76p (b9,hng crack) 30.00

GOSS,N S-Revised Catalogue of the Birds of Kansas-Topeka-1886-8vo-(1),76p-cl (y8,edge wn) 35.00

GOSS,WILLARD-Isle of the Lakes-Elgin-(1903)-David C Cook Publ-95p-cl & mrbld bds,dbl cols (l1) 17.50

GOSSE,EDMUND-Books on the Table-Lond-(1921)-Heinemann-x,348p-blnd stmpd cl-1st ed (dd10,sl soil cov) 30.00

GOSSE,P H-History of the British Sea Anemones and Corals-1860-Van Voorst-362p-g dec bds & sp,12 plts(11 col) (bb3,rub) 75.00

GOSSE,PHILIP H-Tenby: a Sea Side Holiday-Lond-1856-John Van Voorst-1/2 grn calf & mrbld bds,g dec sp,23 col lithos (p6,sl sun sp) 200.00

GOSSE,SIR EDMUND-Silhouettes-NY-(1925)-1st Amer ed (r2,uncut) 30.00

GOTLIEB,PHYLLIS-Oh Master Caliban!-NY-(1976)-Harper & Row-1st ed (h3,f,dj) 10.00

GOTTESMAN,RONALD-Upton Sinclair-Kent-1973-KSU Pr-1st ed (x9,f) 20.00

GOTTFREDSON,PETER-History of Indian Depredations in Utah-SLC-1919-352p+16p suppl-pict cl,plts-scarce wi suppl (z1,f) 115.00

GOUDGE,ELIZABETH-Green Dolphin Street-NY-(1944)-Coward-McCann-1st ed (b10,dj) 25.00

GOUDGE,ELIZABETH-Smoky House-NY-(1940)-Coward McCann-286p-pict cl,illus,R Floethe-1st US ed (r3,dj wn,chip & sp drknd) 50.00

GOUGH,BARRY-ED.-To the Pacific and Arctic with Beechey-Cambridge-1973-Hakluyt Soc-8vo-272p-blu cl,fldg map,plts (p1) 40.00

GOUGH,JOHN B-An Autobiography-Bost-1845-publ by auth-172p+ads-cl-scarce-1st ed (a1,few sm holes uppr joints) 75.00

GOUGH,JOHN B-Sunlight and Shadow-Lond-1881-401p-cl (a1) 15.00

GOUGH,JOHN-Temperance Address-NY-nd(1870s?)-Amer Tract Soc-24p-wrps (a1) 10.00

GOULART,RON-Cheap Thrills-1972-Arlington-1st ed (s10,dj fox) 20.00

GOULD,CHESTER-Dick Tracy, Ace Detective-Racine-1943-Whitman-1st ed (f4,yel pgs) 12.50

GOULD,D W-Top: Universal Toy, Enduring Pastime-NY-1973-Potter-8vo-274p-120 illus-1st ed (s1,f,dj) 40.00

GOULD,GEORGE M-Concerning Lafcadio Hearn-Phila-1908-Jacobs-photos-1st ed (t4) 35.00

GOULD,HOWARD-Sporting Library of ...-1940-Parke-Bernet-8vo-25p-wrps-auction catlg (m3) 15.00

GOULD,JOHN-Birds of Europe-Lond-1966-Methuen-321p-160 col plts (b9,f,f dj) 50.00

GOULD,JOHN-Monstrous Depravity-1953-Morrow-224p-drwngs (q8,sl fray dj) 10.00

GOULD,MAURICE M-1960 Catalog of Hawaiian Coins, Tokens and Paper Money-Racine-(1960)-Whitman-8vo-45p-blk cl,plts-1st ed (t10) 25.00

GOULD,R T-Captain Cook-Lond-1978-Duckworth-8vo-128p-text illus-new ed wi intro (nn1,dj) 25.00

GOULD,R T-Case for the Sea Serpent-(Lond)-1930-Philip Allan-xii,291p-cl,pict e.p.,frntis,plts,illus-1st ed (dd10,sl soil cov,edge fox) 35.00

GOURMET MAGAZINE EDITORS-Gourmet Cookbook-NY-(1959,60)-thk 4to-2 vols-g dec brwn cl,col photos (q8) 50.00

GOURMET'S BOOK OF FOOD AND DRINK-NY-1935-Macmillan-278p-orng bds,papr sp labl,col dec by Henty-Bitting 558 (k6,rub labl) 32.00

GOVE,CAPT JESSE A-Utah Expedition, 1857 to 1858: The Letters of...-Concord-1928-NH Hist Soc-8vo-442p-orig buckrm,frntis port,illus-Howes G279-1st ed (aa3,f) 95.00

GOVER,ROBERT-Here Goes Kitten-1964-Grove-1st ed (r9,sl wn dj) 15.00

GOVER,ROBERT-Here Goes Kitten-NY-(1964)-Grove-1st ed (b5,dj) 20.00

GOVER,ROBERT-Maniac Responsible-NY-(1963)-Grove-1st ed (bb1,f,dj) 25.00

GOVER,ROBERT-One Hundred Dollar Misunderstanding-NY-(1962)-Grove-auth 1st bk-1st ed (bb1,f,dj) 30.00

GOVER,ROBERT-Poorboy at the Party-NY-1966-Trident-1st ed (hh5,dj) 12.50

GOW,R M-Jersey-NY-1936-Amer Jersey Cattle Cl-xviii+539p-blu cl,illus-1st ed (dd1) 30.00

GOWANLOCH,JAMES N-Sea Fishes and Sea Fishing in Louisiana-New Orleans-1932-8vo-wrps,illus,photos (m3) 17.50

GOWANS,A-Images of American Living-Phila-1964-illus-1st ed (h10,sl chip dj) 45.00

GOYEN,WILLIAM-Collected Stories of ...-GC-1975-1st ed (e5,as new in dj) 20.00

GOYEN,WILLIAM-Come, the Restorer-1974-Dbldy-1st ed (q9,f,sl rub dj) 25.00

GOYEN,WILLIAM-Faces of Blood Kindred-NY-1960-1st ed (r5,f,dj) 40.00

GOYEN,WILLIAM-Fair Sister-NY-1963-DD-1st ed (y1,f,f dj) 75.00

GOYEN,WILLIAM-Ghost and Flesh-NY-1952-1st ed (r5,dj) 50.00

GOYEN,WILLIAM-House of Breath-NY-1950-auth 1st bk-1st ed (r5,sl chip dj) 75.00

GRABER,RALPH-ED.-Baseball Reader-1951-Barnes-1st ed (ff2,dj) 25.00

GRACE,D-I Am Still Alive-NY-1931-8vo-256p-cl,frntis,12p plts,illus e.p.-1st ed (t2,sl wn sp) 25.00

GRACE,D-Squadron of Death-GC-1929-8vo-xii,304p-cl,frntis,16p plts,illus e.p.-1st ed (t2) 35.00

GRACIE,ARCHIBALD-Truth about Chickamauga-Bost-1911-462p-illus,maps-1st ed (c4) 175.00

GRACQ,JULIEN-Balcony in the Forest-NY-1959-Braziller-1st ed (w5,f,sl tn dj) 20.00

GRACQ,JULIEN-Dark Stranger-NY-nd-New Directions-1st ed (w5,f,dj) 30.00

GRACY,DAVID B-Littlefield Lands-Austin-1968-U of Tex Pr-161p-cl,photos-1st ed (w3,f,dj) 20.00

GRACY,DAVID-Littlefield Lands-Austin-1968-161p-photos,maps-1st ed (t7,f,dj) 12.50

GRAEBNER,A L-Trial and Self Conviction of the Pope of Rome-Milan-nd-Rail Splitter Pr-31p-wrps (n1) 12.50

GRAEME,BRUCE-Epilogue-1934-Lippincott-1st Amer ed (s10,f,f dj) 60.00

GRAEME,BRUCE-Epilogue-Phila-1934-Lippincott-Variant grn cl wi dj wi add text on sp & frnt panel-1st Amer ed (e4,dj) 40.00

GRAEME,DAVID-Monsieur Blackshirt-Phila-1933-Lippincott-1st US ed (h4) 10.00

GRAEME,THEODORE-ED.-An Angling Bibliography-San Diego-1962-4to-22p-wrps (m3) 22.50

GRAESER,ANDREAS-Plotinus and the Stoics-Leiden-1972-E J Brill-wrps-1st prtg (n8,f) 25.00

GRAF,A B-Exotica International. Ser.4-1982-Roehrs-4to-2 vols-photos,drwngs (bb3,f,dj) 145.00

GRAF,ALFRED-Exotic Plant Manual-NY-1974-Roehrs-842p-cl-3rd ed (x6,as new in dj) 20.00

GRAF,EVERETT D-Catalog of...Collection of Western Americana by Colton Storm-Chig-1968-854p-frntis-1st ed (t7,dj) 45.00

GRAFTON,C W-Rat Began to Gnaw the Rope-1943-Farrar-1st ed (s10,slant,dj) 25.00

GRAFTON,C W-Rat Began to Gnaw the Rope-NY-1943-F&R-1st ed (z9,sl sun sp) 10.00

GRAFTON,CHARLES S-Canadian "Emma Gees"-Lond,Ont.-1938-Can Mach Gun Corps Assn-218p-pict cl,illus,port,maps-Dornsbusch #34 (k10) 125.00*

GRAFTON,SUE-A is for Alibi-NY-1982-Holt-1st ed (e4,f,dj) 500.00

GRAFTON,SUE-A is for Alibi-1982-HRW-1st ed (x7,f,dj) 595.00

GRAFTON,SUE-Kezia Dane-Lond-1968-P Owens-auth 1st bk-1st Brit ed (gg8,f,sl rub dj) 150.00

GRAFTON,SUE-Keziah Dane-NY-(1967)-Macmillan-auth 1st bk-1st ed (b5,dj,autg) 350.00

GRAFTON,SUE-Keziah Dane-NY-1967-Macmillan-auth 1st bk-1st ed (j4,f,dj) 250.00

GRAHAM,A-Alligators-1979-Delacorte-130p-illus-1st ed (bb3,f,dj) 12.00

GRAHAM,C A L-History of the Indian Mountain Artillery-Aldershot-1957-470p-maps,illus-1st ed (b7,f,dj) 150.00

GRAHAM,COL W A-Custer Myth, a Source Book of Custeriana-Harrisburg-(1953)-Stackpole-4to-413p-photos-1st ed (d3,dj) 70.00

GRAHAM,COL W A-Custer Myth-Harrisburg-(1953)-413p-illus-1st ed (c7,f,poor dj) 85.00

GRAHAM,COL W A-Custer Myth-Harrisburg-(1953)-illus,col illus e.p.-1st ed (n3,dj) 50.00

GRAHAM,COL W A-Reno Court of Inquiry-Harrisburg-(1954)-305p-e.p. maps,fldg map-Dowd #395 (c7,f,dj) 65.00

GRAHAM,COL W A-Story of the Little Big Horn-Harrisburg-(1952)-fldg map-Dowd 399-rprnt (j7,chip dj) 30.00

GRAHAM,COL W A-Story of the Little Big Horn-Harrisburg-(1952)-Military Serv Publ-4th prtg (v3) 35.00

GRAHAM,CUNNINGHAME-Reincarnation, the Best Short Stories of...-NY-1980-Ticknor & Fields-1st US ed (y1,f,dj) 25.00

GRAHAM,DOUGLAS-Practical Treatise on Massage-NY-1884-286p-scarce-1st ed (dd3) 100.00

GRAHAM,F P-He's in the Air Corps Now-NY-(1942)-8vo-218p-cl,frntis,plts-1st ed (t2) 30.00

GRAHAM,FRANCES W-1874 to 1894-(Oswego)-(1894)-83,(5)p-cl (a1,soil covs) 15.00

GRAHAM,FRANK,JR.-Casey Stengel-1958-John Day (q7,dj) 25.00

GRAHAM,FRANK-Baseball Extra-1954-Barnes-photos-1st ed (s8,f,dj) 40.00

GRAHAM,FRANK-Baseball Wit and Wisdom-1962-McKay-1st ed (q7,dj) 17.50

GRAHAM,FRANK-Baseball Wit and Wisdom-1962-McKay-1st ed (s8,f,dj) 20.00

GRAHAM,FRANK-Brooklyn Dodgers-1945-Putnam-1st ed (s8,dj) 45.00

GRAHAM,FRANK-Dodgers-1945-Putnam-1st ed (p7,dj) 50.00

GRAHAM,FRANK-Lou Gehrig, A Quiet Hero-1942-Putnam (r7,dj) 30.00

GRAHAM,FRANK-N Y Yankees-1943-Putnam-1st ed (s7,lacks dj) 30.00

GRAHAM,FRANK-N Y Yankees-1948-Putnam-rvsd ed (ff2,dj) 37.50

GRAHAM,FRANK-New York Giants-1952-Putnam-1st ed (ff2,dj) 75.00

GRAHAM,GEORGE W-Mecklenburg Declaration of Independence, May 20, 1775, and Lives of Its Signers-NY-1905-Neale Publ-205p-red cl-1st ed (oo5,sl rub,fray) 125.00

GRAHAM,GID-Animal Outlaws-Collinsville-1938-236p-frntis,photos-1st ed (t7) 35.00

GRAHAM,HARVEY-Eternal Eve-NY-1951-699p-illus-1st ed (g10,sl wn dj) 50.00

GRAHAM,HARVEY-Eternal Eve: the Story of Gynecology-GC-1951-699p-1st Amer ed (dd3) 60.00

GRAHAM,J B-Handset Reminiscences-SLC-1915-307p-frntis-1st ed (t7) 60.00

GRAHAM,JANETTE-Challenge of the Coulee-1954-Longmans-197p-illus-1st ed (r8,edge wn dj) 12.00

GRAHAM,JOHN R-History of Carpets and Carpet Weaving-Bridgeton-1879-40p-wrps,port (aa6) 50.00

GRAHAM,JOHN-Farmers' and Mechanics' Assistant and Companion-Eaton-1824-prntd by S Tizzard-218,(1)p-lea-rare (k1) 150.00

GRAHAM,JOSEPH A-Sporting Dog-NY-1904-8vo-324p-photos-1st ed (m3,frnt hng crckd) 20.00

GRAHAM,MARGARET-Swing Shift-NY-(1951)-Citadel-auth 1st bk-1st ed (a10,dj) 25.00

GRAHAM,MRS E JEFFERS-Etchings from a Parsonage Veranda-Cin/NY-1895-Crnstn & Crts/Hnt & Etn-187p-cl (d1) 15.00

GRAHAM,SHEILA-College of One-1967-Viking-1st ed (s9,f,dj) 20.00

GRAHAM,STEPHEN-With Poor Immigrants to America-NY-1914-Macmillan-xviii,306p-32 photos-1st ed (o2,sl rub) 17.50

GRAHAM,W A-Custer Myth-(1953)-Stackpole-413p-illus,maps-1st ed (r8) 45.00

GRAHAM,W A-Custer Myth-NY-nd-Bonanza Bks-413p-illus (o7,dj) 10.00

GRAHAM,W-Marnie-1961-Dbldy-1st ed (x7,f,dj) 35.00

GRAHAM,WILLIAM A-General Joseph Graham and His Papers on North Carolina Revolutionary History-Raleigh-1904-Edwards & Broughton-385p-grn cl-1st ed (oo5,bump,rub) 135.00

GRAHAME,KENNETH-Dream Days-Lond-(1902)-J Lane-228p+ads-pict grn cl,illus by M Parrish-2nd ed(1st wi Parrish illus) (hh9,sl spot cov) 100.00

GRAHAME,KENNETH-Wind in the Willows-NY-1908-Scribner's-1st Amer ed (y2,sp brwnd) 150.00

GRAHAME,KENNETH-Wind in the Willows-NY-1940-LEC-ltd to 2020c,autg,16 tip in col plts by A Rackham (w1,f,lacks box) 650.00

GRAHAME-WHITE,C-Aircraft in the Great War-Chig-1915-8vo-346p-cl-1st ed (t2,lacks frntis) 50.00

GRAHAME-WHITE,C-Heroes of the Air-NY-nd(ca.1915)-roy 8vo-272p-illus cl,col frntis,5p col plts & 6p b&w plts,C Cuneo (t2,rear cov stnd) 45.00

GRAHAME-WHITE,C-Our First Airways-Lond-1919-sm 12mo-185p-ports,11 plts (a3,sp lttrng wn) 22.50

GRAHAME-WHITE,C-Story of the Aeroplane-Bost-(1911)-Small,Maynard-thk 8vo-xii,390p-cl,frntis,35 illus,tbls-1st ed (t2,uncut) 125.00

GRANBY,MARQUESS OF-Trout-Lond-1898-8vo-272p-deluxe lg pap ed,1/4 vel bndg,ltd 157c,nbrd,12p illus (m3) 125.00

GRAND,GORDON-Colonel Weatherford's Young Entry-Derrydale-1935-8vo-214p-one of 1350c,illus by P Brown (m3,f) 75.00

GRAND,GORDON-Horse for Christmas Morning & Other Stories-NY-1970-8vo-115p-one of 1450c,illus (m3,vf,box) 50.00

GRAND,GORDON-Silver Horn-Lond-1934-Cntry Life Ltd-grn cl,drwngs-1st ed (gg7,sl soil cov) 30.00

GRAND,GORDON-Southboro Fox-Derrydale-1939-8vo-239p-one of 1450c,autg,orig glassine wrapper,illus (m3,f) 80.00

GRAND,SARAH-Our Manifold Nature-Lond-1894-Heinemann-8vo-271p+ads-orig cl-1st ed (w6) 95.00

GRAND,W JOS-Illustrated History of the Union Stock Yards-Chig-1896-Thos Knapp Ptg-362p+ads-illus cl-Rampaging Herd #915,"scarce"-1st ed (b6) 165.00

GRANDVILLE'S ANIMALS-(NY,Lond)-(1981)-Thames & Hudson-oblng 8vo-63p-blu cl,72 illus(23 col)-1st ed (t10,f,dj) 10.95

GRANGE,WALLACE B-Those of the Forest-Babcock-1953-Flambeau Publ-314p-cl,illus,O J Murie (z7) 22.50

GRANGE,WALLACE B-Way to Game Abundance-NY-1949-8vo-365p-illus (m3) 10.00

GRANGE,WALLACE B-Wisconsin Grouse Problems-Madison-1948-8vo-318p-illus,photos (m3) 25.00

GRANT,BLANCHE C-One Hundred Years Ago in Old Taos-Taos-1925-8vo-31p-wrps,6 illus-1st ed (aa3) 45.00

GRANT,BLANCHE-Taos Indians-Taos-1925-127p-pict wrps,frntis,photos-Rader #1646-1st ed (t7) 45.00

GRANT,BLANCHE-Taos Indians-Taos-1925-Santa Fe NM Publ-wrps,photos-1st ed (oo9) 60.00

GRANT,BLANCHE-When Old Trails Were New-NY-1934-344p-pict cl,frntis,photos-Rittenhouse #250-1st ed (t7,cor wn,hng rprd) 25.00

GRANT,BLANCHE-When Old Trails Were New-NY-1934-Pr of Pioneers-photos-1st ed (oo9,chip dj) 125.00

GRANT,C L-Hour of the Oxrum Dead-GC-1977-Dbldy-1st ed (p3,f,sl rub dj) 60.00

GRANT,ED-Tame Trout-SF-1939-Grabhorn Pr-12mo-7p-wrps,wi orig mailing envelope-scarce (m3,vf) 65.00

GRANT,EMMA F-Remembrances of a Pioneer Woman-SF-1926-16p-bds,frntis (bb9,sp wn) 40.00

GRANT,GEORGE-Art of Weaving Hair Hackles-1971-priv prntd-4to-81p-wrps-illus,auth-1st prntng (m3) 42.50

GRANT,GEORGE-Master Fly Weaver-Portland-1980-4to-234p-ltd to 1950c,nbrd-col plts in pckt at end of bk-scarce (m3,vf) 70.00

GRANT,GEORGE-Montana Trout Flies-1972-priv prntd-4to-unpgd-wrps-illus,auth-1st prntng (m3,vf) 55.00

GRANT,GEORGE-Montana Trout Flies-Portland-1981-Champoeg Pr-4to-col plts rear pckt,w/o dj as issued-ltd to 1950c,nbrd (nn3,f) 50.00

GRANT,J B-Our Common Birds and How to Know Them-NY-1894-oblng 12mo-224p-cl,64 b&w plts-4th ed (y8,chip,soil,dmpstng) 10.00

GRANT,J D-Redwoods & Remembrances-SF-1973-4to-216p-photos (m3,vf) 45.00

GRANT,JAMES E-Green Shadow-1935-Hartney-1st ed (s10,dj) 50.00

GRANT,JAMES J-More Single Shot Rifles-NY-1959-8vo-322p-illus,photos-1st ed (m3,dj) 30.00

GRANT,JAMES-British Battles on Land and Sea-Lond-nd(ca.1900)-8 vols-red dec cl,engrvngs,maps (kk2) 200.00

GRANT,JAMES-Scottish Soldiers of Fortune-Lond-1889-331p-brwn dec cl,illus-1st ed (gg2) 35.00

GRANT,JESSE R-In the Days of My Father General Grant-NY-1925-329p-frntis-1st ed (t7) 45.00

GRANT,JOAN-Many Lifetimes-GC-1967-Dbldy-cl-1st ed (n8,f,dj) 16.50

GRANT,JOY-Harold Monro & the Poetry Bookshop-Lond-1967-Routledge & K Paul-1st Brit ed (x9,t.e. spot,dj soil) 12.50

GRANT,JULIA D-Personal Memoirs of...-NY-(1975)-346p-illus-1st ed (c4,dj) 32.50

GRANT,KAREN A-Hummingbirds & Their Flowers-NY-1968-Columbia U Pr-115p-30 col photo plts (c9,dj) 40.00

GRANT,MARIA M-Artiste-Lond-1871-Hurst & Blackett-8vo-3 vols-3/4 calf & mrbld bds,auth 1st bk-1st ed (w6) 325.00

GRANT,MAXWELL-Norgil the Magician-NY-1977-Mysterious-1st trd ed (f4,f,dj) 20.00

GRANT,MAXWELL-Shadow Laughs-NY-(1931)-Street & Smith-pict papr cov bds,w/o dj as iss-1st ed (bb1,rub,pgs brwnd) 100.00

GRANT,N B-Records of Alaska Big Game-AK-1971-111p-photos (gg3,f,dj) 35.00

GRANT,ROBERT-Jack in the Bush-NY-1893-12mo-374p-illus,F T Merrill (m3) 12.50

GRANT,U F-Tricks with a One Way Deck-(Pittsfield)-(1935)-23p-wrps (l1) 10.00

GRANT,U S-Personal Memoirs of...-NY-1885,1886-cl,2 vols (c1) 50.00

GRANT,U S-Personal Memoirs of...-NY-1885-Webster-2 vols-1st ed (z2,sl wn) 75.00

GRANT,ULYSSES S,3RD-Ulysses S Grant, Warrior and Statesman-NY-1969-480p-illus-1st ed (n3,f,dj) 32.50

GRANT,VERNON-Mr.Mixie Dough-Racine-1934-Whitman Publ-folio-unpgd(38)-bds wi tip on illus,drwngs,V Grant (l6,chip bds & tip on) 45.00

GRAPE JUICE AS A THERAPEUTIC AGENT-Westfield-(1921)-Welch Grape Juice Co-28p-sm bklt,cl bds,frntis (n6) 20.00

GRAPES-Chig-1945-Whitman/WPA-46p-cl,2 col illus (x6,dj) 15.00

GRAPHIC ARTS-Production Yearbook-Ninth-NY-1950-Colton Pr-lg thk 4to-750p-qtr leatherette & cl,col fldg plts,papr samples (l10) 37.50

GRASS,GUNTER-Cat and Mouse-Lond-(1963)-Secker & Warburg-1st Brit ed (d10,f,sl soil dj) 35.00

GRASS,GUNTER-Dog Years-(1965)-HB&W-1st US ed (m9,sl soil,dj sl tn) 35.00

GRASS,GUNTER-Dog Years-NY-(1965)-Harcourt Brace-1st US ed (e3,dj) 25.00

GRASS,GUNTER-Flounder-1978-Harcourt-1st Amer ed (m9,f,dj) 15.00

GRASS,GUNTER-Flounder-NY,Lond-(1978)-HBJ-1st ed (b5,f,dj) 20.00

GRASS,GUNTER-Local Anaesthetic-NY-(1970)-HBW-1st ed (b5,as new in dj) 25.00

GRASSES OF THE SOUTHWEST-nd-Dept of Agri-4to-3/4 lea,100p plts (a9,cov wn) 50.00

GRATTAN,THOMAS C-Civilized America-Lond-1859-Bradbury & Evans-8vo-2 vols in later cl,g sp titles,2 maps(incl lg col fldg map)-Howes G319-1st ed (mm1) 160.00

GRATTEN,J H G-Anglo Saxon Magic and Medicine-Lond-1952-234p-illus-1st ed (dd3) 100.00

GRAU,SHIRLEY ANN-Condor Passes-NY-1971-Knopf-1st ed (a5,f,dj) 20.00

GRAU,SHIRLEY ANN-Keepers of the House-NY-1964-Knopf-1st ed (a5,sl wn dj) 30.00

GRAUER,JACK-Mount Hood-Ore-1975-4to-300p-wrps,illus (o10,f) 15.00

GRAUMONT,R-Encyclopedia of Knots & Fancy Rope Work-NY-1945-Cornell Maritime Pr-4to-663p-332 plts (hh1) 27.50

GRAUWIN,DR PAUL-Doctor at Dienbienphu-NY-(1955)-John Day-8vo-304p-8p photos-1st US ed (cc5,dj) 30.00

GRAVES,J A-My Seventy Years in California 1857 to 1927-LA-1927-Times-Mirror Pr-478p-photos-1st ed (cc4) 45.00

GRAVES,J A-My Seventy Years in California-LA-1927-8vo-478p-photos-1st ed (m3) 32.50

GRAVES,J A-My Seventy Years in California: 1857 to 1927-LA-1927-Times Mirror-478p-1st ed (d3) 75.00

GRAVES,J A-Out of Doors California & Oregon-LA-1912-8vo-122p-photos-1st ed (m3,sp labl badly chip) 30.00

GRAVES,JACKSON A-California Memories-LA-1930-Time Mirror Pr-lg 8vo-330p-illus-1st ed (bb4) 35.00

GRAVES,JOHN-From a Limestone Ledge-1980-Knopf-228p-maps,illus-1st ed (t8,dj) 25.00

GRAVES,JOHN-Goodbye to a River-NY-1960-306p-illus (t7,f,dj) 17.50

GRAVES,JOHN-Goodbye to a River-NY-1960-Knopf-1st ed (oo9,sl chip dj) 75.00

GRAVES,JOHN-Hard Scrabble-1974-Knopf-267p-maps-1st ed (t8,sl tn dj) 25.00

GRAVES,JOHN-Hard Scrabble-NY-1974-Knopf-1st ed (b10,f,dj) 20.00

GRAVES,RALPH H-Triumph of an Idea-GC-1934-184p-cl-1st ed so stated (e1) 10.00

GRAVES,RICHARD S-Oklahoma Outlaws-(Okla City)-(1915)-(State Prtg)-131p-wrps,photos-Howes G322-1st ed (ee4,wn) 25.00

GRAVES,ROBERT J-Clinical Lectures Delivered During the Sessions of 1834,5 and 1836,7-Phila-1838-A Waldie-xii+408p-1/2 lea-Duglison's Amer Med Libr-1st Amer ed (a2,sl fox) 75.00

GRAVES,ROBERT-5 Pens in Hand-GC-1958-Dbldy-1st ed (q2,dj rub) 55.00

GRAVES,ROBERT-5 Pens in Hand-GC-1958-Doubleday-1st ed (e10,sl spot,dj sl wn) 40.00

GRAVES,ROBERT-Adam's Rib-NY-(1958)-Yoseloff-qto-red bds,engrvngs-1st Amer ed (bb2,f,dj) 50.00

GRAVES,ROBERT-An Ancient Castle-Lond-(1980)-Owen-66p-cl,illus,E Graves-1st ed (s3,as new in dj) 15.00

GRAVES,ROBERT-Antigua Stamp-NY-(1937)-Random-russet bds,postage stamp labl-1st Amer ed (bb2,dj wn) 125.00

GRAVES,ROBERT-But It Still Goes On-NY-1931-Cape & Smith-1st US ed (w5,dj sl wn,chip) 85.00

GRAVES,ROBERT-Claudius the God and His Wife Messalina-NY-1935-Smith & Haas-583p+fldg chart-cl-1st Amer ed (m1,dj) 25.00

GRAVES,ROBERT-Claudius the God and his Wife Messalina-NY-1935-Smith & Haas-583p-plus fldng chart-cl-1st US ed (e1,dj) 25.00

GRAVES,ROBERT-Collected Poems-GC-1961-Dbldy-1st US ed (b10,dj) 35.00

GRAVES,ROBERT-Crowning Privelege, The Clark Lectures 1954,55-Lond-1955-1st ed (y7,dj) 40.00

GRAVES,ROBERT-Hebrew Myths-GC-1964-Dbldy-1st ed (q2,dj) 45.00

GRAVES,ROBERT-Homer's Daughter-GC-1955-Doubleday-1st US ed (e10,f,dj) 30.00

GRAVES,ROBERT-Infant with the Globe-NY-1959-Yoseloff-orng bds-1st Amer ed (bb2,f,dj chip) 40.00

GRAVES,ROBERT-Islands of Unwisdom-GC-1949-Dbldy-1st US ed (x9,bump,dj tn,chip) 25.00

GRAVES,ROBERT-Islands of Unwisdom-GC-1949-Dbldy-8vo-328p-1st US ed (bb5,dj) 30.00

GRAVES,ROBERT-Love Respelt Again-(1969)-Dbldy-8vo-blk cl,ltd to 1000c,nbrd,autg-1st ed (v10,f,f dj) 45.00

GRAVES,ROBERT-Occupation: Writer-Lond-1951-Cassell-8vo-cl-1st ed (kk8,vf,dj) 45.00

GRAVES,ROBERT-Penny Fiddle-GC-(1960)-Dbldy-8vo-64p-cl,col illus,Ardizzone-1st US ed (s3,skinned area on dj) 30.00

GRAVES,ROBERT-Poems 1938 to 1945-Lond-(1946)-Cassell-8vo-grn cl-1st ed (v10,dj) 40.00

GRAVES,ROBERT-Sergeant Lamb's America-1940-Random-pict dj-1st ed (x2,sl fade sp,dj sl chip) 65.00

GRAVES,ROBERT-Siege and Fall of Troy-Lond-1962-Cassell-1st Brit ed (y1,f,f dj) 50.00

GRAVES,ROBERT-Watch the Northwind Rise-NY-1949-Creative Age Pr-1st ed (bb1,f,dj) 45.00

GRAVES,ROBERT-Watch the Northwind Rise-NY-1949-Creative Edge-1st US ed (o3,edge wn dj) 15.00

GRAVES,ROBERT-White Goddess-NY-1948-Creative Age Pr-1st Amer ed (bb2,f,dj rub,chip) 60.00

GRAVES,SAMUEL-Discourse on the Occasion of the Twenty Fifth Anniversary of the Central Baptist Church ...-Norwich-1865-Bulletin Job Office-35p-wrps (h1) 15.00

GRAVES,THOMAS-DESPATCHES OF...1781-NY-1916-NHS-268p-vel & bds-ltd to 650c (gg2,f) 100.00

GRAVES,WM W-Protestant Osage Missions 1820 to 1837-Oswego-1949-272p-1st ed (t7) 12.50

GRAY,A P-Bird Hybrids-Farnham Royal-1958-8vo-390p-cl (y8,dmpstnd,dj wn) 35.00

GRAY,A P-Mammalian Hybrids-Farnham Royal-1954-8vo-144p-cl (y8,water damgd cov,dj) 25.00

GRAY,A-Elements of Botany for Beginners and Schools...-1887-Ivison Blakeman-(2 vols in one)-589 figs (bb3) 18.00

GRAY,ARTHUR-Toasts and Tributes-NY-1904-Rohde & Haskins-301p-dec red bds (n6) 45.00

GRAY,ASA-Darwiniana-NY-1876-396p-1st ed (dd3) 150.00

GRAY,ASA-Gray's School and Field Botany-NY,Chig-(1887)-iv,386p+ads-589 engrvngs (x5,ex-lib) 20.00

GRAY,ASA-Manual of the Botany of the Northern United States-NY-(1889)-760p-25 plts-6th ed,rev (x5,sl wn,fray) 20.00

GRAY,C-Great Experiment-1962-Abrams-257 plts(incl 24 col & tip-in)-1st ed (h10,dj) 250.00

GRAY,C-Great Experiment: Russian Art 1863 to 1922-1962-Abrams-257 plts(24 col & tip-in)-1st ed (ee1,dj) 200.00

GRAY,CECIL-Bed-Lond-(1946)-Nicholson & Watson-280p-bds,decs (k6) 22.00

GRAY,DAVID-Gallops 1,Gallops 2 & Mr.Carteret-Derrydale-1929-8vo-3 vols,ltd to 750sets,nbrd,vol#1 autg-scarce (m3) 200.00

GRAY,DULCIE-Epitaph for a Dead Actor-Lond-1960-Barker-1st ed (h4,dj) 15.00

GRAY,DULCIE-Murder on the Stairs-Lond-1957-Barker-1st ed (e4,dj missing sm chips) 15.00

GRAY,ELIZABETH J-Cheerful Heart-NY-(1959)-Viking-176p-cl,b&w illus,K Mizumura-1st ed (r3,f,dj) 20.00

GRAY,ELIZABETH J-Cheerful Heart-NY-(1959)-Viking-8vo-176p-beige pict cl,pict e.p.,illus by K Mizumura-1st ed (nn8,chip dj) 18.00

GRAY,ELIZABETH J-Penn-NY-(1938)-Viking-8vo-298p-crimson emboss cl,pict e.p.,illus by G G Whitney-1st ed (nn8,sl tn sp,dj tn) 40.00

GRAY,FRANK S-Pioneer Adventures-Cherokee-1948-photos-Herd 919-1st ed (oo9,dj chip & soil) 60.00

GRAY,JAMES-History of the Royal Medical Society 1737 to 1937-Edinburgh-1952-355p-illus (g10) 50.00

GRAY,JOHN A C-Amerika Samoa-Annapolis-(1960)-U.S. Naval Inst-8vo-xx,295p-beige cl,illus,map e.p.-1st ed (t10,dj) 20.00

GRAY,JOHN C-War Letters-Bost-1927-Houghton Mifflin-vi+532p-maroon cl-ltd to 1275c-1st ed (k2,tn dj) 45.00

GRAY,JOHN M-Lord Selkirk of Red River-1964-Mich State U Pr-388p-illus-1st Amer ed (ff4,dj) 25.00

GRAY,NICHOLAS S-Killer's Cookbook-Lond-(1976)-Dobson-184p-blk cl-1st Brit ed (q8,dj) 12.50

GRAY,P N-African Game Lands, a Graphic Itinerary-Bost-1930-33p-wrps,photos-Vol.VIII,#IV (gg3,soil) 15.00

GRAY,PRENTISS N-African Game-Lands a Graphic Itinerary-Bost-1930-folio-33p-wrps,photos,maps (m3,vf) 60.00

GRAY,RALPH D-National Waterway-1967-U of Illinois-illus-1st ed (pp4,dj) 15.00

GRAY,ROBERT F-Family Estate in Africa-Lond-(1964)-Routledge & K Paul-8vo-265p-cl-1st ed (y5,dj) 25.00

GRAY,SIMON-An Unnatural Pursuit and Other Pieces-NY-1985-St.Martins-1st ed (w5,f,sl tn dj) 20.00

GRAY,VIRGINIA-Mud, Space & Spirit-Santa Barbara-1976-oblng-95p-wrps,photos-1st ed (u7,f) 10.00

GRAY,W C-Camp-Fire Musings-NY-1894-12mo-304p-illus-1st ed (m3,pres cpy) 35.00

GRAY,W C-Musings by Campfire & Wayside-Chig-1902-8vo-337p-illus (m3) 15.00

GRAY,W-Hidden Civil War-NY-1942-314p-illus,maps,ports (z10) 35.00

GRAY,WILLIAM R-Voyages to Paradise-Wash D.C.-1981-Nat'l Geographic Scty-215p-blu leatherette,photos,G W Gahan,Drwngs & reprdctns (nn1) 20.00

GRAYBILL,FLORENCE C-Edward Sheriff Curtis: Visions of a Vanishing Race-NY-(1976)-Crowell-sm folio-303p-photos-1st ed (oo8,f,dj) 150.00

GRAYMONT,BARBARA-Iroquois in the American Revolution-1972-Syracuse U Pr-x,359p-frntis,illus,map-1st ed (bb7,dj) 25.00*

GRAYSON,CHAS-ED.-Sportsman's Hornbook-NY-1933-8vo-169p-one of 500c,1/4 lea & bds,dec by E Smythe (m3) 22.50

GRAYSON,HARRY-They Played the Game-1944-Barnes (r7,dj) 20.00

GRAYSON,RICHARD-Monterant Affair-NY-1980-St.Martin's-1st US ed (f4,f,dj) 12.50

GREAT BATTLES OF THE BRITISH ARMY-Lond-nd(ca.1870)-565p-brwn lea,g dec sp,mrbld edges & e.p.,8 col plts (gg2) 125.00

GREAT WESTERN RAILWAY CO-Haunts & Hints for Anglers-Lond-1925-8vo-156p-wrps,fldg map,illus (m3) 27.50

GREATHOUSE,CHARLES H-Ranch Life in the Old West-Hollywood-(1971)-286p-photos,ltd to 1000c,autg-1st ed (v7,dj) 25.00

GREELEY,HORACE-Recollections of a Busy Life-NY-1868-J B Ford-624p-drwngs (dd4) 20.00

GREELEY,WILLIAM R-Essence of Architecture-NY-1927-photos-1st ed (r2) 30.00

GREELY,A W-Handbook of Alaska-NY-1909-Scribner's-280p-maps,illus,fldg map rear pckt (dd4) 45.00

GREELY,A W-Reminiscences of Adventure and Service-NY-1927-Scribners-356p-frntis,illus (cc6,dj chip,tn & soil) 100.00

GREELY,A W-Three Years of Arctic Service-NY-1886-Scribner's-2 vols-illus,43 plts,maps-Ricks p.112-1st ed (oo1) 325.00

GREELY,JOHN N-War Breaks Down Doors-Bost-(1929)-Hale Cushman & Flint-8vo-red cl-1st ed (x10,f,f dj) 35.00

GREEN KIRTLED SPRING-Lond-1924-Elkin Mathews Ltd-4to-cl backd bds,tip-in illus-1st ed (w2,sl wn) 35.00

GREEN,ALAN A-Jottings From a Cruise-Seattle-1947-Kelly Print-blu illus cl,illus (b6,pres cpy) 10.00

GREEN,ALMA-Forbidden Voice-Lond-nd(ca.1970s)-Hamlyn-8vo-157p-illus & cov design by G McLean,illus e.p.-1st ed (aa7,dj) 20.00*

GREEN,ANNA K-Agatha Webb-1899-Putnam-1st ed (s10,sp lettrng fade) 25.00

GREEN,ANNA K-Amethyst Box-1905-BM-298p-paste on col illus identical to front dj panel,harrison Fisher dj,2 illus-1st ed (x7,f,sl chip dj) 250.00

GREEN,ANNA K-Chief Legatee-1906-A.N.A.-4 col plts-1st ed (x7) 15.00

GREEN,ANNA K-Circular Study-NY-1900-dec grn g cl-1st ed, 1st bndg (r2) 75.00

GREEN,ANNA K-Circular Study-NY-1900-McClure,Phillips-8vo-269p-grn cl-1st ed (w6,f,uncut) 100.00

GREEN,ANNA K-Dark Hollow-NY-1914-Dodd-1st ed (d4) 20.00

GREEN,ANNA K-Difficult Problem-1900-Lupton-pict cov-1st ed (s10) 45.00

GREEN,ANNA K-Filigree Ball-1903-BM-1st ed (x7) 12.00

GREEN,ANNA K-Filigree Ball-Indpls-1903,March-1st ed,1st iss wi printer's slug prtd in red (r2,f) 60.00

GREEN,ANNA K-Golden Slipper & Other Problems for Violet Strange-1915-Putnams-1st ed (x7) 22.00

GREEN,ANNA K-Hand and Ring-NY-1883-1st ed (r2,sl rub) 150.00

GREEN,ANNA K-Miss Hurd: An Enigma-NY-1894-Putnam's-357p-cl-Wright 4659-1st ed (e1) 25.00

GREEN,ANNA K-Sword of Damocles-NY-1881-Putnam-1st ed (d4) 85.00

GREEN,ANNA K-Three Thousand Dollars-1910-R Badger-1st ed (x7) 25.00

GREEN,ANNA-They Died Laughing-1952-S&S-1st ed (x7,f,dj) 18.00

GREEN,ASA T-Eureka-Cin-1883-A G Collins-141,(4)p-cl-"Now published for the first time" (c1) 40.00

GREEN,BEN A-Biography of the Tennessee Walking Horse-Nashville-1960-Parthenon Pr-1st ed (h9) 60.00

GREEN,BEN K-Ben Green Tales-Flagstaff-(1974)-Northland Pr-4 vols-ltd to 1250c,nbrd,autg-v scarce (f9,box) 150.00

GREEN,BEN K-Horse Tradin'-NY-1967-304p-cl-illus,L Bjorklund-1st ed so stated (d1,dj) 40.00

GREEN,BEN K-Horse Tradin-NY-1967-Knopf-1st ed (h9,dj) 45.00

GREEN,BEN K-Last Trail Drive Through Downtown Dallas-Flagstaff-1971-Northland-4to-ltd to 1750c (a9,dj) 75.00

GREEN,BEN K-Last Trail Drive Through Downtown Dallas-Flagstaff-1971-Northland-illus by J Beeler-ltd 1st ed (oo9,dj) 95.00

GREEN,BEN K-Some More Horse Tradin'-NY-1972-Knopf-(iv),255p-cl,illus,J Beeler-1st ed (v1,dj) 65.00

GREEN,BEN K-Thousand Miles of Mustangin'-Flagstaff-1972-Northland Pr-145p-cl,illus,J Beeler,deluxe & espec bnd ed,ltd to 150c,two autg (w3,vf,vf box) 195.00

GREEN,BEN K-Wild Cow Tales-NY-1969-Knopf-306,(2)p-brn cl,illus-1st ed so stated (b6,f,dj) 28.00

GREEN,BEN K-Wild Cow Tales-NY-1969-Knopf-illus-1st ed (h9,dj) 45.00

GREEN,C H-Birds of the South-Chapel Hill-1933-8vo-277p-cl,32 col plts (y8,dj stuck cov) 17.00

GREEN,CHARLOTTE H-Trees of the South-Chapel Hill-1939-xiv,551p-half tones-1st ed (j10,sl soil) 15.00

GREEN,DAVID-Blenheim-NY-1974-162p-illus-1st ed (b7,dj) 35.00

GREEN,EDITH P-Perfect Fools-NY-(1982)-Dutton-1st ed (l3,f,dj) 15.00

GREEN,EDWARD L-Manual of the Botany of the Region of San Francisco Bay-SF-1894-Cubery-xiii,342p-scarce-1st ed (mm4,cov wn & soil,hng weak) 55.00

GREEN,FRANCES-Analytical Class Book of Botany-NY-1855-Appleton-228p (x6,sp rub) 30.00

GREEN,G G-Green's Pictorial Almanac, 1878 & 9-(Woodbury)-(1878)-36p-wrps,illus (aa6) 35.00

GREEN,GORDON-Heritage of Canadian Handicrafts-Tor-1967-M&S-8vo-xv,222p-43 illus-1st ed (bb7,dj) 20.00*

GREEN,HENRY-Nothing-NY-1950-Viking-1st US ed (hh5,dj) 20.00

GREEN,J H-Gamblers' Tricks with Cards, Exposed and Explained-NY-Dick & Fitzgerald-114p+ads-(1859?)date not clearly prntd-wrps (g1,sl chip) 35.00

GREEN,J-Biology of Crustacea-1961-Witherby-180p-4 plts-1st ed (bb3,dj) 18.00

GREEN,JAMES A-William Henry Harrison-Richmond-(1941)-Garrett & Massie-lg 8vo-xiv+536p-tan cl,illus-1st ed (e2) 45.00

GREEN,JERRY-Year of the Tiger-1969-Coward McCann (r7,f,dj) 20.00

GREEN,JOHN-Birds of Britain-NY-1967-Macmillan-lg 4to-unpgd-photos-1st US ed (bb5,sl tn dj) 25.00

GREEN,JOHN-Birds of Britain-NY-1967-Macmillan-lg 4to-unpgd-photos-1st US ed (gg5,sl tn dj) 25.00

GREEN,MARTIN-Earth Again Redeemed-NY-(1977)-Basic Bks-1st ed (e3,f,dj) 25.00

GREEN,PETER-Kenneth Grahame-Cleve-(1959)-World-400p-cl,illus-1st ed (nn10,dj) 30.00

GREEN,ROGER L-Story of Lewis Carroll-Lond-(1949)-Methuen-179p-cl,illus-1st ed (oo10,cov speckled,dj) 25.00

GREEN,ROLAND-Treatise on the Cultivation of Ornamental Flowers-Bost-1828-Russell-60p-cl sp,prtd bds-scarce (x6) 850.00

GREEN,SAMUEL-Popular Fruit Growing-St.Paul-1914-Webb-328p-cl,illus-5th ed (x6) 16.00

GREEN,SETH-Fish Hatching & Fish Catching-Rochester-1879-12mo-245p-illus-1st ed (m3,f) 50.00

GREEN,W-Famous Bombers of the Second World War-GC-(1959)-roy 8vo-134p-cl,plts & text illus,G W Heumann-1st ed (t2) 25.00

GREEN,W-Famous Fighters of the Second World War-NY-(1958)-roy 8vo-128p-cl,plts & text illus,G W Heumann-1st ed (t2) 25.00

GREEN,W-Jet Aircraft of the World-GC-(1956)-4to-176p-cl,plts,text illus-1st ed (t2,fade) 25.00

GREENAN,EDITH-Of Una Jeffers-np-1939-Ward Ritchie Pr-4to-blu cl,ltd to 250c (x3) 45.00

GREENAWAY,KATE-Kate Greenaway's Almanack for 1884-1884-Routledge & Sons-wrps,col illus,auth,deluxe ed-1st ed (x2,sl soil) 85.00

GREENAWAY,KATE-Kate Greenaway's Almanack for 1885-1885-Routledge & Sons-bds,col illus,auth-1st ed (x2) 95.00

GREENAWAY,KATE-Kate Greenaway's Birthday Book for Children-(1880)-Routledge & Sons-col illus,auth-1st ed (x2) 120.00

GREENBAUM,FLORENCE-Jewish Cook Book-1939-Bloch-488p-grn cl-13th prtg (q8,cov fray) 18.50

GREENBERG,CAROL A-Day Before Cookbook-(1968)-Little,Brown-274p-orng cl-1st ed (q8,f,dj) 15.00

GREENBERG,D B-Raising Game Birds in Captivity-NY-1949-tall 8vo-224p-cl,photos (y8) 35.00

GREENBERG,DAVID-Trout Farming-Phila,NY-1960-4to-197p-illus,photos-1st ed (m3,f,dj) 20.00

GREENBERG,JOANNE-King's Ransom-NY-1963-auth 1st bk-1st ed (p5,dj) 20.00

GREENBERG,MARTIN-ED.-Coming Attractions-NY-(1957)-Fantasy Pr-1st ed (k9,dj) 17.50

GREENBIE,SYDNEY-Frontiers & the Fur Trade-NY-(1929)-235p-8 illus-scarce-1st ed (d7) 90.00

GREENBIE,SYDNEY-Gold of Ophur-NY-1925-frntis,photos,map e.p.-1st ed (t7,dj) 15.00

GREENBURG,DAVID-Countryman's Companion-NY-1947-Harper-412p (x6,sp sun) 12.00

GREENE & HANFF-ET AL-Bibliographia Oziana-1976-Intl Wizard of Oz Club-wrps,illus-1st ed (pp10,f) 15.00

GREENE,A C-Personal Country-NY-1969-Knopf-auth 1st bk,drwngs by A Nunn-1st ed (b10,f,dj) 50.00

GREENE,A C-Personal Country-NY-1969-Knopf-auth 1st bk,drwngs-1st ed (ff6,f,dj) 50.00

GREENE,AELLA-Rhymes of Yankee Land-Springfield-1872-Whitney & Adams-83p-cl (g1,sl wn) 15.00

GREENE,ALBERT-Recollections of the Jersey Prisonship-Providence-1829-H H Brown-3/4 lea,ltd to 100c (l9) 400.00

GREENE,ANNE B-Dipper Hill-NY-1925-Century-1st ed (j9) 20.00

GREENE,ANNE B-Lambs in March-NY-1928-Century-1st ed (j9) 15.00

GREENE,ANNE B-Lone Winter-NY-1923-Century-1st ed (h9) 10.00

GREENE,CHARLES S-Thrilling Stories of the Great Rebellion...-NY-(1891)-Internat'l Bk Co-494p-cl (c1,sl rub,rear cov sl discol) 15.00

GREENE,CHAS W-ED.-Sketch of Kingston & It Surroundings-Kingston-1883-48p-wrps-cov title begins,"The Mine of Kingston..."-rare pamphlet-1st ed (u7,chip backstrip) 600.00

GREENE,DOUGLAS G-W W Denslow-(Mt.Pleasant)-(1976)-225p-cl (b1) 17.50

GREENE,E R-ET AL-Birds of Georgia-Athens-1945-8vo-111p-cl,tip-in frntis,1 map (y8,bump) 19.00

GREENE,EVARTS B-Guide to the Principal Sources for Early American History in New York City-NY-1929-Columbia U Pr-1st ed (v4,f) 40.00

GREENE,FELIX-Vietnam! Vietnam! in Photographs and Text-Palo Alto-1966-Fulton Publ-175p-dec wrps,photos,map (c3) 40.00

GREENE,FRANCIS B-History of Boothbay,Southport, and Boothbay Harbor,Maine-Portland-1906-Loring,Short & Harmon-693p-brwn cl,plts,fldg maps-1st ed (k2,sl rub) 85.00

GREENE,GEORGE W-Nathanael Greene-Bost-1866-Ticknor & Fields-vi,86p-1st ed (n2,ex-libr,lacks sp pc) 30.00

GREENE,GRAHAM-21 Stories-NY-1955-Viking-1st ed (f8,f,dj) 40.00

GREENE,GRAHAM-British Dramatists-Lond-1942-Wm Collins-1st ed (dd2,sp rub dj) 45.00

GREENE,GRAHAM-Burnt Out Case-Lond-(1961)-Heinemann-1st ed (hh5,dj) 30.00

GREENE,GRAHAM-Burnt Out Case-Lond-(1961)-Heinemann-1st ed (v5,f,dj) 60.00

GREENE,GRAHAM-Comedian-Lond-(1966)-Bodley Head-1st ed (cc2,f,dj) 50.00

GREENE,GRAHAM-Complaisant Lover-NY-1961-patterned bds-1st US ed (r5,dj) 22.50

GREENE,GRAHAM-Doctor Fischer of Geneva or the Bomb Party-Lond-(1980)-Bodley Head-1st ed (cc2,f,dj) 30.00

GREENE,GRAHAM-End of the Affair-NY-1951-Viking-1st US ed (v5,f,dj) 35.00

GREENE,GRAHAM-Heart of the Matter-1948-Viking-1st ed (x7,dj) 25.00

GREENE,GRAHAM-Honorary Consul-1973-Bodley Head-1st ed (x7,f,dj) 27.00

GREENE,GRAHAM-In Search of a Character-NY-1962-1st US ed (q5,sl chip dj) 25.00

GREENE,GRAHAM-Little Fire Engine-Lond-(1973)-Bodley Head-oblng 8vo-48p-glossy bds,illus,Ardizzone-1st ed thus (s3,f) 25.00

GREENE,GRAHAM-Little Horse Bus-NY-(1954)-LL&S-sq 8vo-35p-illus by D Craigie-1st US ed (nn10,f,sl chip dj) 60.00

GREENE,GRAHAM-Living Room-NY-1954-Viking-1st Amer ed (dd2,f,dj) 50.00

GREENE,GRAHAM-May We Borrow Your Husband-Lond-(1967)-Bodley Head-1st ed (cc2,f,dj) 60.00

GREENE,GRAHAM-May We Borrow Your Husband-NY-1967-1st US ed (s5,dj) 20.00

GREENE,GRAHAM-Ministry of Fear-1943-Viking-1st Amer ed (x7,dj) 150.00

GREENE,GRAHAM-Our Man in Havana-Lond-1958-Heinemann-1st ed (v5,f,dj rprd,sl drknd) 75.00

GREENE,GRAHAM-Potting Shed-NY-1957-Viking-ltd to 4000c-1st Amer ed (dd2,f,dj) 60.00

GREENE,GRAHAM-Quiet American-Lond-(1955)-Heinemann-1st Brit ed (e6,dj) 150.00

GREENE,GRAHAM-Quiet American-NY-1956-Viking-1st US ed (ff3,edgewn dj) 45.00

GREENE,GRAHAM-Quiet American-NY-1956-Viking-1st US ed (j3,f,dj) 40.00

GREENE,GRAHAM-Selected Essays-NY-(1969)-Viking-1st Amer ed (dd2,f,dj) 40.00

GREENE,GRAHAM-Sense of Reality-NY-(1963)-1st US ed (p5,dj) 30.00

GREENE,GRAHAM-Sense of Reality-NY-(1963)-Viking-1st US ed (q2,dj) 45.00

GREENE,GRAHAM-Third Man-NY-1950-1st ed (t5,sl wn dj) 85.00

GREENE,GRAHAM-Travels with My Aunt-Lond-(1969)-Bodley Head-1st ed (e3,f,dj) 60.00

GREENE,GRAHAM-Travels with My Aunt-NY-(1969)-1st Amer ed (t5,dj sp sl sunned) 15.00

GREENE,GRAHAM-Travels With My Aunt-NY-(1970)-Viking-1st Amer ed (s9,dj) 20.00

GREENE,HARRY P-Where the Bright Waters Meet-Lond-1924-8vo-253p-photos,e.p. map-1st ed (m3) 70.00

GREENE,HENRY-Listen In: Radio Health Talks-Bost-1923-144p-wrps-1st ed (dd3) 25.00

GREENE,HUGH-ED.-Cosmopolitan Crimes-NY-1971-Pantheon-1st US ed (f4,f,sl wn dj) 12.50

GREENE,KATHERINE G-Winchester, Virginia and Its Beginnings 1743 to 1814-Strasburg-1926-Shenandoah-8vo-441p-grn cl,illus-1st ed (s1) 35.00

GREENE,LAURENCE-Filibuster. The Career of William Walker-Indpls-1937-Bobbs Merrill-8vo-350p-blu cl,map e.p.,maps,illus-1st ed (mm1) 45.00

GREENE,SAMUEL S-An Introduction to the Study of English Grammar-Phila-(1868)-Cowperwait-240p-pict bds (k1) 15.00

GREENE,SIR HUGH-Further Rivals of Sherlock Holmes-1973-Pantheon-1st Amer ed (n9,sl tn dj) 15.00

GREENER,W W-Breech Loader and How to Use It-Lond-1892-288p+ads-rebacked wi orig pict bds,illus (ee3,rbkd) 75.00

GREENER,W W-Modern Shot Guns-Lond-1888-192p-blu cl,illus (ee3,sl tn) 75.00

GREENER,W W-Sharp Shooting for Sport & War-Lond-1900-181p+ads-illus papr wrps,dec (ee3,f) 45.00

GREENEWALT,CRAWFORD-Hummingbirds-GC-1960-4to-250p-tip-in photos,rare (m3,f,dj) 300.00

GREENFELD,JOSH-Harry and Tonto-1974-Sat Review Pr-1st ed (s9,f,dj) 20.00

GREENHILL,BASIL-Schooners-Annapolis-1980-Naval Inst Pr-4to-160p-141 plts-1st ed (p8,as new in dj) 30.00

GREENING,C R-Not as Briefed-St.Paul-(ca.1946)-Brown & Bigelow-sm 4to-114p-illus cl wi spiral sp,illus t.p.,50p col plts & 7 col text illus by auth-ltd ed (t2) 100.00

GREENLAW,O S-Lady and the Tigers-NY-1943-8vo-318p-cl,frntis,14p plts,e.p. maps-1st ed (t2,chip dj) 35.00

GREENLEAF,STEPHEN-Death Bed-NY-1980-Dial-1st ed (e4,f,dj) 20.00

GREENLEAF,STEPHEN-Grave Error-1979-Dial-auth 1st bk-1st ed (x7,f,dj) 35.00

GREENLEAF,STEPHEN-State's Evidence-NY-1982-Dial-1st ed (h4,f,dj) 15.00

GREENOUGH,SARAH-Alfred Stieglitz, Photographs and Writings-Wash D.C.-1983-Nat Gallery Art/Callaway-248p-73 photos,orig packing case as iss-1st ed (cc9,as new in dj,packng case) 100.00

GREENOUGH,WILLIAM P-Canadian Folk Life and Folk Lore-NY-1897-Geo H Richmond-tall 8vo-xii,199p-orig dec cl,illus-Watters p.872-1st ed (pp2) 45.00*

GREENSLET,FERRIS-Under the Bridge-Bost-1943-8vo-237p-illus-1st ed (m3,f,dj) 17.50

GREENWALD,SHANER-Treasured Jewish Recipes-(1969)-Hawthorn-159p-blu cl,illus-1st prtg (q8,wn dj) 15.00

GREENWALL,H J-I'm Going to Maxim's-Lond-(1958)-Allen Wingate-200p (l6,dj) 30.00

GREENWALT,C H-Hummingbirds-1960-Amer Mus Nat Hist-4to-70 tip in col photos,drwngs,maps (bb3,vf) 300.00

GREENWAY,JOHN-Down Among the Wild Men-Bost-(1972)-Atlanta/Little,Brown-8vo-361p-24 illus-1st ed (jj5,dj) 20.00

GREENWAY,JOHN-Folklore of the Great West-Palo Alto-1969-453p-illus-1st ed (t7,dj) 15.00

GREENWAY,JOHN-Folklore of the West-Palo Alto-(1969)-453p-drwngs-1st ed (r8,dj) 25.00

GREENWAY,NELLIE-How to Become Beautiful-NY-nd-J S Ogilvie Publ Co-128p-wrps (d1,sl wn) 15.00

GREENWICH-HISTORY OF THE ... AREA-Greenwich-1979-Grnwch Area Hist Soc-128p-photos (e1,wrps) 12.50

GREENWOOD,ANNIE P-We Sagebrush Folks-NY-1934-Appleton Century-8vo-xii,482p-illus-1st ed (y4,dj) 50.00

GREENWOOD,ERNEST-Prometheus U.S.A.-NY-1929-Harper-8vo-213p-9 illus-1st ed (dd5,sl chip dj) 30.00

GREENWOOD,HAROLD S-Pictorial Album of Wireless and Radio 1905 to 1928-1962-223p-wrps-999 photos-1st ed (h6,f) 35.00

GREENWOOD,JAMES-Wild Sports of the World-NY-1870-8vo-474p-old 1/2 mor,147 engrvngs (m3,badly wn bndg) 35.00

GREENWOOD,ROBERT-California Outlaw, Tiburcio Vasquez-Los Gatos-1960-296p-illus,e.p. maps-ltd ed-scarce-1st ed (f7,f,dj) 80.00

GREER,ANDREW-Reckless-NY-1955-Dutton-1st ed (h9,dj) 25.00

GREER,GEORGEANNA H-Meyer Family: Master Potters of Texas-S.A.-1971-Trinity U Pr-97p-photos-scarce-1st ed (a9,vf) 200.00

GREER,JAMES K-Colonel Jack Hays Texas Frontier Leader and California Builder-NY-1952-429p-col frntis,photos,map e.p.-1st ed (t7) 50.00

GREEVER,WILLIAM-Arid Domain-Stanford-(1954)-174p-maps-1st ed (v7,dj) 45.00

GREEVER,WILLIAM-Bonanza West-Norman-(1963)-U of Okla Pr-430p-illus,maps-1st ed (cc4,dj) 40.00

GREEVER,WILLIAM-Bonanza West-Norman-(1963)-U of Okla Pr-430p-illus-1st ed (f9,dj) 25.00

GREGG,FRANK M-Founding of a Nation-Cleve-1915-2 vols-t.e.g.,illus-v scarce-1st ed (c7,f) 150.00

GREGG,JOSIAH-Commerce of the Prairies-Chig-1926-Donnelley & Sons-frntis,map-Lakeside Classics (ff4) 30.00

GREGG,JOSIAH-Commerce of the Prairies-Dallas-1933-SW Pr-scarce rprnt (oo9,dj chip) 75.00

GREGG,KATE L-Road to Santa Fe-1952-UNM Pr-8vo-viii,280p-map e.p.,frntis port-1st ed (aa3,f,dj) 45.00

GREGG,KATE L-Road to Santa Fe-Albuq-(1952)-208p-cl-1st ed (z1,f,dj) 50.00

GREGG,W H-Where,When & How to Catch Fish on the East Coast of Florida-NY-1902-8vo-267p-12 col plts,tip-in fld-out map (m3,hngs cracked) 22.50

GREGORICH,JOSEPH-Apostle of the Chippewas-Chig-1932-Bishop Baraga Assoc-8vo-104p-g brgndy cl,frntis,illus-1st ed (aa7,wn cl) 25.00*

GREGORY,ANNIE-San Francisco Chronicle Blue Ribbon Cook Book-Chig-(1906)-Monarch-promo bk identical to "Women's Favorite Cook Book" except for cov (q8) 45.00

GREGORY,ANNIE-Women's Favorite Cook Book-(Chig)-(1902)-610p-pict tan cl,photos,col plts (q8) 50.00

GREGORY,DICK-Dick Gregory's Bible Tales-NY-(1974)-Stein & Day-8vo-187p-1st ed (gg5,f,dj) 15.00

GREGORY,DICK-Nigger-NY-1964-Dutton-224p-1st ed (ff1,dj) 30.00

GREGORY,HUGH M-Sea Serpent Journal-Charlottesville-1975-U Pr of Va-142p-blu cl,g titles,map e.p.,fldg drwng-1st ed (p8,as new in dj) 25.00

GREGORY,JACK-Sam Houston with the Cherokees 1829 to 1833-Austin-1967-206p-photos,maps-1st ed (t7,f,dj) 15.00

GREGORY,JAMES J H-Onion Raising-Mass-1909-Gregory-66p-wrps (x6,sp wn) 40.00

GREGORY,LADY-Kiltartan Poetry Book-NY-1919-Putnam-8vo-112p-1st US ed (w6,sl soil cov) 45.00

GREGORY,W K-In Quest of Gorillas-New Bedford-1937-8vo-241p-cl,photos,map (y8,wn cor) 35.00

GREGORY,WILLIAM-Letters to a Candid Inquirer on Animal Magnetism-Lond-1851-Taylor,Walton & Maberly-thk 12mo-(xxiv)+528p-emboss blu cl-1st ed (y9,sp & edge drknd) 100.00

GREIFF,C M-Princeton Architecture-Princeton-1967-4to-vii,200p-cl,illus (aa6) 35.00

GREIFF,CONSTANCE-John Notman, Architect-Phila-1979-Athenaeum of Phila-4to-253p-pict wrps,photos-1st ed (r10,sl rub) 17.50

GREIG,IAN-Silver King Mystery-NY-1930-Holt-1st US ed (f4) 10.00

GREIG,MAYSIE-Professional Lover-NY-1933-Dbldy,Doran-8vo-282p-1st ed (w6,dj) 35.00

GREINER,J-Wager With the Wind-Chig-1974-256p-1st ed (o10,f,dj) 25.00

GREINER,T-How to Make the Garden Pay-Phila-1890-Maule-272p-cl,illus (x6) 25.00

GRENDON,STEPHEN-Mr.George and Other Odd Persons-Sauk City-1963-Arkham-239p-ltd to 2546c-(auth a pseudonym of August Derleth)-1st ed (k5,f,dj) 35.00

GRENFELL,WILFRED T-Down North on the Labrador-NY-1911-Revell Co-8vo-229p-frntis,11 illus (cc7,dj) 35.00*

GRESHAM,GRITS-Complete Book of Bass Fishing-NY-1966-8vo-264p-photos,illus-1st ed (m3,f,dj) 10.00

GRESHAM,GRITS-Complete Wildfowler-NY-1973-8vo-294p-photos (m3,vf,dj) 25.00

GRESHAM,WM LINDSAY-Nightmare Alley-NY,Tor-(1946)-Rinehart-auth 1st bk-1st ed (e10,f,dj) 50.00

GREW,DAVID-Beyond Rope and Fence-1922-Boni & Liveright-1st ed (d3) 25.00

GREW,SIDNEY-Art of the Player Piano...-Lond,NY-1922-Kegan Paul/Dutton-8vo-333p wi index,tbls & chrts-1st Amer ed (u1,f,chip dj) 60.00

GREY OF FALLODON-Charm of Birds-NY-1927-Stokes-286p-woodcts by Robt Gibbings (d9) 15.00

GREY OWL-Men of the Last Frontier-Lond-(1935)-Country Life Ltd-253p-illus,illus e.p. (dd4) 25.00

GREY OWL-Pilgrims of the Wild-Lond-(1935)-Lovat Dickson & Thompson-281p-illus (dd4) 20.00

GREY,ELIZABETH-ED.-Noise of Drums and Trumpets-NY-1971-255p-illus-1st ed (b7,f,dj) 15.00

GREY,HUGH-ED.-Field & Stream Treasury-NY-1955-8vo-351p-photos (m3) 12.00

GREY,J T-Handbook for the Margaree-PA-1976-199p-photos (gg3,autg,vf,box) 45.00

GREY,R C-Adventures of a Deep Sea Angler-1930-Harpers-224p-photos,photo e.p. (ee3,sl fray,sp tn) 110.00

GREY,R-Cruise of the Fisherman, Adventures in Southern Seas-NY-1929-268p-photos,(son of Zane Grey)-scarce (gg3,f) 125.00

GREY,SIR EDWARD-Fallodon Papers-Bost,NY-1926-12mo-169p-ltd to 550c,nbrd,illus-scarce (m3,uncut,f,wn box) 90.00

GREY,SIR EDWARD-Fly Fishing-Lond-1899-8vo-276p-col plts-dec by A Rackham-scarce-1st ed (m3) 80.00

GREY,SIR EDWARD-Fly Fishing-Lond-1930-8vo-244p-illus,E F Daglish (m3,sl fray dj) 45.00

GREY,SIR EDWARD-Recreation-Bost,NY-1920-12mo-43p-1st ed (m3,vf) 17.50

GREY,ZANE-30,000 on the Hoof-NY-1940-Harper-1st ed (k4,dj sp sl fray) 30.00

GREY,ZANE-Arizona Ames-NY-(1932)-Harper & Bros-1st ed (bb2,f,dj) 125.00

GREY,ZANE-Desert Gold-1913-Harpers-1st ed (x2,sl wn sp) 65.00

GREY,ZANE-Desert of Wheat-NY/Lond-1919-Harper & Bros-1st ed (z9,sl cocked,sp sun) 25.00

GREY,ZANE-Forlorn River-NY-1927-Harper-8vo-cl-1st ed (x3,dj sl tn & chip) 175.00

GREY,ZANE-Ken Ward in the Jungle-(1912)-G&D-12mo-309p-frontis (m3) 17.50

GREY,ZANE-Ken Ward in the Jungle-Tor-1912-309p-1st Canadian ed (m3) 40.00

GREY,ZANE-Mysterious Rider-NY-1921-Harper & Bros-336p-cl,illus,F B Hoffman-1st ed (w3,f) 20.00

GREY,ZANE-Redheaded Outfield-1948-G&D-12mo-238p (m3,vf,fray dj) 25.00

GREY,ZANE-Roping Lions in the Grand Canyon-(1924)-G&D-12mo-191p (m3,f,dj) 25.00

GREY,ZANE-Shortstop-1937-G&D-12mo-310p (m3,badly fray dj) 12.50

GREY,ZANE-Shortstop-NY-1914-G&D-310p (v3,sl wn) 28.00

GREY,ZANE-Tales of Fishes-1919-G&D-8vo-267p-photos (m3,sl drknd sp) 55.00

GREY,ZANE-Tales of Fishing Virgin Seas-1925-Harpers-216p-photos,illus (gg3,vf) 110.00

GREY,ZANE-Tales of Fresh Water Fishing-1971-Barnes-8vo-277p-photos (m3,sl soil dj) 50.00

GREY,ZANE-Tales of Swordfish & Tuna-1927-Harpers-4to-203p-t.p. say Harpers,but bndg say G&D-orng cl,photos (m3,rear cov stnd) 80.00

GREY,ZANE-Tales of Tahitian Waters-NY,Lond-1931-Harper & Bros-303p-cl-scarce-1st ed so stated (d1,sl fox,dj wn) 350.00

GREY,ZANE-U.P. Trail-1918-Harpers-12mo-409p-code letters a-s,frontis-1st ed (m3,f) 35.00

GREY,ZANE-Wanderer of the Wasteland-1923-Harper & Bros-1st ed (t9) 25.00

GREY,ZANE-Wildfire-NY-(1917)-Harpers-illus-1st ed (m4,sp rub) 30.00

GREY,ZANE-Young Lion Hunter-NY-1911-G&D-12mo-278p (m3) 10.00

GREY,ZANE-Young Pitcher-NY-(1911)-G&D-248,(1)p+ads-cl (n1,sl wn,cov sl soil) 12.50

GREY,ZANE-Zane Grey Cookbook-New Jersey-1976-4to-239p-photos-1st ed (m3,vf,dj) 40.00

GREY,ZANE-Zane Grey's Adventures in Fishing-1952-Harpers-8vo-later prntng (m3,creased t.p.& dedctn pg) 65.00

GRIBBLE,FRANCIS-Early Mountaineers-Lond-1899-388p-g title & cov dec of mtn,t.e.g.,48 plts-1st Brit ed (o10) 225.00

GRICE-HUTCHINSON,MARJORIE-Malaga Farm-Westminster-1957-Newman Pr-8vo-168p-29 illus-1st US ed (gg5,dj) 10.00

GRIDLEY,MARION E-Indian Legends of American Scenes-Chig-(1939)-Donohue & Co-127p-11 col illus (dd4,dj) 20.00

GRIDLEY,MARION E-Indians of Yesterday-Chig-1940-Donohue-4to-63p-prntd bds,illus,Lone Wolf (z4) 25.00

GRIDLEY,MARION-Indians of Yesterday-Chig-1940-Donohoe-lg 4to-illus-1st ed (oo9,dj edgewn) 50.00

GRIEF,MARTIN-New Industrial Landscape-Clinton-(1978)-Main St Pr-4to-192p-illus-1st ed (ee5,f,sl tn dj) 20.00

GRIER,SARAH A-Few Hints About Cooking-Bost-1887-Wright & Potter Prtg-321p-Bitting p.201 (a8,sl wn) 65.00

GRIER,THOMAS G-Pueblo Indians-1912-priv prtd-sm-33p-tied wrps,photos-v scarce-1st ed (v7,f) 75.00

GRIERSON,EDWARD-Crime of One's Own-1967-Putnam-1st Amer ed (s10,dj) 12.50

GRIERSON,J-Challenge to the Poles-Lond-(1964)-8vo-696p-cl,48p plts,27 maps,e.p. maps-1st ed (t2,dj) 45.00

GRIEVE,MRS M-Culinary Herbs and Condiments-Lond-1933-Heinemann-209p-brn bds,papr labls (m6) 25.00

GRIFFIN,A R-Ship to Remember-NY-(1943)-8vo-302p-cl,14p plts-1st ed (t2,sl chip dj) 20.00

GRIFFIN,CHARLES E-Four Years in Europe with Buffalo Bill-Albia-1908-94p-pict cl,frntis,photos-1st ed (t7,flaking,hng loose) 30.00

GRIFFIN,H L-An Official in British Guinea...Harrow and the Royal Artillery-Lond-nd(ca.1925)-Palmer-8vo-xi,252p-orig cl,16 plts,1 map-1st ed (bb6,sl soil cov) 15.00

GRIFFIN,JAMES B-Fort Ancient Aspect-Ann Arbor-1943-U of Mich-4to-xvi+392p-blu cl,157 plts,18 text figs,10 maps(incl fldg)-1st ed (d2) 125.00

GRIFFIN,WALTER T-Homes of Our Country-NY-1882-640p-cl (g1,sl wn) 17.50

GRIFFITH,A KINNEY-Mickey Free, Manhunter-Caldwell-1969-Caxton-239p-1st ed (dd4,dj) 40.00

GRIFFITH,CORINNE-I Can't Boil Water-NY-(1963)-Messner-sm 8vo-140p-grn cl-1st prtg (q8,dj) 15.00

GRIFFITH,G W E-My 96 Years in the Great West-LA-1929-Geo W E Griffith-289p-port-1st ed (dd4) 35.00

GRIFFITH,G-Brothers of the Chain-1900-F V White-pict stmpd cl-1st ed (x7) 100.00

GRIFFITH,R EGLESFELD-Medical Botany-Phila-1847-704p-woodcut illus-1st ed (dd3,rbnd,new e.p.) 225.00

GRIFFITHS,JULIA-ED.-Autographs for Freedom-Auburn-1854-Alden,Beardsley-1st ed (w5,sp fray) 75.00

GRIFFITHS,THOMAS S-History of Baptists in New Jersey-Highstown-1904-xvii,542p-cl,port (aa6) 30.00

GRIGGS,GEORGE-History of Mesilla Valley-Mesilla-1930-124p-cl,sm map on t.p.-rare-1st ed (u7,rbnd,undrlines,marg notes) 300.00

GRIGGS,ROBERT F-Valley of Ten Thousand Smokes-1922-Nat Geog Soc-341p-233 illus(incl fldg view),9 maps(incl fldg) (bb3,cor wn) 110.00

GRIGGS,ROBERT F-Valley of Ten Thousand Smokes-1922-Nat'l Geographic-341p-photos(incl col),2 fldg col maps-1st ed (u8,sl wn cor) 90.00

GRIGGS,WILLIAM C-ED.-Pictorial History of Lubbock Texas, 1880 to 1950-Lubbock-1976-Lubbock Cnty Hist Comm-80p-cl,photos-1st ed (w3,vf) 20.00

GRIGSBY,MELVIN-Smoked Yank-Sioux Falls-1888-227p-pict cl-Dornbusch W18-scarce-1st ed (t7,cor bump) 100.00

GRIGSON,GEOFFREY-Wild Flowers in Britain-Lond-1944-W Collins-47p-pict bds,col plts,illus-1st ed (dd10,f,dj) 15.00

GRIGSON,JANE-ED.-World Atlas of Food-(1974)-S&S-folio-319p-tan cl,col plts,65 col maps-1st Amer ed (q8,dj) 35.00

GRIGSON,JANE-Food with the Famous-Lond-(1979)-M Joseph-photos-1st prtg (q8,dj) 18.50

GRIMBLE,ARTHUR-Return to the Islands-1957-Morrow-215p-1st Amer ed (u8,dj chip & spot) 10.00

GRIMBLE,ARTHUR-We Chose the Islands-NY-1952-Morrow-8vo-340p-illus-1st US ed (jj5,f,dj) 15.00

GRIMBLE,AUGUSTUS-Salmon Rivers of England and Wales-Lond-1913-8vo-310p-photos,fldg map (m3) 40.00

GRIMBLE,AUGUSTUS-Salmon Rivers of Ireland-Lond-1913-8vo-296p-1/4 vel bndg,fldg map,photos-scarce (m3,pres cpy) 75.00

GRIME,KITTY-Jazz Voices-Lond,Melbourne,NY-(1983)-Quartet Bks-photos-1st Brit ed (bb1,f,dj) 22.50

GRIMES,ABSALOM-Absalom Grimes, Confederate Mail Runner-New Haven-1926-Yale U Pr-xii+216p-blu cl,plts-1st ed (h2) 40.00

GRIMES,JOHN F-Romance of the American Camp Meeting-Cin-1922-196p+fldg plt-cl (b1) 20.00

GRIMES,ROY-ED.-300 Years in Victoria County-1968-Victoria Advocate-649p-photos-1st ed (a9,dj) 100.00

GRIMM,WILLIAM C-Book of Trees-Harrisburg-1961(1957)-4to-xiii,363p-drwngs (jj7,f,dj) 25.00

GRINNELL,DIXON-Fur Bearing Mammals of California-Berkeley-1937-4to-2 vols,photos,col illus by A Brooks-scarce-1st ed (m3) 85.00

GRINNELL,G B-ET AL-Hunting Big Game-Out of Door Library-1897-Scribners-327p-photos (gg3) 35.00

GRINNELL,GEORGE B-American Game Bird Shooting-NY-1910-8vo-558p-illus-1st ed (m3) 40.00

GRINNELL,GEORGE B-Beyond the Old Frontier-NY-1913-Scribner's-xii,374p-dec cl,map,illus,ads-1st ed (v1) 95.00

GRINNELL,GEORGE B-Beyond the Old Frontier-NY-1920-374p-pict cl,illus-Smith #3880 (t7,f) 30.00

GRINNELL,GEORGE B-Blackfoot Lodge Tales-NY-1892-310p+4p ads-silv & blk dec red bds-1st ed (h7) 60.00

GRINNELL,GEORGE B-By Cheyenne Campfires-New Haven-1926-Yale U Pr-305p-photos-1st ed (ff4) 150.00

GRINNELL,GEORGE B-Cheyenne Indians-New Haven-1923-Yale U Pr-2 vols-photos,fldg map-1st ed (ff4,autg) 300.00

GRINNELL,GEORGE B-Fighting Cheyennes-Norman-(1956)-453p-illus-1st Okla ed (e7,f,dj) 40.00

GRINNELL,GEORGE B-Fighting Cheyennes-NY-1915-Scribner-x,431p-dec cl,maps-Howes G433-1st prtg (v1) 150.00

GRINNELL,GEORGE B-Jack the Young Explorer-NY-1908-12mo-308p-illus (m3) 15.00

GRINNELL,GEORGE B-Punishment of the Stingy & Other Indian Stories-NY-1901-Harper-mrbld cov wi g edges,illus-1st ed (oo9) 65.00

GRINNELL,H W-Synopsis of the Bats of California-Berkeley-1918-8vo-(223-)404p-11 plts (y8) 40.00

GRINNELL,HON J B-Cattle Industries of the United States-NY-1882-Joseph H Reall-74p+2p ads-blu wrps-Herd 936-rare (ee4,cov chip) 300.00

GRINNELL,J-Directory to Bird Life of San Francisco Bay Region-Berkeley-1927-8vo-160p-wrps,col frntis,map (y8) 30.00

GRINNELL,J-Directory to the Bird Life of the San Francisco Bay Region-Berkeley-1927-Cooper Ornith Club. Pac Coast Avifauna,No.18-8vo-160p-wrps,col frntis,1 map (jj10) 35.00

GRINNELL,J-Distributional List of the Birds of California-Hollywood-1915-Cooper Ornith Club-8vo-217p-wrps,3 maps(1 lg col fldg)-Pac Coast Avifauna,No.11 (jj10,uncut) 45.00

GRINNELL,JOSEPH-Gold Hunting in Alaska...-Elgin,Chig-(1901)-David C Cook-96p-cl & mrbld bds-Smith 3904,Wickersham 31 (e1) 50.00

GRINNELL,JOSEPH-Gold Hunting in Alaska...-Elgin-1901-David C Cook-sq 12mo-96p-3/4 red cl,mrbld bds,photos-Graff 1678-1st ed (aa3,cov wn) 75.00

GRINNELL-LADIES OF...-COMP.-Free Library Cook Book-Grinnell-1896-Ray & MacDonald Prntrs-90p+30p catlg-bds (o6,soil bds) 45.00

GRINNELL-MILNE,DUNCAN-Wind in the Wires-Lond-nd(ca.1933)-Aviation Bk Club ed-288p-red cl,illus (kk2) 45.00

GRINSLEY,WILL-Football: The Greatest Moments in the Southwest Conference-Bost-1968-Little,Brown-152p-1st ed (v3,chip dj) 26.00

GRINSTEIN,HYMAN B-Rise of the Jewish Community of New York, 1654 to 1860-Phila-1945-JPSA-xiv+645p-grn cl,plts-1st ed (b2) 20.00

GRISCOM,L-ET AL-Warblers of America-1957-Devin Adair-356p-33 col plts-1st prtg (bb3,f,chip dj) 45.00

GRISCOM,LUDLOW-Birds of Concord-Cambridge-1949-Harvard U Pr-340p-photos (c9,chip dj) 15.00

GRISCOM,LUDLOW-Modern Bird Study-Cambridge-1945-Harvard-190p (c9,dj) 12.50

GRISSOM,IRENE W-Under Desert Skies-Caldwell-1935-Caxton-12mo-cl,photos,drwngs-1st ed (ee9,dj) 15.00

GRISWOLD,DON L-Carbonate Camp Called Leadville-Denver-1951-277p-photos,map-1st ed (v7,sl chip dj) 45.00

GRISWOLD,DON-Colorado's Century of "Cities"-(1958)-Griswold & Mazzulla-307p-illus (cc4,dj) 25.00

GRISWOLD,FRANK G-After Thoughts-1936-Harpers-8vo-202p (m3,f,chip dj) 40.00

GRISWOLD,FRANK G-After Thoughts-1936-priv prtg-202p-ltd to 150c,autg (gg3,cov dmpstnd) 45.00

GRISWOLD,FRANK G-Cascapedia Club-1920-priv prntd-12mo-27p-photos-scarce-1st ed (m3,pres cpy) 125.00

GRISWOLD,FRANK G-El Greco-Derrydale-1930-8vo-98p-one of 300c,illus,Frazier State G-19-A,scarce (m3) 225.00

GRISWOLD,FRANK G-Fish Facts and Fancies-1925-priv prntd-102p-vol.2(only),photos (gg3,autg,f) 20.00

GRISWOLD,FRANK G-Horse & Buggy Days-1936-priv prntd-12mo-161p-one of 150c,frontis photo,scarce-1st ed (m3) 80.00

GRISWOLD,FRANK G-Horses & Hounds-NY-1926-8vo-275p-one of 300c,lea,illus (m3,sl wn) 60.00

GRISWOLD,FRANK G-Life History of the Atlantic & Pacific Salmon of Canada-NY-1930-8vo-179p-frontis,map,photos-1st ed (m3) 200.00

GRISWOLD,FRANK G-Memoirs of a Salmon-1931-priv prtg-44p-red lea,illus (gg3,sp tn,cov wn,pres cpy) 75.00

GRISWOLD,FRANK G-Observations on a Salmon River-1921-priv prntd-12mo-52p-photos,map frontis,scarce-1st ed (m3,vf) 135.00

GRISWOLD,FRANK G-Salmon River-NY-1928-8vo-239p-one of 250c,photos,maps,col frontis (m3) 85.00

GRISWOLD,FRANK G-Salmon Score of F. Gray Griswold for Ten Seasons 1920-1929-1930-priv prntd-12mo-16p-scarce (m3,f,autg) 80.00

GRISWOLD,FRANK G-Some Fish and Some Fishing-NY-1921-251p-photos (gg3,f) 10.00

GRISWOLD,FRANK G-Some Fishing & Some Fishing-NY-1921-8vo-251p-illus (m3) 15.00

GRISWOLD,P R-Colorado's Loneliest Railroad: San Luis Southern-Boulder-1980-190p-1st ed (n4,f) 24.00

GRISWOLD,WESLEY S-Train Wreck-Brattleboro-1969-150p-illus-1st ed (n4,f,dj) 15.00

GRISWOLD,WESLEY S-Work of Giants-NY-1962-367p-1st ed (n4,f,dj) 22.00

GROAT,DICK-World Champion Pittsburgh Pirates-1961-Coward McCann-photos-1st ed (s8,f,dj) 25.00

GROCER'S COMPANION AND MERCHANT'S HANDBOOK-Bost-(entered 1883)-New England Grocer Office-240p-blk bds (l6,bds faded) 50.00

GROENE,BERTRAM H-Tracing Your Civil War Ancestor-Winston Salem-(1973)-124p-illus-1st ed (n3,f,dj) 15.00

GROGAN,EMMETT-Final Score-NY-(1976)-1st ed (e5,as new in dj) 20.00

GROGAN,EMMETT-Ringolevio-Bost,Tor-(1972)-auth 1st bk-photos-1st ed (e5,as new in dj) 45.00

GROGAN,EWART S-From the Cape to Cairo-Lond-1902-Hurst & Blackett-8vo-xix,402p-blu cl,frntis,illus,2 col fldg maps-rvsd ed (t10) 100.00

GROHMANN,WILL-Paul Klee-NY-nd-tall 4to-447p-40 tip in col plts (l10,f,dj) 60.00

GROMME,O J-Birds of Wisconsin-Madison-1963-4to-219p-cl,105 col plts,maps-1st ed (y8,dj chip) 45.00

GRONOW,REES H-Reminiscences and Recollections of Captain Gronow-Lond-1889-qto-2 vols-3/4 brwn calf,mrbld bds & e.p.,t.e.g.,ribbon mrkr,25 handcol plts(iss in dupl b&w)-ltd to 870c,nbrd-1st collected ed (b7) 450.00

GRONSETH,H E-Suttons Bay Michigan, Our First Century, 1854 to 1954-Suttons Bay-1954-Chamber of Comm-32p+ads-wrps,photos (z7,ex-libr) 30.00

GROOCH,S W-Skyway to Asia-NY-1937-8vo-xii,206p-cl,frntis,15p plts,e.p. maps (t2,sl chip dj) 40.00

GROOM,ARTHUR-Old London Coaching Inns...-Lond-nd-Midland & Scottish Railwy-sm 4to-43p-illus (h9) 40.00

GROPIUS,WALTER-New Arch. & the Bauhaus-NY-1936-MOMA-16 plts-1st ed (kk4,dj) 100.00

GROPIUS,WALTER-Rebuilding Our Communities-Chig-1945-P Theobald-4to-61p-illus wrps,42 plts (cc10) 125.00

GROSBOIS,CHARLES-Shunga: Images of Spring-Geneva-1965-Nagel Publ-folio-157p-tip in col plts,monochromes & b&w-1st ed (c3,f,sl tn dj,box) 85.00

GROSE,GEORGE R-James W Bashford, Pastor, Educator, Bishop-NY-(1922)-252p-cl (h1) 12.50

GROSE,PARLEE C-Five Fairies-NY-(1917)-223p-cl-1st ed(& only ed) (b1,f,dj) 15.00

GROSS,A O-Heath Hen-Bost-1928-Bost Scty,Vol.6,#4-4to-(3),(491-)588p-cl,11 plts (y8,ring stain cov) 75.00

GROSS,HENRY-Simplified Bookbinding-NY-(1976)-Scribner's-8vo-xiv,176p-cl,illus-1st ed (x4,dj) 30.00

GROSS,MICHAEL-Book Windows That Sell-NY-(1948)-Amer Bk Publ Council-8vo-(iv),43p-stiff papr wrps,illus (x4) 20.00

GROSS,MILTON-Yankee Doodles-1948-House of Kent-1st ed (r7,f,dj) 50.00

GROSS,MILTON-Yankee Doodles-1948-House of Kent-drwngs-1st ed (s8,f,dj) 45.00

GROSS,MIRIAM-ED.-World of George Orwell-NY-(1971)-S&S-4to-182p-photos-1st US ed (r1,dj) 30.00

GROSS,MIRIAM-ED.-World of George Orwell-NY-(1971)-S&S-photos-1st US ed (bb1,as new in dj) 20.00

GROSS,MIRIAM-ED.-World of Raymond Chandler-1978-A&W-1st Amer ed (q9,vf,dj) 20.00

GROSS,MIRIAM-World of Raymond Chandler-NY-1978-A&W-illus-1st Amer ed (p4,f,dj) 25.00

GROSS,SAMUEL D-History of American Medical Literature from 1776 to the Present Time-NY-1972-(facs of 1876 ed) (dd3) 50.00

GROSS,SIDNEY-How to Run a Paperback Bookshop-NY-1963-R R Bowker-8vo-xi,135p-stiff papr wrps,illus-1st ed (x4,cov chip) 15.00

GROSSINGER,JENNIE-Art of Jewish Cooking-(1958)-Random-229p-pict wht cov,e.p. & drwngs by L Fox-1st ed (q8,sl wn dj) 20.00

GROSSMAN,M L-Birds of Prey of the World-NY-1964-tall 4to-496p-cl,70 photos,maps-1st ed (y8,dj tn) 50.00

GROSSMAN,M L-Birds of Prey of the World-1964-Potter-4to-496p-70 col & 283 b&w photos,illus,maps (bb3,f,dj) 55.00

GROSSMAN,M L-Our Vanishing Wilderness-NY-1969-4to-324p-photos (m3,vf,dj) 12.50

GROSSMAN,WILLIAM-Heart of Jazz-1956-NYU Pr-1st ed (w1,f,dj) 25.00

GROSSVOGEL,DAVID I-Mystery & Its Fictions-Balt,Lond-1979-Johns Hopkins Univ-1st ed (r4,f,dj) 35.00

GROSVENER,GILBERT-ED.-Book of Birds-Wash D.C.-1937-Nat'l Geo Soc-2 vols-grn cl wi gilt,col & b&w plts,maps (o2,sl fox) 35.00

GROSVENOR,JEWETT-Wooden Architecture of the Lower Delaware Valley-St.Paul-1920-White Pine Monos-4to-16p-wrps,photos (l10) 9.50

GROSZ,GEORGE-Little Yes and a Big No-NY-1946-Dial-4to-cl,illus-1st ed (oo6,dj tape mrkd) 65.00

GROTH,JOHN-Studio:Europe-NY-1945-Vanguard-illus by auth-1st ed (a10) 35.00

GROVE,ALVIN-Lure & Lore of Trout Fishing-Harrisburg-1951-8vo-318p-illus-1st ed (m3,vf,sl soil dj) 40.00

GROVE,FRED-Running Horses-1980-Dbldy-1st ed (p9,dj) 15.00

GROVE,LEE E-Of Brooks & Books-Mpls-(1945)-U of Minn-ix,85p-dec bds-ltd to 1500c,nbrd-1st ed (dd10,f,dj) 45.00

GROVE,LEE E-Of Brooks & Books-Mpls-(1945)-U of Minn-ltd to 1500c-1st ed (w1,f,dj) 30.00

GROVER,FRANK R-Brief Early History of Les Cheneaux Islands-Evanston-1911-140p-wrps-Streeter 1996 (b1) 25.00

GROVER,R-Art Glass Nouveau-1968-Tuttle-231p-425 col plts-3rd prtg (cc8,dj,box) 65.00

GROVER,R-Carved and Decorated European Art Glass-1970-Tuttle-243p-424 col plts (cc8) 65.00

GROVES DICTIONARY OF MUSIC AND MUSICIANS-NY-1911-MacMillan-5 vols-t.e.g.-2nd ed (u4,sl wn) 75.00

GROVES DICTIONARY OF MUSIC AND MUSICIANS-NY-1946-Macmillan-5 vols-plus Amer Spplmnt-3rd ed (u4) 95.00

GROVES,PERCY-History of the Second Dragoons, the Royal Scots Greys-Edinburgh-1893-sm folio-30p text+4 col plts-pict bds-1st ed (gg2) 125.00

GRUBAR,FRANCIS-William Ranney, Painter of the Early West-1962-Clarkson Potter-4to-65p+plts-1st ed (d3,dj) 27.50

GRUBB,DAVIS-Night of the Hunter-NY-1953-auth 1st bk-1st ed (r5,dj) 40.00

GRUBB,E H-Potato-GC-1912-Dbldy,Page-545p-Bitting 204 (a8,sun,fox sp,hng weak) 35.00

GRUBB,SARAH-Selection from the Letters of the Late...-Sudbury-1848-J Wright-8vo-451p-lea-1st ed (y6,sl scuff,fox) 28.00

GRUBER,FRANK-Brass Knuckles-(1966)-Shelbourne Pr-383p-1st ed (g9,dj) 35.00

GRUBER,FRANK-Brass Knuckles-LA-(1966)-Sherbourne-1st ed (j4,f,sl wn dj) 25.00

GRUBER,FRANK-Etruscan Bull-NY-1969-Dutton-1st ed (e4,dj) 10.00

GRUBER,FRANK-Limping Goose-NY-1954-1st ed (s5,dj sl chip & sp sunned) 25.00

GRUBER,FRANK-Little Hercules-1965-Dutton-1st ed (s10,dj sp fade) 10.00

GRUBER,FRANK-Little Hercules-NY-1965-1st ed (p5,rub dj) 15.00

GRUBER,FRANK-Murder '97-NY-1948-Farrar-1st ed (l4,dj) 35.00

GRUBER,FRANK-Pulp Jungle-LA-1967-Sherbourne Pr-1st ed (d4,f,dj) 25.00

GRUBER,FRANK-Pulp Jungle-LA-1967-Sherbourne-1st ed (w9,f,dj) 45.00

GRUBER,FRANK-Spanish Prisoner-NY-1969-Dutton-1st ed (c10,dj) 20.00

GRUBER,L FRITZ-Famous Portraits-NY-1960-Ziff Davis-1st ed (v5,f,sl tn dj) 25.00

GRUBER,O VON-ED.-Photogrammetry-Bost-1932-Amer Photo Publ-xii+454p-red cl,353 text figs,inset map,addenda slip-1st ed (d2,sl smudged cov) 75.00

GRUELLE,JOHNNY-Raggedy Ann and Andy and the Camel with the Wrinkled Knees-Joliet-(1924)-Volland (r3,tips wn,edge rub) 45.00

GRUEN,JOHN-New Bohemia-NY-1967-wrps-1st ed (v9) 25.00

GRUMMOND,JANE L DE-Baratarians and the Battle of New Orleans-Baton Rouge-1961-180p-illus-1st ed (b7,f,dj) 45.00

GRUNER,O CAMERON-Treatise on the Canon of Medicine of Avicenna, Incorporating a Translation of the First Book-Lond-1930-612p-rare-1st ed (dd3) 200.00

GRUNIGER,URSULA-Cooking with Fruit-Lond-(1971)-Allen & Unwin-220p-brwn cl,drwngs-1st Brit ed (q8) 16.50

GRUNWALD,HENRY-ED.-Salinger-NY-1962-H&R-1st ed (z9,dj) 10.00

GRUVER,SUZANNE CARY-Cape Cod Cook Book-Bost-1930-Little,Brown-214p-yel bds,papr labls,illus-1st ed (o6) 25.00

GRZIMEK,B-He and I and the Elephants-NY-1967-8vo-208p-30p photos (y8,dj) 30.00

GRZIMEK,B-No Room for Wild Animals-NY-1957-8vo-(8),271p-cl,20 photos,3 maps (y8,dj) 15.00

GRZIMEK,BERNHARD-Serengeti Shall Not Die-NY-1961-8vo-344p-photos-1st US ed (m3,vf,dj) 30.00

GRZYBOWSKI,J A-Oklahoma Ornithology-1984-U of Okla-175p-1st ed (bb3,f) 20.00

GUBELIN,EDWARD J-Internal World of Gemstones-Zurich-1979-ABC Editions-234p-pict cov,360 col photos-2nd ed (u5,f,dj) 160.00

GUBERLET,MURIEL L-Seaweeds at Ebb Tide-Seattle-1956-U of Wash-8vo-182p-87 drwngs-1st ed (gg5,dj) 20.00

GUDERIAN,GEN HEIN-Panzer Leader-NY-1952-Dutton-photos,maps,chrts (z2) 30.00

GUE,BENJAMIN F-History of Iowa-NY-1903-Century Hist Co-4 vols-frntis,illus (v2) 200.00

GUENON,M F-Treatise on Milch Cows-1854-McElrath-88p-cl,illus (bb3,rbnd,t.p. soil,chip) 42.00

GUENON,RENE-Introduction to the Study of the Hindu Doctrines-Lond-1945-Luzac & Co-cl-1st ed (l8,wn dj) 95.00

GUENON,RENE-Symbolism of the Cross-Lond-1975-Luzac & Co-cl-2nd ed (l8,f,dj) 35.00

GUENTHER,HERBERT V-Royal Song of Saraha-Seattle-1969-U of Wash Pr-cl-1st prtg (o8,dj) 20.00

GUENTHER,KONRAD-Naturalist in Brazil-Bost-1931-400p-32 plts-1st Engl ed (hh7,sl fox) 44.00

GUERARD,MICHEL-Michel Guerard's Cuisine Munceur-(1976)-Morrow-320p-blu cl,16 col plts-1st prtg (q8,sl fray dj) 15.00

GUERNSEY,CHARLES A-Wyoming Cowboy Days-NY-1936-Putnam's-288p-illus-Six Guns 880-Herd 940-1st ed (bb4,chip dj) 75.00

GUERRA,FRANCISCO-American Medical Bibliography 1639 to 1783-NY-1962-885p (dd3) 175.00

GUERRA,FRANCISCO-American Medical Bibliography, 1639 to 1783-NY-1962-Lathrop C Harper-885p-blu cl,plts-1st ed (d2) 125.00

GUEST,JUDITH-Ordinary People-NY-1976-auth 1st bk-1st ed (t5,f,dj) 20.00

GUEVARA,CHE-Che Guevara on Guerilla Warfare-NY-1961-Praeger-85p (r1,f,dj) 30.00

GUGAS,CHRIS-Silent Witness-Englewood-(1979)-Prentice Hall-8vo-254p-1st ed (dd5,dj) 12.50

GUGGISBERG,CAPT F C-Shop-Lond-1900-276p-red mor,linen bds,g dec sp,mrbld e.p.,t.e.g.,photos,fldg plans,8 col plts-1st ed (gg2,f) 200.00

GUIDICI,D-Tragedy of the Italia-NY-1929-8vo-xvi,208p-g cl,frntis,32p plts,1 dblpg map-1st ed (t2) 65.00

GUIDRY,RON-Guidry-1980-Prentice Hall-1st ed (s8,dj) 12.50

GUILD HOUSE COMMITTEE OF ALL SAINT'S CATHEDRAL-ED.-Choice Receipts-(Albany)-1898-"Albania Pr"-16mo-94p+20p ads-wrps-Bitting 529 (u6) 35.00

GUILD,CURTIS-Abroad Again-Bost-1877-Lee & Shepard-8vo-474p-1st ed (jj5) 25.00

GUILD,LURELLE V A-Geography of American Antiques-GC-1935-283p-cl (j1) 12.50

GUILLAUME,P-Primitive Negro Sculpture-NY-1926-41 illus-1st ed (h10,dj) 150.00

GUILLIERMOND,ALEXANDRE-Cytoplasm of the Plant Cell-Waltham-1941-Chronica Botanica-x+247p-blu cl,152 text figs-1st ed (l2) 25.00

GUINEY,LOUISE I-Lovers' Saint Ruth's-1895-Copeland & Day-8vo-yel dec cl-1st ed (v10,sl soil cov) 30.00

GUITEAU,CHARLES J-Truth-Chig-1879-Donnelley,Gassette & Loyd-98p-cl (c1,covs flecked) 32.50

GULICK,BILL-Snake River country-Caldwell-1978-Caxton-folio-xiv+199p-leatherette,photos,Earl Roberge,map e.p. (z4,f,dj) 20.00

GULLASON,THOMAS-ED.-Stephen Crane's Career-NY-1972-NYU Pr-1st ed (z9,f,sl rub dj) 15.00

GULLIVER,JOE-Gulliver Travels Again-nd-priv prntd-8vo-61p-one of 100c-rare (m3,vf,autg) 150.00

GULLIVER,P H-Neighbours and Networks-Berkeley-1971-U of Cal Pr-8vo-366p-cl,maps (y5,dj) 40.00

GUNCKEL,JOHN E-Early History of the Maumee Valley-Toledo-1902-101p-cl-1st ed (j1,sl rub,reinfrcd innr hngs) 17.50

GUNDER,CLAUDE A-Life of...-Marion-1908-auth-70p-wrps (a1,sl chip) 20.00

GUNDY,ELIZABETH-Cat on a Leash-NY-1978-Viking-1st ed (ee9,f,dj) 15.00

GUNDY,ELIZABETH-Cat on a Leash-NY-1978-Viking-1st ed (w5,f,f dj) 20.00

GUNDY,ELIZABETH-Naked in a Public Place-NY-1975-Harper-auth 1st bk-1st ed (w5,f,dj) 25.00

GUNN,GERTRUDE-Political History of Newfoundland, 1832 to 1864-Tor-1966-U of Tor Pr-249p-map (k10) 20.00*

GUNN,JAMES-Breaking Point-NY-(1972)-Walker-1st ed (j3,f,dj) 15.00

GUNN,JAMES-End of the Dreams-NY-1975-Scribners-1st ed (w5,f,dj) 25.00

GUNN,JAMES-Some Dreams are Nightmares-NY-(1974)-Scribner's-1st ed (j3,f,dj) 15.00

GUNN,JOHN C-Gunn's Domestic Medicine, or Poor Man's Friend...-NY-1842-893p-lea,port (dd3) 200.00

GUNN,JOHN C-Gunn's New Domestic Physician-Cin-1864-1129-lea (dd3) 200.00

GUNN,JOHN M-Schat chen-(Albuq)-(1917)-222(223)p-photos,drwngs-scarce (v7,pres by step-son,cov spot) 100.00

GUNN,JOHN M-Schatchen-Albuq-1917-priv publ-223p-cl,illus-Rader 1713 (z1,f) 125.00

GUNNISON,ALMON-Rambles Overland-Bost-1884-12mo-245p-dec cov-1st ed (r8,sp wn) 50.00

GUNNISON,ALMON-Rambles Overland-Bost-1884-Universalist-245p-1st ed (d3) 65.00

GUNNISON,ALMON-Wayside and Fireside Rambles-Bost-1894-Universalist-241p-cl-9 illus by Remington (g1) 25.00

GUNSAULUS,HELEN C-Japanese Textiles-NY-1941-Priv Prtd for Japan Soc-4to-94p-col & b&w plts-ltd to 1000c (c3) 75.00

GUNTER,A Y-Big Thicket a Challenge for Conservation-Austin-1971-Jenkins Publ-172p-cl,photos-1st ed (w3,f,dj) 12.00

GUNTHER,ERNA-Art in the Life of N W Coast Indian-Seattle-(1966)-275p-illus-1st ed (h7,f,sl tn dj) 35.00

GUNTHER,ERNA-Indian Life on the Northwest Coast of North America-Chig,Lond-(1972)-sm 4to-277p-illus-1st ed (e7,dj) 35.00

GUNTHER,ERNA-Klallam Folk Tales-Seattle-1925-50p-wrps-1st ed (t7) 15.00

GURLEY,F G-New Mexico and the Santa Fe Railway-1950-Newcomen Soc-32p-wrps,map-2nd ed (d3) 15.00

GURNEY,G-War in the Air-NY-1962-4to-352p-cl,dblpg illus t.p.,illus (t2,dj) 35.00

GURNEY,IVOR-Poems 1890 to 1947-Lond-1973-1st ed (y7,dj) 20.00

GURNEY,JOSEPH J-Winter in the West Indies-Lond-1840-John Murray-8vo-xvi,282p+15 ads-orig cl wi g titles-Sabin 29312 (p8,fade,edgewn) 175.00

GUSSOW & ODELL-Mushrooms & Toadstools-Ottawa-1927-Agric-274p-cl,3 col plts,photos (x6) 25.00

GUSSOW,ALAN-Sense of Place-SF-1971-Friends of Earth-lg 4to-col illus (oo9,dj wn,chip) 75.00

GUSSOW,H T-Mushrooms and Toadstools-Ottawa-1927-274p-g stmpd grn cl,2p col plts,125 hlf tones,1 plt drwngs (x5,wn,soil) 30.00

GUSTAFSON,A M-ED.-John Spring's Arizona-Tucson-1966-UAP-326p-1st ed (d3,dj) 20.00

GUSTE,ROY F,JR.-Antoine's Restaurant Since 1840 Cookbook-New Orleans-1979-4to-186p-grn cl,col illus-rvsd ed (q8,f,dj) 25.00

GUSTE,ROY F,JR.-Antoine's Restaurant Since 1840 Cookbook-New Orleans-1979-Carbery Guste-186p-illus-rvsd Amer ed (l6,dj) 30.00

GUTENMAKHER,L I-Electronic Information, Logic Machines-NY-1963-Intersci Publ-x+170p-grn cl,50 figs-1st Amer ed (j2) 25.00

GUTHRIE,A B,JR.-Big Sky-NY-(1947)-Wm Sloane-386p-cl,map-1st ed (v1,sl wn dj) 45.00

GUTHRIE,A B,JR.-Blue Hen's Chick-1965-McGraw Hill-261p-1st ed (r8,dj sl tn & soil) 42.00

GUTHRIE,A B,JR.-Blue Hen's Chick-NY,Tor-(1965)-McGraw Hill-1st ed (ff6,f,dj) 30.00

GUTHRIE,A B,JR.-Genuine Article-Bost-1977-Houghton-1st ed (d4,dj) 20.00

GUTHRIE,A B,JR.-Genuine Article-Bost-1977-Houghton-1st ed (q4,f,dj) 25.00

GUTHRIE,A B,JR.-These Thousand Hills-Bost-(1956)-Houghton Mifflin-Tan cl-1st ed (f2,dj) 20.00

GUTHRIE,A B,JR.-Way West-NY-(1949)-Wm Sloane-(viii),340p-cl-1st ed (v1,sl wn dj) 40.00

GUTHRIE,A B,JR.-Wild Pitch-Bost-1973-Houghton-1st ed (s4,dj) 30.00

GUTHRIE,GEORGE M-Child Rearing and Personality Development in the Philippines-Univ Prk & Lond-1966-lg 8vo-223p-cl-1st ed (y5,dj tn) 15.00

GUTMAN,BILL-Modern Baseball Superstars-1973-Dodd,Mead-photos-1st ed (s8,f,dj) 12.00

GUTMAN,WALTER-Gutman Letter-NY-1969-photos (x8,dj) 75.00

GUYOT'S GEOGRAPHICAL SERIES-NY-1869-Scribner-118p-pict bds (d1) 20.00

GUZMAN,MARTIN L-Memoirs of (Pancho Villa)-Austin-(1975)-U of Tex Pr-512p-map,illus (cc4,dj) 25.00

GUZZO,LOUIS-Is It True What They Say About Dixy-Mercer Island-1980-234p-red cl (b6,dj) 7.50

GWALTNEY,FRANCIS I-Day the Century Ended-NY-1955-1st ed (q5,sl chip dj) 30.00

GWALTNEY,FRANCIS I-Destiny's Chickens-Indpls-1973-1st ed (q5,dj) 12.50

GWALTNEY,FRANCIS I-Step in the River-NY-1960-1st ed (q5,dj) 20.00

GWATHMEY,JOHN H-Fly Fishing in the South-Richmond-1942-12mo-74p-wrps,scarce (m3) 65.00

GWATHMEY,JOHN H-Justice John: Tales from the Courtroom of the Virginia Judge-1934-Dietz-147p-port by L P Pinder-ltd to 1000c,nbrd (dd9) 40.00

GWYNN,STEPHEN-Fishing Holidays-Lond-1904-8vo-299p (m3) 20.00

GWYNN,STEPHEN-Garden Wisdom-NY-1922-Macmillan-149p-cl (x6) 18.00

GWYNN,STEPHEN-River to River-Lond-1937-4to-210p-illus,R Beddington-1st ed (m3) 15.00

GWYNNE,A E-Practical Treatise on the Law of Sheriff and Coroner...-Cin-1849-H W Derby-620p-lea (d1,sp chip,sl dmpstnd pgs) 75.00

GWYNNE,PAUL-Along Spain's River of Romance, the Guadalquivir-NY-1912-McBride, Nast-8vo-356p-45 illus-1st ed (jj5) 25.00

GYMNASTICS-MANUAL OF...-Chig-nd-A Flanagan-30,(2)p-wrps (k1) 12.50

GYSIN,BRION-To Master, a Long Goodnight-NY-(1946)-Creative Age-auth 1st bk-1st ed (u10,f,sl wn dj) 75.00

H D-By Avon River-NY-1949-Macmillan-1st ed (w6,f,dj) 75.00

H D-Hyman-NY-1921-H Holt-Pelican Pr-47p-grn wrps,prntd in UK,but t.p. a cancel stmpd "Made in the U.S.A"-scarce-1st ed (w6) 225.00

H D-Tribute to the Angels-Lond & NY-1945-Oxford-8vo-42p-1st ed (w6) 45.00

HAAN,ENO R-Radio Trouble Shooting-1928-317p-90 photos,166 illus-1st ed (h6) 25.00

HAARDT,GEORGES-MARIE-Black Journey: Across Central Africa with the Citroen Expedition-NY-(1927)-Cosmopolitan-lg 8vo-316p-photos-1st Amer ed (u1,vf,dj) 50.00

HAAS,IRVIN-Bibliography of Material Relating to Private Presses-Chig-1937-Black Cat Pr-8vo-xvi,57p-buckrm-ltd to 250c (w2,sp lettrng rub) 85.00

HAAS,RICHARD-Richard Haas, an Architecture of Illusion-1981-Rizzoli-187 illus(incl 46 col)-1st ed (h10,dj) 45.00

HAAS,ROBERT B-Muybridge, Man in Motion-Berkeley-1976-U of Cal Pr-207p-95 photos-1st ed (cc9,as new in dj) 35.00

HABBERTON,JOHN-Bowsham Puzzle-NY-1884-222p-cl,dec frnt cov & sp-Wright 2343-1st ed (c1) 25.00

HABELER,PETER-Lonely Victory-NY-1979-223p-1st US ed (o10,f,dj) 28.00

HACHTEN,HARVA-Kitchen Safari-NY-1970-Atheneum-274p-1st ed (o6) 20.00

HACKETT,CHARLES W-ED.-Revolt of the Pueblo Indians of New Mexico and Otermin's Attempted Reconquest-Albuq-1970-2 vols-cl,ltd to 1000 sets-facs rprnt of 1942 ed (z1,f) 175.00

HACKETT,CHARLES W-Revolt of the Pueblo Indians of New Mexico & Otermin's Attempted Reconquest-Albuq-1942-part(vols 8 & 9)of Coronado Cuarto Cent Publ-scarce-1st ed (u7,f,unopened,djs) 250.00

HACKETT,L W-Malaria in Europe, an Ecological Study-Oxford-1937-336p (dd3) 40.00

HACKLE,SPARSE GREY-Fishless Days-1954-Angler's Club of NY-8vo-147p-one of 591c,illus by Chas De Feo-scarce (m3,vf) 200.00

HADDONFIELD-The Two Hundredth Anniversary of Settlement of...New Jersey-Haddonfield-1913-58p-cl backd bds,plts (aa6,soil) 30.00

HADFIELD,A M-Time to Finish the Game-Lond-(1964)-Phoenix Hs-8vo-228p-20 illus-1st ed (jj5,rub dj) 12.50

HADFIELD,CHARLES-Atmospheric Railways-Newton Abbot-1967-David & Charles-240p-blu cl,24 plts-1st ed (dd1,dj) 25.00

HADFIELD,MILES-Gardens of Delight-Bost-(1964)-Little,Brown-192p-col plts-1st Amer ed (m6,rprd dj) 25.00

HADFIELD,MILES-Gardens of Delight-Bost-(1964)-tall 8vo-192p-45 b&w & col plts-1st Amer ed (j10,bump,dj chip) 30.00

HAEBERLIN & GUNTHER-Indians of Puget Sound-Seattle-1952-wrps,illus-rprnt of 1930 U of Wash ed (c7) 25.00

HAFEN,ANN W-Reports From Colorado-Glendale-1961-333p-frntis,illus,lg fldg map-1st ed (t7,f) 40.00

HAFEN,LEROY R-Colorado and Its People-NY-1948-Lewis Hist Publ-3 vols,orig grn cl wi g sp titles,map e.p.,illus (mm1) 225.00

HAFEN,LEROY R-Colorado Gold Rush Contemporary Letters and Reports 1858 to 1859-Phila-1974-SW Hist Ser, Vol X-386p-frntis,illus,fldg map (t7,f) 20.00

HAFEN,LEROY R-ED.-Far West & the Rockies Historical Series 1820 thru 1875-Glendale-1954 to 1961-15 vols-fldg maps,ports,plts-1st eds (u7) 850.00

HAFEN,LEROY R-ED.-Pike's Peak Gold Rush Guidebooks of 1859-Phila-1974-SW Hist Ser,Vol IX-346p-frntis,illus,fldg map (t7,f) 20.00

HAFEN,LEROY R-ED.-Powder River Campaigns and Sawyers Expedition 1865-Glendale-1961-386p-illus,fldg map-Farwest & Rockies Ser,Vol.XII-1st ed (c7,f) 85.00

HAFEN,LEROY R-Fort Laramie-Glendale-1938-Arthur H Clark Co-429p-illus,map-Six Guns #888-1st ed (cc4) 200.00

HAFEN,LEROY R-Old Spanish Trail-Glendale-(1968)-377p-illus,fldg map-Far West & Rockies Ser,Vol.1-3rd prtg (f7,vf) 45.00

HAFEN,LEROY R-Overland Mail 1849 to 1869-Cleve-1926-Arthur Clark Publ-361p-illus,fldg map-1st ed (c7,f) 175.00

HAFEN,LEROY R-Overland Mail, 1849 to 1869-Cleve-1926-Arthur H Clark-8vo-361p-illus,fldg map-Howes H11-1st ed (aa3,vf) 250.00

HAFEN,LEROY R-Overland Routes to the Gold Fields, 1859 Contemporary Diaries-Phila-1974-SW Hist Ser, Vol XI-320p-frntis,illus (t7,f) 20.00

HAFEN,LEROY R-Ruxton of the Rockies-Norman-1950-325p-photos-1st ed (t7,dj) 32.50

HAFEN,LEROY R-Utah Expedition 1857 to 1858-Glendale-1958-Arthur H Clark-8vo-375p-grn cl,10 illus,fldg map-1st ed (mm1,cors wn) 95.00

HAFEY,JOHN-Platinum Print-Rochester-1979-Roch Inst of Tech-1st ed (t3) 30.00

HAGAN,ARTHUR P-Day the Bookies Took a Bath-LA-1982-Sherbourne-1st ed (r9,f,dj) 15.00

HAGAN,ARTHUR-Day the Bookies Took a Bath-LA-1971-Sherbourne-1st ed (r4,f,dj) 20.00

HAGAN,WILLIAM T-Sac and Fox Indians-Norman-(1958)-U of Okla Pr-287p-illus-1st ed (cc4,dj) 35.00

HAGE,GEORGE S-Newspapers on the Minnesota Frontier 1849 to 1860-St.Paul-1967-Minn Hist Soc-176p-illus-1st ed (cc4,dj) 15.00

HAGEDORN,HERMAN-Roosevelt in the Badlands-Bost,NY-1921-8vo-475p (m3) 20.00

HAGEMANN,E R-Comprehensive Index to Blask Mask 1920 to 1951-Bowling Green-1982-Popular Pr-wrps-1st ed (v5,f) 10.00

HAGEMANN,E R-ED.-Fighting Rebel and Redskins-Norman-1969-U of Okla Pr-355p-1st ed (d3,dj) 30.00

HAGEN,TONI-ET AL-Mount Everest-Lond-1963-195p-fldg map in pckt-1st ed (a4,vf,vf dj) 110.00

HAGEN,TONI-Nepal-Berne-1961-4to-119p-71 plts-1st ed (q10,f,dj) 65.00

HAGEN,WALTER-Walter Hagen Story-NY-1956-photos-1st ed (ll7,dj) 45.00

HAGERTY,HARRY J-Jasmine Trail-1936-Lothrop-1st ed (s10,sp chip dj) 35.00

HAGERUP,A T-Birds of Greenland-Bost-1891-8vo-62p-wrps (y8,sp chip) 15.00

HAGGARD,ANDREW C P-Louis XI and Charles the Bold-NY-1913-Moffat Yard-8vo-412p-16 illus-1st US ed (jj5) 25.00

HAGGARD,H RIDER-Allan Quartermain-Lond-1887-Longmans,Green-blu cl wi gold lttrng,20 wood engrvngs-1st Brit ed (aa8,sl fox) 750.00

HAGGARD,H RIDER-Allan the Hunter-Bost-1898-12mo-111p-illus (m3) 12.50

HAGGARD,H RIDER-Allan's Wife & Other Tales-Lond-1889-Spencer Blackett-brwn pebbld cl,34 plts-1st Brit trd ed (aa8,sl wn & fray) 175.00

HAGGARD,H RIDER-Ancient Allan-NY-1920-col frntis-1st Amer ed (r2,sl fox) 45.00

HAGGARD,H RIDER-Ayesha, the Return of She-Lond-1905-Ward,Lock & Co-32 plts by Greiffenhagen-1st Brit ed (bb1,e.p. brwnd,sl fox) 150.00

HAGGARD,H RIDER-Ayesha-NY-1905-Dbldy,Page-red cl,frntis-1st Amer ed (dd6) 60.00

HAGGARD,H RIDER-Beatrice-Lond-1890-Longmans,Green-312p-blu cl,bev bds-1st Brit ed (e10,sp brwnd,sl wn) 75.00

HAGGARD,H RIDER-Belshazzar-NY-1930-Doran-blu cl-1st US ed (d4) 20.00

HAGGARD,H RIDER-Bretheren-Lond et al-(1904)-Cassell-1st Brit ed (aa8,sp sl fade) 75.00

HAGGARD,H RIDER-Colonel Quaritch, V.C.-Lond-1888-Longmans,Green-3 vols-1st Brit ed (aa8,sp fade,cocked,sl fox pgs 300.00

HAGGARD,H RIDER-Dawn-1887-Appleton-2 vols,wrps-rare-1st Amer ed (x2,sp sl chip,covs sl fox) 2,750.00

HAGGARD,H RIDER-Doctor Therne-Lond,NY,Bombay-1898-Longmans,Green-1st Brit ed (aa8,sp drknd,bndg soil) 50.00

HAGGARD,H RIDER-Dr.Therne-1898-Longmans,Green-variant state wi unprtd wht e.p.-1st ed (x2) 185.00

HAGGARD,H RIDER-Fair Margaret-Lond-1907-Hutchinson-15 plts by J R Skelton-1st Brit ed (aa8,sp fade,e.p. brwnd) 40.00

HAGGARD,H RIDER-Gardener's Year-Lond-1905-Green-404p (x6,sp sun) 15.00

HAGGARD,H RIDER-Ghost Kings-Lond et al-1908-Cassell-blu cl,8 plts by A C Michael-1st Brit ed (aa8,sp fade,e.p. brwnd) 40.00

HAGGARD,H RIDER-Heart of the World-1895-Longmans,Green-pict cov,illus-1st ed (x2,sl fade sp) 100.00

HAGGARD,H RIDER-Heu Heu or the Monster-1924-Dbldy,Page-1st Amer ed (x2,dj sl wn & tn) 265.00

HAGGARD,H RIDER-Jess-Lond-1887-Smith,Elder-1st Brit ed (aa8,sl spot cov,sp wn,fade) 125.00

HAGGARD,H RIDER-King Solomon's Mines-Lond et al-1905-Cassell-red & gold pict bndg,32 illus by R Flint,(incl fldg col map)-rvsd ed (aa8,sl fade sp,sl fox) 250.00

HAGGARD,H RIDER-Maiwa's Revenge-Lond,NY-1888-Longmans,Green-scarcer bndg of blu grn bds-1st Brit ed (aa8,sp wn,e.p. brwnd) 100.00

HAGGARD,H RIDER-Marie-1912-Longmans,Green-1st ed (x2) 75.00

HAGGARD,H RIDER-Mr Meeson's Will-1888-Spencer Blackett-pict cl-1st ed (x7) 325.00

HAGGARD,H RIDER-Mr.Meeson's Will-Lond-1881-Spencer Blackett-xvii+286p-orig pict red cl,16 illus-1st ed,1st iss (kk5,cov sl mrkd,uncut) 235.00

HAGGARD,H RIDER-Mr.Meeson's Will-Lond-1888-Spencer Blackett-red,blk & gld pict bndg,16 plts-1st Brit ed (aa8,sp sl fade,rub) 200.00

HAGGARD,H RIDER-Nada the Lilly-Lond,NY-1895-Longmans,Green-maroon & silv bndg,illus-New ed (aa8,cors fray,sp edge wn) 50.00

HAGGARD,H RIDER-People of the Mist-1894-Longmans,Green-pict stmpd cl,illus-1st ed (x2) 115.00

HAGGARD,H RIDER-People of the Mist-NY-1894-Longmans,Green-16 plts by A Layard-1st US ed (aa8,sl stnd cov) 50.00

HAGGARD,H RIDER-Queen of the Dawn-Lond-nd(1925)-Hutchinson-1st ed,1st iss (aa8,sl bump) 65.00

HAGGARD,H RIDER-She-Lond-1887-Longmans,Green-2 col plts at frnt-1st Brit ed (bb1,sl nick sp) 225.00

HAGGARD,H RIDER-She-Lond-1887-Longmans,Green-317p-blu cl,bev bds,2 col plts-1st Brit ed (e10,rprd sp chips) 225.00

HAGGARD,H RIDER-Smith and the Pharaohs & Other tales-Bristol,Lond-1920-Arrowsmith-1st Brit ed (aa8) 125.00

HAGGARD,H RIDER-Virgin of the Sun-Lond et al-(1922)-Cassell-1st Brit ed (aa8,sl drknd sp,e.p. brwnd) 45.00

HAGGARD,H RIDER-Way of the Spirit-Lond-1906-Hutchinson-1st Brit ed (aa8,bndg dull,sp drknd) 35.00

HAGGARD,H RIDER-Witches Head-Lond-nd(1890)-Spencer Blackett-16 plts by Chas Kerr-Brit rprnt (aa8,sp wn) 35.00

HAGGARD,H RIDER-Yellow God-Lond-1911-1st ed (r2,papr brwnd) 30.00

HAGGARD,WILLIAM-Bitter Harvest-Lond-1971-Cassell-1st ed (s4,dj) 22.50

HAGUE,ELEANOR-Spanish American Folk Songs-Lancaster,NY-1917-Am Folk Lore Soc,Vol.X-111p+4p bibliog-1st ed (u7) 35.00

HAHN,EMILY-Diamond-NY-1956-Dbldy-314p-e.p. maps-1st ed (u5,f,dj edgewn,chip) 20.00

HAHN,EMILY-Mabel-Bost-1977-228p-photos-1st ed (t7,f,dj) 15.00

HAHN,EMILY-Romantic Rebels-Bost-1967-HMCo-8vo-318p-16p photos-1st ed (bb5,f,f dj) 20.00

HAHN,PAUL-Where is that Vanished Bird?-Tor-1963-Roy Ontarian Mus-347p-wrps (b9) 20.00

HAHN,W L-Mammals of Indiana-Indpls-1909-8vo-(1),(418-)663p-wrps,6 plts (y8,sp wn) 25.00

HAIG-BROWN,R L-Canada's Pacific Salmon-Ottawa-1952-8vo-23p-wrps,illus by T Brayshaw-scarce-1st ed (m3) 75.00

HAIG-BROWN,R L-Come Wade the River-Seattle-1971-folio-unpgd-photos,R Wahl-trd ed (m3,f,sl wn dj) 35.00

HAIG-BROWN,R L-Fabulous Fishing in Latin America, That Other Trout Season-NY-1956-Pan Am World Airlines-99p-wrps,photos-scarce (gg3,vf) 45.00

HAIG-BROWN,R L-Fisherman's Fall-1964-Morrow-279p-1st ed (gg3,vf,vf dj) 40.00

HAIG-BROWN,R L-Fisherman's Spring-NY-1951-8vo-222p-illus,L Darling-1st ed (m3,vf) 50.00

HAIG-BROWN,R L-Fisherman's Summer-NY-1959-8vo-253p-illus,L Darling-1st ed (m3,f) 45.00

HAIG-BROWN,R L-Fisherman's Winter-NY-1954-8vo-288p-illus,L Darling-1st ed (m3,fade sp) 45.00

HAIG-BROWN,R L-Living Land-Tor-1961-4to-269p-photos,illus,map in rear pocket-1st ed (m3,f,dj) 75.00

HAIG-BROWN,R L-Master and His Fish-(Tor)-(1981)-200p-1st ed (f7,dj) 25.00

HAIG-BROWN,R L-Measure of the Year-Tor-1950-8vo-279p-1st Canadian ed (m3,badly fray dj) 30.00

HAIG-BROWN,R L-Mounted Police Patrol-Lond-1960-191p (gg3) 15.00

HAIG-BROWN,R L-Primer of Fly Fishing-NY-1964-8vo-189p-illus,L Darling-1st ed (m3,vf,sl soil dj) 50.00

HAIG-BROWN,R L-Return to the River-1941-Morrow-8vo-259p-ltd to 520c,nbrd,two autg,illus by Chas De Feo (m3) 225.00

HAIG-BROWN,R L-Return to the River-NY-1941-8vo-248p-1st trd ed (m3,f,dj) 45.00

HAIG-BROWN,R L-Return to the River-Tor-c.1946-McClelland & Stewart-248p-illus,map-1st Can ed (k10,chip dj) 30.00*

HAIG-BROWN,R L-River Never Sleeps-NY-1946-8vo-352p-illus,L Darling-1st ed (m3,f) 45.00

HAIG-BROWN,R L-River Never Sleeps-NY-1946-Morrow-1st ed (f8,f,dj missing lg sp chip) 85.00

HAIG-BROWN,R L-Salmon-Ottowa-1974-4to-79p-wrps,photos (m3,vf) 40.00

HAIG-BROWN,R L-Saltwater Summer-Lond-1957-192p-illus (gg3,f,chip dj) 20.00

HAIG-BROWN,R L-Saltwater Summer-NY-1948-8vo-256p-col frontis-1st ed (m3,dj) 45.00

HAIG-BROWN,R L-Starbuck Valley Winter-Tor-1948-8vo-310p-illus,Chas De Feo (m3,sl fray dj) 22.50

HAIG-BROWN,R L-Timber-NY-1942-Morrow-8vo-410p-pict e.p.s-1st ed (m3) 50.00

HAIG-BROWN,R L-Western Angler-Derrydale-1939-4to-2 vols,ltd to 950c,nbrd,photos,illus by T Brayshaw,fldg map opp pg 3 in vol 1 (m3,partially uncut) 600.00

HAIG-BROWN,R L-Western Angler-NY-1947-8vo-356p-1st trd ed (m3,f) 70.00

HAIG-BROWN,R L-Western Angler-NY-1947-Morrow-8vo-356p-1st trd ed (y4,f,dj) 75.00

HAIG-BROWN,R L-Whale People-Lond-1962-Collins-184p-illus,map (k10,dj) 15.00*

HAIG-BROWN,R L-Woods and River Tales-(Tor)-(1980)-192p-1st ed (f7,dj) 25.00

HAIG-BROWN,R L-Writings & Reflections-Tor-1982-8vo-222p-1st ed (m3,vf,dj) 25.00

HAIGHT,A D-Biography of a Sportsman-NY-1939-209p-grn cl,wht linen cl sp,g dec bds,illus (ee3,vf,box) 32.00

HAIGHT,ANNE L-Banned Books-NY-1935-Bowker-1st ed (w1) 25.00

HAILE,BERARD-Learning Navaho-St.Michaels-1941,1942,1947 & 1948-4 vols-wrps-1st eds (v7,f) 175.00

HAILEY,ARTHUR-Flight into Danger-Tor-1958-Ryerson-auth 1st bk-1st ed (gg8,f,tn dj) 65.00

HAIN,JOHN A-COMP.-Side Wheel Steamers of the Chesapeake Bay 1880 to 1947-1947-Glendale-unpgd-spiral bnd,prtd on recto only,illus (dd9) 25.00

HAINES,A L-ED.-Valley of the Upper Yellowstone-(1965)-U of OK-79p-illus,maps,fldg map-1st ed (r8,dj) 20.00

HAINES,A-Mountain Fever-Portland-1962-255p-wrps,illus,maps-1st ed (o10,f) 20.00

HAINES,ALANSON A-History of the Fifteenth Regiment, New Jersey Volunteers-NY-1883-388p-cl,illus,port (aa6) 200.00

HAINES,ANNA-Health Work in Soviet Russia-NY-1928-177p-1st ed (dd3) 40.00

HAINES,AUBREY-ED.-Osborne Russell's Journal of a Trapper-Lincoln-nd-190p-frntis,maps(incl fldg)-Graff #3611 (t7,f) 20.00

HAINES,DONAL H-Luck in All Weathers-NY-1941-8vo-290p-illus,R Boyer-1st ed (m3,vf,dj) 17.50

HAINES,EDITH K-Tried Temptations Old and New-(1935)-Farrar-229p-blu cl-2nd ed (q8,wn dj) 16.50

HAINES,FRANCIS-Buffalo-NY-1970-Crowell-8vo-242p-1st ed (z4,dj) 35.00

HAINES,FRANCIS-Bufffalo-1970-Crowell-242p-photos-1st ed (bb3,f,dj) 19.00

HAINES,FRANCIS-Horses in America-NY-1971-Crowell-8vo-213p-1st ed (z4,sl stnd dj) 20.00

HAINES,FRANCIS-Nez Perces-Norman-(1955)-U of Okla-xviii,329p-cl,photos,illus,maps-1st ed (v1,dj) 75.00

HAINES,FRANCIS-Red Eagles of the Northwest-Portland-1939-361p-e.p. & text maps-1st ed (e7) 75.00

HAINES,JENNIE D-Christmasse Tyde-SF-(1907)-Paul Elder-111p-decs,S Wright,frntis,G Ross,prntd on Norman vel at Tomoye Pr (n6) 45.00

HAINES,JENNIE-De Gardeyne Boke-NY-1906-Elder-72p-cl (x6,rub,wn) 35.00

HAINES,RICHARD-Ancestry of the Haines, Sharp, Collins, Wills, Gardiner, Prickitt, Eves, Evans...-Camden-1902-(2),456p-cl,plts (aa6,spot,new e.p.) 175.00

HAINES,WILLIAM P-History of the Men of Co. F-Mickleton-1897-(3),vi-vii,293p-cl (aa6,ex-libr) 200.00

HAINING,JOHN-Ploughing by Steam-Hemel Heamstead-1970-Model & Allied Publ-360p-cl-1st ed (dd1,dj) 30.00

HAINING,PETER-ED.-Lucifer Society-1972-Taplinger-1st ed (t4,f,f dj) 20.00

HAINING,PETER-Movable Books-Lond-(1979)-New English Libr-obl lg 4to-140p-cl,illus-1st Brit ed (s3,f,dj) 95.00

HAINING,PETER-Sherlock Holmes Scrapbook-NY-1974-Potter-illus-1st Amer ed (p4,f,dj) 30.00

HAJ,FAREED-Disability in Antiquity-NY-1970-188p-1st ed (dd3,dj) 45.00

HAKLUYT,RICHARD-Principal Navigations Voyages Traffiques & Discoveries of...-Glasgow-1903-James MacLehose & Sons-12 vols-blu cl,vel sp,fldg maps-ltd to 100c,nbrd (p8,sl wn) 1,200.00

HAKLUYT,RICHARD-Principal Navigations, Voyages, Traffiques & Discoveries of the English Nation...-Glasgow-1903 to 1905-James MacLehose & Sons-8vo-12 vols-blu cl,t.e.g.,frntis,95 plts incl fldg maps,plans,chrts-1st collected ed (t10) 650.00

HAKOLA,JOHN W-ED.-Frontier Omnibus-Missoula-(1962)-Montana St U Pr-436p-buckskin,e.p. & many illus by C M Russell-ltd to 298c-1st ed (gg4) 150.00

HALBERSTAM,DAVID-Making of a Quagmire-NY-1965-1st ed (o5,dj) 22.50

HALBERSTAM,DAVID-Noblest Roman-Bost-1961-auth 1st bk-1st ed (s5,dj sp sl chip) 25.00

HALBERSTAM,DAVID-Powers That Be-1979-Knopf-1st ed (r9,f,dj) 20.00

HALDANE,A R B-By Many Waters-Lond-1940-8vo-223p-photos (m3,f) 12.50

HALDANE,ELIZABETH-Scots Gardens in Old Times-Lond-1934-Maclehose-243p-cl,illus (x6,dj wn) 25.00

HALDANE,J W C-3800 Miles Across Canada-Lond-1900-S,M,H,K & Co-sm 8vo-xxiii,344p-g blu cl,frntis,44 illus,fldg map at rear-1st ed (mm8,bump,hngs weak) 40.00*

HALDANE,J W C-3800 Miles Across Canada-Lond-1908-S,M,H,K & Co-sm 8vo-xxiii,344p,spplmntry chptr,23p,10p ads-g dec blu cl,frntis,44 illus,2 fldg maps(1 col) (cc7,bump,sp soil) 60.00*

HALDEMAN,JOE-Infinite Dreams-NY-(1978)-1st ed (k5,f,dj) 10.00

HALDEMAN-JULIUS,E-ED.-K K K-Girard-(1924)-Haldeman-Julius-64p-wrps-Little Blu Bk 650 (g1) 12.50

HALDEMAN-JULIUS,MARCET-Girl in the Snappy Roadster-Girard-nd-Haldeman Julius-32p-wrps,Little Blu Bk 1605 (d1) 10.00

HALDENE,CHARLOTTE-Last Great Empress of China-NY-1965-303p-1st ed (b7,dj) 25.00

HALE,A R-Rooseveltian Fact & Fable-NY-1908-8vo-198p-frontis port (m3) 25.00

HALE,CHRISTOPHER-Rumor Hath It-NY-1945-Dbldy CC-1st ed (g4,f,dj) 12.50

HALE,EDWARD E-Man Without a Country-Mount Vernon-(1938)-Peter Pauper-59p-cl-ltd to 1450c-dec by V Angelo (j1,sl wn box) 15.00

HALE,EDWARD E-Memories of a Hundred Years-NY-1902-Macmillan-2 vols-col pict cl,frntis,illus-scarce-1st ed (f9,fade) 85.00

HALE,EDWARD E-One Hundred Years Ago-Bost-1875-40p-prntd wrps (n1) 12.50

HALE,JOHN-ED.-Settlers-Lond-1950-Faber-408p-frntis,illus,maps,port (k10,dj) 30.00*

HALE,KATHLEEN-Henrietta's Magic Egg-Lond-(1973)-Allen & Unwin-oblng 8vo-32p-pict bds,col & b&w illus,auth-1st ed (r3) 35.00

HALE,MABEL-Beautiful Girlhood-Anderson-(1922)-224p-cl (d1) 15.00

HALE,MRS.S J-Northwood-Bost-1827-Bowles & Dearborn-12mo-2 vols-lea bckd mrbl bds-scarce-BAL 6776-1st ed (w6,hngs loose,sl wtrstnd) 325.00

HALE,NANCY-Life in the Studio-(1969)-Little,Brown-209p-1st ed (dd9,dj) 12.00

HALE,NANCY-Mary Cassatt-NY-1975-Dbldy-8vo-333p-beige cl,illus-1st ed (r10,wn dj) 12.50

HALES,A G-Campaign Pictures of the War in South Africa 1899 to 1900-Lond-1900-303p-red cl,frntis-1st ed (b7) 100.00

HALES,PHILIP-Madonna-Bost-1908-Bates & Guild-4to-74p-20 plts-1st ed (bb5) 25.00

HALEY,ALEX-Roots-GC-1976-1st ed (n5,dj) 45.00

HALEY,ALEX-Roots-GC-1976-Dbldy-1st ed (cc1,dj) 35.00

HALEY,J EVETTS-Charles Goodnight's Indian Recollections-Canyon-1928-128p-Panhandle Plns Hist Rev, Vol.I,No.I-128p-map pict wrps-1st ed (t7,sl chip) 35.00

HALEY,J EVETTS-Earl Vandale on the Trail of Texas Books-Canyon-1965-prtd by Carl Hertzog-44p-cl,ltd to 500c (w3,vf) 150.00

HALEY,J EVETTS-ET AL-Some Southwestern Trails-El Paso-1948-Carl Hertzog-unpgd(30)-cl,frntis,illus,H Bugbee-Herd #2125 (w3,f,box coming apart) 225.00

HALEY,J EVETTS-Fort Concho and the Texas Frontier-San Angelo-1952-SA Standard Times-8vo-352p-illus by H Bugbee,6 maps-1st trd ed (aa3,f,f dj) 250.00

HALEY,J EVETTS-Fort Concho and the Texas Frontier-San Angelo-1952-Standard Times-352p-Hertzog design,illus by Bugbee-1st ed (a9,f,dj,box) 300.00

HALEY,J EVETTS-George W Littlefield: Texan-1943-U of Okla Pr-8vo-xiv,287p-drwngs by H Bugbee-1st ed (aa3,f,sl chip dj) 85.00

HALEY,J EVETTS-Jeff Milton-Norman-1948-U of Okla-xiv,430p-cl,photos,1st prtg wi upside down type on pg 421-1st ed (v1,dj) 95.00

HALEY,J EVETTS-Jeff Milton: a Good Man with a Gun-1948-U of Okla Pr-8vo-xiii,430p-photos,drwngs by H Bugbee-Herd 965-1st ed,1st state(wi line inverted pg 421) (aa3,f,chip dj) 85.00

HALEY,J EVETTS-Life on the Texas Range-Austin-1952-112p-cl,frntis port,photos-1st ed (z1,f,lacks box) 90.00

HALEY,JAY-ED.-Advanced Techniques of Hypnosis and Therapy-NY-(1967)-Grune & Stratton-hvy 8vo-(x)+(558)p-blu cl-1st prntg (y9,sl rub,dj chip) 76.50

HALEY,MOLLIE A-Gardens and You-Joliet-1925-Volland-16mo-unpgd-pict bds,dblfld leaves wi col illus,M H Myers-1st ed (r3,f,box drknd & chip) 45.00

HALEY,NELSON C-Whale Hunt,The Narrative of a Voyage-NY-1948-Ives Washburn-8vo-304p-blu cl,map e.p.,illus (nn1,sl fade sp) 30.00

HALFORD,F M-An Angler's Autobiography-Lond-1903-8vo-286p-photos-scarce-1st ed (m3,sm gouge at sp edge) 400.00

HALFORD,F M-Making a Fishery-Lond-1895-8vo-212p-illus-1st ed (m3) 100.00

HALIBURTON,THOMAS C-Sam Slick, the Clockmaker-NY-1887-John B Alden-84p-wrps,dbl cols (j1) 12.50

HALKETT,ANDREW-Checklist of the Dominion of Canada & Newfoundland-Ottawa-1913-folio-138p-plts-scarce (m3) 85.00

HALL & OSBORNE-COMPS.-Ordinances of the City of Seattle Published by Order of the Common Council-Seattle-1880-Hanford-176p+index,wrps-v rare-1st prtg in book form (w1,two lg chips fr wrp) 750.00

HALL,ADAM-9th Directive-1966-S&S-1st Amer ed (r9,f,dj) 25.00

HALL,ADAM-Berlin Memorandum-Lond-1965-Collins-1st ed (s4,f,sl wn & mrkd dj) 30.00

HALL,ADAM-Kobra Manifesto-1976-Dbldy-1st Amer ed (q9,f,dj) 20.00

HALL,ADAM-Mandarin Cypher-1975-Dbldy-1st ed (r9,dj) 15.00

HALL,ADAM-Pekin Target-Lond-1981-Collins-1st ed (q4,f,dj sp sl fade) 30.00

HALL,ADAM-Sinkiang Executive-1978-Dbldy-1st Amer ed (q9,f,dj) 20.00

HALL,ADAM-Tango Briefing-1973-Dbldy-1st Amer ed (q9,dj) 20.00

HALL,AMANDA B-Cinnamon Saint-Bost-(1937)-Humphries-8vo-153p-1st ed (w6,dj) 35.00

HALL,ANNA G-Nansen-NY-(1940)-Jr Lit Guild/Viking-165p-cl,illus in blu by Artzybasheff-1st ed thus (oo10) 25.00

HALL,B P-An Atlas of Speciation in African Passerine Birds-Lond-1970-folio-423p-cl,col frntis,col maps (y8,dj) 100.00

HALL,B P-ED.-Birds of the Harold Hall Australian Expedtions 1962 to 70-Lond-1974-8vo-396,(2)p-wrps,col frntis,10 plts,fldg map (y8) 48.00

HALL,B-One Man's War-NY-(1929)-8vo-viii,354p-g cl,frntis,12p plts-1st ed (t2,fade) 65.00

HALL,BASIL-Accounts of a Voyage of Discovery to the West Coast of Corea...-Lond-1818-John Murray-4to-3/4 calf,bands,chrts,col plts (gg6,rbnd) 800.00

HALL,BERT-En L'air-NY-(1918)-New Library-sm 8vo-cl,frntis,plts (t2,wn,wtrstnd margins) 25.00

HALL,C G-Skyways-NY-1938-8vo-144p-illus cl,text illus,illus e.p.-1st ed (t2,sl wn sp,cor bump) 20.00

HALL,DON-On Top of Oregon-Corvallis-1975-180p-wrps,illus,maps-1st ed (o10,f) 9.00

HALL,DONALD-Playing Around-1974-Little,Brown-photos-1st ed (s8,dj) 12.00

HALL,EDWARD H-Appleton's Hand Book of American Travel-NY-1867-456p+51p ads,fldg maps-9th Annual ed-Graff #1726-1st ed (t7) 100.00

HALL,ELTON W-Sperm Whaling from New Bedford-New Bedford-1982-Old Dartmouth Hist Soc-221p-red cl,125 photos by C W Ashley (pp1,as new in dj) 28.50

HALL,FREDERICK T-Pedigree of the Devil-Lond-1883-Trubner-8vo-256p,illus+80p ads,blk cl-1st ed (t1) 125.00

HALL,GEORGE F-Plain Points on Personal Purity or Startling Sins of the Sterner Sex-Chig,Phila-nd-Amer Bible Hs-317p+ads-cl (l1) 20.00

HALL,GEORGE F-Study in Bloomers-Chig,Phila,Stockton-1895-Amer Bible Hs-272p-cl,frntis,Wright 2401 (d1) 75.00

HALL,H M-Gathering of Shore Birds-NY-1960-242p-illus (gg3,f,dj) 20.00

HALL,H M-Gathering of Shore Birds-NY-1960-8vo-242p-cl,drwngs (y8,dj tn) 35.00

HALL,H M-Woodcock Ways-NY-1946-4to-84p-illus,R Ray-1st ed (m3,vf,dj) 35.00

HALL,H M-Woodcock Ways-NY-1946-84p-illus (gg3) 22.00

HALL,HENRY-ED.-Tribune Book of Open Air Sports...-NY-1887-Trib Assoc-500p-cl (a1,cov sl rub,soil,hng rprd) 225.00

HALL,INEZ A E-Romance of Lake Conneaut or All is Well That Ends Well-Bost-(1932)-193p-cl (b1) 15.00

HALL,J N-Flying with Chaucer-Bost-1930-8vo-vi,56p-illus cl-1st ed (t2,sp fade) 25.00

HALL,J N-High Adventure-Bost-1918-Houghton Mifflin-8vo-xxiv,238p-illus cl,frntis,plts,4 dblpg plts-1st ed (t2) 100.00

HALL,JAMES B-Ralph Eugene Meatyard-(Millerton)-1974-Aperture-136p-100 photos-1st ed (cc9,as new in dj) 45.00

HALL,JAMES N-High Adventure-Bost-1918-red cl,photos-1st ed (gg7) 15.00

HALL,JAMES N-Under a Thatched Roof-Bost-1942-HMCO-1st ed (y1,f,f dj) 40.00

HALL,JAMES-Palaeontology of New York-Albany-1847,52-C Van Benthuysen-4to-2 vols-plts-Part VI of Nat Hist of NY-1st ed (c2,sl fox) 100.00

HALL,JAMES-Western Reader-Cin-1834-Corey & Fairbank-216p-prntd bds-Amer Imprnts 24793-rare (k1,rub,sp chip) 250.00

HALL,JOHN E-Autobiography and Experiences of John E Hall-Blanchester-nd-auth-97p-wrps (a1) 20.00

HALL,JOHN F-Daily Union History of Atlantic City and County, New Jersey-Atlantic City-1900-4to-517p-cl,illus,fldg map (aa6,rbnd) 250.00

HALL,L-Sinister House-1919-H-M-1st ed (x7,rprd hng,rnfrcd dj) 65.00

HALL,MARTIN H-Confederate Army of New Mexico-Austin-1978-392p-lea,photos,maps,deluxe ed ltd to 35c,autg,prtd on spec papr-1st ed (v7,f,box) 85.00

HALL,MARTIN H-Confederate Army of New Mexico-Austin-1978-Presidial Pr-lg 8vo-422p-1st ed (dd4) 45.00

HALL,MRS. S C-ED.-Juvenile Forget-Me-Not-Lond,Phila-1833-224p-3/4 lea & mrbld bds,frntis,7p engrvngs (n1) 25.00

HALL,RADCLYFFE-Sixth Beatitdude-Lond-(1936)-Heinemann-8vo-261p-pict dj-1st ed (w6,dj chip,wn & sl wtrstnd) 125.00

HALL,RADCLYFFE-Well of Loneliness-NY-1929-Covici & Friede-2 vols-ltd to 225c,autg-Victory ed (l9) 300.00

HALL,RICHARD-Stanley-Bost-1975-Houghton Mifflin-8vo-400p-gry cl,map e.p.,illus-1st Amer ed (dd7,dj) 40.00

HALL,ROBERT L-Exit Sherlock Holmes-Lond-1977-Murray-1st Brit ed (r4,f,dj) 22.50

HALL,ROBERT L-Exit Sherlock Holmes-NY-1977-Scribners-1st ed (f4,f,dj) 15.00

HALL,ROBERT L-King Edward Plot-NY-1980-McGraw-1st ed (q4,vf,dj) 27.50

HALL,RONALD-Frederick the Great and His Seven Years War-Lond-1915-240p-red cl,maps-1st ed (jj2) 50.00

HALL,SHARLOT M-Cactus and Pine: Songs of the Southwest-Phoenix-1924-250p-illus-2nd,enlgd ed (bb9) 45.00

HALL,SUSAN-Gentlemen of Leisure-NY-(1972)-Prairie Hs-sm 4to-192p-photos by Adelman (y4,dj) 25.00
HALL,THOMAS S-Ideas of Life and Matter-Chig-(1969)-U of Chig Pr-2 vols-1st ed (a2,dj) 35.00
HALL,TREVOR-Sherlock Holmes & His Creator-Lond-1978-Duckworth-1st ed (q4,dj) 20.00
HALL,W W-Guide Board to Health, Peace and Competence-Springfield-1869-752p-grn pebbld papr cov bds,frntis (g10) 45.00
HALLAHAN,WILLIAM-Catch Me, Kill Me-Lond-1978-Gollancz-1st Brit ed (s4,f,dj) 25.00
HALLE,FANNINA-Women in the Soviet East-NY-1938-Dutton-8vo-363p-77 illus-1st US ed (dd5,tape rnfrcd dj) 35.00
HALLE,LOUIS F,JR.-Birds Against Men-NY-1938-Viking-8vo-228p-illus by L Ward-1st ed (aa5,dj) 30.00
HALLENBECK,CLEVE-Journey of Fray Marcos de Niza-Dallas-1949-U Pr-illus by Cisneros-ltd 1st ed (oo9,sl tn dj) 200.00
HALLENBECK,CLEVE-Land of the Conquistadors-Caldwell-1950-367p-drwngs,maps(1 fldg)-1st ed (u7,f,dj) 50.00
HALLENBECK,CLEVE-Legends of the Spanish SW-Glendale-1938-327p+index-illus,fldg map-1st ed (u7) 75.00
HALLENBECK,CLEVE-Spanish Missions of the Old Southwest-NY-1926-Dbldy-4to-184p+plts-119 half tones,11 illus-1st ed (d3,sl wn) 100.00
HALLENBECK,CLEVE-Spanish Missions of the Old Southwest-NY-1926-Dbldy-lg 4to-maps,photos,drwngs-1st ed (oo9) 85.00
HALLER,JAMES-Blue Strawberry Cookbook-np-(1975)-Harvard Common Pr-150p-illus wrps (l6) 12.00
HALLER,JOHN-Physician and Sexuality in Victorian America-Chig-1974-331p-1st ed (dd3,dj) 35.00
HALLET,JEAN-PIERRE-Animal Kitabu-NY-1967-8vo-292p-1st prntng (m3,vf,dj) 15.00
HALLETT,JEAN-PIERRE-Pygmy Kitabu-NY-(1973)-Random-8vo-434p-cl,illus (y5) 22.00
HALLGARTEN,PETER-Liqueurs-Lond-(1967)-Wine & Spirit Publ-135p-grn cl,pict e.p.-1st ed (q8,dj) 15.00
HALLIDAY & NOBLE-Hows and Whys of Cooking-1928-U of Chig Pr (v6,dj) 12.00
HALLIDAY,BRETT-Die Like a Dog-1959-Torquil-1st ed (s10,sp chip dj) 10.00
HALLIDAY,BRETT-Dolls are Deadly-NY-1960-Torquil-1st ed (f4,dj) 12.50
HALLIDAY,BRETT-Marked for Murder-1945-Dodd-1st ed (s10,dj) 22.50
HALLIDAY,BRETT-Murder and Wanton Bride-NY-1958-Torquil-1st ed (f4,sp chip dj) 10.00
HALLIDAY,BRETT-Taste for Violence-NY-1949-Dodd-1st ed (f4,dj) 15.00
HALLIDAY,F E-Cult of Shakespeare-NY-1960-Yoseloff-1st US ed (x9,f,dj) 15.00
HALLIDAY,W E-Forest Classification for Cananda-Ottawa-1950-Resource-50p-wrps (x6,wrps soil) 10.00
HALLOCK,CHARLES-An Angler's Reminiscences-Cin-1913-8vo-135p-photos-scarce (m3) 120.00
HALLOCK,CHARLES-Fishing Tourist-NY-1873-12mo-239p-illus (m3) 27.50
HALLOCK,CHARLES-Fishing Tourist-NY-1873-Harpers-1st ed (gg7) 65.00
HALLOCK,CHARLES-Our New Alaska-NY-1886-Forest & Stream Publ-209p-fldg map-1st ed (dd4) 50.00
HALLOCK,CHARLES-Sportsman's Gazetteer & General Guide-NY-1877-12mo-688p+208p index-illus,port frontis,brn cl-1st ed (m3,lacks fldg map) 25.00
HALLOCK,CHARLES-Sportsman's Gazetteer and General Guide-NY-1877-Forest & Stream-dec blu cl,2 fldg maps,rear pckt map-1st ed (dd6,sl rub) 45.00
HALLOCK,WILLIAM A-Memoir of Harlan Page-NY-(1835)-230p-lea-Sabin 29909 (n1) 17.50
HALLOWELL,RICHARD P-Quaker Invasion of Massachusetts-Bost-1883-Houghton Mifflin-12mo-227+16p (y6,sp chip,fade,papr brwng) 16.00
HALPER,ALBERT-Good Bye, Union Square-Chig-1970-Quadrangle-1st ed (w5,f,f dj) 20.00
HALSELL,H H-Cowboys and Cattleland-Dallas-nd-Wilkinson Prtg Co-237p-illus-Six Guns #978-3rd ed (cc4,sl wn dj) 60.00
HALSELL,H H-My Autobiography-(Dallas)-(1948)-(Wilkinson Prtg Co)-253p-illus,map-1st ed (cc4,dj,autg) 125.00
HALSELL,H H-My Philosophy of Life-Ft.Worth-1946-sm oblng-129p-1st ed (n10,f,dj,autg) 20.00
HALSEY,EDMUND D-Rockaway Township in the War of the Rebellion-Dover-1892-16p-wrps (aa6) 50.00
HALSEY,R T-Pictures of Early New York on Dark Blue Staffordshire Pottery-NY-1899-Dodd,Mead-vel,orig dj,ltd to 268c (l9) 500.00
HALSMAN,PHILIPPE-Halsman Sight and Insight-GC-1972-Dbldy-4to-cl-1st ed (y3,cor bump,f dj) 50.00
HALSMAN,PHILIPPE-Jump Book-NY-1959-photos-1st ed (r5,sl chip dj) 60.00
HALSMAN,PHILIPPE-Jump Book-NY-1959-Simon-4to-cl-1st ed (y3,fox dj) 55.00
HALSTEAD,MURAT-Our Country in War and Relations with All Nations-np-(1898)-611,(1);xl pgs-cl-illus,incl 24p col plts (j1) 15.00
HALSTEAD,MURAT-Story of Cuba-Akron-(1898)-Werner-649p-cl-6th ed (n1) 12.50
HALSTED,BYRON H-Barn Plans and Outbuildings-NY-1881-Orange Judd-235p-g dec cl,257 illus (x6,hngs rub) 125.00
HAMBLETON,JACK-Fisherman's Paradise-Tor-1946-8vo-172p-illus (m3,vf,dj) 15.00
HAMBLETON,JACK-Hunter's Holidays-Tor-1947-8vo-207p-photos (m3) 12.00
HAMBLIN,ROBERT W-Selections from the William Faulkner Collection of Louis Daniel Brodsky-1979-U Pr of Va-1st ed (q2,f,f dj) 35.00
HAMBY,W B-Case Reports and Autopsy Records of Ambroise Pare-Springfield-1960-214p-1st Engl transl (dd3,dj) 100.00
HAMID,GEORGE A-Circus-(1950)-Sterling-253p-illus-1st ed (v8,sl wn dj) 25.00
HAMIL,FRED C-Lake Erie Baron-Tor-1955-Macmillan-ix,326p-plts,ports (k10,fray dj) 30.00*
HAMIL,FRED C-Michigan in the War of 1812-Lansing-1960-Mich Hist Comm-44p-wrps,ltd to 1600c,photos,No.4 prtg (z7,ex-libr) 15.00
HAMILTON,ALEXANDER-Industrial and Commercial Correspondence of...Anticipating his Report on Manufactures-Chig-1928-A W Shaw-xxx+334p-blu cl-1st ed (e2) 25.00
HAMILTON,ALICE-Elements of John Updike-Grand Rapids-(1970)-Eerdmans-1st ed (h3,dj) 10.00
HAMILTON,ANTHONY-Hamilton's Campaign with Moore and Wellinton-Troy-1847-163p-brwn cl-1st ed (b7) 150.00

HAMILTON,BOB-Gene Autry and the Redwood Pirates-Racine-(1946)-Whitman-illus (m4,f,dj) 10.00

HAMILTON,BRUCE-To Be Hanged-NY-1930-Dbldy CC-1st US ed (g4) 12.50

HAMILTON,CHARLES W-Early Day Oil Tales of Mexico-Houston-(1966)-Gulf Publ-(viii)+246p-orng cl,drwngs-1st ed (j2,dj) 20.00

HAMILTON,CHARLES W-Early Day Oil Tales of Mexico-Houston-1966-246p-illus-1st ed (t7,f,dj) 15.00

HAMILTON,CHARLES-Auction Madness...-NY-(1981)-Everest Hs-1st ed (w1,dj) 20.00

HAMILTON,CHARLES-Book of Autographs-NY-(1978)-S&S-1st ed (w1,f,f dj) 20.00

HAMILTON,CHARLES-Collecting Autographs and Manuscripts-Norman-(1961)-269p-cl-illus-1st ed so stated (e1,sl fox,sl wn dj) 22.50

HAMILTON,COL J P-Travels Through the Interior Provinces of Columbia-Lond-1827-John Murray-12mo-2 vols,mod 1/2 mor & mrbld papr,5 raised bnds,sp labls,fldg map,7 engrvd plts-1st ed (mm1,rbnd,e.p. renewed) 495.00

HAMILTON,DONALD-Cruises with Kathleen-NY-1980-McKay-247p-blu papr over bds,illus-1st ed (p8,sl soil dj) 7.50

HAMILTON,DOUGLAS T-Shrapnel Shell Manufacture-NY-1915-Industrial Pr-296p-maroon cl,illus-1st ed (dd1) 25.00

HAMILTON,EDMOND-Star Kings-NY-(1949)-Frederick Fell-1st ed (e10,sp chip dj) 100.00

HAMILTON,EDWARD-Recollections of Fly Fishing for Salmon,Trout & Grayling-Lond-1884-12mo-190p-illus-1st ed (m3) 40.00

HAMILTON,G H-Art & Architecture of Russia-1954-Penguin Bks-plts-1st ed (h10,dj,box) 50.00

HAMILTON,GAIL-Twelve Miles From a Lemon-NY-1874-Harper & Bros-320p-cl-BAL 4727-1st ed (d1,cov sl flecked) 15.00

HAMILTON,GAIL-Twelve Miles from a Lemon-NY-1874-Harper & Bros-320p-cl-BAL 4727-1st ed (f1,cov sl flecked) 17.50

HAMILTON,GEORGE H-Art and Architecture of Russia-Balt-1954-Penguin Bks-4to-320p+180p plts,red cl-1st ed (r10,sl wn dj & box) 40.00

HAMILTON,HENRIETTA-Two Hundred Ghost-Lond-1956-Hodder-1st ed (e4,dj) 25.00

HAMILTON,HENRY W-Sioux of the Rosebud-Norman-(1971)-U of Okla Pr-320p-photos-1st ed (cc4,dj) 30.00

HAMILTON,IAN-Gallipoli Diary-NY-1920-2 vols-red cl,maps,illus-1st Amer ed (b7) 50.00

HAMILTON,J ARNOTT-Byzantine Architecture and Decoration-Lond-1956-Batsford-cl,illus-2nd ed (m8,f) 55.00

HAMILTON,J T-Beginnings of the Moravian Mission in Alaska-Phila-1890-23p-scarce-Wickersham 1240 (bb9) 95.00

HAMILTON,JAMES M-From Wilderness to Statehood-Portland-(1957)-620p-chapt decs,e.p. maps-1st ed (g7) 35.00

HAMILTON,JAMES-PWO Karen-St.Paul-(1960)-8vo-354p-cl-AES No.60-v scarce-1st ed (y5) 25.00

HAMILTON,RAPHAEL N-Marquette's Explorations-Bloomington-1970-275p-maps-1st ed (t7,dj) 20.00

HAMILTON,ROSS-ED.-Prominent Men of Canada, 1931 to 32-Montr-(1931)-Nat Publ Co-640p (k10) 30.00*

HAMILTON,THOMAS M-Young Pioneer-Wash D.C.-(1932)-284p-one illus-Adams Guns#908,Dykes#184-1st ed (v7,sp chip dj) 50.00

HAMILTON,W T-My Sixty Years on the Plains-Columbus-1951-244p-frntis,illus by C M Russell-Graff #1759 (t7,f) 37.50

HAMILTON,W T-My Sixty Years on the Plains-NY-1905-Forest & Stream-244p-pict cl,port,plts,incl 6 illus by C M Russell-1st ed (v1) 150.00

HAMLIN,T-Benjamin Henry Latrobe-NY-1955-OUP-104 illus,42 drwngs-1st ed (h10,dj) 50.00

HAMMER,ELLEN-Vietnam Yesterday and Today-NY-(1966)-282p-cl (h1) 10.00

HAMMER,H S-Dolomites-NY-1910-305p-16 col illus-1st US ed (q10,hng weak) 60.00

HAMMERSTEIN,OSCAR-Lyrics-NY-1949-S&S-1st ed (w1,f,f dj) 50.00

HAMMETT,DASHIELL-Battle of the Aleutians-(Adak)-(1944)-oblng 8vo-stapled blu illus wrps-1st ed (v10,cor creased,sl wn & soil) 100.00

HAMMETT,DASHIELL-Battle of the Aleutians-Adak-1944-oblng-24p-blu wrps,drwngs,maps-1st ed (c5,sl dampstnd f.e.p.) 275.00

HAMMETT,DASHIELL-Big Knockover-1966-Random-1st ed (s9,dj chip,sl tn) 30.00

HAMMETT,DASHIELL-Big Knockover-NY-1966-Random-1st ed (q2,dj) 60.00

HAMMETT,DASHIELL-Continental Op-Lond-1975-Macmillan-1st Brit ed (q4,pgs brwng,dj) 20.00

HAMMETT,DASHIELL-Continental Op-NY-(1974)-Random-1st ed (bb1,f,dj) 40.00

HAMMETT,DASHIELL-Continental Op-NY-1974-Random-1st ed (w9,f,sl creased dj) 30.00

HAMMETT,DASHIELL-Dain Curse-1929-Knopf-1st ed (x7) 385.00

HAMMETT,DASHIELL-Dain Curse-NY-1929-Knopf-8vo-tan cl stmpd in red & blk-1st ed wi "dopped in" on page 260,line 19 (x3) 125.00

HAMMETT,DASHIELL-Dashiell Hammett Story Omnibus-Lond-1966-Cassell-1st Brit ed (e8,f,f dj) 75.00

HAMMETT,DASHIELL-Glass Key-NY-nd-G&D-photoplay dj (u2,sl discol pgs,dj) 30.00

HAMMETT,DASHIELL-Maltese Falcon-1930-Knopf-1st ed (x7,sl stnd cov) 750.00

HAMMETT,DASHIELL-Man Called Spade-(Tor)-(1945)-Dell(map-back)-"Printed in Canada" on t.p.-(from 3rd Amer ed)-1st Can ed (gg8,sm sp rub) 30.00

HAMMETT,DASHIELL-Man Named Thin and Other Stories-NY-1962-Joseph W Ferman-wrps-1st ed (w5,sl wn) 50.00

HAMMETT,DASHIELL-Red Harvest-NY-(1929)-Grosset-reprint (h4,yel pgs,dj) 12.50

HAMMETT,DASHIELL-Red Harvest-NY-1929-Knopf-1st ed (e4,weak inner hnge,sp fade) 125.00

HAMMETT,DASHIELL-Red Harvest-NY-1929-Knopf-red cl-auth 1st bk-1st ed (gg7,sl sun,sp sl wn) 200.00

HAMMETT,DASHIELL-Thin Man-NY-(1934)-Grosset-reprint (h4,yel pgs,dj) 12.50

HAMMETT,DASHIELL-Woman in the Dark-NY-1951-Lawrence E Spivak Publ-prntd blu wrps,Jonathan Press Mystery,Softbound Orig-1st ed (q5) 45.00

HAMMITZSCH,HORST-Zen in the Art of the Tea Ceremony-NY-1980-St.Martin's-cl-1st Amer ed (o8,dj) 10.00

HAMMOND,CLARA T-Amarillo-Amarillo-1971-Geo Autry-369p-cl,illus,photos-1st ed (w3,f,autg) 55.00

HAMMOND,CLEON E-John Hart-Newfane-1977-xv,357p-cl,illus (aa6) 40.00

HAMMOND,GEORGE-Adventures of Alexander Barclay Mountain Man-Denver-1976-Old West Publ/Rosenstock-256p-illus (ee4,dj) 50.00

HAMMOND,GEORGE-Adventures of Alexander Barclay, Mountain Man-Denver-1976-246p-plts,3 fldg maps in pckt-1st ed (h7,f,dj) 75.00

HAMMOND,GEORGE-Coronado's Seven Cities-Albuq-1940-82p-stiff wrps,photos-1st ed (t7) 12.50

HAMMOND,GEORGE-Coronado's Seven Cities-Albuq-1940-82p-wrps,illus-1st ed (u7) 15.00

HAMMOND,GEORGE-Don Juan De Onate, Colonizer of New Mexico: 1595 to 1628-1953-U of NM Pr-4to-2 vols-maps-1st ed (d3,uncut) 200.00

HAMMOND,GEORGE-ED.-Larkin Papers for the History of California-Berkeley-1951 to 1964-UCP-10 vols (d3,uncut,f,dj) 600.00

HAMMOND,GEORGE-Gallegos Relation of Rodriguez Expedition to New Mexico-Santa Fe-1927-Hist Soc NM Publ,Vol.IV-66p-wrps,illus-scarce (u7,chip) 100.00

HAMMOND,GILBERT R-Wilfred Glenn or the Struggle with Wealth-Dayton-(1911)-Drury Prtg Co-269p-cl (b1) 20.00

HAMMOND,I B-Reminiscences of Frontier Life-Portland-1904-priv prtd-stiff wrps,illus-Six Guns #912-rare-1st ed (t7) 300.00

HAMMOND,JASON E-School Law of Michigan-Lansing-1895-126p-wrps (k1) 15.00

HAMMOND,JASON E-School Law of Michigan-Lansing-1896-126p-linen-2nd ed (j1) 12.50

HAMMOND,JOHN F-Surgeon's Report on Socorro New Mexico, 1852-Santa Fe-1966-47p-frntis,illus,ltd ed (t7,f,dj) 35.00

HAMMOND,JOHN M-Quaint and Historic Forts of North America-Phila-1915-Lippincott-308p-illus-1st ed (ee4) 125.00

HAMMOND,JOHN-On Record-NY-1977-Summit-1st ed (w1,f,dj) 20.00

HAMMOND,R B-Training & Hunting the Brittany Spaniel-S Brunswick-1971-8vo-166p-photos-1st ed (m3,vf,dj) 35.00

HAMMOND,S H-Hills,Lakes, and Forest Streams-NY-1854-J C Derby-1st ed (w8,edge wn) 65.00

HAMMOND,S H-Wild Northern Scenes-NY-1857-Derby & Jackson-brwn cl-1st ed (w8,edgw wn) 90.00

HAMMOND,S H-Wild Northern Scenes-NY-1967-Abercrombie & Fitch Libr-12mo-341p-illus (m3,vf,dj) 25.00

HAMMOND,S H-Wild Northern Scenes-Phila-1863-J E Potter-blu cl (gg7,rbnd) 50.00

HAMMOND,S T-My Friend the Partridge-NY-1908-Forest & Stream-148p-gry cl,photos-1st ed (ee3,sl drknd sp) 125.00

HAMMOND,WILLIAM A-Lal-NY-1884-D Appleton-466p+ads-cl-Wright 2430 (g1,sl wn) 25.00

HAMMOND,WILLIAM A-Strong Minded Woman-NY-1885-503p-cl,Wright 2434 (d1) 25.00

HAMOVITCH,MITZI B-Hound & Horn Letters-Athens-(1982)-U of Ga-1st ed (k7,f,f dj) 20.00

HAMPTON,J F-Hampton on Pike Fishing-Lond-1947-8vo-160p-illus (m3,f,dj) 12.50

HAMPTON,TAYLOR-Nickel Plate Road-Cleve-(1947)-World-366p-cl,frntis,illus,plts-1st ed (hh8,fox,autg) 20.00

HAMPTON,TAYLOR-Nickle Plate Road-(1947)-World-8vo-366p-illus (nn7,sl wn dj) 35.00

HAMSUN,KNUT-Women at the Pump-NY-1978-FSG-1st ed (f8,f,f dj) 30.00

HANAFORD,PHEBE A-Daughters of America-Augusta-nd-730p-cl (n1,sm sp snag,sl wn) 15.00

HANBY,BRAINERD O-Widow-Mt.Vernon-nd-43,(1)p-wrps (d1) 25.00

HANCHETT,WILLIAM-Irish-Syracuse-(1970)-208p-map-1st ed (n3,dj) 22.50

HANCOCK COUNTY-HISTORY OF...OHIO...-Chig-1886-880p-mor (pp6,sl wn sp) 100.00

HANCOCK,H IRVING-Jiu Jitsu Combat Tricks-NY,Lond-(1904)-Putnam-151p-cl,32 photos (m1) 15.00

HANCOCK,J-Herons of the World-1978-Harper Row-4to-304p-41 col plts,maps-1st US ed (bb3,f,dj) 85.00

HANCOCK,MRS W S-Reminiscences of Winfield Scott Hancock by His Wife-NY-1887-340p-lea,g edges,illus-1st ed (n3) 75.00

HANCOCK,RALPH-Fabulous Boulevard-NY-(1949)-Funk & Wagnalls-8vo-322p-1st ed (gg5,dj) 15.00

HANCOCK,SAMUEL-Narrative of...-NY-1927-217p-Map-Tweney #26-1st ed so stated (d7,f,chip dj) 60.00

HANDBOOK OF AMERICAN GLASS INDUSTRIES-1936-Brooklyn Mus-117p-wrps,illus (cc8) 75.00

HANDBOOK OF RHODODENDRONS-1946-U of Wash Arboretum Fndtn-vii,198p-photo onlay-ltd to 700c,nbrd (x5) 20.00

HANDFORTH,THOMAS-Tranquilina's Paradise-NY-(1930)-Minton,Balch-4to-cl/pict bds,illus-(text by Susan Smith) (pp10,cor wn,dj sl wn) 45.00

HANDKE,PETER-Goalie's Anxiety at the Penalty Kick-NY-(1972)-FS&G-1st bk publ in Engl-1st ed (b5,as new in dj) 30.00

HANDKE,PETER-Moment of True Feeling-NY-(1977)-FS&G-1st US ed (b5,as new in dj) 20.00

HANDKE,PETER-Sorrow Beyond Dreams-NY-(1975)-FS&G-1st US ed (bb1,as new in dj) 20.00

HANDLER,HANS-Spanish Riding School-NY-1972-McGraw Hill-folio-1st US ed (h9,dj) 195.00

HANDWRITING ON THE WALL OR REVOLUTION IN 1907-St.Louis-(1903)-P H Roberts-337p-cl (f1) 20.00

HANDY,AMY L-War Time Breads and Cakes-Bost-1918-Houghton Mifflin-66p-oil cl bds-Axford 414 (m6) 35.00

HANDY,MARY O-History of Fort Sam Houston-San Antonio-1951-Naylor-111p-photos-1st ed (a9,dj) 40.00

HANDY,NORMAN H-Savage South Seas-Lond-1907-Black-211p-blu cl,g dec cov,68 col pntngs by Handy,text by E W Elkington-1st ed (u8,sl rub,sunned sp & t.e.) 60.00

HANENKRAT,W F-Education of a Turkey Hunter-NY-1974-8vo-216p-illus,J M Roever (m3,f,dj) 14.50

HANESWORTH,ROBERT D-Daddy's of `Em All-Cheyenne-1967-168p-frntis,photos,illus-1st ed (t7,f) 35.00

HANEY,RBT-ET AL-Woodstock Handmade Houses-NY-1974-wrps,col illus-1st prtg (h10) 25.00

HANFF,HELENE-84, Charing Cross Road-NY-1970-Grossman-1st ed (w1,f,f dj) 45.00

HANFF,HELENE-Duchess of Bloomsbury Street-1973-Lippincott-1st ed (w4,dj) 35.00

HANFF,HELENE-Q's Legacy-1985-Little,Brown-1st ed (w4,dj) 15.00

HANFORD,C H-ED.-Seattle and Environs 1852 to 1924-Chig,Seattle-1924-Pioneer Hist Co-3 vols-photos,ports-Smith 4041-1st ed (w1) 150.00

HANFORD,H C-General Claxton-NY-1917-Neal Publ-blu cl-Smith #4038-1st ed (b6) 40.00

HANFT,ROBERT M-Pine Across the Mountain...California's McCloud River Railroad-San Marino-1972-224p-2nd ed (n4,f,dj) 25.00

HANKS,EPHRAIM K-Scouting for the Mormons on the Great Frontier-(SLC)-(1948)-298p-port-1st ed (bb8,sp sun dj) 35.00

HANKS,S W-Crystal River Turned upon the Black Valley Railroad and Black Valley Country-Bost-(1879)-213p-cl,illus(incl dbl pg col illus)-Wright 2443-1st ed (a1) 40.00

HANLE,ZACK-Cooking with Flowers-LA-(1971)-PS&S-sq 16mo-93p-dec pnk cl,col illus (q8,dj) 15.00

HANLEY,J FRANK-Day in the Siskiyous-Indpls-1916-Art Pr-4to-154p-cl,photos-1st ed (q3) 100.00

HANLEY,J FRANK-Day in the Siskiyous-Indpls-1916-sm 4to-154p-g pict cov,3 col frntis,38 photos (o10) 45.00

HANLEY,JAMES-Against the Stream-NY-(1981)-Horizon Pr-publ in Engl as "The House in the Valley"-1st ed (z8,vf,dj) 16.50

HANLEY,JAMES-An End and a Beginning-NY-(1958)-Horizon-1st ed (d10,sl soil dj) 35.00

HANLEY,JAMES-Dream Journey-NY-(1976)-Horizon Pr-1st Amer ed (z8,vf,sl scuff dj) 12.50

HANLEY,JAMES-Kingdom-Lond-1978-1st ed (y7,dj) 35.00

HANLEY,JAMES-Ocean-NY-1941-Morrow-1st ed (cc2,f,chip dj) 45.00

HANNA,BARRY-Two Stories-(1982)-Nouveau Pr-wrps-ltd to 200c,autg-1st ed (j3,f,wrps & dj) 50.00

HANNA,HILTON E-Pat Gorman Story...-Yonkers-1960-Amer Inst of Soc Science-416p-photos-1st ed (j8,f) 25.00

HANNAFORD,E-History and Description of our Philippine Wonderland and Photographic Panorama of Hawaii...-Springfield-1899-256p-cl-fldg map,illus (g1) 17.50

HANNAH,BARRY-Airships-NY-1978-Knopf-1st ed (a5,as new in dj) 60.00

HANNAH,BARRY-Black Butterfly-Winston Salem-(1982)-Palaemon-ltd to 150c,nbrd,autg-1st ed (s6,f,wrps) 75.00

HANNAH,BARRY-Geronimo Rex-NY-1972-auth 1st bk-1st ed (p5,f,dj) 100.00

HANNAH,BARRY-Nightwatchmen-NY-1973-1st ed (s5,dj) 45.00

HANNAH,BARRY-Ray-1980-Knopf-1st ed (p9,vf,dj) 15.00

HANNAH,BARRY-Ray-NY-1980-Knopf-1st ed (a5,as new in dj) 20.00

HANNAU,ILSE-ED.-Costanzo Pucillo's Recipes of the Famous Petite Marmite-Miami-(1970)-Argos-80p-pict bds,col & b&w photos-1st prtg (q8) 18.50

HANNAVY,JOHN-Roger Fenton of Crimble Hall-Bost-1975-Godine-sm folio-184p-cl,duotone illus-1st ed (t3) 40.00

HANNAY,JAMES-History of the War of 1812-St.John-1901-John A Bowes-8vo-400p-orig cl,9 maps in text-1st ed (u3,rub,sp fade) 120.00

HANNAY,JAMES-History of the War of 1812...-Tor-1905-Morang-xvi+372p-olive cl,illus,maps-1st ed (m2) 65.00

HANNEMAN,AUDRE-Ernest Hemingway-1969-Princeton Univ-2nd prtg (y10,f) 50.00

HANNON,JESSIE G-Boston Newton Company Venture-Lincoln-1969-Univ of Nebr-xvi+224p-red cl,illus,7 maps-1st ed (e2,dj) 25.00

HANNUM,ALBERTA-Paint the Wind-NY-1958-206p-col illus-1st ed (v7,f,dj) 20.00

HANO,ARNOLD-Sandy Koufax-1964-Putnam-1st ed (p7,dj) 10.00

HANO,ARNOLD-Willie Mays, the Say Hey Kid-1961-Bartholomew Hs-pbk orig-Sport Mag Libr #6-1st ed (s8) 12.50

HANO,ARNOLD-Willie Mays, the Say Hey Kid-1961-Bartholomew Hs-wrps (ff2,f) 15.00

HANOTEAU,GUILLAUME-Alps I Love-NY-1963-4to-photos(incl col)-1st ed (p10,f,dj) 12.00

HANS,FRED M-Great Sioux Nation-Chig-1907-575p-pict cl,frntis,illus-Graff #1771-1st ed (t7) 85.00

HANS,FRED M-Great Sioux Nation-Mpls-(1964)-Ross & Haines-586p-illus-ltd to 2000c-Howes H166 (cc4,wn dj) 25.00

HANSCOMBE,GILLIAN-Art of Life-Athens-1982-OU Pr-1st ed (z3,f,dj) 11.00

HANSEL,FRENCH K-Allergy of the Nose and Paranasal Sinuses-St.Louis-1936-820p-3 col plts (g10) 20.00

HANSELL,J E-Men Hunters of the North-Tacoma-1928-Tacoma Star-152p-red wrps wi illus of NW Mounty,port-rare (b6) 45.00

HANSEN,CHARLES-My Heart is in the Hills-Phila-1925-8vo-205p-photos (m3) 25.00

HANSEN,JOSEPH-Fadeout-1970-Harper-1st ed (m9,dj sp sl fade,sl rub & wn) 60.00

HANSEN,JOSEPH-Man Everybody Was Afraid Of-1978-Holt-1st ed (m9,f,dj) 20.00

HANSEN,JOSEPH-Skinflick-NY-(1979)-Holt-1st ed (f4,as new in dj) 15.00

HANSEN,JOSEPH-Skinflick-NY-(1979)-HR&W-1st ed (j3,f,dj) 20.00

HANSEN,MARCUS L-Old Fort Snelling 1819 to 1858-Iowa City-1918-Hist Soc of Iowa-270p-1st ed (dd4) 50.00

HANSEN,MARCUS L-Old Fort Snelling 1819 to 1858-Mpls-1958-Ross & Haines-270p-illus,map e.p.-ltd to 1500c (gg4,dj) 20.00

HANSEN,RON-Assassination of Jesse James by the Coward Robert Ford-NY-1983-Knopf-1st ed (dd2,f,dj) 30.00

HANSEN,RON-Desperadoes-NY-1979-Knopf-auth 1st bk-1st ed (b5,as new in dj) 35.00

HANSEN,T-Arabia Felix-1964-Harper Row-381p-illus,maps-1st ed (bb3,f,dj) 25.00

HANSEN,WOODROW J-Search of Authority in California-Oakland-1960-192p-illus,lg fldg map rear e.p.-1st ed (t7,f) 17.50

HANSER,RICHARD-Glorious Hour of Lt.Monroe-NY-1976-170p-cl-1st ed so stated (g1,f,dj) 12.50

HANSHEW,THOMAS W-Riddle of the Purple Emperor-NY-1919-Dbldy-1st US ed (d4,sp top wn) 25.00

HANSON,A E-Rolling Hills-Rolling Hills-1978-illus-ltd ed (h10) 45.00

HANSON,CHARLES E,JR.-Northwest Gun-Lincoln-1956-85p-frntis,photos-1st ed (t7,pres) 45.00

HANSON,E D-Origin and Early Evolution of Animals-1977-Wesleyan Univ-670p-illus-1st ed (bb3,f,dj) 35.00

HANSON,ELISABETH-My Poor Arthur-Lond-1959-Secker & Warburg & Chatto-300p-1st Brit ed (j8,f,dj) 25.00

HANSON,JAMES A-Buckskinners Cook Book-Chadron-1979-Fur Pr-60p-wht wrps,plastic comb bndg (n6) 20.00

HANSON,JAMES A-Metal Weapons, Tools, and Ornaments of the Teton Dakota Indians-Lincoln-(1975)-oblng-114p-dbl col,photos-1st ed (u7,f,dj) 25.00

HANSON,JOSEPH M-Conquest of the Missouri-Chig-1909-458p-pict bds,illus,fldg map-1st ed (g7,sl fade sp,sm edge stn) 75.00

HANSON,LAWRENCE-Noble Savage-NY-1955-Random-8vo-pict brwn cl (p8,f) 10.00

HANSON,RAUS M-Virginia Places Names, Derivations, Historical Uses-(1969)-McClure Pr-1st ed (dd9,dj) 20.00

HANSON,S C-Merry Songs for the School Room ...a Text book for the Teacher and an Instructor to the Pupil-Chig-(1889)-A Flanagan-117,(1)p-bds (h1,sl edge wn) 15.00

HAPGOOD,CHARLES H-Voices of Spirit-1975-Delacourt Pr/priv prtd-8vo-xii,336p-photos-1st prtg (aa7,dj) 15.00*

HAPGOOD,OLIVE C-School Needlework-Bost-1893-Ginn & Co-162p-illus bds,illus (u6) 25.00

HAPGOOD,RICHARD L-History of the Harvard Dental School-Bost-1930-Harvard U Dental Schl-xii+343p-red cl,plts-1st ed (d2,spot on cov) 35.00

HARADA,JIRO-Japanese Gardens-Lond-1956-Studio-160p-cl,photos (x6,f,dj) 25.00

HARADA,JIRO-Lesson of Japanese Architecture-Lond-1936-Studio-4to-192p-grn cl,illus (r10,sp drknd,sl wn) 50.00

HARBISON,P-ET AL-Irish Art & Architecture-Lond-1978-316 illus(incl 40 col) (h10,dj) 35.00

HARBOUR,DAVE-Hunting the American Wild Turkey-Harrisburg-1975-8vo-256p-photos (m3,vf,dj) 15.00

HARCOURT,HELEN-Florida Fruits and How to Raise Them-Louisville-1886-347p-orig g dec cl-rvsd & enlgd ed (jj7) 72.50

HARCOURT,ROBERT-Elementary Forge Practice-Peoria-1920-Manual Arts Pr-2nd ed (h9) 28.00

HARDAWAY,W A-Essentials of Vaccination-St.Louis-1886-46p-1st ed (dd3) 75.00

HARDEMAN,BENEDICT E-Everybody Called Him Cedric-Mpls-1971-Serendipity (v3,dj) 23.00

HARDEMAN,N P-Wilderness Calling-(1977)-U of TN-357p-illus,maps-1st ed (r8,f,f dj) 18.00

HARDEMAN,NICHOLAS-Wilderness Calling-(Knoxville)-(1977)-357p-cl,illus-1st ed (z1,f,dj) 30.00

HARDER,WARREN J-Daniel Drawbaugh-Phila-(1960)-Univ of Penn Pr-228p-brwn cl,61 illus-1st ed (j2,dj) 20.00

HARDIE,MARTIN-Our Italian Front-Lond-1920-Black-203p-dec blu cl,fldg map,50 col plts-1st ed (b7) 50.00

HARDIN,JOHN WESLEY-Life of...-Seguin-1896-Smith & Moore-144p-orig wrps,ports,illus-Adams,Guns 919-1st ed (v1) 150.00

HARDING,A B-Deadfalls and Snares-Columbus-(1907)-218,xv p-cl (n1) 15.00

HARDING,A B-Ginseng and Other Medicinal Plants-Columbus-(1908)-367p-cl (n1) 15.00

HARDING,BERTITA-Land Columbus Loved, the Dominican Republic-NY-(1949)-Coward McCann-8vo-246p-1st ed (ff5,sl tn dj) 12.50

HARDING,G LANKESTER-Antiquities of Jordan-NY-(1959)-Crowell-8vo-206p-31 plts-1st US ed (jj5,dj) 20.00

HARDING,LEE-ED.-Rooms of Paradise-NY-(1979)-St.Martin's-1st ed (h3,F,dj) 15.00

HARDING,STANLEY-Amateur Trapper-Chig-1917-12mo-135p+ads-wrps,illus (m3) 15.00

HARDING,THOMAS G-Voyagers of Teh Vitiaz Strait-Seattle-(1967)-U of Wash Pr-1st ed (y5,sl tn dj) 25.00

HARDING,WARREN-Downward Bound-Englewood-1975-204p-1st hdbk ed (o10,f,dj) 65.00

HARDWICK,ELIZABETH-Ghostly Lover-NY-(1945)-Harcourt-auth 1st bk-1st ed (j6,dj) 200.00

HARDWICK,ELIZABETH-Simple Truth-NY-(1955)-Harcourt,Brace-1st ed (a5,f,sl soil dj) 75.00

HARDWICK,ELIZABETH-Simple Truth-NY-(1955)-Harcourt,Brace-1st ed (u10,dj sl chip & tn) 50.00

HARDWICK,MICHAEL-Jolly Toper-Lond-(1961)-Jenkins-126p-blu cl,drwngs-1st ed (q8,dj) 15.00

HARDWICK,MICHAEL-Prisoner of the Devil-Lond,NY-1979-Proteus-1st ed (r4,f,dj) 25.00

HARDWICK,MICHAEL-Sherlock Holmes Companion-Lond-1962-John Murray-1st ed (w9,f,dj) 45.00

HARDY,CAPT CAMPBELL-Forest Life in Acadie-Lond-1869-Chapman & Hall-8vo-ix,371p-1/2 blk mor,11 plts-Sabin 30349 (u3,sl rub) 285.00

HARDY,CAPT H F H-Good Gun Dogs-Lond-1930-92p-16 plts (ee3,vf) 60.00

HARDY,LADY DUFFUS-Through Cities and Prairie Lands-NY-1890-338p-cl (b1,one leaf missng sm cor pc) 15.00

HARDY,RENE-Sword of God-GC-1954-Dbldy-pict dj-scarce-1st ed (ff3,sl tn dj) 65.00

HARDY,ROBIN-Wicker Man-NY-1978-Crown-1st ed (j4,f,dj) 20.00

HARDY,SIR W B-Collected Papers-Cambridge-1936-Cambridge U Pr-xii+922p-maroon cl,14 plts(incl col)-1st ed (a2,cov spot,sl bump) 85.00

HARDY,THOMAS-Group of Noble Dames-Lond-1891-Osgood,McIlvaine-orig g buff cl-1st ed,1st iss (kk5) 125.00

HARDY,THOMAS-Group of Noble Dames-NY-1891-g dec covs,illus-1st Amer ed (r2,f) 60.00

HARDY,THOMAS-Laodicean-1881-Holt-released same day as Brit ed,preceded by 2 unauthorized eds in wrps-1st Amer hdbk ed (x2,sl soil & wn) 150.00

HARDY,THOMAS-Late Lyric and Earlier-Lond-1922-Macmillan-gold stmpd olive grn cl-1st ed (cc2,sl chip dj) 125.00

HARDY,THOMAS-Life and Art-NY-1925-Greenberg-ltd to 2000c-1st ed (cc2,f,sl chip dj) 65.00

HARDY,THOMAS-Life's Little Ironies-Lond-1894-Osgood,McIlvaine-orig g grn cl-1st ed (kk5) 135.00

HARDY,THOMAS-Under the Greenwood Tree-NY-1940-Macmillan-sm 4to-x,236,(2)p-cl,engrvngs by C Leighton-1st US ed thus (w2,dj) 65.00

HARDY,THOMAS-Wessex Tales-Strange, Lively & Commonplace-1888-MacMillan-2 vols,3/4 lea wi g tooled dec sp,raised bands,marbld e.p.,t.p.e. in g gilt-1st ed (x2, rbnd) 850.00

HARDY,THOMAS-Winter Words-Lond-1928-Macmillan-1st ed (cc2,bump,sp sunned) 50.00

HARDY,THOMAS-Winter Words-NY-1928-vel sp,g lttrng-ltd to 500c,nbrd-1st Amer ed (r2,sp sun,rub,box rub,tn) 75.00

HARDY,WAL-Saltwater Angler-Sydney-1966-8vo-304p-photos,illus (m3,vf,dj) 25.00

HARDY,WILLIAM-Little Sin-NY-1958-Dodd-1st ed (h4,dj) 10.00

HARE,C E-Language of Field Sports-Lond-1949-8vo-276p-illus (m3) 15.00

HARE,CYRIL-Death Walks the Woods-1954-Little,Brown-1st Amer ed (s10,dj) 20.00

HARE,CYRIL-Untimely Death-NY-1958-Macmillan-1st US ed (g4,dj) 15.00

HARE,LLOYD C M-Salted Stories, the Story of the Whaling Fleets of San Francisco-Mystic-1960-Marine Hist Assn-lg 8vo-ix,114p-blu papr wrps,frntis,5 plts-1st ed (p8,sm stn rear cov) 30.00

HARE,LLOYD C M-Thomas Mayhew-NY-1932-D Appleton-4to-xiv+231p-blk cl,plts-1st ed (h2,sl spot & stnd cov,dj tn) 50.00

HARE,T LEMAN-ED.-National Gallery-NY-nd-Dodge Publ-quarto-2 vols,cl,100 tip in col plts (m1) 35.00

HARESNAPE,BRIAN-Railway Design Since 1830-Lond-1968-130p-Vol 1:1830 to 1914-1st ed (n4,f,dj) 26.00

HARESNAPE,BRIAN-Railway Design Since 1830-Lond-1969-128p-Vol.2: 1914 to 1969-1st ed (n4,f,dj) 25.00

HARESNAPE,BRIAN-Stanier Locomotives: a Pictorial History-Lond-1970-128p-1st ed (n4,f,dj) 16.50

HARGREAVES,REGINALD-Bloodybacks-NY-1968-368p-red cl-1st ed (gg2,f) 40.00

HARGREAVES,REGINALD-Red Sun Rising: the Siege of Port Arthur-NY-1962-210p-1st ed (b7,f,dj) 35.00

HARGRETT,LESTER-Gilcrease-Hargrett Catalogue of Imprints-Norman-1972-U of Okla Pr-400p-illus-1st ed (cc4,dj) 50.00

HARING,C H-Buccaneers in the West Indies in the XVII Century-NY-1910-Dutton-1st ed (z2,sp fade,sl fray) 45.00

HARK,ANN-Blue Hills and Shoofly Pie-(1952)-Lippincott-284p-blu cl,13 drwngs-1st ed (q8,chip dj) 15.00

HARKINS,PHILIP-Bomber Pilot-NY-1944-HB-1st ed (x1,dj edgewn) 30.00

HARLAN,J R-Iowa Fish & Fishing-1951-8vo-237p-col plts by M Reece-1st ed (m3,fray dj) 14.50

HARLAN,JACOB W-California '46 to '88-SF-1888-Bancroft-242p-frntis-Howes H198-1st ed (nn6) 150.00

HARLAND,MARIAN-Dinner Year Book-NY-(c.1878)-Scribner's-713p-grn bds,6 col plts-Bitting p.214 (a8,wn bds,hng weak) 45.00

HARLAND,MARION-Common Sense in the Household-Tor-1879-Belfords,Clarke & Co-319p-bds-Bitting 214 (n6,sl wn) 45.00

HARLAND,MARION-Common Sense in the Nursery-NY-1885-Scribners-205p wi index+ads,dec brwn cl-1st ed (w1) 50.00

HARLAND,MARION-Cookery for Beginners-Bost-(1884)-Lothrup-157p-Bitting 214 (k6,wn) 75.00

HARLAND,MARION-Dinner Year Book-(1878)-Scribners-713p-grn cl,6 col plts-1st ed (q8,sl wn,bndg weak,plt loose) 85.00

HARLAND,MARION-Dinner Year Book-NY-(1878)-Scribner's-713p-grn bds,dec sp,6 col plts-Bitting 214 (n6) 50.00

HARLING,ROBERT-Home:a Victorian Vignette-NY-1939-illus-1st ed (pp4,rprd dj) 15.00

HARLOW,ALVIN-Old Bowery Days-NY-1931-Appleton-565p-red cl,g titles,illus-1st ed (ee7) 75.00

HARLOW,ALVIN-Old Waybills-NY-1934-Appleton Century-504p-illus-Six Guns #924-1st ed (ee4) 50.00

HARLOW,ALVIN-Serene Cincinnatians-NY-1950-442p-cl-1st ed so stated (d1,sl wn dj) 25.00

HARLOW,ALVIN-Steelways of New England-NY-1946-461p-2nd prtg (n4,f,dj) 20.00

HARLOW,DANA D-Prairie Echoes-Aberdeen-1961-436p-1st ed (t7) 45.00

HARMON,GEORGE D-Sixty Years of Indian Affairs-Chapel Hill-1941-U of NC Pr-428p-1st ed (dd4) 30.00

HARMON,R W-Bibliography of Animal Venoms-Gainesville-1943-340p (dd3) 30.00

HARMSEN,DOROTHY-Harmsen's Western Americana-Flagstaff-1971-Northland-4to-col plts-1st ed (oo9,dj) 85.00

HARMSWORTH,LORD CECIL-Little Fishing Book-Lond-1942-16mo-126p-1st ed (m3,dj) 25.00

HARPENDING,ASBURY-Great Diamond Hoax...-SF-1913-James H Barry-283,(1)p-illus-1st ed (n2) 50.00

HARPER'S PICTORIAL HISTORY OF THE CIVIL WAR-Chig-(1866)-2 vols-illus,maps,fldg col map-1st ed (c4,fldg map tn) 250.00

HARPER,H W-Universal Recipe Book-Bost-1869-Geo Oakes & Co-292p-blu bds (n6,wn bds) 75.00

HARPER,H-Flying Witness-Lond-1958-8vo-272p-cl,frntis,10p plts-1st ed (t2,dj) 30.00

HARPER,H-Twenty-Five Years of Flying-Lond-nd(ca.1929)-roy 8vo-292p-cl,frntis,62p plts-1st ed (t2,sp fade) 75.00

HARPER,HENRY H-Library Essays About Books, Bibliophiles, Writers & Kindred Subjects-(1924)-priv prtd/Torch Pr-194p-blu cl,vel sp (w10,uncut) 25.00

HARPER,J RUSSELL-People's Art-1974-U of Tor Pr-4to-(x),176p-1st ed (aa7,sl chip dj) 50.00*

HARPER,JOHN W-An Old Fly Book & Other Stuff-Hartford-1913-12mo-154p-frontis (m3) 45.00

HARPER,MINNIE-Old Ranches-Dallas-1936-Dealey & Lowe-8vo-101p-stiff pict wrps,photos-Herd 994-1st ed (aa3) 45.00

HARPER,R S-Lincoln and the Press-NY-1951-418p-illus,ports (z10,dj) 30.00

HARPER,RALPH-World of the Thriller-1969-Case Western-1st ed (s10) 12.50

HARPER,RALPH-World of the Thriller-Cleve-1968-Case Wstrn Resrv U-139p-1st ed (g9,dj) 35.00

HARPER,VINCENT-Mortgage on the Brain-1905-Dbldy-pict cov,Bleiler-1st Amer ed (s10,hngs rprd) 20.00

HARRELSON,KEN-Hawk-1969-Viking-photos-1st ed (s8,f,dj) 20.00

HARRER,H-Seven Years in Tibet-NY-1954-Dutton-314p-photos,map-1st ed (bb3,dj) 10.00

HARRER,HEINRICH-Seven Years in Tibet-Lond-1953-1st Brit ed (o10,sp chip dj) 45.00

HARRER,HEINRICH-Seven Years in Tibet-NY-1954-314p-plts,map-rprnt (o10,f,dj) 15.00

HARRER,HEINRICH-White Spider-Lond-1977-310p-rvsd 2nd impr (o10,as new in dj) 50.00

HARRIMAN ALASKA EXPEDITION-NY-1901-vols 1 & 2,t.e.g.,col illus,photos by Curtis-1st ed (d7) 400.00

HARRIMAN,E ROLAND-ET AL-Gold Spike-NY-1969-118p-wrps-1st ed (n4) 12.50

HARRIMAN,MARGARET C-And the Price is Right-Cleve-(1958)-World-8vo-318p-1st ed (gg5,f,dj) 12.50

HARRINGTON,FRED H-Fighting Politician, Major General N P Banks-Phila-1948-301p-e.p. maps,illus-1st ed (c4,f,sl chip dj) 55.00

HARRINGTON,FRED H-Hanging Judge-Caldwell-(1951)-Caxton-204p-map e.p.-Six Guns #931-1st ed (dd4,dj) 50.00

HARRINGTON,H D-Manual of the Plants of Colorado-Denver-1954-sm 4to-x,666p-1st ed (j10,tattrd dj) 80.00

HARRINGTON,J P-Ethnogeography of the Tewa Indians-1916-Bur Amer Ethnol 29th Ann Rept-4to-21 plts,30 maps (bb3) 65.00

HARRINGTON,JOSEPH-Last Doorbell-Phila-1969-Lippincott-1st ed (e4,dj) 12.50

HARRINGTON,RICHARD-Face of the Arctic-NY-1952-Henry Schuman-369p-photos,maps-1st ed (j8,f,rprd dj) 35.00

HARRIS,A C-Alaska and the Klondike Gold Fields-(1897)-(G B Bertron)-566p-pict cl,illus,fldg map (gg4) 40.00

HARRIS,A C-Alaska and the Klondike Gold Fields-np-(1897)-528p-pict cov,illus,fldg map (u8,lacks 1/2 map,discol cov) 45.00

HARRIS,A C-Alaska and the Klondike Gold Fields-np-(1897)-528p-red sculpted lea,map (h2,sl wn,sm tear in map) 65.00

HARRIS,A-Bomber Offensive-NY-1947-8vo-288p-cl,e.p. maps-1st ed (t2) 25.00

HARRIS,ALBERT W-Cruise of a Schooner-Chig-1911-priv prtd-266p-pict cl,plts,map-Howes H221-scarce-1st ed (t7,autg) 65.00

HARRIS,ALBERT-Blood of the Arab-Chig-1941-AHC-4to-1st ed (j9) 125.00

HARRIS,BENJAMIN B-Gila Trail-Norman-(1960)-U of Okla Pr-175p-illus-1st ed (gg4,dj) 25.00

HARRIS,BURTON-John Colter, His Years in the Rockies-NY,Lond-1952-180p-e.p. maps-1st ed (c7,f,chip dj) 45.00

HARRIS,CHARLES T-Memories of Manhattan-1928-Derrydale-8vo-125p-ltd to 1000c,illus (m3) 45.00

HARRIS,CHARLES T-Memories of Manhattan-NY-1928-Derrydale-125p-illus,ltd to 1000c (gg3,f) 65.00

HARRIS,CHARLES W-Cowboy-Norman-1976-U of Okla-sm 4to-viii+167p-bds-rprnt ed (z4,dj) 25.00

HARRIS,CHAUNCY D-Salt Lake City-Chig-1940-priv ed,U of Chig Libr-xv,206p-orig prtd wrps,17 fldg maps rear pckt-1st ed (dd10) 65.00

HARRIS,CREDO F-Microphone Memoirs of the Horse and Buggy Days of Radio-(1937)-Bobbs Merrill-1st ed (kk9,f,dj) 35.00

HARRIS,EDWARD-Up the Missouri with Audubon. The Journal of...-Norman-(1951)-222p-cl-1st ed so stated (a1,dj) 30.00

HARRIS,FLORA-One Burner Cookery-NY-(1940)-Farrar & Rinehart-184p (u6,dj) 18.00

HARRIS,FOSTER-Look of the Old West-NY-1955-316p-illus-1st ed (c4,dj) 27.50

HARRIS,FRANK-"A Greene Countrie Towne"-Greenfield-1954-180p-cl-1st ed (h1) 15.00

HARRIS,FRANK-Bomb-NY-1909-M Kennerley-1st ed (w5,sp lettrng flake) 50.00

HARRIS,FRANK-Contemporary Portraits Fourth Series-NY-(1923)-1st ed (m4) 20.00

HARRIS,FRANK-Contemporary Portraits Second Series-NY-1919-ports-1st ed (m4,pres) 25.00

HARRIS,FRANK-Contemporary Portraits-1915-M,K-1st ed (x2) 25.00

HARRIS,FRANK-Hometown Chronicles-Greenfield-1955-246p-cl (h1,pres cpy) 17.50

HARRIS,FRANK-Mad Love-NY-1920-12mo-wrps-1st ed (m4,pres) 20.00

HARRIS,FRANK-Montes the Matador and Other Stories-NY-1910-M Kennerley-orig glassine dj-1st ed (k8,sl nick dj) 25.00

HARRIS,FRANK-My Reminiscences as a Cowboy-NY-1930-Chas Boni-12mo-217p-illus wrps,date on t.p.-Rampaging Herd #998-scarce (b6) 45.00

HARRIS,H-Robert Ridgway with a Bibliography of His Published Writings and Fifty Illustrations-1928-Condor-118p-wrps,photos (bb3) 10.00

HARRIS,JAMES E-X Raying the Pharaohs-NY-1973-Scribners-illus-1st ed (y10,sl tn dj) 28.00

HARRIS,JOEL C-Aaron in the Wildwoods-Bost-1897-Houghton Mifflin-dec tan cl,illus by Herford-1st ed (k8,sl drknd sp) 75.00

HARRIS,JOEL C-Evening Tales Done Into English from the French of Frederic Ortoli-NY-1893-Scribners-8vo-dec tan cl-BAL #7127-1st ed (p1) 75.00

HARRIS,JOEL C-Plantation Pageants-Bost,NY-1899-Houghton Mifflin-sm 4to-dec cl,illus by E Boyd Smith-BAL #7142-1st ed (p1) 85.00

HARRIS,JOEL C-Uncle Remus, His Songs and His Sayings-NY-1881-Appleton-8vo-231p-orig pict stmpd brick red cl,frntis,7 plts,text illus,8p ads in rear-auth 1st bk-BAL 7100-1st ed,1st issue (hh4,sl wn) 1,500.00

HARRIS,JOHN-Old Trade of Killing-1966-Sloane-1st Amer ed (s10,dj) 12.50

HARRIS,L-Butterflies of Georgia-1972-U of Okla-326p-10 col & 14 b&w plts-1st ed (bb3,f,dj) 15.00

HARRIS,MARK-Bang the Drum Slowly-1956-Knopf-1st ed (ff2,dj) 100.00

HARRIS,MARK-Goy-NY-1970-Dial-1st ed (a10,f,dj) 10.00

HARRIS,MARK-It Looked Like For Ever-1979-McGraw Hill-1st ed (n9,edgewn dj) 15.00

HARRIS,MARK-It Looked Like Forever-1979-McGraw Hill-1st ed (ff2,f,dj) 25.00

HARRIS,MARK-It Looked Like Forever-1979-McGraw Hill-1st ed (s8,f,dj) 20.00

HARRIS,MARK-Mark the Glove Boy-1964-Macmillan-1st ed (s9,f,sl stnd dj) 25.00

HARRIS,MARK-Something About a Soldier-NY-1957-Macmillan-1st ed (x1,sl soil dj) 30.00

HARRIS,MARK-Southpaw-1953-Bobbs Merrill-1st ed (ff2,dj) 125.00

HARRIS,MARK-Ticket for a Seamstich-1957-Knopf-1st ed (p7,dj) 40.00

HARRIS,MARK-Trumpet to the World-NY-1946-auth 1st bk-1st ed (t5,sl chip dj) 45.00

HARRIS,MARK-Wake Up Stupid-Lond-1960-Andre Deutsch-1st Brit ed (y1,dj) 20.00

HARRIS,MEL-Naked Hollywood-NY-(1953)-Pellegrini-4to-cl-1st ed (y3,f,dj) 75.00

HARRIS,NATHANIEL E-Autobiography-Macon-1925-J W Burke Co-(ii)+550p-grn cl,illus-1st ed (h2) 75.00

HARRIS,REV W S-Capital and Labor-Harrisburg-1907-Minter Co-illus by P Krafft-1st ed (w5) 45.00

HARRIS,SEALE-Woman's Surgeon-NY-1950-Macmillan-xx+432p-gry cl,plts-1st ed (c2,dj) 20.00

HARRIS,T M-Assassination of Lincoln, a History of the Great Conspiracy-Bost-(1892)-Amer Cit-424p-blu cl,plts-1st ed (mm10) 125.00

HARRIS,THOMAS-Red Dragon-(1981)-Putnam-1st ed (n9,f,f dj) 45.00

HARRIS,THOMAS-Red Dragon-NY-(1981)-Putnam's-1st ed (a5,f,dj) 65.00

HARRIS,TIMOTHY-Kronski/McSmash-GC-1970-auth 1st bk-1st ed (n5,f,f dj) 65.00

HARRIS,TOWNSEND-Complete Journal of...-Rutland,Tokyo-(1959)-616p-illus-rvsd ed (j7,f,dj) 40.00

HARRIS,W JEFFERSON-History of Bourbon King 1788-(Cleve)-(1934)-221p-cl (a1) 15.00

HARRIS,W S-Sermons by the Devil-np-(1904)-304p-cl (f1) 12.50

HARRIS,W T-Springs of Mende Belief and Conduct-Freetown-1968-Sierra Leone U Pr-8vo-152p-cl,illus-1st ed (y5,f,f dj) 25.00

HARRIS,WILLIAM W-Battle of Groton Heights...on the Sixth of September, 1781-New London-1882-Chas Allyn-399p-blu cl,illus,maps-revsd & enlgd-2nd ed (m2,frnt inner hng sl exposed) 80.00

HARRISON,BENJAMIN S-Fortune Favors the Brave-LA-1953-307p-photos-1st ed (t7,cor bump) 15.00

HARRISON,BENJAMIN S-Fortune Favors the Brave-LA-1953-W Ritchie Pr-xvi+307p-red/brwn cl,plts-1st ed (k2,dj) 35.00

HARRISON,BENJAMIN-Speeches of...-NY-1892-U.S. Book-lg 12mo-580p-1st ed (p2) 20.00

HARRISON,C-Gold Mine in the Front Yard-1905-Webb-279p (x6) 10.00

HARRISON,ERIC-Riding-Lond-1949-Lehman-illus,J Board-1st ed (j9,dj) 18.00

HARRISON,F-Painted Glass of York-Lond,NY-1927-253p-56 illus(incl col)-1st ed (cc8,tn dj) 65.00

HARRISON,FRED-Hell Holes and Hangings-Clarendon-1968-Clarendon Pr-(xiv),170p-cl,photos-1st ed (v1,dj) 45.00

HARRISON,G B-Trial of the Lancaster Witches A.D. MDCXII-Lond-1929-Peter Davies-sm 8vo-(xlviii)+188+(4)p-cream buckrm-1st ed (y9) 45.00

HARRISON,GEN SIR RICHARD-Recollections of a Life in the British Army-Lond-1908-382p-red cl,illus-1st ed (jj2) 200.00
HARRISON,GEORGE-I Me Mine-NY-1980-1st US ed (r5,dj) 22.50
HARRISON,HARRY-ED.-Nova 4-NY-(1974)-Walker-1st ed (h3,f,dj) 15.00
HARRISON,HARRY-Skyfall-NY-1977-Atheneum-1st ed (k3,f,dj) 25.00
HARRISON,JIM-Farmer-NY-(1976)-1st ed (d5,as new in dj) 30.00
HARRISON,JIM-Good Day to Die-NY-(1973)-S&S-1st ed (l7,dj) 225.00
HARRISON,JIM-Good Day to Die-NY-(1973)-S&S-scarce-1st ed (bb1,sl cocked sp,f dj) 200.00
HARRISON,JIM-Legends of the Fall-Lond-1980-Collins-1st Brit ed (a10,f,dj) 40.00
HARRISON,JIM-Legends of the Fall-Lond-1980-Collins-1st Brit ed (s9,f,dj) 35.00
HARRISON,JIM-Legends of the Fall-NY-1979-1st ed (t5,sl stnd dj) 40.00
HARRISON,JIM-Letters to Yesenin-Fremont-1973-Sumac Pr-wrps-ltd to 1126c of which 1000c are in wrps-1st ed (b8,sl soil cov) 150.00
HARRISON,JIM-Locations-NY-(1968)-Norton-1st ed (a10,f,dj) 125.00
HARRISON,JIM-Locations-NY-1968-1st ed (s5,vf,dj) 75.00
HARRISON,JIM-Selected & New Poems 1961 to 1981-(NY)-(1982)-ltd to 250c,nbrd,autg-1st ed (m5,as new in box) 100.00
HARRISON,JIM-Warlock-(NY)-(1981)-1st ed (d5,as new in dj) 30.00
HARRISON,JIM-Wolf-NY-(1971)-1st ed (h5,f,dj) 45.00
HARRISON,KENNETH-Windows of Kings College Chapel-1952-Cambridge Univ Pr-90p-1st ed (cc8,dj) 25.00
HARRISON,MERTON E-Autobiography of Dan Patch-1912-Priv Prtd-186p-wrps-1st prtg (f10,cov soil) 65.00
HARRISON,MICHAEL-In the Footsteps of Sherlock Holmes-NY-1960-illus-1st ed (r2,f,dj) 30.00
HARRISON,MICHAEL-Theatrical Mr.Holmes-1974-Covent Gardens-wrps,ltd to 750c (s10) 25.00
HARRISON,MICHAEL-World of Sherlock Holmes-NY-1975-Dutton-illus-1st US ed (h4,f,dj) 15.00
HARRISON,PELEG D-Stars and Stripes and Other American Flags-Bost-1906-Little,Brown-8vo-g dec blu cl,illus,incl col-1st ed (t1) 50.00
HARRISON,W P-ED.-Gospel Among the Slaves-Nashville-1893-394p-cl (b1) 50.00
HARRISON,WALTER M-War Years-Okla City-1945-priv prtd-plain wraparound dj (z2,f,dj) 40.00
HARRISON,WILLIAM-Africana-NY-1977-1st ed (q5,dj) 12.50
HARRISON,WILLIAM-In a Wild Sanctuary-NY-1969-Morrow-1st ed (a5,f,dj) 20.00
HARRISON,WILLIAM-Lessons in Paradise-NY-1971-1st ed (q5,dj) 22.50
HARRISON,WILLIAM-Savannah Blue-NY-1980-1st ed (q5,f,dj) 12.50
HARRISON,WILLIAM-Theologian-NY-(1965)-Harper & Row-1st ed (a5,f,dj) 40.00
HARRON,ROB'T-Rockne-NY-1931-Burt-240p+stats,photos (p2,sl spot,fade) 10.00
HARSHBERGER,JOHN W-Vegetation of the New Jersey Pine Barrens-Phila-1916-xi,329p-cl,illus,fldg maps (aa6) 100.00
HART,ALBERT B-Salmon Portland Chase-Bost-1899-Amer Statesmen Ser-465p+ads-1st ed (n3) 30.00
HART,B H LIDDELL-ED.-Letters of Private Wheeler-Lond-1951-287p-1st ed (gg2,f,dj) 30.00
HART,CAROLYN-Settling of Accounts-NY-1976-Dbldy CC-1st ed (l4,f,sl wn dj) 20.00
HART,FRANCES N-Pigs in Clover-GC-1931-Dbldy,Doran-297p (k6,soil,wn) 14.00
HART,FRANCIS R-Siege of Havana 1762-Bost-1931-54p-blu cl,illus,fldg map-ltd to 675c-1st ed (kk2,box) 75.00
HART,GEORGE-Violin-Lond-1880-Dulau-sm 8vo-310p-g dec brwn cl,illus-"Popular Edition" from 1st ed of 1875 (s1) 50.00
HART,HAROLD H-Big Time Baseball-NY-1950-Hart-lg 8vo-192p-wrps,illus,photos (y4,sl wn) 30.00
HART,HERBERT M-Old Forts of the Northwest-(1963)-Superior-192p-photos,map-1st ed (r8,dj) 35.00
HART,HERBERT M-Old Forts of the Southwest-(1964)-Superior-4to-192p-illus-1st ed (t8) 18.00
HART,HERBERT M-Old Forts of the Southwest-Seattle-(1964)-192p-illus,maps-1st ed (n3,f,dj) 22.50
HART,HERBERT M-Pioneer Forts of the West-(1967)-Superior-192p-photos-1st ed (r8,dj) 35.00
HART,HERBERT M-Pioneer Forts of the West-Seattle-(1967)-Superior-192p-photos,drwngs-4th in Wstrn Forts ser-1st ed (cc4,sl wn dj) 20.00
HART,JERREMS C-Cruising Guide to the Caribbean and the Bahamas-NY-1976-Dodd,Mead-8vo-578p-blu cl over bds,chrts,maps (p8) 9.50
HART,JOHN-14000 Feet-Denver-1925-53p-wrps-1st ed (o10,f) 90.00
HART,MOSS-Winged Victory-NY-1943-Random-1st ed (v5,f,sl tn dj) 35.00
HART,WILLIAM S-Golden West Boys-Bost-1921-278,(1)p-cl,illus,H Cue-1st ed (c1,sl rub) 15.00
HART,WILLIAM S-My Life East and West-Bost-1929-Houghton Mifflin-8vo-col frntis port by C M Russell,photos-Herd 1005-1st ed (aa3,sl chip dj) 85.00
HART,WILLIAM S-My Life East and West-Bost-1929-Houghton Mifflin-cl,photos,col frntis,-1st ed (v1) 65.00
HART,WILLIAM S-Pinto Ben...-NY-1919-illus-1st ed (d3) 15.00
HARTE,BRET-Barker's Luck, Etc-1896-C&W-39 illus-1st Brit ed (x2) 35.00
HARTE,BRET-Bell Ringer of Angel's and Other Stories-Bost-1894-Blanck 7372-1st ed (d3) 25.00
HARTE,BRET-Condensed Novels-1902-Houghton-1st ed (s10) 67.50
HARTE,BRET-On the Frontier-Bost-1884-Houghton,Mifflin-12mo-blu cl-BAL 7327-1st ed (f2) 25.00
HARTE,BRET-Salomy Jane-Bost-1910-Houghton Mifflin-blu dec bds-1st ed (h8) 50.00
HARTE,BRET-Salomy Jane-NY-1910-78p-dec cl,col illus,illus by H Fisher & A Keller (t7,f) 22.50
HARTE,BRET-Tales of the Argonauts-Bost-1875-James R Osgood-grn cl-Blanck's prntg A-BAL 7280-1st ed (f2) 30.00
HARTE,BRET-Tales of the Gold Rush-NY-1944-Heritage Pr-223p-cl & bds,illus-1st ed thus (t7) 15.00
HARTE,BRET-Wild West-1930-Harrison of Paris-col illus-ltd to 840c,nbrd (d3) 125.00
HARTE,GEOFFREY-Island in the Sun-Bost-1937-Little,Brown-8vo-319p-illus-1st ed (cc5,dj) 30.00
HARTLAND,EDWIN S-Primitive Paternity-Lond-1909-David Nutt-2 vols-cl-1st ed (o8) 95.00

HARTLEY,HOWARD H-Tragedy of Sand Cave-Louisville-1925-Standard Prntng Co-159,(3)p-wrps (h1,rprd sm tears) 20.00

HARTLEY,L P-Travelling Grave and Other Stories-Sauk City-1948-Arkham Hs-ltd to 2047c-1st ed (ee6,dj) 75.00

HARTLEY,OLIVER-Hunting Dogs-Columbus-1909-12mo-251p-illus-1st ed (m3) 14.00

HARTMAN,JOAN-Chines Jade of Five Centuries-Rutland-1969-Tuttle-172p-drk grn emboss silk cl,g sp,45 b&w photos,10 col plts-1st prtg (u5,f,f dj) 35.00

HARTMAN,S B-Confidential Physician-Columbus-(1898)-220,(2)p-wrps-rvsd ed (l1) 15.00

HARTNETT,MICHAEL-Poems in English-Dublin-(1977)-Dolmen Pr-1st ed (z8,vf,dj) 50.00

HARTNEY,H E-Up and At 'Em-Harrisburg-(1940)-roy 8vo-334p-cl,frntis,6p plts-1st ed (t2,sl stnd) 50.00

HARTWELL,JONATHAN-Plants Used Against Cancer-Lawrence-1982-Qtrmn Publ-8vo-viii,440p-1st ed (ff9,as new in dj) 75.00*

HARTWIG,G-Dwellers in the Arctic Regions-Lond-1887-Longmans-8vo-158p-red calf wi raised bands & g floral decs,blk lea labl,g dentelles,mrbld e.p. & edges,28 plts-1st ed (u1,sl fox) 125.00

HARTWIG,G-Polar and Tropical Worlds-Columbus-1876-Geo G Watrous-811p-3/4 lea-illus-2 vols in one as issued (j1,joints reinfrcd wi blk tp) 20.00

HARTWIG,G-Polar and Tropical Worlds-Springfield-1873-Bill Nichols-xx,803p-200 illus-New ed (o2,sl dull) 35.00

HARTZ,RUTHERFURD S-Airplane Mechanics Rigging Handbook-NY-(1930)-Ronald Pr-267p-cl,illus (m1,dj) 15.00

HARVARD,ANDREW-Mountain of Storms-1974-NYU Pr-4to-(8),(2),210p-photos(incl 16 col),2 maps-1st ed (ll1,sl chip dj) 40.00

HARVARD,ANDREW-Mountain of Storms-NY-1974-210p-1st ed (p10,f,dj) 25.00

HARVEY,A K P-In the Glow of the Camp Fire-Bost-1903-12mo-159p-illus (m3) 35.00

HARVEY,A N-Tales and Trails of Wakarusa-Topeka-1917-Crane & Co-96p-cl (m1,autg) 15.00

HARVEY,A-Journey in Ladakh-Bost-1983-236p-1st US ed (o10,f,dj) 20.00

HARVEY,B-Portfolio of New Zealand Birds-Wellington-1970-folio-60p-cl,25 col plts (y8,dj) 65.00

HARVEY,BASIL-Rifle Brigade-Lond-1975-130p-illus-Famous Regiment ser-1st ed (gg2,f,dj) 25.00

HARVEY,BYRON-Ritual in Pueblo Art-NY-1970-Heye Found-plts-1st ed (oo9,dj) 65.00

HARVEY,CLARA T-Not So Wild the Old West-Denver-1961-398p-1st ed (t7,f) 37.50

HARVEY,E NEWTON-Nature of Animal Light-Phila-(1920)-Lippincott-x+182p-red cl-1st ed (c2) 20.00

HARVEY,N P-Medieval Gardens-Beaverton-1981-Timber Pr-sm 4to-199p-11 col plts,maps,illus-1st ed (mm4,f,dj) 40.00

HARVEY,PEGGY-Horn of Plenty-(1964)-Little,Brown-284p-prpl cl (q8,dj) 15.00

HARVEY,PEGGY-Season to Taste-1957-Knopf-268p-gry cl-1st ed (q8,wn dj) 16.50

HARVEY,WILLIAM,M.D.-Works of...Translated from the Latin with a Life of the Author by Robert Willis-Lond-1847-624p-1st ed (dd3) 300.00

HARVEY,WILLIAM-Anatomical Exercises of Dr.William Harvey-Lond-1928-Nonesuch Pr-gilt mor-ltd to 1450c (dd3) 325.00

HARVEY,WILLIAM-De Motu Locali Animalium, 1627-Cambridge-1959-4to-163p-ltd ed (dd3,dj) 100.00

HARVEY,WILLIAM-Movement of the Heart and Blood in Animals-Springfield-1957-209p-ltd ed (dd3,dj) 60.00

HARVIE,K G-Tramways of South London & Croydon 1899 to 1949-Lond-1968-122p-wrps-4th ed (n4) 30.00

HARVIE-BROWN,J A-Wonderful Trout-Edinburgh-1898-12mo-173p-illus (m3) 35.00

HARWELL,RICHARD B-ED.-Union Reader-NY-(1958)-362p-illus-1st ed (c4,dj) 30.00

HARWELL,RICHARD-Lee: An Abridgement in One Volume of the Four Volume R E Lee by D S Freeman-NY-1961-Scribners-1st ed (o7,tn dj) 25.00

HARWELL,RICHARD-War They Fought-NY-1960-Longmans,Green-362p-1st ed thus (o7,f,f dj) 25.00

HARWOOD,ALAN-Witchcraft, Sorcery, and Social Categories among the Safwa-Lond-1970-OUP-8vo-160p-cl,illus-1st ed (y5,f,dj) 22.50

HARWOOD,HERBERT H,JR.-Blue Ridge Trolley-San Marino-1970-144p-1st ed (n4,f,dj) 22.00

HASHAGEN,ERNST-U Boats Westward-NY-1931-247p-illus-1st ed (jj2,f,dj) 60.00

HASKELL,BARBARA-Arthur Dove-(1974)-NYGS-sq 4to-136p-cl,63 col & 43 b&w illus-1st ed (l10,f,dj) 27.50

HASKELL,FRANK A-Battle of Gettysburg-Nov 1908-Wisc Hist Comm-185p-ltd to 2500c-Nevins I,31 (bb4,sl soil cov) 50.00

HASKELL,H C-City of the Future-KC-(1950)-Glenn-193p-illus-1st ed (u8,sl wn) 30.00

HASLUCK,PAUL-ED.-Harness Making-Phila-1904-McKay-12mo-illus-1st ed (h9,cor & sp wn) 85.00

HASLUCK,PAUL-Saddlery-Phila-1904-McKay-1st ed (h9,hng crack) 65.00

HASLUND,HENNING-Tents in Mongolia-1934-Dutton-366p-64 photos,map (bb3,f) 45.00

HASLUND,HENNING-Tents in Mongolia-NY-1934-366p-64 plts,map-1st US ed (o10) 25.00

HASSANEIN,A M-Lost Oases-NY-(1925)-Century-8vo-363p-91 illus-1st US ed (jj5,f,dj) 45.00

HASSLER,EDGAR W-Old Westmoreland-Pitt-1900-J R Weldin-grn cl-Howes H286-1st ed (mm10) 100.00

HASSLER,W W-A P Hill:Lee's Forgotten General-Richmond-1957-249p-illus,maps,ports-1st ed (z10) 45.00

HASSRICK,ROYAL B-George Catlin Book of American Indians-NY-(1977)-Watson Guptill-sm folio-207p-col illus-1st ed (gg4,dj) 40.00

HASSRICK,ROYAL B-Sioux-Norman-(1964)-U of Okla Pr-337p-illus-1st ed (bb4,dj) 50.00

HASTINGS,FRANK S-Ranchman's Recollections-Chig-1921-Breeders Gazette/Lakeside-12mo-xiii,235p-pict cl,illus,photos-Howes H287-1st ed (aa3,tan spot sp,pg bent) 175.00

HASTINGS,MACDONALD-Cork on the Water-NY-1951-8vo-186p-map frontis (m3,f,dj) 20.00

HASTINGS,SALLY-Poems on Different Subjects-Lancaster-1808-Wm Dickson-12mo-220p-contemp calf-Sabin 30826-1st ed (w6,sp chip,joints tender) 375.00

HASTINGS,SAMUEL D-ED.-People Versus the Liquor Traffic...Speeches of John B Finch...-Chig-(1883)-285p-cl-6th ed (a1,cov spot) 15.00

HASTON,DOUGAL-In High Places-NY-1973-Macmillan-12mo-168p-blk cl,photos-1st prtg (ll1,f,dj) 20.00

HATCH,A-Glenn Curtiss. Pioneer of Naval Aviation-NY-1942-roy 8vo-x,294p-cl,frntis,22p plts-1st ed (t2,chip dj) 45.00

HATCH,ALDEN-American Express a Century of Service-1950-287p-pict cl,photos,illus-1st ed (t7) 10.00

HATCH,ALDEN-Byrds of Virginia-(1969)-HR&W-535p-illus-1st ed (dd9,dj) 20.00

HATCH,JOHN-History of Britain in Africa-NY-1969-Praeger-8vo-320p-1st US ed (ff5,f,f dj) 15.00

HATCH,P L-Notes on the Birds of Minnesota-1892-Minn Nat Hist Survey-487p-cl (bb3,rbnd) 30.00

HATCH,P L-Notes on the Birds of Minnesota-Mpls-1892-Geo & Nat Hist Sur-8vo-487p-half mor (y8,scuff) 33.00

HATCH,TED-American Wine Cook Book-(1941)-Putnam-315p-tan cl-1st ed (q8,dj tn) 20.00

HATCHER,HARLAN-Century of Iron and Men-Indpls-(1950)-295p-cl-1st ed (h1,sl wn dj) 15.00

HATCHER,JOHN B-Ceratopsia-Wash D.C.-1907-GPO/USGS Mono Vol.49-4to-xxx+300p+ii-brwn cl,51 plts-1st ed (g2) 135.00

HATCHER,JULIAN-Book of the Garand-Wash D.C.-1948-8vo-292p-illus,photos-1st ed (m3) 30.00

HATFIELD,AUDREY W-Pleasures of Herbs-NY-(1965)-186p-45 drwngs by auth-1st ed (x5,dj chip,tn) 17.00

HATFIELD,EDWIN A-History of Elizabeth, New Jersey-NY-1868-701p-cl,plts (aa6,cl sl spot,stnd) 150.00

HATHAWAY,CYNTHIA-Two Bridgets-GC-1941-Dbldy,Doran-4to-unpgd-cl bckd pict bds,col & b&w illus-1st ed (r3) 20.00

HATTAWAY,HERMAN-How the North Won-Urbana-(1983)-762p-illus,maps-1st ed (n3,dj) 25.00

HATTAWAY,HERMAN-How the North Won-Urbana-1983-U of Ill Pr-762p-illus,maps (o7,dj) 25.00

HAUCK,RICHARD B-Crockett, a Bio Bibliography-Westport-1982-Greenwood-169p-1st ed (a9) 25.00

HAUGE,EILIV-Flight From Dakar-NY-(1954)-Dutton-8vo-200p-photos-1st US ed (jj5,dj) 12.50

HAUS,ANDREAS-Moholy-Nagy, Photographs & Photograms-NY-1980-Pantheon-(227)p-150 photos-1st Amer ed (cc9,as new in dj) 50.00

HAUSCHILD,HENRY-ED.-Victoria Sesquicentennial "Scrapbook",1824 to 1974-Victoria-1974-Advocate Prtg-95p-cl,photos-1st ed (w3,vf) 25.00

HAUSHALTER,WALTER M-Mrs.Eddy Purloins from Hegel-Bost-1936-A A Beauchamp-viii+126p+14p facs-blu cl-1st ed (b2) 25.00

HAUSMAN,GERALD A-No Witness-Harrisburg-1980-Stackpole-8vo-223p-1st ed (z4,dj) 12.50

HAUSMAN,GERALD-Sitting on the Blue Eyed Bear-Westport-(1975)-130p-drwngs-1st ed (v7,f,dj) 20.00

HAUSMAN,L A-Birds of Prey of Northeastern North America-New Brunswick-1948-8vo-(1),164p-cl,col frntis,31 drwngs (y8,dj chip) 35.00

HAUSMAN,L A-Birds of Prey of Northeastern North America-Petersborough-1966-Smith-drwngs-2nd ed,rvsd & enlgd (b9) 12.50

HAVEN,CHARLES T-History of the Colt Revolver...-NY-1940-Morrow-xxiv+711p-grn cl,illus-Howes H308-1st ed (mm10,dj) 125.00

HAVEN,E O-Common Schools Unsectarian-Ann Arbor-1853-Washtenaw Whig Pr-21p-prntd wrps (k1,sl wn & soil) 25.00

HAVERSCHMIDT,F-Birds of Surinam-Edinburgh,Lond-1968-4to-cl,1 fldg map,30 plain & 40 col plts-scarce (y8,dj chip) 465.00

HAVERSTOCK,MARY S-An American Bestiary-NY-1979-Abrams-248p-orng cl,illus (mm1,as new in dj) 45.00

HAVERTY,MARTIN-History of Ireland-NY-(1885)-Thos Kelly-lg 8vo-(22),882,34p-1/2 lea,g stmpd,mrbld e.p.,col lithos,2p col map (m4,rub) 95.00

HAVIGHURST,WALTER-Land of Promise-NY-1946-384p-map e.p.-1st ed (t7) 7.50

HAVIGHURST,WALTER-Land of Promise-NY-1946-Macmillan-384p-map e.p.-1st ed (cc4,dj rprd & chip) 20.00

HAVIGHURST,WALTER-Long Ships Passing-NY-1942-Macmillan-291p-map,drwngs-1st ed (o2,autg) 20.00

HAVIGHURST,WALTER-Upper Mississippi-NY-1944-305p-illus-River of Amer Ser-1st ed (t7) 7.50

HAVILAND,MAUD D-Summer on the Yenesei-Lond-1915-Edw Arnold-photos-1st ed (ll8,sl tn sp) 50.00

HAWAII-REPORT OF HISTORICAL COMMISSION OF TERRITORY OF...-Honolulu-1927-57p-wrps (u8,chip cor) 10.00

HAWBAKER,S STANLEY-Trapping North American Furbearers-1944-priv prntd-8vo-216p-dec wrps,illus-revsd ed (m3,vf) 15.00

HAWES,CHARLES B-Whaling-NY-1924-Dbldy,Page-8vo-358p-blu cl,g titles,t.e.g.,8 col plts-1st ed (p8,f) 165.00

HAWES,HARRY B-My Friend the Black Bass-NY-1939-12mo-288p-photos-1st ed (m3,f) 22.50

HAWGOOD,JOHN A-America's Western Frontiers-NY-1967-Knopf-8vo-xxiii,440p-98 illus,19 maps(incl 4 dbl-pg)-1st Amer ed (aa3,f,dj) 30.00

HAWGOOD,JOHN A-America's Western Frontiers-NY-1967-Knopf-sm 4to-xxiii+440p-cl-1st Amer ed (z4,dj) 35.00

HAWK,DAVE-100 Years on Bass-San Antonio-1970-8vo-134p-illus-scarce (m3,as new in dj) 40.00

HAWKER,PETER-Colonel Hawker's Shooting Diaries-Derrydale-nd-8vo-300p-illus (m3) 150.00

HAWKES,CLARENCE-Shovelhorns, the Biography of a Moose-Phila-(1909)-Geo W Jacobs-270p-cl,frnts+4p plts,Chas Copeland-1st ed (l1) 15.00

HAWKES,ERNEST W-Inviting In Feast of the Alaska Eskimo-Ottawa-1913-20p+13 plts wi tiss-Dept of Mines Memoir #45-scarce-1st ed (e7,sl crack sp) 50.00

HAWKES,ERNEST W-Inviting In Feast of the Alaskan Eskimo-Ottawa-1913-Govt Prtg Bur-20p-orig gry prtd wrps,13 guarded plts-Arctic Biblio 6776 (dd7,hngs rnfrcd) 75.00

HAWKES,JACQUETTA-History in Earth and Stone-Cambridge-1952-Harvard U Pr-8vo-312p-20 illus,5 maps-1st US ed (gg5,sl tn dj) 25.00

HAWKES,JACQUETTA-Man and the Sun-NY-(1962)-Random-8vo-277p-1st US ed (gg5,f,dj) 20.00

HAWKES,JOHN-Death, Sleep & the Traveler-(NY)-(1974)-New Directions-1st ed (bb1,pub comp cpy,as new in dj 35.00

HAWKES,JOHN-Death,Sleep & the Traveler-Lond-1975-Chatto & Windus-1st Brit ed (k7,dj) 25.00

HAWKES,JOHN-Passion Artist-NY-(1979)-Harper & Row-1st ed (bb1,as new in dj) 15.00

HAWKES,JOHN-Passion Artist-NY-1979-H&R-1st ed (x9,f,dj tn) 10.00

HAWKES,JOHN-Providence Island-1959-Random-1st ed (x2,vf,dj) 15.00

HAWKES,JOHN-Travesty-(NY)-(1976)-New Directions-1st ed (bb1,as new in dj) 20.00

HAWKES,JOHN-Virginie-NY-1982-H&R-1st trd ed (x9,dj) 10.00

HAWKEYE,HARRY-Dalton Brothers and Their Gang-Balt-(1908)-187p-col pict wrps,frntis,illus-1st ed (t7) 35.00

HAWKEYE,HARRY-Dalton Brothers and Their Gang-Balt-(1908)-Ottenheimer-187p+ads-pict wrps (n1) 20.00

HAWKEYE,HARRY-Rube Burrow, the Outlaw-Balt-1908-172p-col pict wrps,frntis-scarce-cheap paper used-1st ed (t7,chip) 40.00

HAWKINS,CORA F-Buggies,Blizzards, and Babies-Ames-(1971)-191p-cl-1st ed so stated (j1,f,dj) 12.50

HAWKINS,HENRY G-Twenty Months in Japan-Nashville-1901-86p-wrps,illus (aa1) 15.00

HAWKINS,LEONARD-Man in the Iron Lung-Kingswood-(1957)-World's Work-8vo-252p-photos-1st Brit ed (gg5,sl tn dj) 12.50

HAWKINS,SIR JOHN-General History of the Science & Practice of Music-NY-1963-Dover-2 vols (u4,dj) 46.00

HAWKINS,WALACE-Case of John C Watrous United States Judge for Texas-Dallas-1950-SMU Pr-109p-cl,illus,Design by C Hertzog-1st ed (w3,f,dj) 25.00

HAWKINS,WALLACE-El Sol Del Ray-Austin-1947-68p-illus,map e.p.-1st ed (t7,f,dj,autg) 75.00

HAWKINS,WATERHOUSE-Anatomy of the Horse-Lond-nd(1865?)-Windsor & Newton-stiff papr cov,24 wdcuts+64p list supplies (j9) 22.00

HAWKS,ELLISON-Pioneers of Wireless-1927-304p-24 photos,45 illus-rare-1st ed (h6,cov fade) 65.00

HAWKS,F-Once to Every Pilot-NY-(1936)-roy 8vo-144p-cl,frntis,23p plts (t2,dj) 45.00

HAWKS,F-Speed-NY-1931-8vo-viii,314p-cl,frntis,20p plts-1st ed (t2) 40.00

HAWKSHAW-Blinky Morgan, the Detective's Foe-Chig-1889-Eagle-217p+ads-pict wrps,Globe Detective Ser. No.5,Oct.1887 (n1,sl wn) 60.00

HAWKSWORTH,FRANK-Biology & Classif. of Dwarf Mistletoes-Wash-1972-USDA-234p-cl (x6) 10.00

HAWLEY,GESSNER-Seeing the Invisible, Story of Electron Microscope-NY-1945-Knopf-204p-cl (x6) 18.00

HAWLEY,W M-ED.-Chinese Folk Design-Hollywood-1949-W M Hawley-sm folio-unpgd-cl,illus-1st ed (kk1,f,dj) 60.00

HAWORTH,CAPT M E-Road Scrapings-Lond-1882-Tinsley-1st ed (f10) 225.00

HAWORTH,PAUL L-George Washington: Farmer-Indpls-1915-Bobbs-336p-cl (x6) 30.00

HAWTHORNE,HILDEGARDE-California's Missions-(NY)-1942-Appleton Century-lg 8vo-237p-Suydam,illus-1st ed (ff5,sl chip dj) 30.00

HAWTHORNE,HILDEGARDE-California's Missions-NY-(1942)-Appleton Century-237p-48p drwngs-1st ed (cc4,dj) 15.00

HAWTHORNE,HILDEGARDE-Lure of the Garden-NY-1911-Century-4to-x,259p-orig g dec cl,48 plts(16 col)-1st prtg (cc10,hng crack) 125.00

HAWTHORNE,HILDEGARDE-Rambles in Old College Towns-NY-1917-Dodd,Mead-8vo-364p-16 sketches-1st ed (cc5,unopened) 12.50

HAWTHORNE,HILDEGARDE-Romantic Cities of California-NY-1939-Appleton Century-456p-col frntis,illus (cc4) 25.00

HAWTHORNE,J-ED.-Lock & Key Library of Classic Mystery and Detective Stories: German-1909-Review of Reviews-1st ed (t4,f) 10.00

HAWTHORNE,JULIAN-ED.-History of Washington, the Evergreen State, From Early Dawn to Daylight-NY-1893-Amer Hist Publ-lg 8vo-2 vols-3/4 lea over cl bds,a.e.g.,ports-Smith 4181-1st ed (w1) 200.00

HAWTHORNE,NATHANIEL-Doctor Grimshaw's Secret-Bost-1883-James R Osgood-dec cl-earliest bndg wi children & spiders-BAL 7642-1st ed (f2) 100.00

HAWTHORNE,NATHANIEL-Marble Faun-Bost-1889-Houghton Mifflin-2 vols-vel-1st ed thus (l9,sl warp) 125.00

HAY,DAVID-Last of the Confederate Privateers-NY-(1977)-178p-illus-1st ed (n3,f,dj) 27.50

HAY,ELIZABETH-Sambo Sahib-Edinburgh-(1981)-Harris-194p-bds-1st ed (s3,f,f dj) 18.00

HAY,GERTRUDE S-ET AL-Roster of Soldiers from North Carolina in the American Revolution-np-1932-NCDAR-709p-blu cl-ltd to 1000c,autg-1st ed (oo5) 95.00

HAY,JAMES-"No Clue!"-NY-1915-Dodd-1st ed (g4) 12.50

HAY,T R-Hood's Tennessee Campaign-Dayton-1976-272p-fldg maps (z10,as new) 20.00

HAYAKAWA,SESSUE-Zen Showed Me the Way...-Indpls-1960-Bobbs-Merrill-cl-1st ed (n8,f,dj) 12.50

HAYCOX,ERNEST-Earthbreakers-Little,Brown-1952-405p-1st ed (r8,sl chip dj) 25.00

HAYDEN,F V-Annual Report of the U.S. Geological and Geographical Survey...Colorado...for the Year 1874-Wash D.C.-1876-x+515p-blk cl,fldg maps,plts,charts (k2,sl wn) 65.00

HAYDEN,F V-Prelim Report of U.S. Geo. Survey of Montana-Wash-1872-538p-illus,6 fldg maps-1st ed (r8) 75.00

HAYDEN,JULIE-Lists of the Past-NY-1976-Viking-auth 1st bk-1st ed (z9,f,tn dj) 7.50

HAYDEN,PROF F V-ED.-North America-Lond-1883-Stanford-thk 8vo-652p wi index,dec g stmpd grn cl,16 prtd col fldg maps-1st ed (t1,innr hng rprd) 225.00

HAYDON,A L-Trooper Police of Australia-Lond-1911-426p-dec grn cl,6 maps,43 plts-scarce-1st ed (b7,sl wn) 95.00

HAYDON,F S-Aeronautics in the Union and Confederate Armies-Balt-1941-421p+plts-illus,map,ports-1st ed (z10,sl soil) 150.00

HAYES,ALICE M-Horsewoman-Lond-1910-Hurst & Blackett-photos-3rd ed (h9) 125.00

HAYES,CAPT M H-Illustrated Horse Breaking-Lond-1905-Hurst & Blackett-3rd ed (j9,edge wn) 25.00

HAYES,CAPT M HORACE-Among Men and Horses-NY-1894-Dodd,Mead-1st US ed (f10,bent cor,sl fox) 45.00

HAYES,I I-Open Polar Sea-NY-1867-Hurd & Houghton-g stmpd pebbld cl,3 col maps,6p engrvngs-1st ed (p6,rebckd,restored) 200.00

HAYES,ISAAC A-Arctic Boat Journey in Autumn of 1854-Bost-1860-Brown,Taggard & Chase-375p-g dec sp & frnt cov,2 fldg maps-1st ed (u8,hngs crckd,chip sp,tn map) 60.00

HAYES,JESS G-Apache Vengeance-Albuq-1954-185p-cl-1st ed (z1,f,dj) 35.00

HAYES,JESS G-Boots and Bullets-1967-U of AZ pr-12mo-xv,139p-illus-1st ed (aa3,as new in dj) 20.00

HAYES,JESS G-Sheriff Thompson's Day-1968-U of AZ Pr-12mo-xiii,190p-photos-1st ed (aa3,as new in dj) 22.50

HAYES,JOHN F-Wilderness Mission-Tor-1969-Ryerson Pr-4to-120p-photos-1st ed (bb7,dj) 25.00*

HAYES,JOHN R-Old Fashioned Garden and Other Verses-Phila-1895-John C Winston-101p-cl (g1) 15.00

HAYES,JOHN R-Old Meeting Houses-Phila-1909-Riddle-8vo-unpgd-wrps,52 photos-1st ed (aa5) 35.00

HAYES,M HORACE-Points of the Horse-Lond-1904-Hurst & Blackett-sm 4to-736p-illus-3rd ed rvsd & enlgd (j9) 65.00

HAYES,OPAL M-State Fair Blue Ribbon Cookbook-(Palm Springs)-(1976)-ETC Publ-123p (n6) 25.00

HAYES,RALPH-Visiting Moon-NY-1971-Lenox Hill-1st ed (j3,f,sl wn dj) 15.00

HAYES,WILLIAM C-Scepter of Egypt-Cambridge-1959-Harvard U Pr-buckram,illus-1st ed (n8,f) 45.00

HAYES,WILMA-Foods the Indians Gave Us-NY-(1973)-Ives Washburn-113p (o6,dj) 15.00

HAYMAN,RONALD-Literature & Living-1972-Covent Garden Press-wrps-ltd to 100c,nbrd,autg-1st ed (m7,sl sunned) 15.00

HAYMON,S T-Ritual Murder-NY-1982-St.Martin's-1st Amer ed (q4,vf,dj) 20.00

HAYNE,COE-Race Grit-Phila-(1922)-Judson Pr-210p-cl-1st ed (j1) 15.00

HAYNE,COE-Red Men on the Bighorn-Phila-(1929)-Judson Pr-(x)+123p-orng cl-1st ed (e2,dj chip & creased) 45.00

HAYNES,E W-History of the Tenth Regiment, Vt. Vols.-Rutland-1894-504p-pict cl,illus,fldg map-2nd ed,rvsd & enlgd (n3,hngs weak) 75.00

HAYNES,GLYNN W-American Paint Horse-Norman-1976-U of Okla Pr-1st ed (f10,dj) 65.00

HAYNES,W-Fisherman's Verse-NY-1919-12mo-312p-1st ed (m3) 40.00

HAYNES,WILLIAM-Stone that Burns-NY-1942-Van Nostrand-xii+345p-yel & blk cl,plts-1st ed (j2,dj) 20.00

HAYNES,WILLIAMS-American Chemical Industry-NY-1945 thru 54-Van Nostrand-6 vols,maroon cl,illus-1st ed (l2) 225.00

HAYS,ALICE N-COMP.-David Starr Jordan, a Bibliography of his Writings 1871-1931-Stanford-1952-8vo-195p-wrps-scarce (m3) 50.00

HAYS,ARTHUR G-Let Freedom Ring-NY-1928-341p-cl-2nd ed (n1,dj) 15.00

HAYS,GEO P-Presbyterians-NY-1892-544p-cl (j1,few spots on rear cov) 17.50

HAYS,H R-Lie Down in Darkness-NY-(1944)-Reynal & Hitchcock-1st ed (hh5,f,dj) 12.50

HAYS,HELEN-Little Maryland Garden-NY-1909-Putnam's-201p-cl,8 col plts (x6,f) 22.00

HAYWARD,CHARLES B-How to Become a Wireless Operator-1918-312p-196 illus-1st ed (h6) 20.00

HAYWOOD,CHARLES-Bibliography of North American Folklore and Folk Song-NY-1951-1292p-ltd ed (a9) 30.00

HAZAN,MARCELLA-Classic Italian Cookbook-Lond-(1980)-Macmillan-414p-pict bds,drwngs-rvsd ed (q8,bump cor,dj) 22.50

HAZARD,JOSEPH-Pacific Crest Trails-(1946)-Superior-317p-illus-1st ed (r8,dj chip,pc missng) 40.00

HAZARD,JOSEPH-Snow Sentinals of the Pacific Northwest-Seattle-1932-249p-1st ed (o10,f) 65.00

HAZARD,LUCY L-Frontier in American Literature-NY-(1927)-308p-cl-Howes H 363-1st ed (h1) 35.00

HAZARD,ROBERT-Hacking New York-NY-1930-Scribners-8vo-213p-red cl-1st ed (b3) 45.00

HAZARD,THOMAS R-Report on the Poor and Insane in Rhode Island-Providence-1851-Joseph Knowles-119p-wrps,frontis-1st ed (j2,chip wrps,sp tips peelng) 65.00

HAZELIUS,ERNEST L-History of the American Lutheran Church ...to the year 1842...-Zanesville-1846-prtd by E C Church-300p-lea (e1,sl cracked joints) 65.00

HAZELTON,NIKA-Ups and Downs-NY-(1989)-Harper & Row-1st ed (l6) 15.00

HAZEN,A T-Bibliography of Strawberry Hill Press...-NY-1973-B&N-new ed of 1942 Yale U Pr ed-1st ed thus (q2,dj) 45.00

HAZEN,MAJ GEN W B-School and the Army in Germany and France-NY-1872-408p-grn cl-1st ed (jj2) 75.00

HAZLEHURST,FRANKLIN H-Jacques Boyceau and the French Formal Garden-(1966)-U of Georgia-xiii,137p-illus-1st ed (m10) 26.00

HAZLETT,W CAREW-Old Cookery Books and Ancient Cuisine-Lond-1903-Elliot Stock-271p-Bitting 221 (m6) 65.00

HAZLITT,W CAREW-Old Cookery Books and Ancient Cuisine-Lond-1902-Elliot Stock-sm 8vo-271p-grn cl-Book Lover's Libr-Popular ed (t10) 45.00

HAZLITT,W CAREW-Old Cookery Books and Ancient Cuisine-NY-1886-Coombes-bev cl bds-1st ed (w1) 45.00

HAZZARD,SHIRLEY-Bay of Noon-Bost-1970-1st ed (n5,f,dj) 20.00

HAZZARD,SHIRLEY-Evening of the Holiday-NY-1966-auth 1st novel-1st ed (n5,dj) 25.00

HEACOX,C E-Complete Brown Trout-Winchester-1974-182p-photos (gg3,f,dj) 15.00

HEACOX,CECIL E-Complete Brown Trout-NY-1974-4to-182p-illus-1st ed (m3,vf,dj) 10.00

HEAD,BRANDON-Food of the Gods-Lond-1903-Johnson-109p-g dec grn cl,photos,maps,chrts,col plts-1st ed (q8) 40.00

HEAD,EDITH-Dress Doctor-Bost-(1959)-Little,Brown-249p-cl,photos-1st ed (z5,dj) 15.00

HEAD,SIR FRANCIS-Narrative-Lond-1839-John Murray-8vo-viii,488,38p-mod 1/2 calf,mrbld bds-2nd ed (u3,rbnd) 150.00

HEADLAND,ISAAC T-Home Life in China-Lond-1914-Methuen-cl,4 col & 12 b&w plts (p6) 75.00

HEAL,AMBROSE-London Tradesmen's Cards of the XVIII Century-Lond-1925-B T Batsford-4to-110p txt-beige cl sp,grn bds,101p plts-ltd to 700c (r10,mottld bds,sl shaken) 65.00

HEALEY,B J-Plant Hunters-NY-(1975)-vii,214p-11 illus (m10,sl wn dj) 25.00

HEALEY,ELIZABETH-History of Alert Bay and District-(Alert Bay)-(1971)-(Alert Bay Mus)-101p-prtd wrps,map e.p.,illus-3rd prtg (k10) 15.00*

HEALEY,LARRY-Hoard of the Himalayas-NY-1981-190p-1st ed (o10,as new in dj) 18.00

HEALING ART-Lond-1887-2 vols-rare-1st ed (dd3) 175.00

HEALY,LAURIN H-Admiral-Chig-(1944)-Ziff Davis-8vo-338p-4p photos-1st ed (ff5,chip dj) 20.00

HEALY,W J-Women of Red River-Winnipeg-1923-Russell,Lang-261p-pict cl,illus,e.p. maps (cc4) 50.00

HEANEY'S PROFESSIONAL CATALOG OF WONDERS-(Berlin)-nd(ca.1920's)-Heaney Magic/Cat#24-96p-wrps,illus (f1) 20.00

HEANEY,SEAMUS-Field Work-Lond-(1979)-Faber-1st ed (z8,vf,dj) 150.00

HEANEY,SEAMUS-Field Work-NY-(1979)-FS&G-1st Amer ed (z8,vf,dj) 40.00

HEANEY,SEAMUS-Fire I' The Flint-1974-Brit Acad/Oxford U Pr-lime grn wrps-1st ed (cc2) 35.00

HEANEY,SEAMUS-Makings of a Music-Liverpool-(1978)-grn wrps,Kenneth Allot Lectures-1st ed (cc2,f) 40.00

HEANEY,SEAMUS-Poems 1965 thru 1975-NY-(1980)-FS&G-1st ed (cc2,f,dj) 30.00

HEANEY,SEAMUS-Selected Poems, 1965 to 1975-Lond-(1980)-Faber-1st ed (z8,as new in dj) 50.00

HEAP,GWINN H-Central Route to the Pacific, From the Valley of the Mississippi to California-Phila-1854-Lippincott,Grambo-8vo-136p+46p ads,orig brwn emboss cl,col frntis,12 plts-Howes H378 "map(not inserted in all copies)"-1st ed (mm1,rbkd wi orig sp,lacks map) 350.00

HEAPS,LEO-Log of the Centurion-NY-1974-Macmillan-264p-blu emboss cl,map e.p.,illus-1st ed (p8,dj) 30.00

HEAPS,WILLARD A-Singing Sixties-Norman-(1960)-423p-illus-1st ed (n3,dj) 30.00

HEARD,GERALD-Is God Evident?-Lond-1950-Faber & Faber-cl-1st ed (n8,tn dj) 15.00

HEARD,H F-Notched Haripin-1949-Vanguard-1st ed (x7,dj) 58.00

HEARD,H L-Doppelgangers-NY-1947-Vanguard-1st ed (v5,f,sl chip dj) 30.00

HEARD,ISAAC V D-History of the Sioux War and Massacres of 1862 and 1863-NY-1863-Harper-354p+2p ads-orig cl,plts,illus-Howes H378a-1st ed (v1,bndg wn) 95.00

HEARN,LAFCADIO-Chita-NY-1889-Harper-1st ed (v5) 75.00

HEARN,LAFCADIO-Creole Cook Book-New Orleans-1967-Pelican-268p-pict blu cl,illus-facs of orig 1885 ed (q8,soil dj) 35.00

HEARN,LAFCADIO-Exotics and Retrospectives-Bost-1899-Little,Brown-(10),299p-emboss floral cl,g stmpd,4p illus-1st ed (m4,rear cov stnd) 85.00

HEARN,LAFCADIO-Exotics and Retrospectives-Bost-1907-Little,Brown-cl,illus-later prtg (n8) 27.50

HEARN,LAFCADIO-Fantastic and Other Fancies-Bost-(1914)-HM Co-(9),242p-qtr cl & papr bds-1st ed (m4) 65.00

HEARN,LAFCADIO-Glimpses of Unfamiliar Japan-Bost-1894-Houghton Mifflin-2 vols-vol one is second state-1st ed (w1,vf) 175.00

HEARN,LAFCADIO-Japan's Religions-New Hyde Park-1966-Univ Bks-cl-1st prtg (n8,dj) 20.00

HEARN,LAFCADIO-Japan: An Attempt at Interpretation, by...-NY-1904-Macmillan-BAL 7941-1st ed (hh4,f,f dj) 450.00

HEARN,LAFCADIO-Kokoro-Bost-1896-Houghton Mifflin-cl-1st ed (o8) 37.50

HEARN,LAFCADIO-When I Was a Flower-1939-Illinois Typesetters-sewn in wraps-BAL 8035 (w5,f) 20.00

HEARNE,SAMUEL-Journey to the Northern Ocean-Tor-1958-301p-illus,fldg map-Pioneer Bk Ser,Vol.7-1st ed thus (h7,f,dj) 40.00

HEARTMAN,CHARLES F-Preliminary Checklist of Almanacs Printed in New Jersey Prior to 1850-Metuchen-1929-priv prtd-39p-wrps-ltd to 200c (aa6) 45.00

HEATH,AMBROSE-Good Jams, Preserves and Pickles-Lond-(1947)-Faber-91p (l6) 18.00

HEATH,DAVE-Dialogue with Solitude-(Culpeper)-1965-Community Pr-unpgd-81 photos-rare-1st ed (cc9,as new in dj) 75.00

HEAVISIDE,JOHN T C-American Antiquities-Lond-1868-Trubner & Co-8vo-45,(1),2p-bnd by Zaehnsdorf in 1/2 lea,mrbld e.p.-Sabin 31196 (mm1) 130.00

HEBARD & BRININSTOOL-Bozeman Trail-Glendale-1960-2 vols in 1-346p & 306p-illus-2nd prtg (e7) 110.00

HEBARD,GRACE R-Washakie-Cleve-1930-337p-frntis,photos & illus wi tiss guards,maps-Howes H384-1st ed (t7,f,TLS tip-in) 200.00

HEBARD,GRACE-Washakie-Cleve-1930-337p-t.e.g.,illus,maps-1st ed (f7,f) 125.00

HEBDEN,MARK-Pel & the Faceless Corpse-Lond-1979-Hamilton-1st ed (q4,f,dj) 22.50

HEBER,REGINALD-From Greenland's Icy Mountains...-Phila-(1884)-John C Winston-unpgd-bds in col-20 illus (g1) 15.00

HEBERDEN,M V-Murder Follows Desmond Shannon-1942-CC-1st ed (s10,dj) 20.00

HEBERDEN,M V-Murder of a Stuffed Shirt-NY-1944-Dbldy CC-1st ed (h4,chip dj) 20.00

HEBERDEN,M V-Vicious Pattern-1945-CC-1st ed (s10,dj) 17.50

HECHT,BEN-Champion From Far Away-1931-C,F-1st ed (x2,sp gilt gone) 17.00

HECHT,BEN-Miracle in the Rain-NY-1943-Knopf-1st ed (hh5,dj) 20.00

HECHT,BEN-Mirage in the Rain-NY-1943-Knopf-1st ed (e3,f,dj) 30.00

HECHT,BEN-Tales of Chicago Streets-Girard-nd-Haldeman Julius-57p-wrps-Little Blu Bk 698 (d1) 10.00

HECHT,BEN-Tales of Chicago Streets-Girard-nd-Haldeman Julius-wrps-Little Blu Bk 698-1st ed (w5,f) 15.00

HECKEL,VILEM-Climbing in the Caucasus-Lond-1958-208p-b&w & col photos-1st ed (p10,f,dj) 185.00

HECKELMANN,CHARLES N-Rawhider-1952-H Holt-1st ed (r9,dj rub & sl tn) 20.00

HECKER,J F C-Epidemics of the Middle Ages-Lond-1846-380p-1st Engl transl (dd3) 150.00

HECKER,W R-Auriculas & Primroses-1971-Branford-216p (x6,as new in dj) 15.00

HECKER,W R-Auriculas and Primroses-Lond-(1971)-216p-40 b&w,12 col illus (x5,dj) 17.00

HECKMAN,HAZEL-Island Year-Seattle,Lond-(1972)-255p-bds (g1) 12.50

HECKMAN,HAZEL-Island Year-Seattle-(1972)-255p-illus (b6,f,dj) 10.00

HEDGECOE,J-ED.-Henry Moore-NY-1968-folio-525 plts-1st ed (h10,sl rub box) 125.00

HEDGES,JAMES B-Browns of Providence Plantations: Colonial Years-Cambridge-1952-Harvard U Pr-xx+379p-gry cl,plts-1st ed (b2,dj chip,tn) 15.00

HEDGPETH,J W-ED.-Treatise on Marine Ecology and Paleoecology-1957-Geol Soc Amer-2 vols-illus,maps (bb3) 55.00

HEDIN,S-Conquest of Tibet-NY-1941-400p (o10,f,dj) 25.00

HEDIN,SVEN-Conquest of Tibet-NY-1934-Dutton-cl,illus-transl by J Lincoln-1st ed (l8) 25.00

HEDIN,SVEN-Jehol: City of Emperors-NY-1933-Dutton-cl-1st ed (o8,sl spot bds) 35.00

HEDIN,SVEN-My Life as an Explorer-NY-1925-544p-165 illus-1st US ed (q10,f) 22.00

HEDIN,SVEN-Riddles of the Gobi Desert-NY-1933-Dutton-382p-24 illus-1st Amer ed (gg6,hng weak,sl fox) 40.00

HEDIN,SVEN-Through Asia-Lond-1898-Methuen-2vols-map,photos-1st Brit ed (gg6,shaken,map tn) 220.00

HEDIN,SVEN-Through Asia-NY,Lond-1899-2 vols-uncut,t.e.g.,g stmpd dec cov & sp,illus,2 col fldg maps-1st ed (q10,f) 250.00

HEDIN,SVEN-Trans Himalaya-NY-1909-2 vols-maps(3 fldg,vol 2)-1st US ed (p10,sp chip) 150.00

HEDLEY,LESLIE W-ED.-Four New Poets-SF-1957-Inferno Pr-1st ed (s5,wrps wn) 175.00

HEDREN,PAUL L-First Scalp for Custer-Glendale-1980-Arthur H Clark-107p-pict cl,illus-ltd to 350c-Hidden Springs of Custeriana ser,Vol.5-1st ed (gg4) 85.00

HEDRICK,U P-Cherries of New York-1915-NY Dept Agric-4to-371p-56 col plts (bb3) 150.00

HEDRICK,U P-History of Agriculture in the State of New York-Albany-1933-Lyon,for NY St Agri Soc-462p (x6,ex-libr) 35.00

HEDRICK,U P-Pears of New York-1921-NY Dept Agric-4to-636p-76 col plts (bb3,f) 150.00

HEDRICK,U P-Plums of New York-1911-NY Dept Agric-4to-616p-97 col plts (bb3) 150.00

HEDRICK,U P-Vegetables of New York. Beans-1931-NY Dept Agric-4to-110p-stiff papr wrps,39 col plts (bb3,as new in orig mail crtn) 55.00

HEDRICK,ULYSSES P-History of Agriculture in the State of New York-(Albany)-1933-NY St Agri Soc-illus-1st ed (y10,dj chip,fade) 85.00

HEDRICK,ULYSSES P-History of Agriculture in the State of New York-np-1933-NYS Agri Soc-462p-grn cl,illus-1st ed (u2) 50.00

HEFELBOWER,SAMUEL G-History of Gettysburg College 1832 to 1932-Gettysburg-1932-Gettysburg College-485p-frntis,illus (n7,sp drknd) 30.00

HEFFERMAN,WILLIAM-Broderick-NY-1980-Crown-auth 1st bk-1st ed (r4,f,dj) 22.50

HEFNER,HUGH-ED.-Best From Playboy-NY-(1954)-Waldorf-sm folio-160p-1st ed (ll9,dj) 75.00

HEGEMANN,ELIZABETH C-Navaho Trading Days-Albuq-(1963)-388p-photos-1st ed (v7,sl wn dj) 45.00

HEGEMANN,ELIZABETH C-Navaho Trading Days-Albuq-1963-UNM Pr-xi,388p-gry cl,photo e.p.,318 photos-1st ed (mm1,dj v chip & wn) 95.00

HEGEMANN,ELIZABETH-Navaho Trading Days-Albuq-1963-cl,photos-scarce-1st ed (z1,f,dj) 75.00

HEILNER,V C-Book on Duck Shooting-Phila-1939-8vo-540p-photos-illus,L B Hunt-scarce-1st ed (m3,f) 100.00

HEILNER,V C-Book on Duck Shooting-Phila-1940-540p-photos (gg3,f,poor dj,pres cpy) 45.00

HEILNER,V C-Book on Duck Shooting-Phila-1943-540p-photos (gg3,f,dj) 35.00

HEILNER,V C-Call of the Surf-GC-1920-12mo-294p-illus,F Stick-scarce-1st ed (m3) 55.00

HEILNER,V C-Our American Game Birds-NY-1947-170p-illus (gg3,f) 15.00

HEILNER,V C-Salt Water Fishing-Phila-1937-8vo-452p-photos-1st ed (m3) 40.00

HEILPRIN,ANGELO-Alaska and the Klondike-NY-1899-315p+ads-cl,3 fldg maps,frntis,34p plts (l1,rear cov stnd,sl wn) 35.00

HEIMSATH,CLOVIS-Pioneer Texas Buildings-(1968)-U of Tex-Sq lg 8vo-158p-illus-1st ed (t8,dj sl soil & chip) 18.00

HEINEMANN,LARRY-Close Quarter-NY-(1977)-FSG-1st ed (ff3,f,dj,pres) 150.00

HEINLEIN,ROBERT A-Citizen of the Galaxy-NY-(1957)-1st ed (bb10,dj creased,rprd) 150.00

HEINLEIN,ROBERT A-Farham's Freehold-NY-(1964)-Putnam-1st ed (l3,f,sl wn sp) 350.00

HEINLEIN,ROBERT A-Menace From Earth-Lond-(1959)-Dobson-8vo-cl-1st Brit ed (x3,dj) 125.00

HEINLEIN,ROBERT A-Moon is a Harsh Mistress-NY-(1966)-Putnam-1st ed (j3,dj sl edge wn) 900.00

HEINLEIN,ROBERT A-Rolling Stones-NY-(1952)-Scribner's-8vo-cl-1st ed wi seal & "A" (x3,dj) 185.00

HEINLEIN,ROBERT A-Time For the Stars-NY-1956-Scribner's-1st ed (p3,f,dj sp sl rub) 300.00

HEINLEIN,ROBERT-Discovery of the Future-1941-Novacious Pr-wrps wi orig mailing envelope,one of 200c,auth 1st bk-1st ed (x2,f) 1,975.00

HEINLEIN,ROBERT-I Will Fear No Evil-NY-(1970)-1st ed (m5,sl wn dj) 65.00

HEINLEIN,ROBERT-I Will Fear No Evil-NY-(1970)-Putnam-1st ed (q2,edges fade,dj rub) 85.00

HEINLEIN,ROBERT-Rocketship Galileo-1947-Scribners-auth 1st commercially publ bk-1st ed (x2,sl dmpstnd rear panel,dj) 475.00

HEINTZELMAN,DONALD S-Manual for Bird Watching in the Americas-NY-1979-8vo-255p-red cl,illus,col photos-1st ed (mm1,dj) 20.00

HEINZ BOOK OF SALADS-Pitt-(1925)-H J Heinz-95p-pict bds,col plts (q8,edge wn) 18.50

HEIRS OF HIPPOCRATES: DEVELOPMENT OF MEDICINE IN A CATALOGUE OF HISTORIC BOOKS...UNIVERSITY OF IOWA-Iowa City-1980-4to-474p (dd3) 60.00

HEISENBERG,W-ED.-Cosmic Radiation-NY-1946-Dover-x+192p-grn cl-1st ed in Engl (dd1,chip dj) 45.00

HEISENBERG,W-Nuclear Physics-NY-(1953)-Philos Libr-viii+224p-gry cl-1st ed (d2,dj) 30.00

HEITMAN,FRANCIS B-Historical Register and Dictionary of the United States Army-Urbana-1965-U of Ill-2 vols (gg4) 50.00

HEIZER,ROBERT F-Natural Worlds of the California Indians-Berkeley-(1980)-U of Cal-sm 8vo-271p-cl,sketches (y5,dj) 20.00

HELD,JULIUS-ET AL-Joseph Floch-NY-1968-Yoseloff-4to-143p-beige cl,b&w & col illus (r10,f dj) 30.00

HELGELAND,G-ED.-Complete Guide to Bow Hunting-NJ-1975-262p-photos (gg3,f,dj) 15.00

HELGESEN,SALLY-Wildcatters-1981-Dbldy-198p-1st ed (a9,dj) 20.00

HELIN TACKLE CO-Ad Catalog-nd-oblng-31p-col illus (gg3,f) 25.00

HELLER'S SECRETS OF MEAT CURING AND SAUSAGE MAKING-Chig-1929-Heller & Co-440p-red bds,illus (l6) 35.00

HELLER,FRANK-Mr.Collins is Ruined-1925-Crowell-1st Amer ed (s10,sp stnd) 22.50

HELLER,FRANK-Perilous Transactions of Mr Collin-Lond-1924-John Lane-1st Brit ed (d4,fade sp) 30.00

HELLER,JOSEPH-Catch 22-NY-1961-auth 1st bk-1st ed (r2,f,sl chip dj) 350.00

HELLER,JOSEPH-Catch 22-NY-1961-Simon-8vo-blu cl-auth 1st bk-1st Amer ed (x3,chip dj) 285.00

HELLER,JOSEPH-Good as Gold-NY-(1979)-S&S-1st ed (b5,as new in dj) 17.50

HELLER,JOSEPH-Good as Gold-NY-(1979)-S&S-1st ed (j3,f,dj) 20.00

HELLER,JOSEPH-Something Happened-NY-(1974)-Knopf-1st ed (b5,as new in dj) 25.00

HELLER,JOSEPH-Something Happened-NY-(1974)-Knopf-1st ed (j3,f,dj) 20.00

HELLER,MORDECAI T-Shameful Decline of the "Truth Seeker"-Girard-(1949)-Haldeman-Julius Publ-24p-wrps-Big Blu Bk B-836 (h1) 15.00

HELLMAN,GEOFFREY T-Smithsonian: Octupus on the Mall-Phila-1967-Lippincott-1st ed (v4,as new in dj) 20.00

HELLMAN,LILLIAN-An Unfinished Woman-Bost,Tor-(1969)-Little,Brown-photos-1st ed (a5,as new in dj) 25.00

HELLMAN,LILLIAN-An Unfinished Woman-Bost-(1969)-Little,Brown-wine red bds,blind stmpd in gold wi navy blu cl,acetate dj as iss-Special ed for friends (ee2,f,dj) 40.00

HELLMAN,LILLIAN-Autumn Garden-Bost-1951-1st ed (r5,dj sl chip & yel) 20.00

HELLMAN,LILLIAN-Children's Hour-NY-1934-auth 1st bk-1st ed (y1,dj sl chip & wn) 550.00

HELLMAN,LILLIAN-Eating Together-Bost-(1984)-Little,Brown-1st ed (y10,dj) 15.00

HELLMAN,LILLIAN-Maybe-Bost-(1980)-106p-1st ed (k9,f,dj) 12.50

HELLMAN,LILLIAN-Maybe-Bost-1980-1st ed (r5,f,dj) 15.00

HELLMAN,LILLIAN-Montserrat-NY-(1950)-1st ed (k9,wn dj) 20.00

HELLMAN,LILLIAN-My Mother, My Father, and Me-1963-Random-1st ed (kk6,dj) 35.00

HELLMAN,LILLIAN-North Star-NY-1943-1st ed (r5,sl chip dj) 40.00

HELLMAN,LILLIAN-Pentimento-Bost,Tor-(1973)-Little,Brown-1st ed (b5,f,dj frnt flap creased) 20.00

HELLMAN,LILLIAN-Scoundrel Time-Bost,Tor-(1976)-Little,Brown-photos-1st ed (a5,as new in dj) 15.00

HELM,THOMAS-Fishing Southern Salt Waters-NY-1972-8vo-393p-photos (m3,vf,dj) 25.00

HELM,THOMAS-Sea Lark-NY-nd-8vo-253p-illus,e.p. maps (m3,dj) 15.00

HELME,ELEANOR-Mayfly-NY-1931-Scribner-10p illus by L Edwards-1st US ed (f10,few cov spots) 25.00

HELME,W C-American Farrier, and Family Medical Companion-Cleve-1852-Smead & Cowles-97,(3)p-bds-rare (c1) 125.00

HELMER,WILLIAM F O-Long Life and Slow Death of the New York, Ontario & Western Railway-Berkeley-1959-Howell-North-xiii+211p-beige cl,illus,2 fldg maps-1st ed (k2,dj) 20.00

HELMER,WILLIAM F-Rip Van Winkle Railroads-Berkeley-1970-146p-1st ed (n4,f,dj) 22.00

HELMERICKS,CONSTANCE-Flight of the Arctic Tern-Bost-(1952)-Little,Brown-8vo-321p-cl-1st ed (pp5,f,sl wn dj) 50.00*

HELMERICKS,CONSTANCE-Hunting in North America-Harrisburg-1956-8vo-298p-illus-1st ed (m3,f,sl fray dj) 12.50

HELMS,MARJORIE N-Early Days in Phoenix, Oregon-Grants Pass-1954-Bull Pub Co-8vo-39p-pict wrps,illus (cc4,autg) 15.00

HELMS,RANDEL-Tolkien's World-Bost-1974-Houghton Mifflin-1st ed (bb1,f,dj) 10.00

HELMS,S W-Jawa-Ithaca-(1981)-Cornell U Pr-8vo-270p-100 figs-1st ed (jj5,vf,vf dj) 17.50

HELPER,HINTON R-Impending Crisis of the South-NY-1857-A B Burdick-420p-1st ed (v2,hng weak) 75.00

HELPER,HINTON R-Impending Crisis of the South-NY-1857-Burdick-420p-1st ed (o7,hng weak) 75.00

HELPRIN,MARK-Dove of the East & Other Stories-NY-1975-Knopf-auth 1st bk-1st ed (bb1,f,dj) 65.00

HELPRIN,MARK-Ellis Island-NY-(1981)-Delacorte/Lawrence-1st ed (bb2,f,dj) 45.00

HELPRIN,MARK-Refiner's Fire-NY-1977-1st ed (p5,dj sl snag) 35.00

HELSTROM,HENNING-Henning's Fishing, Hunting & Vacation Guide to the Pacific Northwest-Portland-1969-4to-624p-photos,maps (m3,vf,dj) 15.00

HEMANS,FELICIA-Records of Woman-NY-1828-Gilley-8vo-324p-linen bkd bds wi pap labl-1st US ed (w6,uncut,wn labl) 35.00

HEMANS,MRS.-Songs of Affections-Cin-1850-J A & U P James-124p-cl (g1) 40.00

HEMENWAY,ROBERT-Girl Who Sang with the Beatles...-NY-1970-Knopf-auth 1st bk-1st ed (b10,f,dj) 25.00

HEMINGWAY,ERNEST-Across the River and Into the Trees-Lond-(1950)-grn cl-preceded 1st US ed by 3 days-1st ed (k5,lt fox,dj sl wn) 100.00

HEMINGWAY,ERNEST-Across the River and Into the Trees-NY-1950-1st ed (t5,sl wn dj) 65.00

HEMINGWAY,ERNEST-Across the River and Into the Trees-NY-1950-Scribner-8vo-cl-1st iss dj(sp yellow)-1st ed wi "A" & seal (x3,dj sl chip,tape rnfrcd) 75.00

HEMINGWAY,ERNEST-Across the River and Into the Trees-NY-1950-Scribners-1st ed (ee2,f,dj sp chip) 40.00

HEMINGWAY,ERNEST-By Line-1967-Scribners-1st ed (x2,f,dj) 60.00

HEMINGWAY,ERNEST-By Line-NY-1967-Scribner's-1st ed (c6,dj) 40.00

HEMINGWAY,ERNEST-Ernest Hemingway, Selected Letters 1917 to 1961-NY-(1981)-Scribner's-1st trd ed (ff6,dj) 35.00

HEMINGWAY,ERNEST-Farewell to Arms-NY-1929-Scribner's-8vo-cl,1st iss dj-1st ed,1st iss (x3,dj sl sunned & chip) 450.00

HEMINGWAY,ERNEST-Farewell to Arms-NY-1929-Scribners-1st iss w/o disclaimer-1st ed (ee2,sl cocked sp,lacks dj) 70.00

HEMINGWAY,ERNEST-Farewell to Arms-NY-1948-Scribner's-iss w/o dj,illus by D Rasmusson-1st illus ed (ff6,f,lacks box) 250.00

HEMINGWAY,ERNEST-Fifth Column & Four Stories of the Spanish Civil War-NY-(1969)-Scribner's-1st ed (b5,f,dj) 100.00

HEMINGWAY,ERNEST-For Whom the Bell Tolls-NY-1940-1st ed (m4,sp dull) 20.00

HEMINGWAY,ERNEST-For Whom the Bell Tolls-NY-1940-Scribner's-1st ed,1st state dj (ff6,dj sl wn & crease) 300.00

HEMINGWAY,ERNEST-For Whom the Bell Tolls-NY-1940-Scribner's-4to-cl,1st state dj(w/o photographer's name)-Hanneman A18A-1st ed (x3,sl chip dj) 225.00

HEMINGWAY,ERNEST-Green Hills of Africa-NY,Lond-1935-Scribner's-1st ed (ff6,sl fade sp,dj sl chip) 700.00

HEMINGWAY,ERNEST-Green Hills of Africa-NY-(1935)-Scribner's-1st ed (aa10,fade,dj rub & fade) 575.00

HEMINGWAY,ERNEST-In Our Time-Paris-1932-Crosby Continental Eds-sm 8vo-wrps-Hanneman A3C (x3,mssng sm sp pc) 225.00

HEMINGWAY,ERNEST-Islands in the Stream-1970-Scribners-1st ed (x2,f,dj,auth photo laid in) 38.00

HEMINGWAY,ERNEST-Islands in the Stream-NY-(1970)-Scribners-1st ed (cc2,f,dj) 40.00

HEMINGWAY,ERNEST-Men Without Women-Cleve-(1946)-World Publ-illus,Groth Hanneman A7e-1st illus rprnt ed (cc2,f,dj) 50.00

HEMINGWAY,ERNEST-Moveable Feast-Lond-(1964)-J Cape-1st Brit ed (b5,f,dj) 40.00

HEMINGWAY,ERNEST-Moveable Feast-Lond-(1964)-Jonathan Cape-1st Brit ed (c10,dj sl soil & sl rub sp) 50.00

HEMINGWAY,ERNEST-Moveable Feast-NY-(1964)-Scribner-1st ed (bb2,f,dj) 45.00

HEMINGWAY,ERNEST-Moveable Feast-NY-1964-photos-1st ed (o5,dj wi sm chip) 30.00

HEMINGWAY,ERNEST-Nick Adams Stories-NY-1972-Scribner's-1st ed (d10,f,dj) 65.00

HEMINGWAY,ERNEST-Nick Adams Stories-NY-1972-Scribners-1st ed (y10,sl wn dj) 48.00

HEMINGWAY,ERNEST-Old Man and the Sea-Lond-(1952)-1st Brit ed (k5,dj sl wn,sm mark bot sp) 65.00

HEMINGWAY,ERNEST-Old Man and the Sea-Lond-(1952)-1st Brit ed (r5,dj sl edgewn) 75.00

HEMINGWAY,ERNEST-Old Man and the Sea-NY-1952-Scribner's-8vo-cl-1st ed (ll10,sl fox cov,dj) 350.00

HEMINGWAY,ERNEST-Old Man and the Sea-NY-1952-Scribners-1st ed (q2,dj sl tn,chip) 225.00

HEMINGWAY,ERNEST-Old Man and the Sea-NY-1952-Scribners-1st ed (x2,dj) 195.00

HEMINGWAY,ERNEST-Sun Also Rises-np(NY)-nd(1930)-G&D-pict dj-1st G&D ed (a10,dj chip & rprd) 40.00

HEMINGWAY,ERNEST-To Have and Have Not-1937-Cape-1st Brit ed (x7,dj,auth photo laid in) 425.00

HEMINGWAY,ERNEST-To Have and Have Not-1937-Scribners-1st ed (x7,dj,auth photos laid in) 575.00

HEMINGWAY,ERNEST-To Have and Have Not-NY-1937-(8),262p-cl-Hanneman 14A-1st ed (o4,f,dj) 750.00

HEMINGWAY,ERNEST-To Have and Have Not-NY-1937-Scribner's-8vo-cl-1st ed (ll10,f,sl wn dj) 450.00

HEMINGWAY,ERNEST-Winner Take Nothing-NY-(1933)-Scribner's-1st ed (aa10,sl chip dj) 600.00

HEMINGWAY,ERNEST-Winner Take Nothing-NY-(1933)-Scribner's-blk cl-"A" on copyright pg-1st ed (s6,dj missing sm pc top sp) 350.00

HEMINGWAY,ERNEST-Winner Take Nothing-NY-1933-Scribners-1st ed (v5,dj rnfrcd,sp wn) 200.00

HEMINGWAY,LEICESTER-My Brother, Ernest Hemingway-Cleve,NY-(1962)-World-photos-1st ed (e10,f,dj) 25.00

HEMLOW,JOYCE-History of Fanny Burney-Lond-1958-Oxford-1st ed (z3,f,sp sun dj) 22.50

HEMMING,JOHN-Red Gold-Cambridge-1978-677p-cl-1st ed (aa1,f,dj) 20.00

HEMMING,JOHN-Red Gold-Cambridge-1978-677p-frntis,photos,illus,maps-1st ed (t7,f,dj) 17.50

HEMON,LOUIS-Maria Chapdellaine-NY-1924-288p-cl-illus,W Jones-1st illus ed (d1) 15.00

HEMPHILL,VIVIA-Down the Mother Lode-Sacramento-1922-Purnell's-91p-bds-scarce-Six Guns 966-1st ed (bb4,dj) 20.00

HENDERSON,ARCHIBALD-Washington's Southern Tour-Bost-1791-Houghton Mifflin-lg 8vo-bds,grn cl sp,plts-1st ed (mm10,dj) 80.00

HENDERSON,CHARLES R-Social Spirit in America-Chig-1904-358p-cl (j1) 12.50

HENDERSON,COL G F R-Civil War, a Soldier's View-Chig-(1958)-323p-maps-1st ed (n3,f,dj) 40.00

HENDERSON,DANIEL-Hidden Coasts-NY-1953-306p-e.p. maps-1st ed (c7,chip dj) 35.00

HENDERSON,DAVID-Men & Whales at Scammon's Lagoon-1972-Dawson's-313p-ltd to 700c (d3) 45.00

HENDERSON,EMMA-ED.-Wind and Waving Grass-Dallas-1976-Taylor Publ-tall 8vo-112p-pict covs,photos (dd4) 20.00

HENDERSON,ERNEST-Blucher and the Uprising of Prussia Against Napoleon-NY-1911-347p-red cl,maps,illus-1st ed (b7) 50.00

HENDERSON,G F R-Stonewall Jackson and the American Civil War-NY-1949-737p-maps(incl fldg),ports (z10) 40.00

HENDERSON,JOHN B-Cruise of the Tomas Barrera-NY,Lond-1916-Putnam's-8vo-320p-g dec blu cl,36 illus(5 col),maps(1 fldg) (p8,f) 50.00

HENDERSON,MARY F-Practical Cooking and Dinner Giving-NY-1877-Harper & Bros-376p-grn bds,illus-Bitting 223 (u6) 40.00

HENDERSON,MARY F-Practical Cooking and Dinner Giving-NY-1882-Harper & Bros-378p-brwn bds,illus-Bitting 223 (k6,wn) 50.00

HENDERSON,PETER-Garden & Farm Topics-NY-1884-Henderson-244p (x6,sp sun) 20.00

HENDERSON,PETER-Gardening for Pleasure-NY-1889-Orange Judd-404p-cl-rvsd (x6,sl wn,brwnd) 25.00

HENDERSON,PETER-Gardening for Profit Guide to Successful Cultivation of the Market and Family Garden-NY-1881-Orange Judd-276p-cl (x6,edge rub) 30.00

HENDERSON,PETER-Gardening for Profit-NY-1867-Orange Judd-243p-cl (x6,vf) 30.00

HENDERSON,PETER-Practical Floriculture-NY-1907-Orange Judd-325p-cl,illus-rvsd (x6,sp rub) 18.00

HENDERSON,RANDALL-On Desert Trails-1961-Wstrnlore-357p-photos,maps-1st ed (d3,dj) 35.00

HENDERSON,ROBERT W-Ball,Bat and Bishop-1947-Rockport Pr-photos,drwngs-1st ed (s8,dj) 85.00

HENDERSON,SAM H-Fred Gipson: Southwest Writers Series, No.10-Austin-1967-Steck Vaughn-12mo-ii,52p-stiff wrps-1st ed (aa3,f) 15.00

HENDRICK,B J-Lees of Virginia-NY-1935-455p-illus,ports (z10,wn dj) 35.00

HENDRICKS,ROBERT J-Bethel and Aurora-NY-1933-Pr of the Pioneers-xviii+324p-olive cl,plts-1st ed (m2) 35.00

HENDRICKSON,JAMES E-Joe Lane of Oregon-New Haven-1976-274p-1st ed (t7,dj) 10.00

HENDRIX,JOHN-If I Can Do It Horseback-1964-U of Tex Pr-8vo-xv,355p-pict cl,illus,dbl pg map-1st ed (aa3,f,f dj) 35.00

HENDRIX,JOHN-If I Can Do It Horseback-Austin-1964-U of Tex Pr-355p-illus-1st ed (f9,dj) 30.00

HENDRON,J W-Frijoles-Santa Fe-1946-Rydal Pr-8vo-89p+indx-photos,6 plts rear pckt,map frnt e.p.-1st ed (aa3,f) 50.00

HENDY,ANNE MARIE-American Railroad Stock Certificates-Lond-(1980)-8vo-168p-illus (nn7,f,f dj) 20.00

HENDY,ANNE MARIE-American Railroad Stock Certificates-Lond-(1980)-Stanley Gibbons Publ-sm 4to-viii,168p-cl,col illus (x4,dj soil) 35.00

HENDY,ANNE MARIE-American Railroad Stock Certificates-Lond-1980-168p-1st ed (n4,f,f dj) 17.00

HENIE,SONJA-Wings on My Feet-NY-1940-Prentice Hall-8vo-177p-photos-1st ed (dd5,dj) 75.00

HENKEL,ALICE-American Root Drugs-Wash-1907-GPO-80p+7p plts-wrps (m6,sl flawed wrps) 25.00

HENKIN,HARMON-Fly Tackle-Phila-1976-Lippincott-1st ed (ff7,f,dj) 17.50

HENNICK,LOUIS C-Louisiana: Its Street and Interurban Railways, Vol.I-1962-Hennick-4to-143p-illus (nn7) 45.00

HENNICK,LOUIS C-Louisiana: Its Street and Interurban Railways, Vol.I-Shreveport-1962-143p-1st ed (n4,f,dj) 15.00

HENRY COUNTY-HISTORY OF...,INDIANA...-Chig-1884-912p-cl (n1,sl dmpstnd,rbnd,rprd pgs) 75.00

HENRY,ALEXANDER-Alexander Henry's Travels and Adventures in the Years 1760 to 1776-Chig-1921-Donnelley-340p-frntis,map-Lakeside Classics (cc4) 35.00

HENRY,FRANCOISE-ED.-Book of Kells-NY-1974-Knopf-lg folio-linen bds,publ box,126 col plts,75 monochromes-1st Amer ed (l8,f,box) 125.00

HENRY,FRANCOISE-Irish Art-Ithaca-1965-Cornell U Pr-2 vols,buckram,col & b&w plts,maps,drwngs-1st ed (l8) 125.00

HENRY,G M-Guide to the Birds of Ceylon-Lond-1955-8vo-432p-cl,27 col & 3 half-tone plts-1st ed (y8,dj chip) 45.00

HENRY,JOHN-Mounted Drill Team-NY-1954-Barnes-1st ed (h9) 18.00

HENRY,JOSEPH-Scientific Writings of...-Wash D.C.-1886-Smithsonian-2 vols,gry cl,text figs-1st ed (j2,sl wn & soil) 85.00

HENRY,MARGUERITE-Boy and a Dog-Chig-1944-Willcox & Follett-4to-pict bds,illus-1st ed (pp10,dj) 15.00

HENRY,MARGUERITE-Dear Readers and Riders-Chig-1969-Rand McNally-sm 4to-1st ed (h9) 25.00

HENRY,MARGUERITE-Justin Morgan Had a Horse-Chig-(1945)-Wilcox & Follett-4to-pict cl,illus-presumed 1st ed (pp10,f,sl rub dj) 35.00

HENRY,MARGUERITE-Misty of Chincoteague-Chig-(1947)-Rand McNally-sm 4to-pict cl,col & b&w illus-1st ed (pp10,dj) 25.00

HENRY,O-Options-NY,Lond-1909-Harper-orig g titled cl-1st ed (aa9,sl fade sp) 40.00

HENRY,O-Postscripts-1923-Harpers-1st ed (x7,sp chip dj) 65.00

HENRY,O-Trimmed Lamp and Other Stories of the Four Million-NY-1907-McClure,Phillips-orig g titled cl-1st ed,1st iss (aa9) 40.00

HENRY,O-Voice of the City-NY-1908-McClure-orig g titled cl-1st ed,1st iss (aa9,sl rub sp) 40.00

HENRY,ROBERT S-This Fascinating Railroad Business-NY-1946-521p-3rd rvsd ed (n4,f,dj) 22.50

HENRY,ROBERT-Armed Forces Institute of Pathology-Wash-1964-422p-1st ed (dd3) 50.00

HENRY,STUART-Conquering Our Great American Plains-NY-(1930)-Dutton-12mo-xvi,395p-illus,map-Howes H427-1st ed (aa3,sl chip dj) 85.00

HENRY,STUART-Conquering Our Great American Plains-NY-(1930)-Dutton-395p-illus-Herd 1026-1st ed (cc4,dj) 50.00

HENRY,VERA-Mystery of Cedar Valley-1964-Avalon-1st ed (s10,dj) 12.50

HENRY,WILL-Death of a Legend-NY-(1954)-Random-1st ed (p1,f,dj) 35.00

HENSEL,W U-Christiana Riot and the Treason Trials of 1851-Lancaster-1911-New Era Prntg Co-4to-x+158p-wht cl,plts-2nd ed (k2,sl soil cov) 65.00

HENSHALL,J A-Bass, Pike, Perch and Other Game Fishes of America...-Cin-1919-Stewart & Kidd-410p+ads-cl-col frontis,19 pg b&w plts-new ed (h1) 15.00

HENSHALL,J A-Favorite Fish & Fishing-NY-1908-8vo-192p-illus-1st ed (m3) 35.00

HENSHALL,J A-More About the Black Bass-Cin-1889-8vo-204p-illus,photos-1st ed (m3) 70.00

HENSON,PAULINE-Founding a Wilderness Capital Prescot, A.T.1864-Flagstaff-1965-261p-fldg map frntis,photos,illus-1st ed (t7,dj,autg) 15.00

HENSON,PAULINE-Founding a Wilderness Capital-Flagstaff-(1965)-Northland Pr-xvi+261p-olive cl,illus,fldg map-1st ed (h2) 20.00

HENSON,TRUMAN-Sporting Rifles & Scope Sights-NY-1950-8vo-204p-photos,illus-1st ed (m3,sl chip dj) 25.00

HENTOFF,NAT-Blues For Charles Darwin-NY-1982-Morrow-1st ed (e3,f,dj) 20.00

HENTOFF,NAT-Blues for Charlie Darwin-NY-1982-Morrow-1st ed (g4,as new in dj) 10.00

HENTOFF,NAT-Jazz Life-1961-Dial-1st ed (m9,f,dj sp sl wn) 35.00

HENTOFF,NAT-Jazz Life-NY-1961-Dial-1st ed (w1,f,dj) 25.00

HENTOFF,NAT-Jazz: New Perspectives on the History...-NY-(1959)-Rinehart-1st ed (w1,f,dj) 30.00

HENWOOD,JAMES N J-Short Haul to the Bay-Brattleboro-1969-48p-1st ed (n4,f,dj) 10.00

HENZELL,H P-Fishing for Sea Trout-Lond-1949-8vo-147p-illus,col frontis (m3,vf) 20.00

HEPPER,F N-West African Herbaria of Isert & Thonning-Kew-1976-Moxon Trust-227p-cl (x6,dj) 25.00

HEPTINSTALL,WILLIAM-Gourmet Recipes from a Highland Hotel-Lond-(1967)-Faber-176p (u6) 25.00

HEPTINSTALL,WILLIAM-Hors D'Oeuvre and Cold Table-Lond-(1959)-Faber-264p (u6) 25.00

HEPWORTH,GEORGE-Brown Studies or Camp Fires & Morals-NY-1895-12mo-332p-illus (m3,sl fade sp) 12.50

HEPWORTH,GEORGE-Starboard & Port-NY-1876-12mo-237p-illus-1st ed (m3,f) 50.00

HERALD-TRIBUNE HOME INSTITUTE-America's Cook Book-1952-Scribner-1154p-grn cl,col plts-1st prtg,rvsd ed (q8,dj) 40.00

HERBERT,APRIL-Tailgate Cookbook-(1970)-Galahad-205p-red cl-1st prtg (q8,dj) 10.00

HERBERT,FRANK-Dune Messiah-NY-(1969)-Putnam-1st ed (e3,dj sp sl chip) 200.00

HERBERT,FRANK-God Emperor of Dune-NY-(1981)-Putnam-1st ed (l3,f,dj) 25.00

HERBERT,FRANK-God Makers-NY-1972-Putnam-1st ed (w5,f,dj) 50.00

HERBERT,FRANK-Jesus Incident-np-(1979)-Berkley-1st ed (b5,as new in dj) 12.50

HERBERT,FRANK-Whipping Star-1970-Putnam-1st ed (o9,sunned dj sp) 75.00

HERBERT,FRANK-White Plague-NY-(1982)-Putnam's-1st ed (b5,as new in dj) 12.50

HERBERT,FRANK-White Plague-NY-(1982)-Putnam-1st ed (e3,f,dj) 20.00

HERBERT,HENRY-Hints to Horse Leepers-NY-(1859)-Orange Judd (j9) 35.00

HERBERT,HENRY-Hints to Horsekeepers-NY-1859-Moore-1st ed (h9) 65.00

HERBERT,IVOR-Queen Mother's Horses-Lond-1967-Pelham-1st ed (j9,dj wn) 25.00

HERBERT,J A-Illuminated Manuscripts-NY,Lond-1911-lg thk 8vo-356p-g dec cl,51 plts(incl illuminated frntis) (a3,uncut) 75.00

HERBERT,LT COL ANTHONY B-Soldier-NY-(1976)-HR&W-1st ed (ff3,f,dj) 40.00

HERBIG,G H-ED.-Spectroscopic Astrophysics...Otto Struve-Berkeley-1970-U of Cal Pr-462p-illus (hh6,chip dj) 50.00

HERBODEAU,EUGENE-George Auguste Escoffier-Lond-(1955)-Practical Pr-138p-prntd in two inks,illus (u6) 22.00

HERBRUCK,EMIL P-Early Years and Late Reflections-Cleve-nd-257p-cl (f1,sl wn dj) 17.50

HEREFORD,J-Flying Years-np-(1946)-roy 8vo-x,114p-cl,illus,2p maps (t2) 30.00

HERFORD,OLIVER-An Alphabet of Celebrities-Bost-1899-Small,Maynard-sq 8vo-unpgd-cl bckd bds,prntd in red & blk,illus-1st ed (r3,t.p. rprd) 50.00

HERGESHEIMER,JOSEPH-Sheridan-Bost-1931-Houghton Mifflin-frntis,maps-1st ed (o7) 30.00

HERIVEL,E B-We Farmed a Desert-Lond-(1957)-Faber & Faber-8vo-280p-illus-1st ed (gg5,dj) 20.00

HERLIHY,JAMES L-Midnight Cowboy-(1965)-S&S-1st ed (m9,dj sl soil & sl tn) 30.00

HERLIHY,JAMES L-Midnight Cowboy-NY-(1965)-S&S-1st ed (u10,vf,vf dj) 45.00

HERLIHY,JAMES L-Sleep of Baby Filbertson-NY-1959-Dutton-1st solo bk-1st ed (e10,fray cor,dj) 25.00

HERMANN'S WIZARD'S MANUAL-Chig-(1916)-Shrewsbury Publ-150p+ads-wrps (m1,sl wn,sl stnd wrps) 15.00

HERMANN,BINGER-Louisiana Purchase-1900-GPO-87p+3 fldg maps & ports-Tweney #28 (h7,cov speckld) 50.00

HERMANN,H-Luftwaffe-NY-(1943)-8vo-xviii,300p-cl-1st ed (t2,chip dj) 40.00

HERMANN,MATTHIAS-Herbs and Medicinal Flowers-NY-(1973)-Galahad-128p-wht cl,221 col plts (q8,dj) 22.50

HERMES,MARGARET-Phoenix Nest-1981-Contemporary-1st ed (s10,dj) 12.50

HERNDON,SARAH R-Days on the Road-NY-1902-xvi,270p-port-Howes H439-Smith 4371 (a7) 125.00

HERNDON,SARAH R-Days on the Road: Crossing the Plains in 1865-NY-1902-Burr Prtg Hs-12mo-xvi,270p-orig cl & dec e.p.,frntis port-Howes H439-1st ed (aa3,cl wn) 150.00

HERNDON,SARAH R-Days on the Road:Crossing the Plains in 1865-NY-1902-Burr Prtg Hs-12mo-xvi,270p-orig brwn cl wi "S.R.H." on sp,frntis-Howes H439-1st ed (mm1) 195.00

HERNDON,WILLIAM H-Herndon's Lincoln-Chig-(1889-Bedford,Clarke-3 vols-blu cl,illus-Howes H440-1st ed (h2,rub) 275.00

HERNER,CHARLES-Arizona Rough Riders-Tucson-1970-U of Ariz-275p-map e.p.-1st ed (dd7,as new in dj) 25.00

HERR,MICHAEL-Dispatches-NY-1977-auth 1st bk-1st ed (s5,f,dj) 90.00

HERR,MICHAEL-Dispatches-NY-1977-Knopf-1st ed (ff3,f,f dj) 125.00

HERRICK,C J-Neurological Foundations of Animal Behavior-1924-Holt-334p-131 figs (bb3) 16.00

HERRICK,C L-Mammals of Minnesota-Mpls-1892-8vo-299,(1)p-cl,8 plts(1 col) (y8) 30.00

HERRICK,FRANCIS H-American Eagle-NY-1934-Appleton Century-266p-photos (c9,sp fade) 65.00

HERRICK,FRANCIS-Audubon the Naturalist-NY-1917-Appleton-2 vols-photos,drwngs-scarce-1st ed (oo9) 175.00

HERRICK,JAMES-Short History of Cardiology-Springfield-1942-258p-illus-1st ed (dd3) 125.00

HERRICK,LEO-Great Balloon Ascension-np-nd(ca.1960)-33p-dbl col,wrps (e1) 17.50

HERRING,FRANCES-Among the People of British Columbia, Red, White, Yellow and Brown-Lond-1903-xvi,299p-illus-Smith 4374 (a7,sl wn) 75.00

HERRIOT,JAMES-James Herriot's Yorkshire-NY-(1979)-St.Martin's-1st US ed (hh5,f,dj) 12.50

HERRLIGKOFFER,KARL-Killer Mountain-NY-1954-Knopf-maps,photos-Neate 365-1st ed (j8,f,sl edge wn dj) 45.00

HERRLIGKOFFER,KARL-Nanga Parbat-NY-1954-263p-1st US ed (q10,f,dj) 22.00

HERRLINGER,ROBERT-History of Medical Illustration from Antiquity to 1600-NY-1970-4to-178p-illus-1st Engl transl (dd3,box) 150.00

HERRMANN,JOHN-Salesman-NY-1939-S&S-1st ed (w5,f) 30.00

HERSEY,JOHN-Hiroshima-NY-1946-1st ed (o5,chip dj) 20.00

HERSEY,JOHN-Hiroshima-NY-1946-Knopf-1st ed (s6,sl wn dj) 30.00

HERSEY,JOHN-Hiroshima-NY-1983-LEC-sm folio-blk aniline lea,8 orig silk screens by J Lawrence,ltd to 1500c,three autg (w1,f,box) 750.00

HERSEY,JOHN-Letter to the Alumni-NY-1970-Knopf-1st ed (y10,dj) 20.00

HERSEY,JOHN-Marmot Drive-NY-1953-Knopf-1st ed (hh5,dj) 15.00

HERSEY,JOHN-Too Far To Walk-NY-1966-Knopf-1st ed (e3,f,sl wn dj sp) 35.00

HERSEY,JOHN-Wall-NY-1950-Knopf-1st ed (x1,f,f dj) 50.00

HERSEY,JOHN-Walnut Door-NY-1977-1st ed (q5,f,dj) 12.50

HERSKOVITS,MELVILLE J-Dahomean Narrative-Evanston-1958-Nrthwstrn U Pr-8vo-African Studies No.1 (y5) 35.00

HERSTLKOVITZ,P-Living New World Monkeys-Chig-1977-4to-1117p-cl,7 col plts-Vol.1 (y8,dj) 110.00

HERT,C-Tracking the Big Cats-ID-1955-330p-photos (gg3,f,dj) 75.00

HERTER,G L-Bull Cook & Authentic Historical Recipes & Practices. Vol.2-Herter's,Waseca-1968-752p-gold cl,illus (b6) 20.00

HERTER,G L-Professional & Amateur Tournament & Hunting Instructions & Encyclopedia-MN-1963-227p-dec e.p.,photos (gg3,f) 45.00

HERTER,G L-Professional Fly Tying Manual-Waseca-1941-8vo-110p-wrps,illus-1st ed (m3,f) 12.50

HERTER,G L-Professional Guide's Manual-MN-1964-for North Star Guide Assn-349p-photos (gg3,f) 12.00

HERTER,G L-Professional Guide's Manual-Waseca-1963-8vo-349p-photos,illus (m3) 15.00

HERTER,G L-Truth About Hunting in Today's Africa-1963-auth publ-314p-photos (gg3,f) 10.00

HERTRICH,WILLIAM-Camellias in the Huntington Gardens-San Marino-1954,1955,1959-Huntington Botanical Gdns-3 vols-7 col plts,photos (m10,ea vol pres,dj wn,rprd) 150.00

HERTZ,EMANUEL-Hidden Lincoln-NY-1938-Viking-xii+461p-tan cl,plts-1st ed (k2) 20.00

HERTZ,HEINRICH-Principles of Mechanics-1899-276p-v rare-1st Engl language ed (h6) 250.00

HERTZ,LOUIS H-Messrs.Ives of Bridgeport-Withersfield-1950-159p-1st ed (n4,f,dj) 22.00

HERTZBERG,HAZEL W-Search for American Indian Identity-Syracuse-(1972)-Syracuse Univ Pr-362p-illus (cc4,dj) 20.00

HERTZEL,BOB-Big Red Machine-1976-Prentice Hall-photos,pict e.p.-1st ed (s8,dj) 12.50

HERTZLER,ARTHUR E-Horse and Buggy Doctor-NY-1938-322p-cl-1st ed so stated (m1,dj) 12.50

HERTZOG,PETER-Directory of New Mexico Desperados-Santa Fe-1965-Pr of Territorian-8vo-44p-stiff wrps-1st ed (aa3,edge fade) 17.50

HERTZOG,PETER-Little Known Facts about Billy, the Kid-Santa Fe-1963-Pr of Territorian-8vo-32p-stiff wrps,illus-1st ed (aa3,f) 22.50

HERVEY,HARRY-Where Strange Gods Call-NY-1924-Century-349p-drwngs,pict dj (c3,dj) 30.00

HERVEY,JOHN-American Trotter-NY-1947-Coward McCann-1st ed (h9,dj) 125.00

HERZOG,M-Annapurna-NY-1953-316p-28 plts,fldg map-rprnt (o10,f,dj) 15.00

HERZOG,TH-Pneumatic Structures-NY-1976-707 illus-1st ed (h10,dj) 50.00

HESELTINE,NIGEL-Madagascar-NY-(1971)-Praeger-8vo-334p-4 maps-Libr of African Affairs ser-1st US ed (dd5,f,sl tn dj) 20.00

HESS,LILO-Shetland Ponies-NY-1964-Crowell-photos-1st ed (h9,dj) 10.00

HESS,STEPHEN-Ungentlemanly Art-NY-(1968)-Macmillan-lg 8vo-252p-blu cl,illus-1st ed (k2,dj) 25.00

HESS,THOMAS B-Barnett Newman-NY-1971-MOMA-4to-158p-pict wrps,b&w & col illus (r10) 12.50

HESSE,HERMAN-Autobiographical Writings-1972-Farrar-1st US ed (kk6,f,dj) 30.00

HESSE,HERMAN-Demian-Lond-(1958)-Owen/Vision Pr-1st Brit ed (x10,dj sl tn & wn) 50.00

HESSE,HERMAN-Gertrude-1969-Farrar-1st US ed (kk6,f,sl tn dj) 30.00

HESSE,HERMAN-Hermann Hesse and Roman Rolland-Lond-1978-Oswald Wolff-155p-1st ed (j8,f,dj) 27.50

HESSE,HERMAN-Klingsor's Last Summer-1970-Farrar-1st ed (kk6,f,dj) 30.00

HESSE,HERMAN-My Belief-NY-(1974)-Farrar Straus-1st US ed (f3,dj) 25.00

HESSE,HERMAN-Narcissus & Goldmund-NY-1968-FSG-1st US ed (x9,pgs brwng,dj) 30.00

HESSE,HERMAN-Peter Camenzind-Lond-(1961)-Owen/Vision Pr-1st Brit ed (x10,dj) 50.00

HESSE,HERMAN-Peter Camenzind-Lond-1961-1st Brit ed (y7,sl fray dj) 20.00

HESSE,HERMAN-Prodigy-Lond-(1961)-Owen/Vision Pr-1st Brit ed (x10,dj) 50.00

HESSE,HERMAN-Reflections-NY-1974-FS&G-1st ed (h8,f,f dj) 30.00

HESSE,HERMAN-Rosshalde-NY-1970-FSG-1st ed (z3,dj) 20.00

HESSE,HERMAN-Stories from Five Decades-(1972)-Farrar-1st US ed (kk6,f,dj) 30.00

HESSE,HERMAN-Stories of Five Decades-NY-(1972)-FS&G-translated by R Manheim-1st ed (s6,sl rub dj) 20.00

HESSE,HERMAN-Tales of Student Life-NY-1976-FS&G-1st ed (h8,f,f dj) 45.00

HESSE,HERMANN-Wandering-NY-1972-FSG-1st ed (c8,f,f dj) 30.00

HESSE,R-Ecological Animal Geography-NY-1937-8vo-xiv,597p-cl,text figs (jj10) 47.50

HESTER,F E-World of the Wood Duck-1973-Lippincott-160p-photos-1st ed (bb3,dj) 25.00

HESTER,HARRIET H-300 Sugar Saving Recipes-NY-(1942)-M Barrows-181p-1st ed (m6) 15.00

HESTON,ALFRED M-ED.-South Jersey. a History, 1664 to 1924-NY-(ca.1924)-4to-546p-cl-vol.5 only(iss sep from 4 vol hist) (aa6) 75.00

HESTON,ALFRED M-ED.-South Jersey. a History, 1664 to 1924-NY-1924-4to-4 vols-(a fifth vol iss separately)-cl,plts (aa6) 200.00

HESTON,ALFRED M-Jersey Waggon Jaunts-(np)-1926-2 vols-cl,plts (aa6) 90.00

HETHERINGTON,A L-Chinese Ceramic Glazes-Cambridge-1937-U Pr & Courtland Inst Art-sm 8vo-76p-14 plts(incl 6 col)-rprnt wi corrections of 1st ed (c3) 95.00

HEUSINGER,EDWARD W-Early Explorations and Mission Establishments in Texas-S.A.-1936-Naylor-202p-illus,maps(1 fldg)-1st ed (a9,dj) 100.00

HEUSSER,ALBERT H-Forgotten General-Paterson-(1928)-4to-ix,(2),216p-cl,plts (aa6) 65.00

HEUSSER,ALBERT H-George Washington's Map Maker-New Brunswick-(1966)-xix,268p-cl,plts-revision of 1928 ed (aa6) 35.00

HEWARD,BILL-Some Are Called Clowns-1974-Crowell-photos-1st ed (s8,dj) 25.00

HEWER,H R-British Seals-1974-Taplinger-256p-photos-1st US ed (bb3,f,fray dj) 18.00

HEWETT,EDGAR-Ancient Life in the American Southwest-Indpls-1930-Bobbs Merrill-e.p. maps,illus-1st ed (v4) 40.00

HEWETT,EDGAR-Handbooks of Archaelogical History-Albuq-1947-204p-dec cl,frntis,photos (t7) 17.50

HEWETT,EDGAR-Landmarks of New Mexico-Albuq-1940-UNM-photos-1st ed (oo9) 50.00

HEWETT,EDGAR-Landmarks of New Mexico: Handbooks of Archaelogical History-1947-UNM Pr-lg sq 8vo-204p-dec cov,map,photos-2nd ed (aa3,dj) 50.00

HEWETT,EDGAR-Mission Monuments of New Mexico-Albuq-1943-269p-cl,illus-1st ed (z1,chip dj) 60.00

HEWETT,EDGAR-Pueblo Indian World-Albuq-1945-UNM-photos,fldg maps-1st ed (oo9,dj chip) 75.00

HEWETT,EDWARD-Convivial Dickens: The Drinks of Dickens & His Times-(1983)-Ohio U Pr-191p-red cl,illus-1st ed (q8,dj) 25.00

HEWINS,CAROLINE-Mid Century Child and Her Books-NY-1926-Macmillan-sm 8vo-136p-cl-1st ed (nn10,f,dj) 35.00

HEWINS,CAROLINE-Midcentury Child and Her Books-NY-1926-Macmillan-illus (a8) 20.00

HEWINS,RALPH-Mr.Five Per Cent-NY-1957-Rinehart-cl,illus-1st ed (m8,f,dj) 13.50

HEWITT,E R-Days From Seventy-Five to Ninety-NY-1957-8vo-131p-scarce-1st ed (m3,f,fray dj) 85.00

HEWITT,E R-Secrets of the Salmon-NY-1925-8vo-158p-photos (m3) 22.50

HEWITT,E R-Those Were the Days-NY-1943-8vo-318p-1st ed (m3) 22.50

HEWITT,E R-Trout & Salmon Fisherman for 75 Years-1966-Ambercrombie & Fitch-8vo-338p-photos (m3,f) 22.50

HEWITT,EMMA C-Corn Products Refining Co-NYC-nd(ca.1905)-52p-pict wrps,col plts (q8) 15.00

HEWITT,J N B-ED.-Contains Seneca Fiction, Legends, and Myths-Wash-1918-GPO/Bur Amer Ethnol-3/4 lea-32nd Annual Report (ff4,ex-libr) 60.00

HEWITT,O H-Wild Turkey & Its Management-1967-Wildlife Soc-589p-col plts (gg3,f,dj) 75.00

HEWITT,W LOVELL-Beagling-Lond-1960-Faber & Faber-1st prtg (f10,dj) 35.00

HEWLETT,RICHARD-ET AL-History of the United States Atomic Energy Commission-Univ Park-1962,69-Penn St Univ Pr-2 vols,gry & slt cl,illus (j2,dj & box) 65.00

HEWLETT,RICHARD-History of the U.S. Atomic Energy Commission-Univ Park-1962,69-Penn St U Pr-2 vols-gry cl-1st ed (c2,e.p. cut,dj) 50.00

HEXT,H-Monster-1925-Macmillan-1st ed (x7,dj) 55.00

HEYEN,WILLIAM-Of Palestine: a Meditation-Omaha-1976-Abattoir Ed-sm 8vo-prtd wrps-ltd to 275c-1st ed (jj8,f) 35.00

HEYER,GEORGETTE-No Wind of Blame-NY-1939-Dbldy CC-1st US ed (g4,f,dj missing sm chips) 25.00

HEYER,P-Architects on Architecture-NY-1966-lg 4to-plans,photos-1st ed (h10,dj sl chip) 65.00

HEYERDAHL,THOR-Aku Aku-Chig-(1958)-Rand McNally-8vo-384p-col photos-1st ed (cc5,dj) 20.00

HEYERDAHL,THOR-American Indians in the Pacific-Lond-1952-821p-illus,fldg map-1st ed (j7) 100.00

HEYERDAHL,THOR-American Indians in the Pacific-Lond-1952-Allen & Unwin-lg 8vo-xv+821p-brwn cl,90 plts,11 maps-1st Brit ed (p8,wn dj) 125.00

HEYERDAHL,THOR-Art of Easter Island-GC-1975-Dbldy-4to-349p-photos(incl 16p col),e.p. maps-1st ed (mm8,dj) 75.00*

HEYERDAHL,THOR-Ra Expeditions-GC-1971-Dbldy-8vo-341p-grn cl over bds,111 col photos (p8,wn dj) 20.00

HEYLIGER,WILLIAM-Big Leaguer-1936-Goldsmith-1st ed (s8,dj) 12.50

HEYMAN,MAX L,JR.-Prudent Soldier-Glendale-1959-418p-illus,maps(incl fldg)-1st ed (c4) 110.00

HEYMAN,MAX L,JR.-Prudent Soldier-Glendale-1959-Arthur H Clark-418p-illus,maps-1st ed (ff4) 95.00

HEYN,MARIE KAHN-Marie Kahn, L'Americaine-Cin-1943-Current Topic Club-35p-wrps (d1) 12.50

HEYNEMAN,J H-Desert Cactus-Lond-1934-10 illus-scarce-1st Brit ed (kk4,dj sl chip) 100.00

HEYSINGER,ISAAC W-Spirit and Matter-Phila-1910-Lippincott-8vo-433p-1st US ed (aa5) 60.00

HEYWARD,DUBOSE-Brass Ankle-NY-1931-orng dj-1st trd ed (o5,sl chip dj) 45.00

HEYWARD,DUBOSE-Carolina Chansons-NY-1922-Macmillan-auth 1st bk-1st ed (z9,cor bump,sl soil) 45.00

HEYWOOD,VALENTINE-British Titles-Lond-(1951)-A & C Black-8vo-xi,188p-red cl (t10,f) 25.00

HEYWOOD-WAKEFIELD COMPANY-Completed Century 1826 to 1926: The Story of...-Bost-1926-prtd for Co(Merrymnt Pr)-4to-112p-maroon cl-photos-1st ed (s1) 40.00

HIATT,J M-Political-Manual...-Indpls-1865-Asher & Adams-276p-cl (j1,sl wn sp) 15.00

HIATT,JAMES M-Voter's Text Book-Indpls-1868-Asher,Ames & Higgins-1st ed (ee6) 15.00

HIBBARD,WHITNEY S-Forensic Hypnosis-Springfield-(1981)-Chas C Thomas Publ-(xx)+(354)p-prntd tan cl-1st ed (y9,chip dj) 27.50

HIBBEN,F C-Hunting in Africa-NY-1962-236p-photos,illus (gg3,f) 35.00

HIBBEN,F D-Hunting American Bears-NY-1950-247p-photos (gg3,f,dj) 28.00

HIBBEN,FRANK C-Treasure in the Dust-Phila-1951-311p-photos,illus-1st ed (t7,dj) 15.00

HIBBEN,SHEILA-Kitchen Manual-(1941)-DS&P-231p-gry cl-1st ed (q8,edgewn dj) 12.50

HIBBERT,CHRISTOPHER-Battle of Arnhem-NY-1962-224p-illus-1st ed (jj2,f,dj) 40.00

HIBBERT,CHRISTOPHER-Corunna-NY-1961-216p-illus-1st ed (gg2,f,dj) 35.00

HIBBETT,HOWARD-ED.-Contemporary Japanese Literature-NY-1977-Knopf-1st ed (z9,dj) 20.00

HIBBITS,JOHN J-Take'er Up Alone, Mister-NY-(1943)-234p-cl (l1,wn dj) 12.50

HICHBORN,FRANKLIN-System-SF-1915-James H Barry-12mo-464,xi p-1st ed (n2) 30.00

HICHENS,ROBERT-Barbary Sheep-NY-1907-Harper-dec pgs-1st ed (hh5) 12.50

HICKEY,JOSEPH J-Guide to Bird Watching-Lond-1943-Oxford U Pr-264p (d9) 10.00

HICKMAN,PAUL-George Fiske, Yosemite Photographer-Flagstaff-1980-Northland Pr-118p-75 photos-1st ed (cc9,as new in dj) 45.00

HICKOK,MARTHA J C-Calamity Jane's Letters to Her Daughter-(San Lorenzo)-(1976)-(Shameless Hussy Pr)-unpgd(46)-wht wrps (l6) 15.00

HICKS,GRANVILLE-Great Tradition-NY-1933-Macmillan-1st ed (v5,f,dj soil,wn) 35.00

HICKS,GRANVILLE-John Reed-NY-1936-Macmillan-x+445p-gry cl-1st ed (b2,edge wn dj) 35.00

HICKS,GRANVILLE-Only One Storm-NY-1942-Macmillan-1st ed (bb1,sl drknd sp,dj) 20.00

HICKS,GRANVILLE-Only One Storm-NY-1942-Macmillan-1st ed (hh5,dj) 15.00

HICKS,GRANVILLE-Part of the Truth-NY-(1965)-314p-cl-1st ed (b1,f,dj) 17.50

HICKS,GRANVILLE-Small Town-NY-1946-Macmillan-1st ed (hh5,dj) 10.00

HIDY,RALPH W-Pioneering in Big Business-NY-(1955)-839p-cl-1st ed so stated (j1,sl wn dj) 17.50

HIDY,VERNON-Pleasures of Fly Fishing-NY-1972-4to-128p-photos (m3,vf,dj) 32.50

HIEBELER,TONI-North Face in Winter-Phila-1963-121p (o10,f,dj) 35.00

HIGBE,KIRBY-High Hard One-1967-Viking (r7,f,dj) 50.00

HIGBE,KIRBY-High Hard One-1967-Viking-1st ed (s8,f,dj) 55.00

HIGGERS,JIM-Adventures of Theodore-Chig-1901-12mo-210p-illus (m3) 15.00

HIGGINBOTHAM,DON-War of American Independence-NY-1971-509p-16 plts,9 maps-1st ed (b7,f,dj) 35.00

HIGGINS,C A-New Guide to the Pacific Coast-Chig-(1894)-Rand,McNally-282p-lg fldg map (ff4) 30.00

HIGGINS,GEORGE V-Cogan's Trade-NY-1974-1st ed (q5,f,dj) 12.50

HIGGINS,GEORGE V-Friends of Eddie Coyle-Lond-1972-auth 1st bk-1st Brit ed (t5,dj) 20.00

HIGGINS,GEORGE V-Friends of Eddie Coyle-NY-1972-auth 1st bk-1st ed (f5,f,dj) 30.00

HIGGINS,GEORGE V-Friends of Eddie Coyle-NY-1972-Knopf-auth 1st bk-1st ed (x7,f,dj) 27.00

HIGGINS,GEORGE V-Judgement of Deke Hunter-Bost,Tor-(1976)-Little,Brown-1st ed (bb1,as new in dj) 15.00

HIGGINS,GEORGE V-Kennedy for the Defense-NY-1980-Knopf-1st ed (bb1,as new in dj) 15.00

HIGGINS,GEORGE V-Patriot Game-NY-1982-Knopf-1st ed (bb1,as new in dj) 15.00

HIGGINS,GEORGE V-Rat on Fire-NY-1981-Knopf-1st ed (bb1,as new in dj) 15.00

HIGGINS,JACK-Eagle Has Landed-Lond-1975-Collins-1st ed (f4,dj) 12.50

HIGGINS,JACK-Luciano's Luck-Lond-1981-Collins-1st ed (q4,f,dj) 37.50

HIGGINS,JACK-Solo-Lond-1980-Collins-1st ed (s4,f,dj) 37.50

HIGGINS,JACK-Stormwarning-Lond-1976-Collins-1st ed (g4,f,dj) 12.50

HIGGINSON,A HENRY-Letters From an Old Sportsman to a Young One-GC-1929-Dbldy-illus-1st ed (h9) 48.00

HIGGINSON,GEORGE-Seventy One Years of a Guardsman's Life-Lond-1916-403p-red cl,illus-1st ed (b7,sl wn) 65.00

HIGGINSON,HENRY A-British & American Sporting Authors-Lond-1951-4to-443p-photos-1st ed (m3,f,chip dj) 100.00

HIGGINSON,THOMAS W-Tales of the Enchanted Islands of the Atlantic-NY-1898-Macmillan-cl,illus,A Herter-1st ed (l8,hngs weak) 25.00

HIGGINSON,THOMAS W-Travellers and Outlaws-Bost-1889-Lee & Shepard-340p+ads-brwn dec dl-BAL 8362-1st ed (k2) 30.00

HIGGINSON,THOMAS W-Women and Men-NY-1888-326p-cl-BAL 8354-1st ed (d1,sl soil,lacks rear f.e.p.) 15.00
HIGHAM,CHARLES-Kate-NY-(1975)-244p-cl-1st ed so stated (d1,dj scrtchd) 12.50
HIGHSMITH,PATRICIA-Boy Who Followed Ripley-NY-1980-1st US ed (r5,f,dj) 12.50
HIGHSMITH,PATRICIA-Cry of the Owl-NY-1962-Harper-1st ed (g4,f,dj) 35.00
HIGHSMITH,PATRICIA-Dog's Ransom-Lond-1972-Heinemann-1st ed (w9,f,dj) 40.00
HIGHSMITH,PATRICIA-Dog's Ransom-NY-1972-Knopf-1st US ed (f4,f,dj) 15.00
HIGHSMITH,PATRICIA-Game for the Living-(1958)-Harpers-1st ed (x7,dj sl chip,sp fade) 55.00
HIGHSMITH,PATRICIA-Game For the Living-NY-(1958)-Harper-1st ed (e10,dj rear panel sl stnd) 35.00
HIGHSMITH,PATRICIA-Glass Cell-1964-Crime Club-1st ed (s9,dj) 20.00
HIGHSMITH,PATRICIA-Slowly, Slowly in the Wind-Lond-1979-Heinemann-1st ed (w9,f,dj) 35.00
HIGHSMITH,PATRICIA-Snail Watcher-1970-Dbldy-1st ed (t4,f,dj) 25.00
HIGHSMITH,PATRICIA-Snail Watcher-1970-Dbldy-1st ed (x7,f,dj) 23.00
HIGHSMITH,PATRICIA-Strangers on a Train-1950-Harper-auth 1st bk-1st ed (x7) 65.00
HIGHSMITH,PATRICIA-Strangers on a Train-NY-1950-Harper & Bros-auth scarce 1st bk-1st ed (bb1,dj sp fade & sl chip) 275.00
HIGHSMITH,PATRICIA-Talented Mr Ripley-1955-CM-1st ed (x7,sl fox dj) 120.00
HIGHSMITH,PATRICIA-Tremor of Forgery-Lond-1969-Heinemann-1st Brit ed (w9,f,dj) 45.00
HIGHSMITH,PATRICIA-Two Faces of January-Lond-1964-Heinemann-1st Brit ed (w5,f,f dj) 35.00
HIGHTOWER,JOHN-Pheasant Hunting-NY-1946-227p-ltd to 350c,nbrd,autg-illus,L B Hunt-scarce (m3,f) 150.00
HIGHWATER,JAMAKE-Journey to the Sky-1978-Crowell-1st ed (t9,dj) 25.00
HIGHWATER,JAMAKE-Ritual of the Wind-NY-(1977)-Viking-sm folio-192p-illus e.p.,drwngs,photos-1st ed (gg4,sl wn dj) 15.00
HIGMAN,HARRY W-Union Bay-Seattle-1951-U of Wash-viii,315p-37 illus-1st ed (o2,sl rub dj) 15.00
HIGUCHI,TADAHIKO-Visual and Spatial Structure of Landscapes-Cambridge-1983-MIT-4to-x,218p-cl,illus,maps,plans (cc10,as new in dj) 40.00
HILBERSEIMER,L-New City: Principles of Planning-Chig-1944-P Theobald-sm folio-192p-illus-1st ed (b3,dj) 50.00
HILBERSEIMER,L-New Regional Pattern-Chig-1949-123 illus-1st ed (h10,dj) 75.00
HILDER,BRETT-Navigator in the South Seas-Lond-1961-Percival Marshall-8vo-232p-blk cl,map e.p.,illus (p8,wn dj,pres) 30.00
HILDER,BRETT-Voyages of Torres-St.Lucia-1980-U of Queensland-sm 4to-col e.p maps,5 col,26 b&w illus (p8,as new in dj) 50.00
HILDRETH,S P-Memoirs of the Early Pioneer Settlers of Ohio, with narratives...in 1775-Cin-1854-H W Derby & Co-539p-cl-Howes H 473 (j1) 75.00
HILDRETH,SAMUEL P-Genealogical and Biographical Sketches of the Hildreth Family from the Year 1652 to the Year 1840-np-nd-334p-cl-rare (d1,covs sl flecked) 100.00
HILDRETH,SAMUEL-Spell of the Turf-Phila-1926-Lippincott-1st ed (f10,sl tn sp) 35.00
HILES,THERON L-Ice Crop-NY-1893(c.1892)-Orng Judd-122p+publ cat-illus (a8) 75.00
HILGARD,ERNEST R-Hypnotic Susceptibility-NY-(1965)-HB&W-sm 8vo-(xiv)+434p-prntd grn cl-1st prntg (y9) 27.50
HILGER,M INEZ-Arapaho Child Life and Its Cultural Background-Wash D.C.-1952-GPO/Bur Ethno Bull No.148-253p-orig blu wrps,40 plts-1st ed (ee7) 37.50
HILGER,SISTER M I-Chippewa Child Life and Its Cultural Background-Wash D.C.-1951-Smithsonian Inst-xvi+204p-wrps,31 plts,Bur Amer Ethnlgy,Bull.#146-1st ed (e2) 20.00
HILL,A-Penobscot Vegetation-1923-Portland Soc Nat Hist-cl wi orig wrps bnd in (x6,rbnd) 25.00
HILL,ALFRED J-History of Company E of the Sixth Minnesota Regiment of Volunteer Infantry-St.Paul-1899-Pioneer Pr-45p-wrps bnd in hdcov,frntis-Howes H478-1st ed (ee4,rbnd) 175.00
HILL,ALICE P-Tales of the Colorado Pioneers-Denver-1884-Pierson & Gardner-319p-illus-Howes H480-1st ed (ee4,autg) 130.00
HILL,AMELIA-Garden Portraits-NY-1923-McBride-230p (x6,sl fox) 15.00
HILL,ANTHONY-ED.-Data-Greenwich-(1978)-NYGS-lg 8vo-302p-100 illus-1st US ed (ee5,f,f dj) 25.00
HILL,ART-I Don't Care If I Never Come Back-1980-S&S-1st ed (r7,f,dj) 20.00
HILL,ART-I Don't Care If I Never Come Back-1980-S&S-photos-1st ed (s8,f,dj) 15.00
HILL,BURTON S-On the Platte and North-np-nd-91p-stiff pict wrps,photos-1st ed (t7) 15.00
HILL,CAROL-Jeremiah 8:20-NY-(1970)-Random-auth 1st bk-1st ed (bb1,f,dj) 35.00
HILL,CAROL-Subsistence USA-NY-1973-HR&W-192p-72 photos by B Davidson-1st ed (cc9,f,soil dj) 35.00
HILL,COL HOWARD G-Riding the Limiteds' Locomotives-Seattle-1972-175p-1st ed (n4,f,dj) 24.00
HILL,FORREST-Roads,Rails, and Waterways-Norman-1957-248p-illus-1st ed (t7,dj) 25.00
HILL,FREDERICK-Salmon Fishing - The Greased Line on Dee,Don & Earn-Lond-1948-12mo-98p-illus (m3,f,dj) 45.00
HILL,GENE-Hill Country-1978-Nat'l Sporting Frat-8vo-166p-ltd to 1000c,nbrd,autg-illus,T Hennessey (m3,vf,box) 100.00
HILL,GENE-Tears & Laughter-LA-1981-8vo-168p-illus,H Strasser-1st ed so stated (m3,f,dj) 12.50
HILL,GENE-Whispering Wings of Autumn-1981-Amwell Pr-8vo-168p-ltd to 1000c,nbrd,autg-illus,Wm Schaldach (m3,as new in box) 80.00
HILL,H-Hunting the Hard Way-NY-1956-318p-photos (ee3,f) 70.00
HILL,H-Wild Adventures-PA-1954-228p-photos (ee3,vf,dj) 70.00
HILL,HARRY C-Dictionary of the Chippewa Indian Language...Never Before Printed-np-(1943)-priv prntd by auth-(15)p-wrps (f1) 15.00
HILL,HEADON-Avengers-NY-1907-Dodge-frontis,dec cov-1st US ed (g4) 15.00
HILL,J L-End of the Cattle Trail-Long Beach-nd(ca.1905 to 1910)-120p-prtd gry wrps,illus (z1) 40.00

HILL,JANET M-Salads, Sandwiches and Chafing Dish Dainties-Bost-1899-Little,Brown-sm 4to-250p-grn bds,gold motif,32 illus-Bitting 228 (u6) 25.00

HILL,JASON-Curious Gardener-Lond-1932-173p-drwngs-1st & only ed (hh7) 59.00

HILL,JASPER S-Letters of a Young Miner-SF-1964-John Howell Bks-xiii,111p-frntis,fldg map-ltd ed (n2,f) 50.00

HILL,JOSEPH J-History of Warner's Ranch & Its Environs-LA-1927-priv prtd-221p-illus-ltd to 1000c,nbrd-1st ed (g7) 45.00

HILL,L B-Joseph E Brown and the Confederacy-Westport-1974-360p-rprnt of 1939ed (z10,f) 30.00

HILL,LARRY D-Emissaries to a Revolution-Baton Rouge-1973-LSU Pr-8vo-xi,394p-beige cl,map,photos (mm1,dj) 30.00

HILL,M F-Permanent Way-Nairobi-1949-582p-1st ed (n4,dj) 39.50

HILL,MARY-Food to Make You Famous-NY-(1953)-Farrar-310p-yel cl-1st ed (q8,dj,pres) 15.00

HILL,MRS AGNES L-Colorado Blue Book, 1892-Denver-1892-James Ives-1st ed (oo9) 150.00

HILL,N N,JR.-History of Knox County, Ohio-Mt.Vernon-1881-854,(2)p-1/2 lea (d1,sp wn) 85.00

HILL,REGINALD-Killing Kindness-NY-1980-1st US ed (r5,f,dj) 15.00

HILL,REGINALD-Pascoe's Ghost-Lond-1979-Collins-1st ed (e4,f,sl rub dj) 30.00

HILL,REGINALD-Pinch of Snuff-NY-1978-1st US ed (r5,f,dj) 20.00

HILL,REGINALD-Spy's Wife-NY-1980-Pantheon-1st Amer ed (s4,vf,dj) 25.00

HILL,REGINALD-Very Good Hater-Woodstock-1982-Foul Play-1st US ed (f4,f,dj) 12.50

HILL,REGINALD-Who Guards the Palace?-NY-1982-Pantheon-1st US ed (f4,f,dj) 12.50

HILL,ROBERT T-Geography & Geology of the Black and Grand Prairies, Texas...-Wash-1901-US Geo Srvy,21st Ann Rprt-666p-71 plts,80 drwngs,7 fldg maps & chrts-1st ed (a9,cov flecked) 100.00

HILL,ROBERT T-Preliminary Annotated Check List of the Cretaceous Invertebrate Fossils of Texas-Austin-1889-Geo Survey of Tex-57p-wrps,Bull No.4-scarce (w3,rnfrcd sp) 20.00

HILL,ROLAND L-I Recommend-Torrance-(1948)-DeLaney-lg 8vo-640p-pbbld red cl-1st prtg (q8,dj) 15.00

HILL,S C-Yusuf Khan-Lond-1914-320p-red cl,maps,illus-1st ed (gg2,f) 85.00

HILL,SARAH J F-Mrs.Hill's Journal, Civil War Reminiscences-Chig-1980-Donnelley & Sons-frntis,illus-Lakeside Classics (ff4) 15.00

HILL,SARAH J F-Mrs.Hill's Journal, Civil War Reminiscences-Chig-1980-Lakeside Pr-xlvii; 343p+ads-cl-Lakeside Classics ed (j1,f) 22.50

HILL,W W-An Ethnography of Santa Clara Pueblo-Albuq-(1982)-391p-mainly dbl col,photos-1st ed (v7,f,dj) 45.00

HILLARD,KATHARINE-My Mother's Journal-Bost-1900-Geo H Ellis-8vo-320p-cl,floral e.p.,frntis port (pp1,cov wn,fade) 150.00

HILLARY,EDMUND-High in the Thin Cold Air-NY-1962-254p-1st US ed (q10,f,dj) 14.00

HILLARY,EDMUND-His Autobiography-NY-1975-1st ed (v9,f,f dj) 45.00

HILLARY,EDMUND-Nothing Venture, Nothing Win-Lond-1975-319p-32 plts-1st Brit ed (o10,f,dj) 30.00

HILLARY,EDMUND-Schoolhouse in the Clouds-NY-1964-180p-1st US ed (p10,f,dj) 15.00

HILLARY,LOUISE-Yak for Christmas-Lond-1968-108p-1st Brit ed (p10,f,dj) 30.00

HILLARY,MAX-Hunted Down-NY-nd-John W Lovell-165p-cl (c1,few spots rear cov) 17.50

HILLEN,WILLIAM-Blackwater River: Toa Thal Kas-Tor-(c.1971)-McClelland & Stewart-169p-illus,map(lining papers)-Edwards & Lort #1730 (k10,dj) 20.00*

HILLER,ELIZABETH O-Fifty-two Sunday Dinners-Chig-1913-Fairbank Co-192p-pict bds-Bitting 229 (u6) 25.00

HILLER,L-Surgery Through the Ages: a Pictorial Chronicle-NY-1944-177p-photos (dd3) 75.00

HILLERMAN,ABBIE B-1888 to 1925. History of the Woman's Christian Temperance Union of Indian Territory, Oklahoma...-Sapulpa-nd(1925?)-Jennings Prtg & Sta-111p-bds-scarce (a1) 27.50

HILLERMAN,TONY-Blessing Way-Lond-1970-Macmillan-auth 1st bk-1st Brit ed (gg8,dj) 400.00

HILLERMAN,TONY-Blessing Way-NY,Evanston,Lond-(1970)-Harper & Row-auth 1st bk-1st ed (bb1,fade dj) 700.00

HILLERMAN,TONY-Dark Wind-NY-1982-1st ed (o5,f,dj) 110.00

HILLERMAN,TONY-Dark Wind-NY-1982-Harper-1st ed (e4,f,dj) 90.00

HILLERMAN,TONY-ED.-Spell of New Mexico-Albuq-1981-105p (t7,f,dj) 15.00

HILLERMAN,TONY-Listening Woman-(Lond)-(1979)-Macmillan-1st Brit ed (ff6,sl soil dj) 125.00

HILLERMAN,TONY-Listening Woman-NY-1978-Harper & Row-1st ed (w9,f,sl tn dj) 250.00

HILLERMAN,TONY-New Mexico-Portland-1974-Chas Belding-photos,D Muench-1st ed (e4,dj) 250.00

HILLERMAN,TONY-Rio Grande-Portland-1975-Chas H Belding-photos,R Reynolds-1st ed (w9,vf,dj) 200.00

HILLES,HELEN T-To the Queens Taste-(1950)-Random-339p-grn cl-rvsd ed (q8,dj) 17.50

HILLIARD,A R-Outlaw Island-NY-1942-Farrar-1st ed (g4,dj) 15.00

HILLIER,B-Decorative Arts of the `40's & `50's-NY-1975-150 b&w & 10 col illus-1st Amer ed (h10,dj) 50.00

HILLIER,J-Japanese Print, a New Approach-Rutland-(1960)-Tuttle-8vo-184p-64 illus-1st ed (bb5,dj) 35.00

HILLIS,MARJORIE-Work Ends at Nightfall-Indpls,NY-(1938)-Bobbs Merrill-8vo-94p-cl,illus-1st ed (ee9) 20.00

HILLIS,NEWELL-Quest of John Chapman-NY-1904-Macmillan-349p-red cl (x6,spot cl) 35.00

HILLS,GEORGE M-History of the Church in Burlington, New Jersey-Trenton-1885-831p-cl,plts-enlgd 2nd ed (aa6) 75.00

HILLS,J W-Dorado-Lond-1932-8vo-190p-photos,maps-1st ed (m3) 55.00

HILLS,J W-Golden River-Lond-1922-8vo-187p-photos (m3) 45.00

HILLS,J W-Summer on the Test-Lond-1924-folio-198p-1/2 vel,gilt,deluxe ed of 25c,nbrd,autg-12 orig dry pnts by N WIlkinson,each autg in pencil-rare (m3,uncut) 1,750.00

HILLSMAN,JOHN B-Eleven Men and a Scalpel-Winnipeg-1948-Columbia Pr-sm 8vo-144p-red cl-Peel 4104-1st ed (mm8,sl wn) 20.00*

HILLYER,V M-Child's History of Art-NY-1933-Appleton Century-lg 8vo-443p-cl,photos-1st ed (s3,sp lttrng flaked,stnd edg) 20.00

HILTON,GEORGE-Electric Interurban Railways in America-1960-Stanford-8vo-463p-illus (nn7,dj tn) 35.00

HILTON,GEORGE-Electric Interurban Railways in America-Stanford-1960-463p-1st ed (n4,f,dj) 24.00

HILTON,JAMES-Good Bye, Mr.Chips-Bost-1934-Little,Brown-1st ed (ff6,f,dj) 250.00

HILTON,JAMES-Random Harvest-Bost-1941-Little,Brown-1st ed (d10,dj sp sl chip) 40.00

HILTON,JAMES-So Well Remembered-Bost-1945-Atlanta/Little,Brown-1st ed (hh5,dj) 12.50

HILTON,JOHN B-Death of an Alderman-NY-1968-Walker-1st US ed (d4,dj) 20.00

HILTON,RICHARD-Indian Mutiny-Lond-1957-232p-maps-1st ed (b7,dj) 35.00

HIMES,CHESTER-Case of Rape-(1980)-Targ-8vo-cl/bds,plain dj-ltd to 350c,autg-1st ed (v10,f,dj) 60.00

HIMES,CHESTER-Case of Rape-NY-(1980)-Targ-8vo-cl bckd bds,glassine dj-ltd to 350c,autg-1st ed (jj8,as new in dj) 100.00

HIMES,CHESTER-Cast the First Stone-NY-1952-1st ed (o5,dj sp sl chip) 125.00

HIMES,CHESTER-Lonely Crusade-NY-1947-1st ed (s5,dj) 110.00

HIMES,CHESTER-Lonely Crusade-NY-1947-Knopf-1st ed (gg8,dj) 85.00

HIMES,CHESTER-Pinktoes-(1965)-Putnam/Stein & Day-1st Amer ed (q9,f,dj) 30.00

HIMES,CHESTER-Pinktoes-NY-(1965)-Putnams-1st Amer ed (f2,ink mrk on e.p.,dj) 30.00

HIMES,NORMAN E-Medical History of Contraception-Balt-1936-Williams & Wilkins-xxxii+521p-grn cl,30 figs,29 tbls-1st ed (l2) 75.00

HIMMELFARB,GERTRUDE-Darwin and the Darwinian Revolution-GC-1959-Dbldy-480p-wht cl-1st ed (a2,dj) 15.00

HIMMELWRIGHT,A L A-Pistol & Revolver Shooting-NY-1915-12mo-223p-illus-1st ed (m3) 20.00

HINCKLEY,BRYANT S-Heber J Grant-SLC-1951-264p-cl,frntis-1st ed (bb8,dj) 20.00

HINCKLEY,G W-Daniel Alexander McDonald-NY-1904-24p-cl (h1,sl spot cl) 10.00

HINCKLEY,HELEN-Rails from the West...a Biography of Theodore D Judah-San Marino-1969-207p-1st ed (n4,f,dj) 18.00

HIND,HENRY Y-Narrative of the Canadian Red River...1857 and of the Assinniboine and Saskatchewan...1858-Edmonton-1971-Hurtig Publ-thk 8vo-xiv,472p-col frntis,13 chromoxylographs,33 woodcts,5 maps-(orig ed 1860,Lond)-1st ed thus (bb7,dj) 75.00*

HIND,HENRY Y-Narrative of the Canadian Red River...Expedition of 1857...Assinniboine and Saskatchewan...1858-Lond-1860-Longman,Green-8vo-2 vols-mod 1/2 red mor,mrbld bds,8 maps,20 plts-Sabin 31934 (u3,rbnd) 785.00

HIND,R RENTON-Spirits Unbroken-SF-1946-John Howell Publ-291p-e.p. maps-1st ed (c3) 22.00

HINDLEY,GEOFFRERY-World Art Treasures-NY-1979-Octopus Bks-4to-320p-cl,illus(incl 200 col)-Mayflower ed (gg6,vf,chip dj) 25.00

HINE,BENJAMIN-Miscellaneous Poetry-NY-1835-273p-cl-Amer Imprnts 32156 (h1,spot cov) 20.00

HINE,C G-Woodside, the North End of Newark, N.J-(np)-1909-(2),iv,308p-cl,plts (aa6) 50.00

HINE,CHARLES-Letters From an Old Railway Official-1904-Rwy Age-12mo-179p (nn7,rub) 25.00

HINE,DARYL-Five Poems 1954-Tor-(1954)-(Emblem Bk No.One)-8vo-13p-wrps-auth 1st bk-v scarce-1st ed (pp2,sl soil wrps) 300.00*

HINE,LEWIS-America & Lewis Hine: Photographs 1904 to 1940-NY-1977-Millerton,Aperture-142p-191 photos-1st ed (cc9,as new in dj) 50.00

HINE,ROBERT V-California's Utopian Colonies-San Marino-1953-Huntington Libr-xii+209p-red/brwn cl,plts-1st ed (h2,chip dj) 50.00

HINE,ROBERT V-Community on the Frontier-Norman-1980-292p-photos-1st ed (t7,f,dj) 10.00

HINE,ROBERT V-ED.-Frontier Experience-Belmont-(1963)-Wadsworth-418p (cc4) 15.00

HINE,ROBERT V-Edward Kern & American Expansion-New Haven,Lond-1962-180p+illus in rear-Yale Wstrn Amer Ser,No.1-1st ed (h7,f,dj) 25.00

HINES,DUNCAN-Food Odyssey-(1955)-Crowell-274p-blu bds-1st ed (q8,dj,autg) 20.00

HINES,GORDON-True Tales of the Old 101 Ranch, and Other Stories-Okla City-1953-Nat Prtg-8vo-v,89p-dec stiff wrps,illus-Herd 1040-1st ed (aa3,f) 25.00

HINES,GUSTAVUS-Voyage Round the World, With a History of the Oregon Mission...-Buffalo-1850-brwn cl-Tweney 30,Smith 4495-1st ed (w1,sl wn & fox) 100.00

HINES,H K-Illustrated History of the State of Washington-1894-Clarke Co-lg 4to-771p-lea (b6) 175.00

HINGSTON,R W G-Meaning of Animal Colour and Adornment-Lond-1933-8vo-411p-cl,illus (y8,ex-lib) 30.00

HINKLE,G-Sierra Nevada Lakes-Indpls-1949-383p-g pict cov,28 photos,6 maps-1st ed (o10,f,dj sl chip) 50.00

HINKLE,G-Sierra Nevada Lakes-Indpls-1949-383p-g pict cov,28 photos,6 maps-1st ed (p10,f,sl chip dj) 65.00

HINKS,DAVID-Fishes of Manitoba-Winnipeg-1943-8vo-102p-illus (m3) 12.50

HINMAN,WILBUR F-Story of the Sherman Brigade-(Alliance)-1897-publ by auth-1104p-cl-scarce (j1,inner hnge rprd,wrnkld sp) 100.00

HINSDALE,B A-American Government, National and State-Chig,NY-(1895)-494p-cl-new & revsd ed (k1) 15.00

HINSDALE,B A-Horace Mann and the Common School Revival in the United States-NY-1900-326p-cl,Great Educators ser (k1) 15.00

HINSDALE,HARRIETT-Confederate Gray-Petersborough-(1963)-102p-e.p. maps,illus-1st ed (n3,dj) 22.50

HINSHAW,GLENNIS-COMP.-Bibliography of Writings and Illustrations by Tom Lea-El Paso-1971-wrps-1st ed (a9) 25.00

HINSHELWOOD,N M-Montreal and Vicinity-Canada-1903-220 photos-1st ed (r2) 40.00

HINTON,H B-Air Victory-NY-(1948)-8vo-xx,428p-cl,32p plts-1st ed (t2,weak hngs) 30.00

HINTON,ISAAC T-History of Baptism, Both from the Inspired and Uninspired Writings-Phila-1840-Am Baptist Publ & S S Soc-12mo-372p-1st ed (gg5) 17.50

HINTON,J W-Story of the Electric Organ-Lond-1909-SMHK-(viii)+124p+ads-blu cl,7 plts-presume 1st ed (c2) 50.00

HINTON,PHYLLIS-British Native Ponies and Their Crosses-Lond-1971-Nelson-1st ed (j9,dj) 18.00

HINTON,RICHARD J-John Brown and His Men-NY-1894-752p-1st ed (c4,sp fade) 35.00

HINTON,S E-Rumble Fish-NY-1975-1st ed (s5,dj) 20.00

HINTON,S.E.-Outsiders-NY-(1967)-Viking-wi scarce wrap around band,auth 1st bk-1st ed (a5,f,dj) 125.00

HINTON,W-Opportunities in Aviation-NY-(1929)-8vo-xiv,256p-illus cl,4p plts,8p maps,text illus-1st ed (t2) 30.00

HINTZ,O S-Trout at Taupo-Lond-1970-8vo-239p-photos,illus-revsd ed (m3,f,dj) 20.00

HIPPOCRATES-Genuine Works of...Translated from the Greek...by Francis Adams-Lond-1849-2 vols-plts-1st ed (dd3,sp chip) 300.00

HIPPOCRATES-On Intercourse and Pregnancy-NY-1952-128p-1st Engl transl (dd3,dj) 100.00

HIRD,RALPH-Colored Plate & Sporting Books-1935-Anderson Galleries-8vo-112p-red cl wi orig pap wrps bnd in-illus-auction catlg (m3,priced) 25.00

HIRES,CHARLES E-Short Historical Sketch of the Old Merion Meeting House, Pa-Merion-1917-12mo (y6) 16.00

HIRSCH,PETER-Last Man in Paradise-GC-1961-8vo-239p-photos-1st ed (m3,dj) 12.50

HIRSH,JOSEPH-1st 100 Years of the Mount Sinai Hospital of New York 1852 to 1952-NY-1952-Random-xv,364p-illus-1st prtg (n2,dj rub,chip) 20.00

HIRSHBERG,AL-Braves,the Pick and the Shovel-1948-Waverly Hs-1st ed (s8,f,dj) 60.00

HIRSHON,STANLEY P-Grenville M Dodge-Bloomington-1967-Indiana U Pr-334p-frntis,illus,maps-1st ed (o7,f,dj) 75.00

HIRSHON,STANLEY-Grenville M Dodge-Bloomington-1967-334p-frntis-1st ed (t7,f,dj) 40.00

HIRST,F W-Early Life and Letters of John Morley-NY-1927-Macmillan-8vo-2 vols-9 illus-1st ed (cc5,sl fox,dj) 50.00

HIRST,F W-Early Life and Letters of John Morley-NY-1927-Macmillan-8vo-2 vols-9 illus-1st ed (jj5,sl fox,dj) 50.00

HIRTH,GEORGE-COMP.-Picture Book of the Graphic Arts 1500 to 1800-NY-1972-Blom-sm folio-6 vols-maroon cl,illus-(reissue of 1882-90 ed) (s1,f) 200.00

HIRTZLER,VICTOR-Hotel St.Francis Cook Book-Chig-(c.1919)-Hotel Monthly Pr-430p-grn bds-Bitting 231 (l6,sl spot) 75.00

HISEY,LEHMANN-Sea Grist-(Pasadena)-(1922)-251p-bds (b1) 20.00

HISS,A EMIL-Standard Manual of Soda and Other Beverages-Chig-1901-G P Engelhard & Co-242p-cl-10th ed (h1,spot cov,fr in hng crkng) 15.00

HISS,A EMIL-Thesaurus of Proprietary Preparations-Chig-1898-Engelhard-286p-blk cl-1st ed (q8,hng crack) 35.00

HISSEY,JAMES J-Drive Through England-Lond-1885-Bentley-1st ed (h9,weak hng) 58.00

HISTORY OF THE SONS OF UNION VETERANS OF THE CIVIL WAR 1881-1939...DAVIS STAR CAMP...PENNSYLVANIA-(Pitt)-(1939)-27p-wrps (j1) 10.00

HISTORY OF THE UNITED STATES...FOR THE USE OF SCHOOLS AND FAMILIES-Keene-1821-J Prentiss-276p-lea-Amer Imprnts 6521-2nd ed (k1) 25.00

HITCHCOCK,EDWARD-Ichnology of New England-Bost-1858-Wm White-4to-xii+220p-brwn cl,60 plts incl col maps-1st ed (g2,f) 225.00

HITCHCOCK,H R,JR.-Rhode Island Architecture-Providence-1939-RI Mus-81 plts (kk4) 125.00

HITCHCOCK,H R-German Rococo-Balt-1968-Penguin Bks-4to-100p+58 photos,beige cl-1st ed (r10,sl wn dj) 25.00

HITCHCOCK,H R-International Architecture Since 1922-NY-1932-illus-1st ed (ee1) 275.00

HITCHCOCK,H R-Modern Architecture-NY-1929-Payson & Clarke-4to-xvii,(1),252,(2)p-cl,58 plts (pp7) 135.00

HITCHCOCK,H R-Modern Architecture-NY-1929-Payson & Clarke-illus-orig ed (h10,edge rub) 125.00

HITCHCOCK,HENRY-Marching with Sherman-New Haven-1927-Yale U Pr-332p-frntis port,fldg map-Coulter 235-1st ed (v2,cl mottld,sl soil) 60.00

HITCHMAN,JANET-Such a Strange Lady-NY-1975-Harper-1st US ed (h4,f,dj) 12.50

HITTEL.JOHN S-Resources of California-SF-1863-A Roman-12mo-464p-cl-Cowan p.284-scarce-1st ed (mm7) 175.00

HITTELL,T-ED.-Adventures of James C Adams...-NY-1911-373p-illus-Howes H543 (e7) 65.00

HITTELL,THEODORE H-Adventures of James Capen Adams, Mountaineer and Grizzly Bear Hunter of California-SF-1860-Towne & Bacon-378p-orig cl,plts-Howes H543-1st ed (v1) 200.00

HITTSON,JACK H-Brazos Broncbuster's Scrapbook-Mineral Wells-1971-Brazos Bks-191p-wrps-1st ed (w3,f,autg) 15.00

HIX,JOHN-Glass House-1974-MIT Pr-208p-cl,illus (x6,dj) 40.00

HIX,THEODORA-DR.SNOOK AND THE MURDER OF...-np-nd-45p-wrps (d1) 32.50

HIXSON,RICHARD F-Isaac Collins, A Quaker Printer in 18th Century America-New Brunswick-1968-1st ed (y7,dj) 6.00

HJORTSBERG,WILLIAM-Alp-NY-1969-S&S-auth 1st bk-1st ed (g8,f,dj) 60.00

HJORTSBERG,WILLIAM-Falling Angel-1978-HBJ-1st ed (x7,dj) 33.00

HJORTSBERG,WILLIAM-Falling Angel-NY-1978-gold foil dj rare in f condition-1st ed (n5,f,f dj) 40.00

HJORTSBERG,WILLIAM-Gray Matters-NY-(1971)-S&S-1st ed (a5,as new in dj) 30.00

HJORTSBERG,WILLIAM-Symbiography-Freemont-(1973)-Sumac-ltd to 1026c in hdcov-1st ed (b5,as new in dj) 35.00

HJORTSBERG,WILLIAM-Toro! Toro! Toro!-NY-1974-1st ed (q5,f,dj) 25.00

HO HUM: NEWSBREAKS FROM THE NEW YORKER-NY-(1931)-Farrar & Rinehart-orig grn bds stmpd in blu-(E B White's scarce 4th bk)-Hall A4-1st ed (dd2) 150.00

HOAGLAND,EDWARD-Cat Man-1956-HMCO-auth 1st bk-1st ed (x10,dj edge-wn,rub) 35.00

HOAGLAND,EDWARD-Cat Man-Bost-1956-Houghton Mifflin-auth 1st bk-1st ed (bb1,f,edge rub dj) 60.00

HOAGLAND,EDWARD-Circle Home-NY-(1960)-Crowell-1st ed (bb1,f,sl wn dj) 35.00

HOAGLAND,EDWARD-Circle Home-NY-(1960)-Crowell-1st ed (e10,f,sl wn dj) 35.00

HOAGLAND,EDWARD-Notes From the Century Before-NY-(1969)-Random-1st ed (b5,as new in dj) 25.00

HOAGLAND,EDWARD-Notes from the Century Before-NY-(1969)-Random-1st ed (bb2,f,dj) 35.00

HOAGLAND,EDWARD-Peacock's Tail-NY et al-(1965)-McGraw-Hill-1st ed (bb1,f,dj) 30.00

HOAGLAND,EDWARD-Red Wolves and Black Bears-NY-(1976)-Random-1st ed (b5,as new in dj) 17.50

HOAGLAND,EDWARD-Walking the Dead Diamond River-NY-(1973)-Random-1st ed (b5,as new in dj) 20.00

HOAGLAND,R W-Blue Book of Aviation-LA-1932-4to-292p-dec cl,text illus,illus e.p.-library ed (t2) 75.00

HOARE,CLEMENT-Practical Treatise on the Cultivation of the Grape Vine on Open Walls-Lond-1841-Longman-210p-cl-3rd ed (x6) 72.00

HOBAN,RUSSELL-La Corona and the Tin Frog-Lond-(1979)-Cape-4to-unpgd-pict glossy bds,no dj as iss,col illus,N Bayley-1st ed (r3,f) 20.00

HOBAN,RUSSELL-Lion of Boaz Jachin and Jachin Boaz-NY-1973-Stein & Day-auth 1st novel-1st ed (y1,f,sl wn dj) 50.00

HOBAN,RUSSELL-Pilgermann-NY-(1983)-Summit Bks-1st Amer ed (x10,f,f dj) 15.00

HOBART,DONALD B-Cell Murder Mystery-NY-1931-Fiction League-1st US ed (f4) 12.00

HOBART,T D-White Deer Lands in the Panhandle of Texas-Pampa-nd(ca.1904)-38p-maps,illus-rare-1st ed (jj1) 95.00

HOBBES,JOHN O-Dream and the Business-Lond-1906-T Fisher Unwin-blu/ivory cl,col illus by A Beardsley-1st ed (u2) 47.50

HOBBS,CAPT JAMES-Wild Life in the Far West-Hartford-1872-Wiley,Waterman & Eaton-488p-col frntis,illus-Howes H550-1st ed (bb4,new innr hngs,wn) 200.00

HOBBS,FRANKLYN-Secret of Wealth-Chig-(1923)-F Hobbs & Co-230p-bds-ltd to 1000c,nbrd,autg (g1) 15.00

HOBBS,RICHARD G-Glamor Valley-(San Benito)-nd-Cameron Cnty News & Farm-96p-wrps-1st ed so stated (h1,sl soil) 17.50

HOBBS,WILLIAM H-Characteristics of Existing Glaciers-NY-1922-Macmillan-xxvi+301p-grn cl,34 plts,140 figs-1st ed (l2) 25.00

HOBBS,WILLIAM H-Exploring about the North Pole of the Winds-NY-1930-Putnam's-viii,376p-blu cl/bds,map e.p.,26 photos & maps-Arctic Biblio 7150-1st ed (oo1,cor bump,dj) 65.00

HOBHOUSE,JANET-Everybody Who Was Anybody-NY-1975-Putnam-1st ed (f8,f,f dj) 20.00

HOBO CAMP FIRE TALES-Erie-(1911)-133p-wrps-14th ed (l1) 15.00

HOBSON,R L-Chinese Art-Lond-1965-Spring Bks-4to-21p text-yel bds,100 col plts (r10,wn dj) 12.50

HOBSON,R L-Chinese Art-NY-1927-Macmillan-4to-15p text-grn cl,untrimmed,100 col plts wi tiss guards (r10,sl wn) 85.00

HOBSON,WILDER-American Jazz Music-NY-(1939)-Norton-8vo-230p-photos-1st ed (p1,f,dj) 125.00

HOCH,PAUL H-ED.-Failures in Psychiatric Treatment-NY-(1948)-Grune & Stratton-sm 8vo-viii+241+(9)p-grn cl-1st ed (y9) 25.00

HOCHBAUM,H A-Travels & Traditions of Waterfowl-Mpls-1955-Univ of Minn Pr-301p-illus-1st ed (m3,f,dj) 27.50

HOCHMAN,SANDRA-Voyage Home-Paris-1960-Two Cities-wrps,auth 1st bk-scarce-1st ed (w6,f) 75.00

HOCHWALT,A F-Bird Dogs-Cin-1922-12mo-128p-illus (m3,vf) 40.00

HOCHWALT,A F-Modern Pointer-Dayton-1923-8vo-260p-photos-2nd ed revsd & enlgd (m3,f) 50.00

HOCHWALT,A F-Modern Setter-Dayton-1935-8vo-285p-companion vol to 1923 ed wi index for both vols-photos (m3,vf,dj) 70.00

HOCKING,ANNE-Finishing Touch-NY-1948-Dbldy CC-1st US ed (j4,yel pgs,dj) 20.00

HOCKNEY,DAVID-Cameraworks-NY-1984-Knopf-unpgd-117 photocollages-1st Amer ed (cc9,as new in dj) 75.00

HODAPP,WILLIAM-Pleasures of the Jazz Age-NY-1948-J Held illus dj-1st ed (s5,sl sunned dj) 45.00

HODEL,MICHAEL-Enter the Lion-Lond-1980-Dent-1st Brit ed (p4,sl bump,dj) 20.00

HODES,ART-Selections From the Gutter: Portraits From the Jazz Record-(1977)-U of Cal Pr-1st ed (w1,f,dj) 15.00

HODGE,EDWIN-Mt Multnomah-Eugene-1925-158p-wrps,illus,photos,fldg map rear pckt-1st ed (p10) 18.00

HODGE,FREDERICK W-ED.-Handbook of American Indians North of Mexico-1959(1907-10)-Pageant-2 vols (d3) 90.00

HODGE,FREDERICK W-History of Hawikuh, New Mexico...-LA-1937-SW Mus/W Ritchie Pr-8vo-xviii,155p-stiff wrps,2 figs,26p plts-1st ed (aa3) 50.00

HODGE,FREDERICK W-Memorial of Fray Alonso De Benavides, 1630-Albuq-1965-Horn & Wallace/Lakeside-309p-photos-1st ed (d3,dj) 35.00

HODGE,GENE M-Kachinas are Coming-LA-1936-Steller Miller-4to-18 col plts-1st ed (oo9) 250.00

HODGE,HERBERT-Cockney on Main Street-Lond-(1945)-M Joseph-154p-Edwards & Lort #1744 (k10,dj) 15.00*

HODGES,HENRY-Technology in the Ancient World-NY-1970-Knopf-8vo-284p-illus-1st US ed (dd5,f,sl tn dj) 20.00

HODGINS,E-Sky High-NY-1929-8vo-xx,336p-cl,frntis,62p plts-1st ed (t2,sl chip dj) 40.00

HODGKINSON,FRANK-Sepik Diary-Northbridge-1984-Reid Bks-lg 4to-emboss grn cl wi g titles,dec e.p. (p8,f,f dj) 65.00

HODGSON,FRED T-Builders' Architectural Drawing Self Taught-Chig-1904-262;55,(3)p-cl,18 fldg plts (d1) 30.00

HODGSON,J E-History of Aeronautics in Great Britain-Lond-1924-Oxford U Pr-4to-x,436p-g cl,t.e.g.,col frntis,150 plts incl 13 col-ltd to 1000c (t2,uncut,dj) 400.00

HODGSON,MRS WILLOUGHBY-Quest of the Antique-Lond-1924-H Jenkins-4to-255p-64p plts-1st Brit ed (gg5,sl wn,fox) 50.00

HODGSON,PAT-Early War Photographs-NY-1974-NYGS-159p-97 photos-1st ed (cc9,f,dj) 30.00

HODGSON,RALPH-Last Blackbird & Other Lines-NY-1907-Macmillan-auth 1st bk-1st US ed (y1) 75.00

HODGSON,W EARL-How to Fish-Lond-1933-12mo-377p-illus (m3,f,sl fray dj) 12.50

HODGSON,W EARL-Trout Fishing-Lond-1904-8vo-276p-col plts,orig bndg-1st ed (m3) 40.00

HODGSON,WM H-Carnacki, The Ghost Finder-1947-M&M-1st publ in U.K. in 1910,this ed contains 3 add stories not in Brit ed-1st Amer ed (x7,dj) 85.00

HODGSON,WM H-Carnacki, The Ghost Finder-Sauk City-1947-Mycroft & Moran-241p-ltd to 3050c-1st ed (k5,sl wn dj) 75.00

HODIER,ANDRE-Toward Jazz-NY-(1962)-Grove-1st Amer ed (w1,f,dj) 20.00

HODKIN & COUSEN-Textbook of Glass Technology-Lond-1929-551p-2nd ed (cc8) 125.00

HOEBEL,E ADAMSON-Law of Primitive Man-Cambridge-(1954)-Harvard U Pr-8vo-356p-cl-1st prtg (y5,dj tattrd) 25.00

HOERMANN,O S B́-Daughter of Tehuan-S.A.-1932(1866)-Standard-orig pict bndg,photo-1st transl ed (a9) 75.00

HOESE,H D-Fishes of the Gulf of Mexico-1977-Tex A&M-327p-illus-1st ed (bb3,f,dj) 23.00

HOFF,EBBE C-Bibliographical Sourcebook of Compressed Air, Diving and Submarine Medicine-Wash-1948-382p-1st ed (dd3) 60.00

HOFF,EBBE C-Bibliography of Aviation Medicine-Springfield-1942-237p-1st ed (dd3,dj) 50.00

HOFF,EBBE C-Bibliography of Aviation Medicine-Springfield-1942-Chas C Thomas-xvi+237p-blu cl-1st ed (c2,dj) 60.00

HOFFMAN,ABBIE-Square Dancing in the Ice Age-NY-1982-Putnam-242p-1st ed (r1,sl tn dj) 25.00

HOFFMAN,ABBIE-Woodstock Nation-NY-1969-Vintage-wrps-1st prtg (q1) 20.00

HOFFMAN,ALICE-Angel Landing-NY-(1980)-Putnam's-1st ed (bb1,as new in dj) 20.00

HOFFMAN,ALICE-Drowning Season-NY-(1979)-Dutton-1st ed (b5,as new in dj) 25.00

HOFFMAN,ALICE-Property of-NY-(1977)-FS&G-auth 1st bk-1st ed (bb1,as new in dj) 35.00

HOFFMAN,ALICE-Property Of-NY-(1977)-FS&G-auth 1st bk-1st ed (l7,f,dj) 45.00

HOFFMAN,ALICE-White Horses-1982-Putnam-1st ed (r9,vf,dj) 15.00

HOFFMAN,ALICE-White Horses-NY-1982-1st ed (n5,dj) 22.50

HOFFMAN,CHARLES F-Wild Scenes in the Forest and Prairie-Lond-1840-R Bentley-2 vols in one-1/2 lea,mrbld bds-Howes H567-2nd Lond ed (dd6,sl rub) 275.00

HOFFMAN,DANIEL-Harvard Guide to Contemporary American Writing-Cambridge,Lond-1979-Belknap-1st ed (b5,as new in dj) 25.00

HOFFMAN,E T A-Selected Letters of...-Chig-1977-U of Chig Pr-1st ed (t4,f,f dj) 20.00

HOFFMAN,FREDERICK J-ED.-Achievement of D H Lawrence-Norman-(1953)-U of Okla-1st ed (b5,sl wn dj) 25.00

HOFFMAN,FREDERICK-William Faulkner-(E Lansing)-1951-Mich St College Pr-1st ed (b10,dj) 60.00

HOFFMAN,R-Birds of the Pacific States-Bost-1927-8vo-353p-cl,col frntis,9 col plts (y8) 25.00

HOFFMAN,ROBERT V-Revolutionary Scene in New Jersey-NY-(1942)-303p-cl,illus (aa6) 35.00

HOFFMAN,W-Gustav Klimt-Greenwich-1974-NYGS-4to-60p txt-blk cl,15 drwngs,82 b&w & col paintings-3rd prtg (r10,sl tattrd dj) 45.00

HOFFMAN,WERNER-Gustav Klimt-(1971)-NYGS-lg 4to-60p text-illus-1st Amer ed (oo8,f,dj) 75.00

HOFFMAN,WILBUR-Sagas of Old Western Travel and Transport-San Diego-1980-Howell North-4to-1st ed (f10,dj) 45.00

HOFFMAN,WILLIAM-Land That Drank the Rain-Baton Rouge-1982-LSU Pr-1st ed (x9,f,dj rub) 10.00

HOFLAND,MRS.-Integrity-Lond-1826-Longman,et al-12mo-264p-3/4 calf & mrbld bds,engrvd frntis-3rd ed (w6) 45.00

HOFLAND,MRS.-Patience-Lond-1827-Longman,et al-12mo-298p-3/4 calf & mrbld bds,engrvd frntis-3rd ed (w6) 45.00

HOFLAND,T C-British Angler's Manual-Lond-1839-8vo-410p-woodcuts-orig bndg-rare-1st ed (m3) 125.00

HOGAN,CHARLES B-Bibliography of Edwin Arlington Robinson-New Haven-1936-Yale U Pr-8vo-xiv,221p-cl-1st ed (w2,dj) 75.00

HOGAN,DESMOND-Children of Lir-NY-(1981)-Braziller-1st Amer ed (z8,vf,dj) 12.50

HOGAN,DESMOND-Diamonds at the Bottom of the Sea...-NY-(1979)-Braziller-1st Amer ed (z8,vf,dj) 12.50

HOGAN,DESMOND-Ikon Maker-NY-(1976)-Braziller-1st Amer ed (z8,vf,dj) 12.50

HOGAN,DESMOND-Seven Irish Plays, 1946 to 1964-Mpls-(1967)-U of Minn Pr-1st ed (z8,vf,dj) 15.00

HOGAN,JAMES P-Genesis Machine-NY-1978-Ballantine-1st ed (y2,f,f dj) 45.00

HOGAN,JOHN J-On the Mission in Missouri, 1857 to 1868-KC-1892-221p-Howes H573-1st ed (t7,f) 65.00

HOGAN,WILLIAM-Quartzsite Trip-NY-1980-Atheneum-auth 1st bk-1st ed (bb1,as new in dj) 25.00

HOGARTH,BASIL-Writing Thrillers for Profit-Lond-(1936)-Black-158p-1st ed (g9) 50.00

HOGARTH,DAVID G-Wandering Scholar in the Levant-Lond-1896-John Murray-illus-2nd ed (m8) 55.00

HOGARTH,WILLIAM-Analysis of Beauty-Pittsfield-1909-Silv Lotus Shop-8vo-241p-3/4 maroon mor/mrbld bds,bands,illus-1st & only prtg this ed (oo8) 125.00

HOGBIN,IAN-Island of Menstruating Men-Scranton-(1970)-Chandler Publ-8vo-203p-wrps (y5) 12.00

HOGG,GARRY-Union Pacific-NY-1969-166p-1st Amer ed (n4,f,dj) 18.00

HOGG,JABEZ-Microscope-Lond-nd(ca.1867)-Routledge-xx+762p-brwn dec cl,8 col plts-6th ed (c2,hngs weak) 65.00

HOGGSON,THOMAS-Squire's Home Made Wines-NY-1924-Pynson-16mo-38p-tan bds-ltd to 1524c,nbrd-rprnt of orig 1765 ed (q8,sp chip) 30.00

HOGNER,DOROTHY C-Herbs-NY-1953-OUP-illus,N Hogner (m6,dj) 15.00

HOGNER,DOROTHY C-Summer Roads to Gaspe-NY-1939-Dutton-8vo-288p-sketches-1st ed (jj5,dj) 25.00

HOGNER,DOROTHY C-Westward High Low and Dry-NY-(1938)-Dutton-310p-illus-1st ed (dd4,wn dj) 20.00

HOHMAN,ELMO P-American Whaleman-NY,Lond-1928-Longmans,Green-355p-gry cl,blk cors,cov & sp labl,illus-1st ed so stated (ee7,sp drknd,cov sl soil) 65.00

HOHMAN,ELMO P-American Whaleman-NY-1928-Longman's-1st ed (z2,f,sl tn dj) 87.50

HOHN,REINHARDT-Curiosities of the Plant Kingdom-NY-(1980)-Universe-4to-212p-col photos-1st US ed (gg5,f,dj) 15.00

HOIG,STAN-Battle of the Washita-NY-1976-268p-photos,map e.p.-1st ed (t7,dj) 30.00

HOIG,STAN-Humor of the American Cowboy-Caldwell-1958-12mo-193p-pict cl & e.p.,illus-1st ed (aa3,f,dj) 40.00

HOIG,STAN-Sand Creek Massacre-Norman-(1961)-217p-illus-1st ed (h7,f,wrnkld dj) 35.00

HOIG,STAN-Western Odyssey of John Simpson Smith-Glendale-1974-254p-illus-Clark Wstrn Frntrsmn Ser,Vol.15-1st ed (e7,f) 35.00

HOKE,HELEN-Rag's Day and Mrs. Silk-NY-1945-Jr Lit Guild & Messner-4to-unpgd-pict cl,illus (r3,sl smudge,dj) 22.00

HOLAND,G A-History of Parker County and the Double Log Cabin-1937-Herald-296p-photos-rare-Herd 1053 (a9,pgs rippled) 95.00

HOLBEIN,HANS-Holbein's Dance of Death and Bible Woodcuts-NY-1947-priv prtd for Sylvan Pr-lg 8vo-150p-blk dec buckrm wi glassine dj-ltd ed (aa7,dj) 100.00*

HOLBEIN,HANS-Holbein's Dance of Death and Bible Woodcuts-NY-1947-Sylvan Pr-4to-150p-ltd ed (dd3) 75.00

HOLBERG,RUTH-Mitty on Mr.Syrup's Farm-GC-1936-Dbldy,Doran-cl bckd bds,col & b&w illus-1st ed (s3,joints wn,dj) 20.00

HOLBROOK,ALFRED-Normal-NY-1860-Barnes & Burr-456p-1/2 lea (k1,lower jnts crckng) 20.00

HOLBROOK,MARION-Crime Wind-NY-1945-Dodd-1st ed (h4,f,dj) 15.00

HOLBROOK,STEWART-ED.-Promised Land-(1945)-Whittlesey-408p-1st ed (r8,chip dj) 20.00

HOLBROOK,STEWART-ED.-Promised Land-NY-(1945)-McGraw Hill-408p-1st ed (gg4,wn dj) 15.00

HOLBROOK,STEWART-Little Annie Oakley and Other Rugged People-NY-1948-Macmillan-12mo-x,238p-pict cl-1st ed (aa3,f,dj) 15.00

HOLCIK,JURAJ-Fresh-Water Fish-Lond-1969-4to-128p-56p col plts (m3,f,rprd dj) 15.00

HOLCOMBE & ADAMS-An Account of the Battle of Wilson's Creek or Oak Hills-Springfield-1883-Dow & Adams-104p-orig pict cl cov pasted over new cl,dbl frntis port-1st ed (o7,rbnd) 100.00

HOLCOMBE AND ADAMS-An Account of the Battle of Wilson's Creek or Oak Hills-Springfield-1961-Green Cnty Hist Soc-111p-maroon cl,dbl frntis ports-Centennial Ed (n7) 25.00

HOLCOMBE,F D-Modern Sea Fishing-Lond-1932-8vo-326p-photos (m3) 10.00

HOLDEN,EDITH-Nature Notes of the Country Diary of an Edwardian Lady-NY-(1984)-wtrcols-1st ed (m10,dj) 12.00

HOLDEN,G P-Idyl of the Split Bamboo-NY-1920-278p-grn cl,g dec,photos (ee3,vf) 135.00

HOLDEN,GEORGE P-Angling Recollection & Practice-NY-1931-12mo-187p-photos-1st ed (m3,fade sp) 25.00

HOLDEN,GEORGE P-Angling-NY & Lond-1931-Appleton-186,(1)p-cl,illus-1st ed (m1) 17.50

HOLDEN,GEORGE P-Streamcraft-Cin-1920-12mo-264p-8 col plts-2nd prntng (m3) 15.00

HOLDEN,WIILIAM C-Alton Hutson-San Antonio-1975-Trinity Univ-4to-xii+152p-photos-1st ed (m2) 30.00

HOLDEN,WILLIAM C-Alton Hutson-San Antonio-1975-Trinity Univ Pr-152p-cl,photos-1st ed (w3,f) 25.00

HOLDEN,WILLIAM C-Ranching Saga-S.A.-1976-T.U.P.-2 vols-1st ed (a9,box) 60.00

HOLDEN,WILLIAM C-Ranching Saga-San Antonio-1976-2 vols,cl,illus,J Cisneros-scarce-1st ed (w3,vf,box,autg) 125.00

HOLDEN,WILLIAM C-Spur Ranch-Bost-1934-Christopher Hs-12mo-229p-map e.p.,chrts,orig glassine dj-Howes H583-1st ed (aa3,vf,dj) 200.00

HOLDEN,WILLIAM C-Spur Ranch-Bost-1934-Christopher-229p-Herd 1051-1st ed (a9,sm cov spot) 175.00

HOLDER,CHARLES F-Big Game at Sea-NY-1908-8vo-352p-photos-1st ed (m3) 32.50

HOLDER,CHARLES F-California Fishing-SF-1908-So Pacific RR-12mo-79p-wrps,photos-rare (m3) 75.00

HOLDER,CHARLES F-Life in the Open-NY-1906-Putnam's-8vo-xv,(1),3-401p-dec grn cl,photogravure frntis,illus,half-tones-1st ed (mm1,sl soil) 65.00

HOLDER,CHARLES F-Recreations of a Sportsman on the Pacific Coast-NY-1910-Putnam's-ix,399p-cl,illus-1st ed (pp8,sl rub) 65.00*

HOLDER,CHARLES F-Salt Water Game Fishing-NY-1923-12mo-163p-photos (m3,f) 25.00

HOLDER,CHARLES F-Treasure Divers-NY-1898-Dodd,Mead-dec cov,illus-1st ed (x1,f) 30.00

HOLDER,EMMY LOU-Mazama Cookbook-Ore-1957-139p-wrps-1st ed (o10) 10.00

HOLDGATE,MARTIN-Mountains in the Sky-Lond-1958-222p-36 photos,lg fldg map-1st ed (a4,f,dj) 45.00

HOLDING,ELISABETH S-Innocent Mrs.Duff-NY-1946-Simon-1st ed (j4,dj) 15.00

HOLDREDGE,HELEN-Firebelle Lillie-NY-(1967)-Meredith-8vo-309p-1st ed (gg5,dj tn,sl soil) 15.00

HOLDREDGE,HELEN-Mammy Pleasant's Cookbook-SF-(1970)-101 Productions-137p-magenta wrps,illus,J B Alexander (u6) 15.00

HOLDREDGE,HELEN-Mammy Pleasant's Cookbook-SF-(1970)-101 Productions-160p-lg pict wrps,drwngs-1st prtg (q8) 16.50

HOLDREN,EARL-Complete Fishing Handbook for New York State's Fabulous Finger Lake Region-Rochester-1962-16mo-188p-wrps,photos,illus-1st ed (m3) 15.00

HOLDRIDGE,BARBARA-Ammi Phillips-NY-1969-C Potter-thin 4to-56p-red cl,b&w & col plts (r10,f,dj) 32.50

HOLDRIDGE,DESMOND-Northern Lights-NY-1939-Viking-240p-cl-1st ed (l1,f,dj) 15.00

HOLE,DONALD-Spiritualism and the Church-Milw-(1929)-Morehouse Publ-12mo-(vi)+122p-emboss tan cl-1st ed (y9,dj) 17.50

HOLE,EDWYN-Andalus, Spain Under the Muslims-Lond-(1958)-Robert Hale-8vo-189p-17 illus-1st Brit ed (gg5,tn dj) 17.50

HOLE,S REYNOLDS-Book About Roses-Lond-1904-Arnold-300p-cl,engrvngs-21st prtg (x6,cl rub) 21.00

HOLE,S REYNOLDS-More Memories-NY-1894-294p-cl (j1) 15.00

HOLE,S REYNOLDS-Our Gardens-Lond-1899-Dent-304p-cl,illus (x6) 18.00

HOLLAND,BOB-Good Shot!-NY-1946-8vo-151p-ltd to 850c,nbrd,3 autg-photos (m3,f,sl soil dj) 85.00

HOLLAND,DAN-Trout Fishing-NY-1949-8vo-420p-illus,Wm J Schaldach (m3) 25.00

HOLLAND,G A-Double Log Cabin-1937-83p-wrps,illus-rare-1st prtg (jj1,sl spot) 250.00

HOLLAND,HENRY-Essays on Scientific and Other Subjects-Lond-1862-499p-1st ed (dd3) 60.00

HOLLAND,JOHN-Memoirs of the Life and Ministry of the Rev. John Summerfield-NY-1846-460p-cl (e1) 20.00

HOLLAND,R P-Bird Dogs-NY-1948-8vo-204p-photos,illus by F McCaleb-1st ed (m3) 20.00

HOLLAND,R P-Master-1946-Barnes-12mo-85p-illus,E Ward-1st ed (m3) 40.00

HOLLAND,R P-My Dog Lemon-1945-Barnes-12mo-86p-illus,W Dennis-1st ed (m3,f,sl chip dj) 40.00

HOLLAND,R P-My Dog Lemon-NY-1945-86p-illus (gg3,f) 17.00

HOLLAND,R P-My Gun Dogs-Bost-1929-8vo-182p-illus,A L Ripley-1st ed (m3) 30.00

HOLLAND,R P-My Gun Dogs-NY-1929-182p-Illus (ee3,vf,dj chip) 45.00

HOLLAND,R P-Nip & Tuck-Phila-1939-8vo-182p-photos,illus by A Fuller-1st ed (m3,fade sp) 17.50

HOLLAND,R P-Now Listen Warden-West Hartford-1946-8vo-130p-ltd to 475c,nbrd,autg-illus,W Dennis-scarce (m3) 80.00

HOLLAND,R P-Scattergunning-NY-1951-Knopf-379p-col frntis,illus (gg3,f) 25.00

HOLLAND,R P-Seven Grand Gun Dogs-NY-1961-4to-152p-illus-1st ed (m3,dj) 35.00

HOLLAND,R P-Shotgunning in the Lowlands-NY-1945-213p-col illus-1st ed (gg3,vf,box) 65.00

HOLLAND,R P-Shotgunning in the Lowlands-NY-1945-4to-213p-illus,L B Hunt-1st prntng (m3) 45.00

HOLLAND,R P-Shotgunning in the Lowlands-NY-1945-Barnes-213p-col illus-2nd ed (gg3,chip dj) 40.00

HOLLAND,R P-Shotgunning in the Uplands-NY-1944-213p-col illus-1st ed (gg3,f) 50.00

HOLLAND,R S-Historic Airships-Phila-(1928)-roy 8vo-344p-illus cl,col frntis,5 col plts,18 b&w illus,text illus,illus e.p. (t2) 30.00

HOLLAND,STEWART S-Landforms of British Columbia-Victoria-1964-Queen's Prtr-138p-prtd wrps,illus,maps(1 in pckt)-Dept of Mines & Petrol Rsrcs,Bull.48 (k10) 15.00*

HOLLAND,W J-Butterfly Book-NY-1902-Dbldy,Page-382p-orig bndg wi lea labl,48p col plts,183 text illus (mm1,ex-libr) 80.00

HOLLEY,EDWARD G-Charles Evans, American Bibliographer-Urbana-1963-U of Illinois Pr-8vo-xii,343p-cl-1st ed (w2,dj) 25.00

HOLLEY,FRANCES C-Once Their Home-Chig-1892-Donohue & Henneberry-419p-pict cl,illus-Howes H592 (gg4) 95.00

HOLLEY,HELEN-Blood on the Beach-NY-1946-Mystery House-1st ed (d4,dj) 20.00

HOLLEY,MARIETTA-Samantha on the Woman Question-NY-(1913)-Revell-192p-tan dec cl,plts-1st ed (k2) 30.00

HOLLIDAY,C W-Valley of Youth-Caldwell-1948-Caxton-357p-cl,col frntis,plts,e.p. map (aa2) 40.00*

HOLLIDAY,ROBERT C-Walking Stick Papers-NY-(1918)-Doran-8vo-309p-cl backd bds,lea sp labl-1st ed (w2,sp labl chip,cov spot) 10.00

HOLLING,HOLLING C-Book of Cowboys-NY-(1936)-Platt & Munk-4to-illus,incl 6 col plts-1st ed (e10,fade sp,sl wn) 12.50

HOLLING,HOLLING C-Book of Indians-NY-(1935)-Platt & Munk-125p-col illus,e.p. maps (dd4) 15.00

HOLLING,HOLLING C-Claws of the Thunderbird-Joliet-(1928)-Volland-128p-pict cl,col illus,auth-1st ed (s3) 40.00

HOLLINGSWORTH,BRIAN-Illustrated Encyclopedia of North American Locomotives-NY-1984-208p-photos,75 col illus-1st ed (n4,dj) 24.00

HOLLINGSWORTH,J B-North American Railways-Lond-1977-190p-1st ed (n4,f,dj) 12.95

HOLLIS,HAROLD-Bass Tackle & Tactics-NY-1945-8vo-147p-photos-1st ed (m3,f,sl fray dj) 25.00

HOLLIS,IRA N-Frigate Constitution-Bost,NY-1901-Houghton Mifflin-16mo-263p-g stmpd dec grn cl (p8,sl wn) 55.00

HOLLISTER,MARY B-Rangoon International Cook Book-Rangoon-1972-Woman's Scty Chrstn Serv-254p-grn cl bds (m6) 35.00

HOLLISTER,OVANDO-Mines of Colorado-Sprngfld-1867-S Bowles-x+450p+ads-terra cotta cl,fldg col map-Howes H602-1st ed (mm10) 300.00

HOLLISTER,PAUL-Beauport at Gloucester-NY-(1951)-Hastings Hs-84p-bds,110 photos(incl 4 col),S Chamberlain (n6,dj) 35.00

HOLLISTER,PAUL-Encyclopedia of Glass Paperweights-NY-1969-312p-col illus-1st ed (cc8,dj) 40.00

HOLLISTER,PAUL-Glass Paperweights at Old Sturbridge Village: the Cheney Wells Collection-Old Sturbridge Village-1969-52p-wrps,50 plts (cc8) 20.00

HOLLISTER,PAUL-Glass Paperweights of the New York Historical Society-1974-Crown-1st ed (cc8,f,dj) 45.00

HOLLISTER,U S-Navajo and His Blanket-Denver-1903-144p-photo illus cov,col illus-Howes H603-1st ed (gg4,pres) 350.00

HOLLISTER,U S-Navajo and His Blanket-Denver-1903-Hollister-144p-cov photo,photos,10 col illus-Howes H603-1st ed (dd4,box,autg) 350.00

HOLLISTER,WILL C-Dinner in the Diner-LA-(1965)-Trans Anglo Bks-144p-photos,maps,drwngs-1st ed (o6,dj) 45.00

HOLLON,EUGENE-Great American Desert-NY-1966-284p-photos,maps-1st ed (t7,dj) 20.00

HOLLON,EUGENE-Lost Pathfinder Zebulon Montgomery Pike-Norman-1949-240p-illus-1st ed (t7,f,autg) 25.00

HOLLON,W E-Frontier Violence-1974-Oxford-274p-photos-1st ed (t8,f,dj) 20.00

HOLLON,W EUGENE-Southwest-NY-1961-Knopf-486p-illus-1st ed (dd4,dj) 35.00

HOLLOWAY,CARROLL-Texas Gunlore-SA-1951-Naylor-Six Guns 1014-scarce-1st ed (oo9,cov fade,dj chip) 50.00

HOLLOWAY,EDWARD S-Practical Book of Furnishing the Small House and Apartment-Phila-1922-Lippincott-296p-illus tan cl,t.e.g.,9 col & 198 b&w illus (r10) 20.00

HOLLOWAY,MARK-Heavens on Earth-NY-(1951)-Libr Publ-240p-blu cl,plts-1st ed (e2,sl wn dj) 22.00

HOLLY,H HUDSON-Modern Dwelling in Town & Country-NY-1878-114 wood engr-1st ed (h10,rear cov rippled) 150.00

HOLM,DON-101 Best Fishing Trips in Oregon-Caldwell-1970-8vo-207p-wrps,photos-1st prntng (m3,as new) 10.00

HOLM,DON-Pacific North-Caldwell-1969-Caxton-4to-283p-illus (m3,as new in dj) 15.00

HOLM,DONALD-Circumnavigators-Englewood Cliffs-(1974)-Prentice Hall-8vo-496p-1st ed (ff5,f,dj) 20.00

HOLMAN,A M-Pioneering in the Northwest-Sioux City-1924-150p-scarce-Smith 4582 (bb9) 75.00

HOLMAN,D-Elephant People-Lond-1967-226p-illus-scarce-1st ed (gg3,f,dj) 65.00

HOLMAN,D-Massacre of the Elephants-1967-Holt-247p-photos-1st ed (bb3,f,dj) 14.00

HOLMAN,DENNIS-Massacre of the Elephants-NY-1967-8vo-247p-photos (m3,vf,chip dj) 27.50

HOLMAN,DENNIS-Sikander Sahib-Lond-1961-275p-illus-1st ed (gg2,dj) 50.00

HOLMAN,FELICE-At the Top of My Voice-NY-1970-Norton-illus by E Gorey-1st ed (y1,f,f dj) 35.00

HOLMAN,FREDERICK V-Dr.John McLoughlin, the Father of Oregon-Cleve-1907-Arthur H Clark-301p-cl,ports-Tweney 31-1st ed (v1) 110.00

HOLMAN,HUGH-Up This Crooked Way-NY-1946-Mill-1st ed (e4,f,dj) 25.00

HOLME,C G-Children's Toys of Yesterday-Lond-1932-Studio-tall 4to-128p-illus(incl col) (a3,sl chip dj) 100.00

HOLME,C-ED.-Peasant Art in Sweden, Lapland & Iceland-Lond-1910-Studio-illus (h10,rear cov stnd) 125.00

HOLME,CHARLES-ED.-Early English Portrait Miniatures-Lond-1917-Studio-4to-44p text-gry bds,tan cl sp,papr sp labl,68 b&w & col plts (r10,sp rub,sl fox) 25.00

HOLMES,BURTON-Burton Holmes Lectures-Battle Creek-1901-Little Preston Co-lg 8vo-10 vols-3/4 lea,mrbld e.p. & cov,t.e.g.,photos-ltd to 1000sets-"Edition Original"-1st ed (ff5,sp sunned) 175.00

HOLMES,CHARLES S-Clocks of Columbus-NY-1972-Atheneum-1st ed (hh5,f,f dj) 10.00

HOLMES,CHARLES-Principles and Practice of Horse Shoeing-Leeds-1949-Farriers' Journal (h9) 45.00

HOLMES,GEORGE S-Lenox China-(Trenton)-(1924)-72,(3)p-cl backd bds (aa6) 50.00

HOLMES,JOHN C-Bowling Green Poems-PA-1977-pict wrps-ltd to 250c,autg (r2,f) 30.00

HOLMES,JOHN C-Get Home Free-NY-1964-Dutton-1st ed (ff6,dj) 45.00

HOLMES,JOHN C-Go-NY-1977-orig publ shrink wrp-2nd ed (x8,f,f dj) 50.00

HOLMES,JOHN C-Horn-NY-1958-1st ed (s5,dj) 65.00

HOLMES,JOHN C-Horn-NY-1958-1st ed (x8,sl wn dj) 75.00

HOLMES,JOHN C-Horn-NY-1958-Random-1st ed (c8,f,dj) 85.00

HOLMES,JOHN C-Nothing More to Declare-Lond-1968-1st Brit ed (q5,dj) 35.00

HOLMES,KENNETH L-Ewing Young Master Trapper-Portland-1967-180p-photos,illus,map e.p.-1st ed (t7,f,dj) 22.50

HOLMES,KENNETH L-Ewing Young, Master Trapper-Portland-1967-Binford & Mort-lg 12mo-viii,180p-map e.p.,photos,illus-1st ed (aa3,f,dj) 25.00

HOLMES,MAURICE-From New Spain by Sea to the Californias 1519 to 1668-Glendale-1963-A H Clark-307p-fldg maps,illus-1st ed (d3) 40.00

HOLMES,MRS.MARY J-Tracy Diamonds-NY-1899-Dillingham-8vo-390p-1st ed (w6) 35.00

HOLMES,OLIVER W,JR.-Touched with Fire-Cambridge-1946-158p-illus-1st ed (n3,sl chip dj) 35.00

HOLMES,OLIVER W-Autocrat of the Breakfast Table Every Man His Own Boswell-Bost-1858-373p-1st ed (dd3,sp & cor wn) 150.00

HOLMES,OLIVER W-Before the Curfew and Other Poems, Chiefly Occasional-Bost-1888-110p-1st ed (dd3) 50.00

HOLMES,OLIVER W-Currents and Counter Currents in Medical Science with Other Addresses and Essays-Bost-1861-406p-1st ed (dd3,sp rub & chip) 175.00

HOLMES,OLIVER W-Currents and Counter Currents in Medical Science-Bost-1861-Ticknor & Fields-xii+406+ads-purple cl-1st ed,1st iss (a2,sl rub) 135.00

HOLMES,OLIVER W-Dissertation on Acute Pericarditis-Bost-1937-Welch Biblio Soc-12mo-39p-vel-1st ed (dd3) 60.00

HOLMES,OLIVER W-Mechanism in Thought and Morals-Bost-1871-James R Osgood-101p-lilac cl-BAL 8876-1st ed,1st prtg (c2,sp fade) 125.00

HOLMES,OLIVER W-New Century and the Building of the Harvard Medical School-Cambridge-1884-55p-1st ed (dd3) 100.00

HOLMES,OLIVER W-One Hoss Shay-Bost,NY-1905-Houghton Mifflin-col plts by Pyle-1st ed thus (p1) 50.00

HOLMES,OLIVER W-One Hundred Days in Europe-Bost-1887-HMCo-1st ed (hh5) 30.00

HOLMES,OLIVER W-Poet at the Breakfast Table-Bost-1872-418p-1st ed (dd3) 100.00

HOLMES,OLIVER-Stagecoach East-Wash-1983-Smithsonian-1st ed (h9,dj) 58.00

HOLMES,PAUL A-Murder Buttoned Up-1948-Dutton-1st ed (s10,dj) 10.00

HOLMES,RICHARD-Naval and Military Trophies & Personal Relics of British Heroes-Lond-1896-folio-unpgd-dec blu cl,a.e.g.,36 col plts-1st ed (gg2) 600.00

HOLMES,S K-Brokenburn: Journal of Kate Stone, 1861 to 1868-Baton Rouge-1955-400p-map-1st ed (z10,dj) 40.00

HOLMES,THOMAS J-Cotton Mather, a Bibliography of His Works-Newton-1974-Crofton Publ Corp-8vo-3 vols-cl,illus-rprnt (w2) 125.00

HOLMES,THOMAS J-Education of a Bibliographer-Cleve-1957-Pr of Wstrn Rsrv Univ-sm 8vo-54p-cl-1st ed (w2,dj) 25.00

HOLMES,TOMMY-Dodger Daze and Knights-1953-McKay-1st ed (s8) 50.00

HOLMES,TOMMY-Dodgers-1975-Rutledge Bks-Baseball's Great Teams series-1st ed (s7,f,dj) 20.00

HOLMES,W D-Safari, R.S.V.P.-NY-1960-179p-photos (gg3,vf,dj) 25.00

HOLMES,W D-Square in the Arctic Circle, an Alaskan Hunt-CN-1960-168p-photos (gg3,ex-libr) 30.00

HOLMES,W H-Aboriginial Pottery of the Eastern United States-1903-Bur Amer Ethnol 20th Ann Rept-4to-237p-cl,177 plts(incl 5 col) (bb3,rbnd) 135.00

HOLMES,WILLIAM D-Safari, R.S.V.P.-NY-1969-8vo-179p-photos-1st ed (m3,f,dj) 25.00

HOLMGREN,ERIC J-2000 Place Names of Alberta-Saskatoon-1972-Modern Pr-8vo-210p-frntis,e.p. map-1st ed (cc7,dj) 20.00*

HOLMSTROM,J-Drake's Modern Blacksmithing and Horseshoeing-NY-1972-Drake (h9) 25.00

HOLROYD,JAMES E-Baker Street By Ways-Lond-(1959)-Allen & Unwin-tiss dj,illus-1st Brit ed (bb1,f,dj) 50.00

HOLROYD,MICHAEL-Lytton Strachey: A Critical Biography-NY,Chig,SF-(1968)-HR&W-2 vols-photos-1st ed (bb1,f,sl tan dj sp,box) 35.00

HOLT,A J-Pioneering in the Southwest-Nashville-1923-304p-pict cl,frntis-Rader #1918-1st ed (t7,cor bump,pres) 60.00

HOLT,EDGAR-Opium War in China-1964-Chester Springs-303p-illus-1st ed (b7,f,dj) 50.00

HOLT,ELIZABETH-Crimean War-E Sussex-1974-128p-illus-1st ed (b7,f,dj) 10.00

HOLT,G-Green Talons-1931-BM-1st ed (x7,wn dj) 18.00

HOLT,HENRY-Scarlet Messenger-NY-1933-Dbldy CC-1st US ed (d4) 10.00

HOLT,ROBERT E-Two Little Devils, a Memoir-Hicksville-1979-Expo Pr-104p-1st ed (z7,dj) 22.50

HOLT,SIMMA-Terror in the Name of God-NY-(1968)-Crown-8vo-312p-illus-1st US ed (jj5,dj) 20.00

HOLTHAUSEN,HENRIETTE-Chicken Goes Around the World-Lond-(1964)-Harrap-lg 8vo-240p-blu cl,drwngs-1st ed (q8,dj) 17.50

HOLTON,LEONARD-Out of the Depths-Lond-1967-Hammond-1st Brit ed (q4,dj sl wn & soil) 20.00

HOLTON,VIRGINIA-Beeps-NY-(1939)-John Day-8vo-192p-8 photos-1st ed (dd5) 15.00

HOLTZMAN,JEROME-ED.-No Cheering in the Press Box-1973-Holt Rinehart-1st ed (ff2,dj) 15.00

HOLTZWORTH,J M-Twin Grizzlies of Admiralty Island-Phila-1932-250p-photos (gg3,f,pres cpy) 50.00

HOLTZWORTH,J M-Wild Grizzlies of Alaska-NY-1930-417p-photos,map e.p. (gg3,f) 40.00

HOLWAY,JOHN-Voices From the Great Black Baseball Leagues-NY-(1975)-Dodd,Mead-photos-1st ed (aa8,f,dj) 25.00

HOLZER,HANS-Alchemist-NY-1974-Stein & Day-cl-1st ed (n8,f,dj) 25.00

HOLZMAN,ROBERT S-Stormy Ben Butler-NY-1954-297p-illus-1st ed (n3,f,dj) 20.00

HOLZMAN,ROBERT S-Stormy Ben Butler-NY-1954-Macmillan-297p-frntis,illus-1st ed (o7,f,dj) 30.00

HOLZWORTH,J M-Wild Grizzlies of Alaska-NY-1930-8vo-(1),417p-cl,col frntis,photos,map-1st ed (y8,spot cov) 75.00

HOME,LORD-Border Reflections Chiefly on the Arts of Shooting & Fishing-Lond-1979-8vo-111p-illus,R McPhail-1st ed (m3,vf,dj) 15.00

HOME,LORD-Reflections on Field & Stream-Bost-1980-Tall 8vo-111p-illus (m3,vf,dj) 12.50

HOMER,RACHEL J-ED.-Legacy of Josiah Johnson Hawes-Barre-1972-Barre Publ-sm folio-131p-cl,photos-1st ed (t3,dj) 65.00

HOMER,WILLIAM I-Alfred Stieglitz and the Photosecession-Bost-1983-NYGS/Little,Brown-4to-103 photos-1st ed (ee6,f,dj) 30.00

HOMES,GEOFFREY-Doctor Died at Dusk-NY-1936-Morrow-1st ed (hh2,f,sl wn dj) 125.00

HONEY,WILLIAM B-Ceramic Art of China and Other Countries of the Far East-NY-(1954)-Beechhurst-lg 8vo-viii,240p+192 photo plts,col plts-1st Amer ed (y4) 50.00

HONEY,WILLIAM B-Ceramic Art of China and Other Countries of the Far East-NY-1954-Beechhurst Pr-238p txt-3 tip in col plts,193 b&w plts-1st Amer ed (c3,f,sl wn dj) 75.00

HONEYMAN,A VAN DOREN-ED.-History of Union County, New Jersey, 1664 to 1923-NY-1923-4to-3 vols-cl,plts (aa6) 150.00

HONEYMAN,A VAN DOREN-ED.-Northwestern New Jersey-NY-1927-4to-(2),223p-cl,ports-vol.5(iss separately from 4 vol set) (aa6) 50.00

HONEYMAN,A VAN DOREN-ED.-Northwestern New Jersey-NY-1927-4to-4 vols-(5th vol iss separately) (aa6) 150.00

HONIG,DONALD-Baseball Between the Lines-1976-Coward,McCann-illus-1st ed (s8,dj) 27.00

HONIG,DONALD-Baseball When the Grass was Real-1975-Coward McCann (r7,f,dj) 20.00

HONIG,DONALD-Man in the Dugout-1977-Follett (r7,f,dj) 15.00

HONIG,DONALD-Man in the Dugout-1977-Follett-photos-1st ed (s8,f,dj) 17.50

HONIG,DONALD-October Heroes-1979-S&S-1st ed (p7,f,f dj) 17.50

HONIG,LOUIS-James Bridger-KC-1951-152p-pict cl,frntis,photos,ltd to 525c,nbrd,autg-v scarce-1st ed (t7,f) 125.00

HONOUR,HUGH-New Golden Land-NY-1975-Pantheon Bks-illus-1st ed (v4,as new in dj) 45.00

HOOBLER,DOROTHY-Voyages of Captain Cook-NY-1983-Putnam's-8vo-206p-1/2 cl,illus-1st ed (nn1,dj) 20.00

HOOD'S PICKLES AND PRESERVES ETCETERA-Lowell-1898-Hood & Co-96p-yel wrps (l6,sl tattrd,soil) 24.00

HOOD,DORA-Side Door-Tor-1958-Ryerson-8vo-ix,238p-frntis-1st ed (cc7,rub dj) 50.00*

HOOD,GRAHAM-American Silver-NY-1971-Praeger-sm 4to-256p-blu cl,illus (r10,f dj) 25.00

HOOD,JOHN B-Advance and Retreat-New Orleans-1880-Hood Orphan Mem Fund-358p-frntis,maps-1st ed (o7,sp split,sl chip) 200.00

HOOD,JOHN-Index of Colonial and State Laws of New Jersey between the Years 1663 and 1903 Inclusive-Camden-1905-(4),1353p-cl-2nd ed (aa6) 90.00

HOOD,ROBERT-Gashouse Gang-1976-Morrow-1st ed (ff2,f,dj) 40.00

HOOD,THOMAS-Epping Hunt-Derrydale-1930-16mo-33p-ltd to 490c,nbrd,hand col plts (m3,f,totally uncut) 100.00

HOOD,W I-Betsy Gaskins (Dimicrat), Wife of Jobe Gaskins (Republican) or Uncle Tom's Cabin Up to Date-Chig-(1897)-Schulte Publ-407p-cl-Wright 2749 (d1) 20.00

HOOKER,RICHARD-M*A*S*H Goes to Maine-NY-1972-Morrow-1st ed (hh5,dj) 10.00

HOOKER,RICHARD-Mash-NY-1968-auth 1st bk-1st ed (g5,dj) 45.00

HOOPER,FREDERICK-Military Horse-So Brunswick-1976-Barnes-4to-1st US ed (j9,dj) 35.00

HOOPER,MARY-Little Dinners-Lond-1891-K Paul-265p+94p cat-red cl-22nd ed (q8) 25.00

HOOPER,ROBERT-Lexicon Medicum-NY-1835-2 vols in one-lea-4th Amer ed (dd3) 100.00

HOOPES,ALBAN W-Road to the Little Big Horn and Beyond-NY-(1975)-Vantage Pr-336p-illus-1st ed (dd4,dj) 20.00

HOOPES,D F-American Impressionists-NY-1972-64 col plts-1st prtg (h10,dj) 50.00

HOOPES,D F-American Watercolor Painting-NY-1977-folio-48 col plts,117 b&w illus-1st prtg (h10,dj) 75.00

HOOPES,D F-Sargent Watercolors-NY-1970-sq 4to-32 col plts-1st ed (h10,dj) 45.00

HOOPES,PENROSE R-Connecticutt Clockmakers of the Eighteenth Century-Hartford-1930-Edw V Mitchell-4to-photos,ltd to 1000c-1st ed (k8) 45.00

HOOPES,ROY-Cain-NY-(1982)-HR&W-1st ed (bb1,f,dj) 25.00

HOOTEN,EARNEST A-Ancient Inhabitants of the Canary Islands-Cambridge-1925-Peabody Mus of Harvard-4to-xxvi+401p-brwn cl sp,pap labl,39 heliotype plts,37 text figs,191 tabls-1st ed (g2) 75.00

HOOTON,EARNEST A-Indians of Pecos Pueblo-New Haven-1930-Yale-4to-390p-plts,tbls,rear pckt plts-1st ed (oo9,sl wn sp) 150.00

HOOVER,DWIGHT W-Pictorial History of Indiana-Bloomington-(1980)-304p-bds-illus (j1,sl wn dj) 12.50

HOOVER,HERBERT-An American Epic-Chig-1959-64-Regnery-8vo-4 vols-1st ed (cc5,f,f dj,box) 75.00

HOOVER,HERBERT-Challenge to Liberty-NY-1934-Scribners-8vo-212p-1st ed (y6) 10.00

HOOVER,HERBERT-Challenge to Liberty-NY-1935-Scribner's-1st ed (p6,sl chip dj) 45.00

HOOVER,HERBERT-Fishing for Fun-NY-(1963)-Random-8vo-86p-1st trd ed (bb5,dj) 10.00

HOOVER,HERBERT-Memoirs of ...-NY-1952-405p-cl-1st ed so stated (g1) 15.00

HOOVER,HERBERT-Remedy for Disappearing Game Fish-NY-1930-8vo-41p-ltd to 950c,nbrd,woodcts (m3,vf,box) 70.00

HOOVER,J EDGAR-Study of Communism-NY-1962-Holt Rinehart-212p (r1,dj) 15.00

HOOVER,MATT-Wild Ginger-NY-1909-8vo-346p-photos (m3,sl fade sp) 35.00

HOOVER,THOMAS N-History of Ohio University-Athens-(1954)-274p-cl (k1,f,dj) 15.00

HOPE,BOB-Five Women I Love-GC-1966-Dbldy-1st ed (ff3,dj) 25.00

HOPE,BOB-They Got Me Covered-Hollywood-1941-B Hope-auth 1st bk-1st ed (x9,soil) 15.00

HOPE,LAURA L-Story of a Nodding Donkey-NY-1920-G&D-Make Believe Stories ser-1st ed (z2,f,dj) 45.00

HOPE,LAURA L-Story of a Stuffed Elephant-NY-1922-G&D-Make Believe Storie ser-1st ed (z2,f,dj) 45.00

HOPE,LAURA L-Story of a Woolly Dog-NY-1923-G&D-Make Believe Stories ser-1st ed (z2,f,dj) 45.00

HOPE,W H-Windsor Castle-Lond-1913-Cntry Life-folio-2 vols-122 plts(incl col)-ltd to 1050c,nbrd (gg6,rbnd) 575.00

HOPKINS,BRIAN-Forest and Savanna Intro to Tropical Plant Ecology...-Lond-1965-Heinemann-100p (x6,dj) 15.00

HOPKINS,CHARLES E-Ohio the Beautiful and Historic...-Bost-(1931)-454p-cl,2 col plts,48 duotone plts,map-1st ed imprssn so stated (m1,sm scratch rear cov) 25.00

HOPKINS,G E-Flying the Line-Wash D.C.-(1982)-8vo-xii,310p-illus bds,32p plts-1st ed (t2) 20.00

HOPKINS,G M-Combined Atlas of the State of New Jersey and the County of Hudson...-Phila-1873-G M Hopkins & Co-lg folio-(8),7-169p-cl,col maps (aa6,rebckd,guarded t.p.) 700.00

HOPKINS,THOMAS S-Colonial Furniture of West New Jersey-Haddonfield-1936-113,(1)p-cl,illus-ltd to 300c (aa6) 150.00

HOPKINS,VIVIAN C-Prodigal Puritan-Cambridge-1959-Harvard Univ Pr-xviii+362p-gry cl,plts-1st ed (k2,dj) 25.00

HOPKINS,WILLIAM J-Telephone Lines and Their Properties-1893-258p-illus-1st ed (h6) 20.00

HOPKINS,WILLIAM S-Labor in the American Economy-NY-1948-McGraw Hill-367p-1st ed (r1) 15.00

HOPLEY,GEORGE-Night Has a Thousand Eyes-1945-Farrar-1st ed (s10,dj) 135.00

HOPLEY,GEORGE-Night Has a Thousand Eyes-NY,Tor-(1945)-Farrar & Rinehart-1st ed (ff6,dj sp sl chip) 200.00

HOPPE,E O-Picturesque Great Britain-NY-(1926)-Brentano's-lg 4to-cl-1st ed (y3,dj sl chip & sunned) 115.00

HOPPER,DEWOLF-Once a Clown, Always a Clown-Bost-1927-238p-cl (h1,sl soil cov) 15.00

HOPPIN,JAMES M-Life of Andrew Hull Foote...-NY-1874-Harper & Bros-411p-brwn cl,plts,maps-1st ed (e2) 50.00

HOPPING,RICHARD C-Sheriff Ranger in Chuckwagon Days-NY-1952-246p-frntis,photos-1st ed (t7,dj) 37.50

HORAN,JAMES D-Across the Cimarron-NY-(1956)-Crown-301p-illus-Herd 1062-1st ed (ee4,dj) 20.00

HORAN,JAMES D-Confederate Agent-NY-(1954)-326p-e.p. maps,illus-1st ed (n3,f,dj) 20.00

HORAN,JAMES D-Desperate Men: Revelations from the Sealed Pinkerton Files-NY-1949-Putnam's-12mo-xx,296p-pict cl,map e.p.,photos,illus-1st ed (aa3,dj) 25.00

HORAN,JAMES D-Desperate Women-(1952)-Putnam-336p-illus-Six Guns #1027-1st ed (r8,dj) 40.00

HORAN,JAMES D-Gunfighters-(1976)-Crown-4to-312p-illus-1st ed (t8,f,dj) 22.00

HORAN,JAMES D-Life and Art of Charles Schreyvogel-NY-(1969)-oblng-63p-plts-1st ed (f7,dj) 85.00

HORAN,JAMES D-Life and Art of Charles Schreyvogel-NY-1969-Crown-long folio-62p text-col port frntis,36 col & 64 gravure illus-1st ed (aa3,chip dj) 125.00

HORAN,JAMES D-Mathew Brady-NY-1955-Crown-244p-453 photos-1st ed (cc9,f,dj) 50.00

HORAN,JAMES D-Pictorial History of the Wild West-NY-(1954)-Crown-254p-illus-Six Guns #1031-1st ed (ee4,dj) 25.00

HORAN,JAMES D-Pinkerton Story-NY-(1951)-Putnam's-xiv,366p-cl,photos-1st ed (v1,sl wn dj) 65.00

HORAN,JAMES D-Pinkerton Story-NY-1951-Putnam's-12mo-xiii,366p-pict cl,illus,photos-1st ed (aa3,f,dj) 40.00

HORAN,JAMES D-Pinkertons-NY-1967-Crown-8vo-xii,564p-blu cl,100 illus,maps (mm1,vf,chip dj) 60.00

HORAN,JAMES D-Timothy O'Sullivan-GC-1966-Dbldy-4to-cl-1st ed (y3,dj sl chip) 50.00

HORBEIN,THOMAS-Everest-SF-1965-4to-201p-89 plts-1st ed (p10,f,dj) 90.00

HORBEIN,THOMAS-West Ridge-SF-1965-4to-201p-89 plts-1st ed (q10,as new in dj) 150.00

HORGAN,PAUL-Centuries of Santa Fe-NY-1956-Dutton-363p-e.p. maps-1st ed (ee4,dj) 20.00

HORGAN,PAUL-Conquistadors in North America-Lond-1963-Macmillan-303p-1st Brit ed (d3,dj) 25.00

HORGAN,PAUL-Conquistadors in North American History-NY-(1963)-295p-1st prtg (u7,f,dj) 30.00

HORGAN,PAUL-Devil in the Desert-NY-1952-Longmans Green-1st ed (ee2,f,dj) 50.00

HORGAN,PAUL-Give Me Possession-1957-FS&C-1st ed (p9,f,dj) 25.00

HORGAN,PAUL-Great River, Vol.I and II-NY-1954-frntis,maps-Herd #1065 (t7) 17.50

HORGAN,PAUL-Great River-1954-Rinehart-2 vols,maps-Herd 1065-1st ed (t8,sl wn box) 45.00

HORGAN,PAUL-Great River-NY-1954-Rinehart-2 vols-maps-Herd 1065-1st ed (ee4,dj) 50.00

HORGAN,PAUL-Great River: The Rio Grande-NY-1965(1954)-HR&W-1020p-1st ed thus (o2) 20.00

HORGAN,PAUL-Heroic Triad-NY-(1970)-248p-1st ed (u7,dj) 25.00

HORGAN,PAUL-Heroic Triad-NY-(1970)-HR&W-256p-e.p. maps-1st ed (ee4,dj) 15.00

HORGAN,PAUL-Josiah Gregg and His Vision of the Early West-NY-1979-116p-frntis-1st ed (t7,f,dj) 12.50

HORGAN,PAUL-Lamy of Santa Fe-NY-(1975)-506p-photos,12 col plts,ltd to 500c,autg,box-1st prtg (u7,f,box) 125.00

HORGAN,PAUL-Lamy of Santa Fe-NY-(1975)-506p-photos-2nd trd ed (v7,f,dj) 30.00

HORGAN,PAUL-Memories of the Future-NY-(1966)-FS&G-1st ed (d10,f,sl soil dj) 12.50

HORKA-FOLLICK,LORAYNE-Vestige of Medievalism in Southwstrn US-LA-1969-222p-photos-1st ed (u7,f,dj) 25.00

HORLACHER,JAMES L-Year in the Oil Fields-Lexington-1929-Pr Ky Kernel-68p-wrps-rare-1st ed (ee10,papr glued to sp) 175.00

HORLER,SYDNEY-Mystery of Mr.X-Lond et al-(1951)-Foulsham-1st Brit ed (bb1,dj sl creased & edgewn) 15.00

HORLER,SYDNEY-Order of the Octopus-NY-1926-Doran-1st US ed (e4,f,f dj) 25.00

HORLER,SYDNEY-Strictly Personal-Lond-nd(ca.1934)-Hutchinson-288p-1st ed (g9,dj wn & tn) 75.00

HORN,CALVIN-ED.-Confederate Victories in the Southwest and Union Army Operations...-Albuq-1961-Stagecoach Pr-2 vols-maps,ltd to 1000c-scarce (z1,f,dj) 125.00

HORN,CALVIN-New Mexico's Troubled Years-Albuq-(1963)-231p-illus-1st ed (u7,dj) 20.00

HORN,COL.-Col. Horn's Hand Book on How to Pick High Bred Horses,Cattle,Sheep,Hogs,Poultry-Lewisburg-nd-Preble Co-200,(4)p (e1,wrps) 20.00

HORN,FLORENCE-Orphans of the Pacific: the Philippines-NY-1941-Reynal-316p-32p photos,e.p. maps (c3,wn dj) 18.00

HORN,MAURICE-Comics of the American West-NY-1977-Winchester-4to-1st ed (oo9,edge fade,dj) 45.00

HORN,STANLEY F-This Fascinating Lumber Business-Indpls,NY-(1943)-328p-34 illus (x5,autg) 15.00

HORN,TOM-Life of...Written by Himself-Denver-(1904)-Louthan Bk-sm 8vo-317p-prtd wrps in col,illus-Six Guns #1033-1st ed (b3) 225.00

HORNADAY,WILLIAM T-Camp Fires in the Canadian Rockies-NY-1907-Scribner's-70 photos,2 maps-1st ed (p6) 100.00

HORNADAY,WILLIAM T-Camp Fires in the Canadian Rockies-NY-1923-Scribner's-lg 8vo-xvii,353p+4p ads-blu cl,g sp titles,70 illus,2 maps (cc7,bump,wn,weak hngs) 125.00*

HORNADAY,WILLIAM T-Thirty Years War for Wildlife-Stamford-1931-Perm Wild Life Prtctn Fnd-xvi+292p+ads,red cl,illus,"Congressional" ed, to precede trd ed (d2,covs fade & sl soil) 35.00

HORNADAY,WM T-American Natural History-NY-1904-4to-449p-illus-1st ed (m3) 60.00

HORNBROOK,ISABEL-From Keel to Kite-Bost-1908-Lothrop,Lee & Shepard-pict cov & illus by F V Smith-1st ed (x1) 20.00

HORNE,BERNARD S-Complete Angler 1653-1967 a New Bibliography-Pitt-1970-4to-350p-ltd to 500c,nbrd-illus-scarce (m3,f,dj) 140.00

HORNE,JOHN-Many Days in Morocco-NY-1927-tall 8vo-60p photos-1st Amer ed (r2) 60.00

HORNER,DAVE-Blockade Runners-NY-1968-Dodd,Mead-241p-illus (o7,dj) 15.00

HORNOR,WILLIAM S-This Old Monmouth of Ours-Freehold-1932-(6),444p-cl,port (aa6) 175.00

HORNSBY,ROGERS-My Kind of Baseball-1953-McKay-1st ed (s8,dj) 45.00

HORNSBY,ROGERS-My War with Baseball-1962-Coward McCann-1st ed (p7,dj) 50.00

HORNUNG,CLARENCE-Wheels Across Africa-So Brunswick-1959-Barnes-4to-1st ed (h9,dj) 35.00

HORNUNG,E W-Amateur Cracksman-1899-Scribners-1st ed (x7,sl discol sp) 85.00

HORNUNG,E W-Camera Fiend-1911-Scribners-1st ed (x7,chip dj) 75.00

HORNUNG,E W-Crime Doctor-1914-BM-illus by F D Steele-1st ed (x7) 25.00

HORNUNG,E W-Mr.Justice Raffles-Lond-1909-Smith Elder-pict cl cov bds,gold stmpd sp titles-1st ed (w9,f) 100.00

HORNUNG,E W-Raffles-1901-Scribners-1st ed (x7,sp fade) 24.00

HORNUNG,E W-Thief in the Night-1905-Scribners-pict cl-1st ed (x7) 19.00

HORNUNG,E W-Thief in the Night-NY-1905-Scribners-1st US ed (f4) 10.00

HORRACKS,JAMES-My Dear Parents-NY-(1982)-188p-illus-1st Amer ed (c4,f,dj) 25.00

HORSLEY,TERENCE-Sporting Pageant-Lond-1947-8vo-208p-photos-1st ed (m3) 15.00

HORST,LOUIS-Modern Dance Forms-SF-1961-Impulse Publ-illus (u4,sl soil) 16.00

HORTICULTURIST AND JOURNAL OF RURAL ART AND RURAL TASTE-NY-1864,1865-Woodward-8vo-2 vols-blndstmpd grn cl,illus (r10,sl stnd cov) 90.00

HOSAKA,EDWARD-Sport Fishing in Hawaii-Honolulu-1944-8vo-198p-illus (m3,vf) 12.50

HOSKIN,BERYL-History of the Santa Clara Mission Library-Oakland-1961-82p-illus-1st ed (t7,f) 10.00

HOSKING,ANNIE S-History of Roxbury Township-(np)-(ca.1965)-184p-wrps,illus,fldg map (aa6) 20.00

HOSKING,F-Antarctic Wildlife-1982-Facts on File-4to-160p-100 col photos,map-1st ed (bb3,f,dj) 24.00

HOSKINS,BARBARA-Men from Morris County, New Jersey, who Served in the American Revolution-(Morristown)-(1979)-197p-wrps,plts (aa6) 20.00

HOSKINS,MARY C-Greene Story 1817 to 1963-Warren-1963-Trumbull Cnty Hist Scty-97p-wrps (d1) 15.00

HOSMER,H L-Early History of the Maumee Valley-Toledo-1858-Hosmer & Harris-(9)-70p-prtd wrps-rare-Howes H659,Sabin 33102 (b1,lacks rear wrps,sp wn) 400.00

HOSMER,J K-History of the Lewis & Clark Expedition-Chig-1902-2 vols-ports,fldg map-1st ed (e7,hng crack,sp tops marred) 150.00

HOSMER,JAMES K-Life of Thomas Hutchinson-Bost-1896-Houghton Mifflin-xxviii+453p-red cl,t.e.g.,plts-1st ed (mm10,sl fade sp) 50.00

HOSMER,JAMES K-Short History of the Mississippi Valley-Bost,NY-1902-230p-cl (f1) 12.50

HOSMER,JAMES-ED.-Gass's Journal of the Lewis and Clark Expedition...-Chig-1904-McClurg-sm 4to-298p-illus-(rprnt of 1811 ed)-1st prtg thus (b3) 125.00

HOSMER,JAMES-ED.-History of the Expedition of Captains Lewis and Clark 1804,5,6-Chig-1902-McClurg-sm 4to-2 vols-illus,(rprnt of 1814 ed)-1st prtg thus (b3) 175.00

HOSMER,JOHN A-Trip to the States by the Way of the Yellowstone and Missouri-1962-MT State Pr-24mo-82p+12p tables-wrps-(facs reprnt of 1867 ed) (r8,f) 35.00

HOSSACK,W C-Account of the Rats of Calcutta-Calcutta-1907-4to-(2),80p-wrps,8 plts(5 col,1 fldg)-Indian Mus Vol.1,No.1 (y8,chip) 35.00

HOSTERMAN,A D-Life and Times of James Abram Garfield...-Springfield-1882-336p-cl (f1) 20.00

HOTCHKISS,WILLIS R-Sketches from the Dark Continent-Cleve-1901-Friends Bible Inst-160p-cl-scarce (g1,sl flecked cov) 22.50

HOTCHNER,A E-Papa Hemingway-NY-(1966)-Random-1st ed (a10,f dj) 25.00

HOTCHNER,A E-Papa Hemingway-NY-(1966)-Random-1st ed (cc2,f,dj) 30.00

HOTCHNER,A E-Treasure-NY-1970-Random-1st ed (x1,f,f dj) 25.00

HOUGH,ALFRED L-Soldier in the West-Phila-1957-250p-illus-1st ed (n3,pc tn dj sp) 30.00

HOUGH,ALFRED L-Soldier in the West-Phila-1957-U of Penn Pr-250p-illus-1st ed (o7,dj) 25.00

HOUGH,E-Story of the Cowboy-NY-1897-Appleton Century-orig brwn cl,stmpd in silv & blk-1st ed (ee2,sl wn) 85.00

HOUGH,EMERSON-Story of the Outlaw-NY-1907-Outing-photos-Howes H764-Dykes 50-rare-1st ed (oo9) 60.00

HOUGH,RICHARD-Captain Bligh & Mr.Christian-NY-1973-320p-illus-1st ed (d7,f,sl tn dj) 35.00

HOUGH,WALTER-Decorative Designs on Elden Pueblo Pottery-Wash D.C.-1932-11p-wrps,10 photo plts-sep prtg no.2930 (v7) 20.00

HOUGHAM,PAUL-Encyclopedia of Archery-NY-1958-8vo-202p-photos (m3,vf,dj) 20.00

HOUGLAND,WILLARD-Santos-NY-(1946)-44p-wrps,dbl col,photos,map-1st ed (u7,f) 35.00

HOUK,RALPH-Ballplayers are Human Too-1962-Putnam-photos-1st ed (s8,f,dj) 16.00

HOULT,NORAH-Poor Women-Lond-1928-Scholartis Pr-8vo-226p-auth 1st bk,ltd to 1000c-scarce-1st ed (w6,sl tn & chip dj) 65.00

HOUSE,BOYCE-Cowtown Columnist-San Antonio-(1946)-Naylor Co-275p-Six Guns #1040-1st ed (cc4) 30.00

HOUSE,BOYCE-Cub Reporter Being Mainly about Mr.Mooney the Commerical Appeal-Dallas-1947-175p-pict cl,frntis-1st ed (t7,f) 12.50

HOUSE,C A-Canaries-Phila-nd-8vo-257p-cl,54 plts(3 col)-2nd ed (y8) 16.00

HOUSE,EDWARD J-Hunter's Campfires-NY-1909-Harpers-lg 8vo-402p-dec tan cl,photos-1st ed (p1,f) 150.00

HOUSE,HOMER-Wild Flowers of New York-Albany-1923-NY Univ-2 vols-cl,262 col plts (x6,sl fox) 40.00

HOUSEHOLD SEARCHLIGHT HOMEMAKING GUIDE-Topeka-1937-Household Mag-320p-orng bds,thumb indexed (n6,bump cor,sl wn) 45.00

HOUSEHOLD,GEOFFREY-Doom's Caravan-1971-Atlantic-1st Amer ed (s10,dj) 12.50

HOUSEHOLD,GEOFFREY-Hostage: London-Bost-1977-Little-1st Amer ed (s4,f,dj) 25.00

HOUSEHOLDER,B-Grand Slam of North American Wild Sheep-AZ-1974-220p-photos (gg3,f,pres,editors postcard) 175.00

HOUSEHOLDER,B-Hunting & Guiding for Desert Bighorn Sheep-AZ-1973-90p-photos-ltd to 500c (ee3,vf) 125.00

HOUSEMAN,JOHN-Front and Center-NY-(1979)-photos-1st ed (g5,as new in dj) 25.00

HOUSMAN,CLEMENCE-Were Wolf-Lond/Chig-1896-Lane/Way & Williams-8vo-124p-blk stmpd brn cl,frntis & 5 plts,L Housman-1st ed,2nd bndg (w6,sl fox e.p.,few nicks) 200.00

HOUSMAN,LAURENCE-Golden Sovereign-NY-(1937)-Scribners-1st US ed (hh5,dj sl tn,soil) 15.00

HOUSSER,F B-Canadian Art Movement-Tor-1926-12 illus (h10,edge rub) 125.00

HOUSTON,CHARLES-K2, the Savage Mountain-Lond-1955-192p-illus,map-1st Brit ed (p10,f,dj) 35.00

HOUSTON,EDWIN J-Dictionary of Electrical Words,Terms, and Phrases-NY-1889-W J Johnston Co-(ii)+iv+640+16p+ads-olive cl,396 text illus-1st ed (l2) 40.00

HOUSTON,EDWIN J-Elements of Physical Geography...-Phila-1896-180p-cl,frntis,wdcuts (k1) 20.00

HOUSTON,JAMES A-Eskimo Prints-Barre-1967-Barre Publ-oblng-112p-48 col prnts-1st ed (bb4,dj) 15.00

HOUSTON,MATILDA-Texas and the Gulf of Mexico-Lond-1844-John Murray-2 vols-10 plts-Howes H693-1st ed (a9,covs chip) 450.00

HOUSTON,MRS-Texas and the Gulf of Mexico-Phila-1845-G B Zieber-288p-orig cl,illus-1st Amer ed (w3,sp wn,lacks fr e.p.) 295.00

HOUSTON,SAM-Autobiography of...-Norman-(1954)-U of Okla Pr-298p-maps,illus-1st ed (cc4,dj) 35.00

HOUSTON,SAM-EVER THINE TRULY. LOVE LETTERS FROM...TO ANNA RAGUET-Austin-1975-157p-cl & papr on bds-ltd to 500c-1st ed (n10,sm holes in papr cov) 75.00

HOUSTON,SAM-THE LIFE OF...-Phila-(1867)-402p-cl,orig bndg-Howes L 271 (n1) 35.00

HOUTS,MARSHALL-From Gun to Gavel-NY-1954-Morrow-246p-map on e.p.s-Six Guns #1044 (cc4,dj) 20.00

HOVEY,C M-Fruits of America-NY-1853-vii,100p-orig g dec mor,innr dentelles,48 col lithos (bb9) 400.00

HOW TO ENTERTAIN AT HOME-Bost-1928-Priscila Publ-401p-red bds,illus (l6,underlining) 18.00

HOWARD & MCGRATH-War Chief Joseph-Caldwell-1958-368p-illus,maps-later prtg (j7) 35.00

HOWARD,BENJ-Report of Decision of Supreme Court... in Case of Dred Scott v Sanford-NY-1857-633p-self wrps-Sabin #3324-rare-1st ed (t7,box) 250.00

HOWARD,C-One Damned Island After Another-Chapel Hill-(1946)-U of N Carolina Pr-roy 8vo-xviii,404p-cl,60 plts,e.p. maps-1st ed (t2,dj) 60.00

HOWARD,CAPT L W-6th Ohio Volunteer Infantry-Toledo-nd-unpgd-orig mor g stmpd frnt cov,photos (d1,f) 75.00

HOWARD,ELIOT-Territory in Bird Life-Lond-1948-Collins (b9,dj) 10.00

HOWARD,ELIOT-Waterhen's Worlds-1940-Cambridge Univ Pr-4to-84p-drwngs,C E Lodge-scarce (m3,f,sl soil dj) 50.00

HOWARD,ELSTON-Catching-1966-Viking-photos-1st ed (s8,f,dj) 20.00

HOWARD,F E-English Church Woodwork-Lond-(1917)-4to-370p-photos (a3,sl rub) 57.50

HOWARD,GENE L-Death at Cross Plains-Univ-(1984)-151p-illus-1st ed (n3,f,dj) 15.00

HOWARD,H W-Salmon Fishing on Puget Sound-Portland-1947-8vo-123p-illus (m3,vf,dj) 13.50

HOWARD,H W-Sport Fishing for Pacific Salmon-Eugene-1954-8vo-148p-wrps,photos,maps-1st ed (m3,f) 27.50

HOWARD,HAROLD P-Sacajawea-Norman-(1973)-218p-illus (f7,dj) 25.00

HOWARD,HELEN A-War Chief Joseph-Caldwell-1941-Caxton-362p-cl,illus,col frntis-1st ed (v1,sl wn dj) 75.00

HOWARD,IRENE-Bowen Island, 1872 to 1972-Bowen Island-1973-Bowen Island Hist-190p-cl,frntis,illus,map (aa2,dj) 25.00*

HOWARD,JAMES H-Warrior Who Killed Custer-Lincoln-(1968)-84p-illus-Dowd #473-1st ed (c7,vf,dj) 50.00

HOWARD,JOSEPH K-ED.-Montana Margins-New Haven-1946-Yale U Pr-lg 8vo-xviii,527p-1st ed (o2) 20.00

HOWARD,JOSEPH K-Strange Empire-NY-1952-Morrow-xiv+601p-blk cl-1st ed (k2,dj) 30.00

HOWARD,JOSEPH,JR.-Life of Henry Ward Beecher-1887-Hubbard Bros-1st ed (dd8) 10.00

HOWARD,LADY WINEFRED...OF GLOSSOP-Journal of a Tour...US,Canada and Mexico-Lond-1897-Sampson Low,Marston-xii,355p-mod 1/4 calf over mrbld bds,5 raised bnds,lea sp labl,speckled edges,frntis wi tiss,35 plts-1st ed (mm1,f,rbnd) 225.00

HOWARD,MAJ GEN O O-My Life and Experiences Among Our Hostile Indians-Hartford-(1907)-Worthington-570p-chromo lithos,plts-Howes H710-1st ed (nn6,cov wn) 125.00

HOWARD,MARIA W-Lowney's Cook Book-Bost-1907-Walter M Lowney-367p-grn bds,10p plts-Bitting 235-1st ed (o6) 35.00

HOWARD,MARIA W-Lowney's Cook Book-Bost-1912-W M Lowney-419p-rvsd ed (v6) 11.00

HOWARD,MARTIN-Victorian Grotesque-Lond-1977-Jupiter Bks-8vo-154p-illus-1st ed (cc7,rub dj) 20.00*

HOWARD,MAUREEN-Before My Time-Bost-1974-Little,Brown-1st ed (w5,f,f dj) 25.00

HOWARD,MAUREEN-Bridgeport Bus-NY-1965-Harcourt-1st ed (w5,f,f dj) 30.00

HOWARD,MAX-People Papers-np-1974-Harlan Quist-sq 4to-unpgd-illus (r3,f,f dj) 20.00

HOWARD,O O-My Life & Experiences Among the Hostile Indians-Hartford-(1907)-570p-col & b&w illus-Howes H710-1st ed (d7) 175.00

HOWARD,O O-My Life Experiences Among our Hostile Indians-Hartford-(1907)-Worthington-570p-grn cl,plts(incl 10 chromlitho plts)-Howes H710-1st ed (h2,sp sunned) 135.00

HOWARD,O O-Nez Perce Joseph-NY-1972-276p-frntis,map-rprnt (t7,f) 50.00

HOWARD,R W-Dawnseekers-1975-Harcourt Brace-314p-illus-1st ed (bb3,f,dj) 18.00

HOWARD,ROBERT E-Almuric-W Kingston-1975-Grant-1st hdbk ed (k3,f,dj) 25.00

HOWARD,ROBERT E-Black Vulnea's Vengeance-W Kingston-1976-Grant-1st ed (g3,f,dj) 25.00

HOWARD,ROBERT E-Coming of Conan-NY-(1953)-Gnome Pr-1st ed (ff6,sl wn dj) 100.00

HOWARD,ROBERT E-Conan the Barbarian-NY-(1954)-Gnome Pr-1st ed (a10,chip dj) 100.00

HOWARD,ROBERT E-Conan the Conqueror-NY-(1950)-Gnome-1st ed (j3,sl soil t.e.,dj) 100.00

HOWARD,ROBERT E-Devil In Iron-W Kingston-1976-Grant-1st ed (k3,f,dj) 25.00

HOWARD,ROBERT E-Garden of Fear & Other Stories of the Bizarre and Fantastic-LA-(1945)-Crawford-pict wrps,cov by A Rogers-1st ed (k7) 35.00

HOWARD,ROBERT E-Hawk of Outremere-W Kingston-1979-Grant-1st ed (k3,f,dj) 25.00

HOWARD,ROBERT E-Iron Man-W Kingston-1976-Grant-1st ed (e3,f,dj) 15.00

HOWARD,ROBERT E-Jewels of Gwahlur-W Kingston-1979-Grant-1st ed (e3,f,dj) 25.00

HOWARD,ROBERT E-King Conan-NY-(1953)-Gnome-1st ed (l3,dj) 75.00

HOWARD,ROBERT E-Marchers of Valhalla-W Kingston-1977-Grant-new ed (e3,f,dj) 15.00

HOWARD,ROBERT E-Mayhem on Bear Creek-W Kingston-1979-Grant-1st ed (g3,f,dj) 25.00

HOWARD,ROBERT E-Queen of the Black Coast-W Kingston-1978-Grant-1st ed (e3,f,dj) 25.00

HOWARD,ROBERT E-Red Blade of Black Cathay-W Kingston-1971-Grant-1st ed (g3,f,dj) 75.00

HOWARD,ROBERT E-Return of Skull Face-West Linn-(1977)-Fax Collector's-S E Leialoha,illus-1st ed (a5,as new in dj) 25.00

HOWARD,ROBERT E-Road to Azarael-W Kingston-1979-Grant-1st ed (k3,f,dj) 25.00

HOWARD,ROBERT E-Singers In the Shadows-W Kingston-1970-Grant-1st ed (g3,f,dj) 125.00

HOWARD,ROBERT E-Skull Face and Others-Sauk City-1946-Arkham-x,475p-ltd to 3004c-1st ed (k5,new col photocopy dj) 175.00

HOWARD,ROBERT E-Son of the White Wolf-(W Linn)-1977-Fax Collector's Eds-illus(incl 3 col plts),M Boas-1st ed (a10,f,dj) 20.00

HOWARD,ROBERT E-Sword of Conan-NY-(1952)-Gnome Pr-1st ed (a10,dj edge-wn) 125.00

HOWARD,ROBERT E-Sword of Conan-NY-(1952)-Gnome-1st ed (k3,dj chip & rnfrcd) 50.00

HOWARD,ROBERT E-Sword of Shahrazar-W Linn-(1976)-Fax-1st ed (g3,f,dj) 20.00

HOWARD,ROBERT E-Tales of Conan-NY-(1955)-Gnome-1st ed (k3,pgs brwnd,dj) 50.00

HOWARD,ROBERT E-Tigers of the Sea-W Kingston-1974-Grant-1st ed (g3,f,dj) 30.00

HOWARD,ROBERT E-Tigers of the Sea-W.Kingston-1974-Donald M Grant-illus,Tim Kirk-1st ed (b5,f,dj) 25.00

HOWARD,ROBERT E-Worms of the Earth-W Kingston-1974-Grant-1st ed (g3,f,dj) 20.00

HOWARD,ROBERT W-Great Iron Trail-NY-1962-376p-1st ed (n4,f,dj,autg) 19.00

HOWARD,ROBERT W-Great Iron Trail-NY-1962-376p-photos,map e.p.-1st ed (t7,dj) 25.00

HOWARD,ROBERT W-Horse in America-Chig-1965-Follett-1st prtg (f10,dj) 25.00

HOWARD-WHITE,F B-Nickel-NY-(1963)-Van Nostrand-xiv+350p-red cl,illus-1st ed (d2,dj) 20.00

HOWARTH,D-We Die Alone-NY-1955-231p-photos,e.p. map-1st US ed (o10,f,dj) 15.00

HOWARTH,DAVID-Shetland Bus-Lond-(1951)-Nelson-8vo-220p-16 photos-1st ed (dd5,dj sp chip,tn) 17.50

HOWARTH,DAVID-Trafalgar, the Nelson Touch-NY-(1969)-254p-illus-1st Amer ed (d7,f,dj) 30.00

HOWARTH,DAVID-Trafalgar: the Nelson Touch-NY-1969-254p-illus-1st Amer ed (b7,f,dj) 20.00

HOWARTH,DAVID-Waterloo-NY-(1968)-239p-e.p. & text maps,col & b&w illus-1st Amer ed (d7,f,dj) 30.00

HOWARTH,DAVID-Waterloo: Day of Battle-NY-1968-239p-maps,col plts,63 b&w illus-1st Amer ed (b7,f,dj) 15.00

HOWARTH,DAVID-We Die Alone-NY-1955-231p-photos,e.p. map-1st US ed (q10,f,dj) 15.00

HOWARTH,T-Charles Rennie Mackintosh & the Modern Movement-Lond-1977-96 plts,28 figs-2nd ed (ee1,dj) 185.00

HOWAT,JOHN K-Hudson River and Its Painters-NY-1972-Viking-maps,100 col plts-1st ed (y10,sl tn dj) 35.00

HOWAY,F W-ED.-Dixon Meares Controversy-Tor,Mont-(1929)-156p-illus-ltd to 500c,nbrd-v scarce (j7,rub sp,dj) 165.00

HOWAY,FREDERIC W-ED.-Voyages of the "Columbia" to the Northwest Coast 1787 to 1790 and 1790 to 1793-Bost-1941-Mass Hist Scty-lg pap 8vo-red lea,raised bnds,g sp titles,illus (nn1,ex-libr) 275.00

HOWAY,FREDERIC W-Voyages of the Columbia-Amsterdam,NY-(1969)-518p-illus-Tweney #32-Bibliotheca Australiana rprnt (e7,f) 175.00

HOWAY,FREDERICK W-Dixon Meares Controversy-Amsterdam-1969-N Israel-(orig publ 1929)-rprnt (p8,as new) 50.00

HOWBERT,IRVING-Memories of a Lifetime in the Pike's Peak Region-NY-1925-298p-frntis-1st ed (u7) 35.00

HOWE,ANN-American Kitchen Directory and Housewife-Cin-1868-Howe's Subscrptn Bk Cncrn-208p-cl-frontis,illus-rare (e1,shaken,cov wn & fades) 65.00

HOWE,CARROL B-Ancient Tribes of the Klamath County-Portland-(1968)-Binfords & Mort-8vo-252p-203 illus-1st ed (cc5,f,sl fade dj,autg) 20.00

HOWE,E W-Plain People-NY-1929-Dodd,Mead-sm 8vo-317p-dec e.p.,frntis port-1st ed (aa3,dj) 50.00

HOWE,FRANCES R-Story of a French Homestead in the Old Northwest-Columbus-1907-Pr of Nitschke Bros-165p-cl-2 fldg maps-Howes H 718-Graff 1986-rare (g1,shakn,cov sl fade,wn,spot) 400.00

HOWE,GRAHAM-Paul Outerbridge, Jr.-NY-1980-Rizzoli-160p-140 photos-1st ed (cc9,as new in dj) 75.00

HOWE,HENRY-Great West-NY-1857(1851)-Geo F Tuttle-xi,576p-blnd stmpd lea over bds wi gilt,23 plts,5 maps,2 t.p.(1 col wi illus)-enlgd ed (p2,sl wn) 85.00

HOWE,IRVING-Leon Trotsky-NY-1978-Viking-214p-1st ed (r1,dj) 20.00

HOWE,JAMES V-Amateur Guncraftsman-NY-1953-8vo-306-illus (m3,f,sl fray dj) 15.00

HOWE,JAMES V-Modern Gunsmith-NY-1934-4to-2 vols,photos-1st ed (m3,f,wn box,pres cpy) 75.00

HOWE,JAMES V-Modern Gunsmith-NY-1954-2 vols-photos (gg3,vf,vf dj) 55.00

HOWE,LOUISE K-Pink Collar Workers-NY-1977-Putnam's-301p (r1,dj sp sun,sl tn) 15.00

HOWE,M A DEWOLFE-Atlantic Monthly and Its Makers-Bost-1919-Atl Monthly Pr-12mo-106p-bds,illus-1st ed (w2,sp chip) 10.00

HOWE,M A DEWOLFE-Life and Labors of Bishop Hare-NY-1911-Sturgis & Walton-417p-illus-1st ed (gg4) 50.00

HOWE,MARTIN-Blue Jazz-Bristol-1934-Perpetua Pr-stiff wrps,photo illus cov-rare-1st ed (ll9) 125.00

HOWE,MARVINE-Prince and I-NY-(1955)-John Day-8vo-252p-1st ed (cc5,dj) 15.00

HOWE,MAUD-Sun And Shadow in Spain-Bost-1908-Little,Brown-8vo-411p-red cl,gilt cov dec,photos-1st ed (gg6) 45.00

HOWE,OCTAVIUS T-Argonauts of '49-Cambridge-1923-Harvard U Pr (v4,sl fade cov) 95.00

HOWE,OCTAVIUS T-Argonauts of `49-Cambridge-1923-Harvard U Pr-(vi)+221p-blu bds,plts-1st ed (k2,dj) 55.00

HOWE,PAUL S-Mayflower Pilgrim Descendants in Cape May County, New Jersey...1620 to 1920-(Cape May)-(1921)-(7),464p-cl,plts (aa6) 100.00

HOWE,R H-Birds of Rhode Island-np-1899-8vo-111p-cl,6 b&w plts (y8,sp tn) 65.00

HOWE,ROBIN-Cook's Tour-Lond-(1958)-Dent-220p-prpl cl,drwngs-1st prtg (q8,dj) 15.00

HOWE,ROBIN-ED.-Mrs.Groundes-Peace's Old Cookery Notebook-Lond-(1971)-David & Charles-123p-red cl,illus e.p.,illus (q8,dj) 22.50

HOWE,ROBIN-Sultan's Pleasure and Other Turkish Recipes-NY-1953-Wyn-152p-grn cl,illus-1st Amer ed (q8,dj) 16.50

HOWE,S L-Philotaxian Grammar...-Lancaster-1838-Wright & Moeller-176p-bds-Amer Imprnts 50902 (k1,sl chip sp,lacks f f.e.p.) 47.50

HOWELL,A B-Birds of the Islands Off the Coast of Southern California-Hollywood-1917-Cooper Ornith Club. Pac Coast Avifauna,No.12-8vo-127p-cl,1 map-scarce (jj10,rbnd) 45.00

HOWELL,A H-Birds of Alabama-Montgomery-1924-8vo-384p-wrps,7 plts (y8,sp tn) 25.00

HOWELL,A H-Birds of Arkansas-1911-USDA-100p-wrps,7 plts-scarce (bb3,sl tn) 15.00

HOWELL,A H-Birds of Arkansas-Wash-1911-8vo-100p-wrps,col fldg map,6 b&w plts (y8) 20.00

HOWELL,A H-Florida Bird Life-Tallahassee-1932-4to-579p-cl,37 col & 2 b&w plts,photos,maps (y8) 55.00

HOWELL,A H-Florida Bird Life-Tallahassee-1932-Fla Dept Gm & Frshwtr Fsh-579p-col plts (d9,dj wn,rprd) 75.00

HOWELL,ARTHUR-Revision of the North American Ground Squirrels-Wash-1938-8vo-256p-wrps,11 col plts (m3) 15.00

HOWELL,P P-Manual of Nuer Law-Lond-1954-OUP-8vo-256p-cl-1st ed (y5,sl sun dj) 18.00

HOWELL,SARAH-Seaside-Lond-(1974)-Studio Vista/Cassell-lg 8vo-208p-illus-1st Brit ed (bb5,f,dj) 20.00

HOWELL,THOMAS R-Breeding Biology of the Egyptian Plover-Berkeley-1979-U Cal Publ Zoology,V.113-76p-15 plts (c9) 17.50

HOWELLS,JOHN M-Architectural Heritage of the Piscataqua-NY-1965-Architect Bk Publ-sm folio-(20),217p-bds,1/4 cl,301 plts (cc10,dj) 45.00

HOWELLS,WILLIAM D-Boy's Town-NY-1890-Harper-247p-cl-scarce 1st iss wi error in caption of illus opp pg 110 & same error in illus list pg v.-BAL 9654-1st ed,1st state (e1) 35.00

HOWELLS,WILLIAM D-Chance Acquaintance-Bost-1873-James R Osgood-12mo-grn cl-BAL 9566-1st ed (f2) 30.00

HOWELLS,WILLIAM D-Criticism and Fiction-NY-1891-188p-grn cl bndg-BAL 9656-1st ed (m1) 15.00

HOWELLS,WILLIAM D-Indian Summer-Bost-1886-Ticknor & Co-395p-cl-BAL 9624-1st ed (g1) 20.00

HOWELLS,WILLIAM D-Lady of Aroostook-Bost-1879-326p-cl-BAL 9584-1st prntg (d1) 22.50

HOWELLS,WILLIAM D-Letters Home-NY-1903-Harper-1st ed (hh5) 10.00

HOWELLS,WILLIAM D-Literature and Life-NY,Lond-1902-322,(1)p-cl-BAL 9749-1st ed (aa1) 20.00

HOWELLS,WILLIAM D-My Mark Twain-NY-1910-bndg A,t.e.g.,illus-BAL 9803-1st ed (r2,uncut,f) 75.00

HOWELLS,WILLIAM D-New Leaf Mills-NY-1913-1st ed (m4) 10.00

HOWELLS,WILLIAM D-Questionable Shapes-NY-1903-Harpers-red cl-1st ed (u2) 30.00

HOWELLS,WILLIAM D-Seven English Cities-NY-1909-Harper & Bros-t.e.g.-1st ed (z9) 20.00

HOWELLS,WILLIAM D-Undiscovered Country-Bost-1880-HMCo-1st ed (hh5) 25.00

HOWELLS,WILLIAM D-Undiscovered Country-Bost-1880-Houghton Mifflin-dec brwn cl-1st ed (u2) 40.00

HOWES,P G-Giant Cactus Forest and Its World-1954-DSP-258p-1 col plt,186 photos & illus-1st ed (bb3) 20.00

HOWES,WRIGHT-U.S.Iana (1650-1950)-NY-1962(1985)-Bowker-652p-cl-2nd ed,rvsd (v1) 65.00

HOWES,WRIGHT-U.S.Iana (1700-1950)-NY-1954-R R Bowker-tall 8vo-x,656p-cl-1st ed (w2,cov rub) 65.00

HOWLAND,ARTHUR-ED.-Materials Toward a History of Witchcraft Collected by Henry Charles Lea-Phila-1939-3 vols-1st ed (dd3,vf) 200.00

HOWLETT,GRAYLE-Tulsa Oilers All Time Texas League Record Book-1950-Tulsa Sports Corp-photos,pbk orig-1st ed (s8) 50.00

HOWLETT,REV W J-Life of the Right Reverend Joseph P Machebeuf D D...Pioneer Priest of New Mexico...-Pueblo-1908-419p-mrbld bds & lea,frntis,photos-Howes H743-1st ed (t7,rbnd) 100.00

HOYLE,FRED-Nicolaus Copernicus-NY-1973-Harper-94p-6 plts-1st US ed (hh6,dj) 19.00

HOYT,EDWIN P,JR.-Germans Who Never Lost-NY-(1968)-Funk & Wagnalls-8vo-247p-1st ed (cc5,dj) 20.00

HOYT,RICHARD-30 for a Harry-NY-1981-Evans-1st ed (d4,dj) 15.00

HOYT,RICHARD-Decoys-NY-1980-Evans-1st ed (d4,dj) 17.50

HOYT,RICHARD-Manna enzyme-NY-(1982)-1st ed (n5,f,f dj) 20.00

HOYT,RICHARD-Manna Enzyme-NY-(1982)-Morrow-1st ed (o3,f,dj) 15.00

HOYT,RICHARD-Trotsky's Run-NY-1982-Morrow-1st ed (h4,f,dj) 10.00

HOYT,RICHARD-Trotsky's Run-NY-1982-Morrow-1st ed (q4,f,dj) 25.00

HRDLICKA,ALES-Alaska Diary 1926 to 1931-Lancaster-1943-Jaques Cattell Pr-lg 8vo-414p-photos-1st ed (p1,wn dj) 75.00

HRDLICKA,ALES-Physiological and Medical Observations among the Indians of Southwestern U.S. and Northern Mexico-Wash D.C.-1908-GPO-Bur Amer Ethn Bull.34-x+460p-olive cl,28 plts,fldg chrts-1st ed (b2) 60.00

HRDLICKA,ALES-Physiological and Medical Observations among the Indians of Southwestern U.S. and Northern Mexico-Wash-1908-450p-illus-1st ed (dd3) 100.00

HU,YUNHUA-Penjing-Beaverton-(1982)-sm 4to-166p-93 col photos plts,58 b&w illus (x5,dj) 25.00

HUBBARD,BERNARD R-Mush, You Malemutes!-NY-1932-179,(10)p-cl,photos-1st ed (e1,sl wn dj) 20.00

HUBBARD,ELBERT-Justinian and Theodora-E Aurora-(1906)-Roycrofters-orng/blk dec,suede gilt,t.e.g.-1st ed (r2,f,uncut) 50.00

HUBBARD,ELBERT-Little Journies to the Homes of the Great-E Aurora-(1916)-Wm Wise/Roycrofters-14 vols-artificial lea-Memorial ed (pp6) 50.00

HUBBARD,ELBERT-Romance of Business-E Aurora-(1917)-Roycrofters-1st ed (r2,sp sun) 30.00

HUBBARD,ELBERT-Twenty O'Clock and Other Droll Stories-East Aurora-(1920)-Roycrofters-125,(1)p-bds (m1) 12.50

HUBBARD,FREEMAN-Great Trains of All Time-NY-1962-156p-1st ed (n4) 15.00

HUBBARD,J M-Notes of a Private-Bolivar-1973-207p-port-facs of 1911 ed (z10) 25.00

HUBBARD,L RON-Kingslayer-LA-1949-Fantasy Publ-1st ed (a10,dj sl chip & wn,soil) 100.00

HUBBARD,L RON-Ole Doc Methuselah-Austin-1970-Theta Pr-1st ed (w5,dj tn) 50.00

HUBBARD,L RON-Triton and Battle of Wizards-LA-1949-Fantasy Publ-1st ed,1st bndg (a10,dj chip,edge-wn,soil) 100.00

HUBBARD,MARGARET A-Sister Simon's Murder Case-Mlwk-1959-Bruce-1st ed (g4,dj) 12.50

HUBBARD,N T-Autobiography with Personal Reminiscences of New York City from 1798 to 1875-NY-1875-John F Trow-xii+235p-lilac cl,frontis-1st ed (h2,sp sunned,sl wn,cov fleck) 30.00

HUBBARD,P M-Flush as May-1963-London Hs-dj designed by E Gorey-1st Amer ed (s10,dj) 15.00

HUBBARD,W P-Notorious Grizzly Bears-Denver-1960-205p-photos (gg3,f,dj) 35.00

HUBBS,CARL-Guide to the Fishes of the Great Lakes & Tributary Waters-Bloomfield Hills-1941-8vo-100p+plts,illus,photos-1st ed (m3) 20.00

HUBER,BERTRAND-Death and the Dowager-NY-1934-Appleton-1st US ed (g4) 10.00

HUBER,L V-ET AL-New Orleans Architecture: the Cemeteries-1974-Gretna-illus-(Ser.,Vol.3)-1st ed (h10,dj) 45.00

HUBIN,ALLEN J-Bibliography of Crime Fiction 1749 to 1975-San Diego-(1979)-697p-cl,w/o dj as issued (g1,f) 25.00

HUBIN,ALLEN J-Bibliography of Crime Fiction 1949 to 1975-Del Mar-1979-Publisher's Inc-iss w/o dj-1st ed (d4) 40.00

HUBLER,R G-Big Eight-NY-(1960)-8vo-xii,244p-cl,16p plts-1st ed (t2,dj) 25.00

HUBLER,R G-Flying Leathernecks-GC-1944-Dbldy,Doran-8vo-xiv,225p-cl,8 plts-1st ed (t2) 35.00

HUBLER,R G-Straight Up-NY-(1961)-DS&P-xii+340p-blu cl,plts-1st ed (a2,dj) 25.00

HUBLER,RICHARD-Cristianis-(1966)-Little,Brown-319p-photos-1st ed (v8,dj) 30.00

HUC,M-Journey Through the Chinese Empire-NY-1855-Harper Bros-2 vols-dec emboss cl,fldg map (c3,sl fox,cor rub) 45.00

HUDLESTON,F J-Gentleman Johnny Burgoyne-Indpls-(1927)-Bobbs Merrill-blk cl-1st ed (b2,chip dj) 15.00

HUDNER,KENNEDY-Heirs of the Kingdom-NY-(1981)-HR&W-1st ed (j3,f,dj) 15.00

HUDSON,ARTHUR P-Folksongs of Mississippi and Their Background-Chapel Hill-1936-U of NC Pr-1st ed (w5) 45.00

HUDSON,CHARLES-Southwestern Indians-Knoxville-1980-573p-photos,illus (t7,as new in dj) 15.00

HUDSON,DEREK-Lewis Carroll-Lond-(1954)-Constable-8vo-354p-cl,illus-1st ed (pp10) 35.00

HUDSON,SUE F-Background of Ho Ho Kus-Ho Ho Kus-(1953)-xi,198p-cl,plts (aa6) 35.00

HUDSON,THOMSON J-Law of Mental Medicine-Chig-1903-McClurg-(xx)+281+(7)p-grn cl-1st ed (y9,sl stnd cl) 35.00

HUDSON,W G-Modern Rifle Shooting-NY-1903-12mo-155p-photos,illus (m3) 25.00

HUDSON,W H-Adventures Among Birds-NY-1915-Kennerley-8vo-315p-1st US ed (jj5) 30.00

HUDSON,W H-Birds of La Plata-Lond,NY-1920-8vo-2 vols-orig cl,22 col plts (y8,djs wn) 175.00

HUDSON,W H-Birds of La Plata-NY-1920-Dutton-2 vols-22 col plts by H Gronvold-Ltd to 1500c prtd for USA (c9,tape rprd djs) 150.00

HUDSON,W H-Hind in Richmond Park-NY-(1913)-Dutton-ltd to 1500c-1st Amer ed (dd2,sl wn sp) 40.00

HUDSON,W H-Land's End-NY-1927-Knopf-1st ed (cc2,f,dj) 50.00

HUDSON,W H-Naturalist in La Plata-1892-Chapman Hall-388p-illus-1st ed (bb3) 75.00

HUEBNER,LOUISE-Never Strike a Happy Medium-LA-(1970)-Nash-8vo-334p-20 illus-1st ed (gg5,dj) 15.00

HUFELAND,OTTO-Westchester County during the American Revolution,1775 to 1783-Wht Plains-1926-Wstchstr Cnty Hist Scty-xxviii+473p-blu cl,4 fldg maps,wi errata slip-1st ed (m2) 65.00

HUFF,EMMA-Memories That Live, Utah County Centennial History-Springville-1947-488p-frntis,photos,map e.p.-1st ed (t7,f) 35.00

HUFF,MARY N-Robert Penn Warren: A Bibliography-NY-1968-David Lewis-1st ed (bb2,f,dj) 30.00

HUFSTADER,ALICE A-Sisters of the Quill-NY-(1978)-329p-cl-1st prntg (d1,f,dj) 15.00

HUGGETT,WILLIAM T-Body Count-NY-(1973)-Putnam's-445p-cl-1st ed (h1,dj) 20.00

HUGGINS,ROY-Lovely Lady, Pity Me-NY-1949-Duell-1st ed (d4,dj sp fade,sl chip) 30.00

HUGGINS,ROY-Too Late for Tears-NY-1947-Morrow-1st ed (h4,f,sl chip dj) 25.00

HUGHAN,WILLIAM J-Encyclopedia of Freemasonry and Its Kindred Sciences...-Chig,NY,Lond-1924-Masonic History Co-2 vol-fabrikoid-illus-new & Revsd ed (j1) 20.00

HUGHES,DELBERT L-Give Me Room-El Paso-1971-255p-photos,errata slip-1st ed (u7,dj) 40.00

HUGHES,DELBERT L-Give Me Room-El Paso-1971-255p-photos,errata slip-1st ed (v7,autg,dj) 45.00

HUGHES,DOROTHY B-Cross Eyed Bear-NY-1940-DS&P-1st ed (u2,dj) 30.00

HUGHES,DOROTHY B-Expendable Man-1963-Random-1st ed (r9,dj) 20.00

HUGHES,DOROTHY-Davidian Report-NY-(1952)-1st ed (k9,dj) 10.00

HUGHES,ELIZABETH-California of the Padres-SF-1875-Choynski-41p-wrps (d3) 35.00

HUGHES,EMMET J-Report from Spain-NY-1947-Holt-323p-1st ed (ff1,chip dj) 20.00

HUGHES,GRAHAM-Modern Jewelry-NY-1968-Crown-256p-415 illus incl col-rvsd ed (u5,edge clip dj) 50.00

HUGHES,H G-Going Fishing-Lond-1925-12mo-223p-frontis (m3,vf,dj) 12.50

HUGHES,HELEN M-Fantastic Lodge, the Autobiography of a Girl Drug Addict-Bost-1961-Houghton Mifflin-1st ed (w5,f,dj) 35.00

HUGHES,JOHN T-Doniphan's Expedition-Cin-1848-J A & U P James-407p-orig blndstmpd blk cl wi g dec,frntis ports wi tiss,fldg map,13 illus-rare-1st prtg of enlgd ed (z1,rprd,box) 575.00

HUGHES,JOHN T-Doniphan's Expedition...-Cin-1848-James-12mo-xii,407p-buckrm,frntis port,fldg map-Howes H769-2nd ed (aa3,rbnd,sl tan & fox) 195.00

HUGHES,LANGSTON-Ask Your Mama-NY-1961-Knopf-1st ed (cc1,dj sp chip) 125.00

HUGHES,LANGSTON-Black Misery-NY-1969-illus-1st ed (r2,f,sl sun dj) 45.00

HUGHES,LANGSTON-ED.-An African Treasury-NY-1960-1st ed (s5,f,dj) 60.00

HUGHES,LANGSTON-ED.-Poetry of the Negro,1746 to 1949-GC-1949-Dbldy-429p-grn cl-1st ed (f2,dj chip & edge-wn) 50.00

HUGHES,LANGSTON-ED.-Poetry of the Negro-GC-1949-Dbldy-1st ed (w5,f,sl tn dj) 75.00

HUGHES,LANGSTON-First Book of Jazz-NY-1955-Franklin Watts-1st ed (v5,pres,f,dj sl chip,rub) 200.00

HUGHES,LANGSTON-Langston Hughes Reader-NY-1958-1st ed (hh10,sl rub dj) 45.00

HUGHES,LANGSTON-Langston Hughes Reader-NY-1958-Geo Braziller-1st ed (c10,sl wn dj) 60.00

HUGHES,LANGSTON-Not Without Laughter-NY-1930-Knopf-scarce-1st ed (y2,dj sp chip,sl fade) 850.00

HUGHES,LANGSTON-One Way Ticket-NY-1949-Knopf-illus by Jacob Lawrence-1st ed (y1,dj sl soil & edgewn) 150.00

HUGHES,LANGSTON-Sweet Flypaper of Life-NY-(1955)-Simon-wrps-1st ed (x3) 80.00

HUGHES,LANGSTON-Sweet Flypaper of Life-NY-1955-photos,Roy Decarva-1st ed (t5,wn dj) 60.00

HUGHES,LANGSTON-Weary Blues-NY-1926-109p-bds,cl sp-auth 1st bk-rare-1st ed (jj1,sp fade,wtrspot cov & pgs 250.00

HUGHES,REV A-Trout Fishing for Beginners-Tiverton-1928-12mo-76p-wrps,photos (m3,f) 20.00

HUGHES,RICHARD B-Pioneer Years in the Black Hills-Glendale-1957-366p-illus-Six Guns #1066-1st ed (c7,f) 80.00

HUGHES,RICHARD-High Wind in Jamaica-1929-C&W-1st ed (x2,f dj) 50.00

HUGHES,RUPERT-Complete Detective-NY-1950-Sheridan-1st ed (z9,dj sl chip) 15.00

HUGHES,RUPERT-George Washington-NY-1926-Morrow-ix,579p-illus-1st ed,1st prtg (n2) 20.00

HUGHES,TED-Cave Birds-NY-(1978)-Viking-drwngs,L Baskin-1st ed (u10,f,f dj) 20.00

HUGHES,TED-Earth Owl and Other Moon People-Lond-1963-illus-1st ed (r2,f,sl nick dj) 50.00

HUGHES,TED-Gaudette-NY-1977-Harper & Row-1st US ed (gg7,dj) 10.00

HUGHES,TED-Lupercal-NY-(1960)-Harper-8vo-cl-1st Amer ed (x3,f,dj) 75.00

HUGHES,TED-Moortown-NY-1979-Harper & Row-1st US ed (x9,f,f dj) 15.00

HUGHES,TED-Season Song-Lond-(1976)-Faber & Faber-1st Brit ed (f3,f,dj) 25.00

HUGHES,TED-Wodwo-NY-1967-Harper-1st US ed (w5,f,sl tn dj) 35.00

HUGHES,W J-Rebellious Ranger, Rip Ford and the Old Southwest-Norman-1964-279p-illus-scarce-1st ed (u7,f,dj) 45.00

HUGHES,W J-Rebellious Ranger-Norman-1964-300p-map,illus-1st ed (n10,f,dj) 75.00

HUGHES,WILLIAM-An Atlas of Classical Geography-Phila-1865-Blanchard & Lea-8vo-viii,76p-brwn buckr,26 plts (t10,ex-libr) 30.00

HUGILL,STAN-Sailortown-Lond-1967-Routledge-360p-illus,maps-1st ed (r8,dj wn) 35.00

HUGILL,STAN-Songs of the Sea-NY-1977-McGraw-Hill-4to-198p-red cl,illus (nn1,dj) 35.00

HUGO,RICHARD-31 Letters and 13 Dreams-NY-1971-Norton-71p-1st ed (j8,f,dj) 45.00

HUGO,RICHARD-Right Madness on Skye-NY-1980-Norton-1st ed (c8,f,f dj) 45.00

HUGO,RICHARD-Road Ends at Tahola-Pitt-1978-Slow Loris Pr-wrps,ltd to 1000c-1st trd ed (c8,f) 50.00

HUGO,RICHARD-What Thou Lovest Well, Remains American-NY-1975-Norton-1st ed (b8,f,f dj) 55.00

HUIE,WILLIAM B-Klansmen-NY-1967-Delacorte-1st ed (oo3,dj) 12.50

HUISH,MARCUS B-Japan & It's Art-Lond-1892-Fine Art Scty-288p,(2)p ads-illus cl incl rear cov,frntis-scarce-New & Enlgd ed (b6,sl tn backstrip,cor wn) 59.00

HUIZENGA,LEE S-Leonard Peter Brink-Grand Rapids-(1937)-66p-one photo-scarce-1st ed (v7,ex-libr) 25.00

HULBERT & HART-Zebulon Pike's Arkansaw Journal-Denver-(1932)-200,xcvi p-illus-Overland to Pacific Ser,Vol.I-1st ed (g7,cov spot) 75.00

HULBERT,ARCHER B-Forty Niners-Bost-1931-340p-cl (g1,sl spot) 15.00

HULBERT,ARCHER B-Forty Niners-Bost-1931-Little,Brown-8vo-340p-illus-1st ed (cc5,sl soil dj) 25.00

HULBERT,ARCHER B-Washington and the West-Cleve-1911-Arthur H Clark-217p-bndg two col prtng,illus (e7) 75.00

HULBERT,ARCHER B-Where Rolls the Oregon-Denver-(1933)-244p-illus-Overland to Pacific Ser,Vol.3-1st ed (g7,f,chip dj) 75.00

HULIT,LEONARD-Fishing With a Boy-Cin-1921-12mo-214p-photos (m3) 17.50

HULIT,LEONARD-Salt Water Angler-NY-1924-8vo-330p-illus,photos-1st ed (m3) 20.00

HULL,DAVID L-Darwin and his Critics-Cambridge-1973-Harvard U Pr-xii+473p-tan cl-1st ed (a2,dj) 20.00

HULL,F M-Bee Flies of the World-1973-Smithsonian-4to-687p-1030 figs (bb3,f,dj) 70.00

HULL,RICHARD-Ghost It Was-NY-1937-Putnam-1st US ed (e4,soil dj) 50.00

HULL,RICHARD-Murder Isn't Easy-NY-1936-Putnam-1st US ed (g4) 15.00

HULL,WILLIAM I-Benjamin Furly and Quakerism in Rotterdam-Swarthmore-1941-Swarthmore College-8vo-314p-coarse linen cov bds-1st ed (y6) 22.00

HULME,F EDWARD-Familiar Wild Flowers-Lond,NY,Tor,Mlbrn-1912-sm 8vo-160p-dec cov,40 col illus (m10) 10.00

HULME,KATHRYN-Annie's Captain-Bost-1961-Little,Brown-330p-1st ed so stated (p8,sl skewed sp) 10.00

HULME,KATHRYN-Look a Lion in the Eye-Bost-1974-Little,Brown-cl-1st ed (n8,f,dj) 16.50

HULME,KATHRYN-Wild Place-Bost-1953-Little,Brown-cl-1st ed (n8,dj) 37.50

HULSE,OLIVE-Salads-1911-Hopewell Pr (v6,cov soil,edgewn) 17.00

HULT,RUBY EL-Steamboats in the Timber-Caldwell-1952-Caxton-209p-tan cl,plts-1st ed (mm10,dj) 35.00

HULT,RUBY-Untamed Olympics-Portland-(1954)-267p-photos,e.p. maps-1st ed (r8,sl chip dj) 30.00

HULTEN,K G P-Machine as Seen at the End of the Mechanical Age-NY-1968-MOMA-metal dec col cov (h10) 100.00

HULTEN,K G PONTUS-Machine-NY-1968-MOMA-4to-218p-illus & sheet metal bndg-1st ed (r10) 45.00

HULTON,PAUL-Work of Jacques De Moyne Les Morgues-Oxford-(1977)-Brit Mus Publ Ltd-tall 4to-2 vols-16 col,144 mono chrome plts (x5,box) 110.00

HULTZ,FRED S-Range Beef Production in the Seventeen Western States-NY-1930-John Wiley & Sons-208p-cl,photos-Herd #1095-1st ed (w3,f) 20.00

HUMBLE,RICHARD-Napoleon's Peninsular Marshalls-NY-1973-Taplinger (z2,f,dj) 20.00

HUMBOLDT,ALEXANDER VON-Aspects of Nature in Different Lands and Different Climates with Scientific Elucidations-Lond-1849-LBG&L & J Murray-2 vols-1/2 lea,a.e. & e.p. mrbld (v4) 75.00

HUMBOLDT,ALEXANDER VON-Letters of...to Varnhagen Von Ense, From 1827 to 1858. With Extracts From Varnhagen's Diaries...-NY-1860-Rudd & Carleton-xv,407p+6p ads-orig emboss cl,transl fr 2nd German ed by F Kapp (nn1,sl wn,sp chip) 75.00

HUMBOLDT,ALEXANDER VON-Personal Narrative of Travels to the Equinoctial Regions of America During the Years 1799 to 1804-Lond,NY-ca.1851-Geo Routledge-3 vols-grn cl (pp1) 195.00

HUMBOLDT,ALEXANDER VON-Views of Nature-Lond-1850-H G Bohn-xxx+452p-red cl,col frntis (c2,sp soil) 45.00

HUME,DAVID-Dangerous Mr.Dell-1935-Appleton-1st Amer ed (s10,dj rear panel stnd) 17.50

HUME,E E-Ornithologists of the U.S. Army Medical Corps-Balt-1942-8vo-583p-cl,frntis,illus-rare (y8,dmpstns) 125.00

HUME,FERGUS-Millionaire Mystery-NY,Lond-1901-Buckles/Chatto & Windus-1st ed (bb1,sl fox e.p.) 75.00

HUME,FERGUS-Miser's Will-1903-Treherne-1st ed (x7,sm cov spot) 85.00

HUME,FERGUS-Mystery of the Hansom Cab...a Startling and Realistic Story of Social Life-NY,Chig-1888-J S Ogilvie & Co-238,(1)p-wrps-Red Cov Series #17,March 1888-rare (g1,frontis tn) 125.00

HUME,FERGUS-Red Money-1911-Dillingham-v scarce in dj-1st ed (x7,rnfrcd dj) 125.00

HUME,FERGUS-Red Window-NY-1904-Dillingham-1st US ed (e4) 15.00

HUME,FERGUS-Sacred Herb-1908-Dillingham-pict cl-1st ed (x7) 85.00

HUME,H-Azaleas-NY-1948-x,199p-8 col photos-1st prtg (m10,ragged dj) 15.00

HUME,H-Camelias in America-Harrisburg-1946-J Horace McFarland-4to-xvi,350p-coated cl,49p col plts-1st ed (mm4,f) 75.00

HUME,H-Gardening in the Lower South-NY-1929-Macmillan-453p-cl (x6) 16.00

HUME,H-Hollies-NY-1953-xi,242p-illus,incl 9 col (x5,wn,tatter dj) 30.00

HUME,MARTIN-Year After the Armada-NY-1896-Macmillan-8vo-388p-blu cl over bds,5 illus (gg6) 25.00

HUMPHREY,G M-Georgia Florida Field Trial Club 1916-NY-1948-Scribners-125p-photos,ltd to 600c (gg3,f) 20.00

HUMPHREY,GRACE-Story of the Williams-Phila-1926-Penn-col frntis,b&w drwngs,H Longstreet-1st ed (s3) 10.00

HUMPHREY,HENRY-ED.-Woman's Home Companion Household Book-(1950)-Collier-958p-blk cl,pict e.p.,plts (q8,edgewn) 18.50

HUMPHREY,SETH K-Indian Dispossessed-Bost-1905-Little,Brown-298p-1st ed (nn6,wn dj) 45.00

HUMPHREY,SETH K-Loafing Through Africa-Phila-1929-Penn-8vo-376p-orig cl,map e.p.,col frntis,plts,illus-1st ed (bb6,sp fade) 12.00

HUMPHREY,WILLIAM-Farther Off From Heaven-NY-1977-Knopf-1st ed (y1,f,dj) 22.50

HUMPHREY,WILLIAM-My Moby Dick-Lond-1978-8vo-96p-photos-1st Brit ed (m3,vf,dj) 10.00

HUMPHREY,WILLIAM-Ordways-NY-1965-Knopf-1st ed (f3,dj) 15.00

HUMPHREY,WILLIAM-Spawning Run-NY-1970-Knopf-illus-1st ed (y1,f,dj) 25.00

HUMPHREY,WILLIAM-Time and a Place-NY-1968-1st ed (n5,dj) 15.00

HUMPHREYS,ANDREW A-Virginia Campaign of '64 and '65-NY-1883-Scribners-451p-fldg maps-1st ed (v2) 30.00

HUMPHREYS,CHARLES A-Field, Camp, Hospital and Prison in the Civil War, 1861 to 1865-Bost-1918-428p-illus-1st ed (c4) 85.00

HUMPHREYS,CHRISTMAS-Sixty Years of Buddhism in England-Lond-1968-Buddhist Scty-cl-1st ed (o8,f,dj) 15.00

HUMPHREYS,GEN A A-Prelim Report Concerning Explor and Surv Principally in Nevada and Arizona-NY-1970-96p-maps(incl fldg)-orig publ in 1871 (t7) 17.50

HUMPHREYS,JOHN-American Racetracks and Contemporary Racing Art-So Bend-1966-So Bend-4to-1st ed (h9) 38.00

HUMPHREYS,P A-Romance of the Airman-Bost-(1931)-8vo-xviii,566p-illus cl,frntis,plts,text illus-1st ed (t2,sp fade) 30.00

HUMPHRIES,JOHN-Rockets and Guided Missiles-Lond-1956-E Benn-229p-illus (hh6,sl wn dj) 30.00

HUND,AUGUST-High Frequency Measurements-1933-491p-373 illus-1st ed (h6) 10.00

HUNDT,SHEILA W-Invitation to Riding-NY-1976-S&S-1st ed (h9,dj,pres) 25.00

HUNGER,F W T-Early Herbals from the Library of...-Amsterdam-1951-Intl Antiq-52p-wrps,illus (x6) 50.00

HUNGERFORD,EDWARD-Locomotives on Parade-1940-Crowell-236p-illus-1st ed (d3) 45.00

HUNGERFORD,EDWARD-Locomotives on Parade-NY-1940-236p-1st ed (n4) 35.00

HUNGERFORD,EDWARD-Pattern for a Railroad for Tomorrow-1960-Kalmbach-8vo-323p-cl,illus-ltd ed-1st ed (nn7) 12.00

HUNGERFORD,EDWARD-Railroad for Tomorrow-Milw-1945-323p-ltd 1st ed (n4,dj) 24.00

HUNGERFORD,EDWARD-Transport for War 1942 to 1943-1943-Dutton-8vo-272p-cl (nn7) 12.00

HUNGERFORD,JOHN-Hawaiian Railroads-1963-Hungerford Pr-8vo-80p-pict hdcov,illus (nn7,f) 35.00

HUNGRY WOLF,BEVERLY-Ways of My Grandmothers-NY-1980-Morrow-8vo-256p-photos-1st ed (bb7,dj) 20.00*

HUNN,C E-Practical Garden Book-NY-1909-Macmillan-250p-cl-7th ed (x6,cl soil) 10.00

HUNN,MAX-Bass Angler's Guide-Harrisburg-1982-8vo-252p-photos (m3,vf,dj) 12.50

HUNT & WILLIS-Genius of the Place-NY-1975-Harper & Row-390p (x6,f,dj) 75.00

HUNT,AURORA-Kirby Benedict, Frontier Federal Judge-Glendale-1961-268p-frntis-1st ed (t7,f) 25.00

HUNT,AURORA-Kirby Benedict, Frontier Federal Judge-Glendale-1961-268p-illus,fldg map-Wstrn Frntrsmn Ser,Vol.8-1st ed (f7,f) 45.00

HUNT,AURORA-Kirby Benedict, Frontier Federal Judge-Glendale-1961-Arthur H Clark Co-268p-illus,fldg map-1st ed (cc4) 35.00

HUNT,AURORA-Major General James Henry Carleton 1814 to 1873-Glendale-1958-Arthur H Clark Co-390p-illus,maps-1st ed (cc4) 95.00

HUNT,DICK-Bygones-Lewes-1948-Baxter-1st ed (j9,few cov spots) 65.00

HUNT,ELVID-History of Fort Leavenworth 1827 to 1937-Ft.Leavenworth-1937-xv,301p-illus,6 fldg maps rear pckt(1 col)-2nd ed (n2) 85.00

HUNT,F J G-Pictorial History of Electric Locomotives-So Brunswick-1970-147p-1st Amer ed (n4,f,dj) 22.00

HUNT,FRAZIER-Cap Mossman-NY-1951-Hastings-illus by R Santee-1st ed (a9,dj) 35.00

HUNT,FRAZIER-I Fought with Custer-NY,Lond-1947-236p-illus-Dowd 481-1st ed (j7,poor dj) 35.00

HUNT,FRAZIER-Long Trail From Texas-1940-Dbldy,Doran-300p-map-Six Guns #1074-1st ed (r8) 50.00

HUNT,FRAZIER-Tragic Days of Billy the Kid-NY-(1956)-Hastings Hs-316p-e.p. maps,maps-Six Guns 1075-1st ed (gg4,dj) 25.00

HUNT,HENRY M-Crime of the Century...-(Chig)-1889-Kochersperger-lg 12mo-xiv,576p-illus-1st ed (o2,sl rub) 25.00

HUNT,HOWARD-East of Farewell-NY-1942-auth 1st bk-1st ed (p5,dj sl wn & chip) 35.00

HUNT,HOWARD-East of Farewell-NY-1942-Knopf-auth 1st bk-1st ed (x1,dj v wn & chip) 40.00

HUNT,JOHN-Ascent of Everest-Lond-1953-Hodder & Stoughton-8vo-300p-blu cl,56 plts(8 col)-1st ed (gg6,dj) 35.00

HUNT,JOHN-Conquest of Everest-NY-1954-Dutton-300p-8 col plts-1st Amer ed (gg6,f,dj) 30.00

HUNT,JOHN-Life is Meeting-Lond-1978-286p-25 photos-1st Brit ed (p10,f,dj) 22.00

HUNT,JOHN-My Favorite Mountaineering Stories-Lond-1978-127p-1st Brit ed (q10,as new in dj) 13.00

HUNT,L B-How to Draw & Paint Birds-CA-nd-30p-wrps (gg3,f) 30.00

HUNT,LEIGH-Old Court Suburb-Phila-1902-2 vols-g dec cov,t.e.g.,illus-1st illus ed (r2,uncut) 75.00

HUNT,LOUIE-Silverton Train-1959-Huntington-4to-70p-pict cov,illus-2nd ed (nn7,f) 52.00

HUNT,LYNN BOGUE-How to Draw & Paint Birds-Laguna Bch-nd-folio-30p-wrps,illus (m3) 30.00

HUNT,MARY-Mary Hunt's Salad Bowl-1942-Barrows-102p-grn cl,dblpg photo-2nd prtg (q8,dj) 15.00

HUNT,PETER-COMP.-Eating and Drinking, An Anthology for Epicures-Lond-(1961)-Ebury Pr-320p-dec pnk cl,drwngs,4 col plts-1st prtg (q8,edgewn dj) 17.50

HUNT,PETER-Peter Hunt's Cape Cod Cookbook-NY-(1954)-Hawthorn Bks-181p-illus-1st ed (k6) 15.00

HUNT,PETER-Peter Hunt's Cape Cod Cookbook-NY-(1962)-Gramercy-190p-red cl,drwngs-2nd ed (q8,f,dj) 15.00

HUNT,ROCKWELL D-Fifteen Decisive Events of California History-LA-1959-Hist Soc of So Cal-91p-illus-1st ed (bb4) 15.00

HUNT,THOMAS-Historical Sketch of the Town of Clermont-Hudson-1928-Hudson Pr-cl sp/papr cov bds,fldg map in rear,map frntis,illus-1st ed (ff7) 85.00

HUNT,W B-Flat Bow-Mlwk-1951-8vo-70p-wrps,photos (m3) 12.50

HUNT,WILSON P-Overland Diary of...-Ashland-1973-Lewis Osborne Pr-67p-cl,illus,maps-1st ed (z1,f) 75.00

HUNTER'S HANDBOOK-Bost-1885-16mo-147p+ads-by "An Old Hunter"-scarce (m3) 35.00

HUNTER,ALAN-Gently Coloured-Lond-1969-Cassell-1st ed (p4,f,dj) 30.00

HUNTER,ALAN-Gently Does It-Lond-1955-Cassell-1st ed (k4,dj) 35.00

HUNTER,ALAN-Honfleur Decision-NY-1980-Walker-1st US ed (e4,f,dj) 15.00

HUNTER,COL GEORGE-Reminiscences of an Old Timer-SF-1887-H S Crocker-454p-pict cl,illus-Six Guns 1081-1st ed (bb4,wn) 125.00

HUNTER,COL WILLIAM C-Frozen Dog Tales and Other Things-Bost-1905-Everett Pr-12mo-dec cl-sketches-1st ed (s1,weak hngs) 45.00

HUNTER,COL. GEORGE-Reminiscences of an Old Timer...A Pioneer, Hunter, Minor and Scout of the Pacific Northwest...-SF-1887-Crocker-454p-brn cl,illus-Graff 2018-1st ed (w1) 300.00

HUNTER,DARD-My Life with Paper-NY-1958-Knopf-8vo-235p+index,photos,papr samples-1st ed (u1,dj) 75.00

HUNTER,DARD-My Life with Paper-NY-1958-Knopf-8vo-cl,paper specimens-1st ed (v10,f,f dj) 100.00

HUNTER,DARD-Papermaking-NY-1943-Knopf-398p-photos,fldg map-1st ed (f9,chip dj) 200.00

HUNTER,E-Find the Feathered Serpent-1952-Winston-auth 1st bk-1st ed (x7,sl tn dj) 70.00

HUNTER,ELEANOR A-Talks to Girls-NY-(1891)-132p-cl (l1) 15.00

HUNTER,EVAN-Horse's Head-NY-1967-Delacorte-1st ed (e4,f,dj) 15.00

HUNTER,EVAN-Matter of Conviction-NY-1959-S&S-1st ed (hh5,papr brwng) 20.00

HUNTER,EVAN-Second Ending-NY-1956-1st ed (g5,dj sp sl wn) 35.00

HUNTER,F W-Stiegel Glass-1950-Dover-272p-12 col plts+149 halftones-rvsd ed (cc8) 50.00

HUNTER,GEORGE-Tapestries-NY-1913-John Lane-ltd ed,autg (l9,cov wn) 250.00

HUNTER,HENRY-How England Got Its Merchant Marine 1066 to 1776-NY-1935-369p-1st ed (gg2,f,dj) 30.00

HUNTER,J A-African Bush Adventures-Lond-1954-252p-photos (gg3,f) 40.00

HUNTER,J A-Hunter's Tracks-NY-1957-8vo-240p-photos-1st ed (m3,vf,sl chip dj) 30.00

HUNTER,J A-Hunter-NY-1952-8vo-263p-photos-1st ed so stated (m3) 13.50

HUNTER,J A-Tales of the African Frontier-NY-1954-308p-photos (gg3,f,dj) 50.00

HUNTER,J MARVIN-Album of Gun Fighters-Bandera-(1951)-sm folio-236p-photos,errata slip-Six Guns 1085-1st ed (gg4) 120.00

HUNTER,J MARVIN-Brief History of Bandera County-Baird-1949-76p-stiff wrps-1st ed (t7) 25.00

HUNTER,J MARVIN-ED.-Trail Drivers of Texas-Nashville-1925-Cokesbury-8vo-(2 vols in one)-photos-2nd ed (aa3,f,dj) 250.00

HUNTER,J MARVIN-Story of Lottie Deno-Bandera-1959-4 Hunters-8vo-viii,199p-photos-1st ed (aa3,f,dj) 40.00

HUNTER,JOHN-Man Behind-NY-1938-Dutton-1st ed (j4,dj) 20.00

HUNTER,MILTON R-Utah Indian Stories-SLC-1946-282p-pict cl,photos,illus-1st ed (t7) 35.00

HUNTER,MILTON R-Utah the Story of Her People-SLC-1946-431p-col frntis,photos-1st ed (t7,f) 30.00

HUNTER,MONICA-Reaction to Conquest-Lond-1964-OUP-8vo-582p-cl-rprnt (y5,dj) 25.00

HUNTER,ROBERT-Labor in Politics-Chig-1915-Soc Party-204p-wrps-1st ed (v5) 30.00

HUNTER,ROBERT-Poverty-NY-1904-Macmillan-1st ed (v5,f) 40.00

HUNTER,THERESA M-Saga of Jean Lafitte-S.A.-1940-Naylor-109p-illus-1st ed (a9,dj) 30.00

HUNTER,THOMAS L-President's Camp on the Rapidan-Richmond-nd-4to-24p-wrps,illus wi map cntrfld & e.p.s,dec pages (m3) 50.00

HUNTER,W A-Fisherman's Pie an Angling Symposium-Lond-1926-8vo-196p-photos,illus (m3) 15.00

HUNTER,W-Letter From...Regarding Voyages of the Vessels "Captain Cook" and "Experiment"...A.D. 1786-(SF)-(1940)-(8)p-wrps-ltd to 125c (bb9) 50.00

HUNTING,WILLIAM-Art of Horse Shoeing-Chig-1920-Amer Vet Publ-later prtg (h9) 25.00

HUNTINGTON,D C-Landscapes of F E Church-NY-1966-oblng 8vo-125 illus(8 col)-1st prtg (ee1,dj sl tn & soil) 125.00

HUNTINGTON,D W-Game Farming for Profit & Pleasure-Wilmington-1915-Hercules-12mo-62p-wrps,illus by C B Davis-scarce (m3,vf) 25.00

HUNTINGTON,D W-Our Big Game-1904-Scribners-347p-photos (bb3) 10.00

HUNTINGTON,ELLSWORTH-Character of Races...-NY-1924-Scribner's-xvi+393p-grn cl-1st ed (j2) 25.00

HUNTINGTON,ELLSWORTH-West of the Pacific-NY,Lond-1925-Scribners-8vo-(1),453p-photos (gg6) 60.00

HUNTINGTON,GEORGE-Robber and Hero-Northfield-1895-Christian Way Co-119p-illus-Six Guns #1087-1st ed (dd4) 125.00

HUNTLEY,PAUL-Cowboy and His Horses-Canon City-1977-auth-141p-wrps,photos,fldg map-1st ed (w3,f) 20.00

HUNTLEY,STANLEY-Mr and Mrs Spoopendyke-NY-(1889)-Hurst & Co-192p-cl (j1) 15.00

HUNTON,JOHN-John Hunton's Diary-Ft.Laramie-nd-L G Flannery-5 vols-maps,illus-ltd to 1500c (nn6) 85.00

HUNTTING,M T-Gold in Washington-Olympia-1955-158p-prntd wrps,2 fldg maps (r8) 15.00

HURD,C W-Boggsville-Las Animas-1957-Boggsville Comm-8vo-89p+indx-pict wrps,photos,illus-Herd 1107-1st ed (aa3) 50.00

HURD,PETER-Lithographs-Lubbock-1968-Baker Gallery Pr-sm folio-81p(incl 58 plts)-1st ed (ee4,dj,autg) 80.00

HURD,PETER-Peter Hurd Portfolio of Landscapes and Portraits-Albuq-1950-NM Artist Ser.No.11-12"x15"-8 loose prnts in col folio-1st ed (t7,f) 135.00

HURD-MEAD,KATE C-History of Women in Medicine from the Earliest Times to the Beginning of the Nineteenth Century-Haddam-1938-569p-1st ed (dd3,ex-libr) 225.00

HURLEY,FRANK-Australia, a Camera Study-Sydney-1956-Angus & Robertson-4to-208p-blu cl,g titles,col photos-2nd prtg (p8) 35.00

HURLEY,FRANK-Pearls and Savages-NY/Lond-1924-Putnam's-Imperial 8vo-xiv,414p-grn cl,g sp & cov titles,t.e.g.,map,80 illus-1st ed (nn1) 250.00

HURLEY,P J-In Search of Australia-Sidney-1943-Dymocks Book Arcade-sm 4to-xi,134p-3 col plts,56 b&w photo plts (p8,papr drknd,dj chip) 25.00

HURLIMANN,BETTINA-Seven Houses-NY-(1977)-Crowell-262p-cl & bds,illus-1st US ed (s3,f,dj) 15.00

HURRY,J B-Vicious Circles in Disease-Lond-1911-J & A Churchill-xiv+186p-grn cl,t.e.g.-1st ed (g2) 65.00

HURST,C C-Mechanism of Creative Evolution-NY-1932-Macmillan-lg 8vo-xxii+365p-red cl,199 illus-1st ed (j2) 25.00

HURST,DAISY-From Pinafores to Politics-NY-1923-359p-illus-1st ed (n2,sl rub,hngs weak) 20.00

HURST,FANNIE-President is Born-NY-1928-Harper-8vo-484p-1st ed (w6,vf,chip dj) 35.00

HURST,IRVIN-46th Star-Okla City-1957-178p-pict cl,photos,illus,maps-scarce-1st ed (t7) 50.00

HURSTON,ZORA N-I Love Myself When I Am Laughing...-(Old Westbury)-(1979)-Feminist Pr-8vo-cl-1st ed (ll10,f,dj) 350.00

HURT,W H-Mammals of Michigan-Ann Arbor-1948-4to-288p-cl,13 col plts,67 maps-rvsd ed (y8) 30.00

HURWITZ,ALFRED-Milestones in Modern Surgery-NY-1958-520p-illus (g10,dj) 65.00

HUSBAND,JOSEPH-Story of the Pullman Car-1917-McClurg-8vo-161p-illus (nn7,sl wn) 31.00

HUSMANN,GEORGE-Cultivation of the Native Grape & Manufacture of American Wines-NY-1870-Woodward-192p-cl (x6) 75.00

HUSON,HOBART-Captain Phillip Dimmitt's Commandancy of Goliad...-Austin-1974-Von Boeckmann-299p-1st ed (a9) 75.00

HUSSEY,J A-Fort Vancouver-nd(1957)-Wash St Hist Soc-256p+54 plts(incl fldg)-glassine dj-ltd to 1000c-Tweney #33 (d7,f,dj) 85.00

HUSTON,HARVEY-Roddis Line-Winnetka-1972-150p-1st ed (n4,f,dj,autg) 20.00

HUTCHENS,JOHN K-One Man's Montana-NY-1964-Lippincott-221p-1st ed (o2,f,dj) 15.00

HUTCHENS,MAJ JAMES M-Beyond Combat-Chig-(1968)-Moody Pr-1st ed (ff3,dj) 40.00

HUTCHESON,ERNEST-Musical Guide to the Richard Wagner Ring of the Nibelung-NY-1940-S&S-1st ed (u4,vf) 18.00

HUTCHINGS,J M-Heart of the Sierras-Yosemite Vly & Oakland-1886-496p-pict cov,26 photos(1 col) (q10,hngs crack) 200.00

HUTCHINGS,J M-In the Heart of the Sierras-Oakland-1886-Pacific Pr-8vo-grn cl stmpd in blk & gilt,28 plts,2 maps(1 fldg)-1st ed,1st iss (y3,stnd rear cov) 245.00

HUTCHINGS,J M-Scenes of Wonder and Curiosity in California-NY,SF-1870-292p-engrvngs (q10,wn) 55.00

HUTCHINGS,J M-Scenes of Wonder and Curiosity in California-NY,SF-1871-grn cl (q10,f) 185.00

HUTCHINS,JAMES-Boots and Saddles at the Little Big Horn-Ft.Collins-1976-81p-stiff pict wrps,photos,illus,maps (t7,f) 20.00

HUTCHINS,ROSS E-Caddis Insects-NY-1966-4to-80p-photos (m3,vf,dj) 20.00

HUTCHINSON,C C-Resources of Kansas: Fifteen Years Experience-Topeka-1871-publ by auth-16mo-vii,287p-40 illus,fldg map rear e.p.-Rader 1994-1st ed (aa3) 150.00

HUTCHINSON,H D-Campaign in Tirah 1897 to 1898-Lond-1898-250p-maps,illus-1st ed (gg2,ex-libr) 125.00

HUTCHINSON,HARRY W-Village and Plantation Life in North Eastern Brazil-Seattle-1957-U of Wash-8vo-199p-papr over bds-AES Publ-1st ed (y5,drknd dj) 25.00

HUTCHINSON,HORACE G-Fellowship of Anglers-Lond-1925-8vo-211p-photos (m3) 25.00

HUTCHINSON,HORACE-ED.-Fishing-Lond-1904-8vo-2 vols,illus,col plts (m3) 80.00

HUTCHINSON,R C-Recollection of a Journey-Lond-1952-Cassell-1st ed (y1,dj) 22.50

HUTCHINSON,THOMAS J-Impressions of Western Africa...-Lond-1858-Longman,Brown,Green-8vo-xvi,313p-orig cl,engrvd t.p.-1st ed (bb6,ex-libr) 175.00

HUTCHINSON,W H-Bar Cross Man-Norman-(1956)-432p-illus-1st ed (j7,fair dj) 30.00

HUTCHINSON,W H-Line of Least Resistance by Eugene M Rhodes-Chico-1958-78p-pict wrps,ltd to 500c,nbrd,autg-1st ed (t7) 65.00

HUTCHINSON,W H-Notebook of the Old West-Chig-1947-122p-pict wrps,illus-1st ed (t7) 45.00

HUTCHINSON,W H-World, the Work & the West of W H D Koerner-1978-U of Okla Pr-4to-xii,243p-100 b&w & 36 col illus-1st ed (aa3,as new in dj) 60.00

HUTCHINSON,W H-World, the Work & the West of W H D Koerner-1978-U of Okla Pr-sm folio-243p-illus-1st ed (cc4,dj) 45.00

HUTCHINSON,WOODS-Doctor in War-Bost-1918-481p-photos-scarce-1st ed (dd3) 100.00

HUTCHISON,BRUCE-Fraser-Tor-1950-8vo-368p-illus,R Bennett-1st ed (m3,f,fray dj) 20.00

HUTCHISON,BRUCE-Fraser-Tor-1950-Clarke,Irwin-368p-illus,map-Rivers of Amer ser (k10,chip dj) 20.00*

HUTCHISON,E R-Tropic of Cancer on Trial-NY-(1968)-Grove-1st ed (w1,f,dj) 15.00

HUTCHISON,JOSEPH C-Treatise on Physiology and Hygiene for Educational Institutions and General Readers-NY-1887-Clark & Maynard-319p-cl-illus (g1) 15.00

HUTSON,H P-ED.-Ornithologists' Guide-Lond-1956-BOU-273p (b9,chip dj) 20.00

HUTTON,EDWARD-In Unknown Tuscany-Lond-(1909)-Methuen-8vo-244p-8 col illus by Ward-1st ed (ff5) 30.00

HUTTON,J ARTHUR-Our Fishing Diary Hampton Bishop 1908-1933-Altrincham-1942-4to-156p-#18 of ltd ed,photos (m3,pres cpy) 100.00

HUTTON,J ARTHUR-Rod Fishing for Salmon on the Wye-Lond-1920-16mo-160p-illus,photos,plts in rear pocket (m3) 50.00

HUTTON,JOHN E-Trout & Salmon Fishing-Lond-1949-8vo-242p-col frontis,illus,photos-1st ed (m3,f,sl fray dj) 27.50

HUTTON,LEN-Just My Story-Lond-1956-Hutchinson-8vo-192p-frntis,41 illus-1st ed (bb7,rub dj) 20.00*

HUTTON,M A-Coeur D'Alenes-(Denver)-1900-246p-photos-Smith 4836 (bb9,wn) 100.00

HUXLEY,ALDOUS-After Many a Summer-Lond-1939-Chatto-1st ed (aa10,dj) 225.00

HUXLEY,ALDOUS-Antic Hay-Lond-1923-Chatto-8vo-cl,t.e. yel-1st ed (x3,dj) 150.00

HUXLEY,ALDOUS-Brave New World-Lond-1932-(6),306,(1)p-cl-1st ed (o4,f,sl tn dj) 600.00

HUXLEY,ALDOUS-Brave New World-Lond-1932-Chatto & Windus-8vo-cl-1st trd ed (kk8,sl cocked,dj sl fox & tn) 750.00

HUXLEY,ALDOUS-Brief Candles-Lond-1930-Chatto & Windus-1st Brit ed (d10,sl bump,fox,dj wn) 50.00

HUXLEY,ALDOUS-Cicadas & Other Poems-GC-1931-Dbldy,Doran-1st US ed (bb1,sl tn dj) 75.00

HUXLEY,ALDOUS-Cicadas and Other Poems-NY-1931-Dbldy Doran-dec bds-1st US ed (h8,edgewn,dj) 50.00

HUXLEY,ALDOUS-Do What You Will-Lond-1929-Chatto & Windus-1st ed (y1,dj soil & sl chip) 100.00

HUXLEY,ALDOUS-ED.-An Encyclopedia of Pacifism-Lond-1937-Chatto & Windus-prtd wrps-1st ed (ll5) 40.00

HUXLEY,ALDOUS-Eyeless in Gaza-Lond-1936-Chatto-8vo-cl-1st ed (x3,f,chip dj) 70.00

HUXLEY,ALDOUS-Genius and the Goddess-NY-(1955)-Harper-8vo-cl-1st ed (x3,dj) 25.00

HUXLEY,ALDOUS-Heaven and Hell-NY-(1956)-Harper-1st ed (x10,f,dj) 15.00

HUXLEY,ALDOUS-Little Mexican & Other Stories-Lond-1924-Chatto & Windus-1st ed (kk5,cov sl spot,dj) 85.00

HUXLEY,ALDOUS-Moksha-NY-1977-Stonehill-cl-1st prtg (o8) 29.00

HUXLEY,ALDOUS-Music at Night and Other Essays-Lond-1931-1st ed (r2,f,dj sp sun,sl chip) 50.00

HUXLEY,ALDOUS-Olive Tree-Lond-1936-Chatto & Windus-grn bev buckram,ltd to 160c,autg-1st ed (ee2,f) 175.00

HUXLEY,ALDOUS-On the Margin, Notes and Essays-Lond-1923-1st ed (y7,sp drknd,cov sl spot) 30.00

HUXLEY,ALDOUS-Science, Liberty and Peace-NY-1946-precedes Brit ed-1st US ed (q5,chip dj) 22.50

HUXLEY,ALDOUS-World of Light-Lond-1931-1st ed (r2,f,dj sl sun,sl chip) 75.00

HUXLEY,E-Murder at Government House-1937-Harpers-auth 1st bk-scarce-1st Amer ed (x7,dj sl wn & chip) 85.00

HUXLEY,ELSPETH-Red Rock Wilderness-NY-1957-Morrow-1st US ed (e10,f dj) 20.00

HUXLEY,ELSPETH-Scott of the Antarctic-NY-1978-Atheneum-8vo-26 illus,3 maps-1st Amer ed (bb7,dj) 25.00*

HUXLEY,FRANCIS-Affable Savages-NY-1957-Viking-8vo-285p-13 photos,map-1st US ed (jj5,creased dj) 15.00

HUXLEY,GERVAS-Tea in Porcelain-1952-Tea Centre-29p-blu wrps (l6) 12.00

HUXLEY,J-ED.-Evolution as a Process-1954-Allen Unwin-367p-1st ed (bb3,sp fade) 20.00

HUXLEY,JULIAN-Man in the Modern World-Lond-1947-1st ed (y7,sl fade,dj sl soil) 20.00

HUXLEY,JULIAN-Problems of Relative Growth-NY-1932-Dial-xx+276p-grn cl,104 figs-1st Amer ed (j2,edgewn dj) 30.00

HUXLEY,JULIAN-Soviet Genetics and World Science-Lond-1949-Chatto & Windus-x+245p-blu cl-1st ed (c2,chip dj) 20.00

HUXLEY,JULIETTE-Wild Lives of Africa-NY-1963-8vo-255p-photos (m3,vf,dj) 12.50

HUXLEY,LEONARD-Life and Letters of Sir Joseph Dalton Hooker-Lond-1918-John Murray-2 vols,blu cl,illus,map-2nd prntg (j2,sm tr on sp tip vol 1) 45.00

HUXLEY,THOMAS-American Addresses, with a Lecture on the Study of Biology-NY-1877-164p-1st ed (dd3) 75.00

HUXLEY,THOMAS-Evidence as to Man's Place in Nature-NY-1863-D Appleton-184p+8p ads-brwn cl,sp labl,32 text figs-1st Amer ed (g2,sl wn cov,sp labl wn) 75.00

HUXLEY,THOMAS-Hume-Lond-1894-Macmillan-xvi+319p+ads-maroon cl-1st ed (c2) 45.00

HUXLEY,THOMAS-Man's Place in Nature and Other Anthropological Essays-1898-Appleton-328p (bb3) 12.00

HUXLEY,THOMAS-Manual of the Anatomy of Vertebrated Animals-NY-1872-Appleton-431p-grn cl,110 text figs-1st Amer ed (d2) 85.00

HUXLEY,THOMAS-Scientific Memoirs of Thomas Henry Huxley...-Lond-1898 to 1902-5 vols-plts(incl fldg)-1st ed (dd3,ex-libr) 400.00

HUXLEY,THOMAS-Social Diseases and Worse Remedies-Lond-1891-Macmillan-128p-brwn cl-1st ed (j2) 30.00

HUXLEY,THOMAS-T H Huxley's Diary of H M S Rattlesnake-NY-1972-Kraus-red cl over bds,g titles,illus-rprnt (p8,as new) 30.00

HUYDA,RICHARD J-Camera in the Interior-Tor-(1975)-Coach Hs Pr-oblng 4to-56p wi fldg map,photos-1st ed (t1,f,dj) 45.00

HUYGHE,RENE-ED.-Larousse Encyclopedia of Prehistoric and Ancient Art-NY-(1962)-4to-414p-col plts (l10,dj) 25.00

HUYSMANS,J K-Against the Grain-NY-1922-1st ed (y7,sl wn) 28.00

HYAMS,EDWARD-Capability Brown and Humphry Repton-NY-(1971)-248p-40 photos (m10,f,dj) 25.00

HYAMS,EDWARD-English Garden-Lond-(1964)-lg 4to-288p-17 tip in col plts,171 photogrvrs-scarce (x5,brwnd pgs,rprd dj) 75.00

HYAMS,EDWARD-English Garden-NY-(1966)-sm 8vo-288p-4 col & 142 b&w plts (j10,tn dj) 20.00

HYAMS,EDWARD-Great Botanical Gardens of the World-(Lond)-(1969)-Nelson-folio-288p-g dec cl,illus(incl col)-1st ed (dd10,f,dj) 50.00

HYAMS,EDWARD-History of Gardens and Gardening-NY-(1971)-4to-ix,345p-33 col & 391 b&w plts,plain box (x5,f,chip dj,box) 60.00

HYAMS,EDWARD-Irish Gardens-Lond-(1967)-lg 4to-160p-15 col & 88 b&w plts (x5,rprd dj) 45.00

HYAMS,EDWARD-Irish Gardens-NY-1967-MacMillan-lg 4to-160p-15 col plts & 88 half tones-1st Amer ed (mm4,dj rprd) 35.00

HYAMS,EDWARD-Ornamental Shrubs for Temperate Zone Gardens-S Brunswick-(1965)-319p-48 col & 48 b&w photo plts (m10,edge fade,dj sl wn) 40.00

HYATT,A-Pseudoceratites of the Cretaceous-1903-US Geol Survevy-4to-351p-47 plts(incl fldg) (bb3) 75.00

HYATT,ALFRED-ED.-Book of Gardens-Lond-1900-Foulis-131p-papr cov bds,6 tip in plts by Waterfield (x6,sp fade) 25.00

HYATT,HARRY M-Folk Lore from Adams County Illinois-NY-1935-723p-map-scarce-1st ed (t7) 35.00

HYDE,CHARLES-Pioneer Days-NY-1939-Putnam's-286p-illus,col pict dj-scarce-1st ed (f9,dj chip,sp fade) 85.00

HYDE,E W-Skew Arches-NY-1875-Van Nostrand-104p+publ catlg-prntd bds (j1,sp wn) 15.00

HYDE,GEORGE E-Early Blackfeet and Their Neighbors-Denver-1933-J VanMale,Publ-45p-orig wrps-ltd to 75c-Howes H858-v scarce-1st ed (gg4) 225.00

HYDE,GEORGE E-Indians of the Woodlands-Norman-(1973)-U of Okla Pr-298p (cc4,dj) 20.00

HYDE,GEORGE E-Life of George Bent-Norman-(1968)-U of Okla Pr-389p-illus-1st ed (dd4,dj) 40.00

HYDE,GEORGE E-Sioux Chronicle-1956-U of Okla Pr-8vo-xix,334p-pict cl,illus,2 maps-1st ed (aa3,f,dj) 40.00

HYDE,GEORGE E-Sioux Chronicle-Norman-(1956)-U of Okla Pr-334p-illus-1st ed (nn6,sl wn dj) 65.00

HYDE,GEORGE E-Spotted Tail's Folk-Norman-(1961)-U of Okla Pr-329p-illus,maps-1st ed (ff4,autg) 50.00

HYDE,GEORGE E-Spotted Tail's Folk-Norman-(1961)-U of Okla Pr-329p-illus-1st ed (gg4,dj) 75.00

HYDE,GEORGE E-Spotted Tail's Folk-Norman-(1961)-U of Okla-8vo-329p-1st ed (z4,dj fr scratched) 20.00

HYDE,H MONTGOMERY-Mr and Mrs Beeton-Lond-(1951)-Harrap-189p-brwn cl,8 photos-1st ed (q8,wn dj) 15.00

HYDE,H MONTGOMERY-Princess Lieven-Bost-1938-Little,Brown-8vo-288p-24 illus-1st ed (ff5,sl cocked,dj sp chip) 20.00

HYDE,H MONTGOMERY-Solitary in the Ranks-NY-1978-1st ed (b7,f,f dj) 35.00

HYDE,WALTER W-Ancient Greek Mariners-NY-1947-Oxford-8vo-360p-3 maps-1st US ed (jj5,f,f dj) 25.00

HYMAN,S-Edward Lear's Birds-1980-Morrow-folio-96p-30 col plts,50 b&w illus (bb3,f,dj) 65.00

HYND,ALAN-Betrayal from the East-NY-(1943)-McBride-8vo-287p-1st ed (gg5,sl wn dj) 15.00

HYNDMAN,J H-Modern Fly Craft-Portland-1938-8vo-76p-true 1st wi tip-in col frontis of trout-1st ed (m3,vf) 30.00

HYNE,C C-Adventures of Captain Kettle-1898-Harpers-1st Amer ed (x7,sl wn & fade sp) 85.00

HYNE,C C-Captain Kettle on the War Path-1916-Methuen-1st ed (x7) 35.00

HYNE,C C-Marriage of Captain Kettle-1912-BM-1st ed (x7) 16.00

HYSLOP,JAMES-Enigmas of Psychical Research-Bost-1906-427p-1st ed (dd3) 75.00

I.E.B.C.-Facts & Useful Hints Relating to Fishing & Shooting-Lond-1866-8vo-115p-illus (m3) 40.00

I.W.W.-Founding Convention of the...-NY-1969-Merit Publ-616p (r1,dj) 25.00

IAMS,JACK-Into Thin Air-NY-1952-Morrow-1st ed (e4,dj) 25.00

IAMS,JACK-Shot of Murder-NY-1950-Morrow-1st ed (e4,f,dj) 25.00

IBSEN,HENRIK-Peer Gynt-Lond-(1936)-Harrap-orig g pict cl,illus by A Rackham-1st trd ed (aa9,sl fade sp) 275.00

ICKES,ANNA W-Mesa Land-Bost-1933-Houghton Mifflin-1st ed (oo9) 17.50

ICKS,COL ROBERT J-Famous Tank Battles-NY-1972-1st ed (z2,f,dj) 25.00

IDE,RICHARD-Possessed with Greatness-Chapel Hill-1980-UNC Pr-1st ed (x9,f,dj) 10.00

IDRIESS,ION L-Flynn of the Inland-Sydney-1934-Angus & Robertson-8vo-xii,306p+ads-brwn cl,map e.p.,35 photos (p8,sl wn) 30.00

IDZERDA,STANLEY J-ED.-Lafayette in the Age of the American Revolution-Ithaca,Lond-1977 to 1983-Cornell U Pr-8vo-5 vols-blu cl,illus-1st eds (dd7,dj) 200.00

IGNATIEFF,MICHAEL-Just Measure of Pain-NY-1978-Pantheon-1st ed (z9,dj) 10.00

IKTOMI-America Needs Indians-Denver-(1937)-425p-illus-1st ed (v7) 35.00

ILLINGWORTH,FRANK-Wild Life Beyond the North-(Lond & NY)-1952-8vo-168p-photos (m3,f,fray dj) 15.00

ILLINOIS STATE BOARD OF FISH COMMISSIONERS-Report for the Years 1900 to 1902-1903-8vo-65p+plts-illus (m3) 35.00

ILLINOIS STATE HISTORICAL SOCIETY-Papers in Illinois History and Transactions for the Year 1940-Springfield-1941-x+217p-blk cl,illus,fldg map-1st ed (k2) 25.00

ILLINOIS-ANNUAL REPORT OF THE ADJUTANT GENERAL OF THE STATE OF...-Springfield-1863-Baker & Phillips (v2) 30.00

ILLINOIS-COMMUNICATION FROM CITIZENS OF THE STATE OF...ON THE SUBJECT OF NATIONAL DEFENCE-(Columbus)-(1842)-14p-Amer Imprnts 42-1233 (b1,dsbnd) 75.00

ILLINOIS-Pictures of...One Hundred Years Ago-Chig-1918-Donnelley-186p-frntis-Lakeside Classics (cc4) 35.00

ILOTT,CHARLES-Book of Asparagus-Lond-1901-Bodley Head-108p-cl-scarce (x6) 30.00

IMHOLTE,JOHN Q-First Volunteers-Mpls-1963-238p-maps-1st ed (c4,f,dj) 40.00

IN-SOB,ZONG-TRANSL.-Folk Tales from Korea-Lond-1952-Routledge & K Paul-cl-1st ed (o8,f,dj) 22.50

INDIAN CAPTIVE-Fostoria-1896-Gray Prtg-70p-prtd cl-Howes B736-rare (a1,soil cov,bnd upside down) 175.00

INDIAN CEREMONIAL DANCES IN THE SOUTHWEST-Santa Fe-(1950)-unpgd(17p)-wrps,7 col block prnts-1st ed (v7,f) 75.00

INDIANA,STATE OF-Biennial Report of the Commissioner of Fisheries-Indpls-1902-4to-617p-full lea,col plts-scarce (m3,head & tail wn) 35.00

INDIANS OF WESTERN NEW YORK-REPORT TO THE PRESBYTERY OF BUFFALO ...CHARGES MADE AGAINST...-Salamanca-1889-Cattaraugus Republ-12p-prntd wrps-rare (h1) 37.50

INFERNAL CONFERENCE-Pitt-1832-Johnston & Stockton-297p-lea-Amer Imprnts 13498 (c1,uppr jnts crckd) 25.00

INFIELD,GLENN B-Unarmed and Unafraid-NY-(1970)-Macmillan-8vo-308p-16p photos-1st ed (dd5,sl tn dj) 15.00

INFLUENZA-STUDIES ON EPIDEMIC...-Pitt-1919-294p+plts-1st ed (dd3) 50.00

INGE,WILLIAM R-God and Astronomers-Lond-1934-Longmans,Green-cl-new ed (l8) 20.00

INGE,WILLIAM-Summer Brave...-NY-(1962)-Random-1st ed (v10,f,dj) 20.00

INGERSOLL,E-Alaskan Bird Life-NY-1914-8vo-72p-cl & bds,7 col plts (y8,ex-libr) 35.00

INGERSOLL,ERNEST-Crest of the Continent-Chig-1885-Donelly-illus-1st ed (oo9,sp sl fox & tn) 35.00

INGERSOLL,ERNEST-Crest of the Continent-Glorieta-1969-Rio Grande Pr-359p-1st publ 1883-1st ed thus (n4) 34.00

INGERSOLL,ERNEST-Rand,McNally & Co.'s Illustrated Guide to the Hudson River and Catskill Mountains...-Chig,NY-1908-Rand,McNally-245,(1)p-col pict wrps-illus,6 fldg maps-15th ed (g1) 15.00

INGERSOLL,ROBERT G-Crimes Against Criminals-E Aurora-1906-Roycrofters-8vo-59p-brgndy suede lea,2p illus-1st ed (mm8,rbnd) 50.00*

INGHAM,MAURICE-Drop Me a Line-Lond-1953-8vo-295p-illus,photos (m3,fray dj) 50.00

INGLEFIELD,CAPT V E-History of the Twentieth Division-Lond-1921-319p-gry papr cov bds,maps,illus-scarce-1st ed (b7) 125.00

INGLIS,ALEX-Northern Vagabond-Tor-1978-M&S-8vo-256p-illus-1st ed (cc7,dj) 25.00*

INGOLDSBY,THOMAS-Ingoldsby Legends or Mirth and Marvels-Lond-1907-J M Dent-1st ed using expanded format & 36 tip in plts,A Rackham (y2) 425.00

INGRAHAM,CHARLES A-Elmer E Ellsworth and the Zouaves of '61-Chig-(1925)-167p-wrps,illus-1st ed (c4,f) 47.50

INGRAHAM,COL PRENTISS-California Joe, the Mysterious Plainsman-NY-1882-15p-pict wrps-Beadle's Boys Libr of Sport & Adventure,Vol III,#54 (t7,f) 15.00

INGRAHAM,HARRY A-American Trout Streams-1926-Angler's Club of NY-4to-139p-ltd to 350c,nbrd,illus,maps (m3,new sp labl) 175.00

INGRAHAM,JOSEPH-Joseph Ingraham's Journal of the Brigantine Hope on a Voyage to Northwest Coast...1790 to 92-Barre-1971-Imprnt Soc-8vo-xxvii,248p-1/2 cl/dec papr-ltd to 1950c,Plantin Pr,20 illus (nn1,sl soil cov) 65.00

INGRAHAM,JOSEPH-Voyage to the Northwest Coast of North America 1791 to 92-Barre-1971-248p-illus-ltd ed (d7) 75.00

INGRAM,ARTHUR-Horse Drawn Vehicles-Poole-1977-Blandford Col Ser-207p-1st prtg (j9,dj) 35.00

INGSTAD,HELGE-Land of Feast and Famine-NY-1933-Knopf-332p-photos,fldg map-1st Amer (o2,sp fade,sl soil) 20.00

INLAND EMPIRE FLY FISHING CLUB-Flies of the Northwest-Spokane-1965-8vo-40p-wrps,illus-1st ed (m3,vf) 20.00

INLAND EMPIRE OF THE NORTH WEST...-(Spokane)-nd-16p-wrps,illus,photos (c1) 17.50

INMAN,HENRY-COMP.-Buffalo Jones' Forty Years of Adventure-Topeka-1899-Crane & Co-xii,469p-dec cl,photos,illus-1st ed (v1) 175.00

INMAN,HENRY-Great Salt Lake Trail-NY-1898-Macmillan-8vo-xiii,529p-pict cl,t.e.g.,frntis port,7p plts,fldg map-Howes I55-1st ed (aa3,cov rub) 60.00

INMAN,HENRY-Old Santa Fe Trail-NY-1897-493p+3p ads-dec tan cl,fldg map,8p plts by Remington-1st ed (h7) 75.00

INMAN,HENRY-Ranch on the Oxhide-NY-1898-Macmillan-dec red cl-scarce-1st ed (gg7) 85.00

INMAN,HENRY-Stories of the Old Santa Fe Trail-KC-1881-291p-drwngs,(Howes:no priority determined of this & 287p prtg)-1st ed (v7,sl wn) 250.00

INN,HENRY-Hawaiian Types-(1945)-Hastings Hs-4to-47 photo plts-1st ed (u8,dj chip & rprd) 35.00

INNES,HAMMOND-Conquistadors-1969-Knopf-4to-336p-col illus-1st ed (d3,dj) 25.00

INNES,HAMMOND-Last Voyage-NY-1979-Knopf-8vo-253p-1/2 cl,map e.p.-1st ed (dd7,f,dj) 25.00

INNES,MICHAEL-Awkward Lie-NY-1971-Dodd-1st US ed (e4,dj) 10.00

INNES,MICHAEL-Big Footprints-Lond-(1977)-Collins-1st ed (f3,f,sl tn dj) 20.00

INNES,MICHAEL-Bloody Wood-1966-DM-1st ed (x7,dj) 18.00

INNES,MICHAEL-Dead Man's Shoes-1954-Dodd-1st Amer ed (s10,sp chip dj) 25.00

INNES,MICHAEL-Honeybath's Haven-NY-1978-Dodd-1st US ed (f4,f,sl wn dj) 12.50

INNES,MICHAEL-Lament for a Maker-NY-1938-Dodd-1st US ed (d4,dj) 60.00

INNES,MICHAEL-Mysterious Commission-NY-1974-Dodd-1st US ed (f4,f,dj) 12.50

INNES,MICHAEL-Operation Pax-Lond-1951-Gollancz-1st ed (e4,dj) 35.00

INNES,MICHAEL-Weight of the Evidence-NY-1943-Dodd-1st US ed (h4,dj) 25.00

INNIS,HAROLD A-Fur Trade in Canada-New Haven-1930-Yale U Pr-8vo-444p-blk cl,2 photos-Peel 3190-1st ed (mm8,scuff,hngs crack) 50.00*

INOGUCHI,R-Divine Wind-Annapolis-(1958)-8vo-xxiii,242p-g cl,frntis,plts,text illus,illus e.p.-1st ed (t2,sl chip dj) 25.00

INVERARITY,ROBERT B-Art of the Northwest Coast Indians-Berkeley,LA-1950-4to-243p-illus-1st ed (j7,poor dj) 30.00

IONESCO,EUGENE-Hermit-1974-Viking-1st ed (s9,f,dj) 25.00

IONESCO,EUGENE-Three Plays-NY-1958-1st US ed (q5,dj) 50.00

IRELAND,M W-ED.-Medical Department of the U.S. Army in the World War-Wash-1921 to 1929-17 vols-photos,col chrts,tbls-only ed (dd3,ex-libr) 750.00

IRISH,FRANK V-Grammar and Analysis Made Easy and Attractive by Diagrams-NY-(1884)-Amer Bk Co-118,(2)p-cl (k1,few spots frnt cov) 15.00

IRISH,WILLIAM-Dancing Detective-Phila,NY-(1946)-Lippincott-1st ed (ff6,dj) 275.00

IRISH,WILLIAM-Dancing Detective-Phila-(1946)-Lippincott-1st ed (ee6,dj) 200.00

IRISH,WILLIAM-Dead Man Blues-Phila,NY-1948-Lippincott-1st ed (ff6,f,dj) 275.00

IRISH,WILLIAM-I Married a Dead Man-Phila-1948-Lippincott-1st ed (j4,sl stnd e.p.,dj) 50.00

IRISH,WILLIAM-If I Should Die Before I Wake-NY-1946-Avon 104-wrps,preceded by appearance as a Murder Mystery Monthly (v5,f) 25.00

IRISH,WILLIAM-You'll Never See Me Again-NY-1951-Dell-pbk orig-Dell 10 cent ser#26-1st ed (h4,wrps) 60.00

IRVINE,JOHN-Treasury of Irish Saints-Dublin-(1964)-Dolmen Pr-drwngs,R Brandt-1st ed (z8,f,dj) 22.50

IRVING,CLIVE-ET AL-Anatomy of a Scandal-NY-1963-Mill,Morrow-8vo-227p-1st US ed (dd5,dj) 15.00

IRVING,HELEN-ED.-Ladies' Wreath-NY-1852-J M Fletcher-3/4 lea,12 col plts,12 engrvngs (l9,spot & wn) 180.00

IRVING,JOHN J-Indian Sketches Taken During an Expedition to the Pawnee Tribes-Phila-1835-2 vols-orig cl (l9,cl spot & sl wn,fox) 375.00

IRVING,JOHN-158 Pound Marriage-NY-(1974)-1st ed (j5,sl mar dj) 85.00

IRVING,JOHN-158 Pound Marriage-NY-(1974)-Random-1st ed (k7,dj sl crease) 100.00

IRVING,JOHN-Hotel New Hampshire-NY-(1981)-1st ed (j5,as new in dj) 15.00

IRVING,JOHN-Hotel New Hampshire-NY-(1981)-Dutton-1st trd ed (b5,as new in dj) 20.00

IRVING,JOHN-Setting Free the Bears-1968-Random-auth 1st bk-1st ed (x2,sl tn dj) 200.00

IRVING,JOHN-Water Method Man-(1972)-Random-1st ed (o9,dj) 75.00

IRVING,JOHN-Water Method Man-NY-(1972)-1st ed (j5,f,sl tn dj) 85.00

IRVING,JOHN-World According to Garp-NY-1978-1st ed (p5,dj) 40.00

IRVING,R L G-Ten Great Mountains-Lond-1947-213p-15 photos,10 maps-rprnt (o10,f) 15.00

IRVING,WASHINGTON-Adventures of Captain Bonneville U.S.A.-Norman-(1961)-424p-illus,fldg map-1st Okla ed (c7,f,nick dj) 45.00

IRVING,WASHINGTON-Angler-1933-Harbor Press-30p-one of 180c (m3) 75.00

IRVING,WASHINGTON-Astoria-Phila-1836-Carey, Lea & Blanchard-285+279p-2 vols-1/4 lea,title g sp,emboss over orig mrbld bds,fldg map-rare-Howes I81-1st ed (z1,hngs crack) 500.00

IRVING,WASHINGTON-Rip Van Winkle-Lond-1905-Heinemann-50 tip in plts,A Rackham-1st trd ed thus (y2,sl fox) 500.00

IRVING,WASHINGTON-Tour of the Prairies-Phila-1835-Carey,Lea & Blanchard-12mo-xv,274,(32)p-orig cl-1st Amer ed (n2,sl rub,lacks sp labl) 200.00

IRVING,WASHINGTON-Tour on the Prairies-Okla City-1955-178p-frntis,photos-rprnt of Howes T86-1st ed thus (t7) 20.00

IRVING,WASHINGTON-Western Journals-Norman-1944-Univ of Okla Pr-xiv+201p-tan cl-1st ed (k2,soil dj) 25.00

IRWIN,DAVID-Alone Across the Top of the World-Chig-1935-Winston-254p-dec grn cl,photos-1st ed (p2) 15.00

IRWIN,GRACE-Trail Blazers of American Art-NY-1930-Harper-8vo-228p-red cl,col & b&w illus-1st ed (r10,sp fade) 15.00

IRWIN,HOWARD S-Roadside Flowers of Texas-Austin-(1961)-293p-illus-1st ed (f9,dj) 30.00

ISAACS,EDITH J R-Negro in the American Theatre-NY-1947-Theatre Arts-1st ed (u4,f,dj sl chip) 22.00

ISAACS,N-Tolkien and the Critics-Notre Dame-1968-UND Pr-1st ed (x9,f,dj) 20.00

ISABELLE,JULANNE-Hemingway's Religious Experience-NY-1964-Vantage-1st ed (e8,f,dj) 40.00

ISE,JOHN-Sod and Stubble-NY-1936-326p-frntis,illus (t7,dj) 35.00

ISHAM,FREDERIC S-Lady of the Mount-Indpls-(1908)-Bobbs Merrill-1st ed (hh5) 10.00

ISHAM,FREDERICK-Under the Rose-Indpls-(1903)-Bobbs Merrill-M Armstrong dec cov-1st ed (hh5) 15.00

ISHAM,NORMAN M-Trinity Church in Newport, Rhode Island-Bost-1936-priv prtd-sm 4to-xi,(1),111p-qtr cl/bds,t.e.g.,frntis,plts (pp7,part uncut) 125.00

ISHERWOOD,CHRISTOPHER-All the Conspirators-NY-1958-1st US ed (s5,dj) 25.00

ISHERWOOD,CHRISTOPHER-Berlin Stories-NY-1945-1st US ed (t5,sl rub dj) 100.00

ISHERWOOD,CHRISTOPHER-Condor and the Cows-NY-(1949)-Random-photos,Wm Caskey-1st Amer ed (cc2,f,dj) 45.00

ISHERWOOD,CHRISTOPHER-Down There on a Visit-Lond-1962-1st ed (y7,dj) 25.00

ISHERWOOD,CHRISTOPHER-Down There on a Visit-NY-1962-1st ed (q5,sp sunned dj) 15.00

ISHERWOOD,CHRISTOPHER-ED-Vedanta for the Western World-Hollywood-1945-Rodd Co-cl-1st ed (n8,dj) 15.00

ISHERWOOD,CHRISTOPHER-Kathleen and Frank-NY-1971-S&S-1st ed (y1,f,f dj) 35.00

ISHERWOOD,CHRISTOPHER-Lions and Shadows-Lond-1938-Hogarth-8vo-cl,1st iss bndg wi blk lettrng-1st ed (x3,sl stnd dj) 250.00

ISHERWOOD,CHRISTOPHER-Lions and Shadows-Norfolk-1947-New Directions-1st ed (q2,t.e. soil,dj chip) 45.00

ISHERWOOD,CHRISTOPHER-My Guru and His Disciple-1980-Farrar-1st ed (o9,vf,dj) 15.00

ISHERWOOD,CHRISTOPHER-People One Ought to Know-1982-Dbldy-illus,S Mangeot-1st ed (o9,vf,dj) 25.00

ISHERWOOD,CHRISTOPHER-Prater Violet-NY-1945-1st ed (q5,tape rnfrcd dj) 40.00

ISHERWOOD,CHRISTOPHER-Ramakrishna and His Disciples-NY-1965-1st ed (y7,dj) 20.00

ISHERWOOD,CHRISTOPHER-Ramakrishna and His Disciples-NY-1965-S&S-cl,frntis,illus-1st ed (n8) 25.00

ISHERWOOD,CHRISTOPHER-World in the Evening-NY-(1954)-1st ed (t5,sl chip dj) 30.00

ISHERWOOD,CHRISTOPHER-World in the Evening-NY-(1954)-Random-1st Amer ed (cc2,f,dj) 40.00

ISINGS,DR CLASING-Antiek Glas-Amsterdam-1966-278p-illus (cc8,dj) 65.00

ISRAEL,PETER-French Kiss-NY-1976-Crowell-1st ed (f4,f,dj) 12.50

ISTHMIAN CANAL COMMISSION-Annual Report for 1912-Wash D.C.-1912-xxii+619p-tan cl,68 plts (l2,cov fade & soil) 40.00

ISYS,COTSWOLD-An Angler's Strange Experiences-Lond-1883-8vo-100p-illus (m3,lacks e.p.s) 40.00

ISYS,COTSWOLD-Handy Guide to Dry-Fly Fishing-Lond-nd-12mo-34p+ads-fld out plts,limp blu cl (m3) 25.00

ITTEN,J-Design & Form-1964-Reinhold-197 illus-1st transl ed (h10,dj) 50.00

IVENS,T C-Still Water Fly Fishing-Lond-1952-8vo-128p-col frontis,illus (m3,f,badly fray dj) 20.00

IVERSON,PETER-Carlos Montezuma and the Changing World of American Indians-Albuq-1982-222p-illus,maps-1st ed (t7,dj) 17.50

IVES,CATHERINE-Homepride Cookery Book-Liverpool-nd(ca.1950)-84p-blu cl,illus (q8) 10.00

IVES,GEORGE-Bibliography of Oliver Wendell Holmes-Bost-1907-322p-1st ed (dd3) 100.00

IVES,LT JOSEPH C-Report Upon the Colorado River of the West-Wash-1861-GPO-8 col plts,maps-Howes 192-Wagner Camp 375 (gg9,rbnd) 525.00

IVINS,WILLIAM M,JR.-Prints and Visual Communications-Cambridge-1953-Harvard U Pr-8vo-xxvi,190p-cl,84 plts-1st ed (w2,sl wn dj) 25.00

IZENBERG,JERRY-Great Latin Sports Figures-1976-Dbldy-photos-1st ed (s8,f,dj) 12.50

JABLONSKI,E-Atlantic Fever-NY-(1972)-roy 8vo-xxiv,326p-cl,illus-1st ed (t2,dj) 30.00

JABLONSKI,E-Knighted Skies-NY-(1964)-roy 8vo-xiv,242p-cl,frntis,plts,text illus-1st ed (t2,sl chip dj) 25.00

JABLONSKI,EDWARD-Harold Arlen-GC-1961-Dbldy-1st ed (w1) 45.00

JACK THE GIANT KILLER-NY-(1889)-McLoughlin Bros-(12)p-col pict wrps,4p col plts (m1) 15.00

JACK,ELLEN E-Fate of a Fairy-Chig-1910-213p-cl,10 illus (d1) 35.00

JACK,ELLEN-Fate of a Fairy, or 27 Years in the Far West-Chig-1910-Donohoe-1st ed (nn9,hng crack,edgewn) 75.00

JACK,MRS ANNIE L-Canadian Garden-Tor-1910-Musson Bk Co-12mo-viii,120p+4 photos,t.e.g. (ff9,cor rub,sp sl shaken,fade 72.00*

JACKMAN,E R-Oregon Desert-Caldwell-1965-407p-frntis,photos,map e.p. (t7,dj) 10.00

JACKMAN,SYDNEY W-Galloping Head-Lond-(1958)-Phoenix-8vo-191p-5 illus-1st Brit ed (jj5,dj,pres) 15.00

JACKS,OLIVER-Man on a Short Leash-Lond-1974-Hodder-1st ed (r4,dj) 27.50

JACKSON & EVANS-New Book of American Ships-NY-1927-Stokes-4to-428p-blu cl-photos,12p col plts-enlgd ed,1st prtg (s1) 50.00

JACKSON,A V WILLIAMS-History of India-Lond-1906,07-Connoisseur Ed,Grolier-8vo-9 vols-1/2 mor,t.e.g.,col frntis,plts-ltd to 200 sets,nbrd (ll1,fade sp,sl wn cor) 600.00

JACKSON,A V WILLIAMS-Zoroaster-NY-1899-Macmillan-cl,illus,lg col fldg map-scarce-1st ed (o8) 145.00

JACKSON,ALLEN W-Half Timber House-NY-1912-McBride, Nast-115p-pict brwn cl,illus (r10,sp dull & wn) 25.00

JACKSON,CHARLES T-Buffalo Wallow-Indpls-1953-Bobbs Merrill-sm 8vo-252p-1st ed (aa3,dj) 12.50

JACKSON,CHARLES T-Fountain of Youth-NY-1914-Outing-8vo-343p-30 photos-1st ed (aa5) 75.00

JACKSON,CHARLES-Fall of Valor-NY,Tor-(1946)-1st ed (e5,dj) 35.00

JACKSON,CHARLES-Fall of Valor-NY-(1946)-Rinehart-1st ed (e3,dj chip & rub) 30.00

JACKSON,CHARLES-Lost Weekend-NY,Tor-(1944)-1st ed (e5,sl wn dj) 65.00

JACKSON,CHARLES-Lost Weekend-NY-1944-1st ed (t5,sl wn dj) 50.00

JACKSON,CHRISTOPHER-Manuel-NY-1964-Knopf-251p-1st ed (n10,dj) 45.00

JACKSON,CLARENCE-Quest of the Snowy Cross-Denver-1952-135p-28 photos-1st ed (o10,f,dj) 35.00

JACKSON,CLYDE-Quanah Parker-NY-1963-Expo-184p-1st ed (a9) 50.00

JACKSON,DONALD-Custer's Gold-New Haven-1966-Yale Univ Pr-8vo-152p-1st ed (z4,wtrstnd dj) 20.00

JACKSON,DONALD-Gold Dust-NY-1980-Knopf-361p-illus-1st ed (cc4,dj) 20.00

JACKSON,EARL-Tumacacori's Yesterdays-Santa Fe-1951-96p-stiff pict wrps,map frntis,photo,maps-1st ed (t7) 10.00

JACKSON,F J-Notes on the Game Birds of Kenya & Uganda-Lond-1926-258p-drk grn ribbed cl,deckld frnt edge,13 col plts (ee3,chip dj) 110.00

JACKSON,FREDERICK G-Thousand Days in the Arctic-NY,Lond-1899-Harper & Bros-thk 8vo-xxiii,940p-dec cov,frntis,15 plts(1 fldg),5 fldg maps-Arctic Biblio 7943-1st ed (oo1) 195.00

JACKSON,GEORGE-Sixty Years in Texas-np-nd(1908?)-322p+errata-red pict cl,31 plts-Herd 1141 (a9,rebckd) 125.00

JACKSON,GEORGE-Soledad Brother-NY-1970-Coward McCann-330p (r1) 15.00

JACKSON,HELEN-Century of Dishonor-Bost-1888-Roberts Bros-514p (dd4) 50.00

JACKSON,HELEN-Ramona-Bost-1884-Roberts Bros-8vo-490p+ads-orig dec red cl-BAL 10456-1st ed (hh9,sl discol cov) 300.00

JACKSON,HELEN-Zeph-Bost-1885-Roberts Bros-grn cl-Bal 10460-1st ed (f2) 30.00

JACKSON,HOLBROOK-Anatomy of Bibliomania-Lond-1930,1931-Soncino Pr-thick 8vo-2 vols-cl,t.e.g.-ltd to 1048c,nbrd-1st ed (w2,dj) 250.00

JACKSON,HOLBROOK-Reading of Books-NY-1947-Scribners-1st Amer ed (ll9,f,dj) 20.00

JACKSON,JAMES-ET AL-Report on Spasmodic Cholera-Bost-1832-190p+fldg map-orig cl bkd bds-1st ed (dd3,ex-libr) 150.00

JACKSON,JAMES-Letters to a Young Physician Just Entering Upon Practice-Bost-1855-344p-1st ed (dd3) 100.00

JACKSON,JOHN W-Pennsylvania Navy, 1775 to 1781-New Brunswick-(1974)-xiv,514p-cl,illus (aa6) 30.00

JACKSON,JOHN-More Than Mountains-Lond-1955-213p-48 halftones,4 maps (o10,f,dj) 26.00

JACKSON,JOHN-Reflections on Peace and War-Phila-1846-T Ellwood Chapman-16mo-108p-2nd ed,enlgd (y6) 14.00

JACKSON,JOSEPH-Anybody's Gold-NY-(1941)-Appleton-Century-468p-illus-1st ed (dd4) 30.00

JACKSON,JOSEPH-Bad Company-NY-1949-Harcourt,Brace-8vo-xx,346p-pict cl,illus-1st ed (aa3,dj) 40.00

JACKSON,JOSEPH-Christmas Flower-NY-(1951)-Harcourt Brace-illus,T Lea-1st ed (e10,f,sl soil dj) 12.50

JACKSON,JOSEPH-Christmas Flower-NY-(1951)-Harcourt,Brace-8vo-31p-illus,Tom Lea-1st ed so stated (z4,dj sunned) 35.00

JACKSON,JOSEPH-Christmas Flower-NY-1951-31p-illus by T Lea-1st ed (t7,dj) 20.00

JACKSON,JOSEPH-Development of American Architecture, 1783 to 1830-Phila-1926-McKay-8vo (h10) 35.00

JACKSON,JOSEPH-Gold Rush Album-NY-1949-Scribner's-ix,239p-photos,maps-1st ed (o2) 20.00

JACKSON,JOSEPH-Tintypes in Gold-NY-1939-Macmillan-191p-illus e.p.,decs-Six Guns #1122-1st ed (ee4,dj) 20.00

JACKSON,MARY E-Life of Nellie C Bailey-Topeka-1885-399p-dec cl,frntis,plts-Six Guns #1123-v scarce-1st ed (t7) 85.00

JACKSON,MARY E-Topeka Pen and Camera Sketches-Topeka-1890-192p-dec cl,frntis,photos-scarce-1st ed (t7) 25.00

JACKSON,MICHAEL-English Pub-NY-(1976)-Harper & Row-illus-1st US ed (y10,dj) 22.00

JACKSON,MICHAEL-World Guide to Beer-Englewood Cliffs-(1978)-Prentice Hall-4to-255p-col illus-1st US ed (gg5,sl tn dj) 20.00

JACKSON,MRS F NEVILL-Ancestors in Silhouette Cut by August Edouart-Lond-1921-John Lane-4to-239p-dec grn cl,t.e.g.,untrimmed,illus (r10,sp drknd,hng broken,fox) 125.00

JACKSON,R-Concise Dictionary of Artists' Signatures-NY-1981-1st ed (h10,dj) 50.00

JACKSON,REGGIE-Inside Hitting-1975-Regnery-photos-1st ed (s8,f,dj) 20.00

JACKSON,REGGIE-Reggie-1975-Playboy-1st ed (s8,dj) 17.50

JACKSON,SHELDON-Alaska and Missions on the North Pacific Coast-(1880)-Dodd Mead-12mo-327p-pict cov,illus,fldg map-1st ed (u8,cov wn,crnkld,,sl soil pg) 55.00

JACKSON,SHELDON-Fourteenth Annual Report on Introduction of Domestic Reindeer into Alaska-Wash-1905-GPO-137p+plts & 2 fldg maps,wrps (cc4) 25.00

JACKSON,SHIRLEY-Bird's Nest-(1954)-FS&Y-1st ed (r9,dj sp drknd & sl wn) 40.00

JACKSON,SHIRLEY-Bird's Nest-NY-(1954)-FS&Y-1st ed (bb1,sl soil dj) 95.00

JACKSON,SHIRLEY-Come Along with Me-NY-(1968)-Viking-1st ed (ee2,f,dj) 35.00

JACKSON,SHIRLEY-Famous Sally-np-(1966)-Quist-cl & bds,col illus,Chas B Slackman-1st ed (s3,f,dj) 45.00

JACKSON,SHIRLEY-Famous Sally-np-1966-Brit iss wi dj price clipped & overstmpd price in Sterling-1st ed (s5,dj) 75.00

JACKSON,SHIRLEY-Hangsaman-(NY)-(1951)-1st ed (d5,dj sl wn,sl creased) 85.00

JACKSON,SHIRLEY-Haunting of Hill House-NY-1959-Viking-1st ed (d10,dj) 175.00

JACKSON,SHIRLEY-Life Among the Savages-NY-(1953)-FS&Y-red cl-1st ed (f2,dj) 65.00

JACKSON,SHIRLEY-Magic of Shirley Jackson-NY-1966-1st ed (s5,f,dj) 40.00

JACKSON,SHIRLEY-Raising Demons-Lond-1957-1st Brit ed (q5,dj soil) 22.50

JACKSON,SHIRLEY-Raising Demons-NY-1957-1st ed (s5,dj) 45.00

JACKSON,SHIRLEY-Raising Demons-NY-1957-FSC-1st ed (f8,f,f dj) 75.00

JACKSON,SHIRLEY-Special Delivery-Bost-1960-Little,Brown-1st ed (v5,sl chip dj) 50.00

JACKSON,SHIRLEY-Sundial-NY-(1958)-1st ed (d5,f,dj) 60.00

JACKSON,SHIRLEY-Sundial-NY-(1958)-1st ed (s5,dj) 45.00

JACKSON,SHIRLEY-We Have Always Lived in the Castle-NY-1962-1st ed (r5,dj) 20.00

JACKSON,SIDNEY L-Libraries and Librarianship in the West-NY-(1974)-McGraw-Hill-8vo-xiv,489p-pict bds,illus (t10,f) 25.00

JACKSON,THOMAS G-Renaissance of Roman Architecture-Cambridge-1921 to 1923-Cambridge U Pr-roy 8vo-3 vols-g dec qtr vel/cl,t.e.g.,frntis,illus,plts(incl col) (pp7,dj) 195.00

JACKSON,W H-Pioneer Photographer-Yonkers on Hudson-1929-xii,314p-illus (bb9) 60.00

JACKSON,W S-Notes of a Fly Fisher-Lond-1933-16mo-195p-illus (m3,vf) 30.00

JACKSON,W TURRENTINE-Twenty Years on the Pacific Slope-New Haven-1965-224p-frntis-1st ed (t7,f,dj) 22.50

JACKSON,W TURRENTINE-Wagon Roads West-Berkeley,LA-1952-422p-text & e.p. maps-1st ed (c7,sl soil,chip dj) 65.00

JACKSON,W TURRENTINE-Wells Fargo Staging Over the Sierra-np-1970-44p-stiff wrps (t7) 10.00

JACKSON,ZEPH-Posthumous Story-Bost-1885-Roberts-8vo-253p-BAL 10460-1st ed (w6) 35.00

JACKSON-STOPS,G-ED.-Writers at Home-Lond-1985-Trefoil Bks-1st ed (z9,f,dj) 12.50

JACOB,H E-Six Thousand Years of Bread-GC-1944-Dbldy,Doran-399p-bds-1st ed (a8,wn bds,soil) 35.00

JACOB,NAOMI-Opera in Italy-Lond-1948-Hutchinson (u4,sl chip dj) 22.00

JACOBI,CARL-Disclosure in Scarlet-Sauk City-1972-Arkham-1st ed (j3,f,dj) 15.00

JACOBI,CARL-Revelations in Black-Sauk City-1947-Arkham-272p-ltd to 3082c-auth 1st bk-1st ed (k5,sl drknd dj) 60.00

JACOBI,LOTTE-Lotte Jacobi-Danbury-1978-Addison Hs-187p-169 photos-1st ed (cc9,f,dj) 50.00

JACOBI,MARY P-Mary Putnam Jacobi, M.D.-NY-1925-Putnam's-xxxii+521p-blu cl,t.e.g.,frontis-1st ed (g2,chip dj) 85.00

JACOBS,HAROLD-Weatherman-NY-1970-Ramparts-wrps-1st ed (v5) 20.00

JACOBS,HARVEY-Egg of the Glak...-NY-(1969)-1st ed (k9,f,dj) 12.50

JACOBS,JANE-Death and Life of Great American Cities-NY-1961-Random-8vo-(10),358,(1)p-cl-1st prtg (cc10,dj) 40.00

JACOBS,MELVIN C-Winning Oregon-Caldwell-1938-261p-dec cl-1st ed (t7,f) 20.00

JACOBS,MICHAEL-Rebel Invasion of Maryland and Pennsylvania and Battle of Gettysburg-Gettysburg-1909-Times Prtg Hs-40p-wrps,fldg map-7th ed (o7,sm sp tr) 35.00

JACOBS,W W-Deep Waters-1919-H&S-1st ed (x2,dj sl wn & tn) 110.00

JACOBS,WILBUR R-Historical World of Frederick Jackson Turner-NY-1968-Yale U Pr-289p-illus-1st ed (dd4,dj) 20.00

JACOBSEN,JOHAN A-Alaskan Voyage 1881 to 1883-(1977)-U of Chig-266p-wht cl,illus-1st ed (u8,sl soil cov) 18.00

JACOBSON,STEVE-Best Team Money Could Buy-1978-Atheneum-1st ed (s7,f,dj) 15.00

JACOBSON,STEVE-Pitching Staff-1975-Crowell-photos-1st ed (s8,f,dj) 17.00

JACOBUS,JOHN M,JR.-Philip Johnson-NY-1962-Braziller-4to-128p-cl-1st ed (t3,dj) 40.00

JACOBY,ARNOLD-Senor Kon Tiki-np-(1967)-Rand McNally-8vo-424p-56 photos-1st ed (cc5,dj) 20.00

JACOUTOT,AUGUSTE-Chocolate and Confectionery Manufacture-Lond-nd(ca.1890)-Joseph Baker & Sons-211p-Bitting p.243 (a8) 175.00

JACQUEMARD-SENECAL-Eleventh Little Indian-NY-1979-Dodd-1st Amer ed (q4,f,dj) 20.00

JACQUES,H E-Plants We Eat and Wear-Mt.Pleasant-(1943)-auth-171p-illus,"Picture Key Nature Ser." (m6) 20.00

JAEGER,B-Life of North American Insects-Providence-1854-Sayles,Miller & Simons-31 handcol litho plts on 6 sewn in leaves-1st ed (p6,sp chip,sl fox & wtrstnd) 150.00

JAEGER,DORIS-Faculty of the College of Physicians & Surgeons Columbia Univ...24 Portraits-NY-1919-folio-frntis-rare-1st ed (dd3,vf) 450.00

JAEGER,ELLSWORTH-Woodsmoke-NY-1953-8vo-228p-illus,auth-1st ed (m3,f,sl chip dj) 10.00

JAGENDORF,M A-Folk Wines, Cordials and Brandies-NY-(1963)-Vanguard-lg 8vo-414p-illus-1st ed (p1,f,dj) 35.00

JAGGAR,T A-Origin and Development of Craters-np-1947-Geol Soc of Amer-xviii+508p-maroon cl,87 plts,14 surveys/maps,(Memoir 21)-1st ed (l2) 45.00

JAHNS,P-Matthew Fontaine Maury & Joseph Henry-NY-1961-308p (z10,dj) 22.50

JAHNS,PATRICIA-Mathew Fontaine Maury & Joseph Henry, Scientists of the Civil War-NY-(1961)-308p-1st ed (n3,dj wn) 25.00

JAHNS,PATRICIA-Violent Years-NY-(1962)-Hastings Hs-309p-map e.p.-1st ed (cc4,dj) 25.00

JAHODA,GLORIA-Trail of Tears-NY-(1975)-356p-illus,e.p. maps (j7,f,f dj) 60.00

JAKES,JOHN-Time Gate-Phila-(1972)-Westminster Pr-1st hdbk ed (o3,f,dj) 10.00

JAMES,AHLEE-Tewa Firelight Tales-NY-1927-248p-10 col drwngs-1st ed (v7,partial dj) 50.00

JAMES,ALLISTON-Attic Light-Santa Barbara-1979-Capra Pr-1st ed (ff3,f,sl tn dj) 35.00

JAMES,BRIAN-Big Burn-(Sydney)-(1965)-Angus & Robertson-231p-cl-1st ed (kk1,f,dj) 30.00

JAMES,DAVID-Scott of the Antarctic-Lond-1948-Convoy Publ-151p-grn papr/bds,illus-Spence 624-1st ed (dd7,sp chip,dj chip & wn) 65.00

JAMES,DON-Butte's Memory Book-Caldwell-1975-Caxton-4to-295p-cl-1st ed (z4,dj sl wn & spot) 12.50

JAMES,DON-Butte's Memory Book-Caldwell-1980-Caxton-sm folio-295p-photos (ee4,dj) 15.00

JAMES,E O-Stone Age-Lond-1927-Sheldon Pr-cl,col frntis,illus-1st ed (n8,f,dj) 25.00

JAMES,EDGAR-Allen Outlaws-Balt-(1912)-Phoenix-191p-prtd wrps,illus-1st ed (v1) 45.00

JAMES,GEN THOMAS-Three Years Among the Indians and Mexicans-Chig-1953-Donnelley & Sons-frntis,illus,map-Lakeside Classics (ff4) 20.00

JAMES,GEORGE W-ED.-California Birthday Book-LA-1909-Arroyo Guild Pr-421,(1)p+ads-bds (g1) 20.00

JAMES,GEORGE W-Grand Canyon of Arizona-1910-Little,Brown-265p-photos,fldg map-1st ed (d3) 25.00

JAMES,GEORGE W-House Blessing Ceremony and Guest Book-Pasadena-1917-Radiant Life Pr-oblng 4to-70p-blk & gold stmpd pict orng cl,t.e.g.-1st ed (u1) 85.00

JAMES,GEORGE W-In & Around the Grand Canyon-Bost-1901-Little,Brown-8vo-346p-gry illus cl,fldg frntis,illus (mm1,vf) 80.00

JAMES,GEORGE W-In and Out of the Old California Missions-Bost-1905-392p-pict cl,frntis,photos-1st ed (t7,f) 42.50

JAMES,GEORGE W-Indian Blankets and Their Maker-Chig-1914-McClurg-213p-pict cl,col illus-Howes J43-1st ed (dd4) 250.00

JAMES,GEORGE W-Indian Blankets and Their Makers-1970-Rio Grande Pr-4to-213p-col plts-1st ed thus (d3) 45.00

JAMES,GEORGE W-Indian Blankets and Their Makers-Chig-1934-A C McClurg-lg 8vo-xvi,213p-pict cl,t.e.g.,photos,32p col plts-Howes J43-2nd prtg (aa3) 95.00

JAMES,GEORGE W-Indian Blankets and Their Makers-NY-1937-213p-pict cl,frntis,col illus-Rader #2050-rvsd & enlgd (t7,f) 80.00

JAMES,GEORGE W-Indians of the Painted Desert Region-Bost-1903-Little,Brown-1st ed (nn9,hng crack,edgewn) 60.00

JAMES,GEORGE W-Indians of the Painted Desert Region-Bost-1907-268p-photos-rprnt of Rader#2051 (v7,f) 35.00

JAMES,GRACE-Green Willow and Other Japanese Fairy Tales-Lond-1923-Macmillan-cl,frntis,16 col illus,W Goble-3rd ed (n8) 37.50

JAMES,H K-Destruction of Mephisto's Greatest Web or, All Grafts Laid Bare...-SLC-1914-Raleigh Publ-8vo-313p-dec grn cl-illus-scarce-1st ed (s1,frnt cov stns) 75.00

JAMES,H L-Acoma-Glorieta-(1970)-96p-col photos every pg,map-1st orig bk of Rio Grande Pr-1st ed (v7,f,dj) 35.00

JAMES,HARRY C-Pages from Hopi History-Tucson-(1974)-245p-photos-1st ed (v7,f,dj) 35.00

JAMES,HARRY C-Red Man White Man-San Antonio-1958-286p-1st ed (v7,dj) 20.00

JAMES,HENRY-Awkward Age-NY-(1899)-Harpers-gold stmpd red bds-1st ed,2nd iss (dd2) 55.00

JAMES,HENRY-Charles W Eliot-Bost-1930-HM-2 vols-t.e.g.-1st ed (x9,sunned sp) 40.00

JAMES,HENRY-Curse of the San Andres-NY-(1953)-163p-photos,map-1st ed (u7,f) 45.00

JAMES,HENRY-Notes & Reviews...-Cambridge-1921-Dunster Hs-bds wi cl sp-1st trd ed (hh1,unopened) 25.00

JAMES,HENRY-Private Life, Lord Dupre, The Visits-NY-1893-Harper & Bros-blu/gry dec cl,Blanck's bndg B(no priority)-BAL 10604-1st ed (f2,sl spot cov) 75.00

JAMES,HENRY-Sense of the Past-1917-Scribners-1st Amer ed (x2) 55.00

JAMES,HENRY-Spoils of Poynton-1897-Houghton,Mifflin-1st Amer ed (x2) 125.00

JAMES,J DAVIS-Iron Peddler-NY-1922-G&D-276p (r1) 18.00

JAMES,JAMES-Guide Book to Women-NY-(1921)-E P Dutton-152p-cl (a1,sl soil) 15.00

JAMES,JESSE S-Early United States Barbed Wire Patents-Maywood-1966-4to-291p-illus-1st ed (a9,dj) 50.00

JAMES,JOHN-My Experience with Indians-Austin-1925-Gammel's Bk Store-12mo-147p-illus,photos,w/o dj as iss-1st ed (aa3) 45.00

JAMES,LIONEL-Indian Frontier War 1897-NY-1898-300p-dec red cl,illus,maps-1st ed (gg2,lacks frntis) 100.00

JAMES,M R-Ghost Stories of an Antiquary-Lond-1904-Edward Arnold-4 plts by J McBryde-auth 1st bk-1st Brit ed (aa8) 250.00

JAMES,M R-More Ghost Stories of an Antiquary-Lond-1911-Edw Arnold-1st Brit ed (ff6,edgewn,bndg soil,e.p. yel 150.00

JAMES,MARQUIS-Andrew Jackson: the Border Captain-NY-1933-Lit Guild-461p-illus,maps-1st ed so stated (o2) 20.00

JAMES,MARQUIS-Cherokee Strip-NY-1945-Viking-1st ed (f8,f,dj) 30.00

JAMES,MARQUIS-History of the American Legion-NY-1923-Wm Green-8vo-320p-32 illus-1st ed (gg5) 30.00

JAMES,MARQUIS-Life of Andrew Jackson-NY-1938-972p-frntis,photos,maps (t7) 12.50

JAMES,MARQUIS-Raven-Indpls-1929-Bobbs Merrill-489p-illus-1st ed (a9) 100.00

JAMES,NORAH C-Greenfingers and the Gourmet-Lond-(1949)-Nicholson & Watson-127p (m6) 12.00

JAMES,NORAH-Sleeveless Errand-Paris-1929-Babou & Kahane-1st ed (r2,sl sun sp) 50.00

JAMES,P D-Cover Her Face-1966-Scribners-1st Amer ed (s10,sp wn dj) 60.00

JAMES,P D-Innocent Blood-Lond-1980-Faber & Faber-1st ed (w9,f,dj) 60.00

JAMES,P D-Innocent Blood-Lond-1980-Faber-1st ed (s10,dj) 35.00

JAMES,P D-Innocent Blood-NY-1980-Scribner's-1st US ed (e4,f,dj) 12.50

JAMES,P D-Innocent Blood-NY-1980-Scribners-1st Amer ed (r9,f,dj) 15.00

JAMES,P D-Shroud For a Nightingale-1971-Scribners-1st Amer ed (x2,dj) 65.00

JAMES,P D-Unnatural Causes-Lond-1967-Faber & Faber-scarce-1st ed (gg8,f,dj) 250.00

JAMES,P D-Unnatural Causes-NY-1967-Scribners-1st Amer ed (n9,dj) 75.00

JAMES,P D-Unnatural Causes-NY-1967-Scribners-1st US ed (l4,f,dj) 60.00

JAMES,SIDNEY V-People Among Peoples-Cambridge-1963-Harvard Univ Pr-8vo-397p-1st ed (y6,stnd cov,dj) 15.00

JAMES,W S-Cow Boy Life in Texas, or 27 Years a Mavrick-Chig-1893-Donohue-12mo-213p-pict cl,illus-Howes J51-2nd issue (aa3) 150.00

JAMES,WILL-American Cowboy-NY-(1942)-Scribner's-1st ed (aa10,f,dj) 300.00

JAMES,WILL-Cowboys North and South-NY-1924-Scribners-gry cl-1st ed (u2) 25.00

JAMES,WILL-Dark Horse-NY-1940-306p-frntis,illus (t7,dj) 30.00

JAMES,WILL-Drifting Cowboy-NY-1925-Scribners-qtr cl-1st ed (u2) 35.00

JAMES,WILL-Home Ranch-NY-(1935)-Scribner's-1st ed (aa10,f,dj) 350.00

JAMES,WILL-Look See with Uncle Bill-NY-1938-Scribners-dec cov,col frntis matches dj,illus-1st ed (y10,dj stnd,chip,sp pcs mssng 200.00

JAMES,WILL-Smoky the Cowhorse-NY-1926-Scribner's-(xiv),310p-grn cl,illus by auth-1st ed (v1) 75.00

JAMES,WILL-Will James Cowboy Book-NY-1938-158p-pict cl,frntis,illus-A Dalgliesh,Ed.-scarce-1st ed (t7,cov soil) 75.00

JAMES,WILLIAM-Principles of Psychology-NY-1890-H Holt-2 vols-olive cl-1st ed,1st iss wi "Psy-chology" in ads,sans serif type on sp,scrambled text pg 307,line 19 (c2,sp fray & sl tn) 1,250.00

JAMESON,EDWIN M-Black Devil of the Bayous-Upper Saddle River-1970-Gregg Pr-8vo-205p-blk cl,silv sp titles (nn1,as new in dj) 25.00

JAMESON,JOHN F-Privateering and Piracy in the Colonial Period-NY-1923-Macmillan-xxviii+619p-red cl-1st ed (h2) 50.00

JAMIESON,F C-Alberta Force Field of 1851-1931-Can NW Hist Soc-8vo-53p-card covs,ports,illus,maps-Vol.1,#7 (cc7) 25.00*

JAMIESON,MRS-Popular Voyages and Travels...-Lond-1820-Whittaker-sm 8vo-2 vols-3/4 blu calf over blu mrbld bds,t.e.g.,g dec sp wi bands,red lea sp labl,hand col frntis,illus (b3) 375.00

JAMMER,MAX-Concepts of Space-Cambridge-1954-Harvard U Pr-xviii+196p-bds-1st ed (a2,sl soil dj) 45.00

JAMMES,ANDRE-William H Fox Talbot-NY-1973-Macmillan-96p-70 photos-1st prtg (cc9,as new in dj) 35.00

JANES,E C-ED.-Fishing with Lee Wulff-NY-1972-8vo-348p-photos-1st prntng (m3,f,sl wn dj) 17.50

JANES,E C-ED.-Fishing with Ray Bergman-NY-1970-8vo-328p-illus-1st ed (m3,vf,dj) 22.50

JANES,E C-Hunting Ducks & Geese-Harrisburg-1954-4to-187p-photos,16 col plts-1st ed (m3,f) 25.00

JANES,E C-Ringneck!-NY-1975-4to-145p-photos (m3,f,dj) 12.50

JANES,E C-Salmon Fishing in the Northeast-Westfield-1973-8vo-110p-photos-1st prntng (m3,vf,dj) 15.00

JANES,EVAN-Citadel in the Wilderness-NY-1966-255p-illus,map-1st ed (n3,f,pc tn dj) 25.00

JANIS,ELSIE-Love Letters of an Actress-NY,Lond-1913-Appleton-97p-cl-1st ed (d1,sl rub,few spot rear cov) 15.00

JANIS,HARRIET-Collage-Phila-1962-Chilton-4to-302p-blk cl,illus-1st ed (r10,wn dj) 20.00

JANNEAU,GUILLAUME-Modern Glass-Lond-1931-Studio-184p-illus (cc8,tn dj) 200.00

JANNOPOULO,HELEN P-And Across Big Seas-Caxton-1949-Caldwell-8vo-353p-illus-1st ed (cc5,dj) 25.00

JANOV,ARTHUR-Primal Scream, Primal Therapy-NY-(1970)-Putnam-8vo-446p-1st ed (gg5,sl tn dj) 15.00

JANOWITZ,TAMA-American Dad-NY-1981-Putnam-auth 1st bk-1st ed (g8,f,sl tn dj) 75.00

JANSSON,TOVE-Moominland Midwinter-Lond-(1958)-Benn-165p-cl,auth illus-1st ed (nn10,papr yel,dj) 40.00

JAPANESE FAIRY TALES-(1960)-Golden Bks-folio-66p-pict glossy bds,col illus,Benvenuti-1st ed (r3,f) 25.00

JAPANESE PHOTOGRAPHY-a Century of...-NY-(1980)-Pantheon-oblng 4to-cl-1st Amer ed (y3,f,box) 55.00

JAQUES,FLORENCE P-As Far as the Yukon-NY-(1951)-243p-illus (gg3) 17.00

JAQUES,FLORENCE P-As Far as the Yukon-NY-(1951)-8vo-243p-illus-1st ed (m3,f,dj) 25.00

JAQUES,FLORENCE P-As Far as the Yukon-NY-(1951)-Harper-8vo-243p-drwngs-1st ed (jj5,dj) 20.00

JAQUES,FLORENCE P-Canoe Country-MN-1958-78p-illus (gg3,f,chip dj) 12.00

JAQUES,FLORENCE P-Snowshoe Country-Mpls-1944-4to-110p-illus-1st ed (m3,f,sl chip dj) 27.50

JARCHOW,H NICHOLAS-Forest Planting-NY-1893-Orange Judd-8vo-238p+illus+8p ads-pict grn cl-1st ed (y4,sl wn) 100.00

JARDINE,DOUGLAS-Mad Mullah of Somaliland-Lond-1923-336p-grn cl,illus-scarce-1st ed (b7,f) 200.00

JARDINE,SIR WILLIAM-Naturalist's Library. Mammalia. Vol.VIII-Edinburgh-1839-W H Lizars-3/4 lea wi mrbld papr over bds,g sp titles & dec,frntis,text drwngs,31 hand-col plts (nn1) 275.00

JARMAN,W-USA, Uncle Sam's Abcess or Hell Upon Earth for US-Exeter-1884-16mo-194p+30p illus,pict cl wi gilt-1st ed (aa3,frnt cov discol,wn) 95.00

JARRATT,VERNON-Spaghetti in My Hair-Lond-(1965)-L Frewin-235p-red cl,drwngs-1st prtg (q8,dj) 15.00

JARRELL,RANDALL-Fly By Night-NY-1976-1st ed (r5,vf,dj) 25.00

JARRELL,RANDALL-Little Friend, Little Friend-1945-Dial-1st ed (kk6,sl chip dj) 100.00

JARRELL,RANDALL-Pictures From an Institution-1954-Knopf-1st ed (kk6,f,dj edgetn,sl rub) 50.00

JARRELL,RANDALL-Pictures From an Institution-NY-1954-1st ed (t5,wn dj) 60.00

JARRELL,RANDALL-Selected Poems-Lond-1956-1st Brit ed (r5,dj) 45.00

JARRELL,RANDALL-Seven League Crutches-NY-(1951)-Harcourt Brace-1st ed (bb2,f,dj) 200.00

JARVES,JAMES J-History of the Hawaiian or Sandwich Islands-Bost-1843-Tappan & Dennet-8vo-xx,(map),407p-orig brwn emboss cl,g titles,25 illus(incl 5p plts & fldg map)-Sabin 35796-1st ed (p8,sl wn,rehngd) 1,500.00

JASMINE FARM-Lond-(1934)-Heinemann-8vo-375p-by the auth of "Elizabeth and her German Garden"-1st ed (w6) 45.00

JASPERS,KARL-General Psychopathology-Chig-(1963)-U of Chig-xxxii+922p-red cl-1st Amer ed (c2,dj) 65.00

JAY,WILLIAM-Review of the Causes & Consequences of the Mexican War-Bost-1849-333p-4th ed (t8,sl fox,sl fray sp) 50.00

JAY,WILLIAM-Review of the Causes and Consequences of the Mexican War-Bost-1849-Benj B Mussey-12mo-333p-1st ed (n2,sl wn) 50.00

JAYNE'S MEDICAL ALMANAC AND GUIDE TO HEALTH...1862-Phila-(1861)-56p-wrps (b1) 15.00

JEANNES,WILLIAM-Gunter's Modern Confectioner-Lond-(1861)-Dean & Son-8vo-xvi,246+2p ads-grn cl,frntis,10 plts-3rd ed (t10,rub) 40.00

JEFFCOTT,PERCIVAL R-Nooksack, Tales & Trails-Ferndale-1949-436p-illus-scarce-1st ed (h7,cor rub,autg) 50.00

JEFFERIS,B G-Search Lights on Health-(1895)-515p-cl (d1) 15.00

JEFFERS,H PAUL-Adventure of the Stalwart Companions-Lond-1979-Cassell-1st Brit ed (q4,f,dj) 22.50

JEFFERS,H PAUL-Rubout at the Onyx-CT-1981-Ticknor & Fields-1st ed (q4,f,dj) 17.50

JEFFERS,ROBINSON-Be Angry at the Sun-NY-(1941)-Random-8vo-cl-1st ed (x3,sl soil,dj) 70.00

JEFFERS,ROBINSON-Be Angry at the Sun-NY-1941-Random-4to-cl & mrbld bds,ltd to 100c,autg-1st ed (x3,f) 625.00

JEFFERS,ROBINSON-Californians-NY-1916-Macmillan-8vo-blu cl stmpd in g & blk,t.e.g.-1st ed (x3,sl wn sp) 225.00

JEFFERS,ROBINSON-Dear Judas and Other Poems-NY-1929-Liveright-1st ed (w1,dj) 100.00

JEFFERS,ROBINSON-Dear Judas-NY-1929-Liveright-8vo-cl/bds-1st ed (x3,f,dj) 60.00

JEFFERS,ROBINSON-Double Axe-NY-(1948)-Random-cl-1st ed (x3,chip dj) 45.00

JEFFERS,ROBINSON-Double Axe-NY-1948-Random-1st ed (e8,sl soil dj) 125.00

JEFFERS,ROBINSON-Give Your Heart to the Hawks-NY-1933-1st ed (q5,dj) 100.00

JEFFERS,ROBINSON-Give Your Heart to the Hawks-NY-1933-Random-8vo-cl-1st ed (x3,sl sunned dj) 70.00

JEFFERS,ROBINSON-Hungerfield-NY-(1954)-Random-4to-cl-1st ed (x3,dj) 75.00

JEFFERS,ROBINSON-Hungerfield-NY-(1954)-Random-blu & wht cl-1st ed (f2,dj) 50.00

JEFFERS,ROBINSON-Medea-NY-1946-1st ed (q5,sl chip dj) 50.00

JEFFERS,ROBINSON-Selected Letters of ... 1897 to 1962-Balt-1968-Johns Hopkins-photos,L Wiener-1st ed (h8,f,f dj) 65.00

JEFFERS,ROBINSON-Solstice and Other Poems-NY-1935-Random-1st ed (h8,sl chip dj) 125.00

JEFFERS,ROBINSON-Such Counsels You Gave To Me-NY-(1937)-Random Hs-1st trd ed (b10,dj) 75.00

JEFFERS,ROBINSON-Such Counsels You Gave To Me-NY-(1937)-Random-8vo-maroon cl wi g lttrng-1st ed (x3,f,dj) 65.00

JEFFERS,ROBINSON-Tamar and other Poems-NY-(1924)-Boyle-sm 8vo-cl-scarce-1st ed (x3) 325.00

JEFFERS,ROBINSON-Thurso's Landing-NY-(1932)-Liveright-8vo-blk cl & mauve bds,g stmpg,untrimmed-1st trd ed (x3,sp drknd dj) 60.00

JEFFERS,ROBINSON-Thurso's Landing-NY-1932-Liveright-ltd to 2570c-1st ed (f8,lacks dj) 65.00

JEFFERSON COUNTY-With Pride in Heritage, History of...-Portland-1966-Prof Publ Ptg-8vo-illus-1st ed (cc5,dj) 20.00

JEFFERSON,THOMAS-Memoir, Correspondence, and Miscellanies from the Papers of...-Charlottesville-1829-F Carr-4 vols-mrbld lea,labls,port,4 facs-1st ed (o2,v.1 covs almost detchd) 300.00

JEFFERSON,THOMAS-Thomas Jefferson's Garden Book, 1766 to 1824-Phila-1944-Amer Philo Soc-xvi+704p-grn cl,36 plts-1st ed (mm10,chip dj) 65.00

JEFFERSON,THOMAS-Writings of...-Wash D.C.-1903-Jefferson Memorial Assoc-20 vols-grn cl,pap sp labls,illus-1st ed (h2,sp labls fade) 250.00

JEFFERSON-BROWN,M J-Daffodil-Lond-1951-264p-yel cl,6 col & 32 b&w plts,16 maps (jj7) 44.00

JEFFERSON-BROWN,M J-Daffodils,Tulips and Other Hardy Bulbs-Lond-(1966)-160p-33 photo plts (x5,f,dj) 18.00

JEFFREYS,J G-Wilful Lady-NY-1975-Walker-1st Amer ed (q4,f,dj) 20.00

JEFFRIES,RICHARD-Field and Farm, Essays-Lond-1957-1st ed (y7,dj) 28.00

JEHL,FRANCIS-Menlo Park Reminiscences-Dearborn-1936-430p-cl,illus (aa6) 40.00

JEHL,FRANCIS-Menlo Park Reminiscences-Dearborn-1937,39-Edison Inst-2 vols-grn wrps,illus-1st ed (a2) 45.00

JEKYLL,GERTRUDE-Annuals & Biennials-Lond-1916-Cntry Life-173p-cl,3 tip in col plts (x6,sl soil cl) 40.00

JEKYLL,GERTRUDE-Colour Schemes for the Flower Garden-Lond-1921-Country Life-xvi,159p-122p illus+4 fldg plts-5th ed (mm4,f) 75.00

JEKYLL,GERTRUDE-Lilies for English Gardens-Lond-1903-Cntry Life-72p-cl-2nd ed (x6,soil cl,sl fox) 55.00

JEKYLL,GERTRUDE-Old West Surrey-Lond-1904-Longmans,Green-xx,320p-orig g dec buckrm,illus,photos-scarce-1st & only ed (mm4,sl dull sp,rear hng weak) 135.00

JEKYLL,GERTRUDE-Wood and Garden-Lond-1901-xvi,286p+ads-blu dec cl wi g stmpg,71 half tones-new ed,9th impr (x5,sl fade) 45.00

JELINEK,GEORGE-Ellsworth, Kansas. 1867 to 1947-nd(ca.1947)-Consolidated-32p-wrps-1st ed (nn9) 60.00

JELLEY,J J-Royal Welcome-Ada-(1885)-Wagner Bros-160p-bds (n1,sl wn cov) 12.50

JELLICOE,ADMIRAL VISCOUNT-Grand Fleet,1914 to 1916-NY-1919-Doran-xiv,510p-plans,illus,diags (nn1,sp scuf & discol,fox) 40.00

JELLICOE,SUSAN-Modern Private Gardens-Lond-1968-Abelard Schuman-oblng 4to-127p-cl,illus,plans-v scarce (cc10,dj) 75.00

JENCKS,C-Adhocism-GC-1972-illus-1st ed (h10,dj) 50.00

JENCKS,CHARLES-Architecture 2000, Predictions & Methods-NY-1971-sq 8vo-illus-1st Amer ed (h10,dj) 45.00

JENISON,MADGE-Sunwise Turn a Human Comedy of Bookselling-NY-(1923)-Dutton-2nd prtg (w1,dj) 20.00

JENKINS,A O-Olives's Last Round Up-(Loup City)-(1930)-12mo-81p-wrps-Howes J90-rare-1st ed (b3,f) 175.00

JENKINS,ALAN-White Horses and Black Bulls-NY-1963-Norton-1st US ed (h9,dj) 15.00

JENKINS,C FRANCIS-Boyhood of an Inventor-Wash D.C.-1931-xx+273p-brwn bds,illus-1st ed (j2,few sm wtr spots) 75.00

JENKINS,C FRANCIS-Vision by Radio, Radio Photographs-1925-140p-35 photos,30 illus-rare-1st ed (h6) 120.00

JENKINS,DAN-Semi Tough-1972-Atheneum-1st ed (s9,f,dj) 25.00

JENKINS,DAN-Sports Illustrated's Best 18 Golf Holes in America-NY-1966-col photos-1st ed (ll7,f,f dj) 65.00

JENKINS,FERGUSON-Inside Pitching-1972-Regnery-photos-1st ed (s8,f,dj) 20.00

JENKINS,FERGUSON-Like Nobody Else-1973-Regnery-photos-1st ed (s8,dj) 30.00

JENKINS,JOHN H-Basic Texas Books-Austin-1983-648p-photos-1st ed (t7,dj) 50.00

JENKINS,JOHN H-Basic Texas Books-Austin-1983-Pemberton-648p-1st ed (a9,dj) 75.00

JENKINS,JOHN H-ED.-Papers of the Texas Revolution, 1835 to 1836-Austin-1973-Presidial Pr-10 vols-1st ed (a9) 300.00

JENKINS,WARREN-School and Township Officer's Manual, and Executor's and Administrator's Guide-Columbus-1839-I N Whiting-310p-lea-Amer Imprnts 56593 (n1,sm pc chip sp top) 65.00

JENKINSON,MICHAEL-Ghost Towns of New Mexico-Albuq-1967-oblng-153p+map-photos-1st ed (u7,dj) 25.00

JENKINSON,MICHAEL-Ghost Towns of New Mexico-Albuq-1967-oblng-156p-cl,photos-1st ed,3rd prtg (z1,f,dj) 35.00

JENKINSON,MICHAEL-Tijerina-(Albuq)-(1968)-103p-wrps,photos-1st ed (u7) 25.00

JENNESS,DIAMOND-Indians of Canada-Ottawa-1963-Nat'l Mus Can-xii,452p-illus,maps,rear pckt map-Bull.65,Anthro Ser 15-6th ed (bb7,minor underlining,rub dj) 50.00*

JENNESS,DIAMOND-People of the Twilight-NY-1928-Macmillan-8vo-247p-cl,illus-1st ed (pp5) 75.00*

JENNESS,DIAMOND-People of the Twilight-NY-1928-Macmillan-8vo-247p-g dec orng cl,e.p. maps,frntis,17 illus,1 map-1st ed (mm8,cov sl spot & warped) 50.00*

JENNEWEIN,L J-Black Hills Booktrails-Mitchell-(1962)-111p-scarce (bb9) 75.00

JENNINGS,A-Through the Shadows with O Henry-NY-(1921)-H K Fly Co-320p-pict cl,illus-Six Guns 1172-1st ed (ff4) 45.00

JENNINGS,GARY-Treasure of the Superstition Mountains-NY-(1973)-247p-photos,maps-1st ed (v7,f,dj) 25.00

JENNINGS,HERMAN A-Provincetown or Odds and Ends from the Tip End-Yarmouthport-(1890)-212p-grn cl,photos-1st ed (m2) 85.00

JENNINGS,LINDA D-COMP.-Washington Women's Cook Book-Seattle-1909-Wash Equal Suffrage Assoc-256p-oilcl bds (n6,wn bds) 120.00

JENNINGS,PRESTON J-Book of Trout Flies-NY-1935-Derrydale-8vo-grn dec cl,illus by Froderstrom-ltd to 850c,nbrd-1st ed (u10,sl drknd sp) 300.00

JENNINGS,PRESTON-Book of Trout Flies-Derrydale-1935-8vo-190p-ltd to 850c,nbrd,7 hand col plts (m3,sl stnd sp & rear cov) 400.00

JENNY,GEORGE F-COMP.-Handbook to Aid in the Study of State & Local History-Columbus-1953-124p-wrps (j1) 10.00

JENSEN,INGEBORG D-Wonderful, Wonderful Danish Cooking-(1965)-S&S-335p-tan & blu cl (q8,dj) 16.50

JENSEN,J MARINUS-History of Provo, Utah-(Provo)-1924-publ by auth-414p-grn cl,illus-Howes J102-1st ed (b2) 85.00

JENSEN,JULIAETTA B-Little Gold Pieces...-SLC-(1948)-242p-illus,port-1st ed (bb8,sl tn dj) 20.00

JENSON,ANDREW-Church Chronology-SLC-1899-259p-orig blk cl-Flake 4400-2nd ed (bb8,few ink mrks) 35.00

JENSON,ANDREW-Church Chronology-SLC-1914-Flake 4401-rvsd & enlgd ed, wi 2 spplmnts (bb8) 47.50

JENSON,BERNIE-Buck & the Cats of Evergreen Acres-1973-Vantage Pr-8vo-135p-photos-1st ed (m3,vf,dj) 20.00

JENYNS,SOAME-Japanese Porcelain-Lond-1979-Faber-352p+120 plts-rprnt (c3,f) 65.00

JEPSON,SELWYN-Angry Millionaire-1968-Harper-1st Amer ed (s10,sp soil dj) 12.50

JEPSON,WILLIS L-Flora of Western Middle California-Berkeley-1901-Encina Publ-sm 8vo-iv,625p+5p ads-orig cl-scarce-1st ed (mm4,hng weak) 42.50

JEPSON,WILLIS L-High School Flora for California-Berkeley-(1935)-Assoc Students Store-223p-cl,illus (m6,sl soil,sunned cl) 16.00

JEREMIAH,EDDIE-Ice Hockey-NY-1942-Barnes-8vo-120p-illus,drwngs (bb7,rub dj) 20.00*

JERNIGAN,C B-From the Prairie to a City Flat-NY-1926-140p-pict bds,frntis,illus-Herd #1172 (t7) 30.00

JERNIGAN,E W-Jewelry of the Prehistoric Southwest-Albuq-1978-pict cl,frntis,col plts-1st ed (t7,f) 30.00

JERNIGAN,E WESLEY-Jewelry of the Prehistoric Southwest-Albuq-1978-UNM Pr-260p-col illus-1st ed (cc4) 35.00

JEROME,JEROME K-American Wives and Others-1904-Stokes-pict cl,illus,G McManus-1st ed (x2) 25.00

JEROME,JEROME K-Paul Kelver-NY-1902-1st ed (m4) 14.50

JEROME,JEROME K-Second Thoughts of an Idle Fellow-NY-1898-Dodd,Mead-gold emboss-1st Amer ed (t4,sl fade sp) 20.00

JEROME,JEROME K-Stage Land-Lond-1889-Chatto & Windus-80p-illus-1st ed (ll2) 15.00

JEROME,JEROME K-Three Men in a Boat-1890-Holt-1st Amer ed (x2,soil) 45.00

JEROME,JOHN-On Mountains-NY-1978-262p-1st ed (p10,as new in dj) 15.00

JEROME,OWEN F-Red Kite Club-1928-Clode-1st ed (s10) 12.50

JEROME,V J-Culture in a Changing World-NY-1947-New Century-94p-wrps-Seidman J53 (r1) 16.00

JEROME,V J-Social Democracy and the War-NY-1940-Workers Libr-wrps-1st ed (w5,f) 20.00

JERSEY CITY-Echoes of the Aesthetic Society of...-NY-1882-xv,255p-cl,frntis-scarce (aa6) 90.00

JERSTAD,LUTHER-Mani Rimdu-Seattle-1969-192p-23 photos-rare-1st ed (o10,f,dj) 45.00

JESSE,DEAN C-ED.-Personal Writings of Joseph Smith-SLC-1984-736p-blk lea,raised bnds,blnd stmpd dec covs,a.e.g.-ltd to 200c (bb8,as new in shrink wrp) 200.00

JESSE,EDWARD-An Angler's Rambles-Lond-1836-12mo-318p (m3,chip sp top) 45.00

JESSEL,GEORGE-Elegy in Manhattan-NY-1961-Holt-198p-1st ed (ll2,dj) 12.50

JESSUP,ELON-Roughing it Smoothly-NY-1923-8vo-247p-photos,illus (m3,f) 15.00

JETT,STEPHEN C-Navajo Architecture-Tucson-(1981)-266p-wrps,photos,maps-1st ed (v7,f) 20.00

JETT,STEPHEN C-Navajo Wildlands-SF-(1967)-sm folio-160p-col photos,pckt map-1st ed (v7,dj) 60.00

JEWETT,CHARLES-Forty Years' Fight with the Drink Demon-NY-1872-407p-cl (a1) 22.50

JEWETT,S G-Birds of Washington State-Seattle-1953-8vo-767p-cl,12 col plts,photos,maps(incl col fldg map rear pckt)-1st ed (y8) 85.00

JEWISH BLACK BOOK COMMITTEE-Black Book-1946-1st ed (z2,sm stn,dj chip) 275.00

JEZREEL,JAMES J-Extracts from the Flying Roll-(Lond)-1879 to 1881-3 vols-cl-v scarce (aa1) 75.00

JHABVALA,R PRAWER-Amritra-NY-1956-auth 1st bk-1st US ed (n5,dj) 40.00

JHABVALA,R PRAWER-Nature of Passion-NY-1957-1st US ed (n5,sl chip dj) 25.00

JHABVALA,RUTH P-Travelers-1973-Harper & Row-1st Amer ed (s9,dj) 15.00

JIMERSON,RANDALL C-ET AL-Guide to the Microfilm Edition of Temperance and Prohibition Papers...-Ann Arbor-(1977)-379p-wrps,illus (a1) 15.00

JOBSON,HAMILTON-Sleeping Tiger-Lond-1982-Hale-1st ed (s4,f,dj) 22.50

JOBSON,HAMILTON-Therefore I Killed Him-Lond-1968-Long-1st ed (q4,f,dj) 22.50

JOCELYN,JULIEN-History of the Royal Artillery-Lond-1911-508p-dec blu cl,fldg maps,illus-1st ed (b7,sp sun) 225.00

JOCELYN-Tripper-NY-1973-Exposition-1st ed (e8,f,f dj) 30.00

JOFFRE-PERSONAL MEMOIRS OF...FIELD MARSHAL OF THE FRENCH ARMY-NY & Lond-1932-Harper & Bros-2 vols,cl-1st ed so stated (m1) 22.50

JOHANNES,R E-Words of the Lagoon-Berkeley-(1981)-U Cal Pr-8vo-245p-photos-1st ed (dd5,f,f dj) 20.00

JOHANNESSON,ERIC O-Novels of August Strindberg-Berkeley-1968-UC Pr-1st ed (x9,f,dj) 12.50

JOHANNSEN,ALBERT-House of Beadle and Adams and Its Dime and Nickel Novels-Norman-1950-3 vols-photos-vol.1 & vol.2 1st eds (t7,f,dj) 125.00

JOHN,EVAN-Atlantic Impact 1861-Lond-(1952)-296p-e.p. maps,illus-1st ed (n3,dj) 25.00

JOHNS,ELIZABETH A H-Storms Brewed in Other Men's Worlds-College Sta-1975-Tex A&M-805p-1st ed (a9,dj) 50.00

JOHNS,RICHARD S-Pet German Shorthaired Pointer-Fond du Lac-1956-8vo-64p-wrps,illus (m3,f) 17.50

JOHNS,W E-Biggles Flies North-Lond-(1939)-OUP-8vo-256p-dec cl,illus-1st ed (pp2,dj) 35.00*

JOHNS,W E-Biggles in the Orient-Tor-1946-Musson Bks-8vo-250p+4p ads-col frntis,12 illus-Venture Bks for Boys (aa7,sl chip dj) 20.00*

JOHNSGARD,P A-Ducks,Geese and Swans of the World-1978-U of Nebr-4to-404p-59 col plts,photos (bb3,f,dj) 35.00

JOHNSGARD,P A-Waterfowl of North America-1975-U of Ind-575p-31 col & 96 b&w photos-1st ed (bb3,f,tn dj) 35.00

JOHNSGARD,P A-Waterfowl-Lincoln-1968-8vo-(1),138p-cl,photos(59 col) (y8,dj wn) 22.50

JOHNSGARD,PAUL A-North American Game Birds of Upland & Shoreline-Lincoln-1975-8vo-183p-illus (m3,vf) 20.00

JOHNSON,A F-One Hundred Title Pages 1500 to 1800-NY-1928-Appleton/Curwen Pr-4to-101p-mrbld papr over bds-1st ed (q3) 150.00

JOHNSON,A N-True Singing School Text Book...-Cin-(1871)-Church & Co-191p-bds (n1,covs wn) 12.50

JOHNSON,A W-Birds of Chile-Buenos Aires-1965 to67-8vo-2 vols-cl,104 col plts (y8,crack,dj chip) 135.00

JOHNSON,ADAM R-Partisan Rangers of the Confederate States Army-Louisville-1904-Geo G Fetter-476p-frntis port,illus-Coulter 257-v scarce-1st ed (v2,sl nick pgs) 300.00

JOHNSON,AMANDUS-Journal and Biography of Nicholas Collin, 1746 to 1831-Phila-1936-368p-cl,plts (aa6) 30.00

JOHNSON,AMANDUS-Swedes on the Delaware, 1638 to 1664-Phila-1927-391p-cl,plts,fldg map-rprnt of 1915 ed (aa6) 60.00

JOHNSON,AMANDUS-Swedish Settlements on the Delaware-(Phila)-1911-2 vols-cl,plts & maps(incl fldg) (aa6) 225.00

JOHNSON,B P-Transactions of the New York State Agricultural Society-Albany-1854-Benthuysen-783p-cl (x6,rub) 25.00

JOHNSON,BRODERICK H-ED.-Stories of Traditional Navajo Life and Culture by Twenty-two Navajo Men and Women-Tsaile-1977-335p-photos-1st ed (v7,f) 20.00

JOHNSON,C N-Tulsa Art Deco-Tulsa-1980-sq lg 4to-illus(incl col)-1st ed (ee1,dj sl rub) 85.00

JOHNSON,C P-British Wild Flowers, Illustrated by John E Sowerby...To Which is Now Added a Supplement...-Lond-1876-186p text+89 hand col plts-grn cl,lea sp & cor,orig title labl laid on (bb3,rbnd) 325.00

JOHNSON,CARL O-History of Byram-(Byram)-(1964)-(4),94p-cl,illus (aa6) 30.00

JOHNSON,CHARLES-Faith and the Good Thing-NY-(1974)-auth 1st bk-1st ed (k5,as new in dj) 50.00

JOHNSON,CHARLES-Oxherding Tale-Bloomington-(1982)-1st ed (k5,as new in dj) 35.00

JOHNSON,CHARLES-Oxherding Tale-Bloomington-(1982)-Indiana U Pr-1st ed (h8,f,dj) 45.00

JOHNSON,CHAS F-Angling in the Lakes of Northern Illinois-Chig-1896-Amer Field Publ-116p-3/4 grn mor wi mrbld bds,illus (w10,rbnd wi old cl in rear) 350.00

JOHNSON,CLIFTON-ED.-District School As It Was-Bost-1897-Lee & Shepard-171,(18)p-cl,illus (k1) 25.00

JOHNSON,CLIFTON-Highways & Byways from the St.Lawrence to Virginia-NY-1913-Macmillan-340p+ads-dec cl,photos-1st ed (p2,hngs weak,rub) 15.00

JOHNSON,CLIFTON-Highways & Byways of New England-NY-1915-Macmillan-299p+ads-dec cl,photos-1st ed (p2) 15.00

JOHNSON,DANIEL H-Hazel Green Man's Story and Other Tales...with a Memoir by Electa Amanda Johson-Mlwk-1904-354p-cl (f1) 15.00

JOHNSON,DENIS-Angels-NY-1983-Knopf-1st ed (bb1,f,dj) 25.00

JOHNSON,DIANE-Dashiell Hammett, A Life-NY-(1983)-Random-1st ed (bb1,f,dj) 17.50

JOHNSON,DIANE-Fair Game-NY-1965-auth 1st bk-1st ed (q5,f,dj) 35.00

JOHNSON,DOROTHY M-Bloody Bozeman-NY-1971-McGraw Hill-8vo-xx,366p-illus,photos,2 maps(1 fldg)-Amer Trails Ser-1st ed (aa3,f,dj) 20.00

JOHNSON,DOROTHY M-Bloody Bozeman-NY-1971-McGraw Hill-xx,366p-illus,maps,ports-Amer Trail ser (k10,dj) 25.00*

JOHNSON,DOROTHY M-Indian Country-NY-(1953)-200p-1st ed (g7,f,dj,autg) 50.00

JOHNSON,DOROTHY M-When You & I Were Young, Whitefish-Missoula-(1982)-164p-1st ed (j7,tn dj) 20.00

JOHNSON,DR FRANK M-Forest Lake & River-Bost-1902-4to-2 vols-ltd to 350c,nbrd,orig ties on orig suede bndg,illus (m3,sl dmpstnd bottom edges) 300.00

JOHNSON,DR FRANK M-Reminiscent Tales of a Humble Angler-Cin-1921-12mo-109p-photos (m3) 25.00

JOHNSON,E PAULINE-Flint and Feather-Tor/Lond-nd(ca.1923)-Musson Bk Co-xx,156p-2 plts (o2,cors wn,sl fox) 20.00

JOHNSON,E PAULINE-Legends of Vancouver-Tor-(1911)-McClelland,Goodchild & St-8vo-165p-7 plts,scarce in dj-"New ed" (bb5,dj) 30.00

JOHNSON,E PAULINE-Legends of Vancouver-Tor-1911-M&S-8vo-xvi,165p-grn cl,g titles,frntis,6 illus-new ed (cc7,rbnd) 35.00*

JOHNSON,EDWARD A-School History of the Negro Race in America from 1619 to 1890...-Chig-1897-Conkey Co-200p-cl-revsd ed (k1,penclng,inner hng rprd) 100.00

JOHNSON,ELMER-Thomas Wolfe-Kent-1970-KSU Pr-1st ed (z9) 12.50

JOHNSON,EMEROY-Church is Planted-Mpls-1948-Lund Pr-386p-illus-1st ed (gg4) 20.00

JOHNSON,EMILY C-Under Quaker Appointment-Phila-1953-Univ of Penn-8vo-211p-1st ed (y6) 12.00

JOHNSON,FRANK E-Professional Wine Reference-NY-(1978)-Beverage Media-16mo-354p-lea-G.E. Handbook (q8) 17.50

JOHNSON,FRIDOLF-ED.-Rockwell Kent-NY-1982-Knopf-1st ed (w5,f,f dj) 50.00

JOHNSON,G WESLEY,JR.-Emergence of Black Politics in Senegal-Stanford-(1971)-Stanford U Pr-8vo-260p-cl-1st ed (y5,dj) 30.00

JOHNSON,G-Peru From the Air-NY-1930-Amer Geo Scty Publ No.12-4to-159p-photos,maps (p10) 45.00

JOHNSON,GENE-Ship Model Building-NY-1961-Cornell Maritime Pr-8vo-300p+ads-blu cl,plans,photos-3rd ed (nn1,chip dj) 30.00

JOHNSON,GEORGE W-Dictionary of Modern Gardening-Phila-1847-Lea-635p-180 woodcts (x6,rebckd) 100.00

JOHNSON,H EARLE-Symphony Hall, Boston-Bost-1950-Little,Brown-1st ed (u4,sl rub dj) 18.00

JOHNSON,HARRY-History of Anderson County Kansas-Garnett-1936-383p-photos,illus-1st ed (t7) 35.00

JOHNSON,HUGH-Wine-NY-(1966)-S&S-sm 4to-264p-photos-1st prtg (o6,dj) 35.00

JOHNSON,IRVING-Westward Bound in the Schooner Yankee-NY-1936-Norton-map e.p.,illus (p8) 25.00

JOHNSON,IVER-Fire Arms-ca.1930's-32p-catalog,photos,illus (gg3,f) 60.00

JOHNSON,J ROSAMOND-Rolling Along in Song-NY-1937-1st ed (r2) 75.00

JOHNSON,JACK-Jack Johnson, In the Ring, and Out-Chig-1927-Nat'l Sports Publ-259p-illus,pict dj-v scarce-1st ed (f9,dj missng sp pc) 85.00

JOHNSON,JAMES D-Lincoln Land Traction-1965-Johnson-4to-147p-illus (nn7,dj wn,tn) 20.00

JOHNSON,JANET H-Demotic Verbal System-Chig-(1976)-Oriental Inst-8vo-xv,344p-prtd wrps-Studies in Ancient Oriental Civil,No.38-1st ed (t10) 25.00

JOHNSON,JOSEPHINE W-Circle of Seasons-NY-1974-Viking-104p-64 col photos by D Stock-1st ed (cc9,as new in dj) 35.00

JOHNSON,JOYCE-Minor Characters-Bost-1983-Houghton Mifflin-1st ed (ff6,as new in dj) 25.00

JOHNSON,KATE-Pioneer Days of Nakusp and the Arrow Lakes-(Nakusp)-1964-the Auth-240p-illus,ports-rprntd wi add (k10,autg) 30.00*

JOHNSON,KENNETH M-K 344 or the Indians of California vs. the U.S.-LA-1966-97p-dec cl,photos-1st ed (t7,f) 30.00

JOHNSON,L F-Famous Kentucky Tragedies and Trials-Louisville-1916-336p-cl-Coleman 1676-1st ed (j1) 50.00

JOHNSON,LES-Sea Run-Portland-1979-4to-76p-photos,col plts (m3,vf,dj) 30.00

JOHNSON,LESTER-Devil's Front Porch-Lawrence-1970-U Pr of Kansas-1st ed (z3,f,dj) 12.50

JOHNSON,LOIS P-I'm Gonna Fly-St.Paul-1959-McAlaster Park Publ-176p-cl-1st ed (z7) 30.00

JOHNSON,M E-Seashore Animals of the Pacific Coast-1935-Macmillan-659p-11 col plts (bb3) 38.00

JOHNSON,M L-Intensely Interesting Little Volume of True History of the Struggle with Hostile Indians...-Dallas-1923-40p-stapled wrps,frntis-Herd #1179-scarce-1st ed (t7) 50.00

JOHNSON,M M-Ammunition, Its History, Development & Use, 1600-1943-NY-1943-374p-photos (gg3,f,dj) 20.00

JOHNSON,M M-Rifles & Machine Guns-NY-1944-390p-photos (gg3,f,chip dj) 25.00

JOHNSON,M-Lion African Adventures with the King of Beasts-NY-1929-281p-photos,fldg map (gg3) 25.00

JOHNSON,M-Over African Jungles-NY-1935-8vo-263p-photos (m3,f,sl fray dj) 30.00

JOHNSON,MARGARET S-Tim-NY-1940-Harcourt Brace-1st prtg (f10,dj) 35.00

JOHNSON,MRS GROVER C-Wagon Yard-Dallas-1938-Wm T Tardy-201p-1st ed (a9,dj) 50.00

JOHNSON,O-Four Years in Paradise-NY-1941-8vo-345p-cl,54 photos (y8,cl fade,dj wn) 23.00

JOHNSON,OLGA W-Early Libby and Troy, Montana-np-1958-110p-spiral pict wrps,photos,maps-1st ed (t7) 15.00

JOHNSON,OVERTON-Route Across the Rocky Mountains-Princeton-1932-(rprnt of 1846 ed) (r8,sp wn,rub) 30.00

JOHNSON,OWEN-Varmint-NY-1910-396p-cl-scarce-1st ed (j1) 65.00

JOHNSON,PAMELA H-Night and Silence Who is Here-NY-(1963)-Scribners-1st Amer ed (dd2,dj,pres) 40.00

JOHNSON,PAMELA H-Night and Silence Who is Here-NY-(1963)-Scribners-1st US ed (hh5,dj) 10.00

JOHNSON,PAMELA H-Unspeakable Skipton-NY-(1959)-Harcourt Brace-1st US ed (hh5,dj) 10.00

JOHNSON,PATRICIA M-Short History of Nanaimo-Nanaimo-c.1958-BC Cent Comm-55p-prtd wrps,illus,port-Edwards & Lort #1920 (k10) 30.00*

JOHNSON,PAUL C-ED.-California Missions-Menlo Park-1964-Sunset Mag-4to-322p-photos-1st ed (d3,dj) 25.00

JOHNSON,PEARL ROSE-King's Daughter-Ft.Scott-nd-Banner Pr-207,(1)p-cl (d1,sl spot frnt cov) 25.00

JOHNSON,PETER H-Parker-America's Finest Shotgun-Harrisburg-1961-8vo-260p-photos,illus-1st ed (m3,vf,dj) 45.00

JOHNSON,PHILIP-Architecture 1949 to 65-NY-1966-sq 4to-illus(incl col)-1st ed (kk4) 85.00

JOHNSON,ROBERT U-ED-Battles and Leaders of the Civil War: Grant, Lee Edition-NY-1887,1888-Century Co-8vols-beige cl,t.e.g.,maps,illus-1st ed thus (o7,sp labls wn,sl soil cov) 225.00

JOHNSON,ROY P-Jacob Horner of the Seventh Cavalry-Bismarck-1949-State Hist Soc-28p-wrps,illus (ff4) 20.00

JOHNSON,SOLOMON-Notes on Travels-Columbus-1915-295p-cl-2nd ed (h1) 15.00

JOHNSON,SPUD-Horizontal Yellow-(Santa Fe)-(1935)-S F Writers Eds,Rydal Pr-84p-ltd to 400c,nbrd-this cpy nbrd out of sequence as #420-rare-1st ed (v7,review cpy,chip dj) 125.00

JOHNSON,STANLEY C-History of Emigration from the United Kingdom to North America, 1763 to 1912-Lond-1913-Routledge-xvi+387p+ads-blu cl-1st ed (b2) 25.00

JOHNSON,STEPHEN L-History of Cardiac Surgery 1896 to 1955-Balt-1970-201p-illus (g10,dj) 45.00

JOHNSON,T B-Sportsman's Cyclopedia-Lond-1831-Sherwood,Gilbert & Piper-1/2 blk lea,engrvngs-1st ed (p6,weak hngs,sl wn) 150.00

JOHNSON,TIMOTHY-Crime Fiction Criticism-NY-1981-Garland-iss w/o dj-1st ed (d4,f) 25.00

JOHNSON,VIRGINIA W-Unregimented General-Bost-1962-Houghton Mifflin-401p-photos,maps-1st ed (gg4,sl wn dj) 50.00

JOHNSON,VIRGINIA W-Unregimented General-Bost-1962-Houghton Mifflin-8vo-401p-illus,photos,6 maps-1st ed (aa3,sl chip dj) 45.00

JOHNSON,W BRANCH-Folktales of Brittany-NY-nd(1927)-Stokes-cl-1st Amer ed (o8,dj) 30.00

JOHNSON,WALTER H-Bay Billy-Seattle-1932-vii,150p-lea (a7,cor wn,pres) 75.00

JOHNSON,WALTER R-Scientific Class Book-Phila-1836-Key & Biddle-478p-lea-Amer Imprints 38310 (e1,upper joints cracking) 25.00

JOHNSON,WALTON R-Worship and Freedom-NY-(1977)-Africana Publ for I.A.I.-8vo-152p-papr over bds-1st ed (y5,dj) 32.00

JOHNSON,WELLWOOD R-Legends of Langley-Langley-1958-Langley Cent Comm-vi,183p-prtd wrps,illus,ports (aa2) 30.00*

JOHNSON,WILLIAM H-Denison University Presidents-Columbus-1915-Champlin Pr-13p-bds,ltd to 50c,nbrd, (k1) 15.00

JOHNSON,WILLIAM W-Kelly Blue-GC-1960-Dbldy-8vo-1st ed (p1,f,dj) 35.00

JOHNSON,WILLIS F-History of the Johnstown Flood-1889-Edgewood Publ-12mo-xiv,459p-map,photos-1st ed (o2,rub,hngs weak) 15.00

JOHNSON,WILLIS F-National Flag, A History-Bost-1930-HMCo-8vo-115p-4 col plts-1st ed (gg5) 15.00

JOHNSTON,ALFRED C-Enchanting Beauty-NY-1937-Swan-4to-spiral bnd wrps,full pg illus-1st ed (y3) 125.00

JOHNSTON,ALVA-Case of Erle Stanley Gardner-NY-1947-1st ed (t5,chip dj) 22.50

JOHNSTON,ALVA-Case of Erle Stanley Gardner-NY-1947-Morrow-1st ed (d4,sp chip dj) 35.00

JOHNSTON,ANNIE F-In League with Israel-Cin,NY-1896-303p-cl-1st ed (n1,sl rub) 15.00

JOHNSTON,ANNIE F-Mildred's Inheritance-Bost-1906-Page-8vo-74p-blu pict cl,illus by D W Horne-Cozy Corner Ser-1st impr (nn8,sl fox) 20.00

JOHNSTON,ANNIE F-Story of Dago-Bost-(1910)-Page-pict cl,illus,Cosy Corner Ser (s3,sl soil) 12.00

JOHNSTON,BERNICE E-California's Gabrielino Indians-1962-SW Mus-198p-illus-1st ed (d3) 25.00

JOHNSTON,CHARLES H L-Famous Cavalry Leaders-Bost-1915-393p-pict cl,frntis,illus (t7,f) 25.00

JOHNSTON,D E-Story of a Confederate Boy in the Civil War-Radford-1980-379p-ports-rprnt of 1914 ed (z10,dj) 20.00

JOHNSTON,H V-Last Roundup-Mpls-(1950)-336p-Six Guns #1187-1st ed (r8,dj) 55.00

JOHNSTON,HANK-Railroad That Lighted Southern California-LA-1965-128p-1st ed (n4,f,dj) 24.00

JOHNSTON,HARRY V-My Home on the Range-St.Paul-(1942)-Webb Publ-313p-illus-Six Guns #1188-1st ed (cc4,dj) 25.00

JOHNSTON,HARRY V-My Home on the Range-St.Paul-1942-313p-frntis,photos-Herd #1184-1st ed (t7,dj) 22.50

JOHNSTON,HARRY-Liberia-NY-(1969)-Negro U Pr-lg 8vo-2 vols-cl,maps,illus-orig publ in 1906 (y5) 55.00

JOHNSTON,HARRY-Nile Quest-NY-(1903)-Stokes-8vo-341p-73 illus-1st US ed (ff5) 85.00

JOHNSTON,HARRY-Story of My Life-Indpls-1923-504p-1st US ed (o10,f) 25.00

JOHNSTON,I H-Birds of West Virginia-Charleston-1923-8vo-138p-wrps,40 col drwngs,photos (y8,dmpstnd wrps) 15.00

JOHNSTON,I H-Crooked Bill, the Life of a Quail-Phila-1937-179p-photos-scarce (ee3,f,autg) 45.00

JOHNSTON,J A-Civil War, 1861 to 1865, In Arkansas and Missouri-Richmond-1967-43p-wrps,maps (z10,f) 20.00

JOHNSTON,J P-What Happened to Johnston-Chig-(1904)-459p-cl (c1) 22.50

JOHNSTON,JENNIFER-Old Jest-GC-1980-Dbldy-1st Amer ed (z8,vf,dj) 16.50

JOHNSTON,JILL-Gullibles Travels-NY-(1974)-Links-1st ed (hh5,f,dj) 10.00

JOHNSTON,JOHN T M-Man with a Purpose-Chig-1906-Donnelley & Sons-176p-Lakeside Pr-cl (f1) 15.00

JOHNSTON,MADELEINE-Death Casts a Lure-1938-CC-1st ed (s10) 15.00

JOHNSTON,MARY-Cease Firing-Bost-1912-Houghton,Mifflin-illus,N C Wyeth-1st ed (k3,weak hngs) 15.00

JOHNSTON,MARY-Cease Firing-Lond-1912-456p-illus-1st Brit ed (n3) 22.50

JOHNSTON,MARY-Long Roll-Bost-1911-683p+ads-pict cl,illus by N C Wyeth,e.p. maps-1st ed (n3) 27.50

JOHNSTON,MARY-Long Roll-Bost-1911-HMCo-1st ed (hh5) 15.00

JOHNSTON,MARY-To Have and To Hold-Bost-1900-HMCo-1st ed (hh5) 15.00

JOHNSTON,RICHARD M-Life of Alexander H Stephens-Phila-1878-Lippincott-619p-brwn cl-1st ed (b2,sl cocked,cov fleck) 50.00

JOHNSTON,S H F-History of the Cameronians 1689 to 1910-Aldershot-1957-308p-maps-1st ed (b7,f,dj) 100.00

JOHNSTON,S P-Horizons Unlimited-NY-(1941)-roy 8vo-vi,354p-cl,frntis,plts,text illus-1st ed (t2,dj) 45.00

JOHNSTON,S-Grim Reapers-NY-(1943)-Dutton-8vo-222p-illus cl,16p plts,2p maps,e.p. maps-1st ed (t2,dj) 35.00

JOHNSTON,S-Queen of the Flat Tops-NY-1942-8vo-280p-illus cl,frntis,10p plts,2 dblpg illus,e.p. maps-1st ed (t2,dj) 50.00

JOHNSTON,WILLIAM-Silent Music-NY-1974-Harper & Row-cl-1st ed (l8,f,dj) 16.50

JOHNSTONE'S,MRS.-...COOK BOOK OF TESTED RECIPES-Butte-(1911)-Miner Publ-154p-wht oilcl-Bitting 148 (o6,few recipes written in) 65.00

JOHNSTONE,G H-Asiatic Magnolias in Cultivation-Lond-1955-4to-160p-cl,14 col & 20 b&w plts,fldg map (jj7,ex-libr) 347.50

JOKELSON,PAUL-Sulphides-NY-1969-Galahad-4to-159p-blu bds,b&w & col illus (r10,f dj) 15.00

JOLAS,EUGENE-ED.-Transition Workshop-NY-(1949)-1st ed (m4) 20.00

JOLAS,EUGENE-ED.-Vertical-NY-(1941)-illus-ltd to 400c-1st ed (m4) 25.00

JOLAS,EUGENE-Planets and Angels-Mt.Vernon-1940-Cornell College-wrps-No.14 in chapbk ser-1st ed (w5,f) 35.00

JOLLY STITCHERS COOK BOOK-Delta-1918-Chronicle-135p-brn wrps (o6,tattrd wrps) 24.00

JONAS,W J-Jack Pine Historical Cookbook-Roscommon-1976-Tee Pee Restaurant-44p-wrps (z7) 17.50

JONES,ALICE DANNER-Poems-Canton-1927-51p-wrps (d1) 10.00

JONES,ARTHUR B-Salem Fire-Bost-1914-Gorham Pr-137p-gry cl-1st ed (h2,cov fade & soil) 30.00

JONES,ARTHUR G-Thornton Rogers Sampson, 1852 to 1915-1917-Richmond Pr-1st ed (a9) 30.00

JONES,B-Habits,Haunts & Anecdotes of the Moose-priv prtg-144p-illus,ltd to 1000c,unsigned-Deluxe ed (gg3,sl soil,lacks autg) 30.00

JONES,BARBARA-Design for Death-Indpls-(1967)-Bobbs Merrill-lg 8vo-304p-illus-1st US ed (gg5,f,dj) 35.00

JONES,BEN-Sam Jones, Lawyer-Norman-1947-218p-illus-1st ed (t7) 10.00

JONES,BESSIE Z-Harvard College Observatory-Cambridge-1971-Harvard Univ Pr-xvi+495p-red cl,56 illus-1st ed (j2,dj) 22.00

JONES,BRADLEY-Elements of Practical Aerodynamics-NY-1936-Wiley & Sons-8vo-vi,398p-cl,text illus-1st ed (t2) 40.00

JONES,BYRON Q-Practical Flying-NY-(1928)-Ronald Pr-210p-cl (m1) 15.00

JONES,C H-Africa-1970-Negro Univ-496p-illus,fldg map-rprnt of 1875 ed (bb3,f) 30.00

JONES,C-Opisthophorus or, the Man Who Walked Backward-Chig-(1909)-Conkey-199p-cl (a1) 25.00

JONES,CECIL K-Hispanic American Bibliographies-1922-tall 8vo-200p-tan cl,frntis port-1st ed (t10,f) 125.00

JONES,CHARLES R-Facsimile-NY-1951-xvi+422p-grn cl-2nd ed (c2,sp fade) 30.00

JONES,CHIEF CHARLES-Queesto-1981-Theytus Bks-8vo-125p-16p photos-1st ed (aa7,dj) 15.00*

JONES,CHRIS-Climbing in North America-Berkeley-1976-391p-1st ed (o10,f,dj) 28.00

JONES,DANIEL W-Forty Years Among the Indians-SLC-1890-blu cl,title stmpd in g on frnt cov & backstrip-Howes J207-1st ed (z1) 150.00

JONES,DAVE-Making and Repairing Western Saddles-NY-1982-Arco-4to-128p-illus,photos,drwngs (h9,dj) 25.00

JONES,DOUGLAS C-Court Martial of George Armstrong Custer-NY-(1976)-291p-1st ed (c4,f,dj) 17.50

JONES,DOUGLAS C-Treaty of Medicine Lodge-Norman-(1966)-237p-illus-1st ed (c7,f,dj) 40.00

JONES,E ALFRED-Loyalists of New Jersey-Newark-1927-346p-cl,port (aa6) 100.00

JONES,ELIZABETH O-Little Child-NY-1946-Viking-oblng 8vo-39p-cl bckd pict bds-1st ed (r3) 15.00

JONES,ERNEST-Essays in Applied Psychoanalysis-Lond-1951-Hogarth Pr-2 vols-grn cl-1st ed thus (a2,tn dj) 40.00

JONES,EVAN-American Food-NY-1975-Dutton-387p-1st ed (k6) 25.00

JONES,EVAN-Citadel in the Wilderness-NY-1966-Coward McCann-255p-illus-1st ed (gg4,dj) 15.00

JONES,EVAN-Citadel in the Wilderness-NY-1966-Coward McCann-8vo-255p-1st ed (z4,wn dj) 10.00

JONES,FAYETTE A-New Mexico Mines and Minerals-World's Fair Editon-Santa Fe-1904-349+(16)p-photos,map-1st of this ed (u7,lacks 1 bio sketch,sp wn) 85.00

JONES,FAYETTE-Old Mining Camps of New Mexico, 1854 to 1904-Santa Fe-1964-92p-frntis,illus-1st ed (t7,f,dj) 35.00

JONES,G WAYMAN-Alias Mr Death-NY-1932-Fiction League-1st ed (e4,dj) 25.00

JONES,GAYL-Corregidora-NY-(1975)-Random-auth 1st bk-1st ed (a10,f,dj) 45.00

JONES,GAYL-Eva's Man-NY-(1976)-Random-1st ed (a10,as new in dj) 35.00

JONES,GAYL-Eva's Man-NY-1976-Random-1st ed (y1,f,dj) 30.00

JONES,GAYL-White Rat-NY-(1977)-Random-8vo-178p-cl-1st ed (ee9,sl soil cov,dj) 20.00

JONES,GAYL-White Rat-NY-1977-1st ed (n5,f,f dj) 35.00

JONES,GUY-Peabody's Mermaid-NY-(1946)-Random-1st ed (e10,dj) 20.00

JONES,H CHAPMAN-Photography of To Day-Lond-1913-Seeley,Service-8vo-342p-cl,illus-1st ed (t3) 60.00

JONES,HOLWAY-John Muir and the Sierra Club-SF-1964-4to-207p-64 photos,7 maps-1st ed (p10,f,dj) 40.00

JONES,IDWAL-High Bonnet-1945-Prentice Hall-184p-prpl cl-1st prtg (q8,fray dj) 15.00

JONES,IDWAL-High Bonnet-NY-1945-Prentice Hall-184p-red bds (u6,dj) 20.00

JONES,IDWAL-Vines in the Sun-1949-Morrow-253p-gry cl,drwngs-1st ed (q8,dj) 20.00

JONES,J W-Salmon-NY-1959-8vo-285p-photos (m3,vf,dj) 17.50

JONES,J-Dirge for a Dog-1939-DD CC-1st ed (x7,rnfrcd dj) 30.00

JONES,JACK-Unfinished Journey-NY-1937-Oxford-8vo-303p-1st US ed (jj5,dj) 25.00

JONES,JAMES-From Here to Eternity-1952-Collins-1st Brit ed (kk6,sl tn dj) 100.00

JONES,JAMES-From Here to Eternity-Lond-1952-1st Brit ed (h5,f,dj) 75.00

JONES,JAMES-Ice Cream Headache-NY-(1968)-Delacorte-1st ed (e3,f,sl fade dj sp) 50.00

JONES,JAMES-Some Came Running-1957-Scribners-1st ed (kk6,dj) 75.00

JONES,JAMES-Some Came Running-1957-Scribners-1st ed (n9,chip & tn dj) 30.00

JONES,JAMES-Thin Red Line-NY-(1962)-Scribners-1st ed (x1,f,dj) 50.00

JONES,JAMES-Viet Journal-NY-1974-Delacorte-1st ed (h8,f,f dj) 50.00

JONES,JAMES-Whistle-NY-(1978)-1st trd ed (d5,as new in dj) 10.00

JONES,JAMES-Whistle-NY-(1978)-Delacorte-1st ed (x1,f,f dj) 30.00

JONES,JAMES-WW II-1975-G&D-col & b&w illus-1st ed (x2,vf,dj) 35.00

JONES,JENKIN L-An Artilleryman's Diary-np-1914-395p-illus-1st ed (c4,ex-libr) 105.00

JONES,JESSIE O-Secrets-1945-Viking-24p-col illus,E O Jones-1st ed (v8,dj chip & wn) 20.00

JONES,JOHN B-Rebel War Clerk's Diary-NY-1958-Sagamore-545p (o7,edge soil,dj) 25.00

JONES,JOHN P-John Paul Jones, Commemorative at Annapolis, April 24,1906-Wash-1907-GPO-4to-blu cl,t.e.g.,36 illus(2 col)-1st ed (p8,sl fade sp) 150.00

JONES,JOHN P-Life and Correspondence of John Paul Jones, Including His Narrative of the Campaign of the Liman-NY-1830-8vo-555p-frntis port (p8,rbckd,few dmpstnd pgs) 125.00

JONES,JOSEPH H-Outline of a Work of Grace in the Presbyterian Congregation at New Brunswick, NJ, During...1837-Phila-1839-148p (aa6) 75.00

JONES,KATHERINE M-Heroines of Dixie-NY-1955-403p-photos-1st ed (t7,ex-libr) 7.50

JONES,LEROI-Black Magic-Indpls-1969-1st ed (t5,dj) 35.00

JONES,LEROI-Dead Lecturer-NY-1964-Grove-wrps-iss simultaneously in cl-1st ed (w5,f) 15.00

JONES,LEROI-Dutchman and the Slave-NY-1964-Morrow-1st ed (q2,dj) 55.00

JONES,LEROI-Home-NY-1966-1st ed (o5,dj) 30.00

JONES,LEROI-Moderns-Lond-1965-MacGibbon & Kee-1st Brit ed (q1,drknd dj) 30.00

JONES,LEROI-Preface to a Twenty Volume Suicide Note...-NY-1961-Totem/Corinth-wrps-1st ed (e8) 40.00

JONES,LEROI-System of Dante's Hell-(1965)-Grove-1st ed (m9,f,dj) 45.00

JONES,LEROI-System of Dante's Hell-NY-(1965)-Grove-1st ed (bb2,dj rub) 60.00

JONES,LOUIS T-Indian Cultures of the Southwest-San Antonio-(1967)-73p-photos,map e.p.-1st ed (v7,f,dj) 10.00

JONES,MADISON-Buried Land-NY-1963-Viking-1st ed (v5,f,f dj) 35.00

JONES,MAJ EVAN R-Lincoln, Stanton and Grant-Lond-c1870-F Warne & Co-342p-3/4 grn lea,steel ports (dd4) 45.00

JONES,MARGARET B-Bastrop-Bastrop-1936-75p-blk wrps,photos-scarce-1st ed (a9) 145.00

JONES,MAX-Louis-1971-Little,Brown-1st Amer ed (o9,f,dj) 25.00

JONES,MOTHER-Autobiography of...-Chig-1925-Chas H Kerr-242p-blu cl,plts-1st ed (k2) 75.00

JONES,MRS AGNES-Kosse Its Past,Its People and Its Churches-Kosse-1970-First Methodist Ch-34p-wrps,photos-1st ed (w3,as new) 15.00

JONES,MRS C S-Household Elegancies-NY-1877-Williams-301p+8p cat,grn cl,illus-5th ed (q8,hng crack) 40.00

JONES,N E-Squirrel Hunters of Ohio-Cin-1898-8vo-pict cl-1st ed (kk7) 45.00

JONES,NARD-Evergreen Land-1947-Dodd,Mead-276p-illus-1st ed (r8,edgewn,bump,dj chip) 12.00

JONES,NARD-Great Command-Bost-(1959)-390p-photos-1st ed (u7,dj,pres) 20.00

JONES,NARD-Island-NY-(1948)-Sloane-1st ed (hh5,sl tn dj,autg) 10.00

JONES,OAKAH L,JR.-Pueblo Warriors & Spanish Conquest-Norman-(1966)-212p-photos,maps-1st ed (u7,f,dj) 25.00

JONES,OWEN-Sport of Shooting-Lond-1911-8vo-285p-photos (m3,vf) 25.00

JONES,PETER-TRANSL.-Collection of Chippeway & English Hyms for the Use of the Native Indians-NY-1847-Methodist-5"x3"-2nd ed (nn9) 75.00

JONES,RALPH F-Longhorns North of the Arkansas-San Antonio-(1969)-Naylor Co-371p-illus,map e.p.,1p brands-1st ed (bb4,dj) 60.00

JONES,RAYMOND F-Son of the Stars-Phila,Tor-(1952)-Winston-1st ed (e10,sl wn dj) 50.00

JONES,ROBERT K-Shudder Pulps-W Linn-(1975)-Fax-1st ed (j3,f,dj) 15.00

JONES,ROBERT-COMP.-Presidents' Own White House Cookbook-Chig-1973-Culinary Arts Inst-4to-112p-g dec ivory cl,col plts (q8,dj) 16.50

JONES,ROBERT-Orthopedic Surgery-NY-1926-699p-712 figs-1st Amer ed (g10) 95.00

JONES,ROY E-Basic Chicken Guide for the Small Flock Owner-NY-(1944)-Morrow-sm 8vo-191p wi index,illus-1st ed (t1,dj) 75.00

JONES,RUFUS-Haverford College-NY-1933-Macmillan-8vo-244p-1st ed (y6) 14.00

JONES,SHERIDAN R-Black Bass and Bass Craft-NY-1924-Macmillan-8vo-xxiv,206p-pict blu cl,g lttrng on sp,illus+15 photo plts-1st ed (u1,sl rub) 65.00

JONES,SHERIDAN-Bait Casting-NY-1927-16mo-86p-wrps,illus (m3,vf) 12.50

JONES,SHERIDAN-Black Bass & Bass Craft-NY-1924-8vo-205p-photos-1st ed (m3,f) 35.00

JONES,SHERIDAN-Fly Casting-NY-1923-16mo-88p-wrps,illus-1st ed (m3) 20.00

JONES,STAN-ED.-British Columbia Fishing Guide-Seattle-1977-4to-78p-photos,maps-1st ed (m3,vf) 12.00

JONES,STAN-ED.-Washington State Fishing Guide-Seattle-1967-8vo-232p-wrps,illus,photos-1st ed (m3,vf) 13.50

JONES,STEPHEN-Drifting-NY-(1971)-Macmillan-8vo-443p-sketches-1st ed (bb5,sl tn dj) 20.00

JONES,T L-From the Gold Mine to the Pulpit...in the Pacific Northwest...-Cin-(1904)-169p-dec cl,photos-Smith 5335-1st ed (w1) 125.00

JONES,THOMAS P-New Conversations on Chemistry...-Phila-1834-332p-lea-frntis,illus-Amer Imprnts 25160 (k1,sl wn) 35.00

JONES,VIOLA M-Peter and Gretchen of Old Nuremberg-Chig-1935-Albert Whitman-4to-96p-cl wi full pasteon,col & b&w illus,H Sewell-1st ed (s3,dj chip & fade) 45.00

JONES,VIRGIL C-Hatfields and McCoys-Chapel Hill-1948-293p-photos,illus-Six Guns #1199-1st ed (t7,f) 32.50

JONES,VIRGIL C-Hatfields and the McCoys-Chapel Hill-(1948)-UNC Pr-xvi+293p-red cl,illus-1st ed (b2,dj wn,chip) 25.00

JONES,VIRGIL-Eight Hours Before Richmond-NY-1957-H Holt-180p-e.p.maps,illus (o7,dj) 30.00

JONES,W F-Memories of...A Deputy Marshall of the Indian Territory-Tulsa-1937-8vo-40p-orig soft wrps,photos-1st ed (aa3,sl tan,spot) 65.00

JONES,W NORTHEY-History of St.Peter's Church in Perth Amboy...-(Perth Amboy)-(1924)-519p-cl,plts (aa6) 125.00

JONES,WILLIAM C-ET AL-Mile High Trolleys-Golden-1965-1st ed (n4,f,dj) 20.00

JONES,WILLIAM-Finger Ring Lore-Lond-1890-Chatto & Windus,Piccdly-xvi,567p+32p publ list,g dec blu cov,illus-scarce-2nd ed,rvsd & enlgd (u5) 185.00

JONES,WILLIAM-Texas History Carved in Stone-Houston-(1958)-Monument Publ-430p-illus-scarce-1st ed (f9,sl tn & spot dj) 40.00

JONG,ERICA-Four Visions of America-1977-Capra-foil dj-1st ed (s9,sl scuff dj) 20.00

JONG,ERICA-How To Save Your Own Life-NY-(1977)-Holt-1st ed (h3,f,dj) 20.00

JONG,ERICA-Loveroot-NY-(1975)-HRW-8vo-114p-1st ed (ee5,f,f dj) 10.00

JOOS,LOUIS D C-Through the Sahara to the Congo-Lond,Glasgow-1961-Blackie-8vo-200p-orig cl,16 plts-1st ed (bb6,dj) 12.00

JORDAN,ALICE M-From Rollo to Tom Sawyer, and Other Papers-Bost-(1948)-Horn Bks-12mo-x,160p-grn cl-1st ed (w2,chip dj) 25.00

JORDAN,D S-American Food & Game Fishes-NY-1902-4to-543p-col plts,photos-1st ed (m3,spot cov) 20.00

JORDAN,D S-Manual of the Vertebrates of Northern U.S.-Chig-1878(1884)-8vo-406p-cl wi lea sp-4th ed (y8,lacks part sp) 18.50

JORDAN,DAVID S-Days of a Man-Yonkers On Hudson-1922-8vo-2 vols,photos (m3,f) 60.00

JORDAN,DAVID S-ED.-Seal & Salmon Fisheries & General Resources of Alaska-1898-GPO-4 vols-red pebble mor,a.e. mrbld,,mrbld e.p.,illus,fldg maps,8 chromoliths (d7,f) 550.00

JORDAN,DAVID S-Foot Notes to Evolution-NY-1898-D Appleton-xviii+392p-blu cl,5 plts,28 text figs-1st ed (g2,cov soil,bumps) 35.00

JORDAN,E L-Hammond's Sports Atlas of America-New Jersey-1956-folio-63p-maps (m3,f,chip dj) 12.50

JORDAN,FRED-Fool's Gold-NY-1960-255p-illus-1st ed (t7,dj) 15.00

JORDAN,GRACE-Home Below Hell's Canyon-NY-1954-243p-frntis,map e.p. (t7,f,dj,autg) 10.00

JORDAN,H J-Elephants & Ivory-NY-1956-250p-photos (gg3,cov spot) 40.00

JORDAN,JOHN A-Elephants and Ivory-NY-(1956)-Rinehart-8vo-250p-1st ed (cc5,dj) 40.00

JORDAN,JOHN E-ED.-Robert Louis Stevenson's Silverado Journal-SF-1954-BC of Cal/Grabhorn Pr-4to-95p-cl-ltd to 400c (mm7,f,dj) 125.00

JORDAN,JUNE-Kimako's Story-1981-Houghton Mifflin-1st ed (p9,vf,dj) 15.00

JORDAN,MILDRED-Distelfink Country of the Pennsylvania Dutch-NY-1978-Crown-xxx,258p-illus-1st ed (o2,dj) 15.00

JORDAN,MRS D M-Rosemary Leaves-Cin-1873-Robt Clarke & Co-158p-cl (j1) 15.00

JORDAN,PAT-False Spring-1975-Dodd,Mead-1st ed (s8,f,dj) 25.00

JORDAN,PAT-Suitors of Spring-1973-Dodd Mead (r7,dj) 15.00

JORDAN,PAT-Suitors of Spring-1973-Dodd,Mead-1st ed (s8,f,dj) 17.50

JORDAN,PHILIP-People's Health-St.Paul-1953-524p-1st ed (dd3,dj) 20.00

JORDAN,ROBERT S-Just Between Us District Managers-Kalamazoo-1964-Sequoia Pr-74p-cl (z7,f,dj) 22.50

JORDAN,THOMAS-Campaigns of Lt Gen N B Forrest and of Forrest's Cavalry-Dayton-1977-Morningside Bkshp-704p-e.p. maps-no index in this ed (o7,f) 30.00

JORDAN,WHITMAN-Feeding of Animals-NY-1908-Macmillan-450p-cl-5th ed (x6) 12.00

JORDAN,WILLIAM L-Ocean-Lond-1873-Longmans,Green-xxvi+344p+ads-14 plts (d2,cov edge sl rub) 60.00

JORDAN-SMITH,PAUL-For the Love of Books-NY-1934-Oxford-1st ed (w1,f,dj) 25.00

JORDANOFF,ASSEN-Jordanoff's Illustrated Aviation Dictionary-NY,Lond-(1942)-Harper & Bros-415p-cl-1st ed so stated (m1,sl wn dj) 15.00

JORDON,JED-Fool's Gold-NY-(1960)-John Day-255p-drwngs-1st ed (nn6,sl wn dj) 15.00

JORGENSEN,JOHANNES-Saint Bridget of Sweden-NY-(1954)-Longmans Green-8vo-2 vols-1st US ed (jj5,chip dj) 25.00

JORGENSEN,P-Dressing Flies for Fresh & Salt Water-NY-1973-192p-photos,illus(some col) (gg3,f,dj) 45.00

JORGENSEN,POUL-Dressing Flies for Fresh & Salt Water-Rockville Cntr-1973-4to-192p-photos-1st ed (m3,fray dj) 22.50

JORGENSEN,POUL-Modern Fly Dressings for the Practical Angler-NY-1976-4to-224p-photos-1st ed (m3,dj) 17.50

JOSEPH,ISYA-Devil Worship-Bost-1919-Richard G Badger-cl-rare-1st ed (n8,dj) 75.00

JOSEPHSON,M-Empire of the Air-NY-(1944)-8vo-xiv,236p-cl,plts,maps-1st ed (s2,sl chip dj) 45.00

JOSEPHSON,MATTHEW-Life Among the Surrealists-NY-1962-Holt-1st ed (v5,f,rprd dj) 35.00

JOSEPHSON,MATTHEW-Sidney Hillman-GC-1952-Dbldy-701p-1st ed (r1) 15.00

JOSEPHY,ALVIN M,JR.-Now That the Buffalo's Gone-NY-1982-Knopf-300p-1st ed (dd4,dj) 25.00

JOSEPHY,ALVIN-Nez Perce & the Opening of the Northwest-New Haven,Lond-1965-lg 8vo-705p+24 illus,maps-Yale Wstrn Amer Ser #10-1st ed (d7,sl tn dj) 75.00

JOSHI,S T-H D Lovecraft and Lovecraft Criticism-Kent-1981-KSU Pr-1st ed (x9,f) 15.00

JOUBERT,PHILIP-Rocket-NY-(1957)-Philos Libr-8vo-190p-22 illus-1st US ed (gg5,dj) 15.00

JOUGHIN,G LOUIS-Legacy of Sacco and Vanzetti-NY-1948-Harcourt,Brace-xviii+598p-grn cl-1st ed (k2,edge-wn dj) 30.00

JOWITT,ROBERT E-Desire of Tramcars-Lond-1969-200p-1st ed (n4,f,dj) 22.00

JOY,CHARLES R-Music in the Life of Albert Schweitzer-NY-1951-Harper & Bros-cl,frntis,illus-1st ed (n8) 15.00

JOYCE,COL JOHN A-Jewels of Memory-Wash D.C.-1896-Gibson Bros-245p-frntis port,illus-Dorn II 369-2nd ed (n7) 50.00

JOYCE,J-Story of Passenger Transport in Britain-Lond-1967-208p-1st ed (n4,f,dj) 24.00

JOYCE,JAMES-Anna Livia Plurabelle-NY-1928-Crosby Gaige-sm 8vo-g dec brwn cl-ltd to 800c,autg-1st ed (ll10,f) 1,100.00

JOYCE,JAMES-Collected Poems-NY-1936-Black Sun Pr-sm 8vo-wht bds lettrd in blu,ltd to 800c,nbrd-1st ed (x3) 550.00

JOYCE,JAMES-Critical Writings-NY-1959-Viking-1st ed (bb2,f,dj) 75.00

JOYCE,JAMES-Exiles-Lond-1918-Grant Richards-1st ed (l3,brwnd pastedwn,ep,sp labl) 125.00

JOYCE,JAMES-Finnegans Wake-Lond-1939-Faber & Faber-ltd to 425c,autg-1st ed (l9,f,box sl soil) 5,000.00

JOYCE,JAMES-Giacomo Joyce-NY-(1968)-Viking-ltd to one prtg-1st ed (b5,as new in box) 25.00

JOYCE,JAMES-Haveth Childers Everywhere-Lond-(1931)-1st Brit ed (bb10,glassine dj) 75.00

JOYCE,JAMES-Letters of...-NY-1957-Viking-1st ed (r2,f,sl chip dj) 50.00

JOYCE,JAMES-Letters-NY-1957-Viking-1st ed (z3,f,dj) 20.00

JOYCE,JAMES-Portrait of the Artist as a Young Man-NY-1916-Huebsch-Slocum & Cahoon 11-1st ed (hh4) 1,000.00

JOYCE,JAMES-Stephen Hero-NY-1944-New Directions-1st ed (q2,erasure mrks,dj chip) 95.00

JOYCE,JAMES-Tales Told of Shem and Shaun-Paris-(1929)-Black Sun Pr-ltd to 500c-1st ed (hh4,f,sl wn box) 1,000.00

JOYCE,JAMES-Two Tales of Shem and Shaun-Lond-1932-1st Brit ed (t5,dj) 75.00

JOYCE,JAMES-Ulysses-NY-(1934)-Random-1st Amer ed (y2,f,dj) 450.00

JOYCE,JAMES-Ulysses-NY-(1934)-Random-thk 8vo-lt tan linen cl-1st Amer ed (y4) 85.00

JOYCE,JAMES-Ulysses-NY-1934-Random-linen type cl stmpd in blk & red-3rd prtg (bb2,dj chip & sp drknd) 50.00

JOYCE,STANISLAUS-My Brother's Keeper-NY-1958-1st ed (r2,f,sl rub dj) 25.00

JOYCE,THOMAS M-South American Archaeology-Lond-1912-Macmillan-8vo-xvi,292p-blu cl,illus,26 plts,fldg map-scarce-1st ed (y4,hng weak) 50.00

JUDD,A N-Campaigning Against the Sioux-NY-1973-Sol Lewis-45p-drwngs-ltd to 500c (bb4) 25.00

JUDD,BERNICE-Voyages to Hawaii Before 1860-Honolulu-1974-U Pr of Hawaii-129p-dec papr over bds-engld & ed by H Y Lind (nn1) 45.00

JUDD,LAURA F-Honolulu-Chig-1966-Donnelley & Sons-frntis,illus,map (ff4) 20.00

JUDD,LAURA F-Honolulu-Chig-1966-Lakeside Pr-12mo-rprnt (nn1,f) 30.00

JUDD,LAURA F-Honolulu-Honolulu-1928-Honolulu Star Bulletin-8vo-xii,209p-red cl-rprnt (p8,f,dj) 75.00

JUDD,LAURA F-Honolulu-NY-c.1880-Randolph & Co-xiv,258p,index-brwn cl wi g titles & sp dec,floral e.p. (nn1,sl wn cov) 200.00

JUDD,N M-Men Met Along the Trail-1968-U of Okla-162p-photos-1st ed (bb3,f,dj) 16.00

JUDD,SYLVESTER D-Relation of Sparrows to Agriculture-1901-GPO-98p-wrps,19 figs,4 plts (x5,sl discol wrps) 12.00

JUDSON,HELEN-Butterick Cook Book-1911-Butterick (v6,cov wn,soil) 12.00

JUDSON,ISABELLA F-ED.-Cyrus W Field-NY-1896-Harper & Bros-(viii)+332p+ads-blu cl-1st ed (a2) 35.00

JUDSON,JEANNE-Legacy of Redfern-1968-Avalon-1st ed (s10,dj) 12.50

JUDSON,KATHERINE B-Myths & Legends of the Pacific NW-Chig-1910-McClurg-photos-scarce-1st ed (nn9,edgewn) 25.00

JUDSON,KATHERINE B-Myths and Legends of British North America-Chig-1917-McClurg-8vo-211p-grn cl,photo laid on frnt bd,18p photos-1st ed (bb7,sl spot cl) 35.00*

JUDSON,PHOEBE G-Pioneer's Search for an Ideal Home-Tacoma-1966-Hist Soc-207p-illus-Tweney #37-rprnt (c7) 40.00

JUDSON,SYLVIA S-For Gardens and Other Places-Chig-(1967)-Regnery-4to-unpgd-85 plts-1st ed (gg5,f,dj) 15.00

JUGLAR,CLEMENT-Brief History of Panics and Their Periodical Occurrence in the United States...-NY,Lond-1893-150p-cl (g1) 20.00

JULLIAN,P-Dreamers of Decadence-NY-1971-149 illus(incl 16 col)-1st ed (h10,sl tn dj) 45.00

JUNG,C G-Flying Saucers-Lond-(1959)-sm 8vo-xiv,184p-cl,frntis,plts-1st ed (t2) 25.00

JUNG,C G-Psychology of the Unconscious-NY-1916-Moffat,Yard-lv+566p-red cl,plts-1st ed in Engl (a2,sp fade,sl soil cov) 90.00

JUNG,C G-Studies in Word Association-NY-1919-Moffat,Yard & Co-lg 8vo-x+575p-1st Amer ed (c2,sp fade,sl soil cov) 85.00

JUNG,C G-Undiscovered Self-1958-Atlantic-Little,Brown-1st Amer ed (t9,f,dj sl chip & tn) 45.00

JUNIOR LEAGUE COOK BOOK-(Roanoak)-nd(ca.1930's)-Walters Prtg & Mfg-152p-wrps (n6,sunned wrps) 32.00

JUNKIN,REV D X-Life of Winfield Scott Hancock-NY-1880-Appleton-398p-frntis,illus (o7) 20.00

JUNOT,MADAME-Memoirs of...-NY-1883-3 vols-3/4 red lea,mrbld bds & e.p.,extra illus wi engrvd plts (b7) 350.00

JUST A COOKBOOK-Chig-(1902)-G M Clark,Amer Stove Co-45p-red illus wrps,illus (n6,sl spot wrps) 22.00

JUST,WARD-Congressman Who Loved Flaubert-Bost-(1973)-Atlanta/Little,Brown-1st ed (hh5,f,dj) 10.00

JUST,WARD-Family Trust-Bost-1978-1st ed (q5,dj) 20.00

JUST,WARD-Honor Power Riches Fame and the Love of Women-NY-1979-1st ed (q5,dj) 12.50

JUST,WARD-Military Men-NY-1970-1st ed (n5,f,dj) 25.00

JUST,WARD-Nicholson at Large-Bost-1975-1st ed (q5,dj) 20.00

JUST,WARD-Soldier of the Revolution-NY-1970-1st ed (r5,f,dj) 35.00

JUST,WARD-Stringer-Bost-1974-1st ed (q5,f,dj) 20.00

JUST,WARD-To What End-Bost-1968-HMCo-auth 1st bk-1st ed (c8,f,sl chip dj) 45.00

JUST,WARD-To What End-Bost-1968-Houghton Mifflin-auth 1st bk-1st ed (q2,dj sp sl fade) 35.00

JUSTEMA,WM-Pattern-Lond-1976-folio-all illus-1st ed (h10,dj) 40.00

KABOTIE,FRED-Fred Kabotie: Hopi Indian Artist-Flagstaff-(1977)-140p-dbl col,photos,33 col paintings-1st ed (u7,f,dj) 40.00

KADANS,JOSEPH M-Encyclopedia of Fruits, Vegetables, Nuts and Seeds for Healthful Living-W Nyack-(1973)-Parker Publ-215p-grn cl-1st prtg (q8,dj) 15.00

KAEL,PAULINE-Reeling-Bost,Tor-(1976)-Little,Brown-1st ed (bb1,as new in dj) 25.00

KAESE,HAROLD-Boston Braves-1948-Putnam-1st ed (r7,f,dj) 60.00

KAESE,HAROLD-Boston Braves-1948-Putnam-photos-1st ed (s8,f,dj) 70.00

KAESE,HAROLD-Milwaukee Braves-1954-Putnam-photos-1st ed (s8,f,dj) 80.00

KAFKA,FRANZ-Trial-Lond-1937-Gollancz-sm 8vo-blu cl,yel dj-transl by E & W Muir-rare-1st Brit ed (ll10,sl fade,dj sp sl tan) 1,500.00

KAGAN,SOLOMON-Contributions of Early Jews to American Medicine-Bost-1934-63p-1st ed (dd3) 50.00

KAHANE,JACK-Memoirs of a Booklegger-Lond-(1939)-Michael Joseph Ltd-8vo-287p-cl-scarce-1st ed (w2,cov fade,dj chip) 65.00

KAHLENBERG,MARY H-Navajo Blanket-LA-(1972)-Praeger Publ-112p-pict wrps,col illus-1st ed (gg4) 20.00

KAHLER,DR.PETER-Dress and Care of the Feet-NY-1910-auth-12mo-48p-dec blu cl,illus-rprnt of 1891 ed (s1,f) 35.00

KAHLO,DOROTHY M-History of the Police and Fire Departments of the City of Seattle-Seattle-1907-Lumberman's Prtg Co-292p-red cl,photos,ports-rare-Smith 5377-1st ed (w1,f) 350.00

KAHN,ARTHUR-Brownstone-NY-1953-Independence-370p-wrps (r1,sp drknd,cov wn) 12.00

KAHN,E J-Voice-NY-(1947)-Harper-1st ed (w1,f,f dj) 25.00

KAHN,ELY J-Design in Art & Industry-NY-1935-illus-1st ed (h10) 85.00

KAHN,FRITZ-Man in Structure and Function-NY-1943-Knopf-8vo-2 vols-illus-1st US ed (bb5,vf,f dj,box) 60.00

KAHN,JAMES-Umpire Story-1953-Putnam-1st ed (ff2,dj) 75.00

KAHN,JOAN-ED.-Some Things Fierce and Fatal-NY-1971-Harper-1st ed (j4,f,dj) 12.50

KAHN,LIAQUAT ALI-Pakistan, The Heart of Asia-Cambridge-1950-Harvard U Pr-8vo-151p-red cl-1st ed (ll1,dj) 15.00

KAHN,R L-Serum Diagnosis of Syphilis by Precipitation-Balt-1925-Williams & Wilkins-xii+237p+ads-grn cl-1st ed (a2,tape rnfrcd dj) 55.00

KAHN,ROGER-Boys of Summer-1972-H & R-1st ed (x2,f,dj) 30.00

KAHN,ROGER-Boys of Summer-1972-Harper & Row-1st ed (s7,dj) 15.00

KAHN,ROGER-How the Weather Was-NY et al-(1973)-Harper & Row-1st ed (b5,as new in dj) 15.00

KAHN,ROGER-Season in the Sun-1977-Harper & Row-photos-1st ed (s8,f,dj) 12.50

KAHN,ROGER-Season in the Sun-NY-(1977)-175p-bds-1st ed so stated (n1,f,dj) 15.00

KAIN,CONRAD-Where the Clouds Can Go-NY-1935-Amer Alpine Club-456p-1st ed (p10,f) 120.00

KAJENCKI,COL FRANCIS C-Stars on Many a Battlefield-Rutherford-(1980)-280p-illus,maps-1st ed (n3,dj) 25.00

KALISH,STANLEY E-Picture Editing-NY-1951-Rinehart-207p-illus-1st ed (cc9,dj tn & chip) 30.00

KALLIR,OTTO-Grandma Moses-NY-(1973)-Abrams-oblng folio-cl,135 col plts-1st ed (oo6,dj) 90.00

KALLIR,OTTO-Grandma Moses-NY-1973-Abrams-oblng 4to-357p-wht cl sp,grn bds,b&w & col illus (r10,f dj) 45.00

KALM,P-Travels into North America-1972-Imprnt Soc-514p-col frntis,plts,fldg panorama & maps-ltd to 1950c (bb3,f,sl rub box) 85.00

KALM,PETER-Peter Kalm's Travels in North America-NY-1937-Wilson Erickson-2 vols-cl,illus,fldg map (z1,wn box) 100.00

KALMAR-RUBY SONG BOOK-NY-(1936)-Random-sm folio-1st ed (w1,f,dj) 250.00

KALMBACH,A C-COMP.-Model Railroader Cyclopedia 1944-Milw-1943-184p+25 plts-5th ed (n4) 37.50

KALMBACH,A C-Model Railroader Cyclopedia-1949-Kalmbach-8vo-184p+27 fldg schematics-6th ed (nn7,sl rub cl) 22.00

KALMBACH,A C-Railroad Panorama-Milw-1944-228p-1st ed (n4) 20.00

KALTENBORN EDITS THE NEWS...-NY-(1937)-Mod Age Bks-sm 8vo-scarce hdbk iss-(ghost writ by Mary McCarthy,her 1st bk)-1st ed (s1,f,dj) 75.00

KALTENBORN,H V-Kaltenborn Edits the News-NY-1937-Modern Age-simultaneous iss wi pbk ed,Mary McCarthy's first bk-1st ed (w1,f,dj) 100.00

KAMBER,GERALD-Max Jacob and the Poetics of Cubism-Balt-1971-Johns Hopkins-1st ed (t4,f,f dj) 15.00

KAMEKURA,YUSAKU-Graphic Design of...-NY,Tokyo-1973-Weatherhill/B Shuppan Sha-sq 8vo-188p-cl-orig publ in Japanese-1st ed (q3,dj) 85.00

KAMINSKY,STUART M-You Bet Your Life-NY-1978-St.Martin's-1st ed (d4,f,dj) 75.00

KAMINSKY,STUART-Bullet For a Star-Lond-1981-Severn-1st Brit ed (q4,f,dj) 30.00

KAMINSKY,STUART-Catch a Falling Clown-NY-1981-St.Martin's-1st ed (e4,f,dj) 20.00

KAMINSKY,STUART-High Midnight-NY-1981-St.Martin's-1st ed (d4,f,dj) 25.00

KAMINSKY,STUART-Murder on the Yellow Brick Road-NY-1977-St.Martin's-1st ed (d4,dj) 50.00

KAMINSKY,STUART-Never Cross a Vampire-NY-1980-St.Martin's-1st ed (e4,dj) 22.50

KAMM,MINNIE W-Old Time Herbs for Northern Gardens-Bost-1938-Little,Brown-256p-32 illus-1st ed (x6,f,dj chip,wn) 30.00

KAMMER,JERRY-Second Long Walk-Albuq-1980-239p-photos,maps-1st ed (t7,f,dj) 15.00

KAMSTRA,JERRY-Frisco Kid-NY-1975-1st ed (x8,dj) 20.00

KAMSTRA,JERRY-Frisco Kid-NY-1975-Harper-1st ed (oo2,f,dj) 25.00

KANDEL,LENORE-Love Book-SF-1966-wrps-1st ed (x8,f) 45.00

KANDER,MRS SIMON-Settlement Cook Book-Milw-1949-623p-pict cl-29th ed (c1) 15.00

KANDER,MRS SIMON-Settlement Cookbook-Milw-1930-Settlement Cook Book Co-624p-bds-Bitting 253,4-18th ed (n6,dj pasted to bds) 40.00

KANDINSKY,WASSILY-Art of Spiritual Harmony-Lond-1914-bds-1st Engl transl (kk4,drknd,edge rub,sl fox) 185.00

KANE,ELISHA K-Arctic Explorations in the Years 1853 to 55-1856-Childs & Peterson-2 vols-engrvngs,fldg map-1st ed,2nd issue (u8,sp fray,sl fox,sl tn map) 90.00

KANE,ELISHA K-Arctic Explorations: The Second Grinnell Expedition in Search of Sir John Franklin,1853, 54, 55-Phila-1857-2 vols-3/4 calf over mrbld bds,col lea sp labls-2nd ed (w1) 150.00

KANE,GEORGE L-Seal Upon My Heart-Mlwk-(1957)-170p-cl,20 sketches (d1,dj) 12.50

KANE,HARNETT T-ED.-Romantic South-NY-(1961)-385p-illus-1st ed (c4,dj wn) 25.00

KANE,HARNETT T-Spies for the Blue and Gray-GC-1954-Hanover Hs-1st ed (o7) 15.00

KANE,JOHN-Sky Hooks-Phila-(1938)-Lippincott-4to-cl-scarce-1st ed (oo6,dj) 150.00

KANE,PAUL-Wanderings of an Artist-Edmonton-1968-Hurtig-8vo-lxiv,329p-fldg frntis,illus-rprnt of 1859 orig (cc7,dj) 50.00*

KANE,THOMAS L-Friend of the Mormons-SF-1937-Gelber-Lilienthal-xii+80p-wht bds,ltd to 500c,prntd at Grabhorn Pr-1st ed (k2,sl fade & wn cov) 65.00

KANER,H-People of the Twilight-Llandudno-1946-Kaner Publ-1st ed (p3,sl chip dj) 15.00

KANIN,GARSON-Blow Up a Storm-NY-1959-Random-1st ed (v5,f,dj) 20.00

KANNER,LEO-Folklore of the Teeth-NY-1928-Macmillan-1st ed (w5,f) 75.00

KANNER,LEO-Folklore of the Teeth-NY-1936-316p (dd3) 45.00

KANNIK,PREBEN-Military Uniforms in Color...-NY-(1968)-278p-cl,128p col illus by auth (c1,sl wn dj) 15.00

KANSAS APPLE-Topeka-1898-229p-wrps,illus (v8,sl chip sp,sun,pgs aging) 25.00

KANSAS CORRAL-Prairie Scout, Vol.I-Abilene-1973-125p-pict cl,photos-1st ed (t7,f) 22.50

KANSAS CORRAL-Prairie Scout, Vol.II-Abilene-1974-136p-pict cl,frntis,photos-1st ed (t7,f) 22.50

KANSAS CORRAL-Prairie Scout, Vol.III-Abilene-1975-198p-pict cl,col frntis by N C Wyeth,photos,illus-1st ed (t7,f) 22.50

KANSAS-Proceedings of the M.W. Grand Lodge of the State of...-Leavenworth-1879-169p-pict wrps-scarce-1st ed (t7) 20.00

KANSAS-TERRITORIAL...-Lawrence-1954-U of Kansas-205p-wrps,maps,tbls-1st ed (ee4) 20.00

KANTOR,MACKINLAY-Arouse and Beware-NY-1936-Coward McCann-1st ed (z2,f dj) 65.00

KANTOR,MACKINLAY-El Goes South-NY-1930-Coward McCann-scarce-1st ed (z2,fox e.p.,dj chip) 125.00

KANTOR,MACKINLAY-Gentle Annie-NY-(1942)-Coward-McCann-1st ed (b10,f dj) 25.00

KANTOR,MACKINLAY-Lobo-Cleve,NY-(1957)-illus,I Layne-1st ed (h5,dj) 12.50

KANTOR,MACKINLAY-Noise of their Wings-NY-1938-Coward McCann-1st ed (z2,f,dj) 50.00

KANTOR,MACKINLAY-Wicked Water-NY-1948-Random-1st ed (z2,f,f dj) 50.00

KAPELNER,ALAN-Lonely Boy Blues-NY-1944-Scribner-auth 1st bk-1st ed (hh5,f,dj) 15.00

KAPLAN,HERBERT-Russia and the Outbreak of the Seven Years' War-Berkeley-1968-165p-1st ed (b7,f,dj) 40.00

KAPLAN,JOHANNA-O My America-NY et al-(1980)-Harper & Row-1st ed (b5,as new in dj) 17.50

KAPLAN,JOHANNA-Other People's Lives-NY-1975-Knopf-auth 1st bk-1st ed (bb1,as new in dj) 30.00

KAPLAN,LEE Z-American Saddle Horses in South Africa-Capetown-1974-folio-456p-photos-ltd to 500c (f10) 795.00

KAPLAN,MOISE N-Big Game Angler's Paradise-NY-1937-8vo-400p-illus (m3,hngs cracked) 20.00

KAPLAN,MOISE N-Big Game Fishermen's Paradise-Tallahassee-1936-priv prntd-8vo-324p-photos,fldg map-scarce-1st ed (m3) 95.00

KAPPEL,A W-British and European Butterflies and Moths-Lond,NY-nd(1896)-4to-273p-dec red cl,a.e.g.,30 chromolitho plts (bb3,new e.p.,sp drknd,sl soil 250.00

KAPPEL,PHILIP-Louisiana Gallery, the River Country and New Orleans-NY-1950-145p-73p illus-1st ed (pp4,pres,dj tn & fray) 25.00

KARAN,PRAYUMNA P-Changing Face of Tibet-Lexington-1976-Univ Pr of Ky-vii,114p-tan cl,map e.p.,photos (ll1,dj) 30.00

KARAS,NICHOLAS-Complete Book of the Striped Bass-NY-1974-8vo-367p-photos,illus (m3,vf,dj) 11.50

KARDEC,ALLAN-Book on Mediums-NY-1970-Samuel Weiser-cl-1st ed thus (n8,vf,dj) 25.00

KARIG,WALTER-Battle Report, Atlantic War-NY-1946-Farrar,Rinehart-8vo-558p-gry cl,80 photos,10 illus/map-1st ed (gg6) 10.00

KARLING,JOHN-Cytology of Chytridiales-1937-Torrey Botanical Cl-92p+plts (x6) 18.00

KARLINS,MARVIN-Gomorrah-GC-1974-Dbldy-1st ed (h3,f,dj) 10.00

KARLSTROM,PAUL J-Louis Michel Eilshemius-NY-(1978)-Abrams-folio-cl-1st ed (oo6,dj) 75.00

KARNES,THOMAS L-William Gilpin: Western Nationalist-1970-U of TX Pr-8vo-383p-frntis port,illus,map-1st ed (aa3,dj) 30.00

KARNS,HARRY J-Luiz De Tierra Incognita-Tucson-1954-303p-photos,maps,fldg map rear pckt-1st publ English transl (t7,f,dj) 30.00

KARNS,HARRY J-TRANSL.-Unknown Arizona and Sonora, 1693 to 1721-Tucson-1954-Ariz Silhouettes-303p-illus,map rear pckt-ltd to 1500c,nbrd (cc4,dj) 60.00

KAROLEVITZ,ROBERT F-Doctors of the Old West-Seattle-(1967)-Superior Publ-4to-192p-yel cl,illus-1st ed (k2,dj) 25.00

KAROLEVITZ,ROBERT-Doctors of the Old West-(1967)-Superior-192p-illus-1st ed (r8,f dj) 30.00

KAROLEVITZ,ROBERT-Newspapering in the Old West-(1965)-Superior-191p-illus-Six Guns #1210-1st ed (r8,dj edgewn,sl chip) 30.00

KARR,JEAN-Zane Grey Man of the West-1949-G&D-12mo-229p (m3,f) 25.00

KARR,JEAN-Zane Grey Man of the West-Lond-1951-218p-1st Brit ed (m3) 30.00

KARSH,YOUSUF-Faces of Destiny-Chig-1946-photos,auth,1st bk-1st US ed (t5,chip dj) 50.00

KARSH,YOUSUF-Faces of Our Time-Tor-1971-U of Tor Pr-4to-202p-cl,photos-1st ed (t3,dj) 50.00

KARSH,YOUSUF-In Search of Greatness-NY-1962-Knopf-210p-17 photos-1st ed (cc9,f,dj) 50.00

KARSH,YOUSUF-Portraits of Greatness-1959-U of Tor Pr-4to-207p-orig card box,96p photos-1st ed (aa7,hng weak,dj,box) 120.00*

KARST,GENE-Who's Who in Professional Baseball-1973-Arlington Hs-1st ed (s8,f,f dj) 35.00

KASSLER,ELIZABETH B-Modern Gardens and the Landscape-NY-1964-MOMA/Dbldy-sm sq 4to-96p-cl,135 illus(6 col)-1st ed (cc10,dj) 65.00

KASSON TOWNSHIP HERITAGE GROUP-Remembering Yesterday-np-nd(ca.1970's?)-4to-82p-wrps (z7) 25.00

KASTNER,ERICH-Annaluise and Anton-NY-1933-Dodd,Mead-illus by W Trier-1st US ed (pp10,dj) 40.00

KASTNER,ERICH-Emil and the Three Twins-Lond-(1935)-Cape-illus by W Trier-1st Brit ed (pp10,fade dj) 40.00

KASTNER,J-Species of Eternity-1977-Knopf-350p-92 illus(incl 20 col)-1st ed (bb3,dj) 20.00

KASTNER,JOSEPH-Species of Eternity-NY-1977-Knopf-350p-cl (x6,dj) 15.00

KASTON,B J-How to Know the Spiders-1953-Brown-220p-552 figs-1st ed (bb3,f) 20.00

KATAYAMA,SEN-Labor Movement in Japan-Chig-(1918)-Kerr-sm 8vo-147p-orng cl-1st ed (s1) 65.00

KATHARINE-Letters from an Oregon Ranch-Chig-1905-McClurg-8vo-212p-12 illus-1st ed (cc5) 25.00

KATZ,FRANK J-Newington Moraine:Maine, New Hampshire & Massachusetts-Wash D.C.-1917-Dept of Interior-29p-papr wrps,photos,2 maps-Prof Papr 108-B (o2) 15.00

KATZ,STEVE-Creamy & Delicious-NY-1970-Random-1st ed (z9,dj) 10.00

KATZ,STEVE-Saw-NY-1972-Knopf-glossy papr bds,cov illus by Walotsky,iss w/o dj-1st ed (y1,f) 35.00

KATZENBERG,DENA S-And Eagles Sweep Across the Sky-Balt-(1977)-oblng-152p-wrps,dbl col,col photos,map-1st ed (v7,f) 20.00

KAUFFELD,CARL-Snakes and Snake Hunting-1957-Hanover Hs-266p-photos-1st ed (bb3,f,dj) 45.00

KAUFFELD,CARL-Snakes and Snake Hunting-GC-(1957)-Hanover House-8vo-266p-photos-1st ed (aa5,dj) 20.00

KAUFFER,E MCKNIGHT-ED.-Art of the Poster-NY-1925-Boni-lg 4to-col illus (h10,edges sl rub) 350.00

KAUFFMAN,HENRY J-Colonial Silversmith-NY-1969-Galahad Bks-176p-dec e.p.,illus (u5,f,f dj) 30.00

KAUFFMAN,HENRY-Pennsylvania Kentucky Rifle-Harrisburg-1960-4to-376p-illus,photos-1st ed (m3,f) 35.00

KAUFFMAN,JANET-Places in a World a Woman Could Walk-NY-1983-Knopf-1st ed (bb1,as new in dj) 20.00

KAUFFMAN,R W-Mark of the Beast-NY-1916-Macaulay-1st ed (e4,dj) 75.00

KAUFFMAN,REGINALD W-Ranger of the Susquehannock-Phila-1927-Penn-illus-1st ed (w5,hngs rprd,dj) 35.00

KAUFMAN,GEORGE S-Dark Tower, A Melodrama-NY-1934-Random-1st ed (w5,f,dj) 35.00

KAUFMAN,LEWIS-ET AL-Moe Berg-1974-Little,Brown-photos-1st ed (s8,f,dj) 35.00

KAUFMAN,LOUIS-ET AL-Moe Berg-1974-Little,Brown-1st ed (ff2,dj) 50.00

KAUFMAN,M-Father of Skyscrapers-Bost-1969-photos-1st ed (kk4,dj) 40.00

KAUFMAN,PAUL-Indian Lore of the Muskingum Headwaters of Ohio-np-(1973)-216p-cl (n1,f,glassine dj) 15.00

KAUFMAN,WILLIAM I-Art of Casserole Cookery-1967-Dbldy-122p-tan cl,photos-1st ed (q8,dj) 17.50

KAUFMAN,WILLIAM I-Cooking in a Castle-(1965)-Holt-224p-g dec wht cl,photos-1st ed (q8,dj) 20.00

KAUFMAN,WOLFE-I Hate Blondes-NY-1946-Simon-1st ed (d4,dj) 30.00

KAULBACK,RONALD-Salween-NY-1939-331p-23 photos,fldg map-1st US ed (o10,f) 40.00

KAUS,GINA-Catherine-NY-1935-Viking-8vo-384p-16 illus,dj by Artzybasheff-1st US ed (cc5,f,dj) 35.00

KAVAN,ANNA-Julia & the Bazooka-NY-1975-Knopf-1st US ed (z9,f,dj) 10.00

KAVAN,ANNA-Julia and the Bazooka-NY-1975-Knopf-1st US ed (b5,as new in dj) 15.00

KAVANAGH,PATRICK-Collected Prose-Lond-(1967)-MacGibbon & Kee-1st ed (z8,vf,dj) 37.50

KAWABATA,YASUNARI-Master of Go-NY-1972-Knopf-1st ed (v5,f,dj) 25.00

KAWABATA,YASUNARI-Sounds of the Mountain-NY-1970-1st US ed (t5,dj) 30.00

KAWABATA,YASUNARI-Thousand Cranes-NY-1959-Knopf-1st ed (w5,f,sl tn dj) 40.00

KAWAI,TATSUO-Goal of Japanese Expansion-Tokyo-1938-Hokuseido Pr-8vo-120p-blu cl-port-1st ed (s1,f,dj) 35.00

KAY,GERTRUDE A-Adventures in Geography-Joliet-(1930)-Volland-lg 8vo-157p-pict cl,col & b&w illus,auth-1st ed (r3) 25.00

KAY,KARL J-History of the National Normal University of Lebanon, Ohio-Wilmington-(1929)-48p-wrps (g1) 12.50

KAY-ROBINSON,DENYS-First Mrs Thomas Hardy-NY-1979-St.Martin's-1st ed (x9,f,dj) 12.50

KAYE,LAMB-ED.-Journals & Letters of Alex. MacKenzie-Cambridge-1970-551p-illus,3 fldg maps-1st ed (c7,dj) 50.00

KAYE-SMITH,SHEILA-Kitchen Fugue-1945-Harper-216p-grn cl-1st ed (q8,dj sp discol) 20.00

KAZANTZAKIS,HELEN-Nikos Kazantzakis-Oxford-1968-Bruno Cassirer-cl,illus-1st ed (l8,dj) 25.00

KAZANTZAKIS,NIKOS-Saviors of God-NY-1960-S&S-1st ed (h8,f,sl wn dj) 50.00

KAZANTZAKIS,NIKOS-Spain-NY-1963-S&S-1st ed (h8,f,dj) 40.00

KAZANTZAKIS,NIKOS-Spain-NY-1963-S&S-1st ed (z2,f,sl wn dj) 25.00

KAZANTZAKIS,NIKOS-Zorba the Greek-NY-1953-S&S-1st Amer ed (oo8,f,dj) 50.00

KEABLE,ROBERT-Tahiti-Lond-nd-254p-cl (d1) 15.00

KEAN,SARAH M-Grandmother's Story-np-nd-priv prntd-177p-cl,not cpyrtd (c1,rub,sl snag sp) 15.00

KEARTON,C-In the Land of the Lion-Lond-1946-250p-coated papr,photos (gg3,f,dj) 20.00

KEARTON,C-Island of Penguins-NY-1933(1931)-8vo-247p-cl,70 photo plts,map (y8,dj wn) 14.00

KEARTON,C-Wild Life Across the World-Lond-(1914)-8vo-286p-cl wi gilt-embossed lion on cov,105 photos (y8,lt wn) 40.00

KEARTON,CHERRY-In the Land of the Lion-Lond-1929-8vo-256p-photos-1st ed (m3) 30.00

KEATING,H R F-Sherlock Holmes-NY-1979-Scribners-1st US ed (h4,f,dj) 15.00

KEATING,H R F-Whodunit?-Lond-1982-Winward-illus-1st ed (q4,vf,dj) 35.00

KEATING,H R F-Whodunit?-NY-1982-Van Nostrand-illus-1st US ed (d4,f,dj) 20.00

KEATING,J M-Yellow Fever Epidemic of 1878 in Memphis, Tenn-Memphis-1879-Howard Assn-454p-grn cl-1st ed (c2,hng rprd) 125.00

KEATING,WILLIAM H-Narrative of an Expedition to the Source of St.Peter's River-Mpls-1959-Ross & Haines-248p+appndx(2 vols in 1)-fldg map,illus-ltd to 1500c-Howes K20 (dd4,dj) 25.00

KEATON,BUSTER-My Wonderful World of Slapstick-GC-1960-Dbldy-8vo-282p-photos-1st ed (y4,dj) 45.00

KEATOR,EUGENE H-Historical Discourse-(np)-(1910)-157p-cl,illus (aa6) 35.00

KEAY,JOHN-When Men and Mountains Meet-Lond-1977-277p-1st Brit ed (a4,f,dj) 30.00

KEBLE,HOWARD-Peculiar Major-NY-1919-Doran-1st ed (t4) 10.00

KEDZIE,J H-Speculations-Chig-1886-Griggs-xii+304+15p-brwn cl-1st ed (d2,sl wn cov) 35.00

KEEGAN,MARCIA-Mother Earth, Father Sky-NY-1974-111p-col photos-scarce-1st ed (v7,f,dj) 25.00

KEELER,HARRIET-Our Native Trees-NY-1915-Scribner-533p-cl,photos (x6) 10.00

KEELER,HARRY S-Man with the Crimson Box-NY-1940-Dutton-1st ed (w9,dj sl wn & tn) 45.00

KEELER,RALPH-Vagabond Adventures-Bost-1870-Fields,Osgood & Co-274p-cl (j1,ex-lib) 22.50

KEEN,A M-Marine Molluscan Genera of Western North America-1963-Stanford-126p (bb3,f,fray dj) 27.00

KEENAN,JACK-Cincinnati & Lake Erie Railroad-1974-Golden West-4to-225p-illus (nn7,dj wn) 35.00

KEENE,CAROLYN-Mysterious Fireplace-NY-1941-G&D-scarce-1st ed (z2,f,sp chip dj) 85.00

KEENE,CAROLYN-Nancy Drew Cookbook-NY-(1978)-G&D-159p-pict bds,drwngs (q8) 10.00

KEENE,H G-History of India-Edinburgh-1906-2 vols-red cl,maps-rvsd ed (gg2) 75.00

KEENE,J HARRINGTON-Boy's Own Guide to Fishing Tackle Making & Fish Breeding-Bost-1894-12mo-200p-illus-1st ed (m3) 50.00

KEENE,JOHN-Boy's Own Guide to Fishing Tackle Making and Fish Breeding-Bost-(1894)-Lee & Shepard-8vo-200,(8)p ads-orig brwn pict cl,82 diagrams (pp8) 85.00*

KEENE,MOLLY-Good Behaviour-NY-1981-Knopf-(auth 1st bk using real name)-1st Amer ed (z8,vf,dj) 40.00

KEENLYSIDE,FRANCIS-Peaks and Pioneers-Lond-1975-4to-248p-165 plts,4 maps-1st ed (p10,f,dj) 40.00

KEENLYSIDE,FRANCIS-Peaks and Pioneers-Lond-1975-4to-248p-165 plts,4 maps-1st ed (q10,f,dj) 40.00

KEEP,J-West Coast Shells-1935-Stanford-350p-334 figs-rvsd ed (bb3) 25.00

KEESING,FELIX M-Pacific Island Peoples in the Postwar World-Eugene-1950-wrps,14 plts,3 maps (v4) 25.00

KEESON,C A CUTHBERT-History & Records of Queen Victoria's Rifles 1792 to 1922-Lond-1923-670p-grn cl,maps,illus-1st ed (b7,f) 125.00

KEILIN,DAVID-History of Cell Respiration and Cytochrome-Cambridge-1966-Cambridge U Pr-xx+416p-grn cl-1st ed (a2) 45.00

KEIM,DE B RANDOLPH-Sheridan's Troopers on the Borders-Phila-1889-McKay-308p-pict cl,engrvngs (gg4) 30.00

KEITH,ARTHUR-Menders of the Maimed-Huntington-1975-335p-(facs of 1919 ed) (dd3) 60.00

KEITH,D-Matter of Iodine-1940-DM-1st ed (x7,dj) 30.00

KEITH,E C-Gun for Company-Lond-1937-202p-col frntis,illus (gg3,f) 12.00

KEITH,E C-Sportsman's Creed-Lond-1938-4to-205p-illus,A Thorburn (m3,f,dj) 25.00

KEITH,E-An Autobiography-Winchester-1974-408p-photos,illus (gg3,f,dj) 40.00

KEITH,E-Big Game Rifles & Cartridges-Onslow County-1936-12mo-161p-photos-1st ed (m3,f,sl fray dj) 100.00

KEITH,E-Big Game Rifles & Cartridges-Samworth-1936-162p-photos-scarce-1st ed (gg3,vf) 110.00

KEITH,E-Elmer Keith's Big Game Hunting-Bost-1948-8vo-420p-illus,B Kuhn-1st ed (m3,f) 90.00

KEITH,E-Elmer Keith's Big Game Hunting-NY-1954-420p-photos,illus (gg3,f) 45.00

KEITH,E-Guns & Ammo for Big Game Hunting-CA-1965-384p-photos (ee3,f,dj) 120.00

KEITH,E-Guns & Ammo for Hunting Big Game and Mr.Rifleman by Whelen & Angier-LA-1965-2 vols-Deluxe ed,leatherette,illus (gg3,vf,box) 225.00

KEITH,E-Hell I Was There-LA-(1979)-308p-dbl col,illus-1st ed (g7,f,dj) 35.00

KEITH,E-Hell, I Was There-LA-(1979)-4to-308p-photos (m3,vf,dj) 25.00

KEITH,E-Keith's Rifles for Large Game-Huntington-1946-8vo-406p-photos,illus,rare-1st ed (m3,f) 600.00

KEITH,E-Shotguns by Keith-NY,Harrisburg-(1950)-Stackpole-307p-illus-1st ed (gg4,chip dj) 50.00

KEITH,E-Shotguns by Keith-PA-1967-340p-photos (gg3,f,dj) 25.00

KEITH,E-Sixgun Cartridges & Loads-Samworth-1936-151p-photos-scarce-1st ed (gg3,vf,dj) 100.00

KEITH,E-Sixguns by Keith-NY-1951-Bonanza ed-335p-illus (gg3,f,dj) 45.00

KEITH,E-Sixguns by Keith-PA-1961-335p-grn cl,photos (ee3,vf,dj) 60.00

KEITH,E-Sixguns-Harrisburg-(1955)-308p-illus-Yost & Renner 114-1st ed (g7,f,dj) 110.00

KEITH,K WYMAND-Long Line Rider-NY-(1971)-McGraw Hill-8vo-229p-1st ed (gg5,sl tn dj) 10.00

KEITHAHN,EDWARD-Monuments in Cedar-Ketchikan-1945-Anderson-photos-1st ed (nn9) 25.00

KEITLEN,TOMI-Farewell to Fear-NY-(1960)-Geis-8vo-286p-16p photos-1st ed (gg5,f,dj) 15.00

KELEHER,JULIA-Padre of Isleta-Santa Fe-(1940)-109p-photos-1st ed (v7,f,dj,2 pres) 35.00

KELEHER,WILLIAM A-Fabulous Frontier-Santa Fe-1945-317p-cl,ports-Howes K37-2nd prtg (z1) 90.00

KELEHER,WILLIAM A-Fabulous Frontier-Santa Fe-1945-Rydal Pr-8vo-ix,317p-map e.p.,illus-ltd to 500c-Howes K37-1st ed (aa3,dj) 125.00

KELEHER,WILLIAM A-Maxwell Land Grant-Santa Fe-(1942)-156p-photos,Howes#K38-scarce-1st ed (u7) 175.00

KELEHER,WILLIAM A-Turmoil in New Mexico, 1846 thru 1868-Albuq-1952-534p-frntis,photos,map e.p.-Rittenhouse #344-1st ed (t7,dj) 60.00

KELEHER,WILLIAM A-Violence in Lincoln County 1869 to 1881-Albuq-(1957)-UNM Pr-390p-e.p. maps,illus-Six Guns 1216-1st ed (gg4,dj) 75.00

KELEHER,WILLIAM A-Violence in Lincoln County, 1869 to 1881-Albuq-(1957)-371p-frntis,map e.p.-1st ed (v7,f,dj) 50.00

KELEHER,WILLIAM-Fabulous Frontier: Twelve New Mexico Items-Santa Fe-1945-Rydal-photos,illus-Howes K37-scarce-1st ed (nn9) 75.00

KELEMAN,P-Medieval American Art-1956-Macmillan-4to-414p+308 plts+33p cat of plts-1st prtg of one vol ed (bb3) 45.00

KELL,RICHARD-Differences-Lond-1969-Chatto & Windus/Hogarth-(Phoenix Living Poets)-1st ed (z8,vf,dj) 17.50

KELLAND,CLARENCE B-Sinister Strangers-1961-Dodd-1st ed (s10,dj) 15.00

KELLAND,CLARENCE B-West of the Law-1958-Harper & Bros-1st ed (r9,f,dj) 15.00

KELLER,DAVID H-Life Everlasting-Newark-1947-Avalon-ltd to 1000c-1st ed (k3,f,sl chip dj) 75.00

KELLER,DAVID H-Tales From Underwood-NY-(1952)-Pellegrini & Cudahy-publ for Arkham by P&C-ltd to 3500c-1st ed (k5,f,dj cov half fade) 30.00

KELLER,DAVID H-Thought Projector-NY-(1929)-Stellar Publ-24p-wrps-Science Fiction Series No.2 (c1) 10.00

KELLER,MORTON-Art and Politics of Thomas Nast-NY-1968-353p-cl-illus-1st ed (h1,dj) 20.00

KELLEY,JOSEPH-Thirteen Years in the Oregon Penitentiary-Portland-1908-142p-stiff pict wrps,frntis,photos-Six Guns #1218-scarce-1st ed (t7) 150.00

KELLEY,WILLIAM M-Drop of Patience-GC-1965-Dbldy-1st ed (bb1,f dj) 50.00

KELLOG,R-Mexican Tailless Amphibians in the United States National Museum-1932-USNM-224p-wrps,illus (bb3) 18.00

KELLOGG,CHARLES-Charles Kellogg the Nature Singer His Book-Morgan Hill-1929-8vo-349p-ltd to 1000c,nbrd,autg,photos by auth (m3) 17.50

KELLOGG,ELLA E-Science in the Kitchen-Battle Creek-(c.1892)-508p-tan cl,illus-rvsd & enlgd ed (q8,hng crack) 50.00

KELLOGG,GEORGE A-History of Whidbey's Island-np-1968-108p-wrps,frnts-3rd rprnt (h7) 40.00

KELLOGG,JAY C-Broncho Buster Busted-Tacoma-(1932)-12mo-54p-pict wrps,2 illus (r8,spot wrps) 90.00

KELLOGG,LOUISE P-British Regime in Wisconsin and the Northwest-Madison-1935-State Hist Soc Wisc-xviii+361p-brwn cl,8 plts,2 maps-Howes K50-1st ed (mm10) 80.00

KELLOGG,LOUISE P-French Regime in Wisconsin and the Northwest-Madison-1925-State Histo Soc Wisc-xvi+474p-brwn cl,30 maps & plts-Howes K51-1st ed (mm10) 85.00

KELLOGG,MARJORIE-Tell Me That You Love Me, Junie Moon-NY-(1968)-FS&G-auth 1st bk-1st ed (a10,dj) 30.00

KELLOGG,ROBERT H-Life and Death in Rebel Prisons-Hartford-1865-399p-cl,frntis,illus-1st ed (t7,rbnd) 25.00

KELLOGG,ROBERT H-Life and Death in Rebel Prisons-Hartford-1865-L Stebbins-400p-illus (v2,cov wn) 30.00

KELLOGG,ROBERT H-Life and Death in Rebel Prisons...-Hartford-1866-423p-cl-Coulter 272 (h1,sl wn) 20.00

KELLOGG,WINTHROP N-Porpoises and Sonar-Chig-(1961)-U Chig Pr-8vo-177p-8 plts-1st ed (dd5,dj) 20.00

KELLS,C EDMUND-Three Score Years and Nine-New Orleans-1926-C Edmund Kells-x+563p-blu cl-1st ed (a2) 25.00

KELLY,CELSUS-ED.-La Australia Del Espiritu Santo-Cambridge-1966-Hakluyt Soc-8vo-2 vols-blu cl,fldg maps,plts (p1) 65.00

KELLY,CHARLES-Miles Goodyear-SLC-1937-Wstrn Prtg(for auths)-8vo-152p+index-photos-ltd to 350c (s1,f,dj) 150.00

KELLY,CHARLES-Salt Desert Trails-SLC-1930-Western Prtg-178,(6)p-dec cl,illus,ports,map e.p.-1st ed (v1) 150.00

KELLY,DANIEL T-Buffalo Head-Santa Fe-1972-272p-photos,map e.p.-1st ed (v7,f,dj) 30.00

KELLY,F C-Wright Brothers-NY-(1943)-8vo-xii,340p-cl,16p plts-1st ed (s2,dj) 40.00

KELLY,FANNY-Narrative of My Captivity Among the Sioux Indians-Cin-1871-Wilstach, Baldwin-8vo-285p-grn cl-illus-Howes K62-scarce-1st ed (s1,rprd sp tear) 200.00

KELLY,FRED C-One Thing Leads to Another-Bost-1936-Houghton Mifflin-105p-17 photos by M Bourke White-1st ed (cc9,chip dj) 40.00

KELLY,FRED C-Seventy Five Years of Hibbard Hardware-Chig-1930-HS&B-95p-orng cl,drwngs (cc3) 35.00

KELLY,FRED C-Wright Brothers-NY-(1943)-Harcourt Brace-8vo-340p-16 photos-1st ed (dd5,dj sp sun,sl tn) 25.00

KELLY,FRED-George Ade-Indpls-1947-BM-1st ed (z9,dj tn) 22.50

KELLY,H H-City of the Dagger and Other Tales from Burma-NY-1971-Frederick Warne-illus,C Price-1st ed (l8,f) 12.50

KELLY,HOWARD-Some American Medical Botanists-Troy-1914-Southworth-216p-cl (x6,sl rub) 60.00

KELLY,J FREDERICK-Early Domestic Architecture of Connecticut-New Haven-1927-Yale-4to-xx,210p-cl,48 plts-2nd prtg (cc10) 85.00

KELLY,LAWRENCE C-Navajo Indians and Federal Indian Policy,1900 thru 1935-Tucson-(1970)-210p-map-2nd prtg (v7,dj) 15.00

KELLY,LAWRENCE C-Navajo Roundup-Boulder-(1970)-181p-pckt map-1st ed (v7,dj) 25.00

KELLY,LUTHER S-Yellowstone Kelly-New Haven-1926-Yale Univ-xiv+268p-blu cl,illus,fldg map-1st ed (m2) 50.00

KELLY,LUTHER S-Yellowstone Kelly-New Haven-1926-Yale-xiv,268p-blu cl,illus,fldg map-1st ed (v1) 65.00

KELLY,MARCELLA R-Behind Eternity-Holyoke-(1973)-priv prtd-v,389p-emboss grn cl wi gilt,photos-only ed (o2) 20.00

KELLY,MRS J E-Early History of Brown County South Dakota-Aberdeen-1965-208p-pict cl,photos,illus-1st ed (t7,f) 27.50

KELLY,PLYMPTON-We Were Not Summer Soldiers-Tacoma-1976-191p-illus,fldg map-1st ed (h7,dj) 20.00

KELLY,R G-More Trails on Six Continents-Charleston-1973-8vo-214p-photos (m3,vf,dj) 55.00

KELLY,R G-Trails,Trouts & Tigers-Charleston-1961-8vo-158p (m3,vf,sl chip dj,pres cpy) 65.00

KELLY,ROBIN-Sky Was Their Roof-Lond-1955-Andrew Melrose-252p-photos,4 maps-Six Guns #1227-1st ed (r8,f,dj) 35.00

KELLY,ROGER E-ET AL-Navaho Figurines Called Dolls-Santa Fe-1972-75p-wrps,photos,drwngs,map-1st ed (v7,f) 20.00

KELLY,WALT-Beau Pogo-NY-1960-S&S-191p-wrps-1st ed (x9) 55.00

KELLY,WALT-I Go Pogo-1952-S&S-wrps-1st ed (x2,sl soil wrps) 18.00

KELLY,WALT-Incompleat Pogo-1954-S&S-wrps-1st ed (m9,wn,sp fade & rub) 15.00

KELLY,WALT-Jack Acid Society Black Book-1962-S&S-lg wrps-scarce-1st ed (dd8) 20.00

KELLY,WALT-Pogo Extra-NY-1960-S&S-144p-wrps-1st ed (x9) 45.00

KELLY,WALT-Pogo Papers-NY-1953-S&S-192p-wrps-1st ed (x9) 50.00

KELLY,WALT-Pogo Party-NY-1956-S&S-191p-wrps-1st ed (x9,sl sunned sp) 50.00

KELLY,WALT-Pogo Sunday Book-NY-1956-S&S-132p-wrps-1st ed (x9) 50.00

KELLY,WALT-Pogo Sunday Parade-NY-1958-S&S-127p-wrps-1st ed (x9) 45.00

KELLY,WALT-Pogo-NY-1951-S&S-182p-wrps,auth 1st bk-Bruccolli var. #4-1st ed (x9,creased) 50.00

KELLY,WALT-Positively Pogo-NY-1957-S&S-189p-wrps-1st ed (x9) 50.00

KELLY,WILLIAM-Stroll Through the Diggings of California-Oakland-1950-206p-illus-Graff #2298-1st ed (t7) 30.00

KELLY,WILLIAM-Stroll Through the Diggins of California-Oakland-1950-Biobooks-paintings-ltd to 750c (ee4) 35.00

KELSEY,D M-History of Our Wild West and Stories of Pioneer Life-Chig-(1901)-Thompson & Thomas-542p-pict cl,drwngs-Six Guns #1228 calls for col frntis, but not in list of illus-1st ed (cc4) 50.00

KELSEY,D M-Our Pioneer Heroes and Their Daring Deeds...-Chig-1900-Thompson & Thomas-sm 8vo-x,542p-pict cl,col frntis-1st ed (aa3,papr brwnd) 40.00

KELSEY,VERA-Young Men So Daring-Indpls-(1956)-Bobbs-Merrill-288p-1st ed (cc4,dj) 20.00

KELSO,LINDA-Mount St.Helens and Other Volcanoes of the West-1980-Beautiful Amer-folio-142p-col photos-1st prtg (r8,sl tn dj) 12.00

KELSON,GEORGE M-Salmon Fly-Lond-1895-4to-510p+ads-8 col plts,text illus-rare-1st ed (m3,rbnd) 425.00

KELTIE,JOHN-ED.-Scottish Highlands-Lond-nd(ca.1890)-5 vols-red dec cl,illus,5 col plts (gg2) 150.00

KEMBLE,FRANCES A-Journal of a Residence on a Georgian Plantation in 1838 to 1839-NY-1863-Harper & Bros-12mo-337,7,(3)p-1st ed (n2,rebckd wi orig sp) 125.00

KEMBLE,JAMES-Idols and Invalids-NY-1936-328p-1st ed (g10) 30.00

KEMBLE,JOHN H-Panama Route 1848 thru 1869-Berkeley,LA-1943-U of Cal Pr-8vo-viii,316p-prtd wrps,frntis,14 plts,2 maps-1st ed (t10) 35.00

KEMBLE,JOHN H-San Francisco Bay-Cambridge-1957-Cornell Maritime Pr-195p-e.p. maps,illus-1st ed (ee4) 15.00

KEMELMAN,HARRY-Friday the Rabbi Slept Late-1964-Crown-1st ed (m9,dj sp sl wn) 20.00

KEMELMAN,HARRY-Nine Mile Walk-NY-1967-Putnam-1st ed (l4,f,dj) 25.00

KEMELMAN,HARRY-Thursday the Rabbi Walked Out-NY-1978-Morrow-1st ed (h4,f,dj) 10.00

KEMELMAN,HARRY-Tuesday the Rabbi Saw Red-1973-Fields-1st ed (s10,dj) 12.50

KEMMERER,DONALD L-Path to Freedom-Princeton-1940-xvi,384p-cl,plts (aa6) 75.00

KEMP,BEN W-Cow Dust and Saddle Leather-Norman-(1968)-300p-cl-1st ed so stated (e1,f,dj) 35.00

KEMP,BEN-Cow Dust and Saddle Leather-(1968)-U of Ok-300p-illus-Six Guns 1229-1st ed (t8,f,dj) 40.00

KEMP,D-Skier's Song Book-Palo Alto-1950-80p-1st ed (o10,f,dj) 15.00

KEMP,HARRY-Don Juan's Note Book-NY-1929-priv prtd-ltd to 1050c,nbrd,iss w/o dj (v5,f,box) 40.00

KEMP,HARRY-ED.-Bronze Treasury-NY-1927-Macaulay-1st ed (v5,dj wn,chip) 50.00

KEMP,OLIVER-Wilderness Homes-NY-1908-8vo-155p-photos,illus,imitation wood covs (m3) 40.00

KEMP,PETER-ED.-History of the Royal Navy-NY-1969-304p-illus-1st Amer ed (b7,f,dj) 30.00

KEMPER,DR.-Night After the Battle...-Cin-(1883)-Peter G Thomson-17p-wrps (h1,sl chip) 17.50

KEMPER,FREDERICK A-Consolations of the Afflicted...-Cin-1831-prntd by Wm J Ferris-258p-lea (c1,sl chip sp,sl crckd joint) 85.00

KEMPER,G W H-Medical History of the State of Indiana-Chig-1911-Amer Med Assoc Pr-393p-cl-errata slip (g1,sl spot cov) 30.00

KENAWELL,WILLIAM W-Quest at Glastonbury-NY-1965-Helix Pr-cl,frntis,illus-1st ed (o8,dj) 22.50

KENDALL,DR. B J-Doctor at Home-Enosburgh Falls-1887-96p-wrps-illus (h1) 15.00

KENDALL,ELIZABETH-Phantom Prince-Seattle-1981-Madrona-1st ed (z9,f,dj) 10.00

KENDALL,GEO WILKINS-Narrative of the Texan Santa Fe Expedition-Chig-1929-Donnelley-585p-frntis,map-Lakeside Classics (cc4) 35.00

KENDALL,P F-Geology of Yorkshire-np-1924-prntd for auth-2 vols,grn cl,plts,maps-1st ed (d2) 65.00

KENDALL,PAUL-Polo Ponies-NY-1933-Derrydale-ltd to 850c-1st ed (h9) 95.00

KENDALL,PHOEBE M-Maria Mitchell-Bost-1896-Lee & Shepard-vi+300p-blu cl-1st ed (l2) 30.00

KENDALL,SIDNEY-Among th Laurentians-Tor-1885-12mo-139p-illus (m3) 40.00

KENDALL,WILKINS-Texan Santa Fe Expedition-NY-1844-Harper & Bros-2 vols-grn buckram,fldg map-rare-1st ed (f9,rbnd,sl wtrstnd) 500.00

KENDRICK,BAYNARD-Death Knell-NY-1945-Morrow-1st ed (f4,dj) 20.00

KENDRICK,BAYNARD-Frankincense and Murder-NY-1961-Dodd-1st ed (j4,f,sl soil dj) 35.00

KENDRICK,BAYNARD-Make Mine Maclain-NY-1947-Morrow-1st ed (k4,f,dj) 35.00

KENDRICK,BAYNARD-Out of Control-1945-Morrow-1st ed (s10,sp chip dj) 15.00

KENDRICK,BAYNARD-Out of Control-NY-1945-Morrow-1st ed (d4,dj) 12.50

KENDRICK,GRACE-Mouth Blown Bottle-Fallon-(1968)-Auth-8vo-200p-ltd ed,nbrd(of unspecified nbr),autg,illus-1st ed (ee5,f,dj) 20.00

KENEALLY,THOMAS-Blood Red, Sister Rose-NY-1975-Viking-1st ed (y1,f,dj) 20.00

KENEALLY,THOMAS-Bring Larks & Heroes-NY-1968-Viking-1st ed (y1,f,dj) 25.00

KENEALLY,THOMAS-Schindler's Ark-Lond-1982-Hodder & Stoughton-1st ed (v5,f,f dj) 30.00

KENNAN,GEORGE-Tragedy of Pelee-NY-1902-Outlook Co/Gilliss Pr-257p-dec brwn cl,t.e.g.,17 photo plts (p8,new e.p.) 45.00

KENNARD,EDWARD A-Hopi Kachinas-NY-1938-J J Augustin-40p+28p col plts by E Earle,cl,v scarce-1st ed (z1) 195.00

KENNEDY,BRUCE L-Safari Koa Chui-nd-priv prntd-12mo-43p-illus,imitation leopard skn covs (m3,vf) 25.00

KENNEDY,E B-Thirty Seasons in Scandinavia-Lond-1903-8vo-278p-photos (m3) 40.00

KENNEDY,ELIJAH R-Contest for California in 1861-Bost-1912-Houghton Mifflin-8vo-361p-maroon cl,illus-1st ed (b3) 45.00

KENNEDY,G W-Pioneer Campfire-Portland-1913-8vo-252p-photos-scarce (m3,f) 40.00

KENNEDY,JOHN F-Profiles in Courage-NY-(1956)-Harper-1st ed (dd2,dj) 250.00

KENNEDY,JOHN F-Why England Slept-Lond,Melbourne-nd-Hutchinson-auth 1st bk-1st Brit ed (b10,sl wn dj) 250.00

KENNEDY,JOSEPH P-I'm For Roosevelt-NY-(1936)-Reynal & Hitchcock-1st ed (w1,f,dj sl chip & rub) 85.00

KENNEDY,LUCY-Sunlit Field-1950-Crown-1st ed (s8,dj) 22.50

KENNEDY,LUDOVIC-Pursuit-NY-(1974)-254p-illus,maps-1st ed (pp4,dj) 15.00

KENNEDY,M-Chickering & Carving of Gunstocks-PA-1962-343p-photos-ed by Samworth (gg3,f,dj) 20.00

KENNEDY,M-Firearm Design & Assembly-1952-Samworth-250p-hard papr cov,photos,fldg patterns (gg3,f) 40.00

KENNEDY,MACLEAN-Great Teams of Baseball-1928-Spink & Son-photos,TP orig-1st ed (s8,wrps sl soil & rub) 75.00

KENNEDY,MARGARET-Together and Apart-NY-1937-Random Hs-1st ed (y1,dj cov sl soil) 30.00

KENNEDY,MARGUERITE W-My Home on the Range-Bost-1951-Little,Brown-12mo-341p-illus-Herd 1272-1st ed (aa3,f,dj) 45.00

KENNEDY,MARY J-Tales of a Trader's Wife-Albuq-1965-61p-pict cl,photos-1st ed (t7,autg) 20.00

KENNEDY,MARY J-Wind Blows Free-(Albuq)-1970-56p-photos-1st ed (v7,autg,f) 20.00

KENNEDY,MICHAEL S-ED.-Cowboys and Cattlemen-NY-(1964)-Hastings Hs-364p-photos,illus by C M Russell(incl pict e.p.)-1st ed (cc4,dj) 50.00

KENNEDY,MICHAEL S-ED.-Cowboys and Cattlemen-NY-1964-Hastings Hs-4to-364p-cl,illus,illus e.p.-1st ed (z4,sl wn dj) 40.00

KENNEDY,MICHAEL S-ED.-Red Man's West-NY-(1965)-Hastings Hs-342p-illus-1st ed (cc4,dj) 35.00

KENNEDY,MICHAEL-Salt Water Angling-NY,Tor,Lond-1956-8vo-376p-illus,photos (m3,sl fray dj) 25.00

KENNEDY,MICHAEL-Sea Angler's Fishes-Lond-1954-8vo-524p-illus,photos (m3,f,sl chip dj) 25.00

KENNEDY,MICHAEL-Trout Flies for Irish Waters-Dublin-nd-8vo-42p-illus (m3,vf) 12.50

KENNEDY,MILWARD-Half Mast Murder-NY-1930-Dbldy CC-1st US ed (e4) 12.50

KENNEDY,MILWARD-Scornful Corpse-NY-1936-Dodd-1st US ed (e4,dj) 30.00

KENNEDY,P G-Birds of Ireland-Edinburgh-1954-8vo-cl,11 b&w plts (y8,dj chip) 100.00

KENNEDY,PROF J C,M.D.-Medical Magician. Part I-Cin,Detr,Louisville-1887-224p-cl,30p illus (c1) 40.00

KENNEDY,R EMMET-Black Cameos-NY-1924-Boni-205p-col pict cl,illus,Tinker,col pict e.p.-v scarce-1st ed (f9,scuff,wn,blurb pasted in) 50.00

KENNEDY,WILLELLA S-Our Heritage-(Marysville)-(1963)-118p-wrps-scarce (f1) 12.50

KENNEDY,WILLIAM-Billy Phelan's Greatest Game-(1978)-Viking-1st ed (o9,f,dj sl wn & rub) 85.00

KENNEDY,WILLIAM-Billy Phelan's Greatest Game-NY-(1978)-King-1st ed (cc2,f,dj) 100.00

KENNEDY,WILLIAM-Ironweed-Lond-1983-1st Brit ed (q5,vf,dj) 85.00

KENNEDY,WILLIAM-Ironweed-NY-1983-Viking-1st ed (q2,sl tn dj) 85.00

KENNEDY,WILLIAM-Legs-NY-1975-1st ed (p5,f,dj) 175.00

KENNELLY,A E-ET AL-Electricity in Daily Life-1890-288p-125 illus-1st ed (h6) 75.00

KENNELLY,BRENDAN-Boats are Home-Dublin-1980-Gallery Pr-1st ed (z8,f,dj) 50.00

KENNER,HUGH-Dublin's Joyce-Bloomington-1956-Indiana Univ-1st Amer ed (x10,f,f dj) 45.00

KENNERLY,WILLIAM C-Persimmon Hill-Norman-1948-U of Okla Pr-273p-illus-1st ed (d3,dj) 35.00

KENNETT,LEE-French Armies in the Seven Years War-Durham-1967-165p-1st ed (b7,f,dj) 50.00

KENNINGTON,E-Drawing the R.A.F.-Lond-1942-8vo-144p-cl,frntis,52p plts incl 4 col-1st ed (t2,dj) 35.00

KENNY,ROBERT-Elizabeth's Admiral-Balt-1970-354p-frntis-1st ed (b7,f,dj) 25.00

KENRICK,TONY-Only Good Body's a Dead One-NY-1971-Simon-auth 1st bk-1st Amer ed (r4,f,dj) 25.00

KENRICK,TONY-Two For the Price of One-Lond-1974-Joseph-1st ed (p4,f,dj) 27.50

KENRICK,TONY-Two Lucky People-Lond-1978-Joseph-1st ed (q4,f,dj) 25.00

KENT,ALEXANDER-Inshore Squadron-NY-1979-1st Amer ed (b7,f,dj) 25.00

KENT,ALEXANDER-Sloop of War-NY-1972-Putnam-1st ed (x1,f,dj) 35.00

KENT,DAVID-Jason Burr's First Case-1941-Random Hs-1st ed (s10,dj) 20.00

KENT,EDWIN C-Isle of Long Ago-NY-1933-8vo-194p-ltd to 1000c,nbrd,photo frontis (m3,fade sp) 55.00

KENT,ELIZABETH-Flora Domestica-Lond-1831-Whittaker-464p-cl,col frntis (x6) 100.00

KENT,JANET-Solomon Islands-Harrisburg-1973-Stackpole Pr-8vo-222p-photos,2 maps-1st Amer ed (p8,f,f dj) 25.00

KENT,JOHN-Racing Life of Lord George Cavendish Bentinck...-Edinburgh-1892-Blackwood-red calf,triple g rule on covs,g dec panelled sp,g innr dentelles & mrbld e.p.-1st ed (p6,wtrstnd cov) 250.00

KENT,LOUISE A-Mrs.Appleyard's Kitchen-Bost-1942-Houghton Mifflin-319p-tan cl-1st prtg (q8,sp tn dj) 20.00

KENT,LOUISE A-With Kitchen Privileges-(1953)-Houghton (q8,dj) 16.50

KENT,NIAL-Divided Path-NY-(1949)-1st ed (m4,dj) 14.50

KENT,NORMAN-ED.-Book of Edward A Wilson-NY-1948-Heritage Pr-4to-108p-orng bds,tip in frntis,col & b&w illus (r10,dj) 40.00

KENT,ROCKWELL-After Long Years-Ausable Forks-1968-Asgaard Pr-sm 8vo-21,(3)p-stiff wrps,illus-1st ed (x4,vf) 20.00

KENT,ROCKWELL-Casanova's Homecoming. by Arthur Schnitzler-NY-1947-Sylvan Pr-153,(1)p-blk cl,illus,ltd ed,unsigned (b6,f) 35.00

KENT,ROCKWELL-N by E-NY-(1930)-Random-dec cl-ltd to 900c,nbrd,autg-1st ed (s6) 200.00

KENT,ROCKWELL-Northern Christmas...-NY-(1941)-Amer Artists Group-illus by auth-1st ed (ll9,dj) 30.00

KENT,ROCKWELL-Rockwellkentiana-NY-1933-Harcourt-illus cl-1st ed (x3,dj chip & wn) 90.00

KENT,ROCKWELL-Salamina-NY-1935-Harcourt-illus by auth-1st ed (b3,f,dj) 50.00

KENT,ROCKWELL-This Is My Own-NY-(1940)-Duell-1st ed (w1,f,f dj) 75.00

KENT,ROCKWELL-To Thee-Manitowoc-(1946)-Rahr Malting-4to-59+(1)p-cl bckd bds,woodcts-1st ed (x4,sp wn box) 75.00

KENT,ROCKWELL-Wilderness-NY-1924-Putnam-4to-217p-yel cl,woodcts-2nd prtg (r10,sl soil) 20.00

KENT,WILLIAM-Reminiscences of Outdoor Life-SF-1929-A M Robertson-305p-cl & papr over bds,frntis is mtnd photo wi tiss,13p plts-1st ed (z1,hng weak) 80.00

KENT,WM W-Life & Works of Baldessare Peruzzi of Siena-NY-1925-89 plts (h10,dj) 75.00

KENYON,G H-Glass Industry of Weald-1967-Leicester Univ Pr-illus-1st ed (cc8,dj) 35.00

KENYON,JAMES B-Remembered Days-NY-1902-8vo-239p (m3) 30.00

KEON,MICHAEL-Durian Tree-Lond-(1960)-Hamish Hamilton-1st Brit ed (b10,f,sl soil dj) 12.50

KEPES,JULIET-Seed that Peacock Planted-Bost-(1967)-Little,Brown-tall 8vo-41p-pict cl,col & b&w illus,auth-1st ed (r3,f,tattrd dj) 15.00

KEPHART,HORACE-Sporting Firearms-NY-1934-12mo-153p-illus (m3) 10.00

KEPPY,FREDERICK-How to Become a Successful Engineer-Bridgeport-1890-46p-pict wrps-17th ed rev (e1,wrps) 15.00

KER,D I-African Adventure-PA-1957-248p-grn cl,dec cov,photos (ee3,f) 75.00

KER,D I-Through Forest & Veldt-Lond-1958-191p-photos (gg3,vf,chip dj) 50.00

KER,D L-African Adventure-PA-1957-248p-photos (gg3,vf,dj) 70.00

KER,HENRY-Travels Through the Western Interior of the United States, from 1808 up to the Year 1816-Elizabethtown-1816-prtd for auth-376p-modern lea,subscribers names on final 4 pgs-Howes K 101,Sabin 37599 (b1,fox) 400.00

KERBEY,MAJOR J O-Boy Spy-Chig-1892-Donohue,Henneberry-557p-cl (e1,fade,sl rub,frnt hng weak) 15.00

KERBY,ROBERT L-Confederate Invasion of New Mexico and Arizona 1861 to 1862-LA-1958-Wstrnlore Pr-159p-illus,maps,map e.p.-ltd to 850c-1st ed (ff4) 50.00

KERENYI,CHARLES-Asklepios-Lond-1960-139p-illus-1st Engl transl (dd3) 125.00

KERFOOT,J B-American Pewter-NY-nd-236p-cl,photos,illus,rprnt of 1924 ed (d1,dj) 15.00

KERHAHAN,COULSON-Captain Shannon-1901-lana-rprnt (s10) 10.00

KEROUAC,JACK-Big Sur-NY-(1962)-Charters A17a-1st ed (x8,dj) 175.00

KEROUAC,JACK-Book of Dreams-SF-1961-prntd in blu on wrps-Charters A15-1st ed (x8) 100.00

KEROUAC,JACK-Book of Dreams-SF-1961-wrps-1st ed (v9,f) 150.00

KEROUAC,JACK-Desolation Angels-NY-(1965)-Coward-McCann-1st ed (a10,dj frnt creased,sl wn) 125.00

KEROUAC,JACK-Dharma Bums-Lond-(1959)-A Deutsch-cpyrt pg incorrectly states "First Published 1950",corrected by publ prntd pasteover-1st Brit ed (ff6,f,dj) 150.00

KEROUAC,JACK-Dharma Bums-NY-1958-Charters A4a-1st ed (x8,dj) 250.00

KEROUAC,JACK-Dharma Bums-NY-1958-Viking-1st ed (a10,dj rub) 175.00

KEROUAC,JACK-Doctor Sax-Lond-1977-Charters A5d-1st Brit ed (x8,f,f dj) 60.00

KEROUAC,JACK-Doctor Sax-NY-(1959)-Grove-(8),245p-cl-ltd to 26c,lttrd,autg-Charters A5c (gg1) 1,500.00

KEROUAC,JACK-Doctor Sax-NY-(1959)-Grove-wrps(iss simultaneously in cl)-1st ed (w5,f) 35.00

KEROUAC,JACK-Doctor Sax-NY-(1959)-Grove-wrps,iss simultaneously wi hdcov ed,variant sp lettrng-Charters A5b-1st ed (q1,sl creased & cor wrnkld) 40.00

KEROUAC,JACK-Doctor Sax-NY-(1959)-wrps,publ simultaneously wi hdbk ed,Charters A5b-1st ed (x8) 50.00

KEROUAC,JACK-Excerpts From Visions of Cody-(NY)-(1959)-(New Directions)-ltd to 750c,autg,acetate dj-1st ed (cc1,publ note laid in,dj) 750.00

KEROUAC,JACK-Excerpts From Visions of Cody-NY-(1959)-New Directions-orig glassine dj,separate insert from New Directions laid in-ltd to 750c,nbrd,autg-Charters A9-1st ed (q1,chip dj) 700.00

KEROUAC,JACK-Lonesome Traveler-NY,Tor,Lond-(1960)-McGraw Hill-drwngs,L Rivers-1st ed (a10,dj rear panel soil) 125.00

KEROUAC,JACK-Lonesome Traveler-NY-(1960)-McGraw Hill-1st ed (x9,dj rub,edge wn) 85.00

KEROUAC,JACK-Maggie Cassidy-NY-(1959)-Avon-pbk,1st iss wi dbl spread t.p.-Charters A7-1st ed (q1,cocked) 25.00

KEROUAC,JACK-Mexico City Blues-NY-1959-Grove-simultaneous pbk iss-Charters A8b-1st ed in wrps (q1,cov sl wn & stnd) 35.00

KEROUAC,JACK-On The Road-NY-1957-1st ed (n5,dj sl tn & sl rub) 600.00

KEROUAC,JACK-On the Road-NY-1957-Viking-310p-blk cl-t.e. red-1st ed (d5,sl cocked sp,dj sl rub) 425.00

KEROUAC,JACK-Pic-NY-1971-wrps-1st ed (x8) 25.00

KEROUAC,JACK-Pull My Daisy-NY-(1959)-Grove-illus wrps-1st ed (qq1,sl soil cov) 180.00

KEROUAC,JACK-Satori in Paris-NY-1966-Charters A21a-1st ed (x8,dj) 90.00

KEROUAC,JACK-Subterraneans-(Lond)-(1960)-A Deutsch-illus dj-1st Brit ed (ff6,dj sp sl wn) 100.00

KEROUAC,JACK-Subterraneans-Lond-1960-1st iss red bds-1st Brit ed (t5,dj) 110.00

KEROUAC,JACK-Subterraneans-NY-1958-wrps,iss simultaneously wi hdbk ed-Charters A3b-1st ed (x8) 65.00

KEROUAC,JACK-Trip Trap-Bolinas-1973-Grey Fox-wrps-1st ed (v5,f) 25.00

KEROUAC,JACK-Tristessa-NY-(1960)-Avon Orig-pict wrps-1st ed (r2,sm crease) 35.00

KEROUAC,JACK-Tristessa-NY-(1960)-Avon T429-orig pbk-1st ed (q1,sl creased cov) 50.00

KEROUAC,JACK-Tristessa-NY-1960-Avon-126p-wrps-1st ed (z3,sl rub) 40.00

KEROUAC,JACK-Vanity of Duluoz-NY-(1968)-Charters A25a-1st ed (x8,dj) 125.00

KEROUAC,JACK-Vanity of Duluoz-NY-(1968)-Coward McCann-1st ed (m7,sp wn,sl wn dj) 85.00

KEROUAC,JACK-Visions of Cody-NY et al-(1972)-McGraw Hill-1st ed (ff6,few sl fox pgs,f dj) 75.00

KEROUAC,JACK-Visions of Cody-NY-(1972)-1st ed (o5,dj) 65.00

KEROUAC,JACK-Visions of Gerard-NY-1963-Farrar Straus-1st ed (d8,f,f dj) 125.00

KEROUAC,JACK-Visions of Gerard-NY-1963-Farrar Straus-illus by J Spanfeller-1st ed (y1,f,f dj) 150.00

KEROUAC,JAN-Baby Driver-NY-1981-1st ed (x8,f,f dj) 19.00

KEROUAC,JOHN-Town and the City-(1950)-Harcourt,Brace-auth 1st bk-1st ed (x2,dj) 425.00

KEROUAC,JOHN-Town and the City-NY-(1950)-Harcourt-1st ed (l5,dj sl tape mrkd) 300.00

KERR,ORPHEUS C-Orpheus C Kerr Papers-NY-1865-3 vols,g stmpd cl-uniform ed (k9) 35.00

KERR,WALTER-Russian Army-NY-1944-Knopf-maps-1st ed (ll9,f,dj) 25.00

KERR,WALTER-Theatre in Spite of Itself-NY-1963-S&S-8vo-319p-1st ed (ee5,f,dj) 12.50

KERR,WALTER-Thirty Plays Hath November-NY-(1969)-S&S-8vo-343p-1st ed (ee5,f,dj) 12.50

KERRIGAN,ANTHONY-At the Front Door of the Atlantic-(Dublin)-(1969)-Dolmen Pr-frntis,Picasso-1st ed (k7,dj sp tn) 15.00

KERRY,KATHERINE-Look What's Cooking-SF-1950-(Fulmer Bros)-136p-illus bds & e.p. (l6) 30.00

KERSEY,RALPH T-Buffalo Jones-GC-1958-184p-1st ed (t7,dj) 12.50

KERSH,GERALD-Faces in a Dusty Picture-NY-1945-Whittlesey HS-1st ed (x1,f,dj) 40.00

KERSH,GERALD-Fowler's End-NY-1957-S&S-1st US ed (hh5,f,dj) 12.50

KERSH,GERALD-Implacable Hunter-Lond,Melb,Tor-(1961)-Heinemann-1st Brit ed (d10,sl wn dj) 20.00

KERSH,GERALD-Sergeant Nelson of the Guards-Phila-1945-Winston-1st ed (x1,f,dj) 40.00

KERSH,GERALD-Weak and the Strong-(NY)-(1946)-1st ed (e5,f,sl soil dj) 20.00

KERSHNER,HOWARD E-Quaker Service in Modern War: Spain & France 1939 to 1940-NY-1950-Prentice Hall-8vo-195p-1st ed (y6,chip dj) 10.00

KERSTEIN,LINCOLN-Elie Nadelman-NY-1973-Eakins Pr-sm folio-360p-cl,cov photo by Frank E Smith,illus & draft catalog raisonne-1st ed (t3,dj,box) 125.00

KERTESZ,ANDRE-Day of Paris-NY-(1945)-Augustin-4to-cl-1st ed (y3,sl soil & stnd cov) 110.00

KERTESZ,ANDRE-Day of Paris-NY-1945-J J Augustin-8vo-148p-cl-scarce-1st ed (q3,dj) 175.00

KERTESZ,ANDRE-Distortions-NY-1976-Knopf-4to-cl,120 gravures,auth-1st ed (y3,f,f dj) 110.00

KERTESZ,ANDRE-Hungarian Memories-Bost-1982-NYGS-lg 4to-195p-cl-1st ed (t3,f,dj) 85.00

KERTESZ,ANDRE-J'Aime Paris-NY-1974-Grossman-4to-224p-cl-1st ed (t3,dj) 125.00

KERTESZ,ANDRE-Of New York-NY-1976-Knopf-4to-cl-1st ed (y3,dj) 125.00

KERTESZ,ANDRE-Sixty Years of Photography 1912 thru 1972-NY-1972-Grossman-oblng 4to-cl-1st ed (y3) 115.00

KESEY,KEN-Day After Superman Died-Northridge-1980-Lord John Pr-patterned bds & cl as iss,ltd to 350c,autg (bb2,f) 75.00

KESEY,KEN-Day Superman Died-Northridge-1980-Lord John-ltd to 300c,autg,w/o dj as iss-1st ed (j3,f) 50.00

KESEY,KEN-Kesey's Garage Sale-NY-1973-1st ed (o5,f,dj) 50.00

KESEY,KEN-Kesey's Garage Sale-NY-1973-illus-1st ed (p5,vf,dj) 60.00

KESEY,KEN-One Flew Over the Cuckoo's Nest-Lond-(1962)-Methuen-1st Brit ed (v10,f,dj) 100.00

KESEY,KEN-Sometimes a Great Notion-NY-1964-1st ed (t5,sl rub dj) 110.00

KESEY,KEN-Sometimes a Great Notion-NY-1964-Viking-1st ed (d8,f,f dj,autg) 375.00

KESSELRING,JOSEPH-Arsenic and Old Lace-NY-1941-Random-1st ed (hh2,f,dj) 385.00

KESTERTON,DAVID-Darkling-Sauk City-1982-Arkham-1st ed (k3,f,dj) 12.95

KESTING,TED-ED.-Bass Fishing-NY-1962-8vo-192p-photos (m3,vf,dj) 10.00

KETCHUM,M,JR.-Shops & Stores-1948-Reinhold (h10) 45.00

KETRING,RUTH A-Charles Osborn in the Anti Slavery Movement-Columbus-1937-95p-cl (m1,f) 15.00

KETTELL,R H-Pine Furniture of Early New England-NY-1929-284 illus (h10,dj) 100.00

KETTON-CREMER,R W-Norfolk in the Civil War-Hamden-1970-382p-illus-1st Amer ed (b7,f,dj) 25.00

KEVERNE,RICHARD-Crook Stuff-Lond-1935-Constable-1st ed (d4,fade sp) 25.00

KEVORKIAN,JACK-Story of Dissection-NY-(1959)-Philo Librsm 8vo-80p-illus-1st ed (b3,f,dj) 45.00

KEYES,DANIEL-Mind of Billy Milligan-NY-(1981)-Random Hs-1st ed (e3,f,dj) 20.00

KEYES,E D-From West Point to California-Oakland-1950-California Biobooks #24-8vo-ix+90p-blu cl over 9x6" bds,2 ports-"1st" (mm1,vf) 30.00

KEYES,FRANCES P-Frances Parkinson Keyes Cookbook-1955-Dbldy-322p-tan cl,illus,sepia e.p.-1st ed (q8,dj) 30.00

KEYNES,G-Jane Austen-Lond-1929-289p-bds,pap labl,plts-ltd to 875p,nbrd (a3,sl dusty bds) 125.00

KEYNES,GEOFFREY-Bibliography of Dr.John Donne-Lond-1973-Oxford Univ Pr-cl,illus-1st ed (n8,f,dj) 45.00

KEYNES,GEOFFREY-Bibliography of Sir Thomas Browne-Oxford-1968-293p (dd3,dj) 200.00

KEYNES,GEOFFREY-Life of William Harvey-Oxford-1966-Clarendon Pr-lg 8vo-483p-maroon cl,32 plts-1st ed (dd1,f,dj) 75.00

KEYNES,R D-ED.-Beagle Record-Cambridge-1980-Cambridge U Pr-409p-brwn cl,g titles,illus-2nd prtg (p8,as new in dj) 100.00

KEYSER,L S-Birds of the Rockies-Chig-1902-8vo-355p-cl,8 plts(4 col) (y8,lt dmpstn) 45.00

KEYSER,L S-Our Bird Comrades-Chig-1907-8vo-197p-cl,16 col plts (y8) 14.00

KEYSER,LEANDER-In Bird Land-Chig-1896-269p-cl (f1) 15.00

KEYSERLING,COUNT HERMANN-Immortality-Lond-1941-OUP-cl-1st ed (n8) 15.00

KHAN,HAZRAT INAYAT-Sufi Message of. Volume I-Lond-1960-Barrie & Rockliff-cl,frntis-1st ed (n8) 20.00

KHAN,HAZRAT INAYAT-Sufi Message of. Volume II-Lond-1960-Barrie & Rockliff-cl,frntis-1st ed (n8) 20.00

KHANNA,Y C-Saser Kangri-Delhi-1980-144p-29 photos-1st ed (q10,as new in dj) 25.00

KHANTIPALO,PHRA-Tolerance-Lond-1964-Rider & Co-cl-1st ed (n8,f,dj) 16.50

KHAYAT,MARIE K-Food From the Arab World-Beirut-1965-(Khayats)-163p-drwngs (m6,sl tattrd dj) 25.00

KHERDIAN,DAVID-Country,Cat City,Cat-(1978)-Four Winds-wdcuts,N Hogrogian-1st ed (u10,f,f dj) 25.00

KHERDIAN,DAVID-Ghost of Shah Mouradian-Fresno-(1975)-Giligia Pr-8vo-string tied wrps-1st ed (x10,sl soil) 10.00

KIBBY,G-Mushrooms and Toadstools-1979-Oxford Univ-256p-1st ed (bb3,f,dj) 20.00

KICHENSIDE,G M-ED.-Loco Spotters Annual for 1968-Lond-1968-64p-1st ed (n4) 15.00

KICHENSIDE,G M-ED.-Steam Portfolio-Lond-1968-1st ed (n4,f,dj) 25.00

KICHENSIDE,G M-Railway Carriages 1839 to 1939-Lond-1964-64p-1st ed (n4) 9.50

KICHENSIDE,G M-Still in Steam-Lond-1969-64p-1st ed (n4) 16.00

KICKNOSWAY,FAYE-Asparagus,Asparagus,Ah Sweet Asparagus-W Brnch Iowa-1981-Toothpaste Pr-ltd to 100c,autg,no dj as iss-1st ed (w6,f) 35.00

KIDD,J H-Personal Recoll of a Cavalryman with Custer's Mich Cavalry...-Alex-1981-476p-pict lea,a.e.g.,frntis,illus (t7,f) 50.00

KIDDER,ALFRED-Introduction to the Study of SW Archaeology-New Haven-1924-Yale-photos,maps-1st ed (nn9) 95.00

KIDDER,GLEN M-Railway to the Moon-1969-184p-ltd to 1500c,nbrd (n4,f,dj) 30.00

KIDDER,TRACY-Road to Yuba City-GC-1974-Dbldy-8vo-317p-auth 1st bk-1st ed (gg5,sl cocked sp,dj) 20.00

KIDDER,TRACY-Soul of a New Machine-1981-Atlantic/Little,Brown-1st ed (q9,vf,dj) 45.00

KIDDLE,CHARLES-Guide to the First Editions of Edgar Wallace-Dorset-(1981)-Ivory Head Pr-88p-pict wrps-1st ed (g9) 25.00

KIEFFER,HARRY M-Recollections of a Drummer Boy-Bost-1883-James R Osgood-332p-pict cl,frntis,illus-1st ed (n7,lg stn rear bd) 50.00

KIEFFER,J M-Pearl-Cleve-(1871)-160p-bds (h1) 12.50

KIEFFER,STEPHEN A-Transit and the Twins-Mpls-1958-60p-wrps-1st ed (n4) 7.50

KIENE,JULIA-Betty Furness Westinghouse Cook Book-NY-(1954)-S&S-487p-1st prtg (u6) 15.00

KIERAN,JOHN-Natural History of New York City-Bost-1959-HMCo-8vo-428p-illus-1st ed (aa5,sl tn dj) 15.00

KIERKEGAARD,SOREN-Training in Christianity-Lond-1941-OUP-cl-1st prtg (l8,pencilng,fray dj) 20.00

KIERMAN,R H-First War in the Air-(Manchester)-1934-sm 8vo-192p-cl,frntis,7p plts-1st ed (t2) 40.00

KIERNAN,THOMAS-Intimate Music-Bost,Tor-(1979)-Little,Brown-1st ed (a10,f,dj) 20.00

KIERNAN,THOMAS-Intimate Music-Bost,Tor-(1979)-Little,Brown-1st ed (e10,f,dj) 20.00

KIERNAN,THOMAS-Secretariat Factor-GC-1979-Dbldy-1st ed (f10,dj) 35.00

KIESTER,J A-History of Faribault County Minnesota, from Its First Settlement to the Close of the Year 1879-Mpls-1896-Harrison & Smith-1st ed (p6) 150.00

KIEWIT,C W DE-Imperial Factor in South Africa-Cambridge-1937-341p-1st ed (b7,f,dj) 40.00

KIKI'S MEMOIRS-Paris-1930-Black Manikin Pr-sm 4to-cream prtd wrps wi mounted illus,photos,orig glassine dj & wraparound band-ltd to 1000c-1st ed in Engl wi add txt (qq1,sl chip dj) 275.00

KILBOURNE,PAYNE K-Sketches and Chronicles of the Town of Litchfield...-Hartford-1859-Case,Lockwood-264p-brwn cl,plts,fldg map-1st ed (k2) 65.00

KILEY,JED-Hemingway-NY-(1965)-Hawthorne-1st ed (cc2,f,dj) 40.00

KILEY,JED-Hemingway: A Title Fight in Ten Rounds-Lond-1965-Methuen-1st Brit ed (d8,dj) 35.00

KILLAM,J C-Annihilationism Examined-Syracuse-1859-J G K Truair-123p-cl (aa1) 20.00

KILMAN,ED-Cannibal Coast-S.A.-1959-Naylor-294p-1st ed (a9,dj) 50.00

KILMAN,ED-Hugh Roy Cullen-NY-1954-376p-frntis,photos,map e.p.-1st ed (t7,dj) 6.00

KILNER,WALTER J-Human Aura-New Hyde Park-1965-Univ Bks-cl-1st prtg (l8,f,dj) 15.00

KILVERT,CORY-Male Chauvinist's Cookbook-(NY)-(1974)-Winchester Pr-273p (q6) 18.00

KIM,RICHARD E-Martyred-NY-1965-GB-auth 1st bk-1st ed (x1,f,dj) 35.00

KIMBALL,MARIE-Martha Washington Cook Book-NY-1940-Coward McCann-212p-wht bds (n6,sl soil sp,wn box) 35.00

KIMBALL,MARIE-Thomas Jefferson's Cook Book-Richmond-(1941)-Garrett & Massie-120p (o6) 35.00

KIMBALL,ROBERT-Gershwins-NY-1973-Atheneum-1st ed (u4,f,dj) 28.00

KIMBALL,SOLOMON F-Thrilling Experiences-SLC-1909-Mag Prtg Co-24mo-157p-frntis port-Howes K139-1st ed (aa3) 150.00

KIMMEL,STANLEY-Mr.Davis's Richmond-NY-1958-Bramhall-214p-illus (v2,f,wn dj) 15.00

KINCAID,JAMAICA-At the Bottom of the River-NY-1983-FS&G-1st ed (y1,f,dj) 35.00

KINDELAN,J-Trackman's Helper-1894-Clark Pub-8vo-333p-cl,iilus-Rvsd 20th Century ed (nn7,sl rub) 35.00

KINERT,R-American Racing Planes and Historic Air Races-Chig-(1952)-4to-144p-cl,col illus t.p.,b&w & col plts-1st ed (t2,chip dj) 30.00

KING COUNTY HISTORICAL SOCIETY-ED.-King County Windmills & Barbed Wire-Quanah-1976-Nortex Pr-465p-cl,photos,brands-1st ed (w3,vf) 35.00

KING,ALAN-Help! I'm a Prisoner in a Chinese Bakery-NY-1964-Dutton-1st ed (hh5,f,dj) 10.00

KING,BEN-Ben King's Southland Melodies-Chig-1911-Forbes-8vo-dec grn cl,photos (y3,sl rub) 85.00

KING,C DALY-States of Human Consciousness-New Hyde Park-1963-Univ Books-cl-1st ed (o8,f,dj) 25.00

KING,C W-Natural History of Gems or Decorative Stones-Lond-1867-Bell & Daldy-377p-frntis,woodcts (u5,ex-libr) 40.00

KING,CAROLINE B-Victorian Cakes-Caldwell-1941-Caxton-273p-blu bds,dec e.p. (o6,tattrd dj,autg) 30.00

KING,CHARLES-Campaigning with Crook and the Stories of Army Life-NY-1890-295p-pict cl,frntis,illus-Luther #37-1st ed (t7,f) 80.00

KING,CHARLES-Captain Blake-1891-Lippincott-495p-illus-1st ed (r8,cov wn,stnd) 15.00

KING,D L-Hunting Big Game in Africa-USA-1926-315p-dec bds,photos (gg3,wn) 15.00

KING,DAVID S-Mountain Meadows Massacre-Wash D.C.-1970-26p-wrps,illus-Potomac Corral, Westerners #8-1st ed (c7,f) 35.00

KING,ELEANOR A-Bible Plants for American Gardens-NY-1941-203p-12p hlftones-1st prntg (x5,wn dj) 10.00

KING,ELEANOR A-Bible Plants for American Gardens-NY-1941-Macmillan-203p-cl (x6) 25.00

KING,ELIZABETH T-Memoir with Extracts from Her Letters and Journal-Balt-1859-Armstrong & Berry-12mo-128p-cl-1st ed (y6,innr hng crackng) 18.50

KING,FRANK H-Farmers of Forty Centuries-Emmaus Penn-nd-Rodale Pr-379p-photos-1st Amer ed (c3,fray dj) 14.00

KING,FRANK M-Mavericks-Pasadena-(1947)-Trail's End Publ-275p-C M Russell,illus,col frntis-Six Guns 1237-1st ed (gg4,sl wn dj) 50.00

KING,FRANK M-Pioneer Western Empire Builders-1946-Trail's End-383p-illus-1st ed so stated (r8) 38.00

KING,FRANK M-Wranglin' the Past-Pasadena-(1946)-284p-photos,illus by Russell-Six Guns 1239-1st ed after priv prtd sm ed for friends (f7,dj) 75.00

KING,FRANK M-Wranglin' the Past-Pasadena-1946-Trails End-C Russell illus,photos-Six Guns 1239-1st rvsd ed after ltd (nn9,dj chip) 45.00

KING,FRANK-Mavericks-Pasadena-(1947)-Trail's End Publ-275p-illus,Russell-1st ed (f9,dj) 35.00

KING,GRACE-Memories of a Southern Woman of Letters-NY-1932-Macmillan-blu cl-1st ed (f2,dj) 25.00

KING,H F-Sopwith Aircraft 1912 to 1920-Lond-(1981)-8vo-cl,frntis,illus (t2,dj) 25.00

KING,IRENE L-Culinary Gems From the Kitchens of Old Virginia-NY-(1952)-Dodd,Mead-224p (o6,dj) 25.00

KING,J C H-Artificial Curiosities From the Northwest Coast of America-Lond-1981-Brit Mus Publ-4to-119p-grn cl,16 col plts,87 monochromes (p8,as new in dj) 75.00

KING,J C-Artificial Curiosities from the Northwest Coast of America-1981-Brit Mus-4to-117p text+16 col & 87 b&w plts-1st ed (bb3,f,dj) 85.00

KING,JOE-San Francisco Giants-1958-Prentice Hall-1st ed (q7,f,dj) 20.00

KING,JOE-San Francisco Giants-1958-Prentice Hall-1st ed (s8,dj) 17.50

KING,JOHN H-Man an Organic Community-Lond-1893-Williams & Norgate-2 vols,grn cl-1st ed (d2,sl tn sp,cov sl wn) 65.00

KING,JULIUS-Wild Flowers at a Glance-Cleve-1935-Harter-63p-papr cov bds,col illus (x6) 10.00

KING,KENNETH-Mission to Paradise-1956-Franciscan Herald-190p-photos-1st ed (d3,dj) 15.00

KING,LESTER-Medical World of the Eighteenth Century-Chig-1958-346p-1st ed (dd3,dj) 40.00

KING,LESTER-Road to Medical Enlightenment, 1650 to 1695-NY-1970-209p-1st ed (dd3) 40.00

KING,MAJOR ROSS-Sportsman & Naturalist in Canada-Tor-1974-8vo-334p-wrps,illus,facs of 1866 ed (m3,vf) 17.50

KING,MOSES-ED.-Notable New Yorkers of 1896 to 1899-NY-1899-Moses King-dec cov,illus-1st ed (y10) 50.00

KING,MRS FRANCIS-Well Considered Garden-NY-1923-Scribner-234p-photos,fldg plt (x6,sp fade) 15.00

KING,RUFUS-Case of the Constant God-1936-CC-1st ed (s10,innr hng shakn,sp chip dj 22.50

KING,RUFUS-Deadly Dove-NY-1945-Dbldy CC-1st ed (e4,f,dj) 10.00

KING,RUFUS-Malice in Wonderland-GC-1958-Dbldy CC-1st ed (w9,f,dj) 60.00

KING,RUFUS-Murder Masks Miami-1939-DM-1st ed (x7,dj) 50.00

KING,RUFUS-Variety of Weapons-NY-1943-Dbldy CC-1st ed (e4,dj) 10.00

KING,SHIRLEY-Dining with Marcel Proust-(Lond)-(1979)-Thames & Hudson-folio-160p-g title,brwn cl,85 illus-1st Brit ed (q8,f,dj) 20.00

KING,STEPHEN-Carrie-1974-Dbldy-auth 1st bk-1st ed (x2,dj) 375.00

KING,STEPHEN-Christine-NY-1983-Viking-1st ed (q2,dj) 45.00

KING,STEPHEN-Cujo-NY-1981-1st ed (o5,f,dj) 20.00

KING,STEPHEN-Danse Macabre-1981-Everest-1st ed (s10,dj) 25.00

KING,STEPHEN-Danse Macabre-NY-1981-1st ed (n5,dj) 45.00

KING,STEPHEN-Dead Zone-NY-1979-1st ed (p5,dj) 40.00

KING,STEPHEN-Dead Zone-NY-1979-Viking-1st ed (w5,f dj) 60.00

KING,STEPHEN-Different Seasons-NY-1982-1st ed (q5,f,dj) 40.00

KING,STEPHEN-Firestarter-NY-1980-1st ed (t5,f,dj) 35.00

KING,STEPHEN-Night Shift-1978-Dbldy-1st ed (x2,dj) 625.00

KING,STEPHEN-Salem's Lot-NY-1975-Dbldy-"Father Cody" dj,clipped to $7.95 price-1st ed (k4,f,dj) 450.00

KING,STEPHEN-Shining-NY-1977-Dbldy-1st ed (y2,f,sl tn dj) 175.00

KING,STEPHEN-Stand-GC-1978-Dbldy-8vo-cl/bds-1st ed (x3,sl chip dj) 150.00

KING,STEPHEN-Stand-NY-1978-Dbldy-1st ed (j4,dj) 200.00

KING,TOM-In the Shadow of the Giants-San Diego-1981-287p-illus-1st ed (p10,as new in dj) 14.00

KING,W A-Rattling Yours...Snake King-1964-priv publ-223p-photos-scarce (bb3) 40.00

KING,W A-Rattling Yours...Snake King-Brownsville-1964-223p-photos-1st ed (a9,dj) 60.00

KING,WILLIAM C-ED.-Woman-Springfield-1902-667p-cl (d1) 25.00

KING,WILLIAM F-Reminiscences-NY-1915-Abingdon-716p (o7,cl scuff) 25.00

KINGDON WARD,F-Field Notes of Rhododendrons and Other Plants Collected by...in 1933-priv prtd-12mo-grn cl (jj7) 22.50

KINGDON WARD,F-Field Notes of Rhododendrons Collected by...in 1926-priv prtd-12mo-81p-brgndy cl (jj7) 22.50

KINGDON WARD,F-Plant Hunter in Manipur-Lond-1952-254p-fldg map,12p photos-1st ed (hh7,dj rprd) 70.00

KINGDON WARD,F-Plant Hunter in Tibet-Lond-1934-317p-illus,fldg map-1st ed (a4,cov wn & sl spot) 75.00

KINGDON WARD,F-Plant Hunter's Paradise-NY-1938-347p-orig grn cl,frntis,12 photos,2 fldg maps (jj7,sp fade) 62.50

KINGDON WARD,F-Plant Hunting on the Edge of the World-Lond-1974-8vo-x,224p-15 plts,3 maps (x5,sl fade,chip dj) 18.00

KINGDON WARD,F-Return to the Irrawaddy-Lond-1956-224p-46 photos,fldg map-1st ed (q10,f,dj) 50.00

KINGDON WARD,F-Return to the Irrawaddy-Lond-1956-224p-red cl,fldg map,46 photos (jj7) 76.00

KINGDON,J-East African Mammals. Vol.I-1984-U of Chig-4to-446p-wrps,9p col illus (bb3,f) 35.00

KINGERY,W D-Introduction to Ceramics-Lond-1960-781p-illus (cc8) 40.00

KINGFISHER-Trout Flies-Lond-1938-8vo-202p-illus,photos-1st ed (m3,vf,sl chip dj) 30.00

KINGMAN,LEE-Peter's Long Walk-NY-1953-Dbldy-oblng 8vo-47p-cl/pict bds,illus by B Cooney-1st ed (oo10,f,dj) 30.00

KINGS OF JAZZ-NY-(1961)-Barnes-11 vols-pict wrps (t1,box) 40.00

KINGSBURY,CARL L-Mystery at Carroll Ranch-Elgin-(1910)-David C Cook-94p-cl & dec bds,dbl cols (d1) 15.00

KINGSBURY,GEORGE W-History of Dakota Territory-Chig-1915-Clarke Publ-2 vols-illus-Herd 1279-1st ed (dd4) 200.00

KINGSBURY,GEORGE W-History of Dakota Territory-Chig-1915-S J Clarke-5 vols-illus-Herd 1279 (nn6) 450.00

KINGSBURY,JOHN M-Poisonous Plants of the United States and Canada-NJ-(1964)-xiii,626p-grn cl,4 col photos,130 figs & b&w photos (x5) 20.00

KINGSFORD,ANNA-Addresses & Essays in Vegetarianism-Lond-1912-J Watkins-227p-prtd wrps (q8,cov wn) 25.00

KINGSFORD,ANNA-Ideal in Diet-Lond-1898-Vege Libr-16mo-176p-red cl (q8) 50.00

KINGSFORD-SMITH,C E-Flight of the Southern Cross-NY-1929-Nat Travel Club-8vo-xvi,296p-cl,frntis,plts,map,illus e.p.-scarce Amer ed (t2) 90.00

KINGSLEY,CHARLES,JR.-Saint's Tragedy-Lond-1848-auth 1st bk-1st ed (r2,sl rub) 150.00

KINGSLEY,CHARLES-At Last: Christmas in the West Indies-NY-1871-Harper-465p-g & blk dec cl,41 woodcts-1st Amer ed (ee7,edgewn) 85.00

KINGSLEY,CHARLES-Westward Ho!-NY-1920-Scribner's-14 col plts,N C Wyeth-1st ed (s3,sp g dull,sl rub cov plt) 85.00

KINGSLEY,GEORGE H-Notes on Sport & Travel-Lond-1900-8vo-544p (m3,f,totally uncut) 50.00

KINGSTON,LYLE-On Behalf of the Hunted-Appleton-1955-8vo-139p-illus,frontis,photos (m3,vf,dj) 35.00

KINGSTON,MAXINE H-China Men-NY-1980-Knopf-1st ed (a10,as new in dj) 25.00

KINGSTON,W H G-Twice Lost-Lond,Edinburgh,NY-1884-T Nelson & Sons-12mo-473p-pict dec cl,46 engrvngs (p8,sl soil) 25.00

KINLOCH,B-Sauce for the Mongoose-1965-Knopf-112p-photos-1st US ed (bb3,f,dj) 10.00

KINMONT,ALEXANDER-Twelve Lectures on the Natural History of Man, and the Rise and Progress of Philosophy...-Cin-1839-U P James-355p-bds-Amer Imprnts 56690 (c1,ex-lib,tn pg) 65.00

KINNELL,GALWAY-Black Light-Bost-1966-Houghton Mifflin-1st ed (q2,sl soil bds,dj) 55.00

KINNELL,GALWAY-Black Light-Bost-1966-Houghton Mifflin-8vo-cl bckd bds-1st ed (jj8,f,sl tn dj) 25.00

KINNELL,GALWAY-How the Alligator Missed Breakfast-1982-Houghton-1st ed (p9,f,dj) 15.00

KINNELL,GALWAY-Mortal Acts,Mortal Words-1980-HMCO-1st ed (x10,f,dj) 15.00

KINNEY,ARTHUR F-Flannery O'Connor's Library-Athens-(1985)-Univ of Georgia Pr-1st ed (c10,f,sl fade dj sp) 25.00

KINNEY,BRUCE-Frontier Missionary Problems-NY-(1918)-Revell-249p-illus (cc4) 15.00

KINNEY,WILLIAM R-Descent of Real Property in Ohio...Various Statutes of Descent...-Cleve-1924-45p-artificial lea (b1) 12.50

KINNISON,WILLIAM A-Building Sullivant's Pyramid-(Columbus)-(1970)-225p-cl (k1,f,dj) 15.00

KINSELLA,THOMAS-Another September-Dublin-1958-Dolmen Pr-1st ed (z8,vf,dj) 32.50

KINSELLA,THOMAS-Downstream-Dublin,Lond-1962-Dolman Pr-1st ed (dd2,f,dj) 50.00

KINSELLA,THOMAS-Fifteen Dead-Dublin-1979-Dolmen Pr-wrps-1st ed (z8,f) 20.00

KINSELLA,THOMAS-New Poems 1973-Dublin-(1973)-Dolmen Pr-1st ed (z8,vf,dj) 70.00

KINSELLA,THOMAS-One, and Other Poems-Dublin-1979-Dolmen Pr/OUP-wrps-1st ed (z8,vf) 17.50

KINSELLA,W P-Shoeless Joe-1982-Houghton Mifflin-1st ed (ff2,dj) 125.00

KINSELLA,W P-Shoeless Joe-1982-Houghton Mifflin-1st ed (s8,dj) 90.00

KINSLEY,H M-One Hundred Recipes for the Chafing Dish-NY-1894-Gorham Mfg,Silversmiths-12mo-182p-orange & blk bds,photo plts-Bitting 260 (u6,sl soil) 50.00

KINZIE,JULIETTE A-Wau Bun, the "Early Day" in the Northwest-Menasha-1930-Geo Banta-12mo-xxii,390p-illus,map e.p.-1st publ 1886-1st ed thus (o2) 25.00

KINZIE,MRS JOHN H-Wau-Bun-Chig-1932-Donnelley-609p-frntis,illus-Lakeside Classics (cc4) 30.00

KIP,JOHN D W-Union Speller-Wash-1830-Hamilton Robb,prntr-204p-bds-rare (k1) 150.00

KIP,LAWRENCE-Indian Council at Walla Walla, May and June, 1855-Eugene-1897-28p-stapled as iss (bb9) 40.00

KIP,W I-Few Days at Nashotah-Albany-1849-31p-wrps-Howes K177-1st ed (t7) 40.00

KIPLING,RUDYARD-Abaft the Funnel-1909-B W Dodge-1st ed (x2,f) 75.00

KIPLING,RUDYARD-Captains Courageous-1897-Century-dec cl over bds-1st US ed (kk6) 110.00

KIPLING,RUDYARD-Courting of Dinah Shadd-1899-Dbldy & McClure-pict cl-1st ed (x2,sl soil) 30.00

KIPLING,RUDYARD-Debits and Credits-Lond-1926-Macmillan-1st Brit ed (d10) 30.00

KIPLING,RUDYARD-Eyes of Asia-NY-1918-101p-1st ed (k9) 15.00

KIPLING,RUDYARD-Incarnation of Krishna Mulvaney-1899-Dbldy & McClure-pict cl-1st ed (x2,sl soil) 30.00

KIPLING,RUDYARD-Irish Guards in the Great War-GC-1923-Dbldy-2 vols-blk cl,t.e.g.,11 maps-1st ed (oo3) 110.00

KIPLING,RUDYARD-Irish Guards in the Great War-NY-1923-2 vols-blk cl,maps-1st Amer ed (gg2) 75.00

KIPLING,RUDYARD-Just So Stories for Little Children-Lond-1902-Macmillan-dec red cl,illus,auth-1st ed (w1) 300.00

KIPLING,RUDYARD-Kipling's Poems-1899-G M HIll-g stmpd pict cl-1st ed (x2,sp sl fade & rub) 85.00

KIPLING,RUDYARD-Maltese Cat-GC-1936-Dbldy Doran-illus-1st US ed thus (h9,bump) 58.00

KIPLING,RUDYARD-Puck of Pook's Hill-1906-Dbldy,Page-4p col illus,A Rackham-1st Amer ed (x2) 125.00

KIPLING,RUDYARD-Puck of Pook's Hill-Lond-1906-Macmillan-xi,306p+ads-orig red cl,gilt,illus by H R Miller-1st ed (hh9) 75.00

KIPLING,RUDYARD-Puck of Pook's Hill-NY-1906-Dbldy,Page-275p-grn dec cl,gilt,t.e.g.,illus by A Rackham-1st Amer ed(and 1st with these illus) (hh9) 75.00

KIPLING,RUDYARD-Puck of Pook's Hill-NY-1906-Dbldy,Page-4 col plts,A Rackham-1st illus ed (s3,cl bubblng,sl wtrstnd pgs) 50.00

KIPLING,RUDYARD-Rewards and Fairies-GC-1910-Dbldy,Page-344p-cl,4 plts,F Craig-1st ed (s3) 35.00

KIPLING,RUDYARD-Rewards and Fairies-GC-1910-Dbldy,Page-344p-g pict cl,4 plts by F Craig-1st US ed (nn10) 25.00

KIPLING,RUDYARD-Rewards and Fairies-NY-1910-illus-1st Amer ed (r2,sl rub) 40.00

KIPLING,RUDYARD-Something of Myself for My Friends Known and Unknown-NY-1937-1st Amer ed (r2,sp sun) 25.00

KIPLING,RUDYARD-Stalky and Co-NY-1899-Dbldy,McClure-cl,8 plts-(precedes Brit ed)-1st ed (nn10) 40.00

KIPLING,RUDYARD-Thy Servant a Dog-GC-1930-Dbldy Doran-95p-cl,b&w drwngs,M Kirmse-1st ed thus (s3) 15.00

KIPLING,RUDYARD-Traffics and Discoveries-Lond-1904-1st ed (d5) 50.00

KIPLING,RUDYARD-Without Benefit of Clergy-1899-Dbldy & McClure-pict cl-1st ed (x2,sl soil) 30.00

KIPNIS,IRA-American Socialist Movement, 1897 to 1912-NY-1912-Columbia Univ Pr-x+496p-blk cl-1st ed (e2,dj) 20.00

KIPPIS,A-Captain Cook's Voyages...-NY-1924-Knopf-8vo-x,(2),404p-drk brwn cl wi papr labls,12 illus (nn1,drknd sp labl,sl wn) 50.00

KIRBY,EDWARD M-Saga of Butch Cassidy and the Wild Bunch-Palmer Lake-1977-116p-stiff pict wrps,frntis,photos,maps-1st ed (t7) 45.00

KIRBY,GEORGIANA B-Years of Experience-NY-1887-Putnam's-(iv)+315p-brwn cl-1st ed (k2) 90.00

KIRBY,MICHAEL-ED.-Happenings-NY-1965-Dutton-photos-1st ed so stated (q1,sl scuff dj) 35.00

KIRBY,RICHARD S-ED.-Inventors and Engineers of Old New Haven-New Haven-1939-New Haven Hist Soc-(vi)+111p-blu cl,illus-1st ed (c2) 15.00

KIRBY,W E-Butterflies and Moths of the United Kingdom-nd(ca. early 1900s)-Routledge-463p-70 col plts (bb3,cor wn) 50.00

KIRBY,W F-European Butterflies and Moths-Lond-1882-Cassell,Petter,Galpin-g dec,dec e.p.,a.e.g.,1 plain & 61 hand col plts (p6,rebckd) 400.00

KIRCHHOFF,THEODORE-Handbook of Insanity for Practitioners and Students-NY-1893-Wm Wood-vi+362p-maroon cl,9 photo plts-1st ed (a2,ex-libr) 40.00

KIRK,RUDOLF-Authors of New Jersey. A Checklist-Trenton-1955-4to-55p-wrps (aa6) 30.00

KIRK,WILLIAM-Right Off the Bat-1911-GW Dillingham-drwngs-1st ed (s8) 125.00

KIRKBRIDE,THOMAS-Pennsylvania Hospital for the Insane-Phila-1845-44p-pnk wrps (d2,sl wn) 50.00

KIRKE,EDMUND-Among the Guerillas-NY-1866-Carleton-purple cl-Wright II, 1002-1st ed (f2,sp fade,sl soil cov) 40.00

KIRKE,EDMUND-Among the Pines-NY-1862-J R Gilmore-310p-cl-Wright 1003 (j1) 22.50

KIRKE,EDMUND-My Southern Friends-NY-1863-Carleton-brwn cl-Wright II, 1005-1st ed (f2,sl fade cov,fox) 35.00

KIRKER,H-California's Architectural Frontier-San Marino-1960-Huntington Libr-64 plts-1st ed (ee1,dj) 125.00

KIRKHAM,STANTON D-In the Open-SF-1908-8vo-223p-photos (m3) 17.50

KIRKLAND,EDWARD C-Men,Cities and Transportation-Cambridge-1948-Harvard Univ-2 vols,grn cl,plts-1st ed (e2) 55.00

KIRKLAND,MRS C M-Spenser and the Faery Queen-NY-1848-Putnam-8vo-246p-BAL 11153-new ed (w6) 35.00

KIRKLAND,MRS E S-Speech and Manners for Home and School-Chig-1884-McClurg & Co-16mo-263p (u6,soil,wn) 50.00

KIRKLAND,MRS-Evening Book-NY-1852-Scribners-312p-g dec blk lea,a.e.g.-1st ed (q8,wn cov,fox) 75.00

KIRKPATRICK,CLIFFORD-Intelligence and Immigration-Balt-1926-Williams & Wilkins-xvi+127p-blu cl-1st ed (j2,dj) 25.00

KIRKPATRICK,D-Eduardo Paolozzi-1971-NYGS-16 col plts-1st ed (h10,dj) 75.00

KIRKUP,THOMAS-History of Socialism-Lond-1900-A & C Black-364p (r1,ex-libr) 15.00

KIRKWOOD,JAMES-American Grotesque-NY-(1970)-S&S-photos-1st ed (c10,sl creased dj) 25.00

KIRKWOOD,JAMES-Hit Me With a Rainbow-NY-(1980)-1st ed (h5,f,sl chip dj) 12.50

KIRKWOOD,JAMES-P S Your Cat is Dead-NY-(1972)-1st ed (h5,sl mar dj) 40.00

KIRKWOOD,JAMES-P.S. Your Cat is Dead-NY-(1972)-1st ed (n5,autg,dj) 30.00

KIRKWOOD,JAMES-Some Kind of Hero-1975-Crowell-1st ed (t9,vf,dj) 15.00

KIRKWOOD,JAMES-There Must Be a Pony-Lond-(1961)-auth 1st bk-1st Brit ed (h5,f,dj) 45.00

KIRSCHNER,B-Everything I Know about Bucks with a Bow-1974-priv prtg-104p-wrps,photos (gg3,f) 20.00

KIRSCHNER,MICHAEL-Forward Freely-So Brunswick-1967-Barnes-1st ed (j9,dj) 15.00

KIRST,HANS H-Night of the Generals-NY-(1963)-Harper & Row-1st US ed (f3,f,dj) 20.00

KIRST,HANS H-Officer Factory-NY-1963-DD-1st US ed (x1,dj) 25.00

KIRST,HANS H-Soldiers' Revolt-NY-1966-H&R-1st US ed (x1,dj) 25.00

KIRST,HANS H-Time For Truth-NY-(1974)-Coward McCann-1st US ed (f3,f,dj) 15.00

KIRST,HANS H-What Became of Gunner Asch-NY-1964-H&R-1st US ed (x1,f,f dj) 25.00

KIRSTEIN,LINCOLN-Dance-NY-1935-Putnam (u4) 18.00

KIRSTEIN,LINCOLN-ET AL-Ballet & Modern Dance-NY-1974-Octupus (u4,as new in dj) 25.00

KITCHEN COOK BOOK...DONATED TO THE LADY FRIENDS OF THE LIMA TEA COMPANY, LIMA,OHIO-nd-212p-wrps (f1,sl wn) 17.50

KITCHENER,L D-Flag Over the North-Seattle-(1954)-349p-illus-1st ed (d7,chip dj) 45.00

KITE,ELIZABETH S-L'Enfant and Washington, 1791 to 1792-Balt-1929-Johns Hopkins Pr-xii+182p-blu bds,cl sp-1st ed (k2) 25.00

KITES,CLIFFORD-Reminiscences of an Old Sportsman-1951-priv prntd-8vo-108p-photos-scarce (m3) 40.00

KITTO,F H-Hudson Bay Region-Ottawa-1929-Dept of Interior-vii,50p-prtd wrps,illus-Arctic Biblio 2741 (dd7,cov sl soil) 35.00

KITTO,F H-Peace River Country, Canada-Ottawa-1930-113p-wrps-3rd ed,revised (g1) 12.50

KITTREDGE,GEORGE L-Old Farmer and His Almanack-Cambridge-1924-Harvard U-xiv,403p-burgundy cl,g lttrng,30 illus (m10,spot cov) 25.00

KITTREDGE,GEORGE L-Witchcraft in Old and New England-Cambridge-1929-Harvard-x+641p-red cl-1st ed (mm10) 50.00

KIZER,CAROLYN-Knock Upon Silence-GC-1965-Dbldy-1st ed (v5,f,sl creased dj) 35.00

KIZER,CAROLYN-Ungrateful Garden-(1961)-U of Indiana Pr-1st ed (u10,f,dj) 60.00

KIZER,CAROLYN-Ungrateful Garden-Bloomington-(1961)-Indiana Univ Pr-wrps-1st paper ed (h8) 25.00

KLAMKIN,CHARLES-Barns-NY-1973-Hawthorn-4to-162p-blu cl,illus-1st ed (r10,dj) 15.00

KLAPPER,C F-Sir Herbert Walker's Southern Railway-Lond-1973-295p-1st ed (n4,f,dj) 18.50

KLAPPER,CHARLES-Golden Age of Tramways-Lond-2nd impr (n4,f,f dj) 20.00

KLAPPHOLZ,LOWELL-ED.-Gold! Gold!-NY-(1959)-McBride-207p-illus-1st ed (bb4,dj) 15.00

KLAUSNER,SAMUEL Z-ED.-Quest for Self Control-NY/Lond-(1965)-Free Pr/Collier,MacMlln-(xiv)+400+(2)p-blu cl-1st ed (y9) 19.00

KLAUSNITZER,B-Beetles-1983-Exeter-214p-210 photos-1st US ed (bb3,f,dj) 24.00

KLEE,PAUL-Diaries of...1898 to 1918-Berkeley-1964-Univ of Cal-1st ed (f8,f,sp chip dj) 50.00

KLEE,PAUL-Inward Vision-1959-Abrams-lg sq folio-col illus,glassine dj as iss (ee1,dj) 100.00

KLEIN,ALEXANDER-ED.-Grand Deception-Lond-(1956)-Faber & Faber-8vo-413p-1st Brit ed (dd5,dj) 15.00

KLEIN,H ARTHUR-Peter Bruegel the Elder-NY-1968-Macmillan-4to-188p-illus grn cl,b&w & col illus (r10,wn dj) 10.00

KLEIN,MAURY-History of the Louisville & Nashville Railroad-NY-1972-Macmillan-xviii+590p-blk cl,illus-Railroad of Amer Ser-1st prtg (b2,red dot bottm edge,dj) 22.00

KLEIN,WILLIAM-New York-Lond-(1956)-Photog Mag-qto-blk cl-scarce (y3) 375.00

KLEIN,WILLIAM-Tokyo-NY-1964-Crown-sm folio-184p-cl,photos-1st ed (q3,sl tn dj) 225.00

KLEIN,WILLIAM-William Klein: Photographs-NY-1981-Aperture-191p-93 photos-1st ed (cc9,as new in dj) 60.00

KLEINPELL,ROBERT M-Miocene Stratigraphy of California-Tulsa-1938-Am Assoc Petro Geologists-8vo-450p-22 plts at end,5 lg fldg tbls & figs rear pckt-1st ed (gg5) 50.00

KLEMENT,FRANK L-limits of Dissent-Lexington-(1970)-351p-illus (c4,f,dj) 27.50

KLICKSTEIN,HERBERT-Wilhelm Konrad Roentgen on a New Kind of Rays, a Bibliographical Study-1966-129p-wrps-1st ed (dd3) 50.00

KLIMT,GUSTAV-Erotic Drawings-NY-(1980)-Abrams-text by H Hofstatter (l9,f,box) 150.00

KLINCK,RICHARD E-Land of Room Enough and Time Enough-Albuq-(1953)-129p-map frnt e.p.,col photos-1st ed (v7) 20.00

KLINE,MARY S-Ferryboats-Seattle-(1983)-Bayless Bks-4to-xii,401p-cl,photos-1st ed (v1,f,dj) 65.00

KLINE,MILTON V-ED.-Hypnodynamic Psychology-NY-1955-Julian Pr-(xii)+367+(5)p-cl-1st ed (y9,dj) 17.50

KLINE,MILTON V-Psychodynamics and Hypnosis-Springfield-(1967)-Chas C Thomas Publ-(xii)+194+(2)p-pebbled crimson cl-1st ed (y9,dj) 25.00

KLINE,OTIS A-Port of Peril-Providence-1949-Grandon-1st ed (f3,f,sl chip dj) 20.00

KLINEBURGER,B-Big Game Hunting Around the World-NY-1969-376p-photos (gg3,vf,dj) 20.00

KLINEFELTER,W A-Fourth Display of Old Maps & Plans-La Cross-1978-Sumac Pr-65p-illus (a3,dj) 12.00

KLONDIKE-Chig-1897-Chicago Record Co-413p+ads-cl-Wickersham 3902-1st ed (h1,sl rub,inner hng reinfrcd) 35.00

KLONDYKE COUNTRY-THE OFFICIAL GUIDE TO THE...AND THE GOLD FIELDS OF ALASKA-Chig-1897-Conkey-295p-g dec red cov,illus,fldg map-1st ed (ll8,cov discol) 150.00

KLONSKY,MILTON-ED.-Fabulous Ego-NY-(1974)-NYT/Quadrangle-8vo-436p-illus-1st ed (cc5,f,sl chip dj) 20.00

KLUCKHOHN,CLYDE-Navaho-Cambridge-1951-Harvard U Pr-258p-illus,map e.p. (cc4) 15.00

KLUCKHORN,CLYDE M-To The Foot of the Rainbow-Glorieta-1967-280p-map e.p.-1st ed (t7) 10.00

KLUGE,P F-Eddie and the Cruisers-NY-1980-Viking-1st ed (y1,f,f dj) 25.00

KNAPP,H S-History of the Maumee Valley commencing with its occupation by the French in 1680-Toledo-1877-685p-cl (j1) 75.00

KNAPPE,K A-Durer: the Complete Engravings Etchings & Woodcuts-1965-Abrams-folio-385 illus-1st ed (h10,dj) 125.00

KNAUSS,JAMES O-First Fifty Years-Kalamazoo-1953-214p-cl-1st ed (k1,sl wn dj,autg) 15.00

KNEALE,ALBERT H-Indian Agent-Caldwell-1950-Caxton-429p-cl,photos-1st ed (ll9,dj) 100.00

KNEELAND,GEORGE J-Commercialized Prostitution in New York City-NY-1913-Century-1st ed (w5) 25.00

KNEISS,GILBERT-Redwood Railways-Berkeley-1957-165p+map-3rd prtg (n4,f,dj) 25.00

KNIGHT,C-Hitch Your Wagon-Drexel Hill-(1950)-8vo-xii,332p-cl,frntis,16p plts,text illus,e.p. maps-1st ed (t2,sp fade) 40.00

KNIGHT,CHARLES-Popular History of England-Lond-(1850)-8 vols-3/4 g dec brwn lea,mrbld bds,edges & e.p.,illus (b7) 250.00

KNIGHT,CHARLES-Shadows of the Old Booksellers-Lond-1865-Bell & Daldy-1st ed (w1,scratch on rear cov) 65.00

KNIGHT,CLIFFORD-Affair of the Heavenly Voice-1937-Dodd-1st ed (s10) 15.00

KNIGHT,CLIFFORD-Dark Abyss-NY-1949-Dutton-1st ed (j4,dj) 10.00

KNIGHT,CLIFFORD-Hangman's Choice-NY-1949-Dutton-1st ed (h4,chip dj) 12.50

KNIGHT,DAMON-Charles Port: Prophet of the Unexplained-GC-1970-Dbldy-cl,illus-1st ed (o8,dj fray) 16.50

KNIGHT,DAMON-ED.-Turning Points-NY-(1977)-Harper & Row-1st ed (h3,f,sl tn dj) 10.00

KNIGHT,DAVID-Natural Science Books in English, 1600 to 1900-NY-1972-262p-illus (dd3,dj) 75.00

KNIGHT,DAVID-Zoological Illustration-Lond-1977-204p-1st ed (dd3) 35.00

KNIGHT,JOHN A-Black Bass-NY-1949-8vo-200p-illus-trd ed (m3,f) 27.50

KNIGHT,JOHN A-Field Book of Fresh-Water Angling-NY-1944-12mo-207p-illus,photos-1st ed (m3,f,dj) 32.50

KNIGHT,JOHN A-Fishing For Trout & Bass-Chig,NY-1949-12mo-128p-photos (m3) 20.00

KNIGHT,JOHN A-Fresh-Water Tackle-Chig,NY-1949-16mo-158p-illus (m3) 20.00

KNIGHT,JOHN A-Modern Angler-NY-1936-8vo-260p-photos-1st ed (m3,fade sp) 25.00

KNIGHT,JOHN A-Moon Up Moon Down-NY-1942-8vo-163p-1st ed (m3,f,badly fray dj) 35.00

KNIGHT,JOHN A-Theory & Technique of Fresh Water Angling-NY-1940-8vo-223p-illus-1st ed so stated (m3,vf) 20.00

KNIGHT,JOHN A-Woodcock-NY-1944-Borzoi-161p-col illus (ee3,f) 45.00

KNIGHT,KATHLEEN M-Birds of Ill Omen-1948-CC-1st ed (s10,edge wn,brwng pgs,dj) 10.00

KNIGHT,KATHLEEN M-Footbridge to Death-1947-CC-1st ed (s10,dj) 12.50

KNIGHT,KATHLEEN M-Port of Seven Strangers-NY-1945-Dbldy CC-1st ed (j4,chip dj) 15.00

KNIGHT,KATHLEEN M-Stream Sinister-NY-1945-Dbldy CC-1st ed (e4,f,dj) 12.50

KNIGHT,KATHLEEN M-Trademark of a Traitor-NY-1943-Dbldy CC-1st ed (j4,dj) 12.50

KNIGHT,MRS.HELEN C-Hannah More-NY-(1862)-282p-cl (n1,lacks f.e.p.,sl wn sp) 15.00

KNIGHT,O W-Birds of Maine-Bangor-1908-8vo-693p-dec cl,map,26 plts (y8) 90.00

KNIGHT,O W-List of the Birds of Maine-Augusta-1897-8vo-184p-wrps (y8,soil) 22.00

KNIGHT,OLIVER-Following the Indian Wars-Norman-(1960)-U of Okla Pr-348p-maps,illus-1st ed (dd4,dj) 35.00

KNIGHT,OLIVER-Fort Worth: Outpost on the Trinity-1953-U of Okla Pr-8vo-xiii,302p-pict cl,illus,photos-Herd 1284-1st ed (aa3,f,rub dj) 45.00

KNIGHT,RICHARD A-Mastering the Shotgun-NY-1975-8vo-127p-photos,illus-1st ed (m3,vf,dj) 20.00

KNIGHT,RICHARD A-Successful Trout Fishing-NY-1968-8vo-166p-photos (m3,vf,dj) 15.00

KNIGHT,WILBUR C-Birds of Wyoming-Laramie-1902-Wy Exper Sta,Bull.#55-174p-1/2 lea on mrbld bds,drwngs by F Bond (b9,hng crack) 35.00

KNITTLE,RHEA M-Early Ohio Taverns ...-(Ashland)-(1937)-39,(1)p-prntd wrps-scarce #1 in "Ohio Frntier Ser"-ltd to 1900c,nbrd-errata slip laid in-2nd ed has 46p-1st ed (h1) 17.50

KNOBLOCK,K T-Murder in the Mind-NY-1932-Harper-1st ed (d4) 12.50

KNOBLOCK,K T-Take Up the Bodies-NY-1933-Harper-1st ed (f4) 10.00

KNOEBL,KUNO-Victor Charlie-NY-(1967)-Praeger-1st ed (ff3,f,dj) 75.00

KNOKE,H-I Flew for the Fuhrer-NY-1954-8vo-viii,214p-cl,frntis,8p plts-1st ed (t2,chip dj) 30.00

KNOPF,ALFRED A-Borzoi 1920-NY-1920-Knopf-patterned bds,photos-1st ed (bb2,bump) 75.00

KNOPF,ALFRED A-Portrait of a Publisher 1915 thru 1965-NY-1965-Typophiles-2 vols-yel box-1st ed (bb2,f,djs,box) 100.00

KNOPF,ALFRED A-Sixty Photographs-NY-1975-1st ed (k5,as new in dj) 20.00

KNOPF,ALFRED A-Sixty Photographs-NY-1975-Knopf-1st ed (dd2,f,dj) 45.00

KNOPF,EDWIN H-Food of Italy and How to Prepare It-1964-Knopf-409p-pict cl-1st ed (q8,dj) 25.00

KNOTTNERUS-MEYER,THEODORE-Birds and Beasts of the Roman Zoo-NY-(1928)-Century-8vo-378p-photos-1st ed (aa5,edgewn dj) 25.00

KNOTTS,ROBERT J-COMP.-Calhoun County in the Civil War-Parsons-1982-116p-cl (f1,f,dj) 17.50

KNOWLES,JOHN-East Windows of Holy Trinity Church, Goodramgate, York-1924-Yorkshire Archae Soc-24p-wrps,illus (cc8) 35.00

KNOWLES,JOHN-Spreading Fires-NY-(1974)-1st ed (j5,dj) 10.00

KNOWLTON,ELIZABETH-Naked Mountain-NY-1934-335p-27 photos,1 plan-1st US ed (a4,sl fox) 70.00

KNOX SOCIETY OF THE FIRST PRESBYTERIAN CHURCH-COMP.-Recipes. Our Own and Our Friends-Beaver Falls-1909-127p-blk cl bds,illus,A D Nichols (n6,wn bds) 35.00

KNOX,BILL-Drum of Ungara-NY-1963-Dbldy CC-1st US ed (h4,f,dj) 20.00

KNOX,BILL-Live Bait-NY-1979-Dbldy-1st Amer ed (q4,f,dj) 25.00

KNOX,BILL-Rally to Kill-NY-1975-Dbldy CC-1st US ed (e4,f,dj) 15.00

KNOX,CAPT DUDLEY W-Eclipse of American Sea Power-NY-(1922)-140p-cl-two fldng maps (e1) 20.00

KNOX,GEORGE W-Japanese Life in Town & Country-NY-1904-Putnam's-275p-dec pict cov,photos,drwngs,fldg map (c3,f) 45.00

KNOX,RONALD-Stil Dead-NY-1934-Dutton-1st US ed (f4,dj sl tn,chip) 85.00

KNUTSON,A J-Thru the Years with Kansas City Since 1861-KC-1937-31p-stiff pict wrps,illus-1st ed (t7,f) 100.00

KNYVETT,CAPT R HUGH-Over There with the Australians-NY-1918-339p-brwn cl,illus-1st ed (b7) 40.00

KOCH,C J-Year of Living Dangerously-NY-1979-St.Martins-1st US ed (w5,f,f dj) 35.00

KOCHANEK,ED-Along an Open Track-Prospect Hts-1972-1st ed (n4,f,dj) 25.00

KOCHER,PAUL-Master of Middle Earth-Bost-1972-Houghton Mifflin-1st ed (bb1,dj) 12.50

KOCHER,PAUL-Reader's Guide to the Silmarillion-Lond-1980-Thames & Hudson-1st ed (z3,f,dj) 10.00

KOEBEL,W H-Argentina Past and Present-Lond-1914-Black-lg 8vo-465p+fldg map,dec cl,photos,wtrcol illus-2nd ed (s1,f) 75.00

KOEHLER,ALAN-Madison Avenue Cook Book-(1962)-Holt-16mo-63p-gry cl,illus (q8,dj) 12.50

KOEHLER,MARY LOU C-Son of a Gun to Sukiyaki-San Antonio-(1971)-Naylor-246p-red cl,drwngs-1st prtg (q8,dj) 15.00

KOEHLER,THOMAS-Songs of a Devotee-Dublin/Lond-1906-Maunsel/B Johnson & Ince-wrps,wi errata,(Tower Pr Bklt No.2)-1st ed (z8,f) 35.00

KOEPPE,CLARENCE E-Canadian Climate-Bloomington-1931-McKnight-8vo-280p-blu cl,g titles,illus,maps-1st ed (cc7) 15.00*

KOERNER,ALBERTA G AURINGER-Detroit and Vicinity before 1900-Wash-1968-Libr of Congress-84p-wrps (h1) 12.50

KOESTER,FRANK-Modern City Planning and Maintenance-NY-1914-McBride,Nast-lg 4to-xix,329p-orig dec cl,plts-1st ed (cc10) 95.00

KOESTLER,ARTHUR-Age of Longing-NY-1951-1st Amer ed (r2,f,sl rub dj) 25.00

KOESTLER,ARTHUR-Invisible Writing-NY-1954-1st Amer ed (r2,f,sl sun dj) 25.00

KOESTLER,ARTHUR-Sleepwalkers-1959-Macmillan-1st Amer ed (t9,sl rub dj) 30.00

KOESTLER,ARTHUR-Spanish Treatment-Lond-1937-Gollancz-flex orng linen wrps-1st ed (v5) 60.00

KOGAN,GEORGES-Ascent of Alpamayo-Lond-134p-1st Brit ed (o10,f,sl chip dj) 35.00

KOHL,J G-History of the Discovery of the East Coast of North America...-Portland-1869-Bailey & Noyes-(xiv)+9-535p-blk cl,22 maps-Vol.1 of Doc Hist of Maine-Howes K246 (b2,innr hng sl exposed) 125.00

KOHT,HALVDAN-Life of Ibsen-Lond-(1931)-Allen & Unwin-2 vols-illus-1st Brit ed (jj9,dj) 50.00

KOIZUMI,KAZUO H-Re Echo...-Caldwell-1957-Caxton-161p-cl,dbl cols,photos,wtrcols-2nd prntg (l1,dj) 15.00

KOLLER,LARRY-Complete Book of Fishing-NY-1955-8vo-144p-photos-1st ed (m3,f,dj) 13.00

KOLLER,LARRY-Sportsman's Workshop-Indpls-1955-8vo-128p-photos (m3,f,dj) 11.00

KOLLER,LARRY-Taking Larger Trout-Bost-1950-8vo-273p-illus-1st ed (m3,f) 70.00

KOLLER,LARRY-Treasury of Angling-NY-1963-4to-252p-illus (m3,vf,dj) 17.50

KOLLER,LARRY-Treasury of Hunting-NY-1965-4to-251p-photos (m3,vf,dj) 15.00

KOLLOCK,HENRY-Sermons on Various Subjects-Savannah-1811-Seymour and Williams-383p-lea-Amer Imprnts 23169 (j1,joints crckng,cor & sp wn) 27.50

KONIZESKI,DICK-ED.-Montanan's Fishing Guide-Missoula-1963-4-8vo-176p-wrps,photos-1st ed (m3,f) 20.00

KONRAD,GEORGE-Case Worker-NY-(1974)-HBJ-1st ed (bb1,dj) 25.00

KONRAD,GEORGE-City Builder-NY,Lond-(1977)-HBJ-1st ed (bb1,as new in dj) 20.00

KONRAD,GEORGE-Loser-SD,NY,Lond-(1982)-HBJ-1st ed (bb1,as new in dj) 15.00

KOOGLER,C V-Aztec-Ft.Worth-1972-242p-cl,photos-1st ed (z1,f,dj,autg) 30.00

KOONTZ,DEAN R-Funhouse-GC-(1980)-Dbldy-1st hdbk ed (p3,f,sp creased dj) 20.00

KOONTZ,DEAN R-Hanging On-NY-(1973)-1st hdbk using his own name-1st ed (d5,dj) 125.00

KOONTZ,DEAN R-Night Chills-NY-1976-Atheneum-1st ed (j3,sl tn dj) 125.00

KOONTZ,DEAN R-Nightmare Journey-NY-1975-Berkley Putnam-1st ed (c8,f,dj) 150.00

KOPP,MARIE E-Birth Control in Practice-NY-1934-McBride-290p-blu cl,tbls-1st ed (d2,edge-wn dj) 55.00

KOPPER,P-National Museum of Natural History-1982-Abrams-4to-496p-324 col plts-1st ed (bb3,f,dj) 55.00

KOPPETT,LEONARD-ED.-New York Times at the Super Bowl-NY-(1974)-Quadrangle-8vo-345p-illus-1st ed (gg5,f,dj) 12.50

KOPPETT,LEONARD-New York Mets-1970-MacMillan-1st ed (ff2,dj) 60.00

KOPPETT,LEONARD-New York Mets-1970-MacMillan-1st ed (r7,dj) 75.00

KOPPETT,LEONARD-Thinking Man's Guide to Baseball-1967-Dutton-1st ed (p7,f,f dj) 20.00

KORG,JACOB-George Gissing-Seattle-1963-U of Wash-1st ed (t4,f,drknd dj) 15.00

KORN,A-Glass in Modern Architecture of the Bauhaus Period-Lond-1967-all illus-1st Brit ed (h10,dj) 75.00

KORN,GRANINO-Electronic Analog Computers-NY-1952-McGraw Hill-xvi+378p-blu cl,figs-1st ed (j2,wn dj) 35.00

KORNBLUTH,C M-Mile Beyond the Moon-GC-1958-Dbldy-1st ed (p3,dj) 10.00

KORNBLUTH,CYRIL M-Best of ...-NY-(1977)-Taplinger-1st ed (d10,as new in dj) 15.00

KORNGOLD,RALPH-Thaddeus Stevens-NY-(1955)-460p-cl-1st ed so stated (a1,dj) 20.00

KORTRIGHT,F H-Ducks, Geese and Swans of North America-Wash-1942-8vo-476p-lea,36 col plts,maps,fldg chrt-ltd to 1000c,2 autg (y8) 135.00

KORTRIGHT,F H-Ducks,Geese & Swans of North America-Wash D.C.-1942-8vo-476p-illus,T M Shortt-1st ed (m3) 25.00

KORTRIGHT,F H-Ducks,Geese & Swans of North America-Wash-1943-Amer Wildlife Inst-476p-illus by Shortt-2nd ed (c9,dj) 25.00

KORTRIGHT,F H-Ducks,Geese and Swans of North America-Harrisburg,Wash-1957(1942)-8vo-476p-cl,36 col plts (y8) 30.00

KOSAMBI,D D-Myth and Reality-Bombay-1962-Popular Prakashan-cl,illus-1st ed (n8,dj) 25.00

KOSINSKI,JERZY-Being There-NY-(1970)-HBJ-1st ed (dd2,f,dj,autg) 30.00

KOSINSKI,JERZY-Blind Date-Bost-1977-1st ed (t5,f,dj) 15.00

KOSINSKI,JERZY-Devil Tree-NY-(1973)-HBJ-1st ed (f3,f,dj) 20.00

KOSINSKI,JERZY-Painted bird-Bost-1965-1st ed (p5,dj chip,sl wn,tape rprd) 100.00

KOSINSKI,JERZY-Painted Bird-Lond-1966-W H Allen-1st Brit ed (d10,f,sl soil dj) 100.00

KOSINSKI,JERZY-Steps-1968-Random-1st ed (t9,f,dj) 35.00

KOSINSKI,JERZY-Steps-NY-(1968)-1st ed (k9,f,dj) 25.00

KOSOFSKY,L J-Moon as Viewed by Lunar Orbiter-Wash D.C.-1970-NASA SP 200-152p-grn cl,illus(incl 4 stereo views),3-D glasses in pckt (hh6,sl fox & soil) 50.00

KOSTASH,MYRNA-All of Baba's Children-Edmonton-1977-Hurtig-414p (k10,dj) 20.00*

KOTSUJI,ABRAHAM-From Tokyo to Jerusalem-NY-(1964)-Geis-8vo-215p-1st US ed (dd5,sl rub dj) 15.00

KOTTURAN,G-Himalayan Gateway-New Delhi-1983-172p-1st ed (o10,f,dj) 20.00

KOTZEBUE,MORITZ VON-Narrative of a Journey into Persia, in the Suite of the Imperial Russian Embassy in the Year 1817-Phila-1820-M Carey & Son-viii,269p-lea wi g sp dec-1st Amer ed (ll1,sl fox) 450.00

KOTZWINKLE,W-Trouble in Bugland-1983-Godine-col illus-1st ed (x7,f,dj) 40.00

KOTZWINKLE,WILLIAM-Christmas at Fontaine's-NY-1982-1st ed (r5,f,dj) 15.00

KOTZWINKLE,WILLIAM-Doctor Rat-NY-1976-Knopf-1st ed (a5,as new in dj) 20.00

KOTZWINKLE,WILLIAM-Dream of Dark Harbor-GC-(1979)-Dbldy-illus by J Servello-1st ed (bb1,f,dj) 17.50

KOTZWINKLE,WILLIAM-Elephant Bangs Train-NY-(1971)-Pantheon-1st ed (b5,as new in dj) 40.00

KOTZWINKLE,WILLIAM-Fata Morgana-NY-1977-Knopf-1st ed (a5,as new in dj) 20.00

KOTZWINKLE,WILLIAM-Hermes 3000-NY-(1972)-Pantheon-1st ed (a5,f,dj) 35.00

KOTZWINKLE,WILLIAM-Hermes 3000-NY-(1972)-Pantheon-1st ed (g6,dj) 45.00

KOTZWINKLE,WILLIAM-Jack in the Box-(1980)-Putnams-1st ed (x2,f,dj) 18.00

KOTZWINKLE,WILLIAM-Jack in the Box-NY-(1980)-Putnam's-1st ed (b5,as new in dj) 15.00

KOUDELKA,JOSEF-Gypsies-NY-1975-Aperture,MOMA-4to-138p-wrps-1st ed (t3) 40.00

KOUFAX,SANDY-Koufax-1966-Viking-1st ed (s8,dj) 25.00

KOURY,MICHAEL-ED.-Diaries of the Little Big Horn-Ft.Collins-1968-82p-pict cl,illus,ltd ed,nbrd,autg (t7,f) 100.00

KOUWENHOVEN,JOHN A-Adventures of America 1857 to 1900-NY-1938-Harper & Bros-4to-illus-1st ed (n2,dj chip,tn) 25.00

KOUWENHOVEN,JOHN A-Columbia Historical Portrait of New York-GC-1953-Dbldy-1st ed (v4,dj wn,rprd) 60.00

KOVACS,ERNIE-How to Talk at Gin-GC-1962-Dbldy-illus-1st ed so stated (q1,dj sl tn & soil) 40.00

KOVACS,ERNIE-Zoomar-1957-Dbldy-auth 1st bk-1st ed (x2,f,sl fox dj) 55.00

KOVACS,ERNIE-Zoomar-GC-1957-GC-auth 1st bk-1st ed (b10,sl wn dj) 40.00

KOWSKY,FRANCIS R-Architecture of Frederick Clarke Withers-Middletown-1980-Wesleyan U Pr-sm 4to-225p-blk cl,illus-1st ed (r10,f dj) 32.50

KOZICKY,EDWARD-Shooting Preserve Management-The Nilo System-E Alton-1967-8vo-311p-photos,illus (m3,dj) 22.50

KPOMASSIE,TETE-MICHEL-An African in Greenland-San Diego,NY,Lond-(1983)-HBJ-photos-1st ed (cc1,as new in dj) 17.50

KRACAUER,S-Offenbach and the Paris of His Time-Lond-(1937)-Constable-24 collotype illus (w1,f,dj) 25.00

KRAFT,HERBERT C-Archaeology of the Tocks Island Area-So Orange-1975-4to-xv,183p-wrps,illus (aa6) 35.00

KRAFT-EBING,RICHARD F VON-An Experimental Study in the Domain of Hypnotism-NY-1889-Putnam's/Knickerbocker-thin 8vo-(xii)+129+(5)p-brwn cl-scarce-1st ed in Engl (y9) 150.00

KRAKEL,DEAN F-Saga of Tom Horn-Laramie-(1954)-Powder River Publ-(x),277p-cl,illus,1st prtg wi orig material intact(pgs 13 & 54 were cut out & replaced in later prtgs)-1st ed (v1,rplcmnts laid in,sl wn dj) 185.00

KRAKEL,DEAN-Tom Ryan-1971-Northland-4to-111p-col illus-1st ed (d3,dj) 15.00

KRAMBLES,GEORGE-Cars of the North Shore Line-Chig-April 1947-Bull.#68-31p-wrps (n4) 10.00

KRAMER,AARON-Roll the Forbidden Drums-NY-1954-Cameron & Kahn-64p (r1,sl tn dj) 25.00

KRAMER,JANE-Allen Ginsberg in America-NY-1969-Charters B40-1st ed (x8,dj) 15.00

KRAMRISCH,STELLA-Art of India-Lond-1954-folio-pict cl,5 col plts-1st ed (r2) 60.00

KRASSO,NICOLAS-ED.-Trotsky-St.Louis-1972-Critics Pr-191p-1st ed (r1,f,f dj) 25.00

KRAUS,HANS P-Sir Francis Drake-Amsterdam-1970-Thistle Pr-folio-236p-facs,lithos-1st ed (d3) 150.00

KRAUS,RENE-Theodora-GC-1938-Dbldy Doran-8vo-337p-1st US ed (gg5,dj) 17.50

KRAUS,ROBERT-Detectives of London-NY-(1978)-Dutton-sm 4to-unpgd-pict cl,illus,R Byrd-1st ed (r3,f,dj chip & creased) 20.00

KRAUS,ROBERT-Reggie Jackson's Scrapbook-1978-Windmill-photos-1st ed (s8,dj) 15.00

KRAUSE,A FRANK-Riding the Ghost Town Trail-Wash D.C.-1969-26p-bds,illus,ltd to 250c,nbrd,autg-Potomac Corral,Westerners #6-1st ltd ed (c7,f) 45.00

KRAUSE,AUREL-Tlingit Indians-Seattle-1956-U of Wash Pr-310p-drwngs,map laid in (bb4,dj) 25.00

KRAUSE,D R-Swiss Shooting Talers & Medals-WI-1965-160p-photos (gg3) 15.00

KRAUSE,ERNST-Erasmus Darwin-NY-1880-Appleton-iv+216p+ads-terra cotta cl-1st Amer ed (d2) 65.00

KRAUSE,IAN-Great Western Branch Line Album-Lond-1969-112p-1st ed (n4,f,dj) 22.00

KRAUSS,BOB-Grove Farm Plantation-Palo Alto-c.1965-Pacific Bks-8vo-xvi,400p-grn cl,map e.p.,photos (p8,dj) 30.00

KREH,LEFTY-Fly Casting with ...-Phila-1974-oblng 8vo-127p-photos-1st ed (m3,vf,dj) 22.50

KREH,LEFTY-Practical Fishing Knots-NY-1972-4to-160p-photos (m3,f,dj) 25.00

KREHBIEL,HENRY E-Afro-American Folksongs-NY,Lond-(1914)-G Schirmer-176p-cl-v scarce (j1,sm spot rear cov) 45.00

KREIDER,CLAUDE-Bamboo Rod & How to Build It-NY-1951-8vo-140p-illus-scarce-1st ed (m3,f,fray dj) 110.00

KREIDER,CLAUDE-Steelhead-NY-1948-8vo-182p-photos (m3,f,fray dj) 32.50

KREIG,MARG-Green Medicine-Chig-1964-Rand-462p (x6,dj wn) 12.00

KREITH,FRANK-Radiation Heat Transfer-Scranton-1962-Intl Textbk Co-236p (dd7,f) 25.00

KREMER,W P-100 Great Battles of the Rebellion-Hoboken-1906-366p-map-1st ed (t7) 75.00

KREPS,E-Science of Trapping-Columbus-(1909)-A R Harding-229; xv p+ads-cl-illus (h1) 15.00

KRESS,PAUL-Isaac Bashevis Singer-NY-(1979)-Dial-1st ed (f3,f,dj) 20.00

KREYMBORG,ALFRED-Funnybone Alley...-NY-(1927)-269p-cl,col frntis & 6 col tip-in illus,Artzybasheff (n1,sl soil cov,sl wrnkld sp) 20.00

KRIDER,JOHN-Krider's Sporting Anecdotes-Phila-1853-8vo-292p+ads-frontis (m3,sp chip) 35.00

KRIDER,JOHN-Price List of Fishing Tackle-Phila-1878-8vo-12p-wrps-rare (m3) 50.00

KRIEGER,B J-Seventy-Five Years of Service-New Orleans-1923-204p-cl (j1) 15.00

KRIEGER,L C-Mushroom Handbook-1936-Macmillan-538p-32 col plts,126 photos & drwngs (bb3) 10.00

KRIM,SEYMOUR-ED.-Beats-1960-Gold Medal-wrps-1st ed (p9,sm cov crease,chip sp) 15.00

KRIM,SEYMOUR-Shake It For the World, Smartass-NY-1970-1st ed (x8,dj) 25.00

KRIM,SEYMOUR-Views of a Nearsighted Cannoneer-NY-1961-Excelsior Pr-wrps,auth 1st bk-1st ed (g8) 35.00

KRIM,SEYMOUR-You & Me-NY-(1974)-1st ed (x8,dj) 20.00

KRIM,SEYMOUR-You & Me-NY-(1974)-HRW-1st ed so stated (q1,sl stnd,dj chip) 15.00

KRIS,ERNST-Catalogue of Post Classical Cameos in the Milton Weil Collection-Vienna-1932-Anton Schroll-sm 8vo-49p text-gry wrps,123 illus (r10,shaken) 20.00

KRISHNA,GOPI-Kundalini-Berkeley-1971-Shambala-cl-1st Amer ed (n8,f,dj) 20.00

KRISHNAMURTI,J-Life in Freedom-NY-1928-Horace Liveright-cl-1st ed (n8,wn dj) 45.00

KROEBER,A L-Sparkman Grammar of Luiseno-Berkeley-1960-Univ of Cal-x+257p-wrps (e2) 30.00

KROEBER,A L-Yurok Myths-LA-1976-488p-1st ed (t7,dj) 22.50

KROEBER,T-Ishi, Last of His Tribe-CA-1964-208p-illus (gg3,f) 20.00

KROEBER,THEODORA-Ishi In Two Worlds-Berkeley-1961-U of Cal Pr-8vo-258p-photos-1st ed (t1,f,dj) 25.00

KROEBER,THEODORA-Ishi, Last of His Tribe-Bost-1964-Houghton Mifflin-1st ed (nn9,dj) 25.00

KROETSCH,ROBERT-World of My Roaring-Tor-1966-MacMillan-8vo-211p-1st ed (cc7,dj rub,chip) 20.00*

KROGER,WILLIAM S-Clinical and Experimental Hypnosis in Medicine, Dentistry and Psychology-Phila-(1963)-Lippincott-lg 8vo-xxii+361+(1)p-1st ed (y9) 30.00

KROLL,CHARLES-Squaretail-NY-1972-8vo-134p-photos (m3,f,dj) 25.00

KROMER,TOM-Waiting for Nothing-NY-1935-Knopf-1st ed (w5,f,dj) 125.00

KRONENBERGER,LOUIS-Republic of Letters-NY-1955-Knopf-1st ed (b5,sl wn dj) 15.00

KRONQUIST,EMIL F-Metalcraft and Jewelry-Peoria-1926-Manual Arts Pr-191p-figs (u5,f,sl chip dj) 28.50

KROPOTKIN,ALEXANDRA-How to Cook and Eat in Russian-1947-Putnam-270p-tan cl-1st ed (q8,dj tn) 18.50

KROPOTKIN,PETER-An Appeal to the Young-NY-1948-Resistance-20p-wrps (r1,tape sp top) 10.00

KROPOTKIN,PETER-Modern Science and Anarchism-NY-1908-Mother Earth Publ-wrps-1st ed (v5) 45.00

KROTT,P-Demon of the North-NY-1959-8vo-260p-40 photos,2 maps (y8) 15.00

KROUSE,JOHN-Rails Through Dixie-San Marino-1965-176p-1st ed (n4,f,dj) 25.00

KRUSE,HORACE-Lure of the Roads in New Mexico-Raton-1921-Swastika Fuel-16p-wrps-1st ed (nn9) 60.00

KRUSSMAN,GERD-Complete Book of Roses-Portland-(1981)-xii,436p-photos,drwngs (x5,f,dj) 35.00

KRUSSMAN,GERD-Roses-Lond-1982-Batsford-4to-xii,436p-16p photos-1st Brit ed (ff9,as new in dj) 50.00*

KRUTCH,J W-ED.-Treasury of Birdlore-NY-1962-8vo-390p-cl,32p illus (y8) 15.00

KRUTCH,JOSEPH W-Baja California-SF-(1967)-Sierra Club-folio-cl-1st ed (y3,f,f dj) 75.00

KRUTCH,JOSEPH W-Desert Year-NY-1952-Sloane-270p (x6,dj) 10.00

KRUTCH,JOSEPH W-Forgotten Peninsula-NY-1961-8vo-277p-photos (m3,vf,dj) 25.00

KU KLUX KLAN SECRETS EXPOSED-Chig-nd(1922?)-Cook,Publ-70p-illus frnt wrps (o1) 30.00

KUBLER,GEORGE A-New History of Stereotyping-NY-1941-362p-bds,illus (c1,sm sp chip) 27.50

KUBLER,GEORGE-Art and Architecture of Ancient America-Balt-(1962)-Penguin Bks-4to-red/brwn cl,168 plts-1st ed (mm10,dj) 50.00

KUBLER,GEORGE-Religious Architecture of New Mexico in the Colonial Period & Since American Occupation-Col Sprngs-1940-Taylor-4to-wrps,photos,fldg maps-ltd to 750c-scarce-1st ed (nn9) 125.00

KUBLER,GEORGE-Religious Architecture of New Mexico-Chig-1962-159p+60p photos & map+index-scarce-rprnt (u7) 25.00

KUBLER-ROSS,ELISABETH-Living with Death and Dying-NY-1981-Macmillan-cl-1st ed (l8,f,dj) 17.50

KUCK,LORAINE E-Hawaiian Flowers-Honolulu-1943-tall 8vo-109p-16 col plts (x5,bump,sl soil) 12.00

KUCK,LORAINE-World of the Japanese Garden-NY,Tokyo-(1968)-lg 8vo-414p-grn silk bndg,45 col photo plts,7 text figs-1st ed (x5,sl stnd cov) 80.00

KUCK,LORIANE-Art of Japanese Gardens-NY-1940-John Day-304p-cl,plts (x6,sl fox,dj tn,wn) 30.00

KUCZYNSKI,J-Economics of Barbarism-NY-1942-Int'l-64p-wrps (r1) 15.00

KUECHLER,O-Practical Fur Ranching-Columbus-1927-12mo-216p-photos,illus-1st ed (m3) 15.00

KUENN,HARVEY-Big League Batting Secrets-1958-Prentice Hall-1st ed (ff2,dj) 30.00

KUENSTER,JOHN-ED.-From Cobb to Catfish-1975-Rand-1st ed (p7,dj) 25.00

KUGLER,JOHN B-History of the First English Presbyterian Church in Amwell-Somerville-1912-x,354p-cl,plts (aa6) 30.00

KUH,KATHARINE-Leger-Urbana-1953-U of Ill-thin 4to-121p-red cl,b&w & col illus (r10,wn dj) 20.00

KUHLMAN,CHARLES-Custer and the Gall Saga-Billings-1940-46p-wrps,fldg map,ltd to 250c-rare-1st ed (t7,f,autg) 185.00

KUHLMAN,CHARLES-Legend Into History-Harrisburg-(1951)-250p-frntis,photos,maps(incl rear pckt)-Luther #110-1st ed (t7,f,dj chip) 125.00

KUHLMAN,CHARLES-Legend into History-Harrisburg-(1951)-250p-illus-Dowd #558-scarce-1st ed (c7,tattrd dj) 110.00

KUHN,LESLEY-ED.-Modern Hypnosis-NY-1947-Psych Libr-(x)+349+(1)p-1st ed (y9) 17.50

KUHNE,FREDERICK-Finger Print Instructor-NY-1916-Munn & Co-g stmpd grn cl wi 11 plts & 2 wanted posters tucked in flap on rear bd-1st ed (w5) 40.00

KUIPERS,C-Zuni Also Prays-np-1946-157p-pict cl,frntis,photos-scarce-1st ed (t7) 45.00

KULISH,JOHN W-Bobcats Before Breakfast-Harrisburg-(1969)-Stackpole-8vo-188p-sketches-1st ed (cc5,sp sun dj) 15.00

KULJIAN,HARRY A-Nuclear Power Plant Design-S Brunswick-(1968)-A S Barnes-4to-xvi+272p-blu cl,illus-1st ed (g2,dj) 25.00

KULL,IRVING S-ED.-New Jersey-NY-1930-(4),442p-cl,ports-Vol.5 only(iss separately from 4 vol set) (aa6) 50.00

KULL,IRVING S-ED.-New Jersey-NY-1930-4to-4 vols-cl,plts (aa6) 100.00

KULP,RANDOLPH L-ED.-History of Lehigh Valley Transit Company: Railway Operations-Allentown-1966-100p-spiral bndg-1st ed (n4) 10.00

KULTURMANN,UDO-ED.-Kenzo Tange, 1946 to 1969-NY-(1970)-Praeger-4to-303p-illus-1st US ed (ee5,vf,f box) 75.00

KUMAR,COL NARINDER-Kanchenjunga-New Delhi-1978-4to-158p-2 maps,col & b&w plts-1st ed (p10,f,dj) 40.00

KUMIN,MAXINE-Halfway-NY-(1961)-HR&W-auth 1st bk-1st ed (u10,f,f dj) 60.00

KUMLIEN,L-Birds of Wisconsin-1951-Wis Ornith Soc-122p-wrps-rvsd ed (bb3,f) 20.00

KUNDERA,MILAN-Farewell Party-Lond-1977-1st Brit ed (o5,f,dj) 35.00

KUNDERA,MILAN-Joke-NY-1969-auth 1st bk-1st US ed (n5,dj) 100.00

KUNDERA,MILAN-Laughable Loves-(Lond)-(1978)-John Murray-1st Brit ed (b5,as new in dj) 35.00

KUNDERA,MILAN-Laughable Loves-1974-Knopf-1st US ed (kk6,f,dj) 45.00

KUNDERA,MILAN-Life is Elsewhere-NY-1974-Knopf-1st Amer ed (oo2,f,dj sl crease,rub) 80.00

KUNDERA,MILAN-Unbearable Lightness of Being-1984-Harper-1st ed (kk6,f,dj) 35.00

KUNDERA,MILAN-Unbearable Lightness of Being-NY-1984-1st US ed (n5,f,dj) 45.00

KUNE,JULIAN-Reminiscences of an Octogenarian Hungarian Exile-Chig-1911-8vo-216p-olive cl-1st ed (kk7) 25.00

KUNEN,JAMES S-Strawberry Statement-NY-1969-Random-1st ed (v5,f,f dj) 25.00

KUNSTLER,WILLIAM-Minister and the Choir Singer-NY-1964-Morrow-8vo-344p-16p photos-1st ed (gg5,dj) 20.00

KUNZ,G F-Gems, Jewelers' Materials, and Ornamental Stones of California-Sacramento-1905-Cal St Mining Bur,Bull.37-gilt,frntis,photos,fldg map (u5,ex-libr) 115.00

KUP,A P-History of Sierra Leone: 1400 to 1787-Cambridge-1961-Univ Pr-8vo-212p-cl-1st ed (y5,dj) 20.00

KUPER,ADAM-Kalahari Village Politics-1970-Cambridge U Pr-8vo-189p-cl,illus,maps-1st ed (y5,dj) 40.00

KUPER,HILDA-African Law-Berkeley-1965-U of Cal Pr-8vo-275p-cl-1st ed (y5,dj) 20.00

KUPER,JESSICA-ED.-Anthropologists' Cookbook-Lond-(1977)-Routledge & K Paul-sm 4to-230p-papr over bds-1st ed (y5,dj) 18.00

KUPER,LEO-Durban-Lond-1958-J Cape-8vo-251p-cl-1st ed (y5,sl sun dj) 15.00

KUPILLAS,MARY C M-House of John Johnson-Balt-1979-ix,98p-cl,plts (aa6) 40.00

KURALT,CHARLES-To the Top of the World-NY-1968-HR&W-8vo-x,193p-photos-1st ed (cc7,dj) 15.00*

KURNITZ,HARRY-Invasion of Privacy-NY-1955-Random-1st ed (f4,f,dj) 12.50

KURTH,DR WILLI-Complete Woodcuts of Albrecht Durer-NY-1946-Crown-4to-gry cl,346 illus (r10,sl wn dj) 12.50

KURTZ,KATHERINE-Saint Camber-NY-(1978)-Ballantine-1st ed (e10,f,dj) 12.50

KURZ,RUDOLPH F-Journal of...-Wash D.C.-1937-382p-wrps,plts-BAE Bull.#115-1st ed (d7) 85.00

KUSHIN,NATHAN-Florida Fishing & Other Stories-1952-Exposition Pr-8vo-137p (m3) 35.00

KUSTOW,MICHAEL-ET AL-Tell Me Lies-Indpls-(1968)-Bobbs Merrill-photos-1st ed (ff3,dj) 125.00

KUTAK,ROSEMARY-Darkness of Slumber-Phila-1944-Lippincott-1st ed (f4,f,sl wn dj) 25.00

KUTUMBIAH,P-Ancient Indian Medicine-Bombay-1962-225p (dd3,dj) 65.00

KUYKENDALL,RALPH S-Hawaiian Kingdom-Honolulu-1938-U of Hawaii Pr-8vo-vii,453p-red cl,e.p. maps (nn1,wn dj) 45.00

KWON,GEORGE I-Oriental Culinary Art-LA-(1933)-Kwon-8vo-115p-red cl-1st ed (t10) 30.00

KYD,THOMAS-Blood is a Beggar-1946-Lippincott-1st ed (s10,sl fade sp,tape rnfrcd dj 40.00

KYD,THOMAS-Blood is a Beggar-Phila-1946-Lippincott-1st ed (h4,stnd dj) 25.00

KYLE,DUNCAN-Green River High-Lond-1979-Collins-1st ed (s4,vf,dj) 27.50

KYLE,R A-Medicine and Stamps-Chig-1970-216p-illus-1st ed (dd3,dj) 40.00

KYNE,PETER B-Cappy Ricks Retires-NY-1922-Cosmopolitan-dj & illus by T D Skidmore-1st ed (x1,dj) 75.00

KYNE,PETER B-Lord of Lonely Valley-NY-1932-1st ed (k9,dj edge wn) 15.00

KYNE,PETER-Kindred of the Dust-NY-1920-Cosmo-illus-1st ed (m4) 9.50

KYNER,JAMES H-End of Track-Caldwell-1937-Caxton-lg 8vo-277p-photos-1st ed (p1,f,dj) 50.00

L'ENGLE,MADELEINE-Wrinkle in Time-Lond-(1963)-Constable Young-182p-bds-1st ed (nn10,few smudges,dj) 65.00

L'HOPITAL,WINEFRIDE DE-Westminster Cathedral and Its Architect-NY-1919-Dodd,Mead-sm 4to-2 vols-grn cl,t.e.g.,illus (r10) 60.00

LA BONNE CUISINE CANADIENNE-Quebec-1927-173p-wrps,10 col plts (q8) 7.50

LA BRANCHE,GEORGE M L-Dry Fly & Fast Water & The Salmon & The Dry Fly-NY-1951-8vo-252p-illus,frontis-1st prntng thus (m3,vf) 40.00

LA CUISINE CREOLE-New Orleans-(1885)-Hansell & Bro-268p-pict blu bds,gold lttrng-2nd ed (u6,wn bds) 75.00

LA FARGE,JOHN-Reminiscences of the South Seas-GC-1912-Dbldy,Page-lg 8vo-480p-grn cl wi col illus pasted on,g titles,48 illus(incl 32 col) (p8) 125.00

LA FARGE,OLIVER-All the Young Men-1935-Houghton Mifflin-1st ed (x2,f,dj) 45.00

LA FARGE,OLIVER-As Long as the Grass Shall Grow-NY-(1940)-Longmans-4to-cl-1st ed (y3,dj sl chip) 50.00

LA FARGE,OLIVER-Santa Fe-Norman-(1959)-U of Okla Pr-436p-illus-1st ed (f9,dj) 40.00

LA FARGUE,THOMAS E-China's First Hundred-Pullman-1942-Wash St U Pr-8vo-176p-28 illus-1st ed (gg5,dj,autg) 30.00

LA FLESCHE,FRANCIS-Dictionary of the Osage Language-Wash-1932-Smithsonian-406p-wrps,BAE Bulletin 109 (l1) 15.00

LA FOLLETTE,ROBERT H-Eight Notches and Other Stories of Nuevo Mejico-Albuq-1950-90p-hdbk-1st ed (v7) 35.00

LA FOLLETTE,ROBERT H-Eight Notches and Other Stories of Nuevo Mejico-Albuq-1950-90p-wrps,illus-1st ed (v7) 25.00

LA FONTAINE,GARY-Challenge of the Trout-Missoula-1976-8vo-243p (m3,f,sl fray dj) 12.50

LA FRANCE,MARSTON-Miami Murder Go Round-Cleve-1951-World-1st ed (g4,dj) 15.00

LA GRANGE,HELEN-Clipper Ships of America Great Britain 1833 to 1869-NY-1936-Putnam's-8vo-381p-3/4 sailcl canvas & woodgrn papr bndg wi g cov dec,37 tip-in col plts,initialed-ltd to 300c,nbrd (p8,f,2 autg) 275.00

LA GRANGE,JACQUES-Clipper Ships of America and Great Britain. 1833 to 1869-NY-1936-Putnam's-xi,(13)-381p-beige cl wi blu & g sp titles & cov decs,over 50 drwngs-trd ed (nn1,fr hng cracked,soil bds) 95.00

LA MAR,ELDEN-Clothing Workers in Philadelphia-Phila-1940-Amalgamated Cl Wrkrs-cl-1st ed (y3,f,f dj) 35.00

LA MONTE,FRANCESCA-Marine Game Fishes of the World-GC-1952-12mo-190p-illus-1st ed (m3,f,dj) 12.50

LA MONTE,FRANCESCA-North American Game Fishes-NY-1945-12mo-202p-illus-1st ed (m3,f,fray dj) 13.50

LA TOURETTE DRIGGS,L-Heroes of Aviation-Bost-1918-8vo-xxvi,302p-cl,frntis,15p plts-1st ed (s2) 50.00

LA WALL,CHARLES-Curious Lore of Drugs and Medicines-GC-(c.1927)-665p-red cl,illus (q8,hng crack) 40.00

LABELLE,JENIJOY-Echoing Wood of Theodore Roethke-Princeton-(1976)-Princeton U Pr-8vo-174p-1st ed (ee5,f dj) 10.00

LABIN,SUZANNE-Hippies, Drugs and Promiscuity-New Rochelle-1972-Arlington-1st ed (f8,f,f dj) 25.00

LABISKY,WALLACE R-Waterfowl Shooting-NY-1954-8vo-150p-illus-1st prntng (m3,vf,dj) 27.50

LACHOUQUE,HENRY-Anatomy of Glory-Lond,NY-(1978)-sm 4to-564p-illus (d7,f,dj) 50.00

LACHOUQUE,HENRY-Anatomy of Glory-Providence-1961-564p-14 maps,173 plts(74 col)-1st ed (b7,f,dj) 125.00

LACK,D-Darwin's Finches-Gloucester-1968(1947)-8vo-204p-cl,5 b&w plts (y8) 12.50

LACK,D-Island Biology-Berkeley-1976-8vo-445p-cl,14 plts (y8,dj) 45.00

LACKEY,BERTRRAM-Outwitting Trout with Fly-LA-1929-8vo-132p-col plts,photos (m3,lettering dull,autg) 75.00

LACKEY,LOUANA M-Pottery of Acatlan, A Changing Mexican Tradition-Norman-1982-U of Okla Pr-8vo-xi,3,4-164p-grn cl,18 col plts,58 b&w photos repro,3 maps-1st ed (mm1,f,f dj) 30.00

LACKEY,W W-Flowers and Fruits-Midland-1940-cl,photos (w3) 15.00

LACOUR,TAGE-Murder Book-NY-(1973)-Herder & Herder-192p-1st ed (g9,bump,dj wn,tn) 40.00

LACROIX,J V-Animal Castration-Chig-1915-Amer Journal Vet Med-8vo-144p-grn cl,photos-1st ed (b3) 45.00

LADA-MOCARSKI,VALERIAN-Bibliography of Books on Alaska Published Before 1868-1969-Yale-567p-1st ed (w1,f,dj) 250.00

LADD,B F-History of Vineland-Vineland-1881-84p-wrps,illus (aa6,sl soil wrps) 90.00

LADD,HORATIO O-Story of the States-Bost-(1891)-465p-drwngs-1st ed (u7,ex-libr) 75.00

LADIES AUXILIARY TO TEMPLE DE HIRSCH FAMOUS COOK BOOK-Seattle-1916-349p+11p index-wht bds,many ads (n6) 40.00

LADIES SOCIAL CIRCLE, SIMPSON M. E. CHURCH-How We Cook in Los Angeles-LA-1894-Commercial Prtg Hs-382p-wrps (n6,chip wrps) 150.00

LADIES' AID SOCIETY-Old Mission Cookbook-Traverse City-1921-Ladies' Aid Soc-164p-wrps (z7,cov wn) 30.00

LADIES' HOME JOURNAL ADVENTURES IN COOKING-(1968)-Prentice Hall-folio-384p-red cl,drwngs,col photos (q8,dj) 17.50

LADY MONTAGUE OF BEAULIEU-To the Manor Born-Lond-(1971)-Gentry-144p-brwn cl,pict e.p.,drwngs,facs-1st ed (q8,dj) 25.00

LAFARGE,OLIVER-Door in the Wall-Lond-1966-Gollancz-1st ed (t4,f,f dj) 15.00

LAFARGE,OLIVER-Long Pennant-Bost-1933-HMCO-1st ed (x1,dj) 30.00

LAFARGE,OLIVER-Pictorial History of the American Indian-NY-(1956)-272p-illus(incl col)-1st ed (c4,dj) 25.00

LAFARGE,OLIVER-Santa Eulalia-Chig-1947-U of Chig-scarce-1st ed (nn9,dj) 65.00

LAFARGUE,PAUL-Social and Philosophical Studies-Chig-1906-Chas H Kerr-blu/gry cl-1st ed (v5,f) 25.00

LAFFAL,KEN-Vivolo and His Wooden Children-Essex-1976-Gallery Pr-8vo-144p-red cl,b&w & col illus (r10,sl soil dj) 15.00

LAFFERTY,R A-Fourth Mansions-Lond-(1972)-Dobson-1st hdbk ed (g3,f,dj) 50.00

LAFFERTY,R A-Not to Mention Camels-Indpls-(1976)-1st ed (bb10,f,dj) 30.00

LAFFERTY,R A-Past Master-NY-(1968)-Ace-wrps-auth 1st bk-1st ed (l3,f) 15.00

LAFFIN,JOHN-Thomas Atkins-Lond-1966-235p-illus-1st ed (b7,f,dj) 35.00

LAFITAU,FATHER JOSEPH F-Customs of the American Indians compared with the Customs of Primitive Times-Tor-1974-Champlain Scty-8vo-2 vols-red cl,23 plts (mm1,f) 160.00

LAGERKVIST,PAR-Herod and Mariamne-NY-1968-Knopf-1st US ed (y1,f,dj) 30.00

LAGERLOF,SELMA-Christ Legends-Lond-1937-T Werner Laurie Ltd-cl,frntis-1st ed (l8) 25.00

LAGLER,KARL F-Freshwater Fishery Biology-Dubuque-1952-8vo-360p-illus-scarce-1st ed (m3,f) 25.00

LAGRANGE,HELEN-Clipper Ships of America and Great Britain 1833 to 1869-NY-1936-Putnam's-xi,381p-col wood engrvngs-1st ed (n2,sp discol) 45.00

LAHNE,HERBERT J-Cotton Mill Worker-NY-1944-Farrar & Rinehart-303p-Labor in 20th Cent Amer ser-Seidman L38 (r1,chip dj) 30.00

LAHONTAN,BARON DE-New Voyages to North America-Chig-1905-McClurg-2 vols-map,illus-(rprnt of 1703 Engl ed) (p8,sm sp split) 150.00

LAIDLER,HARRY W-British Labor's Rise to Power-NY-1945-League Indstrl Dmcrcy-39p-wrps (r1) 15.00

LAIDLER,HARRY W-Road Ahead-NY-1932-Crowell-86p-illus (ff1,sl sun) 25.00

LAIDLER,HARRY W-Socialism of Our Time-NY-1929-Indstrl Dmcrcy/Vanguard-377p (r1,dj tn,soil,chip) 30.00

LAIDLER,K-River Wolf-1983-Allen Unwin-178p-photos-1st ed (bb3,f,dj) 20.00

LAIDLER,L-Otters in Britain-1982-David Charles-200p-photos-1st ed (bb3,f,dj) 25.00

LAIDLER,PERCY-South Africa, Its Medical History 1652 to 1898-Cape Town-1971-536p-1st ed (dd3) 100.00

LAING,ALEXANDER-Clipper Ship Men-NY-1944-DS&P-8vo-279p-blu cl,illus,A Sperry-1st ed (nn1) 15.00

LAING,ALEXANDER-Methods of Dr.Scarlett-NY-1937-Farrar-1st ed (e4,dj) 25.00

LAING,DILYS B-Birth is Farewell-NY-(1944)-DSP-8vo-53p-1st US ed (ee5,f,f dj) 15.00

LAING,MARGARET-Josephine and Napoleon-NY-1974-196p-illus-1st Amer ed (b7,f,dj) 15.00

LAITHWAITE,E R-Propulsion Without Wheels-NY-1968-Hart Publ-x+273p-grn cl,illus-1st Amer ed (g2,dj) 25.00

LAKE,A-Killers in Africa-GC-1953-8vo-290p (m3,f,dj) 20.00

LAKE,A-Killers in Africa-NY-1953-290p-photos (gg3,f,dj) 22.00

LAKE,RICHARD-Grayling-Shrewsbury-1943-12mo-50p-wrps,illus (m3) 15.00

LAKE,STUART N-Wyatt Earp, Frontier Marshal-Bost-1931-Houghton,Mifflin-xiv,392p-orng cl,illus,col illus dj-1st ed (v1,sl chip dj) 65.00

LAKE,STUART N-Wyatt Earp-Bost-1931-Houghton Mifflin-sm 8vo-xiv,392p-photos,illus-Howes L27-1st ed,1st state wi "ellby" at line 18,pg 54-1st ed (aa3,f,chip dj) 195.00

LALIBERTE,NORMAN-History of the Cross-NY-1960-72p-illus-1st ed (t7,dj) 25.00

LAMANTIA,PHILIP-Blood of the Air-SF-1970-Four Seasons-wrps-1st ed (v5,f) 15.00

LAMANTIA,PHILIP-Narcotica-SF-1959-Auerhahn Pr-8vo-wrps-1st ed (m4) 20.00

LAMANTIA,PHILIP-Narcotica-SF-1959-Auerhahn Pr-wrps-1st ed (v5) 35.00

LAMANTIA,PHILIP-Selected Poems-SF-1967-City Lights-wrps-Pckt Poets No.20-1st ed (v5,f) 15.00

LAMANTIA,PHILIP-Touch of the Marvelous-1966-Oyez-wrps-1st ed (v5,f) 15.00

LAMB,ARTHUR H-Tragedies of the Osage Hills-Pawhuska-nd(ca.1935)-Osage Pr-203p-pict wrps-Six Guns #1274-scarce-1st ed (cc4) 150.00

LAMB,ARTHUR-Osage People-Pawhuska-nd-32p-pict wrps,frntis,photos,illus-scarce-1st ed (t7) 45.00

LAMB,CHARLES-Letters of...(and) Mary Lamb-New Haven-1935-Yale U Pr-3 vols-1st ed thus (z9,ex-libr) 50.00

LAMB,CHARLES-Tales from Shakespeare-Phila-1922-McKay-lg 8vo-377p-g dec cl wi sm pict pasteon,pict title,11 col plts (r3,few spot pgs,sl fox) 65.00

LAMB,D S-ET AL-History of the Medical Society of the District of Columbia 1817 to 1909-Wash-1909-501p-illus-1st ed (dd3) 50.00

LAMB,D-Enchanted Vagabonds-NY-1938-415p-photos,maps (gg3,f) 15.00

LAMB,DANA-Bright Salmon & Brown Trout-Barre-1964-8vo-111p-one of 1500c,illus (m3) 35.00

LAMB,DANA-Fishing's Only Part of It-1982-Amwell Pr-8vo-171p-ltd to 1000c,nbrd,3 autg,illus by E Hardie-scarce (m3,as new in box) 175.00

LAMB,DANA-Quest for the Lost City-NY-1951-8vo-340p-photos-scarce (m3,vf,dj) 35.00

LAMB,DANA-Where the Pools are Bright & Deep-NY-1973-8vo-145p-illus,E Hardie (m3,vf,sl soil dj) 11.00

LAMB,HAROLD-Crusades-GC-1930-Dbldy Doran-1st ed (hh5,dj chip,tn) 25.00

LAMB,HAROLD-Marching Sands-NY-1920-Appleton-1st ed (e4,cov spot,fox,dj chip) 50.00

LAMB,HAROLD-Three Palladins-W Kingston-1977-Grant-1st ed (g3,f,dj) 25.00

LAMB,HUGH-ED.-Cold Fear-NY-(1977)-1st ed (bb10,f,dj) 25.00

LAMB,JACK-How to Catch Game Fish-Ft.Worth-1937-12mo-190p-wrps,photos (m3) 35.00

LAMB,LYBTON-Drawing for Illustration-Lond-1962-OUP-8vo-xviii,211p-cl-1st ed (x4) 35.00

LAMB,MAJ A-Horse Facts-NY-nd(1935)-Greenburg-1st US ed (j9,dj wn) 25.00

LAMB,P S-Where Pools are Bright & Deep-Winchester-1973-145p-illus (gg3,f,dj) 9.00

LAMB,RICHARD B-In Celebration of Wine and Life-SF-1980-Wine Appr Guild-4to-255p-red cl,col & b&w illus-rvsd ed (q8,dj) 25.00

LAMB,SIR JAMES B-Birth and Triumph of Love-Lond-1823-8vo-g dec calf,a.e.g.,raised bnds,25 hand col engrvngs,P W Tompkins-1st ed (v10,sl wn bndg) 250.00

LAMB,W KAYE-ED.-Simon Fraser, Letters & Journals,1806-08-Tor-(1966)-292p-text maps (g7,f,f dj) 40.00

LAMB,W KAYE-ED.-Voyage of George Vancouver 1791 to 1795-Lond-1984-Hakluyt Soc-4 vols-illus,fldg maps-1st ed (j7,vf,f dj) 125.00

LAMB,WALLACE E-Lake George-(Glens Falls)-(1934)-52p-fldg map,frontis,10 plts,wrps (d1) 15.00

LAMBERT,A W-Modern Archery-NY-1929-306p-photos (gg3,f) 20.00

LAMBERT,ELISABETH-Sleeping House Party-1951-Coward-1st Amer ed (s10,dj) 20.00

LAMBERT,F-Bygone Days of the Old West-Ft.Worth-(1970)-Wstrn Heritage Pr-488p-illus by auth (f9) 200.00

LAMBERT,GAVIN-Dangerous Edge-Lond-1975-Barrie-1st ed (p4,dj) 25.00

LAMBERT,GAVIN-Dangerous Edge-NY-1976-Grossman-1st ed (y1,f,f dj) 35.00

LAMBERT,MRS ALMEDA-Guide to Nut Cookery-Battle Creek-1899-J Lambert & Co-451p-illus bds,illus-Bitting 271 (k6) 85.00

LAMBERT,OSMUND-Angling Literature in England & Descriptions of Fishing...Books on Other Piscatorial Subjects-Lond-1881-12mo-87p-prntd prchmnt bds-scarce (m3) 95.00

LAMBERT,ROSA-Mystery of the Golden Wings-NY-1936-Macaulay-1st US ed (j4,f,dj) 25.00

LAMBERT,S-ET AL-Three Vesalian Essays to Accompany the Icones Anatomicae of 1934-NY-1952-130p-1st ed (dd3,dj) 50.00

LAMBERT,SAMUEL-When Mr.Pickwick Went Fishing-NY-1924-12mo-83p-illus,Rbt Seymour (m3,f,dj) 65.00

LAMBERTON,W M-COMP.-Fighter Aircraft of the 1914 to 1918 War-Letchworth-1960-4to-224p-cl,col frntis,illus (s2,dj) 45.00

LAMBUTH,LECTHER-Anglers Workshop-Portland-1979-4to-217p-ltd to 1250c,nbrd,photos,illus (m3,vf) 80.00

LAMBUTH,LETCHER-Angler's Workshop-Portland-1979-Champoeg Pr-4to-cl-ltd to 1250c,nbrd-1st ed (gg7,f) 65.00

LAMMON,DAD-Outdoors with "Dad" Lammon-Coleraine-1936-8vo-381p-illus-scarce-1st ed (m3,vf,fray dj) 60.00

LAMNECK,JOHN H-From Lamplight to Satellite-Bost-(1961)-390p-cl (c1,f,dj) 17.50

LAMON,H M-Ducks and Geese-NY-1929-12mo-231p-cl,frntis,55 photos (y8,sp split) 22.00

LAMOND,HENRY-Loch Lomond-Glasgow-1931-8vo-340p-photos,fldg map (m3) 30.00

LAMONT,CORLISS-Soviet Russia Versus Nazi Germany-NY-1941-Amer Council Soviet Rltns-45p-wrps (r1) 15.00

LAMOTT,ANNE-Hard Laughter-1980-Viking-1st ed (t9,f,dj) 20.00

LAMOTTE-FOUQUE,HEINRICH-Ondine-Paris-1912-Hachette-vel bds,15 tip in col plts,A Rackham,ltd to 390c-1st French ed (l9,soil,sl fox) 500.00

LAMPE,DAVID-tunnel-Lond-(1963)-Harrap-224p-wht cl,plts-1st ed (d2,dj) 15.00

LAMPHERE,LOUISE-To Run After Them-Tucson-(1977)-218p-maps-1st ed (v7,f,dj) 20.00

LAMPMAN,ARCHIBALD-Selected Poems-Tor-1947-Ryerson Pr-8vo-xxvii,176p-frntis photos-1st ed (aa7,dj) 20.00*

LAMPMAN,BEN HUR-At the End of the Car Line-Portland-1942-8vo-192p-frontis-1st ed (m3,vf,dj,autg) 30.00

LAMPMAN,BEN HUR-Centralia, Tragedy and Trial-Seattle-1965-80p-stiff wrps,ring fldr,illus-ltd facs ed of 100c-scarce (d7) 60.00

LAMPMAN,BEN HUR-Coming of the Pond Fishes-Portland-1946-8vo-177p-illus (m3,as new in dj) 16.00

LAMPMAN,BEN HUR-How Could I Be Forgetting-Portland-1926-8vo-196p-illus-1st ed (m3,f,tn dj,pres cpy) 37.50

LAMPMAN,BEN HUR-Leaf From French Eddy-Portland-1965-12mo-109p-ltd to 950c,nbrd,illus-scarce (m3,as new in dj) 150.00

LAMPMAN,BEN HUR-Leaf from French Eddy-Portland-1965-Touchstone-12mo-109p-illus-1st trd ed (bb5,f,f dj) 35.00

LAMPMAN,BEN HUR-Tramp Printer-Portland-1934-4to-58p-ltd to 500c,nbrd,illus-1st ed (m3,f,pres cpy) 65.00

LAMPMAN,BEN HUR-Wild Swan-NY-1947-8vo-205p-illus-1st ed (m3,vf,dj) 26.00

LAMPMAN,HERBERT S-Northwest Nature Trails-Portland-1933-8vo-288p-illus,Q Scott-1st ed (m3,vf,dj,autg) 25.00

LAMPRECHT,DOROTHY-Proceedings Forty-Fourth Annual State Conference the Ohio State...Daughters of American Revolution-(Greenfield)-(1943)-268p-wrps (d1) 12.50

LAMSON-SCRIBNER,F-Fungus Diseases of the Grape and Other Plants and Their Treatment-Little Silver-1890-J T Lovett Co-134p+index & illus ads-brn bds (n6,sl wn) 50.00

LANCASTER,CLAY-Old Brooklyn Heights-Rutland-1961-Tuttle-8vo-183p-photos-1st ed (r10,f dj) 25.00

LANCASTER,O-Sailing to Byzantium-Bost-1969-illus-1st prtg (h10,dj) 40.00

LANCE,MARY-Lynn Ford Texas Artist and Craftsman-S.A.-1978-Trinity U Pr-109p-illus-1st ed (a9,dj) 15.00

LAND O' LAKES KITCHENS-Land O Lakes Cookie Lover's Cookbook-Mpls-1979-42p-wrps (mm6,f) 12.50

LAND,H C-Birds of Guatemala-Wynnewood-1970-8vo-381p-cl,44 col plts,5 maps (y8,dj wn) 45.00

LAND,MARY-Mary Land's Louisiana Cookery-NY-(1954)-Bonanza-xviii,376p-illus-1st ed thus (o2,f,dj) 15.00

LANDAU,HENRY-All's Fair-NY-1934-Putnam's-8vo-329p-brwn cl,6 illus (gg6,autg) 22.50

LANDES,RUTH-Ojibwa Woman-NY-1938-Columbia Univ Pr-8vo-viii,247p+ads-burgandy cl,g sp titles-1st ed (mm1) 60.00

LANDESS,THOMAS-Larry McMurtry-Austin-(1969)-Steck-Vaugh Co-wrps-Southwest Writers Ser #23-1st ed (c10,f) 25.00

LANDGREN,M E-Years of Art-NY-1940-illus,72 plts-1st ed (h10,dj sl chip & rub) 50.00

LANDIS,C S-Rifle Craft-Cin-1923-124p-dec bds,wrps,illus-scarce (gg3,vf) 100.00

LANDIS,C S-Woodchucks & Woodchuck Rifles-NY-1951-402p-photos (gg3,f,dj) 65.00

LANDIS,CHARLES K-Carabajal, the Jew-Vineland-(1894)-priv prtd-27p-wrps-scarce-Wright III, 3200-1st ed (aa6,f) 150.00

LANDMAN,J H-Human Sterilization-NY-1932-Macmillan-xviii+341p-blck cl-1st ed (a2,dj) 55.00

LANDON,FRED-An Exile from Canada to Van Diem's Land-Tor-1960-Longman's,Green-facs rprnt (k10,f,dj) 25.00*

LANDON,MELVILLE D-Eli Perkins Thirty Years of Wit and Reminiscences of the Witty,Wise and Eloquent Men-Akron-1899-Werner-305p-cl (g1) 15.00

LANDON,PERCIVAL-Opening of Tibet-NY-1905-484p-grn cl,photos-1st ed (gg2,sl stnd edges) 75.00

LANDOR,HENRY S-In the Forbidden Land-NY,Lond-1909-2 vols-fldg map (q10,vf) 75.00

LANDRUM,CHARLES H-COMP.-Michigan in the World War-Lansing-nd-Mich Hist Comm-247p-blu cl (cc3) 40.00

LANDY,JACOB-Architecture of Minard Lafever-NY-1970-Columbia U Pr-sm 4to-313p-gry/tan cl,illus (r10,sl wn dj) 32.50

LANE,HARRISON-Long Flight, History of Nez Perce War-(Havre)-(1982)-24p-wrps,illus,map-1st ed (f7) 20.00

LANE,JOHN-ED.-Love of an Unknown Soldier-Tor-1918-MG&S-8vo-viii,207p-red cl-1st ed (cc7,wtr spot frnt cov) 20.00*

LANE,M-Life with Ionides-NY-1963-180p-photos (gg3,cov spots) 15.00

LANE,MARK-Code Name "Zorro"-Englewood Cliffs-1977-Prentice Hall-314p-1st ed (r1,dj) 30.00

LANE,ROGER-Violent Death in the City-1979-Harvard U Pr-1st ed (t4,f,sl rub dj) 15.00

LANE,ROSE-Peaks of Shala-NY-1923-349p-1st US ed (p10) 20.00

LANE,SAMUEL-Journal for the Years 1739 to 1803...-Concord-1937-NH Hist Scty-vi+115p-red cl-1st ed (h2) 25.00

LANE,WHEATON J-From Indian Trail to Iron Horse-Princeton-1939-xviii,437p-cl,plts(incl fldg) (aa6) 75.00

LANG,ANDREW-Book of Princes and Princesses-NY,Lond-1908-Longmans,Green-pict g blu cl,a.e.g.,plts incl 8 col & cov design by H J Ford-1st ed (r3,sl wn,sl fade sp) 90.00

LANG,ANDREW-Book of Romance-Lond-1902-Longmans,Green-384p-pict g blu cl,a.e.g.,8 tip in col plts by H J Ford+b&w plts-1st ed (r3,few spot pgs) 95.00

LANG,ANDREW-Letters to Dead Authors-Lond,NY-1892-8vo-194p-one of 113c lg pap deluxe 1st ed-scarce (m3) 90.00

LANG,C-Buffalo, The Lone Trail of a Big Game Hunter-Lond-1934-310p-photos,map e.p.-scarce (gg3,cov soil,cov relettrd) 125.00

LANG,DANIEL-Casualties of War-NY-(1969)-McGraw Hill-scarce hdcov-1st prtg (ff3,f,f dj) 100.00

LANG,DANIEL-Man in the Thick Lead Suit-NY-1954-Oxford-1st ed (nn9,dj chip) 22.50

LANG,LINCOLN A-Ranching with Roosevelt-Phila-1926-8vo-367p-pict cl,24 illus-Herd 1304-1st ed (aa3,f,dj) 95.00

LANG,LINCOLN-Ranching with Roosevelt-Phila-1926-Lippincott-photos-1st ed (nn9,sl chip dj) 75.00

LANG,PAUL H-Pictorial History of Music-NY-1960-Norton-illus-1st ed (u4,f,dj tn) 26.00

LANG,W-History of Seneca County, from the close of the Revolutionary War to July, 1880-Springfield-1880-691,(1);xii p-mod cl (j1,rebnd) 85.00

LANG,WALTER-First Overland Mail-np-1940-163p-stiff pict wrps,illus-1st ed (t7) 35.00

LANGDON,ALLAN G-Tuberous Begonia-Bath-nd(1940's)-92p-28 b&w photos,engrvngs (j10,tattrd dj) 15.00

LANGDON,WILLIAM C-Everyday Things in American Life 1607 to 1776-NY-1937-xx,353p-illus,incl 4 col plts-1st ed (x5,wn,sp scuff) 25.00

LANGE,ALGOT-Lower Amazon-NY-1914-Putnam's-xxv,468p+ads-blu cl wi g titles & cov dec,109 illus,6 maps(1 fldg) (mm1,dj chip & drknd) 65.00

LANGE,CHARLES H-Cochiti, a New Mexico Pueblo, Past & Present-Austin-(1959)-585p-photos-1st ed (v7,f,dj) 45.00

LANGE,CHARLES-ED.-Southwestern Journals of Adolf F Bandelier 1883 to 1884-Albuq-1970-528p-illus,maps,map e.p.-1st ed (t7,dj) 40.00

LANGE,CHARLES-ED.-Southwestern Journals of Adolph F Bandelier: 1880 to 1882-Albuq-1965-UNM-462p-21 photos,2 maps,drwngs-1st ed (d3,dj) 30.00

LANGER,PAUL F-North Vietnam and the Pathet Lao-Cambridge-1970-Harvard-1st ed (e8,f,f dj) 35.00

LANGEWIESCHE,W-I'll Take the High Road-NY-1939-8vo-x,254p-cl,frntis,22p plts-1st ed (s2) 25.00

LANGEWIESCHE,W-Stick and Rudder-NY-(1944)-8vo-vi,390p-cl,illus-1st ed (s2,chip dj) 35.00

LANGFORD,G B-Out of the Earth-1954-U of Tor Pr-8vo-xiv,125p-14 photos,fldg map-1st ed (bb7,dj chip,discol) 20.00*

LANGFORD,N P-Discovery of Yellowstone Park 1870-1905-publ by auth-122p-blu cl-Graff 2389-1st ed (w1) 50.00

LANGFORD,N P-Discovery of Yellowstone Park-np-(1905)-122p-t.e.g.,illus (c7,f) 75.00

LANGFORD,N P-Vigilante Days and Ways-Bost-1890-2 vols-pict bds,illus-Howes L78-v scarce-1st ed (g7) 300.00

LANGFORD-SMITH,F-Radiotron Designer's Handbook-1953-1482p-illus-4th ed (h6,f) 40.00

LANGGUTH,A J-Jesus Christs-NY-1968-Harper-1st ed (w5,f,dj) 25.00

LANGGUTH,A J-Macumba-NY et al-(1975)-Harper & Row-1st ed (bb1,f,dj) 12.50

LANGIE,ANDRE-Cryptography-Lond-1922-Constable-viii+192p-grn cl,illus-1st Brit ed (l2,dj) 40.00

LANGILLE,J H-Our Birds in Their Haunts-Bost-1884-8vo-624p-cl,engvngs (y8,sp tn) 25.00

LANGLEY,HAROLD D-ED.-To Utah with the Dragoons and Glimpses of Life in Arizona and California 1858 to 1859-SLC-1974-230p-frntis,photos,maps-1st ed (t7,f,dj) 25.00

LANGLEY,LEE-Dead Center-1968-CC-1st ed (s10,dj) 10.00

LANGLOIS,THOMAS H-South Bass Island and Islanders-(Columbus)-1948-Ohio St Univ-x; 139p-wrps-#10 of Franz Theodore Stone Lab. (h1) 15.00

LANGSETH-CHRISTENNSEN,LILLIAN-Instant Epicure Cookbook-(1963)-Coward,McCann-1st ed (q8,edgewn dj) 15.00

LANGSTRAND,ROLF-Long Pony Race-NY-1966-Knopf-4to-1st US ed (h9,dj) 10.00

LANGTON,JANE-Dark Nantucket Noon-NY-1975-Harper-1st ed (f4,f,dj) 35.00

LANGTON,JANE-Natural Enemy-New Haven-1982-Ticknor-1st ed (j4,f,dj) 15.00

LANGWORTHY,DANIEL A-Reminiscences of a Prisoner of War and His Escape-Mpls-1915-Byron Prtg-74p-frntis,illus (o7,lacks ffep) 50.00

LANIER,H W-A B Frost-NY-(1933)-Derrydale-lg 4to-tan bndg-ltd to 950c,illus-1st ed (u10) 400.00

LANIER,H W-Far Horizon-NY-1933-8vo-xvi,286p-illus cl,frntis-1st ed (t2,sp fade) 30.00

LANIER,H W-Romance of Piscator-NY-1904-12mo-227p-illus (m3) 50.00

LANIER,HENRY-Greenwich Village-NY-(1949)-Harper-4to-cl-1st ed (y3,sl chip dj) 125.00

LANIER,LEE-Golden Phantoms-NY-1952-Comet Pr Bks-64p-1st ed (bb4,dj) 25.00

LANIER,SIDNEY-Boy's Froissart-NY-1879-Scribner's-422p-cl,illus,A Kappes-1st ed (s3) 60.00

LANIER,SIDNEY-Florida-Phila-1876-Lippincott-steel engrvngs,fld-out map-BAL 11247-1st ed (b10,frnt innr hng crckd,sl wn 300.00

LANK,DAVID M-Once Upon A Tyne-Montreal-1977-oblng 12mo-105p-ltd to 1000c,nbrd,autg (m3,vf) 75.00

LANKESTER,E RAY-Extinct Animals-NY-1906-H Holt-xxiv+331p-maroon cl,illus-1st ed (c2) 45.00

LANNING,JOHN T-Brief Description of the Province of Carolina on the Coasts of Florida-1944-Tracy W McGregor Libr-23p-wrps,map-ltd to 1100c (dd9,sl soil cov) 25.00

LANNOY,RICHARD-India-Lond-1955-Thames & Hudson-4to-200p-red cl,cov dec,plts(6 col) (gg6) 30.00

LANNUZZI,J NICHOLAS-What's Happening-NY-1963-A S Barnes-1st ed (g8,f,dj missing sm chip) 25.00

LANSDOWNE,J F-Birds of the Eastern Forest-Bost-1968,70-tall 4to-2 vols-cl,112 col plts (y8) 145.00

LANSDOWNE,J F-Birds of the Eastern Forest. Vol.1-1968-Houghton Mifflin-folio-231p-52 col plts (bb3,f,dj) 75.00

LANSDOWNE,J F-Birds of the Northern Forest(Canada)-Bost-1966-4to-247p-cl,56 col plts (y8,dj) 65.00

LANSDOWNE,J F-Birds of the Northern Forest-Tor-1966-M&S-4to-247p-56p col plts-1st ed (aa7,dj) 65.00*

LANSDOWNE,J F-Birds of the West Coast. Vol.1-Bost-1976-folio-175p-cl,52 col plts(incl 4 fldg) (y8,dj) 70.00

LANSDOWNE,J F-Birds of the West Coast. Vol.2-1980-Feheley-folio-167p-96 illus(incl 48 col) (bb3,f,dj) 75.00

LANTERNARI,VITTORIO-Religions of the Opressed-NY-1963-Knopf-8vo-356p-cl-1st Amer ed (y5,sl wn dj) 15.00

LANTIS,M-Alaskan Indian Ceremonialism-1966-U of Wash-127p-2nd prtg (bb3,f,dj) 20.00

LANTIS,MARGARET-ED.-Ethnohistory in Southwestern Alaska & the Southern Yukon-(1970)-U of Ken-311p-illus,text maps & graphs-1st ed (j7,f,dj) 35.00

LANTIS,MARGARET-Eskimo Childhood and Interpersonal Relationships-Seattle-1960-U of Wash Pr-8vo-xv,215p+ads-map (dd7,sl rub,bump) 22.50

LAPHAM,MACY H-Criss Cross Trails-Berkley-1949-246p-photos-1st ed (t7) 10.00

LAPIERRE,CHARLES J-Care & Repair of Fishing Reels and Rods-NY-1945-16mo-16p-wrps,photos (m3) 12.50

LAPIUS,S Q-Current Coins-Columbus-1893-Hann & Adair-192p-cl-auth(James Ball Naylor) 1st bk-rare (e1,rub,lacks rear f.e.p.) 50.00

LAPPIN,S S-Where the Long Trail Begins-Cin-(1913)-Standard Publ-65p-cl (b1,sl rub) 12.50

LARCOM,LUCY-Childhood Songs-Bost-1875-Osgood-8vo-202p-gold stmpd bev blu cl-BAL 11335-1st ed (w6,sl rub) 45.00

LARDEN,WALTER-Recollections of an Old Mountaineer-Lond-1910-320p-1/2 lea,t.e.g.,17 plts-1st ed (a4,f) 110.00

LARDEN,WALTER-Recollections of an Old Mountaineer-Lond-1910-320p-17 plts-1st ed (p10,f) 140.00

LARDNER,JOHN-Strong Cigars and Lovely Women-NY-1951-drwngs,W Kelly-1st ed (s5,dj wn) 20.00

LARDNER,RING-Bib Ballads-NY,Chig,Tor-(1915)-Volland-auth 1st bk-illus,iss w/o dj-ltd to 500c-1st ed (ff6,f,lacks box) 350.00

LARDNER,RING-Bib Ballads-NY,Chig-(1915)-P F Volland-orig brwn bds gold stmpd,ltd to 500c,auth 1st bk-1st ed (bb2,rprd) 175.00

LARDNER,RING-First and Last-NY-1934-Scribner's-grn & blu cl-1st ed (f2,sl wn dj) 75.00

LARDNER,RING-Lose with a Smile-1933-Scribners-1st ed (x2,f,dj) 250.00

LARDNER,RING-Love Nest and Other Stories-NY-1926-1st ed (m4) 10.00

LARDNER,RING-Portable...-NY-1946-1st ed (n5,dj) 22.50

LARDNER,RING-Round Up-NY-1929-1st ed (r2,f) 35.00

LARDNER,RING-Round Up-NY-1929-Scribner's-1st ed (aa8,sl fade sp) 40.00

LARDNER,RING-Shut Up, He Explained-1962-Scribners-1st ed (x2,f,dj) 45.00

LARDNER,RING-You Know Me Al, A Busher's Letters-1916-Doran-1st ed (x2,sp lettrng sl dull) 125.00

LARGE,R G-Prince Rupert-Vancouver-1960-Mitchell-4to-210p-illus,errata slip-1st ed (u8,dj) 25.00

LARGE,R G-Skeena, River of Destiny-Vancouver-1957-180p-frntis,photos,map e.p.-1st ed (t7,dj) 15.00

LARIAR,LAWRENCE-Day I Died-NY-1952-Appleton-1st ed (d4,dj) 20.00

LARISON,CORNELIUS W-Ancient Village, Amwell-Flemington-1916-8p-wrps-ltd to 100c (aa6) 35.00

LARISON,CORNELIUS W-Clas Abrod-Ringoes-1888-Larison's Fonic Publ Hs-79p-mod cl,phonetic type (aa6,rbnd) 100.00

LARISON,CORNELIUS W-Iz the Sol a Substans-Ringoes-1904-vii,(1),188p-cl (aa6) 50.00

LARISON,CORNELIUS W-Larisun Famili-Ringos-1888-Fonic Publ Hs-472p-mod cl (aa6,rbnd) 175.00

LARISON,CORNELIUS W-Reminissensez ov Scul Lif-Ringoes-1896-510p+ads-cl (aa6) 90.00

LARISON,CORNELIUS W-Silvia Dubois-Ringoes-1883-124p+ads-cl,plts (aa6,innr hngs broken) 125.00

LARISON,CORNELIUS W-Tenting School-Ringos-1883-viii,292p-cl,illus (aa6) 100.00

LARKEY,S-An Herbal, 1525 of Bancke's-NY-1941-NYBG-86p-cl-ltd to 500c (x6) 50.00

LARKIN,DAVID-ED.-Art of Nancy Ekholm Burkert-NY-1977-Harper & Row-4to-wht cl,40 col plts (r10,f dj) 22.50

LARKIN,DAVID-ED.-Giants-NY-(1979)-Abrams-4to-192p-1st US ed (gg5,dj) 20.00

LARKIN,PHILIP-All What Jazz: a Record Diary 1961 to 1968-Lond-(1968)-Faber-1st ed (b3,f,dj) 65.00

LARMOTH,JEANINE-Murder on the Menu-NY-(1972)-Scribner's-268p-1st ed (u6,dj) 20.00

LARMOTH,JEANINE-Passionate Palate-1975-Morrow-263p-brwn bds-1st ed (q8,dj) 20.00

LARNED,LINDA H-Hostess of Today-1901-Scribners-303p-pict grn cl,illus (q8) 25.00

LAROQUE,FRANCOIS-Journal of...-Fairfield-1981-102p-illus,ltd ed,nbrd-rprnt of Howes L107 (t7,dj) 20.00

LARPENTEUR,CHARLES-Forty Years a Fur Trader on the Upper Missouri-Chig-1933-Donnelley-388p-frntis,map-Lakeside Classics (cc4) 35.00

LARSON,A KARL-Diary of Charles Lowell Walker-Logan-1980-Utah St-8vo-2 vols (z4,dj) 16.00

LARSON,ARTHUR-Eisenhower, the President Nobody Knew-NY-(1968)-Scribner's-210p-cl-1st ed (m1,f,dj) 12.50

LARSON,E E-Tales From the Minnesota Forest Fires-St.Paul-(1912)-94p-illus-scarce (bb9) 75.00

LARSON,JAMES-Reason & Experience Representation of Natural Order in the Work of Carl Von Linne'-Berkeley-1971-U of Ca-171p (x6,dj sun) 18.00

LARSON,JOHN A-Lying and its Detection-Chig-(1932)-U of Chig-xxii+453p-blu cl,fldg plts-1st ed (c2,dj) 45.00

LARSON,L-Lighting & Its Design-1964-Whitney Libr-sq 4to-illus-1st ed (kk4,dj) 65.00

LARSON,ROBERT W-New Mexico's Quest for Statehood-(Albuq)-(1968)-384p-1st ed (u7,f,dj) 20.00

LARSON,T A-History of Wyoming-Lincoln-1965-U of Neb Pr-619p-maps,chrts,illus-1st ed (cc4,dj) 20.00

LARZELERE,CLAUDE S-Story of Michigan-Lansing-1929-424p-cl-2nd ed (k1) 10.00

LASH,JOSEPH P-Helen & Teacher-NY-1980-Delacorte-811p-1st ed (r1,dj) 20.00

LASKI,HAROLD J-Trade Unions in the New Society-NY-1949-Viking-182p-1st ed (r1,edgewn dj) 20.00

LASSWELL,MARY-ED.-Rags and Hope-NY-1961-280p-1st ed (n10,dj) 45.00

LASSWELL,MARY-High Time-(1944)-Houghton Mifflin-174p-tan cl,frntis (q8,sl tn dj) 12.50

LASSWELL,MARY-I'll Take Texas-1958-HM-376p-brwn bds,illus-1st ed (q8,dj) 25.00

LASSWELL,MARY-Mrs.Rasmussen's Book of One Arm Cookery-Bost-1946-Houghton Mifflin-101p-decs & e.p.,G Price (m6) 15.00

LASSWELL,MARY-Mrs.Rasmussen's Book of One Arm Cookery-Bost-1946-Houghton Mifflin-12mo-ix,101p-1st ed (aa3,f dj) 50.00

LASSWELL,MARY-Tio Pepe-1963-HM-118p-brwn cl,illus-1st prtg (q8,dj) 16.50

LASSWELL,MARY-Wait for the Wagon-1951-HM-185p-tan cl,illus-1st ed (q8,dj) 16.50

LASSWELL,MAY-John Henry Kirby, Prince of the Pines-Austin-1967-Encino-203p-photos-1st ed (a9,dj) 50.00

LAST RIVET-NY-1940-Columbia U-4to-grn suede cl cov bds illus wi silver outline of rivets,illus e.p.,photos-1st ed (y3,sl stnd cov,dj) 100.00

LAST,JEF-Spanish Tragedy-Lond-1939-Routledge-288p (ff1,dj sp sun,sl tn) 35.00

LATHAM,JOHN W-British Military Swords-NY-1967-91p-photos-1st Amer ed (b7,dj) 30.00

LATHAM,R M-Complete Book of Wild Turkey-PA-1956-265p-illus-1st ed (ee3,f) 45.00

LATHAM,RUTH-Check List of American Revolutionary War Pamphlets in the Newberry Library-Chig-1922-(Newberry Libr)-tall 8vo-viii,115p-stiff wrps (w2,cov chip) 65.00

LATHEM,EDWARD C-ED.-76 United Statesiana-Wash D.C.-1976-1st ed (w1,f,f dj) 17.50

LATHEN,EMMA-Ashes to Ashes-NY-1971-Simon-1st ed (f4,f,sl wn dj) 15.00

LATHEN,EMMA-Death Shall Overcome-1966-Macmillan-1st ed (s10,f,dj) 65.00

LATHEN,EMMA-Double, Double, Oil and Trouble-NY-1978-S&S-1st ed (z9,dj) 10.00

LATHEN,EMMA-Going For the Gold-NY-1981-Simon-1st ed (s4,vf,dj) 25.00

LATHEN,EMMA-Green Grow the Dollar-NY-1982-Simon-1st ed (r4,vf,dj) 25.00

LATHEN,EMMA-Longer the Thread-1971-Inner Sanctum-1st ed (o9,dj) 15.00

LATHEN,EMMA-Murder Against the Grain-Lond-1967-Gollancz-1st Brit ed (q4,f,dj) 25.00

LATHEN,EMMA-Pick Up Sticks-NY-1970-S&S-1st ed (z3,f,dj) 15.00

LATHEN,EMMA-Sweet and Low-NY-1974-S&S-1st ed (z9,f,dj) 10.00

LATHEN,EMMA-Sweet and Low-NY-1974-Simon-1st ed (f4,f,sl wn dj) 12.50

LATHEN,EMMA-When in Greece-NY-1969-Simon-1st ed (l4,dj) 25.00

LATHROP,AMY-Tales of Western Kansas-Norton-(1948)-152p-photos-scarce (v8) 50.00

LATHROP,CORNELIA P-Black Rock-New Haven-1930-Morehouse & Taylor-xii+214p-grn cl,illus,maps-1st ed (m2) 45.00

LATHROP,ELISE-Early American Inns and Taverns-NY-1926-McBride-4to-365p-cl,illus e.p.,90 halftones-1st ed (cc10) 50.00

LATHROP,ELISE-Early American Inns and Taverns-NY-1936-365p-cl,photos-Tudor ed (a1) 15.00

LATHROP,WILLIAM G-Brass Industry in the United States-Mt.Carmel-1926-Wm G Lathrop-12mo-viii+174p-plts-rvsd ed (a2) 45.00

LATIMER,CAROLINE W-Girl and Woman-NY,Lond-1912-331p-cl (d1,f) 15.00

LATIMER,JOHN-Red Gardenias-GC-1939-Dbldy CC-1st ed (w9,f,dj sl tn & wn) 300.00

LATIMER,JONATHAN-Black is the Fashion for Dying-1959-Random-1st ed (x7,f,dj) 40.00

LATIMER,JONATHAN-Black is the Fashion for Dying-NY-1959-1st ed (r5,sl chip dj) 30.00

LATIMER,JONATHAN-Red Gardenias-1939-CC-1st ed (s10,sp chip dj) 75.00

LATIMER,JONATHAN-Sinners and Shrouds-NY-1955-1st ed (r5,dj) 30.00

LATON,FRANCIS M-Old Zuni Mission-St.Anthony's Mission-nd-unpgd(41p)-wrps,photos,maps (v7) 15.00

LATORRE,DOLORES L-Cooking and Curing with Mexican Herbs-(Austin)-(1977)-Encino Pr-wdcut illus,B M Whitehead (m6) 22.00

LATOUR,HARRY-Magical Suggestions...-Lond-1921-47,(1)p-cl,illus (c1) 15.00

LATTA,F F-Black Gold in the Joaquin-Caldwell-1949-Caxton-344p-blk cl,plts-1st ed (mm10,dj) 50.00

LATTA,FRANK F-Dalton Gang Days-Santa Cruz-(1976)-Bear State Bks-lg 8vo-(xx),293p-illus,e.p. map-1st ed (v1) 35.00

LATTA,FRANK F-Joaquin Murrieta and His Horse Gangs-Santa Cruz-(1980)-Bear State Bks-beige cl wi g sp titles & cov dec,photo frnt e.p.,photos,facs,drwngs-1st ed (mm1,f) 45.00

LATTA,FRANK F-Joaquin Murrieta-Santa Cruz-(1980)-Bear State Bks-tall 8vo-685p-illus-1st ed (ee4,dj) 25.00

LATTA,WILLIAM-Ascent of the Lion Fifth September & Subsequent Days 1903-Vancouver-1953-22p-wrps,illus (q10,f) 50.00

LATTIMORE,ELEANOR F-Beachcomber Boy-NY-1960-Morrow-124p-pict cl-1st ed (s3,dj) 15.00

LATTIMORE,RICHMOND-TRANSL.-Acts and Letters of the Apostles-NY-1982-FS&G-cl-1st ed (l8,f,dj) 10.00

LATTIMORE,RICHMOND-TRANSL.-Four Gospels and the Revelation-NY-1979-FS&G-cl-1st ed (l8,f,dj) 10.00

LAUBIN,REGINALD-American Indian Archery-Norman-(1980)-U of Okla-xii,179p-cl,illus,col photos,drwngs-1st ed (v1) 30.00

LAUBIN,REGINALD-Indian Tipi Its History, Construction and Use-Norman-1970-208p-col frntis,photos (t7,dj) 10.00

LAUDE,G A-Kansas Shorthorns-Iola-1920-Laude Prtg-647p-illus-Herd 1310-1st ed (dd4) 35.00

LAUDER,SIR HARRY-Roamin' in the Gloamin'-Phila-1928-Lippincott-1st Amer ed (w1,f,dj) 25.00

LAUER,HENRI-Radio Engineering Principles-1920-300p-12 photos,241 illus-1st ed (h6) 30.00

LAUFER,BERTHOLD-Sino Iranica Chinese Contributions with Special Reference to History of Cultivated Plants & Products-Chig-1919-Field Mus-630p-wrps (x6,ex-libr) 35.00

LAUGHLIN,EDWARD D-Yaqui Gold-San Antonio-1943-Naylor Co-80p-illus-1st ed (ee4,dj) 25.00

LAUGHTER,VICTOR H-Operator's Wireless Telegraph and Telephone Hand Book-1909-180p-30 photos,56 illus-1st ed (h6,f) 40.00

LAUGHTON,CATHRINE-ED.-Mary Cullen's Northwest Cook Book-Portland-(1946)-Binsford & Mort-340p-grn cl,illus-1st prtg (q8) 17.50

LAUGHTON,J K-Nelson and His Companion in Arms-Lond-1899-351p-blu cl,col frntis,illus-2nd ed (gg2) 50.00

LAUMER,KEITH-House in November-NY-(1970)-Putnam-1st ed (g3,f,dj) 40.00

LAUMER,KEITH-World Shuffler-NY-(1970)-Putnam-1st ed (k3,f,dj) 25.00

LAURENCE,F S-Color in Architecture-NY-1924-Nat Terra Cotta Soc-64p-brwn bds,blk cl sp,12 plts (r10) 30.00

LAURENCE,MARGARET-Diviners-Tor-1974-M&S-382p-1st ed (aa2,dj) 25.00*

LAURENCE,MARGARET-Fire Dwellers-NY-1969-Knopf-1st US ed (pp2,f,sl rub dj) 65.00*

LAURENCE,MARGARET-Stone Angel-NY-1964-Knopf-1st US ed (pp2,dj) 185.00*

LAURENTS,ARTHUR-Home of the Brave-NY-(1946)-Random-auth 1st bk-1st ed (e10,sl bump,dj) 50.00

LAURITZREN,JONREED-Arrows in the Sun-NY-1943-Knopf-auth 1st bk-1st ed (hh5,dj) 30.00

LAUT,A C-Cadillac-Indpls-(1931)-Bobbs Merrill-298p-map e.p.,illus-1st ed (dd4,wn dj) 25.00

LAUT,A C-Conquest of Our Western Empire-1927-McBride-363p-illus,maps-1st ed (r8,discol cov,sp fray) 45.00

LAUT,A C-Conquest of the Great Northwest-NY-1908-Outing-2 vols,cl,plts,maps(incl fldg)-1st ed (v1) 90.00

LAUT,A C-Fur Trade in America-NY-1921-Macmillan-8vo-341p-cl,photos,tbls-1st ed (t1,sl soil) 75.00

LAUT,A C-Heralds of Empire-NY-1902-Appleton-372p-pict cl-1st ed (dd4) 25.00

LAUT,A C-Heralds of Empire-Tor-1902-Wm Briggs-red cl-1st ed (u2) 30.00

LAUT,A C-Lords of the North-NY-1900-J F Taylor-442p-pict cl-1st ed (ee4) 25.00

LAUT,A C-Overland Trail-NY-1929-358p-dec cl,frntis,photos,map e.p. (t7,sunned sp,fleck) 17.50

LAUT,A C-Overland Trail-NY-1929-Stokes-358p-maps,illus-1st ed (dd4) 35.00

LAUT,A C-Pathfinders of the West-NY-1904-380p-pict cl,frntis,photos,illus-Rader #2209-1st ed (t7) 50.00

LAUT,A C-Pathfinders of the West-NY-1904-Macmillan-380p-illus-1st ed (dd4) 35.00

LAUT,A C-Pioneers of the Pacific Coast-Tor-1915-Glasgow,Brook-12mo-viii,139p-col frntis,col fldg map,plts,ports-Chron of Can ser,Vol.22-Strathern #310 (k10,sp fade) 15.00*

LAUT,A C-Romance of the Rails-NY-1936-Tudor-photos,illus-rprnt (nn9) 37.50

LAVANTURE,PAULINE-So, Indian Legend About the Blue Bonnet-1941-Naylor-col illus (a9,dj) 30.00

LAVENDER,DAVID-Bent's Fort-NY-1954-Dbldy-450p-e.p. maps-1st ed (dd4,dj) 30.00

LAVENDER,DAVID-California Land of New Beginnings-NY-1972-464p-map e.p.-1st ed (t7,dj) 17.50

LAVENDER,DAVID-Climax at Buena Vista-Phila-(1966)-Lippincott-252p-maps-1st ed (cc4,dj) 25.00

LAVENDER,DAVID-Fist in the Wilderness-GC-(1964)-Dbldy-490p-map e.p.-Amer Trail Ser-1st ed (gg4,chip dj) 50.00

LAVENDER,DAVID-Fist in the Wilderness-NY-(1964)-Dbldy-1st ed (nn9,dj) 55.00

LAVENDER,DAVID-Great Persuader-GC-1970-Dbldy-sm 4to-ix+444p-cl,map e.p.-1st ed (z4,sl fade dj) 20.00

LAVENDER,DAVID-Land of Giants-1958-Dbldy-468p-6 dbl pg maps-1st ed (r8) 14.00

LAVENDER,DAVID-Land of Giants-GC-1958-Dlbdy-468p-maps-Mainstream of Amer Ser-Six Guns #1292-1st ed (cc4,dj) 25.00

LAVENDER,DAVID-Rockies-NY-(1968)-Harper & Row-404p-maps,illus e.p.-Six Guns #1293-1st ed (cc4,dj) 25.00

LAVENDER,DAVID-Westward Vision-NY-1963-424p-illus-1st ed (t7,dj) 20.00

LAVERTY,MAURA-Feasting Galore-(1961)-Holt-144p-pict bds,drwngs-1st ed (q8) 17.50

LAVIGNAC,ALBERT-Music Dramas of Richard Wagner...-NY-1930-Dodd,Mead-rprnt of 1898 ed (u4) 22.00

LAVIN,MARY-At Sallygap-Bost-1947-Little,Brown-1st Amer ed (dd2,f,dj) 25.00

LAVIN,MARY-Collected Stories-Bost-1970-Houghton Mifflin-1st ed (cc2,f,dj) 30.00

LAVIN,MARY-Collected Stories-Bost-1971-Houghton Mifflin-1st ed (z8,vf,dj) 20.00

LAVIN,MARY-In the Middle of the Fields-Lond-(1967)-Constable-1st ed (dd2,f,dj) 35.00

LAVIN,MARY-Shrine, and Other Stories-Bost-1977-Houghton Mifflin-1st Amer ed (z8,vf,scuff dj) 16.50

LAVINE,SIGMUND-Horses the Indians Rode-NY-1974-Dodd,Mead-4to-78p-illus (h9,dj) 25.00

LAWFORD,JAMES-Napoleon: the Last Campaigns 1813 to 15-NY-1977-folio-160p-illus-1st ed (gg2,f,dj) 25.00

LAWLESS,HON. EMILY-Grania-Lond-1892-Smith Elder-8vo-2 vols,maroon cl,map frntis in vol 1-1st ed (w6,lacks fr fly in both vols) 135.00

LAWN TENNIS MANUAL FOR 1889-NY-1889-Spalding-47p+(17)p ads-orig illus wrps (a7) 35.00

LAWRENCE,ALEXANDER A-James Johnston, Georgia's First Printer-Savannah-1956-Pigeonhole Pr-8vo-(vi),54,(2)p-bds,illus-1st ed (w2,dj) 45.00

LAWRENCE,CHARLES-History of the Philadelphia Almshouses and Hospitals-(Phila)-1905-398p-photos-v scarce-1st ed (dd3) 150.00

LAWRENCE,D H-Apocalypse-NY-1932-Viking-1st Amer ed (bb2,f,dj chip,sp drknd) 95.00

LAWRENCE,D H-Birds,Beasts and Flowers-NY-1923-Seltzer-rare dj-1st ed (hh4,vf,dj) 950.00

LAWRENCE,D H-Body of God-1970-Ark Pr-illus-1st ed (jj6,f,dj) 40.00

LAWRENCE,D H-Boy in the Bush-NY-1924-Seltzer-8vo-cl-1st ed (x3) 40.00

LAWRENCE,D H-Complete Plays of...-NY-1965-Viking-1st ed (x9,f,dj) 25.00

LAWRENCE,D H-David, A Play-1926-Knopf-1st ed (x2,dj sl soil & wn) 130.00

LAWRENCE,D H-England, My England-Lond-(1924)-Martin Secker-8vo-brwn cl-1st Brit ed (x3) 40.00

LAWRENCE,D H-Escaped Cock-Paris-1929-Black Sun Pr-lettrd wrps,col dec by auth,orig glassine dj-ltd to 450c,nbrd (x3,f,sl chip dj,box) 475.00

LAWRENCE,D H-Kangaroo-NY-1923-T Seltzer-1st US ed (x9,sp rub) 70.00

LAWRENCE,D H-Lady Chatterley's Lover-NY-(1959)-Grove-8vo-368p-1st unexpurgated US prtg-1st US ed thus (bb5,f,dj) 25.00

LAWRENCE,D H-Letters of...-NY-1932-Viking-1st Amer ed (u9,wn dj) 95.00

LAWRENCE,D H-Letters of...-NY-1932-Viking-893p-1st Amer ed (bb2,sp fade,bump,dj) 65.00

LAWRENCE,D H-Lost Girl-NY-1982-Viking-1st ed thus (z9,f,dj) 12.50

LAWRENCE,D H-Man Who Died-1931-Secker-ltd to 2000c-1st ed (kk6,dj) 150.00

LAWRENCE,D H-Modern Lover-NY-1934-Viking-1st Amer ed (bb2,dj chip) 65.00

LAWRENCE,D H-Mornings in Mexico-NY-1927-Knopf-orng bds-1st ed (cc2) 95.00

LAWRENCE,D H-My Skirmish with Jolly Roger-NY-1929-Random-ltd to 600c,nbrd-1st ed (q2,sl wn sp) 55.00

LAWRENCE,D H-Nettles-Lond-1930-Faber & Faber-30p-wrps-scarce-1st ed (u9,wn wrps) 65.00

LAWRENCE,D H-Pansies-(Lond)-1929-priv prtd-stiff wrps,glassine dj-ltd to 500c,nbrd,autg (jj4) 225.00

LAWRENCE,D H-Pansies-Lond-(1929)-M Secker-1st trd ed(after ltd of 500c) (u9) 85.00

LAWRENCE,D H-Pansies-Lond-(1929)-Secker-slim 8vo-cl bkd pattrnd bds-1st ed (x3,chip dj) 100.00

LAWRENCE,D H-Pornography and Obscenity-1929-Faber & Faber-orng wrps-1st ed (x2,sl soil,sp rub) 30.00

LAWRENCE,D H-Pornography and Obscenity-1929-Faber-cl,tissue dj as iss-scarce-1st ed (jj6,dj) 210.00

LAWRENCE,D H-Selected Letters of...-NY-(1958)-FS&C-1st ed (b10,f,sl soil dj) 20.00

LAWRENCE,D H-St.Mawr-1925-Knopf-222p-1st separate ed (v8) 45.00

LAWRENCE,D H-Touch & Go-NY-1920-T Seltzer-1st US ed (u9,wn dj) 100.00

LAWRENCE,D H-Touch and Go-Lond-1920-Daniel-sm 8vo-limp papr bds,orig glassine dj-1st ed (x3,sl sunned,sl soil,dj) 160.00

LAWRENCE,D H-Triumph of the Machine-Lond-1930-Faber & Faber-sm wrps-Roberts A58b-Special ed (u9) 25.00

LAWRENCE,D H-Twilight in Italy-NY-1916-Huebsch-1st US ed (mm5,lacks dj) 75.00

LAWRENCE,D H-Virgin & the Gypsy-NY-1930-Knopf-1st US ed (u9) 45.00

LAWRENCE,D H-Widowing of Mrs.Holroyd-NY-1914-Kennerley-red bds,ltd to 500c,precedes Brit ed-1st ed (bb2) 85.00

LAWRENCE,EDWARD-Clover Passage-Caldwell-1954-8vo-260p-illus (m3,vf,dj) 15.00

LAWRENCE,EDWARD-Spiritualism Among Civilised and Savage Races-Lond-1921-A & C Black,Ltd-cl,frntis,illus-1st ed (l8) 25.00

LAWRENCE,ELIZABETH-Southern Garden-Chapel Hill-1942-U of NC-241p-cl-1st prtg (x6) 12.00

LAWRENCE,FRIEDA-Not I, But the Wind...-Santa Fe-(1934)-Rydal Pr-lg 8vo-cl,prtd sp labl-ltd to 1000c,autg-1st ed (ll10,cor bump,dj sl wn & soil 150.00

LAWRENCE,HILDA-Pavilion-NY-1946-S&S-8vo-279p-1st ed (w6,dj) 25.00

LAWRENCE,JEANNIE-My Life with Sydney Lawrence-Seattle-1974-Salisbury Pr-160p-1st ed (oo4,dj) 95.00

LAWRENCE,JEROME-Inherit the Wind-NY-(1955)-Random-1st ed (bb1,dj sp brwnd,sl chip) 20.00

LAWRENCE,LARS-Morning Noon and Night-NY-1954-Putnam-1st ed (w5,f,dj) 25.00

LAWRENCE,LARS-Morning,Noon & Night-NY-1954-Putnam's-1st ed (nn9,dj) 37.50

LAWRENCE,LARS-Old Father Antic-Lond-1961-J Calder-1st Brit ed (nn9,dj) 50.00

LAWRENCE,MARGERY-Number Seven, Queer Street-Sauk City-1969-Mycroft & Moran-236p-ltd to 2027c-1st ed (k5,as new in dj) 35.00

LAWRENCE,MARY C-Captain's Best Mate-Providence-1966-Brown Univ Pr-8vo-drk brwn cl,illus-1st ed (nn1,dj) 40.00

LAWRENCE,T E-Mint-Lond-(1955)-J Cape-lea sp,ltd to 2000c (l9,lacks box) 200.00

LAWRENCE,T E-Mint-Lond-(1955)-Jonathan Cape-sm 4to-mor bkd cl,sp g,t.e.g.,other edges untrmmd,t.p. prntd in blk & red-ltd to 2000c,nbrd (s2,box) 225.00

LAWRENCE,T E-Revolt in the Desert-Lond-1927-J Cape-1st ed (c8,sp chip dj) 500.00

LAWRENCE,T E-Revolt in the Desert-NY-1927-Dbldy Doran-1st US ed (h8,f,sl chip dj) 100.00

LAWRENCE,T E-Seven Pillars of Wisdom-GC-(1935)-Doubleday-1st US trd ed (g6,sl tn dj) 100.00

LAWRENCE,W H-New Mexico Territorial Bureau of Immigration-Silver City-1881-31p-wrps,removed from bk of bnd pamphlets-rare-Adams Herd#1320-1st ed (v7,lacks rear wrpr,sp chip) 400.00

LAWRENCE,WILLIAM B-Colonization and Subsequent History of New Jersey-Somerville-1843-31p (aa6) 45.00

LAWRIE,W H-All Fur & Flies & How To Dress Them-Lond-1967-8vo-162p-col frontis,illus (m3,vf,dj) 20.00

LAWRIE,W H-Book of the Rough Stream Nymph-Edinburgh-1947-8vo-103p-col plts-1st ed (m3,vf,dj) 20.00

LAWRIE,W H-English & Welsh Trout Flies-Lond-1967-8vo-152p-col plts,illus-1st ed (m3,vf,dj) 20.00

LAWRIE,W H-English Trout Flies-S Brunswick-1969-8vo-392p-photos (m3,vf,dj) 25.00

LAWRIE,W H-Reference Book of English Trout Flies-Lond-1967-8vo-392p-col plts,illus-1st ed (m3,vf,dj) 35.00

LAWRIE,W H-Scottish Trout Flies-Lond-1966-8vo-126p-col plts,photos-1st ed (m3,vf,dj) 25.00

LAWS,M E S-Battery Records of the Royal Artillery 1716 to 1859-Woolrich-1952-oblng folio-313p-dec blu cl-1st ed (b7) 200.00

LAWSON,ELIZABETH-Thaddeus Stevens-NY-1941-Int'l-wrps-1st ed (w5) 30.00

LAWSON,ELIZABETH-Thaddeus Stevens-NY-1962-publ by auth-32p-wrps (r1) 13.00

LAWSON,G W-Plant Life in West Africa-Lond-1966-OUP-150p-cl (x6) 20.00

LAWSON,J H W-Four Five Five-Melbourne-(1951)-sm 8vo-208p-cl,plts (t2,dj) 225.00

LAWSON,JOHN C-Modern Greek Folklore and Ancient Greek Religion-New Hyde Park-1964-Univ Bks-cl,illus-1st ed thus (n8) 45.00

LAWSON,ROBERT-Rabbit Hill-1944-Viking-128p-illus,e.p. maps-1st ed (v8,dj sl chip & soil) 55.00

LAWSON,ROBERT-Tough Winter-NY-(1954)-Viking-pict cl,auth illus-1st ed (pp10,dj wn) 45.00

LAWSON,THOMAS W-Path Pointer for Delegates to the National Republican Convention-Bost-1916-48p-flex cl-scarce (j1) 17.50

LAWSON,WILLIAM P-Log of a Timber Cruiser-NY-1915-Duffield-scarce-1st ed (nn9) 75.00

LAWTON,CHARLES-Clarkville's Battery-1937-Cupples & Leon-1st ed (s8,dj) 25.00

LAWTON,MARY-Queen of Cooks, And Some Kings-NY-1925-Boni Liveright-208p-red cl,illus (u6,soil,wn) 25.00

LAY,CHARLES-Garden Book for Autumn and Winter-NY-1924-Duffield-303p-cl (x6,rub) 25.00

LAYCOCK,G-Sign of the Flying Goose-NY-1965-8vo-(3),299p-cl,e.p. maps,25 plts,maps (y8,dj chip) 15.00

LAYCOCK,GEORGE-Hunting With Bow & Arrow-NY-1965-8vo-111p-photos (m3,vf,sl wn dj) 15.00

LAYHEW,JANE-RX for Murder-Phila-1946-Lippincott-1st ed (j4,dj) 15.00

LAYMAN,RICHARD-Dashiell Hammett-Pitt-1979-Univ of Pitt-iss w/o dj-1st ed (d4) 40.00

LAYMAN,RICHARD-Shadow Man-Lond-1981-Junction-illus-1st Brit ed (r4,f,dj) 35.00

LAYMAN,RICHARD-Shadow Man-NY,Lond-(1981)-HBJ-photos-1st ed (l5,f,dj) 20.00

LAYTON,T A-Wine and Food Society's Guide to Cheese and Cheese Cookery-(Cleve)-(1967)-World-254p-col plts (o6,dj) 30.00

LAYTON,T A-Wines and Castles of Spain-Lond-(1959)-M Joseph-246p-blk cl-1st ed (q8,dj,pres) 25.00

LAYTON,T A-Wines of Italy-Lond-1961-Harper Trd Journals-221p-red cl,map e.p.,plts-1st ed (q8,dj) 30.00

LAZAREV,VIKTOR-Old Russian Murals & Mosaics-Lond-1966-folio-265 illus(9 col)-1st ed (r2,dj) 65.00

LAZELERE,CLAUDE-Government of Michigan-NY-1951-Hillsdale Sch Supply-176p-cl,photos (z7,pencil notes) 20.00

LE BLANC,MAURICE-Confessions of Arsene Lupin-1913-Dbldy-1st Amer ed (s10) 35.00

LE BLANC,MAURICE-Golden Triangle-1917-Macaulay-1st Amer ed (s10) 20.00

LE BLANC,MAURICE-Golden Triangle-NY-1917-Macaulay Co-rare pict dj-1st Amer ed (gg8,sl chip dj) 65.00

LE BON GENRE: A SELECTION OF 100 PLATES OF THE FAMOUS `GAZETTE DU BON GENRE'-NY-(1923)-Foreign Publ-4to-pattrnd papr bds,100 col plts each on a hngd leaf (p1,f) 1,100.00

LE BON,GUSTAVE-Psychology of Revolution-Lond-(1913)-Unwin-336p-cl,t.e.g.-1st Brit ed (dd10,sl fox) 25.00

LE BON,GUSTAVE-Psychology of the Great War-NY-1917-Macmillan-480p-cl-1st Amer ed (dd10,sl fox) 30.00

LE CARRE,JOHN-Honourable Schoolboy-NY-1977-Knopf-1st trd ed (a5,f,dj) 25.00

LE CARRE,JOHN-Little Drummer Girl-Lond-1983-Hodder-1st ed (q4,sl bump cov,dj) 45.00

LE CARRE,JOHN-Little Drummer Girl-NY-1983-Knopf-1st ed (bb1,as new in dj) 25.00

LE CARRE,JOHN-Looking Glass War-Lond-1965-Heinemann-1st ed (z2,f,f dj) 125.00

LE CARRE,JOHN-Murder of Quality-1962-Gollancz-scarce-1st ed (x2,dj sp missing sm pc) 1,475.00

LE CARRE,JOHN-Murder of Quality-1962-Walker-scarce-1st Amer ed (x7,f,dj) 450.00

LE CARRE,JOHN-Small Town in Germany-Lond-1968-Heinemann-1st ed (gg8,f,dj) 75.00
LE CARRE,JOHN-Small Town in Germany-NY-1968-1st Amer ed (r5,f,dj) 25.00
LE CARRE,JOHN-Small Town in Germany-NY-1968-CM-1st Amer ed (x7,dj) 18.00
LE CARRE,JOHN-Smiley's People-(1980)-Hodder and Stoughton-1st ed (ee2,f,dj) 40.00
LE CARRE,JOHN-Smiley's People-NY-1980-Knopf-1st trd ed (a5,as new in dj) 30.00
LE CARRE,JOHN-Spy Who Came in From the Cold-Lond-1963-Gollancz-1st ed (gg8,dj) 400.00
LE CARRE,JOHN-Tinker, Tailor, Soldier, Spy-1974-Knopf-1st Amer ed (x7,dj) 23.00
LE CLERQ,TANAQUIL-Ballet Cook Book-(1966)-Stein & Day-424p-tan bds,photos-1st ed (q8,dj) 27.50
LE CORBUSIER-Athens Charter-NY-1973-sq 8vo-1st transl ed (ee1,dj) 50.00
LE CORBUSIER-Concerning Town Planning-1948-Yale-illus-1st Amer ed (ee1,dj) 50.00
LE CORBUSIER-Creation is a Patient Search-NY-1960-Praeger-1st ed (d8,f,tn dj) 125.00
LE CORBUSIER-Four Routes-Lond-1947-1st Brit ed (ee1,dj) 50.00
LE CORBUSIER-Home of Man-Lond-1948-illus-1st transl ed (kk4) 75.00
LE CORBUSIER-Radiant City-NY-1967-oblng 4to-illus-1st transl ed (h10,dj) 85.00
LE CORBUSIER-When the Cathedrals were White-NY-1947-1st transl ed (h10,sl chip dj) 50.00
LE CORBUSIER-When the Cathedrals were White-NY-1947-1st transl ed (kk4) 45.00
LE COUTEUR,J D-English Mediaeval Painted Glass-Lond-1926-184p-162 illus (cc8,sl fox) 35.00
LE COUTEUR,JOHN-On the Varieties, Properties and Classification of Wheat-Jersey-1836-Payn-122p-1/2 calf wi mrbld bds,5 plts,fldg tabl-scarce (x6,rbnd) 300.00
LE FANU,J SHERIDAN-Evil Guest-Lond-nd(1895)-Downey-drk grn & gld dec cl wi March 1895 ads in rear,t.e.g.,30 illus,Brinsley Le Fanu-1st Brit ed (a10,chip sp cor) 600.00
LE FANU,J SHERIDAN-House By the Churchyard-Lond,NY-1899-Macmillan-rprnt (a10,sl soil bndg,discol sp) 40.00
LE FANU,J SHERIDAN-Purcell Papers-Sauk City-1975-Arkham-1st ed (k3,f,dj) 12.00
LE FANU,J SHERIDAN-Purcell Papers-Sauk City-1975-ltd to 4288c-1st ed (k5,as new in dj) 10.00
LE FANU,J SHERIDAN-Watcher & Other Weird Stories-Lond-nd(1894)-Downey-gry,silv & blk pict bndg,21 illus by Brinsley Le Fanu-1st Brit ed (aa8) 700.00
LE FEURE,GEORGES-An Eastern Odyssey-Bost-1935-368p-40 illus,fldg map-1st ed (o10,f) 25.00
LE GALLIENNE,EVA-Flossie and Bossie-NY-(1949)-Harper-210p-pict cl,illus,G Williams-1st ed (r3,chip dj) 40.00
LE GUIN,URSULA K-Beginning Place-NY et al-(1980)-1st ed (m5,f,dj) 12.50
LE GUIN,URSULA K-Beginning Place-NY-(1980)-Harper & Row-1st ed (e3,f,dj) 25.00
LE GUIN,URSULA K-City of Illusions-1978-Harper & Row-new intro by auth-1st ed thus (p9,f,dj) 45.00
LE GUIN,URSULA K-Dispossessed-NY-1974-H&R-1st ed (y1,dj) 100.00
LE GUIN,URSULA K-Eye of the Heron-NY-(1978)-Harper & Row-1st Separate US ed (h3,f,dj) 17.00
LE GUIN,URSULA K-Wind's Twelve Quarters-NY-1975-Harper & Row-1st ed (h8,f,sl wn dj) 30.00
LE MASTER,RICHARD-Wildlife in Wood-Chig-1978-oblng 8vo-247p-illus,photos-1st ed (m3,vf,creased dj) 27.50
LE MAY,ALAN-Searchers-NY-1954-Harpers-ltd to 800c,autg-1st ed (z2,f,dj) 225.00
LE PAGE,W L-ABC of Flight-NY-1928-sm 8vo-x,142p-illus cl,6p plts-1st ed (s2,dj) 25.00
LE PRAT,THERESE-Faces and Destinies-W Germ-1963-Overseas Publ Vaduz-folio-104p-prtd bds,ports-1st ed (t3,f) 40.00
LE QUEUX,W-Doctor of Pimlico-1920-Macaulay-1st ed (x7,f,sp chip dj) 35.00
LE QUEUX,W-Spies of the Kaiser-1909-Hurst & Blackett-1st ed (x7) 65.00
LE QUEUX,W-Treasure of Israel-1910-Eveleigh Nash-1st ed (x7) 65.00
LE WARNE,CHARLES P-Utopias on Puget Sound 1885 to 1915-Seattle-1975-UW Pr-8vo-323p wi photos,index-1st ed (t1,dj) 35.00
LEA,AURORA LUCERO-WHITE-Literary Folklore of Hispanic SW-San Antonio-(1953)-243p-1st ed (u7,dj) 35.00
LEA,HENRY-An Historical Sketch of Sacerdotal Celibacy in the Christian Church-Phila-1867-Lippincott-xx,601+(2)p ads-orig cl-1st ed (dd10,cov soil & fade) 35.00
LEA,HOMER-Valor of Ignorance-NY,Lond-1909-Harper & Bros-8vo-(2),344p-blu cl-1st ed (gg6) 80.00
LEA,TOM-Brave Bulls-Bost-1949-270p-illus,auth-1st ed (t7,dj) 17.50
LEA,TOM-Brave Bulls-Bost-1949-Little,Brown-1st ed (u9,edgewn dj) 35.00
LEA,TOM-Bullfight Manual for Beginners-Juarez-(1949)-24p-wrps (j7) 20.00
LEA,TOM-Bullfight Manual for Spectators-Ciudad Juarez,Chihuahua-1949-Plaza De Toros-16mo-24p-pict wrps,illus-1st ed (aa3) 27.50
LEA,TOM-Hands of Cantu-Bost-(1964)-Little,Brown-(iv),244p-cl,illus,auth-1st ed (v1,sl wn dj) 50.00
LEA,TOM-King Ranch-Bost-(1957)-Little,Brown-2 vols-maps,drwngs-Herd 1318-1st iss(chptr heading p507 vol.2 changed to read Alice in latr prtgs)-1st ed (cc4,box) 200.00
LEA,TOM-Picture Gallery-Bost-1968-Little,Brown-2 vols-1st ed (u9,box) 150.00
LEA,TOM-Primal Yoke-(1960)-Little,Brown-illus,Lea-1st ed (t8,dj chip,sl wn,rprd) 18.00
LEA,TOM-Wonderful Country-Bost-1952-Little,Brown-387p-cl,illus by auth-1st ed (w3,f,dj) 25.00
LEACH,A J-Early Day Stories-Norfolk-1916-244p-frntis,photos-Smith #5779-scarce (t7,dj) 40.00
LEACH,A J-Early Day Stories-Norfolk-1916-Huse-v scarce dj-Howes 162a-2nd ed (u9,dj chip & soil) 100.00
LEACH,GLEN-Artificial Propagation of Brook Trout & Rainbow Trout with Notes on Three Other Species-Wash-1939-8vo-74p-wrps,illus (m3,vf) 12.50
LEACH,JOSEPH-Typical Texan-Dallas-1952-SMU Pr-178p-illus (cc4,dj) 25.00
LEACOCK,STEPHEN-Canada's War at Sea-Montreal-1944-Alvah M Beatty Publ-4to-(vols I & II in one vol)-blu cl,g titles & decs,col illus-1st ed (cc7,sl bump) 75.00*
LEACOCK,STEPHEN-Canada, The Foundations of its Future-1941-Seagrams-illus-1st ed (x2,dj) 35.00

LEACOCK,STEPHEN-Garden of Folly-NY-1924-Dodd,Mead-1st ed (z9,sl edgewn) 12.50

LEACOCK,STEPHEN-Hellements of Hickonomics-NY-1936-Dodd,Mead-(12),84p-illus-1st ed (m4) 12.50

LEACOCK,STEPHEN-Here Are My Lectures-1937-D,M-1st ed (x2,f,dj missing 2 sm chips) 65.00

LEACOCK,STEPHEN-Last Leaves-NY-1945-1st US ed (n5,chip dj) 22.50

LEACOCK,STEPHEN-Literary Lapses-Montreal-1910-Gazette Prtg-125p-cl/bds,papr labl-1st ed (pp2,sl rub) 150.00*

LEACOCK,STEPHEN-My Discovery of England-Lond-1922-1st ed (r2,dj chip,rub) 30.00

LEACOCK,STEPHEN-My Discovery of the West-Bost-1937-1st US ed (n5,dj) 35.00

LEACOCK,STEPHEN-Our Heritage of Liberty-Lond-(1942)-J Lane,Bodley Head-1st ed (pp2,dj sl soil & chip) 45.00*

LEACOCK,STEPHEN-Sunshine Sketches-NY-1912-John Lane-1st ed (w5) 30.00

LEACOCK,STEPHEN-Winnowed Wisdom-Lond-1926-J Lane,Bodley Head-1st Brit ed (pp2) 50.00*

LEADVILLE,COL-Ballenger and Richards 11th Annual Leadville City Directory...for 1890-Leadville-1890-287p-orig bds wi new sp-1st ed (t7,rprd) 125.00

LEAF,MUNRO-Gordon the Goat-(1944)-Lippincott-8vo-grn cl-1st ed (u10,f,sl wn dj) 25.00

LEAHY,C-Birdwatcher's Companion-NY-(1982)-917p-illus-1st prtg (w10,dj) 15.00

LEAKEY,JOHN-West That Was-Dallas-(1958)-SMU Pr-271p-illus-1st ed (ee4,dj) 35.00

LEAKEY,LOUIS B-Animals of East Africa-Wash D.C.-1973-4to-199p-photos (m3,f,dj) 10.00

LEAR,EDWARD-Owl and the Pussycat-GC-1961-Dbldy-sm 8vo-pict cl,col illus,Wm P du Bois-1st ed (s3,f,dj) 30.00

LEAR,EDWARD-Pobble Who Has No Toes-NY-(1978)-Viking-sm 4to-unpgd-pict bds,col illus,K Maddison-1st US ed (r3,f,f dj) 15.00

LEAR,PETER-Spider Girl-Lond-1980-Cassell-1st ed (p4,vf,dj) 30.00

LEAROYD,C G-Physicians' Fare-NY-1939-Longmans-1st US ed (d4) 30.00

LEARY,FRANCIS-Golden Longing-NY-(1959)-Scribner-8vo-358p-17 illus-1st ed (dd5,dj) 15.00

LEARY,TIMOTHY-Changing My Mind, Among Others-Englewood Cliffs-1982-1st ed (x8,dj) 22.00

LEARY,TIMOTHY-High Priest-NY-1968-1st ed (r5,dj) 30.00

LEARY,TIMOTHY-Jail Notes-NY-1970-1st ed (x8,dj) 25.00

LEASOR,J-Millionth Chance-NY-(1957)-8vo-x,244p-cl,6p plts,1 dblpg plt-1st ed (s2,dj) 25.00

LEASOR,JAMES-Clock with Four Hands-NY-(1959)-Reynal-8vo-314p-8p photos-1st US ed (aa5,dj sl chip & tn) 17.50

LEASOR,JAMES-Passport in Suspense-Lond-1967-Heinemann-1st ed (gg8,sl rub dj) 30.00

LEATHERMAN,LEROY-Martha Graham-NY-1966-Random-photos-1st ed (u4,f,dj) 30.00

LEAVITT,DUDLEY-Leavitt's Farmer's Almanack, Improved...for the year of our Lord 1887...-Concord-(1886)-Edson C Eastman-48p-wrps (g1) 12.50

LEAVITT,ROBERT G-Noah's Ark, New England Yankees and the Endless Quest-Springfield-1947-106p-wrps (n1) 12.50

LEBESON,ANITA L-Pilgrim People-NY-(1950)-Harper-8vo-624p-illus-1st ed (cc5,sl tn dj) 20.00

LEBLANC,M-Arsene Lupin Gentleman Burglar-1910-Donahue-1st ed (x7) 14.00

LEBLANC,M-Arsene Lupin-1909-DP-1st ed (x7) 12.00

LEBLANC,MAURICE-Arsene Lupin Versus Herlock Sholmes-NY-1910-J S Ogilvie-dec olive cl-1st ed (u2) 35.00

LEBLANC,MAURICE-Eight Strokes of the Clock-NY-1922-Macaulay-frontis,pict cov-1st US ed (j4) 35.00

LEBLOND,AUBREY-True Tales of Mountain Adventure-NY-1903-299p-pict cov,t.e.g.,photos-1st US ed (a4) 48.00

LECK,C-Birds of New Jersey-New Brunswick-1975-8vo-190p-cl,40 illus,3 maps (y8) 25.00

LECKIE,ROBERT-Challenge for the Pacific-GC-1965-Dbldy-8vo-372p-maps-1st ed (cc5,dj) 20.00

LECKIE,WILLIAM H-Buffalo Soldiers-Norman-(1967)-290p-illus,maps-2nd prtg (n3,f,dj) 40.00

LECKIE,WILLIAM H-Unlikely Warriors-Norman-1984-368p-illus-1st ed (n3,f,dj) 27.50

LECLER,RENE-Sahara-NY-1954-Hanover Hs-8vo-280p-photos-1st ed (dd5,dj) 17.50

LECONTE,EMMA-When the World Ended-NY-1957-124p-1st ed (n3,f,dj) 37.50

LECONTE,JOSEPH-Autobiography of...-NY-1903-1st ed (o10,ex-libr) 45.00

LECONTE,JOSEPH-Journal of Ramblings Through the High Sierra of California by the Univ. Excursion Party-SF-1960-Sierra Cl-ltd to 2500c (o10,f,dj) 40.00

LECONTE,JOSEPH-Journal of Ramblings Through the High Sierra of California by the University Excursion Party-SF-1930-148p-5 photos,ltd to 1500c-rprnt (p10,f) 125.00

LECRON,LESLIE M-ED.-Experimental Hypnosis-NY-1952-Macmillan-(xx)+(484)p-prntd blu cl-1st ed (y9) 25.00

LECRON,LESLIE M-Techniques of Hypnotherapy-NY-1961-Julian Pr-(xxii)+261+(5)p-1st ed (y9) 26.50

LECTURESS: OR WOMAN'S SPHERE-Bost-1839-Whipple & Damrell-124p+(2)p ads-cl-1st ed (n1,fox) 85.00

LEDIN,R BRUCE-Compositae of South Florida-Coral Gables-1951-U of Miami-154p-wrps (x6) 18.00

LEDWIGE,FRANCIS-Complete Poems-Lond-1919-H Jenkins-cl-1st ed (z8,vf) 45.00

LEDWIGE,FRANCIS-Songs of Peace-Lond-(1916)-H Jenkins-cl-1st ed (z8,f) 40.00

LEDYARD,JOHN-John Ledyard's Journey Through Russia and Siberia 1787 to 1788-Madison-1966-U of Wisc Pr-8vo-xiv,294p-cl,illus-1st ed thus (y4,dj) 25.00

LEDYARD,JOHN-Journal of Captain Cook's Last Voyage...-Chig-1963-Quadrangle Bks-16mo-208p-blu cl-(facs of 1783 ed) (p8,f,f dj) 25.00

LEE,ALFRED P-Bibliography of Christopher Morley-Ann Arbor-1971-Gryphon Bks-8vo-x,277,(8)p-cl,papr sp labl,facs of t.p. not in orig ed-rprnt (x4) 40.00

LEE,ALFRED-Fine Art of Propaganda-NY-1939-Harcourt-wrps-1st ed (w5) 20.00

LEE,BABS-Measured for Murder-1944-Scribners-1st Amer ed (s10,dj) 22.50

LEE,BOB-Last Grass Frontier-Sturgis-1964-Black Hills Publ-456p-illus-1st ed (ee4) 30.00

LEE,BOURKE-Death Valley-NY-1930-MacMillan-blk cl,photos-1st ed (u2) 30.00

LEE,BRIAN N-British Bookplates, a Pictorial History-Lond-1979-David & Charles-sm folio-160p-cl,illus-1st ed (w2,dj) 45.00

LEE,CARSON J-Oswald Langdon or, Pierre and Paul Lanier-Chig-1900-Lakeside Pr-413p-cl (f1) 15.00

LEE,CHARLES A-COMP.-Alaska Indian Dictionary...-Seattle-1896-Lowman & Hanford-12mo-23p-prtd wrps-rare-1st ed (p1) 110.00

LEE,CHIP-On Edge-Bost-1982-291p-1st ed (p10,f,dj) 18.00

LEE,FRANCIS B-ED.-Genealogical and Memorial History of the State of New Jersey-NY-1910-4to-4 vols-mod buckrm,plts (aa6,rbnd) 250.00

LEE,FRANCIS B-Genealogical and Personal Memorial of Mercer County, New Jersey-NY-1907-4to-2 vols-mod buckrm (aa6,rbnd) 200.00

LEE,FRANCIS B-History of Trenton, New Jersey-(Trenton)-1895-4to-335,(1)p-cl,illus (aa6) 150.00

LEE,FRANCIS B-New Jersey as a Colony and as a State-NY-1902-4 vols-cl,illus,plts (aa6) 75.00

LEE,FRED-ET AL-Azalea Handbook-Wash-1952-Amer Hort Soc-148p-wrps (x6) 18.00

LEE,GEORGE J-Selected Far Eastern Art in the Yale University Art Gallery-New Haven-1970-Yale U Pr-4to-285p-wht cl,illus (r10,dj) 20.00

LEE,H-Octopus-1875-Chapman Hall-114p-13 figs (bb3) 15.00

LEE,HARPER-To Kill a Mockingbird-Lond-(1960)-Heinemann-8vo-bds-1st Brit ed (v10,f,f dj) 150.00

LEE,HARPER-To Kill a Mockingbird-Phila-1960-Lippincott-auth 1st & only bk-scarce-1st ed (d8,f,dj) 1,250.00

LEE,HENRY-Memoirs of the War in the Southern Department of the United States-NY-1869-620p-brwn 1/2 calf,mrbld bds & e.p.,plts,maps-Howes L202 (jj2,sl wn) 100.00

LEE,HENRY-Memoirs of the War in the Southern Department of the United States-Phila-1812-Bradford & Inskeep-2 vols-1/2 lea & mrbld bds-1st ed (oo5,rbnd,sl chip & tn frntis) 250.00

LEE,HENRY-Octopus-Lond-1875-Chapman & Hall-sm 8vo-114p wi illus+ads,brn cl-1st ed (u1,sm scratch fr cov) 100.00

LEE,IVY-Present Day Russia-NY-1928-Macmillan-204p (ff1,dj chip,tn) 30.00

LEE,JACK-Powder River Let'er Buck-Bost-(1930)-65p-drwngs-scarce-1st ed (r8) 35.00

LEE,JENNETTE-Uncle William, the Man who was Shif'less-NY-1906-Century-298p-cl-1st ed (g1) 15.00

LEE,JOHN A-Simple on a Soap Box-Lond-1964-Collins-285p-cl-1st ed (kk1,f,dj) 30.00

LEE,JOHN D-Journals of...1846,7 and 1859-SLC-1938-priv prtd for Watt-244p-plts,port-ltd to 250c,nbrd-scarce-1st ed (bb8,dj) 275.00

LEE,JONATHAN-Fate of the Grosvenor-NY-1938-Covici Friede-8vo-348p-blu cl wi papr labls,illus-1st ed (p8,sp fade) 30.00

LEE,L P-ED.-History of the Spirit Lake Massacre-New Britain-1857-48p-pict wrps,illus-1st ed (c4,sl stnd) 185.00

LEE,LAURIE-As I Walked Out One Midsummer Morning-NY-1969-1st US ed (q5,dj) 15.00

LEE,LLOYD-Story of Yale-np-nd-priv prntd-216p-cl-(New Haven,1878)auth is Edward Blair-Wright 560-scarce (j1,corners wn,pres cpy) 27.50

LEE,MABEL B-Cripple Creek Days-GC-1958-Dbldy-12mo-xvi,270p-photos-1st ed (aa3,dj) 25.00

LEE,MABEL B-Cripple Creek Days-NY-1958-270p-photos-1st ed (t7) 10.00

LEE,MARY-It's a Great War-Bost-1929-HMCO-1st ed (x1,dj) 35.00

LEE,NELSON-Three Years Among the Comanches-Norman-1957-179p-1st ed thus (t7,dj) 15.00

LEE,R M-Safari Today-PA-1960-227p-photos,zebra dj (gg3,f,dj) 15.00

LEE,REBECCA S-Mary Austin Holley, a Biography-Austin-1962-UT-447p-1st ed (a9,dj) 30.00

LEE,RICHARD H-Letters of...1762 to 1794-NY-1911-Macmillan-2 vols-red cl-1st ed (mm10,sp lttrng fade,sl soil) 50.00

LEE,SHERMAN E-History of Far Eastern Art-Englewood Cliffs-(1964)-Prentice Hall-cl,col & b&w illus-1st prtg (n8,f,dj) 45.00

LEE,SUSAN E-These Also Served-Los Lunas-1960-priv prtd-8vo-xiv,208p-pict cl,photos,maps-1st ed (aa3,as new in dj) 35.00

LEE,TANITH-Unsilent Night-Cambridge-1981-NESFA-one of 1000c-1st ed (h3,f,dj) 15.00

LEE,VERNON-Pope Jacynth ...-Lond-1904-1st ed (k5,f.e.p. creased,sp fade) 75.00

LEE,W A-Catalogue of Books in the Liverpool Medical Institution Library to the End of the Nineteenth Century-Liverpool-1968-569p-1st ed (dd3) 40.00

LEE,W STORRS-Great California Deserts-1963-Putnam-1st ed (q9,sl wn dj) 25.00

LEE,W STORRS-Washington State, a Literary Chronicle-(1959)-Funk & Wagnalls-514p-illus,e.p. map (r8,dj sl soil & chip) 25.00

LEE,WAYNE C-Scotty Philip-Caldwell-1975-Caxton-xx+334p-orng cl,illus-1st ed (m2,dj) 30.00

LEE,WAYNE-Scotty Philip the Man Who Saved the Buffalo-Caldwell-1975-334p-frntis,photos-1st ed (t7,dj) 15.00

LEE,WILLIAM H-Standard Domestic Science Cook Book-Chig-(1908)-Laird & Lee-552p-wht oil cl bds,thumb index-Bitting 279 (u6,recipes laid in & writ in) 30.00

LEE,WILLIS T-Water Resources of the Rio Grande Valley in New Mexico and Their Development-Wash-1907-56; vi p +2 fldg maps,7 plts (c1,disbnd) 17.50

LEECH,SAMUEL V-Raid of John Brown at Harper's Ferry as I Saw It-Wash D.C.-1909-publ by auth-24p-cl (aa1) 40.00

LEECH,SAMUEL-Thirty Years from Home, or a Voice from the Main Deck...-Bost-1844-Tappan & Dennet-12mo-xvi,(17)-305p,ad-orig brwn cl,3 engrvngs (nn1,fox,cl wn & soil) 150.00

LEECHMAN,DOUGLAS-Indian Summer-Tor-1949-Ryerson Pr-sm 8vo-182p-3 ports-1st ed (bb7,sl chip dj) 20.00*

LEEDS,JOSIAH W-Primitive Christians' Estimate of War and Self-Defense-New Vienna-1876-Peace Assoc of Friends-58,(6)p-cl (j1,sp wn) 15.00

LEEK,SYBIL-Inside Bellevue-NY-(1976)-Mason Charter-8vo-210p-1st ed (gg5,dj) 10.00

LEELANAU TOWNSHIP HIST WRITERS GROUP-History of Leelanau Township-Chelsea-1982-Book Crafters-sm 4to-288p-cl,illus,ltd to 1000c (z7) 65.00

LEEPA,ALLEN-Abraham Rattner-NY-c.1979-Leepa-folio-cl-1st ed (oo6,dj) 75.00

LEEPER,D R-Argonauts of Forty Nine-Columbus-1950-Long's College Bk Co-146p+appndx-drwngs-Howes L226 (cc4,lt spot t.p.,dj) 25.00

LEEPER,WESLEY T-Rebels Valiant-Little Rock-(1964)-328p-1st ed (n3,f) 45.00

LEES,HERBERT-New Iris Syrett Cookery Book-Lond-(1973)-Faber-392p-blu cl-1st ed (q8,dj) 20.00

LEFANU,WILLIAM-Bio Bibliography of Edward Jenner 1749 to 1823-Lond-1951-176p-1st ed (dd3) 60.00

LEFANU,WILLIAM-English Books Printed Before 1701 in the Library of the Royal College of Surgeons of England-Edinburgh-1963-28p-1st ed (dd3) 30.00

LEFANU,WILLIAM-Notable Medical Books from the Lilly Library Indiana University-Indpls-1976-275p-illus-1st ed (dd3) 50.00

LEFF,DAVID N-Uncle Sam's Pacific Islet-(1940)-Stanford U-71p-stiff dec wrps,9 maps-1st ed (u8,sl wn) 10.00

LEFFLAND,ELLA-Love Out of Season-NY-1974-Atheneum-1st ed (v5,f,f dj) 35.00

LEFINGWELL,WILLIAM B-Art of Wing Shooting-Chig-1894-12mo-240p-illus-1st ed (m3,sl soil cov) 70.00

LEFORS,JOE-Wyoming Peace Officer, An Autobiography-Laramie-1953-Laramie Prtg-200p-cl-Guns #1315-scarce-1st ed (w3,f,dj missng sm pcs) 175.00

LEGALLIENNE,RICHARD-Wagner's Tristan & Isolde-1909-Stokes-4to-g & blu dec blk cl,7 col plts by G A William wi tiss guards (v8,sl wn) 65.00

LEGAT,A W-ET AL-Design & Construction of Reinforced Concrete Bridges-Lond-1948-illus(incl fldg)-1st ed (ee1) 85.00

LEGENDRE,M-Exotic Cage Birds-NY-1958-12mo-95p-cl,40 col plts (y8,dj chip) 13.00

LEGGE,EDWARD-Empress Eugenie 1870 to 1910-NY-1910-Scribner-8vo-409p-17 illus-1st US ed (jj5) 25.00

LEGHORN,LISA-Woman's Worth-Bost-1981-RKP-356p (r1,dj) 15.00

LEGION OF LIBERTY!-NY-1857-Amer Anti-Slavery Society-336p-cl-separate t.p. on pg 276-woodcts-Sabin 39867 (j1) 35.00

LEGMAN,G-Horn Book-New Hyde Park-1964-Univ Bks-cl-1st prtg (l8,f,edge wn dj) 16.50

LEGMAN,G-Love & Death-Breaking Point-1949-95p-wrps-scarce (d1) 50.00

LEGROS,LUCIEN-Typographical Printing Surfaces-Lond-1916-Longmans,Green-lg thk 8vo-xxiv,732p-cl-1st ed (w2) 395.00

LEHMAN,VW-Forgotten Legions-El Paso-1969-UTEP-illus-1st ed (u9,dj) 35.00

LEHMANN,JOHN-Thrown to the Woolfs-NY-1978-HRW-1st ed (t4,f,f dj) 15.00

LEHMANN,ROSAMOND-Invitation to the Waltz-1932-Holt-1st Amer ed (x2,f,sl tn dj) 65.00

LEHMANN-HAUPT,HELLMUT-Gutenberg and the Master of the Playing Cards-New Haven-1966-Yale U Pr-4to-xii,83p-cl,38 illus(incl col)-1st ed (w2) 50.00

LEHMANN-HAUPT,HELLMUT-Peter Schoeffer of Gernsheim and Mainz with a List of His Surviving Books...-Rochester,NY-1950-L Hart-1st ed (w1,f,f dj) 20.00

LEHNER,ERNST-Fantastic Bestiary-NY-1969-Tudor Publ-4to-192p-illus-1st ed (ff9,f,sl wn dj) 40.00*

LEHRMAN,STEVE-Your Career in Harness Racing-NY-1976-Atheneum-1st ed (j9,f,f dj) 15.00

LEHRMANN,CHARLES-Jewish Element in French Literature-Rutherford-1971-Fairleigh Dickinson U Pr-1st US ed (z9,rub dj) 12.00

LEHRS,MAX-Late Gothic Engravings of Germany & the Netherlands-NY-1969-Dover-4to-367p-pict wrps,682 illus (r10) 12.50

LEIB,CHARLES-Nine Months in the Quartermaster's Dept.-Cin-1862-200p-pict mor,raised sp bnds,frntis,illus-Coulter #288-rare-1st ed (t7) 185.00

LEIBER,FRITZ-Night's Black Agents-Jersey-(1975)-Neville Spearman-1st Brit ed (j3,f,sl rub dj) 25.00

LEIBER,FRITZ-Night's Black Agents-Sauk City-1947-Arkham Hs-auth 1st bk-ltd to 3084c (bb1,sl wn sp) 125.00

LEIBER,FRITZ-Two Sought Adventure-NY-(1957)-Gnome-1st ed,1st bndg (o3,pgs brwnd,chip dj) 40.00

LEIBLING,A J-Chicago the Second City-NY-1961-Knopf-1st ed (y1,f,f dj) 50.00

LEIBOWITZ,J-History of Coronary Heart Disease-Lond-1970-227p-1st ed (dd3) 75.00

LEIBY,ADRIAN C-Revolutionary War in the Hackensack Valley-New Brunswick-(1962)-ix,329p-cl,illus,plts (aa6) 30.00

LEICESTER,HENRY-Sourcebook in Chemistry, 1400 to 1900-Cambridge-1952-554p-1st ed (dd3,dj) 45.00

LEIGH,H-Planes of the Great War-Lond-nd(ca.1920)-roy 8vo-112p-cl,49p plts,auth-1st ed (s2,chip dj) 100.00

LEIGH,LEOTI-Nonie-(Cin)-(1899)-Editor Publ Co-306p-cl-Wright(3270) (b1) 30.00

LEIGH,WILLIAM R-Frontiers of Enchantment-NY-1938-299p-illus (gg3,f,dj) 12.00

LEIGH,WILLIAM R-Frontiers of Enchantment-NY-1938-8vo-299p-illus,auth-1st ed (m3,vf,sl chip dj) 55.00

LEIGH,WILLIAM R-Western Pony-NY-(1933)-Harper & Bros-sm folio-116p-6 col tip in plts by auth-Herd 1325 (cc4,sm sp hole,spot cov) 150.00

LEIGHTON,ANN-American Gardens in the Eighteenth Century-Bost-1976-Houghton-xxi,514p-cl (x6,vf,dj) 35.00

LEIGHTON,ANN-Early American Gardens-Bost-1970-Houghton Mifflin-441p-scarce in cl (x6,dj wn) 35.00

LEIGHTON,ANN-Early American Gardens-Bost-1970-xviii,441p-84 illus-1st prtg (m10,sl wn,tattrd dj) 25.00

LEIGHTON,CAROLINE C-Life at Puget Sound with Sketches of Travel in Washington Territory...and California-Bost-1884-ix,258p-orig cl-Lowther 663 (a7) 85.00

LEIGHTON,CAROLINE C-Life at Puget Sound-Bost,NY-1884-258p+6p ads-Tweney #43-1st ed (h7,e.p. split,autg) 85.00

LEIGHTON,CLARE-Southern Harvest-NY-1942-Macmillan-157p-illus,auth-1st prntg (u6) 40.00

LEIGHTON,CLARE-Southern Harvest-NY-1942-Macmillan-lg 4to-157p-engrvngs,auth-1st ed (u1,dj) 125.00

LEIGHTON,DOROTHEA C-People of the Middle Place-(New Haven)-(1966)-160p+31 photo plts+frntis map,wrps-1st ed (v7) 10.00

LEIGHTON,MARGARET-Sword and the Compass-Bost-(1951)-Houghton Mifflin-264p-cl,line drwngs,J Leighton (s3,dj) 12.00

LEINSTER,MURRAY-Last Space Ship-NY-(1949)-Fell-1st ed (f3,chip dj) 25.00

LEINWAND,RITA-ET AL-How to Beat Those Cordon Bleus-Pasadena-(1974)-Ward Ritchie-288p-pict bds,drwngs-1st prtg (q8) 22.50

LEIPNIK,F L-History of French Etching from the 16th Century to Present-Lond-1924-106 photos-1st ed (r2,sl rub) 100.00

LEISENRING,JAMES E-Art of Tying the Wet Fly-NY-1941-12mo-81p-photos-scarce-1st ed (m3,f) 200.00

LEISER,ERIC-Complete Book of Fly Tying-NY-1977-8vo-241p-photos,illus-1st ed (m3,vf,dj) 20.00

LEISING,W-Arctic Wings-GC-(1959)-8vo-336p-cl,illus,e.p. maps-1st ed (s2,dj) 25.00

LEITCH,GORDON B-Chinese Rugs-NY-1935-Tudor Publ-cl,col frntis,illus-new ed (l8) 25.00

LEITER,SAMUEL L-Kabuki Encyclopedia-Westport-1979-Greenwood Pr-cl,illus-1st prtg (n8,f) 20.00

LEITFRED,ROBERT H-Death Cancels the Evidence-NY-1938-Green Circle-1st ed (h4,dj) 15.00

LEITHAUSER,JOACHIM G-Worlds Beyond the Horizon-NY-1955-Knopf-8vo-412p-59 plts+maps,drwngs-1st US ed (jj5,f,dj) 17.50

LEITNER,IRVING-Baseball, Diamond in the Rough-1972-Criterion-photos-1st ed (s8,f,dj) 30.00

LEJAREN A'HILLER-Surgery Through the Ages-NY-1944-Davis & Heck-4to-178p-cl,photos-1st ed (q3,sl chip dj) 175.00

LELAND,CHARLES G-Have You a Strong Will-Lond-1899-Geo Redway-12mo-xxxii+232+(5)p-maroon cl-1st ed (y9) 25.00

LELAND,E H-Farm Homes-NY-1881-Orange Judd-12mo-204p-g & blk dec grn cl,illus (a3,sl spot) 67.50

LELYVELD,TOBY-Shylock on the Stage-Cleve-(1960)-Wstrn Rsrv U-8vo-149p-6 illus-1st ed (ee5,f,dj) 20.00

LEM,STANISLAW-Futurological Congress-NY-1974-Seabury-1st ed (w5,f,f dj) 25.00

LEM,STANISLAW-Investigation-NY-1974-Seabury-1st ed (w5,f,sp crease dj) 25.00

LEM,STANISLAW-Return From the Stars-NY,Lond-(1980)-HBJ-1st ed (bb1,as new in dj) 10.00

LEM,STANISLAW-Return From the Stars-NY-(1980)-Harcourt Brace-1st US ed (h3,f,dj) 15.00

LEMARCHAND,ELIZABETH-Change for the Worse-1981-Walker-1st Amer ed (s10,dj) 12.50

LEMARCHAND,ELIZABETH-Cyanide with Compliments-Lond-1972-MacGibbon-1st ed (p4,dj) 25.00

LEMARCHAND,ELIZABETH-Troubled Waters-NY-1982-Walker-1st Amer ed (r4,vf,dj) 22.50

LEMASSENA,R A-Colorado's Mountain Railroads Volume I-1963-Smoking Stack-8vo-112p-wrps,illus (nn7) 24.00

LEMASSENA,R A-Colorado's Mountain Railroads Volume II-1965-Smoking Stack-8vo-unpgd-wrps,illus (nn7) 24.00

LEMASSENA,ROBERT A-Articulated Steam Locomotives of North America, Vol 1-SLC-1979-416p-pict lea & bds,photos-1st ed (t7,f) 45.00

LEMASTERS,E E-Blue Collar Aristocrats-Madison-1975-U of Wisc-218p (r1,sl tn dj) 17.00

LEMAY,REGINALD-An Asian Arcady-Cambridge-1926-Heffer-274p-blu cl,cov dec,col frntis,col fldg map,photos (gg6,sp wn) 75.00

LEMCKE,GESINE-Chafing Dish Recipes-NY-1896-Appleton-82p-gnr bds (u6) 35.00

LEMON,ROBERT-COMP.-Catalogue of a Collection of Printed Broadsides in the Possession of Soc. of Antiquaries of Lond.-Lond-1866-Soc of Antiq of Lond-4to-xi,228p-orig maroon cl,illus-1st ed (t10,f) 125.00

LENEVE,LANS-Hello, Sportsmen-NY-1954-8vo-213p-photos-1st ed (m3,vf,fray dj) 12.50

LENHOFF,H M-ED.-Biology of Hydra and Some Other Coelenterates-1961-U of Miami-467p-photos (bb3,f,dj) 25.00

LENIN,N-Letter to American Workingmen-NY-1918-Socialist Publ Soc-15p-stapled wrps-rprntd from "Class Struggle" (r1,sl curled pgs) 20.00

LENIN,V I-Will the Bolsheviks Retain State Power-NY-1932-Int'l-47p-wrps-Little Lenin Libr,Vol.12 (r1) 14.00

LENNON,JOHN-In His Own Write-Lond-1964-illus bds,illus by auth-1st ed (r2,sl wn) 65.00

LENNON,JOHN-Spaniard in the Works-1965-Cape-1st ed (x7,f) 78.00

LENS,SIDNEY-Crisis of American Labor-NY-1959-Sagamore-318p (r1,dj wn,sunned) 15.00

LENS,SIDNEY-Forging of the American Empire-NY-1971-Crowell-462p (r1,dj) 27.00

LENS,SIDNEY-Futile Crusade-Chig-1964-Quadrangle-256p-1st ed (r1,dj) 30.00

LENS,SIDNEY-Labor Wars-GC-1973-Dbldy-366p (r1,dj edge tn) 27.00

LENS,SIDNEY-World in Revolution-NY-1956-Praeger-250p (r1,chip dj) 20.00

LENTRICCHIA,FRANK-Robert Frost: A Bibliography, 1913 to 1974-Metuchen-1976-Scarecrow Pr-(8),238p-cl-1st ed (m4,f) 20.00

LENZ,E C-Muzzle Flashes-WV-1944-813p-photos (gg3,f,chip dj) 30.00

LENZ,E C-Rifleman's Progress-WV-1946-162p-photos (gg3,f) 15.00

LEON-PORTILLA,MIGUEL-Pre Columbian Literatures of Mexico-Norman-1969-U of Okla Pr-8vo-red cl,9 illus-1st ed (mm1,f,f dj) 30.00

LEONARD,ARTHUR G-How We Made Rhodesia-Lond-1896-356p-dec grn cl-1st ed (b7,sl rub sp) 300.00

LEONARD,CHARLES-Expert in Murder-NY-1945-Dbldy CC-1st ed (j4,dj) 12.50

LEONARD,ELIZABETH J-Buffalo Bill, King of the Old West-NY-1955-Libr Publ-8vo-320p-41 illus-1st ed (ff5,f,sl tn dj) 25.00

LEONARD,ELIZABETH J-Buffalo Bill-NY-(1955)-Libr Publ-320p-illus,map e.p.-Six Guns #1319 (cc4,dj) 15.00

LEONARD,ELMORE-Cat Chaser-1982-Arbor Hs-1st ed (r9,f,dj) 17.50

LEONARD,ELMORE-Cat Chaser-NY-(1982)-Arbor Hs-1st ed (j3,f,sl chip dj) 12.00

LEONARD,ELMORE-City Primeval-NY-(1980)-Arbor Hs-1st ed (j3,f,sl tn dj) 20.00

LEONARD,ELMORE-Fifty Two Pickup-1974-Delacorte-1st ed (q9,dj) 200.00

LEONARD,ELMORE-Fifty Two Pickup-Lond-1974-1st Brit ed (o5,vf,dj) 100.00

LEONARD,ELMORE-Split Images-NY-(1981)-Arbor-1st ed (g3,f,dj) 20.00

LEONARD,ELMORE-Stick-NY-(1983)-1st ed (bb10,f,dj) 15.00

LEONARD,ELMORE-Swag-1976-Delacorte-1st ed (o9,chip corner,f dj) 60.00

LEONARD,ELMORE-Swag-NY-1976-Delacorte-1st ed (z2,f,dj) 85.00

LEONARD,ELMORE-Unknown Man No.89-Lond-1977-1st Brit ed (o5,f,dj) 100.00

LEONARD,HENRY-Fisherman's Allegories...-Dayton-1887-305p-cl (j1) 15.00

LEONARD,IRVING A-Mercurio Volante of Don Carlos De Siguenza Y Gongora-LA-1932-136p-pict bds,frntis,photos,ltd ed-1st ed (t7,f) 150.00

LEONARD,J EDSON-Essential Fly Tier-NJ-1976-8vo-262p-fldg plts,illus-1st ed (m3,vf,dj) 17.50

LEONARD,J EDSON-Flies-NY-1950-8vo-340p-col frontis,illus-1st ed (m3,fray dj) 16.50

LEONARD,JACOB C-Southern Synod of the Evangelical and Reformed Church-Lexington-1940-373p-cl (b1) 20.00

LEONARD,JOHN W-Gold Fields of the Klondike Fortune-Lond,Chig-(1897)-215p-orig cl,plts,maps,illus-Smith 5862 (a7) 150.00

LEONARD,JOHN-Black Conceit-GC-1973-Dbldy-1st ed (bb1,f,dj) 20.00

LEONARD,R-I Flew for China-GC-1942-8vo-xxii,296p-cl,e.p. maps-1st ed (s2,dj) 35.00

LEONARD,THOMAS H-From Indian Trail to Electric Rail-Atlantic Highlands-1923-xvii,665p-cl,illus,plts (aa6) 100.00

LEONARD,ZENAS-Narrative of the Adventures of...-Chig-1934-Donnelley-278p-fldg map-Lakeside Classics (cc4) 30.00

LEONARDI,DELL-Reincarnation of John Wilkes Booth-Old Greenwich-(1975)-180p-1st ed (n3,f) 20.00

LEONHART,RUDOLPH-Treasure of Montezuma-Canton-1888-Cassidy-279p-cl-Wright 3282-scarce (a1,sp top wn,hngs weak) 25.00

LEONTYEV,A-Work Under Capitalism & Socialism-NY-1942-Int'l-62p-wrps (r1) 11.00

LEOPOLD,A-Game Management-NY-1933-Scribner's-drwngs-1st ed (c9,dj) 20.00

LEOPOLD,A-Game Survey of the North Central States-Madison-1931-Sprtng Arms & Amm Mfg Ins-299p (c9) 15.00

LEOPOLD,A-North American Game Birds & Mammals-NY-1981-4to-198p-illus (m3,vf,dj) 17.50

LEOPOLD,A-Round River-NY-1953-173p-illus (ee3,f,dj) 30.00

LEOPOLD,A-Sand County Almanac-(NY)-1949-OUP-226p-illus (gg3,f) 35.00

LEOPOLD,A-Sand County Almanac-NY-1949-OUP-8vo-bds,illus by Chas W Schwartz-1st ed (kk8,f,dj) 100.00

LEQUEUX,WM-Mademoiselle of Monte Carlo-NY-1921-Macaulay-1st US ed (d4,f.e.p. fox) 15.00

LEQUEUX,WM-Money Spider-Bost-1911-Badger-pict cov-1st US ed (e4) 15.00

LERNER,ALAN JAY-Camelot-NY-(1961)-Random Hs-1st ed (a10,sp chip dj) 20.00

LERNER,ROBERT E-Heresy of the Free Spirit in the Later Middle Ages-Berkeley-1972-U of Cal Pr-8vo-257p-cl-1st ed (y5,f,f dj) 25.00

LEROUX,GASTON-Lady Helena or the Mysterious Lady-1931-Dutton-1st Amer ed (s10) 20.00

LEROUX,GASTON-Man with the Black Feather-Bost-1912-Small-pict cov,illus-1st US ed (f4) 20.00

LEROUX,GASTON-Missing Men-NY-1923-Macaulay-1st US ed (g4) 10.00

LEROUX,GASTON-Mystery of the Yellow Room-NY-1908-Brentano's-auth 1st bk-1st US ed (ff6,fray cor,sl soil bndg) 50.00

LEROUX,GASTON-Mystery of the Yellow Room-NY-1908-Brentanos-1st US ed (g4) 35.00

LEROUX,GASTON-Nomads of the Night-NY-1925-Macauley-312p-pict bds-1st US ed (z9,sp sun) 20.00

LEROUX,GASTON-Perfume of the Lady in Black-NY-1909-Brentanos-1st US ed (f4) 35.00

LEROUX,GASTON-Phantom of the Opera-NY-(1911)-Grosset-photoplay ed-dbl pg col illus by A Castaigne (d4) 45.00

LEROY,BRUCE-ED.-H M Chittenden, a Western Epic-1961-Wash State Hist Soc-lg 8vo-136p-illus,ltd to 1000c-1st ed (r8) 18.00

LESBERG,SANDY-Master Chef's Cookbook-(1980)-McGraw Hill-folio-180p-blu cl,col plts-1st ed (q8,f,dj) 16.50

LESKE,G I-I Was a Nazi Flier-NY-1941-8vo-352p-cl-1st ed (s2,chip dj) 20.00

LESKO,LEONARD H-King Tut's Wine Cellar-Berkeley-(1977)-B C Scribe Publ-sm 4to-48p-pict wrps,col & b&w plts-1st ed (q8) 10.00

LESKY,ERNA-Vienna Medical School of the 19th Century-Balt-(1976)-Johns Hopkins U-xvi+604p-blu cl,100 illus on plts-1st ed (g2) 40.00

LESLEY,LEWIS B-ED.-Uncle Sam's Camels-Cambridge-1929-Harvard U Pr-298p-plts,fldg map-1st ed (d3,dj) 100.00

LESLEY,ROBERT W-History of the Portland Cement Industry in the United States-Chig-(1924)-Int'l Trd Pr-(xiv)+330p-grn cl,illus-1st ed (l2) 50.00

LESLIE,C E-Joy Bells of Heaven-Chig-(1886)-Chig Music Co-124p-bds (h1,sl wn) 12.50

LESLIE,JEAN-One Cried Murder-NY-1945-Dbldy CC-1st ed (k4,dj) 25.00

LESLIE,MISS-ED.-Gift 1840-Phila-1840-Carey & Hart-dec drk red lea,a.e.g. (u2,sl rub) 125.00

LESLIE,MRS.MADELINE-Prairie Flower-Bost-(1861)-Henry Hoyt-147p-cl (l1) 15.00

LESLIE,R F-In the Shadow of a Rainbow-1974-Norton-190p-1st ed (bb3,f,dj) 18.00

LESLIE,SHANE-Shane Leslie's Ghost Book-Lond-(1956)-Hollis & Carter-2nd ed (bb1,dj) 15.00

LESLIE,SUSAN-In the Western Mountains-Victoria-1980-lg 8vo-75p-wrps-1st ed (q10,f) 10.00

LESLIE,WARREN-Dallas, Public & Private-NY-1964-Grossman-1st ed (u9,f,sl wn dj) 25.00

LESQUEREAUX,L-Contribution to the Fossil Flora of the Western Territories. Part III-1883-US Geol Surv of Terr-283p-59 duotone plts (bb3,cov wn,sl soil pgs) 110.00

LESQUEREUX,L-Contribution to the Fossil Flora of the Western Territories. Part I-1874-US Geol Surv of Terr-4to-136p-30 duotone plts (bb3,cor wn,sl soil pgs) 95.00

LESQUEREUX,L-Contribution to the Fossil Flora of the Western Territories. Part II-1878-US Geol Surv of Terr-4to-366p-65 duotone plts (bb3,cov wn) 110.00

LESSA,WILLIAM A-Drake's Island of Thieves,Ethnological Sleuthing-Honolulu-1975-U of Hawaii Pr-xviii,289p-dec e.p.,11 maps,35 illus,5 tbls-1st ed (nn1,dj) 30.00

LESSER,MARY-Art of Learning Medicine-NY-1974-4to-343p-1st ed (dd3) 75.00

LESSING,DORIS-Briefing For a Descent Into Hell-NY-1971-1st US ed (r5,f,dj) 15.00

LESSING,DORIS-Briefing For a Descent Into Hell-NY-1971-Knopf-1st US ed (g3,f,dj) 25.00

LESSING,DORIS-Four Gated City-NY-1969-Knopf-1st ed (hh5,f,dj) 20.00

LESSING,DORIS-Golden Notebook-NY-1962-1st US ed (s5,chip dj) 22.50

LESSING,DORIS-Habit of Loving-NY-1957-Crowell-1st US ed (hh5,f,sl rub dj) 20.00

LESSING,DORIS-Man and Two Women-1963-S&S-1st ed (x2,f,dj) 30.00

LESSING,DORIS-Man and Two Women-NY-1963-S&S-8vo-316p-1st ed (w6,f,sl wn dj) 35.00

LESSING,DORIS-Memoirs of a Survivor-NY-1975-Knopf-1st US ed (hh5,f,f dj) 15.00

LESSING,DORIS-Particulary Cats-1967-S&S-1st Amer ed (x2,vf,dj) 38.00

LESSING,DORIS-Small Personal Voice-1974-Knopf-1st Amer ed (x10,f,f dj) 20.00

LESSING,DORIS-Stories-NY-1978-Knopf-1st ed (bb1,as new in dj) 25.00

LESSING,DORIS-Stories-NY-1978-Knopf-1st ed (x9,f,dj) 20.00

LESSING,DORIS-Summer Before the Dark-Lond-(1973)-Cape-8vo-241p-1st ed (w6,f,dj) 35.00

LESSING,DORIS-Summer Before the Dark-NY-1973-Knopf-1st US ed (bb1,f,dj) 20.00

LESSING,DORIS-Temptation of Jack Orkney & Other Stories-NY-1972-Knopf-1st US ed (bb1,as new in dj) 25.00

LESSNER,ERWIN-Danube-GC-1961-Dbldy-8vo-529p-1st ed (bb5,f,dj) 15.00

LESTER,ANNIE J-ED.-Ohio State History of the Daughters of the American Revolution-np-nd-640,(3)p-fabricoid-15p suplmnt & errata laid in (g1) 20.00

LESTER,C E-Glory and the Shame of England-1841-Harpers-2 vols,orig cl-1st ed (x2) 150.00

LETCHER,JOHN S-Self Steering for Sailing Craft-Camden-1974-Int'l Marine-262p-red cl,drwngs,photos (p8,sl rub dj) 10.00

LETHABY,W R-Westminster Abbey Re Examined-Lond-1925-Duckworth-8vo-298p-red cl,illus-1st ed (u10,f,edgewn dj) 35.00

LETHBRIDGE,T C-Painted Men-Lond-(1954)-Melrose-8vo-208p-36 illus-1st ed (gg5,chip dj) 20.00

LETHBRIDGE,T C-Witches-NY-(1962)-Citadel-8vo-162p-16 figs-1st US ed (gg5,dj) 15.00

LETOURNEAU,GENE-Sportsmen Say-Augusta-1975-8vo-217p-photos (m3,f,dj) 20.00

LETTERMAN,EDWARD J-From Whole Log to No Log-Mpls-(1969)-291p-frntis,photos,illus-1st ed (t7,dj) 10.00

LETTERMANN,EDWARD J-From Whole Log to No Log-Mpls-(1969)-Dillon Pr-291p-illus-1st ed (ee4,dj) 20.00

LETTERS FROM THE MOUNTAINS-Bost-1809-Greenough & Stebbins-2 vols-contemp 3/4 calf-1st Amer ed frm 3rd Lond ed (w6,rub) 150.00

LETTS,J M-Pictorial View of California-NY-1853-Henry Bill-vii,224,(1)p-g dec,blnd stmpd cl,48p lithos (p2,rebckd,new e.p.,sl fox) 200.00

LEUPP,FRANCIS E-In Red Man's Land-NY,et al-161p-Revell-161p-cl,frnts+8 pg plts (l1) 15.00

LEUPP,FRANCIS E-Indian and His Problem-NY-1910-Scribner's-369p-1st ed (bb4,sl spot cov) 25.00

LEUTZ,CHARLES R-Modern Radio Reception-1928-383p-254 illus-3rd ed (h6) 55.00

LEVARIE,NORMA-Art & History of Books-NY-(1968)-Heineman-quarto-illus-1st ed (w1,f,dj) 50.00

LEVEL,MAURICE-Tales of Mystery and Horror-NY-1920-1st ed (k5,sl wn sp) 100.00

LEVERAGE,HENRY-Whispering Wires-NY-1918-Moffat-1st ed (e4) 15.00

LEVERTOV,DENISE-Jacob's Ladder-1965-Cape-1st ed (kk6,f,dj) 50.00

LEVERTOV,DENISE-Pig Dreams-Woodstock-(1981)-Countryman Pr-illus-1st ed (k7,f,dj) 25.00

LEVERTOV,DENISE-Relearning the Alphabet-NY-(1970)-New Directions-8vo-cl bckd bds-1st ed (jj8,vf,dj) 25.00

LEVERTOV,DENISE-Sorrow Dance-NY-(1966)-New Directions-8vo-cl bckd bds-1st ed (jj8,few spots,dj) 35.00

LEVERTOV,DENISE-With Eyes at the Back of Our Heads-1959-New Directions-1st ed (kk6,dj) 45.00

LEVI,ELIPHAS-Transcendental Magic-Lond-1958-Rider-cl-3rd ed,rvsd (n8,f,dj) 65.00

LEVI,PRIMO-Monkey's Wrench-NY-1978-Summit Bks-1st ed (b8,f,f dj) 35.00

LEVI,W M-Pigeon-Columbia-1945-4to-(1),512p-cl,illus(2 col plts)-2nd ed (y8,sl stnd) 65.00

LEVI,W M-Pigeon-Sumpter-1969(1957)-4to-667p-buckr,col frntis,1 col plt-revsd ed (y8,scuff,dmpstnd rear cov) 65.00

LEVIN,ERNEST M-Phase Diagrams for Ceramists-1956-Amer Ceramic Soc-2 vols-illus (cc8) 75.00

LEVIN,HARRY-Memories of the Moderns-(NY)-(1980)-New Directions-1st ed (a10,as new in dj) 20.00

LEVIN,IRA-Kiss Before Dying-1953-Simon-auth 1st bk-1st ed (s10,pgs brwng,dj chip,soil) 100.00

LEVIN,IRA-Perfect Day-NY-(1970)-Random-1st ed (j3,dj) 10.00

LEVIN,IRA-Rosemary's Baby-NY-1967-Random-1st ed (v5,f,sl tn dj) 50.00

LEVIN,IRA-This Perfect Day-NY-(1970)-Random-1st ed (l3,dj) 10.00

LEVIN,MEYER-My Father's House-NY-1947-Viking-1st ed (w5,sp wn dj) 25.00

LEVINE,DAVID-Fables of Aesop-Bost-1975-Gambit-drwngs-1st ed (bb1,f,dj) 25.00

LEVINE,DAVID-No Known Survivors-Bost-1970-Gambit-drwngs-1st ed (bb1,as new in dj) 35.00

LEVINE,DONALD-Greater Ethiopia-Chig-(1974)-U of Chig Pr-8vo-cl,maps-1st ed (y5,f,f dj) 18.00

LEVINE,ED-Adventures of Red Perkins-Lakemont-1976-N Country Bks-66p-wrps-1st ed (dd6) 15.00

LEVINE,I D-Mitchell. Pioneer of Air Power-Cleve-(1944)-8vo-xii,420p-cl,10 plts (s2,chip dj) 35.00

LEVINE,ISAAC D-Mind of an Assassin-NY-(1959)-FSC-8vo-232p-12p photos-1st ed (jj5,dj) 17.50

LEVINE,RABBI RAPHAEL H-Israel: a Frank Appraisal-Seattle-(1959)-McCaffrey-8vo-141p-photos-1st ed (s1,dj) 15.00

LEVINGE,RICHARD G A-Historical Records of the Forty Third, Monmouthshire Light Infantry-Lond-1868-352p-red cl,col frntis-scarce-1st ed (b7,sl chip) 250.00

LEVY,BERNARD-HENRI-Barbarism with a Human Face-NY-1977-Harper & Row-210p-1st ed so stated (r1,dj) 20.00

LEVY,MERVYN-Drawings of L S Lowry-Lond-1976-Jupiter Bks-4to-tan cl,282 illus (r10,dj) 40.00

LEVY,MRS.ESTHER-Jewish Cookery Book-Garden Grove-(1982)-210p-grn buckrm-facs of 1871 first Amer ed (q8,f,dj) 25.00

LEVY,PAUL E-Rational Education of the Will-Lond-1913-Wm Rider & Son-12mo-scarce-1st ed (y9,chip dj) 27.50

LEWER,H W-Book of Simples-1908-Sampson Low,Marston & Co-225p-g dec grn vel papr bds,t.e.g.,others uncut (m6) 165.00

LEWES,GEORGE H-On Actors and the Art of Acting-NY-1892-237p-cl (n1,sl dmpstnd frnt cov) 15.00

LEWIN,ESTHER-Stewed to the Gills-LA-(1971)-Nash-168p-wht bds,col drwngs-1st prtg (q8,dj) 40.00

LEWIN,MICHAEL Z-Enemies Within-Lond-1974-Hamilton-1st Brit ed (q4,dj) 22.50

LEWIN,MICHAEL Z-Missing Woman-NY-1981-Knopf-1st ed (e4,dj) 12.50

LEWIN,MICHAEL Z-Night Cover-Lond-1976-H Hamilton-1st Brit ed (w5,f,f dj) 35.00

LEWIN,MICHAEL Z-Outside In-NY-1980-Knopf-1st ed (h4,as new in dj) 15.00

LEWIN,MICHAEL Z-Way We Die Now-NY-1973-Putnam-1st ed (d4,dj) 35.00

LEWINE,RICHARD-Songs of the American Theatre-NY-1973-Dodd,Mead-lg 8vo-820p-1st ed (p1,f,dj) 35.00

LEWINS,ROBERT-Life and Mind on the Basis of Modern Medicine-Lond-1877-66p-1st ed (dd3) 75.00

LEWIS & CO,J H-Wholesale Manufacturers of Coffins and Caskets-(Cin)-(1867)-4p leaflet,incl pricelist,unbnd as iss,trade catlg,illus (o1,unbnd) 20.00

LEWIS & DRYDEN-Marine History of the Pacific Northwest-NY-1961-494p-illus,clear dj-ltd to 750c-Tweney #87-2nd ed (e7,f,dj) 135.00

LEWIS,A H-Apaches of New York-1912-Dillingham-illus-1st ed (x7) 45.00

LEWIS,ALFRED H-Confessions of a Detective-NY-1906-Barnes-illus-1st ed (f4,sl fade cov) 75.00

LEWIS,ALFRED H-Faro Nell & Her Friends-NY-1913-Dillingham-rare dj-1st ed (u9,wn dj) 200.00

LEWIS,ALFRED H-Peggy O'Neal-NY-(1903)-R F Fenno-494p-cl-1st ed (a1) 15.00

LEWIS,ALFRED H-Sandburrs-NY-(1900)-318p-cl-Wright 3289-1st ed (h1) 17.50

LEWIS,ALFRED H-Wolfville Nights-NY-1902-Stokes-pict cov-1st ed (u9) 85.00

LEWIS,ALFRED H-Wolfville-1897-Stokes-337p-illus by F Remington-1st ed (d3) 75.00

LEWIS,ARTHUR M-Ten Blind Leaders of the Blind-Chig-1909-Chas H Kerr-blu/gry cl-1st ed (v5,f) 15.00

LEWIS,B A-Murle-Oxford-1972-Clarendon Pr-8vo-166o-cl-1st ed (y5) 16.00

LEWIS,BENJAMIN-Riding-Derrydale-1936-4to-141p-one of 1250c,photos (m3,f) 70.00

LEWIS,BERKELEY R-Notes on Ammunition on the American Civil War-1959-Amer Ordnance Assn-unpgd-stiff papr wrps,illus (dd9) 25.00

LEWIS,BERNARD-Behind the Type-Pitt-1941-Carnegie Inst-ltd to 1600c-1st ed (w1) 30.00

LEWIS,C DAY-Otterbury Incident-NY-1949-Viking-160p-pict cl,col dj & 22 b&w drwngs,Ardizzone-1st US ed (r3,rear e.p. crease,dj) 40.00

LEWIS,C S-Broadcast Talks-Lond-1942-1st Brit ed (s5,dj) 35.00

LEWIS,C S-Christian Reflections-Lond-1967-G Bles-1st ed (z9,f,dj chip,tn) 30.00

LEWIS,C S-Letters to an American Lady-(1967)-Wm Eerdmans-1st ed (x10,dj) 20.00

LEWIS,C S-Letters to an American Lady-Grand Rapids-(1967)-Eerdmans-1st ed (z8,f,sp fray dj) 12.50

LEWIS,C S-Poems-Lond-1964-G Bles-1st ed (z8,vf,dj) 30.00

LEWIS,C S-Poems-NY-(1965)-HB&W-1st Amer ed (x10,f,rub dj) 15.00

LEWIS,C S-Problem of Pain-Lond-1940-Centenary Pr-1st ed (z9,f,sl rub dj) 35.00

LEWIS,C S-Surprised by Joy-NY-(1956)-Harcourt Brace-1st ed (cc2,f,dj) 35.00

LEWIS,C S-Till We Have Faces-1956-Bles-1st ed (x2,dj) 135.00

LEWIS,C-Sagittarius Rising-NY-(1936)-8vo-xii,302p-cl-1st ed (s2,chip dj) 35.00

LEWIS,CARROLL-Treasures of Galveston Bay-Waco-1966-59p-cl,maps-1st ed (z1,f,dj) 25.00

LEWIS,CARROLL-Treasures of Galveston Bay-Waco-1966-Texian-59p-1st ed (a9,dj) 30.00

LEWIS,CHARLES L-Admiral Franklin Buchanan - Fearless Man of Action-Balt-1929-Norman,Remington-8vo-xvi,285p-blu cl wi g titles & cov dec,map e.p.,col frntis,photos,reprodctns (nn1,sl scuff) 45.00

LEWIS,CLIFFORD M-Spanish Jesuit Mission in Virginia, 1570 to 1572-Chapel Hill-1953-Univ of No Carolina-8vo-xviii+294p-tan cl,19 plts-1st ed (e2,dj) 50.00

LEWIS,DIO-Gypsies-Bost-1881-Eastern Bk Co-dec blu cl,drwngs-1st ed (ee6,f) 75.00

LEWIS,DIO-Our Digestion-Phila-1872-407p-cl (n1) 17.50

LEWIS,DIO-Our Girls-NY-1885-Dio Lewis Publ Co-202p-cl (d1,sl spot cov) 22.50

LEWIS,DR E J-ED.-Lewis' American Sportsman-Phila-1857-8vo-510p-orig bndg,illus (m3,f) 80.00

LEWIS,DR E J-Youatt on the Dog-Phila-nd-8vo-403p+ads-illus (m3,vf) 30.00

LEWIS,EUGENE W-Motor Memories-Detr-1947-Alved Publ-xxvi+258p-gry bds,cl sp,illus-1st ed (h2,dj) 25.00

LEWIS,FAYE C-Nothing to Make a Shadow-1971-Iowa State U Pr-8vo-viii,155p-drwngs-1st ed (aa3,dj) 15.00

LEWIS,FAYE C-Nothing to Make a Shadow-Ames-1971-155p-cl-1st ed so stated (f1,f,sl wn dj) 12.50

LEWIS,GEORGE A-Practical Treatment of Stammering and Stuttering...-Detr-1902-G A Lewis-8vo-416p-g dec grn cl,t.e.g.-1st ed (y4,weak hng) 25.00

LEWIS,GEORGE W-Ape I Knew-1961-Caxton-263p-illus-1st ed (v8,dj) 35.00

LEWIS,H H-ED.-Gunner Aboard the "Yankee"-NY-1898-Dbldy & McClure-xv,312p-dec blu cl,photos,4 col plts-1st ed (o2,sl wn cors) 30.00

LEWIS,H R-Poultry Keeping-Phila-1919-8vo-365p-cl,col frntis-2nd rvsd ed (y8,crack) 18.00

LEWIS,I M-Pastoral Democracy-Lond-1961-OUP-1st ed (y5,dj) 40.00

LEWIS,J-Graphic Reproduction & Photography of Works of Art-Lond-1969-illus-1st ed (h10,dj) 40.00

LEWIS,JAMES C-World of the Wild Turkey-Phila-1973-4to-158p-photos-1st ed (m3,vf,dj) 25.00

LEWIS,JAMES-Photographing the Horse and Rider-So Brunswick-1977-Barnes-4to-138p-1st ed (f10,dj) 35.00

LEWIS,JEFFERSON-Something Hidden-Tor-1981-311p-illus-1st ed (g10,dj) 25.00

LEWIS,JOHN-Collecting Printed Ephemera-(Lond)-(1976)-Studio Vista-4to-160p-cl,col illus-1st ed (w2,sl chip dj) 55.00

LEWIS,JOHN-Handbook of Type and Illustration-Lond-1956-1st ed (y7,dj) 45.00

LEWIS,JOHN-Twentieth Century Book, Its Illustration and Design-(NY)-(1967)-Reinhold Publ-4to-270p-cl,28 col illus-1st US ed (w2,dj) 75.00

LEWIS,LLOYD-Oscar Wilde Discovers America-NY-1936-462p-frntis,illus-Six Guns #1328-scarce (t7) 37.50

LEWIS,LLOYD-Sherman, Fighting Prophet-NY-(1932)-690p-illus-1st ed (c4,dj chip & sp fade) 45.00

LEWIS,M M-Infant Speech-NY-1936-Harcourt Brace-xii+335p-drk grn cl-1st ed (d2,chip dj) 20.00

LEWIS,MERIWETHER-Journals of Lewis and Clark-Bost-(1953)-Houghton Mifflin-503p-maps,map e.p. (dd4,wn dj) 15.00

LEWIS,MERIWETHER-Journals of the Expedition Under the Command of Lewis & Clark-NY-1962-Heritage-4to-2 vols (z4,box) 100.00

LEWIS,MERIWETHER-Lewis & Clark Expedition-Phila,NY-(1961)-sm 8vo-3 vols-text map-1814 ed unabridged-1st ed thus (c7,box) 60.00

LEWIS,MICHAEL-Napoleon and His British Captives-Lond-1962-317p-maps,illus-1st ed (b7,f,dj) 25.00

LEWIS,MONTGOMERY-Legends That Libel Lincoln-NY-(1946)-239p-1st ed (c4,dj) 18.50

LEWIS,OSCAR-Bay Window Bohemia-SF-1956-Dbldy-1st ed (t4,f,dj) 15.00

LEWIS,OSCAR-California Heritage-NY-(1949)-Crowell-186p-e.p. maps,illus-1st ed (ee4,dj) 25.00

LEWIS,OSCAR-Family of Builders-SF-1961-priv prntd(Grabhorn Pr)-4to-x+72p-mottled bds,cl sp,plts-1st ed (k2) 35.00

LEWIS,OSCAR-George Davidson: Pioneer West Coast Scientist-Berkeley-1954-U of Cal Pr-x+146p-grn cl,plts-1st ed (dd1,dj) 20.00

LEWIS,OSCAR-Here Lived the Californians-NY-(1957)-Rinehart-265p-photos-1st ed (bb4,dj) 25.00

LEWIS,OSCAR-Lost Years-NY-1951-Knopf-1st ed (hh5,dj) 10.00

LEWIS,OSCAR-San Francisco: Mission to Metropolis-1966-Howell North-274p-illus-1st ed (d3,dj) 20.00

LEWIS,OSCAR-Sea Routes to the Gold Fields-NY-1949-Knopf-photos-1st ed (u9,dj) 25.00

LEWIS,RICHARD S-From Vinland to Mars-NY-(1976)-NYT Quadrangle-8vo-436p-16p photos-1st ed (cc5,f,dj) 12.50

LEWIS,ROY H-Cracking of Spines-1981-St.Martin's-auth 1st bk-1st Amer ed (s9,vf,dj) 15.00

LEWIS,ROY H-Cracking of Spines-Lond-1980-Hale-1st ed (w5,f,dj) 25.00

LEWIS,ROY H-Cracking of Spines-NY-1981-St.Martin's-1st US ed (j4,as new in dj) 17.50

LEWIS,ROY H-Fine Bookbinding in the Twentieth Century-NY-(1985)-Arco-4to-151p-cl,33 col illus-1st US ed (w2,dj) 29.95

LEWIS,ROY-Wolf by the Ears-NY-1972-World-1st US ed (e4,f,sl wn dj) 14.00

LEWIS,SINCLAIR-Bethel Merriday-NY-1940-1st ed (r5,tape reinfrcd dj) 15.00

LEWIS,SINCLAIR-Cass Timberlane-Lond-1946-J Cape-1st Brit ed (y1,dj) 50.00

LEWIS,SINCLAIR-Cass Timberlane-NY-(1945)-Random-1st ed (ee2,f,dj) 35.00

LEWIS,SINCLAIR-Dodsworth-NY-March 1929-1st ed (r2) 45.00

LEWIS,SINCLAIR-Elmer Gantry-1927-Harcourt Brace-1st ed (x2,dj sl chip & soil) 125.00

LEWIS,SINCLAIR-Gideon Planish-NY-(1943)-Random-1st ed (ee2,f,dj) 50.00

LEWIS,SINCLAIR-God Seekers-NY-(1949)-1st ed (m4,edge wn dj) 15.00

LEWIS,SINCLAIR-It Can't Happen Here-Lond-1935-J Cape-1st Brit ed (y1,dj) 75.00

LEWIS,SINCLAIR-John Dos Passos' "Manhattan Transfer"-NY,Lond-1926-ltd to 975c,nbrd-1st ed (k5,inner hng sl cracked) 60.00

LEWIS,SINCLAIR-Kingsblood Royal-Lond-1948-J Cape-1st Brit ed (y1,dj) 50.00

LEWIS,SINCLAIR-Prodigal Parents-1938-D,D-1st ed (x2,dj) 45.00

LEWIS,SIR THOMAS-Clinical Disorders of the Heart Beat-Lond-131p-55 figs-6th ed (g10) 30.00

LEWIS,T PERCY-Catering by Confectioners-Lond-nd(ca.1910)-MacLaren & Sons-sm 8vo-177p-bds (o6) 30.00

LEWIS,TRACY H-Along the Rio Grande-NY-1916-Lewis-215p-illus-scarce-1st ed (a9) 60.00

LEWIS,VIRGIL-Story of the Louisiana Purchase-St.Louis-1903-300p-pict cl,frntis,illus-1st ed (t7,f) 20.00

LEWIS,WALKER-Without Fear or Favor-Bost-1965-HMCo-8vo-556p-1st ed (cc5,f,sl tn dj) 20.00

LEWIS,WILLIE N-Between Sun and Sod-Clarendon-1939-244p-cl,illu (v3) 55.00

LEWIS,WILLIE N-Tapadero-(1972)-U of Tx-189p-illus,map-1st ed (t8,f,dj) 25.00

LEWIS,WILMARTH-Collector's Progress-NY-1951-Knopf-1st Amer ed (w1,dj) 20.00

LEWIS,WYNDHAM-America, I Presume-(NY)-(1940)-Howell,Soskin-8vo-red cl,dj wi $2.00 cov price-1st ed (x10,e.p.s brwnd,dj sl wn) 50.00

LEWIS,WYNDHAM-Filibusters in Barbary-NY-1932-Nat'l Travel Club-1st Amer ed (x10,f,f dj) 125.00

LEWIS,WYNDHAM-Revenge for Love-Chig-1952-Regnery-1st US ed (w5,dj) 35.00

LEWITT,SOL-Autobiography 1980-Bost,NY-1980-Multiples & Torf-wrps in dj-1st ed (w5,f,f dj) 30.00

LEY,MADELINE-Enchanted Eve-np-(1946)-Howell,Soskin-4to-unpgd-cl,illus,E Legrand-1st US ed (r3,speckld cov,dj) 40.00

LEY,WILLY-Rockets-NY-1944-Viking-8vo-287p-illus-1st ed (aa5,dj) 25.00

LEYDA,JAY-Melville Log-NY-1951-Harcourt,Brace-8vo-2 vols-blu cl,map e.p.,15 plts-1st ed (ee7,sp drknd,v wn box) 125.00

LEYDET,FRANCOIS-Time and the River Flowing: Grand Canyon-SF-1965-Sierra Club-folio-176p-map e.p.,col photos-1st ed (aa3,f,sl chip dj) 65.00

LEYLAND,J-Adventures in the Far Interior of Africa...-1972-Struik-289p-illus-ltd to 1000c,nbrd-rprnt of 1866 ed (bb3,f,rub dj) 45.00

LEYLAND,JOHN-ED.-Gardens Old & New-Lond-Cntry Life/Geo Newnes-folio-3 vols-publ gilt dec cl,a.e.g.,photos-4th ed (cc10,ex-libr) 375.00

LEYS,JAMES F-Better Earth-SF-1940-Olympic Pr-204p-cl,pict papr cov labl,illus-1st ed (kk1,f) 25.00

LHALUNGPA,LOBSANG P-Tibet, the Sacred Realm: Photographs 1880 to 1950-NY-1983-Aperture-oblng 4to-1st ed (gg7,f,dj) 30.00

LI PO-Works of...-NY-1922-illus-transl by S Obata-1st Amer ed (r2,sl sun sp,sl rub) 30.00

LIBBY,BILL-Catfish-1976-Coward,McCann-1st ed (s8,dj) 11.00

LIBBY,BILL-Charlie O. and the Angry A's-1975-Dbldy-photos-1st ed (s8,f,dj) 12.50

LIBBY,BILL-Reggie Jackson Story-1979-Lothrop (r7,f,dj) 10.00

LIBBY,BILL-Reggie Jackson Story-1979-Lothrop,Lee & Sheperd-photos-1st ed (s8,f,dj) 18.00

LIBBY,BILL-Thurman Munson-1978-Putnam-1st ed (p7,dj) 12.50

LIBBY,BILL-Vida, His Own Story-1972-Prentice Hall-photos-1st ed (s8,f,dj) 12.50

LIBBY,LEONA M-Uranium People-NY-(1979)-Russak & Scribner's-x+341p-red cl,illus-1st ed (dd1,dj) 25.00

LIBBY,O G-ED.-Arikara Narrative of the Campaign Against the Hostile Dakotas, June 1876-NY-1973-219p-illus-ltd ed (f7) 65.00

LIBERMAN,ALEXANDER-Artist in His Studio-NY-(1960)-Viking-folio-cl-1st Amer ed (y3,sl soil cov) 45.00

LIBERMAN,ALEXANDER-ED.-Art and Technique of Color Photography-NY-1951-S&S-226p-195 col photos-1st ed (cc9,f,dj) 90.00

LICART,JEAN-Start Riding Right-Princeton-1966-Van Nostrand-1st US ed (f10,dj) 22.00

LICHT,HANS-Sexual Life in Ancient Greece-NY-1953-557p-1st ed (dd3) 40.00

LICHTEN,FRANCES-Folk Art of Rural Pennsylvania-NY-(1946)-Scribner-4to-276p-32p col illus-1st ed (ee5) 25.00

LICHTENSTEIN,BEN W-Textbook of Neuropathology-Phila-1949-474p-illus-1st ed (g10) 35.00

LICK OBSERVATORY-METEORS AND SUNSETS OBSERVED BY THE ASTRONOMERS OF THE...IN 1893,1894 AND 1895-Sacramento-1895-A J Johnston-vi+86p-blk cl,17 plts-1st ed (j2) 20.00

LIDDY,JAMES-Blue Mountains-Dublin-(1968)-Dolmen Pr-1st ed (z8,vf,dj) 100.00

LIDDY,JAMES-In a Blue Smoke-Dublin-(1964)-Dolmen Pr-1st ed (z8,vf,dj) 100.00

LIDELL,KEN-Alberta Revisited-Tor-1960-Ryerson Pr-8vo-xiv,234p-30 illus-1st ed (cc7,dj) 15.00*

LIEB,FRED-Baseball as I Have Known It-1977-Coward McCann-1st ed (r7,dj) 35.00

LIEB,FRED-Baseball, As I Have Known It-1977-Coward McCann-photos-1st ed (s8,f,dj) 25.00

LIEB,FRED-Boston Red Sox-1947-Putnam-1st ed (q7,f,dj) 65.00

LIEB,FRED-Boston Red Sox-1947-Putnam-photos-1st ed (s8,nick & chip dj) 60.00

LIEB,FRED-Connie Mack-1948-Putnam-rvsd ed (ff2,dj) 50.00

LIEB,FRED-Connie Mack-NY-(1945)-Putnam-276p-pict dj,photos-1st ed (f9,dj chip,stnd) 25.00

LIEB,FRED-Detroit Tigers-1946-Putnam (q7,dj) 35.00

LIEB,FRED-Detroit Tigers-1946-Putnam-photos-1st ed (s8,dj) 50.00

LIEB,FRED-St.Louis Cardinals-1944-Putnam-photos-1st ed (s8,dj) 50.00

LIEB,FRED-Story of the World Series-1949-Putnam-photos-1st ed (s8,sl wn dj) 35.00

LIEBERG,OWEN S-First Air Race-NY-1974-Dbldy-8vo-cl,illus-1st ed (s2,dj) 30.00

LIEBERMAN,HERBERT-Night Call From a Distant Time Zone-NY-(1982)-Crown-1st ed (p3,f,dj) 15.00

LIEBLING,A J-Back Where I Came From-NY-(1938)-Sheridan Hs-auth 1st bk-1st ed (a10,dj) 275.00

LIEBLING,A J-Chicago-NY-1952-1st ed (c5,edge rub,dj sp sl chip) 45.00

LIEBLING,A J-Sweet Science-NY-1956-Viking-1st ed (f8,f,dj missing sm chip) 100.00

LIEBOW,AVERILL-Encounter with Disaster-NY-1970-209p-illus-1st ed (dd3,dj) 75.00

LIENHARD,HEINRICH-From St.Louis to Sutter's Fort 1846-Norman-(1961)-204p-illus-1st ed (e7,vf,vf dj) 45.00

LIENHARD,HEINRICH-From St.Louis to Sutter's Fort, 1846-Norman-(1961)-U of Okla Pr-xx,204p-cl,illus-1st ed (ll9,f,dj) 35.00

LIFE AND DEATH OF LADY JANE GREY-NY-nd-Amer Tract Scty-16p-wrps,wdcut illus on t.p. & verso (d1) 10.00

LIFSHEY,EARL-Housewares Story-Chig-(1973)-Nat Hswrs Mfg Assoc-4to-384p-illus-1st ed (gg5,f,dj rub,sl tn) 25.00

LIGHT,RICHARD-Focus on Africa-NY-1944-228p-323 photos-1st ed (a4,f) 65.00

LIGHT,ROBERT E-Cuba vs the C.I.A.-NY-1961-Marzani & Munsell-wrps-1st ed (w5) 20.00

LIGHTBODY,CHARLES W-Judgements of Joan-Cambridge-1961-Harvard U Pr-cl,frntis,illus-1st Amer ed (n8,f,dj) 25.00

LIGON,J S-New Mexico Birds and Where to Find Them-1961-UNM-360p-33 col plts,photos,drwngs-1st ed (bb3,f,wn dj) 65.00

LIGON,J S-New Mexico Birds-Albuquerque-1961-8vo-360p-cl,34 col plts,photos,maps (y8,fray dj) 75.00

LIGON,J S-Wildlife of New Mexico-Santa Fe-1927-State Game Comm-wrps,photos,maps (u9) 40.00

LIJSEN,H J-Mounted Quadrilles, Carrousels and Other Equestrian Manoeuvres-Lond-1957-Allen-12mo-1st Brit ed (h9) 35.00

LIKINS,W M-Trail of the Serpent-np-(1928)-123p-wrps (g1) 22.50

LILIENTHAL,META S-Women of the Future-NY-1916-Rand School-wrps-1st ed (v5,f) 35.00

LILIUOKALANI-Hawaii's Story by Hawaii's Queen...-Bost-1898-Lee & Shepard-8vo-viii,409p-g dec red cl,t.e.g,photos (nn1) 250.00

LILIUOKALANI-Hawaii's Story-Rutland-1971-Tuttle-8vo-blu cl,photos-5th prtg (p8,dj) 30.00

LILLARD,MRS REESE-Tennessee Cookbook-Nashville-1913-M E Church,South-267p-grn bds-rvsd ed (u6,sp wn,rear hng broken) 50.00

LILLARD,RICHARD G-Desert Challenge-NY-1942-398p-frntis,fldg map,photos-1st ed (t7,pres) 25.00

LILLARD,RICHARD G-Desert Challenge-NY-1942-Knopf-8vo-viii,388,ix p-beige cl,fldg map,52 illus on 32 pgs-1st ed (mm1,dj chip & wn) 65.00

LILLARD,RICHARD G-Desert Challenge-NY-1949-Knopf-388p+index-map,illus (cc4,dj) 25.00

LILLEY,W OSBORNE-Bound for Australia on Board the Orient-Lond-1885-Andrew Crombie-12mo-133p+ads-g dec & imprntd blu cl,frntis,illus (p8,sl wn) 60.00

LILLICH,MEREDITH P-Stained Glass of Saint Pere De Chartres-1978-Wesleyan Univ Pr-1st ed (cc8,dj) 40.00

LILLY,J K-Medicine: An Exhibition of Books Relating to Medicine and Surgery from the Collection Formed by...-Indpls-c.1962-100p-wrps,illus-1st ed (dd3) 25.00

LILLY,WILLIAM E-Set My People Free-NY-(1932)-Farrar & Rinehart-269p-cl-1st ed (m1) 15.00

LIMA,E DA CRUZ-Mammals of Amazonia, Vol.1-Rio de Janeiro-1945-folio-(5),274p-orig wrps,42 col plts-vol.1(all publ),scarce-English ed ltd to 975c (y8) 185.00

LINCKE,J R-Jenny Was No Lady-NY-(1970)-8vo-288p-cl,illus t.p.,plts,illus e.p.-1st ed (s2,dj) 45.00

LINCOLN STORIES-NY-1926-Wm E Rudge-dec covs-1st ed (r2,f) 35.00

LINCOLN,A H-Familiar Lectures on Botany-1847-Huntington Savage-246p+220p appndx-lea,8 plts (bb3,sl fox) 35.00

LINCOLN,ABRAHAM-Uncollected Letters of...-Bost-1917-Houghton,Mifflin-xxii+264p-grn bds,cl sp-ltd to 500c-1st ed (k2,few pgs bent) 35.00

LINCOLN,CHARLES M-ED.-Narratives of the Indian Wars, 1675 to 1669-NY-1913-316p+ads-maps-1st ed (c4,cov stnd,sl wn,hngs weak) 50.00

LINCOLN,E S-Electric Home-NY-1934-Electric Home Publ-454p-blu cl,283 text illus (a2) 25.00

LINCOLN,EDMOND E-Results of Municipal Electric Lighting in Massachusetts-Bost-1918-Houghton Mifflin-xx+484p-maroon cl-1st ed (dd1) 20.00

LINCOLN,EVELYN-My Twelve Years with John F Kennedy-NY-(1965)-David McKay-371p-cl (l1,dj) 12.50

LINCOLN,F S-Charleston, Photographic Studies-1946-Corinthian Publ-unpgd-photos-1st ed (dd9,dj) 25.00

LINCOLN,FREDERICK-Migration of North American Birds-Wash D.C.-1935-8vo-72p-wrps,photos,maps (m3) 12.50

LINCOLN,JOSEPH C-Big Mogul-NY-1926-D Appleton-red cov-1st ed (f2,f,sl wn dj) 20.00

LINCOLN,JOSEPH C-Blair's Attic-1929-Coward-illus dj & e.p.,N C Wyeth-1st ed (s10,hng weak,soil pgs,dj) 25.00

LINCOLN,JOSEPH C-Blair's Attic-NY-1929-Coward McCann-369p-cl,N C Wyeth e.p.-1st ed (m1) 12.50

LINCOLN,JOSEPH C-Blowing Clear-NY-1930-Appleton Century-1st ed (y1,f,sl tn dj) 35.00

LINCOLN,JOSEPH C-Christmas Days-NY-1938-Coward McCann-1st ed (y1,f,dj) 50.00

LINCOLN,JOSEPH C-Christmas Days-NY-1939-illus by H Brett-ltd to 1000c,nbrd,2 autg (r2,uncut,sp sun,sl chip) 40.00

LINCOLN,JOSEPH C-Rugged Water-NY-1924-1st ed (m4) 15.00

LINCOLN,JOSEPH C-Rugged Water-NY-1924-Appleton Century-1st ed (y1,dj sl chip & wn) 35.00

LINCOLN,JOSEPH C-Storm Signals-NY-1935-D Appleton-blu cl-1st ed (f2,f,sl wn dj) 20.00

LINCOLN,LOUISE-ED.-Southwest Indian Silver from the Doneghy Collection-Mpls-(1982)-189p-dbl col,photos,map-1st ed (v7,f,dj) 30.00

LINCOLN,MARY-Bost Cook Book-Bost-1891-Roberts-536p+8p ads,brwn bds (q8,cov wn) 75.00

LINCOLN,MRS D A-Mrs. Lincoln's Boston Cook Book-Bost-1889-Roberts Bros-527p (k6) 150.00

LINCOLN,NATALIE S-Swan-Island Murders-1930-Farrar-1st ed (s10,sp chip dj) 25.00

LINCOLN,ROBERT P-Black Bass Fishing-Harrisburg-1952-8vo-376p-illus-1st prntng (m3,vf,dj) 35.00

LINCOLN,ROBERT P-Musky Fishing-Harrisburg-1952-8vo-127p-wrps,photos (m3,f) 25.00

LINCOLN,ROBERT P-Pike Family-Harrisburg-1953-8vo-274p-illus,F Everett-1st ed (m3,f,dj) 25.00

LINCOLN,ROBERT P-Sportsmen's Manual-Greenwich-1935-8vo-146p-wrps,illus (m3,f) 10.00

LINCOLN,VICTORIA-Private Disgrace-NY-(1967)-Putnam's-317p-blu cl-1st ed (h2,dj) 30.00

LINCOLN,VICTORIA-Swan Island Murders-NY-1930-Farrar-1st ed (g4) 10.00

LINCRAFT BOOK OF FENCES & FURNITURE-Burlington-ca.1920's-NJ Fence Co-8vo-43p-tan wrps,illus-trade cat (r10) 20.00

LIND,ERNIE-Complete Book of Trick & Fancy Shooting-NY-1972-8vo-159p-photos (m3,f,dj) 12.50

LIND,JAKOV-Counting My Steps-(NY)&Lond-(1969)-Macmillan/Collier-McMlln-1st ed (bb1,as new in dj) 20.00

LIND,JAMES-Story of the Fabulous Muskie-Chig-1964-8vo-204p-photos,illus (m3,vf) 40.00

LIND,L R-Studies in Pre Vesalian Anatomy-Phila-1975-344p-1st ed (dd3) 75.00

LINDBERGH,ANNE M-Listen! the Wind-NY-(1938)-8vo-xii,276p-cl,illus,3 maps,e.p. maps-1st ed (s2,dj) 30.00

LINDBERGH,ANNE M-North to the Orient-NY-(1935)-8vo-256p-cl,frntis,maps,e.p. maps-1st ed (s2) 35.00

LINDBERGH,CHARLES-Spirit of St.Louis-NY-1953-Scribner-8vo-xiv,562p-illus cl,12p plts,2 dblpg plts,illus e.p.-1st ed (s2,chip dj) 40.00

LINDBERGH,CHARLES-We-NY-1927-Putnam-8vo-318p-48 illus-1st trd ed (ff5,sp chip dj) 30.00

LINDBURG,D G-ED.-Macaques-1980-Van Nostrand-384p-photos-1st ed (bb3,f,dj) 30.00

LINDEBOOM,G A-Dutch Medical Biography-Amsterdam-1984-1122p-1st ed (dd3,dj) 125.00

LINDEMAN,M H-Quarter Horse Breeder-Wichita Falls-1959-Priv Prtd-4to (f10,dj) 95.00

LINDERMAN,FRANK B-American-NY-(1930)-John Day-xii,313p-cl,illus-1st ed (v1,sl wn dj) 85.00

LINDERMAN,FRANK B-Blackfeet Indians-St.Paul-1935-Great Northern Ry-65p-49 col ports-1st ed (gg4) 195.00

LINDERMAN,FRANK B-Indian Why Stories-NY-1915-Scribner's-xvi,236p-dec cl,col plts,illus by Russell,col dec title-scarce-1st ed (v1,sl wn,sp sl sunned) 150.00

LINDERMAN,FRANK B-Kootenai Why Stories-NY-1926-166p-illus by C L Bull-1st ed (g7,fade sp) 50.00

LINDERMAN,FRANK B-Lige Mounts, Free Trapper-NY-1922-330p-pict cl,frntis,illus-1st ed (t7,f) 75.00

LINDERMAN,FRANK B-On a Passing Frontier-NY-1920-Scribner-(vi),214p-cl-1st ed (v1) 45.00

LINDERMAN,FRANK B-Recollections of Charley Russell-Norman-(1963)-148p-illus-1st ed (e7,f,dj) 50.00

LINDESTROM,PETER-Geographia Americae, with an Account of the Delaware Indians...-Phila-1925-xliv,418,(1)p-cl,plts (aa6) 75.00

LINDFORS,BERNTH-Black African Literature in English-Detr-1979-Gale Rsrch-8vo-xxx,482p-cl-1st ed (ee7,f) 25.00

LINDGREN,ASTRID-Springtime in Noisy Village-(1966)-Viking-oblng 8vo-cl & bds,col illus,I Wikland-1st US ed (s3,f,lg pc tn dj rear panel) 25.00

LINDIG,OTTO-100 Years Historical Recollections of Gillespie County, 1870 to 1970-Stonewall-1970-Otto Lindig-138p-cl,photos-1st ed (w3,f) 35.00

LINDLEY,HARLOW-ED.-Indiana Centennial 1916-Indpls-1919-441p-cl (j1) 15.00

LINDLEY,WALTER-California of the South-NY-1888-Appleton-12mo-viii,402,(6)p-maps(3 fldg incl 2 col),illus-1st ed (n2,sl wn,spot rear) 50.00

LINDQUIST,EMORY K-Smoky Valley People-Lindsborg-1953-Bethany College-x+269p-red cl,plts-1st ed (mm10,dj) 20.00

LINDQUIST,G E E-Red Man in the United States-NY-1923-Doran-1st ed (u9,sp tn) 50.00

LINDSAY,DAVID-Voyage to Arcturus-NY-1963-Macmillan-1st US ed (g3,f,dj) 50.00

LINDSAY,ETHEL-Here Be Mystery and Murder-Scotland-1982-priv prtd-unpgd-ltd to 100c (g9) 25.00

LINDSAY,J S-Iron & Brass Implements of the English House-Lond-1927-folio-cl (ff10) 100.00

LINDSAY,JACK-Storm at Sea-Lond-1935-Golden Cockerel Pr-1/2 blu mor & dec cl,g sp lttrng,t.e.g.,woodengrvngs-ltd to 250c (p8,sp fade,sl rub,autg) 140.00

LINDSAY,NORMAN-Cousin From Fiji-NY-(1946)-Random-8vo-286p-1st ed (jj5,dj) 10.00

LINDSAY,PHILIP-Great Buccaneer-NY-(1951)-W Funk-8vo-305p-1st US ed (gg5,f,dj) 25.00

LINDSAY,VACHEL-Candle in the Cabin-NY,Lond-1926-pict cl,illus-scarce-1st ed (t4,f,dj pcs missng) 30.00

LINDSAY,VACHEL-Every Soul is a Circus-NY-1929-Macmillan-decs by auth & Richards-1st ed (y1,f,dj) 75.00

LINDSAY,VACHEL-Going to the Sun-NY-1923-Appleton-8vo-blk cl-1st ed (x10,f,dj sl chip & edge-wn) 65.00

LINDSAY,VACHEL-Going to the Sun-NY-1923-Appleton-emboss cov,illus by auth-1st ed (t4) 25.00

LINDSEY,ALMONT-Pullman Strike-Chig-(1942)-Univ of Chig Pr-xii+385p-red cl,8 plts-1st ed (k2,chip dj) 30.00

LINDSEY,ROBERT-Travels of Robert and Sarah Lindsey-Lond-1886-189p-cl-illus (h1,sl wn sp) 22.50

LINDSTROM,THAIS-Concise History of Russian Literature-NY-1966-NYU Pr-233p-gry cl-1st ed (x9,f,dj) 12.50

LINE,LES-Audubon Society Book of Marine Wildlife-NY-1980-Abrams-4to-240p-123 col plts-1st ed (ff9,as new in dj) 40.00*

LINEWEAVER,T H-Natural History of Sharks-1970-Lippincott-256p-photos-1st US ed (bb3,fray dj) 15.00

LING,TREVOR-Buddha-NY-(1973)-Scribner-8vo-287p-1st US ed (dd5,dj) 15.00

LINGG,ANNE M-Mozart, Genius of Harmony-NY-1946-Holt-1st prtg (u4,chip dj) 12.00

LINK,MARTIN-Navajo-Window Rock-1968-Navajo-4to-photos-1st ed (u9) 25.00

LINKLATER,ERIC-Conquest of England-GC-1966-Dbldy-8vo-318p-1st US ed (jj5,f,dj) 15.00

LINKLATER,ERIC-Juan in China-NY-(1937)-F&R-1st US ed (hh5,dj) 15.00

LINKLATER,ERIC-Voyage of the Challenger-1972-Dbldy-288p-28 col plts,photos (bb3,f,dj) 35.00

LINKLATER,ERIC-Voyage of the Challenger-GC-1972-Dbldy-288p-drwngs,photos,reprdctns(28 col) (nn1,sl wn dj) 30.00

LINN,ED-Steinbrenner's Yankees-1982-HRW-1st ed (s8,f,dj) 10.00

LINNEHAN,JOHN-Driving Clubs of Greater Boston-Bost-1914-priv prtd-4to-291p+ads-photos (j9) 125.00

LINSDALE,JEAN M-Birds of Nevada-Berkeley-1936-8vo-145p-wrps (y8) 20.00

LINSDALE,JEAN M-Birds of Nevada-Berkeley-1936-Cooper-145p-wrps-Pac Coast Avifauna No.23 (b9,f) 30.00

LINSON,CORWIN K-My Stephen Crane-Syracuse-1958-Syracuse U Pr-1st ed (z9,dj) 12.50

LINTHURST,RANDOLPH-1947 Trenton Giants-np-(1982)-43,(3)p-wrps (c1,sl wn) 8.50

LINTON,E LYNN-Ourselves-Lond-1893-Chatto & Windus-282,(1)+ads-cl-"New Edition" (d1) 20.00

LINTON,RALPH-ED.-Acculturation in Seven American Indian Tribes-NY-(1940)-520p (v7) 25.00

LINTZ,DR WILLIAM-ED.-European Clinics-Phila-1928-Lippincott-xviii+347p-blk fabrikoid,plts,ltd to 500c,nbrd-1st ed (c2) 35.00

LION-GOLDSCHMIDT,DAISY-Chinese Art-NY-1962-lg folio-428p-65 col plts-3rd ed (ff10,dj) 150.00

LIONEL GOLDEN ANNIVERSARY YEAR-(NY)-(1950)-43p-wrps,col illus,trade catalogue (b1) 35.00

LIONNI,LEO-In the Rabbitgarden-NY-(1975)-Pantheon-4to-cl & bds-1st ed (s3,f,sl stnd dj) 35.00

LIONNI,LEO-Tico and the Golden Wings-NY-1964-Pantheon-4to-unpgd-cl bckd pict bds,illus,auth-1st ed (r3,dj) 25.00

LIONS CLUB-Lions Stunt Book and Toastmaster's Guide-Chig-(1950)-Int'l Ass'n Lions Clubs-8vo-224p-1st ed (dd5,sl tn dj) 12.50

LIOTTA,ERNEST,JR.-Technique of Bait Casting-Chig-1949-16mo-127p-photos,illus (m3,f) 14.50

LIPMAN,JACOB G-Bacteria in Relation to Country Life-NY-1908-8vo-xx,486p+ads-71 figs (m10,wn) 12.00

LIPMAN,JEAN-American Folk Art in Wood, Metal, and Stone-NY-1948-Pantheon-4to-193p-orng cl,183 illus(incl 4 tip in col plts) (r10,dj) 45.00

LIPMAN,JEAN-Rufus Porter-NY-(1968)-Clarkson N Potter-4to-x+202p-red cl,illus-1st ed (g2,dj) 35.00

LIPPINCOTT,B E-From Fiji Through the Philippines-NY-(1948)-Macmillan-oblng 4to-xxiv,194p-illus cl,97p plts,maps,e.p. maps (s2,chip dj) 200.00

LIPPINCOTT,JOSEPH W-Wilderness Champion-Phila-1944-8vo-195p-illus,P Bransom (m3,f,chip dj) 15.00

LIPSET,SEYMOUR M-Social Stratification & "Right-Wing Extremism"-Berkeley-1960-Inst Indstrl Relations-38p-wrps-Brit Journal of Soc. Rprnt #141 (r1) 12.00

LIPTON,LAWRENCE-Holy Barbarians-NY-(1959)-1st ed (x8,dj) 50.00

LIPTON,LAWRENCE-Holy Barbarians-NY-(1959)-Messner-photos-1st ed (bb1,sl wn dj) 25.00

LISH,GORDON-Dear Mr.Capote-NY-(1983)-HR&W-auth 1st bk-1st ed (bb1,as new in dj) 20.00

LISS,HOWARD-Boston Red Sox-1982-S&S-1st ed (q7,f,dj) 20.00

LISS,HOWARD-Boston Red Sox-1982-S&S-photos-1st ed (s8,f,f dj) 15.00

LISS,HOWARD-Sandy Koufax Album-1966-Hawthorn-50p photos-1st ed (s8,f,nick dj) 35.00

LIST,HERBERT-Nigeria-Munchen-1961-Stadtische Galerie-4to-214p-wrps,photos-rare-1st ed (t3,f) 100.00

LITERARY ILLUSIONS COOKBOOK-Nashville-1982-Women's Nat'l Bk Assoc-296p-wrps,comb bndg (q6) 35.00

LITTAUER,VLADIMIR-Common Sense Horsemanship-NY-1951-Van Nostrand-1st ed (h9,wn dj) 25.00

LITTAUER,VLADIMIR-Horseman's Progress-1962-Van Nostrand Sporting Bk-1st ed (f10,dj) 45.00

LITTAUER,VLADIMIR-More About Riding Forward-Syosset-1938-priv prtd-1st ed (h9,dj) 45.00

LITTAUER,VLADIMIR-Schooling Your Horse-Princeton-1956-Van Nostrand (j9,dj) 25.00

LITTAUER,VLADIMIR-Schooling Your Horse-Princeton-1956-Van Nostrand-1st ed (h9,dj) 45.00

LITTELL,ROBERT-October Circle-Lond-1976-Hodder-1st Brit ed (q4,dj) 20.00

LITTLE BOOK OF EXCELLENT RECIPES-(Hoboken)-(1932)-(R B Davis Co)-98p-illus wrps,Davis Baking Powder promo (l6) 12.00

LITTLE GIRL'S DIAMOND-Cin-(1852)-Onken's Lithography-85p-bds,hand-col frontis,t.p. & 5 full pg illus-scarce (e1,frnts miss pc,cov wn,fade) 75.00

LITTLE,B M-National Old Trails Road and the Part Played by Lexinton in the Westward Movement-Lexington-(1928)-(28)p-wrps (h1) 12.50

LITTLE,BRYAN-Life and Work of James Gibbs: 1682 to 1754-Lond-1955-B T Batsford-8vo-210p-blu cl,36 illus-1st ed (r10,f,dj) 32.50

LITTLE,CONYTH-Black Stocking-Lond-1947-Collins CC-1st Brit ed (e4,dj) 25.00

LITTLE,GEORGE-American Cruisers Own Book-Phila-1859-J B Smith-orig emboss cl,g sp titles,illus,Billings (nn1,interior badly fox) 75.00

LITTLE,MAY-Year's Dinners-Lond-nd(ca.1920)-Harrods-438p-pict blu cl (q8,dj) 25.00

LITTLEFIELD,DANIEL F,JR.-Chickasaw Freedmen-Westport-1980-248p-1st ed (t7,f) 12.50

LIU,ALLAN-American Sporting Collector's Handbook-NY-1976-4to-239p-illus-1st ed (m3,vf,dj) 20.00

LIVE STOCK OWNERS' DIRECTORY OF BRANDS & TATTOO MARKS, STATE OF WASHINGTON, 1935,6-128p-grn wrps-(looks like first official brand bk for state under "Brand Law" of 1935)-rare (b6) 85.00

LIVELY,ROBERT A-Fiction Fights the Civil War-(1957)-UNC-230p (dd9,dj fade & sl chip) 45.00

LIVELY,W IRVEN-Mystic Mountains-1955-Lively Publ-29p-wrps (bb4) 15.00

LIVERMORE,ABIEL A-War with Mexico Reviewed-Bost-1850-Am Peace-Tutorow 3223-1st ed (u9) 100.00

LIVERMORE,MARY A-Story of My Life-Hartford-1899-730p+ads-cl (aa1) 30.00

LIVERMORE,MARY A-Story of My Life...-Hartford-1898-730p-1st ed (dd3) 75.00

LIVERMORE,MARY-My Story of the War-Hartford-1890-700p-plts,chromolithos-scarce-1st ed (dd3) 150.00

LIVESAY,DOROTHY-Documentaries-(Tor)-(1968)-(Ryerson)-1st ed (pp2,f,dj) 35.00*

LIVESY,PETER-Rock Climbing-Seattle-1978-116p-photos-1st US ed (q10,f) 10.00

LIVINGSTON,A D-Fly-Rodding for Bass-Phila-1976-8vo-203p-photos,illus (m3,vf,sl wn dj) 10.00

LIVINGSTON,ARMSTRONG-Night of Crime-1938-Sovereign Hs-1st ed (s10,dj) 50.00

LIVINGSTON,ARMSTRONG-Trackless Death-Indpls-1930-Bobbs-1st ed (f4,f) 15.00

LIVINGSTON,GEORGE-Field Crop Production-NY-1914-Macmillan-424p-cl-Rural Text Bk Ser (x6) 18.00

LIVINGSTON,JOHN A-Birds of the Eastern Forest:1 & 2-Bost-1968,1970-Houghton Mifflin-2 vols-illus by Lansdowne-1st ed (c9) 100.00

LIVINGSTON,JOHN A-Birds of the Northern Forest-Bost-1966-Houghton Mifflin-painting by Lansdowne-1st ed (c9) 50.00

LIVINGSTON,WALTER-Mystery of Burnleigh Manor-NY-1930-Mystery League-1st ed (f4,f,dj) 12.50

LIVINGSTON,WALTER-Mystery of Villa Sineste-1931-Mystery League-1st ed (s10,sp chip dj) 12.50

LIVINGSTON-LITTLE,D E-An Economic History of North Idaho 1800 to 1900-1965-Journal of West-133p-photos,maps (r8) 35.00

LIVINGSTON-The Story of a Community...-(Livingston)-1939-Fed Writer's Prjct/WPA-viii,166p-cl,plts (aa6) 35.00

LIVINGSTONE,DAVID-Missionary Travels and Researches in South Africa-NY-1858-732p+fldg maps & plts-1st Amer ed (dd3) 150.00

LLOSA,MARIO V-Aunt Julia and the Scriptwriter-NY-1982-1st US ed (q5,dj) 27.50

LLOSA,MARIO V-Captain Pantoja and the Special Service-(1978)-Harper-1st US ed (kk6,f,sl tn dj) 30.00

LLOSA,MARIO V-Captain Pantoja and the Special Service-NY et al-(1978)-Harper & Row-1st US ed (a10,f,dj) 40.00

LLOSA,MARIO V-Green House-NY,Evanston-(1968)-Harper & Row-1st ed (a10,dj) 40.00

LLOSA,MARIO V-Green House-NY-1968-1st US ed (q5,dj) 35.00

LLOSA,MARIO V-Time of the Hero-1966-Grove-auth 1st bk-1st ed (t9,f,dj) 35.00

LLOSA,MARIO V-Time of the Hero-NY-(1966)-Grove-1st US ed (e3,f,dj) 40.00

LLOYD'S REGISTER OF AMERICAN YACHTS 1965 (WI SUPPLEMENT)-NY-1965-Lloyd's Register-oblng 12mo-1191p-68 col plts (o2) 20.00

LLOYD,ANNE-Antiques and Amber-NY-1928-Derrydale Pr-bds,papr labls-ltd to 250c(of 400) (a3) 65.00

LLOYD,CHRISTOPHER-Capture of Quebec-NY-1959-175p-illus-1st ed (b7,f,dj) 45.00

LLOYD,CHRISTOPHER-Clematis-Lond-(1977)-8vo-208p-16p col plts-rvsd & enlgd ed (m10,dj) 17.00

LLOYD,CHRISTOPHER-Well Tempered Garden-NY-(1971)-478p-25 col photos-1st US ed (m10,wn dj) 21.00

LLOYD,CLEM-Australia's National Collections-Melbourne-1980-Cassell-4to-320p-blu cl,b&w & col illus (r10,f dj) 20.00

LLOYD,FRANCIS E-Carnivorous Plants-NY-1942-Ronald-352p-cl,illus (x6,cl rub & soil) 35.00

LLOYD,FREEMAN-All Spaniels-NY-1930-8vo-72p-illus,photos-later prntng (m3,f,sl fray dj) 27.50

LLOYD,J U-Drugs and Medicines of North America. Volume 1, Ranunculaceae-Cin-1885-304p-1st ed (dd3,f) 150.00

LLOYD,J U-Etidorhpa or the End of the Earth-Cin-1895-376p-cl-"Author's Edition, Ltd"-1st ed (pp6,sl wn) 175.00

LLOYD,J U-Warwick of the Knobs-NY-1901-305p-cl-1st ed (e1) 15.00

LLOYD,L-Field Sports of the North of Europe-Lond-1830-8vo-2 vols,full calf,gilt,illus-rare-1st ed (m3) 100.00

LLOYD,NATHANIEL-History of the English House from Primitive Times to the Victorian Period-Lond-1949-Architect Pr-lg 4to-ix,487p-cl,illus-New ed (cc10,dj) 50.00

LLOYD,P C-City of Abadan-Cambridge-1967-Univ Pr-8vo-280p-cl,map,plts-1st ed (y5,sl sun dj) 18.00

LLOYD,PETERS-Lionhead Lodge-Fairfield-1976-Ye Galleon Pr-sm 4to-180p-presumed 1st ed (z4,dj) 12.50

LLOYD,SELWYN-Suez-NY-(1978)-Mayflower-8vo-282p-28 photos-1st US ed (jj5,vf,f dj) 12.50

LLOYD,W A-Agriculture of Ohio-Wooster-1918-441p-cl-Ohio AES Bull.326 (g1) 15.00

LLOYD-JONES,W-K A R-Lond-1926-296p-dec blu cl,illus-scarce-1st ed (b7,f) 375.00

LO,KENNETH-ED.-Encyclopedia of Regional Chinese Cooking-Lond-1984-Octupus-folio-watercol e.p.,col photos-1st ed (q8,f,dj) 25.00

LOBB,ALLAN-Indian Baskets of the Northwest Coast-(Portland)-(1978)-119p-photos-auth 1st bk-1st ed (e7,f,dj) 50.00

LOCHHEAD,R N-With Rod Well Bent-Lond-1951-8vo-176p-photos-1st ed (m3,fray dj) 17.50

LOCKE,E W-Three Years in Camp and Hospital-Bost-1870-408p-scarce-1st ed (dd3,t.p. soil & spot) 225.00

LOCKE,EDWIN-Tuberculosis in Massachusetts-Bost-1908-223p-photos-1st ed (dd3) 75.00

LOCKE,JOHN-Letters Concerning Toleration-Lond-1765-Millar,Woodfll,Whitson...-lg 4to-g red mor,a.e. mrbld,frntis port-1st ed (ll10,sl rub,stns,frnt cov wn) 500.00

LOCKE,LT. COL. A-Tigers of Trengganu-NY-1954-Scribner's-photos,maps-1st ed (e8,f,dj) 45.00

LOCKE,W J-Joyous Adventure of Aristide Pujol-NY-1912-Lane-1st US ed (e4,cov stns) 35.00

LOCKET,G H-British Spiders-1951-Ray Soc-310p-142 figs (bb3,f,dj) 40.00

LOCKETTE,H C-Along the Beale Trail-Window Rock-1940-56p-stiff pict wrps,photos (t7) 20.00

LOCKHART,GEORGE B-New Harmony Movement-NY-1905-404p-cl-1st ed (c1) 22.50

LOCKHART,J G-Blenden Hall-NY-1930-Appleton-8vo-grn cl,g sp titles,illus (nn1) 30.00

LOCKHART,ROBERT B-My Rod My Comfort-Lond-1949-4to-75p-ltd to 50c,nbrd,autg,grn niger mor,wdcuts by J Gaastra-rare (m3,vf,chip dj,cracked box) 350.00

LOCKIE,LAURENCE D-Pharmacy on the Niagara Frontier-E Aurora-(1968)-Stewart-viii+264p-blu cl,illus-1st ed (d2) 25.00

LOCKLEY,FRED-Vigilantes Days at Virginia City-Portland-(1924)-19p-wrps-1st ed (f7) 20.00

LOCKLEY,R M-Puffins-NY-1953-8vo-186p-cl,col frntis,16p b&w photos,maps (y8,dj chip) 40.00

LOCKRIDGE,FRANCES-Catch as Catch Can-Phila-1958-Lippincott-1st ed (f4,f,dj) 15.00

LOCKRIDGE,FRANCES-Dead as a Dinosaur-Phila-1952-Lippincott-1st ed (f4,f,chip dj) 17.50

LOCKRIDGE,FRANCES-Death Takes a Bow-1943-Lippincott-1st ed (s10,dj) 37.50

LOCKRIDGE,FRANCES-Death Takes a Bow-Phila-1943-Lippincott-1st ed (k4,f,dj) 45.00

LOCKRIDGE,FRANCES-Dishonest Murderer-Phila-1949-Lippincott-1st ed (d4,sp soil dj) 25.00

LOCKRIDGE,FRANCES-Golden Man-Phila-1960-Lippincott-1st ed (w9,sl drknd pgs,dj) 35.00

LOCKRIDGE,FRANCES-Long Skeleton-NY-1958-Lippincott-1st ed (e4,dj) 20.00

LOCKRIDGE,FRANCES-Murder & Blueberry Pie-1959-Lippincott-1st ed (s10,dj) 12.50

LOCKRIDGE,FRANCES-Murder in a Hurry-1950-Lippincott-1st ed (s10,dj) 30.00

LOCKRIDGE,FRANCES-Murder is Served-1948-Lippincott-1st ed (s10,dj) 30.00

LOCKRIDGE,FRANCES-Murder is Suggested-Phila-1959-Lippincott-1st ed (j4,dj) 12.50

LOCKRIDGE,FRANCES-Murder Within Murder-Phila-1946-Lippincott-1st ed (g4,dj missing sm chips) 25.00

LOCKRIDGE,FRANCES-Night of Shadows-Phila-1962-Lippincott-1st ed (f4,f,dj) 20.00

LOCKRIDGE,FRANCES-Norths Meet Murder-NY-1941-Grosset-photos-Photoplay ed (j4) 15.00

LOCKRIDGE,FRANCES-Payoff for the Banker-Phila-1945-Lippincott-1st ed (v5,f,sl chip dj) 30.00

LOCKRIDGE,FRANCES-Ticking Clock-1962-Lippincott-1st ed (s10,sl brwnd pgs,dj) 25.00

LOCKRIDGE,FRANCES-Voyage into Violence-Phila-1956-Lippincott-1st ed (f4,f,dj) 20.00

LOCKRIDGE,FRANCES-With One Stone-Phila-1961-Lippincott-1st ed (d4,dj) 15.00

LOCKRIDGE,FRANCIS-Tangled Cord-Phila-1957-Lippincott-1st ed (d4,dj) 20.00

LOCKRIDGE,RICHARD-Accent on Murder-Phila-1958-Lippincott-1st ed (e4,f,dj) 20.00

LOCKRIDGE,RICHARD-Death on the House-Phila-1974-Lippincott-1st ed (h4,f,dj) 10.00

LOCKRIDGE,RICHARD-Murder in False Face-Phila-1968-Lippincott-1st ed (f4,f,sl wn dj) 15.00

LOCKRIDGE,RICHARD-Practice to Deceive-Phila-1957-Lippincott-1st ed (f4,dj) 15.00

LOCKRIDGE,RICHARD-Risky Way to Kill-Phila-1959-Lippincott-1st ed (e4,f,dj) 15.00

LOCKRIDGE,RICHARD-Something Up a Sleeve-Phila-1972-Lippincott-1st ed (f4,f,dj) 15.00

LOCKRIDGE,RICHARD-Streak of Light-Phila-1976-Lippincott-1st ed (h4,f,dj) 12.00

LOCKRIDGE,RICHARD-Troubled Journey-Phila-1970-Lippincott-1st ed (f4,f,dj) 15.00

LOCKRIDGE,RICHARD-Twice Retired-Phila-1970-Lippincott-1st ed (f4,f,dj) 15.00

LOCKRIDGE,RICHARD-Write Murder Down-Phila-1972-Lippincott-1st ed (f4,f,dj) 20.00

LOCKWOOD & ADAMSON-Tragedy at Honda-Phila,NY-(1960)-243p-illus,e.p. maps-1st ed so stated (c7,f,chip dj) 50.00

LOCKWOOD,BELVA A-Peace and the Outlook-Wash D.C.-1899-8vo-20p-prtd wrps-1st ed (oo7) 135.00

LOCKWOOD,CHARLES-Bricks & Brownstone-NY-1972-McGraw HIll-lg 4to-xxv,262p-cl,illus-1st ed (cc10,dj discol,chip) 65.00

LOCKWOOD,CHARLES-Tragedy at Honda-Phila-(1960)-Chilton-8vo-243p-16p photos-1st ed (ff5,dj) 30.00

LOCKWOOD,DOUGLAS I-Aboriginal-Adelaide-1980-Rigby-200p-map e.p.,45 illus(some col),A Roberts-1st illus ed (nn1,dj) 25.00

LOCKWOOD,FRANK C-Arizona Characters-LA-1928-Times Mirror-12mo-xiv,230p-photos-Howes L416-1st ed (aa3) 65.00

LOCKWOOD,FRANK C-Life in Old Tucson, 1854 to 1864-LA-1943-Tucson Civic Comm-255p-illus-Herd 1342 (cc4,dj) 75.00

LOCKWOOD,FRANK C-Life in Old Tucson, 1854 to 1864-LA-1943-Ward Ritchie Pr-12mo-xx,255p-illus-Herd 1342-1st ed (aa3,f,dj) 65.00

LOCKWOOD,FRANK C-Life in Old Tucson, 1854 to 1864-LA-1943-Ward Ritchie Pr-xx+255p-blu cl,plts-Adams,Herd 1342-1st ed (mm10,dj) 60.00

LOCKWOOD,FRANK C-Pioneer Days in Arizona-NY-1932-Macmillan-8vo-xiv,387p-illus-Howes L417-1st ed (aa3,f,dj) 195.00

LOCKWOOD,FRANK C-Pioneer Days in Arizona-NY-1932-MacMillan-photos,illus-1st ed (u9,dj wn,chip) 125.00

LOCKWOOD,FRANK C-With Padre Kino on the Trail-Tucson-1934-142p-wrps,photos-1st ed (t7,cov taped) 27.50

LOCKWOOD,GEORGE R-New Harmony Movement-NY-1905-Appleton-1st ed (v5) 25.00

LOCKWOOD,JAMES D-Life and Adventures of a Drummer Boy, or Seven Years a Soldier-Albany-1893-John Skinner-12mo-191p-pict cl,frntis illus-Howes L418-1st ed (aa3,sp wn,sl soil cov) 135.00

LOCKWOOD,MRS G H-Mrs.Lockwood's Book of Favorite Recitations-Kalamazoo-nd-Lockwood Publ Co-31,(1)p-wrps,illus,3p photos (d1) 20.00

LOCKWOOD,MYNA-Mouse is Miracle Enough-NY-(1965)-FSG-8vo-184p-1st ed (dd5,dj) 10.00

LOCKWOOD,SARAH M-Decoration Past, Present & Future-NY-(1934)-198p-cl (m1) 15.00

LOCKWOOD,T D-Electrical Measurement and the Galvanometer-1887-137p-32 illus-rare-2nd ed (h6) 65.00

LOCKWOOD,THOMAS D-Electricity, Magnetism, and Electric Telegraphy-1883-377p-152 illus-1st ed (h6) 40.00

LOCOMOTIVE CYCLOPEDIA 1950 TO 1952-Simmons Boardman-8vo-1028p-cl,illus-14th ed (nn7,rub,bump) 111.00

LODGE,JOHN C-I Remember Detroit-Detr-1949-Wayne U Pr-208p-cl,photos-1st ed (z7,dj) 20.00

LODGE,OLIVER-Pioneers of Science-Lond-1893-Macmillan-8vo-404p-g dec blu cl,illus-1st ed (p1) 45.00

LODGE,OLIVER-Talks About Radio-1925-267p-1st ed (h6) 30.00

LODGE,OLIVER-Work of Hertz and some of his Successors-1894-58p-32 illus-v rare-1st ed (h6) 290.00

LODGE,R C-ED.-Manitoba Essays-Tor-1937-Macmillan-8vo-xiii,432p-frntis,8 illus-1st ed (cc7,dj) 35.00*

LOEB,HAROLD-Way It Was-NY-1959-photos-1st ed (t5,dj) 30.00

LOEB,JACQUES-Artificial Parthenogenesis and Fertilization-Chig-c.1913-312p (g10) 85.00

LOEB,ROBERT H-How to Wine Friends and Affluent People-Chig-1965-Follett Publ-131p-illus,J Buelow-1st prtg (m6,dj) 20.00

LOEB,ROBERT H-She Cooks To Conquer-NY-(1952)-Wilfred Funk-121p (m6) 23.00

LOEBER,R-Biographical Dictionary of Architects in Ireland 1600 to 1720-Lond-1981-1st ed (h10,dj) 45.00

LOENING,G C-Military Aeroplanes-(Bost)-1918-roy 8vo-viii,202p-cl,frntis,plts incl 6 fldg-1st ed (s2,sl wn sp) 200.00

LOENING,G C-Monoplanes and Biplanes-NY-1911-8vo-illus cl,frntis,plts-1st ed (s2) 200.00

LOENING,G-Our Wings Grow Faster...Personal Episodes of a Lifetime in Aviation...-GC-1935-sm 4to-vi,204p-cl,illus t.p.-1st ed (s2,dj) 35.00

LOESELL,CLARENCE M-History of Kiwanis in Michigan-np-1956-Kiwanas-218p-cl,photos (z7) 25.00

LOESSER,ARTHUR-Men, Women & Pianos-NY-1954-S&S-1st prtg (u4,f,dj) 20.00

LOESSER,FRANK-Frank Loesser Songbook-1971-S&S-1st ed (u4,dj tn) 25.00

LOEWENBERG,ROBERT J-Equality on the Oregon Frontier-Jason Lee and the Methodist Mission 1834 to 43-Seattle/Lond-1976-U of Wash Pr-8vo-xi,287p-blk cl-1st ed (mm1,as new in dj) 30.00

LOEWINSOHN,RON-Magnetic Fields-NY-1983-Knopf-1st ed (y1,f,f dj) 25.00

LOEWY,RAYMOND-Industrial Design-NY-1979-Overlook Pr-4to-250p-cl,col illus-1st ed (q3,dj) 75.00

LOEWY,RAYMOND-Industrial Design-Woodstock-1979-illus(incl 1 fldg col)-1st ed (ee1,dj) 85.00

LOEWY,RAYMOND-Locomotive-Lond-1937-New Vision ser-1st ed (n4) 20.00

LOEWY,RAYMOND-Never Leave Well Enough Alone-NY-1951-8vo-illus (ee1) 175.00

LOFT,ABRAM-Violin and Keyboard, the Duo Repertoire-NY-1973-Grossman-2 vols (u4,dj) 25.00

LOFTS,NORAH-Women in the Old Testament-NY-1949-Macmillan-cl-1st ed (n8,dj) 12.50

LOFTS,W O G-British Bibliography of Edgar Wallace-Lond-(1969)-Howard Baker-264p-1st ed (g9,sl wn dj) 35.00

LOGAN,DANIEL-History of the Hawaiian Islands-NY,Chig-1907-Lewis Publ-sm 4to-viii,259p-blck lea (p8,rbnd,sl dmpstnd) 150.00

LOGAN,HERSCHEL C-Buckskin and Satin-Harrisburg-(1954)-Stackpole-xiv+218p-beige cl,illus-1st ed (e2,sl wn dj) 25.00

LOGAN,HERSCHEL-Hand Cannon to Automatic-Huntington-1944-oblng 8vo-unpgd-illus-1st ed (m3) 30.00

LOGAN,L B-Practical Carp Culture-(Youngstown)-nd-ca 1888-136p-cl-not cpyrtd (j1,pres) 35.00

LOGAN,MRS JOHN A-Thirty Years in Washington-Hartford-(1901)-752p-cl (d1) 22.50

LOGAN,RAYFORD W-Howard University: the First Hundred Years-NY-1969-NYU Pr-xviii+658p-blu cl-1st ed (b2,dj) 25.00

LOGAN,RAYFORD-ED.-Memoirs of a Monticello Slave as Dictated to Charles Campbell in the 1840's by Isaac...-1951-U Va Pr-45p-ltd to 1000c-1st ed (dd9,dj) 35.00

LOHSE,REMIE-Miniature Camera in Professional Hands-NY-1933-Studio Publ-119p-spiral bndg,cardbd covs,48 photos-1st ed (cc9) 35.00

LOHSE,REMIE-Modern Way in Picture Making-NY-1907-Eastman Kodak-190p-photos-rvsd ed (cc9,sp wn) 35.00

LOKKE,CARL L-Klondike Saga-1965-Norwgn Amer Hist Assoc-211p-illus-1st ed (u8,sl chip dj) 25.00

LOKKE,CARL L-Klondike Saga-Mpls-1965-U of Minn Pr-8vo-lt blu cl,photos,3 maps (oo1,dj wn,tn) 30.00

LOMAX,ALAN-Mister Jelly Roll-NY-1950-Duell-1st ed (w1,f,dj) 45.00

LOMBROSO,CAESAR-Female Offender-NY-1899-Appleton-313p-cl (l1) 22.50

LOMBROSO,CAESAR-Female Offender-NY-1903-Appleton-313p+ads-cl (d1) 17.50

LONDON,CHARMIAN K-Our Hawaii-1917-MacMillan-345p+ads-g dec cov,photos-1st ed (u8) 80.00

LONDON,JACK-Adventure-1911-Nelson-1st ed (x2,sp sl flaking) 135.00

LONDON,JACK-Assassination Bureau-1963-MH-ltd to 2500c-1st ed (x7,dj) 88.00

LONDON,JACK-Cruise of the Snark-NY-1911-MacMillan-blu cl wi pasteon cov illus,t.e.g.-BAL 11929-1st ed (hh4,sl rub) 325.00

LONDON,JACK-Game-NY-1905-Macmillan-grn cl-BAL 11886-1st ed (f2,one cor sl bump) 75.00

LONDON,JACK-Human Drift-NY-1917-Macmillan-8vo-"Published February 1917" on cpyrt page-BAL 11972-1st ed (x3) 300.00

LONDON,JACK-John Barleycorn-NY-1913-Century-8vo-g dec drk grn cl,1st iss wi blank leaf at rear-BAL11945-1st ed (x3) 90.00

LONDON,JACK-John Barleycorn-NY-1913-Century-gold stmpd blk bds,"Published, August, 1913" on cpyrt pg-1st ed (bb2) 125.00

LONDON,JACK-Letters From...-NY-1965-Odyssey Pr-1st ed (y1,dj) 50.00

LONDON,JACK-Little Lady of the Big House-NY-1916-Macmillan-pict bndg,col frntis-1st ed (ff6,sp wn,hng crack) 175.00

LONDON,JACK-London's Essays of Revolt-NY-1926-Vanguard-1st ed (e10,sl bump cov) 20.00

LONDON,JACK-London's Essays of Revolt-NY-1926-Vanguard-1st ed (y1,lacks dj) 40.00

LONDON,JACK-Love of Life and Other Stories-1908-Everett-1st Brit ed (x2,sl fade sp) 65.00

LONDON,JACK-Martin Eden-NY-1909-Macmillan-8vo-blu cl-BAL 11912-1st ed (x3,weak hngs) 135.00

LONDON,JACK-Martin Eden-NY-1909-Macmillan-blu cl-BAL 11912-1st ed (f2,covs sl soil,sl bump text) 75.00

LONDON,JACK-Martin Eden-NY-1909-Macmillan-blu dec cl,frntis-Woodbridge #66-1st ed (ll9,f) 500.00

LONDON,JACK-Revolution-NY-1910-Macmillan-1st ed (z2,f) 200.00

LONDON,JACK-Star Rover-NY-1915-Macmillan-gold stmpd blu dec cl-BAL 11963-1st Amer ed (hh4,f) 150.00

LONDON,JACK-White Fang-NY-1906-Macmillan-1st ed (e3,cracked hngs) 35.00

LONG BRANCH-Entertaining a Nation. The Career of...-Long Branch-1940-Fed Writer's Prjct/WPA-xiv,211p-cl,plts,fldg map (aa6) 40.00

LONG,BRYANT A-Mail by Rail-NY-1951-414p-1st ed (n4,f,dj) 26.00

LONG,C CHAILLE-Central Africa-Lond-1876-Sampson,Low,Marston-8vo-xvi,330p-orig cl,frntis,20 illus(incl 8 full pg),1 col fldg map-1st ed (bb6,ex-libr) 175.00

LONG,E B-Saints and the Union-Urbanna-(1981)-310p-illus,map e.p.-1st ed (c4) 17.50

LONG,FRANK B-Horror From the Hills-Sauk City-1963-Arkham-1st ed (g3,f,dj) 75.00

LONG,FRANK B-Hounds of Tindalos-Sauk City-1946-Arkham-316p-ltd to 2602c-1st ed (k5,dj sp sl wn) 100.00

LONG,FREDERIC J-Dictionary of the Chinook Jargon-Seattle-c.1909-Lowman & Hanford-orig brwn prtd wrps (dd7,sl chip) 65.00

LONG,HUEY P-My First Days in the White House-Harrisburg-1935-146p-cl-illus-1st ed so stated (h1) 20.00

LONG,JOE-Papa Was a Fisherman-Barre-1969-8vo-98p (m3,f,dj) 17.50

LONG,JOHN D-ED.-Republican Party-NY-(1900)-447p-cl (j1,sl wn sp) 15.00

LONG,JOHN-John Long's Voyages and Travels in the Years 1768 to 1788-Chig-1922-Donnelley-238p-map-Lakeside Classics (cc4) 35.00

LONG,JOHN-Voyages and Travels of an Indian Interpreter and Trader...-Lond-1791-prtd for auth-4to-x,errata,engrvd fldg map,295p-orig bds,uncut-1st ed (mm1,bds wn,few stns,prt unopn 1,800.00

LONG,JULIUS-Keep the Coffins Coming-NY-1947-Messner-1st ed (h4,dj) 15.00

LONG,KATHERINE W-Yuma From Hell Hole to Haven-Yuma-1950-Yuma Cnty COC-64p-wrps-Six Guns #1359 (ee4) 15.00

LONG,LILY A-Apprentices to Destiny-NY-(1893)-348p-cl-Wright 3391 (n1) 15.00

LONG,MARGARET-Shadow of the Arrow-Caldwell-1941-Caxton-310p-gry cl,plts-1st ed (e2,dj) 30.00

LONG,MASON-Life of...the Converted Gambler-Chig-1878-256p-brwn cl-1st ed (jj4) 40.00

LONG,PHILIP S-Dreams,Dust and Depression-Calgary-(1972)-Cypress Publ-228p (bb4,dj) 25.00

LONG,RAPHAEL-Pacific Electric's Big Red Cars-1966-Phillips-4to-unpgd-wrps,illus (nn7,f) 17.00

LONG,RAPHAEL-Pacific Electric's Big Red Cars-Universal City-1966-wrps-1st ed (n4) 12.00

LONG,STEPHEN H-Voyage in a Six Oared Skiff to the Falls of Saint Anthony in 1817-Phila-1860-Henry B Ashmead-8vo-88p-mod cl-Howes L415 (mm1,f,rbnd) 125.00

LONG,W H-Medals of the British Navy...-Lond-1895-450p-blu cl,21 col plts,11 woodcts-v scarce-1st ed (b7,recased,sl fox plts) 450.00

LONG,W J-Fowls of the Air-Bost-1901-8vo-310p-cl,illus (y8,sp fade) 18.00

LONGACRE,EDWARD G-From Union Stars to Top Hat-Harrisburg-1972-Stackpole Bks-320p-illus,maps-1st ed (v2,dj) 25.00

LONGACRES,EDWARD G-From Union Stars to Top Hat-Harrisburg-(1972)-320p-illus-1st ed (c4,f,dj) 40.00

LONGACRES,EDWARD G-Man Behind the Guns-NY-(1977)-294p-illus-1st ed (n3,f,dj) 30.00

LONGFELLOW,FANNY A-Mrs.Longfellow:Selected Letters and Journals of...-NY-1956-255p-cl-1st ed so stated (d1,dj) 15.00

LONGFELLOW,HENRY W-Courtship of Miles Standish, and Other Poems-Bost-1858-Ticknor & Fields-215p+ads-cl,single leaf adv for Waverly Novels inserted at front-BAL 12122-1st Amer ed,1st prntg (o1) 125.00

LONGFELLOW,HENRY W-Courtship of Miles Standish-Bost-1920-Houghton Mifflin-4to-dec grn cl,cov plt & 8p col plts by N C Wyeth-1st ed thus (oo8) 100.00

LONGFELLOW,HENRY W-Evangeline-NY-(1913)-Stokes-lg 8vo-cl,pict pasteon,12 col plts incl cov,M L Kirk-1st ed thus (s3,cov sl scratched) 40.00

LONGFELLOW,HENRY W-New England Tragedies...-Bost-1868-179p-cl-earlier ed iss for priv distr-1st state bndng-BAL 12150-1st ed (e1) 20.00

LONGFELLOW,HENRY W-Song of Hiawatha-Bost-1855-all points per Merle Johnson-1st Amer ed (m4,sp bump) 150.00

LONGFELLOW,HENRY W-Song of Hiawatha-Lond-(1911)-Harrap-frnt cov inlay by M Parrish,illus,Remington,Parrish & Wyeth-1st ed thus (y2,cor bump) 225.00

LONGFELLOW,HENRY W-Tales of a Wayside Inn-Bost-1863-Ticknor & Fields-drk grn cl-1st ed,1st iss (gg7,sp sl dull & wn) 50.00

LONGLEY,MICHAEL-No Continuing City-Dublin-(1969)-Gill & Macmillan-1st ed (z8,vf,dj) 50.00

LONGMATE,NORMAN-Socialist Anthology-Lond-1953-Phoenix Hs-256p (ff1,dj edgewn,tn) 35.00

LONGRIDGE,C NEPEAN-Cutty Sark-Lond-nd(c.1933)-Percival Marshall-2 vols-blu cl,vol.I:85 illus,3 fldg plts,vol.II:83 photos & drwngs,2 fldg plts (nn1,v wn djs) 125.00

LONGRIGG,ROGER-English Squire & His Sport-Lond-1977-8vo-302p-illus (m3,vf,dj) 20.00

LONGRIGG,ROGER-History of Horse Racing-NY-1972-Stein & Day-folio-320p-32 col plts,130 illus-1st ed (f10,dj) 45.00

LONGSTREET,STEPHEN-Canvas Falcons-NY-(1970)-World-8vo-365p-16p photos-1st ed (dd5,dj) 20.00

LONGSTREET,STEPHEN-Century on Wheels-NY-1952-Holt-1st ed (h9) 65.00

LONGSTREET,STEPHEN-Sportin' House-LA-1965-Sherbourne Pr-1st ed (w5,sl sunned t.e.,f dj) 25.00

LONGSTREET,STEPHEN-Sportin' House-LA-1965-Sherbourne Pr-illus,auth-1st ed (w1,f,dj) 30.00

LONGWORTH,ALICE R-Crowded Hours-NY-1933-Scribner-8vo-355p-24 photos-1st ed (ff5,sl chip dj) 25.00

LOO,MIRIAM B-Miriam B Loo's Family Favorites Cookbook-Colorado Springs-1977-92p-pict stiff wrps,spiral bnd,drwngs-1st prtg (q8) 10.00

LOOK ON THIS PICTURE - AND ON THIS-(NY)-nd-ca.1889-32p-pict wrps (c1) 22.50

LOOK,AL-1,000 Million Years on the Colorado Plateau-Denver-1955-Bell-photos-1st ed (u9,dj chip) 35.00

LOOK-Santa Fe Trail-NY-1946-271p-pict cl,illus-Rittenhouse #371-1st ed (t7) 12.50

LOOMIS,ALFRED F-Ranging the Maine Coast-NY-1939-274p-cl,illus by E A Wilson-1st trd ed (d1,sl wn dj) 20.00

LOOMIS,CHARLES B-Araminta and the Automobile-NY-(1907)-Crowell-93,(1)p-cl,dec frnt cov,illus,O Lang (n1) 17.50

LOOMIS,ELISHA S-Life and Appreciation of Dr.Aaron Schuyler...-np-(1936)-190p-cl,ltd to 150c,nbrd (k1,sl flecked cov) 32.50

LOOMIS,FREDERIC B-Hunting Extinct Animals in the Patagonian Pampas-NY-1913-Dodd,Mead-141p-red cl,plts-1st ed (c2) 55.00

LOOMIS,L M-Review of the Albatrosses, Petrels, and Diving Petrels-SF-1918-8vo-187p-wrps,17 plts(1 fldg) (y8,sp wn) 27.00

LOOMIS,MARY T-Radio Theory and Operating-1925-848p-635 illus incl photos-1st ed (h6) 30.00

LOOMIS,NOEL M-Pedro Vial and the Roads to Santa Fe-Norman-1967-U of Okla Pr-569p-1st ed (d3,dj) 30.00

LOOMIS,NOEL-Pedro Vial & the Roads to Santa Fe-Norman-1967-U of Okla-1st ed (u9,dj) 37.50

LOOMIS,SAMUEL L-Modern Cities and Their Religious Problems-NY-(1887)-Baker & Taylor-219+ads-cl (b1) 17.50

LOONEY,RALPH-Haunted Highways-NY-(1968)-214p-dbl col,photos-1st ed (u7,dj) 25.00

LOOS,ANITA-Mouse is Born-GC-1951-Dbldy-8vo-214p-drwngs,F Pallavicini-1st ed (w6,dj) 45.00

LOPATE,CAROL-Women in Medicine-Balt-1968-204p-1st ed (dd3,dj) 25.00

LOPEZ,BARRY-Of Wolves and Men-NY-(1978)-Scribners-1st ed (bb2,f,dj) 80.00

LOPEZ,BARRY-River Notes-KC-1979-Andrews & McMeel-1st ed (c8,f,f dj) 75.00

LOPEZ,BARRY-River Notes-KC-1979-Andrews & McMeel-1st ed (q2,dj) 55.00

LOPEZ,BARRY-Winter Count-NY-1981-1st ed (n5,f,f dj) 22.50

LOPEZ,VINCENT-What's Ahead?-Phila-(1944)-McKay-1st ed (w1,f,dj) 20.00

LORAC,E C R-Bats in the Belfry-NY-1937-Macaulay-1st US ed (f4,f) 35.00

LORANT,STEFAN-ED.-New World: The First Pictures of America...-(1946)-DS&P-292p-illus-1st ed (dd9) 45.00

LORANT,STEFAN-Lincoln-NY-(1941)-DS&P-4to-160p-cl,photos-1st ed (k2,chip dj) 30.00

LORANT,STEPHEN-Glorious Burden-NY-(1968)-959p-cl-illus (h1,sl wn dj) 15.00

LORD,ELIOT-Comstock Mining and Miners-Wash D.C.-1883-GPO/US Geo Survey-4to-xiv,451p-3 maps(2 fldg) (o2) 85.00

LORD,ELIOT-ET AL-Italian in America-NY-1905-B F Buck-x+268p-brwn cl-1st ed (h2,sl rub) 22.00

LORD,JOHN-Frontier Dust-Hartford-1926-198p-ltd ed-scarce-1st ed (g7) 40.00

LORD,JOHN-Frontier Dust-Hartford-1926-E V Mitchell-198p-ltd to 1000c-Six Guns 1362-1st ed (gg4,dj) 50.00

LORD,W R-First Book Upon the Birds of Oregon and Wash-Portland-1913-12mo-308,(8)p-cl,17 illus-revsd ed (y8,sp tn) 16.00

LORD,WALTER-Night to Remember-NY-1955-H Holt-209p-1st ed (j8,f,edge wn dj) 20.00

LORD,WALTER-Night to Remember-NY-1955-H Holt-8vo-209p-illus e.p.,photos-1st ed (bb7,sl chip dj) 45.00*

LORD,WALTER-Time to Stand-NY-(1961)-255p-illus-1st ed so stated (e7,f,dj) 40.00

LORING,GEORGE B-Farm Club of Jotham-Bost-1876-Lockwood, Brooks-8vo-xvi,604p-g dec pict blu cl,illus-1st ed (y4,sl wtrstnd cov) 45.00

LORING,J ALDEN-African Adventure Stories-NY-1914-Scribners-8vo-301p-dec cl,illus-1st ed (s1,sp lttrng flake) 50.00

LORNE,MARQUIS OF-Memories of Canada and Scotland-Montreal-1884-xi,360p (a7) 40.00

LOSE,CHARLES-Vanishing Trout-Altoona-1931-8vo-318p-grn/brn sim lea,gold emboss trout on cov (m3,vf) 30.00

LOSE,G W-Esther and Other Poems-Columbus-1883-Lutheran Bk Concern-116p-cl (c1) 15.00

LOSSING,BENSON J-History of the Civil War 1861 to 65-NY-(1912)-512p-wrps,col frntis ports,photos (c4) 125.00

LOSSING,BENSON J-Martha Washington-NY-1865-24p+ads-wrps (d1,sl chip wrps) 15.00

LOSSING,BENSON J-Mount Vernon & Its Associations-NY-1859-W A Townsend-376p-g emboss red cl,engrvngs-1st ed (n2,rebckd wi orig sp) 75.00

LOSSING,BENSON J-Mount Vernon and Its Associations-Cin-1883-Yorston-448p-dec blnd stmpd cl,160 engrvngs (o2) 20.00

LOTHROP,GLORIA R-ED.-Recollections of the Flathead Mission-Glendale-1977-256p-map frntis,photos-1st ed (t7,f) 25.00

LOTT,VIRGIL-Kingdom of Zapata-S.A.-1953-Naylor-254p-photos-1st ed (a9) 55.00

LOTZ,WOLFGANG-Champagne Spy-NY-(1972)-St.Martin's-8vo-240p-illus-1st ed (cc5,dj) 10.00

LOUDON,J C-Landscape Gardening and Landscape Architecture of the Late Humphrey Repton-Lond-1890-Longman-619p-new ed wi hist intro (x6,rbnd) 210.00

LOUDON,J-Encyclopedia of Gardening-Lond-1834-Spottiswoode-418p-buckrm-New ed (x6,rbnd) 60.00

LOUDON,J-Gardening for Ladies-NY-1874-Wiley-430p-grn cl-2nd Amer ed (x6,sl wn) 45.00

LOUDON,J-Ladies' Companion to the Flower Garden-Lond-1853-Bradbury-355p-6th ed (x6,rebckd) 65.00

LOUIS PHILLIPE-Diary of My Travels in America-NY-(1977)-oblng-202p-col & b&w illus-1st Amer ed (e7,f,dj) 30.00

LOUISVILLE COOK BOOK-Louisville-nd(ca.1890)-Guide Prtg & Publ Co-133p-Young Ladies' Missionary Scty of First Christian Church (n6) 65.00

LOUNSBERRY,ALICE-Guide to the Trees-NY-(1900)-xvii,313p-164 b&w,55 diagrms-2nd ed (x5,sl wn sp) 23.00

LOUNSBERRY,C A-Early History of North Dakota-Wash D.C.-1919-Liberty Pr-645p-pict covs,illus,maps-Howes L516-1st ed (cc4) 200.00

LOUNSBERRY,C A-North Dakota, History & People-1917-S J Clarke Publ-thk 4to-3 vols-scarce (b6) 425.00

LOUPE,ROBERT-Martyr in Tibet-NY-1956-234p-1st ed (p10,f,dj) 15.00

LOUYS,PIERRE-Aphrodite-np-1925-priv prntd-269p-bds,ltd to 1500c,nbrd (m1,sl rub) 15.00

LOVE,ANNIE C-History of Navarro County-Dallas-1933-Southwest-photos-1st ed (a9) 100.00

LOVE,PAULA-COMP.-Will Rogers Book-Indpls-(1961)-Bobbs-Merrill-218p-illus-1st ed (cc4,dj) 25.00

LOVE,ROBERTUS-Rise and Fall of Jesse James-NY-1926-Putnam's-446p-frntis-Six Guns #1366 (cc4,sl fade & wn sp) 50.00

LOVECRAFT,H P-Dagon and Other Macabre Tales-1965-Arkham-ltd to 3500c-1st ed (w4,dj) 100.00

LOVECRAFT,H P-Dark Brotherhood & Other Pieces-Sauk City-1966-Arkham-x,321p-ltd to 3460c-1st ed (m5,dj) 85.00

LOVECRAFT,H P-Dark Brotherhood and Other Pieces-1966-Arkham-ltd to 3460c-1st ed (w4,sl stnd,dj) 100.00

LOVECRAFT,H P-Dreams and Fancies-1962-Arkham-ltd to 2000c-1st ed (w4,dj) 115.00

LOVECRAFT,H P-Dreams and Fancies-Sauk City-1962-Arkham-1st ed (k7,f,dj) 95.00

LOVECRAFT,H P-Lovecraft at Last-Arlington-(1975)-Carrollton-Clark-photos-ltd to 1000c,nbrd (bb1,f,dj,box) 125.00

LOVECRAFT,H P-Lurker at the Threshold-1945-Arkham-ltd to 3000c-1st ed (w4,f,dj) 150.00

LOVECRAFT,H P-Lurker at the Threshold-Sauk City-1945-Arkham-196p-one of 3,041c-1st ed (d5,f,sl soil dj) 125.00

LOVECRAFT,H P-Lurking Fear-W Warwick-1977-Necronomicon-wrps,illus by C A Smith-ltd to 550c-1st ed (j3,f) 30.00

LOVECRAFT,H P-Selected Letters IV-1976-Arkham-ltd to 5000c-1st ed (w4,dj) 25.00

LOVECRAFT,H P-Supernatural Horror in Literature as Revised in 1936-Arlington-(1974)-Carrollton-Clark-ltd to 2000c,nbrd (b10,f,wrps) 25.00

LOVECRAFT,H P-Survivors and Others-Sauk City-1957-Arkham-161p-ltd to 2096c-1st ed (h5,f,dj) 90.00

LOVECRAFT,H P-To Quebec and the Stars-W Kingston-1976-1st ed (m5,as new in dj) 20.00

LOVEJOY,ESTHER P,M.D.-Certain Samaritans-NY-1927-Macmillan-8vo-302p-photos-1st ed (gg5,pc mssng dj) 30.00

LOVELL,JOSEPHINE-Eight Little Indians-NY-(1936)-Platt and Munk-pict cl,col illus,R Vernam-early ed (s3) 12.00

LOVELL,MRS F S-History of...Rockingham, Vt...Bellows Falls, Saxton's River...Cambridgeport & Bartonsville-Bellows Falls-1958-553p-illus (a3) 37.50

LOVELOCK,JAMES-Climbing-Lond-1971-185p-16 plts-1st ed (q10,f,dj) 12.00

LOVESEY,PETER-Abracadaver-NY-1972-Dodd-1st US ed (f4,dj) 15.00

LOVESEY,PETER-Swing,swing together-NY-1976-Dodd-1st US ed (h4,dj) 10.00

LOVESEY,PETER-Waxwork-Lond-1978-Macmillan-1st ed (s4,f,dj) 25.00

LOVESEY,PETER-Waxwork-NY-1978-Pantheon-1st US ed (h4,f,dj) 15.00

LOVESEY,PETER-Wobble to Death-NY-1970-Dodd-1st US ed (e4,soil dj) 15.00

LOVETT,JAMES D-Old Boston Boys and the Games They Played-1906-Riverside Pr-priv prntg-emboss cov-1st ed (s8) 400.00

LOVETTE,LELAND P-Naval Customs and Usage-Annapolis-1934-US Naval Inst-8vo-371p-blu cl over bds wi,g cov dec,48 illus (p8,sl wtr mrkd) 9.50

LOVING,J C-Loving Brand Book-Austin-1965-Pemberton Pr-Ing 4to-118p-illus-1st trd ed (aa3,f,dj) 100.00

LOVING,JEROME M-ED.-Civil War Letters of George Washington Whitman-Durham-1975-Duke U Pr-1st ed (dd6,dj) 15.00

LOVOOS,JANICE-Frederick Whitaker, an Illus Biog-Flagstaff-1972-115p-col frntis,illus-1st ed (t7,f,dj) 27.50

LOW,FRANCIS-Fishing is For Me-NY-1963-8vo-161p-photos (m3,dj) 17.50

LOW,GARY-North American Marsh Birds-NY-(1983)-sm folio-192p-col illus-1st ed (w10,dj) 25.00

LOW-Ye Madde Designer-Lond-1935-Studio-lg 8vo-128p-1st ed (m4) 15.00

LOWE,E J,ESQ.-Ferns: British and Exotic-Lond-1872-Geo Bell-8vo-8 vols-3/4 grn mor over mrbld bds,aprox. 480 chromolith plts-New ed (w1) 500.00

LOWE,E J-Natural History of British Grasses-Lond-1868-Grommbridge & Sons-cl,74p col plts (p6,sl tn rear cov,sl wn) 150.00

LOWE,JUDGE J M-National Old Trails Road-Kansas City-1925-284p+ lg fldg map-cl-revsd ed (h1,sl tn map) 35.00

LOWE,KENNETH-Catalyst-1958-CC-1st ed (s10,dj) 10.00

LOWE,PERCIVAL G-Five Years a Dragoon and Other Adventures on the Great Plains-KC-1906-F Hudson-12mo-417p-pict cl,46 photos & illus-Howes L526-1st ed (aa3,soil,wn) 95.00

LOWELL,AMY-Ballads for Sale-Bost-1927-Houghton Mifflin-8vo-311p-purple cl-BAL 13013-1st ed (w6,sp fade) 45.00

LOWELL,AMY-East Wind-Bost,NY-1926-Houghton Mifflin-12mo-240p-1st ed (b3,f,dj) 45.00

LOWELL,AMY-Legends-Bost-1921-Houghton Mifflin-red orng cl,prntd tan dj,state A of the adv on pgs (268),(269),no priority-BAL 12989-1st ed (w6,dj) 75.00

LOWELL,G-More Small Italian Villas & Farm Houses-NY-1920-lg folio-illus (ee1) 125.00

LOWELL,G-Smaller Italian Villas & Farmhouses-NY-1916-lg folio-illus (h10) 145.00

LOWELL,GUY-American Gardens-Bost-1902-Bates & Guild-17p wi 112p photos,cl (x6,innr hng rprd) 125.00

LOWELL,GUY-American Gardens-Bost-1902-lg 4to-unpgd-dec cl,t.e.g.,112 photo plts (jj7,cor wn,sl soil) 195.00

LOWELL,JAMES R-Three Memorial Poems-Bost-1877-92p-cl-BAL 13154-1st ed (m1) 17.50

LOWELL,ROBERT-Day by Day-NY-(1977)-FS&G-1st ed (u10,f,f dj) 20.00

LOWELL,ROBERT-Dolphin-NY-(1973)-FS&G-1st ed (c10,as new in dj) 30.00

LOWELL,ROBERT-Dolphin-NY-(1975)-FS&G-1st ed (bb2,f,dj) 35.00

LOWELL,ROBERT-ED.-Randall Jarrell, 1914 to 1965-NY-1967-FSG-photos-1st ed (q2,dj) 75.00

LOWELL,ROBERT-For Lizzie and Harriet-NY-(1973)-FS&G-1st ed (v10,f,f dj) 20.00

LOWELL,ROBERT-For the Union Dead-Lond-(1964)-Faber & Faber-1st Brit ed (bb2,f,dj) 45.00

LOWELL,ROBERT-For the Union Dead-NY-(1964)-FS&G-1st ed (v10,vf,vf dj) 75.00

LOWELL,ROBERT-For the Union Dead-NY-(1964)-FS&G-8vo-cl-1st ed (jj8,vf,dj) 50.00

LOWELL,ROBERT-History-NY-(1973)-FS&G-1st ed (c10,as new in dj) 25.00

LOWELL,ROBERT-Life Studies-NY-(1959)-FS&C-1st ed (v10,vf,vf dj) 100.00

LOWELL,ROBERT-Life Studies-NY-(1959)-FS&C-8vo-1st ed (jj8,f,dj) 75.00

LOWELL,ROBERT-Lord Weary's Castle-NY-(1946)-Harcourt Brace-blk bds stmpd in gold-1st ed (cc2,dj) 225.00

LOWELL,ROBERT-Mills of the Kavanaughs-NY-(1951)-Harcourt,Brace-1st ed (v10,vf,vf dj) 200.00

LOWELL,ROBERT-Notebook 1967 to 1968-NY-(1969)-FS&G-1st ed (bb2,f,dj) 35.00

LOWELL,V W-Airline Safety is a Myth-np-(1967)-8vo-236p-cl,14p plts-1st ed (s2,dj) 20.00

LOWENFELS,WALTER-ED.-Where is Vietnam-GC-1967-Dbldy Anchor-wrps-1st ed (v5,f) 15.00

LOWENFISH,LEE-Imperfect Diamond-1980-Stein & Day-photos-1st ed (s8,f,dj) 25.00

LOWENSTEIN,ELEANOR-Bibliography of American Cookery Books. 1742 to 1860-Worcester-1972-Amer Antiquarian Scty-132p (m6) 40.00

LOWER,ARTHUR R M-Unconventional Voyages-Tor-1954-Ryerson-xii,156p (k10,wn dj) 15.00*

LOWERY,F W-History of a Fishing Trip Written to Order by the Keeper of the Records-nd-priv prntd-8vo-130p-one of 100c-rare (m3) 350.00

LOWERY,G-Louisiana Birds-1974-LSU-651p-14p col plts,photos-3rd ed,rvsd (bb3,f,dj) 30.00

LOWERY,G-Louisiana Birds-Baton Rouge-1955-8vo-556p-cl,col frntis,40 col plts,photos-1st ed (y8,dj chip) 35.00

LOWIE,ROBERT H-Indians of the Plains-NY-1954-222p-photos,illus,maps-1st ed (t7) 20.00

LOWMAN,AL-Printing Arts in Texas-np-(1975)-Roger Beacham Publ-107p-illus-ltd to 395c (jj1) 200.00

LOWNDES,A G-ED.-South Pacific Enterprise-Sydney-(1956)-Angus & Robertson-xviii+500p-beige cl,plts-1st ed (j2) 20.00

LOWNDES,MARIE B-Why It Happened-NY-1938-Longmans-1st US ed (h4,dj) 12.50

LOWREY,LAWSON G-Orthopsychiatry 1923 to 1948-np-(1948)-Amer Orthopsych Assn-viii+623p-red cl (c2) 25.00

LOWREY,WOODBURY-Descriptive List of Maps of Spanish Possesions within...United States,1502 to 1820-Wash-1912-GPO-8vo-567p-red cl cov bds,frntis port,col t.p & half t (mm1,cov streaked,sl dmpstnd) 340.00

LOWRY,MALCOLM-Dark as the Grave Wherein My Friend is Laid-1968-NAL-1st ed (x2,vf,dj) 45.00

LOWRY,MALCOLM-Hear US O Lord from Heaven thy Dwelling Place-Lond-1962-J Cape-1st Brit ed (d8,dj) 85.00

LOWRY,MALCOLM-October Ferry to Gabriola-NY-1970-World-8vo-338p-1st ed (bb7,sl wrnkld dj) 25.00*

LOWRY,ROBERT W-Joyful Lays-NY-(1884)-192p-bds (h1) 12.50

LOWRY,ROBERT-Casualty-NY-1946-1st ed (q5,dj) 20.00

LOWRY,ROBERT-Find Me In Fire-GC-1948-1st ed (r5,chip dj) 20.00

LOWRY,ROBERT-Party of Dreamers-NY-1982-1st ed (r5,f,dj) 15.00

LOWRY,ROBERT-What's Left of April-GC-1956-1st ed (r5,chip dj) 15.00

LOWTH,ROBERT-Short Introduction to English Grammar-Phila-1799-prntd by R Aitken-132p-lea (k1,sl wn) 75.00

LOWTHER,CHARLES C-Dodge City, Kansas-Phila-(1940)-Dorrance-213p-cl,frntis,plts-1st ed (v1,dj chip & tn) 65.00

LOY,MINA-Last Lunar Baedeker-Highlands-1982-Jargon-1st ed (v5,f,f dj) 35.00

LOZIER,J H-Forty Rounds from the Fighting Chaplain-Mt.Vernon-nd(1887?)-auth publ-61p-wrps,illus (o7) 30.00

LUARD,G D-Fishing Adventures in Canada & U S A-Lond-1950-8vo-157p-illus (m3,vf,dj) 10.00

LUBBOCK,BASIL-Bully Hayes, South Sea Pirate-Bost-1931-322p-cl,col frontis+16 b&w illus-scarce (d1,sl spot cov) 50.00

LUBELL,CECIL-ED.-An Illustrated Guide to Textile Collections in French Museums-NY-(1977)-4to-240p-32p col illus (l10) 27.50

LUCAS,A M-Atlas of Avian Hematology-Wash-1961-U.S.D.A. Mon.25-4to-271p-cl,illus(many col) (y8) 40.00

LUCAS,CHARLES-Pitcairn Island Register Book-NY-1977-AMS Pr-181p-brwn cl,fldg map-rprnt of 1929 ed (dd7,f) 80.00

LUCAS,DIONE-Dione Lucas Book of French Cooking-(1973)-Little,Brown-4to-925p-g title on blu cl,illus-1st ed (q8,dj) 30.00

LUCAS,DIONE-Gourmet Cooking School Cook Book-Lond-(1964)-Oldbourne-4to-367p-red bds,drwngs-2nd prtg (q8,dj) 20.00

LUCAS,E V-Luck of the Year-1923-Doran-1st ed (x2,dj sl wn & tn) 45.00

LUCAS,F L-Tragedy-Lond-1927-Hogarth Pr-8vo-cl-Hogarth Lectures No.2-1st ed (x3,sl soil cov) 55.00

LUCAS,FREDERIC A-Animals Before Man in North America-NY-1902-Appleton-viii+291p+ads-grn cl,illus-1st ed (d2) 20.00

LUCAS,JIM G-Dateline: Viet Nam-NY-1966-Award Hs/Crwn-334p-1st ed (j8,dj) 50.00

LUCAS,WALTER A-ED.-Locomotives and Cars since 1900-NY-1959-119p-illus-1st ed (n4,f,dj) 22.00

LUCAS,WALTER A-From the Hills to the Hudson-(np)-(1944)-(viii),319p-cl,illus,fldg map (aa6) 45.00

LUCAS,WALTER-100 Years of Steam Locomotives-1957-Simmons Boardman-4to-278p-illus (nn7,dj tn) 29.00

LUCE,CAPT E S-Keogh, Comanche and Custer-Ashland-1974-148p-photos-rprnt Howes L553 (t7,f) 125.00

LUCE,R DUNCAN-ET AL-Developments in Mathematical Psychology-Glencose-(1960)-Free Pr-(viii)+294p-blu cl-1st ed (a2,dj) 20.00

LUCH,BILL-Steelhead Drift Fishing & Fly Fishing-Seattle-1970-8vo-125p-wrps,photos-1st ed (m3) 10.00

LUCIA,ELLIS-Saga of Ben Holladay-NY-(1959)-Hastings Hs-x,374p-pict cl,illus,map e.p.-1st ed (v1,dj) 35.00

LUCIA,ELLIS-Saga of Ben Holladay-NY-1959-Hastings Hs-1st ed (f10,dj) 65.00

LUCIA,S P,M.D.-Comment on the Wines Served at a Dinner of the Medical Friends of Wine-SF-Nov.19, 1944-Bohemian Club-wrps (l6) 45.00

LUCIE SMITH,E-Waking Man-1975-Knopf-folio-216 plts-1st Amer ed (h10,dj) 60.00

LUCKY,ROCHELLE-Treatise on the Art & Antiquity of Cookery in the Middle Ages-Fallbrook-1978-V Gerry,Weather Bird Pr-2 vols,ltd to 200c (o6,as new in box) 75.00

LUDGATE,H J-Trot Line Fishing for Pleasure and Profit-Toledo-1950-8vo-48p-illus,photos-1st ed (m3) 8.00

LUDLUM,DAVID M-Early American Winters. II-Bost-1968-Amer Meteorological Soc-4to-x+257p-blu cl,tbls,maps-1st ed (b2,dj) 35.00

LUDLUM,ROBERT-Chancellor Manuscript-NY-1977-1st ed (q5,f,dj) 20.00

LUDLUM,ROBERT-Chancellor Manuscript-NY-1977-Dial-1st ed (a5,dj) 35.00

LUDLUM,ROBERT-Matarese Circle-1979-Marek-1st ed (r9,dj) 20.00

LUDLUM,ROBERT-Osterman Weekend-NY-1972-orig prntd acetate dj-1st ed (s5,sl chip dj) 40.00

LUDLUM,ROBERT-Rhinemann Exchange-NY-1974-1st ed (q5,f,dj) 20.00

LUDLUM,ROBERT-Scarlatti Inheritance-Lond-1971-auth 1st bk-1st Brit ed (p5,dj) 30.00

LUDWIG,COY-Maxfield Parrish-NY-1973-Watson Guptill-4to-224p-blu cl,b&w & col illus (r10,f,f dj) 15.00

LUDWIG,EMIL-Goethe-NY-1928-Putnam's-1st US ed (z9,bump,sp sunned) 12.50

LUDWIG,EMIL-Stalin-NY-(1942)-Putnam-8vo-248p-1st US ed (ff5,sl tn dj) 25.00

LUEBKE,FREDERICK C-Immigrants and Politics-Lincoln-1969-220p-maps-1st ed (t7,dj) 12.50

LUEDY,ART-Christmas Rose-Ohio-1948-Auth-44p (x6,dj rub) 24.00

LUFKIN,ARTHUR W-History of Dentistry-Phila-1938-Lea & Febiger-255p-blu cl,90 illus-1st ed (l2) 55.00

LUHAN,MABEL D-Edge of Taos Desert-NY-1937-Harcourt Brace-vol.4 of her memoirs-2nd ed (u9,dj wn,chip) 60.00

LUHAN,MABEL D-Intimate Memories Background-NY-1933-290p-frntis-1st ed (t7) 60.00

LUHAN,MABEL D-Intimate Memories-NY-(1933)-290p-frntis-1st ed (v7,sl chip dj) 85.00

LUHAN,MABEL D-Lorenzo in Taos-NY-1932-Knopf-8vo-cl-1st ed (x10,f,dj edge wn & tn) 50.00

LUHAN,MABEL D-Lorenzo in Taos-NY-1932-Knopf-photos-1st ed (u9,dj wn,chip) 100.00

LUHAN,MABEL D-Movers and Shakers-NY-1936-542p-frntis,photos-Vol III of Intimate Mem.-1st ed (t7,dj,autg) 85.00

LUHAN,MABEL D-Taos & Its Artists-NY-1947-57 illus-1st ed (h10,sl chip dj) 150.00

LUHAN,MABEL D-Winter in Taos-NY-1935-Harcourt Brace-photos-1st ed (u9) 100.00

LUHRS,VICTOR-Great Baseball Mystery-1966-Barnes-1st ed (p7,dj) 60.00

LUK,CHARLES-Ch'an and Zen Teaching-Lond-1960-Rider & Co-cl,frntis-1st ed (o8,dj) 45.00

LUKAN,KARL-ED.-Alps & Alpinism-Lond-1968-4to-184p-239 photos,8 tip in col photos-1st Brit ed (p10,as new in dj) 45.00

LUKAN,KARL-ED.-Alps and Alpinism-Lond-1968-Thames & Hudson-4to-grn cl,col plts,tip in photos (gg6) 35.00

LUKE,HARRY-Cyprus-Lond-1957-Harrap & Co-cl,illus-1st ed (n8,dj) 15.00

LUKE,HELEN M-Inner Story-NY-1982-Crossroad-cl-1st ed (n8,vf,dj) 20.00

LUKEMAN,ADAMS-Eevalu-NY-(1963)-Avalon-1st ed (h3,dj) 15.00

LUKINS,A H-COMP.-Book of Miles Aircraft-Leicester-nd(ca.1940)-4to-88p-cl,illus-rare (t2) 150.00

LUM,EDWARD H-Genealogy of the Lum Family-Somerville-(1927)-270p-cl (aa6) 90.00

LUMHOLTZ,CARL-Among Cannibals-Firle-1979-Caliban Bks-8vo-383p+map at end,4 b&w plts,illus-rprnt ed (p8,vf,dj) 50.00

LUMHOLTZ,CARL-Among Cannibals-NY-1902-Scribner's-8vo-xx,395p-grn cl,g & blck titles,port,maps,4 chromos & woodcts (p8,sl soil,pres) 90.00

LUMHOLTZ,CARL-New Trails in Mexico-NY-1912-Scribner's-411p-orig pict cl,illus,rear pckt map-1st ed (ff4,ex-libr) 135.00

LUMHOLTZ,CARL-New Trails in Mexico-NY-1912-Scribner's-4to-2 maps-1st ed (u9,edgewn) 175.00

LUMLEY,BRIAN-Beneath the Moors-Sauk City-1974-Arkham-1st ed (l3,f,dj) 10.00

LUMLEY,BRIAN-Beneath the Moors-Sauk City-1974-ltd to 3842c-1st ed (k5,as new in dj) 25.00

LUMLEY,BRIAN-Horror at Oakdeene and Others-(Sauk City)-1977-ltd to 4162c-1st ed (k5,as new in dj) 10.00

LUMLEY,BRIAN-Horror at Oakdeene-Sauk City-1977-Arkham-1st ed (g3,f,dj) 20.00

LUMMIS,CHARLES F-Bronco Pegasus-Bost-1928-150p-photos-1st ed (v7,dj) 30.00

LUMMIS,CHARLES F-Bullying the Moqui-Prescott-1968-129p-photos,map-1st ed (v7,f,dj) 20.00

LUMMIS,CHARLES F-Dateline Fort Bowie-Norman-(1979)-206p-illus-1st ed (e7,f,dj) 35.00

LUMMIS,CHARLES F-Enchanted Burro-Chig-1897-277p-drwngs-v scarce-1st ed (v7) 100.00

LUMMIS,CHARLES F-Flowers of Our Lost Romance-Bost-1929-288p-drwngs-1st ed (v7,sl wn dj) 45.00

LUMMIS,CHARLES F-General Crook and the Apache Wars-Flagstaff-(1966)-148p-illus,deluxe ed,ltd to 250c,3 autg-1st ed (v7,f,box) 50.00

LUMMIS,CHARLES F-General Crook and the Apache Wars-Flagstaff-(1966)-148p-illus-1st ed (t7,dj) 32.50

LUMMIS,CHARLES F-General Crook and the Apache Wars-Flagstaff-(1966)-1st trd ed (v7,f,dj) 20.00

LUMMIS,CHARLES F-Gold Fish of Gran Chimu-Chig-1911-126p-drnwgs-2nd ed(not so indicated,1st ed as Bost, 1896) (v7,pres) 30.00

LUMMIS,CHARLES F-King of the Bronchos-NY-1897-254p-illus-Adams Herd#1361 (v7) 65.00

LUMMIS,CHARLES F-Land of Poco Tiempo-NY-1893-310p-photos,drwngs-1st ed (u7,f) 75.00

LUMMIS,CHARLES F-Land of Poco Tiempo-NY-1928-Scribner's-photos (u9,wn dj) 50.00

LUMMIS,CHARLES F-Man Who Married the Moon-NY-1894-239p-drwngs,v scarce-1st ed (v7,lacks f.e.p.,hng rprd) 100.00

LUMMIS,CHARLES F-Mesa, Canon and Pueblo-NY-(1925)-517p-col frntis,photos,fldg map-1st ed (v7) 35.00

LUMMIS,CHARLES F-Mesa, Canon and Pueblo-NY-(1925)-Century-517p-photos,map,errata-1st ed (bb4) 40.00

LUMMIS,CHARLES F-New Mexico David...-NY-1891-Adams Herd 1362-1st ed (u9) 75.00

LUMMIS,CHARLES F-Pueblo Indian Folk Stories-NY-1910-257p-drwngs-1st prtg (v7) 50.00

LUMMIS,CHARLES F-Some Strange Corners of Our Country-NY-1892-NY-270p-col frntis-1st ed (v7) 60.00

LUMMIS,CHARLES F-Spanish Pioneers-Chig-1893-292p-illus-1st ed (v7) 65.00

LUMMIS,CHARLES F-Tramp Across the Continent-NY-1892-270p-1st ed (v7) 75.00

LUMPKIN,GRACE-Wedding-NY-1939-Lee Furman-1st ed (v5,f,dj) 75.00

LUMPKIN,KATHERINE D-Child Workers in America-NY-1937-McBride-292p-1st ed (r1,sl drknd sp) 25.00

LUMPKINS,WILLIAM-La Casa Adobe-Santa Fe-1961-sm folio-7p dbl col text+34p drwngs,plans,spiralbnd wrps-1st ed (u7,f) 45.00

LUMPKINS,WILLIAM-Modern Spanish-Pueblo Homes-np(Santa Fe)-nd(1946)-102p-thin papr wrps,drwngs-1st ed (u7,cov rprd) 35.00

LUMSDEN,PETER-Lumsden of the Guides-Lond-1898-333p-brwn cl,maps,plts-1st ed (b7,sl soil cov,sl fox) 175.00

LUND,MARSHA-Indian Jewelry, Fact & Fantasy-(Boulder)-(1976)-159p-pict wrps,col photos,maps-1st ed (v7,f) 10.00

LUNDBORG,E-Arctic Rescue-NY-1929-8vo-222p-cl,frntis,plts,e.p. maps-1st ed (s2) 45.00

LUNDE,KARL-Anuszkiewicz-NY-(1977)-Abrams-folio-cl-1st ed (oo6,dj) 75.00

LUNDGREN,WILLIAM R-Across the High Frontier-NY-1955-288p-1st ed (nn2,f,dj) 12.50

LUNDIN,LEONARD-Cockpit of the Revolution-Princeton-1940-(xvii),463p-cl,plts (aa6) 75.00

LUNDQUIST,JAMES-Chester Himes-NY-(1976)-Ungar Publ-1st ed (cc1,f,dj) 15.00

LUNN,ARNOLD-Complete Ski Runner-Lond-1930-223p-1st Brit ed (a4,dj) 75.00

LUNN,ARNOLD-Matterhorn Centenary-Chig-1965-144p-1st US ed (p10,f,dj) 20.00

LUNT,DUDLEY C-Taylors Gut in the Delaware State-NY-1968-8vo-303p-1st ed (m3,f) 20.00

LUNT,JAMES-Charge to Glory-Lond-1961-265p-illus-1st ed (kk2,dj) 25.00

LUNT,JAMES-John Burgoyne of Saratoga-NY-1975-369p-1st ed (b7,f,dj) 35.00

LUPOFF,RICHARD A-Edgar Rice Burroughs-NY-1965-Canaveral-ltd to 150c,autg & dated-1st ed (k3,f,dj) 125.00

LURIE,ALISON-Imaginary Friends-Lond-1967-1st ed (r5,sl chip dj) 25.00

LURIE,ALISON-Nowhere City-Lond-1965-1st Brit ed (r5,dj) 40.00

LURIE,ALISON-Only Children-1979-Random-1st ed (s9,vf,dj) 15.00

LURIE,ALISON-Real People-NY-(1969)-1st US ed (q5,dj) 20.00

LURIE,ALISON-Real People-NY-(1969)-Random-1st ed (e3,dj) 30.00

LURIE,ALISON-War Between the Tates-NY-(1974)-Random-1st ed (ee2,f,dj,autg) 40.00

LUSCOMB,SALLY-Collector's Encyclopedia of Buttons-NY-(1967)-Bonanza-xii,242p-col illus (u5,f,dj) 45.00

LUSTGARTEN,EDGAR-One More Unfortunate-NY-1947-Scribners-1st US ed (g4,dj) 15.00

LUSTGARTEN,EDGAR-Woman in the Case-NY-1955-Scribner-8vo-218p-1st ed (oo7,f,dj) 25.00

LUTES,DELLA T-Country Kitchen-1936-Little,Brown-264p-dec red/wht cl-7th prtg (q8,cov soil,hng weak) 10.00

LUTES,DELLA T-Country Kitchen-Bost-1936-Little,Brown-red check cl-1st ed (k6,dj) 20.00

LUTES,DELLA T-Home Grown-Bost-1937-Little,Brown-272p-grn check cl bds,papr labls-1st ed (k6) 20.00

LUTES,DELLA-Table Setting and Service for Mistress and Maid-NY-(1928,1934)-Barrows-155p-b&w photos (l6) 18.00

LUTZ,B-Brazilian Species of Hyla-1973-U of Tex-4to-260p-7 col plts (bb3,f,dj) 45.00

LUTZ,CORA-Essays on Manuscripts and Rare Books-(Hamden)-1975-Archon-177p-cl,frntis,illus-1st ed (dd10,f,dj) 15.00

LUTZ,JOHN-Buyer Beware-NY-(1976)-Putnam-1st ed (j3,f,sl tn dj) 25.00

LUTZ,JOHN-Lazarus Man-NY-1979-Morrow-1st ed (j3,f,dj) 20.00

LUVAAS,JAY-Military Legacy of the Civil War-Chig-(1959)-253p-illus-1st ed (c4,dj) 30.00

LUXTON,NORMAN K-Tilikum,Luxton's Pacific Crossing-Sidney-1971-Gray's Publ-8vo-159p-photos-1st ed (cc5,f,sl tn dj) 15.00

LYALL,GAVIN-Secret Servant-NY-1980-Viking-1st Amer ed (p4,f,dj) 25.00

LYALL,GAVIN-Wrong Side of the Sky-1961-Scribners-1st Amer ed (s10,dj) 15.00

LYCEUM OF NATURAL HISTORY OF N Y-ANNALS OF...VOL.6-NY-1858-8vo-443p-half lea,9 plts,errata (y8,ex-libr) 135.00

LYDEKKER,R-ED.-Libray of Natural History-NY-1902(1901)-lg 8vo-6 vols-cl,72 col plts (y8,edges wn) 135.00

LYDON,JAMES G-Pirates,Privateers, and Profits-Upper Saddle River-1970-Gregg Pr-8vo-303p-blk cl,7 tabls,illus (nn1,f,rub dj) 30.00

LYELL,CHARLES-Travels in North America-Lond-1845-John Murray-2 vols in one-fldg col panorama & maps-1st ed (p6) 450.00

LYFORD,CARRIE A-Ojibway Crafts-1943-Bureau of Indian Affairs-tall 8vo-216p-wrps,illus (cc4) 18.00

LYFORD,CARRIE A-Quill and Beadwork of the Western Sioux-(July 1954)-Bureau of Indian Affairs-tall 8vo-116p-wrps,photos,drwngs (cc4) 15.00

LYMAN,CHESTER S-Around the Horn to the Sandwich Islands and California 1845 to 1850-New Haven-1924-Yale U Pr-8vo-g dec blck cl wi e.p. maps,16 plts (p8) 160.00

LYMAN,GEORGE D-Ralston's Ring-NY-1937-Scribner's-368p-illus e.p.,illus-1st ed (gg4) 40.00

LYMAN,GEORGE D-Ralston's Ring-NY/Lond-1937-Scribner's-8vo-red cl,g sp & cov titles,photo e.p.,illus-1st ed (mm1) 45.00

LYMAN,GEORGE D-Saga of the Comstock Lode-NY-1934-Scribner's-1st ed (v4,as new in dj) 50.00

LYMAN,GEORGE D-Saga of the Comstock Lode-NY-1934-Scribner's-399p-pict e.p.,illus-Six Guns 1377-1st ed (bb4,dj) 35.00

LYMAN,H S-History of Oregon-NY-1903-4 vols-illus-1st ed (d7) 200.00

LYMAN,HENRY-Artificial Anaesthesia and Anaesthetics-NY-1881-338p (dd3) 150.00

LYMAN,HENRY-Bluefishing-Bost-1952-8vo-98p-photos (m3,f) 12.50

LYMAN,WILLIAM D-Columbia River-NY-1909-Putnam's-409p-blu cl wi gilt,applied photo,t.e.g.,2 fldg maps in rear,photos,prnts-1st Amer ed (o2,hngs weak,sl rub cors) 55.00

LYMAN,WILLIAM D-Columbia River-NY-1909-Putnam's-blu cl,pict cov,80 illus,fldg map-1st ed (pp3) 45.00

LYNAM,EDWARD-British Maps and Map Makers-Lond-1947-Collins-8 col plts,22 b&w illus-3rd impr rvsd (v4,f,dj) 30.00

LYNAM,EDWARD-Mapmaker's Art-Lond-(1953)-Batchworth Pr-8vo-ix,140p-roy blu cl,52 figs-1st ed (t10,dj) 45.00

LYNCH,ARTHUR-Case Against Einstein-NY-1933-Dodd,Mead-xxx+275p-red cl-1st Amer ed (dd1) 20.00

LYNCH,JEREMIAH-Three Years in the Klondike-Chig-1967-Donnelley & Sons-frntis,illus,map-Lakeside Classics (ff4) 20.00

LYNCH,JEREMIAH-Three Years in the Klondike-Lond-1904-280p-mod cl-Wickersham 4356-1st ed (g1,ex-lib,rbnd) 15.00

LYNCH,V E-Thrilling Adventures-NP-1928-priv prtd-pict grn cl,photos-1st ed (ee6) 20.00

LYND,STAUGHTON-Other Side-NY-1966-1st ed (v9,f,f dj) 40.00

LYNN,ETHEL-Adventures of a Woman Hobo-NY-(1917)-296p-cl (d1) 35.00

LYNN,MRS ALMA W-Helpful Hints for the Young Wife-KC-1922-Wstrn Baptist Publ-145p-wrps,cord bndg-Bitting 296 (n6) 15.00

LYNN-ALLEN,E H-Leaves From a Game Book-NY,Lond-1946-8vo-176p-illus (m3,f) 20.00

LYNN-ALLEN,E H-Rough Shoot-Lond-1942-8vo-160p-illus,pict e.p.s-1st ed (m3,fray dj) 20.00

LYNNHURST CONGREGATIONAL COOK BOOK-Mpls-1913-179p+18p ads-wht cl (q8,edgewn,hng weak) 20.00

LYON,EUGENE-Search for the Atocha-NY-(1979)-Harper Row-246p-1st ed (ee8,f,dj) 19.00

LYON,G F-Brief Narrative of an Unsuccessful Attempt to Reach Repulse Bay..in the Year MDCCCXXIV-Lond-1825-J Murray-orig papr bds,6p engrvngs,1 fldg map-1st ed (p6,sp chip & sl split,uncut) 300.00

LYON,I W-Colonial Furniture of New England-Bost-1891-4to-illus-1st ed (ff10,hngs weak) 50.00

LYON,PETER-Wild, Wild West-NY-1969-Funk & Wagnalls-8vo-156p-1st ed (z4,dj) 20.00

LYON,PETER-Wild, Wild West-NY-1969-Funk & Wagnalls-8vo-156p-40 photos & illus-1st ed (aa3,f,chip dj) 25.00

LYON,W E-Youth in the Saddle-NY-nd(1955)-Barnes-1st ed (h9,dj) 10.00

LYONS,A B,M.D.-Plant Names Scientific and Popular...-Detr-1900-Nelson,Baker-469p-blu bds (m6,sl wn) 35.00

LYONS,ARTHUR-All God's Children-NY-1975-Mason-1st ed (d4,cor bump,dj) 250.00

LYONS,ARTHUR-All God's Children-NY-1975-Mason/Charter-1st ed (w5,dj) 125.00

LYONS,ARTHUR-Dead are Discreet-NY-1974-Mason-1st ed (d4,sl wn dj) 250.00

LYONS,ARTHUR-Dead Ringer-NY-1977-Mason-1st ed (j4,f,dj) 35.00

LYONS,ARTHUR-Hard Trade-NY-1981-Holt-1st ed (e4,f,dj) 12.50

LYONS,ARTHUR-Killing Floor-NY-1976-Mason-1st ed (d4,t.e. soil,dj) 225.00

LYONS,JIMMY-Dizzy, Duke, the Count and Me-SF-1978-Cal Living-1st ed (w5,f,dj) 30.00

LYONS,NAN-Someone is Killing the Great Chefs of Europe-NY-1976-Harcourt-1st ed (f4,as new in dj) 10.00

LYONS,NATHAN-Notations in Passing-Cambridge-1974-MIT Pr/Light Impr-121p-96 photos-1st ed (cc9,as new in dj) 40.00

LYONS,NATHAN-Photography in the Twentieth Century-NY-(1967)-Horizon-4to-cl-1st ed (y3,dj) 50.00

LYONS,NATHAN-Under the Sun-NY-1960-Braziller-unpgd-36 photos-1st ed (cc9,dj chip & sl tn) 50.00

LYONS,NICK-ED.-Fisherman's Bounty-NY-1971-8vo-352p-illus-"deluxe" ed (m3,vf,sl tn dj) 35.00

LYONS,NICK-Fishing Widows-NY-1974-8vo-154p-1st ed (m3,vf,dj) 20.00

LYONS,NINETTE-Fish for All Occasions-(1967)-Rand McNally-271p-grn cl,photos-1st Amer ed (q8,dj) 15.00

LYREN,CARL-365 Ways to Prepare Chicken-(1974)-Dbldy-232p-grn cl-orig ed (q8,dj) 15.00

LYSAGHT,A M-Joseph Banks in Newfoundland and Labrador, 1766-1971-U of Cal-4to-512p-12 col plts,91 illus,maps (bb3,f,dj) 48.00

LYSAGHT,EDWARD E-Irish Eclogues-Dublin-1915-Maunsel-g stmpd papr cov bds,vel sp-1st ed (z8,f) 45.00

LYSNAR,FRANCES B-New Zealand the Dear Old Maori Land-Auckland-1915-Brett Prtg-8vo-xii,268p-blu cl,85 photo illus (p8,sl wn,spot) 45.00

LYTHE,H-How to Win Field Trials-NY-1950-229p-photos (gg3,f,dj) 25.00

LYTHE,H-Point, A Book About Bird Dogs-NY-1941-Derrydale-197p-drk red cl,gold stmpd pointer on frnt cov-ltd to 950c,nbrd (ee3,f) 125.00

LYTLE,ANDREW-Name For Evil-Indpls-1947-1st ed (p5,dj sl chip & soil) 150.00

LYTLE,ANDREW-Novel, a Novella and Four Stories-NY-1958-1st ed (q5,dj) 40.00

LYTLE,ANDREW-Velvet Horn-NY-1957-1st ed (r5,dj) 45.00

LYTLE,HORACE-Bird Dog Days-NY-1926-8vo-191p-photos frontis (m3) 20.00

LYTLE,HORACE-Breaking a Bird Dog-NY-1924-8vo-167p-photos (m3) 15.00

LYTLE,HORACE-Gun Dogs Afield-NY-1942-8vo-277p-col frontis by L B Hunt,illus-1st ed (m3) 17.50

LYTLE,HORACE-How to Win Field Trials-NY-1950-8vo-229p-photos-1st ed (m3,f,fray dj) 55.00

LYTLE,HORACE-Point-1941-Derrydale-8vo-197p-ltd to 950c,nbrd,illus,photos (m3,tape stnd e.p.s) 100.00

LYTLE,HORACE-Point-Harrisburg-1954-8vo-232p-illus (m3,f,dj) 30.00

LYTLE,J HORACE-Story of Jack-Dayton-(1917)-44p-cl (c1) 12.50

LYTTON,EDWARD-Billy Bub, the Double-Prize Detective-NY-1899-16p-self wrps-Beadle's Half Dime Library No.1093 (j1) 15.00

L'HEUREUX,JOHN-Clang Birds-NY-(1972)-Macmillan-1st ed (b10,dj) 20.00

M'CLINTOCK,F L-Narrative of the Discovery of the Fate of Sir John Franklin and His Companions-Lond-1859-xxvii,403p-orig cl,illus,maps (a7,smudge cov,sl fox pgs) 200.00

M'CLINTOCK,FRANCIS L-Narrative of the Discovery of the Fate of Sir John Franklin and His Companions-Edmonton-1972-Hurtig-sm 8vo-xi,375p-frntis,18 illus,fldg maps (bb7,dj) 65.00*

M'CLINTOCK,SIR F LEOPOLD-Voyage of the `Fox' in the Arctic Seas in Search of Franklin...-Lond-1875-John Murray-336p+32p ads-blu cl-4th ed (p8,wn,fox) 40.00

M'CLURE,ROBERT LE M-Discovery of the North West Passage-Edmonton-1969(1856)-Hurtig-sm 8vo-xxxv,405p-frntis,fldg map,4 illus (bb7,dj) 50.00*

M'COLLESTER,SULLIVAN H-Round the Globe-Bost-1890-Universalist Publ Hs-354p-cl-4th ed (g1) 17.50

M'DOUGAL,JOHN-Farmer's Assistant-Chillicothe-1813-Fredonian Pr-271,(1)p-orig bds,rvsd & corrctd,wi addtns-Amer Imprnts 29012-2nd ed (n1,lacks frnt cov,t.p. soil) 200.00

M'LEOD,JOHN-Voyage of His Majesty's Ship Alceste, to China, Corea, and the Island of Lewchew...-Lond-1818-John Murray-323p-mod lea bndg wi e.p. renewed,port,fldg map,5 handcol plts-2nd ed (ll1,rbnd,few pgs dmpstnd) 350.00

MAAS,PETER-Rescuer-NY-(1967)-H&R-8vo-239p-1st ed (jj5,f,dj) 15.00

MAASS,DAVID-Gallery of Waterfowl & Upland Birds-LA-1978-oblng 4to-121p-paintings by Maass-1st ed (m3,f,badly fray dj) 60.00

MABBUTT,J A-Lands of the Port Moresby Kairuku Area, Territory of Papua and New Guinea-Melbourne-1965-Commwlth Sci-crwn 4to-184p-prtd wrps,orig envelope,12 photo plts,illus,separate lg col fldg map-Land Rsrch Ser No.14 (p8,vf,sl wn envelope) 35.00

MABIE,HAROLD W-ED.-Young Folk's Treasury-NY-1918-Univ Soc-12 vols-dec cov & sp,g dec e.p.,col plts-later prtg (y10,sp fade,few vol sl dmpstn 85.00

MACARTHUR,JAMES-ED.-Bookman Literary Year Book 1898-NY-1898-Dodd, Mead-8vo-iv,263p-cl backd bds wi papr cov sp (w2,cov rub) 20.00

MACASKILL,W R-Out of Halifax-Derrydale-1937-folio-unpgd-ltd to 950c,nbrd,photos (m3) 70.00

MACAULAY,JAMES,M.D.-Grey Hawk-Lond-1883-Hodder & Stoughton-11 b&w engrv-blu & gld illus bndg wi a.e.g.-1st Brit ed (e10,frontis loose) 25.00

MACAULAY,LORD-Critical and Historical Essays Contributed to the Edinburgh Review-Lond-1866-Longmans,Green-sm 8vo-4 vols-polished tan calf,g sp wi red lea labls-"New Edition" (oo8) 175.00

MACAULAY,ROSE-Letters to a Sister-NY-1964-Atheneum-1st ed (z3,f,dj) 10.00

MACAULAY,ROSE-Potterism-NY-(1920)-Boni & Liveright-1st Amer ed (u10,dj) 50.00

MACAULEY,ROSE-World My Wilderness-Bost-1950-Atlanta/Little,Brown-1st US ed (hh5,f,dj) 12.50

MACBETH,R G-Policing the Plains-NY-nd-Doran-320p-illus (bb4) 30.00

MACBRIDE,MACKENZIE-ED.-With Napoleon at Waterloo-Lond-1911-249p-red cl,illus-1st ed (kk2) 125.00

MACCAS,LEON-German Barbarism-Lond-1916-Hodder & Stoughton-12mo-228p-1st ed (aa5,dj) 20.00

MACCLINTOCK,DORCAS-Natural History of Zebras-NY-1976-Scribner-picts by U Mochi-1st prtg (f10,dj) 25.00

MACCLOUD,MALCOLM-Tera Beyond-NY-1981-Atheneum-1st ed (h3,f,dj) 15.00

MACCORKLE,WILLIAM A-White Sulphur Springs-NY-1916-Neale Publ-x,410p-g orng cl,t.e.g,48 photo plts-1st ed (n2,sl soil,rub) 65.00

MACCRACKEN,HAROLD-Frank Tenney Johnson Book-GC-1974-207p-padded lea,cl cov emboss box,all in gold gift box-ltd to 4000c,nbrd-1st ed (f7,as new in boxes) 115.00

MACDIARMID,HUGH-Lucky Poet-Berkeley-1972-UC Pr-1st ed thus (z9,f,dj) 10.00

MACDOANDL,ROSS-Chill-1964-Knopf-1st ed (x7,vf,f dj) 200.00

MACDONAGH,THOMAS-Poems...-Dublin-(1924)-Talbot Pr-wrps-1st ed (z8,covs sl mrkd) 60.00

MACDONAGH,THOMAS-Poetical Works of...-Lond-1916-T Fisher Unwin-papr cov bds wi cl sp-1st ed (z8,f) 50.00

MACDONALD,ALEXANDER-Design for Angling-Bost-1947-8vo-145p-illus (m3,vf,fray dj) 20.00

MACDONALD,ALEXANDER-In Search of El Dorado-Lond-1910-Unwin-291p-cl,frntis port+32 photo plts-3rd prtg (p8,sp fade) 45.00

MACDONALD,ALEXANDER-On Becoming A Fly Fisherman-NY-1959-8vo-168p-illus (m3,f,sl chip dj) 20.00

MACDONALD,BETTY-Anybody Can Do Anything-Phila-1950-Lippincott-1st ed (e8,f,sl wn & chip dj) 45.00

MACDONALD,ELEANOR D-San Juan Basin-Denver-(1970)-239p-photos,map-1st ed (v7,f,dj) 45.00

MACDONALD,GEORGE-Paul Faber-Surgeon-1879-Lippincott-1st Amer ed (x2) 175.00

MACDONALD,GEORGE-Within and Without-1872-Scribners & Armstrong-auth 1st bk-1st Amer ed (x2) 185.00

MACDONALD,H H-Big Game Management-Dallas-1934-12mo-183p-photos (m3) 35.00

MACDONALD,J D-Seven-1974-Hale-1st ed (x7,vf,dj) 40.00

MACDONALD,JOHN D-Ballroom in the Skies-NY-1952-Greenberg-1st ed (h4,sl wn dj) 35.00

MACDONALD,JOHN D-Brass Cupcake-1974-Hale-auth 1st bk-1st hdcov ed (x7,vf,dj) 65.00

MACDONALD,JOHN D-Brass Cupcake-NY-1950-Gold Medal-wrps-auth 1st bk-1st ed (w5,f) 50.00

MACDONALD,JOHN D-Bright Orange for the Shroud-1972-Lippincott-1st ed (x7,dj) 135.00

MACDONALD,JOHN D-Cinnamon Skin-NY-1982-Harper-1st ed (j4,dj) 10.00

MACDONALD,JOHN D-Condominium-Lond-1977-Hale-1st Brit ed (q4,f,dj) 25.00

MACDONALD,JOHN D-Contrary Pleasure-NY-1954-Appleton Century Crofts-1st ed (gg8,dj) 65.00

MACDONALD,JOHN D-Crossroads-NY-1959-Simon-1st ed (d4,brwnd pgs,dj) 75.00

MACDONALD,JOHN D-Dead Low Tide-Lond-1976-Hale-1st Brit hdbk ed (s4,vf,dj) 55.00

MACDONALD,JOHN D-Deep Blue Good By-Phila-1975-Lippincott-1st hdbk ed (d4,sp slant,dj) 75.00

MACDONALD,JOHN D-Dress Her in Indigo-1971-Lippincott-1st hdcov ed (x7,vf,f dj) 175.00

MACDONALD,JOHN D-Executioners-NY-1958-Simon-1st ed (f4,sl fade t.e.,dj chip) 75.00

MACDONALD,JOHN D-Free Fall in Crimson-1981-Harper-1st ed (n9,sl tn dj) 15.00

MACDONALD,JOHN D-Free Fall in Crimson-NY-1981-Harper-1st ed (d4,f,dj) 12.50

MACDONALD,JOHN D-Girl in the Plain Brown Wrapper-1968-Lippincott-1st hdcov ed (x7,f,dj) 125.00

MACDONALD,JOHN D-Good Old Stuff-NY-1982-Harper-1st ed (e4,f,dj) 15.00

MACDONALD,JOHN D-Green Ripper-NY-1979-Lippincott-1st ed (f4,f,dj) 15.00

MACDONALD,JOHN D-House Guests-1965-Dbldy-1st ed (x7,f,dj) 85.00

MACDONALD,JOHN D-Last One Left-1967-Dbldy-1st ed (x7,dj) 40.00

MACDONALD,JOHN D-Long Lavender Look-1972-Lippincott-1st Amer hdcov ed (x7,vf,f dj) 165.00

MACDONALD,JOHN D-Murder for the Bride-Lond-1977-Hale-1st Brit hdbk ed (s4,vf,dj) 55.00

MACDONALD,JOHN D-No Deadly Drug-NY-1968-Dbldy-1st ed (g4,f,dj) 20.00

MACDONALD,JOHN D-One Fearful Yellow Eye-Phila-1977-Lippincott-1st hdbk ed (e4,dj) 110.00

MACDONALD,JOHN D-Please Write for Details-1959-S&S-1st ed (x7,f,dj) 85.00

MACDONALD,JOHN D-Purple Place for Dying-Phila-1976-Lippincott-1st hdbk ed (j4,dj) 50.00

MACDONALD,JOHN D-Quick Red Fox-1974-Lippincott-1st Amer hdcov ed (x7,vf,f dj) 175.00

MACDONALD,JOHN D-Scarlet Ruse-NY-1973-Lippincott-1st US hdbk ed (e4,f,sl wn dj) 110.00

MACDONALD,JOHN D-Seven-Lond-1974-1st Brit,1st hdbk ed (s5,vf,dj) 35.00

MACDONALD,JOHN D-Seven-Lond-1974-Hale-1st Brit & 1st hdbk ed (s4,vf,dj) 50.00

MACDONALD,JOHN D-Tan and Sandy Silence-Phila-1979-Lippincott-1st hdbk ed (f4,dj) 60.00

MACDONALD,JOHN D-Turquoise Lament-1973-Lippincott-1st ed (x7,f,dj) 125.00

MACDONALD,JOHN D-Wine of the Dreamers-NY-(1951)-Greenberg-1st ed (v5,f,sl wn dj) 100.00

MACDONALD,JOHN D-Wine of the Dreamers-NY-(1951)-Greenberg-auth 1st hdbk bk-1st ed (a5) 125.00

MACDONALD,JOHN D-You Live Once-Lond-1976-Hale-1st Brit & 1st hdbk ed (s4,vf,dj) 50.00

MACDONALD,JOHN ROSS-Ivory Grin-NY-1952-Knopf-1st ed (bb1,sl chip dj) 150.00

MACDONALD,MURRAY-Watercolor Painting: A Dialogue-Edmonton-1982-U of Alberta-lng 8vo-xvi,57p-wtrcol illus-1st ed (aa7,dj) 25.00*

MACDONALD,PHILIP-Crime Conductor-1931-CC-1st Amer ed (s10) 15.00

MACDONALD,PHILIP-Dark Wheel-NY-1948-Morrow-1st ed (f4,f,chip dj) 10.00

MACDONALD,PHILIP-Link-NY-1930-Dbldy CC-1st US ed (e4,dj) 45.00

MACDONALD,PHILIP-List of Adrian Messenger-GC-1959-Dbldy CC-1st ed (w5,f,sl wn dj) 35.00

MACDONALD,PHILIP-Menace-NY-1933-Dbldy CC-1st US ed (g4) 20.00

MACDONALD,PHILIP-Noose-NY-1930-Dial-1st US ed (h4) 25.00

MACDONALD,PHILIP-Polferry Riddle-NY-1931-Dbldy CC-1st US ed (d4,sp slant,sp chip dj) 60.00

MACDONALD,PHILIP-Polferry Riddle-NY-1931-Dbldy-1st Amer ed (p4,sl wn) 25.00

MACDONALD,PHILIP-Rasp-NY-1925-MacVeagh-1st US ed (f4) 20.00

MACDONALD,ROSS-Barbarous Coast-1956-Knopf-1st ed (x2,dj) 250.00

MACDONALD,ROSS-Black Money-1966-Knopf-1st ed (x7,vf,f dj) 165.00

MACDONALD,ROSS-Black Money-NY-(1966)-Knopf-1st ed (s6,sl wn dj) 75.00

MACDONALD,ROSS-Blue Hammer-1976-Knopf-1st ed (x7,dj) 17.00

MACDONALD,ROSS-Far Side of the Dollar-NY-1965-Knopf-1st ed (f4,f,sl wn dj) 75.00

MACDONALD,ROSS-Goodbye Look-1969-Knopf-1st ed (s10,dj) 22.50

MACDONALD,ROSS-Goodbye Look-1969-Knopf-1st ed (x7,f,dj) 50.00

MACDONALD,ROSS-Instant Enemy-1968-Knopf-1st ed (p9,vf,dj) 90.00

MACDONALD,ROSS-Instant Enemy-1968-Knopf-1st ed (s9,f,dj) 60.00

MACDONALD,ROSS-Lew Archer,Private Detective-NY-1977-Mysterious-ltd to 250c,nbrd,autg-acetate dj-1st ed (e4,as new in dj & box) 150.00

MACDONALD,ROSS-Meet Me at the Morgue-1953-Knopf-1st ed (x7,f,dj) 400.00

MACDONALD,ROSS-Self Portrait-Santa Barbara-1981-Capra Pr-1st ed (bb2,f,dj) 35.00

MACDONALD,ROSS-Self Portrait-Santa Barbara-1981-Capra-1st ed (r4,f,dj) 25.00

MACDONALD,ROSS-Sleeping Beauty-NY-1973-1st ed (q5,dj) 22.50

MACDONALD,ROSS-Sleeping Beauty-NY-1973-Knopf-1st ed (f4,f,dj) 15.00

MACDONALD,ROSS-Trouble Follows Me-1946-DM-scarce-1st ed (x7,dj sl tn & chip) 1,000.00

MACDONALD,ROSS-Underground Man-NY-1971-Knopf-1st ed (bb2,f,dj) 50.00

MACDONALD,ROSS-Underground Man-NY-1971-Knopf-1st ed (w5,f,f dj) 35.00

MACDONALD,ROSS-Wycherly Woman-NY-1961-Knopf-1st ed (e4,dj sl tn,fray) 75.00

MACDONALD,ROSS-Zebra Striped Hearse-1962-Knopf-1st ed (x7,vf,dj) 225.00

MACDONNELL,KEVIN-Eadweard Muybridge-Bost-1972-Little,Brown-160p-photos-1st ed (cc9,as new in dj) 35.00

MACDOUGALL,ALICE F-...COOK BOOK-Bost-1935-Lothrup,Lee & Shepard-292p-silv bds,frntis,photos-Bitting 298 (l6) 25.00

MACDOUGALL,ALICE F-Coffee and Waffles-GC-1926-Dbldy,Page-115p-floral bds,papr labls (l6,wn bds) 15.00

MACDOUGALL,ALICE F-Secret of Successful Restaurants-NY-1929-Harper & Bros-245p-blu bds,frntis,illus (n6,soil bds) 18.00

MACDOUGALL,ALLAN R-Gourmet's Almanac-NY-1930-Covici-316p-orng cl,illus (q8,sp fade) 16.50

MACDOUGALL,ARTHUR R-Dud Dean & His Country-NY-1946-8vo-171p-ltd to 450c,nbrd,autg,illus by M Weiler (m3) 85.00

MACDOUGALL,ARTHUR R-Trout Fisherman's Bedside Book-NY-1963-12mo-224p-illus-1st prntg (m3,vf,dj) 15.00

MACDOUGALL,ARTHUR R-Under a Willow Tree-NY-1946-8vo-200p-illus (m3,vf,fray dj) 17.50

MACDOUGALL,ARTHUR R-Where Flows the Kennebec-NY-1947-8vo-181p-illus,M Weiler (m3,f,dj) 22.50

MACDOWELL,SYL-Western Trout-NY-1948-8vo-261p-photos-1st ed (m3,f,dj) 25.00

MACE,JEAN-History of a Mouthful of Bread-NY-1868-399p-1st Amer ed (dd3) 75.00

MACENTEE,MAIRE-Heart Full of Thought-Dublin-1959-Dolmen Pr-wrps-1st ed (z8,f) 15.00

MACFADDEN,BERNARD-Hair Culture-NY-1922-Phys Culture Corp-sm 8vo-xii,199p-blu cl,frntis,38 illus-1st ed (mm8,bump) 25.00*

MACFADDEN,HARRY A-Rambles in the Far West-Hollidaysburg-(1906)-278p-grn cl-Howes M94-1st ed (jj4) 50.00

MACFADDEN,MARY-Dumbbells and Carrot Strips-(1953)-Holt-245p-brwn bds-1st ed (q8,dj) 12.50

MACFARLAN,ALLAN A-Modern Hunting with Indian Secrets-Harrisburg-1971-8vo-223p-illus (m3,vf,dj) 10.00

MACFIE,HARRY-Wasa,Wasa-NY-1951-8vo-288p-1st ed (m3,f,sl chip dj) 15.00

MACGRATH,HAROLD-Blue Rajah Murder-NY-1930-Dbldy CC-1st ed (e4,f,dj) 25.00

MACGREGOR,BRUCE A-South Pacific Coast-Berkeley-1968-280p-1st ed (n4,f,dj) 25.00

MACGREGOR,DANIEL A-Memoir of...-Tor-1891-Tor Baptist College-8vo-248p-blu cl,frntis-1st ed (mm8,hngs crack) 35.00*

MACGREGOR,DAVID R-Tea Clippers-Annapolis-1983-Naval Inst Pr-4to-256p-chrts,drwngs-2nd ed (pp1,sl rub dj) 30.00

MACGREGOR,FRANCES C-Twentieth Century Indians-NY-1941-Putnam's-4to-127p-map e.p.-1st ed (cc4) 20.00

MACGREGOR,J C-Peter Fidler-Tor-1966-M&S-8vo-xix,265p-e.p. maps,illus,maps-1st ed (cc7,dj) 50.00*

MACGREGOR,J G-Blankets and Beads-Edmonton-1949-Inst of Applied Arts-8vo-278p-wrps,illus-1st ed (cc7,scuff,autg) 15.00*

MACGREGOR,J G-Edmonton Trader-Tor-1963-M&S-8vo-262p-e.p. maps,18p illus,-1st ed (cc7,dj) 65.00*

MACGREGOR,J G-Paddle Wheels to Bucket Wheels-Tor-1974-M&S-8vo-xii,190p-e.p. maps & illus,illus-1st ed (cc7,dj) 50.00*

MACGREGOR,JESSIE-Gardens of Celebrities and Celebrated Gardens in and Around London-Lond-1918-Hutchinson-326p-cl,20 col plts (x6) 35.00

MACGREGOR,JOHN-Tibet-NY-1970-373p-28 plts,8 maps-1st ed (p10,as new in dj) 45.00

MACGREGOR-MORRIS,PAMELA-Spinners of the Big Top-Lond-1960-Chatto & Windus-140p-photos-1st ed (v8,sl soil cov) 25.00

MACH,ELYSE-Great Pianists Speak for Themselves-Lond-1981-Robson-1st ed (u4,as new in dj) 12.00

MACHARDY,CHARLES-Ice Mirror-Lond-1971-380p-1st ed (q10,as new in dj) 20.00

MACHARG,WILLIAM-Affairs of O'Malley-NY-1940-Dial-1st ed (c10,dj chip,edge wn) 75.00

MACHEN,ARTHUR-Dog and Duck-NY-1924-Knopf-cl-precedes Brit ed-1st ed (n8) 25.00

MACHETANZ,SARA-Howl of the Malemute-NY-1961-Sloane-xiv,204p-photos-1st ed (ll8,dj) 25.00

MACINNES,C M-In the Shadow of the Rockies-Lond-1930-Rivingtons,Convent Grdn-8vo-viii,347p-g dec blu cl,frntis,8 illus,2 fldg col maps rear e.p.-Peel 3203-scarce-1st ed (mm8,cov sl dmpstnd & bump) 200.00*

MACINNES,C M-In the Shadow of the Rockies-Lond-1930-viii,347p-2 maps-Peel 3203 (bb9) 225.00

MACINNES,COLIN-Absolute Beginners-NY-1960-Macmillan-1st US ed (hh5,dj) 15.00

MACINNES,COLIN-City of Spades-NY-1958-Macmillan-1st US ed (hh5,tn dj) 15.00

MACINNES,HAMISH-Call Out-Lond-1974-1st ed (v9,f,sl sun dj) 27.50

MACINNES,HAMISH-High Drama-Seattle-1980-208p-1st US ed (p10,as new in dj) 20.00

MACINNES,HELEN-Horizon-Bost-1946-223p-1st US ed (q10,f,dj) 20.00

MACINNES,HELEN-Salzburg Connection-1968-Harcourt-1st ed (s10,soil dj) 10.00

MACINNES,HELEN-Snare of the Hunter-NY-1974-Harcourt-1st US ed (j4,f,dj) 10.00

MACINNES,JOE-Underwater Man-NY-1975-Dodd,Mead-142p-cl,photos-1st ed (z7,dj) 30.00

MACINTYRE,CAPT DONALD-Narvik-NY-(1959,60)-Norton-8vo-224p-12p photos-1st US ed (cc5,dj) 20.00

MACINTYRE,NIEL-Great Heart-NY-(1919)-Wm Edwin Rudge-242,(1)p-cl (d1) 25.00

MACK,CONNIE-My 66 Years in the Big Leagues-1950-Winston-1st ed (p7,pg brwng,dj) 40.00

MACK,CONNIE-My 66 Years in the Big Leagues-1950-Winston-1st ed (s8,dj) 45.00

MACK,EDWARD C-Peter Cooper, Citizen of New York-NY-(1949)-DS&P-8vo-432p-16p photos-1st ed (cc5,f,dj sl chip,tn) 25.00

MACK,EDWIN F-Old Monroe Street-Chig-1914-83p-bds (n1,sl soil bds) 10.00

MACK,EFFIE M-Mark Twain in Nevada-NY-1947-Scribner's-398p-drwngs,photos-1st ed (ff4,chip dj) 35.00

MACK,GENE-Hall of Fame Cartoons of Major League Ball Parks-1947-Globe-drwngs,TP orig-1st ed (s8) 80.00

MACK,GENE-Hall of Fame Cartoons of Major League Ball Parks-1947-Globe-oversize papr (ff2,f) 100.00

MACKANESS,GEORGE-Life of Vice Admiral William Bligh R.N,F.R.S.-NY,Tor-ca.1931-Farrar & Rinehart-8vo-2 vols in one,grn cl,369p,348p+bibliog,index & fldg map at rear,chrts,engrvngs (nn1,sl fade) 50.00

MACKANESS,GEORGE-Life of Vice Admiral William Bligh R.N.,F.R.S.-NY,Tor-ca.1931-F&R-2 vols in one-fldg map at end,illus (p8,wn dj) 65.00

MACKAY,H H-Fishes of Ontario-Tor-1963-8vo-300p-illus-1st ed (m3,f) 45.00

MACKAY,JOHN-Mark!-NY-1956-4to-121p-illus,photos (m3,f,dj) 27.50

MACKAY,M S-Cow Range & Hunting Trail-NY-1925-243p-photos,illus,C M Russell-scarce (gg3,f,chip dj) 350.00

MACKAY,SAMPSON-Picturesque Boulder-Boulder-1901-folio-44p-wht & silv dec cl,photos(incl dbl pg) (bb9) 125.00

MACKAYE,BENTON-Expedition Nine-Wash D.C.-1969-8vo-50p-illus (m3,vf) 15.00

MACKAYE,MILTON-Dramatic Crimes of 1927-NY-1928-CC-1st ed (x9) 25.00

MACKELLAR,JEAN S-Hawaii Goes Fishing-1956-8vo-160p-illus (m3,vf) 12.50

MACKENTY,JOHN G-Duck Hunting-NY-1953-8vo-206p-photos (m3,vf,sl fray dj) 16.00

MACKENZIE RIVER TRIBES-(Ottawa)-1938-Nat Mus of Can-6p-prtd wrps,illus,map-anthro lflt #3 (k10) 10.00*

MACKENZIE,ALEXANDER-Alexander Mackenzie's Voyage to the Pacific Ocean in 1793-Chig-1931-Donnelley-384p-frntis,map-Lakeside Classic (cc4) 30.00

MACKENZIE,ALEXANDER-Voyages From Montreal...in 1789 and 1793...Rise and State of the Fur Trade-NY-1902-New Amsterdam Bk-12mo-2 vols-gry cl,fldg map-rprnt (p8,sp drknd) 40.00

MACKENZIE,COMPTON-Cats' Company-NY-1961-Tapinger-photos-1st US ed (y1,f,dj) 25.00

MACKENZIE,COMPTON-Gallipoli Memoirs-Lond-(1929)-Cassell-8vo-blk cl-1st ed (x10,sl fox,dj sp drknd) 50.00

MACKENZIE,COMPTON-Lunatic Republic-Lond-1959-Chatto & Windus-1st ed (e3,dj) 30.00

MACKENZIE,COMPTON-Old Men of the Sea-NY-1924-Stokes-1st ed (x1,weak hng,dj) 30.00

MACKENZIE,COMPTON-Rival Monster-Lond-1952-1st ed (y7,dj,pres) 50.00

MACKENZIE,COMPTON-Savoy of London-Lond-(1953)-Harrap-142p-pict bds,col & b&w photos-1st prtg (q8) 16.50

MACKENZIE,G MUIR-Turks,the Greeks, & the Slavons-Lond-1867-thk 8vo-687p-3/4 tan calf,illus,maps (a3,rbnd) 175.00

MACKENZIE,J P-Birds in Peril-1977-Houghton Mifflin-191p-20 col plts-1st ed (bb3,f,dj) 14.00

MACKENZIE,JEANNE-Murder of Maria Marten...-NY-1948-Pellegrini & Cudahy-1st ed thus (z3,rear bds wtrstnd) 12.50

MACKENZIE,MURDO-View of the Salmon Fishery of Scotland-Edinburgh,Lond-1860-8vo-182p (m3) 50.00

MACKEY,W F-American Bird Decoys-1979-Schiffer-4to-256p-8 col plts,illus (bb3,f,dj) 20.00

MACKIE,PAULINE B-Ye Little Salem Maide-Bost-1898-Lamson,Wolffe-gry cl,t.e.g.,illus-1st ed (nn3) 12.50

MACKINNEY,LOREN-Early Medieval Medicine with Special Reference with France and Chartres-Balt-1937-247p-1st ed (dd3) 75.00

MACKINNON,ALLAN-Assignment in Iraq-NY-1960-Dbldy CC-1st US ed (e4,f,sl wn dj) 12.50

MACKINNON,ALLAN-Cormorant's Isle-NY-1962-Dbldy CC-1st US ed (f4,f,dj) 12.50

MACKINNON,ALLAN-Money on the Black-NY-1946-Dbldy CC-1st US ed (f4,yel pgs,dj) 15.00

MACKINNON,ALLAN-Summons from Baghdad-NY-1958-Dbldy CC-1st US ed (e4,f,dj) 12.50

MACKINNON,COL DANIEL-Origin and Services of the Coldstream Guards-Lond-1833-2 vols-1/2 blu cl,mrbld bds,2 maps,14 plts-rare-1st ed (kk2,rbnd) 350.00

MACKSEY,KENNETH-Tanks-Lond-1979-304p-illus-1st ed (b7,f,dj) 25.00

MACKWORTH-PRAED,C W-African Handbook of Birds-Lond-(1952)&(1955)-Longmans-2 vols-1st ed (b9,dj) 150.00

MACKWORTH-PRAED,C W-Birds of the Southern Third of Africa: African Handbook of Birds, Series Two-Lond-1962,1963-Longmans-2 vols (c9,as new in djs) 140.00

MACKWORTH-PRAED,C W-Birds of West Central and Western Africa-1970,73-Longmans-2 vols-93 col plts,maps-1st ed (bb3,dj) 150.00

MACLACHLAN,PATRICIA-Arthur, For the Very First Time-NY-(1980)-Harper & Row-117p-cl & bds,illus,L Bloom-1st ed (r3,f,dj) 12.00

MACLANE,JOHN F-Sagebrush Lawyer-NY-(1953)-Pandick Pr-x+177p-tan cl,plts-1st ed (e2,few cov spots) 65.00

MACLAREN-ROSS,J-Memoirs of the Forties-Lond-1965-1st ed (y7,dj) 35.00

MACLAURIN,W RUPERT-Invention and Innovation in the Radio Industry-NY-1949-Macmillan-xxii+304p-gry cl,plts,text illus-1st ed (j2,dj) 45.00

MACLAY,EDGAR S-History of American Privateers-NY-1899-519p-cl-Howes M 149-1st ed (h1,cov spot,sm sp snag) 25.00

MACLEAN,ALISTAIR-Bear Island-Lond-1971-Collins-1st ed (p4,dj) 35.00

MACLEAN,ALISTAIR-Captain Cook-GC-1972-Dbldy-8vo-193p-map e.p.,col plts-1st ed (p8) 30.00

MACLEAN,ALISTAIR-Golden Gate-Lond-1976-Collins-1st Brit ed (bb1,f,dj) 20.00

MACLEAN,ALISTAIR-Golden Rendevous-Lond-1962-Collins-1st ed (e4,f,dj) 20.00

MACLEAN,ALISTAIR-Guns of Navarone-Lond-1957-Collins-1st ed (r4,dj) 40.00

MACLEAN,ALISTAIR-Ice Station Zebra-1963-Dbldy-1st Amer ed (x7,dj) 25.00

MACLEAN,ALISTAIR-Puppet on a Chain-Lond-1969-Collins-1st ed (q4,f,dj) 40.00

MACLEAN,ALISTAIR-Satan Bug-1962-Scribners-1st Amer ed (x7,dj) 55.00

MACLEAN,ALISTAIR-Where Eagles Dare-1967-Dbldy-1st ed (s10,dj) 12.50

MACLEAN,DAVID G-ED.-Prisoner of the Rebels in Texas-Decatur-1978-178p-cl (c1,f,dj) 25.00

MACLEAN,DAVID G-Gene Stratton Porter-Decatur-1976-117p-cl,ltd to 1500c,nbrd,autg (n1,sl wn dj) 37.50

MACLEAN,GEORGE M-Elements of Somatology-NY-1859-John Wiley-124p+ads-blk cl,37 text figs-1st ed (j2,sl wn sp) 25.00

MACLEAN,NORMAN-River Runs Through It-Chig-1976-Univ of Chig Pr-auth 1st bk-1st ed (g8,f,dj) 100.00

MACLEAN,VIRGINIA-Much Entertainment-NY-(1973)-Liveright-oblng qto-86p-blk cl,photos-1st US ed (q8,f,dj) 20.00

MACLEAR,MICHAEL-Ten Thousand Day War-NY-(1981)-St.Martin's-368p-bds-1st ed (h1,f,dj) 15.00

MACLEISH,ARCHIBALD-America was Promises-NY-1939-1st ed (r2,f,sp sun dj) 25.00

MACLEISH,ARCHIBALD-Collected Poems,1917 to 1952-Bost-1952-Houghton Mifflin-1st ed (dd2,f,dj) 25.00

MACLEISH,ARCHIBALD-Fall of the City-NY-(1937)-Farrar and Rinehart-orng bds-1st ed (dd2) 35.00

MACLEISH,ARCHIBALD-Great American Fourth of July-(1975)-U of Pitt Pr-1st ed (dd2,f,dj) 35.00

MACLEISH,ARCHIBALD-Irresponsibles-NY-(1940)-DS&P-1st ed (d10,sl soil dj) 40.00

MACLEISH,ARCHIBALD-Letters of...1907 to 1982-Bost-1983-1st ed (m4,f,dj) 12.50

MACLEISH,ARCHIBALD-Panic, a Play in Verse-Bost-1935-HMCo-8vo-102p-1st ed (ee5,dj) 25.00

MACLEISH,ARCHIBALD-Poems 1924 to 1933-Bost-(1933)-1st ed (r2,f,dj sl chip & sp sun) 30.00

MACLEISH,ARCHIBALD-Riders on the Earth-Bost-1978-Houghton Mifflin-1st ed (dd2,f,dj,autg) 45.00

MACLEISH,ARCHIBALD-Riders on the Earth-Bost-1978-Houghton Mifflin-8vo-cl-1st ed (ll10,f,dj) 25.00

MACLEISH,ARCHIBALD-Time to Speak-Bost-1941-Houghton Mifflin-1st ed (dd2,f,sl wn dj) 30.00

MACLENNAN,HUGH-Precipice-Tor-(1948)-Collins-1st ed (pp2,f,dj) 50.00*

MACLENNAN,HUGH-Scotchman's Return and Other Essays-Tor-1960-Macmillan-1st Can ed (hh5,f,dj) 10.00

MACLENNAN,HUGH-Thirty and Three-Tor-1954-Macmlln of Can-1st Can ed (hh5,dj) 15.00

MACLEOD,CHARLOTTE-Next Door to Danger-1965-Avalon-1st ed (s10,dj) 160.00

MACLEOD,DAWN-Down to Earth Women-Edinburgh-1982-Wm Blackwood-xx,86p-photos-1st ed (mm4,as new) 28.00

MACLEOD,ROBERT-Iron Sanctuary-NY-1966-Holt-1st US ed (f4,f,dj) 15.00

MACLEOD,ROBERT-Place of Mists-NY-1970-McCall-1st Amer ed (s4,dj sl wn & sl soil) 25.00

MACMICHAEL,WILLIAM-Gold Headed Cane-NY-1932-Froben Pr-xxxii+223p-grn cl-1st ed thus (c2,dj) 25.00

MACMILLAN,C-Metaspermae of Minnesota Valley-1892-Minn Nat Hist Survey-826p-cl (bb3,rbnd) 40.00

MACMILLAN,DONALD-Four Years in the White North-NY-(1918)-Harper-8vo-426p-cl,illus-1st US ed (pp5,sp fade) 50.00*

MACMILLAN,JAMES-15 New Mexico Santos-Santa Fe-1941-Rydal Pr-7p text+15 col plts by Ewing+15 t.p. plts,ltd to 200c,French wrapper & box by Dreis-rare-1st ed (u7,box) 450.00

MACMILLAN,N-An Hour of Aviation-Phila-(1930)-sm 8vo-158p-cl-1st ed (s2) 25.00

MACMILLAN,THOMAS C-Inter Ocean Curiosity Shop for the Year 1888-Chig-1889-174p-dec cl-1st ed (t7) 30.00

MACMINN,EDWIN-On the Frontier with Colonel Antes-Camden-1900-Chew & Sons-513p-illus-ltd to 1000c-1st ed (bb4) 200.00

MACMULLEN,JERRY-Paddle Wheel Days in California-(1944)-Stanford U Pr-xiv+157p-grn & red cl-2nd prtg (b2,dj) 20.00

MACMULLEN,JERRY-Paddle Wheel Days in California-(1944)-Stanford Univ Pr-tall 8vo-xiv,157p-cl,illus,photos-1st ed (v1,dj) 40.00

MACMULLEN,JERRY-Star of India-Berkeley-1961-Howell North-8vo-133p-illus-1st ed (cc5,sp fade dj) 15.00

MACNAB,GORDON-Century of News & People in the East Oregonian 1875 to 1975-Pendleton-1975-397p-illus-1st prtg (r8,f,dj) 25.00

MACNEICE,LOUIS-Burning Perch-Lond-(1963)-Faber-1st ed (z8,vf,dj sp sl fade) 40.00

MACNEICE,LOUIS-Collected Poems, 1925 to 1948-Lond-(1949)-Faber-1st ed (z8,f,dj) 75.00

MACNEICE,LOUIS-Out of the Picture-Lond-(1937)-Faber-1st ed (z8,f,dj) 75.00

MACNEICE,LOUIS-Springboard, 1941 to 1944-NY-(1945)-Random-1st Amer ed (z8,f,dj sp pcs missng) 45.00

MACNEICE,LOUIS-Visitations-Lond-(1957)-Faber-1st ed (z8,vf,sl fray dj) 25.00

MACNEIL,NEIL-Hoover Report 1953-1955-NY-1956-344p-cl-1st ed so stated (n1,f,dj) 12.50

MACNICOL,MARY-Flower Cookery-NY-1967-Fleet Pr Corp-263p-grn cl,dec e.p. (m6) 35.00

MACOBOY,STIRLING-What Flower is That?-NY-(1973)-tall 8vo-317p-over 1000 col photos (j10,dj) 20.00

MACON MOORE, THE SOUTHERN DETECTIVE-NY-(1881)-Ogilvie-161p+ads-cl-Wright 2412 (n1) 60.00

MACOUN,JOHN-Manitoba and the Great North West-Lond-1882-lg 8vo-xxii,687p-orig cl,col frntis,maps,plts (bb9) 175.00

MACPHAIL,IAN-Thomas Nuttall-1983-Morton Arboretum-35p-wrps (x6,as new) 15.00

MACPHERSON,BYRON-Picturesque Washington-Seattle-(1945)-4to-44p-pict bds,240 drwngs,maps (r8) 12.00

MACQUARRIE,GORDON-Stories of Old Duck Hunters & Other Drivel-Harrisburg-1967-8vo-223p (m3,f,dj) 22.50

MACQUARRIE,HECTOR-Tahiti Days-(1920)-Geo Doran-266p-pict pastedown,photo plts-1st ed (u8,covs sl wn & sl soil) 35.00

MACSELF,A J-Plant Portraits and Plant Names-Lond-nd-Amateur Grdng-2 vols-cl,photos-scarce (x6,spot,soil cl) 30.00

MACVEIGH,SUE-Grand Central Murder-Bost-1939-Houghton-1st ed (k4,dj) 25.00

MADDEN,DAVID-Beautiful Greed-1961-Random-1st ed (m9,f,sp drknd dj) 60.00

MADDEN,HENRY M-German Travelers in California-SF-1958-Roxburghe Club-sm 8vo-cl sp over dec bds,col title leaf-ltd to 125c (p1) 60.00

MADDEN,R R-Mussulman-Lond-1830-Colburn & Bently-16mo-3 vols-1/2 lea & mrbld bds-1st ed (ll1) 225.00

MADDEN,R R-Phantasmata-Lond-1857-T C Newby-2 vols-Victorian cl-1st ed (y9,fox) 350.00

MADDOW,BEN-Faces-Bost-1977-NYGS-lg 4to-cl-1st ed (y3,f,f dj) 80.00

MADDOX,JOHN L-Medicine Man-NY-1923-Macmillan-330p-illus,errata (bb4) 75.00

MADEIRA,CRAWFORD C-Delaware and Raritan Canal-E Orange-1941-xi,96,(1)p-cl backd bds,2 plts-ltd to 175c,nbrd-v scarce (aa6) 150.00

MADELBAUM,DAVID G-Society in India-Berkeley-(1970)-U of Cal-8vo-2 vols-wrps-1st ed (y5) 25.00

MADISON,VIRGINIA-Big Bend Country-1955-UNM-illus,Six Guns 1434-1st ed (t8,some pnclg,sl chip dj) 30.00

MADISON,VIRGINIA-Big Bend Country-Albuq-1955-UNM-263p-photos-1st ed (a9,dj) 35.00

MADSEN,BRIGHAM-North of Montana-SLC-(1980)-298p-illus-1st ed (g7,f,dj) 35.00

MADSEN,DAVID-Black Plume-NY-1980-Simon-1st ed (g4,f,dj) 15.00

MADSON,JOHN-Ring Necked Pheasant-E Alton-1962-8vo-104p-wrps,cov by M Reece,photos,illus (m3,f) 20.00

MADSON,JOHN-Ruffed Grouse-Winchester-1969-103p-cov dec,wrps,coated papr,photos (gg3,sl crease) 20.00

MADSON,JOHN-Up on the River-NY-1985-276p-illus-1st ed (t7,dj) 12.50

MAEDER,HERBERT-Mountains of Switzerland-NY-1969-288p-b&w & col photos,2 fldg-1st US ed (p10,f,dj) 30.00

MAEGRAITH,BRIAN-Pathological Processes in Malaria and Blackwater Fever-Springfield-(1948)-Chas C Thomas-xii+430p-brwn cl,22 text figs-1st ed (d2) 25.00

MAERTH,OSCAR K-Beginning was the End-NY-(1974,71)-Praeger-8vo-236p-photos-1st US ed (gg5,dj tn) 12.50

MAERZ,A-Dictionary of Color-NY-1930-56 col plts-1st ed (kk4) 125.00

MAETERLINCK,MAURICE-Old Fashioned Flowers-Lond-1906-Allen-115p-cl,6 col plts by Elgood (x6,cl wn,innr hngs rnfrcd) 22.00

MAETERLINCK,MAURICE-Ruysbroeck and the Mystics-Lond-1894-Hodder & Stoughton-cl-1st ed (o8,sp wn) 45.00

MAFFITT,E M-Life and Services of John Newland Maffitt-NY,Wash-1906-Neale Publ-436p-illus,ports-v scarce-1st ed (z10,hngs rprd,scuff) 200.00

MAGALANER,MARVIN-Joyce: The Man, The Work, The Reputation-NY-1956-NYU Pr-1st ed (z8,f,dj) 25.00

MAGAN,WILLIAM-Umma-More, The Story of an Irish Family-Salisbury-(1983)-Element Bks-8vo-447p-41 photos-1st ed (cc5,f,f dj) 15.00

MAGGIO,JOE-Company Man-NY-(1972)-Putnam-1st ed (ff3,f,f dj) 50.00

MAGIDOFF,ROBERT-Russian Science Fiction-Lond-(1963)-Allen & Unwin-1st ed in Engl (j3,sl rub dj) 10.00

MAGILL,MARCUS-Murder Out of Tune-Phila-1931-Lippincott-1st US ed (g4,f,dj) 35.00

MAGNER,D-Art of Taming and Educating the Horse...-Battle Creek-1887-1088p-lea (h9) 85.00

MAGNER,D-Magner's ABC Guide to Sensible Horseshoeing-NY-1899-Werner-illus-1st ed (h9,cors bump) 85.00

MAGNIFICENT FORAGERS-Wash-1978-Nat Mus Natural Hist-4to-223p-illus (p8,f,f dj) 45.00

MAGNUS,HUGO-Superstition in Medicine-NY-1905-205p-1st Engl transl (dd3) 65.00

MAGNUSON,JAMES-Rundown-1977-Dial-1st ed (s7,f,dj) 25.00

MAGNUSSEN,DANIEL O-Peter Thompson's Narrative of the Little Bighorn Campaign 1876-Glendale-1974-Arthur Clark-fldg map-1st ed (u9,f) 75.00

MAGNUSSON,SIGURDUR-Stallion of the North-Rekjavik-1978-Iceland Review (h9,f) 35.00

MAGOFFIN,R V D-Magic Spades-NY-(1929)-150 illus-1st ed (d5,dj sp sl wn) 35.00

MAGOFFIN,SUSAN S-Down the Santa Fe Trail and Into Mexico-New Haven-1926-Yale U Pr-294p-illus-Howes M211-Rittenhouse 392-1st ed (d3) 125.00

MAGUIRE,JOHN F-Irish in America-NY-1868-Sadlier-1st ed (dd6) 50.00

MAGUIRE,ROBERT-Red Virgin Soil-Princeton-1968-PU Pr-1st ed (z9,t.e. spot,dj soil) 20.00

MAHAN,A T-Influence of Sea Power Upon History 1660 to 1783-Bost-1911-557p-blu cl-22nd ed (b7) 75.00

MAHAN,A T-Influence of Sea Power Upon the French Revolution and Empire 1793 to 1812-Bost-1894-Little,Brown-8vo-2 vols-blu cl,t.e.g.,g title & dec,maps-3rd ed (p8) 150.00

MAHAN,A T-Story of the War in South Africa-Lond-1900-322p-dec blu cl,frntis,fldg map-1st ed (b7) 150.00

MAHER,WILLIAM H-On the Road to Riches or How to Succeed in Life-Chig-1898-377,(12)p-cl (g1) 15.00

MAHON,DEREK-Poems, 1962 to 1978-Oxford-1979-OUP-1st ed (z8,vf,dj) 27.50

MAHON,MICHAEL P-Ireland's Fairy Lore-Bost-1919-Thomas J Flynn-cl,frntis-1st ed (o8) 65.00

MAHON,P J-Trials and Triumphs of the Catholic Church in America-Chig-(1907)-J S Hyland-4to-2 vols-3/4 lea,mrbld e.p.,illus-1st ed(?) (ff5) 75.00

MAHONING VALLEY-HISTORICAL COLLECTIONS OF THE...-Youngstown-1876-524p-cl,vol 1(all publ)-1st ed (l1,sl wn) 60.00

MAHONY,BERTHA-COMP.-Realms of Gold in Children's Books-NY-1929-Dbldy-796p-bds,illus-1st ed (s3) 40.00

MAHONY,D A-Prisoner of State-NY-1863-Carleton-414p (o7) 75.00

MAHOOD,RUTH I-ED.-Photographer of the Southwest Adam Clark Vroman 1856 to 1916-1961-Ward Ritchie Pr-4to-126p-clear dj,photos-1st ed (p1,f,dj) 65.00

MAHOOD,RUTH-ED.-Photographer of the Southwest: Adam Clark Vroman, 1856 to 1916-1961-Ward Ritchie-4to-125p-1st ed-1st ed (d3,cov soil) 50.00

MAIDEN,CECIL-Lighted Journey-(Vancouver)-(c.1948)-BC Electric Co-170p-illus,ports-Edwards & Lort #2443-Lother #1885 (k10,dj) 30.00*

MAILER,NORMAN-Advertisements for Myself-NY-1959-1st ed (q5,dj) 20.00

MAILER,NORMAN-American Dream-NY-1965-Dial-1st ed (ee2,f,dj) 35.00

MAILER,NORMAN-An American Dream-1965-Dial-1st ed (t9,dj sp rub) 20.00

MAILER,NORMAN-Armies of the Night-1968-NAL-1st ed (o9,dj) 20.00

MAILER,NORMAN-Barbary Shore-NY-(1951)-Rinehart-blk bds-1st ed (f2,edge-rub dj) 45.00

MAILER,NORMAN-Cannibals and Christians-NY-1966-Dial-1st ed (j3,f,dj sl tn & sp scuff) 15.00

MAILER,NORMAN-Existential Errands-Bost-(1972)-Little,Brown-1st ed (dd2,f,dj) 35.00

MAILER,NORMAN-Genius and Lust-NY-(1976)-Grove-1st ed (h3,f,dj) 15.00

MAILER,NORMAN-Marilyn: A Biography-NY-1977-illus-1st ed (z6,vf,sl rub dj) 50.00

MAILER,NORMAN-Naked and the Dead-NY-(1948)-Rinehart-auth 1st bk-1st ed (x1,dj) 300.00

MAILER,NORMAN-Naked and the Dead-NY-(1948)-Rinehart-wi publ colophon on cpyrt pg-1st ed (dd2,rprd dj) 175.00

MAILER,NORMAN-Of A Fire on the Moon-Bost-(1970)-1st ed (bb10,f,sl scuff dj) 20.00

MAILER,NORMAN-Prisoner of Sex-Bost-(1971)-Little,Brown-1st ed (dd2,f,dj) 35.00

MAILER,NORMAN-St.George and the Godfather-1972-Signet-wrps-1st ed (o9,f) 15.00

MAILER,NORMAN-Why are We in Vietnam-NY-(1967)-Putnam-1st ed (ff3,dj) 35.00

MAILS,THOMAS E-Mystic Warriors of the Plains-GC-(1972)-Dbldy-618p-col illus-1st ed (cc4,sl fox pgs,dj) 100.00

MAILS,THOMAS E-People Called Apache-(1974)-Prentice-Hall-4to-447p-illus-1st ed (cc4,dj) 90.00

MAILS,THOMAS E-Pueblo Children of the Earth Mother-GC-1983-lg format-2 vols-illus-1st ed (h7,f,dj) 90.00

MAILS,THOMAS-Mystic Warriors of the Plains-GC-1972-lg 4to-618p-illus-1st trd ed (g7,f,nick dj) 85.00

MAINE HISTORICAL SOCIETY-Collections, Volume III-Portland-1853-xvi+447p-blk cl,maps-1st ed (mm10) 65.00

MAINE,RENE-Trafalgar-Lond-1957-1st ed (b7,f,dj) 40.00

MAIR,CHARLES-Through the Mackenzie Basin...also Notes on the Mammals and Birds of Northern Canada by R MacFarlane-Tor-1908-Wm Briggs-494p-frntis,plts,ports,fldg map,errata slip-Peel #2004 (k10,wn,soil bndg) 40.00*

MAIR,LUCY P-Native Policies in Africa-NY-(1969)-Negro U Pr-8vo-303p-cl,6 maps-rprnt (y5) 18.00

MAIR,LUCY P-Studies in Applied Anthroplogy-Lond-1957-Athlone Pr-8vo-81p-cl-Lond Sch Econ Mono on Soc Anthro No.16-1st ed (y5,dj) 20.00

MAIROWITZ,DAVID Z-Radical Soap Opera-Lond-1974-Wildwood Hs-289p-1st ed (r1,pg edges brwng,dj) 30.00

MAISEL,ALBERT-Miracles of Military Medicine-NY-1943-373p-1st ed (dd3,dj) 30.00

MAISEL,ALBERT-Wounded Get Back-NY-1944-230p-1st ed (dd3,dj) 45.00

MAISSEN,EUGENE-French in Mexico & Texas-Salado-1961-Anson Jones-4to-illus-1st ed in Engl (u9) 75.00

MAITLAND,L J-Knights of the Air-NY-1929-roy 8vo-xvi,338p-buckram,frntis,31 plts,illus e.p. (s2,uncut) 50.00

MAJOR LEAGUE BASEBALL FACTS AND FIGURES-NY-(1948)-Dell-128,(2)p-wrps (n1) 15.00

MAJOR,CLARENCE-Reflex and Bone Structure-NY-(1975)-Fict Collective-1st ed (b5,as new in dj) 25.00

MAJOR,HARLAN-Basic Fishing From the Worm to the Fly-NY-1947-8vo-176p-illus (m3,vf,sl chip dj) 12.50

MAJOR,HOWARD-Domestic Architecture of the Early American Republic-Phila-1926-Lippincott-4to-(1),236,(2)p-cl,illus (cc10) 110.00

MAJOR,LETTIE N-C W Post, the Hour and the Man...-Wash-1963-Judd & Detweiler-4to-318p-cl,illus (cc3,f,dj) 75.00

MAJOR,RALPH H-Classic Descriptions of Disease, With Biographical Descriptions of the Authors-Springfield-1932-Chas C Thomas-xxviii+630p-blu cl,illus-1st ed (d2,dj soil & edge-wn) 90.00

MAJOR,RALPH-Fatal Partners, War and Disease-NY-1941-342p-1st ed (dd3) 50.00

MAJOR,RALPH-History of Medicine-Springfield-1954-2 vols-1st ed (dd3) 175.00

MAJORS,ALEXANDER-Seventy Years on the Frontier-Chig-1893-Rand,McNally-325p-blu cl,frntis,port,plts,ads-1st ed (v1,sl wn) 165.00

MAJORS,ALEXANDER-Seventy Years on the Frontier-Columbus-1950-Long's College Bk Co-325p-illus-Howes M232 (cc4,dj) 20.00

MAJORS,ALEXANDER-Seventy Years on the Frontier-Mpls-1965-325p-frntis,illus-Rittenhouse #394 (t7,dj) 17.50

MAKIN,WILLIAM J-Red Sea Nights-NY-1933-McBride-8vo-327p-17 illus-1st ed (jj5,f,dj) 30.00

MAKSIC,S-Primitive Art of New Guinea-Worcester-1973-sq 8vo-108 illus-1st ed (h10,dj sl tn & soil) 45.00

MALAMUD,BERNARD-Assistant-NY-1957-1st ed (s5,sl chip dj) 100.00

MALAMUD,BERNARD-Assistant-NY-1957-FS&C-1st ed (z2,f,f dj) 85.00

MALAMUD,BERNARD-Dubin's Lives-NY-(1979)-Farrar,Straus-1st trd ed (e3,f,dj) 20.00

MALAMUD,BERNARD-Fixer-NY-1966-FSG-1st ed (q2,dj) 45.00

MALAMUD,BERNARD-Idiots First-NY-1963-1st ed (q5,dj) 15.00

MALAMUD,BERNARD-New Life-NY-1961-1st ed (q5,dj) 15.00

MALAMUD,BERNARD-Tenants-(1971)-FS&G-1st ed (q9,sl chip dj) 15.00

MALAMUD,BERNARD-Tenants-NY-(1971)-Farrar,Straus-1st ed (e3,f,dj) 20.00

MALARTIC,Y-Tenzing of Everset-NY-1954-285p-illus-1st US ed (o10,f,dj) 15.00

MALET,CAPT-Annals of the Road-Lond-1876-Longmans Green-10 col plts-1st ed (h9,edge wn,ffep detached) 295.00

MALET,COL HAROLD-Historical Memoirs of the XVIIIth Hussars-Lond-1907-345p-dec blu cl,mrbld e.p.,15 plts(7 col)-1st ed (b7,f) 225.00

MALIN,MARIE C W-Legends of Le Detroit...-Detr-1884-317p-cl-2nd ed (l1,sl wn sp,sm stn on sp) 20.00

MALING,ARTHUR-Decoy-NY-1969-Harper-auth 1st bk-1st ed (d4,dj) 20.00

MALING,ARTHUR-Go Between-NY-1970-Harper-1st ed (f4,f,dj) 10.00

MALING,ARTHUR-Koberg Link-NY-1979-Harper-1st ed (e4,f dj) 12.50

MALING,ARTHUR-Lucky Devil-NY-1978-Harper-1st ed (e4,dj) 13.50

MALING,ARTHUR-Rheingold Route-Lond-1979-Gollancz-1st Brit ed (q4,vf,dj) 22.50

MALING,ARTHUR-Schroeder's Game-NY-(1977)-Harper & Row-1st ed (g3,f,dj) 30.00

MALING,ARTHUR-Snowman-NY-1973-Harper-1st ed (e4,dj) 15.00

MALINOWSKI,BRONISLAW-Crime and Custom in Savage Society-Lond-(1966)-Routledge & K Paul-8vo-132p-cl-8th prtg (y5,dj) 25.00

MALINOWSKI,BRONISLAW-Sex, Culture, and Myth-Lond-1963-R Hart-Davis-8vo-356p-papr over bds (y5,dj) 18.00

MALINS,PETER-Peter Malins' Rose Book-NY-(1979)-258p-55 photos-1st ed (x5,f,wn dj) 12.00

MALLAN,LLOYD-Day in the Life of a Supersonic Project Officer-np-1958-8vo-xiv,178p-cl,illus (s2) 30.00

MALLESON,G B-History of the French in India-Edinburgh-1909-John Grant-8vo-614p-red cl,3 maps(1 fldg)-reprnt (gg6) 40.00

MALLESON,G B-History of the French in India-Lond-1868-583p-grn cl,maps (kk2) 125.00

MALLESON,G B-Indian Mutiny of 1857-Lond-1891-Seeley-421p+ads-orig cl (gg6) 35.00

MALLESON,G B-Life of Warren Hastings-Lond-1894-Chapman & Hall-563p-blu cl,frntis (gg6,weak hng) 30.00

MALLET,CAPT THIERRY-Glimpses of Barren Lands-NY-1930-8vo-142p-illus (m3) 20.00

MALLET,CAPT THIERRY-Glimpses of the Barren Lands-NY-1930-142p-bds,illus-1st ed (t7,sp tn) 10.00

MALLET,CAPT THIERRY-Plain Tales of the North-NY-1925-8vo-136p-illus (m3) 17.50

MALLEY,JAMES-Beautiful Victim of Elm City-NY-1881-Ivers & Co-64p-pnk prtd wrps-2nd ed (ee6) 85.00

MALLIS,ARTHUR-American Entomologists-New Brunswick-(1971)-Rutgers U Pr-8vo-549p-211 illus-1st ed (dd5,sl tn dj) 30.00

MALLISON,SAM T-Great Wildcatter-Charleston-1953-Educ Fndtn-528p-1st ed (a9,dj) 35.00

MALLISON,SAM-Great Wildcatter-Charleston-1953-Educ Fndtn of WV-528p-cl,photos-1st ed (w3,f,dj) 37.50

MALLOCH,ARCHIBALD-Short Years-Chig-1938-Normandie Hs-xx+344p-beige cl,14 illus-1st ed (c2) 20.00

MALLOCH,P D-Life History & Habits of the Salmon Sea-Trout & Other Freshwater Fish-Lond-1912-4to-294p-photos (m3) 50.00

MALMSBURY,C A-Life, Labors and Sermons of Rev Charles Pitman...of the New Jersey Conference-Phila-(1887)-xvi,352p-cl,port (aa6) 35.00

MALONE,DOROTHY-How Mama Could Cook!-NY-1946-A A Wynn-178p (n6) 10.00

MALONE,MICHAEL P-Battle for Butte-Seattle-(1981)-U of Wash Pr-281p-illus (bb4,dj) 15.00

MALONE,MICHAEL-Dingley Falls-NY,Lond-(1980)-1st ed (k5,f,dj) 50.00

MALONE,MICHAEL-Painting the Roses Red-NY-(1974)-Random-auth 1st bk-1st ed (bb1,f,dj) 125.00

MALONE,P V-Sam Houston's Indians-San Antonio-1960-63p-1st ed (t7,f,dj) 12.50

MALONEY,T J-ED.-U S Camera 1935-NY-1935-Morrow-201p-spiral bnd cardbd covs,no dj as publ,214 photos-1st ed (cc9) 60.00

MALONEY,TOM-U S Camera 1953-NY-1952-US Camera Publ-384p-photos-1st ed (cc9,f,dj) 40.00

MALRAUX,ANDRE-Felled Oaks-NY-(1972)-HR&W-1st US ed (e3,f,sl chip dj) 15.00

MALTZ,ALBERT-Underground Stream-Bost-1940-Little,Brown-1st ed (v5,f,dj) 75.00

MALTZ,ALBERT-Way Things Are and Other Stories-NY-1938-Int'l-1st ed (w5,f) 30.00

MALTZ,MAXWELL-Evolution of Plastic Surgery-NY-1946-368p-illus-v rare-1st ed (dd3) 350.00

MALVERN,GLADYS-Curtain Going Up-NY-(1943)-Messner-8vo-239p-34 photos-1st ed (ee5,dj) 12.50

MALZBERG,BARRY-Guernica Night-Indpls-(1974)-Bobbs-Merrill-1st ed (h3,f,dj) 20.00

MALZBERG,BARRY-Screen-NY-1968-Olympia Pr-1st ed (v5,f,dj wn,tn) 15.00

MAMET,DAVID-Lakeboat-1981-Grove-1st ed (m9,vf,dj) 20.00

MAMOULIAN,ROUBEN-Abigayil-Greenwich-1964-NYGS-cl,illus,M Goodman-1st ed (m8,dj wn) 15.00

MAN RAY-Photographic Image-Woodbury-(1980)-Barron's-4to-cl-1st US ed (qq1,sl chip dj) 65.00

MAN RAY-Self Portrait-Bost-(1963)-Little,Brown-4to-cl-1st ed (qq1,f,dj) 95.00

MAN RAY-Self Portrait-Bost-(1963)-Little,Brown-8vo-cl-1st ed (y3,f,dj) 85.00

MANCHESTER ANGLER'S ASSOCIATION-Angler's Evenings - Second Series-Manchester-1882-8vo-283p-1/2 grn mor,mrbld bds & e.p.s,t.e.g.,illus (m3,f) 60.00

MANCHESTER,D W-Historical Sketch of the Western Reserve Historical Society-Cleve-1888-Williams Publ-39p-wrps-scarce-reprntd from Mag of Western Hist. (h1) 15.00

MANCHESTER,WILLIAM-Death of a President-NY-1967-Harper & Row-xvi,710p-maps-1st ed (o2,dj) 15.00

MANCHESTER,WM-Shadow on the Monsoon-GC-1956-1st ed (j5,dj) 25.00

MANCINI,J-Prostitutes and Their Parasites-Lond-(1963)-Elek-8vo-109p-1st Brit ed (oo7,f,dj) 20.00

MANDEL,OSCAR-ED.-Theatre of Don Juan-1963-U of Nebr Pr-8vo-731p-7 illus-1st ed (ee5,f,dj) 20.00

MANDEL,WILLIAM-Man Bites Dog-NY-1952-Nat'l Guard-22p-wrps (r1,pgs brwnd) 11.00

MANDELBAUM,DAVID G-Plains Cree-Saskatchewan-1979-Can Plains Res Cent-8vo-400p-wrps,illus (y5) 16.00

MANDELSTAM,OSIP-Journey to Armenia-Lond-(1980)-Faber & Faber-spiral bnd stiff prtd wrps-1st ed (cc2,f) 50.00

MANDERS,OLGA-Mrs.Manners' Cook Book-1968-Viking-178p-brwn cl,-orig ed (q8,dj) 18.50

MANDEVILLE,JOHN-Mandeville's Travels, Two Volumes-Cambridge-1953-Hakluyt Soc-8vo-blu cl,illus,maps-Ser.II,Vol CI,CII (pp1) 95.00

MANERO,NICK-Cook Out Barbecue Book-NY-(1962)-Arco-144p-red cl,photos-orig ed (q8,edgewn dj) 15.00

MANFORD,ERASMUS-Twenty Five Years in the West...-Chig-1885-Manford-413p-cl-rvsd ed (l1,sl rub & flecked) 25.00

MANFRED,FREDERICK-Riders of Judgment-NY-(1957)-Random-368p-1st ed (cc4,dj) 50.00

MANFRED,FREDERICK-Sons of Adam-1980-Crown-1st ed (t9,f,dj) 20.00

MANGAM,WILLIAM D-Clarks of Montana-np-1939-8vo-221p-stiff wrps-Six Guns #1439-rare-1st ed (oo8) 650.00

MANGAN,FRANK J-Bordertown, the Life and Times of El Paso Del Norte-El Paso-1964-Carl Hertzog-121p-1st ed (a9) 45.00

MANGELSDORF & REEVES-Origin of Indian Corn and Its Relatives-1939-Tex Ag Exp St-315p-wrps (x6,vf) 45.00

MANGELSDORF,PAUL-Corn Its Origin Evolution & Improvement-Cambridge-1974-Harvard-262p (x6,sl wn dj) 25.00

MANGUM,CHARLES S,JR.-Legal Status of the Negro-Chapel Hill-1940-UNC Pr-xii+436p-blu cl-1st ed (b2,dj) 25.00

MANHEIM,FRANK J-Garland of Weights-1967-FS&G-45 col illus-ltd to 1000c (cc8,dj) 65.00

MANIFOLD,LAURIE F-Christmas Window-Bost-1971-Houghton,Mifflin-cl-auth 1st bk-1st ed (aa9,f,f dj) 20.00

MANISCHEWITZ CO-Tempting Kosher Disher-Cin-1930-16mo-170p-pict bds,col photos-3rd ed (q8,hng weak) 16.50

MANKIEWICZ,DON-See How They Run-NY-1951-Knopf-auth 1st bk-1st ed (hh5,f dj) 25.00

MANKOWITZ,WOLF-Expresso Bongo-NY-(1961)-Yoseloff-1st US ed (hh5,dj) 10.00

MANKOWITZ,WOLF-Laugh Till You Cry-NY-1955-Dutton-1st US ed (hh5,dj) 10.00

MANLY,A STEWART-Hit and Miss or the Mystery of Nellie Clare-Chig-1889-Rhodes & McClure-428p-cl-first publ in 1883 under diff title-Wright 3597 (e1) 25.00

MANLY,HAROLD P-Radio and Electronic Dictionary-1931-300p-550 illus-1st ed (h6,f,dj) 10.00

MANLY,JOE-Fishing in the Great Smoky Mountains National Park & Adjacent Waters-Gatlinburg-1938-priv prntd-12mo-79p-photos-rare (m3) 65.00

MANLY,WILLIAM L-Death Valley in '49-Chig-1927-Donnelley-307p-frntis,map-Lakeside Classics (cc4) 35.00

MANLY,WILLIAM L-Death Valley in '49-NY-1929-524p-frntis,illus,map e.p.-rprnt Howes M255 (t7) 30.00

MANLY,WILLIAM L-Death Valley in '49-San Jose-1894-Pac Tree & Vine-498p-pict cl,illus-Howes M255-1st ed (cc4) 200.00

MANLY,WILLIAM L-Death Valley in '49-San Jose-1894-Pac Tree & Vine-octavo-498p-orig dec cl,port,illus-Graff 2670-1st ed (mm1) 225.00

MANLY,WILLIAM L-Jayhawkers' Oath and Other Sketches-LA-1949-W Lewis-168p-illus,fldg map-1st ed (d3,dj) 40.00

MANN,ARTHUR-Branch Rickey-1957-Houghton Mifflin-photos-1st ed (s8,dj) 20.00

MANN,ARTHUR-How to Play Winning Baseball-NY-(1953)-158p-cl-1st ed (n1,wn dj) 15.00

MANN,ARTHUR-Jackie Robinson Story-1950-G&D (ff2,dj) 17.50

MANN,CHARLES E-In the Heart of Cape Ann-Gloucester-(1896)-71p-cl,cpyrt date at bot of last pg of text (d1) 15.00

MANN,F W-Bullet's Flight from Powder to Target-Huntington-1942-8vo-384p-illus (m3) 40.00

MANN,F W-Bullet's Flight-WV-1948-384p-photos (gg3,f) 35.00

MANN,FELIX-Acupuncture-NY-1963-174p-1st ed (dd3,dj) 25.00

MANN,HEINRICH-Diana-NY-1929-1st Amer ed (m4,sl wn dj) 20.00

MANN,JACK-Decline and Fall of the New York Yankees-1967-S&S-1st ed (r7,f,dj) 15.00

MANN,JESSICA-Deadlier Than the Male-1981-Macmillan-1st ed (r9,vf,dj) 20.00

MANN,THOMAS-Joseph the Provider-NY-(1944)-Knopf-1st ed (s6,sl wn dj) 25.00

MANN,THOMAS-Letters of ...-NY-1971-Knopf-photos-1st US ed (b5,f,dj) 25.00

MANN,THOMAS-Letters of...to Caroline Newton-1971-priv prtd/Princeton U-orig glassine dj-1st ed (r2,f,sl tn dj) 25.00

MANN,THOMAS-Magic Mountain-NY-1939-1st US one vol ed (t5,sl chip dj) 35.00

MANN,THOMAS-Thomas Mann Diaries 1918 to 1939-NY-1982-Abrams-1st ed (z3,f,dj) 25.00

MANN,THOMAS-Transposed Heads-NY-1941-Knopf-1st US ed (a10,f,dj) 40.00

MANNIN,ETHEL-Dark Forest-Lond-(1946)-Jarrolds-1st ed (z8,f,dj) 13.50

MANNING,HARVEY-ED.-Mountaineering-Seattle-1960-430p-1st prtg (o10,f) 22.00

MANNING,HARVEY-North Cascades National Park-Seattle-(1969)-Superior-4to-142p-100 photos(incl 16 col)-1st ed (bb5,f,dj) 25.00

MANO,D KEITH-Bridge-GC-1973-Dbldy-1st ed (k3,f,dj) 25.00

MANO,D KEITH-Proselytizer-1972-Knopf-1st ed (x2,f,dj) 23.00

MANSFIELD,E D-Personal Memories-Cin-1879-Robt Clarke-viii+348p-grn cl-Howes M265-1st ed (b2) 75.00

MANSFIELD,EDWARD-Mexican War-NY-1848-Barnes-v scarce-Tuterrow 3225-Haferkorn p15-1st ed (u9,v wn cov) 160.00

MANSFIELD,H-Challenge-Lond-(1958)-8vo-236p-cl,frntis,10p plts-1st ed (s2,dj) 30.00

MANSFIELD,HAROLD-Vision-NY-(1956)-DSP-8vo-389p-8p photos-1st ed (gg5,dj sl chip,tn,autg) 15.00

MANSFIELD,KATHERINE-Dove's Nest and Other Stories-Lond-(1923)-Constable-2nd iss lacking the 't',line 8,pg 64,(after a 1st iss of 25 travelers' copies)-1st ed (w6) 35.00

MANSFIELD,KATHERINE-Dove's Nest and Other Stories-NY-1923-Knopf-1st US ed (w6) 20.00

MANSFIELD,KATHERINE-Journal-Lond-1927-Constable-orig cl-1st ed (aa9,sl rub sp,e.p. brwnd) 20.00

MANSFIELD,KATHERINE-Kathernine Mansfield's Letters to John Middleton Murry 1913 to 1922-NY-1951-Knopf-1st US ed (x9,dj tn,chip) 12.50

MANSFIELD,KATHERINE-Letters of...-Lond-1928-Constable-2 vols-1st ed (w6) 50.00

MANSFIELD,KENNETH-ED.-Trout & How to Catch Them-NY-1972-12mo-283p-illus (m3,vf,dj) 12.50

MANSFIELD,LOUIS C S-Solution of Codes and Ciphers-Lond-1936-A Maclehose-xii+162p-grn cl,text illus-1st ed (l2,fade sp,dj) 30.00

MANSFIELD,LOUISE-An Artist's Herbal-NY-1937-Macmillan-76p-38 plts (m6) 35.00

MANSFIELD,LOUISE-An Artist's Herbal-NY-1937-xiv,76p-38 plts-1st ed (x5,pastedowns brwng,sl soil) 21.00

MANSFIELD,ROBERT S-Towboats to the Orient-(Seattle)-(1970)-(PAC)-wrps-1st ed (ff3) 75.00

MANSFIELD,T C-Alpines in Colour and Cultivation-NY-1945-Dutton-278p-cl,80 col plts (x6,dj) 22.00

MANSFIELD,T C-Carnations in Colour and Cultivation-Lond-1951-Collins-243p-cl,64 col photos (x6,as new in dj) 25.00

MANTELL,GIDEON A-Petrifactions and Their Teachings...-Lond-1851-Henry G Bohn-xii+496p-red cl,115 text illus-1st ed (j2) 75.00

MANTER,ETHEL-Rocket of the Comstock-Caldwell-1950-Caxton-256p-blu cl,illus-1st ed (m2,dj) 25.00

MANTLE,BURNS-ED.-Best Plays of 1936,37 and the Year Book of Drama in America-NY-1937-Dodd,Mead-549p-cl (l1) 12.50

MANTLE,MICKEY-Education of a Baseball Player-1967-S&S-photos-1st ed (s8,dj) 17.50

MANTLE,MICKEY-Quality of Courage-1964-Dbldy-1st ed (s8,dj) 20.00

MANTON,JO-Elizabeth Garrett Anderson-NY-1965-382p-illus-1st ed (g10,dj) 25.00

MANUAL FOR STABLE SERGEANTS-Wash-1917-GPO-12mo-219p-1st prtg (h9) 45.00

MANUILSKY,D Z-Social Democracy, Stepping Stone to Facism...-NY-1934-Workers Libr-64p-wrps (r1) 20.00

MANVILLE,BILL-Saloon Society-NY-1960-DS&P-4to-125p-cl,photos by D Attie-1st ed (q3,chip dj) 75.00

MANYAN,GLADYS-Country Seasons Cookbook-(1974)-Crown-182p-grn cl,drwngs (q8,dj) 15.00

MAONGHAN,JAY-Chile,Peru and the California Gold Rush of 1849-Berkeley-U of Cal-1st ed (jj4,f,dj) 15.00

MAPLE SUGAR COOKBOOK-Battleboro-nd(ca.1890)-Vermont Mpl Sugar Exchng-16mo-43p-wrps,ads (k6,sl tn,soil) 50.00

MARAINI,FOSCO-Karakoram: the Ascent of Gasherbrum IV-NY-1961-319p-1st US ed (a4,f,dj tn) 70.00

MARAINI,FOSCO-Secret Tibet-Lond-1954-Readers Union-8vo-254p-yel dec cl,photos (gg6) 35.00

MARAINI,FOSCO-Secret Tibet-NY-1952-306p-60 photos-1st US ed (o10) 30.00

MARAINI,FOSCO-Where Four Worlds Meet-Lond-1965-290p-100 plts,fldg map-RU ed (p10,f,dj) 25.00

MARAINI,FOSCO-Where Four Worlds Meet-NY-1964-1st US ed (p10,f,dj) 30.00

MARBAKER,THOMAS D-History of the Eleventh New Jersey Volunteers from its Organization of Appomattox...-Trenton-1898-viii,364p-cl,illus (aa6) 200.00

MARBLE,M S-Die by Night-NY-1947-Rinehart-1st ed (g4,f,dj) 20.00

MARBURY,MARY O-Favorite Flies and Their Histories-Bost-1892-Houghton Mifflin-col plts-1st ed (ff7) 425.00

MARCANTONIO,VITO-We Accuse! The Story of Tom Mooney-NY-1938-Int'l Labor Def-wrps-1st ed (v5,f) 15.00

MARCH,FRANCIS A-History of the World War-Chig-1919-736p-cl (e1) 15.00

MARCH,J-Jolly Angler-Lond-1833-12mo-96p-orig bndg,illus-scarce-1st ed (m3) 110.00

MARCHAM,F G-ED.-Louis Agassiz Fuertes & the Singular Beauty of Birds-1971-Harper Row-folio-220p-60 col plts-1st ed (bb3,f,dj) 150.00

MARCHAM,FREDERICK G-Louis Agassiz Fuertes and the Singular Beauty of Birds-NY-1971-Harper & Row-220p-60 col plts (d9,as new in dj) 100.00

MARCHANT,WILLIAM-Privilege of His Company-Indpls-1975-BM-1st ed (x9,f,rub dj) 15.00

MARCIN,MAX-Wife He Never Saw-1911-E Nash-v scarce in dj-1st Brit ed (x7,fade sp,dj) 70.00

MARCONI WIRELESS TELEGRAPH COMPANY-Yearbook of Wireless Telegraphy-1914-742p-photos,fldg map in rear-rare-1st ed (h6,hng weak) 65.00

MARCONI,DEGNA-My Father Marconi-(1962)-320p-23 photos-1st ed (h6,f,dj) 25.00

MARCONI,DEGNA-My Father, Marconi-NY-(1962)-McGraw Hill-x+321p-bds-1st ed (a2,fray dj) 35.00

MARCOSSON,ISAAC F-Anaconda-NY-1957-310p-photos,map e.p.-1st ed (t7,f,dj) 15.00

MARCOSSON,ISAAC F-Wherever Men Trade-NY-1945-Dodd,Mead-263p-1st ed (e1,sl wn dj) 15.00

MARCUS,ADRIANNE-Chocolate Bible-(1975)-Putnam-279p-choc cov & e.p.,8p col plts,87 halftones-1st ed (q8,dj) 18.50

MARCY,COLONEL R B-Thirty Years of Army Life on the Border-NY-1866-Harper-442p-orig cl,plts-Howes M280-1st ed (v1,bndg spotted,sp wn) 150.00

MARCY,MARY E-Shop Talks on Economics-Chig-1911-Chas H Kerr-58p-stapled wrps (r1) 25.00

MARCY,MARY-Women as Sex Vendors-Chig-1918-Kerr-1st ed (w5) 60.00

MARCY,RANDOLPH-Border Reminiscences-NY-1872-396p+ads-pict cl,illus-2nd prtg (c4) 85.00

MARCY,RANDOLPH-Border Reminiscences-NY-1872-396p-pict cl,frntis,illus-Smith #6508 (t7) 125.00

MARCY,RANDOLPH-Exploration of the Red River of Louisiana in the Year 1852-Wash-1854-Tucker-Senate ed wi maps in separate case (u9,sl wn cov) 495.00

MARDEN,PHILIP S-Sailing South-Bost & NY-1921-303p-cl-1st ed (b1) 15.00

MARDEN,WILLIAM-Exile of Ellendon-GC-1974-Dbldy-1st ed (k3,f,dj) 20.00

MARDIKIAN,GEORGE-Dinner at Omar Khayyam's-(1952)-Viking-150p-dec red cl-4th prtg (q8) 20.00

MARDIKIAN,GEORGE-Dinner at Omar Khayyam's-NY-1944-Viking-cl-1st ed (m8,wn dj) 25.00

MARDSEN,E W-Greek and Roman Artillery-Oxford-1969-218p-illus,14 plts-1st ed (kk2,dj) 35.00

MAREAN,BEATRICE-Tragedies of Oak Hurst-Chig-1891-Donohue,Henneberry-401p-cl-Wright 3602 (l1,sl creased sp) 40.00

MARETT,R R-Psychology and Folk-Lore-Lond-1920-Methuen-cl-1st ed (l8) 25.00

MARGOLIN,VICTOR-American Poster Renaissance-(NY)-(1975)-Castle Bks-4to-cl-1st ed (oo6,dj) 55.00

MARGRETHE-After Confirmation...-Mpls-1900-Augsburg Publ-8vo-274p-1st US ed (w6) 65.00

MARIACHER,GIOVANNI-Italian Blown Glass-1961-McGraw Hill-285p-84 pasted in col photos (cc8,dj) 95.00

MARIL,LEE-Savor and Flavor-NY-(1944)-63p-dec bds,7 plts (x5,dj wn) 12.00

MARIN,JOHN-Letters of...-NY-1931-Priv Prtg for Amer Place-4to-114p-cl-ltd to 400c,nbrd-1st ed (t3) 150.00

MARINARO,V C-In the Ring of the Rise-NY-1976-184p-photos (gg3,f,dj) 25.00

MARINARO,VINCENT-Modern Dry Fly Code-NY-1950-8vo-269p-blu bndg variant,illus-1st ed (m3) 85.00

MARINGER,JOHANNES-Art in the Ice Age-NY-1953-Praeger-lg 4to-168p-buckrm,illus,col plts-1st ed (y4) 20.00

MARIO,THOMAS-Midnight Cookbook-(Chig)-(1971)-Cowles Bk Co-252p-blu bds (l6) 20.00

MARION,F-Wonderful Balloon Ascents-NY-1870-8vo-cl,frntis,39p plts-1st ed (s2,sp fade & wn) 150.00

MARION,J H-Notes of Travel Through the Territory of Arizona-Tucson-62p-map-1st ed (t7) 22.50

MARIPOSA-Hollywood Glamour Cook Book-Miami-(1940)-427p-dec grn cl-1st ed (q8,dj) 15.00

MARIUS,RICHARD-Coming of Rain-NY-1969-Knopf-auth 1st bk-1st ed (bb1,f,dj) 35.00

MARK,NORMAN-Mayors,Madams, and Madmen-Chig-(1979)-240p-bds-1st ed so stated (m1,f,dj) 12.50

MARKAM,VIRGIL-Death in the Dusk-NY-1928-Knopf-1st ed (j4,sl spot cov) 12.50

MARKEVITCH,MARIE A-Epicure in Imperial Russia-1941-Colt Pr-103p-pict red cl-ltd to 500c-1st ed (q8,f) 100.00

MARKHAM,CLEMENTS-Fighting Veres-Bost-1888-508p-blu cl,maps,illus-1st ed (b7) 100.00

MARKHAM,EDWIN-California the Wonderful-NY-1914-400p-dec brwn cl,col map frntis,64 illus-1st ed (p2) 30.00

MARKHAM,EDWIN-Children in Bondage-NY-1914-Hearst's Int'l Libr-411p-frntis-1st ed (r1,sp wn) 35.00

MARKHAM,GERVASE-Country Contentments-Lond-1631-12mo-118p-mod 1/4 brn calf,gilt,mrbld bds-rare-4th ed (m3,rbnd,f) 350.00

MARKHAM,GERVASE-Pleasures of Princes-Lond-1927-8vo-111p-ltd to 650c,nbrd,prchmnt bkd bds-scarce (m3) 65.00

MARKHAM,ROBERT-Colonel Sun-NY-1968-Harper-1st Amer ed (q4,f,dj) 25.00

MARKHAM,ROBERT-Colonel Sun-NY-1968-Harper-1st US ed (k4,sl spot edge,dj) 12.50

MARKINO,YOSHIO-Recollections & Reflections of a Japanese Artist-Phila-(1913)-Jacobs-262p-15 tip in plts(9 col) (v8,uncut,dj) 40.00

MARKINO,YOSHIO-When I Was a Child-Lond-1912-Constable-red cl,illus-1st ed (ll9) 50.00

MARKLAND,GEORGE-Pteryplegia-Derrydale-1931-4to-44p-ltd to 500c,nbrd,1/4 imit vel,blu bds,illus by R Ball (m3,f) 150.00

MARKS,ELAINE-Colette-New Brunswick-1960-RU Pr-1st ed (x9,dj tn,chip) 10.00

MARKS,ROWENA M-California Cooks-LA-(1970)-Ward Ritchie-166p-pict red cl,prntd on multicol stock,photos-1st ed (q8,f,dj) 20.00

MARLATT,DAPHNE-Here & There-Lantzville-1981-Island Writing Ser-(16)p-prtd wrps-ltd to 500c (aa2) 10.00*

MARLEN,GEORGE-Earl Browder-NY-1937-auth-1st ed (w5,f,sl wn dj) 50.00

MARLETT,MELBA-Escape While I Can-NY-1944-Dbldy CC-1st ed (k4,f,sl wn dj) 15.00

MARLETTE,JERRY-Electric Railroads of Indiana-Indpls-1959-158p+map-papr wi spiral bndg-1st ed (n4) 22.00

MARLOWE,GEORGE F-Coaching Roads of Old New England-NY-(1946)-Macmillan (f10,dj) 35.00

MARLOWE,HUGH-Candle for the Dead-NY,Lond-1966-Abelard-1st ed (g4,f,sl wn dj) 15.00

MARLOWE,KENNETH-Mr.Madam-LA-(1964)-Sherbourne Pr-8vo-246p-photos-1st ed (dd5,sp cocked,dj) 20.00

MARMELSZADT,WILLARD-Musical Sons of Aesculapius-NY-1946-116p-scarce-1st ed (dd3) 150.00

MARQUAND,J P-Black Cargo-NY-1925-Scribners-scarce-1st ed (x1,lacks dj) 35.00

MARQUAND,J P-Last Laugh, Mr.Moto-Lond-(1943)-Robt Hale-scarce-1st Brit ed (ff6,dj) 200.00

MARQUAND,J P-Mr.Moto is So Sorry-Bost-1938-Little,Brown-1st ed (w9,f,dj sp drknd & chip,wn) 325.00

MARQUAND,J P-Mr.Moto is So Sorry-Bost-1938-Little,Brown-scarce-1st ed (ff6) 45.00

MARQUAND,J P-Repent in Haste-Bost-1945-Little,Brown-1st ed (x1,f,dj) 25.00

MARQUAND,J P-Stopover:Tokyo-Bost-1957-LB-1st ed (x7,f,chip dj) 18.00

MARQUAND,J P-Stopover:Tokyo-Bost-1957-Little-1st ed (e4,f,dj) 12.50

MARQUETTE,DAVID-History of Nebraska Methodism. First Half-Century 1854-1904-Cin-1904-Wstrn Meth Bk Concern Pr-564p-cl (b1) 35.00

MARQUEZ,GABRIEL G-Autumn of the Patriarch-Lond-1977-1st Brit ed (s5,vf,dj) 75.00

MARQUEZ,GABRIEL G-In Evil Hour-NY et al-(1979)-Harper & Row-1st ed (a10,as new in dj) 45.00

MARQUEZ,GABRIEL G-Innocent Erendira-Lond-1979-J Cape-1st Brit ed (h8,f,f dj) 75.00

MARQUEZ,GABRIEL G-Innocent Erendira-NY-(1978)-Harper & Row-1st ed (k7,f,f dj) 45.00

MARQUEZ,GABRIEL G-Leaf Storm and Other Stories-Lond-(1972)-J Cape-orig bds-1st Engl transl (aa9,f,dj) 25.00

MARQUEZ,GABRIEL G-No One Writes to the Colonel & Other Stories-NY,Evanston,Lond-(1968)-Harper & Row-auth 1st bk-1st ed (b5,f,dj) 400.00

MARQUEZ,GABRIEL G-One Hundred Years of Solitude-NY-1970-1st US ed,1st iss (p5,sl chip dj) 450.00

MARQUEZ,GABRIEL G-One Hundred Years of Solitude-NY-1970-1st US ed,1st iss (r2,f,dj) 600.00

MARQUIS,DON-Almost Perfect State-GC-1927-Dbldy,Page-blk & red bds-1st ed (f2,edge-wn dj) 25.00

MARQUIS,DON-Best of...-GC-1946-Dbldy-1st ed (z3,dj sp sun,chip) 27.50

MARQUIS,DON-Chapters for the Orthodox-GC-1934-Dbldy-314p-1st ed (ll2) 15.00

MARQUIS,DON-Danny's Own Story-NY-1912-illus by E W Kemble-auth 1st bk-1st ed (r2,sl rub sp) 65.00

MARQUIS,DON-Hermione and Her Little Group of Serious Thinkers-NY-1916-Appleton-187p-1st ed (ll2) 15.00

MARQUIS,DON-Prefaces-NY-1919-Appleton-276p-illus-1st ed (ll2) 15.00

MARQUIS,T G-Canada's Sons on Kopje and Veldt-Tor-1900-490p-illus-scarce-1st ed (gg2,cov wn,sp v wn) 50.00

MARQUIS,THOMAS B-Keep the Last Bullet for Yourself-NY-1976-203p-frntis,maps-1st ed (t7,dj) 25.00

MARQUIS,THOMAS B-Sitting Bull & Gall, the Warrior-Hardin-1934-Marquis-8p-scarce-1st ed (u9) 25.00

MARR,JAMES PRATT-Pioneer Surgeons of the Woman's Hospital-Phila-1957-F A Davis-x+149p-brwn cl,nbrd cpy(#860)-1st ed (d2,box) 20.00

MARRIC,J J-Gideon's Badge-NY-1965-Harper-1st US ed (f4,dj) 10.00

MARRIC,J J-Gideon's Lot-NY-1964-Harper-1st ed (g4,as new in dj) 12.50

MARRIC,J J-Gideon's March-NY-1962-Harper-1st US ed (h4,f,dj) 10.00

MARRIC,J J-Gideon's Ride-NY-1963-Harper-1st US ed (h4,as new in dj) 12.50

MARRIOTT,ALICE-American Indian Mythology-NY-(1968)-211p-photos-1st prtg (v7,dj) 15.00

MARRIOTT,ALICE-Indians of the Four Corners-NY-1952-229p-1st ed (n10,dj) 45.00

MARRIOTT,ALICE-Marla: the Potter of San Ildefonso-Norman-1948-U of Okla-illus-1st ed (u9,dj wn,chip) 75.00

MARRIOTT,ALICE-Ten Grandmothers-Norman-1945-306p-cl-1st ed so stated (j1,sl wn dj) 15.00

MARRIOTT,ALICE-Valley Below-Norman-1949-243p-drwngs-1st ed (j7,dj) 30.00

MARRIOTT,ALICE-Valley Below-Norman-1949-U of Okla Pr-243p-drwngs-1st ed (cc4,dj) 35.00

MARRIOTT,ELSIE F-Bainbridge Through Bifocals-Seattle-1941-Gateway Co-8vo-292p-blu buckrm-1st ed (y4) 65.00

MARRON,EUGENIE-Albacora-NY-1957-8vo-214p-photos-1st prntg (m3,f,dj) 12.50

MARROW,EUGENE-Albacora-NY-1957-Random-1st prtg (nn5,f,f dj) 17.50

MARRYAT,CAP'T-Diary in America...-Phila-1839-Carey & Hart-12mo-263p-1 vol ed-papr cov bds-Howes M300 (n2,sl rub,spot,fox) 65.00

MARRYAT,CAPT FREDERICK-Diary in America-NY-1962-Knopf-8vo-487p-1st ed thus (ff5,f,dj) 15.00

MARRYAT,FLORENCE-There is No Death-NY-1973-Causeway Bks-8vo-vii,248p-frntis-1st ed (aa7,dj) 15.00*

MARRYAT,FREDERICK-Children of the New Forest-NY,Lond-(1927)-Scribner's-orig cl,pict cov labl,illus by S Good (aa9) 75.00

MARS,FLORENCE-Witness in Philadelphia-Baton Rouge-1977-LSU-296p-cl (v3,dj) 22.00

MARSDEN,PETER-Wreck of the Amsterdam-NY-1975-Stein & Day-8vo-290p-1/2 cl,photos-1st ed (pp1,dj) 35.00

MARSELLA,ELENA M-Quest for Eden-NY-1966-Philo Libr-cl-1st ed (o8,f,dj) 10.00

MARSH,CHARLES L-Not on the Chart-NY-1902-Stokes-col pict cov,frntis,map-1st ed (x1) 25.00

MARSH,CHARLES W-Recollections, 1837 to 1910-Chig-1910-Farm Implmnt News-xvi+299p-grn cl-1st ed (mm10,cov sl wn & rub) 85.00

MARSH,J B T-Story of the Jubilee Singers-Bost-nd-265p-cl-revsd ed (g1,back cov sl fleck) 15.00

MARSH,NGAIO-Black Beech and Honeydew-Bost-(1965)-Little,Brown-343p-1st ed (g9,sl fade,dj wn,tn) 45.00

MARSH,NGAIO-Clutch of Constables-Lond-1968-Collins-1st ed (p4,dj) 20.00

MARSH,NGAIO-Death in Ecstasy-NY-1941-Sheridan-1st US ed (f4,wn dj) 10.00

MARSH,NGAIO-Final Curtain-Bost-1947-Little-1st US ed (e4,f,dj) 30.00

MARSH,NGAIO-Grave Mistake-Lond-1978-Collins-1st ed (r4,vf,dj) 25.00

MARSH,NGAIO-Hand in Glove-Bost-1962-Little-1st US ed (g4,f,dj) 12.50

MARSH,NGAIO-Last Ditch-1977-Little,Brown-1st Amer ed (s10,dj) 12.50

MARSH,NGAIO-Light Thickens-1982-Little,Brown-1st Amer ed (s10,dj) 12.50

MARSH,NGAIO-Light Thickens-Lond-1982-Collins-1st ed (q4,f,dj) 25.00

MARSH,NGAIO-Night at the Vulcan-Bost-1951-Little-1st ed (e4,dj) 25.00

MARSH,NGAIO-Photo Finish-Lond-1980-1st ed (y7,dj) 10.00

MARSH,NGAIO-Spinsters in Jeopardy-Bost-1953-Little-1st ed (e4,dj) 15.00

MARSH,NGAIO-Vintage Murder-1940-Sheridan-1st ed (s10) 20.00

MARSH,NGAIO-When in Rome-Bost-1971-Little-1st US ed (j4,f,dj) 10.00

MARSH,O C-Odontornithes-1880-US Geol Explor 40th Para-201p-34 plts(incl fldg) (bb3,ex-libr) 125.00

MARSH,PATRICK-Breakdown-NY-1953-Longmans-1st US ed (f4,dj) 10.00

MARSH,PHILIP M-Works of Philip Freneau-Metuchen-1968-197p-cl (aa6) 30.00

MARSH,REV JOHN-Hannah Hawkins, the Reformed Drunkard's Daughter...-NY-1846-Amer Temp Union-72p-cl-4th ed (a1) 35.00

MARSH,RICHARD-Datchet Diamonds-NY-nd(1898?)-Amsterdam Bk Co-cancel title-scarce-1st Amer ed (gg8) 40.00

MARSH,RICHARD-Joss: A Reversion-1901-F V White-pict cl-1st ed (x7,sl fox e.p.) 195.00

MARSH,T W-Early Friends in Surrey and Sussex-Lond-1886-S Harris-8vo-162p-papr cov bds (y6,wn,soil,sp drknd,sl fox) 18.00

MARSH,WINIFRED P-People of the Willow-Tor-1976-63p-col plts-1st ed (t7,f,dj) 12.50

MARSH,WINIFRED P-People of the Willows-Tor-1976-OUP-63p-wtrcols-1st ed (ee4,dj,autg) 30.00

MARSHALL,A J-Darwin and Huxley in Australia-Sydney,Lond-1970-Hodder & Stoughton-8vo-142p-blk cl,illus-1st ed (p8,f,sl rub dj) 65.00

MARSHALL,ARCHIBALD-Dragon-NY-(1967)-Dutton-oblng 8vo-pict bds,illus,Ardizzone-1st US ed (r3,dj) 35.00

MARSHALL,ARCHIBALD-Mote House Mystery-NY-1926-Dodd-1st US ed (f4) 10.00

MARSHALL,BRENDA-Mr.Pickwick's Plentiful Portions-Lond-(1980)-Muller-176p-red cl,facs illus-1st ed (q8,dj) 20.00

MARSHALL,C F DENDY-History of the Southern Railway-Lond-1936-So Railway Co (Curwen Pr)-lg 8vo-xiv+708p-grn cl,illus(incl col),maps-1st ed (g2) 150.00

MARSHALL,DAVID T-Recollections of Boyhood Days in Old Metuchen-(np)-(1930)-253p-cl,illus,fldg map (aa6) 35.00

MARSHALL,DONALD-Ra'Ivavae-GC-c.1961-Dbldy-8vo-301p-map e.p.,26 photos (p8,tapemrks,wn dj) 25.00

MARSHALL,E-Shikar & Safari-MA-1947-263p-photos (gg3,f,dj) 20.00

MARSHALL,EDISON-Heart of the Hunter-NY-1956-8vo-328p-illus (m3,f,sl fray dj) 15.00

MARSHALL,GEORGE S-History of Music in Columbus, Ohio 1812 to 1953-Columbus-1956-(8)193p-2 ports-1st ed (l10) 15.00

MARSHALL,HOWARD-Men Against Everest-Lond-1954-64p-29 photos-1st ed (q10,f,dj) 25.00

MARSHALL,HOWARD-Reflections of a River-Lond-1967-8vo-153p-photos-1st ed (m3,f,dj) 12.50

MARSHALL,JAMES-Santa Fe-NY-(1945)-449p-maps,photos,ltd pres ed-1st prtg (v7,pres,box) 50.00

MARSHALL,JAMES-Santa Fe: the Railroad that Built an Empire-(1945)-Random-465p-photos-1st ed (d3) 30.00

MARSHALL,JIM-Swinging Doors-Seattle-1949-267p-photos-1st ed (t7,dj) 42.50

MARSHALL,LOGAN-Life of Theodore Roosevelt...-np-(1910)-424p-cl (h1) 15.00

MARSHALL,M E-Delectable Egg-NY-(1968)-Trident Pr-319p-dec olive cl,drwngs-1st prtg (q8,dj) 16.50

MARSHALL,M-Steelhead-Winchester-1973-186p-photos (gg3,f,dj) 15.00

MARSHALL,MAJ F C-Elements of Hippology-KC-1925-Franklin Hudson-4th rvsd ed (j9) 28.00

MARSHALL,MEL-Care & Repair of Fishing Tackle-NY-1976-4to-237p-1st ed (m3,vf,dj) 20.00

MARSHALL,MEL-Steelhead-NY-1973-8vo-186p-illus-1st ed (m3,as new in dj) 12.50

MARSHALL,N L-Mushroom Book-1901-Dbldy Page-167p-48 col & b&w plts (bb3) 45.00

MARSHALL,NINA L-Mushroom Book-NY-1903-Dbldy,Page-sm 4to-167p-brn linen,lea labl,t.e.g.,untrmmd edges,col & b&w illus,photos (u6,scuff,sl wn) 45.00

MARSHALL,ORSAMUS H-Historical Writings of...-Albany-1887-buckrm,frntis,map-1st ed (pp4,rbnd) 75.00

MARSHALL,OTTO M-Wham Paymaster Robbery-Pima-1967-Pima COC-79p-wrps,illus,photos-1st ed (w3,vf) 25.00

MARSHALL,PETER-Let's Keep Christmas-NY-(1953)-McGraw Hill-pict bds-1st ed (s3,f,dj) 15.00

MARSHALL,ROBERT E-Onza-NY-1961-8vo-202p-photos-1st ed (m3,vf,dj) 25.00

MARSHALL,ROBERT-Arctic Wilderness-Berkeley-1956-UC Pr-xii,171p-photos-1st ed (ll8,dj) 27.50

MARSHALL,RODERICK-William Morris and His Earthly Paradise-NY-1981-Braziller-frntis-1st Amer ed (t4,f,f dj) 20.00

MARSHALL,ROGER-Race to Win-NY-1980-Norton-8vo-270p-half cl,illus-1st ed (nn1,f,dj) 15.00

MARSHALL,S L A-Battles in the Monsoon-NY-1967-1st ed (v9,f,sl chip dj) 65.00

MARSHALL,S L A-Fields of Bamboo-NY-1971-1st ed (v9,f,f dj) 75.00

MARSHALL,WILLIAM I-Acquistion of Oregon-Seattle-1911-2 vols-frntis-Smith 2381,Tweney #48 (d7,f) 185.00

MARSHALL,WILLIAM I-Acquistion of Oregon...-Seattle-1911-Lowman & Hanford-2 vols-Howes M322 (nn6,sl tn sp) 145.00

MARSHALL,WILLIAM-Gelignite-NY-1977-Holt-1st US ed (f4,f,dj) 15.00

MARSHALL,WILLIAM-Hatchet Man-NY-1977-Holt-1st US ed (h4,f,dj) 15.00

MARSHALL,WILLIAM-Skullduggery-NY-1980-Holt-1st US ed (e4,dj) 15.00

MARSHALL,WILLIAM-Thin Air-Lond-1977-Hamilton-1st ed (g4,f,sl wn dj) 15.00

MARSHALL,WILLIAM-Yellowthread Street-NY-1975-Holt-1st US ed (e4,dj) 20.00

MARSHALL-CROMWELL,JAMES-Grant as a Military Commander-NY-(1970)-244p & maps-1st Amer ed (c4,f,dj wn) 30.00

MARSHALL-HARDY,E-Mirror of Angling-Lond-1937-8vo-128p-illus (m3,vf,dj) 12.50

MARSTON,E-An Old Man's Holidays-Lond-1900-12mo-140p+ads-ltd to 250c,nbrd,initialed,1/4 prchmnt bndg,photos-scarce (m3,sp dull,sl fox) 70.00

MARSTON,E-By Meadow & Stream-Lond-1896-12mo-134p-ltd to 250c,nbrd,illus,photos (m3) 65.00

MARSTON,E-Fishing for Pleasure & Catching It-Lond-1906-12mo-152p-illus (m3) 25.00

MARSTON,E-On a Sunshine Holiday-Lond-1897-12mo-140p-ltd to 250c,nbrd,initialed,frontis,illus (m3) 75.00

MARTEKO,V-Mushrooms-1980-Norton-290p-30 col photos-1st ed (bb3,f,dj) 10.00

MARTELLI,GEORGE-Livingstone's River-NY-(1969)-S&S-8vo-286p-maps-1st US ed (cc5,f,sl tn dj) 20.00

MARTIN,A C-Food of Game Ducks in the U.S. and Canada-Wash-1939-8vo-157p-wrps,col frntis,152 plts (y8,cov stnd) 23.00

MARTIN,A C-Food of the Game Ducks in the United States & Canada-Wash D.C.-1939-8vo-157p-wrps,col frontis,photos (m3) 35.00

MARTIN,ALEX-Fishing Tackle-Glasgow-1960-oblng 12mo-63p-wrps,illus (m3,f) 15.00

MARTIN,BILL-Smoky Poky-KC-(1947)-Tell Well Pr-pict bds-1st ed (aa9) 20.00

MARTIN,BILL-Wild Horse Roundup-KC-1950-Tell Well Pr-pict bds-1st ed (aa9) 25.00

MARTIN,BILLY-Number 1-NY-(1980)-272p-bds-1st ed so stated (n1,f,dj) 15.00

MARTIN,COLIN-Full Fathom Five-NY-(1975)-Viking-8vo-288p-photos-1st US ed (cc5,dj) 20.00

MARTIN,CY-Saga of the Buffalo-NY-1973-188p-photos-1st ed (t7,dj) 10.00

MARTIN,DARREL-Imitations Methods in Fly Tying and Trouting-Seattle-1980-12mo-161p-wrps,illus (m3,vf) 12.50

MARTIN,DAVID-Crying Heart Tattoo-NY-1982-1st ed (n5,f,f dj) 20.00

MARTIN,DOUGLAS D-Earps of Tombstone...-Tombstone-(1959)-Tombstone Epitaph-65p-dbl cols-wrps-Six-Guns 1453-1st ed so stated (h1) 12.50

MARTIN,DOUGLAS D-Lamp in the Desert-Tucson-1960-U of Ariz Pr-304p-illus-1st ed (bb4,dj) 15.00

MARTIN,DOUGLAS D-Tombstone's Epitaph-Albuq-(1951)-U of NM Pr-272p-illus-1st ed (f9,dj fade,sl tn) 35.00

MARTIN,DOUGLAS D-Yuma Crossing-Albuq-1954-UNM Pr-(x),243p-cl,illus,map-1st ed (v1,sl wn dj) 40.00

MARTIN,DOUGLAS D-Yuma Crossing-Albuq-1954-UNM Pr-243p-illus-1st ed (cc4,dj) 25.00

MARTIN,DR.FRANKLIN H-Joy of Living-GC-1933-2 vols,cl-1st ed so stated (b1) 20.00

MARTIN,E-Run Rhino Run-1982-Chatto Windus-4to-136p-photos-1st ed (bb3,f,dj) 18.00

MARTIN,EVA-COMP.-Reincarnation-New Hyde Park-1963-Univ Bks-cl-1st Amer ed (n8,f) 15.00

MARTIN,F-Sea Bears-1960-Chilton-201p-photos-1st ed (bb3,dj) 11.00

MARTIN,I T-Voice From the West-St.Louis-1908-256p-cl (b1) 15.00

MARTIN,ISAAC-Journal of the Life, Travels, Labours, and Religious Exercises-Phila-1834-Wm P Gibbons-12mo-160p-lea-1st ed (y6,wn,fox,tn f.e.p.) 26.00

MARTIN,J L-ED.-Circle-NY-(1971,37)-Praeger-sm 4to-291p-119 illus-new ed (ee5,f,f dj) 30.00

MARTIN,J W-My Fishing Days & Fishing Ways-Lond-(1906)-8vo-190p-nbrd,autg,photos-1st ed (m3) 45.00

MARTIN,JANE W-Cooking as You Like It-NY-(1963)-Macmillan-306p-blu cl,col woodcts,photos-1st prtg (q8,dj) 17.50

MARTIN,JOHN H-Manual of Microscopic Mounting...-Lond-1872-J & A Churchill-viii+200p+ads-grn cl,10 plts,102 figs-1st ed (j2) 55.00

MARTIN,MILTON F-Trout Lore-NY-(1942)-DS&P-4to-96p-photos-1st ed (bb5,f,dj) 25.00

MARTIN,MILTON F-Trout Lore-NY-(1942)-folio-96p-photos-1st ed (m3) 11.50

MARTIN,R D-ED.-Breeding Endangered Species in Captivity-Lond-1975-8vo-420p-cl,illus (y8,dj) 95.00

MARTIN,ROLAND-One Hundred & One Bass-Catching Secrets-Tulsa-1980-8vo-411p-photos-1st ed (m3,vf,dj) 15.00

MARTIN,SIDNEY W-Florida's Flagler-Athens-(1949)-U of Georgia Pr-xii+280p-grn cl-1st ed (h2,dj) 25.00

MARTIN,STUART-Trial of Scotland Yard-NY-1930-Harper-1st US ed (j4,f) 12.50

MARTIN,TROY K-Beat on a Damask Drum-NY-1960-Dutton-auth 1st bk-1st ed (ff3,t.e. pgs sl spot,dj) 90.00

MARTINEAU,HARRIET-Retrospect of Western Travel-NY-1942-Harper & Bros-2 vols-emboss cl,papr sp labls,prtd box-rprnt of 1838 ed (dd7,f,dj,box) 50.00

MARTINELL,C-Gaudi, His Life, His Theories, His Work-1967-MIT-555 illus-1st transl ed (h10,dj) 150.00

MARTINEZ,ANDRES-True Narrative...of Those Who Sailed on the Voyage to the Rio De La Plata-NY-1946-priv prtd-unpgd-grn cl sp,papr over bds,orig protective dj,ltd to 200c-Americanum Nauticum Number 1 (nn1,dj) 75.00

MARTINEZ,E-Viva La Raza-GC-(1974)-Dbldy-8vo-353p-1st ed (cc5,dj) 15.00

MARTINEZ,OSCAR J-Fragments of the Mexican Revolution-Albuq-(1983)-U of NM Pr-316p-illus-1st ed (cc4) 25.00

MARTINEZ-ALIER,VERENA-Marriage, Class and Colour in Nineteenth Century Cuba-Cambridge-(1974)-Cambridge U Pr-8vo-202p-papr over bds-1st ed (y5,dj) 21.00

MARTON,GREGORY-Boy and His Friend the Blizzard-NY-(1962)-Harper & Row-126p-cl,e.p. & 2-col text illus by Wildsmith-1st US ed (r3,f,f dj) 25.00

MARTY,SID-Men for the Mountains-NY-1978-270p-1st US ed (p10,dj) 18.00

MARTYN,WYNDHAM-Trent Trail-NY-1930-McBride-pict cov-1st US ed (g4) 12.50

MARTYR,WESTON-Southseaman-Edinburgh,Lond-1928-Wm Blackwood-8vo-394p-blu cl,frntis,text illus-New ed (p8,sl wn) 30.00

MARTZOLFF,C L-Synopsis of Ohio History with more than 1500 Topical References-Athens-1908-52p (e1,wrps) 12.50

MARVIN,CHARLES-Training the Trotting Horse-Franklin-1907-5th ed (h9) 40.00

MARVIN,FREDERIC R-Excursions of a Book Lover-Bost-1910-Sherman,French-331p-cl,t.e.g.-1st ed (dd10,sl spot cov) 25.00

MARVIN,ISABEL B-Bon Appetit-1947-Houghton Mifflin-269p-blu cl-1st ed (q8,dj) 15.00

MARWICK,ALICE-Northland Post-Cochrane-(1950)-(Auth)-341p-illus,map,port (k10) 25.00*

MARWICK,M G-Sorcery in its Social Setting-Manchester-(1965)-Univ Pr-8vo-339p-cl,maps,plts-1st ed (y5,sl chip dj) 20.00

MARX,GROUCHO-Groucho Letters-1967-S&S-1st ed (r9,sl chip dj) 20.00

MARX,ROBERT F-Still More Adventures-NY-(1976)-Mason/Charter-8vo-256p-illus-1st ed (jj5,dj) 17.50

MASEFIELD,JOHN-Chaucer-NY-1931-Macmillan-1st ed (q2,soil e.p.) 20.00

MASEFIELD,JOHN-Conway-NY-1933-Macmillan-orig g titled cl-1st Amer ed (aa9,sl fade sp) 15.00

MASEFIELD,JOHN-Eggs and Baker or the Days of Trial-Lond-(1936)-Heinemann-orig g titled cl-1st ed (aa9,sp drknd dj) 25.00

MASEFIELD,JOHN-Hawbucks-Lond-1929-Heinemann-orig g titled cl-1st trd ed (aa9,sl spot,fox,dj sl tn) 25.00

MASEFIELD,JOHN-Midsummer Night and Other Tales in Verse-Lond-(1928)-Heinemann-orig g titled cl-1st ed (aa9,sl fox e.p.,dj sl wn) 20.00

MASEFIELD,JOHN-Recent Prose-Lond-1924-Heinemann-1st Brit ed (hh5) 12.50

MASEFIELD,JOHN-Right Royal-Lond-1920-Heinemann-orig g titled bds-1st ed (aa9,sp fade dj) 25.00

MASEFIELD,JOHN-So Long to Learn-NY-1952-Macmillan-1st US ed (hh5,sl tn dj) 10.00

MASEFIELD,JOHN-Tristan and Isolt-Lond-(1927)-Heinemann-orig g titled cl-1st ed (aa9,sp chip dj) 20.00

MASEFIELD,JOHN-Wanderer of Liverpool-NY-1930-Macmillan-139p-grn cl,col frntis,plts,4 plans(3 fldg)-1st Amer trd ed (gg6) 30.00

MASIN,HERMAN L-How to Star in Baseball-NY-(1960)-63,(1)p-wrps (n1) 10.00

MASKELYNE,J N-Further Selection of Locomotives I Have Known-Lond-1962-71p-drwngs-1st ed (n4,dj) 16.00

MASLOWSKI,PETER-Treason Must Be Made Odious-Millwood-(1978)-171p-1st ed (n3,f,dj) 17.50

MASON,A E W-At the Villa Rose-Tor-1910-MacLeod & Allen-illus-1st Can ed (h4,f) 20.00

MASON,A E W-Dean's Elbow-Lond-1930-Hodder-1st ed (f4,sl soil dj) 25.00

MASON,A E W-Dilemmas-NY-1935-Dbldy-1st US ed (e4,f,dj) 35.00

MASON,A E W-Four Corners of the World-NY-1917-Scribners-1st US ed (g4) 25.00

MASON,A E W-House in Lordship Lane-NY-1946-Dodd-1st US ed (e4,f,dj) 20.00

MASON,A E W-House of the Arrow-1924-Doran-1st Amer ed (n9,f) 40.00

MASON,A E W-No Other Tiger-NY-1927-Doran-1st US ed (h4,f,chip dj) 35.00

MASON,A E W-Prisoner in the Opal-NY-1928-Dbldy CC-1st US ed (f4) 10.00

MASON,A E W-Three Gentlemen-NY-1932-Dbldy-1st US ed (e4,dj) 20.00

MASON,BERNARD S-Drums, Tom Toms and Rattles-NY-1938-206p-drwngs-1st ed (v7,dj) 35.00

MASON,BOBBIE ANN-Shiloh & Other Stories-NY-(1982)-Harper-1st ed (a5,f,dj) 65.00

MASON,BOBBIE ANN-Shiloh and Other Stories-NY-(1982)-Harper & Row-1st ed (u10,as new in dj) 100.00

MASON,FRANCES N-ED.-John Norton & Sons Merchants of London & Virginia...1750 to 1795-Richmond-1937-Deitz Pr-thk 8vo-573p-illus-1st ed (s1,f) 35.00

MASON,GEORGE-Newport Illustrated in a Series of Pen and Pencil Sketches-1854-Appleton-110p-engrvngs-scarce (v3,edges wn) 65.00

MASON,JERRY-ED.-Sportsman's Wilderness-1974-Ridge Pr-4to-253p-photos (m3,f) 10.00

MASON,KENNETH-Abode of Snow-NY-1955-Dutton-8vo-372p-grn cl,maps,20 plts-1st Amer ed (gg6,wn dj) 45.00

MASON,KILPATRICK-Pirates of the Prairies or the Trail Hunter-Cleve-1927-182p-col pict wrps,frntis-1st ed (t7) 25.00

MASON,LOUIS B-Life and Times of Major John Mason of Connecticut-NY-1935-Putnam's-350p-blu cl,plts-1st ed (h2,dj) 25.00

MASON,PHILIP-Skinner's Horse-NY-1979-241p-1st Amer ed (b7,f,dj) 25.00

MASON,RICHARD O-Considerations of the Reasons That Exist for Reviving the Use of the Long Bow with the Pike-Lond-1798-8vo-59p-orig bd covs,fld out illus-rare (m3,cov wn) 130.00

MASON,STUART-Bibliography of the Poems of Oscar Wilde-NY-1908-Mitchell Kennerley-ltd to 475c (l9,sl fox) 150.00

MASON,VAN WYCK-Deadly Orbit Mission-NY-1968-Dbldy-1st ed (j4,f,dj) 12.50

MASON,VAN WYCK-Himalayan Assignment-NY-1952-Dbldy-1952 (e4,f,dj) 20.00

MASON,VAN WYCK-Maracaibo Mission-NY-1965-Dbldy-1st ed (j4,f,dj) 12.50

MASON,VAN WYCK-Rio Casino Intrigue-NY-1941-Reynal-1st ed (h4,dj) 20.00

MASON,VAN WYCK-Sulu Sea Murders-NY-1933-Dbldy CC-1st ed (j4) 10.00

MASON,VAN WYCK-Trouble in Burma-NY-1962-Dbldy-1st ed (g4,f,dj) 12.50

MASON,WILLIAM A-History of the Art of Writing-NY-1920-Macmillan-thk 8vo-(vi),502p-cl-1st ed (w2) 55.00

MASONIC HISTORY OF THE N.W.-1902-History Publ Co-hvy lg 4to-574p+41p biogr.(viii)-lea,g edges,ports-scarce (b6,sl crack) 225.00

MASS HIST SOC-Lectures Delivered...before Lowell Institute, in Boston...relating to Early History of Massachusetts-Bost-1869-viii+498p-grn cl-BAL 8868-1st ed (b2) 55.00

MASSACHUSETTS STATE COMMISSIONERS OF ZOOLOGY & BOTANY-Reports on the Fishes,Reptiles & Birds of Massachusetts-Bost-1839-8vo-426p-1/2 mor & mrbld bds,g lettering,illus-scarce (m3) 75.00

MASSACHUSETTS-JOURNALS OF EACH PROVINCIAL CONGRESS OF...IN 1774 AND 1775...-Bost-1838-Dutton & Wentworth-lx+778p-full calf-1st ed (k2,edge wn) 35.00

MASSAR,PHYLLIS D-Presenting Stefano Della Bella-NY-1971-Metro Mus Art-4to-141p-brwn cl,illus (r10,wn dj) 12.50

MASSEE,GEORGE-European Fungus Flora Agaracaceae-Lond-1902-12mo-274p-grn cl-1st ed (x5) 25.00

MASSEY,RUTH-Death in the Wind-NY-(1932)-Nelson-1st US ed (e4,f,sl wn dj) 20.00

MASSIE & CHRISTIAN-Descriptive Guide Book of Virginia's Old Gardens-Richmond-ca.1915-Gard Club of Va-88p-cl (x6) 20.00

MASSIE,SUSANNE W-ED.-Homes and Gardens in Old Virginia-Richmond-1932-Garrett & Massie-4to-dec cl,132p plts-2nd prtg (cc10,sp sun) 50.00

MASSIE,SUZANNE-Land of the Firebird-NY-1980-S&S-lg 8vo-493p-64p col illus-1st ed (jj5,f,f dj) 45.00

MASSINGHAM,H J-Birds of the Sea Shore-Lond-1936-8vo-309p-illus,plts (m3,dj) 20.00

MASSY,CARL-Fly-Fishing for Trout-Sydney-1976-8vo-175p-photos,illus-1st ed (m3,vf,dj) 30.00

MAST,REV ISAAC-Gun,Rod & Saddle-Phila-1875-16mo-278p-illus-scarce-1st ed (m3) 60.00

MASTERMAN,WALTER S-Wrong Letter-NY-1926-Dutton-1st US ed (f4) 15.00

MASTERS OF MYSTERIES-1912-BM-illus,publ anon(G Burgess)-1st ed (x7) 150.00

MASTERS,DEXTER-ED.-One World or None-NY-1946-McGraw Hill-4to-xii+79p-wrps-1st ed (c2) 25.00

MASTERS,EDGAR L-Poems of People-NY-1936-D Appleton-blu cl-1st ed (f2,edge-wn dj) 20.00

MASTERS,EDGAR L-Whitman-NY-1937-1st ed (k5,dj) 35.00

MASTERS,FRANK M-History of Baptists in Kentucky-Louisville-1953-Kntcky Baptist Hist Scty-vi+639p-blu cl-1st ed (k2,writing on e.p.) 30.00

MASTERS,JOHN-Venus of Konpara-NY-(1960)-1st ed (m5,sl wn dj) 10.00

MASTERS,R E L-Pscychedelic Art-Lond-1968-30 col plts,110 b&w illus-1st Brit ed (h10,dj) 50.00

MASTERSON,JAMES R-Bering's Successors,1745 to 1780-Seattle-1948-U of Wash Pr-96p-maps-1st ed in book form (bb4) 20.00

MASTERSON,V V-Katy Railroad and the Last Frontier-Norman-1952-U of Okla Pr-312p-cl,photos,illus-Herd #1451-1st ed (w3,f,chip dj) 25.00

MASTERSON,V V-Katy Railroad and the Last Frontier-Norman-1952-U of Okla Pr-xvi+312p-red/brwn cl,maps,plts,text illus-1st ed (h2,edge-tn dj) 30.00

MASTERSON,W B-Famous Gunfighters of the Western Frontier-Monroe-1982-182p-wrps,photos-1st ed (t7,f) 15.00

MASTERTON,ELSIE-Blueberry Hill Cookbook-NY-(1950)-Crowell-302p (l6,dj) 15.00

MATEER,ADA H-Siege Days-NY-1903-411p-blk cl,illus-1st ed (b7,f) 100.00

MATHE,JEAN-Leonardo Da Vinci: Anatomical Drawings-Barcelona-1978-4to-122p-1st ed (dd3,dj) 60.00

MATHER,CHARLES O-Billfish-Sidney-1976-4to-272p-photos-1st ed (m3,f,dj) 25.00

MATHER,COTTON-Magnalia Christi Americana-Hartford-1820-2 vols-brwn cl wi papr labls-1st Amer ed (w10,rbnd,sl fox) 100.00

MATHER,FRED-Modern Fish Culture-NY-1900-12mo-333p-illus (m3,hngs cracked) 15.00

MATHER,FRED-My Angling Friends-NY-1901-Forest & Stream-grn cl-Plum #6707-1st ed (w8,sl fade,discol) 50.00

MATHER,W W-Second Annual Report of the Geological Survey of the State of Ohio-Columbus-1838-286p-19 plts,incl rare fldg plt of the Trilobite-Amer Imprnts 52044 (c1,dsbnd) 150.00

MATHERS,POWYS-RENDERED BY-Love Songs of Asia-NY-1946-Knopf-cl-1st Amer ed (n8,f,dj) 15.00

MATHES,CAPT J HARVEY-General Forrest-NY-1902-Appleton-395p-frntis,illus,maps-Great Commanders Ser-1st ed (cc6,sl soil,uncut) 125.00

MATHES,W MICHAEL-ED.-Spanish Approaches to the Island of California 1628 to 1632-SF-1975-Bk Club of Cal-tall 8vo-xviii,78p-pict papr bds,illus-ltd to 400c (y4,f) 65.00

MATHESON,RICHARD-Hell House-NY-(1971)-Viking-1st ed (ff6,sl creased dj) 150.00

MATHESON,RICHARD-I Am Legend-NY-(1970)-Walker-1st hdcov ed (bb1,f,sl tn dj) 175.00

MATHESON,RICHARD-I Am Legend-NY-1954-Gold Medal Bks-pbk orig-1st prtg (bb1,cov cor creased) 45.00

MATHESON,RICHARD-Shock III-NY-(1966)-Dell-wrps-1st ed (k9,f) 17.50

MATHESON,RICHARD-Shrinking Man-Lond-(1973)-David Bruce & Watson-orig publ as a pbk orig-1st Brit & 1st hdcov ed (aa8,f,dj) 200.00

MATHESON,RICHARD-Stir of Echoes-Phila,NY-(1958)-1st ed (e5,f,sl soil dj) 95.00

MATHEWS,CATHARINE V-Andrew Ellicott-NY-(1908)-Grafton Pr-x+256p-blu cl,illus,maps-ltd to 1000c-1st ed (e2) 55.00

MATHEWS,F SCHUYLER-Field Book of American Trees and Shrubs-NY,Lond-(1915)-Putnam's-465p-cl-plts,incl 16 col (j1) 12.50

MATHEWS,J H-Toward the Poetics of Surrealism-1976-Syracuse U-1st ed (t4,f,f dj) 15.00

MATHEWS,JOHN J-Talking to the Moon-Chig-(1945)-U of Chig Pr-243p-line drwngs-1st ed (cc4,dj) 25.00

MATHEWS,JOHN J-Wah'Kon Tah-Norman-1932-359p-illus,maps-1st ed (c4,sl chip dj) 30.00

MATHEWS,SCHUYLER-Book of Wild Flowers for Young People-NY-1923-397p-37 col plts (x6) 10.00

MATHEWS,T S-Under the Influence-Lond-1979-Cassell-cl-1st ed (l8,vf,dj) 16.50

MATHEWS,WILLIAM-Oratory and Orators-Chig-1882-456p-cl (j1) 15.00

MATHEWSON,CHRISTY-First Base Faulkner-1916-G&D (q7) 35.00

MATHEWSON,CHRISTY-Pitching in a Pinch-1912-G&D-Boy Scout ed (ff2) 50.00

MATHIAS,MILDRED-Studies in Umbelliferae III-St.Louis-1930-MoBot-230p-wrps (x6) 25.00

MATHIESON,WILLIAM D-My Grandfather's War-Tor-1981-Macmillan of Can-338p-cl (aa2,dj) 20.00*

MATINEAU,MRS.PHILIP-More Caviar and More Candy-Lond-1938-Cobden Sanderson-262p (r6,dj) 15.00

MATISSE,HENRI-Jazz-1983-Braziller-folio (ee1,as new in dj & shppng box 125.00

MATLACK,LUCIUS C-Life of Rev Orange Scott-NY-1847-Prindle & Matlack-307p-blk cl-1st ed (b2) 40.00

MATSON,DANIEL-Friar Bringas Reports to the King-Tucson-1977-U of Az-2 maps-1st ed (u9,dj) 30.00

MATSON,RUTH A-Cooking by the Garden Calendar-GC-1955-Amer Grdn Guild/Dbldy-258p-1st ed (m6,sl soil) 12.00

MATTERA,JOANNE-Navajo Techniques for Today's Weaver-NY-(1975)-158p-photos,col e.p. & flyleaves-1st prtg (v7,f,dj) 25.00

MATTERN,J R-Handloading Ammunition-1926-Samworth-380p-photos (gg3,wn) 15.00

MATTES,MERRILL-Indians, Infants & Infantry-Denver-1960-Old West-1st ed (u9,dj) 25.00

MATTHES,FRANCOIS-Incomparable Valley-Berkeley-1950-1st ed (o10,f,sl chip dj) 35.00

MATTHEWS,BRANDER-An Introduction to the Study of American Literature-NY-(1896)-Amer Bk Co-256p-cl (k1) 12.50

MATTHEWS,J H-Surrealism, Insanity, and Poetry-1982-Syracuse-1st ed (t4,f,f dj) 15.00

MATTHEWS,JACK-Collecting Rare Books for Pleasure and Profit-NY-(1977)-Putnam's-317p-cl (e1,sl wn dj) 15.00

MATTHEWS,JAMES-ED.-Black Voices Shout-Austin-1976-Troubadour Pr-wrps-1st US ed (v5,f) 15.00

MATTHEWS,JAMES-Voices-NY-1983-Atheneum-photos-1st ed (bb1,as new in dj) 25.00

MATTHEWS,L H-ET AL-Whale-NY-1968-oblng 4to-287p-cl,col illus (y8,dj) 35.00

MATTHEWS,LESLIE-History of Pharmacy in Britain-Edinburgh-1962-427p-1st ed (dd3) 75.00

MATTHEWS,PATRICK-ED.-Pursuit of Moths and Butterflies-Lond-1957-Chatto & Windus-sm 4to-141p-67 photos(11 col)-1st ed (bb5,sl soil dj) 25.00

MATTHEWS,R S-Retail Butcher-(Memphis)-(1911)-H W Dixon-8vo-101p-maroon cl-1st ed (oo8,sl soil) 45.00

MATTHEWS,WILLIAM-COMP.-American Diaries-Bost-1959-J S Canner-xiv+383p-red cl-2nd prntg (e2,sl fade sp) 45.00

MATTHIESSEN,PETER-At Play in the Fields of the Lord-NY-1965-1st ed (p5,f,dj) 40.00

MATTHIESSEN,PETER-Blue Meridian-1971-Random-204p-col photos-1st ed (bb3,dj) 17.00

MATTHIESSEN,PETER-Cloud Forest-NY-1961-Viking-1st ed (q2,rub dj) 75.00

MATTHIESSEN,PETER-Far Tortuga-NY-1975-Random-1st ed (h8,f,dj) 45.00

MATTHIESSEN,PETER-In the Spirit of Crazy Horse-NY-(1983)-Viking-1st ed (q1,f,f dj) 135.00

MATTHIESSEN,PETER-In the Spirit of Crazy Horse-NY-(1983)-Viking-628p-maps-1st ed (nn6,dj) 175.00

MATTHIESSEN,PETER-Oomingmak-NY-(1967)-Hastings Hs-1st ed (dd2,f,dj) 45.00

MATTHIESSEN,PETER-Oomingmak-NY-1967-Hastings Hs-photos-1st ed (q2,dj) 55.00

MATTHIESSEN,PETER-Partisans-Lond-1956-Secker & Warburg-8vo-bds-1st Brit ed (jj8,f,sl tn dj) 100.00

MATTHIESSEN,PETER-Race Rock-NY-(1954)-Harper-auth 1st bk-1st ed (m7,sl wn dj) 125.00

MATTHIESSEN,PETER-Raditzer-1961-Viking-1st ed (o9,dj wn & chip) 40.00

MATTHIESSEN,PETER-Raditzer-NY-1961-Viking-1st ed (cc2,sl chip dj) 45.00

MATTHIESSEN,PETER-Sal Si Puedes-NY-1969-1st ed (p5,dj) 25.00

MATTHIESSEN,PETER-Sand River-NY-1981-photos,H Van Lawick-1st ed (q5,f,dj) 22.50

MATTHIESSEN,PETER-Sand Rivers-NY-1981-4to-213p-photos (m3,f,dj) 17.50

MATTHIESSEN,PETER-Shorebirds of North America-NY-1967-folio-270p-32p col plts,Robt V Clem (m3,f) 60.00

MATTHIESSEN,PETER-Snow Leopard-NY-(1978)-Viking-1st ed (bb2,f,dj) 40.00

MATTHIESSEN,PETER-Snow Leopard-NY-(1978)-Viking-1st ed (e10,f,dj) 30.00

MATTHIESSEN,PETER-Tree Where Man was Born-NY-1972-Dutton-folio-cl-1st ed (y3,f,f dj) 45.00

MATTHIESSEN,PETER-Under the Mountain Wall-1962-Viking-1st ed (x2,f,dj) 55.00

MATTHIESSEN,PETER-Under the Mountain Wall-NY-(1962)-Viking-1st ed (dd2,f,sl rub dj) 40.00

MATTHIESSEN,PETER-Wildlife in America-NY-1959-8vo-304p-cl,8 col plts,16p photos-1st ed (y8,dj) 85.00

MATTHIESSEN,PETER-Wildlife-NY-1959-drwngs,B Hines-1st ed (r5,dj) 75.00

MATTISON,RAY H-Henry A Boller, Missouri River Fur Trader-Bismarck-1966-171p-stiff pict wrps,photos (t7) 12.50

MAUBORGNE,J O-Practical Uses of the Wave Meter in Wireless Telegraphy-1913-74p-42 illus-1st ed (h6,cov stnd) 40.00

MAUDSLAY,ALFRED P-Life in the Pacific Fifty Years Ago-Lond-1930-Routledge & Sons-8vo-ix,261p-blu cl,2 plts,map (nn1) 95.00

MAUDSLAY,ROBERT-Texas Sheepman-Austin-1951-U of Tex Pr-138p-illus-1st ed (cc4,dj) 50.00

MAUGHAM,ROBIN-Nomad-Lond-1947-1st ed (y7,dj rub) 26.00

MAUGHAM,ROBIN-Servant-NY-1949-Harcourt-1st Amer ed (t4,f,dj wn) 15.00

MAUGHAM,ROBIN-Wrong People-Lond-1970-1st ed (y7,dj) 22.00

MAUGHAM,W SOMERSET-Ah King-GC-1933-1st ed (c5,dj) 55.00

MAUGHAM,W SOMERSET-Books and You-Lond-(1940)-Heinemann-xx,78p-dec cl-1st ed (dd10) 20.00

MAUGHAM,W SOMERSET-Cakes and Ale-Lond-1930-Heinemann-1st ed (w5,sl fox,dj) 50.00

MAUGHAM,W SOMERSET-Cakes and Ale-NY-1930-Dbldy,Doran-orig g titled cl-1st Amer ed (aa9,sp dull,sl rub) 20.00

MAUGHAM,W SOMERSET-Circle-Lond-1921-Heinemann-500c bnd in cl,the rest(1500) in wrps-Stott 40-1st ed (bb2,fox e.p.) 195.00

MAUGHAM,W SOMERSET-Explorer-1909-Baker & Taylor-1st Amer ed (x2) 85.00

MAUGHAM,W SOMERSET-Gentleman in the Parlour-GC-1930-1st ed (c5,wn cor & sp,dj) 65.00

MAUGHAM,W SOMERSET-Gentleman in the Parlour-Lond-(1930)-Heinemann-gold stmpd blk cl-Stott A40-1st ed (ee2,lacks dj) 50.00

MAUGHAM,W SOMERSET-Lady Frederick-1912-Heinemann-wrps-1st ed (x2) 125.00

MAUGHAM,W SOMERSET-Making of a Saint-Lond-1898-Unwin-1st ed (ee2,rprd) 125.00

MAUGHAM,W SOMERSET-Maugham's Encore-1952-Dbldy-1st Amer ed (p9,f,sl rub dj) 40.00

MAUGHAM,W SOMERSET-Moon and Sixpence-1919-Doran-variant ed wi auth name misspelled "Maughan" on cov & sp-1st Amer ed (x2) 135.00

MAUGHAM,W SOMERSET-Narrow Corner-Lond-(1932)-Heinemann-1st ed (ee2,f,sp chip dj) 65.00

MAUGHAM,W SOMERSET-Razor's Edge-GC-(1944)-Dbldy-buckrm-ltd to 750c,nbrd,autg-1st ed (aa10,f,box sl fade,rub) 375.00

MAUGHAM,W SOMERSET-Razor's Edge-GC-1944-Dbldy-precedes Brit ed by 4 months-1st ed (ee2,dj wn & tape rprd) 35.00

MAUGHAM,W SOMERSET-Razor's Edge-NY-(1944)-383,(1)p-wrps,dbl cols,Armed Service ed (n1,sl wn) 10.00

MAUGHAM,W SOMERSET-Unknown-Lond-1920-Heinemann-orig wrps-1st ed (ee2) 50.00

MAUGHAM,W SOMERSET-Writer's Notebook-NY-1949-Cosmo Mag-no dj as iss-1st ed (dd2,f) 75.00

MAULDIN,BILL-Sort of Saga-NY-(1949)-Wm Sloane Assoc-illus,auth-1st ed (b10,sl wn dj) 25.00

MAUNSELL,G W-Fisherman's Vade Mecum-Lond-1933-16mo-474p-illus-1st ed (m3) 17.50

MAURER,M-ED.-Air Force Combat Units of World War II-Wash D.C.-1961-roy 8vo-xii,506p-g cl,text illus-1st ed (s2) 35.00

MAUREY,ED B-Where the West Began-Coraopolis-1930-75p+ads-papr wrps,frntis (p2) 10.00

MAURICE,FREDERICK-An Aide De Camp of Lee Being the Papers of Col Charles Marshall...-Bost-1927-287p-pcit cl,frntis,photos,fldg map-1st ed (t7,ex-libr) 20.00

MAUROIS,ANDRE-Next Chapter-NY-(1928)-Dutton-orig cl,papr sp & cov labls-1st ed (aa9,sl wn dj) 15.00

MAUROIS,ANDRE-Voyage to the Island of the Articoles-NY-1929-transl by Garnett-wood engrvngs-1st Amer ed (m4,dj) 12.50

MAUROIS,ANDRE-Women of Paris-Lond-(1954)-photos by Nico Jesse-1st ed (c5,e.p. brwnd,dj sl tn) 20.00

MAURY,GEN.DABNEY H-Recollections of a Virginian in Mexican,Indian, and Civil Wars-NY-1894-279p-frntis-Howes#M440-1st ed (u7) 100.00

MAURY,M F-Physical Geography of the Sea-NY-1855-Harper & Bros-xxiv,25-287p-orig blu ribbed cl wi g cov dec,12 plts(incl 8 fldg)-Sabin 46969-3rd ed (p8,sp fade,bds rub,sl fox) 175.00

MAURY,M F-Physical Geography of the Sea-NY-1855-Harper & Bros-xxiv,25-287p-orig cl wi g ship vignette cov dec,12 plts(8 fldg)-Sabin 46969-2nd ed (nn1,fade sp,rub,soil,e.p. fox 350.00

MAURY,MATTEW F-Physical Geography of the Sea-Lond-1856-Sampson,Low-Basic Geog Libr No.475-fldg chrts,ads-New ed(6th ed) (v4) 225.00

MAURY,MATTHEW F-Physical Geography of the Sea-1856-Harper-348p-cl,13 plts(incl fldg)-6th ed (dd9,cov v wn,stnd e.p.,fox) 225.00

MAUSS,MARCEL-General Theory of Magic-Lond-(1972)-Routledge & K Paul-8vo-148p-cl (y5,dj) 17.00

MAVERICK,MARY A-Memoirs of Mary A Maverick, San Antonio's First American Woman-S.A.-1921-Alamo-136p-wrps-1st ed (a9) 100.00

MAWSON,THOMAS H-Art & Craft of Garden Making-Lond/NY-1907-Batsford/Scribner's-sm folio-xx,310p-g dec cl,t.e.g.,illus e.p.,218 illus(incl frntis)-3rd ed,rvsd & enlgd (pp7,sl shaken,cov rub,sun) 325.00

MAXIM,HUDSON-Lake Hopatcong the Beautiful-Landing-(1913)-65p-wrps,fldg map-3rd ed (aa6) 60.00

MAXIM,HUDSON-Reminiscences and Comments-GC,NY-1924-Dbldy,Page-vii,350p-cl,t.e.g.,frntis,plts-1st ed (dd10,hng crack,dj wn,rprd) 40.00

MAXIMOV,G P-ED.-Political Philosophy of Bakunin-Glencoe-1953-Free Pr-434p (r1,dj) 35.00

MAXON,P B-Waltz of Death-1941-Mystery Hs-1st ed (s10,dj cut & tn) 20.00

MAXWELL,AYMER-Pheasants & Covert Shooting-Lond-1913-12mo-332p-col plts (m3) 30.00

MAXWELL,D FYFE-Low Road-Lond-1927-vi,105p-7 col plts (x5,fade sp) 30.00

MAXWELL,G-Rocks Remain-1963-Dutton-209p-photos-1st ed (bb3,f,dj) 10.00

MAXWELL,GAVIN-Harpoon Venture-NY-1952-Viking-8vo-304p-82 photos-1st US ed (aa5,dj sl fade,tape rprd) 25.00

MAXWELL,GAVIN-Seals of the World-Bost-(1967)-HMCo-lg 8vo-153p-16p photos-1st US ed (gg5,f,sp tn dj) 12.50

MAXWELL,H-British Fresh Water Fishes-nd-Hutchinson-320p-25 col plts (bb3) 35.00

MAXWELL,JAMES C-An Elementary Treatise on Electricity-1888-208p-53 illus-rare-2nd ed (h6,wn sp,sp top split) 115.00

MAXWELL,JOHN C-World Makers-NY-(1969)-Arcadia-1st hdbk ed (h3,dj) 10.00

MAXWELL,M-Elephants and Other Big Game Studies from the Times-Lond-1930-oblng 8vo-cl,28 plts (y8,cov stnd) 50.00

MAXWELL,M-Stalking Big Game with a Camera in Equatorial Africa-Lond-1925(1924)-4to-206p-cl,113 plts(4 fldg) (y8,sl edge wn) 125.00

MAXWELL,ROBERT S-Whistle in the Piney Woods-Houston-1963-Tex Gulf Coast Hist Assoc-77p-wrps,photos-1st ed (w3,f) 35.00

MAXWELL,SIR HERBERT-Salmon and Sea Trout-Lond-nd-12mo-272p+ads-photos,col plts,fldg plts (m3,f) 40.00

MAXWELL,WILLIAM-Ancestors-NY-1971-1st ed (t5,f,dj) 20.00

MAXWELL,WILLIAM-Ancestors-NY-1971-Knopf-1st ed (b5,f,dj) 30.00

MAXWELL,WILLIAM-Chateau-NY-1961-1st ed (t5,dj) 35.00

MAXWELL,WILLIAM-Heavenly Tenants-NY-(1946)-Harper-4to-57p-dec cl,illus,I Karasz-1st ed (r3,dj chip & creased) 50.00

MAXWELL,WILLIAM-Old Man at the Railroad Crossing...-NY-1966-Knopf-1st ed (b10,f,dj) 35.00

MAXWELL,WILLIAM-Old Man at the Railroad Crossing...-NY-1966-Knopf-1st ed (w5,f,dj) 50.00

MAXWELL,WILLIAM-Over By the River and Other Stories-NY-1977-Knopf-1st ed (w5,f,f dj) 40.00

MAXWELL,WM AUDLEY-Crossing the Plains, Days of '57-SF-(1915)-Sunset Co-179p-wrps-Graff 2728-1st ed (s1) 90.00

MAY,CLIFF-Western Ranch Houses-SF-1946-Sunset Bks-illus-1st prtg (h10,dj) 45.00

MAY,EARL C-Principio to Wheeling, 1715 to 1945-NY-(1945)-Harper & Bros-xvi+335p-gry cl,illus-1st ed (k2,dj) 15.00

MAY,FLORENCE L-Hispanic Lace & Lace Making-NY-1939-Hispanic Soc-photos-1st ed (u9) 75.00

MAY,GEORGE S-Michigan and the Civil War Years 1860 to 1866-Lansing-1964-Mich Civ War Cent Obs Com-124p-wrps (v2) 15.00

MAY,GEORGE W-Massac Pilgrimage-Ann Arbor-1964-115p-cl-ltd,nbrd ed (j1,f) 15.00

MAY,JOHN R-Hawks of North America-NY-1935-Nat Assoc Audubon Soc-140p-illus (c9,cors bump) 35.00

MAY,MARGARET-TRANSL-Galen on the Usefulness of the Parts of the Body-Ithaca-1968-2 vols-1st Engl transl (dd3,box) 150.00

MAYBECK,BERNARD R-Palace of Fine Arts & Lagoon-SF-1915-P Elder-dec g wrps,tip in frntis-Pac Int Expo (h10) 175.00

MAYDON,H C-Big Game of Africa-NY-1935-254p-illus (gg3,f) 100.00

MAYER,A G-Medusae of the World-1910-Carnegie Inst-4to-3 vols-76 col plts (bb3,cor wn,bump) 325.00

MAYER,ALFRED M-ED.-Sport with Gun and Rod in American Woods and Waters-NY-(1883)-Century-8vo-892p-illus,precedes two vol Brit ed-1st ed (bb5) 150.00

MAYER,C-Jungle Beasts I Have Captured-GC-1924-8vo-(1),269p-cl,17 plts (y8,cor wn) 20.00

MAYER,CHARLES-Jungle Beasts I Have Captured-GC-1924-8vo-269p-illus (m3) 15.00

MAYER,CHARLES-Jungle Beasts I Have Captured-GC-1924-Dbldy Page-8vo-269p-Stinemetz drwngs-1st ed (ff5) 25.00

MAYER,CHARLES-Trapping Wild Animals in Malay Jungles-GC-1921-8vo-207p-illus (m3) 12.50

MAYER,FRANK B-With Pen & Pencil on the Frontier in 1851-St.Paul-1932-Minn Hist Soc-illus-1st ed (pp4,sp lttrs fade) 15.00

MAYER,FRANK B-With Pen and Pencil on the Frontier in 1851-St.Paul-1932-Minn Hist Soc-xiv+214p-red cl,plts,vol.1 of MHS Narratives and Docs ser-1st ed (h2) 35.00

MAYER,RONALD-1937 Newark Bears-1980-Wm Wise-photos-1st ed (s8,sl wn,sm stn to dj) 45.00

MAYER,TOM-Weary Falcon-Bost-1971-HM-1st ed (ff3,f,dj) 125.00

MAYER,W-ED.-Physiological Mammalogy-Academis-2 vols-illus (bb3,dj) 15.00

MAYFIELD,H-Kirtland's Warbler-Bloomfield Hills-1960-8vo-242p-cl,col frntis,photos (y8) 55.00

MAYFIELD,JULIAN-Hit-NY-1957-auth 1st bk-1st ed (n5,dj) 25.00

MAYHALL,MILDRED P-Kiowas-Norman-(1962)-U of Okla Pr-315p-illus-1st ed (cc4) 35.00

MAYHALL,MILDRED P-Kiowas-Norman-1962-U of Okla Pr-315p-1st ed (a9,dj) 45.00

MAYHEW,AUBREY-World's Tribute to John F Kennedy in Medallic Art-NY-1966-Morrow-4to-197p-cl (v3,tn dj) 25.00

MAYHEW,IRA-Mayhew's Practical Book Keeping Key-Bost-1871-Nichols & Hall-120p-prntd bds (k1,f) 15.00

MAYHEW,RALPH-Second Bubble Book-NY-(1918)-Harper-oblng 12mo-col illus by R Chase,3 sm records in pckts (nn10) 30.00

MAYNARD,C J-Butterflies of New England, with Original Descriptions of One Hundred and Six Species-Newtonvlle-1891-C J Maynard-10 handcol plts,handcol figs-2nd ed (p6,ex-libr) 200.00

MAYNARD,CHARLES J-Manual of North American Butterflies-Bost-1891-De Wolfe,Fiske-10p handcol plts,woodcts-1st ed (p6) 125.00

MAYNARD,SAMUEL T-Small Country Place-Phila-1908-Lippincott-8vo-320p-dec bds,100 illus-1st ed (cc10,sp drknd) 75.00

MAYNARD,SAMUEL-Landscape Gardening Applied to Home Decoration-NY-1914-Wiley-338p-cl-1st ed (x6) 18.00

MAYNE,PETER-Journey to the Pathans-GC-1955-Dbldy-8vo-315p-1st ed (jj5,dj edgewn) 15.00

MAYNE,PETER-Narrow Smile-Lond-1955-John Murray-8vo-264p-grn cl-1st ed (ll1,sl chip dj) 20.00

MAYO CLINIC-SKETCH OF THE HISTORY OF THE...AND THE MAYO FOUNDATION-Phila-1926-185p-1st ed (dd3) 40.00

MAYO,GERTRUDE-Coue For Children-Tor-1923-S B Gundy-sm 8vo-prntd blu cl-1st Can ed (y9) 27.50

MAYO,J H-Medals and Decorations of the British Army and Navy-Westminster-1897-2 vols-red cl,55 col plts-scarce-1st ed (b7,recased,sp sun) 350.00

MAYO,KATHERINE-Face of Mother India-Lond-nd-H Hamilton-41p-red cl,400 photos (gg6,soil cl) 30.00

MAYO,KATHERINE-Isles of Fear-(1925)-Harcourt,Brace-372p-photo plts-1st ed (u8,cov sl wn,soil) 10.00

MAYO,WILLIAM J-Collection of Papers Published Previous to 1909-Phila & Lond-1912-W B Saunders-2 vols-blu cl,71 figs on plts-1st ed (j2) 65.00

MAYOKOK,ROBERT-Eskimo Customs-1959-Nome Nugget-sm 8vo-37p-blu card cov,illus (mm8) 25.00*

MAYOR,A HYATT-Popular Prints of the Americas-NY-1973-Crown-folio-183p-grn cl,195 illus(incl 47 col) (r10,dj) 32.50

MAYR,ERNST-Birds of the Southwest Pacific-NY-1945-Macmillan-316p-col plts-2nd prtg (d9) 12.00

MAYS,WILLIE-Born to Play Ball-1955-Putnam-photos-1st ed (s8,f,sl wn & sunned dj) 50.00

MAYS,WILLIE-My Life In and Out of Baseball-1966-Dutton-1st ed (r7,f,dj) 25.00

MAZET,HORACE-Shark Fishing off the Great Barrier Reef-NY-1957-12mo-215p-illus (m3,vf,chip dj) 25.00

MAZIERE,FRANCIS-Expedition Tumac Humac-GC-1955-Dbldy-8vo-249p-30 photos,dj design by Edw Gorey-1st ed (ff5,sl tn dj) 20.00

MAZOR,JULIAN-Washington and Baltimore-NY-1968-Knopf-auth 1st bk-1st ed (a10,f,dj) 25.00

MAZZA,IRMA G-Accent on Seasoning-Bost-(1959)-Little,Brown-305p-cl bds-1st ed (m6) 18.00

MAZZA,IRMA G-Herbs for the Kitchen-Bost-1940-Little,Brown-312p-auth 1st bk (m6) 20.00

MAZZANOVICH,ANTON-Trailing Geronimo-LA-1926-Gem Publ-1st ed (mm10,sl fade sp) 100.00

MAZZANOVICH,ANTON-Trailing Geronimo-LA-1926-Gem Publ-277p-cl,col frntis,photos-1st ed (v1) 75.00

MAZZUCHELLI,SAMUEL-Memoirs of Father Mazzuchelli O.P.-Chig-1915-375p-3/4 lea,frntis,fldg map-Howes M457-1st ed (t7) 40.00

MC.,J-Witch-Woman's Revenge-Oswego-1882-R J Oliphant-16p-pict wrps-rare-Wright 3452 (e1,sl stnd back wrpr) 35.00

MCADOO,WILLIAM-Procession to Tyburn-NY-1927-Boni & Liveright-1st ed (w5) 15.00

MCALEXANDER,U G-History of the Thirteenth Regiment United States Infantry-np-1905-Regimental Pr-328p-lea,illus,maps (c4,cov sl wn,sp fade) 150.00

MCALLESTER,DAVID P-TRANSL.-Hogans. Navajo Houses & House Songs-Mddltwn-(1980)-113p-photos-1st ed (v7,dj) 20.00

MCALLISTER,PAM-Bedside,Bathtub and Armchair Companion to Agatha Christie-NY-1979-Ungar-illus-1st ed (h4,as new in dj) 15.00

MCALLISTER,WARD-Society as I Have Found It-NY-(c.1890)-Cassell-469p (a8,sl soil) 50.00

MCALMON,ROBERT-Hasty Bunch-Carbondale-(1977)-SIU Pr-1st ed (j6,f,dj) 20.00

MCALMON,ROBERT-Portrait of a Generation-Paris-(1926)-Contact eds-8vo-wrps,ltd to 200c (x3,sl chip & sunned) 550.00

MCARTHUR,ALEXANDER-Pianoforte Study-Phila-1897-Presser-dec brn cl-1st ed (w1,f) 20.00

MCARTHUR,E D-Electronics and Electron Tubes-1936-173p-89 illus-1st ed (h6) 10.00

MCARTHUR,LEWIS A-Oregon Geographic Names-1952-Binfords & Mort-686p-rvsd & enlgd ed (ff4,dj) 60.00

MCARTHUR,PETER-Around Home-Tor-1925-Musson Bk Co-8vo-250p-illus,dec e.p.-1st ed (bb7,dj) 20.00*

MCATEE,W L-Birds of the Vicinity of the Univ of Indiana-np-1905-8vo-(1),(65-)202p-wrps,32 photos (y8,sp wn) 15.00

MCATEE,W L-Wildfowl Food Plants-Ames-1939-8vo-141p-photos (m3,f) 24.00

MCAULEY,JAMES J-After the Blizaard-Columbia-1975-U of Missouri Pr-cl,iss w/o dj-1st ed (z8,vf) 12.50

MCAULEY,JAMES J-Recital-Dublin-(1982)-Dolmen Pr-wrps-1st ed (z8,f) 45.00

MCBAIN,ED-87th Precinct-1959-S&S-1st ed (x7,vf,vf dj) 60.00

MCBAIN,ED-87th Squad-1960-S&S-1st ed (x7,vf,dj) 65.00

MCBAIN,ED-April Robin Murders-1958-Random-(started by C Rice,finished by McBain)-1st ed (q9,sp chip dj) 20.00

MCBAIN,ED-Ax-1964-S&S-1st ed (x7,f,dj) 65.00

MCBAIN,ED-Blood Relatives-NY-1975-Random-1st ed (h4,f,dj) 12.50

MCBAIN,ED-Eighty Million Eyes-NY-1966-Delacorte-1st ed (f4,dj) 20.00

MCBAIN,ED-Give the Boys a Great Big Hand-1960-S&S-1st ed (x7,f,dj) 60.00

MCBAIN,ED-Goldilocks-1977-Arbor-1st ed (s10,sp chip dj) 15.00

MCBAIN,ED-Guns-NY-1976-Random-1st ed (e4,f,dj) 12.50

MCBAIN,ED-Hail to the Chief-NY-1973-Random-1st ed (f4,dj) 10.00

MCBAIN,ED-Hail, Hail the Gang's All Here-1971-Dbldy-1st ed (x7,f,dj) 35.00

MCBAIN,ED-King's Ransom-1959-S&S-1st ed (x7,f,dj) 80.00

MCBAIN,ED-Lady, Lady, I Did It-1961-S&S-1st ed (x7,f,dj) 55.00

MCBAIN,ED-Sadie When She Died-NY-1972-Dbldy-1st ed (e4,dj) 15.00

MCBAIN,ED-See Them Die-1960-S&S-1st ed (x7,vf,f dj) 70.00

MCBAIN,ED-Til Death-1959-S&S-1st ed (x7,f,dj) 75.00

MCBRIDE,H A-Trains Rolling-NY-1953-269p-237 illus-1st ed (n4,f,dj) 22.00

MCBRIDE,H W-Rifleman Went to War-Plantersville-1935-398p-frntis-1st ed (kk2,sl shaken) 75.00

MCBRIDE,JOHN R-History of the 33rd Indiana Veteran Volunteer Infantry-Indpls-1900-W B Burford-280p-frntis port,illus (n7) 175.00

MCBRIDE,MARY M-America For Me-NY-1941-Macmillan-sm 8vo-102p-1st ed (s1,f,dj) 15.00

MCBRIDE,MARY M-Encyclopedia of Cooking-Evanston-(1958)-Homemakers Rsrch Inst-12 vols,dbl col pgs,illus (o6) 60.00

MCCABE,JOSEPH-History of Satanism-Girard-(1948)-Haldeman-Julius-31,(1)p-wrps,Big Blue Bk B-768 (n1) 12.50

MCCAFFREY,ANNE-Dragondrums-NY-1979-1st ed (j5,f,dj) 20.00

MCCAFFREY,ANNE-Moreta-NY-1983-Del Rey-1st ed (w5,f,sl tn dj) 15.00

MCCAFFREY,ANNE-Ship Who Sang-NY-(1969)-Walker-1st ed (h3,f,sl brwnd & sl tn dj) 150.00

MCCAFFREY,FRANK-Campus Memories-Seattle-1933-Dogwood Pr-sm 8vo-97p-photos (y4,vf) 90.00

MCCAFFREY,P R-From Dusk to Dawn-NY-1932-300,(1)p-cl (d1) 12.50

MCCAGUE,JAMES-Moguls and Iron Men-(1964)-Harper & Row-392p-illus,maps-1st ed (r8,dj) 25.00

MCCAGUE,JAMES-Moguls and Iron Men-NY-1964-392p-1st ed (n4,f,dj) 22.00

MCCAIN,CHARLES W-History of the S S Beaver-Vancouver-1894-99p-illus-scarce-1st ed (e7,wrnkld cov) 100.00

MCCALEB,WALTER F-Conquest of the West-NY-(1947)-Prentice Hall-336p-maps-1st ed (cc4,wn dj) 15.00

MCCALL'S COOK BOOK-(NY)-(1963)-Random-786p-blu bds,dec e.p.-1st prtg (o6) 22.00

MCCALL,COL GEORGE A-New Mexico in 1850: a Military View-Norman-1968-U of Okla-1st ed (u9,dj) 25.00

MCCALL,DOROTHY L-Ranch Under the Rimrock-Portland-(1968)-166p+photos-1st ed so stated (r8,dj) 15.00

MCCALL,SAMUEL W-Life of Thomas Brackett Reed-Bost,NY-(1914)-303p-cl (g1) 15.00

MCCALLUM,HENRY-Wire That Fenced the West-Norman-(1965)-U of Okla Pr-8vo-285p-16p illus-1st ed (gg5,sl tn dj) 30.00

MCCALLUM,JOHN-Everest Diary-NY-1966-213p-28 photos-1st ed (q10,f,dj) 30.00

MCCALLUM,JOHN-Port Angles, U.S.A.-Seattle-(1961)-Wood & Reber-8vo-197p-32p photos-1st ed (cc5,dj,2 autg) 25.00

MCCALLUM,JOHN-Tiger Wore Spikes-1956-Barnes (q7,dj) 40.00

MCCALLUM,JOHN-Ty Cobb-1975-Praeger-photos-1st ed (s8,f,dj) 20.00

MCCAMPBELL,COLEMAN-Texas Seaport-NY-1952-305p-photos,illus,fldg map-1st ed (t7) 20.00

MCCANN,EDSON-Preferred Risk-NY-1955-1st ed (bb10,brwnd pgs,sl chip dj) 25.00

MCCARRY,CHARLES-Miernik Dossier-Lond-1974-Hutchinson-1st Brit ed (p4,f,dj) 27.50

MCCARRY,CHARLES-Miernik Dossier-NY-1973-Saturday Rev-1st ed (e4,dj) 25.00

MCCARRY,CHARLES-Secret Lovers-1977-Dutton-1st ed (s10,dj) 15.00

MCCARTER,MARGARET H-Winning the Wilderness-Chig-1914-404p-col frntis-1st ed (t7,dj) 20.00

MCCARTER,ROBERT H-Memories of a Half Century at the New Jersey Bar-(np)-1937-xii,178p-cl,plts-ltd to 150c,nbrd,autg-"Autographed Ed." (aa6) 45.00

MCCARTHY,CORMAC-Child of God-Lond-1975-Chatto & Windus-1st Brit ed (m7,bk & dj sp bump) 60.00

MCCARTHY,CORMAC-Child of God-Lond-1975-Chatto-1st Brit ed (kk6,f,dj) 65.00

MCCARTHY,CORMAC-Child of God-NY-(1973)-Random-1st ed (j6,sl wn dj) 150.00

MCCARTHY,CORMAC-Child of God-NY-1974-1st ed (z6,vf,dj) 200.00

MCCARTHY,CORMAC-Orchard Keeper-Lond-1966-full col pict dj-scarce-1st Brit ed (z6,vf,dj) 300.00

MCCARTHY,CORMAC-Suttree-1980-Chatto-1st Brit ed (kk6,f,dj) 45.00

MCCARTHY,EUGENE-Familiar Fish-NY-1900-8vo-216p-illus-1st ed (m3,vf) 17.50

MCCARTHY,JAMES R-New Pioneers-Indpls-(1934)-343p-cl-1st ed so stated (j1,few sm checkmrks) 15.00

MCCARTHY,JOE-Days and Nights at Costello's-(1980)-Little,Brown-281p-blu bds-1st ed (q8,dj) 15.00

MCCARTHY,JOSEPH-McCarthyism-NY-1952-Devin Adair-4to-104p-wrps,illus-1st ed (e2) 25.00

MCCARTHY,JOSEPH-Treason in Washington-St.Louis-1950-stapled prntd wrps-1st ed (q5) 25.00

MCCARTHY,MARGUERITE G-Aunt Ella's Cook Book-Bost-1949-Little,Brown-205p-red check bds-1st ed (n6,sl wn) 18.00

MCCARTHY,MARY-Cannibals and Missionaries-NY-1979-1st ed (r2,f,dj,autg) 35.00

MCCARTHY,MARY-Group-NY-1963-Harcourt-1st ed (w5,f,f dj) 25.00

MCCARTHY,MARY-Groves of Academe-NY-(1952)-Harcourt,Brace-8vo-302p-1st ed (w6,f,dj) 35.00

MCCARTHY,MARY-On the Contrary-NY-(1961)-FS&C-1st ed (hh5,dj) 15.00

MCCARTHY,MARY-On the Contrary-NY-(1961)-FS&C-gry cl-1st ed (f2,dj) 25.00

MCCARTHY,MARY-Theatre Sights and Spectacles-NY-(1956)-FS&C-1st ed (cc2,f,dj) 40.00

MCCARTHY,MARY-Venice Observed-NY-1956-Reynal-col photos,I Morath-1st ed (e8,f,dj missing 2 chips) 50.00

MCCARTHY,MARY-Winter Visitors-NY-(1970)-HBJ-special ltd ed publ for friends of auth & publ (hh5) 12.50

MCCARTHY,PATRICK-Celine-NY-(1976)-Viking-1st ed (bb1,f,dj) 15.00

MCCARTHY,THOMAS-First Convention-Dublin-1978-Dolmen Pr-wrps,auth 1st bk-1st ed (z8,vf) 35.00

MCCARTNEY,CLARENCE E-Mr Lincoln's Admirals-NY-1956-335p-illus,map-1st ed (n3,dj) 27.50

MCCARVER,NORMAN-Hearne on the Brazos-1958-Century-369p-1st ed (a9) 75.00

MCCAULEY,LENA-Joy of Gardens-NY-1911-McNally-239p-cl (x6) 12.00

MCCAUSLAND,ELIZABETH-George Inness-NY-1946-Amer Artists Group-4to-cl-1st ed (oo6,dj) 65.00

MCCAWLEY,E S-Shotguns & Shooting-NY-1965-8vo-146p-photos (m3,vf,dj) 12.50

MCCLANE,A J-101 of the World's Best Fishing Spots-E Hartford-1952-4to-unpgd-wrps (m3) 25.00

MCCLANE,A J-American Angler-NY-1954-8vo-207p-photos-1st ed (m3,f,sl fray dj) 15.00

MCCLANE,A J-ED.-McClane's New Standard Fishing Encyclopedia-NY-1974-4to-1156p-illus,photos,col plts-1st ed (m3,vf,dj) 40.00

MCCLANE,A J-ED.-Wise Fishermen's Encyclopedia-NY-1951-8vo-1336p-illus (m3,f,chip dj) 17.50

MCCLANE,A J-Spinning for Fresh & Saltwater Fish in North America-NY-1952-8vo-280p-illus (m3,f,dj) 10.00

MCCLARY,JANE M-Portion for Foxes-NY-1972-S&S-1st ed (h9,wn dj) 12.00

MCCLELLAN,ELISABETH-Historic Dress in America 1607 thru 1800; Historic Dress in America 1800 thru 1870-Phila-(1904 & 1910)-2 vols-photo,drwngs,col plts-1st eds (u7) 125.00

MCCLELLAN,GEORGE B-McClellan's Own Story-NY-1887-Webster & Co-678p-pict cl,illus,maps-Nevins I,124-1st ed (bb4,sl wn sp) 75.00

MCCLELLAN,GEORGE B-Report on the Organization and Campaigns of the Army of the Potomac-NY-1864-Sheldon-480p-cl (j1) 35.00

MCCLELLAN,GEORGE B-Report on the Organization and Campaigns of the Army of the Potomac-NY-1864-Sheldon & Co-480p-purple cl,maps-1st ed (k2,sl wn sp) 75.00

MCCLELLAN,H B-Life and Campaigns of Major General J E B Stuart-Bost-1885-Houghton Mifflin-468p-7 fldg maps-1st ed (dd4,rbnd,sp lettrng faded) 175.00

MCCLENAGHAN,JACK-Fiordland-Wellington-(1966)-Reed-8vo-180p-41 illus-1st NZ ed (jj5,dj edgewn,sl tn) 10.00

MCCLERNAND,EDWARD J-With the Indian and the Buffalo in Montana, 1870 to 1878-Glendale-1969-Arthur H Clark-176p-maps,illus-ltd to 300c (ee4) 250.00

MCCLINTOCK,JAMES-Mormon Settlement in Arizona-Phoenix-1921-307p-illus-1st ed (d3) 35.00

MCCLINTOCK,JOHN S-Pioneer Days in the Black Hills-Deadwood-(1939)-336p-illus-Six Guns #1391-1st ed (cc4) 225.00

MCCLINTOCK,WALTER-Old Indian Trails-Bost-1923-326p-col frntis,illus-1st ed (u7,e.p. clipped) 45.00

MCCLINTOCK,WALTER-Old North Trail...-Lond-1910-Macmillan-xxvi,540p-orig g dec blu cl,col frntis,fldg map,photo plts-Howes M45-1st ed (v1) 175.00

MCCLINTON,K M-Art Deco, a Guide for Collectors-NY-1972-275 b&w & 16 col plts-1st ed (h10,dj) 50.00

MCCLOSKEY,MICHAEL-Formative Years of the Missionary College of Santa Cruz of Queretaro: 1683 to 1733-1955-Acad Amer Francscn Hist-128p-1st ed (d3,dj) 30.00

MCCLOW,L L-Tumbling Illustrated-NY-1931-illus-1st ed (r2) 30.00

MCCLUNG,NELLIE-Three Times and Out-Tor-1918-T Allen-cl,illus-Watters p.577-1st Can ed (pp2,sl soil & rub) 35.00*

MCCLUNG,ROBERT H-Otus, the Story of a Screech Owl-NY-1959-Morrow-unpgd-pict cl,col & b&w illus,L Sandford-1st ed (r3,f,dj) 25.00

MCCLURE,A K-Three Thousand Miles Through the Rocky Mountains-Phila-1869-Lippincott-456p-orig cl,3 plts-Smith 6231-1st ed (v1) 150.00

MCCLURE,H E-Migration & Survival of the Birds of Asia-Bangkok-1974-4to-(1),476,(1)p-illus (y8,cor wn) 38.00

MCCLURE,J B-Edison and His Inventions-Chig-1879-Rhodes & McClure-171p+ads-red cl,engrvngs-1st ed (d2,drknd sp,few spots) 100.00

MCCLURE,J B-Edison and His Inventions...-Chig-1879-Rhodes & McClure-171p+ads-red cl-1st ed (dd1) 85.00

MCCLURE,JAMES-Blood of an Englishman-NY-1981-Harper-1st Amer ed (s4,vf,dj) 27.50

MCCLURE,JAMES-Caterpillar Cop-NY-1972-1st US ed (r5,f,dj) 25.00

MCCLURE,JAMES-Gooseberry Fool-NY-1974-1st US ed (r5,f,dj) 22.50

MCCLURE,JAMES-Spike Island-Lond-1980-Macmillan-1st ed (s4,f,dj) 35.00

MCCLURE,JAMES-Steam Pig-NY et al-(1971)-Harper & Row-auth 1st bk-1st US ed (a10,dj) 35.00

MCCLURE,MICHAEL-Beard-SF-1967-wrps-1st ed (x8) 20.00

MCCLURE,MICHAEL-For Artaud-(NY)-(1959)-(Totem Pr)-8vo-wrps-1st ed (jj8,f) 20.00

MCCLURE,MICHAEL-Freewheelin' Frank, Secretary of the Angels-NY-1967-1st ed (t5,f,dj) 15.00

MCCLURE,MICHAEL-Meat Science Essays-(SF)-(1963)-City Lights-sm 8vo-pict wrps-1st ed (jj8,f) 15.00

MCCLURE,MICHAEL-Plane Pomes-NY-1969-Phoenix Bk Shop-wrps-ltd to 100c,nbrd,autg-1st ed (cc1,f) 50.00

MCCLURE,MICHAEL-Scratching the Beat Surface-SF-1982-North Point-1st ed (k7,f,dj) 15.00

MCCONKEY,HARRIET E B-Dakota War Whoop-Chig-1965-Donnelley & Sons-frntis,illus-Lakeside Classics (ff4) 20.00

MCCONNELL,H H-Five Years a Cavalryman-Jacksboro-1888-319p-prntd on pink papr-Howes M59-rare-1st ed (t7) 375.00

MCCONNELL,J R-Flying for France-GC-1917-8vo-xiv,158p-illus cl,frntis,5p plts-1st ed (s2) 50.00

MCCONNELL,JOSEPH C-West Texas Frontier-Jacksboro Palo Pinto-1933,1939-2 vols-photos-Rader #2281-1st ed (t7,pres) 275.00

MCCONNELL,LELA G-Hitherto and Henceforth in the Kentucky Mountains-np-(1949)-221p-cl (d1,sl wn dj) 15.00

MCCONNELL,W J-Early History of Idaho-Caldwell-1913-Caxton-8vo-420p-cl,frntis port-Howes M62-1st ed (v1) 150.00

MCCORD,DAVID-Andrew Wyeth-Bost-(1970)-Mus Fine Arts-oblng 4to-cl-1st ed (oo6,sl soil dj) 35.00

MCCORD,WILLIAM B-ED.-Souvenir History of Ye Old town Salem, Ohio...-Salem-1906-128p-cl,dbl cols (n1) 20.00

MCCORKLE,JILL-July 7th-Chapel Hill-1984-Algonquin Bks-auth co 1st bk wi "The Cheer Leader"-1st ed (cc1,sl tn dj,autg) 100.00

MCCORMICK,CALVIN-Memoir of Miss Eliza McCoy-Dallas-1892-publ by auth-162p-cl (c1) 45.00

MCCORMICK,DONALD-Who's Who in Spy Fiction-Lond-1977-Elm Tree-1st ed (p4,f,dj) 25.00

MCCORMICK,ESTHER-Sunbury's Part in Ohio History-np-(1966)-158p-wrps (g1) 12.50

MCCORMICK,HARRIET-Landscape Art Past and Present-NY-1923-Scribner-4to-31p+56p plts,cl-ltd to 1200c (x6,rub,sl fox) 125.00

MCCORMICK,LEANDER-Fishing Round the World-NY-1937-8vo-307p-photos (m3) 22.50

MCCORMICK,RICHARD P-Experiment in Independence-New Brunswick-1950-xiii,338p-cl,fldg map (aa6) 35.00

MCCORMICK,RICHARD-Visit to the Camp Before Sevastopol-NY-1855-212p-fldg map,7 plts(2 fldg)-1st ed (b7,sp sun,sl fox) 90.00

MCCORMICK,WILFRED-Bases Loaded-1950-Putnam-1st ed (q7,dj) 25.00

MCCORMICK,WILFRED-Go Ahead Runner-1965-McKay-#13 in Bronc Burnett ser-1st ed (s8,f,f dj) 30.00

MCCORMICK,WILFRED-Legion Tourney-1948-G&D (q7,dj) 15.00

MCCORMICK,WILFRED-Three Two Pitch-1948-Putnam-#1 in Bronc Burnett ser-1st ed (s8,dj) 35.00

MCCOWAN,P-Animals of the Canadian Rockies-Tor-1938(1936)-8vo-302p-cl,frntis,19 plts (y8,sp fade,pres cpy) 35.00

MCCOY,ALFRED C-Politics of Heroin in Southeast Asia-NY-1972-Harper-464p-1st ed (r1,f,dj sl tn,spot) 35.00

MCCOY,DELL-Crystal River Pictorial-Denver-1972-224p-1st ed (n4) 29.50

MCCOY,HORACE-I Should Have Stayed Home-NY-1938-1st ed (r5,dj) 125.00

MCCOY,HORACE-Kiss Tomorrow Good Bye-NY-(1948)-Random-1st ed (ff6,sl wn dj) 100.00

MCCOY,HORACE-Scalpel-NY-(1952)-Appleton-1st ed (w1,f,f dj) 50.00

MCCOY,HORACE-They Shoot Horses, Don't They-NY-1935-1st ed (q5,sl fox bds,lacks dj.) 45.00

MCCOY,ISAAC-History of Baptist Indian Missions-Wash-1840-Wm M Morrison-611p-cl-Howes M68-1st ed (ee4,ex-libr,rbnd) 300.00

MCCOY,JOSEPH G-Historic Sketches of the Cattle Trade of the West and Southwest-Columbus-1951-Long's College Bk Co-427p-illus-Howes M72 (cc4,dj) 65.00

MCCRACKEN,HAROLD-American Cowboy-GC-1973-Dbldy-4to-198p-cl,illus-1st ed (z4,sl wn dj) 50.00

MCCRACKEN,HAROLD-Beast that Walks Like Man-NY-1955-319p-photos (gg3,f,dj) 35.00

MCCRACKEN,HAROLD-Beast That Walks Like Man-NY-1955-8vo-319p-illus-1st ed (m3) 25.00

MCCRACKEN,HAROLD-Charles M Russell Book-GC-1957-Dbldy-sm folio-236p-pict cl,illus e.p.,col illus,acetate cov-Herd 1387-1st trd ed (gg4) 50.00

MCCRACKEN,HAROLD-Frederic Remington Book-GC-1966-Dbldy-4to-284p (z4,dj) 35.00

MCCRACKEN,HAROLD-George Catlin and the Old Frontier-1959-Dial-folio-216p-36 col & 131 b&w plts-1st ed (d3,dj) 50.00

MCCRACKEN,HAROLD-Portrait of the Old West-NY-(1952)-McGraw Hill-sm folio-232p-illus-1st ed (gg4,dj) 30.00

MCCRACKEN,HAROLD-Son of the Walrus King-Phila,NY-(1944)-Lippincott-cl,drwngs by L B Hunt-1st ed (aa9,sp fade) 25.00

MCCRACKEN,M C-Hidalgo, Home Life at West Lawn-Chig-1904-Donohue-222p-cl,photos (z7) 35.00

MCCRARY,J R-First of the Many-NY-1944-8vo-xxxii,242p-illus cl,196 text illus incl plts-1st ed (s2,chip dj) 50.00

MCCREIGHT,M I-Firewater and Forked Tongues-Pasadena-(1947)-Trail's End Publ-180p-2 col illus,C M Russell-1st ed (dd4,wn dj) 35.00

MCCULLERS,CARSON-Clock Without Hands-Bost-1961-Houghton Mifflin-1st ed (w6,vf,dj) 75.00

MCCULLERS,CARSON-Member of the Wedding, a Play-NY-(1951)-New Directions-1st ed (w5,f,dj) 125.00

MCCULLERS,CARSON-Member of the Wedding-Bost-1946-Houghton Mifflin-1st ed (a5,rub dj wi sm tape mrks) 85.00

MCCULLERS,CARSON-Mortgaged Heart-Bost-1971-1st ed (r5,dj) 15.00

MCCULLERS,CARSON-Reflections in a Golden Eye-Cambridge-1941-Houghton,Mifflin-1st issue dj wi cellophane window-1st ed (a5,sl soil cov,dj cel puckrd) 150.00

MCCULLERS,CARSON-Square Root of Wonderful-Bost-1958-Houghton Mifflin-8vo-159p-1st ed (w6,f,dj) 75.00

MCCULLERS,CARSON-Square Root of Wonderful-Lond-1958-Cresset Pr-1st Brit ed (a5,sl soil dj) 50.00

MCCULLEY,JOHNSTON-Black Star Murders-NY-1921-Chelsea-1st ed (h4) 15.00

MCCULLOUGH,COLLEEN-Thorn Birds-NY et al-(1977)-Harper & Row-1st ed (c10,f,dj) 17.50

MCCULLOUGH,EDO-Good Old Coney Island-NY-1957-Scribner's-344p-illus-1st ed (p2,f,dj) 15.00

MCCULLOUGH,ROBERT-Pennsylvania Main Line Canal-York-1973-wrps,illus (pp4) 15.00

MCCULLY,ANDERSON-American Alpines in the Garden-NY-1931-Macmillan-251p-cl (x6) 18.00

MCCULLY,HELEN-Cooking with Helen McCully Beside You-(1970)-Random-oblng 8vo-321p-grn cl (q8,dj) 15.00

MCCULLY,HELEN-Nobody Ever Tells You These Things-(1967)-Holt-308p-pict wht cl,illus e.p.,illus-1st ed (q8,dj) 15.00

MCCULLY,HELEN-Things You've Alway Wanted to Know About Food & Drink-(1972)-Holt-248p-blk/wht cl-1st ed (q8,dj) 15.00

MCCUNE,ALICE P-History of Juab County, 1847 to 1947-(Nephi)-1947-301p-maroon bds,illus-1st ed (mm10) 65.00

MCCURDY,H W-Marine History of the Pacific Northwest-Seattle-1966 & 1977-folio-2 vols-illus-1st ed (c7,f,vol.2 box) 375.00

MCCURDY,JAMES G-Indian Days at Neah Bay-Seattle-(1961)-123p-illus-ltd ed-1st ed (h7,chip dj) 35.00

MCCURDY,ROBERT-Book of Garden Flowers-NY-1931-Dbldy-311p-cl,col illus (x6) 6.00

MCCUTCHAN,JOSEPH-Mier Expedition Diary-Austin-1978-U of Tex-1st ed (u9,dj) 25.00

MCCUTCHAN,PHILIP-Drakotny-Lond-1971-Harrap-1st ed (p4,f,dj) 25.00

MCCUTCHAN,PHILIP-Man from Moscow-Lond-1963-Harrap-1st ed (e4,f,sl wn dj) 20.00

MCCUTCHEON,G-Daughter of Anderson Crow-1907-DM-1st ed (x7) 20.00

MCDADE,THOMAS M-Annals of Murder-Norman-(1961)-U of Okla Pr-359p-illus-Six Guns 1398-1st ed (gg4,dj) 75.00

MCDANIEL,RUEL-One More Sunrise-Port Lavaca-1965-Tex Hist Publ-165p-photos-1st ed (v3) 38.00

MCDANIEL,RUEL-Vinegarron-Kingsport-1936-So Publ-143p-1st ed (ff8) 37.00

MCDERMAND,CHARLES-Waters of the Golden Trout Country-NY-1946-8vo-162p-illus-1st ed (m3) 15.00

MCDERMAND,CHARLES-Yosemite & Kings Canyon Trout-NY-1947-8vo-178p-illus (m3,dj fade & Wn) 20.00

MCDERMOTT,ALICE-Bigamist's Daughter-NY-1982-auth 1st bk-1st ed (t5,f,dj) 60.00

MCDERMOTT,CHARLES H-History of the Shoe and Leather Industries of the U.S.-Bost-1918-John W Denehy-4to-(viii)+404p-red dec cl,ports-1st ed (c2) 75.00

MCDERMOTT,JOHN F-Captain Philip Pittman's the Present State of the European Settlements on the Mississippi-Memphis-1977-123p-pict cl,frntis,maps,fldg maps-1st ed thus (t7,f) 22.50

MCDERMOTT,JOHN F-ED.-Before Mark Twain-Carbondale-1968-298p-illus,map e.p.-1st ed (t7,dj) 10.00

MCDERMOTT,JOHN F-ED.-Travelers on the Western Frontier-Urbana-1970-351p-photos,illus,maps-1st ed (t7,dj) 15.00

MCDERMOTT,JOHN F-ED.-Western Journals of Dr.George Hunter 1796 to 1805-Phila-1963-APS-4to-133p-wrps (x6,as new) 30.00

MCDERMOTT,JOHN F-ED.-Western Journals of Washington Irving-Norman-1954-201p-illus-1st ed (t7,dj) 25.00

MCDERMOTT,JOHN F-Seth Eastman, Pictorial Historian of the Indian-Norman-1961-U of Okla Pr-sm 4to-270p-116p illus(8 col)-1st ed (a9,dj) 45.00

MCDONALD,ARCHDEACON R-Grammar of the Tukudh Language-Lond-1911-201p-orig cl-Smith 6301 (a7) 350.00

MCDONALD,CLEVELAND-History of Cedarville College-Cedarville-(1966)-170p-wrps (j1,f,autg) 12.50

MCDONALD,DANIEL-History of Freemasonry in Indiana from 1806 to 1898-Indpls-1898-473p-cl (c1) 30.00

MCDONALD,FREDERIC W-Recreations of a Book Lover-Lond-1911-Hodder & Stoughton-viii,216p-g dec cl,t.e.g.-1st ed (dd10,sl rub,rear cov stnd) 25.00

MCDONALD,GREGORY-Fletch & the Widow Bradley-Lond-1981-Gollancz-1st Brit & 1st hdbk ed (r4,vf,dj) 45.00

MCDONALD,GREGORY-Fletch-NY-1974-Bobbs-Merill-1st ed (d4,f,dj) 150.00

MCDONALD,GREGORY-Running Scared-1964-Obolensky-1st ed (x7,f,sl rub dj) 75.00

MCDONALD,GREGORY-Running Scared-1964-Obolensky-auth 1st bk-1st ed (s10,dj) 50.00

MCDONALD,GREGORY-Who Took Toby Rinaldi?-NY-(1980)-Putnam-1st ed (h3,f,dj) 20.00

MCDONALD,JOHN D-Brass Cupcake-Lond-1974-Hale-auth 1st bk-1st Brit hdbk ed (s4,vf,dj) 55.00

MCDONALD,JOHN-ED.-Complete Fly Fisherman-NY-1947-8vo-551p-illus,Robt Ball-1st ed (m3,f) 70.00

MCDONALD,JOHN-Origins of Angling-GC-1953-4to-273p-illus-1st ed (m3,f,dj) 40.00

MCDONALD,JOHN-Quill Gordon-NY-1972-4to-196p-col plts-1st ed (m3,vf,dj) 35.00

MCDONALD,LUCILE-Coast Country-1966-Binfords & Mort-184p-photos-1st ed (r8,dj chip) 20.00

MCDONALD,LUCILLE-Swan Among the Indians-Portland-(1972)-233p-illus,e.p. maps-1st ed so stated (g7,vf,dj) 30.00

MCDONALD,VIRGINIA-How I Cook It-KC-(1949)-Glenn-256p-grn cl-1st ed (q8,dj) 15.00

MCDONOUGH,JAMES L-Chattanooga-Knoxville-(1984)-298p-illus,maps-1st ed (n3,f,dj) 20.00

MCDONOUGH,JAMES L-Five Tragic Hours-Knoxville-(1983)-217p-illus-1st ed (n3,f,dj) 25.00

MCDOUALL,ROBIN-Collins Pocket Guide to Good Cooking-Lond-1955-Collins-256p-red cl,4 col plts,16p photos-1st ed (q8,dj) 12.50

MCDOUGALL,J-Saddle, Sled and Snowshoe: Pioneering on the Saskatchewan in the Sixties-Cin-(1896)-282p-illus-1st US ed (a7,rub sp lttrng) 75.00

MCDOWELL,CATHERINE-ED.-Now You Hear My Horn-Austin-1967-212p-frntis,photos,map e.p.,illus-1st ed (t7,f,dj) 30.00

MCDOWELL,CATHERINE-ED.-Now You Hear My Horn-Austin-1967-U of Tex-1st ed (u9,dj) 37.50

MCELROY,JOSEPH-Ancient History-NY-1971-1st ed (r5,f,dj) 25.00

MCELROY,JOSEPH-Hind's Kidnap-NY-1969-H&R-1st ed (y1,f,dj) 40.00

MCELROY,JOSEPH-Letter Left to Me-NY-1988-1st ed (o5,f,dj) 20.00

MCELROY,JOSEPH-Lookout Cartridge-NY-1974-1st ed (o5,f,dj) 25.00

MCELROY,JOSEPH-Plus-NY-1977-Knopf-1st ed (w5,f,dj) 35.00

MCELROY,LUCY C-Juletty, a Story of Old Kentucky-NY-(1901)-280p-cl (e1,sl rub,sm dmpstn frnt cov) 17.50

MCELWAINE,EUGENE-Truth About Alaska-(Chig)-1901-the Auth-445p-grn cl,g sp,photos-1st ed (w1,sp g fade) 150.00

MCENNIS,JOHN T-ED.-Clan Na Gael and the Murder of Dr.Cronin-Chig-1889-Johns Publ-526p-cl (a1) 35.00

MCEWAN,IAN-Cement Garden-NY-(1978)-S&S-1st ed (bb1,as new in dj) 25.00

MCEWAN,IAN-In Between the Sheets & Other Stories-NY-(1978)-S&S-1st ed (bb1,as new in dj) 20.00

MCFADDEN,DOROTHY-Touring the Gardens of Europe-NY-(1965)-sm 8vo-xiii,306p-yel cl,maps (j10) 10.00

MCFADDEN,ROY-Flowers For a Lady-Lond-(1945)-Routledge-1st ed (z8,vf,wn dj) 40.00

MCFADDEN,ROY-Garryowen-Lond-1971-Chatto & Windus,Hogarth-(Phoenix Living Poets)-1st ed (z8,vf,dj) 40.00

MCFADDEN,ROY-Swords and Ploughshares-Lond-(1943)-Routledge-card covs wi shelf wrps-scarce-1st ed (z8,f) 85.00

MCFARLAND,D-ED.-Oxford Companion to Animal Behavior-1982-Oxford Univ-653p-illus-1st ed (bb3,f,dj) 30.00

MCFARLAND,J HORACE-Rose in America-NY-(1923)-x,233p-grn cl,5 col photos(incl cov onlay),16 sepia photos-1st ed (m10,wn) 10.50

MCFARLAND,RAYMOND-History of the New England Fisheries, with Maps-NY-1911-U of Penn-grn cl-1st ed (mm10) 65.00

MCFARLAND,WILLIAM L-Salmon of the Atlantic-NY-1925-8vo-156p-photos-1st ed (m3,f,badly wn box) 45.00

MCFARLING,LLOYD-ED.-Exploring the Northern Plains 1804 to 1876-Caldwell-1955-441p-maps-1st ed (f7,dj) 45.00

MCFEE,WILLIAM-Harbourmaster-GC-1932-Dbldy,Doran-v scarce glassine dj overlay-1st ed (bb1,sp dull,dj & overlay) 45.00

MCFEE,WILLIAM-In the First Watch-NY-1946-Random-1st ed (x1,dj tn) 32.50

MCFEE,WILLIAM-North of Suez-NY-1930-Dbldy,Doran-orig linen bckd bds,papr labls,t.e.g.,publ box wi papr sp labl-ltd to 350c,autg-1st ed (aa9,box) 75.00

MCFEE,WILLIAM-North of Suez-NY-1930-DD Doran-papr labls-ltd to 350c,autg (x1) 50.00

MCFEELY,WILLIAM S-Grant-NY-(1981)-592p-illus-1st ed (c4,dj) 25.00

MCFEELY,WILLIAM S-Grant-NY-(1981)-Norton-592p-illus-1st ed (o7,dj) 20.00

MCGAFFEY,ERNEST-Outdoors-NY-1907-12mo-271p-1st ed (m3) 14.00

MCGAFFEY,ERNEST-Poems of Gun & Rod-NY-1892-8vo-140p-illus (m3) 20.00

MCGAHERN,JOHN-Getting Through-NY-(1980)-Harper & Row-1st Amer ed (z8,vf,dj) 14.50

MCGAHERN,JOHN-Nightlines-Bost-(1971)-Little,Brown-1st Amer ed (z8,vf,sl wn dj) 12.50

MCGAVIN,E C-Mormon Pioneers-SLC-1947-236p-pict cl-1st ed (t7) 22.50

MCGAW,WILLIAM C-Savage Scene-NY-(1972)-242p-illus-1st ed (c4,f,dj) 25.00

MCGERR,PAT-Death in a Million Living Rooms-NY-1951-Dbldy CC-1st ed (e4,f,dj sp sl wn) 25.00

MCGERR,PAT-Follow, as the Night-NY-1950-Dbldy CC-1st ed (g4,yel pgs,dj) 15.00

MCGIFFEN,LEE-Horse Hunters-NY-1963-Dutton-1st ed (f10,dj) 18.00

MCGILL,PATRICK-Soldier Songs-Lond-1918-H Jenkins-1st trd ed (z8,f) 50.00

MCGILLICUDDY,T D-Proceedings of ...the Department of Ohio Grand Army of the Republic for the First Fourteen Years...-Columbus-1912-175p-cl (j1) 17.50

MCGILLYCUDDY,JULIA B-McGillycuddy Agent-(1941)-Stanford U Pr-291p-Six Guns #1404-1st ed (cc4) 75.00

MCGIRR,EDMUND-Bardel's Murder-Lond-1973-Gollancz-1st ed (p4,dj) 20.00

MCGLASHEN,C F-History of the Donner Party-nd-Stanford-261p+LVII p-Stanford Univ facs rprnt of 1881 ed (h7,f,dj) 20.00

MCGOODWIN,H-Architectural Shades & Shadows-Bost-1904-illus-2nd ed (h10,sp top sl tn) 50.00

MCGOODWIN,HENRY-Architectural Shades and Shadows-Bost-1904-folio-118p-buckrm,drwngs,photos-1st ed (ff10) 32.50

MCGOWAN,DAN-Animals of the Canadian Rockies-NY-1936-8vo-302p-1/4 lea,frontis,photos-scarce-1st ed (m3) 25.00

MCGOWAN,DAN-Tidewater to Timberline-Tor-1951-8vo-205p-photos-1st ed (m3,fray dj) 12.50

MCGRAIL,JOIE-Catch & the Feast-NY-1969-4to-196p-col photos (m3,vf,dj) 25.00

MCGRANE,REGINALD C-William Allen, a Study in Western Democracy-(Columbus)-(1925)-279p-cl (g1) 17.50

MCGRAW,ELOISE J-Merry Go Round in Oz-Chig-1963-Reilly & Lee-scarce-1st ed (z2,f,dj chip,creased) 300.00

MCGRAW,JOHN-My Thirty Years in Baseball-NY-(1923)-Boni & Liveright-265p-photos-1st ed (f9,fade,spots) 45.00

MCGRAW,PEG-Assignment: Prison Riots-NY-1954-Holt-270p-cl,photos (cc3,dj) 40.00

MCGRAW,TUG-Screwball-1974-Houghton Mifflin-1st ed (s8,f,dj) 12.00

MCGREGOR,ALEXANDER-Counting Sheep-(1982)-U of Wash-482p-photos,maps-1st ed (r8,f,f dj) 35.00

MCGREGOR,JAMES H-Wounded Knee Massacre-Mpls-(1950)-140p-stiff wrps,illus (c7,autg) 30.00

MCGROARTY,JOHN S-California Its History and Romance-LA-1911-393p-frntis,photos-1st ed (t7,f,pres) 35.00

MCGROARTY,JOHN S-California of the South-Chig-1933-S J Clarke-5 vols-cl,mrbld edges,frntis port,illus-1st ed (kk1,cov sl soil) 125.00

MCGROARTY,JOHN S-California-LA-(1924)-Grafton Publ-393p-illus (cc4) 15.00

MCGUANE,THOMAS-An Outside Chance-NY-(1980)-FS&G-1st ed (c10,f,dj) 50.00

MCGUANE,THOMAS-An Outside Chance-NY-1980-1st ed (p5,dj) 40.00

MCGUANE,THOMAS-Bushwacked Piano-NY-(1971)-S&S-1st ed (c10,f,dj sp sl drknd,sl soil) 100.00

MCGUANE,THOMAS-Missouri Breaks-1976-Ballantine-wrps-1st ed (p9) 15.00

MCGUANE,THOMAS-Ninety Two in the Shade-Lond-(1974)-Collins-1st Brit ed (s6,dj) 40.00

MCGUANE,THOMAS-Ninety Two in the Shade-NY-(1973)-FS&G-1st ed (n9,vf,dj) 60.00

MCGUANE,THOMAS-Ninety-Two in the Shade-NY-(1973)-FS&G-1st ed (c10,f,dj) 60.00

MCGUANE,THOMAS-Nobody's Angel-NY-1981-1st ed (q5,f,dj) 35.00

MCGUANE,THOMAS-Nobody's Angel-NY-1981-Random-1st ed (h8,f,dj) 45.00

MCGUANE,THOMAS-Panama-(1978)-Farrar-1st ed (p9,dj) 25.00

MCGUANE,THOMAS-Panama-NY-(1978)-FS&G-1st ed (b5,as new in dj) 20.00

MCGUANE,THOMAS-To Skin a Cat-NY-(1980)-Dutton/Lawrence-1st ed (ee2,f,dj) 25.00

MCGUFFEY'S ALTERNATE SIXTH READER-Cin,NY-(1889)-Van Antwerp,Bragg-432p-cl (k1) 22.50

MCGUFFEY'S FIFTH ECLECTIC READER-NY,Cin,Chg-(1896)-Amer Bk Co-352p-cl-revsd ed (k1,rub,sl edge-wn) 12.50

MCGUFFEY'S NEWLY REVISED ECLECTIC SPELLING BOOK...ENGLISH ORTHOEPY-Cin-(1846)-Winthrop B Smith-144p-bds-Imprvd stereotype ed (k1,sl wn) 50.00

MCGUFFEY'S SIXTH ECLECTIC READER-NY,Cin,Chg-(1921)-Amer Bk Co-464p-bds-revsd ed (k1,f) 8.50

MCGUFFEY,A H-McGuffey's Rhetorical Guide-Cin-(1844)-Winthrop B Smith-480p-mod lea-Stereotype ed (k1,rbnd) 125.00

MCGUFFEY,WM H-Eclectic Fourth Reader-Cin-1841-Truman & Smith-324p-lea-19th ed (k1) 65.00

MCGUFFEY,WM H-McGuffey's New Third Eclectic Reader-Cin,NY-(1865)-Wilson,Hinkle-242p-pict bds (k1,sl wn) 17.50

MCGUFFEY,WM H-McGuffey's Newly Revised Eclectic Second Reader-Cin-(1848)-Winthrop B Smith-192p-prntd bds (k1,wn,lacks f f.e.p.,sl chip) 35.00

MCGUFFEYS'S NEWLY REVISED ECLECTIC PRIMER-Cin,NY-(1867)-Wilson,Hinkle-34p-pict wrps (k1,wn wrps) 15.00

MCGUFFIE,T H-ED.-Rank and File-NY-1966-424p-illus-1st ed (b7,dj) 25.00

MCGUIRE,J A-In the Alaska-Yukon Gamelands-Cin-1921-8vo-215p-1/2 grn mor,5 raised bnds,g decs,illus (m3) 100.00

MCGUIRK,KATHLEEN L-Diary of Thomas A Edison-1970-72p-25 photos-1st ed (h6,f,dj) 15.00

MCHUGH,ROLAND-Sigla of Finnegans Wake-Austin-(1976)-U of Tex-1st US ed (bb1,as new in dj) 15.00

MCHUGH,TOM-Time of the Buffalo-NY-1972-Knopf-339p-pict e.p.,illus-1st ed (bb4,dj) 30.00

MCHUGH,TOM-Time of the Buffalo-NY-1972-Knopf-8vo-illus e.p.,4 maps,photos,illus-1st ed (bb7,dj) 35.00*

MCILHANY,EDWARD-Recollections of a Forty Niner-KC-1908-Hailman-212p-1st ed (d3,sp wn) 40.00

MCILVAINE,CHARLES-One Thousand American Fungi-Indpls-(1900,1902)-Bowen Merrill-729p-34 col plts,drwngs (l6,hngs breaking) 75.00

MCILVAINE,JANE-Cammie's Challenge-Indpls-1962-Bobbs Merrill-illus,W Dennis-1st ed (h9,dj) 45.00

MCILVAINE,MABEL-INTRO-Reminiscences of Early Chicago-Chig-1912-Lakeside Pr-xxxiv+174p-grn cl-1st ed (b2) 35.00

MCINERNY,RALPH-Bishop as Pawn-NY-1978-Vanguard-1st ed (g4,f,dj) 15.00

MCINERNY,RALPH-Her Death of Cold-NY-1977-Vanguard-1st ed (h4,f,dj) 20.00

MCINERNY,RALPH-Rest in Pieces-1985-Vanguard-1st ed (s10,dj) 12.50

MCINERNY,RALPH-Second Vespers-NY-1980-Vanguard-1st ed (h4,f,dj) 15.00

MCINERNY,RALPH-Seventh Station-NY-1977-Vanguard-1st ed (j4,f,sl tn dj) 15.00

MCINNES,TOM-Romance of the Lost-1908-Montreal Desbarats-auth 1st bk-Watters p.126-1st ed (pp2,hng weak) 75.00*

MCINTOSH,BURR-Little I Saw of Cuba-Lond,NY-(1899)-173p-cl,photos (aa1) 20.00

MCINTOSH,W C-Resources of the Sea-Lond-1899-C J Clay-xvi+248p-blu cl,plts,fldg tbls-1st ed (g2,sm margin tr on 25pgs) 65.00

MCINTURFF,ROY-Wilderness Fishing for Salmon & Steelhead-S Brunswick-1974-8vo-197p-photos-1st ed (m3,vf,dj) 37.50

MCINTYRE,NANCY F-It's a Picnic-(1969)-Viking-150p-grn bds,col dec-1st ed (q8,dj) 12.50

MCINTYRE,PETER-Peter McIntyre's West-Menlo Park-1970-350p-56 tip in col plts-1st ed (t7,dj) 35.00

MCINTYRE,RBT C-Martin Johnson Heade, 1819 to 1904-NY-1948-24 plts-1st ed (h10,dj tn) 100.00

MCINTYRE,VONDA N-Fireflood and other Stories-1979-Houghton Mifflin-1st ed (p9,vf,dj) 25.00

MCKAIG,THOMAS H-Building Failures-NY-(1962)-McGraw Hill-viii+261p-figs-1st ed (j2,dj) 30.00

MCKAY,CLAUDE-Banjo-NY-1929-dec bds & e.p.s-scarce-1st ed (t5,dj sl tn & sp drknd) 175.00

MCKAY,CLAUDE-Selected Poems of...-NY-1953-Bookman Assoc-1st ed (w5,f,sl tn dj) 35.00

MCKAY,DOUGLAS-Honourable Company-NY-1938-Tudor Publ-396p-illus (dd4) 25.00

MCKAY,H C-Principles of Stereoscopy-Bost-1948-Amer Photo Publ-191p-illus-1st ed (cc9,f) 40.00

MCKAY,RICHARD-Some Famous Sailing Ships and their Builder Donald McKay-NY-1928-Putnam's-xxviii+395p-blu cl,58 illus(10 col)-1st ed (l2) 70.00

MCKAY,W J STEWART-History of Ancient Gynaecology-NY-1901-302p (g10) 80.00

MCKEARIN,HELEN-Two Hundred Years of American Blown Glass-1950-Dbldy-382p-10 col plts-1st ed (cc8,dj,box) 50.00

MCKEE,I-Ben Hur Wallace-Berkeley-1947-301p-illus,ports (z10,dj) 40.00

MCKEE,LANIER-Land of Nome-NY-(1902)-Grafton Pr-260p-dec blu cl-1st ed (w1) 75.00

MCKEE,MAJ JAMES C-Narrative of the Surrender of a Command of US Forces at Fort Filmore, New Mexico, in July 1861-Bost-1886-J Lowell-stpld wrps-ltd to 300c-3rd ed (u9) 325.00

MCKEE,PHILIP-Big Town-NY-(1931)-John Day Co-1st ed (ff6,sp brwnd,cov soil,f dj) 15.00

MCKEE,ROBERT E-Zia Company in Los Alamos-El Paso-1950-71p-photos,map-scarce Hertzog-1st ed (v7) 125.00

MCKEE,RUTH K-Mary Richardson Walker-Caldwell-1945-357p-frntis,illus-1st ed (t7,dj) 27.50

MCKEE,THOMAS H-Gun Book-NY-1918-12mo-362p-photos (m3) 15.00

MCKELVEY,SUSAN D-Botanical Exploration of the Trans Mississippi West-1955-Harvard-xxxviii,1144p-2 fldg maps,orig glassine dj (x6,as new in dj) 225.00

MCKELVEY,SUSAN D-Lilac-NY-1928-qto-xvi,581p-172 half tone plts,4 col chrts in pckt (jj7,sp fade,cor wn,sl fox) 299.00

MCKELVIE,MARTHA-Lawman of the West-Phila-1971-70p-photos-1st ed (t7) 12.50

MCKENDRY,MAXINE-Seven Centuries Cookbook-(1973)-McGraw Hill-240p-red cl,illus-1st Amer ed (q8,dj) 15.00

MCKENNA,JAMES A-Black Range Tales-NY-1936-300p-illus-Howes#M127-1st ed (u7,f,dj) 50.00

MCKENNA,JAMES A-Black Range Tales-NY-1936-Wilson Erickson-300p-woodcts-Howes M127-1st trd ed (ee4) 45.00

MCKENNEY & HALL-History of the Indian Tribes of North America-Kent-1978-2 vols-lea,a.e.g.,col illus,maps,cl cov box-ltd ed (d7,f,box) 275.00

MCKENNEY,RUTH-Jake Home-NY-1943-Harcourt-1st ed (v5,f,dj rnfrcd,taped) 60.00

MCKENNEY,THOMAS L-Sketches of a Tour to the Lakes-Barre-1972-Imprint Soc-414p-29 illus-Howes M132 (gg4,box) 40.00

MCKENNEY,THOMAS L-Sketches of a Tour to the Lakes...-Mpls-1959-Ross & Haines-493p-illus-Howes M132 (bb4,dj) 25.00

MCKENNEY,THOMAS-Indian Tribes of North America-Edinburgh-1933,34-John Grant-3 vols-ltd to 200c (l9,bump,dj sl scuff & fade) 595.00

MCKENNY,MARGARET-Mushrooms of Field and Wood-NY-1929-Day-193p-photos,drwngs (x6,dj wn) 12.00

MCKENNY,MARGARET-Wild Garden-GC-1936-Dbldy-123p-cl (x6,dj) 14.00

MCKENNY,THOMAS L-Indian Tribes of North America-Edinburgh-1933,1934-John Grant-lg 8vo-3 vols-blu cl,emboss cov,123p col plts,2 fldg col map in rear of vol.III (mm8,sl bump) 425.00*

MCKEON,NEWTON F-Amherst, Massachusetts Imprints 1825 to 1876-Amherst-1946-Amherst College Libr-191p-blu cl-1st ed (m2,dj) 25.00

MCKEOWN,MARTHA F-Trail Led North-NY-1948-Macmillan-222p-maps-Six Guns #1419-1st ed (cc4,wn dj,autg) 20.00

MCKIM,RANDOLPH H-Soldier's Recollections-NY-1911-Longmans,Green-362p-illus (dd4,cov spot,sl tn sp) 75.00

MCKINLEY,EARL-Geography of Disease-Wash-1935-495p-1st ed (dd3) 50.00

MCKINNEY,FRANCIS F-Education in Violence-Detr-1961-Wayne State U Pr-530p-illus,maps,pckt map (ee4,dj) 75.00

MCKINNEY,ROLAND-Thomas Eakins-NY-(1942)-Crown-4to-cl-1st ed (oo6,dj) 50.00

MCKINNEY,WILSON-Fred Carrasco: the Heroin Merchant-Austin-1975-Heidelberg-310p-photos-1st ed (a9,dj) 125.00

MCKINSEY,J C C-Introduction to the Theory of Games-NY-1952-McGraw-Hill-x+371p-gry cl-1st ed (c2) 30.00

MCKITTRICK,MYRTLE M-Vallejo-Portland-(1944)-Binfords & Mort-377p-illus (cc4) 25.00

MCKNIGHT,CHARLES-Our Western Border...100 Years Ago-Phila-1876(1875)-McCurdy-xi,756p-illus-Howes M143-2nd prtg (n2,hngs weak,sl rub,fox) 45.00

MCKNIGHT,H P-Prison Poetry-(Columbus?)-(1896)-194p-cl (b1,sl chip sp) 20.00

MCKNIGHT,J C-Conditions and Remedies-Oklahoma City-1917-439p (g1) 20.00

MCKONE,W J-Michigan State and Local Government-Lansing-1911-Hammond Publ-226p-cl-8th ed (z7) 20.00

MCLAIN,DENNY-Nobody's Perfect-1975-Dial-1st ed (r7,f,dj) 15.00

MCLAIN,JOHN S-Alaska and the Klondike-NY-1905-McClure-8vo-330p wi index-grn cl,photos-1st ed (t1) 90.00

MCLANATHAN,RICHARD-Art of Marguerite Stix-NY-1977-Abrams-4to-192p-wht cl,col & b&w illus (r10,sl soil dj) 45.00

MCLAREN,CHARLES-Fishing for Salmon-Edinburgh-1977-8vo-99p-photos (m3,vf,dj) 15.00

MCLAREN,L L-Pan Pacific Cook Book-SF-1915-Blair Murdock-170p-flowered bds,illus-Bitting 302 (o6) 30.00

MCLAREN,MORAY-Fishing As We Find It-Lond-1960-8vo-151p-illus,L Paterson (m3,as new in dj) 12.50

MCLAREN,MORAY-Fishing the Waters of Scotland-Lond-1972-8vo-264p-photos (m3,vf,dj) 15.00

MCLAREN,MORAY-Singing Reel-Lond-1953-8vo-191p-illus-1st ed (m3) 12.50

MCLAUGHLIN,JAMES-My Friend the Indian-Bost-1910-Houghton Mifflin-8vo-417p,dec cl wi mntd cov port,photos,index-2nd prtg (t1) 50.00

MCLAUGHLIN,JAMES-My Friend the Indian-Bost-1926-Houghton Mifflin-8vo-xiv,418p-orng cl wi papr pastedown,16 plts-Howes M147 (y4) 50.00

MCLAUGHLIN,JAMES-My Friend the Indian-Seattle-1970-Superior-4to-ltd to 3005c,nbrd (z4,lacks box) 20.00

MCLAUGHLIN,P A-Comparative Morphology of Recent Crustacea-Freeman-4to-177p-53 figs-1st ed (bb3,f) 25.00

MCLAUGHLIN,REDMOND-Royal Army Medical Corps-Lond-1972-121p-illus-1st ed (b7,f,dj) 25.00

MCLAURIN,JOHN J-Sketches in Crude Oil-Harrisburg-1896-x+406p-beige cl,illus-1st ed (c2,hng weak) 50.00

MCLAVERTY,MICHAEL-In This Thy Day-NY-1947-Macmillan-1st Amer ed (z8,vf,sl wn dj) 15.00

MCLEAN,ALEXANDER-History of Jersey City...-Jersey City-1895-sm folio-462,(2)p-mod cl,illus,plts (aa6,rbnd) 250.00

MCLEAN,BETH B-Complete Meat Cookbook-Peoria-(1953)-Bennett-559p-dec tan cl,photos,drwngs-1st ed (q8,dj) 16.50

MCLEAN,RUARI-Jan Tschichold: Typographer-Bost-(1975)-David Godine-sm 4to-160p-cl,illus-1st US ed (w2,dj) 45.00

MCLEAN,RUARI-Joseph Cundall, a Victorian Publisher-Dollar-1976-Ruari McLean Assoc-sm 4to-viii,96p-cl-1st ed (w2,dj) 25.00

MCLELLAN,ISAAC-Haunts of Wild Game-NY-1896-12mo-207p+ads-photos (m3,f) 30.00

MCLEMORE,RICHARD A-ED.-History of Mississippi-Jackson-(1981)-Univ Pr of Miss-2 vols-brwn cl,plts-3rd prtg (b2,dj) 50.00

MCLEOD,JAMES-Theodore Roethke: A Manuscript Checklist-Kent-1971-KSU Pr-1st ed (z9) 10.00

MCLOGHLEN,DIANA-Last Headlands-Lond-1972-Chatto & Windus,Hogarth-(Phoenix Living Poets)-1st ed (z8,vf,f dj) 25.00

MCLOUGHLIN,DENIS-Wild & Wooley-GC-1975-Dbldy-8vo-570p-1st ed (z4,dj) 30.00

MCLOUGHLIN,DR.JOHN-Letters of...-Portland-(1948)-Binfords & Mort-376p-map e.p.-1st ed (nn6,wn dj) 40.00

MCLOUGHLIN,DR.JOHN-Letters of...-Portland-(1948)-Oregon Hist Soc-1st ed (w1,f,dj) 45.00

MCMAHON,J R-Wright Brothers-Bost-1930-8vo-viii,308p-cl,frntis,plts (s2,chip dj) 35.00

MCMAHON,THERESA S-Women and Economic Evolutions-Madison-1912-U of Wisc,Bull. No.496-wrps-1st ed (w5) 30.00

MCMANAWAY,JAMES G-Joseph Quincy Adams Memorial Studies-Wash-1948-Folger-8vo-x,808p-red cl,frntis port-1st ed (t10) 40.00

MCMANIS,J ALLEN-Flesh of My Brother-Hollywood-1946-Murray & Gee-8vo-281p-red cl,map e.p.,62 photos-1st ed (p8,wn dj,pres) 35.00

MCMANUS,PATRICK-Fine & Pleasant Misery-NY-1978-8vo-209p-1st ed (m3,vf,dj) 12.50

MCMASTER,GARY J-International Trout and Salmon Cookbook-S Brunswick-1970-4to-137p (m3,f,dj) 15.00

MCMECHEN,PETER-Shining Mountains-Denver-1935-56p-pict wrps,frntis,illus,maps-scarce-1st ed (t7) 35.00

MCMICHAEL,JOHN-ED.-Circulation: Proceedings of the Harvey Tercentenary Congress-Springfield-1958-503p-1st Amer ed (dd3) 100.00

MCMINN,HOWARD E-An Illustrated Manual of California Shrubs-SF-1939-sm 4to-xi,689p-photos (m10,bump) 27.00

MCMINN,HOWARD E-An Illustrated Manual of Pacific Coast Trees-Berkeley-1935-U of Cal Pr-sm 8vo-409p-e.p. maps,col frntis,figs-1st ed (mm4) 35.00

MCMORRIS,W BRUCE-Real Book of Mountaineering-NY-1958-217p-illus (q10,f,dj) 10.00

MCMULLEN,ROY-World of Marc Chagall-NY-1968-Dbldy-folio-268p-cl,col illus,photos by Izis-1st ed (t3,dj) 100.00

MCMURRAY,W J-History of the 20th Tennessee Regiment Volunteer Infantry CSA-Nashville-1976-Elder's Bookstore-520p-ports-(rprnt of 1904 ed) (o7,f) 40.00

MCMURRY,RICHARD M-John Bell Hood and the War for Southern Independence-Lexington-(1982)-239p-illus,maps-1st ed (n3,f,dj) 20.00

MCMURTRIE,DOUGLAS C-Alphabets. A Manual of Letter Design...-NY-(1926)-Bridgman-1st ed (w1,f,f dj) 25.00

MCMURTRIE,DOUGLAS C-American Type Design in the Twentieth Century with Specimens...-Chig-1924-Ballou-1st ed (w1,sp wn) 30.00

MCMURTRIE,DOUGLAS C-Bibliography of Peoria Imprints 1835-1860-Springfield-1934-priv prntd-30p-wrps-one of 200c, reprntd from Journal of the Illinois St Hist Society (h1) 17.50

MCMURTRIE,DOUGLAS C-Earliest New Jersey Imprint-Newark-1932-14p-stitched,facs (aa6) 30.00

MCMURTRIE,DOUGLAS C-Golden Book-Chig-1927-Covici-thk 8vo-xvi,406p-orig g stmpd blu cl,t.e.g.-ltd to 2000c-1st ed (x4,sp sl fade,wn,shaken) 65.00

MCMURTRIE,DOUGLAS C-Gutenberg Documents-NY-1941-Oxford Univ Pr-239p-unbound sheets,wi plain back & frnt wrps-ltd to 900c (g1) 20.00

MCMURTRIE,DOUGLAS C-Imprints Advertised in the Whitestone Gazette 1796-1798-Chig-1935-priv prntd-6p-wrps-ltd to 200c (g1) 12.50

MCMURTRIE,DOUGLAS C-John Bradford, Pioneer Printer of Kentucky-Springfield-1931-priv prntd-11p-wrps-200c reprntd from Nat'l Prntr Journalist (g1) 15.00

MCMURTRIE,DOUGLAS C-Notes in Supplement to "The First Printers of Chicago"-Chig-1931-priv prntd-14p-ltd to 250c (f1,wrps) 15.00

MCMURTRIE,DOUGLAS C-Preliminary Check List ... Relating to the History of Printing in Argentina-Chig-1942-Chig Clb Prntg Hs Crftmn-14p-wrps (g1) 12.50

MCMURTRIE,DOUGLAS C-Price of Printing in Philadelphia, 1774-Chig-1928-priv prntd-6p-wrps-ltd to 250c (h1,f) 12.50

MCMURTRIE,DOUGLAS C-Royalist Printers at Shelburne, Nova Scotia-Chig-1933-priv prntd-16p-wrps-one of 250c, reprinted from Amer Bk Collector (h1) 15.00

MCMURTRIE,DOUGLAS C-Two Early Issues of the Council Bluffs Press-Des Moines-1935-priv prntd-8p-wrps-one of 200c, reprntd from Annals of Iowa (h1) 20.00

MCMURTRY,LARRY-All My Friends are Going to be Strangers-NY-(1972)-S&S-1st ed (g6,sl rub dj) 75.00

MCMURTRY,LARRY-All My Friends are Going To Be Strangers-NY-(1972)-S&S-1st ed (j3,f,dj) 100.00

MCMURTRY,LARRY-All My Friends Are Going To Be Strangers-NY-1972-1st ed (q5,f,dj) 125.00

MCMURTRY,LARRY-Cadillac Jack-NY-1982-1st ed (r2,f,dj) 25.00

MCMURTRY,LARRY-Cadillac Jack-NY-1982-1st ed (r5,dj) 40.00

MCMURTRY,LARRY-Horseman, Pass By-NY-(1961)-Harper-auth 1st bk-1st ed (c5,cor bump,dj sl rub) 900.00

MCMURTRY,LARRY-Last Picture Show-NY-1966-Dial-1st ed (aa8,f,dj) 325.00

MCMURTRY,LARRY-Leaving Cheyenne-1963-H&R-1st ed (x2,dj) 650.00

MCMURTRY,LARRY-Moving On-(1970)-S&S-1st ed (p9,vf,dj) 125.00

MCMURTRY,LARRY-Moving On-NY-(1970)-S&S-1st ed (bb2,f,dj) 100.00

MCMURTRY,LARRY-Somebody's Darling-NY-(1978)-S&S-1st ed (o3,dj) 20.00

MCMURTRY,LARRY-Terms of Endearment-NY-1975-S&S-1st ed (h8,f,dj) 125.00

MCMURTRY,R GERALD-My Lifelong Pursuit of Lincoln-Ft.Wayne-1981-127p-wrps (b1,pres cpy) 15.00

MCNALLY,DENNIS-Desolate Angel-NY-(1979)-Random-1st prtg (q1,vf,sl rub dj) 30.00

MCNALLY,DENNIS-Desolate Angel-NY-(1979)-Random-photos-1st ed (ff6,f,dj) 25.00

MCNALLY,TOM-Fly Fishing-NY-1978-4to-420p-illus,T Beecham-1st ed (m3,f,sl chip dj) 17.50

MCNALLY,WARD-Smithy-NY-(1967)-8vo-190p-cl,illus-1st Amer ed (t2,dj) 35.00

MCNAMARA,KATHERINE-Landscape Architecture a Classified Bibliography-Cambridge-1934-Harvard-209p-cl,typescript of preliminary ed-scarce (x6,cl wn) 100.00

MCNEAL,T A-When Kansas Was Young-NY-1922-Macmillan-287p-Six Guns #1426-1st ed (cc4) 30.00

MCNEER,MAY-Waif Maid-NY-1930-Macmillan-orig cl,papr sp & cov labls-1st ed (aa9) 35.00

MCNEILE,H C-Bulldog Drummond at Bay-NY-1935-Dbldy CC-1st US ed (g4) 12.50

MCNEILE,H C-Bulldog Drummond Returns-NY-1932-Dbldy CC-1st US ed (g4,f) 12.50

MCNEILE,H C-Dinner Club-Lond-(1923)-Hodder-1st ed (l4) 15.00

MCNEILE,H C-Guardians of the Treasure-NY-1931-Dbldy CC-1st US ed (h4,f) 12.50

MCNEILE,H C-Jim Maitland-NY-1924-Doran-1st US ed (d4) 15.00

MCNEILL,DON-Moving Through Here-1970-Knopf-1st ed (q9,f,dj) 20.00

MCNEILL,DON-Moving Through Here-NY-1970-Knopf-1st ed (z9,f,dj) 10.00

MCNICKLE,D'ARCY-They Came Here First-Phila-(1949)-Lippincott-325p-illus-1st ed (cc4) 25.00

MCNICOL,DONALD-Radio's Conquest of Space-1946-374p-20 photos,53 illus-1st ed (h6,f) 45.00

MCNIFF,WILLIAM J-Heaven on Earth-Oxford-1940-Miss Valley Pr-262p-1st ed (cc4,dj,autg) 45.00

MCPHEE,JOHN-Alaska, Images of the Country-SF-1981-4to-145p-102 col photos,G Rowell-1st ed (q10,f,dj) 35.00

MCPHEE,JOHN-Annals of the Former World-NY-(1983)-FSG-2 vols-nbrd,autg-1st ed thus (ee2,f,box) 85.00

MCPHEE,JOHN-Coming Into the Country-Lond-1978-H Hamilton-1st Brit ed (y1,f,f dj) 45.00

MCPHEE,JOHN-Coming Into the Country-NY-(1977)-FS&G-1st ed (bb2,f,dj) 65.00

MCPHEE,JOHN-Coming Into the Country-NY-(1977)-FS&G-4 maps-1st ed (a10,f dj) 50.00

MCPHEE,JOHN-Crofter & the Laird-NY-(1970)-FS&G-drwngs,Graves-1st ed (b5,as new in dj) 60.00

MCPHEE,JOHN-Crofters and the Laird-NY-1970-Farrar-1st ed (w5,f,f dj) 45.00

MCPHEE,JOHN-Curve of Binding Energy-NY-1974-1st ed (r5,f,dj) 45.00

MCPHEE,JOHN-Deltoid Pumpkin Seed-1973-Farrar-1st ed (m9,f,sl drknd dj) 25.00

MCPHEE,JOHN-Deltoid Pumpkin Seed-NY-(1973)-FS&G-1st ed (a10,dj) 35.00

MCPHEE,JOHN-Encounters with the Archdruid-1971-FS&G-1st ed (m9,f,dj sl soil,sp drknd) 60.00

MCPHEE,JOHN-Giving Good Weight-NY-(1979)-1st ed (h5,f,dj rear flap creased) 17.50

MCPHEE,JOHN-Giving Good Weight-NY-(1979)-FS&G-1st ed (h3,f,sl tn dj) 20.00

MCPHEE,JOHN-Headmaster-NY-(1966)-Farrar-1st ed (w5,f,f dj) 50.00

MCPHEE,JOHN-Headmaster-NY-(1966)-FS&G-1st ed (dd2,f,sl rub dj) 75.00

MCPHEE,JOHN-In Suspect Terrain-NY-(1983)-FS&G-1st ed (bb2,f,dj) 35.00

MCPHEE,JOHN-John McPhee Reader-NY-1976-Farrar-1st ed (w5,f,f dj) 35.00

MCPHEE,JOHN-Levels of the Game-NY-(1969)-1st ed (t5,dj) 40.00

MCPHEE,JOHN-Levels of the Game-NY-(1969)-FS&G-1st ed (bb2,f,dj) 50.00

MCPHEE,JOHN-Oranges-Lond-(1967)-Heinemann-1st Brit ed (cc2,f,dj) 60.00

MCPHEE,JOHN-Oranges-NY-(1967)-1st ed (h5,f,dj) 60.00

MCPHEE,JOHN-Oranges-NY-1967-FSG-1st ed (q2,sl fade cov,dj sl tn) 70.00

MCPHEE,JOHN-Pieces of the Frame-1975-FS&G-1st ed (m9,f,dj) 45.00

MCPHEE,JOHN-Pine Barrens-NY-(1968)-1st ed (h5,f,dj) 85.00

MCPHEE,JOHN-Survival of the Bark Canoe-(1975)-FS&G-1st ed (m9,f,dj sp sl drkdnd) 100.00

MCPHEE,JOHN-Survival of the Bark Canoe-NY-(1975)-FS&G-illus-1st ed (d10,f,sl tn dj) 100.00

MCPHEE,JOHN-Wimbledon-NY-(1972)-FSG-oversized-photos,Eisenstadt-1st ed (ee2,f,dj) 50.00

MCPHEE,JOHN-Wimbledon-NY-(1972)-photos,A Eisenstaedt-1st ed (q5,f,dj) 35.00

MCPHEE,WILLIAM-Six Hour Shift-GC-1920-Dbldy-ltd to 377c,nbrd,autg-1st ed (ee2) 50.00

MCPHERREN,IDA-Imprints on Pioneer Trails-Bost-1950-380p-illus-Six Guns #1430-1st ed (r8,sl tn dj) 60.00

MCQUEEN,IAN-Sherlock Holmes Detected-Newton Abbot-1974-David & Charles-illus-1st ed (q4,vf,dj) 25.00

MCREYNOLDS,EDWIN C-Oklahoma-Norman-(1954)-U of Okla-xii+461p-plts,maps-1st ed (e2,dj) 30.00

MCREYNOLDS,EDWIN-Oklahoma-Norman-(1954)-U of Okla Pr-461p-illus-1st ed (cc4,dj) 35.00

MCREYNOLDS,EDWIN-Seminoles-Norman-1957-397p-photos-1st ed (t7,dj) 17.50

MCSPADDEN,J WALKER-California-NY-(1926)-127p-cl,illus,H L Hastings,full col pict frnt cov (l1) 15.00

MCTAGGART,M F-Art of Riding-NY-1931-Scribner-1st US ed (h9) 25.00

MCTAGGART,M F-Horse and His Schooling-Lond-1932-Methuen-1st ed (h9) 25.00

MCTAMMANY,JOHN-History of the Player-NY-1913-(x)+83p-brwn cl,ltd to 1000c,nbrd(#154)-1st ed (d2) 65.00

MCTAVISH,GEORGE S-Behind the Palisades-Sidney-1963-priv publ-8vo-(8),249p-brgndy cl,photos (ee7,dj tn & wn) 45.00

MCTAVISH,GEORGE S-Behind the Palisades-Victoria-1963-E Gurd-249p-illus,ports (k10) 35.00*

MCVAUGH,ROGERS-Edward Palmer-1956-U of Okla-430p (x6,dj) 20.00

MCVAUGH,ROGERS-Edward Palmer-Norman-(1956)-U of Okla-xviii+430p-beige cl,plts-1st ed (l2,dj) 22.00

MCVEY,E E-Crow Scout WHo killed Custer-Billings-1952-32p-pict wrps,illus-Luther #120-scarce (t7) 40.00

MCVICKER,MARY L-Writings of J Frank Dobie: A Bibliography-Lawton-(1968)-Mus of the Grt Plains-(xvi),258p-cl,photos-1st ed (v1,dj) 65.00

MCVOY,LIZZIE C-Bibliography of Fiction by Louisianians and Louisiana Subjects-Baton Rouge-1935-LSU Pr-87p-wrps-1st ed (f2,title written on sp) 15.00

MCWATTERS,GEORGE S-Knots Untied...-1871-Burr-1st ed (s10,sp wn & fade,hngs reglued 35.00

MCWHINEY,GRADY-ED.-Grant, Lee, Lincoln and the Radicals-Chig-1964-117p-1st ed (c4,sl soil cov,dj) 20.00

MCWHIRTER,GEORGE-Bloodlight for Malachi McNair-SF-(1947)-Kachenjunga Pr-wrps-ltd to 250c-1st ed (z8,vf) 20.00

MCWHORTER,L V-Crime Against the Yakimas-Yakima-(1913)-57p-wrps,photos-1st ed (e7,sl soil & peeling) 75.00

MCWHORTER,L V-Crime Against the Yakimas-Yakima-(1913)-Republic Prnt-57p-pict wrps,photos-Smith 6474-1st ed (v1,sl wn & soil wrps) 85.00

MCWHORTER,L V-Hear Me My Chiefs-Caldwell-1952-640p-illus,fldg map-v scarce-1st ed (e7) 225.00

MCWHORTER,L V-Hear Me, My Chiefs!-Caldwell-1952-Caxton-xxvi,640p-cl,illus,photos,maps,map e.p.-1st ed (v1,chip dj) 250.00

MCWHORTER,L V-Yellow Wolf-Caldwell-1940-324p-variant blu bndg,illus,e.p. maps-scarce-1st ed (e7) 150.00

MCWILLIAMS,CAREY-California-NY-1949-Current Bks-377p-1st ed (bb4,wn dj) 15.00

MCWILLIAMS,CAREY-New Regionalism in American Literature-Seattle-1930-UW Chapbks-wrps-ltd to 500c-scarce (b3) 45.00

MEACHAM,HENRY H-Empty Sleeve-Springfield-nd-24p-wrps (j1) 35.00

MEAD JOHNSON COLLECTION OF PEDIATRIC ANTIQUES-Evansville-c.1945-48p-wrps-1st ed (dd3) 20.00

MEAD,CHARLES W-Old Civilizations of Inca Land-NY-1972-Cooper Sq Publ-8vo-141p-red cl,g sp titles,illus-rprnt ed (mm1) 35.00

MEAD,EDGAR T,JR.-Busted and Still Running-Brattleboro-1968-58p-illus-1st ed (n4,f,dj) 12.50

MEAD,EDGAR T,JR.-Over the Hills to Woodstock-Brattleboro-1967-44p-1st ed (n4,f,dj) 12.00

MEAD,GEORGE H-Philosophy of the Act-Chig-(1938)-Univ of Chig-lxxxiv+696p-blu cl-1st ed (l2,dj) 65.00

MEAD,MARGARET-Growing Up in New Guinea-1930-Morrow-372p-photo plts-1st ed (u8,sp sunned,fray) 15.00

MEAD,ROBERT D-Journies Down the Line-1978-Dbldy-609p-1st ed (oo4,dj sl tn & wn) 20.00

MEAD,WILLIAM-Even the Browns-1978-Contemporary-1st ed (ff2,dj) 25.00

MEADE,JULIAN-Adam's Profession and Its Conquest by Eve-NY-1936-Longmans-261p (x6,sl fade sp) 10.00

MEADER,J W-Merrimack River, its Sources and its Tributaries-Bost-1869-B Russell-307p-grn cl,fldg map-Howes M463-1st ed (b2) 65.00

MEADMORE,C-Modern Chair-NY-1975-illus-1st Amer ed (h10,dj) 125.00

MEAKIN,ANNETTE-What America is Doing-Lond-1911-Blackwood & Sons-blu cl-1st ed (dd6,auth card wi pres laid in 35.00

MEANLEY,B-Waterfowl of the Chesapeake Bay Country-1982-Tidewater-210p-photos,maps-1st ed (bb3,f,dj) 30.00

MEANLEY,BROOKE-Natural History of Swainson's Warbler-Wash-1971-GPO/No Amer Fauna No.69-90p-wrps (e9) 12.50

MEANS,PHILIP A-Ancient Civilizations of the Andes-NY-1931-Scribner's-xviii,586p-cl,col frntis,plts,illus-1st ed (kk1) 65.00

MEANS,PHILIP A-Fall of the Inca Empire, and the Spanish Rule in Peru: 1530 to 1780-NY-1932-Scribner's-xii,351p-cl,frntis,plts-1st ed (kk1,vf,dj soil) 75.00

MEANS,WM GORDON-My Guns-Dedham-1941-8vo-178p-illus (m3) 20.00

MEANY,EDMOND S-Mountain Campfires-Seattle-1911-12mo-90p-pict cov-scarce-1st ed (a4,f) 70.00

MEANY,EDMOND S-Origin of Washington Geographic Names-Seattle-1923-U of W Pr-8vo-357p-grn cl-1st ed (p1) 225.00

MEANY,EDMOND S-Vancouver's Discovery of Puget Sound-NY-1907-Macmillan-344p wi index,blu cl-Smith 6671-1st ed (w1,sl stnd fr cov) 75.00

MEANY,EDMOND S-Vancouver's Discovery of Puget Sound-NY-1907-MacMillan-344p-illus,4 maps,dbl pg chrt-1st ed (r8,edge wn,bump) 100.00

MEANY,EDMOND S-Vancouver's Discovery of Puget Sound-Portland-1942-344p-illus (h7,dj) 30.00
MEANY,EDMOND S-Vancouver's Discovery of Puget Sound-Portland-1957-344p + 47p-illus,e.p. maps (c7,f,chip dj) 45.00
MEANY,EDMOND S-Vancouver's Discovery of Puget Sound...-Portland-1957-Binfords & Mort-8vo-344p wi index+spplmnt-rprnt (t1,dj) 40.00
MEANY,TOM-Artful Dodgers-1954-G&D (s7,dj) 25.00
MEANY,TOM-Babe Ruth-1951-G&D (ff2,dj) 15.00
MEANY,TOM-Baseball's Greatest Pitchers-1951-Barnes (s7,f,dj) 25.00
MEANY,TOM-Incredible Giants-1955-Barnes-1st ed (r7,lacks dj) 15.00
MEANY,TOM-Magnificent Yankees-1952-Barnes-1st ed (q7,lacks dj) 15.00
MEANY,TOM-Magnificent Yankees-1952-Barnes-photos-1st ed (s8,f,dj) 45.00
MEANY,TOM-Milwaukee's Miracle Braves-1954-Barnes-1st ed (p7,dj) 40.00
MEANY,TOM-Mostly Baseball-NY-(1958)-Barnes-441p-cl-1st ed (n1,f,dj) 17.50
MEANY,TOM-Yankee Story-1960-Dutton (p7,f,dj) 40.00
MEARES,JOHN-Voyages Made in the Years 1788 and 1789...-Amsterdam-1967-N Israel-596p-port,27 maps & plts-(orig publ Lond, 1790)-rprnt (p8,as new) 115.00
MEARS,HELEN-Year of the Wild Boar-Phila-(1942)-Lippincott-8vo-346p-1st ed (jj5,dj) 15.00
MEARS,J H-Racing the Moon-NY-1928-8vo-320p-cl,frntis,plts-1st ed (s2,chip dj) 25.00
MECH,L O-Wolf-NY-1970-384p-photos (gg3,f,dj) 12.00
MECHEM,KIRKE-ED.-Kansas Historical Quarterly. Vol.VIII-Topeka-1939-Kansas Hist Soc-1st ed (u9) 27.50
MECK,CHARLES R-Meeting & Fishing the Hatches-NY-1977-4to-194p-photos,illus (m3,f,dj) 17.50
MEDICAL CLASSICS-Balt-1936 to 1941-5 vols-1/2 lea-v scarce-1st & only ed (dd3) 900.00
MEDICAL ESSAYS:COMPILED...BY MEDICAL OFFICERS OF THE U.S. NAVY-Wash-1873-345p-scarce-1st ed (dd3) 350.00
MEDICAL LEAVES 1939-Chig-1939-4to-1st ed (dd3) 100.00
MEDSGER,OLIVER P-Edible Wild plants-NY-1939-Macmillan-323p-blu cl,photos,drwngs (m6,sl sunned) 22.00
MEDVED,EVA-Food in Theory and Practice-Fullerton-(1978)-Plycon-596p-blu cl (q8,dj) 15.00
MEDWIN,THOMAS-Angler in Wales-Lond-1834-8vo-2 vols,1/2 strght grn mor,mrbld bds & e.p.s,t.e.g.,illus-scarce (m3) 175.00
MEDWIN,THOMAS-Journal of the Conversations of Lord Byron-Lond-1824-for Henry Colburn-3/4 mor,g sp,raised bnds,t.e.g. (aa9,sl rub cov) 200.00
MEEHAN,WILLIAM E-Fish Culture-NY-1913-12mo-287p-photos,illus (m3) 15.00
MEEK,BASIL-Twentieth Century History of Sandusky County, Ohio and Representative Citizens-Chig-1909-Richmond-Arnold-934p-mor,dbl cols (j1,poorly rebkd) 85.00
MEEKER,E-Hop Culture in the United States Being a Practical Treatise on Hop Growing in Washington...-Puyallup-(1883)-publ by auth-170p wi index,brwn cl,illus-Smith 6699-1st ed (w1) 350.00
MEEKER,EZRA-Busy Life of Eighty Five Years-Seattle-(1916)-publ by auth-399p-pict cl,illus-1st ed (ee4,autg) 35.00
MEEKER,EZRA-Busy Life of Eighty Five Years-Seattle-(1916)-sm 8vo-399p+4p ads-brwn pict cl,illus-1st ed thus (kk7) 40.00
MEEKER,EZRA-Busy Life of Eighty Five Years-Seattle-1916-xii+399p-brwn cl,illus,expanded from 1909 ed-1st ed (e2,sl wn) 55.00
MEEKER,EZRA-Ox Team or the Old Oregon Trail-1896-Indpls-(1906)-publ by auth-248p+ads-cl (n1) 25.00
MEEKER,EZRA-Ox Team or the Old Oregon Trail-Omaha-(1906)-publ by auth-248p+ads-blu cl-1st ed (b2) 55.00
MEEKER,EZRA-Personal Experiences on the Oregon Trail 60 Years Ago-Seattle-1912-16mo-red illus wrps,photos (b6,news clippings laid in) 35.00
MEEKER,EZRA-Pioneer Reminiscences of Puget Sound-Seattle-(1905)-Lowman & Hanford-559p-illus-Howes M477-1st ed (bb4) 100.00
MEEKER,EZRA-Pioneer Reminiscences of Puget Sound: The Tragedy of Leschi...-Seattle-1905-Lowman & Hanford-555p-blu cl-1st ed (w1,f) 100.00
MEEKER,EZRA-Seventy Years of Progress-Seattle-1921-381,(1),52p appendix-lt brn cl,illus fldg post card of Oregon Tr Expo (b6) 60.00
MEEKS,A S-Naturalist in Cannibal Land-Lond-1913-8vo-g dec cl,frntis,35 photos-scarce (jj10) 75.00
MEIER,LILI-Auschwitz Album-NY-1982-Random-illus-1st ed (y10,sl soil,dj) 35.00
MEIER-GRAEFE,JULIUS-Vincent Van Gogh-NY-1933-Lit Guild-61 plts (gg6,chip & wn dj) 20.00
MEIGHN,MOIRA-Magic Ring for the Needy and Greedy-Lond-1936-Oxford U Pr-115p-drwngs (m6) 15.00
MEIGS,CORNELIA-Clearing Weather-Bost-1928-Little,Brown-313p-pict cl,col & b&w illus,F Dobias-1st ed (s3) 12.00
MEIGS,CORNELIA-Scarlet Oak-NY-1938-Macmillan-198p-cl,col & b&w illus,E O Jones-1st ed (s3,dj) 30.00
MEIGS,JOHN-Cowboy in American Prints-Chig-(1972)-Swallow-oblng 4to-cl-1st trd ed (oo6,dj) 45.00
MEIGS,JOHN-Cowboy in American Prints-Chig-1972-Swallow-folio-184p-ltd to 5000c-1st ed (d3,dj) 40.00
MEINECKE,CONRAD-Your Cabin in the Woods-Buffalo-1945-4to-187p-illus (m3,f) 17.50
MEINERTZHAGEN,COLONEL R-Birds of Arabia-Edinburgh-1954-Oliver & Boyd-624p-photos,maps,col plts-scarce (b9,f,f dj) 500.00
MEINERTZHAGEN,FREDERICK-Art of the Netsuke Carver-Lond-(1956)-Routledge-4to-80p+photos-1st ed (ll9) 75.00
MEINIG,D W-Great Columbia Plain-(1968)-U of Wash-576p-illus,52 maps,1 fldg map-1st ed (r8,few pgs highltd,dj chip) 28.00
MEIRING,DESMOND-Brinkman-Bost-1965-HMCo-1st ed (c8,f,sl scuff dj) 65.00
MEISS,MILLARD-Great Age of Fresco-1970-Metro MOA-4to-1st ed (004,sl bump,dj) 70.00
MELADY,THOMAS-Idi Amin Dada-KC-(1977)-Sheed Andrews McMeel-8vo-184p-photos-1st ed (dd5,f,f dj) 12.50
MELDGAARD,JORGEN-Eskimo Sculpture-NY-(1960)-Clarkson Potter-48p-75 plts-1st Engl ed (ll8,dj) 25.00
MELENDY,MARY R-Perfect Womanhood for Maidens, Wives, Mothers-np-(1903)-448p-cl,plts(incl col) (l1,sl spot cov) 20.00
MELINE,JAMES F-Two Thousand Miles on Horseback-NY-1867-317p-blndstmpd cl,fldg map-1st ed (z1) 150.00

MELLEN,KATHLEEN D-In a Hawaiian Valley-(1947)-Hastings-126p-ports,M Tennett-1st ed (u8,sl chip dj) 20.00

MELLERSH,H.E.-Fitzroy of the Beagle-np-1968-Mason & Lipscomb-sm 8vo-308p-blu cl,illus (nn1,dj) 40.00

MELLICK,ANDREW D-Story of an Old Farm-Somerville-1889-Unionist-Gazette-xxvi+743p-grn cl,plts,Howes M498-1st ed (k2) 150.00

MELLICK,ANDREW D-Story of an Old Farm-Somerville-1889-xxiv,743,(1)p-cl,plts (aa6) 225.00

MELLINKOFF,RUTH-Something Special Cookbook-(1959)-Ward Ritchie-255p-pict bds,illus-1st ed (q8,dj) 18.50

MELLON,J-African Hunter-NY-1975-HBJ-522p-cl,382 photos,maps-1st ed so stated (ee3,vf,dj) 175.00

MELLON,JAMES-African Hunter-NY,Lond-1975-4to-522p-photos,maps-1st ed (m3,as new in dj) 200.00

MELTZER,DAVID-ED.-San Francisco Poets-NY-1971-Ballantine-wrps,pbk orig-1st ed (w5,rmndr line) 20.00

MELVILL,ANDREW-Memoirs of Sir..., and the Wars of the 17th Century-Lond-1918-John Lane-8vo-297p-9 illus-1st ed (jj5) 20.00

MELVILLE,HERMAN-Omoo-NY-1847-Harper-1/2 mor wi mrbld bds,lea sp labl,map-1st Amer ed (aa9,fox) 500.00

MELVILLE,HERMAN-Portable Melville-NY-1952-Viking-746p-1st ed (j8,f,chip dj) 20.00

MELVILLE,HERMAN-Selected Poems-Norfolk-1944-New Directions-wrps,"Poets of the Year"-1st ed thus (d8,f) 20.00

MELVILLE,JENNIE-Come Home and Be Killed-NY-1964-London House-1st US ed (f4,f,dj) 25.00

MELVILLE,LEWIS-Stage Favourites of the 18th Century-Lond-nd(1928)-Hutchinson-8vo-288p-1 col & 16 b&w plts-1st Brit ed (ee5) 20.00

MELVIN,ROY-Hawaiian Tramways-1976-Golden West-4to-31p-wrps,illus (nn7,f) 20.00

MEMOIRS OF AN AMERICAN LADY-Lond-1817-Newman & Co-2 vols in one(322p;344p)-Howes G303 (cc4,rbnd) 85.00

MENABONI,A-Menaboni's Birds-NY-1950-4to-132p-cl,31 col plts (y8,dj chip) 25.00

MENCKEN,AUGUST-ED.-By the Neck-NY-(1942)-Hastings Hs-264p-illus-Six Guns 1476-1st ed (gg4,sl chip dj) 25.00

MENCKEN,H L-Artist: A Drama Without Words-Bost-1912-Luce-12mo-dec papr bds-scarce-1st hdbk iss (y4) 125.00

MENCKEN,H L-Bathtub Hoax-1958-Knopf-1st ed (x2,vf,vf dj) 60.00

MENCKEN,H L-Bathtub Hoax-NY-1958-Knopf-1st ed (y1,f,dj) 75.00

MENCKEN,H L-Carnival of Buncombe-Balt-(1956)-John Hopkins Pr-blu & red cl-1st ed (f2,dj) 35.00

MENCKEN,H L-Christmas Story-NY-1946-illus,B Crawford-1st ed (t5,dj) 35.00

MENCKEN,H L-Christmas Story-NY-1946-Knopf-illus,B Crawford-1st ed (h8,dj) 40.00

MENCKEN,H L-George Bernard Shaw, His Plays-1905-Luce-1st ed (x2) 125.00

MENCKEN,H L-H L Mencken on Music-NY-1961-Knopf-1st ed (y1,vf,vf dj) 65.00

MENCKEN,H L-Mencken Chrestomathy-NY-1949-Knopf-blu cl-1st ed (f2,dj) 35.00

MENCKEN,H L-Minority Report-NY-1956-Knopf-1st ed (z9,dj) 20.00

MENDELSON,OSCAR A-Salute to Onions-(1966)-Hawthorn-190p-brwn cl,illus-1st Amer ed (q8,dj) 10.00

MENDOZA,GEORGE-Secret Places of Trout Fisherman-NY-1977-8vo-112p-photos-1st ed (m3,as new in dj) 14.00

MENGEL,R M-Birds of Kentucky-Lawrence-1965-8vo-581p-cl,4 col plts,map (y8,spots) 20.00

MENNINGER,EDWIN A-Flowering Trees of the World-NY-1962-xv,336p-col photos,drwngs (jj7,dj) 57.50

MENOTTI,GIAN CARLO-Amahl and the Night Visitors-NY-(1952)-McGraw Hill-col illus,R Duvoisin-1st ed (s3,vf,dj) 35.00

MENZIES,SIR ROBERT-Afternoon Light-Lond-(1967)-Cassell-8vo-384p-1st Brit ed (jj5,f,f dj) 10.00

MENZIES,W J M-Sea Trout and Trout-Lond-1936-8vo-230p-photos-1st ed (m3,f,sl chip dj) 30.00

MERA,H P-Alfred I Barton Collection of Southwestern Textiles-Santa Fe-(1949)-99p-bds,3 col photo plts,ltd to 250c,nbrd,autgs-rare-1st ed (v7,f) 150.00

MERA,H P-Navajo Textile Arts-Santa Fe-nd-102p-bds,96 photo plts-scarce-1st ed (v7,f) 100.00

MERA,H P-Rain Bird-Santa Fe-1937-Lab of Anthro, vol.II-4to-113p-wrps,48p plts-1st ed (a9) 450.00

MERCER,A S-Banditti of the Plains-Cheyenne-1894-8vo-139p-plain blk cl-Six Guns #1478-Howes M522-Smith 6735-rare-1st ed (oo8,sl damaged sp) 2,350.00

MERCER,A S-Banditti of the Plains-Norman-1954-U of Okla-12mo-195p-illus-1st prtg thus (p2) 20.00

MERCER,A S-Banditti of the Plains-SF-1935-Grabhorn Pr-4to-136p-cl & bds-Howes M522-3rd ed (z4,f) 150.00

MERCER,CAVALIE-Journal of the Waterloo Campaign-Lond-1969-388p (gg2,f,dj) 40.00

MERCER,P-Life of the Gallant Pelham-Georgia-1958-180p-illus,map,ports (z10) 45.00

MERCIER,CHARLES A-Astrology in Medicine-Lond-1914-Macmillan-12mo-(viii)+100p-ruled mauve pebbled cl-1st ed (y9) 45.00

MERCIER,LOUIS S-Memoirs of the Year 2500-Bost-1977-Gregg Pr-w/o dj as iss-1st ed thus (j3,f) 20.00

MERCK & CO-Merck's Manual of the Materia Medica-NY-1923-581p-wrps-5th ed (g10) 20.00

MEREDITH,GEORGE-An Essay on Comedy-NY-1897-Scribner-1st ed (t4,sl fox) 15.00

MEREDITH,GEORGE-Lord Ormont and His Aminta-1894-C&H-3 vols-1st ed (x2) 60.00

MEREDITH,GEORGE-Modern Love-NY-1909-M Kennerley-t.e.g.,port frntis-1st Amer ed (r2,uncut,rub) 30.00

MEREDITH,GRACE E-Girl Captives of the Cheyennes-LA-1927-123p-frntis,photos-1st ed (t7,pres) 100.00

MEREDITH,JAMES-Three Years in Mississippi-Bloomington-1966-Indiana-1st ed (t6,dj) 40.00

MEREDITH,RICHARD-At the Narrow Passage-NY-(1973)-Putnam-1st ed (j3,edge rub dj) 10.00

MEREDITH,ROY-Face of Robert E Lee in Life and Legend-NY-1947-143p-illus-1st ed (c4,f,dj wn) 45.00

MEREDITH,ROY-Mr.Lincoln's Camera Man-NY-1946-Scribner's-368p-284 photos-1st ed (cc9,f,dj) 50.00

MEREDITH,ROY-Storm Over Sumter-NY-1957-S&S-214p-illus,maps-1st prtg so stated (o7,wn dj) 20.00

MEREDITH,ROY-World of Mathew Brady-LA-(1976)-240p-illus-1st ed (c4,dj) 32.50

MERFIELD,F G-Gorilla Hunting-NY-1956-238p-photos (gg3,f,dj) 12.00

MERILLAT,LOUIS A-Veterinary Military History of the United States-Kansas City-1935-Haver-Glover Labs-2 vols,red cl,illus-1st ed (k2) 110.00

MERINGTON,MARGUERITE-ED.-Custer Story-NY-1950-339p-illus-1st ed (j7,dj) 20.00

MERINGTON,MARGUERITE-ED.-Custer Story-NY-1950-Devin Adair-339p-illus-1st ed (gg4,sl wn dj) 35.00

MERIWETHER,LEE-Tramp at Home-1889-Harper-296p-illus-1st ed (v8,sl wn) 55.00

MERIWETHER,LEE-Tramp Trip-NY-1887-Harper & Bros-276p+publ catlg-cl (m1,cov sl fleck & wn) 15.00

MERK,FREDERICK-History of the Westward Movement-NY-1978-Knopf-(xx),660p-cl,maps,illus-1st ed (v1,dj) 40.00

MERK,FREDERICK-Oregon Question-Cambridge-1967-427p-1st ed (g7,f,dj) 35.00

MERK,FREDERICK-Slavery and Annexation of Texas-NY-1972-Knopf-290p-1st ed (a9,dj) 30.00

MERKIN,RICHARD-Velvet Eden-NY-1979-Methuen-144p-150 photos-1st Amer ed (cc9,f,wn dj) 50.00

MERKLEY,CHRISTOPHER-Biography of...-SLC-1887-J H Parry & Co-orig pink prtd wrps-Graff 2755 (mm1,fade sp,wn,sl soil) 125.00

MERMAN,ETHEL-Who Could Ask for Anything More-1955-Dbldy-1st ed (dd8,dj) 10.00

MERRIAM,FLORENCE-Birds of Village & Field-Bost-1898-Houghton Mifflin-drwngs-1st ed (u9,edges rub) 75.00

MERRIAM,H G-ED.-Way Out West-(1969)-U of OK-296p-1st ed (r8,f,f dj) 28.00

MERRIAM,ROBERT L-ET AL-History of the John Russell Cutlery Company, 1833 to 1936-Greenfield-(1976)-Bete Pr-4to-vi+120p-blu bds,illus (b2) 20.00

MERRICK,GEORGE B-Old Times on the Upper Missippi-Cleve-1909-Arthur H Clark Co-323p-illus,map-Howes M539-1st ed (cc4) 150.00

MERRICK,HENRIETTA S-Caucus Race-NY-1938-Putnam-8vo-272p-29 photos-1st ed (cc5,tape rprd dj) 20.00

MERRICK,HENRIETTA-Sands: Caucasus Race-NY-1938-272p-29 photos,2 maps-1st ed (o10,f) 35.00

MERRIL,JUDITH-Shadow on the Heart-GC-1950-Dbldy-1st ed (h3,chip dj) 30.00

MERRILL,J M-Target Tokyo-Chig-(1964)-8vo-208p-cl-1st ed (s2,dj) 25.00

MERRILL,JAMES M-Rebel Shore-Bost-(1957)-Little,Brown-8vo-245p-8p illus-1st ed (cc5,dj fade) 25.00

MERRILL,JAMES M-Spurs to Glory-NY-(1967)-Rand McNally-302p-illus (bb4,dj) 20.00

MERRILL,JAMES-Country of a Thousand Years of Peace-NY-1959-Knopf-8vo-cl-1st ed (x10,dj edge-rub & sp drknd) 50.00

MERRILL,JAMES-Seraglio-NY-1957-1st ed (p5,f,dj) 60.00

MERRILL,SAMUEL-Moose Book-NY-1916-399p-dec cov,photos (gg3,f) 50.00

MERRILL,SAMUEL-Moose Book-NY-1916-Dutton-xii,366p-illus grn cl,fldg map,photos,illus-1st ed (bb7,sl bump) 90.00*

MERRILL,SAMUEL-Moose Book-NY-1920-8vo-399p-illus-2nd ed (m3) 30.00

MERRITT,A-Creep Shadow Creep-1943-Avon Murder Myst Montly-col pict wrps-1st wrps ed (x7) 15.00

MERRITT,A-Seven Footprints to Satan-1929-G&D-photo play ed (x7) 20.00

MERRITT,RAYMOND H-Creativity, Conflict, and Controversy-Wash D.C.-nd(ca.1975)-USGPO-4to-461p-pict bds,illus (b2) 20.00

MERRITT,W W,SR.-History of the County of Montgomery from the Earliest Days to 1906-Red Oak-1906-343,(1)p-cl (a1) 60.00

MERRYMAN,BRYAN-Midnight Court-Dublin-1945-M Fridberg-Frank O'Connor,transl.-1st ed (z8,vf,dj) 25.00

MERSHON,WM B-Recollections of My 50 Years Hunting & Fishing-Bost-1923-8vo-253p-illus (m3,f,autg) 100.00

MERTON,THOMAS-Disputed Questions-NY-(1960)-FS&C-1st ed (cc2,f,dj) 45.00

MERTON,THOMAS-Disputed Questions-NY-1960-1st ed (r2,f,dj) 30.00

MERTON,THOMAS-Ishi Means Man-Greensboro-(1976)-Unicorn Pr-1st ed (dd2,f) 60.00

MERTON,THOMAS-Life and Holiness-Lond-(1963)-Herder & Herder-1st Brit ed (bb2,f,dj) 40.00

MERTON,THOMAS-Literary Essays of...-NY-(1981)-New Directions-1st ed (ee2,f,dj) 40.00

MERTON,THOMAS-Living Bread-NY-(1956)-FSC-1st ed (ee2,f,dj) 40.00

MERTON,THOMAS-My Argument with the Gestapo-GC-1969-Dbldy-1st ed (dd2,f,dj) 40.00

MERTON,THOMAS-Original Child Bomb-np-1962-New Directions-w/o dj as iss-ltd to 8000c-1st ed (z9,sl bump,rub) 40.00

MERTON,THOMAS-Secular Journal of...-NY-(1958)-FS&C-1st ed (dd2,f,dj) 35.00

MERTON,THOMAS-Seeds of Contemplation-1949-New Directions-1st ed (x2,f,dj) 90.00

MERTON,THOMAS-Seeds of Contemplation-Norfolk-1949-New Directions-hvy burlap cov,papr labls-1st ed (y1,f,soil dj) 100.00

MERTON,THOMAS-Silent Life-Lond-(1957)-Burns & Oates-1st ed (cc2,f,dj) 60.00

MERTON,THOMAS-Tears of the Blind Lions-NY-(1949)-New Directions-1st ed (x3,dj) 40.00

MERTZ,BARBARA-Temples,Tombs and Hieroglyphs-NY-(1964)-Coward McCann-illus-auth 1st bk-1st ed (d10,dj sp sl wn) 50.00

MERWIN,JOHN-ED.-Stillwater Trout-GC-1980-Dbldy-4to-1st ed (ff7,dj) 20.00

MERWIN,JOHN-Stillwater Trout-GC-1980-Dbldy-4to-1st ed (gg7,f,dj) 20.00

MERWIN,SAMUEL-Discourse on the Completion of Fifty Years Service in the Ministry of the Gospel-New Haven-1855-72p-wrps-Sabin 48036 (j1) 15.00

MERWIN,W S-Animae-1969-Kayak Pr-wrps,illus-ltd to 1200c (kk6) 25.00

MERWIN,W S-Dancing Bears-New Haven-1954-Yale U Pr-1st ed (v10,f,f dj) 75.00

MERWIN,W S-Miner's Pale Children-NY-1970-Atheneum-1st ed (b5,as new in dj) 35.00

MERWIN,W S-Moving Target-NY-1963-Atheneum-1st ed (v10,f,f dj) 40.00

MERWIN,W S-Unframed Originals-NY-1982-Atheneum-1st ed (v10,f,f dj) 20.00

MERYMAN,R-Andrew Wyeth-Bost-1968-oblng 4to-all illus-1st prtg (h10,dj sl tn & rub) 250.00

MESSLER,ABRAHAM-Centennial History of Somerset County-Somerville-1878-190,8p-buckrm-scarce (aa6,rbnd) 150.00

MESSLER,ABRAHAM-Forty Years at Raritan-NY-1873-viii,327p-cl (aa6) 50.00

MESSNER,REINHOLD-7th Grade-NY-1974-164p-illus-1st US ed (p10,f,dj) 70.00

MESSNER,REINHOLD-Challenge-NY-1977-205p-1st US ed (o10,f,dj) 70.00

MESSNER,REINHOLD-Everest: Expedition to the Ultimate-Lond-1979-254p-32 col plts-1st ed (a4,f,dj) 70.00

MESSNER,REINHOLD-Solo Nanga Parbat-NY,Lond-1980-268p-illus-1st ed (p10,as new in dj) 55.00

METALIOUS,GRACE-Peyton Place-NY-(1956)-J Messner-auth 1st bk-1st ed (e10,sl cocked sp,e.p.mrks,dj) 60.00

METALIOUS,GRACE-Return to Peyton Place-NY-(1959)-J Messner-1st ed (e10,f,dj) 20.00

METCALF,E W,JR.-Paul Lawrence Dunbar, a Bibliography-Metuchen-1975-193p-cl (g1,f) 17.50

METCALF,M M-Opalinid Ciliate Infusorians-1923-USNM-484p-cl,258 figs (bb3,rbnd,rprd t.p.) 55.00

METCALFE,CHARLES T-ED.-Two Narratives of the Mutiny in Delhi-Westminster-1898-259p-brwn cl,illus-1st ed (b7,f) 250.00

METCALFE,JEAN-Sunnylea-Lond-(1980)-Joseph-4to-60p-cl,26p watercolors,auth-1st ed (s3,f,f dj) 15.00

METCALFE,JOHN-Feasting Dead-Sauk City-1954-Arkham-1st ed (j3,dj) 50.00

METCHNIKOFF,ELIE-Nature of Man, Studies in Optimistic Philosophy-Lond-1903-309p-1st Engl transl (dd3) 100.00

METEOROLOGY AND ATOMIC ENERGY-Wash D.C.-1955-4to-169p-wrps,text figs-1st ed (c2) 15.00

METZ,LEON-Pat Garrett-Norman-1974-328p-cl,illus-1st ed (z1,f,dj) 40.00

METZ,LEON-Pat Garrett-Norman-1974-328p-photos,map-1st ed (n10,f,dj) 50.00

MEW,JAMES-Drinks of the World-NY-1892-Scribner's-362p-bds (l6,wn bds) 120.00

MEYER DE SCHAUENSEE,RODOLPHE-Guide to the Birds of South America-Wynnewood-1970-Livingston Publ-470p-illus-publ for Acad Nat Sci of Phila-scarce-1st ed (c9,f,dj) 100.00

MEYER,ADRIAN C-Caste and Kinship in Central India-Lond-(1960)-Routledge & K Paul-8vo-295p-cl-1st ed (y5,dj tn) 30.00

MEYER,ARTHUR-An Analysis of De Generatione Animalium of William Harvey-Stanford-1936-167p-1st ed (dd3,dj) 50.00

MEYER,CLARENCE-American Folk Medicine-(1973)-Crowell-296p-grn cl,decs-1st ed (q8,dj) 12.50

MEYER,DR M WILHELM-End of the World-Chig-1905-Chas H Kerr-140p (r1) 25.00

MEYER,E A-Pen Drawings of St.Augustine and Other Views of Florida-(St.Augustine)-(1940)-(72)p-wrps (l1) 15.00

MEYER,F W-Rock and Water Gardens-Lond-1910-Country Life-227p-cl,photos (x6) 25.00

MEYER,HAZEL-Gold in Tin Pan Alley-Phila-(1958)-Lippincott-8vo-258p-1st ed (dd5,dj) 20.00

MEYER,HERBERT W-History of Electricity and Magnetism-Norwalk-1972-Burndy Libr-xviii+325p-gry cl,illus-1st ed (d2,dj) 25.00

MEYER,JOSEPH E-Herbalist-Hammond-(1934)-narrow 12mo-40p-col plts (j10,wn,sl soil) 15.00

MEYER,JOSEPH-Nature's Remedies-Hammond-1934-200p-1st ed (dd3) 40.00

MEYER,LORENZO-Mexico and the United States in the Oil Controversy, 1917 to 1942-Austin-(1977)-U of Tex Pr-367p (cc4,dj) 20.00

MEYER,LUCY A-Kinnelon-Kinnelon-(1976)-4to-(1),219p-cl,illus (aa6) 25.00

MEYER,NICHOLAS-Seven-Per-Cent Solution-1974-Dutton-true 1st wi "1" on nmbr line-1st ed (s10,dj) 15.00

MEYER,ROBERT-Autobiography of Dr...-NY-1949-Schuman-126p-cl (z7) 40.00

MEYER,ROY W-History of the Santee Sioux-Lincoln-(1967)-U of Nebr-434p-e.p. maps,illus-1st ed (gg4,dj) 30.00

MEYER,ROY W-Village Indians of the Upper Missouri-Lincoln,Lond-(1977)-354p-cl-1st ed (a1,f,dj) 20.00

MEYEROWITZ,JOEL-Wild Flowers-Bost-1983-NYGS-63p col photos-1st prtg (cc9,f,dj) 35.00

MEYERS,WILLIAM H-Journal of a Cruise to California and the Sandwich Islands...1841 to 1844-SF-1955-Grabhorn Pr-1/2 mor & cl,11 col plts-ltd to 400c (p8,rub) 325.00

MEYERS,WILLIAM H-Sketches of California and Hawaii by...-SF-1970-Grabhorn-Hoyem-104p-cl over bds,papr sp labl,22 col illus-ltd to 450c (p8) 250.00

MEYNELL,ALICE-Children-NY-1897-John Lane-12mo-134p-grn stmpd cl bndg,t.e.g.,cov & t.p. decs,W Bradley-1st ed (w6,uncut) 75.00

MEYNELL,ALICE-Hearts of Controversy-Lond-(1917)-Burns & Oates-8vo-115p-1st ed (w6,sp drknd) 35.00

MEYNELL,ALICE-Wares of Autolycus-Lond-1965-Oxford U Pr-frntis-1st ed (t4,f,f dj) 20.00

MEYNELL,FRANCIS-My Lives-NY-(1971)-Random-1st Amer ed (w1,f,f dj) 25.00

MEYNELL,LAURENCE-Hooky & the Prancing Horse-Lond-1980-Macmillan-1st ed (r4,dj) 20.00

MEYNELL,VIOLA-Alice Meynell: Memoir-NY-1929-Scribner-photos-1st ed (t4,uncut) 20.00

MEYNELL,VIOLA-Francis Thompson & Wilfred Meynell-Lond-1952-Hollis & Carter-col frntis,illus-1st ed (t4,f,dj) 25.00

MEZZROW,MEZZ-Really the Blues-NY-1946-Random-1st ed (mm9,dj chip) 35.00

MIALL,L C-Natural History of Aquatic Insects-Lond-1895-12mo-395p-illus (m3) 25.00

MIAMI IN A COCO-NUT...LAND OF PALMS AND SUNSHINE-(St.Augustine)-nd(1923)-prtd by Record Co-(16)p-col pict wrps (aa1) 15.00

MICHAEL,G-African Fury-Lond-1954-220p-photos (ee3,f,dj) 70.00

MICHAEL,G-Michaels in Africa-Lond-1959-232p-photos (gg3,f,dj) 12.00

MICHAEL,HELEN A-Studies in Plant and Organic Chemistry and Literary Papers-Cambridge-1907-Riverside-(iv)+423p-blu cl-1st ed (d2) 35.00

MICHAEL,HENRY-ED.-Lt Zagoskin's Travels in Russian America,1842 thru 1844-Tor-(1967)-360p-fldg map-1st ed (f7,f,dj) 45.00

MICHAELIS,R-From Bird Cage to Battle Plane-NY-(1943)-8vo-viii,248p-cl,18 illus-1st ed (s2,chip dj) 35.00

MICHAELS,BARBARA-Ammie, Come Home-NY-1968-Meredith-1st ed (l4,dj) 25.00

MICHAELS,BARBARA-Greygallows-NY-1972-Dodd-1st ed (j4,f,dj) 40.00

MICHAELS,BARBARA-Patriot's Dream-NY-1976-Dodd-1st ed (e4,dj) 35.00

MICHAELS,BARBARA-Someone in the House-NY-1981-Dodd-1st ed (e4,edge wn dj) 35.00

MICHAELS,BARBARA-Sons of the Wolf-NY-1967-Meredith-1st ed (w9,vf,dj) 125.00

MICHAELS,BARBARA-Wait for What Will Come-NY-1978-Dodd-1st ed (h4,f,dj sp sl fray) 30.00

MICHAELS,BARBARA-Walker in Shadows-NY-1979-Dodd Mead-1st ed (w9,f,dj sp sl wn) 85.00

MICHAELS,DUANE-Visit with Magritte-Providence-1981-Matrix-wrps in dj(iss simultaneously wi cl ed)-1st ed (w5,f,f dj) 20.00

MICHAELS,LEONARD-Going Places-NY-(1969)-FS&G-auth 1st bk-1st ed (b5,as new in dj) 30.00

MICHAELS,LEONARD-Going Places-NY-(1969)-FS&G-auth 1st bk-1st ed (bb1,as new in dj) 30.00

MICHAELS,LEONARD-I Would Have Saved Them If I Could-NY-(1975)-FS&G-1st ed (bb1,as new in dj) 20.00

MICHALAK,DAVID-Fly Fishing-S Brunswick-1976-8vo-159p-illus-1st ed (m3,vf,dj) 12.50

MICHALS,DUANE-Real Dreams-NY-1976-1st ed (z6,vf,dj tn & chip) 75.00

MICHEL,W-Wyndham Lewis: Painting & Drawing-Berkeley-1971-UC Pr-781 illus(incl 16 col plts)-1st ed (h10,dj) 150.00

MICHELET,JULES-Bird-NY-1869-Nelson & Sons-lea,210 illus by Giacomelli (l9) 300.00

MICHELET,JULES-Insect-Lond-1875-Nelson & Sons-lea,140 illus by Giacomelli (l9) 400.00

MICHELI,SILVIO-Mongolia, in Search of Marco Polo-NY-1967-Harcourt,Brace-8vo-366p-tan cl,map,38 photos-1st Engl ed (gg6,dj) 20.00

MICHELL,E B-Art and Practice of Hawking-Lond-1972-Holland Pr-291p-7th impr (c9,dj) 30.00

MICHELL,JOHN-City of Revelation-Lond-1972-Garnstone Pr-cl-1st ed (l8,dj) 25.00

MICHELSON,HERB-Charlie O-Indpls-(1975)-331p-cl-1st ed so stated (n1,f,dj) 15.00

MICHELSON,HERB-Sportin' Ladies, Confessions of the Bimbos-Radnor-(1975)-Chilton-8vo-216p-1st ed (gg5,dj soil,sl chip) 7.50

MICHENER,C D-Social Behavior of Bees-1974-Harvard-404p-photos,illus (bb3,f,dj) 25.00

MICHENER,JAMES A-Bridge at Andau-1957-S&W-1st Brit ed (x2,dj) 45.00

MICHENER,JAMES A-Bridge at Andau-NY-(1957)-Random-8vo-1st ed (x3,f,dj) 35.00

MICHENER,JAMES A-Chesapeake-NY-(1978)-Random-1st ed (e10,f,dj) 30.00

MICHENER,JAMES A-Covenant-NY-(1980)-Random-1st ed (p3,dj sp sl fray) 15.00

MICHENER,JAMES A-Drifters-1971-Random-1st ed (x2,dj) 22.00

MICHENER,JAMES A-Hawaii-Lond-1960-Secker & Warburg-1st Brit ed (e10,dj sl fade,rub) 50.00

MICHENER,JAMES A-Hawaii-NY-(1959)-Random-4to-wht cl-1st ed (x3,sl chip dj) 55.00

MICHENER,JAMES A-Hawaii-NY-1959-Random Hs-1st ed (e8,f,f dj) 65.00

MICHENER,JAMES A-Michener on Sport-Lond-(1976)-Secker & Warburg-1st Brit ed (k3,f,dj) 20.00

MICHENER,JAMES A-Rascals in Paradise-NY-(1957)-Random-1st ed (ee2,f,sl tn dj) 35.00

MICHENER,JAMES A-Report of the County Chairman-NY-1961-RH-1st ed (x9,f,sl rub dj) 35.00

MICHENER,JAMES A-Return to Paradise-NY-1951-Random-orig g titled cl-1st ed (aa9,dj rprd,sl wn) 50.00

MICHENER,JAMES A-Sayonara-NY-(1954)-Random-orig cl bckd bds-1st ed (aa9,dj sp fade) 75.00

MICHENER,JAMES A-Source-NY-(1965)-Random-ltd to 500c,autg-1st ed (l9,f,box) 200.00

MICHIE,A A-Air Offensive Against Germany-NY-(1943)-8vo-xiv,176p-cl,18p plts,3 dblpg plts-1st ed (s2) 25.00

MICHIGAN LAKES AND STREAMS DIRECTORY-Lansing-1941-Robt McCarthy-4to-82p+9p-wrps,9p maps (cc3) 27.50

MICHIGAN-Biennial Report of the Attorney General of the State of...1933 to 34-Lansing-1934-DeKline-cl (z7) 20.00

MICKLE,ISAAC-Gentlemen of Much Promise-(Phila)-1977-2 vols-cl backd bds,illus (aa6,box) 35.00

MIDDLEBROOK,LOUIS F-Captain Gideon Olmsted...-Salem-1933-Newcomb & Gauss-x+172p-blu cl,gry bds,7 plts,deckle edges (m2,dj) 65.00

MIDDLEBROOK,LOUIS F-Mariktime Connecticut During the American Revolution 1775 to 1783-Salem-1925-Essex-2 vols-ltd to 1250c-1st ed (z2,f,f djs) 150.00

MIDDLETON,A H-Records of the Stirlingshire Militia-Stirling-1904-255p-red cl-1st ed (gg2) 150.00

MIDDLETON,DOROTHY-Victorian Lady Travellers-NY-1965-182p-bds-1st ed so stated (d1,dj) 20.00

MIDDLETON,E-Glorious Exploits of the Air-NY-1918-8vo-256p-cl,frntis,3p plts-1st ed (s2) 20.00

MIDDLETON,JOHN-ED.-Witchcraft and Sorcery in East Africa-Lond-1964-Routledge & K Paul-8vo-302p-cl-2nd impr (y5,dj) 30.00

MIDDLETON,JOHN-Lugbara Religion-Lond-1960-OUP-8vo-276p-cl,illus-1st ed (y5,dj sun) 47.00

MIDDLETON,LAMAR-Rape of Africa-Lond-1936-Hale-8vo-xi,288p-orig cl,frntis,4 maps,1 graph,4 plts-1st ed (bb6) 12.00

MIDDLETON,MAY-Flowers of Bermuda-Tucker-nd-wrps,12 tip in col cards (x6,spot wrps) 15.00

MIDDLETON,R-Day Before Yesterday-1912-T Fisher/Unwin-1st ed (x2,dj sl wn & tn) 125.00

MIDDLETON,WM D-Interurban Era-1961-Kalmbach-4to-431p-illus (nn7,dj wn) 43.00

MIDDLETON,WM-When the Steam Railroads Electrified-1974-Kalmbach-4to-439p-illus (nn7,wn dj) 85.00

MIDLAND NOTES NO.40-Ohio Valley in Fact and Fiction...-Mansfield-(1948)-apprx 46p-wrps (l1) 10.00

MIERE,EARL S-Great Rebellion-Westport-1971-Negro U Pr-369p-(rprnt of 1958 ed) (o7,f) 15.00

MIERS,EARL S-Composing Sticks & Mortar Boards-New Brunswick-1941-Rutgers U Pr-(12),97p-1st trd ed (m4) 14.50

MIERS,EARL S-Great Rebellion-Cleve-(1958)-369p-1st ed (n3,dj) 20.00

MIERS,EARL-ED.-Bookmaking & Kindred Amenities-New Brunswick-1942-Rutgers/Haddon Craftsman-lg 8vo-147p-cl-ltd to 1500c-1st ed (dd10,cor bump,dj) 32.00

MIGDALSKI,EDWARD C-Angler's Guide to Salt Water Game Fishes-NY-1958-8vo-506p-illus,photos (m3,f,dj) 25.00

MIGDALSKI,EDWARD C-Angler's Guide to the Fresh Water Sport Fishes-NY-1962-8vo-431p-illus (m3,f) 22.50

MIGEL,J MICHAEL-ED.-Masters on the Nymph-GC-1979-4to-272p-illus by D Whitlock,photos-1st ed (m3,vf,dj) 25.00

MIGEL,PARMENIA-Titania-NY-1967-Random-1st ed (x9,chip dj) 10.00

MILBANK,JEREMIAH,JR.-First Century of Flight in America-Princeton-(1943)-Princeton Univ Pr-8vo-x,248p-g cl,plts (s2,dj) 100.00

MILBANK,JEREMIAH,JR.-First Century of Flight in America-Princeton-(1943)-Princeton Univ-x+248p-beige cl,plts-1st ed (l2,sp drknd) 25.00

MILBANK,JEREMIAH-Turkey Hill Plantation-1966-priv prntd-8vo-128p-1/4 lea & bds,map e.p.s,photos (m3) 65.00

MILBANK,K-Flighty Prince-NY-1963-priv prtd-66p-prchmnt bkd grn papr,cov bds,a.e.g.,g stmpd turkey on cov,photos (ee3,vf) 75.00

MILBURN,GEORGE-ED.-Casey at the Bat and Other Humorous Favorites-Girard-(1926)-Haldeman-Julius-64p-wrps-Little Blue Bk 1025 (n1) 10.00

MILBURN,GEORGE-Oklahoma Town-NY-1931-Harcourt-1st ed (w5,f,dj) 60.00

MILES,ARTHUR-Land of the Lingam-Lond-1933-Hurst & Blackett-cl,frntis,illus-4th prtg (l8,bds wn) 25.00

MILES,NELSON A-Personal Recollections and Observations of General...-Chig-1896-Werner-lg 8vo-(viii),590p-dec cl,illus,plts-Howes M595-1st iss wi rank on port given as "General"-1st ed (v1,weak hngs) 200.00

MILES,NELSON A-Personal Recollections of...-Chig,NY-1896-lg qto-591p-dec brwn cl,illus (h7,f) 125.00

MILES,NELSON A-Serving the Republic-NY,Lond-1911-340p-illus-1st ed (h7) 85.00

MILES,W H-Early History of Frontier County Nebraska-Maywood-1911-40p-stiff pict wrps-rprnt Howes M596-rare (t7) 75.00

MILFORD,LOUIS LECLERC DE-Memoir-Chig-1956-Donnelley & Sons-map-Lakeside Classics (ff4) 20.00

MILFORD,NANCY-Zelda-NY-(1970)-Harper & Row-cl-1st ed (aa9,f,dj) 20.00

MILITARY MOUNTAINEERING-Wash D.C.-1976-sm 4to-140p-wrps,91 illus (a4,f) 12.00

MILLAIS,J G-Life of Frederick C Selous,D.S.O.-NY-1919-387p-14p illus (ee3) 85.00

MILLAIS,J G-Life of Frederick Courtenay Selous-NY-1919-8vo-387p-photos (m3,sl fade sp) 65.00

MILLAIS,J G-Newfoundland and Its Untrodden Ways-1907-Longmans,Green-340p-g dec frnt bd,t.e.g.,photos,illus-1st ed (bb3) 175.00

MILLAIS,JOHN G-Newfoundland and Its Untrodden Ways-Lond-1907-Longmans,Green-8vo-xvi,340p-orig pict cl,2 maps,6 gravures,6 col plts (u3,sl rub) 120.00

MILLAR,KENNETH-Blue City-NY-1947-Knopf-1st ed (w9,dj sl wn & tn) 200.00

MILLAR,KENNETH-Three Roads-NY-1948-Knopf-1st ed (d4,sl soil dj) 200.00

MILLAR,KENNETH-Trouble Follows Me-1946-Knopf-1st ed (s10,sp chip dj) 1,100.00

MILLAR,MARGARET-An Air That Kills-NY-1957-Random-1st ed (h4,f dj) 12.50

MILLAR,MARGARET-Birds and the Beasts Were There-1967-Random-1st ed (kk6,f,dj) 25.00

MILLAR,MARGARET-Cannibal Heart-1949-Random-1st ed (s10,sl soil dj) 40.00

MILLAR,MARGARET-Do Evil in Return-NY-1950-Random-1st ed (f4,dj) 12.50

MILLAR,MARGARET-Experiment in Springtime-NY-1947-Random-1st ed (e4,dj) 30.00

MILLAR,MARGARET-Fiend-NY-1964-Random-1st ed (e4,dj) 15.00

MILLAR,MARGARET-How Like an Angel-NY-1962-1st ed (t5,dj) 20.00

MILLAR,MARGARET-How Like an Angel-NY-1962-Random-1st ed (w5,f,f dj) 25.00

MILLAR,MARGARET-Iron Gates-NY-1945-Random-1st ed (x9,dj) 30.00

MILLAR,MARGARET-Iron Gates-NY-1945-Random-1st ed (z9,dj) 35.00

MILLAR,MARGARET-It's All in the Family-NY-1948-Random-1st ed (d4,dj) 25.00

MILLAR,MARGARET-Murder of Miranda-NY-(1979)-Random-1st ed (h3,f,dj) 20.00

MILLAR,MARGARET-Stranger in My Grave-1960-Random-1st ed (s10,dj) 20.00

MILLAR,MARGARET-Wives and Lovers-1954-Random-1st ed (s10,dj) 20.00

MILLAR,MARGARET-Wives and Lovers-NY-1954-1st ed (t5,dj) 22.50

MILLAR,WILLIAM-Plastering Plain & Decorative-NY-1929-Dodd,Mead-sm 4to-351p-illus-4th ed (r10,wn dj) 80.00

MILLARD,BAILEY-She of the West-NY-1898-264p-dec cl (bb9) 20.00

MILLARD,OLIVE-Under My Thumb-Lond-(1952)-C Johnson-8vo-236p-6 photos-1st ed (dd5,dj) 30.00

MILLARD,S T-Opaque Glass-1953-Central Pr-325 plts-3rd ed (cc8) 45.00

MILLAY,EDNA ST.VINCENT-Collected Sonnets-NY,Lond-1941-Harper-orig g titled cl,orig publ box-1st ed (aa9,sp drknd,box sl wn) 20.00

MILLAY,EDNA ST.VINCENT-Collected Sonnets-NY-1941-Harper Bros-1st ed (cc2,box) 35.00

MILLAY,EDNA ST.VINCENT-Fatal Interview-NY-1931-Harper-8vo-cl & bds-1st ed (x3,dj) 25.00

MILLAY,EDNA ST.VINCENT-Harp Weaver-NY,Lond-1923-Harper-orig g titled cl-1st ed (aa9) 25.00

MILLAY,EDNA ST.VINCENT-Harp Weaver-NY-1923-Harper-1st ed (z3) 12.50

MILLAY,EDNA ST.VINCENT-Huntsman, What Quarry-NY-1939-Harper-8vo-94p-1st ed (w6,f,tn dj) 30.00

MILLAY,EDNA ST.VINCENT-Huntsman, What Quarry-NY-1939-Harper-8vo-limp lea-1st ed (x3) 40.00

MILLAY,EDNA ST.VINCENT-King's Henchman-NY,Lond-1927-Harper-orig cl bckd bds,papr sp labl-1st ed (aa9) 20.00

MILLAY,EDNA ST.VINCENT-King's Henchman-NY-1927-Harper & Bros-ltd to 500c,autg-Artists' ed (l9) 165.00

MILLAY,EDNA ST.VINCENT-Letters of ...-NY-(1952)-1st ed (m5,f,dj) 17.50

MILLAY,EDNA ST.VINCENT-Letters-NY-(1949)-Harper & Bros-1st ed (cc2,f,2 djs) 30.00

MILLAY,EDNA ST.VINCENT-Mine the Harvest-NY-(1954)-Harper-cl bckd bds-1st ed (aa9,f,sl wn dj) 30.00

MILLAY,EDNA ST.VINCENT-Murder of Lidice-NY-1942-Harper-8vo-wrps-1st ed (x3) 25.00

MILLAY,EDNA ST.VINCENT-Princess Marries the Page-NY-1932-Harper & Bros-beige & grn bds-decs by J Paget-Fredericks-1st ed (f2,sl wn dj) 25.00

MILLAY,EDNA ST.VINCENT-Wine From These Grapes-1934-Harpers-1st ed (x2,f,dj) 30.00

MILLER,ALFRED J-Braves and Buffalo Plains Indian Life in 1837-(1973)-U of Tor-oblng 4to-176p-wtrcols by auth-1st ed (e7,chip dj) 40.00

MILLER,ALFRED J-West of...-Norman-(1951)-4to-unpgd-200 paintings-1st ed (h7,f,sl chip dj) 100.00

MILLER,ALICE D-Are Women People-NY-(1915)-Doran-8vo-94p-orig yel cl wi papr title inset-1st ed (z5,sl soil cov) 30.00

MILLER,AMY B-Shaker Herbs-NY-(1976)-tall 8vo-272p-cl bkd pap cov bds,110 illus,incl 8 col-1st ed (x5,dj) 30.00

MILLER,ARTHUR-An Enemy of the People-NY-1951-Viking-1st ed (y1,dj) 65.00

MILLER,ARTHUR-Death of a Salesman-NY-1949-1st ed (n5,dj) 125.00

MILLER,ARTHUR-I Don't Need You Anymore-NY-1967-Viking-1st ed (q2,dj) 25.00

MILLER,ARTHUR-Incident at Vichy-NY-(1965)-Viking-1st ed (c10,f,dj) 25.00

MILLER,ARTHUR-Misfits-NY-1961-1st ed (n5,dj) 40.00

MILLER,ARTHUR-Misfits-NY-1961-Viking-1st ed (y1,dj) 50.00

MILLER,CAPT E D-Modern Polo-Lond,NY-1902-Hurst,Blackett,Scribner-2nd rvsd ed (j9) 35.00

MILLER,CAREY D-ET AL-Some Fruits of Hawaii-(Honolulu)-(1936)-Paradise of Pacific Pr-133p-wrps,illus (a8,sl sun) 22.00

MILLER,CAROLYN P-Captured-Chappaqua-(1977)-Christian Herald Bks-288p-cl-1st ed so stated (g1,dj) 12.50

MILLER,CHARLES C-Black Borneo-NY-(1942)-Mod Age Bk-8vo-278p-photos-1st ed (cc5,dj) 20.00

MILLER,D C-ED.-Americans 1942-NY-1942-MOMA-ltd ed (h10,sl chip dj) 25.00

MILLER,D HENRY-Baptists of Trenton 1787...1867-Trenton-1867-prntd at True Amer Office-48p-wrps (h1,sl chip wrps) 15.00

MILLER,D HENRY-Baptists of Trenton, 1787 to 1867-Trenton-1867-48p-prtd wrps (aa6) 25.00

MILLER,D L-Other Half of the Globe-Elgin-1906-398p-cl,illus-1st ed so stated (l1) 15.00

MILLER,DAVID E-Golden Spike-SLC-1973-159p-frntis,photos-1st ed (t7,f) 30.00

MILLER,DAVID H-Custer's Fall-(1957)-DS&P-271p-illus,e.p. maps-1st ed (r8,dj sp creased,edge wn) 45.00

MILLER,DAVID H-Custer's Fall-NY-(1957)-DS&P-271p-e.p. maps,illus by auth-1st ed (gg4,dj) 50.00

MILLER,DAYTON C-Sparks,Lightning,Cosmic Rays-NY-1939-Macmillan-xviii+192p-blu cl,89 text figs-1st ed (d2,dj) 15.00

MILLER,DONALD C-Ghost Towns of the Southwest-Boulder-(1980)-127p-dbl col,photos,maps-1st ed (u7,dj) 20.00

MILLER,DOROTHY-Life and Work of David G Blythe-Pitt-(1950)-U Pitt Pr-8vo-142p-21 illus-1st ed (ee5,dj wn,chip) 17.50

MILLER,EDMUND W-Bergen and Jersey City-Jersey City-1910-34,(2)p-wrps,plts,fldg map (aa6) 30.00

MILLER,EDNA-Mousekin's Christmas Eve-(1965)-Prentice Hall-g pict cl-1st ed (aa9,f,f dj) 20.00

MILLER,ELIZABETH C-Young Trajan-NY-1931-Dbldy,Doran-pict cl,illus by M & M Petersham-1st ed (aa9) 15.00

MILLER,ELIZABETH-Yoke-Indpls-(1904)-Bobbs-Merrill-619p+ads-cl,Egyptian motif dec frnt cov by M Armstrong (n1) 15.00

MILLER,ERNEST C-John Wilkes Booth, Oilman-NY-(1947)-Exposition Pr-78p-blu cl,plts-1st ed (e2,sl wn dj) 40.00

MILLER,F T-Byrd's Great Adventure-Chig-(1930)-8vo-384p-illus cl,col frntis,plts,col e.p. maps (t2) 25.00

MILLER,F T-ED.-Photographic History of the Civil War-NY-(ca.1970)-10 vols-illus,maps,port (z10,djs) 100.00

MILLER,F T-ED.-Photographic History of the Civil War-NY-1911-10 vols-issued w/o djs-1st ed (k5,sl wn) 275.00

MILLER,F T-ED.-Photographic History of the Civil War: Prisons and Hospitals-NY-1957-352p-(facs of 1911 ed) (dd3,dj) 75.00

MILLER,F T-Fight to Conquer the Ends of the Earth-Phila-(1930)-Winston-8vo-384p-dec cl,col frntis,plts,col e.p. maps (t2) 50.00

MILLER,F T-Portrait Life of Lincoln-Springfield-1910-Patriot Publ-g stmpd illus cl-1st ed (y3) 65.00

MILLER,F T-World in the Air-NY-(1930)-4to-2 vols,cl,illus,illus e.p. (s2,sp fade & sl wn) 125.00

MILLER,F T-World in the Air-NY-1930-2 vols-g pict folio,illus,photos-1st ed (r2) 150.00

MILLER,F T-World in the Air-NY-1930-Putnam's-2 vols-cl,illus-1st trd ed (aa1,dj sl wn,chip) 125.00

MILLER,FLORENCE H-COMP.-Memorial Album of Revolutionary Soldiers, 1776-Crete-1958-auth-8vo-406p-375 illus-1st ed(?) (cc5,f,dj) 20.00

MILLER,FRANK E-Indian Club,Swinging-Akron-1900-Saalfield-182p+ads-cl,frontis port,illus (h1) 15.00

MILLER,G S,JR.-Directions for Preparing Specimens of Mammals-Wash-1932-USNM/Smiths Bull.39,Prt N-8vo-20p-cl,text figs-scarce (jj10) 10.00

MILLER,G S-American Bats of the Genera Myotis and Pizonyx-Wash-1928-8vo-218p-wrps,1 plt,13 maps (y8,ex-libr) 37.00

MILLER,G S-Families and Genera of Bats-Wash-1907-8vo-282p-wrps,14 plts-Bull. U.S. Nat.Museum No.57 (y8,wrps chip,soil) 60.00

MILLER,GENEVIEVE-Adoption of Inoculation for Smallpox in England and France-Phila-1957-355p-1st ed (dd3) 50.00

MILLER,GENEVIEVE-Bibliography of the Writings of Henry E Sigerist-Montreal-1966-112p-1st ed (dd3,dj) 20.00

MILLER,HAZEN L-Old Au Sable-Grand Rapids-1963-Eerdmans-164p-cl,photos-1st ed (z7,dj) 35.00

MILLER,HENRY-Air Conditioned Nightmare-Norfolk-(1945)-New Directions-1st issue dj-1st ed,1st issue (mm5,f,sl chip dj) 70.00

MILLER,HENRY-Art & Outrage-Lond-1959-1st Brit ed (s5,dj) 40.00

MILLER,HENRY-Black Spring-NY-1963-Grove-1st trd ed (f8,f,sl spot dj) 45.00

MILLER,HENRY-Book of Friends-Santa Barbara-1976-Capra Pr-illus-1st ed (r2,f,dj sl rub,sl tn) 25.00

MILLER,HENRY-Books in My Life-Lond-(1952)-Peter Owen-gry buckram,blu stmpng-1st Brit ed (v10,f,dj wn & tn) 100.00

MILLER,HENRY-Books in My Life-Norfolk-(1952)-New Directions-1st iss wi 4 photos-1st ed (e8,dj) 125.00

MILLER,HENRY-Colossus of Maroussi-SF-(1941)-Colt Pr-4to-cl-1st ed (x3,dj) 185.00

MILLER,HENRY-Cosmological Eye-Lond-1945-Poetry London-1st Brit ed (h8,chip dj) 125.00

MILLER,HENRY-First Impression of Greece-Santa Barbara-1973-Capra Pr-12mo-47p-g dec cl,papr sp labl,frntis,illus,pic of auth tip in at rear-ltd to 250c,nbrd,autg-1st ed (dd10,as new) 75.00

MILLER,HENRY-Greece-NY-1964-drwngs-1st ed (v9,sl tn dj) 65.00

MILLER,HENRY-Hamlet-Santurce-(1939)-Carrefour-12mo-prntd wrps-ltd to 500c-1st ed (v10,f) 150.00

MILLER,HENRY-Just Wild About Henry-Lond-1964-MacGibbon & Kee-1st Brit ed (y1,f,dj) 40.00

MILLER,HENRY-Lawrence Durrell & Henry Miller:A Private Correspondence-NY-1963-Dutton-1st ed (f3,dj) 30.00

MILLER,HENRY-Letters to Anais Nin-NY-1965-Putnam-1st ed (c8,f,dj) 60.00

MILLER,HENRY-MY Life and Times-np-nd-Playboy-4to-photos-1st ed (b5,f,dj) 35.00

MILLER,HENRY-My Life and Times-NY-(1971)-Playboy Press-1st ed (h3,dj) 30.00

MILLER,HENRY-Notes on "Aaron's Rod"-Santa Barbara-1980-dec bds,acetate dj,ltd to 750c-1st trd ed (t5,f,dj) 15.00

MILLER,HENRY-Plexus-NY-1965-1st US ed (s5,f,dj) 20.00

MILLER,HENRY-Plexus-Paris-(1953)-Olympia Pr-12mo-2 vols-prntd wrps-ltd to 2000c,nbrd-1st Engl lang ed (v10) 175.00

MILLER,HENRY-Quiet Days in Clichy-NY-(1965,56)-Grove-wrps as iss-1st US ed (hh5) 10.00

MILLER,HENRY-Remember to Remember-Lond-1952-Grey Walls Pr-1st Brit ed (h8,f,f dj) 100.00

MILLER,HENRY-Remember to Remember-NY-1947-New Directions-8vo-cl-1st ed (x3,sl chip dj) 125.00

MILLER,HENRY-Stand Still Like a Hummingbird-Norfolk-1962-New Directions-1st ed (c8,f,dj) 75.00

MILLER,HENRY-Sunday After the War-NY-1945-1st ed (v9,f,sl chip dj) 125.00

MILLER,HENRY-Tropic of Capricorn-NY-1961-Grove Pr-1st ed (q2,dj) 45.00

MILLER,HENRY-Tropic of Capricorn-NY-1961-Grove-1st trd ed (f8,f,dj sp sl sunned) 50.00

MILLER,HENRY-What Are You Going To Do About Alf-Berkeley-(1944)-Bern Porter-prtd wrps,frntis-1st ed (r2,f) 60.00

MILLER,HUGH-Cruise of the Betsey-Bost-1865-Gould & Lincoln-xiv,(15)-524p-orig brwn cl-"Authorized Ed." (nn1,sp wn) 45.00

MILLER,J MARTIN-ED.-Discovery of the North Pole-np-(1909)-428p-cl (f1) 20.00

MILLER,JAMES K P-Road to Virginia City-Norman-(1960)-142p-illus-1st ed (j7,dj) 30.00

MILLER,JOACHIN-Baroness of New York-NY-1877-G W Carleton-grn cl-BAL 13771-1st ed (f2) 25.00

MILLER,JOAQUIN-An Illustrated History of the State of Montana-Chig-1894-Lewis-2 vols,half lea,engrvngs,illus,ports-1st ed (v1) 350.00

MILLER,JOAQUIN-Building of the City Beautiful-Trntn-1905-Brandt-gold emboss red cl,photogravure frntis-1st ed (t4,f) 30.00

MILLER,JOAQUIN-California Diary Beginning in 1855 & Ending in 1857-Seattle-1936-Dogwood Pr-#47 of 700c-1st ed (h8,box) 75.00

MILLER,JOAQUIN-Danites in the Sierras-Chig-1881-Jansen,McClurg-16mo-258p-cl-1st ed (mm7,sl fade) 65.00

MILLER,JOAQUIN-First Families of the Sierras-Chig-1876-Jansen,McClurg-16mo-258p-cl-1st ed (mm7,sl rub,few spots) 45.00

MILLER,JOAQUIN-In Classic Shades and Other Poems-Chig-1890-1st ed (d3) 25.00

MILLER,JOAQUIN-Poetical Works of...-NY-1923-g stmpd cl,photos frntis-1st ed (m4) 15.00

MILLER,JOAQUIN-Songs of Summer Lands-Chig-(1893)-Conkey-cl-BAL 13900 (c1) 12.50

MILLER,JOAQUIN-True Bear Stories-Chig,NY-(1900)-Rand,McNally-v scarce dj,bndg "C"-BAL #13848-1st ed,3rd prtg (w1,f,dj) 100.00

MILLER,JOAQUIN-Unwritten History,Life Among the Modocs-Hartford-1874-445p+3p ads-illus-1st Amer ed (g7,sl wn,edge stnd plts) 90.00

MILLER,JOHN T-Applied Character Analysis-Bost-1922-Gorham Pr-8vo-223p-8 photos-1st ed (aa7,scuff bds) 35.00*

MILLER,JOSEPH-Arizona Indians-NY-(1941)-59p-photos-1st ed (v7,f,dj) 15.00

MILLER,JOSEPH-Arizona-(1956)-Hastings-350p-illus-1st ed (d3,dj) 20.00

MILLER,JOSEPH-Arizona-NY-(1956)-Hastings Hs-350p-drwngs,e.p. maps-Six Guns #1491-1st ed (cc4,dj) 30.00

MILLER,JOSEPH-Descendants of Capt Thomas Carter of "Barford", Lancaster County, Virginia-(Thomas)-(1912)-388p-scarce (jj3,f) 125.00

MILLER,JOSEPH-ED.-Arizona Cavalcade-NY-(1962)-Hastings Hs-306p-Ross Santee,illus-Six Guns 1492-1st ed (gg4,dj) 25.00

MILLER,KELLY-Negro Soldier in Our War(cov title)-np-1919-"Kelly Miller's History of the World War for Human Rights"-1st ed (w5) 50.00

MILLER,KEMPSTER B-American Telephone Practice-1899-458p-357 illus-1st ed (h6) 25.00

MILLER,L C-Handsprings for Hamburgers-Hollywood-1929-sm 8vo-204p-cl,9p plts-1st ed (s2,sl chip dj) 35.00

MILLER,L-On Top of the World-US-1976-222p-1st ed (o10,as new in dj) 22.00

MILLER,LEWIS B-Crooked Trail-Bost-(1911)-Dana Estes & Co-413p-cl-2nd ed,enlgd (b1) 65.00

MILLER,LEWIS B-Crooked Trail-Pitt-(1908)-184p-prtd wrps-rare-Howes M 611-1st ed (b1,rbkd) 85.00

MILLER,LIDA B-Round the World with Note Book and Camera-Chig-1897-A B Kuhlman-318p-orng cl wi silv titles & blk cov decs (ll1,hngs weak) 25.00

MILLER,M-Daybreak for our Carrier-NY-(1944)-8vo-184p-illus cl,frntis,plts,text illus-1st ed (s2) 25.00

MILLER,MADELAINE H-Ernie-NY-(1975)-Crown-1st ed (cc2,f,dj) 30.00

MILLER,MRS S G-Sixty Years in the Nueces Valley-S.A.-1930-Naylor-374p-Frntis,photos-Herd 1491-1st ed (a9) 150.00

MILLER,NAOMI-Heavenly Caves-NY-1982-Braziller-sm 4to-141p-maroon bds,illus-1st ed (r10,f,dj) 22.50

MILLER,NATHAN-Roosevelt Chronicles-GC-1979-377p-cl-1st ed so stated (h1,sl wn dj) 12.50

MILLER,NATHAN-U.S. Navy, an Illustrated History-NY-1977-Amer Heritage-4to (p8,dj) 25.00

MILLER,NINA-Shutters West-(1962)-Sage-oblng 16mo-152p-photos by A C Hull-1st ed (r8,f dj) 50.00

MILLER,NYLE H-Why the West was Wild-Topeka-1963-Ks State Hist Soc-685p-illus,e.p. maps-1st ed (cc4,dj) 125.00

MILLER,O T-Birdways-Bost-1885-12mo-(2),227p-half lea (y8,sp wn) 15.00

MILLER,OLIVE B-My Book House-Chig-(1930)-Bk Hs for Chldrn-12 vols-blu covs,gold lttrng,pict pastedowns,illus-later ed (y10) 185.00

MILLER,ORLANDO-Frontier in Alaska & the Matanuska Colony-1975-Yale-329p-1st ed (u8,dj) 27.00

MILLER,PAMELA-And the Whale is Ours-Bost/Sharon-1979-Godine/Kendall Whalng Mus-8vo-201p-grn cl,illus (ee7,dj) 25.00

MILLER,RAY J-Lure of the Roca Grande-1950-Hennel Locke-1st ed (r9,dj) 15.00

MILLER,RICHARD-Bohemia-Chig-1977-Nelson Hall-1st ed (w5,f,f dj) 25.00

MILLER,RICK-Train Robbing Bunch-College Sta-1983-Creative Publ-175p-illus-1st ed (bb4,dj) 15.00

MILLER,ROBERT R-Cyprinodont Fishes of the Death Valley System of Eastern California & Southwestern Canada-Ann Arbor-1948-4to-155p-wrps,photos (m3) 12.50

MILLER,RONALD D-Shady Ladies of the West-LA-1964-Westernlore Pr-224p-illus-Six Guns #1499-1st ed (cc4,dj) 35.00

MILLER,RONALD-Death of an Army-Bost-1970-323p-illus-1st Amer ed (b7,f,dj) 35.00

MILLER,S C-Neon Signs-NY-1935 (h10) 45.00

MILLER,S C-Neon Signs: Manufacture, Installation, Design-1935-McGraw Hill-288p-illus-8th impr (cc8) 75.00

MILLER,SAMUEL-Life of...-Phila-1869-2 vols-cl,port (aa6) 40.00

MILLER,SIDNEY-Tomorrow in West Texas-Lubbock-1956-643p-1st ed (t7,f) 20.00

MILLER,STEWART-Florida Fishing-NY-1931-8vo-320p-illus (m3) 20.00

MILLER,T L-History of Hereford Cattle...with...History of the Herefords in America, by Wm H Sotham-Chillicothe-1902-T F B Sotham-4to-592p-purple cl,341 illus-1st ed (a2,cov wn,sl soil text) 75.00

MILLER,T L-Public Lands of Texas 1519 to 1970-(1972)-U of Ok-341p-wrps,maps,illus-1st ed so stated (t8,sl wn) 15.00

MILLER,T-Lindbergh. His Story in Pictures-NY-1929-Putnam-8vo-320p-g cl,372 photos,F A Barber,illus e.p. (s2,sl wn sp) 40.00

MILLER,TOM-North Cascades-Seattle-1964-4to-94p-67 photos-1st ed (p10,f,f dj) 75.00

MILLER,W HENRY-Pioneering North Texas-San Antonio-1953-Naylor Co-303p-cl,illus,photos-Herd #1496-1st ed (w3,f,dj) 75.00

MILLER,W T-Birds at Home-Cape Town-1947-8vo-100,(2)p-cl,50 photos (y8) 18.50

MILLER,WADE-Deadly Weapon-NY-1946-Farrar-1st ed (f4,rprd dj) 20.00

MILLER,WARREN H-Rifles & Shotguns-NY-1917-8vo-233p-photos (m3) 15.00

MILLER,WARREN-Cool World-1959-Little,Brown-1st ed (n9,f,sl wn dj) 35.00

MILLER,WARREN-Flush Times-1962-Little,Brown-1st ed (m9,dj wi sm tr & sp drknd) 25.00

MILLER,WICK R-Acoma Grammar and Texts-Berkeley-1965-U of Cal Publ-Vol.40-259p-wrps-1st ed (v7,f) 20.00

MILLER,WILLIAM D-Silversmiths of Little Rest-Kingston-1928-Merrymount Pr-sm 4to-rust cl sp,brwn bds,t.e.g.,untrimmed (r10,f) 90.00

MILLET,SAMUEL A-Whaling Voyage in the Bark "Willis" 1849 to 1850-Bost-1924-priv prtd/Thomas Perkins-vi,(3),46p-mrbld papr over bds,8 illus-ltd to 50c-1st prtg (p8,sl fox e.p.) 250.00

MILLETT,KATE-Elegy for Sita-(NY)-(1979)-Targ Eds-oblng 4to-cl-ltd to 350c,autg-1st ed (jj8,vf,dj) 50.00

MILLETT,KATE-Sexual Politics-GC-1970-Dbldy-8vo-393p-auth 1st bk-1st ed (bb5,f,dj) 17.50

MILLHAUSER,STEVEN-Portrait of a Romantic-NY-1977-Knopf-1st ed (bb1,as new in dj) 20.00

MILLICHAP,JOSEPH-Steinbeck and Film-NY-1983-Ungar-1st ed (x9,f,dj) 15.00

MILLIGAN,ALICE-Hero Lays-Dublin-1908-Maunsel-limp covs-1st ed (z8,f) 150.00

MILLIGAN,ALICE-Poems-Dublin-1954-Gill & Son-1st ed (z8,f,soil dj) 40.00

MILLIKEN,HENRY-Hunting in Maine-Freeport-1947-8vo-186p-illus-1st ed (m3) 15.00

MILLS,CLARENCE A-Climate Makes the Man-NY-(1942)-Harper-8vo-320p-1st ed (dd5,sl tn dj) 25.00

MILLS,DONALD-Southwest Impressions by Mills-Glorieta-1973-Rio Grande-folio-b&w & col illus-1st ed (u9) 25.00

MILLS,ENOS A-Grizzly: Our Greatest Wild Animal-Bost-1909-Houghton Mifflin-8vo-289p wi index,photos-1st ed (w1) 85.00

MILLS,ENOS-Adventures of a Nature Guide-GC-1927-8vo-271p-photos (m3) 12.50

MILLS,ENOS-Rocky Mountain Wonderland-Bost-1915-363p-plts,illus-1st ed (q10,2 pgs chip) 25.00

MILLS,JAMES-Airborne to the Mountains-NY-1961-261p-22 photos-1st US ed (q10,f,dj) 15.00

MILLS,JOHN-Radio Communication: Theory and Methods-1918-205p-10 photos,110 illus-1st ed (h6) 20.00

MILLS,LADY DOROTHY-Through Liberia-Lond-(1926)-Duckworth-8vo-240p-40 illus-1st Brit ed (cc5,sl box & fox) 40.00

MILLS,OSMINGTON-At One Fell Swoop-NY-1963-Roy-1st US ed (d4,dj) 12.50

MILLS,OSMINGTON-Enemies of the Bride-NY-1966-Roy-1st US ed (d4,f,dj) 15.00

MILLS,RANDALL-Railroads Down the Valley-1950-Pacific Bks-8vo-151p (nn7,dj wn) 45.00

MILLS,RANDALL-Stern Wheelers up Columbia-Palo Alto-(1947)-212p-photos,maps-1st ed (r8,dj chip,wn) 40.00

MILLS,RANDALL-Stern Wheelers up Columbia-Palo Alto-(1947)-Pacific Bks-(x)+212p-tan cl,plts,maps-1st ed (mm10,dj) 45.00

MILLS,S E-Sourdough Sky-NY-(1960)-4to-176p-cl,frntis,illus t.p.,plts (s2,dj) 35.00

MILLS,W JAY-Historic Houses of New Jersey-Phila-1903-348p-cl,plts (aa6,sl soil cl) 50.00

MILLS,W W-Forty Years at El Paso, 1858 to 1898-np-1901-166p-port-Howes M633-rare-1st ed (a9) 200.00

MILLSPAUGH,C F-Descriptive List of the Weeds of West Virginia-Charleston-1892-(96)p-stapled as iss,illus,WV Agri Experiment Sta Bulletin 23 (b1) 17.50

MILNE,A A-By Way of Introduction-Lond-1929-Methuen-1st Brit ed (q2,dj) 150.00

MILNE,A A-Christopher Robin Birthday Book-Lond-(1930)-Methuen-orig g pict cl,dec by E H Shepard-1st ed (aa9,sl fade) 100.00

MILNE,A A-Four Days Wonder-Lond-(1933)-Methuen-8vo-cl-1st ed (jj8,vf,dj) 125.00

MILNE,A A-Gallery of Children-Phila-(1925)-McKay-125p-pict cl,125 drwngs,A H Watson-1st US ed (s3,sl drknd,tatterd dj) 35.00

MILNE,A A-Ivory Door-Lond-1929-Chatto-slim 8vo-cl-1st ed (x3,f,sl chip dj) 35.00

MILNE,A A-Michael and Mary-Lond-1930-Chatto & Windus-cl,papr sp labl-1st ed (aa9) 50.00

MILNE,A A-Now We are Six-Lond-(1927)-Methuen-g pict cl,t.e.g.,illus by E H Shepard-1st ed (aa9,sl rub) 125.00

MILNE,A A-Perfect Alibi-1929-S French-wrps-1st ed (x7) 38.00

MILNE,A A-Red House Mystery-NY-1922-Dutton-1st US ed (k4) 50.00

MILNE,A A-Secret and Other Stories-NY-1929-Fountain Pr-cl,papr sp labl-1st Amer ed (aa9,autg) 125.00

MILNE,A A-Two People-Lond-(1931)-Methuen-cl stmpd in gilt & grn-1st ed (aa9) 25.00

MILNE,A A-Winnie the Pooh-Lond-1926-g pict cl,t.e.g.,illus by E H Shepard-1st ed (r2) 350.00

MILNE,A A-Year In, Year Out-NY-(1952)-Dutton-1st US ed (hh5,chip dj) 20.00

MILNE,CHRISTOPHER-Path Through the Trees-1979-Dutton-1st Amer ed (w4,dj) 20.00

MILNE,E A-Relativity, Gravitation and World Structure-Oxford-1935-Clarendon Pr-x+365p-blu cl,4 plts,21 text figs-1st ed (j2,dj) 75.00

MILNE,EWART-Diamond Cut Diamond-Lond-(1950)-Bodley Head-1st ed (z8,f,dj) 37.50

MILNE,EWART-Garland for the Grenn-Lond-(1962)-Hutchinson-1st ed (z8,f,dj) 22.50

MILNE,EWART-Jubilo-Lond-(1944)-F Muller-1st ed (z8,f,dj) 37.50

MILNE,L J-Time to be Born-1982-Sierra Club-218p-illus-1st ed (bb3,f,dj) 14.00

MILNE,MALCOM-Book of Modern Mountaineering-NY-1968-4to-304p-photos(incl col)-1st ed (p10,f,tn dj) 15.00

MILNE,PETER-Motion Picture Directing-NY-(1922)-Falk Publ-8vo-230p-maroon buckram,photos (u1) 125.00

MILNER,DOUGLAS-Mountain Photograhy-Lond-1945-238p-photos-1st Brit ed (q10) 20.00

MILNER,DOUGLAS-Rock For Climbing-Lond-1950-lg 8vo-128p-96 photos-1st Brit ed (p10,dj chip) 20.00

MILNER,JOE E-California Joe-Caldwell-1935-Caxton-396p-cl,illus-Howes M635-1st ed (v1,chip dj) 125.00

MILNER,JOE E-California Joe-Caldwell-1935-Caxton-8vo-396p-grn cl,illus-Six Guns #1507-1st ed (p1) 100.00

MILNER,REV THOMAS-Gallery of Geography-Glasgow-1864-W R M'Phun & Son-lg 8vo-2 vols-1/2 grn lea,mrbld e.p.,illus,5 plts,12 maps-1st ed (mm8,wn,hngs weak) 125.00*

MILNOR,WILLIAM-Memoirs of the Gloucester Fox Hunting Club near Philadelphia-NY-1927-E R Gee/Derrydale Pr-(9),47p-bds,2 plts-ltd to 375c,nbrd-rprnt of 1830 ed (aa6,bds fade,sp chip) 125.00

MILORADOVICH,MILO-Art of Cooking with Herbs and Spices-GC-1950-Dbldy-304p (m6) 15.00

MILSTEN,DAVID-Thomas Gilcrease-San Antonio-(1969)-Naylor-468p-photos,pict dj-1st ed (f9,sl spot dj) 35.00

MILTON,GEORGE F-Abraham Lincoln and the Fifth Column-NY-1942-364p-illus-1st ed (n3,f,dj) 40.00

MILTS,M H-Only a Gringo Would Die for an Anteater-1979-Norton-225p-photos-1st ed (bb3,f,dj) 12.00

MILWARD,MARGUERITE-Artist in Unknown India-Lond-(1948)-Werner Laurie-8vo-274p-98 illus-1st ed (jj5,dj soil) 20.00

MINARD,JNO S-Recollections of the Log School House Period and Sketches of Life and Customs in Pioneer Days-Cuba,N.Y.-1905-Free Press-137,(3)p-cl-scarce (k1) 35.00

MINCHIN,C C-Sea Fishing-Lond-1911-306p+ads-pict cl & sp-1st ed (jj4) 40.00

MINCHIN,C O-Sea Fishing-Lond-1911-8vo-306p+ads-illus (m3) 15.00

MINER,JACK-Jack Miner & the Birds-Chig-1932-8vo-176p-photos-1st ed (m3) 15.00

MINETTA-Art of Tea Cup Fortune Telling-NY-1958-Foulsham-sm 8vo-155p-drwngs-1st ed (aa7,sl rub dj) 20.00*

MINGE,WARD A-Acoma, Pueblo in the Sky-Albuq-(1976)-173p-col photos-1st ed (v7,f,dj) 35.00

MINGUS,CHARLES-Beneath the Underdog-1971-Knopf-1st ed (n9,dj sp tn & sl wn) 35.00

MINNEAPOLIS INSTITUTE OF ARTS-Art Deco-Mpls-1971-4to-224p-wrps,dec e.p.,illus,16 col plts (pp7) 45.00

MINNEGERODE,MEADE-Fabulous Forties, America's Awkward Age 1840 to 1850-NY-1924-345p-frntis,illus (t7,dj) 7.50

MINNESOTA ARROWHEAD COUNTRY-Chig-1941-WPA/Amer Guide Ser-233p-frntis,photos,map e.p.-1st ed (t7,dj) 25.00

MINNESOTA'S TIMBER LAND-St.Paul-nd(ca.1908)-Minn St Bd of Immigration-47,(1)p-wrps (e1,sl soil wrps) 15.00

MINNESOTA-Annals of the...Historical Society-St.Paul-1850-James M Goodhue-32p-wrps-Howes M641-2nd ed (a1,sl wn) 40.00

MINNESOTA. BRIEF SKETCHES OF ITS HISTORY ...FOR DISTRIBUTION AT THE WORLD'S FAIR, ST.LOUIS, 1904-np-1904-99,(1)p-wrps (h1,frnt labl remvd, sl soil) 15.00

MINOGUE,ANNA-Loretto: Annals of the Century-NY-1912-America-photos-1st ed (u9) 37.50

MINOR WHITE-Living Remembrance-Millerton-1984-Aperture-1st ed (w5,f,sl tn dj) 30.00

MINOR,B B-Southern Literary Messenger, 1834 to 1864-NY,Wash-1905-Neale Publ-252p-illus (z10,sl wn & soil) 75.00

MINOR,ROBERT-Lynching and Frame Up in Tennessee-NY-1946-New Century-wrps-1st ed (w5,cor crease) 20.00

MINTON,BRUCE-Men Who Lead Labor-NY-1937-Modern Age-wrps in dj-1st ed (v5,rnfrcd dj) 20.00

MINTON,S A-Giant Reptiles-1973-Scribners-345p-photos-1st ed (bb3,f,dj) 35.00

MINUTES OF CANADA YEARLY MEETING OF FRIENDS HELD AT PICKERING, ONTARIO 1914-Pickering-(1914)-35p-wrps (h1) 12.50

MIRKSEY,JEANETTE-Westward Crossings-Chig-1970-378p-photos,maps (t7,f,dj) 10.00

MIRRLEES,HOPE-Paris-Richmond-1919-Hogarth-12mo-dec wrps,prtd cov labl-ltd to 175c,handprtd by L & V Woolf wi 2 corrections in V Woolf's hand-1st ed (ll10,sl wn sp) 500.00

MIRZA,YOUEL-Myself When Young-GC-1929-Dbldy-1st ed (s3,pres cpy) 15.00

MISCELLANEOUS NOSTRUMS-Chig-1919-140p-wrps-scarce-4th ed (dd3) 50.00

MISCIATELLI,PIERO-Piccolomini Library in the Cathedral of Siena-Siena-1924-Bentivolglio-8vo-blu cl,64 illus(incl col)-ltd to 500c (r10) 22.50

MISHIMA,YUKIO-After the Banquet-NY-1963-Knopf-271p-blk cl & blu papr over bds-1st Amer ed (ll1,wn dj) 35.00

MISHIMA,YUKIO-Confessions of the Mask-Norfolk-1958-1st US ed (p5,dj) 35.00

MISHIMA,YUKIO-Decay of the Angel-1974-Knopf-1st Amer ed (p9,dj) 15.00

MISHIMA,YUKIO-Five Modern No Plays-NY-1957-1st US ed (p5,dj) 30.00

MISHIMA,YUKIO-Forbidden Colors-NY-1968-1st US ed (t5,f,dj) 30.00

MISHIMA,YUKIO-Runaway Horses-1973-Knopf-1st Amer ed (t9,f,sl tn dj) 20.00

MISHIMA,YUKIO-Runaway Horses-1973-Knopf-1st Amer ed (x2,f,dj) 30.00

MISHIMA,YUKIO-Sound of the Waves-NY-1956-Knopf-1st Engl transl of auth 1st bk-1st Amer ed (g8,sl chip dj) 85.00

MISHIMA,YUKIO-Sun & Steel-Lond-1971-1st Brit ed (t5,f,dj) 40.00

MISHIMA,YUKIO-Sun & Steel-Tokyo,Palo Alto-(1970)-Kodansha Intl-sm 4to-104p-photo dj-1st ed (oo8,vf,dj) 100.00

MISHIMA,YUKIO-Temple of the Golden Pavilion-NY-1959-1st US ed (s5,dj) 35.00

MISHIMA,YUKIO-Thirst for Love-NY-1969-Knopf-1st ed (d8,f,f dj) 50.00

MITCHAM,GILROY-Man From Bar Harbour-Lond-1958-Dobson-1st ed (j4,dj) 15.00

MITCHELL,ANNIE-Jim Savage and the Tulareno Indians-1957-Wstrnlore-118p-illus-1st ed (d3,dj) 20.00

MITCHELL,ARTHUR-Labour in Irish Politics 1890 to 1930-NY-1974-Harper-317p (r1,dj) 20.00

MITCHELL,B W-Trail Life in the Canadian Rockies-NY-1924-Macmillan-8vo-xii,269p-32 illus-1st ed (cc7,dj) 50.00*

MITCHELL,C AINSWORTH-Vinegar-Lond-1916-Chas Griffin-xvi+201p-maroon cl,5 plts-1st ed (a2) 40.00

MITCHELL,CARLETON-Islands to Windward-NY-(1948)-287p-cl,photos(incl col) (aa1) 20.00

MITCHELL,DONALD G-Works of...-NY-1907-Scribner's-16 vols-brwn cl-ltd to 240 sets,nbrd,autg port (f2,few discol sp,sl fox,spot) 225.00

MITCHELL,EDWIN V-Morocco Bound: Adrift Among Books-NY-(1929)-Farrar & Rinehart-xiv,232p-blind dec cl,frntis,plts,illus-1st ed (dd10,f) 20.00

MITCHELL,EMERSON B-Miracle Hill-Norman-(1967)-223p-1st ed (v7,f,dj) 20.00

MITCHELL,EMERSON B-Miracle Hill-Norman-(1967)-U of Okla Pr-230p-1st ed (cc4,dj) 15.00

MITCHELL,ERHMAN-MFH:Ponies for Young People-Princeton-1960-Van Nostrand-1st ed (h9,dj) 15.00

MITCHELL,F A-Marketing the Apple-1909-Mich State Grange-8p-self wrps (z7) 22.50

MITCHELL,GEN BILLY-Skyways:a Book on Modern Aeronautics-Phila-1930-Lippincott-1st ed (ll9,f,sp fade dj) 75.00

MITCHELL,GLADYS-Dancing Druids-Lond-1948-Joseph-1st ed (h4,dj) 35.00

MITCHELL,GLADYS-Death-Cap Dancers-Lond-1981-Joseph-1st ed (f4,f,dj) 20.00

MITCHELL,GLADYS-Longer Bodies-1930-Gollancz-1st ed (s10,fox pgs & e.p.) 30.00

MITCHELL,GLADYS-Man Who Grew Tomatoes-NY-1959-London House-1st US ed (d4,f,dj) 30.00

MITCHELL,GLADYS-Noonday and Night-Lond-1977-Joseph-1st ed (q4,f,dj) 22.50

MITCHELL,GLADYS-Speedy Death-NY-1929-MacVeagh/Dial-1st Amer ed (w9,f,dj sl tn,wn & sp faded) 350.00

MITCHELL,GLADYS-Spotted Hemlock-Lond-1958-Joseph-1st ed (e4,f,dj) 25.00

MITCHELL,GLADYS-Twelve Horses and the Hangman's Noose-Lond-1956-Joseph-1st ed (h4,dj) 25.00

MITCHELL,GLADYS-Uncoffin'd Clay-Lond-1980-Joseph-1st ed (f4,f,dj) 20.00

MITCHELL,GLADYS-Watson's Choice-Lond-1955-Michael Joseph-1st ed (e4,dj) 30.00

MITCHELL,J B-Badge of Gallantry-NY-1968-194p-illus,ports-1st ed (z10,soil dj) 25.00

MITCHELL,J L-Colt, the Man, the Arms, the Company-1959-Stackpole-265p-photos (gg3,f,chip dj) 40.00

MITCHELL,JAMES C-Tennessee Justice's Manual, and Civil Officer's Guide...-Nashville-1834-Mitchell & Norvell-534p-lea,1 vol,in 3 prts-Amer Imprnts 25783 (c1,lacks f f.e.p.,fox,sl rub) 100.00

MITCHELL,JOE H-One Room Shack-1973-NRU Publ-wrps-1st ed (w5) 15.00

MITCHELL,JOHN D-Lost Mines and Buried Treasure along the Old Frontier-Palm Desert-(1953)-233p-illus,maps-1st ed (u7,wn,rprd dj) 60.00

MITCHELL,JOHN G-Losing Ground-SF-1975-Sierra Club-227p (z7,dj) 25.00

MITCHELL,JOSEPH-Bottom of the Harbor-Bost,Tor-(1959)-Little,Brown-1st ed (a10,f,dj) 75.00

MITCHELL,JOSEPH-Bottom of the Harbor-Bost-(1959)-Little,Brown-1st ed (cc2,f,dj) 60.00

MITCHELL,JOSEPH-Joe Gould's Secret-NY-1965-1st ed (n5,dj) 40.00

MITCHELL,JOSEPH-Old Mr.Flood-NY-1948-1st ed (n5,sl chip dj) 50.00

MITCHELL,LT.COL.SIR T L-Journal of an Expedition into the Interior of Tropical Australia...-NY-1969-Greenwood-8vo-xiv,(2),437p-brwn cl,plts,maps(4 fldg)-rprnt (p8,as new) 35.00

MITCHELL,MARGARET-Gone With the Wind-NY-1939-Macmillan-391p-dbl col,pict wrps-12 pg col plts-Motion Pict Ed-1st prntng (e1) 75.00

MITCHELL,MARGARET-Gone with the Wind-NY-1939-Macmillan-391p-pict wrps,dbl cols,12p col plts-"Published December, 1939" on cpyrt pg & t.p. dated 1939-1st prtg Motion Pict Ed (a1) 75.00

MITCHELL,MARIE-Navajo Peace Treaty 1868-NY-1973-145p-illus-(Great Events in World History ser)-1st ed (c4,f,dj) 17.50

MITCHELL,RICHARD-Mountain Experiences-Chig-1983-1st ed (o10,f,dj) 25.00

MITCHELL,S A-Eclipses of the Sun-NY-1923-Columbia Univ-xviii+425p-grn cl,plts-1st ed (d2) 45.00

MITCHELL,S AUGUSTUS-An Easy Introduction to the Study of Geography-Phila-1846-Thomas,Cowperthwait-176p-pict bds,120 engrvngs,14 col maps (k1,sl wn) 37.50

MITCHELL,S AUGUSTUS-System of Modern Geography...-Phila-1857-Cowperthwait-336p-bds (k1,covs wn) 22.50

MITCHELL,S WEIR-Mary Reynolds-Phila-1889-Wm J Dornan,prntr-(ii)+(20)p-prntd gry wrps-scarce-1st seprt prntg (y9) 185.00

MITCHELL,S WEIR-Some Recently Discovered Letters of William Harvey...Bibliography...by Charles Perry Fisher-Phila-1912-59p-wrps-1st ed (dd3) 100.00

MITCHELL,S WEIR-Venture in 1777-Phila-1908-Jacobs-1st ed (hh5) 20.00

MITCHELL,S WEIR-When All the Woods are Green-NY-1894-Century Co-419p-cl-BAL 14160-1st ed (b1) 15.00

MITCHELL,SUSAN L-Aids to the Immortality of Certain Persons in Ireland...-Dublin-1913-Maunsel-papr cov bds,prchmnt sp-new ed wi poems added-1st ed thus (z8,sl fox e.p.) 45.00

MITCHELL,SUSAN L-Living Chalice...-Dublin-1913-Maunsel-papr cov bds,vel sp-new ed wi poems added-1st ed thus (z8) 50.00

MITCHELL,W O-Jake and the Kid-Tor-1961-Macmillan-8vo-184p-1st ed (bb7,sl chip dj) 50.00*

MITCHELL,W O-Kite-Tor-1962-Macmillan-8vo-210p-1st ed (bb7,dj) 35.00*

MITCHELL,W O-Vanishing Point-Tor-1973-Macmillan-8vo-393p-1st ed (bb7,chip dj) 35.00*

MITCHELL,W-Memoirs of World War I-NY-(1960)-roy 8vo-xvi,314p-cl,13 plts (s2,chip dj) 35.00

MITCHELL,W-Skyways-Phila-1930-8vo-314p-illus cl,frntis,60p plts-1st ed (s2,sl chip dj) 45.00

MITCHELL,W-Winged Defense-NY-1925-8vo-xxiv,262p-cl,frntis,15p plts,illus e.p. (s2) 50.00

MITCHELL-HEDGES,F A-Battles with Giant Fish-Bost-1924-8vo-300p-photos (m3) 30.00

MITCHELL-HEDGES,F A-Battles with Monsters of the Sea-NY-1937-8vo-349p-photos (m3) 25.00

MITCHENER,C H-Ohio Annals-Dayton-1876-358p-cl-Howes M 701 (o1,cov wn) 45.00

MITCHISON,NAOMI-Small Talk-Lond-1973-Bodley Head-1st ed (y1,f,dj) 22.50

MITFORD,B-Fordham's Feud-1897-Ward Lock-pict cl,stmpd in gold,red,blu,brwn & red,illus-1st ed (x7,sl tn sp) 75.00

MITFORD,BERTRAM-John Ames, Native Commissioner-Lond-1900-F V White-dec drk grn & red cl,3 plts-1st Brit ed (ff6,e.p. brwnd) 50.00

MITFORD,BERTRAM-Sign of the Spider-Lond-1896-Methuen-grn & blk pict bndg,4 plts-1st Brit ed (ff6) 50.00

MITFORD,MARY R-Our Village...Illustrated-Lond-1879-Sampson,Low-4to-xi,170p-g grn mor,a.e.g.,mrbld e.p.,frntis,plts,illus (dd10,vf) 235.00

MITFORD,NANCY-Blessing-Lond-1951-1st ed (y7,fray dj) 20.00

MITFORD,NANCY-Don't Tell Alfred-Lond-(1960)-1st ed (y7,fray dj) 18.00

MITFORD,NANCY-Don't Tell Alfred-Lond-(1960)-H Hamilton-1st ed (v10,dj) 15.00

MITTELL,B E G-Continuous Wave Wireless Telegraphy-1922-114p-58 illus-1st ed (h6) 30.00

MITTON,SIMON-ED.-Cambridge Encyclopedia of Astronomy-NY-1977-Crown-481p-illus (hh6,sl fox,dj) 35.00

MIURA,YUICHIRA-Man Who SKied Down Everest-SF-1978-illus-1st ed (p10,f,dj) 12.00

MIVART,ST.GEORGE-Man and Apes-NY-1874-Appleton-viii+200p-grn cl,61 figs on plts-1st Amer ed (c2) 65.00

MIVART,ST.GEORGE-On the Genesis of Species-NY-1871-Appleton-314p+ads-terra cotta cl,63 text illus-1st Amer ed (d2,sl wn,sl soil text) 55.00

MIX,PAUL E-Life and Legend of Tom Mix-So Brunswick-(1972)-Barnes-206p-illus-1st ed (cc4,dj) 25.00

MIYAKAWA,T SCOTT-Protestants and Pioneers-Chig-(1964)-U of Chig Pr-306p-1st ed (cc4,dj) 15.00

MIZE,JOHHNY-How to Hit-1953-Holt-1st ed (p7,dj) 25.00

MIZENER,ARTHUR-Saddest Story-NY,Cleve-(1971)-World-1st ed (bb1,as new in box) 30.00

MJELDE,MICHAEL J-Glory of the Seas-Middleton-(1970)-303p-illus-Wesleyan's Amer Maritime Libr,Vol.1-1st ed so stated (f7,f,dj) 50.00

MJELDE,MICHAEL J-Glory of the Seas-Middletown-1970-Wesleyan U-303p-photos-ltd to 500c,nbrd-Amer Maritime Libr (p8) 70.00

MOATS,LEONE B-Thunder in Their Veins-NY-1922-279p-cl,illus-1st ed (n10,sp fade) 30.00

MOATS,LEONE-Off to Mexico-NY-1935-Scribner-8vo-186p-10 dbl pg col maps-1st ed (jj5,dj) 20.00

MOCHI,U-Hoofed Mammals of the World-1953-Scribners-unpgd-dec bds,silhouettes-Scribners"A" (gg3,f) 225.00

MOCHI,U-Hoofed Mammals of the World-1971-Scribners-rprnt (gg3,vf,dj) 35.00

MOCHI,U-Natural History of Giraffes-1973-Scribners-134p-illus (bb3,f,dj) 30.00

MOCHI,U-Natural History of Zebras-1976-Scribners-134p-illus-1st ed (bb3,f,dj) 30.00

MODERN BOOK PRODUCTION-Lond-1928-Studio-4to-vel sp,dec bds,t.e.g.,untrim,b&w & col plts(incl tip-in) (r10,sl soil,wn & fox) 85.00

MODERN GLADIATOR-Chig-1889-Athletic Publ-(iv)+384p-blu cl,illus-1st ed (b2,sp lettrng fade,sl wn) 75.00

MODERN GUERRILLA WARFARE-NY-(1962)-Free Pr of Glencoe-1st ed (ff3,dj) 50.00

MODOC COUNTY BRAND BOOK-np-nd-23p-pict wrps,illus,intro by W Rodman (t7,f) 30.00

MOFFIT,ELLA B-Elias Vail Trains Gun Dog-NY-1937-8vo-219p-photos-1st ed (m3,f,sl fray dj) 25.00

MOFFIT,F H-Upper Chitina Valley, Alaska-1918-US Geo Srvy,Bull.675-82p-wrps,1 fldg photo plt,2 fldg maps in text,2 fldg maps in rear pckt (u8,pckt split) 25.00

MOGELEVER,JACOB-Death to Traitors-GC-1960-429p-illus-1st ed (c4,dj) 37.50

MOHERMAN,T S-History of the Church of the Bretheren-Elgin-1914-366p-cl (h1) 15.00

MOHOLY-NAGY,L-Vision in Motion-Chig-1947-Paul Theobald-371p-440 illus-1st ed (cc9,few cov stns) 75.00

MOHR,FREDERICK-Grape Vine-NY-1867-Orange Judd-129p-cl (x6,sl rub) 100.00

MOJTABAI,A G-Autumn-Bost-1982-Houghton Mifflin-1st ed (b5,as new in dj) 10.00

MOJTABAI,A G-Mundome-NY-(1974)-S&S-auth 1st bk-1st ed (bb1,as new in dj) 30.00

MOJTABAI,A G-Stopping Place-NY-(1979)-S&S-1st ed (b5,as new in dj) 15.00

MOLDENKE,CHARLES E-New York Obelisk, Cleopatra's Needle-NY-1891-202p-cl (e1,sm hole in free e.p.) 35.00

MOLENAAR,DEE-Challenge of Rainier-Seattle-1973-lg 8vo-332p-photos-2nd prtg (o10,f,dj) 30.00

MOLESWORTH,MRS-Children of the Castle-Lond-1890-Macmillan-8vo-pict cl,cov title & 7 b&w plts,W Crane-1st ed (s3,fade,hngs cracked) 20.00

MOLESWORTH,MRS.-Bolted Door and Other Stories-NY-1906-Dutton-8vo-dec blu cl,illus-1st ed (t1,f,dj) 45.00

MOLLER,F PECKEL-Cod Liver Oil and Chemistry-Lond-1895-Moller-4to-508p-g dec (x6) 35.00

MOLLO,JOHN-Uniforms of the American Revolution-NY-1975-228p-80 col plts-1st Amer ed (b7,f,dj) 15.00

MOLLOY,PAUL-Pennant for the Kremlin-1964-Dbldy-1st ed (p7,dj) 20.00

MOLONEY,TED-Oh, For a French Wife-(1953)-Abelard-124p-dec tan cl,drwngs (q8,dj) 10.00

MOMADAY,N SCOTT-House Made of Dawn-NY-1968-1st ed (s5,f,dj) 80.00

MOMADAY,N SCOTT-Names-NY-1976-Harper Row-photos-1st ed (u9,f dj) 40.00

MON-GAS-YAH-Life and Experiences of ...-Paulding-1886-Paulding County Gazette-55p-pict wrps-rare (e1,sl wn wrps) 750.00

MONAGHAN,JAY-Australians and the Gold Rush-1966-U of Cal-317p-illus-1st ed (d3,dj) 20.00

MONAGHAN,JAY-Civil War on the Western Border, 1854 thru 1865-Bost-1955-Little,Brown-454p-1st ed (o7,wn dj) 50.00

MONAGHAN,JAY-Custer-Bost-(1959)-Little,Brown-469p-map e.p.-1st ed (dd4,wn dj) 50.00

MONAGHAN,JAY-Great Rascal-NY-(1951)-Bonanza-353p-1st ed (g9,dj wn & soil) 40.00

MONAGHAN,JAY-Last of the Bad Men-(1946)-Bobbs Merrill-293p-illus-Six Guns #1526-1st ed (r8,edgewn,sl spot) 35.00

MONAHAN,M-ED.-Text Book of True Temperance...-NY-1911-US Brewers' Assoc-323p-cl-2nd ed,rvsd & enlgd (a1) 15.00

MONCRIEFF,G SCOTT-ED.-Scottish Country-Bristol-1935-12mo-281p-illus (m3,f) 20.00

MONCURE,BLANCHE E-Aunt Jane's Souvenir Cookbook and Some Old Virginia Recipes-Williamsburg-(1937)-87p-grn overhang wrps,frntis (n6) 75.00

MONCUS,HERMAN H-Prairie Schooner Pirates-Ft.Worth-(1963)-191p-photos-1st ed (u7,f,dj,autg) 25.00

MONDEY,D-ED.-International Encyclopedia of Aviation-NY-(1977)-folio-480p-cl,col & b&w plts (s2,dj) 25.00

MONEY,CAPT A W-Pigeon Shooting-NY-1896-Shooting & Fishing Publ-101p-g cov dec,photos-scarce (ee3,sp tn,cov wn) 175.00

MONEY,DON-Man Who Made Milwaukee Famous-1976-Agape-photos-1st ed (s8,f,dj sp sl chip) 22.50

MONK,MARIA-Awful Disclosures, by ..., of the Hotel Dieu Nunnery of Montreal-NY-1855-DeWitt & Davenport-261p-cl-Sabin 49992 (d1,sl wn,prt of sp reglued) 35.00

MONKMAN,NOEL-Quest of the Curly Tailed Horses-Lond-(1963)-Angus & Robertson-8vo-212p-illus-1st Brit ed (aa5,f,dj rub,sl chip) 20.00

MONKS,NOEL-Squadrons Up-Cleve-(1942)-8vo-x,260p-cl,tip in photos (s2,sl wn) 45.00

MONKS,NOEL-Squadrons Up-NY-1941-260p-illus-1st ed (jj2,dj) 50.00

MONONGALIA CO.,W VIR-SESQUI-CENTENNIAL OF...OCT.20,21,22,23,1926...-Morgantown-(1928)-(prntd Charleston)-275p-cl (o1,cov spot) 27.50

MONROE,ANNE S-World I Saw-NY-1928-Dbldy,Doran-8vo-331p-1st ed (w6,dj) 30.00

MONROE,HARRIET-Poet's Life-NY-1938-Macmillan-photos-1st ed (t4,f,chip dj) 30.00

MONROE,ROBERT A-Journeys Out of the Body-GC-1971-Dbldy-cl-1st ed (l8,f,dj) 25.00

MONROE,W S-Turkey and the Turks-Lond-1908-G Bell & Sons-cl,illus-1st ed (m8,frnt hng tender) 35.00

MONSON,KAREN-Alban Berg-Bost-1979-Houghton Mifflin-1st ed (u4,f,sl chip dj) 12.00

MONSON-FITZJOHN,G J-Drinking Vessels of Bygone Days from the Neolithic Age to the Georgian Period-1937-Herbert Jenkins-144p-illus (cc8,tape mrkd cov,sl fox) 45.00

MONTAGU,G-Ornithological Dictionary of British Birds-Lond-1831-8vo-592p-calf,28 wdcuts-2nd ed (y8,ex-libr,cov detched) 75.00

MONTAGUE,JOHN-Chosen Light-Lond-(1967)-MacGibbon & Kee-1st ed (z8,f,dj) 60.00

MONTAGUE,JOHN-Great Cloak-Dublin-(1978)-Dolmen Pr-wrps-1st ed (z8,vf) 25.00

MONTAGUE,JOHN-Rough Field-Dublin-(1972)-Dolmen Pr-stiff wrps-1st trd ed (z8,f) 20.00

MONTAGUE,JOHN-Slow Dance-Dublin-(1975)-Dolmen Pr-wrps-1st ed (z8,vf) 25.00

MONTAGUE,JOHN-Tides-Dublin-(1970)-Dolmen Pr-1st ed (z8,vf,rear fade dj) 40.00

MONTAGUE,LADY MARY W-Letters and Works of...-Lond-1837-Bentley-3 vols-bnd in calf by Sangorski & Sutcliffe,raised bnds,g stmpd sp-1st ed (w6) 325.00

MONTAIGNES,FRANCOIS DE-Plains-Norman-1972-182p-illus-1st ed (t7,dj) 17.50

MONTAIGNES,FRANCOIS DES-Plains-Norman-1972-U of Okla-1st ed (u9,dj) 25.00

MONTANA HISTORICAL SOC-Contribution to...Vol V-Helena-1904-467p-col frntis,photos,maps-1st ed (t7) 85.00

MONTANA, A STATE GUIDE BOOK-NY-1939-Viking-(xxiv);430;(12)p+fldg map in back pckt-WPA,Amer Guide Ser-cl-illus-Selvaggio 316-1st ed,1st prntng (f1,sl wn dj) 50.00

MONTANA-Constitution of the State of...-Helena-(1889)-Independ Publ-76p-wrps-1st ed (ee4) 125.00

MONTANA-CONTRIBUTIONS TO THE HISTORICAL SOCIETY OF...VOL.1-Helena-1876-357p-cl,port,map-v scarce (z1,soil,rub) 150.00

MONTANA-HISTORY OF...1739 TO 1885-Chig-1885-Warner,Beers-4to-1367p-orig half lea,lg fldg col map,scarce wi map-Howes L228-1st ed (v1) 750.00

MONTCLAIR-Story of...-Montclair-1930-xi,202p-cl,plts,maps (aa6) 30.00

MONTEIRO,MARIANA-Legends and Popular Tales of the Basque People-NY-1891-Stokes-cl,photogravures,H Copping-2nd ed (l8) 65.00

MONTER,E WILLIAM-Witchcraft in France and Switzerland-Ithaca-(1976)-Cornell Univ-232+(8)p-blk cl-1st ed (y9,dj) 30.00

MONTEREY PENINSULA-Stanford-1946-WPA/Amer Guide Ser-200p-pict cl,photos (t7) 22.50

MONTESSORI,MARIA-Pedagogical Anthropology-NY-1913-Stokes-xii+508p-blu cl,plts-1st ed (c2,fox,cov sl soil) 65.00

MONTGOMERY,BERNARD L-Memoirs of Field Marshall Montgomery-Lond-1958-Collins-1st ed (z2,sl crease,dj) 25.00

MONTGOMERY,CHARLES F-American Furniture, the Federal Period, in the Henry Francis du Pont Winterhur Museum-NY-1966-Viking-lg stout 4to-497p-g dec cl,illus,27 plts(most col) (pp7,dj) 135.00

MONTGOMERY,DOUGLASS W-Collected Writings of ...-SF-1943-2 vols,blu cl,illus-1st ed (j2) 45.00

MONTGOMERY,HORACE-Johnny Cobb-Athens-1964-104p-stiff wrps-1st ed (t7,wtrstns) 12.50

MONTGOMERY,JAMES-Chimney Sweeper's Friend-Lond-1824-blu mor,3 illus by Cruikshank-1st ed (l9,sl wn & spot) 150.00

MONTGOMERY,L M-Anne of Green Gables-Bost-1908-Page-auth 1st bk-1st ed (y2) 275.00

MONTGOMERY,L M-Emily of New Moon-Tor-(1925)-McClelland & Stewart-1st ed (pp10) 30.00

MONTGOMERY,L M-Jane of Lantern Hill-Tor-(1937)-M&S-Watters p.347-1st ed (pp2,f,sl wn dj) 50.00*

MONTGOMERY,L M-Rilla of Ingleside-NY-(1921)-Stokes-370p-cl wi pict pasteon,col frntis,M L Kirk-1st US ed (s3,sp lttrng dull) 40.00

MONTGOMERY,R G-Pechuck-Caldwell-1948-8vo-291p-illus (m3,f) 22.50

MONTGOMERY,RICHARD-White Headed Eagle-1935-MacMillan-358p-illus-1st ed (r8) 30.00

MONTGOMERY,RICHARD-Young Northwest-(1948)-Binfords & Mort-318p-illus-2nd ed rvsd (r8,sl chip dj) 18.00

MONTGOMERY,ROBERT H-Fifty Years of Accountancy-np-1939-Ronald Pr-xii+678p-blu cl-1st ed (d2) 30.00

MONTGOMERY,RUTH-Flowers at the White House-NY-1967-104p-cl (h1) 12.50

MONTGOMERY,RUTHERFORD-High Country-Derrydale-1938-8vo-248p-ltd to 950c,nbrd,photos (m3) 80.00

MONTHAN,DORIS-R C Gorman, the Lithographs-Flagstaff-1978-170p-col frntis,col plts-1st ed (t7,dj,pres) 50.00

MONZERT,L-Independent Liquorist-NY-1866-Trow-1st ed (q8,lacks ffep,tips wn) 15.00

MOODIE,MRS SUSANNA-Roughing It in the Bush or, Forest Life in Canada-NY-1913-8vo-569p-col illus,R A Stewart (m3,sl fade sp) 27.50

MOODIE,ROY L-Roentgenologic Studies of Egyptian and Peruvian Mummies-Chig-1931-Field Mus Nat Hist-4to-66p-gry wrps,76 plts-1st ed (l2,sl wn) 85.00

MOODY,D W-Life of a Rover, 1865 to 1926-np-(1926)-(D W Moody)-116p+ads-pict bds,frntis,drwngs-1st ed (cc4) 40.00

MOODY,GEORGE R-South Worthington Parish-S Worthington-nd-oblng-103p-cl,dbl cols,photos (l1,sl edge-wn) 15.00

MOODY,LINWOOD-Maine Two Footers-1959-Howell North-8vo-203p-illus,maps (nn7,dj) 20.00

MOODY,LINWOOD-Maine Two Footers-Berkeley-1959-Howell North-photos,2 maps rear pckt-1st ed (k8,dj) 25.00

MOODY,RALPH-Horse of a Different Color-(1968)-Norton-272p-1st ed (t8,edge wn dj) 35.00

MOODY,RALPH-Horse of a Different Color-NY-(1968)-272p-1st ed (t7,f,dj) 15.00

MOODY,RALPH-Man of the Family-NY-(1951)-Norton-272p-cl,illus by E Shenton-1st ed (nn10,f,dj) 30.00

MOODY,RALPH-Old Trails West-NY-1963-318p-illus,maps-Rittenhouse #417 (t7,dj) 12.50

MOODY,RALPH-Stagecoach West-(1967)-Promontory-341p-illus (r8,dj) 15.00

MOON,SHEILA-Magic Dwells-Middletown-1970-Wesleyan-1st ed (u9,dj) 20.00

MOON,WILLIAM LEAST HEAT-Blue Highways-Bost-(1982)-Little,Brown-1st ed (hh5,dj) 30.00

MOON,WM LEAST HEAT-Blue Highways-Bost,Tor-(1982)-auth 1st bk-1st ed (c5,sl rub dj) 45.00

MOONEY,JAMES-Ghost Dance Religion and the Sioux Outbreak of 1890-Chig-(1965)-U of Chig Pr-lg 8vo-359p-wrps,illus-1st ed (y5) 16.00

MOONEY,JAMES-Sacred Formulas of the Cherokees-Wash-(1891)-Smithson Bur of Ethnol-illus-1st ed (y10,rbnd) 60.00

MOONEY,JAMES-Trail of the Barrow-NY,Chig-(1888)-Ogilvie-216p-cl-Wright 3808 (n1) 50.00

MOONEY,TED-Easy Travel to Other Planets-NY-(1981)-FS&G-auth 1st bk-1st ed (a10,f,dj) 25.00

MOOR,J H-Notices of the Indian Arcipelago and Adjacent Countries, Being a Collection of Papers...-Singapore-1837-modern mor in dec archival box,6 engrvd fldg maps & chrts(5 col in outline)-2 parts in one vol-rare-1st ed (ll1,rbnd,restored,few spots) 7,500.00

MOORCOCK,MICHAEL-An Alien Heat-NY-(1972)-Harper & Row-1st US ed (h3,f,dj) 15.00

MOORCOCK,MICHAEL-ED.-England Invaded-Lond-1977-1st ed (bb10,f,dj) 20.00

MOORCOCK,MICHAEL-ED.-England Invaded-Lond-1977-Allen-1st ed (j3,dj) 15.00

MOORCOCK,MICHAEL-English Assassin-NY et al-(1972)-Harper & Row-illus-1st US ed (bb1,f,dj) 25.00

MOORE,ALBERT C-Iconography of Religions-Phila-1977-Fortress Pr-cl,illus-1st ed (l8,f,dj) 20.00

MOORE,ALISON-Louisiana Tigers-Baton Rouge-1961-183p-illus-1st ed (n3,addenda laid in) 75.00

MOORE,B-First Five Million Miles-NY-(1955)-8vo-xii,276p-cl,frntis,8p plts-1st ed (s2,dj) 35.00

MOORE,BRIAN-Doctor's Wife-NY-(1976)-FS&G-1st ed (z8,vf,f dj) 20.00

MOORE,BRIAN-Feast of Lupercal-Bost,Tor-(1957)-Little,Brown-1st ed (a10,dj) 75.00

MOORE,BRIAN-Fergus-NY-(1970)-HR&W-1st ed (z8,vf,dj) 25.00

MOORE,BRIAN-Great Victorian Collection-NY-(1975)-FS&G-1st ed (z8,vf,dj) 22.50

MOORE,C L-Black God's Shadow-West Kingston-1977-1st trd ed (d5,f,dj) 30.00

MOORE,C L-Doomsday Morning-GC-1957-Dbldy-1st ed (k3,sl soil,dj) 50.00

MOORE,C L-Scarlet Dream-West Kingston-1981-1st trd ed (d5,f,dj) 25.00

MOORE,C L-Shambleau-NY-(1953)-1st ed (bb10,sl tn dj) 60.00

MOORE,CHARLES W-Timing a Century-Cambridge-1945-Harvard-362p-red cl,illus-1st ed (dd1,dj) 30.00

MOORE,CHARLES-Daniel Burnham, Architect, Planner of Cities-Bost-1921-Houghton Mifflin-4to-2 vols-grn cl,112 plts(incl 13 col) (c2,f,dj,sl wn box) 150.00

MOORE,CHARLES-Daniel H Burnham, Architect, Planner of Cities-Bost-1921-Houghton Mifflin-4to-2 vols-dec cl,t.e.g.,66 plts(incl col) (cc10,dj) 250.00

MOORE,CHARLES-Daniel H Burnham-Bost-1931-Houghton Mifflin-2 vols-g dec grn cl,t.e.g.,col frntis,illus (r10,sl tn sp) 140.00

MOORE,CLEMENT-Night Before Christmas-Chig-1912-Donohue-lg 8vo-(10)p-pict cl,4p col illus,prtd on linen (hh4,f) 165.00

MOORE,CLEMENT-Night Before Christmas-Worcester-nd-Achille J St.Onge-lea,illus by T Tudor (l9,f,dj) 100.00

MOORE,DEAN W-Washington's Woods-Parsons-1971-389p-cl (j1) 30.00

MOORE,F-Garden of Peace-NY-1920-Doran-300p-cl (x6,rub) 15.00

MOORE,FRANK-Women of the War-Hartford-1866-596p-ports-1st ed (dd3) 100.00

MOORE,GENE D-Killing at Ngo Tho-NY-(1967)-Norton-1st ed (ff3,dj) 65.00

MOORE,GEORGE H-Notes on the History of Slavery in Massachusetts-NY-1866-Appleton-iv+256p+ads-lilac cl-1st ed (mm10,few stnd pgs,unopened) 125.00

MOORE,GEORGE H-Treason of Charles Lee...-NY-1860-xii,115,(1)p-cl,plts,fldg facs (aa6) 60.00

MOORE,GEORGE-Aphrodite in Aulis-NY-1931-Brentano-1st Amer ed (t4,chip dj) 15.00

MOORE,GEORGE-Celibate Lives-Lond-1927-Heinemann-orig cl bckd mrbld bds,papr sp labl (aa9,unopened) 40.00

MOORE,GEORGE-Evelyn Innes-Lond-1898-T Fisher Unwin-orig g titled cl,t.e.g.,(this cpy w/o ads at end)-1st ed (aa9,sl rub,sm cov mrks) 100.00

MOORE,GEORGE-Making of an Immortal-NY-1927-Bowling Grn Pr-orig bds,lea sp labl-ltd to 1240c,autg-1st ed (aa9,unopened) 45.00

MOORE,GEORGE-Story Teller's Holiday-NY-1918-priv prtd for subscribers-orig cl,papr sp labl-ltd to 1250c-1st Amer ed (aa9) 30.00

MOORE,H E-African Violets, Gloxinias and Their Relatives-1957-Macmillan-323p-5 col plts-1st prtg (bb3,dj) 17.00

MOORE,HARRY-Public Health in the United States, an Outline with Statistical Data-NY-1923-557p-1st ed (dd3) 50.00

MOORE,HELEN W-Camouflage Cookery-NY-1918-Duffield & Co-106p-Bitting 330 (m6) 35.00

MOORE,ISABEL-Complete Oriental Cookbook-Lond-(1982)-Cavendish-thk folio-422p-blk cl,col plts-3rd prtg (q8,f,dj) 22.50

MOORE,ISABEL-ED.-Supercooks Cookbook-Lond-(1976)-Cavendish-lg 4to-384p-blk cl,col photos-1st ed (q8,dj) 15.00

MOORE,J BERNARD-Skagway in Days Primeval-NY-1968-Vantage-202p-1st ed (j8,f,dj) 20.00

MOORE,J HAMILTON-Young Gentleman and Lady's Monitor...-Phila-1813-prntd by W Howard-368,(4)p-lea-Amer Imprnts 29194 (d1) 35.00

MOORE,JAMES-Narrative of the Campaign of the British Army in Spain-Lond-1809-521p-1/2 brwn calf,mrbld bds,2 fldg maps-3rd ed (gg2,rebkd) 275.00

MOORE,JOANNE R-Nahanni Trailhead-Ottawa-1980-Deneau & Greenberg-228p-illus,maps (k10,dj) 15.00*

MOORE,JOHN M-West-(1935)-Wichita Pr-147p+1p trib-illus-Six Guns #1538 (r8,dj wn,soil,tape rnfrcd) 75.00

MOORE,JOHN-Gift of the Grass-Bost-1911-Little,Brown (f10) 15.00

MOORE,JOSEPH-Queen's Empire-Phila-1886-Lippincott-280p-dec orng cl,fldg map,illus (gg6) 75.00

MOORE,MARIANNE-Complete Poems of...-NY-1967-Viking-1st ed (f8,f,sl scuff dj) 35.00

MOORE,MARIANNE-Idiosyncrasy & Technique-Berkeley-1958-27p-prntd wrps-scarce-1st ed (n5,f) 30.00

MOORE,MARIANNE-Like a Bulwark-NY-1956-Viking-1st ed (w6,f,dj) 45.00

MOORE,MARIANNE-Nevertheless-NY-1944-Macmillan-1st ed (v5,f,sl tn dj) 75.00

MOORE,MARIANNE-Predilections-NY-1955-Viking-1st ed (v10,f,dj) 20.00

MOORE,MARIANNE-Predilections-NY-1955-Viking-blu cl-1st ed (f2,f,dj) 35.00

MOORE,MARIANNE-Tell Me, Tell Me-NY-(1966)-Viking-8vo-cl bckd bds-1st ed (jj8,f,dj) 35.00

MOORE,MARIANNE-What Are Years-NY-1941-1st ed (r2,f,sl tn dj) 150.00

MOORE,MERILL-Illegitimate Sonnets-NY-(1950)-Twayne-E Gorey illus e.p.s-1st ed (u10,f,f dj) 35.00

MOORE,MRS.JOHN H-Memories of a Long Life in Virginia-Staunton-(1920)-McClure-183p-brwn cl,plts-1st ed (h2) 40.00

MOORE,N HUDSON-Collector's Manual-NY-(1935)-Tudor Publ-329p-blu bds wi emboss title,dec sp-new ed (n6,sl sunned sp) 45.00

MOORE,NICOLAS-Tall Bearded Iris-Forest Hills-1956-120p-col frntis,10 photos (hh7,f,dj) 29.00

MOORE,NORMAN-History of the Study of Medicine in the British Isles-Oxford-1908-202p-1st ed (dd3) 100.00

MOORE,PHIL-With Rod & Gun in Canada-Lond-1922-8vo-261p-photos (m3) 15.00

MOORE,R LAURENCE-In Search of White Crows-NY-1977-Oxford U Pr-cl-1st ed (n8,f,dj) 20.00

MOORE,R-Universal Assistant & Complete Mechanic...Over One Million Industrial Facts...-NY-(1907)-1024p+20p ads-500 illus (a3,sl brwnd papr) 15.00

MOORE,ROBERT A-Life for the Confederacy-Jackson-1959-McCowat Mercer Pr-182p-frntis,illus-1st ed (o7,f,wn dj) 40.00

MOORE,SUSANNA-My Old Sweetheart-Bost-1982-Houghton Mifflin-auth 1st bk-1st ed (w5,f,f dj) 25.00

MOORE,TEX-West-(1935)-(Wichita Prtg Co)-v scarce-Six Guns 1538-1st ed (gg4,sl spot cov) 60.00

MOORE,THOMAS-Epitome of Gardening-Scotland-1881-Black-444p-cl (x6,rub,hngs weak) 35.00

MOOREHEAD,ALAN-African Trilogy, a Personal Account 1940 to 43-Lond-1944-1st ed (y7,dj fray,sl soil) 30.00

MOOREHEAD,ALAN-Darwin and the Beagle-NY-1969-Harper & Row-4to-280p-col & monotone illus (nn1,dj) 30.00

MOOREHEAD,ALAN-Fatal Impact-NY-1966-Harper & Row-8vo-230p-blu cl over bds,28 illus,4 maps,chrt-1st ed (p8,f,dj) 17.50

MOOREHEAD,WARREN K-American Indian in the United States... 1850 to 1914-Andover-1914-lg 8vo-440p-illus,fldg map-scarce-1st ed (f7) 200.00

MOOREHEAD,WARREN K-American Indian in the United States..1850 to 1914-Andover-1914-Andover Pr-8vo-440p-cl,fldg maps,photos,photogravure plts by R Wanamaker-Howes M781-1st ed (v1) 250.00

MOORHEAD,MAX L-Apache Frontier-Norman-1968-U of Okla-1st ed (u9,dj) 30.00

MOORHEAD,MAX L-New Mexico's Royal Road-Norman-1958-234p-cl,illus,maps-1st ed (z1,lt wn dj) 60.00

MOORHEAD,MAX-Presido-(1975)-U of Ok-288p-maps-1st ed (t8,f,dj) 20.00

MOORHEAD,ROBERT L-Story of the 139th Field Artillery, American Expeditionary Forces...-Indpls-(1920)-Bobbs-Merrill-468p-cl-Dornbusch 1186 (l1) 30.00

MOORHOUSE,GEOFFREY-India Britannica-NY-1983-288p-illus-1st ed (b7,f,dj) 20.00

MOORMAN,LEWIS J,M.D.-Pioneer Doctor-Norman-(1951)-U of Okla Pr-252p-photos-1st ed (bb4) 25.00

MOORMAN,MADISON B-Journal of Madison Berryman Moorman 1850 to 1851-SF-1948-Cal Hist Soc-150p-frntis,fldg map (dd4) 35.00

MOOSO,JOSIAH-Life and Travels of...-Winfield-1888-400p-frntis-Howes#M784-1st ed (u7,sp wn) 350.00

MOOSO,JOSIAH-Life and Travels of...-Winfield-1888-Telegram Print-400p-cl,port-Howes M784-1st ed (nn6,new e.p.) 500.00

MORA,JO-Californios-GC-1949-Dbldy-sm 4to-1st ed (f10,dj) 45.00

MORA,JO-Trail Dust and Saddle Leather-NY-1946-Scribner's-8vo-246p-cl-1st ed (mm7,f,sl wn dj) 65.00

MORAN,JAMES-Printing Presses-LA-(1973)-U of Cal Pr-sm 4to-1st ed (w1,f) 35.00

MORANG,ALFRED-Santa Fe-Denver-1947-Sage-32p-wrps,drwngs-1st ed (u9) 35.00

MORANT,G M-Bibliography of Statistical and Other Writings of Karl Pearson-Cambridge-1939-119p-1st ed (dd3) 60.00

MORANTE,ELSA-Arturo's Island-NY-1959-1st US ed (q5,dj) 25.00

MORANTE,ELSA-History-NY-1977-1st US ed (q5,vf,dj) 12.50

MORANTE,ELSA-House of Liars-NY-1951-auth 1st bk-1st US ed (q5,sl chip dj) 60.00

MORANTZ-SANCHEZ,REGINA-Sympathy and Science, Women Physicians in American Medicine-NY-1985-464p-1st ed (dd3,dj) 35.00

MORAUTA,LOUISE-Beyond the Village-Lond-1974-Athlone Pr-8vo-192p-cl,plts,maps-1st ed (y5,dj) 30.00

MORAVETZ,BRUNO-Big Book of Mountaineering-NY-1980-lg 4to-284p-108 plts-1st US ed (q10,f,dj) 38.00

MORAVETZ,BRUNO-Big Book of Mountineering-NY-1980-lg 4to-284p-108 plts-1st US ed (p10,f,dj) 38.00

MORAVIA,ALBERTO-Wheel of Fortune-NY-1937-Viking-1st US ed (g3,dj) 20.00

MORDAUNT,ELINOR-Venture Book-(1926)-Century-328p-photo plts,drwngs-1st ed (u8,sl chip dj) 10.00

MORDECAI,D-Himalaya-Calcutta-1966-28p-illus bds,30 photos,1 fldg panorama-scarce (q10,f) 135.00

MORDELL,ALBERT-Frank Harris and Haldeman-Julius-Girard-(1950)-Haldeman-Julius Publ-31p-wrps,dbl cols-Big Blu Bk B-873 (g1) 15.00

MORE SECRET REMEDIES-Lond-1912-282p-1st ed (dd3) 75.00

MORE,HANNAH-Works of...-Dublin-1803-Graisberry-4 vols,lea bkd bds-1st Irish ed (w6) 250.00

MOREAU,GENEVIEVE-Restless Journey of James Agee-NY-1977-320p-1st ed (mm3,f,dj) 17.50

MOREAU,JEFFREY-ED.-Pacific Electric Pictorial: Vol.I-LA-1964-69p-wrps-1st ed (n4) 16.00

MOREAU,JEFFREY-Los Angeles Railway Pictorial-LA-1964-ltd to 1000c,nbrd (n4) 14.00

MOREAU,JEFFREY-Mount Lowe Pictorial-LA-1964-wrps-1st ed (n4) 12.00

MORECROFT,J H-Principles of Radio Communication-1921-935p-26 photos,610 illus-1st ed (h6) 30.00

MORECROFT,JOHN H-History and Operation of the Vacuum Tube-1924-E I Co.-48p-wrps,21 illus-1st ed (h6,few pencil mrkngs) 10.00

MOREL,J J-Progressive Catering-Lond-(1952)-Caxton-4 vols-col & b&w plts-2nd prtg (q8) 85.00

MOREY,SYLVESTER-Respect for Life...-GC-nd(1974)-202p-wrps,photos-1st ed (v7) 10.00

MOREY,WALT-Gentle Ben-NY-(1965)-illus,J Schoenherr-1st ed (j5,dj) 15.00

MORGAN HORSE SHOW YEARBOOK 1975-Vol.II-San Jose-1976-Logan-4to (h9) 45.00

MORGAN,BRYAN-ED.-Great Trains-1973-Crown-folio-259p-col illus-1st ed (d3,dj) 20.00

MORGAN,C L-Animal Life and Intelligence-Bost-1891-8vo-xvi,512p-cl,frntis (y8,pencil,hf sl tn) 60.00

MORGAN,DALE-ED.-Overland Diary of James A Pritchard from Kentucky to California in 1849-Denver-1959-221p-pict bds,frntis,maps(incl fldg),rear pckt-1st ed (t7) 85.00

MORGAN,DALE-ED.-Overland Diary of James A Pritchard...-Denver-1959-221p-frntis,fldg maps,chrt in rear pckt-1st ed (h7,f,nick dj) 110.00

MORGAN,DALE-ED.-Overland in 1846-Georgetown-1963-Talisman-2 vols,cl,map-1st ed (v1,dj) 165.00

MORGAN,DALE-ED.-Rocky Mountain Journals of William Marshall Anderson-San Marino-1967-Ward Ritchie Pr-lg 8vo-430p-illus-ltd to 1500c (a7,f,dj) 75.00

MORGAN,DALE-ED.-West of William H Ashley: 1822 to 1838-1964-Rosenstock:Old West-folio-341p-fldg map-1st ed (d3) 250.00

MORGAN,DALE-Jedediah Smith and the Opening of the West-(1953)-Bobbs Merrill-458p-illus,e.p. map-1st ed (r8,cov wn) 55.00

MORGAN,DALE-Jedediah Smith and the Opening of the West-Indpls-(1953)-Bobbs Merrill-458p-cl,illus,map e.p.s-1st ed (v1,dj) 75.00

MORGAN,DAVID P-ED.-Canadian Steam-Milw-1961-1st ed (n4,f,dj) 22.00

MORGAN,GARY-Sugar Tramp-1975-Centennial-4to-96p-illus-1st ed (nn7,f,f dj) 26.00

MORGAN,GENE-Westward the Course of Empire-Chig-1945-Lakeside Pr-57p-dec bds w/o dj as issued-1st ed (j8,f) 12.50

MORGAN,J M-Recollections of a Rebel Reefer-Bost-1917-491p-illus,ports (z10,scuff,soil) 75.00

MORGAN,JAMES O-Field Crops for the Cotton Belt-NY-1917-Macmillan-456p-cl-Rural Text Bk ser (x6,wn,soil) 18.00

MORGAN,JOHN-Life and Adventures of William Buckley-Sussex-1979-Caliban-12mo-238p-illus (p8,as new in dj) 30.00

MORGAN,JOHNNIE R-History of Wichita Falls-Wichita Falls-1931-221p-emboss cl,photos-Six Guns #1544-scarce-1st ed (t7,f) 150.00

MORGAN,LADY-France-Lond-1817-Colburn-8vo-2 vols,calf-2nd ed (w6,hngs tender) 135.00

MORGAN,LEWIS H-American Beaver and His Works-Phila-1868-Lippincott-330p-cl,maps(1 fldg),23 plts-1st ed (z1,sp wn,spot cov) 175.00

MORGAN,LEWIS H-Houses and House Life of the American Aborigines-Chig-(1965)-U of Chig-lg 8vo-319p-wrps,illus-1st ed thus (y5) 15.00

MORGAN,LEWIS H-Houses and House Life of the American Aborigines-Wash D.C.-1881-Dept of Interior-4to-xiv+281p-maroon cl,56 figs-1st ed (h2,sl wn cov) 125.00

MORGAN,LEWIS H-Indian Journals 1859 to 62-Ann Arbor-(1959)-U of Mich Pr-232p-16 col illus-1st ed (ee4,dj) 50.00

MORGAN,LEWIS H-Lewis Henry Morgan-Ann Arbor-(1959)-U of Mich Pr-qto-233p-col illus-1st ed (bb4,dj) 50.00

MORGAN,MANIE-New Stars-(Yellow Springs)-1949-Antioch Pr-301p-cl (b1,dj) 15.00

MORGAN,MURRAY-Dam-1954-Viking-162p-illus,e.p. map-1st ed (r8,dj) 20.00

MORGAN,MURRAY-Last Wilderness-1955-Viking-275p-illus,e.p. map-1st ed (r8,dj,autg) 22.00

MORGAN,MURRAY-Last Wilderness-NY-1955-Viking-8vo-xiv,276p-grn cl,map e.p.,photos-1st ed (y4,dj) 20.00

MORGAN,MURRAY-Skid Road-1951-Viking-280p-e.p. maps-Six Guns #1546-1st ed (r8,dj) 25.00

MORGAN,MURRAY-Skid Road-NY-1951-Viking-1st ed (kk9,dj) 35.00

MORGAN,MURRAY-Viewless Winds-NY-(1949)-Dutton-8vo-220p-1st ed (bb5,dj) 20.00

MORGAN,PHILLIP-Glass Reinforced Plastics-Lond-1955-248p-illus (cc8) 55.00

MORGAN,SHERLEY W-Architectural Drawing-NY-1950-McGraw Hill-4to-227p-red cl,col frntis,illus-1st ed (r10,sl fade sp) 20.00

MORGAN,THOMAS H-Critique of the Theory of Evolution-Princeton-1916-197p-1st ed (dd3) 75.00

MORGAN,THOMAS H-Theory of the Gene-New Haven-1926-Yale U Pr-xvi+343p-blu cl,156 illus-1st ed (a2) 85.00

MORGAN,WILLARD D-Leica Manual-NY-1935-Morgan & Lester-502p-illus-2nd prtg,Nov.1935 (cc9) 45.00

MORGAN,WILLIAM J-Captains to the Northward-Barre-1959-xvi+260p-maroon cl-1st ed (m2,dj) 40.00

MORGAN,WILLIAM-Bucks County-(NY)-1974-Horizon Pr-112p-86 photos by Siskind-1st ed (cc9,as new in dj) 50.00

MORIARTY,GERALD-TRANSL.-Paris Law Courts-Lond-1894-Seeley & Co-8vo-293p-illus-1st Brit ed (aa5) 50.00

MORICE,ANNE-Hollow Vengeance-NY-1982-St.Martin's-1st US ed (d4,f dj) 15.00

MORICE,ANNE-Murder in Outline-Lond-1979-Macmillan-1st ed (p4,dj) 20.00

MORICE,ANNE-Scared to Death-NY-1977-St.Martin's-1st US ed (h4,f,dj) 15.00

MORICE,ANNE-Sleep of Death-NY-1982-St.Martin's-1st US ed (d4,f,dj) 12.50

MORIN,MICHELINE-Everest-NY-(ca.1955)-John Day-8vo-205p-13 col illus,maps-1st US ed (jj5,f,dj) 20.00

MORIN,MICHELLE-Everest From the First Attempt to the Final Victory-Lond-1955-205p-55 photos-1st ed (q10,f) 13.00

MORIN,RELMAN-Circuit of Conquest-NY-1943-Knopf-361p-1st ed (c3,f) 18.00

MORISON,SAMUEL E-Caribbean as Columbus Saw It-Bost-(1964)-Atl/Little,Brwn-lg 8vo-252p-photos-1st ed (ff5,f,sl tn dj) 15.00

MORISON,SAMUEL E-Caribbean as Columbus Saw it-Bost-(1964)-Little,Brown-xxxvi+252p-blu cl,photos-1st ed (m2,dj) 25.00

MORISON,SAMUEL E-Life and Letters of Harrison Gray Otis, Federalist, 1765 to 1848-Bost-1913-Houghton Mifflin-2 vols-grn cl,plts-1st ed (h2) 55.00

MORISON,SAMUEL E-Maritime History of Massachusetts 1783 to 1860-Bost-1921-Houghton Mifflin-1st ed (z2,f) 85.00

MORISON,SAMUEL E-Vistas of History-NY-1964-Knopf-8vo-181p-3 illus-1st ed (jj5,sl tn dj) 10.00

MORISON,STANLEY-Likeness of Thomas More-NY-(1963)-Fordham U Pr-4to-xii,96p-red buckr,col frntis port,plts-1st ed (t10,f) 75.00

MORKEL,B-Hunting in Africa-UK-1980-252p-photos,illus (gg3,vf,dj) 20.00

MORLAND,NIGEL-Background to Murder-1955-Laurie-1st ed (s10,dj) 12.50

MORLAND,NIGEL-Hangman's Clutch-1954-Laurie-1st ed (s10,dj) 10.00

MORLEY,CHRISTOPHER-Back to Haverford and-Haverford-(1920)-4to-16p (mm3) 10.00

MORLEY,CHRISTOPHER-ED.-Ex Libris-NY-1936 (gg7,dj) 17.50

MORLEY,CHRISTOPHER-ED.-Murder with a Difference-1946-Random-1st ed thus (s10,f,dj) 12.50

MORLEY,CHRISTOPHER-Goldfish Under the Ice-Lond-1929-Elkin Mathews & Marrot-Woburn Bks No.14-ltd to 530c,nbrd,autg (kk5,dj) 30.00

MORLEY,CHRISTOPHER-History of an Autumn-Phila-1938-frntis-1st ed (hh10,dj sl tn & chip) 30.00

MORLEY,CHRISTOPHER-History of an Autumn-Phila-1938-frntis-1st ed (r2,dj sl sp sun,sl chip) 25.00

MORLEY,CHRISTOPHER-Man Who Made Friends with Himself-GC-1949-Dbldy-1st ed (hh5,dj) 15.00

MORLEY,CHRISTOPHER-Middle Kingdom-NY-1944-1st ed (r2,dj sp sun,rub) 25.00

MORLEY,CHRISTOPHER-Mince Pie-1919-Doran-1st ed (x2,sl soil) 15.00

MORLEY,CHRISTOPHER-Morley's Variety-Cleve-(1944)-t.e.g.-Special ed, ltd to 875c,nbrd,for priv distrib (r2,uncut,sl rub & sun) 75.00

MORLEY,CHRISTOPHER-Preface to "Bartlett"-Bost-1937-illus-1st ed (r2,uncut,f) 30.00

MORLEY,CHRISTOPHER-Preface to "Bartlett"-Bost-1937-Little,Brown-photos-1st ed (u9) 25.00

MORLEY,CHRISTOPHER-Romany Stain-NY-1926-Dbldy,Page-orig cl bckd bds,papr sp & cov labls,drwngs by W J Duncan (aa9,sp labl drknd) 40.00

MORLEY,CHRISTOPHER-Seacoast of Bohemia-GC-1929-Dbldy Doran-1st ed (ee2,f,sl chip dj) 35.00

MORLEY,CHRISTOPHER-Sherlock Holmes and Dr.Watson-NY-1944-Harcourt,Brace-12mo-366p-1st ed (f4,f) 100.00

MORLEY,CHRISTOPHER-Translations From the Chinese-NY-(1922)-dec cov-1st ed (r2,sl rub,sl sun) 25.00

MORLEY,CHRISTOPHER-Trojan Horse-1941-Random-1st ed (jj6,e.p. fox,dj) 30.00

MORLEY,F V-East South East-NY-(1929)-Harcourt-8vo-8p (two col)woodcts-1st ed (s1,f,dj) 35.00

MORLEY,JIM-Gold Cities, Grass Valley and Nevada City-1965-Howell North-4to-96p-photos,maps-1st ed (d3,dj) 25.00

MORLEY,SYLVANUS G-Guide Book to the Ruins of Quirigua-Wash-1935-Carnegie-wrps,photos-1st ed (u9) 25.00

MORMONS-Lond-1852-publ at 227 Strand-320p-40 engrvngs-scarce-3rd ed (ff4) 75.00

MORNEWECK,EVELYN F-Chronicles of Stephen Foster's Family-Pitt-1944-U of Pitt Pr-2 vols-gry cl,plts-1st ed (mm10,box) 40.00

MORRELL,BENJAMIN-Narrative of Four Voyages, to the South Sea,North and South Pacific Ocean...Antarctic Ocean-Upper Saddle River-1970-Gregg Pr-8vo-492p+ds-dec cl-rprnt of 1832 ed (nn1) 35.00

MORRESSY,JOHN-Atarbrat-NY-(1972)-Walker-1st ed (j3,dj) 10.00

MORRESSY,JOHN-Nail Down the Stars-NY-(1973)-Walker-1st ed (l3,f,dj) 15.00

MORRESSY,JOHN-Under a Calculating Star-GC-1974-Dbldy-1st ed (h3,f,dj) 15.00

MORRILL,CLAIRE-Taos Mosaic-Albuq-1973-UNM-4to-photos-1st ed (b4,dj) 40.00

MORRILL,G L-Devil in Mexico-(Mpls)-(1917)-346p+ads & add illus (g1,sm sp chip) 32.50

MORRIS COUNTY-History of...-(Morristown)-1967-4to-407p-cl,illus-rprnt of Munsell,1882 ed (aa6) 65.00

MORRIS COUNTY-History of...-NY-1882-W W Munsell-4to-407p-mod buckrm,plts (aa6,rbnd) 200.00

MORRIS,B F-Life of Thomas Morris-Cin-1856-Moore,Wilstach,Key & Ovrd-408p-cl (b1,sl dmpstnd) 35.00

MORRIS,CORA-Gypsy Story Teller-NY-1931-Macmillan-206p-cl,col frntis,16 b&w illus-1st ed (s3,dj fade & chip) 30.00

MORRIS,D-Mammals-1965-Harper Row-448p-photos-1st ed (bb3,f,dj) 20.00

MORRIS,DONALD-Washing of the Spears-NY-1965-655p-illus-1st ed (b7,f,dj) 65.00

MORRIS,EDITA-Flowers of Hiroshima-NY-1959-Marzani & Munsell-187p-wrps (r1) 15.00

MORRIS,EDWIN B-Report of the Commission on the Renovation of the Executive Mansion-Wash-1952-GPO-4to-109p+illus,red cl (r10) 22.50

MORRIS,F BAYARD-TRANSL.-Hernanado Cortes Five Letters, 1519 to 1526-Lond-1928-Routledge-388p-illus,3 maps-1st ed (a9) 40.00

MORRIS,F O-History of British Butterflies-1865-Groombridge-168p+29p-g dec lea sp & cor over mrbld bds,71 handcol plts (bb3,rebkd,cor wn) 275.00

MORRIS,F O-History of British Butterflies-Lond-1864-Groombridge & Sons-g stmpd grn imitation lea,71 col plts (p6) 200.00

MORRIS,F O-Natural History of the Nests and Eggs of British Birds-1896-Nimmo-3 vols-248 litho col plts-4th rvsd ed (bb3,sl wn,scuff,stnd) 270.00

MORRIS,F O-Natural History of the Nests and Eggs of British Birds-Lond-1879-Geo Bell & Sons-3 vols-329p col plts-2nd ed (p6,sl fox cov) 300.00

MORRIS,F T-Birds of Prey of Australia-Melbourne-1973-176p-lea,gilt back,24 col & 24 b&w plts-ltd to 500c,autg,nbrd (y8,f) 950.00

MORRIS,FRANK-Our Wild Orchids Trails and Portraits-NY-1929-Scribner-464p-cl,4 col photos (x6,rub cl,sl fox) 25.00

MORRIS,GEORGE F-Portraitures of Horses-Shrewsbury-1952-Fordacre-oblng 4to-1st & only ed (f10) 450.00

MORRIS,GEORGE S-Bottlers Formulary-KC-(c.1910)-Morris Chemical Co-87p-Noling p.297 (a8,wn bds,stnd pgs) 50.00

MORRIS,H S-Indians in Uganda-Chig-1968-U of Chig Pr-230p-1st ed (y5,dj) 30.00

MORRIS,HELEN-Portrait of a Chef-Cambridge-1938-Univ Pr-221p-illus (u6) 30.00

MORRIS,HENRY C-Desert Gold and Total Prospecting-Wash D.C.-1955-60p-photos,map-Six Guns #1549-scarce-1st ed (t7,dj) 47.50

MORRIS,J-German Air Raids on Great Britain. 1914 to 1918-Lond-nd(ca.1920)-roy 8vo-cl,17p plts,5 fldg map (s2,sl fox,uncut) 100.00

MORRIS,JAMES-Coronation Everest-Lond-1958-145p-1st Brit ed (q10,dj) 30.00

MORRIS,JAMES-Presence of Spain-NY-1964-Harcourt,Brace-sm folio-120p-cl,photos by E Hofer-1st ed (t3,dj) 50.00

MORRIS,JAN-Conundrum-Lond-1974-1st ed (y7,dj) 18.00

MORRIS,JAN-Venetian Bestiary-NY-1982-Thames & Hudson-8vo-128p-77 illus(16 col)-1st US ed (ff9,as new in dj) 25.00*

MORRIS,JOHN W-Historical Atlas of Oklahoma-Norman-(1965)-U of Okla Pr-89p-70 maps-1st ed (bb4,dj) 30.00

MORRIS,JOHN W-Historical Atlas of Oklahoma-Norman-1965-Univ of Okla-red-brwn cl,70 maps-1st ed (k2,dj) 35.00

MORRIS,JOHN-Age of Arthur-NY-1973-Scribner's-cl,illus-1st ed (l8,dj) 20.00

MORRIS,JOSEPH-Songs For Fishermen-Cin-1922-8vo-330p (m3,vf) 15.00

MORRIS,L-Ceiling Unlimited-NY-1953-8vo-x,418p-illus cl,plts-1st ed (s2) 35.00

MORRIS,LEWIS-Papers of...-NY-1852-NJ Hist Soc,IV-xxxii,336p-cl,port (aa6) 75.00

MORRIS,PAUL C-American Sailing Coasters of the North Atlantic-Chardon-1973-Bloch & Osborn-4to-xvi,224p-blu cl,map e.p.,fldg drwng,photos (pp1) 60.00

MORRIS,THOMAS A-Sermons on Various Subjects-Cin-1842-Wright & Swormstedt-355p-lea (l1,fox) 50.00

MORRIS,W OD'CONNOR-Campaign of 1815-NY-1900-Dutton-1st ed (z2,sl wn) 85.00

MORRIS,W W-An Angler in Arcadia-Edinburgh-1934-8vo-271p-photos (m3) 15.00

MORRIS,W W-Blameless Sport-Lond-1929-12mo-208p-photos-1st ed (m3,f,autg) 25.00

MORRIS,W-North Toward Home-1967-Houghton Mifflin-auth 1st bk-1st ed (x2,vf,dj) 45.00

MORRIS,WILLIAM-Architecture and History, and Westminster Abbey-Lond-1900-Longmans-8vo-50p-cl sp/papr bds (pp7) 150.00

MORRIS,WILLIAM-Hopes & Fears for Art-Lond-1901-Longmans,Green-217p-1st ed (r1,sp labl wn) 50.00

MORRIS,WILLIE-Good Old Boy-NY-1971-Harper-1st ed (t6,dj) 35.00

MORRIS,WILLIE-James Jones: A Friendship-GC-(1978)-Doubleday-1st ed (e6,f,dj) 45.00

MORRIS,WILLIE-Last of the Southern Girls-NY-(1973)-Knopf-1st ed (e6,dj) 45.00

MORRIS,WILLIE-North Toward Home-Bost-1967-HM-auth 1st bk-1st ed (g8,f,dj) 45.00

MORRIS,WILLIE-North Towards Home-Bost-1967-Houghton Mifflin-auth 1st bk-1st ed (bb2,f,dj) 50.00

MORRIS,WILLIE-Terrains of the Heart-Oxford-1981-Yoknapatawpha Pr-1st ed (x9,f,dj) 15.00

MORRIS,WILLIE-Yazoo-NY-(1971)-Harper's Mag-1st ed (a5,as new in dj) 25.00

MORRIS,WRIGHT-About Fiction-NY-1975-Harper & Row-182p-1st ed (j8,f,dj) 35.00

MORRIS,WRIGHT-Cause for Wonder-NY-1963-1st ed (bb10,f,sl fray dj) 30.00

MORRIS,WRIGHT-Ceremony in Lone Tree-NY-1960-Atheneum-1st ed (f8,f,dj) 40.00

MORRIS,WRIGHT-Ceremony in Lone Tree-NY-1960-Atheneum-1st ed (ff6,f,dj) 45.00

MORRIS,WRIGHT-Fork River Project-NY-(1977)-Harper & Row-1st ed (j3,f,dj) 25.00

MORRIS,WRIGHT-God's Country and My People-NY,Evanston,Lond-(1968)-Harper & Row-4to-cl-1st ed (y3,sl tn dj) 45.00

MORRIS,WRIGHT-God's Country and My People-NY-(1968)-Harper & Row-unpgd-83 photos-1st ed (cc9,f,dj) 50.00

MORRIS,WRIGHT-Inhabitants-NY-1946-Scribners-4to-cl,photos-1st ed (v10,f,f dj) 150.00

MORRIS,WRIGHT-Inhabitants-NY-1946-Scribners-sm folio-photos-1st ed (u1,f,dj) 135.00

MORRIS,WRIGHT-Love Affair-NY-1972-Harpers-photos-1st ed (y1,f,f dj) 65.00

MORRIS,WRIGHT-Love Among the Cannibals-NY-(1957)-Harcourt,Brace-1st ed (c10,sl rub dj) 40.00

MORRIS,WRIGHT-My Uncle Dudley-NY-1942-HB-auth 1st bk-1st ed (z9,dj sl tn,chip,soil) 650.00

MORRIS,WRIGHT-One Day-NY-1965-Atheneum-8vo-cl-1st ed (u10,f,f dj) 20.00

MORRIS,WRIGHT-Photographs & Words-Carmel-1982-Friends of Photog-4to-120p-cl-1st ed (t3,f,dj) 45.00

MORRIS,WRIGHT-Plains Song-NY-1980-Harper & Row-1st ed (f8,f,dj) 30.00

MORRIS,WRIGHT-Real Losses, Imaginary Gains-NY-1976-Harper & Row-1st ed (z9,dj) 12.50

MORRIS,WRIGHT-What a Way To Go-NY-1962-1st ed (s5,dj) 20.00

MORRIS,WRIGHT-Will's Boy-NY et al-(1981)-Harper & Row-1st ed (c10,f,dj) 10.00

MORRIS,WRIGHT-Works of Love-NY-1952-Knopf-blk cl-1st ed (f2,f,f dj) 35.00

MORRISEY,LOUISE L-An Odd Volume of Cookery-Bost-1949-Houghton Mifflin-215p (l6) 25.00

MORRISON,A-Chronicles of Martin Hewitt-1896-Appleton-1st Amer ed (x7) 80.00

MORRISON,A-Dorrington Deed Box-1897-New Amsterdam-New Amsterdam t.p. bnd in the Ward Lock bndg-scarce-1st ed (x7) 185.00

MORRISON,A-Red Triangle-1903-Page-pict cl-1st ed (x7,sl wn,sp soil) 95.00

MORRISON,A-Tales of Mean Streets-1895-Roberts-1st Amer ed (x7) 125.00

MORRISON,ARTHUR-Green Diamond-Bost-1904-Page-gilt pict cov-illus-1st US ed (g4) 35.00

MORRISON,TONI-Bluest Eye-Lond-1979-Chatto & Windus-auth 1st bk-1st Brit ed (a10,as new in dj) 100.00

MORRISON,TONI-Bluest Eye-NY,Chig,SF-(1970)-scarce,auth 1st bk-1st ed (c5,dj frnt flap creased) 450.00

MORRISON,TONI-Tar Baby-NY-1981-1st ed (c5,as new in dj) 25.00

MORRISON,TONY-Tar Baby-NY-1981-Knopf-1st ed (x10,f,dj) 20.00

MORRISON,WILLIAM M-Morrison's Strangers' Guide to the City of Washington-Wash-1842-Wm M Morrison-16mo-grn lea,port,17 views (dd6) 100.00

MORRISON,WM B-Military Posts and Camps in Oklahoma-Okla City-1936-180p-pict cl,frntis,photos-Ltd to 200c-Six Guns #1554-v scarce-1st ed (t7) 300.00

MORROW,BRADFORD-Bibliography of the Black Sparrow Press 1966 to 1978-Santa Barbara-1981-Black Sparrow-illus,acetate dj-1st ed (hh10,f,dj) 30.00

MORROW,ELIZABETH-Beast,Bird, and Fish-NY-1933-Knopf-illus,D'Harnoncourt-1st ed (s3,f,dj wn & chip) 40.00

MORROW,FELIX-Civil War in Spain-NY-1936-Pioneer Publ-64p-pamphlet (r1,fade edges,sl tn sp) 25.00

MORROW,JAMES-Wine of Violence-NY-(1981)-Holt & Winston-1st ed (o3,f,dj) 15.00

MORROW,JOSEPH-ED.-Life and Speeches of Thomas Corwin, Orator, Lawyer and Statesman-Cin-1896-477p-1/2 cl (g1,sl scuff sp) 17.50

MORROW,MABLE-Indian Rawhide-Norman-(1975)-240p-drwngs,col photos-v scarce-1st ed (u7,dj) 75.00

MORROW,SUSAN-Murder May Follow-NY-1959-Dbldy CC-1st ed (e4,dj) 15.00

MORROW,SUSAN-Rules of the Game-NY-1964-Dbldy CC-1st ed (e4,dj) 15.00

MORSBERGER,ROBERT E-Lew Wallace, Military Romantic-NY-(1980)-560p-illus-1st ed (n3,f,dj) 22.50

MORSCH,LUCILLE-Check List of New Jersey Imprints, 1784 to 1800-Balt-1939-WPA Amer Imprnts Inv,No.9-4to-(xix),189p-wrps,prtd on rectos only (aa6,sp partly chip away) 90.00

MORSE,BRICK-California Football History-Berkeley-(1937)-Gillick Pr-223p+sponsor list,illus-presumed 1st ed (k2) 25.00

MORSE,EDWARD L-ED.-Samuel F B Morse: His Letters and Journals-Bost-1914-Houghton Mifflin-2 vols-grn cl,t.e.g.,plts-1st ed (a2,sp drknd,sm hole rear cov) 65.00

MORSE,EDWARD L-ED.-Samuel F B Morse:His Letters and Journals-1914-2 vols-illus,28 photos-1st ed (h6) 95.00

MORSE,EDWARD S-Japanese Homes and Their Surrounding-NY-1889-Harper & Bros-8vo-372p-dec blu cl,t.e.g.,illus (r10,chip,pg stnd,wn) 65.00

MORSE,EDWARD S-Mars and its Mystery-Bost-1906-Little,Brown-xiv+192p+ads-red cl,9 plts-1st ed (j2) 22.00

MORSE,FRANK P-Cavalcade of the Rails-NY-1940-370p-1st ed (n4) 32.00

MORSE,H B-In the Days of the Taipings-Salem-1927-Essex Inst-8vo-yel cl,frntis port,photos-1st ed (dd7) 60.00

MORSE,HOSEA-In the Days of the Taipings-Salem-1927-1st ed (b7,f) 35.00

MORSE,JEDEDIAH-Geography Made Easy-Bost-1807-Thomas & Andrews-432p-lea,dbl-pg fldg map-Amer Imprnts 13144-11th ed,corrected by auth (k1,sl wrnkld map) 50.00

MORSE,MARY G-Lore of the Olympic Land-np-(1924)-157p-illus (r8,sl wtrstnd) 25.00

MORSE,R G-Canada: the Mountains-Edmonton-1980-4to-127p-photos-1st ed (a4,f,dj) 35.00

MORSE,R G-Naked Mountain-Tor-1982-193p-1st ed (o10,as new in dj) 32.00

MORSE,REBECCA F-Young Women-Chig-(1901)-92p-cl (d1) 12.50

MORSE,SIDNEY-Siege of University City-St.Louis-1912-Univ City Publ-xii+21-772p-maroon cl,plts-1st ed (b2) 45.00

MORSE,WILLIAM G-Pardon My Harvard Accent-NY-(1941)-F&R-8vo-364p-illus-1st ed (dd5,dj wn,chip) 15.00

MORSE,WILLIAM R-Chinese Medicine-NY-1934-185p-16 illus (g10,ex-libr) 50.00

MORTANE,JACQUES-Guynemer. The Ace of Aces-NY-1918-sm 8vo-xxxiv,268p-cl,frntis,28 illus (t2,sl fade) 40.00

MORTENSEN,WILLIAM-Model-SF-1946-Camera Craft-262p-193 photos-6th prtg (cc9) 25.00

MORTENSEN,WILLIAM-Pictorial Lighting-SF-1940-Camera Craft-115p-41 photos-6th prtg (cc9,dj) 30.00

MORTENSEN,WILLIAM-Print Finishing-SF-1938-Camera Craft-127p-89 photos-1st ed (cc9,dj) 30.00

MORTON,H V-This is Rome-NY-1960-Hawthorn-143p-70 photos by Karsh-1st ed (cc9,dj) 30.00

MORTON,LESLIE T-Medical Bibliography-(Lond)-(1970)-A Deutsch-872p-brwn cl-3rd ed (a2,tattrd dj,ex-libr) 50.00

MORTON,LESLIE-Medical Bibliography-Hampshire-1983-1000p-4th ed (dd3,dj) 75.00

MORTON,OHLAND-Teran and Texas-Austin-1948-Tex St Hist-191p-3 maps-1st ed (a9,dj) 100.00

MORTON,THOMAS G-History of the Pennsylvania Hospital 1751 to 1895-Phila-1895-573p-engrvd frntis-1st ed (dd3) 175.00

MORTON,W L-One University-1957-M&S-8vo-200p-5 illus-1st ed (cc7,sl chip dj) 25.00*

MORTON,WILLIAM A-COMP.-Utah and Her People-SLC-1899-Geo G Cannon-(56)p-cl-illus-Flake 5633 (g1) 35.00

MORTON,WILLIAM J-X-Ray, or Photography of the Invisible and its Value in Surgery-1896-196p-orig silv stmpd grn cl,38 photos,91 illus-v rare-1st US prtg (h6) 210.00

MORWOOD,WILLIAM-Traveler in a Vanished Landscape-NY-1973-Potter-244p-cl (x6,as new in dj) 25.00

MOSBY,H S-Wild Turkey in Virginia-Richmond-1943-8vo-281p-illus,F Everett (m3,sl rub sp) 110.00

MOSEDALE,JOHN-Greatest of All, the 1927 N.Y. Yankees-1974-Dial-1st ed (ff2,dj) 35.00

MOSELEY,SYDNEY-John Baird-1952-256p-11 photos-rare-1st ed (h6,f,dj) 40.00

MOSELEY,SYDNEY-Television, a Guide for the Amateur-1936-144p-31 photos,50 illus-1st ed (h6,f,dj) 55.00

MOSELEY,SYDNEY-Television, Today & Tomorrow-1930-130p-48 photos,38 illus-rare-1st ed (h6) 90.00

MOSELEY,SYDNEY-Television, Today & Tomorrow-1933-198p-78 photos,48 illus-rare-3rd ed (h6) 85.00

MOSELEY,SYDNEY-Television, Today and Tomorrow-NY-1940-Pitman-xx+179p-grn cl,34 plts,56 text illus-5th ed (d2,cov edge-wn & soil) 30.00

MOSELY,MARTIN-British Caddie Flies-Lond-1939-lg 8vo-320p-photos,line drwngs-1st ed (m3,vf,dj) 110.00

MOSER,C A-Bighorn Sheep of Colorado-CO-1962-state publ-49p-wrps,photos (gg3,f) 10.00

MOSER,DON-Peninsular-(1962)-Sierra Club-4to-171p-prchmnt dj,80 photos wi facing text (r8,dj chip,tn) 50.00

MOSER,JEFFERSON-Salmon & Salmon Fisheries of Alaska-Wash-1899-4to-178p-illus,fldg maps,photos (m3) 60.00

MOSER,REV. CHAS-Reminiscences of the West Coast of Vancouver Island-(Victoria)-(1926)-(Acme Pr)-193p-wrps,photos (w1) 65.00

MOSES,GRANDMA-My Life's History-NY-(1952)-Harper Bros-g stmpd lea sp,pap cov bds,ltd to 250c,autg,illus (u1) 350.00

MOSES,ROBERT-Theory and Practice in Politics-Cambridge-1939-Harvard-8vo-vi,78p-cl-1st ed (cc10) 50.00

MOSES,ROBERT-Working for the People-NY-1956-Harper & Bros-8vo-283p-cl,illus-1st ed (cc10,dj) 35.00

MOSGROVE,GEORGE D-Kentucky Cavaliers in Dixie-Louisville-1957-281p-illus-rprnt (c4,f,dj) 75.00

MOSHER,EDITH-ED.-From Indian Legends to the Modern Book Shelf-Ann Arbor-1931-Geo Wahr-395p-cl,photos (cc3) 35.00

MOSHER,REV. R C-Baptist in History-Albert Lea,Mn-1900-193p-cl (h1) 15.00

MOSKOWITZ,SAM-Under the Moons of Mars-NY-(1970)-Holt-1st ed (h3,dj) 15.00

MOSLEY,LEONARD-Backs to the Wall-NY-1971-430p-illus-1st Amer ed (jj2,f,dj) 15.00

MOSLEY,MAY P-Little Texas Beginnings in Southeastern New Mexico-Rosell-(1973)-123p-photos,map e.p.-1st ed (v7,f) 35.00

MOSORIAK,ROY-Curious History of Music Boxes-Chig-(1943)-Lightner-sm folio-242p-g dec cl,illus (dd10) 50.00

MOSS,ARTHUR-Legend of the Latin Quarter-1946-Beech Hurst Pr-1st ed (dd8,dj) 10.00

MOSS,C SCOTT-Hypnotic Investigation of Dreams-NY-(1967)-John Wiley & Sons-(xii)+290+(2)p-prntd grn cl-1st ed (y9,dj) 32.50

MOSS,FRANK T-Modern Saltwater Fishing Tackle-Camden-1976-4to-322p-photos,illus-1st ed (m3,vf,dj) 25.00

MOSS,G LAWTON-How to Build & Repair Your Own Fishing Rods-Lond-(1969)-96p-illus (mm2,dj) 24.00

MOSS,GEORGE H-Nauvoo to the Hook-Locust-1964-lg 4to-128p-cl,illus (aa6) 35.00

MOSS,H W-Elements of Fly Fishing for Trout and Grayling-Lond-1951-8vo-118p-illus,G Lawton Moss (m3,f,sl fray dj) 15.00

MOSS,HOWARD-Instant Lives-NY-1974-drwngs,E Gorey-1st ed (s5,dj) 30.00

MOSS,HOWARD-Whatever is Moving-Bost,Tor-(1981)-Little,Brown-1st ed (bb1,as new in dj) 20.00

MOSSER,MARJORIE-Foods of Old New England-1957-Dbldy-428p-gry cl-(enlgd & rvsd ed of "Good Maine Food")-1st prtg (q8,dj) 17.50

MOSTERT,NOEL-Supership-NY-1974-Knopf-8vo-ix,332p-blk cl (nn1,sl wn dj) 12.50

MOTHER STORK'S BABY BOOK-NY-(1904)-Dodge Publ-unpgd(90)-blu bds,illus by A R Wheelan (a8,wn bds) 75.00

MOTHERSHEAD,HARMON R-Swan Land and Cattle Company, Ltd-Norman-1971-U of Okla Pr-203p-cl,photos-1st ed (w3,f,dj) 25.00

MOTLEY,JOHN L-Rise of the Dutch Republic-Lond-(1929,1889)-Allen & Unwin-8vo-2 vols-12th prtg (cc5,f,dj) 40.00

MOTLEY,WILLARD-Let No Man Write My Epitaph-NY-(1958)-Random-1st ed (b10,sl bump,dj) 35.00

MOTLEY,WILLARD-Let Noon Be Fair-NY-(1966)-Putnam's-1st ed (b5,f,dj) 20.00

MOTOLINIA,FRAY TORIBIO DE-History of the Indians of New Spain-Wash D.C.-1951-Acad Amer Franciscan Hist-xx+358p-blu cl,plts-1st ed (e2,sl wn dj) 45.00

MOTORBOAT AND YACHTING MANUAL-Lond-1954-Temple Pr Ltd-420p-illus-15th ed (p8) 9.50

MOTT,FRANK L-Golden Multitudes-NY-1947-Macmillan-8vo-xii,358p-cl-1st ed (w2,dj chip) 10.00

MOTTEL,S-Charas, the Improbable Dome Builders-NY-1973-illus-1st ed (h10,dj) 45.00

MOTTO,SYTHA-No Banners Waving-NY-1966-Vantage-1st ed (b4,dj sl wn & tn) 35.00

MOTTO,SYTHA-Old Houses of New Mexico & People Who Built Them-Albuq-(1972)-sm folio-112p-photos-1st ed (u7,f,dj,review cpy) 50.00

MOTTRAM,J C-Fly Fishing-Lond-nd-12mo-272p-orig blu cl,illus-1st ed (m3) 85.00

MOTTRAM,J C-Sea Trout & Other Fishing Studies-Lond-nd-12mo-157p-illus (m3,some underlining) 22.50

MOTTRAM,J C-Thoughts on Angling-Lond-nd-12mo-144p-illus-1st prtg so stated (m3,dj) 20.00

MOTTRRAM,J C-Trout Fisheries,Their Care & Preservation-Lond-1928-8vo-186p-illus-1st ed (m3) 30.00

MOULIN-ECKERT-Cosima Wagner-NY-1930-Knopf-lg 8vo-2 vols-1st Amer ed (s1,f,box) 75.00

MOULT,MARGARET M-Escaped Nun-Lond,NY-1914-299,(1)p-cl (d1) 12.50

MOUNT VERNON LADIES' ACCOCIATION-Mount Vernon Gardens-Mt.Vernon-(1941)-auth-40p-blu wrps,photos,diagrams (m6) 10.00

MOUNTAINS OPERATIONS FM 70-10-1947-War Dept-12mo-264p-wrps (a4) 20.00

MOUNTENEY-JEPHSON,A J-Emin Pasha and the Rebellion at the Equator-NY-1891-Scribner-8vo-xxiv,490p-orig cl,a.e.g.,23 plts,25 illus,map & facs letter rear pckt (bb6,rub,sl fray,map & lttr tn 65.00

MOUNTFIELD,D-History of Polar Exploration-1974-Dial-4to-208p-illus & maps (bb3,f,dj) 35.00

MOUNTFORD,CHARLES P-Brown Men and Red Sand-NY-(1952)-Praeger-8vo-184p-illus-1st US ed (ff5,chip dj) 20.00

MOURNING GLORY-Co Ge We A, The Half Blood-1927-Four Seasons Co-302p-red cl,frontis port,tip in errata-scarce (b6,autg) 65.00

MOUTON,LEO-Epernon of Old France-GC-1935-Dbldy Doran-8vo-300p-4 illus-1st US ed (jj5,edgewn dj) 15.00

MOWAT,FARLEY-Dog Who Wouldn't Be-Bost-(1957)-Little,Brown-238p-cl,illus-1st ed (nn10,f,dj) 25.00

MOWAT,FARLEY-Never Cry Wolf-Tor-1963-M&S-8vo-247p-1st ed (cc7,dj) 35.00*

MOWAT,FARLEY-Ordeal by Ice-Lond-1961-M Joseph-8vo-327p-map,e.p. maps-1st ed (cc7,dj) 35.00*

MOWAT,FARLEY-Snow Walker-Tor-1975-M&S-8vo-222p-1st ed (cc7,sl chip dj,autg) 50.00*

MOWAT,FARLEY-West Viking-Bost-(1965)-Little,Brown-xviii+494p-blk cl,maps-1st ed (mm10,dj) 25.00

MOWAT,JEAN-Meals for Small Families-Chig-(1929)-Laidlaw Bros-bds,e.p. & text illus by E M Hubbard-Bitting 333 (m6) 30.00

MOXON,JAMES-Volta-NY-(1969)-Praeger-8vo-256p-18 photos,maps-1st US ed (dd5,dj) 15.00

MOYER,H P-History of the Seventeenth Regiment Pennsylvania Volunteer Cavalry-Lebanon-(1911)-472p-pict cl,illus-1st ed (n3) 110.00

MOYER,JOHN W-Famous Indian Chiefs-Chig-(1957)-Donohue-4to-86p-bds-1st ed (cc4) 15.00

MOYES,PATRICIA-Death and the Dutch Uncle-NY-1968-Holt-1st US ed (f4,dj) 10.00

MOYES,PATRICIA-Murder a la Mode-NY-1963-Holt-1st US ed (d4,dj) 20.00

MOYES,PATRICIA-Murder Fantastical-NY-1967-Holt-1st US ed (j4,f,sl wn dj) 20.00

MOYES,PATRICIA-Season of Snows and Sins-Lond-1971-Collins CC-1st ed (j4,f,sl wn dj) 25.00

MOYES,PATRICIA-Season of Snows and Sins-NY-1971-Holt-1st US ed (g4,f,dj) 15.00

MOYNIHAN,RUTH B-ED.-So Much To Be Done-Lincoln-(1900)-U of Nebr Pr-325p-illus-1st ed (ee4,dj) 32.00

MOZINO,JOSE M-Noticias De Nootka-Seattle,Lond-(1970)-141p-illus-1st ed (j7,f,dj) 35.00

MRABET,MOHAMMED-Lemon-NY-1969-P Bowles,ed & transl-1st US ed (t5,f,dj) 15.00

MRAZEK,COL JAMES-Art of Winning Wars-NY-1968-Walker & Co-1st ed (z2,f,dj) 15.00

MT.HOOD: A GUIDE-1940-DS&P/WPA-132p-illus,e.p. map,1st iss dj-1st ed (r8,wn,dj sp chip,wn) 45.00

MT.HOOD: A GUIDE-1940-WPA-132p-44 photos,3 maps-1st ed (q10,f,dj) 35.00

MUCHNIC,HELEN-From Gorky to Pasternac-NY-1961-Random-1st ed (z9,f,sl soil dj) 12.50

MUDGE,ISADORE G-Guide to Reference Books-Chig-1936-Amer Libr Assoc-504p-cl-6th ed (b1) 17.50

MUDRICK,MARVIN-Nobody Here But Us Chickens-New Haven,NY-1981-Ticknor & Fields-1st ed (bb1,as new in dj) 15.00

MUELLER,HANS-Woodcuts & Wood Engravings-NY-1939-Pynson Pr-4to-188p-cl,col illus-1st ed (x4,sl rub) 85.00

MUELLER,LARRY-Calculating Fisherman-Collinsville-1975-8vo-192p-photos (m3,vf) 20.00

MUENCH,JOYCE-West Coast Portrait-(1946)-Hastings-168p photos,drwngs,etchngs-1st ed (r8,dj wn,chip) 25.00

MUENSCHER,W C-Flora of Whatcom County, Washington-Ithaca-1941-134p-illus-1st ed (e7,sl mar cov,autg) 30.00

MUIR,ANDREW F-ED.-Texas in 1837-Austin-1958-232p-1st ed (n10,f,sl chip dj) 125.00

MUIR,JOHN-Cruise of the Corwin-Bost-1917-278p-spec lg papr ed,ltd to 550c,nbrd-scarce-1st ed (o10,uncut,unopened,vf) 325.00

MUIR,JOHN-Cruise of the Corwin-Bost-1917-278p-tip in fr cov pict,t.e.g.-1st ed (o10,vf) 190.00

MUIR,JOHN-ED.-Picturesque California-SF-1888-J Dewing Publ-folio-10 vols-pict gry/blu cl,120 plts,prtd tissues (mm7,f) 1,500.00

MUIR,JOHN-Mountains of California-1911-Century-389p-photos-new & enlgd ed (d3) 25.00

MUIR,JOHN-Mountains of California-NY-1894-Century-8vo-381p-dec cl-1st ed (oo8,lacks fep) 225.00

MUIR,JOHN-Our National Parks-Bost-1929(1901)-Houghton Mifflin-382p-dec grn cl,map,photos-Illus Holiday ed (p2,dj chip,fade) 35.00

MUIR,JOHN-Steep Trails-1918-Houghton Mifflin-391p-pict pastedown on cov,12 illus (r8,fade sp lettrng) 35.00

MUIR,JOHN-Steep Trails-Bost-1918-382p-tip in pic fr cov,12 photos-1st ed (q10) 135.00

MUIR,JOHN-Story of My Boyhood and Youth-Bost-1913-293p-gold stmpd cov & sp,t.e.g.,10 illus-1st ed (o10,f) 150.00

MUIR,JOHN-Thousand Mile Walk to the Gulf-Bost-1916-219p-tip in pic fr cov,t.e.g.-1st ed (q10,sl fade) 115.00

MUIR,JOHN-Travels in Alaska-Bost-1915-326p-tip in pic fr cov,t.e.g.-1st ed (q10) 140.00

MUIR,JOHN-Yosemite and the Sierra Nevada-Cambridge-1948-Houghton-4to-cl-1st ed (y3,sp rub,dj chip) 115.00

MUIR,P H-Book-Collecting as Hobby-NY-1947-Knopf-181;x p-cl-1st ed so stated (b1,sl wn dj) 15.00

MUIR,PERCY H-Just in Time-Christmas 1954-priv prtd-10p-stitched prtd wrps-ltd to 250c (kk5,sl fade & soil) 60.00

MUIR,WILLA-Women:An Inquiry-NY-1926-Knopf-sm 8vo-76p-1st ed (w6,f,sl chip dj) 45.00

MUKERJEE,R-Culture and Art of India-NY-1959-Praeger-447p+54 plts-red cl (gg6,dj) 30.00

MUKERJI,DHAN G-Fierce Face-NY-1936-Dutton-cl,illus by D P Lathrop-1st ed (aa9,sl yel sp) 40.00

MUKERJI,DHAN GOPAL-Gay Neck-NY-(1927)-Dutton-197p-vel sp,patterned bds,ltd to 1000c,two autg,illus,Artzybasheff,Newbery Medal Bk (s3,fade,soil cov,seal on sp) 60.00

MUKERJI,DHAN GOPAL-Master Monkey-NY-1932-Dutton-cl,illus,F Weber-1st ed (n8,chip dj) 20.00

MUKERJI,DHAN GOPAL-Song of God-NY-1931-Dutton-cl-1st ed (n8,bds wn) 15.00

MULDOON,G-Leopards in the Night-NY-1955-306p-photos (gg3,f,dj) 30.00

MULDOON,G-Trumpeting Herd-Lond-1957-182p-illus (gg3,f) 32.00

MULDOON,PAUL-Knowing My Place-Belfast-(1971)-Ulsterman Publ-wrps,auth 1st bk-scarce-1st ed (z8) 150.00

MULFORD,CLARENCE E-Buck Peters, Ranchman-NY-1912-McClurg-8vo-vii+367p-cl,4 col illus,M Dixon-1st ed (z4,joints cracked,cov sl wn) 45.00

MULFORD,CLARENCE E-Corson of the JC-1927-Dbldy,Page-1st ed (r9,sp sl tn & soil) 20.00

MULFORD,CLARENCE E-Hopalong Cassidy Returns-GC-1924-Dbldy,Page-8vo-310p-cl-1st ed so stated (z4,sp cocked,cov soil) 12.50

MULFORD,ISAAC S-Civil and Political History of New Jersey-Phila-1851-500p+(1)p ad-cl-1st publ 1848-2nd ed (aa6,sl wn) 90.00

MULFORD,WILLIAM C-Historical Tales of Cumberland County, New Jersey-Bridgeton-(1941)-197,(3)p-cl,frntis,illus (aa6) 75.00

MULGARDT,LOUIS C-Architecture & Landscape Gardening of the Exposition-SF-1915-P Elder-202p(10p text+tip-in photos)-g linen bds-1st ed (mm4,f,uncut) 50.00

MULGREW,PETER-I Hold the Heights-NY-1965-203p-1st US ed (o10) 18.00

MULLAHY,PATRICK-Oedipus, Myth and Complex-NY-(1948)-Hermitage-8vo-538p-1st ed (gg5,dj chip,tn) 12.50

MULLAN,JOHN-Report on Construction of a Military Road from Fort Walla Walla to Fort Benton-Wash-1863-363p-orig stmpd cl,errata,4 lg fldg maps,10 col plts-1st ed (z1,rprd) 495.00

MULLER,DAN-My Life with Buffalo Bill-(1948)-Reilly & Lee-303p-illus by auth,e.p. map-Herd 1586-1st ed (r8,dj wn,chip) 35.00

MULLER,MARCIA-Edwin of the Iron Shoes-NY-1977-McKay-auth 1st bk-1st ed (e4,few creased pgs,f dj) 40.00

MULLER,MARGARETHE-Carla Wenckebach, Pioneer-Bost,Lond-1908-289,(1)p-cl-1st ed (d1) 20.00

MULLER,PAUL-Danger, Dame at Work-1968-Roy-1st Amer ed (s10,dj) 12.50

MULLER,PAUL-Lady is Lethal-1968-Roy-1st Amer ed (s10,dj) 12.50

MULLER,PAUL-Slay Time-1968-Roy-1st Amer ed (s10,dj) 12.50

MULLER,W MAX-Mythology of All Races. Vol XII:Egyptian, by...Indo-Chinese, by James George Scott-NY-1964-Cooper Sq Publ-cl,col frntis,plts,drwngs-2nd ed (l8,f) 25.00

MULLER-FREIENFELS,RICHARD-Evolution of Modern Psychology-New Haven-1935-Yale U Pr-xvi+513p-grn cl-1st ed (c2,chip dj) 25.00

MULLETT,CHARLES-Public Baths and Health in England, 16th to 18th Century-Balt-1946-85p-wrps-1st ed (dd3) 35.00

MUMEY,NOLIE-Edward Dunsha Steele 1829 to 1865...A Diary of His Journal...-Boulder-1960-81p-ltd to 500c,autg,views-1st ed (t7,box) 65.00

MUMEY,NOLIE-Epitome of the Semi Centennial History of Colorado's Air Mail-Denver-1977-179p-pict bds,photos-ltd to 200c,autg-1st ed (t7,f) 125.00

MUMEY,NOLIE-Estelle Philleo 1881 to 1936-Denver-1955-21p-stiff pict wrps,frntis-1st ed (t7,autg) 17.50

MUMEY,NOLIE-History and Laws of Nevadaville-Boulder-1962-61p-pict bds-ltd ed,nbrd,autg-1st ed (t7) 27.50

MUMEY,NOLIE-James Pierson Beckwourth an Enigmatic Figure of the West 1856 to 1866-Denver-1957-188p-illus,fldg map-ltd to 750c,autg-1st ed (t7,dj) 165.00

MUMEY,NOLIE-Leyes Del Territoria De Neuva Dejica...-Denver-1970-38p-wrps,photos (t7,f,box) 30.00

MUMEY,NOLIE-Old Forts and Trading Posts of the West-Denver-1956-239p-illus,fldg maps incl lg fldg map rear bd-ltd to 500c,nbrd,autg-1st ed (f7,f,dj) 200.00

MUMEY,NOLIE-Pioneer Denver-Denver-1948-44p-illus,lg fldg illus-ltd to 240c,nbrd,autg-rare-1st ed (t7) 150.00

MUMFORD,JAMES G-Surgical Memoirs and Other Essays-NY-1908-Moffat,Yard-x+358p-blu cl,plts-1st ed (g2,fade sp lttrng) 35.00

MUMFORD,JAMES-Narrative of Medicine in America-Phila-1903-508p (dd3) 100.00

MUMFORD,JAMES-Surgical Memoirs and Other Essays-NY-1908-358p (dd3) 75.00

MUMFORD,LEWIS-City in History-NY-1961-HB&W-thk 4to-cl,64 plts-1st ed (cc10,dj) 50.00

MUMFORD,LEWIS-Culture of Cities-NY-1938-Harcourt Brace-sm,thk 4to-xii,586p-cl,illus-1st ed (cc10) 45.00

MUNBY,A N L-Formation of the Phillipps Library up to the Year 1840-Cambridge-1954-U Pr-Phillipps Studies No.3-1st ed (w1,f) 35.00

MUNBY,A N L-History and Bibliography of Science in England-Berkeley,LA-1968-U of Cal-tall 8vo-41p-prtd wrps (t10,f) 15.00

MUNDAY,DON-Mt Garibaldi Park-1922-priv prtd-12mo-47p-wrps,pict cov,fldg map,photos-1st ed (o10,as new) 95.00

MUNDAY,DON-Unknown Mountain-Lond-1948-268p-illus-1st ed (a4,chip dj) 45.00

MUNDAY,DON-Unknown Mountain-Lond-1948-268p-illus-1st ed (o10,dj chip) 40.00

MUNDAY,DON-Unknown Mountain-Lond-1948-Hodder & Stoughton-xx,268p-cl,frntis,illus,maps(1 fldg) (aa2,dj) 60.00*

MUNDELL,E H-List of the Original Appearances of Dashiell Hammett's Magazine Work-Kent-(1968)-52p-cl (l1) 10.00

MUNDELL,E H-List of the Original Appearances of Dashiell Hammett's Magazine Work-Kent-(1968)-KSU Pr-52p-grn cl-1st ed (z3) 15.00

MUNDT,ERNEST-Birth of a Cook-1956-Knopf-244p-yel cl,illus-1st ed (q8,dj) 12.50

MUNDY,GODFREY C-Our Antipodes-Lond-1852-Richard Bentley-8vo-3 vols-orig g dec blu cl-2nd ed (p8,spot,soil) 700.00

MUNDY,TALBOT-Black Light-Indpls-1930-Bobbs-1st ed (g4) 15.00

MUNDY,TALBOT-Jimgrim and Allah's Peace-NY,Lond-1936-Appelton Century-pict dj-1st ed (ff6,dj sl chip & soil) 175.00

MUNDY,TALBOT-Purple Pirate-Hicksville-(1959)-1st ed (d5,f,dj) 30.00

MUNEMITSU,MUTSU-Kenkenroku-Princeton-(1982)-Princeton U Pr-8vo-318p-illus-1st ed (jj5,f,f dj) 15.00

MUNGER,ALBERT J-Those Old Fishing Reels-Phila-1982-8vo-120p-wrps,photos-1st ed (m3,f) 25.00

MUNGO,RAYMOND-Tropical Detective Story, The Flower Children Meet the Voodoo Chiefs-1972-Dutton-1st ed (x2,dj) 35.00

MUNITZ,MILTON K-ED.-Theories of the Universe-Glencoe-1957-Free Pr & Falcon's Wing-cl-1st ed (l8,f,dj) 10.00

MUNK,J A-Southwest Sketches-NY-1920-311p-pict cl,frntis,photos-Rader #2458-1st ed (t7) 40.00

MUNN,H WARNER-Banner of Joan-W Kingston-1975-Grant-1st ed (g3,f,dj) 15.00

MUNRO,ALICE-Dance of the Happy Shades-1968-Ryerson Pr-auth 1st bk-scarce-1st ed (x2,as new in dj) 250.00

MUNRO,ALICE-Moons of Jupiter-Tor-(1982)-Macmillan-1st Can ed (pp2,f,dj) 25.00*

MUNRO,E-Originals: American Women Artists-NY-1979-illus-1st ed (h10,dj) 35.00

MUNRO,G C-Birds of Hawaii-Rutland-1960-8vo-192p-cl,20 col plts-rvsd ed (y8,dj tn) 25.00

MUNSON,THURMAN-Thurman Munson-1978-Coward McCann-photos-1st ed (s8,dj) 20.00

MUNSTERBERG,HUGO-Arts of Japan-Rutland-(1957)-Tuttle-sm folio-xviii,201p-dec cl,col frntis,plts(incl col)-1st ed (kk1,f,sl soil dj) 32.00

MUNSTERBERG,HUGO-Landscape Painting of China and Japan-Rutland-1955-Tuttle-144p-col frntis,101p plts-1st ed (c3,box) 37.00

MUNSTERBERG,HUGO-Zen & Oriental Art-Rutland-1969-Tuttle-cl,illus-2nd prtg (l8,f,dj) 25.00

MURALS BY AMERICAN PAINTERS AND PHOTOGRAPHERS-NY-1932-MOMA-thin 4to-orng wrps,illus-ltd to 2000c (r10) 30.00

MURBARGER,NELL-Ghosts of the Adobe Walls-LA-1964-398p-photos,illus-1st ed (t7,f,dj) 30.00

MURCH,A E-Development of the Detective Novel-NY-(1958)-Philos Libr-272p-1st ed (g9,sl wn dj) 45.00

MURDOCH,IRIS-An Unofficial Rose-NY-(1962)-Viking-8vo-344p-1st US ed (ee5,dj) 25.00

MURDOCH,IRIS-Henry and Cato-Lond-1976-1st ed (hh10,f,dj sp sl sun) 25.00

MURDOCH,IRIS-Italian Girl-NY-(1964)-Viking-1st US ed (hh5,dj) 15.00

MURDOCH,IRIS-Red and the Green-NY-1965-1st US ed (q5,f,dj) 22.50

MURDOCH,IRIS-Sandcastle-NY-1957-1st US ed (q5,dj sl chip,sp sunned) 25.00

MURDOCH,IRIS-Severed Head-Lond-1961-Chatto & Windus-1st ed (w5,f,sl wn dj) 65.00

MURDOCH,IRIS-Three Arrows & the Servants and the Snow-NY-1974-1st US ed (r5,dj) 30.00

MURDOCH,IRIS-Under the Net-1954-Viking-1st US ed (jj6,f,dj sl rub,edgewn & tn) 45.00

MURDOCH,IRIS-Unicorn-1963-Viking-1st US ed (kk6,f,sl nick dj) 25.00

MURDOCH,IRIS-Unicorn-NY-1963-1st US ed (t5,dj) 20.00

MURDOCH,IRIS-Word Child-(1975)-Viking-1st US ed (kk6,vf,sl tn dj) 20.00

MURDOCK,G P-Ethnographic Bibliography of North America-1960-Human Relations-4to-393p-wrps,maps-3rd ed (bb3) 45.00

MURFIN,JAMES V-Gleam of Bayonets-NY-(1965)-451p-maps-1st ed (c4,dj) 40.00

MURIE,ADOLPH-Naturalist in Alaska-NY-1961-Devin Adair-8vo-302p-photos,illus-1st ed (ff5,f,dj) 20.00

MURIE,ADOLPH-Wolves of Mount McKinley-Wash D.C.-1944-Dept of Interior-8vo-238p-wrps,58 illus-1st ed (aa5,sp creased) 40.00

MURIE,MARGARET E-Island Between-1977-U of Alaska-228p-drwngs-1st ed (u8,sl rub dj) 15.00

MURIE,MARGARET E-Two in the Far North-NY-1962-8vo-438p-illus,O Murie-1st ed (m3,f,dj) 15.00

MURIE,O J-Elk of North America-WY-1979-376p-photos (gg3,f,dj) 15.00

MURIE,O J-Field Guide to Animal Tracks-Bost-1958(1954)-12mo-374,(1)p-cl,illus (y8,dj) 10.00

MURPHY,BEATRICE-ED.-Negro Voices-NY-1938-H Harrison-scarce-1st ed (v5,dj) 125.00

MURPHY,DERVLA-In Ethiopia with a Mule-Lond-(1968)-J Murray-8vo-281p-22 photos-1st Brit ed (cc5,dj) 30.00

MURPHY,E F-They Struck Opal-Sydney-1948-Assoc Gen Publ-191p-frntis,3 col plts,illus,maps-scarce (u5) 55.00

MURPHY,E J-Movement West-Denver-(1958)-178p-illus,col fldg plt-1st ed (r8,f,dj chip) 22.00

MURPHY,GWENDOLYN-Cabinet of Characters-Lond-1925-11 illus-1st ed (k9) 12.50

MURPHY,J MORTIMER-Sporting Adventures in the Far West-NY-1880-Harpers-dec cov-1st US ed (b4) 125.00

MURPHY,LAWRENCE-Philmont-Albuq-1972-261p-photos-1st ed (t7,dj) 30.00

MURPHY,MARK-83 Days: Survival of Seaman Izzi-NY-1943-Dutton-12mo-124p-11 illus-1st ed (cc5,f,sl tn dj) 17.50

MURPHY,MICHAEL-Golf in the Kingdom-NY-1972-Viking-1st ed (c8,dj) 40.00

MURPHY,P C-Shadows of the Gallows-np(Caldwell)-nd(1928)-192p-illus-1st ed (h7) 30.00

MURPHY,R C-Bird Islands of Peru-1925-Putnams-362p-t.e.g.,photos-1st ed (bb3,f) 145.00

MURPHY,R C-Land Birds of America-1953-McGraw Hill-4to-240p-221 col & 43 b&w photos-2nd prtg (bb3,f,wn dj) 18.00

MURPHY,R C-Land Birds of America-NY-1953-McGraw Hill-240p-col photos (b9) 17.50

MURPHY,R C-Oceanic Birds of South Amer-NY-1936-4to-2 vols-cl,16 col plts (y8) 175.00

MURPHY,R C-Oceanic Birds of South America-1936-Macmillan-2 vols-16 col plts,72 photos,figs,maps (bb3,stnd e.p.) 190.00

MURPHY,R C-Oceanic Birds of South America-NY-1936-Amer Mus of Nat Hist-2 vols-16 col inserts,photos,maps-ltd to 1200c,nbrd (b9,frntis loose) 240.00

MURPHY,R C-Peregrine Falcon-Bost-1964-Houghton Mifflin-157p-illus-1st prtg (d9,dj) 10.00

MURPHY,R C-Peregrine Falcon-NY-1964-157p-illus (gg3,f) 15.00

MURPHY,RICHARD-Sailing to an Island-Lond-(1963)-Faber-1st ed (z8,vf,dj) 30.00

MURPHY,THOMAS D-On Sunset Highways-Bost-1915-Page Co-(3),376,(4)p-dec cl,40 photo plts,16 col plts,fldg map-1st ed,1st prtg (o2) 45.00

MURRAY,ALAN E-Shoes and Feet to Boot-Chapel Hill-1950-Orange Prntsp-xxvi+139p-grn cl,plts-1st ed (g2,sl fade sp) 20.00

MURRAY,ALBERT-Omni Americans-NY-1970-Outerbridge & Dientsfrey-auth 1st bk-1st ed (v5,f,dj) 20.00

MURRAY,ALBERT-South to a Very Old Place-1971-McGraw-Hill-1st ed (t9,f,dj) 20.00

MURRAY,ALBERT-Train Whistle Guitar-NY-1974-McGraw-1st ed (v5,f,f dj) 35.00

MURRAY,AMELIA M-Letters from the United States, Cuba, and Canada-NY-1856-Putnam-(2 vols in one)-1st Amer ed (p6,sp wn) 75.00

MURRAY,CROMWELL-Day of the Dead-Phila-1946-McKay-1st ed (g4,f,dj) 15.00

MURRAY,F ALISTER-Book of Ted or Roosevelt and the Railroads in Scripture-np-(1907)-38,(1)p-wrps (g1) 35.00

MURRAY,HON CHARLES A-Travels in North America During the Years 1834, 1835 & 1836-NY-1839-Harper & Bros-2 vols-Howes M913-1st Amer ed (cc4,wn) 150.00

MURRAY,JAMES R-Dainty Songs for Little Lads and Lasses...-Cin-(1887)-John Church-160p-bds (h1) 15.00

MURRAY,KEITH A-Modocs and Their War-Norman-(1969)-343p-illus,maps-2nd prtg (n3,f,dj) 35.00

MURRAY,KEITH-Pig War-1968-Wash State Hist Soc-84p-stiff wrps,illus,map (r8) 10.00

MURRAY,LINDLEY-Compendium of Religious Faith and Practice-NY-1817-Samuel Wood & Sons-87p-bds-Amer Imprnts 41509 (k1,sl dmpstnd) 35.00

MURRAY,LINDLEY-English Grammar-NY-1807-Collins & Perkins-332p-lea-frm 15th Engl ed (k1,sl wn) 25.00

MURRAY,LINDLEY-English Reader-Binghamton-1828-J & C Orton-252p-cl (e1) 25.00

MURRAY,LINDLEY-English Reader-Cin-1826-N & G Guilford-204p-bds-Amer Imprnts 25453 (k1,covs wn) 50.00

MURRAY,LINDLEY-English Reader-Utica-1820-prntd by Wm Wlliams-263p-orig calf bndg-Amer Imprnts 2373 (k1,f) 30.00

MURRAY,LINDLEY-Introduction to the English Reader-Cin-1829-N & G Guilford-156p-bds (k1) 50.00

MURRAY,LINDLEY-Sequel to the English Reader-Phila-1803-prntd for B & J Johnson-388p-lea-Amer Imprnts 4703-2nd Phila ed (k1,wn,lacks f.e.p.s) 32.50

MURRAY,MARGARET-Bibliography of the Research and Tissue Culture 1884 to 1950-NY-1953-2 vols-1st ed (dd3) 50.00

MURRAY,PAUL-Ritual Poems-Dublin-(1971)-New Writers' Pr-wrps-1st ed (z8,vf) 30.00

MURRAY,PHILIP A-Fishing in the Carolinas-Chapel Hill-1941-8vo-183p-illus-1st ed (m3,f,dj) 50.00

MURRAY,REV THOMAS B-Pitcairn-Lond-1853-Soc Promo Chrstn Knwldg-12mo-xiv,280p-12 illus (p8,rbnd,pres) 150.00

MURRAY,ROBERT-Army Moves West-Ft.Collins-1981-22p-pict wrps,illus-1st ed (t7,f) 17.50

MURRAY,W H H-Adirondack Tales-Bost-1877-Golden Rule-Plum #7326-1st ed (gg7,few cov spots) 50.00

MURRAY,W H H-Busted Ex Texan and Other Stories-Bost-1890-DeWolfe, Fiske & Co-112p-cl,illus-1st ed (w3,vf) 30.00

MURRAY,W H H-Lake Champlain and Its Shores-Bost-1890-DeWolfe,Fiske-brwn cl-Plum #352-1st ed (gg7) 30.00

MURRAY,W H-Perfect Horse-Bost-1873-Osgood-1st ed (f10) 95.00

MURRAY,W H-Story of Everest 1921 to 1952-NY-1953-193p-23 photos,14 maps-1st US ed (q10,f,dj) 19.00

MURRAY,W H-Story of Everest-Lond-1953-Dent-8vo-218p-blu cl,photos,maps-4th ed (gg6,dj) 25.00

MURRAY,WILLIAM H H-Adventures in the Wilderness-Bost-1869-Fields,Osgood-236p+ads-grn cl,plts-1st ed (h2,cov rub & sl flecked) 65.00

MURRAY,WILLIAM-Horse Fever-1976-Dodd,Mead-1st ed (r9,f,dj) 35.00

MURRY,J MIDDLETON-Critic in Judgement or Belshazzar of Baronscourt-Richmond-nd(1918)-Hogarth Pr-26p-blk wrps,wht labl-ltd to 200c-Woolmer 6-1st ed (nn4,uncut) 250.00

MURSELL,WALTER A-Byways in Bookland-Bost,NY-1914-Houghton Mifflin-vii,205p-pict bds-1st Amer ed (dd10) 20.00

MURTY,T S-Seismic Sea Waves, Tsunamis-Ottawa-1977-Dept of Fish & Environmnt-x+337p-red cl,maps,photos,drwngs-Bull 198-1st ed (j2) 22.00

MUSCATINE,DORIS-Cook's Tour of Rome-(1964)-Scribners-369p-gry cl,maps,drwngs (q8,dj) 15.00

MUSCHAMP,E A-Audacious Audubon-1929-Brentanos-312p-illus (bb3) 17.00

MUSCIANO,W A-Eagles of the Black Cross-NY-(1965)-8vo-xiv,302p-cl,frntis,illus-1st ed (s2,dj) 35.00

MUSCROFT,COMRADE S J-Drummer Boy-Mansfield-1872-L D Myers & Bro.-31p-wrps (c1) 35.00

MUSEUM OF MODERN ART FIRST LOAN EXHIBITION-NY-Nov,1929-MOMA-4to-yel wrps,illus-ltd to 3000c-1st ed (r10,sl fade) 12.50

MUSGROVE,JACK W-Waterfowl in Iowa-Des Moines-1943-8vo-124p-illus,M Reece-1st ed (m3) 40.00

MUSIAL,STAN-Stan Musial, the Man's Own Story-1964-Dbldy-1st ed (p7,dj) 35.00

MUSMANO,MICHAEL-After Twelve Years-1939-Knopf-1st ed (s10,chip dj) 15.00

MUSSAEUS,THOMAS A-Lure of Cave Lore-(Strasburg)-1939-65p-wrps,photos (e1,sl wn wrps) 15.00

MUSSOLINI,BENITO-John Huss-NY-1929-Boni-225p-1st ed (r1) 20.00

MUSTARD,HARRY-Rural Health Practice-NY-1936-603p (dd3) 50.00

MUSTERS,GEORGE C-At Home with the Patagonians-NY-1969-Greenwood Pr-8vo-brwn cl,fldg map,illus-rprnt of 1897 ed (mm1,as new) 25.00

MUUSMANN,C-Sherlock Holmes at Elsinore-1956-BSI-wrps-1st ed (x7) 45.00

MUYBRIDGE,EADWEARD-Human Figure in Motion-NY-(1955)-Dover-4to-cl,194 illus (y3,dj sl chip & sunned) 45.00

MY FARM OF EDGEWOOD: A COUNTRY BOOK-NY-1864-x,319p (j10,edge wn,sl stnd) 20.00

MYATT,FREDERICK-Royal Berkshire Regiment-Lond-1968-136p-illus-Famous Regiments ser-1st ed (b7,f,dj) 30.00

MYERS,B S-German Expressionists-NY-1957-74 col & 173 b&w plts,64 gravure plts-1st ed (h10,dj) 175.00

MYERS,CHARLES E-Memoirs of a Hunter-Davenport-1948-priv prntd-8vo-309p-photos (m3,vf,dj) 60.00

MYERS,CHARLES E-Memoirs of a Hunter-Davenport-1948-Shaw & Borden Co-309p-red cl-Smith #7201-v scarce (b6,f,tn dj,pres cpy) 85.00

MYERS,ELLA-Gardening in Virginia-1936-Dietz-208p-cl (x6) 15.00

MYERS,F W H-Human Personality and its Survival of Bodily Death-New Hyde Park-1961-Univ Bks-cl-1st prtg (n8,f,dj) 20.00

MYERS,FRANK-Soldiering in Dakota Among the Indians in 1863,4,5-Fairfield-1975-Ye Galleon Pr-48p-pict e.p.-ltd to 300c-Howes M929 (ee4) 20.00

MYERS,GARY-House of the Worm-Sauk City-1975-Arkham-1st ed (j3,f,dj) 10.00

MYERS,GUSTAVUS-History of Bigotry in the United States-NY-(1943)-Random-504p-cl-1st ed (dd10,f,dj) 35.00

MYERS,JOHN M-Alamo-NY-1948-240p-pict cl,maps (t7) 12.00

MYERS,JOHN M-Death of the Bravos-Bost-(1962)-Little,Brown-467p-map e.p.-1st ed (bb4,dj) 20.00

MYERS,JOHN M-Death of the Bravos-Bost-1962-467p-e.p. maps-1st ed (c4,dj wn) 25.00

MYERS,JOHN M-Doc Holliday-Bost-(1955)-Little,Brown-287p-Six Guns #1586-1st ed (ee4,dj,autg) 30.00

MYERS,JOHN M-Doc Holliday-Bost-(1955)-Little,Brown-viii+287p-tan cl-1st ed (e2,dj wn & tn) 20.00

MYERS,JOHN M-I, Jack Swilling-NY-1961-Hastings-1st ed (b4,sl tn dj) 25.00

MYERS,JOHN M-Pirate, Pawnee & Mountain Man-Bost-1963-Little,Brown-1st ed (b4,dj) 35.00

MYERS,JOHN M-Pirate, Pawnee and Mountain Man-Bost-(1963)-237p-1st ed (n3,dj) 25.00

MYERS,JOHN M-San Francisco's Reign of Terror-GC-1966-Dbldy-301p-illus-1st ed (bb4,dj) 20.00

MYERS,JOHN M-San Francisco's Reign of Terror-NY-1966-301p-1st ed (t7,dj) 10.00

MYERS,JOHN M-Westerners-(1969)-Prentice Hall-258p-1st ed (r8,dj) 28.00

MYERS,JOHNNIE J-Texas Electric Railway-Chig-1982-256p-Bull.#121-1st ed (n4,f,f dj) 30.00

MYERS,L H-Clio-NY-1925-Scribner's-1st Amer ed (o8) 15.00

MYERS,L M-Television Optics-Lond-1936-Sir Isaac Pitman-x+338p+ads-blu cl,214 text illus-1st ed (g2,owners sp labl rmvd) 35.00

MYERS,LEWIS A-History of New Mexico Baptists-NM-1965-Baptist Convention-1st ed (b4,dj) 45.00

MYERS,N-Long African Day-NY-1972-404p-photos (ee3,f,dj) 40.00

MYERS,ROBERT M-Children of Pride-New Haven-(1972)-1841p-e.p. maps-1st ed (n3,f,dj sl wn,chip) 55.00

MYERS,ROBERT M-ED.-Children of Pride-New Haven-1972-Yale U Pr-xxvi+1845p-gry cl-1st ed (b2,dj) 45.00

MYERS,ROBERT M-Handel's Messiah-NY-1948-Macmillan-8vo-338p-13 illus-1st ed (ee5,chip dj) 20.00

MYERS,SAMUEL D-Permian Basin, Petroleum Empire of the Southwest-El Paso-1977-624p-cl,illus,photos-(Regular ed)-1st ed (ee10,as new in dj) 40.00

MYERS,WILLIAM S-Story of New Jersey-NY-(1945)-4to-5 vols-cl,illus (aa6) 100.00

MYERSON,JOEL-Margaret Fuller: a Descriptive Bibliography-Pitt-(1978)-163p-cl (a1) 15.00

MYERSON,MICHAEL-These are the Good Old Days-NY-1970-Grossman-1st ed (v5,dj sl rub,tn) 20.00

MYLES,EUGENIE L-Airborne From Edmonton-Tor-1959-Ryerson Pr-8vo-xii,280p-29 illus-1st ed (cc7,dj) 35.00*

MYRES,DWIGHT-ED.-In Celebration of the Book-Albuq,Santa Fe-1982-222p-cl,mrbld e.p.-ltd to 500c,nbrd,autg by all-scarce (n10,f,box) 350.00

MYRES,SAMUEL D-Permian Basin Petroleum Empire of the Southwest-El Paso-1977-Permian Pr-624p-cl,photos,drwngs by J Cisneros,ltd ed wi brass engrvngs set into cov (w3,f,box) 150.00

MYRES,SAMUEL D-Southwestern Portfolio-El Paso-1968-Ex Students Assoc UTEP-portfolio wi 12 b&w & col prnts, 16 1/2 x 21 1/4 inches,designed by C Hertzog (w3,f,sl wn cov) 125.00

MYRICK,DAVID F-New Mexico's Railroads-an Historical Survey-(Golden)-1970-197+3p-photos,maps-1st ed (v7,dj) 25.00

MYRICK,THOMAS-Gold Rush-Mount Pleasant-(1971)-priv pr of John Cumming-117p-cl (c1) 22.50

MYSTIC,BLACKSTONE AND CHARLES RIVERS-REPORT OF A COMMISSION...DRAINAGE FOR THE VALLEYS OF...-Bost-1886-Wright & Potter-lxxxiv+243p-brwn cl,fldg maps,7 photo plts (d2) 50.00

MYTINGER,CAROLINE-Headhunting in the Solomon Islands Around the Coral Sea-NY-1942-Macmillan-8vo-416p-blk cl,illus-1st prtg (nn1,f,dj) 25.00

NABOKOV,PETER-Tijerina and the Courthouse Raid-Albuq-(1969)-274p-photos-1st ed (u7,f,dj) 35.00

NABOKOV,VLADIMIR-Ada-NY-1969-1st ed (q5,dj) 25.00

NABOKOV,VLADIMIR-Annotated Lolita-NY-1970-1st ed (n5,f,dj) 60.00

NABOKOV,VLADIMIR-Bend Sinister-NY-(1947)-H Holt-scarce-1st ed (ee2,f,sl rub dj) 165.00

NABOKOV,VLADIMIR-Conclusive Evidence-1951-Harper-1st ed (x2,sl soil dj) 195.00

NABOKOV,VLADIMIR-Conclusive Evidence-NY-1951-Harpers-1st ed (y1,dj edgewn) 175.00

NABOKOV,VLADIMIR-Despair-1966-Putnam-1st Amer ed (s9,sl tn dj) 30.00
NABOKOV,VLADIMIR-Details of a Sunset-NY-1976-McGraw Hill-1st ed (h8,f dj) 30.00
NABOKOV,VLADIMIR-Eye-1965-Phaedra-1st US ed (kk6,f,dj) 85.00
NABOKOV,VLADIMIR-Glory-(1971)-McGraw Hill-1st ed (j3,f,dj) 25.00
NABOKOV,VLADIMIR-Invitation to a Beheading-NY-(1959)-1st US ed (s5,sl chip dj) 40.00
NABOKOV,VLADIMIR-Invitation to a Beheading-NY-(1959)-Putnam-1st US ed (j3,chip dj) 25.00
NABOKOV,VLADIMIR-King,Queen,Knave-1968-McGraw Hill-1st Amer ed (n9,f,dj) 30.00
NABOKOV,VLADIMIR-Laughter in the Dark-1960-New Directions-1st ed thus (kk6,sl wn dj) 50.00
NABOKOV,VLADIMIR-Lectures on Literature-NY-1980-1st ed (s5,f,dj) 25.00
NABOKOV,VLADIMIR-Lectures on Russian Literature-NY,Lond-(1981)-HBJ/Bruccoli Clark-1st ed (b5,as new in dj) 35.00
NABOKOV,VLADIMIR-Life of Sebastian Knight-Norfolk-(1959)-New Directions-1st ed (ee2,f,dj) 45.00
NABOKOV,VLADIMIR-Lolita-NY-1958-1st US ed (p5,chip dj) 40.00
NABOKOV,VLADIMIR-Mary-1970-M,H-1st US ed (x2,f,dj) 25.00
NABOKOV,VLADIMIR-Mary-NY-1970-1st US ed (q5,f,dj) 20.00
NABOKOV,VLADIMIR-Nabokov's Dozen-1958-Dbldy-1st ed (n9,dj wn & rprd) 45.00
NABOKOV,VLADIMIR-Nabokov's Dozen-GC-1958-1st ed (q5,dj) 75.00
NABOKOV,VLADIMIR-Nabokov's Dozen-GC-1958-Dbldy-1st ed (ee2,f,sl wn dj) 85.00
NABOKOV,VLADIMIR-Nabokov's Quartet-NY-1966-Phaedra-1st US ed (kk6,f,sl chip dj) 40.00
NABOKOV,VLADIMIR-Nabokov's Quartet-NY-1966-Phaedra-1st US ed (z2,f,sl tn dj) 30.00
NABOKOV,VLADIMIR-Nikolai Gogol-Norfolk-(1944)-New Directions-12mo-gry bds-1st ed (x10,f,dj) 75.00
NABOKOV,VLADIMIR-Nikolai Gogol-Norfolk-1944-New Directions-1st bndg,1st state dj-1st ed (v5,f,dj) 125.00
NABOKOV,VLADIMIR-Pale Fire-NY-1962-NY-1st ed (q5,dj) 65.00
NABOKOV,VLADIMIR-Poems-NY-1959-Dbldy-8vo-blu cl,drwngs,R Jacques-1st ed (v10,f,dj) 100.00
NABOKOV,VLADIMIR-Real Life of Sebastian Knight-Lond-(1945)-Editions Poetry-1st Brit ed (x10,dj edge-tn) 35.00
NABOKOV,VLADIMIR-Speak Memory-Lond-1951-Gollancz-gold stmpd blu bds,2nd iss dj wi Welty & Behrman blurbs-1st ed (dd2,sl rub dj) 175.00
NABOKOV,VLADIMIR-Strong Opinions-NY-1973-1st ed (p5,f,dj) 40.00
NABOKOV,VLADIMIR-TRANS.-Three Russian Poets-Norfolk-(1944)-New Directions-1st ed (t1,dj) 100.00
NABOKOV,VLADIMIR-Transparent Things-NY-(1972)-McGraw Hill-1st ed (ee2,f,dj) 35.00
NABOKOV,VLADIMIR-Waltz Invention-NY-1966-Phaedra-var "b" wi non acidic papr-1st ed (q2,dj) 65.00
NADAL,E S.-Virginian Village-1917-Macmillan-277p (dd9) 35.00
NADAUD,M-Flying Poilu-NY-(1918)-8vo-218p-illus cl,frntis,9p plts-1st ed (s2) 30.00
NADEAU,REMI-Fort Laramie and the Sioux Indians-Englewood Cliffs-(1967)-Prentice-Hall-335p-illus,map e.p.-1st ed (cc4,dj) 50.00
NADEAU,REMI-Ghost Towns and Mining Camps of California-1965-Ward Ritchie-278p-1st ed (d3,dj) 25.00
NADEL,S F-Black Byzantium-Lond-1965-OUP-8vo-420p-cl,illus,maps-rprnt (y5,dj) 45.00
NADEL,S F-Nupe Religion-Lond-(1954)-Routledge & K Paul-8vo-288p-cl,illus (y5,dj) 40.00
NAEF,WESTON J-Era of Exploration-Bost-(1975)-NYGS-oblng 8vo-cl (y3,f,dj sl chip) 75.00
NAEF,WESTON J-Truthful Lens-NY-1980-Grolier Club-lg 4to-blk cl,red lea sp labl,orig box,ltd to 1000c-scarce-1st ed (y3,f,box) 275.00
NAFTALIN,ROSE-Grandma Rose's Book of Sinfully Delicious Cakes, Cookies, Pies...-(1975)-Random-255p-maroon cl,drwngs-1st ed (q8,dj) 15.00
NAFTALIN,ROSE-Grandma Rose's Book of Sinfully Delicious Snacks, Nibbles, Noshes & Other Delights-(1978)-Random-259p-grn cl,drwngs-1st ed (q8,dj) 15.00
NAHAS,REBECCA-New Couple-NY-(1979)-Seaview-8vo-viii,291p-cl-1st ed (z5,f,f dj) 15.00
NAHM,MILTON C-Las Vegas & Uncle Joe-Norman-1964-U of Okla-1st ed (b4,dj) 45.00
NAHOUM,CHEF ALDO-Art of Israeli Cooking-Lond-(1970)-Gifford-152p-wht bds,col photos-1st ed (q8,dj) 15.00
NAIL,A F-Drummer Boy or the "Spy of Shiloh"-np-nd-74p-stiff wrps (l1,sm pc missing cor t.p.) 25.00
NAIPAUL,V S-Among the Believers-NY-1981-1st US ed (r5,f,dj) 20.00
NAIPAUL,V S-An Area of Darkness-NY-1965-Macmillan-1st US ed (v5,f,dj) 50.00
NAIPAUL,V S-Loss of El Dorado-NY-1970-Knopf-1st US ed (bb1,f,dj) 35.00
NAIPAUL,V S-Miguel Street-NY-1960-1st US ed (r5,f,dj) 50.00
NAIPAUL,V S-Mr.Stone and the Knight's Companion-NY-1963-1st US ed (r5,f,dj) 45.00
NAIPAUL,V S-Mystic Masseur-NY-(1959)-auth 1st bk-1st US ed (o5,dj) 90.00
NAIPAUL,V S-Mystic Masseur-NY-(1959)-Vanguard-auth 1st bk-1st US ed (b5,dj sl tn,sl wn) 60.00
NAIPAUL,V S-Overcrowded Barracoon-NY-1972-1st US ed (q5,dj) 45.00
NAIPAUL,V S-Return of Eva Peron-NY-1980-1st US ed (s5,f,dj) 20.00
NAKAMURA,KYOKO M-Miraculous Stories from the Japanese Buddhist Tradition-Cambridge-1973-Harvard U Pr-cl-1st prtg (n8,vf,dj) 30.00
NAKANE,CHIE-Japanese Society-Lond-(1970)-Weidenfeld & Nicholson-8vo-157p-cl-1st ed (y5,dj) 15.00
NAKAYA,U-Snow Crystals, Natural and Artificial-1954-Harvard-510p-photos (bb3,f,fray dj) 48.00
NAKAYA,UKICHIRO-Snow Crystals Natural and Artificial-Cambridge-1954-Harvard Univ Pr-xiv+510p-blk cl,188p illus,514 text figs-1st ed (l2,chip dj) 50.00
NALLE,OUIDA F-Fergusons of Texas or "Two Governors for the Price of One"-San Antonio-1946-Naylor Co-272p-cl,fldg chrt-1st ed (w3,f,chip dj) 45.00
NAMMACK,GEORGINA C-Fraud, Politics, and the Dispossession of the Indians-1969-U of Okla Pr-xix,128p-g brwn cl,11 maps & illus-1st ed (bb7) 15.00

NANDRIS,MABEL-Folk Tales from Roumania-NY-1953-Roy Publ-cl,illus-1st ed (n8) 25.00

NANSEN,FRIDTJOF-In Northern Mists-Lond-1911-Wm Heinemann-4to-2 vols-blu cl,illus-1st ed (pp5,sl wn) 300.00*

NANSEN,FRIDTJOF-Through Siberia-NY/Lond-1914-Stokes/Heinemann-8vo-xvi,478p-3 fldg maps,photos (ll1) 100.00

NANSON,F-Hunting & Adventure in the Arctic-NY-1925-462p-photos (gg3,cov sl wn) 45.00

NANTON,PAUL-Arctic Breakthrough-Tor-1970-Clarke Irwin-8vo-xi,262p-frntis,8p illus,map,e.p. maps-1st ed (cc7,dj) 25.00*

NANTON,PAUL-Arctic Breakthrough-Tor-1970-Clarke,Irwin-8vo-262p-1st Can ed (ff5,f,dj) 20.00

NAPHEYS,GEO H-Physical Life of Women-Phila,NY &Bost-1872-Geo MacLean-322p-cl-enlgd & rvsd ed (d1,sl spot cov) 20.00

NAPIER,HENRY E-New England Blockaded 1814-Salem-1939-Peabody Mus-8vo-xxi,88p-orig cl,t.e.g.,fldg chrt,8 plts-ltd to 1200c (u3,sl tn dj) 50.00

NAPIER,MILES-Thoroughbred Pedigrees Simplified-Lond-1973-Allen-1st ed (j9,dj) 18.00

NAPIER,WILLIAM-History of the War in the Peninsula-Lond-1867-6 vols-3/4 g dec red lea,mrbld bds & e.p.,red ribbon mrkr,t.e.g.,maps (b7,f,lacks one plt) 400.00

NAPIER,WILLIAM-War in the Peninsula-Lond-1973-Folio Soc-331p-illus (d7,f) 40.00

NAPTON,WILLIAM-Over the Santa Fe Trail 1857-Santa Fe-1964-73p-frntis,ltd ed-Rittenhouse #428 (t7,f,dj) 40.00

NAPTON,WILLIAM-Over the Santa Fe Trail-Santa Fe-1964-Stagecoach Pr-73p-cl,ltd to 99c,10 illus,reiss of 1905 ed-v scarce (z1,vf,dj) 60.00

NARAMORE,E-Principles & Practices of Loading Ammunition-1954-Samworth-952p-photos (gg3) 35.00

NARAMORE,EARL-Handloader's Manual-Onslow Cnty-1937-12mo-369p+ads-photos (m3,sp & cov lttrng dull) 20.00

NARAYAN,R K-Guide-NY-1958-Viking-1st US ed (hh5,f,sp fade dj) 12.50

NARAYAN,R K-Waiting for the Mahatma-1955-Mich State-1st US ed (hh5,f,dj fade,soil) 12.50

NARBOROUGH,JOHN-An Account of Several Late Voyages and Discoveries to the South and North-Amsterdam/NY-1970-N Israel-442p-19 plts,2 fldg maps,tbl-facs of 1694 ed (p8,f) 110.00

NASATIR,ABRAHAM-Borderland in Retreat-(1979)-U of NM-175p-maps-1st ed (t8,f,f dj) 15.00

NASH,E-Farmer's Practical Horse Farriery...-Auburn-1858-Nash-frntis (f10) 45.00

NASH,JAY R-Look for the Woman-NY-1981-Evans-1st ed (z3,f,sl tn dj) 12.50

NASH,JOSEPH-Relations Between Capital and Labor in the U.S.-Bost-1878-Lee & Shepard-wrps-1st ed (w5) 20.00

NASH,MRS F B-Lessons on the Gentle Art of Cookery-Fargo-1892-Commonwealth Publ-79p+index & errata,bds-Bitting 339 (k6) 125.00

NASH,OGDEN-Adventures of Isabel-Bost-(1963)-Little,Brown-4to-30p-pict cl,illus by W Lorraine-1st ed thus (nn10,edge fade,dj wn,yel) 20.00

NASH,OGDEN-Ave Ogden! Nash in Latin-Bost-1973-LB-1st ed (y1,f,dj) 25.00

NASH,OGDEN-Christmas That Almost Wasn't-Bost-1957-Little,Brown-illus-1st ed (gg7,dj) 15.00

NASH,OGDEN-Free Wheeling-NY-1931-S&S-grn cl-illus,O Soglow-1st ed (f2,dj chip & edge-wn) 50.00

NASH,OGDEN-Private Dining Room-Bost-(1953)-Little,Brown-1st ed (d10,f,sl spot dj) 12.50

NASH,PAUL-Fertile Image-Lond-(1951)-Faber-4to-cl-1st ed (y3,dj) 65.00

NASH,RAY-American Penmanship, 1800 to 1850-Worcester-1969-Amer Antiquarian Soc-xii+303p-blk cl-1st ed (b2) 30.00

NASH,WALLIS-Two Years in Oregon-NY-1882-311p-dec cl,frntis,illus-Smith #7217 (t7) 30.00

NASMITH,GEORGE G-Timothy Eaton-Tor-1923-M&S-312p-cl,frntis port,illus,port (aa2) 25.00*

NASON,EMMA H-Old Colonial Houses in Maine Built Prior to 1776-Augusta-1908-priv prtd-4to-x,(2),106p-cl,t.e.g.,23 plts (cc10) 60.00

NATHAN,JOAN-Jewish Holiday Kitchen-(1979)-Schocken-280p-red cl,drwngs,photos-1st prtg (q8,dj) 16.50

NATHAN,JOHN-Mishima-Bost-1974-Little,Brown-1st ed (t4,f,f dj) 25.00

NATHAN,ROBERT-Bishop's Wife-(1928)-Bobbs Merril-Laurence A8-1st ed (w1,f,dj) 85.00

NATHAN,ROBERT-Morning in Iowa-NY-1944-Knopf-blnd stmpd cl-1st ed (aa9,dj) 20.00

NATHAN,ROBERT-Mr.Whittle and the Morning Star-1947-Knopf-1st ed (x2,f,sl tn dj) 15.00

NATHAN,ROBERT-Peter Kindred-NY-1919-Duffield-red stmpd blu cl,auth 1st bk-Laurence A1-1st ed (w1,lacks dj) 35.00

NATHAN,ROBERT-Portrait of Jennie-NY-1940-1st ed (s5,dj) 30.00

NATHAN,ROBERT-Portrait of Jennie-NY-1940-Knopf-Laurence A20-1st ed (w1,f,dj) 45.00

NATHAN,ROBERT-River Journey-1949-Knopf-1st ed (x2,f,dj) 15.00

NATHAN,ROBERT-So Love Returns-NY-1958-Knopf-1st ed (t4,f,f dj) 20.00

NATHAN,ROBERT-Tapiola's Brave Regiment-NY-1941-Knopf-1st ed (hh5,dj sl tn,soil) 10.00

NATHAN,ROBERT-There is Another Heaven-(1929)-Bobbs Merrill-Laurence A10-1st ed,1st state (w1,dj) 75.00

NATION,CARRY A-Use and Need of the Life of ...-Topeka-1908-396p-cl-rvsd ed (d1,rub) 20.00

NATIONAL BANK OF COMMERCE OF SEATTLE-Palo Alto-1972-Pacific Bks-277p-gry cl,illus,ltd ed-1st ed (b6,as new in dj,pres card) 10.00

NATIONAL GEOGRAPHIC SOCIETY-Book of Fishes-Wash D.C.-1924-8vo-243p-imitation lea,gilt,photos,illus-1st ed (m3,f) 20.00

NATIONAL ROAD IN SONG AND STORY-(Columbus)-(1940)-WPA-48p-wrps (c1) 25.00

NATKIN,MARCEL-Photography and the Art of Seeing-Lond-1935-Fountain Pr-70p-37 photos-1st ed (cc9) 50.00

NATL GEOGR MAGAZINE-JAN 1926. CONTAINS ILLUS-PIGEONS-wrps (y8,sl fade,wn) 12.50

NAUDE,GABRIEL-Advice on Establishing a Library...-Berkeley,LA-1950-U of Cal Pr-110p-g dec cl-1st ed (dd10,f,dj) 25.00

NAUMAN,ST.ELMO-ED.-Exorcism Through the Ages-NY-1974-Philo Libr-cl-1st ed (n8,f,dj) 15.00

NAUMBURG,E M B-Birds of Matto Grosso, Brazil-NY-1930-8vo-432p-cl,17 plts(5 col),5 maps-Bull Amer Nat Hist,Vol.60 (y8,rbnd) 95.00

NAVAJO SERVICE-1937 directory for the...-(Gallup)-(1937)-48p-wrps,ads on most pgs,maps (v7) 25.00

NAVAL HISTORY, THE MIDDLE AGES TO 1815-Lond-1976-Nat Maritime Mus-209p-12 plts-1st ed (p8,as new in dj) 50.00

NAVARRETE,FRIAR DOMINGO-Travels and Controversies of...1618 to 86-Cambridge-1962-Hakluyt Scty-8vo-475p-blu cl,gilt,18 plts & sketch maps (ll1) 60.00

NAVE,JOHANN-Handy Book to the Collection & Preparation of Freshwater & Marine Algae,Diatoms,Desmids...-Lond-1867-Hardwicke-203p-3/4 lea (x6,wn,rub,hngs weak) 45.00

NAY,CAROL-Timmy Rides the China Clipper-Chig-1939-Whitman-sm 4to-96p-cl wi pasteon,col & b&w illus,auth-1st ed (s3,f,dj) 20.00

NAYLOR,GLORIA-Women of Brewster Place-NY-(1982)-Viking-auth 1st bk-1st ed (k7,dj) 325.00

NAYLOR,JAMES B-Book of Buckeye Verse-Chig-1927-253p-cl (b1) 25.00

NEAGLE,ANNA-Anna Neagle Says "There's Always Tomorrow"-Lond-1974-W H Allen-8vo-236p-cl,illus-1st ed (ee9,dj) 15.00

NEAGOE,PETER-ED.-Americans Abroad-The Hague-1932-Servire Pr-2nd bndg of yel cl-scarce tiss cov-1st ed (e10,f,dj & tiss cov) 300.00

NEAL,ALICE-Patient Waiting No Loss-NY-1863-Appleton-182p-chromo frntis (x6) 20.00

NEAL,DOROTHY J-Captive Mountain Waters-El Paso-1961-103p-pict wrps,illus-Six Guns #1592 (t7,f,Hertzog autg) 45.00

NEAL,DOROTHY J-Cloud-Climbing Railroad-Alamagordo-1966-76p-photos,maps-scarce-1st ed (v7,f,dj,2 autgs) 45.00

NEAL,E-Natural History of Badgers-1986-Facts on File-238p-20 col photos-1st US ed (bb3,f,dj) 23.00

NEAL,J C-Root Knot Disease of the Peach, Orange, and Other Plants in Florida, due to the Work of Anguillula-Wash-1889-USDA Div. of Entomology-31p+21plts,wrps,Bull 20 (l1) 12.50

NEAME,J A-Among the Meadow and Alpine Flowers of Northern Italy-Lond-1937-Mortiboy-192p-cl,16 watercols (x6,sl fox) 25.00

NEARING,SCOTT-Tragedy of Empire-NY-1945-Island Pr-wrps-1st ed (v5,sl wn) 25.00

NEASHAM,V AUBREY-Wild Legacy-Berkeley-1973-8vo-178p-illus (m3,as new in dj) 12.50

NEATBY,LESLIE H-In Quest of the Northwest Passage-NY-(1958)-Crowell-194p-fldg map,illus-1st Amer ed (ll8,dj) 25.00

NEATBY,LESLIE H-Search for Franklin-Edmonton-1970-Hurtig-8vo-281p-13 photos,5 maps-1st ed (cc7,sl chip dj) 20.00*

NEBESKY-WOJKOWITZ,R-Where the Gods are Mountains-NY-1956-256p (o10,f,dj) 28.00

NEBLETTE,C B-Photographic Lenses-Hastings on Hudson-1965-Morgan & Morgan-152p-illus-1st ed (cc9,f,dj) 35.00

NEBRASKA-History of the State of...-(1975)-sm folio-2 vols-illus-orig publ in 1882 by Wstrn Hist Co (bb4) 95.00

NEBRASKA-STANDARD ATLAS OF DIXON AND DAKOTA COUNTIES,...-Chig-1911-117;xxii pgs-cl,31 col maps-LeGear L 2212 (e1,rebkd,soil t.p.,wn cors) 100.00

NECKER,CLAIRE-Four Centuries of Cat Books-Metuchen-1972-Scarecrow Pr-8vo-viii,512p-1st ed (ff9,as new) 20.00*

NEEDHAM,J G-Life of Inland Waters-Ithaca-1916-8vo-438p+errata slip,illus,photos-scarce-1st ed (m3,some underlining) 40.00

NEEDHAM,JOSEPH-Biochemistry and Morphogenesis-Cambridge-1942-Cambridge U Pr-xvi+787p-grn cl,35 plts-1st ed (a2,sl wn) 75.00

NEEDHAM,JOSEPH-Great Amphibium-NY-1932-Scribner's-180p-blu cl-1st Amer ed (a2,sl wn dj) 20.00

NEEDHAM,JOSEPH-History of Embryology-NY-(1959)-Abelard Schuman-304p-red cl,18 plts-2nd ed,rvsd (c2,dj) 65.00

NEEDHAM,JOSEPH-History of Embryology-NY-1959-304p-illus-2nd ed (dd3,ex-libr) 75 00

NEEDHAM,P R-Trout Streams-NY-1938-233p-photos (ee3,dj chip) 55.00

NEEDHAM,PAUL-Rainbow Trout In Mexico & California-Berkeley-1959-4to-123p-wrps,photos (m3,vf) 40.00

NEEDHAM,RODNEY-Belief, Language, and Experience-Oxford-(1972)-Blackwell-8vo-269p-papr over bds-1st ed (y5,dj) 20.00

NEELY,HAROLD G-Wildcatting from Pennsylvania to Texas-Ft.Worth-1976-auth-54p-wrps,photos-ltd to 500c (ee10) 50.00

NEF,J U-Rise of the British Coal Industry-Lond-1932-Routledge & Sons-2 vols,maroon cl,fldg maps-1st ed (j2) 50.00

NEFF,ISABEL H-Text Book of Cookery for the Use of Schools-(Cin)-1899-57p+ads-pict bds-Brown 3707 (k1,sl wn) 15.00

NEFF,WALLACE-Architecture of Southern Calif-Chig-1964-illus-1st ed (h10,dj) 125.00

NEGRI,N C-Valley of Shadows-Lond-1956-196p-plts,maps-1st ed (q10,f) 18.00

NEIDER,CHARLES-Authentic Death of Hendry Jones-NY-(1956)-Harper & Bros-1st ed (b10,sl wn dj) 40.00

NEIHARDT,JOHN G-All is But a Beginning-NY-1972-HBJ-1st ed (y1,f,dj) 25.00

NEIHARDT,JOHN G-Black Elk Speaks-NY-1932-Morrow-280p-col illus-1st ed (dd4,wn) 40.00

NEIHARDT,JOHN G-River and I-NY-1927-199p-plts-later ed (t7,dj) 35.00

NEIHARDT,JOHN G-Splendid Wayfaring-NY-1920-290p-frntis,photos,maps-Rader #2476-1st ed (t7,f) 45.00

NEIL,MARION H-How to Cook in Casserole Dishes-NY-(c.1912)-David McKay-252p-illus bds-Bitting p.340 (a8) 25.00

NEILL,EDWARD D-Effort and Failure to Civilize the Aborigines-Wash-1868-GPO-15p-wrps-1st ed (bb4) 75.00

NEILL,EDWARD D-History of Minnesota-Phila-1858-Lippincott-xlviii,628p-4 maps(1 fldg)-1st ed (o2,sl wn,sp chip,fldg map tn) 95.00

NEIMAN,LEROY-Art & Life Style-NY-1974-Felicie-folio-300 col illus-1st prtg (h10,dj) 50.00

NELSON,BEATRICE-State Recreation Parks Forests and Game Preserves-Wash D.C.-1928-Nat Conference State Prks-436p-wrps (x6) 30.00

NELSON,BRUCE-Land of the Dacotahs-Mpls-(1946)-U of Minn Pr-354p-illus-1st ed (gg4,dj) 20.00

NELSON,BRYAN-Seabirds-Lond-1980-Hamlyn-224p (c9,f,f dj) 30.00

NELSON,DALE,CO.-Nelson's Home Comforts-Lond-1895-126p-red cl-16th ed,rvsd & enlgd by Mary Hooper (q8) 25.00

NELSON,E W-Report upon Natural History Collections Made in Alaska...-Wash-1887-Henshaw,ed.-4to-337p-cl,12 col plts (y8,crack) 140.00

NELSON,E W-Wild Animals of North America-Wash D C-1918-8vo-227p-photos (m3) 17.50

NELSON,E W-Wild Animals of North America-Wash-1930-Nat'l Geographic Scty-254p-fabrikoid,col illus (l1) 15.00

NELSON,EDNA-California Dons-1962-Appleton Century-309p-1st ed (d3,dj) 25.00

NELSON,FREDERICK-Beyond the Horizon-Portland-1930-publ by auth-12mo-292p-grn cl-Smith #7262-v scarce (b6) 37.00

NELSON,HERBERT-Literary Impulse in Pioneer Oregon-Corvallis-1948-86p-wrps,illus (r8) 30.00

NELSON,J BRYAN-Sulidae: Gannets and Boobies-1978-U of Abrdeen/Oxford U Pr-1012p (e9,as new in dj) 125.00

NELSON,J RALEIGH-Lady Unafraid-Caldwell-1952-Caxton-278p-cl,illus (z7,tattrd dj) 40.00

NELSON,JAMES-ED.-Complete Murder Sampler-NY-1946-Dbldy CC-1st ed (f4,chip dj) 25.00

NELSON,JOHN L-Rhythm for Rain-Bost-1937-Houghton Mifflin-272p-photos,pntngs-1st ed (ee4,dj) 30.00

NELSON,LINDSEY-Backstage at the Mets-1966-Viking-1st ed (s8,dj) 17.50

NELSON,LOWRY-Mormon Village-SLC-1952-U of Utah Pr-296p-photos,maps-1st ed (d3) 35.00

NELSON,MARY C-Masters of Western Art-NY-1982-Watson Guptill-4to-176p-cl,col & b&w illus-1st ed (z4,f,sl wn dj) 15.00

NELSON,MARY-Pablita Velarde-1971-Dillon Pr-58p-illus-1st ed (d3) 15.00

NELSON,NARKA-Western College for Women-Oxford-1967-295p-cl (d1,sl wn dj) 15.00

NELSON,RICHARD K-Hunters of the Northern Ice-(1969)-U of Chig Pr-xxiv,429p-photos-1st ed (ll8,dj) 15.00

NELSON,RICHARD K-Hunters of the Northern Ice-1969-U of Chig-429p-illus-1st ed (u8,dj) 22.00

NELSON,W-Eskimo About Bering Strait-1899-Bur Amer Ethnol 18th Ann Rept-4to-518p-107 plts (bb3,cov sl wn) 45.00

NELSON,WILLIAM-Beginnings of the Iron Industry in Trenton, New Jersey, 1723 to 1750-Phila-1911-16p-wrps-ltd to 100c-rprntd from Penn Mag of Hist & Biog (aa6) 35.00

NELSON,WILLIAM-Fees in Criminal Cases of Justices of the Peace and Constables in New Jersey...-Paterson-1888-33p-wrps (aa6,sl chip) 45.00

NELSON,WILLIAM-Founding of Paterson as the Intended Manufacturing Metropolis of the United States-Newark-1887-17p-wrps (aa6) 35.00

NELSON,WILLIAM-History of the City of Paterson and the County of Passaic, New Jersey-Paterson-1901-4to-viii,448p-cl-Vol.I all publ-text on last pg ends in mid-sentence (aa6,frnt pastedwn mrkd) 450.00

NELSON,WILLIAM-Nelson's Biographical Cyclopedia of New Jersey-NY-1913-4to-2 vols-mod cl,port (aa6,rbnd) 175.00

NELSON,WILLIAM-Personal Names of Indians of New Jersey-Paterson-1904-83p-cl-ltd to 250c (aa6) 50.00

NELSON,WILLIAM-Records of the Paterson Fire Association, 1821 to 1854-Paterson-1894-(4),263p-wrps,plts-ltd to 100c (aa6,wrps brittle) 75.00

NELSON,WILLIAM-Some New Jersey Printers and Printing in the Eighteenth Century-Worcester-1911-44p-prtd wrps (aa6) 50.00

NEMECEK,OTTOKAR-Virginity-NY-(1958)-Philo Libr-8vo-vi,129p-cl,illus (z5,dj) 20.00

NEMEROV,HOWARD-Guide to the Ruins-NY-1950-dec bds-1st ed (s5,sl chip dj) 30.00

NEMEROV,HOWARD-Melodramatists-NY-1949-1st ed (o5,sl chip dj) 40.00

NEMEROV,HOWARD-Western Approaches-Chig-1975-Univ of Chig-1st ed (h8,f,dj) 20.00

NEPRUD,ROBERT E-Flying Minute Men-NY-(1948)-DSP-8vo-243p-16p photos-1st ed (gg5,dj edgewn,chip) 15.00

NERN,D-Black as Night-1958-Beacon Pr-auth 1st bk-1st ed (x2,lt tape mrkd e.p.,dj) 35.00

NERNST,WALTER-Theoretical Chemistry from the Standpoint of Avogadro's Rule & Thermodynamics-Lond-1895-697p-1st Engl transl (dd3,f) 200.00

NERUDA,PABLO-Captain's Verses-1972-New Directions-1st Amer ed (x2,f,dj) 30.00

NERUDA,PABLO-Fully Empowered-NY-1975-bilingual ed-1st US ed (q5,f,dj) 25.00

NERUDA,PABLO-Fully Empowered-NY-1975-FS&G-bilingual ed-1st US ed (h8,f,dj) 30.00

NERUDA,PABLO-Let the Rail Splitter Awake and Other Poems-NY-1950-Masses & Mainstreams-prtd wrps-1st Amer ed (r2,sl rub) 25.00

NERVI,PIER L-Aesthetics & Technology in Building-1965-Harvard U Pr-oblng 8vo-1st ed (h10,dj) 50.00

NESBITT,PAUL H-Ancient Mimbrenos-Beloit-1931-Logan Mus-photos-1st ed (b4) 65.00

NESS,F C-Practical Dope on the Big Bores-PA-1948-436p-photos (gg3,sl loose) 95.00

NESSMUK-Woodcraft-NY-1936-12mo-188p-wrps,illus (m3,f) 18.50

NESTLER,AL-Al Nestler's Southwest-Flagstaff-1970-92p-dec cl,col frntis,col plts-ltd ed (t7,f) 10.00

NESTOR,SARAH-ED.-Spanish Textile Tradition of New Mexico and Colorado-Santa Fe-(1979)-oblng-259p-wrps,dbl col,col photos,maps-1st ed (u7,f) 35.00

NETBOY,ANTHONY-Atlantic Salmon,a Vanishing Species??-Bost-1968-8vo-457p-photos-1st prntg (m3,f,dj) 35.00

NETBOY,ANTHONY-Columbia River Salmon & Steelhead Trout-Seattle-1980-8vo-180p-photos-1st ed (m3,vf,dj) 13.50

NETBOY,ANTHONY-Columbia River Salmon and Steelhead Trout-1980-U of Wash-180p-photos (bb3,f,dj) 20.00

NETBOY,ANTHONY-ED.-Pacific Northwest-GC-1963-8vo-191p-photos (m3,f,dj) 12.50

NETBOY,ANTHONY-Salmon of the Pacific Northwest-Portland-1958-8vo-122p-illus (m3,vf,dj) 13.00

NETBOY,ANTHONY-Salmon the World's Most Harassed Fish-NY-1980-8vo-304p-photos,maps-1st ed (m3,vf,dj) 15.00

NETBOY,ANTHONY-Salmon,Their Fight for Survival-Bost-1973-8vo-612p-photos-1st prntg (m3,vf,dj) 30.00

NETHERTON,CLIFF-Angling & Casting-S Brunswick-1977-8vo-157p-photos-1st ed (m3,vf,dj) 12.00

NETTLES,GRAIG-Balls-1984-Putnam-1st ed (ff2,f,dj) 10.00

NEUBURG,VICTOR E-Penny Histories-Lond-1968-OUP-illus-1st ed (ll5,f,dj) 35.00

NEUBURGER,MAX-British Medicine and the Vienna School, Contacts and Parallels-Lond-1943-134p-1st ed (dd3) 75.00

NEUFELD,CHARLES-Prisoner of the Khaleefa-Lond-1899-365p-red cl,illus (gg2) 150.00

NEUGEBOREN,JAY-Corky's Brother-1969-FS&G-1st ed (s8,f,dj) 20.00

NEUGEBOREN,JAY-Sam's Legacy-1974-HRW-1st ed (s8,f,dj) 25.00

NEUHAUS,EUGENE-History & Ideals of American Art-1931-Stanford U Pr-4to-cl-1st ed (oo6,vf,dj) 180.00

NEUMAN,J J-Polyporaceae of Wisconsin-Madison-1914-State/Geol Nat Hist Survy-207p-cl,25 plts (x6) 40.00

NEUMANN,A H-Elephant Hunting in East Equatorial Africa-NY-1966-455p-photos,col plts,fldg map-A & F Libr rprnt (gg3,vf) 100.00

NEUMANN,E-ED.-Bauhaus & Bauhaus People-NY-1970 (ee1,dj) 85.00

NEUMANN,ERWIN-Wilhelm Thony-Vienna-1957-Bruder Rosenbaum-4to-14p text-blu cl,24 col plts (r10,f dj) 15.00

NEUMANN,RUTH V-Cooking with Spirits-Chig-(1961)-Reilly & Lee-249p-blu cl-1st ed (q8,dj wn) 12.50

NEURER,RONI-UKIYO-E-NY-1981-Mayflower-4to-390p-blk cl,col illus (r10,f dj) 45.00

NEUSTADT,DR EGON-Lamps of Tiffany-1970-Fairfield Pr-220p-300 plts(238 col) (cc8) 195.00

NEVADA-Check List of...Imprints, 1859 to 1890-Chig-1939-Hist Rec Survey/WPA-4to-127p-stiff wrps-No.7 of Amer Imprnts Invntry (x4,lacks frnt cov) 45.00

NEVADA-Cook Book of the Womens Art and Industrial Association of...-(1973)-Valley Bank of Nev-168p-blk cl-facs of orig 1887 Carson City ed (q8,f) 25.00

NEVE,ARTHUR-Picturesque Kashmir-Lond-1899-163p-gold stmpd sp & cov,54 illus,3 diags-1st ed (a4) 140.00

NEVILL,JOHN T-Wanderings-NY-1956-Expo-216p-cl (z7,dj) 30.00

NEVILL,RALPH-British Military Prints-Lond-1909-72p+24 col plts & 127 b&w illus-dec red cl-1st ed (b7) 175.00

NEVILLE,A W-Red River Valley Then & Now-Paris,Tx-(1948)-278p-illus,e.p. maps-ltd to 2000c-Six Guns #1604 (cc4,dj) 125.00

NEVILLE,A W-Red River Valley Then and Now-Paris-(1948)-No Tex Publ-278p-pict dj,illus,map e.p.,ltd to 2000c (f9,dj) 150.00

NEVILLE,RALPH-Old English Sporting Prints and Their History-Lond-1923-Studio-4to-ltd to 1500c (f10) 175.00

NEVINS,ALLAN-John D Rockefeller-1940-Scribner's-2 vols-cl,photos-1st ed (ee10) 45.00

NEVINS,ALLAN-Ordeal of the Union-NY-1947 to 1971-8 vols-illus (n3,dj) 150.00

NEW AMERICAN PRIMARY SPELLER-NY,Cin,Chig-(1872)-Amer Bk Co-72p-pict bds,illus (k1) 15.00

NEW BRUNSWICK DIRECTORY, FOR 1877-'8-by Babcock & Johnson-New Brunswick-1877-x,(17)-308p+ads-lea backd bds (aa6,sp wn) 125.00

NEW DIRECTIONS 16-NY-1957-New Directions-1st ed (v5,dj) 20.00

NEW EMPIRES IN THE NORTHWEST-NY-(1889)-Tribune Assoc-Libr of Trib Extras, Vol.I, No.8-1st ed (e1,sl wn sp,wrps sl dmpstnd) 50.00

NEW ENGLAND AVIATORS 1914 TO 1918-Bost-1919,1920-thk 8vo-2 vols-cl,ports (s2,sm hole sp of vol.2) 750.00

NEW HAMPSHIRE FISH & GAME COMMISSIONER-Report-Concord-June 1884-8vo-71p-illus (m3) 25.00

NEW JERSEY AND THE NEGRO-A Bibliography, 1715 to 1966...-(np)-1967-196p-cl (aa6) 30.00

NEW JERSEY-Archives of the State of... Subset-Newark-1880 to 1886-10 vols-cl-vol.I thru X (aa6) 175.00

NEW JERSEY-Archives of the State of...-1800-1949-48 vols-cl-complete first & second ser (aa6) 1,500.00

NEW JERSEY-Atlas of...-(np)-(1888)-lg folio-(2)p+19 dbl pgd col maps-orig lea backed cl (aa6,sl chip sp) 400.00

NEW JERSEY-Collecting...Antiques-Union City-(1978)-x,374p-cl,illus,col plts (aa6) 35.00

NEW JERSEY-Early Furniture Made in.... 1690 to 1870-Newark-1958-Newark Mus-89p-wrps,illus (aa6) 45.00

NEW JERSEY-Geological Survey of...-Trenton-1856-viii,248p-plts,2 fldg maps (aa6) 60.00

NEW JERSEY-State Atlas of...-NY-1872-folio-122,(12)p-mor backd cl,hand col maps (aa6,sp broken) 550.00

NEW JERSEY-The Industrial Directory of...-Trenton-1906-xxiv,534p-cl,fldg map (aa6) 50.00

NEW JERSEY-Work in...-(np)-(1936)-4to-(5),81,vii p-wrps,plts (aa6) 30.00

NEW MEXICO FOLKLORE RECORD-VOL IX,1954 THRU 1955-wrps-scarce (u7) 65.00

NEW MEXICO-Directory of Churches and Religious Organizations in...1940-Albuq-1940-NM Hist Rec Survey(WPA)-341p-wrps,maps-v scarce-1st ed (v7) 60.00

NEW MEXICO-Otherwise, the Voyage of Anthony of Espero, Who in the Year 1883...-(Lancaster)-(1928)-51p-ltd to 200c,autg-1st ed thus (v7,sl chip) 200.00

NEW MEXICO-Report of Gov of New Mex to Sec of Int-Wash-1894-45p-wrps-1st ed (t7) 65.00

NEW MEXICO-Report of Gov of New Mex-Wash-1902-wrps,maps(incl fldg)-1st ed (t7) 75.00

NEW MEXICO-Resources of...-Santa Fe-1881-64p incl ads-wrps,errata slip-Adams Herd#1658-rare-1st ed (v7,sp v chip) 350.00

NEW MEXICO-Spanish & Indian New Mexico-Denver-1882-sm oblng-26 views on 18 panels in orig cl folder-1st ed (u7,f) 100.00

NEW MEXICO-Territorial Bur of Immigr Report as to Socorro Co-Socorro-1881-6p-wrps-rare-1st ed (t7) 150.00

NEW SYSTEM OF DOMESTIC COOKERY FOR THE USE OF PRIVATE FAMILIES. BY A LADY-Lond-nd(ca.1870)-Milner & Sowerby-16mo-376p+16p ads-g stmpd 3/4 calf,engrvngs (q8,rbnd) 65.00

NEW SYSTEM OF DOMESTIC COOKERY...-Lond-nd(ca.1890)-Milner-16mo-376+16p ads-brwn cl,illus (q8,cov wn,bndg weak) 40.00

NEW TESTAMENT OF OUR LORD AND SAVIOUR JESUS CHRIST, TRANSLATED OUT OF THE ORIGINAL GREEK-Steubenville-1845-Abner L Frazer-287,(1)p-bds-prntd by L. Harper,Cadiz (j1) 85.00

NEW YORK AT GETTYSBURG-Albany-1900 to 1902-3 vols-pict cl,illus,maps,col maps e.p. pckts-1st ed (c4) 150.00

NEW YORK CENTURY RAILROAD 1831 TO 1915-np-nd(1915)-NY Central RR-31p-flex blk lea,illus (ee6) 40.00

NEW YORK CITY GUIDE-NY-(1939)-Random-thk 8vo-670p wi index,pckt map-1st ed (w1,f,dj) 75.00

NEW YORK MEDICAL JOURNAL. VOLUME 25-NY-1877-672p-1/2 lea (dd3) 45.00

NEW YORK SPORTING GOODS CO.-Sportsmen's Handbook-NY-1915-12mo-472p-wrps,illus (m3) 40.00

NEW YORK TIMES BOOK OF BASEBALL HISTORY-1975-Quadrangle-oversize-1st ed (ff2,dj) 25.00

NEW YORK YANKEES-Play Ball With the Yankees-1950-NY Yankees-photos,TP orig-1st ed (s8,wrps cov wn) 55.00

NEW ZEALAND PILOT-np(Lond)-1919-Hydrographic Dpt,Adm-8vo-578p-purple cl,fldg map-9th ed (p8,sl dmpstnd) 50.00

NEWALL,CAPTAIN J T-Hog Hunting in the East-Lond-1867-8vo-466p-full calf,gilt,illus-scarce (m3,rebkd) 85.00

NEWARK-Directory of the City of...for 1844 to 45. By B T Pierson-Newark-240p-lea backd prtd bds (aa6,wn) 175.00

NEWARK-Holbrook's...City and Business Directory for the Year Ending May 1, 1889-Newark-1888-1444p+ads-mod cl (aa6,rbnd) 125.00

NEWBERRY,MIKE-Yahoos-NY-1964-Marzani & Munsell-wrps-1st ed (v5,sp sunned) 20.00

NEWBORN,MONROE-Computer Chess-NY-1975-Academic Pr-xiv+200p-blk cl-1st ed (c2) 25.00

NEWBY,ERIC-Great Ascents-NY-1977-illus-1st ed (p10,f,dj) 30.00

NEWBY,ERIC-Great Ascents-NY-1977-Viking-photos-1st ed (e8,f,f dj) 40.00

NEWCOMB,COVELLE-Silver Saddles-NY-1943-Longmans Green-1st ed (f10,dj) 25.00

NEWCOMB,FRANC J-Navaho Neighbors-Norman-(1966)-230p-photos-1st ed (v7,f,dj) 20.00

NEWCOMB,REXFORD-Colonial and Federal House-Phila-1933-Lippincott-sm 4to-174p-illus blu cl,100 illus-1st ed (r10,dj sl spot,wn) 45.00

NEWCOMB,REXFORD-Spanish House for America-Phila-1927-97 plts-1st ed (h10,sl stnd cov) 125.00

NEWCOMB,W W,JR.-Rock Art of Texas Indians-Austin-1967-folio-239p-illus by Kirkland-scarce-1st ed (n10,f,dj) 125.00

NEWELL,A DONALD-Gunstock Finishing & Care-Georgetown-1949-8vo-444p-illus-1st prntg (m3) 35.00

NEWELL,CHARLES M-Kamehameha, the Conquering King-NY,Lond-1885-Putnam's-8vo-viii,399p-olive grn cl,frntis-1st ed (t10) 75.00

NEWELL,CHESTER-History of the Revolution in Texas-1838-Wiley & Putnam-215p-Howes N115-1st ed (a9,lacks fldg map) 250.00

NEWELL,GORDON-Pacific Tugboats-Seattle-1957-Superior Publ-4to-191p-ltd to 2000c,autg,pres by Henry Broderick wi "HB" signature-Autographed Ed (b6,dj,pres cpy) 37.50

NEWELL,GORDON-Paddlewheel Pirate-NY-1959-Dutton-8vo-248p-6 illus-1st ed (cc5,dj) 15.00

NEWELL,GORDON-Ships of the Inland Sea-(1951)-Binfords & Mort-241p-illus-1st ed (r8,dj chip,pcs missng) 25.00

NEWELL,GORDON-Westward to Alki-Seattle-1977-Superior-sm 4to-122p wi index,photos-1st ed (t1,dj) 20.00

NEWELL,ROBERT-Robert Newell's Memoranda-Portland-1959-Champoeg-1st ed (b4) 60.00

NEWELL,ROBERT-Roebert Newell's Memoranda-(Portland)-1959-4to-159p-illus-ltd to 1000c (bb9) 100.00

NEWELL,WILLIAM W-Games and Songs of American Children-NY-(c.1883,1903)-Harper & Bros-282p-new & enlgd ed (a8) 50.00

NEWHALL,BEAUMONT-Airborne Camera-NY-1969-Hastings Hs-4to-144p-cl,photos-1st ed (q3,f,dj) 55.00

NEWHALL,BEAUMONT-Discovery of Photography-NY-1967-Dbldy-8vo-148p-cl-1st ed (q3,dj) 65.00

NEWHALL,BEAUMONT-History of Photography-NY-(1964)-MOMA-blu cl,g sp lettrng-rvsd & enlg ed (y3,dj) 50.00

NEWHALL,BEAUMONT-History of Photography-NY-1949-MOMA-4to-cl-1st ed (y3,f,dj) 65.00

NEWHALL,BEAUMONT-In Plain Sight: The Photographs of...-SLC-1983-1st ed (ff10,dj) 22.50

NEWHALL,BEAUMONT-Masters of Photography-NY-1958-Braziller-4to-cl-1st ed (y3,pgs sl brwnd,dj rub,chip) 60.00

NEWHALL,LOUIS C-Minor Chateaux and Manor Houses of France of the XV and XVI Century-NY-1914-Arch Bk Publ-4to-beige cl sp,tan bds,illus (r10,sp drknd) 40.00

NEWHALL,NANCY-Pageant of History in Northern California-SF-1954-Amer Trust-folio-spiral bnd wrps-1st ed (y3) 85.00

NEWHALL,NANCY-Paul Strand. Photographs 1915 to 1945-NY-1945-MOMA-4to-32p-cl-1st ed (t3) 45.00

NEWHALL,NANCY-Photographs of Edward Weston-NY-1946-MOMA-36p-wrps,23 photos-rare-1st ed (cc9) 60.00

NEWHALL,RUTH W-Newhall Ranch-San Marino-1958-Huntington Libr-viii+120p-dec bds,plts-1st ed (k2,dj) 22.00

NEWHAN,ROSS-California Angels-1982-S&S-1st ed (s7,dj) 12.50

NEWHOUSE,S-Trapper's Guide and Manual of Instructions for Capturing all Kinds of Fur Bearing Animals...-NY-1894-Forest & Stream-205p+appndx-9th ed,rvsd (nn6,sl wn sp) 50.00

NEWKIRK,NEWTON-Stealthy Steve-Bost-1904-Luce-pict cov,illus-1st ed (j4) 15.00

NEWMAN,A-Rondeaux of Boyhood-Lond-1923-ltd to 250c-1st ed (y7,unopened) 125.00

NEWMAN,ARNOLD-Faces USA-GC-1978-Amphoto-111p-92 photos-1st ed (cc9,dj tn) 30.00

NEWMAN,CHARLES-Evolution of Medical Education in the Nineteenth Century-Lond-1957-340p-1st ed (dd3) 100.00

NEWMAN,GEORGE-Interpreters of Nature-NY-1927-296p-1st ed (dd3,dj) 25.00

NEWMAN,SAMUEL P-Practical System of Rhetoric-Portland/Andover-1829-Shirley & Hyde/M Newman-252p-bds-Amer Imprnts 39481-2nd ed (k1) 27.50

NEWMARK,HARRIS-Sixty Years in Southern California 1853 to 1913-Bost-1930-Houghton Mifflin-xxxv,744p-illus-3rd,rvsd ed (n2) 45.00

NEWMARK,MAXIM-Dictionary of Spanish Literature-NY-1956-Philo Libr-1st ed (z3,dj) 10.00

NEWPORT,DAVID-Indices, Historical and Rational, to a Revision of the Scriptures-Phila-1871-Lippincott-16mo-220p-1st ed (y6) 12.00

NEWSHOLME,ARTHUR-Evolution of Preventive Medicine-Balt-1927-226p-1st Amer ed (dd3) 75.00

NEWSHOLME,SIR ARTHUR-Story of Modern Preventive Medicine-Balt-1929-Williams & Wilkins-xii+295p+ads-grn dec cl-1st ed (a2,sl fox,dj) 55.00

NEWSOM,DAVID-Western Observer 1805 to 1882-1972-OR Hist Soc-299p-wrps,illus,7 maps (r8,f) 16.00

NEWTON,A EDWARD-Amenities of Book Collecting and Kindred Affections-Bost-1918-Atlantic-1st ed (w1) 25.00

NEWTON,A EDWARD-Bibliography and Psuedo Bibliography-Phila-1936-U of Penn Pr-116p-cl bckd bds,frntis,illus-1st ed (dd10,f,dj) 25.00

NEWTON,A EDWARD-Derby Day and Other Adventures-Bost-1934-col frontis,24 b&w illus-1st ed (h5,sp brwnd,sp tan dj) 45.00

NEWTON,A EDWARD-Magnificent Farce and Other Diversions of a Book Collector-Bost-(1921)-t.e.g.,illus-1st ed (hh10,sl rub) 30.00

NEWTON,A EDWARD-Newton on Blackstone-Phila-1937-U of Penn-ltd to 2000c,nbrd,autg-1st ed (w1,dj) 20.00

NEWTON,A EDWARD-Rare Books Original Drawings Autograph Letters and Manuscripts Collected by...Sale Catalogue-NY-1941-3 vols-illus-1st ed (hh10,djs sl chip & tn) 100.00

NEWTON,A EDWARD-Tourist in Spite of Himself-Bost-1930-Little,Brown-1st trd ed (w1,f,dj) 17.50

NEWTON,HELMUT-Sleepless Nights-NY-1978-Congreve Publ-4to-172p-cl,photos-1st ed (t3,dj) 75.00

NEWTON,HELMUT-World Without Men-NY-(1984)-Xavier Moreau-4to-cl-1st ed (qq1,f,f dj) 60.00

NEWTON,HUEY P-Revolutionary Suicide-NY-(1973)-Harcourt-1st ed (v5,f,dj) 45.00

NEWTON,HUEY P-Revolutionary Suicide-NY-(1973)-HBJ-333p-1st ed (r1,f,sl tn dj) 25.00

NEWTON,PETER-County of Oxford-Lond-1979-Corpus Vitrearum-246p-50 plts(incl col) (cc8,dj) 125.00

NEWTON,W-Twenty Years on the Saskatchewan, N.W. Canada-Lond-1897-viii,184p-6 illus (a7,stamp on e.p.s) 125.00

NEYMAN,JERZY-Selection of Early Statistical Papers of...-Berkeley-1967-Univ of Cal Pr-4to-x+429p-grn cl-1st ed (j2,dj) 30.00

NIALL,IAN-Country Blacksmith-Lond-1966-Heinemann-1st ed (h9,dj) 45.00

NICE,MARGARET M-Watcher at the Nest-NY-1939-Macmillan-8vo-159p-sketches-1st ed (dd5,sl chip dj) 20.00

NICHOL,J R-Stepping Stones to the South Pole-Sydney-(1948)-Angus & Robertson-xxi,199p-illus-1st ed (ll8,dj) 25.00

NICHOLAS,DONALD-ED.-Intercepted Post-Lond-1956-152p-frntis-1st ed (b7,f,dj) 30.00

NICHOLS,ALICE-Bleeding Kansas-NY-1954-Oxford U Pr-307p-map-2nd prtg (v2,dj) 20.00

NICHOLS,BEVERLEY-Cats' ABC-NY-(1960)-Dutton-sm 4to-124p-pict bds,col & b&w drwngs,D Sayer-1st US ed (r3,f,dj) 25.00

NICHOLS,BEVERLEY-Death to Slow Music-1956-Dutton-1st Amer ed (s10,dj) 12.50

NICHOLS,BEVERLEY-Forty Favorite Flowers-Lond-1964-Studio Vista-87p-40p photos-1st ed (mm4,f,dj) 30.00

NICHOLS,BEVERLEY-Green Grows the City-Lond-1930-J Cape-258p-8p photos-1st & only ed (mm4,dj rprd) 40.00

NICHOLS,BEVERLEY-Merry Hall-NY-1953-319p-drwngs-1st ed (m10,dj) 17.00

NICHOLS,BEVERLEY-Moonflower Murder-1955-Dutton-1st Amer ed (s10,soil dj) 20.00

NICHOLS,BEVERLEY-Thatched Roof-Lond-1933-J Cape-285p-pict dj-1st ed (mm4,f,dj) 35.00

NICHOLS,BOB-Shotgunner-NY-1949-373p-frntis (t7,dj) 10.00

NICHOLS,FREDERICK D-Early Architecture of Georgia-Chapel Hill-1957-UNC Pr-sm folio-xvi,292p-cl,illus (cc10) 150.00

NICHOLS,FREDERICK D-Thomas Jefferson Landscape Architect-(1978)-U Pr of Va-196p-illus-1st ed (dd9,f,dj) 30.00

NICHOLS,G W-Soldier's Story of His Regiment and Incidently of the Lawton Gordon Evans Brigade-Kennesaw-1961-291p-ports-rprnt of 1898 ed (z10,sl speckld bds) 27.50

NICHOLS,GEORGE W-Story of the Great March-NY-1865-394p+ads-pict cl,illus,fldg map-1st ed (n3,cov sl chip & soil) 65.00

NICHOLS,HENRY W-Standard Cotton Cloths and Their Construction-Fall River-1927-Dover-160p incl 32p wi 124 swatches-gry cl-presume 1st ed (dd1) 75.00

NICHOLS,HERBERT-Our Notions of Number and Space-Bost-1894-Ginn & Co-vi+201p-brwn cl-1st ed (d2,sl edge-wn) 20.00

NICHOLS,JOHN T-Fishes and Shells of the Pacific World-NY-1945-Macmillan-201p-blu cl,16 plts-1st prtg (pp1,dj) 22.50

NICHOLS,JOHN T-Representative North American Fresh-Water Fishes-NY-1942-oblng 32mo-128p-illus,A Janson (m3,f,box) 20.00

NICHOLS,JOHN-Ghost in the Music-NY-(1979)-HR&W-1st ed (g3,f,dj) 25.00

NICHOLS,JOHN-Ghost in the Music-NY-(1979)-HR&W-cl bckd bds-1st ed (aa9,f,dj) 30.00

NICHOLS,JOHN-Milagro Beanfield War-(1974)-HRW-1st ed (x2,vf,vf dj) 185.00

NICHOLS,JOHN-Milagro Beanfield War-NY,Chig,SF-(1974)-illus,R Templeton-1st ed (h5,f,dj) 175.00

NICHOLS,JOHN-Wizard of Loneliness-Lond-1966-1st Brit ed (s5,rub dj) 40.00

NICHOLS,JOHN-Wizard of Loneliness-NY-(1966)-1st ed (c5,sp dull,dj sl wn,sl tn) 60.00

NICHOLS,JOHN-Wizard of Lonliness-NY-(1966)-Putnam's-1st ed (z2,sl fade sp,dj sl rub) 45.00

NICHOLS,NELL-Good Home Cooking-Ames-1952-Iowa St College Pr-560p-blu bds (o6,wn bds) 20 00

NICHOLS,PETER-Science Fiction at Large-NY-(1976)-Harper & Row-1st US ed (l3,f,dj) 15.00

NICHOLS,ROGER L-General Henry Atkinson-(1965)-U of Okla-243p-illus,maps-1st ed (u8,dj) 25.00

NICHOLS,ROGER L-General Henry Atkinson-Norman-(1965)-243p-illus,maps-1st ed (c4,dj) 32.50

NICHOLS,ROSE S-English Pleasure Gardens-NY-1902-Macmillan-4to-xxii,(2),324p-orig dec wht cl,t.e.g.,frntis,65 plts,11 plans-1st prtg (cc10,cov sl soil) 95.00

NICHOLS,ROSE S-Spanish & Portugese Gardens-Bost-1924-Houghton Mifflin-4to-304p-cl,t.e.g.,231 illus-1st ed (cc10) 75.00

NICHOLSON,B E-ET AL-Oxford Book of Garden Flowers-Lond-1963-tall 8vo-207p-pict cl,96 col plts (x5,sl wn dj) 20.00

NICHOLSON,MEREDITH-Main Chance-Indpls-(1903)-Bobbs Merrill-419p-cl-1st ed (d1) 15.00

NICHOLSON,MEREDITH-Poet-Bost,NY-1914-Houghton,Mifflin-t.e.g.,4 col plts-1st ed (bb1) 35.00

NICHOLSON,MEREDITH-Zelda Dameron-Indpls-(1904)-411p-cl-1st ed,2nd state (j1) 15.00

NICHOLSON,PETER-Principles of Architecture, Volume the Second-Lond-1797-8vo-81p+fldg illus-qtr calf (b6,fox) 195.00

NICHOLSON,WILLIAM G-Pete Gray-Pleasantville-(1976)-(32)p-wrps (n1) 12.50

NICODEMUS OF THE HOLY MOUNTAIN-ED.-Unseen Warfare-Lond-1963-Faber & Faber-cl-1st prtg (n8,f,dj) 45.00

NICOL,C W-From the Roof of Africa-1972-Knopf-362p-col & b&w photos-1st ed (bb3,f,dj) 19.00

NICOL,ERIC-Sense & Nonsense-Tor-(1947)-Ryerson-auth 1st bk-1st Can ed (hh5,dj soil,sl chip) 10.00

NICOL,HUGH-Plant Growth Substances-NY-1938-Chemical-108p-cl (x6) 15.00

NICOLAS,J-Rose Odyssey-NY-1937-Dbldy-238p (x6,dj) 15.00

NICOLL,HENRY-Salmon and Other Things-Lond-1923-12mo-168p-illus,photos (m3) 25.00

NICOLL,M J-Three Voyages of a Naturalist-Lond-1908-Witherby & Co-56p photo plts,4 maps-1st ed (p6) 75.00

NICOLLET,JOSEPH N-Journals of...-St.Paul-(1970)-Minn Hist Soc-288p-map e.p.-ltd to 2000c-1st ed (cc4,dj) 30.00

NICOLLS,WILLIAM J-Story of American Coals-Phila-1897-Lippincott-405p-blu cl-1st ed (c2,cov sl spot) 40.00

NICOLSON,BENEDICT-Joseph Wright of Derby-Lond-1968-P Mellon Fndtn Brit Art-4to-2 vols-grn cl,b&w & col illus (r10,f,dj) 75.00

NICOLSON,HAROLD-English Sense of Humor-NY-1968-Funk & Wagnalls-1st ed (z9,dj) 15.00

NICOLSON,JOHN-ED.-Arizona of Joseph Pratt Allyn, Letters from a Pioneer Judge-Tucson-1974-U of Ariz-284p-1st ed (dd7,as new in dj) 18.50

NICOLSON,JOHN-ED.-Arizona of Joseph Pratt Allyn-Tucson-1974-U of Ariz Pr-sm 4to-xviii+284p,cl-1st ed (z4,dj) 15.00

NICOLSON,MARJORIE H-Voyages to the Moon-NY-1948-Macmillan-8vo-1st ed (s1,f,dj) 45.00

NICOSIA,GERALD-Memory Babe-NY-(1983)-Grove-767p-1st ed (q1,vf,dj) 30.00

NIECKS,FREDERICK-Frederick Chopin as Man and Musician-Lond-1890-Novello-2 vols (u4) 22.00
NIEDERER,FRANCIS J-Town of Fincastle-(1965)-U Pr of Va-68p-illus,fldg pckt map-1st ed (dd9) 25.00
NIEDIECK,P-With Rifle in Five Continents-Lond-1908-426p+ads-32 full-pg photos-transl fr German by Ward (gg3) 175.00
NIEDRACH,R J-Birds of Denver and Mountain Parks-np-1959(1939)-8vo-(3),203p-cl,fldg map,photos (y8) 18.50
NIELSEN,HELEN-Crime is Murder-NY-1956-Morrow-1st ed (d4,dj) 20.00
NIELSON,D-ED.-Saga of the U.S. Air Mail Service. 1918 to 1927-np-1962-sm 4to-xiv,128p-cl & illus bds,plts (s2) 25.00
NIEMCEWICZ,JULIAN U-Under Their Vine and Fig Tree-Elizabeth-(1965)-Coll of NJ Hist Soc,#14-398p-cl,plts (aa6) 35.00
NIETHAMMER,CAROLYN-American Indian Food and Lore-NY-(1974)-Macmillan-4to-191p-brn bds,illus-1st prtg (u6) 35.00
NIEZYCHOWSKI,COUNT ALFRED VON-Cruise of the Kronprinz Wilhelm-NY-1938-Sun Dial-8vo-blu cl,photos (p8,wn dj) 25.00
NIGHTINGALE,FLORENCE-Notes on Nursing-Lond-(1860)-79p-"the right of Translation is reserved" on t.p.,printers errors in text not corrected-1st ed (dd3) 400.00
NIGHTINGALE,FLORENCE-Selected Writings of...-NY-1954-Macmillan-cl-1st prtg (o8,f,dj) 19.00
NIKOLAIDIS,GEORGE-Japanese Nudes and the Amateur Photographer-Rutland/Tokyo-(1965)-Tuttle-110p-pict wrps,illus-1st ed (kk1,cov sl soil) 25.00
NIKOLAYEVA,GALINA-Harvest-Moscow-1953-Foreign Lang Publ-8vo-622p-frntis,port-1st ed in Engl (w6,f,dj) 45.00
NIKOLSKY,ALEXANDER A-Helicopter Analysis-NY-(1951)-John Wiley & Sons-xii+340p-blu cl-1st ed (l2,dj) 25.00
NILES,BLAIR-James-NY,Tor-(1939)-359,(13)p-cl-"Second Large Printing" on dj flap (c1,dj) 17.50
NIMROD-My Horses...-Edinburgh/NY-1928-Blackwood/Scribner-1st US ed (f10,dj) 65.00
NIMS,MARION-Woman in the War: a Bibliography-Wash-1918-77p-wrps-1st ed (dd3) 35.00
NIN,ANAIS-Anais Nin Reader-Chig-1973-Swallow-1st ed (e8,f,f dj) 45.00
NIN,ANAIS-Children of the Albatross-1947-Dutton-1st ed (x2,sl rub dj) 95.00
NIN,ANAIS-Collages-Chig-1964-sftbnd orig,wrps-1st ed (s5) 15.00
NIN,ANAIS-D H Lawrence-Lond-1961-1st Brit ed (s5,dj) 45.00
NIN,ANAIS-Delta of Venus-NY-(1977)-Harcourt Brace-1st ed (dd2,f,dj) 30.00
NIN,ANAIS-Ladders to Fire-NY-1946-Dutton-1st ed (dd2,f,dj) 50.00
NIN,ANAIS-Ladders to Fire-NY-1946-Dutton-8vo-213p-engrvngs,I Hugo-1st ed (w6,dj sl chip & wn) 45.00
NIN,ANAIS-Ladders to Fire-NY-1946-Dutton-8vo-cl-1st ed (x3,f dj) 75.00
NIN,ANAIS-Little Birds-NY-1979-1st ed (r5,f,dj) 15.00
NIN,ANAIS-Novel of the Future-NY-1968-1st ed (s5,f,dj) 25.00
NIN,ANAIS-On Writing-Yonkers-(1947)-Alicat Bk Shop-8vo-stapled wrps-ltd to 1000c-1st ed (x10) 35.00
NIN,ANAIS-Realism and Reality-Yonkers-1946-Alicat Bk Shop-8vo-stapled prntd wrps-ltd to 750c-1st ed (x10) 25.00
NIN,ANAIS-Winter of Artifice-np-nd-pict bds,engrvngs by Ian Hugo-1st ed (dd2) 65.00
NININGER,H H-Nininger Collection of Meteorites-Winslow-1950-Amer Meteorite Mus-144p-tan cl,38 plts (a2) 25.00
NISSEN,HARTVIG-A B C of the Swedish System of Educational Gymnastics-NY,Bost,Chig-(1892)-Educ Publ Co-107p+ads-cl,illus (b1) 20.00
NIVEN,LARRY-Lucifer's Hammer-(Chig)-(1977)-Playboy Pr-1st ed (a5,sl wn dj) 40.00
NIX,E D-Oklahombres-St.Louis-(1919)-auth-280p-cl,plastic dj (z1,wn dj) 65.00
NIX,E D-Oklahombres-St.Louis-(1929)-xx,280p-cl,photos-1st ed (v1,chip dj) 85.00
NIX,JAMES E-Mission Among the Buffalo-Tor-1960-Ryerson Pr-8vo-viii,123p-2 maps,10 illus-1st ed (aa7,sl rub dj) 45.00*
NIXON,O W-Whitman's Ride Through Savage Lands-Winona-1905-186p-pict cl,frntis,photos-Smith #7330-1st ed (t7,f) 17.50
NIXON,O W-Whitman's Ride Through Savage Lands-Winona-1905-186p-pict cov,17 illus (r8) 45.00
NIXON,PAT I-Medical Story of Early Texas, 1528 to 1853-1946-Mollie B Lupe Mem Fund-507p-1st ed (a9) 145.00
NIXON,RICHARD-Challenges We Face-NY-(1960)-McGraw Hill-auth 1st bk-1st ed (hh5,f,dj) 50.00
NIXON,ROBERT B,JR.-Corner Druggist-NY-1941-291p-1st ed (g10) 25.00
NOBBS,P E-Salmon Tactics-Lond-1934-8vo-147p-illus-1st ed (m3,f) 70.00
NOBILE,U-My Polar Flights-Lond-(1961)-8vo-288p-cl,frntis,12p plts-1st ed (s2,sp fade) 25.00
NOBLE,JOSEPH-From Cab to Caboose, 50 Years of Railroading-Norman-1964-U of Okla Pr-205p-photos-1st ed (d3,dj) 25.00
NOBLE,PETER-Bette Davis-Lond-(1948)-Skelton-sm 8vo-231p-blk buckram,illus-1st ed (u1,f) 40.00
NOBLE,SAM-Sam Noble, Able Seaman `Tween Decks in the Seventies-NY-1926-Stokes-blu cl,g sp & cov titles,frntis (nn1) 40.00
NOCK,O S-Algoma Central Railway-Lond-1975-A & C Black-sm 4to-190p-col frntis,col illus,maps (k10,dj) 30.00*
NOCK,O S-British Steam Railways-Lond-1961-326p-1st ed (n4,f,dj) 22.00
NOCK,O S-Pocket Encyclopedia of British Steam Locomotives in Colour-Lond-1964-192p-1st ed (n4,f,dj) 10.00
NOCK,O S-Railway Enthusiast's Encyclopedia-Lond-1968-341p-1st ed (n4,f,dj) 22.00
NOCK,O S-Railways at the Turn of the Century: 1895 to 1905-1969-Macmillan-186p-col illus-1st ed (d3,dj) 20.00
NOCK,O S-Railways at the Turn of the Century: 1895 to 1905-Lond-1969-186p-1st ed (n4,f,dj) 12.00
NOCK,O S-Railways at the Zenith of Steam: 1920 to 40-1970-Macmillan-186p-col illus-1st ed (d3,dj) 20.00
NOCK,O S-Railways Then and Now: World History-NY-1975-215p-1st ed (n4,f,dj) 27.50
NOCK,O S-World Atlas of Railways-NY-1979-224p-maps,photos-1st ed (n4,dj) 29.00
NOCK,PETER-Rock Climbing-Lond-1963-96p-1st ed (p10,f) 18.00
NOCKOLDS,H-Magic of a Name-Lond-nd(ca.1949)-8vo-282p-cl,col frntis,5 col tip in plts (s2,sl wn) 40.00
NOEL HUME,IVOR-1775: Another Part of the Field-1966-Knopf-465p-illus-1st ed (dd9,dj) 35.00
NOEL HUME,IVOR-Here Lies Virginia-1968-Knopf-316p-illus-1st ed (dd9,dj) 35.00

NOEL,JOSEPH-Footloose in Arcadia-NY-1940-Carrick & Evans-1st ed (z2,f,dj sl fade) 75.00

NOEL,SYBILLE-Magic Bird of Chomo Lung Ma-GC-1931-Dbldy,Doran-cl,illus,A Avinoff-1st ed (n8) 25.00

NOEL,THEOPHILUS-Autobiography & Reminiscences of...-Chig-1904-Theo Noel Co-rare-1st ed (b4,edge wn,hng breaking) 325.00

NOGGLE,ANNE-Silver Lining-Albuq-1983-UNM-oblng 4to-photos-1st ed (b4,dj) 45.00

NOGUCHI,ISAMU-Sculptor's World-NY-1968-13 col & 255 b&w plts-scarce-1st Amer ed (h10,dj) 325.00

NOLAN,FREDERICK W-ED.-Life & Death of John Henry Tunstall-Albuq-(1965)-U of NM-480p-illus-Six Guns #1614-1st ed (cc4,dj) 50.00

NOLAN,WILLIAM F-Dashiell Hammett: A Casebook-(1969)-McNally & Loftin-189p-1st prtg (g9,dj) 40.00

NOLAN,WILLIAM F-Psuedo People-LA-(1965)-Shelbourne-1st ed (k3,dj) 15.00

NOLEN,JOHN-City Planning-NY-1916-Appleton-447p-cl (x6,soil cl,sl fox) 30.00

NOLING,A W-Beverage Literature-Metuchen-1971-Scarecrow Pr-865p (o6) 75.00

NOMAD-George A Custer in Turf, Field and Farm-Austin-(1980)-174p-illus-1st ed (n3,f,dj) 27.50

NORBERG,INGA-COMP.-Good Food from Sweden-Lond-(1938)-Chatto & Windus-180p-grn cl-Phoenix Libr Food & Drink #7-3rd prtg (q8,dj) 12.50

NORBU,THUBTEN J-Tibet is My Country-Lond-1960-Rupert Hart Davis-cl,19 col photos-1st ed (o8,dj) 15.00

NORDEN,PIERRE-Conan Doyle-NY-1967-Holt-illus-1st Amer ed (p4,f,dj) 25.00

NORDENSKIOLD,A E-Voyage of the Vega Round Asia and Europe...North Coast of the Old World-Lond-1882-Macmillan-8vo-xxvi,756p-orig grn cl,5 ports,10 fldg maps-Arctic Biblio 12443 (pp1,hng crack,few mrks) 125.00

NORDENSKIOLD,E-History of Biology-1928-Tudor-629p-illus (bb3) 25.00

NORDENSKIOLD,G-Ruiner of Klippboningar; Mesa Verde's Canons-Stockholm-(1893)-193p+index & map+15 litho plts,maps-text in Swedish-v rare-1st ed (v7) 750.00

NORDHOFF, OJAI VALLEY, CALIFORNIA-(LA)-nd-(LA Engrvng Co)-(32)p-pict wrps (l1,sm indent top of leaves) 15.00

NORDHOFF,C-Falcons of France-Bost-1929-8vo-cl,col frntis,3p col plts,A Vimnera (s2) 30.00

NORDHOFF,CHARLES-Botany Bay-Bost-1941-Little,Brown-N C Wyeth dj-1st ed (x1,dj) 40.00

NORDHOFF,CHARLES-Hurricane-Bost-1936-blu bndg,N C Wyeth dj-1st ed (x1,fade bndg,dj) 40.00

NORDHOFF,CHARLES-Men Against the Sea-Bost-1934-Little,Brown-1st ed (x1,dj) 50.00

NORDHOFF,CHARLES-Peninsular California-NY-1888-Harper & Bros-1st ed (l9,sl fox,sm smudge t.p.) 200.00

NORDHOFF,CHARLES-Politics for Young Americans-NY-1886-200p-lea-bckd cl (k1,sl wn sp) 15.00

NORDIN,D SVEN-Rich Harvest-Jackson-(1974)-273p-cl (d1) 15.00

NORDIN,D SVEN-Rich Harvest-Jackson-(1974)-U Pr of Miss-ix,273p-tan cl,photos-1st ed (p2,f,f dj) 17.50

NORDYKE,LEWIS-Cattle Empire-NY-1949-273p-cl,illus,map-1st ed (z1,lacks dj,pres cpy) 45.00

NORDYKE,LEWIS-Great Roundup-NY-1955-Morrow-1st ed (f10,dj wn) 65.00

NORELLI,M R-American Wildlife Painting-NY-1975-224p-col plts (gg3,f,dj) 25.00

NORMAN,CHARLES-Ezra Pound-NY-1960-Macmillan-8vo-493p-1st ed (ee5,dj) 12.50

NORMAN,DOROTHY-Alfred Stieglitz-NY-(1973)-Random-4to-cl-1st ed (y3,f,dj) 45.00

NORMAN,FRANK-Dead Butler Caper-NY-1979-St.Martin's-1st Amer ed (r4,vf,dj) 20.00

NORMAN,HILDA L-Swindlers and Rogues in French Drama-Chig-(1928)-U of Chig-8vo-259p-sketches-1st ed (ee5) 12.50

NORMAN,J R-History of Fishes-Lond-1947-8vo-463p-illus (m3,f) 17.50

NORMAN,OSCAR E-Romance of the Gas Industry-Chig-1922-McClurg-(xvi)+203p-red cl,plts-1st ed (l2,sl stnd dj) 15.00

NORRIE,H S-Electric Gas Lighting-NY-1901-Spon & Chamberlain-12mo-viii+101p+ads-grn dec cl,57 text figs-1st ed (d2) 40 00

NORRIS,FRANK-Letters of...-SF-1956-BC of Cal/Grabhorn Pr-port frntis-ltd to 350c (r2,f) 100.00

NORRIS,FRANK-Pit-NY-1903-Dbldy,Page-orig gold stmpd red bds-1st ed (ee2) 65.00

NORRIS,FRANK-Tower in the West-NY-(1957)-Harper & Bros-ltd ed of unspecified number,nbrd,autg,frnt cov stmpd "Presentation Edition"(iss w/o dj?)-1st ed (cc1) 35.00

NORRIS,KENNETH S-ED.-Whales,Dolphins, and Porpoises-Berkeley,LA-1966-xvi+789p-blu cl,illus-1st ed (l2,dj) 40.00

NORRIS,THAD-American Angler's Book-Phila-1865-8vo-701p-illus-2nd ed wi spplmnt (m3) 140.00

NORRIS,THAD-American Fish Culture-Phila-1868-12mo-304p-illus (m3) 30.00

NORRIS-NEWMAN,CHARLES L-In Zululand with the British Throughout the War of 1879-Lond-1880-343p-grn cl,lg fldg map,8 fldg maps & plans,3 plts,photos-rare-1st ed (kk2) 600.00

NORTH COUNTRY ANGLER-Coquet-Dale Fishing Songs-Edinburgh,Lond-1852-12mo-168p-orig cl-1st ed (m3) 75.00

NORTH COUNTRY-Tourist's Handbook of Northern New York-Watertown-nd(ca.1930)-Santway Photocraft-tall,narrow 8vo-col wrps,fldg map,col & b&w photos (ee6,sl wn & soil) 12.50

NORTH DAKOTA-Fargo-1938-WPA/Amer Guide Ser-371p-photos,maps,fldg map rear pckt-scarce-1st ed (t7,f) 75.00

NORTH DAKOTA-OFFICIAL BRAND BOOK OF THE STATE OF...FOR 1956-456p + spplments-grn flex cov-scarce (b6) 65.00

NORTH,ARTHUR W-Camp and Camino in Lower California-NY-1910-364p-cl,pict cov,illus,maps(1 fldg)-1st ed (z1) 40.00

NORTH,ARTHUR W-Camp and Camino in Lower California-NY-1910-Baker & Taylor-346p-pict hd cov,illus,fldg map in rear-1st ed (bb4) 45.00

NORTH,HENRY RINGLING-Circus Kings-1960-Dbldy-383p-illus-1st ed (v8,sl soil dj) 20.00

NORTH,LUTHER-Man of the Plains-Lincoln-1961-350p-text maps-1st ed (g7,f) 35.00

NORTH,STERLING-Wolfling-NY-1969-Dutton-drwngs,J Schoenherr-1st ed (r3,f,dj) 25.00

NORTHCUTT,DR. W D-Longview, Texas Centennial-Longview-1970-Hudson Pr-76p-wrps,photos-1st ed (w3,vf) 25.00

NORTHEND,CHARLES-Little Orator-NY,Chig-(1859)-Barnes-178p-cl (c1) 20.00

NORTHERN ELECTRIC & MFG CO LTD-How to Build Rural Telephone Lines-Montr-1910-93p-cl,illus (k10) 20.00*

NORTHEY,SUE-American Indian-Springfield-1939-Milton Bradley-216p-illus-1st ed (gg4) 35.00

NORTHROP,STUART A-Minerals of New Mexico-Albuq-1959-U of NM Pr-xvi,665p-rear pckt map-rvsd ed (u5) 25.00

NORTHWEST PLOWING, GRADING AND HEAVY TRACTION ENGINE-Stillwater-1907-12mo-78p-illus (v8,sl soil cov) 18.00

NORTON,ANDRE-Day of the Ness-NY-(1975)-Walker-illus,M Gilbert-1st ed (v10,f,f dj) 25.00

NORTON,ANDRE-Defiant Agents-Bost-1978-Gregg Pr-rprnt (e3,f,dj) 12.00

NORTON,ANDRE-Huon of the Horn-NY-1950-Harcourt Brace-illus,J Krush-1st ed (q2,dj) 145.00

NORTON,ANDRE-Huon of the Horn-NY-1951-Harcourt-1st ed (y2,f,sl wn dj) 125.00

NORTON,ANDRE-Iron Cage-NY-(1974)-1st ed (h5,f,dj sl chip & tn) 35.00

NORTON,ANDRE-Judgement of Janus-NY-(1963)-HB&W-1st ed (k3,dj,autg) 75.00

NORTON,ANDRE-No Night Without Stars-NY-1975-Atheneum-1st ed (d10,f,dj) 40.00

NORTON,ANDRE-Opal Eyed Fan-NY-(1977)-Dutton-1st ed (d10,f,dj) 30.00

NORTON,ANDRE-Star Ka'At World-NY-(1978)-Walker-illus-1st ed (bb1,f,dj) 35.00

NORTON,ANDRE-Star Ka'Ats and the Plant People-NY-(1979)-Walker-illus-1st ed (bb1,f,dj) 35.00

NORTON,ANDRE-Trey of Swords-NY-1977-G&D-1st ed (y2,f,f dj) 25.00

NORTON,BOYD-Snake Wilderness-(1972)-Sierra Club-159p-col photos,map (r8,rub dj) 12.00

NORTON,F J-Descriptive Catalogue of Printing in Spain and Portugal, 1501 to 1520-Cambridge-1978-Cambridge U Pr-600p (v4,as new in dj) 300.00

NORTON,FREDERICK C-Yankee Post Office-New Haven-1935-Tuttle,Morehouse & Taylor-(x)+140p-blu cl-1st ed (k2) 22.00

NORTON,FREDK C-Governors of Connecticut-Htfd-1905-lg sq 8vo-385p-t.e.g.,44 ports-ltd to 1000c,nbrd (a3) 35.00

NORTON,HERMAN-Record of Facts Concerning the Persecutions at Madeira in 1843 and 1846-NY-1849-Am & Foreign Chrstn Union-18mo-228p-orig brwn emboss cl,g sp titles & decs,2 ports-Sabin 55878-2nd ed (mm1,sl fox,sp wn) 125.00

NORTON,MARY-Borrowers Afield-NY-(1955)-Harcourt,Brace-illus,B & J Krush-1st ed (e10,f,dj) 35.00

NORTON,MARY-Borrowers Afloat-Lond-(1959)-Dent-pict cl,col frntis,drwngs-1st ed (pp10,sl fade) 25.00

NORTON,MARY-Borrowers Afloat-NY-(1959)-Harcourt,Brace-illus,B & J Krush-1st ed (e10,f,dj) 25.00

NORTON,MARY-Borrowers Aloft-NY-1961-HB&W-8vo-193p-red cl,illus by B & J Krush-1st Amer ed (nn8,f,dj) 45.00

NORTON,MARY-Borrowers-NY-(1953)-Harcourt,Brace-8vo-180p-blu pict cl,illus by B & J Krush-1st ed (nn8,f,dj sl scuff) 50.00

NORTON,MARY-Borrowers-NY-(1953)-Harcourt,Brace-illus,B & J Krush-1st ed (e10,f,dj) 75.00

NORVELL-Miracle Power of the I Ching-West Nyack-1980-Parker Publ-cl-1st ed (l8,f,dj) 12.50

NORWELL,SAUNDERS-Forty Years of Hardware-NY-(1924)-Hardware Age-(iv)+443p-blk cl,illus-Six Guns 1624-1st ed (mm10) 65.00

NORWOOD,HAYDEN-Death Down East-1941-Phoenix-1st ed (s10,dj) 25.00

NOSTRUMS AND QUACKERY-Chig-c.1911-509p-illus-1st ed (dd3) 100.00

NOTMAN,WILLIAM-Portrait of a Period-1967-McGill U Pr-lg 4to-unpgd-174 photos(incl fldg)-1st ed (aa7,sl rub dj) 125.00*

NOTT,DAVID-Angels Four-Englewood Cliffs-1972-191p-illus,maps-1st ed (o10,f,dj) 18.00

NOTT,DAVID-Into the Lost World, a Descent into Prehistoric Time-Englewood Cliffs-(1975)-Prentice Hall-8vo-186p-8p photos-1st ed (jj5,f,sl tn dj) 10.00

NOTT,STANLEY C-Chinese Jade in the Stanley Charles Nott Collection-W Palm Bch-1942-Norton Gallery-4to-xvi,536p+8p prospectus laid in,118 halftone plts,123 line engrvngs-ltd to 1000c,nbrd (c3,dh chip,sun,adv laid in) 195.00

NOUGIER,LOUIS-RENE-Cave of Rouffignac-Lond-1958-Geo Newnes-8vo-(x),230p+24p photos,cl-1st ed (y4,dj) 25.00

NOURISSIER,FRANCOIS-Cartier Bresson's France-NY-(1970)-Viking-folio-wht cl,cardboard box-1st Amer ed (y3,f,f dj,box) 75.00

NOVA SCOTIA BUREAU OF INFORMATION-Haunts of Fish and Game Nova Scotia-Halifax-1937-8vo-32p-wrps,photos (m3) 30.00

NOVA,CRAIG-Geek-NY-(1975)-NY et al-drwngs,Holland-1st ed (b5,as new in dj) 20.00

NOVA,CRAIG-Good Son-(NY)-(1982)-Delacorte/Lawrence-1st ed (bb1,as new in dj) 12.50

NOVA,CRAIG-Incandescence-NY et al-(1979)-Harper & Row-1st ed (b5,as new in dj) 15.00

NOVA,CRAIG-Turkey Hash-NY-1972-auth 1st bk-1st ed (p5,f,dj) 25.00

NOVAK,JOSEPH-Future is Ours, Comrade-NY-1960-Dbldy-auth 1st bk-1st ed (f8,f,dj) 200.00

NOVELTY COOK BOOK-Phila-1913-Abram Cox Stove Co-80p-wht oil-cl bds,illus,cntrfld of "The Handy Kitchen" (n6) 35.00

NOYCE,WILFRID-ED.-World Atlas of Moutaineering-1970-4to-224p-photos(58 col),32 maps-1st US ed (a4,f,dj) 65.00

NOYCE,WILFRID-Springs of Adventure-NY-1958-255p-1st ed (a4,f,dj) 18.00

NOYCE,WILFRID-Unknown Mountain-Lond-1962-183p-1st Brit ed (a4,f,dj) 40.00

NOYES CARRIAGE CO-Catalog 22-Elkhart-nd(ca.1910)-oblng-64p-illus (h9,f) 85.00

NOYES,A J-In the Land of Chinook, Story of Blaine County-Helena-(1917)-152p-illus-1st ed (d7,f) 175.00

NOYES,AL J-In the Land of Chinook or the Story of Blaine County-Helena-(1917)-State Publ Co-g stmpd grn cl-Graff 3051-1st ed (w1,f) 165.00

NOYES,AL-Dimsdale's Vigilantes of Montana & History of Southern Montana by Noyes-Helena-nd-State Publ-290p-blu cl,illus-Howes #D345 "Best Edition"-5th ed (b6,f) 45.00

NOYES,ALFRED-Forest of Wild Thyme-Edinburgh,Lond-1911-Blackwood-orig g titled cl,t.e.g.-1st ed (aa9,sl fox) 40.00

NOYES,JOHN H-History of American Socialisms-NY-(1961)(1870)-Hillary Hs-8vo-678p-ltd to 500c-rprnt (cc5,dj) 17.50

NOYES,KATHERINE M-ED.-Jesse Macy: An Autobiography-Springfield-1933-Chas C Thomas-192p-frntis,illus (o7) 30.00

NOZAKA,AKIYUKI-Pornographers-NY-1968-1st US ed (t5,dj) 15.00

NULL,MARION M-Forgotten Pioneer-NY-1954-Vantage Pr-138p-cl,photos-1st ed (w3,f,dj) 17.50

NUMBER FOUR JOY STREET-NY-1926-Appleton-lg 8vo-228p-cl,plts,incl 8 tip in col plts-1st US ed (s3) 35.00

NUNIS,DOYCE B,JR.-ED.-Hudson's Bay Company's First Fur Bridgade to the Sacramento Valley-Sacramento-1968-59p-map-ltd to 310c-1st ed (t7,f) 60.00

NUNIS,DOYCE B,JR.-ED.-Hudson's Bay Company's First Fur Brigade to the Sacramento Valley-1968-Sacramento Bk Coll Cl-royal oct-59p-errata (d3) 75.00

NUNIS,DOYCE B,JR.-Huse Journal-Santa Barbara-1977-279p-frntis,photos,map e.p.-ltd to 500c (t7) 35.00

NUNN,LOTTIE-Ada Greenwood-Cin-1882-200p-cl-6th ed (a1,sp fade) 15.00

NUNNERY,GENE-Old Pro Turkey Hunter-Meridian-1980-8vo-144p-illus (m3,vf,dj) 20.00

NURGE,ETHEL-Life in a Leyte Village-Seattle-1964-U of Wash Pr-8vo-157p-cl,photos,maps-AES Mono-1st ed (y5,dj) 15.00

NUSBAUM,AILEEN-Seven Cities of Cibola-NY-1926-Putnam's-167p-col picts-1st ed (bb4,sl wn sp) 35.00

NUTE,GRACE L-Voyageur's Highway-St.Paul-1941-113p-stiff pict wrps,photos,maps,map e.p.-1st ed (t7) 12.50

NUTE,GRACE L-Voyageur-NY/Lond-1931-Appleton-burgandy cl,g sp titles & cov dec,map e.p.,illus,C W Bertsch-1st ed (mm1) 60.00

NUTE,GRACE L-Voyageur-St.Paul-1955-289p-frntis,illus,map e.p. (t7,dj) 20.00

NUTTALL,DAVID-Mooching-Vancouver-1980-8vo-180p-photos (m3,dj) 12.50

NUTTALL,T-Journal of Travels into Arkansas Territory during the Year 1819-1980-U of Okla-361p-maps-1st ed thus (bb3,f,dj) 29.00

NUTTALL,T-Journal of Travels into the Arkansas Territory during the Year 1819...-1966-AMS Pr-366p-illus,fldg map-rprnt of 1821 ed (bb3,f) 27.00

NUTTALL,T-Popular Handbook of Birds of the United States-1929-Little,Brown-904p(2 vols in one)-20 col plts-rvsd ed (bb3) 135.00

NUTTING,RUFUS-Practical Grammar of the English Language-Montpelier-1828-E P Walton-144p-bds-Amer Imprnts 34592-4th ed,revsd by auth (k1,sl wn) 22.50

NUTTING,WALLACE-Clock Book-GC-1935-Garden City Publ-sm 4to-312p-tan cl,illus (r10) 30.00

NYBERG,BJORN-Return of Conan-NY-1957-Gnome-1st ed (b5,sl tn dj) 75.00

NYE,CAPT W S-Carbine and Lance-Norman-1937-U of Okla Pr-441p-illus-1st ed (cc4) 45.00

NYE,ELWOOD L-Marching with Custer-Glendale-1964-Arthur H Clark-53p-pict fabrikoid,col frntis,illus-ltd to 300c-Hidden Springs of Custerian ser,Vol.I-1st ed (gg4) 300.00

NYE,NELSON-ED.-Western Roundup-1961-MacMillan-1st ed (t8,dj sl chip & sl soil) 18.00

NYE,WILBUR S-Carbine and Lance-Norman-1937-U of Okla Pr-441p-illus-1st ed (gg4) 45.00

NYE,WILBUR S-Plains Indian Raiders-Norman-(1968)-407p-photos-1st ed (u7,dj) 35.00

NYGAARD,NORMAN E-Lew Reese and His Scio Pottery-NY-(1948)-176p-cl (f1,dj lacks sm pc) 17.50

O'BALLANCE,EDGAR-Wars in Vietnam-NY-1975-1st ed (v9,f,f dj) 40.00

O'BRIEN,CLARA V-God's Country-Sylvan Bch-1982-N Cntry Bks-1st ed (dd6,dj) 27.50

O'BRIEN,EDNA-August is a Wicked Month-Lond-(1965)-Cape-8vo-bds-1st ed (jj8,f,dj) 45.00

O'BRIEN,EDNA-Casualties of Peace-NY-(1966)-1st Amer ed (bb10,sl tn dj) 20.00

O'BRIEN,EDNA-James and Nora-1981-Lord John Pr-8vo-cl,iss w/o dj-ltd to 250c,nbrd,autg-1st ed (x10,f) 35.00

O'BRIEN,EDNA-Lonely Girl-Lond-(1962)-Cape-8vo-bds-1st ed (jj8,f,sl wn dj) 45.00

O'BRIEN,EDNA-Mother Ireland-Lond-(1976)-Weidenfeld & Nicholson-photos,F Bourke-1st ed (z8,vf,sp rprd dj) 27.50

O'BRIEN,EDNA-Night-NY-1973-Knopf-1st Amer ed (t4,f,f dj) 15.00

O'BRIEN,EDNA-Night-NY-1973-Knopf-1st Amer ed (z8,vf,dj) 17.50

O'BRIEN,EDNA-Scandalous Woman, and Other Stories-NY-(1974)-HBJ-1st ed (z8,vf,dj) 17.50

O'BRIEN,EDNA-Virginia-NY,Lond-(1981)-HBJ-1st US ed (e10,as new in dj) 10.00

O'BRIEN,EDNA-Virginia-NY-(1981)-HB&J-1st ed (l7,dj) 15.00

O'BRIEN,ELMER-Varieties of Mystic Experience-NY-1964-HR&W-cl-1st ed (l8,f,dj) 13.50

O'BRIEN,FLANN-Dalkey Archive-NY-(1965)-Macmillan-1st Amer ed (z8,vf,dj tn & sm pc missng) 45.00

O'BRIEN,FLANN-Hard Life-(1962)-Pantheon-1st Amer ed (s9,f,sl wn dj sp) 65.00

O'BRIEN,FLANN-Hard Life...-NY-(1962)-Pantheon-1st Amer ed (z8,vf,dj) 45.00

O'BRIEN,FLANN-Poor Mouth...-NY-(1974)-Viking-illus,R Steadman-1st Amer ed (z8,vf,dj) 20.00

O'BRIEN,FLANN-Stories and Plays-NY-(1976)-Viking-1st ed (z8,vf,dj) 25.00

O'BRIEN,FREDERICK-Atolls of the Sun-1922-Century-508p-pict cov,illus-1st ed (u8) 15.00

O'BRIEN,FREDERICK-Mystic Isles of the South Seas-NY-1921-Century-1st ed (v4) 35.00

O'BRIEN,FREDERICK-White Shadows in the South Seas-NY-1921-Century-8vo-450p-pict dec grn cl,63p photos (p8,sl wn) 25.00

O'BRIEN,GEOFFREY-Hardboiled America-NY-1981-Van Nostrand-illus-1st ed (p4,vf,dj) 50.00

O'BRIEN,KATE-Farewell Spain-GC-1937-Dbldy, Doran-8vo-243p-13 illus-1st US ed (jj5,sl discol dj) 30.00

O'BRIEN,ROBERT-California Called Them-NY-(1951)-McGraw Hill-251p-e.p. maps,illus-Six Guns 1630-1st ed (gg4,wn dj) 25.00

O'BRIEN,SIR EDWARD-Shooting at Dromoland-Dublin-1961-8vo-14p-wrps,illus by auth (m3) 10.00

O'BRIEN,TIM-Going After Cacciato-Lond-1978-1st Brit ed (s5,vf,dj) 35.00

O'BRIEN,TIM-If I Die in a Combat Zone-Lond-1973-Calder Boyars-auth 1st bk-1st Brit ed (g8,f,f dj) 100.00

O'BRIEN,TIM-If I Die in a Combat Zone-np-(1973)-Delacorte-1st ed (ff3,f,f dj) 100.00

O'BRIEN,TIM-Northern Lights-Lond-(1976)-Marion Boyars-1st Brit ed (a10,as new in dj) 75.00

O'CALLAGHAN,SEAN-Slave Trade Today-NY-1961-Crown-189p-1st ed (j8,dj) 15.00

O'CASEY,SEAN-Green Crow-NY-1956-precedes Brit ed-1st ed (r2,f,dj) 30.00

O'CASEY,SEAN-Oak Leaves and Lavender-Lond-1946-Macmillan-g titled cl-1st ed (aa9,dj sp sl fade) 40.00

O'CASEY,SEAN-Sunset and Evening Star-Lond-1954-1st ed (r2,f,dj sl rub,nick) 25.00

O'CONNELL,JOHN-Railroad Album-Chig-1954-160p-1st ed (n4,f,dj) 18.00

O'CONNELL,MARGARET J-Pennington Profile-(np)-(1966)-289,(14)p-cl,plts (aa6) 40.00

O'CONNER,KATHRYN K-Theatre in the Cow Country-So Bend-1966-Albuq Little Theatre-1st ed (b4,dj) 37.50

O'CONNOR,FLANNERY-Complete Stories-1971-FS&G-1st ed (m9,f,dj sp drknd & sl tn) 75.00

O'CONNOR,FLANNERY-Complete Stories-NY-(1971)-FS&G-1st ed (s6,f,dj) 90.00

O'CONNOR,FLANNERY-Complete Stories-NY-1971-FS&G-1st ed (dd2,f,dj) 100.00

O'CONNOR,FLANNERY-Death of a Child-Lond-(1961)-Catholic Bk Club-1st Brit ed (l7,sl tn dj) 60.00

O'CONNOR,FLANNERY-Everything That Rises Must Converge-NY-(1965)-FS&G-1st ed (dd2,f,f dj) 125.00

O'CONNOR,FLANNERY-Habit of Being-NY-(1979)-FSG-1st ed (ee2,f,dj) 65.00

O'CONNOR,FLANNERY-Habit of Being-NY-(1979)-FSG-1st ed (m7,sl wn dj) 45.00

O'CONNOR,FLANNERY-Mystery and Manners-NY-(1969)-FS&G-1st ed (dd2,f,dj) 65.00

O'CONNOR,FLANNERY-Mystery and Manners-NY-(1969)-FSG-1st ed (q2,dj) 75.00

O'CONNOR,FLANNERY-Violent Bear it Away-1960-Farrar-1st ed (jj6,f,dj) 190.00

O'CONNOR,FLANNERY-Violent Bear It Away-Lond-1960-1st Brit ed (p5,dj) 90.00

O'CONNOR,FLANNERY-Wise Blood-1955-N Spearman-auth 1st bk-1st Brit ed (x2,f,dj sl wn & soil) 275.00

O'CONNOR,FLANNERY-Wise Blood-Lond-(1955)-Neville Spearman-8vo-orng bds-1st Brit ed (u10,f,dj) 300.00

O'CONNOR,FLANNERY-Wise Blood-NY-(1952)-Harcourt,Brace-auth 1st bk-1st ed (l7,chip dj) 400.00

O'CONNOR,FRANK-An Only Child-Lond-1961-Macmillan-1st ed (z8,vf,rprd & sl rub dj) 20.00

O'CONNOR,FRANK-Backward Look-Lond-1967-Macmillan-1st ed (z8,f,dj) 25.00

O'CONNOR,FRANK-Collected Stories-NY-1981-Knopf-1st ed (z8,f,dj) 20.00

O'CONNOR,FRANK-Domestic Relations-NY-1957-Knopf-1st ed (t4,f,f dj) 40.00

O'CONNOR,FRANK-Midnight Court-Lond,Dublin-1946-Maurice Frieber-1st ed (dd2,f,sl chip dj) 35.00

O'CONNOR,FRANK-Mirror in the Roadway-NY-(1956)-Knopf-1st ed (z8,vf,sl wn dj) 35.00

O'CONNOR,FRANK-My Father's Son-NY-1969-Knopf-1st US ed (bb1,as new in dj) 25.00

O'CONNOR,FRANK-Set of Variations-NY-1969-Knopf-1st ed (bb1,as new in dj) 25.00

O'CONNOR,FRANK-Shakespeare's Progress-Cleve-(1960)-World-1st Amer ed (z8,f,dj) 20.00

O'CONNOR,FRANK-Three Old Brothers...-Lond-(1936)-T Nelson-1st ed (z8,f,dj) 80.00

O'CONNOR,FRANK-Towards an Appreciation of Literature-Dublin-1945-Metro Publ-1st ed (z8,vf,f dj) 12.50

O'CONNOR,FRANK-TRANSL.-Kings, Lords & Commons...-NY-1959-Knopf-precedes Brit ed-1st ed (z8,vf,sl wn dj) 60.00

O'CONNOR,G W-Railroads of New York-NY-1949-144p-scarce-1st ed (n4) 60.00

O'CONNOR,JACK-Art of Hunting Big Game in North America-1967-Borzoi-8vo-404p-130 photos (m3,f,dj) 20.00

O'CONNOR,JACK-Art of Hunting Big Game in North America-NY-1967-404p-photos (gg3,f,dj) 15.00

O'CONNOR,JACK-Best of Jack O'Connor-1984-Amwell-192p-photos (gg3,f,box) 15.00

O'CONNOR,JACK-Big Game Animals of North America-NY-1961-folio-264p-illus,D Allen-1st ed (m3) 24.00

O'CONNOR,JACK-Complete Book of Rifles & Shotguns-NY-1961-8vo-477p-illus-1st ed (m3,vf,dj) 20.00

O'CONNOR,JACK-Complete Book of Shooting-NY-1965-8vo-385p-illus-1st ed (m3,vf,dj) 12.50

O'CONNOR,JACK-Conquest-NY-1930-12mo-293p-scarce-1st ed (m3) 185.00

O'CONNOR,JACK-Game in the Desert Revisited-1977-306p-illus-book club ed (gg3,f) 20.00

O'CONNOR,JACK-Game in the Desert-NY-1939-Derrydale-298p-grn simulated lizard skin,col frntis,b&w plts,photos,ltd to 950c,nbrd (ee3,vf) 500.00

O'CONNOR,JACK-Game in the Desert-NY-1939-Derrydale-298p-simulated lizard skin bndg,col frntis-scarce when autg (gg3,f,pres cpy) 525.00

O'CONNOR,JACK-Horse & Buggy West-NY-1969-8vo-302p-illus,I Boker-1st ed (m3,f,dj) 150.00

O'CONNOR,JACK-Hunting in the Rockies-NY-1947-8vo-297p-photos-scarce-1st ed (m3,f,sl chip & soil dj) 225.00

O'CONNOR,JACK-Hunting Rifle-Winchester-1970-314p-photos (gg3,f,dj) 15.00

O'CONNOR,JACK-Jack O'Connor's Big Game Hunts-NY-1963-415p-photos,illus (gg3,vf,dj) 22.00

O'CONNOR,JACK-Jack O'Connor's Big Game Hunts-NY-1963-8vo-415p-photos-1st ed (m3,f,dj) 35.00

O'CONNOR,JACK-Rifle Book-NY-1949-8vo-352p-photos-1st ed (m3) 55.00

O'CONNOR,JACK-Sheep & Sheep Hunting-Winchester-1974-308p-photos (gg3,vf,dj) 75.00

O'CONNOR,JACK-Shotgun Book-NY-1965-8vo-332p-photos-1st ed (m3,vf,dj) 25.00

O'CONNOR,JACK-Sportsman's Arms & Ammunition Manual-NY-1952-8vo-256p-photos,illus-1st ed (m3,vf,fray dj) 27.50

O'CONNOR,JOHN E-William Paterson-New Brunswick-(1979)-xv,351p-cl (aa6) 40.00

O'CONNOR,JOHN F-Adobe Book-Santa Fe-(1973)-132p+20p photos,drwngs-1st ed (u7,f,dj) 20.00

O'CONNOR,JOHN J-Chaplain Looks at Vietnam-Cleve & NY-(1968)-World-256p-cl-1st ed so stated (h1,sl rub dj) 15.00

O'CONNOR,PHILIP F-Stealing Home-NY-1979-Knopf-1st ed (b5,f,dj) 25.00

O'CONNOR,RICHARD-Bat Masterson-GC-1957-Dbldy-263p-Six Guns #1632-1st ed (cc4,dj) 25.00

O'CONNOR,RICHARD-High Jinks in the Klondike-Indpls-(1954)-284p-pict e.p.-1st ed (jj1,chip dj) 20.00

O'CONNOR,RICHARD-Pat Garrett-GC-1960-Dbldy-286p-Six Guns 1634-1st ed (gg4,dj) 20.00

O'CONNOR,RICHARD-Wild Bill Hickok-GC-1959-Dbldy-282p-Six Guns #1635-1st ed (cc4,dj) 20.00

O'CONNOR,ULICK-Life Styles-Lond-(1973)-Dolmen Pr-wrps-1st ed (z8,f) 27.50

O'CONOR,NORREYS J-Beside the Backwater-Dublin-1914-Maunsel-1st ed (z8,f,few holes dj sp) 75.00

O'CORK,SHANNON-End of the Line-NY-1981-St.Martin's-1st ed (q4,f,dj) 17.50

O'CROULEY,PEDRO A-Description of the Kingdom of New Spain: 1774-1972-John Howell Bks-4to-148p-fldg map in pckt-1st ed (d3,dj) 50.00

O'DELL,BOB-Aerobatics Today-NY-(1980)-St.Martin's-8vo-208p-illus-1st ed (gg5,f,f dj) 12.50

O'DONNELL,GEORGENE-Miniaturia-Chig-(1943)-Lightner-viii,329p-cl,illus-1st ed (dd10,autg) 40.00

O'DONNELL,LILLIAN-Falling Star-NY-1979-Putnam-1st ed (q4,f,dj) 20.00

O'DONNELL,PETER-Modesty Blaise - I, Lucifer-Lond-1967-Souvenir-1st ed (p4,f,dj) 25.00

O'DONNELL,PETER-Modesty Blaise-1965-Souvenir-auth 1st bk-1st ed (x7,sl fox,dj) 55.00

O'DONNELL,PETER-Sabre Tooth-1966-Dbldy-1st Amer ed (s10,dj) 10.00

O'DONNELL,PETER-Sabre Tooth-NY-1966-Dbldy-1st Amer ed (e4,f,sl wn dj) 20.00

O'DUFFY,EIMAR-King Goshawk and the Birds-Lond-1926-Macmillan-1st ed (w5,f,tape rprd dj) 65.00

O'DUFFY,EIMAR-Spacious Adventures of the Man in the Street-Lond-1928-Macmillan-1st ed (w5,f,sl chip dj) 60.00

O'FAOLAIN,SEAN-I Remember! I Remember!-Bost-(1961)-Little,Brown-precedes Brit ed-1st ed (z8,f,dj) 50.00

O'FAOLAIN,SEAN-I Remember! I Remember!-Lond-1962-Hart Davis-1st Brit ed (z8,vf,dj) 17.50

O'FAOLAIN,SEAN-Man Who Invented Sin-NY-1948-illus-1st Amer ed (r2,f,dj) 30.00

O'FAOLAIN,SEAN-Vive Moi-Bost-(1964)-Little,Brown-cl-1st ed (aa9,f,dj) 30.00

O'FAOLIN,SEAN-Finest Stories of...-Bost-(1957)-Little,Brown-1st ed (z8,vf,dj) 25.00

O'FLAHERTY,LIAM-Assassin-Lond-1928-1st Brit ed (r5,dj) 40.00

O'FLAHERTY,LIAM-Insurrection-Lond-1950-Gollancz-8vo-cl-1st ed (x3,f,dj) 40.00

O'FLAHERTY,LIAM-Land-Lond-(1946)-1st ed (r2,f,dj sp sl sun) 50.00

O'FLAHERTY,LIAM-Land-NY-(1946)-Random-8vo-cl-1st ed (x3,dj sl chip & creased) 40.00

O'FLAHERTY,LIAM-Martyr-NY-1933-Macmillan-1st Amer ed (z8,vf,dj) 65.00

O'FLAHERTY,LIAM-Skerrett-NY-1932-Long & Smith-cl-1st ed (z8) 18.50

O'FLAHERTY,LIAM-Spring Sowing-Lond-1924-1st Brit ed (r5,sp drknd dj) 50.00

O'GRADY,DESMOND-Dark Edge of Europe-Lond-(1967)-MacGibbon & Kee-1st ed (z8,vf,sl rub dj) 40.00

O'GRADY,DESMOND-Dying Gaul-Lond-(1968)-MacGibbon & Kee-1st ed (z8,vf,dj) 30.00

O'GRADY,DESMOND-Limerick Rake-Dublin-(1978)-Gallery Pr-cl-1st ed (z8,vf,dj) 40.00

O'GRADY,DESMOND-Off License-Dublin-(1968)-Dolmen Pr-1st ed (z8,vf,f dj) 30.00

O'GRADY,DESMOND-Sing Me Creation-Dublin-1977-Gallery Pr-1st ed (z8,f,dj) 40.00

O'HANLON,JAMES-Murder at Horsethief-NY-1941-Phoenix-1st ed (k4,dj) 20.00

O'HARA,DWIGHT-Air Borne Infection-NY-1943-Commonwealth Fund-xii+114p-grn cl,11 chrts-1st ed (d2) 15.00

O'HARA,FRANK-Nakian-NY-1966-MOMA-wrps,illus-1st ed (m8,f) 10.00

O'HARA,JOHN-Big Laugh-NY-(1962)-1st ed (o5,f,dj) 15.00

O'HARA,JOHN-Big Laugh-NY-(1962)-Random-1st ed (hh5,f,f dj) 10.00

O'HARA,JOHN-Butterfield 8-NY-(1935)-scarce in dj-1st ed (t5,sl chip dj) 150.00

O'HARA,JOHN-Cape Cod Lighter-NY-(1962)-1st ed (r2,f,dj sl sp sun) 25.00

O'HARA,JOHN-Doctor's Son and Other Stories-NY-(1935)-Harcourt-1st ed (w1,sp lttrs flaked,sl tn dj) 200.00

O'HARA,JOHN-Family Party-NY-(1956)-Random-8vo-cl & pattrnd bds-1st ed (x3,f,dj) 45 00

O'HARA,JOHN-Farmer's Hotel-NY-(1951)-1st ed (r5,dj) 22.50

O'HARA,JOHN-Farmers Hotel-NY-(1951)-Random Hs-1st ed (a10,dj sl chip,creased & tn) 15.00

O'HARA,JOHN-From the Terrace-NY-(1958)-1st ed (o5,f,sl wn dj) 20.00

O'HARA,JOHN-From the Terrace-NY-(1958)-Random-1st ed (hh5,dj rub,edgewn) 15.00

O'HARA,JOHN-Hat on the Bed-NY-(1963)-Random-1st ed (e8,f,dj) 45.00

O'HARA,JOHN-Here's O'Hara-NY-(1946)-DS&P-1st ed (cc2,f,dj) 45.00

O'HARA,JOHN-Hope of Heaven-NY-(1938)-1st ed (q5,wn dj) 100.00

O'HARA,JOHN-Hope of Heaven-NY-(1938)-Harcourt,Brace-1st ed (a10,sl tn & wn dj) 85.00

O'HARA,JOHN-Horse Knows the Way-NY-(1964)-1st ed (k9,f,dj) 10.00

O'HARA,JOHN-Instrument-NY-(1967)-Random-1st ed (e3,f,sl tn dj) 35.00

O'HARA,JOHN-Lovey Childs-NY-(1969)-Random-249p-cl-1st ed so stated (c1,f,dj) 15.00

O'HARA,JOHN-Ourselves to Know-NY-(1960)-1st ed (r5,f,dj) 22.50

O'HARA,JOHN-Rage to Live-NY-(1949)-1st ed (k9,sp chip dj) 35.00

O'HARA,JOHN-Rage to Live-NY-(1949)-Random-8vo-cl-1st ed (x3,sl chip dj) 55.00

O'HARA,JOHN-Selected Letters of...-NY-1978-Random-1st ed (z9,f,dj) 10.00

O'HARA,JOHN-Sermons and Soda Water-1961-Cresset-1st one vol ed-1st Brit ed (x2,f,dj) 35.00

O'HARA,JOHN-Sermons and Soda Water-NY-1960-Random-3 vols-1st ed (z9,f,bump box) 17.50

O'HARA,JOHN-Sweet and Sour-NY-(1954)-Random-1st ed (j5,f,dj) 20.00

O'HARA,JOHN-Time Element & Other Stories-NY-1972-Random-1st ed (e8,f,f dj) 35.00

O'HARA,JOHN-Waiting for Winter-NY-1966-Random-1st ed (e8,f,f dj) 40.00

O'HARE,KATE R-What Happened to Dan-(KC)-(1904)-63p-wrps (d1,sl chip frnt wrps) 30.00

O'HARRA,CLEOPHAS C-O'Harra's Handbook of the Black Hills-Rapid City-1927-175p-pict wrps,frntis,photos,maps (t7,few underlinings) 30.00

O'KANE,WALTER C-Hopis-Norman-(1953)-267p-col photos-1st ed (v7,dj) 25.00

O'KEEFE,GEORGIA-Georgia O'Keefe-1976-Viking-folio-(this ed wi fldg plt #106)-1st prtg (h10,dj) 200.00

O'KEEFE,J J-Sport Fishing in Canada-Ottawa-1946-8vo-48p-wrps,photos (m3) 20.00

O'KEEFE,REV J J-Buildings and Churches of the Mission of Santa Barbara-SB-1886-40p-wrps-1st ed (d3) 45.00

O'KEEFE,SPECS-Men Who Robbed Brinks-NY-1961-RH-1st ed (z9,f,dj chip) 10.00

O'KIEFFE,CHARLEY-Western Story-Lincoln-1960-U of Nebr Pr-224p-1st ed (bb4,dj) 20.00

O'LEARY,JEREMIAH A-My Political Trial and Experiences-NY-1919-illus-1st Amer ed (r2,f) 45.00

O'MALLEY,AUSTIN-Ethics of Medical Homicide and Mutilation-NY-1922-285p (dd3) 75.00

O'MALLEY,C D-Michael Servetus-Phila-1953-208p-1st ed (dd3) 75.00

O'MALLEY,HENRY-Artificial Propagation of the Salmons of the Pacific Coast-Wash D.C.-1920-8vo-32p-wrps,photos (m3,f) 15.00

O'MEARA,WALTER-Daughters of the Country-NY-1968-Harcourt,Brace-1st ed (b4,dj) 45.00

O'MEARA,WALTER-Guns at the Forks-Englewood-(1965)-275p-illus-Amer Forts Ser,Vol.1-1st ed (e7,f,dj) 30.00

O'MEARA,WALTER-Minnesota Gothic-NY-(1956)-Holt-314p-1st ed (m4,dj) 12.50

O'MEARA,WALTER-Savage Country-Bost-1960-308p-illus,map e.p.-1st ed (t7,dj) 17.50

O'NEAL,BILL-Encyclopedia of Western Gun Fighters-Norman-1979-U of Okla-photos-1st ed (b4,dj) 50.00

O'NEALL,JOHN B-Annals of Newberry, Historical, Biographical and Anecdotical-Charleston-1859-413;viii p-cl-scarce-1st ed (n1,rbnd,sl dmpstnd pgs) 60.00

O'NEIL,JAMES B-They Die But Once-NY-1935-228p-Herd 1718-1st ed (t8,dj) 70.00

O'NEIL,JAMES B-They Die But Once-NY-1935-Knight Publ-228p-Six Guns #1650-1st ed (cc4) 50.00

O'NEILL,C-Wild Train: Story of the Andrews Raiders-NY-1956-482p-illus,maps,ports-1st ed (z10,dj) 35.00

O'NEILL,EDWARD-Biography by Americans, 1658 to 1936-Phila-1939-U of Penn Pr-x,465p-cl-1st ed (w2) 45.00

O'NEILL,EUGENE-Beyond the Horizon-NY-(1920)-Boni & Liveright-cl bckd bds-1st ed,1st iss (aa9,sl rub sp) 50.00

O'NEILL,EUGENE-Complete Works-NY-1924-Boni-4to-2 vols-cl/bds,ltd to 1200 sets,nbrd,autg (x3,cors wn,weak joint) 125.00

O'NEILL,EUGENE-Days Without End-NY-(1934)-Random-lea,ltd to 325c,autg-1st ed (l9,sp wn & scuff) 150.00

O'NEILL,EUGENE-Desire Under the Elms-NY-1925-Boni & Liveright-blk cl-1st separate ed (hh4,f,sl wn dj) 225.00

O'NEILL,EUGENE-Dynamo-NY-1929-Horace Liveright-orig g titled cl-1st trd ed (aa9,sp dull) 35.00

O'NEILL,EUGENE-Emperor Jones. Diff'rent. The Straw-NY-(1921)-Boni & Liveright-cl bckd bds-1st ed (aa9,sl rub sp) 45.00

O'NEILL,EUGENE-Gold-1920-B & L-1st ed (x2) 40.00

O'NEILL,EUGENE-Great God Brown...-NY-1926-Boni,Liveright-blu grn bds-1st ed (hh4,f,f dj) 200.00

O'NEILL,EUGENE-Iceman Cometh-NY-(1946)-Random-8vo-cl-1st ed (x3,f,dj) 50.00

O'NEILL,EUGENE-Lazrus Laughed-NY-1927-Boni & Liveright-ltd to 775c,autg-1st ed (l9,sp fade) 170.00

O'NEILL,EUGENE-Lost Plays of...-NY-1950-New Fathoms-gry cl-1st ed (f2,edge-wn dj) 45.00

O'NEILL,EUGENE-Marco Milions-NY-1927-Boni & Liveright-1st ed (l9,spot,fade,dj sp sl fade) 85.00

O'NEILL,EUGENE-Moon for the Misbegotten-NY-(1952)-1st ed (c5,dj sp sl chip) 35.00

O'NEILL,EUGENE-Mourning Becomes Electra, a Trilogy-NY-1931-Horace Liveright-1st ed (l9,fade,wn,dj chip) 150.00

O'NEILL,EUGENE-Strange Interlude-NY-1928-Boni & Liveright-g titled cl-1st ed,1st iss (aa9) 30.00

O'NEILL,EUGENE-Ten "Lost" Plays-NY-(1964)-1st ed (c5,f,dj) 25.00

O'NEILL,EUGENE-Thirst-Bost-(1914)-Gorham Pr-auth 1st bk-1st ed (a10,sp drknd,sl brnd e.p.s) 225.00

O'NEILL,EUGENE-Touch of the Poet-1957-Yale U Pr-1st ed (r2,f,sl nick dj) 25.00

O'NEILL,REV. P-Sermon on the Mystery of the Real Presence...-Pitt-1831-Johnston & Stockton-80p-cl cov wrps-Amer Imprnts 8583 (c1) 40.00

O'NEILL,ROSE C-Loves of Edwy-Bost-(1904)-Lothrop-8vo-dec cl,illus-1st ed (oo8) 60.00

O'NEILL,TIM-And We, the People. Ten Years with the Primitive Tribes of New Guinea-NY-c.1960-P J Kenedy-8vo-xiii,248p-map e.p.,photos (nn1) 17.50

O'NEILL,WILLIAM L-Last Romantic-NY-1978-Oxford-339p (r1,sl tn dj) 15.00

O'RELL,MAX-Jonathan and His Continent-NY-1889-Cassell-12mo-ix,313p-dec cov (n2,sl soil cov) 35.00

O'RELL,MAX-Rambles in Womanland-Lond-1903-Chatto & Windus-8vo-298p-calf/mrbld bds-1st ed (oo7,uncut) 65.00

O'ROURKE,FRANK-Catcher and the Manager-1953-Barnes-1st ed (s8,brwnd pgs,dj) 20.00

O'ROURKE,FRANK-Greatest Victory and Other Stories-1950-Barnes-1st ed (ff2,dj) 40.00

O'ROURKE,FRANK-Heavenly World Series-1952-Barnes-1st ed (ff2,dj) 45.00

O'SHAUGHNESSY,EDITH-Diplomat's Wife in Mexico-NY-1917-Harper & Bros-8vo-356p-red cl,g titles,illus (mm1,sp fade) 25.00

O'SHEA,ELENA Z-El Mesquite-Dallas-1935-Mathis (a9) 125.00

O'SULLIVAN,MAURICE-Twenty Years A Growing-NY-1933-1st ed (y7,dj) 85.00

O'SULLIVAN,MAURICE-Twenty Years A Growing-NY-1933-Viking-scarce-1st US ed (hh5,dj) 60.00

O'SULLIVAN,SEAMUS-Collected Poems-Dublin-1940-Orwell Pr-ltd to 300c,autg-scarce-1st ed (z8,f,dj) 210.00

O'SULLIVAN,SEAN-Legends From Ireland-Lond-(1977)-Batsford-drwngs,J Skelton-1st ed (z8,vf,dj) 17.50

O'SULLIVAN,SEUMAS-Poems-Dublin-1912-Maunsel-8vo-101p+2p ads-1st ed (bb7,chip dj) 35.00*

O'SULLIVAN,SEUMAS-Rosses, and Other Poems-Dublin-1918-Maunsel-papr cov bds-v scarce-1st ed (z8) 165.00

O'SULLIVAN,VINCENT-Some Letters to A J A Symons-Edinburgh-1975-Tragara Pr-wrps,ltd to 130c,nbrd,prtd on Strathmore papr-1st ed (y7) 45.00

O'TOOLE,GEORGE B-Case Against Evolution-NY-1925-Macmillan-xvi+408p-maroon cl-1st ed (a2) 20.00

O.V.I.-REUNION MINUTES AND ROSTER OF 125TH ... 1900-np-1900-17p-wrps-reunion at Hawley House (f1) 50.00

OAKES,MAUD-Two Crosses of Todos Santos-NY-1951-Pantheon-4to-photos,illus-1st ed (b4) 75.00

OAKLEY,AMY-Kaleidoscopic Quebec-NY-1947-Appleton Century-278p-e.p. maps,illus-1st ed (p2,chip dj) 12.50

OAKLEY,GRAHAM-Hetty and Harriet-NY-1982-Atheneum-oblng 8vo-unpgd-pict cl,col illus,auth-1st US ed (r3,f,f dj) 20.00

OATES,E W-Fauna of British India Including Ceylon and Burma. Birds-1889 to 98-Taylor & Francis-4 vols (bb3,cor wn,bds spot) 135.00

OATES,JOYCE C-Angel of Light-1981-Dutton-1st ed (x2,f,dj) 15.00

OATES,JOYCE C-Assassins-NY-(1975)-Vanguard-1st ed (ee2,f,dj) 35.00

OATES,JOYCE C-Bellefleur-NY-1980-1st ed (y7,dj) 12.00

OATES,JOYCE C-Childworld-NY-1976-1st ed (r5,f,dj) 20.00

OATES,JOYCE C-Crossing the Border-NY-1976-1st ed (r5,f,dj) 20.00

OATES,JOYCE C-Cybele-Santa Barbara-1979-Black Sparrow-cl,acetate dj-ltd to 300c,autg-1st ed (w6,f,dj) 50.00

OATES,JOYCE C-Cybele-Santa Barbara-1979-dec bds,acetate dj,ltd to 1000c-1st trd ed (t5,f,dj) 15.00

OATES,JOYCE C-Do With Me What You Will-NY-(1973)-Vanguard-1st ed (b5,as new in dj) 25.00

OATES,JOYCE C-Do With Me What You Will-NY-1973-1st ed (r5,f,dj) 20.00

OATES,JOYCE C-Goddess and Other Women-NY-1974-1st ed (t5,dj) 20.00

OATES,JOYCE C-Hostile Sun: Poetry of D H Lawrence-LA-1973-Black Sparrow-ltd to 300c,nbrd,autg-1st ed (ee2,f) 75.00

OATES,JOYCE C-Hungry Ghosts-LA-1974-Black Sparrow-4to-cl/bds,ltd to 350c,nbrd,autg (x3,f) 55.00

OATES,JOYCE C-New Heaven: New Earth-NY-(1974)-Vanguard-1st ed (ee2,f,dj) 45.00

OATES,JOYCE C-Son of the Morning-NY-1978-Vanguard-1st ed (h3,f,dj) 20.00

OATES,JOYCE C-Step Father-Northridge-1978-Lord John Pr-ltd to 300c,autg,iss w/o dj-1st ed (cc1,as new) 40.00

OATES,JOYCE C-Them-NY-(1969)-Vanguard-1st ed (b3,f,dj) 50.00

OATES,JOYCE C-Wheel of Love-NY-1970-1st ed (r5,dj) 15.00

OATES,JOYCE C-Wonderland-NY-(1971)-Vanguard-1st ed (ee2,f,dj) 35.00

OATES,STEPHEN B-Visions of Glory-Norman-1970-217p-1st ed (t7,f,dj) 15.00

OATMAN,EDWARD L-Diagnostics of the Fundus Oculi-Troy-1913-Southworth-3 vols(1 text+2 portfolios)-blu cl,234 illus,4 col plts,79 stereograms,8 diagnostic cards-1st ed (a2) 75.00

OBER,F A-Camps in the Caribbees-Bost-1880-8vo-366p-orig brwn cl,gilt vign frnt & back cov,34 engrvngs (y8,hng weak) 150.00

OBER,WILLIAM B-Boswell's Clap and Other Essays-Carbondale-(1979)-SIU Pr-xviii+291p-brwn cl-1st ed (j2,dj) 20.00

OBERG,KALERVO-Social Economy of the Tlingit Indians-Seattle-1973-U of Wash Pr-xvi,146p-1 map,4 figs,8 photos-1st ed (bb7,dj) 35.00*

OBERHOLSER,H C-Bird Life of Louisiana-1938-La Conserv Dept-834p-wrps,8 col plts,37 photos (bb3) 45.00

OBERHOLSER,H C-Bird Life of Texas-1974-U of Tex-4to-2 vols-34 col & 36 b&w plts by Fuertes,photos,maps (bb3,f) 135.00

OBERHOLSER,HARRY C-Bird Life of Texas-Austin-1974-U of Tex-2 vols-paintings,maps (c9,box) 125.00

OBERHOLSER,HARRY C-Birds of the Anamba Islands-Wash-1917-USNM,Bull.98-76p-wrps (b9,uncut) 10.00

OBERHOLSER,HARRY C-Birds of the Natuna Islands-Wash-1932-USNM,Bull.159-137p (b9) 12.50

OBERLIN,JOHN F-Memoirs of ...-Pitt-1832-Luke Loomis-246p-cl-1st US ed (e1,lacks frnt f.e.p.,sl wn) 27.50

OBERSTE,WILLIAM H-Texas Irish Empresarios and Their Colonies-Austin-1953-Von Boeckmann-Jones-310p+title list-fldg maps-ltd to 300c,nbrd,autg (a9) 350.00

OBOJSKI,ROBERT-All Star Baseball Since 1933-1980-Stein & Day-photos-1st ed (s8,f,f dj) 11.00

OBOJSKI,ROBERT-Bush League-1975-MacMillan-1st ed (ff2,dj) 35.00

OBREITER,JOHN-77th Pennsylvania at Shiloh-Harrisburg-1908-Harrisburg Publ-341p-frntis,illus,maps-rvsd ed (o7) 75.00

OCEAN COUNTY-Tides of Time in...-(np)-1940-4to-(8),192,(4)p-cl,illus (aa6) 30.00

ODDO,SANDRA-Home Made-NY-1972-Atheneum-504p-1st ed (k6) 22.00

ODETS,CLIFFORD-Golden Boy-Lond-1938-Gollancz-wrps in dj-1st Brit ed (v5,f,dj) 35.00

OELGART,ISAAC-Borzoi Books for Sportsmen-Litchfield-1982-8vo-12p-ltd to 75c,nbrd,autg,hndsewn wrps (m3,as new) 20.00

OESTERLEN,F-Medical Logic-Lond-1855-437p-1st Engl transl (dd3) 75.00

OESTERREICH,TRAUGOTT-Possession and Exorcism-NY-1974-Causeway Bks-8vo-400p-1st transl ed (aa7,dj sl rub,chip) 15.00*

OETTINGER,ANTHONY G-Automatic Language Translation-Cambridge-1960-Harvard Univ Pr-xx+380p-grn cl,95 figs-1st ed (j2,dj) 30.00

OFFICER,H R-Australian Honeyeaters-1965-Bird Observers Club-83p-8 col plts,map (bb3,cor bump,dj) 35.00

OFFICIAL BASE BALL RULES...HOW TO PITCH-Cin-nd(1922)-P Goldsmith's Sons Mfg-48p-wrps (b1,sl wn) 17.50

OGDEN,JOHN-Science of Education-Cin-1859-Moore,Wilstach,Keys-478p-cl-3rd ed (k1) 20.00

OGDEN,PETER S-Snare Country Journal's 1824 to 26-Lond-1950-Hudson Bay Record Soc-Vol.XIII-283p-t.e.g.,fldg map in rear pckt-ltd ed (g7,unopened,f) 125.00

OGDEN,W A-Anthem Choir...-Toledo-(1872)-W W Whitney-206,(2)p-bds (g1) 15.00

OGDEN-History of...-Ogden City-1940-WPA-77p-pict wrps,frntis,photos-scarce-1st ed (t7) 40.00

OGLESBY,CATHARINE-Modern Primitive Arts of Mexico, Guatemala & the Southwest-NY-1939-McGraw Hill-photos,illus-1st ed (b4) 35.00

OGLESBY,RICHARD E-Manual Lisa and the Opening of the Missouri Fur Trade-Norman-(1963)-246p-cl-1st ed so stated (aa1,pencil mrks,dj) 15.00

OHIO ARCHAEOLOGICAL AND HISTORICAL PUBLICATIONS. VOL.VIII-Columbus-1900-488p-cl,fldg map (c1) 17.50

OHIO FARMERS ALMANAC 1881-(Cleve)-(1880)-Ohio Farmers Insurance-(32)p-wrps (d1) 15.00

OHIO-BIOGRAPHICAL ENCYCLOPEDIA OF ... OF THE NINETEENTH CENTURY-Cin,Phila-1876-Galaxy-672p-mor (g1) 100.00

OHIO-INVENTORY OF THE COUNTY ARCHIVES OF ...-Cleve-1937-Cuyahoga Cnty Archvs Srvy-347p-wrps-WPA No.18 (d1) 20.00

OHIO-OFFICIAL ROSTER OF THE SOLDIERS OF...IN THE WAR OF THE REBELLION,VOL.IV: 37TH-53RD REG INFANTRY-Akron-1887-Werner Prtg & Mfg-820p-3/4 lea (v2) 30.00

OHIO: AN EMPIRE WITHIN AN EMPIRE-Columbus-1944-Ohio Dvlpmnt & Publ Comm-212p-cl,map(incl 2 fldg),chrts (aa1) 15.00

OKA,HIDEYUKI-How to Wrap 5 Eggs-NY-1967-Harper-1st ed (e8,rprd dj) 85.00

OKAKURA-KAKUZO-Awakening of Japan-NY-1921-Japan Soc-12mo-255p-rprnt of orig 1904 ed (c3,fray dj) 12.00

OKLADNIKOV,A P-Soviet Far East in Antiquity-Tor-1965-U of Tor Pr-280p-orig blu prtd wrps (ee7,sp fade) 45.00

OKRENT,DANIEL-ED.-Ultimate Baseball Book-1979-Houghton Mifflin-1st ed (p7,f,dj) 50.00

OKRENT,DANIEL-ED.-Ultimate Baseball Book-1979-Houghton Mifflin-photos+col section not incl in pbk eds-1st ed (s8,f,dj) 60.00

OLANDER,JOSEPH-ED.-Robert A Heinlein-NY-(1978)-Taplinger-wrps-1st ed (h3,f) 15.00

OLCOTT,ANTHONY-Murder at the Red October-Chig-1981-Academy-auth 1st bk-1st ed (q4,f,dj) 17.50

OLD ENGLISH COFFEE HOUSES-(1954)-Rodale Pr-16mo-32p-prtd bds,col plts-1st ed (q8) 8.50

OLD TESTAMENT MINIATURES-NY-1975-Braziller-folio-209p-beige cl,col illus (r10,wn dj) 40.00

OLDEN,SARAH E-Little Slants of Western Life-NY-1927-Harold Vinal-1st ed (b4) 50.00

OLDERMAN,MURRAY-Nelson's 20th Century Encyclopedia of Baseball-1963-Nelson-drwngs by auth,photos-1st ed (s8,f,dj) 22.50

OLDROYD,I S-Marine Shells of the West Coast of North America-1924 to 27-Stanford-4 vols-cl,165 plts (bb3,rbnd) 235.00

OLDROYD,OSBORN H-Assassination of Abraham Lincoln-Wash D.C.-1901-xviii+305p+ads-brwn cl,photos,fldg map-1st ed (b2,sp fray,hng crack) 50.00

OLDS,ELIZABETH-Feather Mountain-Bost-1951-Houghton Mifflin-oblng 8vo-pict cl,col & b&w illus,auth-1st ed (s3,sl fade,few pg soil,dj) 45.00

OLDS,IRVING S-Bits and Pieces of American History...by a Collection of American Naval and... Historical Prints...-NY-1951-4to-xxv,463p-beige gry cl,g cov & sp titles,132 illus-one of 500c (nn1,f) 350.00

OLDS,R-Helldiver Squadron-NY-1944-8vo-xiv,226p-g cl,plts,maps-1st ed (s2,sl chip dj) 35.00

OLENDORFF,R R-Golden Eagle Country-NY-1975-4to-202p-cl,map,drwngs (y8,pres cpy) 45.00

OLENDORFF,RICHARD R-Golden Eagle Country-NY-1975-Knopf-4to-202p-illus-1st ed (aa5,f,dj) 18.00

OLENIUS,ELSA-ED.-Great Swedish Fairy Tales-NY-(1973)-Delacorte-238p-pict cl,45p col illus,2 half pg,J Bauer-1st US ed (r3,f,dj) 35.00

OLESKER,HARRY-Impact-NY-1961-Random-1st ed (e4,f,dj) 12.50

OLIPHANT,J ORIN-On the Cattle Ranges of the Oregon Country-(1968)-U of Wa-372p-e.p. map-Herd 1709-1st ed (r8,dj) 40.00

OLIPHANT,MRS MARGARET-Literary History of England in the End of the Eighteenth and Beginning of the Nineteenth Century-Lond-1882-Macmillan-3 vols-g blu cl-1st ed,2nd iss (kk5) 125.00

OLIPHANT,MRS. W O W-Autobiography and Letters of...-NY-1899-Dodd,Mead-8vo-451p-3/4 mor & mrbld bds,raised bnds,t.e.g.-1st US ed (w6,uncut,mostly unopened) 75.00

OLIVER,ANDREW,JR.-Ancient Glass in the Museum of Natural History, Pittsburgh-1980-Carnegie Inst-153p-illus(incl col) (cc8) 45.00

OLIVER,CHAD-Another Kind-NY-(1954)-Ballantine-1st ed (k3,pgs brwnd,sl soil dj) 125.00

OLIVER,CHAD-Edge of Forever-LA-(1971)-Shelbourne-1st ed (e3,sl tn dj) 25.00

OLIVER,CHARLES-Dinner at Buckingham Palace-Englewood Cliffs-1972-Prentice Hall-256p-1st ed (j8,f,dj) 30.00

OLIVER,DOUGLAS L-Pacific Islands-Cambridge-1958-Harvard U Pr-8vo-x,313p-tan cl,map e.p.,maps,decs-3rd prtg (p8,f,sl wn dj) 45.00

OLIVER,F W-ED.-Natural History of Plants-Lond-1894-Blackie & Sons-4to-2 vols-1/2 lea,g emboss ribbed sp,mrbld bds & e.p.,a.e.g.,woodcts,16 col plts-1st ed (mm8,sl rub & wn) 450.00*

OLIVER,HERMAN-Gold and Cattle Country-1961-Binfords & Mort-312p-illus-1st ed (r8,dj) 30.00

OLIVER,HERMAN-Gold and Cattle Country-Portland-1961-Binfords & Mort-312p-photos,illus e.p.-1st ed (bb4) 25.00

OLIVER,RAYMOND-French at Table-Lond-(1967)-Wine & Food Soc-4to-335p-blk cl,illus e.p.,col & b&w plts-1st ed (q8,cov fade) 35.00

OLIVER,ROBERT-An Apple a Day-Lond-(1963)-Hutchinson-271p-red cl,photos-1st ed (q8,edge tn dj) 15.00

OLIVIA,LEO E-Soldiers on the Santa Fe Trail-Norman-(1967)-226p-illus,fldg map-1st ed (n3,f,dj) 35.00

OLLARD,RICHARD-This War Without an Enemy-NY-1976-224p-illus-1st Amer ed (b7,dj) 35.00

OLLEY,G P,CAPT.-Million Miles in the Air-Lond-nd(ca.1934)-8vo-320p-cl,frntis,16p illus-1st ed (s2) 25.00

OLLIVANT,ALFRED-Owd Bob-Lond-1898-Methuen-orig g titled cl-1st ed (aa9,sl fade sp) 45.00

OLMSTED,MILDRED-Land of Never Was-Phila-(1908)-Jacobs-8vo-148p-cl,pict pasteon,12 col plts-1st ed (nn10,cov plt sl rub,nick) 65.00

OLMSTED-Walks and Talks of an American Farmer in England-NY-1852-Putnam-246p-cl (x6,edge wn,soil cov,sl fox) 90.00

OLNEY,EDWARD-Complete School Algebra...-NY-(1870)-Sheldon-390p-lea-bckd cl (k1) 15.00

OLNEY,JUDITH-Judith Olney's Entertainments-NY-(1981)-Barron's-4to-307p-tan cl,col photos (q8,dj) 25.00

OLSCHAK,BLANCH-Bhutan-Lond,NY-1971-63p-80 col photos-1st ed (q10,f,dj) 25.00

OLSCHAK,BLANCH-Bhutan: Land of Hidden Treasures-NY-1971-63p-80 col photos-1st ed (a4,f,dj) 45.00

OLSEN,BRUCE M-I Did Not Kill Bob Neville-Victoria-1975-Pac Coast Publ-8vo-xi,235p-1st ed (cc7,dj) 15.00*

OLSEN,D B-Enrollment Canceled-NY-1952-Dbldy CC-1st ed (f4,sl yel pgs,dj) 25.00

OLSEN,D B-Gallows for the Groom-NY-1947-Dbldy CC-1st ed (j4,dj) 20.00

OLSEN,D B-Something About Midnight-NY-1950-Dbldy CC-1st ed (j4,yel pgs,dj) 20.00

OLSEN,D B-Ticking Heart-NY-1940-Dbldy CC-1st ed (f4,f,sl wn dj) 50.00

OLSEN,JACK-Climb Up to Hell-NY-1962-Harper & Row-8vo-212p-blk cl,photos-1st ed (gg6,wn dj) 20.00

OLSEN,TILLIE-Tell Me a Riddle-NY-(1978)-Delacorte-8vo-cl-ltd to 100c,autg-1st ltd autg ed (jj8,vf,box) 100.00

OLSEN,TILLIE-Yonnondio-Lond-1975-1st Brit ed (t5,dj) 20.00

OLSEN,TILLIE-Yonnondio-NY-1974-1st ed (p5,f,dj) 40.00

OLSON,CHARLES-Archeologist of Morning-NY-1970-Cape Goliard/Grossman-1st ed,1st iss (q1,f,sl creased dj) 300.00

OLSON,CHARLES-Call Me Ishmael-NY-(1947)-Reynal & Hitchcock-auth 1st bk-1st ed (y4,dj) 100.00

OLSON,CHARLES-Mayan Letters-Lond-1968-J Cape-1st Brit ed (v5,f,sl tn dj) 50.00

OLSON,CHARLES-Proprioception-SF-1965-Four Seasons-wrps-1st ed (v5,f) 15.00

OLSON,CHARLES-Stocking Cap-SF-1966-Four Seasons Fndtn-wrps-1st ed (m7,f) 20.00

OLSON,CHARLES-Y & X-(Wash D.C.)-1948-Black Sun Pr,C Crosby-4to-glassine wrps,papr envelope,box(issued wi only sm part of edition)-ltd to 500c-scarce-1st ed (ll10,f,sl wn & split box) 450.00

OLSON,D B-Cat Wears a Mask-1949-CC-1st ed (s10,brwnd pgs,soil dj) 20.00

OLSON,D B-Devious Design-1948-CC-1st ed (s10,dj) 20.00

OLSON,FRED-Exciter Fishing-NY-1978-8vo-270p-photos-1st ed (m3,vf,dj) 12.50

OLSON,JAMES C-History of Nebraska-Lincoln-1955-Univ of Nebr-xii+372p-brwn cl,illus-1st ed (m2,dj) 20.00

OLSON,JAMES C-Red Cloud and the Sioux Problem-Lincoln-(1965)-U of Neb Pr-375p-e.p. maps,illus-1st ed (dd4,dj) 45.00

OLSON,K E-Music and Musket-Westport-1981-299p-illus (z10,f,dj) 25.00

OLSON,SIGURD-Runes of the North-NY-1964-Knopf-256p-cl,illus (z7,dj) 25.00

OLSON,TED-Ranch on the Laramie-Bost-1973-240p-1st ed (t7,dj) 12.50

OLSSON,JAN-Welcome to Tombstone-Lond-1956-Elek-164p-cl,photos-Guns #1649-scarce-1st ed (w3,f,dj) 40.00

OMAN,CHARLES-History of the Art of War in the Sixteenth Century-Lond-1937-784p-red cl,12 plts,13 maps-1st ed (b7) 200.00

OMAN,JOHN C-Brahmans,Theists and Muslims of India-Phila-nd(c.1900)-G W Jacobs-buckrm,photos,drwngs-scarce-1st Amer ed (o8) 75.00

OMAR KHAYYAM-Rubaiyat of Omar Khayyam-Bost-(1912)-Houghton Mifflin-orig cl bckd bds,papr sp labl,pict cov labl,drwngs by Vedder-transl by Edw Fitzgerald (aa9) 25.00

OMMANNEY,F D-Fishes-Sacramento-1967-4to-192p-photos (m3,vf) 12.50

OMORI-ET AL-TRANSL.-Diaries of Court Ladies of Old Japan...-Bost,NY-1920-Houghton Mifflin-xxxii,200p-cl/bds,col frntis wi guard,plts(1 col)-1st ed (kk1,bump) 45.00

OMWAKE,JOHN-Conestoga Six Horse Bell Teams of Eastern Pennsylvania-Cin-1930-Omwake-4to-136p-1st ed (j9,pres) 225.00

ONDAATJE,MICHAEL-Coming Through Slaughter-NY-nd-Norton-1st US ed (c10,f,dj) 40.00

ONE HUNDRED SIXTEEN UNCOMMON BOOKS ON FOOD AND DRINK-Berkeley-(1975)-Friends of Bancroft Libr-84p-wrps,illus (m6) 50.00

ONO,YOKO-Grapefruit-NY-(1970)-S&S-sq 16mo-orig publ in Tokyo in an ed of 500c-1st prtg trd ed (k9,dj wn) 35.00

OPDYKE,CHARLES W-Op Dyck Genealogy-NY-1889-(xlii),499p-cl (aa6) 200.00

OPERATION CROSSROADS-NY-1946-Wm H Wise-roy 8vo-224p-cl,illus (s2) 125.00

OPHULUS,M-Sorrow and the Pity-1972-Outerbridge & Lazard-illus-1st ed (x2,f,dj) 38.00

OPLER,MORRIS E-Grenville Goodwin Among the Western Apache-Tucson-1973-103p-1st ed (t7,f,dj) 12.50

OPLER,MORRIS E-Memoirs of the Amer Anthropological Assoc, Dirty Boy, a Jicarilla Tale of Raid and War-Menasha-1938-80p-wrps-1st ed (t7) 15.00

OPPEN,GEORGE-Collected Poems-(NY)-(1975)-New Directions-1st ed (a10,f,dj) 35.00

OPPENHEIM,E PHILLIPS-Envoy Extraordinary-Tor-1937-McClelland & Stewart-1st Can ed (f4,f,dj) 12.50

OPPENHEIM,E PHILLIPS-Great Impersonation-Bost-1920-Little-1st US ed (h4) 12.50

OPPENHEIM,E PHILLIPS-Harvey Garrard's Crime-Bost-1926-Little-precedes Brit ed-1st ed (d4,sl tn dj) 25.00

OPPENHEIM,E PHILLIPS-Mayor on Horseback-Tor-1937-McClelland-1st Can ed (k4,f,dj) 20.00

OPPENHEIM,E PHILLIPS-Michael's Evil Deeds-Bost-1923-Little-wrap-around dj-1st ed (g4,sl tn dj) 35.00

OPPENHEIM,E PHILLIPS-NIcholas Goade,Detective-Bost-1929-Little-1st US ed (f4) 10.00

OPPENHEIM,E PHILLIPS-Spymaster-Bost-1938-Little-1st US ed (e4,dj) 15.00

OPPENHEIM,JAMES-Solitary-NY-1919-Huebsch-1st ed (w5) 20.00

OPPENHEIMER,JOEL-Dutiful Son-(Highlands)-1956-J Williams/Jargon 16-8vo-blu wprs wi prtd labl-ltd to 200c-scarce-1st ed (jj8,sl drknd) 450.00

ORANGES-Atlas of the...by J M Lathrop and T Flynn-Phila-1911-A H Mueller-folio-2 prtd lvs + 27 dblpg col maps,all linen backd as iss,lea backd cl (aa6,outer hngs broken) 450.00

ORCHARD,VINCENT-Tattersalls-Lond-1954-Hutchinson-2nd prtg (j9,dj) 35.00

ORCUTT,HIRAM-Gleanings from School-Life Experience-Rutland-1858-Tuttle-72p-cl (k1,sl wn sp) 25.00

ORCUTT,WILLIAM D-Magic of the Book-Bost-1930-Little,Brown-g dec cl,t.e.g.,col frntis guarded,plts-1st trd ed (dd10) 65.00

ORCUTT,WILLIAM D-Master Makers of the Book-Lond-nd(ca.1928)-Allen & Unwin-8vo-272p-cl-1st Brit ed (x4,sl fox dj) 45.00

ORCUTT,WILLIAM D-Robert Cavelier-Chig-1904-g pict cov,illus-auth 1st bk-1st ed (r2,uncut,sl rub) 55.00

ORCZY,BARONESS-Man in the Corner-NY-1909-Dodd-1st US ed (g4,cov fade) 85.00

ORCZY,BARONESS-Noble Rogue-NY-1912-Hodder-1st US ed (h4) 12.50

ORCZY,BARONESS-Triumph of the Scarlet Pimpernel-1922-Doran-1st Amer ed (s10,sp lettrng fade,cov stnd) 15.00

OREGON ALMANAC-Salem-1915-320p-pict wrps,maps-scarce-1st ed (t7) 25.00

OREGON STATE-5th & 6th Annual Reports of the Fish & Game Protector of the State of Oregon 1897-1898-Salem-1898-8vo-138p+index-illus,photos-scarce (m3) 65.00

OREGON, END OF THE TRAIL-(1940)-Binfords & Mort-549p-photos,e.p. map,lg fldg map rear pckt,Amer Guide Ser-1st ed (r8,few stnd pgs,dj chip) 50.00

OREM,PRESTON D-Baseball 1845 to 1881-1961-self publ-photos,scarce-1st ed (s8,f) 70.00

ORFORD,HENRY-Lens Work for Amateurs-Lond-1944(1931)-Sir Isaac Pitman-230p-blu cl,illus-5th ed,rvsd (hh6,cor bump) 50.00

ORLEANS,DUKE OF-Hunters & Hunting in the Arctic-Lond-1911-204p-photos,illus (gg3,f) 15.00

ORLOFF,N W-Armenian Folk Tales-Phila-1946-Colonial Hs-cl,col frntis,col & b&w illus-1st ed (n8,vf,dj) 35.00

ORMES,ROBERT M-Railroads and the Rockies-Denver-1963-406p-1st ed (n4,f,dj) 37.50

ORMES,ROBERT-Guide to the Colorado Mountains-1955-231p-4th rvsd ed (q10,as new in dj) 20.00

ORMOND,CLYDE-Hunting Our Biggest Game-Harrisburg-1956-8vo-197p-illus,photos (m3,f,dj) 13.00

ORMOND,R-John Singer Sargent-NY-1970-152 plts(incl 32 col)-1st Amer ed (kk4,dj) 200.00

ORMSBY,MARGARET A-British Columbia: a History-(Tor)-1958-Macmillan-x,558p-cl,illus(incl col),col maps,ports (aa2,dj) 35.00*

ORMSBY,WATERMAN-Butterfield Overland Mail-1960(1942)-1960-Huntington Libr-179p-map e.p. (d3,dj) 50.00

ORMSBY,WATERMAN-Butterfield Overland Mail-San Marino-1955-179p-map e.p. (t7,dj) 30.00

ORNDUFF,DONALD R-First 49-Kansas City-1981-Lowell Pr-281p-cl,photos-1st ed (w3,vf,dj) 17.50

ORNITZ,SAMUEL-Bride of the Sabbath-NY-1951-Rinehart-1st ed (v5,f,dj) 35.00

ORNSTEIN,ROBERT E-Psychology of Consciousness-NY-1972-Viking-cl-1st ed (n8,vf,dj) 15.00

ORPEN,A E-Memories of the Old Emigrant Days in Kansas, 1862 to 1865-Edinburgh-1926-ix,324p (bb9) 75.00

ORR,H WINNETT-On the Contributions of Hugh Owen Thomas, Sir Robert Jones, and John Ridlon...-Springfield-1949-253p-1st ed (dd3) 75.00

ORR,MARY M-12,000 Miles by Land Rover-Grand Rapids-1957-Zondervan Publ-8vo-192p-drwngs-1st ed (aa7,dj) 15.00*

ORR,MYRON D-Citadel of the Lakes-NY-1952-Dodd,Mead-287p-cl (z7,dj) 30.00

ORR,PHIL-Prehistory of Santa Rosa Island-Santa Barbara-1968-253p-photos-1st ed (d3) 15.00

ORR,R T-Birds of Lake Tahoe Region-SF-1971-8vo-150p-col frntis (y8) 20.00

ORR,R T-Mammals of Lake Tahoe-SF-1949-8vo-(8),127p-cl,illus (y8,wn dj) 14.00

ORR,R T-Rabbits of California-SF-1940-8vo-(3),227p-wrps,10 plts (y8) 18.50

ORR,ROBERT T-Wildflowers of Western America-NY-1974-270p-291 col photos-1st ed (hh7,dj) 27.50

ORTIZ,ALFONSO-Tewa World-Chig-(1969)-186p-1st prtg (v7,f,dj,review cpy) 25.00

ORTNER,SHERRY-Sherpas Through Their Rituals-Cambridge-1978-194p-1st ed (o10) 25.00

ORTON,HOY D-Orton's Lighting Calculator and Accountant's Assistant...-Balt-1875-216p-cl-new ed (k1,sl wn sp) 15.00

ORTON,HOY D-Orton's Lightning Calculator, and Accountant's Assistant-Shelby-(1866)-H D Orton-194p-prtd bds (k1) 17.50

ORTON,JAMES-Andes and the Amazon-1870-Harper-356p-illus,map (bb3,cov wn,sl fox,map tn) 35.00

ORTON,JAMES-Andes and the Amazon-NY-(1875)-Harper & Bros-g stmpd pebble cl,engrvngs,2 fldg maps-3rd ed,rvsd & enlgd (p6) 75.00

ORTON,JAMES-Underground Treasures-Hartford-1872-137p-cl,"illuminated t.p. precedes reg t.p.,frntis,4 plts-1st ed (aa1,cov sl spot) 100.00

ORVIS,CHARLES-Fishing With the Fly-Manchester-1883-12mo-299p-15 col plts-scarce-1st ed (m3,frnt hng cracked & weak) 130.00

ORWELL,GEORGE-Animal Farm-NY-(1946)-Harcourt Brace-1st US ed (ff6,dj sl wn & sl soil) 100.00

ORWELL,GEORGE-Dickens,Dali & Others-NY-1946-1st US ed (s5,dj sl chip & sl stnd) 45.00

ORWELL,GEORGE-English People-Lond-1947-Collins-pict bds,8 col plts,17 b&w illus-1st ed (kk5,f,dj) 65.00

ORWELL,GEORGE-English People-Lond-1947-Collins-sm 4to-bds,illus-1st ed (jj8,f,dj) 50.00

ORWELL,GEORGE-Keep the Apidistra Flying-(1956)-Harcourt-1st US ed (jj6,f,dj sl tn & rub) 65.00

ORWELL,GEORGE-Keep the Aspidistra Flying-NY-(1956)-Harcourt-1st US ed (aa10,dj) 100.00

ORWELL,GEORGE-Lion and the Unicorn-Lond-1941-Secker & Warburg-8vo-wht cl-1st ed (u10,dj sl soil & edge tn) 75.00

ORWELL,GEORGE-Nineteen Eighty Four-Lond-1949-Secker & Warburg-8vo-cl,variant grn dj(no priority)-1st ed (kk8,dj sl tn & edgewn) 750.00

ORWELL,GEORGE-Orwell Reader-NY-1956-Harcourt Brace-1st ed (e8,f,f dj) 45.00

ORWELL,GEORGE-Shooting an Elephant & Other Essays-NY-1950-HB-ltd to 4000c-1st ed (y1,f,f dj) 100.00

ORWELL,GEORGE-Shooting an Elephant-Lond-(1950)-Secker-1st ed (aa10,dj) 100.00

OSBORN,ARTHUR W-Meaning of Personal Existence in the Light of Paranormal Phenomena-Wheaton-1966-Theosoph Publ Hs-cl-1st ed (l8,f,dj) 15.00

OSBORN,E B-ED.-Anthology of Sporting Verse-Lond-1930-12mo-288p (m3) 15.00

OSBORN,HENRY F-Titanotheres of Ancient Wyoming,Dakota and Nebraska-Wash D.C.-1929-GPO/US Geo Srvy,Mono.55-4to-2 vols-brwn cl,236plts-1st ed (g2) 350.00

OSBORN,HERBERT-Fragments of Entomological History-Columbus-1937-publ by auth-viii+393p-blu cl,plts-1st ed (mm10) 35.00

OSBORN,HERBERT-Pediculi and Mallophaga Affecting Man and the Lower Animals-Wash-1891-56p-wrps (f1) 12.50

OSBORNE,DOUGLAS-River Basin Surveys Papers,No.8...McNary Reservoir...Oregon-Wash D.C.-1957-GPO/Bur Ethno Bull No.166-258p-orig olive cl,g titles,40 plts,19 maps-1st ed (ee7) 20.00

OSBORNE,HAROLD-South American Mythology-Middlesex-1968-P Hamlyn-cl,col & b&w illus on every pg-1st ed (l8,vf,dj) 10.00

OSBORNE,NEWELL Y-Select School-np-(1967)-645p-bds (k1,f,dj) 17.50

OSBORNE,W H-Red Mouse-1909-DM-auth 1st bk-1st ed (x7) 20.00

OSBOURNE,KATHARINE D-Robert Louis Stevenson in California-Chig-1911-McClurg-emboss ship,sp labl,frntis,69 illus-1st ed (ee7,f) 60.00

OSBUN,ALBERT G-To California and the South Seas-San Marino-1966-Huntington Libr-8vo-xiii,233p-1st ed (mm1,f,sl wn dj) 40.00

OSBURN,ARTHUR W-Axis and the Rim-NY-1963-Nelson & Sons-cl-1st Amer ed (n8,dj) 20.00

OSBURN,BURL-Constructive Design-Milw-(1948)-Bruce-4to-94p-illus-1st ed (ee5) 20.00

OSGOOD,CORNELIUS-Chinese, a Study of a Hong Kong Community-Tucson-(1975)-U Arizona Pr-lg 8vo-3 vols-1st ed (ff5,vf,f dj,f box) 75.00

OSGOOD,E S-Field Notes of Capt William Clark 1803 to 05-New Haven,Lond-1964-folio-335p-photo repro of Clark's notes-1st ed (h7,vf,vf dj) 325.00

OSGOOD,ERNEST S-Day of the Cattleman-Mpls-1929-Univ of Minn-xiv+283p-tan cl,14 plts & maps-1st ed (e2,sl drknd sp) 135.00

OSGOOD,HENRY O-So This is Jazz-Bost-1926-illus-1st ed (r2,sp chip dj) 75.00

OSGOOD,HENRY O-So This is Jazz-Bost-1926-Little,Brown-1st ed (w1,lacks dj) 35.00

OSGOOD,LUCIUS-Osgood's Progressive Speller-Pitt-(1868)-A H English-170p-bds (k1,sl chip sp) 15.00

OSGOOD,W H-Results of a Biological Reconnoissance of the Yukon River Region-Wash-1900-100p-wrps (bb9) 50.00

OSKISON,JOHN M-Texas Titan-NY-1929-Dbldy,Doran-331p-cl-1st ed (w3,vf,sp chip dj) 30.00

OSLER,E B-Man Who Had to Hang Louis Riel-Tor-1961-Longmans,Green-8vo-320p-1st ed (cc7,dj sl scuff,chip) 15.00*

OSLER,W-An Alabama Student and Other Biographical Essays-NY-1908-334p-1st ed,1st prtg (dd3) 225.00

OSLER,W-Concise History of Medicine-Balt-1919-66p-1st ed (dd3) 125.00

OSLER,W-Evolution of Modern Medicine-New Haven-1921-243p-1st ed (dd3) 250.00

OSLER,W-Evolution of Modern Medicine-New Haven-1921-Yale Univ Pr-1st ed (p6) 200.00

OSLER,W-Incunabula Medica, a Study of the Earliest Printed Medical Books 1467 to 1480-Oxford-1923-137p-linen wi papr cov bds,16 plts & frntis (g10,ex-libr) 450.00

OSLER,W-Old Humanities and the New Science-Bost-1920-64p-port (dd3) 100.00

OSLER,W-Principles and Practice of Medicine-NY-1892-1079p-orig brwn cl-1st ed,2nd prtg (dd3,f) 1,250.00

OSLER,W-Principles and Practice of Medicine-NY-1913-1225p-8th ed (dd3) 75.00

OSLER,W-Unity, Peace, and Concord-Oxford-1905-22p-wrps-scarce-1st ed (dd3) 150.00

OSMOND,R-John Singer Sargent-NY-1970-lg 4to-152 plts(incl 32 col)-1st Amer ed (ee1) 250.00

OSSMAN,DAVID-Sullen Art-NY-1963-Corinth-wrps-1st ed (w5,f) 15.00

OSTEN,EARL-Tournament Fly & Bait Casting-NY-1946-8vo-145p-photos (m3,f,sl fray dj) 17.50

OSTENSO,MARTHA-White Reef-NY-1934-Dodd-1st ed (v5,dj sl chip,wn) 25.00

OSTERWEIS,R G-Myth of the Lost Cause, 1865 to 1900-Hamden-1973-188p (z10,f,dj) 12.50

OSTOR,AKOS-Play of the Gods-Chig-(1980)-U of Chig Pr-8vo-241p-cl-1st ed (y5,f,f dj) 27.00

OSTRANDER,A B-After 60 Years-Seattle-(1925)-120p-wrps,illus-1st ed (c4) 100.00

OSTRANDER,ISABEL-Clue in the Air-NY-1917-Watt-1st ed (e4) 15.00

OSTRANDER,ISABEL-Neglected Clue-NY-1925-McBride-1st ed (f4) 10.00

OSTRIKER,ALICIA-Songs-NY-1969-Holt-1st ed (w5,f,dj) 35.00

OSTROGORSKY,GEORGE-History of the Byzantine State-New Brunswick-1957-Rutgers U Pr-8vo-548p-illus,8 col maps-1st US ed (cc5,f,dj) 45.00

OSTROVSKY,ERIKA-Celine and His Vision-NY/Lond-1967-NYU Pr/U of Lond Pr-1st ed (bb1,f,dj) 20.00

OSTROVSKY,ERIKA-Voyeur Voyant-NY-(1971)-Random-photos-1st ed (bb1,f,dj) 20.00

OSWALD,FELIX-Vaccination a Crime, with Comments on Other Sanitary Superstitions-NY-1901-195p-1/2 lea-1st ed (dd3) 75.00

OTERO,MIGUEL A-My Life on the Frontier 1864 to 1882-NY-1935-Pr of Pioneers-293p-cl,iss w/o illus,(first of 3-vol ser)-scarce-1st trd ed (z1,cov tape mrks) 75.00

OTERO,MIGUEL A-My Life on the Frontier. Vol.2-Albuq-1939-UNM-photos-1st ed (b4,dj) 95.00

OTERO,MIGUEL A-My Nine Years as Governor-Albuq-1940-UNM-vol.3 of memoirs-1st ltd ed (b4,edgewn dj) 125.00

OTERO,MIGUEL A-Real Billy the Kid with new Light on the Lincoln County War-NY-1936-200p-photos-Adams Guns#1661-1st ed (v7) 100.00

OTERO,MIGUEL A-Real Billy the Kid with New Light on the Lincoln County War-NY-1936-R R Wilson-200p-cl,illus-Guns #1661-1st ed (w3,f) 110.00

OTERO,NINA-Old Spain in Our Southwest-NY-(1936)-192p-drwngs-1st ed (u7,dj,autg) 35.00

OTIS,JAMES-Toby Tyler, or Ten Weeks with a Circus-NY-1881-Harper & Bros-265p+ads-orig pict cl,gilt,coated e.p.,illus-scarce-1st ed (hh9,rub,spots,sl shaken) 150.00

OTIS,JAMES-Toby Tyler-(1937)-Winston-212p-illus,E Shinn,pict pastedown-1st ed thus (v8,sl wn dj) 50.00

OTIS,MAJ GEN E S-Report of...US Army, Commanding Division of Phillipines, Military Governer-Wash-1900-GPO-8vo-365p-brwn cl,6 fldg maps (p8,rbnd) 75.00

OTIS,RAYMOND-Indian Art of the Southwest-(Santa Fe)-(1931)-unpgd-wrps,4 plts-1st ed (v7) 20.00

OTT,ELEANORE-Plantation Cookery of Old Louisiana-New Orleans-(1938)-Harmanson Publ-96p-wrps-1st ed (u6) 15.00

OTTLEY,ROI-White Marble Lady-NY-(1965)-FS&G-1st ed (b5,dj) 20.00

OUOLOGUEM,YAMBO-Bound to Violence-NY-(1971)-HBJ-1st ed (b5,as new in dj) 25.00

OUR COOK BOOK-Wichita-1896-Presbytrn Ch of Okla City-69p+ads-wrps (l1,wn sp,sl stnd) 50.00

OURSLER,WILL-Departure Delayed-NY-1947-Simon-1st ed (h4,dj) 10.00

OUSLEY,CLARENCE-Galveston in Nineteen Hundred-Atlanta-1900-Wm Chase-346p-illus-1st ed (a9) 85.00

OUSPENSKY,P D-Fourth Way-Lond-1957-Routledge & K Paul-cl-1st ed (n8,vf,dj) 65.00

OUSPENSKY,P D-In Search of the Miraculous-NY-1949-Harcourt,Brace-cl-1st ed (n8,sm scratch frnt bd) 27.50

OUSPENSKY,P D-New Model of the Universe-NY-1931-Knopf-cl-1st ed (o8) 52.00

OUSPENSKY,P D-Strange Life of Ivan Osokin-NY-1955-Hermitage Hs-cl-2nd ed (l8,f,dj) 25.00

OUTDOOR LIFE'S-Gallery of N Amer Game-NY-1946-folio-142p-cl,31 col plts (y8,bndg sl wn) 45.00

OUTDOOR LIFE'S-Gallery of North American Game-NY-1958-oversized-photos,31 col paintings (gg3,f,dj) 25.00

OUTDOOR LIFE-EDS.-Story of American Hunting & Firearms-NY-1959-folio-172p-illus-1st ed (m3,vf,dj,box) 15.00

OUTLETTERS OF THE CONTINENTAL MARINE COMMITTEE AND BOARD OF ADMIRALTY 1776 TO 1780-NY-1914-Naval Hist Soc-2 vols-cl bds,vel sp-ltd to 500 sets (gg2,f) 100.00

OUTRAM,JAMES-In the Heart of the Canadian Rockies-NY-1905-Macmillan-8vo-xiv,466p+2p ads-orig pict cl,fldg map,illus-1st ed (u3,sl rub) 85.00

OUVRY,COL H A-Cavalry Experiences-Lymington-1892-235p-red cl,fldg maps,drwngs-1st ed (kk2,f) 125.00

OVER,W H-Birds of South Dakota-Vermillion-1946-8vo-200,(10)p-wrps,frntis,54 photos-rvsd ed (y8,chip) 20.00

OVER,WILLIAM H-Birds of South Dakota-Vermillion-1920-SD Geo & Nat Hist Srvy-SD Geo & Nat Hist Srvy,Ser.XXI,No.9-142p-wrps,col frntis,b&w photos (b9) 25.00

OVER,WILLIAM H-Birds of South Dakota-Vermillion-1946-U of SD Mus/Nat Hist St#1-200,(10)p-wrps,65 illus-rvsd ed wi new records & add illus (a1) 17.50

OVERFIELD II,LOYD J-COMP.-Little Big Horn 1876-Glendale-1971-Arthur H Clark Co-203p-pict cl,illus-ltd to 300c-Hidden Spgs of Custeriana Ser,Vol.3-1st ed (cc4) 200.00

OVERLAND MOTOR CARS MODEL 79...-(Toledo)-nd-Willys Overland Co-(24)p-wrps-trade cat-illus (g1) 30.00

OVERTON,RICHARD C-Burlington Route-1965-Knopf-8vo-623p-illus (nn7,dj wn) 30.00

OVERTON,RICHARD C-Burlington Route-NY-1965-Knopf-623p-cl,maps-1st ed (z7) 35.00

OVERTON,RICHARD C-Gulf to Rockies-Austin-1953-U of Tex Pr-410p-illus,maps,illus e.p.,sketches by R Marsh-1st ed (bb4) 35.00

OVERTON,RICHARD C-Gulf to Rockies-Austin-1953-U of Tex Pr-xiv+410p-beige cl,plts,maps,charts-1st ed (h2,chip dj) 45.00

OVINGTON,RAY-How to Take Trout on Wet Flies & Nymphs-Bost-1952-8vo-231p-illus-1st ed (m3,f,dj) 40.00

OVINGTON,RAY-Tactics on Trout-NY-1969-8vo-328p-illus,auth-1st ed (m3,f,dj) 10.00

OWEN,A R G-Psychic Mysteries of the North-NY-1975-Harper & Row-8vo-xii,242p-1st Amer ed (aa7,dj) 15.00*

OWEN,CATHERINE-Catherine Owen's New Cook Book-1885-Cassell-pict cov (v6,wn,sl fade,hng loose,spot) 45.00

OWEN,DAVID D-Report of a Geological Survey of Wisconsin, Iowa, and Minnesota-Phila-1852-638p+plts & map-cl-engrvd frontis,69 wdcuts + 27pg plts,17 col fldg sects,col map-Sabin 58009 (h1,fade,sl wn) 100.00

OWEN,DYLIS-Leo Possessed-NY-(1975)-HBJ-150p-cl,8p illus,S Gammell-1st US ed (r3,f,f dj) 15.00

OWEN,EDGAR W-Trek of the Oil Finders-Tulsa-1975-Amer Assoc of Petro Geol-xvi+1647p-blu cl,maps,glossy paper (d2) 75.00

OWEN,MAGGIE-Book of...-Indpls-(1941)-Bobbs Merrill-8vo-262p-1st ed (dd5,dj chip,tn) 25.00

OWEN,MAJ JOHN-Journals and Letters of...Pioneer of the Northwest 1850 to 1871-NY-1927-Eberstadt-8vo-2 vols-red cl,t.e.g.,2 fldg maps,30 plts-ltd to 550c-Tweney 58 (y4,f,box) 250.00

OWEN,MAJ JOHN-Journals and Letters of...Pioneer of the Northwest 1850 to 1871-NY-1927-Edw Eberstadt-2 vols-fldg maps & plts-ltd ot 500c-Howes O163-1st ed (ee4) 200.00

OWEN,MARY A-Folk Lore of Musquakie, Indians of North America & Catalogue of Musquakie Beadwork,etc-Lond-1904-147p-8 plts(2 col)-1st ed (u7,hngs crack) 100.00

OWEN,MRS DE WITT C-Chafing Dish Delicacies-Dixon-nd(ca.1900)-Tri Weekly Star-16p-gry wrps (u6,sl ink stnd wrps) 15.00

OWEN,MRS DE WITT-Chafing Dish Delicacies-Dixon-nd(ca.1900)-silv/blk wrps,cartoon on t.p. (q8) 10.00

OWEN,PAULA-Lamb Favorites, Old and New-(1970)-Random-246p-tan bds,col photos-1st ed (q8,dj) 17.50

OWEN,REV. RICHARD-Life of Richard Owen-NY-1894-Appleton-2 vols,red cl-1st Amer ed (d2,covs sl fleck & wn) 50.00

OWENS,ADAIR A B-Some of Her Life Experiences-Portland-nd-537p-pict cl,frntis,photos-1st ed (t7) 55.00

OWENS,CATHERINE-Choice Cookery-NY-1889-Harper & Bros-316p-blu bds-Bitting 351 (k6,sl wn) 65.00

OWENS,CLAIRE M-Zen and the Lady-NY-1979-Baraka Bks-wrps-1st ed (n8) 15.00

OWENS,HUBERT-Georgia's Planting Prelate-Athens-1945-U of Ga-57p-cl (x6) 45.00

OWENS,OSCAR L-Fighting Men of Oklahoma-Okla City-1946-Victory-2 vols-photos-1st ed (b4) 75.00

OWINGS,N A-Spaces in Between-Bost-1973-1st prtg (h10,sl tn dj) 45.00

OWINGS,NATHANIEL-American Aesthetic-NY-1969-Harper & Row-199p-wht cl,photos-1st ed (r10,sl wn dj) 12.50

OWSLEY,F L-King Cotton Diplomacy-Chig-1931-617p-1st ed (z10,ex-libr) 30.00

OYABE,JENICHIRO-Japanese Robinson Crusoe-Bost-(1898)-Pilgrim Pr-12mo-219p-sketches-1st(?) (dd5,f) 45.00

OZICK,CYNTHIA-Art & Ardor-NY-1983-Knopf-1st ed (a10,as new in dj) 20.00

OZICK,CYNTHIA-Levitation-NY-1982-1st ed (p5,f,dj) 20.00

OZICK,CYNTHIA-Pagan Rabbi-Lond-1972-1st Brit ed (p5,dj soil) 25.00

OZICK,CYNTHIA-Pagan Rabbi-NY-1971-Knopf-1st ed (a10,dj) 45.00

OZICK,CYNTHIA-Trust-np(Lond)-(1966)-MacGibbon & Kee-auth 1st bk-1st Brit ed (a10,sl soil dj) 75.00

PABOR,WILLIAM E-Colorado as an Agricultural State-NY-1883-213p-drwngs-1st ed (u7,rub) 50.00

PACE,ANTONIO-Luigi Castiglioni's Viaggio-1983-Syracuse U Pr-xli,487p-cl (x6,dj) 40.00

PACEY,DESMOND-ED.-Letters of Frederick Philip Grove-1976-U of Tor Pr-8vo-xxix,584p-27 illus-1st ed (cc7,dj) 25.00*

PACIFIC COAST TRIBES-(Ottawa)-1939-Nat Mus of Can-17p-prtd wrps,illus,map-Anthro lflt #6 (k10) 10.00*

PACIFIC LOGGING CONGRESS-Men of Timber-Peoria-1954,5,9-Caterpiller Tractor-12mo-3 vols,cl,port (b6,f) 35.00

PACIFIC TYPESETTING CO-Specimen Book,Linotype Faces & Decorative Material-Seattle-1927-4to-mostly unpgd-tan wrps,illus-scarce (b6) 35.00

PACK,CHARLES-Trees as Good Citizens-Phila-1922-Lippincott-257p-cl,illus (x6) 10.00

PACKARD,FRANCIS-Some Account of the Pennsylvania Hospital from its First Rise to the Beginning of the Year 1938-Phila-1938-133p-1st ed (dd3) 75.00

PACKARD,FRANK L-Adventures of Jimmie Dale-Tor-1917-Copp Clark Co-1st Can ed (gg8) 17.50

PACKARD,FRANK L-Doors of the Night-1922-Doran-scarce in dj-1st ed (x7,dj) 40.00

PACKARD,FRANK L-Hidden Door-Tor-1933-Dbldy CC-1st Can ed (k4,sl fox,dj sl wn) 20.00

PACKARD,FRANK L-Jimmie Dale and the Blue Envelope Murder-NY-1930-Dbldy-1st ed (k4,f,dj) 35.00

PACKARD,FRANK L-Night Operator-Tor-1919-Copp,Clark-1st Can ed (k4,f,dj) 35.00

PACKARD,FRANK L-Shanghai Jim-Tor-1928-Copp Clark-1st Can ed (gg8,chip dj) 35.00

PACKARD,FRANK L-Two Stolen Idols-NY-1927-Doran-1st ed (e4,dj) 40.00

PACKARD,S S-New Bryant and Stratton Common School Book-Keeping-NY,Cin,Chig-(1878)-Amer Bk Co-208p-cl (k1) 15.00

PADDLEFORD,CLEMENTINE-How America Eats-(1960)-Scribners-4to-495p-dec brwn cl,col & b&w photos-2nd prtg (q8,dj) 18.50

PADDOCK,MRS A G-In the Tolls-Chig-1879-Shepard,Tobias-301p-1st ed (d3,cov wn) 15.00

PADEN,IRENE D-Wake of the Prairie Schooner-NY-1943-Macmillan-514p-cl,maps-scarce-1st ed (z1,chip dj) 75.00

PADEN,IRENE D-Wake of the Prairie Schooner-NY-1943-Macmillan-514p-drwngs-1st ed (dd4) 30.00

PADOVER,SAUL-Letters of Karl Marx-Englewood Cliffs-(1979)-(27),576p-1st ed (m4,f,dj) 17.50

PAETOW,LOUIS J-Guide to the Study of Medieval History-NY-1931-F S Crofts-8vo-643p-red buckr-rvsd ed (t10,few ink mrkngs) 30.00

PAEZ,DON R-Wild Scenes in South America-NY-1862-Scribner-frntis photo,illus-1st ed (u2) 85.00

PAGE,DREW-Drew's Blues-Baton Rouge-1980-LSU Pr-1st ed (mm9,dj) 10.00

PAGE,E B-Master Chefs-NY-(1951)-St.Martin's Pr-248p (l6) 35.00

PAGE,ELIZABETH M-In Camp and Tepee-NY-1915-245p+ads-cl-frontis+15 pg plts-Rader 2567-1st ed (f1) 22.50

PAGE,GERALD W-ED.-Nameless Places-Sauk City-1975-ltd to 4160c-1st ed (k5,as new in dj) 10.00

PAGE,H S-Over the Open-NY-1925-8vo-155p-ltd to 1000c,nbrd,illus-scarce (m3) 35.00

PAGE,R C-Air Commando Doc-NY-(1945)-Bernard Ackerman-8vo-186p-cl,plts (s2) 25.00

PAGE,SUSANNE-Hopi-NY-(1982)-sm folio-240p-dbl col,col photos,maps-1st prtg (v7,as new in dj,2 autg) 75.00

PAGE,THOMAS N-Old South-NY-1894-344p+ads-cl (h1) 15.00

PAGE,THOMAS N-Robert E Lee, the Southerner-NY-1908-312p+ads-illus-1st ed (n3) 32.50

PAGE,THOMAS N-Santa Claus's Partner-NY-1899-Scribners-g dec cov & sp,red dec covs wi blind dec brdrs,t.e.g.,8 col illus,W Glackens-1st ed (y10,sp fade) 50.00

PAGE,V W-Everybody's Aviation Guide-NY-1928-8vo-cl,140 illus-1st ed (s2,fade,sl stnd) 20.00

PAGE,V W-Modern Aircraft-NY-1928-8vo-cl,frntis,plts (s2,sl wn) 50.00

PAGE,VICTOR W-Model T Ford Car-NY-1917-288p+4p ads-pict cl,illus,fldg diag (mm2,sl rub) 32.50

PAGE,WARREN-Accurate Rifle-NY-1973-8vo-238p-photos-1st ed (m3,vf,dj) 15.00

PAGE,WARREN-One Man's Wilderness-NY-1973-256p-photos (gg3,vf,dj) 17.00

PAGE,WARREN-One Man's Wilderness-NY-1973-8vo-256p-photos-1st ed (m3,vf,sl wrnkld dj) 25.00

PAHER,STANLEY W-Nevada: An Annotated Bibliography-Las Vegas-1980-S W Paher-558p-prpl cl,illus,iss w/o dj-1st ed (ee7,f) 50.00

PAIN,C E-Fifty Years on the Test-Lond-1934-198p-photos (gg3,cov sl wn) 50.00

PAINE,ALBERT B-Captain Bill McDonald, Texas Ranger-NY-1909-Little & Ives-448p-illus,Spec subscrptn ed-Six Guns #1669-1st ed,2nd bndg(deep red cl) (dd4,hng crack) 100.00

PAINE,ALBERT B-Car That Went Abroad-NY-(1921)-Harper-8vo-340p-sketches (ff5,chip dj) 20.00

PAINE,ALBERT B-Mystery of Evelin Delorme-Bost-1894-Arena Publ-129p-cl-auth 1st bk-Wright 4079 (h1) 50.00

PAINE,ALBERT B-Short Life of Mark Twain-GC-1925-Garden City Publ-343,(1)p-cl (j1) 10.00

PAINE,ALBERT B-Tent Dwellers-NY-1908-8vo-280p-illus,Hy Watson-1st ed (m3) 20.00

PAINE,ALBERT B-Thomas Nast-NY-1904-Macmillan-xxii+583+xx pgs-blu cl,illus-1st ed (b2) 75.00

PAINE,MARTYN-Letters on the Cholera Asphyxia, as it Appeared in the City of New York-NY-1832-160p-1st ed (dd3) 150.00

PAINE,MARTYN-Physiology of the Soul and Instinct, as Distinguished from Materialism-1872-Harper & Bros-707p+ads-brwn cl-1st ed (c2,ex-libr) 40.00

PAINE,RALPH D-Lost Ships and Lonely Seas-NY-1921-Century-411p-17 illus (ee8,sp fade) 29.00

PAINE,RALPH D-Story of Martin Coe-NY-1906-Outing Co-gold stmpd cov & sp,illus-1st ed (x1) 30.00

PAINE,ROBERT T-Art and Architecture of Japan-Balt-1955-Penguin Bks-cl,173p plts-1st ed (o8) 35.00

PAINE,THOMAS-Rights of Man-NY-(1961)-lg 4to-illus by L Ward (m4,box) 14.50

PAKENHAM,THOMAS-Mountains of Rasselas, An Ethiopian Adventure-NY-(1959)-Reynal-8vo-192p-24 photos,13 drwngs-1st US ed (cc5,sl chip dj) 20.00

PALEY,GRACE-Enormous Changes at the Last Minute-NY-(1974)-FS&G-1st ed (l7,f,dj) 30.00

PALEY,GRACE-Enormous Changes at the Last Minute-NY-1974-1st ed (o5,f,dj) 20.00

PALEY,GRACE-Little Disturbances of Man-NY-1968-1st reissued ed of auth 1st bk (n5,dj) 20.00

PALGRAVE,FRANCIS-ED.-Children's Treasury of English Song-NY-1898-Macmillan-12mo-cl (s3) 10.00

PALLADINO,L B-Indian and White in the Northwest-Lancaster-1922-512p-emboss pict bd,a.e. mrbld,illus-Howes P40-2nd ed (d7) 65.00

PALLIS,MARCO-Peaks & Lamas-NY-1940-428p-1 col plt,95 photos,3 maps-1st US ed (q10) 35.00

PALLISER,JOHN-Solitary Hunter-Lond-nd(c.1860)-Routledge-xii,264p+2p ads-illus (bb7) 50.00*

PALMER,BERTHA R-Beauty Spots in North Dakota-Bost-(1928)-R C Badger-266p-illus-1st ed (gg4) 30.00

PALMER,C H-Salmon Rivers of Newfoundland-Bost-1928-8vo-271p-wrps,photos,fldg map-scarce-1st ed (m3,f) 65.00

PALMER,DAVE R-River and the Rock-NY-(1969)-Greenwood Publ-4to-xii+395p-gry cl,maps,illus-1st ed (b2,box) 50.00

PALMER,EDWARD E-Forty Years of Hustling-(Wooster)-(1942)-363p-wrps (j1) 17.50

PALMER,H R-This Was Air Travel-Seattle-(1960)-4to-190p-cl,frntis,plts,text illus-1st ed (s2,dj) 35.00

PALMER,HARRY-ET AL-Athletic Sports in America,England and Australia-1889-Hubbard Bros-711p-4 col plts,b&w photos-1st ed (s8,sl weak hngs,brwng pgs) 550.00

PALMER,HERBERT E-Judgement of Francois Villon-Lond-1927-Hogarth Pr-8vo-143p-cl,t.e.g.-ltd to 400c,nbrd,autg-Woolmer 140-1st ed (nn4,f dj) 125.00

PALMER,HOWARD-Mountaineering & Exploration in the Selkirks-NY-1914-437p-139 photos,3 fldg maps(1 col)-1st ed (a4,f) 295.00

PALMER,JIM-Pitching-1975-Atheneum-photos-1st ed (s8,dj) 20.00

PALMER,JOEL-Journal of Travels over the Rocky Mountains, to Columbia River During 1845 and 1846...-Cin-1847-J A & U P James-189p-prtd papr cov,lacks errata slip(ink corr)-Howes P54 (z1,sl stnd,fox,f box) 1,250.00

PALMER,LTC DAVE R-Readings in Current Military History-West Point-(1969)-US Military Acad-4to-wrps-1st ed (ff3) 50.00

PALMER,LYNDE-Help Over Hard Places-Bost-(1862)-Amer Trct Scty-224p-cl (d1) 20.00

PALMER,R S-ED.-Handbook of North Amer Birds...Vol.1-New Haven-1962-lg 8vo-(1),567p-cl,6 col plts(incl dbl-pg col chrt),maps-1st prtg (y8,dj) 60.00

PALMER,ROBERT-Deep Blues-NY-(1981)-Viking-1st ed (v5,f,f dj) 15.00

PALMER,ROBERT-Deep Blues-NY-(1981)-Viking-1st ed (w1,f,f dj) 20.00

PALMER,STUART-Miss Withers Regrets-NY-1947-Dbldy CC-1st ed (j4,sl yel pgs,sl wn dj) 45.00

PALMER,STUART-Murder on the Blackboard-1932-Brentano-1st ed (s10,tape rnfrcd dj) 150.00

PALMER,STUART-Nipped in the Bud-1951-Mill-1st ed (s10,dj) 45.00

PALMER,STUART-People Vs. Withers and Malone-NY-1963-Simon-1st ed (f4,sl yel pgs,dj) 35.00

PALMER,T S-Index Generum Mammalium-Codicote(Wash,1904)-1968-8vo-984p (y8) 120.00

PALMER,TRUMAN-Sugar Beet Seed History and Development-NY-1918-Wiley-120p-cl (x6) 20.00

PALMER,W T-English Lakes-NY-1932-281p-1st ed (o10,f,dj) 9.00

PALMQUIST,PETER-With Nature's Children-Eureka-1976-Interface Cal-sq 4to-134p-wrps-1st ed (t3) 30.00

PALOCZI-HORVATH,GEORGE-Undefeated-Bost-(1959)-Atl/Little,Brown-8vo-305p-1st ed (jj5,dj) 12.50

PALTENGHI,MADELENA-Rumpus Rabbit-NY-1939-Harper-pict cl,illus by C W Anderson-1st ed (aa9) 45.00

PALUDAN,PHILLIP S-Victims-Knoxville-(1981)-144p-1st ed (c4,f,dj) 17.50

PAN AMER PETROL AND TRANSPORT CO-Mexican Petroleum-NY-1922-xiv+300p-flex fabrikoid bds,illus,fldg map pckt (c2) 20.00

PANAMA ROSE-Hashish Cookbook-1966-Gnaoua Pr-wrps-1st ed (v5,f) 25.00

PANASSIE,HUGUES-Louis Armstrong-1971-Scribners-1st Amer ed (o9,f,dj) 35.00

PANASSIE,HUGUES-Real Jazz-NY-(1942)-Smith-1st Amer ed (w1,f,dj) 45.00

PANCOAST,CHALMERS L-Our Home Town Memories-(Newark)-(1958)-96p-cl,dbl cols,photos (j1,pres cpy) 17.50

PANCOAST,S-Pancoast's Tokology and Ladies' Medical Guide-Chig-(1903)-508p-cl,illus (d1) 20.00

PANGBORN,EDGAR-West of the Sun-GC-1953-Dbldy-1st ed (e3,chip dj) 25.00

PANGBORN,J G-World's Railway-NY-1974-165p-(facs of 1894 ed) (n4,f,dj) 25.00

PANKHURST,CHRISTABEL-Plain Facts About a Great Evil-NY-1913-Soc Fund Med Rev of Revs-8vo-157p+ads-cl-1st ed (z5) 40.00

PANKHURST,E SYLVIA-Suffragette-Bost-1911-Woman's Journal-photos-1st ed (p6) 125.00

PANKHURST,EMMELINE-My Own Story-NY-(1914)-Hearst's Int'l Libr-blu wrps,photos-1st ed (p6,sl wn) 100.00

PANKHURST,RICHARD-Sylvia Pankhurst, Artist and Crusader-NY-(1979)-Paddington-4to-224p-col illus-1st US ed (ee5,f,f dj) 20.00

PANNELL,WALTER-Civil War on the Range-LA-(1943)-Welcome News-12mo-48p-wrps-Rampaging Herd 1754-1st ed (h2) 15.00

PANOFSKY,DORA-Pandora's Box-NY-1956-Pantheon-buckram,illus,Bollingen Ser.LII-1st ed (l8,f) 45.00

PANOVA,VERA-Train-NY-1949-Knopf-281p-cl-1st Amer ed so stated (c1,f,dj) 20.00

PANUM,PETER-Observations Made During the Epidemic of Measles on the Faroe Islands in the Year 1846-NY-1940-111p-1st Engl transl (dd3) 60.00

PAPACHRISTOU,T-Marcel Breuer: New Buildings & Projects-1970-Praeger-sq 4to-illus(incl col)-1st ed (ee1,dj) 150.00

PAPADAKI,S-ED.-Le Corbusier: Architect, Painter, Writer-NY-1948-illus-1st prtg (h10,dj) 85.00

PARACELSUS-Four Treatises of Theophrastus Von Hohenheim called...-Balt-1941-256p-1st ed (dd3) 100.00

PARACELSUS-Selected Writings-NY-1951-347p-1st Engl transl (dd3) 75.00

PARACELSUS-Selected Writings-NY-1951-Pantheon-cl,frntis,illus,Bollingen Ser.XXVIII-transl by N Guterman-1st ed (l8,dj) 125.00

PARAMORE,EDWARD E,JR.-Ballad of Yukon Jake-NY-1928-Coward-12mo-prtd pap bds,illus,"Hogarth, Jr."(Rockwell Kent)-1st ed (w1) 35.00

PARCHER,EMILY-Shady Gardens-NY-(1955)-vi,282p-photos (m10,wn,tattrd dj) 14.00

PARDEE,R G-Complete Manual for the Cultivation of the Strawberry-NY-1854-thin 8vo-144p+10p ads-red stmpd cl-scarce-1st ed (jj4,sl chip sp,sl fox & soil) 45.00

PARDEE,R G-Complete Manual for the Cultivation of the Strawberry-NY-1865-OJ-158p-cl-rvsd (x6,fade) 30.00

PARE,AMBROISE-Apologie and Treatise of Ambroise Pare...-Chig-1952-227p-1st ed (dd3) 50.00

PAREDES,AMERICO-With His Pistol in His Hand-Austin-(1958)-UTP-262p-1st ed (a9,dj) 40.00

PARENT,GAIL-David Meyer is a Mother-NY-1976-1st ed (r5,dj) 12.50

PARENT,GAIL-Sheila Levine is Dead and Living in New York-NY-1972-auth 1st bk-1st ed (n5,f,dj) 20.00

PARER,DAVID-Douglas Mawson, the Survivor-Victoria-1983-Alella-lg 8vo-160p-map e.p.,160 photos-1st ed (dd7,as new in dj) 40.00

PARES,BIP-Himalayan Honeymoon-Lond-1940-301p-16 monochromes-1st ed (p10) 80.00

PARGETER,EDITH-Assize of the Dying-NY-1958-Dbldy CC-1st US ed (k4,f,dj) 25.00

PARIS EXPOSITION-Reports of U.S. Comm to Paris Universal Expo,1867-Wash D.C.-1870-GPO-6 vols-brwn cl,fldg plts (c2) 165.00

PARIS REVIEW-BEST SHORT STORIES FROM...-NY-1959-1st ed (s5,dj) 40.00

PARIS,BEN-Hunting & Fishing Guide to the Northwest-Seattle-1946-8vo-304p-wrps,photos (m3) 17.50

PARIS,DOMINIC P-ED.-Heritage of Livonia-Livonia-1962-73p-wrps (e1,wrps) 10.00

PARISH,ELIJAH-New System of Modern Geography-Newburyport-1814-E Little-366,(2)p-lea-2 fldg maps-Amer Imprnts 32432-3rd ed (k1) 50.00

PARISH,JOHN C-Man with the Iron Hand-Bost,NY-1913-Houghton Mifflin-288,(1)p-cl (e1) 17.50

PARISOT,REV P F-Reminiscences of a Texas Missionary-San Antonio-1899-St.Mary's Church-227p-1st ed (a9) 90.00

PARK,BERTRAM-Collins Guide to Roses-Lond-1956-288p-64 col plts (j10,dj soil & edge wn) 20.00

PARK,CLYDE W-Morgan the Unpredictable-np-(1959)-C J Krehbiel Co-40p-pict cl,illus,map,Christmas gift of Krehbiel Co-1st ed (c4,f) 60.00

PARK,FRANCIS E,JR.-Deer Hunting-NY-1954-8vo-96p-illus-1st ed (m3,dj) 12.50

PARK,HELEN-List of Architectural Books Available in America Before the Revolution-LA-1973-Hennessey & Ingalls-8vo-79p-grn cl,illus (r10,as new in dj) 20.00

PARK,HELEN-List of Architectural Books Available in America before the Revolution-LA-1973-new ed,rvsd & enlgd (h10,dj) 25.00

PARK,ORLANDO-Sherlock Holmes,Esq. and John H Watson,M.D.-Chig-1962-Northwestern U-1st ed (e4,edge rub,dj) 25.00

PARKE,JUDGE J E-Recollections of Seventy Years and Historical Gleanings of Allegheny, Pennsylvania-Bost-1886-Rand,Avery & Co-xii+385p-grn cl,port-Howes P72-1st ed (b2) 65.00

PARKE,URIAH-Key to the Farmers' & Mechanics' Practical Arithmetic-Zanesville-1840-A Lippitt-130,(1)p-bds (k1,covs wn,few pgs bent) 40.00

PARKER GUNS-Catalog for 1926-32p-orig catalog,frnt cov geese in flight,photos-scarce (gg3) 115.00

PARKER,ARTHUR C-An Analytical History of the Seneca Indians-Rochester-1926-NY State Arch Assoc-162p-gry wrps,25 plts,11 text figs (k2) 25.00

PARKER,BENJAMIN S-Poets and Poetry of Indiana-NY-(1900)-464p-cl (g1) 20.00

PARKER,CHARLES W-Lawn-Bost-(1939)-Hale Cushman & Flint-8vo-118p-12 illus-1st ed (dd5,dj) 15.00

PARKER,CHARLES W-Shipley-(np)-1931-24p-wrps,illus (aa6) 20.00

PARKER,DOROTHY-After Such Pleasures-NY-1933-Viking-1st ed (w5,f,dj) 50.00

PARKER,DOROTHY-Constant Reader-NY-1970-Viking-1st ed (q2,dj) 35.00

PARKER,DOROTHY-Death and Taxes-NY-1931-Viking-1st prtg stated on dj panel-1st trd ed (bb1,sl chip dj) 100.00

PARKER,DOROTHY-Here Lies-NY-1939-art deco e.p.s-1st ed (q5,sl chip dj) 60.00

PARKER,DOROTHY-Not So Deep as a Well-NY-1936-1st ed (p5,wn dj) 45.00

PARKER,G H-Animal Colour Changes and Their Neurohumours-Cambridge-1948-8vo-377p-cl,illus (y8,dj wn) 40.00

PARKER,G M N-Mountain Massacre-Bluefield-1930-Cntry Life-97p-blu cl-1st ed (oo5,soil,sun) 30.00

PARKER,GEORGE C-Proud Beginnings: a Pictorial History of Red Deer-Red Deer-1981-Red Deer & Distr Mus-oblng 4to-361p-illus,maps,ports (aa2,wn dj) 25.00*

PARKER,GILBERT-An Adventurer of the North-NY-1896-Stone & Kimball-orig g paneled cl-1st ed (aa9,few cov spots) 45.00

PARKER,GILBERT-Seats of the Mighty-NY-1898-D Appleton-376p-cl (g1) 12.50

PARKER,I-Ivory Crisis-Lond-1983-184p-photos (gg3,f,dj) 75.00

PARKER,J M-An Aged Wanderer-Bryan-nd-pict wrps,ltd ed-Herd #1757 (t7,f) 20.00

PARKER,MAUDE-Invisible Red-NY-1953-Rinehart-1st ed (j4,dj) 10.00

PARKER,PROF HARLEY-Lady's Toilet Table-Lond-nd(ca.1900s)-auth-151p (a8) 30.00

PARKER,REV SAMUEL-Parker's Exploring Tour-Mpls-1967-380p-map-Smith #7894 (t7,f,dj) 10.00

PARKER,RICHARD D-Historical Recollections of Robertson County Texas-Salado-1955-Anson Jones Pr-254p-pict e.p.,fldg map,illus-ltd to 1000c-1st ed (ee4) 50.00

PARKER,ROBERT B-Ceremony-NY-1982-Delacorte-1st ed (h4,as new in dj) 20.00

PARKER,ROBERT B-Early Autumn-1981-Delacorte-1st ed (x7,f,dj,autg) 38.00

PARKER,ROBERT B-Early Autumn-NY-1981-Delacorte-1st ed (d4,dj) 10.00

PARKER,ROBERT B-God Save the Child-Bost-1974-Houghton Mifflin-185p-cl-1st ed so stated (a1,f,dj) 200.00

PARKER,ROBERT B-God Save the Child-Bost-1974-Houghton Mifflin-1st ed (w9,f,dj sl tn,sl sp fade) 225.00

PARKER,ROBERT B-God Save the Child-Lond-1975-1st Brit ed (p5,f,dj) 90.00

PARKER,ROBERT B-Godwulf Manuscript-1974-HM-auth 1st bk-1st ed (x7,f,dj) 250.00

PARKER,ROBERT B-Godwulf Manuscript-Bost-1974-Houghton Mifflin- 1st Spenser bk-1st ed (cc1,dj,autg) 300.00

PARKER,ROBERT B-Godwulf Manuscript-Bost-1974-Houghton Mifflin-1st ed (w9,vf,dj) 275.00

PARKER,ROBERT B-Judas Goat-(Lond)-(1982)-Andre Deutsch-1st Brit ed (a10,as new in dj) 25.00

PARKER,ROBERT B-Judas Goat-Bost-1978-Houghton-1st ed (e4,f dj) 50.00

PARKER,ROBERT B-Promised Land-Bost-1976-Houghton Mifflin-1st ed (bb2,f,dj) 85.00

PARKER,ROBERT B-Promised Land-Boston-1975-Houghton-1st ed (h4,as new in dj) 75.00

PARKER,ROBERT B-Savage Place-1981-Delacorte-1st ed (s9,dj) 20.00

PARKER,ROBERT B-Savage Place-NY-1981-Delacorte-1st ed (h4,as new in dj) 25.00

PARKER,ROBERT B-Three Weeks in Spring-Bost-1978-HMCo-1st ed (h8,f,dj) 40.00

PARKER,ROBERT B-Wilderness-Lond-1980-1st Brit ed (q5,f,dj) 45.00

PARKER,SAMUEL-Journal...Tour Beyond the Rocky Mountains...1835,'36,and '37...map of Oregon Territory-Mpls-(1967)-380p-cl,fldg map laid in-ltd to 2000c-rprnt of 1838 ed (aa1,f,dj) 20.00

PARKER,TONY-Lighthouse-NY-(1976)-Taplinger-8vo-288p-1st US ed (gg5,f,dj) 20.00

PARKER,W GORDON-Rival Boy Sportsmen-Bost-1905-8vo-363p-illus (m3) 15.00

PARKER,W K-Monograph on the Structure and Development of the Shoulder-Girdle and Sternum in the Vertebrata-Lond-1868-Ray Scty-folio-(1),237,(1)p-orig bds,30 col plts (y8,wn,rear cov dtchd) 90.00

PARKER,WATSON-Deadwood-Lincoln-(1981)-U of Neb Pr-302p-illus-1st ed (dd4,dj) 25.00

PARKER,WATSON-Gold in the Black Hills-Norman-(1966)-U of Okla Pr-259p-illus-1st ed (bb4,dj) 30.00

PARKER,WILLIAM-William Parker: Mounted Policeman-Calgary/Edmonton-1973-Glenbow Albrta Inst/Hrtg-xviii,163p-illus,ports (k10,dj) 20.00*

PARKHILL,FORBES-Wildest of the West-NY-1951-H Holt-310p-cl,photos,Guns #1684-1st ed (w3,f,fade dj) 25.00

PARKHILL,HARRIET R-Mission to the Seminoles in the Everglades of Florida-Orlando-nd-Sentinel Print-21p-wrps-illus (h1) 22.50

PARKHURST,MINNIE-Louise Olivereau Case-Seattle-(1918)-Auth-64p-gry prtd wrps-1st ed (ll9) 40.00

PARKISON,EDWARD-Guide to the Country Home-NY-1909-Outing-155p-cl (x6,fade) 12.00

PARKMAN,FRANCIS-Half Century of Conflict-NY-1892-2 vols-1st ed (a7) 75.00

PARKMAN,FRANCIS-Historical Handbook of the Northern Tour-Bost-1885-180p-illus (a7) 60.00

PARKMAN,FRANCIS-History of the Conspiracy of Pontiac...-Bost-1863(1851)-Little,Brown-xxiv,632p-3/4 lea,mrbld bds,4 maps(2 fldg)-3rd ed (o2,sl rub) 100.00

PARKMAN,FRANCIS-Journals of...-NY-1947-Harper & Bros-2 vols-map e.p.,illus,maps-1st ed (nn6) 65.00

PARKMAN,FRANCIS-Journals of...-NY-1947-Harper & Bros-2 vols-map e.p.-Wade Mason,ed.-1st ed thus (b4) 50.00

PARKMAN,FRANCIS-Oregon Trail-Bost-1925-364p-cl,frnts+4p col illus,N C Wyeth,illus e.p.,illus mntd on frnt cov (l1,sl wn dj) 15.00

PARKMAN,FRANCIS-Works-Bost-1894,5-12 vols-gilt dec 1/2 grn lea,t.e.g.,mrbld bds & e.p. (jj2,sl rub) 350.00

PARKS,DAVID-G I Diary-NY-1968-Harper & Row-scarce-1st ed (e8,f,f dj) 50.00

PARKS,GEORGE B-Richard Hakluyt and the English Voyages-NY-1925-Amer Geo Soc-289p-orig cl,32 illus-1st ed (p8,sl soil) 65.00

PARKS,GEORGE B-Richard Hakluyt and the English Voyages-NY-1928-Amer Geographic Scty-xvii,289p-orig gry cl,32 illus incl fldg map-Spec. Publ. No.10 (nn1,sp drknd,sl soil) 60.00

PARKS,GORDON-Choice of Weapons-NY-1966-Harper & Row-1st ed (q2,dj) 35.00

PARKS,GORDON-Learning Tree-NY-1963-Harper & Row-1st ed (q2,sp rub,dj) 65.00

PARKS,GORDON-To Smile in Autumn-NY,Lond-(1979)-Norton-photos-1st ed (cc1,f,dj) 35.00

PARKS,GORDON-Whisper of Intimate Things-NY-1971-col photos-1st ed (s5,dj) 20.00

PARKS,JAMES H-History of the Scotch Plains Baptist Church from its Organization...1747 to...1897-Scotch Plains-1897-74p-cl,plts (aa6) 35.00

PARKS,PAT-Railroad That Died at Sea-Brattleboro-1968-44p-1st ed (n4,f,dj) 9.50

PARKS,STEPHEN-R C Gorman-Bost-1983-143p-frntis,photos,col plts-1st ed (t7,f,dj,Gorman autg) 40.00

PARKYN,MAJ H G-Shoulder Belt Plates and Buttons-Aldershot-1956-341p-illus-1st ed (gg2,f,dj) 45.00

PARLEY,PETER-Adventures of Billy Bump-NY-1865-16mo-192p-g sp dec,illus (v8) 32.00

PARLIN,S W-American Trotter-Bost-1905-Amer Horse Breeder-1st ed (j9) 40.00

PARLOA,MARIA-Home Economics-1898-Century-378p-g dec red cl-1st ed (q8) 75.00

PARLOA,MISS M-Camp Cookery-Bost-(c.1878)-Graves,Locke-sm 16mo-91p-bds illus wi camp scene-Bitting 356 (k6) 75.00

PARLOA,MISS M-Original Appledore Cook Book-Bost-(1872,1881)-Chas E Brown-230p-emboss bds-Bitting 356 (k6,sl rub,wn) 45.00

PARLOUR MAGIC-Lond-1858-W Kent-sm sq 8vo-g pict cl,engrvd & prtd t.p.s,illus-4th ed,enlgd (jj9) 150.00

PARMELE,CLAUDE-How To Be a Crack Shot with Rifle & Shotgun-NY-1950-4to-78p-photos (m3,vf,sl fray dj) 20.00

PARMELEE,DAVID F-Birds of West Central Ellesmere Island and Adjacent Areas-Ottawa-1960-Nat Mus of Can,Bull.169-103p-wrps (b9) 10.00

PARMELIN,HELENE-Picasso: Women-Amsterdam-1964-Abrams-4to-203p-beige cl,tip in col plts (r10,dj) 75.00

PARMET,HERBERT S-Eisenhower and the American Crusades-NY-1972-Macmillan-xi,660p-photos-1st prtg (o2,dj) 15.00

PARRAMORE,DOCK D-Scenes and Stories of Early West Texas-El Paso-1975-93p-dec bds,illus-1st ed (t7,f) 15.00

PARRIS,GUICHARD-Blacks in the City-Bost-1971-Little,Brown-534p-photos-1st ed so stated (r1,dj tn,edgewn) 25.00

PARRISH,HENRY M-Poisonous Snakebites in the United States-NY-(1980)-Vantage Pr-xiv+469p-blck bds,72 figs,tbls-1st ed (a2,dj) 25.00

PARRISH,R-Gift of the Desert-1922-McClurg-frntis & col frnt dj panel,J Allen St.John-1st ed (x2,dj sl wn & tn) 85.00

PARRISH,RAIN-Woven Holy People-Santa Fe-1982-unpgd(61p)-wrps,col photos-1st ed (v7,f) 15.00

PARRISH,RANDALL-Great Plains-Chig-1907-399p-pict bds,illus-1st ed (j7,weak hng) 45.00

PARROTT,HAROLD-Lords of Baseball-1976-Praeger-1st ed (ff2,f,dj) 40.00

PARRY,ALBERT-Tattoo-NY-1933-171p-cl wi pict papr labl,29 plts(3 col) (w10) 145.00

PARRY,GARETH-Birds of Prey-NY-1979-S&S-sm folio-120p-maps,photos,35 paintings (c9) 27.50

PARRY,J H-Disocvery of the Sea-Berkeley-1981-U of Cal-8vo-279p-blu cl,maps,chrts-1st ed (p8,as new in dj) 22.50

PARRY,SIR W E-Three Voyages for the Discovery of a Northwest Passage from the Atlantic to the Pacific...-NY-1840-Harper & Bros-2 vols-prtd cl-Family Libr ser-Amer Imprnts 40-5257 (a1) 45.00

PARS,H H-Pictures in Peril-NY-1957-Oxford-1st ed (z9,edge spot,dj) 10.00

PARSONS,ALFRED-Notes in Japan-NY-1896-Harpers-xiv,226p-g dec cov,118 drwngs-1st ed (c3) 45.00

PARSONS,DAVID-Comprehensive Collection of Classified Geographical Topics-Columbus-1856-62p+fldg chrt,prtd wrps (b1,sl soil wrps) 20.00

PARSONS,E C-I Flew with the Lafayette Escadrille-Indpls-(1963)-8vo-xvi,336p-cl,frntis,79 illus (s2,dj) 30.00

PARSONS,ELSIE C-ED.-American Indian Life-NY-1922-419p-drwngs by LaFarge-1st ed scarce-1st ed (u7) 85.00

PARSONS,ELSIE C-Folk Lore from the Cape Verde Islands. Part I & Part II-Cambridge-1923-Amer Folk Lore Soc-2 vols-cl-1st ed (o8) 85.00

PARSONS,ELSIE C-Folklore of the Sea Islands, South Carolina-Cambridge-1923-Amer Folk Lore Soc-Memoirs Vol.XVI-1st ed (w5,sl sunned sp) 85.00

PARSONS,ELSIE C-Pueblo of Jemez-New Haven-1925-144p+8 plts rear pckt-photos,col plts,map-v scarce-1st ed (v7) 125.00

PARSONS,ELSIE C-Taos Tales-NY-1940-J J Augustin-1st ed (b4) 65.00

PARSONS,ELSIE C-Zuni Conception and Pregnancy Beliefs-Wash D.C.-1917-separate prtg 19th Int'l Cong Americanists,pgs 379 thru 383-wrps (v7) 20.00

PARSONS,GEORGE F-Life and Adventures of James W Marshall, the Discoverer of Gold in California-SF-1935-Geo Fields/Grabhorn Pr-xvi+145p-grn bds,3 plts-ltd to 500c-Howes P105-1st ed (b2,sl soil,sl tn plt) 75.00

PARSONS,HERBERT C-Puritan Outpost-NY-1937-Macmillan-546p-g blu cl,frntis,fldg map+26 plts-ltd to 500c,nbrd,autg (p2) 85.00

PARSONS,J E-First Winchester-NY-1955-207p-coated papr,photos (gg3,vf,dj) 35.00

PARSONS,JACK-Land and Cattle-Albuquerque-1978-U of N Mexico-brwn cl,photo e.p.,photos-1st ed (mm1,as new in dj) 25.00

PARSONS,JOHN E-Henry Deringer's Pocket Pistol-NY-1952-8vo-255p-photos-1st ed (m3,f,dj) 40.00

PARSONS,JOHN E-West of the 49th Parallel-NY-1963-208p-photos,map e.p.-1st ed (t7,dj) 27.50

PARSONS,MARION R-Old California Houses-(1952)-U of Cal Pr-143p-auth illus-1st ed (pp4,autg) 25.00

PARSONS,S,JR.-How to Plan the Home Grounds-NY-1899-Dbldy-249p (x6,sp drknd) 30.00

PARSONS,SAMUEL,JR.-Landscape Gardening-NY,Lond-1891-lg 8vo-329p-177 illus,photo,engrvng-1st prtg (m10,soil,sp rub,few pgs wn) 35.00

PARSONS,WILLIAM B-Robert Fulton and the Submarine-NY-1922-Columbia U Pr-xiii,154p-plum col cl,g title & dec,20 illus-1st ed (p8) 95.00

PARSONS,WILLIAM B-Robert Fulton and the Submarine-NY-1922-Columbia U Pr-xiv+154p-Maroon cl,20 plts-1st ed (g2) 75.00

PARTON,JAMES-Life of Horace Greeley-Bost-1872-James R Osgood-548p-cl-Miles 570 (j1,sl spot cov,weak rear hng) 15.00

PASHA,RUDOLPH S-Fire and Sword in the Sudan-Lond-1896-636p-dec grn cl,maps,illus-1st ed (b7,f) 150.00

PASIONARIA-People's Tribune of Spain-NY-1938-Workers Libr-wrps-1st ed (v5) 25.00

PASLEY,VIRGINIA-You Can Do Anything with Crepes-(1970)-S&S-174p-blu cl-1st ed (q8,f,dj,autg) 10.00

PASSER,HAROLD C-Electrical Manufacturers, 1875 to 1900-Cambridge-1953-Harvard Univ Pr-xx+412p-gry cl,11 illus-1st ed (j2,dj) 40.00

PASSERON,R-Impressionist Prints-NY-1974-folio-99 illus(24 col)-1st Amer ed (h10,dj) 125.00

PASSION FLOWERS-Bost-1854-Ticknor,Reed & Fields-8vo-187p-blind stmpd brwn cl(state B,no priority),publ 8p cat date Nov 1853 in rear,1st bk of Julia W Howe-1st ed (w6,sl chip sp) 135.00

PASTERNAK,BORIS-Dr Zhivago-(NY)-(1958)-Pantheon-cl-1st Amer ed (aa9,sl wn dj) 50.00

PASTERNAK,BORIS-I Remember-NY-1959-Pantheon-1st ed (z9,f,sl rub dj) 10.00

PASTERNAK,BORIS-Three Letters From...-1967-HBW-glassine dj,given out as a seasonal gift by publ-1st ed (x2,f,dj) 55.00

PASTIER,JOHN-Cesar Pelli-NY-1980-Whitney Libr of Design-sq 8vo-120p-grn bds,illus-Contemp Arch ser (r10,f dj) 20.00

PASTON,GEORGE-At John Murray's-Lond-(1932)-J Murray-1st ed (w1) 30.00

PATCHEN,KENNETH-Before the Brave-NY-1936-Random-auth 1st bk-1st ed (w5,f,sl chip dj) 250.00

PATCHEN,KENNETH-Dark Kingdom-NY-(1942)-ltd to 775c-1st ed (r2) 50.00

PATCHEN,KENNETH-Famous Boating Party...-NY-1954-New Directions-1st ed (q2,sl wn sp,dj sl tn) 95.00

PATCHEN,KENNETH-Hurrah for Anything-Highlands-1957-Jargon Soc 21-8vo-pict wrps-1st ed (jj8,f) 65.00

PATCHEN,KENNETH-Outlaw of the Lowest Planet-Lond-1946-Grey Walls Pr-1st ed (r2,f,dj) 30.00

PATCHEN,KENNETH-Red Wine and Yellow Hair-NY-(1949)-New Directions-8vo-yel cl-1st ed (x10,f,sl soil dj) 50.00

PATCHEN,KENNETH-See You in the Morning-NY-(1947)-1st ed (r2,dj chip,sl tn) 60.00

PATCHEN,KENNETH-See You in the Morning-NY-(1947)-Padell-8vo-blu cl-1st ed (x10,f,dj) 50.00

PATCHEN,KENNETH-They Keep Riding Down All the Time-NY-(1946)-Padell-8vo-dec wrps-1st ed (x10) 35.00

PATCHIN,FRANK G-Pony Rider Boys with the Texas Rangers-Akron-1920-Saalfield-212p-cl,illus,col illus dj-1st ed (w3,f,dj) 15.00

PATE,JANET-Book of Sleuths-Chig-1977-Contemporary-1st ed (d4,dj) 20.00

PATERNAK,JOSEPH-Cooking with Love and Paprika-(1966)-Geis-375p-gry cl,drwngs (q8,dj) 12.50

PATERNOSTER,G S-Cruise of the Conqueror-1906-Page-pict cov-1st ed (x7,sl soil cov) 35.00

PATILLO,T R-Moose Hunting,Salmon Fishing & Other Sketches of Sport-Lond-1902-12mo-299p (m3) 35.00

PATON,LUCY A-TRANSL.-Sir Lancelot of the Lake-NY-1929-Harcourt Brace-cl,frntis,illus-1st prtg (l8) 25.00

PATRI,ANGELO-Schoolmaster of the Great City-NY-1917-221p-cl-1st ed (k1) 15.00

PATRICK,Q-Cottage Sininter-1931-Swain-1st ed (s10) 25.00

PATRICK,Q-S S Murder-1933-Farrar-1st ed (s10) 20.00

PATRICK,TED-Thinking Dog's Man-NY-(1964)-Random Hs-illus,R McKie-1st ed (a10,f,dj) 35.00

PATRICK,VINCENT-Pope of Greenwich Village-NY-(1979)-auth 1st bk-1st ed (m4,sl tn dj) 20.00

PATRICK,VINCENT-Pope of Greenwich Village-NY-(1979)-Seaview-1st ed (f3,f,dj) 20.00

PATTEE,FRED L-History of American Literature Since 1870-NY-1917-449p-cl (b1) 15.00

PATTEN,DONALD W-Long Day of Joshua and Six Other Catastrophes-Seattle-1973-Pac Meridian-8vo-328p-43 figs-1st ed (gg5,f,dj) 12.50

PATTEN,GILBERT-Frank Merriwell's "Father"...-Norman-(1964)-331p-cl-1st ed so stated (e1,sl wn dj) 25.00

PATTEN,MARGUERITE-Epicure's Book of Steak and Beef Dishes-Lond-(1979)-Barrie & Jenkins-sq 4to-168p-g titled grn cl,col photos-1st ed (q8,f,dj) 20.00

PATTEN,MARGUERITE-Round the World Cookery-Lond-(1964)-Hamlyn-190p-pict bds,col & b&w photos (q8,chip dj) 17.50

PATTEN,MRS. FRANCIS J-Our New England Family Recipes-(NY)-1910-Tobias A Wright-134p-wht bds wi red lttrng & sp-Nat'l Scty of New England Women (n6) 65.00

PATTEN,WILLIAM-Book of Baseball-1911-Collier-illus,pict cov-1st ed (s8,hngs rprd) 475.00

PATTENGILL,HENRY R-Civil Government of Michigan-Lansing-(1887)-92p-cl cov wrps (k1) 12.50

PATTERSON'S SPELLER AND ANALYZER...-NY-(1875)-Sheldon-176p-bds (k1,rub bds) 15.00

PATTERSON,ARTHUR W-Heaviest Pipe-Phila-1921-Jacobs-1st ed (f4,sl fox) 10.00

PATTERSON,BESSIE-History of Deaf Smith County-Hereford-(1964)-167p-pict wrps,illus-1st ed (jj1,sl spot) 50.00

PATTERSON,C L-History and Directory of Bandera County-np-nd-18p+ads-wrps (a9) 45.00

PATTERSON,C L-Two Conspiracies-Bost-1928-Christopher Publ-226p-15 photos-1st ed (a9,dj) 50.00

PATTERSON,E PALMER,II-Canadian Indian-1972-Collier MacMlln,Don Mills-210p-grn cl,illus,map-1st ed (bb7,sl scuff) 15.00*

PATTERSON,F B-African Adventures-NY-1928-83p-photos,e.p. photo (gg3,f,dj) 35.00

PATTERSON,H W-Small Boat Building-NY-1943-144p-10 fldg plts,plans,illus (gg3,vf,dj) 12.00

PATTERSON,HARRY-Valhalla Exchange-Lond-1977-Hutchinson-1st ed (r4,f,dj) 30.00

PATTERSON,INNIS-Standish Gaunt Case-1931-Farrar-1st ed (s10,dj) 25.00

PATTERSON,ISABELLA I-Eppworth Case-NY-1930-Farrar-1st ed (g4) 10.00

PATTERSON,J H-In the Grip of the Nyika-NY-1909-Macmillan-8vo-389p-photos-1st US ed (ff5,hngs weak) 90.00

PATTERSON,J H-Man Eaters of Tsaro & Other East African Adventures-Lond-1921-351p-photos,g stmpd lion head frnt cov-see 1989 UBPG (gg3) 50.00

PATTERSON,JAMES-Thomas Berryman Number-Bost-1976-Little-1st ed (g4,as new in dj) 12.50

PATTERSON,JOSEPH M-Little Brother of the Rich-Chig-1908-Reilly & Britton-1st ed (w5,sl shaken,sp rub) 60.00

PATTERSON,MAUREEN L P-South Asia: An Introductory BIbliography-Chig-1962-Univ of Chig-8vo-412p-orig prtd orng wrps (ee7,sp fade,cov sl soil) 35.00

PATTERSON,NANCY LOU-Canadian Native Art-1973-Collier MacMillan-180p-15 col plts,1 col map,55 b&w illus,1 chrt-1st ed (bb7,sl chip dj) 15.00*

PATTERSON,R L-Sage Grouse in Wyoming-CO-1952-341p-photos (ee3,f,dj) 50.00

PATTERSON,R M-Buffalo Head-NY-1961-Wm Sloane-273p-e.p. maps,illus-1st ed (cc4,dj) 20.00

PATTERSON,RICHARD N-Outside Man-Bost-1981-Little-1st ed (s4,f,dj) 25.00

PATTERSON,ROBERT L-Sage Grouse in Wyoming-Denver-1952-Wy Game & Fish Comm-xxiv+341p-grn cl,plts,maps-1st ed (c2,dj) 20.00

PATTIE,JAMES O-Personal Narrative of...of Kentucky-Chig-1930-Donnelley-428p-frntis,illus-Lakeside Classics (cc4) 30.00

PATTON,ORION E-Aircraft Instruments-NY-1941-220p-cl,photos,drwngs-1st ed (m1) 15.00

PATTON,WALTER S-Insects, Ticks, Mites, and Venomous Animals of Medical & Veterinary Importance-Croyden-1929,31-H R Grubb-lg 8vo-2 vols-grn dec cl,117 plts-1st ed (a2,sl rub & wn) 125.00

PATTULLO,GEORGE-Tight Lines-NY-1938-8vo-171p-ltd to 300c,nbrd,illus by G R DePew (m3,f) 50.00

PAUL,ELLIOT-Black and the Red-NY-1956-Random-1st ed (hh2,f,dj) 45.00

PAUL,ELLIOT-Black Gardenia-NY-1952-Random-1st ed (d4,dj) 15.00

PAUL,ELLIOT-Desperate Scenery-(1954)-Random-302p-1st prtg (r8,dj edgewn,rub) 35.00

PAUL,ELLIOT-Ghost Town on the Yellowstone-NY-1948-341p-Herd #1763-1st ed (t7,dj) 12.50

PAUL,ELLIOT-Life and Death of a Spanish Town-NY-(1937)-Random Hs-1st prntg wi "H Wolff Book Mfg. Co." on copyright pg-1st ed (b10,sl fade sp,f dj) 40.00

PAUL,ELLIOT-Life and Death of a Spanish Town-NY-1937-Random Hs-427p-red cl over bds (gg6,dj) 25.00

PAUL,ELLIOT-Mayhem in B Flat-NY-1940-Random-1st ed (d4,dj) 25.00

PAUL,ELLIOT-Murder on the Left Bank-NY-(1951)-Random-1st ed (a5,rprd dj) 25.00

PAUL,ELLIOT-Waylaid in Boston-NY-1953-Random-1st ed (w5,f,dj) 25.00

PAUL,ELLIOT-With a Hays Nonny Nonny-NY-(1942)-Random-65 drwngs,L Quintanilla-1st ed (e10,dj) 25.00

PAUL,J HARLAND-Last Cruise of the Carnegie-Balt-1932-Williams & Wilkins-331p+ads-blu cl,198 illus-1st ed (dd1) 25.00

PAUL,JOHN-Scriptural Revelations of the Universal Apostasy...-np-nd(ca.1900?)-4p-self wrps-Flake 6160-1st ed (bb8) 30.00

PAUL,RAYMOND-Thomas Street Horror-NY-(1982)-Viking-1st ed (bb1,f,sl creased dj) 12.50

PAUL,RODMAN W-California Gold Discovery-Georgetown-1967-Talisman Pr-sm 4to-237p-illus-2nd prtg (d3) 75.00

PAUL,SHERMAN-Hart's Bridge-Urbana,Chig,Lond-(1972)-U of Ill Pr-1st ed (bb1,as new in dj) 20.00

PAUL,VIRGINIA-This Was Cattle Ranching-1973-Superior-4to-192p-photos-1st ed (t8,rub dj) 40.00

PAUL,WILLIAM P-ED.-History of the 6th Argylls 93rd Anti Tank Regiment-Lond-1949-134p-maps,illus-1st ed (b7,dj) 75.00

PAULCKE,DUNBAR-Hazards in Mountaineering-Lond-1973-159p-1st ed (p10,f,dj) 20.00

PAULDING,HIRAM-Journal of a Cruise of the United States Schooner Dolphin Among the Islands of the Pacific Ocean...-Honolulu-1970-U of Miami Pr-xxi,iv,258p-map e.p.-(rprnt of 1831) (p8,f,sl wn dj) 35.00

PAULDING,HIRAM-Journal of a Cruise of the United States Schooner Dolphin, among the Islands of the Pacific Ocean-NY-1831-258p-contemp speckld calf,fldg map-scarce-Howes P131-1st ed (o4) 1,750.00

PAULEY,ART-Henry Plummer Lawman and Outlaw-White Sulphur Springs-1980-Meagher Cnty News-289p-cl,photos-1st ed (w3,f,dj) 35.00

PAULLIN,CHARLES O-Atlas of the Historical Geography of the United States-(Wash D.C.)-1932-Carnegie & Amer Geog Scty-lg 4to-166p-grn cl,162 plts mntd on cl stubs-1st ed (e2) 75.00

PAULLIN,CHARLES O-Commodore John Rodgers-Cleve-1910-Arthur H Clark-thk 8vo-434p-blu cl-illus-1st ed (s1) 75.00

PAUSE,WALTER-Salute the Skiers-Lond-1963-8vo-211p-100 photos-1st ed (o10,f,dj) 30.00

PAUST,G-Fighting Wings-NY-(1944)-roy 8vo-256p-cl,illus t.p.,plts,e.p. maps (s2,dj) 30.00

PAVIERE,SYDNEY-Dictionary of British Sporting Painters-Leigh on Sea-1980-Lewis-folio-93p text & 43p plts-corrected ed (h9,dj) 60.00

PAVLIK,MILAN-Dialogue of Forms, Prague Baroque Architecture-NY-(1976)-St.Martin's-lg 4to-unpgd-117 plts-1st US ed (gg5,dj) 35.00

PAVLOV,I P-Selected Works-Moscow-1955-Foreign Lang Publ Hs-654p-olive cl-1st Engl ed (c2) 35.00

PAVY,F W-Treatise on Food and Dietetics,Physiologically and Therapeutically Considered-Phila-1874-Henry C Lea-xii+17-574p+ads-brwn cl-1st ed (d2,fade cov) 55.00

PAWLEY,MARTIN-Mies van der Rohe-NY-1970-S&S-sm 4to-134p-blk cl,60 photos-1st US prtg (r10,f dj) 12.50

PAWLING,J R-Dr.Samuel Guthrie-Watertown-1947-Brewster Pr-123p-grn cl,illus-1st ed (dd1) 25.00

PAWSEY,J L-Radio Astronomy-Oxford-1955-Clarendon Pr-x+361p-blu cl,150 text figs,23 plts in rear-1st ed (g2,sl wn dj) 50.00

PAXSON,FREDERIC L-History of the American Frontier 1763 to 1893-Bost-1924-Houghton Mifflin-598p-maps-Howes P145-1st ed (bb4) 50.00

PAXTON,HARRY-Whiz Kids-1950-McKay (r7,f,dj) 75.00

PAXTON,J G-ED.-Civil War Letters of General Frank `Bull' Paxton-Hillsboro-1978-102p-illus,ports (z10,f,scuff dj) 30.00

PAYER,JULIUS-New Lands Within the Arctic Circle-NY-1877-Appleton-8vo-xxiv,400p-g stmpd pict grn cl,drwngs,auth,col frntis,dbl pg map-scarce-1st ed (u1) 175.00

PAYETTE,B C-Northwest-Montreal-1964-732p-illus,maps,lg fldg map (r8) 55.00

PAYETTE,B C-Oregon Country Under the Union Jack-Montreal-1961-197p-dec wrps,illus (r8) 35.00

PAYNE,ABRAHAM-Reminiscences of the Rhode Island Bar-Providence-1885-Tibbitts & Preston-xii+277p-brwn cl-1st ed (h2) 20.00

PAYNE,CHARLES E-Josiah Bushnell Grinnell-Iowa City-1938-338p-cl (j1,f) 15.00

PAYNE,CHARLES E-Josiah Bushnell Grinnell-Iowa City-1938-St Hist Soc-338p-frntis-Iowa Bio Ser (o7,sp sunned) 20.00

PAYNE,DORIS P-Captain Jack, Modoc Renegade-Portland-(1938)-Binford & Mort-(viii),261p-cl,illus,map e.p.-1st ed (v1,dj sl wn & stnd) 85.00

PAYNE,H T-Game Birds & Game Fishes of the Pacific Coast-LA-1913-12mo-181p+ads-illus (m3) 13.00

PAYNE,L G S-Air Dates-Lond-(1957)-8vo-viii,566p-cl-1st ed (s2,dj) 40.00

PAYNE,LEONIDAS W,JR.-When the Woods Were Burnt-Austin-1946-27p-bds-1st ed (t7) 45.00

PAYNE,SELMA-Cooking with Exotic Fruit-Lond-(1979)-Batsford-144p-brwn cl,drwngs-1st prtg (q8,dj) 17.50

PAYNE,STEPHEN-Where the Rockies Herd-Denver-1965-358p-photos,map e.p.-1st ed (t7) 10.00

PAYNE-GALLWEY,R-Crossbow, Medieval & Modern Military & Sporting-Lond-1958-328p (gg3,f,dj) 45.00

PAYSON,EDWIN-Monograph of the Section Oreocarya of Cryptantha-St.Louis-1927-Mo Bot-148p-wrps,illus (x6) 20.00

PAYSON,EDWIN-Monographic Study of Thelypodium and Its Immediate Allies-St.Louis-1923-Mo Bot-91p-wrps (x6) 18.00

PAYTIAMO,JAMES-Flaming Arrow's People by an Acoma Indian-NY-(1932)-158p-col illus-v scarce-1st ed (v7,fade) 100.00

PAYTIAMO,JAMES-Flaming Arrow's People, By an Acoma Indian-NY-1932-Duffield & Green-col serigraphs-1st ed (b4) 125.00

PEABODY,ROBERT-Hospital Sketches-Bost-1916-91p-1st ed (dd3) 45.00

PEACH,ARTHUR W-Country Rod & Gun Book-Weston-1938-12mo-224p-illus,F Tolman-1st ed (m3,f,dj) 10.00

PEACOCK,ANGUS-Journey Through the Valley of Pearls and the City Beyond-Greenfield-1925-28p-wrps-5th ed (g1) 12.50

PEACOCK,BASIL-Royal Northumberland Fusiliers-Lond-1970-128p-illus-1st ed (b7,f,dj) 25.00

PEAKE,JAMES-Rudimentary Treatise on Ship Building, for the Use of Beginners-Lond-1849-John Weale-vi,132p-orig flex grn cl,paste on cov labl,6 fldg plts-1st ed (nn1,sl spot cov) 175.00

PEAKE,MERVYN-Titus Groan-NY-1946-Reynal & Hitchcock-1st ed (u2,dj) 50.00

PEAKE,ORA B-Colorado Range Cattle Industry-Glendale-1937-Arthur Clark Co-357p-cl,frntis,illus,fldg maps-1st ed (w3,f) 135.00

PEAKE,ORA B-History of the United States Indian Factory System 1795 to 1822-Denver-1954-Sage Bks-340p-illus-1st ed (gg4,dj) 30.00

PEARCE,DONN-Cool Hand Luke-NY-(1965)-Scribner's-auth 1st bk-1st ed (ff6,dj sp sl wn) 75.00

PEARCE,HAMILTON-Story of the Kidnaping of Billy Whitla-Cleve-1909-Wells Publ-205p-red cl-1st ed (x9,sp sunned) 45.00

PEARCE,W M-Matador Land and Cattle Company-Norman-(1964)-U of Okla Pr-244p-illus,maps-1st ed (ff4) 45.00

PEARCE,W M-Matador Land and Cattle Company-Norman-1964-UOP-244p-Six Score 86-1st ed (a9,dj) 35.00

PEARS,SIR EDWIN-Forty Years in Constantinople. The Recollections of...1873 to 1915-Lond-1916-H Jenkins-cl,frntis,illus-2nd ed (l8) 65.00

PEARSALL,RONALD-Conan Doyle-Lond-1977-Weidenfeld-illus-1st ed (p4,dj) 20.00

PEARSE,JOHN B-Concise History of the Iron Manufacture of the American Colonies...and of Pennsylvania...-Phila-1876-282p+ads-cl,lg fldg map (e1,sl wn sp) 40.00

PEARSE,PADRIAC H-Political Writings & Speeches-Dublin-1952-Talbot Pr-271p (r1,dj wn,chip) 20.00

PEARSON,BILLY-Never Look Back-NY-1958-S&S-1st prtg (f10,dj) 25.00

PEARSON,CAROL-Emily Carr as I Knew Her-Tor-1954-Clarke,Irwin-8vo-x,162p-col frntis-1st ed (cc7,dj wn,chip) 35.00*

PEARSON,EDMUND-Murder at Smutty Nose and Other Murders-GC-1926-Dbldy,Page-xii+330p-blu cl,plts-1st ed (k2,dj soil & chip) 30.00

PEARSON,EDMUND-Studies in Murder-NY-1924-Macmillan-1st ed (x9) 15.00

PEARSON,EDWIN-Angler's Garland & Fisher's Delight for 1871-Westminster-1871-8vo-28p-wrps,one of 350c,wdcts by T Bewick (m3) 50.00

PEARSON,F S-Butchered Baseball-1952-Barnes-illus-1st ed (s8,f,dj) 12.00

PEARSON,FRANCIS B-Reveries of a Schoolmaster-NY-(1917)-203p-cl (k1) 12.50

PEARSON,GEORGE W-Fifty Years as a Newspaper Reporter-(Van Wert)-(1953)-39p-wrps,dbl cols (c1) 10.00

PEARSON,GRANT H-My Life of High Adventure-Englewood Cliffs-1962-Prentice Hall-8vo-xviii,238p-cl,photos-1st ed (u1,dj) 30.00

PEARSON,HAYDEN S-Country Flavor-NY-(1945)-Whittlesey-112p-bds,illus-1st prtg (o6) 15.00

PEARSON,HENRY J-Three Summers Among the Birds of Russian Lapland...-Lond-1904-sm 4to-216p+68 photo plts(fldg map & plt).t.e.g.-1st ed (hh1) 135.00

PEARSON,HENRY-An American Railroad Builder John Murray Forbes-1911-Houghton Mifflin-8vo-196p (nn7,dj wn) 35.00

PEARSON,HESKETH-Conan Doyle-NY-1977-Tapplinger-illus-1st Amer ed (r4,dj) 20.00

PEARSON,HESKETH-Henry of Navarre-NY-1963-Harper & Row-8vo-249p-blu cl,5 plts-1st ed (gg6,wn dj) 15.00

PEARSON,JIM B-Maxwell Land Grant-Norman-(1961)-294p-photos,maps-1st ed (u7,f,dj) 50.00

PEARSON,JIM B-Maxwell Land Grant-Norman-1961-305p-cl,maps,photos-1st ed (z1,dj) 45.00

PEARSON,JOHN-Life of Ian Fleming-Lond-1966-Cape-illus-1st ed (q4,dj) 35.00

PEARSON,KARL-Ethic of Freethought and Other Addresses and Essays-Lond-1901-431p-2nd ed (dd3) 30.00

PEARSON,KARL-Grammar of Science-Lond-1900-548p-2nd ed (dd3) 60.00

PEARSON,L-Diseases and Enemies of Poultry-Harrisburg-1897-8vo-2 vols in 1-three qtr lea,95 col & 8 b&w plts (y8,scuff) 165.00

PEARSON,LEONARD-Psychologists' Eat Anything Diet-NY-(1973)-Wyden-276p-yel cl-1st ed (q8,dj) 12.50

PEARSON,LU-Elizabethans at Home-1957-Stanford Univ-630p-red cl,illus-1st ed (gg6) 16.00

PEARSON,T G-Adventures in Bird Protection-NY-1937-8vo-459p-cl,frntis,10 photos (y8) 18.50

PEARSON,T G-Birds of North Carolina-1942-NC Mus-416p-20 col plts,drwngs-rvsd ed (bb3,f,tn dj) 60.00

PEARSON,T G-Birds of North Carolina-Raleigh-1919-8vo-380p-cl,24 col plts-1st ed (y8,cor wn,pres cpy) 85.00

PEARSON,T G-Birds of North Carolina-Raleigh-1959-8vo-434p-cl,47 plts(24 col)-3rd ed,rvsd (y8,dj chip) 45.00

PEART,LANCELOT-South Country Fisherman-Lond-1935-8vo-283p-frontis (m3,fray dj) 25.00

PEARY,ROBERT E-Nearest the Pole-NY-1907-Dbldy,Page-sm 4to-xx,411p-g dec cov,t.e.g.,65 plts,2 fldg maps-1st ed (ll8) 125.00

PEARY,ROBERT E-Nearest the Pole-NY-1907-lg 8vo-411p-illus,fldg map-1st ed (d7,f) 100.00

PEARY,ROBERT E-Northward Over the Great Ice-NY-1898-Stokes-2 vols-dec blu cl,lg fldg map,illus-1st ed (w1) 175.00

PEASE,ARTHUR-Vascular Flora Coos County New Hampshire-Bost-1924-Nat Hist Soc-388p-bnd wi orig wrps,10 plts (x6,rbnd) 25.00

PEASE,ARTHUR-Vascular Flora of Coos County New Hampshire-Bost-1924-Nat Hist Soc-388p+11 plts (x6,sp sun) 30.00

PEASE,HOWARD-Long Wharf-NY-1930-Dodd,Mead-219p-cl,pict t & map e.p.,M. de V. lee-1st ed (s3) 20.00

PEATTIE,DONALD C-ED.-Audubon's America-Bost-1940-4to-328p-illus (m3) 25.00

PEATTIE,R-Mountain Geography-Cambridge-1936-Harvard U Pr-257p-63 illus (o10,f) 27.00

PEATTIE,RODERICK-ED.-Black Hills-NY-(1952)-310p-photos-1st ed (u7,dj) 20.00

PEATTIE,RODERICK-ED.-Friendly Mountains-NY-1942-341p-1st ed (o10,f,dj) 20.00

PEATTIE,RODERICK-Pacific Coast Range-NY-1964-402p-1st ed (q10,f,dj) 12.00

PECK,ANNE M-March of Arizona History-Tucson-1962-373p-map e.p.-1st ed (d3) 20.00

PECK,ANNIE-Industrial and Commercial South America-NY-1922-1st ed (o10,unopened,f) 15.00

PECK,ANNIE-Roundabout South America-NY-1940-359p-1st ed (q10,f) 32.00

PECK,ANNIE-Search for the Apex of America-NY-1911-370p-pict cov,64 plts,fldg map-1st US ed (o10,sm wtrmrk rear cov) 425.00

PECK,ANNIE-South American Tour-NY-1913-398p-pict cov,fldg map-1st ed (q10,sl dmpstnd) 40.00

PECK,CHARLES H-Jacksonian Epoch-NY-1899-472p-cl (b1) 22.50

PECK,GEORGE W-Peck's Bad Boy with the Cowboys-Chig-1907-Thompson & Thomas-gry pict cl-1st ed (f2,few sm sp spots) 25.00

PECK,MORTON E-Manual of the Higher Plants of Oregon-Portland-(1961)-936p-2nd ed (m10,sl shaken) 35.00

PECK,PAULA-Art of Fine Baking-(1961)-S&S-320p-gry cl,drwngs (q8,dj) 12.50

PECK,R D-Fly-Fishing for Duffers-Lond-1944-12mo-82p-illus,H M Bateman (m3,f,dj) 15.00

PECK,ROBERT N-Day No Pigs Would Die-NY-(1972)-Knopf-150p-cl-1st ed (r3,dj) 16.00

PECKHAM,ETHEL A S-ED.-Alphabetical Iris Check List, 1939-Balt-1940-Amer Iris Soc-vii,582p-grn cl,frntis (hh7) 85.00

PECKHAM,HOWARD-War for Independence-Chig-1958-227p-1st ed (gg2,f,dj) 30.00

PECKHAM,JAMES-Gen Nathaniel Lyon and Missouri in 1861-NY-1866-Amer News-447p-frntis,illus (cc6,sl wn sp) 65.00

PECKOVER,W S-Birds of New Guinea and Tropical Australia-1976-Reed-160p-117 col photos,map-1st ed (bb3,f,dj) 45.00

PEEK,S W-Nursery and the Orchard-1885-Harrison-208p-128 figs (bb3) 55.00

PEEKE,HEWSON L-Standard History of Erie County, Ohio-Chig,NY-1916-Lewis Publ-2 vols,mor (d1,sl wn) 100.00

PEEL,BRUCE-Steamboats on the Saskatchewan-Saskatoon-1972-Prairie Bk Serv,Wstrn Pro-238p-cl,frntis,illus,map e.p. (aa2,chip dj) 20.00*

PEEL,BRUCE-Steamboats on the Saskatchewan-Saskatoon-1972-Prairie Bks,Wstnr Prod-8vo-238p-frntis,61 illus,5 maps,e.p. maps-1st ed (mm8,dj) 40.00*

PEEL,DAVID-Peetie Wheatstraw Stomps-Burlington-1972-Belltower Bks-wrps-1st ed (w5,f) 35.00

PEET,LOUIS H-Trees and Shrubs of Prospect Park-NY-(1902)-12mo-x,237p-13 diags,map (m10) 30.00

PEET,STEPHEN D-Ashtabula Disaster-Chig-1877-Goodman,Louis Lloyd-illus-1st ed (p6) 60.00

PEETS,ELBERT-On the Art of Designing Cities-Cambridge-1968-MIT Pr-oblng 4to-xiii,234p-cl,146 illus,plans (cc10,dj) 40.00

PEHNT,W-Expressionist Architecture-NY-1973-519 illus-1st Amer ed (h10,dj) 85.00

PEIRCE,PARKER I-Antelope Bill-Mpls-1962-Ross & Haines-196p-drwngs-ltd to 550c-Howes P180 (cc4,box) 35.00

PEIRSON,ERMA-Mojave River and Its Valley-1970-Arthur H Clark-229p-illus-1st ed (d3,dj) 20.00

PEISSEL,M ZANSKAR-Hidden Kingdom-NY-1979-205p-col photos-1st US ed (o10,as new in dj) 15.00

PEISSEL,MICHAEL-Tiger for Breakfast-NY-1968-282p-2nd prtg (p10,f,dj) 15.00

PEISSEL,MICHEL-Mustang, Forbidden Kingdom-NY-1967-Dutton-8vo-318p-grn cl,photos,4 maps-2nd prtg (gg6,wn dj) 45.00

PEIXOTTO,E-Pacific Shores From Panama-NY-1913-285p-g pict cov,t.e.g.,80 illus-1st ed (o10,hngs loose) 15.00

PELET,JEAN J-French Campaign in Portugal 1810 to 1811-Mpls-1973-570p-maps,illus-1st ed (b7,f,dj) 50.00

PELL,S MORRIS-Scribblings of an Outdoor Boy-Princeton-1945-8vo-75p-etchings,photos (m3) 40.00

PELLAPRAT,HENRI-PAUL-Everyday French Cooking-(1968)-World-4to-562p-blu cl,80 col photos (q8,edgewn dj) 18.50

PELLAPRAT,HENRI-PAUL-Good Food From France-Lond-(1953)-F Muller-248p-blu cl,drwngs-1st ed (q8,wn dj) 12.50

PELLAPRAT,HENRI-PAUL-Pellaprat's Great Book of French Cuisine-Lond-(1979)-Collins-4to-952p+57p spplmnt,g dec red cl,col plts-rvsd ed (q8,dj) 40.00

PELLETT,FRANK C-Practical Tomato Culture-NY-1930-A T de la Mare-154p-cl,illus (m1,sl wn) 12.50

PELTIER,EUGENE-History of the Plainfield Fire Department...1827 to 1901-Plainfield-(1901?)-(40)p-bds,plts (aa6,wn,chip) 35.00

PELTON,C-Key to Pelton's Hemispheres...-Phila-1851-Sower & Barnes-176p-pict bds (k1) 35.00

PEMBERTON,ROBERT L-History of Pleasants County, West Virginia-St.Mary's-1929-1st ed (jj4) 60.00

PEMBERTON,W BARING-Battles of the Crimean War-NY-1962-239p-illus-1st ed (b7,f,dj) 35.00

PEMBLE,JOHN-Invasion of Nepal-Lond-1971-389p-blu cl,illus-1st ed (b7,f) 100.00

PEMBLE,JOHN-Raj, the Indian Mutiny, and the Kingdom of Oudh, 1801 to 1859-Sussex-1977-303p-maps,illus-1st ed (b7,f,dj) 30.00

PENDER,WILLIAM D-General to His Lady-Chapel Hill-1965-UNC Pr-271p-gry cl-1st ed (oo5,dj sl rub,chip & tn) 45.00

PENDERGAST,A W-Cigar Store Figures in Amer. Folk Art-Chig-1953-68 illus-1st ed (kk4,dj sl tn & soil) 35.00

PENDERGAST,JAMES F-ET AL-Cartier's Hochelaga and the Dawson Site-Montreal-1972-Queen's U Pr-xxvii,388p-illus,chrts(incl fldg),maps-1st ed (bb7,dj) 40.00*

PENDLETON ROUND UP...OREGON SEPTEMBER, 24,25,26 1914.-Let'Er Buck-np-nd-14p-wrps,illus (bb9) 40.00

PENDLETON,MARY-Navajo and Hopi Weaving Techniques-NY-(1975)-157p-col photos-2nd prtg (v7,dj) 15.00

PENDLETON,WILLIAM C-History of Tazewell County and Southwest Virginia, 1748 to 1920-1920-W C Hill-700p (dd9,hng tn,fox) 85.00

PENN,I GARLAND-Afro American Press and Its Editors-Springfield-1891-Wiley & Co-569p+ads-yel dec cl,illus-scarce-1st ed (k2,text & cov soil) 165.00

PENN,IRVING-Moments Preserved-NY-(1960)-Simon-4to-cl-1st ed (y3,f,dj sl creased,box) 400.00

PENN,IRVING-Moments Preserved-NY-1960-S&S-folio-184p-cl,photos-1st ed (t3,box) 350.00

PENN,WILLIAM-Fruits of Solitude-Chig-1906-Donnelley/Lakeside Clssc-sm 8vo-130p-drk grn cl,port-1st ed (ll9) 125.00

PENNELL,ELIZABETH R-Guide for the Greedy-Lond-(1923)-Lane-179p-dec orng cl-rvsd ed (q8,sl fox) 25.00

PENNELL,ELIZABETH R-My Cookery Books-(Lond)-(1983)-(Holland Pr)-ltd to 500c-facsimile ed (m6) 65.00

PENNELL,ELIZABETH R-My Cookery Books-Bost-1903-171p-mrbld bds,tip in facs & illus-ltd to 330c-Bitting 363 (m6,sl wn) 400.00

PENNELL,ELIZABETH R-Nights-Phila-1916-Lippincott-312p-bds,illus (u6,sl shaky & fox) 20.00

PENNELL,JOSEPH-Works of Charles Keene-NY-1894-R H Russell-folio-289p-red cl,t.e.g.,illus (r10,sp drknd,sl wn & fox) 125.00

PENNEY,CLARA L-List of Books Printed 1601 to 1700 in the Library of the Hispanic Society of America-NY-1938-Hispanic Soc-thk sm 8vo-xxvi,972p-cl-1st ed (w2) 85.00

PENNING-ROWSELL,EDMUND-Wines of Bordeaux-NY-(1969,1970)-Stein & Day-320p-1st Amer ed (o6,dj) 30.00

PENNINGTON,EDGAR L-Apostle of New Jersey-Phila-(1938)-xiii,217p-cl (aa6) 30.00

PENNSYLVANIA AT CHICKAMAUGA AND CHATTANOOGA-Harrisburg-1897-499p-1/2 lea,g edges,illus (n3) 35.00

PENNSYLVANIA DUTCH AND OTHER ESSAYS-Phila-1872-Lippincott-207p+ads-grn cl-1st ed (k2) 40.00

PENNSYLVANIA,STATE OF-Report of the State Commissioners for the Year 1896-Harrisburg-1897-8vo-457p-1/2 calf,gilt,mrbld bds & e.p.s,a.e.g.,col plts,photos (m3) 65.00

PENNSYLVANIA-A SHORT INTRODUCTION TO LATIN GRAMMAR, FOR THE USE OF THE UNIVERSITY AND ACADEMY OF...-Bost-1790-John W Folson-127,(1)p-lea-4th ed,revsd (k1,lacks f.e.p.s,wn cor) 85.00

PENNY,M-Birds of Seychelles and Outlying Islands-1974-Taplinger-160p-12 col plts,map-1st US ed (bb3,f,dj) 25.00

PENNYPACKER,ISSAC R-General Meade-NY-1901-Appleton-402p-frntis,illus,maps-1st ed (cc6,sl tn sp) 35.00

PENNYPACKER,MORTON-General Washington's Spies on Long Island and in New York-Brooklyn-1939-L I Hist Scty-xiv+302p-red cl,plts-1st ed (m2,chip dj) 45.00

PENNYPACKER,SAMUEL W-Autobiography of a Pennsylvanian-Phila-1918-Winston-564p-g blu cl,frntis,plts-1st ed (p2) 20.00

PENNYPACKER,SAMUEL W-Historical and Biographical Sketches-Phila-1883-Robt A Tripple-416p-brwn buckram wi sp labl-Howes P212-1st ed (k2,sl rub cov) 90.00

PENROSE,CHARLES B-Rustler Business-Douglas-(1959)-Douglas Budget-56p-pict wrps-Six Guns 1712-1st ed (oo8,f) 75.00

PENROSE,ROLAND-Man Ray-Bost-1975-NYGS-154 illus(incl 20 col)-1st ed (t4,f,dj) 45.00

PENTECOST,HUGH-24th Horse-NY-1940-Dodd-1st ed (h4,f,sl wn dj) 25.00

PENTECOST,HUGH-Cancelled in Red-1939-DM-auth 1st bk-1st ed (x7,dj) 50.00

PENTECOST,HUGH-Champagne Killer-NY-1972-Dodd-1st ed (j4,f,dj) 12.00

PENTECOST,HUGH-Dead Woman of the Year-Lond-1967-Macdonald-1st Brit ed (j4,f,dj) 12.50

PENTECOST,HUGH-Deadly Joke-NY-1971-Dodd-1st ed' (l4,dj) 10.00

PENTECOST,HUGH-Hide Her from Every Eye-Lond-1966-Boardman-1st Brit ed (j4,f,dj) 12.50

PENTECOST,HUGH-Honeymoon with Death-Lond-1976-Hale-1st Brit ed (h4,f,dj) 10.00

PENTECOST,HUGH-Judas Freak-1974-DM-1st ed (x7,f,dj) 20.00

PENTECOST,HUGH-Plague of Violence-Lond-1972-Hale-1st Brit ed (f4,dj) 12.00

PENTECOST,HUGH-Shadow of Madness-NY-1950-Dodd-1st ed (j4,f,dj) 20.00

PENTECOST,HUGH-Target for Tragedy-NY-1982-Dodd-1st ed (g4,f,dj) 12.50

PENTECOST,HUGH-Twenty Fourth Horse-NY-1940-Dodd-1st ed (l4,f,chip dj) 25.00

PENTECOST,HUGH-Walking Dead Man-NY-1973-Dodd-1st ed (g4,dj) 12.50

PENZER,N M-Poison,Damsels-1952-C Sawyer/Grafton Hs-1st ed (x7,f,dj) 45.00

PENZER,NORMAN M-Poison Damsels-Lond-1952-priv prtd for Chas Sawyer-8vo-319p-red cl-1st ed (t10) 35.00

PENZLER,OTTO,ET AL-ED.-Detectionary-(Woodstock)-(1977)-Overlook Pr-illus-1st trd ed (a10,dj) 25.00

PENZLER,OTTO-ED.-Great Detectives-1978-Little,Brown-1st ed (o9,f,dj) 15.00

PEOPLE OF IMPORTANCE-Lond,NY-(1934)-Cntry Life,Scribner's-4to-72p text+83p drwngs by J E Dowd-cl/bds-1st ed (pp10) 30.00

PEPE,PHIL-Wit and Wisdom of Yogi Berra-1974-Hawthorn-1st ed (s7,f,dj) 15.00
PEPIN,JACQUES-La Technique-(1976)-NY Times-folio-470p-yel bds,photos-5th prtg (q8,dj) 40.00
PEPLE,EDWARD-An Auto-Biography-NY-1915-Moffat-sm 8vo-dec cl bndg-1st ed (p1,vf,dj) 45.00
PEPLOW,BONNIE-Roundup Recipes-Cleve-(1951)-World-278p-dec e.p.-1st ed (o6) 25.00
PEPPAR,ALBERT H-Mysteries of Angling Revealed-Vancouver-1937-12mo-98p-illus-scarce (m3,vf) 60.00
PEPPER,ADELINE-Glass Gaffers of New Jersey and their Creations from 1739 to the Present-NY-(1971)-xx,331p-cl,illus,col plts (aa6) 90.00
PEPPER,ART-Straight Life-NY-(1979)-Schirmer-1st ed (w1,f,dj) 20.00
PEPPER,BEVERLY-Potluck Cookery-1955-Dbldy-284p-tan cl,illus-1st ed (q8,edgewn dj) 15.00
PEPPER,BEVERLY-See Rome and Eat-1960-Dbldy-4to-256p-pict bds,map e.p.,drwngs,photos-1st ed (q8,dj) 20.00
PEPPER,CHARLES M-Life-Work of Louis Klopsch-NY-(1910)-395p-cl (h1) 17.50
PEPPER,JOHN H-Boy's Playbook of Science-Lond-1869-Routledge-440p-g illus prpl cl,a.e.g.,engrvngs (hh6,sp fade,cor bump,sl fox) 50.00
PEPPER,O H PERRY-Medical Etymology-Phila-1949-263p-1st ed (dd3,sl rub) 75.00
PEPYS,SAMUEL-Diary and Correspondence of-Lond-1875-Bickers & Son-12 vols-lea,extra illus (l9) 4,000.00
PERAGALLO,EDWARD-Origin and Evolution of Double Entry Bookkeeping-NY-1938-Amer Inst Publ Co-4to-xiv+156p-brwn bds,cl sp-1st ed (j2) 40.00
PERCEVAULT,DORIS A-Rock Ridge Remembered-(np)-(1974)-(2),162p-wrps,illus (aa6) 20.00
PERCIVAL,ELEANOR H-Duck Creek Acres-Columbus-1952-150p-felt wrps-rare (c1) 45.00
PERCIVAL,MACIVER-Fan Book-Lond-(1920)-Unwin-344p-pict cl,frntis,31 plts-1st ed (dd10,f,wn dj) 75.00
PERCY,WALKER-Lancelot-NY-1977-1st ed (q5,f,dj) 20.00
PERCY,WALKER-Last Gentleman-NY-(1966)-FS&G-1st ed (a5,f,dj) 125.00
PERCY,WALKER-Last Gentleman-NY-1966-1st ed (s5,f,dj) 100.00
PERCY,WALKER-Love in the Ruins-1971-FS&G-1st ed (m9,f,dj) 60.00
PERCY,WALKER-Love in the Ruins-NY-(1971)-FS&G-1st ed (a5,f,dj) 50.00
PERCY,WALKER-Message in the Bottle-NY-(1975)-FS&G-1st issue wi t.e. unstained-1st ed (a5,as new in dj) 60.00
PERCY,WALKER-Message in the Bottle-NY-1975-1st ed (p5,f,dj) 75.00
PERCY,WALKER-Second Coming-1980-FS&G-1st ed (m9,f,dj) 30.00
PERCY,WALKER-Second Coming-NY-(1980)-1st ed (j5,as new in dj) 25.00
PERDUE,THEDA-Slavery and Evolution of Cherokee Society-Knoxville-1979-207p-1st ed (t7,f,dj) 12.50
PERDUE,VIRGINIA-Alarum and Excursion-NY-1944-Dbldy CC-1st ed (j4,chip dj) 20.00
PERDUE,VIRGINIA-Singing Clock-NY-1941-Dbldy CC-1st ed (k4,dj) 15.00
PERELMAN,S J-Acres and Pains-1947-Reynal & Hitchcock-illus-1st ed (jj6,f,dj) 75.00
PERELMAN,S J-Acres and Pains-NY-1947-Reynal & Hitchcock-1st ed (w5,f,dj) 45.00
PERELMAN,S J-Baby, It's Cold Inside-1970-S&S-1st ed (t9,f,dj) 20.00
PERELMAN,S J-Crazy Like a Fox-Lond-1945-1st Brit ed (q5,dj) 40.00
PERELMAN,S J-Dream Department-NY-(1943)-Random-lt blu cl-1st ed (f2,dj) 65.00
PERELMAN,S J-Eastward Ha!-NY-(1977)-1st ed (d5,f,dj) 20.00
PERELMAN,S J-Eastward Ha-NY-1977-1st ed (q5,dj) 12.50
PERELMAN,S J-Ill Tempered Clavichord-NY-1952-1st ed (q5,chip dj) 25.00
PERELMAN,S J-Keep It Crisp-NY-1946-1st ed (q5,chip dj) 30.00
PERELMAN,S J-Listen to the Mockingbird-NY-1949-S&S-1st ed (hh5,f,dj chip,sl soil) 20.00
PERELMAN,S J-Most of S J Perelman-NY-1958-S&S-1st ed (hh5,dj) 17.50
PERELMAN,S J-One Touch of Venus-1944-Little Brown-1st ed (x2,dj sl wn & tn) 90.00
PERELMAN,S J-Perelman's Home Companion-NY-1955-1st ed (t5,dj) 35.00
PERELMAN,S J-Rising Gorge-1961-S&S-1st ed (x2,f,dj) 30.00
PERELMAN,S J-Rising Gorge-NY-1961-S&S-1st ed (ll5,dj) 50.00
PERELMAN,S J-Road to Miltown-NY-1957-S&S-1st ed (oo3,dj sp mssng sm pc) 12.50
PERELMAN,S J-Swiss Family Perelman-NY-1950-illus,Hirschfeld-1st ed (q5,chip dj) 30.00
PERELMAN,S J-Vinegar Puss-1975-S&S-1st ed (q9,f,dj) 15.00
PERIAM,JONATHAN-Groundswell, a History of the Farmer's Movement-Cin-1874-Hannaford-576p-cl-scarce (x6,wn) 20.00
PERIAM,JONATHAN-Groundswell-Cin-1874-576p-grn cl-1st ed (mm10,sl rub) 65.00
PERKIN,ROBERT L-First Hundred Years-GC-1959-Dbldy-624p-e.p. maps,illus-1st ed (gg4,dj) 20.00
PERKIN,ROBERT L-First Hundred Years-GC-1959-Dbldy-sm 4to-624p-cl,32p photos-1st ed so stated (z4,sl spot t.e.,dj) 12.50
PERKIN,ROBERT-1859 to 1959-NY-1959-624p-illus,map e.p.-1st ed (t7,dj) 10.00
PERKINS,D A W-History of O'Brien County, Iowa...-Sioux Falls-1897-485p-lt blu cl (a3,rbnd) 65.00
PERKINS,ELISHA D-Gold Rush Diary-Lexington-1967-U of KY-xxv,206p-maps,illus-1st ed (o2,f,dj sl rub,chip) 37.50
PERKINS,FREDERIC B-Scrope-Bost-1874-Roberts-1st ed (j4) 300.00
PERKINS,JOHN-To the Ends of the Earth-NY-1981-Pantheon-oblng 4to-184p-blk cl,photos-1st ed (ll1,dj) 30.00
PERKINS,LUCY F-Belgian Twins-Bost-1917-Houghton Mifflin-scarce dj-1st ed (z2,dj sl stnd & tn) 75.00
PERKINS,LUCY F-Filipino Twins-Bost-1923-Houghton Mifflin-151p-drwngs,pict dj-1st ed (c3,sl chip dj sp) 25.00
PERKINS,MAXWELL-Editor to Author-1977-Dunwoody. Norman Berg-scarce Berg ed (cc2,f,dj) 35.00
PERKINS,MAXWELL-Editor to Author-NY-1950-Scribners-1st ed (cc2,f,dj) 35.00
PERKINS,WILLIAM-Three Years in California-Berkeley,LA-1964-424p-illus (j7,dj) 35.00
PERL,LILA-Rice, Spice and Bitter Oranges-(1967)-World-272p-yel cl,illus-1st ed (q8,dj) 20.00
PERLES,ALFRED-My Friend Henry Miller-NY-(1956)-John Day-1st ed (e3,f,dj) 20.00

PERLES,PAUL-Planning, Design and Production of the Modern Scientific Book-Brklyn-(1949)-Geo McKibbin-8vo-31p-cl,illus-1st ed (x4) 12.50

PERLMAN,WILLIAM J-ED.-Movies on Trial-NY-1936-Macmillan-8vo-254p-1st ed (s1,f,dj) 65.00

PERMUTT,CYRIL-Collecting Old Cameras-NY-1976-Da Capo-199p-200 photos-1st Amer ed (cc9,as new in dj) 45.00

PERMUTT,CYRIL-Collecting Old Cameras-NY-1976-Da Capo-4to-illus-1st US ed (mm9,f,dj) 25.00

PERNIN,H M-Phrase Book in Pernin Phonography for Teachers,Reporters,Amanuenses,Students...-Detr-1907-146p-cl-revsd ed (k1) 12.50

PERNOUD,REGINE-Retrial of Joan of Arc-NY-1955-Harcourt,Brace-cl-1st Amer ed (n8,f,dj) 25.00

PEROWNE,BARRY-Raffles of the M C C-NY-1979-St.Martin's-1st ed (r4,f,dj) 20.00

PERRIN,J NICK-Perrin's History of Illinois-(Springfield)-(1906)-231p-cl (h1) 12.50

PERRIN,JIM-ED.-Mirror in the Cliffs-Lond-1983-688p-1st ed (o10,as new in dj) 25.00

PERRIN,W G-British Flags, Their Early History and Development at Sea-Cambridge-1922-207p+ads-col illus (gg6,chip dj) 95.00

PERROTT,ROY-Aristocrats, a Portrait of Britain's Nobility-Lond-1968-1st ed (y7,dj) 12.00

PERROW,GEO L-Hoosier Editor-Indpls-1877-Tilford & Carlon-223,(1)p-cl-Wright 4188 (j1,wn sp ends) 15.00

PERRY,BLISS-Fishing with a Worm-Bost,NY-1916-12mo-24p (m3,f) 25.00

PERRY,BLISS-Life and Letters of Henry Lee Higginson-Bost-1921-Atlantic Monthly-557p-frntis,ports (o7,sl fox) 40.00

PERRY,BLISS-Pools and Ripples-Bost-1936-12mo-102p-photos-2nd prntg (m3,vf,sl wn & soil dj) 30.00

PERRY,FRANCIS-Woman Gardener-NY-nd(1955)-384p-photos (m10) 15.00

PERRY,GAYLORD-Me & the Spitter-1974-Dutton-1st ed (ff2,dj) 35.00

PERRY,GEORGE S-ED.-Roundup Time-NY,Lond-(1943)-Whittlesey Hs-1st ed (d10,dj) 30.00

PERRY,GEORGE S-Where Away-NY-(1944)-Whittlesey Hs-249p-illus,,map e.p.,col pict dj-1st ed (f9,few pgs loose,dj chip) 65.00

PERRY,NORA-Another Flock of Girls-Bost-1890-Little,Brown-sq 8vo-194p-g emboss,dec grn cl,illus-1st ed (hh9,f) 45.00

PERRY,ORAN-COMP.-Indiana in the Mexican War-Indpls-1908-496p-cl (j1,sl wn sp) 35.00

PERRY,R-Life in Desert and Plain-1977-Taplinger-253p-illus-1st ed (bb3,f,dj) 14.00

PERRY,R-World of the Tiger-NY-1965-261p-col photos (gg3,f,dj) 27.00

PERRY,R-World of the Tiger-NY-1965-8vo-(9),261p-cl,col frntis,plts,1 map (y8,cor soil,dj wn) 35.00

PERRY,RITCHIE-Bishop's Pawn-Lond-1979-Collins-1st ed (r4,vf,dj) 22.50

PERRY,ROBERT E-Treaty City-Bradford-1945-201p-cl (n1,f,dj) 15.00

PERRY,VINCENT-Boston Terrier-1928-Judy-153p-blu cl wi g terrier,photos,drwngs-1st ed (v8,sl wn) 25.00

PERRY,W A-American Game Fishes-Chig,NY-1892-8vo-580p-illus,col plts-1st ed (m3,wn) 25.00

PERRY,W-Bucks & Bows-PA-1953-223p-photos (gg3,f,dj) 15.00

PERRYMAN,F M-Pioneer Life in Illinois-Pana-1908-Kerr's Prtg Hs-104p-wrps-2nd ed rewritten (b1) 25.00

PERSHING,JOHN J-My Experiences in the World War-NY-1931-Stokes-2 vols,cl-1st ed so stated (m1,sl spot sp) 20.00

PERSHING,JOHN J-My Experiences in the World War-NY-1931-Stokes-8vo-2 vols-illus,maps-1st ed (cc5,f) 30.00

PERSISTENCE OF BEAUTY, PORTFOLIO #1-Carmel-1969-Friends of Photo-ltd to 2500 sets (y3,f) 125.00

PERTWEE,R-Hell's Loose-1929-HM-col wrap around pict dj-1st Amer ed (x7,dj) 65.00

PESATOVA,ZUZANA-Bohemian Engraved Glass-Prague-1968-132 plts (cc8) 45.00

PESETSKY,BETTE-Author From a Savage People-NY-1983-Knopf-1st ed (bb1,as new in dj) 20.00

PESETSKY,BETTE-Stories Up to a Point-NY-1981-Knopf-auth 1st bk-1st ed (bb1,f,dj) 25.00

PESKETT,WILLIAM-Survivors-Lond-(1980)-Secker & Warburg-1st ed (z8,vf,dj) 18.50

PETERKIN,JULIA-Roll, Jordan, Roll-Indpls-(1933)-Bobbs Merrill-251p-Ulmann,photos,pict dj-scarce-1st ed (f9,dj chip,spot) 125.00

PETERS,DEWITT C-Kit Carson's Life and Adventures...-Hartford-1874-604p-cl (f1,wn,sp reinfrcd) 15.00

PETERS,ELIZABETH-Crocodile on the Sandbank-1975-DM-1st ed (x7,sl stnd,dj) 85.00

PETERS,ELIZABETH-Murder of Richard III-NY-1974-Dodd Mead-1st ed (w9,f,dj) 85.00

PETERS,ELIZABETH-Night of the Four Hundred Rabbits-NY-1971-Dodd-1st ed (j4,f,dj) 35.00

PETERS,ELLIS-Black is the Colour of My True Love's Heart-NY-1967-Morrow-1st Amer ed (w9,f,dj) 45.00

PETERS,ELLIS-Borrower of the Night-1974-Cassell-1st Brit ed (x7,f,dj) 55.00

PETERS,ELLIS-City of Gold and Shadows-Lond-1973-Macmillan-1st ed (w9,f,dj) 75.00

PETERS,ELLIS-Horn of Roland-NY-1974-Morrow-1st Amer ed (w9,f,dj) 45.00

PETERS,ELLIS-Leper of St.Giles-NY-1982-Morrow-1st US ed (d4,f dj) 25.00

PETERS,ELLIS-Monk's Hood-1981-Morrow-1st Amer ed (s10,f,f dj) 25.00

PETERS,ELLIS-Monk's Hood-NY-1981-Morrow-1st Amer ed (f4,as new in dj) 15.00

PETERS,ELLIS-Mourning Raga-1970-Morrow-1st Amer ed (x7,f,sl soil dj) 50.00

PETERS,ELLIS-One Corpse Too Many-NY-1980-Morrow-1st US ed (e4,f,dj) 35.00

PETERS,ELLIS-Rainbow's End-NY-1979-Morrow-1st US ed (e4,dj) 35.00

PETERS,ELLIS-Sanctuary Sparrow-NY-1983-Morrow-1st ed (v5,f,f dj) 20.00

PETERS,ELLIS-St.Peter's Fair-NY-1981-Morrow-1st Amer ed (q4,f,dj) 27.50

PETERS,ELLIS-St.Peter's Fair-NY-1981-Morrow-1st US ed (e4,f,dj) 30.00

PETERS,FREDERICK G-Robert Musil, Master of the Hovering Life-NY-1978-Columbia Univ Pr-1st ed (bb1,f,dj) 20.00

PETERS,FRITZ-Boyhood with Gurdjieff-NY-1964-Dutton-cl-1st ed (n8,f) 42.50

PETERS,FRITZ-Descent-NY-1952-FS&Y-cl-1st ed (o8,fray dj) 27.50

PETERS,H S-Birds of Newfoundland-1951-Nwfndlnd Nat Res Dept-431p-32 col plts,map (bb3,e.p. stnd,dj fray,tn) 135.00

PETERS,HANNAH-Ovary-Berkeley-(1980)-U Cal Pr-8vo-175p-illus-1st US ed (dd5,f,f dj) 20.00

PETERS,HAROLD S-Birds of Newfoundland-Bost-1951-Houghton Mifflin-431p-illus by R T Peterson-1st ed (d9,dj) 75.00

PETERS,HARRY T-California on Stone-NY-1976-Arno Pr-4to-227p-illus-ltd to 501c,nbrd-(facs of 1935 orig ed) (n2,sl wn,soil) 95.00

PETERS,HARRY T-Currier & Ives, Printmakers to the American People-GC-(1942)-41p+192plts(incl 32 col)-cl (h1,dj) 17.50

PETERS,JEAN-ED.-Book Collecting: A Modern Guide-NY,Lond-1977-Bowker-1st ed (aa8,f,dj) 25.00

PETERS,SAMUEL A-General History of Connecticut-Lond-1781-(x)+436p-calf-Sabin 61209-1st ed (k2,rbckd,edge-wn bds) 750.00

PETERS,W AUSTIN-Feathers Preferred-Harrisburg-1951-8vo-198p-illus (m3,vf,dj) 17.50

PETERSEN,H-Old Bones-1943-DS&P-1st ed (x7,dj) 25.00

PETERSEN,MARCUS-Fur Traders & Fur Bearing Animals-Buffalo-1914-Hammond Pr-8vo-(xii),372p-pict brn cl,illus,chrts,map-1st ed (u1,sm spot fr cov) 75.00

PETERSEN,WILLIAM J-Steamboating on the Upper Mississippi-Iowa City-1937-St Hist Soc of Ia-576p-orig g dec grn cl,t.e.grn-1st ed (n2,f) 125.00

PETERSEN,WILLIAM J-Steamboating on the Upper Mississippi-Iowa City-1968-State Hist Soc Iowa-576p-grn cl,plts-2nd ed(1st wi plts) (mm10,dj) 35.00

PETERSEN,WILLIAM-Hippocratic Wisdom-Springfield-1946-263p-1st ed (dd3) 50.00

PETERSHAM,MAUD-Auntie and Celia Jane and Miki-NY-1932-Jr Lit Guild,Dbldy Doran-4to-cl,soft col lithos,cov title "Auntie"-scarce-1st ed (s3,wn,fade,hng cracked) 30.00

PETERSHAM,MAUD-David-Phila-(1938)-Winston-g pict cl,col & b&w illus (s3,f,dj) 20.00

PETERSHAM,MAUD-Jesus' Story-NY-1942-Macmillan-119p-pict cl,col illus-1st ed (r3,f,dj) 35.00

PETERSHAM,MAUD-Silver Mace-NY-(1956)-Macmillan-sm 4to-40p-cl,col illus-1st ed (s3,dj) 25.00

PETERSHAM,MAUD-Story Book of Corn-Chig-c.1936-Winston-unpgd(34)-bds (a8,dj) 27.00

PETERSON,ALVAH-Fishing with Natural Insects-Columbus-1956-8vo-176p-illus,photos (m3,vf,dj) 50.00

PETERSON,ANNA J-Mrs. Anna J Peterson's Simplified Cooking-Chig-1924-Peoples Gas Light & Coke-255p-brn bds,illus-Home Service Ed (n6,soil & wn) 20.00

PETERSON,CHARLES S-Take Up Your Mission-Tucson-1973-photos,maps,map e.p.-1st ed (t7,f,dj) 12.50

PETERSON,H L-American Knives-NY-1958-178p-photos (gg3,f) 20.00

PETERSON,H L-American Knives-NY-1958-8vo-178p-photos (m3,f,dj) 30.00

PETERSON,H L-Arms & Armor in Colonial America-PA-1956-350p-illus (gg3,f) 10.00

PETERSON,HAROLD-Man Who Invented Baseball-1973-Scribners-1st ed (s8,f,f dj) 20.00

PETERSON,HOUSTON-Lonely Debate-NY-(1938)-Reynal & Hitchcock-8vo-310p-1st ed (ee5,dj) 15.00

PETERSON,P D-Through the Black Hills and Bad Lands of South Dakota-Pierre-1929-J Fred Olander-189p-dec grn cl,photos (p2) 37.50

PETERSON,R T-Birds Over America-NY-1950(1948)-lg 8vo-342p-cl,105 photos (y8,fox,dj wn) 15.00

PETERSON,R T-Field Guide to the Birds-Bost,NY-1934-12mo-(2),167p-cl,53 plts(4 col)-1st ed,4th state (y8) 25.00

PETERSON,R T-Field Guide to the Birds-Bost-12mo-(1),290p-cl,col & b&w plts-2nd ed,35th prtg (y8,dj) 12.50

PETERSON,ROGER T-Bird Watchers Anthology-NY-1957-Harcourt Brace-drwngs-1st trd ed (d9,chip dj) 20.00

PETERSON,ROGER T-Wildlife in Color-Bost-1951-12mo-191p-450 col illus by auth (m3,f,chip dj) 17.50

PETERSON,WILLIAM J-Iowa History Reference Guide-Iowa City-1952-St Hist Soc-192p (o7,f) 15.00

PETHICK,DEREK-S S Beaver-Vancouver-(1970)-Mitchell Press-sq 8vo-xii,160p-photos,illus,map e.p.-1st ed (v1,wn dj) 45.00

PETHICK,DEREK-S S Beaver-Vancouver-(1970)-Sq-160p-illus,e.p. maps-1st ed (e7,fade dj) 30.00

PETRE,F LORAINE-Napoleon and the Archduke Charles-Lond-1919-413p-red cl,fldg maps,illus-1st ed (b7) 100.00

PETRE,F LORAINE-Napoleon at Bay 1814-Lond-(1972)-219p-2 fldg maps in rear (d7,f,peeled dj) 30.00

PETREMENT,SIMONE-Simone Weil-NY-1976-Pantheon-cl,illus-1st ed (o8,vf,dj) 13.50

PETROFF,IVAN-Report on the Population, Industries and Resources of Alaska-Wash-1884-GPO-189p-cl,2 lg fldg col maps,8 col plts (dd7,rbnd,sl soil cov,sl fox) 100.00

PETRY,ANN-Country Place-Bost-1947-1st ed (t5,dj) 30.00

PETTEE,JULIA-Rev.Jonathan Lee and his Eighteenth Century Salisbury Parish-Salisbury-1957-Salisbury Assn-x+242p-grn cl,illus-1st ed (m2,sl wn,dj) 20.00

PETTEY,GEORGE E-Narcotic Drug Diseases and Allied Ailments-Phila-1913-F A Davis-1st ed (v5,sp wn) 50.00

PETTIGREW,THOMAS F-Profile of the Negro American-Princeton-(1964)-Van Nostrand-8vo-250p-1st ed (gg5,dj) 15.00

PETTIGREW,THOMAS-On Superstitions Connected with the History and Practice of Medicine and Surgery-Lond-1844-167p-1st ed (dd3) 200.00

PETTINGILL,E R-Penguin Summer-1960-Potter-197p-photos,map-1st ed (bb3,dj) 23.00

PETTINGILL,O S-Ornithology in Laboratory and Field-Mpls-(1970)-lg 8vo-524p-cl,col frntis,maps-4th ed (y8) 25.00

PETTY,J W-Victor Rose's History of Victoria-Victoria-1961-249p-rprnt of Howes R455-1st ed thus (t7,f) 40.00

PETULENGRO,GIPSY-Romany Remedies and Recipes-Lond-(1935)-Methuen-47p-orng cl-4th ed (q8,dj) 10.00

PETZOLDT,PATRICIA-On Top of the World-NY-1953-248p-1st ed (o10,f,dj chip) 25.00

PETZOLDT,PATRICIA-On Top of the World-NY-1953-Crowell-248p-photos-Neate 615-1st ed (j8,sl wn dj) 35.00

PEYTON,GREEN-San Antonio, City in the Sun-NY-1946-McGraw-292p-1st ed (a9,dj) 20.00

PEYTON,K M-Sea Fever-Cleve-1963-World-240p-pict cl,b&w illus,V Ambrus-1st US ed (r3,f,dj) 35.00

PHARR,ROBERT D-Book of Numbers-GC-1969-auth 1st bk-1st ed (q5,f,dj sl rub) 40.00

PHELAN,RICHARD-Texas Wild-(1976)-Dutton-4to-276p-col photos,J Bones,maps,drwngs-1st ed (t8,sp chip dj) 25.00

PHELPS,ELIZABETH S-Chapters From a Life-Bost,NY-1896-278p-cl-1st ed (d1) 15.00

PHELPS,HARRIET J-Newport in Flower-Newport-1979-Preserve Soc-153p-cl (x6,f,dj) 60.00

PHELPS,MRS.-Botany for Beginners-NY-1841-Huntington-216p-cl-9th ed (k1,sl wn) 20.00

PHELPS,NETTA S-Valiant Seven-1941-Caxton-221p-dec cov,illus by H H Wilson-1st ed (r8,sl dmpstnd) 30.00

PHELPS,T S-Indian Attack on Seattle Jan. 26,1856-Seattle-1932-57p-wrps,frntis,plan of Seattle-Tweney #61-2nd ed (e7,top sp split) 75.00

PHELPS,T T-Fishing Dreams-Lond-1949-8vo-242p-photos (m3,sl chip dj) 20.00

PHETO,MOLEFE-And Night Fell-Lond-1983-Allison & Busby-illus,auth 1st bk-1st ed (y10,f,f dj) 35.00

PHILADELPHIA-Atlas of...and Environs-Phila-1877-G M Hopkins-folio-72,(2)p-lea backd cl,hand col maps (aa6,cov wn) 500.00

PHILHOWER,CHARLES A-History of Town Westfield, Union County, New Jersey-NY-1923-4to-(6),96p-cl,plts (aa6) 45.00

PHILIPS,CHRISTOPHER-Steichen at War-NY-1981-Abrams-256p-photos-1st ed (cc9,as new in dj) 35.00

PHILIPS,JUDSON-Black Glass City-NY-1965-Dodd-1st ed (j4,f,dj) 15.00

PHILIPS,JUDSON-Death Syndicate-NY-1938-Washburn-1st ed (e4,chip dj) 25.00

PHILIPS,JUDSON-Murder Clear, Track Fast-NY-1961-Dodd-1st ed (k4,dj) 12.50

PHILIPS,JUDSON-Target for Tragedy-NY-1982-Dodd-1st ed (j4,f,dj) 12.50

PHILIPS,JUDSON-Whisper Town-NY-1960-Dodd-1st ed (k4,f,sl wn dj) 20.00

PHILIPS,JUDSON-Wings of Madness-NY-1966-Dodd-1st ed (f4,f,sl wn dj) 15.00

PHILIPS,LANCE-Yonder Comes the Train-NY-1965-395p-1st ed (n4,f,dj) 35.00

PHILIPS,SHINE-Big Spring-NY-1942-Prentice-Hall-231p-Herd 1797-1st ed (cc4,dj) 20.00

PHILLIPPS,G JENKIN-System of Mining Coal and Metalliferous Veins Fully Explained...-Phila-1858-auth publ-86p+ad-brwn cl,5 fldg plts (c2,tn plt,stnd text) 35.00

PHILLIPS,A J-Birds of Arizona-Tucson-1978(1964)-4to-212p,(8p index)-cl,col frntis,12 col plts,51 col photos,maps (y8,dj) 45.00

PHILLIPS,A-ET AL-Birds of Arizona-1983-U of Ariz-4to-212p-51 col photos,126 maps,col illus (bb3,f,dj) 40.00

PHILLIPS,ARTHUR S-My Wilderness Friends-Fall River-1910-16mo-81p-photos,maps-scarce (m3,vf) 150.00

PHILLIPS,CATHERINE C-Cornelius Cole, California Pioneer and United States Senator-SF-1929-prtd by J H Nash-379p-vel-Howes P 308-1st ed (f1,covs sl warped) 60.00

PHILLIPS,ERNEST-Trout in Lakes & Reservoirs-Lond-1914-12mo-136p-photos (m3) 20.00

PHILLIPS,ETHEL C-Wee Ann-Bost-1919-Houghton Mifflin-4 col plts,E Butler-1st ed (s3,dj) 20.00

PHILLIPS,J A-Thompson's Turkey and Other Christmas Tales...-Montreal-1873-J Lovell-12mo-256p-orig g dec cl-v scarce-1st ed (pp2,sp fade,sl wn) 150.00*

PHILLIPS,J C-American Waterfowl-Riverside-1930-312p-illus (gg3,f) 40.00

PHILLIPS,J C-Natural History of the Ducks-Bost-1922 thru 1926-Riverside Pr-4 vols-linen backed papr hard bd & papr labls,74 col plts,28 b&w plts,118 maps(19 fldg) (ee3,vf) 1,100.00

PHILLIPS,JAYNE ANNE-Black Tickets-Lond-(1980)-Allen Lane-1st Brit ed (b5,as new in dj) 50.00

PHILLIPS,JAYNE ANNE-Black Tickets-NY-(1979)-Delacorte/Lawrence-1st ed (cc2,f,dj) 50.00

PHILLIPS,JAYNE ANNE-How Mickey Made It-St.Paul-1981-Bookslinger Ed-ltd to 1000c,autg,pict wrps-1st ed (l7) 75.00

PHILLIPS,JOHN C-American Waterfowl-Bost,NY-1930-8vo-312p-illus,A Brooks & A L Ripley-scarce-1st ed (m3) 60.00

PHILLIPS,JOHN C-American Waterfowl-Bost-1930-Houghton Mifflin-312p (c9) 45.00

PHILLIPS,JOHN C-Sportsman's Second Scrapbook-Bost,NY-1933-8vo-197p-illus,A L Ripley-1st ed (m3,fade sp) 25.00

PHILLIPS,JULIUS-Life History Studies on 10 Species of Rockfish-Sacramento-1964-8vo-70p-wrps,photos-Cal Dept of Fish & Game Bulletin #126 (m3,f) 10.00

PHILLIPS,LEROY-Bibliography of the Writings of Henry James-NY-(1968)-Franklin-(18),285p-facs of 1930 ed (m4) 20.00

PHILLIPS,P L-Alaska and the Northwest Part of North America 1588 to 1898-Wash-1898-119p-wrps (bb9,chip wrps) 75.00

PHILLIPS,PAUL C-Fur Trade-1961-U of Okla Pr-8vo-2 vols-beige cl,cardbd box,34 illus,13 maps-1st ed (mm8,discol sp,box) 200.00*

PHILLIPS,PHILIP L-ED.-Lowery Collection-Wash-1912-GPO/Libr of Congr-sm 4to-x,567p-orig red cl,frntis port,col t.p.-1st ed (t10,ex-libr) 175.00

PHILLIPS,PHILIP L-List of Geographical Atlases in the Library of Congress with Bibliographical Notes-Wash-1909 to 1920-GPO-sm 4to-4 vols-orig red cl-complete as iss by Phillips-1st ed (t10) 500.00

PHILLIPS,TOM-Sketches of...-KC-1971-188p-illus-1st ed (t7,dj) 40.00

PHILLIPS,W A-Labor, Land & Law-NY-1886-Scribner's-471p (r1) 45.00

PHILLIPS,WALTER J-Colour in the Canadian Rockies-Tor-1937-T Nelson-x,125p-illus,32 col plts,map(lining papers)-1st ed (k10,sl rub sp,dj wn,rprd) 100.00*

PHILLPOTTS,EDEN-Children of the Mist-Lond-1898-A D Innes-orig g titled cl-1st ed,1st iss (aa9,sl drknd sp,sl rub,fox) 65.00

PHILLPOTTS,EDEN-Jig Saw-1926-MacMillan-1st Amer ed (s10,innr hng started,dj) 40.00

PHILLPOTTS,EDEN-Red Redmaynes-NY-1922-Macmillan-1st ed (h4) 15.00

PHILLPOTTS,EDEN-Voice From the Dark-1925-Macmillan-1st Amer ed (s10) 15.00

PHILPS,J E-Solomons Sojourn-Hobart-1978-Tasmanian Hist Rsrch Assn-8vo-207p-grn cl,illus-ltd to 550c (dd7,as new in dj) 30.00

PHIN,JOHN-Open Air Grape Culture-NY-1876-266p-g dec grn cl,figs (jj7) 75.00

PHIPPEN,GEORGE-Life of a Cowboy-Tucson-1969-104p-col frntis,col illus-ltd ed (t7,f,dj) 30.00

PHOENIX-Lond-1630-R Meighen-lea (l9,weak sp) 500.00

PIAF,SIMONE B-Piaf-NY-1975-Harper-1st ed (u4,f,dj) 20.00

PIATT,DONN-Memoirs of the Men Who Saved the Union-NY-1887-Belford,Clarke-302p-frntis,ports (o7,sl wn) 20.00

PICARD,MAX-Human Face-NY-(1930)-Farrar & Rinehart-(xvi)+221+(3)p+30 hlftone ports,prntd blk cl-1st ed in Engl,1st prntg (y9) 32.50

PICASSO,PABLO-Picasso 347-NY-(1970)-Maecenas Pr/Random-oblng folio-2 vols-1st ed (l9,f,box) 300.00

PICAYUNE ORIGINAL CREOLE COOK BOOK-New Orleans-1947-Times Picayune-446p-pict red cl-11th ed (q8,dj) 18.50

PICHIERRI,LOUIS-Music in New Hampshire-NY-1960-Columbia U Pr-8vo-297p-1st ed (ee5,tape rprd dj) 25.00

PICHOT,AMEDEE-Les Mormons-Paris-1854-Hachette-292p-lea sp,raised bands,text in French-scarce-1st ed (z1) 150.00

PICKARD,F W-Sixteen British Trout Rivers-NY-1936-124p-photos (gg3) 15.00

PICKARD,F W-Trout & Salmon Fishing in Ireland-NY-1938-8vo-142p-photos (m3,fray dj) 35.00

PICKARD,MADGE-Midwest Pioneer-NY-1946-339p-1st ed (dd3,dj) 40.00

PICKENS,A-Golf Bum-1970-Crown-1st ed (x2,f,dj) 20.00

PICKERELL,JAMES-Vietnam in the Mud-1966-Bobbs Merrill-1st ed (c8,f,f dj) 45.00

PICKERING,MARIE L-Tropical Cookery Simplified-Lond-(1963)-Faber & Faber-180p-new ed (m6) 15.00

PICKTHALL,MARMADUKE-TRANSL.-Meaning of the Glorious Koran-NY-1930-Knopf-cl-1st Amer ed (n8) 35.00

PICKWARD,F W-Sixteen British Trout Rivers-NY-1936-8vo-124p-photos (m3,dj) 20.00

PICKWICK PORTRAIT GALLERY-Lond-(March 1936)-Chapman & Hall-illus-1st ed (cc2,f,dj) 50.00

PICOT,LEONCE-ED.-Great Restaurants of the United States and Their Recipes-Ft.Lauderdale-1966-316p-pict bds,col illus (q8) 15.00

PICTORIAL PHOTOGRAPHY IN AMERICA 1920-NY-1920-Pict Photogs of Amer-qto-cl/bds,photos (y3,sl sunned & soil) 75.00

PICTORIAL PHOTOGRAPHY IN AMERICA 1921-NY-1921-Pict Photogs of Amer-4to-cl & bds (y3) 75.00

PICTORIAL PHOTOGRAPHY IN AMERICA-Vol.5-NY-1929-Pict Photog 1929-folio-cl/bds,58 photos-ltd to 1500c (y3,f) 75.00

PIDGIN,CHARLES F-Blennerhassett-Bost-1901-C M Clark-1st ed (hh5) 12.50

PIDGIN,CHARLES F-Climax-Bost-1902-C M Clark-1st ed (hh5,sp sun) 12.50

PIDGIN,CHARLES F-Little Burr-Bost-1905-Luce-1st ed (hh5) 12.50

PIEPENBURG,ROBERT-Raku Pottery-NY-1972-Macmillan-4to-160p-cl,col illus-1st ed (y4,dj) 35.00

PIER,GARRETT C-Temple Treasures of Japan-NY-1914-F F Shrman-cl,frntis,illus-1st ed (l8,pres cpy) 20.00

PIERCE,AUGUSTUS B-Knocking About...-New Haven-1924-Yale U Pr-8vo-xiv,176p-red cl,illus by auth-1st ed (y4,dj) 35.00

PIERCE,DONN-Master in the Kitchen-1964-Knopf-556p-drwngs-1st ed (q8,dj) 16.50

PIERCE,EARL-Cherokee People-Phoenix-1973-col frntis,photos,maps-Indian Tribal Ser-1st ed (t7,f) 20.00

PIERCE,GEORGE W-Songs of Insects-Cambridge-1948-Harvard U Pr-viii+329p-grn cl-1st ed (c2,dj) 40.00

PIERCE,HENRY C-American Historical & Sporting Library of H C Pierce-1928-Anderson Galleries-8vo-109p-wrps (m3,f,priced) 30.00

PIERCY,CAROLINE B-Valley of God's Pleasure-NY-1951-Stratford Hs-(viii)+247p-blu cl,plts-1st ed (mm10,pres) 22.00

PIERCY,FREDERICK H-Route from Liverpool to Great Salt Lake Valley-Cambridge-1962-313p-illus-Howes P359 (j7,vf,dj) 45.00

PIERCY,MARGE-Braided Lives-NY-(1982)-Summit-1st ed (e3,f,sl tn dj) 20.00

PIERCY,MARGE-Going Down Fast-NY-(1969)-1st ed (s5,f,dj) 40.00

PIERCY,MARGE-Going Down Fast-NY-(1969)-Trident-1st ed (hh5,dj) 25.00

PIERCY,MARGE-High Cost of Living-1978-Harper & Row-1st ed (r9,f,dj) 15.00

PIERRE,W A-Canterbury Provincial Railways-Wellington-1964-190p-1st ed (n4,f,dj) 16.00

PIERREPONT,EDWARD-Fifth Avenue to Alaska-NY-1884-Putnam-8vo-329p-blk cl,fldg maps-1st Amer ed (t1) 165.00

PIERS,CHARLES-Sport & Life in British Columbia-Lond-1923-8vo-159p-photos (m3) 50.00

PIERSON,DAVID L-History of the Oranges to 1921-NY-1922-4to-3 vols-(a 4th vol was iss separately)-cl,plts (aa6) 150.00

PIERSON,DAVID L-Narratives of Newark from the Days of its Founding, 1666 to 1916-Newark-(1917)-x,387p-cl,plts,illus (aa6) 45.00

PIERSON,DAVID L-Narratives of Newark-Newark-(1917)-illus-1st ed (pp4) 25.00

PIERSON,REV HAMILTON W-In the Brush...-NY-1881-D Appleton-iv+321p+ads-olive cl,plts-1st ed (b2) 75.00

PIESSE,CHARLES H-Olfactics and the Physical Senses-Lond-1887-Piesse & Lubin-viii+157p-red cl-1st ed (d2) 35.00

PIGAFETTA,ANTONIO-Voyage of Magellan-Englewood Cliffs-1969-Prentice Hall-4to-emboss cl,facs maps (p8,f,f dj) 125.00

PIGNEY,JOSEPH-For Fear We Shall Perish-NY-1961-Dutton-312p-grn cl-1st ed (e2,dj) 18.00

PIGNEY,JOSEPH-For Fear We Shall Perish-NY-1961-Dutton-312p-maps-1st ed (dd4,dj) 25.00

PIKE COUNTY-INVENTORY OF THE COUNTY ARCHIVES OF OHIO. NO.66...-Columbus-1942-Ohio Hist Rcds Srvy-296,(2)p-wrps (d1) 20.00

PIKE,JAMES-Scout and Ranger-Princeton-1932-164p-pict cl,frntis,illus-Graff #3286 (t7,f) 30.00

PIKE,NICHOLAS-New and Complete System of Arithmetic-Worcester-1797-Pr of Isaiah Thomas-516p-lea-extra leaf nbrd (5)-6 as called for in Karpinski,pg 90-2nd ed,enlarged (g1) 100.00

PIKE,NICOLAS-New and Complete System of Arithmetic...-Newburyport-1788-John Mycall-512p-modern bds wi lea sp-scarce-1st ed (k1,rbnd) 250.00

PIKE,NICOLAS-Sub Tropical Rambles in the Land of the Aphanapteryx-NY-1873-Harper & Bros-48 engrvngs,4 fldg maps-1st ed (p6,sm stn frnt cov) 125.00

PIKE,NICOLAS-Sub Tropical Rambles in the Land of the Aphanapteryx-NY-1873-Harper & Bros-red cl,fldg map-1st ed (gg7) 85.00

PIKE,WARBURTON-Barren Ground of Northern Canada-1917-Dutton-334p-photos,fldg map (bb3,hngs rprd) 55.00

PIKE,WARBURTON-Barren Ground of Northern Canada-NY-1917-Dutton-8vo-ix,334p-grn cl,frntis,16 illus,1 fldg map-1st Amer ed (mm8) 50.00*

PIKE,ZEBULON M-Exploratory Travels Through the Western Territories of North America-Denver-1889-Lawrence & Co-394p-blu cl,bevel bds,4 maps (z1,scuffs) 250.00

PIKE,ZEBULON M-Journals of...with Letters and Related Documents-Norman-(1966)-Univ of Okla-2 vols,60 plts,fldg maps-1st ed thus (e2,box) 100.00

PIKE,ZEBULON M-Southwestern Expedition of...-Chig-1925-Donnelley-239p-frntis,map-Lakeside Classics (cc4) 35.00

PILAT,OLIVER-Sodom by the Sea-GC-1941-Dbldy,Doran-ix,334p-photo plts (n2,sl rub) 25.00

PILCHER,LEWIS-List of Books by ...Old Masters of Medicine and Surgery Together with Books on the History...-Brooklyn-1918-201p-ltd to 250c (dd3,vf) 250.00

PILKINGTON,ROGER-Small Boat Through Germany-NY-1964-St.Martin's-8vo-214p-sketches-Small Boat ser-1st US ed (bb5,f,f dj) 15.00

PILLING,JAMES C-Bibliography of the Eskimo Language-Wash-1887-GPO-116p-orig prntd wrps,Bur of Amer Ethno Bull No.1 (ll1,chip & soil wrps) 65.00

PILLSBURY,ANN-ED.-Pillsbury Best 1000 Recipes-Chig-(1959)-Consol Bk-608p-pict bds-1st ed (q8) 30.00

PILLSBURY,DOROTHY L-Adobe Doorways-Albuq-(1952)-197p-1st ed (u7,f,dj) 25.00

PILLSBURY,DOROTHY L-No High Adobe-Albuq-1950-198p-illus-1st prtg (u7,f,dj) 25.00

PILLSBURY,DOROTHY L-Roots in Adobe-Albuq-(1959)-232p-illus-1st ed (u7,dj) 25.00

PILLSBURY,DOROTHY L-Star Over Adobe-Albuq-1963-208p-frntis,illus-1st ed (t7,dj) 17.50

PILLSBURY,PARKER-Acts of the Anti-Slavery Apostles-Concord-1883-503p-grn cl-1st ed (b2) 40.00

PILLSBURY,PARKER-Mortality of Nations-NY-1867-Robt J Johnston-13,(3)p-wrps (d1,sl wn) 40.00

PINCHBECK,IVY-Children in English Society-Lond-1969-2 vols-1st ed (dd3,dj) 75.00

PINCHOT,ANN-52 West-NY-1962-FS&C-1st ed (y1,f,dj) 25.00

PINCHOT,GIFFORD-Just Fishing Talk-NY,Harrisburg-1936-Telegraph Pr-238p-photos (w10) 25.00

PINCHOT,GIFFORD-To the South Seas-Phila-1930-John C Winston-8vo-xiii,500p-blu cl wi g titles & sailing ship cov dec,maps,wood engrvngs & 250 photos (nn1,autg) 65.00

PINCHOT,GIFFORD-To the South Seas-Phila-1930-John C Winston-dec blu cl,photos,engrvngs-1st ed (gg7,f) 35.00

PINCHOT,GIFFORD-White Pine a Study-NY-1896-Century-x,102p-cl-scarce (x6) 35.00

PINELLI,BABE-Mr.Ump-1953-Guild-1st ed (ff2,dj) 35.00

PINEY,A-ED.-Recent Advances in Microscopy-Phila-1931-P Blakiston's Son-viii+260p-blu cl-1st ed (a2) 25.00

PINKERTON,A F-Saved at the Scaffold or Nic brown, the Chicago Detective-Chig-(1888)-Laird & Lee-161p+ads-cl-rare (n1,weak innr hngs,cov spots) 50.00

PINKERTON,FRANK-Dyke Darrell,the Railroad Detective...-Chig-(1886)-Laird & Lee-155p-cl-wi "Won by Crime" starting on pg 122-Wright 4257 (n1,fade cov,few sm sp holes) 27.50

PINKERTON,FRANK-Life for a Life or the Detective's Triumph-Chig-(1886)-Laird & Lee-157p-cl (g1,wn sp & cor,cov sl spot) 40.00

PINKERTON,KATHRENE G-Woodcraft for Women-NY-1916-12mo-174p-one of "Outing Handbooks"-1st ed (m3,f) 17.50

PINKERTON,ROBERT-Hudson's Bay Company-NY-(1931)-Holt-357p-photos-1st ed (ll9,f,dj) 45.00

PINKHAM,LYDIA E-This Treatise on the Diseases of Women is Dedicated to the Women of the World-(Lynn)-(1907)-47p-wrps (d1,sl chip wrps) 17.50

PINKOWSKI,BOB-Muskie Fever-NY-1961-8vo-127p-photos-1st ed (m3,f,sl chip dj) 35.00

PINKOWSKI,EDWARD-History of Bridgeport, Pa.-Bridgeport-(1951)-South Side Pr-47p-wrps (a1) 12.50

PINNEO,T S-Pinneo's Primary Grammar of the English Language, for Beginners-Cin-(1854)-Smith-160p-prntd bds-"Stereotype by C F O'Driscoll, Cincinnati" on cpyrt pg (k1,wn bds) 15.00

PINNERY,MARGARET-Miniature Rose Book-1964-Van Nostrand-149p-cl (x6,dj) 10.00

PINNEY,PETER-Dust on My Shoes-Indpls-(1951)-Bobbs-Merrill-8vo-371p-25 photos-1st ed (cc5,sl tn dj) 20.00

PINTARD,JOHN-Letters from...to his Daughter, Eliza Noel Pintard Davidson, 1816 to 1833-NY-1940-41-NY Hist Soc,#70-73-4 vols-cl,ports (aa6) 75.00

PINTER,HAROLD-Landscape & Silence-NY-1970-1st US ed (q5,f,dj) 15.00

PIONEER WOMEN-True Stories by Daughters of Pioneers of Washington-np-nd-blu wrps-Amer Rev Bicentennial ed (b6) 10.00

PIONEERS IN GOD'S HILLS-Austin-1960-Von Boeckmann-2 vols-1st ed (a9,dj) 85.00

PIPER,EVELYN-Bunny Lake is Missing-NY-1957-Harper-1st ed (g4,f,dj) 20.00

PIPER,H BEAM-Murder in the Gunroom-NY-1953-Knopf-1st ed (k4,f,chip dj) 60.00

PIPER,MARION J-Dakota Portraits-(1964)-231p-photos,e.p. maps-1st ed (dd4,dj,autg) 15.00

PIPER,MARION J-Dakota Portraits-Bismarck-1964-231p-photos,illus,map e.p.-1st ed (t7,dj,autg) 20.00

PIPER,PETER-Corpse That Came Back-NY-(1954)-Random-1st US ed (bb1,sl soil dj) 15.00

PIRNIE,M D-Michigan Waterfowl Management-Lansing-1935-8vo-328p-photos,fldg maps-1st ed (m3,ex-lib) 30.00

PIRSIG,ROBERT M-Zen and the Art of Motorcycle Maintenance-NY-1974-Morrow-1st ed (y1,f,f dj) 100.00

PIRSIG,ROBERT-Zen and the Art of Motorcycle Maintenance-NY-1974-Morrow-1st ed (g8,f,dj) 95.00

PISANO,R G-William Merritt Chase-NY-1982-sm folio-wrps-1st ed (ff10,f) 25.00

PITKIN,T M-Captain Departs-Carbondale-1973-164p-illus,ports (z10,f,dj) 15.00

PITMAN,I-And Clouds Flying-Lond-1947-8vo-152p-cl,10 plts(2 col) (y8) 25.00

PITMAN,ISAAC-Manual of Phonography-NY-1844-John Donlevy-32p+3 fldg chrts prntd on both sides-bds-3rd Amer ed(wi addtns) (c1) 17.50

PITSEOLAK,PETER-People From Our Side-Edmonton-1975-Hurtig-4to-157p-card covs,photos-1st ed (bb7,sl soil covs) 15.00*

PITT,GIORDANO-Scandinavian Fairy Tales-(1962)-Golden Bks-folio-148p-pict glossy bds,col illus,F Santin (r3,f) 25.00

PITT,LEONARD-Decline of the Californios-Berkeley-1966-UCP-324p-photos-1st ed (d3,dj) 35.00

PITTENGER,PEGGY-Morgan Horses-So Brunswick-1976-Barnes-1st ed (h9,dj) 65.00

PITTS,ZASU-Candy Hits-(1963)-Duell-93p-bds,photos-1st ed (q8,dj) 22.50

PITZ,H C-200 Years of American Illustration-NY-1977-illus-1st ed (h10,dj) 75.00

PITZ,HENRY-Brandywine Tradition-Bost-1969-Houghton Mifflin-4to-240p-cl,col & b&w plts-1st ed (s3,f,dj) 55.00

PITZ,HENRY-Illustrating Children's Books-NY-(1963)-Watson Guptil-205p-cl,b&w illus (s3,f,dj) 35.00

PITZER,JOHN E-Three Days at Gettysburg-(Gettysburg)-nd-"News" Press-100p (e1,wrps) 30.00

PIXLEY,ARISTENE-Green Mountain Cook Book-Brattleboro-(1941)-Stephen Daye Pr-sm 8vo-90p-1st ed (o6) 20.00

PIZZETTI & COCKER-Flowers-NY-1975-Abrams-2 vols-cl,col illus (x6,as new in box) 80.00
PLACE,MARION T-Retreat to the Bear Paw-NY-(1969)-190p-illus,e.p. maps-1st ed (c7,f,chip dj) 35.00
PLAIDY,JEAN-Beyond the Blue Mountains-NY-(1947)-Appleton Century-auth 1st bk-1st ed (hh5,sm cov stn,dj) 35.00
PLAINFIELD-Atlas of the City of...Union County, and Borough of North Plainfield, Somerset County, N.J. 1894-Plainfield-1894-F A Dunham-folio-lea backd cl,13 dblpg linen backd col maps (aa6,rebackd) 600.00
PLAINS INDIANS-(Ottawa)-1938-Nat Mus of Can-10p-prtd wrps,illus,map-Anthro lflt #4 (k10) 10.00*
PLANCK,MAX-Treatise on Thermodynamics-Lond-1903-Longman's,Green-xii+272p-gry cl,errata slip-1st Brit ed (a2,cov rub & wn) 175.00
PLATH,SYLVIA-Ariel-NY-(1966)-Harper & Row-1st ed (u10,f,sl soil dj) 50.00
PLATH,SYLVIA-Bell Jar-1971-Harper-1st US ed (kk6,f dj) 45.00
PLATH,SYLVIA-Bell Jar-NY-1971-1st US ed (o5,dj) 75.00
PLATH,SYLVIA-Johnny Panic and the Bible of Dreams-NY-(1979)-Harper-8vo-313p-1st ed (w6,dj) 35.00
PLATH,SYLVIA-Letters Home-NY-1975-Harper & Row-1st ed (z3,dj chip) 12.50
PLATH,SYLVIA-Three Women-Lond-1968-Turret-4to-ltd to 150c,nbrd-1st ed (w6,f) 200.00
PLATH,SYLVIA-Winter Trees-Lond-(1971)-Faber & Faber-1st ed (k7,vf dj) 50.00
PLATT,CHARLES D-Ballads of New Jersey in the Revolution-Morristown-1896-vi,(2),167,(1)p-cl,fldg map (aa6) 50.00
PLATT,JUNE-...NEW ENGLAND COOK BOOK-NY-1971-Atheneum-239p-dj-1st ed (o6,dj) 18.00
PLATT,JUNE-Cook Book-NY-1958-Knopf-475p (r6) 10.00
PLATT,JUNE-June Platt Cook Book-1958-Knopf-497p-pict yel cl,drwngs (q8) 15.00
PLATT,JUNE-June Platt's Dessert Cook Book-1942-Houghton Mifflin-250p-red cl-1st ed (q8,dj) 16.50
PLATT,RUTHERFORD-Wilderness the Discovery of a Continent of Wonder-NY-1961-310p-map frntis,illus-1st ed (t7,dj) 12.50
PLATT,WARD-Frontier-NY-(1908)-Eaton & Mains-292p-illus,fldg maps (dd4) 15.00
PLATTS,W CARTER-Light Lines & Tight Lines-Lond-nd-12mo-234p+ads-photos (m3) 50.00
PLATTS,W CARTER-Trout Streams & Salmon Rivers Their Management & Improvement-Lond-1930-8vo-218p-photos (m3,fade sp) 25.00
PLAUT,JAMES S-Steuben Glass-1951-Bittener & Co-28p-68 plts (cc8,dj) 65.00
PLAYER,I-White Rhino Saga-1973-Stein Day-254p-photos-1st US ed (bb3,f,dj) 15.00
PLAYFAIR,JOHN-Elements of Geometry, Containing the First Six Books of Euclid, with a Supplement...-Bost-1814-T B Wait-xxx+316+52p-lea-2nd Amer ed (d2,wn cov,fox) 50.00
PLAYFAIR,W S-Systematic Treatment of Nerve Prostration and Hysteria-Phila-1883-111p (g10) 75.00
PLE,A-ET AL-Mystery and Mysticism-NY-1956-Philosophical Libr-1st ed (n8,f,fray dj) 20.00
PLEAS,ELWOOD-Henry County-New Castle-1871-Pleas Bros-148p-bds.,orig wrps bound in-errata bottom pg 148-Howes P 420 calls for 2 plts,but no indication of any (g1,rbnd,soil wrps,sl chip) 75.00
PLEASANTS,HENRY,JR.-Inferno at Petersburg-Phila-(1961)-181p-illus-1st ed (c4,pc tn dj) 20.00
PLEASANTS,HENRY-Death of a Music-Lond-1961-Gollancz-1st ed (w1,f,f dj) 25.00
PLENN,J H-Saddle in the Sky-Indpls-(1940)-287p-cl-Six-Guns 1737-Rampaging Herd 1805-1st ed so stated (g1,sl wn sp,pres cpy) 35.00
PLETCHER,DAVID M-Diplomacy of Annexation-(1975)-U of Missouri-656p-maps (e7,f,dj) 30.00
PLIMPTON,GEORGE-ED.-Writers at Work, Fourth Series-NY-1976-Viking-1st ed (c8,f,f dj) 50.00
PLIMPTON,GEORGE-ED.-Writers at Work,Fifth Series-NY-1981-Viking-1st ed (d8,f,f dj) 45.00
PLIMPTON,GEORGE-Out of My League-1961-Harper-1st ed (q7,f,dj) 20.00
PLOMER,WILLIAM-ED.-Kilvert's Diary 1870 to 1879-NY-1947-xvi,407p-1st prtg (m10,tattrd dj) 12.00
PLOMER,WILLIAM-Paper Houses-1929-C,M-1st Amer ed (x2,dj sl wn) 70.00
PLOWDEN,DAVID-Farewell to Steam-VT-1966-Stephen Greene Pr-sm folio-154p-cl,photos-1st ed (t3,dj) 45.00
PLUM,D A-Adirondack Bibliography-NY-1958-354p (gg3,f) 15.00
PLUMB,CHARLES S-Little Sketches of Famous Beef Cattle-Columbus-1904-auth publ-tall 8vo-99p-cl,Adams #1806-scarce (b6) 75.00
PLUMB,CHARLIE-Last Domino-(Independence)-(1975)-Independence Pr-scarce-1st ed (ff3,f,dj) 75.00
PLUMLEY,LADD-With the Trout Fly-NY-1929-Stokes-grn cl-1st ed (ff7) 25.00
PLUMMER,WILLIAM-Holy Goof-1981-Prentice Hall-1st ed (oo2,f,dj) 30.00
PLUMMER,WILLIAM-Holy Goof-Englewood Cliffs-(1981)-Prentice Hall-photos-1st ed (d5,as new in dj) 20.00
PLUTARCH-Lives of the Noble Grecians and Romanes...-Stratford,Bost-(1928)-Shakespeare Hd Pr/HM Co-8 vols-blu cl sp over papr cov bds,g stmpd lea sp labls-ltd to 500 sets for Amer (p1) 275.00
PLUTO,TERRY-Greatest Summer-Englewood Cliffs-(1979)-179p-cl-1st ed (n1,f,dj) 12.50
PLYMOUTH CONGREGATIONAL CHURCH-LADIES' AID SOCIETY OF THE...-Plymouth Cook Book-Colfax-nd(ca.1910?)-Bramwell Bros-70p-oil cl wrps (n6,wn) 30.00
POATE,ERNEST M-Murder on the Brain-NY-1930-Chelsea-1st ed (g4,sl fox) 10.00
POCHIN MOULD,DAPHNE D C-Celtic Saints-NY-1956-Macmillan-cl-1st ed (l8,f) 22.50
POCHIN,W F-Angling & Hunting Guide in British Columbia-Vancouver-1946-8vo-204p-2 col plts,illus (m3,vf,fray dj) 27.50
POCOCK,ROGER-Following the Frontier-1903-McClure,Phillips-338p+ads-dec cov-Six Guns #1740-1st ed (r8,f) 75.00
PODMORE,FRANK-Modern Spiritualism-Lond-1902-Methuen-2 vols-prntd red cl-1st ed (y9,sl fox) 125.00
PODMORE,HARRY J-Trenton Old and New-Trenton-1927-166p-cl,illus (aa6) 45.00
PODOLSKY,EDW,M.D.-Transvestism Today-NY-1960-Epic Publ-8vo-128p-photos,illus,photo dj-1st ed (y4,dj) 45.00
POE,EDGAR A-Bells and Other Poems-NY,Lond-nd-Hodder & Stoughton-4to-blnd stmpd beige cl,28 col illus by E Dulac (r10,sl soil,spot,loose illus) 120.00
POE,EDGAR A-Fall of the House of Usher-Paris-1928-Black Sun Pr-4to-wrps,orig glassine dj,ltd to 300c (x3,sl chip dj) 375.00

POE,EDGAR A-Fall of the House of Usher-Paris-1928-Black Sun Pr-red cov,illus by Alastair,ltd to 300c,nbrd (cc2) 350.00
POE,EDGAR A-Journal of Julius Rodman-1947-Grabhorn-4to-76p-plain brwn dj as iss,col wood engrvngs by M Dean,ltd to 500c (r8,dj) 90.00
POE,EDGAR A-Monsieur Dupin-1904-MP-illus-1st ed (x7,sl lttrng wn) 55.00
POE,JOHN W-Death of Billy the Kid-Bost-1933-Houghton Mifflin-59p-cl,photos,illus,Guns #1741-1st ed (w3) 50.00
POE,JOHN-Death of Billy the Kid-NY-1933-frntis,photos,illus-Six Guns #1741-scarce-1st ed (t7,f,dj) 75.00
POE,SOPHIE A-Buckboard Days-Caldwell-1936-292p-illus-1st ed (z1,f,dj) 85.00
POESCH,J-Titian Ramsay Peale & Journals of the Wilkes Expedition-Phila-1961-tall 4to-214p-pict cov,illus,fldg map-1st ed (e7,f,dj) 50.00
POESCH,JESSIE-Art of the Old South-NY-1983-folio-1st ed (ff10,dj) 65.00
POGSON,BERYL-Maurice Nicoll-NY-1961-T Nelson & Sons-cl-1st Amer ed (o8,f,dj) 47.50
POGZEBA,WOLFGANG-New Vision, Photographs of the American West-Flagstaff-1977-109p-qtr lea,box,photos,ltd to 100c,nbrd,orig hand done wtrcol,autg-1st ed (t7,f,box) 400.00
POGZEBA,WOLFGANG-New Vision-Flagstaff-1977-Northland Pr-oblng 8vo-110p-blk/gry cl,photos-1st ed (r10,f dj) 15.00
POHL,FREDERICK-Way the Future Was-Lond-1979-Gollancz-1st Brit ed (j3,f,dj,autg) 20.00
POINT,FATHER NICHOLAS-Wilderness Kingdom-NY-1967-HR&W-4to-285 paintngs(incl col)-1st ed (b4,dj) 45.00
POINTDEXTER,MILES-Ayar Incas-NY-1930-Horace Liveright-2 vols-cl,frntis(vol 2 in col),illus-scarce-1st ed (o8,f) 65.00
POINTER,MICHAEL-Public Life of Sherlock Holmes-Newton Abbot-1975-David & Charles-illus-1st ed (r4,f,dj) 35.00
POINTER,MICHAEL-Sherlock Holmes File-NY-1976-Potter-175 illus-1st Amer ed (s4,f,dj) 27.50
POISONOUS SNAKES OF THE WORLD-Wash D.C.-nd-Dept of Navy-lg 8vo-viii+212p-120 text illus,8 col plts,11 maps (g2) 25.00
POKER: HOW TO WIN-NY-nd(1890s)-Richard K Fox Publ-90p+ads-pict wrps (b1,sl wn sp) 25.00
POLACK,J S-New Zealand-Lond-1838-Richard Bently-12mo-2 vols-qtr blck lea wi mrbld papr,1 fldg map,6 plts-1st ed (p8) 750.00
POLAND,WILLIAM-Laws of Thought or Formal Logic-NY-1896-104p-cl (j1) 15.00
POLHEMUS,B M-History and Manual of the Second Reformed Church of Somerville,N.J.-Somerville-1883-65,(1)p-wrps (aa6,brittle) 40.00
POLITES,N-Architecture of Leandro V Locsin-NY-1977-sq 4to-illus-1st ed (h10,dj) 75.00
POLITI,LEO-Song of the Swallows-NY-1949-Scribner's-1st ed (d8,sl chip dj) 50.00
POLK'S NEW BRUNSWICK CITY DIRECTORY...-NY-1940-996p-cl (aa6) 35.00
POLLACK,PETER-Picture History of Photography-NY-(1958)-Abrams-624p-photos-1st ed (cc9,f,sl tn dj) 90.00
POLLACK,PETER-Picture History of Photography-NY-(1958)-Abrams-sq 4to-blu & g stmpd blk cl-1st ed (y3) 45.00
POLLARD,H B C-British & American Game Birds-1939-Scribners-48p-rose col bds,beige cl backstrip,20 col plts wi tiss-scarce (ee3,sl discol sp) 300.00
POLLARD,H B C-British and Amer Game Birds-Lond-1945-4to-48p-cl,20 col plts (y8,dj) 65.00
POLLARD,JOSEPHINE-History of the Battles of America in words of one syllable-NY-(1889)-228,(1)P-col pict bds (h1,sl soil bds) 15.00
POLLARD,LANCASTER-History of the State of Washington-Portland-(1941)-222p-photos,e.p. maps-1st ed (r8,dj) 30.00
POLLARD,REBECCA S-Pollard's Synthetic Speller-Chig-1895-100p-bds (d1) 15.00
POLLOCK,A L-Wings Over Land and Sea-Seattle-1930-8vo-(6),139,(1)p-cl,frntis,30 photos-2nd ed (y8,yel pgs) 28.00
POLLOCK,FRANK L-Mirador Treasure-NY-1927-Chelsea-1st ed (e4,dj) 12.50
POLLOCK,J C-Way to Glory-Lond-1957-270p-map,illus-1st ed (gg2,f,dj) 35.00
POLLOCK,SIMON O-Russian Bastille-Chig-1908-Kerr-drk brwn cl-1st ed (w5,sl spot cov) 15.00
POLLOK,COL F T-Wild Sports of Burma and Assam-Lond-1900-Hurst & Blackett-dec grn cl,illus,maps-1st ed (u2) 175.00
POLLOK,ROBERT-Course of Time, a Poem...with a memoir of the Author...-Cin-1842-U P James-256p-lea (c1,sp chip,upper jnts crckng) 40.00
POLNER,MURRAY-Branch Rickey-1982-Atheneum-1st ed (p7,f,f dj) 40.00
POLO,MARCO-Travels of...-Lond-1929-Argonaut Pr-lg 8vo-381p+colophon-1/4 vel sp,red coat of arms dec yel cl,col frntis,11 maps(1 fldg)-ltd to 1050c,nbrd (ll1,soil bds) 275.00
POLUNIN,NICHOLAS-Botany of the Canadian Eastern Arctic-1947-Canada/Dept Mines-573p-maps-Pt.II, Thallophyta & Bryophyta (x6,sl wrnkld sp) 30.00
POLUNIN,NICHOLAS-Botany of the Canadian Eastern Arctic-Ottawa-1948-Nat Mus Can-8vo-viii,306p-wrps,rear pckt map,108 photos,errata slip (ff9,as new) 30.00*
POLVAY,MARINA-Dracula Cookbook-NY,Lond-1978-Chelsea Hs-253p-blk cl,red e.p.,red/blk illus-1st ed (q8,f,dj) 20.00
POMERANZ,HERMAN-Medicine in the Shakespearean Plays and Dicken's Doctors-NY-1936-416p-1st ed (dd3) 100.00
POMEROY,SETH-Journals and Papers of...-np-1926-Scty of Colnl Wars in NY-vi+180p-red cl-1st ed (k2,few bent pgs) 35.00
POMFRET,JOHN E-ED.-California Gold Rush Voyages, 1848 to 1849-San Marino-1954-Huntington Libr-x+246p-cl sp-1st ed (b2,dj) 35.00
POMFRET,JOHN E-Province of East New Jersey, 1609 to 1702-Princeton-1962-(xiii),407p-cl,frntis (aa6) 60.00
POMFRET,JOHN E-Province of West New Jersey, 1609 to 1702-Princeton-1956-xii,298p-cl (aa6) 35.00
PONCHAUD,FRANCOIS-Cambodia: Year Zero-NY-(1977)-HRW-1st ed (ff3,f,dj) 35.00
PONCINS,GONTRAN DE-Ghost Voyage Out of Eskimo Land-GC-1954-Dbldy-8vo-222p-blu cl,e.p. maps-1st Amer ed (ee7,dj chip & wn) 25.00
POND,B-Sampler of Wayside Herbs-1974-Chatham-4to-126p-32 col plts-1st ed (bb3,f,dj) 22.00
PONICSAN,DARRYL-Goldengrove-NY-1971-Dial-1st ed (a10,f,dj) 20.00
PONICSAN,DARRYL-Last Detail-NY-1970-auth 1st bk-1st ed (q5,dj) 30.00

PONTING,HERBERT G-In Lotus Land Japan-Lond/NY-1922-Dent/Dutton-8vo-xii,306p-g dec blu cl,8 col illus,80 monochromes-new & rvsd ed (ll1,hngs cracked) 95.00

POOL,EUGENE H-Surgery at the New York Hospital One Hundred Years Ago-NY-1930-188p-24p plts (g10) 30.00

POOL,J L-Izaak Walton-1976-priv prntd-8vo-134p-one of 2000c,illus-1st ed (m3,vf,dj) 20.00

POOL,MARIA L-Golden Sorrow-Chig,NY-1898-Herbert S Stone-441p-cl-Wright 4283 (h1) 15.00

POOL,RAYMOND J-Marching with the Grasses-1948-U of Nebr Pr-11 tbls(5 fldg maps)-1st ed (j10) 30.00

POOL,RAYMOND J-Marching with the Grasses-Lincoln-1948-U Nebr Pr-8vo-210p-84 figs,incl fldg-1st ed (gg5) 20.00

POOLE COLLECTION-New Orleans-1980-Kurt Schon-oblng sm 4to-catalogue-66 col plts (h9,dj) 65.00

POOLE,E L-Pennsylvania Birds-Narberth-1964-8vo-(1),94p-cl,maps (y8,dj) 22.50

POOLE,ERNEST-Nurses on Horseback-NY-1932-Macmillan-12mo-viii,168p-photos-1st ed (o2) 20.00

POOLE,ERNEST-Nurses on Horseback-NY-1932-Macmillan-168p-illus-1st ed (bb4) 35.00

POOLE,JOSEPH-Practical Telephone Handbook-1891-288p-227 illus-1st ed (h6) 30.00

POOLEY,T-Discoveries of a Crocodile Man-1982-Collins-213p-col & b&w photos (bb3,f,dj) 30.00

POOLMAN,KENNETH-Alabama Incident-Lond-(1958)-203p+ads-illus-1st ed (c4,f,dj) 17.50

POOR,CHARLES L-Men Against the Rule-Derrydale-1937-8vo-157p-ltd to 950c,nbrd,photos (m3,f) 70.00

POOR,CHARLES L-Men Against the Rule-NY-(1937)-Derrydale-8vo-illus-ltd to 950c,nbrd-1st ed (u10,f,clear dj) 125.00

POOR,CHARLES L-Men Against the Rule-NY-(1937)-Derrydale-xviii+157p-blu cl,illud-ltd to 950c-1st ed (e2) 110.00

POPE & YOUNG CLUB-Bow Hunting Big Game Records of North America-WI-1981-253p-photos (gg3,f,dj) 25.00

POPE,CLARENCE-Oil Scout in the Permian Basin, 1924 to 1960-El Paso-1972-Permian-150p-photos-1st ed (a9,dj) 50.00

POPE,DUDLEY-Black Ship-NY-1964-367p-illus-1st Amer ed (b7,f,dj) 25.00

POPE,DUDLEY-Great Gamble-NY-1972-579p-illus-1st Amer ed (b7,f,dj) 40.00

POPE,EDWIN-Baseball's Greatest Managers-1960-Dbldy-1st ed (r7,f,dj) 15.00

POPE,EDWIN-Baseball's Greatest Managers-1960-Dbldy-1st ed (s8,f,dj) 20.00

POPE,FRANK L-Modern Practice of the Electric Telegraph-NY-1888-Van Nostrand-160p-grn cl-12th ed (dd1,sl nick cov) 35.00

POPE,FRANKLIN L-Evolution of the Electric Incandescent Lamp-1889-91p-20 illus-v rare-1st ed (h6,sp tn) 85.00

POPE,JOSEPH-Tour of Their Royal Highnesses Duke and Dutchess of Cornwall and York-Ottawa-1903-S E Dawson,King's Prntr-8vo-x,372p-dec cl wi g titles,frntis,36 illus-1st ed (cc7,sl bump) 65.00*

POPE,S-Hunting with Bow & Arrow-NY-1930-257p-ribbed grn cl,photos (ee3) 65.00

POPE-HENNESSY,JAMES-Verandah, Some Episodes in the Crown Colonies 1867 to 1889-NY-1964-Knopf-8vo-387p-8 plts,map-1st US ed (jj5,f,dj) 17.50

POPOWSKI,BERT-Crow Hunting-NY-1946-8vo-216p-illus-1st ed (m3) 10.00

POPOWSKI,BERT-Hunting Pronghorn Antelope-Harrisburg-1959-8vo-227p-photos-1st ed (m3,vf,sl chip dj) 25.00

POPOWSKI,BERT-Olt's Hunting Handbook-Omaha-1948-12mo-167p-photos-1st ed (m3,vf) 25.00

POPP,ADELHEID-Autobiography of a Working Woman-Lond-1912-Unwin-8vo-135p-2 ports-rare-1st Brit ed (oo7,uncut) 85.00

POPPER,F-Agam-NY-1976-Abrams-133 col plts(incl fldg)-1st ed (h10,dj) 75.00

PORCINE POETRY-THE CENTURY ANTHOLOGY OF...-np-1924-priv prtd-unpgd(12)-wht bds wi 4 capering pigs,col frntis (l6) 35.00

PORSILD,A E-Illustrated Flora of the Canadian Arctic Archipelago-Ottawa-1957-Nat Mus Can-8vo-iv,214p-wrps,maps,figs-1st ed (ff9,as new) 25.00*

PORTER,A TOOMER-Led On! Step by Step-1898-Putnam-462p-1st ed (dd9) 45.00

PORTER,ANDREW-Music of Three Seasons, 1974 to 1977-NY-1978-McGraw Hill-1st ed (u4,f,dj) 15.00

PORTER,CLYDE-COMP.-Matt Field on the Santa Fe Trail-Norman-(1960)-U of Okla Pr-322p-1st ed (gg4,dj) 30.00

PORTER,CLYDE-Ruxton of the Rockies-(1950)-U of Okla-xxii,325p-cl,illus-1st ed (v1,dj) 45.00

PORTER,DAVID D-Naval History of the Civil War-NY-1886-Sherman Publ-843p-frntis,ports,maps (o7,rbnd) 75.00

PORTER,DENNIS-Pursuit of Crime-1981-Yale-1st ed (s10,dj) 12.50

PORTER,EBENEZER-Rhetorical Reader...-Andover-1831-Flagg & Gould-300p-lea-scarce-Amer Imprnts 8803-1st ed (k1) 22.50

PORTER,EDWIN H-Fall River Tragedy-Fall River-1893-Buffinton-1st ed (d4,new e.p.,1 pg tn,sl wn sp) 450.00

PORTER,EDWIN H-Fall River Tragedy-Fall River-1893-Geo Buffinton-(iv)+3-312p-grn cl,plts-1st ed (e2,inner hng crckd,sp fade) 475.00

PORTER,ELIOT-Antarctica-NY-(1978)-(Dutton)-oblng lg 4to-col photos-1st ed (w10,dj sp sl fray) 22.50

PORTER,ELIOT-Forever Wild-Blue Mt.Lake/NY-1966-Adirondack Mus/H&R-4to-photos-1st ed (dd6,dj) 95.00

PORTER,FANNIE C-ED.-History of the Texas Federation of Women's Clubs, 1918 to 1938-Denton-1941-403p (v3) 22.00

PORTER,GENE STRATTON-Laddie-GC-1913-Dbldy-illus,Pfeifer-MacLean 178B-1st ed (w1,f,dj) 125.00

PORTER,GENE STRATTON-Laddie-NY-1913-Dbldy,Page-scarce early dj-1st ed (z2,f,sl tn dj) 225.00

PORTER,GENE STRATTON-Michael O'Halloran-NY-1915-Dbldy,Page-grn dec bds-1st ed (e8) 100.00

PORTER,JOYCE-Dover and the Unkindest Cut of All-NY-1967-Scribner's-1st US ed (e4,f,dj) 20.00

PORTER,JOYCE-Dover One-NY-1964-Scribners-1st US ed (g4,dj) 25.00

PORTER,JOYCE-Dover Strikes Again-NY-1973-McKay-1st US ed (g4,f,dj) 25.00

PORTER,JOYCE-Dover Two-NY-1965-Scribners-1st US ed (g4,f dj) 20.00

PORTER,JOYCE-It's Murder with Dover-NY-1973-McKay-1st US ed (f4,sl yel pgs,dj) 20.00

PORTER,JOYCE-Meddler and Her Murder-NY-1972-McKay-1st US ed (h4,dj) 15.00

PORTER,JOYCE-Neither a Candle nor a Pitchfork-NY-1970-McCall-1st US ed (e4,f,dj) 17.50

PORTER,KATHERINE A-Collected Essays-NY-(1970)-Delacorte,Lawrence-1st ed (g6,f,dj) 35.00

PORTER,KATHERINE A-Collected Essays...-NY-(1970)-Lawrence/Delacorte-blk cl cov,red cl sp-1st ed (a5,f,sl rub dj) 20.00

PORTER,KATHERINE A-Collected Stories-1965-HB&W-1st Amer ed (t9,f,dj) 75.00

PORTER,KATHERINE A-Days Before-NY-(1952)-Harcourt,Brace-1st ed (c10,dj) 45.00

PORTER,KATHERINE A-Flowering Judas-NY-1930-cl bkd bds,orig glassine dj-ltd to 600c-1st ed (w6,f,wn dj) 250.00

PORTER,KATHERINE A-Hacienda-Paris-(1934)-Harrison-orig cl,t.e.g.-ltd to 895c-1st ed (aa9) 100.00

PORTER,KATHERINE A-Leaning Tower and Other Stories-(1944)-Harcourt Brace-1st ed (n9,dj sp chip & drknd) 75.00

PORTER,KATHERINE A-Leaning Tower-NY-(1944)-Harcourt Pr-1st ed (w6,f,dj) 45.00

PORTER,KATHERINE A-Pale Horse, Pale Rider-NY-(1939)-Harcourt-8vo-cl-1st ed (x3,dj) 95.00

PORTER,M R-Scotsman in Buckskin-NY-(1963)-306p-illus-1st ed (d7,f,f dj) 25.00

PORTER,MILLIE J-Memory Cups of Panhandle Pioneers-Clarendon-1945-648p-1st ed (a9) 150.00

PORTER,ROBERT P-Report on Population and Resources of Alaska at the Eleventh Census:1890-Wash D.C.-1893-GPO-4to-xii,282p-orig cl,chromolith plts,photos,2 fldg maps in pckt-scarce-1st ed (v1,wn bndg) 200.00

PORTER,RUSSELL W-Arctic Diary of...-Charlottesville-1976-U Pr of Va-172p-blu cl-1st ed (oo1,f,dj) 37.50

PORTIS,CHAS-True Grit-NY-(1968)-S&S-1st ed (b5,dj) 20.00

PORTLOCK,NATHANIEL-Voyage Round the World...To the Northwest Coast of America Performed in 1785, 1786, 1787 and 1788...-Lond-1789-Stockdale-4to-384p-mod calf,lea sp labls,6 lg fldg maps,2 ports,chrts,12 plts(incl 4 hand col)-1st ed (w1,rbnd) 2,850.00

PORTRAIT OF A PERIOD-Collection of Notman Photographs from 1856 to 1915-Montreal-1967-McGill Univ-folio-scarce-1st ed (y3,dj sl chip & rub) 165.00

PORTSMOUTH,EARL OF-British Farm Stock-Lond-1950-Brit in Pict Ser-1st prtg (f10,dj) 35.00

POST,A-Skycraft-NY-1930-8vo-xvi,276p-dec cl,frntis,41p plts-1st ed (s2,sl chip dj) 50.00

POST,AUSTIN-Glacier Ice-Seattle-1971-4to-110p-130 photos-1st ed (a4,f) 85.00

POST,CHARLES J-Little War of Private Post-Bost-(1960)-Little,Brown-8vo-340p-4 col illus-1st ed (cc5,f,dj) 25.00

POST,M D-Corrector of Destinies-1908-Clode-1st ed (x7) 115.00

POST,M D-Dwellers in the Hills-1901-Putnam-1st ed (x7) 30.00

POST,M D-Sleuth of St.James's Square-NY-1920-Appleton-1st ed (f4,sl stnd cov) 25.00

POST,M D-Uncle Abner-1972-T Stacey-1st Brit ed (x7,f,dj) 15.00

POST,W-Around the World in Eight Days-NY-(1931)-8vo-322p-cl,14p plts,1 dblpg plt,e.p. map-1st ed (s2,sl wn sp) 35.00

POSTAL, SILVER AND SILVER-Encyclopedia of Jews in Sports-NY-(1965)-Bloch-4to-525p-illus-1st ed (gg5,f,dj) 30.00

POSTER,WILLIAM Z-Great Steel Strike and Its Lessons-NY-1920-prtd wrps,photos-1st ed (r2,sl chip) 30.00

POSTGATE,RAYMOND-Ledger is Kept-Lond-1953-Joseph-1st ed (h4,dj) 20.00

POSTGATE,RAYMOND-Portugese Wine-Lond-1969-Dent-102p-dec gry cl,5 maps-1st ed (q8,dj) 12.50

POSTGATE,RAYMOND-Verdict of Twelve-NY-1940-Dbldy CC-1st US ed (j4,sl stnd cov,dj chip) 20.00

POSTMA,C-Plant Marvels in Miniature-NY-1961-folio-173p-gry cl,77 photo plts-1st Amer ed (x5,wn dj) 35.00

POTTER,BEATRIX-Tale of Pigling Bland-1913-F Warne-1st ed (x2,sl mrkd f.e.p.) 295.00

POTTER,CLARKSON N-An Address Before the Literary Societies of Roanoke College, Va-1878-Darby & Duvall-29p-wrps (dd9,wrps sl wn & soil) 15.00

POTTER,DAVID M-ED.-Trail to California-New Haven-1945-Yale U Pr-xiv+266p-grn cl,map-1st ed (h2,sl wn dj) 30.00

POTTER,EDGAR R-Cowboy Slang-Seattle-1971-Superior-4to-64p-illus bds,col illus,photos-1st ed (z4,spot cov) 15.00

POTTER,JEAN-Flying North-NY-1947-Macmillan-8vo-261p-35 photos-1st ed (ff5,dj chip,tn) 25.00

POTTER,JEREMY-Dance of Death-NY-1968-Walker-1st Amer ed (gg8,f,dj) 45.00

POTTER,MARGARET Y-At Home on the Range-(1947)-Lippincott-214p-blu cl-1st ed (q8,dj) 15.00

POTTERY AND PORCELAIN OF NEW JERSEY PRIOR TO 1876-Newark-1915-Newark Mus-32p-wrps-exhibit catlg (aa6) 50.00

POTTINGER,SIR HENRY-Flood,Fell & Forest-Lond-1905-8vo-2 vols,illus (m3,sl fox) 40.00

POTTS,JEAN-Footsteps on the Stairs-1966-Scribners-1st ed (s10,dj) 12.50

POTTS,JEAN-Home is the Prisoner-NY-1960-Scribners-1st ed (f4,f,dj) 10.00

POTTS,MERLIN-Fish & Fishing in Lassen Volcanic National Park-Mineral-1953-8vo-61p-wrps,illus (m3,f) 15.00

POUCHER,WILLIAM A-Perfumes,Cosmetics and Soaps-NY-1932-xv,599p-photos,engrvngs-Vol.II Manufacture & Preparation-4th ed (m10,sl wn,pamphlet laid in) 50.00

POUGH,R H-Audubon Bird Guide-GC-1946-12mo-(2),312p-cl,48 col plts-1st ed (y8,dj wn) 15.00

POUGH,R H-Audubon Water Bird Guide-GC-1951-12mo-352p-cl,48 col plts-1st ed (y8,dj wn) 12.50

POUGH,R H-Audubon Western Bird Guide-GC-1957-12mo-316p-cl,32 col plts (y8,dj) 42.00

POULSON,HOMER C-History of the Village of Deersville, Ohio 1815-1952-np-nd-168,(1)p-cl-not copyrighted (j1,pres) 25.00

POUND,ARTHUR-Johnson of the Mohawks-NY-1930-556p-e.p. maps,illus-1st ed (c4) 32.50

POUND,ARTHUR-Turning Wheel-GC-1934-Dbldy Doran-8vo-517p-sketches-1st ed (gg5,chip dj) 15.00

POUND,EZRA-ABC of Reading-Lond-1934-Routledge-red cl-1st ed,1st issue (hh4,sl fox,dj sl chip & soil) 275.00

POUND,EZRA-ABC of Reading-New Haven-1934-Yale Pr-1st ed (y1,f,tn dj) 150.00

POUND,EZRA-Imaginary Letters-Paris-1930-Black Sun Pr-8vo-orig wraps,glassine dj-ltd to 300c on Navarre papr out of total ed of 375c-1st ed (kk8,f,sl drknd dj,box) 750.00

POUND,EZRA-Lustra-Lond-1916-Elkin Matthews-8vo-buff cl,frntis by A L Coburn-Gallup A11b-1st ed,2nd imprssn (x3) 195.00

POUND,EZRA-Make it New-1934-Faber & Faber-1st ed (x2,dj sl chip & sp sunned) 200.00

POUND,EZRA-Pisan Cantos-NY-(1948)-New Directions-blk cl stmpd in silv-Gallup A60-1st ed (cc2,f,sl brwnd dj) 150.00

POUND,EZRA-Selected Prose 1909 to 1965-NY-1973-New Directions-1st ed (h8,f,f dj) 100.00

POUND,EZRA-Thrones 96-109 De Los Cantari-NY-(1955)-New Directions-silv stmpd blk bds-Gallup A77-1st ed (bb2,f,dj sp sunned) 95.00

POUND,EZRA-Translations of Ezra Pound-NY-nd-H Kenner-1st ed (r2,dj) 25.00

POUND,LOUISE-Nebraska Folklore-Lincoln-1959-U of Neb Pr-243p-1st ed (dd4,dj) 25.00

POUND,MERRITT B-Benjamin Hawkins Indian Agent-Athens-1951-U of Ga Pr-270p-cl-1st ed (w3,vf,dj) 17.50

POUND,ROSCO-Lawyer from Antiquity to Modern Times-St.Paul-1953-West Publ-xxxii+404p-brwn cl-1st ed (b2,sl wn sp) 25.00

POURADE,RICHARD F-Glory Years-San Diego-1966-274p-frntis,photos,col illus,maps (t7,dj) 10.00

POURADE,RICHARD-Anza Conquers the Desert-1971-Copley-4to-216p-illus-1st ed (d3,dj) 35.00

POURADE,RICHARD-Silver Dons-1963-Union Trib-4to-286p-illus-1st ed (d3,dj) 35.00

POWELL,A M-Trailing and Camping in Alaska-1910-Hurst Blackwell-379p-photos (bb3) 50.00

POWELL,AARON M-Personal Reminiscences of the Anti Slavery and Other Reforms and Reformers-Plainfield-1899-xx,279p-cl,illus (aa6) 30.00

POWELL,ADAM CLAYTON,JR.-Marching Blacks-NY-1945-Dial-218p (r1,dj) 35.00

POWELL,ANTHONY-Faces in My Time-NY-1980-1st ed (y7,dj) 20.00

POWELL,ANTHONY-Hearing Secret Harmonies-Lond-1975-1st ed (y7,dj) 40.00

POWELL,ANTHONY-Soldier's Art-Lond-1966-Heinemann-1st Brit ed (c8,f,dj) 85.00

POWELL,C FRANK-Life of Major General Zachary Taylor-NY-1846-Appleton-96p-frntis-Howes P522-1st ed (gg4,ex-libr) 50.00

POWELL,COL A N N-Call of the Tiger-NY-1958-222p (gg3,f,dj) 15.00

POWELL,DONALD M-Peralta Grant-Norman-(1960)-U of Okla Pr-186p-illus-1st ed (dd4,dj) 30.00

POWELL,E ALEXANDER-End of the Trail-1941-Scribner-462p-g dec cov,illus,fldg map-1st ed (r8,bump,sl edgewn) 35.00

POWELL,E ALEXANDER-End of the Trail-NY-1922-Scribner's-462p-illus,fldg map (cc4,sl wn) 15.00

POWELL,E ALEXANDER-Marches of the North from Cape Breton to the Klondike-NY-(1931)-Century-tall 8vo-x,311p-cl,illus,fldg map-1st ed (pp5) 40.00*

POWELL,E ALEXANDER-Marches of the North, From Cape Breton to the Klondike-NY-(1931)-311p-pict cl,frntis,photos,map e.p.-1st ed (t7) 17.50

POWELL,E ALEXANDER-Thunder Over Europe-NY-1931-Washburn-8vo-288p-1st ed (jj5,dj) 20.00

POWELL,E H-San Francisco's Heritage in Art Glass-Seattle-1976-folio-photos-1st ed (h10,dj) 45.00

POWELL,E P-Orchard and Fruit Garden-NY-1905-xv,322p-24 photo plts-1st ed (x5,drknd cov) 20.00

POWELL,FATHER PETER J-People of the Sacred Mountain-SF-(1981)-Harper & Row-2 vols,wht canvas cl,photos,col plts-1st ed (v1,box) 150.00

POWELL,FLORENCE L-In The Chinese Garden-NY-(1943)-112p-grn cl,74 half tones,5 drwngs (j10,dj chip & yel) 35.00

POWELL,JOHN W-Down the Colorado-NY-1969-168p-col photos-1st ed (e7,f,dj) 75.00

POWELL,JOHN-Bring Out Your Dead-Phila-1949-304p-1st ed (dd3) 35.00

POWELL,LAWRENCE C-Act of Enchantment-Santa Fe-1961-Stagecoach Pr-yel papr covs,ltd to 575c for N.M. Hist Soc members-1st ed,1st iss (z1) 25.00

POWELL,LAWRENCE C-Bookman's Progress-1968-Ward Ritchie Pr-1st ed (w1,f,f dj) 20.00

POWELL,LAWRENCE C-Books, West Southwest-LA-(1957)-Ward Ritchie Pr-8vo-x,157p-cl backd dec bds-1st ed (w2) 45.00

POWELL,LAWRENCE C-From the Heartland-Flagstaff-(1976)-Northland-1st ed (w1,f,f dj) 20.00

POWELL,LAWRENCE C-Great Constellations-1977-El Paso Publ Libr Assoc-wrps (a9) 30.00

POWELL,LAWRENCE C-Landscapes and Bookscapes of California-Berkeley-(1958)-Friends Bancroft Libr-8vo-(ii),15p-stiff wrps-1st ed (w2,cov yel) 20.00

POWELL,LAWRENCE C-Southwestern Book Trails-1963-Horn & Wallace-91p-1st ed (d3,dj) 50.00

POWELL,LAWRENCE C-Voices From the Southwest-Flagstaff-1976-Northland Pr-159p-cl,photos-1st ed (w3,f,dj) 20.00

POWELL,LAWRENCE C-Voices From the Southwest-Flagstaff-1976-Northland Pr-8vo-xvi,159p-cl-1st ed (w2,dj) 15.00

POWELL,MICHAEL-200,000 Feet, the Edge of the World-NY-(1938)-Dutton-8vo-334p-32 illus-1st ed (ff5,dj) 30.00

POWELL,PETER J-Sweet Medicine-Norman-(1979)-2 vols-illus(incl col)-2nd prtg (e7,f,rprd box) 70.00

POWELL,RICHARD-And Hope to Die-NY-1947-Simon-1st ed (e4,pgs brwng,dj sp sl fade) 20.00

POWELL,RICHARD-Lay That Pistol Down-1945-Simon-1st ed (s10,dj) 15.00

POWELL,RICHARD-Shoot if You Must-NY-1946-S&S-1st ed (e4,f,dj) 20.00

POWELL,TALMAGE-Smasher-NY-1959-Macmillan-1st ed (j4,sl yel pgs,sl tn dj) 20.00

POWELL-PRICE,J C-History of India-Lond-1955-Thos Nelson & Sons-lg 8vo-679p-brgndy cl,maps,illus (gg6,chip dj) 30.00

POWER,D'ARCY-Medicine in the British Isles-NY-1930-84p-1st ed (dd3) 45.00

POWER,ETHEL B-Smaller American House-Bost-1927-Little,Brown-4to-x,(2),100p-cl wi pastedowns on sp & cov,halftones,plans (cc10) 65.00

POWER,F D-Sketches of Our Pioneers-Cleve-(1898)-148p-cl-Bethany C E Reading Courses/Hand book Ser (e1) 15.00

POWERS AUTOMATIC TEMPERATURE REGULATOR-(Chig)-(1899)-24p-wrps-trade cat (g1) 15.00

POWERS,ALFRED-Long Way to Frisco-Bost-1951-Little,Brown-186p-pict cl,b&w illus,J Daugherty-1st ed (s3,f,dj) 20.00

POWERS,ALFRED-Marooned in Crater Lake-Portland-1930-177p-1st ed (r8) 20.00

POWERS,J F-Morte D'Urban-GC-1962-Dbldy-1st ed (c10,dj sp sl drknd) 40.00

POWERS,J F-Presence of Grace-GC-1956-Dbldy-1st ed (cc2,f,dj) 40.00

POWERS,LAURA B-Old Monterey-SF-1934-San Carlos Pr-299p-illus,e.p. maps-Six Guns #1754-1st ed (cc4,wn dj) 50.00

POWERS,MRS.O A-Maple Dell of `76...-Phila-1887-95p-cl-13th ed (a1,sl wn) 15.00

POWERS,NICK-Civil Wah Cookbook from Boggar Hollow-Lindale-1972-Country Originals-unpgd(32p)-wrps,illus (o6) 9.00

POWERS,STEPHEN-Afoot and Alone-Hartford-1872-Columbian Book Co-(vi)+11-327p-brwn cl,12 plts+ads-Howes P537-1st ed (m2) 115.00

POWERS,STEPHEN-Afoot and Alone-Hartford-1872-Columbian-327p-illus-Graff 3339-1st ed (d3) 125.00

POWERS,THOMAS-Diana: the Making of a Terrorist-Bost-1971-1st ed (v9,f,f dj) 25.00

POWICKE,F M-ED.-Handbook of British Chronology-Lond-1939-Royal Hist Soc-8vo-xii,424p-red cl (t10) 45.00

POWLEY,EDWARD-Naval Side of King William's War-NY-1972-392p-17 plts-1st Amer ed (b7,f,dj) 35.00

POWNALL,C T-Patches of Memory-Knaresborough-1956-85p-cl (g1) 15.00

POWNALL,THOMAS-Topographical Description of the Dominions of the U.S.A.-Pitt-1949-U of Pitt Pr-4to-xvi+236p-beige cl,2 fldg maps-ltd to 2000c-Howes P543-1st ed thus (b2) 50.00

POWYS,JOHN C-Art of Forgetting the Unpleasant-Girard-(1928)-Little Blu Bk No.1264-prtd wrps-1st ed (r2,edge sun) 20.00

POWYS,JOHN C-Autobiography-NY-1934-1st Amer ed (r2,f,dj chip,rub,sl tn) 35.00

POWYS,JOHN C-Ducdame-GC-1925-embossd frnt bd,map e.p.s-1st US ed (t5,dj sp sl chip) 35.00

POWYS,JOHN C-Enjoyment of Literature-NY-1938-1st Amer ed (r2,f,dj sp sun,sl tn) 30.00

POWYS,JOHN C-In Defence of Sensuality-Lond-1930-1st ed (y7,lacks dj) 30.00

POWYS,JOHN C-John Cowper Powys. A Selection from his Poems-Lond-(1964)-Macdonald-8vo-cl-1st ed (kk8,f,sl rub dj) 50.00

POWYS,JOHN C-Mandragora-NY-1917-G Arnold Shaw-1st Amer ed (r2,sl rub) 75.00

POWYS,JOHN C-Rabelais-Lond-1948-1st ed (r2,f,dj sl tn,edge rub) 25.00

POWYS,JOHN C-Sailor and a Homosexual-Girard-1923-Little Blu Bk No.453-prtd wrps-1st ed (r2,sl brwnd pgs) 20.00

POWYS,JOHN C-Verdict of Bridlegoose-Lond-1927-ltd to 900c,nbrd-1st ed (y7,dj sl wn & tn) 35.00

POWYS,JOHN C-Wolf Solent-NY-1929-S&S-2 vols-1st US ed (hh5,dj sp fade,box) 30.00

POWYS,LLEWELYN-Apples Be Ripe-NY-1930-1st Amer ed (r2,dj sl tn,sp sun) 35.00

POWYS,LLEWELYN-Baker's Dozen-Herrin-(1939)-Trovillion Priv Pr-8vo-cl,illus-ltd to 493c,two autg-1st ed (jj8,f,sl rub box) 75.00

POWYS,LLEWELYN-Pathetic Fallacy-Lond-1930-1st ed (r2) 25.00

POWYS,T F-An Interpretation of Genesis-NY-1929-Viking-99,(1)p-bds,t.e.g.-ltd to 260c,autg (dd10,sp drknd,cov sl soil) 110.00

POWYS,T F-White Paternoster and Other Stories-NY-1931-1st Amer ed (r2,sp sun,edge rub) 25.00

POYNTER,F N L-Medicine and Culture-Lond-1969-322p-1st ed (dd3) 40.00

POYNTER,F N L-Short History of Medicine-Lond-1961-160p-1st ed (dd3,dj) 40.00

POZOS,ROBERT-Hypothermia-Piscataway-1982-173p-1st ed (p10,f,dj) 15.00

PRABHAVANANDA,SWAMI-Religion in Practice-Hollywood-1968-Vedanta Pr-cl-1st Amer ed (n8,f,dj) 15.00

PRACTICAL HOUSEKEEPING-Mpls-1885-Buckeye Publ Co-688p-grn bds,illus-Bitting 593 (n6,hngs weak,fr jnt splttng) 75.00

PRAGER,ARTHUR-Rascals at Large-NY-1971-Dbldy-334p-1st ed (g9,dj) 40.00

PRANCE,CLAUDE A-Peppercorn Papers-Cambridge-1964-Golden Head-1st ed (w1,f,dj) 20.00

PRASSEL,FRANK R-Western Peace Officer-Norman-(1972)-320p-photos-1st ed (u7,f,dj) 25.00

PRATT & WHITNEY AIRCRAFT STORY-np-(1950)-sm 4to-174p-cl,b&w & col plts,illus e.p.-1st ed (s2,sp fade) 35.00

PRATT,E J-Towards the Last Spike-Tor-1952-Macmillan-53p-1st ed (gg4,dj) 20.00

PRATT,F-Navy Has Wings-NY-(1943)-8vo-x,224p-cl,32p plts-1st ed (s2,sl chip dj) 30.00

PRATT,FLETCHER-Man and His Meals-(1947)-Holt-252p-blu cl,drwngs-1st prtg (q8,chip dj) 10.00

PRATT,HARRY E-Lincoln 1809 to 1839-Springfield-(1941)-256p-illus,maps-1st ed (n3,f) 32.50

PRATT,J LOWELL-Baseball's All Stars-1967-Dbldy-photos-1st ed (s8,f,dj wn,creased,chip) 15.00

PRATT,JOHN C-Laotian Fragments-NY-1974-1st ed (v9,f,f dj) 60.00

PRATT,ORSON-Series of Pamphlets...-SLC-1884-314p-orig blu cl-Flake 6544-3rd ed (bb8,sl mottled cov,edgewn) 50.00

PRATT,RICHARD-Picture Garden Book-NY-1943-Howell & Soskin-134p-cl,photos by Edw Steichen (x6,dj) 15.00

PRAY,LEON-Taxidermy-NY-1913-12mo-113p-illus,Outing Hndbk #47-1st ed (m3,f) 25.00

PREECE,HAROLD-Dalton Gang-NY-(1963)-Hastings Hs-320p-illus-Six Guns 1757-1st ed (gg4,dj) 25.00

PREECE,HAROLD-Living Pioneers-Cleve-(1952)-World-317p-1st ed (dd4,dj) 25.00

PREECE,W H A-North American Rock Plants(1st Ser)-NY-1937-204p-100 plts (m10,sl fade) 27.00

PREECE,W H A-North American Rock Plants-NY-1937-204p-100 half tones-1st prtg (j10,fade,dj wn & tn) 32.00

PREIST,DR MICHAEL-Medical Companion Treating According to the Most Successful Practice of the Diseases...-Exeter-1838-Gerrish-214p-lea (x6,lea rub,wn) 90.00

PRENDERGAST,JOHN-Prender's Progress-Lond-1979-256p-maps,illus-1st ed (b7,dj) 25.00

PRENSTIS,A N-My Vineyard at Lakeview-NY-1866-OJ-143p-cl-scarce (x6,sl wn) 95.00

PRENTIS,JOHN H-Case of Doctor Horace-NY-1907-Baker & Taylor-1st ed (d4,sp fade) 25.00

PRENTIS,NOBLE L-Kansas Miscellanies-Topeka-1889-Ks Publ Hs-vi+199p-red cl-1st ed (m2) 35.00

PRENTISS,MRS.E-Pemaquid-NY-(1877)-Randolph-8vo-370p-orig cl-Wright III,4376-1st ed (w6) 25.00

PRENTISS,SEARGENT SMITH-Memoir-NY-1855-Scribner-2 vols-brwn cl-Howes P571-1st ed (b2) 75.00

PRESBYTERIAN REUNION-NY-1871-568p-cl (j1) 17.50

PRESCOTT,GEORGE B-History, Theory, and Practice of the Electric Telegraph-1866-508p-111 illus-rare-4th ed (h6,sp fade,cov wn) 95.00

PRESCOTT,GEORGE B-Speaking Telephone,Electric Light, and other Recent Electrical Inventions-NY-1879-Appleton-616p-grn cl,319 text illus,1 fldg plt in rear-1st ed (l2,sl loose frnt e.p.) 85.00

PRESCOTT,L H-History of Criterion Lodge, No.68 Knights of Pythias-Cleve-1899-Imperial Pr-167p-cl-ltd to 550c,nbrd-t.p. in red & blk (g1) 20.00

PRESCOTT,PHILANDER-Recollection of...-Lincoln-(1966)-272p-1st ed (n3,f,dj) 20.00

PRESCOTT,PHILANDER-Recollections of...-Lincoln-(1966)-U of Nebr Pr-272p-illus,maps-1st ed (ff4,dj) 25.00

PRESCOTT,WILLIAM H-Biographical and Critical Miscellanies-NY-1845-Harper & Bros-x+638p-grn cl-1st ed (b2,sl fox) 50.00

PRESCOTT,WILLIAM H-Conquest of Mexico...-GC-1934-594p-cl,illus,K Henderson (c1) 15.00

PRESCOTT,WILLIAM H-History of the Conquest of Mexico-Phila-1895-3 vols-illus-ltd to 1500c,nbrd (r2) 75.00

PRESCOTT,WINWARD-Bibliography of Book Plate Literature-1914-Princeton-g bds-ltd to 250c-1st ed (hh10,f) 35.00

PRESCOTT,WINWARD-Bibliography of Book Plate Literature-np-1914-Amer Bkplt Soc-8vo-70p-bds-ltd to 250c (w2,papr cov sp split) 55.00

PRESIDENT VANISHES-1934-F&R-Rex Stout novel publ anon-1st ed (x7,dj) 595.00

PRESS PHOTOGRAPHY-COMPLETE BOOK OF...-NY-(1950)-Nat'l Pr Photog Assoc-206p-cl-photos (j1) 15.00

PRESTON,HOWARD-Trust Banking in Washington-Seattle-1953-Univ of Wash Pr-145p-blu cl (b6) 15.00

PRESTON,KERRISON-ED.-Blake Collection of W Graham Robertson-Lond-1952-Faber-4to-263p-red cl,64 illus (r10,sl wn dj) 25.00

PREUS,CAROLINE D M K-Linka's Diary, On Land and Sea 1845 to 1864-Mpls-(1952)-Augsburg-8vo-xiv,288p-cl,frntis port,illus-1st ed (z5,dj) 45.00

PREUSS,CHARLES-Exploring with Fremont-Norman-(1958)-162p-illus-1st ed (c7,f,dj) 45.00

PREVIN,DORY-Bog Trotter-GC-1980-Dbldy-8vo-383p-cl-1st ed (z5,f,dj) 12.00

PREZZOLINI,GUISEPPE-Spaghetti Dinner-NY-(1955)-Abelard Schuman-148p-illus (q6) 30.00

PRICE,A GRENFELL-Western Invasions of the Pacific and Its Continents-Westport-1980-Greenwood Pr-viii,236p-grn cl,maps,photos-1st Amer prtg (nn1,as new) 35.00

PRICE,ALFRED-Rail Life a Book of Yarns-Tor-(1925)-T Allen-Watters P.369-1st ed (pp2,f) 45.00*

PRICE,ALFRED-Rail Life-Tor-(1925)-Thomas Allen-286p-1st ed (cc4) 25.00

PRICE,ANTHONY-Our Man in Camelot-Lond-1975-Gollancz-1st ed (w9,f,dj) 100.00

PRICE,CON-Memories of Old Montana-Hollywood-(1945)-154p-illus by Russell,photos-scarce-1st ed (f7,chip dj) 65.00

PRICE,DOUGHBELLY-Doughbelly's Scrap Book-(Taos)-(1951)-95p-wrps,2 photos-scarce-1st ed (u7) 25.00

PRICE,E HOFFMAN-Far Lands Other Days-Chapel Hill-1975-1st ed (bb10,f,dj) 40.00

PRICE,ELEANOR C-Cardinal De Richelieu-Lond-(1912)-Methuen-8vo-306p-12 illus-1st Brit ed (jj5) 25.00

PRICE,EMERSON-Inn of That Journey-Caldwell-1939-auth 1st bk-1st ed (m4,f,dj) 20.00

PRICE,HARRY-Royal Tour, 1901-NY-1980-Morrow-col drwngs-facs (p8,vf,dj) 30.00

PRICE,PAMELA V-Art of the Table-Lond-(1962)-Batsford-4to-186p-tan cl,col & b&w photos-1st ed (q8,dj) 20.00

PRICE,REYNOLDS-Generous Man-1966-Atheneum-1st ed (x2,f,dj) 35.00

PRICE,REYNOLDS-Long and Happy Life-1962-Atheneum-1st ed (jj6,f,dj sp sl drknd) 85.00

PRICE,REYNOLDS-Long and Happy Life-Lond-1962-Chatto & Windus-8vo-bds-auth 1st bk-1st Brit ed (jj8,f,sl soil dj) 45.00

PRICE,REYNOLDS-Names & Faces of Heroes-NY-1963-Atheneum-8vo-cl-1st ed (jj8,f,dj) 85.00

PRICE,REYNOLDS-Palpable God-NY-1978-1st ed (s5,dj) 20.00

PRICE,REYNOLDS-Permanent Errors-NY-1970-Atheneum-1st ed (cc2,f,dj) 40.00

PRICE,REYNOLDS-Source of Light-NY-1981-1st ed (n5,f,f dj) 20.00

PRICE,REYNOLDS-Surface of Earth-NY-1975-Atheneum-red cl-1st ed (b5,as new in dj) 25.00

PRICE,REYNOLDS-Things Themselves-1972-Atheneum-1st ed (jj6,vf,dj) 35.00

PRICE,REYNOLDS-Things Themselves-NY-1972-Atheneum-1st ed (dd2,f,dj) 40.00

PRICE,RICHARD-Bloodbrothers-Bost-1976-Houghton Mifflin-1st ed (b5,as new in dj) 15.00

PRICE,RICHARD-Ladies' Man-Bost-1978-Houghton Mifflin-1st ed (b5,as new in dj) 15.00

PRICE,RICHARD-Wanderer-Bost-1974-Houghton Mifflin-auth 1st bk-1st ed (cc2,f,dj) 50.00

PRICE,RICHARD-Wanderers-1974-Houghton Mifflin-auth 1st bk-1st ed (p9,vf,dj) 30.00

PRIEST,ALAN-Japanese Costume-NY-1935-Met Mus Art-v,42p text,45 illus-prtd wrps-ltd to 1000c-1st ed (kk1,sl tn sp) 75.00

PRIEST,CHRISTOPHER-Darkening Island-NY-(1972)-Harper & Row-1st ed (o3,dj) 15.00

PRIEST,CHRISTOPHER-Indoctrinaire-NY-(1970)-Harper & Row-1st US ed (o3,dj) 15.00

PRIESTLEY,ANNA F-How to Know Japanese Color Prints-NY-1927-col plts-1st ed (r2) 45.00

PRIESTLEY,J B-Black Out in Gretley-NY-1942-Harpers-1st ed (x1,f,edgewn dj) 30.00

PRIESTLEY,J B-Doomsday Men-1938-Harpers-1st Amer ed (x7,sl tn dj) 70.00

PRIESTLEY,J B-English Humor-NY-(1976)-Stein & Day-1st US ed (e3,dj) 15.00

PRIESTLEY,J B-Outcries and Asides-Lond-1974-1st ed (y7,dj) 12.00

PRIESTLEY,J B-Salt is Leaving-1966-Harper-1st Amer ed (s10,dj) 20.00

PRIESTLEY,RAYMOND E-Antarctic Adventure-Tor-1974-M&S-8vo-x,382p-frntis,148 illus-reissue of 1914 ed (cc7,dj) 65.00*

PRIESTLY,JOSEPH-History and Present State of Electricity, with Original Experiments-Lond-1775-Bathurst & Lowndes-2 vols,contemp half blk calf,mrbld bds,8 fldg plts-3rd ed,corrected & enlgd (j2,vol 1 sp chip,frnt jnt wn) 450.00

PRIME,MARGUERIETE-Catalogue of the H Winnett Orr Historical Collection and Other Rare Books...-Chig-1960-198p-1st ed (dd3,ex-libr) 90.00

PRIME,SAMUEL I-Life of Samuel F B Morse-NY-1875-Appleton-8vo-cl-1st ed (oo6) 125.00

PRIME,W C-I Go A Fishing-NY-1873-Harper & Bros-1st ed (p6) 125.00

PRIMITIVE CHURCH-AN ORIGINAL DRAUGHT OF THE ...,IN ANSWER TO A DISCOURSE...OF THE CHURCH OF ENGLAND-Columbus-1833-Isaac N Whiting-305p-cl-1st Amer ed (d1,sl wn sp & upper joints) 75.00

PRINCE,L BRADFORD-Historical Sketches of New Mexico from the Earliest Records to the American Occupation-NY & KC-1883-327p-v scarce-1st ed (v7,autg card tip-in) 125.00

PRINCE,L BRADFORD-Historical Sketches of New Mexico from the Earliest Records to the American Occupation-KC-1883-329p-pict cl,illus-2nd ed (t7,pres) 75.00

PRINCE,L BRADFORD-Stone Lions of Cochiti-Santa Fe-1903-Hist Soc of NM-21p-wrps,photo plt-scarce-1st ed (v7,fade) 35.00

PRINCE,WALTER F-Noted Witnesses for Psychic Occurrences-New Hyde Park-1963-Univ Bks-cl-1st prtg (o8,f,dj) 12.50

PRINCE,WALTER F-Psychic in the House-Bost-1926-Soc for Psychic Rsrch-8vo-284p-brgndy cl-1st ed (aa7,bump) 35.00*

PRINCE,WILLIAM-Short Treatise on Horticulture-NY-1828-Swords-196p-orig bds & sp,papr labl (x6,lacks ffep,fox,wn) 250.00

PRINDLE,EDWARD J-Art of Curve Pitching-Phila-1911-A J Reach-64p-wrps (pp6) 25.00

PRINGLE,HENRY F-Life and Times of William Howard Taft-NY-(1939)-Farrar & Rinehart-2 vols-grn cl-1st ed (b2,sp fade & soil,e.p. brwnd) 30.00

PRINGLE,JACOBI-Dermochromes-1905-Rebman-2 vols+spplmnt,lea,a.e.g.,231 col illus-2nd ed,rvsd,enlgd (v8,edge wn covs,vol 1 chip) 200.00

PRINZING,FRIEDRICH-Epidemics Resulting from Wars-Oxford-1916-340p-1st ed (dd3,ex-libr) 150.00

PRISCILLA COOK BOOK-(Berkeley)-(1923)-Gullick-240p-wht oil cl bds-First Congregational Church of Berkeley (n6,wn bds) 45.00

PRITCHARD,ALAN-Alchemy: a Bibliography of English Language Writings-Lond-1980-439p-1st ed (dd3,dj) 100.00

PRITCHARD,JAMES B-Ancient Near East-1958-Princeton Univ Pr-cl,illus-1st ed (m8) 15.00

PRITCHARD,W T-Polynesian Reminiscences-Lond-1866-Chapman & Hall-pebble cl,photo lithos-1st ed (p6,restored) 300.00

PRITCHETT,V S-Cab at the Door-NY-1968-Random-244p-1st ed (j8,edge wn dj) 20.00

PRITCHETT,V S-Camberwell Beauty-1974-Random-1st ed (n9,f,dj) 25.00

PRITCHETT,V S-Key to My Heart-NY-1964-Random-illus-1st ed (y1,f,dj) 35.00

PRITCHETT,V S-Midnight Oil-1972-Random-1st Amer ed (n9,f,dj) 20.00

PRITCHETT,V S-New York Proclaimed-NY-1965-HBW-4to-116p-cl,gravure prtgs by E Hofer-1st ed (t3) 60.00

PRITCHETT,V S-Spanish Temper-1954-Knopf-1st ed (n9,f,dj sl rub & wn) 45.00

PRITCHETT,V S-When My Girl Comes Home-NY-1961-1st Amer ed (k9,f,dj) 20.00

PRITT,T E-Book of the Grayling Being a Description of the Fish and the Art of Angling for Him...-Leeds-1888-Goodall & Suddick-4to-64p-maroon cl,3 col plts-1st ed (p1,f) 125.00

PRIVATE SMITH'S JOURNAL-Chig-1963-Donnelley & Sons-Lakeside Classics (ff4) 20.00

PROBERT,THOMAS-Lost Mines & Buried Treasures of the West-Berkeley-1977-U of Cal-4to-1st ed (b4,dj) 45.00

PROBERT,THOMAS-Lost Mines and Buried Treasures of the West-Berkeley-1977-512p+81p index-1st ed (u7) 25.00

PROCTER,MAURICE-Devil's Due-NY-1960-Harper-1st US ed (g4,f,sl wn dj) 10.00

PROCTER,MAURICE-Graveyard Rolls-NY-1964-Harper-1st US ed (f4,f,dj) 10.00

PROCTER,MAURICE-Hideaway-NY-1968-Harper-1st Amer ed (p4,f,sl wn dj) 25.00

PROCTER,MAURICE-Midnight Plumber-Lond-1957-Hutchinson-1st ed (j4,dj) 12.50

PROCTER,MAURICE-Two Men in Twenty-NY-1964-HARPER-1st US ed (d4,dj) 12.50

PROCTOR,B H-Not Without Honor-Austin-nd-361p-wrps,illus,ports-rprnt of 1962 ed (z10) 12.50

PRODDOW,PENELOPE-TRANSL.-Demeter and Persephone: Homeric Hym Number Two-NY-(1972)-Dbldy-4to-unpgd-pict cl,col illus,B Cooney-1st ed (r3,rub dj) 45.00

PROGRESSIVE MEN OF NORTHERN OHIO-Cleve-1906-264p-mor (a1,sl chip sp) 25.00

PROHET,DON-Saga of Slade-NY-1958-221p-1st ed (t7,dj) 15.00

PROHIBITION AND ITS ENFORCEMENT-Waterville-nd(1923)-35,(1)p (a1) 12.50

PROKOSCH,FREDERIC-Carnival-Lond-1938-Chatto & Windus-8vo-1st ed (jj8,f,dj) 35.00

PROKOSCH,FREDERICK-Wreck of the Cassandra-NY-(1966)-FSG-1st ed (hh5,f dj) 12.50

PROLETARIAN LITERATURE IN THE UNITED STATES-NY-1935-1st ed (r5,dj sp sl drknd) 75.00

PRONZINI,BILL-Acts of Mercy-NY-1977-Putnam's-1st ed (z9,dj) 10.00

PRONZINI,BILL-Games-1976-Putnam-1st ed (s9,f,dj) 15.00

PRONZINI,BILL-Gun in Cheek-NY-1982-Coward-1st ed (e4,as new in dj) 20.00

PRONZINI,BILL-Masques-NY-1981-Arbor Hs-1st ed (x9,f,dj) 10.00

PRONZINI,BILL-Night Screams-Chig-(1979)-Playboy Pr-1st ed (j3,f,dj) 20.00

PRONZINI,BILL-Panic-NY-1972-Random-1st ED (e4,dj) 15.00

PRONZINI,BILL-Running of Beasts-NY-1976-Putnam-1st ed (h4,f,dj) 10.00

PRONZINI,BILL-Scattershot-1982-St.Martin's-1st ed (r9,vf,dj) 10.00

PRONZINI,BILL-Snowbound-NY-1974-Putnam-1st ed (f4,as new in dj) 15.00

PRONZINI,BILL-Stalker-NY-1971-Random-1st ed (e4,dj) 20.00

PRONZINI,BILL-Stalker-NY-1971-Random-auth 1st bk-1st ed (l4,f,sl wn dj) 35.00

PRONZINI,BILL-Undercurrent-1973-Random Hs-1st ed (s10,dj) 35.00

PROPPER,MILTON-Blood Transfusion Murders-NY-1943-Harper-1st ed (e4,dj) 25.00

PROPPER,MILTON-Family Burial Murders-1934-Harper-1st ed (s10,dj) 25.00

PROPPER,MILTON-Hide the Body-NY-1939-Harper-1st ed (e4) 12.50

PROPPER,MILTON-Student Fraternity Murder-Indpls-1932-Bobbs-1st ed (j4) 15.00

PROSCH,CHARLES-Reminiscences of Washinton Territory-Fairfield-1969-128p+7p index-illus-Tweney #62-rprnt (j7) 30.00

PROSCH,THOMAS W-David S Maynard and Catherine T Maynard-Seattle-1906-Lowman & Hanford-80p-red cl,2 ports-Howes P634-1st ed (b2) 110.00

PROSE,FRANCINE-Glorious Ones-NY-1974-Atheneum-1st ed (j6,f,sl creased dj) 30.00

PROSE,FRANCINE-Judah the Pious-1973-Atheneum-1st ed (s9,dj) 20.00

PROSSER,WM-History of the Puget Sound Country-1903-Lewis Publ-thk 4to-2 vols-scarce (b6,cov cracked) 285.00

PROUST,MARCEL-Marcel Proust, Selected Letters 1880 to 1903-GC-1983-Dbldy-photos-1st ed (bb1,f,dj) 20.00

PROUST,MARCEL-Vision of Paris-NY-1963-Macmillan-4to-cl,photos by E Atget-1st ed (y3,f,dj) 195.00

PROUTY,LORENZO-Fish-Bost-1883-12mo-115p (m3,ex-lib) 25.00

PROWSE,D W-ED.-Newfoundland Guide Book-Lond-1905-12mo-182p-photos,illus,fldg map (m3) 40.00

PRUDDEN,T MITCHELL-Story of the Bacteria and Their Relations to Health and Disease-NY-1889-143p-1st ed (dd3) 75.00

PRUDENCE PENNY'S COOKBOOK-NY-1939-Prentice Hall-385p-bds,frntis (n6,sl wn bds,spot text) 16.00

PRUDENCE PENNY-Coupon Cookery-Hollywood-1943-Murray & Gee-128p-bds,cartoon illus (n6,dj) 24.00

PRUDHOMME,E C-Gun Engraving Review-LA-1961-145p-col illus-scarce (ee3,f,autg) 150.00

PRUNIER,MADAME-Prunier's-NY-1957-Knopf-298p (l6) 25.00

PRUSSING,EUGENE E-Estate of George Washington, Deceased-Bost-1927-Little,Brown-xiv+512p-maroon cl,plts,maps-1st ed (m2,sl soil cov) 35.00

PRYDE,D-Nunga-1971-Walker-285p-col photos-1st ed (bb3,f,dj) 10.00

PRZERWA-TETMAJER,KAZIMIERZ-Tales of the Tatras-Lond-1941-Minerva Publ-cl,drwngs-1st ed (o8) 40.00

PUCKETT,J L-History of Oklahoma and Indian Territory and Homeseekers' Guide-Vinita-1906-149p-qtr lea & brnw cl,frntis,photos-Herd #1844-1st ed (t7,f) 300.00

PUECHNER,RAY-LSD & Sex & Censorship & Vietnam Cookbook-(Jacksonville)-(1968)-(Harris-Wolfe)-1st ed (ff3,dj) 50.00

PUGH,P D G-Nelson and His Surgeons-Edinburgh-1968-68p-1st ed (dd3) 45.00

PUGSLEY,RADM A F-Destroyer Man-Lond-(1957)-Weidenfeld & Nicholson-8vo-224p-1st ed (cc5,dj) 20.00

PUIG,MANUEL-Betrayed by Rita Hayworth-NY-1971-Dutton-auth 1st bk-1st ed (e8,f,f dj) 85.00

PUIG,MANUEL-Eternal Curse on the Reader of these Pages-NY-(1982)-Random-1st ed (b5,as new in dj) 17.50

PUIG,MANUEL-Kiss of the Spider Woman-NY-1979-Knopf-1st US ed (b5,as new in dj) 30.00

PULITZER,R-Over the Front in an Aeroplane-NY-(1915)-8vo-xiv,170p-cl,frntis,14 illus-1st ed (s2) 35.00

PULLAR,GEORGE-Historical Sketch of the 4th...-Edinburgh-1907-46p-grn cl,4 plts-scarce-1st ed (jj2,f) 75.00

PULLAR,PHILIPPA-Consuming Passions-Bost-(1970)-Little,Brown-278p-1st Amer ed (k6) 25.00

PULLEN,JOHN J-Shower of Stars-Phila-(1966)-269p-illus-1st ed (c4,f,dj) 35.00

PULLEN,JOHN J-Shower of Stars-Phila-1966-Lippincott-269p-illus-1st ed (o7,dj) 30.00

PULLEN,JOHN J-Transcendental Boiled Dinner-(1972)-Lippincott-sm 8vo-92p-blk cl,red e.p.-1st ed (q8,dj) 12.50

PULLEN,JOHN J-Transcendental Boiled Dinner-Phila-(1972)-Lippincott-92p-1st ed (k6) 20.00

PULLMAN,ANNIE K-Experiences of a Pretty Type Writer Girl in Chicago-Chig-(1903)-I Whiteson-79,(1)p-wrps (d1,sl wn,rprd tr rear wrps) 45.00

PULTE,J H-Woman's Medical Guide...-Cin-1863-336p-cl-prntd slip wi imprnt of Smith & Worthington pasted over orig imprnt of Sargent,Wilson & Hinkle-4th ed,rvsd (d1) 25.00

PUMPELLY,RAFAEL-Across America and Asia-NY-1870-Leypoldt & Holt-8vo-470p-brwn cl wi world globe vignet in gilt,12 plts,4 maps(1 col & fldg)-3rd ed,rvsd (ll1,edgw wn & bump) 125.00

PUNSHON,E R-Bath Mysteries-NY-1938-Hillman-Curl Clue Club-1st US ed (l4,dj sl fray,chip) 25.00

PUNSHON,E R-There's a Reason for Everything-1946-Macmillan-1st Amer ed (s10,chip dj) 12.50

PUPIN,MICHAEL-From Immigrant to Inventor-1924-396p-11 photos-1st ed (h6) 20.00

PURCELL,J-Flights to Glory-NY-1944-8vo-184p-cl,illus t.p.,22p plts-1st ed (s2,fade,dj chip) 35.00

PURDY,JAMES C-Moorestown, Old and New-Moorestown-1886-359,(5)p-cl (aa6) 60.00

PURDY,JAMES-Cabot Wright Begins-1964-FSG-1st ed (x2,f,dj) 40.00

PURDY,JAMES-Color of Darkness-1957-New Directions-1st ed (x2,f,dj) 75.00

PURDY,JAMES-Eustace Chisholm and the Works-NY-(1967)-1st ed (k9,f,dj) 17.50

PURDY,JAMES-I Am Elijah Thrush-GC-1972-Dbldy-1st ed (b10,f,dj) 25.00

PURDY,JAMES-Mourners Below-NY-(1981)-Viking-1st ed (j3,f,dj) 20.00

PURDY,JAMES-Mourners Below-NY-1981-1st ed (t5,f,dj) 12.50

PURDY,JAMES-Nephew-NY-(1960)-FS&C-1st ed (b10,f,dj) 45.00

PURPLE,EDWIN R-In Memoriam-NY-1881-12p-bds,frntis-Graff #3403-scarce-1st ed (t7,autg) 125.00

PURRINGTON,PHILIP F-4 Years A Whaling-New Bedford-1972-Barre Publ-oblng 4to-33 plts(9 col) (p8,wn dj) 25.00

PURSLEY,LOUIS H-Toronto Trolley Car Story 1921 to 1961-LA-1961-164p-wrps-Interurban Spec #29-1st ed (n4) 18.00

PURTELL,JOSEPH-Tiffany Touch-NY-(1971)-Random-309p-col illus e.p.,photos-1st ed (u5,f,dj) 35.00

PURVIANCE,ELDER LEVI-Biography of Elder David Purviance, with his Memoirs...-Dayton-1848-B F & G W Ells-304p-cl-scarce-1st ed (c1,rbnd) 100.00

PUSEY,WILLIAM A-History of Dermatology-Springfield-1933-223p-illus (g10,ex-libr) 50.00

PUSHKIN,ALEXANDER-Captain's Daughter and Other Stories-NY-1971-LEC-ltd to 1500c,autg,illus,Chas Mozley (w1,f,box) 50.00

PUTER,S A D-Looters of the Public Domain-Portland-1908-4to-495p-orig dec cl,illus-scarce-Smith 8441 (a7,edgewn) 150.00

PUTNAM COUNTY-FARM JOURNAL ILLUSTRATED DIRECTORY OF...OHIO-Phila-1916-256,(2)p-bds (j1) 15.00

PUTNAM,ANNE E-Madami, My Eight Years of Adventure with the Congo Pigmies-NY-(1954)-Prentice Hall-8vo-303p-8p photos-1st ed (cc5,dj) 20.00

PUTNAM,F W-Archaeological and Ethnological Collections from...Santa Barbara...Arizona and New Mexico-1879-US Geol Srvys West of 100th Meridian-497p-col litho frntis,20 plts (bb3,rbnd,sl fox) 125.00

PUTNAM,G P-Soaring Wings-NY-(1939)-8vo-x,294p-cl,frntis,22p plts (t2,dj) 25.00

PUTNAM,GEORGE G-Salem Vessels and Their Voyages. A History of the "Astrea"...Reminiscences of Salem Shipmasters-Salem-1925-Essex Inst-iv,164p-papr over bds,cl sp,g sp titles,pict paste-on,illus (nn1) 55.00

PUTNAM,GEORGE G-Salem Vessels and Their Voyages. A History of the "George","Glide"...and the Philippine

Islands-Salem-1924-Essex Inst-iv,168p-papr over bds,cl sp,pict paste-on,illus (nn1) 55.00

PUTNAM,GEORGE H-Memories of My Youth 1844 to 1865-NY-1914-447p+ads-illus-1st ed (n3,f,dj) 42.50

PUTNAM,GEORGE P-Andree-NY-1930-Brewer & Warren-8vo-cl,port,map,plts-1st ed (t2,t.p. fox,dj) 45.00

PUTNAM,GEORGE P-In the Oregon Country-NY-1915-Putnam's-12mo-xxi,169p-dec cov,t.e.g.,52 photos-1st ed (o2) 25.00

PUTNAM,JAMES W-Illinois and Michigan Canal-Chig-1918-U of Chig Pr-xiv+213p-cl sp,papr sp labl,plts-Chig Hist Soc Collection, Vol.X-1st ed (b2,f,unopened) 35.00

PUTNAM,MRS WILLIAM L-Happiness of Our Garden-NY-1926-tall 8vo-31p-cl bkd bds,cov labl,ltd to 750c,6 half tones (m10,soil,sm cov stn) 25.00

PUTNAM,MRS-Primary Cook Book By...For New Beginners in Housekeeping-Bost-1862-Loring-84p-yel papr bds-Brown 1493-second thousand (n6,bds wn) 75.00

PUTNAM,R-Birds of Prey-1979-Cntry Life-folio-120p-35 col plts,photos-1st ed (bb3,f,dj) 40.00

PUTNAM,ROBERT-Early Sea Charts-NY-1983-Abbeville Pr-folio-143p-76 plts(incl col) (p8,as new) 45.00

PUTNAM,SAMUEL-Marvelous Journey-NY-1948-Knopf-1st ed (v4,wn dj) 20.00

PUTNAM,SAMUEL-Sequel to the Analytical Reader...-Dover-1831-E French-300p-lea-Amer Imprnts 8912-2nd ed (k1) 22.50

PUTTI,VITTORIO-Historic Artificial Limbs-NY-1930-63p-1st ed (dd3) 75.00

PUZO,MARIO-Dark Arena-NY-(1955)-auth 1st bk-1st ed (c5,f,dj sp sl fade) 60.00

PUZO,MARIO-Godfather-NY-1969-1st ed (n5,dj) 100.00

PUZO,MARIO-Godfather-NY-1969-Putnam's-1st ed (z2,f,sl rub & tn dj) 65.00

PUZO,MARIO-Runaway Summer of Davie Shaw-NY-1966-1st ed (s5,dj) 30.00

PYCRAFT,W P-Camouflage in Nature-Lond-(1925)-8vo-280p-cl,illus(4 col) (y8,cor wn) 35.00

PYLE,HOWARD-Howard Pyle-NY-(1975)-Scribner-4to-unpgd-43 col illus-1st ed (ee5,f,dj) 25.00

PYLE,HOWARD-Merry Adventures of Robin Hood-1929-Scribners-pict dj (x2,dj sl wn & tn) 58.00

PYLE,HOWARD-Otto of the Silver Hand-NY-1888-Scribner's-170p-pict stmpd olive grn cl,16p publ ads in rear,auth illus-1st ed (nn10,rbkd in mor,cor rub) 250.00

PYLE,HOWARD-Rejected of Men-NY-1903-Harper-8vo-grn cl,"Published June 1903" on cpyrt pg-1st ed (x3,weak hng) 50.00

PYLE,HOWARD-Rose of Paradise-NY-1888-Harper-orig g titled cl-1st ed (aa9,sl rub,sl fox) 75.00

PYLE,J G-ED.-Picturesque St.Paul-St.Paul-(1888)-Northwestern Photo-1/2 lea & pebbld bds,g stmpd,a.e.g.,105 photo plts (p6,cov wn) 350.00

PYM BARBARA-Less Than Angels-NY-(1957)-Vanguard-1st ed (j6,dj) 50.00

PYM,BARBARA-An Unsuitable Attachment-NY-(1982)-Dutton-1st ed (j6,f,f dj) 25.00

PYM,BARBARA-Few Green Leaves-NY-(1980)-Dutton-1st ed (j6,dj) 20.00

PYM,BARBARA-Less Than Angels-NY-(1957)-1st US ed (o5,sl fox e.p.,dj) 55.00

PYM,BARBARA-Less Than Angels-NY-(1957)-Vanguard-1st US ed (m7,sl wn,dj wn & soil) 50.00

PYM,BARBARA-No Fond Return of Love-NY-1982-Dutton-1st ed (v5,f,f dj) 25.00

PYM,BARBARA-Sweet Dove Died-NY-(1978)-Dutton-1st US ed (hh5,f,sl tn dj) 10.00

PYM,BARBARA-Very Private Eye-NY-1984-Dutton-1st ed (x9,bump,dj) 10.00

PYNCHON,THOMAS-Crying of Lot 49-Phila,NY-(1966)-Lippincott-1st ed (a10,dj) 200.00

PYNCHON,THOMAS-Crying of Lot 49-Phila-(1965)-Lippincott-8vo-cl/bds-1st ed (x3,f,dj) 225.00

PYNCHON,THOMAS-Gravity's Rainbow-NY-(1973)-Viking-1st ed (j6,dj) 425.00

PYNCHON,THOMAS-Gravity's Rainbow-NY-1973-pict wrps-publ simultaneously wi hdbnd ed-1st ed (r2,f) 50.00

PYNCHON,THOMAS-Gravity's Rainbow-NY-1973-wrps iss simultaneously wi hdbk-1st ed (t5) 25.00

PYNCHON,THOMAS-Low Lands-(Lond)-(1978)-Aloes-wht wrps-no stmnt of 1st ed-ltd to 1500c-1st ed (k5,f) 45.00

PYNCHON,THOMAS-Mortality and Mercy in Vienna-Lond-nd(1976)-Aloes-1st issue wi smooth wht wrps-1st ed (k5,f) 65.00

PYNCHON,THOMAS-Secret Integration-Lond-1980-Aloes Bks-ltd to 2500c-wrps-1st Brit ed (m7,f) 30.00

PYNCHON,THOMAS-Secret Integration-Lond-1980-Aloes Bks-wrps-one of 2500c-1st ed (s1,f) 25.00

PYNCHON,THOMAS-Small Rain-Lond-1982-Aloes-wrps-1st ed (v5,f) 15.00

PYNCHON,THOMAS-V-Phila-1963-Lippincott-auth 1st bk-1st ed (g8,dj) 500.00

PYNE,HENRY R-History of the First New Jersey Cavalry-Trenton-1871-350p-lea,port,col pl (aa6,rbnd,outr hngs brokn) 150.00

PYNE,HENRY R-Ride to War-New Brunswick-(1961)-xxxiii,340p-cl-rprnt of 1871 ed (aa6) 40.00

PYPER,GEORGE D-Romance of an Old Playhouse-SLC-1937-406p-frntis,ports,illus-2nd ed (bb8) 25.00

QUACKENBOS,G P-Practical Arithmetic...Upon the Basis of the Works of Geo. R. Perkins-NY-1868-Appleton-336p-cl (k1) 15.00

QUACKENBOS,JOHN D-Hypnotic Therapeutics in Theory and Practice-NY/Lond-1908-Harper & Bros-(ii)+(viii)+335+(3)p-grn cl,illus-1st ed (y9) 50.00

QUACKENBOS,JOHN D-Hypnotism in Mental and Moral Culture-NY-1900-Harper & Bros-12mo-(xii)+290+(2)p-red cl-1st ed (y9) 30.00

QUAIFE,M M-Chicago in the Old Northwest, 1673 to 1835-Chig-(1913)-U of Chig pr-viii+480p-blu cl,10 plts,map-Howes Q1-1st ed (b2,sl fade sp) 110.00

QUAIFE,M M-Chicago's Highways Old and New, From Indian Trail to Motor Road-Chig-1923-D F Keller-278p-blu cl,plts,fldg maps (mm10) 50.00

QUAIFE,M M-ED.-Pictures of Gold Rush California-NY-(1967)-Citadel Pr-383p-frntis map,drwngs (ff4,sl wn dj) 20.00

QUAIFE,M M-ED.-Yellowstone Kelly-New Haven-1926-Yale Univ-8vo-xiv,268p-blu cl,illus,fldg map,pict dj-1st ed (u1,dj) 85.00

QUAIFE,M M-This is Detroit-Detr-1951-198p-wrps,illus (l1) 12.50

QUAIFE,M M-Wisconsin: Its History and Its People, 1634 to 1924-Chig-1924-S J Clarke-4to-2 vols-grn cl,illus-1st ed (b2) 100.00

QUAIFE,MILO-ED.-Journals of Capt Meriwether Lewis and Sergeant John Ordway...1803 to 1806-Madison-1916-444p-frntis,photos,fldg map-Howes L318-1st ed (t7,f) 125.00

QUAIFE,MILO-Forty Six Years-Detr-1956-Algonquin Club-8vo-52p-cl (cc3,dj) 55.00

QUAIFE,MILO-Narrative of the Adventures of Zenas Leonard-Chig-1934-Lakeside Classic-278p-g cl,map frntis,t.e.g.-Graff #2461 (t7) 35.00

QUAM,ALVINA-TRANSL.-Zuni People-Albuq-(1972)-245p-photos-1st ed (v7,f,dj) 20.00

QUARANTINE AND SANITARY CONVENTION-PROCEEDINGS AND DEBATES OF THE THIRD NATIONAL...-NY-1859-728p-1st ed (dd3) 75.00

QUARLES,E A-American Pheasant Breeding & Shooting-NY-1916-8vo-128p-wrps,illus (m3) 10.00

QUARRIE,GEORGE-Within a Jersey Circle-Somerville-(1910)-332p-cl,plts (aa6) 75.00

QUAYLE,ERIC-Collector's Book of Books-NY-1971-Clarkson Potter-lg format-1st Amer ed (w9,f,dj) 85.00

QUAYLE,ERIC-Collector's Book of Children's Books-Lond-1971-Studio Vista-illus(incl col)-1st ed (ll5,dj sl nick) 95.00

QUAYLE,ERIC-Collector's Book of Detective Fiction-Lond-1972-Studio Vista-illus-1st ed (hh2,f,sl tn dj) 100.00

QUAYLE,ERIC-Early Children's Books-Lond/Ottowa-1983-David & Chas/Brns & Noble-illus-1st ed (s3,as new in dj) 30.00

QUAYLE,ERIC-Old Cook Books-NY-(1978)-Dutton-illus-1st ed (m6) 50.00

QUAYLE,WILLIAM A-Beside Lake Beautiful-NY-1914-Abingdon Pr-4to-240p-cl,illus-1st ed (q3) 25.00

QUEBBEMAN,FRANCES E-Medicine in Territorial Arizona-Phoenix-1966-Ariz Hist Fndtn-423p-illus-1st ed (cc4) 50.00

QUEBEC MISSION-Notices & Voyages of the Famed...to the Pacific Northwest-1956-Ore Hist Soc-243p+index-pict bndg,illus,fldg map-ltd ed (e7,unopened) 95.00

QUEEN MARY, CUNUARD WHITE STAR QUADRUPLE SCREW LINER-NY-1979-Bonanza-288p-fldg plts,photos,drwngs (p8,dj stnd) 20.00

QUEEN,ELLERY-Adventures of Ellery Queen-NY-1934-Stokes-1st ed (e4) 35.00

QUEEN,ELLERY-American Gun Mystery-1933-Stokes-1st ed (s10) 30.00

QUEEN,ELLERY-American Gun Mystery-NY-1933-Stokes-1st ed (k4,sp sl fade,soil) 20.00

QUEEN,ELLERY-And On the Eighth Day-NY-1964-Random-1st ed (g4,chip dj) 12.50

QUEEN,ELLERY-Calamity Town-1942-Little,Brown-1st ed (s10,chip dj) 65.00

QUEEN,ELLERY-Calamity Town-Bost-1942-Little,Brown-1st ed (gg7,dj sl wn) 75.00

QUEEN,ELLERY-Chinese Orange Mystery-NY-1934-Stokes-1st ed (g4) 15.00

QUEEN,ELLERY-Devil to Pay-NY-1938-Stokes-1st ed (gg8,cor fly clip,dj wn) 50.00

QUEEN,ELLERY-Double,Double-1950-Little,Brown-1st ed (q9,f,sl rub dj) 60.00

QUEEN,ELLERY-Dutch Shoe Mystery-NY-1931-Stokes-1st ed (f4) 25.00

QUEEN,ELLERY-ED.-Alfred Hitchcock's Fireside Book of Suspense-NY-1947-Simon-1st ed (e4,dj) 30.00

QUEEN,ELLERY-ED.-Misadventures of Sherlock Holmes-1944-LB-1st ed (x7,f,dj) 400.00

QUEEN,ELLERY-ED.-Misadventures of Sherlock Holmes-1944-LB-1st ed,2nd prtg (x7,dj) 90.00

QUEEN,ELLERY-ED.-Misadventures of Sherlock Holmes-1944-Little,Brown-1st ed (s10,rub rear cov,dj) 450.00

QUEEN,ELLERY-Ellery Queen Master Detective-NY-1941-Grosset-1st ed (g4,f,dj) 25.00

QUEEN,ELLERY-Face to Face-1967-NAL-1st ed (x7,f,dj) 27.00

QUEEN,ELLERY-Finishing Stroke-NY-1958-Simon-1st ed (j4,f,dj) 15.00

QUEEN,ELLERY-Glass Village-Bost-1954-Little-1st ed (f4,dj) 25.00

QUEEN,ELLERY-In the Queens' Parlor-NY-1957-S&S-182p-1st prtg (g9,dj wn,tape rprd) 30.00

QUEEN,ELLERY-Inspector Queen's Own Case-NY-1956-Random-1st ed (k4,dj) 15.00

QUEEN,ELLERY-King is Dead-1952-LB-1st ed (x7,f,dj) 25.00

QUEEN,ELLERY-Penthouse Mystery-NY-1941-Grosset-1st ed (j4,dj) 10.00

QUEEN,ELLERY-Player on the Other Side-NY-1963-Random-1st ed (g4,f,sl wn dj) 15.00

QUEEN,ELLERY-Queen's Bureau of Investigation-1952-LB-1st ed (x7,f,dj) 55.00

QUEEN,ELLERY-Roman Hat Mystery-1929-Stokes-1st ed (x7) 45.00

QUEEN,ELLERY-Scarlet Letters-Bost-1953-Little-1st ed (j4,dj) 25.00

QUEEN,ELLERY-Ten Days' Wonder-Bost-1948-Little-1st ed (j4,sl wn dj sp) 15.00

QUEEN,ELLERY-There Was an Old Woman-Bost-1943-Little-1st ed (e4,weak inner hnge,dj) 65.00

QUEEN,ELLERY-Tragedy of X-1932-Viking-1st ed (x7) 23.00

QUEEN,ELLERY-Tragedy of Z-1942-LB-1st ed (x7,sl tn dj) 55.00

QUEENY,E M-Cheechako-NY-1941-133p+1p bibliog,tan linen cl,papr labl on sp & cov,col photos,ltd to 1200c (ee3,vf,box) 100.00

QUEENY,E M-Prairie Wings-1947-Lippincott-4to-256p-col frntis,photos-scarce-2nd ed (bb3,f) 125.00

QUEENY,E M-Spirit of Enterprise-NY-1943-8vo-267p (m3,vf,sl chip dj) 25.00

QUELCH,MARY T-Herb Garden-Lond-(1951)-234p-8 b&w illus-1st ed (j10,edgewn,dj tattrd) 15.00

QUENNELL,PETER-ED.-Marcel Proust 1871 to 1922-NY-(1971)-S&S-1st US ed (h3,f,chip dj) 15.00

QUENNELL,PETER-Letter to Mrs.Virginia Woolf-Lond-1932-Hogarth Pr-wrps-Hogarth Letters No.12-1st ed (j6,sun wrps) 35.00

QUENNELL,PETER-Who's Who in Shakespeare-NY-1973-Morrow-1st ed (z3,f,dj) 20.00

QUENTIN,PATRICK-Family Skeletons-1965-Random Hs-1st ed (s10,soil dj) 12.50

QUENTIN,PATRICK-Man with Two Wives-NY-1955-Simon-1st ed (j4,yel pgs,dj) 12.50

QUENTIN,PATRICK-Ordeal of Mrs.Snow...-1962-Random Hs-1st Amer ed (s10,dj) 30.00

QUENTIN,PATRICK-Puzzle for Fiends-NY-1946-Simon-1st ed (l4,dj) 15.00

QUENTIN,PATRICK-Puzzle for Puppets-NY-1944-Simon-1st ed (e4,dj) 20.00

QUEVLI,NELS-Cell Intelligence...-Mpls-1917-Colwell Pr-(viii)+460p-brwn cl-1st ed (a2) 20.00

QUICK,H-Brown Mouse-1915-BM-illus-1st ed (x7,sp lttrng flake,dj chip) 90.00

QUICK,HERBERT-Fairview Idea-Indpls-(1919)-Bobbs-Merrill-285p-cl-Hanna 2951-1st ed (j1) 15.00

QUICK,HERBERT-Vandemark's Folly-Indpls-1922-Bobbs Merril-illus,N C Wyeth-1st ed (y2,f,dj) 200.00

QUICK,JIM-Fishing the Nymph-NY-1960-4to-139p-illus (m3,f,dj) 17.50
QUICK,JIM-Trout Fishing & Trout Flies-Woodstock-1957-8vo-252p-photos-1st ed (m3,vf,dj) 17.50
QUIETT,GLENN C-They Built the West-NY-1934-Appleton Century-569p-illus-1st ed (bb4,dj) 35.00
QUIETT,GLENN C-They Built the West-NY-1934-Appleton Century-569p-illus-1st ed (ee4,dj) 35.00
QUIGLEY,MARTIN-Original Colored House of David-1981-Houghton Mifflin-1st ed (s8,f,f dj) 20.00
QUIGLEY,MARTIN-Original Colored House of David-Bost-1981-245p-bds-1st ed (n1,f,dj) 15.00
QUILL,MONICA-Let Us Prey-NY-1982-Vanguard-1st ed (j4,f,dj) 15.00
QUILLER-COUCH,ARTHUR-Lecture on Lectures-Lond-1927-Hogarth Pr-8vo-cl,Hogarth Lectures No.1-1st ed (x3,sp sunned) 55.00
QUILLER-COUCH,ARTHUR-Splendid Spur-NY-(1927)-Doran-lg 8vo-cl wi pict pasteon,3 inserted col plts,12p b&w drwngs,pict e.p.-1st ed thus (r3) 20.00
QUIMBY,GEORGE I-Indian Culture and European Trade Goods-Madison-1966-U of Wisc Pr-217p-1st ed (cc4,dj) 20.00
QUIN,MIKE-More Dangerous Thoughts-SF-1941-People's World-wrps-1st ed (v5) 20.00
QUIN,MIKE-On the Drumhead-SF-1948-Pac Publ Fndtn/Plantin Pr-wrps-1st ed (v5) 20.00
QUINBY,E J-Interurban Interlude-Ramsey-1968-92p-1st ed (n4,sl tn dj) 12.00
QUINCY,ELIZA S M-Memoir of the Life of...-Bost-1861-priv prtd-(2),270p-cl-ltd to 200c (aa6) 100.00
QUINN,DAVID B-Last Voyage of Thomas Cavendish 1591 to 1592-Chig,Lond-1975-Chig Pr-ix,165p-beige cl,12 illus incl frntis & fldg chrt (nn1,vf,vf dj) 35.00
QUINN,DAVID B-New Found Land of Stephen Parmenius-1972-U of Tor Pr-8vo-xii,250p-11 illus-1st ed (cc7,dj) 25.00*
QUINN,DAVID B-New Found Land-Providence-1965-Assoc of J C B Libr-wrps (v4,as new) 25.00
QUINN,JOHN P-Gambling and Gambling Devices-Canton-(1912)-J P Quinn-306,(2)p-cl-scarce (g1) 65.00
QUINN,NIALL-Brigitte, and Other Stories-NY-(1981)-Braziller-1st Amer ed (z8,vf,dj) 14.50
QUINN,VERNON-Beautiful Mexico-NY-1924-Stokes-398p-frnt cov photo,col frntis-1st ed (bb4) 30.00
QUINN,VERNON-Seeds-NY-(1936)-188p-marg illus-1st ed (m10,tn dj) 15.00
QUINN,VERNON-Shrubs in the Garden-NY-1940-x,308p-illus,M Lawson-1st ed (x5,spot frnt cov) 10.00
QUINN,VERNON-War Paint and Powder Horn on the Old Santa Fe Trail-NY-1929-Stokes-298p-col frntis,3 illus-Six Guns #1782-1st ed (dd4) 20.00
QUINT,ALONZO H-Potomac and the Rapidan-Bost-1864-Crosby & Nichols-407p-fldg map-Nevins I,149-1st ed (ee4,sl fray sp) 50.00
QUINTON,CAPTAIN-Strange Adventures of Captain Quinton...Among the Cannibals-Bible House-1912-Christian Herald-dec cov (ee7,sl spot) 50.00
QUIRARTE,JACINTO-Mexican American Artists-Austin/Lond-1973-U of Tex Pr-4to-xxv,149p-grn cl,map (dd7,dj) 25.00
QUIRKE,T T-Disappearance of the Huronia-1930-F A Acland/Geo Srvy 160-8vo-129p-gold emboss titles on red cl cov bds,15 plts & figs,2 fldg maps rear pckt (bb7,bump,sp wn) 45.00*
QURESHI,MOHAMMED I-First Punjabis-Aldershot-1958-484p-maps,illus-1st ed (b7,f,dj) 150.00
R.C.A.F. OVERSEAS-Tor-1944-Oxford U Pr-roy 8vo-xvi,418p-cl,frntis,plts (s2,sl chip dj) 45.00
RABAN,JONATHAN-Soft City-NY-1974-Dutton-8vo-229p-1st US ed (cc5,dj) 15.00
RABE,DAVID-Streamers-NY-1977-Knopf-1st ed (v5,f,f dj) 45.00
RABIN,AL-Peddler in Paradise-NY-1956-Dutton-8vo-240p-5 col photos-1st ed (bb5,f,dj) 15.00
RABKIN,ERIC S-Fantastic Worlds-NY-1979-OUP-1st ed (e3,f,dj) 15.00
RACE,HENRY-Contributions to Hunterdon County History-Paterson-1892-7p-wrps (aa6) 30.00
RACHLEFF,OWEN S-Occult Conceit-NY-1961-Bell Publ-8vo-xvii p-1st ed (aa7,dj) 10.00*
RACKHAM,ARTHUR-Arthur Rackham's Book of Pictures-Lond-1913-Heinemann-44 tip in plts-1st trd ed (y2) 500.00
RACKHAM,BERNARD-Book of Porcelain-Lond-1910-Black-95p-dec grn cl,gilt,28 tip-in col plts-Franklin 3031 (u5) 95.00
RACKHAM,BERNARD-Catalogue of English Porcelain Earthenware Enamels and Glass Collected by Charles Schreiber...-Lond-1924-102p-48 plts (cc8,hng crack) 85.00
RADAM,WILLIAM-Microbes and the Microbe Killers-NY-1890-publ by auth-xiv+369p-red cl,plts-1st ed (dd1) 45.00
RADCLIFF,PETER-Land of Mountains-Seattle-1979-4to-160p-photos(incl col),maps-1st ed (a4,f,dj) 38.00
RADCLYFFE,C E-Round the Smoking Room Fire-Lond-1933-8vo-230p-photos-1st ed (m3,f) 15.00
RADEK,KARL-Portraits and Pamphlets-NY-nd-McBride-306p-1st ed (v5) 35.00
RADER,JESSE L-South of Forty-Norman-1947-336p-1st ed (t7) 100.00
RADFORD'S ARTISTIC HOMES-Chig-1908-Radford Arch Co-4to-261p+ads-illus cl,illus (r10,cov stnd & wn) 40.00
RADIGUET,RAYMOND-Devil in the Flesh-Paris,Wash-1948-Crosby Cont Ed,Black Sun-1st ed (w5,f,dj sp fade) 45.00
RADIN,EDWARD D-Lizzie Borden-NY-1961-S&S-xii+269p-red & wht bds,illus-1st ed (k2,dj) 25.00
RADIN,PAUL-ED.-Crashing Thunder-NY-1926-Appleton-202p-1st ed (bb4) 40.00
RADIN,PAUL-Story of the American Indian-NY-1944-Liveright-cl,6 col & 24 b&w illus-3rd ed (n8,fray dj) 25.00
RADIN,PAUL-Trickster-NY-1956-Philo Libr-cl-1st ed (n8,dj) 45.00
RADIO STARS OF TODAY-np-nd(ca.1931)-Nat Union Radio Corp-sm folio-32p-wrps,photos (p1) 45.00
RADKEY,OLIVER H-Sickle Under the Hammer-NY-(1963)-Columbia U Pr-8vo-525p-1st ed (jj5,dj) 20.00
RADLEY,SHEILA-Chief Inspector's Daughter-Lond-1981-Constable-1st ed (s4,f,dj) 27.50
RADLEY,SHEILA-Death & the Maiden-Lond-1978-Hamilton-1st ed (p4,dj) 25.00
RADOVSKY,M-Alexander Popov-Moscow-1957-Foreign Lang Publ Hs-130p-blu cl,plts-1st ed (l2) 40.00
RADZIWELL,PRINCESS MARIE-This Was Germany-Lond-(1937)-Murray-8vo-403p-5 illus-1st Brit ed (jj5) 100.00
RADZIWILL,PRINCESS CATHERINE-Firebrand of Bolshevism-Bost-1919-Small,Maynard-1st ed (v5,f,dj sl tn,chip) 35.00

RAE,JOHN-Contemporary Socialism-NY-1889-Scribners-455p-presumed 1st ed (ff1,sl rub) 65.00

RAE,W F-Westward by Rail-Lond-1870-Longmans-8vo-391p+ads-frntis map-1st ed (s1,sp fade) 125.00

RAE,W FRASER-Newfoundland to Manitoba-NY-1881-Putnam's-x,294p,6p ads-plt,fldg maps(incl frntis) (k10,ex-lib,lacks fldg map can 60.00*

RAEMAEKERS,LOUIS-Kultur in Cartoons...-NY-1917-Century-quarto-219p-cl,illus-1st ed (m1) 17.50

RAFFEL,BURTON-Robert Lowell-NY-1981-Ungar-1st ed (y10,f,sl soil dj) 15.00

RAFINESQUE,C S-Life of Travels-Waltham-1944-4to-67p-wrps,illus-rprnt (m3) 40.00

RAGAN,ALLEN E-History of Tusculum College 1794-1944-(Bristol)-(1945)-274p-cl (k1) 15.00

RAGG,L M-Women Artists of Bologna-Lond-1907-20 illus-1st ed (h10) 65.00

RAGON,MICHEL-Space of Death-Charlottesville-(1983,81)-U Pr of Va-lg 8vo-328p-illus-1st US ed (gg5,f,f dj) 17.50

RAGUIN,VIRGINIA C-Stained Glass in Thirteenth Century Burgundy-1982-Princeton Univ-182p-161 illus (cc8) 45.00

RAHT,CARLYSLE G-Romance of Davis Mountains and Big Bend Country-El Paso-1919-Rahtbooks-381p-map,photos-Howes R16-1st ed (a9,vf) 110.00

RAIGERSFELD,JEFFREY-Life of a Sea Officer-Lond-1929-Cassell-210p-illus (p8,sl fox) 30.00

RAIKES,G A-History of the Honourable Artillery Company-Lond-1878-2 vols-dec blu cl,maps & plts(incl col)-1st ed (gg2) 175.00

RAILROAD RIOTS IN JULY, 1877-Report of the Committee Appointed to Investigate the...-Harrisburg-1878-Lane S Harte-(ii)+1000p-brwn cl-1st ed (b2) 125.00

RAILWAY LITERATURE-Wash,D.C.-(1942)-Assoc of Amer Railroads-40p-wrps (l1) 8.50

RAINE,W-Bird Nesting in Northwest Canada-Tor-1892-8vo-(2),197p-cl,6 col plts,34 tinted plts (y8) 125.00

RAINE,WILLIAM M-Cattle-GC-1930-Dbldy,Doran-340p-photos-Herd 1852-1st ed (dd4) 50.00

RAINE,WILLIAM M-Famous Sheriffs and Western Outlaws-GC-1929-Dbldy,Doran-294p-Six Guns 1784-1st ed (gg4,dj) 30.00

RAINE,WILLIAM M-Sons of the Saddle-NY-1938-276p-dec cl-1st ed (t7) 10.00

RAINE,WILLIAM M-They Call Him Blue Blazes-Bost-(1941)-Houghton Mifflin-1st ed (aa10,dj) 75.00

RAINES,C W-ED.-Speeches and State Papers of James Stephen Hogg-Austin-1905-State Prtg-453p-1st ed (a9,hngs weak) 100.00

RAINES,HOWELL-My Soul is Rested-NY-(1977)-Putnam's-auth 1st bk-1st ed (aa8,as new in dj) 25.00

RAINES,HOWELL-Whiskey Man-NY-1977-Viking-1st ed (z9,f,dj) 10.00

RAINES,ROBERT-Marcellus Laroon-Lond-1966-P Mellon Fndtn Brit Art-4to-219p-yel cl,col frntis,illus (r10,sl wn dj) 45.00

RALBOVSKY,MARTIN-Destiny's Darlings-1974-Hawthorn-1st ed (p7,dj) 15.00

RALPH,JULIAN-Our Great West-NY-1893-Harper & Bros-pict cl,Remington frntis,drwngs-Six Guns #1793-1st ed (dd4) 50.00

RALSTON,J K-Rhymes of a Cowboy-Billings-(1969)-Rimrock-4to-xxii,101p-cl,col plts & b&w drwngs,auth-1st ed (v1,chip dj) 45.00

RAMALEY,F-Colorado Plant Life-1927-U of Colo-299p-3 col plts,133 photos & drwngs-1st ed (bb3) 35.00

RAMATI,ALEXANDER-Barbed Wire on the Isle of Man-NY-(1980)-HBJ-8vo-231p-1st US ed (gg5,f,f dj) 10.00

RAMAZANI,NESTA-Persian Cooking-NY-(1974)-Quadrangle-296p-maps,drwngs,col plts (o6) 20.00

RAMON Y CAJAL,S-Degeneration & Regeneration of the Nervous System-Birmingham-1984-2 vols-lea-(facs of 1928 ed) (dd3) 125.00

RAMSAY,DAVID-History of the Revolution of South Carolina...-Trenton-1785-Isaac Collins-2 vols-blk lea,fldg maps-Howes R36aa-1st ed (oo5,rbkd,cor wn,sl fox) 950.00

RAMSAY,W M-Everyday Life in Turkey-Lond-1897-Hodder & Stoughton-1st ed (m8) 55.00

RAMSAYE,TERRY-ED.-1936,37 International Motion Picture Almanac-NY-(1936)-Quigley-thk 8vo-1346p+ads (s1,sl wn) 35.00

RAMSBOTTOM,JOHN-Poisonous Fungi-Lond-(1945)-King Penguin-16mo-32p text+16p col plts,pict bds-1st ed (q8) 15.00

RAMSDELL,C W-Behind the Lines in the Southern Confederacy-Baton Rouge-1944-136p-port,v scarce dj-1st ed (z10,dj) 50.00

RAMSEY,FREDERIC,JR.-Guide to Long Play Jazz Records-NY-1954-Long Player Publ-photos-1st prtg (u4,sl chip dj) 20.00

RAMSEY,RICHARD D-Edmund Wilson:A Bibliography-NY-1971-David Lewis-8vo-345p-brwn cl-1st ed (mm1,f,dj) 25.00

RAMSON'S FAMILY RECIPT BOOK-1901-Baker Jones (v6,sl fade,sl soil,brwnd) 20.00

RAND,A L-American Water & Game Birds-NY-1956-oversized-239p-col photos (gg3,vf,dj) 15.00

RAND,A L-Birds from Nepal-1957-Chig Nat Hist Mus-218p-wrps,6 maps (bb3,f) 12.00

RAND,A L-Birds of the Philippine Islands-Chig-1960-8vo-221p-wrps (y8) 23.00

RAND,AUSTIN-American Water & Game Birds-NY-1956-4to-239p-silhouettes by Ugo Mochi,200 illus (m3,vf,dj) 32.50

RAND,AYN-Atlas Shrugged-NY-(1957)-Random-1st ed (a10,dj sp sl wn) 200.00

RAND,AYN-For the New Intellectual-NY-(1961)-1st ed (t5,sl chip dj) 45.00

RAND,AYN-For the New Intellectual-NY-(1961)-Random-1st ed (e10,dj) 60.00

RAND,AYN-Night of January 16th-NY-1968-World-1st ed (c8,f,f dj) 85.00

RAND,AYN-Philosophy:Who Needs It-Indpls-1982-Bobbs-Merrill-1st ed (h8,sl rub dj) 30.00

RAND,AYN-Romantic Manifesto-NY-1969-World-1st ed (f8,f,f dj) 75.00

RAND,AYN-Virtue of Selfishness-(NY)-(1965)-NAL-1st ed (a10,dj) 100.00

RAND,AYN-We the Living-NY-1936-Macmillan-1st ed (z2,sl soil,lacks dj) 250.00

RAND,EDWARD-All Aboard for the Lakes and Mountains-Chig-(1885)-Donohue,Henneberry-385p-col pict bds (f1,loose f.e.p.,rprd hngs) 17.50

RANDALL,DAVID A-Dukedom Large Enough-NY-(1969)-Random-lg 8vo-368p-photos-1st ed (s1,f,dj) 35.00

RANDALL,K C-Wild Hunter-NY-1951-8vo-236p-illus (m3,f,fray dj) 20.00

RANDALL,L W GAY-Footprints Along the Yellowstone-San Antonio-1961-Naylor-186p-photos-1st ed (d3,dj) 30.00

RANDALL,RICHARD N,JR.-Cloisters Bestiary-NY-1960-Metro Museum of Art-cl,col frntis,illus,prntd in two cols-1st ed (l8) 12.50

RANDALL,RUTH P-Mary Lincoln-Bost-(1953)-399p-1st ed (n3,dj wn) 22.50

RANDEL,WILLIAM P-Ku Klux Klan-Phila-(1965)-300p-illus-1st ed (n3) 20.00

RANDOLF,L-Garden Irises-Missouri-1959-Amer Iris Soc-575p-cl (x6,f,dj chip,rub) 25.00

RANDOLPH,ANSON-Leaf and Flower Pictures, & How to Make Them-NY-1859-69p-cl,7 col prtd,hand finished lithos-scarce-rvsd ed (x6,cl wn,innr hngs rnfrcd) 90.00

RANDOLPH,EDMUND-Hell Among the Yearlings-Chig-1978-Donnelley & Sons-frntis,map,illus-Lakeside Classics (ff4,sl spot cov) 15.00

RANDOLPH,ELLEN-Secret of Graytowers-1968-Avalon-1st ed (s10,dj) 12.50

RANDOLPH,JOHN-World of Wood,Field & Stream-NY-1962-8vo-177p-illus,J Groth-1st ed (m3,f,dj) 15.00

RANDOLPH,MARION-Breathe No More-NY-1940-Holt-auth 1st bk-1st ed (g4,f,dj) 25.00

RANDOLPH,PASCHAL B-Seership-Toledo-1892-Randolph Publ-sm 8vo-84p+24p ads-g brgndy cl,dec e.p.-1st ed (aa7) 50.00*

RANDOLPH,VANCE-Americans Who Thought They Were Gods-Girard-(1943)-Haldeman-Julius-24p-wrps (n1,sl dmpstnd) 15.00

RANGER,T O-Historical Study of African Religion-Berkeley-1972-U of Cal Pr-8vo-307p-cl,maps-1st ed (y5,f,sl sun dj) 37.00

RANKE,LEOPOLD VON-History of the Popes-NY-1901-Colonial Pr-3 vols,3/4 maroon lea wi mrbld bds & eps-rev ed (e8,f) 65.00

RANKIN,MELINDA-Twenty Years Among the Mexicans-Cin-1875-Chase & Hall-grn cl-Howes R64-1st ed (k8) 50.00

RANKIN,MILO W-Reminiscences of Frontier Days Including an Authentic Account of the Thornburg and Meeker Massacre-Denver-(1935)-priv prtd-4to-(7),140p-illus-rare-Howes R63aa (a7) 225.00

RANSOME,ARTHUR-Swallowdale-NY-1932-Jr Lit Guild-393p-pict cl,illus,H Carter (s3,f,dj) 35.00

RANSOME,WALLIS P-Last Steam Locomotives of British Railways-Lond-1966-191p-1st ed (n4,f,dj) 30.00

RANSOME,WALLIS P-Southern Album-Lond-1968-128p-1st ed (n4,f,dj) 20.00

RANSOME,WALLIS P-Train Ferries of Western Europe-Shepperton-1968-289p-photos,pull out map-1st ed (n4,sl tn dj) 18.00

RAPHAELIAN,H M-Signs of Life-NY-1957-Anatol Sivas-cl,illus-1st ed (n8,f,dj) 45.00

RASCOE,BURTON-Belle Starr "The Bandit Queen"-NY-1941-Random Hs-340p-illus-1st ed (dd4) 35.00

RASCOE,BURTON-Dalton Brothers-NY-1954-F Fell-251p-illus-1st ed (f9,chip dj) 30.00

RASKY,FRANK-Polar Voyages-Tor-1976-McGraw Hill Ryerson-8vo-320p-e.p. maps,illus-Explorers of the North Ser (cc7,sl chip dj) 20.00*

RASMUSSEN,STEEN E-Towns and Buildings Described in Drawings and Words-Cambridge-1969-MIT Pr-4to-203p-cl,illus-1st US ed (cc10) 30.00

RASWAN,CARL-Black Tents of Arabia-NY-1947-Creative Age-2nd prtg (j9) 45.00

RATCLIFF,J D-Yellow Magic, the Story of Penicillin-NY-1945-173p-1st ed (dd3) 30.00

RATCLIFFE,FRANCIS-Flying Fox and Drifting Sand-Lond-1938-Chatto & Windus-8vo-339p-40 photos-1st Brit ed (aa5) 17.50

RATH,IDA E-Rath Trail-Wichita-(1961)-McCormick Armstrong Co-204p-1st ed (f9,dj) 40.00

RATH,VIRGINIA-An Excellent Night for Murder-1937-CC-1st ed (s10,cov stnd,edge wn) 15.00

RATH,VIRGINIA-Death of a Lucky Lady-NY-1940-Dbldy CC-1st ed (j4,dj) 30.00

RATHBUN,M J-Grapsoid Crabs of America-1918-USNM-461p-cl,161 plts (bb3,rbnd) 65.00

RATHBUN,M J-Spider Crabs of America-1925-USNM-613p-cl,283 plts (bb3,rbnd) 65.00

RATHENAU,ERNEST-Orientals-NY-1945-J J Augustin-4to-108p-cl,photos-1st ed (t3,dj) 65.00

RATHER,LELAND-Genesis of Cancer, a Study in the History of Ideas-Balt-1978-262p-1st ed (dd3,dj) 60.00

RATIGAN,WILLIAM-Young Mister Big-Grand Rapids-1955-Eerdmans-152p-cl (z7,autg) 30.00

RATTAN,VOLNEY-Popular California Flora-SF-1892-xxviii,128p-engrvngs-8th rvsd ed (m10,sl wn) 22.00

RATTI,ABATE-Mountaineer, Now Pope Pius XI, Climbs on Alpine Peaks-Bost-1923-139p-1st US ed (p10,f) 12.00

RATTRAY,ALEX-Vancouver Island and British Columbia...-Lond-1862-viii,182p-orig cl,4 lithos,2 fldg maps,fldg tbl-Lother 185 (a7,cl sl spot,plts sl fox) 400.00

RAUFER,SISTER MARIA I-Black Robes and Indians on the Last Frontier-Milw-(1968)-Bruce Publ-489p-illus (ee4,dj) 20.00

RAULSTON,MARION C-Memories of Owen Humphrey Churchill and His Family-np-1950-priv prtd-pnk bds,frntis,photos,col plts-Herd #1864-scarce-1st ed (t7,wn,pres) 35.00

RAUM,JOHN O-History of New Jersey...-Phila-(1877)-2 vols-cl,frntis (aa6) 90.00

RAUM,JOHN O-History of the City of Trenton...-Trenton-1871-ix,448p-cl,plts,fldg map (aa6,rbnd,sl stnd pgs) 50.00

RAVENEL,HARRIOTT-Eliza Pinckney-NY-1896-Scribner-331p-cl (x6) 45.00

RAVENEL-ED.-Charleston Murders-NY-1947-Duel-8vo-216p-1st ed (b3,f,dj) 25.00

RAVIN,ABE-International Bibliography of Cardiovascular Auscultation and Phonocardiography-NY-1971-318p-1st ed (dd3) 50.00

RAVITCH,MARK-ED.-Papers of Alfred Blalock-Balt-1966-2 vols-illus-1st ed (dd3) 100.00

RAVITCH,MICHAEL-Romance of Russian Medicine-NY-1937-352p-1st ed (dd3,dj) 35.00

RAVOUX,MONSIGNOR A-Reminiscences, Memoirs and Lectures of Monsignor A Ravoux, V. G.-St.Paul-1890-Brown,Treacy-223p-Howes R75-1st ed (bb4,sl wn sp) 75.00

RAWLINGS,MARJORIE K-Cross Creek Cookery-NY-1942-2nd issue (j5,chip dj) 75.00

RAWLINGS,MARJORIE K-Cross Creek Cookery-NY-1942-Scribner's-230p-dec bds,drwngs,R Camp,Scribner's "A"-1st ed (u6) 35.00

RAWLINGS,MARJORIE K-Cross Creek-NY-1942-Scribner's-1st ed (j8,dj creased & edge wn) 60.00

RAWLINGS,MARJORIE K-Cross Creek-NY-1942-Scribners-1st ed (cc2,f,f dj) 100.00

RAWLINGS,MARJORIE K-Golden Apples-NY-1935-1st ed (k5,dj sl creased,sp wn) 95.00

RAWLINGS,MARJORIE K-Marjorie Rawlings Reader-NY-1956-Scribner's-1st ed (z3,sl chip dj) 20.00

RAWLINGS,MARJORIE K-Secret River-NY-1955-Scribner's-8vo-unpgd-tan pict cl,illus by L Weisgard-1st ed("A") (nn8,tape rprd dj) 50.00

RAWLINGS,MARJORIE K-Sojourner-NY-1953-1st ed (s5,dj sl chip & sl tn) 25.00

RAWLINGS,MARJORIE K-Sojourner-NY-1953-Scribner's-1st ed (c10,dj) 30.00

RAWLINGS,MARJORIE K-Yearling-NY-1938-Scribner's-428p-pict cl,illus,E Shenton-1st ed (r3,dj) 45.00

RAWNSLEY,KENNETH-Health Giving Brews-Lond-(1955)-Thorsons Publ-79p-1st ed (o6,dj) 20.00

RAWSON,CLAYTON-Death From a Top Hat-NY-1938-Putnam-1st ed (f4) 35.00

RAWSON,CLAYTON-No Coffin for the Corpse-Lond-1972-Stacey-1st Brit ed (r4,vf,dj) 25.00

RAWSON,PHILIP S-Indian Painting-Paris/NY-1961-Tisne/Universe-169p-beige cl,col tip in plts (gg6) 35.00

RAWSTORNE,LAWRENCE-Gamonia-Phila-1930-4to-256p-15 col plts (m3,f) 25.00

RAY,CYRIL-ED.-Gourmet's Companion-Lond-1963-Eyre & Spottiswoode-503p-red cl-1st ed (q8,dj) 17.50

RAY,DIXIE LEE-ED.-Marine Boring and Fouling Organisms-Seattle-1959-U of Wash Pr-8vo-536p-illus-1st ed (dd5,dj sl tn,chip) 35.00

RAY,DOROTHY J-Artists of the Tundra & the Sea-1961-U of Wash-170p-drwngs,photos,map-1st ed (u8,dj) 35.00

RAY,DOROTHY J-Eskimo Art-Seattle-1977-U of Wash Pr-4to-xi,298p-blu cl,dec e.p.,305 illus-1st ed (oo1,dj) 95.00

RAY,JOSEPH-New Elementary Algebra-NY,Cin,Chig-(1866)-Amer Bk Co-240p-cl wi lea sp (k1) 15.00

RAY,JOSEPH-Ray's New Higher Arithmetic-NY,Cin,Chig-(1880)-Amer Bk Co-408p-lea-bkd cl-rvsd ed (b1) 15.00

RAY,JOSEPH-Three Thousand Test Examples in Arithmetic-Cin,NY-(1862)-Wilson,Hinkle-136p-bds-Electrotype ed (k1,wn) 17.50

RAY,MICHELE-Two Shores of Hell-NY-1968-1st ed (v9,dj) 45.00

RAY,P C-Surrealist Movement in England-Ithaca-1971-Cornell UP-1st ed (h10,dj) 30.00

RAY,TOM-Yellowstone Red-(1948)-Dorrance-1st ed (r8,dj,pres) 15.00

RAY,WORTH S-Down in the Cross Timbers-Austin-(1947)-Worth S Ray-160p-illus by auth-ltd to 500c-Six Guns #1822-1st ed (dd4) 75.00

RAY-JONES,TONY-Day Off-Bost-1974-NYGS-144p-wrps,120 photos-1st Amer ed (cc9,f) 40.00

RAYBOLD,GEORGE A-Reminiscences of Methodism in West Jersey-NY-1849-202,(6)p-cl (aa6) 85.00

RAYFIELD,D-Dream of Lhasa-Lond-1976-221p-1st ed (a4,f,dj) 35.00

RAYMOND,ALEX-Flash Gordon in the Caverns of Mongo-NY-(1936)-G&D-frntis,Beebe-pict dj-1st ed (b5,fray cor,dj sl wn,chip) 200.00

RAYMOND,DANIEL-Elements of Constitutional Law-Cin-1845-J A James-120p-bds (c1,sp wn,jnts crckng) 40.00

RAYMOND,DORA N-Captain Lee Hall of Texas-Norman-(1940)-U of Okla Pr-350p-illus-1st ed (f9,sl spot,dj rprd,chip) 75.00

RAYMOND,STEVE-Kamloops-NY-1971-4to-209p+biblio & index-illus-scarce-1st ed (m3,vf,dj) 70.00

RAYMOND,STEVE-Year of the Angler-NY-1973-4to-205p-illus,D Whitlock-1st ed (m3,vf,sl soil dj) 27.50

RAYMOND,W-Raymond's Vacation Excursions-Bost-1884-Raymond-80p-promo bklt (b4) 40.00

RAYNE,MRS M L-What Can a Woman Do-Petersburgh-(1893)-Eagle Publ-528;(24)p-cl (d1) 20.00

RAYNE,MRS. M L-Against Fate-Chig-1876-Keen,Cooke-Lakeside Pr-8vo-251p-publ cl-Wright III,4452-1st ed (w6,dust faded cl) 65.00

RAYNER,JOHN A-First Century of Piqua, Ohio...-Piqua-1916-Magee Bros-372p-cl (n1) 32.50

RCA INSTITUTES-Television, Vol.I-1936-452p-wrps,100 photos,320 illus-1st ed (h6,f) 35.00

RCA VICTOR COMPANY-RCA Victor Service Notes for 1923 to 1928-1928-280p-unabridged-1st ed (h6) 65.00

RCA-Radio at Ultra High Frequencies-NY-1940-RCA Inst Tech Pr-viii+448p,blu wrps,illus-1st ed (j2) 35.00

READ,HERBERT-English Stained Glass-1973-Kraus Reprint Co-260p-illus-facs of orig 1926 ed (cc8) 75.00

READ,HERBERT-In Retreat-Lond-1925-Hogarth Pr-43p-wrps(designed by V Bell)-Hogarth Essays,1st Ser.,No.6-Woolmer 74-1st ed (nn4) 60.00

READ,MISS-Miss Clare Remembers-1963-Houghton-1st US ed (kk6,f,dj) 25.00

READ,MISS-Miss Read's Country Cooking-Lond-(1969)-M Joseph-223p-orng cl,illus-1st Brit ed (q8,dj) 18.50

READ,MISS-Over the Gate-1965-Houghton-1st US ed (kk6,f,dj) 25.00

READ,OPIE-An Arkansas Planter-1896-R,M-cov & illus,W Denslow-1st ed (x2) 58.00

READ,OPIE-An Arkansas Planter-Chig,NY-(1896)-Rand,McNally-illus,W W Denslow & I Morgan-pic bndg wi gld lettering-1st ed (e10) 75.00

READ,STANLEY E-Ardent Angler & Artist-Vancouver-1977-U of Brit Col-ltd to 2000c,nbrd (nn5,vf) 30.00

READ,STANLEY-Tommy Brayshaw-1977-Univ of B.C. Pr-8vo-94p-ltd to 2000c,nbrd,illus (m3,as new) 35.00

READER'S DIGEST-Book of British Birds-Lond-1969-4to-471,(1)p-cl,col drwngs,maps (y8) 30.00

REAGAN,ROCKY-Rocky's Yarns-S.A.-1973-Naylor-160p-illus-1st ed (a9,dj) 30.00

REAL KRUGER AND THE TRANSVAAL-NY-1900-218p-pict brwn cl,fldg map-1st ed (b7,fade,soil) 45.00

REAMAN,G ELMORE-Trail of the Huguenots in Europe, the U.S., So Africa and Canada-Tor-1963-T Allen-318p-frntis port,illus,map(lining papers) (k10,dj) 30.00*

REAUMUR,R A F-Memoirs on Steel and Iron-Chig-(1956)-Univ of Chig-xxxvi+396p-brwn cl,17 plts-1st ed (d2,f,dj) 40.00

REBELLION-New Orleans-1866-Commercial Prnt-8vo-231p-3/4 lea over cl,port-1st ed (p1) 90.00

REBOK,HORACE M-Last of the Mus Qua Kies and the Indian Congress 1898-Dayton-1900-70p-wrps,photos-scarce (d1,sl spot wrps) 35.00

REBUFFAT,GASTON-Between Heaven & Earth-Lond-1965-183p-104 b&w & 8p col plts-1st Brit ed (o10,f,dj) 50.00

REBUFFAT,GASTON-Mont Blanc Massif, the 100 Finest Routes-NY-1975-1st US ed (a4,f,dj) 120.00

REBUFFAT,GASTON-On Snow & Rock & Ice-Lond-1971-lg 8vo-187p-56 col & 20 b&w photos (o10,f,pasted on dj) 45.00

REBUFFAT,GASTON-Starlight & Storm-NY-1957-189p-1st US ed (p10,f,dj) 50.00

RECENT POLAR VOYAGES-Lond-1877-T Nelson & Sons-orig g dec cl sp & bds,wood engrvngs,plts,fldg col map (bb7) 50.00*

RECHY,JOHN-City of Night-NY-1963-Grove-auth 1st bk-1st ed (g8,f,dj) 55.00

RECHY,JOHN-Fourth Angel-1973-Viking-1st ed (kk6,f,sl tn dj) 20.00

RECHY,JOHN-Numbers-NY-1967-Grove-1st ed (x9,f,dj) 15.00

RECHY,JOHN-This Day's Death-NY-1969-Grove-1st ed (y1,f,sl soil dj) 25.00

RECINOS,ADRIAN-Annals of the Cakchiquels + Title of the Lord of Totonicapan-Norman-1953-U of Okla Pr-8vo-grn cl-2nd prtg (mm1,f,f dj) 30.00

RECK,FRANKLIN M-On Time-1948-184p-1st ed (n4,dj) 12.00

RECTOR,FRANK-Health and Medical Service in American Prisons and Reformatories-NY-1929-282p-1st ed (dd3) 50.00

RED RIVER VALLEY-History of the...Past and Present...-Grand Forks-1909-Herald Prtg-2 vols-3/4 lea,illus (bb4) 150.00

RED,GEORGE P-Medicine Man in Texas-Houston-1930-Standard P&L-photos-1st ed (b4) 150.00

REDDICK,DAVID V-Fishing is a Cinch-Tor-1950-M&S-1st ed (pp8,dj) 35.00*

REDDICK,DAVID-Mighty Muskellunge-NY-1962-8vo-206p-illus,G Goss-1st ed (m3,f,fray dj) 27.50

REDDING,CYRUS-History and Description of Modern Wines-Lond-1851-Henry G Bohn-440p-3/4 lea,mrbld bds,frntis,etchings-3rd ed wi addtns & corrections (n6,rbnd) 225.00

REDFORD,POLLY-Billion Dollar Sandbar-NY-1970-Dutton-8vo-306p-1st ed (gg5,dj) 12.50

REDFORD,ROBERT-Outlaw Trail-NY-1978-G&D-4to-222p-cl-1st ed (mm7,f,dj) 65.00

REDINGER,DAVID H-Story of Big Creek-LA-1949-Angelus Pr-182p-photos-(So Cal Edison Co) (ff8) 38.00

REDMOND,E G-Bank Thieves-Chig-nd-97p-wrps,illus (t7,3p loose,sp rprd) 45.00

REDMOND,OREGON-Redmond-nd(ca.1912)-Redmond Comm Club-32p-wrps,illus (f1) 15.00

REDOUTE,P J-Roses-(1978)-Miller Graphic-sm 4to-wht cl,57 wtrcol plts (x5,dj) 45.00

REECE,EILEEN-French Farmhouse Kitchen-Lond-(1979)-Treasure Pr-4to-175p-pict bds,col plts-New ed (q8,dj) 16.50

REECE,MAYNARD-Fish & Fishing-Des Moines-1963-4to-224p-illus,auth-1st ed (m3,vf,dj) 15.00

REED BOOKS-Darwin's Forgotten World-1978-4to-176p-189 col plts,photos-1st ed (bb3,f,dj) 15.00

REED,A H-Gumdiggers-Wellington-(1972)-Reed-8vo-193p-24p illus-ltd to 2500c,nbrd,autg-1st ed (gg5,dj) 30.00

REED,ANN-Ladies Who Lunch-1972-Scribners-174p-prpl cl,drwngs-1st ed (q8,dj) 15.00

REED,ANNA Y-Seattle Children in School and In Industry...-Seattle-1915-Board of Schl Dirctrs-sm 8vo-103p-wrps,scarce (t1) 50.00

REED,BRIAN-Locomotives in Profile: Volume Two-GC-1972-288p-1st Amer ed (n4,f,dj) 22.00

REED,C A-North American Bird Eggs-1904-Dbldy,Page-356p-photos-1st ed (bb3,sl soil cov) 55.00

REED,C A-North American Birds Eggs-NY-1965(1904)-8vo-372p-wrps,photos-rvsd ed (y8) 12.50

REED,DAVID-Up Front in Vietnam-NY-(1967)-Funk & Wagnalls-1st ed (ff3,dj) 55.00

REED,EARL H-Dune Country-NY-1916-J Lane-288p-60 illus-1st ed (o2,sl wn,cors rub) 37.50

REED,ELIOT-Sky Tip-NY-1950-Dbldy-(precedes Brit ed)-1st ed (gg8,pgs brwng,dj) 45.00

REED,H H,JR.-Golden City-GC-1959-illus-1st ed (h10,dj) 40.00

REED,HENRY M-A B Frost Book-Rutland-1967-folio-149p-illus,Frost-1st ed (m3,vf,dj) 180.00

REED,HENRY-Map of Verona and Other Poems-NY-(1947)-Reynal & Hitchcock-1st Amer ed (w1,f,f dj) 75.00

REED,ISHMAEL-Conjure-Amherst-1972-U of Mass Pr-1st ed (v5,f,sl tn dj) 25.00

REED,ISHMAEL-Flight to Canada-NY-(1976)-1st ed (k5,as new in dj) 20.00

REED,ISHMAEL-Free Lance Pallbearers-GC-1967-Dbldy-auth 1st bk-1st ed (v5,f,dj) 85.00

REED,ISHMAEL-Last Days of Louisiana Red-NY-(1974)-Random-1st ed (b5,dj) 20.00

REED,JOHN F-Campaign to Valley Forge: July 1,1777 to December 19,1777-Phila-(1965)-U of Penn Pr-448p-beige cl,maps,illus-1st ed (b2) 20.00

REED,JOHN-Ten Days That Shook the World-NY-1919-Boni & Liveright-8vo-xxiv,372p-grn cl,illus-1st ed (u1) 150.00

REED,LIEUT.HUGH T-Cadet Life at West Point-Chig-(1896)-publ by auth-236+xx pgs+ads,maroon cl,plts-1st ed (h2,sl rub) 25.00

REED,R D-Geology of California-1933-Amer Assn Pet Geol-355p-60 illus (bb3,cov stns) 25.00

REED,ROBERT C-Train Wrecks-Seattle-1968-183p-1st ed (n4,f,f dj) 27.50

REED,S B-House Plans for Everybody-NY-1882-Orange Judd-243p-cl-scarce (x6,cl rub,stnd) 85.00

REED,S G-History of the Texas Railroads...-Houston-1941-822p-cl-ltd ed,nbrd,autg-1st ed (n10,sp soil,cov wn) 200.00

REED,WALT-ED-Illustrator in America 1900 to 60's-NY-1966-illus-1st ed (h10,dj) 85.00

REED,WALT-Harold O. Schmidt Draws and Paints the Old West-Flagstaff-1972-Northland Pr-4to-xvii+230p-cl,50 col & 170 b&w illus-1st ed so stated (z4,dj sl rub & tn) 50.00

REED,WALTER-Propagation of Yellow Fever Based on Recent Researches-Balt-1901-priv prtd-31p-wrps-scarce-1st ed (dd3) 125.00

REED,WILLIAM-Phantom of the Poles-NY-1906-W S Rockey-8vo-281p-grn cl,21 illus-Ricks p.181 (oo1,hngs weak,cov wn & soil) 125.00

REEDER,COL RED-Northern Generals-NY-1964-DS&P-205p-illus,maps-1st ed (o7,dj) 10.00

REEMAN,DOUGLAS-Prayer for the Ship-NY-1973-Putnam's-1st Amer ed (z2,f,f dj) 20.00

REEMAN,DOUGLAS-Surface with Daring-NY-1977-Putnam's-1st Amer ed (z2,f,dj) 20.00

REEMAN,DOUGLAS-To Risks Unknown-NY-1970-Putnam's-1st Amer ed (z2,f,f dj) 30.00

REES,ALFRED-Ianto the Fisherman & Other Sketches of Country Life-Lond-1904-8vo-349p-photos,illus (m3) 25.00

REES,ALWYN-Celtic Heritage-NY-1961-Grove Pr-cl,illus-1st prtg (o8,dj) 29.00

REES,CLAIR-Matching the Gun to the Game-NJ-1982-4to-302p-photos-1st ed (m3,vf,dj) 20.00

REES,L E RUUTZ-Personal Narrative of the Siege of Lucknow-Lond-1858-380p-red cl,frntis,fldg map-1st ed (b7) 175.00

REESE,ALICE-Hurrah for America-Dayton-1898-U B Publ Hs-204p-cl (c1) 25.00

REESE,M M-Royal Office of Master of the Horse-Lond-1976-Threshold-4to (j9,dj) 65.00

REESE,REV JOHN B-Some Pioneers & Pilgrims on the Prairies of Dakota-Mitchell-1920-94,(1)p-tan cl-rare (b6,stnd cl) 25.00

REESE,TERENCE-Story of an Accusation-NY-(1966)-S&S-8vo-246p-1st ed (aa5,dj) 15.00

REEVE,A B-Dream Doctor-1915-Van Rees Pr-1st ed (x7) 22.00

REEVE,ARTHUR B-Guy Garrick-NY-1914-Hearst-1st ed (f4) 10.00

REEVE,BRYANT-Flying Saucer Pilgrimage-1957-Amherst Pr-8vo-304p-illus-1st ed (cc7,chip dj) 25.00*

REEVE,FRANK D-History of New Mexico-NY-(1961)-Lewis Hist Publ-3 vols-photos-1st ed (v7,f) 275.00

REEVE,MARY-Every Woman's Flower Garden-Lond-1915-Jenkins-353p-cl,5 tip in col plts (x6) 20.00

REEVES,IRA L-A B C of Rifle,Revolver & Pistol Shooting-KC-1913-16mo-198p-photos,illus (m3) 25.00

REEVES,J H-Orange County Stud Book-NY-1880-Tuttle-1st ed (h9) 45.00

REFUGE-Lond-1801-Whittingham for Button-12mo-255p-calf,engrvd frntis-rare-4th ed (w6,weak hngs) 235.00

REGLER,GUSTAV-Owl of Minerva-NY-1959-FS&C-375p-1st ed (r1,dj chip,tn) 18.00

REGNERY,HENRY-Memoirs of a Dissident Publisher-NY-(1979)-HBJ-1st ed (w1,f,f dj) 15.00

REGULATIONS FOR THE INSTRUCTION,FORMATIONS, AND MOVEMENTS OF THE CAVALRY-Lond-1st Jan,1844-rvsd & corrected ed (j9) 95.00

REGULATORS OF NORTHERN INDIANA-HISTORY OF...-Indpls-1859-Indpls Journal Co,Prntrs-67p-prntd wrps (c1,sm stns frnt wrp,wn sp) 850.00

REHMANN,ELSA-Small Place-NY-1918-Putnam's-164p-cl (x6,cl soil) 20.00

REHOR,JOHN-Nickel Plate Story-1978-Kalmbach-4to-483p-illus-5th prtg (nn7,sl wn dj) 69.00

REICHARD,GLADYS A-Analysis of Coeur D'Alene Indian Myths-Phila-1947-Amer Folklore Soc-cl-1st ed (o8,sp lettrng wn) 27.50

REICHARD,GLADYS A-Navajo Shepherd and Weaver-NY-(1936)-215p-burlap cl,photos-1st ed (v7,pres) 100.00

REICHARD,GLADYS A-Spider Woman-NY-1934-MacMillan-photos(1 col)-1st ed (b4,wn & soil cov,sl fox) 95.00

REICHENBACH,WILLIAM-Sixguns & Bullseyes-Onslow Cnty-1936-12mo-145p-1st ed (m3) 15.00

REICHERT,MILTON S-ED.-Fishning Guide to the Northwest-Seattle-1935-8vo-192p-wrps,illus (m3,f) 30.00

REICHLER,JOE-Baseball's Unforgettable Games-1960-Ronald-1st ed (ff2,dj) 20.00

REICHLER,JOE-ED.-Baseball Encyclopedia-1969-MacMillan-1st ed (ff2,f,box) 30.00

REICHLER,JOE-ED.-Baseball Encyclopedia-1969-MacMillan-1st ed (s8,f,box) 45.00

REICHLER,JOE-ED.-Game and the Glory-1976-Prentice hall-1st ed (p7,dj) 25.00

REICHLER,JOE-ED.-Game and the Glory-1976-Prentice Hall-photos(incl col)-1st ed (s8,f,dj) 30.00

REICHLER,JOE-ED.-World Series, 75th Anniversary-1978-S&S-1st ed (r7,f,dj) 22.50

REID,ACE-More Cowpokes-San Antonio-(1960)-Naylor-56p-1st ed (t8) 20.00

REID,AGNES J-Letters of Long Ago-SLC-(1973)-93p-illus (r8,f,dj) 35.00

REID,FORREST-Private Road-Lond-(1940)-Faber-cl-1st ed (z8,f) 25.00

REID,FORREST-Tom Barber-NY-(1955)-Pantheon-1st ed (z8,f,fray dj) 20.00

REID,H-Extra South-Susquehanna-1964-144p-ltd to 1000c,nbrd-1st ed (n4,f,dj) 25.00

REID,H-Virginian Railway-1961-Kalmbach-4to-208p-illus,map (nn7,dj) 31.00

REID,JOHN H-Adopted by the United States-np-1960(on cover)-166p-blu cl,illus (b6,f) 10.00

REID,KENNETH-Louis C Rosenberg-Lond,NY-(1930)-lg 4to-vol.10 of American Etchers ser,12 etchngs-1st ed (t1,f,dj) 45.00

REID,MAYNE-Rifle Rangers-NY-1899-Hurst-sm 8vo-432p-cl,illus-1st ed (ff8,cov sl bent) 95.00

REID,S G-Birds of Bermuda-Wash-1884-8vo-(163-)279p-wrps (y8,sp chip) 35.00

REID,WEMYSS-William Black, Novelist-NY-1902-Harper-1st ed (hh5) 15.00

REID,WILLIAM J-Through Unexplored Asia-Bost-1899-Dana Estes-499p-grn dec cl,g titles,illus,fldg pckt map-1st ed (gg6) 150.00

REIGER,BARBARA-Zane Grey Cookbook-(1976)-Prentice Hall-lg 8vo-238p-tan cl,20p photos-1st prtg (q8,dj) 20.00

REIGER,GEORGE-ED.-Fishing with McClane-Englewood Cliffs-1975-8vo-332p-photos,illus (m3,vf,dj) 14.00

REIGER,GEORGE-ED.-Zane Grey, Outsdoorsman-Englewood Cliffs-(1972)-349p-cl,illus-later prtg (z1,dj) 30.00

REIGER,GEORGE-Profiles in Salt Water Fishing-NY-1973-Prentice Hall-qto-photos-1st ed (cc2,f,dj) 50.00

REIGER,GEORGE-Zane Grey Cookbook-NJ-1976-4to-239p-photos-1st ed (m3,vf,dj) 40.00

REIGER,J I-American Sportsman & the Origins of Conservation-1975-Winchester-316p-photos (ee3,f,dj) 10.00

REIK,THEODOR-Ritual Psycho Analytic Studies-Lond-1931-Hogarth/Inst Psycho An-lg 8vo-367p-Int'l Psycho Analytical Libr,No.19-1st Brit ed (s1,vf,dj) 175.00

REIK,THEODOR-Unknown Murderer-Lond-1936-Hogarth Pr-260p-ltd to 1100c,grn cl-Woolmer 392-1st ed (j2,dj) 75.00

REILLY,ANN-Park's Success with Seeds-Greenwood-(1978)-364p-col photos (m10,wn dj) 18.00

REILLY,EDGAR M,JR.-Audubon Illustrated Handbook of American Birds-NY-1968-McGraw Hill-524p-400 photos(incl 35 col),drwngs (b9,dj) 20.00

REILLY,HELEN-Certain Sleep-1961-Random Hs-1st ed (s10,dj) 12.50

REILLY,HELEN-Day She Died-NY-(1962)-Random-1st ed (k3,dj sl rub & tn) 15.00

REILLY,HELEN-Ding Dong Bell-NY-1958-Random-1st ed (f4,dj) 12.50

REILLY,HELEN-Lineup-NY-1934-Dbldy CC-1st ed (h4) 10.00

REILLY,HELEN-Man with the Painted Head-NY-1931-Farrar-1st ed (k4) 15.00

REILLY,HELEN-Not Me, Inspector-NY-1959-Random-1st ed (f4,f,dj) 15.00

REILLY,HELEN-Tell Her It's Murder-NY-1954-Random-1st ed (j4,f,sl wn dj) 15.00

REIMANN,CHARLES-Game Warden & the Poachers-Ann Arbor-1959-8vo-196p-illus (m3,f) 17.50

REIMANN,LEWIS C-Hurley, Still No Angel-Ann Arbor-(1954)-Northwoods Publ-(iv)+124p,red cl,illus-1st ed (h2,dj) 20.00

REINFELDER,AL-Bait Tail Fishing-S Brunswick-1969-8vo-168p-illus (m3,f,dj) 15.00

REINHARDT,RICHARD-Out West on the Overland Train-Palo Alto-1967-207p-1st ed (n4,f,dj) 27.50

REINHARDT,RICHARD-Out West on the Overland Train-Palo Alto-1967-Amer West Publ-4to-207p-cl,illus (z4,sl wn) 12.50

REINHART,C S-History of the Supreme Court of the State of Washington-np-nd(ca.1931)-8vo-148p-flex maroon buckram,photos-Smith#8598 (t1) 50.00

RELANDER,CLICK-Drummers and Dreamers-1956-Caxton-345p-photos-1st ed (d3,dj) 75.00

RELANDER,CLICK-Drummers and Dreamers-Caldwell-1956-345p-illus-Tweney #63-scarce-1st ed (f7,f,dj,autg) 225.00

RELANDER,CLICK-Strangers on the Land-Yakima-1962-100p-wrps,illus-1st ed (h7) 25.00

REMARQUE,ERICH-All Quiet on the Western Front-Bost-1929-Little,Brown-1st Amer ed (ee2,sl chip dj) 100.00

REMARQUE,ERICH-Flotsam-Bost-1941-Little,Brown-1st US ed (x1,sl wn dj) 40.00

REMARQUE,ERICH-Road Back-1931-Little,Brown-wht dj-1st Amer ed (x2,f dj) 60.00

REMARQUE,ERICH-Road Back-Bost-1931-Little,Brown-1st Amer ed (x1,sl wn dj) 50.00

REMARQUE,ERICH-Time to Love and a Time to Die-NY-1954-HB-1st ed (x1,dj) 25.00

REMAULT,J EDWARDS-Car Hook Tragedy-Phila-1873-Barclay-prtd wrps,3 fldg plts,illus (ff7,sl wn) 135.00

REMINGTON,FREDERIC-Collected Writings of...-NY-1979-Dbldy-649p-illus (ee4,rprd dj) 25.00

REMINGTON,FREDERIC-Crooked Trails-NY-1898-Harper & Bros-150p-pict cl,illus by auth-Howes R203-1st ed (dd4,spot cov) 150.00

REMINGTON,FREDERIC-Done in the Open-NY-1903-Collier-folio-drwngs,auth (z4,fr hng cracked,cov wn,rub) 160.00

REMINGTON,FREDERIC-Frederic Remington's Own West-NY-1960-Dial-4to-254p-cl,illus(1 col) by auth-1st ed (z4,sl wn dj) 25.00

REMINGTON,FREDERIC-Men With the Bark On-NY-1900-Harper-pict bds-BAL 16495-1st ed,1st iss (ee2,few spot pgs) 165.00

REMINGTON,FREDERIC-Pony Tracks-Norman-(1961)-176p-bds,illus by auth-1st prntg thus (n1,f,dj) 12.50

REMINGTON,FREDERIC-Pony Tracks-NY-1895-266p-col pict cl,illus-auth 1st bk-1st ed (jj1,sl wn & spot) 400.00

REMINGTON,FREDERIC-Pony Tracks-NY-1895-Harper-illus,auth 1st bk-1st ed (aa10) 500.00

REMINGTON,FREDERICK-Done in the Open-NY-1902-Collier-lg folio-drwngs-early ed (b4) 200.00

REMINGTON,FREDRIC-Done in the Open-NY-1902-Collier & Sons-"Frederic" spelled wi "k" on cov-1st ed (l9,sl soil & wn) 300.00

REMISE,J-Golden Age of Toys-Lausanne-1967-586 illus(incl col) (h10,sl tn dj) 125.00

REMLAP,L T-ED.-Life of General U.S. Grant-Chig-1885-Fairbanks & Palmer-766p-illus,plts,ports,map-Nevin II,80-1st ed (ee4) 35.00

REMLEY,DAVID A-Crooked Road-(1976)-McGraw Hill-251p-illus-1st ed (u8,dj) 15.00

REMY,NICOLAS-Demonolatry-Lond-1930-John Rodker,Publ-(xliv)+188p-prchmnt bkd bds-scarce-1st ed in Engl (y9) 150.00

RENAULT,MARY-Bull From the Sea-NY-1962-Pantheon-1st ed (v5,f,f dj) 40.00

RENAULT,MARY-Fire From Heaven-NY-1969-Pantheon-1st US ed (y1,f,dj) 30.00

RENAULT,MARY-Last of the Wine-NY-1956-Pantheon-1st ed (v5,f,dj) 50.00

RENAULT,MARY-Mask of Apollo-NY-1966-Pantheon-1st US ed (y1,f,dj) 30.00

RENDELL,RUTH-Lake of Darkness-Lond-1980-Hutchinson-1st ed (s4,dj) 32.50

RENDELL,RUTH-Master of the Moor-NY-1982-Pantheon-1st US ed (g4,f,dj) 12.50

RENDELL,RUTH-Wolf to the Slaughter-NY-1967-Dbldy CC-1st US ed (h4,dj) 25.00

RENEAU,J-Colorado's Biggest Bucks & Bulls-CO-1983-275p-photos (ee3,vf) 25.00

RENFREW,JANE M-Palaeoethnobotany-NY-1973-lg 8vo-xviii,248p-48 plts (x5,sl wn dj) 30.00

RENICK,WILLIAM-Memoirs, Correspondence and Reminiscences of...-Circleville-1880-Union-Herald-115p+sm erratum slip-cl-Rampaging Herd 1879-rare (n1,sm spot rear cov) 600.00

RENNER,FREDERIC G-Charles M Russell-Austin-1966-U of Tex Pr-sm folio-148p-col & b&w plts-1st ed (nn6,sl wn dj) 75.00

RENNER,FREDERIC-Charles Marion Russell Greatest of All Western Artists-Wash D.C.-1968-25p-wrps,illus-Potomac Corral,Westerners #2-1st ed (c7,f) 35.00

RENNIE,JAMES-Alphabet of Angling-Lond-1833-16mo-138p-orig bndg,illus-rare-1st ed (m3) 65.00

RENOIR,JEAN-My Life and My Films-NY-1974-illus-1st ed (g5,as new in dj) 25.00

RENOWNED PLACES IN THE UNITED STATES-np-nd(1880s?)-14p views,fldg style,bds (o1,sp wn) 17.50

RENSCH,H E-Historic Spots in California-Stanford-(1933)-Stanford U Pr-597p-map-Six Guns 1838-1st ed (gg4) 35.00

RENWICK GALLERY-Boxes and Bowls-Wash D.C.-1974-4to-93p-wrps,photos-1st ed (c7) 40.00

RENWICK,JAMES-Syllabus of Lectures on Chemistry-NY-1831-55p-wrps-1st ed (d2,sl wn,fox) 45.00

RENZ,LOUIS T-History of the Northern Pacific Railroad-Fairfield-1980-Ye Galleon Pr-288p-map e.p.,illus (ee4) 35.00

REPLINGER,JOHN G-Jewelry Repairer's Handbook-Peoria-1914-Bradley Polytech Inst-102p+6p appndx+1p ad (u5) 20.00

REPORT ON INDIANS TAXED AND INDIANS NOT TAXED IN THE UNITED STATES...AT THE ELEVENTH CENSUS-Wash-1894-GPO-4to-683p-orig blk cl,25 fldg maps,over 150 photos plts,col chromolith plts-1st ed (v1) 850.00

REPP,ED EARL-Radium Pool-LA-1949-Fantasy Publ-1st ed (k3,sl soil,dj wn) 15.00

REPPLIER,AGNES-Americans and Others-Bost,NY-(1912)-297,(1)p-cl (n1) 15.00

REPS,JOHN W-Making of Urban America-1965-Princeton U Pr-oblng 4to-xv,(1),574p-cl,illus,maps,plans (pp7,dj) 125.00

REPS,PAUL-Zen Flesh,Zen Bones-Rutland-1958-Tuttle-cl,publ box,illus-2nd prtg (l8,box) 15.00

REQUA,R S-Old World Inspiration for American Architecture-LA-1929-folio-144 plts,all illus (h10) 225.00

RESTANY,PIERRE-Chryssa-NY-1977-Abrams-4to-274p-blu cl,illus(incl col & fldg) (r10,f dj) 50.00

REUSSILLE,LEON-Steam Vessels Built in Old Monmouth, 1841 to 1894-(np)-(1975)-4to-(10),160,(1)p-cl,illus (aa6) 40.00

REUSSWIG,WILLIAM-Picture Report of the Custer Fight-(1967)-Hastings-lg 8vo-184p-illus,e.p. maps-1st ed (r8) 18.00

REVELL,LOUISA-See Rome and Die-NY-1957-Macmillan-1st ed (f4,dj) 25.00

REVI,A C-American Cut and Engraved Glass-1965-Schiffer Publ-illus-8th ed (cc8,f,dj) 35.00

REVI,A C-Nineteenth Century Glass-1967-Thos Nelson & Sons-270p-illus (cc8,dj) 35.00

REXROTH,KENNETH-An Autobiographical Novel-1966-Dbldy-1st ed (x2,f,sl tn dj) 37.00

REXROTH,KENNETH-Beyond the Mountains-1951-New Directions-1st ed (kk6,dj) 60.00

REXROTH,KENNETH-Excerpts from a Life-Santa Barbara-1981-Conjunctions-8vo-cl,frntis photo by Man Ray-ltd to 350c,auth-1st ed (jj8,vf,dj) 75.00

REXROTH,KENNETH-Phoenix and the Tortoise-1944-New Directions-1st ed (r2,f,dj sl sun,tn) 125.00

REXROTH,KENNETH-Signature of All Things-(NY)-(1950)-New Directions-cl & dec bds-1st ed (x10,f,dj sl tn & chip) 60.00

REYMOND,LIZELLE-Dedicated-NY-(1953)-John Day-8vo-374p-1st ed (gg5,dj) 15.00

REYNER,J H-Gurdjieff in Action-Lond-1980-Allen & Unwin-cl-1st ed (n8,as new in dj) 20.00

REYNOLDS,BARRIE-Magic Divination and Witchcraft among the Barotse of Northern Rhodesia-Berkeley-1963-U of Cal Pr-181p-1st Amer ed (y9) 22.50

REYNOLDS,CHARLES B-Standard Guide St.Augustine...-St.Augustine-(1890)-E H Reynolds-91p+ads-pict wrps,illus,4 fld-out views (b1,sl wn) 20.00

REYNOLDS,F J-ED.-Marvels of 1924-NY-1925-sm 8vo-viii,184p-cl,col frntis,8p plts-1st ed (s2) 25.00

REYNOLDS,G W-Aloes of South Africa-Johannesburg-1950-520p-77 col plts,maps (bb3,sl wn cov) 125.00

REYNOLDS,HELEN B-Gold, Rawhide and Iron-Palo Alto-(1955)-Pacific Bks-191p-illus-1st ed (gg4,dj) 25.00

REYNOLDS,J RUSSELL-Epilepsy-Chig-1981-360p-(facs of 1861 ed) (dd3) 50.00

REYNOLDS,JAMES-Fabulous Spain-NY-(1953)-Putnam-8vo-319p-illus-1st ed (bb5,f,dj) 20.00

REYNOLDS,JOHN E-In French Creek Valley-Meadville-1938-Crawford Cnty Hist Soc-xiv+352p-red cl,plts-1st ed (mm10) 25.00

REYNOLDS,JOHN N-Twin Hells...-Chig-1890-Bee Publ-331p-cl,illus-Guns #1840-1st ed (w3) 35.00

REYNOLDS,W F R-Fly & Minnow-Lond-1930-4to-156p-illus (m3) 25.00

REZANOV,NIKOLAI P-Rezanov Reconnoiters California, 1806-SF-1972-Bk Club of Cal-xix,map,74p-illus,plain papr dj,one of 450c,orig mailing pcs laid in (mm1,f,dj drknd & sl soil) 115.00

REZNIKOFF,CHARLES-Nine Plays-NY-1927-Auth-1st ed (v5,f,dj) 40.00

RHEAD,L-Fisherman's Lures & Game Fish Food-NY-1920-186p-pict cl,plts (incl col) (mm2) 27.50

RHEAD,LOUIS-Bait Angling for Common Fishes-NY-1907-8vo-152p-illus,auth-1st ed (m3) 20.00

RHEES,WILLIAM-Smithsonian Institution Documents Relative to its Origin and History-Wash-1901-2 vols-1st ed (dd3) 100.00

RHEIMS,MAURICE-Flowering of Art Nouveau-NY-(1966)-Abrams-sm folio-450p-dec cl,tip in col illus-1st Amer ed (ll9) 75.00

RHOADS,SAMUEL N-Mammals of Pennsylvania and New Jersey-Phila-1903-(2),266p-cl,plts,col map (aa6) 50.00

RHODE,IRMA-Viennese Cookbook-NY-1951-Wyn-360p-tan cl-1st ed (q8,edgewn dj) 15.00

RHODE,J-Death in Harley Street-1946-DM-1st ed (x7,f,dj) 45.00

RHODE,JOHN-Body Unidentified-1938-Dodd-1st Amer ed (s10) 17.50

RHODE,JOHN-Claverton Affair-1933-Dodd-1st Amer ed (s10) 15.00

RHODE,JOHN-Claverton Mystery-Lond-1933-Collins-1st ed (g4,sl fox,dj chip,sl stn) 150.00

RHODE,JOHN-Corpse in the Car-1935-Dodd-1st Amer ed (s10,sl fox) 20.00

RHODE,JOHN-Death Invades the Meeting-Lond-1944-Collins CC-1st ed (g4,dj) 45.00

RHODE,JOHN-Dr.Priestley Investigates-NY-1930-Dodd-1st US ed (e4,soil sp) 15.00

RHODE,JOHN-Ellerby Case-NY-1927-Dodd-1st US ed (f4) 25.00

RHODE,JOHN-Murders in Praed Street-1928-Dodd-1st Amer ed (s10) 35.00

RHODE,JOHN-Open Verdict-Lond-1956-Bles-1st ed (g4,yel pgs,chip dj) 35.00

RHODE,JOHN-Secret Meeting-NY-1950-Dodd-1st US ed (j4,dj) 15.00

RHODE,JOHN-Shot at Dawn-NY-1935-Dodd-1st US ed (e4) 20.00

RHODE,JOHN-Tragedy on the Line-1931-CCC-1st ed (s10) 20.00

RHODE,JOHN-Tragedy on the Line-NY-1931-Dodd-1st US ed (f4,sl fade cov,dj sl chip) 100.00

RHODE,JOHN-Venner Crime-Lond-1933-Odhams-1st ed (e4,fox,dj chip) 25.00

RHODES,DANIEL-Kilns-1968-Chilton-240p-illus-1st ed (cc8,dj) 35.00

RHODES,DAVID-Rock Island Line-NY-1975-1st ed (q5,f,dj) 15.00

RHODES,EUGENE M-Bransford in Arcadia-NY-1914-236p-dec cl,frntis (t7) 30.00

RHODES,EUGENE M-Little World Waddies-Chico-1946-Pass on the Rio Bravo-234p-cl,illus,H Bugbee,ltd to 1000c (w3) 135.00

RHODES,EUGENE M-Rhodes Reader-Norman-(1957)-U of Okla Pr-316p-frnt e.p. map-Six Guns #1097-1st ed (cc4,dj) 45.00

RHODES,FREDERICK L-Beginnings of Telephony-NY-1929-Harper & Bros-xviii+261p-blu cl,54 illus-1st ed (a2,tn dj) 50.00

RHODES,IRWIN S-Papers of John Marshall-Norman-1969-U of Okla-2 vols-col frntis-1st ed (o2,f,box split) 30.00

RHODES,J F-History of the Civil War, 1861 to 1865-NY-1927-454p-col fldg maps (z10,sl soil,scuff) 30.00

RHODES,JAMES F-Lectures on the American Revolution-NY-1913-296p-col fldg map-1st ed (n3) 25.00

RHODES,MARYLOU-Landmarks of Richmond-Richmond-(1938)-Garrett and Massie-155p-cl (l1) 12.50

RHODES,RAPHAEL H-ED.-Therapy Through Hypnosis-NY-(1952)-Citadel-xiv+274p-1st ed (y9) 17.50

RHYS,HEDLEY H-Maurice Prendergast-Cambridge-1960-Harvard U Pr-sq 8vo-cl,tip in plts-1st ed (oo6,dj,box) 75.00

RHYS,HORTON-Theatrical Trip for a Wager-Lond-1861-140p-5 tinted lithos(2 ports,3 scenes) (a7,sl chip sp) 350.00

RHYS,JEAN-Sleep It Off, Lady-1976-Harper & Row-1st Amer ed (s9,f,rub dj) 20.00

RHYS,JEAN-Wide Sargasso Sea-NY-1966-1st US ed (n5,dj) 30.00

RIABCHIKOV,EVGENY-Russians in Space-GC-1971-Dbldy-viii+300p-blk cl-1st ed (d2,dj) 18.00

RIBALOW,HAROLD U-Tie That Binds-1980-1st ed (y1,f,dj) 30.00

RIBEIRO,JOAO U-Sergeant Getulio-Bost-1978-Houghton Mifflin-auth 1st bk-1st US ed (e10,as new in dj) 25.00

RIBMAN,RONALD-Final War of Olly Winter-np-1967-CBS-wi orig promo flyer-1st ed (f8,f,lacks glassine dj) 75.00

RICARDO,DON-Early California and Mexico Cook Book-Toluca Lake-(1968)-Pacifica Hs-120p-red cl,illus (q8,dj) 18.50

RICCI,JAMES-Cystocele in America-Phila-1950-436p-scarce-1st ed (dd3,sp fade) 125.00

RICCI,L-Anonymous 20th Century-NY-1962-1st prtg (h10,sl chip dj) 25.00

RICCIUTI,EDWARD-Wild Cats-1979-Ridge Pr-238p-photos (m3,f,dj) 20.00

RICE,ALICE H-Mr Pete & Co-NY-1933-Appleton Century-1st ed (y1,dj edgewn & chip) 40.00

RICE,ALICE H-Romance of Billy Goat Hill-NY-1912-Century-1st ed (hh5) 15.00

RICE,ALICE H-Romance of Billy Goat Hill-NY-1912-Century-illus & dj by Geo Wright-1st ed (y1,bump,dj sl chip) 100.00

RICE,ANNE-Cry to Heaven-NY-1982-1st ed (h5,f,dj) 40.00

RICE,ANNE-Cry to Heaven-NY-1982-1st ed (r5,dj) 35.00

RICE,ANNE-Feast of All Saints-NY-(1979)-S&S-1st ed (k3,f,sl nick dj) 50.00

RICE,ANNE-Interview with the Vampire-Lond-1976-auth 1st bk-1st Brit ed (o5,f,dj) 250.00

RICE,ANNE-Interview with the Vampire-NY-(1976)-Knopf-1st ed (f6,f,dj) 750.00

RICE,ANNE-Vampire Lestat-NY-1985-Knopf-1st ed (ff6,f dj) 125.00

RICE,CRAIG-Knocked for a Loop-1957-S&S-1st ed (x7,vf,sl tn dj) 50.00

RICE,CRAIG-Knocked for a Loop-1957-Simon-1st ed (s10,pgs brwng,dj) 30.00

RICE,CRAIG-Lucky Stiff-NY-1945-Simon-1st ed (j4,dj) 25.00

RICE,CRAIG-Thursday Turkey Murders-NY-1943-Simon-1st ed (h4,chip dj) 12.50

RICE,DAMON-Season's Past-1976-Praeger-1st ed (ff2,f,dj) 50.00

RICE,ELMER-We, the People-NY-1933-Coward-1st ed (w5,f,dj) 45.00

RICE,F PHILIP-America's Favorite Fishing-NY-(1964)-Outdoor Life/Harper Row-285p-cl,illus-1st ed (pp8,f,dj) 35.00*

RICE,F PHILIP-How to Catch Bass-NY-1958-8vo-178p-illus-1st ed (m3,f) 20.00

RICE,GRANTLAND-Tumult and the Shouting-1954-Barnes-1st ed (p7,dj) 20.00

RICE,HOWARD C,JR.-American Campaigns of Rochambeau's Army 1780,1781,1782,1783-Princeton/Providence-1972-Princeton U/Brown U-4to-2 vols,blk cl,illus,col plts,maps-1st ed (mm1,f,dj,box) 150.00

RICE,JOHN H-Memoir of James Brainerd Taylor...-NY-(1833)-Amer Tract Society-441p-lea backed cl-vol 15 of Evangelica Family Libr-Sabin 70844,Amer Imprnts 20955-2nd stereotype ed (j1) 15.00

RICE,JOSIAH H-Cannoneer in Navajo Country-Denver-1970-illus,map-ltd to 1500c-1st ed (c4,f,dj) 50.00

RICE,MARGARET S-Sun on the River-Concord-1955-xvi+146p-grn cl,photos-1st ed (c2) 25.00

RICE,MRS MCKAY-Moody Texas Past Present Future!-Moody-1973-27p-wrps,photos-1st ed (w3,as new) 17.50

RICE,NATHAN-Trials of a Public Benefactor, as Illustrated in the Discovery of Etherization-NY-1859-460p-3 engrvd plts-v scarce-1st ed (dd3,rbnd,new e.p.) 350.00

RICE,THOMAS J-Virginia Woolf, a Guide to Research-NY-1984-Garland Publ-8vo-xix,258p-cl-1st ed (w2) 30.00

RICH & JOHNSON-ED.-Journal of a Voyage From Rocky Mountain Portage in Peace River to the Sources of Finlays Branch...-Lond-1955-Hudson's Bay Soc-260p-blu cl,fldg map (w1) 75.00

RICH,ADRIENNE-Of Woman Born-NY-1976-Norton-1st ed (w5,f,f dj) 20.00

RICH,ADRIENNE-Poems: Selected and New, 1950-1974-1975-Norton-1st ed (x2,f,dj) 35.00

RICH,PROF GEORGE E-Artistic Horse Shoeing-NY-1887-Richardson-1st prtg (h9) 65.00

RICH,VIRGINIA-Baked Bean Supper Murders-(1983)-Dutton-267p-tan bds-1st ed (q8,f,dj) 16.50

RICH,VIRGINIA-Cooking School Murders-NY-1982-Dutton-1st ed (f4,f,dj) 15.00

RICH,VIRGINIA-Cooking School Murders-NY-1982-Dutton-1st ed (w9,vf,dj) 25.00

RICH,WALTER H-Feathered Game of the Northeast-NY-1907-8vo-432p-illus (m3) 27.50

RICH,WALTER H-Swordfish & Sword Fishery of New England-Portland-1947-8vo-102p-photos,fldg map (m3,vf) 25.00

RICHARD,COLETTE-Climbing Blind-Lond-1965-159p-1st ed (p10,dj) 20.00

RICHARD,COLETTE-Climbing Blind-Lond-1966-1st ed (v9,f,dj) 35.00

RICHARD,EVA A-Arctic Mood-Caldwell-1949-282p-illus,map e.p.-1st ed (t7,dj) 7.50

RICHARD,LOUIS-Eleven Days in the Militia During the War of the Rebellion-Phila-1883-Collins-12mo-53p-maroon cl-1st ed (u2,sp rprd) 45.00

RICHARD,RHYS-Whaling and Sealing at the Chatham Islands-Canberra-1982-J S Cumpston-e.p. maps,illus (dd7,f,rub dj) 35.00

RICHARDS,CARA E-Oneida People-Phoenix-1974-frntis,photos,Indian Trails Ser-1st ed (t7,f,autg) 20.00

RICHARDS,COOMBE-Salmon, How to Catch Them-Lond-1956-12mo-94p-illus-1st ed (m3,f,dj) 12.50

RICHARDS,COOMBE-Tight Lines-Lond-1949-12mo-206p-illus (m3) 10.00

RICHARDS,HORACE G-Book of Maps of Cape May, 1610 to 1878-Cape May-1954-lg 4to-28p-wrps,illus,fldg plt (aa6) 50.00

RICHARDS,J M-High Street-Lond-(1938)-Curwen Pr for Cntry Life-24 lithos by E Ravilious-1st ed (p6,f) 750.00

RICHARDS,LAURA E-Elizabeth Fry-NY-1916-Appleton-12mo-206p-1st ed (y6,sp fade,edges wn) 12.50

RICHARDS,LAURA E-Silver Crown...-Bost-1906-Little,Brown-8vo-105p-illus cov & t.p.-1st ed (w6,sl soil sp) 30.00

RICHARDS,LAURA E-When I Was Your Age-Bost-(1894)-Dana Estes-8vo-210p-illus-1st ed (oo7) 25.00

RICHARDS,MILTON-Dick Kent with the Eskimos-Akron-1927-Saalfield-8vo-227p (bb7,discol pgs,sl chip dj) 10.00*

RICHARDS,P W-Tropical Rain Forest-Cambridge-1964-xviii,450p-red cl,43 text figs,15 plts-2nd ed (j10,sl wn,dj edgewn) 60.00

RICHARDS,PAUL-Modern Baseball Strategy-1955-Prentice Hall-1st ed (p7,dj) 27.50

RICHARDS,WALTER-Her Majesty's Army-Lond-ca.1890-2 vols-brwn lea,mrbld bds & e.p.,31 col plts-(3rd vol was issued later) (gg2,sl wn,hngs rprd) 250.00

RICHARDSON & CO-Texas Almanac for 1870 and Emigrants Guide to Texas-Galveston News-288p-orig prtd wrps-1st ed (a9) 500.00

RICHARDSON,ALBERT D-Beyond the Mississippi-Hartford-1867-Amer Publ-572p-illus-1st ed (dd4) 75.00

RICHARDSON,ALBERT D-Beyond the Mississippi-Hartford-1867-Amer Publ-xvi,572p-illus-1st ed (o2,sl rub) 55.00

RICHARDSON,ALBERT D-Personal History of Ulysses S Grant-Hartford-1868-Amer Publ-560p+ads-26 engrvngs,6 maps,facs-1st ed (n2,top sp wn) 40.00

RICHARDSON,BENJAMIN W-Biological Experimentation-Lond-1896-170p-1st ed (dd3) 100.00

RICHARDSON,BENJAMIN W-Disciples of Aesculapius-NY,Lond-1901-2 vols-t.e.g.,illus (g10,new e.p.) 175.00

RICHARDSON,BENJAMIN-Diseases of Modern Life-NY-1882-288p-1st Amer ed (dd3) 35.00

RICHARDSON,BOBBY-Bobby Richardson Story-1965-Revell-1st ed (s8,dj) 10.00

RICHARDSON,CHARLES F-Choice of Books-NY-1885-208p-cl (n1) 15.00

RICHARDSON,DAVID-Pig War Islands-Eastsound-1971-362p-illus-1st ed (j7,f,sl nick dj) 35.00

RICHARDSON,E RAMSAY-Little Aleck-Indpls-1932-Bobbs Merrill-359p-frntis port,illus (v2) 30.00

RICHARDSON,EDGAR P-Washington Allston-Chig-(1948)-U of Chig Pr-4to-cl-1st ed (oo6,vf,dj) 75.00

RICHARDSON,HENRY H-Ultima Thule-NY-1929-Norton-1st US ed (v5,f,dj) 75.00

RICHARDSON,HESTER D-Side Lights on Maryland History-Balt-1913-Williams & Wilkins-2 vols-blk cl,102 plts,2 errata leaves-1st ed (mm10) 110.00

RICHARDSON,JAMES D-Compilation of the Messages & Papers of the Confederacy...-Nashville-1905-U.S. Publ-2 vols-3/4 lea,plts-1st ed (n2,sp rub,chip) 125.00

RICHARDSON,JAMES-ED.-Wonders of the Yellowstone-NY-1873-Scribner,Armstrong-256p-drwngs,fldg map (cc4) 20.00

RICHARDSON,JOHN M-Steamboat Lore of the Penobscot-Augusta-(1941)-Kennebec Journal Prnt Shp-4to-(xii)+3-141p,blu cl,illus-1st ed (h2,sl flecked cov) 45.00

RICHARDSON,LEE-B.C.-Tales of Fishing in British Columbia-Forest Grove-1978-8vo-169p-one of 2000c,map (m3,as new in dj) 60.00

RICHARDSON,MAURICE-Fascination of Reptiles-Lond-1972-A Deutsch-8vo-240p-8 col plts,33 drwngs-1st ed (ff9,dj) 20.00*

RICHARDSON,ROBERT H-Tilton Territory-Phila & Ardmore-(1977)-300p-cl-Rieger 1938 (j1,f,dj,autg) 10.00

RICHARDSON,ROBERT S-Getting Acquainted with Comets-NY-1967-McGraw Hill-306p-70 illus-1st ed (hh6,tn dj) 20.00

RICHARDSON,RUPERT N-Adventuring with a Purpose-San Antonio-1951-114p-photos-Herd #1888-1st ed (t7) 60.00

RICHARDSON,RUPERT N-Comanche Barrier to South Plains Settlement-Glendale-1933-397p-photos-Rader#2783-v scarce-1st ed (u7) 225.00

RICHARDSON,RUPERT N-Frontier of Northwest Texas 1846 to 1876-Glendale-1963-Arthur H Clark Co-332p-maps,illus-1st ed (cc4) 150.00

RICHARDSON,WILLIAM H-Federalist Fathers and the Founding of Jersey City-(Jersey City)-1927-Hist Soc of Hudson Cnty-47,(1)p-wrps,plts (aa6) 40.00

RICHDALE,L E-Sexual Behavior in Penguins-Lawrence-1951-U of Ks Pr-316p-photos (c9,chip dj) 25.00

RICHEY,P-Fighter Pilot-NY-1941-8vo-xii,178p-cl,frntis,15p plts-1st ed (s2,sp fade) 20.00

RICHLER,MORDECAI-Cocksure-Tor-1968-M&S-8vo-250p-1st ed (bb7,fade dj) 25.00*

RICHLER,MORDECAI-Joshua Then and Now-NY-1980-Knopf-1st ed (bb1,as new in dj) 17.50

RICHLER,MORDECAI-Notes on an Endangered Species and Others-NY-1974-Knopf-1st US ed (b5,as new in dj) 20.00

RICHLER,MORDECAI-Stick Your Neck Out-NY-1963-S&S-1st US ed (hh5,f,sl chip dj) 12.50

RICHLER,MORDECAI-Stick Your Neck Out-NY-1963-S&S-8vo-189p-1st Amer prtg (bb7,dj) 25.00*

RICHMOND,A B-Hawk in an Eagle's Nest-np-1881-575p-cl-Wright 4537 (a1,sl wn) 40.00

RICHMOND,LEONARD-Technique of Oil Painting-NY-nd-Pitman Publ-143,(1)p-cl,47p tip in col plts (m1) 20.00

RICHMOND,MARY L-Shaker Literature-Hanover-1977-Shaker Comm-sm 4to-2 vols-cl-1st ed (w2) 45.00

RICHTER,CONRAD-Brothers of No Kin and Other Stories-NY-(1924)-HH&E-g titled cl,auth 1st bk-1st ed (aa9,sl rub sp,autg) 125.00

RICHTER,CONRAD-Simple Honorable Man-NY-1962-Knopf-1st Amer ed (ee2,f,rub dj) 35.00

RICHTER,CONRAD-Town-NY-1950-Knopf-1st Amer ed (ee2,f,sl wn dj) 35.00

RICHTER,ED-View From the Dugout-1964-Chilton-1st ed (s8,f,dj) 20.00

RICHTER,FRANCIS C-ED.-Reach Official American League Base Ball Guide for 1918-Phila-1918-A J Reach-12mo-352p-red cl,photos,ads (kk9,cov wn) 75.00

RICHTER,HANS-Hans Richter-Lond-1971-sq lg 4to-193 illus(incl 33 col)-1st Brit ed (ee1,dj) 125.00

RICHTOFEN,BARON VON-Red Knight of Germany-GC-1927-8vo-viii,384p-illus cl,frntis,7p plts,C Knight-1st ed (s2) 45.00

RICKARD,MRS TEX-Everything Happened to Him-NY-1936-Stokes-368p-frntis-1st ed (f9,edge wn,sl spot) 50.00

RICKENBACKER,E V-Seven Came Through-GC-1943-sm 8vo-x,118p-illus cl,8p plts-1st ed (s2,dj) 20.00

RICKETT,H W-Botanic Manuscript of Jane Colden-NY-1963-Gard Clb Orng & Dtchss Co-205p-facs wi notes-ltd to 1500c,nbrd,autg (x6,dj wn) 35.00

RICKETT,H W-Wild Flowers of the U.S. Northeastern States-NY-1966-McGraw-2 vols (x6,fade sp,rprd box) 75.00

RICKETT,H W-Wild Flowers of the United States: Texas, Part Three, Vols. 1 & 2-NY-1969-McGraw-col photos-1st ed (a9,spot box) 350.00

RICKETT,H W-Wildflowers of the United States. Vol.2-1975-NY Botanical Grdn-4to-2 vols-241 col plts-2nd prtg rvsd of 1st ed (bb3,f) 165.00

RICKETT,H W-Wildflowers of the United States. Vol.4-1970-NY Botanical Grdn-4to-3 vols-248 col photo plts-1st ed (bb3,f) 185.00

RICKETT,H W-Wildflowers of the United States. Vol.6-1973-NY Botanical Grdn-4to-3 vols-262 col plts-1st ed (bb3,f) 185.00

RICKETTS,BENJAMIN-Surgery of the Heart and Lungs-NY-1904-510p-87 plts-rare-1st ed (dd3,ex-libr) 400.00

RICKETTS,CHARLES-Letters to `Michael Field'-Edinburgh-1981-Tragara Pr-ltd to 145c,nbrd-1st ed (y7,dj) 65.00

RICKEY,BRANCH-American Diamond-1965-S&S-1st ed (q7,f,chip dj) 125.00

RICKHOFF,J-ED.-Hunting the World's Mountains-1984-Amwell-2 vols-powder blu lea,a.e.g.,orig col plts by Skirka,ltd to 1000 sets,publ autg (gg3,vf,box) 175.00

RICKLI,EHRW S S-A B C Buch-Columbus-1848-Whiting & Huntington-32p-prntd bds,wdcuts (k1) 75.00

RICKMERS,W RICKMER-Ski-ing For Beginners & Mountaineers-Lond-1910-Fisher Unwin-175p-113 photos-scarce-1st ed (q10) 200.00

RICORD,FREDERICK W-History of Union County, New Jersey-Newark-1897-xiii,656p-orig mor,illus,plts (aa6,wn,outr hngs crackng) 150.00

RIDDELL,FRANCIS A-ET AL-Archaeological Excavations on the Farallon Islands, California-Berkeley-1955-U of Cal Arch Survey-38p-orig wrps,1 map,6 plts,2 figs-Papers No.34,35,36 (mm1,papr aged) 15.00

RIDDELL,J-In the Forests of the Night-NY-1946-230p-photos (gg3,f) 15.00

RIDDELL,JOHN-In the Worst Possible Taste-NY,Lond-1932-Scribner's-14 illus,M Covarrubias-1st ed (a10,dj) 50.00

RIDDELL,JOHN-John Riddell Murder Case-1930-Scribners-illus,Covarrubias,seal remains unbroken-1st ed (x2,sl soil dj) 175.00

RIDDLE,JEFF C-Indian History of the Modoc War and the Causes That Led to It-np-1914-295p-cl,photos-Adams,Guns 1852-1st ed (v1) 90.00

RIDEAL,SAMUEL-Glue and Glue Testing-Lond-1900-144p-14 engrvngs (cc8,fray sp,wn) 45.00

RIDGELY,R S-Guide to the Birds of Panama-1976-Princeton-394p-32 col plts-1st ed (bb3) 40.00

RIDGEWAY,RICK-Last Step-Seattle-1980-301p-1st ed (a4,as new in dj) 26.00

RIDGWAY,R-Birds of North and Middle Amer. Part 1-Wash-1901-8vo-(1),715p-half lea,20 plts (y8,scuff) 35.00

RIDGWAY,R-Birds of North and Middle Amer. Part 10-Wash-1946-8vo-484p-wrps (y8) 32.00

RIDGWAY,R-Birds of North and Middle Amer. Part 2-Wash-1902-8vo-834p-half lea,22 plts (y8,scuff) 35.00

RIDGWAY,R-Birds of North and Middle Amer. Part 3-Wash-1904-8vo-801p-half lea,19 plts (y8,scuff,crack) 35.00

RIDGWAY,R-Birds of North and Middle Amer. Part 5-Wash-1911-8vo-859p-wrps,33 plts (y8,chip) 40.00

RIDGWAY,R-Birds of North and Middle Amer. Part 6-Wash-1914-8vo-882p-grn cl,36 plts (y8,spot) 32.00

RIDGWAY,R-Birds of North and Middle Amer. Part 7-Wash-1916-8vo-543p-buckr,24 plts (y8,rbnd) 35.00

RIDGWAY,R-Birds of North and Middle Amer. Part 8-Wash-1919-8vo-852p-wrps,34 plts (y8,poor) 18.50

RIDGWAY,R-Birds of North and Middle Amer. Part 9-Wash-1941-8vo-254p-wrps (y8,chip) 23.00

RIDGWAY,R-Humming Birds-Wash-1891-U.S. Mus. rprt for 1890-8vo-(253-)383p-half cl,46 plts (y8,rbnd) 65.00

RIDGWAY,R-Ornithology of Illinois-Springfield-1889,95-lg 8vo-2 vols-orig cl,col frntis,65 plts (y8,crack,ex-libr) 75.00

RIDING,LAURA-Trojan Ending-NY-(1937)-red bndg-1st ed (r2,dj sl sun,rub) 60.00

RIDINGS,SAM P-Chisholm Trail-Guthrie-(1936)-591p-pict frnt bd,illus,fldg map-Howes R281-scarce-1st ed (c7,f) 175.00

RIDINGS,SAM P-Chisholm Trail-Guthrie-1936-Co-op-photos,illus- scarce in dj-Howes R281-1st ed (b4,dj) 200.00

RIDLER,ANNE-Shadow Factory, a Nativity Play-Lond-1946-1st ed (y7,dj sl rub) 20.00

RIDLEY,HELEN-Ritz-Carlton Cook Book-(1968)-Lippincott-436p-blk cl,water cols-1st ed (q8) 17.50

RIEDY,JAMES L-Chicago Sculpture-1981-Ill U Pr-300 photos-1st ed (h10,dj) 45.00

RIEFENSTAHL,L-Coral Gardens-1978-Harper Row-4to-223p-col photos-1st US ed (bb3,f,dj) 25.00

RIEGEL,E C-Barnum and Bunk-NY-(1928)-147,(4)p-pict bds (b1,sl rub) 15.00

RIEGEL,ROBERT E-America Moves West-NY-(1930)-H Holt-595p-maps-Herd 1898-1st ed (gg4) 25.00

RIES,ESTELLE-Mother Wit-NY-(1930)-Century-8vo-301p-18 illus-1st ed (gg5) 15.00

RIESE,WALTHER-History of Neurology-NY-1959-223p-1st ed (dd3,dj) 50.00

RIESEN,RENE-Jungle Mission-NY-(1957)-Crowell-photos-1st ed (ff3,dj) 85.00

RIFKIND,C-Main Street-NY-1977-259 illus-1st ed (h10,dj) 40.00

RIGBY,DOUGLAS-Lock, Stock and Barrel-Phila-1944-Lippincott-xix,570p-cl,frntis,plts,illus-1st trd ed (dd10,fray dj) 28.00

RIGGS,ARTHUR S-Spanish Pageant-Indpls-(1928)-Bobbs Merrill-8vo-416p-illus-1st ed (jj5,dj rub,chip) 20.00

RIGGS,DAVID F-East of Gettysburg-Bellevue-(1970)-78p-illus,maps-1st ed (c4,f,dj) 22.50

RIGGS,STEPHEN R-Dakota Grammar, Texts & Ethnography-Wash-1893-GPO-4to-USGS Survey,contrib No Amer Ethno,Vol.IX-1st ed (b4) 95.00

RIGGS,STEPHEN R-Dakota Grammar, Texts, and Ethnography-Wash-1893-GPO-qto-239p-Contrib to N Amer Ethnol,Vol.9 (dd4,edges wn) 65.00

RIGNANO,EUGENIO-Upon the Inheritance of Acquired Characters-Chig-1911-Open Court Publ-vi+411p-red cl-1st Amer ed (j2,sl soil) 35.00

RIGNEY,FRANCIS J-Real Bohemia-NY-1961-1st ed (x8,dj) 45.00

RIIS,JACOB A-Making of an American-NY-1901-Macmillan-8vo-443p-cl,photos-1st ed (q3) 40.00

RIIS,JACOB A-Old Town-NY-1909-Macmillan-269p-1st ed (r1) 15.00

RIIS,JACOB A-Theodore Roosevelt, the Citizen-NY-1904-Outlook-1st ed (v5,f) 30.00

RIIS,JACOB-Battle with the Slum-NY-1902-Macmillan-4to-g dec blu cl,photos-1st ed (x3) 135.00

RIKER,BEN-Pony Wagon Town-Indpls-1948-Bobbs Merrill-1st ed (j9,dj) 65.00

RILEY,C V-Destructive Locust-Wash-1891-62p+12 plts & maps,wrps,USDA Div of Entomology Bulletin 25 (c1) 15.00

RILEY,JAMES W-Flying Islands of the Night-Indpls-(1913)-Bobbs Merrill-4to-124p-16 tip in col plts by F Booth-1st ed (oo8) 125.00

RILEY,JAMES W-His Pa's Romance-Indpls-(1903)-168p-cl-1st ed (e1,sl wn,few cov spots) 15.00

RILEY,JAMES W-Riley Child Verse-Indpls-(1906)-Bobbs Merrill-sm 4to-unpgd-cl wi full pict pasteon,8 inserted col plts,E Betts (r3,sp lttrng flaked,sl soil) 65.00

RILEY,JAMES W-Riley Farm Rhymes-Indpls-(last cpyrt 1905)-187p-cl (b1) 15.00

RILEY,JAMES W-Riley Love Lyrics-Indpls-(last cpyrt 1899)-190p-cl-1st ed,2nd state (b1) 15.00

RILEY,JAMES W-While the Hearts Beat Young-(1906)-Bobbs Merrill-110p-pict pastedown on cov,illus by E F Betts-1st ed (v8,sl wn & chip cov) 75.00

RILEY,R C-Brightion Line Album-Lond-1967-112p-1st ed (n4,f,dj) 22.00

RILEY,R C-Great Eastern Album-Lond-1968-1st ed (n4,f,dj) 19.50

RILEY,R C-Great Western Album No.2-Lond-1970-112p-1st ed (n4,f,dj) 18.50

RILING,R-Powder Flask Book-1953-Bonanza ed-495p-photos (gg3,f,chip dj) 125.00

RILING,R-Powder Flask Book-NY-1953-Bonanza ed-495p-photos (ee3,f,dj chip) 100.00

RILING,RAY-Guns & Shooting-NY-1951-8vo-434p-photos,illus-1st ed (m3,vf,sl chip dj) 125.00

RILKE,R M-Selected Poems-Lond-1941-New Hogarth Libr Vol.3-1st ed (y1,f,f dj) 50.00

RILKE,RAINER M-Letters to a Young Poet-NY-1934-Norton-cl,transl by M D Herter Norton-1st prtg (l8) 25.00

RILKE,RAINER M-Life of the Virgin Mary-NY-1951-Philosophical Libr-cl-1st Amer ed (n8,f,dj) 45.00

RIMBAUD,ARTHUR-Arthur Rimbaud:Complete Works-NY et al-(1975)-Harper & Row-1st ed (b10,as new in price clip dj) 17.50

RIMBAUD,ARTHUR-Complete Works-NY-1975-Harpers-1st ed (y1,f,dj) 30.00

RIMBAUD,ARTHUR-Rimbaud Complete Works,Selected Letters-Chig,Lond-(1966)-Univ of Chig Pr-bi-lingual ed-1st ed (b10,dj) 25.00

RINE,JOSEPHINE Z-Dog Owner's Manual-NY-(1944)-446p-cl (c1) 15.00

RINEHART,MARY R-Alibi for Isabel ...-NY-1944-Farrar-1st ed (l4,sl stnd dj) 20.00

RINEHART,MARY R-Alter of Freedom-Bost-1917-Houghton Mifflin-12mo-48,(6)p-1st ed (o2,few cov spots) 10.00

RINEHART,MARY R-Kings,Queens and Pawns-NY-(1915)-Doran-368p-cl (d1) 20.00

RINEHART,MARY R-Long Live the King-Bost-1917-Houghton-1st ed (d4) 12.50

RINEHART,MARY R-Out Trail-(1923)-Doran-246p-g cov dec,illus-1st ed (r8,sl edgewn,chip) 18.00

RINEHART,MARY R-Red Lamp-NY-1925-Doran-1st ed (e4,rprd dj) 35.00

RINEHART,MARY R-Sight Unseen and the Confession-1921-Doran-scarce in dj(pict)-1st ed (x7,sl chip dj) 70.00

RINEHART,MARY R-Tenting To Night-1918-Houghton Mifflin-188p-pict cov,illus-1st ed (r8) 25.00

RINEHART,MARY R-This Strange Adventure-GC-1929-Dbldy Doran-1st ed (gg8,sl chip dj) 30.00

RINEHART,MARY R-Tish Marches On-1937-F&R-1st ed (x7,sl tn dj) 25.00

RINEHART,MARY R-Tish Plays the Game-NY-1926-Doran-1st ed (k4) 10.00

RINEHART,MARY R-Window at the White Cat-1910-BM-1st ed (x7) 15.00

RINEHART,MARY R-Writing is Work-Bost-(1939)-Writer,Inc.-1st ed (bb1,dj crease,sp chip) 20.00

RINEHART,MARY R-Yellow Room-NY-1945-Farrar & Rinehart-1st ed (gg8,f,dj) 17.50

RINGGOLD,JENNIE P-Frontier Days in the Southwest-S.A.-1952-Naylor-197p-photos-1st ed (a9) 45.00

RINGWALD,DONALD C-Hudson River Day Line-Berkeley-1965-Howell-North Bks-gry cl,blk cov & sp titles,dec e.p.,illus (nn1,dj) 45.00

RINHART,FLOYD-American Daguerreian Art-NY-(1967)-Potter-1st ed (y3,dj) 90.00

RINK,HENRY-Tales and Traditions of the Eskimo...-Edinburgh,Lond-1875-Wm Blackwood & Sons-8vo-xii,(2),472p-orig dec brwn cl,6 plts(2 fldg)-Ricks p.183-1st Brit ed (oo1,cl wn,hng weak) 550.00

RINPOCHE,RECHUNG-Tibetan Medicine, Illustrated in Original Texts-Lond-1973-340p-1st ed (dd3) 60.00

RIPAULT,CHRISTINE-Children's Gastronomique-(1968)-Crown-376p-tan cl-1st Amer ed (q8,dj) 12.50

RIPLEY,DILLON-Paddling of Ducks-Lond-1959-8vo-256p-illus (m3,dj) 20.00

RIPLEY,DILLON-Search for the Spiny Babbler-Kathmandu-1978 (o10,f,dj) 20.00

RIPLEY,JACK-My God How the Money Rolls In-Lond-1972-Hamilton-1st ed (p4,dj) 22.50

RIPLEY,O-Quail & the Quail Dog-OH-1924-110p-wrps (gg3,f) 12.00

RIPLEY,OZARK-Bass & Bass Fishing-Cin-1924-12mo-148p-photos-1st ed (m3) 35.00

RIPLEY,OZARK-Modern Bait & Fly Casting-NY-1928-12mo-250p-illus-1st ed (m3,vf,sl chip dj) 20.00

RIPLEY,OZARK-Quail & the Quail Dog-Cin-1924-12mo-114p-illus-1st ed (m3) 37.50

RIPLEY,S D-Rails of the World-1977-Feheley-folio-406p-41p col plts,17 maps-1st ed (bb3,as new in orig ship crtn) 145.00

RIPLEY,THOMAS-Green Timber-Palo Alto-(1968)-126p-photos-1st ed (r8,f) 12.00

RIPLEY,THOMAS-They Died with Their Boots On-1935-Dbldy,Doran-285p-illus-1st ed (t8,sl soil cov) 45.00

RIPPERGER,HELMUT-Spice Cookery-NY-(1942)-Geo W Stewart-95p-1st ed (u6,dj) 12.50

RIPPINGALE,O H-Queensland and Great Barrier Reef Shells-Brisbane-1961-Jaacaranda Pr-4to-210p-29 col plts-1st ed (p8,sl soil bds) 30.00

RISER,N W-ED.-Biology of the Turbellaria-1974-McGraw Hill-530p-photos-1st ed (bb3,f,tn dj) 20.00

RISTER,CARL C-Comanche Bondage-Glendale-1955-A Clark-1st ed (b4) 195.00

RISTER,CARL C-Fort Griffin on the Texas Frontier-(1956)-U of Okla-216p-photos-1st ed (v3,sl fade,dj tn) 24.00

RISTER,CARL C-Fort Griffin on the Texas Frontier-Norman-(1956)-U of Okla Pr-216p-illus-Six Guns 1861-1st ed (gg4,dj) 30.00

RISTER,CARL C-Land Hunger-Norman-1942-U of Okla Pr-245p-cl,photos-1st ed (w3,f,dj) 37.50

RISTER,CARL C-Oil! Titan of the Southwest-Norman-1949-U of Okla Pr-467p-cl,photos,fldg map & chrt-1st ed (ee10,dj) 37.50

RISTER,CARL C-Southern Plainsmen-Norman-1938-U of Okla Pr-289p-illus-Howes R317-1st ed (d3,dj) 150.00

RISTER,CARL C-Southern Plainsmen-Norman-1938-UOP-289p-illus-1st ed (a9,dj) 120.00

RITCH,W G-Aztlan-Bost-1885-250p-cl,illus(2 fldg),fldg map-scarce-6th ed,rvsd,enlgd (v7,map rprd) 250.00

RITCH,W G-COMP.-Legislative Blue Book, of the Territory of New Mexico-Santa Fe-1882-154p+46p-rare-1st ed (v7,sl rub) 300.00

RITCH,W G-Illustrated New Mexico-Santa Fe-1883-140p+corrctn pg,wrps,illus(1 fldg),2 fldg maps-Adams Herd#1910-scarce-3rd ed (v7,chip) 250.00

RITCH,W G-Illustrated New Mexico-Santa Fe-1883-140p+corrctn pg,wrps,illus,no fldg map-scarce-4th ed (v7,backstrip chipped away) 225.00

RITCH,WILLIAM G-Aztlan-Bost-1885-Lothrop/Bur of Immigr-illus,fldg maps-scarce-6th ed (b4,cov wn,1 map tn) 300.00

RITCHIE,A C-Charles Demuth-NY-1950-MOMA (h10,dj) 40.00

RITCHIE,ANNA C-Fairy Fingers-NY-1865-Carlton-8vo-460p-Wright III,2046-1st ed (w6) 45.00

RITCHIE,MOORE-With Botha in the Field-Lond-1915-68p-brwn cl,papr cov bds,plts-1st ed (kk2) 50.00

RITCHIE,ROBERT W-Hell Roarin' Forty Niners-NY-(1928)-J H Sears-298p-illus-1st ed (nn6,sl wn dj) 30.00

RITCHIE,WILLIAM A-Archaeology of Martha's Vineyard-GC-1969-Natural Hist Pr-xviii+253p-blk & blu cl,56 plts,18 text figs-1st ed (m2,dj) 40.00

RITCHIE,WILLIAM A-Archaeology of New York State-NY-1965-Nat Hist Pr-sm 4to-355p-135 illus-1st ed (dd5,f,sl soil dj) 40.00

RITTENHOUSE,JACK D-American Horse-Drawn Vehicles...-LA-1948-Dillon Litho-4to-(iv)+101p-wht cl,illus,ltd to 1000c,nbrd(#849)-1st ed (d2,dj) 40.00

RITTENHOUSE,JACK D-Man Who Owned Too Much-Houston-1958-52p-illus,ltd to 450c-scarce-1st ed (u7,box) 75.00

RITTENHOUSE,JACK D-Santa Fe Trail-Albuq-(1971)-U of NM Pr-271p-1st ed (dd4,dj) 75.00

RITTER,CHRISTIANE-Woman in the Polar Night-Lond-1954-Allen & Unwin-map,line drwngs-1st Brit ed (ee7,sl fox,dj) 22.50

RITTER,E A-Shaka Zulu-NY-1957-383p-illus-1st Amer ed (b7,dj) 40.00

RITTER,LAWRENCE-100 Greatest Baseball Players of All Time-1981-Crown-photos-1st ed (s8,f,f dj) 30.00

RITTER,LAWRENCE-Image of Their Greatness-1979-Crown-illus-1st ed (s8,f,dj) 25.00

RITTER,MARY B-More Than Gold in California 1849 to 1933-Berkeley-1933-451p (bb9,dj) 75.00

RITTER,MARY B-More Than Gold in California 1849 to 1933-Berkeley-1933-Professional Pr-8vo-451p-grn cov-1st ed (mm1,f,wn dj) 95.00

RITTER,W E-California Woodpecker and I-1938-U of Cal-340p-col frntis,28 figs & maps-1st ed (bb3,f,dj) 35.00

RITTER,WILLIAM E-Charles Darwin and the Golden Rule-Wash D.C.-1954-Sci Service-xxiv+400p-red cl-1st ed (j2,cov cor sl stnd,dj) 20.00

RITZ,CHARLES-Fly Fisher's Life-Lond-1960-4to-230p-photos (m3,fray dj) 20.00

RITZ,DAVID-Man Who Brought the Dodgers Back to Brooklyn-1981-S&S-1st ed (r7,dj) 15.00

RITZ,MARIE L-Cesar Ritz-Phila-(1938)-Lippincott-360p-red bds,illus (l6,sl wn bds) 35.00

RIVER,J PAUL DE-Sexual Criminal-Springfield-(1949)-Chas C Thomas-xvii,281p-cl,illus-1st ed (dd10,dj sl chip & soil) 40.00

RIVER,W L-Malta Story-NY-1943-8vo-222p-illus cl,e.p. maps (s2,dj) 25.00

RIVERA,BETTY-Inkstands and Inkwells-1973-Crown-216p-illus (cc8,dj) 35.00

RIVERA,DIEGO-My Art, My Life-NY-1960-Citadel Pr-8vo-318p-wht cl,illus-1st ed (r10,dj) 15.00

RIVERS,LARRY-Drawings and Digressions-NY-1979-folio-1st ed (ff10,dj) 85.00

RIVERS,W H R-Kinship and Social Organization-Lond-1968-Athlone Pr-8vo-1116p-cl-Sch Econ Mono on Soc Anthro No.34-1st ed (y5,dj) 34.00

RIVES,AMELIE-Barbara Dering-Phila-1893-Lippincott-285p-cl-Wright 5569-1st ed (e1) 15.00

RIVES,HALLIE E-Smoking Flax-Lond,NY-(1897)-F Tennyson Neely-232p+ads-cl-2nd ed (d1) 20.00

RIVIERE,BILL-L L Bean Guide to the Outdoors-NY-1981-4to-299p-illus (m3,vf,dj) 10.00

RIVOIRA,G T-Lombardic Architecture-Lond-1910-folio-2 vols-t.e.g.,illus (ee1) 175.00

RIVOIRA,G T-Moslem Architecture-1918-OUP-dec cov,340 illus-1st Brit ed (h10) 250.00

RIX,MARTYN-Art of the Plant World-1981-Overlook-folio-224p-64 col plts,illus-1st US ed (bb3,as new in dj) 100.00

RIX,MARTYN-Art of the Plant World-NY-1983-Overlook-224p-cl (x6,dj) 50.00

RIZZUTO,PHIL-Miracle NY Yankess-1962-Coward McCann-1st ed (q7,f,f dj) 40.00

ROBB,ISABEL H-Nursing-Cleve-1906-565p-3rd ed (dd3) 125.00

ROBB,JOHN D-Hispanic Folk Music of New Mexico and the SW-Norman-(1980)-874p-photos-1st ed (u7,dj) 45.00

ROBBE-GRILLET,ALAIN-Djinn-NY-(1982)-Grove-1st ed (b5,as new in dj) 12.50

ROBBE-GRILLET,ALAIN-La Maison De Rendez-Vous-1966-Grove-1st Amer ed (t9,f,dj) 25.00

ROBBINS,ANN R-Treadway Inns Cook Book-(1958)-Little,Brown-397p-tan cl,map e.p.-1st ed (q8,dj) 16.50

ROBBINS,CHRISTINE C-David Hosack, Citizen of New York-Phila-1964-Amer Philos Soc-246p (x6,dj sl soil) 30.00

ROBBINS,CLIFTON-Dusty Death-NY-1932-Appleton-1st US ed (k4,f,dj) 25.00

ROBBINS,CLIFTON-Mystery of Mr.Cross-NY-1933-Appleton-1st US ed (l4,f,dj) 25.00

ROBBINS,HAROLD-Adventurers-NY-1966-Trident Pr-1st ed (a10,f,dj) 12.50

ROBBINS,MAJ ROBERT A-91st Infantry Division in World War II-Wash-(1947)-lg 8vo-423p-cl-1st ed (kk7) 40.00

ROBBINS,TOM-Another Roadside Attraction-Lond,NY-1973-Allen-auth 1st bk-1st Brit ed (bb1,f,dj) 225.00

ROBBINS,TOM-Even Cowgirls Get the Blues-Bost-1976-Houghton Mifflin-1st ed (bb1,sl tn dj) 175.00

ROBBINS,TOM-Even Cowgirls Get the Blues-Lond-1977-pbk orig-1st Brit ed (p5) 20.00

ROBBINS,TOM-Skagit Valley Artists-1974-Seattle Art Mus-4to-50p-wrps,photos (l10) 9.50

ROBBINS,TOM-Still Life With Woodpecker-NY et al-(1980)-Bantam-1st ed (e10,f,dj) 65.00

ROBBINS,TOM-Still Life With Woodpecker-NY-1980-1st ed (r5,f,dj) 45.00

ROBBINS,W W-Ethnobotany of the Tewa Indians-Wash-1916-GPO-124p-cl (x6,rprd t.p. tear) 30.00

ROBENSON,ANTHONY-Alpine Roundabout-Lond-1947-214p-1st ed (q10,f,dj) 15.00

ROBERSON,JOHN-Chafing Dish Cookbook-NY-(1950)-Prentice Hall-238p-1st ed (u6,f,dj) 18.00

ROBERT-ROBERT-Paris Restaurants-NY-nd-Brentano's-127p (l6,sl fox) 15.00

ROBERTS,B H-Defense of the Faith and the Saints, Vol.I-SLC-1907-532p-orig dk grn cl-scarce-Flake 7316-1st ed (bb8,sl scuff sp) 150.00

ROBERTS,B H-Falling Away...-SLC-1931-253p-orig grn cl,port,illus-1st ed (bb8,hng loose) 37.50

ROBERTS,B H-New Witness for God, Vols.1 thru 3-SLC-1950,1951-3 vols-blue cl-rprnt (bb8,vf) 100.00

ROBERTS,B H-Seventy's Course in Theology...First Year Book...-SLC-1931-235p-1st ed thus (bb8,tattrd dj) 17.50

ROBERTS,CHARLES G D-Heart That Knows-Bost-1906-Page-1st ed (pp2,sp fade) 45.00*

ROBERTS,D-Mountain of My Fear-NY-1968-157p-1st ed (o10,f,dj) 35.00

ROBERTS,DAN W-Rangers and Sovereignty-San Antonio-1914-Wood Prtg & Engrvng Co-190p-Howes R339-1st ed (gg4,sl spot cov) 75.00

ROBERTS,DAVID-Deborah: a Wilderness Narrative-NY-1970-188p-15 photos,3 maps-1st ed (a4,f,dj) 38.00

ROBERTS,DAVID-Mountain of My Fear-NY-1968-157p-1st ed (p10,f,dj) 35.00

ROBERTS,DONALD-Flyfishing in Still Waters-Portland-1978-4to-75p-photos,illus (m3,f,dj) 20.00

ROBERTS,EDWARDS-Shoshone and Other Western Wonders-NY-1888-275p-cl-1st ed (b1) 50.00

ROBERTS,EDWARDS-With the Invader-SF-1885-Samuel Carson & Co-156p-pict wrps-Rampaging Herd 1917 (g1) 75.00

ROBERTS,GEORGE S-Old Schenectady-Schenectady-nd(1904)-Robson & Adee-red cl wi photo cov,illus-1st ed (ee6,few pgs soil) 65.00

ROBERTS,H ARMSTRONG-Farmer His Own Builder-Phila-1918-McKay-1st ed (h9) 35.00

ROBERTS,JANE-Emir's Education in the Proper Use of Magical Powers-NY-(1979)-Delacorte-138p-cl,b&w illus,L Cherry-1st ed (r3,dj) 15.00

ROBERTS,KENNETH D-Eli Terry and the Connecticut Shelf Clock-Bristol-1973-Ken Roberts Publ Co-4to-xvi+320p-blu bds,illus-1st ed (e2) 30.00

ROBERTS,KENNETH-Battle of Cowpens-NY-1958-111p-maps,illus-1st ed (b7,dj) 35.00

ROBERTS,KENNETH-Battle of Cowpens-NY-1958-Dbldy-1st ed (z2,dj) 30.00

ROBERTS,KENNETH-Boon Island-GC-1956-Dbldy-275,(1)p-cl-1st ed so stated (f1,dj) 25.00

ROBERTS,KENNETH-Boon Island-NY-1956-DD-1st ed (x1,f,dj) 40.00

ROBERTS,KENNETH-Oliver Wiswell-NY-1940-Dbldy,Doran-1st trd ed (bb1,dj sl chip & tn) 25.00

ROBERTS,KENNETH-Seventh Sense-GC-1953-Dbldy-8vo-337p-illus-1st ed (aa5,dj) 25.00

ROBERTS,LESLIE-Chief-Tor-1963-Clarke,Irwin-ix,205p-illus (k10,dj) 25.00*

ROBERTS,LIEUT E M-Flying Fighter-NY-(1918)-Harper & Bros-8vo-xx,340p-cl,frntis,20 illus-1st ed (s2,sp wn) 40.00

ROBERTS,LORD-41 Years in India-Lond-1897-Richard Bentley & Son-2 vols-blu cl,g titles & cov decs,tissue guarded ports,fldg plans,ads (gg6) 150.00

ROBERTS,LORD-41 Years in India-Lond-1901-601p-tree calf bndg,g dec sp,mrbld edges & e.p.-one vol ed (gg2) 150.00

ROBERTS,MAJ N-Breech Loading, Single Shot Match Rifle-NY-1967-293p-photos-scarce 1st ed (gg3,f,dj) 35.00

ROBERTS,MARTHA M-Public Gardens and Arboretums of the U.S.-NY-(1962)-4to-x,148p-half tones,10 col illus (x5,e.p. fox,sp wn) 14.00

ROBERTS,MORLEY-Humble Fisherman-Lond-1932-8vo-260p-photos (m3) 20.00

ROBERTS,MORLEY-On the Earthquake Line-Lond-1924-Arrowsmith-8vo-310p-blu cl,6 tip in col illus (dd7,sl fox) 45.00

ROBERTS,O M-Description of Texas, Its Advantages and Resources...-St.Louis-1881-Gilbert Bk Co-133p+5 maps(4 col)+8 litho col plts-gilt emboss brwn cl-Howes R344-scarce-1st ed (a9) 500.00

ROBERTS,O W-Narrative of Voyages and Excursions on the East Coast and Interior of Central America-1965-U of Fla-302p-fldg map-rprnt of 1827 ed (bb3,f) 25.00

ROBERTS,R W-Tramp to the Klondike or How I Reached the Gold Field of Alaska-(Vaughnsville)-nd(1898?)-43p-prtd wrps-v rare (b1,fox,sl wn,text fox & stnd) 300.00

ROBERTS,S C-Adventures with Authors-Cambridge-1966-CUP-1st ed (ll5,dj) 45.00

ROBERTS,S C-Holmes & Watson-1953-Oxford Univ Pr-1st ed (x7,f,dj) 45.00

ROBERTS,T S-Bird Portraits in Color-1934-U of Minn-4to-90 col plts (bb3) 30.00

ROBERTS,T S-Birds of Minnesota-Mpls-1936-4to-2 vols-cl,92 col plts,maps-2nd rvsd ed (y8,rub) 135.00

ROBERTS,THOMAS S-Birds of Minnesota-1936-U of Minn Pr-2 vols-92 col plts-2nd ed,rvsd (e9) 150.00

ROBERTS,W ADOLPHE-French in the West Indies-Indpls-(1942)-Bobbs Merrill-8vo-335p-9 illus-1st ed (dd5) 25.00

ROBERTS,WARREN-Bibliography of D H Lawrence-Lond-1963-port frntis,illus-1st ed (r2,f,sl chip dj) 60.00

ROBERTSON,ARCHIE-Slow Train to Yesterday-1945-Somerset Bks-189p-photos-1st ed (d3) 15.00

ROBERTSON,ARCHIE-Slow Train to Yesterday-NY-1945-189p-1st ed (n4) 22.00

ROBERTSON,B-Aircraft Camouflage and Markings 1907 to 1954-Letchworth,Herts-1964-4to-232p-cl,col frntis,col plts,b&w illus (s2,dj) 45.00

ROBERTSON,B-ED.-Air Aces of the 1914 to 1918 War-Letchworth, Herts-1959-4to-212p-cl,col frntis,b&w illus (s2,dj) 35.00

ROBERTSON,B-Spitfire, The Story of a Famous Fighter-Letchworth,Herts-1960-4to-212p-cl,col frntis,plts,text illus-1st ed (s2,sp fade) 30.00

ROBERTSON,DAVID-George Mallory-Lond-1969-279p-1st ed (a4,vf,f dj) 85.00

ROBERTSON,FRANK C-Boom Towns of the Great Basin-Denver-(1962)-Sage Bks-331p-illus-1st ed (cc4,dj) 45.00

ROBERTSON,FRANK C-Fort Hall-NY-(1963)-318p-illus-1st ed (j7,f,dj) 35.00

ROBERTSON,FRANK C-Fort Hall-NY-(1963)-Hastings Hs-318p-illus,map-1st ed (gg4,dj) 30.00

ROBERTSON,FRANK C-Soapy Smith-NY-(1961)-Hastings Hs-244p-illus-1st ed (cc4,dj) 25.00

ROBERTSON,GEORGE-Chitral: the Story of a Minor Siege-Lond-1898-368p-dec red cl,maps,illus-1st ed (b7) 95.00

ROBERTSON,GEORGE-Discovery of Tahiti-Lond-1948-Hakluyt Soc-Ser.2,No.98 (v4,f) 150.00

ROBERTSON,GEORGE-General View of the Agriculture of the County of Mid Lothian-Edinburgh-1795-prtd by F Ruthven & Sons-223;135;(4);15p-lea,engraved plts,fldg charts,col map (f1) 100.00

ROBERTSON,HEATHER-Terrible Beauty-Ottawa-1977-Nat'l Mus of Man-8vo-240p-104 illus-1st ed (aa7,sl scuff dj) 35.00*

ROBERTSON,JAMES A-Bibliography of the Philippine Islands: Printed and Manuscript-NY-1970-Krause Rprnt Co-437p-rprnt of orig 1908 ed (c3,f) 35.00

ROBERTSON,JAMES I,JR.-ED.-Rank and File-San Rafael-(1976)-194p-illus-1st ed (n3,f,dj) 15.00

ROBERTSON,JAMES I-Stonewall Brigade-Baton Rouge-1963-LSU Pr-271p-illus-1st ed (n7,sl discol,dj chip) 50.00

ROBERTSON,JOHN-Handbook of Angling for Scotland & the Border Countries-Lond-1861-12mo-184p-fldg map (m3,wn sp top) 40.00

ROBERTSON,P D-Panhandle Pilgrimage-Canyon-1976-Staked Plains Pr-369p-cl,photos-1st ed (w3,f,dj) 40.00

ROBERTSON,PAULINE D-Cowman's Country-Amarillo-1981-Paramount Publ-184p-cl,photos,illus-1st ed (w3,vf) 45.00

ROBERTSON,PRISCILLA-Lewis Farm-Norwood-(1950)-priv publ-x,214,(19)p-illus-only ed (o2) 20.00

ROBERTSON,R MACDONALD-Angling in Wildest Scotland-Lond-1936-8vo-320p-photos,maps (m3,fray dj) 30.00

ROBERTSON,R MACDONALD-In Scotland with a Fishing Rod-Lond-1935-8vo-279p-photos-1st ed (m3) 20.00

ROBERTSON,R MACDONALD-Wade the River,Drift the Loch-Lond-1948-8vo-176p-photos (m3,f,sl chip dj) 24.00

ROBERTSON,R R-Of Sheep and Men-NY-(1957)-Knopf-8vo-307p-12p illus-1st US ed (aa5,f,dj) 25.00

ROBERTSON,THOMAS A-Southwestern Utopia-LA-1947-Ward Ritchie Pr-261p-photos,e.p. maps-1st ed (gg4,dj) 25.00

ROBERTSON,WILLIAM-Hoofprints of the Century-np-nd(1975)-4to-580p+ads (j9) 65.00

ROBESON,KENNETH-Quest of the Spider-NY-(1933)-Street & Smith-pict papr cov bds,iss w/o dj-1st ed (bb1,pgs brwnd,sl wn,rub) 100.00

ROBESON,PAUL-For Freedom and Peace-NY-1949-Council African Affrs-wrps-1st ed (v5,f) 25.00

ROBIDOUX,ORRAL M-Memorial to the Robidoux Brothers-KC-1924-311p-pict cl,frntis,photos,ltd ed,Rittenhouse #491-1st ed (t7) 275.00

ROBIN HOOD-NY-nd(ca.1860)-John McLoughlin-24mo-36p-handcol pict pnk wrps,text illus-scarce (hh9,hng sl separated) 90.00

ROBINS,EDWARD-Twelve Great Actors-NY,Lond-1900-Putnam's-orig g pict cl,frntis port,illus-1st ed (jj9) 40.00

ROBINS,F W-Story of the Lamp-Lond-1939-Oxford U Pr-xiv+155p-gry cl,27 plts-1st ed (dd1) 30.00

ROBINS,JOHN D-Incomplete Anglers-Tor-1943-8vo-229p-illus-1st ed so stated (m3,vf) 17.50

ROBINS,R H-Yurok Language-Berkeley-1958-Univ of Cal-xiv+300p-wrps-1st ed (e2,sl yel wrps) 30.00

ROBINSON'S CRAWFORD COUNTY ROAD BOOK...-Meadville-1892-Robinson-112p+fldg map (l1,sl tn map) 60.00

ROBINSON,ALBERT G-Old New England Houses-NY-1920-Scribner's-4to-viii,29p-dec cl,98 plts-1st prtg (cc10) 75.00

ROBINSON,ALBERT-Old New England Doorways-NY-1919-21p text-dec cl,photos-1st ed (ff10) 20.00

ROBINSON,BEN C-Muskellunge Fishing-NY-1925-12mo-116p-photos-scarce-1st ed (m3,sl spot cov,sl fray dj) 50.00

ROBINSON,BEN C-Pond,Lake & Stream Fishing-Phila-1941-8vo-370p-illus,photos (m3,vf,dj) 14.00

ROBINSON,BEVERLEY-Practical Treatise on Nasal Catarrh-NY-1880-Wm Wood-x+182p-grn cl-1st ed (a2) 45.00

ROBINSON,BROOKS-Putting it All Together-1971-Hawthorn-photos-1st ed (s8,f,f dj) 17.50

ROBINSON,BROOKS-Third Base is My Home-1974-Word-1st ed (p7,f,f dj) 25.00

ROBINSON,CECIL-With the Ears of Strangers-Tucson-1963-U of Az-1st ed (b4,dj) 37.50

ROBINSON,CHANDLER A-ED.-J Evetts Haley and the Passing of the Old West-Austin-1978-Jenkins Publ-239p-frntis,errata slip-1st ed (gg4) 35.00

ROBINSON,CHARLES M-Improvement of Towns and Cities-NY-1901-Putnam-8vo-309p-bds-1st prtg (cc10,ex-libr) 75.00

ROBINSON,CHARLES N-Old Naval Prints-Lond-1924-Studio,Ltd-4to-36p text+96 plts,24 tip in col plts wi guards,g dec blu cl-ltd to 1500c (pp1,sl fox) 650.00

ROBINSON,DAVID M-Baalbek Palmyra-NY-1946-J J Augustin-4to-136p-cl,photos by Hoyningen-Huen-1st ed (t3) 65.00

ROBINSON,DOANE-History of the Dakota or Sioux Indians-Mpls-1956-Ross & Haines-523p-maps & illus (cc4,dj) 30.00

ROBINSON,DOANE-South Dakota-Chig-1930-Amer Hist Soc-3 vols-illus-1st ed (bb4) 150.00

ROBINSON,DOROTHY F-Navajo Indians Today-San Antonio-(1966)-80p-photos,map e.p.-1st ed (v7,f,dj) 15.00

ROBINSON,EDWARD A-Tristram-NY-1927-1st trd ed (m4) 10.00

ROBINSON,EDWIN A-Glory of the Nightingales-NY-1930-Macmillan-1st trd ed (aa9,sp sl dull) 15.00

ROBINSON,EDWIN A-Nicodemus-NY-1932-Macmillan-g titled cl-1st trd ed (aa9) 20.00

ROBINSON,EDWIN A-Talifer-NY-1933-Macmillan-8vo-98p-1st trd ed (ee5,dj) 20.00

ROBINSON,EDWIN A-Talifer-NY-1933-Macmillan-cl-1st trd ed (aa9,f) 15.00

ROBINSON,EDWIN A-Tilbury Town-NY-1953-Macmillan-silv titled cl-1st ed (aa9,f) 15.00

ROBINSON,ELWYN B-History of North Dakota-Lincoln-1966-U of Nebr Pr-599p-map e.p.-1st ed (gg4,dj) 20.00

ROBINSON,EMMA B-History, Department of Iowa Woman's Relief Corps...1884 to 1934-np-1933-64p text-photos (o7) 20.00

ROBINSON,FLORENCE-Palette of Plants-Champaign-1950-Garrard-214p-cl (x6) 22.00

ROBINSON,FRANK B-Strange Autobiography of ...,Founder of Psychiana, Moscow, Idaho-Moscow-1949-274p-cl (d1) 15.00

ROBINSON,FRANK-Frank, The First Year-1976-Holt Rinehart-1st ed (s7,dj) 13.00

ROBINSON,FRANK-My Life Is Baseball-1968-Dbldy-photos-1st ed (s8,dj) 13.50

ROBINSON,GERTRUDE-Bringing Up Raffles-NY-1940-Dutton-pict cl,illus by G Latimer-1st ed (aa9) 30.00

ROBINSON,GIL-Old Wagon Show Days-Cin-1925-250p-2nd prntg (v8) 35.00

ROBINSON,H PERRY-Of Distinguished Animals-Lond-1910-Heinemann-8vo-234p-50 photos-1st ed (aa5) 20.00

ROBINSON,JACKIE-I Never Had it Made-1972-Putnam-1st ed (r7,dj) 20.00

ROBINSON,JACKIE-My Own Story-1948-Greenberg-photos,TP orig,publ simul wi hdbk-scarce-1st ed (s8,wrps sp wn) 125.00

ROBINSON,JOHN-Sailing Ships of New England. Series Three-Salem-1928-Marine Rsrch Soc-45p text-blu cl,plts(nbrd 557 thru 770)-1st ed (dd7) 145.00

ROBINSON,KENNETH-Wilkie Collins-NY-1952-Macmillan-1st ed (z9,f,dj chip,tn) 12.50

ROBINSON,L E-History of Illinois-NY,Cin,Chig-(1909)-288p-cl (k1) 10.00

ROBINSON,MARILYNNE-Housekeeping-1980-FS&G-1st ed (q9,f,dj) 35.00

ROBINSON,PHIL-Sinners and Saints-Bost-1883-370p-orig yel cl-Flake 7392-1st ed (bb8) 100.00

ROBINSON,R S-Shots at Mule Deer-UT-1970-305p-wrps,spiral bndg,photos (gg3,f) 25.00

ROBINSON,RAY-Ted Williams-1962-Putnam-1st ed (q7,dj) 40.00

ROBINSON,ROWLAND E-Sam Lovel's Boy-Bost-1901-12mo-259p (m3) 10.00

ROBINSON,ROWLAND E-Uncle Lisha's Outing-Bost,NY-1897-12mo-308p (m3,f) 15.00

ROBINSON,SARA-Kansas-Lawrence-1899-xi,438p-10th ed (bb9) 45.00

ROBINSON,TOM-Greylock and the Robins-NY-1946-Viking-4to-32p-pict bds,wtrcol illus-1st ed (r3,dj wn & chip) 55.00

ROBINSON,VICTOR-An Essay on Hasheesh-NY-1930-91p-scarce-2nd ed (dd3,dj) 75.00

ROBINSON,W W-Lawyers of Los Angeles-LA-1959-Ward Ritchie-370p-illus-1st ed (d3,dj) 35.00

ROBINSON,W-Gleanings From French Gardens-Lond-1869-Warne-291p-cl (x6,innr hng rnfrcd) 125.00

ROBINSON,WILL H-Story of Arizona-Phoenix-(1919)-Berryhill Co-458p-Six Guns #1877-1st ed (dd4) 65.00

ROBINSON,WILL H-Story of Arizona-Phoenix-1919-458p-frntis,photos,map-Six Guns #1877,scarce-1st ed (t7) 55.00

ROBINSON,WILL H-Under Turquoise Skies-NY-1928-Macmillan-8vo-xvi+538p-cl,photos-1st ed (z4,sp cocked) 40.00

ROBINSON,WILLARD-People's Architecture-Austin-1983-Tex St Hist Assn-4to-365p-photos-1st ed (a9,dj) 35.00

ROBINSON,WILLIAM A-To the Great Southern Sea-NY-1956-Harcourt,Brace-8vo-e.p. maps,plts,diags-1st ed (nn1,wn dj) 35.00

ROBINSON,WILLIAM J-Law Against Abortion-NY-1933-Eugenics Publ-123p+ads-blu cl-1st ed (d2,sl wn) 35.00

ROBINSON,WILLIAM M,JR.-Confederate Privateers-New Haven-1928-Yale U Pr-372p-frntis,ports-1st ed (o7,wn dj) 100.00

ROBINSON,WILLIAM-English Flower Garden-Lond-1883-Murray-303p-cl,illus (x6,rub,pencilng) 95.00

ROBINSON,WILLIAM-Garden Beautiful-Lond-1909-Murray-176p-cl,papr labl (x6,chip labl) 50.00

ROBINSON,WILLIAM-Hardy Flowers-Lond-1900-Grdng Illus-341p-cl (x6) 25.00

ROBISON,CAPT S S-Manual of Wireless Telegraphy 1913-1913-241p-117 illus,photos-3rd ed (h6) 55.00

ROBISON,CAPT S S-Robison's Manual of Radio Telegraphy and Telephony 1918-1918-256p-30 photos,121 illus-4th ed (h6) 50.00

ROBISON,JAMES-Recollections of Rev. Samuel Clawson-Pitt-1883-246p-cl (c1) 25.00

ROBISON,MARY-An Amateur's Guide to the Night-NY-1983-Knopf-1st ed (bb1,as new in dj) 12.50

ROBISON,MARY-Days-NY-1979-Knopf-auth 1st bk-1st ed (bb1,f,dj) 30.00

ROBISON,MARY-Oh-NY-1981-Knopf-1st ed (bb1,as new in dj) 15.00

ROBOTTI,FRANCES D-Whaling and Old Salem-NY-1962-Fountainhead Publ-8vo-xxi,292p-1/2 cl,illus-1st prtg (pp1,dj) 40.00

ROBOTTI,FRANCES D-Whaling and Old Salem-Salem-1950-Newcomb & Gauss-xvi+192p+ads-cl sp,red bds,illus-1st ed (m2) 40.00

ROBOTTI,PETER J-Much Depends on Dinner-NY-(1961)-Fountainhead Publ-306p-tan cl,photos-1st ed (q8) 15.00

ROBSJOHN-GIBBINGS,T H-Homes of the Brave-NY-1954-illus-1st ed (h10,dj) 25.00

ROBY,MARY L-Still as the Grave-NY-1964-Dodd-1st ed (g4,f,dj) 10.00

ROBYNS,GWEN-Mystery of Agatha Christie-NY-1978-Dbldy-illus-1st US ed (h4,f,sl soil dj) 12.50

ROBYNS,GWEN-Potato Cookbook-Owings Mills-1976-Stemmer Hs-4to-136p-pict tan cl,col photos & drwngs-1st ed (q8) 10.00

ROCH,ANDRE-Climbs of My Youth-Lond-1949-159p-1st ed (q10,dj chip) 30.00

ROCH,ANDRE-On Rock & Ice-Lond-1940-lg 8vo-80p-81 photos-1st ed (a4,f,dj) 45.00

ROCHE,ARTHUR S-Ransom-NY-1918-Doran-col illus e.p.-1st ed (l4,dj sl spot,sl chip & tn) 25.00

ROCHE,F J-Historic Locomotive Drawings in 4mm Scale-Lond-1967-104p-spiral bndg-1st ed (n4) 24.00

ROCK,JAMES L-Southern and Western Texas Guide for 1878-St.Louis-1878-A H Granger-282p-illus-1st ed (a9) 300.00

ROCK,JOSEPH F-Indigenous Trees of the Hawaiian Islands-Lawai,Rutland-1974(1913)-lg 8vo-xx,548p-215 photo plts-rvsd ed (hh7,dj,box) 79.00

ROCK,JOSEPH F-Monographic Study of the Hawaiian Species of the Tribe Lobelioideae Family Campanulaceae-Honolulu-1919-B P Bishop Museum-394p+errata,gry cl,blk sp labl wi g titles,frntis,217 plts (nn1,f) 225.00

ROCKEFELLER,JOHN D,JR.-Colorado Industrial Plan...-np-1916-94,(1)p-wrps,prtd slip reading "Compliments of John D Rockefeller, Jr., 26 Broadway,New York" is laid in (b1) 15.00

ROCKEFELLER,MICHAEL C-Asmat of New Guinea-NY-1967-Mus Primitive Art-4to-349p-blck cl,prtd acetate dj,fldg col map,90 col & 510 b&w photos-1st ed (p8,f,dj rub,chip,tn) 185.00

ROCKIES-How to See and Enjoy the Pike's Peak Region from Colorado Springs and Manitou-Colo Spgs-1927-Vol III,No.11-56p-pict wrps,photos,maps (t7,f) 12.50

ROCKLEY,ALICIA-Historic Gardens of England-Lond-1938-Country Life-261p-96 photos (x6) 35.00

ROCKMORE,NOEL-Preservation Hall Portraits-Baton Rouge-1968-LSU Pr-text by Borenstein & Russell-1st ed (w5,f,dj) 35.00

ROCKWELL,F-Home Garden Handbook Peonies-NY-1933-Macmillan-73p (x6,wn dj) 10.00

ROCKWELL,HELEN P-Amateur Epicure's Cook Book-NY-(1958)-Roy-274p-red cl,illus-1st ed (q8,dj) 15.00

ROCKWELL,NORMAN-My Adventures as an Illustrator-GC-1960-Dbldy-8vo-cl,illus,box wi scarce 45 rpm of "Norman Rockwell Reminisces" in sleeve-1st ed (ll10,vf,dj,box) 150.00

ROCKWELL,NORMAN-Norman Rockwell Storybook-NY-(1969)-Windmill/S&S-24 col illus by auth-1st ed (d10,f,sl soil dj) 20.00

ROCKWELL,PAUL A-American Fighters in the Foreign Legion-Bost-1930-376p-tan cl,illus-1st ed (gg2) 40.00

ROCKWELL,ROBERT H-My Way of Becoming a Hunter-NY-1955-8vo-285p-photos (m3,vf,sl chip dj) 15.00

ROCKWELL,WILSON-ED.-Memoirs of a Lawman-Denver-1962-Sage Bks-378p-illus-Six Guns #1881-1st ed (dd4,dj) 50.00

ROCKWELL,WILSON-ED.-Memoirs of a Lawman-Denver-1962-Sage Bks-378p-illus-Six Guns 1881-1st ed (gg4,dj) 50.00

ROCKWELL,WILSON-New Frontier-Denver-1945-World Pr-215p-photos,drwngs,e.p. maps-Six Guns #1879 (dd4,dj) 45.00

ROCKWELL,WILSON-Sunset Slope-Denver-(1956)-Big Mtn Pr-290p-e.p. maps,illus-Six Guns 1880-1st ed (gg4,dj) 45.00

ROCKWOOD,HARRY-Harry Sharpe, the New York Detective-NY-nd(1880s?)-Ogilvie Publ Co-215p-cl (o1,cov soil) 27.50

ROCKWOOD,HARRY-Walt Wheeler, the Scout Detective-NY-(1884)-Ogilvie-124p+ads-cl (l1) 45.00

ROCQ,MARGARET M-California Local History-1970-Stanford U Pr-brwn cl,map-2nd ed,rvsd,enlgd (dd7,as new in dj) 75.00

RODDIS,LOUIS H-Indian Wars of Minnesota-Cedar Rapids-(1956)-Torch Pr-311p-map e.p.,illus-1st ed (ff4,ex-libr,dj) 30.00

RODDIS,LOUIS-Short History of Nautical Medicine-NY-1941-359p (dd3) 80.00

RODEE,MARIAN E-Old Navajo Rugs-Albuq-(1980)-U of NM Pr-113p-pict e.p.col illus-1st ed (gg4,dj) 15.00

RODEE,MARIAN E-Southwestern Weaving-Albuq-(1977)-176p-col photos-1st ed (v7,f,dj) 35.00

RODEE,MARIAN E-Southwestern Weaving-Albuq-(1977)-UNM Pr-176p-col plts-1st ed (ff4,dj) 30.00

RODELL,MARIE-Mystery Fiction-NY-1943-Duell-1st ed (g4,chip dj) 20.00

RODEN,CLAUDIA-Book of Middle Eastern Food-NY-1972-Knopf-453p-1st Amer ed (o6,dj) 20.00

RODENBAUGH,THEO F-From Everglade to Canon with the 2nd Dragoons-NY-1875-561p-pict cl,col frntis,chromolitho's wi tiss guards-Howes R395-rare-1st ed (t7,box) 1,500.00

RODGER,ELLA-Aberdeen Doctors at Home and Abroad, the Narrative of a Medical School-Edinburgh-1893-355p-1st ed (dd3) 75.00

RODGERS,RICHARD-Me and Juliet-NY-1953-1st ed (q5,dj) 20.00

RODGERS,RICHARD-Oklahoma-NY-(1942)-Random-1st ed (dd2,f,dj rprd,chip) 50.00

RODGERS,W R-Europa and the Bull...-Lond-1952-Secker & Warburg-1st ed (z8,vf,f dj) 25.00

RODIN,AUGUSTE-Cathedrals of France & Later Drawings-Bost-1965-2 vols-70 illus(40 col)-1st Engl transl (r2,box) 100.00

RODMAN,SELDEN-Horace Pippin-NY-1947-Quadrangle Pr-4to-cl,illus-1st ed (oo6,dj chip) 180.00

RODNEY,GEORGE B-As a Cavalryman Remembers-Caldwell-1944-297p-photos,illus-1st ed (t7,chip dj) 55.00

RODNEY,THOMAS-Diary of Captain Thomas Rodney, 1776 to 1777...-Wilmington-1888-Hist Soc of Del, VIII-53p-wrps (aa6,chip) 40.00

RODNEY,WILLIAM-Joe Boyle-Tor-1974-McGraw Hill Ryerson-8vo-xiii,368p-12 illus,3 maps-1st ed (cc7,dj) 25.00*

ROE,EDW P-Success with Small Fruits-NY-1880-sq 8vo-313p-dec cl,illus (w10) 24.50

ROE,F G-Indian And the Horse-Norman-(1955)-434p-illus-1st ed (n3) 32.50

ROE,F G-Indian and the Horse-Norman-1955-U of Okla Pr-434p-1st ed (d3,dj) 35.00

ROE,F G-North American Buffalo-Tor-1972-991p-frntis,fldg map rear pckt (r8,f,dj) 30.00

ROE,FRANCES-Army Letters from an Officer's Wife, 1871 to 1888-NY-1909-D Appleton-x+387p-blu cl,10 plts-Howes R403-1st ed (b2,sl soil) 65.00

ROE,MARY E-E P Roe, Reminiscences of His Life-NY-1899-235p-illus-1st ed (n3,ex-libr) 30.00

ROEBLING,JOHANN A-Diary of My Journey from Muehlhausen in Thuringia via Bremen to the U.S. of North America...1831-Trenton-1931-124p-cl,port (aa6) 50.00

ROEBURT,JOHN-Lunatic Time-NY-1956-Simon-1st ed (h4,f,dj) 10.00

ROEDEL,PHIL-Common Marine Fishes of California-Sacramento-1948-8vo-153p-wrps,photos (m3) 17.50

ROEDER,BILL-Jackie Robinson-1950-Barnes-1st ed (ff2,dj) 75.00

ROEDER,HELEN-ED.-Ordeal of Captain Roeder-NY-1961-248p-illus-1st Amer ed (b7,dj) 30.00

ROEDER,RALPH-Catherine De Medici and the Lost Revolution-Lond-1937-Viking-629p-dec wht cl,16 plts-1st Amer ed (gg6,chip dj) 15.00

ROEDIGER,VICTORIA M-Ceremonial Costumes of the Pueblo Indians-Berkeley-1941-251p-40 col plts,25 figs-v scarce-1st ed (v7,f,dj) 175.00

ROEMER,DR FERDINAND-Texas with Particular Reference to German Immigration and the Physical Appearance of the Country-San Antonio-1935-Standard-301p-fldg map-1st ed in Engl (a9,dj) 110.00

ROENIGK,ADOLPH-Pioneer History of Kansas-(Denver)-(1933)-Great Wstrn Publ-illus-Six Guns #1884 (cc4) 150.00

ROESSEL,ROBERT A,JR.-Pictorial History of the Navajo from 1860 to 1910-Rough Rock-1980-240p-photos-1st ed (v7,f) 25.00

ROESSEL,RUTH-COMP.-Papers on Navajo Culture and Life-Tsaile-1970-193p-spiral wrps,photos,maps-1st ed (v7,f) 20.00

ROETHEL,H S-Kandinsky-NY-1979-folio-48 tip in col illus-1st Amer ed (h10) 60.00

ROETHKE,THEODORE-Collected Poems of...-1966-Dbldy-1st ed (u10,f,f dj) 65.00

ROETHKE,THEODORE-Party at the Zoo-NY-(1963)-Crowell Collier-illus bds,illus by A Swiller-1st ed (b8,sm tr,edgewn) 50.00

ROETHKE,THEODORE-Party at the Zoo-NY-(1963)-Crowell Collier-tll 4to-dec cl,no dj as iss,illus,Al Swiller-1st ed (t1) 40.00

ROETHKE,THEODORE-Words For the Wind-Lond-1957-Secker & Warburg-precedes Amer ed-1st ed (u1,f,f dj) 135.00

ROGERS,AGNES-From Man to Machine, a Pictorial History of Invention-Bost-1941-Little,Brown-4to-157p-illus,photos-1st ed (dd5,dj) 20.00

ROGERS,BRUCE-PI-Cleve,NY-1953-185p-facs (a3,dj) 24.00

ROGERS,BRUCE-PI-Cleve-1953-World-1st ed (u2,dj) 40.00

ROGERS,CAPT WOODES-Cruising Voyage Round the World-Amsterdam-1969-N Israel-8vo-5 fldg maps & tbls-(facs rprnt of Lond 1712 Bell ed) (p8,as new) 80.00

ROGERS,DOROTHY-Highways Across the Horizon-Lond-(1966)-Hale-8vo-192p-24 photos-1st Brit ed (cc5,dj) 15.00

ROGERS,GARET-Scandal in Eden-1963-Dial-1st ed (s9,f,dj) 25.00

ROGERS,GEORGE-Universalism Vindicated...-np(Cin ?)-nd(1839?)-36p-orig blnk wrps (b1) 50.00

ROGERS,H C B-British Army of the Eighteenth Century-NY-1977-252p-maps,illus-1st ed (b7,f,dj) 30.00

ROGERS,H C B-Mounted Troops of the British Army-Lond-1959-256p-33 plts(incl 17 col)-1st ed (b7,f,dj) 60.00

ROGERS,H C B-Weapons of the British Soldier-Lond-1960-259p-illus-1st ed (gg2,f,dj) 50.00

ROGERS,HENRY D-Report on the Geological Survey of the State of New Jersey-Phila-1836-174,(1)p-wrps,fldg col geo sect-v scarce (aa6,fox) 400.00

ROGERS,J E-Shell Book-1936-Branford-503p-8 col & 96 b&w plts (bb3,f,fray dj) 22.00

ROGERS,J SMYTH-Catalogue of a Cabinet of Materia Medica-NY-1826-Swords-44p-new salmon col wrps (u2,rbnd) 100.00

ROGERS,JOEL T-Red Right Hand-NY-1945-Simon-1st ed (g4,dj) 20.00

ROGERS,JOHN W-Finding Literature on the Texas Plains-Dallas-1931-Southwest-57p-1st ed (a9) 100.00

ROGERS,JOHN W-Lusty Texans of Dallas-NY-1951-Dutton-384p-frntis,e.p. maps-Six Guns 1889-1st ed (bb4,sl wn dj) 30.00

ROGERS,R VASHON,JR.-Law of the Road or the Wrongs and Rights of a Traveler-Edinburgh,Tor-1881-Carswell-sm 8vo-322p-red cl-1st ed (s1) 75.00

ROGERS,ROBERT-Great Whitetails of North America-Corpus Christi-1981-8vo-223p-photos,maps-rvsd ed (m3,vf) 20.00

ROGERS,SAMUEL-You Leave Me Cold-NY-1946-Harper-1st ed (g4,f,sl wn dj) 20.00

ROGERS,STANLEY-Freak Ships-Lond-(1936)-Bodley Head-8vo-244p-110 illus by auth-1st Brit ed (dd5,dj tn,chip) 35.00

ROGERS,THOMAS-Pursuit of Happiness-(NY)-(1968)-NAL-auth 1st bk-1st ed (bb1,dj) 40.00

ROGERS,W G-Wise Men Fish Here-NY-(1965)-Harcourt Brace-1st ed (bb2,f,dj) 40.00

ROGERS,WILL-Will Roger's Illiterate Digest-NY-1924-Boni-1st ed (hh5,f) 20.00

ROGIN,GILBERT-Fencing Master and Other Stories-NY-(1965)-Random-auth 1st bk-1st ed (hh5,f,f dj) 15.00

ROGOFF,HARRY-An East Side Epic-NY-(1930)-Vanguard-vi+311p-blk cl-1st ed (k2,dj) 25.00

ROHDE,ELEANOUR S-Garden of Herbs-Lond-1921-P L Warner-ix,232+(4)p ads-cl,illus-1st ed (dd10) 22.00

ROHDE,ELEANOUR S-Gardens of Delight-NY-1934-Flint-307p-cl (x6,fade,sl fox) 16.00

ROHDE,ELEANOUR S-Old English Herbals-Lond-1922-Longmans-xii,243p-cl,col frntis,b&w plts (x6,sl fox) 110.00

ROHDE,ELEANOUR S-Oxford's College Gardens-Lond-(1932)-xii,193p-blu cl,g sp,24 col,1 b&w,7 monotone illus (x5) 45.00

ROHDE,ELEANOUR S-Rose Recipes-(Lond)-(1939)-Routledge-94p (m6,dj) 25.00

ROHDE,ELEANOUR S-Scented Garden-Bost-1936-Flint-311p-cl (x6,cl soil) 15.00

ROHMER,SAX-Bimbashi Baruk of Egypt-NY-1944-McBride-1st ed (x7,sl chip dj) 135.00

ROHMER,SAX-Bimbashi Baruk of Egypt-NY-1944-McBride-pict dj-1st ed (bb1,dj sl chip & wn) 175.00

ROHMER,SAX-Book of Fu Manchu-NY-1929-McBride-1st ed thus (j4,sl spot cov) 20.00

ROHMER,SAX-Day the World Ended-1930-DD-1st ed (x7,dj sp pc missing) 75.00

ROHMER,SAX-Day the World Ended-NY-1930-Dbldy CC-1st US ed (d4) 15.00

ROHMER,SAX-Drums of Fu Manchu-1939-CC-1st Amer ed (s10,f,sl tn dj) 225.00

ROHMER,SAX-Fu Manchu's Bride-1933-DD-1st ed (x7) 33.00

ROHMER,SAX-Fu Manchu's Bride-NY-(1933)-Burt-reprint (e4,f,dj) 25.00

ROHMER,SAX-Golden Scorpion-1919-Methuen-1st ed (x7) 75.00

ROHMER,SAX-Grey Face-1924-DD-1st ed (x7,sl fray sp) 25.00

ROHMER,SAX-Hand of Fu Manchu-1917-McBride-1st ed (x7,weak hng) 55.00

ROHMER,SAX-Hangover House-1949-Random-1st ed (x7,f,dj) 45.00

ROHMER,SAX-Island of Fu Manchu-1941-CC-1st Amer ed (s10,dj) 250.00

ROHMER,SAX-Quest of the Sacred Slipper-Lond-1919-Pearson-1st ed (g4) 25.00

ROHMER,SAX-Romance of Sorcercy-NY-1973-Causeway Bks-8vo-xviii,320p-frntis,11 illus (aa7,rub dj) 15.00*

ROHMER,SAX-She Who Sleeps-NY-1928-Dbldy,Doran-1st ed (m4,f,dj sl wn,creased) 95.00

ROHMER,SAX-Sumuru-1951-Fawcett-wrps-1st ed (x7,f) 20.00

ROHMER,SAX-Tales of East and West-NY-1933-Dbldy CC-1st US ed (f4,f,sl rprd dj) 250.00

ROHMER,SAX-Tales of Secret Egypt-NY-1919-McBride-1st US ed (d4,sp drknd) 25.00

ROHMER,SAX-White Velvet-NY-1936-Dbldy-1st US ed (h4) 15.00

ROHMER,SAX-Yellow Shadows-NY-1926-1st ed (k9) 10.00

ROHMER,SAX-Yu'an Hee See Laughs-NY-1932-Dbldy CC-1st US ed (e4) 20.00

ROHN,ARTHUR H-Culture Change and Continuity on Chapin Mesa-Lawrence-(1977)-306p-photos,maps-1st ed (v7,f,dj) 20.00

ROJAS,ARNOLD R-Lore of the California Vaquero-Fresno-1958-Acad Libr Guild-162p-illus-1st ed (bb4,dj) 35.00

ROKITANSKY,CARL-Manual of Pathological Anatomy-Phila-1855-4 vols in 2-brwn cl (g10,sp fade,sl wn) 185.00

ROLF,EDWIN-Lincoln Battalion-NY-1939-Vets Lincoln Brigades-312p-1st ed (ff1) 35.00

ROLFE,D-Airplanes of the World-NY-1954-8vo-320p-cl,illus by auth,illus e.p.-1st ed (s2,chip dj) 45.00

ROLFE,EDWIN-Permit Me Refuge-LA-1955-Cal Qtrly-ltd to 1000c,nbrd-1st ed (w5,f,sp tn dj) 35.00

ROLLE,ANDREW F-ED.-Road to Virginia City-Norman-1960-143p-photos-1st ed (t7,f,dj) 25.00

ROLLE,ANDREW F-ED.-Road to Virginia City-Norman-1960-U of Okla Pr-sm 4to-xxiii+143p-cl,photos,map-1st ed so stated (z4,f,sp fade dj) 20.00

ROLLER,DAVID C-Encyclopedia of Southern History-Baton Rouge-(1979)-1421p-illus,maps-1st ed (n3,dj) 55.00

ROLLESTON,HUMPHRY-Internal Medicine-NY-1930-92p-1st ed (dd3) 60.00

ROLLINS,PHILIP A-Cowboy-1922-Scribner-353p-Six Guns #1891-1st ed (r8,sp fray) 45.00

ROLLINS,PHILIP A-Gone Haywire-NY-1939-Scribners-(xii),269p-dec cl,illus,P Hurd,pict dj-1st prtg (v1,sl chip dj) 65.00

ROLLINS,PHILIP A-Jinglebob-NY-1927-Scribner's-262p-cl,4 plts,J DeYong-1st ed (r3) 25.00

ROLLINS-GRIFFIN,RAMONA-Chaco Canyon Ruins-Flagstaff-(1971)-95p-col frntis,photos-1st ed (v7,f,dj) 15.00

ROLLINSON,JOHN K-Wyoming Cattle Trails-1948-Caxton-illus,maps-Six Guns #1894-3rd prtg (r8) 55.00

ROLLO,W KEITH-Art of Fly Fishing-Lond-1931-8vo-224p-photos,illus-1st ed (m3) 22.50

ROLPH,C H-Books in the Dock-(Lond)-(1969)-Andre Deutsch-144p-bds-1st ed (dd10,dj) 20.00

ROLPH,GEORGE M-Something About Sugar-SF-1917-John J Newbegin-341p-photo plts-Bitting p.403 (a8,sl wn cov) 75.00

ROLT,H A-Grayling Fishing in South Country Streams-Lond-1901-72p-illus (gg3,f) 15.00

ROLT,H A-Grayling's Fishing-Lond-1905-12mo-164p-photos-rvsd & enlgd ed (m3,f) 25.00

ROLT-WHEELER,F-Wonder of War in the Air-Bost-(1917)-Lothrop,Lee & Shepard-8vo-illus cl,frntis,41p plts-1st ed (s2) 35.00

ROLT-WHEELER,FRANCIS-Boy with the U.S. Weather Men-Bost-1917-Lothrop,Lee & Shepard-336p-pict blu cl,photos-1st ed (hh6,cor bump) 10.00

ROLT-WHEELER,FRANCIS-Science History of the Universe-NY-1910-Curr Lit Publ-10 vols-g sp lettrng,illus-early prtg (y10) 50.00

ROLVAAG,O E-Giants in the Earth-NY-1927-Harper & Bros-465p-cl-1st ed so stated (a1) 20.00

ROLVAAG,O E-Giants in the Earth-NY-1927-Harper & Bros-yel/olive cl-1st ed (f2,dj rub & edgewn) 40.00

ROMAN LETTER-Chig-1952-Lakeside Pr-wrps,illus-1st ed (r2) 25.00

ROMAN,ERL-Fishing for Fun in Salty Waters-Phila-1940-12mo-173p-photos (m3,f,dj) 15.00

ROMAN,JEAN-Paris Fin De Siecle-NY-1960-Golden Griffin Bks-bds,photos-1st ed (t3,dj) 40.00

ROMANCE OF TEA-NY-1934-Irwin,Harrison,Whitney-119p-wrps,illus,maps (a8) 16.00

ROMANES,GEORGE J-Mental Evolution in Man-NY-1889-Appleton-x+452p+ads-maroon cl-1st Amer ed (dd1) 65.00

ROMBAUER,IRMA S-Cookbook for Girls and Boys-(1952)-Bobbs-sm 4to-245p-check red/wht cl-rvsd ed (q8) 16.50

ROMBAUER,IRMA S-Joy of Cooking-(1936)-Bobbs Merrill-628p-dec yel cl,illus-4th prtg (q8) 75.00

ROMBAUER,IRMA S-Joy of Cooking-(1953)-Bobbs-1113p-blu cl,illus by Hoffman-new ed,enlgd (q8) 25.00

ROMBAUER,IRMA S-Joy of Cooking-Indpls-1946-Bobbs-Merrill-illus,M R Becker (u6,dj) 55.00

ROMBAUER,IRMA S-Joy of Cooking-Phila-(c.1931-1943)-Blakiston Co-685p (k6,dj) 50.00

ROMBAUER,IRMA S-Streamlined Cooking-Indpls-(1939)-Bobbs Merrill-210p-blu buckram bds (m6) 15.00

ROMBOLA,JOHN-Rombola by Rombola-NY-1965-Barnes-4to-160p-col illus bds,col & b&w illus (r10,f dj) 12.50

ROMER,FRANK-100 Years of Books...To Celebrate the 100th Anniversary of the Davey Company-Jersey City-(1942)-Davey-prtd by Wm Rudge-1st ed (w1) 20.00

ROMER,JOHN-Valley of the Kings-NY-1981-Morrow-lg 8vo-293p-16 col plts,150 b&w illus-1st US ed (gg5,sl tn dj) 20.00

ROMERO,P B-Mexico & Africa from the Sights of My Rifle-Mexico-1960-priv prtg of 1000c-322p-red imitation lea,gilt jaguar head on cov,photos-scarce (gg3) 215.00

ROMERO,P B-My Adventure with Tigers & Lions-Mexico-1960-priv prtg of 1000c-234p-photos-scarce (gg3,vf,dj) 215.00

ROMIG,EMILY C-Pioneer Woman in Alaska-Caldwell-1948-140p-illus-scarce-Smith 8763 (a7,f,sl fade dj) 50.00

RONALD,MARY-Luncheons-NY-1906-Century-223p-pict bds,photos (a8,bds soil & wn) 25.00

RONALDS,ALFRED-Fly-Fisher's Entomology-Cin-nd-8vo-152p-20 col plts (m3,vf) 75.00

RONALDSHAY,EARL OF-Life of Lord Curzon-Lond-1928-Ernest Benn-3 vols-blu cl,photos (gg6,rub,sp fade) 45.00

RONAN,PETER-History of the Flathead Indians-Mpls-(c1965)-Ross & Haines-85p+index,illus-Howes R428 (cc4,dj) 20.00

RONAYNE,E-Ronayne's Reminiscences-Chig-1900-Free Methodist Publ Hs-445p-cl-1st ed (mm10) 25.00

RONTE,DIETER-ET AL-Batuz-NY-1981-Rizzoli-4to-175p-tan cl,b&w & col illus (r10,f dj) 45.00

ROOF,KATHARINE M-Life and Art of William Merritt Chase-NY-1917-Scribner's-8vo-cl/bds-1st ed (oo6,sl rub) 85.00

ROOKE,LEON-Broad Back of the Angel-NY-(1977)-Fict Collective-1st ed (bb1,as new in dj) 20.00

ROOKER,WILLIAM A-Fruit Pectin-NY-1928-Ari Publ-170p-grn bds-Bitting p.405 (a8) 20.00

ROOME,J WILLIAM-Tramping Through Africa-NY-1930-Macmillan-8vo-xii,330p-orig cl,plts(1 fldg)-1st ed (bb6,sl tn sp,sl fox) 115.00

ROOME,WILLIAM-Early Days and Early Surveys of East New Jersey-Morristown-1883-56p-wrps (aa6,lacks rear wrps) 45.00

ROONEY,FRANK-Courts of Memory-NY-(1954)-Vanguard-auth 1st bk-1st ed (bb1,sl soil dj) 35.00

ROONEY,FRANK-Shadow of God-NY-(1967)-HB&W-1st ed (bb1,dj) 25.00

ROONEY,JAMES-Autopsy of the Horse-Huntington-1976-Krieger (j9) 20.00

ROONEY,JAMES-Biomechanics of Lameness in Horses-Balt-1969-Williams & Wilkins-1st ed (f10) 40.00

ROONWAL,M L-Primates of South Asia-1977-Harvard-421p-illus (bb3,f,dj) 35.00

ROOS,K-Made Up to Kill-1940-DM-auth 1st bk-1st ed (x7,sl spot cov,rnfrcd dj) 50.00

ROOS,KELLEY-Blonde Died Dancing-NY-1956-Dodd-1st US ed (d4,dj) 15.00

ROOS,KELLEY-Grave Danger-Lond-1966-Eyre-1st Brit ed (e4,dj) 12.50

ROOS,KELLEY-Suddenly One Night-1970-Dodd-1st Amer ed (s10,dj) 12.50

ROOS,KELLEY-To Save His Life-Lond-1969-Cassell-1st Brit ed (e4,dj) 12.50

ROOSEVELT PANAMA LIBEL CASE AGAINST THE NEW YORK WORLD AND INDIANAPOLIS NEWS-(NY)-1910-NY World-109p (e1,sl wn wrps) 45.00

ROOSEVELT,A E-Hunting Big Game in the Eighties-NY-1933-182p (gg3,cov spot) 20.00

ROOSEVELT,ELEANOR-India and the Awakening East-NY-(1953)-Harper-8vo-237p-photos-1st ed (jj5,dj) 15.00

ROOSEVELT,KERMIT-Sentimental Safari-NY-1963-8vo-286p-photos-1st ed (m3,vf,chip dj) 25.00

ROOSEVELT,NICHOLAS-Philippines: a Treasure and a Problem-NY-1926-Sears-315p-frntis & e.p. maps (c3) 24.00

ROOSEVELT,Q-Quentin Roosevelt. A Sketch with Letters-NY-1921-8vo-xii,282p-cl,frntis,4p plts (s2) 40.00

ROOSEVELT,R B-Superior Fishing-NY-1865-304p+ads-illus (gg3,rbnd) 15.00

ROOSEVELT,THEODORE-African Game Trails-1910-Scribners-583p-dec cov,photos (gg3,vf) 80.00

ROOSEVELT,THEODORE-African Game Trails-NY-1924-12mo-2 vols (m3) 25.00

ROOSEVELT,THEODORE-California Addresses-SF-1903-153p-19 photos-1st ed (d3) 45.00

ROOSEVELT,THEODORE-East of the Sun & West of the Moon-NY-1927-8vo-284p-photos (m3) 20.00

ROOSEVELT,THEODORE-Fear God and Take Your Own Part-1916-Doran-1st ed (x2,innr hng crackng,dj) 125.00

ROOSEVELT,THEODORE-Historic Towns, New York-Lond-1891-Longmans,Green-1st ed (l9,sp chip,sm spot on t.p.) 200.00

ROOSEVELT,THEODORE-Hunting Adventures in the West-NY-1927-372p-photos (gg3,vf) 45.00

ROOSEVELT,THEODORE-Hunting and Exploring Adventures of...,Told in His Own Words-NY-1955-Dial-8vo-431p-1st ed thus (jj5,dj tn) 10.00

ROOSEVELT,THEODORE-Hunting the Grizzly and Other Stories-ny-1910-8vo-296p-frontis (m3) 25.00

ROOSEVELT,THEODORE-Hunting the Grizzly-NY-1900-12mo-247p-illus (m3) 17.50

ROOSEVELT,THEODORE-Hunting Trips of a Ranchman-NY-1909-Knickerbocker Pr-328p-brwn cl,g dec,t.e.g.,illus-Allegheny ed (ee3,f) 165.00

ROOSEVELT,THEODORE-Hunting Trips of a Ranchman-NY-1910-8vo-348p-frontis (m3) 10.00

ROOSEVELT,THEODORE-Outdoor Pastimes of an American Hunter-NY-1922-8vo-409p-photos (m3,vf) 17.50

ROOSEVELT,THEODORE-Outdoor Pastimes of an American Hunter-NY-1926-409p (gg3,f) 15.00

ROOSEVELT,THEODORE-Ranch Life & the Hunting Trail-NY-1915-187p-illus by Remington (gg3) 55.00

ROOSEVELT,THEODORE-Ranch Life & the Hunting Trail-NY-1966-187p-simulated lea cov,illus by Remington (gg3,vf) 22.00

ROOSEVELT,THEODORE-Roosevelt's Hunting Adventures in the West-NY-1927-372p-illus by Frost,Remington,others (gg3,f) 45.00

ROOSEVELT,THEODORE-Rough Riders-NY-1922-8vo-320p-photos (m3,vf) 17.50

ROOSEVELT,THEODORE-Theodore Roosevelt's Letters to His Children-NY-1919-Scribner-1st ed (hh5) 15.00

ROOSEVELT,THEODORE-Through the Brazilian Wilderness-Lond-1914-John Murray-49 photos,2 maps-1st Brit ed (p6,sun,sp sl wn) 150.00

ROOSEVELT,THEODORE-Through the Brazilian Wilderness-NY-1914-8vo-(1),383p-cl,frntis,2 maps(1 fldg),48 photo plts-1st ed (y8,lt soil) 75.00

ROOSEVELT,THEODORE-Through the Brazilian Wilderness-NY-1914-Scribner's-383p-photos,fldg map-1st ed (f9,sl spot,fade,uncut) 50.00

ROOSEVELT,THEODORE-Through the Brazilian Wilderness-NY-1929(1914)-8vo-(8),410p-cl,frntis,2 maps(1 fldg),8 photos (y8,dj tn) 30.00

ROOSEVELT,THEODORE-Wilderness Hunter-8vo-1893-8vo-472p-frontis,A B Frost (m3) 35.00

ROOSEVELT,THEODORE-Winning of the West-NY-1889-Putnam's-2 vols-maroon & grn cl,maps-Howes R433-1st ed,1st iss(wi "diameter" split between pgs 160 & 161) (b2,sp fade,cov soil,flecked) 110.00

ROOT & CONNELLY-Overland Stage to Calfornia-Columbus-1950-630p-illus,fldg map-rprnt of rare 1901 1st ed (f7) 65.00

ROOT,A I-ABC and XYZ of Bee Culture-1929-Root-815p-Illus (bb3) 13.00

ROOT,CHARLES P-Automobile Troubles and How to Remedy Them-Chig-1910-Chas C Thompson Co-219p+ads-cl-5th ed-revsd (j1,sl soil) 12.50

ROOT,E MERRILL-Frank Harris-NY-1947-324p-cl-1st ed so stated (n1,sl wn dj) 15.00

ROOT,FRANK-Overland Stage to California-Topeka-1901-publ by auth-630p-100 illus,31 ports,fldg map-Howes R434-Graff 3562--1st ed (d3,sl wtrstnd,hngs crack) 75.00

ROOT,JONATHAN-Halliburton, the Magnificent Myth-NY-(1965)-Coward McCann-8vo-288p-8p photos-1st ed (ff5,sl tn dj) 35.00

ROOT,L C-Quinby's New Bee-Keeping-NY-1883-Orange Judd-270p-cl,illus (d1) 20.00

ROOT,WAVERLEY-Food of France-1958-Knopf-maps,photos,drwngs-1st ed (q8,cov wn) 15.00

ROOT,WAVERLY-Best of Italian Cooking-NY-(1974)-G&D-271p-illus-1st prtg (q6) 30.00

ROPER,ALLEN-Ancient Eugenics-Mpls-1975-76p-(facs of 1913 ed) (dd3) 30.00

ROPER,LANNING-Gardens in the Royal Park at Windsor-GC-1959-4to-128p-32 col photos,59 hlf tones (x5,rprd dj) 25.00

ROPER,LANNING-Gardens in the Royal Park at Windsor-Lond-1961-Reprint Soc-4vo-128p-col photos (x6,dj) 30.00

ROPER,LANNING-On Gardens and Gardening-NY-1969-Harper & Row-4to-240p-cl,16 col plts-1st US ed (cc10,dj) 40.00

ROPER,W F-Experiments of a Handgunner-PA-1949-NRA Libr Bk-202p-photos (gg3,f,dj) 40.00

ROREM,NED-Paris Diary of Ned Rorem-NY-(1966)-Geo Braziller-photos-1st ed (a10,sl rub dj) 17.50

RORER,MRS S T-Dainties-(1904)-Arnold-16mo-90p+8p ads-brwn cl-(enlgd from 1894 1st ed)-1st ed thus (q8) 20.00

RORER,MRS S T-Mrs.Rorer's Philadelphia Cook Book-(1914)-Arnold-591p-dec brwn cl (q8,cov fade,hng crack) 15.00

ROSBOROUGH,E H-Tying & Fishing the Fuzzy Nymphs-Chiloquin-1965-12mo-88p-wrps,illus,photos-scarce-1st ed (m3,pres cpy) 50.00

ROSCOE,D T-Mountaineering-Lond-1976-181p-1st ed (q10,f,dj) 18.00

ROSCOE,THEODORE-Only in New England, the Story of a Gaslight Crime-NY-(1959)-241p-cl (n1,tn dj) 12.50

ROSCOE,THEODORE-To Live and Die in Dixie-NY-1961-Scribners-1st ed (j4,f,dj) 20.00

ROSCOE,THEODORE-United States Destroyer Operations in World War II-Annapolis-(1953)-sm 4to-xviii,582p-frntis,plts,text illus,e.p. maps (s2) 75.00

ROSCOE,THEODORE-Web of Conspiracy-Englewood Cliffs-(1959)-562p-illus,errata slip-1st ed (c4) 50.00

ROSCOE,THEODORE-Wonderful Lips of Thibong Linh-W Kingston-1981-Donald M Grant-illus-1st ed (bb1,as new in dj) 20.00

ROSE,ALFRED-ED.-Register of Erotic Books-NY-1965-Jack Russell-2 vols (e3,f) 40.00

ROSE,BARBARA-Alexander Liberman-NY-(1981)-Abbeville-folio-cl-1st ed (oo6,dj) 75.00

ROSE,BARBARA-Claes Oldenburg-NY-1970-MOMA-oblng 8vo-222p-soft vinyl wrps,b&w & col illus (r10) 65.00

ROSE,CAPT T D-Pro Le Gome Na Ry Preliminary, Introductory-Dayton-(1903)-225+ads-cl (k1) 27.50

ROSE,EUGENE-High Odyssey-Berkeley-1974-160p-1st ed (p10,f,dj) 25.00

ROSE,JOHN-United States' Arithmetician-Bridgeton-1830-John Richards-ix,(3),240p (aa6) 150.00

ROSE,LISLE A-Assault on Eternity-Annapolis-1980-Naval Inst Pr-8vo-292p-blu cl,illus-1st ed (dd7,f,f dj) 30.00

ROSE,PETE-Pete Rose Story-1970-World-photos-1st ed (s8,f,dj) 17.50

ROSE,PETE-Pete Rose, My Life in Baseball-1979-Dbldy-1st ed (s7,f,dj) 15.00

ROSE,PETE-Pete Rose, My Life in Baseball-1979-Dbldy-photos-1st ed (s8,f,f dj) 20.00

ROSE,ROBERT R-Advocates and Adversaries-Chig-1977-lxiii;328p-cl-Lakeside Classics ed (h1) 15.00

ROSE,RONALD-Living Magic-NY-1956-Rand McNally-8vo-240p-8p illus-1st ed (cc7,rub dj) 20.00*

ROSE,RONALD-Living Magic-NY-1956-Rand McNally-8vo-240p-b&w photos-1st prtg (nn1) 12.50

ROSE,SIR ALEC-My Lively Lady-NY-(1969,68)-McKay-8vo-187p-16p photos-1st US ed (jj5,f,dj) 12.50

ROSEBERRY,C R-Challenging Skies-GC-1966-4to-viii,534p-illus cl,illus-1st ed (s2,dj) 40.00

ROSEBORO,JOHN-Glory Days with the Dodgers-1978-Atheneum-1st ed (ff2,dj) 20.00

ROSEBURY,THEODOR-Life on Man-NY-(1969)-Viking-8vo-239p-1st ed (gg5,dj) 12.50

ROSEN,HAROLD-Hypnotherapy in Clinical Pyschiatry-NY-1953-Julian Pr-1st ed (y9,dj) 19.00

ROSEN,M W-Viking Rocket Story-Lond-(1956)-8vo-248p-cl,frntis,28p plts-1st ed (s2,dj) 20.00

ROSENBACH,A S W-Book Hunter's Holiday-Bost-1936-Houghton Mifflin-1st trd ed (w1,sl soil) 25.00

ROSENBACH,A S W-Books and Bidders-Bost-1927-Little,Brown-1st trd ed (w1,f,dj) 35.00

ROSENBACH,A S W-Early American Children's Books-Portland-1933-Southworth Pr-8vo-lix,354p-qtr maroon mor,dec bds,t.e.g.,col illus,ltd to 585c,nbrd,autg (t10,f,box) 400.00

ROSENBACH,A S W-First Theatrical Company in America-Worcester-1939-Amer Antiq Soc-prtd wrps,plt-1st ed (jj9,f) 30.00

ROSENBACH,A S W-Unpublishable Memoirs-Lond-1924-Castle-frntis-1st Brit ed (kk5,f,dj) 120.00

ROSENBAUM,ART-Giants of San Francisco-1963-Coward McCann-photos-1st ed (s8,f,dj) 20.00

ROSENBAUM,ROBERT A-Earnest Victorians-NY-1961-Hawthorn Bks-8vo-383p-blk cl,illus-1st ed (nn1,dj) 15.00

ROSENBERG,BETTY-Checklist of the Published Writings of Lawrence Clark Powell-LA-1966-U of Ca-pap wrps-1st ed (w1,f) 17.50

ROSENBERG,HAROLD-Saul Steinberg-NY-1978-Knopf-4to-256p-illus wrps,274 illus(incl 64 col) (r10) 10.00

ROSENBERG,JAMES N-50 Lithographs-NY-1964-Abrams-oblng folio-unpgd-beige cl,50 lithos-ltd to 1000c,autg (r10,f dj) 45.00

ROSENBERG,JOHN-Dorothy Richardson-NY-1973-Knopf-1st US ed (x9,f,dj) 10.00

ROSENBERG,SAMUEL-Naked is the Best Disguise-Indpls-1974-Bobbs-1st ed (f4,dj) 15.00

ROSENBLAT,JULIA C-Dining with Sherlock Holmes-Indpls-1976-Bobbs Merrill-1st ed (w9,f,dj) 90.00

ROSENBLUM,L A-ED.-Squirrel Monkey-1968-8vo-451p (y8,casebound) 99.00

ROSENBURG,JOHN M-Story of Baseball-NY-(1964)-178p-cl (n1,sl wn dj) 12.50

ROSENDAHL,C E-What About the Airship-NY-1938-8vo-x,438p-cl,16p plts-1st ed (s2,sp fade,dj) 50.00

ROSENDAHL,CARL O-Trees and Shrubs of the Upper Midwest-Mpls-1955-U of Minn Pr-411p-cl,photos,drwngs,maps (z7) 22.50

ROSENE,W-Bobwhite Quail-NJ-1969-418p-photos (ee3) 40.00

ROSENFIELD,ISAAC-An Age of Enormity-Cleve-1957-1st ed (s5,dj) 30.00

ROSENGARTEN,FREDERIC-Book of Spices-Wynnewood-1969-Livingston Publ-489p-dec e.p.,illus (o6) 45.00

ROSENTHAL & ZACHARY-EDS.-Jazzways-NY-(1947)-Greenberg-sm 4to-109p-photos(incl col)-1st ed (kk9,f,dj) 75.00

ROSENTHAL,HAROLD-Baseball is Their Business-1952-Random (q7,dj) 20.00

ROSENTHAL,HAROLD-Baseball's Best Managers-NY-(1961)-160p-wrps-1st ed so stated (n1) 12.50

ROSEVEAR,D R-Carnivores of West Africa-Lond-1974-8vo-548p-cl,11 col plts (y8,dj) 70.00

ROSEVEAR,D R-Rodents of West Africa-Lond-1969-8vo-604p-cl,11 col plts (y8,dj) 65.00

ROSEVEAR,JOHN-Pot-New Hyde Prk-1967-Univ Bk-1st ed (w5,f,f dj) 30.00

ROSKE,RALPH-Lincoln's Commando-NY-(1957)-310p-illus,col e.p. maps-1st ed (c4) 20.00

ROSKO,MILT-Fishing From Boats-NY-1968-272p-photos (m3,as new in dj) 12.50

ROSMAN,ABRAHAM-Feasting with Mine Enemy-NY-1971-Columbia U Pr-(x),221p-1st ed (bb7) 30.00*

ROSMAN,ALICE G-Nine Lives-(1941)-Putnam-238p-drwngs,D Thorne-1st ed (v8,dj sl wn wi sm tr) 15.00

ROSNER,FRERD-Modern Medicine and Jewish Law-NY-1972-216p-1st ed (dd3) 50.00

ROSNER,JAKOB-Palestine Picture Book-NY-1947-Schocken Bks-4to-142p-cl-1st ed (t3) 50.00

ROSS'S STATISTICAL AND ILLUSTRATED ALMANAC FOR THE YEAR 1880-Trenton-(1879)-Philip Ross-(72)p-wrps,illus (aa6) 30.00

ROSS,ALEXANDER-Adventure of the First Settlers on the Oregon-NY-(1969)-Citadel Pr-388p-map-Howes R448 (cc4,dj) 15.00

ROSS,ALEXANDER-Adventures of the First Settlers on the Oregon or Columbia River 1810 to 1813-Cleve-1904-Arthur H Clark Co-332p-fldg map-Early Wstrn Trav 1748 to 1846,Vol.VII-Howes R448 (cc4) 60.00

ROSS,ALEXANDER-Adventures of the First Settlers on the Oregon or Columbia River-Chig-1923-Donnelley-388p-map-Lakeside Classics (cc4) 35.00

ROSS,ALEXANDER-Adventures of the First Settlers on the Oregon or Columbia River-Chig-1923-Lakeside Pr-12mo-xxviii,388p,index,map,drk grn cl,g lettrng-Lakesides Classic-1st ed thus (y4) 45.00

ROSS,ALEXANDER-Fur Hunters of the Far West-Chig-1924-Donnelley-317p-frntis-Lakeside Classics (cc4) 35.00

ROSS,ALEXANDER-Fur Hunters of the Far West-Norman-(1956)-304p-illus-Howes R449-1st Okla ed (j7) 35.00

ROSS,BARNABY-Tragedy of X-NY-1932-Viking-1st ed (h4,f) 20.00

ROSS,BARNABY-Tragedy of Z-NY-1933-Viking-1st ed (f4,f) 25.00

ROSS,CHARLEY-LIFE, TRIAL AND CONVICTION OF WILLIAM H WESTERVELT, FOR THE ABDUCTION OF LITTLE...-Phila-(1875)-Barclay-112p-pict wrps (n1,sl soil,sl wn wrps) 65.00

ROSS,CHRISTIAN K-Charley Ross-Lond-1877-Hodder & Stoughton-431p+ads-cl (d1,sl wn) 35.00

ROSS,CHRISTIAN K-Father's Story of Charley Ross, the Kidnapped Child-Phila-(1876)-431p-cl (e1,cov flecked) 30.00

ROSS,DOROTHY-Stranger to the Desert-Lond-1958-Jarrolds-1st ed (b4,chip dj) 35.00

ROSS,DUDLEY T-Devil on Horseback-Fresno-1975-Valley Publ-vi+185p-red cl,illus-1st ed (k2,dj) 20.00

ROSS,EDWARD H-Reduction of Domestic Flies-Phila-1913-Lippincott-viii+102p-beige cl,18 illus-1st ed (j2) 22.00

ROSS,I-Rebel Rose-NY-1954-294p-illus,ports-1st ed (z10) 20.00

ROSS,LILLIAN-Portrait of Hemingway-NY-1961-S&S-1st ed (e10,sl soil dj) 20.00

ROSS,MARVIN C-Art of Karl Faberge and His Contemporaries-Norman-(1965)-U of Okla Pr-8vo-238p-col illus-scarce-1st ed (bb5,f,dj) 175.00

ROSS,MARVIN C-West of Alfred Jacob Miller-Norman-(1951)-U of Okla-lg 8vo-(54)p-cl,col frntis,200p plts ea wi facing pg of explanation-1st ed (v1) 75.00

ROSS,MRS.ALEXANDER-Legend of the Holy Stone-Montreal-(1878)-A A Stevenson-8vo-473,(3)p ads-orig dec prpl cl-Watters p.381-1st ed (pp2,f) 125.00*

ROSS,NANCY W-Three Ways of Asian Wisdom-NY-1966-S&S-222p-brwn cl,124 plts-1st prtg (ll1,wn dj) 12.50

ROSS,NANCY W-Waves-NY-(1943)-Holt-8vo-214p-24p photos-1st ed (dd5,sl wn dj,pres) 20.00

ROSS,ROBERT E-Wings Over the Marsh-Lond-1948-152p-photos (gg3,cov spots) 20.00

ROSS,ROBERT E-Wings Over the Marshes-Lond-1948-8vo-152p-photos-1st ed (m3,sl fray dj) 27.50

ROSS,RONALD-Studies on Malaria-Lond-1928-196p-1st ed (dd3) 100.00

ROSS,WALTER S-Last Hero-NY-(1968)-402p-cl (l1,dj) 15.00

ROSS,WALTER-Immortal-NY-1958-S&S-Warhol dj & cov-1st ed (q2,dj chip & rub) 45.00

ROSSELL,LEONARD-Tracks & Trails-NY-1928-8vo-137p-illus-1st ed (m3,f,chip dj) 15.00

ROSSET,BARNEY-ED.-Evergreen Review Reader-NY-(1968)-Grove-1st ed (hh5,f,dj sp tn) 20.00

ROSSETTI,CHRISTINA-New Poems-Lond-1896-Macmillan-orig g dec cl-1st ed (aa9,hngs weak) 85.00

ROSSETTI,DANTE G-Ballads and Sonnets-Lond-1881-Ellis & White-orig g dec cl-1st ed (aa9) 100.00

ROSSITER,JOHN-Murder Makers-NY-1977-Walker-1st US ed (g4,f,dj) 10.00

ROSSLYN,EARL OF-Twice Captured-Lond-1900-237p-blu cl,illus-1st ed (b7) 150.00

ROSSMAN,EARL-Black Sunlight-1926-Oxford-12mo-231p-illus,fldg map-1st ed (u8,sl chip dj) 25.00

ROSTAND,EDMOND-Chanticler-NY-1910-Duffield-8vo-289p-1st US ed (ee5) 20.00

ROSTAND,EDMOND-L`Aiglon-NY-(1900)-R H Russell-8vo-262p-1st US ed (ee5) 20.00

ROSTEN,LEO C-Hollywood-NY-(1941)-Harcourt Brace-436p-cl-1st ed so stated (l1,sl wn dj) 15.00

ROSTENBERG,LEONA-Between Boards-Montclair-(1977)-Allanheld & Schram-1st ed (w1,f,f dj) 17.50

ROSVALL,TOIVO D-Mazarine Legacy-NY-(1969)-Viking-8vo-244p-17 illus-1st ed (jj5,f,dj) 12.50

ROSWELL,A K-Stars of Yesteryear-Sharpsburg,Pitt-(1951)-Fort Pitt Brewing Co-78p-wrps (n1,sl dmpstnd) 17.50

ROTERS,E-ET AL-Berlin 1910 to 33-NY-1982-Rizzoli-illus-1st ed (h10,dj) 65.00

ROTH,HENRY-Nature's First Green-NY-1979-Targ-ltd to 350c,autg,pln yel dj-1st ed (g8,f,dj) 40.00

ROTH,JOSEPH-Job-NY-1931-Viking-1st ed (y1,dj) 50.00

ROTH,MARGARET B-ED.-Well Mary-Madison-1960-U of Wisc Pr-165p-maps,illus-1st ed (v2,f,dj) 35.00

ROTH,PHILIP-Breast-NY,Chig,SF-(1972)-HR&W-1st ed (bb1,as new in dj) 15.00

ROTH,PHILIP-Ghost Writer-NY-(1979)-FS&G-1st ed (b5,as new in dj) 15.00

ROTH,PHILIP-Great American Novel-NY,Chig,SF-(1973)-HR&W-1st ed (b5,as new in dj) 15.00

ROTH,PHILIP-Letting Go-1962-Random-1st ed (p9,dj) 25.00

ROTH,PHILIP-Letting Go-NY-(1962)-Random-1st ed (ee2,f,dj) 45.00

ROTH,PHILIP-My Life as a Man-NY,Chig,SF-(1974)-HR&W-1st ed (b5,as new in dj) 20.00

ROTH,PHILIP-Our Gang-NY-(1971)-Random-1st ed (b5,f,dj) 15.00

ROTH,PHILIP-Philip Roth Reader-NY-(1980)-FS&G-1st ed (b5,as new in dj) 15.00

ROTH,PHILIP-Portnoy's Complaint-NY-(1969)-Random-1st ed (bb1,f,dj) 25.00

ROTH,PHILIP-Professor of Desire-NY-(1977)-FS&G-1st ed (bb1,as new in dj) 15.00

ROTH,PHILIP-Reading Myself and Others-NY-1975-1st ed (s5,f,dj) 20.00

ROTH,PHILIP-When She Was Good-1967-Random-1st ed (n9,f,dj) 45.00

ROTH,PHILIP-Zuckerman Unbound-NY-(1981)-FS&G-1st ed (b5,f,dj) 20.00

ROTH,ROBERT-Sand in the Wind-Bost-1973-Atlantic-Little,Brown-1st ed (g8,sl stnd dj) 30.00

ROTH,W E-Additional Studies of the Arts, Crafts and Customs of the Guiana Indians...-1929-Bur Amer Ethnol Bull.91-110p-34 plts (bb3,f) 20.00

ROTH,W E-ED.-Richard Schomburgk's Travels in British Guiana 1840 to 1844-Georgetown-1922-4to-2 vols-illus,10 fldg maps (bb3,cor wn,fray,stns,1 map tn 195.00

ROTHENSTEIN,WILLIAM-Twenty Four Portraits-Lond-1923-Chatto & Windus-cl backd bds,papr sp & cov labls-2nd Ser-Ltd to 1500c-1st ed (aa9,sl rub sp) 25.00

ROTHSTEIN,ARTHUR-Photojournalism-NY-(1956)-Amer Photo Bk Publ-4to-cl/bds-1st ed (y3,dj) 55.00

ROTHWELL,C F SEYMOUR-Printing of Textile Fabrics-Lond-1897-Chas Griffin-x+312p-maroon cl,109 col swatches,50 text illus(incl fldg plts)-1st ed (g2) 135.00

ROUGHEAD,W-Evil That Men Do-1929-DD-2 vols-1st ed (x7,vf,f djs & box) 125.00

ROUGHHEAD,WILLIAM-Malice Domestic-GC-1929-Dbldy-8vo-285p-1st ed (b3,f,dj) 35.00

ROUGHLEY,T C-Fish & Fisheries of Australia-Sydney-1955-4to-343p-65 col & 21 b&w plts (m3) 35.00

ROULE,LOUIS-Fishes Their Journeys and Migrations-NY-1933-8vo-270p-illus-1st ed (m3) 12.50

ROUND,THORTON E-Good of it All-Cleve-(1957)-Lakeside Prntg Co-(xviii)+243p-gry cl,illus-1st ed (e2) 25.00

ROUNDS,GLEN-Whitey's First Round Up-NY-(1942)-Grosset-unpgd-pict bds,col & b&w illus,auth,Story Parade Picture Bk (r3,dj) 40.00

ROUNSEVELLE,P-Archery Simplified-NY-1931-120p-dec bd,photos (gg3,f,dj) 25.00

ROURKE,C-Charles Sheeler-NY-1938-48 illus-1st ed (h10,dj) 185.00

ROURKE,CONSTANCE-Audubon-NY-(1936)-342p-col frntis & plts-1st ed (t7) 15.00

ROURKE,CONSTANCE-Audubon-NY-(1936)-Harcourt Brace-342p-cl,12 col plts (l1,sl tn dj) 15.00

ROUSE,J J-Pioneer Work in Canada-Kilmarnock-nd-John Ritchie,Ltd-182p (dd4) 15.00

ROUSH,JOHN H,JR.-Successfully Fishing Lake Tahoe-Chig-1976-Adams-1st ed (nn5,f,dj) 20.00

ROUSSELOT,JEAN-Medicine in Art: a Cultural History-NY-1966-4to-333p-1st ed (dd3,dj) 175.00

ROUSSEVE,CHARLES B-Negro in New Orleans-New Orleans-1969-Archives of Negro Hist-wrps-1st ed (w5,f,one line struck out) 15.00

ROUX,ALBERT-New Classic Cuisine-(1984)-Barron's-4to-256p-red cl,col illus & photos-1st US ed (q8,f,dj) 18.50

ROUX,ANTOINE-Ships and Shipping-Salem-1925-Marine Research Scty-270p-red cl over 7x10" bds,118 illus-1st ed thus (nn1,sl soil fr bd) 150.00

ROUX,WILLIAM C-Fried Coffee & Jellied Bourbon-Barre-1967-Barre Publ-111p-pict tan cl,drwngs-1st ed (q8,dj) 12.50

ROWAN,CARL T-Wait Till Next Year-1960-Random-photos-1st ed (s8,dj) 27.50

ROWAN,M K-Doves, Parrots, Louries and Cuckoos of Southern Africa-1983-Philip-429p-8 col plts (bb3,f,dj) 40.00

ROWAN,RICHARD W-Pinkertons-Bost-1931-Little,Brown-350p-illus-Six Guns #1911-1st ed (ee4) 35.00

ROWAN,STEPHEN A-They Wouldn't Let Us Die-Middle Village-(1973)-J David-1st ed (ff3,f,dj) 65.00

ROWAN-ROBINSON,MAJ GEN H-Onward From Today-Lond-nd-Hutchinson (z2,sl discol sp) 20.00

ROWANS,VIRGINIA-Oh, What a Wonderful Wedding-NY-1953-illus,N M Bodecker-1st ed (r5,sl chip dj) 25.00

ROWE,MRS.M F-Master's Messenger...-SF-1884-Winterburn-12mo-97p-publ cl-1st ed (w6) 45.00

ROWE,VIVIAN-Basque Country-Lond-1955-Putnam-8vo-247p-16 photos-1st Brit ed (dd5,sl chip dj) 15.00

ROWELL,GALEN-High & Wild-SF-1979-159p-col plts-1st ed (q10,f,dj) 30.00

ROWELL,GALEN-In the Throne of the Mountain Gods-SF-1977-4to-326p-col photos,maps-1st ed (p10,f,dj) 40.00

ROWELL,GALEN-Vertical World of Yosemite-Berkeley-1974-4to-201p-photos,auth 1st bk-1st ed (o10,f,dj) 80.00

ROWELL,GEORGE P-Forty Years an Advertising Agent, 1865 to 1905-NY-1926-Franklin Publ-517p-maroon cl,illus-1st ed (b2,cov soil & sl wn) 35.00

ROWLAND,HELEN-Sayings of Mrs.Solomon-NY-(1913)-Dodge Publ-122p-cl wi col onlay (d1) 15.00

ROWLANDS,J J-Cache Lake Country-NY-1947-8vo-272p-illus,H B Kane (m3,fray dj) 12.50

ROWLANDS,J J-Cache Lake Country-NY-1947-Norton-272p-grn cl,map e.p.,illus by Henry B Kane-1st ed (bb7,dj wn,chip) 35.00*

ROWLEY,C E-Apples of Gold-Findlay-(1925)-C E Rowley-257p-cl (n1,f) 17.50

ROWLEY,CLINTON W-Pacific Northwest Sportsman's Guide Book-Seattle-1930-12mo-182p-wrps,photos,illus (m3) 25.00

ROWNTREE,B SEEBOHM-Poverty-Lond-1902-Macmillan-xxii+452p-blu cl,fldg map,3 plans-3rd ed (d2) 35.00

ROWNTREE,LESTER-Flowering Shrubs of California and their Value to the Gardener...-(1939)-Stanford U Pr-xii,317p-pict cl,illus-1st ed (dd10) 25.00

ROWNTREE,LESTER-Flowering Shrubs of California-Stanford-(1939)-xii,317p-56 half tones-1st ed (m10,sp wn,tattrd dj,autg) 50.00

ROWNTREE,LESTER-Hardy Californians-NY-1936-Macmillan-255p-cl,photos (x6,bump) 22.00

ROWSE,A L-Man of the Thirties-Lond-1979-1st ed (y7,dj,autg) 30.00

ROWSE,A L-William Shakespeare-Lond-1963-1st ed (y7,dj) 25.00

ROWSOME,FRANK-Trolley Car Treasury-NY-1956-200p-1st ed (n4,f,dj) 30.00

ROXBOROUGH,HENRY-One Hundred, Not Out-Tor-1966-Ryerson Pr-252p-24 illus-1st ed (bb7,dj) 20.00*

ROY,JULES-Battle of Dienbienphu-NY-(1965)-H&R-1st ed (ff3,dj) 50.00

ROY,MIKE-Mike Roy Cook Book-(1966)-Ward Ritchie-135p-dec yel cl,drwngs-1st prtg (q8,dj) 15.00

ROY,R H-Ready for the Fray-Vancouver-1958-Trustees,Can Scot Reg-xiii,509p-red cl,illus,ports,fldg maps-Dornbusch #41 (k10) 40.00*

ROYAL COLLEGE OF PHYSICIANS OF LONDON-Catalogue of the Libray-Lond-1912-Spottiswood-(vi)+1354p-grn cl-1st ed (d2) 50.00

ROYAL,BRIAN J-Star Chase-NY-(1979)-Elsevier/Nelson-1st ed (h3,f,dj) 15.00

ROYAL,C-Trail of a Sourdough-1919-M&S-1st ed (x2,innr rear hng startng,dj) 25.00

ROYAL,WILLIAM R-Man who Rode Sharks-NY-(1978)-Dodd,Mead-8vo-254p-16p photos-1st ed (aa5,dj) 17.50

ROYALL,ANNE-Letters from Alabama on Various Subjects-Wash-1830-232;6p-lea & mrbld bds (j1,one lf missing sm pc) 250.00

ROYCE,JOSIAH-American Commonwealths-NY-1984-513p-fldg col map-Howes R487 (t7) 35.00

ROYCE,SARAH-Frontier Lady-New Haven-1932-144p-1st ed (t7,cov soil) 20.00

ROYCROFT BOOKS: A CATALOGUE AND SOME COMMENT CONCERNING THE SHOP AND WORKERS AT EAST AURORA-NY-1910-30p text-grn suede cov,gravure illus,orig box (kk9,f,sl wn box) 85.00

ROYDEN,A MAUDE-Women at the World's Crossroads-NY-1922-Womans Pr-139p-cl (d1) 15.00

ROYER,JOHN S-Book of Model Solutions-Columbus-1903-(64)p-wrps (k1) 10.00

ROYKO,MIKE-Slats Gronik and Some Other Friends-NY-1973-1st ed (n5,dj) 22.50

ROYLE,SELENA-Pheasants for Peasants-(1956)-Ward Ritchie-127p-dec stiff wht wrps-1st ed (q8) 10.00

RUARK,ROBERT-Grenadine Etching-GC-1947-Doubleday-1st ed (a5,dj sp fade,chip) 50.00

RUARK,ROBERT-Grenadine's Spawn-GC-1952-1st ed (c5,sl wn dj) 45.00

RUARK,ROBERT-Grenadine's Spawn-GC-1952-dj (s5,dj) 30.00

RUARK,ROBERT-Honey Badger-NY-(1965)-McGraw Hill-1st ed (v10,f,f dj) 20.00

RUARK,ROBERT-Horn of the Hunter-GC-1953-8vo-315p-photos,illus by auth-1st ed (m3,vf,rprd dj) 100.00

RUARK,ROBERT-Old Man & the Boy-NY-(1957)-303p-illus by Dower-1st ed so stated (gg3,f,chip dj) 45.00

RUARK,ROBERT-Old Man and the Boy-NY-(1957)-Holt-drwngs-1st ed (m4,vf,dj) 75.00

RUARK,ROBERT-Old Man's Boy Grows Older-NY-(1961)-1st ed (k9,dj rprd) 45.00

RUARK,ROBERT-One For the Road-GC-1949-1st ed (s5,sl wn dj) 25.00

RUARK,ROBERT-One for the Road-GC-1949-8vo-253p-illus,R Taylor-1st ed (m3,f,chip dj) 20.00

RUARK,ROBERT-Poor No More-NY-1959-8vo-705p-1st ed (m3,dj) 15.00

RUARK,ROBERT-Something of Value-1955-Dbldy-1st ed (x2,f,sl tn dj) 27.00

RUARK,ROBERT-Use Enough Gun-NY-1966-1st ed (o5,f,dj) 50.00

RUARK,ROBERT-Women-NY-1967-NAL-1st ed (h8,f,f dj) 50.00

RUARK,ROBT-Honey Badger-NY,Tor,Lond-(1965)-McGraw Hill-1st ed (d10,f,dj) 35.00

RUBASEM,FRED-Grenzerleben, Bilder und Skizzen aus dem "Wilden Westen"-Chig-1894-Koelling & Klappenbach-167p-cl-rare (d1,covs spot & flecked) 300.00

RUBIAO,MURILO-Ex-Magician & Other Stories-NY et al-(1979)-Harper & Row-auth 1st bk in English-1st ed (a10,f,dj) 20.00

RUBIN,JACOB H-I Live to Tell-Indpls-1934-Bobbs-Merrill-330p-1st ed (r1,dj edgewn) 25.00

RUBIN,W-Frank Stella-NY-1970-MOMA (h10,dj) 25.00

RUBIN,W-Frank Stella-NY-1970-MOMA-4to-176p-gry cl,83 illus(18 col) (r10,sl soil dj) 10.00

RUBINSTEIN,CHARLOTTE S-American Women Artists-NY-1982-Avon-8vo-560p-illus wrps,illus-1st ed (r10) 10.00

RUBINSTEIN,HELENA-Food for Beauty-NY-(1938)-Ives Washburn-245p-dec tan cl,illus-1st ed (q8,dj) 16.50

RUBLOWSKY,JOHN-Black Music in America-NY-1971-Basic Bks-1st ed (v5,f,rprd dj) 25.00

RUBY & BROWN-Chinook Indians-Norman-(1976)-349p-illus-1st ed (g7,vf,dj) 35.00

RUBY,R H-Myron Eells and the Puget Sound Indians-(1976)-Superior-127p-photos,drwngs,map-1st ed (r8,f) 15.00

RUBY,ROBERT H-Cayuse Indians-Norman-1972-345p-photos,illus,maps-1st ed (t7,f) 17.50

RUBY,ROBERT H-Chinook Indians-Norman-(1976)-349p-cl-1st ed so stated (a1,f,dj) 30.00

RUBY,ROBERT H-Chinook Indians-Norman-(1976)-U of Okla Pr-349p-illus-1st ed (ee4,dj) 25.00

RUCK-PAUQUET,GINA-Little Hedgehog-Lond/NY-(1959)-Constable/Hastings-4to-cl,col & b&w illus-1st ed (s3,f,dj) 25.00

RUDD,JOHN C-Compendium of Geography...-Auburn-1826-Dbldy/Lindsly & Ball-220p-lea-Amer Imprnts 25980-3rd ed (k1,lacks f f.e.p.,sl wn) 32.50

RUDKIN,MARGARET-...PEPPERIDGE FARM COOKBOOK-NY-(1963)-Atheneum-440p-illus,E Blegvad-1st ed (l6) 25.00

RUDOFSKY,B-Prodigious Builders-NY-1977-311 illus-1st ed (h10,dj) 50.00

RUDOLPH,G A-COMP.-Kansas State University Receipt Book and Household Manual-Manhattan-1968-KSU Libr-230p-prpl wrps-Bibliog ser #4 (q8) 15.00

RUDOLPH,KURT-Gnosis-SF-(1983)-Harper & Row-8vo-xii,411p-lt blu cl,52 plts(4 col),fldg map-1st ed in English (t10,dj) 20.00

RUE,L L-World of the White Tailed Deer-Phila-(1962)-lg 8vo-137p-cl,photos (y8) 9.00

RUEHLMANN,WM-Saint with a Gun-NY-1974-NYU-1st ed (d4,dj) 30.00

RUFFNER,E H-Annual Report Upon Explorations and Surveys in the Department of the Missouri-Wash-1878-GPO-120p-orig wrps,maps,illus (ee4) 75.00

RUFFNER,WILLIAM H-Report on Washington Territory-NY-1889-242p-12 plts,6 maps(2 fldg in pckt) (hh8,sl spot cov,fox) 75.00

RUGGLES,ELEANOR-West Going Heart-NY-(1959)-Norton-8vo-448p-8p photos-1st ed (ee5,dj) 15.00

RUGGLES,WILLIAM-History of the Texas League-np-(1951)-408p-photos-update of 1932 first ed (f9,sl spot,some underlining) 50.00

RUGOFF,MILTON-Beechers-NY-(1981)-653p-bds-1st ed so stated (d1,f,dj) 15.00

RUHEMANN,H-Cleaning of Paintings-1968-Praeger-1st ed (h10,dj) 100.00

RUHEN,OLAF-Tangaroa's Godchild-Bost-1962-Little,Brown-8vo-346p-blu cl,map e.p.-1st ed (p8,wn dj) 25.00

RUHMER,ERNST-Wireless Telephony-1908-Van Nostrand-224p+64p ads,drwngs,photos (v8) 20.00

RUHRAH,JOHN-Pediatrics of the Past-NY-1925-592p-scarce-1st ed (dd3,hng crack,sp dull) 250.00

RUIZ,JUAN-Book of Good Love-Chapel Hill-1968-UNC Pr-269p-gry cl-1st ed thus (z3,f) 10.00

RUKEYSER,MURIEL-29 Poems-Lond-1972-1st ed (r2,f,dj) 25.00

RUKEYSER,MURIEL-Body of Waking-NY-1958-Harper-1st ed (v5,f,dj) 25.00

RUKEYSER,MURIEL-I Go Out-NY-1961-Harper & Row-illus,L Kessler-1st ed (q2,dj) 20.00

RUKEYSER,MURIEL-Life of Poetry-1949-Current Bks-1st ed (jj6,f,dj) 70.00

RUKEYSER,MURIEL-Mazes-NY-(1970)-S&S-4to-pict bds,photos,M Charles-1st ed (u10,f) 20.00

RUKEYSER,MURIEL-One Life-1957-Simon-1st ed (kk6,dj) 25.00

RUKEYSER,MURIEL-Orgy-Lond-1966-1st ed (r2,dj) 25.00

RUKEYSER,MURIEL-Speed of Darkness-NY-1968-1st ed (r2,f,dj) 25.00

RUKEYSER,MURIEL-Theory of Flight-New Haven-1935-Yale Univ Pr-8vo-86p-tan cl,auth 1st bk-scarce-1st ed (w6,dj sl fade & bled to sp) 300.00

RUKEYSER,MURIEL-Waterlily Fire-NY-1962-Macmillan-1st ed (u10,f,f dj) 35.00

RULES FOR GOOD LIVING-np(New London)-1894-WCTU-61p-papr wrps (n6) 50.00

RUMLEY,CHARLES-Diary of...From St.Louis to Portland 1862-Missoula-1939-Sources of NW Hist No.28-12p-wrps (r8) 20.00

RUNNING,CORINNE-When Coyote Walked the Earth-NY-(1949)-H Holt-pict cl,illus by R Bennett-1st ed (aa9) 25.00

RUNYAN,HARRY-Faulkner Glossary-NY-(1964)-1st ed (c5,sl wn dj) 20.00

RUNYON,DAMON-All Horse Players Die Broke-np-(1946)-12mo-brwn lea,tiss dj,ltd ed for patrons of opening day,Del Mar Turf Club,1946-1st ed (x10,edge stns,dj) 25.00

RUNYON,DAMON-My Old Man-1939-Stackpole-1st ed (n9,chip dj) 25.00

RUNYON,DAMON-Poems for Men-NY-(1947)-DS&P-1st ed (bb1,f,dj sp sl chip) 60.00

RURAL RADIO'S ALBUM OF FAVORITE RADIO STARS-np-nd-(16)p-wrps-vol.1-photos (f1) 10.00

RUSCHA,EDWARD-Guacamole Airlines-NY-1980-Abrams-sq 4to-96p-gry cl,col & b&w illus (r10,f dj) 22.50

RUSCHENBERGER,W S W-An Account of the Institution of the College of Physicians of Philadelphia-Phila-1887-336p-1st ed (dd3) 90.00

RUSCHENBURGER,WILLIAM S W-Three Years in the Pacific-Lond-1835-Richard Bentley-8vo-2 vols,3/4 lea & mrbld papr bndg-Sabin 74195-1st Brit ed (mm1) 650.00

RUSH'S ALMANAC AND GUIDE TO HEALTH...-NY-1870-A H Flanders,M.D.-37p-col pict wrps (h1) 15.00

RUSH,BENJAMIN-Lectures on the Mind-Phila-1981-735p-1st ed (dd3) 45.00

RUSH,PHILIP-Some Old Ranchos and Adobes-San Diego-1965-121p-brand on e.p.,photos-1st ed (d3) 30.00

RUSH,W M-Wildlife of Idaho-Caldwell-1942-299p-photos-1st ed (m3) 15.00

RUSHDIE,SALMAN-Grimus-Woodstock-1979-Overlook Pr-auth 1st bk-1st US ed (v5,rmndr line,f dj) 85.00

RUSHDIE,SALMAN-Midnight's Children-NY-1981-1st US ed (p5,f,dj) 100.00

RUSHDIE,SALMAN-Midnight's Children-NY-1981-Knopf-1st ed (p3,f,dj) 75.00

RUSHING,LILITH-Cake Cook Book-(1965)-Chilton-201p-tan cl-1st ed (q8,dj) 15.00

RUSHMORE,HELEN-Dancing Horses of Acoma and Other Acoma Indian Stories-Cleve-(1965)-163+1p-col drwngs-1st ed (v7,dj,2 autg) 65.00

RUSKIN,JOHN-Pearls for Young Ladies-NY,Bost-(1878)-287p-cl (d1) 15.00

RUSKIN,JOHN-Political Economy of Art-NY-1858-Wiley & Halsted-8vo-g cl-1st Amer ed (v10,sl fox pgs) 100.00

RUSS,CAROLYN H-Log of a Forty Niner-Bost-1923-B J Brimmer-183p-illus-1st ed (dd4) 50.00

RUSS,CAROLYN H-Log of a Forty-Niner-Bost-1923-B J Brimmer Co-183p-1/2 cl,tip-on sp & cov labls,illus,auth-1st ed (mm1,wn dj,part unopened) 65.00

RUSS,JOANNA-And Chaos Died-NY-1970-Ace-wrps-1st ed (v5) 25.00

RUSS,JOANNA-Picnic on Paradise-NY-1968-Ace-wrps,auth 1st bk-1st ed (v5,f) 30.00

RUSS,MARTIN-Happy Hunting Ground-NY-1968-Atheneum-1st ed (e8,f,dj) 75.00

RUSS,MARTIN-Last Parallel-NY,Tor-(1957)-333p-bds (j1) 10.00

RUSSELL,A P-Thomas Corwin-Cin-1881-128p-cl (n1,sl wn sp) 15.00

RUSSELL,A-Grizzly Country-NY-1974-302p-photos (gg3,vf,dj) 30.00

RUSSELL,A-Horns in the High Country-NY-1973-259p-photos (gg3,vf,dj) 40.00

RUSSELL,ANDY-Andy Russell's Adventures with Wild Animals-NY-1978-8vo-176p-illus-1st Amer ed (m3,vf,dj) 12.50

RUSSELL,ANNA-Anna Russell Song Book-NY-(1960)-Citadel-drwngs,Folkes-1st Amer ed (w1,f,dj) 25.00

RUSSELL,ASHLEY H-Siskiyou Trail-Portland-(1959)-Binfords & Mort-8vo-195p-photos-1st ed (bb5,f,dj) 12.50

RUSSELL,BERTRAND-How Near is War-Lond-1952-Derricke Ridgway-wrps-1st ed (v5,f,dj) 25.00

RUSSELL,BERTRAND-Justice in War Time-Chig-1916-port frntis-1st Amer ed (r2,sl sun) 30.00

RUSSELL,BERTRAND-My Philosophical Development-Lond-(1959)-Allen & Unwin-280p-red cl-1st ed (j2,dj) 35.00

RUSSELL,CARL P-Firearms, Traps & Tools of the Mountain-NY-1967-448p-illus-1st ed (f7,f,f,dj) 50.00

RUSSELL,CARL P-Guns on the Early Frontiers-Berkeley,LA-1957-395p-illus-1st ed (e7,chip dj) 45.00

RUSSELL,CARL P-Guns on the Early Frontiers-Berkeley-1957-U of Cal Pr-xvi,395p-cl,dec e.p.,illus-1st ed (v1,sl wn dj) 50.00

RUSSELL,CHARLES E-A Rafting on the Mississippi-NY-(1928)-Century-357p-e.p. maps,illus,fldg map-1st ed (dd4,fade sp lettrng) 50.00

RUSSELL,CHARLES E-Greatest Trust in the World-NY-1905-Ridgway-Thayer-252p-cl (j1,sm dmpstn cor frnt cov) 35.00

RUSSELL,CHARLES M-Bibliography of Published Works of...-Lincoln-1971-317p-lea,ltd ed,col frntis,illus-1st ed (t7,f,dj) 75.00

RUSSELL,CHARLES M-Good Medicine-GC-1930-162p-dec e.p.,col illus-Howes 527-1st ed so stated (d7,chip dj) 295.00

RUSSELL,CHARLES M-Good Medicine-NY-(1930)-GC Publ-4to-162p-col illus (cc4,chip dj) 40.00

RUSSELL,CHARLES M-Good Medicine: The Illustrated Letters of...-GC-1930-Dbldy,Doran-162,(2)p-dec cl,col illus,dec e.p.-1st trd ed (v1,sl chip dj) 350.00

RUSSELL,CHARLES M-More Rawhides-Pasadena-1946-60p-illus-v scarce-Trails End ed (g7,f,dj) 100.00

RUSSELL,CHARLES M-Paper Talk-Ft.Worth-1962-Amon Carter-12 col illus (b4) 120.00

RUSSELL,CHARLES M-Rawhide Rawlins Rides Again-Pasadena-(1948)-Trails End Publ-61+1p-lea,gold stmpd back cov,ltd to 300c,nbrd,pres ,illus (v7,pres) 300.00

RUSSELL,CHARLES M-Trails Plowed Under-GC,NY-1927-210p-col & b&w illus-v scarce-1st ed (g7) 100.00

RUSSELL,CHARLES M-Trails Plowed Under-NY-(1927)-Dbldy-lg 8vo-210p-col illus by auth-Howes R532-Herd 1975 (bb4,dj) 60.00

RUSSELL,CHARLOTTE M-Dreadful Reckoning-1941-CC-1st ed (s10,chip dj) 22.50

RUSSELL,CHARLOTTE M-Murder at the Old Stone House-1935-CC-1st ed (s10) 20.00

RUSSELL,DON-Custer's Last-Ft.Worth-(1968)-Amon Carter Mus-67p-illus-1st ed (ee4,dj) 30.00

RUSSELL,F S-Seas-Lond,NY-1975-F Warne-8vo-283p-48 plts(24 col)-4th ed (p8,dj) 10.00

RUSSELL,F S-Seas-Lond-1928-16mo-379p-illus (m3) 15.00

RUSSELL,FRANCIS-Tragedy in Dedham-1962-McGraw-1st ed (s10,dj soil) 15.00

RUSSELL,FRANK-ED.-Art Nouveau Architecture-NY-1979-Rizzoli-lg 4to-1st ed (ee1,dj) 150.00

RUSSELL,G OSCAR-Vowel-Columbus-1928-Ohio St U Pr-xliv+353p-gry cl,illus-1st ed (c2) 35.00

RUSSELL,GEORGE-Hoofprints in Time-So Brunswick-1966-Barnes-4to-1st prtg (f10,dj) 65.00

RUSSELL,GEORGE-House of Titans...-Lond-1934-Macmillan-1st ed (z8,f,dj) 32.50

RUSSELL,ISRAEL C-North America-NY-1904-435p-cl,illus,maps(incl 8 col) (n1) 17.50

RUSSELL,JACK-Gibraltar Beseiged 1779 to 1783-Lond-1965-308p-illus-1st ed (b7,dj) 30.00

RUSSELL,JERVIS-Jimmy Come Lately-Port Angeles-1971-631p-photos,maps-1st ed (t7,dj) 30.00

RUSSELL,MARIA-Beer Makes it Better Cook Book-(1971)-S&S-1160p-pict bds,drwngs-1st ed (q8,dj) 12.50

RUSSELL,MILDRED B-Lowndes Court House-Montgomery-(1951)-Paragon Pr-(viii)+293p,brwn cl-1st ed (h2,dj) 22.00

RUSSELL,MRS D STOBART-Cookery for Small Craft-Lond-(1939)-Blackie & Son Ltd-69p (m6) 12.00

RUSSELL,MRS HAL-Land of Enchantment-Evanston-1954-155p-pict cl,frntis,photos,map e.p.,ltd to 750c,nbrd-Rittenhouse #497-1st ed (t7) 65.00

RUSSELL,OSBORNE-Journal of a Trapper-1955-Oregon Hist Soc-178p+index-frntis,fldg map,ltd to 750c (c7,f) 60.00

RUSSELL,PROF WILLIAM-Scientific Horseshoeing-Cin-1899-Clarke-4th ed rvsd & enlgd (h9,sl spot bndg) 65.00

RUSSELL,ROSS-Sound-NY-1961-Dutton-1st ed (v5,f,sl soil dj) 25.00

RUSSELL,SCOTT-Mountain Prospect-Lond-1946-244p-1st ed (p10,dj) 28.00

RUSSELL,VALERIE-Judging Horses and Ponies-Lond-1978-Pelham-1st ed (j9,dj) 15.00

RUSSELL,W CLARK-Copsford Mystery-NY-1896-New Amsterdam-1st US ed (d4,weak frnt hnge) 35.00

RUSSELL,WILLIAM H-Complete History of the Russian War-NY-1856-181p-brwn dec cl,16 plts,3 fldg chrts-1st Amer ed (jj2) 80.00

RUSSELL,WILLIAM-Spelling Book-Bost-(1844)-Tappan,Whittemore & Mason-160p-prntd bds (k1,rub) 22.50

RUSSELL-WOOD,A J R-Fidalgos and Philanthropists-Berkeley-1968-U of Cal-8vo-429p-8p illus,w/o dj as iss-1st US ed (jj5,f) 20.00

RUSSIAN COOK BOOK FOR AMERICAN HOMES-NY-(1943)-Russian War Relief-95p-wrps-5th prtg (q6) 16.00

RUSSIAN ICONS-NY-1955-Oxford U Pr-cl,14 col plts,12p illus-1st Amer ed (l8,fray dj) 29.00

RUSSIAN REVOLUTION, ITS ORIGIN AND OUTCOME-Manitoba-1948-Soc Prty of Can-wrps-1st ed (w5,f) 15.00

RUSSO,DOROTHY-Bibliographical Studies of Seven Authors of Crawfordsville, Indiana-Indpls-1952-486p-cl-1st ed (e1) 22.50

RUSSO,DOROTHY-Bibliography of George Ade 1866-1944-Indpls-1947-314p-cl (e1) 25.00

RUSSO,J P-Desert Bighorn Sheep in Arizona-1956-Ariz Game & Fish-153p-wrps,photos (bb3) 25.00

RUSSWURM,A D-Aberrations of British Butterflies-1978-Classey-151p-40 col plts (bb3,f,dj) 30.00

RUST,ART-Get That Nigger Off the Field-1976-Delacorte Pr-1st ed (p7,dj) 65.00

RUST,ORTON G-Mad River Country and the Old Skating Pond...-Dayton-(1915)-153p-cl (g1) 15.00

RUTGERS,A-Birds of Asia-NY-1969-Taplinger-160 col plts by Gould (c9,dj) 50.00

RUTGERS,A-Birds of Europe-Lond-1966-8vo-(9),321p-cl,160 col plt lithos,J Gould (y8,dj chip) 45.00

RUTGERS,LISPENARD-On & Off the Saddle-NY-1894-16mo-201p-photos-1st ed (m3,pres cpy) 15.00

RUTH,GEORGE H-Babe Ruth's Own Book of Baseball-1928-Putnam-1st ed (s8,sl wn cov,pgs brwng) 135.00

RUTH,KENT-Touring the Old West-Brattleboro-1971-218p-illus,maps-1st ed (t7,f,dj) 20.00

RUTH,MRS.BABE-Babe and I-1959-Prentice Hall-1st ed (p7,f,dj) 35.00

RUTHER,FRERDERICK-Lond Island To Day-Hicksville-(1909)-publ by auth-271p-maroon cl,illus-1st ed (k2,sm stn rear cov) 35.00

RUTLEDGE,A-Days Off in Dixie-Lond-1925-298p-photos (ee3,vf,vf dj) 70.00

RUTLEDGE,A-From the Hills to the Sea, Fact & Legend of the Carolinas-NY-1958-201p-illus (ee3,vf,dj) 60.00

RUTLEDGE,A-God's Children-NY-1947-159p-photos (gg3,vf,dj,autg) 45.00

RUTLEDGE,A-Home by the River-NY-1941-167p-photos (ee3,vf) 19.00

RUTLEDGE,A-Hunter's Choice-NY-1946-210p-illus-ltd to 5000c (ee3) 30.00

RUTLEDGE,ARCHIBALD-Home By The River-Indpls-1941-4to-167p+photos-1st ed (m3,f) 20.00

RUTLEDGE,ARCHIBALD-Life's Extras-NY-1928-12mo-25p-1st ed (m3) 15.00

RUTLEDGE,ARCHIBALD-World Around Hampton-(1960)-Bobbs Merrill-192p-illus-1st ed (dd9,dj) 35.00

RUTLEDGE,HOWARD-In the Presence of Mine Enemies 1965-1973-Old Tappan-(1973)-Revell-124,(1)p-cl (h1,sl stnd fore-edge,dj) 12.50

RUTLEDGE,HOWARD-In the Presence of Mine Enemies-Old Tappan-(1973)-Revell-1st ed (ff3,dj) 35.00

RUTSCH,EDWARD S-Smoking Technology of the Aborigines of the Iroquois area of New York State-Rutherford-1973-Fairleigh Dickinson Univ-illus-1st ed (y10,f,f dj) 80.00

RUTT,J T-ED.-Diary of Thomas Burton-Lond-1828-4 vols-3/4 grn lea,mrbld bds & e.p.,t.e.g.-1st ed (b7,lacks sp labls) 200.00

RUTTER,JOHN-Culture and Diseases of the Peach-Harrisburg-1880-95p-g dec blk cl (hh7) 35.00

RUTTER,OWEN-Triumphant Pilgrimage-Phila-(1937)-Lippincott-8vo-296p-2 illus,map-1st US ed (jj5,f,dj) 20.00

RUTTLEDGE,HUGH-Everest 1933-Lond-1934-Hodder & Stoughton-blu cl,4 maps(2 fldg),59 photos-1st ed (dd7,dj chip & wn) 150.00

RUTTLEDGE,HUGH-Everest: the Unfinished Adventure-Lond-1937-295p-2 lg fldg maps,63 photos,dj scarce (a4,f,dj) 275.00

RUTTLEDGE,R F-Ireland's Birds-Lond-1966-8vo-207p-cl,11 plts,1 map (y8,dj chip) 35.00

RUXTON,GEORGE F-In the Old West-Oyster Bay-1915-12mo-345p (m3) 15.00

RUXTON,GEORGE F-Life in the Far West-1972-Rio Grande-235p-dec cov,iss w/o dj,fldg map-(facs of 1849 1st ed) (r8,f) 25.00

RUXTON,GEORGE F-Life in the Far West-Norman-(1951)-U of Okla Pr-252p-illus-1st ed (bb4,dj) 35.00

RYAN,ALONZO-Free Lance Political Caricature in Canada-Montr-1904-A T Chapman-4to-112p-illus-ltd ed (k10,covs loose) 40.00*

RYAN,CHARLES C-ED.-Starry Messenger-(1979)-St.Martin's-1st ed (h3,f,dj) 15.00

RYAN,CORNELIUS-ED.-Across the Space Frontier-1952-Viking-147p-silv/g illus grn cl,illus-1st ed (hh6,bump) 25.00

RYAN,DANIEL J-Masters of Men-Columbus-1915-64p-cl (f1) 15.00

RYAN,DOROTHY-Kennedy Family of Massachusetts-Westport-(1981)-200p-cl (c1,f) 25.00

RYAN,FRANCES B-Early Days in Escondido-1970-priv prtd-royal 8vo-175p-illus-1st ed (d3,dj) 25.00

RYAN,J C-Revolt Along the Rio Grande-San Antonio-1964-Naylor-1st ed (b4,dj) 30.00

RYAN,JESSICA-Man Who Asked Why-NY-1945-Dbldy CC-1st ed (l4,dj) 12.50

RYAN,MARAH E-Flute of the Gods-NY-(1909)-Stokes-338p-cl,24 photos,E S Curtis-1st ed (n1) 25.00

RYAN,R N-Spin in Dumbwhacks-Phila-(1943)-8vo-154p-illus cl-1st ed (s2,chip dj) 20.00

RYAN,RACHEL-Dinner for Beginners-Lond-(1934)-H Hamilton-304p-illus-Bitting 412-2nd impr (m6,sl drknd sp) 22.00

RYAN,STELLA-Death Never Weeps-NY-1946-Coward-1st ed (g4,rprd dj) 12.50

RYDEN,HOPE-Mustangs-NY-1972-Viking-long 8vo-111p-photos-1st ed (z4,dj) 12.50

RYDER,DAVID W-Memories of the Mendocino Coast-SF-1948-Taylor & Taylor-80p-illus-1st ed (dd4) 45.00

RYDER,JONATHAN-Cry of the Halidon-1974-Delacorte-1st ed (o9,f,rub dj) 35.00

RYDER,JONATHAN-Cry of the Halidon-NY-1974-Delacorte-1st ed (e4,sl rub dj) 25.00

RYDER,JONATHAN-Trevayne-NY-(1973)-Delacorte-1st ed (bb1,f,sl tn dj) 85.00

RYDER,TOM-High Stepper-Lond-1961-Allen-1st prtg (f10) 25.00

RYDON,JOHN-Oysters with Love-(Lond)-(1968)-P Owen-144p-red cl,drwngs-1st ed (q8,dj) 20.00

RYE,EDGAR-Quirt and the Spur-Chig-(1909)-Conkey-363p-col pict cl,frntis-1st ed (f9,scuff,spot,hngs weak) 175.00

RYE,EDGAR-Quirt and the Spur-Chig-(1909)-W B Conkey-363p-illus cl,illus-Howes #R559-1st ed (w3) 275.00

RYERSON,LOUIS J-Genealogy of the Ryerson Family in America, 1646 to 1902-NY-1902-89p-cl,frntis (aa6) 100.00

RYHLICK,FRANK-Congress & You-NY-1943-Workers Libr-64p-stapled wrps-Seidman R276 (r1,cov wn) 15.00

RYLANDS,GEORGE-Poems-Lond-1931-Hogarth Pr-dec bds,labl,tissue dj-ltd to 350c,nbrd,autg-(early state wi comma after Leonard's initial in imprt)-Woolmer 269-1st ed (nn4,f,f dj) 325.00

RYNNING,CAPT THOMAS H-Gun Notches-NY-(1931)-Burt-332p-Six Guns 1924-Herd 1983 (bb4) 15.00

RYNNING,CAPT THOMAS H-Gun Notches-NY-1931-Stokes-xx,332p-cl,illus e.p.,pict dj-1st ed (v1,dj) 95.00

RYSIA-Old Warsaw Cook Book-(NY)-(1958)-(Roy Publ)-304p-illus (o6,dj) 20.00

RYUS,W H-Second William Penn-KC-(1913)-176p-wrps-Rittenhouse 500 (g1) 15.00

RYWELL,MARTIN-Gun That Shaped American Destiny-Harriman-1957-8vo-156p-illus (m3,f,dj) 25.00

SAARINEN,EERO-Eero Saarinen on His Work-New Haven-1962-Yale U Pr-108p-plts (r10,broken box) 50.00

SABATINI,RAFAEL-Lost King-Bost-1937-HMCo-1st ed (hh5,edgewn dj) 20.00

SABIN,JOSEPH-Bibliography of Bibliography-Ann Arbor-1966-150p-facs of 1877 ed (m4) 14.50

SABINE,LORENZO-Notes on Duels and Dueling-Bost-1859-Crosby-8vo-426p-blk cl-3rd ed (w1) 110.00

SABINE,LORENZO-Notes on Duels and Duelling-Bost-1855-Crosby,Nichols-viii+394p-brwn cl-Howes S4-1st ed (mm10) 125.00

SABLOFF,JEREMY A-Ancient Civilization and Trade-Albuquerque-1975-UNM Pr-8vo-xiv,485p-blu cl,41 text figs,17 tabls-1st ed (ll1,f,sl wn dj) 40.00

SACHER-MASOCH,LEOPOLD-Venus in Furs-NY-1928-illus by C Raymond-ltd to 1250c,nbrd (r2) 50.00

SACHS,CURT-History of Musical Instruments-NY-1940-Norton-cl,illus-1st ed (l8,f,dj) 27.50

SACHS,H B-Heine in America-(Phila)-1916-Univ of Penn-193p-grn cl,Amer Germanica No.23-1st ed (e2) 20.00

SACHS,MAURICE-Decade of Illusion, Paris 1918 to 1928-NY-1933-Knopf-1st ed (j8,wn dj) 50.00

SACHSE,L-Full Color Uniforms of the Prussian Army-NY-1981-72 col plts-(rprnt of 1830 ed) (gg2,f,dj) 35.00

SACK,JOHN-Butcher-NY-1952-213p-16 photos,map-1st ed (p10,f,sl chip dj) 25.00

SACK,JOHN-Butcher-NY-1952-Rinehart-213p-Neate 678-later ed (j8,chip dj) 35.00

SACK,JOHN-Man Eating Machine-NY-1973-FSG-1st ed (c8,dj) 35.00

SACKETT,WILLIAM E-Modern Battles of Trenton-Trenton-1895-501p-cl,illus (aa6) 20.00

SACKETT,WILLIAM E-Modern Battles of Trenton. Volume II-NY-1914-423p-cl,ports (aa6,sp fade) 45.00

SACKLER,HOWARD-Great White Hope-NY-1968-Dial-1st ed (a10,dj rub & sl creased) 25.00

SACKVILLE-WEST,VITA-All Passion Spent-Lond-1931-Hogarth Pr-12mo-296p-cl-1st ed (mm4,sl discol sp) 90.00

SACKVILLE-WEST,VITA-An Other World Than This...an anthology compiled by...and Harold Nicholson-Lond-(1945)-Joseph-8vo-247p-1st ed (w6,f,wn dj) 25.00

SACKVILLE-WEST,VITA-Challenge-NY-nd-Doran-1st US ed (w5,f,dj sl wn,tn) 75.00

SACKVILLE-WEST,VITA-Country Notes in Wartime-NY-1941-Dbldy,Doran-12mo-viii,85p-1st Amer ed (mm4) 35.00

SACKVILLE-WEST,VITA-Dark Island-Lond-1934-Hogarth Pr-8vo-317p-1st ed (w6,dj sl soil & chip) 150.00

SACKVILLE-WEST,VITA-Daughter of France-GC-1959-Dbldy-1st ed (q2,cov spot,dj soil,stnd) 35.00

SACKVILLE-WEST,VITA-Dearest Andrew-NY-1979-Scribner-1st ed (t4,f,f dj) 15.00

SACKVILLE-WEST,VITA-Easter Party-Lond-(1953)-Michael Joseph-8vo-239p-1st ed (w6,f,dj) 75.00

SACKVILLE-WEST,VITA-Edwardians-Lond-1929-Hogarth Pr-8vo-349p-cl-Woolmer 235B-1st trd ed (nn4,sl wn,fox,dj sl chip,tn) 125.00

SACKVILLE-WEST,VITA-Faces-GC-1962-Dbldy-4to-unpgd-photos-1st US ed (dd5,f,tn dj) 20.00

SACKVILLE-WEST,VITA-Garden-NY-1946-DD-1st ed (y1,f,sl tn dj) 40.00

SACKVILLE-WEST,VITA-Garden: A Poem-Lond-1946-M Joseph-134p-1st trd ed (mm4,f,sl wn dj) 55.00

SACKVILLE-WEST,VITA-In Your Garden Again-Lond-1953-M Joseph-178p-illus,pict dj-1st ed (mm4,as new in dj) 65.00

SACKVILLE-WEST,VITA-In Your Garden-Lond-1951-M Joseph-8vo-237p-cl,8 plts-3rd prtg (cc10) 50.00

SACKVILLE-WEST,VITA-Joy of Gardening-NY-1958-xiii,210p-cl sp,bds,illus-1st ed (jj7) 25.00

SACKVILLE-WEST,VITA-King's Daughter-Lond-1929-Hogarth Pr-41p-bds,orng wraparound band-Living Poets Ser No.11-Woolmer 207-1st ed (nn4,sl fade,wraparound) 155.00

SACKVILLE-WEST,VITA-Land-Lond-(1933)-Windmill Libr-12mo-107p (m10,wn dj) 12.00

SACKVILLE-WEST,VITA-Land-Lond-1939(1926)-Heinemann-cl,papr sp labl-Windmill ed (mm4) 32.00

SACKVILLE-WEST,VITA-No Signposts in the Sea-NY-1961-DD-1st ed (y1,f,f dj) 35.00

SACKVILLE-WEST,VITA-Nursery Rhymes-Lond-1947-Dropmore Pr-lg 8vo-66p-g dec cl-ltd to 550c,nbrd-1st ed (dd10,vf,dj,box) 165.00

SACKVILLE-WEST,VITA-Pepita-Lond-1937-Hogarth Pr-8vo-282p-1st ed (w6,f,sl soil dj) 200.00

SACKVILLE-WEST,VITA-Seducers in Ecuador-NY-(1925)-Doran-1st ed (t4,f,chip dj) 35.00

SACKVILLE-WEST,VITA-Seducers in Ecuador-NY-(1925)-Doran-8vo-cl & dec papr cov bds-1st ed (x10,f,sl tn dj) 25.00

SACKVILLE-WEST,VITA-Sissinghurst-Lond-1931-Hogarth Pr-orig mrbld bds,prtd by hand by L & V Woolf-ltd to 500c,autg (aa9) 300.00

SACKVILLE-WEST,VITA-Solitude A Poem-Lond-1938-Hogarth Pr-8vo-56p+4p ads-cl-Woolmer 438B-1st ed (nn4,dj crease,sl tn) 75.00

SADLER,MARK-Falling Man-NY-1970-Random-1st ed (f4,f,dj) 12.50

SAFFORD,C-America's Quilt and Coverlets-NY-1974-Weathervane-4to-313p-blu cl,col & b&w illus (r10,dj) 22.50

SAFFORD,WILLIAM H-Blennerhassett Papers...-Cin-1861-MWK-665p+ads-blk cl,4 plts-1st ed (e2,sl fox,sl wn sp tips) 125.00

SAFFORD,WILLIAM H-Life of Harman Blennerhassett-Chillicothe-1850-Ely,Allen & Locke-239p-blk cl,frnts-Howes S-13-1st ed (m2) 135.00

SAGE,DANA-Moon Was Red-NY-1944-Simon-1st ed (g4,f,dj) 15.00

SAGE,LEE-Last Rustler-1930-Little,Brown-303p-illus-Six Guns #1930-1st ed (r8) 33.00

SAGE,RUFUS B-Rocky Mountain Life-Bost-1858-Wentworth & Co-xiv+29-363p+ads-lilac cl,plts-Howes S16-later ed (b2,sp fade,text fox) 50.00

SAGENDORPH,ROBB-America and Her Almanacs-Dublin-1970-Yankee-318p-illus-1st ed (o2,dj) 15.00

SAGINAW & BAY COUNTIES-PORTRAIT AND BIOGRAPHICAL RECORD OF...MICHIGAN...-Chig-1892-Bio Publ Co-1044p+5p index-mor,dbl cols-Streeter 5847 (n1) 100.00

SAGLE,LAWRENCE W-Book of Rules for Model Railroaders-Ramsey-1943-191p-1st ed (n4) 35.00

SAHADI,LOU-Pirates-1980-Times-1st ed (q7,dj) 25.00

SAHADI,LOU-Pirates-1980-Times-photos-1st ed (s8,f,dj) 20.00

SAIGN,RAY S-ET AL-Stagecoach Museum Gun Collection-Mpls-(1978)-Colwell Pr-4to-207p-pict e.p.,col illus-1st ed (ff4,dj) 25.00

SAINSBURY,HARRINGTON-Drugs and the Drug Habit-Lond-(1909)-Methuen-xvi+308p-red cl,11 illus-1st ed (d2,cov soil & sl edge-wn) 35.00

SAINT-AMAND,IMBERT DE-Women of the Valois Court-NY-1894-356p-cl (d1) 17.50

SAINT-ANDRE,CLAUD-King's Favourite-Lond-1915-Jenkins-8vo-338p-17 illus-1st Brit ed (jj5) 20.00

SAINT-EXUPERY,ANTOINE DE-Flight to Arras-NY-(1942)-Reynal & Hitchcock-8vo-256p-cl,13p plts,col illus e.p.-1st ed (t2,sl wn) 35.00

SAINT-EXUPERY,ANTOINE DE-Little Prince-NY-1943-Reynal & Hitchcock-ltd to 525c,autg (y1,dj sl chip,soil,edgewn) 750.00

SAINT-EXUPERY,ANTOINE DE-Night Flight-1932-Century-auth 1st bk-1st Amer ed (x2,sl wn dj) 70.00

SAINT-EXUPERY,ANTOINE DE-Night Flight-NY-1932-Century-1st ed (dd6,edgewn dj) 45.00

SAINTSBURY,NOEL-Cracker Stanton-1934-Cupples & Leon-drwngs-1st ed (s8,dj) 18.50

SAKURAI,TADAYOSHI-Human Bullets-Lond/Bost-1907-Constable/Houghton-8vo-(1),270p-orig brwn cl (gg6) 55.00

SALAMAN,REDCLIFFE N-History and Social Influence of the Potato-Cambridge-1949-Univ Pr-685p-grn cl (a8,sl sun sp) 85.00

SALAMANCA,J R-Lost Country-NY-1958-auth 1st bk-1st ed (g5,edge wn dj) 50.00

SALAS,FLOYD-Tattoo the Wicked Cross-NY-(1967)-Grove Pr-auth 1st bk-1st ed (a10,f,dj) 25.00

SALE,ROGER-On Not Being Good Enough-NY,Oxford-1979-Oxford Univ-1st ed (e10,as new in dj) 20.00

SALE,WILLIAM M-Samuel Richardson-Ithaca-1950-Cornell U Pr-8vo-x,389p-cl-1st ed (w2) 45.00

SALEEBY,C-Surgery and Society, a Tribute to Listerism-NY-1912-395p (dd3) 50.00

SALETORE,R N-Indian Witchcraft-Atlantic Highlands-1981-Humanities Pr-cl-1st Amer ed (n8,f,dj) 20.00

SALINGER,J D-Catcher in the Rye-Bost-1951-Little,Brown-1st iss dj wi auth photo on rear panel-1st ed (q5,dj sl edgewn & sp chip) 800.00

SALINGER,J D-Catcher in the Rye-Bost-1951-Little,Brown-auth 1st bk-1st ed (e10,sl bump,dj sl wn,sm hole) 1,200.00

SALINGER,J D-Complete Uncollected Short Stories of...-np-nd(1974)-no publ-2 vols-glossy pict wrps-1st ed,2nd issue (ff6,f) 350.00

SALINGER,J D-Franny & Zooey-Bost,Tor-(1961)-Little,Brown-1st ed (ff6,dj) 85.00

SALINGER,J D-Raise High the Roof Beam, Carpenters and Seymour: An Introduction-Bost-1963-Little,Brown-1st ed,2nd state (w5,f,dj sl sun,soil) 35.00

SALINGER,M-Flowers-NY-(1949)-Harper & Bros-4to-27p-dec cl,40 col plts,illus-1st Amer ed (dd10,cor bump,shaken) 30.00

SALINGER,PIERRE-America Held Hostage-GC-1981-Dbldy-349p-1st ed (r1,sl tn dj) 25.00

SALISBURY,ALBERT-Here Rolled the Covered Wagons-(1948)-Superior-4to-264p-223 photos,e.p. map-3rd ed rvsd (r8,dj) 30.00

SALISBURY,ALBERT-Two Captains West-Seattle-(1950)-Superior-qto-235p-photos,map e.p.,drwngs-1st ed (bb4,dj) 30.00

SALISBURY,HARRISON E-Black Night, White Snow-GC-Dbldy-8vo-746p-1st trd ed (cc5,sl tn dj) 20.00

SALLEY,A S,JR.-Happy Hunting Ground-Columbia-1926-83p-photos-scarce (gg3,vf) 100.00

SALMON,RICHARD-Fly Fishing for Trout-NY-1952-8vo-240p-illus-1st ed (m3,f,chip dj) 60.00

SALMONS,C H-COMP.-Burlington Strike-Aurora-1889-Bunnell & Ward-480p-illus (bb4) 25.00

SALOMON,JULIAN H-Book of Indian Crafts and Indian Lore-NY-(1928)-Harper & Row-418p-map e.p. (cc4,dj) 15.00

SALPOINTE,J B-Soldiers of the Cross-Banning-1898-296p-photos-Howes#S55-1st ed (v7) 200.00

SALSBURY,CLARENCE G-Salsbury Story-Tucson-(1969)-271p-photos-1st ed (v7,f,dj) 25.00

SALT,W RAY-Birds of Alberta-Edmonton-1958-8vo-511p-cl,col illus (y8) 40.00

SALT,W RAY-Birds of Alberta-Edmonton-1976-Hurtig Publ-8vo-xiv,498p-photos,303 col & 13 b&w illus,288 maps-updated & enlgd ed (bb7,vf) 25.00*

SALTEN,FELIX-Bambi's Children-Indpls-(1939)-Bobbs-Merrill-315p-cl,b&w illus,E Pinner-1st US ed (s3,f,dj) 15.00

SALTEN,FELIX-Bambi-NY-1928-S&S-cl,b&w illus,K Wiese-1st US ed (s3,sp fade,g dull) 10.00

SALTEN,FELIX-Forest World-Indpls-(1942)-Bobbs Merrill-274p-b&w illus,B Kuhn-1st US ed (r3,f,dj) 15.00

SALTER,EDWIN-History of Monmouth and Ocean Counties-Bayonne-1890-(6),xiii,442,lxxx p-cl,plts (aa6) 200.00

SALTER,HARRY B-ED.-Who's Who in Trenton-(Trenton)-1908-4to-(177)p-cl,illus-ltd to 125c,nbrd (aa6) 90.00

SALTER,JAMES-Light Years-1975-Random-1st ed (q9,dj) 15.00

SALTER,JAMES-Light Years-NY-1975-1st ed (n5,f,f dj) 30.00

SALTER,JAMES-Solo Faces-1979-220p-1st ed (q10,f,dj) 25.00

SALTER,JAMES-Sport and a Pastime-GC-(1967)-Paris Rev Eds-1st ed (x10,f,f dj) 40.00

SALTER,MARJORIE-Delightful Food-Lond-(1957)-Sidgwick & Jackson-148p-pnk cl,6 col plts-1st ed (q8,sl spot,dj) 16.50

SALTER,STEFAN-From Cover to Cover-Englewood Cliffs-(1969)-Prentice-Hall-1st ed (bb1,f,rprd dj) 15.00

SALTER,T F-Angler's Guide-Lond-1815-8vo-217p-extra illus,lg pap,1/4 grn cl,gilt (m3,rbnd) 125.00

SALTER,WILLIAM T-Endocrine Function of Iodine-Cambridge-1940-Harvard U Pr-xviii+351p-red cl-1st ed (c2) 25.00

SALTUS,EDGAR-Imperial Purple-Chig-1892-Morrill Higgins-234p-dec cl-Wright III 4748-1st ed (hh9,hng crack) 25.00

SALTY SAYINGS FROM CYNICAL MEN-Mt.Vernon-(1959)-Peter Pauper Pr-60p-bds-illus,H R Martin (j1,dj) 10.00

SAMPSON,ARTHUR-Important Range Plants-Wash-1917-63p-wrps,illus (t8,one chip & sl soil wrps) 12.00

SAMPSON,ARTHUR-Plant Succession in Relation to Range Management-Wash-1919-76p-wrps,drwngs,photos,4 lg fldg illus (t8,sl wn) 12.00

SAMPSON,EZRA-Beauties of the Bible-Hudson-1802-338,(2)p-prnted by Sampson,Chittenden & Crosswell-lea-Amer Imprints 1871-2nd Hudson ed (e1,tn frnt flylf) 35.00

SAMPSON,HENRY-ED.-Jane's World Railways 1967 to 68-Great Missenden-1968-522p-10th ed (n4,dj) 65.00

SAMPSON,HENRY-ED.-World Railways 1956 to 57-Great Missenden-1957-502p-4th ed (n4,f,dj) 65.00

SAMPSON,HENRY-ED.-World Railways 1960-Great Missenden-1960-412p-6th ed (n4,f,dj) 65.00

SAMPSON,HENRY-ED.-World Railways-NY-1954-462p-3rd ed (n4,f,dj) 75.00

SAMPSON,HENRY-History of Advertising from the Earliest Times-Lond-1874-Chatto & Windus-thk 8vo-616p-tan calf,g sp wi red lea sp labl,fldg col frntis,illus,facs-scarce-1st ed (b3) 375.00

SAMSON,J G-ED.-Worlds of Ernest Thompson Seton-1976-Knopf-4to-204p-57 illus(incl 36 col),71 drwngs (bb3,f,dj) 45.00

SAMSON,J-ED-Best of Corey Ford-NY-1975-266p-illus (gg3,vf,dj) 30.00

SAMSON,JACK-Bear Book-Clinton-1982-8vo-238p-illus (m3,vf) 20.00

SAMSON,JACK-Grizzly Book-1981-Amwell Pr-8vo-304p-ltd to 1000c,nbrd,two autg,illus by Al Barker (m3,vf,box) 90.00

SAMSON,LEON-Toward a United Front-NY-1933-Farrar & Rinehart-276p-1st ed (ff1,pg top soil,dj chip,soil) 25.00

SAMSON,WILLIAM-Passionate North-Lond-1950-Hogarth Pr-8vo-250p-cl-1st ed (nn4,f,f dj) 50.00

SAMSON,WILLIAM-Something Terrible, Something Lovely-Lond-1948-Hogarth Pr-8vo-232p-cl-1st ed (nn4,dj) 55.00

SAMUEL,CHERYL-Chilkat Dancing Blanket-(Seattle)-(1982)-234p-col & b&w illus,photos-1st ed (h7,vf,vf dj) 40.00

SAMUEL,MAURICE-Blood Accusation-NY-1966-Knopf-8vo-286p-1st ed (gg5,sl chip dj) 15.00

SAMUELS,CAPTAIN S-From the Forecastle to the Cabin-NY-1887-Harper & Bros-xviii,308p+ads-blu cl,g titles & decs,illus (nn1,bump,cl v wn) 35.00

SAMUELS,E A-With Fly Rod & Camera-NY-1890-8vo-477p-illus-1st ed (m3) 65.00

SAMUELS,E A-With Rod & Gun in New England & the Maritime Provinces-Bost-1897-4to-540p-illus,photos-scarce-1st ed (m3) 70.00

SAMUELS,L-Hemingway Check List-1951-Scribners-1st ed (x2,f,sl wn dj) 60.00

SAMUELS,NANCY-Old Northwest Texas-Ft.Worth-(1980)-Geneal Soc-2 vols-maps,chrts,ltd to 250c-1st ed (f9) 200.00

SAMUELS,PEGGY-Contemporary Western Artists-1982-SW Arts-4to-col illus-1st ed (b4,dj chip & tn) 75.00

SAMWELL,DAVID-Captain Cook and Hawaii-SF/Lond-1957-D Magee/F Edwards-x,42p-illus-ltd to 750c (pp1,f) 125.00

SAN FRANCISCO OFFICIAL STREET RAILWAY DIRECTORY...1903 EDITION-SF-(1902)-Hoag-240p-wrps,fldg map (n1) 20.00

SAN FRANCISCO-ERADICATING PLAGUE FROM...-SF-1909-vi+313p-maroon cl,photos-1st ed (j2,pgs sl creased & soil) 50.00

SANBORN,F B-ED.-Life and Letters of John Brown-Bost-1885-Roberts Bros-645p-yel cl-1st ed (dd6,sl dmpstnd cov) 50.00

SANBORN,KATE-Truthful Woman in Southern California-NY-1894-Appleton-12mo-192p-pict cl (cc4) 20.00

SANBORN,RUTH B-Murder By Jury-1932-Little,Brown-1st ed (s10,sp fade) 10.00

SANCEAU,ELAINE-Land of Prester John-NY-1944-Knopf-1st Amer ed (v4) 25.00

SANCHEZ,GEORGE I-Forgotten People-Albuq-1940-cl-1st ed (z1) 40.00

SANCHEZ,THOMAS-Rabbit Boss-NY-1973-auth 1st bk-1st ed (q5,dj) 35.00

SANCHEZ,THOMAS-Zoot Suit Murders-NY-(1978)-Dutton-1st ed (b5,f,dj) 25.00

SANCHO,PEDRO-An Account of the Conquest of Peru-NY-1917-Cortes Soc-ltd to 250c,nbrd-v scarce (v4,f,uncut) 75.00

SAND,GEORGE-Consuelo-NY-1889-3 vols-g stmpd cl (m4,f) 20.00

SAND,GEORGE-Consuelo-NY-1889-Dodd,Mead-8vo-four vols bnd in two in 3/4 mor-1st US ed (w6,rbnd) 45.00

SAND,GEORGE-Devil's Pool-Bost-1894-Little,Brown-DeVinne Pr-8vo-197p-etching by E Abot-ltd to 750c-1st US ed (w6,f,dj) 75.00

SAND,GEORGE-Marquis de Villemer-Bost-1871-130p-cl,dbl cols,R Keeler,translator (m1,sl spot cov,sm wn spot) 17.50

SAND,GEORGE-Tales of a Grandmother-Phila-1930-Lippincott-304p-cl,12p col illus,H W Hess-1st ed thus (r3,sl damaged frntis,sl fade) 25.00

SANDBURG,CARL-Abraham Lincoln, the Prairie Years & the War Years-NY-(1957)-Sangamon ed-6 vols-illus (c4,f) 95.00

SANDBURG,CARL-Abraham Lincoln-NY-(1954)-Harcourt,Brace-762p-cl-one vol ed. (h1,dj) 15.00

SANDBURG,CARL-Always the Young Strangers-NY-(1953)-Harcourt,Brace-ltd to 600c,autg (cc1,box) 175.00

SANDBURG,CARL-American Songbag-NY-(1927)-Harcourt,Brace-illus-1st ed (d10,sl chip dj) 125.00

SANDBURG,CARL-Cornhuskers-1918-Holt-brn bds-1st ed (x2) 20.00

SANDBURG,CARL-Early Moon-NY-1930-1st ed (f5) 45.00

SANDBURG,CARL-Home Front Memo-NY-1943-1st ed (s5,dj) 22.50

SANDBURG,CARL-Honey and Salt-NY-(1963)-Harcourt,Brace-g titled cl-1st ed (aa9) 15.00

SANDBURG,CARL-Letters of...-NY-(1968)-Harcourt Brace-575p-1st ed (bb2,f,dj) 40.00

SANDBURG,CARL-Mary Lincoln-NY-1932-Harcourt Brace-1st ed (f8,f,edgetn dj) 100.00

SANDBURG,CARL-People, Yes-NY-(1936)-Harcourt,Brace-cl-1st ed (aa9,chip dj) 30.00

SANDBURG,CARL-Potato Face-NY-1930-1st ed (r2,f,dj sp sun,sl chip,tn) 60.00

SANDBY,GEORGE-Mesmerism and its Opponents-Lond-1844-LBG&L-sm 8vo-x+278p-emboss brwn cl-scarce-1st ed (y9,sl chip) 125.00

SANDEMAN,FRASER-By Hook & By Crook-Lond-1892-4to-255p-ltd to 100c,nbrd,autg,15 full pg plts,text illus-scarce (m3) 300.00

SANDER,AUGUST-Photographs of an Epoch, 1904 to 1959-Millerton-1980-Aperture-125p-104 photos-1st ed (cc9,as new in dj) 40.00

SANDER,ELLEN-Trips: Rock Life in the Sixties-NY-1973-Scribners-1st ed (f8,f,dj) 40.00

SANDERS,ALVIN-Cattle of the World-Wash-1926-Nat Geog Soc-paintings,photos-1st ed (f10) 65.00

SANDERS,ALVIN-In Winter Quarters-Chig-1920-Breeder's-220p-cl-scarce (x6) 25.00

SANDERS,ALVIN-Red White & Roan-Chig-1936-Amer Shrthorn Breeders-illus-1st ed (b4,soil dj) 650.00

SANDERS,ALVIN-Shorthorn Cattle-Chig-1918-Sanders Publ-thk 8vo-1021p-grn cl,g titles,photo inlaid frnt bd,illus-1st ed (bb7,scuff cl) 60.00*

SANDERS,ALVIN-Story of the International Livestock Expo-Chig-1942-I.L.S.E.A.-362p-orng cl-1st ed (c2,spot cov) 15.00

SANDERS,CHARLES W-Sanders' Pictorical Primer-NY-(1846)-Ivison & Phinney-48p-bds,illus (k1,fox) 25.00

SANDERS,CHARLES W-Sanders' Young Ladies Reader...-NY-1866-Ivison,Phinney & Blakeman-500p-1/2 lea (k1,sl wn) 27.50

SANDERS,CHARLES W-School Reader. Third Book-Cin-1844-Wm H Moore-250,(2)p-bds (k1,wn covs) 37.50

SANDERS,ED-Tales of Beatnik Glory-NY-1975-1st ed (x8,dj) 22.00

SANDERS,GEORGE-Stranger at Home-NY-1946-Simon-1st ed (d4,sp tn dj) 15.00

SANDERS,HELEN F-History of Montana-Chig-1913-Lewis-4to-3 vols,half lea,photos illus,ports-1st ed (v1) 500.00

SANDERS,HELEN F-Trails Through Western Woods-NY,Seattle-1910-311p-illus-1st ed (g7) 75.00

SANDERS,JOHN-Early History of Schenectady-Albany-1879-Van Benthuysen-3 engrvd ports-1st ed (mm9) 150.00

SANDERS,LAWRENCE-Anderson Tapes-NY-1970-Putnam-auth 1st bk-1st ed (g4,dj) 12.50

SANDERS,LAWRENCE-Pleasures of Helen-NY-1971-1st ed (s5,dj) 25.00

SANDERS,MILLARD-Two Minute Horse-Cleve-1922-220p-wrps,photos-1st prtg (j9) 95.00

SANDERS,RONALD-Days Grow Short-NY-1980-Holt-1st ed (u4,dj) 18.00

SANDERS,T H-My Japanese Year-Lond-(1915)-Mills & Boon-8vo-345p wi photos+ads,maroon cl-1st ed (s1) 45.00

SANDERS,T W-Encyclopedia of Gardening-Lond-nd(1919)-sm 8vo-xv,482p+ads-brwn pict cl (m10) 11.00

SANDERS,T W-Grapes, Peaches, Melons and How to Grow Them-Lond-(1924)-150p-grn cl,19 b&w photos plts,34 text illus (j10,sl spot) 15.00

SANDERSON,E D-Insect Pests of Farm, Garden and Orchard-NY-1921-Wiley-707p-cl,illus (x6) 20.00

SANDERSON,EDGAR-Fight for the Flag in South Africa-Lond-1900-136p-blk cl,maps,illus-1st ed (gg2) 60.00

SANDERSON,G C-Wild Turkey Management-MO-1973-355p-photos (gg3,f,dj) 35.00

SANDERSON,I T-Dynasty of Abu-1962-Knopf-376p-illus-1st ed (bb3,f,rprd dj) 20.00

SANDERSON,IVAN-Dynasty of Abu-NY-1962-8vo-376p-illus-1st ed (m3,vf,chip dj) 25.00

SANDERSON,WILLIAM-Horses are for Warriors-Caldwell-1954-Caxton-illus,P Crowell-1st ed (h9) 15.00

SANDFORD,JEREMY-In Search of the Magic Mushroom-NY-1973-Clarkson N Potter-cl,illus-1st ed (n8,f,dj) 20.00

SANDO,JOE S-Nee Hemish-Albuq-(1982)-248p-photos,maps-1st ed (v7,f,dj) 20.00

SANDO,JOE S-Pueblo Indians-SF-(1976)-247p-wrps,photos,maps-1st ed (v7,f) 15.00

SANDOZ,MARI-Battle of Little Big Horn-Phila-(1966)-191p-maps-1st ed (c4,f,dj) 35.00

SANDOZ,MARI-Battle of the Little Big Horn-NY-(1966)-191p-e.p. maps (c7,f,dj) 25.00

SANDOZ,MARI-Battle of the Little Big Horn-Phila-(1966)-Lippincott-191p-map e.p.-1st ed (dd4,dj) 40.00

SANDOZ,MARI-Beaver Men-NY-(1964)-Hastings Hs-335p-e.p. maps-1st ed (nn6,wn dj) 20.00

SANDOZ,MARI-Crazy Horse-NY-1942-Knopf-(xiv),428p-cl,fldg map-1st ed (v1,chip dj) 75.00

SANDOZ,MARI-Crazy Horse-NY-1942-Knopf-428p-fldg map-1st ed (nn6,wn dj) 95.00

SANDOZ,MARI-Horsecatcher-Phila-1956-1st ed (q5,dj) 15.00

SANDOZ,MARI-Love Songs to the Plains-NY-(1961)-Harper-1st ed (dd2,f,dj) 35.00

SANDOZ,MARI-Miss Morissa-NY-1955-1st ed (q5,dj) 20.00

SANDOZ,MARI-Old Jules Country-NY-1965-Hastings Hs-1st ed (d10,f,dj) 20.00

SANDOZ,MARI-Old Jules-Bost-1935-Little,Brown-424p-cl-Rampaging Herd 2005-1st ed (m1,lacks sm pc dj sp) 17.50

SANDOZ,MARI-Old Jules-Bost-1935-Little,Brown-424p-illus-Herd 2005-1st ed (cc4,dj wn & taped) 35.00

SANDOZ,MARI-Sandhill Sundays...-Lincoln-(1970)-U of Nebr Pr-165p-1st ed (bb4,dj) 25.00

SANDOZ,MARI-Son of the Gamblin' Man-NY-1960-333p-1st ed (t7,dj) 20.00

SANDOZ,MARI-Story Catcher-Phila-1963-175p-pict cl,illus-1st ed (t7) 15.00

SANDOZ,MARI-These Were the Sioux-NY-(1961)-Hastings Hs-118p-illus-1st ed (cc4) 20.00

SANDS,L-Bird, the Gun, the Dog-NY-1939-494p-photos,col illus (gg3,vf) 15.00

SANDWICH ISLAND NOTES-1854-Harper-illus-1st ed (u8,sl fox pgs,discol e.p.s) 190.00

SANFORD,BISHOP-Waterfowl Family-NY-1903-8vo-598p-illus-1st ed (m3,f) 40.00

SANFORD,MARCELLINE H-At the Hemingways-Lond-1963-Putnam-1st Brit ed (d8,f,wn & tn dj) 35.00

SANFORD,MARCELLINE H-At the Hemingways-Lond-1963-Putnam-1st Brit ed (q2,cor bump,dj) 30.00

SANFORD,PAUL-Sioux Arrows and Bullets-San Antonio-(1969)-171p-1st ed (n3,f,dj) 22.50

SANFORD,TRENT E-Architecture of the Southwest-NY-(1950)-299p-photos,maps-scarce-1st ed (u7,f,dj) 65.00

SANGER,MARGARET-Woman and the New Race-NY-(1920)-Brentano's-8vo-234p-1st ed (oo7) 45.00

SANGER,MARGARET-Woman and the New Race-NY-(1920)-Truth Publ-234p-cl (d1) 15.00

SANGER,WILLIAM,M.D.-History of Prostitution-NY-1906-Medical Publ Co-8vo-709p wi index,blu cl-3rd ed (t1) 50.00

SANGSTER,MARGARET E-Winsome Womanhood-NY-1900-260p-cl (d1,fade,sl rub,wk innr hngs) 15.00

SANITARY ECONOMY: ITS PRINCIPLES AND PRACTICE-Edinburgh-1850-320p-1st ed (dd3) 100.00

SANKHALA,K-Tiger-1978-Collins-220p-photos-1st ed (bb3,f,dj) 25.00

SANKHALA,K-Tiger-NY-1977-220p-photos (gg3,f,dj) 15.00

SANSOM,WILLIAM-South-Lond-Hodder & Stoughton-1st Brit ed (y1,f,dj) 25.00

SANTA ANNA,ANTONIO L DE-Eagle-Austin-1967-Pemberton Pr-299p-illus (cc4,dj) 50.00

SANTA FE CENTRAL RAILWAY-Prospectus-Albuq-1901-15+1p,2p map,wrps-rare-1st ed (v7) 45.00

SANTA FE-CALENDAR OF ANNUAL EVENTS IN...-Santa Fe-1937-Amer Guide Ser-32p-hvy papr cov,13 wdblcks(ea in 3 cols)-1st ed (z1,f) 50.00

SANTA FE-Dude Ranch Country-Chig-1938-34p-pict wrps-scarce promo (t7) 50.00

SANTAYANA,GEORGE-Letters of...-NY-1955-Scribner's-1st ed (e8,f,dj) 45.00

SANTEE,ROSS-Cowboy-1928-Cosmopolitan-257p-illus,auth-Herd 2008-1st ed (t8,cov wn,sp fray) 30.00

SANTEE,ROSS-Cowboy-NY-1928-Cosmo Bk Corp-257p-pict cl-Herd 2008-1st ed (dd4) 35.00

SANTEE,ROSS-Lost Pony Tracks-NY-1953-Scribner's-303p-illus by auth-Herd 2009-1st ed (dd4,dj) 50.00

SANTEE,ROSS-Men & Horses-NY-1926-Century-illus-auth 1st bk-v scarce-1st ed (b4) 100.00

SANTEE,ROSS-Rummy Kid Goes Home-NY-1965-160p-illus-1st ed (t7,dj) 17.50

SANTINI,PIERO-Riding Reflections-Derrydale-1932-8vo-118p-one of 850c,illus,photos (m3) 60.00

SANTOLI,AL-Everything We Had-NY-(1981)-Random-265p-bds-1st ed so stated (h1,sl soil cov,dj sl wn & tn) 12.50

SAPIR,EDWARD-Yana Dictionary-Berkeley-1960-Univ of Cal-xii+267p-wrps-1st ed (e2) 30.00

SAPPINGTON,JOHN-Theory and Treatment of Fevers-Arrow Rock-1844-216p-lea-1st ed (dd3,sp chip) 250.00

SARATOGA FAVORITE-Saratoga Springs-1891-Cozzens & Waterbury-171p-Young Women's Mission Circle of the First Baptist Church (n6) 75.00

SARBER,MARY A-Photographs from the Border-El Paso-1977-Publ Libr-folio-ltd to 3000c-1st ed (a9) 75.00

SARCHET,FANCHER-Murder and Mirth-Denver-(1956)-Sage Bks-8vo-261p-1st ed (gg5,f,dj) 15.00

SARDI,VINCENT,JR.-Curtain Up at Sardi's-(1957)-Random-237p-dec wht cl-1st prtg (q8,dj) 16.50

SARDI,VINCENT-Sardi's-NY-(1953)-H Holt-244p-1st ed (l6,dj) 17.00

SARGEANT,HON.LEONARD-Trial,Confessions, and Conviction of Jesse and Stephen Boorn for the Murder of Russell Colvin...-Manchester-1873-Journal Bk & Job Office-48p-wrps-1st ed (k2) 75.00

SARGEANT,WINTHROP-Geniuses, Goddesses and People-NY-1949-Dutton-1st ed (w1,f,dj) 25.00

SARGEANT,WINTHROP-Jazz: Hot and Hybrid-NY-1946-Dutton-1st prtg,rvsd ed (w1,f,dj) 45.00

SARGENT,A J-Seaports & Hinterlands-Lond-1938-188p-cl (b1,sl spot cov) 12.50

SARGENT,C E-Our Home or the Key to a Nobler Life...-Springfield-1885-W C King-432p+15p testimonials-cl,12p plts (d1) 17.50

SARGENT,EPES-Etymological Reader-Phila-(1872)-J H Butler-480p-lea-backed cl,10p plts (c1) 15.00

SARGENT,FREDERICK-Corn Plants Their Uses and Ways of Life-Bost-1899-Houghton Mifflin-106p-cl (x6,ex-libr) 50.00

SARGENT,MRS.JOHN T-ED.-Sketches and Reminiscences of the Radical Club of Chestnut Street-Bost-1880-James R Osgood-xii+418p-blu cl-1st ed (k2) 60.00

SARGENT,PAMELA-Golden Space-NY-(1982)-1st ed (d5,f,dj) 15.00

SARGENT,SHIRLEY-Galen Clark: Yosemite Guardian-SF-1964-176p-1st ed (o10,f,dj) 45.00

SARGENT,WINTHROP-Life and Career of Major John Andre-Bost-1861-Ticknor & Fields-471p-brwn cl,map,port-1st ed (e2,sl fox) 125.00

SAROYAM,ARAM-Rest-1971-Telegraph Bks-pict wrps-1st ed (r2,sl soil) 20.00

SAROYAN,ARAM-Genesis Angels-NY-1979-1st ed (x8,f,f dj) 12.00

SAROYAN,WILLIAM-Adventures of Wesley Jackson-NY-1946-Harcourt-8vo-cl-1st ed (x3,sl chip dj) 40.00

SAROYAN,WILLIAM-Assyrian-Lond-1950-1st Brit ed (q5,dj sl chip) 40.00

SAROYAN,WILLIAM-Beautiful People-NY-(1941)-Harcourt,Brace-1st ed (u10,f,sp sunned dj) 45.00

SAROYAN,WILLIAM-Bicycle Rider in Beverly Hills-NY-1952-Scribner's-cl-1st ed (m8,f,dj) 25.00

SAROYAN,WILLIAM-Boys and Girls Together-NY-1963-HBCo-1st ed (h8,f,f dj) 40.00

SAROYAN,WILLIAM-Daring Young Man on the Flying Trapeze-NY-1934-Random-gry cl,blk sp,g labl-1st ed (x3,sp chip dj) 95.00

SAROYAN,WILLIAM-Days of Life and Death and Escape to the Moon-NY-1970-Dial-1st ed (y1,f,sl tn dj) 40.00

SAROYAN,WILLIAM-Fat Man in a Famine-NY-1947-Harcourt,Brace-cl-1st ed (m8,dj soil & tn) 15.00

SAROYAN,WILLIAM-Get Away Old Man-NY-1944-HBCo-1st ed (j8,f,f dj) 60.00

SAROYAN,WILLIAM-Human Comedy-Lond-1943-Faber & Faber-1st Brit ed (h8,f,f dj) 85.00

SAROYAN,WILLIAM-I Used to Believe I Had Forever, Now I'm Not So Sure-NY-1968-cl-1st ed (m8,f,chip dj) 20.00

SAROYAN,WILLIAM-Inhale & Exhale-NY-(1936)-Random-8vo-cl-1st ed (x3,dj) 55.00

SAROYAN,WILLIAM-Jim Dandy-NY-(1947)-Harcourt,Brace-1st ed (x10,f,dj) 45.00

SAROYAN,WILLIAM-Laughing Matter-GC-1953-Dbldy-cl-1st ed (m8,f,chip dj) 15.00

SAROYAN,WILLIAM-Little Children-NY-(1937)-Harcourt,Brace-1st ed (d10,sl soil dj) 200.00

SAROYAN,WILLIAM-Look at Us-(NY)-(1967)-Cowles Educ Corp-lg 8vo-blk & wht cl-1st ed (y3,f,f dj) 45.00

SAROYAN,WILLIAM-Look at Us...-NY-(1967)-Cowles-204p-101 photos by Rothstein-1st ed (cc9,f,dj) 40.00

SAROYAN,WILLIAM-Love, Here is My Hat-NY-1938-Modern Age Bks-wrps-1st ed (m8) 22.50

SAROYAN,WILLIAM-My Name is Aram-NY-(1940)-Harcourt Brace-1st ed (dd2,f,dj) 75.00

SAROYAN,WILLIAM-Not Dying-NY-1963-HB&W-cl,drwngs,auth-1st ed (m8,f,dj) 15.00

SAROYAN,WILLIAM-Papa, You're Crazy-Bost-1957-Little,Brown-cl-1st ed (m8,dj) 15.00

SAROYAN,WILLIAM-Places Where I've Done Time-1972-Praeger-1st ed (x2,f,dj) 20.00

SAROYAN,WILLIAM-Razzle Dazzle-NY-1942-Harcourt Brace-1st ed (h8,f,dj) 175.00

SAROYAN,WILLIAM-Short Drive,Sweet Chariot-(NY)-1966-1st ed (f5,f,dj) 12.50

SAROYAN,WILLIAM-Three Plays-NY-1941-Harcourt,Brace-cl-1st ed (m8,sp sunned dj) 20.00

SAROYAN,WILLIAM-Tracy's Tiger-GC-1951-drwngs,H Koerner-1st ed (f5,dj) 30.00

SAROYAN,WILLIAM-William Saroyan Reader-NY-1958-1st ed (f5,sl soil dj) 15.00

SARTON,GEORGE-Appreciation of Ancient and Medieval Science During the Renaissance-Phila-1955-234p-1st ed (dd3) 27.50

SARTON,GEORGE-History of Science and the New Humanism-Cambridge-1937-196p-1st ed (dd3) 30.00

SARTON,GEORGE-History of Science: Ancient Science through the Golden Age of Greece-Cambridge-1952-646p-1st ed (dd3) 40.00

SARTON,GEORGE-Six Wings-Bloomington-1957-318p-1st ed (dd3) 25.00

SARTON,MAY-Anger-NY-(1982)-Norton-8vo-223p-1st ed (w6,f,dj) 10.00

SARTON,MAY-As We Are Now-1973-Norton-1st ed (n9,f,dj) 15.00

SARTON,MAY-Fur Person-NY-1957-illus,B Knox-1st ed (n5,dj) 25.00

SARTON,MAY-Joanna and Ulysses-NY-(1963)-Norton-8vo-127p-illus,J Spanfeller-1st ed (w6,dj) 35.00

SARTON,MAY-Journal of a Solitude-NY-1973-Norton-1st ed (j8,f,dj) 27.50

SARTON,MAY-Journal of Solitude-NY-(1973)-Norton-photos-1st ed (a10,dj) 15.00

SARTON,MAY-Land of Silence and Other Poems-NY-1953-1st ed (t5,dj) 60.00

SARTON,MAY-Miss Pickthorn and Mr.Hare-NY-(1966)-8vo-92p-1st ed (w6,dj) 25.00

SARTON,MAY-Plant Dreaming Deep-1968-Norton-1st ed (m9,f,sl wn dj) 30.00

SARTON,MAY-Private Mythology-1966-Norton-1st ed (n9,f,dj sp wn,sl tn) 35.00

SARTON,MAY-Shadow of Man-NY-1950-1st ed (t5,f,sl rub dj) 50.00

SARTON,MAY-Shower of Summer Days-NY-1952-1st ed (o5,sl chip dj) 35.00

SARTON,MAY-Small Room-1961-Norton-1st ed (n9,dj chip,tn & rub) 30.00

SARTON,MAY-Small Room-NY-1961-8vo-249p-1st ed (w6,dj) 20.00

SARTON,MAY-World of Light-NY-1976-Norton-1st ed (j8,f,dj) 25.00

SARTRE,JEAN-PAUL-Age of Reason-NY-1947-1st US ed (q5,dj sp sl chip) 22.50

SARTRE,JEAN-PAUL-Devil and the Good Lord-NY-1960-Knopf-1st Amer ed (x10,f,sl wn dj) 20.00

SARTRE,JEAN-PAUL-Existentialism-NY-(1947)-Philo Libr-1st ed (x10,f,f dj) 35.00

SARTRE,JEAN-PAUL-No Exit & The Flies-NY-1947-auth 1st bk in U.S.-1st US ed (t5,wn dj) 30.00

SARTRE,JEAN-PAUL-Reprieve-NY-1947-Knopf-1st ed (x10,f,sl wn dj) 30.00

SARTRE,JEAN-PAUL-Situations-NY-1965-1st US ed (s5,rub dj) 15.00

SARTRE,JEAN-PAUL-Three Plays-NY-1949-Knopf-1st Amer ed (x10,f,sl wn dj) 35.00

SARTRE,JEAN-PAUL-Troubled Sleep-NY-1951-1st US ed (q5,dj) 25.00

SARTRE,JEAN-PAUL-Troubled Sleep-NY-1951-Knopf-1st US ed (x10,f,soil & edge tn dj) 20.00

SARTRE,JEAN-PAUL-Wall and Other Stories-NY-1948-dec bds-1st US ed (t5,wn box) 22.50

SASS,HERBERT R-Adventures in Green Places-NY-1935-Putnam-297p-illus (x6,sp fade) 25.00

SASSOON,P-Third Route-GC-1929-8vo-xvi,280p-cl,frntis,plts-1st ed (s2) 35.00

SASSOON,SIEGFRIED-Memoirs of a Fox Hunting Man-Lond-(1938)-Faber & Gwyer-only 1500c publ,publ omitted auth's name-1st ed (cc2,f,sl wn dj) 75.00

SASSOON,SIEGFRIED-Memoirs of an Infantry Officer-Lond-(1936)-Faber & Faber-1st ed (cc2,f,f dj) 45.00

SASSOON,SIEGFRIED-Memoirs of an Infantry Officer-NY-1930-Coward McCann-1st ed (cc2,dj sl chip) 50.00

SASSOON,SIEGFRIED-Old Century and Seven More Years-Lond-(1938)-Faber & Faber-1st ed (bb2,f,dj) 50.00

SASSOON,SIEGFRIED-Road to Ruin-Lond-(1933)-Faber & Faber-bds-1st ed (aa9,drknd bds,dj) 45.00

SASSOON,SIEGFRIED-Satirical Poems-Lond-1926-Heinemann-8vo-cl-1st ed (jj8,sl fox,dj sl wn & soil) 45.00

SASSOON,SIEGFRIED-Sequences-Lond-(1956)-Faber & Faber-cl-1st ed (aa9,dj) 50.00

SASSOON,SIEGFRIED-Sherston's Progress-Lond-(1936)-Faber & Faber-1st ed (cc2,f,f dj) 45.00

SATAN IN SOCIETY-Cin,NY-1873-C F Vent-412p-cl (d1,sl wn) 22.50

SATO,SHOZO-Art of Arranging Flowers-NY-1965-Abrams-4to-366p-grn silk bds,papr labl,b&w & tip in col illus (r10) 35.00

SATTERFIELD,ARCHIE-Lewis and Clark Trail-Harrisburg-1978-224p-photos,illus,maps-1st ed (t7) 22.50

SATTERLEE,L D-American Gun Makers-Buffalo-1940-8vo-186p (m3,f) 30.00

SATTLER,ROLF-Organogenesis of Flowers-(1973)-U of Tor Pr-lg sq 8vo-xxvi,207p-over 1200 b&w photos (j10,dj chip & scraped) 25.00

SATTLER,ROLF-Organogenesis of Flowers-Tor-(1973)-U of Tor-4to-207p-photos-1st Can ed (aa5,dj) 30.00

SAUER,CARL O-Geography of the Ozark Highland of Missouri-Chig-1920-U of Chig-xviii,245p-photo plts,maps-1st ed (o2) 22.50

SAUL,JOHN-God Project-NY-(1982)-Bantam-1st ed (l3,f,dj) 10.00

SAUNDERS,CHARLES F-Finding the Worth While in the Southwest-NY-1928-231p-dec cl,frntis,photos (t7) 7.50

SAUNDERS,CHARLES F-Southern Sierras of California-Bost,NY-1923-367p-cl,illus-1st ed (m1) 17.50

SAUNDERS,CHARLES F-Southern Sierras of California-Bost-1923-Houghton Mifflin-xii,367p-32 photo plts-1st ed (o2) 35.00

SAUNDERS,CHARLES F-Trees and Shrubs of California Gardens-1926-Robt McBride-323p-photos-1st ed (d3) 30.00

SAUNDERS,CHARLES F-Western Wild Flowers-GC-1938-xiv,320p-57 illus-4th ed (x5,dj soil,tn) 30.00

SAUNDERS,HILARY ST.GEORGE-Per Ardua.-Lond-1945-8vo-xii,356p-cl,plts,9 maps(incl 1 dblpg)-1st ed (s2,chip dj) 35.00

SAUNDERS,HILARY ST.GEORGE-Red Beret-Lond-1950-336p-illus-1st ed (b7,dj) 50.00

SAUNDERS,ROY-Queen of the River-Lond-1961-8vo-160p-photos (m3,f,dj) 25.00

SAURAT,DENIS-Literature and Occult Tradition-NY-1930-Lincoln MacVeagh,Dial Pr-viii+245+(3)p-1st Amer ed (y9,chip dj) 25.00

SAVAGE,C-Mandarin Duck-1952-Black-4to-78p-col frntis,16 photo plts,41 drwngs-1st ed (bb3) 48.00

SAVAGE,C-Mandarin Duck-Lond-1952-4to-78p-cl,col frntis,16 b&w plts (y8,dj wn,pres cpy) 55.00

SAVAGE,ERNEST-Two If By Sea-NY-1982-Scribner-auth 1st bk-1st ed (r4,f,dj) 17.50

SAVAGE,EROS M-Prospecting for Gold and Silver-NY/Lond-1934-McGraw-Hill-12mo-xii,307p-grn cl wi g,photos,diags-1st ed (mm1,f) 95.00

SAVAGE,GEORGE-French Decorative Art 1638 to 1793-NY-(1969)-tall 4to-(12),189p+113 plts-cl (l10,f,dj) 27.50

SAVAGE,MAJOR RICHARD HENRY-Our Mysterious Passenger-NY-1899-Street & Smith-pict cov,illus-1st ed (j4) 25.00

SAVAGE,WILLIAM W,JR.-ED.-Indian Life-Norman-(1977)-U of Okla Pr-286p-photos-1st ed (dd4,dj) 25.00

SAVAGE,WILLIAM W,JR.-Singing Cowboys and All that Jazz-Norman-(1983)-U of Okla Pr-185p-illus-1st ed (cc4,dj,autg) 20.00

SAVAGE-LANDOR,A HENRY-Everywhere-NY-1924-Stokes-8vo-2 vols-30 photos,6 maps-1st US ed (ff5,f) 85.00

SAVAGE-LANDOR,HENRY-Tibet & Nepal-Lond-1905-233p-dec cov,fldg map,75 col illus-1st ed (a4,few cov spots) 110.00

SAVIGNY,ANNE-Romance of Toronto-Tor-1888-Wm Briggs-sm 8vo-229p-orig dec cl-Watters p.387-1st ed (pp2,sl rub) 150.00*

SAVILLE-KENT,W-Great Barrier Reef of Australia-1893-Allen-folio-387p-16 col & 48 b&w photo plts,fldg map (bb3,sp ends rprd,cor bump) 185.00

SAVOY,GENE-On the Trail of the Feathered Serpent-Indpls-(1974)-Bobbs Merrill-8vo-216p-photos-1st ed (jj5,dj) 12.50

SAWTELLE,MARY P-Heroine of '49-SF-1891-248p-illus-2nd ed (bb9) 35.00

SAWYER,FRANK-Nymphs & the Trout-Lond-1958-8vo-175p-photos-1st ed (m3,sl chip dj) 40.00

SAWYER,RUTH-Christmas Anna Angel-NY-1944-Viking-48p-cl,col illus by K Seredy-1st ed (oo10,f,dj) 45.00

SAWYER,RUTH-My Spain-NY-(1967)-Viking-8vo-160p-1st ed (jj5,f,dj) 10.00

SAWYER,RUTH-Roller Skates-NY-(1937)-Viking-cl,illus,V Angelo-2nd prtg (s3,vf,dusty dj,autg) 35.00

SAWYER,RUTH-This is the Christmas-Bost-1945-Horn Bk-unpgd(40)-dec bds (n6) 25.00

SAXE,MARY S-Our Little Quebec Cousin-Bost-1919-Page-8vo-122,(10)p ads-pict cl,illus by Chas E Meister-1st ed (pp2,f,chip dj) 65.00*

SAXON,JOHN A-Half Past Mortem-NY-1947-Mill-1st ed (d4,soil pg tops,dj) 85.00

SAXON,LYLE-Father Mississippi-NY-(1927)-Century-427p-illus-1st ed (bb4) 60.00

SAXTON,ALEXANDER-Great Midland-NY-1948-Appelton-1st ed (v5,f,dj) 40.00

SAXTON,C M-American Rose Culturist-NY-1852-Saxton-96p-blndstmpd cl wi dec (x6) 45.00

SAYERS,DOROTHY-Busman's Honeymoon-NY-1937-Harcourt-1st US ed (f4,dj) 125.00

SAYERS,DOROTHY-ED.-Second Omnibus of Crime-NY-1932-Coward-1st US ed (j4) 20.00

SAYERS,DOROTHY-Man Born to be King-Lond-1943-Gollancz-1st ed (k7,dj sp sunned) 50.00

SAYERS,DOROTHY-Whose Body-1923-B&L-auth 1st bk-1st ed (x7,sm cov stn) 375.00

SAYLES,JOHN-Anarchists Convention-Bost-1979-Atlantic-Monthly-1st ed (h8,f,dj) 45.00

SAYLES,JOHN-Anarchists' Convention-Bost-1979-1st ed (q5,dj) 35.00

SAYLES,JOHN-Pride of the Bimbos-Bost-(1975)-Atlantic-auth 1st bk-1st ed (cc2,f,dj) 125.00

SAYLES,JOHN-Union Dues-Bost,Tor-(1977)-Little,Brown-1st ed (b10,f,sl wn dj) 30.00

SAYLES,JOHN-Union Dues-Bost-(1977)-1st ed (t5,sl rub dj) 20.00

SAYLOR,DAVID J-Jackson Hole, Wyoming-Norman-1970-268p-photos,maps-1st ed (t7,dj) 15.00

SAYRE,WOODROW W-Four Against Everest-Englewood Cliffs-1964-259p-1st ed (o10,f,dj) 40.00

SAYWELL,JOHN T-Office of Lieutenant Governor-Tor-1967-U of Tor Pr-xii,302p (k10,dj) 35.00*

SCAGNETTI,JACK-Movie Stars in Bathtubs-Middle Village-(1975)-Jonathan David-4to-160p-photos-1st ed (aa5,sl tn dj) 15.00

SCAMEHORN,HOWARD L-ED.-Buckeye Rovers in the Gold Rush-Athens-1965-Ohio U Pr-195p-1st ed (bb4,dj) 15.00

SCAMMAN,EDITH-Ferns and Fern Allies of New Hampshire-Durham-1947-NH Acad Sci,Bull.#2-98p-wrps,illus (x6) 20.00

SCAMMELL,R E-Thistle Eaters Guide-Lafayette-1970-Floreat Pr-112p-6th ed (m6) 10.00

SCANDLAND,JOHN M-Life of Pat F Garrett-(Colo Spgs)-(1952)-42p-stiff red wrps,illus,facs rprnt of 1st ed-Six Guns #1951 (c7,f) 50.00

SCANLAN,A B-Mountain of Maortland-New Plymouth-1949-4to-115p-49 photos-1st ed (q10,f,dj) 45.00

SCANLON,MARION S-Trails of the French Explorers-San Antonio-(1956)-Naylor Co-79p-photos,map e.p.-1st ed (bb4,dj) 20.00

SCANLON,WILLIAM T-God Have Mercy On Us-Bost-1929-HMCO-1st ed (x1,dj chip,rprd) 50.00

SCANNELL,JOHN J-ED.-Scannell's New Jersey's First Citizens-Paterson-(1917)-xi,564p-cl,ports (aa6) 30.00

SCARBOROUGH'S OFFICIAL TOUR BOOK 1916 NEW YORK, NEW JERSEY, CANADA AND THE EAST-Indpls-1916-1034p+fldg map-flex cl (f1,sl wn,few pg corners stnd) 17.50

SCARBROUGH,CLARA S-ED.-125 Years of Williamson County, 1848 to 1973-Georgetown-1973-Sun Publ-44p-wrps,photos-1st ed (w3,vf) 22.50

SCARFE,LAURENCE-Alphabets an Introductory Treatise...-Lond-(1954)-Batsford-4to-1st ed (w1,f,dj) 45.00

SCARGILL,M H-TRANSL.-Three Icelandic Sagas-NY-1950-Princeton U Pr-cl,col frntis,illus,H G Glyde-also transl by M Schlauch-1st ed (l8,f,dj) 13.50

SCARR,JOSEPHINE-Four Miles High-Lond-1966-188p-1st ed (o10) 30.00

SCEARCE,STANLEY-Northern Lights to Fields of Gold-Caldwell-1939-Caxton-8vo-390p-blu cl,illus-Ricks p.192 (oo1,dj chip) 70.00

SCHACHT,AL-My Own Particular Screwball-1965-Dlbdy-1st ed (p7,f,dj) 25.00

SCHACT,AL-G.I. Had Fun-1945-Putnam-photos-1st ed (s8,dj) 30.00

SCHAEFER,JACK-An American Bestiary-Bost-1975-Houghton Mifflin-sm 4to-xxvii+287p-cl,illus,L K Powell-1st ed (z4,dj) 15.00

SCHAEFER,JACK-Collected Stories of...-Bost-1966-Houghton Mifflin-8vo-xi+520p-cl,illus e.p.-1st ed so stated (z4,sl soil dj) 25.00

SCHAEFER,JACK-Shane-Bost-(1954)-Houghton Mifflin-1st illus ed (aa10,dj) 200.00

SCHAEFFER,A A-Taxonomy of the Amebas with Descriptions of Thirty Nine New Marine and Freshwater Species-1926-Carnegie Inst-4to-116p-binder bd cov,12 col plts (bb3,f) 35.00

SCHAEFFER,CASPER-Memoirs and Reminiscences together with Sketches of the Early History of Sussex County...-Hackensack-1907-187p-cl,plts-ltd to 250c (aa6,sl soil) 100.00

SCHAEFFER,J PARSONS-Nose, Paranasal Sinuses, Nasolacrimal Passageways, and Olfactory Organ in Man-Phila-(1920)-P Blakiston-lg 8vo-xii+370p-maroon cl,204 illus(incl 18 col)-1st ed (a2,cov sl wn,soil & spot) 35.00

SCHAEFFER,SUSAN F-Rhymes & the Runes of the Toad-NY-(1975)-Macmillan-1st ed (g3,f,dj) 25.00

SCHAFER,EDWARD H-Golden Peaches of Samarkand-Berkeley-1963-U of Cal Pr-sm 4to-399p-blu & gold bds (o6) 45.00

SCHAFFNER,JOHN-Field Manual of the Flora of Ohio-Columbus-1928-Adams-638p-cl (x6,sl tn text) 16.00

SCHAFFNER,VAL-Algonquin Cat-NY-(1980)-Delacorte-133p-cl,b&w illus,H Knight-1st ed (s3,f,f dj) 25.00

SCHALDACH,W J-Coverts & Casts, Currents & Eddies-1970-Freshet Pr-4to-2 vols,illus by auth,reprnts of 1943 & 1944 eds (m3,vf,box) 30.00

SCHALDACH,W J-Coverts & Casts-NY-1943-4to-138p-ltd to 160c,nbrd,autg,illus by auth-scarce (m3) 175.00

SCHALDACH,W J-Coverts & Casts-NY-1946-136p-illus-2nd prtg (gg3,vf,dj,autg) 55.00

SCHALDACH,W J-Coverts and Casts-NY-1943-137p-maroon/red cl,g titles & dec,4 col plts-1st prtg (ee3,f,dj chip) 40.00

SCHALDACH,W J-Currents & Eddies-1944-Countryman Press-4to-138p-illus by auth-1st trd ed (m3) 20.00

SCHALDACH,W J-Currents & Eddies-1944-Countryman Press-4to-138p-ltd to 250c,nbrd,autg,illus by auth-scarce (m3) 175.00

SCHALDACH,W J-Currents & Eddies-NY-1944-138p-illus,col frntis-1st prtg so stated (gg3) 30.00

SCHALDACH,W J-Path to Enchantment-1963-Macmillan-4to-226p-176 illus-1st ed (bb3,f,dj) 40.00

SCHALDACH,W J-Wind on Your Cheek-Rockville Centre-1972-4to-160p-illus,auth-1st ed (m3,vf,dj) 27.50

SCHALLER,GEORGE B-Deer and the Tiger-Chig-(1967)-U of Chig Pr-8vo-370p-30 plts-1st ed (aa5,f,dj) 25.00

SCHALLER,GEORGE-Stones of Silence-NY-1980-292p-col photos,6 maps-1st ed (o10,f,dj) 20.00

SCHAPERA,O-Government and Politics in Tribal Societies-Lond-(1956)-Watts-8vo-238p-cl-1st ed (y5,sl soil dj) 35.00

SCHAPPES,MORRIS U-Letters From the Tombs-NY-1941-Schappes Defns Comm-wrps-1st ed (v5) 15.00

SCHARFF,ROBERT-Complete Duck Shooter's Handbook-NY-1957-8vo-250p-illus (m3,vf,chip dj) 22.50

SCHARFF,ROBERT-Standard Handbook of Saltwater Fishing-NY-1959-8vo-374p-photos,illus-1st ed (m3,f,sl fray dj) 20.00

SCHARP,CAPTAIN HAL-Shark Safari-S Brunswick-1975-4to-224p-photos (m3,f,dj) 25.00

SCHAUFFLER,ROBERT H-Franz Schubert, the Ariel of Music-NY-(1949)-Putnam-8vo-427p-25 illus-1st ed (ee5,tape rprd dj) 15.00

SCHEE,GEO W-Biographical Data and Army Records of Old Soldiers Who Have Lived in O'Brien County, Iowa-Primghar-1909-priv prtd-199p-v scarce (o7,vf) 100.00

SCHEER,GEORGE F-Rebels and Redcoats-Cleve-(1957)-572p-cl-1st ed (a1,sl wn dj) 15.00

SCHEFFER,V B-Seals,Sea Lions, and Walruses-Stanford-1958-8vo-179p-buckram,32 plts (y8) 17.50

SCHEIKEVITCH,MARIE-Time Past, Memories of Proust and Others-Bost-1935-HMCo-1st US ed (hh5,dj tn) 17.00

SCHEITHAUER,W-Hummingbirds-NY-1967-lg 8vo-176p-cl,76 col photos (y8,dj chip) 100.00

SCHELL,HERBERT-History of Clay County, South Dakota-Vermillion-1976-293p-map frntis,photos,maps-1st ed (t7,dj,pres) 30.00

SCHELL,JONATHAN-Village of Ben Suc-NY-1967-Knopf-auth 1st bk-1st ed (ff3,dj sl stnd,sm chip) 35.00

SCHENK,J C-Barbers' Recipe Book...-Buffalo-1884-Matthews,Northrup-12mo-192p-bds (u6,soil & wn bds) 50.00

SCHERER,FRANCINE-Soho Charcuterie Cookbook-(1983)-Morrow-272p-gry cl,col plts-1st ed (q8,f,dj) 17.50

SCHERER,JAMES A B-Lion of the Vigilantes-Indpls-(1939)-Bobbs Merrill-335p-brwn cl,plts-1st ed (h2,edge-tn dj) 22.00

SCHERF,MARGARET-Always Murder a Friend-1948-CC-1st ed (s10,pgs brwng,dj) 20.00

SCHERF,MARGARET-Curious Custard Pie-NY-1950-Dbldy CC-1st ed (f4,sl yel pgs,dj) 25.00

SCHERF,MARGARET-Don't Wake Me Up While I'm Dreaming-NY-1977-Dbldy CC-1st ed (f4,f,dj) 15.00

SCHERF,MARGARET-Judicial Body-NY-1957-Dbldy CC-1st ed (g4,f,sl wn dj) 20.00

SCHERMAN,KATHARINE-Spring on an Arctic Island-1956-Little,Brown-8vo-xviii,334p+16 photos,e.p. map-1st ed (ff9,dj) 25.00*

SCHERMAN,KATHERINE-Two Islands-Bost-1971-8vo-256p-illus-1st ed (m3,f) 15.00

SCHERMERHORN,WILLIAM E-History of Burlington, New Jersey...-Burlington-1927-vii,388p-cl,plts (aa6) 90.00

SCHICK,FRANK L-Paperbound Book in America-NY-(1958)-R R Bowker-8vo-xviii,262p-cl-1st ed (w2) 50.00

SCHIECK,PAUL-Trolleys of Lower Delaware Valley Pennsylvania-Forty Fort-1970-86p-wrps,fldg map-1st ed (n4) 14.00

SCHIEL,JACOB H-Journey Through the Rocky Mountains and Humboldt Mountains to the Pacific Ocean-Norman-(1959)-U of Okla Pr-114p-illus-1st ed (cc4,dj) 25.00

SCHIELE,ERIKA-Arab Horse in Europe-Alhambra-1970-Borden-4to-1st US ed (f10,dj) 65.00

SCHIFFER,DON-ED.-World Series Encyclopedia-1961-Nelson-photos,drwngs-1st ed (s8,f,dj) 12.50

SCHILDT,JOHN W-Roads From Gettysburg-Chewsville-1979-Auth-174p-illus,maps-1st ed (o7,f,dj) 40.00

SCHILLER,ZOE-Candle for a Star-1952-MacMillan-1st prtg (r8,dj) 8.00

SCHILLINGS,C G-With Flashlight & Rifle-NY-1905-421p-photos (gg3) 30.00

SCHINDLER,HAROLD-Orin Porter Rockwell-SLC-(1983)-U of Utah Pr-417p-frntis,illus-rvsd 2nd ed (bb4,dj) 35.00

SCHINDLER,HAROLD-Orrin Porter Rockwell-SLC-1966-399p-frntis,illus (t7,dj) 30.00

SCHIWETZ,E M-Buck Schiwetz' Texas-Austin-1960-U of Tex-oblng 4to-illus,1 col plt-1st ed (b4) 35.00

SCHLAUCH,MARGARET-TRANSL.-Saga of the Volsungs-NY-1930-Amer Scandi Fndtn-cl-1st ed (l8) 20.00

SCHLEGEL,H-World of Falconry-1979-Vendome-4to-179p-177 illus(incl 50 col),photos (bb3,f,dj) 80.00

SCHLEGELMILCH,C W-Memoirs of a Hunter-PA-1967-priv prtg-189p-blu/grn cl,photos (gg3,f) 25.00

SCHLEY,FRANK-American Partridge & Pheasant Shooting-NY-1967-8vo-222p-illus,Abercrombie & Fitch Libr (m3,vf,dj) 20.00

SCHLEY,WINFIELD S-Forty Five Years Under the Flag-NY-1904-Appleton-8vo-blu cl,g sp & cov titles,g cov dec,illus (nn1,frnt hng sl weak) 65.00

SCHLOTTERBECK,LEO-History of Twin Valley Grange No.657-(Lewisburg)-(1924)-19p-wrps (c1) 15.00

SCHLUTER,HERMANN-Brewing Industry & the Brewery Worker's Movement in America-Cin-1910-IUUBW-331p (ff1) 65.00

SCHMIDLY,D-Texas Mammals East of the Balcones Fault Zone-1983-Tex A&M-400p-wrps,photos-1st ed (bb3,f) 14.00

SCHMIDT,DANA A-Journey Among Brave Men-Bost-(1964)-Little,Brown-8vo-298p-8p photos-1st ed (jj5,dj) 17.50

SCHMIDT,EDWARD C-ET AL-Comparative Tests of Six Sizes of Illinois Coal on a Mikado Locomotive-Urbana-1917-U of Ill-101p-wrps,illus-Eng Exper Sta Bull.101 (a1) 10.00

SCHMIDT,HUBERT G-Press in Hunterdon County, 1825 to 1925-Flemington-(1962)-(4),82p-cl,port-ltd to 250c (aa6) 35.00

SCHMIDT,HUBERT G-Rural Hunterdon-New Brunswick-1946-xiv,331p-cl,plts (aa6) 30.00

SCHMIDT,STANLEY-Newton and the Quasi Apple-GC-1975-Dbldy-1st ed (l3,f,dj) 15.00

SCHMITT,JO ANN-Fighting Editors-San Antonio-(1958)-Naylor-227p-drwngs-Six Guns 1959-1st ed (bb4,dj) 30.00

SCHMITT,MARTIN F-ED.-General George Crook: His Autobiography-Norman-1960-U of Okla Pr-8vo-xx+326p-cl,map e.p.-1st rvsd ed (z4,sl fade dj sp) 30.00

SCHMITT,MARTIN F-Fighting Indians of the West-NY-1948-Scribner's-qto-362p-photos,e.p. maps-1st ed (bb4,dj) 65.00

SCHMITT,MARTIN F-Settlers' West-NY-1955-Scribner's-4to-258p-photos-Herd 2024-1st ed (cc4,dj) 30.00

SCHMITT,MARTIN F-Settlers' West-NY-1955-Scribner's-4to-xxx+258p-grn cl,illus-1st ed (m2,dj) 35.00

SCHMITZ,JOSEPH W-Thus They Lived-San Antonio-1936-Naylor-cl (w3,f,dj) 55.00

SCHMOE,F-Our Greatest Mountain-NY-1925-366p-64 photos,dj scarce-1st ed (a4,f,dj) 65.00

SCHMOE,F-Our Greatest Mountain-NY-1925-366p-64 photos-1st ed (q10,f) 30.00

SCHMOE,FLOYD-For Love of Some Islands-NY-(1964)-H&R-8vo-226p-photos-1st ed (bb5,f,dj) 15.00

SCHMOE,FLOYD-Year in Paradise-NY-1959-233p-1st ed (q10,f,dj) 18.00

SCHNECK,JEROME M-ED.-Hypnosis in Modern Medicine-Springfield-(1953)-Chas C Thomas Publ-xvi+323+(5)p-blu cl-1st ed (y9,wn dj) 30.00

SCHNECK,JEROME M-Studies in Scientific Hypnosis-NY-1954-Nrvs & Mntl Dis Monos-xvi+333+(3)p-1st ed (y9) 50.00

SCHNEDER,ANNA M-O Mura San-Phila-1905-Bd of F M R Church in US-107p-cl (d1) 15.00

SCHNEIDER,GEO A-ED.-Freeman Journal-San Rafael-(1977)-Presidio Pr-(vi),104p-cl,photos,map-1st ed (v1) 45.00

SCHNEIDER,ISADORE-Temptation of Anthony-NY-1928-Boni & Liveright-1st ed (w5) 20.00

SCHNEIDER,RUSSELL J-Frank Robinson, Making of a Manager-1976-Coward,McCann-photos-1st ed (s8,f,dj) 13.50

SCHNELL,FRED-Rodeo-Chig-1971-Rand McNally-4to-1st prtg (f10,dj) 25.00

SCHOENBERG,W P-Paths to the Northwest-(1982)-Loyola-lg 8vo-647p-illus (r8,sl chip dj) 42.00

SCHOENHOLTZ,LARRY-New Directions in the I Ching-Secaucus-1975-Univ Bks-cl-1st ed (n8,f,dj) 15.00

SCHOFIELD,LT GEN JOHN M-Forty Six Years in the Army-NY-1897-Century-577p-1st ed (ff4) 85.00

SCHOLEY,JEAN-Dead Past-1962-Macmillan-1st Amer ed (s10,dj) 20.00

SCHOOLCRAFT,HENRY R-Narrative Journal of Travels from Detroit Northwest through the Great Chain of American Lakes...1820-Albany-1821-Hosford-419p-1/2 lea,mrbld bds,maps,illus,errata-Howes S186-1st ed (ee4,rbnd,fox) 400.00

SCHOOLCRAFT,HENRY R-Narrative of an Expedition-NY-1834-Harper & Bros-308p-5 maps(incl 2 fldg)-Howes S187-1st ed (gg4,sl fox) 300.00

SCHOONMAKER,FRANK-American Wines-NY-(1941)-312p-cl-1st ed so stated (d1,wn & tn dj) 20.00

SCHOONMAKER,FRANK-Complete Wine Book-Lond-1938-Routledge-262p-red cl,maps-2nd prtg (q8) 15.00

SCHOONMAKER,FRANK-Frank Schoonmaker's Encyclopedia of Wine-(1965)-Hastings Hs-442p-red cl,maps,drwngs-2nd ed,rvsd (q8,edgewn dj) 12.50

SCHOONMAKER,W J-World of the Grizzly Bear-Phila-1968-4to-190p-photos (m3,dj) 30.00

SCHOONMAKER,W J-World of the Woodchuck-1966-Lippincott-146p-photos-1st ed (bb3,f,fray dj) 15.00

SCHOONOVER,CORTLAND T-Frank Schoonover-NY-(1976)-207p-col illus-1st ed (g7,f,dj) 50.00

SCHOONOVER,CORTLANDT-Frank Schoonover-NY-(1976)-Watson Guptill Pub-sm folio-207p-1st ed (dd4,dj) 50.00

SCHOONOVER,T J-Life and Times of Gen'l John A Sutter-Sacramento-1895-D Johnston-136p-pict cl,illus pckt ed-Howes S196-1st ed (ee4,cov soil) 35.00

SCHOOR,GENE-Billy Martin-1980-Dbldy-photos-1st ed (s8,f,f dj) 12.50

SCHOOR,GENE-Jim Thorpe Story-1951-Messner-1st ed (ff2,dj) 17.50

SCHOOR,GENE-Joe DiMaggio-1980-Dbldy-1st ed (ff2,f,dj) 35.00

SCHOOR,GENE-Lew Burdette of the Braves-1960-Putnam-1st ed (s8,f,dj) 20.00

SCHOOR,GENE-Mickey Mantle of the Yankees-1958-Putnam-4th prtg (ff2,dj) 40.00

SCHOOR,GENE-Pee Wee Reese Story-1956-Messner-1st ed (s8,dj sp fade,sl chip & tn) 40.00

SCHOOR,GENE-Stan Musial Story-1955-Messner-1st ed (s7,dj) 20.00

SCHORGER,A W-Passenger Pigeon-Norman-1973-U of Okla Pr-424p-reissue of 1955 ed (c9,dj) 40.00

SCHORGER,A W-Wild Turkey-OK-1966-625p-photos (gg3,f) 40.00

SCHOUTEN,J-Rod and Serpent of Asklepios-Amsterdam-1967-260p-illus-1st Engl transl (dd3,dj) 90.00

SCHRABISCH,MAX-Archaeolgy of Warren and Hunterdon Counties-Trenton-1917-88p-bds,fldg map (aa6) 35.00

SCHRAMM,JACK E-Detroit's Street Railways, Volume I: City Lines 1865 to 1922-Chig-1978-192p-Bull.#117-1st ed (n4,f,dj) 28.00

SCHRAMM,JACK E-Detroit's Street Railways, Volume II:City Lines 1922 to 1956-Chig-1980-271p-Bull.#120-1st ed (n4,f,dj) 24.00

SCHREIBEIS,CHARLES-Pioneer Education in Pacific Northwest 1789 to 1847-Portland-nd(ca.1930s)-illus (r8,f) 45.00

SCHREIBER,G R-Concise History of Vending in the USA-Chig-1961-Vend Mag-8vo-46p-cl,illus (p1) 30.00

SCHREIBER,GEORGES-Bambino the Clown-NY-1947-Viking-4to-32p-pict bds,col illus,auth-1st ed (s3,wn dj) 40.00

SCHREINER,OLIVE-So Here Then Are Dreams-(E Aurora)-(1901)-(Roycrofters)-sm 4to-(viii),84,(4)p-orig qtr suede wi brwn lea sp labl,brwn bds,t.e.g,others uncut,spread t.p. orng ink-1st ed (x4,sp wn) 85.00

SCHREINER,OLIVE-Track to the Water's Edge-NY-(1973)-Harper & Row-198p-1st US ed (gg10,dj) 20.00

SCHREINER,OLIVE-Trooper Peter Halket of Mashonaland-1897-Robert Bros-1st state frntis of 3 hanging African natives-1st Amer ed (x2,sl soil) 95.00

SCHREINER,OLIVE-Trooper Peter Halket of Mashonaland-Bost-1897-grn cl-1st Amer ed (b7) 50.00

SCHREINER,OLIVE-Undine-NY-1928-Harper-374p-1st US ed (gg10,dj sl soil,sm chip) 100.00

SCHRENCK-NOTZING,FRHRN V-Therapeutic Suggestion in Psychopathia Sexualis...-Phila-1895-F A Davis Co-(ii)+(xx)+320+(2)p-grn cl-1st ed in Engl (y9) 50.00

SCHRENKEISEN,RAY-Field Book of Fresh-Water Fishes of North America North of Mexico-NY-1938-12mo-312p-illus-1st ed (m3,fray dj) 35.00

SCHRENKEISEN,RAY-Fishing For Bass,Muskalonge,Pike & Panfishes-GC-1937-12mo-181p-illus-1st ed (m3,sl fray dj) 15.00

SCHRENKEISEN,RAY-Fishing for Salmon & Trout-GC-1937-8vo-185p-illus-1st ed (m3,f) 17.50

SCHREPFER,FRANK-Hardy Evergreens-NY-1928-OJ-127p (x6) 10.00

SCHREUDERS,PIET-Paperbacks, U.S.A.-1981-Blue Dolphin-wrps-1st Amer ed (t9,f) 20.00

SCHRIEVER,J B-ED.-Complete Self Instructing Library of Practical Photography-Scranton-1909-Amer Sch of Art & Photog-4to-10 vols-grn cl,g sp dec,a.e.mrbld-Popular ed (y3) 250.00

SCHROEDER,ALBERT H-Changing Ways of Southwestern Indians-Glorieta-1973-289p-pict cl,photos-1st ed (t7,f) 10.00

SCHROEDER,HENRY A-Shirt Tail and Pigtail-NY-1930-Minton,Blach-8vo-316p-olive grn cl,photos-1st ed (gg6) 35.00

SCHROEDER,HENRY-History of Electric Light-1923-95p-wrps-95 illus(incl photos)-v rare-1st ed (h6,f,uncut) 85.00

SCHRYVER,ALICE-Complete Hors d'Oeuvres Cookbook-(1958)-Coward-McCann-246p-dec tan cl-1st ed (q8,dj) 15.00

SCHUBERT,H R-History of the British Iron and Steel Industry from c.450 B.C. to A.D.1775-Lond-(1957)-Routledge & K Paul-lg 8vo-445p-blu cl,11 maps,26 plts-1st ed (dd1) 55.00

SCHUBERT,H-Modern Theatres-NY-1971-Praeger-273 plts-1st Amer ed (h10,dj) 75.00

SCHUETTE,C H L-State, the Church, and the School-Columbus-1883-381p-cl (k1) 15.00

SCHULBERG,BUDD-Harder They Fall-NY-(1947)-Random-1st ed (d10,sl wn dj) 45.00

SCHULBERG,BUDD-Harder They Fall-NY-(1947)-Random-1st ed (hh5,dj) 35.00

SCHULBERG,BUDD-Sanctuary-NY,Cleve-(1969)-World-cl-1st ed (aa9,f,dj) 20.00

SCHULER,FREDERICK-Flameworking-1968-Chilton-131p-illus (cc8) 35.00

SCHULLIAN,DOROTHY-Catalogue of Incunabula and Manuscripts in the Army Medical Library-NY-1950-361p-1st ed (dd3) 90.00

SCHULLIAN,DOROTHY-ED.-Baglivi Correspondence from the Library of Sir William Osler-Ithaca-1974-531p-1st ed (dd3) 40.00

SCHULTZ,J W-Bird Woman-Bost-1918-Houghton Mifflin-(x),235p-dec cl,plts,ads-1st ed (v1) 110.00

SCHULTZ,J W-Blackfeet and Buffalo-Norman-(1962)-384p-illus-1st ed (g7,f,chip dj) 45.00

SCHULTZ,J W-Blackfeet Tales of Glacier National Park-Bost-1916-Houghton Mifflin-(xii),242p-dec cl,photo plts-1st ed (v1) 85.00

SCHULTZ,J W-Friends of My Life As an Indian-Bost-1923-Houghton Mifflin-(viii),299p-dec cl,photos-1st ed (v1) 50.00

SCHULTZ,J W-In the Great Apache Forest-Bost-1920-Houghton Mifflin-(vi),225p-dec cl,plts-1st ed (v1,sl sunned cov) 65.00

SCHULTZ,J W-My Life as An Indian-NY-1907-Dbldy-(xiv),426p-dec cl,photos-Howes S203-1st ed (v1) 85.00

SCHULTZ,J W-On the Warpath-Bost,NY-1914-245p-illus bds,illus by G Varian-1st ed (f7,speckled cov) 75.00

SCHULTZ,J W-Quest of the Fish Dog Skin-Bost,NY-1913-219p-illus frnt bd,illus by G Varian-1st ed (f7,f) 75.00

SCHULTZ,J W-Quest of the Fish Dog Skin-Bost-1913-Houghton Mifflin-(iv),219p-dec cl,illus-1st ed (v1) 65.00

SCHULTZ,J W-Signposts of Adventure-Bost-1926-Houghton Mifflin-(viii),225p-dec cl,fldg map,plts-1st ed (v1) 65.00

SCHULTZ,J W-Trail of the Spanish Horse-Bost,NY-1922-213p-illus by G Varian-1st ed (f7) 60.00

SCHULTZ,J W-William Jackson Indian Scout-Bost-1926-Houghton Mifflin-(iv),201p-cl,4 plts,F Schoonover-Howes S204-1st ed (v1,chip dj) 75.00

SCHULTZ,J W-With the Indians in the Rockies-Bost,NY-1912-228p+2p ads-illus frnt bd,illus by G Varian-1st ed (f7) 75.00

SCHULTZ,LEONARD P-Fishes of Glacier National Park Montana-Wash D.C.-1941-8vo-42p-wrps,illus (m3) 17.50

SCHULTZ,R A-ED.-Portrait of Sheep & Sheep Hunting-MN-1980-167p-Foundation for N Amer Wild Sheep-photos (gg3,f,dj) 45.00

SCHULZ,BRUNO-Sanatorium Under the Sign of the Hourglass-NY-1978-Walker-1st ed (t4,tn dj) 15.00

SCHULZ,CHARLES-Charlie Brown's All Stars-1966-World-1st ed (ff2,dj) 15.00

SCHULZ,CHARLES-Sandlot Peanuts-1977-Holt Rinehart-1st ed (p7,dj) 25.00

SCHULZ,ELLEN-500 Wild Flowers of San Antonio and Vicinity-San Antonio-1922-272p-41 photos-1st ed (a9,wn) 35.00

SCHULZ,ELLEN-Texas Wildflowers-Chig-1928-Laidlaw-505p-col frntis,illus (a9) 50.00

SCHUMACHER,LUDWIG-Major General the Earl of Stirling-NY-1897-57p-cl,plts-ltd to 150c (aa6,sp drknd) 45.00

SCHUMACHER,LUDWIG-Somerset Hills-NY-(1900?)-133p-cl,plts (aa6,sl soil sp) 45.00

SCHUON,FRITHJOF-Dimensions of Islam-Lond-1970-Allen & Unwin-cl-1st Brit ed (n8,f,dj) 35.00

SCHUSSLER,EDITH-Doctors,Dynamite and Dogs-1956-Caxton-8vo-189p (nn7,dj) 17.00

SCHUTZ,ALBERT J-Diaries and Correspondence of David Cargill, 1832 to 1843-Canberra-1977-Austrln Nat'l Univ Pr-8vo-xvi,255p-3 maps (nn1,dj) 40.00

SCHUYLER,EUGENE-Peter the Great-NY-1884-Scribner's-2 vols-g pict cl,t.e.g.,frntis,plts,fldg col map,fldg tbl-1st ed (kk1,sl soil cov) 50.00

SCHUYLER,HAMILTON-Historical Sketch of Trinity Church, Trenton, New Jersey-Trenton-1910-37p-cl,plts (aa6) 40.00

SCHUYLER,JAMES-Alfred & Guinevere-NY-1958-auth 1st bk-1st ed (n5,chip dj) 35.00

SCHUYLER,K C-Bow Hunting for Big Game-PA-1974-256p-photos (gg3,f,dj) 15.00

SCHUYLER,MONTGOMERY-American Architecture-NY-1892-Harper & Bros-8vo-(8),211,(5)p-blnd stmpd dec calf,t.e.g.,illus-1st ed (pp7,f) 300.00

SCHWARTZ,C W-Prairie Chicken in Missouri-(Jefferson City?)-1944-4to-(182)p-cl,col frntis,pgs(12-179) of half-tone photos on both sides,map (y8) 75.00

SCHWARTZ,C W-Prairie Chicken in Missouri-1944-Mo Conserv Comm-4to-179p-simulated emboss lea,illus e.p.,photos (bb3) 65.00

SCHWARTZ,CHARLES W-Prairie Chicken in Missouri-1944-Missouri Cnsrvtn Comm-folio-unpgd-photos-1st ed (m3,sl fox pgs) 60.00

SCHWARTZ,DELMORE-In Dreams Begin Responsibilities-Norfolk-(1938)-New Directions-8vo-cl-ltd to 1000c-auth 1st bk-scarce-1st ed (kk8,cov sl wn,dj wn) 85.00

SCHWARTZ,DELMORE-Last and Lost Poems of...-NY-(1979)-Vanguard-1st ed (bb2,f,dj) 50.00

SCHWARTZ,DELMORE-Shenandoah-Norfolk-(1941)-New Directions-blu wrps-1st ed (bb2) 100.00

SCHWARTZ,DELMORE-Shenandoah-Norfolk-(1941)-New Directions-blu wrps-1st ed (dd2) 100.00

SCHWARTZ,DELMORE-Summer Knowledge-NY-1959-Dbldy-1st ed (h8,f,dj) 125.00

SCHWARTZ,HELEN-New Jersey House-New Brunswick-(1983)-oblng 4to-x,(2),179p-cl,illus (aa6) 35.00

SCHWARTZ,JACOB-Is Book Publishing a Racket-Brklyn-1947-J Schwartz-8vo-(iv),71p-stiff wrps-1st ed (x4) 17.50

SCHWARTZ,JONATHAN-Almost Home-GC-1970-Dbldy-auth 1st bk-1st ed (bb1,f,dj) 25.00

SCHWARTZ,JONATHAN-Distant Stations-GC-1979-Dbldy-1st ed (bb1,f,dj) 15.00

SCHWARTZ,LYNNE S-Balancing Acts-NY-(1981)-Harper-1st ed (m7,dj) 20.00

SCHWARTZ,LYNNE S-Rough Strife-NY et al-(1980)-Harper & Row-auth 1st bk-1st ed (bb1,f,dj) 30.00

SCHWARTZ,MARIE S-Gold and Name-Bost-1871-Lee & Shepard-tall 8vo-210p-1st US ed (w6) 45.00

SCHWARTZ,NANCY L-Hollywood Writers' War-NY-1982-Knopf-1st ed (v5,f,dj) 20.00

SCHWARTZ,RANDALL-Carnivorous Plants-NY-1974-Praeger-128p-cl,photos,flip book illus (x6) 18.00

SCHWARTZ,STUART B-Sovereignty and Society in Colonial Brazil-Berkeley-(1973)-U of Cal-8vo-438p-10 plts-1st US ed (jj5,f,dj) 20.00

SCHWATKA,F-Military Reconnaissance in Alaska in 1883-1885-GPO-121p-3/4 lea,mrbld bds & e.p.,20 fldg maps,illus-Senate Ex Doc 2 (e7,sl peel lea) 100.00

SCHWATKA,FREDERICK-Summer in Alaska-St.Louis-1893-J W Henry-72 plts (p6,sl wn) 150.00

SCHWATKA,FREDERICK-Summer in Alaska-St.Louis-1894-J W Henry-418p-drwngs (cc4,sl wn sp) 60.00

SCHWIEBERT,ERNEST G-History of the U.S. Air Force Ballistic Missiles-NY-(1965)-Praeger-264p-gry cl,illus-1st ed (dd1,dj) 25.00

SCHWIEBERT,ERNEST G-Remembrances of Rivers Past-NY-1972-8vo-287p-illus-1st ed (m3,as new in dj) 20.00

SCHWIEBERT,ERNEST-Death of a Riverkeeper-NY-1980-Dutton-1st ed (ff7,f,dj) 20.00

SCIENCE OF BAKING-(Yukon)-nd-Yukon Mill & Grain-24p-wrps (h1) 12.50

SCIENTIFIC AMERICAN-Handbook of Travel-NY-1910-Munn & Co-grn dec cl,fldg maps,illus (gg6) 65.00

SCIFRES,BILL-Indiana Outdoors-1976-Indiana Univ Pr-8vo-376p-illus,photos-1st ed (m3,as new in dj) 25.00

SCIGLIANO,ROBERT-South Vietnam: Nation Under Stress-Bost-(1964)-HM-1st ed (ff3,f,dj) 35.00

SCLATER,W L-History of the Birds of Colorado-Lond-1912-8vo-576p-cl,17 plts,map (y8,lt stns) 90.00

SCOBEE,BARRY-Old Fort Davis-San Antonio-(1947)-Naylor-101p-illus-Six Guns 1965-1st ed (bb4,dj) 35.00

SCOPES,JOHN T-Center of the Storm-NY-(1967)-Holt,Rinehart-viii+277p-cl-1st ed (d2) 18.00

SCOTSON-CLARK,G F-Half Hours in the Kitchenette-NY-1927-Appleton-144p-Bitting 424 (m6) 18.00

SCOTT,AUSTIN-Influence of the Proprietors in Founding the State of New Jersey-Balt-1885-26p+ads-wrps (aa6) 30.00

SCOTT,C W A-Scott's Book-Lond-1934-8vo-264p-cl,frntis,14p plts,1 dblpg plt,1 fldg map-1st ed (s2,dj) 65.00

SCOTT,COL ROBERT L-Between the Elephant's Eyes-NY-1954-Dodd Mead-8vo-243p-1st ed (ff5,dj) 17.50

SCOTT,COMMANDER-Romance of the Highways of California-Glendale-1946-320p-photos,illus,maps-1st ed (t7,dj) 10.00

SCOTT,DAVID W-John Sloan-Bost-1971-Bost Bk & Art-4to-col & b&w illus-1st ed (b4,rub dj) 50.00

SCOTT,DUNCAN C-In the Village of Viger-Tor-1945-Ryerson-illus-1st Can ed (z3,dj) 12.50

SCOTT,DUNCAN C-Witching of Elspie-Tor-(1923)-M&S-1st Can ed (pp2) 45.00*

SCOTT,ELIZA J P-Farm Life and Christian Citizenship-Cin-1914-Pr of Jennings & Graham-348p-cl (j1) 20.00

SCOTT,EMMETT J-Scott's Official History of the American Negro in the World War-np-1919-auth-1st ed (w5) 50.00

SCOTT,EVELYN-Wave-NY-(1929)-Cape/Smith-1st ed (j6,f,dj sp sun,sl chip) 35.00

SCOTT,GENIO C-Fishing in American Waters-NY-1869-Harpers-grn cl,illus-1st ed (dd6) 100.00

SCOTT,HILDA-Does Socialism Liberate Women?-Bost-1974-Beacon-240p-1st ed (r1,dj) 15.00

SCOTT,HUGH L-Some Memories of a Soldier-NY-1928-673p-dec cl,frntis,photos-Dustin #245-1st ed (t7) 100.00

SCOTT,J M-Man Who Made Wine-NY-(1954)-Dutton-16mo-125p-red cl,drwngs-1st ed (q8,dj) 10.00

SCOTT,J W-ED.-Pacific Northwest Themes-Bellingham-1978-138p-pict wrps (r8,f) 10.00

SCOTT,J W-Glass Workers of Carmaux-1974-Harvard-8 plts,6 photos-1st ed (cc8,dj) 35.00

SCOTT,J-At the Sign of the Split Cane-Lond-1934-176p-photos (gg3,f) 75.00

SCOTT,JOCK-Game Fish Records-Lond-1936-8vo-316p-photos,illus (m3) 15.00

SCOTT,JOCK-Greased Line Fishing for Salmon-Phila-nd-8vo-221p-photos,illus-1st Amer ed (m3,fade sp) 40.00

SCOTT,JOCK-Lake Fishing for Salmon,Trout & Pike-Lond-1932-12mo-192p-illus-1st ed (m3,fade sp) 20.00

SCOTT,JOCK-Salmon & Trout Fishing Up to Date-Lond-1960-8vo-236p-photos-1st ed (m3,f,dj) 25.00

SCOTT,JOCK-Salmon & Trout Rivers-Leeds-nd-8vo-156p-wrps,photos,fldg maps (m3,f) 30.00

SCOTT,LIEUT GEN-Memoirs of Lieut General Scott-NY-1864-Sheldon-2 vols-frntis-Howes S242-1st ed (cc4,sp chip & wn) 150.00

SCOTT,LIONEL T-Twists and Fancies of the Modern Magician...-(Kansas City)-nd-A M Wilson-27p-wrps (l1) 15.00
SCOTT,MANSFIELD-Spider's Web-NY-1929-Clode-1st ed (j4, stnd cov,dj) 12.50
SCOTT,MANSFIELD-Sportsman ,Detective-NY-1930-Clode-1st ed (f4,dj missing sm chips) 30.00
SCOTT,MARIA L-World of Pasta-(1978)-McGraw-4to-226p-red cl,drwngs-1st ed (q8,dj) 16.50
SCOTT,MARION-Dead Hands Reaching-NY-1932-Macmillan-1st ed (j4,edge fade cov,dj) 15.00
SCOTT,MILTON R-Henry Elwood, a Theological Novel-Newark-1892-Newark Amer Prnt-324p-cl-Wright 4829 (g1) 20.00
SCOTT,MILTON-Dear Dead Harry-NY-1949-Phoenix-1st ed (g4,f,dj) 15.00
SCOTT,MORGAN-Rival Pitchers of Oakdale-1911-Hurst-drwngs,E Colborne-1st ed (s8,wn cov) 20.00
SCOTT,NATALIE A-Little Stockade-NY-1954-Dutton-1st ed (hh5,dj) 10.00
SCOTT,P-Birds of Paradise-1962-Morrow-1st Amer ed (x2,dj) 32.00
SCOTT,P-Coloured Key to Wildfowl of the World-NY-1961-sm 8vo-91p-cl,23 col plts-rvsd (y8,dj chip) 20.00
SCOTT,P-Male Child-1957-Dutton-1st Amer ed (x2,dj) 55.00
SCOTT,P-Peter Scott Observations of Wildlife-NY-1980-112p-photos,col illus (gg3,vf,dj) 16.00
SCOTT,P-Swans-Bost-1972-4to-242p-cl,col frntis,48p photos (y8,dj tn) 30.00
SCOTT,P-Wild Chorus-Lond-1938-tall 4to-119p-blu buckram,24 col plts,ltd ed of 1250c prtd,autg-v scarce-1st ed (y8,sp fade) 400.00
SCOTT,PAUL-Day of the Scorpion-NY-1968-1st US ed (s5,f,dj) 22.50
SCOTT,PAUL-Divison of the Spoils-NY-1975-1st US ed (s5,dj) 15.00
SCOTT,PAUL-Jewel in the Crown-1966-Morrow-1st Amer ed (n9,sl wn dj) 45.00
SCOTT,PAUL-Six Days in Marapore-GC-1953-Dbldy-8vo-319p-1st US ed (ee5,dj) 60.00
SCOTT,PAUL-Towers of Silence-NY-1972-1st US ed (s5,vf,dj) 20.00
SCOTT,PETER-Eye of the Wind-Bost,Cambridge-1961-8vo-679p-photos,illus-1st ed (m3,f,dj) 40.00
SCOTT,PETER-Eye of the Wind-Bost-1961-Houghton Mifflin-679p-1st Amer ed (c9) 30.00
SCOTT,PETER-Wild Geese and Eskimos-Lond-1951-Country Life-254p-col frntis (b9,sp fade) 20.00
SCOTT,R L-Between the Elephant's Eyes-NY-1954-243p-photos (gg3,f,dj) 15.00
SCOTT,R T M-Agony Column Murders-NY-1946-Dutton-1st ed (g4,f,dj) 15.00
SCOTT,ROBERT J-Birch Bark Talking-Tor-1940-J Evans Cent Comm-28p-prtd wrps-Peel #37442 (k10) 20.00*
SCOTT,SUTHERLAND-Bllod in Their Ink-Lond-(1953)-Stanley Paul-200p-1st ed (g9,dj sl wn,soil) 50.00
SCOTT,WALTER S-White of Selborne-Lond-(1950)-Falcon Pr-8vo-260p-12 illus-1st ed (gg5,dj) 20.00
SCOTT,WALTER-Gospel Restored-Cin-1836-prntd by O H Donogh-576p-lea-Amer Imprnts 40097 (g1,fr cov detchd,sl stnd pgs) 75.00
SCOTT,WALTER-Halidon Hill-Edinburgh-1822-for Archibald Constable-orig prtd wrps-1st ed (aa9,sl chip,fox) 150.00
SCOTT,WALTER-Poetical Works of...-Edinburgh-nd(ca.1880)-Gall & Inglis-12mo-(16),624p-ornate g stmpd mor,a.e.g.,8 engrvngs (m4) 20.00
SCOTT,WALTER-Quentin Durward-NY-1923-Scribner's-9 col plts-(Illus Classics) (oo10) 35.00
SCOTT,WILLIAM B-History of Land Mammals in the Western Hemisphere-NY-1913-Macmillan-xvi+693p-blu dec cl,304 text illus-1st ed (j2) 75.00
SCOTT,WILLIAM F-Story of a Cavalry Regiment-NY-1893-602p-frntis,plts,fldg map-Dornbusch I #26-1st ed (t7,hngs weak) 275.00
SCOTT,WILLIAM W-History of Passaic and its Environs-NY-1922-4to-3 vols-cl,plts (aa6) 175.00
SCOTT,WILLIAM-Lessons in Elocution-Concord-1820-prntd by Hill & Moore-384p-lea-Amer Imprnts 3151 (c1,sl wn cov) 20.00
SCOTT,WILLIAM-Lessons in Elocution-Worcester-1803-I Thomas-406p+1p ad-lea,4 hand-col plts-Amer Imprnts 5029-12th Amer ed (k1) 75.00
SCOTT-ELLIOTT,W-Story of Atlantis and the Lost Lemuria-Lond-1925-Theosoph Publ-6 fldg maps in e.p. pckt (v4,f) 75.00
SCOTT-TAGGART,JOHN-Thermionic Tubes in Radio Telegraphy and Telephony-1921-424p-344 illus-1st ed (h6) 55.00
SCOULLER,R E-Armies of Queen Anne-Oxford-1966-420p-1st ed (gg2,f,dj) 65.00
SCOVILLE,WARREN C-Revolution in Glassmaking-Cambridge-1948-Harvard U Pr-xviii+398p-red cl,illus-1st ed (c2) 25.00
SCRIBBLINGS & SKETCHES, DIPLOMATIC, PISCATORY, & OCEANIC-Phila-1844-sm 8vo-blnd stmpd cl-scarce-2nd ed wi add (mm2,sl wn sp) 150.00
SCRIBNER,J M-Scribner's Lumber & Log Book-Rochester-1890-158,(2)p-bds,rvsd,illus ed (n1) 15.00
SCRIPPS,JAMES E-Five Months Abroad...-Detr-1882-458p-cl (l1,frnt inner hng rnfrcd) 20.00
SCRIPTURE CLUB OF VALLEY REST...-NY-1877-188p-cl-Wright 2354 (g1,sl soil cov) 15.00
SCROGGS,GEORGE-Summer Sketching-Champaign-1873-Gazette Stm Bk & Job Offc-40p-cl-rare (g1) 75.00
SCROPE,WILLIAM-Days & Nights of Salmon Fishing in the River Tweed-Lond-1885-8vo-317p+ads-illus-3rd ed (m3) 145.00
SCUDAMORE,SIR CHARLES-Treatise on the Nature and Cure of Gout and Rheumatism-Phila-1819-335p-linen-Austin #1714-1st Amer ed (g10,recased) 95.00
SCUDDER,RALPH E-Custer Country-Portland-(1963)-Binfords & Mort-4to-63p-dec cl,photos-1st ed (p1) 40.00
SCUDDER,RALPH E-Custer Country-Portland-(1963)-Binfords & Mort-63p-e.p. map,photos-1st ed (ee4) 35.00
SCUDDER,S H-Adephagous and Clavicorn Coleoptera from the Tertiary Deposits of Florissant, Colorado...-1900-US Geol Survey Mono-4to-148p-11 plts (bb3,cor wn) 90.00
SCUDDER,S H-Tertiary Insects of North America-1890-US Geol Survey of Terr-4to-734p-28 duotone plts (bb3,cor wn) 105.00
SCULL,ANDREW-ED.-Madhouses,Mad Doctors,and Madmen-Phila-1981-384p-1st ed (dd3,dj) 25.00
SCULL,E MARSHALL-Hunting in the Arctic & Alaska-Lond-1914-8vo-304p-photos,maps-scarce (m3,f) 125.00
SCULLY,FRANK-Behind the Flying Saucers-NY-(1950)-230p-cl-1st ed so stated (l1) 12.50
SCULLY,VINCENT-Pueblo Architecture of the Southwest-Ft.Worth-1971-Amon Carter-4to-photos-1st ed (b4,dj) 45.00

SCWIEBERT,ERNEST G-Matching the Hatch-NY-1955-8vo-221p-illus,auth-2nd prntg so stated (m3) 30.00

SCWIEBERT,ERNEST-Death of a Riverkeeper-NY-1980-8vo-287p-illus,auth-1st ed (m3,vf,dj) 20.00

SEABROOK,WILLIAM-These Foreigners-NY-(1938)-Harcourt Brace-1st ed (hh5,f,dj) 20.00

SEABURY,GEORGE-An Ode to Lake Bass-NY-1890-oblng 12mo-unpgd-every pg illus-scarce (m3) 125.00

SEABURY,REV SAMUEL-American Slavery Distinguished from the Slavery of English Theorists...by the Law of Nature-NY-1861-Mason Bros-cl-1st ed (u2) 90.00

SEAGER,ALLAN-Equinox-NY-1943-S&S-1st ed (hh5,dj) 30.00

SEALE,BOBBY-Seize the Time-NY-1968-Random Hs-429p-1st ed (r1,sl tn dj) 25.00

SEALOCK,RICHARD B-Long Island Bibliography-Balt-1940-4to-xii,338p-cl (w2) 125.00

SEALY,J ROBERT-Revision of the Genus Camellia-Lond-1958-4to-240p-grn cl,col frntis,6 maps,chrt,drwngs (jj7,sl wn cov) 149.00

SEAMAN,N G-Indian Relics of the Pacific Northwest-Portland-(1946)-157p-illus (j7,f,chip dj) 20.00

SEARBROOK,W B-Magic Island-NY-1929-Harcourt Brace-drwngs,A King-1st ed (h8,f,wn & chip dj) 50.00

SEARIGHT,FRANK T-Doomed City, a Thrilling Tale...-Chig-(1906)-Laird & lee-186p-pict bds (f1) 35.00

SEARIGHT,THOMAS B-Old Pike-Uniontown-1894-Auth publ-384p-orig orng/tan cl wi gilt,illus-Howes S257-1st ed (o2,sl rub) 100.00

SEARIGHT,THOMAS B-Old Pike-Uniontown-1894-Auth publ-384p-orig orng/tan cl wi gilt,ports,views-Howes S257-1st ed (n2) 100.00

SEARLE,A G-Comparative Genetics of Coat Colour in Mammals-1968-8vo-308p (y8,casebound) 90.50

SEARLE,RONALD-Paris Sketchbook-NY-1958-Brazillier-4to-cl-1st Amer ed (x10,f,dj) 25.00

SEARS,ALFRED B-Thomas Worthington, Father of Ohio Statehood-Columbus-(1958)-260p-cl (j1,f,dj) 15.00

SEARS,CLARA E-COMP.-Bronson Alcott's Fruitlands. with: Transcendental Wild Oats by L M Alcott-Bost-1915-Houghton Mifflin-xviii+185p-gry cl-1st ed (b2) 50.00

SEARS,ROEBUCK AND CO-Special Vehicle Catalogue-Chig-1896-7" x 10"-64p-illus (h9,edge wn,chip cov) 125.00

SEATON,ALBERT-Crimean War-NY-1977-232p-illus-1st Amer ed (b7,f,dj) 40.00

SEATTLE & KING COUNTY WASHINGTON TERRITORY - STATISTICAL AND DESCRIPTIVE REPORT...TO THE GOVERNOR...-Seattle-Dec. 1884-Hanford-12mo-16p-dec wrps,photo frntis-rare (w1,f) 350.00

SEATTLE AND KING COUNTY-VOLUME OF MEMOIRS AND GENALOGY OF REPRESENTATIVE CITIZENS OF...INCLUDING...-NY,Chig-1903-Lewis-lg thk 8vo-773p-brwn mor,g stmpd sp-1st ed (w1,f) 125.00

SEATTLE ARCHITECTURAL YEAR BOOK, 1910...IN CONNECTION WITH THE FIRST ANNUAL EXHIBITION...-(Seattle)-(1910)-(Lowman & Hanford)-sm 4to-94p-prntd bds,illus,photos-1st ed (w1) 100.00

SEATTLE COOK BOOK-Seattle-1906-Lowman,Hanford-sm 8vo-133p-grn stiff wrps,ads-Ladies Aid Soc of First Christian Church (ll9) 35.00

SEATTLE U.S.A.-Seattle-1906-West & Wheeler-32p-wrps,photos,chrts (w1,f) 45.00

SEAVER,GEORGE-Edward Wilson of the Antarctic-NY-1937-Dutton-8vo-301p-17 illus-1st US ed (ff5) 30.00

SEAVER,TOM-How I Would Pitch to Babe Ruth-1974-Playboy-1st ed (s8,f,dj) 12.00

SEAVER,TOM-Perfect Game-1970-Dutton-1st ed (r7,f,dj) 15.00

SEAWELL,MOLLY E-Ladies' Battle-NY-1911-119p-cl-1st ed (d1) 17.50

SEAWELL,MOLLY E-Midshipman Paulding-NY-1891-133p-cl-illus,Geo Wharton Edwards-1st ed (h1) 15.00

SEC OF WAR FOR YEAR 1877-Annual Report of the Chief of Engineers, Part II-Wash-1877-1438p-chrts,grphs,fldg maps-Luther #248-1st ed (t7) 300.00

SECKER,THOMAS-Lectures on the Catechism of the Protestant Episcopal Church-Columbus-1835-Isaac N Whiting-351p-cl,not cpyrtd-Amer Imprnts 34166-1st Amer ed frm 14th Lond (d1,sl wn) 50.00

SEDGWICK,CATHARINE M-Life and Letters of...-NY-1871-Harper-8vo-446p+ads-cl-BAL 17428-1st ed (w6) 50.00

SEDGWICK,CATHARINE M-Memoir of Joseph Curtis-NY-1858-Harper-8vo-200p-orig cl-BAL 17421-1st ed (w6) 45.00

SEDGWICK,MABEL C-Garden Month by Month-GC-(1907)-xvii,516p-hlf tones,fldng col chrt (x5,sl fox & stnd) 17.00

SEDGWICK,MRS.WILLIAM T-Acoma, the Sky City-Cambridge-1926-305p-illus,map e.p.-1st ed in 2nd ed dj (v7,dj) 45.00

SEDGWICK,MRS.WILLIAM T-Acoma, the Sky City-Chig-1963-318p (t7) 15.00

SEDGWICK,STEPHEN D-Salmon Handbook-Lond-1982-8vo-247p-illus,R Ade (m3,vf,dj) 15.00

SEE,CAROLYN-Blue Money-1974-McKay-1st ed (o9,f,dj) 30.00

SEEDS KE DEE-Tales of The...-Denver-(1963)-Big Mtn Pr-386p-ltd to 1000c,photos,grn cl (t8,sm cov stn) 60.00

SEEDS OF PINE-Tor-1922-Musson Bk-8vo-301p-grn dec cl-1st ed (cc7,discol pgs) 25.00*

SEELER,MARGARET-Art of Enameling-1969-Van Nostrand-128p-illus (cc8,dj) 35.00

SEELEY,MABEL-Chuckling Fingers-1941-DD-1st ed (x7,f,dj) 45.00

SEELEY,MABEL-Eleven Came Back-NY-1943-Dbldy CC-1st ed (g4,f,dj) 12.50

SEELY,J E B-Adventure-NY-1930-Stokes-8vo-326p-17 illus-1st US ed (ff5,dj) 25.00

SEEMANN,BERTHOLD-Viti, an Account of a Gov't Mission to the Vitian or Fijian Islands-Lond-1862-MacMillan-8vo-447p-lea,frntis,fldg map,3 col plts-1st ed (p8,rprd,sl fox) 260.00

SEGAL,LORE-Lucinella-NY-(1976)-FS&G-1st ed (bb1,as new in dj) 25.00

SEGAL,RONALD-Leon Trotsky-NY-1979-Pantheon-406p-1st US ed (r1,dj) 22.00

SEGAR,CHARLES-ED.-Official History of the National League-1951-Jay-illus,photos-1st ed (s8,f,dj) 35.00

SEGHERS,CARROL-Peak Experience-Indpls-1979-302p-illus (o10,as new in dj) 15.00

SEIBOLD,FRANK M-Tales Form the Sonoita-San Antonio-1973-Naylor-90p-cl-1st ed (w3,f,dj) 10.00

SEIDEL,HEINRICH-Magic Inkstand-Lond-(1982)-Cape-11 col plts,W Anderson-1st ed (s3,f,f dj) 20.00

SEIGER,H F-Complete German Shorthaired Pointer-Silver Spring-1951-8vo-432p-illus (m3) 45.00

SEISS,JOSEPH A-Voices from Babylon-Phila-1879-Porter & Coates-cl-1st ed (n8) 45.00

SEITZ,DON C-Braxton Bragg-Columbia-1924-State Co-544p-1st ed (dd4,ink name on cov) 200.00

SELAES,F C-Hunter's Wanderings in Africa-Lond-1925-504p-illus (gg3,f) 125.00

SELBY,HUBERT-Last Exit to Brooklyn-NY-1964-auth 1st bk-1st ed (q5,sl tn dj) 50.00

SELBY,JOHN-Balaclava: Gentlemen's Battle-NY-1970-247p-illus-1st Amer ed (b7,f,dj) 25.00

SELDEN,GEORGE-Cricket in Times Square-NY-(1960)-FS&G-illus,G Williams-1st ed (s3,dj) 45.00

SELDEN,GEORGE-Genie of Sutton Place-NY-(1973)-FSG-175p-cl-1st ed (r3,f,dj) 25.00

SELDEN,GEORGE-Tucker's Countryside-NY-(1969)-FSG-illus,G Williams-1st ed (r3,dj) 25.00

SELDES,L-Legacy of Mark Rothko-NY-1978-illus-1st ed (h10,dj) 30.00

SELER,E-ET AL-Mexican and Central American Antiquities...-1904-Bur Amer Ethnol Bull.28-682p-49 plts (bb3) 25.00

SELF,HUBER-Environment and Man in Kansas-Lawrence-1978-Regents Pr-4to-xvi+288p-blu cl,illus,maps-1st ed (k2,dj) 20.00

SELF,MARGARET C-Morgan Horse in Pictures-No Hollywood-1975-Wilshire-wrps (h9) 35.00

SELFRIDGE,THOMAS O,JR.-Memoirs of...Rear Admiral, U.S.N.-NY-1924-288p-illus,maps-1st ed (n3) 40.00

SELIGMAN,JANET-TRANSL.-Chinese Painting-NY-1983-Rizzoli-folio-linen,40 col plts,160 b&w illus-1st ed (n8,as new in dj) 75.00

SELIGSON,MARCIA-Eternal Bliss Machine-NY-1973-Morrow-8vo-304p-1st ed (gg5,f,dj) 10.00

SELL,FRANCIS E-American Deer Hunter-Harrisburg-1950-8vo-174p-photos (m3,f,dj) 22.50

SELL,FRANCIS E-American Shotgunner-Harrisburg-1962-301p-frntis,photos-1st ed (t7) 25.00

SELL,FRANCIS E-Practical Fresh Water Fishing-NY-1960-8vo-198p-photos (m3,f,dj) 17.50

SELL,FRANCIS E-Sure Hit Shotgun Ways-Harrisburg-1967-8vo-160p-illus (m3,sl fray dj) 20.00

SELLERS,CHARLES C-Lorenzo Dow, the Bearer of the Word-NY-1928-Minton,Balch & Co-275p-cl (g1) 15.00

SELLERS,HAZEL C-Old South Carolina Churches-Columbia-1941-Crowson Prtg Co-unpgd-tan cl-ltd to 1500c-1st ed (oo5,dj sun & sl soil) 100.00

SELLERY,G C-E A Birge-Madison-1956-Univ of Wisc Pr-viii+221p-blu cl,plts-1st ed (j2,dj) 18.00

SELLS,A LYTTON-ED.-Memoirs of James II-Bloomington-1962-301p-illus-1st ed (b7,dj) 45.00

SELMAN,ROBERT-Once Upon a Crime-NY-1947-Morrow-1st ed (h4,dj) 15.00

SELOUS,E-Bird Watching-Lond-1901-8vo-347p-dec grn cl by Rackham,head & tail pcs by Rackham,14 illus-1st trd ed (y8) 48.00

SELOUS,EDMUND-Bird Watcher in the Shetlands-NY-1905-Dutton-t.e.g.,10 illus by J Smit (c9,sl warp,sp & cors wn) 50.00

SELOUS,FREDERICK C-Sunshine and Storm in Rhodesia-Lond-1896-290p-brwn cl,illus,fldg map-1st ed (jj2) 200.00

SELOUS,FREDERICK C-Travel and Adventure in South East Africa-Lond-1893-Rowland Ward-frntis port,22 plts,35 woodcts,1 col fldg map-1st ed (p6,sl wn & soil) 175.00

SELOUS,P-Travel & Big Game-NY-1897-4to-195p-illus-scarce (m3) 150.00

SELTMAN,CHARLES-Wine in the Ancient World-Lond-(1957)-Routledge & Kegan Paul-196p (n6) 45.00

SELWYN-BROWN,ARTHUR-Physician Throughout the Ages-NY-1938-Capehart Brown Co-4to-2 vols-brwn cl,illus-2nd ed (dd1) 100.00

SELZ,PETER-Alberto Giacometti-NY-1965-MOMA-4to-119p-illus (r10,dj) 10.00

SELZ,PETER-Art Nouveau-NY-1959-MOMA-8vo-tan cl,col frntis,illus (r10,chip dj) 20.00

SELZ,PETER-Funk-Berkeley-1967-Univ Art Mus-wrps,illus-exh cat (h10) 35.00

SEMENOV,S A-Prehistoric Technology-(1964)-Barnes & Noble-tall 8vo-211p (cc4,dj) 20.00

SEMMES,R-Service Afloat-Balt-1887-833p-pict cov,col plts,port (z10,hngs rprd,scuff) 100.00

SEMMES,RAPHAEL-Memoirs of Service Afloats-Balt-1869-Kelly,Piet-833p-cl wi lea sp labl,6 col illus,ports,b&w illus,map-1st Amer ed (dd9,recased,new e.p.,pgs brwn 125.00

SEMSCH,O F-ED.-History of the Singer Building Construction-NY-1908-(Shumway & Beattie)-sm folio-117p-grn cl,photos-1st & only ed (oo8,sl shaken) 125.00

SEN,SURENDRA N-Eighteen Fifty Seven-Delhi-1957-Minis of Info-beige cl,paste on label,illus,fldg maps-1st ed (gg6,dj) 40.00

SENCOURT,ROBERT-T S Eliot, A Memoir-NY-(1971)-Dodd Mead-8vo-266p-16p photos-1st ed (ee5,dj) 12.50

SENDAK,JACK-King of the Hermits and Other Stories-NY-(1966)-FS&G-sq 4to-107p-cl,b&w illus,M Zemach-1st ed (r3,f,f dj) 30.00

SENDAK,MAURICE-Some Swell Pup-NY-1976-FSG-illus-1st ed (y10,dj) 30.00

SENECA-Hints & Points for Sportsmen-NY-1889-12mo-224p-illus (m3) 17.50

SENIOR,WILLIAM-Lines in Pleasant Places-Lond-1920-12mo-276p-photos (m3) 20.00

SENIOR,WILLOUGHBY F-Smoke Upon the Winds-Denver-(1961)-144p-illus-1st ed (v7,f,dj) 20.00

SENN,C HERMAN-Pocket Dictionary of Foods & Culinary Encyclopedia-Lond-(1908)-Food & Cookery Publ-sm 8vo-158+(2)p ads-red cl-1st ed (t10) 25.00

SENNETT,A R-Garden Cities in Theory & Practice-Lond-1905-2 vols-350 illus(incl fldg plts) (h10) 350.00

SENZAKI,NYOGEN-ED.-Buddhism and Zen-NY-1953-Philosophical Libr-cl-1st prtg (n8) 12.50

SENZEL,HOWARD-Baseball and the Cold War-1977-Harcourt-1st ed (ff2,dj) 25.00

SERAFIN,DAVID-Christmas Rising-Lond-1982-Collins-1st ed (r4,vf,dj) 20.00

SERANNE,ANN-Best of Near East Cookery-1964-Dbldy-158p-red cl,map e.p.,photos-1st ed (q8,dj) 15.00

SERANNE,ANN-Delectable Desserts-1952-Little,Brown-252p-dec pnk cl,drwngs-1st ed (q8,dj) 15.00

SERANNE,ANN-Epicure's Companion-NY-(1969)-McKay-484p (m6) 25.00

SEREDY,KATE-White Stag-NY-1937-Viking-sq sm 4to-blind stmpd pict cl,illus,auth-1st ed (s3,f,dj rub & sl chip) 60.00

SERGEANT,J-Frank Lloyd Wright's Usonian Houses-NY-1976-200 illus-1st prtg (h10,dj sl tn) 50.00

SERLING,ROBERT J-Only Way to Fly-GC-1976-Dbldy-8vo-x,494p-cl bkd bds,illus-1st ed (s2,dj) 30.00

SERLING,ROD-Patterns-NY-1957-S&S-auth 1st bk,photos-1st ed (a10,dj) 60.00

SERLING,ROD-Season to be Wary-Bost-1967-Little,Brown-1st ed (y2,f,f dj) 125.00

SERRA,VICTORIA-Tia Victoria's Spanish Kitchen-Lond-(1963)-N Kaye-319p-red cl-1st Brit ed (q8,dj) 17.50

SERT,JOSEP L-Can Our Cities Survive-Cambridge-1942-Harvard-sm oblng folio-cl,illus (cc10) 225.00

SERVEN,JAMES E-Conquering the Frontiers-(La Habra)-(1974)-Foundation Pr-qto-256p-illus-1st ed (bb4,dj) 25.00

SERVENTY,V-Koala-1975-Dutton-80p-photos-1st ed (bb3,f,dj) 12.00

SERVICE,ROBERT-Ballads of a Cheechako-Lond-1909-T Fisher Unwin-blu cl sp/mottled blu papr bds-scarce-1st Brit ed (pp2,f) 150.00*

SERVICE,ROBERT-Ballads of a Cheechako-NY-(1909)-Barse & Hopkins-orig pict lea grained cl stmpd in blind,t.e.g.-1st Amer ed (aa9,sl rub,few short tears) 50.00

SERVICE,ROBERT-Ballads of a Cheechako-Tor-1909-137p-1st ed (a7) 60.00

SERVICE,ROBERT-Rhymes of a Red Cross Man-NY-1916-Barse & Hopkins-dec red cl,8 col plts by Chas L Wrenn-1st US ed (dd6) 50.00

SERVICE,ROBERT-Rhymes of a Rolling Stone-Tor-1912-195p-1st ed (a7) 45.00

SERVICE,ROBERT-Song of the Campfire-Tor-(1978)-McGraw Hill-illus-1st separate ed (pp2,f,dj) 20.00*

SERVICE,ROBERT-Trail of '98-Tor-1911-Wm Briggs-blu/gry cl wi heartshaped design-1st Can ed (pp2) 50.00*

SERVICE,ROBERT-Trail of Ninety Eight-Tor-1928-xi,514p-pict dj,4 illus-later prtg (a7,f,dj) 40.00

SERVICE,ROBERT-Why Not Grow Young-NY-(1928)-Barse & Co-scarce-1st ed (pp2,lacks dj) 50.00*

SETNICKA,TIME-Wilderness Search & Rescue-Bost-1980-640p-photos-1st ed (o10,as new) 25.00

SETON,ERNEST T-Arctic Prairies-NY-1912-415p-photos (ee3,f) 35.00

SETON,ERNEST T-Lives of the Hunted-NY-1901-8vo-360p-illus-scarce-1st ed (m3) 20.00

SETON,ERNEST T-Lives of the Hunted-NY-Oct 12,1901-Scribner's-8vo-364p-sketches,drwngs-1st impr (ff9,fade,wn) 40.00*

SETON,ERNEST T-Monarch the Big Bear of Tallac-NY-1904-8vo-214p-illus-1st ed (m3) 17.50

SETON,ERNEST T-Trail of the Sandhill Stag-1899-Scribners-g pict stmpd cl,60 illus-1st ed (x2,sl rub) 55.00

SETON,ERNEST T-Two Little Savages-NY-1903-Dbldy,Page-dec lt grn cl,drwngs-1st ed (dd6) 35.00

SETON,ERNEST T-Two Little Savages...-Tor-1903-Wm Briggs-drwngs-1st Can ed (pp2) 65.00*

SETON,ERNEST T-Woodmyth & Fable-NY-1905-Century-8vo-red dec cl,illus-1st ed (jj8,f) 65.00

SETON,GRAHAM-Eye for an Eye-NY-1933-Farrar-1st US ed (j4,dj) 12.50

SETON,JULIA M-Pulse of the Pueblo-Santa Fe-1939-249p-brwn cl,illus-1st ed (v7,f) 25.00

SETTLE,MARY L-All the Brave Promises-NY-(1966)-1st ed (g5,dj) 35.00

SETTLE,MARY L-Blood Tie-Bost-1977-1st ed (c5,dj) 20.00

SETTLE,MARY L-Empire on Wheels-Stanford-(1949)-Stanford U Pr-153p-map e.p.-1st ed (ff4,dj) 20.00

SETTLE,MARY L-Fight Night on a Sweet Saturday-NY-(1964)-1st ed (c5,dj) 35.00

SETTLE,MARY L-Kiss of Kin-NY-(1955)-Harper-code "G-E"-1st US ed (b5,dj sl wn,sm chip) 125.00

SETTLE,MARY L-Know Nothing-NY-1960-1st ed (c5,dj sp sl fade) 75.00

SETTLE,RAYMOND W-ED.-March of the Mounted Riflemen-Glendale-1940-Arthur H Clark Co-380p-cl-1st ed (a1) 100.00

SETTLE,RAYMOND W-Overland Days to Montana in 1865-Glendale-1971-232p-frntis,fldg map-1st ed (t7,f) 25.00

SEURRE,E-New Practical Cookery Guide-Lond-1913-Horace Cox-548p-grn bds-Bitting 430-2nd ed of Multum in Parvo(enlarged) (m6,bds wn,hngs breaking) 45.00

SEUSS,DR-500 Hats of Bartholomew Cubbins-NY-(1938)-Vanguard-illus-1st ed (e10,rprd dj) 125.00

SEUSS,DR-Seven Lady Godivas-(1939)-Random-unpgd-1st ed (v8) 65.00

SEUSS,DR-Seven Lady Godivas-NY-(1967)-Random-ltd to 300c,autg-Commem ed (dd2,f,box) 135.00

SEVAREID,ERIC-Not So Wild a Dream-NY-1946-Knopf-auth 1st bk-1st ed (a10,dj) 20.00

SEVERIN,TIM-African Adventure-NY-1973-Dutton-4to-288p-red cl,illus-1st Amer ed (ee7,f,dj) 40.00

SEVERIN,TIMOTHY-Golden Antilles-NY-1970-Knopf-8vo-336p-24p illus-1st ed (ff5,f,f dj) 20.00

SEVERSKY,A P DE-Victory Through Air Power-NY-1942-8vo-xiv,354p-cl,24p plts,4p maps,1 dblpg map-1st ed (s2,sl chip dj) 25.00

SEWALL,WILLIAM W-Bill Sewall's Story of T.R.-NY,Lond-(1919)-115,(1)p-cl-Rampaging Herd 2035 (j1,t.p. fox) 22.50

SEWARD,WILLIAM H-Autobiography of...from 1801 to 1834-NY-1877-822p+ads-lea,illus-1st ed (c4,cov sl wn & soil) 20.00

SEXTON,ANNE-45 Mercy Street-Bost-1976-Houghton Mifflin-wht cl-1st ed (f2,dj) 20.00

SEXTON,ANNE-All My Pretty Ones-1962-HMCO-8vo-cl & bds-1st ed (x10,sl tn dj) 25.00

SEXTON,ANNE-Awful Rowing Toward God-Bost-1975-HMCO-1st ed (y1,f,f dj) 25.00

SEXTON,ANNE-Awful Rowing Toward God-Bost-1975-Houghton Mifflin-8vo-86p-1st ed (w6,f,dj) 12.50

SEXTON,ANNE-Book of Folly-1972-HMCO-8vo-cl & bds-ltd to 500c,autg,deluxe ed-1st ed (x10,as new in dj,box) 50.00

SEXTON,ANNE-Book of Folly-Bost-1972-1st ed (m4,f,dj) 15.00

SEXTON,ANNE-Book of Folly-Bost-1972-Houghton,Mifflin-1st ed (w6,dj) 20.00

SEXTON,ANNE-Book of Folly-Bost-1972-Houghton,Mifflin-ltd to 500c lg pap,autg-1st ed (w6,f,box) 50.00

SEXTON,ANNE-Death Notebooks-Bost-1974-HMCO-1st ed (y1,f,f dj) 25.00

SEXTON,ANNE-Selected Poems-1964-Oxford U Pr-1st ed (kk6,f,dj) 40.00

SEXTON,ANNE-To Bedlam and Part Way Back-1960-Houghton-auth 1st bk-1st ed (jj6,f,sl tn dj) 100.00

SEXTON,ANNE-Transformations-Bost-1971-Houghton Mifflin-8vo-cl,tissue dj-ltd to 500c,autg-1st ed (jj8,vf,dj,box) 75.00

SEXTON,ANNE-Words for Dr Y-1978-Houghton-1st ed (kk6,vf,dj) 20.00

SEXTON,GROVER F-Arizona Sheriff-np-1925-46p-pict wrps,plts,map-Six Guns #1979-scarce-1st ed (t7) 75.00

SEXTON,LYDIA-Autobiography of ...-Dayton-1882-United Brethren Publ Hs-655p-cl (d1) 50.00

SEXTON,R W-American Theatres of Today-NY-1927-Arch Publ-4to-175p-blu cl,photos,plans (r10) 150.00

SEXTON,R W-Logic of Modern Architecture-NY-1929-Arch Bk Publ-lg 4to-(4),133p-dec cl,illus (pp7,dj) 150.00

SEXTON,R W-Spanish Influence on American Architecture & Decoration-NY-1927-illus-1st ed (ee1,rub) 175.00

SEYMOUR,E S-Sketches of Minnesota, the New England of the West-NY-1850-Harper & Bros-blndstmpd cl,1 fldg map-1st ed (p6,sl wn sp) 250.00

SEYMOUR,FLORA W-Indian Agents of the Old Frontier-NY-1941-Appleton-1st ed (b4,dj chip,sl tn) 37.50

SEYMOUR,FLORA W-Lords of the Valley-Lond-1930-Longmans,Green-brwn cl-1st ed (ee6,sl rub) 30.00

SEYMOUR,FLORA W-Story of the Red Man-Lond,NY-1929-Longmans,Green-421p-illus,map e.p.-1st ed (gg4) 40.00

SEYMOUR,HAROLD-Baseball, The Early Years-1960-Oxford-photos-1st ed (s8) 45.00

SEYMOUR,HAROLD-Baseball:The Golden Age-1971-Oxford-photos-1st ed (s8,f,dj) 45.00

SEYMOUR,HENRY-Reproduction of Sound-1910-324p-86 illus-rare-1st ed (h6) 95.00

SEYMOUR,RALPH F-Some Went This Way-Chig-(1945)-Seymour (w1,t.e. bump,dj) 30.00

SEYMOUR,WILLIAM W-Cross-NY-1898-Putnam's-cl,frntis,illus-1st ed (n8) 125.00

SFIKAS,GEORGE-Mountains of Greece-Athens-1979-204p-col photos,maps (o10,as new) 25.00

SHA ROCCO-Masculine Cross and Ancient Sex Worship-NY-1904-Commonwealth-sm 8vo-65p+30p ads-g grn cl,drwngs-1st ed (aa7) 40.00*

SHACKLETON,EDWARD-Nansen the Explorer-Lond-1959-Witherby Ltd-8vo-xii,209p-frntis,13 illus,2 maps-1st ed (cc7,dj) 45.00*

SHADWELL,ARTHUR-Industrial Efficiency-1906-Longmans,Green-2 vols-blu cl-1st ed (g2) 75.00

SHAFER,GEORGE D-Ways of a Mud Dauber-(1949)-Stanford U Pr-8vo-78p-10 plts-1st ed (aa5,f,dj soil,sl tn) 20.00

SHAFER,HENRY-American Medical Profession, 1783 to 1850-NY-1936-271p-1st ed (dd3) 75.00

SHAFFER,E-Carolina Gardens-1939-U of NC-326p-cl,photos-garden club ed (x6) 25.00

SHAFFER,NEWTON M-Selected Essays on Orthopaedic Surgery-NY-1923-Putnam's-xii+636p-blu cl,illus-1st ed (c2,sp drknd) 125.00

SHAFFER,PETER-Equus and Shrivings-NY-1974-1st US ed (r5,f,dj) 20.00

SHAFFER,PETER-Equus and Shrivings-NY-1974-Atheneum-1st US ed (b5,f,dj) 35.00

SHAH,IDRIES-Learning How to Learn-Lond-1978-Octagon Pr-cl-1st ed (l8,f,dj) 25.00

SHAKESPEARE,WILLIAM-As You Like It-Lond-nd-Hodder & Stoughton-4to-143p-40 tip in col plts,H Thomsen,wi prntd guards (s3) 75.00

SHAKESPEARE,WILLIAM-Merchant of Venice-Lond-nd(ca.1914)-Hodder & Stoughton-4to-144p-16 tip-in col plts by Linton-rprnt (bb5) 35.00

SHAKESPEARE,WILLIAM-Plays of...-Lond-1800-Bensley-sm 8vo-12 vols-red lea sp & tips over mrbld bds (t1,sl wn & fox) 375.00

SHAKESPEARE,WILLIAM-Sonnets of...-NY-1941-Heritage Pr-cl,prntd in 3 cols,decs,V Angelo (l8) 15.00

SHALER,N S-Story of Our Continent-Bost-1897-Ginn & Co-290p-cl (k1) 12.50

SHAND,WILLIAM-Tempest in a Tea Cup-NY-1959-Roy-1st US ed (g4,f,dj) 10.00

SHANE,SUSANNAH-Lady in a Million-1943-Dodd-1st ed (s10,chip dj) 20.00

SHANGE,NTOZAKE-Three Pieces-NY-1981-1st ed (hh10,dj) 25.00

SHANKLAND,PETER-Byron of the Wager-NY-1975-288p-illus-1st Amer ed (b7,f,dj) 15.00

SHANNON,BILL-Ball Parks-1975-Hawthorn-1st ed (ff2,dj) 175.00

SHANNON,BILL-Ball Parks-1975-Hawthorn-photos-1st ed (s8,f,dj sl tn) 165.00

SHANNON,DAVID L-Socialist Party of America-NY-1955-Macmillan-273p-1st ed (ff1,dj edgewn & sl soil) 30.00

SHANNON,DEL-Cold Trail-NY-1978-1st ed (c5,f,dj) 12.50

SHANNON,DELL-Case Pending-NY-1960-auth 1st bk-1st ed (r5,chip dj) 40.00

SHANNON,DELL-Cold Trail-NY-1978-Morrow-1st ed (bb1,f,dj) 12.50

SHANNON,DELL-Deuces Wild-NY-1975-1st ed (f5,f,dj) 20.00

SHANNON,DELL-Double Bluff-NY-1963-1st ed (r5,dj) 30.00

SHANNON,DELL-Extra Kill-1962-Morrow-1st ed (s10,dj) 45.00

SHANNON,DELL-Knave of Hearts-NY-1962-Morrow-1st ed (z2,f,dj sl wn & tn) 50.00

SHANNON,DELL-Mark of Murder-NY-1964-Morrow-1st ed (w9,f,dj) 30.00

SHANNON,DELL-Motive on Record-NY-1982-Morrow-1st ed (q4,vf,dj) 20.00

SHANNON,DELL-Murder Most Strange-NY-1981-Morrow-1st ed (f4,as new in dj) 10.00

SHANNON,DELL-Root of All Evil-NY-1964-1st ed (r5,dj) 30.00

SHANNON,DELL-Schooled to Kill-NY-1969-1st ed (r5,sp chip dj) 12.50

SHANNON,DELL-Unexpected Death-NY-1970-Morrow-1st ed (bb1,f,dj) 25.00

SHANNON,JAMES P-Catholic Colonization on the Western Frontier-New Haven-1957-Yale U Pr-302p-illus-1st ed (ee4,dj) 25.00

SHAPIRO,H-ED.-Physician to the West: Selected Writings of Daniel Drake on Science & Society-Lexington-1970-419p-1st ed (dd3,dj) 50.00

SHAPIRO,HARRY L-Heritage of the Bounty-1936-S&S-329p-photos-1st ed (u8,cov spots) 12.00

SHAPIRO,HARRY L-Heritage of the Bounty-NY-1936-326p-e.p. map,illus-1st ed (d7) 40.00

SHAPIRO,KARL-V Letter and Other Poems-Lond-1945-Secker & Warburg-1st Brit ed (d10,dj rub,sl soil) 40.00

SHAPIRO,MILTON-Warren Spahn Story-1958-Messner (r7,f,dj) 40.00

SHAPIRO,MILTON-Willie Mays Story-1960-Messner-1st ed (s8,dj) 45.00

SHAPIRO,S R-ED.-United States Cumulative Book Auction Records 1945 to 50-NY-1951-1814p-cl (g1) 35.00

SHAPLEY,HARLOW-Inner Metagalaxy-New Haven-1957-Yale U Pr-xiv+204p-grn cl,59 illus-1st ed (dd1,dj) 25.00

SHARFMAN,I HAROLD-Jews on the Frontier-Chig-1977-Regnery-8vo-xii+337p (z4,dj) 15.00

SHARP,D-ED.-Rationalists-Lond-1978-illus-1st ed (ee1,dj) 100.00

SHARP,D-Modern Architecture & Expressionism-NY-1966-illus-1st Amer ed (h10,sl tn dj) 45.00

SHARP,HAL-An Angler's Corner-Lond-1930-12mo-160p-photos-1st ed (m3,f) 10.00

SHARP,MARGERY-Rescuers-Bost-1959-Little,Brown-149p-blu cl,illus by G Williams-1st US ed (nn8,dj sp sl tn) 75.00

SHARP,MRS ABBIE G-History of the Spirit Lake Massacre and Captivity of Miss Abbie Gardner-Des Moines-1902-Iowa Prtg Co-372p-drwngs,photos-Howes S330 (dd4) 50.00

SHARP,PAUL F-Whoop Up Country-Mpls-(1955)-U of Minn Pr-xiv,347p-cl,illus-Best Montana Bks #30-1st ed (v1,dj) 85.00

SHARP,R FARQUHARSON-Reader's Guide to Everyman's Library-Lond-1932-Dent (w1,f,dj) 20.00

SHARP,WILLIAM S-Address...Delivered before the Students of the Trenton Business College, April 22, 1874-Trenton-1875-11p-wrps (aa6) 35.00

SHARPE,DR WILLIAM-Brain Surgeon-NY-1952-Viking-8vo-271p-1st ed (gg5,dj sp sl fade) 20.00

SHARPE,JOHN-Sermon Preached at Trinity Church in New York, in America, August 13, 1706-Lond-(1706?)-H Hills-16p-1/2 mor (aa6,frnt hng crack) 200.00

SHARPE,P B-Complete Guide to Handloading-NY-1947-465p+72p suppl (gg3,f) 20.00

SHARPE,P B-Rifle in America-NY-1953-800p-photos,illus-3rd ed (gg3,f) 45.00

SHARPSTEEN,HAROLD-Life of John Henry Burke-Kalamazoo-1948-Ihling Bros Everard Co-199p-cl,photos (z7) 35.00

SHARTS,ELIZABETH-Cradle of the Trotter-Goshen-1946-Book Mill-1st ed (j9,sp wn) 35.00

SHATTOCK,E H-An Experiment in Mindfulness-NY-1960-Dutton-cl-1st ed (l8,f,dj) 10.00

SHATTUCK,CYRUS-Explanations of Shattuck's Common School Scientific Apparatus...-Dundee-1852-E Hoogland,prntr-49p-prntd bds-2nd ed (k1) 17.50

SHATTUCK,LEMUEL-Report of the Sanitary Commission of Massachusetts 1850-Cambridge-1948-321p-(facs of 1850 ed) (dd3) 70.00

SHAUGHNESSY & GOODENOUGH-Skeet & Trapshooting-NY-1950-8vo-180p-photos-1st ed (m3,f,fray dj) 15.00

SHAUGHNESSY,JIM-Deleware & Hudson-1974-Howell North-4to-476p-illus (nn7,dj wn) 32.00

SHAW,BERNARD-Rationalization of Russia-Bloomington-1964-IU Pr-1st ed (x9,dj) 10.00

SHAW,C E-Snakes of the American West-1974-Knopf-330p-74 col photos-1st ed (bb3,dj) 40.00

SHAW,CLIFFORD R-Jack Roller-Chig-1930-U of Chig Pr-1st ed (v5,sl tn dj) 45.00

SHAW,FRED G-Science of Dry Fly Fishing-Lond-1906-8vo-illus,photos (m3) 40.00

SHAW,FRED G-Science of Fly Fishing for Trout-NY-1925-8vo-341p-photos (m3) 25.00

SHAW,FRED G-Science of Fly Fishing For Trout-NY-1925-Scribners-lg 8vo-341p wi index+ads,g stmpd blu cl,illus-1st ed (t1) 65.00

SHAW,FREDERIC-Oil Lamps and Iron Ponies-SF-1949-187p-deluxe ltd ed,3 autg-1st ed (n4,f,dj) 40.00

SHAW,FREDERICK-Oil Lamps and Iron Ponies-1949-Bay Bks-187p-illus-1st ed (d3) 40.00

SHAW,GARY-Meat on the Hoof-NY-1972-St.Martin's Pr-234p-cl,photos-1st ed (w3,vf,dj) 12.50

SHAW,GEO C-Chinook Jargon and How to Use It-Seattle-1909-65p-pict wrps,cov port pastedown (r8,cor missng cov port) 40.00

SHAW,GEORGE B-Apple Cart-Lond-1930-Constable-g titled cl-1st ed (aa9,sl drknd sp) 15.00

SHAW,GEORGE B-Plays:Pleasant and Unpleasant-Chig,NY-1905-Stone-2 vols,cl (m1) 12.50

SHAW,GEORGE B-Saint Joan-Lond-1924-Constable-g titled cl-1st trd ed (aa9) 20.00

SHAW,GEORGE B-Translations and Tomfooleries-Lond-1926-Constable-g titled cl-1st ed (aa9) 15.00

SHAW,GEORGE C-Chinook Jargon and How to Use It-Seattle-1909-Rainier Prtg Co-65p+ads-red cl-1st ed (w1) 75.00

SHAW,HELEN-Fly Tying-NY-1963-8vo-281p-photos (m3,vf) 25.00

SHAW,HENRY-Alphabets Numerals and Devices of the Middle Ages-Lond-1845-Wm Pickering-dec lea bndg,over 50 col plts-1st ed (l9,sl rub) 2,000.00

SHAW,IRWIN-Act of Faith-NY-(1946)-Random-1st ed (d10,f,dj) 35.00

SHAW,IRWIN-Evening in Byzantium-NY-(1973)-1st ed (l5,f,dj) 12.50

SHAW,IRWIN-In the Company of Dolphins-np-(1964)-Bernard Geis Assoc-1st ed (a10,f,dj) 12.50

SHAW,IRWIN-Lucy Crown-NY-(1956)-Random Hs-1st ed (a10,dj) 20.00

SHAW,IRWIN-Mixed Company-NY-(1950)-Random-1st ed (d10,f,sp chip dj) 25.00

SHAW,IRWIN-Nightwork-NY-(1975)-Delacorte-1st ed (a10,f,dj) 15.00

SHAW,IRWIN-Rich Man, Poor Man-NY-(1970)-Delacorte-1st ed (a10,chip dj) 15.00

SHAW,IRWIN-Sailor Off the Bremen & Other Stories-NY-(1939)-Random Hs-pict dj-1st ed (a10,soil dj) 125.00

SHAW,IRWIN-Troubled Air-NY-(1951)-Random-cl-1st ed (aa9,dj sl soil,edgewn) 20.00

SHAW,IRWIN-Two Weeks in Another Town-1960-Random-1st ed (s9,dj) 20.00

SHAW,IRWIN-Voices of a Summer Day-1965-Delacorte-1st ed (q7,dj) 25.00

SHAW,IRWIN-Voices of a Summer Day-NY-(1965)-Delacorte-1st ed (a10,f,dj) 15.00

SHAW,JAMES C-North From Texas-1952-Branding Iron Pr-109p-illus,2 ports,map,brand pg-ltd to 750c,nbrd-Herd 2041 (r8,f) 60.00

SHAW,JAMES-Physiognomy of Mental Diseases and Degeneracy-Bristol/Lond-1903-Wright/SMHK&Co-16mo-xii+(84)p+18p hlftones,prntd brwn cl-1st ed (y9) 75.00

SHAW,JOSEPH T-ED.-Hard Boiled Omnibus-NY-1946-1st ed (r5,dj) 75.00

SHAW,JOSEPH T-ED.-Hard Boiled Omnibus-NY-1946-Simon-1st ed (g4,chip dj) 45.00

SHAW,JOSEPH T-Hard Boiled Omnibus-NY-1952-Pocket Bk-wrps-1st prntg (p4,sl wn wrps) 20.00

SHAW,L H-Snipe & Woodcock-NY-1903-298p-dec cov,illus (gg3,f) 20.00

SHAW,LLOYD-Cowboy Dances-Caldwell-1949-Caxton-417p-photos-rvsd ed (bb4) 15.00

SHAW,ROBERT B-Down Brakes-Lond-1961-487p-1st ed (n4,f,dj) 19.00

SHAW,THURSTAN-Igbo Ukwu-Evanston-1970-Northwestern-4to-2 vols-gry cl,vol.1:chrts,col photos;vol.2:514 plts on glossy papr (dd7,dj) 150.00

SHAW,WILLIAM H-History of Essex and Hudson Counties, New Jersey-Phila-1884-4to-2 vols-buckrm,illus,plts,fldg maps (aa6,rbnd) 250.00

SHAWN,TED-One Thousand and One Night Stands-NY-1960-Dbldy-1st ed (u4,dj rub) 18.00

SHAWNEE HIGH SCHOOL GIRLS LOUISVILLE, KENTUCKY-Flood Stories-Louisville-1937-92p-cl (c1,f) 15.00

SHEA,JOHN G-ED.-Fallen Brave-NY-1861-224p-8 ports-1st ed (c4,ex-libr) 75.00

SHEARMAN,MONTAGUE-Athletics and Football-Lond-1887-Longmans,Green-4to-446p-Badminton Libr ser,lg papr ed-ltd to 250c bnd in 3/4 g stmpd blu lea over cl (p1) 100.00

SHEBL,JAMES-King, of the Mountains-Stockton-1974-76p-1st ed (o10,f) 30.00

SHECKLEY,ROBERT-Crompton Divided-NY-(1978)-HR&W-1st US ed (j3,f,dj) 25.00

SHECTER,LEONARD-Roger Maris Home Run Hero-1961-Bartholomew-pbk orig,Sport Mag Libr #11-1st ed (s8) 14.00

SHEEHAN,DONALD-Essays in American Historiography-NY-1960-Columbia U Pr-320p-frntis-1st ed (bb4,dj) 20.00

SHEEHAN,DONALD-This Was Publishing-Bloomington-1952-Indiana U-1st ed (w1,f,f dj) 17.50

SHEEHAN,SUSAN-Welfare Mother-Bost-1976-Houghton Mifflin-8vo-xiv,109p-cl-1st ed (z5,f,dj) 12.00

SHEEHY,JEANNE-Rediscovery of Ireland's Past-Lond-(1980)-Thames & Hudson-4to-208p-177 illus(incl 25 col)-1st Brit ed (jj5,f,dj) 17.50

SHEELER,CHARLES-Paintings Drawings Photographs-NY-1939-MOMA-4to-wrps-1st ed (y3) 45.00

SHEERAN,REV JAMES B-Confederate Chaplain-Milw-1960-168p-illus-1st ed (n3,dj) 37.50

SHEFFIELD,CHARLES-Selkie-NY-(1982)-Macmillan-1st ed (k3,f,dj) 20.00

SHEFFY,LESTER F-Francklyn Land & Cattle Comapny-Austin-1963-UTP-402p-photos-1st ed (a9,dj) 50.00

SHEIR,MORLEY-Fireside Mining-(Vancouver)-nd(1958)-78p-illus,ports-Edwards & Lort #3234 (k10) 25.00*

SHELDON,CHARLES-Wilderness of Denali, Wilderness of North Pac Coast, Wilderness of Upper Yukon-1983-Amwell-3 vols-navy blu lea,a.e.g.,ltd to 1000c,2 autg (gg3,vf,box) 300.00

SHELDON,CHARLES-Wilderness of Denali-NY-1960-8vo-412p (m3,fray dj) 22.00

SHELDON,CHARLES-Wilderness of the Upper Yukon-NY-1911-8vo-354p-photos,col frontis by C Rungius-scarce-1st ed (m3,vf) 300.00

SHELDON,CHARLES-Wilderness of the Upper Yukon-NY-1919-Scribner's-xxiii,364p-52 plts(incl col),4 maps(1 fldg)-Ricks p.198-2nd ed,rvsd (oo1,f) 275.00

SHELDON,G W-American Painters-NY-1879-Appleton-g dec cov & sp,a.e.g.,illus-1st ed (h10,sl fox,edges rub) 225.00

SHELDON,H P-Sportsman's Guide to Wild Ducks-Wash D.C.-1946-8vo-35p-wrps,col illus by F Everett (m3,vf) 17.50

SHELDON,H P-Tranquility Revisited-NY-1945-186p-illus (gg3,f,dj) 15.00

SHELDON,H P-Tranquility Revisited-NY-1945-8vo-186p-ltd to 5000c,illus by A Fuller (m3) 17.50

SHELDON,H P-Tranquility Stories-NY-1974-4to-288p-photos (m3,vf,dj) 40.00

SHELDON,H P-Tranquility, Tranquility Revisited, Tranquility Regained-NY-1945-3 vols-ltd to 5000c (gg3,vf,box) 50.00

SHELDON,H P-Tranquility,Tranquility Regained,Tranquility Revisited-1945-Countryman Pr-8vo-3 vols,ltd to 475sets,nbrd,two autg,illus by A Fuller (m3) 300.00

SHELDON,H P-Tranquillity-NY-1936-Derrydale Pr-illus-ltd to 950c,nbrd (r2) 150.00

SHELDON,H P-Wild Ducks-Wash D.C.-1941-8vo-35p-wrps,col illus by F Everett-1st ed (m3,vf) 22.50

SHELDON,W G-Book of the American Woodcock-MA-1971-227p-col frntis,photos (gg3,vf,dj) 25.00

SHELDON,W G-Exploring for Wild Sheep in British Columbia in 1931 & 1932-NJ-1981-Amwell Pr-246p-blu bonded lea wi yel silk e.p.,a.e.g.,col frntis,photos,ltd to 1000c,autg (ee3,vf,box) 175.00

SHELDON,W G-Wilderness Home of the Giant Panda-1975-U of Mass-196p-photos,drwngs (bb3,f,dj) 25.00

SHELDON,WILLIAM G-Wilderness Home of the Giant Panda-Amherst-1975-U Mass Pr-8vo-196p-photos-1st ed (aa5,f,dj sl tn,rub,sl sun) 15.00

SHELF OF OLD BOOKS-1894-Scribners-drwngs,photos-1st ed (x2,sl fade & wn sp) 50.00

SHELLER,ROSCOE-Courage and Water-Portland-(1952)-263p-photos-1st ed (r8,dj tn,chip) 36.00

SHELLY,ER M-Bird Dog Training Today & Tomorrow-NY-1947-8vo-140p-photos,illus-1st ed (m3) 15.00

SHELTON,LOLA-Charles Marion Russell-NY-1962-231p-4p col illus-1st ed (f7,dj) 40.00

SHELTON,LOLA-Charles Marion Russell-NY-1962-Dodd,Mead-xviii,231p-4 col plts & other illus,C M Russell-1st ed (v1,dj) 45.00

SHELTON,LOUISE-Beautiful Gardens in America-NY-1924-Scribner's-4to-xviii,(2),560,(2)p-cl,8 col plts,275 illus (cc10) 85.00

SHELTON,LOUISE-Continuous Bloom in America-NY-1915-Scribner's-sm 4to-xvii,(3),145p-dec cl,16 plts,7 chrts-1st ed (cc10,sl fox) 45.00

SHELTON,LOUISE-Seasons in a Flower Garden-NY-1906-x,117p-col pict cov,4 hlf tones-1st ed (x5,sp rub) 25.00

SHELTON,WILLIAM R-Winning the Moon-Bost-1970-Little,Brown-230p-illus-1st ed (hh6,sl chip dj) 18.00

SHELVOCKE,CAPT GEORGE-Voyage Round the World by Way of the Great South Sea...-NY-1971-N Isreal-8vo-4 plts(2 fldg),fldg map-rprnt facs (dd7,as new) 70.00

SHENSTONE,W A-Methods of Glass Blowing and Working Silica in the Oxy Gas Flame-1918-Longmans Green-98p-illus-3rd ed (cc8,sl fray sp) 25.00

SHENTON,E-Riders of the Winds-Phila-(1929)-8vo-206p-g cl,illus t.p.,16p b&w & 16p col plts,illus e.p.-1st ed (s2) 30.00

SHENTON,JAMES P-ED.-Reconstruction-NY-(1963)-314p-1st ed (n3,sl chip dj) 22.50

SHEPARD,ERNEST A-Drawn From Life-NY-(1962)-Dutton-illus,auth-1st US ed (s3,dj) 25.00

SHEPARD,ERNEST-Fun and Fantasy-Lond-(1927)-Methuen-4to-dec pict bds,1/4 lea g dec box-1st ed (u10,f,dj,box) 250.00

SHEPARD,ISABEL S-Cruise of the U.S. Steamer "Rush" in Behring Sea, Summer of 1889-SF-1890-Bancroft-8vo-257p-dec maroon cl,photos,maps-scarce-1st ed (kk9) 150.00

SHEPARD,LESLIE-ED.-Dracula Book of Great Vampire Stories-Secaucus-1977-Citadel Pr-8vo-269p-1st ed (cc7,vf,dj) 15.00*

SHEPARDSON,FRANCIS W-Irregularities in Presidential Counts-(Granville)-(1896)-17p-wrps (g1) 15.00

SHEPARDSON,MARY-Navajo Mountain Community-Berkeley-1970-269p-map-1st ed (v7,f,dj) 25.00

SHEPHARD,MICHAEL-Come & Fish-Lond-1952-8vo-240p-photos-1st ed (m3,fray dj) 15.00

SHEPHARD,ODELL-Thy Rod & Thy Creel-Hartford,NY-1930-123p-1st ed (m3,rprd dj) 80.00

SHEPHARD,RICHARD HERNE-ED.-Waltoniana-Lond-1878-12mo-unpgd-every pg dec-1st ed (m3,mostly uncut) 50.00

SHEPHEARD,PETER-Modern Gardens-NY-1954-4to-144p-291 photos,plans & sketches (hh7,dj wn,chip) 95.00

SHEPHERD,JACK-Adams Chronicles-Bost-1975-Little,Brown-xxxi,448p-illus-1st ed (n2,dj) 17.50

SHEPHERD,JEAN-Ferrari in the Bedroom-NY-1972-Dodd,Mead-1st ed (e8,f,f dj) 35.00

SHEPHERD,JEAN-Ferrari in the Bedroom-NY-1972-Dodd-1st ed (w5,f,dj sl tn) 25.00

SHEPHERD,JEAN-In God We Trust, All Others Pay Cash-NY-1966-1st ed (r2,sl chip dj) 25.00

SHEPHERD,JEAN-In God We Trust, All Others Pay Cash-NY-1966-Dbldy-1st ed (g8,sp chip dj) 40.00

SHEPHERD,MAJOR W-Prairie Experiences in Handling Cattle and Sheep-Lond-1884-Chapman & Hall-(vi)+266p+ads,map,8 plts-grn pict cl-Howes S389-1st ed (h2) 175.00

SHEPHERD,RICHARD H-Bibliography of Thackeray-Lond-(1880)-Elliot Stock-sm 8vo-viii,62,(2)p-orig cl-1st ed (w2) 45.00

SHEPHERD,ROY E-History of the Rose-Lond-(1978)-8vo-viii,264p-13 plts-(1st publ in 1954) (m10,dj) 21.00

SHEPHERD,WILLIAM-Prairie Experiences in Handling Cattle and Sheep-Lond-1894-Chapman & Hall-266p+publ catlg(32p)-pict grn cl,fldg map,9 illus-Howes S389-1st ed (z1,sp rprd) 175.00

SHEPPARD,L A-TRANSL.-Memoirs of Lorenzo de Ponte, Mozart's Librettist-Bost-1929-Houghton Mifflin-8vo-373p-illus-1st Amer ed (ll9,f,dj) 30.00

SHEPPARD,S E-Investigations on the Theory of the Photographic Process-1907-Longmans,Green-x+342p-grn cl,65 text figs,1 fldg plt-1st ed (d2) 25.00

SHEPPERSON,ARCHIBALD B-John Paradise and Lucy Ludwell, of London and Williamsburg-Richmond-1942-Dietz Pr-8vo-501p-16 illus-1st ed (ff5,dj) 25.00

SHERATON,MIMI-Seducer's Cookbook-NY-(1961)-Random-214p-1st prtg (q6) 20.00

SHERBURNE,JAMES-Death's Clenched Fist-1982-Houghton Mifflin-1st ed (s9,vf,dj) 15.00

SHERFEY,FLORENCE E-This Was Their Time-Fairfield-1975-Ye Galleon Pr-188p-pict e.p.,illus,map (bb4) 15.00

SHERIDAN,J B-Baseball for Beginners-NY-(1924)-Amer Sports Publ Co-56p+ads-wrps-Spalding Athletic Libr (n1,sl wn cor) 25.00

SHERIDAN,JUANITA-Waikiki Widow-NY-1953-Dbldy-1st ed (d4,dj) 20.00

SHERIDAN,P H-Personal Memoirs-NY-1888-Chas L Webster-2 vols-grn cl-1st ed (u2) 100.00

SHERIDAN,THOMAS-Course of Lectures on Elocution-Troy-1803-prntd by O Penniman-185,(1)p-lea-Amer Imprnts 5046-2nd Amer ed (k1,upper jnts tender) 50.00

SHERIDAN,WYOMING-np-nd(ca.1920's)-42p-wrps,plts,map-scarce promo (t7) 17.50

SHERINGHAM,H T-Coarse Fishing-Lond-1912-8vo-326p-illus-1st ed (m3) 30.00

SHERINGHAM,H T-Trout Fishing Memories & Morals-Bost,NY-nd-8vo-296p-photos (m3) 20.00

SHERINGHAM,H T-Where to Fish-Lond-nd-12mo-270p+ads (m3) 17.50

SHERLOCK,CHESLA C-Successful Rose Culture-Des Moines-(1924)-163p-cl (h1) 15.00

SHERLOCK-Layman's Apology-Albany-1834-Hoffman & White-314p-lilac bds,papr sp labl-1st ed (b2,fox) 50.00

SHERMAN,ANDREW M-Historic Morristown, New Jersey-Morristown-1905-lvi,444p-cl,plts (aa6) 75.00

SHERMAN,DEAN-ED.-Alaska Cavalcade-Seattle-(1943)-Alaska Life-304p-illus,e.p. maps-1st ed (u8,covs wn) 20.00

SHERMAN,HAROLD M-Bases Full-1928-G&D-1st ed (q7,dj) 12.50

SHERMAN,HAROLD M-Last Man Out-Akron-(1937)-Saalfield-unpgd-pict bds (n1) 15.00

SHERMAN,HAROLD M-Strike Him Out-1931-Goldsmith-1st ed (q7,dj) 12.50

SHERMAN,JAMES E-Ghost Towns of Arizona-1969-U of Okla Pr-8vo-208+1p-cl,photos,maps-1st ed (z4,rub cov) 10.00

SHERMAN,PADDY-Cloud Walkers-Tor-1965-161p-1st ed (a4,f,dj) 20.00

SHERMAN,PADDY-Expeditions to Nowhere-Seattle-1981-1st ed (v9,f,f dj) 35.00

SHERMAN,PADDY-Expeditions to Nowhere-Seattle-1981-226p-photos-1st US ed (p10,f,dj) 20.00

SHERMAN,W C-Air Warfare-NY-(1926)-8vo-x,308p-cl,6p plts,10 text illus-1st ed (s2) 65.00

SHERRILL,CHARLES H-Purple or the Red-NY-1924-Doran-318p-tip in photos-1st ed (ff1,dj) 30.00

SHERRINGTON,CHARLES-Endeavour of Jean Fernel-Cambridge-1946-223p-1st ed (dd3,dj) 60.00

SHERRINGTON,CHARLES-Selected Writings of Sir...-Lond-1939-532p-1st ed (dd3,dj) 250.00

SHERROD,R-History of Marine Corps Aviation in World War II-Wash-(1952)-thk 8vo-xvi,496p-cl,plts,maps,text illus-1st ed (s2) 45.00

SHERRY,EDNA-Tears for Jessie Hewitt-NY-1958-Dodd-1st ed (g4,dj) 10.00

SHERWIN,MARK-One Week in March-NY-(1961)-Putnam-8vo-254p-16p photos-1st ed (dd5,dj) 12.50

SHERWOOD,DONALD H-Fishing Years-1982-priv prntd-4to-102p-one of 500c,maps (m3,f) 50.00

SHERWOOD,JOHN-Ambush for Anatol-NY-1952-Dbldy CC-1st US ed (e4,dj) 15.00

SHERWOOD,JOHN-Death at the BBC-NY-(1982)-Scribner's-1st US ed (p3,f,sl tn dj) 10.00

SHERWOOD,JOHN-Dr.Bruderstein Vanishes-NY-1949-Dbldy CC-1st US ed (j4,yel pgs,dj) 10.00

SHERWOOD,JOHN-Hour of the Hyenas-Lond-1979-Macmillan-1st ed (p4,dj) 22.50

SHERWOOD,KATE B-Camp Fire, Memorial Day, and Other Poems-Chig-1885-212p-cl (d1) 15.00

SHERWOOD,M E W-An Epistle to Posterity-NY,Lond-1899-Harper & Bros-380p-cl (d1,frnt cov sl bent) 32.50

SHERWOOD,MARRIEM-Road to Cathay-NY-1928-Macmillan-251p-cl,illus,Wm Siegel-1st ed (s3,wn dj) 20.00

SHERWOOD,MRS-Babes in the Woods of the New World-NY-1831-Mahlon Day-67p+3p ads-orig papr bckd prntd bds,frntis-rare (hh9,rub,soil,sl chip sp,fox) 325.00

SHERWOOD,MRS.-Lady of the Manor-Lond-(1860)-Houlston & Sons-5 vols-orig cl,a.e.g.-new ed (w6) 125.00

SHERWOOD,ROBERT E-Roosevelt and Hopkins-NY-(1948)-Harper-979p-cl-1st ed so stated (e1,wn dj) 12.50

SHERWOOD,ROBERT E-There Shall Be No Night-NY-1941-1st ed (m4,f,dj) 20.00

SHIEL,M P-Invisible Voices-NY-1936-Vanguard Pr-1st US ed (a10,dj soil & rub) 125.00

SHIEL,M P-Prince Zaleski and Cummings King Monk-Sauk City-(1977)-Arkham-1st ed (g3,f,dj) 20.00

SHIEL,M P-Prince Zaleski and Cummings King Monk-Sauk City-(1977)-ltd to 4036c-1st ed (k5,as new in dj) 10.00

SHIEL,M P-Xelucha and Others-Sauk City-1975-Arkham-1st ed (k3,f,dj) 20.00

SHIEL,M P-Xelucha and Others-Sauk City-1975-ltd to 4283c-1st ed (k5,as new in dj) 17.50

SHIELDS,G O-ED.-Big Game of North America-Chig-1890-Rand,McNally-27p plts-1st ed (p6) 150.00

SHIELDS,G O-Rustlings in the Rockies-Chig-1883-Bedford,Clarke-306p-illus-1st ed (d3) 45.00

SHIELDS,GEORGE O-Battle of the Big Hole-Chig-1889-Rand,McNally-120p+4p ads-blk cl,papr sp labl wi auth as "Coquina",frntis,6p plts-Howes S412-1st ed (z1,f) 175.00

SHIELDS,JAMES-Monozygotic Twins, Brought up Apart and Brought up Together-Lond-1962-OUP-x+264p-red cl,4 plts,39 tbls-1st ed (j2,wn dj) 40.00

SHIELS,ARCHIE W-COMP.-Little Journeys into the History of Russian America and the Purchase of Alaska-Bellingham-Christmas 1949-lg qto-Priv Ed of The Journeys,ltd to 100c,nbrd,autg (bb4) 50.00

SHIGERU,NAKAYAMA-History of Japanese Astronomy-Cambridge-1969-Harvard Univ-xvi+329p-tan cl,29 illus-1st ed (d2,dj) 20.00

SHILOH'S WISDOM-Benton Harbor-nd-Israelite Hs of David-3 vols-wrps (aa1) 35.00

SHILTON,NEALE-Million Miles Ago-Somerset-(1982)-Haynes-8vo-300p-photos-1st Brit ed (gg5,f,dj) 25.00

SHINGLETON,ROYCE G-John Taylor Wood: Sea Ghost of the Confederacy-Athens-1982-U of GA Pr-242p-illus,maps (v2,as new in dj) 15.00

SHINKLE,JAMES D-Robert Casey and the Ranch on the Rio Hondo-Roswell-(1970)-186p-photos-1st ed (u7,f) 20.00

SHINN,CHARLES H-Mining Camps-NY-1948-Knopf-8vo-291p-1st ed so stated (z4,sl wn dj) 20.00

SHINN,HENRY C-History of Mount Holly-Mount Holly-(1957)-182p-cl,plts (aa6) 50.00

SHIPLEY,J W-Pulp and Paper Making in Canada-Tor-1929-Longmans,Green-sm 8vo-x,139p-cl,illus-1st ed (x4) 30.00

SHIPLEY,NAN-James Evans Story-Tor-1966-Ryerson Pr-8vo-219p-1st ed (aa7,sl bump,dj) 15.00*

SHIPP,J E D-Giant Days, or Life and Times of William H Crawford-Americus-1909-Southern Prnt-266p-grn cl,fldg map,illus-1st ed (mm10) 30.00

SHIPP,JOHN-MEMOIRS OF THE EXTRAORDINARY MILITARY CAREER OF...LATE A LIEUT. IN HIS MAJESTY'S 87TH...-Lond-1890-386p-cl,new illus ed (l1,sl wn sp) 17.50

SHIPTON,CLIFFORD K-Isaiah Thomas, Printer, Patriot and Philanthropist, 1749 to 1831-NY-1948-Prtg Hs of Leo Hart-8vo-xiv,94p-red cl-1st ed (w2,dj chip) 35.00

SHIPTON,ERIC-Mount Everest Reconnaissance Expedition-NY-1952-4to-128p-92 photos-1st ed (a4,f,dj) 45.00

SHIPTON,ERIC-Mountain Conquest-NY-1966-153p-157 photos(36 col)-1st ed (q10,f,dj) 13.00

SHIPTON,ERIC-Upon That Mountain-Lond-1943-222p-31 photos,4 maps-1st Brit ed (a4,f,dj chip) 60.00

SHIRAEFF,PETER-Flattery's Foal-NY-1938-Knopf-1st US ed (f10,dj) 25.00

SHIRAHATA,SHIRO-Alps-NY-1980-30p text,104 col photos-1st ed (p10,vf,vf dj) 120.00

SHIRAI,SHOHEI-Story of Pearls-Tokyo-1970-Japan Publ-132p-63 col & 62 b&w plts-1st prtg (u5,f,f dj) 30.00

SHIRAKAWA,YOSHIKAZU-Alps-NY-1973-col photos-1st ed (p10,as new in dj) 40.00

SHIRAKAWA,YOSHIKAZU-Himalayas-NY-1972-300p-hvy papr,col photos-1st ed (a4,f,f dj) 190.00

SHIRCLIFFE,ARNOLD-Edgewater Beach Hotel Salad Book-Chig-(1926)-Hotel Monthly Pr-lg 8vo-265p-g stmpd grn buckrm,col photos-1st ed (oo8,f) 75.00

SHIRCLIFFE,ARNOLD-Edgewater Beach Hotel Salad Book-Chig-(1946)-306p-dec grn cl,col plts-7th prtg (q8,dj) 25.00

SHIRK,DAVID-Cattle Drives of David Shirk-1956-Champoeg Pr-148p-illus-ltd 1st ed (f7,sl stnd cov) 100.00

SHIRK,DAVID-Cattle Drives of...-Portland-1956-Champoeg Pr-148p-ltd to 750c-1st ed (bb4) 65.00

SHIRK,LUCYL-Oklahoma City-OKC-1957-Bd of Educ-252p-blu cl,illus-1st ed (ff8) 26.00

SHIRLEY,GLENN-Belle Starr and Her Times-Norman-(1982)-U of Okla Pr-324p-illus-1st ed (dd4,dj) 25.00

SHIRLEY,GLENN-Buckskin and Spurs-NY-(1958)-Hastings Hs-191p-illus-Six Guns 2008-1st ed (bb4,dj) 20.00

SHIRLEY,GLENN-Buckskin and Spurs-NY-(1958)-Hastings Hs-xiv,191p-cl,photos-1st ed (v1,dj) 25.00

SHIRLEY,GLENN-Buckskin Joe Being the Unique and Vivid Memoirs of Edward Jonathan Hoyt...1840 to 1918-Lincoln-(1966)-U of Nebr-(xiv),194p-cl-1st ed (v1,dj) 35.00

SHIRLEY,GLENN-ED.-Buckskin Joe-Lincoln-1966-187p-Six Guns #2016-1st ed (t7,f,dj) 25.00

SHIRLEY,GLENN-Heck Thomas-Phila-(1962)-Chilton-231p-map,photos-1st ed (dd4,wn dj) 25.00

SHIRLEY,GLENN-Henry Starr-NY-(1965)-David McKay-208p-illus-Six Guns #2010-1st ed (cc4,dj) 25.00

SHIRLEY,GLENN-Pawnee Bill-Albuq-1958-UNM-256p-cl,illus-1st ed (v1,dj) 40.00

SHIRLEY,GLENN-Six Gun and Silver Star-Albuq-1955-U of NM Pr-235p-Six Guns #2104-1st ed (cc4,dj) 20.00

SHIRLEY,GLENN-Temple Houston-Norman-(1980)-U of Okla Pr-239p-illus-1st ed (ee4,dj) 20.00

SHIRLEY,GLENN-Toughest of Them All-Albuq-(1953)-U of NM Pr-245p-col pict dj-1st ed (f9,dj fade,chip) 35.00

SHIRLEY,RALPH-Mystery of the Human Double-NY-1965-Univ Bks-8vo-x,189p-1st ed (aa7,dj) 15.00*

SHIRLEY,RODNEY W-Early Printed Maps of the British Isles, a Bibliography 1477 thru 1650-(Lond)-(1980)-Holland Pr-8vo-xxv,188p-drk grn cl,88 plts-Cartographica,#5-rvsd ed (t10) 45.00

SHIRLEY-FOX,JOHN-Angling Adventures of an Artist-NY-1923-8vo-162p-illus,auth (m3,f,sl soil dj) 12.50

SHISHIDO,MISAKO-Folk Toys of Japan-Rutland-(1963)-Japan Publ Trdng Co-71p+(1)p glossary-pattrnd cl,col & b&w illus-1st ed (dd10,f,dj) 35.00

SHISTER,JOSEPH-Readings in Labor Economics & Industrial Relations-Chig-1951-Lippincott-650p (r1,sl soil dj) 30.00

SHIVERS,LOUISE-Here to Get My Baby Out of Jail-Lond-1983-Collins-auth 1st bk-1st Brit ed (bb1,f,dj) 20.00

SHNEIDMAN,EDWIN S-ED.-Essays in Self Destruction-NY-(1967)-Sci Hs-8vo-554p-1st ed (gg5,f,taped rnfrcd dj) 15.00

SHOCK,NATHAN-Classified Bibliography of Gerontology and Geriatrics-Stanford-1951-599p-1st ed (dd3,dj) 125.00

SHOCKLEY,ANN A-Black and White of It-(Iowa City)-1980-Naiad Pr-103p-cl (d1) 10.00

SHOEMAKER,H-Pennsylvania Deer & Their Horns-Reading-1915-120p-photos-scarce (gg3) 75.00

SHOEMAKER,J J-Shoemaker's Battery, Stuart Horse Artillery, Pelham's Battalion-Gaithersburg-nd-108p-port (z10,as new) 20.00

SHOEMAKER,M E-Fresh Water Fishing-NY-1942-8vo-218p-8 col plts-1st ed (m3,f,fray dj) 25.00

SHOEMAKER,MYRON-My Fish Friends-Laceyville-1941-4to-32p-wrps,illus (m3,vf) 35.00

SHOEMAKER,ROBERT-Best in Baseball-1949-Crowell-1st ed (ff2,dj) 17.50

SHOLOMIR,JACK-Beachcombers of the African Jungle-GC-1958-Dbldy-8vo-279p-16p photos-1st ed (cc5,dj chip) 15.00

SHOOK,CHARLES A-True Origin of the Book of Mormon-Cin-(1914)-187p-orig grn cl,plts,ports,illus-v scarce-Flake 7700-1st ed (bb8,sp sun,hng crack,stnd) 60.00

SHOR,ELIZABETH N-Fossil Feud Between E.D. Cope and O.C. Marsh-Hicksville-(1974)-Exposition Pr-xii+340p-blu bds,plts-1st ed (j2,dj) 22.00

SHORE,W TEIGNMOUTH-Dinner Building-Lond-(1929)-Batsford-16mo-180p-orng cl-1st ed (q8) 15.00

SHORT,JOHN T-North Americans of Antiquity-NY-1880-Harper & Bros-544p-cl-scarce-1st ed (m1,sl wn sp) 50.00

SHORTER,DORA S-New Poems-Dublin-1912-Maunsel-cl-1st ed (z8) 75.00

SHORTT,A H-Treasury of Waterfowl-1957-Prentice Hall-folio-142p-36 col plts (bb3,f,dj) 33.00

SHOTEN,KADOKAWA-Pictorial Encyclopedia of the Oriental Arts-NY-1969-Crown-4to-4 vols-brwn cl,685 col & b&w photos (r10) 40.00

SHOTWELL,JOHN B-History of the Schools of Cincinnati-Cin-1902-608p+index,cl-scarce (a1,rprd sp snag) 25.00

SHOWALTER,GRACE I-Music Books of Ruebush & Kieffer, 1866 to 1942, a Bibliography-Richmond-1975-Virginia St Libr-8vo-xii,40p-stiff wrps (x4) 20.00

SHOWALTER,MARY E-Mennonite Community Cookbook-Phila-(1950)-Winston-494p-pict tan cl,drwngs,8 col photos-3rd prtg (q8) 17.50

SHRADER,W A-Fifty Years of Flight-Cleve-(1953)-4to-178p-cl bkd col illus bds,plts,text illus,(this ed, orig prepared for priv circ by Eaton Mfg Co)-1st ed (s2,chip dj) 50.00

SHRADER,WELMAN-Fifty Years of Flight-Cleve-(1953)-Eaton Mfg-4to-178p-cl sp,pict bds,illus-1st ed (dd1) 45.00

SHREVE,BENFORD T-Poems of Elizabeth Shreve Chambers, Sketches of Her Life and Reminiscences-Bayard-1919-138p-cl (d1) 20.00

SHRINER,CHARLES A-Paterson, New Jersey-Paterson-1890-4to-326p-mod buckrm,illus (aa6,rbnd) 90.00

SHRINER,CHARLES A-William Paterson-(Paterson)-1940-96p-cl,port (aa6) 30.00

SHRYOCK,RICHARD-Medicine and Society in America, 1660 to 1860-NY-1960-182p-1st ed (dd3,dj) 40.00

SHRYOCK,RICHARD-Medicine in America, Historical Essays-Balt-1966-346p-1st ed (dd3,dj) 45.00

SHUCK,OSCAR T-California Scrap Book-NY-1869-H H Bancroft-8vo-704p-rbnd in calf wi orig sp labl,illus (ee7,rbnd,pgs brwng) 150.00

SHUCK,OSCAR T-COMP.-California Anthology-SF-1880-A J Leary-471p-orig cl-Cowan p.585-1st ed (kk1,rub) 85.00

SHUCK,OSCAR T-History of the Bench and Bar of California-LA-1901-Comm Prtg Hs-8vo-1151p-1st ed (cc5,rprd hng) 50.00

SHUFELDT,R W-Osteology of Birds-Albany-1909-8vo-381p-wrps,plts (y8,wrps chip,cov spots) 37.00

SHUFELDT,ROBT W-Reports of Explorations & Surveys...Ship Canal between the Atlantic & Pacific Oceans...-Wash-1872-4to-151p-orig cl,20 fldg maps,chrts,11 litho view plts (a3,rebckd) 115.00

SHULDHAM,MOLYNEAUX-DESPATCHES OF...-NY-1913-NHS-330p-vel & cl-ltd to 300c (gg2) 100.00

SHULER,MARJORIE-Passenger to Adventure-NY-1939-Appleton Century-8vo-261p-15 illus-1st ed (ff5,dj sl chip,tn) 25.00

SHULL,MARION-Rainbow Fragments Garden Book of the Iris-NY-1931-Dbldy-317p-cl,col plts (x6) 25.00

SHULMAN,ALIX K-Memoirs of an Ex Prom Queen-NY-1972-Knopf-1st ed (bb1,f,dj) 25.00

SHULMAN,IRVING-Amboy Dukes-GC-1947-Dbldy-auth 1st bk-1st ed (x9,f,dj chip,tn) 27.50

SHULMAN,IRVING-Short End of the Stick...-GC-1959-Dbldy-1st ed (e10,dj wi sm rub spot) 20.00

SHULMAN,MAX-Many Loves of Dobie Gillis-GC-1951-Dbldy-1st ed (b10,sl soil dj) 30.00

SHULMAN,MAX-Rally Round the Flag, Boys-GC-1957-Dbldy-1st ed (b10,dj) 15.00

SHULMAN,MAX-Sleep Till Noon-1950-Dbldy-1st ed (u10,f,dj) 15.00

SHULTZ,EARLE-Offices in the Sky-Indpls-(1959)-Bobbs Merrill-8vo-328p-20 illus-1st ed (ee5,f,dj sl tn,chip) 20.00

SHULTZ,GLADYS D-How Many More Victims?-Phila-(1965)-363p-cl-1st ed (c1,f,sl wn dj) 15.00

SHUMAKER,ARTHUR W-History of Indiana Literature-np-1962-Indiana Hist Scty-x+611p-wrps-1st ed (f2,sl soil cov) 20.00

SHUMAN,EDWIN L-How to Judge a Book-Bost,NY-(1910)-Houghton Mifflin-237p-cl (f1) 17.50

SHUMARD,GEORGE-Billy the Kid-Las Cruces-1969-Cambray-64p-wrps,drwngs,photos-1st ed (ee4) 25.00

SHUMWAY,GEORGE-Conestoga Wagon 1750 to 1850-York-1968-Shumway-3rd ed (j9,dj) 68.00

SHURCLIFF,SIDNEY N-Jungle Islands-NY-1930-Putnam's-4to-xv,(1),errata,298p-g dec blu cl,90 illus(incl col plts),2 maps-1st ed (p8,hng weak,sm dmpstn) 75.00

SHURCLIFF,W A-Bombs at Bikini-NY-1947-Wm H Wise-x+212p-gry cl,photos-1st ed (c2,cov soil,wtrstnd) 25.00

SHUTE,NEVIL-Breaking Wave-NY-1955-1st US ed (t5,sl wn dj) 20.00

SHUTE,NEVIL-In the Wet-Lond-1953-Heinemann-1st ed (ll5,dj) 45.00

SHUTE,NEVIL-Landfall-NY-1940-Morrow-1st ed (e8,f,f dj) 75.00

SHUTE,NEVIL-On the Beach-Lond-(1957)-Heinemann-1st ed (kk5,f,dj) 85.00

SHUTE,NEVIL-On the Beach-Melb,Lond,Tor-(1957)-1st ed (e5,dj) 75.00

SHUTE,NEVIL-On the Beach-NY-1957-Morrow-1st US ed (hh5,dj tn,sl soil) 35.00

SHUTE,NEVIL-Rainbow and the Rose-1958-Morrow-1st US ed (kk6,dj) 20.00

SHUTE,NEVIL-Stephen Morris-NY-1961-1st US ed (s5,f,dj) 25.00

SHUTE,NEVIL-Stephen Morris-NY-1961-Morrow-8vo-x,304p-cl bkd bds-1st US ed (s2,dj) 30.00

SHUTE,NEVIL-Trustee From the Toolroom-NY-1960-Morrow-1st ed (x1,dj) 35.00

SHUTE,NEVIL-Vinland the Good-NY-1946-Morrow-1st ed (f8,f,dj) 60.00

SHUTES,MILTON H-Lincoln & California-Stanford-(1943)-269p-1st ed (c4,f,dj) 30.00

SIBERELL,LLOYD E-Tecumseh His Career-Chillicothe-1944-Ross Cnty Hist Scty-14p-wrps,frntis tip in-ltd to 1000c (w3,f) 20.00

SIBLEY,GEORGE C-Road to Santa Fe-Albuq-1952-UNM-1st ed (b4,chip dj) 37.50

SIBLEY,MARILYN M-Lone Stars and State Gazettes, Texas Newspapers before the Civil War-College Sta-1983-Tex A&M-408p-illus-1st ed (ff8,dj) 30.00

SIBLEY,W G-Story of Freemasonry-Gallipolis-1904-Lion's Paw Club-114p-cl-scarce (b1,sl soil covs) 15.00

SICKLER,JOSEPH-History of Salem County, New Jersey-Salem-(1937)-vii,390,(1)p-cl (aa6) 100.00

SICKLER,JOSEPH-Old Houses of Salem County-(Salem)-1934-(56)p-wrps,illus (aa6) 40.00

SICKLER,JOSEPH-Old Houses of Salem County-Salem-1949-110,(3)p-cl,illus-2nd ed,rvsd & enlgd (aa6) 90.00

SICKLER,JOSEPH-Tea Burning Town-NY-(1950)-xiv,125p-cl,illus (aa6) 50.00

SICKLES,ALICE L-Around the World in St.Paul-Mpls-1945-U of Minn Pr-262p-gry cl,photos (cc3,dj) 20.00

SIDAR,JEAN W-George Hammell Cook-New Brunswick-(1976)-xvi,282p-cl,plts (aa6) 25.00

SIDERS,JAMES B-Off On Pegasus-Dayton-1896-39; 124p-cl (g1) 15.00

SIDGWICK,ELEANOR M-Phantasms of the Living-New Hyde Park-1962-Univ Bks-cl-1st prtg (o8,dj) 20.00

SIDNEY-FRAYER,DONALD-Clark Ashton Smith Bibliography-W Kingston-1978-Grant-1st ed (f3,f,dj) 30.00

SIDRAN,BEN-Black Talk-NY-(1971)-Holt-1st ed (w1,f,dj) 20.00

SIEBEL'S MANUAL FOR BAKERS AND MILLERS-Chig-1924-Siebel Inst of Tech-332p+30p ads-g dec lea-2nd ed,rvsd & enlgd (q8) 40.00

SIEBENHELLER,NORMA-P D James-NY-1981-Ungar-1st ed (s4,f,sl soil dj) 30.00

SIEBER,ROY-African Textiles and Decorative Arts-NY-1972-MOMA-4to-240p-illus wrps,col & b&w illus (r10,f) 45.00

SIEBERT,DICK-How to Improve Your Baseball-1957-Athletic Istitute-trd pbk orig,Motorola promo wi B Feller on frnt cov-1st ed (s8) 11.00

SIEGE OF DETROIT IN 1763-Chig-1958-Donnelley & Sons-frntis,illus,maps-Lakeside Classics (ff4) 20.00

SIEGEL,CHRIS-Early History of Ferndale and Ten Mile Townships-Bellingham-1948-110p-stiff pict wrps,photos-scarce (r8,Chief Sea speech laid in) 25.00

SIEGEL,STANLEY-Poet President of Texas-Austin-1977-Jenkins-176p-cl-1st ed (w3,f,dj) 15.00

SIEGEL,STANLEY-Political History of the Texas Republic, 1836 to 1845-Austin-1956-Univ of Tex-xiv+281p-red cl,map,illus-1st ed (e2,dj) 18.00

SIEMENS,DR W J-Wo De Hombe-Port Orchard-(1972)-oblng 8vo-511p+photos-prntd on tan papr-ltd to 1000c (h7,dj,autg) 40.00

SIERMERING,AUGUST-Hermit of the Cavern-S.A.-1932-Naylor-1st ed (a9,dj) 40.00

SIGERIST,HENRY-American Medicine-NY-1934-316p-1st Engl transl (dd3,sp fade & sl tn) 95.00

SIGERIST,HENRY-Great Doctors-NY-1933-436p-1st Engl transl (dd3) 100.00

SIGERIST,HENRY-Letters of Jean De Carro to Alexandre Marcet, 1794 to 1817-Balt-1950-78p-wrps-1st ed (dd3) 15.00

SIGERIST,HENRY-Man and Medicine-NY-1932-340p-1st Engl transl (dd3) 75.00

SIGERIST,HENRY-On the Sociology of Medicine-NY-1960-397p-1st ed (dd3) 50.00

SIGGERS,PHILIP-Truth About Reno-Reno-1934-64p-stiff pict wrps,plts-1st ed (t7) 20.00

SIGLER,W F-Fishes of Utah-Ann Arbor-1963-8vo-203p-col frontis,col text illus by M Reece (m3) 20.00

SILBERRAD & LYALL-Dutch Bulbs and Gardens-Lond-1909-Black-176p-cl,24 water cols (x6,sl fox) 18.00

SILBERRAD,UNA-Dutch Bulbs and Gardens-Lond-1909-viii,176p+ads-pict g cov,illus (x5) 30.00

SILL,VAN RENSSELAER-American Miracle-NY-1947-Odyssey-8vo-301p-64p photos-1st ed (jj5,dj edgewn,chip) 22.50

SILLAR,F C-Elephants-Lond-1968-8vo-255p-cl,79 plts(13 col) (y8,dj chip) 45.00

SILLITOE,ALAN-Key to the Door-1961-Allen-1st ed (kk6,f,rprd dj) 30.00

SILLOWAY,P M-Summer Birds of Flathead Lake and Additional Notes-Missoula-1901 to 03-U of Mont Series-8vo-83,(2),(293-)308p-cl,21 plts (y8) 23.00

SILSBURY,CAPT JOHN-Journal of the Siege of Gibraltar 1779 to 1783-Gibraltar-1908-143p-grn cl,34 plts & maps-1st ed (b7) 75.00

SILVER,ARTHUR P-Farm Cottage, Camp & Canoe in Maritime Canada-Lond-ca.1900-249p+4p ads,g pict cl,a.e.g.,97 illus (a3) 77.50

SILVER,H-History of New Hampshire Game & Furbearers-Concord-1957-8vo-466p-photos (m3,vf) 11.00

SILVERBERG,ROBERT-Dying Inside-NY-(1972)-Scribner's-1st ed (h3,f,sl fray dj) 15.00

SILVERBERG,ROBERT-ED.-Galactic Dreamers-NY-(1977)-Random-1st ed (h3,f,dj) 10.00

SILVERBERG,ROBERT-ED.-Infinite Jests-Radour-(1974)-Chilton-1st ed (h3,f,dj) 10.00

SILVERBERG,ROBERT-ED.-Other Dimensions-NY-(1973)-Hawthorne-1st ed (h3,f,dj) 10.00

SILVERBERG,ROBERT-Mound Builders of Ancient America-Greenwich-(1968)-NYGS-369p-1st ed (dd4,dj) 25.00

SILVERBERG,ROBERT-New Dimensions 10-NY-(1980)-Harper & Row-1st ed (k3,f,sp fade dj) 10.00

SILVERBERG,ROBERT-World of a Thousand Colors-NY-(1982)-Arbor Hs-1st ed (h3,f,dj) 15.00

SILVERMAN,AL-Joe DiMaggio, the Golden Year 1941-1969-Prentice Hall-1st ed (ff2,f,dj) 40.00

SILVERMAN,DAVID-Pitcairn Island-Cleve-1967-World-1st ed (z2,f,f dj) 35.00

SILVEUS,W A-Texas Grasses, Classification and Description-San Antonio-1933-publ by auth-photos,drwngs-1st ed (a9,hngs rnfrcd) 75.00

SIMAK,CLIFFORD D-Fellowship of the Talisman-NY-(1978)-1st ed (j5,f,dj) 15.00

SIMAK,CLIFFORD-Project Pope-NY-(1981)-Ballantine-1st ed (h3,f,dj) 20.00

SIMAK,CLIFFORD-Special Deliverance-NY-(1982)-Ballantine-1st ed (h3,f,dj) 20.00

SIMAK,CLIFFORD-Visitors-NY-(1980)-Ballantine-1st ed (h3,f,dj) 15.00

SIMENON,GEORGES-Act of Passion-NY-1952-Prentice-1st US ed (e4,f,dj sp sl wn) 20.00

SIMENON,GEORGES-Big Bob-NY-1981-Harcourt-1st US ed (k4,f,dj) 10.00

SIMENON,GEORGES-Disappearance of Odile-NY-1972-Harcourt-1st Amer ed (p4,vf,dj) 30.00

SIMENON,GEORGES-Escape in Vain-NY-1944-Harcourt Brace-1st Amer ed (gg8,dj) 60.00
SIMENON,GEORGES-First Born-NY-1947-Reynal & Hitchcock-1st Amer ed (gg8,f,dj) 35.00
SIMENON,GEORGES-Girl in His Past-NY-1952-Prentice-1st US ed (g4,f,dj) 15.00
SIMENON,GEORGES-Hatter's Phantoms-NY-1976-Harcourt-1st US ed (g4,f,dj) 10.00
SIMENON,GEORGES-Inspector Maigret and the Dead Girl-NY-1955-Dbldy CC-1st US ed (g4,f,dj) 20.00
SIMENON,GEORGES-Inspector Maigret and the Strangled Stripper-NY-1954-Dbldy CC-1st US ed (l4,f,dj) 25.00
SIMENON,GEORGES-Intimate Memoirs-SD,NY,Lond-(1984)-HBJ-1st US ed (bb1,as new in dj) 25.00
SIMENON,GEORGES-Letter to My Mother-Lond-(1976)-H Hamilton-91p-1st ed (g9,dj) 20.00
SIMENON,GEORGES-Maigret & the Informer-1973-Harcourt-1st Amer ed (s10,dj) 10.00
SIMENON,GEORGES-Maigret & the Toy Village-NY-1979-Harcourt-1st Amer ed (p4,f,dj) 22.50
SIMENON,GEORGES-Maigret and the Headless Corpse-NY-1968-Harcourt-1st US ed (j4,f,dj) 10.00
SIMENON,GEORGES-Maigret and the Loner-NY-1975-Harcourt-1st US ed (j4,f,dj) 10.00
SIMENON,GEORGES-Maigret and the Wine Merchant-1971-HBJ-1st Amer ed (t9,f,dj) 20.00
SIMENON,GEORGES-Maigret Keeps a Rendezvous-NY-1941-Harcourt-1st US ed (f4,f,dj fray & sp rprd) 60.00
SIMENON,GEORGES-Maigret to the Rescue-NY-1941-Harcourt-1st US ed (f4,f,rprd dj) 65.00
SIMENON,GEORGES-Maigret Travels South-NY-1940-Harcourt-1st US ed (f4,wn dj) 50.00
SIMENON,GEORGES-Maigret's Christmas-1977-HBJ-1st Amer ed (m9,f,sl tn dj) 15.00
SIMENON,GEORGES-Maigret's Pipe-Lond-1977-Hamilton-1st Brit ed (k4,dj) 20.00
SIMENON,GEORGES-Maigret's Pipe-NY,Lond-(1978)-HBJ-1st US ed (bb1,as new in dj) 10.00
SIMENON,GEORGES-Maigret's Rival-NY,Lond-(1980)-HBJ-1st US ed (bb1,as new in dj) 10.00
SIMENON,GEORGES-Man on the Bench in the Barn-1970-HBW-1st Amer ed (x7,f,dj) 15.00
SIMENON,GEORGES-None of Maigret's Business-NY-1958-Dbldy CC-1st US ed (d4,f,dj) 20.00
SIMENON,GEORGES-Patience of Maigret-NY-1940-Harcourt-1st US ed (f4,f,sl soil dj) 150.00
SIMENON,GEORGES-Rich Man-NY-1971-Harcourt-1st US ed (g4,f,dj) 10.00
SIMENON,GEORGES-Simenon's Paris-NY-1970-Dial-oversized pict cov-iss w/o dj-drwngs by F Franck-1st US ed (h4) 15.00
SIMENON,GEORGES-Teddy Bear-1972-HBJ-1st Amer ed (x7,f,dj) 20.00
SIMENON,GEORGES-Tidal Wave-NY-1954-Dbldy-1st US ed (h4,dj) 15.00
SIMENON,GEORGES-Tropic Moon-1943-HB-1st US ed (x7,sl discol cov,rnfrcd dj) 65.00
SIMENON,GEORGES-Tropic Moon-NY-(1943)-Harcourt-1st US ed (l4,f,dj sp sl wn) 60.00
SIMENON,GEORGES-Venice Train-1974-HBJ-1st Amer ed (x7,f,dj) 17.00
SIMEON,CORNWALL-Stray Notes on Fishing & Natural History-Cambridge,Lond-1860-12mo-263p-illus (m3) 20.00
SIMIC,CHARLES-Return to a Place Lit by a Glass of Milk-NY-(1974)-Brazillier-1st ed (u10,f,f dj) 35.00
SIMMONDS,P L-Sir John Franklin & the Arctic Regions-Buffalo-1852-Derby-396p-illus-1st Amer ed (u8,rbkd,new e.p.,sl fox,soil) 200.00
SIMMONS,ALBERT D-Wing Shots-NY-(1936)-Derrydale-4to-photos by auth-ltd to 950c,nbrd-1st ed (u10,sp lettrng dull) 90.00
SIMMONS,DOUGLAS A-Schweppes-Wash D.C.-(1983)-Acropolis-4to-160p-col photos-1st ed (y4,f,dj) 15.00
SIMMONS,GEORGE F-Birds of the Austin Region-Austin-1925-U.T.-387p-illus-1st ed (a9) 85.00
SIMMONS,LT. COL. T M-Horizon Book of Railway-Lond-(1961)-159,(1)p-cl (m1,dj) 12.50
SIMMONS,MARC-Border Comanches-Seven Spanish Colonial Documents 1785 to 1819-Santa Fe-1967-41p-1st ed (t7) 20.00
SIMMONS,MARC-Little Lion of the Southwest-Chig-(1973)-257p-frntis,photos,map-1st prtg (u7,f,dj) 25.00
SIMMONS,MARC-People of the Sun-Albuq-1979-142p-frntis,photos-1st ed (t7,dj) 10.00
SIMMONS,MARC-Sena Family-Santa Fe-1981-10p+3p,block illus,ltd to 200c-scarce-1st ed in book format (u7,f) 30.00
SIMMONS,MARC-Southwestern Colonial Ironwork-Santa Fe-(1980)-oblng-196p-dbl col,photos-1st ed (u7,f,dj) 25.00
SIMMONS,MARC-Two Southwesterners-(Cerillos)-1968-33p-wrps,photos-1st ed (u7,f) 15.00
SIMMONS,T M-ET AL-Horizon Book of Railways-Lond-1961-160p-1st ed (n4,dj) 24.00
SIMMONS,WILLIAM S-Eyes of the Night-Bost-(1971)-Little,Brown-8vo-169p-wrps-1st prtg (y5,f,pres) 20.00
SIMMS,E-Natural History of British Birds-1983-Dent-367p-16p col plts,137 drwngs-1st ed (bb3,f,dj) 17.00
SIMMS,JEREMIAH H-Last Night and Last Day of John Morgan's Raid-E Liverpool-1963-Wilson Hs-76p+58p ads-wrps,port,illus-rprnt of 1913 ed (v2) 25.00
SIMON,ANDRE-Andre Simon's French Cook Book-1938-Little,Brown-370p-red cl,5 col plts-1st ed (q8) 15.00
SIMON,ANDRE-Drink-Lond-(1948)-Burke-272p-tan cl,33 illus(incl 7 col plts)-1st ed (q8,cov soil) 10.00
SIMON,ANDRE-Great Wines of Germany-(1963)-McGraw-4to-192p+8p col maps,grn cl,col & b&w plts-1st ed (q8,dj) 17.50
SIMON,JAMES R-Yellowstone Fishes-Wyoming-1939-8vo-39p-wrps,illus-1st ed (m3) 22.50
SIMON,N-Last Survivors-NY-1970-8vo-275p-cl,44 col plts (y8,dj fade) 40.00
SIMON,OLIVER-Printing of Today-Lond-1928-P Davies-folio-wht cl,t.e.g.-ltd to 300c,nbrd (r10,sl soil cov) 100.00
SIMON,ROGER-Big Fix-SF-1973-stiff wrps,sftbnd orig-1st ed (r5) 20.00
SIMON,ROGER-Peking Duck-NY-1979-1st ed (r5,f,dj) 15.00
SIMONDS,JOHN O-Landscape Architecture-NY,Tor,Lond-(1961)-244p-photos,diagrams (j10) 36.00
SIMONDS,JOHN O-Landscape Architecture-NY-(1961)-McGraw Hill-4to-244p-gry cl,photos,sketches (r10,sl wn dj) 15.00
SIMONDS,OSSIAN C-Landscape Gardening-NY-1920-Macmillan-sm 4to-x,338p-cl,photos,plans-1st ed (cc10) 90.00
SIMONDS,WILLIAM A-Henry Ford, His Life, His Work, His Genius-Indpls-1943-Bobs,Merrill-365p-cl-1st ed (z7,scuff) 30.00
SIMONOV,KONSTANTIN-Living and the Dead-NY-1960-DD-1st ed (x1,f,dj) 30.00

SIMONS,ALBERT-Charleston-NY-1927-Amer Inst of Arch-4to-grn cl,photos-Octagon Libr of Early Amer Arch,Vol.I (r10) 75.00

SIMPSON,CAPT-Report and Map of Wagon Road Routes in Utah Territory-Wash-1859-GPO/Sen Doc.40-84p-buckrm,fldg maps-Howes S499 (cc4,rbnd,few maps split) 200.00

SIMPSON,CHARLES-Blazing Forest Trails-Caldwell-1967-Caxton-8vo-384p-151 photos-1st ed (gg5,dj sl tn,chip) 20.00

SIMPSON,COLIN-Lusitania-Bost-(1972)-Little Brown-303p-1st Amer ed (ee8,dj) 15.00

SIMPSON,E M-Bluegrass Houses & Their Traditions-Lexington-1932-illus (h10) 85.00

SIMPSON,GEORGE G-Horses-NY-1951-Oxford U Pr-1st ed (j9,dj) 45.00

SIMPSON,GEORGE-Fur Trade and Empire-Cambridge-1968-Belknap Pr-lxii,370p-frntis map-rvsd ed (bb7,sl rub dj) 65.00*

SIMPSON,GEORGE-Narr of Voyage to Calif Ports in 1841,42...-SF-1930-Thos C Russell-232p-1/2 linen & bds,papr sp labl,facs,2 ports,fldg map-ltd to 250c (p8,dj sp fade) 325.00

SIMPSON,GEORGE-Narrative of a Journey Round the World, During the Years 1841 and 1842-Lond-1847-Henry Colburn-8vo-2 vols-orig cl,port,fldg map-1st ed (u3,rub,1 vol rebkd,sl fox) 585.00

SIMPSON,HAZEL B-ED.-Under Four Flags-Woodbury-(1965)-4to-xi,125p-cl,illus (aa6) 30.00

SIMPSON,JOHN L-Holiday in Wartime and Other Stories-np-(1956)-Lawton Kennedy-lg 8vo-(6),36p-cl,frntis-1st ed (m4) 10.00

SIMPSON,R C-Dry Fly Fishing for Beginners-Lond-1929-12mo-85p-illus (m3,fade sp) 15.00

SIMS,E H-American Aces in Great Fighter Battles of World War II-NY-(1958)-8vo-xxvi,256p-cl,illus t.p.,plts (s2,dj) 30.00

SIMS,E H-Fighter Tactics and Strategy 1914 to 1970-NY-(1976)-8vo-xviii,266p-cl,16p plts-1st ed (s2,dj) 25.00

SIMS,E H-Greatest Fighter Missions of the Top Navy and Marine Aces of World War II-NY-(1962)-8vo-xii,250p-cl,illus-1st ed (s2,dj) 25.00

SIMS,GEORGE-Sand Dollar-Lond-1969-Gollancz-1st ed (r4,dj) 25.00

SINCLAIR,A R-African Buffalo-1977-U of Chig-355p-41 photos-1st ed (bb3,f,dj) 20.00

SINCLAIR,A T-Tattoing of the North American Indians-39p-rprntd frm Amer Anthro of 1909-wrps (h7) 30.00

SINCLAIR,ANDREW-Facts in the Case of Edgar Allan Poe-NY-1980-Holt-1st US ed (h4,as new in dj) 12.50

SINCLAIR,ANGUS-Development of the Locomotive Engine-Cambridge-1970-708p-1st publ 1907-1st ed thus (n4,f,dj) 26.00

SINCLAIR,DONALD A-Civil War and New Jersey. A Bibliography-New Brunswick-(1968)-186p-cl (aa6) 35.00

SINCLAIR,J-Instructions for Collecting and Preserving Valuable Lepidoptera-1917-priv publ-112p-wrps,53 illus (bb3) 25.00

SINCLAIR,LISTER-Play on Words-Tor-1948-J M Dent-8vo-297p-dec e.p.-1st ed (cc7,dj) 25.00*

SINCLAIR,UPTON-100% the Story of a Patriot-Pasadena-1920-auth-1st ed (w5,f,sl wn dj) 50.00

SINCLAIR,UPTON-American Outpost-Girard-(1948)-Haldeman Julius-127p-wrps-Gottesman A1377-Big Blue Bk B-706-2nd ed (f1) 15.00

SINCLAIR,UPTON-Another Pamela-NY-1950-1st ed (l5,dj) 10.00

SINCLAIR,UPTON-Enemy Had it Too-NY-1950-1st ed (l5,sl soil dj) 20.00

SINCLAIR,UPTON-Enemy Had It Too-NY-1950-Viking-127p-cl-Gottesmann A2078-1st ed (f1,dj) 17.50

SINCLAIR,UPTON-Giant's Strength-Girard-(1948)-Haldeman-Julius-52p+4p ads-wrps-Big Blu Bk B-666-Gottesman A2059 (g1) 20.00

SINCLAIR,UPTON-Hell-Pasadena-1923-Auth-wrps-1st ed (v5) 35.00

SINCLAIR,UPTON-I, Governor of California, and How I Ended Poverty-LA-1933-Auth-wrps-1st ed (v5,f) 25.00

SINCLAIR,UPTON-Jungle-NY-1906-Jungle Publ-socialist seal on frnt bd-1st ed (w5,sl wn & rub) 50.00

SINCLAIR,UPTON-Money Changers-NY-1908-Dodge-1st ed (w5,f) 35.00

SINCLAIR,UPTON-No Pasaran-Girard-nd-Haldeman Julius-94p-wrps (f1) 17.50

SINCLAIR,UPTON-One Clear Call-NY-1948-Viking-1st ed (h3,sl chip dj) 20.00

SINCLAIR,UPTON-Singing Jailbirds-Pasadena-1924-auth-wrps-1st ed (w5) 45.00

SINCLAIR,UPTON-Wide is the Gate-1943-Viking-1st ed (kk6,dj) 25.00

SINCLAIR-STEVENSON,CHRISTOPHER-Inglorious Rebellion-NY-1972-212p-maps,illus-1st Amer ed (b7,f,dj) 35.00

SINGER,CHARLES-From Magic to Science-Lond-1928-253p-illus-1st ed (dd3) 100.00

SINGER,CHARLES-Greek Biology & Medicine-Oxford-1922-128p-1st ed (dd3) 50.00

SINGER,CHARLES-Short History of Medicine-NY-1928-368p-1st ed (dd3) 50.00

SINGER,DOROTHEA-Catalogue of Latin and Vernacular Alchemical Manuscripts in Great Britain and Ireland...-Brussels-1928 to 31-1179p-wrps-1st ed (dd3) 150.00

SINGER,DOROTHEA-Selections from the Works of Ambroise Pare with Short Biographical...-Lond-1924-246p-1st ed (dd3) 75.00

SINGER,HOWARD-Wake Me When It's Over-NY-(1959)-Putnam's-auth 1st bk-1st ed (bb1,dj) 15.00

SINGER,ISAAC B-Alone in the Wild Forest-NY-1971-FS&G-illus-Ariel Bk-1st ed (y1,f,dj) 35.00

SINGER,ISAAC B-An Isaac Bashevis Singer Reader-NY-(1971)-FS&G-1st ed (b5,f,dj) 30.00

SINGER,ISAAC B-Crown of Feathers-NY-(1973)-FSG-1st ed (ee2,f,dj) 35.00

SINGER,ISAAC B-Day of Pleasure-Lond-(1980)-Julia McRae-1st Brit ed (f3,f,dj) 20.00

SINGER,ISAAC B-Day of Pleasure-NY-1969-FS&G-photos-1st ed (y1,dj) 50.00

SINGER,ISAAC B-Friend of Kafka-NY-(1970)-FS&G-1st ed (b5,f,dj) 35.00

SINGER,ISAAC B-Isaac Bashevis Singer on Literature & Life-Tucson-1979-U of Ariz-wrps-1st ed (y1,f) 15.00

SINGER,ISAAC B-Manor-NY-1967-FS&G-1st ed (z2,f,dj) 50.00

SINGER,ISAAC B-Naftali the Storyteller and His Horse, Sus-NY-1976-FS&G-illus-1st ed (y1,f,f dj) 50.00

SINGER,ISAAC B-Nobel Lecture-(1979)-Farrar-1st ed (r9,f,dj) 15.00

SINGER,ISAAC B-Nobel Lecture-NY-(1979)-FS&G-bilingual ed-1st ed (bb1,as new in dj) 10.00

SINGER,ISAAC B-Passions-NY-(1975)-Farrar,Straus-1st ed (f3,f,sl tn dj) 20.00

SINGER,ISAAC B-Power of Light-NY-(1980)-FS&G-sm 4to-87p-bds,col illus-1st ed (nn10,f,f dj) 20.00

SINGER,ISAAC B-Satan in Goray-NY-1955-Noonday-1st ed (v5,f,dj) 60.00

SINGER,ISAAC B-Seance-NY-1968-FS&G-1st ed (y1,f,f dj) 40.00

SINGER,ISAAC B-Short Friday-NY-1964-FS&G-1st ed (y1,sl soil dj,autg) 75.00

SINGER,ISAAC B-Spinoza of Market Street-NY-1961-Jewish Publ Soc-1st ed (y1,sl fade dj) 50.00

SINGER,ISAAC B-When Shlemiel Went to Warsaw-NY-1968-FS&G-illus-1st ed (y1,f,dj) 50.00

SINGER,LOREN-Parallax View-1970-Dbldy-1st ed (s10,f,dj) 20.00

SINGER,R-Middle Stone Age at Klasies River Mouth in South Africa-1982-U of Chig-4to-234p-72 plts-1st ed (bb3,f,dj) 18.00

SINGH,A-Tiger Haven-1973-Harper Row-239p-photos-1st US ed (bb3,f,dj) 25.00

SINGH,KHUSHWANT-Sikhs-Lond-(1953)-Allen & Unwin-8vo-215p-14p illus-1st Brit ed (dd5,dj) 25.00

SINGH,MADANJEET-Ajanta-NY-1965-Macmillan-quarto-cl,82 col plts,22 figs-1st ed (l8,f,dj) 25.00

SINGLETON,C C-Railways of Australia-Sydney-1963-160p-1st ed (n4,f,dj) 22.00

SINGLETON,ESTHER-Switzerland as Described by Great Writers-NY-1908-346p-42 plts (q10) 20.00

SINKANKAS,JOHN-Gem Cutting-NY-1962-Van Nostrand Reinhold-xix,297p-blue cl,g,col frntis,illus-2nd ed (u5,f,dj chip) 25.00

SINNOTT,E W-Meetinghouse & Church in Early New England-NY-1963-221 illus-1st ed (h10,dj) 45.00

SIPLE,PAUL-Boy Scout with Byrd-NY-1931-Putnam's-viii,165p+ads-photos-1st ed (ll8) 20.00

SIPLEY,LOUIS W-Photography's Great Inventors-Phila-(1965)-Amer Mus of Photog-8vo-red cl-1st ed (y3,f) 45.00

SIRINGO,CHARLES A-Cowboy Detective-Chig-1912-W B Conkey-519p-dec cl,photos-scarce-1st ed (v1,sl wn bndg) 250.00

SIRINGO,CHARLES A-Lone Star Cowboy-Santa Fe-1919-auth-292p-red cl,illus,photos-Howes S518-rare-1st ed (z1,cov gilt fade) 350.00

SIRINGO,CHARLES A-Riata and Spurs-Bost-1927-276p-brwn cl,plts,suppressed 1st ed-rare (z1) 175.00

SIRINGO,CHARLES A-Riata and Spurs-Bost-1927-Houghton Mifflin-8vo-xiv+260p-cl,b&w photos-revsd ed (z4,hng rprd,cov wn,pgs stnd) 30.00

SIRINGO,CHARLES A-Texas Cow Boy-Chig-(1888)-Rand,McNally-347p+ads-pict wrps,frntis,one plt,ex-rare-Globe Libr ed(newsstand ed)-Globe Libr ed (z1,sl chip,hng mended) 275.00

SIRINGO,CHARLES-Texas Cowboy-Chig-(1886)-Rand McNally-347p-orig pict cl,col frntis,illus-rare-3rd prtg (f9,hngs rnfrcd) 850.00

SISKIND,AARON-Aaron Siskind Photographs-NY-1959-Horizon-tall 4to-cl-1st ed (y3,dj creased,sl chip) 125.00

SISKIND,AARON-Places-NY-1976-Light/Farrar-1st ed (w5,f,f dj) 45.00

SISLER,GEORGE-Sisler On Baseball-1954-McKay-1st ed (s8,dj) 22.50

SISSON,EVA B-Story of Tenafly-(Tenafly)-(1939)-74,(12)p-bds,illus (aa6) 30.00

SISSON,SEPTIMUS-Text Book of Veterinary Anatomy-Phila,Lond-1910-Sanders-826p-1/2 lea-1st ed (j9) 85.00

SITGREAVES,LORENZO-Report of an Expedition Down Zuni and Colorado Rivers-Wash-1853-Armstrong-198p-3/4 lea & mrbld bds,lg fldg map,Sen. Exec. Doc.59-rare-Howes S521-1st ed (z1,sp wn,hngs weak) 650.00

SITTE,C-Art of Building Cities-NY-1945-sq 4to-1st ed (h10,dj fade) 75.00

SITWELL,EDITH-Canticle of the Rose-NY-(1949)-Vanguard-gold & rose stmpd blk bds-1st Amer ed (bb2,f,dj sl chip) 45.00

SITWELL,EDITH-COMP.-Book of Flowers-Lond-1952-MacMillan-x,314p-1st ed (mm4,f,dj) 25.00

SITWELL,EDITH-Crusade of the Rose-NY-(1949)-Vanguard-1st ed (cc2,f,sl chip dj) 45.00

SITWELL,EDITH-English Eccentrics-Lond-(1933)-Faber-8vo-332p-16 plts-1st ed (w6,uncut,part unopened) 65.00

SITWELL,EDITH-Facade and Other Poems 1920 to 1935-Lond-(1950)-12mo-1st ed thus (m4,sp fade) 10.00

SITWELL,EDITH-Gardeners and Astronomers-Lond-1953-MacMillan-45p-1st ed (mm4,f,dj) 30.00

SITWELL,EDITH-Old Coast Customs-Bost-1929-Houghton Mifflin-sm oct-gold bds bckd in blk cl-1st Amer ed (dd2) 30.00

SITWELL,EDITH-Queens and the Hive-Bost-1962-Little,Brown-1st ed (x9,dj soil) 12.50

SITWELL,EDITH-Rustic Elegies-Lond-1927-Duckworth-1st ed (m4) 9.50

SITWELL,EDITH-Song of the Cold-NY-(1948)-Vanguard-1st ed (cc2,f,sl chip dj) 35.00

SITWELL,GEORGE-On Making of Gardens-1949-Dropmore Pr-xvi,113p-ltd to 100c(out of 1000)bnd in grn niger mor(#101-1000 bnd in buckram),nbrd,two autg,illus,J Piper (j10) 250.00

SITWELL,OSBERT-Escape with Me, An Oriental Sketch Book-NY-1940-Harrison Hilton-8vo-322p-16 illus-1st US ed (ff5,f,sl tn dj) 35.00

SITWELL,OSBERT-Noble Essences-Bost-1950-Atlanta/Little,Brown-1st US ed (hh5,edgewn dj) 10.00

SITWELL,OSBERT-Scarlet Tree-Lond-1946-Macmillan-1st Brit ed (hh5,dj) 20.00

SITWELL,SACHEVERALL-Old Fashioned Flowers-Lond-1939-Country Life-sm 4to-193p-cl,col dec t.p.,col frntis+11 col plts,pict dj-1st ed (mm4,f,dj) 60.00

SITWELL,SACHEVERELL-Hunters and the Hunted-NY-1948-Macmillan-1st US ed (hh5,dj) 12.50

SITWELL,SACHEVERELL-Poltergeists-NY-(1959)-Univ Bks-1st ed (a5,dj) 20.00

SITWELL,SACHEVERELL-Poltergeists-NY-(1959)-Univ Bks-8vo-418p-illus-1st ed (gg5,f,dj) 25.00

SIZER,THEODORE-Works of Colonel John Trumbull-New Haven-1951-Yale U Pr-4to-117p-blk cl,46 illus-2nd prtg (r10,dj tn & sl soil) 45.00

SJOMAN,VILGOT-I Was Curious, the Diary of the Making of a Film-NY-(1968,67)-Grove-8vo-217p-16p photos-1st US ed (gg5,f,f dj) 12.50

SJOWALL,M-Murder at the Savoy-1971-Pantheon-1st Amer ed (x7,f,dj) 33.00

SJOWALL,MAJ-Man Who Went Up in Smoke-NY-1969-Pantheon-1st US ed (g4,dj) 15.00

SJOWALL,MAJ-Man Who Went Up in Smoke-NY-1969-Pantheon-1st US ed (w5,sl tn dj) 25.00

SJOWALL,MAJ-Murder at the Savoy-1971-Pantheon-1st ed (m9,vf,dj) 15.00

SJOWALL,MAJ-Roseanna-1967-Pantheon-1st ed (s10,sp rub dj) 50.00

SKAGGS,WILLIAM H-Southern Oligarchy-NY-1924-Devin Adair Co-xiv+472p+ads-maroon cl-1st ed (b2) 40.00

SKALLEY,MICHAEL-Ferry Story-(Seattle)-(1983)-152p-wrps,illus-1st ed (c7) 30.00

SKARSTEN,M O-George Drouillard-Glendale-1964-356p-illus,fldg map-1st ed (h7,f) 65.00

SKELLEY,LELOIS D-Modern Fine Glass-GC-1942-144p-97 photos (cc8,dj) 45.00

SKELLY,ALAN R-Victorian Army at Home-Montreal-1977-366p-1st ed (b7,f,dj) 20.00

SKELTON,J-Plea for the Botanic Practice of Medicine-1853-Watson-278p (bb3,cov wn) 80.00

SKELTON,PETER-ED.-Animals All-NY-(1956)-John Day-8vo-253p-1st US ed (dd5,dj) 12.50

SKELTON,R A-ET AL-Vinland Map and the Tartar Relation-New Haven-1965-Yale U Pr-1st ed (v4,as new in dj) 35.00

SKELTON,R A-Explorers' Maps: Chapters in the Cartographic Record of Geographical Discovery-Lond-1970-Spring Bks-Basic Geog Libr No.232 (v4,as new) 50.00

SKENE,JAMES H-With Lord Stratford in the Crimean War-Lond-1883-352p-grn cl-1st ed (b7,f,pg unopened) 150.00

SKIFF,FREDERICK W-Landmarks and Literature-Portland-1937-8vo-318p-photos,illus (m3,vf) 22.50

SKILLINGS,HELEN W-We're Standing on Iron!-Duluth-1972-69p-cl (j1,f,dj,autg) 15.00

SKINNER,A M-Little Child's Book of Stories-NY-1922-Duffield-sm 4to-258p-orng cl wi pict pasteon,8 col plts,J W Smith-1st ed (r3) 120.00

SKINNER,ALANSON-Preliminary Report of the Archaeological Survey of the State of New Jersey-Trenton-1913-Geo Survey of NJ,Bull.9-94p-bds,fldg map (aa6) 35.00

SKINNER,CONSTANCE-Adventurers of Oregon-1920-Yale-290p-dec cov,illus-1st ed (r8) 30.00

SKINNER,J S-Dog and the Sportsman-Phila-1845-Lea & Blanchard-illus-1st ed (u2,sl fox) 95.00

SKINNER,M P-Birds of Yellowstone Natl Park-Syracuse-1925-8vo-192p-2 fldg maps,4 col plts,photos (y8) 18.50

SKINNER,M P-Guide to Winter Birds of North Carolina Sandhills-Albany-1928-8vo-301p-cl,12 col plts,col chrt,30 b&w plts (y8) 45.00

SKOLFIELD,W K-Century of Electric Fans-Bridgeport-(1957)-Gen Elect Co-8vo-152p-drwngs,photos-1st ed (oo8,f,dj) 45.00

SKUES,G E M-Angling Letters of ...-Lond-1956-8vo-153p-photos frontis-1st ed (m3,vf,dj) 55.00

SKUES,G E M-Nymph Fishing for Chalk Stream Trout-Lond-1939-Tall 8vo-136p-photos-1st ed (m3) 65.00

SKUTCH,A F-Birds of Tropical American-1983-U of Tex-305p-photos,illus-1st ed (bb3,f,dj) 30.00

SKUTCH,A F-Life of the Hummingbird-NY-1973-lg 8vo-95p-cl(emboss stamp),col illus (y8,dj) 25.00

SKUTCH,A F-Parent Birds and Their Young-Austin-1976-4to-503p-cl,plts (y8,dj) 45.00

SKVORECKY,JOSEF-Bass Saxophone-NY-1979-1st ed (g5,as new in dj) 25.00

SKVORECKY,JOSEF-Swell Season-(Tor)-(1982)-Dennys-1st ed (bb1,as new in dj) 20.00

SLACK,J H-Practical Trout Culture-NY-1872-12mo-143p-illus (m3) 17.50

SLADE,DANIEL D-Evolution of Horticulture in New England-NY-1895-Putnam-180p-3/4 lea-scarce (x6,sl fox) 48.00

SLADEK,JOHN-Black Aura-NY-1979-Walker-1st US ed (h4,dj) 12.50

SLADEK,JOHN-Invisible Green-NY-1979-Walker-1st US ed (e4,as new in dj) 15.00

SLATER,J H-Illustrated Sporting Books-Lond-1899-12mo-203p (m3) 125.00

SLATER,J HERBERT-How to Collect Books-Lond-1905-Geo Bell-brwn cl stmpd in gilt & blk,t.e.g.-1st ed (w5,ex-libr) 35.00

SLAUGHTER,CHARLES E-Golden Tusk-NY-1931-Knopf-orig cl,illus by F H Horvath-1st ed (aa9,sp fade) 15.00

SLAUSON,H W-Everyman's Guide to Motor Efficiency-NY-1920-288,(12)p-flex cl (l1,fade cov,sl soil,penclng) 15.00

SLAVIN,NEAL-When Two or More are Gathered Together-NY-1976-FS&G-unpgd-64 photos-1st prtg (cc9,as new in dj) 35.00

SLAVITT,DAVID-Cold Comfort-NY-(1980)-Methuen-1st ed (e3,f,dj) 20.00

SLAVITT,DAVID-Rachelle or Virtue Rewarded-NY-(1966)-Delacorte-auth 1st bk-1st ed (e3,f,sl soil dj) 30.00

SLAYMAKER,S R-Simplified Fly Fishing-NY-1969-8vo-142p-illus,N Smith (m3,vf,dj) 10.00

SLEEPER,M B-Radio Hook Ups-1920-71p-86 illus-1st ed (h6) 20.00

SLEMONS,J MORRIS-John Whitridge Williams-Balt-1935-John Hopkins Pr-xiv+109p-cl sp-1st ed (c2) 15.00

SLESAR,HENRY-Enter Murderers-NY-1960-Random-1st ed (f4,dj) 15.00

SLESSER,M-Andes are Prickly-Lond-1966-254p-31 photos,4 maps (o10,f,dj chip) 30.00

SLESSER,MALCOM-Red Peak-NY-1964-256p-20 plts-1st US ed (p10,f,dj) 15.00

SLOAN,J A-Reminiscences of the Guilford Grays-Wendell-1978-130p-rprnt of 1883 ed (z10,f) 25.00

SLOAN,SAMUEL-Sloan's Constructive Architecture-Phila-1866-lg 4to-148p-cl,lea sp labl,66 litho plts(incl col frntis) (o4,rbnd) 700.00

SLOANE,ERIC-Eric Sloane's Americana-NY-1956-Funk & Wagnalls-8vo-3 vols-5th prtg (r10,dj,tattrd box) 20.00

SLOANE,ERIC-For Spacious Skies-NY-1978-Crowell-79p text-beige cl,16 col plts,illus-1st ed (r10,sl tn dj) 30.00

SLOANE,T O'CONOR-Electric Toy Making for Amateurs-NY-1897-Norman W Henry & Co-140p-cl-illus (h1,spot cov & few pgs) 15.00

SLOANE,T O'CONOR-Electric Toy Making-1897-138p-53 illus-2nd ed (h6) 40.00

SLOANE,T O'CONOR-Standard Electrical Dictionary-NY-1892-Norman W Henley-624p-blu cl,350 text illus-1st ed (g2) 35.00

SLOANE,WILLIAM-Life of Napoleon Bonaparte-NY-1909-4 vols-dec red cl,plts (b7) 100.00

SLOBODIN,RICHARD W H R-Rivers-NY-1978-Columbia U Pr-8vo-295p-yel cl-1st ed (ll1,as new in dj) 17.50

SLOCUM,EUGENE E-Ye Gods & Little Fishes-NY-1927-8vo-312p-1st ed (m3) 15.00

SLOCUM,JOHN J-Bibliograpy of James Joyce-1953-Yale U Pr-illus-1st ed (hh10,dj sp sun,sl rub) 125.00

SLOSSON,ANNIE T-Fishin' Jimmy-NY-1889-12mo-53p-illus (m3) 10.00

SLOSSON,ELVENIA-Pioneer American Gardening-NY-1951-xvi,306p-photos (o2,sl rub dj) 15.00

SLUD,PAUL-Birds of Costa Rica-NY-1964-AMNH,Bull.128-420p-wrps,map (b9,f) 50.00

SLUDER,DANNY-ED.-Whitesboro Centennial History, 1873 to 1973-Gainesville-1973-Gainesville Pr-97p-wrps,photos-1st ed (w3,vf) 20.00

SLUMAN,NORMA-Poundmaker-Tor-1967-Ryerson Pr-8vo-viii,301p-frntis-1st ed (aa7,sl rub dj) 15.00*

SMAIL,J L-With Shield and Assegai-Cape Town-1969-172p-photos-1st ed (jj2,f,dj) 100.00

SMALL,A J-Death Maker-1926-Doran-scarce in dj-1st ed (x7,chip dj) 75.00

SMALL,A J-Man They Couldn't Arrest-1925-Doran-1st ed (x7,dj rnfrcd,sl chip) 85.00

SMALL,A-Birds of California-1974-Winchester-310p-photos (bb3,f,dj) 30.00

SMALL,ANNE-Masters of Decorative Bird Carving-Tulsa-1981-4to-147p-photos (m3,f,dj) 20.00

SMALL,ANNE-Masters of Decorative Bird Carving-Tulsa-1981-Winchester Pr-4to-147p-16p col illus-1st ed (gg5,tape rprd dj,pres) 25.00

SMALL,CHARLES S-Rails to the Rising Sun-San Marino-1965-135p-1st ed (n4,f,dj) 28.00

SMALL,JOE A-ED.-Best of the True West-NY-(1964)-Messner-317p-illus-1st ed (ee4,dj) 20.00

SMALL,JOHN K-Flora of Lancaster County-NY-1913-Auth-336p-cl-scarce (x6) 65.00

SMALLWOOD,J R-New Newfoundland-NY-1931-MacMillan-8vo-xvi,277p-g brwn cl,frntis,48 illus-1st ed (aa7,sl wn) 20.00*

SMALLZREID,KATHLEEN-More Than You Promise-NY-1942-Harper-1st ed (h9,dj,2 autg) 65.00

SMALLZRIED,KATHLEEN ANN-Everlasting Pleasure-NY-(1956)-Appleton,Century,Crofts-344p-illus (m6) 30.00

SMART,JAMES H-Manual of Free Gymnastic and Dumb-Bell Exercises-Cin,NY-(1864)-Van Antwerp,Bragg-64p-pict bds (k1) 50.00

SMART,T H-Pre Columbian Historical Treasures-Lond-1906-Norroena-4to-1st ed (b4,wn cov,sl fox) 125.00

SMEDLEY,HAROLD-Accuracy Fly Casting-Chig-1949-12mo-128p-illus,photos-1st ed (m3,f) 17.50

SMEDLEY,HAROLD-Fly Patterns & Their Origins-Muskegon-1943-12mo-114p-illus,errata slip-scarce-1st ed (m3) 85.00

SMEETON,GEORGE-Doings in London-Lond-1828-gilt crimson mor,t.e.g.,extra illus wi 4 hand col engrvngs,illus by R & G Cruikshank-1st ed (y7,sl stnd e.p.) 325.00

SMELSER,MARSHALL-Life That Ruth Built-1975-Quadrangle-photos-1st ed (s8,f,dj) 45.00

SMILES,SAMUEL-Robert Dick Baker of Thurso-Lond-1878-J Murray-8vo-xxii,444p-frntis+53 illus-1st ed (ff9,unopened) 45.00*

SMILEY,F J-Weeds of California and Methods of Control-Sacramento-1922-Dept of Agri,State of Cal-360p-buckram bds,illus,plts,Monthly Bulletin (m6) 20.00

SMILEY,JAMES B-ED.-Household Cook Book-Chig-(1902)-Frederick J Drake-656p-wht pict bds,illus (u6,soil,wn,loose joints) 35.00

SMILLIE,WILSON-Public Health Administration in the United States-NY-1935-458p-1st ed (dd3) 50.00

SMILLIE,WILSON-Public Health, Its Promise for the Future: a Chronicle...in the U.S., 1607 to 1914-NY-1955-501p-1st ed (dd3) 75.00

SMITH,A CROXTON-British Dogs-Lond-1946-Brit in Pict Ser (f10,dj) 28.00

SMITH,A D-Through Unknown African Countries-1897-Arnold-471p-lea sp,mrbld bds,photos,6 fldg maps-1st ed (bb3,rbkd,sl chip pgs) 250.00

SMITH,A M-On To Alaska with Buchanan-LA-1937-8vo-124p-photos (m3) 15.00

SMITH,A P R-Salmon Secrets Shared-Lond-1950-8vo-79p-illus,photos (m3) 25.00

SMITH,AARON-Atrocities of the Pirates...-NY-1824-Robt Lowry-(3),6-158p-orig prtd bds-scarce-Sabin 82298-1st Amer ed (o4,rebckd,sl rub,uncut) 650.00

SMITH,ALBERT-Pottle of Strawberries to Beguile a Short Journey of a Long Half Hour-Lond-1848-D Bogue-12mo-62p-orig pict wrps,frntis,illus-scarce-1st ed (ll2) 40.00

SMITH,ALEXANDER H-Mushroom Hunter's Field Guide-Ann Arbor-1971-U of Mich Pr-264p-cl,col photos (z7) 17.50

SMITH,ALEXANDER-Books and Gardens-Herrin-1946-Trovillion-xiv,33p-cl-ltd to 807c,nbrd (x6,as new) 20.00

SMITH,ALICE R H-Dwelling Houses of Charleston, South Carolina-Phila-1917-Lipincott-lg 8vo-386p-orig dec tan cl,t.e.g.,frntis,128 illus-ltd 1st ed (z5,sp fade,cov soil) 80.00

SMITH,ALICE U-Trees in a Winter Landscape-NY-(1969)-tall 8vo-x,207p-1st ed (j10,dj) 21.00

SMITH,ALSON J-Brother Van-NY-1948-240p-frntis,map e.p.-Six Guns #2042-1st ed (t7) 27.50

SMITH,ALSON J-Men Against the Mountains-NY-(1965)-320p-illus-1st ed (d7,dj) 65.00

SMITH,ALSON J-Men Against the Mountains-NY-(1965)-320p-photos-1st ed (t7,dj) 40.00

SMITH,ALSON J-View of the Spree-NY-(1962)-John Day-8vo-305p-10 illus-1st ed (dd5,dj) 15.00

SMITH,BERNARD-European Vision and the South Pacific. 1768 to 1850-Oxford-1960-Oxford U Pr-xviii,287p+plts-blu cl,g sp titles,171 plts (nn1,wn dj) 125.00

SMITH,BETTY-Tree Grows in Brooklyn-NY,Lond-(1943)-1st ed (l5,dj) 30.00

SMITH,BRADLEY-Horse in the West-NY-1969-World-4to-1st prtg (j9,dj wn) 45.00

SMITH,BRADLEY-Japan a History in Art-1964-GC-4to-1st ed (oo4,dj) 40.00

SMITH,BRADLEY-Japan-NY-(1964)-Dbldy-sm folio-295p-cl,col illus-1st prtg (w10,dj) 24.00

SMITH,BRADLEY-Mexico-GC-(1968)-Dbldy-lg qto-cl,col illus-1st ed (o8,dj) 27.50

SMITH,C ALPHONSO-O. Henry Biography-NY-1916-Dbldy-258p-1st ed (a9) 35.00

SMITH,C W-Country Music-NY-(1975)-FS&G-1st ed (b10,as new in dj) 35.00

SMITH,C W-Thin Men of Haddam-NY-1973-Grossman Publ-auth 1st bk-1st ed (b10,dj) 75.00

SMITH,CAPT.EDGAR C-Short History of Naval and Marine Engineering-Cambridge-1937-Univ Pr-xx+376p-red cl,16 plts,46 text figs (d2,sl sunned sp) 60.00

SMITH,CATHARINE C-In Defense of Magic-Lond-1931-Rider & Co-cl-1st ed (o8) 22.50

SMITH,CHARLES M-Reverend Randollph & the Avenging Angel-1977-Putnam-1st ed (s10,dj) 20.00

SMITH,CHARLES W-Check List of Books and Pamphlets Relating to the History of the Pacific Northwest...-Olympia-1909-E L Boardman-191p-rbnd in cl-1st ed (v1,rbnd) 65.00

SMITH,CLARK A-Other Dimensions-Sauk City-1970-ltd to 3144c-1st ed (k5,as new in dj) 45.00

SMITH,CLARK A-Tales of Science and Sorcery-Sauk City-1964-Arkham Hs-ltd to 2482c-1st ed (l7,f,dj) 95.00

SMITH,CLYDE-Adirondacks-NY-1976-Viking-4to-photos-1st ed (dd6,dj) 25.00

SMITH,CORNELIUS C,JR.-Emilio Kosterlitzky, Eagle of Sonora and the Southwest Border-Glendale-1970-344p-illus,plain dj-1st ed (c4,f,dj) 50.00

SMITH,CORNELIUS C,JR.-Emilio Kosterlitzky-Glendale-1970-A H Clark Co-344p-illus-1st ed (dd4,autg) 40.00

SMITH,COURTLAND L-Salmon Fishers of the Columbia-Corvallis-1979-4to-117p-illus,photos (m3,vf,dj) 17.50

SMITH,CURT-America's Dizzy Dean-1978-Betheny-1st ed (p7,f,f dj) 20.00

SMITH,DAVID C-History of Papermaking in the United States-NY-1970-Lockwood Publ-(x)+693p-brwn cl,illus-1st ed (l2,dj) 50.00

SMITH,DECOST-Martyrs of the Oblong and Little Nine-Caldwell-1948-Caxton-310p-illus-ltd to 1000c-1st ed (nn6,part unopened,dj) 75.00

SMITH,DECOST-Martyrs of the Oblong and Little Nine-Caldwell-1948-frntis,illus-1st ed (t7,dj) 10.00

SMITH,DECOST-Martyrs of the Oblong and Little Nine-Caldwell-1948-ltd to 1000c-1st ed (jj4,dj) 20.00

SMITH,DONIAN-By the River of No Return-Nashville-1967-16mo-111p-illus (m3,f,dj) 10.00

SMITH,DUANE-Rocky Mountain Mining Camps-(1967)-U of N-304p-photos-1st ed (r8,dj) 25.00

SMITH,E B-Architectural Symbolism of Imperial Rome & the Middle Ages-1956-Princeton U Pr-175 illus-(Prnctn Monographs Art & Arch.#30)-1st ed (h10,dj) 85.00

SMITH,E BOYD-My Village-NY-1896-Scribner's-8vo-pict blu cl,auth 1st bk-1st ed (u10) 200.00

SMITH,EARL R-Days of My Years-1968-Oregon Hist Soc-314p-wrps,illus (r8) 20.00

SMITH,EDGAR N-American Naval Broadsides-NY-1974-Phila Maritime Mus-4to-225p-blu cl,117 illus(incl 92 col)-1st ed (r10,wn dj) 45.00

SMITH,EDGAR N-American Naval Broadsides-NY-1974-Phila Maritime Mus-4to-xix,225p-lt blu cl,117 plts(92 col)-1st ed (dd7,dj) 65.00

SMITH,EDGAR W-ED-Adventure of the Blue Carbuncle-1948-BSI-1st trd ed (s10) 12.50

SMITH,EDGAR W-ED.-Profile by Gaslight-NY-1944-Simon-var bndg & wi plain e.p.-1st ed (l4,f,dj) 100.00

SMITH,EDMUND W-Further Adventures of the One-Eyed Poacher-NY-1947-8vo-219p-ltd to 750c,nbrd,autg,illus by A L Ripley (m3) 140.00

SMITH,EDMUND W-One Eyed Poacher of Privilege-NY-(1941)-Derrydale Pr-pict cov,gilt,illus by Ripley,glassine dj-ltd to 750c,nbrd (r2,f,dj) 125.00

SMITH,EDMUND W-One Eyed Poacher of Privilege-NY-1941-Derrydale-8vo-red cl-ltd to 750c,nbrd-1st ed (u10) 165.00

SMITH,EDMUND W-Tomatoe Can Chronicle-Derrydale-1937-8vo-189p-ltd to 950c,nbrd,illus by R Boyer (m3,f) 150.00

SMITH,EDMUND W-Upriver & Down-NY-1965-8vo-240p-illus-1st ed (m3,f,dj) 40.00

SMITH,EDWARD C-Borderland in the Civil War-NY-1927-412p-1st ed (c4,f) 30.00

SMITH,EDWARD E-First Lensman-Reading-1950-Fantasy-1st ed (g3,sl fray & chip dj) 40.00

SMITH,EDWARD E-Galactic Patrol-Reading-1950-Fantasy Pr-1st ed,1st state bndg (k3,dj) 55.00

SMITH,ELMER L-Amish Today-Allentown-1961-x+346p-wht cl,plts-Penn German Folklore Soc,vol.24-1st ed (k2) 65.00

SMITH,FLORENCE P-These Entertaining People-NY-(1966)-Macmillan-350p-grn cl-1st ed (q8,dj) 16.50

SMITH,FREDERICK-History of the Royal Army Veterinary Corps 1796 to 1919-Lond-1927-268p-dec blu cl,illus(10 col plts)-1st ed (b7) 275.00

SMITH,FREDRIKA S-Fire Dragon-NY-1956-Rand McNally-174p-cl,illus-1st ed (z7,dj,autg) 20.00

SMITH,G E KIDDER-Sweden Builds-NY,Stockholm-1950-A Bonnier-tall 4to-279p-cl,illus(1 col)-1st ed (cc10,dj) 60.00

SMITH,G ELLIOT-Egyptian Mummies-NY-1925-tall 8vo-t.e.g.,photos,illus-1st Amer ed (r2) 125.00

SMITH,G F HERBERT-Gemstones-Lond-1935-Methuen-xvi,314p-3 col & 29 b&w plts-7th ed (u5) 25.00

SMITH,GENE-High Crimes & Misdemeanors-NY-1977-320p-illus-1st ed (c4,f,dj) 22.50

SMITH,GEORGE E-P.O.W. Two Years with the Vietcong-Berkeley-1971-1st ed (v9,dj) 50.00

SMITH,GEORGE G-ED.-Spencer Kellogg Brown-NY-1903-Appleton-380p-illus (o7,vf) 65.00

SMITH,GEORGE W-Chronicles of the Gringos-Albuq-1968-523p-illus,maps-1st ed (t7,dj) 45.00

SMITH,GEORGE W-Life in the North During the Civil War-Albuq-(1966)-397p-illus-1st ed (n3,dj) 30.00

SMITH,GEORGE,JR.-Sporting & Colored Plate Books-1937-Anderson Galleries-8vo-192p-wrps,orig drwngs-1st ed (m3) 25.00

SMITH,GEORGE-Armchair Mountaineer-NY-1968-lg 8vo-361p-14 plts,illus-1st ed (q10,f,dj) 10.00

SMITH,GEORGE-Assyrian Discoveries-NY-1875-Scribner,Armstrong-461p-qtr grn lea,29 plts(incl fldg map frntis) (gg6,cov tn) 60.00

SMITH,GEORGE-Oldest London Bookshop-Lond-1928-Ellis-sm folio-141p-illus-1st ed (b3) 85.00

SMITH,GEORGIANA R-Table Decoration-Rutland-(1968)-Tuttle-288p-rose watered silk bndg,over 180 plts incl 15 col-1st prtg (l6,dj) 45.00

SMITH,GORDON-John Brown in Cedar County-Tipton-nd-Cedar County Hist Soc-17p-wrps,illus,map (o7,cov soil) 10.00

SMITH,H ALLEN-Compleat Practical Joker-NY-1953-Dbldy-Chas Addams designed dj-1st ed (mm5,f,dj) 15.00

SMITH,H ALLEN-Great Chili Confrontation-NY-(1969)-Trident-1st ed (q8,dj) 16.50

SMITH,H ALLEN-Lost in the Horse Latitudes-GC-1944-Dbldy Doran-1st ed (hh5,sl tn dj) 10.00

SMITH,H ALLEN-Rhubarb-1946-Dbldy-1st ed (p7,dj) 15.00

SMITH,H ALLEN-Three Men on Third-GC-1951-250p-cl-1st ed so stated (n1,dj) 12.50

SMITH,H CLIFFORD-Jewellery-Yorkshire-1973-EP Publ-xlvii,410p-54p plts-rprnt of 1908 ed (u5,f,f dj) 80.00

SMITH,H L-Airways-NY-1942-8vo-xiv,430,xviiip-cl,32p plts,incl 1 fldg chrt-1st ed (s2,wn) 35.00

SMITH,H M-Fresh Water Fishes of Siam or Thailand-1965-USNM-622p-9 plts (bb3) 45.00

SMITH,HAMILTON L-Natural Philosophy, for the Use of Schools and Academies...-Cleve-1847-M C Younglove-352;8p-lea,woodcts (a1) 50.00

SMITH,HAMILTON L-World-Cleve-1848-M C Younglove-324p-cl-illus (f1) 50.00

SMITH,HAMPTON,JR.-Tramp Reporter-1937-Caxton-1st ed (t4,f,sl chip dj) 25.00

SMITH,HARRY B-First Nights and First Editions-Bost-1931-illus-1st ed (hh10) 30.00

SMITH,HARRY W-Life and Sport in Aiken...-NY-1935-Derrydale Pr-ltd to 950c (f10,dj) 165.00

SMITH,HARRY W-Sporting Family of the Old South-Albany-1936-8vo-477p-illus (m3,vf,dj) 120.00

SMITH,HELEN K-ED.-With Her Own Wings-Portland-1948-Beattie & Co-(x)+248p-yel cl-1st ed (k2,dj) 35.00

SMITH,HELENA H-War on the Powder River-NY,Lond-(1966)-320p-illus-2nd prtg (c7,f,dj) 40.00

SMITH,HERNDON-ED.-Centralia, the First Fifty Years 1845 to 1900-Centralia-(1942)-Daily Chronicle-8vo-368p-16p photos-1st ed (dd5) 35.00

SMITH,HOMER-Black Man in Red Russia-Chig-1964-Johnson-8vo-221p-1st ed (gg5,dj) 15.00

SMITH,HORACE W-Nuts for Future Historians to Crack...-Phila-1856-90p-1/2 mor (aa6) 60.00

SMITH,HORACE-Horseman Through Six Reigns-Lond-1955-Odhams-1st ed (h9,wn dj) 40.00

SMITH,HOWARD M-Principles of Holography-NY-(1969)-Wiley-Interscience-xiv+239p-blck cl,illus-1st ed (a2,dj) 20.00

SMITH,HUGH-Fishes of the Yellowstone National Park-Wash-1921-8vo-30p-wrps,illus (m3,vf) 10.00

SMITH,HUSTON-Forgotten Truth-NY-1976-Harper & Row-cl-1st ed (n8) 25.00

SMITH,IRA L-Low & Inside-1949-Dbldy-drwngs,Hershfield-1st ed (s8,f,dj) 20.00

SMITH,IRA L-Three Men on Third-1951-Dbldy-drwngs,L Hershfield-1st ed (s8,dj) 17.50

SMITH,IRA-Baseball's Famous Pitchers-1954-Barnes-drwngs,L Hershfield-1st ed (s8,dj) 27.50

SMITH,IRA-Low and Inside-1949-Dbldy-1st ed (ff2,tape rnfrcd dj) 12.50

SMITH,ISABEL C-Blue Book of Cookery-NY-(1929)-Lit Digest-650p+4p ads-blu cl,tiss guard col frntis,illus-3rd prtg (q8) 17.50

SMITH,J BUCKNALL-Treatise upon Cable or Rope Traction as Applied to the Working of Street and Other Railways-Lond-1887-Engineering-xii+195p+ads-blu cl,76 illus(incl 4 fldg plts)-1st ed (c2) 175.00

SMITH,J V-Natural History of the Fishes of Massachusetts-1970-Freshet-400p-illus (bb3,f,box) 20.00

SMITH,JEROME V C-Natural History of the Fishes of Massachusetts-Bost-1833-16mo-399p+errata,illus,orig bndg-rare (m3) 175.00

SMITH,JEROME V C-Trout & Angling-1929-Derrydale-8vo-64p-ltd to 325c,illus-scarce (m3) 150.00

SMITH,JESSE G-Heroes of the Saddle Bags-San Antonio-1951-Naylor-234p-cl-1st ed (w3) 30.00

SMITH,JOHN-Fruits and Farinacea-NY-1854-Fowlers-314p-cl,col frntis-scarce-from 2nd Lond ed (x6,cl wn,sp fade,sl fox) 75.00

SMITH,JOHN-Fruits and Farinacea-NY-1892-Fowler & Wells-314p+8p ads,blk cl-from 2nd Lond ed (q8) 35.00

SMITH,JOHN-Irish Diamonds-Lond-1847-Chapman & Hall-175p-a.e.g.,frntis,plts,illus by "Phiz"-1st ed (ll2) 29.50

SMITH,JOSEPH C-Charles Hovey Pepper-Portland-1945-Southworth Anthoensen-4to-cl/bds-1st ed (oo6) 50.00

SMITH,JULIE-Death Turns a Trick-NY-1982-Walker-auth 1st bk-1st ed (hh2,f,dj) 75.00

SMITH,JUSTIN H-War with Mexico-Gloucester-1963(1919)-Peter Smith-2 vols-Howes S634-rprnt (a9) 50.00

SMITH,JUSTIN H-War with Mexico-NY-1919-Macmillan-2 vols-1st ed (j8) 200.00

SMITH,KAY N-Catching Fire-NY-(1982)-1st ed (j5,f,sl creased dj) 20.00

SMITH,KEN-Baseball's Hall of Fame-1947-Barnes-photos-1st ed (s8,dj) 17.50

SMITH,KEN-Baseball's Hall of Fame-1952-Barnes (q7,dj) 15.00

SMITH,L B-American Game Preserve Shooting-1933-Windward Hse-8vo-200p-illus-1st ed (m3) 20.00

SMITH,L B-Fur or Feather-NY-1946-4to-144p-illus,P Brown-1st ed (m3,vf,dj) 13.50

SMITH,L B-Modern Shotgun Shooting-NY-1935-8vo-171p-photos-1st ed (m3,vf,sl chip dj) 25.00

SMITH,L D-Hiram and Other Cats-NY-(1941)-Grosset-4to-unpgd-cl/pict bds,illus-1st ed (oo10) 15.00

SMITH,L WALDEN-Saddles Up-San Antonio-1937-Naylor Co-276p-illus-Herd 2096-1st ed (ff4,dj) 45.00

SMITH,LAWRENCE B-Dude Ranches and Ponies-NY-1936-Coward McCann-1st ed (f10) 25.00

SMITH,LEE-Black Mountain Breakdown-NY-1980-1st ed (o5,f,dj) 35.00

SMITH,LILLIAN-Killers of the Dream-NY-(1949)-Norton-1st ed (a5,sl crease dj) 20.00

SMITH,LILLIAN-Our Faces Our Words-NY-1964-Norton-128p-photos-1st ed so stated (r1,dj) 15.00

SMITH,LOGAN P-Prospects of Literature-Lond-1927-Hogarth Pr-wrps-Hoagarth Essays,2nd Ser.,No.8-Woolmer 148 (nn4,f) 75.00

SMITH,LOGAN P-Saved from the Salvage-Edinburgh-1982-Tragara Pr-wrps,ltd to 110c,nbrd-1st ed (y7) 50.00

SMITH,LYMAN-Bromeliads-S Brunswick,NY-(1969)-4to-55p-32 col plts-1st ed (m10,sp fade,dj tattrd) 25.00

SMITH,M L-New Orthography-Columbus-1888-Wm G Hubbard-146p-cl (k1) 15.00

SMITH,M-East Coast Marine Shells-1951-Edwards-4to-314p-77 plts-rvsd ed (bb3,tn dj) 30.00

SMITH,MARK-Toyland-1965-Little,Brown-auth 1st bk-1st ed (t9,f,dj) 25.00

SMITH,MARTIN-Canto for a Gypsy-1972-Putnam-1st ed (s10,dj) 12.50

SMITH,MARY S-Virginia Cookery Book-NY-1885-Harper & Bros-353p-brn bds-Bitting 440 (u6,wn bds) 75.00

SMITH,MAURICE L-Who Cares-NY-(1968)-Carlton Pr-1st ed (ff3,dj) 125.00

SMITH,MICHAEL-ED.-Duchess of Duke Street Entertains-Lond-1977-Allen-254p-tan cl,illus-1st ed (q8,dj) 15.00

SMITH,MICHAEL-Times & Locutions-Dublin-(1972)-Dolmen Pr-1st ed (z8,vf,dj) 25.00

SMITH,MRS.W J J-Centennial History of the Baptist Women of Texas 1830 to 1930-Dallas-1933-186p-illus (t8,sl spot) 30.00

SMITH,NICOL-Bush Master-Indpls-(1941)-Bobbs Merrill-8vo-315p-23 illus-1st ed (jj5,sl tn dj) 30.00

SMITH,NICOL-Golden Doorway to Tibet-Indpls,NY-c.1949-Bobbs Merrill-8vo-288p-blu cl,photos (gg6,autg) 45.00

SMITH,NICOL-Golden Doorway to Tibet-NY-1949-288p-photos,e.p.map-1st ed (p10,dj) 25.00

SMITH,NORMAN K-Prolegomena to an Idealist Theory of Knowledge-Lond-1924-Macmillan-xiv+240p-red cl-1st ed (l2) 40.00

SMITH,NORMAN L-Return of Billy the Kid-1977-Coward McCann (q7,dj) 10.00

SMITH,O W-Casting Tackle & Methods-Cin-1920-8vo-257p-photos-1st ed (m3,vf,badly fray dj) 30.00

SMITH,O W-Musings of an Angler-NY-1942-8vo-187p-frontis (m3,f) 15.00

SMITH,O W-Trout Lore-NY-1917-8vo-203p-illus (m3) 12.50

SMITH,OLGA W-Gold on the Desert-Albuq-(1956)-UNM Pr-249p-photos-1st ed (bb4,dj) 30.00

SMITH,PAUL J-On Strange Altars-NY-1924-Boni-293p-cl-1st ed (dd10,sl fade sp) 20.00

SMITH,PHILIP C F-Frigate Essex Papers-Salem-1974-Peabody Museum-xx,334p-cl sp,mrbld papr over bds,4 fldg plans in pckt,63 illus-1st ed (nn1,f) 50.00

SMITH,R BOSWORTH-Life of Lord Lawrence-NY-1883-Scribners-8vo-2 vols-1st US ed (cc5,hng split) 85.00

SMITH,R K-Airships Akron & Macon-Annapolis-(1965)-US Naval Inst-4to-xxii,232p-cl,illus (s2,dj) 35.00

SMITH,R K-First Across-Annapolis-(1973)-8vo-282p-cl,frntis,plts,e.p. maps-1st ed (s2,dj) 25.00

SMITH,R M-Story of Pope's Barrels-PA-1960-203p-illus (gg3,f,dj) 85.00

SMITH,RED-Red Smith on Fishing Around the World-NY-1963-181p-1st ed (mm2,dj) 12.50

SMITH,RED-Red Smith on Fishing-GC-1963-8vo-181p-1st ed (m3,vf,dj) 30.00

SMITH,RED-Red Smith Reader-NY-(1982)-Random-1st ed (e10,as new in dj) 20.00

SMITH,RED-Views of Sport-1954-Knopf-1st ed (s8,dj) 30.00

SMITH,REX-ED.-Biography of the Bulls-NY-1957-Rinehart-384p-1st ed (j8,f,dj) 40.00

SMITH,ROBERT-Babe Ruth's America-1974-Crowell-1st ed (p7,f,dj) 17.50

SMITH,ROBERT-Babe Ruth's America-1974-Crowell-photos-1st ed (s8,dj) 25.00

SMITH,ROBERT-Baseball-1947-S&S (p7,dj) 20.00

SMITH,ROBERT-Heroes of Baseball-1952-World-1st ed (ff2,f,dj) 20.00

SMITH,ROBERT-Heroes of Sport-1952-World-1st ed (r7,f,dj) 30.00

SMITH,ROBERT-Pioneers of Baseball-1978-Little,Brown-1st ed (p7,f,f dj) 25.00

SMITH,ROBERT-Pioneers of Baseball-1978-Little,Brown-photos-1st ed (s8,f,dj) 30.00

SMITH,ROBERT-World Series-1967-Dbldy-photos-1st ed (s8,f,dj) 17.50

SMITH,ROSS-14,000 Miles Through the Air-NY-1922-photos-1st ed (r2,sp sun,sl rub & soil) 75.00

SMITH,ROSWELL C-English Grammar on the Productive System-Cin-1845-W T Truman-192p-bds (d1,rub) 50.00

SMITH,S BAYLISS-British Waders in Their Haunts-Lond-1950-G Bell-162p-photos (d9) 15.00

SMITH,SAMUEL J-Miscellaneous Writings of the Late...of Burlington, N.J.-Phila-1836-222p-frntis (aa6) 75.00

SMITH,SAMUEL-History of the Colony of Nova Caesaria, or New Jersey-Burlington-1765-James Parker-x,573,(1)p-contemp calf-1st ed (o4,rebckd) 1,200.00

SMITH,SARAH B-Bending Tree-LA-1933-John Murray-bds,w/o dj as iss-1st ed (z2,pres) 65.00

SMITH,SHELLEY-Game of Consequences-Lond-1978-Macmillan-1st ed (p4,sl bump,dj) 17.50

SMITH,SHELLEY-Lord Have Mercy-NY-1956-Harper-1st US ed (e4,f,dj) 12.50

SMITH,STEPHEN-City That Was-NY-1911-211p-1st ed (dd3) 100.00

SMITH,STEVIE-Best Beasts-NY-1969-Knopf-1st ed (z9,f,dj sl tn,sunned) 20.00

SMITH,STEVIE-Me Again-Lond-1981-Virago-1st ed (m9,f,dj) 30.00

SMITH,STUART-Birds Fighting-Lond-(1955)-Faber & Faber-8vo-128p-photos-1st ed (aa5,f,sl tn dj) 25.00

SMITH,T MURRAY-Nature of the Beast-NY-1963-8vo-206p-photos (m3,f,dj) 15.00

SMITH,THOMAS H-Mapping of Ohio-(1977)-Kent St U Pr-252p-bds,plts-1st ed (e1,f,dj) 22.50

SMITH,THOMAS-French Gardening-Lond-1909-Fels-128p-cl (x6) 20.00

SMITH,THOMAS-Life of a Fox Written by Himself...-Lond,NY-1896-Edw Arnold-sp labl,col plts wi tissue guards-new ed (gg6) 65.00

SMITH,THOMAS-Life of a Fox-Lond-1920-Arnold-sm 4to-1st ed (h9) 35.00

SMITH,THORNE-Biltmore Oswald-NY-(1918)-pict covs,31 illus by R Dorgan,auth 1st bk-1st ed (r2,sl rub) 40.00

SMITH,THORNE-Lazy Bear Lane-GC-1931-Dbldy,Doran-240p-pict cl,illus by G Shank-1st ed (nn10,tattrd dj) 35.00

SMITH,THORNE-Passionate Witch-GC-1941-drwngs,H Rose-1st ed (o5,brwnd pstdwns,sl chip dj) 85.00

SMITH,VIAN-Grand National-So Brunswick-(1970,69)-Barnes-8vo-207p-photos-1st US ed (dd5,f,dj) 12.50

SMITH,VIAN-Horses in the Green Valley-GC-1971-Dbldy-1st US ed (f10,dj) 18.00

SMITH,W A-Anson Guards, Co. C-Wendell-1978-368p-ports-rprnt of 1914 ed (z10,f) 30.00

SMITH,W D A-Under the Influence: a History of Nitrous Oxide and Oxygen Anaesthesia-Lond-1982-188p-1st ed (dd3,dj) 75.00

SMITH,W EUGENE-Minamata-NY-1975-HR&W-4to-1st ed (gg7,dj sl chip) 100.00

SMITH,W EUGENE-Pittsburgh-NY-1964-Dbldy-sm folio-520p-cl,photos-1st ed (q3) 50.00

SMITH,W H-Drunkard-NY-nd(ca.1850s)-Samuel French-64p-wrps-French's Standard Drama No.LXXXVI (a1) 15.00

SMITH,WALKER C-Everett Massacre-Chig-(1917)-IWW Publ Bureau-maroon cl,photos-Smith 9609-1st ed (w1,f) 90.00

SMITH,WALKER C-Everett Massacre-Chig-nd(ca.1919)-302p-illus-scarce (e7,poor bndg) 40.00

SMITH,WALKER C-Was It Murder-Centralia-nd-47p-pamphlet,illus-v scarce-1st ed (e7,loose t.p.) 65.00

SMITH,WALTER-Examples of Household Taste-NY-(1876)-R Worthington-lg 8vo-520p-brwn cl,illus (p1) 100.00

SMITH,WARREN S-London Heretics 1870 to 1914-NY-1968-Dodd,Mead-319p-1st ed (r1,edge rub dj) 15.00

SMITH,WILBUR A-When the Lion Feeds-NY-(1964)-Viking-auth 1st bk-1st ed (a10,dj) 65.00

SMITH,WILLIAM C-Queen City Yesterdays-Crawfordsville-1959-R E Banta-66p-wrps-ltd to 1000c (j1) 12.50

SMITH,WILLIAM F-Diamond Six-1958-Dbldy-383p-e.p. maps-Six Guns 2057-1st ed (t8,dj) 25.00

SMITH,WILLIAM H-Evolution of "Dodd"-Chig-(1884)-Rand,McNally-153p-wrps (k1,sl wn) 20.00

SMITH,WILLIAM-British Heroism-Sunderland-1815-114p-blu wrps-1st ed (b7,rbnd) 50.00

SMITH,WILLIE THE LION-Music On My Mind-GC-1964-Dbldy-1st ed (w1,f,f dj) 35.00

SMITH,WM H-Early Days in Seward County, Nebraska-Seward-1937-111p-stiff pict wrps,frntis,photos-1st ed (t7) 45.00

SMITH-VANIZ,WILLIAM F-Freshwater Fishes of Alabama-Auburn-1968-8vo-211p-photos-1st ed (m3,vf) 20.00

SMITHE,FRANK B-Birds of Tikal-NY-1966-Nat Hist Pr(AMNH)-351p-31 col plts,fldg map (b9,cors bump) 15.00

SMITHERMAN,MRS.JAMES E-Louisiana Plantation Cook Book-E Feliciana Parish,Glencoe Pl-nd-Ina Scott Thompson-274p-red bds,Bitting 441 (o6,wn bds) 55.00

SMITHERMAN,P H-Uniforms of the British Army-Lond-1970-folio-45p col plts-1st ed (b7,f,dj) 60.00

SMITHERMAN,P H-Uniforms of the Royal Artillery 1716 to 1966-Lond-1966-folio-20p col plts-1st ed (gg2,f,dj) 45.00

SMITHERMAN,P H-Uniforms of the Yeomanry Regiments 1783 to 1911-Lond-1967-folio-20p col plts-1st ed (b7,f,dj) 50.00

SMITHSON,ALISON-ED.-Team 10 Primer-Cambridge-1968-MIT Pr-sm 4to-112p-cl,131 illus-1st US ed (cc10,dj) 50.00

SMITHWICK,NOAH-Evolution of a State-Gammel-1900-354p-orig blu cl,illus-Howes S726-1st ed (a9,f) 300.00

SMITTER,WESSEL-F.O.B. Detroit-NY-1938-Harper-1st ed (w5,f) 15.00

SMOLE,WILLIAM J-Yanoama Indians-Austin-(1976)-U of Tex Pr-272p-illus (cc4,dj) 20.00

SMOODIN,ROBERTA-Ursus Major-NY-1980-Knopf-auth 1st bk-1st ed (bb1,as new in dj) 30.00

SMUCKER,ISAAC-History of the Welsh Settlements in Licking County,Ohio...April 7th,1869-Newark-nd-Wilson & Clark-22p-prntd wrps-Thomson 1074 (e1,sp wn,ex-lib) 35.00

SMUCKER,ISAAC-Our Pioneers-Newark-1872-Clark & King-33p-Thomson 1076 (e1,wrps,ex-lib) 35.00

SMURTHWAITE,WILLIAM-Reminiscences...Coal Mining in Steubenville and Vicinity...-np-nd-78p-cl,not cpyrghtd,prntd in a pattern of 2 pg text followed by 2 blank unnmbrd pgs-rare (l1,rbkd) 150.00

SMYTH,C PIAZZI-Teneriffe-Lond-1858-Lovell Reeve-8vo-1/2 mor & mrbld bds,tip in photos-1st ed (y3) 550.00

SMYTH,HENRY D-Atomic Energy for Military Purposes-1945-Princeton-264p-illus (hh1) 50.00

SMYTH,HENRY D-Atomic Energy for Military Purposes-Princeton-1945-Princeton U Pr-xii+264p-gry cl,plts(first ed wi illus)-1st commercial ed (a2,chip dj) 75.00

SMYTH,JOSEPH H-To Nowhere and Return-NY-(1940)-Carrick & Evans-8vo-311p-sketches-1st ed (jj5,dj) 20.00

SMYTHE,F S-Kangchenjunga Adventure-Lond-1930-Gollancz-8vo-464p-grn cl,48 plts (gg6,fade) 50.00

SMYTHE,F S-Mountain Scene-Lond-1938-A & C Black-4to-(3),153p-blu cl,plts-2nd ed (gg6,wn,sp fade) 40.00

SMYTHE,FRANK-British Mountaineers-Lond-1942-48p-8 col plts,24 illus-1st ed (q10,f,dj) 25.00

SMYTHE,FRANK-Camp Six-Lond-1937-307p-36 photos-1st ed (p10) 95.00

SMYTHE,FRANK-Climbs in the Canadian Rockies-Lond-(1950)-ix,260p-illus-1st prtg (bb9,f,sl chip dj) 45.00

SMYTHE,FRANK-Climbs in the Canadian Rockies-NY-nd-Norton-ix,260p-col frtnis,41 illus & maps-1st ed (aa7,sl discol,dj sl chip) 150.00*

SMYTHE,FRANK-Edward Whymper-Lond-1940-330p-27 illus,2 fldg maps-1st ed (p10) 85.00

SMYTHE,FRANK-Kamet Conquered-Lond-1932-420p-48 plts,fldg map-1st ed (a4,f,dj chip) 120.00

SMYTHE,FRANK-Rocky Mountains-Lond-1948-149p-frntis,col plts,48 photos-1st ed (t7,dj) 10.00

SMYTHE,FRANK-Valley of Flowers-NY-1949-325p-16 col plts-1st US ed (a4,f,dj) 38.00

SMYTHE,FRANK-Valley of Flowers-NY-1959-Norton-325p-16 col plts,map (gg6,dj) 30.00

SMYTHE,GONZALVO-Medical Heresies Historically Considered-Phila-1880-228p-1st ed (dd3) 100.00

SMYTHE,MRS.-Ten Months in the Fiji Islands-Oxford,Lond-1864-H & J Parker-grn cl,g vigntt fr cov,g sp lttrng,chromolitho frntis & 3 chromo plts,9 wdcut plts,4 maps(2 fldg)-1st ed (nn1,rbkd, orig sp,new e.p.) 400.00

SMYTHE,MRS.-Ten Months in the Fiji Islands-Oxford-1864-Henry & Parker-g stmpd,pattrnd pebble cl,4 chromolithos,9 woodcts,4 maps-1st ed (p6,part unopened,sl wn) 450.00

SMYTHE,P M-Diary of an All-Round Angler-Lond-1956-8vo-222p-photos (m3,sl fray dj) 15.00

SMYTHE,R H-Horse-Lond-1967-Allen-1st prtg (j9,dj) 25.00

SMYTHIES,BERTRAM E-Birds of Borneo-Kota Kinabalu-1981-Sabah Soc-473p-map,47 col plts-3rd ed,rvsd (c9,cors bump) 75.00

SMYTHIES,E A-Big Game Shooting in Nepal-Calcutta-1942-174p-photos (gg3,cov spotted) 65.00

SNAPP,S S-Some Simple Sunday Suppers-(St.Paul)-(c.1895)-(Wm E Banning)-63p-grn bds-Axford 370 (a8,bds stnd) 45.00

SNEDEKER,CAROLINE D-Town of the Fearless-NY-1931-349p-pict cl,frntis,illus-1st ed (t7) 15.00

SNELL,E-Blue Murder-1933-Lippincott-1st Amer ed (x7,sl tn dj) 68.00

SNELL,GEORGE D-Root,Hog, and Die-Caldwell-1936-Caxton-8vo-418p-cl-1st ed (z4,spot sp,ends wn,cov rub) 20.00

SNELL,J B-Britain's Railways Under Steam-Lond-1965-224p-1st ed (n4,f,dj) 23.00

SNELL,J B-Early Railways-NY-1964-128p-1st ed (n4,f,dj) 23.00

SNELL,JAMES P-History of Sussex and Warren Counties, New Jersey...-Phila-1881-4to-xi,9-748p-mod buckrm,illus,plts (aa6,rbnd) 200.00

SNELLER,ANNE G-Vanished World-1964-Syracuse U Pr-365p-drwngs-1st ed (p2,dj) 12.50

SNELLGROVE,DAVID-Cultural History of Tibet-NY-1968-lg 8vo-291p-118 photos,2 maps-1st US ed (a4,f,dj) 50.00

SNELLGROVE,DAVID-Himalayan Pilgrimage-Oxford-1961-304p-44 plts,12 maps-1st Brit ed (a4,f,dj) 85.00

SNELLING,HENRY H-Memoirs of a Boyhood at Fort Snelling-Mpls-1939-priv prtd-36p-illus (cc4) 25.00

SNELLING,O F-Rare Books and Rarer People-(Lond)-(1982)-Shaw-1st ed (w1,f,f dj) 25.00

SNELLING,O F-Rare Books and Rarer People-(Lond)-(1982)-Werner Shaw-8vo-256p-cl-1st ed (w2,dj) 35.00

SNELLING,WM J-Tales of the Northwest-Mpls-1971-254p-rprnt Howes S738 (t7,dj) 10.00

SNIDER,DENTON J-Lincoln at Richmond-St.Louis-(1914)-388p+ads-1st ed (n3) 27.50

SNIDER,DENTON J-Lincoln in the Black Hawk War-St.Louis-nd(ca.1910)-375p+ad-1st ed (c4) 20.00

SNODGRASS,KATHERINE-Margarine as a Butter Substitute-(c.1930)-Stanford U:Food Rsrch Inst-333p (a8) 18.00

SNOW & HUNTER-More Destructive Grasshoppers of Kansas-Topeka-1897-11p+5 plts-wrps (t8,sl chip) 10.00

SNOW,C P-Death Under Sail-1932-DD CC-auth 1st bk-1st Amer ed (x7) 48.00

SNOW,C P-Strangers and Brothers-NY-1972-3 vols-Omnibus ed-1st ed thus (y7,dj) 50.00

SNOW,CHARLES E-Early Hawaiians-Lesington-1974-U of Ky Pr-4to-179p-photos (p8,f) 35.00

SNOW,EDWARD R-Mysteries and Adventures Along the Atlantic Coast-NY-1948-Dodd & Mead-xiv+352p-grn cl,plts-1st ed (h2,wn dj) 20.00

SNOW,MRS.MARY B-Mrs. Snow's Practical Cook Book-Denver-1903-(A J Ludditt Pr)-195p-blu bds (n6,soil) 30.00

SNOWDEN,RICHARD-American Revolution-Clinton-1815-Smith & M'Ardle-170;38;(7)p-lea-rare (f1,fox) 350.00

SNOWDEN,W H-Some Old Historic Landmarks of Virginia and Maryland...Mount Vernon Electric Railway-1904-G H Ramey-124p-wrps,illus,ltd to 5000c-5th ed (dd9,wrps sl tn & soil) 35.00

SNOWMAN,A KENNETH-Art of Carl Faberge-Lond-(1962)-Faber-4to-186p-col illus-1st prtg,rvsd ed (p1) 50.00

SNYDER,C-Flaw in the Sapphire-1909-Metropolitan Pr-pict cl-1st ed (x7) 25.00

SNYDER,GARY-Earth House Hold-NY-(1969)-New Directions-1st ed (cc2,f,dj) 50.00

SNYDER,GARY-Old Ways-SF-(1977)-City Lights-16mo-wrps-1st prtg (m4) 15.00

SNYDER,GARY-Real Work-NY-1980-New Directions-1st ed (y1,f,dj) 25.00

SNYDER,GARY-Six Selections from Mountains and Rivers Without End-SF-1965-Four Seasons Fndtn-wrps-1st ed (e8,f) 65.00

SNYDER,GERALD-In the Footsteps of Lewis and Clark-Wash D.C.-1970-col frntis,photos,maps-1st ed (t7,f,dj) 22.50

SNYDER,HOWARD-Hall of the Mountain King-NY-1973-207p-1st ed (p10,f,dj) 42.00

SNYDER,JOHN O-Salmon of the Klamath River California-Sacramento-1931-8vo-130p-illus,maps-1st ed (m3) 30.00

SNYDER,JOHN P-Mapping of New Jersey-New Brunswick-(1973)-xiv,234p-cl,illus (aa6) 30.00

SNYDER,JOHN P-Story of New Jersey's Civil Boundaries,1606 to 1968-Trenton-1969-4to-xiii,294p-cl,maps (aa6) 35.00

SNYDER,L L-Arctic Birds of Canada-Tor-1957-8vo-310p-cl,drwngs,maps (y8,scuff,dj wn) 85.00

SNYDER,LEON-Gardening in the Upper Midwest-1978-U of Minn-292p-cl (x6,as new) 15.00

SOBIN,DENNIS P-Working Poor-Port Wash-1973-Kennikat Pr-194p (r1,dj) 15.00

SOBY,JAMES T-Ben Shahn-NY-1963-Braziller-4to-2 vols-cl-1st ed (oo6,dj,box) 85.00

SOBY,JAMES T-Joan Miro-NY-1959-MOMA-8vo-164p-tan cl,b&w & col illus (r10,sl tn dj) 10.00

SOCIETY OF NAVAL ARCHITECTS AND MARINE ENGINEERS-Historical Transactions, 1893 to 1943-NY-1945-SNAME-4to-vi+544p-blu cl,photos,illus-1st ed (dd1) 50.00

SOHL,JERRY-Altered Ego-NY,Tor-(1954)-Rinehart-1st ed (a5,sl soil dj) 20.00

SOKOLOFF,ALICE H-Hadley-NY-(1973)-photos-1st ed (d5,f,dj) 20.00

SOKOLOFF,ALICE H-Kate Chase for the Defense-NY-(1971)-315p-cl-1st ed (d1,f,dj) 20.00

SOKOLOFF,BORIS-Story of Penicillin-Chig-1945-167p-1st ed (dd3) 30.00

SOKOLOV,RAYMOND-ED.-Great Recipes from the New York Times-(1973)-Quadrangle-331p-blk cl,illus-1st ed (q8,dj) 15.00

SOKOLOV,RAYMOND-Fading Feast-(1981)-Farrar-276p-dec crm cl-1st ed (q8,dj) 16.50

SOLDIERS' MEMORIAL BUILDING, TOLEDO, OHIO, IN HONOR OF THOSE WHO FOUGHT... THE WAR OF THE REBELLION-Toledo-1886-B F Wade-67p-cl-col frontis (j1) 15.00

SOLEY JAS R-Sailor Boys of '61-Bost-(1887)-sq 8vo-381p-pict cov,red cl,illus,plts (a3) 32.50

SOLLY,SAMUEL-Human Brain-Phila-1848-496p-calf,lea labl,illus-1st Amer ed from 2nd Lond ed (g10,ex-libr) 150.00

SOLLY,V-Gardens for Town and Suburb-Lond-1926-Benn-112p-cl,39 photos (x6) 20.00

SOLMS-BRAUNFELS,PRINCE CARL OF-Texas 1844 to 1845-1936-Anson Jones-141p-4 maps-ltd to 750c-1st ed in Engl (a9) 200.00

SOLOMON,L-Caddis & the Angler-PA-1977-224p-photos (gg3,f,dj) 50.00

SOLOMON,LOUIS-Ma & Pa Murders & Other Perfect Crimes-1976-Lippincott-1st ed (s10,dj) 15.00

SOLOTAROFF,THEODORE-ED.-New American Review #1-NY,Tor-(1967)-NAL-1st ed (b5,f,dj) 45.00

SOLTES,MORDECAI-Yiddish Press-NY-1925-Teachers College-(iv)+242p-blu cl-1st ed (e2) 30.00

SOLZHENITSN,ALEXANDER-Cancer Ward-Lond-1968-1st ed (y7,dj tape,fray) 18.00

SOLZHENITSN,ALEXANDER-Lenin in Zurich-NY-1976-1st ed (y7,dj) 18.00

SOLZHENITSYN,ALEKSANDR-Letter to the Soviet Leaders-NY-(1974)-Harper & Row-silv titled cl-1st ed (aa9,f,dj) 25.00

SOLZHENITSYN,ALEXANDER-August 1914-1972-FS&G-1st Amer ed (r9,sl tn dj) 15.00

SOLZHENITSYN,ALEXANDER-For the Good of the Cause-1964-Praeger-1st ed (x2,vf,dj) 45.00

SOLZHENITSYN,ALEXANDER-One Day in the Life of Ivan Denisovich-1963-Dutton-1st ed (x2,f,dj) 45.00

SOLZHENITSYN,ALEXANDER-One Day in the Life of Ivan Denisovich-1963-FS&G-auth 1st bk-1st Amer ed (m9,f,sl tn dj) 20.00

SOME EARLY AMERICAN HUNTERS-NY-1928-Derrydale-41p-handcol frntis,ltd to 375c (gg3,f) 125.00

SOMERS,JANE-Diary of a Good Neighbor-NY-1983-Knopf-1st US ed (bb1,as new in dj) 25.00

SOMERS,PAUL-Beginner's Luck-NY-1958-Harper-1st US ed (f4,f,dj) 12.50

SOMERVILE,WILLIAM-Chase-Lond-1896-Geo Redway-navy & gold pict bndg,t.e.g.,illus by H Thomson-(rprnt of orig 1735 ed) (ff6,hng crack,sl fox) 100.00

SOMERVILLE,GEORGE B-Lure of Long Beach-(Long Bch)-1914-80p-bds,plts (aa6,rub) 30.00

SOMMER,F-Man & Beast in Africa-NY-1954-206p-photos,foreword by Hemingway (gg3,sp fade) 45.00

SOMMERFIELD,JOHN-Volunteer in Spain-NY-1937-Knopf-1st US ed (a10,dj) 25.00

SONN,HAROLD A-History of Colonel Joseph Beavers-Short Hills-1948-(7),153,xviii,(3)p-cl,mimeo,prtd on rectos only (aa6,lttrng flaked) 150.00

SONNICHSEN,C L-Billy King's Tombstone-Caldwell-1942-233p-pict cl,frntis,photo,map-Six Guns #2068-scarce-1st ed (t7) 50.00

SONNICHSEN,C L-Cowboys and Cattle Kings, Life on the Range Today-Norman-1950-UOP-316p-1st ed (a9,dj) 50.00

SONNICHSEN,C L-El Paso Salt War of 1877-El Paso-1961-68p-pict wrps,frntis,illus-1st ed (t7) 37.50

SONNICHSEN,C L-Grave of John Wesley Hardin-(1979)-Texas A & M-90p-1st ed (t8,f,sl chip dj) 12.00

SONNICHSEN,C L-I'll Die Before I Run-NY-1951-294p-photos,map e.p.-Six Guns #2067-1st ed (t7,dj,pres) 60.00

SONNICHSEN,C L-Mescalero Apaches-Norman-1958-303p-cl,illus-1st ed (z1,dj) 40.00

SONNICHSEN,C L-Pass of the North-1968-UTEP-467p-illus-1st ed (e7,dj,autg) 85.00

SONNICHSEN,C L-Pass of the North-El Paso-1980-Tex Wstrn Pr-8vo-4th prtg (z4,dj) 25.00

SONNICHSEN,C L-Roy Bean, Law West of the Pecos-NY-1943-207p-frntis,photos-1st ed (t7) 20.00

SONNICHSEN,C L-Ten Texas Feuds-Albuq-1957-248p-scarce-1st ed (n10,f,dj sp fade) 90.00

SONNTAG,CHARLES F-Morphology and Evolution of the Apes and Man-Lond-1924-John Bale-xii+364p-olive cl-1st ed (a2,sp lttrng fade) 30.00

SONTAG,SUSAN-Benefactor-1963-Farrar-auth 1st bk-1st ed (kk6,f,dj sp sl drknd) 45.00

SONTAG,SUSAN-Benefactor-NY-1963-auth 1st bk-1st ed (q5,dj) 30.00

SONTAG,SUSAN-Duet for Cannibals-NY-(1970)-FSG-Noonday Orig Scrnply-1st ed (m7,f,sl soil dj) 15.00

SONTAG,SUSAN-I, Etcetera-NY-(1978)-FSG-1st ed (b5,as new in dj) 15.00

SONTAG,SUSAN-I, Etcetera-NY-(1978)-FSG-1st ed (m7,f,f dj) 10.00

SONTAG,SUSAN-Illness as Metaphor-NY-(1978)-FS&G-1st ed (b5,as new in dj) 15.00

SONTAG,SUSAN-On Photography-NY-(1977)-FS&G-1st ed (b5,as new in dj) 20.00

SONTAG,SUSAN-Styles of Radical Will-1969-Farrar-1st ed (kk6,f,dj) 30.00

SONTAG,SUSAN-Under the Sign of Saturn-NY-(1980)-FS&G-1st ed (b5,as new in dj) 12.50

SONTAG,SUSAN-Under the Sign of Saturn-NY-1980-Farrar Straus-203p-1st ed (r1,dj) 15.00

SOOTHILL,W E-Lotus of the Wonderful Law-Lond-1930-OUP-cl,col frntis,illus-1st ed (o8) 45.00

SOPER,J DEWEY-Mammals of Alberta-Edmonton-1964-Hamly Pr-sm 8vo-402p-frntis,67 col plts,e.p. maps-1st ed (cc7,rub dj) 20.00*

SOPHIE'S COOK BOOK-(Oakland)-(1951)-(Sophie & Emil Gwerder)-64p-gold wrps,plastic comb bndg (l6) 12.00

SORENSON,AL-Hands Up-College Sta-(1982)-Creative Publ-147p-illus-ltd to 1000c-Howes S766 (ee4) 25.00

SORENSON,ALFRED-Early History of Omaha-Omaha-1876-Daily Bee-248p-illus-Howes S765-1st ed (ee4) 85.00

SORIN,SCOTA-Blackbird, a Story of Mackinac Island-Detr-1907-Citator Publ-142p-pict cl,illus (cc3) 65.00

SORRENTINO,GILBERT-Aberration of Starlight-(1980)-Random-1st ed (r9,vf,dj) 15.00

SORRENTINO,GILBERT-Aberration of Starlight-NY-(1980)-Random-1st ed (b5,as new in dj) 12.50

SORRENTINO,GILBERT-Black and White-NY-1964-Totem/Corinth-wrps-1st ed (v5) 15.00

SORRENTINO,GILBERT-Crystal Vision-SF-1981-N Point Pr-1st ed (r2,f,dj) 25.00

SORRENTINO,GILBERT-Imaginative Qualities of Actual Things-NY-(1971)-Pantheon Bks-1st ed (bb1,as new in dj) 35.00

SORRENTINO,GILBERT-Steelwork-NY-(1970)-Pantheon Bks-1st ed (bb1,as new in dj) 25.00

SOSEY,FRANK H-Robert Devoy-Palmyra-1903-Pr of Sosey Bros-173p-frntis,illus-1st ed (n7,f) 75.00

SOSIN,MARK-Practical Black Bass Fishing-NY-1974-4to-216p-illus-1st ed (m3,vf,dj) 14.00

SOSIN,MARK-Through the Fishes Eye-NY-1973-8vo-249p-illus-1st ed (m3,vf,sl chip dj) 11.00

SOTBENE,OSWOLD-Shrine of Aesculapius-Cleve-1905-277p-4 illus (dd3) 100.00

SOUCHERE,DOR DE LA-Picasso in Antibes-NY-1960-Pantheon-oblng 4to-beige cl,b&w & col illus (r10,f box) 60.00

SOURIAN,PETER-Gate-NY-1965-Harcourt,Brace-cl-1st ed (m8,f,chip dj) 15.00

SOUSA,JOHN P-Fifth String-Indpls-(1902)-auth 1st bk-1st ed (hh5) 15.00

SOUSTELLE,JACQUES-Four Suns-NY-1971-Grossman Publ-8vo-xii,256p-blu cl,illus (mm1,dj) 20.00

SOUTH DAKOTA GUIDE-Pierre-1938-Fed Writers Prjct-441p-illus,frnt e.p. map,lg fldg map rear pckt-Amer Guide Ser-Six Guns 44-scarce-1st ed (bb4) 150.00

SOUTH DAKOTA-Historical Collections, Vol II-Aberdeen-1904-523p-frntis,photos,maps-1st ed (t7,t.p. cut,hngs weak) 75.00

SOUTH,R-Moths of the British Isles-1980-Warne-2 vols-289 plts(incl 159 col) (bb3,f,dj) 35.00

SOUTHARD,CHARLES Z-Evolution of Trout & Trout Fishing in America-NY-1928-4to-254p-col plts-scarce (m3) 60.00

SOUTHARD,CHARLES Z-Evolution of Trout and Trout Fishing in America-NY-1928-Dutton-9 col plts,2 maps-1st ed (y10,sl cov spot,pg yel,autg) 125.00

SOUTHARD,CHARLES Z-Treatise on Trout for the Progressive Angler-NY-1931-8vo-267p-illus-1st ed (m3,chip dj) 25.00

SOUTHCOTT,JOANNA-Letters and Communications of...-Stourbridge-1804-Heming-8vo-128p-mod mrbld bds-scarce-1st ed (w6,rbnd) 350.00

SOUTHERN BATTLEFIELDS-Nashville-1906-Nshvll,Chat & St.L Rlwy-48p-wrps,illus,fldg map (v2) 20.00

SOUTHERN,TERRY-Blue Movie-NY,Cleve-(1970)-1st ed (h5,dj) 12.50

SOUTHERN,TERRY-Blue Movie-NY,Cleve-(1970)-World-1st ed (a10,dj) 15.00

SOUTHERN,TERRY-Candy-NY-1964-1st US ed (o5,f,dj) 25.00

SOUTHERN,TERRY-Flash and Filagree-NY-1958-auth 1st bk,wi 1st iss dj-1st US ed (o5,dj) 65.00

SOUTHERN,TERRY-Flash and Filigree-NY-1958-1st US ed (x8,dj) 50.00

SOUTHERN,TERRY-Magic Christian-NY-1960-1st ed (q5,dj) 40.00

SOUTHERN,TERRY-Magic Christian-NY-1960-Random-1st ed (j8,f,dj) 35.00

SOUTHERN,TERRY-Red Dirt Marijuana & Other Tastes-(NY)-(1967)-NAL-1st ed (d10,dj) 25.00

SOUTHESK,EARL OF-Saskatchewan and the Rocky Mountains-Edmonton-1969-Hurtig-8vo-xxxviii,448p,errata & addenda,frntis,6 woodcts,2 lithos,2 fldg col maps-rprnt of orig (cc7,sl chip dj) 65.00*

SOUTHGATE,HENRY-Things a Lady Would Like to Know-Lond-1875-Nimmo-543p+16p cat,dec blu cl,illus-3rd ed (q8) 75.00

SOUTHWICK,MARCIA-Build with Adobe-Denver-(1965)-183p-photos,plans-1st ed (u7,f,dj) 15.00

SOUTHWORTH,MAY E-Let Me Fix It-1927-Morrow-240p-red cl-1st prtg (q8,dj) 15.00

SOWELL,A J-Early Settlers and Indian Fighter of Southwest Texas-NY-1964-Argosy Antiquarian Ltd-2 vols-cl,photos-ltd to 750c (w3,f,box) 125.00

SOWERBY,E MILLICENT-Rare People and Rare Books-Lond-1967-Constable-1st ed (ll5,dj) 65.00

SOWERBY,GINA-Gay Book-Poughkeepsie-(1935)-Artists & Writers Guild-8vo-pict bds,illus,incl 12p col plts,M Sowerby (s3,tips wn) 15.00

SOWERS,ROBERT-Language of Stained Glass-Forest Grove-1981-Timber Pr-col illus (cc8,dj) 30.00

SOWLS,L K-Prairie Ducks-1955-Stackpole/Wldlf Mgmt Inst-193p-46 photos & figs-1st ed (bb3,fray dj) 40.00

SOWLS,LYLE K-Prairie Ducks-Harrisburg-1955-8vo-193p-col frontis by P Scott,illus-1st ed (m3,vf,sl chip dj) 27.50

SOYER,NICHOLAS-Soyer's Paper Bag Cookery-Lond-1911-Melrose-16mo-112p+6p ads,red cl (q8) 18.50

SOYER,NICHOLAS-Soyer's Standard Cookery-1912-Melrose-435p-red cl,6 photos,4 col plts-1st ed (q8) 50.00

SOYINKA,WOLE-Madmen and Specialists-1971-Hill & Wang-1st ed (m9,f,dj) 25.00

SPACKLING,HELEN-Customs on the Table Top-Sturbridge-(1958)-22p (l6) 10.00

SPACKLING,HELEN-Setting Your Table-NY-(1941)-Barrows-dj wi M Bourke White photo (l6,dj) 25.00

SPACKMAN,W H-Heyday-NY-1953-Ballantine Bks-auth 1st bk-scarce hdcov ed-1st ed (y1,papr brwnd,dj) 75.00

SPAETH,SIGMUND-At Home With Music-GC-1945-Dbldy-1st ed (w1,f,dj) 20.00

SPALDING'S ATHLETIC LIBRARY-Canoes & Canoeing-NY-1910-12mo-48p+ads-wrps,photos (m3) 10.00

SPALDING,ALBERT G-Baseball, America's National Game-1911-American Sports-fld out photos-1st ed (s8,sl wn sp,hngs rprd) 425.00

SPALDING,C C-Annals of the City of Kansas-Columbia-(1950)-Stephens for F Glenn Publ-116p-illus-rprnt of 1858 ed-Howes S805 (bb4) 25.00

SPANGLER,A M-Nearby Fresh & Salt Water Fishing or Angling Within a Radius of One Hundred Miles of Philadelphia-Phila-1889-12mo-96p-illus,map (m3) 40.00

SPANIER,GINETTE-It Isn't All Mink-NY-(1960)-Random-8vo-233p-photos-1st ed (gg5,f,dj) 12.50

SPANISH PORTRAITS-(NY)-(c.1940)-4to-wrps (oo6) 50.00

SPANISH VOYAGE TO TO VANCOUVER AND THE NW COAST OF AMER...IN THE YEAR 1792...-Amsterdam-1971-N Israel-156p-5 plts,2 fldg maps-transl by Cecil Jane-orig publ Lond 1930-rprnt (p8,as new) 45.00

SPANISH-AMERICAN SONG AND GAME BOOK-NY-(1942)-WPA-87p-drwngs-scarce-1st ed (u7,sl rub) 50.00

SPARGO,JOHN-Applied Socialism-NY-1912-Huebsch-1st ed (w5,f,sl chip dj) 40.00

SPARGO,JOHN-Marx He Knew-Chig-1909-Kerr-gry papr cov bds wi unprntd cl bkstrp-1st ed (w5,f) 15.00

SPARGO,JOHN-Potters and Potteries of Bennington-Bost-1926-Houghton,Mifflin-Ltd to 800c (l9,sl bump) 200.00

SPARK,MURIEL-Abbess of Crewe-1974-Viking-1st US ed (kk6,f,dj) 20.00

SPARK,MURIEL-Comforters-1957-Lippincott-1st US ed (jj6,dj sl wn & nick) 40.00

SPARK,MURIEL-Driver's Seat-(Lond)-(1970)-Macmillan-1st ed (x10,f,f dj) 15.00

SPARK,MURIEL-Go Away Bird-1960-Lipincott-1st Amer ed (x2,f,dj) 30.00

SPARK,MURIEL-Hothouse by the East River-1973-Macmillan-1st ed (kk6,vf,dj) 20.00

SPARK,MURIEL-Loitering with Intent-1981-Coward-1st US ed (kk6,vf,dj) 20.00

SPARK,MURIEL-Loitering with Intent-NY-(1981)-Coward,McCann-1st US ed (e3,f,dj) 25.00

SPARK,MURIEL-Mandelbaum Gate-NY-1965-1st ed (m4,f,dj) 20.00

SPARK,MURIEL-Takeover-1976-Viking-1st US ed (kk6,f,dj sl chip) 20.00

SPARK,MURIEL-Voices at Play-1962-Lippincott-wht dj-1st Amer ed (x2,f,dj) 30.00

SPARKS,ELIZABETH H-North Carolina and Old Salem Cookery-Kernersville-(1955)-226p-red cl-1st ed (q8,dj) 25.00

SPARNON,NORMAN J-Japanese Flower Arrangement-Rutland-1961-Tuttle-linen,col plts & figs-2nd prtg (l8,f) 30.00

SPARRMAN,ANDERS-Voyage Round the World with Capt James Cook in H.M.S. Resolution-Lond-(1953)-214p-drwngs,fldg map in rear-1st trd ed (f7,f,dj) 40.00

SPARROW,WALTER S-Book of Sporting Painters-Lond,NY-1931-Lane,Scribners-4to-1st US ed (h9,dj) 225.00

SPARROW,WALTER S-British Sporting Artists from Barlow to Herring-Lond,NY-1922-Lane,Scribner-4to-1st US ed (h9) 185.00

SPAULDING,EDITH R-An Experimental Study of Psychopathic Delinquent Women-NY-1923-Rand McNally/Bur Soc Hygn-8vo-368p-illus-1st ed (oo7) 25.00

SPAYTH,HENRY-Checker Player...-NY-(1895)-Fitzgerald-128p+publ catlg-cl (f1) 17.50

SPEAIGHT,ROBERT-Life of Eric Gill-NY-(1966)-1st ed (y7,fray dj) 20.00

SPEAIGHT,ROBERT-Life of Eric Gill-NY-(1966)-Kenedy-8vo-323p-illus-1st ed (ee5,dj rub,sl soil) 35.00

SPEAKMAN,HAROLD-Hilltops in Galilee-NY-(1923)-Abingdon-8vo-259p-8 col illus-1st ed (jj5,dj soil,autg) 20.00

SPEAR,PERCIVAL-India-Ann Arbor-1961-U of Mich Pr-x,491,xix p-blk cl,maps (ll1,v wn dj) 10.00

SPEARS,RAYMOND S-Camping on the Great River-NY,Lond-1912-401,(1)p-cl (l1,pres cpy) 15.00

SPEARS,RAYMOND S-Camping on the Great River-NY-1912-12mo-402p-illus (m3) 30.00

SPECK,GORDON-Breeds and Half Breeds-NY-(1969)-361p-illus-1st ed (n3,dj) 30.00

SPECK,GORDON-Northwest Explorations-Portland-(1954)-394p-illus-1st ed (f7,f,dj) 35.00

SPECTORSKY,A C-ED.-Book of the Mountains-NY-1955-Appleton Century Crofts-lg 8vo-492p-pict cl over bds,photos-1st ed (gg6) 35.00

SPECTORSKY,A C-ED.-College Years-NY-1958-Hawthorn-1st ed (z3,dj) 17.50

SPEER,WILLIAM-Encyclopedia of the New West-Marshall-1881-lea,blnd stmpd,photos-1st ed (f9,sl rub,glassine dj) 750.00

SPEERT,HAROLD-Obstetrics and Gynecology in America: a History-Chig-1980-264p-wrps,illus-1st ed (dd3) 50.00

SPEIR,JERRY-Ross Macdonald-NY-1978-Ungar-1st ed (g4,f,dj) 15.00

SPENCE,BASIL-Phoenix at Coventry-1962-Geo Bles Ltd (cc8,tn dj) 25.00

SPENCE,BILL-Harpooned, the Story of Whaling-Greenwich-1980-Conway Maritime Pr-192p-gry papr over bds,g titles,photos,drwngs,maps-1st ed (p8,as new in dj) 15.00

SPENCE,H-Guide to Early Canadian Glass-1966-Longmans-112p-72 plts(6 col) (cc8,dj) 35.00

SPENCE,HARTZELL-For Every Tear a Victory-NY-1964-McGraw Hill-312p-photos-1st ed (c3,chip dj) 30.00

SPENCE,HARTZELL-Portrait in Oil-NY-(1962)-McGraw-Hill-357p-cl-1st ed (z7) 30.00

SPENCE,HARTZELL-Portrait in Oil-NY-(1962)-McGraw-Hill-357p-cl-1st ed so stated (g1,sl wn dj) 12.50

SPENCE,LEWIS-Mexico and Peru-Bost-nd-David D Nickerson-cl,spec ed of 1000c,nbrd,col frntis,plts (l8) 20.00

SPENCER,C-Civil War Marriage in Virginia-Boyce-1956-267p-illus,maps,ports-v scarce (z10,sl scuf & soil) 85.00

SPENCER,CLAIRE-Gallows Orchard-NY-1930-Cape-1st US ed (g4,f,sl wn dj) 15.00

SPENCER,CLARISSAN Y-One Who Was Valiant-Caldwell-1940-Caxton-8vo-279p-cl,photos-1st ed (mm7,f,dj) 40.00

SPENCER,ELIZABETH-Crooked Way-NY-(1952)-1st ed (f5,sl soil dj) 125.00

SPENCER,ELIZABETH-Knights & Dragons-(1965)-McGraw Hill-1st ed (kk6,f,dj) 40.00

SPENCER,ELIZABETH-Knights and Dragons-NY-(1965)-McGraw Hill-1st ed (cc2,f,dj) 50.00

SPENCER,ELIZABETH-Light in the Piazza-1960-McGraw Hill-1st ed (kk6,f,dj) 45.00

SPENCER,ELIZABETH-Light in the Piazza-NY-1960-McGraw Hill-1st ed (q2,dj) 35.00

SPENCER,ELIZABETH-No Place For an Angel-NY-(1967)-McGraw Hill-1st ed (a5,sl sp spot dj) 22.50

SPENCER,ELIZABETH-This Crooked Way-NY-(1952)-Dodd,Mead-1st ed (a10,dj sl chip & soil) 125.00

SPENCER,ELMA R-Green Russell and Gold-Austin-1966-239p-illus-1st ed (t7,dj) 15.00

SPENCER,JOHN-Terrell's Texas Cavalry-Austin-(1982)-199p-e.p. maps,illus-1st ed (n3,vf,dj) 17.50

SPENCER,O M-Indian Captivity of...-Chig-1917-Donnelley-188p-frntis,map-Lakeside Classics (cc4) 35.00

SPENCER,ORSON-Letters Exhibiting the Most Prominent Doctrines of the Church...-SLC-1891-232p-brwn lea (bb8,sl wn,sp sun) 25.00

SPENCER,SCOTT-Endless Love-NY-1979-Knopf-1st ed (b5,as new in dj) 25.00

SPENCER,SCOTT-Last Night at the Brain Thieves' Ball-Bost-1973-auth 1st bk-1st ed (t5,dj) 30.00

SPENCER,SCOTT-Preservation Hall-NY-1976-1st ed (p5,f,dj) 30.00

SPENCER,SCOTT-Preservation Hall-NY-1976-1st ed (z6,vf,dj) 25.00

SPENCER,SHARON-Collage of Dreams-Chig-1977-Swallow Pr-1st ed (d8,f,f dj) 30.00

SPENCER,SIDNEY-Newly From the Sea-Lond-1969-8vo-250p-photos (m3,vf,dj) 25.00

SPENCER,SIDNEY-Pike on the Plug-Lond-1936-12mo-183p-photos-1st ed (m3,f) 17.50

SPENCER,WILBUR D-Pioneers on Maine Rivers-Portland-1930-Lakeside Prtg-414p-blu cl,illus-1st ed (b2) 60.00

SPENDER,BRENDA-On'y Tony and the Dragon-Lond,NY-1938-Country Life,Scribner-1st US ed (h9) 18.00

SPENDER,BRENDA-On'y Tony's Circus-Lond-1936-Country Life-1st ed (h9,sl wn dj) 20.00

SPENDER,BRENDA-On'y Tony-Lond-1936-Country Life (h9,wn dj) 15.00

SPENDER,HAROLD-Through the High Pyrenees-Lond-1898-365p-maps,lg col fldg map-scarce-1st ed (a4) 130.00

SPENDER,STEPHEN-Poems of Dedication-NY-(1947)-Random-cl backd dec bds-1st Amer ed (aa9,f,sl wn dj) 30.00

SPENDER,STEPHEN-Poems-Lond-(1933)-Faber-8vo-cl-1st ed (jj8,f,sl soil dj) 225.00

SPENDER,STEPHEN-Vienna-1935-Random-1st Amer ed (x2,f,soil dj) 65.00

SPENSER,EDMUND-Shepheard's Calendar-NY-1898-Harper-107p-pict cl,12p illus,W Crane (r3,hngs rprd) 75.00

SPERRY,ARMSTRONG-Pacific Islands Speaking-NY-1955-Macmillan-220p-map e.p.,maps & drwngs,auth-1st prtg (nn1,wn dj) 20.00

SPERRY,L-Botanic Family Physician or the Secret of Curing Diseases-Cornwall-1843-Auth-60p-lea sp,bds (x6,sl fox) 140.00

SPERRY,NEIL-Complete Guide to Texas Gardening-Dallas-1982-Taylor-497p-col illus-1st ed (a9,dj) 22.00

SPEWACK,SAMUEL-Skyscraper Murder-NY-1928-Macaulay-1st ed (g4) 10.00

SPICE ISLAND CO-Spice Islands Cook Book-Menlo Park-(1961)-Lane Bk-208p-pict red cl,watercol illus-1st prtg (q8,chip dj) 15.00

SPICE ISLANDS COOK BOOK-Menlo Park-(1961)-Lane Bk Co-208p-illus,A Harth-1st ed (m6,dj) 24.00

SPICE ISLANDS HOME ECON STAFF-Spice Islands Cookbook-1961-Lane Bk Co-1st ed (v6,dj) 10.00

SPICER,JACK-Book of Music-SF-1969-White Rabbit Pr-pict wrps-1st ed (r2,f) 25.00

SPIEGEL,HERBERT-Trance and Treatment-NY-(1978)-Basic Bks-xiv+382+(4)p-red cl-1st ed (y9,dj) 28.50

SPIELMAN,JEAN E-Stool-Pigeon and the Open Shop Movement-Mpls-(1923)-240p-cl (b1) 25.00

SPIER,JERRY-Raymond Chandler-NY-1981-Unger-1st ed (r4,vf,dj) 25.00

SPIERS,A-ET AL-Bacon's Essay and Wisdom of the Ancients-Bost-1884-Little,Brown-423p-cl (x6) 15.00

SPIERS,REV WILLIAM-Rambles and Reveries of a Naturalist-Lond-1890-Chas H Kelly-8vo-256p-64 illus-1st ed (ff9) 65.00*

SPIKE,PAUL-Bad News-NY,Chig,SF-(1971)-HR&W-auth 1st bk-1st ed (bb1,as new in dj) 20.00

SPIKE,PAUL-Photographs of My Father-NY-1973-Knopf-photos-1st ed (bb1,as new in dj) 15.00

SPILLANE,MICKEY-Bloody Sunrise-NY-1965-Dutton-1st ed (f4,f,sl rprd dj) 25.00

SPILLANE,MICKEY-Body Lovers-NY-1967-Dutton-1st ed (g4,f,dj) 20.00

SPILLANE,MICKEY-By Pass Control-NY-1966-Dutton-1st ed (e4,dj) 15.00

SPILLANE,MICKEY-Day of the Guns-NY-1964-Dutton-1st ed (l4,f,dj) 20.00

SPILLANE,MICKEY-Deep-NY-(1961)-1st ed (l5,dj) 20.00

SPILLANE,MICKEY-Erection Set-NY-1972-Dutton-1st ed (e4,dj) 40.00

SPILLANE,MICKEY-Girl Hunters-1962-Dutton-1st ed (s10,dj) 20.00

SPILLANE,MICKEY-Last Cop Out-NY-1973-Dutton-1st ed (e4,dj) 40.00

SPILLANE,MICKEY-My Gun is Quick-NY-1950-Dutton-1st ed (pp3,dj) 125.00

SPILLANE,MICKEY-Snake-NY-1964-Dutton-1st ed (f4,sl wn dj) 25.00

SPILLANE,MICKEY-Twisted Thing-NY-1966-Dutton-1st ed (e4,rub dj) 20.00

SPILLANE,MICKEY-Vengeance is Mine-1950-Dutton-1st ed (x7,sl tn dj) 165.00

SPILLANE,MICKEY-Vengeance is Mine-NY-1950-Dutton-scarce-1st ed (bb1,dj sp chip,edge rub) 225.00

SPILLARD,WILLIAM-Needle in a Haystack-NY-1945-McGraw Hill-1st ed (z9,f,dj chip) 15.00

SPILLER,BURTON-Drummer in the Woods-NY-1962-239p-photos (ee3,vf,dj) 80.00

SPILLER,BURTON-Grouse Feathers-NY-1947-4to-207p-illus,L B Hunt-1st trd ed (m3) 17.50

SPILLER,BURTON-Hunt-NY-1935-g pict cov wi recessed col illus,illus by L Bogue-ltd to 950c (r2) 150.00

SPILLER,BURTON-More Grouse Feathers-NY-1938-Derrydale-238p-maroon cl,col medallion on cov,ltd to 950c,nbrd (ee3,vf) 225.00

SPILLER,BURTON-More Grouse Feathers-NY-1972-4to-238p-illus,L B Hunt (m3,f,dj) 18.00

SPILLER,BURTON-Thoroughbred-NY-(1936)-Derrydale-4to-illus by L B Hunt,cov medallion by Burke-ltd to 950c,nbrd-1st ed (u10,f) 275.00

SPILLER,ROBT E-Descriptive Bibliography of the Writings of James Fenimore Cooper-NY-1934-260p-facs,illus-ltd to 500c (a3) 75.00

SPINDEN,HERBERT J-Songs of the Tewa-(NY)-(1933)-125p-1st ed (u7,f) 35.00

SPINK,J G TAYLOR-Judge Landis and 25 Years of Baseball-NY-(1947)-illus-1st ed (k5,sl tan sp,dj sp sl chip) 20.00

SPINK,WESLEY-Infectious Diseases-Mpls-1978-577p-1st ed (dd3,dj) 35.00

SPINRAD,NORMAN-Bug Jack Barron-NY-(1969)-Walker-1st ed (k3,f,sl wn dj) 25.00

SPINRAD,NORMAN-Men in the Jungle-GC-1967-Dbldy-1st ed (g3,f,sl creased dj) 75.00

SPIRIT OF THE SOVIET UNION-Lond-1942-Pilot Pr-illus-1st ed (e8,sl chip dj) 30.00

SPIRIT OF WASHINGTON-NY-1863-C D Tracy-16p-pict wrps-"for sale by Miss Flora E Simmons" (e1,sl fox) 50.00

SPIRO,GEORGE-Paris on the Barricades-NY-1929-Workers Libr-1st ed (w5,sl stnd edges) 25.00

SPIVAK,JOHN-Medical Trust Unmasked-NY-1929-170p-1st ed (dd3) 75.00

SPOERRI,DANIEL-Mythology & Meatballs-Berkeley-(1982)-Aris Bks-238p-blu cl,illus-1st prtg (q8,dj) 18.50

SPONENBERG,D P-Horse Color-College Sta-1983-Tex A&M-4to-col illus-1st ed (f10,f,f dj) 35.00

SPOONER,WALTER-Back Woodsmen or Tales of the Borders-Cin-nd-453p-pict cl,frntis,illus-rprnt Howes S841 (t7,hngs weak) 15.00

SPORES,RONALD-Mixtec Kings and Their People-Norman-1967-U of Okla Pr-1st ed (v4,as new in dj) 20.00

SPORTS AND PASTIMES FROM THE FOURTEENTH THROUGH THE EIGHTEENTH CENTURY-NY-1946-P Morgan Libr/Gallery Pr-8vo-47p-self papr wrps (w2,yel) 15.00

SPORTS OF CHILDHOOD-New Haven-nd(ca.1840)-S Babcock-8p-prtd yel wrps,illus (hh9,sl fox) 95.00

SPORTSMAN'S DICTIONARY-Lond-1800-4to-542p-full mottled calf gilt,copper plts-scarce-4th ed,revsd & enlgd (m3,f) 250.00

SPORTSMAN'S PORTFOLIO OF AMERICAN FIELD SPORTS-Derrydale-1929-oblng 8vo-43p-one of 400c-illus-scarce (m3,f) 165.00

SPRADBERY,J P-Wasps-1973-U of Wash-408p-col & b&w photos-1st ed (bb3,f,dj) 35.00

SPRAGUE,MARSHALL-Cheyenne Mountain Ranch-np-nd-28p-stiff pict wrps,photos (t7) 25.00

SPRAGUE,MARSHALL-Great Gates-Bost-1964-Little,Brown-illus,maps-1st ed (v4,as new in dj) 45.00

SPRAGUE,MARSHALL-Money Mountain-Bost-(1953)-Little,Brown-342p-e.p. maps,illus-1st ed (bb4,dj) 25.00

SPRAGUE,REV DELOS E-Descriptive Guide of the Battlefield of Saratoga-Ballston Spa-1930-Battlefield Publ-blu cl,map e.p.,photos,orig glassine dj-1st ed (gg7,f,dj) 20.00

SPRATLING,WILLIAM-Little Mexico-NY-1932-Cape & Smith-198p-yel cl,g sp,ports-1st ed (u5,sp top wn,sl fade) 35.00

SPRIGG,C ST.JOHN-Great Flights-Lond-(1935)-8vo-viii,232p-cl,frntis,9p plts-1st ed (s2,fade,sl stnd) 20.00

SPRIGGE,S SQUIRE-Physic and Fiction-Lond-1921-307p-1st ed (dd3) 40.00

SPRING,AGNES W-Buffalo Bill and His Horses-Ft.Collins-1953-23p-pict wrps,frntis,photos-1st ed (t7,autg laid in) 15.00

SPRING,AGNES W-Caspar Collins, the Life and Exploits of an Indian Fighter of the Sixties-NY-1927-187p-illus-1st ed (g7,f,chip dj) 100.00

SPRING,AGNES W-Caspar Collins-NY-1927-187p-illus-1st ed (n3,f,dj) 75.00

SPRING,AGNES W-Cheyenne & Black Hills Stage & Express Routes-Glendale-1949-418p-plts,fldg map-Six Guns #2084-1st ed (c7,f,unopened) 110.00

SPRING,AGNES W-Cow Country Legacies-KC-1976-Lowell Pr-123p-cl,photos-1st ed (w3,vf,dj) 17.50

SPRING,AGNES W-William Chapin Deming of Wyoming-Glendale-1944-A H Clark Co-531p-illus-Herd 2139-1st ed (dd4) 50.00

SPRING,BOB-High Adventure-Seattle-1951-115p-photos-1st ed (p10,f,dj) 35.00

SPRING,BOB-High Adventure-Seattle-1951-Superior Pr-115p-photos-1st ed (j8,fade dj) 30.00

SPRING,BOB-North Cascades National Park-Seattle-1969-143p-100 photos(16 col),text by H Manning-1st ed (p10,f,dj) 40.00

SPRINGS,E W-Leave Me with a Smile-NY-(1928)-8vo-288p-cl,illus e.p.,B Crawford-1st ed (s2) 25.00

SPRINGS,E W-Nocturnal Militaire-NY-(1927)-8vo-288p-cl,frntis,7 illus,C Knight (s2,dj) 20.00

SPRINGS,F W-Rise and Fall of Carol Banks-GC-1931-Dbldy,Doran-roy 8vo-xii,308p-cl,prntd sp labl,ltd to 200c,autg,prntd on linen sheets (t2,soil,sp wn) 75.00

SPRINGS,W-Above the Bright Blue Sky-GC-1928-8vo-276p-cl bkd col illus bds,illus e.p.-1st ed (s2) 25.00

SPROAT,IAIN-Wodehouse at War-New Haven-1981-Ticknor and Fields-167p-1st ed (g9,dj) 25.00

SPRUNGMAN,ORMAL I-Photography Afield-Harrisburg-(1951)-Stackpole-4to-(15)449p-col photos-1st ed (l10) 17.50

SPRUNT,A-Album of Southern Birds-Austin-1953-4to-103p-buckr,4 col plts (y8) 25.00

SPRUNT,A-Florida Bird Life-1954-Coward McCann-527p-56 col plts,maps (bb3,f) 80.00

SPRUNT,A-Florida Bird Life-NY-1954-Coward McCann/Nat Audubon-527p-col plts (d9) 70.00

SPRUNT,A-North Amer Birds of Prey-NY-1955-8vo-227p-cl,46 col plts (y8,dj wn) 55.00

SPRUNT,A-South Carolina Bird Life-1949-U of SC-585p-34 col plts,photos-1st ed (bb3) 85.00

SPRUNT,A-South Carolina Bird Life-Columbia-1949-585p-cl,frntis,34 col plts,48 photos-1st ed (aa1) 60.00

SPRUNT,A-South Carolina Bird Life-Columbia-1949-8vo-(1),585p-cl,34 col plts,48 photos (y8,2 autgs) 80.00

SPRY,CONSTANCE-Hostess-Lond-(1961)-Dent-126p-drwngs,L Branch (l6) 35.00

SPUNGEON,DEBORAH-And I Don't Want to Live This Life-NY-1983-Villard-8vo-386p-photos-1st ed (gg5,dj) 15.00

SPUNT,GEORGES-Place in Time-NY-(1968)-Putnam-8vo-378p-1st ed (dd5,dj) 12.50

SPURLING,R GLEN-ED.-Surgery in World War II. Neurosurgery Volume I-Wash-1958-466p-illus-1st ed (dd3) 40.00

SPURR,RUSSELL-Glorious Way to Die-NY-(1981)-New Mrkt Pr-roy 8vo-x,342p-cl bkd bds,plts-1st ed (s2,dj) 25.00

SPURZHEIM,J G-Anatomy of the Brain with a General View of the Nervous System-Lond-1826-S Highley-xxiv+234+(2)p+11 litho plts,orig cl bkd drab bds-1st ed (y9,hngs crckd,sl loose) 375.00

SPYRI,JOHANNA-Heidi-NY-(1923)-McKay-356p-cl wi pict pasteon,8 col plts,A Anderson (s3) 25.00

SQIBB'S MATERIA MEDICA-NY-1919-Squibb & Son-544p-yel cl (m6,soil) 15.00

SQUIER,LOUISE S-Sketches of Southern Scenes-NY-1885-J W Pratt-203p-brwn cl-1st ed (oo5,bump,sl rub & wn) 16.50

SQUIERS,GRANVILLE-Secret Hiding Places-Lond-1934-Stanley Paul-8vo-288p+8p ads-tan cl,photos,sketches (r10) 50.00

SQUIRE,J L-Sport Fishing in Hawaii,Guam and American Samoa-Rutland-1979-4to-53p-wrps,illus,maps (m3) 17.50

SQUIRE,JOHN-Cheddar Gorge-NY-1938-Macmillan-sm 4to-181p-illus,E H Shepard-1st ed (o6,wn dj) 35.00

SQUIRE,JOHN-ED.-Cheddar Gorge-Lond-(1937)-Collins-qto-181p-cl,illus by E H Shepard-1st ed (dd10,sl soil dj) 45.00

SQUIRE,LORENE-Wildfowling with a Camera-Phila-1938-4to-217p+photos (m3,f,sl chip dj) 45.00

SQUIRE,LORENE-Wildfowling with a Camera-Phila-1938-4to-217p-cl,illus (y8,sp chip,dj chip) 75.00

SQUIRE,MARIAN-Stag at Ease-Caldwell-1938-Caxton-164p-blu bds,dec e.p. (l6) 35.00

SQUIRES,W AUSTIN-104th Regiment of Foot 1803 to 1817-New Brunswick-1962-246p-illus-1st ed (b7,f,dj) 75.00

ST.ALPHONSUS PARISH, DEARBORN-A CENTURY OF CONQUEST 1852-1952...-Dearborn-1952-196p-cl (b1) 15.00

ST.AMANT,L S-Louisiana Wildlife Inventory and Management Plan-New Orleans-1959-8vo-329p-cl,23 plts (y8,dj fade & chip) 30.00

ST.JOHN,BRUCE-John Sloan-NY-1971-Praeger-4to-col & b&w illus-1st ed (b4,dj) 50.00

ST.JOHN,D-Diabolus-1971-W&T-1st ed (x7,f,dj) 25.00

ST.JOHN,H C-Notes and Sketches from the Wild Coasts of Nippon...Cruising after Pirates in Chinese Waters-Edinburgh-1880-David Douglas-11p plts,5 col maps-1st ed (p6,unopened) 350.00

ST.JOHN,LARRY-Practical Bait Casting-NY-1918-12mo-181p-illus-1st ed (m3,vf) 30.00

ST.JOHN,LARRY-Practical Fly Casting-NY-1920-12mo-175p-photos,illus-1st ed (m3,f) 27.50

ST.JOHNS,ADELA R-Final Verdict-GC-1962-512p-cl-1st ed so stated (d1,sl spot cov,dj) 12.50

ST.JOHNS,ADELA R-Honeycomb-NY-1969-Dbldy-1st ed (aa9,f,dj) 15.00

ST.PIERRE,PAUL-Chilcotin Holiday-Tor-1970-McClelland & Stewart-8vo-(vi),138p-illus-1st ed (bb7,dj) 20.00*

ST.SIMON'S MISSION, SHERIDAN PARK-Cook Book-(Chig)-1904-(Rogerson Pr)-73p+ads-illus grn limp bds-1st ed (n6) 45.00

STACEY INTERNATIONAL PUBLISHERS-Wild Life of Saudi Arabia and its Neighbors-1981-4to-96p-col photos ea pg,map (bb3,f,dj) 45.00

STACKPOLE,EDWARD J-Sheridan in the Shenandoah-Harrisburg-(1961)-413p-illus,maps-1st ed (c4,f,dj) 45.00

STADTFELD,C K-Whitetail Deer, a Year's Cycle-NY-1975-163p-illus (gg3,f,dj) 20.00

STAENDER,GILBERT-Adventures with Arctic Wildlife-Caldwell-1970-Caxton-8vo-260p-col photos-1st ed (aa5,f,sl wn dj) 20.00

STAFFORD,JEAN-Boston Adventure-1944-Harcourt-auth 1st bk-1st ed (kk6,f) 20.00

STAFFORD,JEAN-Boston Adventure-NY-1944-auth 1st bk-1st ed (t5,sl chip dj) 35.00

STAFFORD,JEAN-Catherine Wheel-NY-1952-1st ed (s5,dj) 22.50

STAFFORD,JEAN-Children are Bored on Sunday-1953-Harcourt-1st ed (kk6,dj) 30.00

STAFFORD,JEAN-Mother in History-NY-(1966)-Farrar,Straus-8vo-121p-1st ed (w6,dj) 35.00

STAFFORD,JEAN-Mountain Lion-NY-1947-Harcourt-1st ed (w5,f,dj) 30.00

STAFFORD,JOS-Canadian Oyster-Ottawa-1913-Mortimer-159p-tan cl (q8,cov wn,lt penciling) 35.00

STAFFORD,MURIEL-X Marks the Dot-NY-1943-Duell-1st ed (h4,f,chip dj) 15.00

STAFFORD,WILLIAM-Eleven Untitled Poems-1968-Perishable Pr-wrps-ltd to 250c,nbrd-1st ed (y1) 200.00

STAFFORD,WILLIAM-Rescued Year-NY-(1966)-Harper & Row-pict bds-1st ed (aa9,f,dj) 25.00

STAGER,WALTER-Tall Bearded Iris-Sterling-(1922)-262p+blank pgs (j10,few fox pgs) 45.00

STAGGE,JONATHAN-Death's Old Sweet Song-NY-1946-Dbldy CC-1st ed (g4,dj) 12.50

STAGGE,JONATHAN-Murder by Prescription-1938-CC-1st ed (s10) 20.00

STAHL,JOHN M-Growing with the West-Lond,NY-1930-Longmans,Green-x,515p-illus-1st ed (o2) 17.50

STAINSBY,WILLIAM-Oyster Industry-Trenton-1902-68p-wrps (aa6) 30.00

STALEY,EUGENE-History of the Illinois State Federation of Labor-Chig-1930-U of Chig Pr-1st ed (v5) 30.00

STALIN,JOSEPH-Foundations of Leninism-NY-1932-Int'l-125p-stapled wrps-10th Annvrsy ed (r1,brwnd pg edges) 15.00

STALIN,JOSEPH-Road to Power-NY-1937-Int'l-48p-wrps (r1) 17.00

STALLINGS,LAURENCE-ED.-First World War: a Photographic History-NY-1933-S&S-lg 4to-297p-1st ed (p1,dj) 75.00

STALSON,J OWEN-Marketing Life Insurance-Cambridge-1942-Harvard-xl+911p-red cl,31 tbls,12 charts,15 illus-1st ed (k2) 45.00

STAMBAUGH,J LEE-Lower Rio Grande Valley of TX-San Antonio-1954-Naylor-344p-map e.p.-1st ed (a9) 75.00

STAMM,SARA-Favorite New England Recipes-1977-Yankee Mag-illus (v6,dj wn) 10.00

STAMP,K M-Era of Reconstruction, 1865 to 1877-NY-1965-229p (z10,ex-libr) 10.00

STANARD,MARY N-Richmond-Phila-1923-239p-pict cl,illus-1st ed (c4,cov fade) 50.00

STANDARD,PAUL-Calligraphy's Flowering Decay, and Restauration, with Hints for Its Wider Use-Chig-1947-Soc Typographic Arts-8vo-38p-cl,illus-1st ed (w2,cov fade) 35.00

STANDEN,MIKA-Reminiscence and Ravioli-NY-1946-Morrow-148p-1st ed (q6) 15.00

STANDING BEAR,CHIEF-My People the Sioux-Bost-1928-Houghton Mifflin-288p-illus-1st ed (ee4,dj wn,chip) 95.00

STANDING BEAR,CHIEF-My People the Sioux-Bost-1928-Houghton Mifflin-288p-pict cl,drwngs,photos-1st ed (nn6) 75.00

STANDISH,BURT-Courtney of the Center Garden-1915-Barse & Hopkins-"Big League Ser."#7-1st ed (s8) 25.00

STANDISH,BURT-Covering the Look In Corner-1915-Barse (q7) 12.50

STANDISH,BURT-Covering the Look In Corner-NY-(1915)-Barse & Hopkins-316p-cl (n1) 15.00

STANDISH,BURT-Grip of the Game-NY-(1924)-Barse & Hopkins-245p+ads-cl,illus by C L Wrenn (e1) 15.00

STANDISH,BURT-Lefty O'the Blue Stockings-1914-Barse-1st ed (q7) 12.50

STANDISH,BURT-Lefty O'the Bush-1914-Barse (q7) 12.50

STANDISH,BURT-Lefty O'the Training Camp-1914-Barse (q7) 12.50

STANDISH,BURT-Man on First-1920-Barse-pict cov (p7) 12.50

STANDLEE,MARY-Great Pulse: Japanese Midwifery and Obstetrics Through the Ages-Rutland-1959-192p-1st ed (dd3) 60.00

STANDLEY,BENOIN-Men of Ormolu-Dallas-1935-88p-1st ed (t7,dj) 10.00

STANFORD,ALFRED-Navigator, the Story of Nathaniel Bowditch-NY-1927-Morrow-8vo-xi,308p-blu cl,g cov & sp titles,tip-in frntis drwng-1st prtg (nn1,sl wn & bump) 22.50

STANFORD,J K-Guns Wanted-NY-1949-8vo-348p-illus,A M Hughes (m3,vf) 22.50

STANFORD,J K-Twelfth-Lond-1953-12mo-85p-illus (m3,f,dj) 25.00

STANFORD,J K-Twelfth-VT-1957-125p-illus (gg3,f,dj) 10.00

STANHOPE,PHILIP-Letters to His Son-Wash-1901-M Walter Dunne-2 vols-3/4 lea (l9) 150.00

STANLEY,E J-Life of Rev L B Stateler-Nashville-1916-Publ Hs of M E Church-356p-pict cl,illus-Howes S879-rvsd ed (bb4,innr hng rprd) 65.00

STANLEY,F-Clovis Story-Pampa-1966-358p-1st ed (t7,dj,autg) 45.00

STANLEY,F-Cuidad Santa Fe Mexican Rule 1821 to 1846-Pampa-1962-3 vols-1st ed (t7,dj,autg) 150.00

STANLEY,F-Dave Rudabaugh-(Denver)-(1961)-(World Pr)-200p-Six Guns 2095-1st ed (gg4,dj,autg) 30.00

STANLEY,F-Early Days of the Oil Industry in the Texas Panhandle-Borger-1973-auth-414p-cl-ltd to 500c-1st ed (ee10,as new) 50.00

STANLEY,F-Railroads of the Texas Panhandle-Borger-1976-Hess Publ-456p-cl-scarce-1st ed (w3,vf,dj) 90.00

STANLEY,F-Rodeo Town-Denver-(1953)-World Pr-418p-illus-ltd to 500c,nbrd,autg (ee4,dj) 75.00

STANLEY,FATHER-Fort Stanton-Pampa-(1964)-Pampa Prnt Shp-263p-ltd to 500c,autg-Six Guns #2101-1st ed (ee4,dj) 65.00

STANLEY,HENRY M-Coomassie and Magdala-NY-1874-510p-grn cl,2 fldg maps-scarce-1st Amer ed (b7,f) 200.00

STANLEY,HENRY M-In Darkest Africa-NY-1890-Scribner-8vo-2 vols-orig cl,2 plts,150 illus,3 fldg maps rear pckt-1st ed (bb6) 85.00

STANLEY,HENRY M-In Darkest Africa-NY-1891-2 vols-dec grn cl,4 pckt maps-2nd ed (b7,f,1 map a facs) 75.00

STANLEY,HENRY M-Through the Dark Continent-1899-Newnes-2 vols-33 full pg illus,7 maps-rvsd ed(wi chronology of explorers 1854 to 1898) (bb3) 135.00

STANLEY,REV E J-Life of Rev L B Stateler-Dallas-1907-356p-pict cl,frntis,photos-Graff #39116,Smith #9807-1st ed (t7,f) 150.00

STANLEY,REVA-Biography of Parley P Pratt, the Archer of Paradise-Caldwell-1937-349p-dec stmpd cl,port,plts-1st ed (bb8,sl fox dj & e.p.) 50.00

STANLEY,RUPERT-Wireless Telegraphy-1918-344p-201 illus-1st ed (h6) 45.00

STANLEY-BROWN,KATHERINE-Young Architects-NY,Lond-1929-Harper-orig cl,papr sp & cov labls,illus-1st ed (aa9,sp fade,labl sl rub) 10.00

STANSBURY,HOWARD-Exploration and Survey of the Valley of the Great Salt Lake of Utah...-Phila-1852-2 vols-fldg maps-Graff #3947,Howes S884-1st ed (t7,vol I rbnd) 225.00

STANTON,MARTIN W-History of Public Poor Relief in New Jersey, 1609 to 1934-NY-1934-126p-wrps (aa6,chip,tape mrks) 45.00

STANTON,ROBERT B-Down the Colorado-Norman-1965-237p-photos,maps-1st ed (n10,f,dj) 45.00

STANWELL-FLETCHER,THEODORA-Tundra World-Bost-1952-Little,Brown-8vo-xiv,266p-frntis-1st ed (ff9,wn dj) 30.00*

STANWORTH,J E-Physical Properties of Glass-Oxford-1953-224p-illus (cc8) 65.00

STAPLES,WILLIAM R-Rhode Island in the Continental Congress-Providence-1870-Prov Pr-xlviii+725p-grn cl-1st ed (e2,ex-lib) 50.00

STAPLETON,DAISY M-Daisy Mae's Favorite Recipes-NY-(1958)-Pageant-150p-blu cl-1st prtg (q8,dj) 15.00

STAR FLEET TECHNICAL MANUAL-NY-(1975)-Ballantine-acetate dj-1st ed (j3,dj) 25.00

STARBUCK,EDITH-Crossing the Plains-Nashville-(1927)-So Publ Assoc-8vo-224p-gry cl,frntis,illus-1st ed (ee9,cov soil,sl edgewn & fox) 50.00

STARK,GEORGE W-City of Destiny-Detr-1943-Arnold-Powers-514p-cl,photos (z7) 22.50

STARK,RICHARD-Damsel-1967-Macmillan-1st ed (n9,sl wn dj) 30.00

STARK,RICHARD-Lemons Never Lie-NY-1971-World-1st ed (j4,f,dj) 45.00

STARK,RICHARD-Slayground-NY-1971-1st ed (q5,dj) 30.00

STARK,RICHARD-Slayground-NY-1971-Random-1st ed (f4,f,sl tn dj) 25.00

STARK,STUART-Oak Bay's Heritage Buildings-Oak Bay-(1968)-Oak Bay Heritage Adv Comm-4to-vi,122p-plastic ring bndg,illus,maps (k10) 20.00*

STARKEY,MARION L-Cherokee Nation-NY-1946-361p-1st ed (t7,dj) 30.00

STARKIE,ENID-Baudelaire-(Norfolk)-(1958)-New Directions-photos-1st ed (b10,sl wn dj) 20.00

STARKMAN & READ-Contemplative Man's Recreation-1970-Univ of B.C. Libr-8vo-138p (m3,as new) 25.00

STARKMAN,S B-Contemplative Man's Recreation-Vancouver-1970-138p-illus,dec e.p. (ee3,f) 30.00

STAROBIN,JOSEPH R-Eyewitness in Indo China-NY-(1954)-Cameron & Kahn-1st ed (ff3,dj) 85.00

STAROBIN,JOSEPH R-Eyewitness in Indo China-NY-1954-1st ed (v9,edge rub,dj) 75.00

STAROKADOMSKIY,L M-Charting the Russian Northern Sea Route-1976-McGill,Queen's Univ-332p-illus-1st ed (u8,dj) 18.00

STARR,FREDERICK-Fujiyama-Chig-1924-Covici McGee-158p-pict e.p.,prnts,photos (c3,sl rub dj) 65.00

STARR,FREDERICK-Some First Steps in Human Progress-Meadville-1895-Flood & Vincent-305p-cl (j1) 15.00

STARR,JOHN W,JR.-One Hundred Years of American Railroading-NY-1928-336p-cl,illus-1st ed (m1) 15.00

STARR,LOUIS M-Bohemian Brigade-NY-1954-367p-1st ed (n3) 30.00

STARR,PAUL-Discarded Army-NY-(1973)-304p-cl (h1,dj) 15.00

STARR,STEPHEN Z-Colonel Grenfell's War-Baton Rouge-(1971)-352p-1st ed (n3,f,dj) 32.50

STARR,STEPHEN-Colonel Grenfell's War-Baton Rouge-(1971)-352p-frntis-1st ed (b7,f,dj) 20.00

STARRETT,VINCENT-221B-NY-1940-Macmillan-1st ed (l4,chip missing dj) 150.00

STARRETT,VINCENT-221B: Studies in Sherlock Holmes-1940-Macmillan-1st ed (x7) 65.00

STARRETT,VINCENT-Autolycus in Limbo-1943-Dutton-ltd to 1500c-1st ed (s10,sp fox,dj soil) 25.00

STARRETT,VINCENT-Blue Door-NY-1930-Dbldy CC-1st ed (k4) 15.00

STARRETT,VINCENT-Bookman's Holiday-NY-(1942)-Random-1st ed (e4,dj) 40.00

STARRETT,VINCENT-Bookman's Holiday-NY-(1942)-Random-1st ed (w1,dj) 20.00

STARRETT,VINCENT-Bookman's Holiday-NY-(1942)-Random-312p-cl,pict papr labls cov & sp,illus-1st ed (dd10,f,sl chip dj) 35.00

STARRETT,VINCENT-Books and Bipeds-NY-1947-Argus-1st ed (e4,f,dj) 37.50

STARRETT,VINCENT-Born in a Bookshop-(1965)-U of Okla-1st ed (u10,f,sl wn dj) 25.00

STARRETT,VINCENT-Born in a Bookshop-Norman-(1965)-U of Okla Pr-1st ed (gg7,dj) 30.00

STARRETT,VINCENT-Coffins for Two-1924-Covici McGee-1st ed (s10) 20.00

STARRETT,VINCENT-Dead Man Inside-NY-1931-Dbldy CC-1st ed (e4,sl stnd cov,dj) 50.00

STARRETT,VINCENT-Dead Man Inside-NY-1931-Dbldy CC-1st ed (h4) 15.00

STARRETT,VINCENT-Flame and Dust-Chig-1924-Covici-8vo-cl/bds-ltd to 450c,nbrd-1st ed (u10,f,dj sl wn,sm chip) 100.00

STARRETT,VINCENT-LAST BOOKMAN: A JOURNEY INTO THE LIFE AND TIMES OF...-NY-1968-Candlelight Pr-sm folio-115p-1st ed (w1,f,dj) 30.00

STARRETT,VINCENT-Penny Wise and Book Foolish-NY-1929-Covici-grn cl-1st ed,1st iss (w1,sp fade) 20.00

STARRETT,VINCENT-Persons From Porlock-Chig-1938-Normandie Hs-8vo-cl/bds-ltd to 399c,autg-1st ed (u10,f,sl wn dj) 100.00

STARRETT,VINCENT-Private Life of Sherlock Holmes-NY-1933-Macmillan-1st ed (e4,dj) 200.00

STARRETT,VINCENT-Quick and the Dead-Sauk City-1965-Arkham Hs-ltd to 2047c-1st ed (kk10,dj) 35.00

STARRETT,VINCENT-Quick and the Dead-Sauk City-1965-Arkham-1st ed (k3,dj soil & chip) 25.00

STARRETT,VINCENT-Seaports in the Moon-1928-DD-1st ed (x7,chip dj) 55.00

STARS OF THE MOVIES AND FEATURES PLAYERS-Hollywood-1927-Hllywd Publicity Co-lg 8vo-wrps,250 ports-1st ed (s1,f) 45.00

STASSEN,HAROLD-Where I Stand-GC-1947-Dbldy-8vo-205p-auth 1st bk-1st ed (gg5,dj) 12.50

STATHAM,REGINALD-Paul Kruger and His Times-Lond-1898-312p-dec grn cl,fldg map-1st ed (gg2) 30.00

STATLER,OLIVER-Japanese Inn, A Reconstruction of the Past-NY-1961-Random-8vo-365p-50 drwngs & illus (ll1,sl fade,dj wn) 15.00

STATLER,OLIVER-Japanese Inn-Lond-(1961)-Secker & Warburg-8vo-365p-50 illus-1st Brit ed (jj5,dj) 17.50

STATLER,OLIVER-Shimoda Story-NY-(1969)-Random-8vo-627p-illus-1st ed (jj5,sl tn dj) 17.50

STAUFER,ALVIN F-Pennsy Power-Carrollton-1962-319p-1st ed (n4,f,dj) 36.00

STAUFER,ALVIN F-Thoroughbreds-Medina-1974-352p-1st ed (n4,f,dj) 40.00

STAUNTON,SCHUYLER-Daughters of Destiny-Chig-1906-Reilly & Britton-col illus-1st ed (y2) 200.00

STAUNTON,SCHUYLER-Fate of the Crown-Chig-(1905)-Reilly & Britton-2nd ed (y2,f) 150.00

STEAD,CHRISTINA-House of All Nations-NY-1938-1st US ed (t5,sl chip dj) 75.00

STEAD,CHRISTINA-Letty Fox-NY-1946-1st US ed (t5,sl soil dj) 75.00

STEAD,CHRISTINA-Puzzleheaded Girl-NY-(1967)-HR&W-1st US ed (z5,f,dj) 20.00

STEAD,CHRISTINE-Salzburg Tales-NY-1934-Appleton-auth 1st bk-1st Amer ed (bb2,scuff,dj chip) 100.00

STEARNS,MARSHAL-Memories & Recollections-1935-priv prntd-8vo-158p-illus-scarce (m3) 100.00

STEARNS,OSBORNE P-Italy on a Platter-(1965)-Ward Ritchie-205p-dec tan cl,col illus-1st ed (q8,dj) 17.50

STEBBING,E P-Diary of a Sportsman Naturalist in India-Lond/NY-1920-J Lane-xvi,298p-grn cl,plts,photos-1st ed (dd7,sp fade) 95.00

STEBBING,E P-Stalks in the Himalayas-Lond-1912-Bodley Head-8vo-321p-sketches-1st ed (ff5) 100.00

STEBBINS,DR HENRY M-How to Select & Use Your Big Game Rifle-Wash D.C.-1952-8vo-237p-1st ed (m3,f,dj) 10.00

STEBBINS,DR HENRY M-Rifles-Another Modern Encyclopedia-Harrisburg-1958-4to-376p-photos-1st ed (m3,vf,dj) 20.00

STEBBINS,G L-Variation and Evolution of Plants-1950-Columbia Univ-643p-55 figs (bb3,f) 35.00

STEBBINS,J E-Fifty Years History of the Temperance Cause-Hartford-1874-500p-cl (a1,sl wn) 25.00

STEBBINS,R C-Field Guide to Western Reptiles and Amphibians-1966-Houghton Mifflin-279p-col & b&w illus-1st prtg (bb3) 20.00

STECHOW,WOLFGANG-Dutch Landscape Painting of the Seventeenth Century-Lond-1966-Phaidon-4to-494p-red cl,370 illus (r10,edge tn dj) 25.00

STECKER,MARGARET L-Intercity Differences in Costs of Living-Wash-1937-USGPO-WPA-Rsrch Mono XII-wrps-1st ed (v5,sl soil) 25.00

STEEGMULLER,FRANCIS-Flaubert in Egypt-Bost,Tor-(1973)-Little,Brown-photos,drwngs-1st US ed (bb1,f,dj) 17.50

STEEL,KURT-Ambush House-NY-1943-Harcourt-1st ed (l4,sl tn dj) 20.00

STEELE,C FRANK-Prairie Editor-Tor-1961-Ryerson Pr-8vo-viii,196p-1st ed (cc7,sl rub dj) 20.00*

STEELE,FLETCHER-Gardens and People-Bost-1964-ix,221p-1st prtg (m10,f,dj scuff,sl tn) 22.00

STEELE,J D-Popular Zoology-NY-1887-8vo-319p-illus (m3) 10.00

STEELE,JAMES W-Frontier Army Sketches-Albuq-(1969)-U of NM Pr-329p (cc4,dj) 20.00

STEELE,JAMES W-Frontier Army Sketches-Topeka-(1969)-329p-rprnt (c4,f,dj) 25.00

STEELE,JAMES W-Rand McNally & Co.'s New Guide to the Pacific Coast-Chig-1893(1888)-212p-illus,fldg map (d3) 80.00

STEELE,JAMES-Colorado Outings-Chig-1898-Chig,Brlngtn & Quncy RR-48p-illus,fldg map (gg9,sl soil,sl chip sp) 50.00

STEELE,JAMES-Old Californian Days-Chig-1889-Belford-Clark Co-227p-sktchs-1st ed (cc4) 40.00

STEELE,JOHN-TRANSL.-I LI-Taipei-1966-Ch'eng-wen Publ-cl,frntis,illus-2nd ed (l8,f) 22.50

STEELE,MATTHEW F-American Campaigns-Wash-1909-Byron S Adams-2 vols-vol.1 text,vol.2 maps-1st ed (o7) 75.00

STEELE,OLIVER G-Steele's Book of Niagara Falls-Buffalo-1840-O G Steele-16mo-lea,fldg map,6 views not in previous eds-7th ed (dd6,sl rub) 75.00

STEELE,PHILLIP-Last Cherokee Warriors-Gretna-(1974)-111p-illus-1st ed (c4,f,dj) 25.00

STEELE,PHILLIP-Last Cherokee Warriors-Gretna-(1974)-111p-photos-1st ed (n10,f,dj) 30.00

STEELE,THOMAS J-Santos and Saints-Albuq-1974-213p-photos-1st ed (u7,f,dj) 30.00

STEELE,THOMAS S-Canoe & Camera-NY-1880-8vo-139p-illus,map in rear pocket,g dec bndg (m3) 80.00

STEELE,ZULMA-Angel in Top Hat-NY-(1942)-Harper-8vo-319p-illus-1st ed (dd5,dj) 25.00

STEEN,HERMAN-O W Fisher Heritage-1961-F McCaffrey:Dogwood Pr-224p+index-1st ed (d3) 45.00

STEER,HENRY-Smedleys of Matlock Bank-Lond-1897-Elliot Stock-sm 8vo-xii+121p-brwn cl,plts-1st ed (j2) 35.00

STEERS,HELEN-Death Will Find Me-NY-1947-Dodd-1st ed (g4,f,chip dj) 20.00

STEFANSSON,VILHJALMUR-Adventure of Wrangel Island-NY-1925-Macmillan-blu cl,35 plts incl ports,maps(1 fldg)-Arctic Biblio 16774-1st Amer ed (dd7,cov sl wn) 125.00

STEFANSSON,VILHJALMUR-Hunters of the Great North-NY-(1922)-Harcourt,Brace-vii,301p-e.p. maps,photos-1st ed (ll8) 30.00

STEFFENS,LINCOLN-Moses in Red-Phila-1926-Dorrance-1st ed (w5,sp fray,sl sun) 30.00

STEFFENS,LINCOLN-Shame of the Cities-NY-1904-McClure,Phillips-306+(6)p ads-cl,illus-auth 1st bk-1st ed (dd10,sp fade) 110.00

STEGMANN,C VON-Architecture of the Renaissance in Tuscany-NY-nd(ca.1924)-lg folio-2 vols-dec & g covs,illus (h10) 300.00

STEGMULLER,FRANCIS-Your Isadora-NY-1974-Random-1st ed (u4,dj sl rub) 18.00

STEGNER,WALLACE-All the Little Live Things-NY-(1967)-1st ed (s5,dj) 20.00

STEGNER,WALLACE-All the Little Live Things-NY-(1967)-Viking-1st ed (l3,f,dj sp sl chip) 25.00

STEGNER,WALLACE-Angle of Repose-GC-1971-Dbldy-1st ed (c10,dj) 40.00

STEGNER,WALLACE-Beyond the Hundredth Meridian-Bost-1954-438p-fldg frntis,photos,maps-1st ed (t7,dj) 60.00

STEGNER,WALLACE-Gathering of Zion,the Story of the Mormon Trail-NY-1964-McGraw Hill-8vo-331p-cl-1st ed (mm7,f,dj) 40.00

STEGNER,WALLACE-Gathering of Zion-NY-1964-1st ed (t5,dj) 35.00

STEGNER,WALLACE-Mormon Country-NY-1942-DS&P-362p-cl-1st ed (w3,f,f dj) 37.50

STEGNER,WALLACE-Recapitulation-1979-Dbldy-1st trd ed (m9,f,dj sp wn & rub) 25.00

STEGNER,WALLACE-Recapitulation-GC-1979-Dbldy-1st ed (q2,dj) 45.00

STEGNER,WALLACE-Shooting Star-NY-(1961)-Viking-1st ed (bb2,sl fade,dj) 45.00

STEGNER,WALLACE-Shooting Star-NY-(1961)-Viking-1st ed (h3,sl chip dj) 20.00

STEGNER,WALLACE-Sound of Mountain Water-NY-1969-Dbldy-286p-1st ed (bb4,dj) 25.00

STEGNER,WALLACE-Uneasy Chair-GC-1974-1st ed (t5,f,dj) 20.00

STEGNER,WALLACE-Wolf Willow-1962-Viking-1st ed (x2,f,dj) 38.00

STEICHEN,EDWARD-ED.-Bitter Years 1935 to 1941-NY-1962-MOMA-wrps,27 photos-2nd prtg (cc9,f) 25.00

STEICHEN,EDWARD-Gardens in Color-GC-1944-GC Publ-4to-cl,col photos-1st ed (t3,chip dj) 35.00

STEICHEN,EDWARD-Life in Photography-GC-1963-Dbldy-lg 4to-cl-1st ed,1st state wi patterned e.p. (y3,f,f dj) 75.00

STEICHEN,EDWARD-Power in the Pacific-NY-1945-US Camera-4to-144p-cl-1st ed (q3,dj) 45.00

STEICHEN,EDWARD-Sandburg-NY-1966-HB&W-113p-116p photos-1st ed (cc9,dj tn) 35.00

STEIFF,FREDERICK P-Eat,Drink and Be Merry in Maryland-NY-(1932)-Putnam's-326p-blk bds dec in gld,wht & red,illus,E Tunis (o6,dj) 55.00

STEIG,WILLIAM-Abel's Island-NY-1976-FS&G-8vo-119p-blu cl,illus by auth-1st ed (nn8,f,f dj) 25.00

STEIG,WILLIAM-Agony in the Kindergarten-NY-(1950)-DS&P-unpgd-bds-1st ed (r3,dj) 50.00

STEIG,WILLIAM-Dominic-NY-(1972)-FS&G-1st ed (nn10,sl chip dj) 35.00

STEIG,WILLIAM-Persistent Faces-NY-(1945)-DSP-1st ed (ee5,dj) 10.00

STEIG,WILLIAM-Rejected Lovers-NY-1951-Knopf-153p-bds-1st ed (r3) 25.00

STEIN,ANNE MARIE-Three Picassos Before Breakfast-NY-1973-Hawthorn-1st ed (z9,f,dj) 10.00

STEIN,BENNETT H-ED.-Tough Trip Through Paradise, 1878 to 1879, by Andrew Garcia-Bost-1967-446p-photos,map e.p.-1st ed (t7,dj) 55.00

STEIN,DAVID L-Living the Revolution-Indpls-1969-Bobbs Merrill-1st ed (w5,f,dj sl rub & tn) 25.00

STEIN,FRED-5th Avenue-NY-1947-Querido-(114)p-100 photos-1st ed (cc9,dj tn) 35.00

STEIN,GERTRUDE-Alphabets & Birthdays-New Haven-1957-Yale U Pr-1st ed (x10,f,f dj) 45.00

STEIN,GERTRUDE-Autobiography of Alice B Toklas-Lond-(1933)-Bodley Head-tan cl-1st Brit ed (f2,dj) 250.00

STEIN,GERTRUDE-Autobiography of Alice B Toklas-NY-1933-1st iss dj & bndg,photos-1st ed (s5,dj) 225.00

STEIN,GERTRUDE-Bee Time Vine and Other Occasional Pieces(1913 to 27)-1953-Yale U Pr-1st ed (q2,dj soil,chip) 45.00

STEIN,GERTRUDE-Bee Time Vine...-1953-Yale U Pr-1st ed (x10,cor bump,dj sl wn & tn) 35.00

STEIN,GERTRUDE-Brewsie and Willie-1946-Random-1st prtg (jj6,f,sl tn dj) 50.00

STEIN,GERTRUDE-Composition as Explanation-Lond-1926-Hogarth-59p-prtd bds-Hogarth Essays,Second Ser.,No.1-1st ed (ll5,cov sl brwnd) 145.00

STEIN,GERTRUDE-Everybody's Autobiography-NY-(1937)-Random Hs-photos,C Van Vechten-1st ed (c10,tan sp,f dj) 100.00

STEIN,GERTRUDE-Flowers of Friendship-NY-1953-Borzoi-1st ed (t4,chip dj) 25.00

STEIN,GERTRUDE-Four in America-1947-Yale U Pr-1st ed (q2,dj) 75.00

STEIN,GERTRUDE-Four Saints in Three Acts-NY-1934-Random-1st ed (h8,f,sp rprd dj) 200.00

STEIN,GERTRUDE-Geographical History of America...-(NY)-(1936)-Random-8vo-207p-1st ed (w6,sl stnd flylvs,soil dj) 300.00

STEIN,GERTRUDE-Geography and Plays-Bost-(1922)-Four Seas-8vo-419p-blu cl bkd gry bds,gry dj,2nd bndg-Wilson A 5b-1st ed (w6,f,sl chip dj) 375.00

STEIN,GERTRUDE-How to Write-Barton-1973-Something Else Pr-8vo-cl-1st Amer ed (jj8,f,dj) 50.00

STEIN,GERTRUDE-Lectures in America-(1935)-Random-1st ed (x2,f,dj sl tn & wn) 110.00

STEIN,GERTRUDE-Lectures in America-NY-(1935)-Random Hs-1st ed (c10,sl wn dj) 175.00

STEIN,GERTRUDE-Lucy Church, Amiably-NY-1969-Something Else Pr-1st Amer ed (bb2,f,dj) 35.00

STEIN,GERTRUDE-Mrs.Reynolds-1952-Yale U Pr-1st ed (x10,f,f dj) 45.00

STEIN,GERTRUDE-Picasso-Lond-1939-Scribners/Batsford-blu stmpd rose cl-1st Brit ed following Paris ed in wrps (bb2,dj sp chip) 165.00

STEIN,GERTRUDE-Stanzas in Meditation-1956-Yale U Pr-1st ed (x10,f,sl tn dj) 45.00

STEIN,GERTRUDE-Two-1951-Yale U Pr-1st ed (x10,f,sl tn dj) 45.00

STEIN,GERTRUDE-Wars I Have Seen-Lond-(1945)-Batsford-8vo-blu cl-Wilson A38b-1st Brit ed (x10,f,dj) 40.00

STEIN,HARRY-Hoopla-1983-Knopf-1st ed (ff2,dj) 17.50

STEIN,HARRY-Tiny Tim-Chig-(1976)-Playboy-8vo-243p-8p photos-1st ed (gg5,f,dj) 20.00

STEIN,LEO-A B C of Aesthetics-NY-1927-Boni & Liveright-1st ed (z9,sl cocked,cor fray) 15.00

STEINBECK,JOHN-Acts of King Arthur and His Noble Knights-NY-(1976)-Farrar-1st ed (w5,f,f dj) 30.00

STEINBECK,JOHN-Acts of King Arthur and his Noble Knights-NY-(1976)-FS&G-364p-rough maroon cl,dk grn e.p.,pict dj-1st ed (j5,sl chip dj) 25.00

STEINBECK,JOHN-America and Americans-NY-(1966)-Viking-4to-136p photos,1st bndg wi sp lettrng reading top to bottom-1st ed (a10,f) 25.00

STEINBECK,JOHN-America and Americans-NY-(1966)-Viking-4to-cl-1st ed (x3,sl chip dj) 40.00

STEINBECK,JOHN-Bombs Away-NY-(1942)-Viking-1st ed (ee2,f,dj) 125.00

STEINBECK,JOHN-Bombs Away-NY-1942-Viking-8vo-illus cl-1st ed (x3,cov spot,dj sp chip,sl wn) 60.00

STEINBECK,JOHN-Burning Bright-NY-1950-Viking-1st ed (a10,dj sl soil) 100.00

STEINBECK,JOHN-Cannery Row-NY-1945-Viking-8vo-yel cl-1st ed (x3,f,dj) 85.00

STEINBECK,JOHN-Cannery Row-NY-1945-Viking-yel bds-1st ed (ee2,dj rub & tape rprd) 45.00

STEINBECK,JOHN-Cup of Gold-Cleve-1944-World Publ-rvsd dj by M Reisman,1st prtg Tower ed Feb 1944-1st ed thus (dd2,f,dj) 60.00

STEINBECK,JOHN-Cup of Gold-NY-(1936)-Covici Friede-blu cl,blind stmpng of scroll & ship,t.e. blu-Goldstone A1c-2nd ed (cc2,f,dj) 125.00

STEINBECK,JOHN-Cup of Gold-NY-(1936)-Covici-8vo-blu cl-2nd ed (x3,sl fox,dj) 100.00

STEINBECK,JOHN-Cup of Gold-NY-1929-Robt M. McBride-269p-yel cl,t.e. blu-auth 1st bk-1st ed (d10,lacks dj) 600.00

STEINBECK,JOHN-East of Eden-NY-1952-Viking-1st ed (cc2,f,dj) 165.00

STEINBECK,JOHN-East of Eden-NY-1952-Viking-1st ed,1st iss (z3,f,dj sl chip,rub) 80.00

STEINBECK,JOHN-East of Eden-NY-1952-Viking-grn cl-1st trd ed (pp3,dj) 75.00

STEINBECK,JOHN-Forgotten Village-1941-Viking-1st ed (x2,f,sl wn dj) 90.00

STEINBECK,JOHN-Forgotten Village-NY-1941-Viking-143p-nat buckram,t.e. grn,136 photos-1st ed (d10,tan sp,brn hngs,dj rnfrcd 125.00

STEINBECK,JOHN-Forgotten Village-NY-1941-Viking-4to-cl,photos-1st ed (y3,dj sl chip) 80.00

STEINBECK,JOHN-Grapes of Wrath-NY-(1939)-Viking-1st ed (cc2,f,dj chip,sl wn) 275.00

STEINBECK,JOHN-Grapes of Wrath-NY-(1939)-Viking-1st ed (u1,f,dj sl wn & sp drknd) 550.00

STEINBECK,JOHN-Journal of a Novel-NY-(1969)-Viking-182p-lt blu cl,t.e. blu-1st trd ed (d10,f,sl wn dj) 50.00

STEINBECK,JOHN-Log From the Sea of Cortez-NY-1951-Viking-1st ed (c10,f,dj) 275.00

STEINBECK,JOHN-Long Valley-NY-1938-Viking-1st ed (a10,dj) 325.00

STEINBECK,JOHN-Long Valley-NY-1938-Viking-1st ed (u1,f,dj sp wi sm rough spot) 300.00

STEINBECK,JOHN-Moon is Down-1942-Heinemann-1st Brit ed (x2,dj) 65.00

STEINBECK,JOHN-Moon is Down-Lond,Tor-(1942)-Heinemann-terra cotta cl-1st Brit ed (e10,sp sl ridged,dj) 85.00

STEINBECK,JOHN-Moon is Down-NY-(1942)-Viking-1st ed,1st iss (cc2,f,dj) 85.00

STEINBECK,JOHN-Moon is Down-NY-(1942)-Viking-1st ed,2nd issue (c6,dj) 35.00

STEINBECK,JOHN-Moon is Down-NY-(1942)-Viking-8vo-illus cl-1st ed,2nd iss (x3,sl chip dj) 45.00

STEINBECK,JOHN-Moon is Down-NY-(1942)-Viking-8vo-illus cl-1st iss wi period between "talk" and "this",p.112-1st ed (x3,sl chip dj) 100.00

STEINBECK,JOHN-Of Mice and Men-(1937)-Covici Friede-186p-1st ed,1st state (v8,dj sp sunned,chip,sl wn) 250.00

STEINBECK,JOHN-Once There Was a War-1959-Heinemann-1st Brit ed (x2,f,dj) 85.00

STEINBECK,JOHN-Pearl-1947-Viking-1st ed (kk6,dj) 125.00

STEINBECK,JOHN-Pearl-NY-1947-Viking-122p-brwn cl,t.e. grn-1st st dj wi auth looking to his left in photo,drwngs by J C Orozco-1st ed (h5,edge tn dj) 100.00

STEINBECK,JOHN-Pearl-NY-1947-Viking-illus,Orozco,var dj wi auth looking rt-G&P A25a-1st ed (w1,f,dj) 50.00

STEINBECK,JOHN-Red Pony-NY-1945-col illus by W Dennis-1st illus ed (r2,box) 30.00

STEINBECK,JOHN-Red Pony-NY-1945-Viking-8vo-cl,illus by W Dennis-1st ed thus (x3,box) 40.00

STEINBECK,JOHN-Red Pony-NY-1945-Viking-col illus,W.Dennis-variant ed prtd by "Rogers Kellogg Stillson,Inc."-1st illus ed (d10,sl spot bndg,box split) 45.00

STEINBECK,JOHN-Russian Journal-NY-1948-Viking-220p-cl-photos,R Capa-1st ed (e1,f,dj) 85.00

STEINBECK,JOHN-Russian Journal-NY-1948-Viking-photos,R Capa-1st ed (a10,sl chip dj sp) 100.00

STEINBECK,JOHN-Sea of Cortez-NY-1941-Viking-277p-grn cl-t.e. orange-map e.p.-photos,drwngs-1st ed (f5,sl wn dj) 325.00

STEINBECK,JOHN-Sea of Cortez-NY-1941-Viking-e.p. maps,photos(incl col),drwngs,chrts-Goldstone A15b-1st ed (p6,f,sl chip dj) 250.00

STEINBECK,JOHN-Short Reign of Pippin IV-1957-Viking-1st ed (x2,f,dj) 37.00

STEINBECK,JOHN-Short Reign of Pippin IV-NY-1957-Viking-1st ed (a10,dj) 50.00

STEINBECK,JOHN-Speech Accepting the Nobel Prize for Literature-NY-(1962)-Viking-ltd to 3200c-1st ed (e10,f,wrps) 100.00

STEINBECK,JOHN-Steinbeck: A Life in Letters-NY-(1975)-Viking-1st ed (dd2,f,dj) 35.00

STEINBECK,JOHN-Steinbeck:A Life in Letters-NY-(1975)-1st ed (h5,f,dj) 20.00

STEINBECK,JOHN-Sweet Thursday-NY-1954-Viking-1st ed (h8,f,dj) 85.00

STEINBECK,JOHN-Sweet Thursday-NY-1954-Viking-273p-beige cl,t.e. red,col pict dj-1st ed (h5,f,sl wn dj) 45.00

STEINBECK,JOHN-To a God Unknown-NY-1933-Covici Friede-1st ed,2nd iss (v5,sp chip dj) 150.00

STEINBECK,JOHN-Tortilla Flat-NY-(1947)-Viking-illus,P Worthington-G&P A4d-1st illus ed (w1,f,dj) 75.00

STEINBECK,JOHN-Tortilla Flat-NY-(1947)-Viking-var grn cl,17 pntngs by P Worthington-1st ed thus (h8,f,dj) 150.00

STEINBECK,JOHN-Travels with Charley-1962-Viking-1st ed (x2,sl tn dj) 38.00

STEINBECK,JOHN-Travels with Charley-NY-1962-Viking-G&P A39a-1st ed (w1,f,dj) 30.00

STEINBECK,JOHN-Wayward Bus-NY-1947-Viking-1st ed (z9,f,dj tn,sl chip) 40.00

STEINBECK,JOHN-Wayward Bus-NY-1947-Viking-1st state bndg-1st ed (c10,sl wn,sl soil dj) 100.00

STEINBECK,JOHN-Wayward Bus-NY-1947-Viking-G&P A23a-1st ed (w1,f,dj) 45.00

STEINBECK,JOHN-Winter of Our Discontent-1961-Heinemann-1st Brit ed (kk6,dj) 40.00

STEINBECK,JOHN-Winter of Our Discontent-1961-Heinemann-1st Brit ed (x2,f,dj) 50.00

STEINBOCK,R TED-Paleopathological Diagnosis and Interpretation-Springfield-1976-423p (dd3) 75.00

STEINBRUNNER,CHRIS-ET AL-Detectionary-1971-Hammermill Paper Co-wrps-one of undetermined number of nbrd copies-1st ed (w5,sl cocked sp,sl crease) 85.00

STEINDLER,R A-Firearms Dictionary-Harrisburg-1970-8vo-illus (m3,vf,dj) 15.00

STEINEM,GLORIA-Beach Book-NY-(1963)-Viking-4to-277p-illus,auth 1st bk-1st ed (gg5,sp chip dj) 25.00

STEINEM,GLORIA-Beach Book-NY-1963-illus,Slackman,dj photo collage,Michaels-auth 1st bk-scarce-1st ed (n5,sl chip dj) 40.00

STEINER,EDWARD A-On the Trail of the Immigrant-NY-1906-Revell-1st ed (w5,f) 30.00

STEINER,GEORGE-Portage to San Cristobal of A.H.-NY-(1981)-S&S-1st ed (bb1,as new in dj) 15.00

STEINER,RUDOLF-Christianity as Mystical Fact, and the Mysteries of Antiquity-West Nyack-1961-Steiner Publ-cl-1st prtg (n8,vf,dj) 17.50

STEINER,RUDOLPH-Triorganic Social Organism-Detr-1923-135p-wrps-1st Amer ed (k9) 10.00

STEINER-SCOTT,ELIZABETH-New Jersey Women, 1770 to 1970-Rutherford-(1978)-167p-cl (aa6) 35.00

STEINGRABEN,ERICH-Antique Jewelry-NY-1957-Praeger-191p-tip-in col frntis,333 illus(8 col)-1st US ed (u5,f,dj tn) 87.50

STEINHEIMER,RICHARD-Western Trains-San Marino-1965-71p-1st ed (n4,f,dj) 19.50

STEINMAN,D B-Wichert Truss-NY-1932-Van Nostrand-x+138p-maroon cl-1st ed (c2) 25.00

STEINMAN,DAVID B-Builders of the Bridge-NY-1945-Harcourt,Brace-8vo-457p-photos (cc3,chip dj) 45.00

STEINMAN,DAVID B-Miracle Bridge at Mackinac-Grand Rapids-1957-Eerdmans-208p-wht cl,dec e.p.,drwngs-2nd prtg (cc3,dj) 35.00

STEINMETZ,CHARLES P-Four Lectures on Relativity and Space-1923-126p-33 illus,7 stereo views rear pckt-rare-1st ed (h6,f) 65.00

STEINMETZ,CHARLES P-General Lectures on Electrical Engineering-Schenectady-(1908)-Robson & Adee-284p-brwn cl,lea sp labl-1st ed (a2,sl rub) 75.00

STEKEL,WILHELM-Impotence in the Male-NY-(1939)-Liveright-2 vols-cl (dd10,f,dj) 40.00

STEKEL,WILHELM-Interpretation of Dreams-NY-(1943)-Liveright-2 vols-cl-transl by E C Paul (a1,cov spot,dj) 15.00

STEKEL,WILHELM-Sadism and Masochism-NY-1929-Liveright-2 vols-cl-Authorized Engl Version by L Brink (a1) 20.00

STEKEL,WILHELM-Sexual Aberrations-NY-(1940)-Liveright-2 vols-cl-Auth Engl Version from first German ed (a1,dj) 20.00

STELLAR,G W-Journal of a Voyage with Bering 1741 to 1742-1988-Stanford-252p-25 figs,map-1st ed (bb3,f,dj) 30.00

STENHOUSE,MRS T B H-Tell It All-Cin-1874-623p-grn stmpd cl,g dec sp,frntis,illus-1st ed (jj4,f) 50.00

STENHOUSE,MRS T B H-Tell It All-Cin-1874-Queen City Publ-623p-cl-Flake 8391 (d1) 35.00

STENHOUSE,MRS T B H-Tell It All-Hartford-1875-Worthington & Co-8vo-xxx,(31)-623p-grn cl,g sp titles & cov dec (mm1,wn,sl fox,rear hng weak) 45.00

STEPHEN,ADRIAN-Dreadnought Hoax-Lond-1936-Hogarth Pr-8vo-47p-pict bds,3 photos-1st ed (nn4,sp drknd) 75.00

STEPHEN,LESLIE-Playground of Europe-Oxford-1946-246p-19 photos-rprnt (o10,f,dj) 40.00

STEPHENS,A RAY-Taft Ranch-Austin-1964-279p-photos-1st ed (n10,dj) 45.00

STEPHENS,A RAY-Taft Ranch-Austin-1964-U of Tex Pr-279p-cl,photos-1st ed (w3,vf,dj) 25.00

STEPHENS,H MORSE-Pacific Ocean in History-NY-1917-Macmillan-8vo-535p-cl-1st ed (mm7,f) 65.00

STEPHENS,J L-Incidents of Travel in Egypt, Arabia Petraea and the Holy Land-1970-U of Okla-473p-illus,maps-1st prtg thus (bb3,f,dj) 20.00

STEPHENS,JAMES-Collected Poems-Lond-1926-Macmillan-1st trd ed (z8,f,dj) 60.00

STEPHENS,JAMES-Collected Poems-Lond-1926-Macmillan-orig vel bckd bds-ltd to 500c,autg-lg papr ed (aa9,sp rub,sl fox e.p.) 50.00

STEPHENS,JAMES-Etched in Moonlight-Lond-1928-Macmillan-1st ed (q9,dj sl chip,sp drknd) 40.00

STEPHENS,JAMES-Five New Poems-Lond-1913-Stevens for Flying Flame-wrps-1st ed (z8,f) 135.00

STEPHENS,JAMES-Insurrections-Dublin-1909-Maunsel-papr cov bds,cl sp-1st ed (z8,sm spot fr cov) 125.00

STEPHENS,JAMES-James Stephens, a Selection-Lond-1962-Macmillan-1st Brit ed (z8,f,dj) 25.00

STEPHENS,JAMES-Outcast-Lond-(1929)-Faber-wrps,(Ariel Poems no.22)-1st ed (z8,f) 30.00

STEPHENS,JAMES-Songs From the Clay-Lond-1915-Macmillan-cl-1st ed (z8,f) 40.00

STEPHENS,JAMES-Strict Joy-Lond-1931-Macmillan-cl-1st ed (z8,f) 22.50

STEPHENS,L D-Joseph Le Conte-1982-U of La-340p-illus-1st ed (bb3,f,dj) 16.00

STEPHENS,PETER J-Perrely Plight-NY-1965-Atheneum-216p-cl,illus,R D Rice-1st ed (r3,sp fade,dj) 25.00

STEPHENS,ROBERT N-Mystery of Murray Davenport-1903-Page-1st ed (s10) 20.00

STEPHENS,ROBERT N-Mystery of Murray Davenport-Bost-1903-Page-illus-1st ed (f4) 25.00

STEPHENS,STEPHEN D-Mavericks-New Brunswick-1950-xx,219p-cl,plts (aa6) 225.00

STEPHENSON,BRIAN-Specials in Steam-Lond-1968-1st ed (n4,f,dj) 16.50

STEPHENSON,DOROTHY-Night it Rained Toys-Chig-(1963)-Follett-4to-32p-cl,col illus,J E Johnson-1st ed (r3,f,tattrd dj) 12.00

STEPHENSON,JOHN-Stephenson's Pocket Farrier or , Every One His Own Horse Doctor-Tecumseh-1872-Record Bk & Job Prtg Hs-80p-flex cl-scarce (a1,sm stn frnt cov & e.p.) 35.00

STERLING,ADALINE W-Book of Englewood-Englewood-1922-x,508p-cl,illus,fldg map (aa6) 75.00

STERLING,BRUCE-Artificial Kid-NY-(1980)-Harper & Row-1st ed (l3,f,dj) 50.00

STERLING,GEORGE E-Radio Manual-1929-666p-273 illus-1st ed (h6) 20.00

STERLING,GEORGE-Evanescent City-SF-1925-Robertson-sq 8vo-illus papr cov semi stiff bds,9 tip in illus by Bruguiere-1st ed (y3) 95.00

STERLING,GEORGE-Robinson Jeffers-NY-1926-Boni & Liveright-1st ed (h8,f,rprd dj) 45.00

STERLING,STEWART-Dead of Night-NY-1950-Dutton-1st ed (j4,dj) 10.00

STERN,BERNHARD-Lummi Indians of Northwest Washington-1969-137p-illus-(rprnt of 1934 first ed) (r8) 18.00

STERN,J P-ED.-World of Franz Kafka-NY-1980-Holt-1st Amer ed (t4,f,dj) 20.00

STERN,MADELEINE B-Heads and Headlines-Norman-(1971)-U of Okla Pr-xx+348p-1st ed (y9,dj) 25.00

STERN,MADELEINE B-Heads and Headlines-Norman-(1971)-U of Okla Pr-xx+348p-yel cl,plts-1st ed (mm10,dj) 30.00

STERN,MADELEINE B-Imprints on History-Bloomington-1956-Indiana U Pr-8vo-xii,492p-cl-1st ed (w2,chip dj) 35.00

STERN,MADELEINE B-Imprints on History-Bloomington-1956-Indiana Univ-xii+492p-beige cl,plts-1st ed (e2,chip dj) 25.00

STERN,MADELEINE B-Louisa's Wonder Book-(Mount Pleasant)-(1975)-52;74p-cl (g1) 15.00

STERN,NORTON B-California Jewish History-Glendale-1967-Arthur H Clark-8vo-175p-lt blu cl,plain dj as iss-1st ed (dd7,as new in dj) 22.50

STERN,SUSAN-With the Weathermen-NY-1975-Dbldy-374p-1st ed so stated (q1,edgewn dj) 40.00

STERN,T-Klamath Tribe-Seattle-1965-xvi,356p (bb9,f,sl wn dj) 30.00

STERNBACH,RICHARD A-ED.-Psychology of Pain-NY-(1978)-Raven Pr-x+271+(5)p-blk cl-1st ed (y9,chip dj) 25.00

STERNBERG,GEORGE M-Malaria and Malarial Diseases-NY-1884-Wm Wood & Co-viii+329p,yel cl-1st ed (j2) 35.00

STERNE,EMMA G-Mary McLeod Bethune-NY-1957-1st ed (c5,f,sl wn dj) 25.00

STERNE,LAURENCE-Sentimental Journey-Paris-1929-Black Sun Pr-illus by P Chentoff,orig glassine dj,ltd to 335c,nbrd,on Arches papr (x3,sp tn dj,box) 185.00

STERNE,MAURICE-Maurice Sterne-NY-1933-MOMA-thin 4to-grn wrps,illus-ltd to 1000c (r10,sp fade) 30.00

STEUART,HENRY-Planter's Guide-NY-1832-Thorburn-422p-orig cl wi lea labl,plts-1st Amer ed (x6) 115.00

STEVENS,ALEXANDER-Plea of Humanity in Behalf of Medical Education-NY-1849-47p-pamphlet-4th ed (dd3) 40.00

STEVENS,BLAMEY-Psychology of Physics-Manchester-(1939)-Sherratt & Hughes-xvi+282p-blu cl-1st ed (l2,dj) 35.00

STEVENS,CHARLES E-Anthony Burns-Bost-1856-John P Jewett-295p-grn cl,illus-1st ed (h2,cov fade,wn,text soil) 55.00

STEVENS,D W-James Boys in Minnesota-NY-1882-14p-pict wrps-Five Cent Wide Awake Libr #479 (t7,f) 15.00

STEVENS,DOROTHY A-COMP.-Table Talk and Tidbits-Phila-(1953)-Judson-158p-g title tan cl,col & b&w plts-1st ed (q8,dj) 15.00

STEVENS,G R-Canadian National Railways-Tor-1960,62-Clark,Irwin-2 vols-frntis,illus,maps,ports (k10,dj) 85.00*

STEVENS,G-Garden Flowers in Color-NY-1934-Macmillan-320p-cl,col photos (x6) 8.00

STEVENS,GEORGE T-First Fighting Campaign of the Seventy Seventh N Y V Address by ...-np-(1915)-9p-wrps (f1) 12.50

STEVENS,HAZARD-First Ascent of Takhoma-Seattle-1965-Shorey Bk Store-18p-wrps (o10) 10 00

STEVENS,HAZARD-Life of General Isaac I Stevens-Bost,NY-1900-2 vols-t.e.g.,illus-Tweney #72-1st ed (j7,sl scratched bds) 125.00

STEVENS,HENRY-An Analytical Index to the Colonial Documents of New Jersey, in State Paper Offices of England...-NY-1858-NJ Hist Soc,V-xxix,504p-cl (aa6,rub) 60.00

STEVENS,HENRY-Recollections of Mr.James Lenox of New York and the Formation of his Library-Lond-1887-H Stevens-sm 4to-ix,211p-orig qtr wht cl,mrbld bds,drk grn mor sp labl,plts wi tiss-1st ed (t10,f) 45.00

STEVENS,JAMES-Green Power-1958-Superior-95p-pict cov,illus-1st ed (r8,dj chip) 25.00

STEVENS,JAMES-Homer in the Sagebrush-1928-Knopf-313p-1st ed (r8) 35.00

STEVENS,JAMES-Paul Bunyan's Bears-1947-Dogwood Pr-8vo-129p-illus (m3,vf,dj) 20.00

STEVENS,JAMES-Saginaw Paul Bunyan-NY-1932-Knopf-8vo-woodcts-1st ed (oo8,f,dj) 45.00

STEVENS,JOHN H-Personal Recollections of Minnesota and Its People and Early History of Minneapolis-Mpls-1890-(Trib Job Prtg Co)-432p+index-illus-Howes S969-1st ed (dd4,rbckd) 95.00

STEVENS,JOHN M-Personal Recollections of Minnesota and its People and Early History of Minneapolis-Mpls-1890-(viii)+432+(xv)p-drk blu cl,7 plts-Howes S969-1st ed (k2) 65.00

STEVENS,LEWIS T-History of Cape May County, New Jersey...-Cape May City-1897-480p-cl,illus (aa6) 200.00

STEVENS,S S-Bibliography on Hearing-Cambridge-1955-599p-1st ed (dd3) 45.00

STEVENS,WALLACE-Harmonium-NY-1923-Knopf-8vo-blu cl,stripe bds,papr sp labl,auth 1st bk-1st ed,2nd bndg (x3) 250.00

STEVENS,WALLACE-Man with the Blue Guitar-NY-1937-Knopf-yel bds,2nd iss dj wi "Conjunctioning" corrected on frnt flap-ltd to 1000c-Edelstein A4a-1st ed (dd2,dj) 250.00

STEVENS,WALLACE-Necessary Angel-NY-1951-Knopf-gold stmpd grn bds-1st ed (bb2,f,dj) 150.00

STEVENS,WALLACE-Opus Posthumous-NY-1957-Knopf-1st ed (v10,vf,vf dj) 100.00

STEVENS,WALLACE-Palm at the End of the Road-NY-1971-Knopf-1st ed (u2,dj) 15.00

STEVENS,WILLIAM O-Pistols at Ten Paces-Bost-1940-Houghton Mifflin-8vo-291p-1st ed (s1,f,dj) 45.00

STEVENS,WILLIAM O-Unbidden Guests-NY-1945-Dodd,Mead-1st ed (n8,dj) 16.50

STEVENS,WILLIAM R-Deadly Intentions-1982-Congdon-1st ed (s10,dj) 10.00

STEVENS,WILLIAM-Peddler-Bost-1966-LB-auth 1st bk-1st ed (y1,f,dj) 30.00

STEVENSON,ALLAN-Problem of the "Missale Speciale"-Lond-1967-Biblio Soc-8vo-xxi,400p-drk blu cl,10 plts-1st ed (t10) 45.00

STEVENSON,C A-Song of the Reel-Nottingham-1914-8vo-74p-photos (m3) 30.00

STEVENSON,D ALAN-World's Lighthouses before 1820-Lond,NY-1959-OUP-lg 4to-xiv,310p-cl,199 illus,7 maps (pp7) 125.00

STEVENSON,ELIZABETH-Lafcadio Hearn-NY-1961-Macmillan-frntis port-1st ed (t4,f,dj) 25.00

STEVENSON,ROBERT L-Across the Plains-Lond-1892-Chatto & Windus-drk blu cl-1st trd ed (gg7) 45.00

STEVENSON,ROBERT L-Ballads-Lond-1890-Chatto & Windus-orig g titled cl over bev bds,t.e.g.-1st Brit ed (aa9,sl brwnd e.p.) 75.00

STEVENSON,ROBERT L-Catriona-Lond,Paris,Melb-1893-Cassell-1st Brit ed in bk form (e10,sl cocked sp) 150.00

STEVENSON,ROBERT L-David Balfour-NY-1924-Scribner's-illus,N C Wyeth-1st ed thus (u10,f,f dj) 200.00

STEVENSON,ROBERT L-Edinburgh. Picturesque Notes-Lond-1954-Hart Davis-4to-cl,23 prnts-1st ed (y3,sl sunned dj) 225.00

STEVENSON,ROBERT L-Island Nights' Entertainments-Lond-1893-pict covs gilt,illus-1st ed,1st issue (r2,sp sun,sl rub) 100.00

STEVENSON,ROBERT L-Memories & Portraits-Lond-1887-Chatto & Windus-orig g titled cl over bev bds-1st ed (aa9,sp rub,sl fray,g dull) 30.00

STEVENSON,ROBERT L-Napa Wine-SF-(1974)-Westwind Bks/Cranium Pr-16mo-38p-dec bds-ltd to 950c (q8,f) 40.00

STEVENSON,ROBERT L-Prince Otto-Bost-1886-1st Amer ed (r2,sp sun,sl rub) 60.00

STEVENSON,ROBERT L-Record of a Family of Engineers-Lond-1912-Chatto & Windus-orig g titled cl over bev bds,t.e.g.-1st ed (aa9) 45.00

STEVENSON,ROBERT L-Silverado Squatters-Ashland-1972-Lewis Osborne-line etchings-ltd to 500c,nbrd (d3,dj) 40.00

STEVENSON,ROBERT L-Silverado Squatters-NY-1895-287p-cl (t7) 35.00

STEVENSON,ROBERT L-Songs of Travel and Other Verses-Lond-1896-Chatto & Windus-orig g titled cl over bev bds,t.e.g.-1st ed (aa9,sp fade,unopened) 65.00

STEVENSON,ROBERT L-St.Ives-Lond-1898-Heinemann-orig g titled cl-1st ed (aa9,sl rub sp,sm hole fr fly) 50.00

STEVENSON,ROBERT L-Story of Monterey-SF-1944-Colt Pr-sm 8vo-56p + 2 plts,grn cl over bds-ltd to 500c (u1) 45.00

STEVENSON,ROBERT L-Treasure Island-NY-1911-Scribner's(Illus Classic)-14 col plts(wi guards)by N C Wyeth-1st ed thus (pp10,cor wn,sl rub,e.p. rub) 75.00

STEVENSON,ROBERT L-Underwoods-Lond-1887-Chatto & Windus-orig g titled cl-1st trd ed (aa9,sp rub) 35.00

STEVENSON,ROBERT L-Valima Letters-Lond-1895-Methuen-orig g pict cl,t.e.g.,frntis port,2 plts-1st trd ed (aa9,sl rub) 50.00

STEVENSON,ROBERT L-Weir of Hermiston-Lond-1896-Chatto & Windus-orig g titled cl,t.e.g.-1st publ ed,1st iss (aa9,f) 150.00

STEVENSON-HAMILTON,MAJ J-Animal Life in Africa-NY-1912-539p-photos (gg3,f) 40.00

STEVENSVILLE HIST SOC-Montana Genesis-Missoula-1971-289p-photos,illus-1st ed (t7,dj) 40.00

STEVERS,MARTIN D-Steel Rails-NY-1933-374p-1st ed (n4,f,dj) 32.00

STEWARD,DR WILLIAM-Steward's Healing Art, Corrected and Improved-Saco-1827-Putnam & Blake-126p;40p;20p-calf (x6,sl fox) 150.00

STEWARD,JOHN F-Reaper-NY-1931-Greenberg-xviii+382p-grn cl,illus-1st ed (c2,ex-libr) 30.00

STEWARD,JULIAN H-ED.-Handbook of South Amer Indians-Wash D.C.-1946 thru 1959-Amer Ethno Bull.#143-7 vols-photos,fldg maps-1st eds (u7) 250.00

STEWARD,JULIAN H-ED.-Handbook of South American Indians-Wash-1946-2 vols-illus,plts,fldg maps (hh1,sl edgewn) 55.00

STEWARD,W AUGUSTUS-War Medals and Their History-Lond-1915-407p-dec red cl,plts-1st ed (b7) 100.00

STEWART JAIL WORKS CO.-Cinn-nd-27,(1)p-trade cat-pict wrps,illus (f1) 50.00

STEWART,E P-Letters on an Elk Hunt by a Woman Homesteader-Bost-1915-162p-scarce (bb9) 75.00

STEWART,EDGAR I-Custer's Luck-Norman-(1955)-U of Okla Pr-522p-illus,maps-1st ed (nn6,dj) 75.00

STEWART,FRANK H-Notes on Old Gloucester County, New Jersey-(np)-1917-342p-cl,illus-Vol.1,Complete in itself (aa6) 60.00

STEWART,FRANK H-Notes on Old Gloucester County, New Jersey-(Woodbury)-1917 thru 1964-4 vols in 3-cl,illus-complete set-1st vol publ cl bnd in 1917,vols 2 thru 4 publ in 12 parts in wrps,rbnd in cl (aa6,rbnd) 225.00

STEWART,GEORGE-Big Trees of the Giant Forest-SF-1930-105p-orig glassine dj-1st ed (o10,f,dj) 40.00

STEWART,GEORGE-Canada Under the Administration of the Earl of Dufferin-Tor-1878-Rose Belford-696p-3/4 lea,mrbld bds,frntis (ee7,cov sl wn) 50.00

STEWART,GEORGE-Committee of Vigilance-Bost-1964-339p-illus-1st ed (t7,dj) 15.00

STEWART,HILARY-Cedar: Tree of Life to the Northwest Coast Indians...-Vancouver-1984-Douglas & McIntyre-oblng 4to-192p-cl,illus,map (aa2,dj) 25.00*

STEWART,HILLARY-Artifacts of the N W Coast Indians-(Saanichton)-(1973)-oblng 4to-172p-photos,drwngs-1st ed (c7,nick dj) 30.00

STEWART,J I M-Eight Modern Writers-np-1963-Oxford Univ Pr-1st ed (b10,dj) 30.00

STEWART,J T-Airpower-NY-(1957)-Van Nostrand-8vo-viii,310p-cl,illus-1st ed (s2) 35.00

STEWART,J-Orchids of Africa-1981-Macmillan-folio-159p-50 col plts (bb3,f,dj) 25.00

STEWART,JOHN D-Gilbraltar, the Keystone-Bost-1967-HMCo-8vo-335p-1st ed (dd5,dj sl rub,tn) 15.00

STEWART,JOHN-Winds in the Woods-Phila-1975-126p-1st ed (o10,f,dj) 15.00

STEWART,LUCY S-Reward of Patriotism-NY-1930-Walter Neale-484p-cl (n1,wn dj lacks sm sp pc) 45.00

STEWART,LUCY S-Reward of Patriotism-NY-1930-Walter Neale-484p-illus,maps-1st ed (dd4) 60.00

STEWART,MARION-One Hundred Favorite Foreign Recipes-LA-1933-Sat Night Publ-153p-gry cl,illus e.p.,12p illus-1st ed (q8,cov soil) 17.50

STEWART,MARY-Ivy Tree-NY-1962-Mill-1st US ed (d4,dj) 20.00

STEWART,MARY-Madam, Will You Talk-NY-1956-Mill-1st US ed (f4,f,dj) 12.50

STEWART,MARY-Moon Spinners-1963-Morrow-1st ed (x7,f,dj) 25.00

STEWART,MARY-Rough Magic-Lond-1964-Hodder-1st ed (k4,f,dj) 20.00

STEWART,MARY-This Rough Magic-1964-Mill-1st Amer ed (s10,dj) 15.00

STEWART,O-Aeolus-NY-(1928)-12mo-92p-cl,sp & cov labls,3 text figs-1st ed (s2,dj) 30.00

STEWART,P F-History of the XII Royal Lancers-Oxford-1950-516p-maps,plts-1st ed (b7,f,dj) 100.00

STEWART,R E-Birds of Maryland and the District of Columbia-Wash-1958-USF&WS,No Amer Fauna #62-401p-wrps (c9) 30.00

STEWART,R E-Breeding Birds of North Dakota-Fargo-1975-4to-(12),295p-cl,col frntis,16 col plts,photos (y8,dj) 45.00

STEWART,R F-...And Always a Detective-Newton Abbot-1980-David & Charles-1st ed (r4,f,dj) 20.00

STEWART,SEUMAS-Book Collecting-1973-Dutton-1st Amer ed (t9,f,dj) 20.00

STEWART,VIRGIL A-History of Virgil A Stewart-NY-1836-Harper & Bros-273p-orig cl-Howes H700-1st ed (gg4,fox) 200.00

STEWART,W C-Practical Angler or the Art of Trout Fishing-Lond-1893-A & C Black-"Tenth Thousand" (pp8) 95.00*

STEWART,W C-Practical Angler-Lond-1919-12mo-212p-illus (m3) 22.50

STEWART,W W-When Steam was King-Wellington-1970-144p-1st ed (n4,dj) 40.00

STEYERMARK,JULIAN A-Spring Flowers of Missouri-St.Louis-1940-8vo-vii,582p-163 b&w plts-1st ed (j10,sl stnd pgs,dj sl tn) 65.00

STICK,FRANK-An Artist's Catch-1981-UNC Pr-oblng 8vo-256p-watercolors by auth-1st ed (m3,vf,box) 30.00

STICKNEY,CHARLES E-Father Toryism and the Father of Sussex County Patriotism, Compared-Sussex,Deckertown-1905-(2),28p-wrps (aa6) 30.00

STIEB,ERNEST-Drug Alteration Detection and Control in 19th Century Britain-Madison-1966-335p-1st ed (dd3,dj) 20.00

STIEGHORST,JUNANN J-Bay City and Matagorda County-Austin-1965-Pemberton-269p-1st ed (a9,dj) 75.00

STIEGLITZ,ALFRED-America & Alfred Stieglitz, a Collective Portrait-NY-1934-Lit Guild-8vo-339p-cl,photos-1st ed (q3) 50.00

STIEGLITZ,RON-Saucy Ladies-NY,Lond-(1977)-Peebles Pr-oblng 8vo-128p-tan cl,60 illus-1st prtg (q8,dj) 15.00

STILES M.D.,HENRY R-Bundling-Albany-1871-Knickerbocker-12mo-138p-1st ed (p2) 22.50

STILES,PAULINE-New Footprints in Old Places-SF-1917-Elder-8vo-202p-18 illus-1st ed (jj5,f) 15.00

STILLE,CHARLES J-How a Free People Conducted a Long War-Phila-1863-40p-wrps (b1,lacks rear wrpr) 17.50

STILLMAN,J D B-An 1850 Voyage: San Francisco to Baltimore by Sea and Land-Palo Alto-1967-L Osborne-ltd to 2350c (v4,f) 150.00

STILLMAN,J D B-Around the Horn to California-Palo Alto-1967-92p-map frnt pastedown & e.p.,illus-ltd to 1950c (ee4) 25.00

STILLMAN,J D B-Gold Rush Letters of...-Palo Alto-1967-L Osborne-4to-75p-cl-ltd to 2350c (mm7,f,dj) 45.00

STILLMAN,J D B-Horse in Motion-Bost-1882-Osgood & Co-sm folio-127p-cl,5 heliotype plts by Muybridge,9 chromolithos,46 lithos (t3,f) 600.00

STILLMAN,J D-Horse in Motion-Bost-1882-Osgood-lg 4to-blk & gilt stmpd brwn cl,heliograph plts by Muybridge-1st ed (y3,ex libr) 500.00

STILLMAN,WILLIAM J-Autobiography of a Journalist-Bost-1901-Houghton Mifflin-2 vols-maroon cl-1st ed (k8) 65.00

STILLSON,BLANCHE-Wings-Indpls-(1954)-Bobbs Merrill-8vo-299p-illus-1st ed (aa5,dj chip & tn) 20.00

STILLWELL,MARGARET-Awakening Interest in Science During the First Century of Printing 1450 to 1550-NY-1970-4to-399p-ltd ed (dd3) 150.00

STILWELL,HART-Fishing in Mexico-NY-1948-Knopf-8vo-296p-cl,illus-1st ed (pp8,f,dj chip) 35.00*

STIMSON,A L-History of the Express Business-NY-1881-Baker & Godwin-388p-illus-Howes S1008 (gg4,sp chip) 125.00

STIMSON,H K-From the Stage Coach to the Pulpit-St.Louis-1874-R A Campbell-grn cl-1st ed (gg7,sp chip) 30.00

STOBART,TOM-Adventurer's Eye-Lond-1958-256p-62 photos-1st Brit ed (q10,f,dj) 28.00

STOBART,TOM-Cook's Encyclopedia-NY-(1980)-Harper & Row-547p-1st US ed (m6) 25.00

STOBART,TOM-I Take Pictures for Adventure-Lond-1958-1st Brit ed (o10,f,dj) 28.00

STOBART,TOM-I Take Pictures for Adventure-NY-1958-288p-photos (o10,f,dj) 14.00

STOCHL,SLAVA-Fisherman's World in Pictures-Lond-1970-4to-239p-photos (m3,vf,dj) 17.50

STOCK,NOEL-Reading the Cantos-NY-1966-Pantheon-1st US ed (x9,f,sl rub dj) 10.00

STOCK,PHYLLIS-Better Than Rubles-NY-(1978)-Putnam-8vo-252p-1st ed (gg5,f,dj) 17.50

STOCK,RALPH-Confessions of a Tenderfoot-NY-(1913)-H Holt-8vo-260p-red cl,photos-Adams Herd #2171-1st Amer ed (y4) 75.00

STOCKBERGER,W W-Drug Known as Pinkroot-Wash-1906-GPO-8p-wrps,2p plts (m6) 8.00

STOCKBRIDGE,FRANK P-So This is Florida-NY-(1938)-McBride & Co-300p+index-cl-63p plts (g1) 12.50

STOCKHAM,ALICE B-Koradine Letters-Chig-1893-A B Stockham & Co-424p-cl (d1,edge & sp rub) 25.00

STOCKLI,ALBERT-Splendid Fare: the Albert Stockli Cookbook-1970-Knopf-396p-pict bds,drwngs-1st ed (q8,dj) 20.00

STOCKTON,FRANK R-Girl at Cobhurst-NY-1898-Scribner's-orig dec cl,bndg design by M Armstrong-1st ed (aa9,sl tn sp) 50.00

STOCKTON,FRANK R-Lady or the Tiger?-NY-1885-Scribner's-201p+ads-cl-BAL 18880-early ed (j1) 10.00

STOCKTON,J-Western Calculator...-Pitt-1832-Johnston & Stockton-203,(1)p-bds (h1) 25.00

STOCKTON,ROY-Gashouse Gang and a Couple of Other Guys-NY-(1947)-Barnes-283p-photos,pict dj-1st ed (f9,bump,dj chip) 30.00

STOCKTON,ROY-Gashouse Gang-1945-Barnes-later prtg (ff2,dj) 45.00

STOCKWELL,ELISHA,JR.-Private...Sees the War-Norman-(1958)-210p-illus-1st ed (c4,dj) 45.00

STODDARD,CHARLES C-Shanks' Mare-NY-(1924)-Doran-8vo-217p-1st ed (aa5) 12.50

STODDARD,CHARLES W-Trip to Hawaii-SF-1892-Pssngr Dpt Oceanic Stmshp-8vo-xv,46p-prtd wrps,frntis,13 figs-new ed (t10) 25.00

STODDARD,CORA F-Science and Human Life in the Alcohol Problem-Waterville-1930-80p-wrps,28p illus (a1) 15.00

STODDARD,CORA F-World's New Day and Alcohol-Westerville-(1929)-32p-wrps,illus-3rd ed (a1) 10.00

STODDARD,ELLWYN R-ED.-Borderlands Sourcebook-Norman-(1983)-U of Okla Pr-qto-445p-1st ed (bb4,dj) 50.00

STODDARD,H L-Bobwhite Quail-1978-Scribners-559p-69 plts(incl col)-1st prtg of new ed (bb3) 55.00

STODDARD,H L-Bobwhite Quail-NY-1931-Scribner's-559p-scarce-1st ed (b9) 250.00

STODDARD,H L-Memoirs of a Naturalist-1969-U of Okla-303p-81 plts(4 col)-1st ed (bb3,f,dj) 30.00

STODDARD,JOHN F-American Intellectual Arithmetic...-NY-(1849)-Sheldon,Blakeman-164,(4)p-prntd bds (h1,sl wn) 17.50

STODDARD,JOHN F-Juvenile Mental Arithmetic-NY,et al-(1849)-Sheldon,Blakeman-72p-bds (k1,sl wn sp) 35.00

STODDARD,JOHN L-Famous Parks and Public Buildings in America-NY-1902-lg rectangular pict cl,photos-1st ed (r2,f) 85.00

STODDARD,JOHN L-Napoleon: From Corsica to St.Helena-Chig-ca.1890-oblng folio-260p-1/2 lea,330 plts (gg2) 100.00

STOKER,BRAM-Personal Reminiscences of Henry Irving-NY-1906-Macmillan-8vo-2 vols-36 illus-1st US ed (bb5) 65.00

STOKES TED-Birds of the Atlantic Ocean-NY-1968-Macmillan-paintings by Shackleton-1st Amer ed (c9,sl tn dj) 40.00

STOKES,HORACE W-ED.-Mirrors of the Year-NY-1928-387p (l1) 12.50

STOKES,I N PHELPS-American Historical Prints-NY-1933-NY Public Libr-sm 4to-235p-blu cl,illus-2nd ed (r10,sl scuff) 165.00

STOKES,JOSEPH-Notes on My Stokes Ancestry-(Moorestown)-1937-v,56p-cl,plts (aa6) 60.00

STOKES,MANNING L-Iron Tiger-NY-1957-Arcadia-1st ed (g4,f,dj) 10.00

STOKES,T-Birds of the Atlantic Ocean-NY-1968-4to-156p-cl,38 col plts,maps (y8,dj tn) 65.00

STOLZ,MARY-Fredou-NY-(1962)-Harper-sm 4to-118p-pict cl,b&w drwngs-presumed 1st ed (r3,f,dj) 35.00

STONE,A-American Pep-1918-Shores-4 illus by F Keane-1st ed (x7) 45.00

STONE,EDWARD D-Edward Durell Stone:Recent & Future Architecture-NY-(1967)-Horizon-sq folio-136p-cl,illus(incl col) (pp7,dj) 150.00

STONE,EDWARD D-Evolution of an Architect-NY-1962-Horizon-lg 4to-288p-cl,400 illus (pp7,dj) 125.00

STONE,EDWIN M-Invasion of Canada in 1775-Providence-1867-Knowles,Anthony-blk cl,2 errata slips (mm10) 90.00

STONE,EDWIN M-Life and Recollections of John Howland...-Providence-1857-Geo H Whitney-348p-blk cl-1st ed (k2,sl chip) 30.00

STONE,ELIZABETH A-Uinta County-(Laramie)-(1924)-(Laramie Prtg Co)-276p-grn cl,plts-1st ed (b2) 125.00

STONE,ELLERY W-Elements of Radio Communication-1923-318p-39 photos,145 illus-2nd ed (h6) 40.00

STONE,ELSE-ED.-Writings of Elliott Carter-1977-Indiana U Pr (u4,as new in dj) 22.00

STONE,FRED-Rolling Stone-NY-(1945)-Whittlesey Hs-8vo-246p-photos-1st ed (ee5,sl chip dj) 20.00

STONE,GEORGE C-Glossary of the Construction, Decoration and Use of Arms and Armor in all Countries and in all Times-NY-(1961)-Jack Brussel-694p-illus (ff4) 50.00

STONE,HERBERT L-America's Cup Races-NY-1930-Macmillan-8vo-359p-blu cl,photo cov,photos-New Rvsd ed (pp1) 35.00

STONE,I F-Hidden History of the Korean War-NY-1952-Monthly Revw-348p (r1,dj edgewn,sl tn) 35.00

STONE,I F-Polemics & Prophecies, 1967 to 1970-NY-1970-Random Hs-497p-1st ed (r1,dj) 20.00

STONE,IRVING-Agony and the Ecstasy-GC-1961-1st ed (l5,dj) 12.50

STONE,IRVING-Lust for Life-Lond,NY,Tor-1934-Longmans,Green-x,489p-cl-1st ed (dd10,cov dusty,chip dj) 65.00

STONE,IRVING-Men to Match My Mountains-GC-(1956)-Dbldy-459p-e.p. maps-1st ed (bb4,dj) 20.00

STONE,IRVING-Opening of the Far West 1840 to 1900-NY-1956-459p-map e.p. (t7,f) 10.00

STONE,JOSEPH R-Praise All the Moons of Morning-NY-1979-Atheneum-1st ed (h3,f,dj) 15.00

STONE,LESLIE F-When the Sun Went Out-NY-(1929)-Stellar Publ-24p-wrps-Science Fiction Ser.No.4 (c1) 10.00

STONE,LIVINGSTON-Domesticated Trout-Bost-1872-12mo-347p-orig bndg,illus-1st ed (m3) 45.00

STONE,MELVILLE E-Fifty Years a Journalist-GC-1921-xiv,371p-photos,drwngs-1st ed (n2) 20.00

STONE,PETER-Legering-Lond-1963-12mo-126p-photos (m3,f,dj) 15.00

STONE,ROBERT-Dog Soldiers-1974-Houghton Mifflin-1st ed (s9,f,dj) 50.00

STONE,ROBERT-Dog Soldiers-Bost-1974-1st ed (p5,f,dj) 75.00

STONE,ROBERT-Flag for Sunrise-NY-1981-Knopf-1st ed (k3,f,dj) 20.00

STONE,ROBERT-Hall of Mirrors-Bost,Cambridge-1967-Houghton Mifflin-auth 1st bk-1st ed (b5,sl bump,dj) 225.00

STONE,WILBUR F-ED.-History of Colorado-Chig-1918-S J Clarke-3 vols-illus-1st ed (bb4) 250.00

STONE,WILLIAM L-Life of Joseph Brant-Albany-1864-J Munsell-2 vols-orig cl-Howes S1040 (ee6) 150.00

STONE,WILLIAM L-Reminiscences of Saratoga-NY-1875-Virtue & Yorston-dec brwn cl,illus-1st ed (u2,sp ends wn) 75.00

STONE,WITMER-Bird Studies at Old Cape May-1937-Del Vlly Ornith Club-4to-2 vols-illus,photos,e.p. maps-ltd to 1400c,nbrd-1st ed (bb3) 185.00

STONE,WITMER-Bird Studies at Old Cape May-Phila-1937-2 vols-cl,illus,plts-ltd to 1400 sets,nbrd (aa6) 175.00

STONE,WITMER-Bird Studies of Old Cape May-Phila-1937-4to-2 vols-cl,2 col plts,1 aquatint,photos-ltd to 1400c (y8,pres cpy) 175.00

STONEBRAKER,J CLARENCE-Unwritten South-Hagerstown-(1903)-193p-bds-scarce-1st ed (n1) 25.00

STONERIDGE,M A-Great Horses of Our Time-GC-1972-Dbldy-sm 4to-543p-1st ed (j9,dj) 30.00

STONG,PHIL-Honk the Moose-NY-1935-Dodd,Mead-cl bckd pict bds,illus by K Wiese-1st ed (aa9,sl rub) 40.00

STONG,PHIL-Horses and Americans-NY-1939-Stokes-sm 4to-333p-col frntis,103 illus-ltd to 500c,autg-Herd 2176-1st ed (cc4,box) 100.00

STONG,PHIL-Young Settler-NY-1938-Dodd,Mead-cl bckd pict bds,illus by K Wiese-1st ed (aa9,sl rub) 35.00

STOPES,MARIE-Contraception-Lond-1924-418p-1st ed,3rd prtg (dd3) 100.00

STOPES-ROE,H V-Marie Stopes and Birth Control-Lond-1974-Priory Pr Ltd-8vo-96p-photos-1st ed (aa7,dj) 15.00*

STOPPARD,TOM-Lord Malquist & Mr.Moon-NY-1968-Knopf-1st US ed (b5,dj) 40.00

STOPPARD,TOM-Travesties-NY-(1975)-Grove-1st ed (b5,as new in dj) 20.00

STORER,D H-Fishes,Reptiles & Birds of Massachusetts-Bost-1839-8vo-426p-1/2 brn mor,illus-scarce (m3) 70.00

STOREY,DAVID-This Sporting Life-1960-Macmillan-auth 1st bk-1st Amer ed (s9,pgs brwng,dj) 45.00

STORING,HERBERT J-ED.-Complete Anti Federalist-(1981)-Univ of Chig-7 vols,blu cl-1st ed (e2) 135.00

STORK,BYRON C-Rawhide and Haywire-NY-1959-William-Frederick Pr-146p-illus-1st ed (cc4,dj) 25.00

STORKE,THOMAS M-California Editor-LA-1958-489p-frntis,photos,pict e.p.-1st ed (t7,f,dj) 12.50

STORM,COLTON-Catalogue of the Everett D Graff Collection of Western Americana-Chig-1968-854p-1st ed (f7,f,dj) 45.00

STORM,COLTON-COMP.-Catalogue of the Everett D Graff Collection of Western Americana-Chig-1968-Newberry Libr-4to-xxvi,854p-cl-1st ed (v1,dj) 50.00

STORME,HYEMEYOHSTS-Seven Arrows-NY-1972-374p-col plts,photos,illus-1st ed (t7,dj) 15.00

STORMS,J C-Oldest Inhabitant-Park Ridge-1934-(66)p-wrps (aa6) 45.00

STORRER,WM A-Architecture of Frank Lloyd Wright: a Complete Catalog-1974-MIT-illus-1st ed (h10,dj) 45.00

STORY,A T-Story of Wireless Telegraphy-1904-215p-57 illus-rare-1st ed (h6) 85.00

STORY,ISABELLE F-Glimpses of Our National Parks-Wash-1941-GPO-sm 4to-iii,107p-wrps,e.p. map,illus-rvsd ed (cc10) 15.00

STOTHERD,MAJOR R H-Notes on Torpedoes,Offensive and Defensive-Wash D C-1872-GPO-7+318p-1/2 drk lea,116 text illus-1st ed (d2,covs edge-wn,lea peeling) 225.00

STOTTER,JAMES-Beauty Unmasked-NY-1936-Raymond Pr-141p-blk bds,plts-1st ed (d2,dj) 20.00

STOUT,G D-ED.-Shorebirds of North America-NY-1967-sm folio-270p-cl,32 col plts (y8,dj) 175.00

STOUT,G D-ED.-Shorebirds of North America-NY-1967-Viking-sm folio-270p-32 plts (c9,f,wn dj) 150.00

STOUT,REX-3 at Wolfe's Door-1960-Viking-1st ed (x7,f,dj) 78.00

STOUT,REX-And Be a Villain-NY-1948-Viking-1st ed (j4,dj wi sm tape mrks) 45.00

STOUT,REX-And Four To Go-1958-Viking-1st ed (s10,sl fade sp,dj rub) 100.00

STOUT,REX-Before Midnight-1955-Viking-1st ed (x7,f,dj) 85.00

STOUT,REX-Black Mountain-NY-1954-Viking-1st ed (d4,dj) 75.00

STOUT,REX-Broken Vase-NY-1941-Farrar-1st ed (l4,f,sp chip dj) 150.00

STOUT,REX-Champagne for One-NY-1958-Viking-1st ed (bb1,dj) 40.00

STOUT,REX-Curtains for Three-1951-Viking-1st ed (x7,sl tn dj) 68.00

STOUT,REX-Death of a Doxy-1966-Viking-1st ed (n9,sp wn dj) 45.00

STOUT,REX-Death of a Dude-1969-Viking-1st ed (x2,f,dj sl wn & tn) 38.00

STOUT,REX-Death of a Dude-NY-(1969)-Viking-1st ed (bb1,dj) 50.00

STOUT,REX-Doorbell Rang-1965-Viking-1st ed (x2,f,dj) 50.00

STOUT,REX-Doorbell Rang-NY-(1965)-Viking-1st ed (bb1,one cor fray,dj) 40.00

STOUT,REX-ED.-Rue Morgue No.1-NY-1946-Creative Age Pr-1st ed (x9) 25.00

STOUT,REX-Family Affair-1975-Viking-1st ed (x2,f,sl tn dj) 35.00

STOUT,REX-Family Affair-NY-1975-Viking-1st ed (d4,dj) 20.00

STOUT,REX-Father Hunt-1968-Viking-1st ed (x2,f,sl chip dj) 45.00

STOUT,REX-Father Hunt-NY-1968-Viking-1st ed (e4,f,dj) 35.00

STOUT,REX-Fer De Lance-1935-Collins-scarce-1st Brit ed (x7,sl wn sp) 195.00

STOUT,REX-Fer De Lance-NY-1934-Farrar-1st ed (e4,cor rub,sp cl creased) 200.00

STOUT,REX-Final Deduction-1961-Viking-1st ed (x7,f,dj) 70.00

STOUT,REX-Forest Fire-NY-1933-Farrar & Rinehart-scarce-1st ed (gg8,f,lacks dj) 100.00

STOUT,REX-Gambit-NY-1962-Viking-1st ed (d4,fade dj) 30.00

STOUT,REX-Gambit-NY-1962-Viking-1st ed (w9,f,dj sl tn & wn) 45.00

STOUT,REX-Golden Spiders-1953-Viking-1st ed (x7,sl chip dj) 65.00

STOUT,REX-How Like a God-NY-1929-Vanguard-auth 1st bk-1st ed (f4,dj missing sm chips,rprd) 200.00

STOUT,REX-If Death Ever Slept-NY-1957-Viking-1st ed (w5,f dj) 40.00

STOUT,REX-In the Best Families-NY-1950-Viking-1st ed (e4,dj sp sl wn) 100.00

STOUT,REX-Justice Ends at Home-1977-Viking-1st ed (x7,f,dj) 25.00

STOUT,REX-Justice Ends at Home-NY-1977-Viking-1st ed (p4,vf,dj) 35.00

STOUT,REX-League of Frightened Men-1935-Farrar-1st ed (s10,slant,sl rub sp) 100.00

STOUT,REX-Might as Well be Dead-1953-Viking-1st ed (x7,f,sl tn dj) 70.00

STOUT,REX-Mother Hunt-NY-1963-Viking-1st ed (j4,dj) 25.00

STOUT,REX-Nero Wolfe Cook Book-NY-(1973)-Viking-203p (u6) 20.00

STOUT,REX-Nero Wolfe Cookbook-NY-1973-Viking-1st ed (d4,dj) 65.00

STOUT,REX-Please Pass the Guilt-1973-Viking-1st ed (o9,dj) 15.00

STOUT,REX-Plot it Yourself-NY-1959-Viking-1st ed (e4,dj sp sl fade) 85.00

STOUT,REX-President Vanishes-1934-F&R-1st ed (x2,dj sp sl fade) 595.00

STOUT,REX-Prisoner's Base-1952-Viking-1st ed (x7,sl tn dj) 85.00

STOUT,REX-Prisoner's Base-NY-1952-1st ed (r5,dj sp sl chip) 75.00

STOUT,REX-Right to Die-1964-Viking-1st ed (n9,sl tn dj) 60.00

STOUT,REX-Royal Flush-1966-Viking-1st ed (n9,dj wn & sp chip) 45.00

STOUT,REX-Seed on the Wind-NY-1930-Vanguard-1st ed (c10,dj sp chip,sl tn,wn,soil) 500.00

STOUT,REX-Silent Speaker-NY-1946-Viking-1st ed (f4,f,dj missing sm chips) 75.00

STOUT,REX-Some Buried Caesar-1939-F&R-1st ed (x7,sl tn dj) 895.00

STOUT,REX-Three Aces-1961-Viking-1st ed thus (s10,dj) 25.00

STOUT,REX-Three at Wolfe's Door-NY-1960-Viking-1st ed (bb1,sl stnd dj) 60.00

STOUT,REX-Three for the Chair-NY-1957-Viking-1st ed (x9,f,dj) 50.00

STOUT,REX-Three Witnesses-NY-1956-Viking-1st ed (d4,sp fade dj) 100.00

STOUT,REX-Too Many Clients-1960-Viking-1st ed (x7,sl fade dj sp) 65.00

STOUT,REX-Too Many Clients-NY-1960-Viking-1st ed (bb1,sp fade dj) 60.00

STOUT,REX-Too Many Clients-NY-1960-Viking-1st ed (f4,f,sp fade dj) 50.00

STOUT,REX-Too Many Cooks-NY-1938-Rinehart-1st ed (d4,sl wn,fox ep,dj mis pc sp) 600.00

STOUT,REX-Too Many Women-NY-1947-Viking-1st ed (d4,f,dj sp sl wn) 200.00

STOUT,REX-Trio For Blunt Instruments-1964-Viking-1st ed (n9,dj chip & tn) 45.00

STOUT,REX-Trio for Blunt Instruments-NY-1964-Viking-1st ed (k8,dj) 60.00

STOUT,REX-Triple Jeopardy-NY-1952-Viking-1st ed (d4,f,chip dj) 140.00

STOUT,REX-Trouble in Triplicate-NY-1949-Viking-1st ed (d4,dj sp sl fade) 150.00

STOUT,W B-So Away I Went!-NY-(1951)-8vo-336p-cl,frntis,29p plts (s2,sm stn frnt cov,dj) 25.00

STOUTENBURGH,JOHN-Dictionary of the American Indian-NY-(1960)-Philo Libr-462p (bb4,dj) 20.00

STOUTENBURGH,JOHN-Dictionary of the American Indian-NY-(1960)-Philo Libr-462p (o2,rub dj) 17.50

STOVER,ELIZABETH M-ED.-Son of a Gun Stew-Dallas-1945-216p-illus-1st ed (n10,dj) 30.00

STOWE,C E-Report on Elementary Public Education in Europe...-Bost-1838-68p-Amer Imprnts 53138-2nd prntg (k1,disbnd) 35.00

STOWE,HARRIET B-Dred, A Tale of the Great Dismal Swamp-Bost-1856-2 vols-BAL 19389-1st ed (r2,sl tn sps) 200.00

STOWE,HARRIET B-Key to Uncle Tom's Cabin-Bost-1853-John P Jewett-262p+(2)p ads-cl-presumed 2nd prntg wi both stereotyper's & prntr's imprnt on cpyrt pg,BAL 19359-1st Amer ed (f1,sl wn) 125.00

STOWE,HARRIET B-Key to Uncle Tom's Cabin-Bost-1853-John P Jewett-scarce-1st ed (y2,cov stnd,fade,sm hole t p) 450.00

STOWE,HARRIET B-Men of Our Times-Hartford-1868-575p-18 ports-1st ed (n2) 27.50

STOWE,HARRIET B-Poganuc People-NY-(1878)-g stmpd emboss cl-1st ed (k9) 20.00

STOWE,HARRIET B-Sunny Memories of Foreign Lands-Bost-1854-2 vols-illus,bndg A-BAL 19375-1st ed (r2,sp sun) 125.00

STOWE,HARRIET B-Uncle Tom's Cabin-Lond-1852-Clarke-8vo-x,329p-publ cl-BAL 19518-rare-"reprinted verbatim from the tenth American edition"-1st Brit ed (w6,lacks rear fep,hng loose) 750.00

STRACHEY,JOHN-Digging for Mrs Miller-NY-1941-Random-1st ed (y1,f,dj) 25.00

STRACHEY,JOHN-End of Empire-NY-1960-Random-351p-tan cl-1st US ed (ll1,wn dj) 10.00

STRACHEY,LYTTON-Books & Characters-Lond-1922-Chatto & Windus-papr sp labl-1st ed (y1,sl fox pgs) 30.00

STRACHEY,LYTTON-Books & Characters-NY-1927-Harcourt Brace-1st ed (t4,f) 15.00

STRACHEY,LYTTON-Really Interesting Question-NY-1973-Coward McCann & Geoghegan-1st US ed (y1,f,dj) 20.00

STRACHEY,LYTTON-Really Interesting Question-NY-1973-Coward McCann-col port frntis-1st ed (t4,f,f dj) 10.00

STRAHORN,CARRIE A-Fifteen Thousand Miles by Stage-NY,Lond-1911-673p-dec cl & e.p.,illus,plts(incl col)-Howes S1054-1st ed (g7,custom made box) 300.00

STRAHORN,ROBERT-Hand Book of Wyoming-Cheyenne-1877-249p-illus,ads-rare-1st ed (jj1,sl spot & wn) 350.00

STRAKACZ,ANIELA-Paderewski as I Knew Him-New Brunswick-(1949)-Rutgers U Pr-8vo-338p-illus-1st ed (ee5,dj) 25.00

STRAND,PAUL-Ghana-Millerton-1976-Aperture-160p-93 photos-1st ed (cc9,as new in dj) 50.00

STRAND,PAUL-Ghana-NY-1976-Aperture-4to-160p-cl-1st ed (t3,f) 60.00

STRAND,PAUL-Sixty Years of Photographs-Millerton-(1976)-Aperture-183p-133 photos-1st ed (cc9,as new in dj) 60.00

STRAND,PAUL-Sixty Years of Photography-Millerton-(1976)-Aperture-4to-cl-1st ed (y3,f dj) 85.00

STRANG,JAMES J-Prophetic Controversy-Lansing-1969-ix;59p-cl-ltd to 100c-wi John Cumming intro-orig ed 1856-1st hdbk ed (f1) 25.00

STRANG,JAMES J-Prophetic Controversy-Lansing-1969-ix;59p-cl-ltd to 500c-wi Stanley Johnson intro-(orig ed 1856)-1st hdbk ed (f1) 20.00

STRANG,LEWIS C-Prima Donnas and Soubrettes of Light Opera and Musical Comedy in America-Bost-1900-Page-12mo-270p-wht cl bndg,g dec cov of a peacock,photos-1st ed (s1) 65.00

STRANG,MARK A-ED.-Diary of James J Strang-E Lansing-1961-Mich State U Pr-78p-cl-1st ed (z7) 30.00

STRANGE MANUSCRIPT FOUND IN A COPPER CYLINDER-NY-1888-(auth is James De Mille)-1st ed (k5) 150.00

STRANGE,L A-Recollections of an Airman-Lond-nd(ca.1933)-8vo-cl,port,18p illus (t2,sl fade sp) 65.00

STRATHERN,ANDREW-One Father, One Blood-Lond-(1972)-Tavistock-8vo-265p-cl,maps-1st ed (y5,dj tn) 21.00

STRATTON,A-Elements of Form & Design in Classic Architecture...-NY-1925-Scribner-folio-100 plts-1st ed (h10) 85.00
STRATTON,ARTHUR-Great Red Island-NY-(1964)-Scribners-8vo-368p-16p photos-1st US ed (dd5,dj) 25.00
STRATTON,R B-Life Among the Indians-SF-1935-Grabhorn Pr-209p-wood engrvngs-ltd to 550c (e7,sl stnd cov) 125.00
STRAUB,ELMER F-Sergeant's Diary in the World War-Indpls-1923-356p-cl-Indiana Hist Collections-Dornbusch 1201 (j1) 20.00
STRAUB,PETER-Ghost Story-Lond-(1979)-Jonathan Cape-priority unknown between Brit & US eds-1st Brit ed (g3,f,dj) 65.00
STRAUB,PETER-Ghost Story-NY-(1979)-Coward,McCann-1st US ed (g3,dj) 25.00
STRAUB,PETER-Ghost Story-NY-1979-Coward McCann & Geoghegan-1st ed (e8,f,f dj) 35.00
STRAUB,PETER-Marriages-NY-1973-1st US ed (o5,sl wn dj) 65.00
STRAUB,PETER-Shadow Land-1980-Coward-1st ed (s10,soil cov,dj) 10.00
STRAUB,S W-Star Singer-Chig-(1879)-Jansen,McClurg-192p-bds (n1) 13.50
STRAUSS,MAURICE-Familiar Medical Quotations-Bost-1968-968p-1st ed (dd3,dj) 60.00
STRAUSS,PRESTON F-History of Harlingen Reformed Church...-(Harlingen)-(1927)-56p-wrps (aa6) 35.00
STRAUSS,RICHARD-Confidential Matter-1977-U of Cal Pr (u4,f,sl chip dj) 12.00
STREET,ALFRED B-Woods and Waters-NY-1860-M Doolady-brwn cl,map,9 engrvngs-Plum #1083-1st ed (gg7,sl chip sp) 110.00
STREET,JAMES-Good Bye, My Lady-Phila-1954-Lippincott-1st ed (f10,dj) 25.00
STREET,JOHN-Composition of Certain Patent and Proprietary Medicines-Chig-1917-274p-1st ed (dd3) 50.00
STREET,JULIAN-Abroad at Home-NY-1915-517p-cl (l1) 15.00
STREET,JULIAN-Mysterious Japan-1921-Dbldy,Page-349p-pict pastedown cov,illus-1st ed (v8,bump cov) 25.00
STREET,JULIAN-Wines-1933-Knopf-214p-red cl,fldg map-1st ed (q8,edgewn dj) 17.50
STREETER,DANIEL-Denatured Africa-GC-1929-8vo-338p-photos (m3) 12.50
STREETER,FLOYD B-Ben Thompson-NY-(1957)-F Fell-217p-illus-Six Guns #2154-1st ed (ee4,dj,Kelleher autg) 35.00
STREETER,FLOYD B-Political Parties in Michigan 1837 to 1860-Lansing-1918-401p-cl (h1) 15.00
STREETER,FLOYD B-Prairie Trails & Cow Towns-NY-1963-Devin Adair-214p-map e.p.,illus-Howes S1072 (ee4,dj) 25.00
STREETER,THOMAS WINTHROP-CELEBRATED COLLECTION OF AMERICANA FORMED BY THE LATE...-NY-1966 to 69-Parke Bernet-8vo-8 vols-blu papr cov bds,illus-1st ed (ll9) 750.00
STREETER,THOMAS-Merryland-NY-1932-Robin Hood Hs-135p-cl/col bds-ltd to 777c (ll2) 29.50
STRETE,CRAIG-If All Else Fails...-1980-Dbldy-1st ed (n9,rmdr mrk,dj) 45.00
STRIBLING,T S-Clues of the Caribbees-NY-1929-Dbldy-1st ed (j4) 25.00
STRICK,MARV-Beatnik Ball-(Van Nuys)-Sept 1961-Pike Bks-pbk orig-1st prtg (bb1,sp cocked) 20.00
STRICKLAND,ARVARH E-History of the Chicago Urban League-Urbana-1966-U of Ill-286p (r1,f,f dj) 30.00
STRICKLAND,W P-Life of Jacob Gruber-NY-1860-Carlton & Porter-384p-cl (pp6,sl wn) 60.00
STRICKLER,THEODORE D-When and Where We Met Each Other on Shore and Afloat-Wash.D.C.-(1899)-National Trib-219,(1)p-wrps (f1) 22.50
STRIEBER,WHITLEY-Black Magic-1982-Morrow-1st ed (n9,f,dj) 30.00
STRIKE AT SHANE'S-Bost-(1893)-Amer Humane Educ Society-91,(10)p-wrps-Gold Mine Ser.#2-scarce-1st ed (f1,sl tn,sp wn,chip) 175.00
STRINDBERG,AUGUST-From an Occult Diary-NY-1965-Hill & Wang-1s US ed (x9,edge spot,dj rub,soil) 10.00
STRINGER,ARTHUR-Gun Runner-NY-1909-B W Dodge-pict cov-1st ed (x1,lacks dj) 20.00
STRINGER,ARTHUR-Prairie Child-Tor-1922-M&S-382p-grn cl,frntis,illus by E F Ward-1st ed (bb7) 15.00*
STRODE,HUDSON-Jefferson Davis-NY-(1955,59,64)-3 vols-e.p. map in vol.2-1st ed (h7,vol.3 sp tn) 65.00
STROHBACH,G-Quacks and Grafters by Ex-Osteopath-Cin-1908-126p-1st ed (dd3) 45.00
STROM,ERLING-Pioneers on Skis-NY-1973-239p-1st ed (p10,as new in dj) 30.00
STROM,S A E-And So to Dine-(1955)-Frederick Bks-16mo-100p-red cl-1st ed (q8,dj,autg) 15.00
STRONG,ANNA L-Soviet World-NY-1936-Holt-8vo-xii,302p-red cl-1st ed (y4,dj missng sp top) 45.00
STRONG,ANNA L-Tomorrow's China-NY-1948-Comm Demo Far Estrn Pol-128p-wrps (r1,sl wn & tn) 15.00
STRONG,CHAS J-Art of Show Card Writing-Detr-1907-Detr School of Lettrng-8vo-209p-tan cl,illus (b6) 24.00
STRONG,GRACE-Worst Foe-Columbus-1887-Hubbard-385p-cl-7th ed (a1,cov rub,sl spot) 15.00
STRONG,GRACE-Worst Foe-Columbus-1888-385p-cl-9th ed (a1) 15.00
STRONG,HERBERT T-Stories of Old Chatham-(np)-1946-55,(1)p-wrps,illus (aa6) 30.00
STRONG,L A G-Bay-Lond-1941-Gollancz-1st ed (z8,f dj) 10.00
STRONG,L A G-Body's Imperfection-Lond-(1957)-Methuen-1st ed (z8,vf,dj) 40.00
STRONG,L A G-Corporal Tune-Lond-1934-Gollancz-1st ed (z8,f dj) 10.00
STRONG,L A G-Darling Tom...-Lond-(1952)-Methuen-1st ed (z8,vf,dj) 14.50
STRONG,L A G-Deliverance-Lond-(1955)-Methuen-1st ed (z8,vf,dj) 17.50
STRONG,L A G-Dr.Quicksilver-Lond-(1955)-Andrew Melrose-184p-grn cl,plts-1st ed (d2) 15.00
STRONG,L A G-Green Memory-Lond-(1961)-Methuen-1st ed (z8,vf,dj) 16.50
STRONG,L A G-Light Above the Lake-(Lond)-(1958)-Methuen-1st ed (z8,vf,dj) 17.50
STRONG,L A G-Sacred River-NY-(1951)-Pelligrini & Cudahy-1st ed (x10,f,dj) 20.00
STRONG,L A G-Sea Wall-Lond-1933-Gollancz-1st ed (z8,f dj) 10.00
STRONG,L A G-Seven Arms-Lond-1935-Gollancz-1st ed (z8,f dj) 10.00
STRONG,L A G-Story of Sugar-Lond-(1954)-Weidenfeld & Nicolson-159p-bds,illus (a8,sl sun bds,tattrd dj) 20.00
STRONG,L A G-Which I Never-Lond-(1950)-Collins Crime Club-1st ed (z8,vf,dj) 20.00

STRONG,R M-Bibliography of Birds-Chig-1939 to 59-8vo-4 parts:prts 1 & 2 bnd together in buckr,prts 3 & 4 in orig wrps (y8,ex-libr) 165.00

STRONG,ROBERT H-Yankee Private's Civil War-Chig-1961-H Regnery-218p-frntis,illus-1st ed (cc6,dj) 20.00

STRONG,THERON G-Joseph H Choate-NY-1917-Dodd,Mead-xviii+390p-Maroon cl-1st ed (b2) 15.00

STRONG,THOMAS N-Cathlamet on the Columbia-Portland-1906-119p-dec cov-1st ed (r8,ex-libr) 30.00

STROUD,R H-Black Bass Biology & Management-Wash D.C.-1975-4to-534p-photos,illus (m3) 12.50

STRUEVER,STUART-Koster-NY-1979-Anchor Pr/Dbldy-281p-illus-1st ed (cc4,dj) 20.00

STRUGATSKY,ARKADY-Space Apprentice-NY-(1981)-Macmillan-1st ed in English (h3,f,dj) 15.00

STRUHSAKER,T T-Red Colobus Monkey-1975-U of Chig-311p-photos (bb3,f,dj) 30.00

STRUHSAKER,T T-Red Colobus Monkey-Chig-1975-8vo-311p-cl,37 plts (y8,dj) 30.00

STRUTHER,JAN-Mrs.Miniver-NY-(1940)-G&D-Photoplay ed (s1,sp fade dj) 15.00

STRYKER,L P-Andrew Johnson-NY-1929-881p-illus,ports (z10,cov soil) 25.00

STRYKER,LLOYD-Courts and Doctors-NY-1932-236p-1st ed (dd3) 40.00

STRYKER,WILLIAM S-Affair at Egg Harbor, New Jersey, October 15, 1778-Trenton-1894-34p-wrps,illus (aa6) 30.00

STRYKER,WILLIAM S-Battle of Monmouth-Princeton-1927-(10),303p-cl,plts (aa6) 75.00

STRYKER,WILLIAM S-Battles of Trenton and Princeton-Bost-1898-xv,514p-cl,illus (aa6) 125.00

STRYKER,WILLIAM S-Capture of the Block House at Toms River, New Jersey, March 24, 1782-Trenton-1883-32p (aa6,disbnd) 30.00

STRYKER,WILLIAM S-Forts on the Delaware in the Revolutionary War-Trenton-1901-51p-wrps,plts (aa6) 50.00

STRYKER,WILLIAM S-Official Register of the Officers and Men of New Jersey in the Revolutionary War-Trenton-1872-878p-cl (aa6) 200.00

STRYKER,WILLIAM S-Record of Officers and Men of New Jersey in the Civil War, 1861 to 1865-Trenton-1876-4to-2 vols-mod buckrm (aa6,rbnd) 300.00

STRYKER-RODDA,HARRIET-Some Early Records of Morris County, New Jersey, 1740 to 1799-New Orleans-1975-4to-xviii,225p-wrps (aa6) 50.00

STUART,D M-English Abigail-Lond-1946-Macmillan-221p-red cl,facs (q8) 20.00

STUART,DAVID-Alan Watts-Radnor-1976-Chilton-cl-1st ed (n8,vf,dj) 15.00

STUART,FRANCIS-Hole in the Head-Nantucket-1977-Longship Pr-1st Amer ed (z8,vf,dj) 35.00

STUART,FRANCIS-Redemption-NY-1950-Devin Adair-1st Amer ed (z8,vf,chip dj) 35.00

STUART,GRANVILLE-Forty Years on the Frontier-Glendale-1925-A H Clark-2 vols,drk blu cl,illus-Howes 1096-1st ed (v1) 300.00

STUART,GRANVILLE-Forty Years on the Frontier-Glendale-1957-2 vols in one-illus(3 b&w by Russell)-Howes S1096-2nd ed (c7) 100.00

STUART,HIX C-Notorious Ashley Gang-Stuart-(1928)-St.Lucie Prtg-80p-illus-Six Guns 2161-1st ed (bb4) 45.00

STUART,HIX C-Notorious Ashley Gang-Stuart-1928-St.Lucie Co-sm 8vo-80p-red cl,photos-Six Guns #2161-scarce-1st ed (b3) 60.00

STUART,J-History of the Zulu Rebellion 1906-Lond-1913-581p-red cl,fldg maps,illus-1st ed (b7) 400.00

STUART,JESSE-Beyond Dark Hills-NY-1939-Dutton-6 decs by Ishmael-1st ed (y1,f,sl wn dj) 150.00

STUART,JESSE-Clearing in the Sky-NY-1950-1st ed (n5,dj) 35.00

STUART,JESSE-Foretaste of Glory-NY-1946-Dutton-1st ed (a5,sl chip dj) 40.00

STUART,JESSE-God's Oddling-NY-1960-1st ed (q5,dj sl chip) 25.00

STUART,JESSE-Head O'W Hollow-NY-1936-1st ed (o5,chip dj) 115.00

STUART,JESSE-Head O'W Hollow-NY-1936-Dutton-beige cl-1st ed (f2,dj) 135.00

STUART,JESSE-Trees of Heaven-NY-1940-Dutton-pnk cl-1st ed (f2,dj) 100.00

STUART,ROBERT-On the Oregon Trail-Norman-(1953)-192p-illus-1st ed (c7,f,chip dj) 40.00

STUBBS,S G B-Sixty Centuries of Health and Physick-Lond-1931-253p-illus (dd3) 50.00

STUCK,HUDSON-Ascent of Denali-NY-1914-fldg map-1st ed (q10,ex-libr) 175.00

STUCK,HUDSON-Ascent of Denali-NY-1918-188p-34 plts,map (a4) 150.00

STUCK,HUDSON-Voyages on the Yukon and Its Tributaries-NY-1917-Scribners-8vo-xvi,397p-blu dec cl,2 lg fldg maps,plts-Ricks p.212 (oo1) 195.00

STUDEBAKER BROS MFG MAKERS OF ALL KINDS OF FARM,FREIGHT TRUCK...SOUTH BEND,INDIANA-(Milw)-nd(1880s?)-16p-wrps (o1) 40.00

STUDLEY,J T-Journal of a Sporting Nomad-Lond-1912-303p-photos (gg3) 25.00

STUMER,HAROLD M-This Was Klondike Fever-Seattle-1978-159p-frntis,photos,illus-1st ed (t7,dj) 17.50

STURGE,JOSEPH-Visit to the United States in 1841-Bost-1842-Dexter S King-235;xciii p-lea (j1) 60.00

STURGE,JOSEPH-Visit to the United States in 1841-Bost-1842-Dexter S King-blk cl-1st Amer ed (mm10) 75.00

STURGEON,THEODORE-Cosmic Rape-NY-(1958)-Dell-wrps-1st ed (m4,f) 20.00

STURGEON,THEODORE-E Pluribus Unicorn-NY-(1953)-1st ed (bb10,chip dj) 40.00

STURGIS,BERTHA B-Field Book of Birds of the Panama Canal Zone-NY-1928-12mo-466p-cl,24 plts(incl col) (y8) 45.00

STURGIS,BERTHA B-Field Book of the Birds of the Panama Canal Zone-NY-1928-Putnam's-466p-photos,col plts (b9) 25.00

STURGIS,RUSSELL-Interdependence of the Arts of Design-Chig-1905-McClurg-sm 4to-227p-cl,100 illus (pp7) 65.00

STURGIS,W B-Fly Tying-NY-1940-Scribner's-8vo-254p-"A" on cpyrght pg-1st prntg (m3,dj) 35.00

STURGIS,WILLIAM B-New Lines for Flyfishers-NY-(1936)-Derrydale-8vo-grn cl,illus by R Boyer-ltd to 950c-1st ed (u10) 100.00

STUTFIELD,HUGH E M-Climbs and Explorations in the Canadian Rockies-Lond-1903-Longmans,Green-8vo-xii,343p-orig cl,frntis,illus,2 maps(1 fldg at rear)-1st ed (cc7,rprd cl,new e.p.) 65.00*

STYLES,SHOWELL-Getting to Know Mountains-Lond-1958-160p-1st ed (q10,f,dj) 16.00

STYLES,SHOWELL-Rock & Rope-Lond-1963-174p-1st ed (p10,f,dj) 20.00

STYRON,WILLIAM-Confessions of Nat Turner-NY-(1967)-Random-1st ed (a5,f,dj) 45.00

STYRON,WILLIAM-Confessions of Nat Turner-NY-1967-1st ed (n5,f,f dj) 25.00

STYRON,WILLIAM-In the Clap Shack-NY-(1973)-Random-1st ed (dd2,f,sl tn dj) 35.00

STYRON,WILLIAM-In the Clap Shack-NY-1973-1st ed (q5,dj wi sm tr) 25.00

STYRON,WILLIAM-Lie Down in Darkness-Indpls-1951-auth 1st bk-1st ed (q5,dj) 100.00

STYRON,WILLIAM-Set This House On Fire-NY-1960-1st ed (q5,dj) 25.00

STYRON,WILLIAM-Sophie's Choice-NY-(1979)-Random-1st trd ed (a5,f,dj) 25.00

STYRON,WILLIAM-This Quiet Dust-NY-(1982)-Random-1st ed (h3,f,dj) 15.00

SUARES,CARLO-Resurrection of the Word-Berkeley-1975-Shambhala-cl-1st ed (n8,f,dj) 15.00

SUBITZKY,SEYMOUR-ED.-Geology of Selected Areas in New Jersey and Eastern Pennsylvania and Guidebook of Excursions-New Brunswick-(1969)-4to-(8),382p-illus,cl (aa6) 25.00

SUCKOW,RUTH-John Wood Case-NY-(1959)-Viking-1st ed (hh5,dj) 10.00

SUDHALTER,RICHARD M-Bix-New Rochelle-1974-Arlington Hs-1st ed (w5,f,dj) 50.00

SUEHSDORF,A D-Great American Baseball Scrapbook-1978-Random(Rutledge)-photos(incl col)-1st ed (s8,f,f dj) 27.00

SUEUR,MERIDEL LE-North Star Country-NY-1945-Book Find Club-8vo-327p-cl (z7) 22.50

SUFRIN,MARK-To the Top of the World-NY-1966-94p-1st ed (p10,f,dj) 10.00

SUGAR,BERT R-Hit the Sign and Win a Free Suit of Clothes from Harry Finklestein-1978-Contemporary (r7,f,dj) 25.00

SUGIMOTO,ETSU I-Daughter of the Samurai-NY-1934-Dbldy-314p-drwngs,C Morley intro (c3,chip dj) 24.00

SUGNET,CHRISTOPHER L-Vietnam War Bibliography-Lexington-(1983)-D C Heath-1st ed (ff3,f) 45.00

SUKSDORFF,A B-Tiger in Sight-NY-1970-110p-photos (gg3,vf,dj) 25.00

SULLIVAN,EDMUND B-Collecting Political Americana-1980-Crown-4to-1st ed (dd8,dj) 22.50

SULLIVAN,EDWARD-Book of Kells-Lond/NY-1955-Studio-4to-111p-cl,24 col plts (ll4) 75.00

SULLIVAN,EDWARD-ET AL-Yachting-Lond-1894-Longmans,Green-2 vols-Badminton Libr of Sports-1/2 navy blu mor & tan cl,g stmpd sp,mrbld e.p.,photos,maps,drwngs (p6,f,box) 450.00

SULLIVAN,FRANCES P-COMP.-Standard Recitations by Best Authors...-NY-1884-48p-wrps (j1,sp wn) 12.50

SULLIVAN,GEORGE-Home Run-1977-Dodd,Mead-1st ed (p7,dj) 15.00

SULLIVAN,GEORGE-Picture History of the Boston Red Sox-1979-Bobbs Merrill-1st ed (ff2,dj) 35.00

SULLIVAN,HARRY S-Collected Works-NY-nd(ca.1965)-Norton-2 vols-grn cl (c2,box) 65.00

SULLIVAN,JOHN T-ED.-Madison County-Richmond-1965-80p-wrps (n1) 12.50

SULZ,CHARLES H-Treatise on Beverages-NY-(1888)-Dick & Fitzgerald-xxvi+818p-brwn buckram,428 text figs (l2) 75.00

SUMMER,GEORGE L-Newberry County South Carolina Historical and Genealogical-(Newberry)-1950-Auth-4to-469+11p-blu cl-1st ed (oo5,sl rub & soil) 60.00

SUMMERHAYES,MARTHA-Vanished Arizona-Phila,NY-1963-258p-facs rprnt of 1908 ed (j7,dj) 20.00

SUMMERHAYES,MARTHA-Vanished Arizona-Tucson-273p-fnrtis,photos,map e.p.-ltd ed-rprnt Howes S1132 (t7,f,dj) 35.00

SUMMERHAYS,R S-Lifetime with Horses-NY-1962-Warne-bds-1st US ed (j9,dj) 22.00

SUMMERING IN COLORADO-Denver-1874-Richard & Co-158p+ads-cl-variant state wi no photos (g1,sl spot cov) 40.00

SUMMERING IN COLORADO-Denver-1874-Richards & Co-158p+ads-cl (n1,sl spot cov) 40.00

SUMMERS,FESTUS P-Baltimore and Ohio in the Civil War-NY-(1939)-Putnam's-304p-16 illus,8 maps-Nevins I,15-1st ed (bb4) 100.00

SUMMERS,HARRY G,JR.-On Strategy-(Novato)-(1982)-224p-bds-1st ed (h1,f,dj) 15.00

SUMMERS,LEWIS P-History of Southwest Virginia, 1746 to 1786, Washington County, 1777 to 1870-1903-J L Hill-911p-1st ed (dd9,fray,weak bndg,pencilng) 85.00

SUMMERS,MONTAGUE-Geography of Witchcraft-NY-1927-Knopf-cl,illus-1st Amer ed (o8,fray dj) 15.00

SUMMERS,MONTAGUE-History of Witchcraft and Demonology-Lon/NY-1926-Kegan Paul/Knopf-(xvi)+353+(3)p+16p catlg,blu cl-1st ed (y9) 100.00

SUMMERS,MONTAGUE-Popular History of Witchcraft-NY-(1973,1936)-Causeway-8vo-276p-illus-rprnt (gg5,dj sp rub) 15.00

SUMMERS,MONTAGUE-Vampire in Europe-Lond-1929-K Paul,Trench,Trubner-red cl-1st ed (y9,fade cl) 75.00

SUMMERS,MONTAGUE-Vampire-NY-1960-Univ Bks-8vo-xxvii,356p+6p ads-7 illus-rprnt of 1928 first ed (aa7,rub dj) 25.00*

SUMMERS,MONTAGUE-Vampire:His Kith and Kin-Lond-1928-K Paul,Trench,Trubner-red cl-1st ed (y9) 75.00

SUMMERS,MONTAGUE-Vampire:His Kith and Kin-New Hyde Park-(1960)-Univ Bks-red cl-reprnt ed (y9) 25.00

SUMMERTON,MARGARET-Nightingale at Noon-1963-Dutton-1st Amer ed (s10,dj) 15.00

SUMMERTON,MARGARET-Ring of Mischief-1965-Dutton-1st Amer ed (s10,dj) 15.00

SUMMERTON,MARGARET-Sea House-1961-Holt-1st Amer ed (s10,dj) 15.00

SUMNER,GEORGE-Compendium of Physiological and Systematic Botany-Hartford-1820-Cooke-300p-calf,8 engrvd plts (x6,rbckd) 100.00

SUMNER,JAMES B-ED.-Enzymes-NY-1950-Academic Pr-4 vols-blu cl-1st ed (a2) 100.00

SUMPTER,JESSE-Paso Del Aguila-Encino-1969-152p-illus-1st ed (a9) 60.00

SUMPTION,D-Archery for Beginners-Phila-1932-12mo-141p-photos (m3) 15.00

SUNDAY,W E-Gah Dah Gwa Stee-Pryor-1953-priv prtd-172p-photos,illus-Six Guns #2166-scarce-1st ed (t7,f) 175.00

SUNDBURG,GEORGE-Hail Columbia-NY-1954-Macmillan-8vo-467p-1st ed (gg5,dj) 15.00

SUNDER,JOHN E-Fur Trade on the Upper Missouri 1840 to 1864-Norman-(1965)-295p-photos,maps-1st ed (t7,f,dj) 40.00

SUNDER,JOHN E-Fur Trade on the Upper Missouri 1840 to 1865-(1965)-U of OK-295p-illus,maps-1st ed (r8,dj sp sunned) 30.00

SUNDER,JOHN E-Joshua Pilcher, Fur Trader and Indian Agent-Norman-(1968)-203p-1st ed (a1,f,dj) 22.50

SUNDERMAN,J F-ED.-World War II in the Air-Europe-(1963)-roy 8vo-xii,346p-cl,frntis,plts (s2,dj) 30.00

SUNDKLER,BENGT G M-Bantu Prophets in South Africa-Lond-1961-OUP-8vo-381p-map,illus-2nd ed (y5,sl soil,dj) 22.00

SUNDMAN,PER OLOF-Flight of the Eagle-NY-1970-Pantheon-8vo-vi,386p-e.p. map-1st US ed (ff9,dj) 25.00*

SUNDMAN,PER OLOF-Flight of the Eagle-NY-1970-Pantheon/Random-8vo-e.p. maps,illus-1st US ed (cc7) 20.00*

SUNSERI,ALVIN R-Seeds of Discord-Chig-1979-Nelson Hall-1st ed (ff8,dj) 28.00

SUPREE,BURTON-Bear's Heart-Phila-1977-Lippincott-oblng 8vo-64p-gry bds,col plts (r10,tattrd dj) 15.00

SUPREY,LESLIE V-Steam Trains of the Soo-Mora-1962-96p-2nd rvsd ed (n4,f,dj) 30.00

SURDAM,LLOYD B-Main Roads & Byways-Prairie City-(1947)-Pr of James Decker-92p-cl (g1,f,dj) 15.00

SURFACE,BILL-Roundup at the Double Diamond-Bost-1974-Houghton Mifflin-1st prtg (f10,dj) 15.00

SURTEE,R S-Hawbuck Grange-Westminster-1955-Folio Soc-8vo-211p-frntis,7 col illus by Phiz (bb7,dj rub,chip) 20.00*

SUTER,JOHN W-American Book of Common Prayer...-NY-1949-OUP-8vo-x,85p-cl-1st ed (x4,sp fade) 25.00

SUTHERLAND,DAN A-Memories of Alaska-np-nd(not before 1955)-47p-wrps (b1) 15.00

SUTHERLAND,HALLIDAY-Time to Keep-NY-1934-Morrow-8vo-281p-1st US ed (cc5,dj) 25.00

SUTHERLAND,JAMES-Adventures of an Elephant Hunter-Lond-1912-8vo-312p-photos-scarce-1st ed (m3) 300.00

SUTHERLAND,L W-Aces and Kings-Lond-nd(ca.1920)-8vo-xii,276p-cl,frntis,illus (s2) 75.00

SUTHERLAND,S K-Venomous Creatures of Australia-1981-Oxford Univ-128p-60 col photos-1st ed (bb3,f,dj) 38.00

SUTLEY,ZACK T-Last Frontier-NY-1930-Macmillan-350p-map-Six Guns 2169-Herd 2204-1st ed (bb4) 45.00

SUTLEY,ZACK-Last Frontier-1930-MacMillan-fldg map-Six Guns 2169-1st ed (t8) 35.00

SUTTON,ERNEST V-Life Worth Living-Pasadena-(1948)-Trail's End Publ-350p-col pict e.p.-ltd to 2000c-Six Guns #2170-1st ed (ee4,dj) 45.00

SUTTON,G M-At a Bend in a Mexican River-1972-Eriksson-4to-184p-12 col & 18 b&w plts,photos (bb3,f,tn dj) 40.00

SUTTON,G M-Birds in the Wilderness-1936-Macmillan-200p-4 col & 8 b&w plts-1st ed (bb3,wn dj) 65.00

SUTTON,G M-Birds of Southampton Island-Pitt-1932-Part II,Zoology,Sec.2-tall 4to-275p-wrps,14 plts(3 col) (y8,chip) 110.00

SUTTON,G M-Exploration of Southampton Island, Hudson Bay-Pitt-1932 to 36-tall 4to-574p-wrps,30 plts(6 col) (y8,wrps tn) 250.00

SUTTON,G M-High Arctic-NY-1971-4to-(2),116,(3)p-11 dbl-pg col plts,16 photos (y8) 45.00

SUTTON,G M-Mammals of Southampton Island-Pitt-1932-tall 4to-111p-wrps,5 plts,Part II,Zoology,Sec.1 (y8,chip wrps) 45.00

SUTTON,G M-Mexican Birds-1951-U of Okla-282p-16 col plts,65 drwngs-scarce-1st ed (bb3,f,dj) 165.00

SUTTON,G M-Oklahoma Birds-Norman-1967-8vo-674p-cl,col frntis,2 maps (y8,dj) 80.00

SUTTON,G M-Oklahoma Birds-Norman-1967-U of Okla Pr-674p-col frntis,drwngs-scarce (c9,dj) 110.00

SUTTON,GEOFFERY-Artificial Aids in Mountaineering-Lond-1962-60p-wrps-1st ed (o10,f) 10.00

SUTTON,GEORGE-Glacier Island-Lond-1957-224p-1st ed (o10,f,dj) 30.00

SUTTON,JACK-110 Years with Josephine-Medford-1966-205p-wrps,illus-1st ed (c7,f) 35.00

SUTTON,JEAN-Lords of the East-Lond-1981-Conway Maritime Pr-176p-illus-1st ed (p8,as new in dj) 19.50

SUTTON,RICHARD L-Lond Trek-St.Louis-1930-8vo-347p-photos-1st ed (m3) 30.00

SUTZKEVER,A-Siberia: a Poem-Lond-1961-Abelard Schuman-4to-48p-cl,8p drwngs by Chagall (y4,dj) 45.00

SUYDAM,C R-American Cartridge-CA-1960-184p-photos (gg3,vf,dj) 12.00

SUYIN,HAN-Lhasa, the Open City-NY-1977-180p-1st US ed (q10,f,dj) 20.00

SUYIN,HAN-Morning Deluge-Bost-1972-Little,Brown-571p-1st ed (r1,sl chip dj) 15.00

SUZUKI,BEATRICE L-Mahayana Buddhism-Lond-1938-Buddhist Lodge-cl-1st prtg (l8) 25.00

SUZUKI,D T-Introduction to Zen Buddhism-NY-1974-Causeway Bks-two vols bnd as one,cl-1st prtg (n8,f,dj) 35.00

SUZUKI,D T-Living by Zen-Lond-1950-Rider & Co-cl-1st ed (l8,wn dj) 25.00

SUZUKI,D T-Shin Buddhism-NY-1970-Harper & Row-cl-1st ed (l8,f) 25.00

SVOBODA,ANTONIN-Computing Mechanisms and Linkages-NY-1948-McGraw Hill-xii+359p-red cl,diag in pckt-M.I.T. Radiation Ser-1st ed (c2) 35.00

SWADOS,HARVEY-On the Line-Bost-1957-1st ed (r5,dj) 20.00

SWADOS,HARVEY-Out Went the Candle-NY-1955-auth 1st bk-1st ed (r5,dj sp sl sunned) 30.00

SWADOS,HARVEY-Standing Fast-NY-1970-Dlbdy-cl-1st ed (aa9,f,dj) 15.00

SWALLOW,ALAN-ED.-Wild Bunch-Denver-(1966)-Sage Bks-136p-cl,port,maps-1st ed (v1,dj) 35.00

SWALLOW,JAY-Pony Care-NY-1976-St.Martin's-1st ed (h9) 10.00

SWAN,BRADFORD F-Gregory Dexter of London & New England:1610 to 1700-Rochester-1949-Leo Hart-115p-facs,illus (a3) 15.00

SWAN,CONRAD-Canada-1977-U of Tor Pr-8vo-xiv,272p-24p col plts,illus-1st ed (cc7,sl rub dj) 35.00*

SWAN,HOWARD-Music in the Southwest 1825 thru 1950-San Marino-1952-300p-photos-1st ed (u7,f,dj) 35.00

SWAN,JAMES-Northwest Coast-NY-1857-435p+4p ads-illus-Tweney #74-1st ed (e7) 275.00

SWAN,JOHN A-Trip to the Gold Mines of California in 1848-1960-Bk Club of Cal-51p-ltd to 400c (d3) 75.00

SWAN,KENNETH D-Splendid was the Trail-Missoula-(1968)-Mtn Pr-173p-photos-1st ed (bb4,dj) 25.00

SWAN,THOMAS B-Queens Walk in the Dark-Forest Park-1977-Heritage-ltd to 2000c,acetate dj-1st ed (k3,f,dj) 50.00

SWANBOROUGH,F G-United States Military Aircraft since 1909-Lond-(1963)-8vo-xii,596p-cl,illus (s2) 50.00

SWANDER,JOHN L-Silent Echoes Beneath the Casket Lid-Tiffin-1920-16p-wrps (h1) 12.50

SWANK,W-African Antelope-1971-Winchester-folio-143p-coated papr,col illus (gg3,vf,box) 175.00

SWANN,PETER C-Chinese Painting-NY-1958-tip in col plts-1st ed (r2) 50.00

SWANSON,JAMES-Superstition Mountain-Phoenix-1981-206p-photos,maps-1st ed (v7,f,dj) 25.00

SWANTON,JOHN R-Early History of the Creek Indians and their Neighbors-1922-Bur Amer Ethnol Bull.73-492p-10 fldg pckt maps (bb3) 65.00

SWANTON,JOHN R-Early History of the Creek Indians and their Neighbors-Wash D.C.-1922-Bureau of Ethnlgy,Bull#73-492p-olive cl,10 plts in rear pckt (m2) 55.00

SWANTON,JOHN R-ED.-Dictionary of the Choctaw Language-Wash-1915-Bur Amer Ethnol,Bull.46-611p (gg4) 35.00

SWANTON,JOHN R-Indians of the Southeastern United States-Wash D.C.-1946-GPO/Bur Ethno Bull No.137-943p-orig blu wrps,107 plts,maps-1st ed (ee7,sl chip) 90.00

SWANTON,JOHN R-Linguistic Material from the Tribes of Southern Texas and Northeastern Mexico-1940-Smithsonian BAE Bull.#127-145p-wrps (a9) 20.00

SWANTON,JOHN R-Tlingit Myths and Texts-Wash-1909-BAE Bull #39-451p-cl (aa1,sl spot sp) 25.00

SWARTH,H S-Birds and Mammals of Stikine River Region of Northern Brit Col and Southeastern Alaska-Berkeley-1922-8vo-(3),(126-)314p-wrps,col frntis (y8,dmpstnd covs) 30.00

SWARTH,H S-Report on a Collection of Birds and Mammals from Vancouver Island-Berkeley-1912-8vo-(2),124; (407-)(417)p-cl,4 plts (y8,lt dmpstng) 25.00

SWARTHMORE COLLEGE FACULTY-Adventure in Education: Swarthmore College Under Frank Aydelotte-NY-1941-Macmillan-8vo-236p-1st ed (y6) 12.50

SWARTHOUT,M FRENCH-Sheldon's Graded Examples in Arithmetic. Second Book-NY,Chig-(1884)-Sheldon-221p-bds (j1) 12.50

SWASEY,WILLIAM F-Early Days and Men of California...-Oakland-(1891)-Pacific Pr-(x)+9-406p,port,2 plts-Streeter 3012-1st ed (k2) 475.00

SWAZEY,JUDITH-Reflexes and Motor Integration: Sherrington's Concept of Integrative Action-Cambridge-1969-273p-1st ed (dd3,dj) 40.00

SWEDISH AMERICAN LINE-The Will to Succeed-Stockholm & NY-1948-Bonniers Publ-12mo-347p+index-tan cl,prntd in Sweden-v scarce (b6) 60.00

SWEDISH CHRISTMAS-NY-nd(ca.1959)-H Holt-259p-illus (n6) 33.00

SWEENEY,JAMES-Alexander Calder-NY-(1943)-MOMA-4to-stiff wrps (oo6) 75.00

SWEENEY,MATTHEW-Dream of Maps-Dublin-1981-Raven Arts Pr-wrps-1st ed (z8,vf) 16.50

SWEENY,SARAH L-Harvest of the Wind-Caldwell-1935-Caxton-1st ed (u2,f,dj) 30.00

SWEET,A E-Sketches from "Texas Siftings"-NY-1882-Tex Siftings Publ-228p-pict cl,illus by W H Caskie-Herd 2218-1st ed (bb4,wn sp & cor) 45.00

SWEET,ALEX E-On a Mexican Mustang, Through Texas, From the Gulf to the Rio Grande-Lond-(1883)-Trubner-lg thk 8vo-672p-g dec bndg,illus-Jenkins#201-1st Brit ed (t1) 250.00

SWEETMAN,JACK-American Naval History-Annapolis-1984-Naval Inst Pr-4to-xii,(2),331p-blu cl,maps,illus-1st ed (p8,f,dj) 30.00

SWEETSER,M F-Views of the White Mountains-Portland-(1879)-Chisholm-folio-cl-scarce in lg format-1st ed (y3,crack,weak hngs) 175.00

SWEETZER,M F-Views in the White Mountains-Portland-1879-Chisholm-sq 8vo-blu grn cl stmpd in blk & gilt-1st ed (y3) 55.00

SWENEY,F-Techniques of Drawing & Painting Wildlife-NY-1959-144p-illus (gg3,f,dj) 75.00

SWENGEL,F M-American Steam Locomotive, Vol.I: the Evolution of the Steam Locomotive-Davenport-1967-267p-1st ed (n4,f,dj) 37.50

SWESSINGER,EARL A-Texas Trail to Dodge City-San Antonio-(1950)-Naylor Co-248p-illus-1st ed (ee4,dj) 25.00

SWETT,IRA L-ED.-Market Street Railway Revisited, the Best of "The Inside Track"-So Gate-1972-208p-Interurban Spec #56-1st ed (n4,f,dj) 16.50

SWETT,IRA L-ED.-Sacramento Northern Album-LA-1963-136p-wrps-Interurban Spec #34-1st ed (n4) 14.00

SWETT,IRA L-Los Angeles Railway's Pre Huntington Cars 1890 to 1902-LA-1962-72p-wrps-Interurban Spec #33-1st ed (n4) 10.00

SWETT,IRA L-Tractions of the Orange Empire-LA-1967-253p-wrps-Interurban Spec #41-1st ed (n4) 18.00

SWETT,IRA-ED.-Pacific Electric Album of Cars-LA-1965-208p-wrps-Interurban Spec #39-1st ed (n4) 14.00

SWETTENHAM,FRANK-British Malaya-Lond-1907-354p-yel cl,photos-1st ed (gg2) 75.00

SWIFT & HERRICK-Feed the Brute-1926-Stokes-173p-1st ed (v6,sl wn) 10.00

SWIFT,H-Zack Jones Fisherman-Philosopher-Chig-1944-8vo-225p (m3,f,chip dj) 20.00

SWIFT,HILDEGARDE H-Little Red Lighthouse and the Great Gray Bridge-NY-(1942)-Harcourt Brace-col illus,Lynd Ward-1st ed (s3,f,dj) 45.00

SWIFT,JONATHAN-Directions to Servants-NY-(c.1964)-Pantheon-125p-illus-1st prtg (a8) 30.00

SWIGER,LORAINE B-Family Sketches of Throckmortons of Southern Ohio-Waverly-1975-289,(6)p-wrps (d1,autg) 20.00

SWIGGETT,CAPTAIN S A-Bright Side of Prison Life-Balt-(1897)-Pr of Fleet,McGinley & Co-254p-cl (g1) 100.00

SWIHART,WALTER-Xavier Langston or Circumstances Change-Ada-1895-Univ Herald Pr-357p-cl (n1) 25.00

SWINBURNE,ALGERNON C-Springtide of Life-Lond-(1918)-Heinemann-orig pict g cl,illus by A Rackham-1st ed (aa9,sl rub) 150.00

SWINBURNE,ALGERON C-Springtide of Life-Phila/Lond-1918-Lippincott/Heinemann-4to-133p-grn cl wi blk stmpng,8 col plts wi prntd guards,e.p. & illus t.p.,A Rackham-1st trd ed (r3) 55.00

SWINNERTON,FRANK-Authors and the Book Trade-1932-Knopf-1st Amer ed (x2,f,dj sl wn & tn) 30.00

SWINNERTON,FRANK-Bookman's London-NY-1952-Dbldy-8vo-x,162p-cl-1st US ed (w2,dj chip) 15.00

SWINTON,WILLIAM-New Word-Analysis-NY,Chig-(1879)-Ivison,Blakeman,Taylor-154p-cl (j1) 12.50

SWISHER,D-Fly Fishing Strategy-NY-1975-4to-184p-illus,D Whitlock (m3,f,dj) 15.00

SWISHER,D-Selective Trout-NY-1971-184p-photos,illus (gg3,f,dj) 25.00

SWISHER,D-Selective Trout-NY-1971-4to-184p-illus,photos-1st ed (m3,vf,sl chip dj) 50.00

SWISHER,D-Tying the Swisher Richards Flies-Harrisburg-1977-4to-48p-wrps,illus,photos-1st ed (m3,f) 20.00

SWISHER,JACOB-Iowa Department of the Grand Army of the Republic-Iowa City-1936-State Hist Soc-194p-illus (o7,f) 25.00

SWISHER,JACOB-Iowa in Times of War-Iowa City-1943-State Hist Soc-395p (o7,f) 30.00

SWISHER,JACOB-Iowa in Times of War-Iowa City-1943-Torch Pr(for St Hist Soc)-8vo-395p-red cl-1st ed (s1) 45.00

SWISHER,JACOB-Iowa-Iowa City-1940-St Hist Soc of Iowa-317p-red cl,plts (e2) 30.00

SWISHER,JACOB-Robert Gordon Cousins-Iowa City-1938-307p-cl (c1) 15.00

SWITZER,STEPHEN-Practical Fruit Gardener-Lond-1724-Thos Woodward-mod panelled calf,3 fldg plans,testimonial leaf-Henrey 1413-Crahan Sale 427-1st ed (o4,rbnd) 450.00

SWORD,WILEY-Shiloh, Bloody April-NY-(1974)-519p-illus,maps-1st ed (c4,dj) 52.50

SYDENHAM,LORD-India and the War-Lond-1915-Hodder & Stoughton-76p-wht cl,fldg col map,illus (gg6,cov rub) 35.00

SYDENHAM,THOMAS-Works of...with a Life of the Author by R G Latham-Lond-1848,1850-2 vols-buckrm-1st ed (dd3,rbnd) 200.00

SYLVESTER,HERBERT M-Indian Wars of New England-Bost-1910-W B Clarke-3 vols,gry cl-Howes S1186-1st ed (k2,sp drknd,soil,vol 1 stnd) 275.00

SYLVESTER,NATHANIEL B-Historical Sketches of Northern New York and the Adirondack Wilderness-Troy-1877-Wm H Young-dec drk grn cl-Plum #53-1st ed (w8) 100.00

SYM,COL JOHN-ED.-Seaforth Highlanders-Aldershot-1962-416p-illus-1st ed (gg2,dj) 90.00

SYMINGTON,FRASER-Canadian Indian-(Tor)-(1969)-4to-272p-col & b&w illus-1st ed (e7,dj) 40.00

SYMMES,FRANK R-History of the Old Tennent Church-Cranbury-1904-472p-cl,illus-2nd ed,enlgd (aa6) 100.00

SYMONDS,JOHN A-Letters of...-Detr-1967-Wayne St-3 vols-illus-1st ed (l10,chip dj) 45.00

SYMONDS,MARGARET-Days Spent on a Doge's Farm-NY-1898-Century/Unwin-8vo-254p-44 illus-1st US ed (jj5,sp cocked) 30.00

SYMONS,ARTHUR-From Catullus, Chiefly Concerning Lesbia-Lond-1924-ltd to 200c,nbrd,autg-1st ed (y7,cov sl soil) 75.00

SYMONS,ARTHUR-Thomas Hardy-Lond-1927-Sawyer-sq 8vo-cl lettrd in gilt,t.e.g.,port by Coburn,ltd to 100c,2 autgs-1st ed (y3,sp sunned) 425.00

SYMONS,HARRY-Ojibway Melody-Tor-1946-Ambassador Bks Ltd-8vo-294p-brwn cl,g dec-2nd prtg (cc7) 20.00*

SYMONS,JULIAN-Blackheath Poisonings-Lond-1978-Collins-1st ed (r4,vf,dj) 22.50

SYMONS,JULIAN-Critical Occasions-Lond-1966-1st ed (y7,dj) 20.00

SYMONS,JULIAN-Great Detectives-NY-1981-Abrams-1st ed (d4,f,dj) 20.00

SYMONS,JULIAN-Man Whose Dreams Came True-Lond-1968-Collins-1st ed (p4,f,dj) 25.00

SYMONS,JULIAN-Mortal Consequences-NY-1972-Harper-1st US ed (d4,f,sl wn dj) 20.00

SYMONS,JULIAN-Object of an Affair and Other Poems-Edinburgh-1974-Tragara Pr-wrps,ltd to 90c,nbrd-1st ed (y7) 45.00

SYMONS,JULIAN-Plot Against Roger Rider-Lond-1973-Collins CC-1st ed (d4,dj) 15.00

SYMONS,JULIAN-Three Pipe Problem-NY-1975-Harper-1st US ed (e4,soil dj) 17.50

SYMONS,R D-Where the Wagon Led-NY-1973-343p-illus-1st ed (t7,dj) 17.50

SYMONS,THOMAS W-Report of an Examination of the Upper Columbia River and the Territory in its Vicinity-Wash-1882-Doc No.186-161p-illus,maps(incl fldg)-1st ed (t7) 65.00

SYMONS,THOMAS W-Report on the Upper Columbia River & the Territory in Its Vicinity in Sept & Oct 1881-Wash-1882-GPO-133p-25 map sheets-Sen Ex Doc 186-Tweney #75-1st ed (e7,spot bds) 95.00

SYMONS,THOMAS W-Symons Report on the Upper Columbia River & the Great Plain of the Columbia-Fairfield-1967-Ye Galleon Pr-133p+maps-ltd to 484c (nn6) 20.00

SYMOUR,WILLIAM W-Cross-NY-1898-Putnam's-cl,frntis-1st ed (l8,ex-libr) 125.00

SYNGE,PATRICK-Mountains of the Moon-NY-1938-227p-scarce in dj-3rd ed (o10,f,dj) 60.00

SYSONBY,RIA-Lady Sysonby's Cook Book-Lond-(1935)-Putnam-311p-pict bds,col dec-1st ed (q8,cov soil) 30.00

SZARKOWSKI,JOHN-Face of Minnesota-Mpls-1958-U of Minn Pr-4to-304p-cl,photos-1st ed (t3,dj) 50.00

SZARKOWSKI,JOHN-New Japanese Photography-NY-1974-MOMA-83p photos-1st ed (cc9,as new in dj) 40.00

SZASZ,KATHLEEN-Petishism-Lond-(1968)-Hutchinson-8vo-227p-1st Brit ed (gg5,dj) 12.50

SZASZ,THOMAS-Ceremonial Chemistry-GC-1974-Dbldy-1st ed (v5,f,f dj) 20.00

SZE,MAI MAI-Tao of Painting-NY-1956-Bollingen Fndtn-4to-2 vols-grn cl,b&w & col illus (r10,sl soil dj & box) 150.00

TABER,C A M-Rhymes From a Sailor's Journal-Cambridge-1873-Prtd for auth-215p-g dec brwn cl,t.e.g.-1st ed (pp1,f) 75.00

TABER,GLADYS-Amber-(1970)-Lippincott-154p-photos-1st ed (v8,dj sl wn wi sm tr) 25.00

TABER,GLADYS-Conversations with Amber-Phila,NY-(1978)-drwngs,P Carroll-1st ed (d5,f dj) 20.00

TABER,GLADYS-Country Chronicle-Phila,NY-(1974)-Lippincott-220p-drwngs,P Johnson-1st ed (d5,few marks,dj sl soil) 20.00

TABER,GLADYS-Daisy and Dobbin-(1948)-MacRae Smith-sq 8vo-unpgd-illus,K Wiese (v8,covs wn,discol rear cov) 12.00

TABER,GLADYS-Harvest of Yesterdays-(1976)-Lippincott-224p-blu bds,drwngs-1st ed (q8,dj) 16.50

TABER,GLADYS-My Own Cape Cod-(1971)-Lippincott-251p-blu cl,photos-2nd prtg (q8,dj) 15.00

TABER,GLADYS-My Own Cook Book-Phila-1972-Lippincott-1st ed (e8,f,rprd dj) 50.00

TABER,GLADYS-Stillmeadow and Sugarbridge-Phila-1953-1st ed (v9,f,f dj) 65.00

TABER,GLADYS-Stillmeadow Cook Book-(1965)-Lippincott-335p-1st ed (v8,dj) 55.00

TABER,GLADYS-Stillmeadow Road-(1962)-Lippincott-287p-dec gry cl,drwngs-2nd prtg (q8,sm spot dj cov) 16.50

TABER,GLADYS-Stillmeadow Road-Phila-1962-Lippincott-1st ed (nn3,wn dj) 10.00

TABER,JOHN-Story of the 168th Infantry-Iowa City-1925-2 vols-red cl,illus-1st ed (kk2) 50.00

TABER,THOMAS T-Rock-a-Bye Bab7-(Muncy)-(1972)-4to-55p-wrps,illus (aa6,wrps stnd) 35.00

TABER,WALLACE-Rifleman in Africa-Denver-1953-4to-92p-photos,illus-1st prntg (m3) 20.00

TABOR,GRACE-Come Into the Garden-NY-1921-Macmillan-324p-cl (x6) 18.00

TABOR,GRACE-Garden Primer-NY-1910-McBride,Winston-8vo-(12),118p-col pastedown on emboss cl,36 halftones-1st ed (cc10) 35.00

TABOR,GRACE-Landscape Gardening Book-Phila-1911-John C Winston-4to-(8),180p-col pastedown on bds,illus,plts-1st ed (cc10) 50.00

TABOR,GRACE-Old Fashioned Gardening-NY-1913-ix,263p-36 half tones & plans (m10,hng crack,sp wn) 30.00

TABOR,GRACE-Old Fashioned Gardening-NY-1913-McBride & Nast-263p-cl (x6,hngs weak) 20.00

TABOR,SILVER DOLLAR-Star of Blood-Denver-1909-74p-pict wrps,photos,illus-Six Guns #2177-rare-1st ed (t7,f) 195.00

TABORI,PAUL-Harry Price-Lond-1950-Atheneum-cl,frntis,illus-1st ed (l8) 13.50

TABOUIS,G R-Private Life of Solomon-NY-1936-McBride-cl-1st ed (l8,f,dj) 13.50

TAFEL,EDGAR-Apprentice to Genius-NY-1979-illus-1st ed (h10,dj) 50.00

TAFEL,EDGAR-Apprentice to Genius-NY-1979-McGraw Hill-4to-(vi),228p-cl,illus-1st ed (y4,f,dj) 40.00

TAFT,ALPHONSO-An Oration Delivered Before the Literary Societies of Marietta College...-Cin-1861-Gazette Steam Prntg Hs-34p-wrps (k1) 20.00

TAFT,L R-Greenhouse Construction-NY-1909-Orange Judd-viii,209p+ads (m10,wn,scuff) 10.00

TAFT,ROBERT-Artists and Illustrators of the Old West:1850 to 1900-NY-1953-Scribners-400p-e.p. maps,illus-1st ed (dd4,sl sun sp) 50.00

TAFT,ROBERT-Artists and Illustrators of the Old West:1850 to 1900-NY-1953-Scribners-lg 8vo-400p wi index & illus-1st ed (t1) 40.00

TAFT,ROBERT-Artists and Illustrators of the Old West:1850 to 1900-NY-1953-Scribners-lg 8vo-xvii,400p-illus-1st ed (y4,chip dj) 75.00

TAFT,ROBERT-Artists and Illustrators of the Old West:1850 to 1900-NY-1975-Bonanza-8vo-400p-rust cl,90 illus (r10,tattrd dj) 17.50

TAFUR,PERO-Pero Tafur, Travels and Adventures, 1435 to 1439-NY-(1926)-Harper-8vo-261p-8 plts-1st US ed (jj5) 17.50

TAGG,BILL-Art of Fly Dressing-Lond-1970-8vo-112p-photos,illus (m3,f,dj) 15.00

TAGGARD,GENEVIEVE-ED.-Circumference-NY-1929-Covici Friede-vel sp & gry papr over bds-ltd to 1050c,nbrd,autg (x9,dj chip,tn,soil) 50.00

TAGGART,WILLIAM C-Fighting Congregation-GC-1943-Dbldy Doran-1st ed (ff8) 34.00

TAGORE,RABINDRANATH-Fugitive-NY-1921-Macmillan-cl-1st ed (o8) 10.00

TAGORE,RABINDRANATH-Home and the World-NY-1919-Macmillan-cl-1st ed (o8) 10.00

TAGORE,RABINDRANATH-Thought Relics-1921-MacMillan-1st ed (x2,dj) 40.00

TAHOURDIN,C B-Native Orchids of Britain-Croydon-(1925)-114p-illus (w10) 25.00

TAIT,DAVID-Konkomba of Northern Ghana-Lond-1961-OUP-8vo-255p-cl,illus-1st ed (y5,dj) 27.00

TAKASHIMA,SHICAN-Child in Prison Camp-NY-1971-Tundra-illus,auth-1st ed (z2,f,f dj) 25.00

TAKIS, MAGNETIC SCULPTURE-NY-1967-H Wise-4to-wrps (oo6) 30.00

TALALAY,PAUL-ED.-Drugs in Our Society-Balt-1964-311p-1st ed (dd3) 25.00

TALBOT,BISHOP ETHELBERT-My People of the Plains-NY-1906-Harper & Bros-264p-frntis,photos-Herd 2229-1st ed (dd4) 25.00

TALBOT,DANIEL-ED.-Treasury of Mountaineering Stories-NY-1954-337p-1st ed (q10,f,dj) 20.00

TALBOT,EDWARD A-Five Years' Residence in the Canadas-Lond-1824-Longman,Hurst-8vo-2 vols-orig bds,papr labls,in cl wrps in box,2 plts,dbl pg plan-Sabin 94229-1st ed (u3,box) 385.00

TALBOT,ETHEL-Book of Baby Animals-Lond-1928-Talbot-4to-189p-gry cl dec in cols-16p col plts-1st ed (s1) 50.00

TALBOT,ETHELBERT-My People of the Plains-NY,Lond-1906-264,(1)p-cl (e1,sl chip sp) 15.00

TALBOT,FREDERICK A-Lightships and Lighthouses-Phila-1913-Lippincott-xii+325p-red cl,plts-1st ed (g2) 35.00

TALBOT,HAKE-Rim of the Pit-NY-1944-Simon-1st ed (e4,sp chip dj) 65.00

TALBOT,P A-In the Shadow of the Bush-1912-Heinemann-500p-photos,fldg map (bb3) 60.00

TALBURT,WM-Potato Processing-Ct-1959-AVI-475p (x6,sp cocked) 25.00

TALL BOOK OF NURSERY TALES-NY-(1944)-Auth & Writers Guild-Narrow 4to-120p-pict bds-1st ed (r3,wn dj) 45.00

TALLENT,ANNIE D-Black Hills-Sioux Falls-(1974)-Brevet Pr-563p-illus-Howes T14 (ee4,wn dj) 40.00

TALLENT,ELIZABETH-In Constant Flight-NY-1983-Knopf-auth 1st bk-1st ed (bb1,as new in dj) 30.00

TALLMADGE,FRANK-ED.-Horseback Riding In and Around Columbus 1774-1924-Columbus-1925-Columbus Riding Club-130p-cl (e1) 27.50

TALLMAN,F-Flying the Old Planes-GC-1973-sm 4to-256p-cl,illus t.p.,22p col plts,b&w plts-1st ed (s2,dj) 25.00

TALLON,ROBERT-Zag, a Search Through the Alphabet-NY-(1976)-HR&W-unpgd-cl-1st ed (s3,f,dj) 25.00

TALMAGE,T DEWITT-Masque Torn Off-Chig-1882-Fairbanks,Palmer & Co-526p-cl (j1) 15.00

TALMAGE,T DEWITT-Social Dynamite...-Newark-1889-Samuel Allison-574p-cl (f1) 17.50

TANGE,KENZO-Ise-Cambridge-1965-MIT Pr-sq 4to-212p-wht cl,illus (r10,sl soil) 40.00

TANGE,KENZO-Katsura-New Haven-1967-Yale U Pr-sq 4to-36p text-blu cl,photos-6th prtg (r10,f,wn dj) 45.00

TANHAM,GEORGE K-War Without Guns-NY-(1966)-Praeger-1st ed (ff3,dj) 55.00

TANIZAKI,JUNCHIRO-Secret History of the Lord of Musashi and Arrowroot-NY-1982-Knopf-1st ed (f8,f,f dj) 40.00

TANIZAKI,JUNICHIRO-Secret History of the Lord of Musashi & Arrowroot-NY-1982-Knopf-1st Engl lang ed (ff6,f,dj) 25.00

TANIZAKI,JUNICHIRO-Some Prefer Nettles-NY-1955-Knopf-1st ed (g8,f,dj) 45.00

TANK DATA-Old Greenwich-nd-241p-photos (jj2,dj) 45.00

TANK,HERB-Communists on the Waterfront-NY-1946-New Century-wrps-1st ed (w5,crease rear wrps) 15.00

TANNEHILL,IVAN R-Hurricanes-1938-Princeton Univ Pr-x+257p-gry cl,114 text illus-1st ed (l2,chip dj) 30.00

TANNENBAUM,SAMUEL A-Handwriting of the Renaissance-NY-1930-Columbia U Pr-8vo-xii,210p-cl,illus-1st ed (w2,dj sp chip) 65.00

TANNER & RICHARDS-Colonization on the Little Colorado-Flagstaff-(1977)-200p-illus-1st ed (h7,f,dj) 30.00

TANNER,EDWIN P-Province of New Jersey, 1664 to 1738-NY-1908-xvi,712p-cl (aa6,sp stnd) 90.00

TANNER,JAMES T-Ivory Billed Woodpecker-NY-1966-Dover-wrps-rprnt of Rsrch Rprt No.1,1942,of Nat Audubon Soc (c9) 20.00

TANNER,JAMES T-Walt Whitman: a Supplementary Bibliography: 1961 to 1967-1968-Kent St Univ-w/o dj as iss (t4,f) 10.00

TANNER,JERALD-Joseph Smith and Polygamy-SLC-1966-243p-spiral wrps-rprnt (t7,f) 10.00

TANNER,JERALD-Joseph Smith's History by His Mother-SLC-1966-300p-spiral wrps-rprnt of orig 1853 ed (t7,f) 10.00

TANTE MARIE-Tanta Marie's French Pastry-Oxford-(1954)-146p-blu cl,drwngs-1st Amer ed (q8,dj) 10.00

TANTE,DILLY-Living Authors, a Book of Biographies-NY-1931-H W Wilson-466p-cl-illus (g1) 22.50

TAPLEY,HARRIET S-Salem Imprints 1768 to 1825-Salem-1927-Essex Inst-thk tall 8vo-x,512p-cl,illus-1st ed (w2) 135.00

TAPLEY,HARRIET S-Salem Imprints, 1768 to 1825-Salem-1927-Essex Institute-x+512p-blu cl,plts,deckle edges-1st ed (b2) 100.00

TAPLEY,W T-ET AL-Vegetables of New York. Cucurbits-1937-NY Educ Dept-4to-131p-stiff papr wrps,50 col plts (bb3,as new in orig mail crtn) 55.00

TAPLEY,W T-ET AL-Vegetables of New York. Sweet Corn-1934-NY Educ Dept-4to-111p-stiff papr wrps,24 col plts (bb3,as new in orig mail crtn) 55.00

TAPLIN,A BETTS-Hypnotism-Liverpool/Lond-1912-Littlebury/SMHK&Co-(viii)+133+(3)p-prntd blu cl-1st ed (y9,sl fox) 22.50

TAPPLY,H G-Fly Tyer's Handbook-NY-1949-8vo-73p-illus (m3) 20.00

TAPPLY,H G-Sportsman's Notebook & Tap's Tips-NY-1964-8vo-333p-illus,W Dower-1st ed (m3,vf,dj) 17.50

TAPPLY,H G-Tackle Tinkering-NY-1946-8vo-214p-illus-1st ed (m3) 10.00

TARBELL,IDA M-In the Footsteps of Lincoln-NY-1924-418p-illus-1st ed (c4) 25.00

TARBOX,INCREASE N-Life of Israel Putnam...-Bost-1876-Lockwood,Brooks-389p-terra cotta cl,plts,map-1st ed (h2) 25.00

TARG,WILLIAM-Adventures in Good Reading-Chig-1940-Black Archer-95p-cl (l1,f,dj) 25.00

TARG,WILLIAM-Bibliophile in the Nursery-Cleve,NY-(1957)-World-dec cl,fldg frntis,plt,illus-1st ed (dd10,vf,dj) 75.00

TARG,WILLIAM-Bibliophile in the Nursery-Cleve-(1957)-World-thk 8vo-503,(4)p-cl-1st ed (w2,dj tn,spot) 45.00

TARG,WILLIAM-Indecent Pleasures-NY-(1975)-Macmillan-1st ed (w1,f,dj) 15.00

TARG,WILLIAM-Lafcadio Hearn-Chig-1935-Blk Archer Pr-8vo-bds,tiss dj-1st ed (v10,f,dj) 125.00

TARKINGTON,BOOTH-Beautiful Lady-NY-1905-McClure,Phillips & Co-143,(1)p-cl-1st ed (j1) 15.00

TARKINGTON,BOOTH-His Own People-NY-1907-Dbldy,Page-orig g dec cl-1st ed (aa9,sl fade sp) 60.00

TARKINGTON,BOOTH-Penrod-GC-1914-Dbldy,Page-illus by G Grant-1st ed,later state in 1st bndg (oo10) 50.00

TARR,R-Alaskan Glacier Studies-Wash D.C.-1914-NGS-498p-184 photos,72 illus,9 col maps in rear pckt-1st ed (q10,f) 200.00

TARSHIS,BARRY-Average American Book-NY-1979-Atheneum-8vo-377p-1st ed (gg5,f,dj) 12.50

TART,CHARLES T-ED.-Altered States of Consciousness-NY-1969-Wiley-1st ed (d8,f,f dj) 25.00

TART,CHARLES T-ED.-Altered States of Consciousness-NY-1969-Wiley-1st ed (v5,f,f dj) 35.00

TASHJIAN,VIRGINIA A-Three Apples Fell from Heaven:Armenian Tales Retold by...-Bost-(1971)-Little,Brown-76p-dec bds,col & b&w illus,Hogrogian-1st ed (r3,vf,dj) 25.00

TASKER,E-D H Lawrence-1936-Knight-1st ed (x2,dj sp sl fade) 55.00

TASKER,JOE-Savage Arena-Lond-1982-Methuen-8vo-270p-24 illus,8 maps-1st ed (cc7,dj) 35.00*

TATE,ALLEN-Collected Essays-Denver-1959-1st ed (s5,f,dj) 40.00

TATE,ALLEN-ED.-Southern Vanguard-NY-(1947)-1st ed (n5,chip dj) 35.00

TATE,ALLEN-ED.-Southern Vanguard-NY-(1947)-Prentice Hall-1st ed (a5,f,sp fade dj) 65.00

TATE,ALLEN-Fathers-NY-1938-1st ed (o5,chip dj) 50.00

TATE,ALLEN-Fathers-NY-1938-Putnam-8vo-blu cl-1st ed (x3,sl chip dj) 60.00

TATE,ALLEN-Forlorn Demon-Chig-1953-1st ed (s5,dj) 25.00

TATE,ALLEN-Jefferson Davis-NY-1929-1st ed,1st state (p5,dj wn) 125.00

TATE,ALLEN-Man of Letters in the Modern World-NY-1955-Meridian Bks-1st ed (y1,f,dj) 50.00

TATE,ALLEN-Memories & Essays Old & New 1926 to 1974-np-(1976)-Carcanet Pr-1st Brit ed (a5,f,dj) 30.00

TATE,ALLEN-Mr.Pope and Other Poems-NY-1928-1st ed (r2,lacks sm pc sp labl) 250.00

TATE,ALLEN-On the Limits of Poetry-1948-Swallow Pr-1st ed (kk6,dj sl nick & smudged) 80.00

TATE,ALLEN-Reactionary Essays on Poetry and Ideas-NY-1936-Scribners-8vo-xiv,240p-red cl wi papr labl-1st ed (y4,dj) 45.00

TATE,ALLEN-Selected Poems-1937-Scribners-1st Amer ed (x2,f,sl chip dj) 70.00

TATE,CHARLES S-Pickway-Chig-1905-150p-frntis,photos,illus-Six Guns #2182-rare-1st ed (t7) 225.00

TATE,ELIZABETH-Little Flower Girl-NY-(1956)-Lothrop,Lee & Shepard-sm 4to-unpgd-cl,col & b&w illus,H Stone (r3,f,f dj) 20.00

TATE,G H H-Mammals of Eastern Asia-NY-1947-8vo-(1),366p-cl,illus (y8,cov sl wn) 50.00

TATTERSALL,W M-Review of the Mysidacea of the United States National Museum-1951-USNM-292p-wrps,103 figs (bb3) 10.00

TATTERSON,CLERISSA H-History and Genealogy of the Poling Family-Parsons-1978-453p-cl (j1) 30.00

TAUT,BRUNO-Houses & People of Japan-Tokyo-1937-551 illus-rare-1st ed (kk4) 750.00

TAUT,BRUNO-Modern Architecture-Lond-1929-Studio-illus (h10) 300.00

TAVERNER,ERIC-Angler's Fishes & Their Natural History-Lond-1957-8vo-284p-Lonsdale Libr-photos,illus (m3,f,dj) 20.00

TAVERNER,ERIC-Angler's Week End Book-Lond-1935-12mo-512p-illus (m3) 15.00

TAVERNER,ERIC-Making of Another Trout Stream-Lond-1953-8vo-140p-ltd to 250c,nbrd,autg,illus,e.p. maps (m3,f,sl wn box) 60.00

TAVERNER,ERIC-Running of the Salmon-Lond-1954-8vo-62p-illus (m3,vf,chip dj) 22.50

TAVERNER,ERIC-Running of the Salmon-Lond-1954-G Bles-62p-cl,illus-1st ed (pp8,f,dj soil & rub) 45.00*

TAVERNER,ERIC-Trout Fishing From All Angles-Lond-1929-8vo-448p-photos,illus-1st ed (m3,f) 40.00

TAVERNER,JOHN-Certaine Experiments Concerning Fish & Fruite-Manchester-1928-4to-24p-scarce-reprnt of v rare 1st ed of 1600 (m3) 175.00

TAVERNER,P A-Birds of Canada-Tor-1947-Musson Bk Co-173 plts (d9,dj) 30.00

TAVERNER,P A-Birds of Canada-Tor-1953(1940)-8vo-(3),446p-cl,173 col illus-rvsd ed (y8) 30.00

TAVERNER,P A-Birds of Western Canada-Ottawa-1926-8vo-(2),380p-half lea,84 col plts-Bull. No.41 (y8,rbnd) 60.00

TAVERNER,P A-Canadian Water Birds, Game Birds, Birds of Prey-1939-Musson-291p-illus (bb3,f,wn dj) 15.00

TAWA,NICHOLAS E-Sweet Songs for Gentle Americans-Bowling Green-(1980)-273p-cl (g1,f,dj) 15.00

TAWES,W I-Creative Bird Carving-Centreville-1981-Tidewater-4to-207p-gry cl (r10,f dj) 15.00

TAWES,W I-Creative Bird Carving-MD-1969-207p (gg3,f,dj,pres) 15.00

TAYLOR,A ELIZABETH-Woman Suffrage Movement in Tennessee-NY-(1957)-Bookman-8vo-150p-1st ed (oo7,dj) 35.00

TAYLOR,ALONZO E-On Fermentation-Berkeley-1907-Univ Pr,Pathology-341p-gry wrps (n6) 50.00

TAYLOR,BAYARD-Echo Club and Other Literary Diversions-Bost-1876-Osgood-drk grn emboss bndg-1st ed (t4,sm cov stn) 45.00

TAYLOR,BENJAMIN F-Between the Gates-Chig-1878-Griggs & Co-292p+ads-orig brwn cl wi blk titles & cov dec-1st ed (mm1,cl wn & soil) 25.00

TAYLOR,BENJAMIN F-Pictures of Life in Camp and Field-Chig-1875-270p+ads (c4) 60.00

TAYLOR,BENJAMIN F-Summer-Savory, Gleaned from Rural Nooks in Pleasant Weather...-Chig-1880-S C Grigg-212p-cl-Flake 8807 (g1,sl wn sp,sl flecked cov) 17.50

TAYLOR,CHARLES B-Early History and War Record of Wilkesville and Salem-Cin-1874-Elm St Prntg Co-89p+ tip-in addenda slip-cl-Howes T46-rare (g1,rebkd) 150.00

TAYLOR,CHARLES-Five Years in China-NY-1860-Derby & Jackson-12mo-xvi,25-413p-brwn cl,col frntis (gg6,fox,cov wn) 125.00

TAYLOR,COLIN-Warriors of the Plains-NY-(1975)-Arco-qto-144p-col illus (cc4,dj) 20.00

TAYLOR,DEMETRIA-ED.-Roundup of Beef Cookery-NY-(1960)-Sterling-204p-yel cl,col illus-1st ed (q8,dj) 15.00

TAYLOR,ELIZABETH-Angel-NY-1957-Viking-1st ed (x9,f,dj sp sl sun) 20.00

TAYLOR,ELIZABETH-Hester Lilly-NY-1954-1st US ed (q5,dj) 15.00

TAYLOR,F J-Democracy's Air Arsenal-NY-(1947)-4to-x,208p-cl,illus t.p.,plts-1st ed (s2,dj) 30.00

TAYLOR,F S-Conquest of Bacteria-NY-1942-178p-1st ed (dd3) 25.00

TAYLOR,FRANCIS H-Pierpont Morgan as Collector and Patron, 1837 to 1913-NY-1957-P Morgan Libr-sm 8vo-39p-stiff wrps,illus-1st ed (w2) 15.00

TAYLOR,FRANK H-Philadelphia in the Civil War-Phila-1913-360p-pict cl,illus,fldg map-1st ed (n3) 45.00

TAYLOR,FRANK J-High Horizons-NY-(1951)-McGraw Hill-8vo-x,198p-cl,illus,e.p. maps-1st ed (s2) 35.00

TAYLOR,FRANK-ET AL-From Land and Sea-SF-(1976)-Chronicle Bks-8vo-288p-illus-1st ed (dd5,f,f dj) 15.00

TAYLOR,FRED G-Saga of Sugar-np-1944-Utah Idaho Sugar Co-(xvi)+234p-red/brwn cl,plts-1st ed (j2,dj) 18.00

TAYLOR,FRED-Angling in Earnest-Lond-1958-12mo-148p-photos (m3,vf,dj) 15.00

TAYLOR,GEORGE-Effect of Incorporated Coal Companies upon the Anthracite Coal Trade of Pennsylvania-Pottsville-1833-prntd by B Bannan-34p-wrps-Amer Imprnts 21435 (c1) 35.00

TAYLOR,GORDON-Sky Beyond-Bost-1963-8vo-xii,370p-cl,17 illus,e.p. maps-scarce Amer ed (s2,dj) 65.00

TAYLOR,GRIFFITH-Urban Geography-Lond,NY-1951-Methuen,Dutton-439p-cl,frntis,191 illus-2nd ed,rvsd (cc10,dj) 35.00

TAYLOR,H BALDWIN-Triumvirate-NY-1966-Dbldy CC-1st ed (g4,f,sl wn dj) 12.50

TAYLOR,HENRY E-Powell River's First 50 Years-Powell River-1960-A H Alsgard-4to-(220)p-prtd wrps,illus,ports,maps-Edwards & Lort #3452 (k10) 30.00*

TAYLOR,J-Man Eaters & Marauders-NY-1960-200p-photos-scarce (gg3,f,dj) 200.00

TAYLOR,JAMES B-ET AL-Tornado-Seattle-(1970)-U of Wash Pr-8vo-191p-8 photos-1st ed (dd5,f,dj) 15.00

TAYLOR,JAMES-Great Historic Families of Scotland-Lond-nd-J S Virtue-2 vols-18p engrvngs,50 coats of arms-2nd ed (p6,sl wn,sp sun) 300.00

TAYLOR,JOE G-Louisiana Reconstructed, 1863 to 1877-Baton Rouge-(1974)-552p-illus-1st ed (c4,f,dj) 35.00

TAYLOR,JOHN M-Witchcraft Delusion in Colonial Connecticut 1647 to 1697-NY-(1908)-Grafton Pr-12mo-(xviii)+172+(2)p+frntis,grn cl-1st ed (y9,flecked cl) 37.50

TAYLOR,JOHN-Mediation and Atonement...-SLC-1892-205p-Flake 8834-2nd ed (bb8,sl bowed) 75.00

TAYLOR,JOHN-Pondoro-NY-1955-8vo-354p-1st prntg (m3,f,dj) 50.00

TAYLOR,JOHN-Science and the Supernatural-NY-1980-Dutton-8vo-ix,180p-1st ed (aa7,dj) 15.00*

TAYLOR,JOSHUA C-Futurism-NY-1961-MOMA-8vo-154p-wht cl,illus (r10,dj sl wn & drknd) 15.00

TAYLOR,JOSHUA-Futurism-NY-(1961)-MOMA-sq 8vo-154p-22 col illus-1st ed (ee5,f,dj) 20.00

TAYLOR,KATHERINE A-Lights and Shadows of Yosemite-SF-(1926)-Crocker-8vo-cl & patterned bds,3 photos,A Adams-1st ed (y3) 95.00

TAYLOR,KATHRYN S-Winter Flowers in the Sunheated Pit-NY-1941-xii,294p-1 col,41 b&w photos,fldg plan-1st ed (m10) 20.00

TAYLOR,LOUISE M-Catalog of Books on China in the Essex Institute-Salem-1926-Essex Inst-8vo-ix,392p-yel cl,blk sp labl-1st ed (t10,f) 100.00

TAYLOR,MARIE H-On Two Continents-NY-1905-309p-pict cl,frntis,photos-1st ed (t7) 10.00

TAYLOR,MORRIS F-First Mail West-Albuq-1971-253p-cl,illus-scarce-1st ed (z1,dj) 40.00

TAYLOR,MORRIS-Sketch of Early Days on the Purgatory-Trinidad-1959-48p-wrps-Rittenhouse #555-1st ed (t7) 12.50

TAYLOR,MORRIS-Trinidad, Colorado Territory-Pueblo-1966-214p-photos,illus,map e.p.-Rittenhouse #556-1st ed (t7,dj) 25.00

TAYLOR,PETER-Collected Stories of...-1969-Farrar-1st ed (kk6,dj) 60.00

TAYLOR,PETER-Collected Stories of...-NY-1969-1st ed (n5,dj) 45.00

TAYLOR,PETER-Happy Families Are All Alike-NY-1959-Obolensky-1st ed (mm5,f,dj) 40.00

TAYLOR,PETER-In the Miro District-Lond-1977-1st Brit ed (p5,f,dj) 25.00

TAYLOR,PETER-In the Miro District-Lond-1977-Chatto-1st Brit ed (kk6,f,dj) 45.00

TAYLOR,PETER-In the Miro District-NY-1977-1st ed (p5,f,dj) 40.00

TAYLOR,PETER-Long Journey and Other Stories-NY-1948-Harcourt-auth 1st bk-1st ed (v5,f,chip dj) 100.00

TAYLOR,PETER-Tennessee Day in St.Louis-NY-1957-Random-1st ed (y1,f,dj) 75.00

TAYLOR,PHOEBE ATWOOD-Criminal C.O.D.-NY-1940-Norton-1st ed (d4,sl wn dj) 50.00

TAYLOR,PHOEBE ATWOOD-Figure Away-NY-1937-Norton-1st ed (g4,sl soil cov) 20.00

TAYLOR,PHOEBE ATWOOD-Perennial Boarder-NY-1941-Norton-1st ed (d4,sp chip dj) 65.00

TAYLOR,PHOEBE ATWOOD-Proof of the Pudding-NY-1945-Norton-1st ed (hh2,dj) 75.00

TAYLOR,PHOEBE ATWOOD-Spring Harrowing-NY-1939-Norton-1st ed (f4,dj sp chip,rprd) 45.00

TAYLOR,PHOEBE ATWOOD-Three Plots for Asey Mayo-NY-1942-Norton-1st ed (e4,f,dj missing sm chips) 85.00

TAYLOR,RICHARD-Destruction and Reconstruction-NY-1955-380p-1st ed (t7,dj) 30.00

TAYLOR,ROB-Breach-NY-1981-254p-1st ed (p10,f,dj) 18.00

TAYLOR,ROBERT L-Two Roads to Guadalupe-GC-1964-Dbldy-8vo-428p-1st ed (z4,dj) 10.00

TAYLOR,SAM S-So Cold My Bed-NY-1953-Dutton-1st ed (d4,dj) 25.00

TAYLOR,SAMUEL W-I Have Six Wives-NY-(1956)-Greenburg-8vo-275p-1st ed (gg5,sp cocked,dj) 20.00

TAYLOR,SAMUEL-Angling In All Its Branches-Lond-1800-12mo-298p+ads-full calf-scarce (m3,rebacked) 175.00

TAYLOR,SIDNEY-All of a Kind Family Downtown-Chig-(1972)-Follett-sm 4to-187p-bds,illus,B & J Krush-1st ed (r3,f,f dj) 25.00

TAYLOR,VIRGINIA H-Franco Texan Land Company-Austin-1969-U of Tex Pr-331p-cl,photos-1st ed (w3,as new in dj) 15.00

TAYLOR,W G LANGWORTHY-Katie Fox-NY/Lond-1933-Putnam's-326+(2)p+14 hlftones,olive cl-1st ed (y9,f) 35.00

TAYLOR,W G LANGWORTHY-Saddle Horse-NY-1925-Holt-1st ed (h9) 35.00

TAYLOR,W H-General Lee, His Campaigns in Virginia-Dayton-1975-rprnt of 1906 ed (z10,f) 30.00

TAYLOR,W H-General Lee, His Campaigns in Virginia-Norfolk-1906-314p-col fldg maps-1st ed (z10,hngs rprd,cov soil) 175.00

TAYLOR,W R-Plants of Bikini...-Ann Arbor-1950-8vo-xv,227p-cl,col frntis+79 plts (jj10) 45.00

TAYLOR,W-Snows of Yesteryear-Tor-1973-182p-1st ed (p10,f,dj) 18.00

TAYLOR,WALTER P-Mammals and Birds of Mount Rainier National Park-Wash-1927-US GPO-249p-wrps,fldg map in rear pckt-1st ed (j8) 20.00

TAYLOR,WILLIAM B-Landlord and Peasant in Colonial Oaxaca-1972-Stanford Univ Pr-8vo-red cl,7 maps,5 figs,3 plts,11 tabls-1st ed (mm1,as new in dj) 30.00

TAYLOR,WM H C-Garde of Happy Valley-(KC)-(1925)-306p-wrps-2nd ed (h1) 15.00

TAYLOR,ZACK-Successful Waterfowling-NY-1974-8vo-276p-photos-1st ed (m3,vf,dj) 25.00

TAYLOR,ZADA-Time for Cooking-1963-Houghton Mifflin-244p-dec tan bds-1st prtg (q8) 12.50

TEAL,JOHN-Life and Death of the Salt Marsh-Bost-(1969)-Atl/Little,Brwn-8vo-278p-drwngs-1st ed (dd5,dj) 15.00

TEAL,ROLETA D-Kiowa County-Boulder-1976-432p-pict cl,photos-1st ed (t7,f) 17.50

TEALE,E W-Audubon's Wildlife-NY-1964-4to-viii,256p-cl,col plts(some dbl pg) (y8,dj) 20.00

TEALE,E W-ED.-Insect World of J Henri Fabre-1949-Dodd,Mead-333p (bb3,wn dj) 14.00

TEALE,E W-Wilderness World of John Muir-Bost-1954-332p-1st ed (o10,dj) 22.00

TEALE,EDWIN W-Golden Throng-NY-1940-Dodd,Mead-85 photos-1st ed (nn3,dj) 15.00

TEALE,EDWIN W-Plant Marvels in Miniature-NY-1960-John Day-folio-172p-cl,photos-1st ed (t3,f,dj) 100.00

TEAS, PARTIES, BUFFETS-Ames-1959-Iowa St Univ-22p-illus wrps,photos (l6) 11.00

TEASDALE,SARA-Collected Poems of...-NY-1937-Macmillan-8vo-311p-1st ed (w6,dj) 25.00

TEASDALE,SARA-Country House-NY-(1932)-Knopf-12mo-4p-orig wrps wi mailing envelope,illus,H Roese-scarce-1st ed (w6,f) 35.00

TEASDALE,SARA-Dark of the Moon-NY-1926-Macmillan-orig g titled cl-1st trd ed (aa9) 45.00

TEASDALE,SARA-Stars To Night-NY-1930-Macmillan-49p-cl,papr labl,col frntis & 16 b&w drwngs by D Lathrop-1st ed (nn10,sp fade,sl wn) 30.00

TEASDALE,SARA-Stars Tonight-NY-1930-Macmillan-cl,papr cov labl,illus by D P Lathrop-1st ed (aa9,sl fade sp,sl rub) 25.00

TEBEAU,CHARLTON W-Florida's Last Frontier-1966-Univ of Miami Pr-278p-col pict bds-rvsd ed (d1) 15.00

TECHNICAL NOTES, R.F.C.-Lond-1916-42p+38 fldg plts-tan cl-mrkd "For Official Use Only"-scarce (ll9,sl wn) 175.00

TEDLOCK,DENNIS-TRANSL.-Finding the Center-NY-1972-298p-maps-1st ed (v7,f,dj) 20.00

TEDLOCK,E W,JR.-Frieda Lawrence Collection of D H Lawrence Manuscripts-Albuq-1947-1st ed (cc2,f) 35.00

TEGETMEIER,W B-Pigeons-Lond-nd-Routledge-190p-lea sp,t.e.g.,16 col chromolithos by Weir-latr prtg (b9,cors bump,sp wn) 175.00

TEICHMANN,HOWARD-Solid Gold Cadillac-NY-(1954)-Random-1st ed (e10,dj sl chip,sl soil) 30.00

TEILHET,DARWIN L-Death Flies High-1931-Morrow-1st ed (s10) 10.00

TEIT,JAMES-Traditions of the Thompson River Indians of British Columbia-Bost-1898-Houghton Mifflin-g brgndy cl-Amer Folk Lore Soc-ltd to 500c,nbrd-1st ed (aa7,ex-libr) 95.00*

TEIXEIRA,BERNARDO-Fabric of Terror-NY-1965-Devin Adair-8vo-176p-illus-1st ed (jj5,f,dj) 12.50

TELEGRAPHY-INSTRUCTION IN ARMY...AND TELEPHONY-Lond-1914-Eyre & Spottiswoode-2 vols-red cl,plts-rprnt (c2) 50.00

TELFORD,EMMA P-Standard Paper Bag Cookery-NY-(1912)-Cupples & Leon-160p+4p ads,wht cl-1st ed (q8,few pgs soil) 20.00

TELLER,DANL W-History of Ridgefield, Ct.-Danbury-1878-238p-3/4 mor,t.e.g.,illus (a3) 75.00

TELLINGHAST,PARDON E-History of the Twelfth Regiment Rhode Island Volunteers in the Civil War, 1862 to 1863-Providence-1904-387p-pict cl,illus-1st ed (n3,cov sl wn & soil) 110.00

TEMKIN,OWSEI-ED.-Ancient Medicine: Selected Papers of Ludwig Edelstein-Balt-1967-496p-1st ed (dd3) 75.00

TEMPLE WORKERS' RECIPES-SF-1907-Tmpl Wrkrs of Plymouth Ch-143p-bds (u6,sl wn,pgs sl wrnkld) 40.00

TEMPLE,NIGEL-Seen and Not Heard-NY-1970-Dial-1st US ed (z9,f,dj) 12.50

TEMPLE,P-Nawok-Lond-1962-189p (o10,f,dj) 30.00

TEMPLE,PHILLIP-ED.-Castles in the Air-New Zealand-1973-168p-illus-scarce-1st ed (q10,f,dj) 60.00

TEMPLE,SETH J-Camp McClellan During the Civil War-Davenport-1928-Contemp Club-50p-wrps,illus (v2,f) 10.00

TEMPLE,W H-Pitching for Pawling-1940-Farrar & Rinehart-1st ed (s8,dj chip & edge wn) 45.00

TEN YEARS A COWBOY-Chig-1889-Rhodes & McClure-471p+ads-cl-Rampaging Herd 1819 (a1) 50.00

TENEICK,VIRGINIA E-History of Hollywood-Hollywood-(1966)-City of Hollywood-xxxiv+412p-blu cl,illus-1st ed (mm10,dj) 35.00

TENNANT,ALAN-Guadalupe Mountains of Texas-Austin-1980-U of Tex-166p-cl,col photos & illus,M Allender-1st ed (w3,f,dj) 30.00

TENNENBAUM,SILVIA-Rachel the Rabbi's Wife-1978-Morrow-1st ed (ff2,dj) 17.50

TENNENT,J E-Story of the Guns-Lond-1864-364p-grn cl,gilt sp,illus (ee3,sl fox) 75.00

TENNESSEE-Reunions of the Society of the Army of the...1872 to 76-Cin-1877-548p-pict cl,illus (n3) 25.00

TENNEY,H K-Vert & Venison-1924-priv prntd-8vo-155p-scarce-1st ed (m3) 350.00

TENNEY,H K-Vert & Venison-1924-priv prtg-155p-scarce (gg3,vf) 200.00

TENNYSON,ALFRED-Enoch Arden-Lond-1864-Edward Moxen-drk grn mor wi 4 raised bnds on sp,a.e.g.-1st Brit ed? (a10,edge wn) 150.00

TENNYSON,ALFRED-Poems-Lond-1857-Edw Moxon-mor,g dec covs & sp,raised bnds,g dentelles,a.e.g.,frntis,54 engrvngs (aa9,sl soil,sl fox) 275.00

TENNYSON,ALFRED-Queen Mary-Lond-1875-Henry S King-g titled mor,a.e.g.-1st ed,1st iss (aa9,sl fox) 75.00

TENNYSON,ALFRED-Works of...-Lond-(1878)-Suttaby-4to-lea,gilt dec,a.e.g.,mrbld e.p.,8 tip in photos by P Jennings (y3,sl wn) 225.00

TENNYSON,JON R-Singleness of Purpose-Chig-1977-sq 4to-127p-photos,maps-1st ed (m3,f,dj) 30.00

TENZING,NORGAY-After Everest-Lond-1977-184p-23 photos-1st ed (p10,as new in dj) 25.00

TENZING,NORGAY-Tiger of the Snows-NY-1955-294p-1st ed (o10,f,dj) 20.00

TERHUNE,ALBERT P-True Dog Stories...-Akron-1936-Saalfield-60,(1)p-pict bds,etchngs,D Thorne (c1) 10.00

TERMAN,FREDERICK E-Radio Engineering-1932-688p-418p-1st ed (h6,f) 10.00

TERRAY,LIONEL-Borders of the Impossible-GC-1961-Dbldy-8vo-(x),350+24p photos,grn cl-scarce-1st Amer ed (u1,dj) 90.00

TERRAY,LIONEL-Borders of the Impossible-NY-1963-Dbldy-Neate 803-1st Amer ed (f8,f,f dj) 55.00

TERRELL,JOHN U-Apache Chronicle-NY-(1972)-World-8vo-411p-1st ed (z4,dj) 20.00

TERRELL,JOHN U-Apache Chronicle-NY-(1972)-World-xviii+411p-red bds,cl sp,illus-1st ed (k2,f,dj) 25.00

TERRELL,JOHN U-Arrow and the Cross-Santa Barbara-1979-253p-1st ed (n3,dj pc mssng) 25.00

TERRELL,JOHN U-Faint the Trumpet Sounds-NY-(1966)-332p-e.p. maps,illus-1st ed (n3,f,dj) 27.50

TERRELL,JOHN U-Faint the Trumpet Sounds-NY-(1966)-McKay-332p-e.p. maps,illus-1st ed (gg4,dj) 35.00

TERRELL,JOHN U-Furs by Astor-NY-1963-490p-text maps-1st ed (h7,sl tn dj) 25.00

TERRELL,JOHN U-Furs by Astor-NY-1964-490p (t7,dj) 12.50

TERRELL,JOHN U-Land Grab-NY-1972-Dial Pr-277p-1st ed (gg4,dj) 35.00

TERRELL,JOHN U-Pueblos Gods and Spaniards-NY-1973-358p-1st ed (t7,f,dj) 17.50

TERRELL,JOHN U-Sioux Trail-NY-(1974)-213p-1st ed (t7,f,dj) 15.00

TERRELL,JOHN U-Sioux Trail-NY-(1974)-McGraw Hill-213p-1st ed (dd4,dj) 20.00

TERRES,JOHN K-ED.-Discovery-Phila,NY-(1961)-Lippincott-338p-cl,wood engrvngs,T W Nason-1st ed so stated (m1,f,dj) 15.00

TERRY,CHARLES-Opium Problem-NY-1928-Comm on Drug Addctn-1st ed (w5) 65.00

TERRY,CHARLES-Opium Problem-NY-1928-Comm on Drug Addctns-xvi+1042p-red cl-1st ed (j2,sl wn & soil,wtr spot) 80.00

TERRY,LIONEL-Border of the Impossible-NY-1964-350p-1st US ed (a4,f,vf dj) 85.00

TERRY,LIONEL-Conquistadors of the Useless-Lond-1963-351p-1st Brit ed (o10,f) 60.00

TERRY,M D-Old Inns of Connecticut-Hartford-1937-folio-qtr lea,blu cl,e.p. maps,illus-1st ed (ff10) 55.00

TERRY,M D-Old Inns of Connecticut-Hartford-1937-Prospect Pr-254p-blu cl,blu lea sp,illus-ltd to 1000c,nbrd (r10,f) 60.00

TERRY,SAMUEL H-How to Keep a Store-NY-1884-406p+publ catlg-cl-8th ed (n1) 17.50

TERRY,T E-Historical Sketch of Moore, Texas-np-1971-127p-wrps,photos-1st ed (w3,vf) 20.00

TESCHEMACHER,J E-Concise Application of the Principles of Structural Botany to Horticulture...-Bost-1840-Chas C Little & J Brown-90p-bds wi labl-Amer Imprnts 40-6487 (d1) 50.00

TESLA,NIKOLA-Experiments with Alternate Currents of High Potential and High Frequency-1904-162p-6 photos,35 illus-v rare-2nd ed (h6,f) 125.00

TETSO,JOHN-Trapping is My Life-Tor-1970-P Martin Assoc-8vo-115p-illus,e.p. maps-2nd & rvsd ed (bb7,dj) 15.00*

TEVIS,REV A H-Beyond the Sierras-1877-Lippincott-259p-g stmpd maroon cl,illus-1st ed (d3,sl fleck cl) 175.00

TEVIS,WALTER-Hustler-NY-(1959)-Harper-auth 1st bk-1st ed (e10,dj sl soil,rprd tr) 125.00

TEVIS,WALTER-Mockingbird-GC-1980-1st ed (n5,f,f dj) 30.00

TEVIS,WALTER-Queen's Gambit-NY-1983-1st ed (q5,f,dj) 12.50

TEWA HI-Short Dictionary of Tewa-(Espanola)-1969-37p-wrps-300c prtd (v7) 5.00

TEWALT,WILL-Improved Milk Goats-NY-1944-Orange Judd (f10) 25.00

TEXAS WORLD WAR HEROES-HISTORY OF...-Dallas-1919-Army & Navy Hist Co-4to-608p+ads-leatherette,coated papr,photos-1st ed (a9) 100.00

TEXAS-INTERNATIONAL BLUE BOOK A DELUXE EDITION OF SOUTHWEST...-San Antonio-1912-M J Sullivan-160p-photos (a9) 75.00

TEXAS-Six Missions of...-Waco-1965-Texian Pr-194p-col illus-1st ed (ee4) 20.00

THACHER,JAMES-American Medical Biography to Which is Prefixed a Succint History of Medical Science in the U.S.-NY-1967-(facs of 1828 ed) (dd3) 40.00

THACHER,JAMES-American New Dispensatory-Bost-1810-calf-Austin #1877-1st ed (g10,sp chip,stns,fox) 85.00

THACKERAY,WILLIAM M-Adventures of Philip on His Way Through the World-Lond-1862-three vols-3/4 lea,orig covs bnd in-1st ed (l9,rbnd,sl wn & soil) 400.00

THACKERAY,WILLIAM M-Early and Late Papers Hitherto Uncollected-1867-Ticknor & Fields-1st ed (x2,innr hngs starting) 60.00

THACKERAY,WILLIAM M-History of Henry Esmond,Esq.-Lond-1842-three vols-lea-1st ed (l9,rbnd,weak hngs) 300.00

THACKERAY,WILLIAM M-Kicklebury's on the Rhine-1850-Smith,Elder & Co-3/4 levant lea & mrbld bds,a.e.g.,g dec sp wi raised bnds,mrbld e.p.,15 col plts,auth-1st ed (x2) 225.00

THACKERAY,WILLIAM M-Virginians-Lond-1858-2 vols-3/4 dec lea-1st ed (l9,sl fox) 500.00

THACKERAY,WILLIAM M-Works of...-NY-(1910)-Harpers-lg 8vo-26 vols-crm col Japan vel sp & tips over bds,tip-in col illus-ltd to 491 sets-Centenary Biographical Ed (p1,sl soil) 375.00

THALHEIMER,M E-Eclectic History of the United States-Cin,NY-(1881)-Van Antwerp,Bragg-353;xl p-lea bkd cl (k1) 15.00

THANE,ERIC-Majestic Land-Indpls-(1950)-Bobbs Merrill-347p-illus,e.p. maps-Six Guns 2196-1st ed (bb4,dj) 25.00

THARP,BENJAMIN C-Texas Range Grasses-Austin-1952-UTP-125p-illus-1st ed (a9,dj) 35.00

THARP,LOUISE H-Company of Adventurers-Bost-1946-302p-pict cl,frntis,illus,map e.p.-1st ed (t7,mar sp) 10.00

THAW,MARY C-Secret Unveiled: a Pamphlet-np-July 1909-priv prtd-12mo-prtd wrps-rare-1st ed (s1) 125.00

THAXTER,CELIA-An Island Garden...-NY-1895-Houghton Mifflin-lg 8vo-126p-orig g dec grn cl,t.p. prtd in grn,pnk & yel,illus by C Hassam-BAL 19923-scarce-2nd prtg (hh9,sp sl drknd,hng crack) 400.00

THAYER,ALEXANDER W-Life of Ludwig Van Beethoven-NY-1921-Beethoven Soc-3 vols (u4,box) 60.00

THAYER,G H-Concealing-Coloration in the Animal Kingdom-NY-1909-4to-260p-cl,16 col plts(plt wi die-cut overlay),illus,photos-1st ed (y8,wn,fray,shaken) 96.00

THAYER,LEE-Alias Dr.Ely-1927-Dbldy-1st ed (s10,fox) 12.50

THAYER,LEE-Within the Vault-1950-Dodd-1st ed (s10,sl fade dj) 15.00

THAYER,THEODORE-Colonial and Revolutionary Morris County-(np)-(1975)-325p-cl,illus (aa6) 35.00

THAYER,WADE W-Trade Wind Tales-Honolulu-(1944)-Tongg-213p-pict cov-1st ed (u8,sl rub) 18.00

THEBERGE,C B-Canadiana on Your Bookshelf-(Tor)-(1976)-Dent-sm 8vo-134p-prtd wrps,illus (k10) 15.00*

THEOBALD,W-Defrauding the Government-1908-Myrtle-v scarce-1st ed (x7,f) 35.00

THEODORIC-Surgery of...ca. A.D.1267-NY-1955,1960-2 vols-1st Engl transl (dd3,vol.1 drknd) 100.00

THEOHAURUS,ANNE-Cooking & Baking the Greek Way-(1977)-Holt-257p-red bds,drwngs (q8,dj) 12.50

THEROUX,ALEXANDER-Darconville's Cat-GC-1981-1st ed (s5,dj) 30.00

THEROUX,ALEXANDER-Master Snickup's Cloak-(1979)-Harper & Row-4to-unpgd-bds,col illus,B Froude-1st US ed (r3,f,f dj) 25.00

THEROUX,ALEXANDER-Schinocephalic Waif-(Bost)-(1975)-Godine-drwngs,Washburn-1st ed (e10,f,dj) 35.00

THEROUX,PAUL-Black House-1974-Houghton Mifflin-1st ed (x2,vf,dj) 45.00

THEROUX,PAUL-Black House-Lond-1974-H Hamilton-1st Brit ed (q2,dj) 30.00

THEROUX,PAUL-Christmas Card-Lond-(1978)-Hamish Hamilton-1st ed (ee2,f,dj) 35.00

THEROUX,PAUL-Family Arsenal-1976-Houghton Mifflin-1st ed (p9,vf,dj) 20.00

THEROUX,PAUL-Fong and the Indians-Bost-1968-1st ed (k5,f,dj) 125.00

THEROUX,PAUL-Great Railway Bazaar-Bost-1975-1st ed (y7,sl fray dj) 28.00

THEROUX,PAUL-Jungle Lovers-1971-Houghton-1st ed (kk6,f,dj) 65.00

THEROUX,PAUL-Kingdom by the Sea-Bost-1983-Houghton Mifflin-1st ed (bb1,f,dj) 15.00

THEROUX,PAUL-London Snow-1980-Houghton-1st Amer trd ed (r9,vf,dj) 15.00

THEROUX,PAUL-London Snow-Bost-1980-HMCO-wood engrvngs-1st ed (y1,f,f dj) 25.00

THEROUX,PAUL-Old Patagonian Express-Bost-1979-HMCo-8vo-404p-1st ed (cc5,f,dj) 25.00

THEROUX,PAUL-Old Patagonian Express-Bost-1979-Houghton Mifflin-8vo-404p-dec grn cl,e.p. maps-1st ed (mm1,f,f dj) 35.00

THEROUX,PAUL-Saint Jack-1973-Houghton Mifflin-1st ed (x2,f,dj) 50.00

THEROUX,PAUL-Sinning with Annie-1972-Houghton Mifflin-1st ed (x2,f,dj) 68.00

THEROUX,PAUL-Sinning with Annie-Bost-1972-Houghton Mifflin-1st ed (dd2,f,dj) 95.00

THEROUX,PAUL-Waldo-Bost-1967-Houghton Mifflin-auth 1st bk-1st ed (bb1,sl rub dj) 150.00

THEROUX,PAUL-Waldo-Bost-1967-Houghton-auth 1st bk-1st ed (cc2,f,f dj) 100.00

THEROUX,PAUL-World's End and Other Stories-1980-Houghton Mifflin-1st ed (p9,vf,dj) 25.00

THEROUX,PAUL-World's End-Lond-(1980)-Hamish Hamilton-1st ed (ee2,f,dj) 40.00

THEROUX,PHYLLIS-California and Other States of Grace-NY-1980-Morrow-auth 1st bk-1st ed (hh5,f,f dj) 15.00

THESIGER,WILFRED-Arabian Sands-Lond-1959-326p-rear pckt map-1st Brit ed (p10,f,dj) 50.00

THESIGER,WILFRED-Arabian Sands-NY-326p-fldg map-1st US ed (q10,f,dj) 25.00

THESIGER,WILFRED-Last Nomad-NY-1980-lg 8vo-304p-maps,illus-1st US ed (p10,f,dj) 25.00

THETFORD,OWEN-Aircraft of the Royal Air Force Since 1918-Lond-1962-581p-photos,sketches-3rd ed (kk2,f,dj) 45.00

THINKER,THEODORE-First Lessons in Botany-NY-1860-Barnes & Burr-141p (x6,sp pcs mssng,few wtrstns) 20.00

THIRKELL,ANGELA-Brandons-NY-1939-1st ed (k9,fray dj) 9.50

THIRKELL,ANGELA-Cheerfulness Breaks In-NY-1941-1st Amer ed (m4,f,dj) 9.50

THOBY-MARCELIN,PHILIPPE-Beast of the Haitian Hills-NY-1946-Rinehart & Co-1st ed (gg8,f,dj) 45.00

THOINET,L-Medicolegal Aspects of Moral Offenses-Phila-1911-F A Davis-xvi+487p-brwn cl,17 illus-1st ed (a2,sl soil) 25.00

THOMAS,ALAN-Daggers Drawn-1930-Brewer-1st Amer ed (s10) 10.00

THOMAS,ALFRED B-Forgotten Frontiers-Norman-1932-420p-cl,maps(1 fldg)-scarce-1st ed (z1,sp fade) 40.00

THOMAS,ALFRED B-Forgotten Frontiers-Norman-1969-U of Okla Pr-8vo-xvii,frntis,420p-blu cl over bds,6 plts incl 2 fldg maps-2nd prtg (mm1,sl rub dj) 30.00

THOMAS,ALFRED-After Coronado-Norman-1935-307p-Rittenhouse #567-1st ed (t7,dj) 45.00

THOMAS,BENJAMIN P-Stanton-NY-1962-Knopf-643,xiii p-frntis,illus-1st ed (o7,bump) 25.00

THOMAS,C-Introduction to the Study of North American Archaeology-1903-Clarke-391p (bb3) 28.00

THOMAS,CAITLIN-Leftover Life to Kill-Bost,Tor-(1957)-1st ed (d5,f,dj) 12.50

THOMAS,CYRUS-Aids to the Study of the Maya Codices-Wash-(1888)-Smithson Bur Ethnol-illus-1st ed (y10,rbnd) 65.00

THOMAS,D M-Flute Player-NY-(1979)-Dutton-1st US ed (bb1,as new in dj) 25.00

THOMAS,D M-White Hotel-1981-Gollancz-1st ed (x2,f,dj) 165.00

THOMAS,D M-White Hotel-1981-Viking-1st US ed (n9,vf,dj) 25.00

THOMAS,D M-White Hotel-NY-1981-1st US ed (q5,f,dj) 30.00

THOMAS,DANIEL D-Poems of Adelphia-Ada-1897-Univ Herald Pr-120p-cl (g1,sl spot cov) 15.00

THOMAS,DONALD-Cardigan-(1975,74)-Viking-8vo-369p-16 illus-1st US ed (cc5,dj) 20.00

THOMAS,DOROTHY S-Spoilage-Berkeley,LA-1946-Univ of Cal-xx+388p-red cl,plts,chrts-1st ed (m2,dj) 45.00

THOMAS,DYLAN-Adventures in the Skin Trade-(1955)-New Directions-cl-1st Amer ed (aa9,f,sl fade dj) 75.00

THOMAS,DYLAN-Adventures in the Skin Trade-Norfolk-(1955)-New Directions-8vo-cl-1st ed (x3,sl fox dj) 70.00

THOMAS,DYLAN-Beach of Falesa-NY-1963-Stein & Day-1st ed (y1,f,f dj) 25.00

THOMAS,DYLAN-Child's Christmas in Wales-(1954)-New Directions-prtd bds-1st separate ed (aa9,f,dj) 85.00

THOMAS,DYLAN-Collected Letters-NY-1985-Macmillan-1st ed (z9,f,dj) 25.00

THOMAS,DYLAN-Conversation About Christmas-1954-New Directions-8p-wrps-ltd to 2000c-Rolph #26-1st separate publ (b3) 85.00

THOMAS,DYLAN-Death and Entrances-Lond-1946-Dent-1st ed (z2,f,sl nicked dj) 225.00

THOMAS,DYLAN-Deaths and Entrances-Lond-(1946)-Dent-1st ed (hh4,f,dj sl chip & soil) 250.00

THOMAS,DYLAN-Doctor and the Devils & Other Scripts-NY-1966-New Directions-1st ed (x7,f,dj) 24.00

THOMAS,DYLAN-Doctor and the Devils-NY-(1953)-New Directions-g titled cl-1st Amer ed (aa9,dj) 40.00

THOMAS,DYLAN-Doctor and the Devils-NY-1966-New Directions-229p-1st Amer ed (j8,f,f dj) 45.00

THOMAS,DYLAN-New Poems-(1943)-New Directions-wrps-1st ed (s1,sl fade) 45.00

THOMAS,DYLAN-New Poems-Norfolk-(1943)-New Directions-8vo-mauve wrps-Rolph B9-1st ed (v10,sl fade) 60.00

THOMAS,DYLAN-Notebooks of...-NY-1967-New Directions-5057c prtd-1st ed (q2,dj chip & soil) 35.00

THOMAS,DYLAN-Quite Early One Morning-Lond-(1954)-Dent-sm 8vo-cl,1st iss(full stop after "sailors"p3 & 11)-1st ed (x3,sl chip dj) 100.00

THOMAS,DYLAN-Quite Early One Morning-Lond-1954-Dent-1st ed,1st iss (kk5,f,dj) 75.00

THOMAS,DYLAN-Quite Early One Morning-NY-(1954)-New Directions-cl-1st Amer ed (aa9,f,dj) 50.00

THOMAS,DYLAN-Quite Early One Morning-NY-1954-New Directions-1st ed (c8,sl tn dj) 75.00

THOMAS,DYLAN-Rebecca's Daughter-1965-Little,Brown-1st ed (kk6,f,dj) 25.00

THOMAS,DYLAN-Selected Writings of Dylan Thomas-1946-New Directions-1st ed (x2,dj sl wn,chip & soil) 85.00

THOMAS,DYLAN-Under Milkwood-Lond-(1954)-Dent-sm 8vo-cl-1st ed (x3,dj) 160.00

THOMAS,DYLAN-World I Breathe-(1939)-New Directions-auth 1st bk publ in Amer-ltd to 700c-1st ed,1st iss (r2,f,sl tn dj) 500.00

THOMAS,E M-Harmless People-1959-Knopf-266p-photos,map-1st ed (bb3,f,dj) 14.00

THOMAS,E-Yellow Magic-1934-Sears-pict dj-1st ed (x7,dj) 80.00

THOMAS,EDWARD H-Chinook: a History and Dictionary of the Northwest Coast Trade Jargon-Portland-1935-Metro-8vo-(viii),181p-cl,illus-1st ed (y4,sl wn dj) 45.00

THOMAS,ELIZABETH M-Harmless People-NY-1959-Knopf-8vo-266p-16p photos-1st ed (jj5,sl chip dj) 17.50

THOMAS,GABRIEL-An Account of Pennsylvania and West New Jersey-Cleve-1903-83p-bds,plts,fldg map-ltd to 250c,nbrd-rprntd from 1698 ed (aa6) 60.00

THOMAS,GEORGE C,JR.-Game Fish of the Pacific-Phila-1930-8vo-293p-illus (m3) 25.00

THOMAS,GEORGE C,JR.-Practical Book of Outdoor Rose Growing-Phila-(1920)-224p-lt grn cl,gold stmpd,col onlay,96 col photos plts,37 half tones-5th ed (m10,fox frntis) 45.00

THOMAS,GEORGE C-Game Fish of the Pacific-Phila-1930-293p-col frntis,89 photos & plts-1st ed (jj4,dj) 45.00

THOMAS,GEORGE-Practical Book of Outdoor Rose Growing for the Home Garden-Phila-1916-Lippincott-164p-cl,col photos (x6,cov stnd) 16.00

THOMAS,GERTRUDE I-Dietary Adventures of Anabil Lee-Phila-1928-F A Davis Co-80p-blu bds wi vignette,drwngs,blank pgs (n6,sl wn,rear e.p. tn) 15.00

THOMAS,GERTRUDE-Gay Thomas Cook Book-Omaha-1937-55p-blu bds,wire bndg (n6,wn & chip bds) 12.00

THOMAS,GILBERT-How to Enjoy Detective Fiction-Lond-1947-Rockliff,Salisbury Sq-108p-1st ed (g9,dj sl wn,tn,soil) 45.00

THOMAS,GORDON-Guernica, the Crucible of World War II-NY-(1975)-Stein & Day-8vo-319p-illus-1st ed (jj5,f,sl tn dj) 12.50

THOMAS,H H-Rockeries How to Make & Plant Them-NY-1917-Funk-142p-cl,photos (x6,cl rub) 12.00

THOMAS,HERBERT-Classical Contributions to Obstetrics and Gynecology-Springfield-1935-265p-1st ed (dd3,dj) 100.00

THOMAS,HOWARD-Marinus Willett-Prospect-1954-Prospect Bks-ltd to 1500c,nbrd-1st ed (u2,dj) 30.00

THOMAS,J J-American Fruit Culturist-Auburn-1849-Derby-410p-blnd stmpd cl (x6,rebkd,fox) 75.00

THOMAS,JANET-ED.-That Day in June-Rexburg-1977-Ricks College-309p-tan cl (b6,f,dj) 12.00

THOMAS,JEAN-Devil's Ditties Being Stories of the Kentucky Mountain People...With the Songs They Sing-Chig-1931-W Wilbur Hatfield-4to-180p-grn cl,illus-scarce-1st ed (oo8) 75.00

THOMAS,JERRY-Bar Tender's Guide-NY-(1887)-Dick & Fitzgerald-16mo-130p+16p ads-grn cl-3rd ed,rvsd (q8) 35.00

THOMAS,JOHN-Scottish Railway History in Pictures-Newton Abbot-1967-112p-1st ed (n4,f,dj) 15.00

THOMAS,JOSEPH-Hounds and Hunting Through the Ages-NY-1929-Derrydale-4to-ltd to 250c-2nd prtg (j9) 375.00

THOMAS,L-European Skyways-Bost-1927-8vo-xvi,524p-illus cl,frntis,62p plts,e.p. maps-1st ed (s2) 25.00

THOMAS,LESLIE-Virgin Soldiers-Bost-1966-Little,Brown-1st Amer ed (gg8,f,sl tn dj) 40.00

THOMAS,LOWELL,JR.-Silent War in Tibet-NY-1959-285p-1st ed (a4,f) 18.00

THOMAS,LOWELL-Magic Dials-NY-1939-Lee Furman-sm folio-147p-blu cl,photos by A Bruehl-1st ed (y4) 85.00

THOMAS,LOWELL-Out of This World-NY-1950-320p-illus,32 col-1st ed (p10,dj) 10.00

THOMAS,MRS THEODORE-Our Mountain Garden-NY-1904-Macmillan-212p (x6,sp discol) 12.00

THOMAS,PIRI-Down These Mean Streets-NY-1967-Knopf-auth 1st bk-1st ed so stated (q1,dj) 50.00

THOMAS,ROSS-Backup Men-NY-1971-Morrow-1st ed (d4,dj) 75.00

THOMAS,ROSS-Brass Go Between-1970-H&S-1st Brit ed (x7,f dj) 95.00

THOMAS,ROSS-Cast a Yellow Shadow-NY-1967-Morrow-1st ed (d4,f,dj) 125.00

THOMAS,ROSS-Chinaman's Chance-NY-1978-1st ed (p5,dj) 25.00

THOMAS,ROSS-Eighth Dwarf-NY-1979-S&S-1st ed (w9,f,dj) 35.00

THOMAS,ROSS-Eighth Dwarf-NY-1979-Simon-1st ed (f4,f,dj) 25.00

THOMAS,ROSS-Fools in Town are on Our Side-NY-1971-Morrow-1st ed (f8,f,f dj) 100.00

THOMAS,ROSS-Fools in Town Are On Our Side-NY-1971-Morrow-1st US ed (d4,dj) 100.00

THOMAS,ROSS-If You Can't Be Good-1973-Morrow-1st ed (x7,f,dj) 100.00

THOMAS,ROSS-Money Harvest-NY-1975-Morrow-1st ed (h4,f,sl rub dj) 35.00

THOMAS,ROSS-Mordida Man-NY-(1981)-S&S-1st ed (s6,dj) 35.00

THOMAS,ROSS-Mordida Man-NY-(1981)-Simon-1st ed (d4,f,dj) 25.00

THOMAS,ROSS-Porkchoppers-1972-Morrow-1st ed (x7,f,dj) 70.00

THOMAS,ROSS-Porkchoppers-NY-1972-Morrow-1st ed (d4,f,dj) 65.00

THOMAS,ROSS-Seersucker Whipsaw-Lond-1968-Hodder & Stoughton-1st Brit ed (gg8,f,sl tn dj) 150.00

THOMAS,ROSS-Yellow Dog Contract-NY-1977-1st ed (q5,dj) 40.00

THOMAS,ROSS-Yellow Dog Contract-NY-1977-Morrow-1st ed (w9,vf,dj) 50.00

THOMAS,SEWELL-Silhouettes of Charles S Thomas-Caldwell-1959-275p-frntis,photos,plts-ltd ed-1st ed (t7) 20.00

THOMAS,VERLIN-Successful Physician-1923-303p-1st ed (dd3) 75.00

THOMAS,WILLIAM S-Trails & Tramps in Alaska & Newfoundland-1913-Putnam-330p-photos,cov photo pastedown of rabbit-1st ed (u8) 45.00

THOMASON,JOHN W,JR.-Lone Star Preacher-NY-1941-296p-cl,illus-1st ed (n10) 55.00

THOMASON,JOHN W-Red Pants-NY-1927-246p-blu cl,illus-1st ed (jj2) 20.00

THOMES,WILLIAM H-Gold Hunter's Adventures-Bost-1874-Lee & Shepard-564p-orig emboss brwn cl,illus (p8,sp wn) 125.00

THOMES,WM H-Whaleman's Adventures in the Sandwich Islands and California-Bost-(1871)-Lee & Shepard-8vo-444p-orig grn cl,gilt,frntis,illus-Wright 2469 (hh9,sl wn sp,sl spot) 50.00

THOMPKINS,COL FRANK-Chasing Villa-Harrisburg-1934-Military Service-270p-photos-1st ed (a9,vf) 75.00

THOMPSON,A G-Greatest Airlift-Tokyo-(1954)-roy 8vo-xii,464p-g cl,illus (s2) 75.00

THOMPSON,ALBERT W-They Were Open Range Days-Denver-1946-194p-photos,maps-ltd to 500c-1st ed (u7,f,rprd dj,box) 75.00

THOMPSON,C J S-Mysteries of Sex-Lond-(1938)-Hutchinson-256p+8p ads-cl,col frntis,plts-1st ed (dd10,sl soil,t.e. fox,sm stns 40.00

THOMPSON,C J S-Mystery and Art of the Apothecary-Lond-1929-287p-1st ed (dd3) 60.00

THOMPSON,C J S-Mystery and Lure of Perfume-Lond-(1927)-xvi,247p-26 illus-1st ed (m10,wn,pgs brwng) 32.00

THOMPSON,CHARLES M-Independent Vermont-Bost-1942-Houghton Mifflin-xviii+574p-red cl,sp labl,plts-1st ed (m2) 30.00

THOMPSON,CHARLES W-Fiery Epoch 1830 to 1877-Indpls-(1931)-367p-1st ed (c4,dj) 20.00

THOMPSON,EARL-Garden of Sand-NY-1970-auth 1st bk-1st ed (q5,dj) 22.50

THOMPSON,EARL-Tattoo-NY-1974-1st ed (q5,dj) 15.00

THOMPSON,FRANCIS-Man Has Wings-NY-1957-Hanover-1st ed (t4,f,f dj) 20.00

THOMPSON,FRANCIS-Murder and Mystery in the Highlands-Lond-(1977)-Robert Hale-8vo-187p-16p photos-1st Brit ed (gg5,dj) 15.00

THOMPSON,FRED-COMP.-I.W.W.-Chig-1955-I.W.W.-203p-red cl-1st ed (h2,dj) 20.00

THOMPSON,FRESCO-Every Diamond Doesn't Sparkle-1964-McKay-1st ed (p7,f,dj) 25.00

THOMPSON,GENE-Lupe-NY-(1977)-Random-1st ed (l3,f,sl wn dj) 15.00

THOMPSON,GEORGE A-Treasure Mountain Home-SLC-1968-268p-photos,map e.p.-1st ed (t7,dj,autg) 25.00

THOMPSON,GEORGE F-Manual of Angora Goat Raising-Chig-1903-Amer Sheep Brdr Pr-1st ed (f10) 58.00

THOMPSON,GEORGE-Prison Life and Reflections-Hartford-1854(1847)-A. Work-12mo-xii,377p-frntis (n2,ex-libr) 80.00

THOMPSON,HUNTER S-Fear and Loathing in Las Vegas-NY-1971-Random-1st ed (v5,f,dj) 100.00

THOMPSON,HUNTER S-Great Shark Hunt-NY-1979-1st ed (s5,f,dj) 30.00

THOMPSON,J E S-Rise and Fall of Maya Civilization-Norman-(1954)-U of Okla Pr-8vo-287p-illus-1st ed (jj5,f,dj) 25.00

THOMPSON,J M-Witchery of Archery-Pinehurst-1928-259p-pict cov,illus (ee3,f) 40.00

THOMPSON,JAMES M-My Winter Garden-NY-1900-Century-xiii,302p-cl (x6) 12.00

THOMPSON,JAMES W-Ancient Libraries-Berkeley-1940-U of Cal Pr-120p-g dec cl,frntis,illus-1st ed (dd10,f,sl soil dj) 15.00

THOMPSON,JIM-Getaway-1959-Signet-wrps-1st ed (s10) 125.00

THOMPSON,JIM-Ironside-1967-Popular Libr-wrps-1st ed (q9,f) 25.00

THOMPSON,JIM-Ironside-NY-1967-wrps,pbk orig,(Pop Libr #60-2244)-1st ed (p5) 35.00

THOMPSON,JIM-Nothing Man-NY-1954-wrps,pbk orig,Dell 1st ed #22-1st ed (p5,f) 200.00

THOMPSON,JIM-Pop. 1280-Greenwich-1964-wrps,pbk orig,Gold Medal #k1438-1st ed (p5) 60.00

THOMPSON,JIM-Savage Night-NY-1953-Lion-pbk orig-1st ed (d4,wrps sl creased,rub) 100.00

THOMPSON,JIM-South of Heaven-Greenwich-1967-wrps,pbk orig,Fawcett #d1793-1st ed (p5) 40.00

THOMPSON,JOSEPH-Travels in the Atlas & Southern Morocco-NY-1889-488p-2 fldg maps,31p illus-scarce-1st US ed (q10) 175.00

THOMPSON,KAY-Eloise in Moscow-NY-1959-S&S-1st ed (z2,f,sl tn dj) 125.00

THOMPSON,KAY-Eloise in Paris-Lond-(1958)-Reinhardt-illus,H Knight-1st Brit ed (s3,sl fade,smudge,dj sl soil) 80.00

THOMPSON,LESLIE-Fishing in New England-1955-Van Nostrand-4to-101p-ltd to 1200c,nbrd,col plts by auth (m3,f) 35.00

THOMPSON,M-Byways and Bird Notes-NY-1885-12mo-179p-orig cl-1st ed (y8) 35.00

THOMPSON,M-Sylvan Secrets-NY-1887-tall 12mo-139p-cl-1st ed (y8,wn) 14.00

THOMPSON,MARGARET J-Capt Nathaniel L Thompson of Kennebunk & the Ships He Built 1811 to 89-Bost-1937-Lauriat-8vo-140p-37 illus-trd ed of 1000c-1st trd ed (ff5) 50.00

THOMPSON,MAURICE-Banker of Bankersville-NY-(1886)-Cassell-323p-cl-Wright 5447-1st ed (h1) 22.50

THOMPSON,MAURICE-By Ways and Bird Notes-NY-1885-John Alden-12mo-179p-1st ed (aa5,sl dmpstnd rear cov) 30.00

THOMPSON,MAURICE-Fortnight of Folly-NY,Lond-(1902)-Street & Smith-140;155p-cl (c1) 15.00

THOMPSON,MORTON-Joe, the Wounded Tennis Player-1945-Dbldy,Doran-208p-dec red cl,illus-1st ed (q8,dj) 20.00

THOMPSON,MORTON-More Thoughts on Food-(1943)-Vanguard-282p-dec gry cl (q8,edgewn dj) 15.00

THOMPSON,NORM-Angler's Guide for Fly Fisherman-Portland-1966-8vo-96p-wrps,illus,photos, (m3) 15.00

THOMPSON,PAUL W-Vegetation and Common Plants of Sleeping Bear-Bloomfield Hills-1967-Cranbrook Inst of Sci-47p-wrps,photos (z7) 20.00

THOMPSON,PETER-Narrative of the Little Big Horn Campaign-Glendale-1974-339p-illus,fldg map,plain dj-1st ed (e7,f,dj) 65.00

THOMPSON,PETER-Peter Thompson's Narrative of the Little Bighorn Campaign 1876-Glendale-1974-339p-illus,map-ltd to 1000c (ff4) 95.00

THOMPSON,PETER-Peter Thompson's Narrative of the Little Bighorn Campaign 1876-Glendale-1974-339p-illus,fldg map-ltd to 1000c-1st ed thus (n3,f) 47.50

THOMPSON,R L-Glimpses of Medical Europe-Phila-1908-236p-photos-1st ed (dd3) 75.00

THOMPSON,R W-History of the Protective Tariff Laws-Chig-1888-R S Peale-547p-cl (e1) 17.50

THOMPSON,ROBERT L-Wiring a Continent-Princeton-1947-544p-photos,illus,maps-1st ed (t7,cov sl wtrstnd) 10.00

THOMPSON,ROBERT T-Colonel James Neilson-New Brunswick-1940-xiii,359p-cl,plts (aa6) 35.00

THOMPSON,RUTH P-Giant Horse of Oz-Chig-(1928)-Reilly & Lee-lg 8vo-281p-cl,pict e.p.s,12 tip in col plts by Neill,early cpy wi "r" in "morning undamaged on pg 116,line 1-1st ed (w6,sl brnd t.p.,heel cl cut) 225.00

THOMPSON,S C-All Time Rosters of Major League Baseball Clubs-1973-Barnes-rvsd ed (q7,f,dj) 35.00

THOMPSON,SILVANUS P-Philipp Reis-Lond-1883-E & F N Spon-brwn cl,48 text figs,2 plts in rear-1st ed (g2) 100.00

THOMPSON,SIR D'ARCY-On Growth and Form-Cambridge-1952-2 vols-554 figs-2nd ed (j10,sl fox,soil,dj wn) 50.00

THOMPSON,SLASON-Short History of American Railways Covering Ten Decades-Chig-1925-473p-cl-400 illus-1st ed (j1) 25.00

THOMPSON,SLASON-Way Back When-Chig-1930-priv prntd,H G Adair-364p-cl (l1,sl wn sp,pres cpy) 17.50

THOMPSON,THEOPHILUS-Annals of Influenza or Epidemic Catarrhal Fever in Great Britain from 1510 to 1837-Lond-1852-406p-1st ed (dd3) 150.00

THOMPSON,THOMAS-Blood and Money-GC-1976-Dbldy-1st ed (h9,dj) 35.00

THOMPSON,W E-Aunt Chloe and Her Birds-Kingsport-1927-8vo-208p-dec cl,col frntis,7 col & 14 b&w illus-1st ed (y8,dj chip) 35.00

THOMPSON,W FLETCHER-Image of War-NY-1960-T Yoseloff-248p-illus (v2,dj) 20.00

THOMPSON,WILLIAM I-Imagination of an Insurrection: Dublin Easter 1916-Oxford,NY-1967-(13),262p-1st ed (k9,dj) 10.00

THOMPSON,WILLIAM-Reminiscences of a Pioneer-SF-1912-(vi)+187p,blu cl,illus-Graff 4138-1st ed (k2,cov soil & few spots) 65.00

THOMPSON,WILLIAM-Reminiscences of a Pioneer-SF-1912-187p-illus-1st ed (g7) 35.00

THOMPSON,WILLIAM-Reminiscences of a Pioneer-SF-1912-187p-illus-Graff 4138-1st ed (d3) 50.00

THOMPSON,ZADOC-Guide to Lake George, Lake Champlain, Montreal and Quebec-Burlington-1845-C Goodrich-16mo-48p-wrps,maps(1 fldg)-scarce-1st ed (dd6,sl fox & soil) 150.00

THOMS,HERBERT-Chapters in American Obstetrics-Springfield-1933-90p-1st ed (dd3) 100.00

THOMS,HERBERT-Doctors of Yale College, 1702 thru 1815, and the Founding of the Medical Institution-Hamden-1960-Shoe String Pr-xxii+199p-blu cl,illus-1st ed (c2,dj) 25.00

THOMSON,A L-ED.-New Dictionary of Birds-NY-1964-lg 8vo-928p-cl,48 plts(16 col) (y8) 85.00

THOMSON,A LANDSBOROUGH-ED.-New Dictionary of Birds-Lond-1974-T Nelson-928p-col plts-scarce (d9,wn dj) 60.00

THOMSON,ANTHONY-Domestic Management of the Sick Room...-Phila-1845-353p-rvsd by R E Griffith (dd3) 100.00

THOMSON,C WYVILLE-Depths of the Sea-Lond-1874-Macmillan-thk 8vo-g dec blu cl,84 woodcts,8 maps & plts (ee7,sl fox) 175.00

THOMSON,E A-ED.-Cartoons and Caricatures of Seattle Citizens-(Seattle)-(1906)-sm folio-200p+index-1st ed (u1,sl soil rear cov) 75.00

THOMSON,E-Letters from Europe-Cinn-1856-Swormstedt & A Poe-299p-cl (e1,sl fox) 35.00

THOMSON,J J-Conduction of Electricity Through Gases-1903-566p-181 illus-rare-1st ed (h6) 125.00

THOMSON,J J-Corpuscular Theory of Matter-Lond-1907-Constable-viii+172p-blu cl,29 illus-1st ed (dd1) 110.00

THOMSON,TOM-Birding in Ohio-Bloomington-(1983)-256p-cl-1st ed (a1,f,dj) 15.00

THORBURN,A-Naturalist's Sketch Book-Lond-1919-royal 4to-orig red cl,24 col & 36 collotype plts (y8,sl wn edges) 775.00

THORBURN,GRANT-Fifty Years' Reminiscences of New York...-NY-1845-Fanshaw-287p-ribbed cl (x6,sl wn sp) 175.00

THORBURN,J M-Annual Descriptive Catalogue of Bulbs-NY-1877-Thorburn-19p-wrps (x6,soil wrps,sl fold) 25.00

THORBURN,JAMES-Annual Descriptive Catalogue of Bulbs-NY-1881-Thorburn-32p-wrps,illus (x6,wrps brwnd) 30.00

THOREAU,HENRY D-Life Without Principle-Stanford-1946-James Ladd Delkin-8vo-cl & bds,illus dj & orig tiss wrps-ltd to 500c (v10,f,dj,tiss wrps) 150.00

THOREAU,HENRY D-Yankee in Canada, with Anti Slavery and Reform Papers-Bost-1866-Ticknor & Fields-1st ed (u2) 400.00

THORINGTON,J MONROE-Early American Ascents in the Alps in the 19th Century-NY-1943-83p-1st ed (a4,f) 95.00

THORINGTON,J MONROE-Survey of Early American Ascents in the Alps in the 19th Century-NY-1943-83p-1st ed (q10,f) 75.00

THORN,C JORDAN-Handbook of American Silver and Pewter Marks-NY-1949-Tudor-xii,289p-illus-Franklin 5025-1st ed (u5,dj wn,tn) 30.00

THORN,JOHN-Baseball's 10 Greatest Games-1981-Four Winds-photos-1st ed (s8,f,f dj) 12.50

THORN,JOHN-Century of Baseball Lore-1976-Galahad-1st ed (p7,f,dj) 15.00

THORN,JOHN-Relief Pitcher-1979-Dutton-1st ed (s7,f,f dj) 12.00

THORN,PERCY-Humane Horse Training-Lond-1949-Hutchinson-rvsd ed (h9,dj) 18.00

THORNBURG,NEWTON-Cutter and Bone-(1976)-Little,Brown-1st ed (r9,dj) 30.00

THORNBURG,NEWTON-Cutter and Bone-Bost-(1976)-Little,Brown-1st ed (x10,f,f dj) 25.00

THORNDIKE,LYNN-History of Magic and Experimental Science During the First Thirteen Centuries of Our Era-NY-1929-Macmillan-2 vols,cl-2nd prtg,wi corrctns (n8) 125.00

THORNE,DIANA-Polo-Edinburgh,Lond-1936-Moray Pr-oblng 8vo-79p-drwngs (f10,stnd cov cor) 45.00

THORNE,EDWARD-Decorative Draperies & Upholstery-GC-1937-GC Publ-4to-255p-tan cl,64 col plts,illus-rvsd ed (r10,sl wn dj) 50.00

THORNTON,ARCHIE-Rock Garden Primer-NY-1929-12mo-viii,132p+12p for notes-plts(incl 2 col),24 figs (x5,chip dj) 12.00

THORNTON,BARRY-Steelhead the Supreme Trophy Trout-Seattle-1978-4to-159p-photos (m3,f,dj) 20.00

THORNTON,FRANCIS-Catholic Shrines in the United States and Canada-NY-(1954)-W Funk-8vo-340p-photos-1st ed (gg5,dj) 15.00

THORNTON,IAN-Darwin's Islands-GC-1971-Nat Hist Pr-8vo-xiv,322p-blck cl,map e.p.,photos,maps (p8,dj) 25.00

THORNTON,JOHN L-Scientific Books, Libraries, and Collectors-Lond-1956-Libr Assn-x+288p-blu cl,12 plts-rprnt (c2) 20.00

THORNTON,JOHN-Medical Book Illustration-NY-1983-4to-142p-55 plts-1st ed (dd3,dj) 40.00

THORNWELL,EMILY-Lady's Guide to Complete Etiquette in Manners,Dress and Conversation...-Chig-nd-Donohue,Henneberry-226p-cl (j1) 15.00

THORP,NATHAN H-Pardner of the Wind-Caldwell-1945-309p-cl,illus-1st ed (z1,chip dj) 50.00

THORP,RAYMOND W-Spirit Gun of the West-Glendale-1957-266p-illus-Wstrn Frntrsmn Ser,Vol.VII-1st ed (c7,f) 65.00

THORP,RAYMOND-Bowie Knife-1948-UNM Pr-8vo-167p-photos,illus-1st ed (m3,f) 45.00

THORPE,CARLYLE-Journey to the Walnut Sections of Europe and Asia-LA-1923-priv prtd-101p-cl bkd papr cov bds,24 photos (m10,sl wtrstnd) 26.00

THORPE,SHELDON B-North Haven Annals-New Haven-1892-422p-illus (a3) 65.00

THORPE,W A-English Glass-Lond-1967-A & C Black-24p-photos-3rd ed (cc8,dj) 35.00

THORPE,W H-Learning and Instinct in Animals-Cambridge-1963-8vo-558p-cl,9 plts-2nd ed (y8) 17.00

THORTON,JOHN L-Medical Books, Libraries, and Collectors-(Lond)-(1966)-A Deutsch-xvi+445p-grn cl,16 plts-2nd,rvsd ed (a2) 30.00

THORWALD,JURGEN-Century of the Surgeon-NY-1957-432p-1st ed (dd3) 40.00

THORWALD,JURGEN-Science and Secrets of Early Medicine-NY-1963-331p-illus (dd3) 50.00

THORWALD,JURGEN-Triumph of Surgery-NY-1960-454p-1st ed (dd3) 25.00

THOUGHTS FOR BUFFETS-Bost-1958-Houghton Mifflin-424p-1st prtg (r6,dj) 12.00

THRAPP,DAN L-Conquest of Apacheria-Norman-1967-405p-photos-1st ed (t7,f,dj) 45.00

THRAPP,DAN L-Victorio and the Mimbres Apaches-Norman-1974-393p-illus,maps-1st ed (n10,f,dj) 50.00

THRAPP,DAN L-Victorio and the Mimbres Apaches-Norman-1974-393p-photos,illus,maps-1st ed (t7,dj) 32.50

THRASHER,FREDERICK-ED.-Okay for Sound-NY-(1946)-Duell-4to-303p-photos-1st ed (s1,dj) 45.00

THRASHER,HALSEY-Hunter & Trapper-NY-1868-12mo-91p+ads-illus-rare (m3) 50.00

THRESHER,R E-Reef Fish-1980-Palmetto-171p-col photos-1st US ed (bb3,f,dj) 18.00

THRILLING EXPERIENCE IN A DAKOTA BLIZZARD-np-nd-15,(1)p-wrps-rare (f1) 75.00

THRONE,MILDRED-Cyrus Clay Carpenter and Iowa Politics 1854 thru 1898-Iowa City-1974-State Hist Soc-302p-illus (o7,f) 10.00

THROOP,MONTGOMERY H-Future-NY-1864-343p-cl (n1,sl fade sp,sm sp wrnkl) 20.00

THRUELSEN,R-Mediterranean Sweep-NY-(1944)-8vo-x,278p-cl,16p col plts,b&w plts,e.p.maps-1st ed (s2,sl chip dj) 30.00

THRUELSEN,R-Transocean-NY-(1952)-8vo-xii,242p-cl,frntis,e.p.maps-1st ed (s2,dj) 35.00

THRUM,THOS G-Hawaiian Almanac and Annual For 1921-Honolulu-1920-Thos G Thrum-169p-bckrm bndg (p8,ex-libr) 60.00

THRUSTON,GATES P-Antiquities of Tennessee & Adjacent States...-Cin-1897-362p-photos-scarce-2nd ed (u7,rbkd) 100.00

THUNBERG,CARL P-Flora Japonica-NY-1975-Oriole Eds-418p-fldg plts,facs of 1784 1st ed (c3,f) 50.00

THUNBERG,CARL P-Flora Japonica-NY-1975-Oriole-8vo-420p-39 plts-(facs of 1784 1st ed) (ff9,as new in dj) 35.00*

THURBER,FRANCIS B-Coffee from Plantation to Cup-1884-Amer Grocer Publ-416p-dec brwn cl-9th ed (q8,cov wn,hng crack) 60.00

THURBER,JAMES-Alarms & Diversions-NY-1957-1st ed (s5,dj) 20.00

THURBER,JAMES-Alarms and Diversions-NY-(1957)-Harper-367p-illus-1st ed (ll2,sl tn dj) 15.00

THURBER,JAMES-Beast in Me & Other Animals-NY-(1948)-Harcourt Brace-drwngs-1st ed (ff6,sp chip dj) 35.00

THURBER,JAMES-Beast in Me and Other Animals-NY-(1948)-Harcourt Brace-grn cl-1st ed (f2,dj) 40.00

THURBER,JAMES-Fables For Our Time-1940-Harpers-1st ed (x2,f,dj) 110.00

THURBER,JAMES-Fables for Our Time-NY-(1940)-Harper-4to-124p-pict bds-1st ed (r3) 40.00

THURBER,JAMES-Further Fables For Our Time-NY-1956-S&S-1st ed (k5,dj) 17.50

THURBER,JAMES-Further Fables for Our Time-NY-1956-S&S-8vo-174p-sketches-1st ed (ee5,dj) 25.00

THURBER,JAMES-Lanterns & Lances-NY-(1961)-Harper & Bros-drwngs-1st ed (ff6,sl rub dj) 25.00

THURBER,JAMES-Lanterns & Lances-NY-1961-1st ed (o5,dj) 20.00

THURBER,JAMES-Men,Women and Dogs-NY-1943-1st ed (q5,chip dj) 35.00

THURBER,JAMES-Middle Aged Man on the Flying Trapeze-NY-1935-Harper & Bros-beige cl-1st ed (f2,dj) 90.00

THURBER,JAMES-My Life and Hard Times-NY-1933-illus bds & e.p.,sp papr labl,rare illus dj wi blurb by Hemingway-1st ed (n5,soil,sp labl chip,dj) 125.00

THURBER,JAMES-Selected Letters of ...-Bost,Tor-(1981)-1st trd ed (k5,as new in dj) 10.00

THURBER,JAMES-Thurber & Company-NY et al-(1966)-Harper & Row-1st ed (k5,dj) 10.00

THURBER,JAMES-Thurber Album-NY-1952-1st ed (p5,dj sl rub) 25.00

THURBER,JAMES-Thurber Album-NY-1952-S&S-1st ed (z3,sl cocked,dj chip) 12.50

THURBER,JAMES-Thurber Country-NY-1953-1st ed (s5,sl wn dj) 30.00

THURBER,JAMES-Thurber's Dogs-NY-1955-1st ed (r5,sl chip dj) 15.00

THURBER,JAMES-Thurber's Dogs-NY-1955-S&S-blk & gry bds-1st ed (f2,dj) 30.00

THURBER,JAMES-Thurber's Men, Women, and Dogs-NY-1943-Harcourt,Brace-blu cl-1st ed (f2,dj) 45.00

THURBER,JAMES-White Deer-NY-1945-illus-1st ed (q5,f,sl tn dj) 35.00

THURBER,JAMES-Wonderful O-NY-1957-1st ed (n5,dj) 25.00

THURMAN,MICHAEL E-Naval Department of San Blas-Glendale-1967-382p-illus,fldg map,plain dj-Spain in the West Ser,Vol.XI-1st ed (g7,f,dj) 40.00

THURMAN,MICHAEL E-Naval Department of San Blas-Glendale-1967-Arthur H Clark-382p+ads-red cl,maps,plts-1st ed (m2) 30.00

THURMAN,VIOLET B-"Old Town" Indianola-San Antonio-1952-Standard Prntg Co-55,(1)p-cl (h1,pres cpy) 17.50

THURMOND,BENTON A-High Hill Centennial History-Schulenburg-1960-Schulenburg Sticker-111p-wrps,photos-1st ed (w3,vf) 17.50

THURSTON,JOHN G-Journal of a Trip to Illinois in 1836-Mount Pleasant-(1971)-priv pr of John Cumming-59p-cl-ltd to 487c (f1) 20.00

THURSTON,LORRIN A-Thurston's Hawaiian Guide Book and Auto Road Guide to the Island of Oahu-Honolulu-1927-141p-cl-3 fldg maps (g1) 15.00

THWAITE,ANTHONY-Japan in Color-NY-(1967)-McGraw Hill-folio-160p-96 tip-in col plts-1st US ed (cc5,f,dj chip,tape rprd) 35.00

THWAITES,R G-Lahontan's Voyages to North America-Chig-1905-2 vols-illus,scarce (d7) 150.00

THWAITES,REUBEN G-ED.-Frontier Defense on the Upper Ohio-Madison-1912-Wisc Hist Scty-329p-brwn cl,12 plts,fldg map,2 facs-1st ed (e2) 135.00

THWAITES,REUBEN G-ED.-Fur Trade in Wisconsin, 1812 to 1825-Madison-1911-497p-illus-Wisc Hist Coll,Vol.20-1st ed (e7) 75.00

THWAITES,REUBEN G-ED.-Revolution on the Upper Ohio,1775 to 1777-Madison-1908-Wisc Hist Scty-xx+275p-brwn cl,9 plts,fldg map-ltd to 1200c-1st ed (e2) 135.00

THWAITES,REUBEN G-How George Rogers Clark Won the Northwest...-Chig-1903-McClurg-xx-378p+ads,plts-grn pict cl-1st ed (h2) 85.00

THWAITES,REUBEN G-Original Journals of the Lewis and Clark Expedition-NY-1969-8 vols-7 vols text,8th vol clam box wi fldg maps (d7,f) 400.00

THWAITES,REUBEN-New Voyages to North American by Baron de la Hontan-Chig-1905-McClurg-8vo-2 vols-cl-1st ed (mm7,f) 150.00

THWING,EUGENE-Red-Keggers-NY-1903-Book-Lover Pr-429p-cl-illus-1st ed (j1) 15.00

TIBBLES,THOMAS H-Buckskin and Blanket Days-GC-1957-336p (f7,f,dj) 25.00

TIBBLES,THOMAS H-Buckskin and Blanket Days-GC-1957-Dbldy-336p-Six Guns 2209-1st ed (dd4,dj) 20.00

TIBBLES,THOMAS H-Buckskin and Blanket Days-NY-1957-Dbldy-336p-Six Guns 2209-1st ed (gg4,dj) 20.00

TIBBLES,WILLIAM-Foods-lond-1912-Bailliere,Tindall & Cox-950p-Bitting 461 (l6) 75.00

TICE,JOHN R-Over the Plains and on the Mountains-St.Louis-1872-262p+6p ads-orig cl (z1,rub,sp tn) 150.00

TICEHURST,C B-Systematic Review of Genus Phylloscopus-Lond-1938-Brit Mus-4to-193p-cl,2 col plts,8 maps-v scarce orig prtg (y8) 72.00

TICHY,HERBERT-Himalaya-NY-1970-175p-61 col & 84 b&w photos-1st ed (a4,vf,f dj) 85.00

TICHY,HERBERT-Tibetan Adventure-Lond-261p-133 photos,2 fldg maps,auth 1st bk-scarce-1st ed (q10,f) 160.00

TICKNER,JOHN-Tickner's Ponies-Lond-1966-Putnam-1st ed (j9,dj) 15.00

TICKNOR,CAROLINE-May Alcott-Bost-1928-Little,Brown-315p-cl,t.p. in red & blk-1st ed (d1) 15.00

TIDY,GORDON-Surtees on Fishing-NY-1931-8vo-63p-one of 500c,7 hand col plts-scarce (m3,mostly uncut,f,fray dj) 60.00

TIDYMAN,ERNEST-Shaft-(NY)-(1970)-Macmillan-1st ed (a10,as new in dj) 20.00

TIEDE,TOM-Coward-NY-1968-Trident Pr-auth 1st bk-1st ed (f8,f,dj) 65.00

TIERNEY,RICHARD L-Collected Poems-(Sauk City)-1981-issued w/o dj-semi flex blk wrps-ltd to 1030c-1st ed (k5,as new in wrps) 20.00

TIETSORT,FRANCIS J-ED.-Temperance, or Prohibition-NY-1929-397p-cl-1st ed so stated (a1) 15.00

TIFFANY STUDIOS COLLECTION OF NOTABLE ORIENTAL RUGS-NY-(1907)-col frntis,illus-ltd to 500c (ll9) 100.00

TIFFANY TABLE SETTINGS-NY-(1960)-Crowell-folio-196p-blk cl,col & b&w photos-orig ed (q8,dj) 15.00

TILGHMAN,ZOE-Marshal of the Last Frontier-Glendale-1949-A H Clark-406p-red cl,fldg map,illus-1st ed (v1) 90.00

TILGHMAN,ZOE-Marshall of the Last Frontier-Glendale-1964-Arthur H Clark Co-406p-illus,fldg map-rvsd ed (c7,sl fade sp) 60.00

TILGHMAN,ZOE-Outlaw Days-np-(1926)-Harlow Publ-138p-pict wrps,illus-Six Guns 2212-1st ed (bb4,sp top chip) 25.00

TILLETT LESLIE-ED.-Wind on the Buffalo Grass-NY-(1976)-Crowell-lg oblng 8vo-xvi,160p-55 col & 61 b&w illus-1st prtg (v1) 45.00

TILLETT,LESLIE-ED.-Wind on the Buffalo Grass-NY-(1976)-Crowell-160p-55 col paintings,61 b&w drwngs (bb4,dj tn) 75.00

TILLEY,NANNIE M-Bright Tobacco Industry-Chapel Hill-(1948)-Univ of N Carolina-xiv+754p-brwn cl,illus-1st ed (e2,edge-wn dj) 75.00

TILLEY,NANNIE M-ED-Federals on the Frontier-Austin-1963-U of Tex Pr-429p (o7,f,dj) 85.00

TILLMAN,H W-Ice with Everything-Sidney-1974-142p-photos,maps (o10,f,dj) 15.00

TILLMAN,H W-Triumph and Tribulation-UK-1977-153p-1st ed (o10,as new in dj) 12.00

TILLMAN,S F-Man Unafraid-Wash D.C.-(1958)-8vo-cl,18p plts-1st ed (s2,sl chip dj) 35.00

TILLOTSON,HARRY S-Equisite Exile-Bost-(1932)-LL&S-8vo-205p-9 illus-1st ed (gg5,edgewn dj) 15.00

TILLSON,CHRISTIANA H-Woman's Story of Pioneer Illinois-Chig-1919-Donnelley-169p-2 ports-Lakeside Classics (cc4) 35.00

TILMAN,H W-Ascent of Nanda Devi-NY-1937-232p-illus,fldg map-1st US ed (p10,f,vf dj) 85.00

TILMAN,H W-China to Chitral-Cambridge-1951-123p-1st Brit ed (p10,f,dj) 85.00

TILMAN,H W-Snow on the Equator-NY-1938-265p-21 photos,4 maps (o10,f) 55.00

TILNEY,F C-Principles of Photographic Pictorialism-Bost-1930-Amer Photo Publ-79 photos-1st Amer ed (cc9) 70.00

TILTMAN,RONALD F-Television for the Home-1927-106p-8 photos-rare-1st ed (h6,f) 110.00

TILTON,CECIL G-William Chapman Ralston, Courageous Builder-Bost-(1935)-Christopher Publ Hs-474p-blu cl,plts-1st ed (b2,chip dj) 35.00

TILTON,THEODORE-Swabian Stories-NY-1882-297p-cl-1st ed (l1) 17.50

TIMBERLAKE,BOB-World of Bob Timberlake-Birmingham-1979-Oxmoor-oblng 4to-141p-beige cl,col illus-1st ed (r10,dj) 35.00

TIMLIN,WILLIAM-Ship That Sailed to Mars-1923-Harrap-orig bndg,papr bds wi dec vel sp,col illus,one of 2000c-1st ed (x2) 1,100.00

TINDALL,GILLIAN-George Gissing-NY-1974-HBJ-1st Amer ed (t4,f,dj) 20.00

TINDALL,K-Great Heads-1969-Grove Pr-auth 1st bk-1st Amer ed (x2,f,dj) 17.00

TINKER,B-Mexican Wilderness & Wildlife-1978-U of Tex-131p-illus-1st ed (bb3,f,dj) 15.00

TINKER,EDWARD L-Horsemen of the Americas and the Literature They Inspired-NY-1953-Hastings Hs-151p-brwn & wht cl,col plts-ltd to 1575c,nbrd-1st ed (e2,dj) 65.00

TINKLE,LON-13 Days to Glory-NY-(1958)-McGraw Hill-8vo-256p-8p photos-1st ed (gg5,dj) 20.00

TINKLE,LON-An American Original, the Life of J Frank Dobie-Bost-(1978)-Little,Brown-264p-photos-1st ed (a9,dj) 25.00

TINKLE,LON-An American Original-Bost-(1978)-Little,Brown-264p-illus-1st ed (gg4,dj) 20.00

TINSLEY,JIM BOB-Sailfish-Florida-1964-4to-216p-deluxe ed of 500c,nbrd,illus,photos-scarce (m3,as new in dj & Box) 100.00

TINSLEY,JOHN D-Drainage and Flooding for the Removal of Alkali-Santa Fe-1902-New Mex Prntg Co-29p-wrps-Bull.#43 of NM Agr Exper Sta (g1) 15.00

TIPPING,H AVRAY-Story of the Royal Welsh Fusiliers-Lond-(1915)-281p-purple cl,maps,illus-1st ed (b7) 100.00

TITLEY,NORAH M-Persian Miniature Painting-Austin-1984-U of Tex-1st ed (oo3,f,dj) 25.00

TITOV,GHERMAN-I Am Eagle!-Indpls-(1962)-Bobbs Merrill-8vo-212p-8p illus-1st ed (gg5,rub dj) 17.50

TITTLE,WALTER-Roosevelt as an Artist Saw Him-NY-(1948)-20 illus-1st ed (l10,sl wn dj) 10.00

TITUS,EVE-Basil of Baker Street-1958-Whittlesey Hs-1st ed (s10,dj) 25.00

TITUSVILLE COOK BOOK-Titusville-nd(ca.1900)-Young Ladies Missionary Scty of the Presbyterian Church-159p-wht oil cl bds wi blk lttrng (n6) 45.00

TIXIER,VICTOR-Tixier's Travels on the Osage Prairies-Norman-1940-U of Okla Pr-309p-illus,maps-Howes T276-1st ed (ee4,dj) 45.00

TIXIER,VICTOR-Tixier's Travels on the Osage Prairies-Norman-1940-U of Okla Pr-309p-illus,maps-Howes T276-1st ed (bb4,dj) 45.00

TOBEY'S 80: A RETROSPECTIVE-Seattle-(1971)-Seattle Art Mus/UW Pr-4to-illus-1st ed (p1,f,dj) 50.00

TOBEY,MARK-World of a Market-Seattle-1964-U of Wash Pr-b&w & col illus-1st ed (ll9,dj) 40.00

TOBIAS,FRITZ-Reichstag Fire-NY-1964-Putnam-348p-photos-1st US ed so stated (r1,dj) 30.00

TOBIE,HARVEY-No Man Like Joe-Portland-1949-320p-frntis,photos-1st ed (t7,f,chip dj) 30.00

TOBIN,R L B-Maps: a Family Scrapbook, 50th Anniversary: 1928 to 1978-San Antonio-1978-4to-wrps,maps-ltd to 500c (d3) 45.00

TODD,CHARLES B-Real Benedict Arnold-NY-1903-Barnes-x+235p+ads-blu cl,plts,t.e.g.-1st ed (m2) 35.00

TODD,CHARLES S-Sketches of the Civil and Military Services of William Henry Harrison-Cin-1840-U P James-168p-cl (j1,sl wn) 60.00

TODD,F P-American Military Equipage, 1851 to 1872. Vol.1-NY-1980-602p-illus (z10,dj) 85.00

TODD,F P-American Military Equipage, 1851 to 1872. Vol.2-1983-729p-illus (z10,f,dj) 60.00

TODD,F S-Waterfowl-1979-Sea World Pr-sq 4to-399p-g dec lea,788 col photos-ltd to 1500c,nbrd,autg (bb3,vf,dj,sl soil box) 175.00

TODD,JOHN-Students Manual...-Northampton-1856-Hopkins,Bridgman-402p-cl-21st ed (k1) 17.50

TODD,LEWIS C-Moral Justice of Universalism-Erie-1845-Joseph M Sterrett,Prntr-192p-bds (c1,sl wn) 32.50

TODD,REV JOHN-Sunset Land-Bost-1870-Lee & Shepard-322p-blndstmpd cl-2nd ed (z1,pres cpy) 85.00

TODD,RUTHVEN-Mantlepiece of Shells-(NY)-(1955)-(Bonaci & Saul)-1st ed (u10,f,dj) 35.00

TODD,RUTHVEN-Until Now-Lond-(1942)-Fortune Pr-8vo-cl-1st ed (ll10,f,sl wn dj) 75.00

TODD,W E C-Birds of Western Pennsylvania-1940-U of Pitt Pr-710p-col plts,fldg map (b9) 100.00

TODD,W E C-Birds of Western Pennsylvania-1940-U of Pitt-710p-22 col plts,1 b&w plt,map (bb3,f,wn dj) 125.00

TOILET-Lond-1874-Warne & Co-96p-brn cl wi tip on illus,a.e.g.,miniature bk (m6) 35.00

TOKLAS,ALICE B-Alice B Toklas Cook Book-Lond-(1954)-M Joseph-288p-tan cl,illus e.p.,illus-1st ed (q8) 75.00

TOKLAS,ALICE B-Aromas and Flavors-(1958)-Harper-154p-blu bds-1st ed (q8,dj) 65.00

TOKLAS,ALICE B-What is Remembered-1963-HRW-1st ed (x2,f,sl tanned dj) 38.00

TOLAND,J-Ships in the Sky-NY-(1957)-roy 8vo-352p-cl,16p plts (s2,dj) 30.00

TOLAND,JOHN-No Man's Land-NY-1980-651p-maps,illus-1st ed (b7,f,dj) 15.00

TOLANSKY,S-History and Use of Diamond-Lond-(1962)-Methuen-166p-gry cl,plts-1st ed (a2,dj) 15.00

TOLBERT,FRANK X-An Informal History of Texas-NY-1961-275p-photos,map e.p.-1st ed (t7,dj) 12.50

TOLBERT,FRANK X-Bowl of Red-GC-1966-Dbldy-120p-1st ed (f9,dj) 25.00

TOLD BY THE PIONEERS-(Olympia)-1937-WPA-3 vols(#1,2 & 3)-illus cl cov (b6,vf) 85.00

TOLD BY THE PIONEERS: TALES OF FRONTIER LIFE AS TOLD BY THOSE WHO REMEMBER...-Olympia-1937,1938-WPA-3 vols-cl-1st ed (w1,f) 125.00

TOLER,SIDNEY-Stage Fright and Other Verses-Portland-1910-Smith & Sale-dec wrps,photo-rare-1st ed (s1) 40.00

TOLKIEN,J R R-Father Christmas Letters-Bost-1976-Houghton Mifflin-1st ed (z2,f,f dj) 65.00

TOLKIEN,J R R-Middle English Vocabulary-1922-Clarendon Pr-auth 1st bk,wrps-1st ed (x2,sp wn & flakng,sl soil) 325.00

TOLKIEN,J R R-Silmarillion-1977-Allen & Unwin-1st ed (r9,f,dj) 35.00

TOLKIEN,J R R-Silmarillion-Bost-1977-Houghton Mifflin-1st US ed (bb1,as new in dj) 15.00

TOLKIEN,J R R-Silmarillion-Lond-(1977)-1st issue(lacks price on dj)-1st ed (r2,f,dj) 125.00

TOLKIEN,J R R-Smith of Wootton Major-1967-Houghton-1st US ed (kk6,f,dj) 65.00

TOLKIEN,J R R-Smith of Wootton Major-Bost-1967-HM-illus-1st US ed (x9,f,sl stnd dj) 40.00

TOLKIEN,J R R-Unfinished Tales of Numenor and Middle Earth-Bost-1980-Houghton Mifflin-1st ed (bb1,f,dj) 20.00

TOLL,ROGER-Mountaineering in the Rocky Mountain National Park-Wash D.C.-1921-105p-wrps,25 plts,2 fldg maps rear pckt (a4,f) 115.00

TOLLEMACHE,LIONEL-Stones of Stumbling-Lond-1891-237p-scarce-1st ed (dd3) 75.00

TOLLER,ERNST-Masses and Man-Lond-1923-Nonesuch-1st ed (v5) 40.00

TOLLES,FREDERICK B-George Logan of Philadelphia-NY-1953-362p-cl-1st ed (h1,sl wn dj) 15.00

TOLLEY,KEMP-Cruise of the Lanikai, Incitement to War-Annapolis-1973-Naval Inst Pr-8vo-345p-grn cl,map e.p.,illus (p8,f,sl wn dj) 25.00

TOLLEY,KEMP-Yangtze Patrol-Annapolis-(1971)-Naval Inst Pr-xvi+330p-red cl,illus-1st ed (m2,dj) 20.00

TOLMIE,WILLIAM F-Physician and Fur Trader-Vancouver-1963-Mitchell-8vo-413p-16 illus-1st Can ed (cc5,dj sl tn,wn) 35.00

TOLSTOI,LEO-Anna Karenina-1886-Crowell-1st ed in English (x2) 175.00

TOLSTOI,LYOF-Where Love is There God is Also-NY-1887-Crowell-sewn in bds-1st ed (w5) 65.00

TOLSTOY,LEO-Diaries of...Youth 1847 to 1852-NY-1907-Dutton-grn cl-transl by Hogarth & Sirnis-1st ed (kk10,dull cl) 20.00

TOLSTOY,LEO-Lift Up Your Eyes-NY-1960-Julian Pr-cl-1st prtg (l8,vf,dj) 15.00

TOLSTOY,LEO-Russian Stories and Legends-NY-nd-Pantheon Bks-cl,col frntis,col & b&w illus,transl by L & A Maude (n8,f,dj) 20.00

TOMKINS,CALVIN-Living Well is the Best Revenge-1962-Viking-1st ed (m9,dj) 25.00

TOMLINSON,D W-Sky's the Limit-Phila-(1930)-roy 8vo-290p-cl,frntis,25p plts,16 text figs-1st ed (s2,fade) 75.00

TOMLINSON,H M-All Our Yesterdays-Lond-(1930)-Heinemann-1st Brit ed (hh5,dj) 30.00

TOMLINSON,H M-London River-NY-1921-Knopf-papr sp labl-ltd to 2000c,nbrd (x1,f,f dj) 40.00

TOMLINSON,H M-Tide Marks-NY-1924-Harper & Bros-295p-g dec red cl,frnt map e.p.,drwngs,K Eby (ll1) 40.00

TOMLINSON,H M-Waiting for Daylight-NY-1922-ltd to 2200c,nbrd (y7) 25.00

TOMPKINS,CALVIN-Lewis and Clark Trail-(1965)-Harper & Row-117p+21 maps,illus-1st ed (r8,f,dj) 30.00

TOMPKINS,COL FRANK-Chasing Villa-(Harrisburg)-1934-Military Serv Pub-270p-pict cl,illus,rosters-1st ed (z1) 125.00

TOMPKINS,PETER-Magic of the Obelisks-NY-1981-Harper & Row-cl,illus-1st ed (o8,dj) 20.00

TOMPKINS,PETER-Mysteries of the Mexican Pyramids-NY-1976-Harpers-cl,drwngs,H Harleston,Jr.,illus-1st ed (l8,f,dj) 15.00

TOMPKINS,PETER-Secrets of the Great Pyramid-NY-1971-Harper & Row-qto-cl,illus-1st ed (o8,fray dj) 20.00

TOMPKINS,STUART R-Alaska-1945-U of Okla-350p-illus-1st ed (u8,dj wn) 45.00

TOMPKINS,WALKER A-Little Giant of Signal Hill-Englewood Cliffs-(1964)-258p-cl (d1) 12.50

TONGKO,CASTOR T-Paradise Cook Book-NY-(1857)-Vantage Pr-96p-1st ed (l6) 15.00

TOOKER,WM W-Significance of John Eliot's Natick and the Name Merrimac-NY-1901-56p-ltd ed (t7,f) 20.00

TOOLE,JOHN K-Confederacy of Dunces-Baton Rouge-1980-LSU Pr-1st ed (y2,f,sl tn dj) 400.00

TOOLEY,R V-Maps and Map Makers-NY-(1978)-140p-illus-1st ed (g7,f,dj) 35.00

TOOLEY,RONALD V-Mapping of Australia-(Lond)-(1979)-Holland Pr-tall 8vo-xix,633p-drk grn cl,239 illus-1st ed (t10,f,dj) 85.00

TOOMBS,SAMUEL-New Jersey Troops in the Gettysburg Campaign from June 5 to July 31, 1863-Orange-1888-Evening Mail Publ Hs-406p-maps-Nevins I,169 (ee4) 60.00

TOOMBS,SAMUEL-New Jersey Troops in the Gettysburg Campaign, from June 5 to July 31, 1863-Orange-1888-xvi,406p-cl,illus,plts,fldg map (aa6) 50.00

TOOMER,JEAN-Wayward and the Seeking. A Collection of Writings by...-Wash D.C.-1980-Howard U Pr-cl,frntis-1st ed (l8,vf,dj) 35.00

TOOZE,RUTH-Cambodia Land of Contrasts-NY-1962-Viking-144p-photos (c3,chip dj) 22.00

TOPE,M-Biography of William Holmes McGuffey-Bowerston-1929-Phrenological Era Print-114p (e1,sl soil wrps,reinfrcd sp) 20.00

TOPOLSKI,FELIKS-Shem, Ham & Japheth, Inc-Bost-1971-Houghton Mifflin-4to-unpgd-tri col cl,illus (r10,dj) 32.50

TOPONCE,ALEXANDER-Reminiscences of Alexander Toponce, 1839 to 1923-Ogden-1923-Mrs.Toponce,publ-248p-emboss fabri,14 plts-scarce-1st ed (z1) 150.00

TOPORCER,GEORGE-Baseball from Backyard to Big Leagues-1954-Sterling-1st ed (ff2,f,dj) 15.00

TOPPING,E S-Chronicles of the Yellowstone-Mpls-1968-Ross & Haines-279p-illus,fldg map-Howes T300 (bb4,dj) 25.00

TOPPING,E S-Chronicles of the Yellowstone-St.Paul-1883-Pioneer Pr-(4),246p-cl,fldg map,illus-scarce-Howes T300-1st ed (v1,lacks fr blank e.p.) 225.00

TORCHIA,JOSEPH-Kryptonite Kid-NY-(1979)-Holt-1st ed (h3,f,dj) 15.00

TORCHIANA,H A-Story of the Mission Santa Cruz-SF-1933-460p-frntis,photos,maps-Six Guns #2227-scarce-1st ed (t7,dj) 100.00

TORDAY,E-Camp & Tramp in African Wilds-Phila-1913-8vo-316p-photos,fldg map (m3) 25.00

TORDAY,R-On Trail of the Bushongo-1969-Negro Univ-286p-photos-rprnt of 1925 ed (bb3,f) 25.00
TORGERSON,EDWIN D-Murderer Returns-1930-Smith-1st ed (s10,dj) 30.00
TORGERSON,EDWIN D-Murderer Returns-NY-1930-Smith-1st ed (h4,dj sl tn,sl chip) 20.00
TORRE,SUSANNA-Women in American Architecture-NY-1977-Whitney Libr-4to-224p-blk cl,illus-2nd prtg (r10,f,f dj) 25.00
TORREY,E FULLER-Roots of Treason-NY-1984-McGraw Hill-1st ed (x9,f,dj) 12.50
TORRY,E NORMAN-Round My Library Fire-Lond-(1947)-Nelson & Sons-243p-cl,t.e.g.-1st ed (dd10,f) 20.00
TOULOUSE-LAUTREC,COUNTESS GUY DE-Chez Maxim's-(1962)-McGraw Hill-folio-258p-red cl,photos,drwngs,tip in col plts (q8,chip dj) 75.00
TOURGEE,ALBION W-Fool's Errand-NY-(1880)-521p-cl,2 prts in one vol as iss,16 illus-new,rvsd & enlrgd ed (l1) 25.00
TOURGEE,ALBION-John Eax and Mamelon...-NY-1882-Fords,Howard & Hulbert-300p+ads-pict brwn cl-1st ed (z9,rub) 12.50
TOUSEY,SANFORD-Val Rides the Oregon Trail-1939-Dbldy,Doran-unpgd-col & b&w drwngs-1st ed (r8,sp chip dj) 25.00
TOVEY,DOREEN-Double Trouble-NY-1972-Norton-1st US ed (f10,dj) 15.00
TOWLER,JOHN-Silver Sunbeam-Hastings on Hudson-1969-Morgan & Morgan-351p-facs rprnt of 1864 1st ed (cc9,f,dj) 35.00
TOWN,HAROLD-Tom Thomson-Tor-1977-McClelland & Stewart-oblng 4to-240p-blk cl,col & b&w illus (r10,dj) 45.00
TOWN,SALEM-An Analysis of the Derivative Words in the English Language...-Cin-1847-Derby,Bradley & Co-164p-prtd bds-21st ed (b1) 40.00
TOWN,SALEM-Second Reader-Portland-1854-Blake & Carter-192p-bds (k1) 15.00
TOWNE,C H-Autumn Loiteries-1917-Doran-illus & e.p.,T Fogarty-1st ed (x2) 20.00
TOWNE,C W-Her Majesty Montana-Butte-Montana Standard-8vo-150p-wrps (cc4,lt spot cov) 25.00
TOWNE,CHARLES W-Cattle & Men-(1955)-U of Okla Pr-8vo-384p-photos-1st ed (p1,f,dj) 65.00
TOWNE,CHARLES W-Cattle & Men-Norman-(1955)-U of Okla Pr-384p-illus,map-1st ed (cc4,dj) 35.00
TOWNEND,HELEN G-History of Findlay's Public Schools-np-nd-priv prntd-64p-cl-scarce (j1) 12.50
TOWNER,WESLEY-Elegant Auctioneers-NY-(1970)-Hill & Wang-1st ed (w1,f,dj) 15.00
TOWNSEND,DORIS M-Culinary Crafting-NY-(1977)-Rutledge Bks-192p-grn cl,col & b&w illus-2nd prtg (q8,dj) 16.50
TOWNSEND,F H-Punch Drawings-Lond-1921-Cassell-226p-red cl,frntis port,illus (r10,sp fade) 40.00
TOWNSEND,WILLIAM H-Lincoln and the Bluegrass-Lexington-(1955)-392p-illus-1st ed (n3,f,dj) 32.50
TOWNSEND,WILLIAM H-Lincoln the Litigant-Bost-1925-117p-illus-ltd to 1050c-1st ed (n3) 30.00
TOWNSHEND,CHARLES-My Campaign in Mesopotamia-Lond-1920-400p-red cl,frntis,fldg maps-1st ed (b7) 75.00
TOWNSHEND,CHAUNCY H-Facts in Mesmerism...-Lond-1844-Hippolyte Bailliere-cl-2nd ed,rvsd & enlgd (o8) 45.00
TOWNSHEND,FREDERICK T-Ten Thousand Miles of Travel, Sport and Adventure-Lond-1869-Hurst & Blackett-275p+ads-buckr,frntis-Howes T32 (z1,rbnd) 150.00
TOWNSHEND,R B-Last Memories of a Tenderfoot-Lond-(1926)-Bodley Head-270p-orig cl,photos-Adams "Herd" 2323-1st ed (z1) 95.00
TOWNSHEND,R B-Last Memories of a Tenderfoot-Lond-(1926)-John Lane-xiv,270p-cl,photo plts-1st ed (v1) 75.00
TOWNSHEND,R B-Tenderfoot in Colorado-Lond-(1923)-John Lane-xvi,282p-cl,photos-1st ed (v1,sl wn) 65.00
TOWNSHEND,R B-Tenderfoot in New Mexico-Lond-(1923)-257p-photos-Adams Guns#2221-1st ed (v7) 65.00
TOWNSHEND,R B-Tenderfoot in New Mexico-Lond-(1923)-John Lane-(xii),257p-red cl,plts-1st ed (v1,sp sunned) 75.00
TOWNSHEND,R B-Tenderfoot in New Mexico-Lond-(1923)-John Lane-257p-cl,illus,photos,(1st Amer 1924)-1st ed (z1) 80.00
TOWNSHEND,R B-Tenderfoot in New Mexico-NY-1929-1st Amer ed (v7) 40.00
TOYNBEE,ARNOLD-ED.-Half the World-NY-c.1973-HR&W-4to-368p-brwn cl,col plts,maps (gg6) 65.00
TOZZER,A M-Excavation of a Site at Santiago Ahuitzotla, D F Mexico-1921-Bur Amer Ethnol Bull.74-55p-19 plts (bb3) 15.00
TRACY,HONOR-Butterflies of the Province-Lond-(1970)-Methuen-1st ed (z8,vf,dj) 20.00
TRACY,HONOR-Spanish Leaves-NY-(1964)-Random (z8,vf,dj) 10.00
TRACY,JACK-Encyclopedia Sherlockiana-NY-(1977)-(19),411p-illus-1st ed (k9,f,dj) 20.00
TRACY,JACK-Encyclopedia Sherlockiana-NY-(1977)-(19),411p-illus-1st ed (m4,f,dj) 17.50
TRACY,JACK-Sherlock Holmes-Bost-1980-Houghton-1st ed (e4,dj) 22.50
TRACY,L-Law of the Tallon-1926-Clode-1st ed (x7,wn dj) 33.00
TRACY,LOUIS-Dangerous Situation-1932-Clode-1st Amer ed (s10,dj) 20.00
TRACY,LOUIS-Great Mogul-NY-1905-Clode-elephant dec bds-1st ed (w5,f) 25.00
TRACY,MARIAN-200 Main Course Dishes-NY-(1964)-Scribner's-219p-1st ed (r6,dj) 12.00
TRACY,MILTON-Colonizer, a Saga of Stephen F Austin-El Paso-1941-381p-pict cl,photo-1st ed (t7,soil,weak hng) 10.00
TRACY,SUZY-Klondike Edition of Scientific Cookery-Seattle-1898-64p-leatherette-cov title "The Miners' Cook Book" (a7,bent cors) 175.00
TRAGER,JAMES-Big, Fertile, Rumbling, Cast Iron Growling, Aching, Unbuttoned Belly Book-NY-1971-Grossman Publ-572p (k6) 35.00
TRAGER,PHILIP-New YOrk-Middletown-1980-Wesleyan Univ Pr-120p-82 photos-1st ed (cc9,f,dj) 50.00
TRAIL OF THE TRAMP-Erie-(1913)-136p-wrps-8th ed (l1) 15.00
TRAILL,SINCLAIR-ED.-Play That Music-Lond-(1956)-Faber-1st ed (w1,f,dj) 20.00
TRAILL,WALTER J S-In Rupert's Land-Tor-1970-M&S-232p-e.p. maps (aa2,dj) 20.00*
TRAIN,ARTHUR-No Matter Where-NY-1933-1st ed (s5,chip dj) 35.00
TRAISTER,JOHN-Professional Care & Finishing of Gun Metal-Blue Ridge Summit-1982-8vo-303p-photos-1st ed (m3,f) 12.50
TRALL,R T-New Hydropathic Cook Book-NY-1854-Fowlers & Wells-226p+ads-red cl-1st ed (c2,soil text) 85.00
TRANSEAU,E L-Army Experiences with Drink-Westerville-nd(ca.1917)-37,(1)p-wrps (a1) 12.50

TRANSPORTATION IN AMERICA-Wash-1947-391p-cl (g1,top of cov sl fade) 15.00

TRANTER,G J-Plowing the Arctic-Tor-1945-311p-1st ed (o10,f,dj wn) 10.00

TRAPIDO,HAROLD-Snakes of New Jersey-Newark-1937-60p-wrps,illus (aa6) 35.00

TRAPROCK,WALTER E-Cruise of the Kawa, Wanderings in the South Seas-NY-1921-Putnam's-gry cl,g titles,map e.p. (p8,sl soil,fade) 10.00

TRAUBEL,HELEN-Metropolitan Opera Murders-NY-1951-Simon-1st ed (f4,dj) 12.50

TRAUTMAN,MILTON B-Birds of Buckeye Lake, Ohio-Ann Arbor-1940-U of Mich-466p-wrps-Misc Publ in Zoology No.44 (c9,sl wn) 35.00

TRAVEN,B-Carreta-NY-(1970)-Hill and Wang-1st ed (bb2,f,dj) 50.00

TRAVEN,B-General from the Jungle-NY-(1972)-Hill & Wang-1st ed (y1,f,dj) 50.00

TRAVEN,B-Government-NY-1971-Hill & Wang-1st ed (h8,f,dj wi sm tr) 45.00

TRAVEN,B-Rebellion of the Hanged-NY-1952-Knopf-1st ed (d8,f,sl tn dj) 175.00

TRAVEN,B-Rebellion of the Hanged-NY-1972-Hill & Wang-1st ed thus (b8,f,sl tn dj) 40.00

TRAVEN,B-To the Honorable Miss S & Other Stories-Westport-1981-Lawrence Hill-1st US ed (y1,f,dj) 25.00

TRAVER,ROBERT-Trouble Shooter-NY-1943-Viking-auth 1st bk-1st ed (bb1,dj) 95.00

TRAVER,ROBERT-Trout Madness-NY-1960-8vo-178p-true 1st ed wi $4.95 price on dj-1st ed (m3,vf,sl chip dj) 24.00

TRAVER,ROBERT-Trout Magic-NY-1974-4to-216p-illus,M Weiler-1st ed (m3,f,dj) 50.00

TRAVERS,P L-About the Sleeping Beauty-NY-1975-McGraw Hill-cl,col frntis,illus,Chas Keeping-1st ed (l8,vf,dj) 25.00

TRAVERS,P L-Culinary Consultant, Mary Poppins in the Kitchen-Lond-(1977)-Collins-122p-g dec red cl,illus-1st Brit ed (q8,dj) 20.00

TRAVERS,P L-Friend Monkey-NY-(1971)-HBJ-294p-cl,frntis & dj,Chas Keeping-1st US ed (r3,f,dj) 15.00

TRAVERS,P L-I Go By Sea, I Go By Land-NY-1941-Harper & Bros-cl,col frntis,drwngs,G Hermes-1st ed (l8,dj wn,pc missing) 35.00

TRAVERS,P L-Mary Poppins in the Park-NY-1952-Harcourt,Brace-8vo-235p-blu pict cl,pict e.p.,illus by M Shepard-1st Amer ed (nn8,sl tn dj) 45.00

TRAVERSE CITY-State of Michigan Charter of the City of...-Traverse City-1913-Herald & Record-74p-wrps (z7) 45.00

TRAVIS,CAROLE A-Star Food-Jackson-(1981)-Teton Publ-340p-pict bds,cartoons-1st ed (q8,f,dj) 35.00

TRAVIS,WILLIAM-Shark for Sale-Chig-(1961)-Rand McNally-8vo-181p-9 illus-1st US ed (ff5,dj) 15.00

TRAYLOR,S W-Out of the Southwest-np-(1936)-255p-illus-1st ed (f9,sl soil,wn,dj chip,fade) 45.00

TRAYNOR,SHAUN-Hardening Ground-Lond-1974-Brian & O'Keefe-1st ed (z8,f,dj) 32.50

TREACY,ERIC-Glory of Steam-Lond-1969-112p-1st ed (n4,f,dj) 16.00

TREACY,ERIC-Portrait of Steam-Lond-1967-200p-1st ed (n4,f,dj) 25.00

TREANOR,THOMAS C-John Treanor-LA-1937-Zamorano Club-85p-frntis-scarce-1st ed (v7,f) 35.00

TREAT,LAWRENCE-T as in Trapped-NY-1947-Morrow-1st ed (e4,f,sl chip dj) 15.00

TREDREE,H L-Strange Ordeal of the Normandier-Bost-(1958)-Little,Brown-8vo-231p-1st ed (cc5,dj sl tn,soil) 15.00

TREE,GREGORY-Case Against Butterfly-NY-1951-Scribner's-1st ed (e4,dj) 25.00

TREECE,HENRY-How I See Apocalypse-Lond-1946-Lindsay Drummond-frntis port-1st ed (t4,f,dj) 75.00

TREECE,HENRY-I Cannot Go Hunting Tomorrow & Other Stories-Lond-1946-Grey Walls Pr-1st ed (t4,f,dj) 50.00

TREGANZA,ADAN E-Fort Ross-Berkeley-1954-U of Cal-26p-orig wrps,1 map,1 plt,3 figs (mm1) 25.00

TREGASKIS,RICHARD-Vietnam Diary-NY-1963-HRW-1st ed (c8,f,sl chip dj) 50.00

TREMLETT,REX-Road to Ophir-Lond-(1956)-Hutchinson-8vo-190p-5 illus-1st ed (jj5,dj sl chip,tn) 25.00

TRENCH,C C-History of Marksmanship-Chig-1972-317p-photos (gg3,vf,dj) 20.00

TRENCH,CHARLES C-History of Angling-Chig-1974-4to-288p-illus (m3,vf,dj) 30.00

TRENCH,JOHN-What Rough Beast-NY-1957-Macmillan-1st US ed (p4,f,sl soil dj) 25.00

TRENCH,JOHN-What Rough Beast-NY-1957-Macmilllan-1st US ed (g4,f,dj) 10.00

TRENHOLM,VIRGINIA C-Shoshonis: Sentinels of the Rockies-Norman-(1964)-367p-cl-1st ed (a1,dj) 35.00

TRENNERT,ROBERT A,JR.-Indian Traders on the Middle Border-Lincoln-(1981)-U of Nebr Pr-271p-illus,maps (ff4,dj) 24.00

TRENT,BILL-Northwoods Doctor-Phila-1962-Lippincott-8vo-320p-1st ed (bb7,chip dj) 15.00*

TRENT,GEORGE-ED.-Gentle Art of Walking-NY-1971-Arno/Random-4to-315p-illus-1st ed (gg5,sl tn dj) 15.00

TRENT,LUCY-John Neely Bryan, Founder of Dallas-Dallas-(1936)-Tardy-80p-illus,col pict dj-1st ed (f9,sl spot,fade dj) 50.00

TRENT,WILLIAM P-ED.-Cambridge History of American Literature-NY,Cambridge-1933-3 vols-cl (a1) 20.00

TRENTON-A History of...1679 to 1929-Princeton-1929-xx,1116p-cl,illus-ltd to 500c (aa6) 90.00

TRENTON-Industrial...and Vicinity-Wilmington-1900-4to-92,(1)p-cl,illus-comp by Geo A Wolf (aa6) 90.00

TRESSELT,ALVIN-What Did You Leave Behind?-NY-(1978)-Lothrop,Lee & Shepard-4to-unpgd-cl,col illus,R Duvoisin-1st ed (r3,f,f dj) 20.00

TRESUNNGAR,HUGO-Dark Justice-LA-(1938)-Sutton Hs-8vo-255p-1st ed (dd5,dj) 20.00

TREUE,WILHELM-Art Plunder-NY-1961-John Day-1st US ed (z9,dj rub) 10.00

TREVANIAN-Loo Sanction-1973-Crown-1st ed (x2,f,dj) 26.00

TREVELYAN,G E-Appius and Virginia-NY-1933-Putnam-1st ed (y1,f,dj) 30.00

TREVES,FREDERICK-Elephant Man and Other Reminiscences-Lond-1924-222p (dd3) 50.00

TREVOR,GLEN-Was it Murder?-NY-1933-Harper-1st US ed (h4) 12.50

TREVOR,WILLIAM-Angels at the Ritz-NY-1976-1st US ed (s5,f,dj) 20.00

TREVOR,WILLIAM-Beyond the Pale-1982-Viking-1st Amer ed (r9,vf,dj) 15.00

TREVOR,WILLIAM-Day We Got Drunk on Cake...-NY-(1967)-Viking-1st Amer ed (z8,f,dj) 17.50

TREVOR,WILLIAM-Fools of Fortune-Lond-(1983)-Bodley Head-1st ed (bb2,f,dj) 35.00

TREVOR,WILLIAM-Fools of Fortune-Lond-(1983)-Bodley Head-1st ed (z8,vf,dj) 40.00

TREVOR,WILLIAM-Love Department-NY-1967-1st US ed (s5,dj) 25.00

TREVOR,WILLIAM-Lovers of Their Time-Lond-(1978)-Bodley Head-1st ed (bb2,f,dj) 45.00

TREVOR,WILLIAM-Lovers of Their Time...-Lond-(1978)-Bodley Head-1st ed (z8,f,dj) 35.00

TREVOR,WILLIAM-Mrs Eckdorf in O'Neill's Hotel-NY-1970-Viking-1st ed (y1,dj) 40.00

TREVOR,WILLIAM-Old Boys-1964-Viking-1st Amer ed (t9,f,sp drknd dj) 110.00

TREVOR,WILLIAM-Old Boys-Lond-(1971)-Davis Poyton-wrps-1st ed (z8) 25.00

TREW,CECIL-Horse Through the Ages-NY-nd(1953)-Roy-1st US ed (j9,dj) 20.00

TRIGG,ELWOOD B-Gypsy Demons and Divinities-Secaucus-1973-Citadel Pr-cl-1st ed (o8,f,dj) 15.00

TRIGGS,OSCAR L-Chapters in the History of the Arts and Crafts Movement-Chig-1902-Bohemia Guild Ind Art Lg-1st ed (w5) 100.00

TRILLIN,CALVIN-Alice, Let's Eat-NY-(1978)-Random-182p-1st ed (m6,dj) 15.00

TRILLIN,CALVIN-Alice, Let's Eat-NY-1978-1st ed (n5,dj) 25.00

TRILLIN,CALVIN-American Fried-GC-1974-1st ed (n5,dj) 35.00

TRILLIN,CALVIN-An Education in Georgia-NY-(1964)-Viking-yel cl bkd bds,auth 1st bk-1st ed,1st state (bb2,f,dj chip) 55.00

TRILLIN,CALVIN-Barnett Frummer is an Unbloomed Flower-NY-(1969)-Viking-1st ed (bb1,as new in dj) 30.00

TRILLIN,CALVIN-Killings-NY-1984-Ticknor & Fields-1st ed (bb1,as new in dj) 15.00

TRILLIN,CALVIN-Runestruck-Bost & Tor-(1977)-Little,Brown-1st ed (b5,as new in dj) 20.00

TRILLIN,CALVIN-Third Helpings-New Haven-1983-Ticknor & Fields-184p-red cl-1st ed (q8,dj) 15.00

TRILLIN,CALVIN-U.S. Journal-NY-1971-1st ed (n5,f,f dj) 40.00

TRILLING,DIANA-Mrs.Harris-NY-(1981)-Harcourt Brace-1st ed (o3,f,dj) 15.00

TRILLING,DIANA-Reviewing the Forties-NY,Lond-(1978)-HBJ-1st ed (bb1,as new in dj) 10.00

TRIMBLE,JOE-Phil Rizzuto-1951-Barnes-1st ed (q7,f,dj) 30.00

TRIMBLE,JOE-Phil Rizzuto-1951-Barnes-photos,(MVP series)-1st ed (s8,dj) 27.50

TRIMBLE,JOSEPH M-Memoir of Mrs.Jane Trimble-Cin-1861-177p-cl (d1) 50.00

TRIMBLE,LOUIS-Murder Trouble-NY-1945-Phoenix-1st ed (d4,dj) 20.00

TRIMBLE,LOUIS-Valley of Violence-Phila-(1948)-Macrae Smith Co-1st ed (b10,sl chip dj) 10.00

TRINKA,ZENA I-North Dakota of Today-St.Paul-1920-Dow Co-259p-124 photos (bb4,sl wn sp) 25.00

TRIPLETT,COL FRANK-Conquering WIlderness-NY-1883-742p-pict cl,frntis,illus-Graff #4195-1st ed (t7) 85.00

TRIPLETT,FRANK-Life, Times and Treacherous Death of Jesse James-Chig-1970-Swallow Pr-344p-illus-Howes T355a (cc4,dj) 35.00

TRISTRAM,W OUTRAM-Coaching Days and Coaching Ways-Lond,NY-1893-Macmillan-4th ed (j9) 85.00

TROBIAND,PHILIPPE R DE-Military Life in Dakota-St.Paul-(1951)-Alvord Mem Comm-395p-map,illus-Howes T356 (bb4,dj) 65.00

TROCCHI,ALEXANDER-Cain's Book-NY-1960-1st ed (t5,f,dj) 50.00

TROTH,L G-South Dakota Facts-Pierre-(ca.1930)-16p-pict wrps,col plts (t7,f) 22.50

TROTSKY,LEON-My Life-NY-1930-Scribner-599p-1st ed (r1,sl sun sp) 25.00

TROTZKY,LEON-Bolsheviki & World Peace-NY-1918-Boni & Liveright-239p (r1) 15.00

TROUP,LORIS-Tasting Spoon-NY-(1955)-Citadel Pr-286p-dec e.p.-1st ed (m6,dj) 15.00

TROUP,LORIS-Tasting Spoon-NY-(1955)-Citadel-286p-grn cl,col e.p.-1st ed (q8,dj) 17.50

TROVILLION,VIOLET-Recipes and Remedies of Early England-Herrin-1946-Trovillion Priv Pr-76p-red bds,ltd ed (m6) 50.00

TROW-SMITH,ROBERT-History of British Livestock Husbandry 1700 to 1900-Lond-1959-Routledge & K Paul-1st ed (f10,dj) 45.00

TROWBRIDGE,J T-South-Hartford-1866-L Stebbins-xii,590p-11 maps,10 plts-1st ed (n2,sl fox,extra t.p.) 85.00

TROWBRIDGE,JOHN-My Own Story-Bost-1903-HMCo-1st ed (hh5,f) 20.00

TROYAT,HENRI-Divided Soul-GC-1973-Dbldy-1st US ed (x9,dj) 10.00

TRUAX,CAROL-Ladies Home Journal Cookbook-1960-Dbldy-1st ed (v6,sl wn dj) 14.00

TRUAX,CAROL-Ladies' Home Journal Cookbook-GC-(1960)-Dbldy-sm 4to-728p-thumb index,dbl cols (u6) 30.00

TRUAX,RHODA-Doctors Warren of Boston-Bost-1968-369p-illus e.p.-1st prtg (g10,dj) 30.00

TRUE,ALFRED C-History of Agricultural Education in the United States, 1785 to 1925-Wash D.C.-1929-GPO-x+436p-blu cl-Dept of Agri,Misc Publ.#36-1st ed (a2) 35.00

TRUE,F W-Whalebone Whales of the Western North Atlantic-Wash-1904-Smiths. Vol.33-4to-332p-cl,50 plts (y8,sl tn,H H Brimley bkplt) 150.00

TRUEBLOOD,TED-Angler's Handbook-NY-1949-8vo-434p-photos-1st ed (m3) 22.50

TRUEBLOOD,TED-Hunter's Handbook-NY-1954-8vo-247p-photos-1st ed (m3,f,dj) 20.00

TRUESDELL,S R-Rifle, Its Development for Big Game Hunting-PA-1947-274p-photos (gg3,f,dj) 115.00

TRUETA,JOSEP-ET AL-Studies of the Renal Circulation-Springfield-1947-187p-83 figs-1st ed (g10,dj wn) 50.00

TRUEX,PHILIP-City Gardener-NY-1964-Knopf-355p-cl (x6,dj) 24.00

TRUMAN,BEN-Santa Monica, Illustrated Souvenir-ca.1897-Daily Outlook-4to-56p-wrps,photos (d3) 45.00

TRUMBO,DALTON-Johhny Got His Gun-Phila-1939-Lippincott-1st ed (c8,dj) 350.00

TRUMBO,DALTON-Remarkable Andrew-1941-Lippincott-1st ed (kk6,dj) 40.00

TRUMBULL,BENJAMIN-Compendium of the Indian Wars of New England-Hartford-1926-Mitchell-63p-stiff wrps-ltd to 400c-1st ed (h2,sl soil) 45.00

TRUMBULL,JAMES H-Natick Dictionary-Wash-1903-GPO/Bur Amer Ethno-347p-Bull.25 (bb4) 25.00

TRUSS,SELDON-Coroner Presides-NY-1932-Minton,Balch-1st US ed (d4,sp chip dj) 50.00

TRUSS,SELDON-Truth About Clair Veryan-NY-1957-Dbldy CC-1st US ed (f4,f,dj) 10.00

TRUZZI,MARCELLO-Caldron Cookery-NY-(1969)-Meredith Pr-115p-bds,illus,V Chess-1st ed (m6,soil dj) 25.00

TRYCKARE,T-Lore of Sportfishing-NY-1976-lg 4to-419p-2500 illus (m3,as new in dj) 40.00

TRYON,R M-ET AL-Ferns and Fern Allies of Wisconsin-Madison-1940-U of Wisc-158p-grn cl wi gilt,maps,illus-1st ed (o2) 15.00

TRYON,WARREN-Mirror for Americans-(1952)-U of Chig-467 to 793p-Amer Travelers,Vol.III,illus (r8,chip dj) 15.00

TSELEMENTES,NICHOLAS-Greek Cookery-NY-1959-Divry-240p-grn cl (q8,dj) 16.50

TUBB,E C-Alien Dust-lond-(1955)-Bordman-1st ed (f3,sl fox edges,dj) 50.00

TUBB,E C-Escape into Space-Lond-(1969)-Sidwick & Jackson-1st ed (f3,f,dj) 25.00

TUCHMAN,BARBARA-Zimmermann Telegram-NY-1958-Viking-1st ed (f8,dj chip,wn) 45.00

TUCK,JAMES A-Onondaga Iroquois Prehistory-1971-Syracuse U Pr-xiii,255p-44 plts-1st ed (bb7,dj) 35.00*

TUCK,L M-Snipes-1972-Can Wldlf Ser-428p-92 figs (bb3,f) 35.00

TUCKER,GLENN-Hancock the Superb-Indpls-(1960)-Bobbs Merrill-368p-Nevins II,95-1st ed (ee4,dj) 50.00

TUCKER,GLENN-Tecumseh-Indpls-(1956)-Bobbs-Merrill-399p-maps-1st ed (cc4,dj) 35.00

TUCKER,PATRICK T-Riding the High Country-Caldwell-1933-Caxton Pr-Adams Herd 2342-1st ed (u1,f,dj) 100.00

TUCKER,TED-Practical Projects for the Blacksmith-Emmaus-1980-Rodale-1st prtg (h9,dj) 18.00

TUCKER,W-Dove-1948-Rinehart-1st ed (x7,f,dj) 45.00

TUDOR,F E-Trout in Troubled Waters-Lond-1955-8vo-152p-photos-1st ed (m3,f,dj) 15.00

TUDOR,TASHA-Snow Before Christmas-Lond,NY,Tor-(1941)-Oxford U Pr-cl,pict cov labl-1st ed (aa9,f,sl brwnd dj) 25.00

TUER,ANDREW W-ED.-Stories from Old Fashioned Children's Books-Lond-1899,1900-Leadenhall Pr-orig g pict cl,t.e.g.,frntis,illus(1 hand col)-1st ed (dd10) 70.00

TUFTS,R W-Birds of Nova Scotia-Halifax-1962-8vo-481p-cl,40 col plts-1st ed (y8,sp dmpstnd,dj wn) 45.00

TUNBRIDGE,B R-Guide to the Inland Angling Waters of Victoria-Victoria-1976-8vo-149p-maps-1st prntg (m3) 10.00

TUNNARD,CHRIS-Man Made America-1963-Yale-479p-cl (x6,dj) 50.00

TUNNARD,CHRISTOPHER-Man-Made America: Chaos or Control-New Haven-1963-Yale-lg 4to-xii,479p-cl,illus,maps,plans (cc10,dj) 50.00

TUNNEY,T-Throttled-1919-SM-photos,scarce in dj-1st ed (x7,wn dj) 95.00

TUNNICLIFFE,C F-Sketchbook of Birds-1979-Holt Rinehart-oblng 4to-123 col plts-1st US ed (bb3,f,dj) 25.00

TUNNICLIFFE,C F-Tunnicliffe's Birds-1984-Little,Brown-folio-160p-78 col plts-1st US ed (bb3,f,dj) 45.00

TURBOTT,E G-ED.-Buller's Birds of New Zealand-1982-Whitcoulls-261p-48 tip in col plts-rprnt of 1888 ed (bb3,as new in dj,box) 75.00

TURCOTT,AGNES W-Land of the Big Goose-(Dryden)-nd(ca.1960)-128,(1)p-wrps (f1) 17.50

TURGEON,CHARLOTTE-ED.-Creative Cooking Course-Balt-1975-Ottenheimer-thk 4to-red/wht cl,col photos (q8) 18.50

TURING,H D-Trout Fishing-Lond-1935-12mo-254p-1st ed (m3) 20.00

TURING,H D-Trout Problems-Lond-1948-8vo-190p-illus (m3,f,dj) 15.00

TURING,H D-Where to Fish-Lond-1936-8vo-442p+ads-col plts,fldg map (m3) 15.00

TURKEY-Being Sketches from Life by the Roving Englishman-Lond-1877-Routledge-2nd ed (m8) 75.00

TURKIN,HY-Vest Pocket Encyclopedia-NY-(1956)-320p-wrps (n1) 15.00

TURNBULL,COLIN M-Wayward Servants-Lond-(1966)-Eyre & Spottiswoode-8vo-390p-papr over bds,maps-1st ed (y5,dj) 40.00

TURNBULL,JAMES-History of Animals-Steubenville-1831-J & B Turnbull-204p-lea,12p col plts-rare (n1,lacks 2 leaves & frnt cov) 250.00

TURNBULL,S R-Samurai, a Military History-NY-(1977)-Macmillan-lg 8vo-304p-27 col plts-1st US ed (gg5,f,f dj) 30.00

TURNER,D C-Vampire Bat-Balt-1975-8vo-145p-cl,15 plts (y8,dj) 17.50

TURNER,D-Vampire Bat-1975-Johns Hopkins-145p-photos (bb3,f,dj) 13.00

TURNER,DAN-Expos Inside Out-1983-McClelland & Stewart (ff2,f,dj) 25.00

TURNER,DICK-Wings of the North-Saanichton-c.1976-Hancock Hs-288p-illus,maps (k10,dj) 15.00*

TURNER,E S-Call the Doctor, a Social History of Medical Men-Lond-1958-320p-1st ed (dd3) 40.00

TURNER,FREDERICK W-ED.-Portable North American Indian Reader-NY-1974-Viking-12mo-628p-1st ed (z4,dj) 10.00

TURNER,GEORGE-Beloved Son-1978-Faber & Faber-1st ed (r9,f,dj) 25.00

TURNER,GEORGE-Vaneglory-Lond-1981-Faber-1st ed (r9,f,dj) 25.00

TURNER,HENRY S-Original Journals of...-Norman-(1966)-173p-illus-1st ed (g7,f,dj) 40.00

TURNER,JAMES-Politics of Landscape-1979-Harvard-8vo-237p-11 figs (j10,f,dj) 11.00

TURNER,JOHN K-Barbarous Mexico-Austin-(1969)-U of Tex-322p-illus (cc4) 20.00

TURNER,JOHN P-North West Mounted Police 1873 to 1893...-Ottawa-1950-2 vols-wrps,fldg map-scarce (a1,sl dmpstnd) 100.00

TURNER,JOHN P-North West Mounted Police-Ottawa-1950-Edmond Cloutier-2 vols-card covs,illus,fldg map-Peel 4226 (cc7) 125.00*

TURNER,KATHARINE C-Red Men Calling on the Great White Father-Norman-(1951)-U of Okla Pr-235p-illus,map-1st ed (bb4,dj) 30.00

TURNER,LORENZO D-Africanisms in the Gullah Dialect-Chig-(1949)-U of Chig Pr-8vo-317p-cl-1st ed (y5,sl chip dj) 25.00

TURNER,LORETTA E-ED.-How Women Earn a Competence-(Oberlin)-(1902)-News Prntg Co-320p-cl,ports (d1) 50.00

TURNER,MARTHA A-Sam Houston and His Twelve Women-Austin-1966-Pemberton-96p-photos-1st ed (a9,dj) 75.00

TURNER,MARTHA-William Barret Travis-Waco-(1972)-Texian Pr-318p-illus-1st ed (f9,dj) 45.00

TURNER,MISS BESSIE-Woman in the Case-NY/Lond-1875-Carleton/Low,Son & Co-288p-cl-Wright 2561 (n1) 50.00

TURNER,NEWMAN-Fertility Pastures-Lond-1955-Faber & Faber-204p-illus-1st ed (t8,chip dj) 15.00

TURNER,NEWMAN-Herdsmanship-Lond-1952-Faber & Faber-236p-photos-1st ed (t8,chip dj) 10.00

TURNER,O-History of the Pioneer Settlement of Phelps and Gorham's Purchase...Pioneer History of Monroe County-Rochester-1851-Erastus Darrow-624p-1st ed (u2,sp sl wn,sl fox) 300.00

TURNER,ROBERT D-Vancouver Island Railroads-San Marino-1973-170p-1st ed (n4,f,dj) 27.50

TURNER,SAMUEL-Siberia-Lond-1905-420p-gold emboss red cov & sp,t.e.g.-1st ed (a4,ex libr) 85.00

TURNER,T HUDSON-Some Account of Domestic Architecture in England-Lond-1851-J H Parker-lg 8vo-4 vols-3/4 grn mor/mrbld bds,bands,illus-1st ed (oo8,vf) 385.00

TURNER,W J-ED.-Panorama of Rural England-NY-nd(ca.1940)-Chanticleer Pr-318p-grn bds,48 col plts (k6) 20.00

TURNER,WM-Transfer Printing on Enamels, Porcelain & Pottery-Lond-1907-175p-t.e.g.,etched frntis,48 glossy plts (a3) 150.00

TURNOR,R-19th Century Architecture in Britain-Lond-1950-127 illus-1st ed (h10,dj sl chip) 35.00

TURPIN,DR. JAMES W-Vietnam Doctor-NY-(1966)-McGraw-Hill-210p-bds-1st ed so stated (h1,tape mrks rear e.p.,dj) 12.50

TUSKA,JON-Billy the Kid-Westport-(1983)-Greenwood-xvi,235p-cl,map,photos-1st ed (v1) 35.00

TUTEN,FREDERIC-Adventures of Mao on the Long March-(NY)-(1971)-Citadel-auth 1st bk-scarce-1st ed (a10,f,dj) 75.00

TUTHILL,MRS.L C-Boarding-School Girl-Bost-1848-Crosby & Nichols-139p-cl (k1) 40.00

TUTTLE,BRUCE R-ED.-Standard Book of Fishing-NY-1950-4to-532p-deluxe ed bnd in full mission lea,col frontis,photos,illus (m3,f) 25.00

TUTTLE,CHARLES R-Alaska-Seattle-1914-Franklin Shuey-8vo-318p-32 illus-1st ed (cc5,sl soil) 25.00

TUTTLE,CHARLES R-COMP.-History of the Border Wars of Two Centuries...-Chig-1874-Wall & Co-608p-drwngs-1st ed (bb4,lacks rear fly leaf) 110.00

TUTTLE,JOSEPH F-Life of William Tuttle, the Self Made Man and Consistent Christian...-NY-(1852)-192p-port-abridged by auth-2nd ed (aa6) 40.00

TUTTLE,WILLIAM-Bottle Hill and Madison-(np)-(1917)-(16),(247)p-cl,illus-ltd to 500c,nbrd (aa6) 75.00

TUTTLE,WILLIAM-Life of..., Compiled from an Autobiography under the Name of John Homespun-NY-1852-304p-cl,port (aa6) 40.00

TUTUOLA,AMOS-Brave African Huntress-NY-1958-1st US ed (n5,f,dj) 35.00

TUTUOLA,AMOS-My Life in the Bush of Ghosts-NY-1954-1st US ed (n5,dj) 40.00

TUTUOLA,AMOS-Palm Wine Drinkard-NY-1953-Grove-auth 1st bk-1st Amer ed (y2,f,dj) 75.00

TWAIN,MARK-$30,000 Bequest-1906-Harpers-1st ed (x2) 175.00

TWAIN,MARK-1,000,000 Pound Bank Note...-NY-1893-Chas L Webster-tan dec cov-BAL 3436-1st ed (f2,sl soil cov) 85.00

TWAIN,MARK-Adventures of Huckleberry Finn-NY-1885-Webster-orig publ sheep bndg-wi all key first issue points-1st ed (kk9,hngs rprd,custom cl box) 1,750.00

TWAIN,MARK-Adventures of Tom Sawyer-Hartford-1898-Amer Publ Co-(275p)-orig blk stmpd,blu dec cl,gilt,illus-later prtg-BAL 3369 (hh9,vf) 85.00

TWAIN,MARK-Adventures of Tom Sawyer-NY-1930-Random-4to-132p-1/2 calf & pict cl,ltd to 2000c,autg,illus,D McKay (s3,sl scuff sp) 50.00

TWAIN,MARK-American Claimant-NY-1892-Webster-8vo-dec cl-1st ed (t1) 110.00

TWAIN,MARK-Christian Science-NY-1907-Harper-1st ed (z2,scrape cov & sp) 45.00

TWAIN,MARK-Christian Science-NY-1907-Harper-1st ed,ltr state (z9) 37.50

TWAIN,MARK-Double Barrelled Detective Story-1902-Harpers-1st ed (x7) 135.00

TWAIN,MARK-English As She Is Spoke-Girard-(1923)-Haldeman-Julius-59p+5p ads-wrps-Little Blue Bk #166 (n1,drknd rear wrps) 10.00

TWAIN,MARK-Following the Equator-Hartford-1897-Amer Publ-dec blu cl-1st ed,1st state (k8) 135.00

TWAIN,MARK-Higher Animals: A Mark Twain Bestiary-1976-Harper & Row-1st ed (x2,f,dj) 22.00

TWAIN,MARK-Horse's Tale-NY-1907-Harper & Bros-red dec covs-1st ed (h8) 65.00

TWAIN,MARK-Innocents Abroad-Hartford-1869-8vo-publ sheep,illus-Bal 3316-1st ed,2nd iss (x3,scuff,rub,weak hngs) 125.00

TWAIN,MARK-Is Shakespeare Dead?-1909-Harpers-1st ed (x2) 80.00

TWAIN,MARK-Letters From the Earth-NY-1962-Harper & Row-1st ed (f8,f,dj) 45.00

TWAIN,MARK-Life on the Mississippi-Bost-1883-James R Osgood & Co-illus,a.e.g.-BAL 3411-1st ed,2nd state (c10,sl rub) 300.00

TWAIN,MARK-Mark Twain Able Yachtsman Interviews Himself on Why Lipton Failed to Lift the Cup-(NY)-(1920)-Merle Johnson-one of 97c(of 109)in wrps-BAL #3529-1st separate prtg (s1,sl soil cov,few spot,stns) 200.00

TWAIN,MARK-Mark Twain's Letters From Hawaii-Lond-1967-Chatto & Windus-1st Brit ed (y1,f,dj) 30.00

TWAIN,MARK-Mark Twain's Letters From Hawaii-NY-1966-Appleton-1st ed (t4,f,f dj) 25.00

TWAIN,MARK-Mark Twain's San Francisco-NY-(1963)-McGraw-Hill-cl sp,gry bds-1st ed (f2,dj) 30.00

TWAIN,MARK-My Father Mark Twain with Hitherto Unpublished Letters of...-NY-1931-Harper's-photos-1st ed (f8,f,f dj) 65.00

TWAIN,MARK-Notebooks and Journals-Berkeley-1975-Univ of Cal Pr-two vols,gry cl,illus (f2,dj) 35.00

TWAIN,MARK-Prince and the Pauper-Bost-1882-James R Osgood-8vo-411p-orig grn cl,dec in blk & gilt,illus-BAL 3402-1st ed,1st state bndg (hh9,sl wn & rub) 175.00

TWAIN,MARK-Roughing It-Hartford-1872-591,(1)p-lea,1st iss wi no words missing on lines 20 & 21 on pg 242,adv present on final unnmbrd pg-BAL 3337-1st Amer ed (n1,rbkd,rnfrcd inner hngs) 50.00

TWAIN,MARK-Roughing It-Hartford-1872-Amer Publ Co-3/4 lea-1st ed (l9,rbnd,sl wn) 500.00

TWAIN,MARK-Roughing It-NY-1913-rprnt Six Guns #443-scarce (t7) 15.00

TWAIN,MARK-Simon Wheeler, Detective-1963-N.Y.P.L.-ltd to 1500c-1st ed (x7,sl spot sp) 60.00

TWAIN,MARK-Tom Sawyer Abroad. By Huck Finn-NY-1894-Chas L Webster & Co-8vo-219p+ads-pict wht cl,prtd in orng & blk,illus by D Beard,bndg state "A"-BAL 3440-1st ed (hh9,cov sl soil) 450.00

TWAIN,MARK-Tragedy of Pudd'nhead Wilson-1894-A.P.C.-1st ed (x2) 350.00

TWAIN,MARK-Tragedy of Pudd'nhead Wilson-Hartford-1894-Amer Publ Co-3/4 lea-1st ed,1st state (l9,sl wn) 500.00

TWAIN,MARK-Tragedy of Pudd'nhead Wilson-Hartford-1894-Amer Publ Co-brwn cl,1st iss (sheets bulk 1 1/8 inches)-BAL 3442-1st ed,1st issue (f2,sl flecking frnt cov) 275.00

TWAIN,MARK-Tramp Abroad-CT-1880-g pict cov,328 illus-2nd issue (r2,sp chip,cors rub) 100.00

TWAIN,MARK-Tramp Abroad-Hartford-1880-631p-1/2 lea,mrbld e.p.,g stmpd emboss sp,328 illus-1st ed,2nd state (q10) 175.00

TWEEDIE,MAJ GEN W-Arabian Horse-Alhambra-1961-Borden-4to-411p-illus (j9,dj) 125.00

TWIGG,ENA-Ena Twigg: Medium-NY-Hawthorn Bks-8vo-xiii,297p-1st ed (aa7,dj) 15.00*

TWINING,ERNEST-Art & Craft of Stained Glass-1928-Pitman-238p-10 plts(5 col),3 sheets of drwngs-1st ed (cc8) 145.00

TWITCHELL,RALPH E-History of the Military Occupation of the Territory of New Mexico from 1846 to 1851-Denver-1909-Smith Brooks-394p-illus-1st ed (d3) 100.00

TWITCHELL,RALPH E-Leading Facts of New Mexican History-Cedar Rapids-1911 thru 17-5 vols-red buckr-Howes T443-rare-1st ed (z1,recent djs) 1,500.00

TWITCHELL,RALPH E-Leading Facts of New Mexico History-Albuq-1963-Horn & Wallace-2 vols-fldg maps,illus-Howes T443-rprnt (d3) 250.00

TWITCHELL,RALPH E-Spanish Archives of New Mexico...-(Cedar Rapids)-1914-2 vols-illus-1st ed (u7,wn djs) 500.00

TWO LEGACIES-Cambridge-1863-Riverside Pr-8vo-71p-publ cl-1st ed (w6,sl wn & fade cl) 45.00

TWO WAY TELEVISION AND A PICTORIAL ACCOUNT OF ITS BACKROUND-(NY)-(1930)-Bell Lab-8vo-40p-prtd wrps in rare pict dj,photos-scarce (b3,f,sl chip dj) 125.00

TWOMBLY,GEORGE F-All American Dropout-1967-self publ-photos-1st ed (s8,dj) 35.00

TWOMBLY,ROBERT C-Frank Lloyd Wright-NY et al-(1973)-Harper & Row-photos-1st ed (bb1,as new in dj) 25.00

TYACKE,SARAH-ED.-English Map Making, 1500 to 1650-Lond-1983-Brit Libr (v4,as new in dj) 75.00

TYAS,ROBERT-Favorite Field Flowers or Wild Flowers of England-Lond-1848-Houlston-196p-12 handcol plts (x6,ex-libr) 75.00

TYERS,PAUL D-Television Reception Technique-1937-144p-85 illus-1st ed (h6) 40.00

TYGIEL,JULES-Baseball's Great Experiment, Jackie Robinson and His Legacy-1983-Oxford U Pr-1st ed (dd8,dj) 18.00

TYGIEL,JULES-Baseball's Great Experiment-1983-Oxford-1st ed (ff2,f,dj) 25.00

TYLER,ANNE-Accidental Tourist-1985-Knopf-1st ed (w4,f,dj) 30.00

TYLER,ANNE-Celestial Navigation-NY-1974-Knopf-1st ed (b10,f,sl tn dj) 150.00

TYLER,ANNE-Dinner at the Homesick Restaurant-NY-1982-Knopf-1st ed (a5,sl soil dj) 35.00

TYLER,ANNE-Earthly Possessions-1977-Knopf-1st ed (m9,dj) 75.00

TYLER,ANNE-Morgan's Passing-1980-Knopf-1st ed (o9,f,sl rub dj) 45.00

TYLER,ANNE-Morgan's Passing-NY-1980-1st ed (s5,f,dj) 30.00

TYLER,ANNE-Searching for Caleb-NY-1976-Knopf-1st ed (ff6,dj) 125.00

TYLER,ANNE-Searching for Caleb-NY-1976-Knopf-1st ed (y1,f,f dj) 150.00

TYLER,ANNE-Slipping Down Life-Lond-(1983)-Severn Hs-1st Brit ed (m7,f,dj) 45.00

TYLER,ANNE-Slipping Down Life-Lond-(1983)-Severn Hs-1st Brit hdbk ed (d10,as new in dj) 50.00

TYLER,ANNE-Slipping-Down Life-NY-1970-Knopf-1st ed (c10,f,dj) 200.00

TYLER,ANNE-Visit with Eudora Welty-Chig-nd-Pressworks-wrps-ltd to 100c-1st ed (v5,f) 100.00

TYLER,DAVID B-Bay & River Delaware-Cambridge-1955-4to-(xi),244p-cl,illus (aa6) 30.00

TYLER,DAVID-Wilkes Expedition-Phila-1968-435p-illus (r8) 30.00

TYLER,DONALD H-Old Lawrenceville-(np)-(1965)-x,106,xi-xx p-cl,illus (aa6) 35.00

TYLER,EDGAR-Dinner at the Homesick Restaurant-Lond-1982-1st Brit ed (q5,dj) 35.00

TYLER,HAMILTON-Pueblo Gods and Myths-Norman-1964-313p-Vol 71,Amer Indian Ser-1st ed (t7,f) 22.50

TYLER,LYON G-ED.-Encyclopedia of Virginia Biography-1915-Lewis Hist Publ-5 vols-blk 1/2 lea (dd9,lea badly rub,chip) 100.00

TYLER,MASON W-Recollections of the Civil War-NY-1912-Putnam's-379p-frntis,ports,fldg maps (o7,part uncut,dj) 65.00

TYLER,MOSES C-History of American Literature-NY-1878,1879-Putnam's-8vo-2 vols-orig cl,t.e.g.-1st ed (w2) 60.00

TYLER,MOSES C-Literary History of the American Revolution, 1763 to 1783-NY-1897-Putnam's-2 vols-maroon cl,t.e.g.-1st ed (f2,sl fade sp,sl sep hng v 2) 50.00

TYLER,RON-ED.-Alfred Jacob Miller-Ft.Worth-1982-480p-119 plts(incl col),fldg map-1st ed (d7,f,dj) 75.00

TYLER,RON-ED.-Alfred Jacob Miller-Ft.Worth-1982-Amon Carter Mus-4to-viii,480p-cl,119 plts(incl col),fldg map-1st ed (v1,dj) 60.00

TYLER,RONNIE C-Mexican War-Austin-1973-90p-col maps-1st ed (t7,f,dj) 12.50

TYLER,SERGEANT DANIEL-Concise History of Mormon Battalion in Mexican War-(SLC)-1881-(10)-376p-orig lea-Howes T447-rare-1st ed (z1,rub,crack) 350.00

TYLER,SYDNEY-San Francisco's Great Disaster...-Phila-1906-Ziegler-424p-illus (d3,hngs broken) 20.00

TYLOR,EDWARD B-Primitive Culture-Lond-1929-John Murray-cl,2 vols-5th ed (l8) 55.00

TYNDALL,JOHN-Essays on the Floating Matter of the Air in Relation to Putrefaction and Infection-NY-1882-Appleton-xx+338p-brwn cl-1st Amer ed (c2) 100.00

TYNDALL,JOHN-Forms of Water-NY-1899-196p-t.e.g.,35 engrvngs (o10,f) 25.00

TYNDALL,JOHN-Hours of Exercise in the Alps-Lond-1871-473p-1st Brit ed (a4,hngs weak) 165.00

TYNDALL,JOHN-Lectures on Light-NY-1873-194p-1st ed (dd3) 75.00

TYNDALL,JOHN-Lessons in Electricity-1883-113p-58 illus-rare-1st ed (h6) 40.00

TYNDALL,RUTH R-Eat Yourself Full-NY-(1967)-McKay-274p-blk cl,dec e.p. (q8,dj) 15.00

TYRE,ROBERT-Saddlebag Surgeon-Tor-1954-Dent-8vo-v,261p-frntis-1st ed (cc7,chip dj) 20.00*

TYREE,MARION C-Housekeeping in Old Virginia-Louisville-1884-John P Morton-528p+25 manuscrpt pgs & ads,illus grn bds-Bitting 469 (n6,soil & wn bds) 110.00

TYREE,MARION C-Housekeeping in Old Virginia-Louisville-1965-Fav Recipes Pr-528p+ads-dec cov-rprnt (mm6) 28.00

TYRELL,IAN R-Sobering Up-Westport-(1979)-350p-cl-1st ed (g1) 15.00

TYSON,JAMES L-Diary of a Physician in California-Oakland-1955-Biobooks-ltd to 500c-(rprnt of 1850 ed)-Howes T451 (p6,f) 37.50

TYSON,JOB R-Discourse on the Surviving Remnant of the Indian Race in the US-Phila-1836-38p-Rader #3169-scarce-1st ed (t7,lacks wrps) 30.00

TYTELL,JOHN-Naked Angels-NY-1976-1st ed (x8,f,dj) 15.00

U.S. COMM OF PATENTS-Report for the Year 1854. Arts and Manufactures-Wash D.C.-1855-A.O.P. Nicholson-2 vols-blk cl,illus (c2,sl stnd) 55.00

U.S. NAVY AMPHIBIOUS TRAINING BASE-U.S.N.A.T.B. Scrap Book-(Solomons)-(1944)-(200)p-wrps,photos (hh8,sl soil,cor bent) 40.00

U.S. SANITARY COMM., CLEVELAND BRANCH-Our Acre and Its Harvest-Cleve-1869-511p-illus-1st ed (c4) 60.00

U.S. STRATEGIC BOMBING SURVEY-Naval Analysis Division-np-(1946)-lg 8vo-2 vols,blu cl,maps,plans-1st ed (k2) 75.00

UCHILL IDA L-Pioneers, Peddlers, and Tsadikim-Denver-(1957)-Sage Bks-327p-map e.p.-1st ed (cc4,dj) 25.00

UDALL,STEWART L-National Parks of America-Waukesha-(1972)-226p-cl,col plts (o1,dj) 12.50

UDDERZOOK MYSTERY!-Phila-(1873)-Barclay-112p-pict wrps (c1,wn) 40.00

UDEN,GRANT-Dictionary of British Ships and Seamen-NY-1981-St.Martin's-thk 8vo-561p-maps,photos,drwngs (nn1,dj) 45.00

UDOLF,ROY-Handbook of Hypnosis for Professionals-NY-(1981)-Van Nostrand Reinhold-(xvi)+366+(2)p-1st ed (y9,dj) 20.00

UHER,VLADIMIR-Dialogue of Forms-NY-1975-St.Martin's Pr-sm folio-174p-cl-1st ed (t3,dj) 75.00

UHNAK,DOROTHY-Bait-1968-Simon-1st ed (s10,dj) 10.00

ULANOV,BARRY-Handbook of Jazz-NY-1957-Viking-1st ed (w1,f,dj) 20.00

ULANOV,BARRY-History of Jazz in America-NY-1952-Viking-1st ed (w1,f,dj) 25.00

ULANOV,BARRY-Incredible Crosby-NY-(1948)-Whittlesley-8vo-336p-16p photos-1st ed (ee5,dj) 15.00

ULLMAN,JAMES R-Age of Mountaineering-Phila-1954-352p-1st impr (p10,f,dj) 20.00

ULLMAN,JAMES R-Americans on Everest-Phila-1964-429p-56 plts,maps-1st ed (p10,dj) 25.00

ULLMAN,JAMES R-High Conquest-Phila-1941-334p-illus,map-1st ed (q10,f,dj) 12.00

ULLMAN,JAMES R-Kingdom of Adventure, Everest-Lond-1948-Collins-8vo-320p-29 plts,4 maps-1st Brit ed (ff5,dj sl chip,tn) 15.00

ULLMAN,JAMES R-Kingdom of Adventure-NY-1947-411p-illus,map-1st ed (q10,f,dj tn) 10.00

ULLMAN,JAMES R-Straight Up-NY-1968-287p-32 plts-1st ed (p10,f,dj) 23.00

ULLMAN,JAMES R-Where the Bong Tree Grows-Cleve,NY-1963-World-8vo-316p-dec grn & blu cl,map e.p.-1st ed (p8,dj) 30.00

ULLOM,,JUDITH C-Folklore of the North American Indians-Wash-1969-126p-pict cl,illus-1st ed (t7) 15.00

ULLSTEIN,HERMAN-Rise and Fall of the House of Ullstein-NY-1943-S&S-8vo-308p-1st ed (aa5,f,dj) 25.00

ULMANN,DORIS-Book of Portraits of the Faculty of the Medical Department of the Johns Hopkins University Baltimore-Balt-1922-folio-untrimmed,36 ports-rare-1st ed (dd3,f) 750.00

ULMANN,DORIS-Portrait of American Editors-NY-1925-Wm Rudge-folio-cl/bds-ltd to 375c (y3) 350.00

UMBERGER,J-Collecting Character Bottles-1969-Corker Bk Co-176p-illus (cc8,dj) 30.00

UMBSTAETTER,H D-Red Hot Dollar-Bost-1911-Page-1st ed (j4) 25.00

UMPLEBY,JOSEPH-Geology & Ore Deposits of Republic Mining District-Olympia-1910-Wash Geo Survey,Bull.#1-65p-13 plts(incl 4 maps,1 fldg) (r8,sp chewed) 25.00

UNDERHILL,EVELYN-Jacopone da Todi-Lond-1919-Dent-cl,frntis.illus-1st ed (n8) 45.00

UNDERHILL,EVELYN-Mystics of the Church-Lond-nd-James Clarke & Co-cl-2nd imprssn (l8) 25.00

UNDERHILL,FRANCIS-Driving for Pleasure-NY-1897-Appleton-4to-1/2 lea & suede (f10,lt stnd cov) 395.00

UNDERHILL,RUTH M-Navajos-Norman-1956-299p-photos,maps-1st ed (t7,dj) 20.00

UNDERHILL,RUTH-Pueblo Crafts-(Lawrence)-(1944)-US Ind Serv,Ind Hndcrft#7-147p-orig cl,photos,map-1st ed (v7) 25.00

UNDERHILL,RUTH-Red Man's Religion-Chig-(1965)-290p-photos-1st prtg (v7,f,dj) 45.00

UNDERHILL,RUTH-Work a Day Life of the Pueblos-Phoenix-1946-US Indian Serv-174p-orig cl,photos-Indian Life & Customs No.4-1st ed (v7) 35.00

UNDERSEA WARFARE-A SURVEY ON HUMAN FACTORS IN...-Wash D.C.-1949-Nat'l Rsrch Cncl-lg 8vo-x+541p-grn cl,figs-1st ed (j2) 40.00

UNDERWOOD,FRANCIS H-Life of Henry Wadsworth Longfellow-Bost-1882-355p-cl (h1) 15.00

UNDERWOOD,JOHN J-Alaska, an Empire in the Making-NY-1913-Dodd,Mead-dec cov,fldg col map,48 plts-1st ed (ee7,map tn) 50.00

UNDERWOOD,JOHN J-Alaska-1913-Dodd,Mead-449p-pict cov,photo plts-1st ed (u8,sl wn sp) 35.00

UNDERWOOD,LAMAR-ED.-Bobwhite Quail Book-1980-Amwell Pr-8vo-442p-ltd to 1000c,nbrd,autg,illus (m3,vf,box) 150.00

UNDERWOOD,LAMAR-ED.-Deer Book-1980-Amwell Pr-8vo-460p-ltd to 1000c,nbrd,autg,illus by A Barker (m3,vf,box) 125.00

UNDERWOOD,LAMAR-ED.-Duck Hunter's Book-1982-Amwell Press-4to-607p-ltd to 1000c,nbrd,autg,illus by T Hennessey (m3,vf,box) 150.00

UNDERWOOD,MICHAEL-Murder with Malice-NY-1977-St.Martin's-1st US ed (e4,dj) 15.00

UNDERWOOD,PETER-Complete Book of Dowsing and Divining-Lond-1980-Rider & Co-cl,illus-1st ed (n8,vf,dj) 20.00

UNDERWOOD,W L-Wild Brother-Bost-1921-8vo-140p-photos (m3) 15.00

UNDSET,SIGRID-Burning Bush-1932-Knopf-1st ed (x10,f,dj) 35.00

UNDSET,SIGRID-Ida Elisabeth-1933-Knopf-1st ed (x10,f,f dj) 35.00

UNGER,FREDERIC W-With "Bobs" and Kruger-Phila-1901-412p-pict grn cl,photos-scarce-1st ed (b7,recased) 150.00

UNGER,FREDERICK W-Roosevelt's African Trip-1909-priv prntd-4to-392p-pict cov,illus,photos (m3) 20.00

UNGERER,MIRIAM-Too Hot to Cook Book-(1966)-Walker-176p-red cl,illus-1st ed (q8,dj) 12.50

UNION ARMY-Madison-1908-Fed Publ-8 vols-3/4 lea,mrbld edges (v2,sl wn cor) 750.00

UNITED STATES ARMY - WAR DEPARTMENT-Provisional Small Arms Firing Manual-Wash-1909-18mo-263p-illus (m3) 30.00

UNITED STATES FISHERIES COMMISSION-Manual of Fish Culture Based on the Methods of the United States Commission of Fish & Fisheries-Wash D.C.-1900-8vo-340p+plts,illus (m3) 25.00

UNITED STATES FISHERIES COMMISSION-Proceedings & Papers of the National Fishery Congress Held at Tampa,Florida,January 19-24,1898-Wash D.C.-1898-4to-222p-photos (m3) 35.00

UNITED STATES FISHERIES COMMISSION-Report of the Commissioner for the Year Ending June 30,1889-Wash D.C.-1892-8vo-902p-illus,fldg maps,charts (m3) 50.00

UNJUST JUDGE-Mansfield-1854-352p-cl-scarce (j1,cov fade,sp wn,fox) 50.00

UNRAU,WM E-Kaw People-Phoenix-1975-104p-cl,frntis,col photos,map-Indian Tribal Ser-1st ed (t7) 20.00

UNSELD,SIEGFRIED-Author and His Publisher-Chig,Lond-(1980)-U of Chig Pr-1st US ed (bb1,f,sl rub dj) 15.00

UNSWORTH,WALT-Encyclopedia of Mountaineering-NY-1975-St.Martin's-Neate 858-1st ed (f8,f,dj) 40.00

UNTERECKER,JOHN-Voyager-NY-(1969)-FS&G-photos-1st ed (bb1,f,dj) 30.00

UNTERMANN,ERNEST-How We Are Robbed-Girard-1903-Wayland-wrps-1st ed (w5) 15.00

UNTERMEYER,LOUIS-Adirondack Cycle-NY-1929-Random-orig wrps-ltd to 475c-1st ed (k8,f) 25.00

UNTERMEYER,LOUIS-ED.-Golden Treasury of Poetry-Lond-1969-illus by Anglund-1st ed (y7,dj) 10.00

UNTERMEYER,LOUIS-Pursuit of Poetry-NY-(1969)-S&S-1st ed (bb1,as new in dj) 15.00

UNTRACHT,OPPI-Enameling on Metal-NY-1957-Greenberg-191p-yel cl,illus-(orig ed w/o col frntis of later prtgs)-1st ed (u5,sl soil,sl fade sp) 37.50

UP DE GRAFF,T S-Camping in the Alleghenies or, Bodines-Phila-1883-279p-dec cov & sp,illus-2nd ed (gg3,vf) 75.00

UPDIKE,DANIEL B-ED.-Updike: American Printer and His Merrymount Press-NY-1947-AIGA-1st ed (w1,f) 35.00

UPDIKE,DANIEL B-Some Aspects of Printing Old and New-New Haven-1941-Wm Rudge-tall 8vo-(vi),74p-cl-1st ed (w2,sl rub) 45.00

UPDIKE,JOHN-Assorted Prose-NY-1965-Knopf-1st ed (u10,f,dj) 40.00

UPDIKE,JOHN-Bech is Back-NY-1982-195p-cl-1st ed so stated (d1,f,dj) 15.00

UPDIKE,JOHN-Bech: A Book-Lond-(1970)-Andre Deutsch-1st Brit ed (bb2,f,dj) 45.00

UPDIKE,JOHN-Bech: A Book-NY-1970-Knopf-1st ed (bb1,as new in dj) 35.00

UPDIKE,JOHN-Bech: A Book-NY-1970-Knopf-1st ed (j3,f,dj) 20.00

UPDIKE,JOHN-Bech: A Book-NY-1970-Knopf-ltd to 500c,autg (cc1,as new in box) 125.00

UPDIKE,JOHN-Beloved-Northridge-1982-Lord John-ltd to 100c,autg,w/o dj as iss-1st ed (j3,f) 100.00

UPDIKE,JOHN-Buchanan Dying-Lond-(1974)-Andre Deutsch-1st Brit ed (ee2,f,dj) 50.00

UPDIKE,JOHN-Buchanan Dying-NY-1974-1st ed (z6,as new in dj) 40.00

UPDIKE,JOHN-Centaur-NY-1963-1st ed (q5,dj) 45.00

UPDIKE,JOHN-Coup-NY-1978-Knopf-1st issue wi t.e. yel-1st ed (b5,as new in dj) 30.00

UPDIKE,JOHN-Couples-Lond-(1968)-Andre Deutsch-1st Brit ed (bb2,f,dj) 35.00

UPDIKE,JOHN-Couples-NY-1968-Knopf-1st ed (a10,f,dj) 45.00

UPDIKE,JOHN-Couples-NY-1968-Knopf-1st ed (k3,dj) 15.00

UPDIKE,JOHN-Cunts-NY-(1974)-Frank Hallman-ltd to 276c,autg,iss w/o dj (a10,as new) 300.00

UPDIKE,JOHN-Hoping for a Hoopoe-Lond-1959-Gollancz-auth 1st bk,publ in US as "The Carpentered Hen"-1st Brit ed (z2,f,f dj) 100.00

UPDIKE,JOHN-Marry Me-NY-1976-Knopf-1st trd ed (z2,f,dj) 20.00

UPDIKE,JOHN-Marry Me-NY-1976-Knopf-blue cl-1st trd ed (b5,as new in dj) 30.00

UPDIKE,JOHN-Midpoint & Other Poems-NY-1969-Knopf-1st ed (b5,as new in dj) 40.00

UPDIKE,JOHN-Midpoint and Other Poems-1969-Knopf-1st ed (n9,f,dj) 45.00

UPDIKE,JOHN-Month of Sundays-NY-1975-Knopf-1st trd ed (b5,as new in dj) 25.00

UPDIKE,JOHN-Museums & Women & Other Stories-NY-1972-Knopf-1st ed (b5,as new in dj) 30.00

UPDIKE,JOHN-Of the Farm-NY-1965-Knopf-1st ed (b5,f,dj frnt flap rub) 65.00

UPDIKE,JOHN-Of The Farm-NY-1965-Knopf-1st ed (q2,dj) 95.00

UPDIKE,JOHN-Picked Up Pieces-NY-1975-1st ed (n5,f,f dj) 25.00

UPDIKE,JOHN-Poorhouse Fair-1959-Knopf-1st ed (x2,f,dj) 200.00

UPDIKE,JOHN-Poorhouse Fair-NY-1959-Knopf-1st ed (w5,f,sl chip dj) 150.00

UPDIKE,JOHN-Poorhouse Fair-NY-1959-Knopf-8vo-cl/bds-1st ed (ll10,f,sl rub dj) 225.00

UPDIKE,JOHN-Problems-NY-1979-Knopf-1st ed (b5,as new in dj) 25.00

UPDIKE,JOHN-Rabbit is Rich-NY-(1981)-Knopf-1st ed (ee2,f,dj) 35.00

UPDIKE,JOHN-Rabbit is Rich-NY-1981-Knopf-1st ed (b5,as new in dj) 25.00

UPDIKE,JOHN-Rabbit Redux-1971-Knopf-1st trd ed (n9,f,dj) 35.00

UPDIKE,JOHN-Rabbit Redux-NY-1971-Knopf-1st ed (j3,f,dj) 25.00

UPDIKE,JOHN-Same Door-NY-1959-Knopf-1st ed (q2,dj sl chip & tn) 175.00

UPDIKE,JOHN-Spring Trio-(1982)-Palaemon Pr-tall 8vo-grn dec wrps-ltd to 150c,nbrd,autg-1st ed (u10,f) 100.00

UPDIKE,JOHN-Talk From the Fifties-Northridge-1979-Lord John Pr-ltd to 300c,autg,orig acetate dj-1st ed (l9,f,dj) 135.00

UPDYKE,JAMES-It's Always Four O'Clock-NY-1956-1st ed (p5,sl chip dj) 25.00

UPFIELD,ARTHUR W-Bone is Pointed-1947-Dbldy-1st ed (x7,dj) 48.00

UPFIELD,ARTHUR W-Bushman Who Came Back-NY-1957-Dbldy CC-1st US ed (e4,dj) 25.00

UPFIELD,ARTHUR W-Death of a Lake-1954-CC-1st Amer ed (s10,pgs brwng,dj sl wn) 35.00

UPFIELD,ARTHUR W-Mountains Have a Secret-1948-Dbldy-1st ed (x7,sl tn dj) 40.00

UPFIELD,ARTHUR W-Sands of Windee-Sydney-1958-Angus & Robertson-1st Aust ed (g4,f,dj) 25.00

UPFIELD,ARTHUR W-Sinister Stones-NY-1954-Dbldy-precedes Brit ed-1st ed (e4,sl fox,dj) 35.00

UPFIELD,ARTHUR W-Valley of Smugglers-1960-Dbldy-1st Amer ed (n9,dj tn & chip) 30.00

UPFIELD,ARTHUR W-Valley of Smugglers-1960-Dbldy-1st Amer ed (x10,f,f dj) 25.00

UPFIELD,ARTHUR W-Will of the Tribe-1962-Dbldy-1st ed (x7,f,dj) 33.00

UPFIELD,ARTHUR W-Will of the Tribe-Lond-1962-Heinemann-1st ed (j4,dj) 35.00

UPHAM,CHARLES W-Salem Witchcraft with an Account of Salem Village and a History of Opinions on Witchcraft...-Bost-1867-Wiggin & Lunt-8vo-2 vols-maroon cl-1st ed (s1) 300.00

UPHAM,CHARLES W-Salem Witchcraft...-Bost-1867-Wiggin & Lunt-2 vols,purple cl,fldg map,facs-Howes U21 (m2,sm slit sp vol 2,sl fade) 225.00

UPSON,WILLIAM H-Keep `Em Crawling-NY-(1943)-F&R-1st ed (hh5,f,sl tn dj) 40.00

UPWARD,A-Bride's Madness-1897-Arrowsmith-1st ed (x7) 55.00

UPWARD,A-Lord Alistair's Rebellion-1909-Rivers-1st ed (x7) 50.00

UPWARD,A-Secret History of To Day-1904-C&H-pict cl,illus (x7) 50.00

URBAN,JOHN W-Battlefield and Prison Pen-Phila-(1882)-486p & testimonials-pict cl-1st ed (c4,cov soil,sp fade) 55.00

URE,S-Hawk Lady-1980-Dbldy-215p-photos-1st ed (bb3,f,dj) 14.00

URIS,LEON-Angry Hills-NY-1955-Random-1st ed (f8,f,f dj) 85.00

URQUHART,JOHN W-Electric Light Fitting-1890-226p-89 illus-rare-1st ed (h6) 65.00

URQUHART,JOHN W-Electric Light-1893-412p-153 illus-rare-5th ed (h6) 65.00

URSIN,M J-Guide to the Fishes of the Temperate Atlantic Coast-1977-Dutton-262p-illus-1st ed (bb3,f,dj) 15.00

USINGER,ROBERT-Aquatic Insects of California-Berkeley-1956-4to-508p-illus-1st ed (m3,f,fray & soil dj) 50.00

USSHER,CLARENCE-An American Physician in Turkey-Bost-1917-339p-1st ed (dd3) 40.00

USTINOV,PETER-We Were Only Human-Bost-1961-1st ed (y7,sl fray dj) 10.00

UTAH, A GUIDE TO THE STATE-NY-1941-Amer Guide Ser-593p-illus,map-1st ed (bb8,sp sun dj) 37.50

UTE INDIAN OUTBREAK-Testimony in Relation to...-1880-Mic Doc No.38-205p-qtr lea-scarce (t7,f) 125.00

UTLEY,ROBERT M-American Heritage History of the Indian Wars-NY-1977-Amer Heritage-4to-352p-cl,photos,illus (z4,sl tn dj) 15.00

UTLEY,ROBERT M-Custer and the Great Controversey-LA-1962-184p-illus,e.p. map-Dowd #3035-1st ed (c7,f,dj) 35.00

UTLEY,ROBERT M-Frontier Regulars-NY-(1973)-Macmillan-462p-illus,maps-1st ed (dd4,dj) 50.00

UTLEY,ROBERT M-Frontier Regulars-NY-(1973)-Macmillan-462p-illus,maps-1st ed (gg4,dj) 50.00

UTTLEY,ALLISON-Grey Rabbit's May Day-Lond-(1963)-Collins-12mo-64p-pict bds,col illus,M Tarrant-1st ed (r3) 15.00

UTTLEY,ALLISON-Knot Squirrel-Lond-(1937)-Collins-12mo-bds wi pict pasteon,col illus,M Tempest-1st ed (r3) 35.00

UZANNE,OCTAVE-Book Hunter in Paris-Lond-1893-Elliot Stock-xii,232,(2)p ads-orig g dec red cl,cov illus laid on,t.e.g.,illus-1st ed in Engl (dd10,sp fade,sl dmpstnd cov) 50.00

UZANNE,OCTAVE-French Bookbinders of the Eighteenth Century-Chig-1904-Caxton Club-sm folio-133p wi illus,ltd to 251c (t1,sp labl fade,mstly unopnd) 550.00

VACARESCO,HELENE-Bard of the Dimbovitza-NY-(1892)-Scribner's-8vo-274p-new & enlgd ed (w6) 50.00

VAIL,R W G-Voice of the Old Frontier-NY-1970-492p (t7) 22.50

VAIL,R W G-Voice of the Old Frontier-Phila-1949-U of Penn Pr-8vo-xii,492p-cl-1st ed (w2) 75.00

VAIL,R W G-Voice of the Old Frontier-Phila-1949-Univ of Penn Pr-xii+492p-grn cl-1st ed (k2) 85.00

VAIL,SHARON-Four Poems-NY-1942-Gemor Pr-tall 4to-11p-wrps,ltd to 100c,designed & edit by C Crosby-1st ed (x3,f) 200.00

VALENTIN-Monks of Mount Athos-Lond-1960-Andre Deutsch-cl,illus-1st ed (o8,f,dj) 12.50

VALENZUELA,LUISA-Lizard's Tail-NY-(1983)-FS&G-1st ed (a10,f,dj) 20.00

VALERY,PAUL-Plays-NY-1960-Pantheon-1st ed (z9,f,dj) 20.00

VALIN,JONATHAN-Day of Wrath-NY-1982-Congdon-1st ed (r4,f,dj) 25.00

VALIN,JONATHAN-Final Notice-NY-1980-Dodd-1st ed (w5,f,f dj) 60.00

VALIN,JONATHAN-Lime Pit-1980-Dodd,Mead-auth 1st bk-1st ed (p9,f,dj wi sm tr) 45.00

VALIN,JONATHAN-Lime Pit-NY-1980-Dodd-auth 1st bk-1st ed (v5,f,dj) 50.00

VALJEAN,NELSON-John Steinbeck:The Errant Knight-SF-(1975)-Chronicle Bks-photos-1st ed (a10,f,dj) 30.00

VALLDEJULI,CARMEN A-Art of Caribbean Cookery-1957-Dbldy-254p-dec grn cl,watrcol frntis,illus-1st ed (q8,dj) 15.00

VALLENTIN-LUCHAIRE,ANTONINA-Stresemann-NY-1931-Richard Smith-8vo-359p-1st US ed (jj5,dj) 20.00

VAN ASH,CAY-Master of Villainy-(1972)-Bowling Grn U Popular Pr-312p (g9,dj) 20.00

VAN ASH,CAY-Master of Villainy-Lond-1972-Stacey-illus-1st Brit ed (q4,sl wn cov,dj) 20.00

VAN ATTA,W-Shock Treatment-1961-Dbldy-1st ed (x7,f,dj) 20.00

VAN CLEVE,CHARLOTTE-Three Score Years and Ten-(Mpls)-1888-(Harrison & Smith)-176p-frntis-Howes V21-1st ed (dd4) 65.00

VAN CLEVE,SPIKE-40 Years' Gatherin's-KC-(1977)-303p-illus-1st ed (r8,as new in dj) 18.00

VAN CLEVE,SPIKE-40 Years' Gatherin's-KC-(1977)-Lowell Pr-303p-photos-1st ed (ee4,dj) 25.00

VAN DE BOE,LOUIS-Planning and Planting Your Own Place-NY-1938-xvii,290p-1st prtg (j10,e.p. brwng,sp fade,sl wn) 11.00

VAN DE WATER,FRED F-In Defense of Worms-NY-1949-12mo-182p-1st ed (m3,f,sl chip dj) 18.00

VAN DE WATER,FREDERIC F-Glory Hunter-1934-Bobbs Merrill-394p-1st ed (d3) 45.00

VAN DE WATER,FREDERIC F-Glory Hunter-Indpls-(1934)-Bobbs Merrill-394p-illus-1st ed (gg4) 50.00

VAN DE WATER,FREDERIC F-Glory Hunter-NY-1963-Argosy Antiq-394p-illus,maps-ltd to 750c-Howes V27 (bb4) 35.00

VAN DE WETERING,JANWILLEM-Death of a Hawker-Bost-1977-Houghton-1st ed (j4,f,sl wn dj) 12.50

VAN DE WETERING,JANWILLEM-Empty Mirror-Bost-1974-Houghton Mifflin-cl-1st Amer ed (o8,dj) 16.50

VAN DE WETTERING,JANWILLEM-Corpse on the Dike-Lond-1977-Heinemann-1st Brit ed (p4,dj) 20.00

VAN DENBURGH,ELIZABETH-My Voyage in the United States Frigate "Congress"-NY-1913-Desmond Fitzgerald-8vo-338p-g dec grn cl,11 illus (nn1,sl wn) 45.00

VAN DER BIJL,H J-Thermionic Vacuum Tube-1920-391p-232p-1st ed (h6) 25.00

VAN DER ELSKEN,ED-Sweet Life-NY-1966-Abrams-sm folio-180p-cl,photos-1st ed (t3,dj) 125.00

VAN DER ELSKEN-ED.-Love on the Left Bank-Holland-Export Prtg Office W Vonk-4to-108p-cl,photos-1st ed (q3) 65.00

VAN DER POST,LAURENS-Face Beside the Fire-Lond-1953-Hogarth-311p-1st ed (gg10,dj) 35.00

VAN DER POST,LAURENS-Face Beside the Fire-NY-1953-Morrow-301p-1st US ed (gg10,dj) 25.00

VAN DER POST,LAURENS-Flamingo Feather-NY-1955-Morrow-cl-1st ed (o8,f,dj wn) 10.00

VAN DER POST,LAURENS-Hunter and the Whale-Lond-1967-Hogarth-318p-1st ed (gg10,dj) 20.00

VAN DER POST,LAURENS-Hunter and the Whale-NY-1967-Morrow-1st US ed (hh5,dj) 12.50

VAN DER POST,LAURENS-Lost World of the Kalahari-NY-1958-Morrow-cl-1st ed (o8,vf,dj) 12.50

VAN DER POST,LAURENS-Yet Being Someone Other-Lond-1982-Hogarth Pr-cl-1st ed (l8,vf,dj) 25.00

VAN DER VEER,JUDY-Brown Hills-Lond-1938-Longmans,Green-8vo-273p-cl,drwngs-1st ed (z5,dj) 12.00

VAN DER ZEE,JACOB-British in Iowa-Iowa City-1922-St Hist Soc-340p-1st ed (n2,uncut) 35.00

VAN DER ZEE,JAMES-ET AL-Harlem Book of the Dead-Dobbs Ferry-1978-Morgan & Morgan-photos-1st ed (q2,dj) 175.00

VAN DERSAL,SAMUEL-Van Dersal's Stock Growers' Directory of Marks & Brands for the State of North Dakota, 1902-(St.Paul)-(1902)-(4)p ads,1-213p,(34)p ads-many ads,some tip-ins-Rampaging Herd #2395-scarce (b6,cov stns) 225.00

VAN DEUSEN,DELLA-Murder Bicarb-Indpls-1940-Bobbs-1st ed (e4,dj) 30.00

VAN DEUSEN,GLYNDON G-William Henry Seward-NY-1967-666p-illus-1st ed (c4,f,dj) 45.00

VAN DINE,S S-Benson Murder Case-NY-1926-Scribners-1st ed (j4) 100.00

VAN DINE,S S-Bishop Murder Case-1929-Scribners-1st ed (m9) 20.00

VAN DINE,S S-Canary Murder Case-1927-G&D-photoplay ed (x7) 12.00

VAN DINE,S S-Canary Murder Case-1927-Scribners-1st ed (s9) 15.00

VAN DINE,S S-Casino Murder Case-1934-Scribners-1st ed (s10,fox,dj rub) 150.00

VAN DINE,S S-Casino Murder Case-NY-1934-Scribners-1st ed (f4,dj) 185.00

VAN DINE,S S-Dragon Murder Case-NY-1933-Scribner's-1st ed (y2) 75.00

VAN DINE,S S-Garden Murder Case-NY-1935-Scribners-1st ed (h4,dj) 150.00

VAN DINE,S S-Gracie Allen Murder Case-NY-1938-Scribner's-1st ed (d4,dj) 125.00

VAN DINE,S S-Greene Murder Case-NY-1928-Scribners-1st ed (h4) 12.50

VAN DINE,S S-Kennel Murder Case-1933-Scribners-1st ed (x2,dj) 125.00

VAN DINE,S S-Kidnap Murder Case-1936-Scribners-1st ed (s10,sl rub dj) 150.00

VAN DINE,S S-Kidnap Murder Case-1936-Scribners-1st ed (x7) 18.00

VAN DINE,S S-Scarab Murder Case-1930-Scribners-1st ed (m9,dj sp drknd & chip) 150.00

VAN DINE,S S-Scarab Murder Case-1930-Scribners-1st ed (x7) 18.00

VAN DINE,S S-Scarab Murder Case-1930-Scribners-1st ed (x7,sl tn dj) 85.00

VAN DINE,S S-Winter Murder Case-NY-1939-Scribner's-1st ed (d4,rprd sl tn dj) 300.00

VAN DOESBURG,THEO-Principles of Neo Plastic Art-Greenwich-(1968)-NYGS-lg 8vo-73p-28p illus-1st ed thus (ee5,sl cocked,dj) 20.00

VAN DOREN,CARL-Benjamin Franklin-NY-1938-845p-1st trd ed (e1,dj) 15.00

VAN DOREN,CARL-Jane Mecom, Franklin's Favorite Sister-NY-1950-Viking-8vo-255p-16p illus-1st ed (gg5,sp tn dj) 15.00

VAN DOREN,HAROLD-Industrial Design, a Practical Guide-NY-1940-McGraw Hill-8vo-388p-cl,illus-1st ed (q3) 45.00

VAN DOREN,MARK-Don Quixote's Profession-NY-1958-Columbia Pr-1st ed (y1,f,dj) 25.00

VAN DORN,HAROLD A-Twenty Years of the Chinese Republic-NY-1932-Knopf-20 halftones-1st ed (c3) 28.00

VAN DUZOR,ALLINE P-Fascinating Foods From the Deep South-(1963)-Gramercy-16mo-117p-tan cl,illus (q8,dj) 12.50

VAN DYKE,HENRY-Blood of Strawberries-NY-(1969)-FS&G-1st ed (c10,dj) 40.00

VAN DYKE,HENRY-Blue Flower-NY-1902-298,(1)p-grn,gold & lt blu dec frnt cov on drk blu cl,cov by M Armstrong-Gullans 273-1st ed (b1) 15.00

VAN DYKE,HENRY-Campfires & Guideposts-NY-1921-12mo-319p-photos-1st ed (m3) 22.50

VAN DYKE,HENRY-Days Off & Other Digressions-NY-1907-12mo-322p-illus-1st ed (m3) 15.00

VAN DYKE,HENRY-Dead Piano-NY-(1971)-FS&G-1st ed (c10,as new in dj) 25.00

VAN DYKE,HENRY-ED.-Creeful of Fishing Stories-NY-1932-8vo-420p-illus-1st ed (m3) 15.00

VAN DYKE,HENRY-Fisherman's Luck-NY-1899-8vo-247p-illus-1st ed (m3,f) 25.00

VAN DYKE,HENRY-Little Rivers-NY-1895-8vo-291p-illus-1st ed (m3) 16.50

VAN DYKE,HENRY-Spirit of Christmas-1905-Scribners-g pict cl wi orig tiss dj wi price of 75 Cents Net on fr dj panel,scarce thus,cov design,M Armstrong-1st ed (x2,f,dj) 85.00

VAN DYKE,HENRY-Travel Diary of an Angler-NY-1929-Derrydale-8vo-cl/bds-ltd to 750c-1st ed (u10,tips sl bump) 250.00

VAN DYKE,HENRY-Works of...-NY-1920 to 27-Scribner's-18 vols-3/4 red cl over pap bds-ltd to 504 sets,autg by auth & publ-Avalon Ed (w1) 350.00

VAN DYKE,THEO S-Flirtation Camp or the Rifle,Rod & Gun in California-NY-1881-12mo-299p (m3,rear hng crack) 20.00

VAN DYKE,THEO S-Game Birds at Home-NY-1895-12mo-219p-1st ed (m3) 20.00

VAN DYKE,THEO S-Southern California-NY,SF-1886-8vo-233p-illus (m3) 25.00

VAN DYKE,THEODORE S-Rifle,Rod, and Gun in California-NY-1889-299p-cl-first ed under this title-Wright 5653-3rd ed (g1,cov sl warped) 15.00

VAN DYKE,THEODORE S-Southern California-NY-1886-FH&H-233p-1st ed (d3) 35.00

VAN DYNE,EDITH-Aunt Jane's Nieces Abroad-Chig-1906-Reilly & Britton-1st ed (y2,sl rub) 100.00

VAN DYNE,EDITH-Aunt Jane's Nieces and Uncle John-Chig-1911-Reilly & Britton-1st ed,1st iss (y2,rub) 85.00

VAN DYNE,EDITH-Aunt Jane's Nieces at Work-Chig-1909-Reilly & Britton-dj scarce-1st ed,1st state (y2,sp slant,dj stnd,sp chip) 375.00

VAN DYNE,EDITH-Aunt Jane's Nieces in Society-Chig-1910-Reilly & Britton-1st ed (y2) 85.00

VAN DYNE,EDITH-Aunt Jane's Nieces on Vacation-Chig-1912-Reilly & Britton-1st ed,1st iss (y2,sl soil cov) 85.00

VAN DYNE,EDITH-Aunt Jane's Nieces Out West-Chig-1914-Reilly & Britton-1st ed,1st iss (y2,f) 100.00

VAN DYNE,EDITH-Aunt Jane's Nieces-Chig-1906-Reilly & Britton-1st ed (y2,few creased pgs) 200.00

VAN DYNE,EDITH-Flying Girl and Her Chum-Chig-1912-Reilly & Britton-1st ed (y2,sl fade sp) 150.00

VAN DYNE,EDITH-Mary Louise Adopts a Soldier-Chig-1919-Reilly & Lee-1st ed (y2,f) 50.00

VAN DYNE,EDITH-Mary Louise and the Liberty Girls-Chig-1918-Reilly & Britton-1st ed (y2,f) 75.00

VAN DYNE,EDITH-Mary Louise Solves a Mystery-Chig-1917-Reilly & Britton-1st ed (y2,sl soil cov) 75.00

VAN DYNE,EDITH-Mary Louise-Chig-1916-Reilly & Britton-1st ed,1st iss (y2) 100.00

VAN EVERY,D-Charles Lindbergh-NY-1927-8vo-cl,frntis,14p plts-1st ed (s2,sp fade) 25.00

VAN EVERY,DALE-Day the Sun Died-Bost-1971-Little,Brown-8vo-316p-cl & bds-1st ed so stated (z4,sl spot dj) 10.00

VAN EVERY,DALE-Men of the Western Waters-Bost-1956-Houghton Mifflin-244p-illus,maps-1st ed (cc4,dj) 20.00

VAN FLEET,J A-Old and New Mackinac-Cin-1874-Wstrn Meth Bk-173p-cl-Streeter 6740-2nd ed (z7) 150.00

VAN GULIK,ROBERT-Chinese Gold Murders-NY-1961-Harper & Bros-1st US ed (w9,f,dj) 85.00

VAN GULIK,ROBERT-Chinese Gold Murders-NY-1961-Harper-10 drwngs-1st US ed (a5,dj sl wn & soil) 75.00

VAN GULIK,ROBERT-Chinese Lake Murders-Lond-1960-Joseph-1st ed (e4,dj) 100.00

VAN GULIK,ROBERT-Chinese Lake Murders-NY-1962-Harper & Bros-1st Amer ed (w9,f,dj) 85.00

VAN GULIK,ROBERT-Chinese Maze Murders-The Hague-1957-Van Hoeve-1st ed (f4,f,sl wn dj) 350.00

VAN GULIK,ROBERT-Chinese Nail Murders-1961-Harper & Row-1st Amer ed (x2,dj) 47.00

VAN GULIK,ROBERT-Chinese Nail Murders-NY-1962-Harper-1st US ed (g4,dj) 35.00

VAN GULIK,ROBERT-Haunted Monastery-Kuala Lumpur-1961-Art Prtg Works-pict card covs,8 drwngs by auth,iss w/o dj-1st ed (gg8,f) 400.00

VAN GULIK,ROBERT-Haunted Monastery-NY-1969-Scribner's-1st Amer ed (w9,f,dj) 50.00

VAN GULIK,ROBERT-Haunted Monastery-NY-1969-Scribners-1st US ed (e4,dj) 20.00

VAN GULIK,ROBERT-Lacquer Screen-1969-Scribners-1st Amer ed (x7,f,dj) 35.00

VAN GULIK,ROBERT-Lacquer Screen-NY-1969-Scribners-1st US ed (h4,f,dj) 30.00

VAN GULIK,ROBERT-Monkey and the Tiger-Lond-1965-Heinemann-1st ed (w9,f,dj) 85.00

VAN GULIK,ROBERT-Monkey and the Tiger-NY-(1966)-Scribner's-8 drwngs-1st US ed (a5,f,dj) 75.00

VAN GULIK,ROBERT-Necklace and Calabash-NY-1971-Scribners-1st Amer ed (w9,f,dj) 35.00

VAN GULIK,ROBERT-Poets and Murder-NY-1972-Scribners-1st US ed (l4,f,dj) 20.00

VAN GULIK,ROBERT-Red Pavilion-1968-Scribners-1st Amer ed (n9,sl chip dj) 40.00

VAN GULIK,ROBERT-Willow Pattern-1965-Scribners-1st Amer ed (x7,dj) 35.00

VAN GYTENBEEK,R P-Way of a Trout-Phila-1972-4to-146p-photos (m3,vf,dj) 12.50

VAN HISE,CHARLES R-Geology of the Lake Superior Region-Wash-1911-GPO-4to-641p-49 col & b&w plts,8 col fldg maps rear pckt (o2,cov sl bowed & rub) 60.00

VAN HOESEN,WALTER H-Early Taverns and Stagecoach Days in New Jersey-Rutherford-(1976)-184p-cl,illus (aa6) 30.00

VAN KIRK,J W-Brotherhood-Youngstown-(1908)-publ by J W Van Kirk-171p-cl (h1) 15.00

VAN LAWICK-GOODALL,H-Innocent Killers-Bost-1971-8vo-222p-cl,33 plts (y8,dj sl chip) 25.00

VAN LIERE,EDWARD J-Doctor Enjoys Sherlock Holmes-1959-Vantage-1st ed (s10,cor bump,f dj) 22.50

VAN LOAN,CHARLES-Score By Innings-1919-Doran-1st ed (s8,dj) 60.00

VAN LOON,HENDRICK-Lives-NY-1942-(22),886p-illus,auth (k9,f,dj) 10.00

VAN LOON,HENDRIK-Adventures and Escapes of Augustus Vasa-NY-1945-Dodd,Mead-136p-cl,illus,auth-1st ed (s3,f,chip & fade dj) 20.00

VAN LOON,HENDRIK-Ships and How They Sailed the Seven Seas-Lond-1935-Geo G Harrap-8vo-304p-blu cl,150 drwngs-1st ed (pp1,dj wn) 65.00

VAN LOON,HENDRIK-Story of Wilbur the Hat-Being a True Account of the Strange Things Which Sometimes Happen...-1925-B&L-papr bds,col illus,auth-1st ed (x2) 45.00

VAN LUSTBADER,ERIC-Ninja-NY-(1980)-Evans-1st ed (bb1,f,sl creased dj) 20.00

VAN MARTER,MARTHA-Primary Teacher-NY,Cin-1893-166p-cl (k1) 12.50

VAN MELLE,P J-Shrubs and Trees for the Small Place-NY-1955-Dbldy-246p (x6,dj wn) 15.00

VAN METRE,T W-Trains,Tracks and Travel-NY-(1936)-296p-cl,illus-4th ed (o1) 12.50

VAN NESS,JOHN R-Spanish & Mexican Land Grants in New Mexico and Colorado-np-1980-116p-wrps,dbl col,photos,maps-1st ed (u7) 25.00

VAN NOSTRAND,J-First 100 Years of Painting in Calif 1775 to 1875-SF-1980-Howell-lg 4to-42 col plts-ltd ed (h10,dj) 85.00

VAN NOSTRAND,JEANNE-California Pictorial...1786 to 1859-Berkeley-1948-U of Cal Pr-4to-159p-cl-1st ed (mm7,f,dj) 50.00

VAN NUYS WOMANS CLUB COOK BOOK-np-nd(ca.1925)-(Van Nuys News)-wrps (o6,sl tn wrps) 25.00

VAN ORMAN,RICHARD-Room for the Night-(1966)-Indiana U-162p-illus-Six Guns #1653-1st ed (r8,f,dj) 20.00

VAN PAASSEN,PIERRE-Pilgrim's Vow-NY-1956-Dial-8vo-344p-1st ed (ff5,dj) 12.50

VAN RENSSELAER,CORTLANDT-Funeral Sermon...-Wash-1841-59p-prntd wrps-Sabin 98540 (j1) 22.50

VAN RENSSELAER,S-Early American Bottles & Flasks-NY-1921-110p-illus-1st ed (cc8) 20.00

VAN RIPER,GUERNSEY-Lou Gehrig, Boy of the Sand Lots-1949-Bobbs Merill-drwngs-1st ed (s8,dj) 17.50

VAN SAHER,LILLA-Exotic Cookery-Cleve-(1964)-World-172p-1st ed (o6,dj) 18.00

VAN SCYOC,SIDNEY J-Star Mother-NY-(1976)-Berkley-1st ed (l3,dj) 10.00

VAN SCYOC,SYDNEY J-Cloud Cry-1977-Berkley-1st ed (q9,f,dj) 15.00

VAN SICKLE,EMOGENE-Old York Road and Its Stage Coach Days-(np)-1936(i.e. 1937)-118,(1)p-cl,illus,photos (aa6) 35.00

VAN SINDEREN,ADRIAN-Our Home in the Country-NY-1957-priv prtd (h9) 38.00

VAN SOMEREN,V G L-Days with Birds-Chig-1956-8vo-520p-wrps,frntis (y8) 45.00

VAN STOKE,MARY R-Los Pastores-(Santa Fe)-(1933)-Gates Pr, Cleve-44p-illus in linoleum-scarce-1st ed (u7,f) 45.00

VAN TRAMP,JOHN C-Prairie and Rocky Mountain Adventures-Columbus-1858-J & H Miller-640p-blk lea,61 plts-1st ed (e2,sl fade sp lttrng) 150.00

VAN TRESS,B D-Practical Key to Harvey's False Syntax-Indpls-1884-Normal Publ-100p-flex cl (k1,sl spot frnt cov) 15.00

VAN URK,J BLAN-Story of Rolling Rock-NY-1950-Scribner-4to-ltd to 750c (j9) 295.00

VAN VOGT,A E-Away and Beyond-Chig-(1952)-Pellegrini & Cudahy-1st ed (f3,chip dj) 50.00

VAN VOGT,A E-Book of Ptath-Reading-1947-Fantasy Pr-1st ed (f3,dj) 50.00

VAN VOGT,A E-Mind Cage-NY-1957-S&S-1st ed (g3,sl brwnd pgs,dj) 20.00

VAN VOGT,A E-Rogue Ship-Lond-(1967)-1st ed (k5,f,dj) 20.00

VAN VOGT,A E-Slan-NY-1951-S&S-rvsd text of auth 1st bk-1st ed thus (a10,dj sl wn & sp chip) 35.00

VAN VOGT,A E-Voyage of the Space Beagle-NY-1950-S&S-1st ed (k3,dj chip & tape rnfrcd) 40.00

VAN VOGT,A E-Weapon Shops of Isher-NY-(1951)-Greenberg-1st ed (j3,dj) 65.00

VAN VOGT,A E-World of A-NY-1948-S&S-1st ed (a10,sl rub dj) 75.00

VAN VOGT,A E-World of Null A-Lond-(1969)-1st ed (k5,f,dj) 20.00

VAN VORST,MRS.JOHN-Letters to Women in Love-NY-1906-309p-1st ed (d1) 15.00

VAN WAGONER,MURRAY D-Street Traffic, City of Detroit 1936 to 1937-Lansing-1937-Mich St Hwy Dept/WPA-4to-313p-cl,maps,photos (z7,dmpstnd) 45.00

VAN WATERS,GEORGE-Poetical Geography...-Mlwk-1848-Wilson & King-96p-wrps (k1,lacks rear wrpr) 50.00

VAN WELL,MARY S-Educational Aspects of the Missions in the Southwest-Milw-1942-154p-wrps-v scarce-1st ed (v7) 45.00

VAN WINKLE,DANIEL-Old Bergen-Jersey City-(1902)-x,319p-cl,illus (aa6) 65.00

VAN WORMER,JOE-World of the Black Bear-Phila-1966-4to-163p-photos (m3,f,dj) 11.00

VAN WORMER,JOE-World of the Pronghorn-Phila-1969-4to-191p-photos (m3,vf,dj) 20.00

VAN YOUNG,ERIC-Hacienda and Market in Eighteenth-Century Mexico...-Berkeley/LA-1981-U of Cal Pr-8vo-xvi,388p-orng cl,2 maps,21 figs,29 tabls-1st ed (mm1,as new in dj) 30.00

VAN ZILE,E S-That Marvel,The Movie,A Glimpse at its Reckless Past...Significant Future-1923-Putnams-1st ed (x2,dj sl wn & tn) 125.00

VAN'T HOFF,JACOBUS-Physical Chemistry in the Service of the Sciences-Chig-1903-Univ of Chig-xviii+126p-maroon cl,10 text figs-1st ed (j2,cov sl flecked) 40.00

VANCE,JACK-Lost Moons-SF-1982-Underwood Miller-1st trd ed (f3,f,dj) 20.00

VANCE,JACK-Maske: Thaery-NY-(1976)-Berkley-1st ed (k3,f,dj) 15.00

VANCE,JAMES-Young Man Foursquare-NY-(1894)-104p-cl (g1) 15.00

VANCE,L J-False Face-1918-DP-pict frnt cl-1st ed (x7) 18.00

VANCE,LOUIS J-Lone Wolf-Bost-1914-Little-illus-1st ed (e4,sl wn sp) 50.00

VANDELEUR,SEYMOUR-Campaigning on the Upper Nile and Niger-Lond-1898-320p+40p cat-dec grn cl,maps,plts-v scarce-1st ed (b7,weak hng) 350.00

VANDEN BERGH,L J-On the Trail of the Pygmies-1969-Negro Univ-264p-photos-rprnt of 1921 ed (bb3,f) 25.00

VANDERCOOK,JOHN W-King Cane-NY-1939-Harper & Bros-xiv+192p-grn bds,cl sp,plts-1st ed (k2,chip dj) 18.00

VANDERGRIFT,GEORGE W,MD-Castor Oil and Quinine-NY-1942-Dutton-8vo-252p-1st ed (gg5,dj wn,sl chip) 15.00

VANDERLIP,WASHINGTON B-Search of a Siberian Klondike-NY-1903-Century-8vo-grey cl,photos-1st ed (ll1) 50.00

VANDERVELL,A-Game and the English Landscape-NY-1980-4to-159p-illus (m3,vf,dj) 35.00

VANDIVEER,CLARENCE A-Fur Trade and Early Western Exploration-Cleve-1929-Arthur Clark-8vo-316p-grn cl,illus-1st ed (y4,weak hng) 125.00

VANDIVER,FRANK E-Their Tattered Flags-NY-1970-362p-maps(1 fldg) (z10,sl soil dj) 30.00

VANDIVER,FRANK E-Their Tattered Flags-NY-1970-362p-maps-1st ed (c4,dj) 40.00

VANDIVER,FRANK E-Their Tattered Flags-NY-1970-Harper's Mag Pr-362p-maps-1st ed (o7,dj) 25.00

VANDIVER,FRANK-Jubal's Raid-NY-(1960)-McGraw Hill-198p-1st ed (ee4,dj) 40.00

VANETTI,DOLORES-Querulous Cook-(1963)-Macmillan-291p-red cl-1st prtg (q8,dj) 15.00

VANN,RICHARD T-Social Development of English Quakerism, 1655 to 1755-Cambridge-1969-Harvard U-8vo-259p-1st ed (y6) 16.00

VAQUERO-Life and Adventure in the West Indies-Lond-1914-J Bale,Sons & Danielsson-xiii,284p+ads-orig burgundy cl,g sp titles,blk cov titles,col frntis,109 photos (mm1,ex-lib) 35.00

VARAGNAC,ANDRE-French Costumes-Paris/Lond-1939-Hyperion-lg 4to-unpgd-40 col plts-1st ed (ee5,f,dj) 95.00

VARLEY,JOHN-Titan-NY-(1979)-Berkley-1st ed (k3,sp creased dj) 25.00

VARNA,ANDREW-Gift of Time-NY-(1956)-Putnam-8vo-207p-1st ed (dd5,dj) 15.00

VASILIEV,A V-Space, Time, Motion-Lond-1924-Chatto & Windus-xxiv+232p-brwn cl,sp labl-1st ed (g2,dj soil & wn) 35.00

VASSILI,COUNT PAUL-France From Behind the Veil-NY-1914-Funk & Wagnalls-8vo-396p-23 illus-1st US ed (jj5) 20.00

VASSILIKOS,V-Z-1968-FS&G-1st Amer ed (x2,f,dj) 45.00

VAUGHAN,BEATRICE-Yankee Hill Country Cooking-Battleboro-1962-Stephen Green Pr-202p (k6) 20.00

VAUGHAN,GEORGE T-Papers on Surgery and Other Subjects-Wash D C-1932-W F Roberts-x+408p-blu cl,illus-1st ed (d2,chip dj) 35.00

VAUGHAN,J W-Battle of Platte Bridge-Norman-(1963)-Norman-132p-illus-1st ed (c7,f,dj) 45.00

VAUGHAN,J W-With Crook at the Rosebud-Harrisburg-(1956)-245p-illus,e.p. map-1st ed so stated (c7,f,dj) 45.00

VAUGHAN,T W-Eocene and Lower Oligocene Coral Faunas of the U.S.-1900-US Geol Survey Mono-4to-205p-24 plts (bb3,cor wn) 65.00

VAUGHAN,THOMAS W-ET AL-International Aspects of Oceanography-Wash D.C.-1937-Nat Acad Sci-qto-xvii,225p-cl,36 plts(incl fldg)-1st ed (kk1,sl rub) 60.00

VAUGHN,J W-Indian Fights, New Facts on Seven Encounters-Norman-1966-250p-photos,maps-Luther #75-1st ed (t7,f,dj) 75.00

VAUGHN,J W-Reynolds Campaign on Powder River-Norman-(1961)-U of Okla Pr-239p-1st ed (dd4,dj) 40.00

VAUGHN,J W-With Crook at the Rosebud-Harrisburg-(1956)-Stackpole-(x),245p-cl,photos,map e.p.-1st ed (v1) 65.00

VAUGHN,J W-With Crook at the Rosebud-Harrisburg-(1956)-Stackpole-245p-illus-1st ed (ff4,sl wn dj) 50.00

VAUGHN,J W-With Crook at the Rosebud-Harrisburg-(1956)-Stackpole-xiv+245p-tan cl,illus-1st ed (m2,chip dj) 45.00

VAUGHN,KATE B-Culinary Echoes From Dixie-Cin-(1914)-McDonald-271p-yel cl bds-Bitting 476 (u6,soil,sl fox) 16.00

VAUGHN,ROBERT-Then and Now-Mpls-1900-Tribune-461p-dec grn cl,photos,paintings,C M Russell-Howes V60-1st ed (v1,innr hngs sl weak) 185.00

VAUX,CALVERT-Villas and Cottages-NY-1864-8vo-348p+1p col tiles,cl,illus (b6,cov wn) 225.00

VAUX,CALVERT-Villas and Cottages-NY-1864-Harper & Bros-8vo-348p-g stmpd brwn cl,illus,col tile plt in rear (r10,sp dull,sl wn) 175.00

VAUX,CALVERT-Villas and Cottages-NY-1867-Harper & Bros-348p-brwn cl,frntis,plts(1 col) (c2,wn,sp chip & tn) 100.00

VEACH,WILLIAM T-Bon Vivant's Cookbook-Bost-(1965)-Little,Brown-236p-1st ed (o6,dj) 18.00

VEBLEN,THORSTEIN-Higher Learning in America-NY-1918-Huebsch-x+286p-grn cl-1st ed (h2) 25.00

VECSEY,ARMAND-Fiddler of the Ritz-NY-(1931)-Payson-1st ed (w1,f,dj) 25.00

VECSEY,GEORGE-Baseball's Most Valuable Players-NY-(1966)-186p-col pict bds (n1) 12.50

VECSEY,GEORGE-Joy in Mudville-1970-McCall (r7,dj) 12.50

VEDDER,ALAN C-Furniture of Spanish New Mexico-Santa Fe-(1977)-96p-photos-1st ed (u7) 25.00

VEDDER,HEINRICH-South West Africa in Early Times-Lond-1938-OUP-photos,3 fldg maps (v4,dj rprd) 75.00

VEECK,BILL-Hustler's Handbook-1965-Putnam-1st ed (ff2,dj) 45.00

VEECK,BILL-Hustler's Handbook-1965-Putnam-1st ed (s8,dj) 50.00

VEECK,BILL-Veeck as in Wreck-1962-Putnam-1st ed (s7,f,dj) 27.50

VEIL,CH-Adventure's a Wench-NY-(1934)-8vo-xii,340p-illus cl,frntis,8p plts,2 text illus,col illus e.p.-1st ed (s2) 25.00

VELARDE,PABLITA-Old Father the Story Teller-Globe-1960-66p-pict cl,col reprod-scarce-1st trd ed (z1,minor dmpstns) 65.00

VELARDE,PABLITA-Old Father the Storyteller-Globe-1960-12"x 9"-63p-col illus-deluxe ed,ltd to 400c-1st ed (v7) 45.00

VELIE,LESTER-Labor, USA-NY-1958-Harper-318p-1st ed (r1,dj) 25.00

VELVIN,ELLEN-Behind the Scenes with Wild Animals-1906-Moffat,Yard-222p-pict cov by Dec Designers,photos-scarce-1st ed (v8,sl edge wn) 40.00

VENABLE,CLARK-Fleetfin-Chig-1925-8vo-66p (m3,vf) 17.50

VENABLES,ROBERT-Experienced Angler-Lond-1969-12mo-136p-illus,facs of 1827 ed wi add 66p (m3,vf) 25.00

VENCE,CELINE-Grand Masters of French Cuisine-(1978)-Putnam-folio-288p-tan buckrm,col photos-1st Amer ed (q8,f,dj) 25.00

VENESZ,JOSEF-Hungarian Cuisine-Budapest-(1958)-Corvina-374p-tan cl,col plts-1st ed (q8,wn dj) 20.00

VENIARD,E LTD-Fly Dresser's Guide-Thorton Heath-1952-4to-256p-col plts-1st ed (m3,f,fray dj) 45.00

VENIARD,JOHN-Fly Tying Problems and Their Answers-Thorton Heath-nd-8vo-61p-wrps,illus-1st ed (m3,f) 17.50

VENIARD,JOHN-Modern Fly-Tying Techniques-Lond-1973-8vo-72p-illus,D Downs (m3,dj) 20.00

VENIARD,JOHN-Reservoir & Lake Flies-Lond-1970-8vo-181p-1st ed (m3,vf,dj) 27.50

VENOSTA,GIOVANNI V-Memoirs of Youth-Bost-1914-HMCo-8vo-463p-1st US ed (jj5) 15.00

VENTH,CARL-My Memories-1939-Alamo Prtg-4to-130p-photos-1st ed (a9) 75.00

VENTURI,LIONELLO-Botticelli-NY-1937-Oxford U Pr-folio-beige cl,105 b&w & col plts (r10,tattrd dj) 12.50

VENTURI,ROBERT-Complexity & Contradiction in Architecture-1966-MOMA(Papers on Arch.#1)-1st ed (h10,dj) 40.00

VERANCE,PERCY-Perpetual Motion-np-(1916)-(20th Cent Spec Enltnmnt)-366p-gry cl-presumed 1st ed (a2,sl soil cov) 85.00

VERDON,RENE-...FRENCH COOKING FOR THE AMERICAN TABLE-GC-1974-Dbldy-614p-1st ed (l6) 50.00

VERDON,RENE-Rene Verdon's French Cooking for the American Table-1974-Dbldy-sm folio-614p-blu cl,8 col plts-1st ed (q8,soil dj) 16.50

VERLAINE,PAUL-Forty Poems-Lond-(1948)-Engl transl by Gant & Apcher-1st ed (m4,f,dj) 15.00

VERLAINE,PAUL-Selected Poems-Berkeley-1948-(20),228p-transl by C F MacIntyre-1st ed thus (m4) 15.00

VERMEULE,CORNELIUS C-Morris Canal and Banking Company-(Trenton)-(1929)-80p-wrps,illus,fldg plts (aa6) 60.00

VERMONT-Essays in the Early History of...-Montpelier-1943-Vermont Hist Soc-beige cl-Collections of VHS, Vol.6 (b2) 20.00

VERNAM,GLENN-man on Horseback-NY-1964-Harper & Row-1st ed (h9,dj) 35.00

VERNE,JULES-Chase of the Golden Meteor-1909-G Richards-pict cl,illus-1st Brit ed (x2) 185.00

VERNE,JULES-In Search of the Castaways-Phila-1873-Lippincott-dec cl,illus-1st ed (gg7) 75.00

VERNEY,G L-Devil's Wind-Lond-1956-176p-maps,illus-1st ed (b7,dj) 35.00

VERNON,ARTHUR-History and Romance of the Horse-Bost-(1939)-Waverly Hs-525p-pict cl,illus-1st ed (nn6) 40.00

VERNON,GRENVILLE-Yankee Doodle Doo-1927-Paysana Clarke,Ltd-1st prtg (u4,sl rub) 16.00

VERNON,IDA S W-Pedro De Valdvia, Conquistador of Chile-Austin-1946-U of Tex Pr-193p-brwn cl-1st ed (mm1,f) 50.00

VERNON,JOSEPH S-ET AL-Along the Old Trail-Cimarron-(1910)-141p-wrps,photos-Rittenhouse#604 (v7) 45.00

VERNON,PAUL E-From Coast to Coast by Motor-Lond-1930-A & C Black-115,(1)p+fldg map-cl (o1) 17.50

VERRILL,A E-Invertebrate Animals of Vineyard Sound and Adjacent Waters-1874-Wash-478p-cl,38 plts (bb3,rbnd) 40.00

VERRILL,A H-Harper's Aircraft Book-NY-1913-8vo-xvi,246p-illus cl gilt,frntis,plts,figs-1st ed (s2) 40.00

VERRILL,A HYATT-Harper's Wireless Book-1913-184p-129 illus-1st ed (h6) 30.00

VERRILL,A HYATT-Lost Treasure, True Tales of Hidden Hoards-NY-1930-Appleton-8vo-279p-12 illus-1st ed (jj5,sl tn dj) 35.00

VERSTEEG,JOHN M-Methodism:Ohio Area(1812-1962)-np-(1962)-372p-cl (g1,dj) 15.00

VERTREES,HERBERT H-Pearls and Pearling-NY-nd-Fur News Publ.-203p+ads-cl (e1,spot rear cov) 15.00

VESALIUS,ANDREAS-Four Hundredth Anniversary Celebration of the De Humani Corporis Fabrica of...-New Haven-1943-67p-1st ed (dd3) 75.00

VESEY-FITZGERALD,B-Game Fish of the World-Lond-1949-8vo-446p-illus,A Fraser-Brunner-1st ed (m3) 35.00

VESEY-FITZGERALD,BRIAN-British Game-Lond-1946-Collins-240p-28 col illus,81 photos (d9) 15.00

VESTAL,STANLEY-Joe Meek-Caldwell-1952-Caxton-336p-illus,map e.p. (bb4) 50.00

VESTAL,STANLEY-Kit Carson-Bost-1928-297p-pict cl,frntis,map e.p.-Smith #10541 (t7) 15.00

VESTAL,STANLEY-Old Santa Fe Trail-Bost-1939-304p-8 plts-scarce-1st ed (z1,dj) 75.00

VESTAL,STANLEY-Old Santa Fe Trail-Bost-1939-Houghton Mifflin-304p-map e.p.-1st ed (dd4) 30.00

VESTAL,STANLEY-Queen of Cowtowns Dodge City-(1952)-Harper-285p-illus-Six Guns 2269-1st ed (v8,sl wn dj) 30.00

VESTAL,STANLEY-Revolt on the Border-Bost-1938-246p-dec cl-scarce-1st ed (t7) 20.00

VESTAL,STANLEY-Sitting Bull-Bost-1932-Houghton Mifflin-350p-illus-Howes V82-1st ed (ee4) 50.00

VESTAL,STANLEY-Warpath and Council Fire-NY-(1948)-Random-xiv,338p-cl,photos,map e.p.-1st prtg (v1,sl wn dj) 65.00

VESTAL,STANLEY-Warpath, The True Story...Biography of Chief White Bull-Bost-1934-Houghton Mifflin-8vo-gry cl,orng cov & sp titles,map e.p.,maps.photos,illus (mm1,dj wn & chip) 65.00

VESTAL,STANLEY-Warpath-NY-1934-291p-frntis,photos,maps-Luther #93-1st ed (t7,f,chip dj) 100.00

VESTIGES OF THE NATURAL HISTORY OF CREATION-Cin-1852-J A & U P James-288p-cl,not cpyrtd (b1,lacks fr f.e.p.) 30.00

VETERAN,A-Golf for Occasional Players-NY-1922-McBride (z2,f,sl chip dj) 85.00

VETTER,GEORGE B-Magic and Religion-NY-1958-Philosophical Libr-cl-1st ed (l8,f,dj) 12.50

VETTERLI,RICHARD-Mormonism, Americanism and Politics-SLC-1961-775p-illus,maps-1st ed (t7,dj) 27.50

VIAZZI,ALFREDO-Alfredo Viazzi's Cucina e Nostalgia-(1983)-Random-337p-brwn cl-1st ed (q8,dj) 16.50

VICKREY,ROBERT-Robert Vickrey: Artist at Work-NY-1979-Watson Guptill-4to-144p-blk cl,col & b&w illus-1st ed (r10,sl tn dj) 20.00

VICTOR,F F-Atlantis Arisen-Phila-1891-412p-illus-Smith 10547 (bb9,sl wn) 85.00

VICTOR,FRANCES F-Atlantis Arisen, or Talks of a Tourist About Oregon and Washington-Phila-1891-Lippincott-412p-blu cl,photos,chrts,drwngs-Smith #10547-1st ed (w1) 75.00

VICTOR,MRS FRANCES F-New Penelope-SF-1877-A L Bancroft & Co-349p-grn cl-scarce (b6) 65.00

VICTOR,MRS.FRANCES F-New Penelope-SF-1877-Bancroft-8vo-350p-blnd stmpd blu cl,g decs-1st ed (u1) 75.00

VIDAL,GORE-1876-NY-(1976)-Random-1st ed (b5,f,dj) 25.00

VIDAL,GORE-City and the Pillar-Lond-1949-1st Brit ed (n5,chip dj) 25.00

VIDAL,GORE-Dark Green, Bright Red-NY-1950-1st ed (n5,chip dj) 45.00

VIDAL,GORE-Homage to Daniel Shays-NY-(1972)-Random-1st ed (b5,f,dj) 20.00

VIDAL,GORE-In a Yellow Mood-NY-(1947)-Dutton-1st ed (aa10,edgewn dj) 225.00

VIDAL,GORE-Judgement of Paris-Lond-1953-1st Brit ed (r5,chip dj) 40.00

VIDAL,GORE-Julian-Bost-1964-1st ed (t5,dj) 20.00

VIDAL,GORE-Matters of Fact and of Fiction-NY-(1977)-Random-1st ed (b5,as new in dj) 20.00

VIDAL,GORE-Messiah-1954-Dutton-1st ed (x2,dj) 33.00

VIDAL,GORE-Messiah-Lond-1955-1st Brit ed (r5,chip dj) 40.00

VIDAL,GORE-Myra Breckinridge-Bost-1968-1st ed (n5,f,f dj) 25.00

VIDAL,GORE-Myron-NY-(1974)-Random-1st ed (g3,f,dj) 20.00

VIDAL,GORE-Reflections Upon a Sinking Ship-1969-Little,Brown-1st ed (x2,f,dj) 20.00

VIDAL,GORE-Reflections Upon a Sinking Ship-Bost-1969-1st ed (r5,dj) 22.50

VIDAL,GORE-Rocking the Boat-Bost-1962-1st ed (t5,sl wn dj) 25.00

VIDAL,GORE-Search for the King-NY-1950-Dutton-1st ed (b5,f,sl wn dj) 100.00

VIDAL,GORE-Season of Comfort-NY-1949-1st ed (q5,sl wn dj) 40.00

VIDAL,GORE-Thirsty Evil-NY-1956-1st ed (n5,dj) 45.00

VIDAL,GORE-Two Sisters-Bost-1970-1st ed (n5,f,f dj) 15.00

VIDAL,GORE-Visit to a Small Planet and Other Television Plays-Bost-1956-Little,Brown-blk & orng cl-1st ed (f2,dj) 35.00

VIDRINE,MERCEDES-Quelque Chose Piquante-Baton Rouge-1966-Clairor's Publ Div-136p-red wrps,comb bndg (l6) 20.00

VIETS,HENRY-Brief History of Medicine in Massachusetts-Bost-1930-194p (dd3) 50.00

VIGILANCE COMMITTEE OF 1856-By a Pioneer California Journalist-SF-1890-James H Barry-12mo-57p-pnk wrps-Howes O84-2nd ed (b2) 85.00

VILLA,JOSE GARCIA-Have Come, Am Here-NY-1942-Viking-151p-1st ed (c3,f,dj) 35.00

VILLARD,HENRY-Early History of Transportation in Oregon-1944-U of Or Pr-8vo-99p-wrps-scarce (nn7,wn wrps) 29.00

VILLASENOR,DAVID-Tapestries in Sand-Healdsburg-1963-112p-cl,16 col plts-1st ed? (v7) 10.00

VILLERS STUART,C M-Spanish Gardens-Lond-1929-Batsford-xvii,139p-g dec pict cl,86 plts(incl 6 col)-1st ed (mm4) 120.00

VILLIERS,A J-Falmouth for Orders-NY-1929-Holt-8vo-xxv,(1),301p-brwn cl,photos (p8,f) 50.00

VILLIERS,ALAN-Monsoon Seas-NY-1952-McGraw Hill-8vo-xi,(1),337p-blu cl,illus,maps-3rd prtg (p8,f,tattrd dj) 25.00

VILLIERS,ALAN-Way of a Ship-NY-1953-Scribner's-photos,drwngs-1st ed (v4,dj rprd) 75.00

VINCENT,BATTY A L-Wild Flowers of Central Saudi Arabia-Milan-(1977)-Auth-4to-114p-col photos-1st ed (dd5,f,dj,pres) 20.00

VINCENT,LEON H-Bibliotaph and Other People-Bost-1898-Houghton Mifflin-1st ed (w1,f) 17.50

VINCENT,LEOPOLD-COMP.-Alliance and Labor Songster-Indpls-1891-Vincent Bros-64p-bds (d1) 20.00

VINCENT,TED-Mudville's Revenge-1981-Seaview-1st ed (ff2,dj) 25.00

VINCENZ,STANISLAW-On the High Uplands-NY-(1955)-Roy Publ-cl,illus,Z Czermanski-1st ed (l8,f,dj) 25.00

VINCENZ,STANISLAW-On the High Uplands-NY-(1955)-Roy-8vo-344p-sketches-1st US ed (dd5,sl chip dj) 25.00

VINELAND, NEW JERSEY-(Vineland)-(ca.1900)-(48)p-wrps,illus-promo viewbk (aa6) 30.00

VINES,SHERARD-Course of English Classicism-Lond-1930-Hogarth Pr-8vo-cl,Hogarth Lectures No.12-1st ed (x3,sp sunned) 55.00

VINEYARD,H K-Woman Neglected in Education and the Causes and Effects-Knoxville-1886-Ogden Bros-146p-cl (l1,sl spot cov) 25.00

VINGE,JOAN D-Psion-NY-(1982)-1st ed (h5,as new in dj) 25.00

VINGE,JOAN D-Snow Queen-NY-(1980)-Dial Pr-1st ed (b10,f,dj) 65.00

VINING,ELIZABETH G-Take Heed of Loving Me-Phila-1964-Lippincott-8vo-352p-1st ed (y6,sl tn dj) 10.00

VIRCHOW,RUDOLF-Disease, Life, and Man-Stanford-1971-273p-1st Engl transl (dd3) 30.00

VIRGINIA COOKERY BOOK-Richmond-1921-Va League of Women Voters-191p-blu dec wht oilcl bds (u6) 65.00

VIRGINIA MILITARY INSTITUTE-Official Register for 1929,1930, Catalogue, 1930,31-Lexington-1931-150p-wrps,fldg map (z10,sp wn,sl soil & fade) 15.00

VIRGINIA:A GUIDE TO THE OLD DOMINION-NY-(1940)-Oxford/WPA-thk 8vo-699p wi fldg map & index-1st ed (t1,f,dj) 60.00

VISHNIAC,ROMAN-Polish Jews-NY-(1947)-Schocken-4to-cl-1st ed (y3) 85.00

VISSCHER,WILLIAM L-Thrilling and Truthful History of the Pony Express...-Chig-(1908)-Rand McNally-98p-illus-1st ed (bb4) 35.00

VISSCHER,WM L-Thrilling and Truthful History of the Pony Express...-Chig-1908-98p-pict cl,frntis,photos,illus-Graff #4493-1st ed (t7) 45.00

VITTORINI,ELIO-In Sicily-(NY)-(1949)-New Directions-1st ed (ff6,dj) 20.00

VIVA-Baby-NY-1975-Knopf-1st ed (x9,dj) 15.00

VIVIAN,A P-Wanderings in a Western Land-Lond-1880-426p-dec bds,8 full-pg engrvngs,fldg map (gg3,f,autg) 150.00

VIVIAN,E C-History of Aeronautics-NY-1921-8vo-x,522p-cl,frntis,50p plts,text illus-1st ed (s2,sp damaged,cor bump,fox) 50.00

VIVIAN,GORDON-Kin Klesto-(Globe)-(1973)-296p-dbl-col,wrps,photos,maps-2nd prtg (v7,sl chip sp) 20.00

VIVIAN,H HUSSEY-Notes of a Tour in America...1877-Lond-1878-Stanford-8vo-260p-g dec grn cl wi cov device of Yosemite Vlly,col fldg map-1st ed (t1) 175.00

VIZENOR,GERALD-Wordarrows-Mpls-1978-164p-1st ed (t7,dj) 12.50

VLACK,D-Art Deco Architecture in New York 1920 to 40-NY-1974-184 illus-1st ed (h10,dj) 85.00

VLIET,MINA A-History of the Early Life and Business Interests of the Village and Township of Leslie...-Leslie-1914-Elijah Grout Chap,DAR-120p-grn cl,photos-Streeter 6769 (cc3) 65.00

VOGAN,SARA-In Shelly's Leg-1981-Knopf-1st ed (q7,f,f dj) 25.00

VOGE,CECIL I B-Chemistry and Physics of Contraceptives-Lond-1933-J Cape-288p-brwn cl,32 text figs,31 tbls-1st ed (j2) 60.00

VOGEL,H W-Progress of Photography since the Year 1879-Phila-1883-Edward L Wilson-347p+ads-blu cl,photo frntis,72 text illus-1st ed (j2,ink wrtng on e.p.) 125.00

VOGEL,VIRGIL J-This Country was Ours-NY-(1972)-Harper & Row-473p-1st ed (bb4,dj) 15.00

VOGEL,VIRGIL-American Indian Medicine-Norman-1977-584p-1st ed (dd3,dj) 90.00

VOGT,EVAN Z-Navaho Means People-Cambridge-1951-159p-photos-1st ed (v7) 25.00

VOGUE'S BOOK OF SMART SERVICE-NY-1930-Conde Nast-90p-b&w photos & drwngs (o6) 15.00

VOIGHT,DAVID-American Baseball, From Gentleman's Sport to the Commissioner System-1968-U of Okla (q7,f,f dj) 35.00

VOISIN,G-Men, Women and 10,000 Kites-Lond-(1963)-248p-frntis,8p plts-1st ed (s2) 30.00

VOLKMAN,DANIEL-Fifty Years of the McCloud River Club-SF-1951-priv prntd-4to-unpgd-ltd to 150c,fldg map-scarce (m3,f) 200.00

VOLNEY,C F-View of the Soil and Climate of the USA...-Phila-1804-J Conrad-xxviii,446p-lea,2 fldg maps,2 plts-1st Amer ed (p2,sl rub & fox) 375.00

VON BLIXEN-FINECKE,BARON-African Hunter-NY-1938-284p-photos-1st Amer ed (gg3,f) 75.00

VON BRAUN,WERNHER-Mars Project-Urbana-1953-U of Ill Pr-91p-36 graphs,9 text illus-1st US ed (hh6,dj chip & taped) 180.00

VON DER GOLTZ,LIEUT GEN-Conduct of War-Lond-1917-Kegan Paul (z2) 45.00

VON ECKARDT,HANS-Ivan the Terrible-NY-1949-Knopf-8vo-421p-1st ed (cc5,f,f dj) 25.00

VON FRIEDEN,LUCIUS-Mushrooms of the World-(1969)-Bobbs-Merrill-1439p-brwn cl,186 col illus (q8,dj,box) 40.00

VON HAGEN,V W-Desert Kingdoms of Peru-1965-NYGS-191p-137 col & b&w photos & illus-1st ed (bb3,f,dj) 18.00

VON HAGEN,V W-Maya Explorer John Lloyd Stephens and the Lost Cities of Central America and Yucatan-1947-U of Okla-324p-40 illus-1st ed (bb3,f,fray dj) 20.00

VON HAGEN,VICTOR W-Frederick Catherwood Archt-NY-1950-OUP-8vo-177p-blu cl,illus (r10,wn dj) 32.50

VON HAGEN,VICTOR-South America Called Them...-Lond-1949-Hale-401p-cl,illus (x6) 38.00

VON KOENIG-WARTHAUSEN-Wings Around the World-NY-1930-8vo-illus cl,frntis,22p plts,e.p. maps-1st ed (s2,chip dj) 25.00

VON KOTZEBUE,OTTO-Voyage of Discovery into the South Sea and Beering's Straits-Amsterdam,NY-(1967)-3 vols-psuedo wht vel wi blu labls,col frntis each vol,fldg maps,facs repro of 1821 Lond ed (e7,f) 250.00

VON KRAFFT-EBING,RICHARD-Psychopathia Sexualis-NY-1965-Bell Publ-8vo-xvi,43p-transl from 12th German ed-1st complete transl in Engl (cc7,dj) 45.00*

VON LANGSDORF,GEORGE-Voyages & Travels in Various Parts of the World-Amsterdam,NY-(1968)-4to-2 vols-psuedo wht vel wi blu tabs,glassine dj,facs rprnt (e7,f,dj) 225.00

VON MARX,ROMER-Three Star Cuisine-NY-(1965)-Heinemann-234p-grn cl,drwngs-1st prtg (q8,dj) 12.50

VON RICHTOFEN,M F-Red Battle Flyer-NY-1918-8vo-viii,222p-col illus cl,frntis,4p plts,transl. by J E Barker-1st ed (s2) 50.00

VONNEGUT,KURT,JR.-Breakfast of Champions-(NY)-(1973)-Delacorte/Lawrence-1st ed (m7,f,dj) 25.00

VONNEGUT,KURT,JR.-Breakfast of Champions-NY-(1973)-Delacorte/Lawrence-1st ed (dd2,f,dj) 35.00

VONNEGUT,KURT,JR.-Dead Eye Dick-NY-(1982)-1st ed (k9,f,dj) 14.50

VONNEGUT,KURT,JR.-Fates Worse Than Death-Nottingham-1982-Spokesman-wrps-1st ed (v5,f) 25.00

VONNEGUT,KURT,JR.-Jailbird-(NY)-(1979)-Delacorte/Lawrence-1st ed (a10,as new in dj) 20.00

VONNEGUT,KURT,JR.-Jailbird-NY-(1979)-Delacorte-ltd to 500c,nbrd,autg-1st ed (d6,f,box) 125.00

VONNEGUT,KURT,JR.-Mother Night-NY-1966-Harper & Row-1st ed thus (z3,f,dj) 65.00

VONNEGUT,KURT,JR.-Mother Night-NY-1966-Holt-1st hdcov ed (w5,f,f dj) 100.00

VONNEGUT,KURT,JR.-Palm Sunday-1981-Delacorte-1st ed (x2,f,dj) 14.00

VONNEGUT,KURT,JR.-Palm Sunday-NY-1981-1st ed (q5,f,dj) 20.00

VONNEGUT,KURT,JR.-Player Piano-1952-Scribners-1st ed (m9,dj sl chip wi brwnd sp) 300.00

VONNEGUT,KURT,JR.-Sirens of Titan-(NY)-(1959)-Dell-pbk orig-pict wrps-1st ed (m7,sl wn) 60.00

VONNEGUT,KURT,JR.-Sirens of Titan-NY-1959-pbk orig-1st ed (q5,sl wn wrps) 35.00

VONNEGUT,KURT,JR.-Slapstick-np(NY)-(1976)-Delacorte/Lawrence-1st trd ed (a10,f,dj) 25.00

VONNEGUT,KURT,JR.-Slapstick-NY-(1976)-1st trd ed (k9,f,dj) 15.00

VONNEGUT,KURT,JR.-Slaughterhouse Five-NY-1969-Delacorte-1st ed (h8,f dj) 175.00

VONNEGUT,KURT,JR.-Sun Moon Star-NY-1980-illus,I Chermayeff-1st ed (q5,f,dj) 25.00

VONNEGUT,KURT,JR.-Utopia 14-NY-(1952)-Bantam-wrps-1st ed (bb2,f) 35.00

VOORSANGER,WILLIAM C-Medical Memoirs-SF-1965-lg 8vo-viii+71p-grn cl-ltd to 500c-1st ed (j2) 25.00

VORONOV,N-Soviet Glass-1973-Aurora Art Publ-178p-illus (cc8) 35.00

VORREN,ORNULV-Lapp Life and Customs-Oslo/Lond-1962-Oslo/Oxford U Pr-8vo-183p-24 plts-1st Brit ed (dd5,scuff,dj) 15.00

VORSPAN,MAX-History of the Jews of Los Angeles-San Marino-1970-Huntington Libr-xii+362p-gry cl,plts-1st ed (mm10,edgewn dj) 20.00

VOYNICH,E L-Gadfly-NY-1897-H Holt-cl-1st ed (o8) 15.00

VROOMAN,HENRY WELLINGTON-Half a Million Insurance-NY-1888-Amer Prntg Co-52p-prntd wrps (n1,frnt wrps wtrstnd,pc mssg) 50.00

VROOMAN,JOHN J-Forts and Firesides of the Mohawk Country-Phila-1943-E E Brownell-4to-lg papr cpy,map e.p.-1st ed (ee6) 100.00

VYSHINSKY,A Y-Trotskyism-NY-1936-Workers Libr-68p-wrps (r1,fold crease) 22.00

WADDELL,L AUSTINE-Buddhism of Tibet or Lamaism-Cambridge-1967-W Heffer & Sons-cl,illus-2nd ed (l8,vf,dj) 55.00

WADDELL,MAJ L A-Among the Himalayas-Lond,Phila-1900-452p-fldg map-2nd ed (a4) 150.00

WADDINGTON,IVAN-Medical Profession in the Industrial Revolution-Dublin-1984-236p-1st ed (dd3,dj) 25.00

WADDINGTON,RICHARD-Salmon Fishing - A New Philosophy-NY-1948-8vo-199p-photos (m3,f,dj) 25.00

WADE,C F-Exmoor Streams-Lond-1903-12mo-161p+index-one of 500c,photos (m3) 30.00

WADE,DAVID-David Wade's Magic Kitchen-Dallas-(1973)-304p-gold cl-1st ed (q8,dj) 15.00

WADE,MASON-ED.-Journals of Francis Parkman-NY,Lond-1947-2 vols-e.p. maps,illus-1st ed (d7,f,dj) 65.00

WADE,MASON-ED.-Journals of Francis Parkman-NY-1947-2 vols-frntis,photos,illus,map e.p.-1st ed (t7,dj,box) 50.00

WADE,RICHARD C-Slavery in the Cities-NY-1964-340p-1st ed (n3,dj) 20.00

WADELTON,MAGGIE O-Maggie No Doubt-Indpls-(1943)-Bobbs Merrill-1st US ed (hh5,dj sl chip) 12.50

WADIA,ARDASER S-Belle of Bali-Lond-1936-Dent-4to-xvi,112p-20 photos-1st ed (p8,sl soil dj) 35.00

WADSWORTH,FRANCES-Maui Cookery-Wailuku-1939-Maui Publ-255p-rvsd ed (o6,dj) 35.00

WAGENHEIM,KAL-Babe Ruth, His Life and Legend-1974-Praeger-1st ed (p7,dj) 22.50

WAGENHEIM,KAL-Babe Ruth, His Life and Legend-1974-Praeger-photos-1st ed (s8,f,dj) 35.00

WAGENHEIM,KAL-Clemente-1973-Praeger-1st ed (q7,f,dj) 25.00

WAGER,W-Telefon-1975-Macmillan-1st ed (x7,f,sl rub dj) 25.00

WAGNER,ABNER M-El Rancho Gumbo-Morongo Valley-1983-Sagebrush Pr-124p-tan cl,ltd to 750c,autg (b6,f,dj) 15.00

WAGNER,ARTHUR L-Campaign of Konniggratz...-Ft.Leavenworth-1889-121p-cl,maps incl 6 fldg,erratum slip between pgs 70 & 71-scarce (c1) 100.00

WAGNER,CLARA E-Cupid in Hell-Columbus-1910-198p-cl,photos (a1) 15.00

WAGNER,F HOL,JR.-Colorado Road-1970-Intermt'n Chapt,NRHS-4to-415p-illus (nn7,f,f dj) 50.00

WAGNER,GLENDOLIN D-Old Neutriment-Bost-(1934)-256p-frntis,photos-Luther #74-1st ed (t7) 100.00

WAGNER,GLENDOLIN D-Old Neutriment-Bost-(1934)-Ruth Hill-8vo-256p-cl,photos,Howes W5-1st ed (v1,dj) 175.00

WAGNER,GLENDOLIN D-Old Neutriment-NY-1973-Sol Lewis-8vo-256p-rprnt ed (z4) 15.00

WAGNER,HENRY R-Bullion to Books-LA-1942-Zamorano Club-370p-cl,frntis port,pls-ltd to 300c-1st ed (dd10,f) 325.00

WAGNER,HENRY R-Cartography of the Northwest Coast of America to the Year 1800-Amsterdam-1968-4to-2 vols-fldg maps-rprnt of 1937 ed (d3) 175.00

WAGNER,HENRY R-Cartography of the NW Coast of America to Year 1800-Amsterdam-1968-543p-fldg map-rprnt of 1937 rare 1st ed (u7) 60.00

WAGNER,HENRY R-ED.-California Voyages: 1539 to 1541-1925-John Howell-95p-maps-1st ed (d3) 175.00

WAGNER,HENRY R-First American Vessel in California, Monterey in 1796-1954-Glen Dawson-33p-ltd to 325c (d3) 50.00

WAGNER,HENRY R-Juan Rodriguez Cabrillo-SF-1941-Cal Hist Soc-94p-ltd to 750c-Howes W8 (dd4) 125.00

WAGNER,HENRY R-Juan Rodriguez Cabrillo-SF-1941-Cal Hist Soc-Spec Publ No.17-ltd to 750c prtd by L Kennedy (d3) 100.00

WAGNER,HENRY R-Plains & the Rockies-SF-1982-John Howell-xx,745p-cl,illus-4th ed,rvsd & enlgd (v1) 150.00

WAGNER,HENRY R-Sir Francis Drake's Voyage Around the World, Its Aims and Achievements-SF-1926-John Howell-qto-543p-maroon cl,maps-1st ed (d3) 325.00

WAGNER,HENRY R-Sir Francis Drake's Voyage Around the World: Its Aims and Achievements-Amsterdam-1969-4to-543p-illus-rprnt (d3) 100.00

WAGNER,HENRY R-Spanish Southwest; 1542 to 1794-1967-Arno-2 vols-fldg map-rprntd from Quivira Soc ed (d3) 100.00

WAGNER,HENRY R-TRANSL-California Voyages 1539 to 1541-SF-1925-John Howell-8vo-95p+index & maps-ltd to 200c cl bnd (p1) 250.00

WAGNER,JACK R-Last Whistle-Berkeley-1974-135p-1st ed (n4,f,dj) 25.00

WAGNER,JACK R-Short Line Junction-Fresno-1956-266p-1st ed (n4,f,dj) 20.00

WAGNER,JOHN P-Boxer-NY-1948-282p-cl (l1) 12.50

WAGNER,LAURA V-Through Historic Years with Eliza Ferry Leary-Seattle-1934-Dogwood Pr-flowered cl-1st ed (w1,f) 40.00

WAGNER,PHILIP M-After Sunrise, or Second Attempts at Poetry-Canal Dover-1909-155,(2)p-cl (g1) 15.00

WAGNER,PHILIP M-American Wines...-NY-1933-Knopf-295,xiv p-fldout synopsis-1st ed (o6,dj) 25.00

WAGNER,R-American Combat Planes-GC-1960-4to-448p-cl,illus t.p.,plts (s2,dj) 40.00

WAGNER,R-North American Sabre-GC-(1963)-roy 8vo-162p-cl,col frntis,plts (s2,dj) 35.00

WAGNER,RICHARD M-Cincinnati Streetcars No.1...-1968-Wagner-4to-24p-wrps,illus (nn7) 16.00

WAGNER,RICHARD-Curved Side Cars-Cin-1965-120p-spiral bndg-1st ed (n4) 27.50

WAGNER,RICHARD-Parsifal,A Mystical Drama-1903-Crowell-illus-1st ed (x2,sl sunned sp) 35.00

WAGNER,RUDOLF-Handbook of Chemical Technology-NY-1872-D Appleton-xvi+745+xvi pgs-brwn cl,illus-1st Amer ed (j2) 50.00

WAGNER,STERLING R-Modern Airport-Syracuse-1931-NY St Coll Forestry-sm 4to-109p-wrps,illus,maps,9 fldg plans & elev-Tech Publ. No.33 (cc10) 30.00

WAGNER,WALTER-Golden Fleecers-GC-1966-Dbldy-8vo-278p-1st ed (gg5,sl chip dj) 12.50

WAGNER-CAMP-Plains and the Rockies-SF-1982-745p-frntis,photos (t7,f) 125.00

WAGONER,DAVID-Man in the Middle-NY-1954-Harcourt Brace-1st ed (y10,f,sl soil dj) 45.00

WAGONER,J J-History of Cattle Industry in Southern Arizona, 1540 to 1940-1952-U of Ariz-132p-wrps,illus-U of Ariz Bull No.20,April,1952-Herd#2417 (t8) 30.00

WAHL,P-Gatling Gun-NY-1965-168p-illus,port (z10,dj) 60.00

WAHL,T R-Guide to Bird Finding in Washington-Bellingham-1974(1973)-4to-(4),97p-wrps,2 maps,drwngs-rvsd ed (y8,sp tn) 13.00

WAHLOO,PER-Assignment-NY-1966-Knopf-1st US ed (f4,dj) 10.00

WAHLOO,PER-Generals-NY-1974-Pantheon-1st US ed (h4,f,dj) 12.50

WAHLOO,PER-Necessary Action-1968-Pantheon-1st Amer ed (s9,dj) 20.00

WAHLOO,PER-Necessary Action-1968-Pantheon-1st Amer ed (x7,f,dj) 45.00

WAHLOO,PER-Steel Spring-Lond-1970-Joseph-1st Brit ed (q4,dj) 17.50

WAHLOO,PETER-Steel Spring-1970-Delacorte-1st Amer ed (s10,dj) 15.00

WAHRMUND,HARRY-History of the Doss Community-Doss-1956-36p-wrps,photos-1st ed (w3,vf) 15.00

WAINWRIGHT,JOHN-An Urge for Justice-NY-1981-St.Martin's-1st US ed (e4,f,dj) 10.00

WAINWRIGHT,SAMUEL H-Beauty in Japan-NY-(1935)-Putnam's-ix,308p-dec cl,col frntis,illus-1st ed (kk1,sl wn dj) 35.00

WAIT,GEORGE W-New Jersey's Money-Newark-1976-4to-x.434p-cl backd bds,illus (aa6) 60.00

WAITE,ARTHUR E-Lamps of Western Mysticism-Lond-1923-K Paul,Trench,Trubner-cl-1st ed (l8) 145.00

WAITE,DIANA-ED.-Architectural Elements-NY-1972-Bonanza Bks-4to-70p-rust bds,illus (r10,f,sl wn dj) 20.00

WAITE,S E-Old Settlers, a Historical and Chronological Record...-Traverse City-1918-86p+ads-tan prntd wrps,photos-scarce (z7,crease,sm holes rear cov) 135.00

WAKEFIELD,DAN-Going All the Way-1970-Delacorte-1st ed (s9,dj) 15.00

WAKEFIELD,DAN-Island in the City-Bost-1959-Houghton Mifflin-auth 1st bk-1st ed (l7,f,dj) 35.00

WAKEFIELD,H R-Clock Strikes Twelve-Sauk City-1946-Arkham Hs-ltd to 4,040c-1st ed (l7,f,sl sunned dj) 45.00

WAKEFIELD,H RUSSELL-Strayers From Sheol-Sauk City-1961-Arkham-186p-ltd to 2070c-1st ed (k5,f,dj sp sl tanned) 35.00

WAKEFIELD,HUGH-Nineteenth Century British Glass-Lond-1982-Faber & Faber-168p-9 col+166 monochrome illus (cc8,f,dj) 45.00

WAKEFIELD,MANVILLE B-To the Mountains by Rail-Grahamsville-1970-415p-1st ed (n4,f,dj) 34.00

WAKEFIELD,PRISCILLA-An Introduction to Botany-Lond-1828-Darton-187p-papr cov bds,engrvngs-9th ed (x6,bds wn) 50.00

WAKEFIELD,PRISCILLA-Excursions in North America...-Lond-1806-Darton & Harvey-8vo-(xii),420,(iv)p-contemp calf,fldg 16"x15"map-Sabin 100980-1st ed (w6,sl wn hng) 425.00

WAKEFIELD,ROBERT-Schwering and the West-Aberdeen-1973-North Plains Pr-4to-xvii+207p-bds,col illus-1st ed (z4,sl wn & scratched dj) 30.00

WAKEMAN,FREDERIC-Shore Leave-NY-1944-F&R-auth 1st bk-1st ed (x1,f,sl wn dj) 35.00

WAKOSKI,DIANE-Coins and Coffins-NY-1962-Hawk's Well Pr-wrps-1st ed (w5,f) 85.00

WAKOSKI,DIANE-Looking for Beethoven in Las Vegas-(NY)-(1981)-(Red Ozier Pr)-loose sheets in papr portfolio-ltd to 200c,autg-1st ed (jj8,as new) 45.00

WAKOSKI,DIANE-Saturn's Rings-(NY)-(1982)-Targ Eds-sq 8vo-glassine dj-ltd to 250c,autg-1st ed (jj8,vf,dj) 65.00

WAKOSKI,DIANE-Virtuoso Literature for Two aaaand Four Hands-GC-1975-Dbldy-1st ed (w5,f,f dj) 25.00

WAKOWSKI,DIANE-Virtuoso Literature for Two and Four Hands-NY-1975-Dbldy-8vo-85p-1st ed (w6,f,dj) 10.00

WALAM OLUM OR RED SCORE-Indpls-1954-379p-cl (f1) 60.00

WALBANK,F A-ED.-Wings of War-Lond-(1943)-roy 8vo-viii,164p-cl,frntis,52 illus (s2,dj) 25.00

WALBRAN,CAPT JOHN T-British Columbia Coast Names-Seattle,Lond-(1971)-546p-illus,e.p. maps-rprnt of 1909 Canadian Gov't ed (h7,f,dj) 40.00

WALBRAN,I M-Grayling & How to Catch Them-Lond-1895-142p-illus (gg3,f) 15.00

WALBRIDGE,WILLIAM S-American Bottles Old & New-1920-US Owens Bottle Co-112p-illus (cc8) 35.00

WALCOTT,CHARLES D-Geologic Atlas of the U.S. Tishomingo Folio, Indian Territory-Wash D.C.-1903-USGS-lg folio-unpgd(19p)-wrps,chrts,col map (ee10,f) 25.00

WALCOTT,DEREK-Fortunate Traveller-NY-1981-illus-1st ed (r2,f,dj) 25.00

WALDEN,ARTHUR T-Dog Puncher on the Yukon-Bost,NY-1928-Houghton Mifflin-289p-photos,map e.p.-Six Guns #2278-1st ed (dd4) 30.00

WALDEN,HOWARD T,II-Big Stony-NY-1940-12mo-401p-illus,M Weiler-1st trd ed (m3,fray dj) 12.50

WALDEN,HOWARD T,II-Familiar Freshwater Fishes of America-NY-(1964)-Harper & Row-xiii,324p-cl,illus-1st ed (pp8,dj) 35.00*

WALDEN,HOWARD T,II-Upstream & Down-Derrydale-1938-12mo-367p-ltd to 950c,nbrd,illus by M Weiler (m3,lettering dulled) 100.00

WALDER,DAVID-Nelson-NY-1978-538p-illus-1st Amer ed (b7,f,dj) 25.00

WALDMAN,MILTON-Americana-NY-1925-illus-1st ed (r2) 75.00

WALDO,EDNA L-TRANSL-Deadwood to the Bighorns 1877-Bismarck-1931-50p-ltd to 50c-v scarce (t7,f) 225.00

WALDO,MYRA-Beer and Good Food-1958-Dbldy-264p-pict wht cl,pict e.p.,decs-1st ed (q8,dj) 17.50

WALDO,MYRA-Complete Book of Gourmet Cooking for the American Table-NY-(1960)-Putnam's-374p-illus (r6,dj) 12.00

WALDO,MYRA-Complete Book of Gourmet Cooking-(1960)-Putnam-374p-dec grn cl,drwngs-1st ed (q8,dj) 16.50

WALDO,TERRY-This is Ragtime-NY-1976-Hawthorn-1st ed (v5,f,f dj) 15.00

WALDO,WALLACE-Glimpses of the Past-St.Louis-1938-35p-wrps-Rittenhouse #615-1st ed (t7) 30.00

WALDRON,MALCOLM-Snow Man-Bost,NY-1931-Houghton Mifflin,Rvrsd Pr-8vo-x,292p-e.p. maps,frntis,27 illus-1st ed (mm8,sl bump) 35.00*

WALES,PHILIP-Report on Yellow Fever in the U.S.S. Plymouth in 1878,9-Wash-1880-85p-6 heliotype photo plts-1st ed (dd3) 150.00

WALES,THOMAS B,JR.-COMP.-Holstein-Freisian Herd Book...-(Davenport)-1886-2 vols-cl-scarce (e1) 27.50

WALEY,ARTHUR-Opium Wars Through Chinese Eyes-NY-1958-257p-1st Amer ed (b7,f,dj) 30.00

WALEY,ARTHUR-TRANSL-Pillow Book of Sei Shonagon-Lond-(1928)-Allen & Unwin-162,(2)p ads-cl-1st ed (kk1,f,dj sl soil & wn) 125.00

WALEY,ARTHUR-Yuan Mei-Lond-1956-Allen & Unwin-cl,frntis-1st ed (o8,f,dj) 12.50

WALFORD,LIONEL A-Marine Game Fishes of the Pacific Coast-Berkeley-1937-4to-205p+plts,illus-scarce (m3) 100.00

WALKER,A H-Conjuring Tricks-Lond-nd(1920)-Routledge & Sons-col pict bds,illus-1st ed (jj9) 20.00

WALKER,ALBERT H-History of the Sherman Law of the U.S.A.-NY-1910-Equity Pr-xiv+320p-red cl-1st ed (b2) 20.00

WALKER,ALEXANDER-Beauty-NY-1840-Langley-8vo-xx,390+6p ads-orig blndstmpd cl-1st ed (y4,sun,sl wn) 50.00

WALKER,ALICE-Color Purple-Lond-(1983)-Women's Pr-1st Brit ed (cc2,f,dj) 45.00

WALKER,ALICE-Color Purple-NY-1982-1st ed (p5,f dj) 165.00

WALKER,ALICE-Color Purple-NY-1982-HBJ-1st ed (e8,f,sl tn dj) 275.00

WALKER,ALICE-Horses Make a Landscape Look More Beautiful-NY-1984-HBJ-1st ed (b8,f,f dj) 35.00

WALKER,ALICE-Meridian-Lond-1976-1st Brit ed (q5,dj) 75.00

WALKER,ALICE-Third Life of Grange Copeland-(1970)-HBJ-1st ed (v8,dj rear panel sl stnd) 200.00

WALKER,ALICE-Third Life of Grange Copeland-NY-(1970)-HBJ-1st ed (c10,sl soil dj) 250.00

WALKER,ALICE-Third Life of Grange Copeland-NY-1970-1st ed (o5,dj sl soil,ink prcs f flp) 150.00

WALKER,C F-Art of Chalk Stream Fishing-Lond-1968-8vo-192p-photos (m3,vf,dj) 22.50

WALKER,E P-ET AL-Mammals of the World-Rev. by Paradiso-Balt-1968-8vo-2 vols-cl,photos-2nd ed (y8,box) 60.00

WALKER,FRANCIS A-Indian Question-Bost-1874-Osgood-268p-fldg map-1st ed (bb4,ex-libr) 150.00

WALKER,FRANKLIN-Literary History of Southern California-Berkeley-1950-U of Cal Pr-282p-illus-1st ed (cc4,dj) 25.00

WALKER,FRED-Destination Unknown, Running Away to Danger-Phila-1935-Lippincott-8vo-285p-1st ed (ff5,dj) 35.00

WALKER,GEN FRANCIS A-General Hancock-NY-1894-Appleton-332p-frntis,maps-Great Commanders Ser-1st ed (cc6) 30.00

WALKER,H M-History of the Northumberland Fusiliers 1674 to 1902-Lond-1919-502p-red cl,maps,illus-1st ed (b7) 100.00

WALKER,HENRY P-Wagonmasters-1968-U of OK-347p-illus,maps-2nd prtg (r8,dj) 22.00

WALKER,J HUBERT-Mountain Days in the Highlands and Alps-NY-1937-Macmillan-8vo-320p+64 photo plts by auth-1st Amer ed (u1,dj) 60.00

WALKER,JAMES R-ED.-Lakota Belief and Ritual-Lincoln-1980-329p-photos,illus-1st ed (t7,as new in dj) 20.00

WALKER,JIM-ED.-Yellow Cars of Los Angeles-Glendale-(1977)-Interurban Publ-4to-318p-photos-1st ed (dd5,ffep stnd,dj rub) 17.50

WALKER,JUDSON E-Campaigns of General Custer-NY-(1966)-Promontory Pr-135p-illus-Howes W40 (ee4,dj) 20.00

WALKER,KENNETH R-Day the Presidents Died-Little Rock-1966-175p-1st ed (n3,f,dj) 15.00

WALKER,KENNETH-Making of Man-Lond-1963-Routledge & K Paul-cl,frntis, wi add photo of Gurdjieff-1st ed (l8,f,dj) 27.50

WALKER,KENNETH-Mystic Mind-NY-1965-Emerson Bks-cl-1st Amer ed (n8,f,dj) 20.00

WALKER,KENNETH-Study of Gurdjieff's Teaching-Lond-1957-J Cape-cl,frntis,illus-1st ed (l8,f,dj) 65.00

WALKER,KENNETH-Venture with Ideas-NY-1952-Pellegrini & Cudahy-cl,frntis-1st ed (l8,vf,dj) 27.50

WALKER,L W-Book of Owls-1974-Knopf-255p-photos-1st ed (bb3,f,dj) 20.00

WALKER,MARGARET-Prophets for a New Day-Detr-1970-Broadside Pr-wrps-1st ed (w5,f) 30.00

WALKER,MICHAEL-ED.-Sport Fishing U.S.A.-Wash D.C.-1971-8vo-464p-illus by B Hines,photos (m3,f) 20.00

WALKER,PEGGY-George Humphreys Cowboy and Lawman-Burnet-1978-Eakin Publ-66p-cl,photos-1st ed (w3,as new in dj) 15.00

WALKER,R-Dastral of the Flying Corps-Lond-nd(ca.1919)-sm 8vo-256p-illus cl,frntis,3p plts (t2) 30.00

WALKER,RICHARD-Stillwater Angling-Lond-1953-8vo-232p-photos,illus (m3) 25.00

WALKER,ROBERT S-As the Indians Left It-Chattanooga-1955-239,(1)p-cl (a1,f) 15.00

WALKER,SIR HOVENDEN-Journal or Full Account of the Late Expedition to Canada-Lond-1720-D Browne-8vo-304p-orig panelled calf,red labl-Sabin 101050 (u3) 785.00

WALKER,THEODORE-Red Salmon, Brown Bear-1971-World-226p-col illus-1st prtg (u8,dj) 18.00

WALKER,W M-Troyville Mounds, Catahoula Parish, Louisiana-1936-Bur Amer Ethnol Bull.113-73p-papr wrps,16 plts (bb3,f) 20.00

WALKER,WINIFRED-All the Plants of the Bible-NY-(1957)-col frntis,114 plts (m10,chip dj) 12.50

WALKINSHAW,LAWRENCE H-Sandhill Cranes-1949-Crnbrk Inst Sci,Bull.29-202p (b9,dj) 40.00

WALKINSHAW,LAWRENCE-Cranes of the World-NY-1973-Winchester Pr-4to-370p-photos (c9,dj) 45.00

WALKINSHAW,ROBERT-On Puget Sound-NY-1929-294p-t.e.g.,20 sketches-1st ed (a4,f) 35.00

WALKLEY,A B-PREFACE-Clarisse, or the Old Cook-Lond-(1926)-Methuen-16mo-178p-pict bds-1st ed in Engl (q8,cov fade,dj chip) 25.00

WALL,COL JOHN F-Famous Running Horses-Wash-1949-Infantry Journal-4to-313p-1st ed (f10) 58.00

WALL,DAVID-Rondoy, an Expedition to the Peruvian Andes-Lond-1965-176p-35 photos,3 maps-1st Brit ed (p10,as new in dj) 27.00

WALL,J TOM-Crossing Old Trails to New in North Central Wyoming-(1973)-Dorrance-242p-illus-1st ed (r8,f,f dj) 15.00

WALL,JOHN P-Chronicles of New Brunswick, New Jersey, 1667 to 1931-New Brunswick-1931-viii,487p-cl,illus (aa6) 100.00

WALL,O A-Sex and Sex Worship-St.Louis-1922-C V Mosby-cl,372 illus-3rd prtg (n8) 65.00

WALL,ROBERT-Ocean Liners-NY-(1977)-folio-256p-400 illus(incl col)-1st ed (pp4,dj) 35.00

WALL,ROY-Contemplative Angler-NY-1948-8vo-215p-Illus,G Don Ray (m3,vf,dj) 13.50

WALLA WALLA COUNTY-Souvenir of 1905-unpgd(approx 120p)-oblng 10" by 7"-cord tied wrps,glossy stock,illus-v scarce (h7,sl tn sp) 45.00

WALLACE,A F-Land Cruising & Prospecting-Columbus-1908-16mo-175p-illus (m3) 20.00

WALLACE,A R-Malay Archipelago-Lond-1890-8vo-(1),515p-cl,drwngs,10 maps(2 fldg & tint)-new ed (y8,hng crack) 55.00

WALLACE,ALEXANDER-Heather in Lore,Lyric and Lay-NY-1903-245p-g dec cl,col frntis,32p half tones (jj7,hng rprd) 41.00

WALLACE,ALFRED R-Darwinism, an Exposition of the Theory of Natural Selection...-Lond-1889-494p-1st ed (dd3) 250.00

WALLACE,ALFRED R-Geographical Distribution of Animals-NY-1876-Harper & Bros-2 vols-brwn cl,7 maps,20 plts-1st Amer ed (c2,ex-libr) 165.00

WALLACE,ANTHONY F C-King of the Delawares-Phila-1949-Univ of Penn Pr-xiv+305p-red cl (k2,dj) 30.00

WALLACE,ANTHONY F C-Religion-NY-(1966)-Random-8vo-300p-cl-1st prtg (y5,chip dj) 26.00

WALLACE,DILLON-Lure of the Labrador Wild-NY-1905-Revell Co-8vo-339p-dec blu cl,gilt,frntis,16 illus,fldg map in rear-1st ed (cc7,sl shaken) 35.00*

WALLACE,EDGAR-Black Abbot-NY-1927-Dbldy-1st US ed (g4) 12.50

WALLACE,EDGAR-Day of Uniting-1930-Mystery League-1st ed (x7,dj) 12.00

WALLACE,EDGAR-Four Just Men-Bost-1920-Small-1st US ed (e4) 20.00

WALLACE,EDGAR-Four Just Men-Lond-1905-Tallis-wi fold-out frontis & competition slip-1st ed (j4,fox) 50.00

WALLACE,EDGAR-Man Who Changed His Name-NY-1934-Dbldy CC-1st ed (f4,dj sl chip,sl tn) 25.00

WALLACE,EDGAR-Mr.Commissioner Sanders-NY-1930-Dbldy-1st US ed (f4) 10.00

WALLACE,EDGAR-Ringer Returns-NY-1931-Dbldy CC-1st US ed (d4,f,dj) 45.00

WALLACE,EDGAR-Ringer-Lond-nd-Hodder-pict wrps-"Yellow Ninepenny" ed (h4) 10.00

WALLACE,EDGAR-Sanders of the River-Lond,Mlbrn,Tor-1911-Lock & Co-tooled dec sp & frnt cov,frntis-1st Brit ed (aa8,brwnd e.p.) 75.00

WALLACE,EDGAR-Sergeant Sir Peter-Tor-1932-Musson-precedes Amer ed by one yr-1st Can ed (f4,f,sl soil dj) 35.00

WALLACE,EDGAR-Silinski, Master Criminal-Cleve-1930-World-1st ed (h4,yel pgs,dj) 20.00

WALLACE,EDGAR-Trial of Patrick Mahon-NY-1928-Scribner's-1st US ed (x9,sp sunned) 30.00

WALLACE,EDGAR-White Face-GC-(1931)-Dbldy,Doran-pict dj-1st ed (bb1,edgewn dj) 50.00

WALLACE,EDWARD S-Great Reconnaissance-Bost-(1955)-Little,Brown-288p-illus-1st ed (ee4,dj) 30.00

WALLACE,ERNEST-Comanches-Norman-(1952)-U of Okla Pr-381p-illus-1st ed (ee4) 45.00

WALLACE,ERNEST-ED.-Ranald S Mackenzie's Official Correspondence Relating to Texas, 1871 to 1873-Lubbock-1967-West Tx Mus-202p-1st ed (a9,dj) 50.00

WALLACE,ERNEST-ED.-Ranald S Mackenzie's Official Correspondence Relating to Texas, 1873 to 1879-Lubbock-1968-West Tx Mus Assn-241p-1st ed (a9,dj) 40.00

WALLACE,ERNEST-Howling Coyote-College Sta-1979-217p-photos,illus-1st ed (t7,f,dj) 15.00

WALLACE,FRANCIS-Dementia Pigskin-NY-(1951)-Rinehart-1st ed (y10,dj sl chip,soil) 22.00

WALLACE,FREDERICK T-Men and Events of Half a Century-Cleve-1882-363p-cl (a1,sl soil) 20.00

WALLACE,H FRANK-Hunting Winds-Lond-1949-8vo-351p-illus,auth (m3,f,fray dj) 40.00

WALLACE,HELEN B-Historic Paxton-1913-Woman's Aid Soc-scarce-1st ed (dd8) 15.00

WALLACE,HILDICK-Bracknell's Law-Lond-1976-Hamilton-1st Brit ed (r4,dj) 20.00

WALLACE,JOSEPHINE-Aunt Josephine's Book of Recipes-Des Moines-1923-Wallace Publ-71p-grn wrps-Bitting 483 (n6) 25.00

WALLACE,LEW-Chariot Race From Ben Hur-NY-1908-Harpers-8vo-132p-dec cl bndg in two col,col illus by Ivanowski-1st ed thus (p1,f,dj) 75.00

WALLACE,LEW-Fair God-1873-Osgood-auth 1st bk-1st ed (x2) 75.00

WALLACE,LILY H-Rumford Complete Cook Book-Providence-(1908)-Rumford Chemical Works-241p-grn bds (r6) 14.00

WALLACE,SUSAN E-Land of the Pueblos-NY-1888-285p-cl-1st ed (d1,cov sl flecking) 50.00

WALLACE,SUSAN E-Land of the Pueblos-NY-1888-285p-illus-1st ed (u7) 60.00

WALLACE,SUSAN E-Repose in Egypt-Troy-1889-Nims & Knight-391p-cl-2nd ed (a1) 17.50

WALLACE,WILLIAM S-Journey Through New Mexico's First Judicial District in 1864-LA-(1956)-Wstrnlore Pr-71p-illus-ltd to 350c of which 300 are for sale-1st ed (dd4) 35.00

WALLACK,L R-American Rifle Design & Performance-NY-1977-4to-213p-photos-1st ed (m3,vf,dj) 15.00

WALLANT,EDWARD L-Children at the Gate-NY-1964-1st ed (q5,dj) 20.00

WALLANT,EDWARD L-Human Season-NY-1960-auth 1st bk-1st ed (q5,wn dj) 40.00

WALLANT,EDWARD L-Pawnbroker-Lond-1962-1st Brit ed (q5,dj) 35.00

WALLANT,EDWARD L-Tenants of Moonbloom-NY-1963-1st ed (q5,dj wi sm tape repair) 15.00

WALLEN,ED G-United Methodism Takes Root in the Black Swamp-Fremont-(1981)-300p-wrps (h1) 12.50

WALLING,EDNA-Cottage and Garden in Australia-Melbourne-1947-Cumberlege/OUP-4to-(8),148,(2)p-bds,col frntis,illus-v scarce-1st ed (pp7) 150.00

WALLING,EDNA-Gardens in Australia-Melbourne-1946-Leighton Hs-8vo-148p-blu cl,blu tone photos-4th prtg (r10,wn dj) 20.00

WALLING,R A J-By Hook or Crook-NY-1941-Morrow-1st US ed (g4,chip dj) 15.00

WALLIS,CHARLES L-Stories on Stone-NY-1954-Oxford U-xv,272p-1st ed (o2,sl chip dj) 20.00

WALLIS,ETHEL E-God Speaks Navajo-NY-(1968)-146p-1st ed (v7,dj) 15.00

WALLIS,J H-Capital City Mystery-1932-Dutton-1st ed (s10,lg chip rear dj panel) 15.00

WALLIS,J H-Murder by Formula-1931-Dutton-1931 (s10,dj) 20.00

WALLIS,J H-Mystery of Vaucluse-NY-1933-Dutton-1st ed (e4,sl chip dj) 20.00

WALLIS,MRS-Life in Feejee or, Five Years Amoung the Cannibals. By a Lady-Ridgewood-1967-Gregg Pr-8vo-xv,(1),422p-dec wht cl,map-rprnt of 1851 ed (nn1,f) 45.00

WALLIS,MRS.GEORGE B, JR.-COMP.-D.R. Recipes-NY-nd(ca.1901)-Willett Pr-55p-blu bds (n6,wn bds) 50.00

WALLIS,RUTH S-No Bones About It-NY-1944-Dodd-1st ed (f4,dj) 20.00

WALLOP,DOUGLASS-Baseball, An Informal History-1969-Norton-photos-1st ed (s8,dj) 11.50

WALLS,GORDON L-Vertebrate Eye and Its Adaptive Radiation-Bloomfield Hills-1942-Cranbrook Inst Sci-xvi+785p-beige cl-1st ed (a2) 50.00

WALPOLE,HORACE-Letter to a Modern Novelist-Lond-1932-Hogarth Pr-handsewn wrps-Hogarth Letters No.9-1st ed (q2) 35.00

WALPOLE,HUGH-All Souls Night-1933-MacMillan-1st ed (x2,vf,dj) 250.00

WALPOLE,HUGH-Jeremy at Crale-NY-(1927)-1st US ed (y7,dj fray,pcs missng) 15.00

WALPOLE,HUGH-Jeremy at Crale-NY-(1927)-Doran-1st US ed (hh5,chip dj) 12.50

WALPOLE,HUGH-Prayer For My Son-1936-MacMillan-1st ed (x2,f,dj) 24.00

WALSDORF,JOHN J-William Morris in Private Press and Limited Edition: A Descriptive Bibliography...1891 to 1981-1983-Oryx Pr-thk 4to-601p (w1,f,box) 45.00

WALSH,CHRISTY-ED.-Baseball's Greatest Lineup-1952-Barnes-1st ed (r7,dj) 25.00

WALSH,CHRISTY-ED.-Baseball's Greatest Lineup-1952-Barnes-photos-1st ed (s8,f,dj) 35.00

WALSH,GEORGE E-Friend of the Seminole-Elgin-(1911)-David C Cook-96p-dbl columns-Gardner 1006-1st ed (e1) 20.00

WALSH,HENRY L-Hallowed were the Gold Dust Trails-1946-U of Santa Clara Pr-559p-maps,illus-1st ed (nn6) 30.00

WALSH,JAMES J-Cures-NY-1924-291p (g10) 25.00

WALSH,JAMES J-Makers of Modern Medicine-NY-1907-362p-frntis-1st ed (g10,ex-libr) 35.00

WALSH,RICHARD-Making of Buffalo Bill-Indpls-(1928)-391p-pict e.p.,illus-1st ed (jj1,sl spot & wn) 30.00

WALSH,ROY-Sanctuary Pond-Barre-1967-8vo-94p-photos-1st ed (m3,as new in dj) 12.50

WALSH,THOMAS-To Hide a Rogue-Lond-1965-Cassell-1st Brit ed (r4,sl bump,dj) 17.50

WALSHAM,WILLIAM J-Deformities of the Human Foot-NY-1895-550p-illus (g10) 85.00

WALSHINGHAM,LORD-Fish-Lond-1926-12mo-158p-photos (m3) 10.00

WALSLEY,LEO-Fishermen at War-GC-1941-Dbldy Doran-8vo-302p-9 illus-1st US ed (gg5,dj) 25.00

WALTER,ELIZABETH-In the Mist-Sauk City-1979-Arkham-1st ed (f3,f,dj) 20.00

WALTER,PAUL A-Papers of the School of American Archaeology-np-1916-53p-wrps,photos-1st ed (t7) 25.00

WALTON,CLYDE-Private Smith's Journal-Chig-1963-Lakeside Classic-253p-pict cl,frntis,illus (t7) 15.00

WALTON,EVANGELINE-Witch House-Sauk City-1945-Arkham Hs-ltd to 2949c-1st ed (l7,vf,vf dj) 75.00

WALTON,ISAAK-Compleat Angler-Bost-1891-8vo-2 vols-blu cl,illus-Horne #152-3rd Lowell rprnt (m3) 35.00

WALTON,ISAAK-Compleat Angler-Bost-1912-8vo-465p-illus-Horne #245 (m3) 20.00

WALTON,ISAAK-Compleat Angler-Lond-1856-12mo-497p-illus-Horne #70-1st Jesse ed (m3,chip sp,sl weak frnt hng) 35.00

WALTON,ISAAK-Compleat Angler-Lond-1895-12mo-245p-Horne #168-1st Scott ed (m3) 15.00

WALTON,ISAAK-Compleat Angler-NY,Lond-1847-Wiley & Putnam-12mo-600p-1/4 calf gilt,illus-Horne #60-1st Amer ed (m3,sl stnd text) 150.00

WALTON,ISAAK-Compleat Angler-NY-1925-8vo-221p-col illus,J Thorpe-Horne #273-7th Thorpe rprnt (m3) 50.00

WALTON,ISAAK-Compleat Angler-NY-1938-4to-241p-illus,R Ball-Horne #309-Heritage Club ed (m3,f,box) 40.00

WALTON,ISAAK-Compleat Angler-NY-1975-4to-224p-Illus,A Rackham-Weathervane ed (m3,vf,dj) 12.00

WALTON,ISAAK-Compleat Angler-Phila-1931-8vo-224p-blu grn cl gilt,12p col illus by A Rackham-Horne #301-1st Amer ed thus (m3) 75.00

WALTON,ISAAK-Complete Angler or the Contemplative Man's Recreation-Bost-1928-Goodspeed/Merrymount Pr-illus by W A Dwiggins-ltd to 600c (p6,f) 100.00

WALTON,ISAAK-Complete Angler-Bost-1867-16mo-445p-orig gilt bndg,illus-Horne #88 (m3) 40.00

WALTON,ISAAK-Lives of Dr.John Donne, Sir Henry Wotton, Mr.Richard Hooker, Mr.George Herbert & Dr.Robert Sanderson-Lond-1825-John Major-12mo-503p-orig bndg,illus-scarce (m3) 60.00

WALTON,J P-Early Recollections of Bloomington and Its Surroundings-np-nd-7p-wrps-scarce (t7) 15.00

WALTON,J P-Early Recollections of Bloomington-np-(1887)-(8)p-self wrps (f1) 17.50

WALTON,JOSEPH-Footprints and Waymarks for the Help of the Christian Traveller-Phila-1894-515p-cl (c1) 20.00

WALTON,W M-Life and Adventures of Ben Thompson-Austin-1956-Steck Co-229p-col woodcts-Six Guns #2302 (cc4,box) 30.00

WAMBAUGH,JOSEPH-Blue Knight-Bost-(1972)-Little,Brown-cl bckd bds-1st ed (aa9,f,dj) 20.00

WAMBAUGH,JOSEPH-Delta Star-NY-1983-Morrow-1st ed (bb1,as new in dj) 10.00

WAMBAUGH,JOSEPH-Onion Field-NY-1973-1st ed (n5,f,dj) 15.00

WAMBOLD,H R-Bowhunting for Deer-Harrisburg-1964-8vo-160p-1st ed (m3,f,fray dj) 15.00

WANDEL,JOSEPH-German Dimension of American History-NY-1979-Nelson Hall-238p-1st ed (ff8,dj) 24.00

WANDREI,DONALD-Strange Harvest-Sauk City-1965-Arkham-1st ed (l3,f,dj) 40.00

WANDREI,DONALD-Web of Easter Island-Sauk City-1948-Arkham Hs-ltd to 3068c-1st ed (l7,f,f dj) 55.00

WANDREI,DONALD-Web of Easter Island-Sauk City-1948-Arkham-191p-ltd to 3068c-1st ed (k5,f,dj) 40.00

WANGENSTEEN,OWEN-Rise of Surgery from Empiric Craft to Scientific Discipline-Mpls-1978-784p-1st ed (dd3) 75.00

WANLESS,ALEXANDER-Angler's Creel-Lond-nd-12mo-207p-photos-1st prtg so stated (m3) 10.00

WANLESS,ALEXANDER-Angling Methods-Lond-1935-12mo-156p-Col plts-1st ed (m3,f) 12.50

WANLESS,ALEXANDER-Fly Fisherman's Alphabet-Lond-1949-8vo-154p-illus-1st ed (m3) 15.00

WANLESS,ALEXANDER-Modern Practical Angler-Lond-1931-12mo-168p-illus-1st prntg (m3,f) 15.00

WANLESS,ALEXANDER-Thread Angling Questions Answered-Lond-1933-12mo-134p-illus,photos-1st ed (m3) 12.50

WAR BIRDS-NY-(1926)-277p-cl,col illus by C Knight (d1,sm spots frnt cov) 17.50

WARBASSE,JAMES P-Warbasse History-Falmouth-1954-Kendall Pr-vi+5-226p-blu cl-1st ed (c2,chip dj) 35.00

WARD,A W-ED.-Cambridge History of English Literature-NY,Cambridge-1933-15 vols,cl (m1) 75.00

WARD,ARCH-ED.-Greatest Sports Stories from the Chicago Tribune-1953-Barnes-1st ed (ff2,dj) 20.00

WARD,ARTEMAS-Encyclopedia of Food, Colored Plates-NY-1941-Peter Smith-unpgd-grn cl,col plts indexed to text vol (q8) 25.00

WARD,ARTEMAS-Encyclopedia of Food-NY-1923-lg thk 4to-596p-grn cl,col & b&w plts-3rd ed,1st prtg rvsd & enlgd ed (q8) 75.00

WARD,CHARLES W-American Carnation-NY-1903(1902)-sm 4to-296p-g dec brwn cl,wht cl sp,frntis port,4 guarded col plts,photos (hh7,sl fox) 47.50

WARD,DON-ED.-Wild Streets-GC-1958-Dbldy-285p-1st ed (gg4,dj) 20.00

WARD,ELIZABETH-No Dudes, Few Women-(Albuq)-(1951)-251p-1st ed (v7,dj) 25.00

WARD,ESTOLV E-Harry Bridges on Trial-NY-1940-Mod Age-240p-wrps (r1) 25.00

WARD,EVELYN D-Children of Bladensfield During the Civil War-(1978)-Sand Dune Pr-141p-illus-1st ed (dd9,dj) 25.00

WARD,FRANCIS-Animal Life Under Water-Lond-1919-8vo-178p-photos (m3) 10.00

WARD,HARRY F-Soviet Spirit-NY-1944-Int'l-160p (r1,pg brwng,dj chip,tn) 30.00

WARD,HERBERT-Five Years Among the Congo Cannibals-NY-1890-Robt Bonner's Sons-79 drwngs-1st ed (p6,hngs weak) 200.00

WARD,J-Colour Harmony & Contrast-Lond-1903-16 col plts,11 diagrams-1st ed (ee1) 150.00

WARD,JOHN-Naturalism and Agnosticism-NY-1899-Macmillan-2 vols,grn cl-1st Amer ed (d2) 35.00

WARD,LYND-Mad Man's Drum-NY-(1930)-Cape-4to-cl & pattrnd bds-1st ed (x3,f) 125.00

WARD,LYND-Storyteller Without Words-1974-Abrams-illus-1st ed (ee1,dj,box) 125.00

WARD,MARGARET-Cousins by the Dozens-np-nd-60p-frntis,photos-1st ed (t7,f,dj) 25.00

WARD,MARION B-Boat Children of Canton-Phila-(1944)-McKay-4to-92p-cl,col & b&w illus,H Sewell-1st ed (r3,f,dj) 30.00

WARD,MARTHA-Steve Carlton-1975-Putnam-1st ed (p7,dj) 12.50

WARD,MICHAEL-In This Short Span-Lond-1972-304p-39 photos,5 maps-1st ed (o10,f,dj) 35.00

WARD,MRS HUMPHRY-Helbeck of Bannisdale-NY-1898-Macmillan-2 vols-g titled cl-1st Amer ed (aa9,sl rub) 35.00

WARD,R-Records of Big Game-Lond-1962-375p-photos-(SEE 1989 UBPG)-11th ed (gg3,f) 115.00

WARD,R-Rowland Ward's Records of Big Game-GB-1981-560p-illus (gg3,vf,dj) 40.00

WARD,WILLIAM-Harry Tracy, the Death Dealing Oregon Outlaw-Cleve-(1908)-Arthur Westbrook-191p-col pict wrps,Six-Guns 2309-1st ed (n1,chip pgs) 15.00

WARD,WILLIAM-Jesse James $100,000 Robbery-Cleve-nd-189p-pict wrps,frntis (t7) 25.00

WARD,WILLIAM-Jesse James Battle for Freedom-Cleve-nd-214p-col pict wrps,frntis-1st ed (t7) 25.00

WARD,WILLIAM-Jesse James Knight Errant-Cleve-nd-188p-col pict wrps,frntis,illus-1st ed (t7) 25.00

WARD,WILLIAM-Jesse James' Fate or the End of the Crimson Trail-Cleve-(1910)-Westbrook-179p+ads-col pict wrps (a1) 15.00

WARD,WILLIAM-Jesse James' Greatest Haul-Cleve-nd-188p-col pict wrps,frntis-1st ed (t7) 25.00

WARD,WILLIAM-Jesse James' Long Chance or the Robbery of the Northfield Bank-Cleve-(1909)-Arthur Westbrook Co-192p-col pict wrps (j1,sl wn) 15.00

WARD,WILLIAM-Jesse James' Revenge-Cleve-nd-190p-col wrps (t7) 25.00

WARD,WILLIAM-Jesse James' Ring of Death or the Fate of the Texas Rangers-Cleve-(1909)-Arthur Westbrook-181p-col pict wrps (n1,sl chip) 15.00

WARD,WILLIAM-Jesse James' Ring of Death-Cleve-nd-181p-col pict wrps,frntis (t7) 25.00

WARD,WILLIAM-Jesse James' Ruse or the Mystery of the Two Highwaymen-Cleve-(1909)-Arthur Westbrook-191p-col pict wrps (n1) 15.00

WARDEN,C F-Battle of Waterloo: a Poem-Lond-1817-48p-3/4 g dec brwn calf,mrbld bds,8 handcol plts-1st ed (b7,f) 600.00

WARDENBURG,F-Operation Safari-1948-priv prtd-191p-tip in frntis,photos,ltd to 250c,autg (gg3,pres) 50.00

WARDER,JOHN A-Hedges and Evergreens-NY-1865-OJ-291p-scarce (x6,fade sp) 60.00

WARDLAW,CHARLES D-Fundamentals of Baseball-NY-1924-Scribner's-94p+8p diagrams+1p list,23p photos plts-cl-Smith 7018 (n1) 22.50

WARDLAW,CHARLES-Fundamentals of Baseball-1924-Scribners-pict cov,photos-1st ed (ff2) 65.00

WARDNER,JOM-Jim Wardner of Wardner, Idaho-NY-1900-Anglo Amer-154p+ads-beige cl,3 photos (dd7,cov soil,sp fray) 45.00

WARE,CAPT EUGENE F-Indian War of 1864-NY-(1960)-St.Martin's Pr-483p-illus,(rprnt of 1911 ed) (o7,wn dj) 45.00

WARE,CAPT EUGENE F-Indian War of 1864-NY-(1960)-St.Martin's Pr-483p-plans,maps (dd4,wn dj) 18.00

WARE,CAROLINE F-Greenwich Village,1920 to 1930-Bost-1935-Houghton Mifflin-xiv-496p-grn cl,chrts,fldg map-1st ed (h2) 35.00

WARE,FRANCIS M-First Hand Bits of Stable Lore-Bost-1903-Little,Brown-1st ed (h9) 85.00

WARE,JEAN-Several Lives of a Victorian Vet-NY-1979-213p-illus-1st ed (b7,f,dj) 20.00

WARE,SARAH F-Captain Jacob Ware, Born, England, 1674, Died Greenwich, N.J., 1775, and Some of His Descendants-Vineland-1935-17p-wrps-ltd to 110c (aa6) 40.00

WARFEL,HARRY R-Charles Brockden Brown: American Gothic Novelist-1949-U of Fla Pr-frntis port-1st ed (t4,f,f dj) 35.00

WARGA,W-Hardcover-1985-Walker-1st ed (x7,as new in dj) 18.00

WARHOL,ANDY-A-NY-1968-1st ed (p5,f,dj) 100.00

WARHOL,ANDY-Index Book-NY-1967-stiff silv dec wrps-1st prtg (h10) 475.00

WARING,EDWARD-Pharmacopoeia of India-Lond-1868-503p-qtr lea-rare-1st ed (dd3,rebkd wi orig sp) 250.00

WARING,GEORGE E-Whip and Spur-Bost-1875-Osgood-245p-1st ed (o7) 75.00

WARING,THOMAS-Treatise on Archery-Lond-1824-16mo-67p-orig bds,illus-5th ed (m3,sl wn) 60.00

WARK,ROBERT R-Early British Drawings in the Huntington Collection, 1650 to 1750-San Marino-1969-Huntington Libr-4to-231p-1st ed (ee5,vf,f dj) 17.50

WARMAN,CY-Frontier Stories-NY-1898-246p-dec cl-Six Guns #2316-scarce-1st ed (t7) 65.00

WARMOTH,HENRY C-War, Politics and Reconstruction-NY-1930-Macmillan-285p-frntis-1st ed (cc6) 50.00

WARMOTH,HENRY C-War, Politics, and Reconstruction-NY-1930-Macmillan-xvi+285p-grn cl-1st ed (b2,sl wn sp) 25.00

WARNER,CHARLES D-Being a Boy-Bost,NY-1897-vi,244p (j10) 10.00

WARNER,EZRA J-Biographical Register of the Confederate Congress-Baton Rouge-(1975)-319p-illus-1st ed (c4,f,dj) 30.00

WARNER,GLENN S-Football for Coaches and Players-Stanford Univ-1927-publ by G S Warner-205p-Artificial lea-1st ed (d1) 20.00

WARNER,JOHN A-Life and Art of the North American Indian-NY-(1975)-Crescent Bks-4to-168p-100 col illus (cc4,dj) 20.00

WARNER,LANGDON-Craft of the Japanese Sculptor-NY-1936-Japan Soc-sm folio-55p+85p photo plts-1st ed (ll9,f,dj) 75.00

WARNER,LANGDON-Craft of the Japanese Sculptor-NY-1936-Morrill Pr-(14)55p+85p plts-1st ed (l10,rub,edge wn) 50.00

WARNER,LOUIS H-Archbishop Lamay An Epoch Maker-Santa Fe-1936-Santa Fe New Mex Publ-316p-cl-1st ed (w3) 45.00

WARNER,LOUIS H-Archbishop Lamy an Epoch Maker-Santa Fe-1936-316p-Rittenhouse #622-scarce-1st ed (t7) 25.00

WARNER,LUCIEN C-Popular Treatise on the Functions and Diseases of Woman...-NY-1874-Manhattan Publ co-345p-cl (d1,sl wn) 30.00

WARNER,MATT-Last of the Bandit Riders-Caldwell-1940-Caxton-337p-dec cl,photos-Howes W112-1st ed (v1) 95.00

WARNER,OLIVER-British Navy-Lond-1975-191p-illus-1st ed (b7,f,dj) 25.00

WARNER,OLIVER-With Wolfe to Quebec-Lond-1972-224p-illus-1st ed (gg2,f,dj) 40.00

WARNER,SYLVIA T-After the Death of Don Juan-Lond-1938-Chatto & Windus-8vo-cl-1st ed (jj8,f,dj) 100.00

WARNER,SYLVIA T-Opus 7-NY-1931-Viking-orig cl bckd bds-1st Amer ed (aa9) 15.00

WARNER,SYLVIA T-Some World Far From Ours-Lond-1929-Mathews & Marrot-8vo-dec bds-ltd to 530c,autg-1st ed (jj8,f,dj) 45.00

WARNER,SYLVIA T-Spirit Rises-Lond-1962-Chatto & Windus-8vo-bds-1st ed (jj8,f,dj) 35.00

WARNER,WM W-History of the Ojibway Indians-St.Paul-1885-535p-frntis-1st ed (t7,ex-libr,rbnd) 45.00

WARRE,CAPT H-Sketches in North America & the Oregon Territory-Barre-1970-Imprint Soc Publ-26p & 72p paintings & drwngs-ltd ed (j7,f,f box) 75.00

WARREN COMMISSION REPORT-THE OFFICIAL...ON THE ASSASSINATION OF PRESIDENT JOHN F KENNEDY-GC-1964-888,(4)p-cl (c1) 15.00

WARREN COUNTY-A HISTORY OF ...INDIANA-np-1966-Warren Cnty Hist Society-184p-cl (h1) 22.50

WARREN,B H-Report on Birds of Pennsylvania-Harrisburg-1888-8vo-260p-orig cl,50 plts(49 col)-1st ed (y8,lt insect) 65.00

WARREN,C E T-Only Four Escaped, the Sinking of the Submarine Thetis-NY-1959-Sloane-8vo-219p-26 illus-1st US ed (jj5,f,f dj) 17.50

WARREN,CHARLES-Jacobin and Junto-Cambridge-1931-Harvard Univ-vi+324p-brwn cl-1st ed (e2,dj) 12.00

WARREN,CHIEF JUSTICE EARL-CHAIRMAN-Report of the President's Commission on the Assassination of President John F Kennedy-Wash D.C.-1964-GPO-888p-photos-1st ed (a9,ex-libr) 75.00

WARREN,ELIZA S-Memoirs of the West: the Spaldings-(Portland)-(1916)-(Marsh Prtg)-153p-grn cl,10 plts-Howes W117-1st ed (b2) 125.00

WARREN,J COLLINS-To Work in the Vineyard of Surgery-Cambridge-1958-Harvard Univ-xii+288p-grn cl,illus-1st ed (l2,dj) 18.00

WARREN,JOHN B L-Guide to the Study of Book Plates-Manchester-1900-Sherratt and Hughes-8vo-viii,228p-orig cl,papr sp labl-2nd ed,rvsd (w2,fox) 85.00

WARREN,JOHN C-Physical Education and the Preservation of Health-Bost-1846-90p-1st ed (dd3) 200.00

WARREN,ROBERT P-At Heavens Gate-NY-1943-1st ed (t5,rub frnt cl,dj sl chip) 250.00

WARREN,ROBERT P-Audubon-NY-(1969)-Random-1st trd ed (a5,as new in dj) 40.00

WARREN,ROBERT P-Band of Angels-NY-1955-Random-1st ed (q2,dj) 45.00

WARREN,ROBERT P-Being Here-NY-1980-Random-1st ed (q2,dj) 25.00

WARREN,ROBERT P-Brother to Dragons-NY-(1953)-Random-1st ed (a5,dj) 75.00

WARREN,ROBERT P-Brother to Dragons-NY-1953-Random-1st ed (f8,f,dj missing sm chip) 65.00

WARREN,ROBERT P-Cave-Lond-1959-1st ed (r2,f,sl tn dj) 35.00

WARREN,ROBERT P-Cave-NY-(1959)-Random-1st ed (a5,dj) 30.00

WARREN,ROBERT P-Democracy and Poetry-Cambridge,Lond-1975-1st ed (f5,f,dj) 45.00

WARREN,ROBERT P-Democracy and Poetry-Cambridge-1974-Harvard U Pr-1st ed (q2,dj) 40.00

WARREN,ROBERT P-ED.-Southern Harvest-Bost-1937-Houghton Mifflin-1st ed (a5,dj sp fade,sl wn) 175.00

WARREN,ROBERT P-Eleven Poems on the Same Theme-Norfolk-1942-New Directions-wrps-(Poet of the Month)-1st ed (q2,dj tn & soil) 45.00

WARREN,ROBERT P-Flood-NY-1964-1st ed (r5,f,dj) 20.00

WARREN,ROBERT P-Homage to Theodore Dreiser-NY-(1971)-Random-1st ed (l9,f,dj,autg) 120.00

WARREN,ROBERT P-Incarnations-NY-1968-1st ed (q5,f,dj) 50.00

WARREN,ROBERT P-Incarnations-NY-1968-Random-1st ed (q2,dj) 45.00

WARREN,ROBERT P-Jefferson Davis Gets His Citizenship Back-Lexington-1980-Kentucky Pr-1st ed (y1,f,f dj) 30.00

WARREN,ROBERT P-John Brown-NY-1929-Payson & Clarke-red bds,t.e. red,auth 1st bk-1st ed (bb2,lacks dj) 600.00

WARREN,ROBERT P-Meet Me In the Green Glen-NY-(1971)-Random-ltd to 350c,nbrd,autg-1st ed (ee2,f,box) 135.00

WARREN,ROBERT P-Meet Me In the Green Glen-NY-1971-Random-1st ed (q2,dj) 30.00

WARREN,ROBERT P-Night Rider-Bost-1939-auth 1st novel-rare-1st ed (s5,sl chip dj) 300.00

WARREN,ROBERT P-Selected Essays-NY-1958-1st ed (r5,f,dj) 45.00

WARREN,ROBERT P-Selected Poems 1923 to 1975-Penn-(1976)-Franklin Libr-lea bds-1st ed (s6) 50.00

WARREN,ROBERT P-Selected Poems-NY-1966-Random-1st ed (q2,sl tn dj) 60.00

WARREN,ROBERT P-Who Speaks for the Negro-NY-1965-1st ed (r5,f,dj) 30.00

WARREN,ROBERT P-Who Speaks for the Negro?-NY-1965-Random-1st ed (q2,dj) 60.00

WARREN,ROBERT P-Wilderness-NY-(1961)-Random-1st ed (l9,sl chip dj,autg) 100.00

WARREN,ROBERT P-World Enough and Time-NY-(1950)-nbrd,unspecified ltd ed for pres to bksellers of Amer-clear plastic dj as issued-1st ed (f5,dj) 60.00

WARREN,ROBERT P-World Enough and Time-NY-1950-1st ed (q5,sl chip dj) 25.00

WARREN,RUTH-Pictorial History of Women in America-NY-(1975)-228p-bds-1st ed so stated (d1,f,dj) 15.00

WARREN,WILLIAM W-History of the Ojibway Nation-Mpls-1957-Ross & Haines-527p-map e.p.-ltd to 1500c,nbrd (cc4,dj) 25.00

WARREN,WILLIAM-Legendary American-Bost-1970-HMCo-8vo-275p-16p photos-1st ed (cc5,dj) 15.00

WARREN-County Atlas of...New Jersey...-NY-1874-F W Beers-folio-92p-lea backd cl,hand col litho maps(incl fldg)-variant of 4p fldg map wi only top half usual area (aa6,f) 650.00

WARRICK, SPENCER & PERRY COUNTIES-HISTORY OF...-Chig-1885-837p-mor (j1) 100.00

WARRICK,SPENCER & PERRY COUNTIES-HISTORY OF...INDIANA...-Chig-1885-837p-mor (c1) 100.00

WARRIOR AND THE PRINCESS AND OTHER SOUTH AMERICAN FAIRY TALES-(1961)-Golden Bks-folio-60p-pict glossy bds,col illus,G de Gaspari (r3,vf) 25.00

WASHBURN,BRADFORD-Among the Alps with Bradford-NY-1927-1st ed (a4,f) 40.00

WASHBURN,FREDERIC-Massachusetts General Hospital: Its Development, 1900 to 1935-Bost-1939-643p-1st ed (dd3) 30.00

WASHBURN,WILCOMBE E-Red Man's Land, White Man's Law-NY-1971-280p-1st ed (t7,dj) 12.50

WASHINGTON CITY AND CAPITAL-Wash-1937-WPA-Amer Guide Ser-1140,(1)p+2 fldg maps in rear pckt-1st ed (m1,sl wn dj) 35.00

WASHINGTON COUNTY D.U.P.-COMP.-Under Dixie Sun, a History of Washington County...-Panguitch-1950-440p-orig brwn cl,illus,map-1st ed (bb8) 50.00

WASHINGTON,BOOKER T-Future of the American Negro-Bost-1899-Small,Maynard-cl,t.e.g.-auth 1st bk-1st ed (u2) 185.00

WASHINGTON,BOOKER T-Story of the Negro-NY-1909-Dbldy-2 vols-maroon cl-1st ed (e2) 175.00

WASHINGTON-A REVIEW OF THE RESOURCES AND INDUSTRIES OF...-Olympia-1905-Bur Stats,Agri & Immigr-208,(2);48p-wrps,fldg map (pp6,sl wn sp) 20.00

WASHINGTON-Check List of...Imprints, 1853 to 1876-Seattle-1942-Wash Hist Rec Survey-4to-89p-stiff papr wrps backd wi tape as iss-Amer Imprnts Inv No.44 (w2) 45.00

WASHINGTON-LAWS OF THE TERRITORY OF...-Olympia-1857-Edw Furste,Publ Prntr-8vo-95p-recent bndg of gry sp over mrbld bds-scarce-1st ed (t1,rbnd) 200.00

WASHINGTON-Portland-(1941)-WPA-687p-grn cl,blk dec & lettrng,illus,lg fldg map rear pckt-probable 2nd ed (r8,dj wn,chip,creased) 40.00

WASHINGTON-Portland-1941-WPA-687p-grn cl cov,2nd state bndg,illus,lg fldg map rear pckt-probable 1st ed (r8,lt spot cov) 40.00

WASHINGTON-UNIVERSITY OF...-Three Quarters of a Century at Washington-1941-650p-alumni directory of grads from beginning thr 1940 (b6) 15.00

WASON,BETTY-Dinners That Wait-1954-Dbldy-217p-grn cl-1st ed (q8,dj) 12.50

WASON,BETTY-Salute to Cheese-(1966)-Hawthorn-4to-288p-tan cl-1st ed (q8,f,dj) 12.50

WASSERMANN,JACOB-Bula Matari-NY-(1933)-Liveright-351p-cl (m1) 12.50

WASSON,GEORGE S-Sailing Days on the Penobscot-Salem-1932-Marine Research Scty-xiv,465p+ads-blu cl,illus,b&w photos-1st ed (nn1,dj wn & soil) 125.00

WATANNA,ONOTO-Japanese Nightingale-NY-1901-Harper & Bros-225,(1)p-grn cl,illus (b6,sp fade) 40.00

WATER,L L-Steel Trails to Santa Fe-Lawrence-1950-Univ of Ks-(xiv)+500p-tan cl,illus-1st ed (m2,dj) 50.00

WATERFIELD,DONALD-Continental Waterboy-Tor-1970-Clarke,Irwin-8vo-250p-1st ed (cc7,dj) 20.00*

WATERFIELD,MARGARET-Corners of Grey Old Gardens-Lond-1922-T N Foulis-150p-8 tip in col plts (x6,wn dj & sp,fox) 50.00

WATERHOUSE,F H-Catalogue of the Library of the Zoological Society of London-Lond-1887-515p-4th ed (dd3) 75.00

WATERHOUSE,KEITH-Jubb-Lond-(1963)-Michael Joseph-1st Brit ed (bb1,f,dj) 15.00

WATERLOO,STANLEY-Man and a Woman-Chig-(1892)-250p+ads-cl-scarce-Wright 5817-1st ed (h1) 25.00

WATERMAN,CHAS F-Fisherman's World-NY-nd-4to-250p-photos (m3,vf,dj) 12.50

WATERMAN,CHAS F-Hunter's World-NY-1976-Ridge Pr,Random-4to-250p-grn cl,illus-1st ed (mm1,sl wn dj) 20.00

WATERMAN,CHAS F-Hunting in America-NY-1973-4to-250p-photos (m3,f,dj) 20.00

WATERMAN,CHAS F-Modern Fresh and Salt Water Fly Fishing-NY-1972-8vo-368p-photos-1st ed (m3,vf,dj) 20.00

WATERMAN,THOMAS T-Domestic Colonial Architecture of Tidewater Virginia-Chapel Hill-1947-UNC-folio-191p-grn cl,illus (r10,sp rub) 75.00

WATERMAN,THOMAS T-Mansions of Virginia-Chapel Hill-1945-UNC-456p-red cl,illus (r10,f,sl wn box) 35.00

WATERS,DAVID W-Art of Navigation in England in Elizabethan and Early Stuart Times...-New Haven-1958-Yale U Pr-thk 8vo-xxxix,696p-drk blu cl,87 plts-scarce-1st ed (t10,f) 150.00

WATERS,FRANK-Colorado-(NY)-(1946)-National Travel Club-400p-cl-special ed (g1) 12.50

WATERS,FRANK-Colorado-1946-Rinehart-400p-illus-Rivers of Amer Ser-1st ed (d3) 40.00

WATERS,FRANK-Colorado-NY-(1946)-396p-illus,Fechin,maps-scarce-1st ed (u7,chip dj) 35.00

WATERS,FRANK-Man Who Killed the Deer-Flagstaff-1965-Northland Pr-pattrnd bds & cl,ltd ed,autg-1st ed (dd2,f,f box) 100.00

WATERS,FRANK-Masked Gods-Albuq-(1950)-438p-1st ed (u7,f) 85.00

WATERS,FRANK-To Possess the Land-Chig-1973-Swallow Pr-viii,287p-map e.p.,illus-1st ed,1st prtg (gg9,wn dj) 35.00

WATERS,FRANK-Wild Earth's Nobility-NY-1935-Liveright-v scarce-1st ed (y1,dj sl wn) 300.00

WATERS,HORACE-Sabbath-School Bell-NY-(1859)-Horace Waters-141,(3)p-bds (j1) 15.00

WATERS,L L-Steel Trails to Santa Fe-Lawrence-1950-U of Kansas Pr-500p-illus,maps-Six Guns #2323-1st ed (cc4,dj) 45.00

WATERS,RUSSELL J-El Estranjero-NY-1910-298p-pict cl,frntis,illus-1st ed (t7,autg) 20.00

WATERTON,CHARLES-Wanderings in South America, the North-West of the United States and the Antilles...Natural History-Lond-1852-B Fellowes-280p-3/4 calf,mrbld papr,mrbld e.p. & edges,g sp titles & decs,frntis,"pocket ed"-5th ed (mm1) 85.00

WATHEN,R J-Bricks-Dublin-(1963)-Dolmen Pr-1st ed (z8,vf,dj) 32.50

WATKINS COOK BOOK-Indpls-1936-Watkins-spiralbnd (v6,sl wn cov) 22.00

WATKINS COOK BOOK-Newark-1938-Watkins Co-288p-wire bndg,col plts,promo book (l6,dj) 15.00

WATKINS,L W-Cambridge Glass 1818 to 1888-1965-Bramhall Hs-199p-illus (cc8) 30.00

WATKINS,S C G-Reminiscences of Montclair...as he Remembers it from 1876-NY-1929-x,148p-cl,plts (aa6) 60.00

WATMOUGH,E C-Scribblings & Sketches, Diplomatic,Piscatory & Oceanic-Phila-1844-12mo-189p-orig cl-scarce-2nd ed wi addtns (m3) 200.00

WATSON,ALDREN-Village Blacksmith-NY-1968-Crowell-4to-125p-1st ed (h9,dj) 35.00

WATSON,ALEXANDER-American Home Garden-NY-1859-Harper-531p-cl,illus (x6,fade) 85.00

WATSON,ARTHUR C-Long Harpoon-New Bedford-1929-Geo R Reynolds-190p-grn cl,illus,auth-1st ed (nn1,few ink mrks,dj) 30.00

WATSON,BURTON-TRANSL.-Japanese Literature in Chinese-NY-1975-Columbia Univ Pr-2 vols,cl-1st ed (l8,f,dj) 16.50

WATSON,COLIN-Coffin, Scarcely Used-NY-1967-Putnam-1st US ed (f4,f,dj) 35.00

WATSON,ELKANAH-Men and Times of the Revolution-NY-1856-Dana & Co-460p-brwn cl-Howes W167-1st ed (b2) 85.00

WATSON,ELKANAH-Men and Times of the Revolution-NY-1857-Dana-brwn cl-Howes W167-2nd ed (ee6) 75.00

WATSON,ELMOS S-Professor Goes West-Bloomington-1954-138p-1st ed (t7,f) 25.00

WATSON,FREDERICK-Century of Gunmen-Lond-1931-Nicholson & Watson-296p-Six Guns #2326-1st ed (dd4) 35.00

WATSON,GEORGE-ED.-New Cambridge Bibliography of English Literature, Volume 2, 1660 to 1800-Lond-1971-Cambridge U Pr-1st ed thus (hh5,dj) 50.00

WATSON,IAN-Alien Embassy-Lond-1977-Gollancz-1st ed (f3,f,dj) 35.00

WATSON,JAMES-DNA Story-SF-1981-4to-605p-1st ed (dd3) 75.00

WATSON,JAMES-Double Helix-NY-1968-226p-1st ed (dd3) 22.50

WATSON,MARGARET G-Silver Theatre-Glendale-1964-Arthur H Clark Co-8vo-387p-blu cl-1st ed (mm1,dj) 30.00

WATSON,MRS S H-Folio of Old Songs-Waxahachie-(1912)-152p-illus-scarce-1st ed (jj1) 50.00

WATSON,RICHARD-Bitters Bottles-NY-1965-304p-illus-1st ed (dd3,dj) 75.00

WATSON,ROBERT-History of Psychology and the Behavioral Sciences: a Bibliographic Guide-NY-1978-241p-1st ed (dd3) 25.00

WATSON,S J-By Command of the Emperor-Lond-1957-238p-illus-1st ed (b7,f,dj) 40.00

WATSON,THOMAS L-Preliminary Report on a Part of the Granites and Gneisses of Georgia-Atlanta-1902-367p-emboss brwn cl wi gilt,mrbld edges,fldg maps,photos (n2) 30.00

WATSON,W J-Bridge Architecture-NY-1927-Helburn-folio-illus-1st ed (ee1,hng weak,edge rub) 150.00

WATSON,WILBUR J-Bridge Architecture-NY-(1927)-Wm Helburn-4to-288p-cl sp,illus-1st ed (g2,sl bump cor) 85.00

WATT,ROBERTA F-4 Wagons West-Portland-1931-Binfords & Mort-390p-blu cl (b6,tn dj) 12.50

WATT,ROBERTA F-Four Wagons West-Portland-1931-390p-Smith #10786-1st ed (t7,f,dj) 10.00

WATTS,ALAN W-Myth and Ritual in Christianity-Lond-1953-1st ed (y7,dj rprd) 20.00

WATTS,ALAN W-Two Hands of God-NY-1963-Braziller-cl,24p illus-1st ed (o8,dj) 11.00

WATTS,ALAN-Book. On the Taboo Against Knowing Who You Are-NY-1966-Pantheon-cl-1st ed (n8,chip dj) 16.00

WATTS,ALAN-Cloud Hidden, Whereabouts Unknown-NY-1973-Pantheon-cl-1st ed (n8,f,dj) 25.00

WATTS,ALAN-Does It Matter-NY-(1970)-Pantheon-1st ed (e6,dj) 30.00

WATTS,ALAN-ED.-Patterns of Myth-NY-1963-Braziller-3 vols,cl-1st ed (n8,vf,dj,box) 35.00

WATTS,ALAN-In My Own Way-1972-Pantheon-1st ed (s9,f,dj sp sunned) 35.00

WATTS,ALAN-Two Hands of God-NY-1963-(21),261p-plts,drwngs-1st ed (m4,vf,dj) 20.00

WATTS,EDITH-Jesse's Book of Creole and Deep South Recipes-1954-Viking-184p-blu cl-1st ed (q8,dj) 15.00

WATTS,MORTON S-Maid of the Alamo or the Incarnation of Chivalry-Mineral Wells-1913-auth-93p-cl,photos-1st ed (w3,sm cov stn) 15.00

WATTS,WILLIAM C-Chronicles of a Kentucky Settlement-NY-1897-Putnam's-xiv+490p-maroon cl-Howes W179-1st ed (mm10) 50.00

WAUGH,A-Nonesuch Dickensiana-1937-Nonesuch Pr-1st ed (x2) 60.00

WAUGH,ALEC-In Praise of Wine-Lond-(1959)-Cassell-280p-red cl-1st ed (q8,dusty dj) 25.00

WAUGH,ALEC-Merchants of Wine-Lond-(1957)-Cassell-135p-grn cl,drwngs-1st ed (q8,dj) 17.50

WAUGH,ALEC-Portrait of a Celibate-GC-1929-dec e.p.s-1st US ed (s5,dj soil & sl wn) 15.00

WAUGH,EVELYN-Brideshead Revisited-Bost-1946-Little,Brown-1st ed (w5,f,sl tn dj) 35.00

WAUGH,EVELYN-Helena-Lond-1950-Chapman & Hall-g titled cl-1st ed (aa9,f,rprd dj) 50.00

WAUGH,EVELYN-Letters-New Haven-1980-1st ed (y7,sl stnd dj) 22.00

WAUGH,EVELYN-Little Learning-Bost-1964-1st US ed (q5,dj) 22.50

WAUGH,EVELYN-Loved One-(Lond)-nd-Chapman & Hall-orig g titled cl-1st ed (aa9,f,dj) 100.00

WAUGH,EVELYN-Ninety Two Days-Lond-(1934)-Duckworth-8vo-cl,fldg map,24 illus,rare dj-1st ed (kk8,f,dj sl soil,chip & wn) 1,000.00

WAUGH,EVELYN-Ordeal of Gilbert Pinfold-Lond-1948-Chapman & Hall-1st ed (cc2,f,dj) 40.00

WAUGH,EVELYN-Tourist in Africa-Bost-1960-Little,Brown-1st ed (f8,f,sp sunned dj) 45.00

WAUGH,EVELYN-Tourist in Africa-Lond-1960-Chapman & Hall-g titled cl-1st ed (aa9,f,dj) 75.00

WAUGH,F A-American Apple Orchard-NY-1913-Orange Judd-215p-cl (x6,ex-libr) 15.00

WAUGH,F-Kemp's Landscape Gardening-NY-1912-Wiley & Sons-292p-cl-orig publ 1850 (x6) 20.00

WAUGH,HARRY-Diary of a Winetaster-(1972)-Quadrangle-photos-1st ed (q8,dj) 15.00

WAUGH,JULIA N-Castro Ville and Henry Castro, Empresario-S.A.-1934-Standard-97p+list-wrps-1st ed (a9) 50.00

WAUGH,LORENZO-Autobiography of...-Oakland-1883-311p-orig blk cl,frntis port,illus-Howes W181-1st ed (t7) 100.00

WAUTON,CHAS A N-Troutfisher's Entomology-Lond-1930-16mo-72p-illus (m3,f,badly fray dj) 35.00

WAVY GRAVY-Hog Farm and Friends-NY,Lond-(1974)-Links Bks-illus,pbk orig-1st ed (e10,sl rub,sl creased wrps) 25.00

WAXELL,SVEN-American Expedition-Lond-1952-236p-frntis,fldg illus & maps-1st ed (t7,dj) 25.00

WAY & LEE-Anatomy of the Horse-Phila-1965-Lippincott-4to-214p (j9,dj) 25.00

WAY,JULIUS-An Historical Tour of Cape May County, New Jersey-Sea Isle City-1930-106p-cl,illus,map (aa6) 50.00

WAYBURN,NED-Art of Stage Dancing...A Manual of Stagecraft-NY-(1925)-Wayburn-lg 8vo-382p-1st ed (u1) 65.00

WAYLAND,FRANCIS-Elements of Political Economy-Bost-1847-Gould,Kendall & Lincoln-406p-cl (k1,sl wn) 22.50

WAYLAND,JOHN W-Art Folio of the Shenandoah Valley-Harrisonburg-1926-J W Wayland-oblng 8vo-unpgd-brwn cl-1st ed (oo5,box wn) 60.00

WAYLAND,JOHN W-Pathfinder of Seas. The Life of Matthew Fontaine Maury-Richmond-1930-Garrett & Massie-8vo-grn cl,map e.p.,illus (nn1) 50.00

WAYMAN,DR JOHN H-Doctor on the California Trail-Denver-1971-Old West Publ Co-4to-frntis,fldg map-1st ed (mm1,f) 39.00

WAYMAN,NORBURY L-Life on the River-NY-1971-Bonanza-4to-338p (z4,f,f dj) 12.50

WAYNE,A T-Birds of South Carolina plus 2nd Suppl-Charleston-1910,31-8vo-254p;37p-wrps,frntis map (y8,chip) 75.00

WAYNE,A T-Birds of South Carolina-Charleston-1910-8vo-254p-wrps,frntis map (y8,chip) 50.00

WAYNE,MATTHEW-ED.-Thirst-NY-1964-Macmillan-Pergamon Pr-viii+570p-grn bds,illus-1st ed (d2,tape rprd dj) 25.00

WAYRE,PHILIP-River People-1976-Taplinger-189p-photos-1st US ed (bb3,f,dj) 20.00

WAYRE,PHILIP-River People-Lond-1976-Collins & Harvill-8vo-189p-24 b&w,6 col photos-1st Brit ed (gg5,dj) 12.50

WEAD,FRANK-Gales, Ice and Men-NY-1937-272p-illus-1st ed (g7,chip dj) 50.00

WEADOCK,JACK-Dust of the Desert-Tucson-1963-Ariz Silhouettes-306p-illus by Van Ryder,illus e.p.-Six Guns 2330 (bb4,dj) 25.00

WEADOCK,JACK-Dust of the Desert-Tucson-1963-Ariz Silhouettes-306p-illus e.p.,illus-Herd 2454 (ee4,dj) 25.00

WEALE,B L PUTNAM-Indiscreet Letters From Peking-NY-1916-Dodd,Mead-447p-g dec red cl,frntis (gg6,hng rprd) 60.00

WEAR,BRUCE-Bronze World of Frederick Remington-Tulsa-1966-Gaylord-4to-plts,photos-1st ed (b4,dj) 75.00

WEARIN,OTHA D-Political Americana-Shenandoah-nd-137p-photos-1st ed (t7,dj) 17.50

WEATHERLY,F E-Punch and Judy-Lond-nd(c.1885)-Marcus Ward-sm 4to-g dec bds,cl sp,12 col illus-1st ed (jj9,fox) 150.00

WEATHERS,JOHN-Bulb Book-Lond-1911-Murray-471p-cl,illus-scarce (x6,cl wn,sp soil) 25.00

WEATHERS,W W-Birds of Southern California's Deep Canyons-1983-U of Cal-266p-28 col photos-1st ed (bb3,f,dj) 30.00

WEATHERWAX,PAUL-Indian Corn in Old America-NY-1954-Macmillan-sm folio-253p-3 col illus-1st ed (ee4,dj) 25.00

WEAVER,DR B F-Weaver's New Illustrated Family Atlas of Human Diseases...-Bucyrus-1896-publ by auth-32p-bds-3 pg plts (j1) 12.50

WEAVER,EARL-Winning-1972-Morrow-1st ed (r7,f,dj) 15.00

WEAVER,JOHN D-Carnation, the First 75 Years-LA-(1974)-Carnation-4to-253p-col illus-1st ed (gg5,dj) 15.00

WEAVER,JOHN-Plant Ecology-NY-1938-McGraw-601p-cl-2nd ed (x6,f) 45.00

WEAVER,L-Lutyens Houses & Gardens-Lond-1921-Cntry Life-144 illus (h10,edge rub) 125.00

WEAVER,LOUISE B-Bettina's Best Salads and What to Serve with Them-(1923)-Burt-215p-blu cl,8 col plts (q8,dj) 16.50

WEAVER,LOUISE B-Bettina's Best Salads...-NY-(1923)-Burt-215p-dec & col plts,E Colborne-1st ed (l6,sp lettrng wn) 35.00

WEAVER,LOUISE B-Thousand Ways to Please a Husband-NY-(1917)-Burt-479p-bds,illus,E Colbourne-Bitting 488 (l6,wn bds,soil,fox) 30.00

WEB,WILLIAM-Garden First in Land Development-Lond-1919-Green-124p-cl,25 collotype plts (x6) 20.00

WEBB,A P-Bibliography of the Works of Thomas Hardy, 1865 to 1915-Lond-1916-F Hollings-8vo-xiii,128p-g stmpd blu cl-1st ed (w2) 65.00

WEBB,ALEXANDER S-Peninsula: McClellan's Campaign of 1862-NY-1881-Scribner's-219p-maps-1st ed (o7) 40.00

WEBB,BEATRICE-Health of Working Girls-Lond-1917-Blackie-8vo-103p-1st ed (oo7) 85.00

WEBB,CECIL S-Odyssey of an Animal Collector-NY-1954(53)-Longmans,Green-8vo-368p-32p photos-1st US ed (aa5,f,dj) 17.50

WEBB,CHARLES-Graduate-(1963)-NAL-1st ed (m9,f,dj sp chip & drknd) 45.00

WEBB,CHARLES-Graduate-(NY)-(1963)-auth 1st bk-1st ed (c5,dj sl rub,sp chip) 50.00

WEBB,CHARLES-Love, Roger-Bost-1969-HMCo-1st ed (hh5,f,f dj) 10.00

WEBB,EDITH B-Indian Life at the Old Missions-LA-1952-W Lewis-4to-326p-photos-1st ed (d3,dj) 50.00

WEBB,EDWARD A-Historical Directory of Sussex County, NJ-(np)-1872-142,(1)p-cl,lg fldg col map (aa6,sp fade,tape rprd map) 175.00

WEBB,GEORGE W-Chronological List of Engagements Between the Regular Army of the US and Various Tribes...-St.Joseph-1939-141p-frntis-1st ed (t7) 135.00

WEBB,GERALD-Tuberculosis-NY-1936-205p-1st ed (dd3) 40.00

WEBB,JACK-Delicate Darling-NY-(1959)-Rinehart-1st ed (h3,brwnd pgs,sl wn dj) 15.00

WEBB,JACK-Delicate Darling-NY-1959-Rinehart-1st ed (g4,yel pgs,dj) 10.00

WEBB,JAMES-Fields of Fire-Englewood Cliffs-1978-auth 1st bk-1st ed (s5,dj) 50.00

WEBB,JAMES-Fields of Fire-NJ-1978-Prentice Hall-auth 1st bk-1st ed (g8,f,dj) 60.00

WEBB,SIDNEY-Prevention of Destitution-Lond-1911-Longmans-8vo-348p+ads-cl-1st ed (oo7) 60.00

WEBB,TODD-Gold Strikes and Ghost Towns-1961-Dbldy-160p-photos-1st ed (d3,dj) 20.00

WEBB,WALTER P-Great Plains-Bost-(1931)-515p-illus,maps-1st ed,1st prtg (v7,lacks f.e.p.) 50.00

WEBB,WALTER P-Great Plains-Bost-1931-Ginn & Co-525p-maps,illus-Howes W193-1st ed,1st iss (dd4) 75.00

WEBB,WALTER P-Great Plains-NY-1931-525p-dec cl,photos,maps-Herd #2455 (t7) 17.50

WEBB,WALTER P-History as High Adventure-Austin-1969-206p-1st ed (t7,dj) 10.00

WEBB,WALTER P-Texas Rangers-Austin-(1982)-U of Tex Pr-583p-drwngs,photos-Six Guns #2332 (cc4,dj) 30.00

WEBB,WALTER P-Texas Rangers-Bost-1935-Houghton Mifflin-584p-drwngs,photos-Howes W194-1st ed (ff4,sp lttrng fade) 75.00

WEBB,WALTER P-Texas Rangers-Bost-1935-Houghton,Mifflin-584p-illus,photos,drwngs by L Rees-Six Guns 2333-1st ed,1st state (t8,sl fade sp) 125.00

WEBB,WILLIAM S-California and Alaska and Over the Canadian Pacific Railway-NY-1891-Putnam-268p-dec brn cl,illus-2nd ed (w1) 125.00

WEBBER,A R-Biography of John Baldwin, Sr. of Berea, Ohio...-np-(1925)-Caxton-279p-cl (a1) 17.50

WEBBER,C W-Shot in the Eye, and Adventures with the Texan Rifle Rangers-Lond-ca.1853-Clarke,Beeton & Co-216p-3/4 lea,raised bnds,mrbld bds,illus (f9,sl wn) 350.00

WEBBER,JUDGE A R-Early History of Elyria and Her People-Elyria-1930-326p-cl,photos-1st ed (jj4,pres) 40.00

WEBBER,WINSLOW L-Book about Books-Detr-1974-Gale Rsrch-sm 8vo-(viii),168p-cl-rprnt (x4) 35.00

WEBBER,WINSLOW L-Books About Books-Bost-1937-Hale,Cushman & Flint-1st ed (w1) 30.00

WEBER,DAVID J-Mexican Frontier 1812 to 1846-Albuq-1982-416p-frntis,photos,maps-1st ed (t7,dj) 30.00

WEBER,ELIZABETH A-Duk Duks-Chig-(1929)-U of Chig-8vo-142p-1st ed (gg5) 35.00

WEBER,F PARKES-Aspects of Death in Art and Epigram-Lond-1914-Unwin & Quaritch-cl,126 illus-2nd ed,rvsd & enlgd (l8) 125.00

WEBER,RICHARD-Lady & Gentleman-Dublin-(1963)-Dolmen Pr-auth 1st bk-1st ed (z8,f,dj) 40.00

WEBER,RICHARD-Stephen's Green Revisited-Dublin-1968-Dolmen Pr-1st ed (z8,f,dj) 32.50

WEBSTER'S NEW INTERNATIONAL DICTIONARY OF THE ENGLISH LANGUAGE-Springfield-1949-Merriam-3 vols-cl,unabridged-2nd ed (w1) 150.00

WEBSTER,DANIEL-Speech of Daniel Webster on the Subject of the Public Lands...January 20,1830-Wash D.C.-1830-Gales & Seaton-28p-Wrps fastened wi string-1st ed (h2,sl wn & fox,sm stn 1st pg) 40.00

WEBSTER,E B-Fishing in the Olympics-Port Angeles-1923-8vo-227p-illus-scarce (m3) 95.00

WEBSTER,JEAN-Much Ado About Peter-NY-1909-illus-1st ed (r2) 30.00

WEBSTER,KIMBALL-Gold Seekers of `49-Manchester-1917-Standard Bk Co-240p-yel & blk cl,plts-1st ed (k2,f) 85.00

WEBSTER,NOAH,JR.-Elements of Useful Knowledge. Vol.1-Hartford-1806-O D Cooke-208p-bds-Amer Imprnts 11382 (k1,lacks f.e.p.) 40.00

WEBSTER,NOAH-Elementary Spelling Book-Cin-(1848)-E Morgan-168p-bds (g1,sp wn,sm cov pc missing) 50.00

WEBSTER,NOAH-Elementary Spelling Book-Wells River-1835-Ira White-168p-bds-Amer Imprnts 35322 (k1) 32.50

WEBSTER,NOAH-Elements of Useful Knowledge. Vol.1-Hartford-1809-prntd by Hudson & Goodwin-208p-bds-Amer Imprnts 19178-4th ed (k1) 32.50

WEBSTER,PAUL-Mighty Sierra-Palo Alto-1972-4to-237p-photos-1st ed (o10,as new in box) 30.00

WEBSTER,WILLIAM G-Sequel to Webster's Elementary Spelling Book-Phila-(1845)-Lippincott-172p-prntd bds (k1) 20.00

WEBSTER.E B-King of the Olympics the Roosevelt Elk-Port Angeles-1920-8vo-227p-photos (m3) 35.00

WECHSBERG,JOSEPH-Avalanche-NY-1958-253p-1st ed (p10,f,dj) 15.00

WECHSBERG,JOSEPH-Red Plush and Black Velvet-Bost-(1961)-Little,Brown-1st ed (w1,f,dj) 20.00

WECHSELMANN,WILHELM-Treatment of Syphilis with Salvarsan-NY-(1911)-Rebman Co-4to-175p-gry cl,16 col plts-1st ed (a2,cov soil,sl tn sp) 35.00

WEDDLE,R S-Plow Horse Cavalry-Austin-1974-210p-illus,map,ports-1st ed (z10,dj) 30.00

WEDDLE,ROBERT S-San Juan Bautista, Gateway to Spanish Texas-Austin-1968-U.T.P.-469p-photos-1st ed (a9,dj) 50.00

WEDDLE,ROBERT S-San Saba Mission-Austin-1964-U.T.P.-238p-1st ed (a9,dj) 85.00

WEDECK,H E-Dictionary of Gypsy Life and Lore-NY-1973-Philosophical Libr-cl,illus-1st ed (n8,f,dj) 20.00

WEDECK,H E-Dictionary of Spiritualism-NY-1971-Philo Libr-cl-1st ed (o8,dj) 10.00

WEDEL,W R-Archaeological Investigations at Buena Vista Lake...-1941-Bur Amer Ethnol Bull.130-194p-papr wrps,57 plts (bb3) 20.00

WEDEL,WALDO R-Prehistoric Man on the Great Plains-Norman-(1970)-U of Okla Pr-355p-illus (cc4,dj) 20.00

WEED,ALFRED-Alligator Gar-Chig-1923-8vo-16p-wrps,frontis,photo (m3,vf) 10.00

WEED,ALFRED-Pike Pickerel & Muskalonge-Chig-1927-8vo-52p-wrps,illus (m3,vf) 35.00

WEED,CLARENCE-Spraying Crops-NY-1910-Orange Judd-136p-cl-4th ed (x6) 22.00

WEED,CORA C-Handbook for Soldiers' and Sailors' Monument-np-1898-111p-wrps,illus (o7,sunned) 20.00

WEEDEN,ROBERT B-Alaska: Promises to Keep-Bost-1978-Houghton Mifflin-254p-1st ed (ff8,dj) 18.00

WEEGEE-Creative Camera-NY-1959-Hanover-4to-cl-1st ed (y3,dj sl tn) 75.00

WEEGEE-Naked City-NY-(1945)-Essential-4to-cl-1st ed (y3,f,dj chip) 165.00

WEEGEE-Naked City-NY-1945-Essential Bks-8vo-246p-cl-1st ed (t3) 75.00

WEEGEE-Weegee's People-NY-(1946)-Duell-4to-cl-1st ed (y3,dj sl soil,chip) 125.00

WEEGEE-Weegee's People-NY-(1946)-Essential Bks/DS&P-photos-1st ed (a10,dj) 100.00

WEEKS,ALVIN G-Massasoit of the Wampanoags with...a Chapter on Samoset, Squanto & Hobamock...-Fall River-1920-priv prtd-12mo-xi,270p-frntis,1 plt (n2) 20.00

WEEKS,EDWARD-Fresh Waters-Bost-1968-Atlantic/Little,Brown-1st ed (nn5,sl soil dj) 20.00

WEEMS,J E-Men Without Countries-Bost-1969-272p-illus,map e.p.-1st ed (t7,f,dj) 12.50

WEEMS,JOHN E-To Conquer a Peace-GC-1974-Dbldy-500p-maps,illus-1st ed (cc4,dj) 20.00

WEES,F-Maestro Murders-1931-Mystery League-1st ed (x7,dj) 12.00

WEHLE,HARRY B-American Miniatures 1730 to 1850-NY-1937-Garden City Publ-4to-127p-blu & crm cl,173 b&w & col illus (r10,sl wn dj) 45.00

WEHMAN,HENRY J-Wehman's Book on Fishing-NY-1898-12mo-141p+ads-wrps,illus-rare (m3) 75.00

WEHRLE,EDMUND S-Britain,China and the Antimissionary Riots 1891 to 1900-Mpls-1966-U of Minn-223p (c3) 18.00

WEICHMANN,LOUIS J-True History of the Assassination of Abraham Lincoln and the Conspiracy of 1865-NY-1979-Knopf-492p-illus (dd4,dj) 15.00

WEIG,MELVIN J-Summit Beacon and Alarm Gun in the Revolutionary War-(Summit)-(1944)-14p-wrps (aa6) 20.00

WEIGLE,MARTA-ED.-Hispanic Arts and Ethnohistory in SW-Santa Fe-(1983)-408p-photos-1st ed (u7,f,dj) 35.00

WEIL,OSCAR-Letters and Papers-SF-1923-Grabhorn Pr-tall 4to-half cl & bds,sp & cov labls,tip in photo frntis,D Lange,ltd to 400c (y3,sl rub) 75.00

WEIL,SIMONE-Letter to a Priest-Lond-1953-Routledge & K Paul-cl-1st Brit ed (n8,dj pc missng) 25.00

WEIL,SIMONE-Need for Roots-NY-1952-Putnam's-cl-1st Amer ed (n8) 27.50

WEIL,SIMONE-On Science, Necessity, and the Love of God-Lond-1968-Oxford U Pr-cl-1st ed (l8,fray dj) 45.00

WEIL,SIMONE-Waiting for God-NY-1951-Putnam's-cl-1st Amer ed (n8,chip dj) 35.00

WEINBAUM,STANLEY-Red Peri-Reading-1952-1st ed (bb10,f,dj) 35.00

WEINER,HENRI-Crime on the Cuff-NY-1936-Morrow-1st ed (k4,dj) 25.00

WEINER,J S-Piltdown Forgery-Lond-1955-OUP-214p-brwn cl,9 photos-1st ed (c2) 20.00

WEINER,J S-Piltdown Forgery-Lond-1955-OUP-214p-maroon cl,plts-1st ed (g2,dj) 65.00

WEINER,REX-Woodstock Census-NY-1979-1st ed (x8,dj) 12.00

WEINSTEIN,ROBERT A-Gray's Harbor 1885 to 1913-NY-(1978)-190p-illus-1st ed (j7,dj) 22.50

WEINSTEIN,ROBERT A-Tall Ships on Puget Sound-Seattle,Lond-(1978)-145p-illus,photos-1st ed (j7,f,dj) 37.50

WEIR,TOM-Camps & Climbs in Arctic Norway-Lond-1953-87p-58 photos,maps-1st Brit ed (q10,f,dj) 20.00

WEIR,TOM-East of Katmandu-Edinburgh-(1955)-Oliver & Boyd-8vo-138p-91 photos-1st Scot ed (ff5,dj chip,tn) 15.00

WEIR,TOM-Ultimate Mountains-Lond-1953-98p-80 photos-1st Brit ed (p10,f,dj) 30.00

WEISEL,GEORGE F-Men & Trade on the Northwest Frontier-(Missoula)-(1955)-291p-illus-1st ed (d7,f,f dj) 50.00

WEISLMANN,JOSEPH-John Barth: a Bibliography-NY-1976-Garland-no dj as iss-1st ed (bb2,f) 40.00

WEISS,HARRY B-Colonel Erkuries Beatty, 1759 to 1823-Trenton-1958-vi,80p-cl backd bds,plts-ltd to 200c,nbrd (aa6) 75.00

WEISS,HARRY B-Country Doctor-Trenton-1953-235p-wrps,illus (aa6) 40.00

WEISS,HARRY B-Early Breweries of New Jersey-Trenton-1963-98p-wrps,illus (aa6) 60.00

WEISS,HARRY B-Early Brickmaking in New Jersey-Trenton-1966-v,85p-wrps,illus (aa6) 60.00

WEISS,HARRY B-Early Hatters of New Jersey-Trenton-1961-75p-wrps,illus (aa6) 60.00

WEISS,HARRY B-Early Promotional Literature of New Jersey-Trenton-1964-82p-wrps,facs (aa6) 50.00

WEISS,HARRY B-Early Snuff Mills of New Jersey-Trenton-1962-117p-wrps,illus (aa6) 60.00

WEISS,HARRY B-Early Sports and Pastimes in New Jersey-Trenton-1960-vii,148p-cl backd bds,illus (aa6) 90.00

WEISS,HARRY B-Early Tanning and Currying in New Jersey-Trenton-1959-74p-wrps,illus (aa6) 60.00

WEISS,HARRY B-Early Woolen Industry of New Jersey-Trenton-1958-100p-wrps,illus (aa6) 60.00

WEISS,HARRY B-Forgotten Mills of Early New Jersey-Trenton-1960-94p-wrps,illus (aa6) 60.00

WEISS,HARRY B-History of Applejack or Apple Brandy in New JErsey from Colonial Times to the Present-Trenton-1954-265p-wrps,illus (aa6) 60.00

WEISS,HARRY B-Rafting on the Delaware River-Trenton-1967-v,72p-wrps,illus (aa6) 60.00

WEISS,HARRY B-They Took to the Waters-Trenton-1962-232p-cl,illus-ltd to 500c (aa6) 75.00

WEISS,HARRY B-Thomas Say-Springfield-1931-Chas C Thomas-8vo-xvi,264p-27 illus-1st ed (ff9) 55.00*

WEISS,HARRY B-Trades and Tradesmen of Colonial New Jersey-Trenton-1965-v,143p-cl,illus (aa6) 75.00

WEISS,HARRY B-Whaling in New Jersey-Trenton-1974-ix,148p-cl,illus (aa6) 60.00

WEISS,JOHN-Advanced Bass Fishing-NY-1976-8vo-257p-photos-1st ed (m3,vf,dj) 10.00

WEISSENBORN,G-American Locomotive Engineering and Railway Mechanism-Felton-1969-225p-(orig publ 1871)-rprnt (n4,f,dj) 25.00

WEITENKAMPF,FRANK-Famous Prints-NY-1926-Scribner-folio-beige/grn cl,t.e.g.,untrim,70 plts-ltd to 1025c,nbrd (r10,sl fade) 75.00

WEITENKAMPF,FRANK-Illustrated Book-Cambridge-1938-Harvard U Pr-1st ed (w1,f) 40.00

WEITZENHOFFER,ANDRE M-Hypnotism-NY/Lond-(1953)-Wiley/Chapman & Hall-(xvi)+380p-prntd blu cl-1st ed (y9) 35.00

WELBORN,C A-Red River Controversy-np-1973-Nortex Offset Publ-107p-cl,illus-1st ed (w3,f) 15.00

WELCH,DENTON-Denton Welch. a Selection from His Published Works-Lond-(1963)-Chapman & Hall-8vo-bds-1st ed (jj8,f,dj) 45.00

WELCH,DENTON-In Youth Is Pleasure-Lond-1944-Routledge-8vo-cl-1st ed (jj8,f,sl rub dj) 150.00

WELCH,DENTON-Journals of...-NY-(1984)-Dutton-1st ed (bb1,as new in dj) 25.00

WELCH,DENTON-Last Sheaf-Lond-1951-Lehmann-8vo-cl,illus-1st ed (jj8,f,dj) 85.00

WELCH,DENTON-Maiden Voyage-NY-1945-illus e.p.s-1st US ed (q5,chip dj) 35.00

WELCH,DESHLER-Bachelor and the Chafing Dish-NY-1896-F Tennyson Neely-133p-grn pict bds,illus-Bitting 490 (u6,soil & wn) 35.00

WELCH,HOLMES-Parting of the Way-Bost-1957-Beacon Pr-cl,frntis-1st ed (o8,dj) 22.50

WELCH,HOLMES-Practice of Chinese Buddhism 1900 to 1950-Cambridge-1967-Harvard U Pr-cl,illus-1st ed (l8,f,dj) 30.00

WELCH,JAMES-Death of Jim Loney-NY-1979-H&R-1st ed (y1,f,f dj) 50.00

WELCH,JAMES-Riding the Earthboy 40-NY,Cleve-(1971)-World-auth 1st bk-1st ed (a10,as new in dj) 150.00

WELCH,JAMES-Winter in the Blood-NY et al-(1974)-Harper & Row-1st ed (a10,f,dj) 75.00

WELCH,JAMES-Winter in the Blood-NY-1974-Harper & Row-1st ed (h8,dj rear panel spot) 60.00

WELCH,STUART C-Room for Wonder-NY-1978-Amer Fed of Arts-sq 4to-191p-brwn cl,b&w & col illus (r10,dj) 30.00

WELCH,WILLIAM-Great Physician and Medical Humanist-1925-26p-wrps-1st ed (dd3) 40.00

WELD,ISAAC-Illustrations of the Scenery of Killarney and the Surrounding Country-Lond-1802-Longman,Hurst,Rees & Orme-qtr calf & mrbld papr bds,17 plts,2 maps (p6,needs rebacking) 400.00

WELLCOME,HENRY S-Story of Metlakahtla-Lond-1887-Saxon-481p-illus-3rd ed (u8,cov wn,sl discol sp) 50.00

WELLES,GIDEON-Lincoln and Seward-NY-1874-Sheldon & Co-215p-grn cl-1st ed (b2,sp wn) 30.00

WELLES,ORSON-Mr.Arkadin-NY-1956-1st ed (p5,dj) 40.00

WELLES,RALPH-Bighorn of Death Valley-Wa-1961-242p-wrps,photos,map-1st ed (d3) 25.00

WELLESLEY-IN-WESTCHESTER-COMP.-Favorite Recipes of Wellesley Alumnae-seventy fifth anniversary fund of Wellesley College. 1875 to 1950-blu wrps,comb bndg (n6) 28.00

WELLESZ,EGON-History of Byzantine Music and Hymnography-Lond-1961-OUP-462p+plts,cl,frntis-1st ed (o8,f,dj) 29.00

WELLMAN,MANLY W-Giant in Gray-NY-1949-Scribner's-387p-illus-1st ed (dd4,chip dj) 50.00

WELLMAN,MANLY W-Rebel Boast-NY-1956-317p-map e.p.-Dornbusch II #821-1st ed (t7,dj) 30.00

WELLMAN,MANLY W-Rebel Boast-NY-1956-H Holt-317p-illus,e.p. maps-1st ed (o7,f,dj) 25.00

WELLMAN,MANLY W-Worse Things Waiting-Chapel Hill-1973-Carcosa-1st ed (l3,f,dj) 60.00

WELLMAN,PAUL I-Death in the Desert-NY-1935-Macmillan-294p-illus,fldg map-1st ed (bb4) 40.00

WELLMAN,PAUL I-Dynasty of Western Outlaws-GC-1961-Dbldy-384p-cl,map,map e.p.-1st ed (v1,dj) 50.00

WELLMAN,PAUL I-Dynasty of Western Outlaws-NY-1961-Dbldy-384p-illus-1st ed (cc4,dj) 25.00

WELLMAN,PAUL I-Glory, God and Gold-NY-1954-Dbldy-402p-map e.p.-1st ed (cc4,dj) 25.00

WELLMAN,PAUL I-Indian Wars of the West-NY-1954-484p (t7,dj) 20.00

WELLMAN,PAUL I-Portage Bay-GC-1957-8vo-240p-illus (m3,dj) 15.00

WELLMAN,PAUL-Trampling Herd-(1939)-Carrick & Evans-433p-illus by F Miller,e.p. maps-Herd 2462-1st ed (r8) 55.00

WELLMAN,W-Aerial Age-NY-1911-8vo-448p-col illus cl g,frntis,48p plts-1st ed (s2,lacks frnt e.p.) 100.00

WELLS,CAPT JAMES M-With Touch of Elbow or Death Before Dishonor-Phila-1909-Winston-362p-pict cl,illus-Howes W249-1st ed (cc4) 85.00

WELLS,CAROLYN-Abeniki Caldwell-NY-1902-R H Russell-1st ed (v5) 75.00

WELLS,CAROLYN-Crime Incarnate-Phila-1940-Lippincott-1st ed (w9,f,dj) 75.00

WELLS,CAROLYN-Doomed Five-Phila-1930-Lippincott-1st ed (gg8,sl wn dj) 22.50

WELLS,CAROLYN-Eyes in the Wall-Phila-1934-Lippincott-1st ed (f4) 12.00

WELLS,CAROLYN-Fuller Earth-1932-Lippincott-1st ed (s10,dj) 30.00

WELLS,CAROLYN-Furthest Fury-Phila-1924-Lippincott-1st ed (w9,f,dj sl soil & tn) 75.00

WELLS,CAROLYN-Ghosts' High Noon-Phila-1930-Lippincott-1st ed (d4,dj missing sm chips) 25.00

WELLS,CAROLYN-Killer-Phila-1938-Lippincott-1st ed (l4,sl stnd t.e.,dj) 25.00

WELLS,CAROLYN-Master Murderer-Phila-1933-Lippincott-1st ed (g4) 10.00

WELLS,CAROLYN-Mother Goose's Menagerie-Bost-1901-Noyes,Platt-8vo-pict cl,12 col plts by P Newell-1st ed (pp10) 65.00

WELLS,CAROLYN-Murder at the Casino-Phila-1941-Lippincott-1st ed (g4,f,dj) 25.00

WELLS,CAROLYN-Murder in the Bookshop-Phila-1936-Lippincott-1st ed (f4) 17.50

WELLS,CAROLYN-Radio Studio Murder-Phila-1937-Lippincott-1st ed (h4,dj) 25.00

WELLS,CAROLYN-Rubaiyat of Bridge-NY-1909-Harper-1st ed (v5,f) 45.00

WELLS,CAROLYN-Tannahill Tangle-Phila-1928-Lippincott-1st ed (h4) 12.50

WELLS,CAROLYN-Technique of the Mystery Story-1913-Home Correspondence Sch-1st ed (s10,fr hng started) 30.00

WELLS,CARVETH-Adventure-NY-1931-338p-1st ed (a4,f) 28.00

WELLS,CARVETH-In Coldest Africa-NY-1931-255p-1st ed (o10,f) 25.00

WELLS,CARVETH-Kapoot-NY-1933-Nat'l Travel Club-cl,illus,map-1st ed (m8) 25.00

WELLS,CHARLES K P-Life and Adventures of Polk Wells, the Notorious Outlaw-(Halls)-(1907)-G A Warnica-259p-blu cl,illus-Howes W243-1st ed (mm10) 150.00

WELLS,CHARLES W-Frontier Life: Sketches and Incidents of Homes in the West-Cin-(1902)-sm 8vo-313p-cl-1st ed (kk7) 50.00

WELLS,DAMON-Stephen Douglas-Austin-1971-342p-frntis,photos-1st ed (t7,dj) 12.50

WELLS,E L-Hampton and His Cavalry in `64-Richmond-1899-429p-illus,ports-1st ed (z10) 125.00

WELLS,EVELYN-49ers-NY-1949-Dbldy-273p-Six Guns #2341-1st ed (dd4,dj) 25.00

WELLS,H G-Adventures of Tommy-Poughkeepsie-(1935)-Artists & Writers-4to-26p-pict wrps,orig manuscript text & auth's col illus-presumed 1st ed (s3,soil cov) 40.00

WELLS,H G-Croquet Player-NY-1937-Viking-1st US ed (p3,sl tn dj) 30.00

WELLS,H G-Experiment in Autobiography-NY-1934-718p-cl-1st Amer ed (m1) 15.00

WELLS,H G-First Men in the Moon-Lond-1901-Geo Newnes-12 plts-1st ed,1st iss (aa8,e.p. brwnd) 375.00

WELLS,H G-Food of the Gods-1904-MacMillan-1st ed (x2) 125.00

WELLS,H G-Future in America-1906-Harpers-illus-1st ed (x2) 95.00

WELLS,H G-History of Mr.Polly-Lond-1910-1st ed (y7) 25.00

WELLS,H G-Island of Doctor Moreau-Lond-1896-Heinemann-ad in rear for "The Time Machine" followed by 32p inserted cat wi pg 1 headed Donovan Pasha-1st Brit ed (ff6,sp drknd,rear cov dmpstnd 250.00

WELLS,H G-New America: the New World-Lond-(1935)-Cresset Pr-8vo-cl-1st ed (jj8,f,dj) 50.00

WELLS,H G-Open Conspiracy-Lond-1928-Gollancz-1st ed (ll9,dj) 50.00

WELLS,H G-Soul of a Bishop-NY-1917-Macmillan-1st US ed (z9,sl cocked) 15.00

WELLS,H G-Tales of Space and Time-1899-Dbldy & McClure-1st Amer ed (s9,sp sunned & wn) 110.00

WELLS,H G-Tono Bungay-1909-MacMillan-1st state ads-1st ed (x2) 110.00

WELLS,H G-You Can't Be Too Carefu;-1942-Putnam-1st Amer ed (s9,dj sl wn,sp chip & sunned) 45.00

WELLS,H P-City Boys in the Woods-Lond-1890-8vo-277p-illus-scarce (m3) 25.00

WELLS,HARRY L-California-LA-(ca.1930s)-Wells-photos-1st ed (y10,stnd e.p.) 22.00

WELLS,HENRY P-American Salmon Fisherman-NY-1886-Harpers-166p+ads-grn cl,illus-1st ed (w1,vf) 85.00

WELLS,HENRY-Fly Rods & Fly Tackle-NY-1885-12mo-364p+ads-illus-scarce-1st ed (m3) 65.00

WELLS,HORACE L-ED.-Studies from the Chemical Laboratory of the Sheffield Scientific School-NY-1901-Scribner's-2 vols-1st ed (l2) 65.00

WELLS,HORACE-DENTIST, FATHER OF SURGICAL ANESTHESIA-Hartford-1948-415p-1st ed (dd3,ex-libr) 125.00

WELLS,J R,M.D.-Family Companion-Bost-1847-prtd for auth-72p-grn wrps-10th ed (n6,sl soil & fox) 75.00

WELLS,JAMES M-Chisolm Massacre-Chig-1877-Agency Chis Monumntl Fund-291p-blu cl,illus-1st ed (cc4,rbnd,sl cov spot) 75.00

WELLS,JOHN C-Gateway to the Polynia-Lond-1873-Henry S King-8vo-xi,355p-3/4 lea,mrbld papr over bds,fldg map,longitudinal drwng (pp1,rprd e.p.,fox map & drwng 300.00

WELLS,KENNETH M-By Jumping Cat Bridge-Tor-nd(ca.1950s)-Brit Bk Serv-illus by L Oille (aa7,dj) 20.00*

WELLS,R L-General Lee: A Great Friend of Youth-NY-1950-356p-illus,ports-scarce (z10) 50.00

WELLS,RICHARD A-Manners, Culture and Dress of the Best American Society-Springfield-1892-502p-grn cl,illus (q8) 20.00

WELLS,ROSA L-General Lee, a Great Friend of Youth-NY-(1950)-356p-illus-1st ed (c4,dj) 17.50

WELLS,WILLIAM F-Airborne Contagion and Air Hygiene-Cambridge-1955-Harvard Univ Pr-xxxii+423p-red cl,plts-1st ed (j2) 30.00

WELSH,WILLARD-Hutchinson, A Prairie City in Kansas-np-1946-166p-frntis,photos-1st ed (t7,f) 20.00

WELTFISH,GENE-Lost Universe-NY-(1965)-Basic Bks-506p-drwngs,map e.p.-1st ed (bb4,dj) 25.00

WELTY,EUDORA-Curtain of Green-GC-1941-Dlbdy-auth 1st bk-1st ed (j6,lacks dj) 150.00

WELTY,EUDORA-Delta Wedding-NY-(1946)-Harcourt-8vo-cl-1st ed (x3,sl chip & creased dj) 165.00

WELTY,EUDORA-Delta Wedding-NY-1946-1st ed (t5,dj) 200.00

WELTY,EUDORA-Eye of the Story-NY-1977-1st ed (p5,f,dj) 40.00

WELTY,EUDORA-Golden Apples-NY-1949-Harcourt-8vo-cl-1st ed (x3,dj sl chip & rub) 120.00

WELTY,EUDORA-Losing Battles-(1970)-Random-1st ed (q9,vf,dj) 45.00

WELTY,EUDORA-Losing Battles-NY-(1970)-Random-1st ed (j3,f,sl tn dj) 30.00

WELTY,EUDORA-On Short Stories-NY-1949-dec bds-1st ed (v9) 125.00

WELTY,EUDORA-One Writer's Beginnings-Cambridge-1984-1st ed (v9,f,f dj) 50.00

WELTY,EUDORA-Optimist's Daughter-NY-(1972)-Random-8vo-cl-1st ed (x3,f,dj) 30.00

WELTY,EUDORA-Optimist's Daughter-NY-1972-1st ed (q5,f,dj) 35.00

WELTY,EUDORA-Optimist's Daughter-NY-1972-Random-1st ed (q2,dj) 45.00

WELTY,EUDORA-Ponder Heart-NY-1954-drwngs,J Krush-1st ed (p5,dj) 90.00

WELTY,EUDORA-Ponder Heart-NY-1954-Harcourt Brace-8vo-156p-drwngs,J Krush-1st ed (w6,dj) 85.00

WELTY,EUDORA-Retreat-Winston Salem-1981-Palaemon-bds/cl-ltd to 150c,nbrd,autg-1st ed (t6,f) 100.00

WELTY,EUDORA-Robber Bridegroom-GC-1942-1st ed (v9,dj sl tn,sm stn) 500.00

WELTY,EUDORA-Robber Bridegroom-GC-1942-Dbldy,Doran-1st ed (l9,cov sl wtrstnd,dj) 375.00

WELTY,EUDORA-Robber Bridegroom-GC-1942-Dbldy-1st ed (m7,dj rub,rear panel drknd) 350.00

WELTY,EUDORA-Robber Bridegroom-Lond-1944-illus e.p.s,drwngs by J Holland-1st Brit ed (t5,chip dj) 125.00

WELTY,EUDORA-Shoe Bird-NY-(1964)-HB&W-illus,B Krush-1st ed (a10,f,dj) 150.00

WELTY,EUDORA-Wide Net-NY-(1943)-Harcourt,Brace-1st ed (l9,sl soil dj) 800.00

WELTY,EUDORA-Wide Net-NY-(1943)-Harcourt-1st ed (v5,dj tape rnfrcd,sp fade) 200.00

WELTY,JOEL C-Life of Birds-NY-1963-Knopf-1st ed (b9,dj) 15.00

WELZL,J-Thirty Years in the Golden North-1932-Macmillan-336p-map (bb3) 10.00

WELZL,JAN-Thirty Years in the Golden North-NY-1932-Macmillan-336p-map-1st Amer ed (cc4) 25.00

WENDORF,FRED-ET AL-Midland Discovery-Austin-1955-U of Tex Pr-viii+139p-blk cl,36 illus-1st ed (g2,dj) 25.00

WENDT,EDMUND-Treatise on Asiatic Cholera-NY-1885-403p-1st ed (dd3) 50.00

WENIGER,DEL-Cacti of the Southwest-Austin-nd-UTP-folio-249p-col plts-scarce (a9) 50.00

WENIGER,DEL-Cacti of the Southwest-Austin-nd-UTP-folio-249p-col plts-scarce (d3,dj) 75.00

WENLEY,ROBERT M-Anarchists Ideal-Bost-1913-Badger-8vo-217p-cl (z7,cov stnd) 35.00

WENNING,ELIZABETH-Christmas Mouse-(1959)-H Holt-pict cl,drwngs by B Remington-1st ed (aa9,tape stns,dj) 12.00

WENTER,JAMES-Laikan-Lond-1934-12mo-241p-frontis (m3) 15.00

WENTWORTH,FRANK L-Aspen on the Roaring Fork-Lakewood-1950-353p-illus,map rear pckt,ltd to 600c-v scarce-1st ed (t7) 80.00

WENTWORTH,G A-Wentworth's Primary Arithmetic-Bost-1891-Ginn & Co-220p-bds,illus (k1) 15.00

WENTWORTH,LADY-Horses in the Making-Lond-1951-Allen & Unwin-1st ed (f10,dj) 35.00

WENTWORTH,M P-Forged in Strong Fires-Caldwell-1948-ltd ed,nbrd,autg-1st ed (g7,unopened,f,dj) 50.00

WENTWORTH,P-Chinese Shawl-1943-Lippincott-1st Amer ed (x7,sl chip dj) 25.00

WENTWORTH,PATRICIA-Alington Inheritance-Phila-1958-Lippincott-1st ed (d4,dj) 20.00

WENTWORTH,PATRICIA-Benevent Treasure-Phila-1954-Lippincott-1st ed (j4,f,dj) 20.00

WENTWORTH,PATRICIA-Eternity Ring-Phila-1948-Lippincott-1st ed (e4,dj) 30.00

WENTWORTH,PATRICIA-Fingerprint-Lond-1959-Hodder-1st Brit ed (f4,f,dj) 25.00

WENTWORTH,PATRICIA-Ladie's Bane-Phila-1952-Lippincott-1st ed (j4,f,dj) 25.00

WENTWORTH,PATRICIA-Latter End-Phila-1947-Lippincott-1st ed (e4,sp chip dj) 25.00

WENTWORTH,PATRICIA-Lonesome Road-1939-Lipincott-1st Amer ed (s10,innr hng tender) 30.00

WENTWORTH,PATRICIA-She Came Back-Phila-1945-Lippincott-1st ed (h4,f,dj) 20.00

WENTWORTH,PATRICIA-She Came Back-Phila-1945-Lippincott-1st ed (z9,f,dj sl rub) 25.00

WENZEL,F-Buzzard-1959-Allen Unwin-4to-86p-col & b&w photos-1st Brit ed (bb3,f,dj) 17.00

WERNER,A-Butterflies and Moths-1956-Random-4to-175p-36 col plts (bb3,f,dj) 25.00

WERNER,E T C-Myths & Legends of China-NY-(1922)-Farrar & Rinehart-cl,32 col illus-1st ed (l8,f,dj) 32.50

WERNER,HERMAN-On the Western Frontier with the US Cavalry Fifty Years Ago-np-1944-98p-stiff wrps,photos-Howes W259-1st ed (t7) 60.00

WERNER,M R-Barnum-(1923)-Harcourt,Brace-381p-illus-1st ed (v8,sl wn dj) 25.00

WERNER,RUTH E-Novice in Navajoland-Scottsdale-1972-171p-photos,map-1st ed (v7,f) 20.00

WERSHUB,LEONARD-One Hundred Years of Medical Progress-Springfield-1967-259p-1st ed (dd3,dj) 40.00

WERSTEIN,IRVING-Kearney the Magnificent-NY-1962-John Day-248p-frntis-1st ed (n7,dj) 30.00

WERTENBAKER,CHARLES C-Invasion-NY-(1944)-Appleton Century-sm 8vo-red cl-1st ed (y3,sl chip dj) 65.00

WERTHAM,FREDERIC-Dark Legend-NY-1941-DS&P-1st ed (z3,f) 15.00

WERTHEIM,MAURICE-Salmon on the Dry Fly-1948-priv prntd-8vo-18p-one of 500c,tip-in photos,orig onionskin dj (m3,f,wn dj) 50.00

WERTHNER,WILLIAM B-Backgrounds of Early Dayton History-Dayton-nd-Torch Club-23p-wrps (l1) 10.00

WESCOTT-JONES,KENNETH-By Rail to the Ends of the Earth-NY-1967-143p-1st ed (n4,f,dj) 27.50

WESSON,MAJ D B-Burning Powder-Springfield-1932-121p-wrps,photos-scarce (ee3,vf) 45.00

WEST,A W-Short History of Ohio-Dayton-1888-68p-wrps (f1) 15.00

WEST,DON-Broadside to the Sun-NY-1946-Norton-1st ed (w5,dj) 20.00

WEST,ELIZABETH-Garden in the Hills-Lond-(1980)-Faber & Faber-8vo-204p-13 illus-1st ed (gg5,f,dj) 12.50

WEST,F J,JR.-Village-NY-(1972)-H&R-1st ed (ff3,dj) 75.00

WEST,GEOFFREY-Charles Darwin a Portrait-1938-Yale-359p-cl (x6,dj fade,wn) 25.00

WEST,GEOFFREY-Charles Darwin-New Haven-1938-Yale U Pr-xvi+359p-blk cl,illus-1st ed (c2) 15.00

WEST,HELEN A-History of Hamilton Township, Mercer County, New Jersey-Trenton-1954-127p-cl,illus (aa6) 35.00

WEST,JESSAMYN-Hide and Seek-NY-(1973)-Harcourt,Brace-1st ed (p3,f,dj) 15.00

WEST,JOAN L-Bookplates of the Los Angeles Public Library-LA-1971-LA Libr Assoc-ltd to 500c-1st ed (w1,f) 25.00

WEST,JOHN A-Serpent in the Sky-NY-1979-Harper & Row-cl,illus-1st ed (o8,as new in dj) 15.00

WEST,JOHN D-Maidenhood and Motherhood-Louisville-1888-711p-cl (d1,inner hngs crackng) 20.00

WEST,JOHN-Tom Lea Artist in Two Mediums-Austin-1967-44p-stiff wrps,illus-1st ed (t7) 15.00

WEST,LEONARD-Natural Trout Fly & Its Imitation-Liverpool-1921-8vo-163p-13 col plts-revsd & enlgd 2nd ed (m3,f) 115.00

WEST,LEOTI-Wide Northwest-Spokane-1927-286p-cl (c1) 30.00

WEST,LEVON-Making an Etching-Lond-1932-Studio-4to-80p-illus silv bds,tip in photos,etchings (r10,sp wn) 25.00

WEST,MRS-Letters to a Young Lady-Troy/NY-1806-Penniman/Riley-503,(1)p-lea-Amer Imprnts 11851-1st Amer ed (d1,ex-libr) 65.00

WEST,NATHANAEL-Cool Million-NY-(1934)-lt tan cl,1st bndng-1st ed (l5,tan sp,sl soil cov) 85.00

WEST,NATHANIEL-Day of the Locust-Lond-(1951)-Grey Walls-8vo-1st Brit ed (x3,sl discol dj) 75.00

WEST,R L-Better Blacks-Balt-1956-Better Blacks Inc-1st ed (f10) 65.00

WEST,RAY B,JR,-Kingdom of the Saints-NY-1957-Viking Pr-389p-illus,map e.p.-1st ed (bb4,dj) 30.00

WEST,REBECCA-Black Lamb and Grey Falcon-Lond-1946-Macmillan-8vo-2 vols-grn cl,illus (gg6) 45.00

WEST,REBECCA-Fountain Overflows-NY-1956-1st ed (l5,sl soil dj sp) 15.00

WEST,RICHARD-Tolkien Criticism-Kent-1981-KSU Pr-rvsd ed (x9,f) 13.75

WEST,WALLACE-Bird of Time-NY-(1959)-Gnome-1st ed (k3,pgs brwnd,sl chip dj) 15.00

WEST,WALLACE-Everlasting Exiles-NY-(1967)-1st ed (k5,f,dj) 12.50

WESTELL,W PERCIVAL-Natural History of the Garden-Lond-(1930)-sm 8vo-vii,88p-blu dec cl,8 col plts (m10,bump,sp wn) 12.00

WESTERHOFF,JOHN H,III-McGuffey and His Readers-Nashville-(1978)-Abingdon-206p-cl (k1,f,dj) 20.00

WESTERMARCK,EDWARD-History of Human Marriage-Lond-1894-644p-2nd ed (dd3) 100.00

WESTERN FARMER'S ALMANAC, FOR...1839-Steubenville-(1838)-Turnbull,publ-36p-wrps-rare (o1,lacks rear wrppr) 75.00

WESTERN SANITARY COMMISSION-Sketch of Its Origin, History, Labors for the Sick and Wounded of the Western Armies...-St.Louis-1864-144p-1st ed (dd3,sp chip) 300.00

WESTERN WRITERS OF AMERICA-Water Trails West-GC-1978-Dbldy-8vo-270p-150 photos-1st ed (z4,dj) 25.00

WESTERN WRITERS OF AMERICA-Wild Streets-GC-1958-285p-1st ed (n10,dj) 30.00

WESTERNER'S BRAND BOOK-LA-(1957)-Los Angeles Corral-293p-illus,Book 7,ltd to 475c (c7,f,nick dj) 65.00

WESTERNER'S BRAND BOOK-LA-(1963)-Los Angeles Corral-241p-illus,Book 10,ltd to 525c (c7,f,nick dj) 50.00

WESTERNERS BRAND BOOK 1946, DENVER POSSE-Denver-1947-242p-dec cl covs,illus,tri fold col repro-ltd to 500c,nbrd-1st ed (r8) 80.00

WESTERNERS BRAND BOOK-1948-Los Angeles Corral-175p-illus e.p.,1 col illus-ltd to 400c-1st ed (ff4,dj) 100.00

WESTERNERS BRAND BOOK-LOS ANGELES CORRAL,1947-(LA)-(1948)-176p-tan cl,lea sp,illus,ltd to 600c(so stated in colophon)-Rampaging Herd #2488-1st ed (b6,f) 95.00

WESTERNERS BRAND BOOK-Los Angeles Corral. Book Five-LA-(1953)-180p-red cl,illus-ltd to 400c-1st ed (k2,dupe of Libr of Congress) 35.00

WESTERVELT,FRANCES A-ED.-History of Bergen County, New JErsey, 1630 to 1923-NY-1923-4to-3 vols-cl,plts (aa6) 175.00

WESTERVELT,W D-Hawaiian Legends of Ghost and Ghost Gods-Bost/Lond-1916-Ellis Pr/Constable-262p+appndx-gry dec cl-2nd ed (pp1,ex-libr) 55.00

WESTERVELT,W D-Legends of Gods and Ghosts-Bost,Lond-1915-12mo-dec gry cl,tip in col plts-1st ed (kk9,f) 50.00

WESTERVELT,W D-Legends of Old Honolulu-Bost-1915-Geo H Ellis-cl,frntis,illus-1st ed (o8) 25.00

WESTING,FRED-Locomotives That Baldwin Built-1966-Superior-4to-192p-photos-1st ed (d3,dj) 25.00

WESTING,FREDERICK-Erie Power-Medina-1970-447p-1st ed (n4,f) 28.50

WESTLAKE,DONALD E-Brothers Keepers-NY-1975-Evans-1st ed (e4,dj) 17.50

WESTLAKE,DONALD E-Cops and Robbers-NY-1972-Evans-1st ed (h4,f,dj) 15.00

WESTLAKE,DONALD E-Enough-NY-(1977)-Evans-1st ed (j3,f,dj) 20.00

WESTLAKE,DONALD E-Enough-NY-1977-Evans-1st ed (e4,as new in dj) 12.50

WESTLAKE,DONALD E-God Save the Mark-NY-1967-Random-1st ed (j4,f,sl soil dj) 25.00

WESTLAKE,DONALD E-Two Much-NY-1975-Evans-1st ed (k4,f,sl wn dj) 15.00

WESTLAKE,DONALD E-Up Your Banners-NY-1969-Macmillan-1st ed (e4,f,dj) 30.00

WESTLAKE,DONALD-Bank Shot-NY-1972-1st ed (q5,f,dj) 20.00

WESTLAKE,DONALD-Blackbird-1969-Macmillan-1st ed (x7,f,dj) 30.00

WESTLAKE,DONALD-Damsel-1967-Macmillan-1st ed (x7,dj) 28.00

WESTLAKE,DONALD-Gangway-NY-1973-1st ed (q5,f,dj) 30.00

WESTLAKE,DONALD-Killy-1963-Random-1st ed (x7,dj) 45.00

WESTLAKE,DONALD-Murder Among Children-1967-Random-1st ed (x7,dj) 27.00

WESTLAKE,DONALD-Under an English Heaven-Lond-1973-1st Brit ed (q5,dj) 25.00

WESTLAKE,DONALD-Wax Apple-1970-Random-1st ed (x7,f,dj) 30.00

WESTMORELAND,RUSTY-Adventures in Climbing-Lond-1964-128p-1st ed (q10,f,dj) 15.00

WESTON,EDWARD-California and the West-NY-(1940)-DS&P-cl-1st ed (q3) 125.00

WESTON,EDWARD-California and the West-NY-(1940)-Duell-lg 4to-blk cl,92 photos-1st ed (y3,dj wn & chip) 135.00

WESTON,EDWARD-Daybooks of...-Millerton-(1973)-Aperture-4to-2 vols-cl-2nd ed (y3,djs) 95.00

WESTON,EDWARD-Daybooks of...-Rochester/NY-(1961)&(1966)-Eastman/Horizon-4to-2 vols-cl-Vol.1(Mexico),Vol.2(California)-1st eds (y3,f,sl chip dj) 165.00

WESTON,EDWARD-Edward Weston Nudes-(Millerton)-1977-Aperture-116p-60 photos-1st ed (cc9,as new in dj) 60.00

WESTON,EDWARD-Edward Weston, Photographer-NY-1965-Grossman-88p-54 photos-1st ed (cc9,sl tn dj) 75.00

WESTON,EDWARD-Photographs of...-NY-1946-MOMA-4to-36p-cl-text by Nancy Newhall-1st ed (t3) 40.00

WESTON,EDWARD-Seeing California with...-np-nd(c.1939)-Westways-4to-(7),8-49p of photos,pict bds (mm1,edge-wn bds) 300.00

WESTON,GARNETT-Murder on Shadow Island-1933-Farrar-1st ed (s10,dj) 25.00

WESTPHALL,VICTOR-Public Domain in New Mexico 1854 to 1891-Albuq-1965-212p-chrts,maps-1st ed (t7,dj) 15.00

WESTROPP,HODDER-Ancient Symbol Worship-NY-1875-J W Bouton-cl,illus-2nd ed (o8) 29.00

WESTWOOD,J O-Butterflies of Great Britain with Their Transformations-Lond-1887-Routledge-140p-handcol half t.p.,19 handcol plts (bb3,cor wn) 465.00

WESTWOOD,THOMAS-Chronicle of "The Compleat Angler" of Izaak Walton & Charles Cotton-Lond-1883-8vo-86p-1/4 mor,gilt-scarce-new ed wi notes & add by T Satchell (m3) 145.00

WET DAYS AT EDGEWOOD-NY-1865-Scribner-324p-grn bds (k6) 50.00

WETHERILL,BENJAMIN A-Wetherills of the Mesa Verde-Rutherford-(1977)-322p-photos,maps-1st ed (v7,f,dj) 25.00

WETMORE,A-Birds of Haiti & Dominican Republic-Wash-1931-8vo-483p-wrps,26 plts (y8,lt fox) 60.00

WETMORE,A-Birds of the Republic of Panama-1968 to 84-Smithsonian-4 vols-4 col & 245 b&w illus (bb3,f,dj) 100.00

WETMORE,A-Song and Garden Birds of North Am and Water,Prey and Game Birds of North Am-Wash-1976(1975)&(1973)-Natl Geog Soc-8vo-2 vols-cl,1109 col illus (y8,djs,box) 30.00

WETMORE,A-Song and Garden Birds of North America-1962-Nat Geog Soc-399p-col illus,record in pckt-1st prtg (bb3,f,dj) 30.00

WETMORE,A-Water,Prey, and Game Birds of North Am-Wash-1965-Natl Geogr Soc-8vo-464p-cl,600 col illus+records rear pckt (y8,dj chip) 19.00

WETMORE,HELEN C-Last of the Great Scouts-NY-(1918)-G&D-333p+ads-cl,illus,title orig publ 1899,this ed added Z Grey material,later prntg of 1st ed wi damaged type (l1) 15.00

WETZEL,C M-Practical Fly Fishing-Bost-1945-283p-blu pebble grained cl,photos-2nd ed (ee3,f) 75.00

WETZEL,CHARLES M-American Fishing Books-Newark-1950-priv prtd-235p-3/4 goatskin,handbnd by auth,illus,facs-ltd to 200c,nbrd,autg (o4,f) 1,500.00

WETZEL,CHARLES M-Trout Flies-Harrisburg-1955-4to-152p-full tan calf gilt,#37 of deluxe ltd ed,12 hand col plts by auth-scarce (m3) 750.00

WEXLEY,JOHN-Judgement of Julius & Ethel Rosenberg-NY-1955-Cameron & Kahn-cov illus by R Kent (r1,edgewn dj) 25.00

WEXLEY,JOHN-Last Mile-NY-1930-French-1st ed (w5,f,rprd dj) 45.00

WEYBRIGHT,VICTOR-Making of a Publisher-NY-(1967)-Reynal/Morrow-1st ed (w1,f,dj) 12.50

WEYER,A-Family Physician...-St.Clairsville-1831-publ by auth-216p-lea-Amer Imprnts 10608 (c1) 225.00

WEYGANDT,CORNELIUS-Down Jersey-NY-1940-352p-cl,plts (aa6) 35.00

WEYL,HERMANN-Symmetry-1952-Princeton Univ Pr-(viii)+168p-gry cl,72 text figs-1st ed (j2,dj) 25.00

WEZEL,JAN-Quest for Polar Treasures-Lond-(1933)-Allen & Unwin-8vo-352p-cl-1st ed in Engl (pp5,discol sp,dj sp chip) 65.00*

WHALE FISHERY OF NEW ENGLAND-Bost-1915-State St Trust Co-63p-orig prntd wrps,9th in bank history ser (nn1,sl fox,bnk lettr laid in) 40.00

WHALE-1968-S&S-oblng 4to-287p-267 illus(incl 87 col)-1st prtg (bb3,f,dj) 35.00

WHALEN,PHILIP-Every Day-1965-Coyote's Journal-wrps-1st ed (v5) 20.00

WHALLEY,GEORGE-Legend of John Hornby-Lond-1962-J Murray-xiv,367p-26 illus,6 maps & figs-1st ed (bb7,sl rub dj) 40.00*

WHARFIELD,COL H B-With Scout and Cavalry at Fort Apache-Tucson-1965-124p-pict cl,illus,e.p. maps-1st ed (n3) 32.50

WHARTON,CLARENCE-San Jacinto-Houston-1930-138p-photos-1st ed (t7,autg) 27.50

WHARTON,CLARENCE-Satanta-Dallas-1935-246p-frntis,illus-1st ed (t7) 100.00

WHARTON,CLARENCE-Wharton's History of Fort Bend County-Houston-1950-250p-map frntis-Six Guns #2374 (t7) 60.00

WHARTON,EDITH-Buccaneers-NY-1938-Appleton Century-1st ed (f8,f,dj) 50.00

WHARTON,EDITH-Crucial Instances-NY-1901-Scribners-1st ed (w5,hngs weak) 75.00

WHARTON,EDITH-Gods Arrive-NY,Lond-1932-1st ed (j5,dull sp) 12.50

WHARTON,EDITH-Gods Arrive-NY-1932-Appleton-1st ed (y1,f,dj) 75.00

WHARTON,EDITH-Greater Inclination-NY-1899-Scribner's-new cl wi orig covs laid on,sp g,t.e.g.,auth 1st bk-ltd to 1250c-1st ed (aa9,rbnd) 150.00

WHARTON,EDITH-House of Mirth-NY-1905-8vo-cl,illus-1st ed (jj8,hng weak,sp dull) 45.00

WHARTON,EDITH-Italian Villas and Their Gardens-Lond-1904-J Lane,Bodley Head-lg 8vo-xii,270p-g pict cov,t.e.g.,52 illus(incl 26 M Parrish),(15 col),photos,engrvngs-early ed (mm4,sp wn,uncut) 190.00

WHARTON,EDITH-Italian Villas and Their Gardens-Lond-Lane-270p-cl,illus by Parrish (x6) 120.00

WHARTON,EDITH-Italian Villas and Their Gardens-NY-1907-Century-lg 4to-270p-dec cl,52 illus(15 col)-later prtg (cc10) 180.00

WHARTON,EDITH-Madame De Treymes-NY-1907-Scribner's-orig g dec cl,t.e.g.,illus-1st ed (aa9) 45.00

WHARTON,EDITH-Old New York False Dawn-NY,Lond-1924-Appleton-e.p.'s by Caswell-1st ed (d10,bump,dj sp chip) 75.00

WHARTON,GRACE-Queens of Society-Phila-nd-Porter & Coates-2 vols,cl,engrvd ports (d1) 20.00

WHARTON,WILL-Graphite From Elsinore-Prairie City-1949-Decker Pr-1st ed (v5,sl wn dj) 20.00

WHARTON,WILLIAM-Birdy-NY-1979-Knopf-auth 1st bk-1st ed (bb1,as new in dj) 35.00

WHARTON,WILLIAM-Dad-NY-1981-Knopf-1st ed (bb1,f,dj) 20.00

WHARTON,WILLIAM-Midnight Clear-NY-1982-Knopf-1st ed (h3,f,dj) 20.00

WHAT SALEM DAMES COOKED IN 1700, 1800 & 1900-Salem-1933-Stetson Pr-40p-wrps-Bitting 618-rprnt of 1910 ed (u6) 20.00

WHATMOUGH,JOSHUA-Dialects of Ancient Gaul-1970-Harvard U Pr (m4,f,dj) 27.50

WHEATCROFT,HARRY-In Praise of Roses-Chig-1970-Regnery-192p-col photos (x6,f,dj chip) 25.00

WHEATLEY,DENNIS-Herewith the Clues-1939-Hutchinson & Co-wrps wi all clues & documentation,seal is unbroken,scarce thus-1st ed (x7,seal unbroken) 70.00

WHEATLEY,DENNIS-Malinsay Massacre-1938-Hutchinson & Co-wrps with all clues & documentation-1st ed (x7) 55.00

WHEATLEY,DENNIS-Murder Off Miami-1936-Hutchinson & Co-wrps wi all clues & documentation-1st ed (x7) 70.00

WHEATLEY,HENRY B-Literary Blunders...-NY-1893-Armstrong & Son-sm 8vo-xi,226p-orig grn cl,bev edges-1st US ed (x4,lacks ffep) 35.00

WHEATON,ELIZABETH L-Texas City Remembers-1948-Naylor-4to-109p-photos-1st ed (a9,dj) 75.00

WHEELER,A O-Selkirk Range, British Columbia-Ottawa-1905-495p-92 photos,vol.1 only(vol.2 is a case of maps)-1st ed (o10,f) 150.00

WHEELER,ALWYNE-Fishes of the British Isles & North West Europe-1969-Mich St-8vo-611-illus (m3,f,sl fray dj) 20.00

WHEELER,BURTON K-Yankee from the West-NY-1962-Dbldy-436p-1st ed (ff8,rub dj) 25.00

WHEELER,EDWARD S-Scheyichbi and the Strand, or Early Days Along the Delaware-Phila-1876-vi,116p-cl,plts (aa6,sl wn) 35.00

WHEELER,H A-Short Catalogue of Books Printed in England...Printed Abroad before 1641...Library of Wadham College-Lond,NY,Tor-1929-Longmans,Green-8vo-xv,101p-orig blu buckr-1st ed (t10,f) 60.00

WHEELER,HAROLD F B-Story of the British Navy-Lond-1922-Geo G Harrap-8vo-384p-blu cl,16 col plts-1st ed (pp1,sl fox & edgewn) 40.00

WHEELER,HOMER W-Buffalo Days-Indpls-(1925)-Bobbs Merrill-369p-illus-1st ed thus (n2,chip dj) 75.00

WHEELER,HOMER W-Buffalo Days-Indpls-(1925)-Bobbs Merrill-369p-illus-Herd 2499 (cc4,sl wn sp) 45.00

WHEELER,JOSEPH-American Public Library Building-NY-1941-Scribner-4to-484p-red cl,photos (r10,tattrd dj) 45.00

WHEELER,KENNETH W-To Wear a City's Crown-Cambridge-1968-Harvard U Pr-222p-cl,photos-1st ed (w3,f,dj) 35.00

WHEELER,OLIN D-Eastward Through the Stories Northwest...Over the Shasta Northern Pacific Route-np-nd-62,(2)p-wrps (l1,sl dmpstnd pg bottoms) 12.50

WHEELER,OLIN D-Lewis & Clark Centennial Exposition-St.Paul-nd-No Pacific RR Publ-64p-photos-promo pamphlet for Portland Expo of 1905 (f7) 40.00

WHEELER,OPAL-Sing for Christmas-NY-1943-Dutton-4to-127p-bds,illus-2nd prtg (r3,f,dj drknd,sl tn & soil) 45.00

WHEELER,R-Sherman's March-NY-(1978)-241p-illus,ports-1st ed (z10,fade dj) 25.00

WHEELER,RICHARD-Sherman's March-NY-(1978)-241p-illus-1st ed (n3,f,dj) 22.50

WHEELER,RICHARD-Siege of Vicksburg-NY-1978-Crowell-257p-illus,maps-1st ed (o7,f,f dj) 20.00

WHEELER,RICHARD-We Knew William Tecumseh Sherman-NY-(1977)-130p-illus,maps-1st ed (c4,f,dj) 25.00

WHEELER,ROBERT-Jim Thorpe-1979-U of Okla-1st ed (p7,dj) 15.00

WHEELER,W M-Ants-1960-Columbia Univ-663p-photos,illus (bb3,f) 35.00

WHEELER,WILLIAM M-ED.-Lamarck Manuscripts at Harvard-Cambridge-1933-Harvard Univ-xxxii+202p-red cl,plts-1st ed (d2,dj) 30.00

WHEELER-JONES,C G-Returned Katchinas-Tucson-1954-58p-hand col frnt wrps,hand col plts & illus-2nd prtg (v7) 20.00

WHEELOCK,JOHN H-Poems Old and New-NY-(1956)-Scribner's-1st ed (bb1,dj) 30.00

WHEELOCK,JULIA-Boys in White-NY-1870-268p-1st ed (dd3,few wtrstnd pgs) 300.00

WHEELOCK,MRS T B-Mrs Wheelock's Choice Recipes-(St.Paul)-(1904)-(Randall Prtg)-147p+13p ads-papr wrps,frntis (n6,wn) 35.00

WHEELWRIGHT,MARY C-Myth of Sontso-Santa Fe-1940-Mus of Navaho Cermnl Art-13p-wrps-Bull.No.2-1st ed (v7) 25.00

WHEELWRIGHT,MARY C-Tleji-Santa Fe-1938-14p-wrps-Bull. No.1-scarce-1st ed (v7) 25.00

WHELAN,R-Flying Tigers-NY-1942-8vo-224p-illus cl,8p plts,e.p. maps (s2,dj) 30.00

WHELEN,TOWNSEND-American Rifle-NY-1923-637p-photos,illus (gg3,crack,mildew) 25.00

WHELEN,TOWNSEND-Big Game Hunting for the Novice & Expert-Denver-1928-12mo-93p-wrps,photos,illus (m3) 17.50

WHELEN,TOWNSEND-Hunting Rifle-Harrisburg-1940-8vo-463p-photos,illus-1st ed (m3) 35.00

WHELEN,TOWNSEND-Mister Rifleman-CA-1965-377p+epilogue-photos (gg3,vf,dj) 30.00

WHELEN,TOWNSEND-Mr.Rifleman & Guns and Ammo for Hunting Big Game by F Keith-LA-1965-2 vols-padded leatherette,illus-Deluxe ed (gg3,vf,box) 225.00

WHELEN,TOWNSEND-Telescopic Rifle Sights-Onslow Cnty-1936-12mo-130p-scarce-1st ed (m3,f,fray dj) 45.00

WHELEN,TOWNSEND-Ultimate in Rifle Precision-PA-1954-Bench Rest Shooters Assoc-376p-photos (gg3,f,dj) 32.00

WHELEN,TOWNSEND-Why Not Load Your Own-Wash D.C.-1949-8vo-215p-illus-1st ed (m3,f,fray dj) 17.50

WHELTON,PAUL-Pardon My Blood-Phila-1950-Lippincott-1st ed (e4,dj) 10.00

WHERRY,JOSEPH H-Indian Masks and Myths of the West-NY-(1969)-257p-photos,map e.p.-1st ed (v7,dj) 15.00

WHIFFIN,E T-Outing Lore-NY-1928-8vo-85p (m3) 14.00

WHIGHAM,HARRY-Report of the Commissioner of Immigration for Colfax County-Santa Fe-1880-13p-wrps,rare-1st ed (v7) 400.00

WHILE,ELIZA O-When Molly Was Six-Bost-1894-Houghton Mifflin-133p-pict cl,b&w illus,K Pyle-1st ed (s3) 25.00

WHILLANS,D-Don Whillans, Portrait of a Mountaineer-Lond-1971-266p-photos-1st Brit ed (p10,f,dj) 65.00

WHIPPLE,A B C-Yankee Whalers in the South Seas-GC-1954-Dbldy-304p-gry cl-1st ed (k2,dj) 22.00

WHIPPLE,A B C-Yankee Whalers in the South Seas-GC-1954-Dbldy-8vo-304p-gry dec cl,drwngs (p8,chip dj) 30.00

WHIPPLE,A B C-Yankee Whalers in the South Seas-GC-1954-Dbldy-8vo-304p-gry dec cl,drwngs,R M Powers (nn1,chip dj) 25.00

WHIPPLE,FRED L-Collected Contributions of...-Cambridge-1972-Smithsn Astrophysical Obs-4to-2 vols-grn cl,illus-1st ed (c2) 65.00

WHIPPLE,HENRY B-Bishop Whipple's Southern Diary 1843 to 1844-Mpls-(1973)-U of Minn Pr-208p-illus (cc4) 20.00

WHIPPLE,HENRY B-Lights and Shadows of a Long Episcipate-NY-1902-Macmillan-576p-illus (gg4) 40.00

WHISTLER,H-Popular Handbook of Indian Birds-1949-Gurney Jackson-560p-7 col & 17 b&w plts (bb3) 48.00

WHISTLER,H-Popular Handbook of Indian Birds-1963-Oliver Boyd-560p-7 col & 17 b&w plts-4th ed,rvsd,enlgd (bb3,f,dj) 55.00

WHISTLER,ROY-Guar-1979-Purdue-124p (x6) 20.00

WHITAKER,ALMA-Bacchus Behave-NY-1933-Stokes-140p-bds (n6,autg) 25.00

WHITAKER,CHARLES H-Rameses to Rockefeller-NY-1934-Random-illus-1st ed (f8,f,sl wn dj) 65.00

WHITAKER,P H-Rough Shooting-Lond-1963-12mo-74p-photos (m3,vf,dj) 12.50

WHITBREAD BOOK OF HORSES-NY-1962-Arco-photos-1st US ed (j9,dj) 20.00

WHITBY,CHARLES-Back to the Sun-Lond-1949-C & J Temple-cl-1st ed (n8,f,dj) 30.00

WHITCOMB,ROYDEN P-First History of Bayonne, New Jersey-Bayonne-1904-123p-cl,illus (aa6) 45.00

WHITE,ANDREW D-AUTOBIOGRAPHY OF...-NY-1906-2 vols,cl (l1) 20.00

WHITE,AURORA L-ED.-New Mexico Folk Lore-(Santa Fe)-(1940)-51p-tall stiff wrps,2 photos,music,text in Engl & Spanish-v scarce-1st ed (u7) 50.00

WHITE,BISHOP ALMA-Ku Klux Klan in Prophecy-Zarephath-(1925)-Good Citizen-144p-wrps,illus (e2,cov soil,wn,sl fox) 65.00

WHITE,BISHOP ALMA-Ku Klux Klan-Zarepath-(1925)-136p (e1,wrps sl wn,sl dmpstnd) 20.00

WHITE,CHARLES-Treatise on the Management of Pregnant and Lying In Women-Lond-1777-462p-2 plts-2nd ed (g10) 500.00

WHITE,DALE-Bat Masterson-NY-(1960)-Messner-191p-1st ed (nn6,dj) 18.00

WHITE,DALE-Tall Timber Pilots-NY-1953-223p-illus-1st ed (e7,chip dj) 60.00

WHITE,DANA-ED-Olmstead South-Westport-(1979)-xxxvi,259p-6 maps-1st ed (m10,as new) 17.00

WHITE,E B-Charlotte's Web-1952-Harpers-1st ed (x2,sl tn dj) 225.00

WHITE,E B-Charlotte's Web-NY-(1952)-Harper-184p-cl,illus by G Williams-1st ed (nn10,sl bump,f dj) 250.00

WHITE,E B-Elements of Style-NY-(1959)-Macmillan-1st ed (cc2,f,sl tn dj) 50.00

WHITE,E B-Here is New York-NY-(1949)-Harper-1st ed (cc2,f,dj) 50.00

WHITE,E B-Poems and Sketches of...-NY-1981-Harper & Row-1st ed (z9,f,dj) 10.00

WHITE,E B-Points of My Compass-(1962)-Harper & Row-1st ed (t9,f,dj) 15.00

WHITE,E B-Points of My Compass-NY-(1962)-H&R-1st ed (hh5,f,dj) 10.00

WHITE,E B-Second Tree From the Corner-(1954)-Harper-1st ed (p9,sl chip dj) 30.00

WHITE,E B-Second Tree From the Corner-NY-(1954)-1st ed (ee2,sl wn dj) 40.00

WHITE,E B-Stuart Little in the School Room-NY-(1945)-Harper & Row-12mo-red bds,as iss (ee2,f) 45.00

WHITE,E B-Stuart Little-NY-(1945)-Harper-lt tan bds-1st ed (bb2,dj sl brwnd & chip) 125.00

WHITE,E E-Experiences of a Special Indian Agent-Norman-1965-340p-illus-1st ed (t7,dj) 15.00

WHITE,E J-COMP.-Port Townsend and Hadlock Directory, 1897-Seattle-(1897)-Metro Pr-sm 8vo-96p+ads-scarce (y4,sl spot cov) 200.00

WHITE,E L-Put Out the Light-1933-Harpers-1st Amer ed (x7,sl tn dj) 28.00

WHITE,EDMUND-Forgetting Elena-NY-1973-auth 1st bk-1st ed (n5,f,dj) 55.00

WHITE,EDWARD L-Lukundoo & Other Stories-NY-(1927)-Doran-pict dj-1st ed (bb1,dj) 225.00

WHITE,ELLEN G-Story of the Patriarchs and Prophets-Wash D.C.-1927-790;(9)p-cl (a1) 15.00

WHITE,ETHEL L-Put Out the Light-1943-Harpers-1st Amer ed (s10,dj) 40.00

WHITE,ETHEL L-Some Must Watch-1941-Harper-1st ed (s10,dj) 35.00

WHITE,ETHEL L-Step in the Dark-1939-Harper-1st ed (s10,dj) 32.50

WHITE,F M-Slave of Silence-1906-LB-1st ed (x7,f) 19.00

WHITE,GABRIEL-Edward Ardizzone, Artist and Illustrator-NY-(1980)-Schocken-1st US ed (r3,dj) 35.00

WHITE,HELEN M-ED.-Ho! For the Gold Fields-1966-Minn Hist Soc-289p-illus,e.p.maps+7 maps-1st ed (r8,dj) 30.00

WHITE,HELEN M-ED.-Ho! For the Gold Fields-St.Paul-1966-Minn Hist Soc-289p-illus,e.p. maps-1st ed (gg4,dj) 20.00

WHITE,ISABELLA M-Scottish Bakehouse Cook Book-np-(1972)-Tashmoo Pr-222p-wrps,wire bndg-1st prtg (l6) 17.00

WHITE,J E GRANT-Garden Art and Architecture-Lond-1968-Abelard Schuman-8vo-110p-gry bds,photos (r10,f dj) 20.00

WHITE,J M-Land God Made in Anger-1969-Rand McNally-308p-photos,map-1st ed (bb3,f,dj) 16.00

WHITE,JAMES E-Life Span and Reminiscences of Railway Mail Service-Phila-(1910)-Deemer & Jaisohn-274p-illus-1st ed (bb4) 50.00

WHITE,JANE-Comet-NY-(1975)-Harper & Row-1st US ed (l3,f,dj) 15.00

WHITE,JOHN H,JR.-American Locomotives: An Engineering History, 1830 to 1880-Balt-1968-504p-1st ed (n4,f,dj) 39.00

WHITE,JOHN H-Cincinnati Locomotive Builders 1845 to 1868-Wash D.C.-1965-167p-1st ed (n4) 20.00

WHITE,JOHN I-American Vignettes-Convent Sta-1976-191p-stiff wrps,illus-1st ed (t7) 12.50

WHITE,JON M-Marshal of France-NY-1962-300p-illus-1st ed (b7,f,dj) 35.00

WHITE,JOSEPH J-Cranberry Culture-NY-1870-Orange Judd-126p-cl (x6) 45.00

WHITE,KOCH-Land Title Study-Santa Fe-1971-261p-wrps-1st ed (u7) 45.00

WHITE,LESLIE A-Pioneers in American Anthropology-Albuq-1940-2 vols-illus,ltd to 400c-1st ed (v7) 100.00

WHITE,LESLIE A-Pueblo of Sia, New Mexico-Wash-1962-BAE Bull.184-358p-cl,11 photo plts,fldg map (a1) 20.00

WHITE,LESLIE-ED.-Lewis Henry Morgan, the Indian Journals 1859 thru 62-Ann Arbor-1959-231p-photos,col illus,maps-Dykes High Spots #94-1st ed (t7,dj) 50.00

WHITE,LIONEL-To Find a Killer-NY-1954-1st ed (n5,dj) 25.00

WHITE,M J-Decoy as Art, Waterfowl in a Wooden Soul-Spain-1985-unpgd-photos by Warner (gg3,vf,dj) 12.00

WHITE,MARGARET E-Decorative Arts of Early New Jersey-Princeton-1964-Van Nostrand-8vo-137p-cl,illus-(NJ Hist Ser.25) (ll4,dj) 34.00

WHITE,MINOR-An Octave of Prayer-NY-1972-Aperture-91p-90p photos-1st ed (cc9,as new in dj) 45.00

WHITE,MINOR-Celebrations-Millerton-1974-Aperture-82p-75 photos-1st ed (cc9,as new in dj) 45.00

WHITE,MINOR-Rites & Passages-Millerton-1978-Aperture-143p-80 photos-1st ed (cc9,as new in dj) 50.00

WHITE,OWEN P-Them was the Days-NY-1925-Minton,Balch-235p-pict cl-Six Guns #2386-1st ed (cc4,sl wn sp) 25.00

WHITE,P S-War of Four Thousand Years...-Phila-1846-Griffith & Simon-295p-cl (a1) 50.00

WHITE,PATRICIA H-Mousse Souffle Cookbook-(1972)-Holt-16mo-83p-yel cl-1st prtg (q8,dj) 10.00

WHITE,PATRICK-Cockatoos-Lond-1974-Cape-1st ed (w5,f,dj) 35.00

WHITE,PATRICK-Riders in the Chariot-Lond-(1961)-Eyre & Spottiswoode-1st Brit ed (a10,dj) 35.00

WHITE,PATRICK-Solid Mandala-Lond-1966-Eyre & Spottiswoode-1st Brit ed (d8,f dj) 60.00

WHITE,PATRICK-Vivisector-NY-1970-Viking-1st US ed (z9,dj) 15.00

WHITE,PHILO-Philo White's Narrative of a Cruize in the Pacific...on the U.S. Sloop of War Dale 1841 to 1843-Denver-(1965)-Old West Publ-4to-84p-illus(2 col)-ltd to 1000c (bb4) 50.00

WHITE,STEWART E-Cabin-GC-1911-8vo-283p-photos-1st ed (m3) 25.00

WHITE,STEWART E-Daniel Boone, Wilderness Scout-GC-(1922)-GC Publ-cl,pasteon,illus,J Daugherty (s3,f) 12.00

WHITE,STEWART E-Gold-GC-1913-437,(1);12,(1)p-cl-1st ed (e1,sl dmpstnd frnt cov) 15.00

WHITE,STEWART E-Land of Footprints-NY-1913-440p-photos (gg3) 20.00

WHITE,STEWART E-Lions in the Path-NY-1926-292p-photos,illus (gg3,f) 40.00

WHITE,STEWART E-Mountains-NY-1904-282p-cl-Rampaging Herd 2512-1st ed (d1) 20.00

WHITE,STEWART E-Mystery-1907-MP-illus-1st ed (x7) 45.00

WHITE,STEWART E-Pass-NY-1906-8vo-199p-photos,text dec-1st ed (m3) 15.00

WHITE,STEWART E-Rediscovered Country-GC-1915-Dbldy-8vo-358p-grn cl-fldg map,photos-1st ed (s1) 50.00

WHITE,STEWART E-Rules of the Game-GC-1910-8vo-644p-frontis-1st ed (m3) 20.00

WHITE,STEWART E-Secret Harbor-1926-Dbldy-1st ed (s10,sp tn dj) 30.00

WHITE,STEWART E-Sign at Six-1912-BM-1st ed (x7,weak hng) 20.00

WHITE,T H-Elephant and the Kangaroo-NY-(1947)-Putnam's-254p-cl-1st ed (nn4,f,dj) 45.00

WHITE,T H-Godstone and the Blackmor-1959-Putnam-1st Amer ed (x2,dj) 38.00

WHITE,T H-Once and Future King-Lond-1958-Collins-1st complete ed (ll5,dj) 125.00

WHITE,T H-Sword in the Stone-NY-1939-Putnam's-312p-cl,pict e.p.,R Lawson-1st ed (r3,sl drknd sp) 30.00

WHITE,W L-Queens Die Proudly-NY-(1943)-8vo-e.p. maps-1st ed (s2,sm stn rear cov,dj) 20.00

WHITE,W L-They Were Expendable-NY-(1942)-8vo-viii,210p-cl-1st ed (s2,dj) 25.00

WHITE,WILLIAM C-Tomb Tile Pictures of Ancient China-1939-U of Tor Pr-cl,32p plts,wi maps-scarce-1st ed (l8) 45.00

WHITEBROOK,ROBERT B-Coastal Exploration of Washington-Palo Alto-(1959)-146p-11 chrts-Tweney #82-1st ed (e7,f,dj) 100.00

WHITECHURCH,V-Templeton Case-1924-Clode-scarce-1st ed (x7) 25.00

WHITECHURCH,VICTOR L-Murder at the Pageant-1931-Duffield-1st Amer ed (s10) 35.00

WHITECHURCH,VICTOR L-Shot on the Downs-NY-1928-Duffield-1st Amer ed (e4,brwng pgs) 25.00

WHITECOTTON,JOSEPH W-Zapotecs-Norman-1977-U of Okla Pr-8vo-xiv,338p-illus,maps,tabls-1st ed (mm1,f,sl wn dj) 35.00

WHITEHEAD, WILLIAM A-Contributions to the Early History of Perth Amboy and Adjoining Country...-NY-1856-viii,428p-cl,illus,plts,fldg maps (aa6) 150.00

WHITEHEAD,CHARLES-Man and His Diamonds-1980-Vantage-photos-1st ed (s8,f,sl wn dj) 60.00

WHITEHEAD,G-Before the Wrights Flew-NY-(1966)-8vo-192p-col illus cl,frntis,text illus-1st ed (s2,dj) 20.00

WHITEHEAD,HENRY S-West India Lights-Sauk City-1946-Arkham Hs-one of 3037c (bb1,sl tan dj sp) 65.00

WHITEHEAD,J H C-Mathematical Works of ...-NY-1963-Macmillan/Pergamon Pr Bk-4 vols-red cl-1st ed (g2,dj) 125.00

WHITEHEAD,JAMES-Joiner-NY-1971-Knopf-1st ed (a5,f,dj) 20.00

WHITEHEAD,JOHN-Judicial and Civil History of New Jersey-(Bost?)-1897-xv,527,611p-cl,ports (aa6,rbnd) 150.00

WHITEHEAD,JOHN-Passaic Valley, New Jersey in Three Centuries-NY-1901-4to-2 vols-orig 1/2 lea,illus,plts (aa6,sp wn,chip) 200.00

WHITEHEAD,JOHN-Washington at Morristown-Newark-(1899)-32p-wrps,frntis (aa6) 30.00

WHITEHEAD,WILLIAM A-East Jersey Under the Proprietary Governments-Newark-1875-viii,(2),486p-cl,fldg maps,facs-rvsd & enlgd 2nd ed (aa6,sp chip) 125.00

WHITEHOUSE,E-Texas Flowers in Natural Colors-1948-priv publ-212p-180 col illus-scarce-2nd ed (bb3,fray dj) 35.00

WHITEHOUSE,EULA-Texas Flowers in Natural Colors-Austin-1936-priv prtd-212p-col illus-1st ed (a9,dj) 30.00

WHITEHOUSE,F C-Sport Fishing in Canada-Vancouver-1948-8vo-188p-ltd to 1200c,nbrd,autg,photos,illus (m3) 50.00

WHITEHOUSE,P B-Main Line Album-Lond-1964-1st ed (n4,f,dj) 16.50

WHITEHOUSE,P B-On the Narrow Gauge-Lond-1964-148p-1st ed (n4,f,dj) 25.00

WHITEHOUSE,P B-Round the World on the Narrow Gauge-Lond-1966-159p-1st ed (n4,f,dj) 30.00

WHITEHOUSE,P B-Steam in Europe-Lond-1966-198p-1st ed (n4,f,dj) 23.00

WHITELAW,RALPH T-Virginia's Eastern Shores: a History of Northampton and Accomack Counties-1968-Peter Smith-2 vols-rprnt of V.H.S. 1951 ed (dd9) 85.00

WHITELY,IKE-Rural Life in Texas-Atlanta-1891-Jas P Harrison-82p+ads-wrps-Graff 50-1st ed (a9,wrps soil,loose) 45.00

WHITEMAN,PAUL-Jazz-NY-1926-Sears-red cl-2nd prtg (w1) 25.00

WHITESIDE,THOMAS-Twiggy & Justin-NY-1968-FS&G-8vo-136p-cl,cov & illus by Avedon-1st ed (t3,dj) 30.00

WHITFIELD,RAOUL-Green Ice-NY-1930-Knopf-1st ed (z9,sunned) 35.00

WHITFIELD,SHELBY-Kiss It Goodbye-1973-Abelard Schuman-photos-1st ed (s8,f,dj) 17.50

WHITING,JOHN W M-Becoming a Kwoma-New Haven-1951-Yale U Pr-8vo-226p-cl,illus-2nd prtg (y5,chip dj) 18.00

WHITING,LILIAN-Canada the Spellbinder-Tor-1917-Dent-318p-g dec grn cl,col frntis,32 illus,fldg map-1st ed (bb7,sl warped) 35.00*

WHITING,LILIAN-Kate Field-Bost-1899-610p-cl (a1) 20.00

WHITING,LILIAN-Land of Enchantment-Bost-1909-Little,Brown-347p-pict cl,photos (bb4) 20.00

WHITING,LILIAN-Land of Enchantment-Bost-1909-Little,Brown-347p-pict cl,photos (dd4) 20.00

WHITLOCK,BRAND-13th District-Indpls-(1902)-Bowen-Merrill-490p+publ catlg(20)p-cl (c1) 17.50

WHITLOCK,BRAND-Orator of the Day-Pemberville-nd-Leader Electric Pr-(16)p-wrps (j1) 22.50

WHITLOCK,R-Rare and Extinct Birds of Britain-Lond-1953-8vo-224p-cl,85 plts (y8,dj) 25.00

WHITLOCK,V H-Cowboy Life on the Llano Estacado-Norman-(1970)-269-photos-scarce-1st ed (v7,f,dj) 30.00

WHITMAN,MALCOLM D-Fly Fishing Up to Date-1924-priv prntd-8vo-26p-illus-scarce (m3) 80.00

WHITMAN,MALCOLM D-Fly Fishing up to Date-np-1924-priv prtd-8vo-26p-g dec cov,photo frntis,illu (mm2) 85.00

WHITMAN,NARCISSA-Journals & Letters of...-Portland-1893-192p-wrps-1st ed (d7) 75.00

WHITMAN,SARAH H-Hours of Life-Providence-1853-Geo H Whitney-12mo-vii,227p-orig g blnd stmpd brwn cl,a.e.g.-1st ed (ee9,cov sl fade,sl fox) 100.00

WHITMAN,T J-Dear Brother Walt-Kent-1984-KSU Pr-1st ed (z9,f,dj) 15.00

WHITMAN,WALT-Calamus-Bost-1897-Laurens Maynard-sm oct-grn bds-1st ed (bb2,bds offset) 150.00

WHITMAN,WALT-Good Bye My Fancy-Phila-1891-McKay-tall 8vo-g stmpd cl-1st ed (hh4) 450.00

WHITMAN,WALT-Leaves of Grass with Autobiography-Phila-(1900)-g cl,photo frntis-1st ed thus (k9) 20.00

WHITMAN,WALT-Leaves of Grass-NY-1930-Random/Grabhorn Pr-folio-423p-orig rustic red goatskin bkd hvy wooden bds,woodcuts,ltd to 400c,nbrd (t10,hngs weak) 1,875.00

WHITMAN,WALT-Leaves of Grass-NY-1940-Dbldy,Doran-burlap bds,col & b&w illus,L C Daniel (o8,box) 12.50

WHITMAN,WALT-November Boughs-Phila-1888-McKay-orig g titled cl,t.e.g.,lg papr cpy-1st ed (aa9,sl rub) 300.00

WHITMAN,WALT-November Boughs-Phila-1888-McKay-tall 8vo-140p+ads-g stmpd cl-1st ed (hh4) 425.00

WHITMAN,WALT-Two Prefaces-NY-1926-intro by C Morley-1st ed (r2,dj sl tn,rub,sp sun) 25.00

WHITMAN,WALT-Walt Whitman's Civil War-NY-1960-335p-16p drwngs by W Homer-first one vol ed-1st ed thus (c4,f,dj) 25.00

WHITMAN,WILLIAM-RETOLD BY-Navaho Tales-Bost-1925-Houghton Mifflin-cl,illus,J P Heins-1st ed (l8) 35.00

WHITNEY,C V-Lone and Level Sands-NY-(1951)-8vo-cl,frntis,plts,text illus,e.p. maps-1st ed (s2,chip dj) 25.00

WHITNEY,C-ET AL-Musk Ox, Bison, Sheep and Goat-1904-Macmillan-284p-photos,illus-1st ed (bb3) 85.00

WHITNEY,ELLIOTT-Blind Lion-Chig-1912-12mo-226p-"The Boy's Big Game Series" (m3) 15.00

WHITNEY,HARRY-Hunting with the Eskimos-NY-1911-Century-8vo-xiv,453p-illus blu cl,frntis,63 illus,fldg map(pg.32)-1st ed (mm8,hng crack,bump) 135.00*

WHITNEY,HENRY C-Life on the Circuit with Lincoln...-Bost-(1892)-Estes & Lauriat-(viii)+601p-maroon cl,67plts-Howes W386-1st ed (m2,fade sp) 150.00

WHITNEY,JOSEPH-Kiss Clara for Me-State College-1969-Carnation Pr-175p-frntis port,illus (v2,soil dj) 15.00

WHITNEY,ORSON-Popular History of Utah-SLC-1916-Deseret News-588p-photos,maps-1st ed (f9,sl wn,spot,bump) 50.00

WHITTAKER,ALBERT J-Historical Sketch of the Trenton Banking Company...-Trenton-1880-25p-prtd wrps (aa6) 35.00

WHITTAKER,FREDERICK-Complete Life of Gen George A Custer-NY-1876-Sheldon-648p-illus,maps-1st ed (gg4) 200.00

WHITTEMORE,EDWARD-Jerusalem Poker-NY-(1978)-HR&W-1st ed (b10,as new in dj) 25.00

WHITTEMORE,EDWARD-Quin's Shanghai Circus-NY-1974-auth 1st bk-1st ed (q5,f,dj) 35.00

WHITTEMORE,HENRY-Founders and Builders of the Oranges-Newark-1896-4to-vi,468p-mod buckrm,illus,plts (aa6,rbnd) 175.00

WHITTEN,NORMAN E,JR.-Class, Kinship and Power in an Ecuadorian Town-Stanford-1965-Stanford U Pr-8vo-238p-cl,illus-1st ed (y5) 28.00

WHITTEN,T-Gibbons of Siberut-1982-Dent-207p-col photos-1st ed (bb3,f,dj) 20.00

WHITTICK,A-Small House: Today & Tomorrow-Lond-1957-96 illus,73 plts-2nd ed (h10,dj) 45.00

WHITTIER,JOHN G-At Sundown-Bost-1892-g stmpd cl-1st trd ed (m4) 20.00

WHITTIER,JOHN G-Literary Recreations and Miscellanies-Bost-1854-Ticknor & Field-brwn cl-1st iss wi 8p ads dated Sept 1854-1st ed (f2,sl wn sp) 60.00

WHITTIER,JOHN-Supernaturalism of New England-NY-1847-Wiley & Putnam-lea-1st ed (l9,sl fox) 350.00

WHITTINGTON,C S-Tall Timber Gobblers-1971-priv prtg-104p-photos (gg3,f) 35.00

WHITTLE,T-Plant Hunters-1970-Chilton-281p-31 photos & illus-1st ed (bb3,f,dj) 26.00

WHITTLE,TYLER-Some Ancient Gentlemen-Lond-1965-Heinemann-sm 4to-x,246p-col frntis,16 plts-1st ed (ff9) 28.00*

WHITTLE,TYLER-Some Ancient Gentlemen-NY-(1966)-x,244p-16p b&w illus-1st US ed (j10,sp lettrng wn,dj sl wn) 25.00

WHITTLESEY,CHARLES-Penokie Mineral Range Wisconsin-Bost-1863-10p-wrps-1st ed (t7,wtrstnd cov) 12.50

WHITTON,F E-Short History of the Prince of Wale's Volunteers-Aldershot-1928-54p-blu cl,10 col plts-1st ed (b7) 100.00

WHITTON,F E-Wolfe and North America-Bost-1929-322p-red cl,illus-1st ed (b7) 65.00

WHITWELL,J R-Historical Notes on Psychiatry-Lond-1936-252p-1st ed (dd3,sp dull) 75.00

WHO'S WHO IN WORLD AVIATION AND ASTRONAUTICS. VOL.2-Wash-1958-Aviation Publ-thk roy 8vo-vi,498p-cl-2nd ed (t2) 40.00

WHORTON,J-Before Silent Spring-Princeton-1974-288p-1st ed (dd3,dj) 15.00

WHYMPER,EDWARD-Scrambles Amongst the Alps and Lady Blanche Murphy Down the Rine-Cleve-1888-164p & 75p-lt blu cl,pict cov,a.e.g. (q10,hng crack) 45.00

WHYMPER,EDWARD-Travels Amongst the Great Andes of the Equator-Lond-1892-John Murray-8vo-orig grn cl wi g,4 maps,118 illus (mm1,sm sp tr,hngs weak) 250.00

WIBBERLEY,LEONARD-Encounter Near Venus-NY-1967-FS&G/Ariel Bk-1st ed (y1,f,f dj) 25.00

WIBBERLEY,LEONARD-Epics of Everest-Lond-1955-217p-1st ed (p10,f,dj) 20.00

WIBBERLEY,LEONARD-Hand of Cormac Joyce-NY-1969-Putnam-1st ed (y1,f,dj) 20.00

WIBBERLEY,LEONARD-Mouse on the Moon-NY-1962-Morrow-1st ed (hh5,dj) 15.00

WIBBERLEY,LEONARD-Mrs Searwood's Secret Weapon-Bost-1954-Little,Brown-1st ed (y1,f,sl wn dj) 30.00

WICHER,EDWARD A-Presbyterian Church in California,1849 to 1927-NY-1927-Hitchcock-xiv+360p-grn cl,plts-1st ed (k2,dj) 35.00

WICK,WARREN C-My Recollections of Old Cleveland-(Cleve)-(1979)-120p+lng fldg plt-wrps-ltd to 2000c-1st ed so stated (aa1) 15.00

WICK,WARREN C-My Recollections of Old Cleveland-(Cleve)-(1979)-120p-wrps,lng fldg frntis plt-2nd prtg (b1,f) 10.00

WICKERSHAM,JAMES-Old Yukon-Wash D.C.-1938-514p-illus-1st ed (g7,f,chip dj) 75.00

WICKERSHAM,JAMES-Old Yukon-Wash D.C.-1938-scarce-1st ed (a4,f,dj) 95.00

WICKERSHAM,JAMES-Old Yukon-Wash-1938-Wash Law Bk Libr-xi,514p-photos,maps-1st ed (ll8) 40.00

WICKES,GEORGE-Americans in Paris-NY-1969-Dbldy-photos-1st ed (h8,f,f dj) 40.00

WICKES,STEPHEN-History of the Oranges, in Essex County, N.J., from 1666 to 1806-Newark-1892-viii,334p-cl,plts (aa6) 75.00

WICKSON,EDWARD J-Second Thousand Answered Questions in California Agriculture-SF-1916-Pacific Rural Pr-sm 8vo-254p+2p ads-1st ed (mm4,soil cl) 18.50

WIDDESS,J D H-An Account of the Schools of Surgery Royal College of Surgeons, Dublin 1789 to 1948-Balt-1949-107p-1st ed (dd3) 30.00

WIDEMAN,JOHN E-Glance Away-NY-(1967)-auth 1st bk-1st ed (s5,dj) 75.00

WIDEMAN,JOHN E-Glance Away-NY-(1967)-HB&W-auth 1st bk-1st ed (c10,dj sl chip & tn) 85.00

WIDEMAN,JOHN E-Lynchers-NY-1973-1st ed (s5,dj) 35.00

WIDENER,P A B-Renowned Collections of Sporting & Colored Plate Books-NY-1944-8vo-148p-wrps,illus (m3,f) 30.00

WIDMER,KINGSLEY-Literary Rebel-Carbondale-1965 (x8,dj) 12.00

WIDTSOE,JOHN A-In the Gospel Net, the Story of Anna K G Widtsoe-Independence-(1941)-priv prtd-119p-orig blu cl,port,illus,map-1st ed (bb8) 35.00

WIDTSOE,JOHN A-Joseph Smith, Seeker After Truth, Prophet of God-SLC-1957-385p-port,illus (bb8,dj) 27.50

WIEBENSON,DORA-Tony Garnier: the Cite' Industrielle-NY-1969-Braziller-4to-(11),127p-qtr cl,bds,81 illus,plans-1st prtg (cc10,f,dj) 35.00

WIEDERSHEIM,R-Structure of Man-Lond-1895-Macmillan-xxii+227p-grn cl-1st Engl ed (c2,sl spot sp) 40.00

WIENER,LIONEL-Articulated Locomotives-1970-Kalmbach-8vo-628p-illus-rprnt (nn7,dj) 35.00

WIENER,LIONEL-Articulated Locomotives-Milw-1970-628p-rprnt (n4,f,dj) 22.00

WIENER,NORBERT-Collected Works-Cambridge-(1976-1985)-M.I.T. Pr-4 vols-1st ed (c2,djs) 150.00

WIENER,NORBERT-Ex Prodigy-NY-1953-S&S-xii+311p-gry cl-1st ed (c2,dj) 15.00

WIESEL,ELIE-Beggar in Jerusalem-NY-(1970)-Random-1st ed (e3,f,rub dj) 20.00

WIESEL,ELIE-Beggar in Jerusalem-NY-(1970)-Random-1st ed (z9,sp chip dj) 10.00

WIESEL,ELIE-Jews of Silence-1966-Holt-1st ed (jj6,f,sl tn dj) 30.00

WIESEL,ELIE-Legends of Our Time-1968-Holt-1st ed (jj6,vf,dj) 25.00

WIESEL,ELIE-One Generation After-1970-Random-1st ed (kk6,f,sl tn dj) 25.00

WIESEL,ELIE-Souls on Fire-NY-1972-Random Hs-cl-1st Amer ed (n8,f,dj) 15.00

WIGGIN,EDITH E-Lessons on Manners-Bost-(c.1884)-Lee & Shepard-80p-dec bds (a8,bds wn) 30.00

WIGGIN,KATE D-My Garden of Memory-Bost-1923-Houghton Mifflin-443p-cl,illus-1st ed (s3,sp lttrng drknd) 25.00

WIGGIN,KATE D-Old Peabody Pew-Bost-1907-Houghton Mifflin-pict gry cl,illus by A B Stephens-1st ed (gg7) 35.00

WIGGIN,KATE D-Penelope's Progress-Bost-1898-Houghton Mifflin-plaid cl-1st ed (dd6) 20.00

WIGGIN,KATE D-Rebecca of Sunnybrook Farm-Bost-1903-Houghton Mifflin-8vo-327p-pict grn cl,1st state of bndg wi sp imprnt 1/16" high-1st ed (w6) 45.00

WIGGIN,MAURICE-Passionate Angler-Lond-1949-8vo-135p-one of 300c of deluxe ed,grn calf gilt,illus-scarce (m3,f) 90.00

WIGGINS,FLORENCE R-Strawberry Point Kitchens-np-(1971)-Graphic Publ-213p-g dec red cl,illus-1st ed (q8,dj) 12.50

WIGGINS,MARIANNE-Separate Checks-NY-(1984)-Random-1st ed (j6,f,dj) 25.00

WIGGINS,WALT-Great American Speedhorse-NY-1978-Sovreign-1st prtg (f10,dj) 35.00

WIGHT,F S-Morris Graves-Berkeley-1956-wrps,illus (h10) 30.00

WIGHT,O W-Maxims of Public Health-NY-1884-176p-1st ed (dd3) 35.00

WIGLEY,HARRY-Ski Plane Adventure-Wellington-(1965)-Reed-8vo-222p-36 photos-1st NZ ed (ff5,f dj) 20.00

WIGLEY,HARRY-Ski-Plane Adventure-Wellington-1977-222p-photos (o10,f,dj) 26.00

WIGMORE,JOHN-ED.-Science and Learning in France-(Chig)-1917-454p-1st ed (dd3) 25.00

WIJEY,MRS.MABEL-ED.-Warne's Model Cookery-Lond-(1937)-Warne-773p-red cl,56p col plts,68p b&w plts-rvsd ed (q8) 45.00

WIJK,OLOF-COMP.-Eat at Pleasure, Drink by Measure-Lond-(1970)-Constable-drwngs-1st ed (q8) 15.00

WILBANKS,ELSIE M-Art on the Texas Plains-Lubbock-1959-So Plains Art Guild-166p-cl,photos,ltd ed-1st ed (w3,f,wn dj) 30.00

WILBUR,J H-Travels of...-Salem-(1975)-159p-illus,facs,map-ltd to 800c,nbrd (r8) 10.00

WILBUR,M E-ED.-Vancouver in California 1792 thru 1794-LA-1954-3 vols in one-274p+16plts & maps-Early Cal Trav Ser Vols 9,10 & 22 (f7,rub sp labl) 60.00

WILBUR,MARGUERITE E-ED.-Raveneau De Lussan's Voyage to South Seas...-Cleve-1930-Arthur H Clark-8vo-303p-red cl,g titles,t.e.g.,dckld edge,facs,map plts-1st Engl ed (p8,f,f dj,unopened) 135.00

WILBUR,MARGUERITE E-John Sutter-NY-(1949)-Liveright Publ-371p-illus-1st ed (cc4,dj) 25.00

WILBUR,RAY-ED.-Medical Care for the American People-Chig-1932-213p-1st ed (dd3) 40.00

WILBUR,RICHARD-Ceremony and Other Poems-NY-1950-rare-1st ed (n5,dj) 60.00

WILBUR,RICHARD-Elizabeth Bishop: A Memorial Tribute-NY-1982-Albodocani Pr-wrps-ltd to 212c,autg (p1,as new) 50.00

WILBUR,RICHARD-Memorial Tribute-NY-1982-Albondocani Pr-mrbld wrps-ltd to 210c,autg-1st ed (dd2,f) 40.00

WILBUR,RICHARD-Mind Reader-(1976)-HBJ-1st ed (x10,f,f dj) 20.00

WILBUR,RICHARD-Walking to Sleep-NY-(1969)-Harcourt Brace-1st ed (cc2,f,sl wn dj) 30.00

WILBY,T W-Motor Tour Through Canada-Lond-1914-J Lane-grn cl,31 photos-1st ed (gg7) 25.00

WILCOCKS,CHARLES-Aspects of Medical Investigation in Africa-Lond-1962-120p-1st ed (dd3,dj) 20.00

WILCOX,COLLIN-Third Figure-NY-1968-Dodd-1st ed (j4,f,sl wn dj) 25.00

WILCOX,ELLA W-Men,Women, and Emotions-Chig-(1893)-304p-cl (pp6) 20.00

WILCOX,L A-Mr.Pepy's Navy-NY-1966-189p-illus-1st Amer ed (b7,dj) 20.00

WILCOX,R TURNER-Mode in Furs-NY-1951-Scribners-tall 8vo-257p-illus-1st ed (w1,f,dj) 50.00

WILDAIR-Rational Horse Shoeing-NY-1873-Wynkoop & Hallenbeck-12mo-1st ed (h9) 45.00

WILDE,OSCAR-An Ideal Husband-Lond-1899-L Smithers-recent g dec lt tan cl-ltd to 1000c-1st ed (aa9,rbnd) 175.00

WILDE,OSCAR-Birthday of the Infanta-NY-1929-Macmillan-tall 8vo-58p-cl,col & b&w illus-1st ed (pp10,fade,dj) 40.00

WILDE,OSCAR-Canterville Ghost-1906-J Luce-illus-1st ed (x2) 150.00

WILDE,OSCAR-De Profundis-Lond-(1905)-Methuen & Co-1st ed (l9) 200.00

WILDE,OSCAR-House of Pomegranates-Lond-1891-James Osgood-orig dec cov-1st ed (l9,sl drknd & wn) 300.00

WILDE,OSCAR-House of Pomegranates-Lond-1891-Osgood-grn cl sp over dec crm col linen bds(rear cov plain),dec & illus by Chas Ricketts,4 plts by Shannon-1st ed (p1,hngs sl split,cov sl wn) 375.00

WILDE,OSCAR-House of Pomegranates-Portland-1908-Mosher-overlapping prchmnt cov-1st Amer ed (z8,f) 30.00

WILDE,OSCAR-Portrait of Mr W H-NY-1921-Kennerley-grained blk bds stmpd in gold,ltd to 1000c-1st ed (cc2) 65.00

WILDE,OSCAR-Soul of Man Under Socialism-Portland-1905-Mosher-wrps,ltd to 600c-1st ed (cc2,fox,sl wn) 50.00

WILDER,CHERRY-Nearest Fire-NY-1980-Atheneum-1st ed (p3,f,dj) 25.00

WILDER,ISABEL-Mother and Four-NY-(1933)-Coward McCann-8vo-1st ed (s1,dj) 90.00

WILDER,LOUISE B-Adventures in Suburban Garden-NY-1931-Macmillan-8vo-250p-cl,16 plts-1st prtg (cc10,sp sun,sl fox) 40.00

WILDER,LOUISE B-Fragrant Path-NY-1932-Macmillan-407p-1st ed (x6,sp sun,t.p. fox) 20.00

WILDER,LOUISE B-Garden in Color-NY-1937-lg 8vo-327p-grn cl,320 col plts-1st ed (m10) 15.00

WILDER,LOUISE B-Garden in Color-NY-1937-Macmillan-327p-cl,col photos (x6,wn cl) 18.00

WILDER,LOUISE B-Pleasures and Problems of a Rock Garden-GC-1928-GC Publ-sm 4to-xii,294p-96 photo plts-1st ed (mm4,f) 55.00

WILDER,LOUISE B-What Happens in My Garden-NY-1935-Macmillan-8vo-257p-cl,18 halftone plts-1st prtg (cc10,sp sun) 25.00

WILDER,MITCHELL A-Santos-Colo Spgs-(1943)-49p+64 photo plts,cl-1st ed (u7) 125.00

WILDER,ROBERT-Wine of Youth-NY-1955-Putnam's-8vo-377p-1st ed (z4,sl tn dj) 10.00

WILDER,THORNTON-Eighth Day-NY-(1967)-Harper-orig g titled cl-1st ed (aa9,f,dj) 40.00

WILDER,THORNTON-Ides of March-NY,Lond-(1948)-Harper-1st trd ed (e10,dj sl wn,sl soil) 40.00

WILDER,THORNTON-Our Town-Avon-1974-Meriden Co(for LEC)-ltd to 2000c,two autg (w1,f,box) 110.00

WILDER,THORNTON-Our Town-NY-(1938)-Coward McCann-cl-1st ed (ll10,dj sl rub & soil) 150.00

WILDER,THORNTON-Woman of Andros-1930-A & C Boni-1st ed (n9,f,dj wi sm tr) 45.00

WILDER,THORNTON-Woman of Andros-NY-1930-Boni-sm 8vo-1st ed (x3,sl chip dj) 55.00

WILDING,GEORGE C-Promoted Pioneer Preachers of the West Virginia Conference of the Methodist Episcopal Church...-Parkersburg-1927-137,(3)p-cl (h1) 15.00

WILDMAN,FREDERICKS,JR.-Wine Tour of France-(1972)-Morrow-336p-blu cl,maps-1st ed (q8,dj) 15.00

WILDMAN,ROUNSEVELLE-Tales of the Malayan Coast-Bost-1899-Lothrop-dec pict cov,drwngs (c3,sp spot) 35.00

WILDRICK,MRS.-Zealot in Tulle-NY-1887-Appleton-309p-cl-Wright 5972 (h1) 20.00

WILDWOOD,WILL-Fishcraft-Cin-1922-16mo-146p+ads-illus (m3) 45.00

WILENSKI,R H-Drawing and Paintings by Joan Manning-Sanders-NY-1929-Wm Rudge-4to-xiv p+32 plts,blu cl (r10,sp fade) 15.00

WILENSKI,R H-Flemish Painters 1430 to 1830-NY-1960-2 vols-v.1:text,v.2:plts (h10,dj) 150.00

WILENTZ,ELIAS-ED.-Beat Scene-NY-1960-Corinth Bks-wrps,photos-1st ed (c10) 30.00

WILEY,BELL I-Embattled Confederates-1964-Harper & Row-290p-illus-1st ed (dd9,dj) 30.00

WILEY,BELL I-They Who Fought Here-NY-1959-273p-frntis,photos-1st ed (t7,dj) 27.50

WILEY,BELL I-They Who Fought Here-NY-1959-273p-illus-1st ed (n3,dj) 40.00

WILEY,F A-Theodore Roosevelt's America-1955-418p-silhouettes (gg3,f,dj) 22.00

WILEY,FARIDA-Ferns of Northeastern United States-NY-1973-Dover-108p-cl,illus (x6,as new) 25.00

WILEY,HARVEY W-Foods and Their Adulteration-Phila-1912-Balkiston's-641p-red cl bds-Bitting 496-2nd ed (l6,hngs weak) 75.00

WILEY,SAMUEL T-Biographical and Portrait Cyclopedia of the Third Congressional District of New Jersey-Phila-1896-4to-1039p-mod buckrm,ports (aa6,rbnd) 200.00

WILFORD,JOHN N-Mapmakers-NY-1981-illus-1st ed (g5,as new in dj) 20.00

WILHELM,HELLMUT-Heaven,Earth, and Man in the Book of Changes-Seattle-1977-U of Wash Pr-cl-1st ed (l8,f,dj) 27.50

WILHELM,KATE-Infinity Box-NY-(1975)-Harper & Row-1st ed (k3,f,dj) 20.00

WILHELM,KATE-Juniper Time-NY et al-(1979)-1st ed (h5,sl wn dj) 15.00

WILHELM,KATE-Juniper Time-NY-(1979)-Harper & Row-1st ed (e3,f,dj) 25.00

WILHELM,KATE-Killer Thing-GC-1967-Dbldy-1st ed (k3,f,sl chip dj) 20.00

WILHELM,KATE-Listen Listen-Bost-1981-Houghton Mifflin-1st ed (h3,f,dj) 20.00

WILK,MAX-Dirty Mind Never Sleeps-NY-1969-Norton-1st ed (y1,f,f dj) 30.00

WILK,MAX-Don't Raise the Bridge (Lower the River)-NY-1960-Macmillan-auth 1st bk-1st ed (a10,dj) 12.50

WILKEN,ROBERT L-Anslem Weber, O.F.M. Missionary to the Navaho 1898 thru 1921-Milw-(1955)-248p-illus-1st ed (v7,dj) 15.00

WILKES,CHARLES-Columbia River to the Sacramento-1958-BioBooks-4to-140p-illus,2 fldg maps,ltd to 600c (r8) 35.00

WILKES,CHARLES-U.S. Exploring Expedition during the Years 1838,1839,1840,1841,1842-NY-1851-5 vols-illus,13 maps-Howes W414 (j7,rub,sp chip,fox) 475.00

WILKINS,CAPT GEORGE H-Flying the Arctic-NY,Lond-1928-Putnam's-8vo-xv,336p-brwn cl,dec e.p.,31 plts-1st prtg (ee7) 65.00

WILKINS,CAPT GEORGE H-Flying the Arctic-NY-1928-8vo-xvi,336p-cl,frntis,30p plts,illus e.p.-1st ed,1st iss (t2) 45.00

WILKINS,CAPT GEORGE H-Flying the Arctic-NY-1928-Putnam's-xv,336p-dec e.p.-2nd prtg (ll8) 30.00

WILKINS,HUBERT-Under the North Pole-np-1931-Brewer,Warren & Putnam-8vo-xvi,347p-dec yel cl,map e.p.,illus (oo1) 100.00

WILKINS,JAMES H-ED.-Great Diamond Hoax...Asbury Harpending-SF-1913-James H Barry-283p-blu cl,illus-1st ed (mm10,cov sl wn) 85.00

WILKINS,JAMES-ED.-Great Diamond Hoax...Asbury Harpending-SF-1913-J Barry-283p-photos-1st ed (d3) 50.00

WILKINS,JOHN H-Elements of Astronomy...-Bost-1834-Hilliard,Gray-152,(8)p-bds,frntis,8p plts+3p plts inserted in text-Amer Imprnts 29742 (k1) 27.50

WILKINS,MARY E-Portion of Labor-NY-1901-Harper-1st ed (w5) 30.00

WILKINS-FREEMAN,MARY E-Collected Ghost Stories-Sauk City-1974-Arkham-1st ed (j3,f,dj) 12.00

WILKINSON,ANDREWS-Plantation Stories of Old Louisiana-Bost-1914-Page-22 b&w plts & col frontis by Chas L Bull-pict bndg-1st ed (e10,edges wn) 20.00

WILKINSON,BARRY-Diverting Adventures of Tom Thumb-NY-(1969)-HBW-auth illus-1st US ed (e10,f,sl wn dj) 25.00

WILKINSON,C J-University Club of Washington-Seattle-1954-220p-illus (r8,chip dj) 8.00

WILKINSON,DOUG-Land of the Long Day-Tor-(1955)-Clarke,Irwin-8vo-261p-cl-1st ed (pp5,f,dj tn) 45.00*

WILKINSON,J R-Canadian Battle Fields and Other Poems-Tor-1901-Wm Briggs-Watters p.212-2nd ed,rvsd & enlgd (pp2,cov sl mrkd) 45.00*

WILKINSON,J R-Canadian Battlefields-Tor-1901-Wm Briggs-8vo-(viii),309p-g brgndy cl-2nd ed,rvsd & enlgd (bb7,bump) 15.00*

WILKINSON,LILY G-Revolutionary Socialism and the Woman's Movement-Glasgow-nd-Soc Labor Prty-wrps-1st ed (v5) 40.00

WILKINSON,O N-Old Glass-Lond-1968-200p-125 illus-1st ed (cc8,dj) 35.00

WILKINSON-LATHAM,R J-Collecting Militaria-NY-(1976)-192p-cl-plts,some col (o1,f,dj) 12.50

WILLARD,FRANCES E-How to Win-NY,Lond-1886-Funk & Wagnalls-125p+ads-cl (d1) 22.50

WILLARD,FRANCES E-Wheel Within a Wheel-Chig-(1895)-Woman's Temperance Publ-75p-cl (c1) 75.00

WILLARD,FRANCES E-Woman and Temperance-Hartford-1883-654p-cl-3rd ed (d1) 20.00

WILLARD,JOHN-CMR Book-Seattle-(1970)-Superior-folio-64p-col illus,iss w/o dj (bb4) 50.00

WILLARD,MADELINE D-King's Highway-LA-1913-199p-bds-Baird & Greenwood 2625-1st ed (e1,dj) 20.00

WILLARD,NANCY-Childhood of the Magician-1973-Liveright-auth 1st bk-1st ed (t9,f,dj) 40.00

WILLEFORD,CHARLES-Cockfighter-1972-Crown-1st hdbk ed (s10,sp wn dj) 85.00

WILLEFORD,CHARLES-Off the Wall-Montclair-1980-Pegasus Rex-1st ed (w5,f,f dj) 60.00

WILLEFORD,CHARLES-Off the Wall-Montclair-1980-Pegasus-1st ed (e4,dj) 55.00

WILLEFORD,CHARLES-Proletarian Laughter-Yonkers-1948-softbnd orig,stapled in prntd wrps,ltd to 1000c,auth 1st bk-rare-1st ed (p5) 125.00

WILLETS,GILSON-Inside History of the White House-NY-1908-Christian Herald-492p-g grn cl,43 photos (p2) 15.00

WILLETTS,JACOB-An Easy Grammar Geography...-Poughkeepsie-1822-Paraclete Potter-215,(1)p-bds-Amer Imprnts 11428-8th ed (k1) 30.00

WILLETTS,PAMELA-Beethoven and England-Lond-1970-Trustees of Brit Mus-illus (u4,f,dj) 25.00

WILLEY,G R-ET AL-Prehistoric Maya Settlements in the Belize Valley-1965-Peabody Mus-4to-589p-fldg map & chrts in separate box (bb3) 70.00

WILLIAM,GEO F-Bullet and Shell-NY-1883-454p+2p ads-dec red cl,illus (g7) 75.00

WILLIAM,WALTER-Mammals & Birds of Mount Rainier National Park-Wash D.C.-1927-249p-wrps,fldg map,109 illus-1st ed (q10) 22.00

WILLIAMS,A BRYAN-Rod & Creel in British Columbia-Vancouver-1919-8vo-144p-pict cl,illus,photos-scarce (m3) 55.00

WILLIAMS,A COURTNEY-Dictionary of Trout Flies-Lond-1961-8vo-378p-col illus (m3,f,dj) 20.00

WILLIAMS,A COURTNEY-Trout Flies-Lond-1932-8vo-224p-6 col plts (m3,sl fade sp) 20.00

WILLIAMS,A D-Spanish Colonial Furniture-Milw-(1941)-133p-dbl col,photos-1st ed (u7) 50.00

WILLIAMS,A-Airpower-NY-(1940)-8vo-x,434p-cl,frntis-1st ed (s2,chip dj) 30.00

WILLIAMS,ALBERT R-76 Questions and Answers on the Bolsheviks and the Soviets-NY-(1919)-Rand School Soc Sci-48p-wrps (a1) 10.00

WILLIAMS,ALBERT R-Through the Russian Revolution-NY-1921-Boni & Liveright-viii,299p-cl,plts,illus-1st ed (kk1,sl stnd cov) 25.00

WILLIAMS,ALLISON-Embassy Cookbook-(1966)-Little,Brown-365p-red cl,drwngs-1st ed (q8,dj) 30.00

WILLIAMS,ALPHEUS F-Some Dreams Come True-Capetown-1948-Howard B Timmins-590p-frntis port,photos,6 col plts (u5,f,dj) 120.00

WILLIAMS,AMELIA-Following General Sam Houston, From 1793 to 1863-Austin-1935-Steck Co-252p-cl,etchings,B Wall-1st ed (w3) 75.00

WILLIAMS,BEN A-Fraternity Village-Bost-1949-8vo-336p-1st ed (m3) 25.00

WILLIAMS,BEN A-Happy End-Derrydale-1939-8vo-240p-ltd to 1250c,nbrd,illus by C Ettinger (m3,vf,clear wrps) 160.00

WILLIAMS,BEN A-Happy End-NY-(1939)-Derrydale Pr-g cov,illus,acetate dj-ltd to 1250c,nbrd (r2,f,sl chip dj) 125.00

WILLIAMS,C R-COMP.-Southern Sympathizers-Parkersburg-nd-priv prtd-32p-wrps,prtd on recto only,mimeo-ltd to 50c,nbrd (aa1) 65.00

WILLIAMS,C S-Honker-Princeton-1967-4to-179p-photos (m3,f) 25.00

WILLIAMS,CARL M-Silversmiths of New Jersey, 1700 to 1825-Phila-1949-xii,164p-cl,illus (aa6) 250.00

WILLIAMS,CHARLES R-Life of Rutherford B Hayes-Bost-1914-Houghton Mifflin-2 vols,blu cl,plts-1st ed (e2) 65.00

WILLIAMS,CHARLES W-On Heat in its Relation to Water And Steam-Phila-1864-H C Baird-278p+ads-brwn cl,65 text illus-from 2nd rvsd Lond ed (dd1) 60.00

WILLIAMS,CHARLES-Arthurian Torso-Lond-1969-Oxford U Pr-cl-later prtg (l8,f,dj) 37.50

WILLIAMS,CHARLES-Dead Calm-NY-1963-Viking-1st ed (f4,dj) 15.00

WILLIAMS,CHARLES-Place of the Lion-NY-nd-Pellegrini & Cudahy-cl-1st Amer ed (l8,f,dj) 25.00

WILLIAMS,CHAUNCEY P-Lone Elk(Part I and II)-Denver-1935-50p & 35p-stiff wrps-Howes W449-v scarce-1st ed (t7) 135.00

WILLIAMS,CLARK-Story of a Grateful Citizen-NY-1934-8vo-2 vols,illus,photos-scarce (m3) 40.00

WILLIAMS,DORIAN-Ponies-Lond-1971-Hamlyn-4to-1st ed (h9,wn dj) 10.00

WILLIAMS,DOROTHY-Historic Virginia Gardens-Charlottesville-1975-U of Va-350p-photos (x6,dj) 22.00

WILLIAMS,EDWARD H-Pine Flat Campfire Tales-NY-1924-12mo-169p-illus-scarce-1st ed (m3,vf,fray dj) 75.00

WILLIAMS,EDWARD T-China Yesterday and Today-NY-1927-Crowell-664p-photos,illus,rear pckt map (c3) 30.00

WILLIAMS,ELIZABETH F-Notes of a Feminist Therapist-NY-(1976)-Praeger-1st ed (z5,f,dj) 12.00

WILLIAMS,FLOS J-New Furrows-Ottawa-1926-Graphic Publ-Watters p.418-1st ed (pp2) 45.00*

WILLIAMS,FRANCES L-Matthew Fontaine Maury, Scientist of the Sea-New Brunswick-1963-720p-illus,ports (z10,soil dj) 50.00

WILLIAMS,FRANCES L-Matthew Fontaine Maury, Scientist of the Sea-New Brunswick-1963-Rutgers U Pr-8vo-half cl,dec papr over bds,illus (nn1,cors bump,dj) 35.00

WILLIAMS,FRANCIS E-Flexible, Participation Lotteries-St.Louis-1938-1st ed (r2,ex-libr) 60.00

WILLIAMS,FREDERICK G-Meet...and his Wife Rebecca Swain Williams Pioneer of 1849...-(Independence)-(1951)-234p-1st ed (bb8,dj) 20.00

WILLIAMS,FREDERICK S-Our Iron Roads-Lond-1852-390p-illus-1st ed (n4,sl tn cl cov) 150.00

WILLIAMS,GARDNER F-Diamond Mines of South Africa-NY-1906-B F Buck-2 vols-drk blu buckrm,g dec sp,t.e.g.,Vol.1:frntis,photos,drwngs,Vol.2:col frntis,2 col plts,col fldg map-2nd ed,rvsd & enlgd (u5) 400.00

WILLIAMS,GERTRUDE M-Passionate Pilgrim-NY-1931-Coward-McCann-cl,frntis,illus-1st ed (n8) 20.00

WILLIAMS,GLEN H-Bucks Camp Log-Oshkosh-1974-8vo-111p-illus,photos-1st ed (m3,vf,dj) 22.50

WILLIAMS,HAROLD A-Western Maryland Railway Story-Balt-1952-134p-1st ed (n4) 30.00

WILLIAMS,HENRY L-Modernizing Old Houses-GC-1948-Dbldy-lg 8vo-xiii,269p-brwn cl,drwngs-1st ed (mm8,sl soil cl) 25.00*

WILLIAMS,HENRY L-Old American Houses and How to Restore them-GC-1946-Dbldy-4to-239p-cl,61 illus,18 plts-1st ed (cc10,dj) 30.00

WILLIAMS,HENRY L-Old American Houses and How to Restore Them-GC-1946-Dbldy-8vo-239p-blu cl,illus-1st ed (r10,wn dj) 12.50

WILLIAMS,HENRY S-Practical Radio-1922-413p-100 photos,60 illus-1st ed (h6) 15.00

WILLIAMS,HERB-Twin Harbors Tales-Tacoma-1967-8vo-104p-wrps,photos (m3,pres cpy) 10.00

WILLIAMS,HOWELL-ED.-Landscapes of Alaska-Berkeley-1958-148p-6 fldg maps,23 photos-1st ed (q10,f,dj) 40.00

WILLIAMS,J D-Compleat Strategyst-NY-1954-McGraw Hill-xvi+234p-gry cl-1st ed (c2,dj) 25.00

WILLIAMS,J H-Mountain that was "God"-Tacoma/NY & Lond-1910-J H WIlliams/Putnam's-tall 8vo-111p-papr cov bds wi pict inset,illus(incl 8 col half tones),dbl pg map laid in-1st ed (mm4,wn,sp rprd,hng crack) 55.00

WILLIAMS,J W-Big Ranch Country-Wichita Falls-1954-Terry Bros-307p-maps,drwngs,photos-Herd #2527-1st ed (dd4,dj) 45.00

WILLIAMS,JACK-Legion of Time-1952-Fantasy Pr-1st ed (p9,f,dj) 25.00

WILLIAMS,JAMES M-From That Terrible Field-Univ,Ala-(1981)-187p-illus,maps-1st ed (n3,f,dj) 20.00

WILLIAMS,JAMES-Seventy Five Years on the Border-KC-1912-Pr of Standard Prtg-207p-frntis-1st ed (bb4,prospectus laid in) 45.00

WILLIAMS,JAMES-Seventy Five Years on the Border-KC-1912-Pr of Standard Prtg-208p-pict papr labl fr bd,frntis,illus-1st ed (o7,f) 75.00

WILLIAMS,JAY P-Alaskan Adventure-Harrisburg-1952-8vo-299p-photos-1st ed (m3,f,sl chip dj) 35.00

WILLIAMS,JOAN-Country Woman-Bost-1982-1st ed (p5,f,dj) 20.00

WILLIAMS,JOAN-Morning and the Evening-NY-1961-auth 1st bk-1st ed (o5,dj) 22.50

WILLIAMS,JOHN A-Night Song-NY-(1961)-FS&C-auth 1st hdbk book-1st ed (c10,sl soil dj) 75.00

WILLIAMS,JOHN A-Sissie-NY-1963-1st ed (r5,pgs sl yel,dj) 50.00

WILLIAMS,JOHN-Guardians of the Columbia-Tacoma-1912-142p-pict cov,191 photos(incl col)-1st ed (p10,f) 35.00

WILLIAMS,JOHN-Guardians of the Columbia-Tacoma-1912-144p-pict hvy papr covs,col photos (r8,chip,edgewn) 30.00

WILLIAMS,JOHN-Mountain That was God-NY/Tacoma-1911-Putnam/Williams-8vo-142p-8 col plts,180 b&w photos-2nd ed,rvsd (ff5,wrps) 75.00

WILLIAMS,JOHN-Mountain that was God-Tacoma-1910-lg 8vo-111p-cov pict pastedown,col photos,fldg map tip in-1st ed (r8,bump,lt scratched cov) 45.00

WILLIAMS,JOHN-Yosemite and Its High Sierra-Tacoma-1914-lg 8vo-145p-pict cov,fldg map,8 col photos-1st ed (o10) 30.00

WILLIAMS,JONATHAN-Blues & Roots Rue & Bluets-NY-1971-pict bds,photos-1st ed (r2,f) 40.00

WILLIAMS,JOY-Taking Care-NY-(1982)-Random-1st ed (o3,f,dj) 15.00

WILLIAMS,L R-Our Pacific County-Raymond-1930-104p-maps-Smith 11049 (bb9,autg) 50.00

WILLIAMS,M B-Banff Jasper Highway-Vancouver-1948-H R Larson Publ-8vo-ix,(136)p,illus-1st ed (cc7,sl chip dj) 20.00*

WILLIAMS,M B-Jasper National Park-Vancouver-1949-H R Larson Publ-8vo-xiv,128p-e.p. maps,illus-1st ed (cc7,sl scuff dj) 35.00*

WILLIAMS,M B-Through the Heart of the Rockies and Selkirks-Ottawa-1924-Acland-110p-illus card covs,frntis,64 illus,fldg map at rear-2nd ed (cc7) 35.00*

WILLIAMS,MARTIN-Jazz Masters in Transition 1957 to 69-NY-(1970)-Macmillan-1st ed (w1,f,f dj) 20.00

WILLIAMS,MARY A B-Fifty Pioneer Mothers of McLean County North Dakota-Washburn-(1932)-Washburn Leader-200p-pict cl,illus-ltd to 500c,nbrd,autg (dd4) 50.00

WILLIAMS,MARY E-Elements of the Theory and Practice of Cookery-NY-1915-Macmillan-347p-yel bds,photos (u6) 45.00

WILLIAMS,MEADE C-Early Mackinac-St.Louis-1898-Buschart Bros-111p-wrps-Streeter 6947 & 6948 cite 2nd ed as 1901-2nd ed (h1,soil,sm holes wrps,sp wn) 20.00

WILLIAMS,META-ED.-Tales From the Mabinogion-NY-1892-Cassell-sm oct-pattrnd bds-1st ed (dd2,brwng,rub) 60.00

WILLIAMS,MONIER-Modern India and the Indians-Lond-1878-Trubner-244p+ads-grn cl-2nd ed (gg6,unopened) 25.00

WILLIAMS,MRS-Notes on the Painted Glass of Canterbury Cathedral-Aberdeen-1897-74p-orig wrps,27 plts,22 plans-1st ed (cc8) 45.00

WILLIAMS,NEVILLE-Knaves and Fools-NY-1960-Macmillan-1st US ed (z9,f,dj soil) 12.50

WILLIAMS,R-Ways of Waterfowl-NY-1971-folio-260p-col illus (gg3,f,dj) 75.00

WILLIAMS,RALPH D-Honorable Peter White-Cleve-1905-Penton Publ-xvi+205p-olive cl,illus-1st ed (b2) 55.00

WILLIAMS,ROBERT-Adventures of an Autograph Collector-NY-(1952)-Exposition-99p-illus-1st ed (w1,f,dj) 15.00

WILLIAMS,ROGER D-Horse and Hound-Lexington-1905-R D Williams-dec cl,illus-1st ed (ff7,sl mrkd cov) 25.00

WILLIAMS,RUSS-Ways of Game Fish-Chig-1972-folio-326p-ltd to 3000c,nbrd,grn lea,illus-scarce (m3,vf,box) 90.00

WILLIAMS,T H-Beauregard Napoleon in Gray-Baton Rouge-1954-345p-frntis,photos-1st ed (t7,f,dj chip) 40.00

WILLIAMS,T HARRY-Huey Long-NY-1969-Knopf-photos-1st ed (b5,f,dj) 25.00

WILLIAMS,T HARRY-Lincoln and His Generals-NY-(1952)-370p-maps-1st ed (c4,dj wn) 22.50

WILLIAMS,TED-Fishing the Big Three-NY-1982-8vo-159p-photos-1st ed (m3,vf,dj) 15.00

WILLIAMS,TED-My Turn at Bat-1969-S&S-1st ed (p7,dj) 20.00

WILLIAMS,TENNESSEE-Androgyne, Mon Amour-NY-(1977)-New Directions-1st ed (cc2,f,dj) 35.00

WILLIAMS,TENNESSEE-Androgyne, Mon Amour-NY-(1977)-New Directions-1st ed (e8,f,f dj) 50.00

WILLIAMS,TENNESSEE-Baby Doll-1956-New Directions-1st ed (x2,sl chip dj) 65.00

WILLIAMS,TENNESSEE-Eight Mortal Ladies Possessed-1974-New Directions-1st ed (x2,vf,dj) 50.00

WILLIAMS,TENNESSEE-Hard Candy-NY-1954-patterned bds,1st ltd ed (n5,f,sl wn box) 75.00

WILLIAMS,TENNESSEE-Hard Candy-NY-1959-1st trd ed (n5,dj) 25.00

WILLIAMS,TENNESSEE-In the Winter of Cities-NY-1956-1st ed (v9,f,dj) 175.00

WILLIAMS,TENNESSEE-Memoirs-GC-1975-Dbldy-1st ed (cc2,f,dj) 30.00

WILLIAMS,TENNESSEE-Memoirs-NY-1975-Dbldy-orig cl bckd bds-1st ed (aa9,vf,dj) 20.00
WILLIAMS,TENNESSEE-Night of the Iguana-NY-1962-New Directions-1st ed (v5,f,f dj) 50.00
WILLIAMS,TENNESSEE-Nightly Quest-Lond-(1968)-Secker and Warburg-1st Brit ed (cc2,f,dj) 50.00
WILLIAMS,TENNESSEE-One Arm and Other Stories-1954-New Directions-1st trd ed (t9,chip dj) 25.00
WILLIAMS,TENNESSEE-Orpheus Descending-Lond-1958-Secker-8vo-cl-1st Brit ed (x3,f,dj) 60.00
WILLIAMS,TENNESSEE-Period of Adjustment-NY-1960-1st ed (s5,f,dj) 40.00
WILLIAMS,TENNESSEE-Roman Spring of Mrs Stone-NY-(1950)-New Directions-1st ed (cc2,hng weak,dj) 40.00
WILLIAMS,TENNESSEE-Roman Spring of Mrs.Stone-(1950)-New Directions-1st ed (x10,f,dj rub & soil) 25.00
WILLIAMS,TENNESSEE-Rose Tattoo-NY-(1951)-New Directions-1st ed,1st bndg (cc2,f,sl chip dj) 50.00
WILLIAMS,TENNESSEE-Steps Must Be Gentle-NY-1980-Targ Eds-8vo-cl bckd mrbld bds,tiss dj-ltd to 350c,autg-1st ed (jj8,as new in dj) 175.00
WILLIAMS,TENNESSEE-Streetcar Named Desire-Lond-(1949)-John Lehman-1st Brit ed (cc2,f,sl soil dj) 55.00
WILLIAMS,TENNESSEE-Suddenly Last Summer-1958-New Directions-1st ed (x2,f,dj) 75.00
WILLIAMS,TENNESSEE-Summer and Smoke-NY-(1948)-1st ed (q5,sl wn bds,dj) 40.00
WILLIAMS,TENNESSEE-Summer and Smoke-NY-(1948)-New Directions-1st ed (bb2,f,edge brwnd dj) 100.00
WILLIAMS,TENNESSEE-Sweet Bird of Youth-NY-1959-1st ed (t5,dj) 45.00
WILLIAMS,THOMAS A-Eliphas Levi-1975-U of Alabama Pr-cl,frntis,illus-1st ed (n8,f,dj) 40.00
WILLIAMS,THOMAS-Fiji and the Fijians-NY-1859-Appleton-551p-orig brwn cl,plts(incl col),fldg map-1st ed (p8,rebckd) 200.00
WILLIAMS,THOMAS-Hair of Harold Roux-NY-(1974)-Random-1st ed (bb1,dj) 30.00
WILLIAMS,TREVOR I-ED.-Biographical Dictionary of Scientists-Lond-1969-592p-1st ed (g10,dj) 30.00
WILLIAMS,WALTER-State of Missouri an Autobiography-St.Joseph-1904 (t7,hg weak) 35.00
WILLIAMS,WILLIAM C-Build Up-(1952)-Random-1st ed (x10,f,dj) 60.00
WILLIAMS,WILLIAM C-Build Up-Lond-1969-MacGibbon & Kee-1st Brit ed (f8,f,f dj) 50.00
WILLIAMS,WILLIAM C-Build-Up-NY-(1952)-Random-orange bds,blk cl sp-1st ed (f2,dj) 50.00
WILLIAMS,WILLIAM C-Complete Collected Poems, 1906 to 1938-Norfolk-(1938)-New Directions-8vo-grn cl-ltd to 506c-1st ed,1st bndg (kk8,f,dj sl discol & nick) 450.00
WILLIAMS,WILLIAM C-Desert Music and Other Poems-NY-(1954)-Random-8vo-cl-1st ed (jj8,f,dj) 125.00
WILLIAMS,WILLIAM C-Dog and the Fever-Hamden-(1954)-Shoe String Pr-1st ed (cc2,f,dj) 65.00
WILLIAMS,WILLIAM C-In the American Grain-Lond-1966-MacGibbon & Kee-1st Brit ed (h8,f,f dj) 50.00
WILLIAMS,WILLIAM C-In the Money. White Mule, Part II-Norfolk-(1940)-New Directions-8vo-cl-1st ed (jj8,f,sl rub dj) 150.00
WILLIAMS,WILLIAM C-Knife of the Times-Ithaca-(1932)-Dragon-8vo-blu cl,papr labls-1st ed (x3) 300.00
WILLIAMS,WILLIAM C-Life Along the Passaic River-Norfolk-(1938)-New Directions-8vo-cl-1st ed (jj8,f,sl drknd dj) 175.00
WILLIAMS,WILLIAM C-Make Light of It-NY-1950-Random-1st ed (q2,dj rub & creased) 60.00
WILLIAMS,WILLIAM C-Selected Essays-NY-1954-Random-1st ed (q2,dj) 75.00
WILLIAMS,WILLIAM C-Selected Letters of...-1957-McDowell,Obolensky-1st ed (p9,f,sp rub dj) 35.00
WILLIAMS,WILLIAM-Mountain Climbing 1899 and 1905-np-nd(ca.1905)-self publ-22p-wrps,string bnd (o10) 75.00
WILLIAMSON,A A-Moses-NY-1950-Philo Libr-cl-1st ed (n8,f) 15.00
WILLIAMSON,CHARLES-Breaking and Training the Stock Horse-Caldwell-1980-Caxton-6th ed (h9,dj) 25.00
WILLIAMSON,F PHILLIPS-ED.-Waterfowl Gunner's Book-Clinton-1979-Amwell Pr-8vo-282p-ltd to 1000c,nbrd (m3,as new in box) 150.00
WILLIAMSON,GEO-Gleanings of Leisure Hours-Detr-1894-301,(1)p-cl (g1) 17.50
WILLIAMSON,HAROLD F-Winchester the Gun That Won the West-NY,Lond-(1952)-494p-photos-1st ed (e7,dj) 45.00
WILLIAMSON,HAROLD F-Winchester, the Gun That Won the West-NY-1952-493p-photos (gg3,f,dj) 25.00
WILLIAMSON,HENRY-Clear Water Stream-NY-1959-8vo-229p (m3,vf,dj) 17.50
WILLIAMSON,HENRY-Gold Falcon or the Haggard of Love-Lond-1933-12mo-415p-scarce-1st ed (m3,fray & tn dj) 25.00
WILLIAMSON,HENRY-Phasian Bird-Lond-1948-12mo-341p-1st ed (m3,f,fray dj) 20.00
WILLIAMSON,HENRY-Salar the Salmon-Lond-1935-8vo-319p-pict map e.p.s-1st ed (m3) 25.00
WILLIAMSON,HENRY-Stumblerleap-np-nd(1926)-Putnam's-tan prntd wrps,iss as greeting for Putnam's (not for sale)-scarce-1st ed (a10) 40.00
WILLIAMSON,HENRY-Village Book-Lond-1930-8vo-342p-illus,photos frontis-1st ed (m3) 30.00
WILLIAMSON,HUGH-Methods of Book Design-Lond-1956-Oxford-430p wi index,illus-1st ed (w1,f,dj) 65.00
WILLIAMSON,JACK-Legion of Time-Reading-1952-Fantasy Pr-1st ed (e10,dj) 25.00
WILLIAMSON,JEFFERSON-American Hotel-NY-1930-Knopf-8vo-324p+index,illus-1st ed (y4,f,dj) 50.00
WILLIAMSON,JOE-Maritime Memories of Puget Sound in Photographs and Text-Seattle-1976-Superior-4to-184p-blu leatherette,photo e.p.-1st ed (pp1,sl wn dj) 30.00
WILLIAMSON,SCOTT G-American Craftsman-NY-1940-343 illus-1st ed (r2,dj) 60.00
WILLIAMSON,T-Hunky-NY-1929-Coward McCann-8vo-312p-1st ed (ee5,f,dj) 25.00
WILLING,GEORGE M-Diary of a Journey to the Pike's Peak Gold Mines in 1859-np-1927-Miss Hist Rev-18p-wrps-Rittenhouse #650 (t7) 30.00
WILLINGHAM,CALDER-Gates of Hell-NY-(1951)-Vanguard-1st ed (x10,f,dj) 25.00
WILLINGHAM,CALDER-Geraldine Bradshaw-NY-1950-1st ed (p5,sl chip dj) 25.00
WILLINGHAM,CALDER-Natural Child-NY-1952-1st ed (p5,dj) 20.00
WILLIS,CARRIE H-Legends of the Skyline Drive and the Great Valley of Virginia-Richmond-1940-Dietz Pr-(6),131p-photos,map-1st ed (o2) 15.00
WILLIS,HENRY A-Fitchburg in the War of the Rebellion-Fitchburg-1866-282p-g grn cl,a.e.g.,frnt pastedown (p2,rub pastedwn) 30.00

WILLIS,MARGARET-ED.-Chechacos All-Mt.Vernon-1973-Skagit Hist Soc-4to-212p-illus-1st ed (c7,f,chip dj) 50.00

WILLIS,N PARKER-Pencillings by the Way-Auburn,Rochester-1853-527p-cl (pp6) 20.00

WILLIS,THOMAS-Anatomy of the Brain and Nerves-Birmingham-1978-lea,illus-(facs of 1681 ed) (dd3) 75.00

WILLIS,W A-Downfall of Lobengula-Lond-(1894)-335p-dec grn cl,fldg maps,illus-scarce-1st ed (b7,sl rub) 300.00

WILLIS,WILLIAM-Gods Were Kind-NY-1955-Dutton-8vo-252p-16p photos,4p maps-1st ed (cc5,dj) 12.50

WILLISON,GEORGE F-Here They Dug the Gold-NY-(1931)-Brentano-299p-illus-Six Guns #2415-1st ed (dd4,dj) 35.00

WILLISON,JOHN-An Example of Plain Catechising...-Pitt-1832-Luke Loomis-288p-lea (e1,sl chip sp,sl tender jnts) 60.00

WILLIUS,FREDRICK-Cardiac Classics-St.Louis-1941-858p-1st ed (dd3) 100.00

WILLIUS,FREDRICK-History of the Heart and Circulation-1948-456p-illus-1st ed (dd3) 150.00

WILLOCK,C-Punt Gun Adventure-Lond-1958-200p-photos (gg3,f,dj) 25.00

WILLOCK,COL ROGER-Lone Star Marine-Princeton-1961-priv prtd-195p-scarce-1st ed (a9,dj) 60.00

WILLOCK,COLIN-Angler's Encyclopedia-Lond-1961-8vo-240p-photos,illus (m3,vf,dj) 12.00

WILLOUGHBY,DAVID-Empire of Equus-So Brunswick-1974-Barnes-sm 4to-475p-1st ed (f10,dj) 45.00

WILLS,GEOFFREY-Glass-Lond-(1973)-Orbis Publ-64p-118 col plts (l6) 15.00

WILLS,GEOFFREY-Ivory-So Brunswick-1969-Barnes-95p-18 plts (u5,f,dj) 25.00

WILLS,GEOFFREY-Jade of the East-NY-1972-Weatherhill/Orientations-196p-dec grn silk cl,two col t.p.,162 photos,6 figs,3 maps,illus box-1st US ed (u5,as new in box) 65.00

WILLS,GEOFFREY-Jade-NY-(1964)-Barnes-121p-illus (u5,f,f dj) 21.50

WILLS,GEOFFREY-Silver for Pleasure and Investment-NY-1969-Arco-175p-16 col plts,100 b&w photos (u5,f,sl chip dj) 18.50

WILLS,MAURY-How to Steal a Pennant-NY-(1976)-252p-cl-1st ed (n1,f,dj) 15.00

WILLSON,LOU-Meals on Wheels-NY-(1937)-Modern Age Bks-168p-bds (m6,sl sunned sp) 20.00

WILMERDING,JOHN-Fitz Hugh Lane-NY-(1971)-Praeger-sq 4to-cl-1st ed (oo6,dj) 55.00

WILSON BULLETIN-Quarterly Journal of Ornithology. Vols.16,17 & 18-1904 to 1906-8vo-418p-cl,photos (y8,ex-libr) 20.00

WILSON,ADRIAN-Design of Books-NY-(1967)-folio-illus-1st ed (r2,dj) 60.00

WILSON,ANDREW-Abode of Snow-NY-1882-Putnams Illus Libr Travel-380p (a4,f) 22.00

WILSON,ANGUS-Middle Age of Mrs.Eliot-Lond-1958-Secker & Warburg-1st ed (w5,f,f dj) 30.00

WILSON,B G-Unusual Railways-Lond-1957-212p-1st ed (n4,f,dj) 24.00

WILSON,BECKLES-Life of Lord Strathcona and Mount Royal-Bost-(1915)-Houghton,Mifflin-2 vols-illus-1st ed (bb4) 100.00

WILSON,BRYAN R-Sects and Society-Berkeley-1961-U of Cal-8vo-397p-cl-1st ed (y5) 30.00

WILSON,C R-Baptized in Blood-Athens-1980-256p (z10,dj) 25.00

WILSON,CHARLES-Ambassadors in White-NY-1942-372p-1st ed (dd3) 40.00

WILSON,CHARLES-Mapping the Frontier-Seattle-(1970)-182p-text maps-1st ed (f7,f,dj) 30.00

WILSON,COLIN-Adrift in Soho-Bost,Cambridge-1961-HM/Riverside-1st US ed (b5,sl fade cov,dj sp tan) 45.00

WILSON,COLIN-Beyond the Outsider-Bost,Cambridge-1965-H-M/Riverside Pr-1st US ed (bb1,dj) 50.00

WILSON,COLIN-Necessary Doubt-NY-1964-Trident Pr-cl-1st Amer ed (n8,f,dj) 35.00

WILSON,COLIN-Personality Surgeon-SF-1976-Mercury Hs-1st ed (z2,f,f dj) 25.00

WILSON,COLIN-Religion and the Rebel-Bost-1957-Houghton Mifflin-1st Amer ed (o8,dj) 10.00

WILSON,COLIN-Ritual in the Dark-Lond-1960-1st ed (r2,f,dj sl sp sun,sl chip) 55.00

WILSON,COLIN-Schoolgirl Murder Case-NY-1974-Crown-cl-1st Amer ed (l8,f,dj) 20.00

WILSON,COLIN-Space Vampires-NY-(1976)-preceded 1st Brit ed-1st ed (l5,dj) 20.00

WILSON,COLIN-Strange Powers-1975-Random-1st Amer ed (t9,vf,dj) 25.00

WILSON,COLIN-Strength to Dream-Bost-1962-HMCO-1st ed (u10,f,f dj) 35.00

WILSON,COLIN-Voyage to a Beginning-NY-1969-Crown-cl-1st Amer ed (n8,f,dj) 25.00

WILSON,COLIN-World of Violence-Lond-1963-Gollancz-272p-1st ed (v8,dj) 45.00

WILSON,DAVID-In Search of Penicillin-NY-1976-298p-1st ed (dd3,dj) 20.00

WILSON,DOROTHY C-Bright Eyes-NY-(1974)-McGraw Hill-396p-1st ed (dd4,dj) 25.00

WILSON,DOROTHY C-Stranger and Traveler-Bost-(1975)-360p-cl-1st ed so stated (d1,f,dj) 15.00

WILSON,E D-Arizona Lode Gold Mines and Gold Mining-Tucson-1934-261p-wrps,maps-1st ed (t7) 15.00

WILSON,E H-Aristocrats of the Garden-Bost-1926-Stratford-312p-cl (x6,frnt hng weak) 45.00

WILSON,E H-Plant Hunting-1927-Stratford-2 vols-t.e.g.,e.p. map,128 illus-Special ed,autg in vol.1 (bb3,poor dj) 110.00

WILSON,E-America's Greatest Garden-1925-Stratford-123p-cl (x6) 10.00

WILSON,EDITH B-My Memoir-Indpls-1939-(4),386p-illus-1st ed (n2) 20.00

WILSON,EDMUND-American Earthquake-NY-1958-1st ed (m4,f,dj) 25.00

WILSON,EDMUND-Bit Between My Teeth-NY-(1965)-Farrar,Straus-1st ed (e3,f,sl wn dj) 30.00

WILSON,EDMUND-Boys in the Back Room-SF-1941-Colt-ltd to 1,500c-1st ed (d10,dj sl chip,sl wn) 150.00

WILSON,EDMUND-Devils and Canon Barham-NY-(1973)-FS&G-1st ed (bb1,as new in dj) 30.00

WILSON,EDMUND-Letters on Literature and Politics 1912 to 1972-NY-(1977)-FS&G-photos-1st ed (bb1,as new in dj) 30.00

WILSON,EDMUND-Letters on Literature and Politics-NY-(1977)-photos-1st ed (m4,f,dj) 17.50

WILSON,EDMUND-Memoirs of Hecate County-NY-1946-Dbldy-orig g titled cl-1st ed (aa9,dj rub,chip) 125.00

WILSON,EDMUND-Night Thoughts-NY-(1961)-1st ed (d5,sl spot dj) 12.50

WILSON,EDMUND-Note Books of Night-SF-1942-Colt Pr-1st ed (t5,dj) 110.00

WILSON,EDMUND-Piece of My Mind-NY-1956-Farrar-1st ed (v5,f,f dj) 30.00

WILSON,EDMUND-Shock of Recognition-NY-(1955)-illus-1st rvsd ed (m4,f,tape dj) 20.00

WILSON,EDMUND-Thirties-NY-(1980)-FS&G-1st ed (b5,as new in dj) 25.00

WILSON,EDMUND-To the Finland Station-NY-(1972)-FS&G-orig publ in 1940-1st ed thus (bb1,as new in dj) 25.00

WILSON,EDMUND-Twenties-NY-(1975)-FS&G-1st ed (bb1,as new in dj) 25.00

WILSON,EDMUND-Undertaker's Garland-1922-Knopf-auth 1st bk-1st ed (x2) 90.00

WILSON,EDMUND-Upstate-NY-(1971)-1st ed (m4,f,dj) 20.00

WILSON,EDMUND-Upstate-NY-(1971)-illus-1st ed (r2,dj sl crease,tn) 30.00

WILSON,EDMUND-Window on Russia-NY-(1972)-Farrar Straus-cl-1st ed (aa9,vf,dj) 45.00

WILSON,EDMUND-Window on Russia-NY-(1972)-FS&G-1st ed (bb1,as new in dj) 25.00

WILSON,EDWARD L-Wilson's Photographics-NY-1881-Edw L Wilson-8vo-368p-cl-1st ed (t3) 75.00

WILSON,EDWARD-Diary of the Discovery Expedition...-Lond-1966-Blandford Pr-lg 8vo-416p-frntis,96 illus(incl col),7 maps(1 fldg)-1st ed (cc7,sl bump,dj rub) 65.00*

WILSON,ELLEN-American Painter in Paris-NY-(1971)-Farrar-8vo-cl-1st ed (oo6,dj) 35.00

WILSON,ERNEST H-More Aristocrats of the Garden-Bost-1928-xiv,288p-43 half tones-1st ed (j10,sl wn) 45.00

WILSON,ERNEST-Aristocrats of the Garden-NY-1917-Dbldy-312p-cl & bds-ltd to 1200c,nbrd (x6,cl rub,bds wn) 22.00

WILSON,EUGENE E-Pilgrimage of Anglers-Hartford-1952-8vo-176p-ltd to 450c,nbrd,autg,1/4 grn calf & mrbld bds,illus by K Wilson (m3,f) 125.00

WILSON,FRANCIS-Francis Wilson's Life of Himself-Bost-1924-HMCo-8vo-463p-illus-1st ed (ee5) 35.00

WILSON,FRAZER E-Fort Jefferson...-(Lancaster)-(1950)-36p-wrps (n1) 12.50

WILSON,GAHAN-ED.-First Fantasy Awards-GC-1977-Dbldy-1st ed (l3,f,dj) 25.00

WILSON,GEOFFREY-Old Telegraphs-(Lond)-(1976)-Phillimore-xvi+252p-brwn cl,plts-1st ed (a2,dj) 35.00

WILSON,GEOFFREY-Old Telegraphs-Lond-(1976)-Phillamore-8vo-252p-90 illus-1st Brit ed (jj5,f,f dj) 25.00

WILSON,GILBERT L-Agriculture of the Hidatsa Indians, an Indian Interpretation-Mpls-Nov.1917-U of Minn-129p-wrps,illus-Studies in Soc Sci,No.9 (cc4,sl wn) 25.00

WILSON,GRANVILLE P-Pioneers of the Magalloway from 1820 to 1904-Old Orchard-1918-publ by auth-64p-brwn cl,plts-1st ed (k2) 45.00

WILSON,H-Silverwork and Jewellery-NY-1903-Appleton-346p-bds,cl sp,gilt,16 plts-1st ed (u5,uncut) 38.50

WILSON,HARRY L-Cousin Jane-NY-1925-Cosmo-1st ed (hh5,tape rprd dj) 25.00

WILSON,HARRY L-Ruggles of Red Gap-NY-1915-Dbldy Page-1st ed (hh5) 20.00

WILSON,HELEN V P-Frangrant Year-NY-1967-Bonanza-306p-cl (x6,sl wn dj) 18.00

WILSON,HERBERT E-Lore and Lure of Yosemite-LA-1930-135p-cl-7th ed (o1,lacks fly) 12.50

WILSON,IRIS H-William Wolfskill 1798 to 1866-Glendale-1965-Clark Publ-268p-illus-Wstrn Frntrsmn Ser,Vol.XIII-1st ed (g7,f) 70.00

WILSON,JAMES A-Life, Travels and Adventures-Austin-(1927)-Gammel's Bk Store-200p-drwngs-1st ed (dd4,chip dj) 35.00

WILSON,JAMES R-San Francisco's Horror of Earthquake and Fire...-np-(1906)-416p-cl (l1) 15.00

WILSON,JIM-Aorangi-Christchurch-1968-253p-1st ed (p10,f,dj) 55.00

WILSON,JOB-An Inquiry into the Nature and Treatment of the Prevailing Epidemic, called Spotted Fever-Bost-1815-Bradford & Read-219p-orig calf,errata slip,6 plts-Austin 2074-1st ed (c2,wn,f.e.p. loose,fox) 325.00

WILSON,JOSEPH R-Santa Fe Trail-Phila-1921-Int'l Prtg-75p-1st ed (dd4) 15.00

WILSON,KEN-Hard Rock-Lond-1975-4to-200p-160 photos-1st ed (p10,f,dj) 45.00

WILSON,M E-Occurrence of Oil and Gas in Missouri-Rolla-1922-Mo. Bur of Geol & Mines-284p-cl-Vol.XVI,2nd ser-fldng map in rear pocket (h1) 15.00

WILSON,MITCHELL-Panic Stricken-NY-1946-Simon-1st ed (h4,f,dj) 15.00

WILSON,MRS.LUCY E-Practical Cockbook-Cedar Rapids-1912-Torch Pr-210p-oilcloth bds-Bitting 500 (n6,shaky,wn) 16.00

WILSON,NANCY T-Mam Papaul's Country Creole Basket-Baton Rouge-(1973)-32p-wrps (n6) 18.00

WILSON,NEILL C-ED.-Deep Roots-SF-1955-priv prntd-(xii)+112p,red/brwn cl,illus-1st ed (k2) 20.00

WILSON,NEILL C-Southern Pacific the Roaring Story of a Fighting Railroad-(1952)-McGraw Hill-8vo-256p (nn7,dj wn) 22.00

WILSON,NEILL C-Southern Pacific-NY-(1952)-McGraw Hill-256p-illus,e.p. maps-Six Guns #2421-1st ed (dd4,2 autgs) 35.00

WILSON,NEILL C-Southern Pacific-NY-(1952)-McGraw-Hill-x+256p-blk cl,plts-1st ed (k2,dj) 20.00

WILSON,NEILL C-Treasure Express-NY-1938-Macmillan-322p-illus-Six Guns #2420-1st ed (dd4,dj) 25.00

WILSON,NEILL-Silver Stampede-1937-Macmillan-map e.p.,photos-1st ed (d3,dj) 30.00

WILSON,R MCNAIR-Beloved Physician Sir James Mackenzie-NY-1926-316p-frntis port (g10) 20.00

WILSON,R MCNAIR-British Medicine-NY-c.1950-48p-28 illus(incl col)-1st ed (dd3,dj) 20.00

WILSON,ROBERT A-Ben K Green a Descriptive Bibliography...-Flagstaff-1977-Northland Pr-158p-illus,ltd to 100c,autg (w3,as new in box) 125.00

WILSON,ROBERT A-Ben K Green-Flagstaff-1977-Northland Pr-158p-illus-1st ed (gg4,dj) 20.00

WILSON,ROBERT A-Modern Book Collecting-NY-1980-Knopf-photos-1st ed (b5,as new in dj) 25.00

WILSON,ROBERT C-Drugs and Pharmacy in the Life of Georgia, 1733 to 1959-Atlanta-(1959)-Foote & Davies-x+443p-grn cl,illus-1st ed (mm10,dj) 45.00

WILSON,RUFUS R-New York: Old and New-Phila-1902-Lippincott-2 vols-dec grn cl,prnts,photos-1st ed (p2,sp fade,hngs weak) 27.50

WILSON,SPENCER-Cumbres & Toltec Scenic Railroad-Albuq-(1980)-166p-col photos,maps-1st ed (v7,f,dj) 25.00

WILSON,THOMAS A-Practice of Collotype-Bost-1935-Amer Photo Publ-tall 12mo-viii,96p-cl-scarce-1st ed (x4,dj) 95.00

WILSON,THOMAS-Arrowpoints, Spearheads and Knives of Prehistoric Times-Wash-1899-165p-cl,photos-from 1897 Smithsonian rprt-1st ed (t7,rbnd) 35.00

WILSON,WALTER-Forced Labor in the United States-NY-1933-Int'l-photo illus bds wi cl bkstrp-1st ed (w5) 30.00

WILSON,WILLIAM S-Birthplace-SF-1982-North Point-1st ed (o3,f,dj) 15.00

WILSON,WILLIAM-LBJ Brigade-(LA)-1966-Apocalypse-scarce-1st ed (ff3,dj) 175.00

WILSON-MURRAY,JOHN-Memoirs of a Great Canadian Detective-Tor-1977-Collins-8vo-xiv,226p-frntis-rprnt of 1904 Brit ed-1st Can Ed (cc7,dj) 15.00*

WILSTACH,PAUL-Tidewater Virginia-Indpls-1929-Bobbs Merrill-326p-photo plts,map (o2) 20.00

WIMHURST,C G E-Book of the Hound-Lond-1964-F Muller-1st ed (f10) 40.00

WINANS,WILLIAM H-Reminiscences and Experiences in Life of an Editor-Newark-1875-200p-cl (aa6) 50.00

WINCH,FRANK-American Hunter-Bost-1923-16mo-150p-photos (m3) 20.00

WINCH,FRANK-Thrilling Lives of Buffalo Bill and Pawnee Bill-NY-1911-S L Parsons-8vo-224p-dec stmpd cov,photos,drwngs,Wenders-2nd ed (z4,sl rub cov) 50.00

WINCH,FRANK-Thrilling Lives of Buffalo Bill...and Pawnee Bill-NY-1911-S L Parson-8vo-224p-publs dec cl,illus-scarce in cl bndg-1st ed (u1) 200.00

WINCHELL,ALEXANDER-Walks and Talks in the Geological Field-NY-1886-Chautauqua Pr-395p (z7,dj) 45.00

WINCHELL,N H-ED.-Aborigines of Minnesota-St.Paul-1911-Pioneer Pr-4to-xvi+761p-1/2 pigskin,61 maps(incl fldg),plts,642 text figs,Howes W550-1st ed (k2) 250.00

WINCHESTER, THE "2000-PROOF" WINCHESTER MODEL 21 DOUBLE SHOTGUN-catalog-1933-24p+order blanks (gg3,f) 75.00

WINCHESTER,BENJAMIN-Synopsis of the Holy Scriptures and Concordance...-Phila-1842-256p-orig lea,g ruled & sp title-v scarce-Flake 9943-1st ed (bb8,sl split hng,sl dmpstnd) 975.00

WINCHESTER,CAPTAIN J D-Captain J D Winchester's Experience...Voyage from Lynn, Mass to San Francisco...Alaska Gold Fields-Salem-1900-Newcomb & Gauss-251p-blu cl-Howes W556-1st ed (b2,sl spot cov,brwng e.p.) 80.00

WINCHESTER-Model 21 Double, Worlds Finest Shotgun-Catalog-New Haven-1948-24p-wrps,photos,col illus(incl cov),order form at back (gg3,f) 55.00

WINCOR,RICHARD-Sherlock Holmes in Tibet-1968-Weybright-1st ed (s10,f,dj) 25.00

WIND,HERBERT W-Story of American Golf-NY-1956-S&S-lg 8vo-564p-illus-1st prtg rvsd ed (bb5,dj sl tn,chip) 30.00

WINDHAM,DONALD-Dog Star-GC-1950-1st ed (r5,dj) 40.00

WINDHAM,DONALD-Hero Continues-NY-1960-1st ed (q5,dj) 22.50

WINDHAM,DONALD-Two People-Lond-1965-1st Brit ed (r5,dj) 15.00

WINDROW,MARTIN-ED.-Aircraft in Profile, Volume One-NY-1969-Dbldy-288p-1st US ed (j8,f,dj) 35.00

WINDROW,MARTIN-ED.-Aircraft in Profile-NY-1968-Dbldy-profile nos. 73 thru 96-1st US ed (j8,f,dj) 35.00

WINDSOR,DAVID B-Quaker Enterprise-Lond-1980-Frederick Muller-8vo-176p-1st ed (y6,f,f dj) 15.00

WINFIELD,CHARLES H-Block House by Bull's Ferry...Including the "Cow Chace" by Major Andre'-NY-1904-8vo-(8),61p-cl,plts,map-ltd to 200c,nbrd,octavo of a total ed of 250c (aa6) 60.00

WINFIELD,CHARLES H-History of the County of Hudson, New Jersey, from its Earliest Settlement to the Present Time-NY-1874-vii,568p-orig 3/4 mor,illus,plts (aa6) 150.00

WINFIELD,CHARLES H-Hopoghan Hackingh-(np)-(1895?)-4to-80p-cl,illus (aa6) 35.00

WINGE,OJVIND-Inheritance in Dogs-Ithaca-1950-8vo-153p-illus (m3,vf,dj) 25.00

WINGE,OJVIND-Inheritance in Dogs...-Ithaca-1950-Comstock-1st ed (f10,dj) 35.00

WINKLER,ERNEST W-Check List of Texas Imprints, 1846 to 1860-Austin-1949-352p-frntis-1st ed (t7,dj) 30.00

WINKLER,FRED A-Railroad Conductor-Spokane-1948-1st ed (n4,dj) 10.00

WINKLER,JURGEN-Nepal-Tokyo-1977-4to-244p-col photos,maps-1st ed (q10,f,dj) 60.00

WINKLER,MAX-Longchamps Cookbook-(1954)-Harper-110p-red cl,drwngs-1st ed (q8,dj) 12.50

WINKLER,MAX-Penny From Heaven-NY-(1951)-ACC-8vo-310p-1st ed (dd5,f,dj,pres) 17.50

WINLOCK,HERBERT E-Excavations at Deir el Bahri 1911 to 1931-NY-1942-Macmillan-8vo-x,235p-maroon cl,96 plts,figs,map e.p.-1st ed (t10,sl wn dj) 50.00

WINN,MARY D-Macadam Trail-NY-1931-Knopf-319p+index-col frntis,illus-Six Guns #2430-1st ed (cc4) 30.00

WINNETKA CONGREGATIONAL CHURCH-WOMAN'S SOCIETY OF THE...-Good Recipes-(Chig)-(1906)-(Lakeside Pr)-52p+ads & Rules blnks wi recipes wrttn in-illus bds (n6,sl wn bds,spots,weak hngs) 35.00

WINSHIP,GEORGE P-Cambridge Press,1638 to 1692-Phila-1945-Univ of Penn-x+385p-brwn cl,plts-1st ed (m2,dj) 45.00

WINSHIP,GEORGE P-Daniel Berkeley Updike and the Merrymount Press of Boston...-Rochester-1947-Leo Hart-1st ed (w1,f,f dj) 30.00

WINSHIP,GEORGE P-Daniel Berkeley Updike and the Merrymount Press-Rochester-1947-Prtg Hs of Leo Hart-8vo-142p-cl-1st ed (t3,f,dj) 40.00

WINSHIP,GEORGE P-TRANSL.-Journey of Coronado, 1540 to 1542-NY-1904-Barnes-251p-map-Trail Makers Ser-1st ed thus (d3) 40.00

WINSLOW,C D-With the French Flying Corps-NY-1917-8vo-x,226p-col illus cl,frntis,15p plts-1st ed (s2) 45.00

WINSLOW,EDITH B-In Those Days-1950-Naylor-184p-1st ed (a9) 60.00

WINSLOW,HELEN M-President of Quex-Bost-(1906)-Lothrop,Lee & Shepard-306p-cl-Hanna 3848-1st ed (d1) 20.00

WINSOR,G MCLEOD-Vanishing Men-NY-1927-Morrow-1st US ed (h4,dj chip,rprd) 12.50

WINSOR,JUSTIN-ED.-Narrative and Critical History of America-Bost,NY-(1889)-Houghton,Mifflin-4to-16 vols,grn cl,illus,maps,t.e.g.-Howes W578 (m2) 325.00

WINSOR,JUSTIN-Narrative and Critical History of America-Bost,NY-1888 to 89-Houghton Mifflin-8vo-8 vols-qtr drk brwn mor & rough grain maroon cl,a.e. mrbld,frntis,illus,maps-1st ed (t10,rub) 175.00

WINSTON,HENRY-Politics of People's Action-NY-1972-New Outlook-wrps-1st ed (v5,f) 15.00

WINSTON,HENRY-What It Means to be a Communist-NY-1971-New Century-wrps-1st ed (v5,f) 15.00

WINSTON,NAT T-Hit Haint the Fish-Kingsport-1949-8vo-131p-illus-2nd prntg (m3,vf,dj) 27.50

WINSTON,R A-Dive Bomber-NY-(1941)-8vo-192p-illus cl,col illus t.p.,illus-1st ed (s2,dj) 25.00

WINSTONE,H V F-Gertrude Bell-NY-1978-1st ed (y7,dj) 12.00

WINTER IN NEW ORLEANS...ISSUED BY GENERAL PASSENGER DEPARTMENT SOUTHERN PACIFIC SUNSET ROUTE...-(Chig)-(1914)-59,(1)p-wht wrps,photos plts (b1,sl soil wrps) 15.00

WINTER,L-Minute Epics of Flight-NY-(1933)-sm 4to-cl,sp & cov labls,illus (s2) 30.00

WINTER,MARIAN H-Art Scores for Music-1939-Brooklyn Mus Bklt-US Works Project (u4,sl soil) 20.00

WINTER,WM-Life of David Belasco-NY-1918-2 vols-frntis,photos wi tiss guard-scarce-1st ed (t7,ex-libr) 25.00

WINTERBLOSSOM,HENRY T-Game of Draw-Poker Mathematically Illustrated-NY-1875-Wm H Murphy-72p-cl-1st ed (n1) 50.00

WINTERICH,JOHN T-Books and the Man-NY-1929-Greenberg-lg 8vo-374p-blk cl,illus-1st ed (w1) 20.00

WINTERICH,JOHN T-Books and the Man-NY-1929-Greenberg-xiv,374p-cl,t.e.g.,frntis,plts,illus-1st ed (dd10,f) 25.00

WINTERICH,JOHN T-Collector's Choice-NY-(1928)-Greenberg-blu cl-1st ed (w1) 15.00

WINTERICH,JOHN T-Collector's Choice-NY-1954-priv prtd/Grolier Club-8vo-16p-papr wrps-ltd to 750c (x4) 10.00

WINTERICH,JOHN T-Romance of Great Books and Their Authors-NY-(1929)-374p-cl (d1) 15.00

WINTERS,JONATHAN-Mouse Breath, Conformity, Etc-Indpls-(1965)-1st ed (m4,dj) 10.00

WINTHER,OSCAR O-Old Oregon Country, a History of Frontier Trade, Transportation, and Travel-Bloomington-1950-Indiana Univ Publ-8vo-348p-wrps,illus-Soc Sci Ser No.7 (dd4) 25.00

WINTHER,OSCAR O-Old Oregon Country-Stanford,Lond-(1950)-348p-illus-Tweney #85-1st hdbk ed (e7,f,dj) 75.00

WINTHER,OSCAR O-Via Western Express & Stagecoach-(1945)-Stanford Univ Pr-xi,158p-cl,illus,map e.p.-1st ed (v1,dj) 50.00

WINTHER,OSCAR O-Via Western Express & Stagecoach-Stanford-(1947)-Stanford U Pr-158p-illus,map e.p.-Six Guns #2435 (cc4,dj) 30.00

WINTHROP CHEMICAL CO-Physicians Handbook-NY-nd-224p (g10) 15.00

WINTHROP,JOHN-Journal of the Transactions and Occurrences in the Settlement of Massachusetts...1630 to 1644-Hartford-1790-Elisha Babcock-calf-Howes W583-1st ed (dd6) 250.00

WINTHROP,THEODORE-Canoe and Saddle-nd-Binfords & Mort-illus-rprnt (r8,sp chip dj) 40.00

WINTHROP,THEODORE-Canoe and the Saddle-Bost-1863-Ticknor & Fields-375p-grn cl-Howes W584-1st ed (m2,sl wn & spot cov) 65.00

WINTHROP,THEODORE-Canoe and the Saddle-Bost-1863-Ticknor & Fields-Howes W584-1st ed (ee6,lacks frnt flylf) 95.00

WINTHROP,THEODORE-Canoe and the Saddle-Tacoma-1913-332p-red bds,vel sp,16 col illus (e7,f) 125.00

WINTHROP,THEODORE-Canoe and the Saddle-Tacoma-1913-8vo-332p-1/4 vel,gilt,16 col plts,text illus-scarce (m3) 80.00

WINTHROP,THEODORE-Canoe and the Saddle-Tacoma-1913-John H Williams-(xxviii),332p-prchmnt backed cl,photos,illus,col plts-Howes W584-1st ed thus (v1) 150.00

WINTROBE,MAXWELL-ED.-Blood, Pure and Eloquent-NY-1980-771p-1st ed (dd3) 100.00

WISCONSIN LIGHT ARTILLERY-HISTORY OF THE SERVICES OF THE THIRD BATTERY ...IN THE CIVIL WAR...-Berlin-nd-Courant Press-102,(2)p-cl-rare (h1) 100.00

WISE ENCYCLOPEDIA OF COOKERY-NY-1948-Wm H Wise-1329p-gnr bds,illus,thumbed index (m6,sl soil) 40.00

WISE FISHERMEN'S ENCYCLOPEDIA-NY-1951-Wm H Wise-1336p (l6) 50.00

WISE,H D-Tigers of the Sea-NY-1937-Derrydale-189p-ltd to 950c,photos (gg3,f) 110.00

WISE,HENRY A-Seven Decades of the Union-Phila-1872-320p-cl-1st ed (h1) 25.00

WISE,HENRY A-Seven Decades of the Union-Phila-1872-320p-cl-1st ed (o1) 22.50

WISE,ISAAC M-Reminiscences-Cin-1901-Leo Wise-367p-cl (l1) 25.00

WISE,JAMES W-Springfield Plan-NY-1945-Viking-136p-61 photos by Alland-1st ed (cc9,chip dj) 40.00

WISE,JENNINGS C-Red Man in the New World Drama-NY-1971-Macmillan-xi,418p-1st prtg (o2,dj) 17.50

WISE,JENNINGS C-Red Man in the New World Drama-Wash-(1931)-628p-cl (j1) 35.00

WISE,JOHN S-Diomed-1897-Lamson,Woolfe-330p-illus-1st ed (dd9,hng tn,soil pgs) 28.00

WISE,THOMAS J-COMP.-Introductions by Richard Curle,Augustine Birrell...to the Catalogue of the Ashley Library-NY-1934-Wm H Smith-72p-prntd bds,ltd to 500c (l1) 15.00

WISEHART,M K-Sam Houston American Giant-Wash-nd-Robt B Luce-12mo-712p-cl-1st ed (mm7,f,dj) 25.00

WISEMAN,RICHARD-Of Wounds, of Gun Shot Wounds, of Fractures and Luxations-Bath-1977-4to (dd3) 50.00

WISHART,ALFRED W-Short History of Monks and Monasteries-Trenton-1900-454p-cl,plts (aa6,sp lettrng dull) 60.00

WISMAN,W H-Amos New: A Story of the Workman Law-Dayton-nd(1896)-Reformed Publ Co-100p-prtd wrps (b1) 30.00

WISTER,FANNY-Owen Wister Out West-(1958)-U of Chig-269p-illus-1st ed (r8,dj) 25.00

WISTER,FRANCES-Twenty Five Years of the Philadelphia Orchestra-1925-Womens Comm Phila Orch (u4,sl rub) 16.00

WISTER,JOHN C-Lilac Culture-1936-Orange Judd-xiv,123p-11 photo plts,12 line drwngs (x5,dj) 12.00

WISTER,JOHN-Bulbs for American Gardens-Bost-1930-Stratford-278p-cl (x6) 25.00

WISTER,JOHN-Bulbs for Home Gardens-NY-1948-OUP-270p-cl (x6) 12.00

WISTER,OWEN-Journey in Search of Christmas-NY-(1904)-8vo-red pict cl,illus by Remington-1st ed (kk7,sl soil cov) 20.00

WISTER,OWEN-When West Was West-NY-(1928)-Macmillan-dj illus by Remington-1st ed (aa10,f,dj soil,sl chip) 150.00

WITCHELL,CHARLES A-Evolution of Bird Song with Observations on the Influence of Heredity and Imitation-Lond-1896-Black-x+253p-blu cl-1st ed (l2) 25.00

WITHERS,CARL-ED.-I Saw a Rocket Walk a Mile-NY-(1965)-HR&W-8vo-160p-pict bds,illus,J E Johnson-1st ed (s3,f,dj) 20.00

WITHERS,E L-Salazar Grant-NY-1959-Rinehart-1st ed (d4,dj) 10.00

WITHERSPOON,GARY-Navajo Kinship and Marriage-Chig-(1975)-U of Chig Pr-137p-1st ed (ff4,dj) 15.00

WITHINGTON,ANTOINETTE-Hawaiian Tapestry-1937-Harper-367p-photos-1st ed (u8,cov sl wn,soil) 10.00

WITHINGTON,PAUL-ED.-Book of Athletics-Bost-(1914)-Lothrop-8vo-512p-dec cl-1st prtg (u1) 65.00

WITHROW,W H-Barbara Heck-Tor-1895-Meth Mission Rms-8vo-338p-orig red dec cl-Watters p.420-1st ed (pp2,f) 45.00*

WITTEMANN,A-San Antonio Illustrated-NY-1892-A Wittemann-illus cl,42 photos-scarce-1st ed (w3,f) 75.00

WITTKE,CARL-ED.-History of the State of Ohio-Columbus-1941 to 1944-11 vols-cl (aa1) 75.00

WOBBER,FLORENCE-Ballads of the Wine Mad Town-SF-(1916)-Sunset Hs-16mo-198p-pict blu cl,col illus-1st ed (q8) 25.00

WODEHOUSE,P G-America, I Like You-1956-S&S-1st ed (x2,dj) 50.00

WODEHOUSE,P G-America, I Like You-1956-Simon-1st ed (s10,sp chip dj) 40.00

WODEHOUSE,P G-Angel Cake-GC-1952-Dbldy-1st Amer ed (ee2,f,dj) 50.00

WODEHOUSE,P G-Author! Author!-1962-S&S-1st US ed (w7,f) 60.00

WODEHOUSE,P G-Bachelors Anonymous-1974-S&S-1st ed (x2,f,dj) 35.00

WODEHOUSE,P G-Bachelors Anonymous-1974-S&S-1st US ed (w7,f,dj) 60.00

WODEHOUSE,P G-Bertie Wooster Sees It Through-1955-S&S-blu bds-1st US ed (w7,sl wn dj) 125.00

WODEHOUSE,P G-Big Money-1931-Jenkins-1st Brit ed (w7,f) 90.00

WODEHOUSE,P G-Bill the Conqueror-(1924)-Doran-1st US ed (w7,sl soil sp,sm cov stn) 115.00

WODEHOUSE,P G-Bill the Conqueror-NY-(1924)-Doran-yel cl,col pict dj-1st Amer ed (ll5,sl chip dj) 350.00

WODEHOUSE,P G-Blandings Castle and Elsewhere-Lond-1935-Jenkins-turq cl,col pict dj-1st prtg (kk5,sp fade,dj rprd) 450.00

WODEHOUSE,P G-Blandings Castle-1935-Dbldy-1st US ed (w7,sl fox eps,sl chip dj) 180.00

WODEHOUSE,P G-Bring on the Girls-NY-1953-S&S-1st Amer ed (w1) 25.00

WODEHOUSE,P G-Brinkley Manor-Bost-1934-Little,Brown-red pict cl,blk lttrng-1st Amer ed (kk5,dj sl chip & soil) 250.00

WODEHOUSE,P G-Brinkmanship of Galahad Threepwood-1964-S&S-1st US ed (w7,vf,vf dj) 52.00

WODEHOUSE,P G-Butler Did It-NY-1957-S&S-1st ed (v10,dj wn & chip) 20.00

WODEHOUSE,P G-Carry on Jeeves-1925-Jenkins-1st Brit ed (w7,pgs sl drknd & fox) 70.00

WODEHOUSE,P G-Cat Nappers-(1974)-S&S-1st US ed (w7,f,dj) 35.00

WODEHOUSE,P G-Cat Nappers-NY-(1974)-S&S-1st US ed (ee2,f,dj) 40.00

WODEHOUSE,P G-Cocktail Time-Lond-1958-Jenkins-red cl,col pict dj-1st ed (kk5,sl chip dj) 95.00

WODEHOUSE,P G-Cocktail Time-NY-1958-S&S-1st ed (x10,f,sl tn dj) 35.00

WODEHOUSE,P G-Code of the Woosters-1938-Dbldy-1st US ed (w7) 95.00

WODEHOUSE,P G-Code of the Woosters-Lond-1938-Jenkins-1st ed (w9,dj rprd,chip,sm pc missng) 125.00

WODEHOUSE,P G-Divots-NY-1927-Doran-orng cl-1st ed (u2) 85.00

WODEHOUSE,P G-Do Butlers Burgle Banks-1968-S&S-1st ed (x2,f,dj) 45.00

WODEHOUSE,P G-Do Butlers Burgle Banks-NY-1968-S&S-1st ed (w5,f,f dj) 25.00

WODEHOUSE,P G-Eggs,Beans and Crumpets-1940-Dbldy-1st US ed (w7,f) 60.00

WODEHOUSE,P G-Enter Psmith-1935-McMillan-1st US ed (w7) 110.00

WODEHOUSE,P G-Few Quick Ones-NY-1959-S&S-1st ed (x10,f,sl soil dj) 40.00

WODEHOUSE,P G-Few Quick Ones-NY-1959-S&S-yel & pnk stripe wht cl over gry bds-1st ed (kk5,dj) 65.00

WODEHOUSE,P G-Fore-New Haven-1983-Ticknor & Fields-1st ed (z9,f,dj) 12.50

WODEHOUSE,P G-Full Moon-1947-Jenkins-1st Brit ed (w7,f,f dj) 98.00

WODEHOUSE,P G-Galahad at Blandings-Lond-1965-Jenkins-red cl,col pict dj-1st Brit ed (ll5,f,dj) 85.00

WODEHOUSE,P G-Girl in Blue-1971-S&S-1st ed (x2,f,dj) 38.00

WODEHOUSE,P G-Golf Omnibus-NY-1973-S&S-1st ed (w5,f,dj) 75.00

WODEHOUSE,P G-Golf Without Tears-NY-(1924)-Doran-grn cl,col dec e.p.-1st Amer ed,1st iss (ll5,cor sl bump) 200.00

WODEHOUSE,P G-Good Morning Bill-1928-Methuen-1st Brit ed (w7) 130.00

WODEHOUSE,P G-Heavy Weather-1933-Little,Brown-1st US ed (w7) 90.00

WODEHOUSE,P G-Ice in the Bedroom-NY-1961-S&S-1st Amer ed (ee2,f,dj) 35.00

WODEHOUSE,P G-If I Were You-1931-Dbldy-1st US ed (w7) 105.00

WODEHOUSE,P G-If I Were You-GC-1931-Dbldy,Doran-orng cl,brwn lttrng,col pict dj-1st ed(precedes Brit ed) (kk5,dj lack sp pc,sl chip,tn) 250.00

WODEHOUSE,P G-Jeeves and the Tie that Binds-(1971)-S&S-1st US ed (w7,f,dj) 55.00

WODEHOUSE,P G-Jeeves and the Tie that Binds-NY-(1971)-S&S-1st US ed (ee2,f,dj) 35.00

WODEHOUSE,P G-Jeeves in the Offing-Lond-1960-Jenkins-red cl,col pict dj-1st Brit ed (ll5,f,dj) 120.00

WODEHOUSE,P G-Jeeves-1923-Doran-1st US ed (w7) 425.00

WODEHOUSE,P G-Joy in the Morning-1947-Jenkins-1st Brit ed (w7,sl stnd cov) 36.00

WODEHOUSE,P G-Laughing Gas-GC-1936-Dbldy,Doran-orng cl,col pict dj-1st Amer ed (kk5,dj) 450.00

WODEHOUSE,P G-Laughing Gas-Lond-(1936)-1st ed (e5,fade cov) 15.00

WODEHOUSE,P G-Laughing Gas-Lond-1936-Jenkins-1st ed (w9,f,tape rprd dj) 175.00

WODEHOUSE,P G-Leave It To Psmith-1923/4-Doran-publ colophon on cpyrt pg-1st US ed (w7,sl fox) 240.00

WODEHOUSE,P G-Little Nugget-1914-Watt-1st Brit ed (w7,lacks sp g) 120.00

WODEHOUSE,P G-Little Warrior-NY-(1920)-Doran-tan cl wi grn lttrng-1st ed (kk5,cov crease,hng weak) 195.00

WODEHOUSE,P G-Lord Emsworth and Others-1937-Jenkins-scarlet cl-1st Brit ed (w7,vf) 380.00

WODEHOUSE,P G-Louder and Funnier-1932-Faber & Faber-2nd bndg-1st Brit ed (w7,f) 290.00

WODEHOUSE,P G-Luck of the Bodkins-1935-Jenkins-1st Brit ed (w7,f,rprd dj) 220.00

WODEHOUSE,P G-Mating Season-NY-1944-Didier-red cl,silv lttrng,H McIntosh illus-1st Amer ed (kk5,f,sl tn dj) 185.00

WODEHOUSE,P G-Meet Mr.Mulliner-1928-Dbldy-1st US ed (w7,soil cov) 30.00

WODEHOUSE,P G-Mike at Wrykyn-NY-(1953)-Meredith Pr-gry cl,col pict dj-1st Amer ed (kk5,f,dj) 75.00

WODEHOUSE,P G-Money For Nothing-1928-Dbldy-orng letters on cambridge blu-1st US ed (w7) 110.00

WODEHOUSE,P G-Money in the Bank-1942-D,D-1st ed (x2,dj sl chip & soil) 195.00

WODEHOUSE,P G-Money in the Bank-1946-Jenkins-1st Brit ed (w7,dj) 110.00

WODEHOUSE,P G-Money in the Bank-GC-1942-Dbldy,Doran-1st Amer ed (ee6,dj sl wn & sp fade) 95.00

WODEHOUSE,P G-Most of P G Wodehouse-NY-1960-1st ed (v9,f,sl crease dj) 75.00

WODEHOUSE,P G-Most of...-NY-1960-S&S-1st ed (x10,f,dj sl wn & soil) 30.00

WODEHOUSE,P G-Mr.Mulliner Speaking-1930-Dbldy-1st US ed (w7,sl soil sp) 60.00

WODEHOUSE,P G-Much Obliged, Jeeves-Lond-(1971)-Barrie & Jenkins-192p-dj illus by O Lancaster-1st ed (v8,dj) 80.00

WODEHOUSE,P G-No Nudes is Good Nudes-(1970)-S&S-1st ed (x2,f,sl discol rear dj panel) 38.00

WODEHOUSE,P G-No Nudes is Good Nudes-NY-(1970)-S&S-1st ed (v10,f,sl wn dj) 35.00

WODEHOUSE,P G-Nothing Serious-1951-Dbldy-1st US ed (w7,dj) 160.00

WODEHOUSE,P G-Pearls, Girls and Monty Bodkin-Lond-1972-Barrie & Jenkins-col pict dj-1st ed (ll5,f,sl tn dj) 75.00

WODEHOUSE,P G-Pearls,Girls, and Monty Bodkin-1972-Barrie & Jenkins-1st Brit ed (w7,vf,f dj) 50.00

WODEHOUSE,P G-Plot That Thickened-1973-S&S-1st US ed (w7,as new in dj) 75.00

WODEHOUSE,P G-Plot That Thickened-1973-S&S-1st US ed (x2,f,dj) 37.00

WODEHOUSE,P G-Plum Pie-1967-S&S-1st US ed (w7,dj) 120.00

WODEHOUSE,P G-Prince and Betty-1912-Watt-1st Brit ed (w7) 250.00

WODEHOUSE,P G-Psmith in the City-1910-Black-bds-1st Brit ed (w7) 900.00

WODEHOUSE,P G-Psmith in the City-Lond-1910-Black-blu pict cl,12p illus by T M R Whitewell,1 adv leaf-1st ed (ll5,cor bump) 800.00

WODEHOUSE,P G-Purloined Paperweight-1967-S&S-1st ed (x2,f,dj) 45.00

WODEHOUSE,P G-Right Ho, Jeeves-Lond-1934-Jenkins-red lttrd & dec tan cl-1st ed (kk5,cov sl soil & stnd) 210.00

WODEHOUSE,P G-Sam in the Suburbs-1925-Doran-1st US ed (w7,soil sp) 95.00

WODEHOUSE,P G-Sam the Sudden-1925-Metheun-1st Brit ed (w7) 110.00

WODEHOUSE,P G-Service with a Smile-1961-S&S-1st ed (x2,tn dj) 25.00

WODEHOUSE,P G-Small Bachelor-1927-Doran-1st US ed (w7,sl soil cov) 80.00

WODEHOUSE,P G-Something New-NY-1915-Appelton-dec red cl-1st ed (u2) 80.00

WODEHOUSE,P G-Stiff Upper Lip, Jeeves-1963-S&S-1st US ed (w7,sl fox,f dj) 80.00

WODEHOUSE,P G-Stiff Upper Lip, Jeeves-NY-1963-S&S-1st US ed (b8,sl tn dj) 45.00

WODEHOUSE,P G-Summer Moonshine-GC-1937-Dbldy,Doran-dec orng cl-1st ed (kk5,f,sl wn dj) 250.00

WODEHOUSE,P G-Sunset at Blandings-NY-(1977)-illus by Ionicus-1st Amer ed (r2,f,dj) 40.00

WODEHOUSE,P G-Sunset at Blandings-NY-(1977)-S&S-1st Amer ed (x10,f,f dj) 25.00

WODEHOUSE,P G-Three Men and a Maid-(1922)-Doran-304p-1st ed (v8,frnt hng weak,sl wn) 100.00

WODEHOUSE,P G-Ukridge-Lond-1924-Jenkins-grn pict cl-1st ed (ll5,sl spot & fox) 245.00

WODEHOUSE,P G-Uncle Dynamite-1948-Didier-1st US ed (w7,dj) 245.00

WODEHOUSE,P G-Uncle Dynamite-NY-1948-Didier-red cl,silv lttrng,H McIntosh illus-1st US ed (kk5,f,dj sl chip & tn) 225.00

WODEHOUSE,P G-Uncle Fred in the Springtime-1939-Dbldy-1st US ed (w7,vf) 75.00

WODEHOUSE,P G-Uncollected Wodehouse-NY-(1976)-1st ed (f5,f,dj) 25.00

WODEHOUSE,P G-Very Good, Jeeves-1930-Dbldy-1st US ed (w7,sl fox,sl sun sp) 36.00

WODEHOUSE,P G-Very Good, Jeeves-GC-1930-Dbldy,Doran-orng cl wi blk lttrng-1st US ed (kk5,sl rub sp,hngs weak) 95.00

WODEHOUSE,P G-Wodehouse at War-1981-Ticknor & Fields-1st Amer ed (s9,f,dj) 15.00

WODEHOUSE,P G-Wodehouse on Crime-New Haven-(1981)-Ticknor & Fields-1st ed (ee2,f,dj) 30.00

WODEHOUSE,P G-World of Mr.Mulliner-NY-(1974)-Taplinger-1st Amer ed (ee2,f,f dj) 35.00

WODEHOUSE,P G-Young Men in Spats-Lond-1936-Jenkins-blu/grn cl,col pict dj-1st ed (ll5,part fade sp,dj rprd) 450.00

WODZICKI,K A-Introduced Mammals of New Zealand-Wellington-1950-8vo-255p-cl,fldg tabl,illus (y8,dj wn,pres cpy) 48.00

WOERENSKJOLD,ELISE-Lady with a Pen-Northfield-1961-Norwegian Amer Hist Assoc-183p-pict bds (cc4) 15.00

WOIWODE,LARRY-Even Tide-NY-1977-FS&G-84p-wrps-1st ed (z7) 35.00

WOIWODE,LARRY-Poppa John-(1981)-Farrar Straus-1st ed (k3,f,dj) 15.00

WOLCOTT,IMOGENE-Yankee Cookbook-NY-(1971)-Washburn-366p-Yel cl,illus-New ed (q8,dj) 16.50

WOLCOTT-Lakes of Washington. Vol.1-Olympia-1961-619p-illus,fldg map (j7) 30.00

WOLDMAN,ALBERT A-Lincoln and the Russians-Cleve-(1952)-311p-1st ed (n3,dj) 17.50

WOLF II,EDWIN-Rosenbach: a Biography-Cleve,NY-1960-World-lg thk 8vo-618p-photos-1st ed (oo8,f,dj) 90.00

WOLF,BILL-Reveries of an Outdoor Man-NY-1946-8vo-181p-ltd to 350c,nbrd,autg,illus (m3) 40.00

WOLF,EMMA-Other Things Being Equal-Chig-1892-McClurg-8vo-275p-cl,auth 1st bk-1st ed (w6) 45.00

WOLF,F-Dolomites and Their Legends-Bolanzo-1930-150p-1st ed (o10) 15.00

WOLF,HOWARD-World, the Flesh, and the Holy Ghost-Caldwell-1933-Caxton-1st ed (v5,f,f dj) 30.00

WOLF,L-John of the Mountains-Bost-1938-459p-1st ed (o10,f) 55.00

WOLF,L-Son of the Wilderness-NY-1945-364p-1st ed (o10,f) 55.00

WOLF,L-Son of the Wilderness-NY-1945-scarce dj-3rd prtg (o10,f,dj) 60.00

WOLF,W-Reveries of an Outdoor Man-NY-1946-181p-tip in col frntis-ltd to 350c,nbrd,autg (gg3,vf) 35.00

WOLFE,BERNARD-Limbo-NY-(1952)-Random-1st ed (p3,chip dj) 30.00

WOLFE,DR N B-Guide Book-Cin-1881-60p-cl (aa1,sl fox) 15.00

WOLFE,DR N B-Guide-Book-Cin-1881-60p-cl (j1,sl fox) 15.00

WOLFE,GENE-Peace-NY-1975-1st ed (t5,sl soil dj) 20.00

WOLFE,HUMBERT-Notes on English Verse Satire-Lond-1929-Hogarth Pr-8vo-Hogarth Lectures No.10-1st ed (x3,sl chip dj) 55.00

WOLFE,LINDA-Literary Gourmet-NY-(1962)-Random-387p-1st prtg (k6) 30.00

WOLFE,MICHAEL-Two Star Pigeon-NY-1975-Harper & Row-1st ed (c8,f,f dj) 40.00

WOLFE,MURIEL S-Montana Pay Dirt-Denver-(1963)-4to-436p-dbl col,illus-1st ed (g7,f,dj) 115.00

WOLFE,PETER-Beams Falling-Bowling Green-(1980)-172p-1st ed (g9) 25.00

WOLFE,PETER-Dreamers Who Live Their Dreams-(1976)-Bowling Grn U Pr-345p-pict cl-1st ed (g9) 25.00

WOLFE,THOMAS-From Death to Morning-NY-1935-Scribners-1st ed (cc2,dj rub,sp chip) 125.00

WOLFE,THOMAS-From Death to Morning-NY-1935-Scribners-1st ed (l9,sl fox,dj sl soil) 195.00

WOLFE,THOMAS-Letters of...-NY-(1956)-1st ed (r2,dj) 30.00

WOLFE,THOMAS-Look Homeward, Angel-1947-Scribners-662p-illus,D Gorsline-1st ed of illus ed (v8,dj) 40.00

WOLFE,THOMAS-Mannerhouse-NY-1948-Harpers-1st ed (bb2,f,dj) 100.00

WOLFE,THOMAS-Of Time and the River-NY-1935-Scribner's-1st ed (a5,dj) 175.00

WOLFE,THOMAS-Short Novels of ...-NY-(1961)-1st ed (h5,sl wn dj) 40.00

WOLFE,THOMAS-Stone, a Leaf, a Door-NY-1945-Scribners-1st ed (cc2,dj rub,sp chip) 75.00

WOLFE,THOMAS-Story of a Novel-1936-Scribners-1st ed (jj6,f,dj sl rub & tn) 125.00

WOLFE,THOMAS-Web and the Rock-NY,Lond-1939-1st ed (h5,sp dull,rub,dj sp sl wn) 125.00

WOLFE,THOMAS-Web and the Rock-NY-1939-Harper & Bros-1st ed (cc2,sp chip dj) 100.00

WOLFE,THOMAS-Welcome to Our City-Baton Rouge-(1983)-LSU Pr-1st ed (dd2,f,dj) 40.00

WOLFE,THOMAS-Western Journal-(Pitt)-1951-U of Pitt Pr-1st ed (l9,bump,dj sl wn) 85.00

WOLFE,THOMAS-You Can't Go Home Again-NY,Lond-(1940)-Harper-g titled cl-1st ed (aa9,sl chip dj) 125.00

WOLFE,THOMAS-You Can't Go Home Again-NY-(1940)-Harpers-8vo-cl-1st ed (v10,f,sl tn dj) 100.00

WOLFE,TOM-Electric Kool Aid Acid Test-NY-(1968)-FS&G-8vo-cl-1st ed (ll10,f,dj) 150.00

WOLFE,TOM-From Bauhaus to Our House-NY-(1981)-1st ed (p5,dj) 20.00

WOLFE,TOM-From Bauhaus to Our House-NY-(1981)-FS&G-ltd to 350c,nbrd,autg-1st ed (s6,f,box) 60.00

WOLFE,TOM-In Our Time-NY-1980-drwngs,auth-1st ed (r5,f,dj) 20.00

WOLFE,TOM-Mauve Gloves & Madmen, Clutter & Vine-NY-(1976)-Farrar,Straus-1st ed (k3,f,dj) 20.00

WOLFE,TOM-Mauve Gloves & Madmen, Clutter & Vine-NY-(1976)-FS&G-drwngs-1st ed (b5,as new in dj) 25.00

WOLFE,TOM-New Journalism-NY-1973-Harper & Row-1st ed (c8,f dj) 100.00

WOLFE,TOM-Painted Word-NY-(1975)-1st ed (e5,sl creased dj) 20.00

WOLFE,TOM-Painted Word-NY-(1975)-Farrar-8vo-cl-1st ed (x3,dj) 30.00

WOLFE,TOM-Pump House Gang-NY-1968-1st ed (q5,dj) 25.00

WOLFE,TOM-Purple Decade-NY-1982-1st ed (r5,f,dj) 20.00

WOLFE,TOM-Radical Chic & Mau Mauing the Flak Catchers-Lond-1971-1st Brit ed (r5,f,dj) 25.00

WOLFE,TOM-Radical Chic & Mau Mauing the Flak Catchers-NY-1970-1st ed (r2,f,dj) 30.00

WOLFE,TOM-Radical Chic & Mau Mauing the Flak Catchers-NY-1970-1st ed (x8,dj) 24.00

WOLFE,TOM-Right Stuff-1979-FSG-1st ed (x2,f,dj) 35.00

WOLFE,TOM-Right Stuff-NY-1979-1st ed (q5,f,dj) 22.50

WOLFENSTINE,MANFRED R-Manual of Brands and Marks-Norman-(1970)-U of Okla Pr-434p-illus-1st ed (ff4) 45.00

WOLFERT,I-Torpedo 8-NY-(1943)-8vo-xvi,128p-cl,col illus e.p.-1st ed (s2,chip dj) 25.00

WOLFERT,IRA-Battle for the Solomons-Bost-1943-1st ed (g5,dj) 10.00

WOLFF,DR PAUL-My Experiences in Color Photography-NY-1948-Grayson-43p text+54 col photos-1st Amer ed (cc9,f,tn dj) 35.00

WOLFF,DR PAUL-My First 10 Years with the Leica-NY-nd(ca.1934?)-B Westerman-56p text+192 photos (cc9,dj soil & sl tn) 50.00

WOLFF,GEOFFREY-Bad Debts-NY-(1969)-auth 1st bk-1st ed (g5,as new in dj) 25.00

WOLFF,GEOFFREY-Black Sun-NY-(1976)-Random-photos-1st ed (bb1,as new in dj) 20.00

WOLFF,GEOFFREY-Duke of Deception-NY-(1979)-photos-1st ed (g5,as new in dj) 15.00

WOLFF,GEOFFREY-Inklings-NY-(1977)-1st ed (g5,as new in dj) 15.00

WOLFF,GEOFFREY-Inklings-NY-(1977)-Random-1st ed (k3,f,dj) 20.00

WOLFF,GEOFFREY-Sightseer-NY-(1973)-1st ed (g5,as new in dj) 20.00

WOLFF,MARITTA-Back of Town-NY-1952-Random-436p-blk cl-1st ed (cc3,dj) 25.00

WOLFF,TOBIAS-Hunters in the Snow-Lond-(1982)-Jonathan Cape-1st Brit ed (b10,as new in dj) 40.00

WOLFF,TOBIAS-Ugly Rumors-Lond-(1975)-Geo Allen-auth 1st bk-1st ed (ff3,dj) 750.00

WOLFF,WERNER-Dream, Mirror of Conscience-NY-1952-Grune & Stratton-viii+348p-blk cl,30 illus-1st ed (c2,dj) 20.00

WOLFF,WERNER-Island of Death-NY-1948-J J Augustin-4to-228p-blck cl,20 plts (p8,dj wn,chip,pres) 100.00

WOLFKILL,GRANT-Reported to be Alive-Lond-1966-1st ed (v9,f,f dj) 50.00

WOLFORD,LEAH J-Play-Party in Indiana-Indpls-1916-120p-cl-1st ed (c1) 20.00

WOLFSON,ALBERT-ED.-Recent Studies in Avian Biology-1955-U of Illinois Pr-479p (b9) 25.00

WOLL,F W-Productive Feeding of Farm Animals-Phila-1915-Lippincott-385p-cl (x6) 15.00

WOLLASTON,TULLIE C-Opal-Lond-1924-T Murby & Co-xi,164p-gilt,col frntis,2 col plts wi tiss,11 photo plts,1 text map-scarce-1st ed,1st prtg (u5,f) 160.00

WOLLE,MURIEL S-Bonanza Trail-1953-Indiana U-lg 8vo-510p-illus,maps-Six Guns #2437-1st ed (r8,sl chip dj) 35.00

WOLLE,MURIEL S-Stampede to Timberline-Boulder-(1952)-M S Wolle-544p-e.p. maps,illus (ff4,autg) 25.00

WOLLHEIM,DONALD-Secret of the Ninth Planet-Phila-(1959)-Winston-1st ed (f3,sl wn dj) 45.00

WOLLIN,DR.NILS G-Modern Swedish Arts and Crafts in Pictures-NY-(1931)-Scribners-sm folio-207p-dec tan cl,col illus-1st Amer ed (s1) 65.00

WOLSELEY,LORD-Life of John Churchill, Duke of Marlborough-Lond-1894-2 vols-1/2 red lea,mrbld bds,g dec sp,t.e.g.,plts-1st ed (kk2,sp fade) 200.00

WOLSELEY,LORD-Story of a Soldier's Life-Westminster-1903-2 vols-1/2 red lea & bds,mrbld e.p.,t.e.g.,illus-1st ed (kk2) 200.00

WOLTERS,RICHARD A-Gun Dog-NY-1961-8vo-150p-photos-1st ed (m3,f,dj) 20.00

WOMACK,BOB-Echo of Hoofbeats-Shelbyville-1973-Walking Horse Publ-1st ed (h9,dj) 125.00

WOMACK,JOHN,JR.-Zapata and the Mexican Revolution-NY-1969-Knopf-435p-illus-1st ed (cc4,dj) 15.00

WOMAN OF NEW ORLEANS. BY A MAN O' THE TOWN-np(New Orleans?)-1889-publ by auth(S H James)-238p-3/4 lea & mrbld bds (b1,sl rub) 50.00

WOMAN'S CENTURY CLUB OF DAYTON,OHIO-Good Things to Eat-Dayton-1904-Nat'l Cash Reg Co-58p+ads & index-papr overhang wrps,illus,prntd in diff cols (n6,sl tattrd wrps) 65.00

WOMAN'S DAY COLLECTOR'S COOK BOOK-NY-1960-dutton-dbl col pgs,illus,J Low-1st ed (o6) 20.00

WOMAN'S HOME COMPANION COOK BOOK-NY-(c.1942,1944)-Collier & Son-951p-yel bds (k6,sl wn) 35.00

WOMAN'S RELIEF CORPS-JOURNAL OF THE TWENTY-THIRD ANNUAL CONVENTION...MASSACHUSSETTS...-Bost-1902-406p-cl (d1) 15.00

WOMAN'S THOUGHTS ABOUT WOMEN-Columbus-1858-Follett,Foster-270p-cl-by the author of "John Halifax, Gentleman"-1st Amer ed (aa1) 50.00

WOMEN OF ALL NATIONS-NY/Lond-1912-Cassell-320p-3/4 mor,grn cl,mrbld e.p.,10 col plts,over 500 photos (ll1,cl damaged at t.e.) 95.00

WOMEN TORCH BEARERS, THE STORY OF THE WOMAN'S CHRISTIAN TEMPERANCE UNION-Evanston-1924-320p-photos-2nd ed (dd3) 75.00

WOO-KEUN,HAN-History of Korea-Honolulu-1971-East West Cntr Pr-551p-maps,photos,col plts (c3) 16.00

WOOD COUNTY FARM AND BUSINESS DIRECTORY 1947-48-(Bowling Green)-(1947)-416p+fldg map-cl (j1) 15.00

WOOD,A D-Plywoods-Edinburgh-1946-Johnston Ltd-sm 4to-472p-tan cl,illus (r10,dj wn) 25.00

WOOD,ALPHA K-Texas Coastal Bend-S.A.-1971-Naylor-156p-1st ed (a9) 30.00

WOOD,BARI-Tribe-NY-(1981)-Nal-1st ed (l3,f,dj) 15.00

WOOD,C A-Art of Falconry by Frederick II-CA-1981-637p-illus-rprnt (gg3,f,dj) 65.00

WOOD,CATHERINE M-Palomar, From Tepee to Telescope-San Diego-1937-prtd by Frye & Smith, Ltd-8vo-149p+index-maps,photos,drwngs (mm1,sl wn dj) 35.00

WOOD,D-Narrow Margin-NY-(1961)-8vo-536p-cl,24p plts,8 maps-1st ed (s2,chip dj) 25.00

WOOD,DEE-ET AL-Padre Island-S.A.-1950-Naylor-222p-1st ed (a9,dj) 45.00

WOOD,DEREK-Narrow Margin-NY-1961-536p-illus-1st ed (kk2,f,dj) 35.00

WOOD,E-Thrilling Deeds of British Airmen-Lond-1917-8vo-318p-illus cl,col frntis,1 col & 1 b&w plt-1st ed (s2,sp fade,fox) 30.00

WOOD,ELIZABETH L-Arizona Hoof Trails-Portland-1956-Binfords & Mort-8vo-82p-1st ed (z4,dj wn wi sm pcs missing) 20.00

WOOD,ELIZABETH L-Long Rope-(1958)-Binfords & Mort-168p-illus-1st ed (r8,dj chip,sp pc missng) 15.00

WOOD,ELIZABETH L-Pete Franch, Cattle King-Portland-1951-Binfords & Morts-229,(1)p-illus orng cl,illus dj,illus (b6,vf,dj) 12.50

WOOD,ELIZABETH L-Trail of the Bear-Portland-1932-8vo-174p-illus (m3) 12.50

WOOD,ERNEST-Study of Pleasure and Pain-Wheaton-1962-Theosophical Pr-sm 8vo-(vi)+(98)p-cl-1st ed (y9,dj) 17.50

WOOD,ERSKINE-Days with Chief Joseph-Portland-nd-8vo-26p (m3,f) 35.00

WOOD,ESTHER-House in the Hoo-NY,Tor-(1941)-Longmans,Green-pict cl,illus by T Kalab-1st ed (aa9) 20.00

WOOD,EVELYN-British Battles on Land and Sea-Lond-1915-2 vols-dec blu cl,illus(incl 24 col)-1st ed (b7) 150.00

WOOD,EVELYN-From Midshipman to Field Marshal-Lond-1907-619p-red cl,maps,illus-1st one vol ed (b7,sl sun) 125.00

WOOD,F W-Six Years a Priest and a Decade a Protestant-Cleve-1876-289p-cl-scarce (aa1) 30.00

WOOD,FRANCES-I Hauled These Mountains in Here-Caldwell-1977-377p-photos,illus-1st ed (t7,dj) 12.50

WOOD,FREDERIC J-Turnpikes of New England and Evolution of the Same through England, Virginia and Maryland-Bost-1919-Marshall Jones Co-4to-xviii+461p-blu cl,97 plts,7 maps-1st ed (b2,cov fade,text soil) 45.00

WOOD,GEORGE-Address on the Occasion of the Centennial Celebration of the Founding of the Pennsylvania Hospital-Phila-1851-141p-2 engrvd plts-1st ed (dd3) 50.00

WOOD,IAN-My Way with Salmon-Lond-1957-8vo-108p-photos (m3,vf) 30.00

WOOD,J A-Tour Round my Garden-Lond-1856-Routledge-332p-g dec cl (x6,rub,shaken) 25.00

WOOD,J C-Animate Creation-NY-1898-4to-6 vols-1/2 lea,34 col plts,rvsd by Holder (y8) 150.00

WOOD,J G-ED.-Episodes of Insect Life-Lond-1879-Geo Bell & Sons-430p-cl,g stmpd & dec frnt cov & sp,illus (l1) 20.00

WOOD,J G-Illustrated Natural History-Lond-1865,1864,1863-3 vols-3/4 lea,illus (a1,sl rub,sl shaken) 50.00

WOOD,J G-Papa's Stories about Animals, Wild and Tame-Phila-nd-84p-cl-frontis + 14pg plts by Wm Bispham (h1) 20.00

WOOD,J G-Stories and Anecdotes of Bears-Phila-1856-Willis P Hazard-96p-cl,3p plts (n1,sl dmpstnd,sl fox) 17.50

WOOD,KERRY-Birds and Animals in the Rockies-Saskatoon-nd-H R Larson-8vo-157p-illus card cov,drwngs (mm8) 35.00*

WOOD,M D-Fruit From the Jungle-Mountain View-1918-Pacific Pr-16mo-331p-photos (ll1,papr aging) 30.00

WOOD,MORRISON-With a Jug of Wine-Lond-(1958)-Muller-288p-red cl-1st Brit ed (q8,dj) 16.50

WOOD,NANCY-When Buffalo Free the Mountains-GC-1980-293p-photos-1st ed (u7,as new in dj) 25.00

WOOD,NORMAN A-Birds of Michigan-Ann Arbor-1951-U of Mich-559p-orig wrps-Misc Publ No.75,Mus of Zoology (c9,wn) 40.00

WOOD,OLIVER E-West Point Scrapbook-NY-1871-Van Nostrand-339p-frntis,illus-1st ed (v2,sp tn,lacks ffep) 50.00

WOOD,RICHARD G-Stephen Harriman Long-Glendale-1966-Arthur H Clark Co-8vo-292p-blu cl,g sp titles,frntis,fldg map,illus-1st ed (mm1) 50.00

WOOD,ROBERT L-Trail Country, Olympic National Park-Seattle-(1968)-Mountaineers-8vo-298p-illus-1st ed (ff5,sl tn dj) 15.00

WOOD,RUTH K-Honeymooning in Russia-NY-1911-Dodd,Mead-8vo-341p-40 photos-1st ed (cc5) 50.00

WOOD,RUTH K-Tourist's California-NY-1914-Dodd,Mead-395p-fldg col map,illus-1st ed (d3) 20.00

WOOD,STANLEY-Over the Range to the Golden Gate-Chig-1889-351p-illus,lg col fldg map-1st ed (d3) 75.00

WOOD,STANLEY-Over the Range to the Golden Gate-Chig-1896-Donnelley-283p-cl (e1) 25.00

WOOD,STANLEY-Over the Range to the Golden Gate-Chig-1903-Donnelley & Sons-283p-blu illus cl,fldg map in rear,illus (b6) 20.00

WOOD,STANLEY-Over the Range to the Golden Gate-Chig-1904-pict cl,frntis,photos-Smith #11178 (t7) 10.00

WOOD,THOMAS-Cobbers, Journey from Essex to Australia-Lond-1938-Oxford U Pr-288p-beige cl-New ed (p8,discol,sl tn sp,autg) 10.00

WOOD,W-Index Entomologicus-Lond-1839-Wood-266p-g dec maroon mor,a.e.g.,54 handcol plts (bb3) 850.00

WOOD,WILLIAM-Captains of the Civil War-NY-1921-423p-pict cl,col fldg maps-1st ed (c4) 22.50

WOOD-ALLEN,MARY-What a Young Girl Ought to Know-Phila-(1897)-Vir Publ-190p-cl (d1,sl spot frnt cov) 17.50

WOODALL,RONALD-Taken By the Wind-Bost-1977-NYGS-4to-unpgd-cl,col photos-1st US ed (z4,dj) 30.00

WOODBERRY,GEORGE E-History of Wood Engraving-NY-1883-Harpers-sm 4to-221p wi index,illus,g dec tan cl (t1) 75.00

WOODBRIDGE,ELIZABETH-Jonathon Papers-Bost,NY-1912-12mo-233p (m3) 12.50

WOODBURY,GEORGE-John Goffe's Legacy-NY-(1955)-Norton-8vo-272p-sketches-1st ed (dd5,dj) 15.00

WOODBURY,GEORGE-John Goffe's Mill-NY-(1948)-Norton-8vo-245p-sketches-1st ed (dd5,dj) 20.00

WOODBURY,RICHARD B-Prehistoric Agriculture at Point of Pines, Arizona-np-1961-Scty for Amer Arch-xiii,(1),48p-prtd wrps,16 figs,4 tabls (mm1) 15.00

WOODCOCK,LOUISE-Wiggles-NY-(1953)-S&S-Little Golden Bk-1st ed (r3) 12.00

WOODFORD,FRANK B-Father Abraham's Sons-Detr-1961-305p-illus-1st ed (n3,dj) 40.00

WOODFORD,JACK-Sin and Such-NY-1930-Panurge-ltd to 1500c,nbrd-1st ed (hh5) 20.00

WOODFORD,M H-Manual of Falconry-Lond-(1961)-Black-192p-rprnt (c9,dj) 20.00

WOODFORDE,C-Stained Glass in Somerset 1250 to 1830-Lond-1946-314p-52 plts(12 col)-1st ed (cc8,dj) 85.00

WOODHAM-SMITH,CECIL-Great Hunger-Lond-(1962)-H Hamilton-8vo-510p-19 illus,fldg map-1st ed (gg5,dj tn) 25.00

WOODHOUSE,PHILIP R-Monte Cristo-Seattle-1979-Mountaineers-307,(1)p-blk cl (b6,f,dj) 10.00

WOODING,F H-Angler's Book of Canadian Fishes-Don Mills-(1959)-Collins-303p-cl,illus-1st ed (pp8,f,sl wn dj) 35.00*

WOODING,F H-Angler's Book of Canadian Fishes-Don Mills-1959-8vo-303p-illus,G Fairbairn-1st ed (m3,vf,dj) 25.00

WOODING,F H-Canada's Atlantic Salmon-Ottawa-1956-4to-23p-dec wrps,photos-2nd ed (m3,f) 25.00

WOODLEY,EDWARD C-Legends of French Canada-Tor-1931-Nelson-vii,105p-illus (k10,pres) 20.00*

WOODLEY,THOMAS F-Thaddeus Stevens-Harrisburg-1934-664p-illus-1st ed (c4) 75.00

WOODMAN,MARION-Addiction to Perfection-Tor-1982-Inner City Bks-wrps-1st ed (n8,f) 11.00

WOODMAN,MARY-Jams and Preserves, Bottled Fruit and Vegetables, Chutneys and Pickles-Lond-nd(1940's)-Foulsham-red bds (l6,sl sunned bds) 20.00

WOODRESS,JAMES-Yankee's Odyssey-Phila-(1958)-Lippincott-8vo-347p-6 illus-1st ed (ff5,f,dj) 12.50

WOODRUFF,GEORGE C-History of Hillside, N.J.-Hillside-(1934)-278,(53)p-cl,illus (aa6) 35.00

WOODRUFF,HIRAM-Trotting Horse of America-Phila-1868-Porter & Coates-12mo-xxxvi,412p-frntis,5 plts-presumed 1st ed (o2,wn edges & cors) 45.00

WOODS,HENRY F-God's Loaded Dice-Caxton-1948-Caldwell-298p-illus-1st ed (pp4,dj sp fade) 18.00

WOODS,JOHN-Two Years' Residence on the English Prairie of Illinois-Chig-1968-Donnelley & Sons-illus,map-Lakeside Classics (ff4) 20.00

WOODS,MACDARA-Early Morning Matins-Dublin-(1972)-Gallery Pr-wrps-1st trd ed (z8,vf) 17.50

WOODS,S D-Lights and Shadows of Life on the Pacific Coast-NY-1910-Funk & Wagnalls-8vo-(viii)+474p+frntis,cl-1st ed (y4) 50.00

WOODS,SARA-An Improbable Fiction-NY-1971-Holt-1st US ed (k4,f,dj) 15.00

WOODS,SARA-And Shame the Devil-NY-1972-Holt-1st US ed (e4,f,dj) 15.00

WOODS,SARA-Bloody Instructions-Lond-1962-Collins CC-1st ed (d4,dj) 40.00

WOODS,SARA-Case is Altered-NY-1967-Harper-1st US ed (f4,sl fox,dj) 15.00

WOODS,SARA-Dearest Enemy-NY-1981-St.Martin's-1st US ed (f4,f,dj) 15.00

WOODS,SARA-Done to Death-NY-1975-HRW-1st US ed (x9,f,dj) 10.00

WOODS,SARA-Error of the Moon-1963-CCC-1st ed (s10,chip dj) 15.00

WOODS,SARA-Exit Murderer-NY-1978-St.Martin's-1st US ed (g4,f,dj) 12.50

WOODS,SARA-Law's Delay-NY-1977-St.Martin's-1st US ed (g4,f,dj) 12.50

WOODS,SARA-Let's Choose Executors-NY-1967-Harper-1st Amer ed (e4,dj) 13.50

WOODS,SARA-Most Grievous Murder-NY-1982-St.Martin's-1st US ed (f4,f,dj) 13.50

WOODS,SARA-My Life is Done-NY-1976-St.Martin's-1st Amer ed (e4,f,dj) 12.50

WOODS,SARA-Tarry and Be Hanged-NY-1971-Holt-1st US ed (f4,f,dj) 20.00

WOODS,SARA-Third Encounter-NY-1963-Harper-1st US ed (d4,dj) 25.00

WOODS,SARA-This Fatal Writ-NY-(1979)-St.Martin's-1st US ed (j3,f,dj) 15.00

WOODS,SARA-Though I Know She Lies-NY-1972-Holt-1st US ed (g4,f,dj) 15.00

WOODS,SARA-Yet She Must Die-NY-1974-Holt-1st Amer ed (e4,f,dj) 12.50

WOODSIDE,MARIE-ED.-Flowering Plants from Cuban Gardens-Havana-1951-cl (x6) 20.00

WOODTHORPE,R C-Necessary Corpse-1939-DD-1st ed (x7,rnfrcd dj) 35.00

WOODWARD,ARTHUR-Feud on the Colorado-LA-(1955)-Westernlore Pr-165p-red cl,plts-1st ed (h2,dj) 25.00

WOODWARD,ARTHUR-Jim Waters-LA-Corral of Wstnrs,Publ #23-15p-pict wrps,illus-wrps,Keepsake #43-scarce (t7) 45.00

WOODWARD,CARL R-Development of Agriculture in New Jersey, 1640 to 1880-New Brunswick-1927-321p-wrps,illus (aa6) 30.00

WOODWARD,CARL R-Ploughs and Politicks-New Brunswick-1941-xxvi,468p-cl,plts (aa6) 35.00

WOODWARD,E M-Bonaparte's Park and the Murals-Trenton-1879-116p-wrps,plts (aa6) 45.00

WOODWARD,E M-Our Campaigns-Phila-1865-Potter-362p (o7,wn & stnd cl,fox) 50.00

WOODWARD,EDWARD-House of Terror-1930-Mystery League-1st US ed (x7,dj) 12.00

WOODWARD,EDWARD-House of Terror-NY-1930-Mystery League-1st US ed (g4,dj) 10.00

WOODWARD,GEO-Woodward's Graperies and Horticultural Buildings-NY-1865-Excelsior-139p-cl,illus-presumed 1st ed (x6) 65.00

WOODWARD,GEORGE E-Woodward's Country Homes-NY-1868-Woodward-sm 8vo-188p-grn cl,150 text illus (c2,sl soil) 75.00

WOODWARD,JOSEPH-Diarrhoea and Dysentery-Wash-1879-869p-col lithos,photos-(vol.1 of part 2 of Med. & Surgical Hist of War of the Rebellion)-1st ed (dd3) 300.00

WOODWARD,JOSEPH-ET AL-Medical and Surgical History of the War of Rebellion, 1861 to 65-Wash-1870 to 83-3 vols-orig grn cl-1st ed,vols 1 & 2 are 1st prtg (dd3,hngs crack) 1,500.00

WOODWARD,MARY D-Checkered Years-Caldwell-1937-Caxton-265p-photos-1st ed (ee4,dj flaps attached,autg) 25.00

WOODWARD,SAMUEL-ET AL-Reports and Other Documents Relating to the State Lunatic Hospital at Worcester, Mass-Bost-1837-200p-cl backed bds,litho-1st ed (dd3,ex-libr) 350.00

WOODWARD,W E-Lafayette-NY-(1938)-Farrar & Rinehart-8vo-472p-18 illus-1st ed (jj5,f,dj) 25.00

WOODWORTH,J-Kodiak Bear--Alaskan Adventure-PA-1958-204p-photos (gg3,f,dj) 65.00

WOODWORTH,JIM-Kodiak Bear-Harrisburg-1958-8vo-204p-photos-1st ed (m3) 70.00

WOODWORTH,JOHN-ET AL-Cholera Epidemic of 1873 in the U.S.-Wash-1875-1025p-1st ed (dd3,hng crack) 125.00

WOOFTER,T J,JR.-ET AL-Landlord and Tenant on the Cotton Plantation-Wash-1936-WPA/Rsrch Mono V-288p-wrps-scarce (aa1) 25.00

WOOLEY,ROGER-Fly-Fisher's Flies-Beckenham-1950-16mo-59p-illus-3rd ed (m3,vf) 40.00

WOOLF,CECIL-ED.-Authors Take Sides on Vietnam-Lond-(1967)-Peter Owen-true 1st ed & only one publ in cl (bb2,f,dj) 160.00

WOOLF,LEONARD-Beginning Again-NY-1964-HBW-1st US ed (x9,dj tn) 10.00

WOOLF,VIRGINIA-Between the Acts-Lond-1941-Hogarth Pr-1st ed (l9,fox,dj soil) 185.00

WOOLF,VIRGINIA-Between the Acts-NY-(1941)-Harcourt-8vo-cl-1st Amer ed (x3,dj) 55.00

WOOLF,VIRGINIA-Books and Portraits-NY-1977-1st Amer ed (r2,f,dj) 25.00

WOOLF,VIRGINIA-Captain's Death Bed and Other Essays-Lond-1950-Hogarth Pr-1st Brit ed (l9,sl fox,dj) 150.00

WOOLF,VIRGINIA-Captain's Death Bed and Other Essays-NY-1950-Harcourt Brace-1st ed (t4,dj tn) 30.00

WOOLF,VIRGINIA-Captain's Death Bed-NY-(1950)-Harcourt Brace-1st ed (ee2,f,sl brwnd dj) 50.00

WOOLF,VIRGINIA-Common Reader-1925-Harcourt Brace-1st Amer ed (x2) 45.00

WOOLF,VIRGINIA-Common Reader-NY-(1948)-Harcourt,Brace-ser.1 & 2 in one vol,Kirkpatrick A18e-1st Amer of Cmbnd Series (x10,f,dj) 35.00

WOOLF,VIRGINIA-Common Reader: Second Series-1932-Hogarth Pr-1st ed (x2,dj sl chip & sp sunned) 190.00

WOOLF,VIRGINIA-Contemporary Writers by...-Lond-1965-Hogarth Pr-160p-cl-1st ed (nn4,f,f dj,f box) 70.00

WOOLF,VIRGINIA-Death of the Moth and Other Essays-Lond-1942-Hogarth Pr-157p-cl,V Bell designed dj-Woolmer 500-1st ed (nn4,dj) 85.00

WOOLF,VIRGINIA-Death of the Moth and Other Essays-NY-(1942)-Harcourt,Brace-1st Amer ed (l9,f,dj sl soil) 100.00

WOOLF,VIRGINIA-Flush-NY-(1933)-Harcourt,Brace-185p-cl-1st Amer ed so stated (l1,dj) 20.00

WOOLF,VIRGINIA-Granite & Rainbow-Lond-1958-Hogarth Pr-wi Bk Society wraparound band-1st ed (m7,f,dj edge wn,sunned sp) 100.00

WOOLF,VIRGINIA-Granite and Rainbow-1958-Harcourt Brace-1st Amer ed (x2,dj) 80.00

WOOLF,VIRGINIA-Granite and Rainbow-NY-1958-V Bell dj-1st Amer ed (r2,sl sun,dj sl tn,sp sun) 40.00

WOOLF,VIRGINIA-Haunted House and Other Short Stories-Lond-1943-Hogarth Pr-1st ed (l9,f,dj sl soil) 200.00

WOOLF,VIRGINIA-Haunted House and Other Short Stories-NY-(1944)-Harcourt,Brace-lg crn 8vo-150p-Blu cl bds-V Bell designed dj-ltd to 4,000c-1st US ed (e5,f,dj) 65.00

WOOLF,VIRGINIA-Haunted House and Other Stories-NY-(1944)-Harcourt Brace-1st Amer ed (cc2,f,dj sp chip,drknd) 75.00

WOOLF,VIRGINIA-Hours in a Library-NY-1957-Harcourt-priv prntd for friends of publ-1st ed (m7,wn glassine dj) 100.00

WOOLF,VIRGINIA-Hours in a Library-NY-1957-HB-tissue dj,wi card laid in,"With Season's Greetings from H,B & Co"-1st ed (f8,f,chip dj) 75.00

WOOLF,VIRGINIA-Letter to a Young Poet-Lond-1932-Hogarth Pr-8vo-pict wrps-1st ed (jj8,sl soil wrps) 125.00

WOOLF,VIRGINIA-Letter to a Young Poet-Lond-1932-Hogarth Pr-wrps-Hogarth Letters No.8-1st ed (j6,sun wrps) 65.00

WOOLF,VIRGINIA-Letters-NY-1956-HBCo-1st ed (b8,f,sl tn dj) 45.00

WOOLF,VIRGINIA-London Scene-NY-1975-Random-1st Amer ed (t4,f,f dj) 10.00

WOOLF,VIRGINIA-Moment and Other Essays-NY-(1948)-Harcourt Brace-1st Amer ed (cc2,f,dj) 50.00

WOOLF,VIRGINIA-Monday or Tuesday-NY-1921-1st Amer ed (r2,uncut,sl chip sp,sl sun) 75.00

WOOLF,VIRGINIA-Mr.Bennett and Mrs.Brown-Lond-1924-Hogarth-prtd wrps-Kirkpatrick A7-1st ed (hh4,f) 325.00

WOOLF,VIRGINIA-Mrs.Dalloway-1925-Harcourt Brace-1st Amer ed (x2,sl soil) 85.00

WOOLF,VIRGINIA-Mrs.Dalloway-Lond-(1925)-Hogarth Pr-8vo-cl-ltd to 2000c-Kirkpatrick A9-1st ed (jj8,sl rub,sl fox) 275.00

WOOLF,VIRGINIA-Orlando, a Biography-NY-1928-Crosby Gaige-ltd to 861c,autg-1st ed (l9,f) 600.00

WOOLF,VIRGINIA-Orlando-NY-1928-Crosby Gaige-ltd to 861c,nbrd,autg-1st ed (j6) 650.00

WOOLF,VIRGINIA-Orlando-NY-1928-Crosby Gaige-sm royal 8vo-blk cl,t.e.g.,ltd to 861c,nbrd,autg-Kirkpatrick A11a-1st ed (w6) 850.00

WOOLF,VIRGINIA-Reviewing-1939-Hogarth-blu gry wrps stmpd in red-Sixpenny Pamphlet,No.4-1st ed (cc2,few pgs brwng) 55.00

WOOLF,VIRGINIA-Room of One's Own-NY/Lond-1929-Fountain Pr/Hogarth Pr-tall 8vo-rose cl-ltd to 492c,autg-1st ed (kk8,f,lacks dj) 1,000.00

WOOLF,VIRGINIA-Second Common Reader-1932-Harcourt Brace-1st Amer ed (x2,dj sp sl fade) 150.00

WOOLF,VIRGINIA-Voyage Out-(1920)-Doran-auth 1st bk-1st Amer ed (x2) 135.00

WOOLF,VIRGINIA-Voyage Out-NY-(1920)-Doran-grn cl bds-auth 1st bk-1st Amer ed (m7,sl cov spot,sl edge wn) 85.00

WOOLF,VIRGINIA-Walter Sickert-Lond-1934-Hogarth Pr-8vo-28p-prntd wrps-Kirkpatrick A20a-1st ed (w6,sl wn) 65.00

WOOLF,VIRGINIA-Waves-NY-(1931)-Harcourt-8vo-cl-1st ed (x3,dj sp chip & sunned) 120.00

WOOLF,VIRGINIA-Writer's Diary-NY-1954-V Bell illus dj-1st US ed (s5,sl chip dj) 30.00

WOOLF,VIRGINIA-Years-NY-(1937)-Harcourt-8vo-blu cl-1st Amer ed (x3,dj chip,sp sun) 50.00

WOOLLCOTT,ALEXANDER-Letters of...-NY-1944-Viking-1st ed (hh5,f,dj) 12.50

WOOLLCOTT,ALEXANDER-Long,Long Ago-NY-1943-1st ed (t5,chip dj) 15.00

WOOLLEN,WILLIAM W-Biographical and Historical Sketches of Early Indiana-Indpls-1883-568p-cl (j1) 50.00

WOOLLEN,WILLIAM W-Inside Passage to Alaska 1792 to 1920-Cleve-1924-Clark Publ-2 vols-t.e.g.,illus,v scarce-1st ed (d7,part uncut,f) 250.00

WOOLLEY,C LEONARD-Development of Sumerian Art-Lond-1935-Faber-140p-gry cl,b&w & col illus-1st ed (r10,sl drknd & wn) 40.00

WOOLLEY,L H-California 1849 to 1913-Glendale-1913-48p-dec wrps wi bds holder,frntis-1st ed (t7) 25.00

WOOLLEY,R-Outer Layers of a Star-Oxford-1953-Clarendon Pr-x+306p-blu cl-1st ed (a2,dj) 20.00

WOOLNER,F-Grouse & Grouse Hunting-NY-1970-192p-photos (gg3,vf,dj) 17.00

WOOLNER,FRANK-Grouse & Grouse Hunting-NY-1970-4to-319p-photos-1st ed (m3,f,dj) 27.50

WOOLNER,FRANK-Trout Hunting-NY-1977-8vo-246p-photos (m3,autg,vf,dj) 12.00

WOOLRICH,CORNELL-Dark Side of Love-1965-Walker-1st ed (x7,f,dj) 175.00

WOOLRICH,CORNELL-Hotel Room-(1958)-Random-1st ed (x7,f,dj) 65.00

WOOLRICH,CORNELL-Hotel Room-NY-(1958)-Random-1st ed (v10,f,sp fade dj) 50.00

WOOLRICH,CORNELL-Night Has a Thousand Eyes-1945-F&R-1st ed (x7,sl flake dj sp) 125.00

WOOLRICH,CORNELL-Nightmare-1956-DM-1st ed (x7,f,dj) 185.00

WOOLRICH,CORNELL-Rendevous in Black-NY-1948-Rinehart-1st ed (g4,chip dj) 50.00

WOOLRICH,CORNELL-Ten Faces of...-Lond-(1966)-T V Boardman-1st Brit ed (ff6,f,sl soil dj) 60.00

WOOLRICH,CORNELL-Time of Her Life-1931-Liveright-1st ed (x7) 65.00

WOOLRICH,CORNELL-Times Square-1929-Liveright-1st ed (x7,f) 95.00

WOOLRICH,CORNELL-Violence-1958-DM-1st ed (x7,f,dj) 185.00

WOOLRICH,CORNELL-Violence-1958-Dodd-1st ed (s10,dj soil,sp fade) 110.00

WORCESTER,A-Small Hospitals-NY-1905-114p (dd3) 100.00

WORCESTER,JOSEPH E-Primary Dictionary of the English Language-Bost-(1860)-Brewer & Tileston-384p-1/2 lea (k1) 20.00

WORCESTER,THOMAS K-Portrait of Colorado-Portland-1976-Ore Mus of Sci & Ind-sq 4to-96p-cl,illus,photos-1st ed (z4,dj) 10.00

WORDSWORTH,WILLIAM-Poetical Works of...-Edinburgh-1882-Paterson-lg 8vo-11 vols-g stmpd blu cl (t1) 225.00

WORK,JOHN M-Why Things Happen to Happen-Chig-nd-Nat'l Office Soc Party-59p-stapled wrps (r1) 25.00

WORK,JOHN-Journal of...-Cleve-1923-209p-t.e.g.,illus-NW Hist Ser,Vol.1-1st ed (g7,unopened,f) 200.00

WORK,JOHN-Snake Country Expedition of 1830 to 1831-Norman-(1971)-172p-illus-1st Okla ed (d7,f,dj) 40.00

WORK,MONROE N-Bibliography of the Negro in Africa and America-NY-1965-Argosy Antiquarian Ltd-tall thk 8vo-xxiv,698p-cl-rprnt of 1928 1st ed (w2,rub) 65.00

WORLEY,LEONARD G-Spiders of Washington-Seattle-1932-U Wash Pr-8vo-63p-wrps-UW Publ in Biol,Vol.1,No.1-1st ed (gg5) 12.50

WORMINGTON,H M-Prehistoric Indians of the Southwest-Denver-1947-Col Mus of Nat Hist-191p-gry cl,58 illus-1st ed (m2,dj) 35.00

WORMSER,RICHARD-Battalion of Saints-NY-1961-249p-1st ed (t7) 15.00

WORRELL,JOHN-Diamond in the Rough-Indpls-1906-Wm B Burford-282p-frntis-Howes W679-1st ed (dd4) 35.00

WORSFOLD,W BASIL-Lord Milner's Work in South Africa-NY-1906-620p-blu cl,illus-1st ed (gg2) 75.00

WORSLEY,F A-Shackleton's Boat Journey-NY-1977-Norton-8vo-220p-39 illus,1 map,e.p. maps-1st ed (cc7,dj) 20.00*

WORSLEY,PETER-Trumpet Shall Sound-Lond-1957-MacGibbon & Keel-8vo-290p-cl,illus-1st ed (y5,chip dj) 22.00

WORSNOP,E M-Nurse's Handbook of Cookery-Lond-1905-Black-106p-bds-2nd ed (n6) 20.00

WORTHAM,LOUIS J-History of Texas-Ft.Worth-1924-5 vols,3/4 lea,illus,maps (t8,sl wn) 150.00

WOUK,HERMAN-Caine Mutiny-GC-1951-1st ed (j5,dj) 85.00

WOUK,HERMAN-Don't Stop the Carnival-GC-1965-Doubleday-1st ed (e10,sl wn dj) 25.00

WOUK,HERMAN-Lomokome Papers-NY-(1968)-Pocket Books-pbk orig,not issued in hdbk-1st ed (k5,wrps) 20.00

WOUK,HERMAN-Natures Way-GC-1958-Dbldy-8vo-cl-1st ed (x3,sl chip dj) 55.00

WOUK,HERMAN-This Is My God-GC-1959-Dbldy-1st ed (b10,f,dj) 30.00

WOUK,HERMAN-War and Remembrance-1978-Little,Brown-1st ed (x2,f,dj) 25.00

WPA AMERICAN GUIDE SERIES-Oregon Trail-NY-(1939)-244p-pict bds,illus,fldg map in rear-1st ed (c7) 45.00

WPA AMERICAN GUIDE SERIES-Oregon-Portland-(1940)-549p-e.p. map,illus,fldg map in rear pckt-1st ed (c7,chip dj) 40.00

WPA-Angler's Guide for Washington & Vicinity-Long Island-1941-8vo-61p-illus (m3,f) 10.00

WPA-Copper Camp-NY-1976-Hastings Hs-308p-red cl,illus-6th prtg (b6,vf,dj) 6.00

WPA-Mission San Xavier Del Bac-NY-(1940)-34p text+photos-scarce-1st ed (j7,sl chip dj) 30.00

WPA-Washington-Portland-1941-Binfords & Mort-687p-grn cl,pckt fldg map,illus-1st ed (b6) 50.00

WRA-Story of Human Conservation-Wash D.C.-(1946)-US Dept of Interior-xvi+212p-wrps,photos (h2,sl soil) 40.00

WRAGG,D W-Flight Before Flying-NY-(1974)-F Fell Publ-sm 4to-192p-cl,illus,illus e.p.-1st ed (s2,dj) 30.00

WRAY,J E-ED.-How to Play First Base-NY-(1905)-38p+92p ads-wrps-scarce-Smith 7461-1st ed (n1,sl wn,rnfrcd sp) 35.00

WREN,M K-Curiosity Didn't Kill the Cat-NY-1973-Dbldy CC-1st ed (j4,f,dj) 25.00

WREN,M K-Nothing's Certain but Death-GC-1978-Dbldy-1st ed (hh2,f,sl wn dj) 25.00

WREN,R C-Potter's New Cyclopedia of Botanical Drugs and Preparations-Rustington-1970-Health-400p (x6,dj wn) 25.00

WRIGHT,A T-Islandia-1942-F & R-auth only bk-1st ed (x2,f,dj sl wn & tn) 100.00

WRIGHT,ALBERT D-Elements of the English Language-Cazenovia-1847-Henry & Sweetlands-126p-bds-4th ed (k1,rub) 17.50

WRIGHT,ALFRED J-Economic Geography of Ohio-Columbus-1953-217p-wrps,dbl cols,Div of Geo Survey,Bulletin 50 (b1) 12.50

WRIGHT,ANNA P-Burton Street Folks-Chig-(1913)-Bible Inst Colprtg Assoc-123p-wrps (a1) 12.50

WRIGHT,B S-Black Duck Spring-1966-Dutton-191p-illus-1st ed (bb3,f,dj) 20.00

WRIGHT,BARTON-Pueblo Shields-(Flagstaff)-(1976)-96p-photos-1st ed (u7,f,dj) 35.00

WRIGHT,BRUCE S-Black Duck Spring-NY-1966-8vo-191p-illus-1st ed (m3,f,dj) 20.00

WRIGHT,BRUCE S-High Tide & East Wind-Wash D.C.-1954-8vo-162p-illus-1st ed (m3,f,sl chip dj) 25.00

WRIGHT,CAROL-Cunard Cook Book-Lond-(1969)-Dent-tall 8vo-188p-g dec pnk cl,4p col plts,8p photos-1st ed (q8) 18.50

WRIGHT,CARROLL D-Industrial Revolution of the United States-Meadville-1895-362p-cl (b1) 20.00

WRIGHT,CHARLES-Absolutely Nothing to Get Alarmed About-NY-(1973)-FS&G-1st ed (c10,f,dj) 35.00

WRIGHT,D MACER-Gardening with Strawberries-NY-1973-Drake-207p-cl (x6,dj) 18.00

WRIGHT,DUDLEY-Vampires and Vampirism-Lond-1924-Wm Rider & Son-12mo-(viii)+220(4)p-red cl,(1st publ in 1914)-enlgd ed (y9) 45.00

WRIGHT,E W-ED.-Lewis & Dryden's Maritime History of the Pacific Northwest-Portland-1895-folio-494p-lea,illus-Tweney #87-Howes 693-1st ed (j7,scuff) 300.00

WRIGHT,ESTHER C-Loyalists of New Brunswick-Fredericton-(1955)-vi+365p-red cl-1st ed (h2,dj) 25.00

WRIGHT,FRANCES-Views of Society and Manners in America...-Cambridge-1963-292p-cl-rprntd from 1821 ed (d1,f,dj) 20.00

WRIGHT,FRANK L-An American Architecture-NY-1955-Horizon-lg 4to-268,(1)p-cl,frntis port,illus (pp7) 100.00

WRIGHT,FRANK L-An Autobiography-1933-Longmans,Green-371p+photos,cl (b6,sl fox) 125.00

WRIGHT,FRANK L-An Organic Architecture-Lond-1939-1st ed (h10,dj sl tn & soil) 250.00

WRIGHT,FRANK L-Architecture & Modern Life-NY/Lond-1937-illus-1st ed (h10) 125.00

WRIGHT,FRANK L-Early Work-NY-1968-Horizon-folio-207 photos & plans-1st ed (h10,box) 125.00

WRIGHT,FRANK L-Future of Architecture-NY-1953-Horizon-sq 4to-326p-cl,illus (pp7,dj) 60.00

WRIGHT,FRANK L-Genius & Mobocracy-NY-1949-1st ed (h10) 100.00

WRIGHT,FRANK L-Industrial Revolution Runs Away-NY-1969-illus-ltd ed,nbrd (h10,box) 225.00

WRIGHT,FRANK L-Japanese Print & Interpretation-NY-1967-folio-380 col plts-1st ed (h10,box) 300.00

WRIGHT,FRANK L-Letters to Apprentices-Fresno-1982 (h10,dj) 15.00

WRIGHT,FRANK L-Living City-NY-1958-Horizon-fldg col map in front tip in as iss,illus-1st ed (h10,dj) 135.00

WRIGHT,FRANK L-Man in Possession of His Earth-NY-1962-folio-illus-1st ed (r2) 45.00

WRIGHT,FRANK L-Natural House-NY-1954-Horizon Pr-4to-223p-cl,illus-Sweeney 992 (cc10) 100.00

WRIGHT,FRANK L-Natural House-NY-1954-Horizon-illus-1st ed (h10,sl chip dj) 75.00

WRIGHT,FRANK L-New House by Frank LLoyd Wright on Bear Run, Pennsylvania-NY-1938-MOMA-sm 4to-(20)p-illus wrps,illus-Sweeney 430-v scarce (cc10,sl wn & crease) 60.00

WRIGHT,FRANK L-Selected Drawings: Portfolio,Vol.1-NY-1977-Horizon-elephant folio-50 col plts,Japanese tyle boxed-ltd to 500c,nbrd (h10,as new in box,shppng box) 3,000.00

WRIGHT,FRANK L-Story of the Tower-NY-1956-Horizon-130 illus,6 col plts-1st ed (h10,dj rub & edge creased) 225.00

WRIGHT,FRANK L-Testament-NY-1957-1st ed (h10,sl rub dj) 125.00

WRIGHT,FRANK L-Testament-NY-1957-Horizon-lg 4to-256p-cl,illus(1 triple fldg)-Sweeney 1149-1st ed (pp7,dj) 150.00

WRIGHT,FRANK L-Two Lectures on Architecture-(1931)-Art Inst of Chig-8vo-red wrps,2000c prtd-1st ed (b6) 90.00

WRIGHT,G FREDERICK-Man & the Glacial Period-NY-1896-385p-1/2 lea & mrbld cov,t.e.g.,3 fldg maps,106 illus-2nd ed (a4) 35.00

WRIGHT,G N-Shores and Islands of the Mediterranean-Lond-(1840)-Fisher-1/2 pebbld lea & mrbld bds,mrbld e.p. & edges,63p engrvngs,t.p. vignette,dbl pg map (p6) 400.00

WRIGHT,GEORGE B-Nikon Manual-NY-1957-Universal Photo Bks-288p-illus-1st prtg (cc9,f) 75.00

WRIGHT,H F-ED.-Murder Manual-San Diego-1936-Wright House (d4,cov stns) 20.00

WRIGHT,H-Rehousing Urban America-1935-Columbia U Pr-illus-scarce-1st ed (h10) 125.00

WRIGHT,HAROLD B-Eyes of the World-Chig-(1914)-464p-cl-1st ed (m1) 15.00

WRIGHT,HENRY H-History of the Sixth Iowa Infantry-Iowa City-1923-539p-pict cl-1st ed (c4) 95.00

WRIGHT,HORACE W-Birds of the Boston Public Garden-Bost-1909-Houghton Mifflin-238p-1st ed (c9,cors bump) 25.00

WRIGHT,HORACE-Sweet Peas-Lond-1910-Jack-116p-papr cov bds,8 col plts-Pres Day Grdn ser (x6,bds wn) 12.00

WRIGHT,J WILLISTON-Lectures on Diseases of the Rectum-NY-1884-Bermingham-sm 8vo-170p-grn cl-1st ed (dd1) 20.00

WRIGHT,JOHN C-Crooked Tree, Indian Legends of Northern Michigan-np-1917-John C Wright-144p-dec cl-Streeter 7051 (z7,sp wn) 50.00

WRIGHT,JOHN C-Ella-Harbor Sprngs-(1911)-priv publ-132p-cl (d1) 50.00

WRIGHT,JOHN L-My Father Who is on Earth-NY-1946-1st ed (h10,dj) 125.00

WRIGHT,JOHN-Some Notable Altars-NY-1908-MacMillan-383p-g dec red cl,illus (r10) 50.00

WRIGHT,JULIA M-Among the Alaskans-Phila-(1883)-Presbyterian Bd of Pub-12mo-351p-dec blu bds,g dec sp,illus-1st ed (u8,sp chip & wn) 45.00

WRIGHT,JULIA M-Complete Home-Phila-(1879)-McCurdy-584p-cl (n1) 35.00

WRIGHT,L-Practical Poultry Keeper-NY-c.1870s-8vo-243p-orig cl,12 full-pg engrvngs-4th ed (y8,wn,lacks e.p.) 25.00

WRIGHT,LAWRENCE-Clean and Decent-NY-(1960)-Viking-xii+282p-wht cl,illus-1st ed (l2) 35.00

WRIGHT,LEONARD M,JR.-Fishing the Dry Fly as a Living Insect-NY-1972-8vo-187p-illus-1st ed (m3,vf,dj) 27.50

WRIGHT,LOUIS B-First Americans in North Africa-Princeton-1945-Princeton U Pr-8vo-227p-10 illus-1st ed (ff5) 25.00

WRIGHT,LOUIS B-Of Books and Men-Columbia-(1976)-U of SC-(20),179p-1st ed (m4,as new in dj) 9.50

WRIGHT,LOUIS B-West and By North-NY-1971-Delacorte-1st ed (v4,as new in dj) 20.00

WRIGHT,LYLE H-American Fiction 1774-1850-San Marino-1969-411p-cl-2nd revised ed (h1,as new in dj) 10.00

WRIGHT,LYLE H-American Fiction 1851-1875-San Marino-1978-438p-cl (h1,as new in dj) 10.00

WRIGHT,LYLE H-American Fiction 1876-1900-San Marino-1978-683p-cl (h1,as new in dj) 15.00

WRIGHT,MABEL O-Garden of a Commuter's Wife-NY-1901-MacMillan-ix,354p-g pict cov,8 photo plts (mm4,f) 25.00

WRIGHT,MABEL-Flowers and Ferns in Their Haunts-NY-1928(1901)-Macmillan-358p-cl,illus,photos (x6,f) 16.00

WRIGHT,MARCUS J-Official and Illustrated War Record...-Wash-1898-560p-dec blu cl wi gilt,4 col plts,maps (p2,lacks frnt e.p.,hngs weak) 150.00

WRIGHT,MICKEY-Playing Golf the Wright Way-NY-1962-photos-1st ed (ll7,f,dj) 15.00

WRIGHT,MRS D GIRAUD-Southern Girl in '61-NY-(1905)-258p-pict cl,illus-1st ed (n3,lacks frntis) 40.00

WRIGHT,MRS.J MCNAIR-Shoe Binders of New York-Phila-(1867)-Presbyterian Bd of Publ-237p-cl (d1,sl wn) 20.00

WRIGHT,O L-Frank Lloyd Wright: His Life, His Work, His Words-NY-1966-Horizon-illus-1st ed (h10,dj sl crease,tear rprd) 125.00

WRIGHT,RICHARD J-ED.-John Hunt Memoirs-Maumee-nd-94p-wrps,dbl cols (j1) 12.50

WRIGHT,RICHARD-Color Curtain-Cleve-1956-World-1st ed (v5,f,dj) 50.00

WRIGHT,RICHARD-Native Son-NY,Lond-1940-Harper-2nd state gry bndg,2nd state (grayish)dj-1st ed (cc1,dj sl chip) 60.00

WRIGHT,RICHARD-Native Son-NY-1940-Harper-1st bndg blu,1st issue dj-1st ed (t6,wn dj) 125.00

WRIGHT,RICHARD-Pagan Spain-NY-1957-Harper-1st ed (v5,sl soil dj) 35.00

WRIGHT,RICHARDSON-ED.-House & Garden's Second Book of Houses-NY-1925-Conde Nast-4to-191p-red cl,illus (r10,sl wn,spot) 20.00

WRIGHT,RICHARDSON-Forgotten Ladies-Phila,Lond-1928-Lippincott-307p-cl,32p plts-1st ed so stated (a1) 20.00

WRIGHT,RICHARDSON-Gardening with the Experts-NY-1941-Macmillan-239p-cl (x6,dj) 10.00

WRIGHT,RICHARDSON-Practical Book of Outdoor Flowers-Phila,Lond-(1924)-Lippincott-319p-cl (m1) 15.00

WRIGHT,ROBERT M-Dodge City the Cowboy Capital and the Great Southwest-(Wichita)-(ca.1930)-R M Wright-342p-pict covs,illus-Six Guns #2456 (dd4) 50.00

WRIGHT,ROY V-ED.-Car Builders' Cyclopedia of American Practices-NY-1943-1324p-16th ed (n4) 75.00

WRIGHT,ROY V-ED.-Car Builders' Dictionary-NY-1912-1025p-7th ed (n4) 135.00

WRIGHT,ROY V-ED.-Car Builders' Dictionary-NY-1916-1066p-8th ed (n4) 125.00

WRIGHT,SEAN-Sherlock Holmes Cookbook-NY-1976-Drake-1st ed (w9,f,dj) 45.00

WRIGHT,THOMAS-Womankind in Western Europe-Lond-1869-Groombridge & Sons-340p-qtr blu lea,mrbld bds,t.e.g.,frntis,9 col plts-1st ed (mm8,rbnd,new e.p.) 250.00*

WRIGHT,WILLIAM C-Directory of New Jersey Newspapers, 1765 to 1970-Trenton-1977-xxi,319p-cl (aa6) 40.00

WRISTON,JENNIE A-Pioneer's Odyssey-Menasha-1943-92p-frntis-1st ed (t7,f) 50.00

WROTH,WILLIAM-Christian Images in Hispanic New Mexico-Colo Spgs-(1982)-Taylor Museum collection-215 intermixed single & dbl col pgs,wrps,photos(some col),map-1st ed (u7,f) 25.00

WROTH,WILLIAM-ED.-Hispanic Crafts of the Southwest-Colo Spgs-1977-118p-wrps,photos-1st ed (u7,f) 20.00

WULFF,LEE-Atlantic Salmon-NY-1958-4to-222p-col plts,photos-1st ed (m3,f,tape reinfrcd dj) 45.00

WULFF,LEE-Atlantic Salmon-NY-1958-Barnes-4to-1st trd ed (gg7,wn dj) 40.00

WUORINEN,JOHN H-Finns on the Delaware-NY-1938-179p-blu cl,frontis port,1 text map (b6,f,dj) 20.00

WURLITZER CENTENNIAL COOK BOOK-No Tonawanda-1956-R Wurlitzer Co-172p-ribbon mrkr,illus (k6) 30.00

WURLITZER,RUDOLPH-Nog-NY-1969-auth 1st bk-1st ed (r5,dj) 20.00

WURLITZER,RUDOLPH-Quake-NY-1972-1st ed (r5,f,dj) 20.00

WYANDOT COUNTY-THE HISTORY OF...OHIO...-Chig-1884-Leggett,Conaway-1065p-new cl (j1,rebnd) 100.00

WYATT,GERALDINE-Buffalo Gold-1948-Longmans,Green-1st ed (v8,dj wn,chip) 10.00

WYCHERLEY,GEORGE-Buccaneers of the Pacific-Indpls-1928-Bobbs Merrill-8vo-444p-brwn cl,dec e.p. (ee7,hng weak,sl fox) 65.00

WYCKOFF,WILLIAM C-Silk Goods of America-NY-1879-156p-cl (aa6) 75.00

WYDENBRUCK,NORA-Doctor Mesmer-Lond-1947-John Westhouse-16mo-208p-russet cl-1st ed (y9,wn dj) 25.00

WYDOSKI,R S-Inland Fishes of Washington-1979-U of Wash-220p-76 col photos (bb3,f,dj) 25.00

WYETH,ANDREW-Four Seasons-NY-nd-Art in Amer-folio-blk/grn cl,12 col illus (r10,f,box) 45.00

WYETH,JOHN A-With Sabre and Scapel-NY-1914-535p-illus-1st ed (c4) 115.00

WYETH,JOHN-An Epitome of Therapeutics with Special Reference to the Laboratory Products of John Wyeth & Brother-Phila-1901-371p-trade cat (dd3) 50.00

WYETH,NATHANIEL-Journal of...1831 to 36-Eugene-1899-262p-wrps,2 fldg maps,1 text map-Sources of Hist of Or,Vol.1,prts 3 to 6-Tweney #89-scarce-1st ed (h7,chip & rprd wrps) 85.00

WYETH,WALTER N-Henrietta Feller and the Grand Ligne Mission-Phila-1898-234p-cl (l1) 17.50

WYKEHAM,P-Santos Dumont-NY-(1963)-8vo-278p-cl,16p plts (s2,dj) 25.00

WYKES,ALAN-Royal Hampshire Regiment-Lond-1968-127p-illus-Famous Regiments ser-1st ed (b7,f,dj) 25.00

WYLER,ROSE-Oil Comes to Us-NY-1937-Georges Duplaix-28p-wrps,col illus-1st ed (ee10) 15.00

WYLER,SEYMOUR B-Book of Old Silver-NY-(1937)-Crown-x,447p-photos-7th ed (u5,dj wn,tn) 28.50

WYLIE,ELINOR-Mr.Hodge and Mr.Hazard-NY-1928-8vo-256p-1st ed (w6,f,sl chip dj) 35.00

WYLIE,ELINOR-Nets to Catch the Wind-Lond-1928-Knopf-slim 8vo-41p-1st Brit ed (w6,dj) 50.00

WYLIE,ELINOR-Nets to Catch the Wind-NY-1921-1st issue,wi unwatermrkd pap-1st bk under her name-1st ed (j5) 75.00

WYLIE,ELINOR-Orphan Angel-NY-1926-Knopf-cl bkd bds,ltd to 160 lg pap copies prntd on Borzoi Rag Pap,autg-1st ed (w6,fade) 200.00

WYLIE,PHILIP-Best of Crunch and Des-NY-1954-Rinehart-1st ed (y1,f,dj) 35.00

WYLIE,PHILIP-Big Ones Get Away-NY,Tor-(1940)-Farrar & Rinehart-drwngs,pict dj-1st ed (bb1,sl chip & tn dj) 150.00

WYLIE,PHILIP-Denizens of the Deep-NY-1953-8vo-222p (m3,f,dj) 13.00

WYLIE,PHILIP-Disappearance-NY-1951-1st ed (o5,sl chip dj) 30.00

WYLIE,PHILIP-Fish and Tin Fish-Tor,NY-(1944)-Farrar & Rinehart-1st ed (bb1,dj sp sl wn) 125.00

WYLIE,PHILIP-Generation of Vipers-NY,Tor-(1942)-Farrar & Rinehart-1st ed (bb1,sp chip dj) 85.00

WYLIE,PHILIP-They Both Were Naked-NY-1965-1st ed (m4,vf,dj) 15.00

WYLIE,PHILIP-Three to be Read-NY,Tor-(1951)-Rinehart-1st ed (bb1,f,sl chip dj) 20.00

WYLIE,PHILIP-Tomorrow-NY-(1954)-1st ed (k9,edge wn dj) 12.00

WYLLIE,H S-Fragmentary History of Saint Augustine-(Saint Augustine)-(1914)-(52)p-wrps,dbl cols (l1) 17.50

WYLLIE,JOHN-Killer Breath-NY-1979-Dbldy CC-1st ed (g4,f,dj) 10.00

WYLLY,COL H C-History of the Manchester Regiment-Lond-1923,5-2 vols-dec grn cl,maps,illus,11 col plts-1st ed (b7,lacks 6 pckt maps) 125.00

WYLLYS,RUFUS K-Arizona-Phoenix-(1950)-Hobson & Herr-408p-pict e.p.,maps,illus-Six Guns 2458-1st ed (bb4,dj) 50.00

WYMAN,DONALD-Hedges,Screens and Windbreaks-NY,Lond-(1938)-xviii,249p-1st ed (x5) 14.00

WYMAN,LELAND C-Mountainway of the Navajo-Tucson-(1975)-262p-photos-1st ed (v7,f,dj) 35.00

WYMAN,LELAND C-Navaho Sandpainting-Colo Spgs-1960-88p-wrps,photos-1st ed (v7) 20.00

WYMAN,LELAND C-Southwest Indian Drypainting-Albuq-(1983)-U of NM Pr-320p-col illus-1st ed (ff4,dj) 25.00

WYMAN,LELAND C-Windways of the Navaho-Colo Spgs-1962-wrps,328p+60 figs(incl 6 col)-1st ed (v7,f) 25.00

WYMAN,LUTHER E-Field Book of Birds of the Southwestern United States-Bost-1925-Houghton Mifflin-1st ed (c9,dj) 30.00

WYMAN,WALKER D-ED.-California Emigrant Letters-NY-(1952)-Bookman Assoc-177p-illus (dd4,dj) 15.00

WYMAN,WALKER D-Wild Horse of the West-Caldwell-1945-348p-illus-1st ed (g7,f,chip dj) 65.00

WYMOND,CHARLES E-Atlas of Railway Traffic Maps-Chig-1923-9th prtg (n4) 60.00

WYNDHAM,JOHN-Midwich Cuckoos-NY-1957-Ballantine hdcov bks-#299-1st ed (y1,sl tn dj) 75.00

WYNN,MARGARET B-My Dining Generation-Greenville-(1962)-Office Sply Co-104p-blu wrps,comb bndg (l6,flawed wrps) 25.00

WYNNE,ANTHONY-Death of a Banker-1934-Lippincott-1st Amer ed (s10,tape rprd dj) 25.00

WYNNE,ANTHONY-Emergency Exit-NY-1944-Messner-1st US ed (l4,dj) 25.00

WYNNE,ANTHONY-Fourth Finger-1929-Lippincott-1st Amer ed (s10,dj sp chip & fade) 25.00

WYNNE,ANTHONY-Green Knife-Phila-1932-Lippincott-1st US ed (f4,dj) 35.00

WYNNE,ANTHONY-Horseman of Death-1928-Lippincott-1st Amer ed (s10) 12.50

WYNNE,ANTHONY-Yellow Crystal-1930-Lippincott-1st Amer ed (s10,dj) 15.00

WYOMING-1941-OUP/WPA-490p-yel pict cl,illus,fldg map rear pckt-Six Guns #49-1st ed (r8) 55.00

WYTHE,MAJOR GEORGE-History of the 90th Division-(NY)-(1920)-259p-cl-Dornbusch 1662 (l1,sl wn sp) 27.50

WYTHES,JOSEPH H-Microscopist-Phila-1852-Lindsay & Blakiston-sm 8vo-191p-grn cl,1 plt-1st ed (dd1,fox) 75.00

X MARKS THE SPOT: CHICAGO GANG WARS IN PICTURES-np-1930-Spot Publ-4to-64p-pict wrps,photos-scarce-1st ed (p1) 75.00

YACOUBI,AHMED-Alchemist's Cookbook-Tucson-1972-Omen Pr-142p-wrps (m6) 17.00

YALMAN,NUR-Under the Bo Tree-Berkeley-(1967)-U of Cal Pr-8vo-406p-cl-1st ed (y5,sl soil) 25.00

YAMASHINA,Y-Birds in Japan-Tokyo-1961-8vo-(7),233p-cl,132 col drwngs,maps (y8,dj chip) 45.00

YARBER,ESTHER-Land of the Yankee Fork-Denver-1963-Sage Books-8vo-207p-1st ed (z4,dj sl tn & wn) 20.00

YARBER,ESTHER-Land of the Yankee Fork-SLC-1970-207p-photos,maps (t7) 15.00

YARBRO,C Q-Ogilvie, Tallant & Moon-1976-Putnam-auth 1st bk-1st ed (x7,f,dj) 35.00

YARBRO,CHELSEA Q-Cautionary Tales-GC-1978-Dbldy-1st ed (g3,f,dj) 25.00

YARD,ROBERT S-Book of the National Parks-NY-1919-Scribner's-maps,photos-1st ed (o2) 17.50

YARD,ROBERT-Book of the National Parks-NY-1926-Scribner-436p-cl,illus (x6,sl fox) 30.00

YARDLEY,MAILI-Hawaii Cooks-Rutland-(1970)-Tuttle-112p-grn cl bds-1st ed (k6,dj) 22.00

YARDLEY,MARGARET T-ED.-New Jersey Scrap Book of Women Writers-Newark-1893-2 vols-cl,plts-ltd to 500c (aa6) 50.00

YARDLEY,PAUL T-Millstones and Milestones-Honolulu-(1981)-U of Hawaii-8vo-330p-illus-1st ed (gg5,f,f dj) 15.00

YARRELL,W-History of British Birds,rvsd-Lond-1871 to 75-8vo-4 vols-half calf,564 wd-engrvngs-4th(last)ed (y8,cov v wn) 145.00

YARROW,C H MIKE-Quaker Experiences in International Conciliation-New Haven-1978-Yale Univ Pr-8vo-308p-1st ed (y6,dj) 14.00

YARROW,WM-ED.-Robert Henri, His Life & Works-NY-1921-tall 4to-40 illus-ltd to 990c,nbrd-scarce (h10,dj sl tn) 250.00

YASHIRODA,KAN-Bonsai Japanese Miniature Trees-Mass-1964-Branford-166p-cl,117 photos (x6,as new in dj) 15.00

YASTRZEMSKI,CARL-Batting-1972-Viking-photos-1st ed (s8,f,dj) 20.00

YASTRZEMSKI,CARL-Yaz-1968-Viking (q7,dj) 12.50

YASTRZEMSKI,CARL-Yaz-1968-Viking-photos-1st ed (s8,f,dj) 15.00

YATES,RAYMOND F-ABC of Television or Seeing by Radio-1929-210p-21 photos,78 illus-rare-1st ed (h6) 145.00

YATES,RAYMOND F-Antique Fakes and Their Detection-1950-Gramercy Publ-229p-illus (cc8) 25.00

YATES,RICHARD-Eleven Kinds of Loneliness-Bost-1962-1st ed (p5,dj) 75.00

YATES,RICHARD-Revolutionary Road-Bost-1961-auth 1st bk-1st ed (s5,dj) 60.00

YAVA,ALBERT-Big Falling Snow-NY-(1978)-179p-photos,map.e.p.-1st ed (v7,f,dj) 20.00

YAZZIE,ETHELOU-ED.-Navaho History. Vol.1-Chinle-1971-100p-photos,13 col illus-1st ed (v7,f,dj) 25.00

YEALLAND,LEWIS R-Hysterical Disorders of Warfare-Lond-1918-Macmillan-xii+252p-olive cl-1st ed (dd1) 25.00

YEATS,W B-Ah, Sweet Dancer-(Lond)-(1970)-Macmillan-1st ed (z8,vf,dj) 12.50

YEATS,W B-Correspondence of Robert Bridges &...-Tor-1977-Macmillan of Can-1st ed (y1,f,f dj) 25.00

YEATS,W B-Fairy and Folk Tales of the Irish Peasantry-1888-W Scott-1st ed (x2,sl soil sp labl) 285.00

YEATS,W B-Herne's Egg...-NY-1938-Macmillan-1st ed (z8,f,f dj) 35.00

YEATS,W B-John Sherman & Dhoya-Detr-1969-Wayne St U Pr-1st ed thus (x9,f,dj) 15.00

YEATS,W B-Letters on Poetry From...To Dorothy Wellesley-Lond-1940-OUP-cl-1st ed (z8,f) 30.00

YEATS,W B-On Baile's Strand-Lond-1908-sm oct-brwn wrps-1st ed (cc2) 50.00

YEATS,W B-On the Boiler-Dublin-(1938)-Cuala Pr-wrps-(only 4c of 1st iss were prtd)-1st ed,2nd iss (z8,f) 125.00

YEATS,W B-On the Boiler-Dublin-(1939)-Cuala Pr-orig pict prtd wrps-(only 4c of 1st ed prtd)-2nd ed (aa9,sp crack,chip,sl fox) 50.00

YEATS,W B-Stories of Red Hanrahan-Lond-1913-A H Bullen-papr cov bds,cl sp (z8,vf) 65.00

YEATS,W B-Wheels and Butterflies-NY-1935-Macmillan-1st US ed (y1,sl soil dj) 125.00

YEE,CHIANG-Silent Traveller in Japan-NY-1972-Norton-lg 8vo-430p-e.p. maps,drwngs,col plts-1st ed (c3) 22.00

YEGEN,CHRISTIAN-Law vs Law, Book I and II-Billings-nd-2 vols-stiff pict wrps-scarce (t7,f) 37.50

YELLOWSTONE NATIONAL PARK-Official Guide to...-St.Paul-1890-140p-bds,plts,maps (t7) 15.00

YERBURY,F R-Lesser Known Architecture of Spain-Lond-1925-E Benn-folio-yel cl sp,beige bds wi ties-portfolio of 48 plts (r10,soil bds,cov wn) 45.00

YERBURY,F R-Modern Dutch Buildings-Lond-1931-E Benn-4to-viii p-cl,100 plts (pp7,sp drknd,sl fray & tn) 100.00

YERBY,FRANK-Saracen Blade-NY-1952-Dial-1st ed (e10,sl wn dj) 20.00

YERKES,R M-Chimpanzee Intelligence and its Vocal Expressions-Balt-1925-8vo-157p-cl,2 plts-1st ed (y8) 55.00

YERKES,ROBERT M-Chimpanzee Intelligence and its Vocal Expressions-Balt-1925-Williams & Wilkins-sm 8vo-157p+ads-blu cl-1st ed (c2) 85.00

YERKES,ROBERT-Psychological Examining in the U.S. Army-Wash-1921-890p-1st ed (dd3,ex-libr) 125.00

YGLESIAS,JOSE-An Orderly Life-NY-1968-Pantheon-1st ed (f8,f,f dj) 20.00

YOAKUM,H-History of Texas from its First Settlement in 1685 to its Annexation to the US in 1846-Austin-1935-Steck-2 vols-blk/wht reptile stmpd lea wi silv leaf foil e.p.-facs rprnt of 1855 ed (a9) 250.00

YOAKUM,H-History of Texas-Austin-1935-Steck Co-2 vols-illus,fldg map-Howes Y10 (ff4) 100.00

YOCUM,CHARLES F-Waterfowl & Their Food Plants in Washington-Seattle-1951-8vo-272p-photos-1st ed (m3,vf,dj) 35.00

YODER,SANFORD C-Horse Trails Along the Desert-Scottdale-(1954)-Herald Pr-181p-frntis,drwngs-1st ed (dd4,dj) 25.00

YOES,JOHN W-Jack Brainard a Romance of the Cherokee Hills-Bost-1904-322p-pict cl,frntis-1st ed (t7,sm hole sp) 10.00

YONGE,CHARLOTTE M-Dove in the Eagle's Nest-NY-1924-Duffield-315p-4 col plts,B Stevens-1st ed thus (s3,f,dj wn & chip) 30.00

YORKE,MARGARET-Hand of Death-NY-1981-St.Martin's-1st US ed (l4,f,dj) 10.00

YORKE,W MILTON-Tales of the Porcupine Trails-Tor-1911-Musson Bk Co-sm 8vo-108p-g dec blu cl,frntis,5p illus-1st ed (aa7,bump) 25.00*

YOST,BILLIE W-Bread Upon the Sands-Caldwell-(1958)-245p-photos-1st ed (v7,f,sl chip dj,pres) 30.00

YOST,C S-Patience Worth, a Psychic Mystery-1916-Holt-1st ed (x7) 25.00

YOST,KARL-Bibliography of the Published Works of Charles M Russell-Lincoln-(1971)-U of Nebr-4to-(xiv),317p-cl,illus(incl col)-1st ed (v1,dj) 45.00

YOST,NELLIE S-Call of the Range-Denver-(1966)-Sage Bks-437p-illus,e.p. maps-1st ed (cc4,dj) 25.00

YOST,NELLIE S-Call of the Range-Denver-(1966)-Sage Bks-lg 8vo-437p-cl,photos,map e.p.-1st ed (v1,dj) 35.00

YOST,NELLIE-Boss Cowman-Lincoln-1969-321p-illus,maps-1st ed (t7,dj) 40.00

YOST,NELLIE-Buffalo Bill-Chig-1979-500p-photos,illus-1st ed (t7,f,dj) 30.00

YOUMANS,ELEANOR-Great Adventures of Jack, Jock and Funny-Indpls,NY-(1938)-Bobbs Merrill-cl,illus by W Rannells-1st ed (aa9) 15.00

YOUNG,AL-Ask Me Now-NY et al-(1980)-McGraw Hill-1st ed (c10,as new in dj) 40.00

YOUNG,AL-Sitting Pretty-NY-(1976)-HR&W-1st ed (c10,f,dj) 35.00

YOUNG,AL-Snakes-NY-1970-Holt-1st ed (v5,f,dj) 20.00

YOUNG,ARTHUR-Six Weeks Tour through the Southern Counties of England and Wales-Lond-1772-W Strahan,W Nicoll-xii+438p+index-orig 1/2 calf,mrbld bds,2 plts-3rd ed (dd1,wn,rub) 200.00

YOUNG,AUGUSTUS-Survival-Dublin-1965-New Writers' Pr-wrps-1st ed (z8,f) 32.50

YOUNG,BOB-Mr Polk's War-NY-1968-176p-illus-1st ed (t7,dj) 12.50

YOUNG,C C-Under Twelve Flags-Waco-1908-216,(2)p-cl (d1,sl wn) 15.00

YOUNG,CATHARINE-Lady Who Loved Herself, the Life of Madame Roland-NY-1930-Knopf-8vo-318p-5 illus-1st ed (jj5,dj) 20.00

YOUNG,CATHERINE-To See Our World-NY-(1980)-Morrow-4to-128p-col photos-1st US ed (aa5,f,dj) 12.50

YOUNG,CHAS F T-Economy of Steam Power on Common Roads...-NY,Lond-nd-417,(5)p-cl (l1) 27.50

YOUNG,CHIC-Blondie's Cook Book-Phila-(1947)-McKay-141p-illus bds (n6) 25.00

YOUNG,COL.BENNETT H-Prehistoric Men of Kentucky-Louisville-1910-John P Morton-4to-xvi+343p-wrps,illus,Filson Club Publ,No.25-1st ed (e2,wn cor & sp tips) 65.00

YOUNG,DAVID-Lectures on the Science of Astronomy...New Jersey, in the Year 1820-Morris Town-1821-J Mann,for the auth-108p (aa6) 135.00

YOUNG,DAVID-Wonderful History of the Morristown Ghost...-Newark-1826-B Olds,for auth-76p-linen backd bds-rewritten from orig 1792 ed (aa6) 175.00

YOUNG,DESMOND-Fountain of the Elephants-NY-(1959)-Harper-8vo-319p-11 illus-1st US ed (jj5,dj) 15.00

YOUNG,DOROTHY W-Life & Letters of J Alden Weir-New Haven-1960-Yale-tall 8vo-cl-1st ed (oo6,dj) 40.00

YOUNG,EGERTON R-By Canoe & Dog Train Among the Cree & Salteaux Indians-NY,Cin-nd-12mo-267p-illus (m3,f) 15.00

YOUNG,EGERTON R-By Canoe and Dog Train Among the Cree and Salteaux Indians-Lond-1892-Chas H Kelly-8vo-x,267p-orig grn pict cl,bev edges,frntis,illus-Watters p.991-"Twelfth Thousand" (pp2,lacks e.p.) 75.00*

YOUNG,EGERTON R-By Canoe and Dog Train Among the Cree and Salteaux Indians-NY-ca.1890-Eaton & Mains-267p-pict cl,illus (bb4) 30.00

YOUNG,EGERTON R-COMP.-Algonquin Indian Tales-NY-1903-Eaton & Mains-258p-pict cl,illus (bb4,wn,autg) 20.00

YOUNG,ELLA-Marzilian & Other Poems-Oceana-(1938)-Harbison & Harbison-cl-ltd to 500c-1st ed (z8,f) 75.00

YOUNG,ELLA-To the Little Princess-SF-(1930)-Johnck & Seeger-wrps-ltd to 400c-1st ed (z8,f) 50.00

YOUNG,ELLA-Weird of Fionavar-Dublin-1922-Talbot Pr-wrps-1st ed (z8,f) 55.00

YOUNG,ERNEST-West of the Rockies-Lond-1949-Edw Stanford Ltd-236p-photos,maps-1st ed (bb4) 15.00

YOUNG,FILSON-With Beatty in the North Sea-Bost-1921-389p-blu cl,illus-1st ed (b7,f) 35.00

YOUNG,GEOFFERY-Mountain Craft-Lond-1921-603p-10 plts-2nd ed (o10,sp fade) 50.00

YOUNG,HARRY Y-Hard Knocks-Chig-(1915)-Laird & Lee-242p-illus-Six Guns #2466-1st ed (cc4,dj) 75.00

YOUNG,HUGH H-Studies on Hyperthophy and Cancer of the Prostate-Balt-1906-J Hopkins Hosp Rprt-Vol.XIV-628p-illus (g10) 50.00

YOUNG,HUGH H-Young's Practice of Urology Based on a Study of 12,500 Cases-Phila-1926-2 vols-20 col plts-1st ed (g10,ex-libr) 135.00

YOUNG,J HARVEY-Toadstool Millionaires-Princeton-1961-282p (dd3) 50.00

YOUNG,J P-Seventh Tennessee Cavalry-Dayton-1976-227p-ports,rprnt of 1890 ed (z10,as new) 17.50

YOUNG,JAMES C-Liberia Rediscovered-GC-1934-Dbldy Doran-8vo-212p-16 illus-1st ed (gg5,dj) 25.00

YOUNG,JAMES-What Price Sex in Hollywood-NY-(1932)-1st ed (m4,dj tape,wn) 12.50

YOUNG,JESS B-What a Boy Saw in the Army-NY-1894-Hunt & Eaton-398,(1)p-lea,g emboss,g edges,illus-1st ed (n2,hng crack) 40.00

YOUNG,JESSE B-Battle of Gettysburg-NY-1913-Harper & Bros-463p-maps,illus-1st ed (ee4) 75.00

YOUNG,JOHN P-Journalism in California and the Pacific Coast-SF-1915-SF Chron Publ-8vo-362p-cl-1st ed (mm7) 45.00

YOUNG,JOHN R-Schooling of the Western Horse-Norman-(1954)-U of Okla Pr-322p-drwngs-1st ed (dd4,spot dj) 30.00

YOUNG,KIMBALL-Isn't One Wife Enough?-NY-(1954)-H Holt-xvi+476p-tan cl,plts-1st ed (e2,dj) 18.00

YOUNG,LAMBTON J H-Sea Fishing as a Sport-Lond-1865-12mo-220p-illus (m3) 40.00

YOUNG,LAMBTON J-Sea Fishing as a Sport-Lond-1872-Groombridge-8vo-xi,220,(20)p ads-orig g dec grn cl,a.e.g.,6 col lithos-2nd ed (pp8,hng crack) 125.00*

YOUNG,LOUISE M-Peters Colonists-Chig-1972,3-2 vols-1st ed (n10,dj) 45.00

YOUNG,M S-American Realists-1977-NYC-sq folio-48 col plts,120 b&w illus-1st ed (h10,dj) 40.00

YOUNG,MARGUERITE-Miss MacIntosh,My Darling-NY-(1965)-1st ed (l5,f,dj) 25.00

YOUNG,MARY E-Redskins, Ruffleshirts and Rednecks-Norman-(1961)-U of Okla Pr-217p-illus-1st ed (bb4,dj) 30.00

YOUNG,MARY E-Redskins, Rufflesshirts and Rednecks-Norman-1961-217p-photos,illus,maps-1st ed (t7,dj) 15.00

YOUNG,OTIS E,JR.-Western Mining-Norman-(1976)-U of Okla Pr-342p-illus (bb4,dj) 20.00

YOUNG,OTIS E-West of Philip St.George Cooke 1809 thru 1895-Glendale-1955-393p-illus-Wstrn Frntrsmn Ser,Vol.5-1st ed (f7,f) 65.00

YOUNG,PAUL-Making & Using the Dry Fly-Birmingham-1935-8vo-81p+appndx,illus-2nd ed (m3) 100.00

YOUNG,PERRY D-Two of the Missing-NY-1975-CM&G-1st ed (b8,f,f dj) 40.00

YOUNG,R-Grizzlies Don't Come Easy-1981-Winchester-108p-photos (gg3,f,dj) 17.00

YOUNG,ROBERT W-ED.-Navajo Yearbook-Window Rock-1957-353p-wrps,photos,maps-6th report (v7) 15.00

YOUNG,ROLAND-Actors and Others-Chig-1925-Covici-4to-pap cov bds-ltd to 550c,autg (w1) 60.00

YOUNG,S P-Bobcat of North America-PA-1958-Wildlife Mgmt Inst-193p-photos (gg3,vf,dj) 35.00

YOUNG,S P-Clever Coyote-PA-1951-Wildlife Mgmt Inst-411p-photos (gg3,f,dj) 35.00

YOUNG,S P-Clever Coyote-Wash D.C.-1951-8vo-411p-illus-1st ed (m3,f,chip dj) 37.50

YOUNG,S P-Hints on Mountain-Lion Trapping-Wash D.C.-1933-8vo-8p-wrps,leaflet #94 of U.S. Dept of Agri,illus (m3) 30.00

YOUNG,S P-Puma-MD-1946-Wildlife Mgmt Inst-358p-photos (gg3,f,tn dj) 30.00

YOUNG,S P-Puma-Wash D.C.-1946-8vo-358p-photos-1st ed (m3) 15.00

YOUNG,S P-Wolf in North American History-ID-1946-149p-photos (gg3,f,dj) 30.00

YOUNG,S P-Wolves of North America-Wash D.C.-1944-8vo-636p-photos-1st ed (m3) 40.00

YOUNG,S P-Wolves of North America-Wash D.C.-1944-Amer Wildlife Inst-xxii+636p-grn cl,131 plts-1st ed (c2,sl fade sp) 35.00

YOUNG,SCOTT-O'Brien-Tor-1967-Ryerson Pr-8vo-249p-30 illus-1st ed (cc7,dj) 25.00*

YOUNG,THOMAS D-Gentleman in a Dustcoat-Baton Rouge-(1976)-LSU-1st ed (m7,f,sl tn dj) 15.00

YOUNG,W E-Shark! Shark!-NY-1934-8vo-287p-photos (m3) 20.00

YOUNGER,EDWARD-John A Kasson, Politics and Diplomacy from Lincoln to McKinley...-Iowa City-1955-450p-cl (j1) 15.00

YOUNGHUSBAND,COL G J-Story of the Guides-Lond-1908-Macmillan-8vo-206p-red cl,frntis,illus-1st ed,3rd prtg (gg6,lacks ffep) 30.00

YOUNGHUSBAND,GEORGE-Soldier's Memories-Lond-1917-355p-red cl,illus-2nd ed (gg2,sp sun) 85.00

YOUNGHUSBAND,SIR FRANCIS-Dawn in India-NY-1931-331p-rprnt (o10,f,dj) 25.00

YOUNGHUSBAND,SIR FRANCIS-Epic of Mount Everest-NY/Lond-1926-Longmans/Arnold-8vo-319p-orig tan cl,photos,2 maps (ll1,sl rub & fade) 50.00

YOUNGHUSBAND,SIR FRANCIS-Everest: The Challenge-NY-1936-Nelson-8vo-243p-16 plts,maps (gg6) 30.00

YOUNGMAN,REV W E-Gleanings From Western Prairies-Cambridge-1882-Jones & Piggott-214p+ads (dd4) 25.00

YU-LAN,FUNG-Spirit of Chinese Philosophy-Lond-1947-K Paul,Trench,Trubner-cl-1st ed (l8) 20.00

YULE-COMP.-Book of Ser Marco Polo-NY-1926-Scribner's-8vo-2 vols-red cl,sp labls,photos,maps-3rd ed (gg6) 180.00

YURICK,SOL-Fertig-NY-(1966)-Trident-1st ed (hh5,f,dj) 15.00

YUSUF-ALI,ABDULLAH-Life and Labour of the People of India-Lond-1907-John Murray-360p-grn cl,illus-1st ed (gg6,sl tn sp) 30.00

YZENDOORN,FATHER REGINALD-History of the Catholic Mission in the Hawaiian Islands-Honolulu-1927-Honolulu Star Bulletin-xvi+264p-brwn bds,plts-1st ed (mm10) 65.00

ZABRISKE,GEORGE-Fisherman's Philosophy-Ormond Bch-1935-priv prntd-8vo-22p-hand col illus-scarce (m3,f) 55.00

ZABRISKIE,LUTHER K-Virgin Islands of the United States of America-NY-1918-Putnam's-xviii+339p-blu cl,109 illus,2 maps (m2) 45.00

ZADAN,CRAIG-Sondheim & Co-NY-1974-Macmillan-1st ed (w5,f,f dj) 35.00

ZAEHNER,R C-Hinduism-Lond-1962-Oxford U Pr-cl-1st ed (n8,f,dj) 15.00

ZAEHNSDORF,JOSEPH W-Art of Bookbinding-Lond-1925-Bell & Sons-10th impr (u2) 35.00

ZAHL,PAUL-Coro Coro-Indpls-(1954)-Bobbs Merrill-8vo-264p-illus-1st ed (aa5,dj) 20.00

ZANGWILL,I-Dreamers of the Ghetto-NY-1898-Harpers-8vo-cl-1st Amer ed (t1) 25.00

ZANGWILL,ISRAEL-Big Bow Mystery-Chig-1895-Rand-1st US ed (h4,sm cov stn,sl fade sp) 50.00

ZANUCK,DARRYL F-Tunis Expedition-NY-(1943)-photos-1st ed (p5,dj) 20.00

ZANUCK,DARRYL F-Tunis Expedition-NY-(1943)-Random-8vo-160p-28 photos-1st ed (dd5,f,dj) 25.00

ZARKIN,RICHARD-Electric Kiln Ceramics-1981-Chilton-242p-illus (cc8,dj) 30.00

ZARN,GEORGE-Above the Forks-1978-priv publ-8vo-160p-photos-1st ed (bb7,dj) 20.00*

ZEIGER,HENRY A-Ian Fleming: The Spy Who Came in with the Gold-1965-Duell-1st ed (s10,f,dj) 15.00

ZEISBERGER,DAVID-Zeisberger's Indian Dictionary-Cambridge-1887-J Wilson & Son-4to-xi,236p-brwn cl-1st ed (ee7) 250.00

ZEITLIN,IDA-TOLD BY-Gessar Khan-NY-1927-Doran-cl,illus-1st ed (o8,dj) 45.00

ZEITLIN,J-For Whispers and Chants-1927-Lantern Pr-ltd to 500c,autg,auth 1st bk-Grabhorn Pr bk-1st ed (x2) 95.00

ZELAZNY,ROGER-Courts of Chaos-GC-1978-Dbldy-1st ed (a5,dj) 12.50

ZELAZNY,ROGER-Dream Master-NY-1966-Ace-wrps-1st ed (v5,f) 30.00

ZELAZNY,ROGER-Eye of Cat-(1982)-Timescape-1st ed (n9,f,dj) 15.00

ZELAZNY,ROGER-Eye of the Cat-NY-(1982)-Timescape-1st ed (f3,f,dj) 20.00

ZELAZNY,ROGER-This Immortal-NY-1966-Ace-wrps,auth 1st bk-1st ed (v5,f) 30.00

ZELLER,BERNHARD-Portrait of Hesse-(NY)-(1971)-Herder & Herder-photos-1st ed (bb1,as new in dj) 15.00

ZERFFI,G G-Spiritualism and Animal Magnetism-Lond-1871-Robt Hardwicke-12mo-148p+frntis,prntd brwn cl-scarce-1st ed (y9) 65.00

ZERN,ED-Fine Kettle of Fish Stories-NY-1972-8vo-122p-illus-1st prntg (m3,vf,dj) 15.00

ZERN,ED-How to Catch Fishermen-NY-1951-8vo-116p-illus,auth (m3,vf,dj) 11.00

ZEUNER,CH.-Ancient Lyre-Bost-1839-Crocker & Brewster-358,(6)p-bds-8th ed revsd (o1,cor & sp wn) 15.00

ZHANG,MINGTAO-Roof of the World-NY,Bejing-1982-227p-138 col photos-1st ed (p10,f,dj) 40.00

ZIEGLER,TOM-Zen of Base and Ball-1964-S&S-1st ed (s7,dj) 15.00

ZIEL,RON-Steam in the Sixties-NY-1967-208p-1st ed (n4,f,dj) 24.00

ZIEL,RON-Steel Rails to the Sunrise-NY-1965-320p-1st ed (n4,f,dj) 27.50

ZIEL,RON-Twilight of Steam Locomotives-NY-(1970)-208p-col pict bds,photos (m1,dj) 15.00

ZIEMAN,HUGO-White House Cook Book-Chig-1898-Werner Co-590p-wht oilcl bds-Bitting 184 (n6) 75.00

ZIEMANN,HUGO-White House Cook Book-Akron-1902-Saalfield-590p+ads-pict cov,frntis,illus (mm6,wn,soil cov,hng crack,fox 95.00

ZIEMANN,HUGO-White House Cook Book-Akron-1905-590p-cl,frntis of Edith C Roosevelt (a1,sl rub,tn flylf rprd) 35.00

ZIEMANN,HUGO-White House Cookbook-NY-1903-Saalfield Co-thk 4to-590p (t1,pap brwnd) 85.00

ZIFF,P-J M Hanson-Ithaca-1962-Cornell UP-32 plts-1st ed (h10) 15.00

ZILBOORG,GREGORY-History of Medical Psychology-NY-1941-606p-1st ed (dd3) 25.00

ZILBOORG,GREGORY-Medical Man and the Witch during the Renaissance-Balt-1935-215p-1st ed (dd3) 50.00

ZIMEN,E-Wolf-1981-Delacorte-373p-42 col photos-1st US ed (bb3,dj) 25.00

ZIMILES,MARTHA-Early American Mills-NY-1973-Clarkson Potter-4to-xiv+290p-gry cl,illus-1st ed (mm10,dj) 30.00

ZIMMER,GEORGE F-Popular Dictionary of Botanical Names & Terms-Lond-1956-Routledge (x6,dj) 25.00

ZIMMER,HEINRICH-Art of Indian Asia-NY-1955-Bollingen,Pantheon-oversize-2 vols-blu cl,614 plts (gg6)	135.00
ZIMMER,HEINRICH-Art of Indian Asia-Princeton-1968-Univ Pr-4to-2 vols-blu cl,614 plts-3rd prtg (r10,dj,wn box)	60.00
ZIMMER,HEINRICH-King and the Corpse-1970-Princeton U Pr-cl-Bollingen Ser.XI-2nd ed(wi index) (l8,f,dj)	45.00
ZIMMERMAN,JOHN L-Where the People Sing, Green Land of the Maoris-NY-1946-Knopf-8vo-blu grn cl,photos-1st ed (nn1,sp fade,sl soil cov,dj wn	25.00
ZIMMERMAN,PAUL-L.A. Dodgers-1960-Coward McCann-1st ed (ff2,dj)	15.00
ZIMMERMAN,PAUL-Year the Mets Lost Last Place-1969-World-1st ed (ff2,dj)	12.50
ZIMNIK,REINER-Jonah the Fisherman-NY-(1956)-Pantheon-narrow 4to-unpgd-cl & bds,drwngs,auth-1st US ed (r3,dj sp fade)	45.00
ZINN,HOWARD-Vietnam: the Logic of Withdrawal-Bost-(1967)-Beacon-1st ed (ff3,dj)	35.00
ZINOVIEV,ALEXANDER-Yawning Heights-Lond-1979-transl by G Clough-1st ed (y7,dj)	20.00
ZINSMEISTER,LEE G-Circle "Z" Guest Ranch-Patagonia-nd-20p-pict wrps,photos,illus-promo (t7)	17.50
ZINSSER,WILLIAM-Weekend Guests-NY-(1963)-Harper-4to-unpgd-cl & bds-1st ed (r3,dj)	25.00
ZOLA,EMILE-Nana-NY-1922-Knopf-408p-cl,ltd to 3000c,nbrd-1st Amer ed (a1)	20.00
ZOLLERS,GEORGE D-Thrilling Incidents on Sea and Land-Mt.Morris-1892-Brethren's Publ (v2)	50.00
ZOLOTOW,CHARLOTTE-Someday-np-(1966)-World's Work-oblng 16mo-unpgd-cl & bds,col illus,A Lobel-1st Brit ed (r3)	20.00
ZOOLOGICAL RECORD, VOLS.1 THRU 82-Lond-1865 to 1948-8vo-82 vols-orig cl (y8,ex-lib)	3,250.00
ZORNOW,WILLIAM F-Kansas-(1957)-U of Ok-417p-illus-Six Guns 2474-1st ed (v8,dj chip,sl soil)	35.00
ZORNOW,WILLIAM F-Kansas-Norman-(1957)-U of Okla Pr-417p-illus,maps-1st ed (dd4,dj)	30.00
ZUCKERMAN,S-Functional Affinities of Man, Monkeys, and Apes-NY-1933-Harcourt,Brace-203p-blu cl,illus-1st ed (dd1,dj)	25.00
ZUGSMITH,ALBERT-Beat Generation-NY-1959-wrps,based on MGM pic-1st ed (x8)	20.00
ZUGSMITH,LEANE-Home is Where You Hang Your Childhood-NY-1937-Random Hs-1st ed (v5,dj)	40.00
ZUKERMAN,NATHAN-Wine of Violence-NY-1947-Assoc Pr-361p (r1,chip dj)	20.00
ZUKOFSKY,LOUIS-A 24-NY-1972-1st ed (s5,f,dj)	25.00
ZUKOFSKY,LOUIS-A 1-12-GC-1967-1st US ed (s5,dj)	30.00
ZUKOFSKY,LOUIS-All-Lond-1966-J Cape-1st Brit ed (q2,dj)	35.00
ZUKOFSKY,LOUIS-Little-1970-Grossman-1st ed (n9,dj)	45.00
ZUKOFSKY,LOUIS-Prepositions-NY-(1968)-Horizon Pr-1st ed (x10,f,sl wn dj)	20.00
ZUKOFSKY,LOUIS-Test of Poetry-Brooklyn-1948-Objectivist Pr-maroon cl-1st ed (f2,dj)	85.00
ZWEIG,STEFAN-Conqueror of the Seas-NY-1938-Viking-335p-frnt paste on,map e.p.,illus-1st ed (p8,dj chip,wn)	25.00
ZWEIG,STEFAN-Mental Healers-NY-1932-Viking-xxvi+363+(3)p-prntd blk cl-1st ed in Engl,1st prntg (y9)	40.00
ZWINGER,ANN-Land Above the Trees-NY-1972-Harper & Row-8vo-xviii,494p-24 col plts-1st ed (ff9,dj)	35.00*

USED BOOK PRICE GUIDE©

(a1) Robert G. Hayman,#145,12/92,Box 188, Carey, OH 43316
(a2) Metacomet Books,#45,3/93, Box 2479, Providence, RI 02906
(a3) Whitlock Farm Booksellers,#601A,4/93,20 Sperry Road, Bethany CT 06524-3599
(a4) J.P.Mountain Books, #10,3/93,Box 10884, Portland,OR 97210
(a5) Steven C. Bernard,#53,10/91,15011 Plainfield Lane, Darnestown, MD 20874
(a6) Parker Books of the West, ABC,10/91,Box 8390, Santa Fe, NM 87504
(a7) Stephen C. Lunsford,#36,9/91,Box 3023,Blaine, Wa 98230
(a8) Household Words, #293,4/93,Box 7231,Berkeley, CA 94707
(a9) Maggie Lambeth,#22,6/91, Star Route 4,Box 361, Blanco, TX 78606
(a10) Steven C. Bernard,#58,8/92,15011 Plainfield Lane, Darnestown, MD 20874

(b1) Robert G. Hayman,#144,9/92,Box 188, Carey OH 43316
(b2) Metacomet Books,#44,12/92, Box 2479, Providence, RI 02906
(b3) Bowie & Company Booksellers, #115,4/93,314 First Ave. South, Seattle, WA 98104
(b4) Parker Books of the West, #21,4/93,Box 8390, Santa Fe, NM 87504
(b5) Steven C. Bernard,#52,7/91,15011 Plainfield Lane, Darnestown, MD 20874
(b6) Edmonds Olde Bookstore,C2,8/91,9679 Firdale Ave, Edmonds, WA 98020
(b7) Owen D. Kubik,#18,11/90,3474 Clar-Von Dr,Dayton,OH 45430
(b8) Gregor Books,#12,3/93,3407 Calif Ave SW,Seattle, WA, 98116
(b9) Buteo Books,#4,7/92,Rt 1, Box#242, Shipman, VA 22971
(b10) Steven C. Bernard,#57,5/92,15011 Plainfield Lane, Darnestown, MD 20874

(c1) Robert G. Hayman,#143,6/92,Box 188, Carey, OH 43316
(c2) Metacomet Books,#43,11/92, Box 2479, Providence, RI 02906
(c3) Best Books Ltd,#4,9/89,2340 Valley St, Berkeley,CA 94702
(c4) Wallace D. Pratt,#15,7/90,1801 Gough St, San Francisco,CA 94109
(c5) Steven C. Bernard,#51, 5/91,15011 Plainfield Lane, Darnestown, MD 20874
(c6) Lemuria,#II-R,3/91,202 Banner Hall, Jackson, MS 39206
(c7) Rip Kirby-Folio Books,#20,3/92,527 1st Ave N. #101,Seattle WA, 98109
(c8) Gregor Books,#11,12/92,3407 Calif Ave SW,Seattle, WA 98116
(c9) Buteo Books,#3, 2/92,Rt 1, Box#242, Shipman, VA 22971
(c10) Steven C. Bernard,#56, 4/92,15011 Plainfield Lane, Darnestown, MD 20874

(d1) Robert G. Hayman,#142, 3/92,Box 188, Carey, OH 43316
(d2) Metacomet Books,#42,7/92, Box 2479, Providence, RI 02906
(d3) Maggie Lambeth #21, 6/91, Star Route 4, Box 361, Blanco, TX 78606
(d4) Dunn & Powell, #2, 12/91, The Hideaway, Bar Harbor, ME 04609-1714
(d5) Steven C. Bernard,#50, 2/91,15011 Plainfield Lane, Darnestown, MD 20874
(d6) Lemuria,#IIQ,12/90, 202 Banner Hall, Jackson, MS 39206
(d7) Rip Kirby-Folio Books,#18,3/92,527 1st Ave N. #101,Seattle, WA 98109
(d8) Gregor Books,#10,10/92,3407 Calif Ave SW,Seattle, WA 98116
(d9) Buteo Books,Winter 91 Cat, 1/92,Rt 1, Box#242, Shipman, VA 22971
(d10) Steven C. Bernard,#55, 1/92,15011 Plainfield Lane, Darnestown, MD 20874

(e1) Robert G. Hayman,#141, 12/91,Box 188, Carey, OH 43316
(e2) Metacomet Books,#41,5/92, Box 2479, Providence, RI 02906
(e3) Duga's Books,#17,8/92,610 Aldama Court,Ocoee, FL 34761
(e4) Dunn & Powell, #1, 10/91, The Hideaway, Bar Harbor, ME 04609-1714
(e5) Steven C. Bernard,#49, 12/90,15011 Plainfield Lane, Darnestown, MD 20874
(e6) Lemuria,#IIP 1st Ed,11/90, 202 Banner Hall, Jackson, MS 39206
(e7) Rip Kirby-Folio Books,#17,3/92,527 1st Ave N. #101,Seattle, WA 98109
(e8) Gregor Books,List G,7/92,3407 Calif Ave SW,Seattle, WA 98116
(e9) Buteo Books,#2, 8/91,Rt 1, Box#242, Shipman, VA 22971
(e10) Steven C. Bernard,#54, 11/91,15011 Plainfield Lane, Darnestown, MD 20874

(f1) Robert G. Hayman,#140, 9/91,Box 188, Carey, OH 43316
(f2) Metacomet Books,#40,1/92, Box 2479, Providence, RI 02906
(f3) Duga's Books,#16,5/92,610 Aldama Court,Ocoee, FL 34761
(f4) Steve Powell,#33,9/91, The Hideaway, Bar Harbor, ME 04609-1714
(f5) Steven C. Bernard,#48, 9/90,15011 Plainfield Lane, Darnestown, MD 20874
(f6) Lemuria,#IIP,11/90, 202 Banner Hall, Jackson, MS 39206
(f7) Rip Kirby-Folio Books,#16,3/92,527 1st Ave N. #101,Seattle, WA 98109
(f8) Gregor Books,List F,6/92,3407 Calif Ave SW,Seattle, WA 98116
(f9) Peters & Isham Company,#31,1/92,8600 Hidden Meadow,Ft Worth, TX 76179
(f10) October Farm,#31,3/93,2609 Branch Rd,Raleigh, NC 27610

(g1) Robert G. Hayman,#138, 6/91,Box 188, Carey, OH 43316
(g2) Metacomet Books,#39,12/91, Box 2479, Providence, RI 02906
(g3) Duga's Books,#15,12/91,610 Aldama Court,Ocoee, FL 34761
(g4) Steve Powell,#32,6/91, The Hideaway, Bar Harbor, ME 04609-1714
(g5) Steven C. Bernard,#47, 7/90,15011 Plainfield Lane, Darnestown, MD 20874
(g6) Lemuria,#II-N,9/90, 202 Banner Hall, Jackson, MS 39206
(g7) Rip Kirby-Folio Books,#14,3/92,527 1st Ave N. #101,Seattle, WA 98109
(g8) Gregor Books,#9,4/92,3407 Calif Ave SW,Seattle, WA 98116
(g9) Gravesend Books,#29,6/91,Box 235,Pocono Pines,Pa 18350
(g10) Edward C Atwater #22,1/92,195 Whitewood Lane, Rochester, NY 14618

(h1) Robert G. Hayman,#137, 3/91,Box 188, Carey, OH 43316
(h2) Metacomet Books,#38,10/91, Box 2479, Providence, RI 02906
(h3) Duga's Books,#14,10/91,610 Aldama Court,Ocoee, FL 34761
(h4) Steve Powell,#31,5/91, The Hideaway, Bar Harbor, ME 04609-1714
(h5) Steven C. Bernard,#46, 5/90,15011 Plainfield Lane, Darnestown, MD 20874
(h6) New Wireless Pioneers, #5,9/89,6270 Clinton St, Elma, NY 14059
(h7) Rip Kirby-Folio Books,#11,1/90,527 1st Ave N. #101,Seattle, WA 98109
(h8) Gregor Books,#8,12/91,3407 Calif Ave SW,Seattle, WA 98116
(h9) October Farm,#30,11/92,2609 Branch Rd,Raleigh, NC 27610
(h10) J.B.Muns,#144,8/91,1162 Shattuck Ave, Berkeley, CA 94707

(j1) Robert G. Hayman,#136, 1/91,Box 188, Carey, OH 43316
(j2) Metacomet Books,#37,7/91, Box 2479, Providence, RI 02906
(j3) Duga's Books,#13,6/91,610 Aldama Court,Ocoee, FL 34761
(j4) Steve Powell,#30,2/91, The Hideaway, Bar Harbor, ME 04609-1714
(j5) Steven C. Bernard,#45, 3/90,15011 Plainfield Lane, Darnestown, MD 20874
(j6) Alice Robbins,#8,3/93,3002 Round Hill Road, Greensboro, NC 27408
(j7) Rip Kirby-Folio Books,#10,1/90,527 1st Ave N. #101,Seattle, WA 98109
(j8) Gregor Books,#7,8/91,3407 Calif Ave SW,Seattle, WA 98116
(j9) October Farm,#27,8/91,2609 Branch Rd,Raleigh, NC 27610
(j10) Carol Barnett,#13,10/91,3562 NE Liberty, Portland, OR 97211-7248

(k1) Robert G. Hayman,#135,11/90,Box 188, Carey, OH 43316
(k2) Metacomet Books,#36,5/91, Box 2479, Providence, RI 02906
(k3) Duga's Books,#12,3/91,610 Aldama Court,Ocoee, FL 34761
(k4) Steve Powell,#29,10/90, The Hideaway, Bar Harbor, ME 04609-1714
(k5) Steven C. Bernard,#44, 1/90,15011 Plainfield Lane, Darnestown, MD 20874
(k6) Household Words,1/93,Box 7231,Berkeley, CA 94707
(k7) Alice Robbins,#7,10/92,3002 Round Hill Road, Greensboro, NC 27408
(k8) Bibliomania,#22,12/91,129 Jay St, Schenectady, NY, 12305
(k9) Artis Books, #20,1/92,Box 822,201 N. Second Ave,Alpena,MI 49707
(k10) Robert Reeves Books,#39,4/92,1606 Candella Place,Victoria,BC,Can V8N 5P4

(l1) Robert G. Hayman,#134,9/90,Box 188, Carey, OH 43316
(l2) Metacomet Books,#35,1/91, Box 2479, Providence, RI 02906
(l3) Duga's Books,#9,7/90,610 Aldama Court,Ocoee, FL 34761
(l4) Steve Powell,#28,8/90, The Hideaway, Bar Harbor, ME 04609-1714
(l5) Steven C. Bernard,#43,11/89,15011 Plainfield Lane, Darnestown, MD 20874
(l6) Household Words,9/92,Box 7231,Berkeley, CA 94707
(l7) Alice Robbins,#6,7/92,3002 Round Hill Road, Greensboro, NC 27408
(l8) Abintra, The Bookseller,#33,8/92,Box 337, Blue Hill, ME 04614
(l9) Yesteryear Book Shop,Of Literary Merit,10/92,3201 Maple DR NE, Atlanta GA 30305
(l10) Artis Books, #19,1/92,Box 822,201 N. Second Ave,Alpena,MI 49707

(m1) Robert G. Hayman,#133,8/90,Box 188, Carey, OH 43316
(m2) Metacomet Books,#34,11/90, Box 2479, Providence, RI 02906
(m3) Gary L Estabrook Bks,#50,4/91,Box 61453, Vancouver WA 98666
(m4) Artis Books, #26,2/93,Box 822,201 N. Second Ave,Alpena,MI 49707
(m5) Steven C. Bernard,#42,8/89,15011 Plainfield Lane, Darnestown, MD 20874
(m6) Household Words,3/92,Box 7231,Berkeley, CA 94707
(m7) Alice Robbins,#5,3/92,3002 Round Hill Road, Greensboro, NC 27408
(m8) Abintra, The Bookseller,List #2,9/92,Box 337, Blue Hill, ME 04614
(m9) Monroe Stahr,#33,12/91, 4420 Ventura Canyon Ave #2, Sherman Oaks, CA 91423
(m10) Carol Barnett Bks, #11,11/90,3562 NE Liberty St, Portland OR 97211

(n1) Robert G. Hayman,#132,6/90,Box 188, Carey, OH 43316
(n2) Woodbridge B Brown,List 54-A,2/93,Box 445,312 Main St, Turner Falls, MA 01376
(n3) Walter D Pratt,#14,5/90,1801 Gough St, San Francisco CA 94109
(n4) David R Spivey,#1, 7/90,1915 W. 45th St, Kansas City, KS 66103
(n5) Pettler & Lieberman, #19,10/92,8033 Sunsset Blvd #977, LA, CA 90046
(n6) Household Words,10/91,Box 7231,Berkeley, CA 94707
(n7) Camp Pope Bookshop, #15,1/93, Box 2232, Iowa City, IA 52244
(n8) Abintra, The Bookseller,#32,5/92,Box 337, Blue Hill, ME 04614
(n9) Monroe Stahr,#32,6/91, 4420 Ventura Canyon Ave #2, Sherman Oaks, CA 91423
(n10) The Wright Collection, #91,11/90,333 Harbin St, Waxahachie, TX 75165

(o1) Robert G. Hayman,#131,4/90,Box 188, Carey, OH 43316
(o2) Woodbridge B Brown,List 47,12/91,Box 445,312 Main St, Turner Falls, MA 01376
(o3) Duga's Books,#8,3/90,610 Aldama Court,Ocoee, FL 34761
(o4) Joseph J Felcone,#60,3/93,Box 366, Princeton NJ 08540
(o5) Pettler & Lieberman, #18,6/92,8033 Sunsset Blvd #977, LA, CA 90046
(o6) Household Words,9/90,Box 7231,Berkeley, CA 94707
(o7) Camp Pope Bookshop, #14,10/92, Box 2232, Iowa City, IA 52244
(o8) Abintra, The Bookseller,#29,1/92,Box 337, Blue Hill, ME 04614
(o9) Monroe Stahr,#31,4/91, 4420 Ventura Canyon Ave #2, Sherman Oaks, CA 91423
(o10) J.P Mountain Books, #7,5/92, Box 10884, Portland, OR 97210

(p1) Bowie & Company Booksellers, #114,2/93,314 First Ave. South, Seattle, WA 98104
(p2) Woodbridge B Brown,List 44,6/91,Box 445,312 Main St, Turner Falls, MA 01376
(p3) Duga's Books,#7,1/90,610 Aldama Court,Ocoee, FL 34761
(p4) Silver Door,#20,6/92,Box 3208, Redondo Beach, CA 90277
(p5) Pettler & Lieberman, #17,12/91,8033 Sunsset Blvd #977, LA, CA 90046
(p6) James & Mary Laurie Booksellers,#42, 8/90 251 S. Snelling Ave, St.Paul, MN 55105
(p7) Wayne Greene Baseball Bks, #7 2/93,945 W End Ave, 5D, NY, NY 10025
(p8) J. Parmer, Booksellers, #39,1/90, 7644 Forrestal Rd, San Diego, CA 92120
(p9) Monroe Stahr,#30,11/90, 4420 Ventura Canyon Ave #2, Sherman Oaks, CA 91423
(p10) J.P Mountain Books, #6,1/92, Box 10884, Portland, OR 97210

(q1) AKA Fine Used Bks, Beat,Lit,Mod Lit,9/91,4142 Brookyln Ave NE, Seattle, WA 98105
(q2) Gordon Beckhorn, #21,9/92,23 Ashford Ave, Dobbs Ferry, NY 10522
(q3) Stephen T. Rose, #14,2/93,Box 55701, Indpls, IN 46205
(q4) Silver Door,#19,6/91,Box 3208, Redondo Beach, CA 90277
(q5) Pettler & Lieberman, #16,8/91,8033 Sunsset Blvd #977, LA, CA 90046
(q6) Household Words,12/89,Box 7231,Berkeley, CA 94707
(q7) Wayne Greene Baseball Bks, #6, 9/92,945 W End Ave, 5D, NY, NY 10025
(q8) Needham Book Finders, #75,2/92,Box 3067, Santa Monica, CA 90408
(q9) Monroe Stahr,#29,10/90, 4420 Ventura Canyon Ave #2, Sherman Oaks, CA 91423
(q10) J.P Mountain Books, #5,10/91, Box 10884, Portland, OR 97210

r1) AKA Fine Used Bks, #1,5/91,4142 Brookyln Ave NE, Seattle, WA 98105
(r2) Polyanthos Park Ave Bks,#17,2/93,Box 343, Huntington, NY 11743
(r3) Cynthia K Fowler Books, #14,5/92,1723 Tyler Parkway Louisville, KY 40204
(r4) Silver Door,#18,9/90,Box 3208, Redondo Beach, CA 90277
(r5) Pettler & Lieberman, #15,12/90,8033 Sunset Blvd #977, LA, CA 90046
(r6) Household Words,9/89,Box 7231,Berkeley, CA 94707
(r7) Wayne Greene Baseball Bks, #5, 7/92,945 W End Ave, 5D, NY, NY 10025
(r8) Bebbah Books, #12,10/92,Box 910, Gleneden Beach, OR 97388-0910
(r9) Monroe Stahr,#28,5/90, 4420 Ventura Canyon Ave #2, Sherman Oaks, CA 91423
(r10) Michael C. Dooling, #28,2/90,72 N. St, Box 1047, Middlebury, CT 06762

(s1) Bowie & Company Booksellers, #113,12/92,314 First Ave. South, Seattle, WA 98104
(s2) Messrs Berkelouw,#10,8/92,830 N Highland Ave, LA, CA 90038
(s3) Cynthia K Fowler Books, #13,9/91,1723 Tyler Parkway Louisville, KY 40204
(s4) Silver Door,#17,7/90,Box 3208, Redondo Beach, CA 90277
(s5) Pettler & Lieberman, #14,9/90,8033 Sunset Blvd #977, LA, CA 90046
(s6) Lemuria, #II-A,7/89,202 Banner Hall, Jackson,MS 39206
(s7) Wayne Greene Baseball Bks, Winter 92, 4/92,945 W End Ave, 5D, NY, NY 10025
(s8) R. Plapinger,#13,11/91,Box 1062, Ashland, OR 97520
(s9) Monroe Stahr,#27,3/90, 4420 Ventura Canyon Ave #2, Sherman Oaks, CA 91423
(s10) Dunn's Mysteries of Choice,#97,8/91,Box 2544, Meriden, CT 06450

(t1) Bowie & Company Booksellers, #110,8/92,314 First Ave. South, Seattle, WA 98104
(t2) Messrs Berkelouw,#9,8/92,830 N Highland Ave, LA, CA 90038
(t3) Stephen T Rose #13,11/92,Box 55701, Indianapolis, IN 46206
(t4) Violet Books, #2,3/91,Box 20610, Seattle, WA 98102
(t5) Pettler & Lieberman, #13,7/90,8033 Sunset Blvd #977, LA, CA 90046
(t6) Lemuria, List Z,7/89,202 Banner Hall, Jackson,MS 39206
(t7) T A Swinford, #29,2/90,Box 93,Paris, IL 61944
(t8) Bebbah Books, #9,9/91,Box 910, Gleneden Beach, OR 97388-0910
(t9) Monroe Stahr,#26,11/89, 4420 Ventura Canyon Ave #2, Sherman Oaks, CA 91423
(t10) Jeff Weber Rare Bks, #18,8/92,Box 3368, Glendale, CA 91221-0368

(u1) Bowie & Company Booksellers, #105,12/91,314 First Ave. South, Seattle, WA 98104
(u2) Bibliomania,#27,4/93,129 Jay St, Schenectady, NY, 12305
(u3) Richard H Adelson,Special List,5/90 N Promfret, VT 05053
(u4) Bancroft Book Mews,#5, 7/92,86 Sugar Lane, Newton, CT 06470
(u5) Twelfth St Booksellers, #12,2/92, Box 3103, Santa Monica, CA 90403
(u6) Household Words,7/89,Box 7231,Berkeley, CA 94707
(u7) T N Luther Bks, #138,5/90, Box 429, Taos, NM 87571
(u8) Bebbah Books, #8,9/91,Box 910, Gleneden Beach, OR 97388-0910
(u9) Parker Books of the West, #20,2/93,142 W. Palace Ave, Santa Fe, NM 87504
(u10) Joseph A Dermont, #48,7/91,Box 654, Onset, MA 02558

(v1) Bowie & Weatherford,Inc, Booksellers, #87,10/90,Box 5, Southworth, WA 98386
(v2) Camp Pope Bookshop,#13, 8/92 Box 2232, Iowa City, Iowa 52244
(v3) Carroll Burcham, #26, 12/91,5546 17th Pl, Lubbock, TX 79416
(v4) Overlee Farm Bks,#7,7/90,Box 1155, Stockbridge, MA 01262
(v5) Beasley Books, #47,10/89,1533 W Oakdale, Chicago,IL 60657
(v6) Cicero's Books,Cookbk Lst #4,9/92,115 Beal St,Canandaigua, NY 14424
(v7) T N Luther Bks, #137,12/89, Box 429, Taos, NM 87571
(v8) Bebbah Books, #7,9/91,Box 910, Gleneden Beach, OR 97388-0910
(v9) Gregor Books,#13,7/93,3407 Calif Ave SW,Seattle, WA, 98116
(v10) Joseph A Dermont, #47,1/91,Box 654, Onset, MA 02558

(w1) M Taylor Bowie Bookseller, #12,1/90,2613 5th Ave, Seattle,WA 98121
(w2) Oak Knoll Bks,#138,12/91,414 Delaware St, New Castle, DE 19720
(w3) Michael Gibbs-Bookseller, #19, 10/91,Box 83,West Chester, OH 45069
(w4) N Stewart & G Haluska, #1,1/92,1188 NW Weybridge Way, Beaverton, OR 97006
(w5) Beasley Books, #46,8/89,1533 W Oakdale, Chicago,IL 60657
(w6) Second Life Books, #89,6/92, Box 242,55 Quarry Rd, Lanesborough, MA 01237
(w7) Bertie Books #14, 11/91,Box 8874, Lowell, MA 01853
(w8) Bibliomania,#26,1/93,129 Jay St, Schenectady, NY, 12305
(w9) Mordida Books, #17,3/92, Box 79322, Houston, TX 77279
(w10) Whitlock Farm Booksellers, #600A,1/93, 20 Sperry Rd, Bethany, CT 06524-3599

(x1) Dinkytown Antiquarian Bkstore,#53,3/92,1316 SE 4th St,Mpls,MN 55414
(x2) The Fine Books Co,#47,1/92,781 E Snell Rd, Rochester, MI 48306
(x3) Caney Booksellers,#14,11/92,Suite 220,One Cherry Hill, Cherry Hill, NJ 08002
(x4) Oak Knoll Bks,#135,9/91,414 Delaware St, New Castle, DE 19720
(x5) Carol Barnett, Bks,#12,5/91,3562 NE Liberty,Portland OR 97211-7248
(x6) The American Botanist Booksellers,#23,11/90,Box 532, Chillicothe, IL 61523
(x7) David Arnovitz,#50,11/92,781 E Snell Rd, Rochester, MI 48306
(x8) Beat Sweep Books,#1,5/90,199 Edward St, Bishop CA 93514
(x9) Archer's Used and Rare Bks,#19,12/92,104 S Lincoln St, Kent,OH 44240
(x10) Joseph A Dermont, #45,8/90,Box 654, Onset, MA 02558

(y1) Dinkytown Antiquarian Bkstore,#54,3/92,1316 SE 4th ST,Mpls,MN 55414
(y2) The Book Treasury, Christmas,12/91,Box 20033,Long Beach,CA 90801
(y3) Caney Booksellers,#13,9/92,Suite 220,One Cherry Hill, Cherry Hill, NJ 08002
(y4) Bowie & Weatherford, #103,9/91,314 First Ave. South, Seattle, WA 98104
(y5) Academic Library Service,#81,5/92,6489 S Land Park Dr, Sacramento CA 95831
(y6) Vintage Bks,#2,9/91,117 Concord Ave,Framingham,MA 01701
(y7) Typographeum ,#58,8/91,Stone Cottage,Bennington Rd, Francestown,NH 03043
(y8) Raymond M Sutton Jr,Spec Cat H,10/89,Box 330,Williamsburg,KY 40769
(y9) John Gach Bks,#135,1/92,5620 Waterloo Rd,Columbia MD 21045
(y10) Kemet Bks,#3,12/92,Box 662,Fairfield,CT 06430-0662

(z1) Jack Rittenhouse,#81,4/90,Box 4422,Albuquerque,NM 87196
(z2) The Book Treasury, #39,9/91,Box 20033,Long Beach,CA 90801
(z3) Archer's Used & Rare Bks,#10,2/91,104 S Lincoln St,Kent,Ohio 44240
(z4) Great NW Bookstore,#36,9/91,1234 SW Stark St,Portland,OR 97205
(z5) Shirley R Gellis,#6,12/91,57 Seafield Lane,Bay Shore,NY 11706
(z6) Bookfinders,#21,9/92,Box 13692,Atlanta GA 30324-0692
(z7) Peninsula Bks,#492,11/92,451 N Madison,Traverse City,MI 49684-2112
(z8) Bay Side Bks,#82,8/91,Box 57,Soquel,CA 95073
(z9) Archer's Used & Rare Bks,#15,2/92,104 S Lincoln St,Kent,Ohio 44240
(z10) Owens Civil War Bks,#36,6/89,2728 Tinsley Dr,Richmond VA 23235

(aa1) Robert G. Hayman,#146,3/93,Box 188, Carey, OH 43316
(aa2) Robert Reeves Bks,#41,4/93,1606 Candella Pl,Victoria,BC,Canada V8N 5P4
(aa3) Burkwood Bks,#47,4/93,Box 172,Urbana,IL 61801
(aa4) Bookworm & Silverfish,#207,1/92,Box 639,Wytheville,VA 24382
(aa5) Aard Books,#10,3/93,3026 NW 60th St,Seattle WA 98107
(aa6) Joseph J Felcone Inc,#61,12/92,Box 366,Princeton,NJ 08540
(aa7) The Edmonton Bk Store Ltd,#15,7/92,8530 109th St,Edmonton,Albert Can T6G 1E5
(aa8) Steven C. Bernard,#61, 1/93,15011 Plainfield Lane, Darnestown, MD 20874
(aa9) Sadlon's,#110,11/91,1207 Fox River Dr,De Pere,WI 54115
(aa10) Len Unger-Rare Bks,#10,4/93,Box 5858,Sherman Oaks, CA 91413

(bb1) Steven C. Bernard,#60,11/92,15011 Plainfield Lane, Darnestown, MD 20874
(bb2) Bev Chaney Jr,list J,10/92,73,Croton Ave,Ossining,NY 10562
(bb3) Melvin Marcher,#13,7/91,6204 N Vermont,Oklahoma City, OK 73112
(bb4) Lien's Book Shop,#14,1/93,57 S 9th St,Mpls,MN 55402
(bb5) Aard Books,#9,12/92,3026 NW 60th St,Seattle WA 98107
(bb6) Worldwide Antiquarian,#103,8/90,Box 391,Cambridge,MA 02141
(bb7) The Edmonton Bk Store Ltd,#14,3/92,8530 109th St,Edmonton,Alberta, Can T6G 1E5
(bb8) Benchmark ,#4,6/91,331 Rio Grande St,Suite 300,Box 9027,Salt Lake City,Ut 84109
(bb9) Stephen C. Lunsford,#35,9/91,Box 3023,Blaine, Wa 98230
(b10) Duga's Books,#18,2/93,610 Aldama Court,Ocoee, FL 34761

(cc1) Steven C. Bernard,#59,10/92,15011 Plainfield Lane, Darnestown, MD 20874
(cc2) Bev Chaney Jr,#17,6/92,73,Croton Ave,Ossining,NY 10562
(cc3) Peninsula Bks,#293,4/93,451 N Madison,Traverse City,MI 49684-2112
(cc4) Lien's Book Shop,#13,9/92,57 S 9th St,Mpls,MN 55402
(cc5) Aard Books,#8,10/92,3026 NW 60th St,Seattle WA 98107
(cc6) Camp Pope Bookshop,#16, 4/93 Box 2232, Iowa City, Iowa 52244
(cc7) The Edmonton Bk Store Ltd,#13,9/91,8530 109th St,Edmonton,Alberta, Can T6G 1E5
(cc8) The Book Exchange,8/90,90 W Market St,Corning,NY 14830
(cc9) Arnold Sadow,#25,9/92,40 Reservoir St,#510,Brockkton,MA 02401
(cc10) James Hodgson Bk,#3,9/92,710 County St,New Bedford MA 02740

(dd1) Metacomet Bks,#32,6/90,Box 2479,Providence,RI 02906
(dd2) Bev Chaney Jr,#16,2/92,73,Croton Ave,Ossining,NY 10562
(dd3) W Bruce Fye,#63,3/92,1607 N Wood Ave,Marshfield,WI 54449
(dd4) Lien's Book Shop,#12,5/92,57 S 9th St,Mpls,MN 55402
(dd5) Aard Books,#7,7/92,3026 NW 60th St,Seattle WA 98107
(dd6) Bibliomania,#21,8/91,129 Jay St,Schenectady NY 12305
(dd7) Parmer Bks,4/93,7644 Forrestal Rd, San Diego,CA 92120-2203
(dd8) The Bishop of Bks,Roger Bertoia,#102,3/92,Box 579,Steubenville,OH 43952
(dd9) The Book Broker.#27,5/91,Box 1283,Charlottesville, VA 22902
(dd10) Wm P Wreden,#79,5/91,Box 56,206 Hamilton Ave,Palo Alto,CA 94302-0056

(ee1) J B Muns, Fine Arts Bks,#147,9/92,1162 Shattuck Ave,Berkeley CA 94707
(ee2) Bev Chaney Jr,#15,10/91,73,Croton Ave,Ossining,NY 10562
(ee3) Game Bag Bks,#7,11/91,2704 Ship Rock Rd,Willow St,PA 17584
(ee4) Lien's Book Shop,#11,3/92,57 S 9th St,Mpls,MN 55402
(ee5) Aard Books,#6,5/92,3026 NW 60th St,Seattle WA 98107
(ee6) Bibliomania,#20,5/91,129 Jay St,Schenectady NY 12305
(ee7) Parmer Bks,5/93,7644 Forrestal Rd, San Diego,CA 92120-2203
(ee8) Dave Mattson Nautical Bks,#3,6/90,Box 803,Cape Coral,FL 33910-0803
(ee9) Shirley R Gellis,#7,6/92,57 Seafield Lane,Bay Shore,NY 11706
(ee10) Michael Gibbs,#22,5/93,Box 83,West Chester OH 45069

(ff1) AKA Fine Used Bks, #17,4/90,4142 Brookyln Ave NE, Seattle, WA 98105
(ff2) Wayne Greene Baseball Bks, #8,5/93,945 W End Ave, 5D, NY, NY 10025
(ff3) Ken Lopez,Vietnam Lit,4/91,51 Huntington Rd,Hadley, MA 01035
(ff4) Lien's Book Shop,#10,11/91,57 S 9th St,Mpls,MN 55402
(ff5) Aard Books,#5,2/92,3026 NW 60th St,Seattle WA 98107
(ff6) Steven C. Bernard,#62, 5/93,15011 Plainfield Lane, Darnestown, MD 20874
(ff7) Bibliomania,#19,3/91,129 Jay St,Schenectady NY 12305
(ff8) Carroll Burcham,#20,3/91,5546 17th Pl,Lubbock,TX 79416
(ff9) Jennifer Inderwick,#5,7/90,Saltspring Island,Box 1526,Ganges,BC,Canada VO5 1E0
(ff10) Russel R DuPont,#3,1/93,41 Star St,Whitman,Ma 02382

(gg1) Joseph J Felcone,#50,11/90,Box 366, Princeton,NJ 08540
(gg2) Owen D Kubik,#16,7/90,3474 Clar-Von Dr, Dayton,OH 45430
(gg3) Game Bag Books,#5,11/89,2704 Ship Rock Road, Willow Street,PA 17584
(gg4) Lien's Book Shop,#9,9/91,57 S 9th St, Mpls,MN 55402
(gg5) Aard Books,#4,11/91,3026 NW 60th St,Seattle WA 98107
(gg6) J Parmer,#37,12/89,7644 Forrestal Rd, San Diego,CA 92120
(gg7) Bibliomania,#18,1/91,129 Jay St,Schenectady NY 12305
(gg8) Alphabet Bkshp,#22,9/92,145 Main St W,Port Colborne,Ontario,Canada L3K 3V3
(gg9) Andre Dumont Maps & Bks,#17,5/93,Box 10117,Santa Fe,NM 87504
(gg10) The Backlist,#21,2/91,Box 871, Torrington,CT 06790

(hh1) Whitlock Farm, #598-A,9/92,20 Sperry Rd,Bethany,CT 06524-3599
(hh2) Buckingham Bks,#5,9/92,8058 Stone Bridge Rd,Greencastle,PA 17225-9786
(hh3) Bookworm & Silverfish,#206,1/92,Box 639,Wytheville,VA 24382
(hh4) Anne & David Bromer,#70,2/92,607 Boylston St,Copley Sq,Boston MA 02116
(hh5) Aard Books,#3,7/91,3026 NW 60th St,Seattle WA 98107
(hh6) Knollwood Bks,#58,1/93,Box 197,Oregon,WI 53575-0197
(hh7) Brooks Books,#11,12/91,Box 21473,Concord CA 94521
(hh8) King & Queen Bks,#28,8/90,Box 15062,Pensacola,FL 32514
(hh9) Harold M Burstein & Co,#126,12/92,36 Riverside Dr,Waltham, MA 02154
(hh10) Polyanthos,Park Ave Bks,#16,9/92,Box 348,Huntington, NY 11743

(jj1) Peter & Isham Co,#33,5/93,8600 Hidden Meadow,Fort Worth,TX 76179
(jj2) Owen D Kubik,#14,7/90,3474 Clar-Von Dr,Dayton,OH 45430
(jj3) Bookworm & Silverfish,#205,1/92,Box 639,Wytheville,VA 24382
(jj4) Joel Stark-Bks,#3,5/90,5815 #C Roche Dr,Columbus,OH 43229
(jj5) Aard Books,#2,2/91,3026 NW 60th St,Seattle WA 98107
(jj6) Nouveau Rare Bks,#23,6/90,Box 12471,Jackson,MS 39211
(jj7) Brooks Books,#9,7/91,Box 21473,Concord CA 94521
(jj8) James S Jaffe,#23,9/91,Box 496,Haverford,PA 19041
(jj9) Dramatis Personae,#26,5/93,71 Lexington Ave,NY,NY 10010
(jj10) Rudolph Wm Sabbot,#41,5/93,6821 Babcock Ave,N Hollywood,CA 91605

(kk1) Wm P Wreden,#80,11/91,Box 56,Palo Alto,CA 94302-0056
(kk2) Owen D Kubik,#13,7/90,3474 Clar-Von Dr,Dayton,OH 45430
(kk3) Bookworm & Silverfish,#204,1/92,Box 639,Wytheville,VA 24382
(kk4) J B Muns, Fine Arts Bks,#141C,9/90,1162 Shattuck Ave,Berkeley CA 94707
(kk5) Limestone Hills Bookshop,#33,10/90,Box 1125,Glen Rose,TX 76043
(kk6) Nouveau Rare Bks,#22,2/90,Box 12471,Jackson,MS 39211
(kk7) Joel Stark-Bks,#2,7/89,7371 Fall Creek Ln,Worthington,OH 43235
(kk8) James S Jaffe,#24,12/91,Box 496,Haverford,PA 19041
(kk9) Bowie & Weatherford,Inc,#90,10/90,314 First Ave. S, Seattle, WA 98104
(kk10) Bibliomania,#16,8/90,129 Jay St,Schenectady,NY 12305

(ll1) Parmer Books,Asia,10/91,7644 Forrestal Rd,San Diego,CA 92120
(ll2) Wm P Wreden,#76,12/89,Box 56,Palo Alto,CA 94302-0056
(ll3) Bookworm & Silverfish,#203,1/92,Box 639,Wytheville,VA 24382
(ll4) Arthur H Minters Inc,#88,5/90,39 W 14th St,Room 401,NY,NY 10011
(ll5) Limestone Hills Bookshop,#32,8/90,Box 1125,Glen Rose,TX 76043
(ll6) Robert Frost Books,#1,12/91,Box 719,Rensselaer,NY 12144
(ll7) Richard Gilbo,List A,10/90,Box 12,Carpinteria,CA 93014
(ll8) Blue Dragon Book Shop,#15,2/92,Box 216,Ashland,OR 97520
(ll9) Bowie & Weatherford,Inc,#88,8/90,314 First Ave. S, Seattle, WA 98104
(ll10) James S Jaffe,#25,2/92,Box 496,Haverford,PA 19041

(mm1) Parmer Books, Americana,8/91,7644 Forrestal Rd,San Diego,CA 92120
(mm2) Whitlock Farm, #590-A,4/91,20 Sperry Rd,Bethany,CT 06525
(mm3) Bookworm & Silverfish,#202,1/92,Box 639,Wytheville,VA 24382
(mm4) Quest Rare Bks,#891,2/90,774 Sant Ynez,Stanford,CA 94305
(mm5) David Holloway,#8,1/90,7430 Grace St,Springfield,VA 22150
(mm6) MCL Associates,#92-1,9/92,Box 26,McClean,VA 22101-0026
(mm7) The Bookmine,#2,9/90,1015 2nd St,Old Sacramento,CA 95814
(mm8) Edmonton Book Store Ltd,#9,3/90,8530 109 St,Edmonton,Alberta,Can T6G 1E5
(mm9) Bibliomania,#15,6/90,129 Jay St,Schenectady,NY 12305
(mm10) Metacomet Books,#46,5/93,Box 2479,Providence,RI 02906

(nn1) Parmer Books,Sea & Ships,8/91,7644 Forrestal Rd,San Diego,CA 92120
(nn2) Bookworm & Silverfish,#201,1/92,Box 639,Wytheville,VA 24382
(nn3) Bibliomania,#14,3/90,129 Jay St,Schenectady,NY 12305
(nn4) Freedom Book Shop,#6,2/91,Box 247,Maple St,Freedom,NH 03836
(nn5) James M Edgar,Angling Bks,4/90,10 Buckeye Way,Kentfield,CA 94904
(nn6) Lien's Book Shop,#15,5/93,57 S 9th St, Mpls,MN 55402
(nn7) Western Book Co,#10,7/91,Box 271,Gaston,OR 97119
(nn8) Treasures From The Castle,#18,9/89,1720 N Livernois,Rochester,MI 48604
(nn9) Parker Books of the West,#18,10/92,142 W Palace Ave,Santa Fe,NM 87501
(nn10) Cynthia K Fowler Books, #15,9/92,1723 Tyler Parkway Louisville, KY 40204

(oo1) Parmer Books,Arctic & Antarctic ,4/93,7644 Forrestal Rd,San Diego,CA 92120
(oo2) Taugher Books,#2,2/93,2550 Somerset Dr,Belmont,CA 94002-2926
(oo3) Bibliomania,#13,2/90,129 Jay St,Schenectady,NY 12305
(oo4) Title Wave Used Books,# Feb 92,1/92,505 E Northern Lights,Anchorage AK 99503
(oo5) The Bookshop,#43,1/90,400 W Franklin St,Chapel Hill,NC 27516
(oo6) Margolis & Moss,#26,11/90,Box 2042,Santa Fe,NM 87504-2042
(oo7) Second Life Books,Inc,#94,3/93,Box 242,55 Quarry Rd,Lanesborough,MA 01237
(oo8) Bowie & Co,#116,6/93,314 First Ave. S, Seattle, WA 98104
(oo9) Parker Books of the West,#17,7/92,142 W Palace Ave,Santa Fe,NM 87501
(oo10) Cynthia K Fowler Books, #12,3/91,1723 Tyler Parkway Louisville, KY 40204

(pp1) Parmer Books,Nautica,1/93,7644 Forrestal Rd,San Diego,CA 92120
(pp2) David Mason,#59,9/92,342 Queen St W,2nd Floor,Toronto Ontario,Canada M5V 2A2
(pp3) Bibliomania,#12,1/90,129 Jay St,Schenectady,NY 12305
(pp4) Heinoldt Bks,#43,6/93,1325 W Central Ave,South Egg Harbor,NJ 08215
(pp5) David Mason,#Short 2,9/92,342 Queen St W,2nd Fl,Toronto Ontario,Can M5V 2A2
(pp6) Robert G. Hayman,#147,6/93,Box 188, Carey, OH 43316
(pp7) James Hodgson Books,#4,9/92,710 County St,New Bedford,MA 02740
(pp8) David Mason,#Short 3,9/92,342 Queen St W,2nd Fl,Toronto Ontario,CanM5V 2A2
(pp9) Parker Books of the West,Spring List,5/92,142 W Palace Ave,Santa Fe,NM 87501
(pp10) Cynthia K Fowler Books, #11,9/90,1723 Tyler Parkway Louisville, KY 40204

(qq1) Caney Booksellers,#16,7/93,One Cherry Hill,Ste 220,1 Mall Dr,Cherry Hill,NJ 08002

GENERAL INFORMATION

Modern 1st editions, press books & fine bindings have to be in perfect condition. Any flaws whatsoever bring values down to very little, with few exceptions.

1st editions - same as above but in less strict sense, according to age, rarity, etc. Some are never found in fine condition and have brought some fancy prices.

Americana is a field in which prices have been rising. Condition is important but not so much so as in 1st editions.

Association points, such as author's autograph, presentation note by author or esteemed personality, etc. raises the value.

A rare book is one that a dealer finds once in about ten years.

A scarce book is one that a dealer finds once in about one year.